Facts About the World's Languages:

An Encyclopedia of the World's Major Languages, Past and Present

Edited by
Jane Garry and Carl Rubino

Contributing Linguistics Editors:
Adams B. Bodomo
Alice Faber
Robert French

The H. W. Wilson Company
New York and Dublin

A New England Publishing Associates Book
2001

NEW ENGLAND
PUBLISHING
ASSOCIATES

Copy Editor: Roberta J. Buland
Design and Page Composition: Ron Formica
Editorial Administration: Chris Ceplenski, Ron Formica, Victoria Harlow and Kristine Schiavi
Proof Reading: Susan L. Paruch of Miccinello Associates

International Standard Book Number 0-8242-0970-2

Library of Congress Cataloging–in–Publication Data
Facts about the world's languages: an encyclopedia of the world's major languages, past and present/ edited by Jane Garry and Carl Rubino.
p.cm.
Includes bibliographic references and index
ISBN 0-8242-0970-2 (alk. paper)
1. Language and languages--Handbooks, manuals, etc. 2. Linguistics--Comparative linguistics.
I. Garry, Jane. II. Rubino, Carl R. Galvez

P371 .F33 2000
403--dc21

00-049430

Printed in the United States of America

Contents

The World's Languages

Contributors

Acehnese: Dr. Mark Durie, University of Melbourne, Parkville, Victoria, Australia
Afrikaans: Professor Paul T. Roberge, University of North Carolina
Akan: Professor Samuel R. Obeng, Indiana University
Akkadian: Dr. Benjamin R. Foster, Yale University
Albanian: Professor Gary Bevington (Retired), Northeastern Illinois University
Amharic: Professor Monica S. Devens, University of Washington
Arabic: Professor Michael G. Carter, Oslo University, Norway
Aramaic: Professor Robert D. Hoberman, State University of New York, Stony Brook, New York
Arapesh: Dr. Lise M. Dobrin, University of Virginia
Armenian: Dr. John A.C. Greppin, Cleveland State University
Assamese: Professor Colin Paul Masica, University of Chicago, and Professor Sanjib Baruah, Bard College
Aymara: Professor Martha J. Hardman, University of Florida
Azerbaijanian: Dr. Lars Johanson, Universitaet Mainz, Mainz, Germany
Balinese: Dr. Adrian Clynes, Brunei Darussalam
Balochi: Carina Jahani, Uppsala University, Sweden
Bangla: Dr. Tanmoy Bhattacharya, Universitaet Leipzig, Germany
Basque: Dr. R. L. Trask, University of Sussex, Brighton, England
Belorussian: Professor Raymond H. Miller, Bowdoin College, Brunswick, Maine
Bemba: Professor Debra Spitulnik, Emory University, and Mubanga E. Kashoki, University of Zambia
Bhojpuri: Professor Shaligram Shukla, Georgetown University
Bikol: Professor Malcolm W. Mintz, Murdoch University, Murdoch, Australia
Bugis: Professor Roger Tol, Royal Institute of Linguistics, Leiden, Netherlands
Bulgarian: Professor Ernest A. Scatton, State University of New York, Albany
Burmese: Dr. F. K. Lehman, University of Illinois
Caribbean Creole English: Professor Ronald Kephart, University of North Florida, Jacksonville
Catalan: Dr. Natàlia Díaz-Insensé (Independent Scholar)
Cebuano: Professor John U. Wolff, Cornell University
Cherokee: Professor William Pulte, Southern Methodist University, Dallas
Chichewa: Professor Sam Mchombo, University of California, Berkeley
Chinese Languages:
Classical Chinese: Professor David Prager Branner, University of Maryland
Gan: Professor Laurent Sagart, CRLAO, École des Hautes Études en Sciences Sociales (UM8563 du CNRS), Paris, France
Hakka: Professor Anne O. Yue, University of Washington
Mandarin: Dr. Xiaonong Zhu, Hong Kong Polytechnic University
Min: Professor David Prager Branner, University of Maryland
Wu: Dr. P.J. Rose, Australian National University, Canberra, Australia
Xiang: Professor You Rujie, Fudan University, Shanghai, China
Yue: Professor Anne O. Yue, University of Washington
Coptic: Professor Antonio Loprieno, University of California, Los Angeles
Creek: Professor Jack B. Martin, College of William and Mary
Czech: Professor Charles Townsend, Princeton University
Dagaare: Dr. Adams Bodomo, University of Hong Kong
Danish: Professor Thomas Lundskaer-Nielsen and Professor Robert Allan, University College, London, England
Dutch: Dr. Theo Janssen, Free University of Amsterdam
Egyptian, Ancient: Professor Antonio Loprieno, University of California, Los Angeles
English: Dr. Jon Erikson, Universitaet zu Koln, Koln, Germany
Etruscan: Dr. Larissa Bonfante, New York University
Ewe: Dr. Felix Ameka, Leiden University, Leiden, Netherlands
Finnish: Dr. Erika Mitchell, Zayed University, Dubai, United Arab Emirates
French: Professor Cynthia A. Fox, University of Albany
Fula: Dr. Carole Paradis, Université Laval, Quebec, Canada
Galician: Dr. Henrique Monteagudo, University Santiago de Compostela
Ge'ez: Professor Monica Devens, University of Washington
Georgian: Karina Vamling, Lund University, Lund, Sweden
German: Professor Terrence McCormick, University of Connecticut
Gĩkũyu: Dr. Kimani Njogu, Kenyatta University, Nairobi, Kenya
Goṇḍi: Dr. Rosanne Pelletier, University of Connecticut
Gothic: Professor Charles Barrack, University of Washington
Greek, Ancient: Professor Brian Joseph, Ohio State University
Greek, Modern: Professor Brian Joseph, Ohio State University
Guarani: Dr. Maura Velazquez-Castillo, Colorado State University, Fort Collins
Gujaratí: Professor P. J. Mistry, California State University, Fresno
Gusii: Professor Lee Bickmore, University of Albany
Haitian Creole: Dr. Flore Zephir, University of Missouri, Columbia
Hausa: Professor Paul Newman, Indiana University
Hebrew, Biblical: Professor Gary Rendsburg, Cornell University
Hebrew, Modern: Monica Devens, University of Washington
Hiligaynon: Dr. David Zorc (Independent Scholar)
Hindi: Professor Michael Shapiro, University of Washington
Hittite: Professor Kenneth Shields, Millersville University
Hungarian: Professor Robert Hetzron (Deceased), University of California, Santa Barbara
Ibibio: Professor Okon Essien, University of Calabar, Calabar, Nigeria
Ìgbo: Professor Victor Manfredi and Ejike Eze, Boston University
Ilocano: Dr. Carl Rubino, University of California, Santa Barbara and Australian National University
Irish: Professor James McCloskey, University of California, Santa Cruz
Italian: Professor Lori Repetti, State University of New York, Stony Brook

Japanese: Professor Tim Vance, Connecticut College
Javanese: Dr. Hein Steinhauer, Leiden University, Leiden, Netherlands
Kam: Professor Jerold Edmondson, University of Texas
Kannada: Professor Shikaripur Sridhar, State University of New York, Stony Brook
Kanuri: Dr. John Hutchinson, Boston University
Kapampangan: Hiroaki Kitano, Aichi University of Education, Aichi-Ken, Japan
Kazakh: Professor Lars Johanson, Universitaet Mainz, Mainz, Germany
Khmer: Dr. Robert Headley (Independent Scholar)
Kikongo Kituba: Professor Salikoko Mufwene, University of Chicago
Kinyarwanda: Professor Alexandre Kimenyi, California State University, Sacramento
Kirghiz: Professor Lars Johanson, Universitaet Mainz, Mainz, Germany
Konkani: Professor Rocky Miranda, University of Minnesota
Korean: Professor Young-Mee Yu Cho, Rutgers University
Kurmanjî Kurdish: Dr. Geoffrey Haig, Universitaet Kiel, Kiel, Germany, and Dr. Ludwig Paul, Universitaet Goettingen, Germany
Lakota: Professor David Rood, University of Colorado
Lao: Professor Thomas Gething, University of Washington
Latin: Professor Rex Wallace, University of Massachusetts
Latvian: Professor Lalita Muizniece, Western Michigan University, Kalamazoo
Lingala: Professor Salikoko Mufwene, University of Chicago
Lithuanian: Professor Jules Levin, University of California, Riverside
Luganda: Professor Francis Katamba, University of Lancaster, Lancaster, England
Macedonian: Professor Victor Friedman, University of Chicago
Madurese: Professor Alan M. Stevens, Queens College (CUNY)
Maithili: Professor Yogendra P. Yadava, Royal Nepal Academy, Kathmandu, Nepal
Malagasy: Professor Edward L. Keenan, University of California, Los Angeles, and Dr. Roger Rabenelaina, University of Antan-anarivo
Malay/Indonesian: Professor Hein Steinhauer, Leiden University, Leiden, Netherlands
Malayalam: Professor Rodney Moag, University of Texas
Maninka-Bambara-Dyula: Professor Jessica Barlow, San Diego State University, San Diego
Manipuri/Meithei: Professor Shobhana Chelliah, University of North Texas, Denton
Marathi: Professor Franklin C. Southworth (Retired), University of Pennsylvania
Maya: Professor Gary Bevington (Retired), Northeastern Illinois University
Mende: Professor David Dwyer, Michigan State University
Minangkabau: Dr. Ismet Fanany, School of Australian/ INTL Studies, Burwood, Victoria, Australia
Mongolian: Professor Robert Binnick, University of Toronto, Ontario, Canada
Moore: Professor Norbert Nikiema, University of Ouagadougou, Ouagadougou, Burkina Faso
Nahuatl: Dr. Frances Karttunen (Retired), University of Texas
Nama: Dr. Wilfred Haacke, University of Namibia, Windhoek, Namibia
Navajo: Professor Margaret Field, San Diego State University
Nepali: Professor Manindra Verma, University of Wisconsin
Nivkh: Professor Johanna Mattissen, University of Cologne
Norwegian: John Weinstock, University of Texas
Occitan: Professor Thomas T. Field, University of Maryland
Oriya: Dr. Subhadra Ramachandran, University of Ottawa, Ontario, Canada
Oromo: Dr. Cynthia Robb Clamons, Hamline University
Pali: Dr. John Peterson, Universitaet Munchen, Munich, Germany
Pangasinan: Dr. Carl Rubino, University of California, Santa Barbara
Pashto: Dr. Igor Inozemtsev, University of Chicago
Persian: Dr. John Perry, University of Chicago
Phoenician/Punic: Dr. Charles Krahmalkov, University of Michigan
Polish: Professor Katarzyna Dziwirek, University of Washington
Polynesian Languages: Dr. Jeff Marck, Australian National University, Canberra, Australia
Portuguese: Dr. Cristina Schmitt, Michigan State University
Pulaar: Fallou Ngom, University of Illinois at Urbana-Champaign
Punjabi: Professor Tej K. Bhatia, Syracuse University
Pwo Karen: Dr. Masahiko Kato, National Museum of Ethnology, Osaka, Japan
Quechua: Professor Serafin Coronel-Molina, University of Michigan
Rajasthani: Dr. J. D. Smith, Cambridge University, Cambridge, England
Romani: Professor Ian Hancock, University of Texas
Romanian: Professor Charles M. Carlton, University of Rochester
Rundi: Professor Patrick Bennett, University of Wisconsin
Russian: Dr. Tom Beyer, Middlebury College
Sango: Professor W. J. Samarin, University of Toronto, Ontario, Canada
Sanskrit: Professor Michael Witzel, Harvard University
Santali: Professor Gregory D. S. Anderson, University of Chicago
Serbo-Croatian: Professor Wayles Browne, Cornell University
Sesotho: Professor Katherine Demuth, Brown University
Shan: Professor David Solnit, University of Michigan
Shona: Professor Hazel Carter, University of Wisconsin
Sindhi: Professor Jennifer Cole, University of Illinois
Sinhala: Dr. Sunil Kariyakarawana (Independent Scholar)
Siraiki: Dr. Christopher Shackle, University College, London, England
siSwati: Mpunga wa Ilunga, Citalde University, Louvain-la-Neuve, Belgium
Slovak: Professor David Short, University College, London, England
Slovene: Dr. Marc Greenberg, University of Kansas
Sogdian: Professor Yutuka Yoshida, Kobe City University of Foreign Studies, Kobe, Japan

Somali: Professor John Saeed, Trinity College, Dublin, Ireland
Spanish: Professor Louis Lopez, University of Illinois
Sukuma: Dr. Herman M. Batibo, University of Botswana
Sumerian: Dr. Daniel Snell, University of Oklahoma
Sundanese: Professor Abigail Cohn, Cornell University
Swahili: Dr. Kimani Njogu, Kenyatta University, Nairobi, Kenya
Swedish: Dr. Kersti Borjars, University of Manchester, Manchester, England
Tagalog: Professor Videa P. DeGuzman, University of Calgary, Alberta, Canada
Tajik: Dr. John Perry, University of Chicago
Tamazight: Professor Ali Alalou, Columbia University, and Professor Patrick Farrell, University of California, Davis
Tamil: Dr. Sanford Steever (Independent Scholar)
Tatar: Professor Lars Johanson, Universitaet Mainz, Mainz, Germany
Tay Nung: Professor Peter A. Ross, Australian National University, Canberra, Australia
Telugu: Dr. Rosanne Pelletier, University of Connecticut
Thai: Dr. Alexander Robertson Coupe, LaTrobe University, Bundoora, Victoria, Australia
Tibetan: Professor Christopher I. Beckwith, Indiana University
Tigrinya: Professor Tesfay Tewolde (Independent Scholar)
Tocharian: Professor Douglas Adams, University of Idaho
Tok Pisin: Professor Suzanne Romaine, Merton College, University of Oxford, Oxford, England
Tshilubà: Dr. Mpunga wa Ilunga, Citalde University, Louvain-la-Neuve, Belgium
Tswana: Professor Karen Mistry, California State University, Fresno
Turkish: Professor Robert Underhill, San Diego State University
Turkmen: Professor Lars Johanson, Universitaet Mainz, Mainz, Germany
Ukrainian: Professor Andrij Hornjatkevye, University of Alberta, Edmondton, Alberta, Canada
UMbundu: Dr. Thilo Schadeberg, Leiden University, Leiden, Netherlands
Urdu: Professor Tashin Siddiqi, University of Michigan
Uyghur: Dr. Arienne Dwyer, Universitaet Mainz, Mainz, Germany
Uzbek: Professor Lars Johanson, Universitaet Mainz, Mainz, Germany
Vietnamese: Professor Dinh-Hoa Nguyen, SIU Center for Vietnamese Studies
Waray-Waray: Dr. Carl Rubino, University of California, Santa Barbara
Warlpiri: Dr. Angela Terrill, Max Planck Institute for Evolutionary Anthropology, Leipzig, Germany
Welsh: Nicholas Kibre, University of California, Santa Barbara, California
Wolaitta: Azeb Amha, University of Leiden, Leiden, Netherlands
Wolof: Professor Omar Ka, University of Maryland
Xhosa: Professor Laura Downing, University of British Columbia, Vancouver, British Columbia, Canada
Yi: Professor David Bradley, La Trobe University, Bundoora, Victoria, Australia
Yiddish: Dr. Paul Glasser, YIVO Institute for Jewish Research, New York, New York
Yoruba: Professor Akinbiyi Akinlabi, Rutgers University
Yup'ik (Central Alaskan Yup'uk Eskimo): Professor George Charles, University of Alaska, and Dr. Carl Rubino, University of California, Santa Barbara.
Zhuang-Bouyei: Professor Jerrold Edmondson, University of Texas
Zulu: Professor Sandra Sanneh, Yale University

Abbreviations Employed in this Volume

The following is a list of general abbreviations employed in this book. Language-specific and nonstandard abbreviations are explained in each entry, as are glosses with multiple definitions.

A	agent	EXCL	exclusive	ORD	ordinal (number)
ABL	ablative	F	feminine	PART	particle; participle
ABS	absolutive	fig.	figurative usage	PASS	passive
ACC	accusative	FUT	future	PERF	perfect; perfective
ACT	active	GEN	genitive	PL	plural
ADJ	adjective	GER	gerund	POSS	possessive
ADV	adverb	H	human	POSTP	postposition
AGENT	agentive	HABIT	habitual	POT	potential
ALT	alternate, variant of	IMP	imperative	PREF	prefix
ANTIPASS	antipassive	IMPERF	imperfect	PREP	prepositional
AOR	aorist	INCH	inchoative	PRES	present
ART	article	INCL	inclusive	PRO	pronoun
ASP	aspect	IND	indirect; indicative	PROG	progressive
ASSOC	associative	INDEF	indefinite	PUNCT	punctual
ATTR	attribute	INDIC	indicative	PURP	purposive
AUX	auxiliary	INF	infinitive	Q	interrogative
BEN	benefactive	INST	instrumental	RECIP	reciprocal
CAUS	causative	INTERR	interrogative	RED(UP)	reduplication
cf.	confer, see	INTJ	interjection	REFL	reflexive
CL, CLASS	classifier	INTR	intransitive	REL	relative
COLL	collective	INV	inverse	REP	repetitive
COMP	complementizer; comparative	IO	indirect object	RES	resultative
COND	conditional	IRR	irrealis	S, SG	singular; Subject (SVO)
CONJ	conjunction	ITER	iterative	s.o.	someone
CONT	continuative	LIG	ligature	SS	Same subject
COP	copula	LNK	linker	s.t.	something
DAT	dative	LOC	locative	STAT	stative
DEF	definite	M(ASC)	masculine	SUB	subject; subordinate
DEIC	deictic	MID	middle	SUBJ	subject; subjective; subjunctive
DEM	demonstrative	N	neuter; Noun; homorganic Nasal	SUFF	suffix
DET	determiner	NEG	negative	syn.	synonym
DIR	direct (object); directional	NH	nonhuman	TERM	terminative
DITR	ditransitive	NOM	nominative	THEM	thematic
DO	direct object	NONTOP	nontopic	TNS	tense
DS	different subject	NP	Noun Phrase	TOP	topic
DU	dual	NUM	numeral	TRANS	transitive
DUR	durative	O	Object	V	verb
EMPH	emphatic	OBJ	object; objective	VEN	venitive
ERG	ergative	OBL	oblique	VOC	vocative
EVID	evidential	OBLIG	obligatory	VP	verb phrase
		OPT	optative		

INTRODUCTION

Then Little Coyote did something bad. He suggested to Old Man that he give the people different languages so they would misunderstand each other and use their weapons in wars. . . Old Man did what Little Coyote said, and the people had different languages and made war on each other.[1]

The passage above is from the cosmology of the Crow, a Plains Indians group of North America. It is one variant of a motif found in creation myths around the world that describes how the ancients lost their ability to understand each other's speech when one language was replaced by many.[2] The mythical time when all peoples could communicate freely with each other and live in peace was portrayed as a lost paradise, succeeded by the babble of tongues and strife among nations.

If this myth were true, we might well be on our way to another golden age, for today the great diversity of languages in the world is rapidly declining. This fact has been known and documented by linguists for some time, but today language disappearance has accelerated to the point where we are witnessing widespread language extinctions. Some estimates project that the current number of languages in the world (perhaps 6,000) will be cut in half by the end of the 21st century.

The disappearance of languages is cause for concern. It has been likened to the extinction of species—an unfortunate cultural analogue to the alarming events we are witnessing in the biological world. European exploration and colonization, begun in the fifteenth century, the industrial revolution, and our current globalization of trade and mass culture, combined with unprecedented demand for consumer goods, have impinged on the natural world and indigenous cultures around the globe. It is ironic that even as we celebrate diversity and multiculturalism we are experiencing homogenization. To cite two examples, Western clothing is replacing ethnic dress around the world, and American pop music is crowding out traditional folk music. Variety in all aspects of life and culture has been a source of wonder and celebration for ages, and the loss of that variety is indeed an unfortunate prospect.

Every language has its own subtleties of expression; it is a well known quandary in translating poetry that one must sacrifice either faithfulness or beauty in rendering verses into another language. Although linguists can study and record a dying language, once it ceases to be spoken, a unique and distinctive worldview is lost forever.

This encyclopedia was undertaken with the aim of gathering not only linguistic descriptions of a selected assortment of languages from renowned scholars, but historical and cultural information as well. For that reason, the book will interest general readers as well as linguistic specialists. We have tried to include nearly all contemporary languages spoken by at least two million people. Smaller languages are also documented to allow for geographical and typological representation. Finally, a number of ancient languages are included, because of our focus on philology, history and culture.

---

[1] Leeming, David and Margaret Leeming. *Dictionary of Creation Myths*. New York: Oxford University Press, 1995.

[2] Motif A1333, "Confusion of Tongues" in Stith Thompson, *Motif Index of Folk Literature: A Classification of Narrative Elements in Folktales, Myths, Ballads, Fables, Medieval Romances, Exempla, Fabliaux, Jest Books, and Local Legends.* Bloomington: Indiana University Press, 1932–36.

The working title of this book was *The Encyclopedia of the World's Languages, Past and Present*, and that is the title under which the contributors submitted their entries. A work as complex and comprehensive as this one is sure to contain errors that escape even the repeated readings of several people, for which we take complete responsibility. It is our hope that with user comments for future editions, this work will continue to be a standard resource in the years to come.

Jane Garry and Carl Rubino
January 2001

How to Use This Book

With over 6,000 "living languages" spoken in the world today, space limitations have required us to be very selective in our choice of languages to be covered in this volume. As a general rule, we have tried to include all languages currently spoken by two million or more people. There are, however, some exceptions to this rule. First, we have included noteworthy ancient languages—such as Latin, Ancient Greek, Classical Chinese, Akkadian, Tocharian, Sumerian, Coptic, Ge'ez, Punic, Etruscan, Biblical Hebrew, Pali, and Sanskrit—because of their importance in early linguistic scholarship and in the development of so many other languages. Second, we have included some languages with smaller populations to provide representation to less frequently described language families and to give a broader typological perspective to our readers. Such languages include Nivkh, Creek, Navajo, Cherokee, Eskimo, Warlpiri, and Arapesh. Third, a few languages with more than two million speakers were omitted either because they were closely related to other languages found in the book or because they have been inadequately researched or documented.

Although linguistics is a highly technical discipline, we have asked our contributors to describe each language as clearly as possible in words a student or layperson can comprehend. Yet, there are a number of technical terms in linguistics that have a precise meaning and simply cannot be dispensed with. The glossary at the end of the volume defines these terms.

Each of the 191 chapters in the book is devoted to a single language and follows a consistent structure. Here are the headings for the component parts of our standard structure with a brief explanation of what information readers will find under each heading.

Language Name

The language name chosen to represent each chapter was that most commonly used and accepted by the English-speaking world. Also included are alternate names, including obsolete or pejorative terms, and the autonym, which is the name speakers use to designate their own language. For the major languages of the world, the names by which they are known are well established in many languages; the French call their language *français* and that term is translated as *French* (in English), *Französisch* (in German), *francés* (in Spanish), etc. For some lesser-known languages the naming conventions are often problematic, especially if the people who speak the language have no autonym. In these cases, there may be a large number of alternate names, which are given in their entirety, as they are known by the contributors and the editors of the encyclopedia.

Location

This section gives the main area where the language is currently spoken plus regions where it has spread in recent times through migration or because of colonization or globalization. When historical records exist, the homelands of migratory groups are also given, as well as areas in which the language was spoken in the past but where it is no longer currently used. In a few cases where the language territory is too fragmented to be clearly conveyed in words, we have included a shaded map.

Family

This section gives the genetic classification accepted by the leading specialists for each family. The terms Family, Subfamily, Branch, Subbranch, Group, etc. are not always used in a parallel way in all articles because of differences in approach to classification and the level of specificity chosen by the contributor to pinpoint a genetic relationship.

Related Languages

The languages that are most closely related to the language under discussion are noted along with more distant relatives. In many cases the closest languages are also considered to be dialects of the language, as the degree of mutual intelligibility is not always well established or documented. Historical and political prestige also contribute to varied dialectal classifications.

Dialects

This section details the recognized dialects for each language, all the forms known by linguists that are mutually intelligible but with varying phonologies, lexicons, and/or grammatical characteristics. As noted in the Related Languages section, the distinction between language and dialect is not always clear-cut. Because of political prestige or historical significance, some mutually intelligible languages that would be classified as 'dialects' by linguists are classified as 'languages' by their speakers. Such is the case with Hindi/Urdu, and Indonesian/Malay. There are also areas in the world where a chain of very closely related languages are mutually intelligible on contiguous points on the spectrum, but not on the ends, as in the Bikol peninsula of the Philippines. For the purposes of this volume, the different dialect groups are given whenever they can be established by the specialist contributors, noting some of the distinguishing phonological, morphological, or lexical characteristics of each.

Number of Speakers

This is a very difficult figure to establish, and should be taken as an estimate at best. In most cases upper and lower limits are given. The number of speakers of a given language is constantly changing because of natural population increase as well as fluctuations due to famine, disease, war, political situations, natural disasters, and immigration. Another complicating factor when estimating speakers of a language is multilingualism; people who claim to speak multiple languages may in fact only be competent in one, but if they have a rudimentary knowledge of another language they may want to be counted (or their government may way them to be counted) as speakers for ethnic, religious, or political reasons.

Origin and History

A brief sketch of the history of the language, beginning with what is known about the pre-written history of the speakers is given here. For languages with long written traditions, the earliest known writing is cited, as well as highlights of literature and the political history of the given ethnic group.

Orthography and Basic Phonology

This section outlines the orthographic (written symbols and spelling) conventions used for each language, as well as the phonological system (the inventory and nature of the sound system). Historical information on the development of the orthographic systems is given wherever applicable, as well as samples of non-Roman scripts. Consonant and vowel charts are provided with each language, showing the phonemic inventory based on either the standardized writing systems of the language or the conventions employed in the article. The IPA (International Phonetic Alphabet) representation for the less frequently occurring phonemes is also provided in the consonant and vowel charts, but is avoided in the body of the articles wherever possible.

Among the many things readers will find in this section are phonological rules, which detail phonemic variation, and information on stress, tone, and syllable structure.

Basic Morphology

This section is perhaps the most technical part of each article in the book. It gives a detailed overview of the word classes of each language and the morphological systems available to them. In most entries, this section is divided based on lexical classes, such as: nominal morphology (illustrating relevant categories such as number, case, class, gender), verbal morphology (such as tense, aspect, mode, mood, person, incorporation), and adjectival morphology (the means of expressing comparatives, superlatives, equalitatives, etc.).

Morphological templates, which schematically illustrate the relative position of affixes, are provided for morphologically complex (synthetic) languages. Morpheme types (prefixes, suffixes, infixes, clitics) are also illustrated in this section, as well as allomorphic variation, wherever applicable.

The glossing conventions given in the morphology and syntax sections are those listed on page iv. Unconventional glosses and more language-specific grammatical terms are provided when applicable.

Basic Syntax

The coverage in this section varies in scope from article to article, depending on the nature of the structure of each language and the contributor. Contributors were at liberty to describe in detail certain peculiar syntactic points in their languages, but all were encouraged to at least briefly address basic constituent order and negation. Because the aim of the encyclopedia is to be descriptive, controversial issues that are more relevant to establishing a particular theoretical viewpoint than to describing the behavior of a language are not addressed in this section.

Contact with Other Languages

This section discusses how the language has been influenced by other languages. Sometimes these are languages that are spoken in geographic proximity and sometimes they are those that were spoken by conquerors or colonizers. Examples of words that have entered the lexicon from other languages are given, as well as grammatical patterns that may have resulted from a linguistic area, or *Sprachbund.*

Common Words

This section of each chapter gives a selected set of English words translated into the subject language. The chosen words are more or less uniform for all the entries to give the reader the chance to see family resemblances, and possible patterns that might emerge from language-specific phonological changes that occur within a family. Wherever applicable, information on dialectal variation in the lexical items in question is provided here for each entry, as are specific notes dealing with semantic scope and usage.

Example Sentences

Contributors were asked to supply three sentences with interlinear glosses and free translations for this part of the article. In some cases, these sentences illustrate points made in the syntax section of each chapter, but usually they were chosen just to give readers a cursory look at the basics of the morphology and syntax of each language.

Efforts to Preserve, Protect, and Promote the Language

Although this section is not always germane, as most of the languages documented in the encyclopedia are vibrantly spoken with some sort of official recognition, this section is included to detail the history and legacy of language history and preservation programs for "endangered" languages. Languages that do not have official status in their respective countries or that have a history of governmental repression are detailed here, as well as national languages with a long literary tradition.

Select Bibliography

This section gives the standard grammars, dictionaries, and linguistic works for each language. Contributors were asked to restrict their entries to works done in English, unless the documented language does not have a good history of scholarship in the English-speaking community.

ACEHNESE

Mark Durie

Language Name: Acehnese. **Alternates:** Achinese, Achehnese. **Autonym:** Basa Acèh.

Location: Northern tip of Sumatra and coastal plains.

Family: Achinese-Chamic subgroup of the Malayic group of the Sundic branch of the Western Mayalo-Polynesian subfamily of the Austronesian language family.

Related Languages: Cham, and other Chamic languages in Vietnam, Cambodia, and on Hainan Island (China). More distantly, MALAY-INDONESIAN.

Dialects: Main dialect areas are (1) West Aceh; (2) South Aceh; (3) Daya; (4) North/East Aceh (the standard); (5) Pidie, and (6) Greater Aceh.

Number of Speakers: 2.5–3.5 million.

Origin and History

Acehnese is one of the major regional languages of Indonesia, spoken by approximately two and a half million people in the Special Region of Aceh, on the northern tip of Sumatra. There are also communities of speakers in Medan, North Sumatra, and Malaysia.

Acehnese is related historically to the Chamic languages, now spoken on the Southeast Asian mainland in Vietnam, Cambodia, and Hainan, China. The members of this family are the linguistic remnants of the ancient Hindu kingdom of Champa, which was located from the 2nd century A.D. on the coast of what is today Vietnam. It is likely that the ancestors of the Acehnese came to Sumatra from Champa, perhaps to establish a trading outpost. After Champa declined in power from c. A.D. 1000 the connection between it and Aceh would have gradually faded from memory. The evidence of present-day dialects suggests that Greater Aceh and Daya on the west coast of the Malay peninsula form the oldest Acehnese-speaking areas, for these are where the greatest dialect variation is to be found.

The Acehnese traditionally divided their region into many small *nanggroe* 'kingdoms'. In 1292 Marco Polo visited six kingdoms in North Sumatra. He named them and described them as each having its own language. Five were on the Acehnese coast: Ferlec (Perlak), Basman, Samara, Dagroian, and Lambri; while the sixth—Daya—was on the west coast. Even today some Acehnese dialects are not mutually intelligible. The dialects of Daya are particularly archaic and idiosyncratic as they are isolated from Greater Aceh by a narrow, rocky stretch of coastland. Dialects in both regions differ even among neighboring villages, but where good roads and transportation exist, linguistic convergence is being accelerated. The speech of the North Aceh region has acquired prestige partly because the speakers tend to use more polite forms of pronominal reference, and the dialect has become something of a standard.

The term *Aceh* first appears in the historical record after 1500, when it was used to refer to the port kingdom of Banda Aceh. The extent of the Acehnese language today owes much to the expansion of that kingdom, which began during the time of Sultan Ali Mughayat Syah in the early sixteenth century. In the space of five years Daya, Pidie, and Pase were subjugated. At least as important for linguistic history as this political expansion was the constant migration to the east and west coasts in succeeding centuries. Many people moved to sparsely settled areas to plant pepper, an important export from Aceh until the late 19th century. This migration was especially marked from Pidie, and up to the present the people of Pidie are renowned for their enterprising trading, which still leads them to migrate to regions outside their own.

The Acehnese have had a long tradition of trilingual literacy in ARABIC, Malay, and Acehnese. From Greater Aceh come several early Malay texts which deal with the activities, customs, and personalities of the port kings in Banda Aceh. The oldest manuscripts in Acehnese date from the 18th century, redactions which appear to derive from as far back as the mid-17th century (Voorhoeve, 1993). Acehnese has a rich written literature, which traditionally was written in an Arabic script. Today Acehnese is also written in Roman script, in agreement with *Bahasa Indonesia*, the national language of the Republic of Indonesia.

Acehnese also has a rich oral literature. The traditional *hikayat* epic poetry is still recited today, especially in less developed areas. Dance forms are accompanied by poetic recitation.

Orthography and Basic Phonology

Most Acehnese manuscripts (and some contemporary printed books) are in the *Jawi*, an Arabic-derived script transmitted via Malay, which was never standardized and is far from the ideal of a phonemic orthography.

A standard orthography has been developed by a team of scholars at Universitas Syriah Kuala. It is based on the orthography of Indonesian. (See consonant table on the following page.)

s is a lamino–alveo–dental obstruent with a wide channel

Table 1: Consonants

		Bilabial	Alveolar	Palatal	Velar	Uvular	Glottal
Stops	Voiceless	p	t	c	k	k	
	Voiced	b	d	j	g		
Fricatives			s	ih			h
Liquids			l			r	
Nasals	Plain	m	n	ny	ng		
	Funny	mb	nd	nj	ngg		
Semivowels		w		y			

area. It is produced with the front part of the tongue (not the tip) close to the alveolar ridge. To English speakers it sounds like a cross between /s/ and /th/. In some dialects of Acehnese, it is pronounced almost like *t*, but it is still perceptually quite distinct from *t*, which is produced with the tongue tip touching the alveolar ridge.

ih is a palatal fricative. It is similar to German *ch* in *ich* and to *h* in English words like *heel* and *huge*. It occurs only word-finally, in stressed syllables, and can be regarded as an allophone of /s/.

r is a uvular approximant. In other dialects it is an apical trill, with a tapped allophone.

Final *k* is a glottal stop.

The "funny" nasals are slightly longer than 'plain' nasals, but the principal perceptual feature that distinguishes 'funny' from 'plain' nasals is that after a 'funny' nasal the following vowel is not nasalized, whereas vowels following plain nasals are themselves nasalized. Acehnese 'funny' nasals correspond diachronically with prenasalized voiced stops in other Austronesian languages. "Funny" nasals occur only in stressed syllables.

Table 2: Vowels

	Front	Back	
	Unrounded	Unrounded	Rounded
High	i	eu	u
Mid–high	é	ë	ô
Mid–low	è		o
Low		a	

Some dialects also have a mid-low back unrounded vowel *ö*.

Nasal vowels are marked by ', e.g., s'uep [sũp] 'lungs'.

Almost all Acehnese vowels have nasal counterparts. These nasalized vowels occur both following plain nasal consonants and in words with no nasal. In addition, there are two kinds of diphthongs in Acehnese. First, /i è u o eu/ can combine with *-e*, producing diphthongs /ie/, etc.; /ie/ is pronounced like English *ear*, as said by speakers who do not pronounce the *r* sound. In addition, /a ë u ô/ can combine with *-i*, producing diphthongs like /ai/, etc.; /ai/ is pronounced like the *i* in English *bike*.

Stress in Acehnese falls on the final syllable of the word. A clear distinction can be made between the sound structure of the stressed, final syllables of words on the one hand, and unstresed syllables on the other hand.

Most Acehnese words are mono- or disyllabic. Words of three or more syllables are usually borrowed, or derived by affixation from mono– or disyllabic words, e.g., *pumiyup* 'bury' from *miyup* 'low' or *pancuri* 'thief' from Malay *pəncuri*.

Syllables may end only in: *p, t, k, ih, h, m, n, ŋ, y*. Final stops are unreleased.

There are very few consonant clusters in Acehnese. These occur word initially, and always have *h, r,* or *l* as their second consonant, e.g., *lhom* 'drop', *pheuet* 'chisel', *dhoe* 'forehead', *trieŋ* 'bamboo', *jroh* 'beautiful', *srah* 'wash' *jlueŋ* 'kick', and *bloe* 'buy'.

Basic Morphology

Acehnese has no inflectional morphology. Corresponding to the verb inflection of other languages, Acehnese has a set of clitics. While these function like verb agreement markers, they are not obligatory in the way agreement suffixes in languages like Spanish are.

Although Acehnese has no inflectional morphology—it does not mark for gender, case, person or number—it does have derivational morphology, using prefixation and infixation to form words from other words. The more basic pattern is that of prefixation: even the infixes are "pre-fixed" in that they insert into the first syllable of a word, never into the final syllable. For example, *peuneugöt* 'something made, product' is derived from the verb *peugöt* 'to make' by infixation of *-eun-* following the initial consonant; the function of *-eun-* is to derive nouns.

Basic Syntax

Acehnese has no fixed order of constituents. Word order is not used to encode grammatical relations. The main single constraint on the ordering of grammatical relations is that a clause only has one Core Topic. A Core Topic may be defined as the core NP preceding its predicate or the subject in Acehnese. There can only be one Core Topic in a sentence. Except for this constraint, any ordering is possible. In particular, a verb may come first followed by its Agent and Undergoer in either order:

ka-lôn-poh lé-lôn ureueng-nyan
IN-1sg-hit agent-1sg person-that
'I hit that person.'

ka-lôn-poh ureueng-nyan lé-lôn
IN-1-hit person-that agent-1sg
'I hit that person.'

Contact with Other Languages

The Acehnese lexicon includes borrowings from a number of languages; among them are Mon-KHMER, SANSKRIT, Malay, Arabic and to a lesser extent, TAMIL, PORTUGUESE, DUTCH, and ENGLISH.

The Mon-Khmer borrowings include terms associated with kinship, hunting, and foraging, which suggest an intimate level of contact that might include intermarriage and shared participation in subsistence activities. This would appear to predate the breakup of the Proto-(Aceh)-Chamic family: most of the Mon-Khmer borrowings that have been identified in reconstructions of Proto-Chamic have regular reflexes in Acehnese. The most plausible context for an early period of borrowing of this nature is an extended period of habitation by the Austronesians on the mainland before the ascendancy of the Kingdom of Champa, thus before the 2nd century A.D.

Sanskrit borrowings date from at least the 2nd century A.D., as may Arabic borrowings. Both these loans are characterized by a relatively narrow semantic domain, encompassing, e.g., religion, the legal code, government, war, the arts and the sciences. In this respect, the contrast with Mon–Khmer borrowings is striking.

For centuries there has been extensive borrowing from Malay, the traditional language of the royal courts and scholarship. Today educated people often sprinkle their speech with Indonesian words and idioms, sometimes because there may be no suitable Acehnese word for a modern concept, but often this is a way of expressing one's educational status.

European words have in many cases come via Malay or Indonesian.

From Mon-Khmer: *keumueun* 'nephew, niece', *ya* 'old man, ancestor', *cah* 'chop, clear forest', *rèt* 'graze'
From Sanskrit: *beuet* 'read', *jeuet* 'become', *yo?* 'yoke', *catô* 'chess'
From Arabic: *maw'ot* 'corpse', *syok* 'doubt, suspicion', *rabu* 'Wednesday', *seudenkah* 'charity, alms'
From Malay: *pancuri* 'thief'
From Persian: *nisan* 'gravestone'
From Dutch: *potr'èt* 'photograph'

Common Words

man:	ureueng agam	long:	panyang
woman:	ureueng inong	small:	ubit
water:	ie	yes:	nyo
sun:	mata uroe	no:	kon
three:	lhèe	good:	got
fish:	eungkôt	bird:	cicém
big:	rayëk	dog:	asèe
tree:	bak kayèe		

Example Sentences

(1) Raja ji–coh lé uleue.
king:3sg -bite subj snake
'The king was bitten by a snake.' (literally: 'The king, a snake bit him.")

(2) Bôh ta–buka treuk pintô.
Do! 2sg-open right.away door
'Open the door right away.'

(3) ta–teubiet treuk gata di sinan.
2-exit right.away you from here
'You come out of there right away.'

Efforts to Preserve, Protect, and Promote the Language

Acehnese has shifted in the past ten to fifteen years from the first language of preference of all Acehnese people to a language often not acquired by children of parents who are fluent in Indonesian. Urbanization, the mass media, and universal education are all causing Indonesian to advance into wealthy and educated Acehnese society at the expense of Acehnese. Increasingly, fluency in Acehnese is a mark of a village upbringing.

Select Bibliography

Bukhari Daud and Mark Durie. 1999. *A Trilingual Acehnese Lexicon and Thesaurus.* Canberra: Pacific Linguistics and Universitas Syiah Kuala Press.

Durie, Mark. 1985. *A Grammar of Acehnese on the Basis of a Dialect of North Aceh.* Dordrecht, Holland: Foris Publications.

____. 1995. "Acehnese." In *Comparative Austronesian Dictionary,* ed. Darrel T. Tryon, 405–418. Trends in Linguistics: Documentation. Berlin: Mouton de Gruyter.

——. Forthcoming. "Aceh: Poetry and Performance." In Ann Kumar, ed., *The Temple of Language.* Jakarta: Lontar.

Voorhoeve, P. with T. Iskandar. 1993. *Catalogue of Acehnese Manuscripts in the Library of the University of Leiden and Other Collections Outside Aceh.* Ed. and trans. M. Durie. Leiden: E.J. Brill and The Leiden University Press.

AFRIKAANS

Paul T. Roberge

Language Name and Autonym: Afrikaans. Formerly Cape Dutch (*Kaapsch-Hollandsch*), Boer Dutch, and *Afrikaansch-Hollandsch* 'African Dutch', from which the current name is derived.

Location: South Africa and Namibia (formerly South West Africa).

Family: Germanic branch of the Indo-European language family.

Related Languages: The European base of Afrikaans lies in dialectal and vernacular Early Modern DUTCH. In its written form, Dutch is understood without great difficulty by educated Afrikaans speakers—and vice versa. With a modicum of effort, speakers can usually follow the spoken standard of the other language. Structurally, Afrikaans does not diverge radically from Dutch, although it has undergone drastic inflectional simplification and there are differences to overcome in the phonemic inventories, segmental rules, and prosody. Afrikaans shows a high degree of lexical correspondence with Dutch, although some words are archaic, dialectal, or semanticaly divergent.

Dialects: (1) Cape Afrikaans extends from Cape Town and the Boland (Stellenbosch, Paarl) along the Atlantic coast to approximately the Olifants River in the north and eastward along the south coast to the Overberg district (east of the Hottentots Holland Mountains) and the Little Karoo. It is represented in its most extreme form by the vernacular of the Cape "Coloureds". The sectarian Cape Muslim community of Cape Town, which numbers perhaps 130,000 or so, is treated in some respects as a separate linguistic subgroup. (2) Orange River Afrikaans, which shows a more pronounced Khoikhoi influence, is spoken by people of color in the northwestern Cape (Namaqualand), in Namibia up to the Etosha Pans, and in the southern Free State (with an offshoot near Kokstad in southeastern KwaZulu-Natal). (3) Eastern Cape Afrikaans emerged among the Voortrekkers along the eastern frontier in the mid nineteenth century and was introduced by them into what became the South African Republic (Transvaal, 1852, and the Orange Free State, 1854).

The standard language developed between roughly 1900–1930 and is drawn mostly from the Eastern Frontier variety, with adlexification from Dutch in learned vocabulary.

A more or less pidginized variety of Afrikaans called *Fly Taal* (Afrikaans *Flaaitaal*) is spoken by thousands of Africans living in townships surrounding Johannesburg, Pretoria, and other industrial cities.

Number of Speakers: Afrikaans is the home language of 6.2 million people in South Africa (out of a total population of about 44 million people). Afrikaans is spoken as a second or third language by an indeterminate but very large number of Black South Africans (who speak Bantu languages), Asians, and English-speaking Whites.

Afrikaans is the first language of about 152,000 speakers in Namibia. It did not retain official status with independence (1990), but it remains the dominant lingua franca of Namibia's total population of about 1.6 million.

Origin and History

Roughly half of the native speakers of Afrikaans are descended from the original Dutch, German, and French settlers at the Cape of Good Hope and have called themselves *Afrikaners* (formerly also *Boere* 'farmers'). The other half are people who trace their ancestry to the indigenous Khoikhoi (whom Europeans called "Hottentots"), Free Blacks, enslaved peoples of African and Asian origin, and Europeans.

In 1652, the Dutch East India Company established a station at the Cape of Good Hope for the servicing of its ships and the refreshment of crews. The European presence expanded gradually through natural increase, emigration from the metropole (including Huguenot refugees from France in 1688–89), and Company employees electing to take their discharge at the Cape—a very large number of whom were from northern Germany. The French and German émigrés were rapidly absorbed into the Dutch stream. From the first quarter of the 18th century, a growing number of Europeans moved inland and established themselves as migrant farmers (*trekboere*). Company rule came to an end in 1795, when Great Britain occupied the Cape. European expansion into the interior intensified when Afrikaner emigrants began leaving the Cape Colony to avoid British rule, culminating in the Great Trek (1835–48).

The Khoikhoi were the first South Africans to confront the Dutch at the Cape of Good Hope. The smallpox epidemic of 1713 decimated their population, by which time their traditional economy, social structure and political order had almost entirely collapsed in the southwestern Cape. The gradual advance of European settlement destroyed independent Khoikhoi groups, absorbed others, and drove still others deeper into the interior. By 1800, there were few Khoikhoi in the colony who were not in the service of the Europeans as farm laborers and domestic servants. Along the northern frontier, the class of Cape Dutch–speaking Khoikhoi who had been in service came to be known as *Oorlams*; one such group pushed into present-day Namibia at the beginning of the 19th century.

Pluralization of the early Cape society was furthered during the 17th and 18th centuries by the importation of slaves from tropical Africa, Madagascar, the Indian subcontinent, Ceylon, and the Indonesian archipelago. The Cape was ill-suited for plantation agriculture, and there were no large individual slaveholders, save for the Company itself.

The *Bastaards* were of mixed European, Khoikhoi, and slave parentage. From this class there emerged in the early 19th century a series of Cape Dutch–speaking communities along and to the north of the Orange River known collectively as *Griqua*. In the mid nineteenth century, a group of Bastaards settled in Rehoboth in Namibia.

Many scholars consider Afrikaans a semicreolized language, although this has long been a matter of controversy. Khoikhoi who had dealings with the settlers spoke jargonized forms of Dutch but continued to speak their own language among themselves until the mid eighteenth century, at which time their dialects began to disappear from the western Cape. The contact languages within the slave community were Creole PORTUGUESE, MALAY, and restructured forms of Dutch. Interethnic communication between slaves and Khoikhoi led to the emergence of a stable Cape Dutch pidgin between 1658 and 1713; this pidgin was introduced into outlying areas by retreating Khoikhoi, manumitted slaves, and maroons. It went to the brink of creolization, only to pull back due to ongoing contact with Europeans, who comprised a very high percentage of the colony's population. The input for first-language acquisition of Afrikaans in the language-shift generations within this non-European group was the variety of Dutch spoken by the settlers alongside the stable pidgin. Europeans accepted features from the substrate vernacular and likewise influenced it. It is customary to date the existence of Afrikaans as a language separate from Dutch to the period between 1750 and 1800.

The first truly Afrikaans texts are some doggerel verse from 1795 and a short dialog transcribed in 1825 by a Dutch traveler. From the 1830s we find letters to newspapers written in the vernacular (usually in a jocular vein) and some comic sketches. At about the same time, a tradition of writing Afrikaans with Arabic orthography arose within the Cape Muslim community, even though the first published text—the *Bayânudîn* ['An Explanation of the Religion'] of Abu Bakr Effendi—was not printed until 1877.

Starting in the 1870s, language served as a unifying factor in the Afrikaner drive for political empowerment. Dutch continued to function as the language of religion, education, and elevated writing; it was the official language of the Boer republics, and from 1882 it was permitted in the Cape parliament. However, Dutch had become a virtual foreign language, and ENGLISH threatened to replace it in most "high" functions. From 1875, the *Genootskap van Regte Afrikaners* ['Society of True Afrikaners'] sought to foster ethnic solidarity among Cape Afrikaners and establish Afrikaans as a written medium. A second language movement arose in the aftermath of the Anglo-Boer War (1899–1902), from which a literature of genuine merit emerged. The *Suid-Afrikaanse Akademie vir Wetenskap en Kuns* ['South African Academy for Science and Art'] was founded in 1909 to advance Afrikaans in scholarship, science, and the arts. As such, it has had a cultural and political mission, as well as a purely scientific one. In 1925 Afrikaans was recognized in lieu of Dutch as the second official language (alongside English) of the Union of South Africa. The first Afrikaans Bible appeared in 1933. The comprehensive *Woordeboek van die Afrikaanse Taal* ['Dictionary of the Afrikaans Language'] is being compiled at Stellenbosch University; ten volumes have appeared to date.

Orthography and Basic Phonology

The *Taalkommissie* ['Language Commission'] of the Academy compiles the *Afrikaanse Woordelys en Spelreëls* ['Afrikaans Wordlist and Spelling Rules', 8th ed., 1991], which is a widely accepted authority on orthographic norms.

Table 1: Consonants

	Labial	Alveolar	Palatal	Velar	Glottal
Stops	p b	t d		k gh/g	
Fricatives	f/v w/v	s		g	
Nasals	m	n		ng/n	
Lateral		l			
Trill		r			
Glides			j		h

Voiceless stops are unaspirated.

The voiced velar stop [g] occurs in loanwords, where it is often written *gh* (e.g., *gholf* 'golf'), variably between *r* or *l* and schwa, where it alternates with [x] (e.g., *berg* 'mountain' with [x] vs. *berge* 'mountains' with [g]), and in isolated words (*nege* 'nine').

A palatal stop occurs in the diminutive suffix *-tjie* [-ci]. Affixation of this suffix also causes the palatalization of certain preceding vowels (*pot* 'pot', *potjie* [pɔici] 'little pot').

The graphic alternation between *v* and *f* (e.g., *vis* 'fish', *fees* 'festival') is historical; both are pronounced [f]. *V* occurs as a voiced labiodental fricative in names and loanwords (*Venezuela, televisie*). [z ʃ ʒ tʃ dʒ w] also occur in foreign words and names.

H is a voiced (murmured) glottal approximant [ɦ]; *j* is a semivowel (as in English *year*); *r* is uvular in some regions. Word-final *t* and *d* are deleted when preceded by an obstruent in the same syllable: *nag* 'night' (cf. Dutch *nacht*), *hoof* 'head' (cf. Dutch *hoofd*); when a suffix is present, the etymological stops are preserved (*nagte* 'nights', *hoofde* 'heads'). In general, obstruents are devoiced word-finally: *hard* [ɦɑrt] 'hard', attributive *harde* [ɦɑrdə]. Loss of intervocalic *d* and *g* has resulted in morphophonemic alternations: *pad* 'road', *paaie* 'roads', *dag* 'day', *dae* 'days'.

The high vowels (see Table 2 on the next page) *ie*, *uu*, and *oe* are phonetically [i], [y], and [u]. The mid vowels *e*, *u*, *i*, and *o* are phonetically [ɛ], [œ], [ə], and [ɔ].

Table 2: Vowels

	Front		Central	Back
	Unrounded	Rounded		
High	ie	uu/u		oe
Mid	e, ê	u, û	i, î	o, ô
Low				a, aa/a

Afrikaans vowels can appear either long or short. The high vowels *ie*, *uu*, and *oe* are long before *r* and short elsewhere. Vowel length is indicated in the orthography in several ways: The long vowels and diphthongs signalled by the digraphs *ee*, *aa*, *uu* (before *r*), and *oo* are represented by single letters in open syllables (e.g., *boom* 'tree', *bome* 'trees'). A consonant letter can be doubled to indicate that the preceding vowel is short (e.g., *potte* [pɔtə] 'pots'). A circumflex accent over *e*, *u*, *i*, or *o* indicates that the vowel has been lengthened due to the loss of sounds (*lê* 'lay', cf. Dutch *leggen*); *û, î,* and *ô* are infrequent.

In addition to the above vowels, Afrikaans has a rich inventory of diphthongs: *ei/y* [əi], *ee/e* [eə], *ui* [œi], *ou* [œu, əu], *oo/o* [oə], *eu* [Øə], *oi* [ɔi], and *ai* [ai]. The vowels in words like *sneeu* 'snow', *draai* 'turn', *gooi* 'throw', and *groei* 'grow' are analyzed as double vowels rather than diphthongs. Diaeresis separates vowels that might otherwise be confused (e.g., *voël* 'bird' [foəl] vs. *voel* 'feel' [ful]).

Low and mid-low vowels are usually nasalized before *n* followed by a fricative, glide, or liquid (*mens* [mɛ̃:s] 'person').

Basic Morphology

Afrikaans shows extensive morphological simplification as compared to Dutch. There is no nominal case or grammatical gender. *Die* is the sole definite article and also functions as a demonstrative, along with the neologisms *hierdie* 'this' (lit. 'here the') and *daardie* 'that' (lit. 'there the').

The plural suffix *-s* is much more frequent in Afrikaans than in Dutch, while *-e* (Dutch *-en*) is correspondingly less frequent in Afrikaans. Afrikaans also has an associative plural, incorporating the third person plural pronoun *hulle* (e.g., *Theresa-hulle* 'Theresa-they, Theresa and her family/friends') or the morpheme *-goed* (e.g., *die baas-goed* 'the master and his people').

The first person plural oblique pronoun *ons* 'us' has replaced nominative *wij* 'we' in the grammatical role of subject.

Afrikaans has no subject-verb agreement. Except for certain auxiliary verbs, there is no preterit tense or distinction between finite and infinitival verb forms. The past participle is formed by adding the prefix *ge-* to the verbal root: *skryf* 'write', *geskryf* 'written'. When the past participle is used as an adjective, it may take a suffix and there may be alternations in the stem vowel: *geskrewe Nederlands* 'written Dutch'.

The major innovation in word formation is reduplication (from Malay): *staan-staan* 'stand-stand, i.e., standing'.

Basic Syntax

In Afrikaans the basic word order is Subject-Object-Verb, with verb-second (V2-) phenomena in main clauses. The order of elements within verb clusters is more fixed than in Dutch.

In simple sentences consisting of a subject and finite verb (and possibly a pronominal object), negation is expressed by the particle *nie* in sentence-final position:

Ek ken haar nie.
I know her NEG
'I don't know her.'

A negative marker is augmented by means of a sentence-final *nie* if the former occurs in the subject noun phrase or if the verb phrase contains a non-pronominal object, a predicate adjective or nominal, an adjunct, an infinitive, or a participle.

Geen mens praat nie.
no person speak NEG
'Not a person is speaking.'

Hulle kan nie lees nie.
they can NEG read NEG
'They cannot read.'

If a following embedded clause falls within the scope of negation, *nie* is normally placed in sentence-final position.

Tense, aspect, and mood are expressed periphrastically. The perfect is expressed by the auxiliary *het* 'have'. There is no pluperfect, although its meaning can be expressed by adverbials such as *al, al klaar* 'already'.

Under the influence of Creole Portuguese, the preposition *vir* 'for' is frequently used as an object marker before a human noun phrase:

Hulle ken vir ons baie goed.
they know OBJ us very good
'They know us very well.'

Contact with Other Languages

The historical contact languages have left their mark on the Afrikaans lexicon.

From Khoikhoi: *kierie* 'cudgel', *gogga* 'insect' *karos* 'skin coat, blanket'
From Malay: *baklei* 'fight', *baie* 'very'
From (Creole) Portuguese: *kraal* 'pen, corral', *tronk* 'jail', *sambreel* 'umbrella', *bredie* 'stew'

Contact with Bantu languages is chronologically secondary. Their influence lies chiefly in lexical borrowing in the spheres of culture (*indaba* 'council'), plant/animal names (*mamba* a kind of snake), and natural phenomena (*donga* 'gully').

Afrikaans has been in close contact with English for nearly two centuries, and today a very high percentage of Afrikaans speakers are bilingual in English. A number of English words have become fully integrated into Afrikaans (*gelling* 'gallon', *motor* 'motor, car', *tjek* 'check'), but many loans have been checked by Afrikaans equivalents (e.g., *hyser* 'elevator' for *lift*; *tiener* for *teenager*). Various bodies have existed to handle technical terminology, notably the *Vaktaalburo* ['Terminol ogy Bureau'], created in 1950 by the Academy and taken over by the state in 1977. Loan translation of English idioms is commonplace, especially in colloquial speech (e.g., *Ons het 'n dag af* 'We have a day off' for *'n vrye dag* 'a free day').

Common Words

no:	nee	man:	man
sun:	son	small:	klein
good:	goed	woman:	vrou
three:	drie	yes:	ja
bird:	voël	water:	water
fish:	vis	big:	groot
long:	lang (attributive), lank (predicative)	dog:	hond
		tree:	boom

Example Sentences

(1) Sy het nie ge-sê dat sy môre gaan
she has NEG PARTICIPLE-said that she tomorrow go

wen nie.
win NEG
'She didn't say that she is going to win tomorrow.'

(2) Dit was die seun-tjie wat beseer is se ouer-s.
it was the boy-DIM who injured is POSS parent-PL
'It was the parents of the little boy who was injured.'

(3) Ons kon hulle ge-help het, maar hulle
we could them PARTICIPLE-help have but they

wou nie ge-help word nie.
wanted NEG PARTICIPLE-help become NEG
'We could have helped them, but they did not want to be helped.'

Efforts to Preserve, Protect, and Promote the Language

Afrikaans was built up, promoted, and celebrated by National Party governments and Afrikaner cultural organizations. It is not astonishing that the result was a symbolic association of Afrikaans with racist nationalism. A watershed was reached on June 16, 1976, when thousands of Black schoolchildren in Soweto demonstrated against the government's mandate that certain primary subjects be taught in Afrikaans—as they saw it, the language of apartheid. The protest raged nationwide over the following year, and as many as 700 people were killed. The image of Afrikaans has not fully overcome this legacy.

South Africa's new constitution recognizes language as a fundamental human right. Afrikaans is today one of eleven official languages at the national level, and it enjoys constitutional protection along with the country's other languages. (Official languages in the provinces are determined according to regional demographics.) As of this writing, the debate over language policy is taking shape: Should there be a government-funded language plan? How can the indigenous languages be elaborated to a level where they can become mediums of commerce and power? Secondary and tertiary education in post-apartheid South Africa poses further language issues. Afrikaans-medium universities are likely to see further drift in the direction of dual- and/or parallel-medium instruction—de facto if not de jure. There is a proposal to establish a national body to coordinate the disparate activities of some 200 organizations that currently serve the Afrikaans language group. At this writing, support for such a body is mixed, and it is not yet clear whether some such entity could emerge as a viable advocate for the language as the debate unfolds.

The international standing of English virtually assures it a prominent role in most public domains in the new South Africa. Whether Afrikaans will maintain a similar status over the long haul remains to be seen.

Select Bibliography

Botha, T.J.R. *et al.* eds. 1989. *Inleiding tot die Afrikaanse Taalkunde* [*Introduction to Afrikaans Linguistics*], 2nd. ed. Pretoria: Academica.

Donaldson, Bruce C. 1993. *A Grammar of Afrikaans*. Berlin and New York: Mouton de Gruyter.

____. 1994. "Afrikaans." In Ekkehard König and Johan van der Auwera (eds.), *The Germanic Languages*. London and New York: Routledge, 478–504.

Ponelis, F.A. 1993. *The Development of Afrikaans*. (Duisburger Arbeiten zur Sprach und Kulturwissenschaft, 18). Frankfurt a. M.: Peter Lang.

Raidt, Edith H. 1983. *Einführung in Geschichte und Struktur des Afrikaans*. Darmstadt: Wissenschaftliche Buchgesellschaft.

____. 1991. *Afrikaans en sy Europese verlede*. [*Afrikaans and Its European Past*]. 3rd. ed. Cape Town: Nasou.

Roberge, Paul T. 1995. "The Formation of Afrikaans." In Rajend Meshtrie (ed.), *Language and Social History: Studies in South African Sociolinguistics*. Cape Town: David Philip, 68–88.

Akan

Samuel Gyasi Obeng

Language Name: Akan. **Alternate:** Twi-Fante.

Location: A large part of the coastal areas and middle belt (forest areas) of Ghana and southeastern Côte d'Ivoire.

Family: A Tano language of the Central Comoe branch of the Kwa subgroup of the Niger-Congo branch of the Niger-Kordofanian language family.

Related Languages: Anyi (Aowin), Sehwi, Nzema, Ahanta, Efutu/Autu, Anum, Kyerepong, and Larteh.

Dialects: The main dialects of Akan are (1) Fante, (2) Akuapem, and (3) Asante. Other minor dialects are Bron, Wasa, Agona, Akyem, Kwahu, Akwamu, Gomua, Ahafo, and Ajumako.

Number of Speakers: 6–9 million.

Origin and History

Speakers of the Akan language inhabit most of the coastal and middle belt (forest areas) of Ghana. They are found in the Brong-Ahafo, Ashanti, and Central Regions, and in parts of the Western and Eastern Regions of Ghana. The Akan peoples trace their ancestry to such places as Ancient Ghana and the Oasis of Djado (Boahen 1966), both of which are quite distant from present-day Ghana. The Akan peoples share the same cultural identity including a common 40-day calendar, marriage system, inheritance system, and religious beliefs.

Orthography and Basic Phonology

The Akan Orthography Committee was set up in 1952 to work out a unified orthography for the Akan language. Although it made a decision in 1978 on the form the unified Akan orthography should take, that decision has not yet been implemented. There are at present three orthographies for the three major dialects (Akuapem, Asante, and Fante). The orthographic notations are: a b d e ɛ f g h i k l m n o ɔ p r s t u w y.

Akan has 35 consonants, including six glides, as is shown in Table 1 below. Only the consonants *m* (all dialects), *ŋ* (Ak), *n* (Fa), and *r* (Fa) occur in word-final positions in the dialects put in parentheses. There are no voiced fricatives in Akan. Only stops and affricates have voiced and voiceless counterparts. The velar, glottal, pre-palatal and palatal consonants have labialized and non-labialized counterparts. All nasals, trills, laterals, and glides are voiced. No verbal, nominal, or adjectival stems begin with *r* or *ŋ*. The alveolar affricates occur only in the Fante dialects.

Akan has ten oral vowels, as shown in Table 3 on the next page. The Fante dialect, though, has nine. Fante has *e* in place of *æ*. The following vowels *i,ɪ,e,ɛ,a,ʊ*, and *u* have nasalized counterparts. Nasalization is contrastive in Akan. Akan has ATR vowel harmony so that in any word of two or more syllables, only vowels from either the +ATR set (*i, e, æ, o, u*) or the -ATR set (*ɪ,ɛ,a,ɔ,ʊ*) occur.

Table 1: Consonants

	Bilabial	Labiodental	Alveolar	Pre-palatal	Palatal	Velar	Glottal
Stops	p b		t d			k k^w g g^w	
Fricatives		f	s s^j s^w	ɕ ɕɥ			h h^w
Affricates			ts dz (Fa)	tɕ tɕɥ dʑ dʑɥ			
Nasals	m	ɱ	n		ɲ	ŋ $ŋ^w$	
Lateral			l				
Trill			r (Ak)				
Glides	w ɥ		ɹ	ɥ	j	w	

Table 2: Verbs

	Singular			Plural		
	Subject	Object	Genitive	Subject	Object	Genitive
First	me, m-	me	me, m'	yen, yɛ- h ɛn (Fa)	yɛn h ɛn (Fa)	yɛn h ɛn (Fa)
Second	wo, w-	wo	wo, w'	mo hom (Fa)	mo hom (Fa)	mo hom (Fa)
Third animate	ɔno, ɔ-	no	ne, n'	wɔn, w' hɔn (Fa)	wɔn hɔn (Fa)	wɔn hɔn (Fa)
Third inanimate	ɛno, ɛ- e-	no	ne, n'	e- ɛ-	Ø	wɔn
Third indefinite	obi			ebinom		

Table 3: Vowels

		Front	Back
High	+ATR	i	u
	-ATR	ɪ	ʊ
Mid-high	+ATR	e	o
Mid-low	-ATR	ɛ	ɔ
Low		æ	a

Akan has two basic tones: high and low. Although tones perform contrastive functions in the language, they are not represented in the orthography. Akan has both downdrift and downstep. Specifically, in any utterance, high tones with intervening low tones have their pitches lowered. In very long utterances, a final high tone may even be realized on a lower pitch than an initial low tone. Two kinds of downstepping, automatic and non-automatic, are found in Akan. The automatic downstep is found in downdrift situations. The non-automatic downstep is symbolized by the exclamation mark [!].

Basic Morphology

Akan does not exhibit overt gender marking on its pronouns. For example *ɔno* or its prefix *ɔ-* stands for 'she' and 'he' as well as for animate nouns. Inanimate objects are represented by the pronoun, *ɛno* or *ɛ-*. Akan has a 'vestigial' noun class system. Its once dynamic noun class system has seen considerable decay. The remnants of the previous nominal class system are seen in the present-day Akan singular and plural prefixes in which either a vowel or a homorganic nasal is used in plural formation: *etire* 'head', *atire* 'heads'; *abofra* 'child', *mmofra* 'children'; *ɔkyeame* 'spokesman', *akyeame* 'spokesmen'.

The plural forms of nouns are marked morphologically by prefixes, suffixes, reduplication, and the zero morpheme as follows:

Prefixes: *ɔ-bɔfo* 'messenger', *a-bɔfoɔ* 'messengers'; *dua* 'tree', *n-nua* 'trees'

Suffixes: *afɛ* 'colleague', *mfɛ-foɔ* 'colleagues'; *wɔfa* 'uncle', *wɔfa-nom* 'uncles'

Reduplication: *akuo* 'group', *akuo-akuo* 'groups'; *ɛpɔ* 'knot', *apɔapɔ* 'knots'

Zero morpheme: *aso* 'ear', *aso* 'ears'; *ani* 'eye', *ani* 'eyes', *anwea* 'sand', *anwea* 'sand pl'

Basically, Akan lacks an extensive concordial system that is based on noun class membership. However, a distinction between human and nonhuman nouns using the numerals two to nine, indicates that there may have been such a system in proto-Akan; for example, *mmofra baanu* 'two children'. The following is unacceptable: **akokɔ baanu* 'two fowls'.

Akan verbs have an obligatory root and optional suffixes. There are three verbal affixes: subject prefixes, tense/aspect affixes, and negative prefixes. The subject-concord prefixes as well as the pronouns are indicated in Table 2 above, with Fante variants indicated with Fa.

Negation is marked by a homorganic nasal which is usually said on a low tone: for example, *ɔfa* 's/he takes it', *ɔmfa* 's/he does not take it'; *ɔrefa* 's/he is taking it', *ɔmfae* 's/he is not taking it',*fa* 'take it', *ɛmfa* 'don't take it'. Tense and aspectual markers are indicated by affixes. The past tense marker is either *i* or *ɪ;* for example, *ɔfaɪ* 's/he took it' *odii* 's/he ate it'. The Asante dialect may in addition to *i* and *ɪ* use *yɛ*/*jɛ*; for example, ɔfaayɛ 's/he took it'. In all dialects when the verb is followed by an object or a complement, the final sound of the verb is prolonged: *ɔfaa nsuo no* 's/he took the water', *ɔtee ankaa no* 's/he plucked the orange', *ɔdɔmm ekuo no* 's/he joined the group'. The future aspect is indicated by *ɛ-* or *bɛ-* for example, *mɛfa* 'I'll take it', *ɔbɛfa* 's/he will take it'. The perfect aspect, however, is indicated by *a-*: *ɔafa*/*wafa* 's/he has taken it'.

Compound words in Akan undergo such phonological processes as homorganic nasal assimilation, vowel harmony, changes in the basic tonal systems, loss of final vowel/syllable, and nasalization of voiced plosives: *ɔhene* ' 'chief' /ɔhɪnɪ/ +

fie 'house' /fie/ becomes *ahimfie* 'palace' /ahiɱfie/ which is homorganic with /f/; the -ATR /ɪ/ vowel changes to +ATR /i/.

Basic Syntax

The basic word order in Akan is SVO, as in *Kofi dɔ Ama* 'Kofi loves Ama'; *Ohia yɛ adammɔ* 'poverty is madness', *ɔbra yɛ ɔko* 'life is war'. However, Akan basic word order may be changed from SVO through the use of emphatic markers, such as *ɔdɔ na Kofi wɔ* 'Kofi has love/It's love Kofi has'. In Akan there is no obligatory subject verb agreement. Adverbial elements may either precede or follow the verb, for example: *Ntɛm na Kofi dae* or *Kofi daa ntɛm* 'Kofi went to bed early.'

The negative marker *n* precedes the verb phrase but follows the subjejct, for example: *Kofi mpɛ basabasa* (Kofi NEG-like trouble) 'Kofi doesn't like trouble.'

Beyond the simple sentence, Akan, like most languages of West Africa, may exhibit more complex sentences in the form of verb serialization and other complex constructions. The following is an example of verb serialization in Akan:

Kofi tɔ-ɔ nsuo nomoeɛ
(Kofi buy-PERF water drink-PERF)
'Kofi bought water and drank it.'

Contact with Other Languages

Akan, ENGLISH, and HAUSA constitute the three major lingua francas in Ghana. Akan has considerably influenced the surrounding indigenous languages, particularly Ga and Dangme, the Guang languages, EWE, and the Togo-Remnant languages, notably Siwu, Buem, and Adele. It has also had some influence on DAGAARE, Dagbane, and other Gur languages.

Akan has long been in contact with English and has borrowed extensively from it. Some of the words borrowed are in the areas of religion, politics, science, and technology. Akan has also borrowed a few words from other Ghanaian languages (notably Ga) as well as from PORTUGUESE.

From English: *poopu* 'pope', *fada* 'Rev. Father', *asɛmbiri* 'assembly', *krakye* 'clerk', *trata* 'tractor'

Common Words

man:	ɔbarima (Ak/As); banyin (Fa)
woman:	ɔbaa (Ak/As); basia (Fa)
water:	nsu
sun:	owia
three:	mmiɛnsa
fish:	apataa
big:	kɛseɛ (As); kɛse (Ak/Fa); bodɛɛ (Fa)
long:	tenten (Ak/As); tsentsen (Fa)
small:	ketewa (Ak/As); ketseketse/kakrabaa (Fa)
yes:	aane (As) Yiw; (Ak) inyew
no:	daabi (all dialects); ooho (Fa)
good:	papa
bird:	anomaa
dog:	ɔkraman (Ak/As); ɔtwea/bɔdɔm (Fa)
tree:	dua

Example Sentences*

(1) Merehwɛ abofra no
I.PROGRESSIVE.observe child the
'I am observing/looking after the child.'

(2) Metɔɔ ntama no maa Kofi
I.buy.PAST cloth the give.PAST Kofi
'I bought the cloth for Kofi.'

(3) Me na medii aduan no
I EMPH I.eat.PAST food the
'I ate the food.'

*All sentences are in Akuapem-Twi

Efforts to Preserve, Protect, and Promote the Language

Akan is one of the major national languages of Ghana; the others are Dagaare, Dagbane, Dangme, Ewe, Ga, Gonja, Guruni, and Nzema. Akan is a major lingua franca, particularly in the fields of religion, commerce, education, and politics. In the Guang- and Ga-speaking areas, it is either used concurrently with the local languages or has replaced them in churches, schools, and law courts.

The Bureau of Ghana Languages, as well as other privately owned publishers, publishes books in the three major dialects of Akan: Akuapem, Asante, and Fante. Akan is taught from the primary school to the university level. The universities of Ghana and Cape Coast award postgraduate degrees in Akan. The non-formal section of the Ministry of Education also teaches Akan to adults.

Select Bibliography

Akrofi, C.A. 1943. *Twi Kasa Mmara* [Twi Grammar]. Longman: London.

Berry, J. 1957. *English, Twi, Asante, Fante Dictionary*. London: McMillan.

Boahen, Adu. 1966. "The Origin of the Akan." In *Ghana Notes and Queries*, 9:3–10.

Dakubu, Kropp M.E., ed. 1988. *The Languages of Ghana*. New York: Kegan Paul International for the International African Institute.

Dolphyne, F.A. 1988. *The Akan (Twi-Fante) Language; Its Sound System and Tonal Structure*. Accra: Ghana Universities Press.

Welmers, W.E. 1946. "A Descriptive Grammar of Fante." In *Language* 22:3.

Akkadian

Benjamin R. Foster

Language Name: Akkadian is the modern term for the Semitic language known from Mesopotamian inscriptions from about 2400 B.C. to the Christian era. The autonym *akkadītu(m)* refers to the Semitic language spoken and written in Mesopotamia from at least the beginning of the second millennium B.C. to the Christian era. The native designation(s) for the Semitic languages known from third-millennium Mesopotamia and neighboring regions are unknown. In the third millennium, *akkadītu(m)*, if in use, probably referred to a regional dialect of a Semitic language spoken in northern Babylonia. Thus the modern term may be broader than the autonym.

Location: Akkadian was spoken and written in ancient Mesopotamia, corresponding roughly to modern Iraq.

Family: East Semitic branch of the Semitic language family of the Afroasiatic language group.

Related Languages: Akkadian is related to the newly discovered North Semitic languages of third-millennium Syria and Mesopotamia (Eblaite, Archaic Mari) and less closely to the West Semitic languages, such as ARAMAIC and BIBLICAL HEBREW, or to the South Semitic languages, such as ARABIC.

Dialects: The oldest attested Akkadian—of the third millennium B.C.—is referred to as "Old Akkadian." This is a blanket term for a relatively small corpus of material from southern Mesopotamia, within which regional features can be detected.

After the turn of the second millennium B.C., Akkadian is divided into two main dialects, Assyrian and Babylonian. The Assyrian dialect, spoken and written in northern Mesopotamia, and centered around the city of Assur, is divided into Old (2000–1750 B.C.), Middle (1500–1000 B.C.), and Neo-Assyrian (1000–600 B.C.). Assyrian disappeared with the destruction of the Assyrian empire by the Medes at the end of the seventh century B.C. The Babylonian dialect, originating in southern Mesopotamia, is divided into Old (1900–1500 B.C.), Middle (1500–1000 B.C.), Neo-Babylonian (1000–600 B.C.), and Late Babylonian (600 B.C. to the beginning of the Christian era). Babylonian was gradually replaced by Aramaic.

There are also two literary dialects, both Babylonian in origin; one is called the "Hymnic-Epic Dialect," from the first half of the second millennium B.C. the other called the "Standard Babylonian Dialect," which was the form of the language favored for formal written expression from the middle of the second millennium on.

Local written dialects are known from specific groups of documents, such as from Mari in Syria (19th–18th centuries B.C.), and Nuzi in Mesopotamia (15th–14th centuries B.C.). The international diplomatic and scholarly language in the form best known from Syria, Palestine, and Anatolia is referred to as "Western Peripheral Akkadian."

Origin and History

The history of Akkadian is long and complicated, spanning two millennia and a wide geographical area. In the last half of the third millennium B.C., several related Semitic languages or dialects were used in northern Syria and Mesopotamia. A people living near the confluence of the Diyala and Tigris rivers called themselves "Akkadians" and their land was known as "Akkad." After about 2300 B.C., the Akkadians established an empire embracing much of Mesopotamia and northern Syria for about 150 years. This was regarded in later Mesopotamia as a turning point in their history. Because of the prestige of the Akkadian dynasty, the names Akkad and Akkadian came to mean the northern half of Babylonia, from roughly the point the Euphrates River enters the Mesopotamian floodplain to an undefined transition line about fifty miles south of present-day Baghdad, between the Tigris and the Euphrates rivers. With the collapse of this empire about 2150 B.C. and subsequent immigration around 2000 B.C. of the Amorites (Semitic-speaking peoples originally from northern Syria), Akkadian came to refer to (1) the Semitic language of Mesopotamia, as opposed to SUMERIAN, and (2) the "native" inhabitants of Mesopotamia, regardless of ethnicity or speech (Sumerian may have ceased to be a living language by then), as opposed to the newcomer Amorites. The language thereafter spoken in Mesopotamia was considered one language by its speakers and called "Akkadian," despite dialectal differences, the most important being the division between Assyrian and Babylonian.

Old Babylonian is often thought of as the "classical" phase of the language. In that period, for example, the cases are in regular and consistent use, but later they tend to disappear, become more simplified, or show inconsistencies.

Akkadian was used as an international diplomatic and scholarly language throughout western Asia as far West as Egypt, Cyprus, Anatolia, and the cities of Syria and Palestine in the second half of the second millennium B.C. (most sources date to the end of the14th and the 13th centuries).

Orthography and Basic Phonology

Akkadian was written using the cuneiform writing system, a syllabic-logographic writing apparently invented by the Sumerians around 3000 B.C. to write their own language, and adapted for Old Akkadian. After substantial reforms, cunei form was used to write both Assyrian and Babylonian until the Christian era. The clay tablet was the most common medium for cuneiform writing. The signs were impressed with a stylus; inscriptions on stone, metal, and waxed writing boards are also known. Towards the end of the second millennium B.C., the cuneiform writing system began to be displaced by the alphabets that appeared in western Asia, especially the Aramaic alphabet. It was forgotten until it was deciphered in the 19th century.

Since Akkadian was written with a system originally intended for another language, the inventory of signs does not correspond well to Semitic or Akkadian phonology. The writing system uses signs for words (logograms), signs for syllables (CV, VC, CVC), and "determinatives," markers for certain broad semantic classes, such as sex, profession, object of wood, stone, metal, clay, or geographical name. Most word signs were Sumerian words intended to be read in Akkadian; for example, the Sumerian sign KA was read as Akkadian *pû(m)*, 'mouth', and inflected according to context. Most word signs can also be syllabic, for example, Sumerian KA can be read as the Akkadian syllable /ka/. Most syllabic signs can also have logographic readings, or "values." Most syllabic signs are polyvalent; for example, the syllabic sign UD can also be read as *ut, u, tam, tu, par, pir, laḫ, liḫ, bir, ḫad, ta*, and others, besides being a word sign for 'day', 'sun', 'dry', and 'white or silver', each standing for a different Sumerian word.

Syllables may be written with more than one sign: over twenty signs can be read GI, for example, though not all in the same period. Most word signs are also polyvalent: the sign used for 'mouth' can also mean 'word', 'tooth', 'speak', or 'nose', with a different word read in each instance as well as a different Akkadian equivalent. Signs may be combined so as to yield a reading different from the constituent parts; for example, UD+DU makes a word sign for 'go out', read in Akkadian as a form of the verb *(w)aṣû(m)*, inflected according to context. For basic literacy, a command of several hundred polyvalent signs is required; for scholarly purposes perhaps 3000 or more readings of 500 signs or more in both Sumerian and Akkadian.

The phonological inventory of Akkadian varies by period and dialect. The Old Babylonian dialect and main literary dialect consonants include:

Table 1: Consonants

		Labial	Dental/ Alveolar	Alveo- palatal	Velar	Uvular
Stops	Voiceless	p	t ṭ		k	q
	Voiced		d		g	
Fricatives	Voiceless		s ṣ	š	ḫ	
	Voiced		z			
Nasals		m	n			
Laterals			l, r			

Akkadian consonants could occur either single or geminate (doubled).

The dental /t/ had an emphatic equivalent /ṭ/, which may have been accompanied by a velar or pharyngeal constriction, as in Arabic, or may have been ejective, as in Ethiopian Semitic languages. Likewise, the emphatic /ṣ/ may have been an affricate [ts], as in English *hoots*. /ḫ/ was a voiceless velar fricative [x]. Older stages of Akkadian had, in addition to the consonants charted above, a voiced labio-velar glide [w] and a voiceless lateral fricative *ś* [ɬ].

Phonetic change, such as assimilation, dissimilation, vowel harmony, and nasalization, varies by dialect and period of the language. Some common changes include: change of intervocalic /w/ to /m/, change of /š/ to /l/, change of /lt/ to /ss/.

Table 2: Vowels

	Front	Central	Back
High	i		u
Mid	e		
Low		a	

Vowel length was phonemic in Akkadian. In transliterations of Akkadian, vowel length is generally indicated with a macron (*ā*). If the long vowel represents the coalescence of two original vowels, a circumflex is used instead (*â*).

Basic Morphology

Akkadian morphology is built on roots. Roots may be nominal and irreducible, such as *kalb-* 'dog', or verbal, such as ŠPUR 'write to'. Verbal roots are groups of consonants, often three, in a fixed order with an associated stem vowel. The verbal root is susceptible to prefixing, infixing, and suffixing.

Nouns, whether from verbal or nominal roots, are marked for number (singular, dual, plural) and case. There are two grammatical genders, masculine and feminine. The various forms of *awīlum* 'man' and *aššatum* 'wife' are illustrated below:

	Masculine		**Feminine**	
Case	Singular	Plural	Singular	Plural
Nominative	awīlum	awīlū	aššatum	aššātum
Accusative	awīlam	awīlī	aššatam	aššātim
Genitive	awīlim	awīlī	aššatim	aššātim

Some feminine nouns, like *erištum* 'wish', have a *t* following the noun stem; others, like *ummum* 'mother', represent female entities. Dual forms are marked by the suffix *-ān* in the nominative and *-īn* in the other cases.

Adjectives generally agree with the nouns they modify in number, gender, and case.

Nouns and adjectives under certain conditions are further marked with a suffixed *-m*, referred to as *mimation*. This is regular in Old Babylonian but unsystematic thereafter. It has no effect on meaning.

Akkadian pronouns have common gender first person singular and plural forms, and second and third person forms distinguish masculine and feminine in most instances. Pronouns exist in independent forms and forms that are suffixed to verbs or, to indicate possession, to nouns.

The Akkadian verbal system is built from four principal verb stems. The same root may occur in more than one stem, but most roots occur in only some stems. (The 'names' of the stems come from the forms of the root *PRUS* 'decide'.)

Stem	Form	Example	Gloss
G (I)	iprus	ikkis	'he cut'
		ibluṭ	'he lived'
D (II)	uparris	unakkis	'he cut (two or more things)'
		uballiṭ	'he revived'
		uraggib	'he roofed' (< *rugbu* 'roof')
Š (III)	ušapris	ušamqit	'he felled' (< MQUT 'fall')
		šumruṣāku	'I am very sick (<MRUṢ 'be sick')
N (IV)	ipparis (<inparis)	ipparik	'it was blocked off'
		ibbašši	'it becomes'

In addition to the above stems, there are additional stems used only in poetry or in some dialects, plus special stems for quadriliteral verbs (those with roots of four consonants).

For each stem there are three aspects or tenses: the preterite, the perfect, and the present-future. A fourth tense, the stative or permansive, marks subject-verb agreement exclusively with suffixes. Some inflected forms of the G (I) stem of *PRUS* 'decide' are illustrated below:

Tense	Form	Gloss
Preterite	iprus	'he decided'
Perfect	iptaras	'he has decided'
Present/Future	iparras	'he will decide'
Stative	parsat	'it was/is decided'

Verbs agree with their subjects in person, number, and gender; agreement is marked by a combination of prefixes and suffixes:

	Singular	Plural
1st person	a-prus	ni-prus
2nd person, m	ta-prus	ta-prus-ā
2nd person, f	ta-prus-ī	
3rd person, m	i-prus	i-prus-ū
3rd person, f	i-prus[1]	i-prus-ā

A verbal infix *ta* may be used with the first three stems and any tense to indicate mutual, passive, separative, or other specialized meanings. From the root MḪUR 'face', the present GB stem is *imaḫḫar* 'he faces'; with infixed *ta*, the form is *imtaḫḫaru* 'they face one another'.

A verbal infix *tan(a)* may be used with all stems to denote iterative or sequential action: from *ŠPUR* 'write', *ašapparakkum* 'I will write to you', *aštanapparakkum* 'I will write to you constantly'.

Verbs may be in the indicative mood, which takes no specific marking, or the subjunctive mood, marked with the suffix *-u* (or *-ni* in some dialects). The subjunctive is required in subordinate clauses, and may also be used to express strong assertions, such as oaths.

Basic Syntax

The basic word order in Akkadian is SOV with variations for emphasis and in poetry. VSO order is typical of narrative poetry. Many sentences do not contain any overt nouns.

Adjectives normally follow the nouns they modify, as do relative clauses: *awīl-um damq-um* (man-NOM.SG good-NOM.SG) 'the good man', *awīl-um ša i-kšud-u* (man-NOM.SG that 3SG.M-come.PRETERITE-SUBJUNCTIVE) 'the man who came'.

Constructs (nominal compounds) are common. In many constructs, the first noun will change form and will lose its case endings: *šipr-um šipir awīl-im* (message-NOM.SG message man-GEN.SG) 'the man's message'.

Sentences are negated by *ul* (older *ula*) in main clauses and *lā* in subordinate clauses and before modal verbs. *Ul* immediately precedes the verb it negates. *ul u-š-erib-šu* (NEG 3SG-CAUSATIVE-enter-ACCUSATIVE.3SG) 'He did not let him enter', *lā ta-šappar-ī* (NEG 2SG-write-2SG.F) 'You must not write.'

Contact with Other Languages

Early Akkadian was heavily influenced by Sumerian, a non-Semitic language in use in Sumer, or southern Babylonia, during the third millennium. Sumerian enjoyed great prestige as a cultural language even long after its disappearance as a living language sometime in the early second millennium, such that Mesopotamian literate culture may be considered bilingual at all periods. Sumerian had significant influence on Akkadian phonology, morphology, syntax, and vocabulary.

Hurrian, a non-Semitic language found in northern Mesopotamia in the second half of the second millennium, contributed various loanwords to the Akkadian of its time.

Numerous words are considered Amorite or West Semitic in origin, entering Akkadian with the Amorite migration in the early second millennium or through conquests by the Assyrians and Babylonians in northern Syria in the late second and first millennia.

Although Akkadian was gradually displaced by Aramaic in the first millennium, the high cultural prestige of Akkadian made it resistant to influences of Aramaic, although these can be documented, especially in vocabulary and syntax. In the Achaemenid and Hellenistic periods, various old PERSIAN and GREEK loanwords, especially in the area of government and administration, entered the latest dialects of the language.

From Sumerian: *ekallu(m)* 'palace'
From Amorite: *niššīku(m)* 'leader'
From Hurrian: *altapipa* 'trunk, coffer'
From Kassite: *allak* 'felly, rim of chariot wheel'
From Elamite: *kidinnu* 'divine protection'
From Aramaic: *sepīru* 'scribe'
From Old Persian: *aḫšadrapannu* 'satrap'
From Greek: *istatirru* 'stater' (a coin)

In the opposite direction, Sumerian borrowed from Akkadian *ma.da* 'land' and *sa.tu* 'mountain'.

Common Words

man:	amēlum (earlier: awīlu(m))
woman:	sinništum
water:	mû

[1] In early and late dialects, *ta-prus*

sun:	šamšum
three:	šalāš
fish:	nūnum
tree:	iṣum
long:	arkum
small:	ṣeḫrum
yes:	anna
no:	ulla
good:	ṭâbum
bird:	iṣṣūrum
dog:	kalbum

Example Sentences

(1) inūmi ta-š-tan-appar-an-ni
when 2SG.M-constantly-write.PRES.FUT-DAT-1SG

a-qbī-šum
1SG-say.PRETERITE.DAT-3SG
'After you kept writing to me so many times, I spoke to him.' (from an Old Assyrian letter)

(2) mimma bēl-ī i-šappar-an-niāšim ni-ppeš
anything lord-1SG 3SG.M-write-DAT-1SG 1PL-do.PRES.FUT
'Whatever my lord writes us, we will do.'

(3) puḫāt-im l-i-ddin-ū-nikkum ul
substitute-M.OBL.PL let-3-give-3PL-DAT.2M.SG NEG

damiq
good:M.SG
'Even if they (=let them) give you substitutes, it is not satisfactory.' (from an Old Babylonian letter)

Efforts to Preserve, Protect, and Promote the Language

Akkadian was rediscovered in the nineteenth century from clay tablets excavated in Iraq and brought back to Europe. A crucial discovery was a trilingual inscription (in Old Persian, Akkadian, and Elamite) of Darius I at Behistun, Iran. The Old Persian enabled decipherment of the cuneiform writing, and when Akkadian was recognized to be a Semitic language, analysis of the language was rapid. The main outlines of its grammar were reconstructed by 1930. Disputes remain on many points including phonology, morphology, and syntax. For many of the most important dialects, there is no descriptive grammar yet available. The first comprehensive grammar was published in 1952; the first comprehensive dictionary was completed in 1981.

Select Bibliography

Gelb, I. 1969. *Sequential Reconstruction of Proto-Akkadian.* (Oriental Institute of the University of Chicago, *Assyriological Studies*, no. 18). Chicago: University of Chicago Press.

Oriental Institute of the University of Chicago. 1959– . *The Assyrian Dictionary*. Glückstadt, Germany: Augustin.

Reiner, E. 1966. *A Linguistic Analysis of Akkadian. (Janua Linguarum, Series Practica* XXI). The Hague: Mouton.

____. 1970. 'Akkadian.' In *Current Trends in Linguistics*. Ed. T. Sebeok, 6:274–303. The Hague: Mouton.

Ungnad, A., and Matouš, L. 1964. *Grammatik des Akkadischen*, 4th ed. Munich: C.H. Beck Verlag.

von Soden, W. 1969. *Grundriss der akkadischen Grammatik.* (*Analecta Orientalia* 33.47). Rome: Pontificium Institutum Biblicum.

Albanian

Gary Bevington

Language Name: Albanian. **Autonym:** *shqip*. The presumed origin of the [*alban/arban*] root from which the English and other foreign designations (albanaise, albanisch, arnavutça, etc.) derive was the name of an Illyrian tribe, the *albanoi*. The root has been lost by the Albanians themselves. However, Albanian speakers in Italy and Greece whose ancestors emigrated during Ottoman times use *arbëresh* and *arvanitika* respectively as autonyms.

Location: The Republic of Albania, adjacent countries of Yugoslavia (Serbia and Montenegro), and Macedonia. Greece and Italy have Albanian-speakers who have been there since Ottoman times as well as modern immigrants. There are also Albanian-speakers in the Middle East (particularly in the cities of Istanbul and Damascus) whose ancestors arrived during Ottoman times. Recent immigrants from Albania are found in Europe (particularly Germany, Italy, Belgium, and France), North America (particularly Boston; Detroit; and Bronx, NY), and Australia.

Family: Albanian comprises a one-language subfamily of Indo-European.

Related Languages: All of the Indo-European languages. In addition, Albanian shares a special non-genetic typological relationship with some of its Balkan neighbors, which together make up the Balkan linguistic union (BLU). (See Contact with Other Languages.)

Dialects: (1) Gheg, spoken in northern Albania and adjacent areas of Yugoslavia and Macedonia, and (2) Tosk, upon which the standard is based, spoken in southern Albania and adjacent Macedonia. The examples in this article are in Standard (or Literary) Albanian, which is Tosk-based.

Number of Speakers: 5–6 million.

Origin and History

While there is virtual unanimity that the Albanians and their language have been present in the Balkans for a very long time, longer indeed than many of their neighbors such as the Slavs and the Romance peoples (Romanians, Vlachs, etc.), it is not clear which of the ancient peoples of the Balkans and their associated languages are the ancestors of the Albanians. Native scholars have long claimed the Illyrians as their ancestors, but non-Albanian scholars feel that the evidence to prove this conclusively has not yet been put forth.

Albanian's place within the Indo-European language family has been intensively investigated and has revealed some unique characteristics. In 1854 the linguist Franz Bopp published *Über das Albanesische in seinen verwandschaftlichen Beziehungen,* in which he showed that while Albanian is a member of the Indo-European family, it is unrelated to any other member of that family in a subgrouping. Albanian has been an esoteric puzzle for specialists who have tried to work out the sound changes and grammatical changes that account for the relationship between the reconstructed IE proto-language and Albanian as it is known.

The earliest documentation of Albanian is a single sentence, a baptismal formula, from the year 1462. Continuous texts in the language begin with a Catholic missal (*Meshari*) by Gjon Buzuku from 1555.

The Ottoman invasion and conquest of the Albanian homeland in the15th century brought about numerous changes for the Albanians and their language. Some Catholic Albanians fled across the Adriatic and settled in enclaves in Sicily and Calabria on land granted to them by local princes. Some Orthodox Albanians migrated south into Greece, settling in enclaves in many areas including the Peloponnese and Thrace. Many Albanians converted to Islam. Some of them came to play leading roles in the political, military, and cultural life of the Ottoman Empire, primarily through the institution of the *devshirme*, or child-harvest, by which non-Turkish communities were required to ante up a certain number of their brightest boys for training and service at the Port. Several grand viziers of the empire as well as many of the Janissaries, the elite fighting forces, were of Albanian origin.

Albanians migrated throughout the region under Ottoman control and, even today, Albanians are found in Istanbul, Damascus, and elsewhere in the Middle East. In the 17th and 18th centuries as the Serbs migrated northward out of the 'old kingdom' in the valley of Metohija and the plain of Kosovo into the Danubian plain, Albanians in substantial numbers migrated into the relatively empty lands. Today in Kosovo, a substantial majority of the population is Albanian.

Sixteenth and 17th century documentation of Albanian is almost exclusively from the Catholic north using a modified Latin alphabet. In the late 18th and early 19th centuries Orthodox and Muslim texts appear, the former written in the Greek alphabet and the latter in Turko-Arabic script. During the 19th century various attempts were made to establish either an autonomous Albanian alphabet (e.g., the alphabet of Veqilharxhi) or a Latin-based one with a number of distinctive additional letters (e.g., the Istanbul alpha-

Table 1: Consonants

		Labial	Interdental	Alveolar	Alveo-palatal	Palatal	Velar	Glottal
Stops	Voiceless	p		t		q	k	
	Voiced	b		d		gj	g	
Fricatives	Voiceless	f	th	s	sh			h
	Voiced	v	dh	z	zh			
Affricates	Voiceless			c	ç			
	Voiced			x	xh			
Nasals		m		n		nj		
Laterals				l		ll		
Tap				r				
Trill				rr				
Glide						j		

bet of the Frashëri brothers and the Jesuit Scutarene alphabet). Two Latin alphabets were promulgated by the Congress of Manastir in 1908. The Agimi alphabet, named after the literary society which promoted it, augmented the basic Latin letters with diacritics, while the Bashkimi alphabet, the product of another literary group, relied primarily on the principle of digraphy (using two letters which the phonotactics of the language generally do not bring together to represent one sound, e.g., English or Albanian *sh*). After the Congress, the Bashkimi system quickly became dominant with only the *ç* and *ë* (see Orthography and Basic Phonology, below) using diacritics.

The changes in the structural features of the language during the period of documentation are modest in quantity and quality, comparing favorably with the changes in written English over the same time frame (i.e., comparing the language of Spenser to the written standard of today).

Orthography and Basic Phonology

As described above, Albanian is written in a lightly-adapted variant of the Latin alphabet.

The Albanian palatals /q gj/ are stops produced with the rear portion of the tongue contacting a relatively broad area of the hard palate. These stops are unlike any in American English.

The Albanian affricates /c x/ are comparable to the sounds represented by the underlined segments in English *ca<u>ts</u>* and *a<u>ds</u>*. The affricates /ç xh/ are pronounced like the initial sounds in English *church* and *judge*.

Albanian is unusual in having two distinct lateral sounds. The alveolar /l/ is very similar to the *l* sound in English *leap*, while the velar /ll/ is very similar to the *l* sound in English *fool*. Unlike in English, the two laterals contrast in Albanian: *djali* 'the boy' has an alveolar lateral, while *djalli* 'the devil' has a velar lateral.

Albanian allows a large number of initial consonant clusters of two and three consonants including nasal+stop(+r), e.g. *mbret* 'king', *ndreq* 'to repair'.

Table 2: Vowels

	Front		Central	Back
	Unrounded	Rounded		
High	i	y		u
Mid	e		ë	o
Low			a	

Albanian /ë/, while generally described as a mid central unrounded vowel, is further back than English /ʌ/ in *cup*.

Stress in Albanian is generally predictable, falling on the final vowel of the word stem.

Basic Morphology

Albanian nouns have two full grammatical genders: masculine and feminine, and a small residual number of neuters. Adjectives (both attributive and predicative) and pronouns agree with the gender of the nouns they modify or have as antecedents.

djali trim
boy brave
'the brave boy'

vajza trim-e
girl brave-FEM
'the brave girl'

Postposed articles are incorporated as inflectional suffixes on the nouns which reflect gender as well as case.

Indefinite	Definite	
një student	student-i	masculine nominative sing.
një student	student-in	masculine accusative sing.
një student-i	student-it	masculine genitive/dative sing.
një student-e	student-ja	feminine nominative sing.
një student-e	student-en	feminine accusative sing.
një student-eje	student-es	genitive/dative sing.
student-ë	student-ët	nominative/accusative plural
ca student-ëve	student-ëvet	genitive/dative plural
student-ësh	student-ëvet	ablative plural

Every noun, therefore, has both a definite and indefinite declension including plurals for count nouns. Albanian has three full cases: nominative, genitive-dative, and accusative, and a partial fourth case: ablative, distinct from the genitive-dative only in the indefinite plural. Case is reflected in noun inflection, adjective and demonstrative agreement, and pronouns, and is determined by sentential function and government of various prepositions of all cases including nominative and ablative.

Albanian has a rich system of verbal inflection. Verbs agree with their subjects in person and number. There are three simple tenses: present, imperfect, and aorist; and four compound tenses: perfect, pluperfect, future, and future perfect. For most verbs, the simple tenses are all based on the same stem, but use different sets of endings; a substantial minority of verbs has two stems, one for the aorist (based on the stem for the optative mood), and one for the other simple tenses. A few verbs have an additional stem for the infinitive. There are also different sets of endings for verbs ending in a vowel and verbs ending in a consonant. The imperfect conjugation of the verb *punoj* 'work' is illustrated below:

	Singular	Plural
first person	puno-ja	puno-nim
second person	puno-je	puno-nit
third person	puno-nte	puno-nin

The first person plural present tense form is *puno-jmë* and the aorist equivalent is *punua-m*. The future tense is built on the auxiliaries *do të* followed by an inflected verb. The future tense endings overlap with those of the present, but are not identical to them. The three perfect tenses are composed of inflected forms of the auxiliary verb *kam* 'have', followed by the participle. Some first person plural forms of *punoj* are illustrated below:

Tense	Form
Perfect	kemi punuar
Pluperfect	kishim punuar
Future Perfect	do të kemi punuar

In addition to indicative and subjunctive moods, Albanian also has an *admirative* mood, used to express the speaker's belief that the action described is true but somehow unexpected: *Gëzim po punuaka* means '(Surprisingly), Gezim is working'.

Also part of the Albanian verbal complex is a set of clitic object pronouns which, although usually separated orthographically from the verb, are phonologically attached to it. Clitics are mostly attached to the beginning of the verb complex (proclitics) but in some cases (e.g., imperatives) are attached at the end (enclitics). The third person clitics may also be present with overt objects generally when these are definite, and also with the 'full' (non-clitic) first and second object pronouns. Their function is then essentially one of agreement.

djal-i	j-a	dha	vajzë-s
boy-M/NOM/SG	DAT/SG-ACC/SG	give-AORIST/3SG	girl-F/DAT/SG

dhuratë-n
present-F/ACC/SG
'The boy gave the girl the present.'

In this sentence, the clitic *ja* is a combination of the dative singular clitic *i* and the accusative singular clitic *e*. Clitics occur not only with nouns but also with pronouns. Both the full pronoun and the clitic are found in *Ty të falenderoj shumë* 'Thank you very much'. The pronoun *ty* can be omitted; however, if the clitic *të* is omitted, the sentence is ungrammatical.

Albanian shows all morphological processes associated with the Indo-European languages: affixation, compounding, vowel gradation (ablaut), and reduplication, although the latter appears not to be inherited from Indo-European but is rather a relatively late innovation. Inflection is predominantly affixation, particularly suffixation, with a residual amount of inherited ablaut in the conjugation, as in English. The derivational morphology is predominantly affixation, with prefixes and suffixes much like English and the Romance languages; the former is relational, numerical, and negative; the latter determines category and general semantic characteristics. Compounding is also used in Albanian word formation, somewhat more heavily than in the Romance languages but less than in the Germanic languages. As in many Indo-European languages, the residue of ablaut in the derivational morphology is slight and so elusive that it is only evident when pointed out by specialists. The reduplication, as mentioned above, is quite transparent involving the successive repetition of a word (rarely a bound morpheme) with usually intensive or distributive significance.

The structural similarities of Albanian morphology with the pattern typical of the Romance languages, particularly in the verbal morphology, are striking enough to have led one early student (G. Meyer) to characterize Albanian as "eine halb romanisierte Mischsprache" (a half-Romanized mixed language).

Basic Syntax

The order of major constituents in Albanian clauses is SVO, although case-marking of noun phrases permits reordering for stylistic and discourse purposes such as focus and topicalization. Placement of adjuncts is generally as free as in common European languages.

Major constituents are almost all head-initial. In noun phrases adjectives and clausal modifiers follow the nouns they modify.

djal-i	[që	po	e	lexo-n	libr-in]
boy-DEF/M/SG	[that	PROG	it:ACC	read-PRES/3SG	book-DEF/M/ACC]

'the boy that is reading the book'

In verb phrases auxiliaries precede the verbs but objects and complements follow. Prepositions precede their objects.

qen-i	[ka	shkuar	(nga	kopsht-i)]
dog-DEF/M/NOM	[has	gone	(from	garden-DEF/M/NOM)]

'The dog has gone from the garden.'

Verbal sentences are negated by the addition of the particle *nuk* (or its clitic variant *s'*) before the verb and any clitics associated with it.

as-kush	nuk	i	tha	as-një	fjalë
NEG-who	NEG	him/her:DAT	say:AORIST.3SG	NEG-a	word

mbi	situatë-n
about	situation-ACC/F

'No one said anything to him about the situation.'

In Albanian, unlike in English, words like 'someone' and 'something' are required to be negative in negative sentences. Prohibition ('don't') uses a different negative marker *mos*.

mos	e	prit	ditë-n	e	fund-it
NEG	it:ACC/SG	await	day-ACC/F	AGR.PARTICLE	end-GEN/M

'Don't wait for the last day!'

Contact with Other Languages

Albanian has been in constant contact with other languages for a very long time, and it has borrowed very heavily from them, with the result that the true native stratum of the vocabulary is almost astonishingly small, perhaps as low as ten percent.

From Greek: *mollë* 'apple'
From Latin: *kalë* 'horse'
From Slavic: *çekan* 'hammer'
From Turkish: *babë* 'father'
From French: *grevë* 'strike'
From Italian: *monedhë* 'coin'
From English: *miting* 'meeting'

The Balkan linguistic union (BLU), of which Albanian is a member, is defined on a set of shared innovative structural (mostly morpho-syntactic) features which are found in varying degrees in the Balkan languages. The primary languages of the BLU, (i.e., those showing a maximal number of so-called balkanisms) are, in addition to Albanian, Romanian (a Romance language) and Bulgarian and Macedonian (Slavic languages). Secondary Balkan languages showing some but not all of the symptomatic features are Serbo-Croatian, particularly the Torlakian dialect, and Modern Greek. The assumption is that the convergences among these languages are the product of long-term contact, particularly multilingualism, characteristic of the central area of the Balkan peninsula.

Except for the possibility that some of the balkanisms are of Albanian origin, the influence of Albanian on other languages has been minimal.

Common Words

man:	burrë	long:	i gjatë
woman:	grua	small:	i vogël
water:	ujë	yes:	po
sun:	diellë	no:	jo
three:	tre	good:	i mirë
fish:	peshk	bird:	zog
big:	i madh	dog:	qen
tree:	dru		

Example Sentences

(1)

kam	etje	dua	ujë
have:1SG/PRES	thirst	want:1SG/PRES	water

'I'm thirsty; I want water.'

(2)

Gjon-i	po	e	lexo-n	libr-in
John-NOM	PROG	it	read-3SG/PRES	book-ACC

'John is reading the book.'

(3)

Mbet-ëm	shumë	të	kënaqur
remain-1PL/PAST	very	AGR.PART	satisfied

'We were very pleased.'

Efforts to Preserve, Protect, and Promote the Language

The socialist period in 20th-century Albania was characterized by intense and largely successful efforts in the area of language standardization. Although a Gheg literary koiné had enjoyed dominance in the public life of the country in the period before World War II, the partisan leadership (largely Tosks) began efforts to promulgate a Tosk-based literary language almost as soon as it came to power with the liberation of the country in 1944. Early efforts were largely in the area of grammar until 1954 when the first normative Albanian dictionary, one of middle school format, appeared. By the late seventies larger and more ambitious lexical studies and preliminary studies for parts of a comprehensive normative grammar began appearing under the auspices of the Academy of Sciences section for linguistics.

The Gheg koiné continued in use as a written language in the Albanian parts of Yugoslavia, principally the Kosmet (later Kosovo) Autonomous region until 1968, when an agreement was reached to use the literary language being promulgated in Albania with Kosovar (and other Albanian-Yugoslav) participation in its development. From 1968 to 1980 Yugoslavia practiced a relatively enlightened policy toward the Albanians, allowing them to develop their own cultural and political institutions within the federal framework of Yugoslavia including a full Albanian-language educational system through university level with professional schools in law, medicine, and economics. Regrettably, disorders in Kosovo beginning in 1980 brought about the rise of Serbian nationalism and the subsequent disintegration of Yugoslavia. The Milosevic-led government of Serbia moved to dismantle the political and cultural institutions of the Albanians in Kosovo. The deteriorating predicament of the Kosovar Albanians led to U.S.-led NATO intervention in 1999, and so the province and its largely Albanian population, although technically still part of Serbia, is now under a military administration involving seven NATO countries and Russia.

Select Bibliography

Bevington, Gary. 1974. *Albanian Phonology*. Wiesbaden: Harrassowitz (Albanische Forschungen; Bd. 13).

Byron, Janet L. 1976. *Selection Among Alternates in Language Standardization: The Case of Albanian Contributions to the Sociology of Language*, no. 12. The Hague: Mouton.

Camaj, N. 1984. *Albanian Grammar*. Wiesbaden: Otto Harrassowitz.

Hysa, Ramazan. 1997. *Albanian Comprehensive Dictionary*. New York: Hippocrene.

Kiçi, Gaspar. 1976. *Albanian-English Dictionary*. Printed in Italy.

Kiçi, Gaspar, and Hysni Aliko. 1969. *English-Albanian Dictionary*. Printed in Italy.

Mann, Stuart. 1977. *An Albanian Historical Grammar*. Hamburg: Buske.

Newmark, Leonard, I. Kostallari, and D. Skendi. 1980. *Spoken Albanian*. New York: Spoken Language Services.

Newmark, Leonard. 1982. *Standard Albanian: A Reference Grammar for Students*. Stanford: Stanford University Press.

Newmark, Leonard (ed). 1998. *Oxford Albanian-English Dictionary*. Oxford: Oxford University Press.

AMHARIC

Monica S. Devens

Language Name: Amharic. **Autonym:** *Amarəňňa.*

Location: The country of Ethiopia located in Northeast Africa.

Family: Ethiopic subgroup of the South Semitic group of the Semitic subfamily of the Afro-Asiatic language family.

Related Languages: Closely related to the other languages of the Ethiopic subgroup: Argobba, Gafat, Gurage, Harari, Tigre, TIGRINYA, and GE'EZ, the language of the Ethiopian Orthodox Church. Distantly related to South Arabian in the South Semitic group, and more distantly still to the other languages in the Semitic subfamily, including ARABIC, HEBREW, ARAMAIC, and AKKADIAN.

Dialects: There are conflicting reports concerning dialectal variation by geographic area. Some claim significant differences in all aspects of the language—phonology, morphology, syntax, and vocabulary—while others maintain that the differences are minimal. In any case, details of these variations have not been sufficiently documented.

Number of Speakers: About 28 million. Of these 10–15 million are native speakers. In addition there are several hundred thousand speakers outside of Ethiopia.

Origin and History

It is generally assumed that a Semitic language—or possibly several different Semitic languages—was brought to Africa by traders from South Arabia sometime in the first millenium B.C. and was established on an originally Cushitic substratum.

The earliest written evidence of any Ethiopian Semitic languages is the inscriptions in Ge'ez found at Axum, Ethiopia's ancient capital, which dates from the 3rd or 4th century A.D. The earliest known Amharic writings—poems in praise of the emperor—are from the 14th century, although Amharic was not used with any regularity as a literary language until the late 19th or early 20th century.

The relationship between the oldest known Ethiopian Semitic language, Ge'ez, and the modern Ethiopian Semitic languages is the subject of considerable debate. Traditionally, Ethiopian Semitic has been understood as falling into two geographically-defined groups: North Ethiopic (Ge'ez, Tigre, and Tigrinya) and South Ethiopic (Amharic, Argobba, Gafat, Gurage, Harari, and many others), but many scholars no longer accept this view. Furthermore, even under the traditional understanding, the relationship between Amharic and Ge'ez was never clear. It is clear, however, that Ge'ez was a spoken language for a very short period of time only, and that it was supplanted by Amharic in the area immediately south of Axum probably by A.D. 1000–1200.

The central importance of Amharic derives from the fact that from its earliest existence until the Revolution of 1974 it was the language of the Ethiopian Court, both unofficially and officially. It was popularly called *ləsanä nəgus* or "the language of the King", and in this capacity served as the lingua franca of the Ethiopian Empire. Although its premiere status was challenged after the Revolution, it remains extremely important, and it is the dominant language in a country in which there are over seventy languages spoken.

Orthography and Basic Phonology

Amharic employs a syllabary system. Each grapheme has seven different shapes which represent a different vowel (or zero) added to the same consonant. Traditionally, these seven shapes are called "orders." The consonantal base of this syllabary is probably derived from the South Arabian writing system. The same syllabary is used by all the Ethiopian Semitic languages which have a written tradition.

The syllabary is deficient in two ways. First, there is no marking for geminated, or lengthened, consonants. Second, the "sixth order" symbol, the sign for consonant + schwa, can also stand for consonant + zero vowel; i.e., it is ambiguous.

Table 1: Consonants

		Labial	Dental	Palatal	Velar	Glottal
Stops	Voiceless	p	t	č	k	'
	Voiced	b	d	ğ	g	
	Ejective	p'	t'	č'	q	
Fricatives	Voiceless	f	s	š		h
	Voiced		z	ž		
	Ejective		s'			
Nasals		m	n	ň		
Liquids			l, r			
Glides		w		y		

The palatal 'stops' /č ğ/ are phonetically affricates corresponding to the initial sounds in English *church* and *judge*, respectively. The palatal nasal /ň/ is comparable to the *ñ* of Spanish *piñata* or the sequence *ni* in English *onion*.

The dental stops /t d/ differ from the corresponding English sounds in that the tongue is a little bit further forward; its tip touches the upper front teeth instead of the alveolar ridge. The liquid /r/ is a tap, similar to the English sound in the middle of the word *petty*.

The ejective stops /p' t' q/ represent an articulation not ordinarily used in English. In the production of /p'/, the oral closure for /p/ is accompanied by a simultaneous glottal closure like that for the glottal stop /'/. Amharic is unusual in that this double articulation is also used for an affricate /č'/ and a fricative /s'/.

All Amharic consonants can occur single or geminated.

Table 2: Vowels

	Front	Central	Back
High	i		u
Mid	e	ə	o
Mid-Low		ä	
Low		a	

The mid-low vowel /ä/ is phonetically [ɐ], like the vowel in the English word *cup*. The mid central vowel /ə/ is intermediate in height between the two vowels in English *brushes*.

All Amharic dental consonants, with the exception of /r/, are palatalized in verb forms when they are followed by a front vowel. Thus, /t/ becomes [č], /n/ becomes [ň], and /l/ becomes [ľ].

Basic Morphology

Amharic nouns can be masculine or feminine. Nouns themselves are not marked for gender, but there are different definite articles and demonstrative pronouns for masculine and feminine. The definite form of *bet* 'house', a masculine noun, is *bet-u* 'the house', and the definite form of *doro* 'hen', a feminine noun, is *doro-wa* 'the hen'. All nouns are pluralized by the addition of *-očč*: *bet-očč* 'houses'. Plural nouns are made definite by the addition of *-u*, regardless of gender: *set-očč-u* 'the women'.

There is no true case system in Amharic. However, definite direct objects are marked with a suffix *-n*.

Amharic pronouns are differentiated for gender in the second and third persons. There are also distinct second and third pronoun forms used for respectful address. The independent personal pronouns are illustrated below

	Singular	Plural	Respectful
First	əne	əňňa	
Second masc	antä	ənnantä	ərswo
Second fem	anči	ənnantä	ərswo
Third masc	əssu	ənnässu	əssaččäw
Third fem	əsswa	ənnässu	əssaččäw

In addition to the independent personal pronouns, Amharic has two sets of suffixed pronouns, one to indicate possession and one for pronominal direct objects. Thus, *bet-e* 'my house', *sämma-t* 'he heard her'.

The Amharic verbal system is quite complex. As with all Semitic languages, it has a system of root consonants which carry a basic meaning and which are then manipulated through a set of derived stems, generally expressed as prefixes, to refine the meaning. All roots do not appear in all stems, however. The resulting verbs agree with their subjects in person, number, and gender.

For example, the biradical root /b-l/ expresses the basic meaning 'to eat'. The third person masculine singular form in the perfect is *bälla* 'he ate'. In the derived *tä*-stem, which expresses a passive meaning, the corresponding form is *tä-bälla* 'it (masc) was eaten'. And, in the derived *a*-stem, which expresses a causative meaning, the corresponding form is *a-bälla* 'he fed' (literally, 'he caused to eat'). The corresponding third person feminine singular forms are: *bälla-čč* 'she ate', *tä-bälla-čč* 'it (fem) was eaten', and *a-bälla-čč* 'she fed'.

As illustrated above, the Amharic perfect is generally used to refer to past tense actions. The most common way of describing present or future actions is the compound imperfect, which incorporates forms of the verb *allä* 'there is'. The imperfect equivalents of the verbs illustrated above are:

	3sg masculine	3sg feminine
Basic	yə-bäl-al	tə-bäl-all-äčč
tä-stem	yəb-bäll-al	təb-bäll-all-äčč
a-stem	ya-bäl-al	ta-bäl-all-äčč

In Amharic, negation is expressed through verbal morphology. Perfect verbs are negated by adding the prefix *al-* and the suffix *-m*: *al-bälla-m* 'he didn't eat'. Negation of present and future actions is expressed by a different verb form, the simple imperfect, with the prefix *a-* and suffix *-m*: *a-y-bäla-m* 'he won't eat'. In subordinate clauses, the *-m* is omitted.

Basic Syntax

The preferred order of constituents in Amharic is SOV. If the direct object is definite, OSV order is also possible. Subordinate clauses precede the verb of the main clause:

astämari-w mäs'haf-očč-u-n əndi-y-mälləs-u
teacher-DEF book-PL-DEF-ACC in order-return/IMPERF-3PL

tämari-očč-u-n t'äyyäqä
student-PL-DEF.ACC ask-PERF/3SG MASC
'The teacher asked the students to return the books.'

Within noun phrases, modifiers precede the nouns they modify. If a noun phrase is definite, only the first element is marked as definite: *təlləq-u bet* (big-DEF house) 'the big house'. Positional relations are expressed by a combination of prepositions and postpositions.

bä-mäkina	kä-dabbo-w	wädä tämari bet
in-car	of-bread-DEF	to student house
'in a car'	'of the bread'	'to school'
bet-u wəst'	tärara-w lay	kä-bet-u wəč'č'
house-DEF in	mountain-DEF	of-house-DEF outside
'in the house'	'on the mountain'	'outside the house'

Contact with Other Languages

The vocabulary of Amharic is essentially made up of those words which have a Semitic base, either common or borrowed, and those which were borrowed from the underlying Cushitic languages. One lexicographical study estimated that almost 75 percent of Amharic roots are Semitic, 12 percent Cushitic, and 13 percent from other sources.

Numerous loanwords in the specific semantic area of religion came into Amharic from Aramaic and Hebrew through Ge'ez. Some of the loanwords from Arabic are ultimately of TURKISH or PERSIAN origin. A large number of animal and plant names are of Cushitic origin.

From Ge'ez: *haymanot* 'faith', *tabot* 'ark', *z-m-r* 'to sing psalms'
From Arabic: *däräga* 'rank', *tarik* 'history', *t'äbänǧǧa* 'rifle'
From Cushitic: *č'äw* 'salt', *zaf* 'tree', *leba* 'thief'
From Greek: *šənkurt* 'onion', *qäläm* 'ink'
From Italian: *mäkina* 'car', *fotograf* 'photograph', *gazet'a* 'newspaper'

Common Words

man:	säw	long:	räǧǧim
woman:	set	small:	tənnəš
water:	wəha	yes:	awo
sun:	s'ähay	no:	yälläm
three:	sost	good:	t'əru
fish:	asa	bird:	wäf
big:	təlləq	dog:	wəšša
tree:	zaf		

Example Sentences

(1) wəšša-w ləǧ-u-n näkkäsä
dog-DEF child-DEF-ACC bite:PERFECT/3SG.MASC
'The dog bit the child.'

(2) məst'ir-u-n lä-ləǧ lä-mən
secret-DEF-ACC to-child for-what

tə-nägr-all-äh
2SG.MASC-tell-IMPERF-2SG.MASC
'Why are you telling the secret to a child?'

(3) mäsob-u-n käft-äh
basket-DEF-ACC uncover-GERUNDIVE/2SG.MASC

dabbo-w-ən wəsäd
bread-DEF-ACC take:IMPER/2SG.MASC
'Having uncovered the basket, take the bread!'

Efforts to Preserve, Protect, and Promote the Language

In Ethiopia, Amharic is the language of national unity, unlike in many sub-Saharan countries where European languages fill that role, e.g., English in Nigeria and French in Ivory Coast. Of indigenous African languages, Amharic has the third largest speakership (after SWAHILI and HAUSA), and among Semitic languages, only Arabic is spoken by more people.

The 1987 Constitution of Ethiopia, inaugurating the People's Democratic Republic of Ethiopia, proclaimed Amharic the official language, restoring it to the position it had enjoyed prior to the Revolution of 1974. However, there is much greater linguistic freedom now than in earlier times when use of other languages was restricted, so that, for example, the courts and the media now use a multiplicity of languages. At present Amharic is the medium of instruction through grade 6 and will be extended to include higher grades as well.

Select Bibliography

Bender, Marvin L. 1976. *Language in Ethiopia.* Oxford: Oxford University Press.
____. 1992. "Amharic." In *International Encyclopedia of Linguistics*, ed. William Bright. 1:51–56. New York: Oxford University Press.
Kane, T. 1975. *Ethiopian Literature in Amharic.* Wiesbaden: Harrassowitz.
____. 1990. *Amharic-English Dictionary.* 2 vols. Wiesbaden: Harrassowitz.
Leslau, W. 2000. *Introductory Grammar of Amharic.* Wiesbaden: Harrassowitz.
____. 1995. *Reference Grammar of Amharic.* Wiesbaden: Harrassowitz.
____. 1976. *Concise Amharic Dictionary.* Berkeley: University of California.
____. 1973. *English-Amharic Context Dictionary.* Wiesbaden: Harrassowitz.

ARABIC

Michael G. Carter

Language Name: Arabic. **Autonyms**: al-ʻArabiyya, al-ʻArabiyya l-fuṣḥā (classical); al-Luġa l-ʻāmmiyya, al-ʻĀmmiyya (colloquial).

Location: The Arabian Peninsula (Saudi Arabia, Yemen, Kuwait, United Arab Emirates, Bahrain, Qatar, Oman); the Fertile Crescent (Jordan, Syria, Israel, Lebanon, Iraq); North Africa (Egypt, Sudan, Libya, Tunisia, Algeria, Morocco, Mauritania). Widely spoken in Muslim countries such as Nigeria, Djibouti, and Somalia, and an important literary language in all Muslim countries, such as Iran, Turkey, Pakistan, Indonesia, Central Asian states of the former Soviet Union, Afghanistan, and parts of India and China. Arabic is also an official language of the United Nations.

Family: West Semitic branch of the Semitic group of the Afroasiatic language family.

Related Languages: Ancient: PHOENICIAN, AKKADIAN, Ugaritic, HEBREW, ARAMAIC/Syriac, Old South Arabian, GEʻEZ (Ethiopia). Modern: AMHARIC, Tigre and TIGRINYA (Ethiopia), MODERN HEBREW and Aramaic/Syriac, Mehri, Soqotri (South Arabia).

Dialects: Modern dialects are extremely varied, even to the point of mutual unintelligibility, and every current geopolitical unit has at least one dialect peculiar to it. The differences are comparable to those found in English, e.g. Cockney (London) vs. Deep Southern (USA) or Australian. All are distinguished by their phonology, morphology and vocabulary, though it is the combination of features, rather than any single one, which characterizes them. The Arabic dialects may be classified as follows: (1) Western group: (i) Maghribi (Morocco and Algeria), Tunisian, Libyan; (ii) Egyptian (with many subvarieties, broadly Cairene, Alexandrian, Delta, Upper Egyptian, Beduin, and various oases); (iii) Sudanese; (2) Eastern group: (i) Palestinian, Jordanian, Syrian, Lebanese; (ii) Iraqi (where differences have also been observed among Muslim, Jewish, and Christian varieties); (iii) Gulf and Trucial States, Saudi, Yemeni. There are also African pidgins such as Ki-Nubi.

The difference between the dialectal and written ('formal') varieties of Arabic is now so extreme that the term 'diglossia' has been applied to the situation, i.e., that two different languages are in parallel use, selected by the context and function, viz. a dialect (=mother tongue) for informal communication and the acquired classical language for formal situations such as public speaking, religious discourse, and writing (there is to date relatively little literature in colloquial; mostly plays, poetry, and the dialogue in cartoons).

Number of Speakers: 150–185 million.

Origin and History

Arabic was originally the language of a small population of tribes in the Arabian Peninsula, for whom Classical Arabic may have served as a *koine* in addition to their own dialects.

Some secondary sources trace the Arabs (and therefore their language) back to the second millennium B.C., although the first unequivocal reference dates to the first millennium B.C. The Arabic writing system is ultimately derived from Aramaic (itself derived from Phoenician and thus distantly related to the Greek alphabet and its European descendants). The earliest inscriptions in Arabic language are all in non-Arabic scripts, the best known (but not the oldest) being the Nemara Inscription of A.D. 328, written in Aramaic script. Tomb inscriptions from the 6th century A.D. show the first clear signs of a specifically Arabic script, which was developed enough by the time of the Prophet Muhammad (died A.D. 632) for the text of the Qur'ān to be written down in the form known as Kūfic, which has striking similarities with the Syriac script.

The advent of Islam made Arabic into a world language and the vehicle of an enormously productive culture. At its peak, the Muslim Empire stretched from Spain to the borders of China, and for several centuries Arabic was the dominant language in all of these regions, and the first language in Islamic Spain (conquered in 711, not definitively reconquered until 1492). All Muslims then, and many still today, preferred to write in Arabic regardless of their ethnic origins, although the native languages (e.g., Persian and Turkish) gradually reasserted themselves as Arab power declined. Unlike Latin, Arabic never split up into discrete (Romance) languages; the Arabic text of the Qur'ān has preserved its spiritual and cultural authority and remains the unifying reference point for all linguistic developments.

Orthography and Basic Phonology

Arabic is written from right to left and has symbols for 28 consonants and three short vowels, the latter being inserted above or below the consonant which forms the onset of the syllable. Long vowels and the two diphthongs are indicated by combinations of the short vowel symbols with the letters /'/, /w/ and /y/, thus /a/ + /'/ = /ā/, /i/ + /y/ = /ī/, /u/ + /w/ = /ū/, /a/ + /w/ = /aw/, /a/ + /y/ = /ay/. There are signs for doubled and vowelless consonants, and to indicate that an initial glottal stop is to be elided in juncture. Syllables are normally either C-V or C-V-C, and no word can begin with a consonant cluster, including the

Table 1: Consonants

	Voi.	Labio-Dental	Labial	Inter-dental	Dental-Alveolar	Alveo-Palatal	Velar	Uvular	Pharyngeal	Glottal
Stops	-				t, ṭ		k	q		’
	+		b		d, ḍ	j				
Fricatives	-	f		ṯ	s, ṣ	š		ḫ	ḥ	
	+			ḏ	z, ẓ			ġ	‘	h
Nasals	+		m		n					
Resonants	+		w		l, r	y				

definite article. This is usually resolved by introducing a vowel (default *–i-* but sometimes *–a-* or *–u-*) to relocate the syllable boundary, e.g., *katabat # l-mu‘allimātu* is realized as *katabatil-mu‘allimātu* "the teachers-FEM wrote" (hyphens mark the new syllable distribution).

The dentals /d t s z/ have emphatic equivalents /ḍ ṭ ṣ ẓ/ in which the center of the tongue is lowered while the back is raised towards the velum. In modern dialects there is a tendency for /ḍ/ and /ẓ/ to merge. The uvular fricative /ġ/ is similar to the Parisian French /r/ and /ḫ/ to the German *ch* in *Bach, acht,* etc. /k/ is a front velar like English /k/ in *keep.* /q/ is pronounced with the back of the tongue and the soft palate, and has no English equivalent. In some dialects /k/ becomes /č/, while /q/ has several reflexes, among them /’/ in urban dialects, e.g., Egypt), /g/ (Bedouin dialects), and even /j/ (Gulf States).

Even though /j/ is charted with the stops its value varies in modern Arabic from /g/ (Cairo and much of Egypt) to /ğ/ as in French *jour* (Lebanon, Morocco), and /j/ as in English *jam,* predominantly in the Peninsula, Jordan, and Iraq. /h/ is voiced, unlike in English.

The fricatives /ḏ/ and /ṯ/ are retained in some modern dialects (especially Bedouin) but in urban dialects often split into /t/-/s/ and /d/-/z/, with the stops occurring in everyday words and the continuants being used for words felt to have a literary status, e.g., *tāni* ‘second’ (Class Ar. *ṯānī)* but *sānawī* ‘secondary’ (Class Ar. *ṯānawī*, a relatively erudite word).

Table 2: Vowels

	Front	Central	Back
High	i		u
Low		a	

All vowels can be long or short, and /a/ has a higher and lower variant according to environment. There are two diphthongs, /aw/ and /ay/, which usually reduce to /ō/ and /ē/ respectively in the colloquials.

Basic Morphology

A characteristic of Arabic morphology is the interplay between root and pattern, roots usually consisting of three consonants denoting the basic semantic notion and the patterns indicating grammatical function. Thus the nouns *kātib* ‘writer, secretary’ and *maktaba* ‘library, bookshop’ both use the radicals K-T-B,

The Arabic Script

Name	Translit.	Free	Final	Med.	Init.	Name	Translit.	Free	Final	Med.	Init.
alif	ā	ا	ـا	ـا	ا	*ẓā’*	ẓ	ظ	ـظ	ـظـ	ظـ
bā’	b	ب	ـب	ـبـ	بـ	*‘ayn*	‘	ع	ـع	ـعـ	عـ
tā’	t	ت	ـت	ـتـ	تـ	*ġayn*	ġ	غ	ـغ	ـغـ	غـ
ṯā’	ṯ	ث	ـث	ـثـ	ثـ	*fā’*	f	ف	ـف	ـفـ	فـ
jīm	j	ج	ـج	ـجـ	جـ	*qāf*	q	ق	ـق	ـقـ	قـ
ḥā’	ḥ	ح	ـح	ـحـ	حـ	*kāf*	k	ك	ـك	ـكـ	كـ
ḫā’	ḫ	خ	ـخ	ـخـ	خـ	*lām*	l	ل	ـل	ـلـ	لـ
dāl	d	د	ـد	ـد	د	*mīm*	m	م	ـم	ـمـ	مـ
ḏāl	ḏ	ذ	ـذ	ـذ	ذ	*nūn*	n	ن	ـن	ـنـ	نـ
rā’	r	ر	ـر	ـر	ر	*hā’*	h	ه	ـه	ـهـ	هـ
zā’	z	ز	ـز	ـز	ز	*wāw*	w	و	ـو	ـو	و
sīn	s	س	ـس	ـسـ	سـ	*yā’*	y	ي	ـي	ـيـ	يـ
šīn	š	ش	ـش	ـشـ	شـ	*lām-alif*	lā	لا	ـلا	ـلا	لا
ṣād	ṣ	ص	ـص	ـصـ	صـ	*tā’ marbūṭa*	*t/h*	ة	ـة	ـتـ	(-)
ḍād	ḍ	ض	ـض	ـضـ	ضـ	*hamza*	’	ء	ـئ ـؤ	ـؤـ	ـئـ ؤ إ أ
ṭā’	ṭ	ط	ـط	ـطـ	طـ	*(hamza also* أ ء *in other positions)*					

which indicate writing, with patterns denoting person who does the action and place where the action occurs respectively. These patterns are symbolized through the verb *fa'ala* 'he did' (note that this is also the citation form for the whole paradigm), hence *kātib* has the pattern *maktaba* and *fā'il* the pattern *maf'ala.* Words of the same pattern will therefore tend to have similar kinds of meaning, thus *mālik* 'owner', *ḥāmil* 'porter, carrier', *madrasa* 'school (place of studying)', *maḥkama* 'court (place of judging)'. Verbs follow the same system (see below).

Arabic nouns and adjectives are inflected for number (singular, dual, plural), gender (masculine, feminine), case (independent/nominative, basic marker *-u*, dependent/accusative, marker *-a*, oblique/genitive, marker *-i*), and definition (definite, indefinite), with masculine singular indefinite broadly being the unmarked form, and the feminine usually marked by the suffix *-at-*, e.g., *kātib-at-u-n* 'female secretary (nominative, singular, indefinite)'.

Definite nouns take the prefix *al-*, e.g., *al-kitāb-u* 'the book (nominative)'; indefinites take the suffix *-n*, after the inflectional vowel, e.g., *kitāb-u-n* 'a book (nominative)'. The *l* of the definite article is assimilated before apicals and dentals, and the *a*, though always present graphically, is always elided in juncture: it either take the vowel of the previous word (hence *bi-al-ra'si* 'with the head' is read and pronounced [bi-r-ra'si]) or a vowel (default *i*) is introduce to break up the consonant cluster (see above).

Dual nouns are marked by the suffix *–ā-*, e.g., *kitāb-ā-ni* 'two books' (DEP./OBL. *-ay-*, *kitāb-ay-ni*) between the stem and the indefinite suffix. Plurals are either sound (regular) or broken (irregular). Masculine sound plurals are formed by suffixing *–ū-* to the stem, e.g., *muslim-ū-na* 'male Muslims' (DEP./OBL. *–ī-*, *muslim-ī-na*); for feminines the suffix is *-āt-*, e.g., *muslim-āt-u-n* 'female Muslims' (DEP./OBL. *muslim-āt-i-n).* The so-called "broken" plurals involve a change of pattern, thus *kitāb* 'book' has the plural *kutub* 'books' and *madrasa* 'school' has the plural *madāris.* It is the change of pattern, not the pattern itself, which indicates plural: although there are some patterns exclusive to singulars or plurals (e.g., *mafā'il*, as in *madāris*, is always plural) many are found in both singular and plural, e.g., *fu'ūl*, as in *wujūd* 'existence' vs. *ẓurūf* 'circumstances' (plural of *ẓarf*).

Arabic has two sets of pronouns, suffixed and free, for first, second and third person in singular, dual (not in first person) and plural number. The free pronouns mostly occur as subjects, and the bound pronouns have possessive meaning when suffixed to nouns and objective meaning when suffixed to verbs. Gender is not marked in the first person or the dual. In the first person singular only there is a difference between possessive *-ī* 'my' and the objective *-nī* 'me'.

Arabic verbs occur in two aspects, perfect and imperfect. Perfect refers to actions either completed or regarded as such and imperfect to incomplete action, in neither case with a specific time connotation. Perfect verbs have only one conjugation, but the imperfect has three, an independent (indicative) for main verbs, dependent (subjunctive) for subordinate verbs, and apocopated (jussive) for certain conditional, negative and prohibitive functions. The future is marked by the prefix *sa-* on the independent/indicative, e.g., *sa-ya-ktub-u* 'he will write', though the unmarked imperfect can also have this meaning.

The perfect is inflected entirely by agent pronoun suffixes:

	Singular	Dual	Plural
1	*katab-tu*		*katab-nā*
2m	*katab-ta*	*katab-tumā*	*katab-tum*
2f	*katab-ti*	*katab-tumā*	*katab-tunna*
3m	*katab-a*	*katab-ā*	*katab-ū*
3f	*katab-at*	*katab-atā*	*katab-na*

The other verb forms are inflected by means of combined prefixes and suffixes:

	Singular	Dual	Plural
1	*'a-ktub-u*		*na-ktub-u*
2m	*ta-ktub-u*	*ta-ktub-ā-ni*	*ta-ktub-ū-na*
2f	*ta-ktub-ī-na*	*ta-ktub-ā-ni*	*ta-ktub-na*
3m	*ya-ktubu-u*	*ya-ktub-ā-ni*	*ya-ktub-ū-na*
3f	*ta-ktub-u*	*ta-ktub-ā-ni*	*ya-ktub-na*

In the dependent/subjunctive forms final *-u* becomes *-a.* and *-na*/*-ni* are dropped, except in the 2nd and 3rd feminine plurals, which remain unchanged in all three paradigms. Apocopated forms drop the *-u* and in all other respects are the same as the dependent.

The passive is formed by changing the vowels of the stem, thus *kataba* 'he wrote', *kutiba* 'it was written', *yaktubu* 'he writes', *yuktabu* 'it is written'.

Verbal derivation is accomplished by extensions of the basic pattern *fa'ala* (conventionally Stem I; the central vowel may vary). Each of the twelve Stems (there are more in Classical Arabic but they are exceedingly rare in Modern Arabic) tends to be associated with a specific range of meanings, though no single verb appears in all the derived forms.

Stem	Form	Example	Meaning
I	*fa'ala*	*kasara*	'break', transitive (basic)
		'alima	'know' (basic)
		karuma	'be noble' (stative)
II	*fa''ala*	*kassara*	'shatter, smash' (intensive)
		'allama	'make know, teach' (factitive)
		sallama	'greet' (delocutive = 'to say *al-salāmu 'alaykum*', i.e., 'Peace upon you' using root letters of *salām*, viz. *s-l-m*)
III	*fā'ala*	*kātaba*	'write to someone' (indir. obj.becomes dir. obj., almost always a person)
IV	*'af'ala*	*'a'lama*	'make know, inform' (causative)
V	*tafa''ala*	*ta'allama*	'be taught, learn' (reflexive)
VI	*tafā'ala*	*takātaba*	'write to one another' (reciprocal)
VII	*infa'ala*	*inkasara*	'get broken' (passive reflexive)
VIII	*ifta'ala*	*ijtama'a*	'gather, come together' (personal interest)
IX	*if'alla*	*iḥmarra*	'go red' (colors & bodily defects)
X	*istaf'ala*	*ista'lama*	'seek knowledge, inquire' (conative)
XI	*if'ālla* [also *if'alalla*] rare except for quadriliteral verbs, see below		
XII	*if'aw'ala*	*iḥlawlaka*	'be very black' (intensive of IX)

If a root has four consonants it uses Stems II and V (*'amraka* 'Americanize', *ta'amraka* 'become Americanized') or a variant of Stem XI, e.g., *iṭma'anna* 'be content', *išra'abba* 'crane the neck').

Basic Syntax

Arabic sentences are of two basic types, Topic-Comment and Verb-Agent-Complement. Topic-Comment sentences have no copula, the Topic is usually definite and the Comment (Predicate) is usually indefinite: *al-kitāb-u qadīm-u-n* (the-book-NOM old-NOM-INDEF) 'The book is old.'

The Predicate agrees in number and gender with the Topic. However, if the Topic is an inanimate plural its grammatical status is feminine singular: *al-kutub-u qadīm-at-u-n* (the-books-NOM old-F.SING-NOM-INDEF) 'The books are old.'

In Verb-Agent sentences, 1st and 2nd person Agents will always be represented by a pronoun: *katab-tu l-kitāb-a* (wrote-1SG the-book-ACC) 'I wrote the book.'

In contrast, in the third person the Verb always remains singular (masc. or fem.) if the Agent is explicitly mentioned as a Noun:

katab-ū *l-kitāb-a*
wrote-3PL.M the-book-ACC
'They wrote the book.' (no explicit Noun Agent)

katab-a *l-rijāl-u* *l-kitāb-a*
wrote-M.SG the-men-NOM the-book-ACC
'The men wrote the book.' (explicit plural Agent)

katab-at *(i)l-mar'atāni* *l-kutub-a*
wrote-F.SG the-woman-DUAL.NOM the-book-ACC
'The two women wrote the books.' (explicit dual Noun Agent)

In a Topic-Comment sentence, the Comment may itself be a Verb-Agent sentence. In such a sentence, the Comment contains a pronominal form referring to the Topic:

hāḏā *l-kitāb-u* *katab-a-hu* *l-rajul-u*
this the-book-NOM wrote-3SG.M-it the-man-NOM
'The man wrote this book.'

Arabic adjectives follow the nouns they modify, and agree with it in number, gender, case, and definiteness:

al-maktab-u *l-jadīd-u*
the-office-NOM the-new-NOM
'the new office' (both masculine singular)

fī jāmi'-at-i-n *mašhūr-at-i-n*
in university-FEM-GEN-INDEF famous-FEM-GEN-INDEF
'in a famous university' (both feminine singular)

Possession is indicated by juxtaposing two nouns or a noun and pronoun suffix. The second element is always oblique/genitive and the head noun has the case required by the function of the unit:

kitāb-u *l-rajul-i*
book-NOM the-man-GEN
'the man's book'

fī *kitāb-i* *l-rajul-i*
in book-GEN the-man-GEN
'in the man's book'

The first element is never marked definite or indefinite; it takes its definiteness from that of the second element:

kitāb-u *rajul-i-n*
book-NOM man-GEN-INDEF 'a man's book'

All prepositions observe this structure: *'ilā maktab-i l-jāmi'-at-i* (to office-GEN the-university-F-GEN) 'to the office of the university'

Negation of Topics is effected by *lā* 'no' followed usually by a single term in the dep/accusative without definition markers:

lā *rajul-a* *fī l-maktab-i*
no man-ACC in the-office-GEN
'there is no man in the office'

Predicates can be negated by *laysa* 'is not'; negated predicates take accusative rather than nominative case: *laysa l-rajul-u ḥasan-a-n* (is.not:SG.MASC the-man-NOM good-ACC-INDEF) 'the man is not good'

Verbs are negated by various preverbal particles depending on the aspect or status of the verb:

Affirmative	Negative
'akal-a 'he ate'	*lam ya'kul* 'he has not eaten'
ta-'mal-u 'she works'	*lā ta-'mal-u* 'she doesn't work'
katab-a 'he wrote'	*mā katab-a* 'he did not write'
u-ktub 'write!'	*lā ta-ktub* 'don't write!'
say-ya-ktub-u 'he will write'	*lan ya-ktub-a* 'he will not write'

Among the various subordinating structures are the nominalizers *'anna* 'that'+ Noun and *'an* 'that'+ dep./subj.Verb: *yajibu 'an taktaba* (is.necessary:INDIC that you.write:SUBJ) 'you must write (clause=Agent)'; *'ankara 'anna l-rajula ḥāḍirun* (he.denied that the-man:ACC present) 'he denied that the man was present (clause=direct object)'.

Contact with Other Languages

As the medium of the Islamic revelation and the administrative language of the Islamic empire for many centuries, Arabic has profoundly influenced all other Muslim languages, and been influenced by them in return. It has also borrowed from other languages from the earliest times, e.g. Akkadian, Aramaic, and Greek.

From Akkadian: *akkār* 'tiller of the soil'
From Aramaic: *tājir* 'merchant', *tarjumān* 'interpreter' (both ultimately Akkadian)
From Greek: *faylasūf* 'philosopher', *qānūn* 'law' (<*kanon*)
From Latin: *qaṣr* 'castle' (< *castrum*), *sirāṭ* 'way' *(<strata)*
From French: *jurnāl* 'newspaper', *ūtūbīs* 'bus'
From Italian: *banādūra* 'tomato' (< *pomo d'oro*), *karafitta* 'necktie'

From English: *warša* 'workshop', *banzīn* 'petrol, benzine'

Modern Arabic has countless such borrowings and shows many syntactical and stylistic reflections of English and French.

Arabic influence on the European languages as a result of contacts both through the crusades and the Arabic civilization of Andalusia is well known. As a result, many words of Arabic origin have come into English (and other European languages). Examples are *admiral, alchemy, alkali, bedouin, nadir, syrup, zenith, tariff, algebra, almanac, alcove, magazine, zero* (note that the original definite article *al-* is often preserved).

Common Words

man:	rajul	long:	ṭawīl
woman:	imra'at	small:	ṣaġīr
water:	mā'	yes:	na'am
sun:	šams	no:	lā
three:	ṯalāṯ	good:	ḥasan
fish:	samak(at)	bird:	ṭayr
big:	kabīr	dog:	kalb
tree:	šajar(at)		

Example Sentences

(1) istaqbal-nā-hu fī l-maṭār-i l-duwaliyy-i
met-we-him in the-airport-GEN the-international-GEN
'We met him at the international airport.'

(2) 'inna l-wazīr-a fī l-maḥkam-at-i l-'ān-a
[verily] the-minister-ACC in the-court-F-GEN the-time-ACC
'The minister is in the court now.'

(3) za'am-a l-ṣuḥufiyy-ūna 'anna siyās-at-a-hu
claimed-M.SG the-journalist-PL.NOM that policy-F-ACC-his

kān-at muḫṭi'-at-a-n
was-F.SG erring-F-ACC-INDEF.
'The journalists claimed that his policy had been wrong.'

Efforts to Preserve, Protect, and Promote the Language

Indigenous grammars and other means of language control started to evolve within a century of the Prophet's death (A.D. 632). They led to the creation of a grammatical system which continues to preserve written Arabic to this day from the kinds of changes observed in European languages over the same period. But now the tension between the increasingly self-assertive dialects and the conservative written media has forced the participants to confront the educationally, religiously and politically difficult choice between maintaining an archaic language which enshrines the religion but is no one's mother tongue and adopting a modernized language which risks cutting ties with the religious sources and rich secular literary heritage. A neutral written language is emerging but it remains closer to Classical Arabic than to any contemporary spoken variety.

On the model of the French Academy, several countries (e.g. Syria, Egypt, Iraq, Morocco) have founded academies and similar institutions whose assignment is to monitor and rule on linguistic developments.

Select Bibliography

Bakalla, M.H. 1980. *An Introduction to Arabic Language and Literature*. Taipei.

____. 1983. *Arab Linguistics, an Introduction and Bibliography, 2d. ed.* London: Mansell.

Bateson, Mary Catherine. 1967. *Arabic Language Handbook*. Washington: Center for Applied Linguistics.

Beeston, A. F. L. 1970. *The Arabic Language Today*. London: Hutchinson University Library.

Bohas, G., J.-P. Guillaume and D. E. Kouloughli. 1990. *The Arabic Linguistic Tradition*. London: Routledge.

Cannon, Garland Hampton, with A.S. Kaye. 1994. *The Arabic Contributions to the English Language: An Historical Dictionary*. Wiesbaden: Harrassowitz.

Carter, M. G. (ed.). 1981. *Arab Linguistics, an Introductory Classical Text with Translation and Notes*. Amsterdam: John Benjamins.

Fischer, Wolfdietrich and Jastrow, Otto (eds). 1980. *Handbuch der arabischen Dialekte*. Wiesbaden: Harrassowitz.

Fischer, Wolfdietrich. Helmut Gätje. (eds). 1982–92. *Grundriß der arabischen Philologie*. Wiesbaden: Reichert.

Fischer, Wolfdietrich 1997. "Classical Arabic." In Hetztron, 1997, 187–219

Hetzron, Robert (ed). 1997. *The Semitic Languages*. London: Routledge.

Holes, Clive. 1995. *Modern Arabic, Structures, Functions and Varieties*. London: Longmans.

Kaye, Alan and Rosenhouse, Judith. 1997. "Arabic Dialects and Maltese." In Hetzron 1997, 263–311.

Stetkevych, Jaroslav. 1970. *The Modern Arabic Literary Language, Lexical and Stylistic Developments*. Chicago: University of Chicago Press.

Versteegh, [C. H. M.] Kees. 1997. *The Arabic Language*. Edinburgh: Edinburgh University Press.

Yushmanov, N. V. 1961. *The Structure of the Arabic Language*, trans. Moshe Perlmann. Washington: Center for Applied Linguistics.

Robert D. Hoberman

Language Name: Aramaic. **Classical Varieties:** Syriac, Mandaic. **Modern Varieties and Alternative Names:** Assyrian, Chaldean. **Autonyms:** ‘ārāmāya, ‘ātūrāya. kaldāya. sūrāya, suryōyo, ṭūrōyo.

Location: The oldest Aramaic inscriptions have been found in what are now northern Syria, adjacent parts of Turkey, and Iraq, in northern Mesopotamia. At its height it was spoken throughout the Fertile Crescent (Israel, Syria, Jordan, Iraq, and parts of Turkey), and used in official communication, inscriptions, and literature in Egypt, Iran and as far as India and China. In the twentieth century Aramaic has been spoken in northern Iraq and adjacent parts of Iran, Syria, and Turkey (the regions known as Kurdistan and Azerbaijan), in three villages near Damascus, and in the towns of Ahwaz and Khorramshahr in Khuzistan province of southwestern Iran. In recent decades most of the speakers have left these areas and are now living in Baghdad, Tehran, Israel, Europe, and North America.

Family: Northwest (or Central) branch of the Semitic family of the Afroasiatic phylum.

Related Languages: ARABIC, HEBREW, PHOENICIAN, AKKADIAN, AMHARIC, TIGRINYA. More distantly OROMO, SOMALI, Berber languages, HAUSA, ANCIENT EGYPTIAN, COPTIC.

Dialects: Aramaic is not a language but a family of languages with a documented history of 3,000 years. The earliest inscriptions show two different Aramaic languages, and in later periods differences proliferated. In ancient and classical times there were seven literary languages, which differed in their writing systems, pronunciation, grammar, and vocabulary. The earliest was (1) Imperial Aramaic, the lingua franca and literary language of the Babylonian and Persian empires, in which parts of the biblical books of Ezra and Daniel were written. Aramaic languages after that period are conventionally divided into Eastern Aramaic and Western Aramaic. Western Aramaic consisted of three closely related languages spoken and written in ancient Palestine: (2) Christian Palestinian Aramaic (or Palestinian Syriac), (3) Jewish Palestinian (or Galilean) Aramaic , and (4) Samaritan Aramaic. The languages usually classed as Eastern are (5) Syriac, the classical language of the Christian churches of the Middle East; (6) Jewish Babylonian Aramaic, the main language of the Babylonian Talmud; and (7) Mandaic. Jewish Babylonian Aramaic and Mandaic were grammatically and phonologically similar, although their scripts and cultural milieus were quite different, while Syriac was in many respects intermediate between Eastern and Western Aramaic.

Modern Aramaic languages fall into four groups. Three are small, in terms of the number of speakers, the geographical spread, and the internal dialectal variation: the Ma‘lūla group, spoken in three villages near Damascus, Syria; the Turoyo group, spoken in southeastern Turkey; and modern Mandaic, spoken in southwestern Iran. The fourth and largest group, Northeastern Neo-Aramaic, is spoken by the Christian and Jewish minorities of Kurdistan and Azerbaijan (where the Muslim majority speaks Kurdish and Azeri Turkish). Turoyo and Northeastern Neo-Aramaic share some important grammatical innovations, and have therefore been grouped together as two branches of Central Neo-Aramaic.

Speakers of Aramaic nowadays usually call their language Assyrian or Chaldean, but these terms do not refer to dialect differences so much as to the religious denomination of the speakers: Chaldeans are affiliated with the Catholic church, while Assyrians are often identified with the Ancient Church of the East (Nestorian).

Number of Speakers: Approximately 200,000; some estimates are as high as one million.

Origin and History

The history of Aramaic is divided into five periods: Old, Imperial, Middle, Late, and Modern.

Old Aramaic was originally the language of desert tribes or small kingdoms in northern Syria. Royal inscriptions in Old Aramaic, from the 10th to the 8th centuries B.C., have been found in the areas which are now in Syria, Turkey, and northern Iraq.

Imperial Aramaic later came to be widely used in Mesopotamia, partly because the Arameans themselves moved there in large numbers and gained power and partly because the Aramaic alphabetic writing system, consisting of 22 letters, was easier to learn and use than Akkadian cuneiform with its hundreds of signs. Eventually Aramaic was adopted as the official language of the Babylonian and Achaemenid Persian empires, in which Imperial Aramaic was used approximately from 700 to 200 B.C. for official communication and for literary writings, among them parts of the biblical books of Daniel and Ezra. During this period Aramaic came to be spoken in an increasingly wider area, including Palestine and all of Mesopotamia, and was a lingua franca in an even wider area; in fact, the most important Imperial Aramaic documents have been found in Egypt.

Middle Aramaic dialects were spoken in the same wide area from about 200 B.C. to A.D. 200. Written works during this period, such as some of the Dead Sea Scrolls, tended to approximate Imperial Aramaic. As Aramaic was the predominant vernacular language of the Jews in northern Israel (the Galilee), it was undoubtedly the mother tongue of Jesus.

Late Aramaic comprises the six literary languages of the first millennium A.D. Syriac, the classical language of the Christian churches of the Middle East; Jewish Babylonian Aramaic, the language of the Babylonian Talmud; Mandaic; and Christian, Jewish, and Samaritan Aramaic, all in Palestine.

Syriac provided an important link in the long journey of ancient Greek learning to western Europe. Middle Eastern Christian scholars translated many works of Greek scholarship, both religious and secular, into Syriac and from Syriac into Arabic. These were later translated into Latin and other Western European languages in the late Middle Ages and during the Renaissance.

With the rise of Islam in the seventh century the Arabic language began to spread throughout the area which had formerly been Aramaic-speaking, and spoken Aramaic began a long, slow decline. Nonetheless, the indigenous Christian communities of the Middle East have continued to use Syriac in their liturgy and continued to produce literature in it to this day. Jews and Mandeans likewise continued to use Aramaic for similar functions. Among Jews, the Babylonian Talmud, written in Late Aramaic (with many quotations in Hebrew and earlier varieties of Aramaic) is still the core of the curriculum in the more traditional seminaries; some of the most widely known elements of the Jewish liturgy, such as the Kaddish and Kol Nidre, are in Aramaic; and at various times Jewish scholars who never heard Aramaic spoken wrote influential works in the language, chief among them the Zohar, which was written in thirteenth century Spain.

Modern Aramaic continues to be spoken. At the beginning of the 20th century there were undoubtedly several hundred thousand speakers, most of them in the area known as Kurdistan, straddling the border area of northern Iraq and adjacent parts of Iran and Turkey. Two social processes have led to the diminution of this number: persecution and education. A series of wars and massacres throughout the20th century, beginning with the genocidal attacks by Turkey during World War I not only on Armenians but also on all Christians, led most of the Aramaic speakers to leave their home villages and towns, settling in some of the large cities of the Middle East and in the United States, Canada, Germany, France, and Sweden. In the most recent events, during the Iran-Iraq War and the Gulf War, the governments of Iran, Iraq, and Turkey have bombed Kurdistan and evacuated nearly all the villages in the border areas. As a result there are probably few, if any, Aramaic-speaking communities still living in their original locations in Kurdistan. As modern public education has become available in the Middle East, children are now educated in the national languages—Arabic, PERSIAN, or TURKISH—rather than in traditional religious schools where Syriac would have been taught. Children of Aramaic-speaking parents in the United States, Canada, and Europe rapidly come to prefer to use the local national languages and lose their Aramaic. Virtually all the Jews have moved to Israel, where their children speak Hebrew rather than Aramaic. Of all the modern Aramaic-speaking groups, only the Ma'lula group, which remains in its three villages near Damascus, Syria, is linguistically stable, in that children continue to speak the language as their first and main means of oral communication.

Since Aramaic languages are so different from each other, it is impossible to describe their linguistic structures all together. Instead, the following sections describe classical Syriac, which is by far the best documented and studied Aramaic language. It is fairly representative of Imperial, Middle, and Late Aramaic in many respects.

The Syriac Alphabet (Estrangela Script)

p, p̄	ܦ	ṭ	ܛ	ɔ	ܐ
ṣ	ܨ	y	ܝ ܝ	b, b̲	ܒ
q	ܩ	k, k̲	ܟ ܟ	g, ḡ	ܓ
r	ܪ	l	ܠ	d, d̲	ܕ
š	ܫ	m	ܡ ܡ	h	ܗ
t, t̲	ܬ	n	ܢ ܢ	w	ܘ
		s	ܣ	z	ܙ
		c	ܥ	ḥ	ܚ

Orthography and Basic Phonology

Syriac, like Hebrew and Arabic, is written in two forms, a basic one which does not represent some of the vowels and various other phonological details, and an augmented form which adds optional diacritical symbols specifying those phonological details and certain morphological properties, especially plural number. The basic form is made up of twenty-two letters, which stand for consonants (and correspond one-to-one to the Hebrew letters, with which they share a common ancestry in Phoenician); these are arranged from right to left, and most of them are connected to the preceding and following letters within a word. The letters *w*, *y*, and ' also represent long vowels: *w* represents /ū/ and /ō/, *y* represents /ī/ and sometimes /ē/ or /ẹ̄/, and ' (always at the end of a word and occasionally in the middle) represents /ā/, /ē/, and /ẹ̄/. The optional diacritical marks added in the augmented form of writing specify vowel qualities, the stop or fricative character of *p*/*p̱*, *b*/*b̲*, *t*/*t̲*, *d*/*d̲*, *k*/*k̲*, *g*/*g̱* and a few more details. Some of these marks are nearly always used (such a a pair of dots indicating plural number), but others are used only in the biblical text and in poetry, and on other occasions when explicit precision is considered necessary. Two sets of vowel diacritics exist, one used in the western Syriac churches (Maronite and Syrian Orthodox) and the other in the east (Nestorian and Chaldean). They represent somewhat different modifications of the early Syriac vowel inventory described above. Thus the word *ʿāḇōḏā* 'creator, maker' can be written in the following three ways, which are (respectively from left to right) the obligatory letters only; with

Table 1: Consonants

		Labial	Dental	Palatal	Velar	Uvular	Pharyngeal	Glottal
Stops	Voiceless	p	t		k	q		ʼ
	Voiced	b	d		g			
	Emphatic		ṭ					
Fricatives	Voiceless	p̱	ṯ		ḵ		ḥ	h
	Voiced	ḇ	ḏ		g̱		ʻ	
Sibilants	Voiceless		s	s				
	Voiced		z					
	Emphatic		ṣ					
Resonants			r, l					
Nasals		m	n					
Glides		w		š				

western vowels; with eastern vowels. The transcription uses capital letters for the obligatory letters, and lower case letters for the vowel diacritics.

	Basic Form	Western Vowels	Eastern Vowels
Vowels		ā u ā	ā o ā
Consonants	ʼDWBʻ	ʼDWBʻ	ʼDWBʻ

The emphatic consonants /ṭ/ and /ṣ/ differed from their non-emphatic counterparts, but there is little evidence as to what this difference consisted of in ancient times. In all the modern Aramaic languages, these sounds are pharyngealized or velarized.

The fricatives *p̱, ḇ, ṯ, ḏ, ḵ, g̱* (phonetically [ɸ β θ ð x ɣ]) originated in Imperial Aramaic as a result of a sound change called spirantization, in which the stops /p b t d k g/, when preceded by a vowel and not geminated (doubled), became fricatives. (The emphatics ṭ and ṣ, as well as *q*, did not undergo spirantization.) In later stages of Aramaic, such as Syriac, vowels were lost while the following consonants in some cases remained fricative. In modern Aramaic languages, the rule is either entirely fossilized or changed almost beyond recognition (see Table 1 above).

Table 2: Vowels

	Front	Central	Back
High	ī		ū u
High-Mid	ẹ̄		
Low-Mid	ē e		ō
Low		ā a	

Short vowels in open syllables were dropped. Thus, corresponding to masculine *kāṯeḇ* 'write' (in which *ṯ* and *ḇ* are fricatives because they follow vowels), when the feminine is formed by adding a suffix *-ā*, the result is not *kāṯeḇā* but *kāṯbā*.

Basic Morphology

The morphology of Aramaic makes use of prefixes, suffixes, and the characteristically Semitic system of discontinuous roots consisting of three (less often, two or four) consonants and stem patterns consisting of vowels. Thus the word *ʻāḇōḏā* 'creator, maker' consists of three elements: (1) the root **ʻ-b-d**, which occurs in a whole family of words having to do with doing, making, or serving, among them *ʻbaḏ* 'did, made', *ʻaḇdā* 'slave', and *ʻḇīḏtā* 'service, work'; (2) the pattern **-ā-ō-**, occurring in many words for an actor or agent: *nāṭōrā* 'watchman', *yārōṯā* 'heir', *ʻāḏōrā* 'assistant'; and the suffix *-ā*, which marks the determinate state of most nouns. The word *meṯʻaḇdānūṯā* 'patienthood' (in grammatical terminology) contains the same root:

m-eṯ-ʻaḇd-ān-ūṯ-ā
NOM-PASSIVE-do-AGENTIVE-NOM-DETERMINATE

Discontinuous root-and-pattern morphology is quite productive in the derivation of nouns, adjectives, and verbs, and also in verbal inflection, while noun and adjective inflection works entirely through suffixation.

Syriac nouns are either masculine or feminine, and nearly all feminine nouns are marked with the suffix *-t* (or *-ṯ*). Nouns are inflected for number (singular or plural) and a category called "state." There are three states: absolute, determinate, and construct. In Old and Imperial Aramaic the absolute state was the basic one, and the determinate state suffix-*ā* functioned much like the English article *the*. In Eastern Aramaic, including Syriac, the determinate state lost its semantically definite character and became the functionally basic state, while the absolute state was limited mainly to predicate adjectives and to nouns preceded by quantifiers. Construct state nouns occur with possessive suffixes or preceding a specifier noun. Adjectives likewise are inflected for gender, number, and state, in agreement with the nouns they modify. Noun-noun compounds are not uncommon.

Syriac verbs have two tenses, known as the perfect and the imperfect, which are inflected with prefixes and suffixes for the gender, number, and person of the subject. In addition, there is an active participle, which functions as a present tense, a perfect (often passive) participle, and an imperative, all of which are inflected for gender and number, and an infinitive. Every verb has a stem of one of three canonical patterns: an unmarked pattern, an intensive pattern marked by gemination of the middle root consonant, and a causative pattern with the prefix *a-*. Any of these preceded by the prefix *et̲-* becomes intransitive, reflexive, or passive. Forms of the verb 'to be' often serve as auxiliaries alongside inflected verbs to form additional tenses and moods.

Basic Syntax

The major constituents of a clause or sentence appear in any order, but heads of phrases generally precede their complements; thus nouns generally precede adjectives, and prepositions precede their objects. There is no case marking other than by prepositions. Since a verb is inflected to show the gender, number, and person of its subject, independent subject pronouns are not usually used. When a direct object or object of a preposition is definite, it is often preceded by a pronoun agreeing with it in gender, number, and person; thus, 'to the king' may be expressed as 'to him to king'.

Sentences expressing 'to be' in the present do not contain a verb but rather occur in either of two constructions. In one, a pronoun agreeing with the subject is attached to the first or major word of the predicate; in the other, the particle *īt̲* 'there is' with a pronominal suffix marking the subject stands in place of the verb.

Contact with Other Languages

Aramaic has been in intimate contact with neighboring languages throughout its history, and has influenced them and been influenced by them. In ancient times the major sources of borrowed words in Aramaic were Akkadian, Persian, Greek, and Hebrew, in different proportions in the different cultural and geographic communities which spoke Aramaic; for instance, Syriac is full of Greek religious and philosophical terminology. Modern Aramaic has borrowed many words from Arabic, Kurdish, Turkish, and Persian, although at least two-thirds of the vocabulary is of Aramaic origin. There are also some important grammatical features that arose due to contact with these languages. Some examples of loanwords in Aramaic (citing their Syriac forms) are:

From Persian: *rāzā* 'secret, mystery, symbol, sacrament', *šrāg̱ā* 'lamp'
From Akkadian: *'ākkārā* 'farmer' (Akkadian had borrowed the word from Sumerian)
From Greek: *parṣōpā* 'face', *ṭeḵsā* 'order', *zawgā* 'yoke, pair'

Because all verbs in Aramaic must have one of the three canonical stem shapes, borrowed verbs retain only their original consonants, while replacing their original vowels and syllabic makeup with canonical Aramaic ones:

zawweg 'to join, marry' (a verb in the intensive pattern)
ṭakkes 'to arrange' (a verb in the intensive pattern)

A number of Aramaic words, especially religious terms, were borrowed into Arabic, perhaps to avoid Arabic words with pagan connotations; these include the roots of the words *Islam*, *Muslim*, and *mosque*, and the words *'īd* 'festival', *masīḥ* 'messiah', *ṣalāt* 'prayer'. Aramaic speakers in the Middle East who met Europeans (perhaps Crusaders) known as Franks began to call all western Europeans *frank* or *frang*; this was borrowed into Persian as *afrang* and *ferang* and into Arabic as *ifranj* and *firanj* and via these languages has spread across Asia, as far as Indonesia and Polynesia. Among the handful of Aramaic words which have made their way into European languages are English *abbot* from Aramaic *'abbā* 'father' and French *mesquin* 'shabby, paltry', which originated in Akkadian and came via Aramaic *meskẹ̄nā* to Arabic *miskīn* and thence to Europe. The *bar* in *bar mitsva* (the Jewish rite of passage for thirteen-year-old boys) is the Aramaic word for 'son', while *mitsva* is Hebrew for 'commandment': a *bar mitsva* is a 'son of the commandment(s)', a person ready to take responsibility.

Common Words

man:	gab̲rā, bar-nāšā	small:	z'ōrā
woman:	'a(n)ttā, *pl.* neššē	yes:	'ẹn
water:	mayyā	no:	lā
sun:	šemšā	good:	ṭāb̲ā
three:	tlāt̲ā	bird:	ṣepprā
fish:	nūnā	dog:	kalbā
big:	rabbā	tree:	'īlānā
long:	'arrīḵā		

Example Sentences

(1) šrāg̱ā y mel-t̲-āḵ l-reg̱l-ay
lamp/MASC she word-FEM-your to-foot-PL/my
'Your word is a lamp unto my feet.'

(2) 'āp̱ kārōz-ē šb̲īq-īn l-ēh l-malkā
even herald-PL left/PASS. PART.-PL to-him to-king

d-n-aḵrz-ūn
that-3RD/IMPERF-proclaim-MASC/PL
'The king has also permitted heralds to proclaim...'

(3) ḥakkīm-ē m-et̲-ḥašb̲-īn (h)waw d-mānā
wise-PL NOM-INTRANS-think-PL were that-what

n-e'bd̲-ūn l-hōn l-mayyā yattīr-ē
3RD-do/IMPERF-MASC/PL to-them to-water/PL abundant-PL

d-ett-awsa (h)waw
that-INTRANS-increase/PERF were
'The wise men were thinking what to do about the floodwater, which had increased.'

Efforts to Preserve, Protect, and Promote the Language

Until the 19th century Aramaic speakers nearly always wrote not in their vernacular, colloquial Aramaic, but in a classical language; for Jews this was Hebrew, and for Christians Syriac. Classical Syriac was documented by medieval scholars in a substantial body of grammatical description and lexicography. No other Aramaic language was cultivated, standardized, and analyzed in the way Syriac was.

In the 19th century, European missionaries working in Persia created a written form in Syriac script of the Aramaic spoken by the Christians of the town of Urmi. This standard written language is widely used and has had great influence on speech among Christians in both Iran and Iraq. It forms the basis for the Iraqi koine which is the most widely spoken form of Aramaic today.

In the Assyrian and Chaldean diaspora since the late twentieth century several organizations have been active in promoting the use of the language. In Sweden, where by law all children are entitled to be educated in their native language, an orthography for Turoyo Aramaic in Latin letters has been developed and teaching materials compiled. In the United States, the Assyrian Academic Society publishes a journal relating to the history and culture of the Aramaic-speaking peoples, linguistic studies, and literary works. Modern Aramaic (the Iraqi koine) is taught in several public schools and colleges, especially in Chicago, and periodicals and radio and television programs have appeared. Despite these efforts, however, few children born outside of the Middle East use the language actively. Fourteen hundred years after the beginning of its decline, it is doubtful whether Aramaic (outside of the three villages of the Ma'lula group) will have another generation of speakers.

Select Bibliography

Beyer, Klaus. 1986. *The Aramaic Language: Its Distribution and Subdivision.* Göttingen: Vandenhoeck & Ruprecht.

Brock, Sebastian. 1980. "An Introduction to Syriac Studies." In *Horizons in Semitic Studies: Articles for the Student.* (University Semitics Study Aids 8.) Birmingham, England: University of Birmingham, Department of Theology.

Fitzmyer, Joseph A. 1979. "The Phases of the Aramaic Language." In *A Wandering Aramean: Collected Aramaic Essays,* by Joseph A. Fitzmyer (Society of Biblical Literature, Monograph Series, 25.), pp. 57–84. Chico, CA: Scholars Press.

Heinrichs, Wolfhart, ed. 1990. *Studies in Neo-Aramaic.* Atlanta, GA: Scholars Press.

Jastrow, Marcus. 1903. *A Dictionary of the Targumim, the Talmud Babli and Yerushalmi, and the Midrashic Literature.* London: Lusac, and New York: Putnam.

Kaufman, Sephen A. 1974. *The Akkadian Influences on Aramaic. Assyriological Studies, 19.* Chicago: University of Chicago Press.

Krotkoff, Georg. 1982. *A Neo-Aramaic Dialect of Kurdistan: Texts, Grammar, and Vocabulary.* (American Oriental Series, 64.) New Haven: American Oriental Society.

Kutscher, Eduard Yechezkel. 1970. "Aramaic." In *Current Trends in Linguistics*, ed. Thomas Sebeok. Vol. 6, *Linguistics in South West Asia and North Africa*, 347–412. The Hague: Mouton. Reprinted in E. Y. Kutscher. 1977. *Hebrew and Aramaic Studies*, 90–155. Jerusalem: Magnes.

Kutscher, Eduard Yechezkel. 1971. "Aramaic." In *Encyclopaedia Judaica* 3.259–287. Jerusalem: Keter.

Muraoka, Takamitsu. 1987. *Classical Syriac for Hebraists.* Wiesbaden: Harrassowitz.

Payne Smith, Jessie. 1903. *A Compendious Syriac Dictionary.* Oxford: Clarendon Press.

Rosenthal, Franz. 1961. *A Grammar of Biblical Aramaic. Porta Linguarum Orientalium, 5.* Wiesbaden: Harrassowitz.

Rosenthal, Franz. 1967. *An Aramaic Handbook. Porta Linguarum Orientalium, 10.* Wiesbaden: Harrassowitz.

Sokoloff, Michael. 1990. *A Dictionary of Jewish Palestinian Aramaic of the Byzantine Period.* Ramat-Gan, Israel: Bar Ilan University Press.

ARAPESH

Lise M. Dobrin

Language Name: The name Arapesh is in common use in the anthropological and linguistic literature; however, for the sake of clarity I will use Arapeshan to refer to the language family as a whole. In Arapeshan, several of the language labels used are variants of *buk*: Bukiyip, Bukip, Buki, Abu'. The southwestern Arapeshan languages, known in the literature as Bumbita and Southern Arapesh, are referred to by their speakers as Weri and Muhian, respectively. The dialect described here is that spoken in Wautogik and Kotai villages, which are located at the northeasternmost border of the Arapeshan-speaking territory. This dialect is known locally as Cemaun, after the traditional war alliance to which its speakers belonged.

Location: Arapeshan is spoken along a 45-kilometer stretch of the New Guinea north coast, between the villages of Banak to the east and Matapau to the west, in the country of Papua New Guinea. It is spoken in the sparse settlements in the Prince Alexander mountain range that runs parallel to the coast, as well as in the much more populous region on the inland side of the mountains, where the terrain levels off into the Sepik plain. There Arapeshan maintains its 45-kilometer east-west span, stretching approximately between the government centers of Maprik to the east, and Drekikir to the west.

Family: Arapeshan is one of two families belonging to the Kombio stock of the Torricelli phylum; the other is the Kombio family. The Torricelli phylum belongs to the Papuan grouping, which designates the non-Austronesian languages indigenous to mainland New Guinea and its neighboring islands. A common genetic relationship unifying all Papuan languages has not been established.

Related Languages: The conventional classification of Arapeshan includes three languages: Mountain Arapesh or Bukiyip, Southern Arapesh or Muhiang, and Bumbita Arapesh or Weri. More recently, Nekitel has carved out from this classification a fourth language, Abu'. It is impossible to delineate a precise geographic boundary which divides Southern from Mountain Arapesh, since there is considerable chaining of phonological, lexical, and grammatical features as one moves from village to village.

Dialects: Arapeshan is best understood as one long dialect chain superimposed upon the language classification above. The most divergent Arapeshan language is Weri, which lacks grammatical gender except in human nouns and shares only a low percentage (less than 60) of probable cognates with the lexicostatistically nearest non-Weri dialect. Abu' stands apart from all other Arapeshan languages in lacking agreement in possessive noun phrases.

Number of Speakers: Mountain Arapesh: 10,300; Southern Arapesh: 10,640; Weri: 2,350. These are census figures from 1970, when vernacular fluency was highly predictable from village of residence. Today, however, in many traditionally Arapeshan-speaking areas the language is in declining use, and is being replaced with the Papua New Guinea lingua franca and local prestige language TOK PISIN (TP). In the entire coastal region in which the Cemaun dialect described here is spoken, children—who constitute the majority of village populations—are at best only passively competent in the vernacular; most fully fluent speakers are over age 40. As a result of these trends, population figures no longer adequately represent number of speakers. The 1990 census counts 258 residents of the traditionally Cemaun-speaking villages Wautogik and Kotai, though my own informal census taken in 1998–99 suggests that that figure is much too low. The official language of Papua New Guinea and the language of schooling is ENGLISH.

Origin and History

While it is known that people have occupied the island of New Guinea for around 50,000 years, prehistoric patterns of internal migration are difficult to reconstruct due to the dearth of archeological evidence and the nearly complete lack of historical records dating from before the late nineteenth century, when European involvement intensified with colonization. The distributions of both linguistic and cultural features show substantial evidence of areal diffusion, further complicating the picture. In the Arapeshan area, it seems likely that migrations have swept northward and eastward, since most other Torricelli languages are spoken to the west, and since the relatively high population density in the inland region has caused pressure on land use that would have encouraged migration into previously unoccupied lands. Linguistic evidence that would bear on this issue remains to be carefully studied.

Orthography and Basic Phonology

Arapeshan languages were all unwritten until SIL translators began developing religious and literacy materials in the 1970s; this project continues through the present. Vernacular literacy remains low despite these efforts, however. The materials use Roman alphabetic symbols without additional characters or diacritics; only apostrophe ' is added to represent glottal stop.

The consonant phoneme inventory of Cemaun Arapesh is given in Table 1 on the next page.

Table 1: Consonants

	Labial	Alveolar	Palato-alveolar	Velar	Glottal
Stops	p b	t d		k, kʷ g, gʷ	
Affricates			c j		
Fricatives		s			h, hʷ
Tap		r			
Approximant		l			
Nasals	m	n	ñ		

The labialized glottal fricative *hʷ* is alternatively treated as a voiceless bilabial glide. The glides *w* and *y* are also present, though their consonantal status is never distinctive, as it depends entirely on syllable position: glides appear in onsets; the high vowels *u* and *i* appear elsewhere. There are also several optional phonetic rules that affect the distribution of glides, including spreading from a V+HIGH to provide an onset for a following V-HIGH: *ehiah* > [ehiyah] 'how, way'; *ruahaep* > [ruwahaep] 'morning'. The phonemes *p* and *b* are often articulated with a marked labial transition when they precede a front vowel: *yabic* > [yabwic] 'rotten, ruined'; *m-ə-tep eiguhʷ* > [mətepʷ eiguhʷ] '1.PL-R-search.for fish'. The bilabial nasal *m* is also subject to this rule: *yarupin-um-ei* > [yarupwinumwei] 'friend-OBL-1.SG.IO; my friend'. The glottal fricative *h* merges phonetically with *hʷ* after a round vowel, resulting in ambiguous surface forms such as [uhʷiñ] 'wind' and [ohʷok] 'coconut palm'; it is impossible to determine whether the glottals in these words should be assigned to an underlying *h* or *hʷ*. In certain cases the morphosyntax provides a resolution, as with e.g. the noun *monokuhʷ* 'wild cinnamon tree', which takes gender agreement forms with *hʷ*, echoing the word-final phoneme, rather than with *h*, as would e.g., the *h*-final noun *ahah* 'shoulder'. When they follow a round vowel in word-final position the labialized phonemes *kʷ* and *gʷ* lose their distinctive release; the labial feature is 'retracted' and coarticulated with the velar: [wautog] 'ironwood.treePL' < *wautogʷ*; cf. [nɨbagʷ] 'dogPL', and [məduk] 'highest horizontal house post, apex of roof' < *mədukʷ*; cf. [merikʷ] 'rattan'.

Arapeshan is spoken along a 45-kilometer stretch of the New Guinea north coast (shaded area).

Cemaun has the basic 7-vowel phonemic system shown in Table 2 below.

Table 2: Vowels

i	ɨ	u
e	ə	o
	a	

In addition, the diphthongs *ai*, *ae*, *au*, *ou*, *oi* and *ei* are found. As with consonants, the major phonetic rules affecting vowels involve labial assimilation. *ə* is realized as [ɔ] (a mid, round central vowel) following *w*, neutralizing with *o*, which is also realized as [ɔ] in this context. The neutralization is absolute in non-alternating forms such as [wɔsik] 'alright, yes', though a unique underlying source is recoverable in e.g., *w-ə-rɨh-buk* > [wɔrɨhɨbuk] '3.F.PL-R-XII.PL.-put.down'. Following *b*, the non-low central vowels *ɨ* and *ə* remain central but acquire rounding: *bɨrɨbɨdɨk* > [bʉrʉbʉdɨk] 'cave'; *utəbər* > [utəbør] 'stones, modern money'.

The morphophonemics are quite complex; only a few common patterns will be mentioned here. The irrealis (IR) mood marker which is prefixed to the verb is underlyingly *ɨ*. It surfaces as [u] before *u* and *kʷ*: *p-ɨ-kwacih* > [pukwacih] '2.PL-IR-untie'; *h-ɨ-u-sop* > [huusop] '3.M.PL-IR-F.PL.-set.living.being.down.on.ground'. Irrealis *ɨ* surfaces as [i] both before and after *y*: *kʷ-ɨ-yapurək* > [kwiyapurək] '3.F.SG-IR-jump'; *y-ɨ-tik* > *yitik* > [itik] '1.SG-IR-see'. Following the subject prefixes *m*, *u*, and *kʷ* it surfaces as [u]; *m-ɨ-tik* > [mutik] '1.PL-IR-see'. The default realis mood marker is most frequently *ə*; however, many verbs instead take *a*: *n-ə-dɨk* '3.M.SG-R-stand.up (TR)' vs. *n-a-dɨk* '3.M.SG-R-shoot'. Nasal assimilation affects voiced obstruents, creating homorganic nasal-obstruent clusters when a nasal occurs in the preceding syllable onset. This rule applies systematically in demonstratives: the underlying form of the proximal demonstrative is *ə-C-ɨdək*; nasal assimilation derives [ənɨndək] 'this hornbill' vs. [ətɨdək] 'this dog'. It applies as well in nouns (e.g., [muŋgu] 'thing', [nɨmbarig] 'garden' vs. [dəbarɨn] 'hornbill') and in words of other lexical categories (e.g., [ənəndai] 'sometimes'; [mɨndai] 'not'; [nɨmbuti-] 'bitter'). Notably, however, it never affects verbs: *m-ɨ-gək* > [mugək], *[muŋgək] '1.PL-IR-die'. The phoneme *k* is uniquely subject to deletion in final position on a lexical, partially optional basis. Final *k*-deletion affects words of all lexical categories but nouns, e.g., [-nətɨtik]/[-nətɨti] 'be afraid' (cf. 'the root' *-cerik* 'beat up, smash', where *k* never deletes), [wak]/[wae] 'no', [ecɨdək]/[ecɨdə] 'these things', [eik]/[ei] '1.SG.PRO'. Note that *k* is also odd in that it fails to predict a nominal gender according to the pattern discussed under Noun Morphology below.

The basic syllable structure pattern is (C)V(V)(C), with a requirement that the coda be filled in one-syllable words: *cər* 'clay pot'; *bai* 'steep uncleared mountainside, village periphery'; *goum* 'type of crab', *ou.riñ* 'coconut sheath', *ei.ur* 'fish'; particles and interjections are exempt, however: *bo* 'yes', *ka* 'about to'. Except for forms affected by the nasal spreading rule mentioned above, consonant clusters are extremely rare (but cf. *cepleñip* 'type of bird'); normally *ə* or *ɨ* is epenthesized to resolve clusters that arise as a result of inflection: *c-ɨ-m-dɨk* > [cɨmudɨk] 'VIII.PL-IR-V.SG.-stand.upright', where the second surface vowel is an epenthetic *ɨ*; *p-ə-jem-r* > [pəjemor] '2.PL-R-catch-X.SG.', where the third surface vowel is an epenthetic *ə* (in both examples the inserted vowel is rounded by a preceding *m*). The voiced alveolar obstruents *d* and *j* do not occur word finally in Cemaun or any other dialect of Arapeshan (but cf. *leij* 'type of yam', possibly borrowed from outside the family). No Cemaun words are known to begin with the vowel *ɨ*.

Basic Morphology

Nouns. A central morphological feature of Arapeshan is an extensive noun classification (here: grammatical gender) system, which is largely semantically arbitrary and is linked closely to noun-final form. For nouns with human referents, gender is predictable from the sex of the referent (M → VII, F → IV), though each of these semantically based genders has clear formal correlates as well. For non-human Cemaun Arapesh nouns, gender is regularly predictable from the final phonological segment of the singular form of the noun. Each of the singular-final elements is associated with a corresponding plural-final form (or a phonologically coherent—if not phonologically reducible—set of forms), producing around 15 (depending on the details of the analysis) canonical SG ~ PL pairings. Thus, e.g., the canonical plural of h^w-final (Gender XII) nouns is *-rɨh* (*nah*^{w} ~ *narɨh* 'tooth'), the canonical plural of *t*-final (Gender XI) nouns is replacive *-g*^{w} or additive *-og*^{w} (*nɨbat* ~ *nɨbag*^{w} 'dog', *nokwat* ~ *nokwatog*^{w} 'mouth'), and the canonical plural of k^w-final (Gender IV) nouns is a formal schema organized around the phonological feature +LABIAL: *-u* (*amәgok*^{w} ~ *amәgou* 'fly'), *-meb* (*nәhok*^{w} ~ *nәhomeb* 'flying fox bone'), *-rib* (*ohok*^{w} ~ *ohorib* 'coconut palm'), *-omi* (*babek*^{w} ~ *babekomi* 'grandmother'), etc. Cognate canonical pairings are found in all Arapeshan languages.

The basic nominal inflectional categories are represented by the independent pronoun system charted. Gender is only distinguished in the third person; dual number only (but obligatorily) in the first.

	SG	PL	DU
1	*eik*	*әpәk*	*ohok*
2	*ñәk*	*ipәk*	
3M(=VII)	*әnәn*	*omom*	
3F(=IV)	*okwokw*	*owou*	
3DEF(=VIII)	*eñeñ*	*ecec*	
I	*әbәb*	*әbәbɨs*	
II	*әbәbәr*	*әrәrɨb*	
III	*әgәg*	*әgәgәs*	
etc.			

In Cemaun (though not in all Arapeshan cultures), the regular use of kinship nouns is reinforced by a strong taboo against uttering personal names, particularly those of one's elders. A morphological distinction that is relevant to kinship nouns is a split between forms referring to a relation of one's own, i.e., a direct relation, as opposed to a relation of another's, i.e., an indirect one. In most cases the two terms are formally related (e.g., *wawen*DIR vs. *waken*IND 'mother's brother', *kasin*DIR vs. *kasinen*IND 'child's spouse's father', *barahok*^{w}DIR vs. *barahokwik*^{w}IND 'granddaughter'), but in some cases the two terms are essentially suppletive (e.g., *yamo*DIR vs. *amakek*^{w}IND 'mother', *abahik*^{w}DIR vs. *acɨkeke*^{w}IND 'woman's elder sister'), and in others the distinction is not realized (e.g., *makik*^{w}DIR/IND 'father's sister', *yamenen*DIR/IND 'great grandfather'). The direct/indirect distinction normally extends to the plural as well, e.g., *wawen*DIR ~ *wawenomi*DIR.PL vs. *waken*IND ~ *wakeñim*IND.PL 'mother's brothers'.

A rule of conversion allows most verb roots to function as numberless nouns, though these are used only rarely in normal speech. The gender of converted nouns is always the default gender VIII: *әnәn n-a-rik* 'he 3.M.SG-R-ask' > *dәbei-ñ-i rik* 'important-VIII.SG-ATTR question'.

Diminutives are derived by way of suffixation, though no one suffix is consistently used. While the otherwise locative suffix *-gɨn* is perhaps most commonly used for this purpose, (*mahiñ-i-gɨn* 'meat-POS-LOC/DIM'), many nouns suffix phonological segments associated with other genders, on a lexical basis, to form the diminutive: *ahur-i-c* 'lime.powder-POS-VIII.PL/DIM', *bur-i-k*^{w} 'pig-POS-IV.SG/DIM', *әrәmir-i-p* 'bird-POS-IX.SG/DIM', *nɨbat-i-h*^{w} 'dog-POS-XII.SG/DIM'. A similar strategy is used for individuating non-count nouns, though in the latter case the individuating suffix usually bears some relation to a semantically appropriate noun; e.g., the names of edible mushrooms are numberless, and are individuated and pluralized by adding a final possessed gender marker apparently referring to the individuating "classifier" *cup* 'leaf': *cukwehәbәr-i-p* 'mushroom.type-POS-IX.SG'. The gender of morphologically diminutive and individuated nouns is determined by the suffix.

Verbs. The basic template for verb inflection is SUBJECT-MOOD-ROOT: *n-ә-cuh* '3.M.SG-R-sleep'. Verbs may be either transitive or intransitive, with transitive verbs distinguished into two classes on the basis of whether pronominal objects are prefixed or suffixed (the suffixing class is the larger): *ñ-ɨ-rɨh rɨhic* '2.SG-IR-boil boiled.foods' ~ *ñ-ɨ-c-rɨh* '2.SG-IR-them-boil' vs. *n-a-tәrɨm oub* '3.M.SG-R-gather.together coconuts' ~ *n-a-tәrɨm-b* '3.M.SG-R-gather.together-them'. Addition of affixes to the basic template has morphophonemic consequences in some verbs. A common pattern involves substitution of *p* for root-final *h* with suffixation, e.g., *batowiñ ñ-ә-reh* 'child 3.N.SG.-R-cry' ~ *ñ-ә-rep-um ñumeb* 'VIII.SG-R-cry-OBL breasts'; *n-a-cecanɨh yah* '3.M.SG-R-grope.in.darkness road' ~ *n-a-cecanɨp-h* '3.M.SG-R-grope.in.darkness-it'. Another pattern involves elision of root-initial *w* with object-prefixation, e.g., *ñ-ɨ-wem gәrɨkit* '2.SG-IR-place.overhead broom' ~ *ñ-ɨ-t-em* '2.SG-IR-XI.SG-place.overhead'. The imperative is formed with an unprefixed root, which may be suffixed (regardless of the class of the verb root) with an object pronoun: *bo-әt*! 'hit-XI.SG!'. The most frequent imperatives are suppletive: *yowi*!

(*nak-i*! see directionals below) 'come here!'; *kokw-ñ*! (**wok-ñ*!) 'eat X!'.

A verbal construction that is growing in importance as more borrowings from TP and English enter the language combines an inflected form of the verb root *-ne* 'do, make' with an uninflected root: *n-ə-ne+gəbok* '3.M.SG-R-make+trouble 'mess things up, cause trouble', *n-ə-ne+pupurik-k^w* '3.M.SG-R-make+kiss-3.F.SG.', 'he kissed her'; *c-ə-ne+statim* 'VIII.PL-R-make+start$_{TP}$', 'they started.' This construction accommodates compound roots as well: *ma ñ-ɨ-ne+wi-təgɨr*! 'Quit going in and out! (=make+enter-exit)'; *əpə m-o-ne+to-bɨh wohɨñ* 'all we do is go up and down mountains (=make+ascend-steep.descend)'.

The element *-um* (glossed OBL) has multiple functions when used as a verbal suffix (and still others when used as a clausal clitic; some of them are discussed below). It is added to transitive verbs as a benefactive marker, allowing an indirect object pronoun to be incorporated within the verb frame: *k^w-ə-rup-c* '3.F.SG-R-boil-VIII-PL', *k^W-ə-rup-c-um-n* '3.F.SG-R-boil-VIII.PL.-OBL-M.SG'. On intransitives, *-um* increases the valency of the verb either by introducing a lexical direct object (*h-ɨ-kworɨh-um ən-ñ yuwa* '3.M.PL-IR-steal- INDEF-VIII.SG shell.ring'), or, more rarely, by introducing a direct object pronominal suffix: *ne+rerei*$_{TP}$ 'be ready' ~ *ne+rerei-um-b* 'prepare-OBL-I.SG' (**ne rerei-b*). Many reflexive and some intransitive verb roots begin with *nə-* or *na-*: *nə-tɨtuk* 'trip', *nə-pupuru* 'get excited', *na-boum* 'unite, cooperate'; however, only a few reflexives are transparently derived from a non-reflexive counterpart by such prefixation : *nə-sagɨrik* 'scratch myself' ~ *sagɨrik* 'itch'; *nə-caiweh* 'burn oneself' ~ *caiweh* 'burn.something'.

Verbs of motion may be suffixed with the directionals *-i* or *-ugu*, which indicate movement toward or away from the speaker, respectively: *kwawic* 'she entered' ~ *kwawic-i* 'she came inside (spoken while inside)' ~ *kwawic-ugu* 'she went inside (spoken while outside)'. When used in address, the meaning of *-ugu* shifts: *ei inak-ugu* 'I will go to where you are', *ñə ñenak-ugu* 'you will go to where a third party is'. The semantic value of the highly frequent suffixes *-ɨk* and *-ɨkɨk* are difficult to pinpoint, though they generally signal an action either intensified (*-ɨk*) or carried to completion (*-ɨkɨk*), loss of control, and above all separation of a patient from the agent of the action it is undergoing: *neminek* 'he heard' ~ *neminek-ɨk* 'he heard and comprehended' ~ *neminek-ɨkɨk* 'he heard, comprehended, and left'; *kwakut-up* 'she dropped it (a knife; intentionality unmarked)' ~ *kwakut-up-ɨkɨk* 'she dropped it without knowing and continued on her way'; *ecah^w gətəburek* 'the netbag slid off' ~ *gətəburek-ɨk* 'it slid off (but was caught) ~ *gətəburek-ɨkɨk* 'it slid off (and fell all the way to the ground)'. Reduplication of the first or only syllable of a verb root has the effect of intensifying or distributing the meaning of the action, often implying carelessness or loss of control on the part of the agent: *su* 'touch, hold' ~ *susu* 'touch all over, paw', *bo* 'hit, strike' ~ *bubo* 'beat up', *rɨpok* 'cut' ~ *rɨrɨpok* 'hack up'.

Basic Syntax

Agreement for person, number, and gender occurs on adjectives, verbs (obligatorily for subjects and for pronominal objects on some verbs), numerals, possessive phrases (which agree with the possessed NP), independent and interrogative pronouns, and three series of demonstratives. Agreement is typically alliterative, echoing the noun-final elements (consonants or CVC-sequences) that are predictive of gender in nouns: *ət-um butum* 'one-V.SG walking.stick$_{V.SG}$', *irukweh^w hw-a-kɨs* 'coconut.husk$_{XII.SG}$ XII.SG-R-lies.resting', *ihi-rɨb warɨb* 'all-II.PL villages$_{II.PL}$'. Exceptions to the alliterative pattern tend to occur in relatively more marked contexts such as with plural nouns (*əpə m-a-pe* '1.PL.PRO 1.PL-R-exist'; *omom h-a-pe* '3.M.PL.PRO 3.M.PL-R-exist'), or with vowel-final nouns, which take default (Gender VIII) agreement (*ət-ñ somo* 'one-VIII.SG flying.fox; *eik-i-ñ wopa* '1.SG.PRO-POS-VIII.SG small.game.trap'). Default agreement morphology is also supplied for conjoined NPs of conflicting genders and for NPs of unknown gender, such as indefinite interrogatives.

Unmarked word order is SVO (1); however, fronting a non-subject NP is a common strategy for topicalization (2). Serial verb constructions in which each verb is fully inflected (3) are commonplace; one also finds serial causatives (4). Repetition of the same verb in a serial construction intensifies and adds continuative aspect to the verb (5). Relative clauses are constructed by means of agreement with the modified NP as appropriate for its syntactic role within the relative, plus clause-final cliticization with the attributivizing element *-i* (6a,b).

(1) *ei ka* *iyagurepum* *eñɨdə* *stori*$_{TP}$
I like I tell about this story
'I would like to tell this story'

(2) *əpəkig^w* *urusag^w* *biog^w* *bo* *marupecog^w*
our houses two already we tore them down
'as for our two houses, we had already torn them down'

(3) *nənaki* *necerikec* *nakotic* *okudə*
he came he pounded them he puts them into this

aburak^w
half coconut shell
'he came and beat them [various medicinal herbs] in this coconut-shell dish'

(4) *necaih* *utom* *mah^w*
he heated in fire stone it was red
'he heated a stone until it became red'

(5) *babokeñic* *cene* *kros*$_{TP}$;
grandparents$_{INDIR}$ they did become angry

cehap, cehap, cehap
they expressed anger at us x 3
'(his) grandparents became angry; they kept chewing us out for a long time'

(6) a. *necɨdək* *c-eyerɨb-i* *cɨnaki*
those(VIII.PL) VIII.PL-danced-ATTR they will come

cuwo *worigɨn*
they will eat food
'those who danced will come and eat'

b. *hagɨrɨk* *rohuh-om-i* *pam*
they scraped sago-V.SG-ATTR adze-V.SG
'the adze they scraped sago with'

Possession is indicated by *-i* on the possessor, followed by a suffix agreeing with the possessed NP (7a). When the possessor is a proper noun, the possessive suffix occurs on a resumptive pronoun agreeing with and following the possessor (7b).

(7) a. *nɨbat-i-p* *hənɨp*
dog-POSS-IX.SG tail
'the dog's tail'

b. *Timoti* *ənən-i-kʷ* *aməkeikʷ*
Timoti 3.SG.PRO-POSS-F.SG motherINDIR
'Timothy's mother'

The element *-um* applied as a domain-final clitic has several functions. Clause-final *-um* is used to mark conditionals (8) and to introduce instrumental/purposive clauses (9). It can also be used to mark adverbial phrases and expressions of time and location.

(8) *ei* *ətə* *ipe-um* *ipə* *pɨna* *pɨgək* *ei*
I FUT I stay-IF you you will go you will die I

mare *itɨrip*
NEG I will see you
'If I stay, you all will go off and die and I won't get to see you.'

(9) *ənən* *yeriwerɨh* *wak-um* *nɨrahañ*
he legs NEG-INST he would walk
'he doesn't have legs for walking'

Several major constructions are marked discontinuously. Comparatives use the elements *abo...morim* (10a,b) around the second constituent. Nonfuture negative clauses use *wa...* or *mundai...(uwe)* around the predicate (11a), future negatives and negative imperatives use *mare...(uwe)* (11b).

(10) a. *ənən* *abo* *ənənin* *yaken* *morim*
he COMP1 his father COMP2
'he is like his father'

b ....*abo* *ecec* *cakərieñ* *morim*
COMP1 they they told you COMP2
'like they told you'

(11) a. *mundai* *cɨnek* *worubaici* *anecənec* *uwe*
NEG1 they make many things NEG2
'they didn't do very many things'

b. *nɨbat* *ətə* *mare* *tɨbu* *awotogʷ* *uwe*
dog FUT NEG1 it kills chickens NEG1
'the dog will not kill the chickens'

Relationships between clauses are marked by connector elements such as *bo* 'so that', *əriə* 'and then', *aka* 'or', *baka/waka* 'while', *abo* 'but, until'. Conjoined clauses may also simply be unmarked (12). Note that NPs are conjoined using a verb *-ni* 'be together with', where the first conjunct serves as subject (13). There is a complex system of time-indicating particles, certain of which appear to be derived from corresponding adverbs of time: *gi*, *(i)gə* < *gənikədai* 'earlier, already (within same day)'; *bo* < *nɨmbokɨhi* 'recently, already (within last month)'.

(12) *cene salimei* *yena* *yato* *Kaboibɨs*
they sent me I went I ascended Kaboibɨs

ei yakih *yape* *əneñ kwar* *gani* *Kaboibɨs*
I ascended I stayed one year at K
'they sent me up to Kaboibɨs, and (so) I went up and spent a year in Kaboibɨs'

(13) *Lise* *kwani* *mohon*DIR *kədə*
Lise she is together with brother-in-law soon

cɨnak
they will go
'Lise and our brother-in-law will be leaving soon'

Contact with Other Languages

A large number of borrowings have entered Arapeshan through TP, and are increasingly doing so now through English. Vernacular speech is marked by regular code switching into TP; nevertheless, the native linguistic structure remains substantially intact. Most nonhuman nouns are adapted to the native morphological system on the basis of their final phonological elements (e.g., *bet* ~ *betogʷ* 'bed, table' → II ; *bin* ~ *binəb* 'string bean' → VI), and verbs are assimilated to the formally least restrictive inflectional pattern (see discussion under Verbs above). Borrowed TP verbs regularly incorporate object pronouns, a pattern which is facilitated by the similarity in sound and placement between the native argument-marking suffix *-um* and the TP marker of transitivity on verbs *-im*: *ei yene ripotim*TP*-om* 'I reported them'. Native clause connectors are frequently replaced with their TP counterparts (1), as are negative elements (2a,b). It is not clear whether the heavily used future particle *ba* is a native form, or an adaptation of the TP future *bai* (< *baimbai*) (3).

(1) *natɨr* *hərɨs* *nau*TP *moni*TP *ñatɨh*
he bought feathers and then money was finished

*na*TP *natanumori*
and he returned
'he bought feathers, which depleted his money, and then he returned'

(2) a. *ino*TP *nɨkərip* *irohokwikʷ* *nənaki* *nəna* *necuh*
NEG he tells wife he came he went he slept
'he did not tell his wife; he came and went [straight] to sleep'

b. *noken*TP *ñɨnak*
NEG.IMP you go
'you may not go'

(3) *əriə* *naka* "*orait*TP, *kwəhik* *copuk* *ba*TP?
and then he said "alright, later today too FUT

muchuh"
we will sleep"
'and then he said, "listen, tonight too we will sleep together"

Common Words

man:	ərəmən	woman:	ərəmatokʷ
water:	əbər	sun:	wah
bird:	ərəmir	dog:	nɨbat
tree:	rowog	big:	dəbei-
no:	wak	yes:	wosik, bo
good:	yopu-	long:	rowi-
small:	coku-	three:	bicetiñ

Example Sentences

(1) omom h-ə-nitək-um mare(gəməg)?
3.M.PL.PRO 3.M.PL-R-argue-OBL what(thing)
'What are they arguing about?'

(2) ei i-nam-eñ gani yous aka wak ?
1.SG 1.SG.IR-accompany-2.SG LOC coast or NEG
'Should I go with you to the coast or not?'

(3) moi-ñ-iə batowiñ ñ-e-nak-i ?
which-VIII.SG child-VIII.SG VIII.SG-R-go-toward.speaker
'Which child is coming?'

Select Bibliography

Alungum, John, Robert J. Conrad, and Joshua Lukas. 1978. "Some Muhiang Grammatical Notes." In *Workpapers in Papua New Guinea Languages 25: Miscellaneous Papers on Dobu and Arapesh.* Ukarumpa, Papua New Guinea: SIL.

Conrad, Robert J. 1978. "A Survey of the Arapesh Language Family of Papua New Guinea." In *Workpapers in Papua New Guinea Languages 25: Miscellaneous Papers on Dobu and Arapesh.* Ukarumpa, Papua New Guinea: SIL.

Conrad, Robert J., and Kepas Wogiga. 1991. "An Outline of Bukiyip Grammar." In *Pacific Linguistics* C–113.

Dobrin, Lise M. 1999. "Phonological Form, Morphological Class, and Syntactic Gender: The Noun Class Systems of Papua New Guinea Arapeshan." University of Chicago doctoral dissertation.

_____. 1999. "Lexical Splitting in the Kinship Vocabulary of the Buki (Arapesh) Languages." In *Language and Linguistics in Melanesia* 28: 99–118.

Fortune, Reo F. 1942. "Arapesh." In *Publications of the American Ethnological Society* 19. New York: J. Augustin.

Laycock, Donald. 1975. "The Torricelli Phylum." In S. Wurm (ed.), *New Guinea Area Languages and Language Study, 1: Papuan Languages and the New Guinea Linguistic Scene.* 767–780. Pacific Linguistics C–38.

Nekitel, Otto. 1986. "A Sketch of Nominal Concord in Abu' (An Arapesh Language)." In *Papers in New Guinea Linguistics* No. 24, Pacific Linguistics A–70.

Nekitel, Otto. 1992. "Culture Change, Language Change: The Case of Abu' Arapesh, Sandaun Province, Papua New Guinea." In Tom Dutton (ed.), *Culture Change, Language Change—Case Studies from Melanesia.* 49–58. Pacific Linguistics C–120.

Nidue, Joseph A. 1990. "Language Use in a New Guinea Village: A Triglossic Profile of Makopin I." In *Language and Linguistics in Melanesia* 21: 47–69.

ARMENIAN

John A.C. Greppin

Language Name: Armenian. **Autonym:** *hayerēn.*

Location: The Eastern dialect of Armenian is spoken in the Republic of Armenia. There are also speakers of the Eastern dialect in the cities of Tehran, Isfahan, Shiraz, and the Charmahal district in central Iran. The Western Armenian dialect is spoken in Lebanon, in the Aleppo region and nearby coastal area of Syria, in Cairo and Alexandria in Egypt, in Cyprus, and in Istanbul, Turkey, where there remains a substantial Armenian colony (Armenian was spoken in Eastern Turkey from the first millennium B.C. until 1915). A special Karabagh dialect has been maintained in Western Azerbaijan since at least the third century A.D.

Language Family: Armenian is the sole member of the Armenian branch of the Indo-European family.

Related Languages: Most closely related genetically to GREEK, although this is only apparent with reconstruction.

Dialects: Modern Armenian has two main dialects, Modern Eastern Armenian (the official language of the Republic of Armenia) and Modern Western Armenian. There are numerous subdialects, many nearly extinct since the Genocide of 1915–18. G.B. Djahakian (1976) divides Armenian into eleven separate dialect groups (summarized in Greppin and Khachaturian 1986). Where not otherwise specified, information in this article is about Classical Armenian, from which both principal modern dialects are derived.

Number of Speakers: 5–6 million, the majority of whom (somewhat less than 4 million) live in Armenia and speak Modern Eastern Armenian.

Origin and History

Armenian falls into three periods: **Classical**, or *Grabar*, which dates from the 5th century, **Middle** (900–1600), and **Modern**, which dates from about 1600 on. The separation of the language into eastern and western dialects occurred at least by the beginning of the Middle Armenian period.

The origin of the Armenians is a puzzle. Because there are Urartian (and quite likely Hurrian and Luwian) loanwords in Armenian, we can assume Armenian presence in Eastern Anatolia certainly by the early first millennium, although there is not one sherd of pottery that identifies the Armenians before they are mentioned by ancient historians. They appear in the cuneiform inscriptions of Darius the Great (c. 525 B.C.) where it is noted that it took three campaigns for the mighty Persians to conquer them. This implies that by this time they were of good number and were unified. The Greek historians mention the Armenians in the late 6th century B.C. The Armenians' own historiography begins shortly after A.D. 400.

For the next millennium Armenia was ruled by a branch of the Arsacid dynasty that ruled in Persia before the Sassanids, and during this period over 600 PERSIAN (Iranian) roots of wide semantic range entered the language.

There followed periods of independence, the partition of Armenia between Persia and Rome in 397, and invasions by Arabs, Seljuk Turks, Mongols, and Ottoman Turks. The Armenians embraced Christianity in the fourth century. About 400 the Armenian alphabet was developed by a cleric, Mesrop Maštocʻ, and shortly afterwards the entire Bible and a large body of religious writing was translated into Armenian from Syriac and GREEK.

The first books printed in Armenian were produced in Venice in 1565. In the 17th century, presses in Paris, Lemberg, Milan, Padua, Leghorn, Amsterdam, Marseilles, Leipzig, Constantinople, and Isfahan (Iran) were also printing books in Armenian.

By the 17th century, overwhelmed by Ottoman rule, the Armenians had fallen into a trough of despair. At this point, Armenian religious groups were instrumental in increasing literacy, and the well-being of the population greatly improved. The Turkish massacres, occurring in the late nineteenth century, and the Genocide of 1915–18, in which between 800,000 and 1,500,000 died, virtually removed the Armenians from what was their ancient homeland. Among the diaspora in North America, South America, and in certain European cities, Armenian is maintained with difficulty and the second generation will frequently know only phrases.

Orthography and Basic Phonology

The Armenian alphabet was subtly derived from Greek and Middle Persian with original characters created for sounds that existed in neither of those languages. Until the 11th century the orthography was a near-perfect reflection of the phonology. After that time, there were slight phonological changes which caused the orthography to be a less perfect representation of the spoken language. In 1922 the Soviet Armenian government instituted orthographical reforms, although some of these were retracted in 1940. Armenian spelling today largely represents the pronunciation of the word, except for the use and non-use of schwa.

The primary phonological differences among modern Ar-

Armenian Alphabet

Capitals	Lower Case	Roman	Capitals	Lower Case	Roman	Capitals	Lower Case	Roman	Capitals	Lower Case	Roman
Ա	ա	a	Ժ	ժ	ž	Ճ	ճ	č	Ռ	ռ	ṛ
Բ	բ	b	Ի	ի	i	Մ	մ	m	Ս	ս	s
Գ	գ	g	Լ	լ	l	Յ	յ	y	Վ	վ	v
Դ	դ	d	Խ	խ	x	Ն	ն	n	Տ	տ	t
Ե	ե	e	Ծ	ծ	c	Շ	շ	š	Ր	ր	r
Զ	զ	z	Կ	կ	k	Ո	ո	o	Ց	ց	c‘
Է	է	ē	Հ	հ	h	Չ	չ	č‘	Ւ	ւ	w
Ը	ը	ə	Ձ	ձ	j	Պ	պ	p	Փ	փ	p‘
Թ	թ	t‘	Ղ	ղ	ł	Ջ	ջ	ǰ	Ք	ք	k‘

menian dialects involve consonant manner of articulation. Classical Armenian, illustrated in the table above, distinguished three consonant manners, voiced (*b*, etc.), voiceless unaspirated (*p*, etc.), and voiceless aspirated (*p‘*, etc.). This three-way distinction is preserved in Modern Eastern Armenian. In Modern Western Armenian, however, the voiceless unaspirated stops become voiced; in addition, the Classical voiced series merges with the voiceless aspirated series, so that only a two-way distinction between voiced and voiceless stops is observed.

Table 1: Consonants

	Labial	Dental	Alveo-Palatal	Velar	Glottal
Stops					
Voiceless	p	t		k	
Voiced	b	d		g	
Aspirated	p‘		k‘	k‘	k‘
Fricatives					
Voiceless	(f)	s	š	x	h
Voiced	w	z	ž		
Affricates					
Voiceless		c		č	
Voiced		j		ǰ	
Aspirated		c‘		č‘	
Nasals	m	n			
Resonants		l, r, ŕ	y	ł	

In Modern Eastern Armenian, the voiceless unaspirated consonants (*p*, etc.) have begun to be pronounced as ejectives [p‘ t‘ k‘ c‘ č‘]. This tendency is most common in speakers with little formal education. The affricates /c/ and /j/ are pronounced [ts] and [dz], respectively.

Table 2: Vowels

	Front	Central	Back
High	i		u
Mid	e ē	ä	o ō
Low		a	

The Classical Armenian length contrast in the mid vowels has been reduced in modern Armenian: word initial /e/ became /ye/, and /ō/ in loanwords became /ov/.

Armenian has some rules of vowel reduction. For example, CēC- and CoyC- roots (where C is any consonant) reduce to CiC- and CuC- respectively when a syllable is added to the root: *ēǰ* ‘page’, *iǰi* ‘of the page’; *hoyz* ‘juice’, *huzi* ‘of the juice’. The vowel in these stems can sometimes reduce further, to /ä/, if an additional syllable is added. This /ä/ was often written in Middle Armenian; in both Classical and Modern Armenian, however, it is usually not written. Thus, *vser* ‘boldness’, from *vēs-anam* ‘be arrogant’, in turn from *vēs* ‘arrogance’ is pronounced /vəser/ (ē > i > ə).

Basic Morphology

Armenian nouns are marked for number and case. The numbers are singular and plural. All eight Indo-European cases are preserved in Armenian: nominative, accusative, genitive, dative, ablative, instrumental, locative, and vocative, although the vocative has no special marking. There are numerous declensions for nouns, depending on features of the noun stem. Examples of two nouns, *cov* ‘sea’ (*u*-declension) and *hayr* ‘father’ (*r*-declension) follow:

	Singular	Plural	Singular	Plural
Nominative	cov	covk‘	hayr	hark‘
Accusative	cov	covs	hayr	hars
Genitive	covu	covuc‘	hawr	harc‘
Dative	covu	covuc‘	hawr	harc‘
Locative	covu	covs	hawr	hars
Ablative	covē	covuc‘	hawrē	harc‘
Instrum.	covu	covuk‘	harb	harbk‘

Armenian verbs agree with their subjects in person and number. There are three indicative tenses, present, imperfect, and aorist (past). Some representative first person forms of the verb *sirel* ‘to love’ are illustrated below:

	Singular	Plural
Present indic.	sirem	siremk‘
Imperfect indic.	serei	sireak‘
Aorist indic.	sirec‘i	sirec‘ak‘

Modern Western Armenian present is formed with a *k-* augment on the Classical Armenian, or Grabar, present stem.

Grabar *asem* 'I say'; Modern Western Armenian *kasem* 'I am saying'. The Modern Western Armenian future is a periphrastic form built with *piti* 'must'; thus *piti asem* 'I will say'.

Modern Eastern Armenian uses a periphrastic participial formation with the verb 'to be'; thus *asum em* 'I (am) saying'; the future is with the *k-* augment, Modern Eastern Armenian *kasem* 'I will say'. Causative verbs are formed by the addition of *c‘uc‘anem*: *sirec‘uc‘anem* 'I cause X to love'.

Basic Syntax

When no particular element is being emphasized, the order of elements is S-O-V:

Hovhannes šun tes-ē
John:NOM dog:ACC see-PRES/3SG
'John sees a dog.'

However, when the direct object is specific (marked with prefixed *z-*), word order is more flexible, depending on which element is being focused on:

Z-šun Hovhannes tes-ē
SPEC-dog:ACC John:NOM see-PRES/3SG
'John sees a dog.'

Adjectives do not occur in a fixed order relative to the nouns they modify, but may precede or follow, depending on such factors as emphasis and the case of the noun. Adjectives do not agree with the nouns they modify in case.

Verbs are negated by the addition of *mi* before the verb:

mi serēk‘
NEG love:2PL
'you (pl) don't love'

Contact with Other Languages

There are a substantial number of loanwords in earliest Armenian from Pahlavi, sufficient to cause the nineteenth-century grammarians to consider Armenian an odd Iranian dialect (disproved by Henrich Hübschmann in 1875). These Pahlavi loans represent words of a high frequency of use, and are not largely specialized vocabulary such as those from Greek and Syriac.

Following the Edict of Milan, Armenians embraced Christianity in A.D. 314, which made them the earliest Christian state. There was an intrusion of Greek (about 500) and Syriac (about 150) words, mostly of a religious or scholarly nature.

Following the late seventh century there began an ARABIC intrusion which in some dialects was extensive, depending on the distance from Arabic influence. In the 12th century the TURKISH intrusion began. And although the Arabic words intruded into the literary dialect, the Turkish vocabulary for the most part entered only the vernacular and by 1600 was pushing out Arabisms.

From Persian: *pahapan* 'guard' (< Pahlavi *paspan*)
From Greek: *ekełec‘i* 'church' (< Gk. *ekklēsía*)
From Syriac: *at‘ut‘ayk‘* 'alphabet' (< Syr. *āθūθa*)
From Hurrian: *xnjor* 'apple' (< Hurr. *hinzuri* '[apple] orchard')
From Luwian: *brut* 'potter' (< Luw. *purut* 'clay')

Common Words

man:	mard, ayr	big:	mec
woman:	kin	long:	erkar
water:	ǰur	yes:	aio
sun:	arew	no:	č‘ē, oč‘
three:	erek‘	good:	bari
fish:	jukn [dzukn]	bird:	t‘ŕč‘un, haw
dog:	šun		

Example Sentences

(1) Ew z-ays as-ac‘-eal hramay-eac‘
and SPEC-this-ACC/SG say-AOR-PAST PFCT order-AOR/3SG

zi z-niwt‘ šin-ac-oy-n
particle SPEC-material-ACC/SG build-NOMINAL-GEN/SG-DEF

vałvał-aki patrast-esc‘-en
quick-ly prepare-AOR/SUBJ-3PL
'Having said this, he ordered them to prepare quickly the material for the building.'

(2) surb hayr-s tesē
holy father-ACC/PL see.1SG
'He sees the holy fathers.'

Efforts to Preserve, Protect, and Promote the Language

In the nineteenth century there was an active movement to remove contemporary foreign vocabulary (most Armenians were at least bilingual, and hence knew if a word was a loan from ARABIC or TURKISH). This was a successful movement, influencing the literary language first, but also effective among the peasant population who were eager to assert their Armenian nationalism. The purge was overwhelmingly successful, and relatively few Arabisms or Turkisms are now used in either Eastern or Western dialect.

The Armenians take great pride in their language, and many firmly believe that Margaret Mead once said that Armenian was the most expressive of the world's languages and should be used in the United Nations as a lingua franca. The language is safe in Armenia, although under socialism some Armenians preferred Russian as a language to get along in the world with, and therefore did not learn to read and write Armenian well. Some even spoke the language poorly. Since independence, however, this is being reversed.

In the diaspora in the West, if a city has a sufficient Armenian population, Armenian day schools will be found which propagate the language, although there are political tensions about which dialect—Eastern or Western—should be taught.

Select Bibliography

Bedrossian, Matthias. 1973. *New Dictionary Armenian-English.* Beirut: Librarie du Liban. (Orig. pub. Venice, 1875–79).

Bardakjian, Kevork, and Robert Thomson. 1977. *A Textbook of Modern Western Armenian.* Delmar, NY: Caravan Books.

Bournoutian, George. 1994. *A History of the Armenian People.* 2 vol. Costa Mesa, CA: Mazda Publishers.

Greppin, John A.C., ed. 1994. *Studies in Classical Armenian Literature.* Delmar, NY: Caravan Books.

Greppin, John A.C., and Amalya Khachaturian. 1986. *A Handbook of Armenian Dialectology.* Delmar, NY: Caravan Books.

Samuelian, Thomas J. 1994. *Armenian Dictionary in Transliteration: Western Pronunciation.* New York: Armenian National Education Committee.

Thomson, Robert W. 1975. *An Introduction to Classical Armenian.* Delmar, NY: Caravan Books.

Zorc, R. David. 1995. *Armenian Newspaper Reader and Grammar.* Kensington, MD: Dunwoody Press.

ASSAMESE

Sanjib Baruah and Colin P. Masica

Language Name: Assamese. **Autonym:** *ɒχamiya*. "Normalized" name used elsewhere in India: *asamiya*.

Location: Spoken mainly in the Brahmaputra Valley of the State of Assam in northeastern India. The hill areas surrounding the Brahmaputra Valley, and parts of the Valley itself, are home to Tibeto-Burman-, Mon-Khmer-, and Tai-speaking peoples. Among these peoples, there are some, especially among those living closer to the Valley, who have traditionally spoken Assamese as a second, or sometimes even as a first language. However, among speakers of Bodo (a Tibeto-Burman language spoken partly in the Valley itself), the younger generation tends to look at this practice with disfavor.

The British province of Assam was larger than the present state, and included additional areas of non-Indo-European speech, some of which are now constituted as separate States of the Indian Union including Meghalaya, Arunachal Pradesh, Nagaland, and Mizoram. There are no large colonies of Assamese-speakers outside Assam.

Family: Eastern subgroup of the Indo-Aryan group of the Indo-Iranian branch of Indo-European. Assamese is the easternmost Indo-European language.

Related Languages: Assamese is most closely related to BANGLA, particularly to the northern dialects of that language. In fact, the (northern) Rajbangshi "dialect" of Bangla could be considered a dialect of Assamese that has come under Bengali cultural hegemony; that is mainly because the area concerned, which was once controlled by independent Koch kings, has in more recent times been politically a part of Bengal. Assamese also shares characteristics with other languages of the Eastern subgroup of Indo-Aryan, namely ORIYA and the "Bihari" dialects (MAITHILI, etc.). It also has features, not merely loanwords, that betray the influence of its immediate non-Indo-Aryan hinterland [see above and below] and thus link it in some respects with Southeast Asian languages.

Dialects: There is a basic East/West dialectal division with three main dialects: (1) Eastern Assamese (the speech of Upper Assam, centering on Sibsagar, on which the modern Standard language is based); and in the Western division, (2) Kamrupi and (3) Goalparia, which are spoken respectively in the (old) Kamrup and Goalpara Districts at the western end of the Valley (corresponding to the reorganized Districts of Kamrup, Nalbari, and Barpeta; and of Goalpara, Dhubri, Bongaigaon, and Kokrajhar), which are differentiated into further subdialects.

The premodern literary language was based on Western Assamese, which shares a number of features of pronunciation and morphology with neighboring so-called Northern dialects of Bengali [see above]. Western and Eastern Assamese dialects show differences in phonology (stress, vowel quality, and aspiration); morphology (plural markers and personal endings of verbs); and especially vocabulary.

There is also a class dialect with differences between Prestige and Vernacular speech being marked in phonology [see below] and usage of forms.

Two other forms of speech are sometimes called dialects of Assamese. Nagamese, a pidginized and subsequently creolized form of Assamese, is used as a lingua franca in Nagaland to the east. Bishnupriya Manipuri, sometimes called Mayang, is spoken by a group of people (est. 160,000) of Indo-Aryan origin formerly (until the 18th century) resident in the (mainly Tibeto-Burman speaking) State of Manipur (next to Burma) and now resettled in nearby parts of Assam, Tripura, and Bangladesh. Some authorities insist Bishnupriya Manipuri is a separate language or a sister, not a dialect of Assamese. In any case, it is not mutually intelligible with other forms of Assamese.

Number of Speakers: 8.9 million in 1971. By 1991 it is estimated that it grew to 13.6 million. The 1991 Census of India language data has not been made public.

Origin and History

Like Bangla, Oriya, and Maithili, Assamese derives from the eastern form of Prakrit (Middle Indo-Aryan) known as Magadhi. It represents the northeasternmost thrust of Magadhi-speakers up the Brahmaputra valley, into an area of Tibeto-Burman (particularly Bodo) and other non-Indo-Aryan speech (which is still present), and many of its special characteristics would appear to derive from the influence of this substratum.

The language of the *Sorjyapada*—poems composed by Buddhist monks between the 10th and 12th centuries and once thought to be the earliest known form of Bangla—has significant similarities with Old Assamese. It has similarities with Old Oriya and Old Maithili as well. It is likely that these poems were written in a language that was a common ancestor of all these languages, or it was a written language used by speakers of a variety of spoken languages. Leaving aside the Sorjyapada, the oldest surviving Assamese written texts are the retelling of tales from the Ramayana and Mahabharata epics by Hem Saraswati, dating most likely from the late 13th

Table 1: Consonants

		Bilabial	Alveolar	Palatal	Velar	Glottal
Stops	Voiceless	p	t		k	
	Voiceless asp.	ph	th		kh	
	Voiced	b	d		g	
	Voiced asp.	bh	dh		gh	
Fricatives	Voiceless		s		χ	h
	Voiced		z			
Affricates				(j)		
Nasals		m	n		ŋ	
Liquid			l,r			
Glides		w			y	

and early 14th centuries. The bulk of "classical" Assamese texts—the highly revered Vaishnava texts and the historical chronicles (*buranjis*) of the Ahoms—were written in the following three centuries.

The name of the language and of the country dates from an earlier version of the name of the medieval dynasty of the Ahoms, a people of Tai (Shan, i.e., Sham, cf. *Siam)* origin who ruled Assam for six centuries from 1228 (the traditional date, presently under minor revision) until the Burmese conquest in 1819, one of the longest-lasting and most stable Indian polities. The Ahoms gradually became Hinduized, and their language has nearly died out. The influence of the original Ahom language on Assamese seems to be limited to loanwords, but the detailed chronicles the Ahoms kept gave rise to a type of historical literature in Assamese, the *buranjis* (itself an Ahom word), which is unique in India.

The modern standard language developed under the influence of missionaries whose headquarters were in the upper part of the Valley; hence it reflects that dialectal bias. Although the "missionary standard" avoided SANSKRIT words in favor of everyday words, the literary language has subsequently been heavily Sanskritized.

Orthography and Basic Phonology

Assamese uses a semi-syllabic alphabetic script of the common Indic type. Word initial vowels and postvocalic vowels constitute syllables and are indicated by independent vowel symbols. Postconsonantal vowels, which combine with consonants to form syllables, are indicated by special signs above, below, to the right, to the left, or both to the right and the left of the consonant symbol, thus forming a syllabic bundle.

The orthography makes a number of distinctions which reflect phonological contrasts that obtained in Old Indo-Aryan but which do not obtain in Assamese. For example, distinct symbols are used to represent long high vowels and short high vowels even though Assamese now has no such phonological contrast. In addition, the orthography retains symbols for retroflex and dental stops even though the sounds these symbols once represented have merged phonologically as alveolars; it has three symbols for sibilants which all now represent the sound /χ/ (or /s/ in certain consonant clusters); and it has four orthographic affricates which now represent the two fricatives /s, z/ (involving the merger of aspirated and unaspirated affricates).

On the other hand, a phonological contrast now exists in Assamese between the mid-front vowels /e/ and /ɛ/, yet the orthography does not provide any means for distinguishing these sounds. Nor did the orthography distinguish the contrasting lower back vowels /ɔ/ and /ɒ/ until recently when an apostro-

Assamese is spoken mainly in the Indian state of Assam (shaded area).

phe was introduced to indicate the former sound. A special symbol has also been developed to represent the phoneme /w/.

Assamese shares with other Indo-Aryan languages the four-way contrast among voiceless unaspirated, voiceless aspirated, voiced unaspirated, and voiced aspirated stops. However, it differs from other Indo-Aryan languages in having only a three-way opposition in stop articulation positions. That is, like the surrounding Tibeto-Burman languages, Assamese lacks the dental/retroflex opposition in the apical stops. These have merged as alveolars in Assamese.

Table 1 on the previous page takes note of a feature of Prestige speech not described previously, namely the asymmetrical presence of /j/ contrasting with /z/ (a corresponding contrast between */c/ and /s/ is absent): *jowa* 'go' versus *zowai* 'son-in-law'. In this dialect there has been a shift from /j/ to /z/ that appears to have affected only part of the domain of [j] thus creating a split. This split is reinforced by borrowings from Sanskrit since Assamese /j/ often, but not exclusively, seems to represent etymological and orthographic "y": *χɒ jja* 'bed' (<Skt. *śayyā*)).

More work needs to be done on the distribution and history of this phenomenon.

/χ/ is a velar fricative without much friction, which has a palatal allophone [ç] before and after the high front vowels /i, e/.

All consonants except /r, χ, h, g/ may occur phonemically geminated (lengthened): *ɒssɒ* 'horse' versus *asɒ* 'thou art'. Many other consonant clusters occur, mainly in words borrowed from Sanskrit (*bhrɒm* 'illusion'), although, as in Bangla, many Sanskrit clusters are simplified as geminates, for example, *tɒttɒ* 'significance' < Skt. **tatva*.

Table 2: Vowels

	Front	Central	Back
	Unrounded		Rounded
High	i		u
Mid High	e		o
Mid Low			ɔ
Low		a	ɒ

All of the vowels except /ɔ/ occur with contrastive nasalization; for example, *sa* 'look!', *sã* 'shade'.

Basic Morphology

Assamese inflection, both nominal and verbal, is through regular (agglutinative) suffixation. Adjectives are not inflected.

The basic case suffixes, added to both singular and plural nouns, are the genitive *-ɒr*, dative *-ɒk*, allative ("motion toward; for") *-lɒi*, instrumental *-ere*, agentive *-e*, and locative *-ɒt*. The initial *-ɒ-* of the genitive, dative, allative, and locative is dropped when the suffix is added to a word ending in a vowel. The same case suffixes are used for singular and plural nouns. Other case notions are expressed by postpositions attached generally to the genitive, for example, *- ɒrχɔite* 'with'/sociative, *- ɒr pɒra* 'from'/ablative.

There is no unique plural suffix. One of a number of different words indicating quantity is suffixed to a noun to indicate plurality, but this is only if plurality would not otherwise be clear on the basis of linguistic context. The principle quantity words are *-bor, -bilak, -χɒkɒl*, and *-hɒt*.

Assamese has no lexical articles and nouns do not have grammatical gender, but Assamese has a system of noun classification that is akin to the numeral-classifier systems of Southeast and East Asia. It has a series of enclitic suffixes which classify nouns according to features such as nature (animate/inanimate), size, shape, physical state (solid/loose/flexible), and attitude (ordinary/respected/fond). When one of these is suffixed to a noun, the noun is understood as definite: *manuh* 'man', *manuhzɒn* 'the (respected) man', and *manuhgɒraki* 'the (highly repected) man'. When one of these is suffixed to the element *e-* (an abbreviated form of *ek* 'one') and is placed before the noun, the noun is understood as indefinite: *ezɒn manuh* 'a (respected) man'.

Except in the first person (*mɒi, ami* 'I, we'), Assamese personal pronouns are differentiated for honorificity rather than number. A gender distinction exists in Assamese in non-honorific third person pronouns: *χi* (masculine)/*tai* (feminine). Number can be indicated by using pluralizing suffixes akin to those of nouns. Unlike nouns, several interrogative, indefinite, and personal pronouns have an oblique form to which case suffixes are attached: *mɒi, mok* 'I, to me'.

Finite verbs agree with their subjects in person and honorificity, but not number: *dɛkhõ* 'I/we see', *dɛkhɒ* 'you (inferior/very familiar) see', *dɛkha* 'you see', and *dɛkhe* 'he/she/they/you-honorific see'.

Unlike a number of other Indo-Aryan languages in which suffixes and/or auxiliaries are used to differentiate aspect from tense/mood, Assamese is perhaps best analyzed as having a simple tense system. The present tense is formed by adding the personal endings to the simple stem. The suffix *-ib-* is used for the future tense (*dekhibi* 'you (inf./very fam.) will see') and *-il-* for the past tense (*dekhili* 'you (inf./very fam.) saw/have seen'). In the past tense, transitive and intransitive verbs show different endings in the third person (*-e* versus ZERO): *ahil* 'he/she/it/they came', *kɔrile* 'he/she/it/they did'.

A periphrastic tense made up of a verbal noun plus a present tense form of the verb 'to be' allows a verb to be interpreted as either present continuous or present perfect, depending on context: *dekhisɒ* 'you (inf./very fam.) are seeing/have seen'. Other periphrastic formations exist for the contrafactual and for the passive, which is based on a verbal noun in *-a, dekha jay*' (it) is seen'.

There is a productive causative formation in *-a, -uwa, -owa*: *kɒre* 'he/she/it/they do', and *kɒroway* 'he/she/it/they cause to do'. Other verb forms include the imperative (second and third persons), present participle and verbal noun (infinitive).

As in other Indic languages, the most productive method for deriving new verbal expressions is by combining a noun, adjective, or onomatopoeic form with the verbs 'to do' and 'to be': *bhojɒn kɒra* 'to eat' [polite].

Basic Syntax

The basic word order of Assamese is SOV. Variations on the basic order are possible, however, for affective and stylistic reasons; and subordinate clauses may follow as well as precede main clauses. Phrases are generally head-final, so that modifiers and complements normally precede their phrasal heads.

Subjects of transitive and some intransitive verbs receive agentive case. Direct objects receive nominative (unmarked) case, as do subjects of certain intransitive verbs.

χikkhok-e satra-χɒkɒl-ɒk path pɔrhay
teacher-AG student-pl-DAT lesson-NOM teach:3sg.PRES
'The teacher teaches the lesson to the students.'

Sentence negation is expressed by prefixing to the finite verb the particle *nɒ-* (the vowel of which assimilates to that of the verbal root): *misamas mas nɒhɒy* 'A shrimp is not a fish'. In addition, there is an invariant negative existential verb *nai* 'there is not; X is/are not present', as in *χi iyat nai* 'He (non-honorific) is not here'.

Contact with Other Languages

Like most other Indo-Aryan languages (except those under predominantly Islamic influence), modern Assamese draws on Sanskrit for its higher vocabulary by borrowing, or more often coining, words from Sanskrit elements, but assimilating the result to Assamese phonological patterns. Because of its geographical position, it has long been exposed to the influence of surrounding non-Indo-Aryan languages, of Tibeto-Burman and other stocks. These, particularly the Bodo language of the plains of Assam, have influenced Assamese structurally as well as in vocabulary. In phonology, they seem to be responsible for the merger of the two sets of apical (T/D) sounds into one alveolar set and for the change of C/J to S/Z. In morphology they seem to be the source of some of the plural markers, for example, *bilak*; and the source or model for the numeral classifier system, a special system of personal affixes attached to nouns referring to kinship (not described here); and a number of derivative and formative suffixes. Their influence may also be felt in the onomatopeic expressions, found, it is true, in other Indic languages, but in which Assamese is peculiarly rich: *zupzupia* 'very wet', *kinkinia boroχun* 'drizzling', *buku hɒmhɒm kɒre* 'anxious'.

From Tibeto-Burman (Bodo): *sɛp* 'squeeze', *bhɛkur* 'get moldy', *laŋi* 'fish trap'
From Mon-Khmer (Khasi): *khamos* 'grasp', *hɛno* 'it is said, they say', *khɒŋ* 'anger'
From Tai (Ahom): *paŋ* 'plan', *hai* 'noise', *zin* 'quiet', *zɛka* 'damp'
From Sanskrit: *akrɒmɒn* 'invasion, attack', *asrɒy* 'refuge'
From Hindustani (Urdu-Hindi): *khɒbɒr* 'news', *kitap* 'book', *sɒrkar* 'government'
From English: *gilas* 'glass', *daktor* 'doctor', *tebul* 'table', *iskul* 'school'

Common Words

man:	puruχ	yes:	hɒy
no:	nɒhɒy	good:	bhal
bird:	sɒrai	dog:	kukur
tree:	gɒs	small:	χoru
woman:	mɒhila	water:	pani
sun:	beli	three:	tini
fish:	mas	big:	daŋɒr
long:	dighɒl		

Example Sentences

(1) tɛkhɛt jetiya ah-i pa-y, mɒi tɛkhɛt-ɒk
He(HON) when come(ABS) reaches, I him-DAT

bisar-i ɒh-a-r khɒbɒr-to di-bɒ.
look(ABS) coming(vbl.n.)-GEN news-the give-FUT-IMPER
'When he arrives, let him know that I came looking for him.'

(2) χei dina mɒi nam-ghɒr-ɒlɔi ja-õte eikhini tha-it
That day I "Name-House"-to go-ing

manuh-ɒr bes bhir dekh-i-sil-õ
this spot-LOC man-GEN quite crowd seen-was-1st P.
'That day on my way to the Nam Ghor (Vaishnavite place of worship), I saw a big crowd of people here.'

(3) man-ɒr akrɒmɒn-ɒr χɒmɒy-ɒt ahom rɒza-r
Burmese-GEN invasion-GEN time-LOC Ahom king-GEN

bohubɒ-r da-daŋɔriyay gowalpara-t
many-GEN high-official Goalpara-LOC

asrɒy lɔi-sil-gɔi.
refuge take-PAST-go-CONJ.PPL
'During the Burmese invasion, many high officials of the Ahom king took shelter in Goalpara.'

Efforts to Preserve, Protect, and Promote the Language

The *Asom Sahitya Sabha* [*ɒχom χahityɒ χɒbha*], or Assam Literary Association, established in 1917, works on the preservation, protection, and promotion of Assamese. (In romanized Assamese the use of the letter "x" to represent the velar fricative is becoming common, but the Assam Literary Association, being a very old organization, has not adopted it, and retains the old pan-Indian transliteration-equivalent system for its romanized Assamese name.) Its publications include a dictionary, *Candrakanto Abhidhan*, and old Assamese texts as well as books by nineteenth and twentieth century pioneers of modern Assamese literature. Publication Board Assam or Axom Prokaxon Porixod also reprints major historical and literary texts. The Asom Sahitya Sabha has campaigned for the use of Assamese in the conduct of official business and as a language of education in Assam. The Assamese Departments of the Gauhati and Dibrugarh Universities in Assam are centers of scholarship on Assamese language and literature.

Insecurity about the status of Assamese culture and language as a result of demographic changes is a theme in successive political campaigns in Assam. Indeed, immigration may be causing the percentage of the population that speaks Assamese to drop. The contraction of the political boundaries of Assam as a result of the formation of new states and residual demands for formation of more states and the specter of further contraction of political boundaries contribute to this feeling of insecurity. In August 1985, an agreement between the government of India and leaders of a campaign demanding controls on immigration included a clause stating that "constitutional, legislative, and administrative safeguards, as may be appropriate, shall be provided to protect, preserve, and promote the cultural, social, linguistic identity, and heritage of the Assamese people." However, there have been no concrete programs implementing this part of the agreement.

Select Bibliography

Barpujari, H.K., ed. 1992– . *The Comprehensive History of Assam*, 5 vols. Guwahati: Publication Board Assa.

Barua, Hem Chandra. 1985. *Hem Kox [Hema Kosha]* [Assamese-English Dictionary], 6th ed. Guwahati: Hemkox Prokaxon.

Baruah, Sanjib. 1999. *India Against Itself: Assam and the Politics of Nationality*. Philadelphia: University of Pennsylvania Press.

Bhattacharyya, Budhindranath. 1988. *The Pronouncing Anglo-Assamese Dictionary*. Guwahati: LBS Publications.

Cantlie, Audrey. 1984. *The Assamese: Religions, Case, and Sect in an Assamese Village*. London: Curzon Press.

Dutta Baruah, P.N. 1975. "Negative Formation in Asamiya and Oriya." In *Indian Linguistics* 36.2:144–51.

Goswami, Golok Chandra. 1966. *An Introduction to Assamese Phonology*. Poona: Deccan College.

AYMARA

M. J. Hardman

Language Name: Aymara. **Alternates:** *Aimara, Jaqi aru.*

Location: Bolivia, southern Peru, and northern Chile; and, by migration, Buenos Aires and the coastal cities of Perú (Tacna, Arequipa, Cañete, and Lima).

Family: Jaqi.

Related Languages: Jaqaru and Kawki, the other extant Jaqi languages.

Dialects: The main dialect divisons are among (1) the area around Lake Titicaca including Huancané, Juli, Socca, and LaPaz; (2) the areas south, primarily the Bolivian Departments of Oruro and Potosí; (3) east in Calacoa and Sitajara in Perú; and (4) the Aymara spoken in northern Chile and southern Perú (Moquegua). While dialectal differences are relatively minor, mutual understanding is virtually always possible, usually with ease.

There are three additional social dialects: the Missionary, the Overlord, and the Radio. These are all a product of contact with SPANISH, the first two dating from the 16th century, the latter more recently. This article gives examples in the dialect from the La Paz region, the one with the largest number of speakers.

Number of Speakers: 3.5 million, according to calculations by native speakers and researchers. Government census numbers are sometimes as low as 1.75 million.

Origin and History

Aymara is the second most widely spoken indigenous language of South America (QUECHUA is the first). It is the first language of approximately one-third of the population of Bolivia. The Aymara-speaking population in Perú is considerably smaller, both in absolute size and in relation to the nation, but Aymara is nonetheless the dominant language of the southern area of that country. In northern Chile there are more than 20,000 persons who speak Aymara. Although the Aymara community is politically divided by the border between Perú and Bolivia which divides Lake Titicaca between the two countries, there is great unity in language and culture.

The Aymara are predominantly farmers and pastoralists, with the marketing of their own or their neighbors' products playing an important economic role. Most of the marketing, both wholesale and retail, domestic and international, is done by women.

Aymara is a member of the Jaqi language group, which includes two other known extant languages: Jaqaru and Kawki, both spoken in Perú. Archaeological and linguistic evidence points to a much wider distribution of the Jaqi languages in prehistoric times, at least as far north as Cajamarca in Perú and deep into Chile and Argentina in the south. The proto language—Proto-Jaqi—would appear to be the language of the Huari expansion, about A.D. 650. Proto-Jaqi became a major imperial language of Perú, serving as a lingua franca for the Huari culture which had an extensive trading network and road system.

Between about A.D. 400 and 800, Proto-Jaqi split and one branch became Proto-Aymara. After the collapse of the Huari culture, around 1000, the various Jaqi languages were isolated from each other. When the Incas, who were Puquina speakers, arrived in Cuzco to establish their own empire, they adopted a coastal language, Quechua, as their empire's lingua franca. (Although Quechua languages belong to a different language family, there has been contact between the two families for a minimum of two millennia.) The switch to Quechua took place less than a century before the European conquest. The bulk of the Aymara population was gradually pushed southward until that language came to occupy the area formerly held by Puquina speakers, around and south of Lake Titicaca. With the coming of the Europeans, most of the Jaqi languages died out, either by population loss or by enforced adoption of Quechua, continuing the process begun by the Incas. Spanish, brought by the Europeans, is the dominant language of South America today.

The first grammar of Aymara was by the Jesuit priest, Ludovico Bertonio (1603). In the same year he published in Rome two books, the *Arte y gramatica muy copiosa de la lengua aymara* and *Arte breve de la lengua aymara, para introduccion del arte grande de la misma lingua.* A second early grammar is that of Padre Diego de Torres Rubio, *Arte de la lengua Aymara*, published in 1616. Subsequent grammars have been largely copied, or miscopied, from these early works. All of the grammars have shared problems arising from an imposed Indo-European world view.

Orthography and Basic Phonology

There are compatible phonemic alphabets for all of the Jaqi languages. Alphabets have been the topic of intense argument, usually based on political and/or religious territories. The points of contention have been (1) the vowels—whether the Aymara

Table 1: Consonants

		Labial	Dental	Palatal	Velar	Postvelar	Pharynegeal
Stops	Unaspirated	p	t	ch	k	q	
	Aspirated	p"	t"	ch"	k"	q"	
	Glottalized	p'	t'	ch'	k'	q'	
Nasals		m	n	ñ	nh		
Fricatives			s			x	j
Laterals			l	ll			
Resonants		w	r	y			

three vowel system should be represented as five vowels so as to look more like Spanish; (2) the representation of the velar and post-velar consonants, using *q* and *c* for the velars and *k*, *cc*, *cq*, *qq* inter alia for the post-velars; (3) the representation of the *x*-*j* contrast, usually with *jj* for the post-velar fricative, which is problematic because both *x* and *j* occur in clusters; and (4) the representation of aspiration and glottalization. (The Aymara prefer to use " to mark aspiration, but the official alphabet uses *h*.)

Ch, ch", ch' are affricates. The Aymara orthography uses " to indicate aspirated stops: *p"* represents $[p^h]$, and so on for the other aspirated stops. A ' following a consonant letter indicates that the consonant is glottalized; that is, it is produced with a glottal closure simultaneous with the main consonant articulation.

Ll and *ñ* represent palatal sounds, similar to (but not identical with) *ll* of English *million* and *ni* of English *onion*. *Nh* represents the velar nasal, spelled *ng* in English. *R* is an alveolar flap, similar to *tt* in English *letter*. *X* is a post-velar fricative, while *j* is a pharyngeal fricative, similar to strongly articulated variants of English *h*.

Table 2: Vowels

	Front	Central	Back
High	i		u
Low		a	

Aymara vowels may be long or short. There are very few lexical roots distinguished solely by vowel length. However, vowel length does serve to distinguish grammatical inflections and derivations. In fact, there are two morphemes whose only expression is vowel length. In addition, part of the expression of a particular morpheme may be to lengthen a vowel in the stem to which it is added.

The precise quality of the Aymara vowels varies depending on consonantal context. Vowels adjacent to post-velar consonants are generally lower and/or further back relative to other instances of the same vowel. For example, *u* is generally perceived by speakers of English or Spanish as [o] preceding or following a post-velar consonant; likewise, *i* may be heard as [e] adjacent to a post-velar.

Aymara stress is fixed on the penultimate vowel in a word.

Basic Morphology

Many Aymara inflectional and derivational morphemes involve deletion of the final vowel of the stem to which they are added. Thus, the 1>3 verbal inflection *ta*, which must follow a consonant, requires the deletion of the final vowel from the verb root *uma* 'drink', producing, with the sentence suffix (see below) *wa*, *umtwa* 'I drink' (< *uma* + *ta* + *wa*).

Aymara does not mark number or gender on nouns. A suffix is now used for translation of the Spanish plural; some Spanish-Aymara bilinguals use this suffix in the manner of the Spanish plural markers.

Aymara has a case-like system for coding the syntactic function of nouns in a sentence. All nouns have a zero complement (indicated with Ø in sentence glosses), formed by dropping the final vowel of the noun stem: the zero complement of *t'ant'a* 'bread' is *t'ant'*. It is sometimes claimed that the zero complement is simply direct object, but the correspondence does not hold up. The *ru* complement (formed by suffixing *ru* to the noun) marks such functions as indirect object and direction.

The distinction between humans and nonhumans is important for many aspects of the morphology. There are two sets of pronouns, one for humans and one for nonhumans. There are four human pronouns: *naya* 'I, we (excluding you)', *juma* 'you', *jupa* 'he, she, they', and *jiwasa* 'you and I, we (including you)'. These pronouns are considered to represent first, second, third, and fourth persons respectively. The nonhuman pronouns are *aka*, *uka*, *k" aya*; these forms also serve as deictics, meaning approximately 'here, this', 'there, that', and 'yonder, yon' respectively.

Aymara verbs are inflected to agree with both subject and object. This agreement is marked by selection of an appropriate suffix that encodes the person of the subject and that of the *ru* complement simultaneously. There are nine combinations of subject and complement that are each encoded by a distinct affix. The following example illustrates some of the nominal and verbal marking described above:

Jupa-w jupa-r t'ant' chur-i
she-ss he-ru bread-Ø give-3>3/PAST SIMPLE
'She gave him bread.'

The suffix *-i* in the example indicates that both the subject and the *ru* complement are third person. (The sentence suffix *-w* will be discussed under syntax, below.)

Such modifications as benefactive and malefactive are indicated by combinations of verbal and nominative affixes;

Juma-taki-w t'ant' chura-rap-sma
you-for-ss bread-Ø give-BENEFACTIVE-1>2/PAST
'I gave her bread for you.'

Most verb roots take, preferentially, human subjects, but may take nonhuman subjects as well. But some verbs, like *achu-ña* 'to produce', take only nonhuman subjects:

Ch'uqi-w ach-u
potato-ss produce-3>3/SIMPLE
'Potatoes are produced.'

These roots may be made human by addition of the person causative affix *-ya*:

Ch'uq-w achu-y-ta
potato-Ø-ss produce-CAUSE-1>3/SIMPLE
'I produce potatoes/I cause potatoes to produce.'

Tense in Aymara involves both time and mode. There are five primary tenses: future, simple (non-future), remote, imperative, and desiderative. In addition to these primary tenses, there are three complex tenses: remonstrator, inferential, and non-involver.

There are two causatives in Aymara, one for the stem and one for the persons. The stem causative affix is *-cha* (such as *yatichaña* 'to teach' [= 'cause knowing'] < *yatiña* 'to know'), and the person causative affix is *-ya* (for example, *yatiyaña* 'to inform' [= 'cause someone to know']). The person causative can be reduplicated (as in, *yatiyayaña* 'to have someone inform someone').

Basic Syntax

Because of the extensive morphological marking of syntactic function both on verbs and on their nominal arguments, word order in Aymara is relatively flexible. More important than word order are sentence suffixes (indicated by ss in the accompanying examples). In addition to coding sentence type (indicative, interrogative, negative, etc.), they also contribute to data source marking. That is, the specific sentence suffix used may indicate whether the speaker is speaking based on his or her direct observation, based on what he or she has been told, or on neither. The *-w(a)* that occurs in many of the examples in this article indicates personal knowledge, for example. In Spanish-influenced Aymara, word order is more consistently Subject-Object-Verb.

Within noun phrases, adjectives and other modifiers precede the nouns that they modify:

Aka-x wawa uta-wa
this-ss child house
'This is the kindergarten.'

ch'uxña uta
green house
'green house'

Negative sentences in Aymara contain the particle *jani*. In addition, different sentence suffixes must be used than those used in the corresponding affirmative suffixes, and the verb in a negative sentence takes a derivational suffix from the complete/incomplete affix class.

Jani-w jupa-x jiwasa-r ch'uq
neg-ss they-ss you & me-RU potato-Ø

chur-k-istani-ti
give-INCOMPLETE-3>4/FUTURE-NEG
'They will not be giving us potatoes.'

Contact with Other Languages

Aymara has borrowed a great deal of vocabulary from Spanish during the 500 years of contact. Vocabulary has also been borrowed from other languages, currently from ENGLISH, and, to a lesser extent, JAPANESE. Some of the early borrowings from Spanish are completely integrated into Aymara; others, more recent, bring with them some of the phonology of Spanish.

From Spanish: *waka* 'cow', *parlaña* 'to speak', *tinta* 'store', *ilisa* 'church', *kujicha* 'harvest, crop', *iwisa* 'sheep', *papila* 'paper', *kasiki* 'chief', *kisu* 'cheese'

Common Words

man:	karmaja	woman:	warmi
water:	uma	sun:	inti
three:	kimsa	fish:	challwa
big:	jach'a	long:	jach'wa, lawq'a
small:	jisk"a	yes:	jisa
no:	jani	good:	suma ('beautiful')
bird:	jamachi'i	dog:	anu
tree:	quqa		

Example Sentences

(1) Aru-s-kipa-si-p-xa-ña
language-VERBAL-DERIV-RECIPROCAL-all involved-COMPLETIVE-NOMINAL

naka-sa-ki-puni-raki-spa-wa
all involved-you & I-just-EMPHATIC-indeed-VERBAL-3>3/DESIDERATIVE-SS

'It is my personal knowledge that all of us, you included, should make the effort to communicate.' (motto of ILCA [Instituto de Lenguaje y Cultura Aymara])

(2) Kuna-s us-tam
what-INTERROGATIVE hurt-3>2/SIMPLE
'What hurts you?'

(3) P'iqi-w us-utu
head-ss hurt-3>1/SIMPLE
'My head aches.'

Efforts to Preserve, Protect, and Promote the Language

At this time, though Aymara would appear to be decreasing as a first language, it is being formally studied by many people. Aymara is now taught at the Universidad Mayor de San Andrés in La Paz, with a degree offered. A number of people are also writing and publishing in the language.

The social dialect known as Radio dialect is the result of direct translations from Spanish, including Spanish syntactic patterns and borrowings to the point that sometimes the only Aymara content is that of the sentence suffixes. There is currently a movement among some Aymara radio personalities to combat the use of the Radio dialect.

The Instituto de Lenguaje y Cultura Aymara (ILCA) was founded in La Paz in 1972 as a private cultural institution to foster knowledge of Aymara. It publishes a newspaper in Aymara called *Yatiñasawa* ('We must be informed'). Its content is informational and cultural, written for Aymara speakers who already know the language. There are now two other Aymara language newspapers. Since 1965, Aymara studies and literary production have advanced, achieving respect for the Aymara language and culture.

Select Bibliography

Briggs, Lucy Therina. 1993. *El idioma Aymara: variantes regionales y sociales*. La Paz: Ediciones ILCA.

Hardman, M. J., Juana Vasquez, y Juan de Dios Yapita, con Lucy T. Briggs, Nora C. England, y Laura Martin. 1988. *Aymara: Compendio de estructura fonológica y gramatical*. La Paz, Bolivia: Editorial ILCA, Gramma Impresión.

Hardman, M. J. 1966. *Jaqaru: Outline of Phonological and Morphological Structure*. The Hague: Mouton.

____. 1978. "Jaqi: The Linguistic Family." In *International Journal of American Linguistics* 44:2.

____. 1978. "Linguistic Postulates and Applied Anthropological Linguistics." In *Papers on Linguistics and Child Language, Ruth Hirsch Weir Memorial Volume*, ed. by Honsa & Hardman. The Hague: Mouton.

____. 1981. "Aymara Language in Its Cultural and Social Context." In *Collection of Essays on Aspects of Aymara* Language *and Culture*. (Social Science Monograph Series, University of Florida), ed. by M. J. Hardman. Gainesville, University Presses of Florida.

____. 1982. "Mutual Influences of Andean Languages and Spanish." In *Word* 33:1–2.

____. 1985. "Aymara and Quechua: Languages in Contact." In *South American Indian Languages, Retrospect* and *Prospect*, ed. by Harriet E. M. Klein and Louisa R. Stark. Austin: University of Texas Press, 1985 (pp. 617–643).

AZERBAIJANIAN

Lars Johanson

Language Name: Azerbaijanian. **Alternate:** Azerbaijani, Azeri (this form is deprecated by many native speakers). **Autonym:** *Azärbayǰanǰa, Azärbayǰan didi.*

Location: Spoken in the Republic of Azerbaijan and in northwestern Iran. Similar dialects are also spoken in eastern Turkey, northern Iraq ("Iraq Turkmen"), Georgia, and Armenia.

Family: Southwestern (Oghuz) branch of the Turkic family.

Related Languages: TURKISH, Khorasan Turkic, and TURKMEN.

Dialects: The Azerbaijanian dialects are mostly divided into three groups: (1) Northern dialects in the Republic of Azerbaijan, (2) Southern dialects in northwest Iran, and (3) East Anatolian dialects in Turkey. Modern Standard Azerbaijanian is based on the dialect of the capital Baku. The Northern and Southern varieties differ partly in vocabulary, for example, northern *stol* 'table', *gäzet* 'newspaper' versus Southern *miz, ruznamä.*

Number of Speakers: About 20 million.

Origin and History

The Azerbaijanians go back to the Turkic-speaking Oghuz confederation of tribes, whose Inner Asian steppe empire collapsed in A.D. 744. One group founded the Saljuk state on the lower Syrdarya in the second part of the 10th century. In the middle of the 11th century, the Saljuk Oghuz left the area and migrated westward to establish a huge empire. Their modern descendants include the Azerbaijanians and the Turks of Turkey. Later on, the Azerbaijanians lived for centuries in relative separation from the Turks of Turkey because of political and religious boundaries. In 1828, Azerbaijan was divided into a northern part ruled by Russia, and a southern part belonging to Persia. In 1991, northern Azerbaijan gained independence under the name of the Republic of Azerbaijan.

The early history of Azerbaijanian as a literary language is closely linked to that of Ottoman Turkish. There was also a strong Turkish impact on modern written Azerbaijanian up to the first decades of the 20th century.

Orthography and Basic Phonology

Azerbaijanian has been written in ARABIC script up to the twentieth century. In 1929, a Roman-based script was introduced for Northern Azerbaijan but soon afterwards was replaced by a Cyrillic-based alphabet. A new Roman-based script was adopted by the Republic of Azerbaijan in 1991. At present, Northern Azerbaijan applies a dual script system with the Cyrilic and Roman alphabets appearing side by side. South Azerbaijanian, which has a limited use as a written language, is still written in Arabic script.

In the Cyrillic-based script, more recent loanwords from RUSSIAN are written according to Russian orthography. Table 2 on the next page shows the standard Azerbaijanian consonant phonemes; the phoneme /ž/ occurs only in loanwords:

The voiceless stops are aspirated. The fricatives /f/ and /v/ are labio-dental. A voiceless back stop back-velar [q] is lacking, except in dialects. The phoneme /k/ is realized as a front-velar [k̯] or as a palatalized variant [k´], whereas /ġ/ occurs as

Table 1: Azerbaijanian Alphabet

Cyrillic-based	Roman-based	Value	Cyrillic-based	Roman-based	Value	Cyrillic-based	Roman-based	Value
Аа	Aa	a	Ыы	Iı	ï	Сс	Ss	s
Бб	Bb	b	Јј	Yy	y	Тт	Tt	t
Вв	Vv	v	Кк	Kk	k	Уу	Uu	u
Гг	Qq	ġ	Кк	Gg	g	Үү	Üü	ü
Ғғ	Ğğ	γ	Лл	Ll	l	Фф	Ff	f
Дд	Dd	d	Мм	Mm	m	Хх	Xx	x
Ее	Ee	e	Нн	Nn	n	һһ	Hh	h
Әә	Əə	ä	Оо	Oo	o	Чч	Çç	č
Жж	Jj	ž	Өө	Öö	ö	Чч	Cc	ǰ
Зз	Zz	z	Пп	Pp	p	Шш	Şş	ş
Ии	İi	i	Рр	Rr	r	'	'	' (glottal stop)

Table 2: Consonants

	Labial	Dental/ Alveolar	Alveo-palatal	Front Velar	Back Velar	Glottal
Stops	p b	t d		k g	 ġ	
Fricatives	f v	s z	š ž		x ɣ	h
Affricates		č ǰ				
Nasals	m	n				
Liquids		l, r				
Glide			y			

a back velar (uvular) [ɢ]. The phoneme /g/ occurs as a front-velar [g] or palatalized [g´]. The phonemes /l/ and /x/ occur as backed variants [ł] and [x] in back syllables, and as fronted variants [l] and [ç] in front syllables. The back-velar fricatives /x/ and /ɣ/ are uvular. A non-phonemic glottal stop [ʻ] occurs in front of initial vowels. Loanwords from Arabic may contain a word-medial glottal stop, sometimes realized as vowel length, for example, *tä'sir* ~ *tä:sir* 'influence'.

Table 3: Vowels

	Front		Back	
	Unrounded	Rounded	Unrounded	Rounded
High	i	ü	ï	u
Mid	e	ö		o
Low	ä		a	

Vowel length is not distinctive, but appears at a subphonemic level. Long vowels appear in the pronunciation of Arabic and PERSIAN loanwords.

The vowels /e/, /o/ and /ö/ do not occur in suffixes. Certain bisyllabic stems lose the high vowel of their final syllable when a suffix with an initial vowel is added, for example, *oɣul* 'son' versus *oɣlum* 'my son'. Devoicing of word-final consonants and suffix-initial consonants after voiceless consonants is usually not reflected in the orthography, for example куч 'force', чыхды 'came out'. A number of stems display final weak obstruents that are voiced before suffix-initial vowels (mostly written *d*, *ǰ* etc.) and more or less voiceless in other positions (mostly written *t*, *č*, etc.) such as *gėdir* 'goes' versus *gėt!* 'go!' Strong obstruents are not subject to this alternation, for example *ata* 'to the horse' versus *at* 'horse'.

Although front versus back harmony is well developed in suffixes, for example *it-lär-imiz-dän* (front) 'from our dogs' versus *at-lar-ïmïz-dan* (back) 'from our horses', some suffixes are invariable, for example *-kän* 'while'. Rounded versus unrounded harmony does not affect low vowels. Thus, the low suffix vowels are /a/ and /ä/. Suffixes affected by both kinds of harmony display the high vowels /ï/, /i/, /u/, /ü/.

Basic Morphology

Azerbaijanian is an agglutinative language with suffixing morphology. Nouns and adjectives are formed from nominal and verbal stems by means of various derivational suffixes, for example, *gir-iš* 'entry' (*gir-* 'enter'), *duz-lu* 'salty' (*duz* 'salt'). Nouns take the plural suffix *-lAr*, possessive suffixes such as *-(I)n* 'your', and case suffixes: genitive *-(n)In*, accusative *-(n)I*, dative ('to') *-(y)A* locative ('in', 'at', 'on') *-DA*, ablative ('from') *-DAn*. (Capital letters are used here to indicate variation.) An example is: *yol-daš-lar-ïm-dan* (road-DERIVATION-PLURAL-POSSESSIVE 1P. SG.-ABLATIVE) 'from my comrades' (*yol-daš* < 'fellow traveler', sharing the same road).

Secondary verbal stems are formed from nominal and verbal stems by means of various suffixes. Deverbal suffixes include passive, cooperative, causative and other elements. Negation is expressed with the suffix *-mA*, for example, *get-mä-* 'not to go'. Finite and infinite verb forms consist of a simple or expanded lexical stem plus aspect/mood/tense suffixes and often person and number suffixes, for example, *bir-läš-sin-lär* [one-DERIVATION-OPTATIVE-PLURAL] 'may they unite'. There is a wide variety of simple and compound aspect/mood/tense forms, as well as numerous converbs and participles.

Azerbaijanian has numerous postpositions, corresponding to English prepositions, such as, *düsmänä ġaršï* (enemy-DATIVE-against) 'against the enemy'.

Basic Syntax

Azerbaijanian is syntactically very similar to other Turkic languages. It has a head-final constituent order, SOV. The order of elements in a nominal phrase is Demonstrative-Numeral-Adjective-Noun, for example, *bu beš gözäl aɣač* 'these five beautiful trees', and the head of a relative clause follows the relative, as in *sän ač-an ġapï* (you open-PARTICIPLE-door) 'the door you opened'. Conjunctions and other functional words copied from Persian and Arabic (via Persian) are frequently used, for example, *ki* (preceding complement and relative clauses).

Contact with Other Languages

Azerbaijanian has for centuries been in close contact with Persian. The modern written language has been influenced by Turkish. Northern Azerbaijanian has been strongly influenced by Russian in its modern vocabulary. The Persian impact on the syntax of Southern Azerbaijanian is considerable. Even loanwords written according to Russian orthography may be pronounced according to indigenous phonotactic rules.

From Persian: *kor* 'blind', *räng* 'color', *pul* 'money'
From Arabic: *kef* 'pleasure', *dua* 'prayer', *ġädär* 'amount'
From Russian (Northern Azerbaijanian): *stul* 'chair', *ġalstuk* 'necktie', *lampa* 'lamp'

Common Words

man:	kiši	woman:	ġadïn
water:	su	sun:	günäš
three:	üč	fish:	balïġ
big:	böyük	long:	uzun
small:	balaǰa	yes:	bäli, hä
no:	yox	good:	yaxšï
bird:	ġuš	dog:	it
tree:	ayač		

Example Sentences

(1) Sän-in ad-ïn nä-dir?
You-GEN. name-POSS.2P.SG. what-COP.3P.SG.
'What is your name?'

(2) Ömr-üm boy-u siz-ä minnätdar ol-aǰaɣ-am
life-POSS.1P.SG. length-POSS.3P.SG. you-DAT. grateful be-FUT.-COP.1P.SG.
'I will be grateful to you all my life.'

(3) Sän ġïz-ïmïz-ï tanï-yïr-san-mï?
you girl-POSS.1P.SG.ACC. know-PRES.-COP.2P.SG.-Q.
'Do you know our daughter?'

Efforts to Preserve, Protect, and Promote the Language

Northern Azerbaijanian has been subject to various standardizing measures. Since the proclamation of an independent republic in 1991, the language has consolidated its position further.

In Iran, where the public use of Azerbaijanian was banned under the Shah government, the social situation of the language is now improving and its status increasing.

Select Bibliography

Doerfer, Gerhard. 1959. "Das Aserbaidschanische." In J. Deny et al. eds. *Philologiae Turcicae Fundamenta, 1.* Wiesbaden: Steiner, 280–307.

Johanson, Lars & Éva Á. Csató, eds. 1998. *The Turkic Languages.* London & New York: Routledge.

Schönig, Claus. 1998. "Azerbaijanian." In Johanson & Csató 1998, 248–260.

Balinese

Adrian Clynes

Language Name: Balinese. **Autonyms:** *omong Bali, raos Bali, basa Bali.*

Location: Island of Bali, Indonesia. There are also smaller numbers of speakers on Nusa Penida (a small island off the southeast coast), in western Lombok (the island immediately to the east of Bali); southern Sumatra (Lampung area), and Sulawesi, the last two because of recent transmigration.

Family: Austronesian.

Related Languages: Balinese is generally sub-grouped with Sasak and Sumbawanese and is more distantly related to JAVANESE, MADURESE, MALAY, and other western Austronesian languages.

Dialects: Most divergent varieties are the minority 'Bali Aga' dialects spoken in isolated villages mainly in the central mountain chain. These are not always comprehensible to speakers of the numerically dominant lowland varieties, which are mutually comprehensible. Lowland varieties are normally further distinguished according to the eight administrative regions (and formerly independent kingdoms): Klungkung speech, Tabanan speech, Karangasem speech and so on. In fact there is lexical and phonological variation from one village to the next, all over the island.

Speech levels: All lowland varieties are characterized by 'speech levels', distinct informal and formal registers which to outsiders can seem like distinct languages; the speaker's perceived relationship with the addressee/person referred to is expressed via complex lexical choices. The Bali Aga varieties lack this feature, originally borrowed from Old Javanese, as well as other innovations found in the lowland varieties.

Number of Speakers: Bali 2.75–3.25 million; Lombok 70,000–80,000; southern Sumatra 35,000–40,000; Sulawesi 40,000–60,000.

Origin and History

Balinese has been spoken continuously on Bali for over 1,000 years. The earliest known written texts are royal decrees inscribed on copper/bronze plaques, dating from the 9th to the 11th centuries, and totaling about 10,000 words. There is clear SANSKRIT and particularly Old Javanese influence in these texts. Javanese cultural and political domination continued over a period of at least 700 years until the end of the 15th century, with profound cultural and linguistic influences, including the borrowing of the speech levels system. There was a more or less total break in cultural relations after that date, with hostility alternating with sporadic warfare between Hindu Bali and an increasingly Islamicized Java. Modern Balinese is as a result both heavily influenced by, and an important source of information about, spoken Old Javanese. Original works in Old Javanese verse forms were still being composed well into the twentieth century, with texts in native Balinese often closely following Old Javanese canons. Written literature until the twentieth century meant verse, although many short stories as well as novels and plays have since been published. At the same time there is a rich oral literature, including a variety of traditional theater genres.

The lowland varieties spoken in the Buleleng (north) and Klungkung (central-south) regions are the basis for the 'Standard Balinese' of education and broadcasting. In the area of the capital, Denpasar (in the south), verbal and nominal suffixes found elsewhere tend to be lost.

Published literature on Balinese is mainly in INDONESIAN, such as Kersten's grammar and dictionary (1984). Clynes (1994) describes the speech styles system and its history, Clynes (1995a) is a general introduction, brief literature survey, plus word list (the latter by Clynes and W. Bawa). Recent dissertations include Artawa (1994), Clynes (1995b), Arka (1998), all dealing with aspects of the grammar. Beratha (1992) is a useful source of data on Old Balinese. The variety described here is based on Singaraja Balinese, and is thus generally identical to standard Balinese.

Orthography and Basic Phonology

There are two scripts, the traditional *aksara* orthography, deriving ultimately from southern India but very closely related to the *aksara* script of Java, and the Latin orthography, introduced in the twentieth century and largely following the conventions of Indonesian orthography. The *aksara* script, although sometimes said to be syllabic, is largely phonemic except that: (a) the 'default' vowel /a/ is not normally represented; (b) in prefixes and word-finally, /ə/ is similarly not written (reflecting an earlier historical stage of the language when present-day /ə/ in this context was /a/); and (c) graphemes originally used to write Sanskrit aspirates and retroflexes are used idiosyncratically, for example, in some personal and place names.

The Latin script is generally phonemic and largely in accord with IPA conventions (see tables on the next page). The main exceptions are that: (a) there is no separate symbol for /ə/: in prefixes and absolute word-finally it is represented by <a>; elsewhere <e> represents both /ə/ and /e/; (b) the digraph <ng>

always represents /ŋ/; and (c) <ny> represents /ɲ/ before vowels, <n> represents /ɲ/ before homorganic stops.

In the rest of this entry, examples are given in the standard (Latin) orthography, with the exception that /e/ is written as <é>. Schwa (/ə/) is represented as indicated in (a) in the paragraph above.

Consonant phonemes are listed in Table 1 with their representation in the standard orthography. Where the IPA value differs, that value is given in brackets.

Table 1: Consonants

	Voicing	Labial	Apical	Laminal	Dorsal/ Back
Stops	-	p	t	c [tʃ]	k
	+	b	d	j [dʒ]	g
Nasals	+	m	n	ny [ɲ]	ng [ŋ]
Fricatives	-			s	h
Liquids	+		l, r		
Glides	+	w		y [j]	

Both apical and laminal series are realized in the alveolar region. /k/ is realized as the glottal stop [ʔ] in syllable codas. In the native lexis all consonants occur in syllable onsets, except /h/. All may occur syllable-finally, except laminal stops and glides. The liquids and glides occur as the second element in syllable-initial clusters.

The six vowel phonemes are listed in Table 2 with their representation in the standard orthography. Where the IPA value differs, that form is given in brackets.

Table 2: Vowels

	Front	Central	Back
High	i		u
Mid	é [e]	e, a [ə]	o
Low		a	

The high and mid (non-central) vowels have lax allophones in word-final closed syllables and are tense elsewhere (in Singaraja). Vowel-vowel sequences occur, with each vowel constituting a distinct syllable nucleus: there are no phonemic diphthongs or long vowels. Absolute restrictions on distribution of individual vowels are (a) /ə/ does not occur immediately before another vowel; (b) underlyingly, /ə/ does not occur in absolute morpheme-final position, although in derived contexts surfaces there, since (c) /a/, while occurring morpheme-finally underlyingly, does not surface absolute *word*-finally, being realized by [ə]. There is thus regular alternation of [a] and [ə] in morpheme-final position: for example, underlying /mata/ 'eye' realized as [matə], but *mata-ne* /mata-ne/ 'eye-DEF: the eye' as [matane]. More than 90% of lexical morphemes are disyllabic. Longer words generally contain derivational affixes as suffixes or prefixes, or both. Morphemes are of preferred shape C(L)VNC(L)VC, where N is a nasal homorganic with a following stop (or N before /s/), L is a glide or liquid, and the only obligatory elements are the vowels. Only one L slot may be filled. Consonant harmony restrictions disprefer the occurrence of more than one consonant of the same place of articulation per simple (non-reduplicated) morpheme. There is a strong tendency to vowel harmony, in that non-central vowels in adjacent syllables generally agree in height. All the above phonotactic restrictions are productively violated in the coining of expressive lexis.

Stress is on the final syllable, including derivational suffixes.

Basic Morphology

Balinese is a morphologically agglutinating language. A limited number of affixes signal a variety of functions; the meaning and syntactic behavior of a derived form is generally predictable from (a) the particular affix(es) used, (b) the semantics of the root.

Case, number, gender, and other such inflectional categories are not signaled. Plurality is optionally signaled by reduplication, on both nouns and verbs: *bé* 'fish' *bé-bé* 'fish (plural)', *mokoh* '(be) fat', *mokoh-mokoh* 'fat (plural)'. The presence of an affix does not necessarily indicate that derivation has occurred: in verbs (a) the presence in the semantic structure of an agent and (b) the semantic role of the undergoer participant of transitive verbs are both obligatorily signaled by affixes, even in underived verbs.

While many lexemes are monomorphemic, the maximal structure of both nouns and verbs is generally (prefix-) (prefix-) root (-suffix): *panyorogan* 'wheelbarrow', /pə-N-sorog-an/ CAUS-AGT-push-NOM, *masasorogan* 'push (vi, plural)' /mə-sə-sorog-an/ VBL-RED-push-LOC.

Clitic pronominals may attach to both verbs and nouns: *panyorogan=né* 'wheelbarrow-3; his/her/their wheelbarrow'; *jagur* 'hit', *jagur=a* [jagurə] 'hit=3; hit by him/her/them'.

Pronouns: Pronouns have exclusively human reference, generally signaling person but not number. Where understood from context, NPs with inanimate reference are simply ellipsed: *jəmak*! 'take [it]!'. Names and titles are often used as 'pro-pronouns', to avoid the more pragmatically charged choices.

awaké, icang	first person singular (familiar)
tiang	first person singular formal, first person plural exclusive
i raga	first person plural inclusive
cai	second person familiar
raga-né	second person formal (literally body-DEF, 'the body')
ia	third person
=a	clitic third person agent pronominal, on verbs
=né	clitic third person pronominal, on nouns: 'his/her/their'
raga-n-né	third person formal (body-GEN-3, literally 'his/her/their body')
ida	third person honorific (high caste referent), also used as second person honorific
ipun	third person humbling (low caste referent)

Definiteness is signaled by the enclitic *=é*, (*=né* after vowels). The latter allomorph is distinct from the invariant 3 clitic pronominal *=né*: *montor=é* 'the car', *montor=né* 'his car'. *=ne* is preceded by the 'genitive' linker *-n-*, though only after vowel-final heads: see *raga-n-né* above.

Principal nominal affixes: *pa-* [pə]: attaches to a variety of roots/stems: *pa-gaé* 'product of work' (*gaé* (vt) 'make'), *pa-dagang* 'merchant' (*ma-dagang* 'sell wares (vi)'), *pa-laib* 'running' (*ma-laib* 'run (vi)').

-an : attaches to a variety of roots/stems: *ajeng-an* 'food' (*ng-ajeng* 'eat (honorific)); *kikih-an* 'grater' (*kikih* 'grate (vt)'); *adeng-an* 'freckle' (*adeng* 'charcoal, noun'); *pules-an* 'bed' (*pules* 'sleep (vi)').

pa-(stem)*-an*: cooccur, producing nouns with meanings similar to those under *pa-* and *-an* above: *panyorogan* 'wheelbarrow', (*-sorog* 'push vehicle (vt)'; *pa-saré-an* 'bed', (*-saré* (vi) 'lie down, sleep'); *pa-lekad-an* 'birthplace, day of birth' (*lekad* 'be born')

Principal verbal affixes: Verbal affixation follows a split-S pattern. The term 'transitive' is used below to refer to a verb which encodes both an undergoer and an agent in its semantic structure: for certain lexemes only one of these is realized in the syntax, such as *ng-lengeh-in* 'be intoxicating' (of drink), carries affixes referencing both agent (the prefix) and generic undergoer (the suffix), yet an NP encoding the undergoer cannot occur in the surface syntax.

/N/-: prefix on both transitive and intransitive verbs where the subject is semantically agentive. Realized as /ŋ/ before sonorant-initial roots: (*ng-omong*, 'talk (vi)', *ng-wel*, 'scold (vi)'), and as a nasal homorganic with, and replacing, root-initial obstruents: *maling* 'steal (vt)' (*/N-paliŋ/*), *negak* 'sit (vi)' (*/N-təgak/*, *nyagur* 'punch (vt), active form (*/N-jagur/*), *ngaé* 'make (vt)', (*/N-gae/*).

'Ø-': the unprefixed root, occurs where the subject is semantically a patient, both on intransitives and transitives: *pules* 'sleep', *jagur* 'be punched' ; otherwise on a small class of non-derived intransitive verbs of motion: *luas* 'leave home', *pesu* 'go out'.

ma- ([mə]): prefix on (a) agentless stative intransitives, derived from transitives: *ma-jagur* 'be hit' (b) some non-derived intransitive verbs of motion *ma-jalan* 'walk', *ma-jujuk* 'stand up'. Allomorph: *m-* before some vowel-initial roots.

pa- ([pə]): causative prefix, the agent is a 'causer': *pa-gedé-nin* 'CAUS-big-LOC': 'enlarge'; *labur* 'whitewash (vt)' *pa-labur-ang* 'have whitewashed'.

ka- ([kə]): prefix on a variety of derived 'passive'-like transitive and intransitive verbs.

-in : suffix on derived and non-derived transitive verbs, where the semantic role of the undergoer NP is 'locative' (location, goal, source): *tegak-in* 'sit on' (*tegak* 'sit (vi)'), *kulit-in* 'skin (vt), (*kulit* 'skin, noun'), *beli-in* 'buy from, (*beli* 'buy, (vt)'). Otherwise, on 'verbs of violence', indicates that the action of the verb is repeated: *jagur* 'punch', *jagur-in* 'punch repeatedly'. Allomorph: *-nin* after some vowel-final roots.

-an : allomorph of *-in*, on derived intransitives: *ma-jagur-an* 'punch repeatedly (vi)' from *jagur-in* 'punch repeatedly (vt)'. Attached to a nominal base *-an* derives verbs with locative sense: 'covered or affected by (base)' e.g. *oong-an* 'covered in fungus', *oong* 'fungus'. Allomorph: *-nan* after some vowel-final roots.

-ang: suffix on transitive verbs, where the semantic role of the undergoer NP is 'circumstantial' (benefactee, causee, instrument, thing transferred): *beli-ang* 'buy for; buy with (*beli* 'buy (vt)'); *tegak-ang* 'cause to sit down'. Allomorphs: *-nang* or *-yang* after some vowel-final roots.

Basic Syntax

Balinese has many typical 'western Austronesian' syntactic features, including marking on the verb of the semantic/thematic role of core NP arguments, patient primacy (in that 'passive' or 'undergoer pivot' clauses seem more basic than 'active/actor pivot' clauses), and restriction of relativization to (mainly) subjects and possessors of subjects. Apart from VPs, NPs and PPs may fill the predicate position. Verbs are not inflected for tense or aspect (aspect only is marked, lexically), or for other inflectional categories. There is little or no evidence for the syntactic relation object and debate as to whether the syntax is nominative-accusative, ergative-absolutive, a mixed system, or none of these.

Word order at clause level is primarily subject-predicate, though predicate-subject order is also common. Balinese is a head-initial language, with these basic orderings:

Verb > 'Object'/Complement	*naar nasi* 'eat rice'
Noun > Stative verb ('adjective')	*anak luh* 'person female: woman'
Noun > Genitive	*panak bikul* 'child (of) mouse'
Noun > Relative clause	*panak-né ané cerik* (child=3 REL small) 'her small child'
Adposition > Noun phrase	*uli buléléng* 'from Buleleng'

Negation: Both verbal and nominal predicates are negated with *sing*: *tiang sing ngelah pipis* 'I don't have (any) money'. Only nominal predicates can be negated with *(ti)dong: ené dong pipis* 'This (is) not money'. NP-internal negators (as in English 'I have no money') do not occur.

Speech Levels: As in Javanese, distinct speech 'levels' or registers are the result of obligatory choices among lexical alternants belonging to distinct pragmatic classes. The choice of functors can indicate social closeness/informality, such as *sing* 'NEGator' (everyday lexis) or distance/formality, as in *nénten* 'NEG' (HI/*alus* lexis). For the lexical classes (nouns, verbs), there are three distinct 'high' subclasses:

(A) general HI/*alus* lexis encodes distance/formality: *peken* 'market (everyday form)' *pasar* 'market, HI';

(B) honorific/*alus singgih* lexis encodes the honorific/higher status of the person referred to, generally with respect to the speaker: *cokor* 'leg (of honored person)' cf *batis* 'leg (everyday)'; *séda* 'dead (of honored person)' cf *mati* 'dead (everyday form)';

(C) deferential or *alus sor* lexis: the humbler status of the person referred to, with respect to the addressee: *titiang* 'first person pronoun, deferential' (*awaké, icang*, everyday forms), *neda* 'eat (of humble person)' cf *ng-rayun-ang* 'eat HON', *ma-daar* 'eat (everyday)'.

For several hundred of the most common meanings, choice among such dyads or triads is required. Generally this is the case even within the family: children should use formal and honorific/deferential lexis when addressing parents and (often) elder siblings, who return everyday/low style. And even in otherwise everyday style, honorifics for third-person reference are used as required.

Contact with Other Languages

As well as the extensive influence of Javanese, there are large numbers of Sanskrit loanwords (particularly in the fields of religion, arts, and government), as well as borrowings from languages such as Malay and in the 20th century DUTCH and (most recently) ENGLISH. Generally borrowings from other languages such as PORTUGUESE and CHINESE have come via Malay. It is likely that the prolonged contact with Javanese and Malay over more than 1,000 years has also influenced the syntax, morphology, and phonology.

From Sanskrit: *drué* 'property HON' (Skt *dravya-*); *raga* 'body HON', (Skt. *ra:ga*); *uga* 'yoke' (Skt *yoga-*); *istri* 'female HON' (Skt *stri:*); *ramayana* 'Hindu epic' (Skt *ra:maya:na*); *agama* 'religion' (Skt. *a:gama*)

From Javanese: *-daar* 'eat' (Jav. *dhahar*); *cokor* 'leg HON' (Jav. *cakar*); *cang* first person (familiar) pronoun, *titiang* first person (deferential) pronoun, both from Jav. *tiang* 'person'

From Dutch: *atrék* 'reverse (a car)' (D. *achteruit*); *nécis* 'smart, well-dressed' (D. *netjes*); *saklek* 'business-like, cold' (D. *zakelijk*); *kapling* 'land division, lot' (D. *kaveling*)

From Malay: *tiga*, 'three HI' (M. *tiga* via Javanese); *ma-kata* 'speak Malay/Indonesian' (M. *kata* 'word'); *baju* 'dress, shirt' ultimately from Portuguese

From English: *turis, toris* 'European' from *tourist*; *baipas* 'by-pass (road)', *ski* 'surfboard'

Common Words

man:	anak muani	long:	lantang
woman:	anak luh	small:	cenik
water:	yéh	yes:	aa, inggih
sun:	mata-n-ai (eye-GEN-sun)	no:	sing
		bird:	kedis
three:	telu	dog:	cicing
fish:	bé	tree:	punya, punya-n kayu
big:	gedé		

Example Sentences

(1) tiang anak bali
1exc person Bali
'I am a Balinese.'

(2) kuluk-é medem [N-pədəm]
dog-DEF AGT-sleep (AGT = subject is agent)
'The dog is sleeping.'

(3) tikeh tiang-é pedem-in-a ajak kuluk-é
mat 1exc-DEF UND.sleep-LOC=3 with dog-DEF
'My mat was slept on by the dog.' (UND = subject is undergoer, LOC = undergoer is location)

Efforts to Preserve, Protect, and Promote the Language

The national language, *Bahasa Indonesia*, which is spoken by most people, has increasing influence, encroaching in many domains where previously only Balinese was spoken. It is common now for urban teenagers to speak only Indonesian with their parents and peers, and there is growing concern that Indonesian will supplant Balinese as the language of the city-raised, with Balinese increasingly restricted to the villages.

Select Bibliography

Arka, I Wayan. 1998. *From Morphosyntax to Pragmatics in Balinese: A Lexical-Functional Approach.* Ph.D. dissertation. University of Sydney.

Artawa, I Ketut. 1994. *Syntactic Ergativity in Balinese.* Ph.D. dissertation. La Trobe University.

Beratha, Ni Luh Sutjiati. 1992. *Evolution of Verbal Morphoplogy in Balinese.* Ph. D. dissertation. Australian National University.

Clynes, Adrian. 1994. "Old Javanese Influence in Balinese: Balinese Speech styles." In Tom Dutton and Darrell T. Tryon, eds. *Language Contact and Change in the Austronesian World.* Berlin: Mouton de Gruyter.

______. 1995a. "Balinese." In Darrell T. Tryon, ed. *Comparative Austronesian Dictionary.* Part 1: Fascicle 1. Berlin: Mouton de Gruyter. 495–509.

______. 1995b. *Topics in the phonology and morphosyntax of Balinese.* Ph.D. dissertation. Australian National University.

Kersten, J. 1984. *Bahasa Bali.* Ende: Nusa Indah.

BALOCHI

Carina Jahani

Language Name: Balochi. **Alternate:** Baluchi (Persian pronunciation). **Autonym:** *Balochi.*

Location: Southwestern Pakistan in the province of Baluchistan, smaller populations also in Punjab and Sind, and a large group in Karachi; Southeastern Iran in the province of Sistan and Baluchistan and smaller populations also in province of Khorasan; southern Afghanistan in the province of Nimruz; the Gulf States and Turkmenistan in the Marw region. After the Islamic Revolution a limited number of mainly well-educated Baloch from Iran took refuge in several European countries, the United States, and Canada.

Family: The West Iranian group of the Iranian branch of the Indo-European family.

Related Languages: Balochi is most closely related to KURDISH and other northwest Iranian languages, such as Tāti and Tālišī. It is also related to PERSIAN (southwest Iranian), although the structure of Balochi is closer to that of Parthian, Middle Persian and Classic New Persian than to Modern New Persian. Balochi is more distantly related to PASHTO, Ossetic and other east Iranian languages. The Middle Iranian language to which Balochi stands in closest relation is Parthian, known mainly from stone inscriptions and religious (Manichean) literature.

Dialects: The main dialect split is among eastern, southern, and western dialects. (1) Eastern Balochi is characterized by a change of stops and affricates, except the retroflex stops, into fricatives in intervocalic and word-final postvocalic position. These dialects are spoken in border areas to Indian languages in Punjab, Sind, and the northeastern parts of Pakistani Baluchistan, and are heavily influenced by Indian languages, for example, SINDHI and Lahnda.

(2) Southern Balochi is spoken in the coastal areas of the Balochi-speaking parts of Iran up to Iranshahr and Pakistan up to the Kech valley and also in Karachi as well as in the Gulf States. These dialects are characterized by a lack of flat fricatives (except /h/) and by strong nasalization (a feature they share with Eastern Balochi).

(3) Western Balochi is spoken in the northern Balochi-speaking area in Iran in and around Zahidan and southwards past Khash as well as in Khorasan, in Pakistan in the central parts of the province of Baluchistan but not in the northeast, in Afghanistan, and in Turkmenistan.

There are also other differences both in phonology, morphology, syntax and lexicon among the different dialect groups. The dialect picture outlined here is a broad division. Within the three groups further dialect divisions can be made. The dialect of Karachi, for example, is characterized by stronger URDU influence than other southern dialects, and the dialect of the Sarawan district in Iran is characterized by heavy Persian influence. In modern times because of mass media and education in other languages than Balochi, the Balochi of Iran as a whole has been more and more strongly influenced by Persian, and the Balochi of Pakistan has been strongly influenced by Urdu and ENGLISH. Presumably the same phenomenon can be observed in ARABIC-speaking countries and in Turkmenistan.

Number of Speakers: 5–8 million. It is difficult to estimate because central governments do not want to stress ethnic identity in census reports. The main populations are in Iran and Pakistan.

Origin and History

The Balochi language is a northwest Iranian language but is now spoken in the southeastern corner of the Iranian linguistic area. According to the epic tradition of the Baloch themselves, they are of Arabic origin and migrated from Aleppo after the battle of Karbala, where they (despite being mainly Sunni Muslims) fought on the side of the Shiah Muslim imam and martyr Hussein. Even if these legends must be seriously questioned, they may carry at least some truth in them. It is likely that the original home of the Baloch was somewhere in the central Caspian region, and that they then migrated southeastwards under pressure from Turkic peoples invading from the Iranian plateau from Central Asia.

The Balochi language has long been regarded as a dialect of Persian and has not until recently been used as a written language. Balochi possesses, however, a rich oral literature in both poetry and prose. As a written language Balochi can be divided into two periods: the colonial period with British rule in India and the period after the Independence of Pakistan. During the first period most of the existing written literature was produced as a result of British influence. The literature of this time on and in Balochi consists of grammar books and collections of oral poetry and tales in order to provide samples of the language and to make it possible for British military and civil officials to learn Balochi.

Balochi was more widely spoken in the nineteenth and early 20th centuries than it is today. Especially in Punjab and Sind there are now many people who recognize themselves as Baloch but speak Indian languages. There are also Baloch both in the Gulf States and in eastern Africa who have switched from speaking Balochi to speaking (and writing) Arabic and

Table 1: Consonants

	Labial	Dental	Alveolar	Retroflex	Palato-Alveolar	Palatal	Velar	Uvular	Glottal
Stops	p b	t d		(ṭ) (ḍ)			k g	(q)	
Fricatives	(f)		s z		š ž		(x) (ġ)		h
Affricates					č j				
Nasals	m	n		(ṇ)					
Resonants			l, r	(ṛ)					
Glides	w					y			

SWAHILI respectively. On the other hand, several Brahui tribes, both in Iran and Pakistan, have switched to speaking Balochi.

With the withdrawal of the British and the independence of Pakistan in 1947, the Baloch themselves became increasingly concerned with the development of their language. Baloch poets, who had previously composed in Persian and Urdu, started to write poetry in their mother tongue. Literary circles were founded and publication of magazines and books in Balochi began. This use of Balochi as a written language has mainly been limited to Pakistan where Quetta and Karachi soon developed into the two main centers of Balochi literary activities. In Iran, Afghanistan, Turkmenistan, and the Gulf States, Balochi is still mainly an oral language despite sporadic attempts at writing and publication. Thus Balochi is mainly a language of the home and the local community.

Orthography and Basic Phonology

Balochi has a very short tradition of writing. The works written in the nineteenth and early twentieth centuries by Englishmen are in Latin script. The orthography used today by the Baloch in Pakistan is based on the Arabic script, using Persian-Urdu conventions. There is no standard written language, and therefore no fixed alphabet. Depending on which dialect is written, the number of letters in a proposed alphabet may vary. Writers of Southern Balochi may not want to employ the letters for some of the fricatives, and writers of Eastern Balochi may add several signs, for example, for aspirated stops.

In the Balochi alphabet there are some phonemes that can be represented by more than one sign, for example /s/ and /z/. This is because the script was originally developed for the Arabic language which has several consonant phonemes not found in Indo-Iranian languages. The complete Arabic alphabet has, however, been adopted for Persian/Urdu and thereby also for Balochi, and Arabic loanwords in Balochi are generally spelled in accordance with their spelling in Arabic. This leads to over-representation of consonant phonemes. Vowel phonemes are, on the contrary, not fully represented.

The retroflex consonants were borrowed from Indian languages; /ṇ/ is found only in Eastern Balochi. The fricative phonemes /f/, /x/, and /ġ/ are found in Western Balochi in non-native loanwords of, for example, Persian origin. In Eastern Balochi, these fricatives occur also as variants of the stops /p/, /k/, and /g/. The phoneme /q/ is found only in learned pronunciations of loanwords, in both Eastern and Western Balochi. Normally it is replaced by /k/.

Because of the large number of loanwords from Indian languages in Eastern Balochi, voiced unaspirated and aspirated stops and fricatives, namely /p^h, b^h, t^h, d^h, k^h, g^h, $\check{c}^h$, j^h/, have entered the phonological system of those dialects.

Both unaspirated and aspirated plosives are voiceless in Western and Southern Balochi. In Eastern Balochi, the voiceless stops and the voiceless affricates are aspirated in word-initial position as well as after consonants in word-medial and word-final position. All the stops and affricates (except /ṭ/ and /ḍ/) become fricatives in intervocalic and word-final post-vocalic position. Only in word-medial position before a consonant are the voiceless unaspirated stops and the voiceless unaspirated affricate kept unchanged.

Because of loanwords, this picture may be disturbed. When a word with an intervocalic stop is borrowed into Eastern Balochi without changing this stop to the corresponding fricative, a phonemic contrast develops, and a separate fricative phoneme must then be established.

Final consonants are often lengthened in one-syllable words with a short vowel, as in *piss* 'father', *duzz* 'thief'. There are minimal pairs such as *čam* 'trick' - *čamm* 'eye' where consonant length is phonemic.

Table 2: Vowels

	Front	Central	Back
High	ī i		u ū
High-mid	ē		ō
Low-mid		a	
Low		ā	

Because of nasalization, five additional phonemes /ā̃ ē̃ ī̃ ū̃ ō̃/ may need to be established for Southern and Eastern Balochi.

In Southern Balochi, *jā̃* 'he hits' (Western *jant*) contrasts with *jā* 'he hit' (Western *jat*).

Stress in Balochi falls on the last syllable of the word, except in vocatives, which carry the stress on the first syllable. Inflectional endings are, however, for the most part unstressed.

Basic Morphology

Nouns in Balochi are inflected for number (singular, plural) and case (nominative, genitive, accusative/dative, general oblique); there is no grammatical gender. The inflected forms of the noun *dračk* 'tree' are illustrated below.

	Singular	Plural
Nominative	dračk	dračk
Genitive	dračk-ē	dračk-ānī
Acc./Dat./Obl.	dračk-ā	dračk-ān
Vocative	dračk	dračk-ān

Nouns in the accusative/dative/oblique case may take the additional ending *-rā* (singular)/*-ā* (plural), especially if the noun is emphasized. The nominative singular and plural forms are identical in Balochi. However, in some dialects of Iranian Balochi, the suffix *-ān* is added to the noun also in the nominative plural under the influence of Persian.

The suffix *-ē* is added to singular nouns to mark indefiniteness, as in *dračk-ē* 'a tree'. Only definite nouns take the case endings *-ā*/*-ān* as direct objects; an indefinite direct object occurs in the nominative, marked with the indefinite ending *-ē* in the singular, and in the nominative without any suffix in the plural. Prepositions govern the oblique case, while postpositions govern the genitive case:

gōn	ē	kalam-ā	
with	this	pen-OBL/SG	'with this pen'

mēz-ē	sar-ā	
table-GEN/SG	on	'on the table'

Pronouns are inflected according to Table 4 on the next page (with dialect forms in parentheses).

In several Balochi dialects there is a first person plural inclusive pronoun *māšmā* 'we' (lit. 'we-you'). It is declined like *šumā*.

When a pronoun refers back to the subject of a sentence, the reflexive pronoun *wat* 'self' (always singular) is used.

Balochi verbs have two stems, one for present tense forms and one for past tense forms. The infinitive is in most dialects derived from the present stem, for example, *kan-ag* 'to do', but in some dialects of Western Balochi from the past stem, as in *kurt-in* 'to do'.

Verbs are inflected for person and number, as illustrated in Table 3 in the Western and Southern present indicative forms of the verb *wānag* 'to read'.

Present subjunctive and imperative forms add the prefix *bi-/bu-/b-* to the present indicative forms. Past tense forms differ from present tense forms in that the third person singular lacks personal endings. Compound past tenses are formed by the past participle (ending in *-ag*) and inflected forms of the verb 'to be'.

There are several periphrastic verbal constructions:

Progressive:	kan-ag-ā	un
	do-INFIN-OBL	be-1SG
	'I am doing'	

Iterative:	kan-ān	un
	do-PRES/PART	be-1SG
	'I keep on doing'	

Obligatory:	raw-ag-ī	un
	go-FUT-PART	be-1SG
	'I must/intend to/will/have to go'	

Potential:	ōdā	šut	na-kan-īn
	there	go-PAST	NEG-do-PRES/1SG
	'I cannot go there'		

Causative verbs are formed by adding the suffix *-ēn* to the present stem of the verb it is formed from, for example, *wān-ēn-ag* 'to educate' from *wān-ag* 'to study'.

There are several suffixes that are used in Balochi word formation. Some of the most common ones are *-ōk*, added to the present stem of a verb to form an agent noun, as in *guš-ōk* 'speaker' from the verb *guš-ag* 'to speak'; *-ānk*, added to the past stem of a verb to form a verbal noun (*guš-t-ānk* 'speech'); *-kār*, denoting a person, like *rad-kār* 'criminal' from *rad* 'mistake'; and *-ī*, to form either an abstract noun, as in *jwān-ī* 'goodness' from *jwān* 'good', or in adjectives like *ṭapp-ī* 'wounded' from *ṭapp* 'wound'.

Basic Syntax

The basic word order in Balochi is SOV. The word order may be altered to OSV to emphasize the object. The relative order of direct and indirect object is also quite free, with the more emphasized object coming earlier in the sentence.

man-ī	mās	ta-rā	kitāb
my-GEN/SG	mother-NOM/SG	you-DAT/SG	book:NOM.PL

dāt
give:PAST.3SG
'My mother gave you books.'

The subject of actively construed verbs stands in the nomi-

Table 3: Present Indicative of *wānag* 'to read'

	Singular	
	Western	Southern
First person	wān-īn	wān-ā̃
Second person	wān-ay	wān-ē
Third person	wān-īt	wān-ī
	Plural	
	Western	Southern
First person	wān-an	wān-ē̃
Second person	wān-it	wān-ē
Third person	wān-ant	wān-ā̃

Table 4: Inflected Pronouns

	Nominative	Genitive	Accusative/ Dative	Oblique
Singular				
First person	man	man-ī (m(i)n-ī)	man-ā	man
Second person	taw (ta, tō)	ta^{y}ī (tī)	ta-rā	taw (ta, tō)
Third person	ā	ā^{y}ī	ā^{h}īyā (ā^{h}i-rā)	ā^{y}ī
Plural				
First person	mā	may (mē)	mā-rā	mā
Second person	šumā	šumay (šumē)	šumā-rā	šumā
Third person	ā	āwān-ī	āwān-ā āhān-rā	āwān

native case; the agent of ergatively construed verbs stands in the oblique case and its patient in the nominative. In Eastern and Southern Balochi, past tenses of verbs are construed ergatively and other tenses are construed actively; in Western Balochi the active construction predominates.

ē mard-ā ta'-ī kitāb want-ā̃
this man-OBL/SG your-GEN/SG book:NOM.PL read-PAST/3PL
'This man read your books.' (Southern Balochi)

Adjectives do not agree with the nouns they modify. Attributive adjectives precede the nouns they modify, and take the suffix *-ēn*:

jwān-ēn kitāb-ē
good-ATTRIB. book-NOM/SG/INDEFIN.
'a good book'

In the negative, the prefix *na-* is added to a verb, except in the subjunctive, imperative, and irrealis, where *ma-* is the negative prefix, replacing *bi-/bu-/b-*.

na-wān-ant
NEG-read-PRES-3PL 'they do not read'

na-šut
NEG-go:PAST.3SG 'he did not go'

ma-kan
NEG-do:PRES 'don't do (stop it)'

Contact with Other Languages

Balochi is surrounded by languages belonging to at least five language families. In the Balochi mainland it meets Persian (Farsi and Dari) in the West and Northwest, Pashto and PUNJABI in the North and Northeast and other Indian languages such as Lahnda and Sindhi in the East. All these languages belong to the Indo-Iranian branch of Indo-European languages. In the Gulf States Balochi stands in contact with Arabic (Semitic) and in East Africa with Bantu languages (most prominently Swahili). In East Africa, however, Balochi is hardly spoken at all nowadays. In central parts of Pakistani Balochistan the Dravidian language Brahui has lived in symbiosis with and been dominated by Balochi for centuries, and in Turkmenistan Balochi meets the Turkic language TURKMEN. In the diaspora, mainly in Europe and North America, Balochi meets new languages, mainly of the Indo-European family.

Balochi has a long history of contact with the dominant literary language Persian, and via Persian also with Arabic. Older loanwords from Persian are often hard to distinguish from common words between the two languages. Words in Balochi like *dil* 'heart' (Pe. *del*) and *dānā* 'wise' (= Pe.) are, however, borrowed at an earlier or later stage, since the northwest Iranian form of these words has a /z/ instead of the /d/ (for example, *zird* 'heart' in some Balochi dialects and the Balochi verb *zānag* 'to know' [Pe. *dānestan*]). Words like *barf* 'snow' (= Pe.) and *xašm* 'anger' (=Pe.) are also borrowed, since they are pronounced with a fricative. The first word is, however, often naturalized to *barp*, at least in Southern Balochi. A number of compound words, for example *xānabadōš* 'nomad' (Pe. *xānebeduš*, lit. 'house-on-back') and *xwārīkašš* (Pe. *zahmatkeš*) are either borrowed as a whole or loan translations from Persian. It may also be noted that in the Balochi of Iran a larger number of loanwords from Persian are used than elsewhere, some of them neologisms created by the Academy of Persian language in Iran and not used in the Persian of Afghanistan (Dari) and Tajikistan (TAJIK), such as *bīmāristān* 'hospital' and *dānišjū* 'university student'.

A large number of Arabic loanwords have entered Balochi via Persian. These words are much easier to identify than Persian loanwords because of their Semitic origin. Among naturalized Arabic loanwords one can mention those found on the next page:

From Arabic: *wahd* 'time' (Ar. *waqt*, colloquial Pe. *vaxt*); *hayāl* 'thought' (Ar./Pe. *xiyāl*); *halk* 'village' (Ar./Pe. *xalq* 'people')

Words like *ġazal* 'ghazal' (a kind of poem), *sūrat* ' face' and *xilāf* 'contrary, opposite, against' normally retain the Persian pronunciation, although without the Arabic velarized consonants but with fricatives. Some Arabic loanwords have entered Balochi via Urdu, which in turn has borrowed them via Persian, but sometimes not exactly with the same meaning as in Persian. The word *mazmūn* 'article' is one such word. It is used in this sense also in Urdu, whereas in Persian it means 'guaranteed sum' or 'contents'. (Persian uses another Arabic loanword, *maqāle*, for 'article'.)

Loanwords from Indian languages are also common, not only in dialects bordering the Indian language area, even if they are more numerous there. Samples of loanwords from Indian languages common in all Balochi dialects: *waṛ* 'kind, manner, way'; *ṭukkur* 'piece'; *ḍaḍḍ* 'strong'.

Balochi and Brahui, a Dravidian language spoken in the central part of Pakistani Baluchistan, also have a number of words in common. Some of these have an established Brahui etymology, but in other cases etymologies are uncertain. Examples of such common Balochi-Brahui words are: *puṭ* 'hair', *ṭū* 'huge', *čāp* 'dance'.

Balochi also contains loanwords from European languages. English loanwords have entered the Balochi mainly via Indian languages. Even though they are more frequently employed in dialects spoken outside Iran, there are English loanwords that are common in all dialects, for example *rēḍyō* 'radio', *jēl* 'jail', *iskūl* 'school', *fēšan* 'fashion' (Southern Balochi normally *pēšan*). In Iran there are also a certain number of loanwords from FRENCH: *līsāns* 'B.A.', *mitr* 'meter', *būrs* 'grant', and words denoting the European months and several European countries. Outside Iran, English equivalents are used in these instances.

No studies have been made of Turkmen and RUSSIAN influence on the Balochi of Turkmenistan, but in the few texts published in Balochi from Afghanistan during the era of the Soviet occupation some loanwords from Russian were found.

Common Words

man:	mard	long:	drāj
woman:	janēn	small:	kisān
water:	āp	yes:	hāw
sun:	rōč	no:	na
three:	say	good:	jwān
fish:	māhī(g)	bird:	murg
big:	mazan	dog:	kučakk
tree:	dračk		

Example Sentences

(1) aga taw balōčistān-ā bi-raw-ay
if you:NOM.SG Balochistan-OBL/SG SUBJ-go-PRES/2SG

guḍa man ham gon taw kāy-īn
then I too with you:OBL.SG come-PRES/1SG
'If you go to Balochistan, I too will come with you.'

(2) ē ham-ā bačakk int ki par ā'ī
this also-that boy:NOM.SG be:3SG that for he:OBL.SG

ē kitāb-ā āwur-t-ay
this book-ACC/SG bring-PAST/2SG
'Is this the boy for whom you brought the book?'

(3) wat-ī mās u piss-ā
self-GEN/SG mother:NOM.SG and father-ACC/SG

biy-ār tānki mā ham
IMPER-bring-2SG in order to we:NOM.SG too

bi-gind-an-iš
SUBJ-see-PRES/1PL/3PL
'Bring your parents, in order for us to meet them, too.'

Efforts to Preserve, Protect, and Promote the Language

Balochi is not an official language in that it is not a language of education and/or administration in any of the countries where it is spoken. Efforts to preserve and promote the language are therefore mainly initiatives taken by individuals, lacking the authority that official decisions would be invested with.

However, a number of educated Baloch, mainly in Pakistan, have since the 1950s actively attempted to preserve the language, creating a literature in it, and promoting it as a literary vehicle and in the area of education. Quetta and Karachi are the main centers of these activities. There is a Balochi Academy in Quetta, founded in 1961, receiving some financial support from the government. Its most important literary activities are publication of books, mainly in Balochi, and arranging literary meetings. There are also other academies, publishing houses and individuals active in these fields. A number of periodicals have been published in Balochi for a shorter or longer period of time. Of those that are published at present one may mention *Monthly Balochi* from Quetta and *Labzānk* from Karachi.

There have also been some attempts at starting primary education in Balochi. In 1991 a state program for mother tongue education in the Province of Baluchistan, Pakistan, was established, but it did not last long; neither did it result in any official decision on matters of language standardization. Private initiatives have also been taken to teach Balochi, especially in the main Baloch residential area of Karachi, Lyari. It is also possible to study Balochi for an M.A. degree at the University of Baluchistan, Quetta.

Some of the Baloch in the diaspora are also active in the preservation and promotion of Balochi by publishing magazines and arranging literacy classes and cultural evenings. However, it is hard to imagine that there will develop a standard norm for written Balochi unless the language gains official status as a language of education and/or administration in at least one of the main countries where it is spoken.

Select Bibliography

Ahmad, Mumtaz. 1985. *A Baluchi-English Glossary: Elementary Level*. Kensington, MD: Dunwoody Press.

Barker, M.A., and A.K. Mengal. 1969. *A Course in Baluchi, I-II*. Montreal: Institute of Islamic Studies, McGill University.

Buddruss, Georg. 1988. *Aus dem Leben eines jungen Balutschen von ihm selbst erzählt*, Abhandlungen fur die kunde des Morgenlandes, Band XL VIII, 4, Deutsche Morgenländische Gesellschaft. Stuttgart: Kommissionsverlag Franz Steiner Wiesbaden GMBH.

Collett, N.A. 1986. *A Grammar, Phrase Book and Vocabulary of Baluchi (as Spoken in the Sultanate of Oman)*, 2nd ed. Cambridge [Eng.]: Abingdon.

Dames, M. Longworth. 1891. *A Text Book of the Balochi Language*. Lahore: Punjab Government Press.

_____. 1907. *Popular Poetry of the Baloches, I–II*. London. Published for the Folk-Lore Society by David Nutt.

Elfenbein, Josef. 1963. *A Vocabulary of Marw Baluchi*. Naples: Istituto Universitario Orientale.

____. 1966. *The Baluchi Language, A Dialectology with Texts*. London: The Royal Asiatic Society of Great Britain and Ireland.

____ 1989. "Balōči." In *Compendium Linguarium Iranicarum*. Rüdiger Schmitt, ed. 350–362. Wiesbaden: Ludwig Reichert Verlag.

____. 1990. *An Anthology of Classical and Modern Balochi Literature, I–II*. Wiesbaden: Otto Harrassowitz.

Farrell, Tim. 1990. *Basic Balochi*. Baluchistan Monograph Series, 1. Naples: Istituto Universitario Orientale.

Jahani, Carina. 1989. *Standardization and Orthography in the Balochi Language*. Uppsala: Acta Universitatis Upsaliensis, Studia Iranica Upsaliensia, 3.

____. 1994. "Notes on the Use of Genitive Construction versus *Iẓāfa* Construction in Iranian Balochi." In *Studia Iranica*, 23:2: 285–298.

_____. 2000. *Language in Society: Eight Sociolinguistic Essays on Balochi*. Uppsala: Acta Universitatis Upsaliensis, Studia Iranica Upsaliensia, 3.

Pierce, E. 1969. "A Description of the Mekranee-Beloochee Dialect." In *Journal of the Bombay Branch of the Royal Asiatic Society* 11(1875):31. Bombay 1876. Reprint Liechtenstein, Nendeln: 1–98.

Rossi, Adriano V. 1979. "Phonemics in Balōči and Modern Dialectology." In *Iranica*, Naples: Istituto Universitario Orientale: 161–232.

Spooner, Brian. 1967. "Notes on the Baluchi Spoken in Persian Baluchistan." In *Iran, Journal of the British Institute of Persian Studies*, 5: 51–71.

BANGLA

Tanmoy Bhattacharya

Language Name: Bangla. The name comes from the term *Bangaalah*, the name of the land comprising the states of West Bengal, part of Assam (both in India), and East Bengal (now Bangladesh) first used about 1200. **Alternate:** Bengali is the Colonial English designation for the language; however, the use of the term Bangla is becoming increasingly common in linguistic English. **Autonym:** *Baŋgla*.

Location: Bangla is the language of the Indian state of West Bengal and is also spoken in the states of Assam, Bihar, and Orissa. Bangla is the national language of the country of Bangladesh.

Family: Part of the Indic group of the Indo-Aryan (IA) branch of the Indo-European family of languages.

Related Languages: The bordering languages are ASSAMESE in the northeast, NEPALI in the north, MAITHILI and Magahi in the west, and ORIYA in the southwest. Several aboriginal languages and dialects also form part of its border. These are the non-related Austro-Asiatic languages SANTALI, Ho and Mundari, and two Dravidian dialects Malto and Oraon (or Kurukh) to the west; a number of dialects belonging to six different groups of the Tibeto-Burman branch of the Tibeto-Chinese family to the North and East like Lepcha, Limbu, Banjong-ka (Sikkim), Lho-ke (Bhutan), Bodo, Garo, Maitei, Lushai, etc. Another Austro-Asiatic language, this time of the Mon-Khmer group, Khasi, is spoken to the east.

Dialects: Bangla is divided first into two main branches, Western and Eastern (or Vaŋga or Eastern Bangla). The Western branch is further divided into (i) Raḍha (South) (ii) Varendra (North Central) (iii) Kamrupa (North Bengal). Raḍha is subdivided into South Western Bangla and Western Bangla, the standard colloquial form of Bangla spoken around Calcutta.

Social Variety. Bangla is divided into codes, classifiable in terms of a High versus Low dichotomy called a diglossia. The H(igh) and L(ow) codes are differentiated in terms of the way the inflectional and pronominal systems in the *Sadhu* or H code of standard written Bangla contrast with those in the *colit* or L code. For example, the *Sadhu* and *colit* versions of the sentence 'They (distal)[1] (are) going[2]' are *tahara jaiteche* and *tara jacche* respectively [here and elsewhere, superscripts represent the sequence in the original]. The use of the H form for written prose became the norm for Bangla in the early nineteenth century as a result of that period's process of Sanskritization. It is rarely in use now. The L written norm uses the South Western morphology.

Number of Speakers: In the 1991 census, Bangla had 58,541,519 speakers in West Bengal (88,752 sq km) plus 11,054,219 other Indian speakers, and an estimated 107 million in Bangladesh (143,998 sq km), a total of 177 million subcontinental speakers in 1991, plus diasporic speakers for whom systematic figures are unavailable. The enthnolinguistic survey of LSA puts the total number of Bangla speakers at 189 million.

Origin and History

Around 600 B.C. outposts of the Aryan colonialization were being set up in the east inhabited by pre-Aryan tribes like Raḍhas and Vaŋgas—ancestors of the people of Bengal. These were considered to be barbarous lands not suitable for high-caste Brahmins of the north and the midland to settle. Bengali toponomy suggests that these earlier tribes were speakers of Dravidian or some Austro-Asiatic language(s). However, by 700 B.C., a distinct Eastern branch (Pracya) of the Old IA was in existence, and by the fourth century Bengal was part of the well-established Aryan kingdom Magadh. The language spoken in these areas had certain distinct characteristics all of which are traceable in its current descendants. For example, the Old IA vowel [ʌ] became the default vowel [ɔ]; epenthesis with /i/, /ʃ/ for IA /*s ʃ ṣ*/; interchangeability of /l/ and /r/; IA /*kṣ* / became /*(k)khy*/, using the affix *-rɔ* for the genitive *-e*, *-ẽ* for the instrumental, *-e* for the locative, *-l-* for the passive participle of the verbal noun and *-b-* for the future, and the roots for the auxiliary being *ho, ah, rah, ach*. This mother-dialect of the current Eastern IA languages was called the *Maagadhii Apabhranʃaa* (MA), the second word meaning 'speech fallen from the norm'. This characterization is consistent with the depiction by the Sanskrit dramatists prior to 100 B.C. of lower caste characters speaking a /ʃ/ dialect. However, by the sixth century, MA was well-established and this is probably the language that the 7th century Chinese traveller Hiuen Tsang described when he said that the whole East India spoke a similar tongue. The following is a rough chronology of the different periods of Bangla:

1. **Pracya** ('Eastern'): 700 B.C.
2. **Middle IA:**
   (i) Early Middle IA: 300 B.C.
   (ii) Transitional Middle IA
   (iii) 2nd Middle IA: A.D. 300
   (iv) Late Middle IA: A.D. 800 (MA)
3. **Old Bangla:** 1100
4. **Early Middle Bangla:** 1400
5. **Late Middle Bangla:** 1600
6. **New Bangla:** 1800

Table 1: Consonants

	Labial	Dental	Alveolar	Retroflex	Palato-Alveolar	Palatal	Velar	Glottal
Stops	p b	t d		ṭ ḍ			k g	
Aspirated	ph bh	th dh		ṭh ḍh			kh gh	
Fricatives			s z		ʃ			h
Affricates						c j		
Aspirated						ch jh		
Nasal	m		n				ŋ	
Lateral			l					
Flap			r	ṛ				
Glide	w					y		

Politically, the Bengali dynasties of Pal (750–1162), Sen/ Barman (1096–1228) and Dev (1170–1260) (years sometime overlapping due to separate independent kingdoms) ruled before the foreign invasion began with the Turkish (1204–1338) and continued with the independent Muslim Sultans (1338–1538), Moghuls (1575–1757) and the British (1757–1947). During the Muslim rule of Bengal the lexicon of Bangla drew heavily on SANSKRIT and (Turko)-Perso-Arabic sources, as the administrative language of the region was PERSIAN.

The earliest specimen of Bangla is found in a set of 47 songs called *Caryas* written by the teachers of a Mahayana Buddhist sect around the first millennium (950–1200). The manuscript was discovered in Nepal in 1907 (and later published in 1916), where some of the scholars possessing older manuscripts escaped after the Turkish invasion of Bengal in 1200—a period marked by destruction of manuscripts and persecution of their authors or possessors.

Fortunately, there is a copious Middle Bangla literature of which the earliest and most important is *Sri-Krishna Kirtan* of Chandi-dasa belonging to the latter half of the 14th century. Late Middle Bangla witnessed the development of the *Vaisnava* literature through the influence of the saint Chaitanya (1483–1533). This period also saw the development of an artificial literary language *Braja-Buli* (the speech of the Vraja, the birthplace of Krishna), which was a curious mix of Maithili, Bangla and Western HINDI.

New or Modern Bangla evolved a prose style due to western influence. Its greatest exponent was Rabindranath Tagore (the English spelling for the surname Thakur) who won the Nobel prize in literature in 1913.

The British departure in 1947 resulted in the partition of the subcontinent where West Bengal was left as part of India and East Bengal as the sole province of East Pakistan. In 1971 the war to free Bangladesh from Pakistan cost the lives of an estimated 3 million speakers of Bangla.

Orthography and Basic Phonology

The Bangla script is originally derived from the Brahmi script current from 400 B.C. to A.D. 300, a derivative of the Semitic branch of ARAMAIC. But it was reshaped by the dominant Devanagari of the Northern and Western India from the seventh century onwards. Below is a sample of five Bangla alphabets on the extreme right as derived from the original Brahmi on the extreme left.

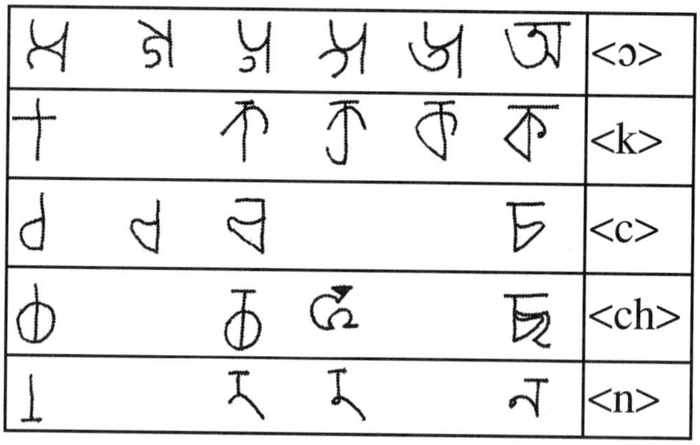

					অ	<ɔ>
					ক	<k>
					চ	<c>
					ছ	<ch>
					ন	<n>

From the Middle Ages, the Indian notion of *Akṣaras*, or the system of words being divided into syllables not closed by a consonant, was always treated somewhat mystically and was a result of the system of writing. The number of primary letters (or *maatṛakṣara*) in Sanskrit, and following that in the vernacular languages, is 50, with 16 vowels and 34 consonants. Vowels include the retroflex /ɽ/, the vocalic /ri/, the *Anusvara* or voiceless /n/ and the *Visarga* /ɦ/ which are not phonemic (apart from the ones used as part of the spelling system) in Bangla. The same holds for the consonant /kṣ/.

Spelling rules for Bangla are extremely unscientific due mainly to the vast gap between the script and the pronunciation, a result of the heavy Sanskritization of Bangla since the twelfth century and carried on vigorously throughout the Middle Ages. For example, although Bangla does not distinguish between */s ʃ ṣ/* (which are phonemically /ʃ/), primary school students are still taught the three different alphabets which in fact bear phonetically descriptive names, namely, *dantya* ('dental') *ʃɔ* for [s], *talbya* ('palatal') *ʃɔ* for [ʃ], and *muṛdhanya* ('retroflex') *ʃɔ* for [ṣ]. The script also marks contrasts now lost between short and long high vowels. That the orthography of particular words uses long vowel symbols has to be rote-learnt, as in <*din*> 'day' and <*diin*> 'poor' (angled brackets indicating graphemes where the default vowel pronunciation associated with consonants is not shown), both phonologically /*din*/. Nasalization has a consistent written correlate, the *candrabindu*, distinguished from the *Anusvara*—the dependent nasal alphabet which is treated as simply a silenced /n/.

Lacking a monographemic symbol of its own, /æ/ is written variously as <e>, <y>, or <yɔ>: <*khela, byaakarŋ̩, byst*> for /*khæla, bækoron, bæsto*/ 'to play, grammar, busy'.

Table 2: Vowels

	Back	Front
Close	u, ũ	i, ĩ
Half-Close	o, õ	e, ẽ
Half-Open	ɔ,ɔ̃	æ, æ̃
Open	a, ã	

The low round /ɔ/ is treated as a default vowel. Thus, a graphic *kh* is to be pronounced as /*khɔ*/. The symbol ~ (tilde) over the vowel indicates a nasalized vowel in the vowel chart above and elsewhere. The half-open back vowel /ɔ/ is pronounced as the English word *awe*. The half-open front *æ* is pronounced as the vowel sound in the English word *bat*.

Phonological Rules. Vowel length is not phonologically significant. In monosyllabic contexts vowels can be phonetically long as the vowel /a/ in *ma:* 'mother' as opposed to *manuʃ* '(hu)man'. No phonologically nasalized vowel occurs before or after a nasal consonant: *nacon* 'dance', *bondhu* 'friend'.

Vowel Lowering applies to a monosyllabic verb stem whose nuclear vowel is /i u e/ and lowers it to /e o æ/: *cin* > *cena* 'to recongnize' *bujh* > *bojha* 'to understand' *dekh* > *dækha* 'to see'. Vowel Raising raises /æ/ to /e/ and /ɔ/ to /o/ in non root-initial position: *ækhon* 'now' versus *ɔnekkhon* 'a long time', *pɔrajito* 'defeated' versus *ɔ-porajito* 'undefeated'.

Regressive Vowel Harmony (RVH) raises a low/ mid vowel by one if the first vowel after it is high with matching roundedness value: *æk* 'one' > *ekuʃ* 'twenty one'. RVH for the verbal paradigm is absolute: *ken-* > *kini* 'I buy', *lekh-* > *likhi* 'I write'. Progressive Vowel Harmony (PVH) turns /a/ into /o/ in a verb stem if the first preceding vocoid is high: *bila* > *bilo* 'distribute-PRES.2', *douṛa* > *douṛo* 'run-PRES.2'. PVH for the non-verbal cases turns /a/ to /e/ as well: *pujo* > *puja* 'worship', *mula* > *mulo* 'radish' *iccha*> *icche* 'desire'. Regressive Assimilation takes place for stop voicing, /r/ assimilation, either across word boundaries or within a single word: *jak ge* > *jagge* 'let it go!', *ḍak ghɔr* > *ḍagghɔr* 'post office' *rag kɔra* > *rakkora* 'to be angry', *tar jonno* > *tajjono* 'for him/ that', *murcha* > *muccha* 'faint', *karjo* > *kajjo* 'work'.

Deaspiration may occur as assimilation: *rɔth tɔla* > *rɔttɔla* 'festival place where decorated carts are drawn', *mukh khani* > *mukkhani* 'that face', *kaṭh phaṭa* > *kaṭphaṭa* 'wood-splitting (spoken of strong sunshine)'. Assimilation across different consonant groups occurs in: *pãc ʃo* > *pãʃʃo* 'five hundred', and finally gemination may be used morphologically to emphasize: *ækebare* 'at once, for good' > *ækkebare* 'for all time, entirely (beyond repair)', *thapoṛ* 'slap' > *thappoṛ* 'series of slaps'.

Basic Morphology

Noun Morphology. Nouns inflect for the following cases: Nominative: *baṛi* 'house'; Accusative-Dative (Objective): *baṛi-ke*; Genitive: *baṛi-r*; Locative: *baṛi-te*. The genitive suffix is *-er* when the noun ends in a consonant as in *bon-er* 'sister's', the locative suffix is *-e* when the noun ends in a consonant and can be either *-e* or *-te* when the noun ends in a non-high vowel as in *ṭebil-e* 'on/ in the table' and *alo-e* or *alo-te* 'in the light' respectively. The Bangla genitive covers some uses of the dative in other Indic languages, as in the experiencer subject construction: *robiner probin-ke bhalo lage* 'Robin likes Probin, lit. Robin-GEN[1] Probin-ACCDAT[2] good[3] feels[4]'.

Non-human nouns, and non-honorific human nouns generally take a Nominative (zero), Objective *-ke*, Genitive *-(e)r*, or Locative *-(t)e* suffix after the enclitic counting expression (or pluralizer *gulo*), if any; *tak-gulo-te* 'on the shelves'. But human nouns even here, resist the locative plural; *chele-gulo-te* for 'among the boys' is not possible.

Nominative *-ra* and objective/genitive *-der* constitute a human plural marker whose use is possible only when the noun is not counted, and is obligatory with personal pronouns; while *chele* means 'boy(s)', *o* means 'that person', never 'those persons'. Its absence signifies singularity also in the case of possessed or pointed-at nouns: *amar bhai* 'my[1] brother[2]', *ei kɔrmocari* 'this[1] employee[2]'. Other human nouns can have a plural meaning without the plural marker: *mee aʃbe na, ʃudhu chele* 'girls[1] won't[3] come[2], only[4] boys[5]'. The plural marker *ra-der* carries an overtone of definiteness, though less consistently than *gulo*. These facts indicate that plurality is less distinct for indefinite nouns.

As a special case of the process of definiteness *gulo* may be used as a definitive plural "general" (not specifically human) suffix, as in *chele-gulo* 'the boys'. But *gulo* is also a classifier, as in : *ɔnek-gulo boi* 'many[1] books[2]', *kɔtok-gulo kɔlom* 'so many[1] pens[2]'.

Classifiers. Barring exceptions like *dui deʃer moittri* 'Two[1] countries'[2] friendship[3]', the relation of a number word (or other quantity) to the noun it counts is mediated by a classifier enclitic like the human classifier *jon* in *du-jon montri* 'Two[1] ministers[2]'. A counted noun never has a plural ending. The other two important classifiers are the general classifier *ṭa* and the piece-classifier *khana* which signals single objects. Compare *æk-ṭa mach* and *æk-khana mach* for 'a[1] fish[2]'. Only the former can refer to a living fish. *ṭi*, a slightly literary version of *ṭa*, carries diminutive and feminine overtones. *ṭo* and *ṭe* are conditioned variants of *ṭa*.

Definiteness/Specificity. Definiteness/Specificity is expressed by either using a Num(eral)/Q(uantifier)-Cla(ssifier): *du-ṭo thala* 'two[1] plates[2]' (Indefinite) versus *thala du-ṭo* 'the two[2] plates[1]'. When the sequence is *æk-ṭa* or *æk-khana*, *æk* 'one' is understood in the definite version: *æk-ṭa thala* 'one/a[1] plate[2]' *thala-ṭa* 'the (one) plate'. A noun followed by an inanimate (animacy-neutral) classifier conveys definiteness: *gramṭa* 'the village', *ciṭhikhana* 'the letter'. The nonhuman classifier *gulo* combines this positional definiteness with plurality:

Table 3: Various Classifiers and Quantifiers

Quantifier	Classifiers			
	-Ta	gulo	khana/ khani	jOn
		[+count]	[+count/mass]	[+human]
Sɔb 'all'	√	√	√	×
kɔtok 'somewhat'	√	√	×	×
kichu 'some'	√	×	×	×
khanik 'a bit'	√	×	×	×
ɔlpek- 'a little'	√	×	×	×
prottek 'every other'	√	×	×	×
ɔnek 'a lot'	√	√	√	√
kɔto 'how/so much'	√	√	√	√
ɔto 'so much'	√	√	√	√
kɔek 'a few'	√	×	√	√
numerals	√	×	√	√

khamgulo 'the envelopes'. Demonstratives may convey definiteness, as in *thala* 'plate' versus *oi thala* 'that[1] plate[2]' and a Q as in *boi* 'book' *kono boi* 'some[1] book[2]'. However, this definiteness is a matter of true or insinuated prior familiarity, not of the demonstrative type. Thus *oi duṭo thala* 'those[1] two[2] plates[3]' and its near paraphrase, *oi thala duṭo* both use demonstratives but only the latter expresses familiarity. Case marking may also indicate specificity: *beṛal* 'cat' (nonspecifc/ generic) versus *beṛal-ke* 'cat-DAT' (definitive/ specific).

Determiners. The *e o ʃe* elements of the third person paradigm serve as invariable determiners: *e boi* 'This[1] book[2]', *o kaj* 'That[1] job[2]', *ʃe jiniʃ* 'That[1] thing[2]'. These determiners optionally add an augment /i/: *ei boi*, *oi kaj*, *ʃei jiniʃ*. The interrogative determiners are: *ki* 'What', *kon* 'Which', *je* 'Which' etc.

Bangla exhibits no case or number agreement, and no grammatical gender phenomena at all. Thus, dependents like demonstratives and adjectives do not agree with the head noun on any grammatical dimension; they carry no inflectional features:

ei/ oi lɔmba chele 'this/that[1] tall[2] boy[3]'
ei/oi lɔmba meye 'this/that tall girl'
ei/oi lɔmba gach 'this/that tall tree'

Personal pronouns express formality. The agreement that the verb exhibits with its subject for Person and Formality conflates 2F(ormal) with 3F (see below).

Pronouns. The first person paradigm is as follows:

	Singular	Plural
Nom	*ami*	*amra*
Acc/Dat	*amake/amay*	*amader*
Gen	*amar*	*amader*

The second person paradigm in terms of formality is as follows:

	Formal (sg/pl)	Neutral (sg/pl)	Intimate (sg/pl)
Nom	*apni/apnara*	*tumi/tomra*	*tui/tora*
Acc/Dat	*apnake/apnader*	*tomake/tomader*	*toke/toder*
Gen	*apnar/apnader*	*tomar/tomader*	*tor/toder*

To define the third person pronoun in Bangla is difficult. If it is a semantic notion based on the properties of expressions like 'Ram[1] and[2] his[3] brother[4]' and 'Sudha[1] won't[3] come[2], she[4] is[7] very[5] busy[6]', then Bangla has two systems. The *Correlative* system for the first (and as a marked option also the second) case and the *Distal* system just for the second case: *ram ar tar bhai*, *ʃudha aʃbe na, o khub bæsto ache*.

Each system has Neutral and Honorific sets.

	Formal (sg/pl)	Neutral (sg/pl)
Correlative:		
Nom	tini/tãra	ʃe/tara
Acc/Dat	tãke/tãder	take/tader
Gen	tãr/tãder	tar/tader
Distal:		
Nom	uni/õra	o/ora
Acc/Dat	õke/õder	oke/oder
Gen	õr/õder	or/oder

If third person pronouns are just pronouns taking third person verbs, then there is yet another system:

Nom	ini/ẽra	e/era
Acc/Dat	ẽke/ẽder	eke/eder
Gen	ẽr/ẽder	er/eder

These words have an emphatic *this*-function, one of pointing at people in "my (our)" orbit as opposed to "yours". Distals point at people in "your" orbit. Correlatives refer to absent people.

Verb Morphology. Finite verbs agree with the nominative subject for person and formality. Thus 'you came' has singular /*apni elen, tumi ele, tui eli*/, plural /*apnara elen, tomra ele, tora eli*/ (see below for verb inflection).

Negative. The negative particle *na* is derived from the old Bangla and the High form but the original sense 'existed not' is now lost. The negative of all verb roots excepting *ach-* 'be' in simple present, past, and future is formed by using *na* postpositionally to the fully inflected verbal forms. The verb *ach-* 'be' forms its negative root as *nei* and is not inflected for person and number.

achi	'be.1'	} + *na* => *nei*
acho	'be.2'	
achiʃ	'be.2.I'	
achen	'be.2.F'	
ache	'be.3'	

The past of 'be' is formed by adding *na* to the past root *chil* which is inflected for person /*chilam* 'be.PST.1', *chile* 'be.PST.2', *chilo* 'be.PST.3' + *na*/. The future root is *thakb* + *na*. The formation of the negative of the imperative and simple future are the same.

tui jabi na	'you[1] do not[3] go.2I[2]'
tumi jabe na	'you do not go.2N'
apni jaben na	'you do not go.2F'

In the perfect aspect the negative is formed by suffixing /*ni*/ in all the tenses, while in the future /*na*/ is used as a separate word postverbally. In the formation of the negative of conjuctives /*na*/ is prefixed in the first and not the second clause: *ʃe na aʃle ami jabo na* 'I[4] shall not[6] go[5] if he[1] does not[2] come[3]'.

Passive. Bangla does not have an inflected passive. The analytical or periphrastic passive is usually formed by the passive participle affix *-a* and the auxiliary verb *ja* 'to go' although a proper passive voice with a nominative object is not natural in the language. The *ja*-passive form is an impersonal construction, e.g., with the verb 'to see': *dækha jay* 'it is seen'. If a promoted object is used, it is in the dative: *ama-ke dækha jay* 'I am seen' (= to me is seen).

A few cases of idiomatic passive formation take place with the verb root *pɔṛ* 'to fall', *gælo* 'went', *cɔl* 'to go', *hɔy* 'to happen' etc., instead of *ja*: *mara pɔṛe* 'gets killed', *mara gælo* 'got killed', *khawa cɔle* 'can be eaten', *amake dækha hɔy* 'I am seen' (=They see me). The oldest form of Bangla used the *-ɔn* suffix (instead of the *-a*) which is lost in standard Bangla but is preserved in some East Bangla dialects. A recent passive form with the auxiliary *ach* is also available for inanimate nouns: *e boi amar pɔra ache* 'this[1] book[2] has[5] been read[4] by me[3]'. Sometimes the impersonal passive is employed for politeness when the use of a particular pronominal form can be avoided: *ki kɔra hɔy* 'What[1] is[3] done[2] (by you) = What do you do?'

Causatives. Bangla has both morphological and periphrastic causatives. The two morphological ways of forming the causative are either adding the affix *-a* to the root as in *kɔr* 'to do', *kɔra* 'to cause to do', *de* > *dewa* 'to cause to give', or with the suffix *-ano* as the passive participle affix for causative and denominative roots: *janano* 'cause to be informed' from *jana* 'to know' (cf. dialectal *-il-* as in *kɔrailo* 'done, cause to be done').

Periphrastic causatives are formed with the verbal noun in *-a-* and the verb *kɔrano* 'to cause to do' and are common in Raḍha: *rakh* 'to keep' versus *rakh kɔrano* 'to cause to keep' and in standard Bangla: *snan kɔrano* 'to cause to take bath'.

Morphological single causatives can syntactically function as double causatives but Bangla has no double causative morphology.

Inflection. Verb inflection is shown in Table 4 for the vowel-final stem (*kha*) verb /*khawa*/ 'to eat, to drink'. 1P, 2P, 3P stand for the three Persons and I(ntimate), N(eutral), F(ormal), formality levels. The Pres[ent], Past, Fut[ure] tenses interact with moods, namely the Imper[ative] and the unmarked Indicative, and with aspects, namely Simp[le], Prog[ressive], Perf[ect], Hab[itual].

Derivation. Productive affixation is rare in the language. Compounding is the only productive word formation process. Causative formation, as above, is one productive strategy: *kena* 'to buy' > *kenano* 'to make (someone) buy'.

In nominals, masculine bases yield feminine nouns in *-i*, as in *mama, mami* 'maternal uncle, auntie', *ʃiŋho, ʃiŋhi* 'lion, lioness'. Some bases use instead the strategy of *ni* or *ini* suffixation, as in *gowala, gowalini* 'milk man, woman' *bagh, baghini* 'tiger, tigress'. A second *-i* forms adjectives and inhabitant/language names from place names and nouns: *gujrat, gujrati* 'Gujarat, Gujarati', *begun, beguni* 'eggplant, purplish'.

Table 4: Verb Inflection for *kha* 'eat, drink'

	1P	2PI	2PN	2/3PF	3PN
Pres Simp	khai	khaʃ	khao	khan	khay
Pres Prog	khacchi	khacchiʃ	khaccho	khacchen	khacche
Pres Perf	kheyechi	kheyechiʃ	kheyecho	kheyechen	kheyeche
Imper Pres	—	kha	khao	khan	khak
Past Simp	khelam	kheli	khele	khelen	khelo
Past Prog	khacchilam	khacchili	khacchile	khacchilen	khacchilo
Past Perf	kheyechilam	kheyechili	kheyechile	kheyechilen	kheyechilo
Past Hab	khetam	kheti(ʃ)	khete	kheten	khete
Fut Simp	khabo	khabi	khabe	khaben	khabe
Imper Fut	—	khaʃ	kheyo	khaben	khabe

A third *-i* nominalizes adjectives: *calak, calaki* 'clever, cleverness'; *bekar, bekari* 'unemployed, unemployment'. Another nominalizing suffix, *-(t)to* <tb> from Sanskrit */tva/*, is productive to form expressions like */panḍitto/* 'erudition' where no other affix is possible.

The *-amo/ami* forms abstract nouns or character/ profession from nouns: *boka, bokami* 'fool, foolishness', *paka, pakami* 'ripe, precocious', *cor, corami* 'thief, thievery'.

The Perso-Arabic privative prefix */be/* of words such as */becal/* 'waywardness' and */beʃamal/* 'not in control of one's faculties' is not productive; but many suffixes are: *khana: ḍaktar-khana* 'dispensary', *khor: ghuʃ-khor* 'bribe-taker', *giri: babu-giri* 'way of a gentleman', *dan: ator-dan* 'attar-holder', *ʃohi: cɔlon-ʃohi* 'agreeable'.

Compounding. Compounds are formed by the addition of a verb root or an auxiliary to a noun in accusative or locative (nominal) or an unaffected verbal conjunctive or a participle (verbal). The verb root or auxiliary takes the agreement morphemes.

(I) Nominals: (i) With Accusative: *jɔl dewa* 'to water (lit: water giving)'; (ii) With Locative: *ga-e makha* 'to smear on the body'; (iii) Locative verbal noun in *-te*: *korte laga* 'to start doing (lit: do-and attaching)'; (iv) With verbal noun in *-i/-a*: *muṛi dewa* 'to wrap oneself up', *hama dewa* 'to crawl'

(II)Verbals: (i) With conjunctive in *-e*: *kheye phæla* 'to eat up (Lit: eat-and drop)'; (ii) With present participle in *-ite*: *dite thaka* 'to keep giving (Lit: give-and stay)'

The normal way to make new verbs is to add a light verb like */kɔra/* 'to do' or */hɔwa/* 'to be' to form a Composite Verb: *ziraks kɔra* 'to xerox', *mægnifai kɔra* 'to magnify', etc.

Basic Syntax

The basic order of major constituents is Adjunct + Subject + Predicate Adjunct + Indirect Object + Direct Object + (Dependents of the complement verb) Complement Verb + Finite Main Verb + Negative. The maximal noun phrase structure is: Possessive + Dem + Num/ Q + Classifier + Adjective + Noun. This also shows that modifying adjectives precede the modified noun. Adpositions follow the noun (postposition): *bakʃer moddhe* 'inside[2] the box[1]'.

Question words (or K-words) are: *kɔkhon* 'when', *kothay* 'where', *kon* 'which', *ki* 'what', *ke/ kara* 'Who-Nom (sg/pl)', *kake* 'Who-Acc', *kar* 'whose'. Questions are formed 'in-situ':

tumi kal baṛi-te mɔdon-ke dekhechile
'yesterday[2] you[1] saw[5] Modon[4] at home[3]'
ke *kal baṛi-te mɔdon-ke dekhechilo*
'yesterday[2] who[1] saw[5] Modon[4] at home[3]?'
tumi ***kɔbe*** *baṛi-te mɔdon-ke dekhechile*
'when[2] did you[1] see[5] Modon[4] at home[3]?'
tumi kal ***kothay*** *mɔdon-ke dekhechile*
'where[3] did you[1] see[5] Modon[4] yesterday[2]?'
tumi kal baṛi-te ***ka-ke*** *dekhechile*
'whom[4] did you[1] see[5] at home[3] yesterday[2]?'

Case Marking of Major Constituents. Subject case can be Nom (zero) (*mɔdon aʃe* 'Modon[1] comes[2]'), Genitive for experiencer subjects (*ama-r matha dhoreche* 'my[1] head[2] is aching[3] (Lit: my head is-held)', Locative (*lok-e bɔle* 'people say'). Objects are marked as Dative for animates (*robin cheleṭa-ke dekhlo* 'Robin[1] saw[3] the boy[2]'), Accusative (zero) (*ami phɔl khacchi* 'I[1] am eating[3] fruits[2]').

Adpositions mark their complement, e.g. (a) Genitive (*ṭebil-er nice/ upore/ paʃe* 'under/ on/ beside[2] the table[1]'); (b) Objective (*-ke* or zero) (*bhai-ke/boi nie/die* 'With/ by[2] brother/ book[1]'); (c) Locative (*hat-e kore* 'with[2] hand[1]').

Bangla exhibits head-initial and head-final, structure. The complementizers can be both initial (*je*) and final (*bole*) (the complements are marked within square brackets):

ami dekhlam [je rɔma baṛi nei]
'I[1] saw[2] that[3] Roma[4] is not[6] at home[5]'
ami [rɔma aʃbe bole] ʃunechi
'I[1] have heard[5] that[4] Roma[2] will come[3]'

Unmarked order inside the VP is head-final but since Bangla is a free word-order language, almost all possible orders may obtain.

Relative Clauses (RC) are formed with the Relative Pronoun (RP) *je* and a 'Co-relative' pronoun (CoP) *ʃe* both at the initial and the final position of their respective clauses. The following points may be noted in connection with the RCs in (1-7):

(a) RP before or inside the RC and CoP is initial in the matrix clause (1-7)
(b) Complete embedding where the identical NP (or the antecedent) is deleted from the RC and retained in the matrix clause (6)
(c) The identical NP is deleted from the matrix clause and is retained in the RC (1,4)
(d) RC without an antecedent (2a,b)
(e) The correlative clause is with (3,5,6) and without (1,2,4,6) an antecedent
(f) RC is embedded in the matrix clause, cop is absent, the antecedent is within the correlative clause (7)

1. *je chele-ṭa amar bondhu, ʃe eʃechilo*
'the boy[2] who[1] is my[3] friend[4], he[5] had come[6]'
2. a. *amar bondhu je, ʃe eʃechilo*
b. *je amar bondhu, ʃe eʃechilo*
3. *je amar bondhu, ʃe chele-ṭa eʃechilo*
4. *ʃe eʃechilo, je chele-ṭa amar bondhu*
5. *ʃe chele-ṭa amar bondhu, je eʃechilo*
6. *chele-ṭa, je amar bondhu, eʃechilo*
7. *amar ækṭa chobi ache, ja dada dieche*
'I[1] have[4] a[2] picture[3], that[5] brother[6] gave[7] me'

Negation. Postverbal in finite and preverbal in non-finites:

robin aʃe na
'Robin[1] does not[3] come[2]' (Finite) versus
robin na ele
'If Robin[1] doesn't[2] come[3]' (Conditional)
robin-er na aʃa
'Robin's[1] not[2] coming[3]' (Gerund)
robin cay probin na aʃe
'Robin[1] wants[2] that Probin[3] doesn't[4] come[5]' (Subjunctive)

In addition, the particles *je, to, naki, ki* roughly corresponding to 'topic/comment that', 'of course', 'apparently', and 'yes/no question marker' when added to a phrase turns it into the given or the topic of the sentence. The rest of the sentence acts as the new information—the peak of this information is marked by a 'focalizer' *-i*/ or *-o* (see example 3 in Example Sentences).

Contact with Other Languages

Apart from the bordering IA languages there is constant emigration to Bengal from speakers of Tibeto-Burman, Austro-Asiatic and Dravidian language families. Needless to say, the contact with ENGLISH continues.

Persian (mainly lexical from the beginning of the thirteenth century until 1836 when English replaced Persian as the language of the courts): *tir* 'arrow', *kaman* 'bow, gun', *kɔtol* 'execution', *kella* 'fort', *lɔʃkor* 'army', *phɔte* 'victory', etc. Standard dictionaries usually list around 2,000 words of Persian origin.

From Portuguese: *khana* 'ditch' (cf Portugese *cano*), *janala* 'window', *almaṛi* 'cupboard'

From French: *kartuj* 'cartridge' (Fr. *cartouche*), *buruʃ* 'brush' (Fr. *barouche*), *kupon* 'coupon', *ollondaj* 'Dutch' (Fr. *Hollandais*)

From Dutch: names of cards: *hɔroton* 'hearts' (Dutch *harten*), *ruitɔn* 'diamonds' (Dutch *ruiten*), *iskabɔn* 'spades' (Dutch *schopen*), *turup* 'trump card' (= *troef*)

From English: Numerous borrowings. Some completely Bengalized English words are: *hãʃpatal* 'hospital', *laṭ* 'lord', *iskul* 'school', *ḍaktar* 'doctor', *gelaʃ* 'glass', *ɔphiʃ* 'office', *ṭebil* 'table, *benci* 'bench', *maʃṭar* 'master', *garod* 'guard'

Common Words

man:	manuʃ, lok	long:	lɔmba
woman:	mohila	small:	choṭo
water:	jɔl	yes:	hæ̃
sun:	ʃurjo	no:	na
three:	tin	good:	bhalo
fish:	mach	bird:	pakhi
big:	bɔṛo	dog:	kukur
tree:	gach		

Example Sentences

(1) ɔthoco robin kal probin-ke boi dite
although Robin tomorrow Probin-DAT book give.CONJ

bolbe na
say.FUT.3 NEG

'Although tomorrow Robin won't tell Probin to give the book.'

(2) amar ei du(koek) jon ghoniʃṭho bondhu ṭebil-er
my this two (some) CLA close friends table-GEN

nice boʃbe
undersit.FUT

'Two/some of my close friends will sit under the table.'

(3) probin-**to** ajkal e baṛi-te-**i** thak-che
Probin-TOP these days this house-LOC-EMP AUX-PROG.3

'As for Probin, these days he is staying in this very house.'

Efforts to Preserve, Protect, and Promote the Language

Early Pakistani language policy (beginning in 1947) favored URDU as a symbol of Muslim identity in Bangladesh. But a movement for giving Bangla equal status, culminating in a major demonstration in Dhaka in 1952 in which seven university students were killed, forced a settlement making Bangla and Urdu the official languages of Pakistan. Ever since, the anniversary, 21 February, has been *bhaʃa dibaʃ* 'language day' in East Bengal.

The Bangla Academy in Bangladesh and the Bengal Sahitya Parishad of Calcutta, India have continued admirable work in the fields of historical research and folk studies. Current efforts to promote the language are much more serious in Bangladesh than in West Bengal, where most of the bureaucratic work is still in English. Even there, college level textbooks and educational materials in various subjects are now available. Since the B.A. exam in 1973 candidates at the University of Calcutta have had the option of writing their answers in Bangla.

Select Bibliography

Bender, Ernest and T. Riccardi. 1978. *An Advanced Course in Bengali*. Philadelphia: South Asia Regional Studies, University of Pennsylvania.

Bhattacharya, Tanmoy. 1999. *The Structure of the Bangla DP*. University College London dissertation.

Biswas, Sailendra. (Compiled by). 1959. *Samsad English-Bengali Dictionary*. Calcutta: Sahitya Samsad. (5th Edition, 1980)

Comrie, Bernard. (ed.). 1990. *The Major Languages of South Asia, the Middle East, and Africa*. London: Routledge.

Dasgupta, Probal. 1980. *Question and Relative and Complement Clauses in Bangla Grammar*. New York: New York University dissertation.

Dimock, Edward C., Somdev Bhattaeharji and Suhas Chatterji. 1964. *Introductory Bengali*, Part 1. Honolulu: East-West Center Press. (Reprinted 1991. New Delhi: Manohar Publications).

Ferguson, Charles A. 1969. "Bibliographic Review of Bengali Studies." In *Current Trends in Linguistics*, vol. 5, Linguistics in South Asia, ed. Thomas A. Sebeok, 85–98. The Hague: Mouton.

Kostic, Djordje and Rhea S. Das. 1972. *A Short Outline of Bengali Phonetics*. Calcutta: Indian Statistical Institute.

Maniruzzaman. 1991. *Studies in the Bangla Language*. Adiabad, Dhaka and Chittagong: Adiabad Sahitya Bhavan and Bhasha Tattva Kendra.

Radice, William. 1994. *Teach Yourself Bengali*. London: Hodder Headline; Lincolnwood (Chicago): NTC Publishing.

Sarkar, Pabitra. 1987. *Bangla Banan Shanshkar: Shomashsha O Shambhabona* (Bangla Spelling Reform: Problems and Possibilities). Calcutta: Chirayat Prakashan Pvt. Ltd.

Basque

R. L. Trask

Language Name: Basque. **Autonym:** *euskara.* (Dialect variants *euskera, eskuara).* In Spanish: vasco *or* vascuence. In French: basque.

Location: The Basque-speaking area (called by Basques *Euskal Herria*) straddles part of the border of northern Spain and southwestern France, along the Bay of Biscay. It extends for about 100 miles from west to east and for about 30 miles from north to south. In Spain, it encompasses the provinces of Navarre, Bizkaia, Gipuzkoa, and Álava. In France it includes the former provinces of Labourd, Basse-Navarre, and Soule.

Family: None. Basque is genetically isolated. Specialists are satisfied that there is no shred of persuasive evidence that Basque is discoverably related to any other living language, and the not infrequent statements to the contrary in the non-specialist literature may be safely disregarded.

Related Languages: None, apart from its ancestral form Aquitanian (see below).

Dialects: The dialectal diversification is fairly substantial, enough to impede communication to some extent. Linguistically, however, the differences are quite superficial, consisting chiefly of differing vocabulary and some rather low-level phonological rules. Non-specialists writing about the language have often greatly exaggerated the degree of dialectal diversification.

The current classification is that of the Basque linguist Luis Michelena, who recognized nine dialect areas; however, the ninth, Roncalese, in the Roncal Valley in Pyrenees, has become extinct within the last few years. One other dialect, called Southern, is attested to in the sixteenth century but is long extinct.

The contemporary dialects are, roughly from west to east (locations cite modern Spanish provinces and former French provinces now incorporated into the *département* of Pyrenees-Atlantique): (1) Bizkaian (or Vizcayan) (B), in Bizkaia and western Gipuzkoa; (2) Gipuzkoan (or Guipuzcoan) (G), in most of Gipuzkoa; (3) High Navarrese (HN), in northern Navarre and eastern Gipuzkoa; (4) Lapurdian (or Labourdin) (L) in Labourd; (5) Low Navarrese (LN), in Basse Navarre; (6) Salazarese (S), in Salazar Valley in Pyrenees; (7) Aezkoan (A), in Aezkoa Valley in Pyrenees; and (8) Zuberoan (or Souletin) (Z), in Soule.

Following are a few of the more prominent dialectal differences: The French Basque varieties (L, LN, and Z) retain the consonant /h/ as well as distinctively aspirated plosives; the aspiration was long ago lost in all Spanish varieties. Z and R retain distinctively nasalized vowels; these have been lost in all other varieties. Z (only) has acquired a contrastive front rounded vowel and contrastive voiced fricatives. The ordinary main verb 'have' is *ukan* in the French varieties but *eduki* in the Spanish ones. There is considerable lexical differentiation between Basque dialects. For example, 'speak' is *berba egin* in B, *itz egin* in G, and *mintzatu* in the French varieties.

There is no significant social variation, save that educated speakers tend to adjust their speech toward the norms of the new standard language and to prefer indigenous words and neologisms to loanwords where possible.

Number of Speakers: 660,000 according to the 1991 census. Fewer than 80,000 of these are on the French side. This figure includes a few thousand people who speak Basque as a second language.

Origin and History

Basque is unquestionably the last surviving pre-Indo-European language in western Europe. In Roman times, while most of Gaul was occupied by Celts, the southwest (roughly the medieval Duchy of Aquitaine) was occupied by a quite distinctive people called Aquitanians. Their Aquitanian language is preserved only in the form of some 400 personal names and 70 divine names in Latin texts, but many of these names are so transparently Basque that specialists are satisfied that Aquitanian (Aq.) was an ancestral form of Basque (Bq.). Examples: Aq. *Cison*, Bq. *gizon* 'man'; Aq. *Andere* Bq. *andere* 'lady'; Aq. *Nescato,* Bq. *neskato* 'young girl'; Aq. *Sembe*, Bq. *seme* 'son' (< **senbe*); Aq. *Ombe* and *Vmme*, Bq. *ume* 'child' (<**unbe*); Aq. *SA.HAR*, Bq. *zahar* 'old'; Aq. *Osso-*, Bq. *otso* 'wolf'. The phonological system of Aquitanian is strikingly similar to that of the pre-Basque of the Roman era reconstructed independently.

Aquitanian is only sparsely attested south of the Pyrenees in Roman times, although it was probably spoken in at least part of the modern Spanish Basque Country. Toponymic evidence shows that it must also have been spoken in the Pyrenees as far east as the valley of Arán, in territory which today is CATALAN-speaking.

There is clear evidence that Aquitanian/Basque co-existed with at least one Indo-European language in Roman times. As

Table 1: Consonants

	Labial	Dental	Alveolar	Palatal	Velar	Glottal
Stops	p, (ph) b	t, (th) d		tt dd, j	k, (kh) g	
Fricatives	f		s/z/x	j	j	(h)
Affricates			ts/tz/tx	j		
Nasals	m		n	ñ		
Liquids			l r, rr	ll		
Glides				j		

far as we can judge, the western part of the modern Basque Country was entirely Indo-European-speaking. Some time after the collapse of the western Roman Empire, Basque was extended into what is now the western part of the Basque-speaking region, and also into much of the Rioja and Burgos, both of which were Basque-speaking in the early medieval period. Since that time, the language has been steadily losing ground to SPANISH (and Catalan) in the south and east. In the sixteenth century, the southern frontier of the language lay in the Ebro Valley; today, the language has disappeared from all but one small corner of Álava, from western Bizkaia, and from the greater part of Navarre. In the north, most of Aquitania was romanized rather early, but Basque survived in what is now the French Basque Country. The Basque-Gascon frontier in the north has been stable for many centuries, although French Basque is now under severe pressure from FRENCH.

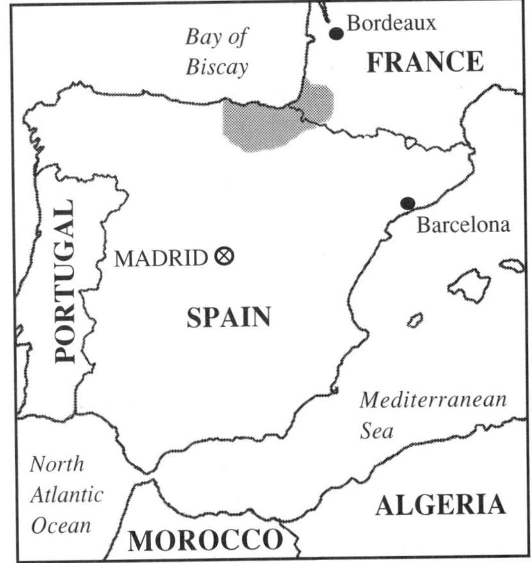

Basque is spoken along the coast of the Bay of Biscay in northern Spain and southwestern France (shaded area).

Aside from the Aquitanian materials, the first documentation of Basque is the Emilian Glosses, usually dated to around 950. Thereafter, we find an increasing number of glosses, glossaries, individual words and phrases, complete sentences, brief inscriptions, personal names, place names, songs, verses, personal letters, and other materials. The first book published in Basque was Bernard Dechepare's *Linguae Vasconum Primitiae*, a collection of poems published in 1545. Since that time, there has been a steady flow of publications in the language.

Orthography and Basic Phonology

Basque has always been written in the Roman alphabet. Before the 1960s, there was no standard orthography, and writers often used Romance spelling conventions supplemented by various additional devices to represent sounds absent from Romance. The modern standard orthography was promulgated by the Royal Basque Language Academy in 1964 and is now almost universally used.

The modern standard alphabet consists largely of the following letters: *a b d e f g h i j k l m n n o p r s t u x z*. The letters *c q v w y* are not considered part of the alphabet, but they are used in writing foreign words and names. The digraphs *dd ll rr ts tt tx tz* represent single segments, but these are regarded as sequences of letters, not as single characters.

A notable feature of Basque orthography is that it rejects Romance conventions which are unmotivated in Basque. So the phoneme /k/ is always written *k* and never as *c* or *qu*; /g/ is always written as *g* and never as *gu*; /s/ is always written *z* and never *c* or *ç*. Hence we have the town names *Gernika* (Sp. *Guernica*) and *Zegama* (Sp. *Cegama*) and provinces *Bizkaia* (Sp. *Vizcaya*) and *Gipuzkoa* (Sp. *Guipuzcoa*).

The letter *h* is written where the French Basques have it word-initially or intervocalically, but not after a consonant. Thus, the standard orthography writes *hau* 'this' and *ehun* '100' rather than the *au* and *eun* traditionally used by Spanish Basques, but it writes *ipar* 'north' rather than the *iphar* traditionally used by French Basques.

There is no standard pronunciation of Basque. The consonantal segments shown in Table 1 are shared by most varieties of Basque, however, with the exception of *tt*, a voiceless palatal stop, which occurs only in some varieties. Segments in parentheses belong to French Basque varieties only.

Among the voiceless alveolar fricatives, *s* is apico-alveolar, *z* is lamino-alveolar, and *x* is palato-alveolar [ʃ]. The same distinctions obtain for the voiceless alveolar affricates. The rhotic *r* is a tap, whereas *rr* is a trill. The letter *j* has diverse phonetic realizations according to region.

Table 2: Vowels

	Front	Central	Back
High	i		u
Mid	e		o
Low		a	

Basque /a/ is phonetically somewhat front and, indeed, behaves phonologically like a front vowel. One variety, Zuberoan, contains the front rounded vowel *ü*. Both Zuberoan and Roncalese have nasalized vowels contrasting with the oral ones. Most varieties also have the diphthongs *ai ei oi ui au eu*. Bizkaian also has the diphthong *ao*. All other vowel sequences constitute two syllables.

There are no significant phonological processes applying across the language. Many western varieties have a pitch-accent, while most other varieties have a stress-accent; the details vary considerably according to region.

Basic Morphology

In Basque, nouns cannot be directly inflected; only full noun phrases (NPs) can be inflected. Basque has no grammatical gender, no classifiers, and no noun classes. Animate NPs form their local cases (only) somewhat differently from inanimate NPs.

The order of elements in an NP is as follows:

complex modifier–Det1–Noun–Adj–Det2–Number–Case

With only minor exceptions, an NP (other than a pronoun) always contains one and only one determiner (Det). The determiners which can occur in the Det2 position are the definite determiners (the definite article and three demonstratives), the indefinite article, the numeral 'one' and some quantifiers. All others occupy the Det1 position. Only an NP containing a definite determiner is marked for number (singular or plural).

Examples, with *gizon* 'man':

gizona 'the man'; *gizonak* 'the men'
gizon hau 'this man'; *gizon hauek* 'these men'
gizon bat 'a man'; *gizon asko* 'lots of men'
zenbat gizon 'how many men'
gizon handia 'the big man'; *gizon handiak* 'the big men'
gizon handi hauek 'these big men'
bi gizon 'two men'; *bi gizon handi* 'two big men'
bi gizonak 'the two men', 'both men'

There are thirteen cases, all but one marked by case-suffixes. Case-marking is ergative: subjects of intransitive verbs and direct objects stand in the Absolutive case, while subjects of transitive verbs stand in the Ergative case. The cases are as follows:

Absolutive: **-Ø**	Intransitive subj.; Dir. obj.,vocative
Ergative: **-k**	Transitive subject
Dative: **-i**	Indirect object; ethic dative
Instrumental: **-z**	Instrument; misc. uses of 'with'
Comitative: **-ekin**	Accompaniment
Genitive: **-en**	Possessor
Locative: **-n**	Location
Allative: **-ra**	Goal of motion
Ablative: **-tik**	Source of motion
Benefactive: **-entzat**	Beneficiary
Directional: **-rantz**	Direction of motion
Terminative: **-raino**	Terminus of motion
Destinative: **-rako**	Inanimate destination

The last four cases are compound, consisting of the Genitive or Allative plus an additional morph.

Most textbooks recognize a further case, the Partitive, suffix *-ik*, which marks the direct object of a negated verb and an unspecified whole of which a part is identified. Neither the Partitive suffix nor the Essive suffix *-tzat*, which expresses capacity, can be added to an NP that contains a Determiner. Most textbooks also recognize a Locative Genitive case in *-ko*, but this is a serious error of analysis. A *-ko* phrase is a complex modifier that consists of any kind of adverbial plus the suffix *-ko*. Genitives and relative clauses are also complex modifiers.

The personal pronouns are *ni* 'I', *hi* 'you' (intimate singular), *zu* 'you' (unmarked singular), *gu* 'we', and *zuek* 'you' (plural). The intimate pronoun *hi* is regularly used only between siblings and between close friends of the same sex and roughly the same age. Some varieties have recently acquired third-person pronouns, in most cases by generalizing the third-person intensive pronouns.

Verbal morphology is overwhelmingly periphrastic; only a handful of verbs have any synthetic forms at all. Most intransitive verbs are conjugated with the auxiliary *izan* 'be'. Transitive verbs (and a small, semantically arbitrary set of intransitive verbs) use the defective verb **edun* 'have', which has an irregular citation form *ukan* in some varieties.

In a periphrastic form, the main verb is marked at most for aspect (perfective, imperfective, future). The finite auxiliary is marked for tense (past or non-past) and mood (several moods distinguished), and it also carries all agreement: *ikus-i n-a-u-zu* (see-PERF 1SG.ABS-PRES-AUX-2SG.ERG) 'you have seen me'. Agreement is extensive; the finite form agrees in person and number with its subject, with its direct object (if any), and with its indirect object (if any). Agreement with the third person is often zero. Agreement is in most cases Ergative: intransitive subjects and direct objects (Absolutives) are marked by prefixes, whereas transitive subjects (Ergatives) are marked by suffixes. Certain past tense forms are exceptions to this pattern.

A causative is derived by suffixing *-erazi* to a simple lexical verb. There is no true passive-with-agent, but any transitive verb can be conjugated intransitively to produce a mediopassive, which is equivalent to an English passive without agent: *Jon-ek lan-a* *egin-go d-u* (John-ERG work-DET do-FUT pres.3ABS-AUX.TRANS) 'John will do the work', *Lan-a egin-go d-a* (work-DET do-FUT PRES.3ABS-AUX.INTRANS) 'The work will be done'.

There is a rich set of non-finite forms, and these are very frequent. Participles and gerunds can take case-marked NP arguments, and a combination of a participle with an ergative NP is functionally equivalent to a passive-with-agent.

Basque is very rich in word-forming suffixes, but it is virtually devoid of prefixes, save for a very few borrowed from, or calqued on, Romance. Compound formation is highly productive for both nouns and verbs and moderately productive for adjectives. For example, the nouns *eliza* 'church' and *txori* 'bird' form *elizatxori* 'sparrow'; the verb *jan* 'eat' and the noun *ordu* 'hour' form *janordu* 'dinnertime'; the noun *larru* 'skin' and the adjective *gorri* 'red' form *larrugorri* 'naked'.

Basic Syntax

Basque is an SOV language, but not a rigid one: phrases may be permuted within a sentence with considerable freedom. Verb-final order is mandatory only in relative clauses. A phrase is focused by placing it immediately before the verb.

Within major phrases, Basque is primarily head-final. Thus, an auxiliary verb follows a main verb and the language is exclusively postpositional. Moreover, an adjective or adverb follows a degree modifier, and within an NP, a noun follows a genitive, a relative clause, a complex adjectival, and some determiners, although it precedes a lexical adjective and certain other determiners.

Question-word questions are formed with a question word like *nor* 'who', *zer* 'what', or *noiz* 'when'; the question word must immediately precede the verb and normally also occurs in sentence-initial position, e.g. *Nor-k eros-i d-it-u liburu hau-ek* (who-ERG buy-PERFECTIVE PRES.3ABS-PL.ABS-AUX.TRANS book this-PL) 'Who has bought these books/Who bought these books (earlier today)?' Yes-no questions may be formed in three ways: (1) by using rising intonation alone (all dialects); (2) by inserting the question particle *al* between the two parts of periphrastic verb-form, or immediately before a synthetic verb-form (usually with rising intonation) (G only); (3) by suffixing *-a* to the finite verb or auxiliary (usually with falling intonation) (L and LN only).

There is an invariable negative *ez*, which immediately precedes the finite verb or auxiliary and induces a change in word order: *Bilbo-n ikusi-ko z-a-it-u-t* (Bilbao-LOC see-FUT 2SG-PRES-PL.ABS-AUX.TRANS-1SG.ERG) 'I will see you in Bilbao', *Ez zaitut Bilbon ikusiko* 'I won't see you in Bilbao'.

A striking characteristic of Basque syntax is the frequency of *-ko* phrases, in which almost any kind of adverbial can be converted to a preposed adnominal modifier. Thus, *atzo* 'yesterday' yields *atzoko egunkaria* 'yesterday's newspaper'; *mendietara* 'to the mountains' yields *mendietarako bidea* 'the road to the mountains; *zu bezala* 'like you' yields *zu bezalako pertsona bat* 'a person like you', *izarra agertu zitzaienean* 'when the star appeared to them' yields *izarra agertu zitzaieneko garaian* 'at the time when the star appeared to them.'

Contact with Other Languages

Basque has been in intense contact with LATIN and its Romance descendants for some 2000 years, and it has borrowed thousands of words from these sources. Words from Latin were clearly borrowed very early, while others show the effect of phonological changes which affected Romance in post-Roman times and must be later. In the last 1000 years or so, contact has chiefly been with Castilian, Navarrese, Aragonese, and OCCITAN (particularly Gascon). Contact with Asturian in the west has had little effect. Contact with French mainly dates only from the French Revolution but has recently been intense in the French Basque Country. Recent loans are very numerous, and indeed almost any Spanish or French word may be borrowed into Basque on occasion. The French-Spanish divide leads to lexical difference, such as southern *kotxe* 'car' and *juez* 'judge', but northern *boitura* 'car' and *juje* 'judge'.

From Latin: *liburu* 'book' (< *librum*), *luku* 'grove' (< *lucum*), *lege* 'law' (< *legem*), *maizter* 'master shepherd' (< *magister*)

From Romance: *zeru* 'sky' (< *caelum*), *deitu* 'call' (participle) (< *dictum*), *putzu* 'well' (< *puteum*)

Common Words

man:	gizon	small:	txiki – ttipi
woman:	emakume	yes:	bai
water:	ur	no:	ez
sun:	eguzki – eki	good:	on
three:	hiru(r)	bird:	(t)xori
fish:	arrai(n)	dog:	zakur – txakur
big:	handi	tree:	zuhaitz
long:	luze		

Example Sentences

(1) Jon-ek liburu hau-Ø idatz-i z-u-Ø-en
John-ERG book this-ABS write-PERF PAST-AUX-3SERG-PAST
'John wrote this book.'

(2) Jon-ek ez z-u-Ø-en liburu hau-Ø
John-ERG NEG PAST-AUX-3SERG-PAST book this-ABS

idatz-i.
write-PERF
'John didn't write this book.'

(3) Jon-ek (gaur goiz-(e)a-n ikus-i d-u-gu-n)
John-ERG (today morning-DET-LOC see-PERF PRES-AUX-1PL-REL)

kotxe-a-Ø eros-i nahi d-u-Ø.
car-DET-ABS buy-PERF want PRES-AUX-3SERG
'John wants to buy the car we saw this morning.'

Efforts to Preserve, Protect, and Promote the Language

Apart from young children, probably all Basques under the age of 70 are bilingual in Spanish or French. Traditionally, children have spoken only Basque before starting school, and this pattern is still the norm in much of the country, although the picture may change due to the influence of the mass media.

For centuries Basque has been a language of little prestige. The rise of a self-conscious Basque nationalism in the late nineteenth century attracted hostility from the Spanish government and at times persecution; this persecution reached its height after the Fascist victory in the Civil War, when the very speaking of Basque was declared illegal.

After World War II, unofficial Basque-language schools called *ikastolas* were set up, and publication in Basque again began to flourish. In 1979, a long-coveted statute of autonomy set up an Autonomous Basque Government in the three provinces of Bizkaia, Gipuzkoa, and Álava (Navarre declined to join, and the French Basque Country was of course automatically excluded). The autonomous government has made strenuous efforts to promote the language, and a knowledge of Basque is required for many jobs.

Today Basque is used for all internal purposes within the territory of the Basque Autonomous Government. Basque-language education is available at all levels, including the university level for some subjects, although everyone is also obliged to be educated in Spanish. There are several Basque-language radio stations as well as a television station and there is abundant publication in the language (although no monoglot daily newspaper). Numerous textbooks, dictionaries, and various other reference works exist in Basque, and a significant amount of scholarly work on the language is now published in Basque.

Select Bibliography

Aulestia, Gorka. 1989. *Basque-English Dictionary.* Reno: University of Nevada Press.

Aulestia, Gorka and Linda White. 1990. *English-Basque Dictionary.* Reno: University of Nevada Press.

King, Alan. 1994. *The Basque Language: A Practical Introduction.* Reno: University of Nevada Press.

Lafitte, Pierre. 1944. *Grammaire basque: navarro-labourdin littéraire.* 3rd ed. (1979). Donostia: ELKAR. [textbook of French Basque].

Saltarelli, Mario. 1988. *Basque.* London: Croom Helm.

Trask, R.L. 1996. *The History of Basque.* London: Routledge.

Belorussian

Raymond H. Miller

Language Name: Belorussian. **Alternates:** Byelorussian, Belarusian, White Russian, belorusskij jazyk (Russian). **Autonym:** *belaruskaja mova.*

Location: Largely coextensive with the newly-independent Republic of Belarus (formerly Belorussia, Byelorussia, or White Russia). There are sizable colonies of Belorussian speakers in Lithuania (its capital Vilnius is a Belorussian cultural center) and Latvia. Most investigators agree that the Belorussian language area extends historically into eastern Poland (Bialystok region), western Russian (most of Smolensk *oblast*), and northern Ukraine.

Family: East Slavic group of the Slavic branch of the Indo-European language family.

Related Languages: Belorussian is extremely closely related to the other East Slavic languages (UKRAINIAN and especially RUSSIAN). Due to centuries of close contact, it now bears certain affinities to POLISH, a West Slavic language. There is also a strong family resemblance to all the other Slavic languages.

Dialects: There are two major dialect groups: Northeastern and Southwestern. The standard language is based on the SW dialects. There is also a fairly thick band of transitional Central dialects transecting Belarus from northwest to southeast; these dialects display a mix of NE and SW features. Scholars also distinguish various other Belorussian dialect groups, including a group in the vicinity of Brest in the southwest corner of Belarus, displaying features shared with neighboring Ukrainian dialects. (Some investigators consider these Brest-area dialects Ukrainian.)

Number of Speakers: 7.5–8 million.

Origin and History

Although the point remains much debated, there was for all intents and purposes one East Slavic language until the 13th century. To be sure, this large language area must have been characterized by considerable dialectal variation, but there is no solid evidence that medieval Eastern Slavs self-consciously considered themselves differentiated nationally by language.

In the Middle Ages, the Eastern Slavs were loosely united in a kind of federation of principalities known as *Rus* or *Kievan Rus*, or simply Kiev after its capital city. *Rus* became Christianized in 988 and inherited the Orthodox/Slavonic culture of the Balkans. Torn by internecine strife, the federation fell apart in the 1200s, and it was conquered in 1240 by the Mongols.

In a period from approximately the mid-1200s to the mid-1300s, Lithuanian warriors swept down from the Baltic and conquered the old principalities of western and southern Rus. It is generally held that this act is what laid the foundation for the development of separate East Slavic languages (Russian, Belorussian, and Ukrainian), because it created a military/political boundary which enabled western and southern 'Rusian' dialects to develop independently from those of the east. It is significant that the isogloss bundle in the Smolensk region of western Russia which demarcates the Belorussian language area corresponds almost exactly to the old eastern Lithuanian frontier.

The conquering Lithuanians were illiterate, while their new subjects had a rich literary tradition which had long flourished in such West Russian cities as Polock and Smolensk. Indeed, the Lithuanians even adopted a standardized form of the West Russian vernacular as their state language. (Western scholars refer to this as the West Russian Chancellery Language but Belorussian scholars call it the 'Old Belorussian Literary Language'.) Printing presses sprang up in several cities in West Russia beginning in the 15th century, and the high point of Lithuanian/Russian literature falls in the late 15th to early 16th centuries.

Gradually the chancellery language became corrupted through a large influx of foreign borrowings. The Grand Duchy of Lithuania became formally united with the Kingdom of Poland through the Union of Lublin in 1569, and Polish culture predominated. With the Union of Brest in 1596, there was total assimilation of the Lithuanian-Russian gentry to Polish culture and the Catholic religion. East Slavic culture, being identified with the Orthodox Church, survived only in the villages where its overt manifestations were often brutally repressed. By 1697 the West Russian Chancellery Language had been banned from courts and offices. The young Belorussian language was left to the peasants whose poor lot meant that the language ceased to exist as a medium of culture.

By 1800 all of the former Grand Duchy of Lithuania had been brought into the Russian empire through the three partitions of Poland. The region was now officially referred to as 'Belorossija', although at this stage it was strictly a regional designation having no overt ethnic content. Revolts throughout historical Poland in 1830–31 and, especially, in 1863, prompted severe counter-measures, including the proscribing of the Polish language; and since Belorussian was viewed at that time as merely a variant of Polish, its fitful use as a written language was effectively curtailed as well. Meanwhile, an aggressive policy of Russification was pursued in Belorussia, as elsewhere in the empire: Polish and Polanized gentry and intellectuals abandoned Catholicism en masse for Orthodoxy. About this time a

Table 1: The Belorussian Alphabet with Transliteration

Аа	a as in **ah**	Тт	t
Бб	b	Уу	u as in b**oo**t
Вв	v	Ўў	post-vocalic - w, as in bo**w**ing
Гг	h	Фф	f, occurs only in very recent borrowings
Дд	d	Хх	hard German or Scottish ch, as in lo**ch**, transliterated by x
Ее	ye	Цц	ts as in bi**ts**, transliterated by c
Ёё	yo; not normally indicated in texts; differs from Ee only under stress; '**yo**ke'	Чч	hard Eng. ch, approx. **ch**urch; harder than in Russian equivalent; transliterated by č
Жж	ž	Шш	English sh, approx. **sh**oot, transliterated by š
Зз	z	ы	a high back unrounded vowel; no equivalent in English; positional variant of i after hard consonant; never used initially
Іі	i as in sweet	ь	soft sign: indicates softness of proceeding consonant
й	post-vocalic -y as in 'bo**y**'; never appears initially	Ээ	e as in b**e**t
Кк	k	Юю	yu
Лл	l (hard); dark or velar l, approx. as in tab**le**	Яя	ya
Мм	m	'	apostrophe used to separate hard consonant from /j/, indicated by following vowel letter (е, ё, и, ю, я): з'езд 'congress' = /z+jezd/
Нн	n		
Оо	pure /o/, as in Br. pronunciation of f**o**r		
Пп	p		
Рр	rolled r		
Сс	s		

group of intellectuals began to write in their own tongue, but the Russian government proscribed the use of Belorussian in 1867, and literary activity ceased until the 1880s when a new group of writers began producing works in Belorussian. Although a great deal of distinctively Belorussian literature was produced between 1880 and the 1917 Russian Revolution, there was no accepted literary standard until around 1906.

The formation of a Belorussian literary norm began with the work of the poets Jakub Kolas and Janka Kupala and the journal *Naša Niva* (Our Soil). The first grammar was B. Taraškevič's *Belaruskaja hramatyka dlja škol* (Belorussian Grammar for Schools), published in 1918 and based on the Southwestern dialect group, arguably the idioms most distinct from Russian and Ukrainian. In 1933 under Stalin, with the publication of a decree entitled 'On the changes and simplification of the Belorussian orthography', another period of Russification was inaugurated. Russification waxed and waned throughout the Soviet period, in connection with Moscow's nationalities policies. Belorussian's position in the Soviet Union was generally weaker than that of the various other languages, because of its close resemblance to Russian. Scholarly interest has always been intense, however. For example, in 1963, Belorussian was the first of the East Slavic languages to publish its dialect atlas, capping years of field work.

Orthography and Basic Phonology

Consonant symbols followed by an apostrophe (') are soft or palatalized consonants.

As in Russian, voiced consonants are devoiced in word-final position and before voiceless consonants. This devoicing is not reflected in the orthography. Thus, /l'od/ 'ice' is pronounced [l'ot]. Likewise, voiceless consonants will become voiced in clusters before voiced consonants: /kas'bá/ 'scything' is pronounced [kaz'bá].

Soft /t'/ and /d'/ are regularly pronounced as soft affricates /c'/ and /dz'/: /brat/ 'brother (NOM.SG)', but /brác'e/ 'brother (LOC.SG)'.

The consonants /l/ and /v/ become /w/ in word-final position and before a consonant: /p'isáw/ 'he wrote', /p'isála/ 'she wrote'.

Table 2: Consonants

	Labial	Dental	Alveo-Palatal	Velar
Stops Voiceless	p p'	t t'		k
Stops Voiced	b b'	d d'		
Fricatives Voiceless	f f'	s s'	š	x
Fricatives Voiced	v v'	z z'	ž	ɣ
Affricates Voiceless		c	č	
Affricates Voiced			dž	
Nasals	m m'	n n'		
Resonants		r	l'	l
Glides			j	

Table 3: Vowels

	Front	Central	Back
High	i		u
Mid	e		o
Low		a	

The spelling of the vowels /i u o a/ differs depending on whether they follow soft (palatalized) or hard (non-palatalized) consonants.

The high front vowel /i/ has a high back unrounded variant

Table 4: Verb Conjugation

Form	brac'	čytac'	s'adz'ec'	rab'ic'
Present				
1sg	b'arú	čytáju	s'adžú	rabl'ú
2sg	b'aréš	čytáješ	s'adz'íš	rób'iš
3sg	b'aré	čytáje	s'adz'íc'	rób'ic'
1pl	b'aróm	čytájem	s'adz'ím	rób'im
2pl	b'arac'ó	čytájec'e	s'adz'ic'ó	rób'ic'e
3pl	b'arúc'	čytájuc'	s'adz'ac'	rób'ac'
Past				
m.sg	braw	čytáw	s'adz'éw	rab'íw
f.sg	bralá	čytála	s'adz'éla	rab'íla
n.sg	brála	čytála	s'adz'éla	rab'íla
pl	brál'i	čytál'i	s'adz'él'i	rab'íl'i

[y] that occurs after hard consonants only. Unstressed non-high vowels (/e o a/) fall together. As a result, the following changes are observed:

/o/ > /a/ following a hard consonant
/e/ > /y/ after /c/
/e/ > /a/ after other hard consonants
/e o/ > /a/ in the first pretonic syllable, following a soft consonant
/o/ > /e/ in other unstressed positions following a soft consonant

Unlike in Russian, these reductions are reflected in Belorussian orthography: /kon'/ 'horse (NOM.SG)', /kan'óm/ 'horse (INSTR.SG)'.

Stress in Belorussian is dynamic; it can occur on any syllable in the word, and its place can shift within paradigms.

Basic Morphology

Nouns in Belorussian inflect for case and number. There are six cases (nominative, accusative, genitive, locative or prepositional, dative, and instrumental) and two numbers (singular and plural). There are three genders (masculine, feminine, and neuter). There are four major declensional classes for nouns. Which class a particular noun falls in depends both on its gender and, for feminine nouns, on its phonological form; the four classes are *a*-stem (mostly feminine), *i*-stem (all feminine), masculine, and neuter. In all four classes, the sets of endings following stem-final soft consonants differ somewhat from those that follow hard consonants.

Adjectives and pronouns decline for the same set of cases and numbers as nouns do. Adjectives agree with the nouns that they modify in number and case and, in the singular, also in gender.

There is no overt marking for definiteness.

As in all the other Slavic languages, there are two lexical verbs for every verbal idea, representing two aspects, the imperfective and the perfective. Perfective verbs focus on the result of the action, or else limit it in time in some way, while imperfectives simply name the action, without making any such comment on it. Imperfective verbs conjugate for three tenses: past, present, and future, while perfectives have forms only for the past and future. As in other Slavic languages, perfective verbs are related to imperfectives by prefixation (impf *rabíc'* 'to work', pf *zrabíc'*), suffixation (pf *padp'icác'* 'to sign', impf *padp'ícvac'*), or suppletion (impf *klasc'is'a* 'lie down', pf *l'eұcy*).

Present tense verbs agree with their subjects in person and number, and past tense verbs agree with their subjects in gender and number. The future tense of imperfectives is formed with the future tense of the verb *byc'* 'to be' and the infinitive. For the inflected tenses, there are two basic conjugation types which are characterized in addition by three different stress patterns: fixed final stress, fixed stem stress, and shifting stress. The conjugations of the first conjugation final stressed verb *brac'* 'to take', first conjugation stem stressed verb *čytac'* 'to read', second conjugation final stressed verb *s'adz'ec'* 'to sit', and second conjugation shifting stress verb *rab'ic'* 'to do' are illustrated in Table 4 above.

In addition to the forms in Table 4, Belorussian verbs have a variety of participles and verbal adverbs. These forms combine with inflected forms of the verb 'to be' and other verbs to form periphrastic tenses (e.g., pluperfect and future perfect). Passive voice can be overtly expressed by use of the past passive participle with a form of *byc'* 'to be':

vaknó	bý-l-a	razb'íta	kúl'a-ju
window:NOM.NEUT.SG	be-PAST-N.SG	smashed	bullet-INST

'The window was smashed by a bullet.'

Alternatively, the so-called reflexive particle *-s'a* can be affixed to a transitive verb; in the third person and infinitive forms, this particle has the form *-cca*.

dom	budúje-cca	májstr-am'i
home:NOM.MASC.SG	build-REFL	skilled workman-INST.PL

'The house is being built by skilled workmen.'

Basic Syntax

Belorussian has a relatively free word order, since grammatical relations can be shown through inflection. New information tends to be held until the end of the sentence. In the following example, the congress is old information, and the professor is new information:

na	zjédz'-e	ɣavar-ýw	praf'éssar
at	congress-LOC	speak-PAST.3SG	professor:NOM.M.SG

'A professor spoke at the congress.'

Otherwise, the preferred order of constituents is SVO. In sentences with both direct and indirect objects, the neutral word order will be subject-verb-dative-accusative. Pronominal forms tend to gravitate towards the front of the sentence following the subject:

jon	mn'e	jaɣó	da-w
3SG.NOM	1SG.DAT	3SG.ACC	give-PAST.3SG

'He gave it to me.'

Within noun phrases, adjectival and pronominal modifiers precede the nouns they modify, and genitive nouns follow the nouns they modify.

Sentences are negated by the particle *n'e* immediately preceding the element being negated: *jon mn'e jayó n'e daw:* 'He didn't give it to me.'

Contact with Other Languages

Belorussian has the same international borrowings as do many of the other Slavic languages. Borrowings are usually completely naturalized. Over the years, many words have been borrowed from Polish. As in Russian, further enrichment of the lexicon is achieved through calquing of Greek or Latinate vocabulary. An example of this is *rúkap'is'* 'manuscript' (< *ruká* 'hand', *p'isac'* 'to write').

From Polish: *pan* 'mister, gentleman', *hának* 'porch'
From Latin: *af'icér* 'officer', *respúbl'ika* 'republic', *arb'ítr* 'referee'

Common Words

man:	čalav'ék	long:	dówɣa
woman:	žančýna	small:	mály
water:	vadá	yes:	tak
sun:	sónca	no:	n'e
three:	try	good:	dóbry
fish:	rýba	bird:	ptax
big:	v'al'ík'i	dog:	sabáka
tree:	dz'érava		

Example Sentences

(1) U	náš-ym	s'al'é	žy-w	adz'ín	čalav'ék
in	our-LOC	village.LOC	live-PAST.3SG	one	man:NOM.M.SG

'A certain man lived in our village.'

(2) ɣéta	dl'a	c'ab'é
this.NEUT	for	2SG.LOC

'This is for you.'

(3) ja	ɣavar-ú	pab'elarúsku
1SG.NOM	speak-1SG	Belorussian

'I speak Belorussian.'

Efforts to Preserve, Protect, and Promote the Language

Efforts to promote Belorussian have been hindered by its close relationship with neighboring languages. For example, it is relatively easy for Belorussians to learn standard Russian, a world language of considerable prestige. By the end of the Brezhnev era in the early 1980s, less than 80% of Belorussians claimed Belorussian as their native tongue; and nearly 98% of all pupils in Belorussian cities received their instruction in Russian. Today, Belorussian nationalists bemoan the fact that so many of their compatriots are Russian speakers, especially in the cities. New teaching materials in Belorussian have been prepared for the nation's schools and universities.

Although most investigators place the eastern boundary of the Belorussian language area well to the east of Smolensk, the political boundary between Belarus and Russia has run well to the west of that city since the creation of the Belorussian republic after the 1917 Russian Revolution. Today, Russian linguists routinely view the dialects spoken in the area between these two borders as 'West Russian' dialects. Although Belorussia did declare its independence when the Soviet Union collapsed in 1991, and it revived symbols from the brief period of Belorussian independence after World War I, it is a fact that Belorussian national identity—and the linguistic awareness nationalism entails—has been far weaker than that of any other East European nation.

Select Bibliography

Carlton, Terence. R. 1991. *Introduction to the Phonological History of the Slavic Languages*. Columbus: Slavic Publishers.

De Bray, R.G.A. 1980. *Guide to the East Slavonic Languages*. Columbus: Slavic Publishers.

Mayo, Peter. 1993. "Belorussian." In *The Slavonic Languages*, eds. B. Comrie and G. Corbett, 887–946. London & New York: Routledge.

Susha, T.M., and A.K. Shchuka. 1989. *English-Byelorussian-Russian Dictionary*. Minsk: Belaruskaja saveckaja encyklapedyja.

Ushkevich, Alexander, and Alexandra Zezulin. 1992. *Byelorussian-English English-Byelorussian Dictionary: With Complete Phonetics*. New York: Hippocrene Books.

Wexler, Paul. 1979. "The Rise (and Fall) of the Modern Byelorussian Literary Language." In *Slavic and East European Review* 57, 4 (October, 1979): 481–508.

Debra Spitulnik and Mubanga E. Kashoki

Language Name: Bemba. **Autonym:** *iciBemba.* **Alternates:** ciBemba, ChiBemba, ichiBemba.

Location: Principally spoken in Zambia, in the Northern, Copperbelt, and Luapula Provinces; also spoken in southern Zaire and southern Tanzania.

Family: Central Bantu subgroup of the Bantu group of the Benue-Congo branch of the Niger-Congo subfamily of Niger-Kordofanian.

Related Languages: Most closely related to the Bantu languages Kaonde (in Zambia and Congo (DRC)), TSHILUBA (in Congo (DRC)), Nsenga and Tonga (in Zambia), and Nyanja/CHICHEWA (in Zambia and Malawi).

Dialects: Principal dialects are: Aushi, Bemba, Bisa, Chishinga, Kunda, Lala, Lamba, Luunda, Ng'umbo, Swaka, Tabwa, and Unga.

Each of these dialects is distinguished by its association with a distinct ethnic group, culture, and territory of the same name. Each dialect exhibits minor differences of pronunciation and phonology, and very minor differences in morphology and vocabulary. Because Bemba is such a widely used *lingua franca*, varieties of the language exist in urban areas. Urban varieties exhibit large lexical input from ENGLISH and have several names, including: chiKopabeeluti [chiCopperbelt], chiTauni [chiTown], and Town Bemba.

Number of Speakers: 5–6 million. An estimated 3.7 million people speak Bemba and related dialects as a first language; other speakers speak Bemba as a second language.

Origin and History

The Bemba people in Zambia originated from the Kola region in present-day Congo (DRC) and are an offshoot of the ancient Luba empire. Oral historical accounts differ slightly, but there is general agreement that the Luba immigrants arrived in the high plateau area of northeastern Zambia (extending from Lake Bangweulu to the Malawi border) sometime during the mid-17th century. This area was already settled by agriculturalists, but by the end of the eighteenth century the Bemba people had established a powerful kingdom under the central authority of Chitimukulu, the paramount chief. Bemba rule continued to expand widely throughout northeastern Zambia up until the end of the 19th century, when the first European missionaries and entrepreneurs began to vie for power in the area. In 1898–99, the British South Africa Company's army wrested control of the Bemba territory, and in 1924 the British colony of Northern Rhodesia was established across the entire region of what is now present-day Zambia. Zambia gained independence from British domination in 1964.

In contemporary Zambia, the word "Bemba" actually has several meanings. It may designate people of Bemba origin, regardless of whether they live in urban areas or in the original rural Bemba area. Alternatively, it may encompass a much larger population which includes some eighteen different ethnic groups, who together with the Bemba form a closely related ethnolinguistic cluster of matrilineal-matrifocal agriculturalists known as the Bemba-speaking peoples of Zambia (*see* Dialects).

Because of the political importance of the Bemba kingdom and the extensive reach of the Bemba language, Bemba was targeted as a major language for the production of religious and educational materials in the early 1900s. The White Fathers missionaries published the earliest written texts on and in Bemba, including the first Bemba grammar in 1907 and the first Bemba translation of the New Testament in 1923. Bemba was also selected by the colonial administration as one of the four main indigenous languages (along with Lozi, Nyanja, and Tonga) to be used in education and mass media. With the extensive migration of Bemba-speaking peoples to the mining areas of the Copperbelt from the late 1920s onward, the language's range expanded further. By the late 1940s, Bemba—and specifically an urban variety known as Town Bemba—had become well-established as the lingua franca of the Copperbelt region. Extensive urban-urban migration, interethnic marriage, and the high degree of multilingualism in the country have yielded a situation where over half of the national population currently speaks Bemba. While Nyanja is still the primary lingua franca of the capital city of Lusaka, Bemba is spoken widely there as well.

Orthography and Basic Phonology

Until the publication of *Zambian Languages: Orthography Approved by the Ministry of Education* (1977), itself the culmination of efforts over a five-year period, attempts at orthographic reform had remained sporadic, uncoordinated, and not officially backed. Among the orthographic rules now officially approved for Bemba, the most notable include: (a) the use of Roman characters (as shown in the Tables 1 and 2); (b) the

Table 1: Consonants

		Bilabial	Labiodental	Alveolar	Alveo-palatal	Palatal	Velar
Stops	Voiceless	p		t			k
	Voiced	(b)		(d)			g
Fricatives	Voiceless		f	s	(s) (sh) [ʃ]		
	Voiced	b [β]					
Affricates	Voiceless				c [tʃ]		
	Voiced				dʒ		
Nasals		m		n		ny [ɲ]	ng', ŋ
Glides		w				y	

symbolization of long vowels with doubled vowel graphemes; (c) the non-symbolization of tone, despite its semantic functions; and (d) the adoption of a conjunctive mode of spelling nouns, verbs, adjectives and other grammatical forms which represents them with their bound affixes (e.g. *ífyakulya* 'foodstuffs', comprised of *ifi-a-ku-lya* 'things-of-to-eat').

Bemba has 19 consonants: p, t, k, b, d, g, tʃ, β, dʒ, f, s, ʃ, l, m, n, ɲ, ŋ, w and y. The alveopalatal voiceless affricate [tʃ] is written as *c*, except in the case of proper nouns, where it is represented as *ch*. The voiced bilabial fricative [β] is represented as *b*, and the velar nasal [ŋ] as ŋ, except before [k] and [g] when *n* is used, as in *íŋŋandá* 'house', *nkaya* 'I shall go (near future)' and *íngála* 'finger nails'. The sound [ʃ] is represented orthographically as *s* or *sh*, and [ɲ] is represented as *ny*.

The sounds [b], [d], and [ʃ] (represented above in parentheses) are allophones of the phonemes /p/, /l/, and /s/ respectively. The consonant [b] occurs only when preceded by the homorganic nasal [m] as in *mbwééle* 'should I return?' (derived from *N-* (1st pers. sg.), *-bwel-* (verb root), *-e* (Subjunctive); where *N-* becomes *m-* in homorganic harmony with the following *b*). The consonant [d] occurs only when preceded by the homorganic nasal [n], as in *ndééyá* 'I shall go' (derived from *N-* (1st pers. sg.), *-lee-* (progressive/future), *-ya* (verb root)). The alveopalatal [ʃ] occurs before [i]. In addition, the consonants [j] and [g] never occur word initially or between vowels; they are always preceded by a homorganic nasal in nasal clusters represented orthographically as *nj* and *ng* (e.g. *njebá* 'tell me' and *ngupá* 'marry me').

Table 2: Vowels

	Front	Central	Back
High	i ii		u uu
Mid	e ee		o oo
Low		a aa	

Bemba has five vowels, as shown in Table 2 above. There is a contrastive semantic distinction between short and long vowels (the doubling of vowels represents vowel length):

ukú-pámá	'to be brave'	ukú-pááma	'to hide'
ukú-shíká	'to be deep'	ukú-shííká	'to bury'
ukú-sélá	'to move'	ukú-séélá	'to dangle'

Long vowels may also result from the fusion of two vowels across morpheme boundaries. For example, *umwééní* 'stranger, guest' is derived from *umu-* + *-eni* (class 1 singular + stem), and its plural *abééní* 'strangers, guests' from *aba-* + *-eni* (class 2 plural prefix + stem).The outcome of vowel fusion is as follows:

followed by:	**i**	**e**	**a**	**o**	**u**
i	ii	yee	yaa	yoo	yuu
e	ee	ee	yaa	yoo	yoo
a	ee	ee	aa	oo	oo
o	wee	wee	waa	oo	oo
u	wii	wee	waa	oo	uu

Tone. Bemba is a tone language, with two basic tones, high (H) and low (L). H is marked with an acute accent while L is unmarked. As with most other Bantu languages, tone (a kind of musical pitch at the syllabic level) can be phonemic and is an important functional marker in Bemba, signaling semantic distinctions between words.

ímbá	'sing!'	imbá	'dig!'
ulúpwá	'family'	úlupwá	'eggplant'

Tonal contrasts also exist at the grammatical level, e.g. in signaling different tenses:

bááfíkílé	'they arrived (yesterday)'
bááfikílé	'they (had) arrived (a long time ago)'

In actual speech, tonal patterns are more complex than these example suggest as they interact with other morpho-syntactic, morpho-phonological, and prosodic processes. For example consider these two sentences:

Tuléélyá buléétí.	'We are eating bread'
Tuléelyá nshí?	'What shall we eat?'

In the first sentence, the tense/aspect marker *-lee-* carries a high tone, and in the second sentence it has a falling tone (H followed by L). Moreover, a high tone can become a low tone at the end of a declarative sentence.

Syllable Structure. As with many other Bantu languages, syllables in Bemba are characteristically open and are of four main types: V, CV, NCV, and NCGV (where V stands for vowel, C stands for consonant, N stands for nasal, and G stands for glide). These types are illustrated by *isá* (*i-sa*) 'come!', *somá* (*so-ma*) 'read!', *yambá* (*ya-mba*) 'begin!' and *ímpwa* (*i-mpwa*) 'eggplants'.

Basic Morphology

Bemba, like most Bantu languages, has a very elaborate noun class system which involves pluralization patterns, agreement marking, and patterns of pronominal reference. There are twenty different classes in Bemba: 15 basic classes, two subclasses, and three locative classes. Each noun class is indicated by a class prefix (typically VCV-, VC-, or V-) and the co-occurring agreement markers on adjectives, numerals and verbs.

umú-ntú	ú-mó	umú-sumá	á-áfíká
person	one	good	(he/she) just arrive

'One good person just arrived.'

abá-ntú	bá-tátú	abá-sumá	bá-áfíká
people	three	good	(they) just arrive

'Three good people just arrived.'

ími-tí	í-tátú	íí-sumá	í-léékula
trees	three	good	(they) grow

'Three good trees are growing.'

The noun consists of a class prefix and a stem: *umú-ntú* 'person' (Class 1), *abá-ntú* 'people' (Class 2). Noun classes have some semantic content, and there are regular patterns of singular/plural pairing and non-count classes. Class 1/2 nouns denote human beings; Class 3/4 nouns tend to be animate, agentive, or plant-like (*úmu-tí* 'tree', *ími-tí* 'trees'); and Class 9/10 nouns represent wild animals (*ín-kalamo* 'lion', *ín-kalamo* 'lions'). Things that occur in pairs or multiples are denoted by Class 5/6 nouns (*i-lúbá* 'flower', *amá-lúbá* 'flowers'); nouns for long objects are in Class 11/10 (*úlu-séngó* 'horn', *ín-sengo* 'horns'); and diminutives are in Class 12/13 (*aká-ntú* 'small thing', *utú-ntú* 'small things'). Class 7/8 is the general class for inanimate nouns (*icí-ntú* 'thing', *ifí-ntú* 'things') and also augmentatives; abstract nouns occur in Class 14 (*ubú-ntú* 'humanity'); and verbal infinitives occur in Class 15 (*úku-lyá* 'eating, to eat').

Some class prefixes have a derivational semantic function; they either replace the basic class prefix or occur as a secondary prefix on the noun form. The locative class prefixes function in an analogous manner.

úmu-tí	'tree', 'medicine'	(Class 3)
áka-tí	'a bit of medicine'	(Class 12)
aká-mu-tí	'little tree'	(Class 12)
icí-mu-tí	'stick', 'pole', 'big tree'	(Class 7)
pá-ci-mu-tí	'on the pole', 'on the big tree'	(Class 16)
íŋ-aŋdá	'house'	(Class 9)
kú-ŋŋandá	'to/from the house', 'at home'	(Class 17)
mú-ŋŋandá	'in the house'	(Class 18)

The Bemba verb has the following basic structure:

Subject Marker + Tense/Aspect/Mood Marker + Object Marker + Verb Root + Extension + Final Vowel + Suffixes

The only obligatory morphemes are the subject marker (except in imperatives), the root, and the final vowel. The final vowel (indicated as FV) marks tense and/or mood, and sometimes co-varies with the preceding tense marker. Some past tense forms are represented by *-ile* or a modified root instead of a single FV. Bemba distinguishes numerous different tenses on the verb form, including: Today Past, Recent Past, Remote Past, Present, Today Future, Later Future.

n-ací-cí-sáng-a	'I found it (today).'
1sg-PAST_{TD}-it(7)-find-FV	('it' = Class 7; e.g. *icípé* 'basket')

n-léé-cí-sáng-a	'I am finding it'
1sg-PROG/FUT_{TD}-it(7)-find-FV	'I will find it (today).'

n-aalíí-cí-sáng-ile	'I found it (a long time ago).'
1sg-PAST_{RM}-it(7)-find-PAST_{RM}	

Basic Syntax

Bemba is an SVO language. The situation is more complex, however, because verb forms themselves must be marked for the subject and may be marked for the object. There is no case marking on nouns. Objects can be pre-posed for emphasis, in which case an object marker (which would be absent in an SVO sentence) co-occurs on the verb form.

Chanda,	u-ací-sáng-a	icúúní	kwî ?
Chanda	2sg-PAST_{TD}-find-FV	bird	where

'Chanda, where did you find the bird (today)?'

icúúní,	u-ací-cí-sáng-a	kwî ?
bird	2sg-PAST_{TD}-it(7)-find-FV	where

'The bird, where did you find it (today)?'

Verbal extensions have syntactic functions (e.g. indicating a relation to an indirect object) and derivational semantic functions, as in these illustrations of the applicative, intensive, and passive extensions:

a-0-lím-a	ifyúmbú
3sg-HAB-farm-FV	sweet potatoes

'S/he grows sweet potatoes.'

a-0-lím-in-a	ábaaná	ifyúmbú
3sg-HAB-farm-APPL-FV	children	sweet potatoes

'S/he grows sweet potatoes for the children.'

a-lá-lím-ísh-á	
3sg-HAB-farm-INTENS-FV	'He/she (always) farms a lot.'

cí-ká-lím-w-á
7-FUT-farm-PASS-FV
'It will be farmed/cultivated.'

Negative sentences are usually formed with the prefix *ta-*. The infix *-shi-* marks the negative when the subject marker on the verb is first person singular or when the verb is in a dependent clause.

n-shi-léé-y-a-kó
1sg-NEG-PROG/FUT$_{TD}$-go-FV-there
'I am not going there.'

ta-bá-lee-y-á-ko
NEG-3pl-PROG/FUT$_{TD}$-go-FV-there
'They are not going there.'

n-aa-món-á ába-shí-lee-y-á-ko
1sg-PRES-see-FV 3PL-NEG-PROG/FUT$_{TD}$-go-FV-there
'I see the ones who are not going there.'

Contact with Other Languages

In the early 1800s, Portuguese and Arab traders were quite active in Bemba-speaking regions, and as a result, present day Bemba has a number of loanwords from these languages. Over the past two centuries, many SWAHILI words have entered into Bemba through direct contact with Swahili speaking peoples and also through Arab and missionary contact. In addition, words originally deriving from PORTUGUESE and ARABIC have entered into Bemba via loans from Swahili. Contact with English speaking people began to intensify in the late 1880s, and since that time a very large number of English-derived words have entered Bemba. Christian evangelization, and specifically Bemba Bible translations, have also resulted in the incorporation of some LATIN words into Bemba. In addition, Bemba has incorporated numerous loanwords from AFRIKAANS and ZULU, via mine workers' pidgins known variously as Fanagalo, Kabanga, Fanakalo, Silunguboi, Isilolo, and Chilapalapa.

Urban varieties of Bemba reflect the very dynamic language situation in Zambia, where multilingualism is high and where Bemba exists side-by-side with several other languages, most prominently English and Nyanja. Town Bemba exhibits an extremely high number of linguistic innovations and adoptions from varieties of British English and American English, which enter into the Zambian arena primarily through international business and imported media such as television programs and recorded music.

From English: *áka-etulo/útu-etulo* 'kettle/kettles', *í-lámpi/amá-lámpi* 'lamp/lamps', *ínsóókoshi* 'socks', *shuga* 'sugar'
From Swahili: *umú-shikáále/abá-shikáále* 'soldier/soliders' (< *askari* or *askikari* < Arabic), *in-sá* 'clock; hour' (< *saa* < Arabic)
From Portuguese: *in-sápátó* 'shoe/shoes' (< *sapato*), *i-péélá/amá-péélá* 'guava/guavas' (< *peera*)
From Afrikaans (via miners' pidgin): *pasóópo* 'beware!' (< *pas op*), *bulúlu* (pl. *ba-bulúlu*) 'relative, relation' (< *broer*), and *fúseeke* 'go away!' (< *voetsak*)
From Latin: *im-mínsá* 'liturgical mass/masses', *katoolika/bakatoolika* 'Catholic/Catholics'

English loans in Town Bemba exist alongside standard Bemba equivalents (indicated in parentheses): *kaa-géélo* 'girl' *(úmu-káshána)*, *kaa-bébi* 'baby' *(úmu-aná)*, *áma-guys* 'guys' *(ába-lúméndo)*, *cééya* 'chair' *(íci-púná)*.

Common Words

man:	úmwaaúmé
woman:	úmwaanakashi
water:	ámeenshí
sun:	ákasuba
three:	-tatu (adj. stem; *abántú bátátú* 'three people')
fish:	ísabi
big:	-kulu (adj.stem; *abántú ábakulu* 'big/elderly/important people')
long:	-tali (adj. stem; *ísabi ílitali* 'long fish')
small:	-ipi (adj. stem; *ísabi íliipí* 'small fish')
yes:	ééya; eendíta
no:	iyóó; ááwe
good:	-suma (adj. stem; *abántú abásumá* 'good people')
bird:	icúúní
dog:	ímbwa
tree:	úmutí

Example Sentences

(1) Mutálé a-0-fwáy-a ukú-y-á kú-ŋŋandá
Mutale 3sg-PRES-want-FV INF-go-FV to(17)-house

kú-á Chanda.
17-POSS Chanda.
'Mutale desires/longs to go to Chanda's house.'

(2) Bá-áá-ilé kwíi uyú mulungu
3pl-PAST$_{RC}$-go[mod.stem, PAST$_{RC}$] where DEM(3) week(3)

u-aa-pít-íle ?
3-PAST$_{RC}$-pass-PAST$_{RC}$
'Where did they go last week?'[Lit. 'the week that just passed']

(3) Naa-tú-lee-y-a nóombá!
PRES-1pl-PROG-go-FV now
'Let's go now!'

Efforts to Preserve, Protect, and Promote the Language

Bemba is one of the seven official Zambian languages (along with Kaonde, Lozi, Lunda, Luvale, Nyanja, and Tonga). These are the only Zambian languages sanctioned for use in education, mass media, and government documents. English is the official national language and is the primary language of government, business administration, and higher education. In the Northern, Luapula, and Copperbelt Provinces, Bemba is the primary medium of instruction in Grades 1–3, and is taught as a subject in Grades 4–12. The Zambian Ministry of Education is very active in Bemba language curriculum development. Other efforts related to preserving and promoting the language include the regular publishing of religious texts; the periodic publishing of novels, poetry, and cultural commentary; and the occasional audio recording of traditional songs. There is no official Bemba language organization, but the dominance of a specific dialect (central Bemba) in educational texts, print media, and radio newscasting serves to create a national standard.

As one of Zambia's major lingua francas (in addition to English and Nyanja), Bemba is an extremely widely-spoken language across different regions of the country and across different ethnic groups. The rate of multilingualism is quite high in Zambia. Bemba is in no danger of losing speakers, but recent history has seen some changes (such as English-derived vocabulary) in the language because of its widespread use as an urban lingua franca. Language purists express concern over this "corruption" of Bemba and the rise of the high prestige urban variety. Others point to the bivalent status of urban and rural varieties—both are positively and negatively valued, depending on context—and argue that urban and rural varieties will continue to co-exist.

Select Bibliography

Givón, Talmy. 1969. "Studies in ChiBemba and Bantu Grammar." In *Studies in African Linguistics*, Supplement 3.

Hoch, E. 1998. *Bemba Pocket Dictionary: Bemba-English and English-Bemba*. New York: Hippocrene Books. (Reprint of 1960 edition by National Educational Company of Zambia).

Hyman, Larry M. 1995. "Minimality and the Prosodic Morphology of Cibemba Imbrication." In *Journal of African Languages and Linguistics* 16 (1):3–39.

Kashoki, Mubanga E. 1968. *A Phonemic Analysis of Bemba*. Zambian Papers, No. 3. Institute for Social Research, University of Zambia. Manchester: Manchester University Press.

____. 1972. "Town Bemba: A Sketch of Its Main Characteristics." *African Social Research* 13:161-86.

____. 1978. "The Language Situation in Zambia." In *Language in Zambia*. Sirarpi Ohannessian and Mubanga E. Kashoki, eds., 9–46. London: International African Institute.

____. 1990. "Sources and Patterns of Word Adoption in Bemba." In *Language Reform: History and Future, Volume V*, ed. Istvan Fodor and Claude Hagege, 31–57. Hamburg: Helmut Buske.

Kasonde, Makasa. 1985. *Contribution á la Description du ChiBemba (Bantu M.42): Aperçu sur le Système verbal*. Paris: Université de la Sorbonne nouvelle.

Mann, Michael. 1977. "An Outline of Bemba Grammar." In *Language in Zambia: Grammatical Sketches, Volume I*. Lusaka: University of Zambia, Institute for African Studies.

Mann, Michael, ed. 1995. *A Vocabularly of Icibemba* (compiled by Malcolm Guthrie). African Languages and Cultures, Supplement 2. London: School of Oriental and African Studies, University of London.

Ministry of Education (Republic of Zambia). 1977. *Zambian Languages: Orthography Approved by the Ministry of Education*. Lusaka: NECZAM.

Oger, Louis. 1982. *IciBemba cakwa Citimukulu (Volume 1): Amasambililo* 43. Ilondola, Chinsali, Zambia: Language Centre.

_____. 1982. *IciBemba cakwa Citimukulu (Volume 2): The English Companion, Learn Bemba the Easy Way*. Ilondola, Chinsali, Zambia: Language Centre.

Spitulnik, Debra. 1998. "The Language of the City: Town Bemba as Urban Hybridity." In *Journal of Linguistic Anthropology* 8(2):30–59.

_____. 1987. *Semantic Superstructuring and Infrastructuring: Nominal Class Struggle in ChiBemba*. Studies in African Grammatical Systems, Monograph No. 4. Bloomington: Indiana University Linguistics Club.

_____. 1988. "Levels of Semantic Structuring in Bantu Noun Classification." In *Current Approaches to African Linguistics, Volume 5*, ed. Paul Newman and Robert D. Botne, 207–20. Dordrecht, The Netherlands: Foris.

White Fathers. 1991. *White Fathers' Bemba-English Dictionary*. Ndola: Mission Press by the Society of the Missionaries of Africa (White Fathers). Reprint of 1954 edition by Longmans, Green and Company (London).

Van Sambeek, J. 1955. *A Bemba Grammar*. London: Longmans, Green and Company.

BHOJPURI

Shaligram Shukla

Language Name: Bhojpuri. **Alternate Names:** Purbi, Banarasi, Bangarboli. **Autonym:** Bhojpuri.

Location: Bhojpuri is spoken in the North Indian states of Bihar, Bengal (in Calcutta), Uttar Pradesh, and the Tarai region of Nepal.

Family: Bhojpuri belongs to the eastern zone of the Indo-Aryan languages, a sub-group of the Indo-European family of languages.

Related Languages: Bhojpuri is most closely related to the five other eastern zone languages: ASSAMESE, BANGLA/Bengali, Magahi and MAITHILI, and ORIYA.

Dialects: Bhojpuri is divided into four dialects: (i) Northern Bhojpuri (districts of Saran, eastern Gorakhpur, western Deoria, in the area and around the river Sarju and in Nepal). (ii) Southern Bhojpuri (in and around the town of Bhojpur in Shahabad district in Bihar; in the district Palamau; and in the south Gangetic portion of the district Ghazipur in Uttar Pradesh). (iii) Western Bhojpuri (districts of western Ghazipur, southeast of Mirzapur, Varanasi, eastern Jaunpur, Azamgarh, and eastern Faizabad). (iv) The Sadani and the Nagpuria dialaect of Bhojpuri (south of the river Son and also parts of the districts of Palamau and Ranchi).

These divisions are based on the geographical distribution of certain phonological features, lexical usages, and syntactic constructions. For example, there is sporadic nasalization in certain lexical items in all other dialects, but not in Southern Bhojpuri. Northern and Southern Bhojpuri keep the final short [i] in many words but not the Western and Nagpuri Bhojpuri. In Southern Bhojpuri, the medial retroflex [ɽ] changes to a non-retroflex apical [r], while all other dialects maintain the retroflex pronunciation. Western and Northern Bhojpuri dialects add a final long [ā] to many lexical items which elsewhere end either with a consonant or with an [o]. Nagpuria dialect of Bhojpuri raises [a] to [o] in words such as *sob* 'all', *tob* 'then', and *job* 'when'. These are just a few of the linguistic peculiarities and variations. The grammatical description that follows is based mainly on Northern Bhojpuri.

Number of Speakers: Bhojpuri is spoken over an area of approximately 43,000 square miles and, according to the latest census, has approximately 60 million speakers. Through immigration, now there are thousands of Bhojpuri speakers in Trinidad, Mauritius, South Africa, the United Kingdom, U.S., and Canada.

Origin and History

The Indo-Europeans came to India from the northwest about four thousand years ago. In India they called themselves *arya* 'noble, honorable'. Because of this ancient reference, the term *Aryan* is used now to refer to these people and their languages. The historical period of Indo-Aryan begins with the composition and compilation of the Rigveda. In the linguistic context, the term Indo-Aryan includes all languages derived from this source from the earliest time to the present day. With regard to its structure and its continuity, the Indo-Aryan languages can be divided into three periods: Old Indo-Aryan, Middle Indo-Aryan, and Modern Indo-Aryan.

Old Indo-Aryan is represented by Vedic and Classical SANSKRIT. With the grammarian Panini's work (4th century B.C.) classical Sanskrit became finally established and change was discouraged. From then on, the history of Indo-Aryan is the history of Middle Indo-Aryan and then of Modern Indo-Aryan. Middle Indo-Aryan is represented by three successive stages of development: PALI, Prakrit, and Apabhransha. Pali is the language of the canonical writings of the Theravada school of Buddhism. The various dialects recorded in the inscriptions of Ashoka (c. 250 B.C.) and other early inscriptions also belong to this first period. Prakrit, found mainly in drama and in the religious writings of the Jains, represents the second stage of development. Apabhransha, though known from the texts of the tenth century A.D., was undoubtedly formed earlier than this date. It represents the final stage of Middle Indo-Aryan. The modern Indo-Aryan languages, such as Assamese, Bhojpuri, Bangla, HINDI, GUJARATI, Kashmiri, MARATHI, NEPALI, Oriya, PUNJABI, SINHALA, SINDHI, and others, show their earliest records from about the end of the 10th century, A.D. From then, their development shows the gradual transformation into their present day form. The evolution of Bhojpuri can be seen in the derivation of the words for 'fire' and 'heated': Sanskrit *agni*, *tapta* > Magadhi Prakrit *aggi*, *tatta* > Magadhi Apabhransha *aggi*, *tatt* > Bhojpuri *āgi*, *tāt*.

Orthography and Basic Phonology

A form of Semitic writing was introduced into northwest India by way of Mesopotamia about 700 B.C. The earliest adaptation of this script, as determined by coins and inscriptions from the 3rd century B.C., is called Brahmi. From Brahmi are descended all the later Indian scripts. The most important of these is the Nagari or Devanagari, which assumed its characteristic shape

Table 1: Consonants

		Labial	Dental	Retroflex	Palatal	Velar	Glottal
Stops and Palatal Affricates	Voiceless	p	t	ʈ	c	k	
	Voiceless, asp.	pʰ	tʰ	ʈʰ	cʰ	kʰ	
	Voiced	b	d	ɖ	j	g	
	Voiced, asp.	bʰ	dʰ	ɖʰ	jʰ	gʰ	
Nasals	Plain	m	n	[ɳ]	[ɲ]	[ŋ]	
	Aspirated	mʰ	nʰ				
Fricatives			s				h
Lateral	Plain		l				
	Aspirated		lʰ				
Trill/Flap	Plain		r	[ɽ]			
	Aspirated		rʰ	[ɽʰ]			
Glides		w			y		

about the middle of the 8th century A.D. Sanskrit is written in this Devanagari script, which is not a true alphabet, but a modified form of syllabary. When the Indian scribes acquired the Semitic writing, they were faced with a script which contained no symbols for vowels. To solve this problem, they decided that each simple consonant sign would stand for that consonant plus the vowel [a]. In this way there were signs available for the vowel [a] in all Devanagari consonants. For Sanskrit this method proved to be more convenient since [a] was by far the most common vowel. Other vowels were depicted by adding marks to the consonants. These marks for vowels were considered dependent since they were attached to the preceding consonant with which they formed a syllable. Vowels which constituted a syllable by themselves were considered independent vowels and were represented by different independent symbols. Finally, there was the problem of a consonant not followed by any vowel. This was solved by placing a small oblique stroke under the consonant (not always followed in writing modern Indo-Aryan languages). The symbols for zero along with the other nine digits and the principle of position value were invented in India approximately 1,200 or 1,500 years ago. We call the notation "Arabic" because it was transmitted from India to Europe by Arabs. Bhojpuri is written in this Devanagari alphabet and uses the same Devanagari symbols for numerals. Not all sounds, however, occurring in Bhojpuri are uniquely represented by its alphabet. In transliteration the order of the Devanagari alphabet as used in Bhojpuri is as follows: *Vowels*: a, ā, i, ī, u, ū, e, ai, o, au. *Consonants*: ka, kʰa, ga, gʰa, ŋa, ca, cʰa, ja, jʰa, ɲa, ʈa, ʈʰa, ɖa, ɖʰa, ɳ, ta, tʰa, da, dʰa, na, pa, pʰa, ba, bʰa, ma, ya, ra, la, wa, sa, ha.

Voiceless, voiced and aspirated (asp.) consonants and vowel phonemes of Bhojpuri are written in a modified form of IPA. A raised ʰ represents aspiration and a centered subscript rightward hook (ą) under the vowel represents nasalization. Elements enclosed in square brackets are allophones of the three phonemes described below.

Vowels. (All oral vowels and diphthongs have corresponding contrasting nasal vowels and diphthongs written with a centered subscript rightward hook under the vowel, e.g., [ą].)

The voiced and the voiced aspirated retroflex stops /ɖ/ and /ɖʰ/, respectively, show variants [ɽ] and [ɽʰ] after a vowel and [ɖ] and [ɖʰ] elsewhere. The nasal /n/ shows three variants: a retroflex [ɳ] before a retroflex consonant, a palatal [ɲ] before a palatal consonant, and an alveolar [n] elsewhere.

Table 2: Vowels

	Front		Central		Back	
	Short	Long	Short	Long	Short	Long
High	i	ī			u	ū
Mid	e	ē			o	ō
		ɛ̄				ɔ̄
Low			a	ā		

Diphthongs:	ai, au, oi, ou, ei, ia, ua

A Bhojpuri syllable consists of an optional onset, a syllabic peak, and an optional coda. It can be either 'weak' or 'strong'. A peak with a long vowel or a diphthong or with a short vowel followed by two consonants is considered a strong syllable. The placement of stress in Bhojpuri (indicated by a superior vertical stroke (') placed as a separate character before the stressed syllable) is determined by the syllable structure of a word: (i) In words with all strong or all weak syllables, the penultimate syllable is stressed, e.g., *'ānand* 'pleasure', *ban'jārā* 'nomad', *uba'hani* 'rope for drawing water from a well'. (ii) In words with both weak and strong syllables, if there is only one strong syllable, that syllable is stressed; if, however, there is more than one strong syllable, the penultimate, if strong is stressed, otherwise the nearest preceding strong syllable receives the stress, e.g., *pahuna'ī* 'the pleasure of being a guest', *lam'ērā* 'wild grass', *pan'cāiti* 'assembly'. A monosyllable word is usually stressed. Bhojpuri has a 'syllable timed rhythm' in the sense that, no matter how many stressed syllables there are, an utterance of ten syllables will take approximately twice as long as one of five syllables.

Basic Morphology

Bhojpuri words are either simple or complex, e.g., *pūt* 'son', *kaputwē* 'the bad sons'. The parts or morphemes which enter into a complex word often show phonemic variations or allomorphy. Usually, a complex Bhojpuri word consists of a stem plus affixes. In order to account for the various distributional facts, Bhojpuri words are classified into parts of speech such as nouns and pronouns, verbs, adjectives, adverbs, and postpositions.

Bhojpuri nouns combine with demonstratives, numerals, possessives, adjectives, and postpositions to form phrases, e.g., *ū mehrārū* 'that woman', *dui laikē* 'two boys', *tōr māī* 'your mother', *nīki laikī* 'good girl', *dewtā kē* 'to a god'. These nouns have inherent grammatical gender, eg., *manaī* 'man', *mehrārū* 'woman', *pānī* 'water (masculine)', *dūbi* 'a kind of soft grass (feminine)'. They can be either singular or plural, e.g., *manaī* 'man', *manaiē* 'men'.

Bhojpuri has a reflexive pronoun *apnē kē* 'myself, yourself, himself, herself, ourselves, yourselves, themselves', and two set of non-reflexive pronouns: subject forms: *ham* 'I', *hamman* 'we', *tū* 'you (singular)' *tę̄* 'you (singular, familiar or impolite)' *tuhan* 'you (plural)' *ū* 'he', *onnʰan* 'they;' and the corresponding object forms: *hammę̄, hamman kē, tuhan, tuhan kē, ōkē, onnʰan kē*, and a set of possessive pronouns: *hamār* 'my, mine', *hamman kē* 'our', *tohār* 'your' (singular) *tōr* 'your (singular familiar or impolite)', *ōkar* 'his, her', and *onnʰan kē* 'their'.

The basic paradigm of the Bhojpuri verb consists of personal forms for indicative, optative, and imperative modes. The indicative mode consists of four subsets: the simple forms, the progressive forms, the imperfective forms, and perfective forms. Each of these four classes show again three contrasting subsets for the present, past, and future tenses. Bhojpuri verbs agree with their subject in number, gender, and person, e.g., *laikā āil* 'boy came', *laikē ailę̄* 'boys came', *laikī āili* 'girl came', *laikiē ailini* 'girls came', *tū ailā* 'you (singular) came', *ham ailı̣̄* 'I came'. Forming a paradigm, they may occur with the many suffixes, such as infinitive *kʰan-ē* 'to dig' imperative *kʰan-u* 'Dig!' present tense *kʰan-īlā* '(I) dig', past tense *kʰan-alı̣̄* '(I) dug', and future tense *kʰn-ab* '(I) will dig'.

Bhojpuri verbs also have causative forms for all modes and tenses, e.g., *kʰanāīlā* '(I) cause to dig'. Bhojpuri also has a number of compound verbs consisting of either a verb stem plus *i* plus an inflected verb, or a noun, adjective, or an adverb stem plus an inflected verb, e.g., (*ū*) *cal-i-āil* '(He) walk-came: He came', (*ham*) *kām karab* '(I) work do-will: I will work'.

Bhojpuri adjectives are either definite or indefinite, e.g., *nīk* 'good' and *nikkā* 'the good'. They agree with the head noun in number and gender, e.g., *nikkā manaī* 'the good man', *nīkkī mehrārū* 'the good woman', *nikkē maniē* 'the good men'. Bhojpuri has no comparative or superlative adjective forms; postpositional phrases are used to mark comparison, e.g., *rām nīk bāy* 'Ram good is: Ram is good', *rām syām sē nīk bāy* 'Ram Syam-than good is: Ram is better than Syam', *rām sab sē nīk bāy* 'Ram all-than good is: Ram is the best'.

Bhojpuri adverbs modify verbs, adjectives, and other adverbs, e.g., *dhīrē bōlu* 'Speak slowly!' *tanik dukʰī* 'slightly sad', *tanik dʰīrē* 'slightly slowly'.

Bhojpuri postpositions refer to location, direction, and instrumental relations and govern the complement noun or pronoun with which they form the postpositional phrase, e.g., *gʰar mę̄* 'in the house', *gʰar sē* 'from the house', *gʰar tarē* 'under the house'.

When a Bhojpuri word involves both derivational and inflectional formations, the inner layer always consists of derivational form(s) and the outer inflectional, e.g., *bimār* 'sick (adjective)', *bimārī* 'sickness (noun)', *bimariē* 'sicknesses'. Notice that when the affixes are attached to a stem, beside meaning and the category changes, phonological changes also often affect the stem and/or the affix.

Bhojpuri compounds are mostly endocentric, in which the final member of the compound functions as the head and determines the part of speech of the whole compound, e.g., *lāl-kilā* 'red fort', *dukʰ-bʰaral* 'sorrow-filled', *umiri-bʰar* 'all one's life'. But not all Bhojpuri compounds are endocentric. Some compounds lack a head, and are known as *bahubrihi* or exocentric, in which the compound functions as an adjective qualifying some other concept, e.g., *mų-jʰaųsā* 'mouth-scorched: villainous' and *buri-jʰaųsī* 'vulva-scorched: a slut'.

Bhojpuri is spoken in the North Indian states of Bihar, Bengal, Uttar Pradesh and the Tarai region of Nepal (shaded area).

Basic Syntax

Although there is a great deal of stylistic flexibility, Bhojpuri is basically a SOV language, and is head-final at all levels of structure. Noun, adjective, postpositional, and verb phrases make up the major constituents of a sentence, e.g., *tōr mehrārū bahut sunnari bāy* 'your woman very beautiful is: Your woman is very beautiful', *ū pānī mę̄ kūdī* 'he water in jump-will: He will jump in water'.

In Bhojpuri a noun occurring in nominative, accusative (with dative), and vocative cases is represented by its *direct form*, while in dative, instrumental, ablative, genitive, and locative cases it is represented by its *oblique form* which is usually followed by a postposition marking a particular case, e.g., *kʰēt lāmē bāy̨* 'field away is: The field is at a distance', *ū kʰētē mę̄ bāy̨* 'he field in is: He is in the field'. Here *kʰēt* is the direct form and *kʰētē* the oblique.

Negation in Bhojpuri is expressed by adding a negative morpheme *nąī* (*na* in imperative and interrogative sentences) immediately before the verb, e.g., *ū kʰētē mę̄ nąī bāy̨* 'He is not in the field', *na jā* '(you) not go: Don't go'.

Polar (yes/no) questions in Bhojpuri begin with the interrogative morpheme *kā*, e.g., *kā pānī barsī* 'question water rain-will: Will it rain?' The other interrogatives which question various phrases use the question morphemes *kē* 'who?' *kā* 'what?' *kab* 'when?' *kahą̄* 'where?' *kaisē* 'how?' *kēkar* 'whose?' and *kāhē* 'why?' In a sentence these question morphemes occur in the same place where the questioned phrases occur, e.g., *kē āī* 'Who will come?', *tū kab jābā* 'you when will go: When will you go?', *tū kahą̄ rahālā* 'you where live: Where do you live?', *tū kaisē aibā* 'you how will come: How will you come?', *tū kēkar ghar phų̄kbā* 'you whose house will burn: Whose house will you burn?', *tū kāhē jābā* 'you why will go: Why will you go?'

Like in all other Indo-Aryan languages, dative subjects occur in Bhojpuri, e.g., *hammē ām cāhį̄* 'me-dative mangoes need: I need mangoes'. Verbs in the dative subject constructions do not inflect for agreement. Since Bhojpuri is a highly inflected language, subjects, especially pronouns, are often dropped, e.g., *gharē jā-tę̄* 'home go-3rd person singular present: He is going home'.

Contact with Other Languages

Hindi has been the primary source for borrowing in Bhojpuri. Words from Sanskrit, PERSIAN, ARABIC, TURKISH, PORTUGUESE, and ENGLISH also occur, but they have mostly entered through Hindi, e.g., *rūp* 'form' (< Sanskrit *rūpa*), *jamīn* 'land (< Persian *zamīn*), *takdīr* 'fate' (< Arabic *taqdīr*), *kącī* 'scissors' (< Turkish *kę̄ci*), *pʰītā* 'shoe-lace' (< Portuguese *fita*), and *ṭīsan* 'station' (< English *station*). These and many other such words occur frequently and have been completely naturalized.

Common Words

man:	manaī	long:	lammā
woman:	mehrārū	small:	cʰōṭ
water:	pānī	yes:	hą̄
sun:	surj	no:	na
three:	tīn	good:	nīk
fish:	macʰarī	bird:	ciraī
big:	baṛā	dog:	kūkur
tree:	pę̄ṛ		

Example Sentences

(1) apnē māī sē kah-ā ki ū bahut
your mother with tell-2.SG.IMP that she very

nīk-i bāy̨
good-FEM be:3.SG.PRES

'Tell your mother that she is very good.'

(2) kalʰiyą̄ jab rāti bhar beyāri
yesterday night the.whole.of wind:FEM

bahali ta tū kahą̄ rah-lā
blow:3SG.PAST:FEM then where remain-2.PAST

'Where were you yesterday when the wind blew all night?'

(3) amrīkā sē duniyą̄ kē kuli atyācarī ḍerā-lę̄
America from world of all tyrants fear-3.PL.PRES

'All tyrants in the world fear America.'

Effort to Preserve, Protect, and Promote the Language

In order to stress its significance and thus continue to receive economic assistance from the central government, many literary and news journals are now being published in Bhojpuri, and it is now regularly heard on radio, television, and in many full feature films.

Although Hindi is widely used in the Bhojpuri-speaking area, Bhojpuri is spoken by everyone, of all social and educational levels, for all face to face discourse, and although there are dialectal differences, they are not sufficient to impair understanding to any significant extent between speakers from any part of the Bhojpuri area. Since there are over 60 million Bhojpuri speakers, the language commands an impressive political and economic prestige in India and there is every likelihood that its use will spread.

Select Bibliography

Henry, Edward O. 1988. *Chant the Names of God: Musical Culture in Bhojpuri Speaking India*. San Diego: San Diego State University.

Jain, Chandra Sen Kumar. 1980. *A Comparative Sudy of Suffixes in Oriya and Bhojpuri*. Cuttack: Purvanchal Prakashan.

Mallik, Bhaktiprasad. 1976. *Dictionary of the Underworld Argot: West Bengal and the Bhojpuri and Magahi Areas of Bihar*. Calcutta: Indian Journal of Linguistics.

Mesthrie, Rajend. 1992. *Language in Indenture: A Sociolinguistic History of Bhojpuri Hindi in South Africa*. London, New York: Routledge.

Neerputh, Naving Coomar. 1986. *Le Systeme Verbal du Bhojpuri de l'île Maurice*. Paris: L'Harmattan.

Ramdin, Suchita. 1980. *Literature of Mauritius (Hindi & Bhojpuri): A Bibliography*. Moka, Mauritius: Mahatma Gandhi Institute.

Shukla, Shaligram. 1981. *Bhojpuri Grammar*. Washington, D.C.: Georgetown University Press.

Singh, Chandramani, co-translator Ronald Amend. 1979. *Marriage Songs from Bhojpuri Region*. Jaipur: Kitab Mahal.

Thiel-Horstmann, Monika. 1969. *Sadani; A Bhojpuri Dialect Spoken in Chotanagpur*. Wiesbaden: Harrassowitz.

Tiwari, U. N. 1960. *The Origin and Development of Bhojpuri*. Calcutta: The Asiatic Society.

Bikol

Malcolm W. Mintz

Language Name: Bikol. **Alternate:** Bicol.

Location: The Philippines, specifically provinces on the southeastern peninsula of the island of Luzon and the offshore islands of Catanduanes, Masbate, Burias, and Ticao.

Family: Central Philippine group of the Philippine subbranch of the (Western) Malayo-Polynesian branch of the Austronesian language family.

Related Languages: Bikol shows an affinity to all of the languages of the Central Philippine subgroup, in particular TAGALOG to the north, and the North Visayan languages HILIGAYNON (Ilongo), WARAY WARAY (Samar-Leyte), and CEBUANO to the south.

Dialects: Dialects of Bikol include the five closely related dialects of standard Bikol (that of Naga City), as well as some dialects which are so diverse that they are not mutually intelligible. To give a clearer idea of the types of differences which are found among the dialects in the Bikol region, sample utterances from a variety of dialects follow. All utterances relate the same information, the translation of the English exchange 'Where did you go/To the market/Were you there a long time?/No, just one hour':

1. Naga City, Camarines Sur (Standard Bikol)
   Nagsa'ín ka? / Sa sa'ód. / Halóy ka dumán? / Da'í, saróng óras saná.
2. Virac, Catanduanes
   Nanga'ín ka? / Sa sa'ód. / Awát ka dumán? / Da'í, sałong óras lang.
3. Pandan, Catanduanes
   Nagpasi'ín ka? / Sa sa'ód. / Huráy ka do'ón? / Ma'í, sadóng óras saná.
4. Gubat, Sorsogon
   Nagkarín ka? / Sa plása. / Awát ka didtó? / Dirí', saró' ka óras hámok.
5. Sorsogon, Sorsogon
   Nagka'ín ka? / Sa sa'ód. / Awát ka didtó? / Lá'in, isád na óras lang.
6. Ticao (Masbateño)
   Nagka'ín ka? / Sa paléngke. / Dúgay ka didtó? / Díli', usád na óras lang.
7. Ligao, Albay
   Napasa'ín ka? / Sa sa'rán. / Eléy ka idtó? / Idí', núsad a óras saná.
8. Libon, Albay
   Napáarin iká? / Sa saod. / Ubán iká adtó? / De', usád a óras saná.
9. Oas, Albay
   Nagsáin iká? / Sa sed. / Eléy iká idtó? / Di', sad na óras lang.
10. Iriga, Camarines Sur (Rinconada Bikol)
    Napasári iká? / Sa sa'rán. / Naebán iká sadtó? / Dirí', esád na óras saná.
11. Buhi, Camarines Sur
    Napasá'ri ka? / Sa sa'rán. / Naeǵéy iká adtó? / Indí', esád a óras saná.

Number of Speakers: 4–6 million.

Origin and History

Based on archaeological evidence such as the Kalanay pottery complex discovered on Masbate and the use of iron in the other Bikol provinces, it is believed that the region has been inhabited by the ancestors of the modern Bikolanos for just over 2,000 years. These people came from mainland Southeast Asia to the Philippines, moving northward through the Visayas to the region currently called Bikol.

The long, narrow Bikol peninsula was particularly exposed to migrating groups, especially from the south across the protected waters of the inland sea. The varied and complex dialect situation in the region and the links these dialects have with the Visayan languages to the south are evidence enough of this. In addition, the general cultural influences found in ancient songs and verse show ties to the south, rather than to the north.

The region was also exposed to Muslim raiders coming from the islands to the south of the Philippines in what are currently Indonesia and Malaysia. These were slave-taking raids that came with such ferocity that some coastal villages were depopulated and unoccupied for generations. These raids continued well into the Spanish period.

Table 1: Consonants

		Labial	Alveolar	Palatal	Velar	Glottal
Stops/ Affricates	Voiceless	p	t	(ts)	k	‘
	Voiced	b	d	(dy)	g	
Fricatives	Voiceless	(f)	s	(sy)		h
	Voiced	(v)	(z)			
Nasals		m	n	ny	ng	
Laterals			l	(ly)		
Tap			r			
Glides				y	w	

The Spanish first came to the Bikol region for gold. They reached the gold mines of Paracale in Camarines Norte in 1571. In 1572 the Spanish began subduing the Bikol provinces, and set up the first permanent settlement in the Bikol River basin in Camarines Sur in 1573. In 1574, they moved on to dominate the remaining Bikol provinces of Albay, Sorsogon, and Catanduanes. The Augustinians arrived with the Spanish conquistadors on Masbate in 1569. The Franciscans arrived in the region in 1577 and were later to dominate the conversion of Bikolanos to Christianity.

At the time of conquest, the Bikolanos used an Indic-based syllabic script to write their language. Similar types of script were in common use throughout the Philippines during pre-Hispanic times and remained in use among some members of the community until the mid-19th century. Father Marcos de Lisboa, a Franciscan friar, was in Bikol from 1602 until 1611; during that time he compiled the *Vocabulario de la lengua Bicol*, probably the finest early dictionary of any Philippine language in existence. It is through the entries in this dictionary that insights into the pre-Hispanic Bikol language and culture can be gained. Lisboa's dictionary is of Standard Bikol, and the modern Bikol examples which are used for comparative purposes in this chapter are also from Standard Bikol, the dialect of Naga City.

From the earliest days of contact, the Spanish used their Roman-alphabet script for the writing of Bikol. Lisboa's dictionary represented all Bikol words in this script, and it remained in common use until after World War II.

Orthography and Basic Phonology

The modern script for Bikol is based on the script adopted for the Philippine national language, Tagalog-based Filipino. No standard orthography is fully in evidence in the Bikol-speaking provinces, and variations in spelling will occur in different articles within the same newspaper or journal. The dominant system is obviously that used for Filipino. The variations generally include spellings used during the Spanish period which are perceived of as not very foreign-looking to modern readers, such as *enot* 'first' and *orig* 'pig', or adaptations of earlier SPANISH spellings to approximate the new system, such as *gawe-gawe* 'habit, manner' from the original Spanish representation, *gaue-gaue*. Spanish loanwords are generally adjusted to the Bikol sound system and spelled as they would be in Filipino, although there is a diminishing number of writers who still prefer to use Spanish orthography for such words.

Mintz & Britanico (1985) in their *Bikol-English Dictionary* attempted to regularize the Bikol spelling system by using the Filipino script with some minor adjustments. These adjustments relate to indicating phonemic (meaningful and non-predictable) stress, writing the glottal stop (‘) in medial and final position, and the representation of the vowels *u* and *o* which show no phonemic (meaningful) distinction. Regularization was also offered for the writing of Spanish loan words. This involved the retention of the original Spanish vowels and vowel sequences, while adjusting all consonants to the Filipino system in an attempt to retain at least some recognition of the Spanish word.

The writing of ENGLISH loanwords is more problematic since the sound systems of English and Bikol are substantially different. To adjust all English words to a modern Bikol script would destroy much of the visual recognition of the word. The solution by Mintz & Britanico was to include in the Bikol alphabet enough foreign letters to allow the writing of words from languages such as English. This writing system is described briefly below.

The full Bikol alphabet has 28 letters. Eight of these (those underlined) are used only in the writing of loanwords borrowed primarily from English:

Aa, Bb, <u>Cc</u>, Dd, <u>Ee</u>, <u>Ff</u>, Gg, Hh, Ii, <u>Jj</u>, Kk, Ll, Mm, Nn, NGng, Oo, Pp, <u>Qq</u>, Rr, Ss, Tt, Uu, <u>Vv</u>, Ww, <u>Xx</u>, Yy, <u>Zz</u>, and ‘ (representing the glottal stop)

Those sounds in parentheses in Table 1 above occur only in loanwords, mostly from Spanish and English. Even though they are listed as stops, the palatals /ts/ and /dy/ are phonetically affricates [č] and [j]. The voiceless stops /p t k/ are always unaspirated.

Table 2: Vowels

	Front	Central	Back
High	i		u
Mid	e		o
Low		a	

Table 3: Tense Inflection

Root	Infinitive	Future	Past	Continuous	Translation
puli'	magpuli'	mapuli'	nagpuli'	nag**pu**puli'	'go home'
sublí'	subli'ón	**su**subli'ón	sinublí'	sin**u**sublí'	'borrow something'
ta'ó	ita'ó	i**ta**ta'ó	itina'ó	i**t**ina**ta**'ó	'give something'
imbitár	imbitarán	**i**imbitarán	inimbitarán	in**i**imbitarán	'invite someone'

The mid vowels /e o/ do not occur in native Bikol words and were not found in the language until after the Spanish Conquest. Bikol also has diphthongs /ay aw oy iw/.

Bikol is a syllable-timed language. This means that each syllable in an utterance takes approximately the same amount of time to pronounce. The Bikol syllable is either a single vowel (V), a combination of a vowel and consonant (VC) or (CV), or a combination of a consonant, vowel and consonant (CVC). Bikol root words most commonly have two syllables, e.g. *i.yó* 'yes', *a.póg* 'lime', *un.tól* 'bounce', *gá.tas* 'milk', *luk.só* 'jump', *big.lá'* 'abruptly'. With the addition of suffixes and sets of prefixes, however, Bikol words can grow to considerable length. The root word in the example below is underlined: *pi.nag.pa.pa.ra.a.ra.dal.an* 'to keep on studying a number of things (object-focus, continuous, repetitive, plural)'.

Stress in Bikol is phonemic and contrastive: *dapít* 'regarding', *dápit* 'to escort the dead (priests)'. Once the stress on the root word is known, then the placement of other stresses due to affixation can be predicted. When a word is suffixed, for example, the stress will move one syllable to the right: *hapót* 'a question', *hapotón* 'to ask someone a question'.

Basic Morphology

Bikol nouns may be either singular or plural. Nouns are pluralized by adding the particle *manga*, written *mga*: *babáyi* 'woman', *mga babáyi* 'women'.

Bikol nouns are not inflected for case, strictly speaking. However, there are four sets of syntactic markers which are functionally equivalent to case markers; for subject, agent, object/goal, indirect object/location. Each set includes singular and plural markers for personal names. Furthermore, each set (with the exception of the indirect object set) has one form used before nouns that have not yet been mentioned in a particular conversation or discourse, and another form used before nouns that have already been mentioned. Thus, *an babáyi* means roughly 'a woman (that we haven't yet mentioned)', and *su babáyi* means roughly 'the woman (we've already talked about)'; both of these are subjects.

Bikol has three sets of personal pronouns, corresponding to subject, agent, and object roles (the pronouns for direct and indirect object are the same): *akó* 'I', *ko* 'by me', *sakúya'* '(to) me'. Bikol also distinguishes between inclusive and exclusive first person plural: *mi* 'by us (excluding the addressee)', *ta* 'by us (including the addressee)'.

Verbs in Bikol are considerably more complex than the nouns. There are three groups of verbs, depending on which of three affixes is used to mark the object as the focus or subject of the sentence. If, instead, the agent is the focus or subject, the prefix *mag-* is used. The three classes are illustrated below, with the verb root underlined in each case:

-on: sublí' 'borrow': magsublí', subli'ón
i-: ta'ó 'give': magta'ó, ita'ó
-an: imbitár 'invite': magimbitár, imbitarán

These forms are all infinitives. Bikol verbs are inflected for tense. The three basic tenses are future, past, and continuous (see Table 3 above). Tense inflection proceeds via reduplication (indicated in bold) and/or infixation.

Bikol verbs do not agree with their subjects. However, in order to emphasize that the subject is plural, the infix *-Vr-* is used (where V is a copy of the first vowel in the verb root): *magpulí'* 'to go home (singular)', *magp**ur**ulí'* 'to go home (plural)'.

Besides the basic verbal affix pairs, which can be called the regular series of affixes, Bikol has a large inventory of additional verbal affixes. These affixes show not only the role of the subject noun phrase, but also add an extra semantic dimension which is not included in the regular series of affixes. These affixes include the instrumental/benefactive prefix *i-*, the locative affix *–an*, the reflexive suffixes *–on*, and *–an*, and those in Table 4 on the next page, shown in relation to the regular affix series which they combine with or replace.

There are three classes of adjectives: those which take the prefix *ma-*, those which take the prefix *ha-*, and those which take no affixation. Adjectives which take the prefix *ha-* are adjectives of measurement showing height, length or depth: *langkáw halangkáw* tall. Examples of other adjectives are: *gayón, magayón* beautiful; *sadít* small. As with the verbs, the plural of adjectives is a matter of emphasis, and not of grammatical necessity.

Adjective plurals are formed in two ways. For adjectives which take the prefix *ha-* and those which take no prefix at all, *-Vr-* in infixed between the first consonant and vowel of the root. If, however, the root begins with an *l* or *r*, the sequence of *Vr* is prefixed to the root: *halangkáw* tall, *haralangkáw* PLURAL; *sadít* small; *saradit* PLURAL. For adjectives which take the *ma-* prefix, the first consonant and vowel of the root is reduplicated. The stress on such adjectives must be penultimate, that is, on the next to the last syllable: *magayón* beautiful, *magagáyon* PLURAL. The superlative is formed by prefixing *pinaka-* to the full adjective form: *magayón* beautiful, *pinakamagayón* most beautiful; *halangkáw* tall, *pinakahalangkáw* tallest; *sadít* small, *pinakasadít* smallest.

Degrees of intensification below the superlative are shown by suffixing *-on: sadíton* very small. Intensification may also be shown through reduplication of the adjective root: *basóg* full; *basóg-básog* very full. The comparative is formed by us-

Table 4:

Function	Basic Affixes			
	mag-	-on	-i	-an
Potential	maka-	ma-	ika-, mai, ma-	ma- -an
Social	maki-	paki- -on	ipaki-	paki- -an
General	mang-	pang- -on	ipang-	pang- -an
Transitional	maghing-	hing- on	ihing-	hing- -an
Intensive	mag(pag)-	pag- -on	ipag-	pag- -an
Repetitive	magpara-	pagpara- -on	ipagpara-	pagpara- -an
Causative	magpa-, pa- -on	ipa-	ipa-	pa- -an
Consequential	-umin-			
Pending	mina-, na-	na-	nai-	na- -an
Reciprocal	mag- -an	(pag-) -an	(pag-) -an	(pag-) -an
Concomitant		ka- -on		
Developmental	magka-	magka-	magka-	magka- -an
Continous State	naka-			
Transitory State	magín			
Collective	mangag-			
Mitigating	Reduplication of Root			

ing the Spanish loan word *mas*, the Bikol particle *pa*, or using the two in combination for emphasis: *mas halangkáw* taller; *sadít pa* smaller; *mas magayón pa* even prettier.

Basic Syntax

Bikol has three basic sentence types: verbal, equational and existential. A verbal sentence has a subject and a predicate. The subject comprises a subject noun phrase. The predicate comprises a verb phrase and a number of non-subject noun phrases. The role of the subject (whether it be the agent, object or goal, indirect object or location), is determined by the affix on the verb in the predicate. The predicate, however, is discontinuous. Unlike English, the subject actually falls between the various predicate phrases. In the following example, the verbal prefix *i-* indicates that the subject of the sentence, that is, the phrase preceded by one of the subject markers, is the goal or object.

Itina'ó	ni Lúdy	an reló	ki Cárlos	sa haróng.
i-verb	agent	object	indirect object	location
	NON-SUBJECT	SUBJECT	NON-SUBJECT	NON-SUBJECT
gave	Ludy	a watch	to Carlos	in the house

'Ludy gave a watch to Carlos in the house.'

The subject of the sentence can be changed by changing the verbal affix. The type of emphasis desired by the speaker will have an effect on the word order used, and on the type of sentence chosen. In the following example, the verbal suffix *-an* indicates that the subject is the indirect object.

Tina'wán	si	Carlos	nin	reló	ni	Lúdy
gave-an	SUBJECT	Carlos	OBJ	watch	AGENT	Ludy

sa	haróng.
LOC	house

'Ludy gave Carlos a watch in the house.'

The subject of the above sentence can be changed to the agent with the affix *mag-*: *Nagta'ó si Lúdy nin reló ki Carlos sa haróng* 'Ludy gave a watch to Carlos in the house'.

An equational sentence comprises a subject and a predicate. The predicate here may be called a *complement* since it presents additional information about the subject, thereby "completing" its meaning. An equational sentence may have two noun phrases, one serving as the subject, and the other as the predicate:

SUBJECT	**PREDICATE** (COMPLEMENT)
Si Cárlos	*an maéstro ko*
noun phrase	noun phrase
Carlos	my teacher

'Carlos is my teacher.'

An equational sentence is emphatic. When a speaker wishes to emphasize a particular phrase in a verbal sentence, he or she will generally change to an equational sentence type where the predicate as well as the subject will be represented as noun phrases. Even though the complete predicate in nominalized, that is, converted into a noun phrase, the prefix on the verb still determines the role of the subject, just as it did in the verbal sentence: *Si Lúdy an nagta'ó nin reló ki Cárlos sa haróng* 'It was Ludy who gave a watch to Carlos in the house'. Equational sentences may also comprise an adjective phrase and a noun phrase: *Halangkáw si Carlos* (tall PERSONAL.ARTICLE Carlos) 'Carlos is tall'.

Existential sentences show either existence or possession. These sentences require the use of either *igwá* or *may*. Existential sentences have a subject and predicate. The predicate in sentences showing existence is a complement giving additional information about the subject. It is possible, however, for existential sentences to comprise only a subject, there being nothing further to be *predicated* or said. The analysis of existential sentences is complex and there is little agreement as to how this sentence type should be divided into a subject and predicate. In the analysis here, if the subject is general, as occurs in sentences showing existence, the particles *igwá* or *may* are part of the subject. If the subject is specific, as is the case with existential sentences showing possession, *igwá* or *may* are part of the predicate, e.g. *May relo* (EXIST watch) 'There is a watch', *May reló si lúdy* (EXIST watch PERSONAL.ARTICLE Ludy) 'Ludy has a watch'.

Existential sentences may also contain verbal phrases. These sentences pattern like the existential sentences showing possession. The predicate, as was the case with the verbal sentences, is discontinuous. The grammatical subject is always the noun phrase marked with one of the subject markers. The role of the subject is always agent. The affix on the verb indicates the role of the noun phrase which has been replaced by *igwá* or *may*. In the example which follows this role is the object or goal.

Igwá-ng	itina'ó	si	Lúdy	ki	Carlos	sa	haróng
EXIST-LINKER	gave	SUBJ	Ludy	OBJ	Carlos	LOC	house

'Ludy gave something to Carlos in the house.'

Bikol word order is difficult to characterize in terms of the relative order of verb, subject, and object. VSO order is common, but the subject can also appear between two nonsubject noun phrases.

Contact with Other Languages

Bikol has undergone dramatic lexical and semantic changes in the almost 400 years since Lisboa described the language. Most noticeable to the observer is the addition of many Spanish loanwords. Bikol borrowed thousands of vocabulary items from Spanish which either replaced native Bikol words, co-existed with a native word to offer an alternative expression, or introduced new words with the introduction of new implements or concepts. Bikol words have also undergone semantic change with old words adapted to new uses and given new meanings. Examples of this are common in the adaption of Christianity as a religion, e.g. *ágaw* (*mag-*, *-on*) 'to cure a person of disease [Old Bikol]' > 'to deliver someone (as from evil) [Modern Bikol]'.

Bikol has also seen the disappearance of hundreds of words associated with concepts that were lost due to the dramatic social changes that occurred after the arrival of the Spanish. Some of these words dealt with religion, mythology and ritual, e.g. *ásog* 'a spiritual leader associated with worship of the *ánito* who dresses and cuts his ears like a woman, imitating women in actions and words in rites and ceremonies; does not usually marry', *átang* a sacrifice offered to the *gugúrang* as a sign of thanksgiving, consisting of one-tenth of the harvest, later eaten by the participants in the ritual'. Others dealt with kinship, marriage and inheritance: *binulahos* 'true, natural; used only to show true blood relations for children and siblings', *hikaw* (*mag-*, *-an*) 'to refuse to marry someone who is lower in social status, or possesses less wealth than oneself', *mu'o'* 'referring to the bequest left to relatives by a couple who die childless'. Others with law and crime: *budhí'* (*mag-*, *-an*) 'to kill someone from another town', *mulong* (*magpa-*, *ipa-*) 'to accuse someone of wrong-doing before a judge or other high official of the town'. And still others with clothing and fiber, with climate and weather, with mining, business, construction and countless other fields of human endeavor.

Bikol numbers are most commonly used when counting from one to ten. Above ten, Spanish numbers are used. While equivalent Bikol numbers are known, they will almost never be heard except in historical reference. Examples are: *dóse* [Spanish *doce*], *sampúlo' may duwá* [Bikol] 'twelve'; *beínte úno* [Spanish *veinte uno*], *duwáng púlo' may saró'* [Bikol] 'twenty one'. There are hundreds of Spanish words which were introduced with new implements or concepts. Examples of these are: *lapis* [Spanish *lapiz*] 'pencil'; *asada* [Spanish *azada*] 'hoe'; *pádi'* [Spanish *padre*] 'priest'.

Bikol has borrowed large numbers of words from English. Some words have been borrowed with the same meanings in the donor language, such as the English words *taxi* and *order*. Other words have undergone dramatic changes in meaning as they have become associated with concepts quite different from that in the donor language:

báksat 'a slingshot comprising a rubber band stretched between two fingers, used for shooting spitballs, paper clips, etc.' [English: *buckshot*]
burlés 'peanuts' (boiled or fried, shelled and skinned) [English: *burlesque*, referring to the naked look of skinned peanuts]
tsánsing 'to make advances to a woman' [English: *chancing*]

Borrowings from Hokkien CHINESE are far fewer in number and are confined primarily to the areas of food, crafts, and gaming: *híbi* 'small, dried shrimp' [Hokkien: he^5 bi^4]; *bakyá'* 'wooden shoes' [Hokkien: ba^5 gia^5]; *huéting* 'the numbers game' [Hokkien: hue^5 $dong^0$].

Common Words

man:	laláki	yes:	iyó
woman:	babáyi	no:	da'i (verbal);
water:	túbig		bakó' (equational);
sun:	aldáw		máyo' (existential)
three:	tuló	good:	maráy
fish:	sirá'	bird:	gamgám
big:	dakúla'	dog:	áyam
long:	halába'	tree:	káhoy
small:	sadít		

Example Sentences

(1) May reló si Lúdy
there is watch SUBJ Ludy
'Ludy has a watch.'

(2) Da'í nagta'ó si Lúdy nin reló ki Cárlos
NEG give.PAST AGENT Ludy DO watch IO Carlos
'Ludy didn't give Carlos a watch.'

(3) Kon kakalabánon mo siya, mada'óg
if fight.FUT you(AGENT) him(SUBJ) lose.FUT

ka
you(SUBJ)
'If you fight with him, you will lose.'

Efforts to Preserve, Protect, and Promote the Language

Efforts to preserve and promote Bikol are centered on the two main urban areas of the Bikol region: Naga City in Camarines Sur and Legazpi City in Albay. In Manila, the Ateneo de Manila University has also been involved in such promotion and preservation, thanks to the dedication of Father James O'Brien, S.J., who initiated such efforts. Some of the groups which are active in the Bikol region are: The Ateneo de Naga Social Science Research Center (ASSRC), Kabikolan, Muklat (Makabikolnon na Ugat sa Kultura, Literatura, Arte asin Teatro), Institute for the Documentation of Bikol Culture and History, the Bicol Culture Group of Bicol University, the Maogmang Lugar Journal (Ateneo de Naga High School), and Cecilio Press.

Select Bibliography

Blair, Emma H. and James A. Robertson, eds. 1903–1909. *The Philippine Islands: 1493–1898*. 55 vols. Cleveland: Arthur H. Clarke Co.

Blust, Robert. 1980. "Austronesian Etymologies." In *Oceanic Linguistics*, 19:1–2, 1–189. Honolulu.

____. 1991. "The Greater Central Philippines Hypothesis." In *Oceanic Linguistics*, 30:2, 73–129. Honolulu.

Chang, Kwang-chih, George W. Grace and William G. Solheim II. 1964. "Movement of the Malayo-Polynesians: 150 B.C. to A.D. 500." In *Current Anthropology*, 5:5 (December), 359–406.

Dery, Luis C. 1991. *From Ibalon to Sorsogon: A Historical Survey of Sorsogon Province to 1905*. Quezon City: New Day Publishers.

Gerona, Danilo M. 1988. *From Epic to History: A Brief Introduction To Bicol History*. Naga City: Ateneo de Naga.

McFarland, Curtis D. 1981. *A Linguistic Atlas Of The Philippines*. Manila: De La Salle University and the Linguistic Society of the Philippines.

Mintz, Malcolm Warren and José Del Rosario Britanico. 1985. *Bikol-English Dictionary*, Quezon City: New Day Publishers (contains English-Bikol Index and introduction to Bikol grammar).

O'Brien, James J. S.J. 1994. *The Historical and Cultural Heritage of the Bicol People*, 3d edition. Naga City: Ateneo de Naga.

Owen, Norman G. 1984. *Prosperity Without Progress: Manila Hemp And Material Life In The Colonial Philippines*. Berkeley: University of California Press.

Realubit, Ma. Lilia. 1983. *Bikols of the Philippines*. Naga City: AMS Press.

Bugis

Roger Tol

Language Name: Bugis. **Autonym:** *Basa Ugiq*. **Alternates:** Buginese; Basa Ogiq, Basa Wugiq; Bahasa Bugis (Indonesian); Boeginees, Buginees (Dutch).

Location: Major part of southwestern arm of the island of Sulawesi, Indonesia (old name: Celebes).

Family: South Sulawesi group of the West Austronesian branch of the Austronesian language family.

Related Languages: Makasarese, Mandarese, Saqdan Toraja

Dialects: Bugis is spoken with great homogeneity. About ten dialects may be distinguished, roughly corresponding to the old Bugis kingdoms, including Boné (the standard), Soppéng, Sinjai, Wajoq, Luwuq, and Sidénréng.

Number of Speakers: 2.5–3.5 million.

Origin and History

As is the case with most other Austronesian languages, very little is known about the early stages of Bugis. Scientific study of the language began only in the mid-19th century through the efforts of the linguist and Bible translator, B. F. Matthes. Until recently, very little serious work had been done since Matthes. New research has been conducted and has resulted in a number of publications, mostly of a descriptive nature.

The Bugis monarchy dates from the 13th or 14th century. Foreign traders came to the island in large numbers beginning with the Malays in the mid 16th century. They were based in Makassar, a free port which became important in the spice trade with the Moluccas. Next came the Portuguese around 1600. Later traders included the English, Danes, French, Spanish, Golconda and Acehnese. From the mid-17th until the mid-20th centuries, the Dutch dominated the political arena. The overwhelming majority of Bugis and other groups on Sulawesi are Muslim, and have been so for over 300 years.

The Bugis possess a very rich literature, which has been transmitted both orally and in written form. These literary products rank among the most interesting of Southeast Asia, in quality as well as in quantity. A wide variety of genres are represented in texts, such as myths, local histories, ritual chants, law books, Islamic legends and tracts, daily registers, genealogies, wise sayings, folk tales and others. The vast epic myth, named *La Galigo*, is one of the most voluminous works in world literature.

Orthography and Basic Phonology

Written Bugis documents date from the 17th century onwards. These are written in three different scripts, more or less chronologically arranged: Bugis (also called Bugis/Makasarese), Arabic, and Roman. It is now assumed that Makasarese and Bugis are derived from the same (now extinct) source, which was close to the Kawi (Old JAVANESE) alphabet. So, contrary to what had been thought for a long time, the Bugis script is not derived from Makasarese. Of course, there was a great overlap in time in the use of these alphabets. Very often we see more than one alphabet used in a manuscript. In particular, Bugis and Arabic occur side by side in religious manuscripts. Presently all three scripts are still in use, although competence in using Bugis script is steadily declining, and the Arabic script is exclusively used for the writing of ARABIC.

Like a number of other indigenous scripts such as Kawi (Java), Batak and Lampung (both from Sumatra), the Bugis script derives from an Indian prototype. Apart from similarities in shapes of letters, evidence for this origin is that the script is semi-syllabic with each character indicating a syllable which consists of a consonant followed by the vowel '*a*'. Other vowels are indicated by putting diacritics on the main character: over ('*i*' and '*e*'), under ('*u*'), before ('*é*'), and after ('*o*'). Furthermore, the traditional sequence of the characters is similar to the Indian alphabetic listing, which is according to the articulatory features of the consonants (the alphabet starts with *k*, *g*, *ng*, *ngk*, etc.).

Bugis Script

ka	pa	ta	ca	ya	sa
ga	ba	da	ja	ra	ʔa
nga	ma	na	ña	la	ha
ngka	mpa	nra	ñca	wa	

Bugis Diacritics (With the Consonant *la*)

li	lu	le	lo	lə

One peculiar feature of the Bugis script is that it is a defective script; i.e., not all phonemes are written. Distinctive phenomena such as geminated consonants (/tt/, /ss/, etc.), glottal stop (/ʔ/) and final nasal (/ŋ/) are never written, and in many cases, also, prenasalization is not indicated. The script is there-

Table 1: Consonants

	Voicing	Labial	Dental/ Alveolar	Alveo- palatal	Velar	Glottal
Stops	-	p	t	c	k	ʔ
	+	b	d	j	g	
Fricatives	-		s			h
Nasals	+	m	n	ñ	ŋ	
Lateral			l			
Trill			r			
Glides		w		y		

fore subject to a variety of interpretations. Theoretically, one character may be interpreted in nine different ways; for instance *pa*, which may be read as /pa/, /ppa/, /paŋ/, /ppaŋ/, /paʔ/, /ppaʔ/, /mpa/, /mpaŋ/, /mpaʔ/, although generally the number of legitimate interpretations is small. This defectiveness sometimes poses huge interpretative problems for the reader. To add to this complexity, separation between words is not indicated, and only one reading sign (represented by three vertical or diagonal dots) is used indicating the border of a syntactic unit.

A Romanized spelling system is not yet standardized. For a transcription table of the individual letters, see the illustration. In addition, the following conventions are employed in actual practice for writing romanized Bugis:

/ñ/ is written *ny*
/ʔ/ is written *q*
/ŋ/ is written *ng*
/e/ is written *e*, sometimes *é*
/ə/ is written *e*
/ʔb/ is written *bb*
/ʔd/ is written *dd*
/ʔj/ is written *jj*
/ʔg/ is written *gg*

All consonants can occur in word-initial position; in word-final position, only /ʔ/ and /ŋ/ are observed. Consonants can occur single, long, or prenasalized. Long voiced stops are preglottalized; thus, /bb/ is [ʔb]. All other long consonants are geminate; thus, /pp/ is [pp]. Pre-nasalized stops are clusters of a stop preceded by the homorganic nasal: /mb/, /mp/, /nd/, etc.

Table 2: Vowels

	Front	Central	Back
High	i		u
Mid	e	ə	o
Low		a	

All vowels except /ə/ can occur freely in words; /ə/ cannot occur in word-final position. In positions other than in the final syllable, /ə/ must be followed by a long or prenasalized consonant.

Basic Morphology

The morphological system is rather complex and not yet fully described. Affixation plays a major role in word formation and transposition between word classes. On the basis of a root morpheme, a set of prefixes and suffixes render, alone or in combination, groups of morphological processes. Affixed morphemes may function as a basis for other mechanisms involving affixation. The meaning of the affixed form is largely dependent on the class of the root morpheme, or base, and the affix.

Common prefixes are: *ma-*, *a-*, *pa-*, *po-*, *ta-* , *ri-*, *si-*, *ké-*, *maka-*, with or without gemination/glottalization or pre-nasalization of the initial consonant of the base. Prefixes to a base with initial vowel may occur with a consonant *ng*, *k*, or *r* before the vowel. (The base may be either a root morpheme or an affixed morpheme.)

The suffixes are: *-eng* and *-i*.

Frequent combinations of affixes (non-pronominal) include: *mappa-*, *makké-*, *ripa-*, *pasi-*, *a-eng*, *pa-eng*, *mappa-eng*, *ripa-eng*.

Examples:

anaq 'child' (noun) - *poanaq* 'to have as a child' (verb, active)
dua 'two' (numeral) - *taddua* 'two each' (adjunct)
elli 'buy' (verb, imperative) - *mangngelli* 'to buy' (verb, active) - *rielli* '(be) bought' (verb, passive)
bicara 'speech' (noun) - *mabbicara* 'to speak' (verb, active) - *pabbicara* 'speaker, judge' (noun)
tudang 'to sit' (verb, active) - *tudangeng* 'seat' (noun) - *tudangi* 'to occupy' (verb, active)
lampéq (adjective) - *malampéq* 'long' (adjective) - *passilampéq* 'to become of the same length' (verb, active, causative) - *mallampéri* 'to lengthen' (verb, active) - *riallampéri* 'to be lengthened' (verb, passive) - *ripallampéq* 'being made long' (verb, passive, causative)

Nouns are not inflected, even for number: *bola* can mean either 'house' or 'houses'.

Reduplication occurs and denotes similarity/diversity/smallness. *manuq-manuq* 'bird' (< *manuq* 'chicken'); *bua-bua* 'all kinds of fruit' (< *bua* 'fruit'); *bola-bola* 'a small house' (< *bola* 'house').

Tense is not marked. However, perfectiveness and futurity may be expressed by the use of clitics:

matinro ko	'you sleep, you will sleep, you slept'
matinro no	'you have slept'
matinro po	'you will sleep'

Sandhi phenomena such as assimilation between words and/or clitics and/or affixes are very frequent: *temmanré* 'not eat' (*teng-* + *manré*); *waramparang* 'goods' (*warang* + *warang*; also spelled *warang-mparang*).

Basic Syntax

The syntax of the Bugis sentence is complicated and is still an almost unexplored field of research. Among the most important factors governing the sentence are: transitivity or intransitivity of the verb, definiteness or indefiniteness of the object, and the occurrence of clitics and function words (both pronominal and non-pronominal). A characteristic phenomenon is pronominal cross-reference, in which a definite nominal constituent (subject or object) is also represented by a pronoun.

The preferred order of the basic sentence seems to be V(O)S, in particular with an intransitive verb or a verb without an object: *matinro kaq* (sleep I) 'I sleep', *mabacca i La Tuppu* (read he La Tuppu) 'La Tuppu is reading', *manré i balé méong éro* (eat he fish cat that) 'That cat eats fish'.

Also frequent is the order SVO, in particular with transitive verbs:

ia mala i tédong-ku
he take it buffalo-mine 'He takes my buffalo.'

arung-é mita i joaq-na
ruler-the see him followers-his
'The ruler sees his followers.'

méong éro manré balé
cat that eat fish 'That cat eats fish.'

Within noun phrases, modifiers tend to follow the nouns they modify. Definiteness is expressed by a suffixed article *-é*, or by suffixed pronouns indicating possession.

A predicate may be negated by either the prefix *teng-* or the word *déq*. *Tania* may be used to express the notion 'not to be'. A prohibition is expressed by *ajaq* 'don't'.

tem-matinro i
not-sleep he
(with assimilation < *teng+matinro)
'He does not sleep.'

déq u-isseng i
not I-know it 'I do not know that.'

tania bola-mu iaé
not.be house-your this
'This is not your house.'

ajaq mu-ala i doiq-é
don't you-take it money-the
'Don't take the money.'

Common Words

man:	oroané	small:	baiccuq
woman:	makkunrai	yes:	iéq
water:	uaé	no:	déq
sun:	mata esso	good:	madécéng
three:	tellu	bird:	manuq-manuq
fish:	balé	dog:	asu
big:	maloppo	tree:	aju
long:	malampéq		

Example Sentences

(1) ma-éloq i lao ri pasaq-é
PREF-wish he go to market-the
'He wants to go to the market.'

(2) bola éro maloppo
house that big
'That house is big.'

(3) mpawa i utti ipaq-na
bring he banana brother-in-law-his
'His brother-in-law brought bananas.'

Contact with Other Languages

Most loans are from MALAY/INDONESIAN and/or Makasarese, and Arabic (mostly via Malay or Makasarese). A small number of words are loans from DUTCH or PORTUGUESE (also in most cases via Malay or Makasarese).

From Malay/Makasarese: *séntéréq* 'flashlight', *kaing* 'cloth'
From Arabic (via Malay/Makasarese): *telleq* 'divorce', *wettu* 'time'
From Dutch: *oto* 'car', *kantoroq* 'office'
From Portuguese: *kadéra* 'chair'

The use of Bugis has been mainly confined to the South Sulawesi area. Although the Bugis are well known as seafarers and traders in the whole archipelago (up to Australia, the Philippines and Malaysia) with settlements on various coasts, no pockets of Bugis seem to have developed in other areas. For contact with members from other language groups they most probably used Malay as their vehicle, whereas settlers generally seem to have adopted the local language.

Efforts to Preserve, Protect, and Promote the Language

In the provincial capital Makassar there is a branch of the National Language Center, which collects language materials from South Sulawesi (both written and oral), and conducts research in the area. Preservation and collection of manuscripts are also stimulated by the local government. Recently a project was carried out aimed at microfilming all extant indigenous manuscripts. However, proficiency among the Bugis in their language is dwindling. This is undoubtedly due to the increasingly dominant position of the national language of Indonesia, *Bahasa Indonesia*, which dominates all media. There are no texts written anymore in Bugis, there are no radio or television broadcasts in Bugis, and the position of the language in the curriculum of primary education is uncertain.

Select Bibliography

Grimes, Charles E., and Barbara D. Grimes. 1987. *Languages of South Sulawesi*. Pacific Linguistics D-78.

Friberg, Timothy, and Barbara Friberg. 1988. "A Dialect Geography of Bugis." In Hein Steinhauer, ed., *Papers in Western Austronesian Linguistics no. 4* (Pacific Linguisitics A-79), 303–30.

Noorduyn, J. 1991. *A Critical Survey of Studies on the Languages of Sulawesi*. Leiden: KITLV Press [Bibliographical series; 18]

Said DM, M. Ide. 1977. *Kamus Bahasa Bugis-Indonesia*. Jakarta: Pusat Pembinaan dan Pengembangan Bahasa, Departemen Pendidikan dan Kebudayaan.

Salim, Muhammad, et al. 1995. *I La Galigo: menurut naskah NBG 188 yang disusun oleh Arung Pancana Toa*. Jilid 1. Jakasrta: Djambatan.

_____. 1995. *I La Galigo: menurut naskah NBG 188 yang disusun oleh Arung Pancana Toa*. Jilid 2. Jakasrta: Djambatan.

Sikki, Muhammad et al. 1991. *Tata bahasa Bugis*. Jakarta: Departemen Pendidikan dan Kebudayaan.

Sirk, Ü. 1996. *The Buginese Language of Traditional Literature*. Moskva: Nauka [2nd edition of translation of *Bugijski yazyk*. Moskva: Nauka, 1975]

Tol, Roger. 1996. "A separate empire: writings of South Sulawesi." In Ann Kumar and John H. McGlynn (eds.), *Illuminations: The Writing Traditions of Indonesia: Featuring Manuscripts from the National Library of Indonesia*. 213–230. Jakarta: The Lontar Foundation/New York: Weatherhill.

Bulgarian

Ernest A. Scatton

Language Name: Bulgarian. **Autonym:** *Bâlgarski (ezik).*

Location: The Republic of Bulgaria. Also spoken in areas of the former Soviet Union (Bessarabia, the vicinity of the Sea of Azov, and Ukraine), in the Danubian region (southwestern Romania, northern Serbia, and southeastern Hungary), and in a few villages near Bucharest, Romania.

Family: East Balkan Slavic subgroup of the South Slavic group of the Slavic branch of Indo-European.

Related Languages: Most closely related to MACEDONIAN, the other member of the East Balkan Slavic subgroup.

Dialects: Within Bulgaria, the principal dialect division is between East and West. There is a compact mass of dialects in the Rhodope Mountains in south-central Bulgaria that retain some features of Old Bulgarian. Besides archaic phonological systems, these dialects preserve nominal case forms lost elsewhere in the language, and show unusual and archaic lexical material.

Standard literary Bulgarian is a hybrid based on northeastern Bulgarian dialects with significant accommodations, especially in phonology, to western dialects. Not spoken naturally anywhere in Bulgaria, the "proper" literary language is more or less learned by all Bulgarians. Written norms of the literary language are fairly well established; spoken norms are less so, and many educated Bulgarians speak with noticeable regional characteristics. Due to the prestige and size of the population of Bulgaria's capital, Sofia, located in the center of the western Bulgarian dialect area, there has developed a recognizable colloquial variant of the literary language used by many educated residents of the city; it is marked by greater use of western dialect features.

Slavic dialects spoken in northern Greece, in the Former Yugoslav Republic of Macedonia, and in isolated areas of Albania are variously claimed to be dialects of Bulgarian and Macedonian. Similarly, the status of dialects in eastern Serbia, transitional between Serbian and Bulgarian, has been the subject of dispute. In general, linguistic issues have played a major role in the often thorny relations between Bulgaria and its modern neighbors.

Number of Speakers: 8–9 million.

Origin and History

Slavic people, speaking Late Common Slavic dialects that would become Bulgarian, crossed the lower Danube from the north and began to spread through the eastern Balkan Peninsula in the beginning of the 6th century. By the middle of the 7th century they reached the Aegean islands and the Greek Peloponnese (from which they were later pushed back or assimilated, in a still on-going process). At the end of the 7th century Slavs living in what is today northeastern Bulgaria were conquered by Turkic Bulgars, led by Khan Asparukh, and the first "Bulgarian Kingdom" was established (approximately 680). In the following two centuries the Turkic Bulgars were entirely assimilated by indigenous Slavs, and the only remnants of the Turkic tongue were a few words, including the name of the state and its ethnic majority population.

Old Bulgarian (the Late Common Slavic dialect spoken in the Eastern Balkans) served as the basis for the first Slavic written monuments: liturgical texts, some original, others translated from the GREEK by Saints Cyril and Methodius and their disciples, used in the Byzantine Christian mission to Moravia beginning in 683. The language of these texts—the first Slavic literary language—is called by many scholars outside of Bulgaria Old Church Slavonic (or Old Church Slavic).

After the deaths of Cyril (869) and Methodius (885) and the collapse of the Moravian Mission, a number of their disciples found refuge in the Bulgarian Kingdom of Prince Boris, who had converted to Christianity. Here, during the First and Second Bulgarian Empires, Medieval Bulgarian literature and learning flourished, exerting significant influence on the cultures of the other Orthodox Slavs—particularly in Serbia and Russia. This "Golden Age" of Bulgarian literature ended with the fall of Bulgaria to the Turks at the end of the 14th century. Although Bulgarian literary traditions were maintained to some extent in the Bulgarian Church during Ottoman rule, a modern, secular literary language did not begin to emerge until the end of the 18th century and beginning of the 19th. By that time, in addition to major phonological changes, the striking morphological and syntactic changes that distinguish Modern Bulgarian (and Macedonian) from the other Slavic languages had already taken place: the replacement of many morphological markers by phrasal syntactic constructions, especially the loss of nominal case forms and the replacement of many of their functions by prepositional phrases; the development of a definite article; the replacement of the Common Slavic infinitive by a verb phrase; the development of future tense forms using an auxiliary from the verb 'want'; and the replacement of comparative and superlative adjectival morphemes by adjectival phrases. In the absence of written records reflecting vernacular Bulgarian during much of the time of the Ottoman

Table 1: Consonants

		Labial	Dental-Alveolar	Alveo-palatal	Palatal	Velar
Stops	Voiceless	p p'	t t'		k'	k
	Voiced	b b'	d d'		g'	g
Fricatives	Voiceless	f f'	s s'	š		x
	Voiced	v v'	z z'	ž		
Affricates	Voiceless		c c'	č		
	Voiced			ǰ		
Nasals		m m'	n n'			
Laterals			l l'			
Trills			r r'			
Glide					j	

rule, the history of these developments remains largely unknown.

The first Bulgarian grammar was published in 1835, the beginning of a national revival marked by a literary renaissance and movement to establish Bulgarian schools. By 1845 there were five presses printing books in Bulgarian and more than fifty Bulgarian schools had been established. In 1878 the Ottoman Turks were defeated and the modern Bulgarian state was created. The codification of modern standard Bulgarian was completed only in the first half of the 20th century, and there still remains some indeterminacy in its norms, especially in pronunciation.

Orthography and Basic Phonology

Traditionally, the Bulgarian phonological (phonemic) inventory is described as in Tables 1 and 2.

Bulgarian labial and alveolar/dental consonants occur in non-palatalized-palatalized pairs. Palatalized consonants, marked with ' in the chart above, are pronounced with a simultaneous additional articulation similar to that of *j*. In Bulgarian, palatalized consonants occur only before *non-front* vowels; non-palatalized consonants occur freely in all environments. The orthographic representation of palatalized consonants is described below.

The consonants *k'*, *g'*, and *ǰ* occur only in foreign words.

Word-final obstruents (stops, fricatives, affricates) are always voiceless. When two obstruents occur in sequence, the first takes on the voicing value of the second (unless the second is followed by *v* or *v'*).

Table 2: Vowels

	Front	Central	Back
High	i	ɨ	u
Mid	e		o
Low		a	

Unstressed non-high vowels tend to be raised towards their high counterparts; there is considerable variation here. The changes in decreasing order of occurrence are:

(1) a > ɨ , (2) o > u, (3) e > i

In a fairly large, but lexically limited, number of words containing *l* or *r* and the vowel *ɨ*, the relative order of the vowel and the liquid depends on the following environment: *dɨrvó* 'tree' vs. *drɨvník* 'chopping block'.

In many words, forms containing *e* or *ɨ* alternate with forms without them: *dén* 'day' vs. *dní* 'days', *málɨk* 'small (m/sg)' vs. *málka* 'small (f/sg)'.

Table 3: The Bulgarian Cyrillic Alphabet

Cyrillic	Latin	Cyrillic	Latin
Аа	a	Пп	p
Бб	b	Рр	r
Вв	v	Сс	s
Гг	g	Тт	t
Дд	d	Уу	u
Ее	e	Фф	f
Жж	ž	Хх	h (x)
Зз	z	Цц	c
Ии	i	Чч	č
Йй	j	Шш	š
Кк	k	Щщ	št
Лл	l	Ъъ	â
Мм	m	Ьь	'
Нн	n	Юю	ju
Оо	o	Яя	ja

Bulgarian uses the Cyrillic alphabet (see Table 3 above), which dates from the end of the 9th century. It is generally accepted that the original Slavic alphabet, devised by Cyril and Methodius for the Moravian Mission, was an unusual alphabet called Glagolitic, believed by some to be derived from the cursive Greek of that time. Cyrillic seems to have been developed later in Bulgaria by disciples of Cyril and Methodius. Cyrillic quickly superseded Glagolitic.

The relationship of the orthographic system to the phonemic system is straightforward. Minor differences between the Bulgarian Academy's transliteration system and the system used in the phonemic inventories given above are indicated parenthetically. Note two important orthographic conventions (transliterated forms in italics):

1. Bulgarian palatalized consonants (and rare palatals) are represented in three instances by special vowel symbols and in one other by the use of a special symbol (not used otherwise) plus a vowel:

a. Before /u/ (rare) — ю, and before /a/ and /ɨ/ — я

бял	*bjál* /b'ál/	'white (m/sg)'
болят	*boljá* /bol'ɨ́t/	'(they) hurt'

b. Before /o/ — ьо:

лéльо	*léljo* /lél'o/	'aunt (voc)'

2. /j/ is indicated in various ways depending upon environment:

a. Before /u/ by ю and before /a/ and /ɨ/ by я:

ю́жен	*júžen* /júžen/	'southern (m/sg)'
я́дене	*jádene* /jádene/	'meal'
пéя	*péja* /péjɨ/	'(I) sing'

b. Otherwise the symbol й is used:

мóй	*mój* /mój/	'my (m/sg)'

c. The phoneme /ǯ/ is spelled дж/dž.

джоб	*džób* /ǯóp/	'pocket (m/sg)'

With few exceptions, the Bulgarian orthographic system provides an accurate representation of broad phonemic transcription. One exception, noted above, is я, which represents one or the other of two vowels. This is, however, limited morphologically: я indicates the vowel /ɨ/ only in first singular and third plural present tense verb forms and in masculine singular definite nominal forms (below). Another is a, which in the same morphological categories represents /ɨ/ after other consonants: for example, пи́ша *píša* /píšɨ/ '(I) write'; otherwise the letter a always represents /a/.

Unless marked otherwise as phonemic, all Bulgarian examples in the following text are transliterated using the system of the Bulgarian Academy as shown above but with *x* for *h* and *ɨ* for *â*.

Basic Morphology

Bulgarian nouns are morphologically marked for number (singular vs. plural) and in the singular for gender (masculine, feminine, neuter). A vocative form is possible in the singular of masculine and feminine nouns, most commonly those denoting persons.

Bulgarian adjectives agree in number and, in the singular, gender with the nouns which they modify:

dobɨ́r mɨ́ž	dobr-á žen-á	dobr-ó det-é
good man	good woman	good child
dobr-í mɨž-é	dobr-í žen-í	dobr-í dec-á
good men	good women	good children

Bulgarian has a definite article, historically derived from the Old Bulgarian demonstrative pronoun 'that', which is postposed to the initial adjective or noun of noun phrases:

kníga-ta	interésna-ta	kníga
book-the	interesting-the	book
'the book'	'the interesting book'	

The form of the definite article changes with respect to the number and gender of the head noun.

Only in local dialects are vestigial case forms for nouns found, most frequently an "objective" form for masculine personal nouns, used as the direct object of transitive verbs and the object of prepositions. However, pronouns, both full (independent) and clitic, are marked for case:

	Full		**Clitic**	
	Subject	Object	Dative	Accusative
lsg	áz	méne	mi	me
2sg	tí	tébe	ti	te
3sg/m	tój	négo	mu	go
3sg/f	tjá	néja	i	ja
3sg/n	tó	négo	mu	go
lpl	níe	nás	ni	ni
2pl	víe	vás	vi	vi
3pl	té	tjáx	im	gi

Bulgarian verbs can occur in three simple tenses: present, imperfect, and aorist. These verbs agree with their subjects in person and number, as illustrated below:

	Singular	Plural
Present	*píš-a* 'I write'	*píš-em* 'we write'
Imperfect	*píš-e-še* 'you (sg)/ he/she/it was/were writing'	*píš-e-xte* 'you (pl) were writing'
Aorist	*písa* 'he/she/it wrote'	*písa-xa* 'they wrote'

Other tenses are compound. The simple future tense is formed with the non-inflected auxiliary *šte*, derived from the verb 'want', together with the present tense of the verb: *šte píš-ete* 'you (pl) will write'. There is also a past future tense, formed from the imperfect of *št-* 'want' and the present tense: *áz štjáx da píša* 'I was about to write'.

Bulgarian also has a series of perfect tenses, based on forms of the verb 'to be' and the past participle, which agrees with the subject in number and gender (see Table 4 on the next page).

The past future perfect tense is rare.

In addition to the indicative verb forms already illustrated, Bulgarian has a subjunctive mood, using a special aorist form of the verb 'to be' and the past participle: *áz bix písal* 'I would write'. In the third person, perfect indicative forms are distinguished from renarrated forms: the perfect *té sa písali* 'they have written' indicates that the speaker cannot personally vouch for the accuracy of the statement.

Table 4: Examples of Bulgarian Perfect Tenses

Tense	Example	Gloss
Perfect	tój e písal	'he has written'
Past Perfect	té bjáxa písali	'they had written'
Future Perfect	níe šte sme písali	'we will have written'
Past Future Perfect	tjá štéše da e písala	'she was to have written'

Bulgarian has two distinct passive formations. First, any tense of 'be' can be combined with the past passive participle of a transitive verb: *béše písano* 'it was written'. Alternatively, any tense of a transitive verb can occur with the reflexive particle *se* 'self': *tó se píše* 'it is written'.

Like other Slavic languages, Bulgarian distinguishes two verbal aspects: perfective, which specifies the accomplishment of the result of a verbal action, and imperfective, which is unmarked in this respect. Generally verb stems come in pairs, one perfective and the other imperfective:

Perfective: *tój napísa pismóto* 'he wrote (and completed) the letter'
Imperfective: *tój písa pismóto* 'he wrote the letter (and it may or may not be finished)'

Basic Syntax

The preferred order of major constituents in Bulgarian sentences is Subject-Verb-Object, but variations are possible in order to change the focus of a sentence:

tjá namér-i kníga-ta na mása-ta
she found-3SG book-the on table-the
'She found the book on the table.'

na mása-ta tjá namér-i kníga-ta
on table-the she found-3SG book-the
'It was on the table that she found the book.'

Within a noun phrase, adjectives precede the nouns they modify.

As illustrated above, Bulgarian has clitics of various sorts (accusative and dative personal pronouns, present tense forms of the verb 'be', and others). Clitics are positioned within noun and verb phrases relative to one another and relative to fully stressed words with which they are associated according to strict rules. The clitics are underlined in the following examples:

tój <u>go</u> <u>e</u> písal; písal <u>e</u> <u>go</u>
he it has written; written has it
'He has written it.'

kníga-<u>ta</u> <u>mi</u>
book-the to.me
'my book'

nóva-<u>ta</u> <u>mi</u> kníga
new-the to.me book
'my new book'

Verbs are generally negated with the preposed clitic particle *ne*: *níe ne píšem* 'we don't write'. For pragmatic purposes, the negative particle may be located elsewhere in the sentence:

áz píš-a ne pismó a státija
I write-1SG NEG letter but article
'I'm not writing a letter but an article.'

The presence in the sentence of any negative pronoun requires the verb to be negated as well:

tój ní-što ne píš-e
he no-thing NEG write-3SG
'He isn't writing anything.'

Contact with Other Languages

Since the end of the first millennium A.D., Bulgarian has been in close contact with TURKISH, Greek, ROMANIAN, Serbian, and ALBANIAN. Turkish aside, these languages show striking patterns of historical convergence (doubtless due to extensive multilingualism), and they constitute a grouping referred to as the "Balkan linguistic union."

Bulgarian has borrowed extensively in the past from Greek and Turkish, although many Turkish borrowings have been purposefully eliminated from the language. For centuries Bulgarian has maintained close ties with Russian and the archaic language of the Russian Orthodox Church, Russian Church Slavonic. There have also been borrowings from GERMAN and FRENCH, and Bulgarian is now borrowing widely from ENGLISH.

From Turkish: *kajmá* 'ground meat'
From French: *bjufét* 'buffet'
From Russian: *podgotóvka* 'preparation'
From German: *shtépsel* 'electric plug'
From English: *ímidzh* 'image'

Common Words

man:	mɨ́zh	long:	dəlɨ́g
woman:	žená	small:	málɨk
water:	vodá	yes:	dá
sun:	slɨ́nce	no:	né
three:	trí	good:	dobɨ́r
fish:	ríba	bird:	ptíca
big:	goljám	dog:	kúče
tree:	dɨrvó		

Example Sentences

(1) Sinɨ́t na náš-ija sɨséd šte otíd-e v
Son-the of our-the neighbor will go-3SG.PERF to

čužbína na specializácija.
foreign.country for specialization
'Our neighbor's son will go abroad for specialized study.'

(2) Kój tŕrsi gospodín Petróv?
who.MSG looks.for.3SG.PRES Mr. Petrov?
'Who's looking for Mr. Petrov?'

(3) Maríjo, elá túka da ti
Maria:VOC come:2SG.IMPERAT here so to.you:SG.DAT

káža néšto mnógo interésno.
tell.1SG something very.NEUT.SG interesting
'Maria, come here so that I can tell you something very interesting.'

Efforts to Preserve, Protect, and Promote the Language

Late in the 19th century and early in the 20th century, conscious efforts were made to replace large numbers of Turkish and to a lesser extent Greek borrowings with native Bulgarian constructs.

There are no particular efforts to preserve regional dialects from extinction. Standard literary Bulgarian is codified in prescriptive grammars and dictionaries, especially those produced by the Institute for Bulgarian Language (Bulgarian Academy of Sciences), the *de facto* authority on the literary norm.

Select Bibliography

Aronson, Howard. 1968. *Bulgarian Inflectional Morphophonology*. The Hague: Mouton.

Atanasova, T., M. Rankova, Rusi Rusev, D. Spasov, and V. Filipov. 1992. *Bâlgarsko-angliiski rechnik/Bulgarian-English Dictionary*. Sofia: Vezni-4.

de Bray, R.G.A. 1980. "Bulgarian." In his *Guide to the Slavonic Languages*, 3rd ed., revised and expanded, Part 1, 77–136. Columbus: Slavica.

Mayer, Gerald. 1988. *The Definite Article in Contemporary Bulgarian*. Wiesbaden: Harrassowitz.

Rudin, Catherine. 1986. *Aspects of Bulgarian Syntax: Complementizers and WH Constructions*. Columbus: Slavica.

Scatton, Ernest. 1975. *Bulgarian Phonology*. Cambridge: Slavica. Reprint: Columbus: Slavica, 1983.

____. 1984. *A Reference Grammar of Modern Bulgarian*. Columbus: Slavica.

____. 1993. "Bulgarian." In *The Slavonic Languages*, ed. B. Comrie and G. G. Corbett, 188–248. London & New York: Routledge.

BURMESE

F. K. L. Chit Hlaing

Language Name: Burmese (nowadays officially Myanmar). **Autonym:** *bama saka:* or *myamma saka:* In reality, 'Burma' is based on an old contraction form (*bəma*) of 'Myanma', so the ideologically motivated claim that they have separate referents, or that 'Burma' is a mere Anglicism, is not correct.

Location: Southeast Asia, between India and Bangladesh (on the west) and Thailand (on the east).

Family: The Burmese-Yi (Burmese-Lolo) subgroup of the Tibeto-Burman family of the Sino-Tibetan superfamily.

Related Languages: Arakanese (almost a dialect of Burmese—the State of Arakan is in the Union of Myanmar), Mru (a tribal language of the far North of Burma), more distantly the YI (Loloish) languages of the China-Southeast Asia borderlands.

Dialects: The only major dialect is, as above, Arakanese (Rakhain) and its variant, Marma (in the Chittagong Hills Tract of easternmost Bangladesh), but numerous, poorly recorded regional dialects within Burma proper abound, such as Yaw (west of the Lower Chindwin Valley; it comes closest to preserving the pronunciation indicated by the Burmese orthography, that approximating Old Burmese), Intha (in the Southern Shan State on the East of Burma Proper), Tavoyan (Dawe—in the peninsular Southern coastal strip in Burma), and Northern Burmese (Upper Irrawaddy/Ayeyawady Valley) are possibly other minor variants.

The Standard dialect in recent times, since the imposition of British colonial rule at the end of the 19th Century, is that of Lower Burma, specifically of the capital, Rangoon (Yangon). The more classical form of Modern Burmese is that of Upper Burma, the former home (until 1885) of the old Royal capitals in and around Mandalay. There is no mutual incomprehensibility between Standard Burmese and the dialects of any part of the whole Irrawaddy Valley, but as one goes east, west and south from this central core region of the country degrees of mutual intelligibility decrease, although nowadays few if any speakers of the more remote dialects (Yaw, Intha, Dawe, Marma and Arakanese) do not know Standard Burmese owing to two factors: within Burma, the increasing universality of national education, and in the case even of Marma, the fact the Buddhist monks tend to be trained in Burma monasteries where they learn Standard Burmese.

Number of Speakers: On the order of 40 million or more. Burmese is increasingly a second language for peoples of Burma whose native languages are distinct from Burmese, and this is in particular the case for those who speak SHAN (a Tai language) and live on the westernmost edge of the Shan State (the so-called *myei-lat* 'intermediate country' between the Shan State core and Burma Proper). Thus the uncertainty of the cited figure.

Origin and History

The oldest record of Burmese is some stone inscriptions dating back to approximately A.D. 1000, and these are in the oldest known form of Old Burmese. At this time the orthography was still incompletely standardized, so that it is not certain how much the very 'different' spellings tell us about the phonology of Old Burmese. They certainly allow us to demonstrate the close relationship of Burmese to its nearest relatives within Tibeto-Burman and give us a good bit of information on the historical phonology of the whole language family. It is thought that the Burmans (native speakers of Burmese, as opposed to 'Burmese', used nowadays to refer to the whole population of the Union of Myanmar regardless of native language) had only come into the Irrawaddy Valley in present-day Burma within a couple of centuries before these early inscriptions.

The inscriptional corpus of **Old Burmese** extends at least throughout the era of the first Burmese imperial kingdom, that of Pagan (the name of the capital near the confluence of the Irrawaddy and Chindwin rivers), which 'fell' in A.D. 1228. Gradually thereafter the inscriptions show increasing changes in the phonology and grammar, changes which eventuate in what we may call **Middle Burmese**, a form of the language during the era from about 1400 to some time towards the end of the 18th century. Of course during this period we begin to get Burmese literature aside from the stone inscriptions: Buddhist religious works, chronicles and court poetry, for instance. However, we have no surviving palm leaf or mulberry paper manuscripts from those early times; possibly the oldest surviving manuscript is at most 500 years old and we have no more than a handful of comparable antiquity. All the rest of the literature from these early times exists now only in the form of copies, and copies of copies, so that we cannot tell how much scribal 'correction' may have crept in during copying. The temporal boundaries between the successive forms of the language are not sharp; for instance, older writers writing early in the 19th century still use archaic (late Middle Burmese) words and syntactic constructions. In any event, Middle Burmese shows little significant grammatical difference from **Modern Burmese**, the differences being mainly those of spelling and lexicon, but one generally refers to archaic words and phrases from both Old Burmese and Middle Burmese under the heading of *Porana* (archaic) Burmese, of which published dictionaries exist.

Orthography and Basic Phonology

The Burmese writing system is alphabetic-syllabic, and is derived from the ancient TAMIL scripts of South Eastern India. There are 33 consonant signs, 4 each in a velar series, a palatal series, a retroflex series (transcribed here with a dot under the consonant but pronounced identically with the dental series, and only used to transcribe borrowed Indian words), a labial series and then glides, liquids, 'h', a retroflex 'l̥'(again only for the spelling of PALI and SANSKRIT words, and a glottal stop. All words begin with one of these, and, if no additional vowel signs are placed on, after, before or below the initial, it bears the inherent vowel *a*—hence it is often said that the last initial, the glottal stop, is the vowel *a* itself. There are five letters in each of the first five series (velar to labial); they are always in the order plain, aspirated, voiced, voiced, nasal (the second voiced letter represents the Indian aspirated voiced sound, but this is not pronounceable in Burmese). In Modern Burmese the palatal series is pronounced as a sibilant series except for the nasal, and the old sibilant, in the mixed series at the end, is now the *th* of English 'thing'; Old Burmese *r* is now, at least for most words, pronounced as *y* and for many speakers this shift from *r* to *y* is total.

Table 1: Consonants

	Labial	Dental	Palatal	Velar	Glottal
Stops	p ph b	t th d		k kh g	?
Fricatives		th s	sh z		h
Nasals	m	n	ny	ng	
Liquids		l, r			
Glides	w		y		

Burmese Script Samples

က	ခ	ဂ	ဃ	င	Velar			
ka.	kha.	ga.	ga.	nga.				
စ	ဆ	ဇ	ဈ	ည	'Palatal'			
sa.	sha.	za.	za.	nya.				
ဋ	ဌ	ဍ	ဎ	ဏ	'Retroflex'			
ṭa.	ṭha.	ḍa.	ḍa.	ṇa.				
တ	ထ	ဒ	ဓ	န	Dental			
ta.	tha.	da.	da.	na.				
ပ	ဖ	ဗ	ဘ	မ	Labial			
pa.	pha.	ba.	ba.	ma.				
ယ	ရ	လ	ဝ	သ	ဟ	ဠ	အ	
ya.	'ra.'	la.	wa.	θa.	ha.	la.	ʔa.	

Vowels. The vowels of Modern Burmese are: a, i, u, ou, o, [ɔ], ei, e, [ɛ]. and the orthographically non-distinctive ə—the toneless vowel of syllables reduced as clitic 'light' syllables in the iambic-footed prosody of this language. Each syllable unless so 'reduced' or weakened, has one of four tones: a creaky tone (high, short, and rapidly falling) marked here with a subscript dot after the syllable, a level tone (mid-pitch, with a slight rise at the end (unmarked in this transcription), a heavy tone (high, long, breathy and falling), marked here with a 'colon' after the syllable, and a final glottal stop, which is how orthographic (and etymological) syllables ending in a final oral stop consonant are pronounced—final consonants are written with one of the initials above which a superscript mark is added to 'kill' the inherent vowel—for example:

လက် (hand) *la.* + 'killed' *ka.* i.e., orthographic *lak* is pronounced (with a predictable vowel shift for all syllables with final velar stops and no vowel signs added) *le?*. The rules for the vocalism of syllables closed with stops or nasals are complicated owing to vowels shifts between Old Burmese and Modern Burmese. They can be summarized (with minor exceptions) as follows: (1) a syllable with no vowel signs and a final velar stop takes the vowel *e*; but takes the vowel *ɪ* when closed with a velar nasal; (2) final dental or labial consonants (stops or nasals) do not change the inherent *a* vowel of a syllable; (3) a final palatal stop turns inherent *a* into *ɪ*; but a final palatal nasal (unpredictably) turns it into either *ɪn*, *e*, *ei*, or *i*. In addition, if a syllable begins with initial or medial *w*, the vowel *a* becomes *u*.

Vowel signs are placed as follows (the initial *ka* is used in the examples):

ကိကီကီး ကုကူကူး ကေကေ့ကေး ကဲကဲ့ကယ်

ကိုကို့ကိုး ကော ကော် ကော့

ki. ki ki: ku. ku ku: kee kei. kei: ke: ke. ke kou lou. kou: ko: ko ko.

Note that pronunciation of syllables with these otherwise unmodified vowel signs follows a rule: the least marked high vowels take the creaky tone, the mid vowels take the level tone and the low vowels take the heavy tone. There are also letters representing vocalic syllables as such, not made by adding diacritic marks to the sign for the initial glottal stop, These are mainly used for the transcription of Indic loanwords or formal, high-flown literary words and formatives. Such letters are mostly called *eʔkhəya*, from the Sanskrit-Pāli word *akṣara/ akkhara*, 'consonant' or 'letter'. For instance, the syllable *ei*, ordinarily written အေး, can be written as ဧ, called *eʔkhəya, ei:*

As a general rule (the details are beyond the scope of this sketch), within a single surface word, a voiced syllable final causes an otherwise unvoiced initial following it to become voiced, e.g., the Realis modal ending for verbs in colloquial Burmese is *-te* but on the verb *θwa:* 'to go', it is *θwa:de* 'goes/ went'. However, after many reduced (clitic) initial syllables, voicing may fail to occur; e.g., *ʔəkhu.* 'now', though many speakers say *ʔəgu.* ; voicing is less likely, however, when the clitic weak syllable is a reduction of a stopped syllable. Thus, for instance, *tiʔ* 'one' + *khu.* 'instance of a class (generalized classifier for inanimates)' = *təkhu.* 'one [of some set of inanimate objects]'.

Finally, in isolation or utterance final position, a nasal syllable coda surfaces as just nasalization of the nuclear vowel. However, there are sandhi rules that assimilate this nasal to the position of articulation of a following syllable initial in the same word; similarly, a syllable final glottal stop followed in the word by an oral stop creates a geminate of the latter, whilst, at least in more rapid speech, a final nasal followed by a stop initial first voices the latter and then, again in rapid speech, forms a geminate of the preceding initial. A nice example of the way all these sandhi rules work is seen in the word meaning 'you' (man speaking), which is spelt *khinphya* but in fully colloquial speech becomes *khimbya* and then *khəmya* (assimilative voicing followed by gemination with weakening).

Basic Morphology

This discussion of morphology as well as the section on syntax, is limited to the colloquial style. Formal Written Burmese uses many forms and words not used in the Colloquial style but has comparatively only a few grammatical differences. It is beyond the scope of this sketch to deal with the latter.

Verbs and Adjectives. In the affirmative, the order of elements is V [one or more roots, possibly compounded] (+auxiliary verb) + aspect particle + modal ending. Preceding the aspectual element there may be inserted the element *pa* indicating explicitness, which serves to mark the utterance as 'polite', though not when it is used with an imperative: *thweʔ θwe: nei ba to. me* (exit go stay ! CHANGE.OF.STATE REALIS) 'will leave now/already', *θwa*[l]*: ba to.* (go ! ASP) 'Go already!'.

Negation is marked by prefixing a clitic *mə* and suffixing an element (*phu:*) etymologically meaning 'ever': *mə θwa:bu:* 'doesn't/didn't go'.

Nouns. Nouns may be compounded and a morphological compound need not be construed as such semantically. Thus, for instance, *mi.* ('mother') + *ba.* ('father') > *mi.ba.* 'parent'; such compounds are not conjunctive but disjunctive — a 'parent' is, after all, literally 'a mother or father'. But many such compounds are indeed transparent, such as *sa-ʔouʔ* 'book' > *sa* 'letter/writing' and *ʔəʔouʔ* 'a cover', indicating writings 'bound' together. Note that *ʔouʔ* is basically a verb root meaning 'to cover', prefixed with the clitic element *ʔə*, which serves to make a deverbal noun, and in such instances the first element of a compound replaces this clitic element. This is also how one compounds a noun with a succeeding adjective, because, in Burmese, adjectives are morphosyntactically ordinary stative verbs. Thus, *lu* ('person') + *ʔəkaun* > *lu-gaun:* 'good person'.

The noun can have a suffix indicating plurality. Suffixing *te* (spelt 'twei' and sometimes so pronounced) indicates definite plurality, whilst suffixing [*ʔə*]*mya:* (from *mya:* 'to be many') indicates indefinite plurality; thus, *lu-mya:* means 'people' (one or more thereof). Marking of number is not however obligatory and, in particular, if a noun is followed by a number-plus classifier indicating a plurality, the plural suffix is not used.

Manner Adverbs and Related Expressions. Ordinarily, a manner adverb is formed by reduplicating an adjective root, as in *myan-myan* 'quickly' from *myan* 'to be fast'. Note that in Burmese and many Tibeto-Burman and Tai languages, reduplication is ordinarily interpreted not as intensification of the root word but rather as having a disjunctive-distributive force; so 'quickly' here means something like 'more or less fast/fast to some degree or other'.

Adverbial expressions signifying intensification are formed by compounding the root for the noun 'strength' + the root for the adjective 'big' giving *a:ji:* meaning 'very much', or more exactly 'in full force' (with a null postposition), the surface form being simply a compound noun + adjective. *Ji:* may similarly be suffixed to a noun to indicate intensification (e.g., *ʔəmya: ji:* 'a lot'); with nouns indicating persons or relationships such suffixing may serve to indicate relative status or importance, or, with an adjective root indicating smallness, lesser status or importance. Thus *lu-ji:* is 'an important person' (also 'adult'), whilst *lu-nge:* (*nge:* = little') is 'an insignificant person'.

Postpositional Phrases and Case Markers. In accordance with the head-final order of the language, Burmese has postpositions. In ordinary colloquial usage there are only three: *kou* ('to', also a dative~oblique case-marker), *hma* (locative), *ne.* ('with', serving also to mark noun phrase co-ordination). For all the rest of what English marks with prepositions, Burmese uses subordinated noun compounding. Thus, to distinguish 'in' from 'on' or 'at', the noun *ʔəthef* is appended to the semantically main noun as in *ʔein-the:hma*, lit. 'at the interior of the house' (*ʔein*); English 'for' (benefactive sense) appends *ʔətweʔ* 'sake', as in *di lu ʔətweʔ* 'for this person', and so on. The indirect object (dative) of verbs such as 'to send' requires that the postposition *kou* be preceded by an 'appended' head noun meaning 'presence' *ʔəshi* (e.g., 'to him' in such contexts is *ɵu.(zi)gou*; note here that personal pronouns and related personal nominals commonly are subordinated to postpositions and the appended elements by taking the creaky tone even if they are on another tone in isolation: *ɵu-* = 'him'/'her' in isolation. (It should be noticed that this order does not violate the head-final order; the morphosyntactic head is indeed the 'appended' element.)

Notice above that one postposition can also serve as a case-marker—*kou.* Most commonly it marks a dative argument, but really this is basically an oblique case, as can be seen from the fact that pronouns and nouns denoting animate beings (including human persons), when they are direct objects also require this marker. We may say technically that in fact *kou* is always a marker of oblique~dative case (which of the two is governed by the main verb of the clause), and that it never literally means 'to' at all. On that view, we can say that there is really no distinction between case markers and postpositions: the distinction is imposed only by the need to translate from languages such as English, and it is simply a fact of the language that case markers follow the noun phrases (more correctly, demonstrative phrases—see below) they mark. As for *ne.*, when it serves as a noun-phrase conjunction, it comes between the conjoined nouns, but, even with conjoined nouns, when it serves as the postposition 'with', it comes after the conjoined noun phrase. For instance, 'pencil and paper' is *khe:dan* <u>*ne.*</u> *sekku* but 'with pencil and paper' is *khe:dan* <u>*ne.*</u> *sekku* <u>*ne.*</u> Analytically this is no great difference; in reality when serving as 'and' *ne.* still means 'with', but is then postposed to the first conjunct only. As will be seen shortly, semantic categories represented by other prepositions in English and other such languages are rendered in Burmese by the demonstrative system.

Demonstratives and Classifiers. Given the strictly head-final order of Burmese, we are obliged to adopt the Demonstrative Phrase (DP) hypothesis for the language: the noun phrase is properly embedded in a superordinate Demonstrative Phrase. We note that a 'complete' nominal expression generally consists of an 'article' (superficially *the* demonstrative itself), followed by a noun, then by an enumerative expression (number + 'classifier'), followed in turn by case-marking postpositions (see above), and ending with elements that are sometimes partial copies of the article, although these last sometimes serve semantically in place of what English etc. does with prepositions.

The written Burmese element *θi* (equivalent to colloquial *di*) meaning 'this' can come both before and after a noun. If it is only after the noun it generally 'points' to an already mentioned or understood antecedent for the noun (discourse anaphora). And because Burmese is a strictly head-final language, we see that the post-nominal one is the true demonstrative, with the pre-nominal one 'specifying' the 'space' in which the one is pointing (technically the specifier of the encompassing Determiner Phrase within which the Noun Phrase is properly contained). One may prefix to this specifier the particle *e:* which intensifies the specification, as in *e: di-lu*, 'this very person', or the *e:* alone. Note that in such simple colloquial expressions the actual determiner is commonly omitted, but may be filled with elements such as *ha*, as in *e:di- lu- ha* , which in effect 'points' to the 'space' of conceptual categories—*ha* meaning 'thing' in the sense of an entity of some named category.

Some common classifiers include: *khu.* ('unit instance') for objects of complex shape or abstractions, *kaung* for animals, *yauʔ* for ordinary human beings, *pa:* for more honored persons (teachers, kings, and so on), *hsu* for sacred things and persons (pagodas, Buddhas), *chaung:* ('stick') for long things (rivers, sticks, trains, etc.), *loun:* ('round') for round, globular things or, more generally, things perceived as enclosing space, and *si:* ('to ride on') for vehicles. There is really no fixed list; one may be fairly inventive in 'choosing' a Burmese classifier, by referring to various different ways of thinking about or looking at something. For instance, one may count houses with the classifier 'house' (*ein*) meaning just 'house', or the classifier *hsaung* 'structure'.

Numeral expressions immediately follow the noun and consist of a number + classifier, as in *lu təyauʔ* (person 1+classifier) 'one person'.

The prenominal specifier of the demonstrative phrase houses '*wh*'- words, understood as question words only when the utterance ends with the content-question marker *le*, as in *be θwa:məle:* (where go future ?) 'Where you you going?' Lacking this sentence final marker, a *wh*-word marks the nominal expression as non-specific, as in *be-θu məshou* (wh-person not-specified) 'whoever'.

Basic Syntax

The most basic fact of the syntax is that Burmese is a Head-final language: the verb and its inflections follow all arguments (subject, object, indirect object) and all adjuncts (adverbials and pospositional phrases); and within a phrase likewise.

Burmese is, however, not a tense-marking language but a mode-cum-aspect marking language. Basically there are two modal endings: *-te* 'realis' (ranging over past and present 'tense') and *-me* 'irrealis' (future and subjunctive). There is, in addition an evidentiary system in Burmese which forces modification of the irrealis modal ending as follows. A distinction is drawn between a 'future' representing what one knows by direct evidence or experience and one representing a prediction made on the basis of only indirect or conventional knowledge. Thus, for instance, if I want to indicate that I will go somewhere, I say (knowing directly my own intention) *cun-no θwa:me* (I go IRREALIS/FUT). But if I want to tell you that the train will leave at five o'clock (assuming I am not in charge of the trains and their schedules), I will say: *mi:yətha: nga: na-yi htweʔlein.me* (train 5 hour leave INDIRECT IRREALIS) 'The train will (supposedly) leave at five o'clock', where *lein.* (contraction of *lei*, an emotive-emphatic particle, and *an.* an archaic irrealis-future ending) has to precede *-me*. The composite future modal *lein.me* has sometimes been rendered in English as 'probably will', but this misses the evidentiary character of the matter. The other major evidentiary element, sometimes called 'quotative', is the particle *te.* suffixed to a finite modal ending, as in *θwa:te-te* ([one] goes *te*) indicating that what one has just said is based on what someone else has told you, or on general knowledge—essentially that you are simply relaying someone else's information.

Unstressed (non-contrastive) pronouns in Burmese are absent in discourse: *hou-go θwa: me* (there to go FUT) 'I'm going there'. Moreover, pronouns of reference and address are often replaced by 'pronoun substitutes' such as the word for 'teacher' (*hsəya*), or kinship relations, e.g., *əphei* 'father' (used in reference to one's actual father) or *u:lei:* 'uncle' (used to address or refer to any older, respectable man). What characterizes a pronoun substitute is that when I use, say, *əphei* in speaking to my father it serves as 'you'; when he uses it in speaking to me it serves as 'I', and when I use it to refer to him, it serves as 'he'. This is to be distinguished from such words as *cun-no* (more carefully, *cun-do*—literally 'royal [*to* an honorific suffix] subject'), which has come to be the ordinary word for specifically the first person singular pronoun, replacing the etymological 'true' pronoun *nga*, which is more informal because it fails to carry any implications of personal status.

Burmese has no passive sentences, save in the literary genre where it is necessary to use a somewhat artificial way of rendering the Pāli or Sanskrit passives (Burma is largely a Theravāda Buddhist nation and those are its 'classical' languages, both Indo-European). Burmese also has no true coordinate conjunction of clauses. Instead it employs participial subordinate conjunction. Thus, the equivalent of English 'I went and she remained' is *cun-no θwa: bi: θu nei-de* (I go finish she remain-REALIS) 'I having gone, she remained' where a bare verb root (here *pi:* 'finish') is always participial, and where the third person singular pronoun *θu* is gender-neutral.

Since Burmese is a head-final language and since, as stated, functional phrases head substantive phrases, we find that markers of sentence type are clause-final. *Wh*-questions are marked with a sentence-final *le:* and a yes/no questions by sentence-final *la:*. Similarly, the final element of a declarative clause is the modal ending, and a negative declarative, having no semantic modality save itself (no realis-irrealis contrast), ends instead with postposed *hpu:* even though the basic negation morpheme is the preverbal clitic *mə* 'non-finite'. Subordinate clauses are likewise marked with clause-final 'complementizers', the complementizer phrase being the ultimate functional phrase as usual informal syntax.

Two remarks about the complementizers are necessary here. First, they are at least commonly cliticized to any immediately preceding 'tense' inflection, which then itself becomes a reduced syllables, as in *θwa: mə la:* (go FUT?) 'Will [you] go?' Second, a distinction is to be drawn between finite and non-finite subordinate clauses and their complementizers. In the former case, the complementizer is cliticized to an inflectional ending; in the latter, to the bare verb root/participle.

Consider the complementizer *lou.*. It can bound a finite 'that' type clause, as in the full form of the colloquial question 'where are you going?' [*be θwa: mə lou. le:*], *viz., be θwa: mə lou. sin:za:θə le:* (wh go FUT COMP intend REALIS-?) 'Where do [you] intend that [you]will go?' But it can also take a non-finite complement clause, where it can be rendered in colloquial English as 'because of' or 'for', sometimes (depending upon the verb of the main clause) simply as participializing the verb of the subordinate clause, or even as 'for' or 'in as much as': *ci.lou. kaun:de* (look-at for good-REALIS) 'good to look at'; *sa:lou. kaun:de* (eat for good-REALIS) 'good to eat [good when or as you eat it—not purposive]'; *di keiʔsa.ne. paθəʔlou. mə twei.ya.bu:* (this affair-with concern -ing not find-get-to) '[I] couldn't find anything concerning this business [in the newspaper]'.

There are other complementizers, but they can take *only* non-finite complement clauses. e.g., *yin* ('if'), *hpou.* 'for' and so on: *ša yin twei.me* (seek-if find FUT) 'if one seeks one will find [something]'; *sa:bou. kaun:de* (eat-for good-REAL) 'good to eat [purposive]'. The complementizer *yin* is commonly used for clauses functioning as topical, sentence adverbial clauses, as in: *di hsou-lou-yin* ... (this say want if ...) 'As for this [lit. if this is what you want to say/have in mind to say...]'.

Note that this leads to a superficial distinction concerning head-attribute order. Ordinarily one expects a rigid modifier-head order, as in such examples as *lu-gaun:* (person-good) 'good person'. However consider the expression *θauʔyei* (drink-water) 'drinking water'. This seems on first view an exception to the usual order, but is not because it is actually a contraction (here a lexicalized contraction) of a relative-clause construction, where *yei*, 'water', is the head noun and *θauʔ* 'drink' is, in open form, *θauʔ bou.* 'for drinking', so that the construction is really 'water [that is for] drinking'. Adjectival attributes, however follow the expected surface order, as we have seen, and are *not* readily paraphrased as reduced relative clauses. For the expression *lu-gaun:* ('good person') means an *inherently* good person, whereas *kaun:de. lu* ('a person who is good') signifies one who is good in a given context only, e.g., who is behaving properly for the time being. Such attributive 'compounds' are actually noun-noun compounds with the expected order; in this example *lu* + *əkaun:* (person + goodness/good-one), the latter really the head of the construction, formed with the clitic prefix *ə* that serves to make a deverbal noun. This leads us directly to a consideration of relative clauses and noun-phrase complement clauses.

First, relative clauses prepose the finite subordinate clause to the head nominal by marking the clause-final modal endings, normally on the level tone, with the derived creaky tone, the general marker of genitive subordination, including possession. Thus we may compare the following: *cun-no. sa-ouʔ* (I GEN book) 'my book ('I' is inherently level tone, *cun-no*)'; *θwa: de. lu* (go REALIS GEN person) '[the] person who goes/went'(the realis ending is inherently level tone *-te*)'.

It will be noted already above that sentential word order is (almost) invariant under question formation, and the same is true, here, for relative clauses—the nominal in the clause controlled for reference by the head nominal of the relative construction is never displaced. As to whether there is any sort of 'relative pronoun', that is anything in the complementizer phrase containing the relative clause, in a way there is, as can be seen from the fact that, once again, the dependent-genitive creaky tone can be, instead, on the 'item' element, presumably itself in the complementizer position: *θwa: de-ye. lu* 'the person who goes/went'. Although this is very stilted usage, it shows that there is something equivalent to the 'that' of 'the man that went', and we can conclude that what happens more ordinarily is that the creaky tone inherently associated with the complementizer, when the latter is phonologically null, is conflated morphologically with the modal ending of the subordinate clause.

Equational sentences are verbless; 'this is a book' is, ordinarily, *di-ha sa-ouʔ* (this-thing [a] book) where *di-ha*, commonly contracted to *da*, is a 'demonstrative noun'. Using this form, one negates an equational expression by embedding the affirmative in a negation of the verb 'to be so' (*houʔ*), as in *di-ha sa-ouʔ məhouʔphu:* (this book not.so) 'this is not a book'.

Finally, concerning sentence types, one must note the existence of a large class of nominalized sentences. These are extremely common in running conversation, where there may be few if any 'verbal' declarative sentences at all, and nominalized sentences are especially common in the context of exclamatory emphasis. One nominalizes a sentence by contracting the modal declarative ending with the generalized noun *ha* 'thing': [*θu*] *θwa:da po.* ([he] go real.+thing certainly) 'He goes, of course'.

In this connection, there is also a fairly large class of formatives that make deverbal nouns (but do not serve to nominalize finite clauses). Perhaps the most common one in colloquial usage is the abstract noun formative *əhmu.* 'deed', 'matter', 'case', as in *win-hmu.* 'the fact or act of entering'. It is somewhat difficult to distinguish this way of forming abstract deverbal nouns from the use of the clitic prefix *ə*. but the latter means something more abstract still, in particular not factive—'going' as an intentional concept.

Contact with Other Languages

Pali and Sanskrit have provided both a considerable corpus of loanwords at all levels of vocabulary (religious and philosophical words, of course, but also common words such as *ding-ga:*

for 'coin' from general India *tangka*) and a model for various construction types in at least the literary register (see remarks on 'passive', above), functioning as 'classical' languages for Burmese culture. Then, because of the position of Burma in the Indian Ocean trading region, vocabulary items have come into Burmese from, for instance, PORTUGUESE, ARABIC and, in particular TAMIL (e.g., the generic Burmese word for a sarong, *loun-ji* from Tamil *lunghi*). ENGLISH has provided a considerable array of words because Burma was under British colonial rule, particularly from 1885 to 1947. Examples are *main* from English 'mile', or even such words as *sain-boʔ* from 'sign-board', which are in common use though they do not appear in any known Burmese dictionary. Many loanwords from Burmese have entered into minority languages within Burma, although Burmese words have not made their way into neighboring languages, nor do they appear in any European languages.

Common Words

man:	yaunʔca
woman:	mein-ma.
water:	yei
sun:	nei
three:	θoun:
fish:	nga:
big:	ci:
long:	hye [še]
small:	nge
yes:	houʔke. (There is no general 'yes'; this means 'right!'. To say 'yes' to, e.g., 'is it good?' one replies 'is good')
no:	məhouʔphu: (There is no general 'no'; this means 'Not so'; one must negate whatever verb is asked about)
good:	kaun:
bird:	hngeʔ
dog:	khwei:
tree:	θiʔpin (lit. 'wood-plant')
house:	ein (lit. 'dwelling')

Example Sentences

(1) bəθu hma. məla: bu:
who even not come
'No one came.' (lit., 'even whoever didn't come')

(2) bəθu ma phyu ka. [Maun Maun myin:de lou.] pyo: θəle:
who [name,f.] subj.emph. [Name,m] see [real.comp] say real-Q
'Who did Ma Phyu say that Maung Maung saw?'

(3) ša yin twei.me
seek-if find.FUT
'If one seeks one will find [something].'

Efforts to Preserve, Protect, and Promote the Language

After independence from colonial rule was achieved in 1947, Burmese became the official language of the country and of the education system. Following the military coup of 1962, in particular, and especially since the imposition of military rule in 1988, Burmese has become the only allowed medium of educational instruction at all levels, even in minority ethnic regions, and an attempt has been made to purge the language of Anglicisms (e.g., the common word *nam-baʔ* from English 'number' has been officially replaced with the Burmese etymon *əhmaʔ* 'mark; indexical signifier', although common usage often results in the compound *əhmaʔ nam-baʔ* when one is referring to item number such-and-such). Along with these language 'reforms' have come increasing attempts to impose a reformed standard of spellings for many words, largely the work of the Language Commission and its several quite excellent dictionaries.

Select Bibliography

Bernot, Denise. 1978–1992. *Dictionnaire Burman-Français* (15 fascicules) Paris: Editions Peters/SELAF.

Department of the Myanmar Language Commission. 1993. *Myanmar-English Dictionary*. Rangoon: Ministry of Education.

Lehman, F. K. 1985. "Ergativity and the Nominal-Verbal Cycle: Internal Syntactic Reconstruction in Burmese." In Arlene R. K. Zide, *et al*, eds. *Proceedings of a Conference on Participant Roles: South Asia and Adjacent Areas*. Bloomington: Indiana University Linguistics Club, pp. 71–81.

Okell, John. 1969. *A Reference Grammar of Burmese*. 2 volumes. London: Oxford University Press. (Contains a thorough bibliography of further references.)

Sawada, Hideo. 1994. "Significance of Pseudo-cleft Construction in Burmese." Pp.723–729 *in* Hajime Kitamura *et al.*, eds. *Current Issues in Sino-Tibetan Linguistics*. Osaka: The Organizing Committee of the 26th International Conference on Sino-Tibetan Language and Linguistics.

Wheatley, Julian K. 1982. *Burmese: A Grammatical Sketch*. Ph. D. Dissertation, Cornell University.

Yabu, Shiro. 1994. "Case Particles *-ka* and *-kou* in Burmese." In Hajime Kitamura *et al.* eds. *Current Issues in Sino-Tibetan Linguistics*, pp. 730–736. Osaka: The Organizing Committee of the 26th International Conference on Sino-Tibetan Language and Linguistics.

Caribbean Creole English

Ronald Kephart

Language Name: Caribbean Creole English (CCE); terms typically used by speakers include Creole, Patwa, Dialect, and Broken English.

Location: Islands of the Caribbean, including Jamaica, Cayman Islands, Virgin Islands, Leeward and Windward Islands, Barbados, Trinidad & Tobago; coastal mainland Central America, especially Belize but also coastal Nicaragua and Panama; South America, especially Guyana and Suriname.

Family: Atlantic Creole English; some scholars refer to the group as Afro-American, reflecting the fact that the languages developed in the context of the African diaspora.

Related Languages: West African creole and "pidgin" English, e.g., Nigerian Pidgin and Cameroon Pidgin; Bahaman Creole; North American "Gullah" (Sea Island Creole), Afro-Seminole, and Black English. Many linguists consider other creole languages of the African diaspora, such as HAITAN CREOLE FRENCH, to be related.

Dialects: There are three major varieties: (1) Western Caribbean Creole English, the most important example of which is Jamaican Creole (JC) but including also Belizean Creole and Miskito Coast Creole; (2) Eastern Caribbean Creole English (EC), including Guyanese, Trinidadian, Barbadian, Grenadian, etc.; (3) the Suriname creoles, which include Sranan Tongo, Saramakan, Ndyuka, etc.

Dialects of CCE vary according to the extent to which they are mutually intelligible with Metropolitan English (ME). Trinidadian and Barbadian, for example, are relatively intelligible; the Suriname creoles on the other hand are virtually unintelligible without extensive study. The term *basilectal* refers to the latter; *mesolectal* is used for the former. The term *acrolectal* is used to describe speech that is essentially Metropolitan English.

In addition to the geographical variation just described, social variation exists within those speech communities where ENGLISH is the official language. Any given speaker of Jamaican Creole fully controls the basilect; depending on schooling, exposure to ME, and other factors, s/he may also be able to produce speech that is mesolectal (incorporating features from ME) and acrolectal (fully ME except perhaps for accent). As an illustration, note the following realizations of 'I am going to town' from Jamaica; note especially the replacement of the basilectal progressive aspect marker *a-* with the ME suffix *-in(g)*.

basilect:	mi a-go a tong
mesolect:	mi goin a tong, a goin na tong
acrolect:	ay am goin tu tong

In Suriname, where the acrolectal language is DUTCH, the mesolect is not present.

Number of Speakers: The total number of speakers of varieties of Caribbean Creole English living in the Caribbean is about six million. Some of these are speakers of more than one variety. Many more Creole English speakers reside as immigrants in metropolitan centers such as London, New York, and Toronto.

Origin and History

Caribbean Creole English had its origin in the European use of African slave labor on plantations in the New World beginning in the early seventeenth century. There are competing models regarding the exact nature of the origin, however. One model suggests that English, FRENCH, and other creole languages all developed from a PORTUGUESE-based pidgin/creole spoken on Portuguese sugar plantations prior to New World settlement. According to this model, slaves who later ended up on plantations dominated by French or ENGLISH relexified the Portuguese pidgin, with the result being modern Haitian Creole (French) and Jamaican Creole (English). This model suggests that English, French, and other creoles are similar to one another because they all have structures inherited from the relexified Portuguese pidgin.

A radically different model proposes that slaves on plantations in the new World spoke pidgin languages among themselves. When they began having children, the children intuitively restructured the relatively grammar-less pidgin into fully natural creole via innate language-acquisition abilities possessed by all humans. This model views similarities among creole languages as reflections of the genetically provided aspects of natural language.

A third model stresses the fact that creole languages were created by speakers of West African languages of the Kwa and

Mande language families. These languages share broad features of phonology, morphology, syntax, and semantics, some of which show up in different varieties of creole.

Orthography and Basic Phonology

Unlike Haitian and some other varieties of Creole French, there is no standardized or even widely accepted orthography for most varieties of CCE. Some who write Jamaican Creole use the phonologically-based system found in Cassidy and Le Page's *Dictionary of Jamaican English.* Most, however, use some form of eye dialect, so that a word like 'mother' (spelled *moda* in the Cassidy–Le Page system) might be spelled *mudder, muddah*, etc. A phonemic spelling system for the variety spoken on Carriacou (Grenada) was used in a creole literacy project in the 1980s; in general, however, literacy via CCE is not encouraged and is sometimes actively discouraged.

All varieties of CCE are syllable-timed (like SPANISH) rather than stress-timed (like American English); this means that vowels are less likely to reduce than consonants in rapid speech. At the word level, stress is not contrastive and stress usually falls on the last syllable of a word.

The Cassidy Le–Page orthography for Jamaican Creole is given in Tables 1 and 2.

Table 1: Consonants

		Labial	Alveolar	Palatal	Velar	Glottal
Stops	Voiceless	p	t	ch [tʃ]	k	
	Voiced	b	d	j [dʒ]	g	
Fricatives	Voiceless	f	s	sh [ʃ]		h
	Voiced	v	z			
Nasals		m	n		ng [ŋ]	
Laterals			l			
Retroflex				r		
Glides				y	w	

Table 2: Vowels

	Front		Back
high long:	ii [iː]		uu [uː]
high short:	i [ɪ]		u [ʊ]
falling diphthongs:	ie [yɛ]		uo [wɔ]
mid short:	e [ɛ]		o [ɔ]
low short:		a [a]	
low long:		aa [aː]	
rising diphthongs:		ai [ay]	ou [ɔw]

Varieties spoken in Eastern Caribbean and Suriname differ most significantly in their vowel systems. In Suriname, most varieties have a five-vowel system similar to Spanish [i e a o u]. In Carriacou and Dominica, a tense-lax contrast is added to the mid vowels resulting in [i e ɛ a ɔ o u], which resembles Creole French and also some West African languages; these varieties also add a voiced palatal fricative, [ʒ].

Basic Morphology

Nouns are forms that can be marked for number and/or occur with the definite/indefinite determiners. Unmarked nouns are generic (*uman* = 'women in general'). Non-generic nouns may be marked for number and definiteness in the following ways:

	Definite	Indefinite
Singular	di uman wan uman	a uman
Plural	di uman-dem	som uman

In EC, *-andem* frequently replaces *-dem: di uman-andem* 'the women'. In CCE, number is not marked redundantly on nouns; a plural determiner or other quantifier is sufficient; *wan kou* 'a cow'; *dem kou* 'these cows'; *faiv kou* 'five cows'.

In the basilect, pronouns are generally invariant (not inflected for gender or case). This is shown in the table below:

	Jamaican Creole		EC (Carriacou)	
	Sing.	Plural	Sing.	Plural
1st Person	mi	wi	a, mi	wi, alwi
2nd Person	yu	unu, aayu	yu	alyu
3rd Person	im	dem	i, shi	de

Verbs are forms which may be marked for tense, mode, and aspect by preverbal clitic forms that resemble to some extent English auxiliary verbs. Note that, unlike English, an unmarked verb usually has a past connected to present meaning, which contrasts with the true past or anterior. The following are examples of verbal markings in Jamaican Creole.

dem guo	'they go' (habitually)
dem a-guo	'they are going'
dem guo	'they've gone'
dem (b)en-guo	'they went'
dem (b)en-a-guo	'they were going'
dem wi-guo	'they will go'
dem kyan-guo	'they can go'
dem kyaan-guo	'they cannot go'

In EC the aspect marker *a-* has been largely replaced by the English progressive suffix *-ing*. Also *doz-* is used to mark habitual: *de guo-in* 'they are going'; *de doz-guo* 'they go' (habitually). Verbs in CCE include forms that are usually classified as adjectives in English, so that *smaat* 'clever' can give: *dem ben smaat* 'they used to be clever'; *dem wi-smaat* 'they will be clever'; etc.

CCE divides the functions of the English verb *be* into two distinct domains. To express location (being-where) and health (being-how), CCE has a special verb *de* as in: *dem de na ruod* 'they are in the road'; *a de gud* 'I am alright'. To introduce a predicate nominate (being-what), JC uses the equating verb *a* (*iz* in the mesolect): *im a di liida* 'she is the leader'; *dat iz a guot* 'that is a goat'.

Basic Syntax

All varieties of CCE are SVO languages. There is no case marking in the basilect, so that syntactic position determines the roles of subject and object: *mi sii im* 'I see her'; *im sii mi* 'she sees me'. In its phrase structure, CCE is strongly head-initial as illustrated by the following:

NP	yo a jus	'pitcher of juice' (EC)
DP	di liida	'the leader'
QP	al dis bad rom	'all this bad rum'
PrepP	pan de tiebl	'on the table'
VP	sii a pikni	'(he) saw a little child'
TenseP	ben-guo	'(someone) went'

The universal negative marker *no* usually precedes the entire predicate in the basilect. In the mesolect it often takes the form *en* and attaches to the preverbal clitics instead of preceding them. In the mesolect predicate nominates are negated with *nat*:

Jamaican	EC (Carriacou)
dem no guo 'they haven't gone'	de en guo 'they haven't gone'
dem no a-guo 'they aren't going'	de en/no/do guo-in 'they aren't going'
dem no ben guo 'they didn't go'	de di-n-guo 'they didn't go'
im no a di liida 'she is not the leader'	she nat di lida 'she is not the leader'

For question formation, CCE shares WH-movement, but no Aux-movement, with English, as shown below:

Creole	English
Jaan a-iit-mango	John is eating mangoes
Jaan a-iit mango?	Is John eating mangoes?
Wa Jaan a-iit?	What is John eating?

CCE makes use of three syntactic processes that are either rare or missing in English, but which occur in many West African languages. These are reduplication, topicalization, and serial verbs. Reduplication is generally performed on adjectives:

di mango swiit swiit
'the mango is really sweet'

Topicalization involves fronting an element of the predicate; the fronted constituent is marked by a form of the equative verb, basilectal *a* or mesolectal *iz:*

iz tiif dem tiif it
'they certainly stole it'

In serial verb constructions two or more verbs are conjoined in a single predicate; sometimes an 'and' is used. The following example is from EC (Carriacou).

i liv guo-in an bring di chayl in dakta
3S leave go-ASP CONJ. take DEF child to doctor
'He went to take the child to the doctor.'

Contact with Other Languages

Most CCE lexicon is from English. All varieties of CCE also have words from various West African languages. The names Quamina [kwamina], Quashie [kwashi], and Cudjoe [kojo] are Twi day-names (Saturday, Sunday, Monday). CCE also acquired some words from Cariban, Arawakan, and other American Indian sources. These include more widely diffused terms such as *hammock* and *hurricane* as well as more restricted ones such as *maniku* 'opossum', *tatu* 'armadillo', and *guti* 'agouti'. CCE that is maintained alongside Creole French uses *wi?* as a sentence tag, as in: *mekin haat, wi?* 'the weather is hot, isn't it?' (Carriacou, etc.). These varieties also contain extensive Creole French vocabulary, especially terms for local plants and animals such as *zwit* 'oysters', *piewo* 'mockingbird', and *zaboka* 'avocado'.

Common Words

The examples reflect Jamaican Creole pronunciation and are spelled in the Cassidy–Le Page system; where an alternative is offered, it is for general Eastern Caribbean unless specified.

man:	man	long:	lang
woman:	uman	small:	smaal; smal
water:	waata; wata	yes:	yes; wi (Grenada etc.)
sun:	son	no:	no
three:	trii; tri	good:	gud
fish:	fish	bird:	bod; brd (Barbados)
big:	big	dog:	daag; dag
tree:	trii; tri		

Efforts to Preserve, Protect, and Promote the Language

Until the 1960s, official attitudes toward CCE were mostly negative, reflecting an ideology that it was merely ungrammatical English and that it was a problem to be solved, rather than a resource to be valued and maximized. Today, due to the activities of a growing number of creolists from both within and outside the region, most Caribbean educational systems recognize varieties of CCE as languages in their own right.

Despite this overall change in official attitudes, vestiges of the old prejudice linger on in the belief that, while CCE is a real language, it is only suitable for use in limited domains such as folklore, and not for formal education, literacy training, or public discourse. This means that children rarely have the opportunity to fully utilize their native language in school, for example in literacy acquisition. Still, even this is changing in some areas, as research is carried out on teaching and learning in CCE and as linguists and others debate how best to write the language and integrate it into the educational process.

Within the officially English-speaking Caribbean, CCE remains the de facto native language of most people, especially in rural areas where effective speaking, storytelling, and singing in CCE are still highly valued. CCE is the language of reggae and calypso music, both of which have achieved worldwide popularity, as have a number of West Indian writers and poets who use the language in their works. In addition, many immigrants use CCE as a symbol of ethnic identity and unity in places such as London and New York. All of this taken together suggests that the language, while besieged at times by Metropolitan forms of English, is in no danger of disappearing.

Select Bibliography

Allsopp, R. 1996. *Dictionary of Caribbean English Usage.* Oxford: Oxford University Press.

Bailey, B. 1966. *Jamaican Creole Syntax.* Cambridge: Cambridge University Press.

Bickerton, D. 1982. *The Roots of Language.* Ann Arbor: Karoma.

Carrington, L. D. (ed.) 1983. *Studies in Caribbean Language.* St. Augustine: Society for Caribbean Linguistics.

Cassidy, F. G. 1961. *Jamaica Talk: Three Hundred Years of the English Language in Jamaica.* McMillan & Company.

____, and R. B. Le Page (eds.). 1980. *Dictionary of Jamaican English.* Cambridge: Cambridge University Press.

Farquhar, B. 1974. *A Grammar of Antiguan Creole.* Ann Arbor: University Microfilms.

Hancock, I. F. 1985. *Diversity and Development in English-related Creoles.* Ann Arbor: Karoma.

Hymes, D. (ed.). 1974. *Pidginization and Creolization of Languages.* Cambridge: Cambridge University Press.

McWhorter, J. 1997. *Towards a New Model of Creole Genesis.* New York: Peter Lang Publishers.

Minderhout, D. J. 1973. *A Sociolinguistic Description of Tobagonian English.* Ann Arbor: University Microfilms.

Romaine, S. 1988. *Pidgin and Creole Languages.* London: Longman.

Valdman, A. 1977. *Pidgin and Creole Linguistics.* Bloomington: Indiana University Press.

CATALAN

Natàlia Díaz-Insensé

Language Name: Catalan. **Autonym:** *Català*.

Location: Catalan is spoken in three autonomous regions in eastern Spain (Catalonia, most of the Valencian Autonomous Community, and the Balearic Islands) as well as in the eastern strip of Aragón. It is also spoken in a small area of southeastern France (Roussillon), in the Principality of Andorra, and in the town of Alghero in Sardinia (Italy). Since Catalan's current linguistic domain spreads over several countries, the name *Països Catalans* (lit. 'Catalan Countries') is often used to identify the area that falls within linguistic, as opposed to national, boundaries.

Family: Romance group of the Italic branch of the Indo-European family.

Related Languages: FRENCH, ITALIAN, OCCITAN (Gascon, Provençal), PORTUGUESE, Rhaeto-Romanic, ROMANIAN, Sardinian, and SPANISH.

Dialects: Catalan has one major dialectal split: Western and Eastern. Western Catalan includes Northwestern Catalan (or *Lleidatà*) and Southern Catalan (or *Valencià*). Eastern Catalan includes Northern Catalan (or *Rossellonès*), Central Catalan, Insular Catalan (or *Balearic*) and the variety spoken in Alghero (or *Aiguerès*). Standard Catalan is mainly based on the Central dialect.

Apart from the common dialectal differences which arise within a language (such as particular vocabulary choices and a few syntactic constructions), the only features which distinguish Catalan dialects are a few phonological and morphological processes. In particular, one major dialectal feature of Western Catalan dialects is the lack of schwa [ə] in their vocalic system.

Number of Speakers: 7–9 million.

Origin and History

Catalan is a descendant of Vulgar LATIN, which was the language spoken by the soldiers, merchants and officials of the Roman Empire who, between the 2nd century B.C. and 4th century A.D., settled and dominated the area which is today covered by Catalan territories. The Roman invasion and colonization had a major linguistic impact on the early inhabitants of the region who were of Ibero-BASQUE and Celtic origin. Their languages were gradually replaced by Vulgar Latin and the only traces of the previous languages in Modern Catalan are a few vocabulary items and place-names.

To a great extent, the breakup of the Roman Empire and subsequent invasions by Germanic peoples (the Visigoths, in 418) and the Arabs (who entered the Iberian peninsula in 711) paved the way to the development of the language. Since the Visigoths adopted the Roman administrative system and spoke Latin, they did not have a major linguistic impact (most words of Germanic origin were introduced via Latin, because of former contacts between the Germanic and the Roman population). However, it was during this period that the variety of Vulgar Latin spoken by the natives became gradually distinctive. Evidence to the effect that these changes were taking place in the vernacular is found in the *Appèndix Probi*, a document dating from the 6th or 7th century, which contains a list of words to be avoided by the local authors when writing in Latin. During the Arab occupation of northern and eastern Catalonia (711–801), the vernacular was not replaced by ARABIC, but by the 9th century it had become so different from Latin that at the Council of Reims (813) the clergy was instructed to preach *in rusticam Romanam linguam*, that is, the local Romance variety. However, words and expressions such as 'Catalan' or 'Catalan language', and documents written in what can be considered to be Catalan, do not appear until the 12th century: a translation of the *Forum Judicum* is the oldest known text entirely written in Catalan, and the *Homilies d'Organyà* is the first literary example.

During the 12th century the natives of northern and western Catalonia began their westward and southward expansion (the so-called *reconquesta*), and in the early 13th century they gained control over València and the Balearic Islands. Since the population in these territories had been under Islamic rule for over four centuries, the influence of Arabic on the Romance variety spoken there (Mozarabic) had been very strong. Catalan quickly supplanted Mozarabic, but a few idiosyncratic words and features of the latter were incorporated. In fact, most of the Arabic words in Catalan were introduced through Mozarabic.

Between the 13th and 14th centuries, Catalans began a period of expansion and trading throughout the Mediterranean, resulting in a flourishing of their culture and language. This cultural dynamism is demonstrated by the fact that a Catalan writer, Ramon Llull (1235–1316), stands out as the first European scholar to produce philosophical essays in a Romance language. The quality and richness of his language has led some researchers to claim that Llull was the creator of the

Table 1: Consonants

		Labial	Labiodental	Dental	Alveolar	Prepalatal	Palatal	Velar
Stops	Voiceless	p		t				k
	Voiced	b		d				g
Fricatives	Voiceless		f		s	ʃ		
	Voiced		(v)		z	ʒ		
Affricates	Voiceless				ts	tʃ		
	Voiced				dz	dʒ		
Nasals		m			n		ɲ	
Lateral					l		ʎ	
Flap					ɾ			
Trill					r			
Glides						(j)	(w)	

standard Catalan language. Although during the medieval ages many Catalan poets often wrote in Provençal (a neighboring language which they called *llemosí*), the number and diversity of literary works and scientific translations in Catalan was significant.

Towards the end of the 15th century, the printing press gave impetus to the standardization and alphabetization processes. This century was the high point for literary production in Catalan. However, after the marriage of the Castilian and the Catalano-Aragonese monarchs (1469), Catalan began a period of decline: Catalan continued to be used by the local administration as well as by the native population, but it started losing prestige, and Castilian (Spanish) became the language of the wealthy and the intellectuals throughout Spain. In the 16th century, Catalan entered the so-called "decadent" period. During the 17th century, hostilities in northern Catalan territories led to Catalan surrender of the Roussillon (*Tractat dels Pirineus*, 1659).

In the 18th century the language reached its lowest point: King Felipe V of Spain abolished Catalan as the official language (*Decreto de Nueva Planta,* 1714), and began enforcing the use of Castilian Spanish; in France, French became the language of legal and public affairs (1700) and languages other than French were seen as a potential threat to French unity; and, in Sardinia, Italian became the official language (1764) shortly after Catalans had lost control over the island (*Tractat d'Utrecht*, 1713). Thus, Catalan became an oppressed minority language excluded from public life, education, and administration and was confined to private use.

During the period of economic growth in the 19th century, Catalonia's middle class began fighting against the centralist government to recover its linguistic identity. This was the birth of the Catalan nationalist movement, or *Catalanism*, that led to the so-called 'Catalan Renaissance' in literature and prompted the first attempts at language codification. After the creation of the *Institut d'Estudis Catalans* (1907), Pompeu Fabra and other collaborators published the first orthographic manual (1913), the first official grammar (1918), and dictionary (1932). During the Spanish republic, Catalan was restored as the official language of Catalonia. However, after the Spanish Civil War (1936–1939), Catalan was again officially banned, and it was not until the end of General Franco's dictatorship (1975) and after democracy was re-established in Spain that Catalan was given special recognition in the Constitution (1978) and was later granted official status within three autonomous regions: Catalonia, the community of València, and the Balearic Islands. Over the last twenty years, because of the standardization efforts of previous generations and current institutional support, Catalan seems to have made substantial progress towards recovery.

Orthography and Basic Phonology

Catalan is written in the Latin alphabet. Some phonemes may be represented by more than one letter. The following is a summary of different orthographic renderings which can be encountered in the written language (where FVs, Vs and Cs stand for front vowels, vowels, and consonants, respectively):

Stops	/b/	b, v
	/k/	qu- (before FVs), c (before non FVs or codas)
	/g/	gu- (before FVs)
Fricatives	/s/	-ss- (bet. Vs), s-, ç, c- (before FVs), -sc-
	/z/	z, -s- (between Vs)
	/ʃ/	-ix, x- (but x- is often realized as [tʃ])
	/ʒ/	g (before FVs) , j
Affricates	/dz/	-tz-
	/tʃ/	tx, -ig, -g
	/dʒ/	-tj-,-tg- (before FVs), -dj-
Nasal	/ɲ/	ny
Lateral	/ʎ/	ll
Flap	/ɾ/	-r- (between Vs), -r (after tautosyllabic Cs)
Trill	/r/	r-, -rr- (between Vs), -r

Apart from these orthographic conventions, it must be noted that *h* is always silent (though in onomatopoeic words it stands for aspiration), and that orthographic *w* is pronounced as [b] or a glide.

In word-final position or prefixes like *ex-*, the letter *x* may sometimes correspond to compound sounds [ks] or [gz] (depending on the phonological rules described below).

The segment /v/ is only phonemic in some varieties of Insular Catalan (*Mallorquí*). The phonemic status of glides is controversial. The alveolar lateral /l/ shows a strong velarization in Catalan [ɫ].

One or more of the following rules can apply to a given sequence of consonants and across word boundaries:

Voiced stops become fricatives (or approximants,[β], [ð], [ɣ]): when they occur between vowels, after laterals and continuants. But [b] and [d] are stops after /f/ and laterals, respectively.

Syllable-final stops agree in voice with a following consonant. Syllable-final fricatives and affricates agree in voice with a following segment.

/n/ assimilates to any following consonant; /m/ assimilates to a following labiodental.

All obstruents are voiceless before a pause. In addition, word final [ʒ] undergoes affrication [tʃ].

Stops are deleted after homorganic nasals and laterals before a pause. Rhotics are usually deleted word-finally before a pause.

Standard Catalan has seven phonological vowels in stressed position (see Table 2).

Table 2: Vowels

	Front	Central	Back
High	i		u
Mid-high	e		o
Mid-low	ɛ		ɔ
Low		a	

High vowels are realized as glides when they are immediately preceded by a stressed vowel (across word boundaries and in word internal position, but not across verbal morpheme boundaries), and after unstressed vowels. Prevocalic glides are found in word-initial position and in combination with orthographic *q* and *g*. Prevocalic glides are also found in other contexts but they are usually discouraged by prescriptive grammars. If two high vowels co-occur in a syllable, the second one is always the glide.

Accent marks are used to indicate stress and to distinguish mid-high from mid-low vowels

Mid-high and mid-low vowels are distinguished in stressed syllables by means of two different accent-marks: è [ɛ],ò [ɔ], *é* [e], *ó* [o].

In certain varieties of Insular Catalan (*Mallorquí*), schwa is also phonemic in stressed position. In Northern Catalan (*Rossellonès*) the stressed vocalic inventory lacks midlow vowels.

Stress in Catalan is not always predictable, but shows the following pattern: words ending in a consonant have stress on the final syllable while words ending in a vowel have penultimate stress. Some words have antepenultimate stress, and certain monosyllabic words (such as clitics and articles) are always unstressed. Verbal paradigms exhibit a different stress pattern.

Orthographic conventions require that stress should always be marked with the appropriate diacritic on words which end in *-a*, *-e*, *-i*, *-o*, *-u*, *-as*, *-es*, *-is*, *-os*, *-us*, *-en*, *-in* and bear final stress; or words which do not end in any of the previous combinations and bear penultimate stress; stress must always be marked on words bearing antepenultimate stress. In addition, some monosyllabic words bear a written mark to distinguish homographs.

The main phonological rule which applies to vowels in Standard Catalan is vowel reduction. This rule reduces the phonological vowels in unstressed position to three: /i/ is realized as [i]; /ɛ e a/ are realized as [ə]; and /ɔ o u/ are realized as [u] (e.g., [ˈkazə] 'house' vs. [kəˈzɛtə] 'little house', and [ˈfosk] 'dark' vs. [fusˈko] 'darkness'). However, in Western Catalan dialects, this rule yields five distinct vocalic segments in unstressed position by merging unstressed mid-low vowels with /e/ and /o/.

Basic Morphology

Catalan nouns belong to one of two gender classes: masculine or feminine. Apart from natural gender which is reflected on words referring to human beings (and some animals), the assignment of nouns to either one of these classes is, by and large, arbitrary. One relatively useful regularity is that nouns which end in *-e* tend to be masculine, and those which end in *-a* are (usually) feminine (e.g., masculine [ˈʎiβɾə] *llibre* 'book' vs. feminine [ˈtarðə] *tarda* 'afternoon'). But phonological rules such as vowel reduction in the spoken language make this pattern much less transparent. Many masculine nouns appear as bare stems (i.e., without gender markers); feminine nouns that are formed by adding *-a* to these stems may look irregular due to the application of phonological processes such as final devoicing of obstruents (e.g. [əˈmik] *amic* 'male friend' vs. [əˈmiɣə] *amiga* 'female friend').

As for number marking, nouns are usually pluralized by adding *-s*. Due to prior application of word-final phonological rules (such as /n/ deletion), some masculine nouns look irregular (e.g., *camió* 'truck'/*camions* 'trucks'). In addition, epenthetic vowels may appear with certain masculine plural forms (e.g., *gos* 'dog' vs. *gossos* 'dogs'). Orthographic conventions require that feminine plural be *-es* instead of *-as* (e.g. singular *casa* 'house' vs. plural *cases* 'houses'). Although irrelevant to spoken Standard Catalan (because of vowel reduction), this convention reflects the realization of feminine plural marking in all Western Catalan dialects.

Catalan has both definite and indefinite articles. They all inflect for gender and number, agree with the noun, and always precede it. The definite article may be realized as *el* (masculine singular), *la* (feminine singular), *els* (masculine plural) or *les* (feminine plural). Definite articles (or a special determiner: *en*, *na*) are also used before a proper name. In addition, some varieties of Catalan make use of a definite article which derives from Latin *ipse* (as opposed to *ille*): *es*, *sa*, *sos*, and *ses*. When definite singular articles are followed by vowels or are preceded by certain prepositions (such as *a* 'to' or *de* 'of, from', *per* 'for, by'), some orthographic conventions apply (e.g., masculine *a l'avi* 'to the grandfather' vs. *al pare* 'to the father'). The four variants of the indefinite article are: *un, una, uns, unes.*

Adjectives must agree with nouns in gender and number; feminine adjectives are obtained by adding *-a* to the masculine form, and plural adjectives by adding *-s* to the corresponding singular. However, some adjectives are invariant in form. Some numerals and a few quantifiers also bear gender and plural marking. In prenominal position, Catalan possessives require overt definite articles:

el	meu	país
the/M/SG	my/M/SG	country/M/SG

'my country'

la	meva	llengua
the/F/SG	my/F/SG	language/F/SG

'my language'

The demonstrative system in most dialects of Catalan shows a two-way distinction: *aquest(-a)* 'this' and *aquell(-a)* 'that' are the masculine (and feminine) singular forms, and *aquests* (*aquestes*) 'these' and *aquelles* (*aquelles*) 'those' are the corresponding plurals. These forms can appear as adjectives or pronouns; but pronominal neuter forms also exist (cf. *això* and *allò*). In some dialects a third intermediate distinction is made based on either of the following masculine singular forms: *eix* or *aqueix.*

Aside from those nouns which are case-marked by means of a preposition, personal pronouns are the only nominal expressions in Catalan which exhibit overt morphological case. Free (nominative) pronouns appear as the subject of the clause, and as the object of a preposition, but in the latter position, two first person singular forms (*mi* and *jo*) are used. Direct and indirect object pronouns are accusative and dative clitics which exhibit a high degree of allomorphy (according to their relative position and phonological environment). First and second person dative clitics are identical. Third person dative clitics (as opposed to accusative ones) do not have gender distinction.

Catalan reflexive pronouns are also clitics. They do not show gender features, and are identical to accusative and dative clitic forms in all but the third person (which uses a special form). Plural reflexive clitics may also have a reciprocal value. Other clitics include the partitive *en*, the neuter *ho*, and the locative *hi*.

Catalan verbs are marked for mood, tense, aspect, person and number features, and are classified into three conjugations according to the spelling of their infinitive ending (*-ar,-er/-re*, and *-ir*). Some verbs are very irregular with respect to this basic classification. All verbs exhibit both simple and compound forms. In their simple forms, all features are realized as a suffix (subject-verb agreement in person and number is obligatory), but suffixes are not discrete units themselves. Compound forms expressing aspect make use of auxiliary verbs and invariable participles: [*haver* 'to have' + past participle] encodes perfective aspect, and [*estar* 'to be' + present participle] yields progressive aspect. Passive voice is also expressed analytically by a verb (*ser* 'to be') and a past participle which agrees with the subject in gender and number features.

For a given verb, the inflectional paradigm involves four different mood features (indicative, conditional, subjunctive and imperative), three basic tenses (present, preterit, and future), aspect features (perfective), three person features (first, second, and third), and two number features (singular and plural). With regard to tense and aspect, Catalan also has a simple past imperfective, and a unique compound preterit made up of an auxiliary verb (*anar* 'to go') with present tense inflection and an infinitive. The compound preterit tense is semantically equivalent to the basic preterit tense and, in fact, it is the preferred one. The following are sample forms of the verb *cantar* 'to sing', inflected for first person singular:

Infinitive: *cantar*
Present participle: *cantant*
Past participle: *cantat*

	Indicative	Subjunctive
Present	canto	canti
Present Perfect	he cantat	hagi cantat
Imperfect	cantava	cantés
Pluperfect	havia cantat	hagués cantat
Preterit	cantí or vaig cantar	
Preterit Anterior	haguí cantat	
Future	cantaré	
Future Perfect	hauré cantat	
Conditional	cantaria	
Conditional Perfect	hauria cantat	

Basic Syntax

Catalan's most basic order of constituents is SVO. When a sentence contains both direct and indirect objects, the direct object usually precedes the indirect object. Other complements usually follow direct and indirect objects. Preverbal pronominal subjects are typically dropped (unless emphasis is intended). Passive constructions and subordinate clauses are also SVO.

Even though word order in Catalan is not fixed, certain changes of this basic SVO order correlate with changes in the discourse structure (postverbal subjects represent 'new' information, and preverbal objects represent 'old' information). When a dislocated constituent appears in preverbal position (e.g., OSV), the appropriate clitic (accusative, dative, partitive or locative) also occurs.

Clitics occupy a fixed position with respect to the verb. Cliticization may take place with direct objects, indirect objects (dative clitics), partitives, locatives, and copular predicates. In fact, cliticization of pronominal direct and indirect objects is always required, but free pronouns may simultaneously appear (with a preposition) to add clarification or emphasis. With regard to their distribution, clitics precede all finite verbs, but follow infinitives, gerunds and imperative forms:

la	cantaré
it/F/SG	sing/FUTURE/1SG

'I will sing it.'

canta-la
sing/IMPERATIVE/2SG-it/F/SG
'Sing it!'

Given these rules, there are two potential positions in some analytic verbal forms:

l'estic	cantant
it/F/SG-be/PRES/1SG	sing/PRES PART

'I am singing it.'

estic	cantant-la
be/PRES/1SG	sing/PRES PART-it/F/SG

Clitic allomorphy is very common and depends on the phonological environment and the clitic's relative position. For example, the second person singular clitic has the form *et* with the future tense of 'telephone' *et trucaré* '(I) will phone you' and *t* with the present perfect *t' he trucat* '(I) have phoned you'. With respect to the relative ordering of clitics, Catalan exhibits the following general pattern, in both preverbal and postverbal position: reflexive or reciprocal clitics precede all others; dative clitics precede accusative or partitive clitics; and, locative clitics follow all others. However, clitic sequences can never be split around the verb.

Other deviations from the SVO order arise within the context of yes-no questions, non-echo questions and relative clauses. Yes-no questions usually require the VOS order, and are always preceded by a special wh-word *que* [kə] which triggers a distinctive intonation (e.g., *que ha trucat el Joan?* 'has John called?').

Some other structures which consistently appear with postverbal subjects include a number of psychological verbs (*agradar* 'to like'), some intransitive verbs with indefinite subjects (e.g., verbs such as *arribar* 'to arrive'), and certain impersonal constructions. Existential and copular constructions also exhibit special patterns. Sentential negation in Catalan is basically expressed with *no*. *No* must precede the verb (including auxiliaries) and all preverbal clitics.

Even though Catalan is a descendant of head-final language, Catalan is basically head-initial: in the noun phrase, attributive adjectives usually follow nouns; in prepositional phrases, complements follow prepositions. However, other noun phrase complements (articles, demonstratives, numerals and quantificational expressions) always precede the noun. Possessives may appear in both prenominal and postnominal position.

Contact with Other Languages

Over the centuries Catalan has borrowed words from a number of languages. Some borrowings entered Catalan directly, but a few words from Germanic, Arabic, GREEK, HEBREW, and Native American languages did so indirectly. Given the long historical contact between Catalan and Spanish, Catalan has acquired a number of words and expressions from this language, which made (early) normalization efforts highly prescriptive. Borrowings from other neighboring languages (French, Italian, and Sardinian) are also common, but often restricted to one particular dialect. Over the course of the twentieth century, Catalan also incorporated many words from ENGLISH, but there are a few borrowings in Insular Catalan which date back to British invasions of Minorca during the eighteenth century (e.g., *pinxa* 'pilchard', *xoc* 'chalk'). Ongoing worldwide scientific research has also given rise to a relatively high number of neologisms in the language based on suffixes, prefixes and words from Latin and Greek (e.g., Latin: *auricular* 'receiver, headphone' or Greek: *telèfon* 'telephone').

Most borrowings have been completely naturalized, that is, they use native sounds, undergo Catalan's phonological processes, and also fall under standard orthographic conventions (certain related pairs may even reflect the various stages in the development of Catalan: Latin *estrictu* > *estret* 'narrow', vs. *estricte* 'strict'). Modern borrowings often compete with native words (e.g., Sp. *sombrero* vs. Cat. *barret* 'hat'; or Sp. *sombra* vs. Cat. *ombra* 'shade') and they are often discouraged by prescriptive grammarians. Due to the fact that speakers of Catalan are bilingual, a few borrowings also maintain sounds which are otherwise foreign to the language (e.g. Sp. *jefe* 'boss' is pronounced as ['xefə]).

From Ibero-Basque: *estalviar* 'to save', *isard* 'wild goat'
From Celtic: *trencar* 'to break', *tancar* 'to close'
From Latin: *rotund* 'definite, clear', *estricte* 'strict'
From Germanic: *blau* 'blue', *guerra* 'war'
From Arabic: *albergínia* 'eggplant', *arròs* 'rice'
From Mozarabic: *baldriga* 'puffin', place names: *Elx, Muro*
From Greek: *església* 'church', *escola* 'school'
From Provençal: *coratge* 'courage', *espasa* 'sword'
From Gascon: *auca* 'goose', *milloc* 'corn'
From French: *jardí* 'garden', *missatge* 'message'
From Sardinian: *anca* 'leg', *murendu* 'donkey'
From Italian: *escopeta* 'shotgun', *partitura* 'musical score'
From Spanish: *borratxo* 'drunk', *xoriço* 'chorizo'
From English: *bistec* 'beef steak', *futbol* 'football'

Common Words

man:	home	long:	llarg
woman:	dona	small:	petit
water:	aigua	yes:	sí
sun:	sol	no:	no
three:	tres	good:	bo
fish:	peix	bird:	ocell
big:	gran	dog:	gos
tree:	arbre		

Example Sentences

[Note: Since all tenses in the examples below are of the Indicative Mood, this feature has been omitted from the glosses.]

(1)

Avui,	el	Pere	anirá	amb	cotxe
Today,	the/M/SG	Peter	go/FUT/3SG	with	car

a	casa	dels	seus	avis.
to	house	of/the/M/PL	his/M/PL	grandparents.

'Today, Peter will go by car to his grandparents' house.'

(2)

Ella	et	va	escriure	una	carta,
She	you/DAT/2SG	go/PRES/3SG	write/INF	a/F/SG	letter

però	no	te	la	va	enviar.
but	not	you/DAT/2SG	it/ACC/3F/SG	go/PRES/3SG	send/INF

'She wrote you a letter, but she didn't send it.'

(3) Quin llibre vols comprar-li
which/M/SG book want/PRES/2SG buy/INF-3SG/DAT

a la Rosa?
to the/F/SG Rose?
'Which book do you want to buy for Rosa?'

Efforts to Preserve, Protect, and Promote the Language

Following Catalan's official recognition by the Spanish Constitution in 1978 and the creation of autonomous administrations, the language received institutional support and legal protection, particularly in Catalonia. During the 1980s, efforts were focused on "normalization," to restore Catalan to public life.

In Catalonia, the initial efforts were directed towards creating an updated grammar. This task (which had been initiated before the Spanish Civil War) was mainly carried out at research institutions such as the *Institut d'Estudis Catalans.* The prescriptive grammar started a lively debate among native speakers and was extensively documented in the press. In order to promote the language, Catalonia's autonomous administration created the 'Directorate General for Linguistic Policy' (1980), an office whose major task was to extend the knowledge and use of Catalan in public and private institutions; it approved the *Llei de Normalització Lingüística* (1983), a law whereby Catalan was given priority as the official language of administration and was promoted as the language of education. It also supported the creation of a center for ongoing terminological research in Catalan, TERMCAT (1985), whose major role has been to extend the knowledge and use of Catalan among the scientific, technical and professional communities. Thanks to these institutional efforts, Catalan has been gradually restored to the public domain, and it is now used in the media and at all levels of instruction. Although knowledge and use of Catalan are not compulsory in Catalonia, the efforts outlined above have made the language accessible to non-native speakers of Catalan, and currently the number of monolingual Spanish speakers living in Catalonia is relatively small. To a certain extent, similar efforts have been made and comparable results achieved in the two other autonomous communities of Spain.

In the Principality of Andorra, Catalan enjoys official protection and status as the national language. In the Catalan-speaking areas of France and Italy, Catalan does not receive comparable official protection. However, there have been efforts by the native communities to establish cultural relations with Catalan-speaking areas of Spain. Local officials from *Perpinyà* (France) and Catalonia's Department of Culture signed a special agreement (1987) to carry out cultural exchanges through the *Museu Puig-CEDACC* (Catalan Culture Documentation and Activities Center). In Alghero (Sardinia), in spite of being the smallest and most isolated of all Catalan-speaking territories, Catalan is still the native language and there have been efforts to offer language instruction at schools (and two universities), and to promote literary production and publications.

At the international level, numerous associations and institutions have been actively engaged in the study of Catalan language and culture for many decades, for example, the *Anglo-Catalan Society* (1954), the *Associació Internacional de Llengua i Literatura Catalanes* (1973), the *North-American Catalan Society* (1978), the *Associazione Italiana di Studi Catalani* (1978), the *Deutsch-Katalanische Gesellschaft* (1983), and the *Association Française des Catalanistes* (1990) among others. The promotion of Catalan abroad has resulted in the European Parliament's official recognition of Catalan as a language of the European Community (1990), and the adoption of Catalan as one of the official languages at the Barcelona Olympic Games (1992) and at the United Nations (1993).

According to 1994 statistics, in Catalonia, while only 30% of people between ages 30 and 50 can write Catalan, 80% of young people between ages 20 and 30 can write it (and 90% of these young people also read it). These figures illustrate not only the remarkable progress made in the teaching of Catalan, but also Catalan's current potential for full recovery.

Select Bibliography

Alcover, A.M., and F. de B. Moll. 1926–1968. *Diccionari Català-Valencià-Balear*. Palma de Mallorca, 10 vols.

Aracil, LL.V. 1982. *Papers de sociolingüística*. Barcelona: La Magrana.

Badia, A. 1962. *Gramàtica Catalana*. Madrid: Gredos.

Cabré, M.T. & G. Rigau. 1985. *Lexicologia i semàntica*. Barcelona: Enciclopèdia Catalana.

Coromines, J. 1980. *Diccionari etimològic i complementari de la llengua catalana*. Barcelona: Curial.

Diccionari de la llengua catalana. 1982. Barcelona: Enciclopèdia Catalana.

Fabra, P. 1983. *Diccionari general de la llengua catalana*, 17th ed. Barcelona: Edhasa.

_____. 1956. *Gramàtica catalana*. Barcelona: Teide.

Gili, J. 1974. *Catalan Grammar*. Oxford Dolphin Book.

Hualde, J.I. 1992. *Catalan*. New York: Routledge.

Massip, A., and C. Duarte. 1981. *Síntesi d'història de la llengua catalana*. Barcelona: La Magrana.

Martí, M. 1985. *Gramàtica catalana: curs superior*. Barcelona: Edhasa.

Mascaró, J. 1987. *Morfologia*. 2nd. ed. Barcelona: Enciclopèdia Catalana.

Nadal, J.M. & M. Prats. 1982. *Història de la llengua catalana*. Barcelona: Edicions 62.

Oliva, S. & A. Buxton. 1983. *Diccionari Anglès-Català*. Barcelona: Enciclopèdia Catalana.

_____. 1985. *Diccionari Català-Anglès*. Barcelona: Enciclopèdia Catalana.

Ruaix, J. 1976–1980. *El català en fitxes*, 3 vols. Moià: J. Ruaix.

Solà, J. 1972–1973. *Estudis de sintaxi catalana*. 2 vols. Barcelona: Edicions 62.

Veny, J. 1989. *Els parlars catalans: síntesi de dialectolgia*. 8th ed. Palma de Mallorca: Moll.

Wheeler, M. 1979. *Phonology of Catalan*. Oxford: Blackwell.

Yates, A. 1984. *Catalan*. London: Teach Youself Books.

Cebuano

John U. Wolff

Language Name: Cebuano. **Alternates:** Visayan, Bisayan, Cebuano Visayan, Sugbuanon. **Autonyms:** *Binisayáʔ, Sibuwánu, sugbuʔánun.*

Location: Central Philippines (islands of Cebu and Bohol, and on the smaller islands in the vicinity).

Family: Bisayan subgroup of the Central Philippine group of the Western Malayo-Polynesian branch of the Austronesian language family.

Related Languages: TAGALOG, HILIGAYNON, BIKOL, and the other languages in the Philippine group. Cebuano is more distantly related to MALAY, outside of the Philippines.

Dialects: Cebuano is marked by a certain amount of dialectal variation which is regionally based. The dialect spoken in Cebu City is the most influential.

Number of Speakers: 12 million.

Origin and History

Cebuano or an ancestor of this language has probably been spoken in the Cebu heartland since Proto-Austronesian times, perhaps 6,000 years ago. This is not to say that Cebuano has likely passed in an unbroken tradition from the earliest times up to the present. Internal evidence and a study of ongoing developments of Cebuano and other languages of the Philippines reveals that Cebuano, like the other languages of the region, has developed by repeated processes of overlay, whereby a closely related language (or even a not so closely related language) comes to the area and replaces the language originally spoken and receives substantial substratal influence from the language replaced. Alternatively, the introduced language does not replace the original language but alters it significantly. Cebuano has spread from its base in Cebu to adjacent areas, probably in the last few hundred years, and has replaced closely related languages which were spoken there. Dialectal differentiation is largely due to the influence of languages which were replaced.

The first recorded text in Cebuano is a word list gathered in Cebu by Pigafetta, the chronicler who accompanied Magellan on his trip westward in search of the Spice Islands in 1521. The Spaniards returned to Cebu in 1564, and beginning a few years after this time, the first catechisms were prepared. The word lists and grammars date from the following century, although the printed versions of these materials appear only in the eighteenth century. None of the indigenous literature has survived in published form, although there is a certain amount of orally transmitted material which has an unbroken history predating the Spanish Conquest. There is almost no published literature prior to the twentieth century, and the only earlier specimens of the languages come from catechisms, or other religious texts, or sample sentences in grammars and dictionaries. Earlier grammars and dictionaries reveal that the language has undergone rapid changes in the course of the last four centuries. The sample sentences in the older sources show numerous grammatical forms which are not known nowadays. Many entries in the earlier dictionaries are for words which no one seems to know today, and many of the old folk songs and older religious texts use grammatical forms which are not part of the colloquial language but, rather, are used in elevated literary styles.

Dialects: The Cebu City dialect is spreading throughout the Cebuano speech area. Cebuano speakers note dialects which drop /l/ between two /a/'s, two /u/'s, between an /a/ and a /u/, or between a /u/ and an /a/, and dialects which retain /l/ in those environments. The isoglosses which mark these phono-

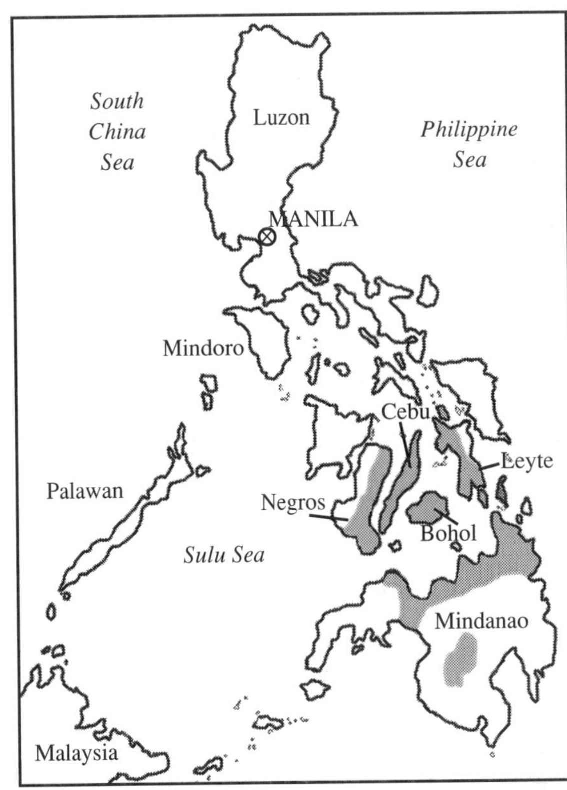

Cebuano is spoken on the islands of Cebu and Bohol as well as in areas of the surrounding islands (shaded areas).

Table 1: Consonants

		Bilabial	Dental	Palatal	Velar	Glottal
Stops	Voiceless	p	t	c	k	ʔ
	Voiced	b	d	j	g	
Fricatives			s			h
Nasals		m	n		ŋ	
Liquids			l, r			
Glides				y	w	

logical features coincide with numerous other isoglosses involving lexical items or morphological features. The l-dropping dialects extend on the island of Cebu from an area immediately to the south of Cebu City northward throughout the island, over the island of Bohol, and over the areas of Leyte which are Cebuano-speaking. The Cebuano areas to the south of Cebu City and those on Mindanao and Negros are l-retaining. There are other dialectal differences which the community does not remark on overtly, but which are important phonologically and distinguish rustic dialects from sophisticated dialects. One of the most important is the merging of /e/ and /u/, which has taken place throughout the Cebuano speech area except in pockets or speech-islands which preserve /e/, although not necessarily in all forms which formerly had /e/. Also, there are areas in which /e/ is preserved in the speech of certain groups or classes. That is, in some areas, /e/ still remains in some words but is a stylistic marker.

Orthography and Basic Phonology

The Cebuano alphabet is based on the Roman one. All sounds are written, with the exception of the glottal stop /ʔ/, which is written with a dash (-), but only following a consonant. Some sounds are written with combinations of two letters: /ŋ/ is written *ng*, as in English; /c/ is written *ts*; and /j/, *dy*. The vowel /i/ can be written either *i* or *e*, and /u/ can be written either *u* or *o*. Stress is not indicated.

The palatals /c/ and /j/ are phonetically affricates [č] and [j].

Table 2: Vowels

	Front	Central	Back
High	i		u
Low		a	

Dialectally there is a central vowel /e/ which is inherited from Proto-Austronesian *e, but in standard Cebuano /e/ has merged with /u/. The height of /i/ and /u/ is variable according to dialect. Also there is a tendency for lower allophones to occur in final syllables. /a/ tends to be pronounced centrally and quite low, although in some dialects there is a slight tendency to front /a/. Backing and rounding of /a/ is not known, except in the speech of speakers who affect an ENGLISH (American) accent.

Stress and Length. Where /l/ has been lost between like vowels (see ***Dialects***, above), there is compensatory lengthening in the penult or final syllable (but not earlier in the word). Dialects with l-loss thus show contrast between long and short vowels in the penult or final syllable, although this does not have a high functional load. For example, in the l-dropping dialects *nagdalá* 'brought' is pronounced *nagdáa* (where writing two vowels indicates length), but if the /l/ is lost in an earlier syllable there is no compensatory lengthening: *ʔuluʔasáwa* 'concubine' is pronounced *ʔuʔasáwa* (with short /u/) in the l-dropping dialects. Since l-loss occurs between two /u/'s and two /a/'s but not between two /i/'s, there is no long /i/. There are only a long /u/ and a long /a/.

Every word has a stress, either on the final syllable or on the penult. All long vowels are stressed. If the penult is closed, the stress is automatically on the penult, except in the case of loan words. Stress on the open penult causes the vowel to be lengthened.

Phonological Rules. With one exception all syllables in forms not recent borrowings from Spanish or English have the shape C_1(r)V(C_2). C_2 may be any consonant but /h/. Further, except in dialects C_2 may not be /ʔ/ except at the end of the word and in reduplicated roots—that is, roots with the shape C_1VʔC_1Vʔ. Phonetically sequences with Cy and Cw also occur, but these are phonologically analyzable as Ciy and Cuw respectively, for there is no contrast between [Cy] and [Ciy] and between [Cw] and [Cuw]. The canonical shape C_1(r)V(C_2) states that no syllable begins with a vowel. There is no contrast between word initial /ʔ/ and its absence, and words that are written with initial vowel do in fact have initial /ʔ/ phonemically and phonetically. The canonical shape C_1(r)V(C_2) also states that no sequences of vowels occur. When a suffix beginning with a vowel is added to roots ending with a vowel, /ʔ/ or /h/ is added to the root before the suffix. (Whether /h/ or /ʔ/ is added depends on the root. In some cases both may be alternatively added; e.g., *gustu* 'like' + *-an* yields *gustuhán* or alternatively *gustuʔán* 'like something'.) Roots are typically disyllabic or occasionally trisyllabic. The exception to the canonical shape of the syllable is that names can be made diminutive and endearing by a morphological process which uses the a single syllable of the name and adds a suffix *-s*. This has produced syllables ending in Cs. /s/ is assimilated to preceding voiced consonants. For example, the name *ʔída* 'Ida' may be shortened to /ʔid/ and then made diminutive by adding *-s* forming /ʔids/ pronounced [ʔidz].

The stress pattern of a morphologically complex form is the same as the stress pattern of the root (except in the case of morphological formations in which the shift of stress from the penult to the end or from the end to the penult is part of the morphological process). Thus *bása* 'read' has penultimate stress, and when it adds *-un* the resulting form is *basáhun* 'read it' where the stress remains on the penult of the resulting word.

Historically, stress was forceful and tended to weaken the

Table 3: Primary Affixes

Voice (case)	Past	Future	Tenseless
active volitional	*mipalít* 'bought'	*mupalít* 'will buy'	*mupalít/ palít* 'buy'
active non-volitional	*nagpalít* 'bought'	*magpalít* 'will buy'	*magpalít* 'buy'
active progressive	*nagapalít* 'is buying'	*magapalít* 'will be buying'	*magapalít* 'be buying'
direct passive	*gipalít* 'bought it'	*palitún* 'will buy it'	*palitá* 'buy it'
local passive	*gipalitán* 'bought from it'	*palitán* 'will buy from it'	*palití* 'buy from it'
conveyance passive	*gipalít* 'used it to buy/buy for him'	*ʔipalít* 'will use to buy, etc.'	*ʔipalít* 'use to buy, etc.'

vowel of a syllable preceding the stressed syllable, which became lost in rapid speech or in morphological processes. This feature reflects itself in the process whereby common forms (pronouns, deictics and the like) tend to lose the first syllable in colloquial speech. (E.g., *kamí* 'we (not you)' tends to be pronounced /mi/, with loss of the /a/ of the first syllable and loss of the initial /k-/ to avoid the resulting non-occurring consonant sequence; *niʔíni* 'this (genitive)' tends to be pronounced /ʔíni/, and so forth. In the morphophonemics of word formation, the same type of phonological rule applies: the vowel of an open penult is lost when the final syllable of the word is stressed, but earlier syllables in the word are not lost. Thus, when *-un* is added to *putúl* 'cut' the resulting form is *pútlun* 'cut it', where the penultimate vowel of the resulting word is lost. The stress then shifts from the final syllable to the penultimate, by the rule that closed penults must have the stress.

Metathesis is common in affixational processes, especially involving nasals, /s/, /ʔ/. and /h/. E.g. *tanúm* 'plant' plus *+an* produces *támnan* (with loss of the /u/ plus metathesis) 'plant on it'; *putús* 'wrap' plus *-un* produces *pústun* 'wrap it'; *gabíʔi* 'night' plus *hi-án* produces *higabiʔhán* 'get overtaken by nightfall (on the road or the like)' dialectally, and in the Cebuano of Cebu City produces metathesized *higabhiʔán*.

Basic Morphology

Noun (and Adjective) Morphology. There is no inflectional noun or adjective morphology—that is, there is no inflection for number, case, agreement, or gender in nouns and adjectives. There is an extensive and productive system of affixes which derive nouns and adjectives from roots of given semantic classes. All forms in the sentence are marked for case: nominative, genitive or dative/locative. In all classes of words except for the pronouns case is indicated by separate particles which precede the word marked. E.g. *babáyi* 'woman' *ʔaŋ babáyi* (nominative) and *sa babáyi* (genitive); *Huwán* 'John' *si Huwán* (nominative), *ni Huwán* (genitive), *kaŋ Huwán* (dative). The pronouns mark case inflectionally—that is, by special case forms, e.g. the first person singular 'I' *akú* or *ku* (nominative), *ku* or *náku?* (genitive), *áku?* (preposed genitive), and *kanáku?* or *náku?* (dative). Case relations are additionally expressed by verbal inflection (see directly below).

Verb Morphology. Verb morphology is elaborate, as is the case of all the Philippine languages, and the Cebuano verb system is in many ways similar to that of other Philippine languages. There is a small series of primary (inflectional) affixes and a fairly large number of productive secondary affixes. Secondary affixes indicate things like causation, potentiality, mutual action (involving two agents whose activities devolve on one another), plurality, accidental action, and other categories not describable in some simple way. The primary affixes indicate tense, aspect (or lack thereof), volitionality or inchoativeness, and case (the relation between the verb and a word to which it is oriented as the location, the direct object of the action, the time of the action, the place of the action, the beneficiary of the action, the thing conveyed in a direction away from the speaker, and other semantic relations not easily characterizable in simple terms). Table 3 above shows the primary affixes added to an unaffixed root. The tense meanings conveyed by the translations here only approximate the Cebuano meanings. The tenseless forms are used when the verb is preceded by another form which shows time or tense (e.g. the deictics, as shown below). We take *palít* 'buy' as our paradigm.

These affixes undergo complicated morphophonemic changes when added to stems which consist of a root plus some of the derivative affixes (but in the case of other derived stems, the inflectional affixes are added agglutinatively; they do not undergo morphophonemic alternations). Tables 4 and 5 on the next page show the paradigm of *papalít* 'cause to buy' (consisting of *pa-* plus *palít*, in which the inflectional affixes are added in an agglutinative way) and the root plus a potential derivative affix (in which the inflectional affixes combine with the derivational affixes with complex morphophonemics, so that neither is recoverable).

Other Information on Morphology: The deictics (particles meaning "here, there, where") are inflected for tense and motion. When following the phrase modified, the deictics distinguish the meaning "motion" from "non-motion" and for expressing the meaning "non-motion" use the form which is the same as the past tense form. When preceding the phrase modified, the deictics have tense meaning, but the meaning "motion" is not distinguished in this position, and the motion form does not occur preceding the word modified:

	Past	Present	Future	Motion
here (near me)	dirí	díʔa	arí	ngarí
here (near you and me)	dinhi	níʔa	ánhi	ngánhi
there (near you)	dihá?	náʔa	ánhaʔ	ngánhaʔ
there (far)	dídtu	túʔa	ádtu	ngádtu
where	diʔín	háʔin	ʔása	(none)

Basic Syntax

The syntax of Cebuano, as is the case of all Philippine languages and in fact most of the Austronesian languages, is such that every word is free to occur in every grammatical construction—that is, there are subjects, predicates, and modifiers

Table 4: The Causative Paradigm with *pa-*

Voice (case)	Past	Future	Tenseless
active	*nagpapalít* 'had someone buy'	*magpapalít* 'will have someone buy'	*magpapalít/papalit* 'have someone buy'
direct passive	*gipapalít* 'had him/her buy'	*papalitún* 'will have him/ her buy'	*papalitá* 'have him/her buy'
local passive	*gipapalitán* 'had someone buy from'	*papalitán* 'will have someone buy from'	*papalití* 'have someone buy from'
conveyance passive	*gipapalít* ' 'had it bought'	*ʔipapalít* 'will have it bought'	*ʔipapalít* 'have it bought'

Table 5: The Potential Paradigm

Voice (case)	Past	Future	Tenseless
active	*nakapalít* 'managed to buy'	*makapalít* 'can buy'	*makapalít* 'can buy'
direct passive	*napalít* 'happened to buy it'	*mapalít* 'can buy it'	*mapalít* 'can buy it'
local passive	*napapalitán* 'happened to buy from'	*mapalitán/kapalitán* 'can buy from'	*mapalitán/kapalitan* 'can buy from'
conveyance passive	*gikapalít* 'managed to use it to buy'	*ʔikapalít* 'can use it to buy'	*ʔikapalít* 'can use it to buy'

of various sorts and each word is free to occur in all three of those types of constructions without undergoing any morphological process. For example, a verb may modify a noun and when it does so it is not morphologically marked (that is, the verb is not transformed into something like a participle, as would be the case in Indo-European languages). There is no morphology which marks case, gender, number, or agreement, except that there are special verb derivations which refer to plural stems of various semantic types.

Cebuano has full words and particles which mark or modify full words. The markers are a small number which show grammatical relations (e.g. case, see above). Other particles are words which precede the full word they modify and those which follow them. Those which precede are the words meaning 'no' *díliʔ* and *waláʔ* and auxiliaries such as *kinahánglan* 'must', *mahímu* 'can', *gústu* 'want to', and a few others. Post-posed modifiers carry time or aspectual meanings or kinds of meanings carried by intonation in English. A sample list of some of these: *pa* 'still', *na* 'completed action', *gayúd* 'for sure', *man* 'because', *bítaw* 'you're right', *lagí* 'it is so the case', and so forth. Full words can only be modified if they are in the predicate.

Case Marking of Major Constituents. Full words can occur in any of the six types of construction which occur in Cebuano sentences: subject or theme, predicate (subject, theme, and predication are marked by the nominative case), attribute or appositive (marked by a linking particle *ŋa* (alternatively *ŋ*), complement (marked by *sa* for specific complements and *ʔug* for nonspecific complements), genitive (marked by *ni* in the case of proper nouns or *sa* for all other forms) and dative/locative (marked by *kaŋ* in the case of the proper nouns or *sa* for all other forms).

The **order of constituents** is free except that length of constituent influences the word order and complements and genitive follow the forms they are in a phrase with. (There is also an alternative genitive which is placed immediately preceding the forms it is in a phrase with). However, there is a normal unmarked order, and other word orders thematicize or topicalize. The normal basic order is predicate + subject +dative/ locative/time phrase: *gipalít ni Huwán ʔaŋ líbru gahápun* (bought–it GEN John NOM book yesterday) 'John bought the book yesterday.'

The other alternative orders are also possible, but they thematicize the element put first: Time Predicate Subject, Time Subject Predicate, Subject Predicate Time, Subject Time Predicate, and Predicate Time Subject (although the latter two are unusual). Further, modifying particles and all pronouns except dative forms must occur immediately following the first word of the predicate or a time/location/dative form which comes ahead of the predicate. Thus for example, the above sentence could also have the Time phrase first (with an appropriate change in the verb form): *gahápun palitá ni Huwán ʔaŋ líbru* (yesterday bought–it GEN John NOM book) 'Yesterday John bought the book.'

If a pronoun is substituted for *ni Huwan*, e.g., *níya* 'he (genitive)', then *níya* must come immediately after *gahápun* 'yesterday' or as close after it as possible: *gahápun níya palitá ʔaŋ líbru* 'Yesterday he bought the book.'

If a modifying particle comes with the predicate, it is placed next to the preceding time-phrase or as close after it as possible: *gahápun pa níya palitá ʔaŋ líbru* (yesterday already bought–it he.GEN NOM book) 'Yesterday he bought the book.' If a pronoun is substituted for *ʔang líbru* 'the book', e.g., *naʔ* 'that (nominative)', then *naʔ* must come immediately after *gahápun* 'yesterday' or as close after it as possible: *Gahápun naʔ níya palitá*. 'It was yesterday he bought that.'

Head Initial or Head-final Nature. For appositions or adjectival constructions there is no set order, and it is impossible to say which of the two or more forms in the phrase is the head. For example, in a phrase meaning 'the big house', the form meaning 'big' can come first or second: *ʔaŋ dakú ŋ baláy* 'the big thing that is a house' or *ʔaŋ baláy ŋ dakúʔ* 'the house that is big.' Another example: for 'the book I asked him to buy', the phrase meaning 'I asked him to buy' can come first or second: *ʔaŋ gipapalít náku? níya ŋ líbru* 'the thing which I had him buy which was a book' or *ʔaŋ líbru ŋ gipapalít náku? níya* 'the book which I asked him to buy.'

Numerals must precede the words they modify, however. In the following phrase the word for 'two' *duhá* must come first: *duhá ka libru* /two linker book/ 'two books.'

Negation. There are two negatives: *waláʔ* (past, present verbs and location) and *díliʔ* (future verbs, adjectives, and nouns). Since *waláʔ* with verbs indicates past time, the tenseless form of the verb follows all verbs modified with *waláʔ*, as for example the form *palitá* 'buy' which is tenseless in the following example: *waláʔ palitá ni Huwán ʔaŋ líbru* (NEG–PAST buy–it GEN John NOM book) 'John didn't buy the book.'

Common Words

water:	túbig	sun:	ʔádlaw
fish:	ʔísdaʔ	big:	dakúʔ
long:	taʔás	good:	maʔáyu
bird:	lánggam	dog:	ʔirúʔ
tree:	káhuy	woman:	babáyi
yes:	ʔúʔu		
no:	waláʔ (past tense, there is not), díliʔ (otherwise)		
man:	laláki (male), táwu (human)		
small:	gamáy (in size), jútay (in amount)		

Contact with Other Languages

Cebuano is in contact with Tagalog, the language of the capital city of the Philippines and one of the national languages of the Philippines, and this language exercises an influence on Cebuano greater than any other. The strongest influence is felt in urban areas, especially where there is a considerable population of Tagalog speakers, immigrants from Luzon or their descendents, as is the case in Davao City. In these areas both Tagalog and Cebuano are widely spoken, and much of the Cebuano-speaking population is bilingual in both languages. Further, Tagalog exercises a strong influence on the Cebuano in urban areas indirectly even where the Tagalog-speaking population is small, as the Tagalog speakers who come to Cebuano areas invariably form the top stratum of society: they are the best off and have the best jobs, and they are thus seen as prestigeful. These Tagalog speakers learn Cebuano, because it is the only language in which one can socialize, but their grammar is always strongly influenced by Tagalog, either in that they fail to make distinctions lacking in Tagalog but present in Cebuano or in that they substitute Tagalog forms for Cebuano. The new forms which arise from this foreign Cebuano get imitated by the local population, as those who speak this way make up the most highly regarded stratum of the community. In this manner urban Cebuano has changed substantially in its grammar over the past forty years.

In comparison with Tagalog, English has had a much more superficial influence. English is widely used in many domains and has the function of the high code in the diglossic situation, so that in social situations its use is confined to code switches. Further, English as spoken in the Philippines has lost much of English phonology and in some ways has been accommodated to Philippines grammar or semantic categories. Thus English influences Cebuano primarily at the lexical level—that is, Cebuano is replete with loan words from English, but there has been no influence from English on any other plane.

In the past, starting with the period of the first Spanish contacts in the sixteeenth century until approximately World War II, Cebuano was in contact with SPANISH. There was a influential population of native speakers of Spanish present in the Cebuano-speaking areas, the mestizos, who were natively bilingual with Cebuano as well. This population had considerable money and power and to be known to be or thought to be Spanish-speaking was a source of great pride. This led to considerable importation of Spanish words, including some of the most intimate and frequently occurring forms, for one could give the impression of being a Spanish speaker by brief code switches into Spanish or by borrowing Spanish words where possible. As a result Cebuano has heavy borrowing from Spanish, especially in the urban dialects, and unlike English, which developed no mestizo community, Spanish provides Cebuano with words for some of the forms which are most frequent in occurrence and most important for the flow of the discourse. As is the case with English, Spanish in the Philippines lost much of its original phonology and was accommodated in some ways to Philippine grammar or semantic categories. Thus the influence of Spanish, like that of English, was mainly in the area of the lexicon.

Cebuano is also in contact with smaller languages because Cebuano is a lingua franca in many of the multi-lingual areas of Mindanao. The smaller languages seem to have exercised little influence on Cebuano, but it is likely that Cebuano has influenced them. The extent of Cebuano influence on these languages has not been studied. In many areas of Mindanao Cebuano immigrants have moved into areas where the population speaks minority languages, and some of these languages have lost a large portion of their speakers to Cebuano.

Cebuano currently borrows from Tagalog and English. Beginning with the first Spanish contacts in the sixteenth century, Cebuano borrowed heavily from Spanish. Prior to the Spanish influence there was influence from Malay via Tagalog and SANSKRIT via JAVANESE, Malay, and Tagalog. There also has been a small amount of borrowing from Hokkien CHINESE.

The earliest Spanish borrowings reveal that Cebuano had a simpler phonology than it currently has, e.g. the phoneme /r/ did not exist. Thus we get *húdnuʔ* 'stove' from Spanish *horno*. (This also shows that the Spanish /h/ was pronounced.) Another example showing the lack of /r/ is *ámbi* 'give me' (from Spanish *a ver* 'let me see'). Later borrowings also tend to be naturalized, but the language now has /r/, /c/, and /j/ which have developed in Cebuano through phonological changes in historical times. Loanwords are also naturalized into the inflectional and derivational system of Cebuano. For example Spanish *maldito* "naughty" is borrowed into Cebuano as *maldítu*. This borrowed root can be affixed to form a verb stem like any adjective of a similar semantic class, e.g. with the infix *-in-* plus shift of stress to form a verb stem *minalditú* 'act naughty'. The verb stem can then have the inflectional affixes added to it, e.g. *nagminalditú* 'is being naughty'. The loan words are also naturalized into the Cebuano semantic system—that is, they are understood to cover the meanings of equivalent native words and often veer strongly from the original range of meanings in the donating language. For example Cebuano *láʔ in* 'another' can also mean 'bad.' When the English word 'another' is borrowed into Cebuano, it can mean 'different, another' or it can mean 'bad': *bíri ʔanádir naʔ si Bíŋbiŋ* (very different[bad] that NOM Bingbing) 'That Bingbing woman is not very nice.'

Recent borrowings reflect the status of English and Tagalog as widely-spoken, over-arching languages. Forms are borrowed not only for items and concepts which have been introduced but also as a reflection of the use of English and Tagalog as communicative codes for much of the population or English as the language of public signs. Thus we get *inrúl* 'enroll (in school)' *ispíliŋ* 'spelling, make sense of something', *blákhart* 'spades (in cards)' *báskit* 'basketball', etc., from cultural or technical domains and *dúnat íntir* 'one-way street' (from 'Do Not Enter'), *diʔín* 'the end' etc. from signs and *istrít* 'vote a straight ticket', *didikít* 'dedicate (a musical number on the radio)', *ríjun* 'region', *ilijibúl* 'civil service eligible', *ʔakampaniʔíŋ* 'family member or servant who stays with a patient in the hospital ward' etc., reflecting the use of English in public life. We also have borrowings from English and Tagalog which are used where native forms exist as well, usually to create a humorous tone or key, as for example *bíri ʔanádir* 'not nice' quoted above, where the native *láʔin kaʔáyu* is also available or Tagalog *waláŋ takwal* 'flat broke', *siráʔ* 'crazy' and so forth. All of these forms set a joking key. The use of English and Tagalog as communicative codes among much of the Cebuano-speaking population is beginning to affect the phonology. Cebuano has added consonant clusters with /l/ and /r/ from English borrowings with these clusters, e.g. *blákhart* 'spades (in cards)', which show a cluster with /l/ and /rC/, formerly not occurring in Cebuano. Tagalog may possibly be affecting Cebuano in a major way: there is some evidence that the Tagalog distinction between /u/ and /o/ and between /i/ and /e/ is being carried over in Tagalog loans used in Cebuano by some younger speakers, at least sporadically, but this matter has not been investigated in detail.

Although Spanish did not have as wide a currency in Cebuano society as English and Tagalog now have, Spanish loan words show analogous characteristics—that is, they reflect not only words in certain technical or cultural domains, but also the fact that Spanish was spoken a second language in certain circles of the Cebuano speech community. Thus we have technical or introduced cultural terms: *dúbla* 'ringing of church bells' *tilipunú* 'telephone', *intabládu* 'stage' *turbinádu* 'granualted brown sugar', *dunsílya* 'virgin' *disgrasyáda* 'woman who had a baby out of wedlock' *báhu disisiyún* 'bound by one's husband's decision', and we also have words for which there existed Cebuano words and which show that Spanish was a second language in some circles: *asyúsu* 'finicky, hoity-toity', *múcu diníru* 'rich', *bunítu* 'good looking', and the adjective formers *-ádu* and *-íru,* which occur in numerous words of Hispanic origin referring to negative personal characteristics and have become productive and added to roots of native origin as well, e.g., *palikíru* 'womanizer' (of Hispanic origin) and *babayíru* 'womanizer' (with a native root). Further, there was a mestizo community in Cebuano areas which spoke Philippine Spanish natively as well as Cebuano. The existence of this group has led to the borrowing of forms of high frequency and high importance for the discourse like *píru* 'but', *purʔísu* 'therefore', *miyíntras tántu* 'in the meantime', *ísti* 'hesitation particle', etc.

From Malay: *putliʔ* 'pure' (<Malay *putri* 'honorable woman', ultimately <Sanskrit), *pangádyiʔ* 'pray', *bárang* 'kind of sorcery involving bugs', *salátan* 'south wind'
From Spanish: *dubla* 'ringing of church bells', *tilipunú* 'telephone', *intabládu* 'stage', *turbinádu* 'granulated brown sugar', *dunsílya* 'virgin'
From English: *báywan tíkwan* 'buy one, get one free', *imbúyis* 'invoice', *dúnat qíntir* 'one-way street', *didikít* 'dedicate (a number on the radio)'
From Chinese (Hokkien): *husí* 'ramie cloth', *búysit* 'bad luck', *púthaw* 'iron', *bákyaʔ* 'wooden slippers'

Efforts to Preserve, Protect, and Promote the Language

Cebuano has traditionally had little prestige and few proponents. There is one Cebuano-language weekly periodical, *Bisaya,* which has had a commercial success over the past forty years, and there has always been a small number of intellectuals who have been committed to developing and preserving Cebuano and have published in this periodical. Most of what is published in this periodical, however, is commercial in nature and aimed at the amusement of the uneducated groups who do not read English easily. The majority of Cebuano intellectuals publish in English, and few in the population have much interest in Cebuano as a language or see its importance as a vehicle of the native culture.

Select Bibliography

Bell, Sarah J. 1979. *Cebuano Subjects in Two Frameworks.* Bloomington: Indiana University Linguistics Series.

Cabonce, Rodolfo. 1983. *An English-Cebuano Visasyan Dictionary.* Manila: National Book Store.

Encarnacion, Juan Felix de la, R.P. Fr. 1885. *Diccionarario Bisaya-Español.* Third Edition. Manila.

Mojares, Resil B. 1977. *Bibliography of Cebuano Linguistics.* University of San CArlos, Cebu City.

Wolff, John U. 1961. *Cebuano Texts with Glossary and Grammar.* Mimeographed, Cebu City.

____. 1966-7. *Beginning Cebuano, Parts I and II.* New Haven: Yale University Press.

____. 1972. *A Cebuano Visayan Dictionary.* Linguistic Society of the Philippines, Monograph No. 3 and Southeast Asian Program, Data Paper No. 84, Cornell University.

____. 1973. "The Character of Borrowings from Spanish and English in the Languages of the Philippines." In *Journal of Philippine Linguistics*, 4.1.

Zorc, David. 1977. "The Bisayan Dialects of the Philippines: Subgrouping and Reconstruction." In *Pacific Linguistics* C.,44. (xiii + 328 pp.)

Cherokee

William Pulte and Durbin Feeling

Language Name: Cherokee. **Autonym:** jalagi, tsalagi.

Location: Cherokee is spoken in northeastern Oklahoma and in the vicinity of Cherokee and Robbinsville, North Carolina.

Family: Cherokee is the only language classified as Southern Iroquoian, one of the two major divisions within the larger Iroquoian family.

Related Languages: Cherokee is distantly related to Mohawk, Seneca, Cayuga, Oneida, Onondaga, and Tuscarora, which belong to the Northern branch of the Iroquoian family.

Dialects: The primary dialect division is between Eastern and Western Cherokee, spoken in North Carolina and Oklahoma, respectively. The differences are primarily in phonology, morphology, and vocabulary, and do not interfere with communication. Sub-dialects exist within both Eastern and Western Cherokee, and consist of relatively minor differences in phonology and vocabulary.

Number of Speakers: There are about 10,000 Cherokee speakers in Oklahoma, and fewer than 1,000 in North Carolina.

Origin and History

Proto-Iroquoian was spoken in the general vicinity of the Great Lakes some 3,500 years ago. Linguistic evidence indicates that a group of Iroquoian speakers left their homeland about 1500 B.C. and gradually migrated southward, eventually settling in the southern ranges of the Appalachians. The form of Iroquoian they spoke gradually became modern Cherokee, the only member of the Southern Iroquoian sub-family. Iroquoian as spoken by the remaining speakers, who did not migrate southward, is known as Northern Iroquoian, which later gave rise to six modern daughter languages: Mohawk, Seneca, Cayuga, Oneida, Onondaga, and Tuscarora.

The Cherokees encountered Euroamerican settlers at an early period, and by 1800 had adopted many aspects of their culture. In 1838–39 they were forced to relocate to Indian Territory, now Oklahoma. Their removal is known as the Trail of Tears. Because they were forced to take a northerly route during the dead of winter, at least one-fourth of the people perished during the march. Several hundred Cherokees resisted relocation, and hid in remote areas of the Great Smoky Mountains. Their descendants live today near Cherokee and Robbinsville, North Carolina.

After the Trail of Tears, an independent Cherokee Nation was established in Indian Territory, and both Cherokee and English were employed in conducting official business, and as languages of education. The Cherokee Nation was soon devastated by the Civil War, however, and the territory of the Cherokee Nation became part of Oklahoma in 1906, marking the end of the Cherokee educational system. The loss of their schools was a severe blow to the Cherokees, who had attained a higher rate of literacy in Cherokee than the English literacy rate of the Euroamerican populations of Texas and Arkansas.

Most Cherokee speakers live today in the areas of northeastern Oklahoma which once formed part of the Cherokee Nation, The modern tribal government, referred to once again as the Cherokee Nation (known as the Cherokee Nation of Oklahoma from 1906 until recent years), conducts tribal business on behalf of Cherokees listed on the tribal rolls.

Orthography and Basic Phonology

The history of native literacy among the Cherokees is unique in its origins, its rapid acceptance by the Cherokee people, and the extent of its use for a variety of purposes.

The Cherokee writing system was developed by Sequoyah, a monolingual Cherokee who is believed to have been born about 1770. Sequoyah had observed Euroamericans reading and writing, and realized that English speakers had devised a method of representing their language with symbols. He decided to develop a similar system for Cherokee, and began to experiment. According to some sources, Sequoyah at first attempted to represent each word with a separate symbol, but decided that this approach was impractical. He eventually arrived at a system of eighty-five symbols, eighty-four of which represented distinct syllables of Cherokee, with one symbol used for the consonant *s*.

The brilliance of Sequoyah's accomplishment is universally recognized. He "discovered" the principle of syllabic writing as well as the principle of alphabetic writing, although he used the latter only to represent *s*. He also discovered the principle underlying ideographic writing systems, the use of one symbol per word, if the reports that Sequoyah began with a word writing system are correct. Sequoyah therefore independently discovered two, and perhaps all three, of the types of writing systems in use throughout the world today.

Sequoyah perfected the syllabary by 1819, and after some initial opposition, his system rapidly gained acceptance. A newspaper, the *Cherokee Phoenix*, was published as early as 1828. After removal, a newspaper called the *Cherokee Advocate*, as well as a number of books, were printed in Indian Territory. The tradition of Cherokee printing came to an end with statehood for Oklahoma in 1906, however, when the federal government confiscated the Cherokee printing press. The syllabary has continued to be used for religious purposes and since about 1970 it has been taught in a number of elementary school bilingual education programs in Northeastern Oklahoma.

The phonetic values of the syllabary symbols can be determined from the following chart. The symbols of Row 1 represent the vowels which serve as the labels for the columns. The sound values for the symbols of Rows 2–13 are arrived at by combining the consonant(s) which label each row, with the vowel labels for the columns. For example, the symbol for the syllable *ha* is found at the intersection of Row 6 and Column 1. The symbol which represents both *da* and *ta* is found in the cell for Row 2, Column 5. The symbol for *ga* is the first symbol in the cell of Row 4, Column 1, followed by the symbol for *ka* in the same cell.

Cherokee Syllabary

	1 (a)	2 (e)	3 (i)	4 (o)	5 (u)	6 (v)
1	Ꭰ	Ꭱ	Ꭲ	Ꭳ	Ꭴ	Ꭵ
2 (d, t)	Ꮣ Ꮤ	Ꮥ Ꮦ	Ꮧ Ꮨ	Ꮩ	Ꮪ	Ꮫ
3 (dl, tl)	Ꮬ Ꮭ	Ꮮ	Ꮯ	Ꮰ	Ꮱ	Ꮲ
4 (g, k)	Ꭶ Ꭷ	Ꭸ	Ꭹ	Ꭺ	Ꭻ	Ꭼ
5 (gw, kw)	Ꮖ	Ꮗ	Ꮘ	Ꮙ	Ꮚ	Ꮛ
6 (h)	Ꭽ	Ꭾ	Ꭿ	Ꮀ	Ꮁ	Ꮂ
7 (j, ch)	Ꮳ	Ꮴ	Ꮵ	Ꮶ	Ꮷ	Ꮸ
8 (l)	Ꮃ	Ꮄ	Ꮅ	Ꮆ	Ꮇ	Ꮈ
9 (m)	Ꮉ	Ꮊ	Ꮋ	Ꮌ	Ꮍ	
10 (n, hn)	Ꮎ Ꮏ	Ꮑ	Ꮒ	Ꮓ	Ꮔ	Ꮕ
11 (s) Ꮝ	Ꮜ	Ꮞ	Ꮟ	Ꮠ	Ꮡ	Ꮢ
12 (w, hw)	Ꮹ	Ꮺ	Ꮻ	Ꮼ	Ꮽ	Ꮾ
13 (y, hy)	Ꮿ	Ᏸ	Ᏹ	Ᏺ	Ᏻ	Ᏼ

Sequoyah appears to have represented contrasts with high functional loads, but not to have represented less important contrasts. This enabled him to keep the number of symbols in the syllabary low, promoting more rapid learning of the system.

There are six vowel phonemes in Cherokee. The mid central vowel is always nasalized; it is represented by *v* traditionally in transliterations of the syllabary, and is still in use today in most Roman practical orthographies.

Table 1: Vowels

	Front	Central	Back
High	i		u
Mid	e	v	o
Low		a	

Word final vowels are generally deleted in casual speech, e.g. *utan asgay* 'big man'; they tend to be retained at the ends of phrases and before pause in consultative and formal speech, e.g. *utan asgaya*; and they are retained on all words of an utterance only in extremely formal or ceremonial style, e.g. *utana asgaya*. Final vowels are generally retained in writing; proficient readers automatically delete them in reading aloud when it is stylistically appropriate to do so.

Vowel length in Cherokee is largely predictable, but long and short vowels contrast in some environments; compare *agi:ʔa* 'he/she's picking it up' and *agiʔa* 'he/she is eating it (a solid food)'. Note that the orthography employed in this article is regularized, i.e. phonemic length and pitch are not represented unless relevant to the point under discussion, as in this instance where vowel length is indicated by a colon following the long vowel.

The consonants shown in Table 2 represent distinct phonemes, with the exception of the voiced stops *d* and *g*, which are non-basic allophones of *t* and *k*, respectively. The voiced stop allophones are included here because they are important orthographically. The practical orthography generally employed by literacy projects in Oklahoma represents the voiced stops and the unaspirated voiceless ones by *d* and *g*, and uses *t* and *k* for sequences of a voiceless stop plus *h*, which yield aspirated *t* and *k* phonetically. This orthographic convention is generally preferred by Cherokee speakers who are readers of English.

For some speakers, the affricates are usually alveolar rather than alveopalatal. For many speakers there is free or stylistic variation between the alveopalatal and alveolar allophones.

Table 2: Consonants

	Voi	Labial	Alveolar	Palatal	Velar	Glottal
Stops	-		t		k	ʔ
	+		d		g	
Fricatives			s			h
Affricates	-			ch		
	+			j		
Nasals		m				
Laterals			l			
Glides				y	w	

Phonetically, Cherokee syllables may have low, mid, or high pitch, represented by the numerals 2, 3, and 4 respectively. There is also a falling pitch from low, a rising pitch from low to mid and a falling pitch from mid to low. These gliding pitches are represented by 1, 23, and 32, respectively. Before pause, a fall from high is always predictable and is indicated by 4. Some examples are:

ka^{2}ma^{2}ma^4 'butterfly, elephant'
ga^{3}hl^{2}ida^4 'arrow'
ga^{23}ga^{3}ma^4 'cucumber'
ga^{2}do^{32}ga^4 'he/she is standing'

Some of these pitch phenomena are predictable, but not all. Cherokee may be a pitch accent language or a tone language. A consensus has not been reached on this point by linguists who have studied Cherokee.

Basic Morphology

Cherokee verbs are extremely complex in their morphology. The minimal verb consists of a stem preceded by a pronominal prefix, and followed by a tense/aspect suffix. For example, *gawoniha* 'he/she is speaking' is made up of the stem *-wonih-*, preceded by the pronominal prefix *ga-* '3rd person singular', and the tense/aspect suffix *-a* 'PRESENT'.

As many as six additional prefixes and ten additional suffixes may also occur in a single verb form, sometimes resulting in very long Cherokee verbs which correspond to English phrases or sentences comprised of long sequences of words. For example, the verb *yiwidogawonisisidolidoha* may be translated as "if he/she is going away randomly making the identical speeches from place to place". Three prepronominal prefixes occur in this form: *yi-* 'if', *-wi-* 'away from', *-do-* 'plural (speeches)'. The pronominal prefix *-ga-* and the verb stem *–woni-* occur next, followed by *–sisi-* 'duplicative', *-do-* 'randomly', *-li-* 'repetitive', *-do-* 'plural (places)', and *–ha-* 'present'. From the same root, can be derived also:

ga-woni-sisi-lo-ʔel-e-ga.
3-speak-DUPLIC-REPET-TRANSLOC-BEN-TENSE/ASPECT
'He/she is going there to make the identical speech repeatedly for him.'

Some additional examples of verbs exhibiting a prepronominal prefix are *yigawoniha* 'if he/she is speaking'; *nigawoniha* 'he/she is speaking with his/her side turned (to the person who makes the statement)'; *igawoniha* 'he/she is speaking again'. The prepronominal prefixes which appear in these examples are *yi-* 'if'; *ni-* 'lateral position'; and *i-* 'again'. These prefixes may also occur together, as in *yiniʔigawoniha* 'if he/she is speaking again with his/her side turned'.

Nouns are derived from verbs by a number of productive processes. The derivational suffix *-i* 'agentive' is used to form nouns by replacing the habitual suffix, e.g. *gawonisgo* 'he/she habitually speaks'; *gawonisgi* 'speaker'. Derived nouns are also formed by replacing the pronoun prefixes used with infinitives, with the corresponding finite verb prefix; e.g. *uwonihisdi* 'to speak', *gawonihisdi* 'speech'. Derived nouns are extremely frequent in Cherokee. In running text, they often exceed the number of non-derived nouns.

Adjectives form a separate word class. They differ from verbs with respect to affixation. The tense/aspect suffixes in verb forms, for example, do not occur with adjectives such as *utana* 'big'. The past tense suffix *-vʔi*, for example, appears with verbs such as *gawonisgvʔi*, but must be suffixed to the copula in adjective phrases such as *utana gesvʔi* 'he/she was big'.

Nouns which refer to humans are marked by the animate prefix *a-*, e.g. *agehya* 'woman', and *ajalagi* 'Cherokee (person)'; cf. *jalagi* 'Cherokee (language)'. Plurality of human nouns is marked by the prefix *-ni-*, which follows the animate prefix; e.g. *anigehya* 'women'.

Nouns which refer to non-humans and which are not derived from verbs, are ordinarily not inflected for number. There are some exceptions, including *gadusi* 'hill', *digadusi* 'hills'; *kanesaʔi* 'box'; *dikanesaʔi* 'boxes'.

Basic Syntax

Cherokee is a Subject Object Verb language, but other orders frequently occur. For example, the sentence "A cat sees a dog" can appear in its basic SOV order, or in OVS order.

wesa gihli agowhtiha
cat dog s/he sees.it
'A cat sees a dog.'

gihli agowhtiha wesa
dog s/he sees it cat
'A cat sees a dog.'

Within noun phrases, adjectives generally precede nouns, and always follow demonstratives, numeral words, and degree words, e.g.

na taʔli udohiyu gvhnage wesa
that two really black cat
'Those two really black cats.'

Within verb phrases, adverbs precede verbs:

udohiyu asdayi gawoniha
very loud he/she speaks
'He/she is speaking very loudly.'

Cherokee is strictly postpositional. Postpositional phrases usually precede the verb, but they may also follow it:

gahljode didla aʔi.
house toward walks
'He/she is walking toward the house.'

Negative sentences are formed by the negative word *hla*, together with the conditional verb prefix *y-*, *yi-*.

agiʔa 'he/she is eating'
hla yagiʔa 'he/she is not eating'

Coordination is marked by the suffix *-hno*, which occurs with the first word of each conjoined element except the first:

asgaya agehya-hno agehyuja-hno aniwoniha
man woman-and girl-and 3p.speak
'A man, a woman, and a child are speaking.'

asgaya gawoniha, agehya-hno dekanogiʔa
man speaks woman-and sings
'A man is speaking and a woman is singing.'

In extremely formal style, the conjunction *ale* is used instead of *-hno*:

asgaya gawoniha, ale agehya dekanogiʔa
man speaks and woman sings
'A man is speaking and a woman is singing.'

Questions are formed by the suffix *-sko*, which usually appears as *-s*; cf. *agehya gawoniha* 'a woman is speaking', *agehyas gawoniha* 'Is a woman speaking?'

Contact with Other Languages

Cherokee speakers have been in intensive contact with English speakers since the early 18th century, but there are very few loans from English. Note *asamadi* 'smart'; *advji* 'German (from "Dutch")'; and *askwani* 'Mexican'. In the last example the English *-ks-* is inverted to *-sk-*, and *w* is inserted before *-an*.

Common Words

man:	asgaya	woman:	agehya
water:	ama	sun:	nvdo
three:	joʔi	fish:	ajatʔdi
big:	utana	long:	ganvhida
small:	usdi	yes:	vʔv
no:	hla	good:	osda
bird:	jisgwa	dog:	gihli
tree:	hlgvʔi	cat:	wesa
person:	yvwi	eye:	akta
six:	sudali	you:	nihi
red:	gigage	leaf:	ugaloga

Example Sentences

(1) Asgaya ahwi ganohalidoha galogwe gvhdi
man deer 3s.hunt.PRES gun with
'A man is hunting a deer with a gun.'

(2) Gajanuli natli uwodigeʔi dagwalela
fast:lateral 3s.run brown car
'A brown car is passing fast.'

(3) Svhi jigesv akdlvgv asehnv osigwu igi kohi
yesterday it.was 1s.sick.PAST but fine be this

iga
day
'I was sick yesterday, but I'm fine today.'

Efforts to Preserve, Protect, and Promote the Language

In traditional Cherokee communities in Oklahoma, most people over 50 are bilingual in both Cherokee and English. Many adults between 20 and 50 are bilingual, but some speak only English although they may understand Cherokee. Most persons under 20 speak only English, although some understand Cherokee.

A number of projects have attempted to promote native language literacy in Oklahoma. In the mid 1960s the Carnegie Cross Cultural Education Project developed materials to help Cherokee speakers who could read English to become literate in Cherokee. A practical Roman orthography was employed as an aid in mastering the syllabary.

Since the early 1970s, bilingual education programs have introduced literacy in Cherokee in the elementary school curriculum in a number of schools in northeastern Oklahoma. The Cherokee Nation has also sponsored community based Cherokee literacy classes for adults in a number of communities.

In the early 1970s, the Cherokee Nation sponsored a major dictionary project, resulting in the publication of the *Cherokee-English Dictionary*. The dictionary was intended as a resource for students in Cherokee literacy classes, and for students learning Cherokee as a second language. All Cherokee entries appear in both the syllabary and in a practical Roman orthography.

Cherokee courses have been offered at Northeastern State University at Tahlequah, Oklahoma, and at Tulsa University. The Cherokee Nation newsletter includes a column in Cherokee, and there are weekly Cherokee radio broadcasts of a religious nature.

Select References

Bradley, Ruth H., and Betty S. Smith. *Beginning Cherokee.* Norman: University of Oklahoma Press.

Crawford, James. 1975. "Southeastern Indian Languages." In *Studies in Southeastern Indian Languages.* James Crawford, editor. Athens: University of Georgia Press.

Feeling, Durbin D. 1975. *Cherokee-English Dictionary.* William Pulte, editor. Tahlequah, Oklahoma: Cherokee Nation of Oklahoma.

Feeling, Durbin D. 1994. *A Structured Approach to Learning the Basic Inflections of the Cherokee Verb.* Foreword by Wilma P. Mankiller. Muskogee, Oklahoma: Indian University Press.

Lounsbury, Floyd. 1961. "Iroquois-Cherokee Linguistic Relations." In *Bureau of American Ethnology Bulletin* 180: 11–17.

Mithun, Marianne. 1979. "Iroquoian." In *The Languages of Native America.* Lyle Campbell and Marianne Mithun, editors. Austin: University of Texas Press.

Pulte, William and Durbin Feeling. 1975. "An Outline of Cherokee Grammar." In Feeling (1975).

Reyburn, William D. 1953–4. "Cherokee Verb Morphology." In *International Journal of American Linguistics.* 19:172–180, 259–273, 20:44–64.

Scancarelli, Janine. 1987. *Grammatical Relations and Verb Agreement in Cherokee.* Ph.D. dissertation, UCLA.

Van Tuyl, Charles D., and Durbin D. Feeling. 1994. *An Outline of Basic Verb Inflections of Oklahoma Cherokee.* Muskogee, Oklahoma: Indian University Press.

Walker, Willard. 1975. "Cherokee." In *Studies in Southeastern Indian Languages.* James Crawford, editor. Athens: University of Georgia Press.

Worcester, Samuel A., Elias Boudinot, et al. 1860. *The Cherokee New Testament.* New York: American Bible Society.

Chichewa

Sam A. Mchombo

Language Name: Chichewa. **Alternates:** Chinyanja or Nyanja.

Location: The African countries of Malawi, Mozambique, Zambia, and Zimbabwe.

Family: Bantu.

Related Languages: Other Bantu languages, especially Tumbuka, Chiyao, and SHONA.

Dialects: None.

Number of Speakers: 4–6 million.

Origin and History

The Chewa, better known as aChewa, the people who speak Chichewa, are descendants of the people known as Malawi or Maravi (according to some Portuguese records). The Malawi migrated from the lower basin on the Congo in Central Africa, moving southeast, and settled in the central region of the modern-day state of Malawi. The label Chewa is, apparently, one they acquired while in Zambia as they made their way, but before they crossed the border, into Malawi. It is claimed that the name derives from the word *cheva* or *sheva* or *seva* which, in the language of the people who called them that, meant 'foreigner'. The language of these foreigners was thus referred to as Chichewa. The Chewa leader who led them into Malawi was called Kalonga and he founded in Malawi what later came to be called the Maravi empire.

As the Chewa spread throughout the central and southern part of the country, into eastern Zambia, and into parts of Mozambique including along the Zambezi River, their language spread too. This dispersion was responsible for the proliferation of regional varieties of the language, varieties which were identified by distinct names creating the impression of the existence of a multiplicity of ethnic groups. Some of the groups identified themselves by reference to significant features of their new habitat. The people who settled along the lakeshores and along the banks of the River Shire called themselves *aNyanja*, the lake people, and their particular variety of Chichewa was called *Chi-Nyanja*, or simply *Nyanja*, the language of the lake people. Those who moved into the interior, the land of tall grass, called themselves *aChipeta*, the dwellers of the savanna land. These names began to obscure the nature of the relationship among these people, and the introduction of yet other labels by Europeans further complicated matters. The multiplicity of labels under which the aChewa came to be identified was remarked on by various scholars. Thus Young (1949:53) says that Nyanja is "the language of a people scattered over a large south-east-central African area, the aMaravi, who today live under at least six different names according to the area in which Europeans found them in the closing decades of the last century".

Greenberg does not mention Chichewa in his classification of African languages, and in the works of Guthrie Chichewa and Chimang'anja are listed as two dialect variations of Nyanja. He classifies Chichewa as belonging to zone N31b, being identified as the second dialect of the main language. The treatment of Chichewa as a dialect of Nyanja was largely because of the fact that missionaries and colonialists from Britain had chosen to use Nyanja over Chichewa (see Efforts to Preserve, Protect, and Promote the Language).

The Chichewa language has spread into the countries of Zimbabwe and even South Africa because of the migrations of Chichewa-speakers to those countries to work in the mines, on European-owned farms, and in hotels and offices.

Orthography and Basic Phonology

Chichewa is written in the Latin alphabet. Table 1 below gives the Chichewa consonants.

Table 1: Consonants

		Labial	Dental	Alveo-palatal	Velar
Stops	Unaspirated	p	t		k
	Aspirated	ph	th		kh
	Voiced	b	d		g
Fricatives	Voiceless	f	s		
	Voiced	v	z		
Affricatives	Unaspirated			ch	
	Aspirated			tch	
	Voiced		dz	j	
Nasals		m	n	ny	ng
Resonants			l, r		
Glides		w		y	

The nasal /m/ may be syllabic: *mpini* 'hoe, axe handle' has three syllables: /m-pi-ni/.

The sequence *ng'* represents the velar nasal /ŋ/. In contrast, the sequence *ng* (without the apostrophe) represents a prenasalized consonant /ŋg/ which is similar to the middle consonant sequence of the English word *finger*.

Table 2: Vowels

	Front	Central	Back
High	i		u
Mid	e		o
Low		a	

Chichewa is a tone language. Its four tones high, mid, low, and rising serve to differentiate meaning. For example, *mténgo* 'tree' vs. *mtengo* 'price' are distinguished by the high tone on the second syllable of *mténgo* as opposed to the mid tone on the second syllable of *mtengo*. And *mawěre* 'yeast' is distinguished from *mawére* 'breasts' by rising vs. high tone in the second syllable. Tone is not generally represented in ordinary Chichewa orthography. In scholarly discussions, diacritic accent marks are used to indicate tone.

Basic Morphology

Like other Bantu languages, Chichewa nouns tend to be grouped into gender-like classes, 17 of which are preserved. These classes influence agreement on adjectives, demonstratives, and verbs. Both noun class and number (singular vs. plural) are indicated by prefixes as illustrated below:

Singular	Plural	Gloss
m-kazi	a-kazi	'woman'
m-tengo	mi-tengo	'tree'
chi-soti	zi-soti	'hat'

The same noun stem can occur in different classes, with different meanings. For instance, from the stem *lemba*, which refers to writing, are derived *chi-lembo* 'character (in an alphabet)', *m-lembo* 'handwriting', and *ma-lembo* 'contents of the written word'.

There are no definite/indefinite articles, which means that definiteness has to be understood from context.

Chichewa verbs are morphologically complex. All inflected verbs must agree with their subject in noun class and may also agree with their objects. Both subject and object agreement are marked with prefixes.

Verbs are inflected for tense (past, present, future, present habitual, past habitual, perfect) as well. Tense is indicated by a prefix immediately following the subject agreement prefix.

Like other Bantu languages, Chichewa has a series of root extension suffixes indicating such meanings as passive, causative, applicative, reciprocal, and stative.

Basic Syntax

The general rule for word order in Chichewa is that in a simple transitive sentence the object follows the verb if there is no object agreement marker on the verb; otherwise the order is free. Both of the sentences below mean 'The lion is selling the hoe handles.' However, *mipini* must follow the verb in the first sentence, but it can be moved to precede the verb in the second sentence.

m-kango u-ku-gulits-a mi-pini
CL-lion CL/SUBJ-PRES-sell-INDIC CL-hoe handle

m-kango u-ku-i-gulits-a mi-pini
CL-lion CL/SUBJ-PRES-CL/OBJ-sell-INDIC CL-hoe handle

Within a Chichewa noun phrase, adjectives and other modifiers follow the nouns that they modify: *m-kango wa-bwino* (CL-lion CL-good) 'a good lion'.

Negation is marked by *si*. This can be treated as a negative copula:

Si m-kango
NEG CL-lion 'it's not a lion'

In a sentence containing a verb, *si* appears as the first prefix in a verb to denote negation:

m-kango si-u-ku-gulits-a mi-pini
CL-lion NEG-CL-PRES-sell-INDIC CL-hoe handle
'The lion isn't selling hoe handles.'

Contact with Other Languages

Loanwords include:

From Shona: *mtsikana* 'girl'
From SOTHO: *zakhali* 'aunt'
From SWAHILI: *ndege* 'airplane'
From PORTUGUESE: *kalata* 'letter' (< *carta*), *chipewa* 'hat' (< *chapéu*), *nsapato* 'shoes' (< *sapato*)
From ENGLISH: *batiza* 'to baptize', *kupopa* 'to pump'

The pace of technological change has seen the infusion of English vocabulary into the language to deal with the new products. Thus expressions such as 'video', 'computer', 'satellite', etc., have made their way into the language with minimal modification to them.

Common Words

man:	mwamuna	long:	-tali
woman:	mkazi	small:	-ng'ono
water:	madzi	yes:	inde
sun:	dzuwa	no:	iyayi
three:	-tatu	good:	-bwino
fish:	nsomba	bird:	mbalame
big:	-kulu	dog:	galu
tree:	mtengo		

Example Sentences

(1) M-kango u-ku-mang-its-a chi-patala
CL-lion CL-PRES-build-CAUS-INDIC CL-hospital
'The lion is getting a hospital built.'

(2) Mkazi a-na-mw-a ma-dzi
woman CL-PAST-drink-INDIC CL-water
'The/A woman drank (some) water.'

(3) Mba-lame zi-ku-sewer-a
CL-birds CL-PRES-play-INDIC
'The birds are playing.'

Efforts to Preserve, Protect, and Promote the Language

When the British moved into Malawi at the turn of the century they made Nyanja the official language of the colonial government. It was taught in schools and knowledge of it was required for government posts. The production of publications in and on Nyanja and of grammars and dictionaries went a long way toward giving Nyanja the profile of a major language while other varieties, including Chichewa, acquired dialect status.

In 1968, four years after Malawi had attained its independence from Great Britain, the question of language was reviewed. The decision was made by the then ruling and sole political power, the Malawi Congress Party, to reassert Chichewa as the main language and to treat Nyanja as a regional variety. Chichewa is now the national language of Malawi; it is used for mass communication and is taught in the schools. There are radio programs designed to discuss various aspects of the language for the benefit of the population. The Chichewa Board oversees work on a dictionary and was instrumental in the production of *Chichewa Orthography Rules*.

Chichewa is taught and researched at the University of Malawi where there are efforts to promote the development of a literary tradition and to make reading material in the language available. Recently, Chichewa has featured prominently in research on theoretical linguistics; studies of it have made notable contributions to progress in linguistic theory and in the study of the linguistic structure of Bantu languages.

Chichewa will continue to serve as the main vehicle for communication for people within the area in which it is spoken. It is a major language in that it crosses political boundaries, hence it serves as a lingua franca.

Select Bibliography

Atkins, G. 1950. "Suggestions for an amended spelling and word division in Nyanja." In *Africa; Journal of the International African Institute* 20:200–218.

Chichewa Board. 1980. *Chichewa Orthography Rules*. Zomba: University of Malawi.

Greenberg, J. 1966. *The Languages of Africa*. Bloomington: Indiana University Press.

Guthrie, M. 1967. *Comparative Bantu: An Introduction to the Comparative Linguistics and Prehistory of the Bantu Languages*. Farnborough, England: Gregg.

Hetherwick, A. 1901. *A Practical Manual of the Nyanja Language*. London.

Kishindo, P. J. 1990. "Historical survey of spontaneous and planned development of Chichewa." In Fodor, I. and C. Hagege, *Language Reform: History and Future*. Vol. V. Hamburg: Helmut Buske Verlag, 59–82.

Made, S. M., M. V. B. Mangoche Mbewe, and R. Jackson. 1976. *One Hundred Years of Chichewa in Writing, 1875–1975*. Zomba: University of Malawi.

Mchombo, Sam A. 1998. "Chichewa." In Spencer, Andrew and Arnold Zwicky eds. *The Handbook of Morphology*. Oxford: Blackwell. 500–520.

Pachai, Bridglal, ed. 1971. *The Early History of Malawi*. London: Longman.

____. 1946. *The Elements of Nyanja*. Malawi: Blantyre.

Ranger, T. O., ed. 1968. *Aspects of Central African History*. Evanston: Northwestern University Press.

Thomson, T. D. 1955. *A Practical Approach to Chinyanja; with English-Nyanja Vocabulary*. 1947. Reprint, Zomba, Malawi: Government Printer, 1955.

Young, Cullen. 1949. Review of *A Practical Approach to Chinyanja*, by T. D. Thomson. *Africa; Journal of the International African Institute* 19:253–54.

CHINESE LANGUAGES: CLASSICAL CHINESE

David Prager Branner

Language Name: Classical Chinese. **Alternate:** Literary Chinese, *wénlǐ.* **Autonym:** Wényán ("literary language"), Wényánwén ("*wényán* writing"), *gǔwén* ("ancient writing"), Gǔdài Hànyǔ ("ancient Chinese").

Location: Taiwan, Mainland China, and Singapore; formerly also in Japan, Korea, Vietnam.

Family: Commonly said to belong to Sino-Tibetan, although strictly speaking Classical Chinese is an exclusively written language, and so it should perhaps not be classified with spoken languages, modern or ancient.

Related Languages: Classical and Literary Chinese have had a great influence on the many varieties of spoken Chinese through history.

Dialects: Certain Classical texts are associated with specific regions of ancient China, and their linguistic peculiarities are sometimes imputed to dialect usage. Examples include the *Analects* of Confucius, said by some to reflect the syntax of the eastern state of Lǔ, and the long poem "Lí sāo", said to use much vocabulary of the southern state of Chǔ.

However, as Classical Chinese is a literary language, it is much more useful to speak of periods and genres. See Origin and History, below.

Number of Speakers: For most of history, literacy in Chinese meant literacy in Literary Chinese. Rawski (1979) estimates that in the 18th and 19th centuries, between 30 and 45 percent of all Chinese men and between 2 and 10 percent of all Chinese women could read and write to some extent. Even such hazy figures as these are difficult to come by for earlier periods. The vernacular language movement, beginning in 1919, has made great inroads into the dominance of the literary standard, however, so that children today learn primarily Mandarin in school. The Mandarin used in Taiwan and southern Mainland China, however, has a markedly more literary component than the Mandarin taught in north China. The reason for this is that native southern dialects are not closely related to Mandarin and so southern Mandarin has a more formal character.

Origin and History

Classical Chinese in the strict sense is the written language appearing in prose texts of the Warring States period (475–221 B.C.), a time of political disunity before the establishment of the first true Chinese empire, that of the Qín and Hàn dynasties (221 B.C–A.D. 220). The conventions of this written language began to be fixed as what we may call Literary Chinese during the first empire, but other styles of writing also arose in that time. To the best of our understanding, it has never reflected a true spoken language, although some of its main varieties may have been influenced in part by real koines. It is often terse, at times telegraphically so.

Literary Chinese was all along the language of historical writing, anecdote, and some philosophy. However, euphuism grew dominant in most other genres, along with the rise of brilliant new forms of poetry, especially those composed within close phonological strictures. In the 8th century, some intellectuals began pressing for a return to the norms of Classical prose (*gǔwén*); this recrudescent style persisted into the eleventh century and greatly influenced much later prose. It was not until the nationalistic "May 4th Movement" of 1919, led by Hu Shih (1891–1962) and others, that writing in even a semi-colloquial style became intellectually respectable. The erosion of literary Chinese as the educated written language of China is, in the broad context of East Asian civilization, culturally comparable to the erosion of Latin in the educated West in the 14th–17th centuries, although the Chinese development took place within a much shorter time and therefore had a vastly more wrenching effect on society.

Orthography and Basic Phonology

The Chinese script has exerted an immensely seductive power on the Western imagination since the 16th century. Consequently much nonsense has been written about it. Chinese characters are not strictly speaking hieroglyphic or pictographic, and most certainly not "ideographic" (meaning fundamentally representative of abstract concepts). They represent the words for things rather than things themselves. Most of the graphs do have their origins in images of concrete objects. However, from an early time, characters were borrowed to represent secondary words: rough homophones for the words they were originally designed to write.

The early script was apparently very diverse, but underwent far-reaching standardization during the period of the first empire, and it is in variations of this form that Classical Chinese has been read for most of subsequent history. The great majority of characters consist of two primary parts. One is a "phonetic element", the other a "semantic element". The phonetic element indicates the approximate sound of the word in question in some early stage of the language. Semantic elements serve to distinguish the various characters that contain the same phonetic elements and that would otherwise be written identically. Semantic elements generally give little more than a clue to the basic nature of the word being written: a certain word is *kɪn* having to do with trees ('root') rather than a homophonous word *kɪn* having to do with the human foot ('heel'). Historically, most phonetic elements are derived from the early forms of the pictographs that were borrowed to write homophonic words. They play a vital role in the modern study of early phonology.

The writing system is introduced in detail in DeFrancis (1984), Boltz (1994) and Qiu (2000).

"Classical Chinese", as a written language, has no phonology readily apparent in it. The phonological system it does reflect is of an early period (or periods), unrelated to the spoken languages of most of Chinese history. Discussion here will cover the formal system of the medieval dictionaries, and what we know of early Chinese.

Medieval Phonology. Medieval dictionaries (those dating from c. A.D. 300–1200) are prescriptive and generally represent more or less standard phonologies of reading pronunciation, rather than speech *per se*. We suspect that the most important of those dictionaries (the *Qièyùn* of A.D 601 and its successors) embodies obsolete phonological distinctions and does so perhaps intentionally, precisely because it was meant to maintain the sound not of speech but of the written language of antiquity in a highly conservative form. Books of the *Qièyùn* tradition document their subject exhaustively; they contain tens of thousands of characters, all taken from various written sources. Many are unknown outside of those dictionaries.

The medieval representation of speech sound is abstract and does not involve realistic phonetics. Much of what we know of the sound of medieval Chinese is reconstructed based on contemporary native reading traditions. Each Chinese character represented a single syllable. The native tradition analyzed the syllable into three elements: [initial] + [rime], and "rime" was subcategorized by tone. Syllable structure as we would analyze it today consisted of [initial] + ([medial]) + [main vowel] + ([secondary vowel]) + ([coda]). The coda could be an oral nasal ending, an oral stop, or a vowel. "Rime" is our word for the rhyming element of the syllable, embracing everything except the initial and, sometimes, the medial. Because the *Qièyùn* dictionaries were concerned primarily with rhyming, the rime is their chief organizing element. It is not defined as closely as would be done in modern linguistic analysis.

There were four tone categories: *píng*, *shǎng*, *qù*, and *rù*. The *rù* tone category contained only syllables ending in oral stops. The other tone categories contained only syllables ending in nasals or open vowels of some sort. The *shǎng* tone category probably featured constriction or an outright glottal stop ending. The *qù* tone category is thought to have had some other sort of laryngeal feature, and the *píng* category was plain. In the present transcription, the *shǎng* tone is marked with *Q* and the *qù* tone with *H*; the *píng* tone is unmarked.

"Medial" refers to a semivowel or liquid that appears between the initial and the main vowel. Modern reconstructions of the medieval vowels and particularly the medials vary greatly. 10th century materials classify the rimes into four types, called *děng* ("rows", "divisions", "grades") and numbered one through four. Below I transcribe the principal syllable-finals (main vowel plus coda) as proposed in Branner (1999), with the *děng* represented as numerical subscripts.

					i_{3a}	i_{3b}	i_{3c}	i_{3d}	
ei_{1a}	ei_{1b}	ei_{2a}	ei_{2b}	ei_{2c}	ei_{3a}	ei_{3b}			ei_{4}
		a_{2}			a_{3}				
e_{1}					e_{3}				
uo_{1}					uo_{3b}	uo_{3c}			
au_{1}		au_{2}			au_{3}				au_{4}
ou_{1}					ou_{3b}	ou_{3c}			
am_{1a}	am_{1b}	am_{2a}	am_{2b}		am_{3a}	am_{3b}			am_{4}
					em_{3}				
an_{1}		an_{2a}	an_{2b}		an_{3a}	an_{3b}			an_{4}
en_{1}					en_{3a}	en_{3b}			
ang_{1}					ang_{3}				
		$eing_{2a}$	$eing_{2b}$		$eing_{3a}$	$eing_{3b}$			$eing_{4}$
eng_{1}					eng_{3}				
		ong_{2}							
ung_{1b}	ung_{1c}				ung_{3b}	ung_{3c}			

Děng 1 generally corresponds to unpalatalized rimes in modern Chinese reading phonologies, and *děng* 3 to heavy palatalization, that is, to medial *i*. The rimes of *děng* 3 encompass fully half of the words in the medieval dictionaries, and the majority of common words in the ancient written language. It has been suggested that all *děng* 3 words were originally plain and phonologically unmarked, but that the entire category underwent palatalization (Norman 1994). Subscript 4 is also palatalized in all of today's reading accents, but is thought to have originated from vowel-raising unrelated to the event that produced *děng* 3. *Děng* 2 is thought once to have been characterized by liquid medials (*l* or *r* of some kind) or by the presence of rhotacized initials. In modern reading accents, *děng* 2 is usually unpalatalized, except after velar and laryngeal initials and then only in northern dialects and reading systems showing heavy influence of northern phonological systems.

Initials are more numerous in the medieval books than in any modern variety of Chinese. They are traditionally subject to a four-way classification: plain, aspirated, voiced, and nasal. Below they are transcribed after Branner (1999).

p	ph	b	m
t	th	d	n
			l
tr	thr	dr	ny
ts	tsh	dz	
s		z	
tsr	tshr	dzr	
sr			
tsy	tshy	dzy	
sy		zy	
k	kh	g	ng
0	h	gh	y

Certain of the voiced initials (*ny*, *z*, *g*, and *y*) and the palatal *tsy*-series only appear in *děng* 3 syllables. The initials of the rhotacized *tr* and *tsr* series only appear in *děng* 2 and 3. Modern dialects of north China, as well as words influenced by northern phonology in southern dialects, have an additional series of initials, *f* and *v*, which apparently began splitting off from the bilabials as early as medieval times.

Karlgren (1923) contains a useful short introduction to Chinese historical phonology. The main Western-language works on medieval Chinese phonology are Karlgren (1915–24) and Pulleyblank (1984). See Branner (2000) on the sources of medieval phonology.

Early Chinese. Chinese people must long have realized that the medieval phonological system did not apply well to the literature of earlier times. Phonological science was highly developed in China by the Sòng dynasty (960–1279), and at this time scholars began to explore alternate systems. Work focused at first primarily on rhyming, but by the early 19th century, it had been discovered that early phonology made sense of the writing system, and that the writing system could therefore be used to unlock the secrets of early phonology. Progress has been great since that time, with the mixture of both traditional native and modern linguistic methods.

Depending on whose research one reads, the typology of early Chinese may have been far different from that of medieval and modern Chinese. It is widely thought to have had no tones. Contour tone must have developed later out of final segmental features: a glottal stop for the *shǎng* tone and *-s* for the *qù* tone. These segments may also have derivational functions. Not only the *rù* but also the *qù* tone could have short syllables ending in oral stops. Initial clusters have been reconstructed involving *s-*, a voicing feature sometimes segmentalized *ɦ-*, a nasalizing feature sometimes segmentalized N-, a medial *-l-*, as well as more daring proposals. The majority of these proposals are intended to resolve problems in the script, namely graphic contacts between medieval initials of different places of articulation. For instance, the character for *ngwan*$_{3a}$ 'head' appears as the phonetic element in the character for *kwan*$_{1}$ < **kon* 'cap,' hence 'head' is reconstructed as **Nkjon*; the *N* prefix accounts for the initial *ng-* in 'head.' The character for *pet*$_{3b}$ 'necessarily' appears as the phonetic element in the character for *sret*$_{3c}$ 'kind of stringed instrument'; the early Chinese form of *sret*$_{3c}$ is therefore reconstructed as *sprjit*, incorporating an *s-* prefix on a *p-* initial base. In addition to the sonorant initials of medieval and modern Chinese, there is evidence of a series of voiceless sonorants (written *hm*, *hn*, *hl*, and *hng*) that produced aspirated stops and *h* in medieval Chinese. The initial system is at present still rather *ad hoc*. Below are the main early Chinese initials, after the presentation of Baxter (1992). Clusters are not shown (forms such as *tr* are considered rhotacized rather than true clusters).

p	ph	b	m	hm
t	th	d	n	hn
	hl	l		
	hr			
tj	thj	dj	nj	hnj
				hlj
				hj
tr	thr	dr	nr	
	hnr	ɦsl	lj	ɦhly
pr		br	r	hrj
			j	
ts	tsh	dz		
s		z		
tsr	tshr	dzr		
sz		zr		
k	kh	g	ng	hng
kr		gr		
ʔ	x	ɦ		

There is also a separate series of labiovelar (and labio-laryngeal) initials. Velar and laryngeal initials constitute a much larger class in early Chinese than they do in medieval Chinese; it is recognized that a fair number of medieval words with palatal initials (*tsy-* etc.) must have had velar-laryngeal initials in earlier times. In fact, the process of palatalization by which *děng* 3 (above) was produced is thought to have altered many aspects of phonology. The only syllables that resisted some of the sweeping effects of palatalization were those not "protected" by various segmental features, such as medial *-rj-* (Pulleyblank) or a pharyngealization (Norman).

The following table of finals (not including "tonogenic" segments) follows Baxter (1992):

in	en	ɨn	an	un	on
it	et	ɨt	at	ut	ot
ij	ej(?)	ɨj	aj	uj	oj
i(?)	e	ɨ	a	u	o
ik>it	ɨk		uk		
ing>in	eng	ɨng	ang	ung	ong
iw	ew		aw		
iwk	ewk		awk		
im	em	ɨm	am	um	om
ip	ep	ɨp	ap	up	op

Few Western-language works on early Chinese phonology are at all comprehensive. Karlgren (1954, 1957) are seminal. Pulleyblank (1962) and Baxter (1992) embody substantial renovations of Karlgren's work but lack proper indexes.

Basic Morphology

The traditional Chinese written language uses one character for each morpheme, thus concealing any morphological behavior that might have been present in earlier forms of speech. Classical Chinese therefore appears to be a strongly isolating language; there are no cases, tenses, or conjugations apparent. Grammar seems to be characterized by semantically loose relations between syntactic elements, and much material must be supplied to make translations clear. When we read, we assign the plain Chinese morphemes mentally to parts of speech that make the text intelligible. (This process is less arbitrary than it sounds, although it usually takes some time to learn.) For instance, we can say *pauH*$_{1}$ *gou*$_{3b}$ "pay back" + "enmity" = 'to take revenge' or *gou*$_{3b}$ *pauH*$_{1}$ "enmity" + "pay back" = 'revenge is taken.' Neither in script nor pronunciation is there any difference between the use of *gou*$_{3b}$ in the two phrases to indicate which is semantically the agent of the verb and which is patient; there is no difference between the use of *pauH*$_{1}$ as a verb to indicate whether it is in its active ("transitive") or inactive ("intransitive") form. Even the boundaries between traditional Western parts of speech such as verb and noun are not necessarily clear; it is very ordinary to find words we might imagine to be "inherently" verbal being used as nouns and other words inherently nominal used as verbs. Traditional native grammatical thinking distinguishes two types of words: the "empty", generally meaning grammar particles, and the "full", meaning everything else. This is no weak-minded analysis; it is an accurate description of the fuzziness of syntactic categories in actual usage. Harbsmeier (1998) discusses this question in great detail as part of his larger study of the logical underpinnings of Chinese.

Basic Syntax

In Classical and Literary Chinese, as in modern spoken Chinese, it is most useful to describe overall syntax by way of the "topic-comment" model. The "topic" is simply the thing being spoken about and the "comment" is what is said about it. The topic may be the agent or subject of the verb, but it need not be; it can also be the patient or object. It can even be what we would expect to call the "predicate", apparently drawn into initial position to expose it and thereby emphasize it.

Pronouns exist in great variety, but are often omitted in places where they might be expected by context, such as the subject or (less so) the object of the verb. Objects can also be omitted from coverb-object phrases, leaving the coverb alone to serve syntactically as an adverb. Below, $yuoQ_{3b}$ is a coverb, $tsyi_{3d}$ is its expected object, and together they form an adverbial phrase modifying mou_{3b} 'to scheme,' e.g. Expected = $yuoQ_{3b}$ $tsyi_{3d}$ mou_{3b} (with him to.scheme) 'to scheme with him'; Actual = $yuoQ_{3b}$ mou_{3b} (together to.scheme) 'to scheme together, scheme with [him].'

A few syntactic generalizations are possible. Modifiers ordinarily precede what they modify; conjunctions are placed between the phrases they join. Objects are ordinarily placed after their verbs, although object-pronouns are placed before the verb when the verb is negated or when they are question words such as 'whom?', 'what?'. There is no tense, mood, or any other overt derivation of the verb in Classical Chinese, however, there are some particles that appear to function as aspect markers. The sentence-final particle yaQ_3 indicates that the sentence conveys a firm statement, or that an action is presently or imminently taking place; $ghiQ_{3d}$ indicates that some state has been achieved, some change has taken place, or some or contrast is being made. There is also an adverb kiH_{3a} that indicates that the action verb has already taken place; it has its own negative form miH_{3a}.

Since Classical Chinese does not have a subjunctive mood, some Western scholars have claimed that it also does not express counterfactual states, but in fact there are words for 'if' such as $nyuo_{3b}$ and $nyak_3$, and particles introducing general contrary-to-fact situations such as $sriQ_{3d}$ and $dzyeing_{3b}$; there is also a negative counterfactual particle, $ywiQ_{3c}$ 'if not for....'

Karlgren's belief in a pronominal case system based on ablaut has not proven viable. But some of the more conspicuously affix-like segments in early Chinese have been identified as having morphological functions. This is a rather contentious area of inquiry, but one of the best attested examples involves the alternation of voiced and unvoiced initials in active and inactive forms of a given verb. For instance, a character glossed 'to break' has an active form $tsyat_{3b}$ 'to cause to break' and an inactive form $dzyat_{3b}$ 'to become broken.' Baxter (1992) assigns this function to the absence or presence of an initial ɦ; Sagart (1999) to an initial *N*.

Few Western language works on Classical grammar are both thorough and reliable, but Pulleyblank (1995) and Gabelenz (1881) are good sources. By far the best materials are written in Chinese. Morphology has received little treatment; the reader should consult Sagart (1999), which includes a useful section etymologizing the basic Classical Chinese lexicon.

Contact with Other Languages

Throughout history, Literary Chinese has had an enormous influence on the spoken Chinese languages.

Common Words

Below are given the most common forms for each meaning. With the exception of $tsywi_{3c}$, all of these survive as common bound forms in modern Chinese; many are also equivalent to the most common spoken forms. Of course, in their transcribed forms they would not be recognizable to the ordinary, literate person, who knows only the characters.

man:	puo$_{3c}$; nyen$_{3b}$	woman:	nuoQ$_{3b}$
water:	sywiQ$_{3c}$	sun:	nyet$_{3b}$
three:	sam$_{1b}$	fish:	nguo$_{3b}$
big:	deiH$_{1b}$	long:	drang$_3$
small:	sauQ$_3$	tree:	muk1$_b$
bird:	tauQ$_4$, tsywi$_{3c}$	dog:	khwanQ$_4$; kouQ$_1$
no:	pi$_3$ yaQ$_3$ (it is not so)		
yes:	dzyiQ$_{3b}$ yaQ$_3$ (it is so); nak$_1$ (I assent)		
good:	hauQ$_1$, dzyanQ$_{3b}$; lang$_3$		

Example Sentences

(1)

uoH$_1$	nyen$_{3b}$	mwen$_{3a}$	tsyi$_{3d}$	kheQ$_1$	yaQ$_3$
to.hate	people	to.hear	[OBJ]	possible	[firm statement]

uoH$_1$	kiQ$_{3d}$	dziH$_{3c}$	mwen$_{3a}$	tsyi$_{3d}$	bwet$_1$
to.hate	self.[PRON]	self. [ADV]	to.hear	[OBJ]	absurd

ghiQ$_{3d}$
[completion]
'It is all right to fear that others should hear it, but to fear hearing it oneself is absurd.'

(2)

pi$_{3a}$	ngou$_{3b}$	pwet$_{3a}$	mwen$_{3a}$	pou$_{3a}$	ghap$_{1a}$
it.is.not	oxen	[NEG+OBJ]	to.hear	[NEG]	to.suit

gi$_{3d}$	nyiQ$_{3d}$	ghiQ$_{3d}$
[POSS]	ear	[completion]

'It isn't that the oxen weren't listening to it, but that it did not agree with their ears.'

(3)

zyemQ$_3$	ghiQ$_{3d}$,	nguo$_1$	pou$_{3b}$	tri$_{3b}$	nyen$_{3b}$
very much	[completion]	I	[NEG]	to.know	person

yaQ$_3$
[firm.statement]

'Extreme, my not knowing others' = 'My inability to judge others is extreme indeed.'

Efforts to Preserve, Protect, and Promote the Language

Although Classical and Literary Chinese are still taught to secondary school students in Chinese parts of the world, they no longer have the influence they once did, even though premodern literature remains very widely read in the original—far more than Classical Latin and Greek are in the West. There has been marked resistance to the use of Literary Chinese during the more ideological periods of the People's Republic of China (1945–).

Select Bibliography

Branner, David Prager. 1999. "A Neutral Transcription System for Teaching Medieval Chinese." In *T'ang Studies* 17:1–170.

____. 2000. "The Suí-Táng Tradition of Fanqiè Phonology" and "The Rime-table System of Formal Chinese Phonology". Articles 6 and 7 of the *Geschichte der Sprachwissenschaften —History of the Language Sciences—Histoire des sciences du language—an International Handbook on the Evolution of the Study of Language from the Beginnings to the Present*, edited by Sylvain Auroux, Konrad Koerner, Hans-Josef Niederehe, and Kees Versteegh.

Boltz, William. 1994. *The Origin and Early Development of the Chinese Writing System*. American Oriental Society.

DeFrancis, John. 1984. *The Chinese Language, Fact and Fantasy*. Honolulu: University of Hawaii Press.

von der Gabelenz, Georg. 1881. *Chinesische Grammatik*. Leipzig: T.O. Weigel.

Harbsmeier, Kristof. 1998. *Science and Civilization in China*. Vol 7, part 2: *Language and Logic*. Cambridge and New York: Cambridge University Press.

Karlgren, Bernhard. 1915–24. *Études sur la Phonologie Chinoise*. Upsala: K. W. Appleberg. In four installments: 1915: Archives D'Études Orientales, No. 12; 1916: No. 13; 1919: No. 19; 1924: No. 24.

____. 1923. *Analytic Dictionary of Chinese and Sino-Japanese*. Paris: Librairie Orientaliste Paul Geuthner. Many reprints.

____. 1954. "Compendium of phonetics in Ancient and Archaic Chinese." In *Bulletin of the Museum of Far Eastern Antiquities* 26: 211–367.

____. 1957. "Grammata serica recensa." In *Bulletin of the Museum of Far Eastern Antiquities* 29: 1–332.

Norman, Jerry. 1994. "Pharyngealization in Early Chinese." In *JAOS* 114:3.397–408.

Pulleyblank, Edwin G. 1962. "The Consonantal System of Old Chinese." In *Asia Major* 9: 58–144, 206–265.

____. 1984. *Middle Chinese*. Vancouver: University of British Columbia Press.

____. 1995. *An Outline of Classical Chinese*. Vancouver: University of British Columbia Press

Rawski, Evelyn Sakakida. 1979. *Education and Popular Literacy in Ch'ing China*. Ann Arbor: University of Michigan Press.

Sagart, Laurent. 1999. *The Roots of Old Chinese*. Amsterdam/ Philadelphia: John Benjamins Publishing Company.

Chinese Languages: Gan

Laurent Sagart

Language Name: Gan.

Location: The center and north of Jiangxi Province, plus adjoining areas in Hunan, Hubei and Anhui provinces of the People's Republic of China.

Family: Sinitic.

Related Languages: Within the Sinitic family, Gan is most closely related to HAKKA (also known as Kejia), spoken in south Jiangxi, north Guangdong and West Fujian. Gan-Hakka as a whole is most closely related to other Sinitic languages like XIANG, YUE (Cantonese) and MANDARIN. Most distant within Sinitic are WU and the MIN supergroup, spoken in Fujian province.

Dialects: The main linguistic divide is between Northern Gan, spoken in the plains area around lake Poyang, and Southern Gan, spoken in the hillier areas further south. Northern Gan dialects have some vowel contrasts which are not found in Southern Gan: thus the vowel in 'silkworm' and 'south' contrasts with the vowel in 'three' and 'blue', usually as low rounded [ɔ] vs. low unrounded [a]. In Southern Gan, the two vowels are merged, usually as low unrounded.

Northern and Southern Gan also show distinct developments among initial consonants. Most Gan dialects have merged the Middle Chinese voiced stops and affricates with their voiceless aspirated counterparts, but while in all southern Gan and in Hakka the merger results in voiceless aspirates, in many northern Gan dialects the outcome is voiced stops and affricates, in all contexts (Hukou, Duchang), or at least in non-initial position in connected speech (Anyi, Nanchang). Secondary voicing of the old voiceless aspirated obstruents (apparently of hypercorrect origin) has brought about a lowering of their tonal onsets, this resulting in secondary tone splits within their high tone register (Middle Chinese voiceless initials), the voiceless unaspirated initials commanding higher tones, and the secondarily voiced initials (from Middle Chinese voiceless aspirates), commanding lower tones.

In Southern Gan, where these developments are not seen, initial /th-/ characteristically shows some instability, shifting to other sounds (especially *h*-), this in turn triggering sound shifts recreating tokens of /th-/ out of other sounds, usually voiceless aspirated affricates. In lexicon, Northern Gan has absorbed more elements of the northern Chinese lexicon than Southern Gan.

Number of Speakers: Approximately 30 million speakers.

Origin and History

Jiangxi province was gradually integrated into China through military conquest and immigration between the 3rd century B.C. and the end of the first millennium A.D. Its inhabitants at the time of the Chinese conquest may have included Miao-Yao speakers, of which the She people of north Guangdong and west Fujian are perhaps descended. Little is known about the settlement patterns of early Chinese immigrants during the Han period (c. 200 B.C.–A.D. 200); they certainly included soldiers and administrative personnel, and possibly craftsmen and peasants. These settlers concentrated in the northern plains and the main river valleys. After a marked demographic increase during the first two centuries A.D., a catastrophic reduction of the population occurred in the third century. This was followed by demographic stagnation until the beginning of the 8th century. Because of the numerical weakness of its speakers, the language of these early Chinese settlers has left few linguistic traces in the modern Gan dialects, especially in Northern Gan. Following the fall of Luoyang, the Chinese capital, to a coalition of foreign powers, in 313, the Chinese ruling classes emigrated south of the Yangzi, opening a period of development for north Jiangxi where large agricultural domains, especially tea plantations, were established. In this period the style of speech associated with the southern aristocracy during the period of division ('Early Middle Chinese', with the vowel distinctions described above) was introduced into north Jiangxi, while more archaic forms of speech, with connections to southern Hunan dialects, continued to prevail in south Jiangxi. Beginning in the 7th century, massive migrations of northern settlers brought to Jiangxi a new style of speech, characteristic of the Tang period ('Late Middle Chinese'). The new settlers outnumbered pre-existing Chinese-speaking populations, in the north, and especially in the south, where agricultural lands were available. It is this layer, the thickest in all of Jiangxi, which provides the unity of Gan. The developments described above in the section of dialects took place within the past millennium.

We now present some facts about the dialect of Nanchang, the provincial capital, a city of over one million, where an influential variety of Northern Gan is spoken. The data are based primarily on Wei Gangqiang and Chen Changyi (1998). Occasional use of Beijing Daxue Zhongguo Yuyan Wenxue Xi Yuyanxue Jiaoyanshi (1964) has been made for lexical matters.

Orthography and Basic Phonology

Gan is not a literary language. Literate speakers of Gan write in Classical Chinese or in Mandarin.

Like other Sinitic languages, Nanchang phonology is syllable-based. Syllables are analyzable into onsets and rhymes. Tone is a property of the rhymes.

Table 1: Onsets

	Labial	Alveolar	Palatal	Velar	Laryngeal
Stops					
Unaspirated	p	t		k	
Aspirated	pʰ	tʰ		kʰ	
Affricates					
Unaspirated		ts	tɕ		
Aspirated		tsʰ	tɕʰ		
Fricatives	f	s	ɕ		h
Liquid		l			
Nasals	m	n	ɲ	ŋ	
Glides	w		jɥ		

Complex onsets include Cj-, Cɥ- and Cw- sequences as follows:

(a) Cj- sequences: pj, pʰj, tj, tʰj, tɕj, tɕʰj, ɕj, kj, kʰj, mj, lj, ɲj
(b) Cɥ- sequences: tɕɥ, tɕʰɥ, ɕɥ
(c) Cw- sequences: kw, kʰw

The aspirated initials are voiceless in isolation, but occasionally voiced and breathy~lax in running speech, except utterance-initially. Among simple onsets, the palatals are always followed by a high front syllabic vowel. They are in complementary distribution with the alveolar sibilants, which are never followed by such a vowel. The palatals may also form complex onsets with a following glide /j/ or /ɥ/, while the alveolar sibilants cannot.

Rhymes. Segmental rhymes are as follows:

ɑ		ɑu		ɑŋ	ɑʔ
	ai		an		
e					
		ɛu	ɛn		ɛʔ
ɵ					
o					
			ɔn	ɔŋ	ɔʔ
ɨ	ɨi	ɨu	ɨn		ɨʔ
i		iu	in		iʔ
y			yn		yʔ
u	ui		un	uŋ	uʔ
m	n	ŋ			

There is complementary distribution between [a] and [ɑ]: the former occurs preceding acute codas, the latter elsewhere. [e] and [o] have lower allophones [ɛ] and [ɔ] respectively when followed by any coda. The rhyme noted as *ɨ* is the so-called 'apical vowel'. It only occurs following alveolar sibilants. The rhymes *m*, *n* and *ŋ* are syllabic nasals which do not combine with any onset: *n*³ 'you'; *ŋ*³ 'five'.

Tones. There are 7 tones, in Y. R. Chao's 5-level notation (Chao 1930):

T1 [42]; T2 [24]; T3 [213]; T5 [45]; T6 [21]; T7 [5ˀ]; T8 [2ˀ]

Tones T1, T2, T3, T5 and T6 contrast on syllables ending in sonorants. All syllables ending in -ʔ have either tone T7 or tone T8, and all T7 and T8 syllables end in -ʔ. Tones T7 and T8 are short and abrupt. In addition, some syllables are toneless (T0). Their actual contour depends on the contour of a preceding tonal syllable: it is mid-high [4] if the preceding syllable ends in a rise (T2, T3, T5) and mid-low [2] otherwise.

The correspondence of Nanchang tones to Middle Chinese (MC) tones (ca. A.D. 600) is shown below:

MC initial types	MC tones PING	SHANG	QU	RU
voiceless unaspirated	42	213	45	5ˀ
voiceless aspirated	42	213	213	5ˀ
voiced obstruents	24	21	21	5ˀ, 2ˀ
sonorants	45	213	21	5ˀ, 2ˀ

There is much variability in Nanchang phonology, in particular regarding final consonants and tones, an indication of change in progress. Earlier descriptions of Nanchang list final oral stops *-t* and *-k*: replacement of *-t* and *-k* by a glottal stop is now near completion. Tones 7 and 8 are merged as a high tone in some reports.

Basic Morphology

As in most modern Sinitic languages, there is little morphology in Gan. Nanchang has no case-marking, no number and gender marking, no articles, no modifier-noun agreement. Noun morphology is limited to a few nominal suffixes: *-tsɨ⁰* (*tau¹ tsɨ⁰* 'knife'; *maŋ³ tsɨ⁰* 'tall person'), *-tʰɛu⁰* (*saʔ⁷ tʰɛu⁰* 'stone'). Suffixed *-li⁰* is rare in Nanchang but much more common in other Gan dialects, for instance Shanggao *mœn⁶ liᴴ* 'mosquito'.

Personal Pronouns. Plural pronouns are formed by suffixing *-ko⁰ li⁰*:

	1	2	3
sg.	ŋo³	n³	tɕjɛ³
pl.	ŋo³ ko⁰ li⁰	n³ ko⁰ li⁰	tɕjɛ³ ko⁰ li⁰

Verbs. There is no verb agreement. Nanchang verb morphology makes use of some aspect suffixes: *-tau⁰* 'continuative'; *-piʔ⁰* 'perfective'; *-kwo⁰* 'experiential'.

Basic Syntax

Gan is SVO and head-final:

tɕiɛ³	*sin¹*	*sɔŋ⁰*	*tsʰɔn1 tau⁰*	*tɕʰjɛn⁶*	*hɛu⁶*	*tʰai⁶ i¹*
3sg	body	on	wear-ASP	CL	thick	overcoat

'on his body he was wearing a thick overcoat'

Verbs and adjectives are negated by *pɨʔ⁷* :

pɨʔ⁷	*ɕi³-fɔn⁰*	*pɨʔ⁷*	*hau³*
NEG	like	NEG	good
'not like'		'not good'	

but *jiu³* 'have' is negated by *mau⁶*, as are verbs in the perfective and experiential aspects.

Contact with Other Languages

Mandarin Chinese is the principal source of borrowings. Examples: *y⁵ mi³* 'corn' (maize); *tɕjɛu³ tsɨ⁰* 'boiled dumplings'

Common Words

man:	lan²ko⁰	water:	sui³
woman:	ɲy³ko⁰	sun:	ɲiʔ⁷ tʰɛu⁰
three:	san¹	fish:	ɲje⁵
big:	tʰai⁶	long:	tsʰɔŋ²
small:	ɕi⁵	yes:	sɨ⁶
good:	hɑu³	no:	pɨʔ⁷
bird:	ɲjɛu³	dog:	kjɛu³
tree:	ɕy⁶		

Example Sentences

(1) lɑʔ⁷ ŋo³ iʔ⁷ pɨn³ ɕy¹
give 1sg one CL book
'Give me a book.'

(2) ko³ tsɑʔ⁷ pi³ he³ tsɑʔ⁷ hɑu³
this CL compared.with that CL good
'This one is better than that one.'

(3) tɕje³ tɕʰje³ kwo⁰ sɔŋ⁶-hai³, ŋo³ mɑu⁶ tɕʰje³ kwo⁰
3sg go ASP Shanghai 1sg haven't go ASP
'He has been to Shanghai, I haven't.'

Efforts to Preserve, Protect, and Promote the Language

No efforts are currently made to preserve, protect, or promote Gan. Gan is not a literary language, and is not taught in schools. The current policy of the Chinese state aims at promoting Putonghua through the eradication of other Sinitic languages ('dialects'), including Gan, rather than through promoting bilingualism with Putonghua. If current trends continue, Gan may find itself an endangered language in a few generations' time.

Select Bibliography

Chao, Y-R. 1930. "A system of tone-letters." In *Le Maître Phonétique* 45: 24–7.

Chen Changyi. 1991. *Gan Fangyan Gaiyao* [Outline of Gan Dialects]. Nanchang: Jiangxi Jiaoyu Chubanshe.

Ho Dah-an. 1986. "Lun Kan Fangyen" [On the Gan dialect]. In *Hanhsueh Yenchiu* 5, 1: 1–28.

Li Rulong and Zhang Shuangqing. 1992. *Ke-Gan fangyan diaocha baogao* [A report on a survey of the Kejia and Gan dialects]. Xiamen: Xiamen University Publishing House.

Luo Changpei. 1940. *Linchuan Yinxi* [The sound system of Linchuan]. Changsha: Shangwu.

Sagart, L. 1988. "On Gan-Hakka." In *Tsinghua Journal of Chinese Studies New Series* Vol. 18 No.1 (June 1988) 141–160.

____. 1993. *Les dialectes gan* [the Gan dialects]. Paris: Langages Croisés.

Xiong Zhenghui. 1995. *Nanchang Fangyan Cidian* [dictionary of the Nanchang dialect]. Nanjing: Jiangsu Jiaoyu Chubanshe.

Yan Sen. 1986. "Jiangxi Fangyan De Fenqu (Gao)" [the subdivisions of Gan (draft)]. In *Fangyan 1986, 1*: 19–38.

Wei Gangqiang and Chen Changyi. 1998. "Nanchang Hua Yin Dang" [Nanchang sound archives]. In Hou Jingyi (ed.) *Xiandai Hanyu Fangyin Yinku*. Shanghai: Shanghai Jiaoyu Chubanshe.

CHINESE LANGUAGES: HAKKA

Anne O. Yue

Language Name: Hakka. **Alternates:** Kejia, Ngaiwa, Makkaiwa

Location: Southern China (eastern and central Guangdong province, western Fujian province, and southern Jiangxi province), but also scattered in various parts of Guangxi, Hunan, Sichuan, Taiwan, Hainan, as well as areas outside China, especially Southeast Asia, such as Malaysia, Singapore, Indonesia, Brunei, South Pacific islands, and to a lesser extent, Europe, America, and Africa.

Family: Sino-Tibetan.

Related Languages: GAN, YUE, MIN, XIANG, WU, MANDARIN (Northern Chinese).

Dialects: There are about thirty Hakka dialects described. A tentative classification based on available materials and taking into consideration the number of tones, the existence of two or one series of sibilants, and the number of consonantal endings as classificatory criteria, gives three major subgroups: (1) Jiāyìng, (2) Outer Inland, and (3) Northern Inland. These dialects are distinguished from other closely related Sinitic languages by several features. These include shifts in the tonal classes of some words and the change of voiced stop and affricate initials into voiceless affricates.

Hakka's most prominent characteristic as a Sinitic language group lies in the development of a number of colloquial words derived from Ancient Chinese syllables with glide or sonorant initial consonants and the rising (*Shang*) Tone into modern syllables with the Upper Even (*Yin-Ping*) Tone, for example, 'horse', 'to buy', 'ear', 'tail', 'to bite', 'to have', 'to dye', 'to be lazy', 'to be warm', 'to be soft', 'two', and 'to be cold'. Since there are a few dialects outside the Hakka group, such as Yixing and Wuxi of Wu and Taiping Xianyuan in Anhui, that manifest the first feature, Hakka may not be defined uniquely by this feature alone, but by the existence of two more important features. One is the development of a number of colloquial words derived from Ancient Chinese syllables with voiced initials and the Rising Tone into modern syllables with the Upper Even Tone, such as 'to sit', 'below', 'pillar', 'younger brother', 'covering', 'maternal uncle', 'insipid', 'to break', 'to be near', 'to ascend', 'to move', and 'to be heavy'. However, this feature is shared with a number of the Gan dialects (Jishui, Duchang, and Nancheng). Another important feature is the development of ancient voiced stop and affricate initials into voiceless aspirates despite tonal distinction of the syllable, another feature that Hakka shares with the Gan language as well as with a number of dialects from other Sinitic languages; for example, Lianzhou of Yue and Shaowu of Min.

Number of Speakers: 35 million, as of the 1982 census.

Origin and History

The Hakka people, whose name in Cantonese, *hak*[7b] *ka*[1], means 'guest' or 'stranger', are believed to have moved from northern China to the South through five major waves of migration from the beginning of the 4th century to the middle of the 19th century, as a result of foreign invasion, civil war, or (linguistic) tribal disputes. Although the exact location of their homeland has yet to be ascertained, the regions of southern Shanxi, northern Henan, and northern Anhui have been suggested. The first wave of migration (317–819) brought the Hakkas across Henan to central and southwestern Anhui as well as northern Jiangxi; the second wave (880–1126) brought them from southern Henan through northern Jiangxi to southern Jiangxi and northern Guangdong; the third wave (1127–1644) brought them from southern Jiangxi through northern Guangdong to central Guangdong and southern Guangxi; the fourth wave (1645–1867) brought them from southern Jiangxi northward through eastern Hunan to central and western Sichuan, from northeastern Guangdong to southern Hunan, central Guangxi and across the Formosa Strait to western coastal Taiwan; and the fifth wave (after 1867) brought them from central Guangdong to western Guangdong and the Hainan island as well as central Guangxi. The scattered distribution of the present-day Hakka speakers is unparalleled among the Sinitic languages, although the major concentration is around a five hundred kilometer radius circling the border area of Guangdong, Fujian, and Jiangxi.

Unlike the Wu, the Min, and the Yue languages, there were no written records in the Hakka language until the 19th century when Western missionaries first transcribed them and compiled dictionaries and textbooks for learning them. Such early materials pertain to the dialects of Lùféng (southeastern coastal Guangdong) as spoken in Brunei, the New Territories (in Hong Kong), and Méixiàn only. Systematic linguistic study of Hakka began around the middle of the 20th century. A complete reconstruction of proto-Hakka based on extant materials has not been fully worked out.

Orthography and Basic Phonology

No orthography has been devised for the Hakka language ex-

Hakka is spoken primarily in the eastern and central Guangdong province (shaded area) of China.

cept romanization. Unless indicated, the following descriptions are of the standard dialect, Méixiàn (East Guangdong).

Table 1: Consonants

		Labial	Dental	Velar	Glottal
Stops	Unaspirated	p	t	k	
	Aspirated	p'	t'	k'	
Fricatives	Voiceless	f	s		h
	Voiced	v			
Affricates	Unaspirated		ts		
	Aspirated		ts'		
Nasals		m	n	ŋ	
Resonants			l		

Hakka has an additional palatal nasal [ɲ] that is in complementary distribution with [n]: [ɲ] only occurs before the high front vowels /i ɪ/, and [n] occurs in other contexts.

Among the above consonants, only the nasals and the oral stops can occur in syllable-final position.

Table 2: Vowels

	Front	Central	Back
High	i ɪ		u
Mid	e [ɛ]	ə	o [ɔ]
Low		a	

The mid vowels /e/ and /o/ are phonetically [ɛ] and [ɔ].

Hakka is a tone language. In open syllables or syllables ending in a nasal consonant, four different tones are possible. In syllables ending in an oral stop, two tones are possible.

Syllable Type	Tone Contour	Traditional Name	Gloss
Open	mid-high level	Yīn-Píng (1)	'higher even'
	low level	Yáng-Píng(2)	'lower even'
	low falling	Shăng (3)	'rising'
	high falling	Qù (5)	'going'
Closed	low checked	Yīn-Rù (7)	'upper entering'
	high checked	Yáng-Rù (8)	'lower entering'

This is the dominant configuration of tonal categories for the Hakka dialects, although a few have as many as seven tones or as few as five.

In a phonetic sequence of sounds, assimilation occurs, both progessive and regressive. For example, the last segment of the bound morpheme 'what' assimilates to the following sound:

maɲ ɲin
what person 'who'

mak kai
what CLASSIFIER 'what'

The Sìxiàn variety of the Xīnzhú dialect (Taiwan) abounds in assimilation. For example, the nominal suffix *-e* takes on different initial consonants in accordance with the preceding sound (D indicates a flapped dental stop):

li^2-e
pear-NOM.SUFF

kit^7-De
small.mandarin.orange-NOM.SUFF

kam^1-me
tangerine-NOM.SUFF

son^1-ne
mango-NOM.SUFF

Basic Morphology

Unless specified otherwise, the Méixián dialect is used here. Like all Sinitic languages, Hakka has no marking for case, number or gender. The only marker for nouns is the classifier, which appears almost obligatorily whenever a noun is used with numbers or demonstratives. Sometimes the classifier signifies the shape of the item it goes with; for example, *ki*^{1} for 'branch like object' and *t'iao*^{2} for 'long thin object'. Examples follow:

jit^{7}	tsak^{7}	ɲin^{2}
one	CLASS	person

jit^{7}	ki^{1}	pit^{7}
one	CLASS	pen

jit^{7}	t'iau^{2}	tsu^{1}
one	CLASS	pig

jit^{7}	lioŋ^{2}	ts'a^{1}
one	CLASS	car

The plural for the personal pronouns is a complex suffixal form consisting of the plural marker *ten*^{3} + *ɲin*^{2} 'person':

ŋai^{2}-ten^{3}-ɲin^{2}	ɲ^{2}-ten^{3}-ɲin^{2}	ki^{2}-ten^{3}-ɲin^{2}
I-PL-person	you-PL-person	s/he-PL-person
'we'	'you plural'	'they'

There are gender markers for animals, which appear as suffixes, a typical feature of Southern Sinitic languages such as Min or Yue. There are several different suffixes for 'male' but only one for 'female':

ke^{1}-kuŋ^{1}	ke^{1}-ma^{2}
chicken-male 'cock'	chicken-female 'hen'

tsu^{1}-ku^{3}/-sjuŋ^{2}	tsu^{1} -ma^{2}
pig-male 'boar'	pig-female 'sow'

There is no verbal morphology strictly speaking. Perfective, progressive/durative, and experiential aspects are expressed with suffixes, while the affirmative present and the past tense are expressed by "prefixing" the existential verb [ju^{1}] 'ex':

ki^{2}	hi^{5}-e	saŋ^{2}-tu^{3}-e
s/he	go-PERF	town-stomach-NOM.SUFF

'S/he has gone to town.'

ki^{2}	ju^{1}	hi^{5}	saŋ^{2}-tu^{3}-e
s/he	VEX	go	town-stomach-NOM.SUFF

'S/he went to town.'

ki^{2}	k'on^{5}-ten^{3}	fa^{1}	
s/he	look-PROG	flower	'S/he is looking at the flowers.'

ki^{2}	k'on^{5}-kuo^{5}	
s/he	look-EXP	'S/he has seen (it).'

Unlike Northern Chinese and similar to Southern Sinitic languages such as Yue and Min, the passive is expressed by the marker *pun*^{1} that goes with the agent and not with the verb, and it is the same marker that expresses the causative, which is identical with the verb 'to give'. The following examples are from the Xīnzhú dialect of Taiwan:

ŋai^{2}	pun^{1}	ki^{2}	ta^{3}	ŋai^{2}	
I	let	s/he	hit	me	'I let her/him hit me.'

ŋai^{2}	pun^{1}	ki^{2}	ta^{3}-to^{3}	
I	PASS	s/he	hit-get	'I was hit by her.'

ŋai^{2}	voi^{5}	pun^{1}	ɲi^{2}	it^{7}	suŋ^{2}	k'uai^{5}-e
I	shall	give	you	one	pair	chopsticks-NOM.SUFF

'I'll give you a pair of chopsticks.'

Basic Syntax

The preferred word order in an unmarked declarative or interrogative sentence is SVO.

maŋ^{7}	ɲin^{2}	k'ok^{8}	mun^{2}	a?
what	person	knock	door	FINAL.PARTICLE

'Who is knocking at the door?'

An OV order indicates topicalization for emphasis or contrast.

ki^{2}	mak^{7}-kai^{5}	su^{1}	tu^{1}	mai^{1}	
s/he	what-CL	book	all	buy	'She'll buy any book.'

With respect to the structure of the noun phrase, Hakka is head-final. All nominal modifiers precede the head noun.

ɲ^{2}	k'on^{5}	ke^{5}	pun^{3}	su^{1}	he^{5}	ŋai^{2}-ke^{5}
you	look	that	CL	book	be	I-NOMINALIZING.SUFF

'The book you are reading is mine.'

The general negative is *m*^{2} while the negative for the perfective is *maŋ*^{2} and the negative for the existential is *mo*^{2} (*m*^{2} + [ju^{1}]).

ts'oi^{5}	ke^{5}-e	m^{2}	ts'oi^{5}	li^{3}-e	
locate	there	NEG	locate	here	'It is there, not here.'

ki^{2}	hi^{5}-e	saŋ^{2}-tu^{3}-e	maŋ^{2}-t'ien^{2}
s/he	go-PERF	town-stomach-NOM.SUFF	NEG-yet

'Has s/he gone to town yet?'

Contact with Other Languages

Depending on locations, the Hakka people have lived for centuries among speakers of other languages such as She (non-Sinitic), Gan, Min, Yue, and Southwestern Mandarin. Loanwords probably abound, although they have not yet been studied. Some examples are:

From Cantonese into Méixiàn: *ŋam*^{1} 'right', *ŋam*^{1}*-ŋam*^{1} 'just now'
From Taiwanese into Xīnzhú: *tsin*^{5} *su*^{3} 'right hand'

There is as yet no systematic study of language contact in China. We can only offer some preliminary observation. The fact that the Hakka people have lived among other peoples for centuries is reflected in every aspect of the language. Early contact with the non-Sinitic She language is unfortunately not documented. The She people are believed to be the aborigines who lived in regions that the Hakka first migrated into—in the hilly parts of Fujian, Zhejiang, Guangdong, Jiangxi, Anhui, for example. Today, it is estimated that only about 1,000 of the Shes still speak the original tongue (believed to be a branch of the Miao language) in some mountainous villages in Boluo, Zengcheng, Huidong, and Haifeng. A detailed description of She is yet to appear. One possible remnant of language contact is the existence of a three-way distinction in the deictics—near, far, farther—which is characteristic of She. This is distinctive neither in Hakka nor in other Sinitic languages, but appears in a nineteenth century record of the Lufeng dialect of Hakka (as well as sporadically in other Sinitic languages):

li, liá = 'this'; li-tse, li-t'ang = 'here'
kai, ká = 'that'; kai-tse, kai-t'ang = 'there'
un = 'yonder'; un-tse, un-t'ang = 'yonder'
(un-tjak/kian-wuk = 'yonder house')

Hakka and Gan not only share an important phonological development from Ancient Chinese (mentioned above under "Dialects"), and have thus been sometimes classified together as a single language group, but also certain vocabulary items, such as 'shrimp' or 'nose' which consist of a Han cognate stem suffixed with a male gender marker (for nonhuman). Hakka also shares some lexical items with both Gan and Xiang, such as 'younger brother'; or 'younger sister', which consists of a Han cognate stem prefixed with a familiar marker derived from the word 'old'. Hakka seems to share even more with the southern dialects of Min and Yue.

In a language contact situation, the direction of borrowing is not always clear. The triple reduplication of stative verbs to indicate an intensive degree is characteristic of S. Min. It is also found in the Xingzhu dialect of Hakka (as well as the Yue dialect of Huazhou in southwestern Guangdong). In addition, it occurs in Vietnamese too. The paucity of available detailed syntactic information in the languages concerned prevents one from drawing significant conclusions.

Common Words

man:	nam^{2}eɲin^{2}	long:	ts'oŋ^{2}
woman:	fu^{5} ɲin^{2}ka^{1}	small:	se^{5}
water:	sui^{3}	yes:	(repeat verb)
sun:	ɲit^{7}t'eu^{2}	no:	(negate verb)
three:	sam^{1}	good:	ho^{3}
fish:	ŋ^{2}	bird:	tiau^{1}e
big:	t'ai	dog:	keu^{3}
tree:	su^{5}		

Example Sentences

(1) pun^{1} it^{7} pun^{3} su^{1} (pun^{1}) ŋai^{2}
give one CL book (give) I
'Give me a book.'

(2) ŋai^{2} pi^{3} ɲ^{2} ko^{1} sam^{1} ts'un^{5}
I compare you tall three inch
'I am three inches taller than you.'

(3) sit^{8}-e fan^{5} tsai^{5} hi^{5} ho^{3} mo^{2}?
eat-PERF rice then go good NEG
'Go after eating, okay?'

Efforts to Preserve, Protect, and Promote the Language

Because of the persecution from "natives" (earlier settlers as well as aborigines), the Hakkas have a strong sense of ethnicity. In addition, because of the "accusation" by other Sinitic language speakers, notably during the Qing dynasty, that they are a non-Sinitic "barbarian" people, the Hakkas indignantly began research into the origin of their people and on their language to prove that both are cognate with the Han stock. However, early studies contained many forced etymologies, and it was not until the middle of the twentieth century that modern linguistic research confirmed the genetic relationship of Hakka with other Sinitic languages and its derivation from Ancient Chinese.

Select Bibliography

Egerod, Søren. 1959. "A sampling of Chungshan Hakka." In *Studia Serica Karlgren Dedicata*. Copenhagen: Ejnar Munksgaard, 36–54.

Hashimoto, Mantaro. 1973. *The Hakka Dialect: A Linguistic Study of its Phonology, Syntax and Lexicon*. Cambridge: Cambridge University Press.

____. 1992. "Hakka in wellentheorie perspective." In *Journal of Chinese Linguistics*. 20–1:1–49.

Henne, Henry. 1964. "Sathewkok Hakka phonology." In *Norsk Tidsskrift for Sprogvidenskap* 20:109–61.

____. 1966. "A Sketch of Sathewkok Hakka Grammatical Strucutre." In *Acta Linguistica Hafniensia*. 10–1:69–108.

Li, Rong, et al. 1987. *Language Atlas of China*. Hong Kong: Longman.

Li, Rulong and Zhang Shuangqing. 1992. *Ke Gan Fangyan Diaocha Baogao* (Report on a Survey of the Gan and the Hakka Dialects). Xiamen: Xiamen University Press.

MacIver, Donald. 1905. *An English-Chinese Dictionary in the Vernacular of the Hakka People in the Canton Province*. Shanghai: American Presbyterian Mission Press.

Mei, Yi, et al, eds. 1988. *Chinese Encyclopedia: Language, Writing*. Shanghai: Chinese Encyclopedia Publisher.

Norman, Jerry. 1989. "What is a Kejia dialect?" In *Proceedings of the 2nd International Confedrence on Sinology*. 324–44. Taiwan: Academia Sinica.

O'Connor, Kevin A. 1976. "Proto-Hakka." In *Journal of Asian and African Studies*. 11:1–24.

Ramsey, Robert S. 1987. *The Languages of China*. Princeton: Princeton University Press.

Rey, Charles. 1901. *Dictionnaire Chinois-Francais Dialecte Hac-ka*. Hong Kong: Imprimerie de la Société des Missions Étrangères.

Sagart, Laurent. 1982. *Phonologie du Dialecte Hakka de Sung Him Tong*. Paris: Centre de Recherches Linguistiques sur l'Asie Orientale.

Yang, Paul Fumien, S.J. 1967. "Elements of Hakka dialectology." In *Monumenta Serica*. 26:305–351.

Yue-Hashimoto, Anne. 1993. *Comparative Chinese Dialectal Grammar: Handbook for Investigators* Paris: École des Hautes Études en Sciences Sociales Centre de Recherches linguistiques sur l'Asie Orientale.

Chinese Languages: Mandarin

Xiaonong Zhu

Language Name: Mandarin is not the name of a language, but refers to a group or 'supergroup' of Chinese dialects. Mandarin is the largest among the seven major Chinese dialect groups. Over 70% of the Chinese-speaking people speak one of the Mandarin dialects.

Mandarin is a translation of *guānhuà* (literally, 'officials' language' or 'public language'), which is now a technical term in Chinese linguistics.

The modern standard Chinese, *putonghua*, is based on the Beijing dialect of Mandarin; specifically, it has the Beijing pronunciation as its standard pronunciation and the exemplary literature written in the modern colloquial of Mandarin as its grammatical model.

The examples cited below are taken from the Beijing dialect using romanized orthography (*pinyin*) and phonetic transcription in square brackets if greater precision is required.

Location: While Mandarin predominates north of the Yangtze River, varieties of Mandarin have native speakers in all the provinces of China except Tibet and the southeast coastal provinces of Shanghai, Zhejiang, Jiangxi (with the exception around Jiujiang City), Fujian (except the city of Nanping), Guangdong, and Hainan. As noted above, the official and educational language of China, *putonghua*, is based on Mandarin, and it is the medium of education throughout China. It is also used in government and on radio and television. There are also native speakers of Mandarin in Taiwan. The official and educational language in Taiwan is Mandarin, which is called *guoyu* ('national language') and is slightly different from *putonghua*.

Family: Mandarin belongs to the Sinitic branch of Sino-Tibetan.

Related Languages: Mandarin is most closely related to other Chinese dialect groups such as WU, XIANG, GAN, Kejia (HAKKA), YUE (Cantonese), and MIN. As some hundred cognates have been recognized, its genetic relationship with Tibeto-Burmese has been reasonably established.

Dialects: Mandarin is generally thought to consist of four mutually intelligible dialect groups: Northern, Northwestern, Southwestern, and Xiajiang (the lower reach of the Yangtze River), each of which contains subgroups.

Recent research (Wurm et al. 1987) suggests eight rather than four groups, splitting Northern into Northeastern, Jiaoliao, Jilu, Beijing, and Zhongyuan. Under this scheme, Northwestern is renamed Lanying and Xiajiang is called Jianghuai. What is controversial in this scheme is that the dialects spoken in Shangxi and Inner Mongolia have been culled out of the Northwestern Mandarin and a new Jin group has been set up for them at the same level as Mandarin, Wu, Yue, etc. This article follows the more conservative view, and takes the Jin-speaking territory into account when talking about the location of Mandarin, including the Jin speakers when counting the number of Mandarin speakers.

It is widely held that the differences among the Chinese dialects are greatest in phonetics and phonology, less in lexicon, and least in syntax. Local vocabulary, as in any other large language group, can be heard everywhere in Mandarin-speaking areas. Syntactic differences mainly lie in functional words. Morphology has drawn the least attention from Chinese linguists because Chinese has little morphology. According to the dialectal data available now, however, the morphological differences within Mandarin are strikingly extensive, at least more than would be expected. The most notable differences within Mandarin are the diverse pitch values of local varieties [e.g., T(one)1 has the highest-level pitch [55] in Beijing but the lowest [11] in neighboring Tianjin] and the redistribution of the words with the Middle Chinese (MC) *rusheng* ('entering-tone'). In fact, the recategorization of old *rusheng* words is the primary criterion for the above-mentioned revision of Mandarin dialect grouping.

Number of Speakers: The Chinese-speaking people constitute 95% of the total Chinese population, and 70% of Chinese speakers have Mandarin as their first language. That is, about two-thirds of the 1.2 billion Chinese people, or some 800 million, are native speakers of Mandarin. Among these Mandarin speakers are not only most of the Han nationals, but also all Hui and Manchu nationals.

There are other native Mandarin speakers who are not included in the above statistics. Some minority ethnics, e.g., most of the Tujia and She nationals, use Mandarin as their mother tongue. Also, many ethnic groups are Mandarin-bilingual speakers. Almost all young Taiwanese speak Mandarin, and some of them use Mandarin as their first language. Before the 1980s, few Hong Kong residents spoke Mandarin. Today the situation is changing rapidly. In recent years, more and more schools and universities in Hong Kong include Mandarin courses in their curricula. Mandarin is one of the official languages in Singapore and is spoken by hundreds of thousands of Chinese overseas.

Table 1: Consonants

		Labial	Dental	Alveo-palatal	Retroflex	Velar
Stops	Aspirated	p [pʰ]	t [tʰ]			k [kʰ]
	Unaspirated	b [p]	d [t]			g [k]
Fricatives		f	s	x [ɕ]	sh [ʂ]	h [x]
Affricates	Aspirated		c [tsʰ]	q [tɕʰ]	ch [tʂʰ]	
	Unaspirated		z [ts]	j [tɕ]	zh [tʂ]	
Nasals		m	n			
Approximants			l		r [ɻ]	

Origin and History

The "Chinese language" is an all-encompassing term that subsumes a great number of linguistic varieties in terms of history, geography, stylistic registers, and social status. Mandarin is considered the 'mainstream' of Chinese language. Of the seven major dialect groups, Mandarin has deviated from the common ancestor the most. For example, Mandarin has more disyllabic compounds than do the other groups. Since most words in Old Chinese were monosyllabic, disyllabic compounds are thought to be innovative in the development of Chinese. Phonologically, too, Mandarin is among the least conservative in three aspects—voicing, endings, and tones.

The earliest Chinese is supposed to have arisen in the Yellow River Valley where two large nations, out of hundreds, met in the second millennium B.C. The two nations, Shang from the east (now Shandong) and Zhou from the west (now Shaanxi), established two successive empires for one and a half millennia (seventeenth century–249 B.C.). Zhou is believed to be a branch of, or to share a common ancestor with, Qiang, which is more closely related to Tibetan than Burmese is.

There is no received periodicization for Mandarin and its predecessors. A rough historical profile is given below. Each period can be further divided into several phases.

Old Chinese
1000+ B.C.–ca. A.D. 200—Late Shang to Eastern Han dynasties
Transition
ca. 200–ca. 600—Three Kingdoms to Nan-Bei dynasties
Middle Chinese
ca. 600–ca. 1100—Sui to Northern Song
Transition
ca. 1100–ca. 1300—Jin(Jurchen) to Southern Song
Old Mandarin
ca. 1300–ca. 1900—Yuan (Mongol) to Qing (Manchu)
Modern Mandarin
from early this century—post-Qing

It is noted that the contrasts between *yayan* ('elegant speech') and *fangyan* ('regional speech'), and between *shuyin* ('literary pronunciation') and *baihua* ('colloquial') have existed throughout the history of the language. Prior to the time of Modern Mandarin in the early twentieth century, *yayan* was based on the *shuyin* of a capital city. From Old to Middle Chinese, the literary pronunciation of Luoyang (in Henan), played a major role in setting norms for the language. From Old Mandarin, Beijing (called Dadu during the Yuan dynasty) became the capital, but its colloquial accent did not gain preeminent status until the Modern Mandarin era. During the Old Mandarin period, the Luoyang *shuyin* was still a prestigious *yayan*, and the Beijing *shuyin* gradually gained its social status.

The most noteworthy change in the course of evolution from Old to Middle Chinese is probably the emergence of distinctive tones, which originally were accompanying features of consonantal voicing and various syllable endings such as [-*Ø, -*ŋ, -*ʔ, -*h, -*s, -*p, -*t, -*k]. Specifically, open syllables and nasal endings are associated with *pingsheng* 'level-tone', the glottal stop ending with *shangsheng* 'rising-tone', the fricative endings with *qusheng* 'departing-tone', and the oral stop endings with *rusheng* 'entering-tone'. Each of these four tones splits into two registers: *yin* 'upper' and *yang* 'lower', according to whether the initial consonant is voiceless or voiced. So there are eight tone categories in Middle Chinese.

The earliest syntactically mature written Chinese dates back to the middle of the second millennium B.C. when primitive characters were first inscribed on oracle bones and shells. The earliest characters were pictographs (*xiangxing*) and representative symbols (*zhishi*). Later on, phonetic borrowing (*jiajie*) and phonetic compounding (*xingsheng*) were gradually developed. Phonetic compounding was/is the most productive means in creating new characters; *xingsheng* words account for more than four-fifths of all Chinese characters. This transtime and transspatial written form has guaranteed the continuity of the Chinese culture and the unity of the Chinese language.

Official romanization, *pinyin*, has been adopted in the People's Republic of China since 1958. The examples cited in this article are written in *pinyin*.

Orthography and Basic Phonology

With few exceptions, each Chinese character represents a syllable-sized morpheme. Traditionally, Chinese was written or printed in vertical style, from right to left.

The *pinyin* (official romanization in the People's Republic of China) spelling represents individual phonemes, with some exceptions.

It is general practice, stemming from a long and venerable

Table 2: Mandarin Finals

Ending		Medial *kai* -Ø-	*qi* -y-	*he* -w-	*chuo* -ɥ-
yin	-Ø	i [ʐ̩ ɹ̩]	i	u	ü
'open'		a	ia [ya]	ua [wa]	
		e [ɤ]	ie [yɛ]		üe [ɥɛ]
		o		uo	er [ɚ]
	-y	ai		uai [way]	
		ei		ui [wey]	
	-w	ao [ɑw]	iao [yɑw]		
		ou	iu [yəw]		
yang	-n	an	ian [yɛn]	uan	üan [ɥɛn]
'closed'		en [ə]	in	un [wən]	ün
	-ŋ	ang [ɑŋ]	iang [yɑŋ]	uang [wɑŋ]	
		eng [əŋ]	ing	uang [wɑŋ]	
		ong [ʊŋ]	iong [yʊŋ]		

tradition in Chinese phonology, to describe phonological structures in terms of syllable-structure constituents rather than phonemes. The Mandarin syllable comprises three constituents: a base or neutralized tone (in modern phonology, the neutralized tone is regarded as toneless); an optional Initial (initial consonant); and a Final (the rest of the syllable).

A zero-initial is usually realized as a glottal stop [ʔ].

The alveo-palatal affricates *j*, *q*, and fricative *x* are phonetically [tɕ], [tɕʰ], and [ɕ] respectively, while their retroflex equivalents *zh*, *ch*, and *sh* are [tʂ], [tʂh], and [ʂ]. Neither *x* nor *sh* is identical with English *sh* /š/. The retroflex *r* is a resonant or approximant [ɻ] rather than a voiced fricative [ʐ].

Mandarin Finals, as illustrated in Table 2 above, may contain an optional Medial element. The three potential Medials are the high, front, unrounded glide [y]; the high, back, rounded glide [w]; and the high, front, rounded glide [ɥ].

Finals can also be grouped in terms of their endings. *Yin*, or open, syllables may be closed by an offglide [y] or [w]. *Yang*, or closed, syllables end in either [n] or [ŋ]. These are the only consonants that can close syllables in Beijing Mandarin.

Tones. Beijing Mandarin has four base tones and a neutralized tone. Using Chao's five-level system (with 5 representing the highest pitch and 1 the lowest), the four base tones are: T1 [55] high level, T2 [35] high rising, T3 [214] fall-rise, and T4 [51] full falling. The actual pitch on a syllable described as having neutralized tone can be predicted from its context. In *pinyin*, T1 is marked by ¯ on the nucleus, T2 by ´, T3 by ˇ, and T4 by `. The neutralized tone is not marked.

One characteristic process in Mandarin phonology is *tone sandhi*. The actual pitch on words that take T3 in isolation depends on the tone of the following word. In a phrase of two syllables bearing T3, the first T3 is realized as a rising pitch, which is undistinguishable from T2:

xiǎo mǎ T3 + T3 > T2 + T3 [35 + 214](=T2+T3)
small horse
'a small horse'

Before a tone other than T3, T3 words are realized with a low-level pitch [11]:

xiǎo zhàn T3 + T4 > [11 + 51]
small station 'a small station'

Basic Morphology

Mandarin is an isolating or analytic language with little morphology. There is no systematic case marking, grammatical number, or gender. Nor is there any modifier-noun agreement. To convey these meanings, Mandarin employs functional particles or word order. For instance, the Mandarin expression meaning 'his grandma's family' is: *tā de lǎolao de jiā* (s/he PT mother's.mother PT family). Either or both instances of the particle *de* can be eliminated, depending on pragmatic context and/or semantic focus.

There is no subject-verb agreement in Mandarin. Nor are verbs inflected for tense, voice, or mood. There are three functional particles that are usually regarded as aspect markers: *zhe* progressive, *le* completed, and *guo* experienced.

Derivational morphology utilizes suffixes and reduplication. Reduplication of a noun or a classifier expresses the meaning of 'every', e.g., *tiān-tiān* ('day-day') 'every day'. Reduplication of a verb often softens the degree of action: *cháng-chang* ('to taste–to taste') 'to have a little taste'.

There are three particles that are commonly regarded as noun suffixes, *zi*, *r*, and *tou*: *lǎo* 'old', *lǎo-zi* 'father', *bàn* 'to accompany', *bànr* [pɐɻ] 'companions'.

Compounding is the most productive method of forming new words in present-day Mandarin. A compound can be made up of any kind of syntactic construction: *tóuténg* 'headache' (subject predicate), *dǎzì* 'to type' (literally, 'type-word', verb object).

Basic Syntax

The basic word order in Mandarin is Subject-Verb or Agent-

Verb-Patient. As with other languages, variation in word order serves pragmatic, semantic, rhetorical, or processing motivations. Mandarin is just more pragmatics motivated. Change in the relative order of subject and verb may indicate whether the subject is definite or not.

kèren	lái	le	
guest(s)	come	PARTICLE	'**The** guest has come.'

lái	kèren	le	
come	guest(s)	PARTICLE	'There came **a** guest.'

yǒu	rén	lái	le
there.is	person(s)	come	PARTICLE

'There is somebody coming.'

Change in word order may also indicate which element in the sentence is being topicalized. In the following examples, the first sentence is unmarked; in contrast, in the other two, 'book' is topicalized.

tā	kàn	wán	nèi	běn	shū	le
s/he	read	finish	that.one	CLASS	book	PARTICLE

'He has read that book.'

nèi	běn	shū	tā	kàn	wán	le
that.one	CLASS	book	s/he	read	finish	PARTICLE

tā	nèi	běn	shū	kàn	wán	le
s/he	that-one	CLASS	book	read	finish	PARTICLE

Within noun phrases, modifiers precede the noun: *hǎo rén* 'good person', *huaì rén* 'bad person'. The modifier can be an adjective, a noun, a possessor, a numeral plus a classifier, or a relative clause.

Mandarin sentences are negated by either *méi*, before the existential or possessive verb *yǒu*, and *bù* before other verbs:

tā	zǒu	le	
s/he	go	PARTICLE	'He has gone.'

tā	bù	zǒu	le	
s/he	NEG	go	PARTICLE	'He is not going anymore.'

tā	méi	(-yǒu)	zǒu	
s/he	NEG		go	'He hasn't gone.'

Contact with Other Languages

Mandarin and its predecessors, Old and Middle Chinese, have long been exposed to the Altaic languages to the north and Austroasiatic languages to the south. The Altaic-speaking peoples occupied North China during the two linguistic transitional periods (to mention the major events) and even ruled all of China in the Yuan and Qing dynasties. However, Mandarin has only marginally absorbed a few foreign words from the north, and even fewer from the south. The same is not true for the languages peripheral to the Chinese language. Some of these languages, such as ZHUANG and Miao, borrowed numerous Chinese loanwords; others became extinct in the long course of contact with Chinese. The systematic borrowing of the Middle Chinese characters and their pronunciations into JAPANESE, KOREAN, and VIETNAMESE makes these languages continue to rely on their rich source of Chinese stems in forming new words.

While not many European loanwords have survived in present-day Chinese, Chinese grammar, especially the written language structure, did change noticeably after Western literature and grammar had been introduced to China.

The earliest documented and well-attested loanwords came from central Asia as early as the Han dynasties (Western, 206 B.C. to A.D. 24; Eastern, A.D. 25 to 220), from or through PERSIAN and SANSKRIT.

Some words were brought in from Sanskrit or via some Central Asian languages, through the large-scale translation of Buddhist classics after the Old Chinese period.

The occupation of China by Mongols (Yuan, 1271–1368) and Manchus (Qing, 1644–1911) left a few loanwords.

From Persian: *shī* 'lion', *pútao* 'grapes' (maybe ultimately from Greek)
From Sanskrit: *zhāntán* 'sandalwood', *mòli* 'jasmine'
From Mongolian: *hútong* 'alley'
From Manchu: *sàgímǎ* 'a sweet pastry made of fried noodle'
From English: *shāfā* 'sofa', *tǎnkè* 'tank', *léidá* 'radar'

The language usually accommodates imported concepts/things by forming new compounds with internal resources, e.g., *huǒchē* 'fire-vehicle' (train) from FRENCH *chemin de fer*. There were many more loanwords in the early part of this century when Western innovations began to flow in, but gradually they have been replaced by native creations. For example, *délüfēng* 'telephone' has been replaced by *diànhuà* 'electric-talk'.

It is interesting to note that many borrowings did not come directly from the West, but entered via Japan around the turn of the century. The Japanese coined new terms for Western concepts and technology using Chinese characters, which they borrowed from China a millennium ago. Then, when borrowing these new terms, the Chinese just borrowed back the characters and pronounced them in Chinese. Thus, English 'nerve' was adopted into Japanese as *shinkei* and is pronounced in Mandarin as *shénjīng*. Words like this are quite different from the loanwords mentioned above; they are completely naturalized.

Common Words

man:	nánren	long:	cháng
woman:	nǚren	small:	xiǎo
water:	shuǐ	yes:	shì
sun:	tàiyang	no:	bù
three:	sān	good:	hǎo
fish:	yú	bird:	niǎo
big:	dà	dog:	gǒu
tree:	shù		

Example Sentences

(1) zhuótiān	Zhāngsān	zài	xiào-mén-kǒu
yesterday	Zhangsan	at	school-gate-mouth

pèngjiàn le Lǐsì.
meet PARTICLE Lisi
'Zhangsan met Lisi at the school gate yesterday.'

(2) tái shàng zuò zhe zhǔxítuán.
platform on sit PARTICLE presidium
'The presidium is sitting on the platform.'

(3) Wáng Miǎn qī-suì shàng si le fùqin.
Wang Mian seven-year on die PARTICLE father
'When Wang Mian was seven years old, his father died.'

Efforts to Preserve, Protect, and Promote the Language

Setting the norm for the pronunciation of *putonghua*, Beijing Mandarin has a superior status sociolinguistically over other Chinese dialects. Yet *putonghua* pronunciation is not entirely identical with vernacular Beijingese.

Reform of the Chinese written language dates from the 1950s. In 1956 the state-run newspapers began to be printed in horizontal style, from left to right, and the Chinese government formally promulgated the Plan for Simplification of Chinese Characters. In the following month the government issued the Directive Concerning Popularization of Putonghua, and the Commission for Writing Reform announced the Draft Plan for Chinese Language Phonetic Spelling (Pinyin), which was eventually adopted and promulgated by the National People's Congress in 1958.

Nowadays, the simplified characters and the *pinyin* spelling are widely taught and used in Mainland China. While no efforts seem likely for further simplification of the characters, the main task for the State Language Commission (replacing the Commission for Writing Reform) is nationwide promotion and dissemination of Mandarin-based *putonghua*, an aim being written into the Chinese Constitution.

Select Bibliography

Chao, Y.R. 1948. *Mandarin Primer*. Cambridge: Harvard University Press.

____. 1968. *A Grammar of Spoken Chinese*. Berkeley: University of California Press.

____. 1976. *Aspects of Chinese Sociolinguistics: Essays*. Stanford: Stanford University Press.

Chao, Y.R. and L.S. Yang. 1952. *Concise Dictionary of Spoken Chinese*. Cambridge, MA: Harvard-Yenching Institute.

DeFrancis, J. 1984. *The Chinese Language: Fact and Fantasy*. Honolulu: University of Hawaii Press.

Kratochivil, P. 1968. *The Chinese Language Today: Features of an Emerging Standard*. London: Huchinson.

Lehmann, Winfed, ed. 1975. *Language and Linguistics in the People's Republic of China*. Austin: University of Texas Press.

Li, C. and S. Thomson. 1981. *Mandarin Chinese: A Functional Reference Grammar*. Berkeley: University of California Press.

Norman, Jerry. 1988. *Chinese*. Cambridge: Cambridge University Press.

Pulleyblank, Edwin G. 1991. *Lexicon of Reconstructed Pronunciation in Early Middle Chinese, Late Chinese, and Early Mandarin*. Vancouver: University of British Columbia Press.

Ramsey, S.R. 1987. *The Languages of China*. Princeton: Princeton University Press.

Seybolt, Peter, and George K. Chiang, eds. 1979. *Language Reform in China: Documents and Commentary*. New York: M.E. Sharpe, Inc.

Wurm, S.A. et al. 1987–1991. *Language Atlas of China*. Hong Kong: Longman.

Zhu, Xiaonong. 1989. *On the Rhyming System in Middle Chinese, AD 960–1126: A Study of Mathematical Statistics*. Beijing: Language Publishing House.

CHINESE LANGUAGES: MIN

David Prager Branner

Language Name: Min. **Alternate:** Miin. **Autonym:** *Mǐn, Hokkien, Hoklo, Teochew, Taiwanese*, (or the name of the country, city, or town where it is spoken).

Location: (1) Mainland China: Provinces of Fújiàn (traditionally spelled Fukien in ENGLISH), eastern and coastal Guǎngdōng (traditionally spelled Kwangtung), Hǎinán. (2) Taiwan: Most of the island, apart from some Hakka-speaking counties in the northwest and Mandarin-speaking areas of the capital, Taipei. (3) Singapore. (4) Overseas Chinese communities in Malaysia, Indonesia, Thailand, Vietnam, Burma, the Philippines, Cambodia, and other countries of the world. Outside of Fújiàn Province, the vast majority of Mǐn speakers speak Southern Mǐn. There are many small S. Mǐn–speaking communities found transplanted in southern China, as well.

Family: Chinese. The Chinese family is considered by many to belong to a larger group called Sino-Tibetan, but at present the formal place of Chinese within Sino-Tibetan is ill-defined.

Related Languages: The other Chinese "dialects." Min belongs to the southern group of dialects (including HAKKA and YUE), which are considered more conservative than the northern and central groups. The subclassification of Chinese is by no means a settled matter yet, but it is safe to say that Min is the most diverse and distinct group within Greater Chinese, while Chinese is the least diverse and most widely spoken subfamily within Sino-Tibetan.

Dialects: The three varieties here are not strictly "dialects" but are better described as separate languages. The primary linguistic division within Min is between Coastal Min and Inland Min. Coastal Min is represented by the Southern and Eastern Min groups, and Inland Min by the Northern Min group.

Southern Min (Chinese *Mǐnnán*). The S. Min dialects are by far the most widely spoken varieties of Min. They are also called *Hokkien* and *Hoklo* (a term of perjorative origin), and are also known by the names of the largest populations that speak them: Taiwanese (Chinese *Táiwānhuà, Táiyǔ*), Amoy (Chinese *Xiàmén*, also *Hagu*), Teochew (Chinese *Cháozhōu*), Swatow (Chinese *Shàntóu*). The best known is Amoy. In Taiwan, the names Zhāngzhōu and Quánzhōu are used to denote differing accents of Taiwanese; Taiwan was settled in large part by S. Min speakers from those areas of Fújiàn, and there is still clear evidence of Zhāngzhōu and Quánzhōu characteristics, in spite of the large-scale synthesis that Taiwanese has undergone. Note that some non–S. Min speakers in Taiwan object to the term "Taiwanese," though it currently has the force of general usage.

The varieties of S. Min spoken in Hǎinán Province and the Léizhōu Peninsula of Guǎngdōng have certain distinctive phonetic features, though there is no doubt that they are indeed Southern Min.

Eastern Min (Chinese *Mǐndōng*). The best known dialect is Fúzhōu (traditionally Foochow in English). Other linguistically important dialects include Lungtu (Chinese *Lóngdū*), Fúān, and (arguably) the transitional dialects of Pútián and Xiānyóu (traditionally called Hinghwa in English). Notes: E. Min has sometimes been referred to popularly as "Northern Min," though linguists do not follow this usage.

True Northern Min (Chinese *Mǐnběi*). The best known dialect is Jiànyáng (traditionally Kienyang in English). N. Min dialects are the most diverse of the Min group, but have the smallest populations of speakers.

Number of Speakers: Recent estimates of the number of S. Min speakers range from 30–60 million. A semiofficial Chinese study published in 1989 arrived at a figure of 40 million speakers of S. Min in Taiwan, Fújiàn, and Hǎinán, based largely on the Mainland Chinese census of 1982. A large proportion of the 4.3 million Min speakers in the provinces of Guǎngdōng, Guǎngxī, Jiāngsū, Jiāngxī, and Zhèjiāng speak S. Min varieties, giving us perhaps 44 million speakers of S. Min in Mainland China and Taiwan. This figure does not include overseas speakers. The same study finds not quite 10 million speakers of E. Min (including Hinghwa) and over 3.5 million for the various N. Min varieties.

Origin and History

The name "Min" is an ancient ethnic term for a non-Chinese civilization, better known as the Mǐn-Yuè, who once lived in the southeastern part of what is now China. The traditional pronunciation of the character Min is the same as Mán, a name for the "savages" of the south, and that is presumably the fundamental meaning of Min. The historical connection of Min-Yuè to modern Min is uncertain. "Min" has long referred to Fújiàn, the homeland of modern Min, and the linguistic name comes from that geographic usage. But it is not clear that modern Min descends from a language spoken by the Min-Yuè peoples. In any case, no direct evidence about the ancient Min-Yuè language survives to the present day.

It has been suggested that certain colloquial Min words, especially in S. Min, may be related to forms in Tai and Miao-

Yao. However, this applies mainly to words that occur in individual branches of Min and only sporadically to words found throughout all the Min dialects. The great majority of words for which phonologically equivalent forms can be found in all three branches of Min are in fact related to known Chinese forms. That suggests modern Min is the result of the imposition of some kind of Chinese onto one or more different languages that have survived as substrates in the various branches of Min.

The early history of Min is not yet known with any certainty, but it is clear that what is now Fújiàn Province (like all of southern China) was settled only gradually by ethnic Chinese, and in waves of migration. Probably the majority of the early waves took place between about A.D. 100 and 600, but influence by both standard and non-standard varieties of Chinese has continued into the present day. These many waves have left countless traces in Min, of which the best documented evidence to date is phonological: etymological doublets and triplets, that is to say, multiple forms of the same recognizable Chinese morpheme. Scholars have identified as many as *seven* distinct forms representing a single etymon in some varieties of S. Min, but in most cases we find only doublets and triplets. Such multiple forms occur in most varieties of Chinese, but they are pandemic in Min, and from them we can discern different strata in the history of the language. The oldest strata represent early forms from Chinese or substrate languages, while later strata reflect borrowings from prestige languages over the centuries, or character readings of a fundamentally artificial nature. The S. Min character readings, for instance, correspond neatly to the outlines of standard Chinese phonology that was codified in the 10th–12th centuries. It is thought that a large proportion of these readings were created by combining the pronunciation formulas in traditional dictionaries with the actual phonetic values of colloquial words. However, even if artificial, dialect reading traditions may be of some antiquity.

Orthography and Basic Phonology

As with essentially all varieties of modern Chinese other than the standard language, Min dialects are not ordinarily written. In traditional times, however, local theater evolved limited traditions of writing dialect, using a combination of standard characters and local coinages. In modern Taiwan, as a result of the fervent native culture movement, there has recently begun to be a corpus of Taiwanese literature written wholly in characters. See Chen (1999: 114–28) for some discussion and references.

Nineteenth- and 20th-century Protestant missionaries developed Roman letter transcriptions for perhaps a dozen Min dialects, but today only that for the "Amoy" variety of S. Min has any currency; it survives primarily in Taiwan, where the influential Taiwanese Presbyterian Church continues to use romanized Bibles and other materials. The Maryknoll Fathers, based in Taichung, have published excellent English-language textbooks and dictionaries of Taiwanese using this system, and the 19th-century Amoy-English dictionary of Carstairs Douglas, arguably still the most thorough Chinese-dialect dictionary ever produced in any language, is frequently reprinted. See Douglas ([1873] 1899), Sprinkle *et al.* (1976), Marsecano *et al.* (1979), and Maryknoll (1984–85). The textbook of Nicholas Bodman is superb, but uses a different system of romanization and is based on Malaysian varieties of S. Min. Other S. Min transcription systems have recently been promulgated. One, devised in the People's Republic of China and derived from standard *Pīnyīn* romanization for Mandarin, is represented in a large dictionary and at least one textbook. It is little used outside of classrooms in Xiàmén, however. A more complicated system has recently been promulgated in Taiwan, designed to serve as the official romanization for several different Taiwanese dialects.

In the present article, IPA is used. Syllable tone is notated here in two distinct ways. First, it is ordinarily written as contrastive tone categories. There are theoretically eight such categories in Chinese, and there exist two widely used but competing ways of numbering them, as diagrammed below:

Upper-register tones	Here	Taiwan
yīnpíng	1	1
yīnshǎng	3	2
yīnqù	5	3
yīnrù	7	4
Lower-register tones	Here	Taiwan
yángpíng	2	5
yángshǎng	4	6
yángqù	6	7
yángrù	8	8

In the present article tonal categories are written in superscript; some scholars write them in subscript.

The actual phonetic values of contour tones may be also represented numerically, shown here in subscript. Imagine the range of the speaking voice to be divided into five parts. The lowest part is represented by 1, the highest by 5, and tone contours are represented by the pitches of the beginning and end of the syllable, together with the "turning point" of bidirectional contours. For instance, 55 would represent a high, level pitch; 24 would represent a rising contour, beginning mid low and ending mid high; 342 would represent a bidirectional contour, rising from the middle point of the register to mid high pitch and then falling to mid low pitch.

Phonologically, no one branch of Min is significantly more conservative than the others, and enormous variation is found. In this article, unless otherwise mentioned, the Zhāngzhōu accent of Taiwanese is taken as the usual representative of the whole dialect family.

Table 1: Consonants

	Stops		Nasals	Fricatives	
	Plain	+Asp		-Voi	+Voi
Labials	p	ph	m ~ b [^{m}b]		
Dentals	t	th	n ~ l [ɾ]		
Sibilants	ts	tsh		s	z
Velar-Laryngeals	k	kh	ŋ~ g [^{ŋ}g]	h	

Phonological inventory. There are 15 initials. There is one important case of allophony: the three "nasal" initials are articulated as true nasals when they appear in words bearing a

Table 2: Finals of Zhāngzhōu accent

Plain								Stop-ending					
			-i	*-u*	*-ŋ*	*-n*	*-m*		*-i*	*-u*	*-k*	*-t*	*-p*
a		a	ai	au	aŋ	an	am	aʔ	aiʔ	auʔ	ak	at	ap
		ã	ãi	ãu				ãʔ	ãiʔ	ãuʔ			
	i-	ia		iau	iaŋ	ɛn	iam	iaʔ		iauʔ	iak	ɛt	iap
		iã		iãu				iãʔ		iãuʔ			
	u-	ua	uai		uaŋ	uan		uaʔ			uak	uat	
		uã	uãi					uãʔ					
i		i			iŋ	in	im	iʔ			ik	it	ip
		ĩ						ĩʔ					
	u-	ui						uiʔ					
		uĩ						uĩʔ					
ə		e		o~ɵ~ɣ				eʔ		oʔ~ɵʔ~ɣʔ			
		ẽ						ẽʔ					
	i-			io, etc.						ioʔ, etc.			
	u-	ue						ueʔ					
ɔ		ɔ			ɔŋ		ɔm				ɔk		ɔp
		ɔ̃						ɔ̃ʔ			iɔk		
	i-				iɔŋ								
u		u			ŋ	un	m	uʔ			ŋʔ	ut	mʔ
	i-	iu						iuʔ					
		iũ											

nasalized vowel or a whole syllabic nasal ending. But elsewhere they are heard as voiced stops, prenasalized in the case of /m/ and /ŋ/, and /ɾ/ for /n/.

There are varying numbers of contrastive finals in the several most common types of Southern Min. Table 2 lists the finals of the Zhāngzhōu accent, analyzed phonemically into a five-main-vowel system.

Comparative-historical phonological features. The primary lexical-phonological feature that identifies the Min dialects is the pattern of aspiration in the initials of words belonging to "lower-register" (even-numbered) tone categories. Among words beginning with obstruents in these tones, essentially all Chinese dialects have either all aspirated initials or all unaspirated in each tone category. Min alone exhibits *two* sets of initial obstruents, aspirated as well as unaspirated, in each even-numbered tone category. Here are examples, representing only the labial initials /p/ and /ph/ in the four even-numbered tone categories.

Unaspirated forms: 'plate' /puã²/; 'female slave' /pi⁶/ (< tone 4); 'to roast' /pue⁶/; 'white' /peʔ⁸/.
Aspirated forms: 'sail' /phaŋ²/; 'to hold in the arms' /pho⁶/ (< tone 4); 'a crack' /phaŋ⁶/; 'hail (falling ice)' /phauʔ⁸/.

All obstruent initials in the lower tone registers exist in aspirated and unaspirated varieties in Min. This extra set of initials does not appear to be due to different strata of Chinese, because we do not find regular sets of doublets exhibiting the alternation. If the extra set of initials is the result of dialect mixture, then that mixture must predate the whole Min group because the pattern of aspiration is generally consistent across all Min dialects. The extra set of initials may reflect an early Chinese phonological distinction that has been lost everywhere else in Chinese, but at present there is no other compelling evidence that Chinese as a whole once had such an extra set of initials. It is just possible that the contrast between aspirated and unaspirated obstruents in lower-register tones derives from some sort of now lost morphological process. A tantalizing clue is the fact that apparently no adjectives have initials in the aspirated group (at least, none of the adjectives found across the whole Min group). A second interesting fact is that in certain northwestern Fújiàn dialects (such as Shàowŭ), these two sets of initials are distinguished not by aspiration but by tone (see Norman 1982). For the moment no decisive explanation of the two sets of lower-register initials has been offered, but it does seem clear that this contrast is the single most reliable diagnostic feature of the Min dialect group (see Branner 2000).

There are a great number of words for which Min dialects have failed to undergo the process of palatalization of initial consonants, as nearly all the rest of Chinese has. Min also lacks palatalized vowels in a great many words for which the rest of Chinese exhibits them. This entire set of features apparently reflects the fact that the varieties of ancient Chinese surviving in modern Min did not undergo the large-scale process of palatalization that all the rest of Chinese underwent, apparently beginning in the eighth or ninth centuries (see Norman 1994).

Another feature, which Min shares only with Hakka, is the use of initials /ts/ and /tsh/ for many words where much of Chinese uses plain sibilants, such as Mandarin *sh* and *x* [ɕ]: 'deep' /tshim¹/ (Mand. *shēn*); 'fresh' /tshĩ¹/ (Mand. *xiān*); 'ringworm' /tshuã³/ (Mand. *xiăn*); 'hand' /tshiu³/ (Mand. *shŏu*); 'few' /tsio³/ (Mand. *shăo*); 'to try' /tshi⁵/ (Mand. *shì*); 'to laugh' /tshio⁵/ (Mand. *xiào*); 'father's younger brother' /tsek⁷/ (Mand. *shú*).

Perhaps because of its long period of relative separation from the rest of Chinese, Min has evidently undergone considerable independent phonological development. For example, there are many examples of allophonic variation in Min, which presumably developed gradually from an earlier unity.

There are two important phonological features that serve to divide Inland from Coastal Min. One is the presence in N. Min dialects of an initial /s/ in some words where Coastal Min has an initial /l/ (in S. Min, this may be articulated as /n/ in nasalized syllables). It is thought that this initial /s/ survives from an earlier voiceless /l/ initial. Some of the words representing this feature are:

Gloss	Jiànyáng	S. Min
basket	/saŋ²/	/nã²/
rice hamper	/sue²/	/lua²/
to remain	/seu²/	/lau²/
six	/su⁸/	/lak⁸/
deaf	/suŋ²/	/laŋ²/
egg	/syŋ⁵/	/nŋ⁶/
old, not young	/seu⁵/	/lau⁶/
rain hat	/seʔ⁸/	/le⁸/

The other feature dividing Inland and Coastal Min is a group of words for which N. Min has a whole extra set of correspondences: 'cup' Jiànyáng /pui¹/ S. Min /pue¹/; 'cake' Jiànyáng /piaŋʔ³/ S. Min /piã³/; 'intestines' Jiànyáng /tɔŋ²/ S. Min /tŋ²/; 'heavy' Jiànyáng /toŋ⁵/ S. Min /taŋ⁶/; 'to run' Jiànyáng /tseuʔ³/ S. Min /tsau³/; 'stove' Jiànyáng /tseu⁵/ S. Min /tsau⁵/; 'near' Jiànyáng /kyeŋ⁵/ S. Min /kin⁶/; 'horn' Jiànyáng /ko⁷/ S. Min /kak⁷/. Examples of the "third series" of initials: 'to collapse' Jiànyáng /vaiŋ⁹/ S. Min /paŋ¹/; 'to reverse' Jiànyáng /vaiŋʔ³/ S. Min /peŋ³/; 'long' Jiànyáng /lɔŋ⁹/ S. Min /tŋ²/; 'to move' Jiànyáng /loŋ⁵/ S. Min /taŋ⁶/; 'early' Jiànyáng /lauʔ³/ S. Min /tsa³/; 'drunken' Jiànyáng /ly⁹/ S. Min /tsui⁵/; 'thick' Jiànyáng /eu⁵/ S. Min /kau⁶/; 'fern' Jiànyáng /yeʔ³/ S. Min /kueʔ⁷/.

Inland Min also has an assortment of characteristic vocabulary that is not found in Coastal Min.

Phonological features of S. Min. One highly distinctive characteristic of mainstream S. Min dialects is associated with nasalization. S. Min dialects vary somewhat in the distribution of the prenasalized stop initials described above, but most have them, and indeed numbers of Fújián-area dialects other than S. Min also have them, including varieties of Hinghwa and E. Min, as well as non-Min dialects such as some of those in Liánchéng and Nínghuà Counties. Some scholars have seen in the prenasalized stops a trace of Táng dynasty Cháng'ān dialect; others have seen them as a typological relic of a pre-Chinese Miáo-Yáo substrate.

A second salient S. Min feature is the so-called "chains" or "cycles" of tone contours involved in tone sandhi. Tone sandhi is quite prevalent in Coastal Min, and operates as follows: A given morpheme tends to be pronounced with its "basic" (i.e., inherent) tonal value only when it is the last syllable of a phrase or juncture unit. In all other environments, it is pronounced with a "sandhi" (morphophonologically alternate) tonal value. Sometimes a given tone category may have several different sandhi forms, each of which is used in a different environment. Many Coastal Min dialects thus have two or more contours associated with each tone category—one basic contour, and one or more sandhi contours.

In many varieties of S. Min, the situation is made still more interesting by the fact that the sandhi values of some or all of the tone categories appear to be the same as the basic values of other tone categories. For example, in the Zhāngzhōu accent of Taiwanese, the following tone contours are used:

Tone category	*Basic contour*	*Sandhi contour*	*Notes*
1	44	33	sounds like 6
2	24	33	sounds like 6
3	53	44	sounds like 1
5	21	53	sounds like 3
6	33	21	sounds like 5

Each of these five tone categories has a sandhi contour that sounds like the basic contour of some other category. Patterns of this kind occur in a number of S. Min dialects, though not all.

Basic Morphology

As with most of Chinese, it appears that no productive morphology survives in Min from the postulated common ancestor of the modern Chinese dialects. Rather, when productive morphology does exist in Min, it is specific to individual modern dialects. There is some evidence in Min of ancient morphological processes that have ceased to be productive. For instance, there are pairs of words in S. Min, related in meaning, that differ only in whether they end in a stop or a nasal that is homorganic with the stop. Here are some Amoy dialect examples: /khim²/ 'to catch, trap' vs. /khip⁷/ 'to grab hold of'; /uan¹/ 'curved' vs. /uat⁷/ 'to make a (left or right) turn'; /phoŋ⁵/ 'to swell up, be convex' vs. /phok⁷/ 'to bulge, to rise in blisters (said of paint on a wall).' Exactly what the basis might be of such doublets is uncertain; other than some lost morphological process, they might derive from dialect mixture.

A second tantalizing suggestion of ancient morphology is the fact that, as noted above, words with aspirated obstruent initials in lower-register tones are never adjectives (at least not those found across the whole Min group).

In the case of individual varieties of Min, there are by all means such things as productive morphological processes, with their own associated phonology. Two examples from S. Min are diminution and nominalization with the suffix /a³/ and intensive retriplication of adjectives.

Grammatically, there is much diversity among the varieties of Min, and it may well be that what we call Min is a mixture of more than one historically dissimilar language. S. Min, featured here, uses lexicon and grammatical particles that are least characteristic of the rest of Min and Chinese.

Basic Syntax

As in most varieties of Chinese, Min grammatical functions are expressed syntactically, by means of "particles," or function words. Particles vary greatly from dialect to dialect. Here, some of those for the Zhāngzhōu accent of S. Min are described.

S. Min, like all major Chinese dialects, uses an aspect system. Syntactically, it follows the S-V pattern, with direct object O appearing variously before or after V, and at times (for reasons of emphasis) before S. As noted by Yuen Ren Chao, it is generally more useful in Chinese to analyze the sentence loosely into "topic" and "comment," and define the individual parts of speech on semantic rather than primarily syntactic grounds.

Many grammatical variations of the S. Min verb are effected with special grammar words, which may be classified into several types:

1. Auxiliary verbs precede the main verb, and supplement its meaning. The great majority of aspect particles are auxiliary verbs. Examples: /u^6/ [completed aspect]; /bo^2/ [uncompleted aspect] note special enclitic uses of /u^6/ and /bo^2/: /u^6/ [successful perception] /bo^2/ [unsuccessful perception]; note also the sentence-final question particle /bɔ/ (tonally unstressed), which is considered by some to be derived from /bo^2/); /aʔ^7 bue^6/ [tentatively uncompleted aspect] (~ 'not yet'), also /iau^5 bue^6/; /beʔ^7/ [aspect of intention] ~ 'want to'; compare: /ai^5/ [desire] ~ 'to want, wish'; /tiʔ^7/ [progressive aspect]; /tiʔ^7 beʔ^7/ [imminent aspect]; /ho^3/ [aspect of imminent necessity]; /e^6/ [aspect of prediction of unfulfilled condition] ~ 'will'; also introduces adjectives describing unpleasant condition; /be^6/ [aspect of negative prediction of unfulfilled condition] ~ 'will not'; also introduces and negates adjectives describing unpleasant condition (note: other auxiliary verbs formed from /e^6/ and /be^6/: /e^6 sai^3/ 'may', be^6 sai^3/ 'may not'; /e^6 hiau^3/ 'know how to', /be^6 hiau^3/ 'don't know how to'—the particles /e^6/ and /be^6/ are further used as infixes in potential resultative compounds); /kam^3/ makes yes-or-no question of a simple declarative sentence.
2. Adverbs precede the main verb of the sentence; certain adverbs (such as adverbs of time-when) may also appear at the beginning of the sentence, before any subject or object. Examples: /loŋ^3/ [totalizer] 'all' (appears at the beginning of the "comment" part of the sentence, after the "topic"); /toʔ^8/ indicates precise equivalence, immediate expected consequence; /tsiaʔ^7/ indicates unexpected result, delayed consequence; /khaʔ^7/ 'more so, relatively'; /khaʔ^7 be^6/ 'less so, relatively not'; /tu^3/ [recent action] 'just now', also heard as /tu^3-tu^3/ or /tu^3-tu^3-a^3/; /koʔ^7/ 'again, further, still, more'; /kan^5-a^3/ 'apparently'; /nã^3/ 'if...'; /nã^3 e^6/ 'why?'
3. Coverbs. A coverb is a secondary verb that takes a direct object and the complex of these two elements modifies the main verb, usually as an adverbial phrase. Coverbs are generally similar in sense to English prepositions. Less often, a coverb may be used by itself, adverbially, without an explicit object; in such cases, the object is assumed to be a third-person pronoun. Examples: /ka^6/ [introduces direct or indirect object], may be used adverbially, with third-person pronoun understood; /kaʔ^7/ 'and, with'; /ti^6/ [introduces place of action], in some areas, /tiʔ^7/ (above) is used; /ui^5/ 'from'; /tau^5/ 'to help [someone do something]' may be used adverbially, with third-person pronoun understood; /hɔ^6/ indicates that the object of /hɔ^6/ is being allowed to perform the action of the main verb. This coverb-object complex can also be used after the verb, in the sense 'on behalf of, for'. Also, it can be used as an enclitic particle to introduce an adjectival result (compare /ka^5/, which generally introduces a verbal result). As an enclitic, /hɔ^6/ is unstressed and undergoes no tone change. Note that in some dialects this enclitic in fact has a distinct vowel and may be a different particle: /ho^6/.
4. Enclitics appear directly after the main verb, and often have to do with the results of the action of the verb. Examples: /tioʔ^8/ [successful accomplishment of the action of the verb, often involving some condition that befalls the subject of the sentence]; /liau^3/ indicates that an action has been fully completed and that the direct object is used up, also appears as /liau^3 liau^3/; /ho^3/ indicates that an action is finished; /suaʔ^7/ indicates that an action has come to a complete end, has much more finality than /ho^3/, and is often used with some impatience; /ka^5/ introduces a result phrase, containing another verb; /ho^6/. See discussion under /hɔ^6/, above.
5. Sentence-final particles are tonally unstressed, i.e. they have no recognizable tonal value, but are not necessarily unstressed with respect to loudness. Example: /a/ [aspect of the attainment of some state or condition]. Examples: /bɔ/ makes a yes-or-no question of an ordinary declarative sentence (see under /bo^2/, above); /bue/ makes a yes or no question, in tentatively uncompleted aspect, of an ordinary declarative sentence (presumably the same particle as in /aʔ^7 bue^6/ and /iau^5 bue^6/, mentioned above); /hɔ̃/ indicates that the speaker expects agreement from the listener.
6. Other miscellaneous particles. Examples: /e^2/ [nominalizing particle], placed after a pronoun or other noun, makes it possessive or the modifier of another noun, but placed after a verb, creates a noun phrase referring to the subject or object of the verb; /m^6/ [general negative for verbs], adjectives tend to use /bo^2/ and /be^6/; /a^3/ [nominalizing and diminutive particle] ("diminutive" may not be quite the right word; many nouns in their most commonly used forms have the /a^3/ suffix, indicating ordinariness; this particle has special morphophonemics associated with it, and when combined with morphemes in certain tones becomes tonally unstressed).

Contact with Other Languages

Language contact involving the Min group is best documented for S. Min, which is widely spoken in Southeast Asia. Most contact involves the borrowing of S. Min lexicon into Southeast Asian languages. Following, for example, is a selection of some common S. Min loanwords in TAGALOG, the national language of the Philippines. Note that most are related to cooking and food: Tagalog *am* 'rice gruel cooked until it is a liquid' (Amoy /am^3/); *bamì* 'noodles cooked with meat' (/baʔ^7 mĩ^6/, lit. 'meat noodles'); *bihon* 'rice noodles' (/bi^3 hun^3/); *dikyám* 'salted, preserved plum' (/li^3 kiam^2/); *guto* 'ox tripe (as food)' (/gu^2 tɔ^6/); *hibí* 'small dried shrimp' (/he^2 bi^3/); *tawgi* 'mung bean sprouts' (/tau^6 ge^2/); *tuwabak* 'kind of large-eyed herring' (/tua^6 bak^8/, lit. 'large eye').

S. Min also plays a role in one apparent creole dialect, Baba Malay, spoken by some ethnic Chinese in Singapore and the Malaysian state of Malacca. Opinions differ as to whether Baba Malay is a S. Min substrate overlayed by MALAY (Ansaldo and Matthews 1999) or a variety of restructured Malay relexified by S. Min (see Pakir 1986). See also the survey of opinions in Holm (1988–89: 577–81).

Few Min loanwords have come into English, but those that are common English words are also of S. Min origin. The most important example is tea, from Amoy /te^2/. Related forms are found in essentially all Western European languages, while Russian and the languages of most of west, south, central, and north Asia apparently use words derived from some form of northern Chinese *chá* 'tea' or possibly *zhāi* 'non-alcoholic.' Another likely Min loanword is *junk* 'small Chinese fishing boat', presumably from Teochew /tɕuŋ^{2}/. The martial-arts weapon *nunchaku*, in origin a two-segmented threshing flail, evidently represents the Japanese form of a Teochew word /nŋ^{6} tɕak^{7}/ 'two segments'. The English names of certain teas (*pe-koe, congou, bohea*) are probably of S. Min origin. Another possible loanword is ketchup, from Changchew /ke^{2} tsiap^{7}/ 'briny sauce made from salted fish' (but note that American ketchup is technically a kind of puréed tomato chutney). The traditional English spellings of several S. Min dialect names reflect dialect pronunciations: Amoy (in Zhāngzhōu, /ɛ^{6} muĩ^{2}/), Hokkien (in Amoy, /hok^{7} kian^{5}/), Swatow (in Amoy, /suã^{1} thau^{2}/), Teochew/Teochiu (in Cháozhōu dialect, /tio^{2} tsiu^{1}/).

In Taiwanese there are a goodly number of JAPANESE loanwords that have now endured half a century past the end of Japanese rule. The majority of them are for things introduced under Japanese rule, and many are themselves originally Western loanwords into Japanese. Two distinctive tonal patterns are found on these words:

(1) Last two syllables high-to-low falling: /bi^{53} lu^{21}/ 'beer' (< J. *bīru* < Eng.); /su^{53} si^{21}/ 'sushi' (< J.); /thɔ^{33} lak^{53} khu^{21}/ 'truck' (< J. *torakku* < Eng.); /sa^{33} si^{53} mĩ^{21}/ 'sashimi" (< J.).

(2) Last two syllables first rising then high-falling: /le^{24} boŋ^{53}/ 'lemon' (< J. *lemon* < Eng.); /o^{33} to^{34} bai^{53}/ 'motorcycle' (< J. *otobai* < Eng. *autobike*); /ɔ^{33} pa^{34} saŋ^{53}/ 'older woman' (respectful term; < J. *obasan* 'aunt, older woman'); /ɔ^{33} zi^{34} saŋ^{53}/ 'older man' (respectful term; < J. *ozisan* 'uncle, older man').

One word evidently of Romance derivation is /sap^{53} bun^{24}/ ~ /siap^{53} bun^{24}/ 'soap', ultimately from a Romance form of LATIN *sāpon-* 'soap' (SPANISH *jabón*, modern PORTUGUESE *sabão*). There are also many place names originating in the Austronesian languages native to Taiwan; these have been adapted to Taiwanese phonology and fitted with characters, and in many cases their non-Taiwanese origins are unknown to ordinary Taiwan people.

Chinese dialect influence on standard MANDARIN is widespread, and generally consists of both lexical and syntactic borrowing, as well as the coopting of Mandarin words as calques to translate dialect particles (grammar words). Such calquing is very common in Min dialects generally, and especially in S. Min, many of whose native grammatical constructions are not the same as those in standard Chinese. The Mandarin spoken in Taiwan shows a number of Taiwanese grammatical influences. Taiwanese has also taken on certain Mandarin grammatical constructions in recent decades.

Common Words

Some miscellaneous common words in S. Min (Taiwan Zhāngzhōu accent) follow (note that at least two forms are given for each entry, an ordinary form, and a character reading, used as a bound form):

	Ordinary	*Character Reading*
man	tsa^{1} pɔ^{1} laŋ^{2}	lam^{2}
woman	tsa^{1} bɔ^{3} laŋ^{2}	li^{3}
water	tsui^{3}	sui^{3}
sun	zit^{8} thau^{2}	zit^{8}
three	sã^{1}	sam^{1} (telephone)
fish	hi^{2}-a^{3}	gi^{2} (rare)^{1}
big	tua^{6}	tai^{6}
long	tŋ^{2}	toŋ^{2}
small	se^{5}	siau^{3} (different word)
good	ho^{3}	hau^{3} (rare, used as bound form)
bird	tsiau^{3}-a^{3}	niãu^{3} (extremely rare)
dog	kau^{3}	kɔ^{3} (extremely rare)
tree	tshiu^{6}	su^{6} (extremely rare)

Other words and expressions:

yes: *si^{6}* affirms certain verbal statements; *e^{6}* affirms certain statements of sensation; *tioʔ^{8}* (lit. 'correct'); *hẽ^{5}* (used in conversation for general affirmation); *hẽ^{1} a^{1}* more emphatic than *hẽ^{5}*. Note: Min speakers generally tend to reply affirmatively to questions by repeating the verb of the original question.

no: *m^{6} si^{6}* denies certain verbal statements; *be^{6}* denies certain statements of sensation; *m^{6} tioʔ^{8}* (lit., 'incorrect'). Note: Min speakers generally tend to reply negatively to questions by repeating the verb of the original question, negated.

I'm sorry/Excuse me: *phãi^{44} se^{21}* (lit. 'bad form/condition').

Example Sentences

Following are some common S. Min expressions, represented again in the Zhāngzhōu accent of Taiwanese.

(1) gau^{33} tsa^{53}
skilled.at early
'You're up early' (~ 'Good morning' said only early in the morning).

(2) li^{44} tsiaʔ^{22} pa^{53} bue
2SG to.eat sated NEG.PAST.EXPERIENCE
'Have you eaten?' (~ 'Hello' – said any time after the early morning). Note: /tsiaʔ^{22} pa^{53}/ is syntactically [verb] + [adjective of result].

(3) lai^{33} tse^{33}
come sit
'Please come and be my guest at my home' (~ 'Goodbye'– said at parting when not at either of the speakers' homes).

Efforts to Preserve, Protect, and Promote the Language

Taiwan and Singapore are the only places where S. Min may ascend to the level of majority national language, although there are political obstacles in both countries. In Mainland China, Min dialects are still widely used by ordinary people, especially in the S. Min area and rural areas. But in China there seems to be no particular interest in preserving or promoting Min, and heavy Mandarin and prestige dialect influence is becoming evident in all rural dialects. Certainly there is nothing in Mainland Chinese Min dialect areas remotely like the nationalism associated with Taiwanese in Taiwan. In the 1980s and 1990s, Taiwanese came into much wider use in government, education, and the media in Taiwan, after decades of official discouragement. A range of dictionaries and textbooks have appeared, and popular interest in Taiwanese seems unlikely to diminish.

Select Bibliography

Ansaldo, Umberto, and Stephen Matthews. 1999. "The Minnan Substrate and Creolization in Baba Malay." In *Journal of Chinese Linguistics* 27/1: 38–68.

Bodman, Nicholas Cleaveland. 1955–58. *Spoken Amoy Hokkien*. Kuala Lumpur: Government, Federation of Malaya. Two volumes.

Branner, David Prager. 1999. "The Classification of Longyan." In *Issues in Chinese Dialect Description and Classification*, edited by Richard VanNess Simmons (Berkeley: Journal of Chinese Linguistics Monograph Series).

_____. 2000. *Problems in Comparative Chinese Dialectology*. Berlin: Mouton de Gruyter.

Chen, Leo and Jerry Norman. 1965. *An Introduction to the Foochow Dialect*. San Francisco: U.S. Office of Education.

Chen, Ping. 1999. *Modern Chinese—History and Sociolinguistics*. Cambridge: Cambridge University Press.

Chiu Bien-ming. 1931. "The Phonetic Structure and Tone Behaviour in Hagu (Commonly Known as the Amoy Dialect) and Their Relation to Certain Questions in Chinese Linguistics." In *T'oung Pao* XXVII/3–5: 245–345.

Douglas, Carstairs. [1873] 1899. *Chinese-English Dictionary of the Vernacular or Spoken Language of Amoy*. London: Presbyterian Church of England.

Holm, John. 1988–89. *Pidgins and Creoles*. Cambridge: Cambridge University Press.

Li, Paul Jen-kuei. 1971. "Two Negative Markers in Taiwanese." In *Bulletin of the Institute of History and Philology, Academia Sinica*. 43/2: 201–20.

Li, Zhuqing. 1998. *Fuzhou-English Dictionary*. Kensington, Maryland: Dunwoody Press.

Maclay, Robert Samuel and Caleb C. Baldwin. [1870] 1944. *An Alphabetic Dictionary of the Chinese Language in the Foochow Dialect*. Foochow, Methodist Episcopal Mission Press. [Reprint, U.S. Government Printing Office, 1944].

Marsecano, Guerrino, et al. 1979. *English/Amoy Dictionary*. Taichung: Maryknoll Fathers.

Maryknoll Language Service Center. 1984–85. *Taiwanese*. Taichung: Maryknoll Language Service Center. Two volumes.

Norman, Jerry. 1977. "A Preliminary Report on the Dialects of Mintung." In *Monumenta Serica* XXXIII (1977–8): 326–348.

_____. 1982. "The Classification of the Shaowu Dialect." In *Bulletin of the Institute of History and Philology, Academia Sinica* (Taiwan) 53: 543–583.

_____. 1985. "The Origin of the Proto-Min Softened Stops." In John McCoy and Timothy Light, eds., *Contributions to Sino-Tibetan Studies*. Leiden: E.J. Brill, 375–384.

_____. 1988. *Chinese*. Cambridge: Cambridge University Press.

_____. 1991a. "Nasals in Old Southern Chinese." In *Studies in the Historical Phonology of Asian Languages*, edited by William G. Boltz and Michael C. Shapiro, 206–214. Amsterdam: John Benjamins Publishing Co.

_____. 1991b. "The Min Dialects in Historical Perspective." In *Languages and Dialects of China*, edited by William S.-Y. Wang. *Journal of Chinese Linguistics*. Monograph series, no. 3, pp. 325–360.

_____. 1994. "Pharyngealization in Early Chinese." In *JAOS* 114: 397–408.

_____. 1996. "Tonal Development in the Jennchyan Dialect." In *Yuen Ren Society Treasury of Chinese Dialect Data* II: 7–41.

Pakir, Anne Geok-in Sim. 1986. "A Linguistic Investigation of Baba Malay." Ph.D. dissertation, University of Hawaii.

Ramsey, S. Robert. 1987. *The Languages of China*. Princeton: Princeton University Press.

Sprinkle, Russell, *et al*. 1976. *Amoy-English Dictionary*. Taichung: Maryknoll Fathers.

Chinese Languages: Wu

Phil Rose

Language Name: Wu refers to a phonologically well-defined group of Chinese dialects. Wu is one of the seven major dialect groups of Chinese, (the others are MANDARIN, MIN, HAKKA, YUE, XIANG, and GAN), and is the second largest in terms of speakers. Shanghai is a Wu dialect. The Wu dialects differ considerably from north to south, where mutual unintelligibility can exist between varieties separated by as little as 200 kilometers. There is no particular overall standard form, although local prestigious standards, e.g., Shanghai, or local koines, e.g., Jinhua, exist. Neither is there a truly representative variety, although some, e.g., Suzhou, are often quoted as such. Because of these factors, and in order to illustrate these differences, examples are given from various localities. Unless otherwise stated, the examples are from the Zhenhai dialect.

Location: Varieties of Wu are spoken in the two eastern coastal provinces of Jiangsu and Zhejiang, with a little overspill to the west into the provinces of northeastern Jiangxi and Anhui. In Jiangsu, Wu is found south of the Yangtze River, except for the region around Nanjing, where varieties of a major subgroup of Mandarin (the River Dialects) are spoken. It is also spoken on Chongming Island in the Yangtze estuary and in a few localities north of the river. All of Zhejiang appears to be Wu speaking with the exception of some extreme southwestern localities. The Wu dialect area is bordered to the south by the Min dialects, to the west by Gan, and to the north by a transition zone between Wu and the River Dialects.

Family: Wu belongs to the Sinitic (Chinese) branch of Sino-Tibetan.

Related Languages: The Wu dialects are of course most closely related to the other dialects of Chinese. Some linguists have drawn parallels between the internal language relationships within Chinese and those within the Romance languages (one of the first-order families of Indo-European, from which languages like FRENCH, ITALIAN, and ROMANIAN have developed). On this basis, the Wu dialects would be comparable to, for example, a subgroup within the Romance dialect continuum. However, the validity of this comparison has yet to be tested since it has yet to be shown that the Chinese dialects constitute a single dialect continuum. The Wu-Min isogloss, for example, is one of the strongest within Chinese, and possibly stronger than anything within the Romance languages. Moreover, the degree of diversity within a particular subgroup like Wu (or even more so in Min) appears greater than that found within any subgroup of Romance. On this basis, then, it may be more accurate to consider the Wu dialects as a separate continuum, and any one variety as a separate language.

Wu is considered conservative in its retention of phonological features, especially of initial consonants and tones. Because of this, there is little evidence of subgrouping with other dialects of Chinese on the basis of shared changes from the protolanguage (Ancient Chinese). Some scholars posit a closer connection with the Old XIANG (or Chu) dialects. From a synchronic typological viewpoint, the Wu dialects appear to constitute, together with Gan and Xiang, a transitional group between a northern (Mandarin) group and a southern (Yue, Hakka, Min) group.

Within Wu, a basic division into Northern (e.g., Shanghai, Shaoxing, and Suzhou) and Southern (e.g., Jinhua, Yongkang, and Wenzhou) groups was demonstrated in the late 1960s on evidence from comparative reconstruction of Wu phonology, although this was based on relatively few (13) sites, especially in the south.

Number of Speakers: 77–87 million.

Origin and History

The Wu dialects are named after an ancient state, the boundaries of which contracted and expanded over time, but which was at various historical times roughly coextensive with the area where the modern dialects are spoken.

The modern Wu dialects are originally the result of the general imperial expansion during the Qin/Han period (200 B.C.–A.D. 200). The Northern Wu area was colonized first, and then later in Qin there was a southwards expansion down the coast to cover roughly the Southern Wu area as well. In the period of political disunity after the fall of the Han dynasty (200–600), the dialectal diversification in the southern dialects of colonized areas was left to develop relatively free from the influence of a central normative standard language. The dialects were also influenced by non-Chinese languages. In particular, it has been hypothesized that many of the phonological peculiarities of Wu such as the retention of Ancient Chinese Initial and Tonal features, the loss of syllable-final contrasts, and the development of sandhi are due to the influence of a Miao substratum. Northern Chinese vernacular and/or literary standards have changed or supplanted older dialect forms at least twice in the history of Wu (and Southern dialects in general). This has resulted in complex stratification of many aspects of the Wu linguistic structure. A similar process can be witnessed today, as the Wu dialects are influenced by another northern standard, namely Modern Standard Chinese.

The phonological development of the Wu dialects from Ancient Chinese is characterized by conservatism in the Initials and loss of contrast in the Finals. Unlike the vast majority

Table 1: Consonants

		Labial	Dental/ Alveolar	Palatal	Velar/ Glottal
Stops	Voiceless, asp	ph	th		kh
	Voiceless, unasp	p	t		k
	Voiced	b	d		g
Fricatives	Voiceless	f	s	ɕ	h
	Voiced	v	z	ʑ	
Affricates	Voiceless, asp		tsh	tɕh	
	Voiceless, unasp		ts	tɕ	
	Voiced		dz	dʑ	
Nasals		m	n	ɲ	ŋ
Lateral			l		

of the Chinese dialects, Wu preserved the Ancient Chinese three-way division of syllable-initial stops and affricates (*ph, *p, *b, etc.), and two-way division of fricatives (*s, *z, etc.). However, the place contrast in the syllable-final stops *p, *t, and *k was lost. These became deoralized to a glottal stop, which disappears in close juncture. Ancient Chinese syllable-final nasals *m, *n, *ŋ, also underwent a merger to a single phonemic nasal, or disappeared after nasalizing the vowel. Under certain conditions, especially in the south, the process is carried further by loss of vowel nasalization. The tones show both conservative and innovative traits. They retain a correspondence, in citation form, between pitch onset height, phonation type, and manner of articulation of syllable-initial consonant, which is taken to reflect an exaggeration of late Ancient Chinese allotony. However, the various types of complex tone sandhi found in Wu are not reconstructable for Ancient Chinese, and must represent a Wu innovation. How they arose—in particular the origin of the left versus right spreading difference—is still a mystery. The individual tones differ considerably among the dialects, but, at least in the north, there is general similarity in the tone sandhi shapes. This suggests that there has been more change over time in the individual tones than in the sandhi shapes.

Orthography and Basic Phonology

There is no accepted romanization, although several systems have been proposed for individual dialects, e.g., Shanghai. Most descriptions use the IPA to indicate sounds, in conjunction with appropriate Chinese characters to indicate morphemes.

Wu, like many south Asian languages, has phonological patterning of a very different sort from that observed in ENGLISH and other Western languages. The only consonants that can occur at the end of the syllable in Wu, for example, are *ŋ* and *ʔ*. This is one of the reasons why it is appropriate to describe the phonological structure of Wu in terms of syllable-structure constituents, rather than phonemes. The Wu syllable consists of three immediate constituents: a Tone; an Initial, i.e., an initial consonant; and a Final, i.e., an optional semivocalic onglide, vowel, and an optional final consonant. (The terms Initial and Final are used in Chinese linguistics; they correspond to what is commonly referred to in modern phonology as onset and rhyme. In traditional terminology, the term "rhyme" refers to the final minus the onglide.) Thus in the Zhenhai word for 'needle' - *tɕɪŋ 41* - the *tɕ* is the Initial, *ɪŋ* is the Final, and 41 indicates the (falling pitch of the) Tone. One important phonological feature of Wu is that the tone is relevant for accounting for the distribution of both Initials and Finals, at least in monosyllabic words.

With the exception of Old Xiang, Wu is the only Chinese dialect group to maintain a three-way distinction among aspirated, voiceless unaspirated, and voiced stops.

The phonetic realization of the voiced stops and fricatives differs depending on where they occur. Word internally, they are modally voiced, but word initially, they are usually voiceless lenis. For example, the palatal affricate in the Zhenhai morpheme 'tide ~ dynasty' is voiceless lenis in the word *dʑɔ sz̤* 11 441 'tide', but modally voiced in the word *mɪŋdʑɔ* 11 441 'Ming dynasty'.

Tones. Most Wu dialects have a rather large inventory of seven or eight tones (Shanghai is unusual in having only five). The table below gives the pitch values of tones from the Northern dialect of Changshu. Tones are notated with the conventional Chao 'tone letters'. These show the pitch of a tone with a five-point scale: 5 is the highest point in a speaker's normal pitch range; 1 is the lowest. Level pitches are usually shown with two integers. Underscoring indicates short pitch.

Tones in Changshu

		SHU		RU
YIN	53	423	324	$\underline{5}$
YANG	33	31	213	$\underline{2}$

Two of the tones in Wu, traditionally called *Ru* or 'entering' tones, are usually very short with short lax vowels, and end in a glottal stop before a pause. They also have a small (circa 3–6) number of contrasting rhymes. The other tones, traditionally called *Shu*, are long, with long finals, and have a much larger number (circa 25) of contrasting rhymes. Wu tones can also be divided into two other natural classes, traditionally called *yin* and *yang*. *Yang* tones have low pitch onset, marked breathy or whispery phonation types, and cooccur with voiceless breathy initial consonants. *Yin* tones have higher pitch onset, model or tense phonation type, and cooccur with voiceless initial consonants, or sonorants with glottal-stop onsets. It is generally believed that the breathy phonation type in the *yang* tones is conditioned by an initial breathy stop. However, breathy phonation occurs on *yang* tones irrespective of the initial consonant: it is found, for example, on syllables with initial fricatives and indeed with no initial consonant. It must, therefore, be considered an independent part of the realization for the *yang* tones.

Tone in Wu is phonemic, but unlike most other tone languages, tonal contrasts often depend on features other than pitch alone, like phonation type, vowel duration, phonation offset, and manner of initial consonant. Wu tones can change drastically depending on morphological and syntactic structure, and this tone sandhi is the most complex of any of the Chinese languages, and probably of any of the world's tone languages. For example, a level pitch on *tsha* 'to fry' and a dipping pitch on *vɛ̃* 'rice' (thus: 33 213) means 'to fry rice', but if the pitch is rising then falling (thus: 334 51) it means 'fried rice'. One extremely important distinction in Wu tone sandhi is so-called left versus right dominance. In left-dominant dialects, the pitch shape of the tones is determined by the tones at the beginning of a word, and tonal contrasts are neutralized towards its end. Right-dominant dialects, which show the opposite behavior, are found in the south, but the exact location of the boundary between left- and right-dominant dialects is not known.

Finals. Finals are composed of a rhyme and an optional semivowel on-glide, usually *j, w,* or *ɥ*. There are two sets of rhymes: one occurs with entering (Ru) tones, and one occurs with Shu tones.

Table 2: Rhymes in Shu Tones

	Front	Central	Back	Diphthongs
Plain				
High	i y		u	
High-mid	e ø			
Low-mid			ɔ	œy, ɛi
Low		a	ɑ	au
Nasal				
High	ĩ iŋ ỹ yŋ		ʊŋ	
Mid	ɛ̃ œ̃			
Low	æ̃	aŋ	ɑ̃	

Syllabic consonants: m̩ l̩ z̩ ŋ̍ z̩̈.

Table 3: Rhymes with Ru Tones

	Front	Central	Back
High	ɪ ʔ		
High-mid	ø ʔ		
Low-mid			ɔ ʔ
Low		a ʔ	

Basic Morphology

As with other varieties of Chinese, Wu dialects are best typologized as isolating/analytic, with a low ratio of morphemes to word. The vast majority of morphemes is realized by syllable-sized allomorphs (this is what is meant by the often-heard comment that "Chinese is a 'monosyllabic' language"). Words are formed primarily by compounding and/or affixal derivation, e.g., Zhenhai:

tsz̩ 334-dœy 51 'paper'
paper-nominal suffix

ɔ̆ $\underline{1}$ -sæ̃ 34 -tsz̩ 51 'student'
study-profession suffix-nominal suffix

a 44-m̩ 31 'mother'
kinship prefix-mother

The same few types of exceptions to the one syllable–one morpheme equivalence exist, as in most other dialects, e.g., monomorphemic polysyllabic words like: *wudiaʔ* 11 $\underline{4}$ 'butterfly', *bibɔ* 11 441 'pipa'. Bimorphemic monosyllabic words involve the diminutive/familiar morpheme, which is signaled by tone change in some dialects. For example in Wenling the 33 tone in the word for 'chicken' changes to 15 to indicate 'little chicken'. Such tone changes probably reflect the effect of a former nasal diminutive suffix that has changed the tone of the root morpheme by tone sandhi and then disappeared. The fossilized remnants of a previously separate diminutive nasal suffix can also be seen in morphophonemic and tonemic variation in some other mid and southern coastal Wu dialects.

There is no complex inflectional morphology. Inflectional morphemes are restricted to a typically small inventory of verbal aspectual suffixes and negative prefixes.

Basic Syntax

Wu syntax, like other varieties of Chinese, reflects pragmatic dimensions like topicality and definiteness. Word order is structured in terms of topic-comment, where the topic can be any constituent, including a full sentence, as in:

n̩ - nau zɑ̃ - ɲĭ - tsz̩ ja - dœy tæ̃ dʑi va hɑ
$\underline{1}$ 114 11 $\underline{34}$ 31 11 24 33 4 $\underline{1}$ 334
you yesterday evening hit him not good
'It wasn't good you hitting him last night.'

The usual order of major constituents within a sentence is SVO, e.g.:

dʑi	a - m̩	le - tɪʔ	dʑæ̃	ɲi - ɕɪŋ - ŋəʔ	i - zɑ̃
24	44 31	11 4	11	11 44 3	33 441
he	mother	PROG	wash	dirty-POSS	clothes

'His mother is washing dirty clothes.'

However, a well-known characteristic of Wu is the preposing of the direct object NP in front of the verb. This is especially common in questions, e.g.:

dʑĭ - laʔ	ʔjɪŋ - vaŋ	wei - taʔ	kɑ̃	vei
1 25	33 441	11 4	334	31
they	English	can	speak	Q

'Can they speak English?'

Contact with Other Languages

Varieties of Chinese generally do not borrow words readily and prefer to form new words with language-internal resources. However, a small number of loanwords or loan blends in some Wu dialects can be attributed to trade and missionary activity in the Ningpo and Shanghai regions in the mid-1800s. Most are no longer in use. Examples attested in Ningpo dialect in 1840 are *law sz̩* 242 1 'roast (beef)', and *pɪŋ phɔ̆ dɪŋ* 33 4 33 'ice cream' (lit. 'ice (*pɪŋ*) pudding'). The word *uŋ dĕ ă sɛ* 11 4 3 21 'Indian policeman (in British concession)' (lit. red head "I say") dates from the Treaty Port era of Shanghai. The economic and cultural importance of Modern Shanghai is reflected in a fairly large number of current English borrowings, e.g., *ɕɔ 51* 'shot' (in basketball); *gɔ* l̩ 13 'goal'; *khɛ sz̩* 44 31 'kiss'.

Common Words

Integers indicate pitch of tones after sandhi rule application.

	Wenzhou Dialect	Zhenhai Dialect
man:	nø31 gei	nei 11 ɲɪŋ 441
woman:	ɲy24 gei	ɲy 224 ɲɪŋ 51
small:	sai 45	ɕɔ 323
water:	sz̩ 45	sz̩̆ 323
yes:	z̩ 24	z̩ 242 gɔʔ 1
sun:	tha 42 i 31 (vai 12)	ɲĭ 1 dœy 23 bu 51
no:	fu 45 z̩ 45	vă 1 z̩ 242
three:	sa44	sɛ̃ 441
good:	xə 45	hɑ323
fish:	ŋœy 31	ŋ 231
bird:	tiɛ 45	tiɔ 323
big:	du 11	dau 213
dog:	kau 45	wɑ̃ 11 ki 441
tree:	z̩ 11	z̩̈ 213

Example Sentences

(1)

vɛ̃	tɕhɥɔ̆ - kau	vă - laʔ
24	5 31	1 1
rice	eat-EXP	Q.

'Hello.' (lit. 'have you eaten yet?')

(2)

ŋɔ - tshz̩̆	tei	z̩ĭ - dœy	ka	hɑ - ləʔ	a	ju
11 441	33	1 242	41	33 4	231	11
tooth	face	tongue	so	good PART	still	exist

ŋɑ - thuŋ
224 441
bite pain

'It still hurts when you bite your tongue, no matter how well it gets on with your teeth.'

(3)

kɪʔ	œy	sɔ̆ - ɕi	laʔ
5	33	5 52	1
this	call	what	Q

'What's this called?'

Efforts to Preserve, Protect, and Promote the Language

Speaking dialect is neither actively encouraged or discouraged, and occurs in sociolinguistically well-defined circumstances. The desire to signal individual identity through dialect is an important factor in maintaining internal diversity. Dialects tend to be primarily heteronymous with respect to local prestigious forms, e.g., Shanghai. However, increasing influence from the National Standard (Mandarin-based *putonghua*) has also been noted.

Although the standard is used for official broadcasts on television (including the news), Wu is used on local radio and television for other programming.

Select Bibliography

Ballard, W.L. 1988. *The History and Development of Tonal Systems and Tone Alternations in South China.* Study of Languages and Cultures of Asia and Africa Monograph Series No. 22. Tokyo: Institute for the Study of Languages and Cultures of Asia and Africa.

Chao Yuen Ren. 1967. "Contrastive Aspects of the Wu Dialects." In *Language 43.1:* 92–101. Also published as "Contrasting Aspects of the Wu Dialects" in Anwar S. Dil, editor *Aspects of Chinese Sociolinguistics-Essays by Yuen Ren Chao,* 34–47 (1976).

____. 1970. "The Changchow Dialect." In *JAOS* 90, 1:45–56. Also in Dil 1976 (op. cit.) 48–71.

Hook, B., ed. 1982. *The Cambridge Encyclopedia of China.* Cambridge: Cambridge University Press.

Ramsey, S.R. 1987. *The Languages of China.* Princeton, New Jersey: Princeton University Press.

Sherard, M. 1979. "Wu Dialect Studies in Western Literature." In *Fangyan* 3: 183–195.

Wurm, S. *et al*, eds. 1987. *Language Atlas of China.* Pacific Linguistics Series C, No. 102. Canberra: Longmans/Australian National University Research School of Pacific Studies.

Zhu, Sean and Phil Rose. 1998. "Tonal Complexity as a Dialectal Feature: 25 Different Citation Tones from Four Zhejiang Wu Dialects." In R. Mannell and J. Robert-Ribes *Proceedings of the 5th International Conference on Spoken Language Processing.* The Austrailian Speech Science and Technology Association, vol. 3: 919–922.

Chinese Languages: Xiang

You Rujie

Language Name: Xiang.

Location: Xiang dialects are mainly located along the rivers Xiangjiang, Yuanshui, and Zishui in Hunan Province, and in Quanzhou, Xingan, Guanyang, and Ziyuan counties in northeastern Guangxi Province.

Family: Xiang belongs to the Sinitic subfamily of Sino-Tibetan.

Related Languages: Xiang dialects are, of course, closely related to other dialects of Chinese. However, the modern Northern variety (or the New Xiang) is more closely related to MANDARIN and the modern Southern variety (or Old Xiang) is more closely related to WU dialects.

Dialects: The Xiang group is divided into three subgroups: (1) Changyi, spoken along the Xiangjiang River; (2) Loushao, spoken in central Hunan Province; and (3) Jixu, spoken in northwestern Hunan Province.

Number of Speakers: 30.85 million.

Origin and History

The precursor of the modern Xiang dialect was the ancient language of Chu. The ancestry of the Chu people traces back to the central plains. During the Warring Kingdoms period (403–221 B.C.), the Chu people moved south, conquering the river valleys of Xiang, Zi, Yuan, and Li, and the Chu language was spoken throughout the region that approximately equals Hunan Province. Under the powerful influence of Chinese, the Chu language became similar to Chinese. This connection can be seen in "Chu Poems". Gradually the Chu language developed into the Proto-Xiang dialect of Chinese. Afterwards, the ancient Xiang dialect was influenced by immigration from the north, so that the modern Xiang dialect, especially the Changyi subgroup, is very similar to Mandarin. Proto-Xiang has not been reconstructed.

Orthography and Basic Phonology

There is no writing system other than Chinese characters. The system used in this article is the transliteration used in scholarly works. This article describes the Xiang of Changsha City.

As is the case with other Chinese languages, Xiang phonology is best described in terms of Initials, Finals, and Tones. The Initials are all consonants. However, a Final may be a vowel or a diphthong, optionally followed by *n* or *ŋ*. The nasals *m* and *n* may likewise serve as Finals.

In the speech of younger Xiang speakers, the retroflex affricates /tʂ tʂh/ and fricative /ʂ/ have merged with the dentals /ts tsh s/.

Table 1: Finals

ɪ	a	o		ai	ei	au	u
i	ia	io	ie			iau	iəu
u	ua		u	uai	uei		
y	ya		ye	yai	yei		
		õ		iẽ	ye		
ən	an	oŋ				m̩	n̩
in	ian	ioŋ					
uən	uan						
yn	yan						

Table 2: Initials

		Labial	Dental	Retroflex	Palatal	Velar
Stops	Aspirated	p	t	ɕ		k
	Unaspirated	ph	th			kh
Fricatives	Voiceless	f	s	ʂ		
	Voiced			ʐ		
Affricates	Unaspirated		ts	tʂ	tɕ	
	Aspirated		tsh	tʂh	tɕh	
Nasals		m	n		ɲ	ŋ
Resonant			l			

Tones. Xiang has six phonemic tones, including five lax (Shu) tones and an abrupt (Ru) tone.

		SHU		RU
YIN	33	41	55	24
YANG	13		11	

The three level tones are low (11), mid (33), and high (55). The two contour Shu tones are low rising (13) and high falling (41). The Ru tone is, like 13, a low-rising tone, but it is somewhat higher in pitch, both at the beginning and the end of the rise.

The Yang tones occur in syllables that had a voiced initial in Middle Chinese. Because of phonological change, some of these have voiceless unaspirated initials in Xiang. Yin tones occur only in syllables with voiceless initials. The Ru tone (24) occurs in syllables that had a final stop in Middle Chinese; even though the stops have been lost in Xiang, the older contrast between closed (CVC) and open (CV) syllables is preserved in the contrast between 24 tone and the other tones.

There are also some syllables in which the tone is weakened. This weakened tone is represented as 0.

Basic Morphology

There is virtually no inflectional morphology in Xiang. Personal pronouns are pluralized by the addition of the suffix *mən*^{0}:

	Singular	Plural
1st	ŋo^{41}	ŋo^{41}mən^{0}
2nd	ɲi^{41}	ɲi^{41}mən^{0}
3rd	tha^{33}	tha^{33}mən^{0}

Possessives are formed by adding *ti*^{0} to the personal pronoun or noun: *tha*^{33} 's/he', *tha*^{33}*ti*^{0} 'his/hers'.

Within the verb system, verbs do not agree with their subjects. Tense and aspect distinctions are indicated lexically. For example, the particle *ka*^{0} following a verb marks perfective aspect:

tɕhia^{24}	ka^{0}	tsa^{13}	ɕia^{11}	tɕi^{11}
drink	PERFECT	tea	play	chess

'Play chess after drinking tea.'

Basic Syntax

The basic order of major constituents within a Xiang sentence is Subject-Verb-Object:

si^{55}-mei^{11}tsɪ^{0}	si^{41}	i^{33}fu^{0}
little-girl	wash	clothes

'The little girl washes clothes.'

Modifiers precede the nouns that they modify:

ɕian^{33}ni^{0}	mei^{11}tsɪ^{0}
countryside	girl

'the girl from the countryside.'

The direct object can precede the indirect object:

tɕie^{55}	san^{33}	khuai^{55}	tɕhie^{13}	ta^{33}
lend	three	dollar	money	3SG

'Lend him three dollars.'

The adverb *pu*^{24} negates a following verb or adjective:

pu^{24}	khuən^{55}	pu^{24}	tai^{11}
NEG	sleep	NEG	big
'not ... sleep'		'not big'	

Contact with Other Languages

As mentioned above, Xiang dialects were influenced by Mandarin. Since the Ming dynasty, because of the successive movements from Jiangxi Province, the Xiang dialects spoken in the eastern border area have been strongly influenced by GAN dialects.

Common Words

man:	lan^{13}zən^{13}ka^{33}	long:	tɪ́an^{13}
woman:	ny^{41}zən^{13}ka^{33}	small:	siau^{41} or si^{55}
water:	ɕyei^{41}	yes:	sɪ̂^{41}
sun:	thai^{55}ian^{13}	no:	pu^{24}
three:	san^{33}	good:	xau^{41}
fish:	y^{13}	bird:	tiau^{41}
big:	tai^{11}	dog:	kəu^{41}
tree:	ɕy^{11}		

Example Sentences

(1)

tsən^{13}	li^{0}	ŋa^{13}tsɪ̂^{0}	tɕhy^{933}	pi^{13}	xai^{13}
city	in	boy	wear	leather	shoes

'The boy wears leather shoes in the city.'

(2)

ŋo^{41}	tɕhia^{24}	ka^{0}	fan^{11}	tɕiəu^{11}	lai^{41}
1SG	eat	PERFECTIVE	meal	as soon as	come

'I ate as soon as I came.'

(3)

ta^{33}	sən^{55}	pən^{41}	ɕin^{33}	ɕy^{33}	no^{41}
3SG	send	CLASSIFIER	new	book	1SG

'He's sending me some new books.'

Efforts to Preserve, Protect, and Promote the Language

At the present time, no protective or promotional efforts have been taken on behalf of the Xiang dialects.

Select Bibliography

Bao Houxing, Cui Zhenheua, Shen Ruoyun, and Wu Yunji. 1993. *Dictionary of the Changha dialect.* Nanjing: Jiangsu Education Publishing House.

Bao Houxing and Yansen. 1986. *The Grouping of the Dialects of Hunan Province, Fangyan.*

Yang, S.F. 1974. *A Report on the Survey of the Dialects of Hunan.* Institute of History and Philology, Academia Sinica, Taipei, special issue, 66.

Chinese Languages: Yue

Anne O. Yue

Language Name: Yue. **Alternates:** Cantonese 'language of Guangdong', 'local language'. Current practice is to use the term "Yue" for the entire language group and "Cantonese" for its standard dialect.

Location: Mainly spoken in central (around the Pearl River Delta) and southwestern Guangdong Province, and southeastern Guangxi (especially along the West River Basin). Secondarily spoken in eastern Guangdong and Guangxi as well as areas outside China, concentrating in North America and to a lesser extent, Southeast Asia, notably although not limited to Singapore. The name Yue nowadays is also a geographical term referring to the regions of both Guangdong and Guangxi, homeland of the Yue speakers.

Family: Sinitic branch of the Sino-Tibetan family.

Related Languages: HAKKA, MIN, WU, XIANG, GAN, and MANDARIN (Northern Chinese).

Dialects: There is now information on about 70 Yue dialects, some of which have been studied in detail in monographs and others have been described in materials dating back to the 19th century. Subclassification of Yue dialects has often been made according to geographical region. But based on linguistic criteria, two major subgroups with further subdivisions can be established: (1) the Delta group, subdivided into North (including dialects along and north of the West River Basin in Guangxi), South (including dialects of southwestern Guangdong and Guangxi), and Gudangfu (including dialects spoken in large cities like Nanning and Maoming); (2) the Siyi Liang-Yang group, divided into Siyi ('Four Districts') and Liang-Yang. This subclassification reflects the settlement pattern of the Yue speakers, with enclaves of diverse dialects around the fertile Pearl River Delta, which is one of the earliest settled regions, and the hilly, formerly less accessible region neighboring the delta. The greater similarity found among dialects of the delta region and those of southwestern Guangdong (also called Nanlu 'the Southern Route') or Guangxi than among the delta dialects themselves recalls the waves of migration radiating from the delta region. Cantonese is the standard dialect of the Yue group, based on the dialect of the city of Guangzhou, which has been the capital of Guangdong Province since the establishment of the republic as well as the administrative center for the region south of the Five Passes in southern China since Qin-Han times (more than 2,000 years) and the cultural center of the region since Southern Song (more than 800 years). It is thus no wonder that it serves also as the socially high dialect and *lingua franca* of Guangdong and the greater part of Guangxi, which constitute the homeland not only for Yue speakers, but also for Hakka and Southern Min speakers, as well as speakers of a number of minority languages. Varieties of Cantonese outside the delta area are often referred to as *pak*^{8}*wa*$^{6>3}$ 'the vernacular', *saŋ*^{3}*(sɛŋ*^{2}*)wa*$^{6>3}$ 'language of the capital', or *kwɔŋ*^{3}*fu*^{3}*wa*$^{6>3}$ 'language of the Guangzhou district'.

Number of Speakers: About 40 million according to the 1982 census.

Origin and History

The name Yue was first used to refer to a group of peoples (*Bai Yue* 'the Hundred Yue') who inhabited the south China coastal region (south of the Yangzi River from the Hangzhou Bay all the way to the northern part of present-day Vietnam) more than 2,000 years ago. It was also the name of a state during the Warring States period (475–221 B.C.). Ethnic and linguistic identification of these peoples (generally believed to be non-Han) as well as their relationship to the present-day inhabitants of this region still awaits research.

Large, scale migration of Han people into this region occurred later during the Qin Dynasty (mid 3rd century B.C.) as a result of military conquest. Subsequent political turmoil in northern China resulted in several major emigrations, especially during the end of the Han (third century A.D.), the Tang (7th-10th centuries), and the Song Dynasties (13th century). Linguistic evidence points to Tang as an important period for the Yue speakers, since they refer to themselves as the "Tang people", to their language as the "Tang language", to their country as the "Tang mountain", to their clothes as the "Tang costumes", and to their food as "Tang cuisine".

However, there is linguistic reason to believe that even as early as the first migration, the Yue language was already being formed, absorbing new elements from the Han languages of subsequent waves of migrations to form the literary stratum of the Yue language, as well as assimilating various aboriginal elements form part of the colloquial stratum.

The migration routes of the Yue speakers from the central plains throughout the ages were mainly two, one from Lake Dongting (present-day northern Hunan Province) through River Xiang, and the other from Lake Boyang (present-day northern Jiangxi Province) through River Gan. The former was probably more popular before the Tang Dynasty because of the mountain barriers imposed on the latter. Linguistically, it is significant to note that areas along these two routes have

Table 1: Consonants

		Labial	Dental	Palato-Alveolar	Velar	Glottal
Stops	Unaspirated	p	t		k	
	Aspirated	p'	t'		k'	
Fricatives		f		s/ʃ		h
Affricates	Unaspirated			ts/tʃ		
	Aspirated			ts'/tʃ'		
Nasals		m	n		ŋ	
Lateral			l			
Glides		(w, ɥ)		(j)		

evolved into homelands of the Xiang and the Gan dialect groups respectively, with which some Yue dialects share prominent features.

Orthography and Basic Phonology

No standard orthography has been devised for Yue except a romanization designed by Western missionaries and a standard romanization system announced by the Administrative Department of Education of the Guangdong provincial government in 1960, both for Cantonese. However, colloquial words without cognates in Mandarin are represented with specially devised dialectal characters through modification of traditional characters. It is difficult to tell when such characters were first coined, since the colloquial language has left no written records earlier than a rime dictionary, *Fenyun Cuoyao* 'Summary of Rimes', compiled by Zhou Guanshan, the earliest extant edition of which dates probably from the 18th century. Another source where such characters occur is the book, *Cantonese Love Songs*, written by Zhao Ziyong, probably around the first part of the 18th century. Works by Western missionaries of the last century, which also contain such characters, are based on these two sources.

Except where indicated, the descriptions in this article are of Cantonese.

All of the consonants in Table 1 above can serve as the initial segment of a syllable (or initial according to traditional Chinese phonology, as opposed to the rest of the syllable, which is called the final or rime). The phonologically nondistinctive glides (in parentheses on the above chart) may either precede or follow the vowel in a syllable. In addition, there are two labio-velars, k^w and k'^w, which may also be interpreted as a sequence of a velar followed by the glide *w*.

The above inventory of initial consonants is typical of most Yue dialects. Like the majority of Sinitic languages, Yue has no voiced consonants except for sonorants (nasals, liquids, glides), although a number of Yue dialects in Guangxi, such as Rongxian, Cenxi, Yulin, Shinan, Sihe, and Binyang, have murmur or breathiness accompanying the pronunciation of obstruents in syllables with the Yang tones (see below for tones).

The sibilants *ts, ts'*, and *s* have alveolar [ts ts' s] and palato-alveolar [tʃ tʃ' ʃ] variants, depending on speakers. In some other Yue dialects such as Yingde, the two series are phonologically distinct, each tracing back to different sources in Ancient Chinese.

Apart from the glides, only six of the consonants—*p, t, k, m, n*, and *ŋ*—occur as final segments. When *p, t*, and *k* occur as final segments, they are unreleased stops. A number of Yue dialects in northern Guangdong, such as Qujiang, Renhua, Lechang, Lianshan, and Lianxian, have only four stop endings, the labials having merged with either the dentals or the velars.

Table 2: Vowels

	Front		Central	Back
	Unrounded	Rounded		
High	i:/ɪ	y:/		u:/ʊ
Mid	/e	/ø	ɐ	/o
Low	ɛ:/	œ:/	a:/	ɔ:/

There are eight distinctive vowels in Cantonese. Except for *y*, all vowels are phonetically paired in a tense/lax contrast; on the chart, tense allophones precede a slash, while lax allophones follow a slash. The lax allophones are usually shorter and centralized, while the tense allophones are longer and located nearer the periphery of the vowel space. In terms of distribution, the lax allophones do not occur alone, but are always followed by a glide or a consonant; the tense allophones are free from such restriction. The two central vowels /ɐ/ and /a:/ are contrastive in Cantonese.

This vowel system is not typical of other Yue dialects, where the tense/lax distinction is at most found with the central vowels, and even there, it is not universal.

In Cantonese and the great majority of Yue dialects, *m* and *ŋ* can also serve in place of a vowel as the nucleus of a syllable.

Tones

	Even	Rising	Going	Entering
Yin	(1) high level/ falling	(3) high rising	(5) mid-high level	(7a) high checked
				(7b) mid checked

Yang	(2) low level/ (falling)	(4) low rising	(6) mid-low level	(8)low checked

Phonologically speaking, the Yue dialects average a greater number of tones than other Sinitic dialects. There are 9 distinctive tones in the majority of the Yue dialects, while a number of them have 8 tones, and a very small number have ten tones, 7 tones, o even 6 tones. The entering tones occur only in syllables endi g with an oral stop, while all other tones occur in open syllables or syllables ending with a nasal.

In Cantonese, in terms of tonal contour, (7a) is identical with the nonfalling variant of (1), except for its shortness; (7b) is identical with (5), and (8) with (6). Tone (1), and, for a dwindling number of older speakers, tone (2), has a level variant and a falling variant. In a sequence of tone 1 or of tone 2, all but the last are of the level variant.

Basic Morphology

Yue nouns are not marked for case, number, or gender. The only marker for nouns is the classifier, which appears almost obligatorily whenever a noun is used with numbers or demonstratives, and it often signifies the shape of the item it goes with.

Cantonese uses a suffix *-tei⁶* to signify the plural of personal pronouns:

	Singular	Plural
1st	ŋɔ⁴	ŋɔ⁴-tei⁶
2nd	nei⁴	nei⁴-tei⁶
3rd	k'øy⁴	k'øy⁴-tei⁶

There are gender suffixes for animals, a typical feature of Southern Sinitic languages:

Masculine	Feminine
kɐi¹-kʊŋ¹	kɐi¹-na³
chicken-male 'cock'	chicken-female 'hen'
ŋɐu²-kʊŋ¹	ŋɐu²-na³
cattle-male 'ox'	cattle-female 'cow'

A special feature of Cantonese and many Yue dialects is the use of tonal change, or *pin⁵ jɐm¹*, to express 'familiarity' and its often associated meaning of 'endearment, dimunition, unimportance, contemptuousness' for high-frequency nouns in common use. In Cantonese, all categories of tones except the high-level/falling (1) and high-rising (3) will change into the high-rising tone in this function:

ɥy²ᐳ³ 'fish', cf. ɥy²syn² 'fishing boat'
hɐu⁶ mun²ᐳ³ 'back door', cf. tai⁶ mun² 'front door'

Yue has no verbal morphology. Aspects are generally expressed with suffixes:

PERFective	-tʃɔ³
PROGressive	-kɐn³
EXPeriential	-kʷɔ⁵

The affirmative present and the past tense are expressed by the existential verb *jɐu⁴* (EXIST) preceding the verb:

k'øy⁴	høy⁵-tʃɔ³	kɔ³-tou⁶	
s/he	go-PERF	there	's/he has gone there'

k'øy⁴	jɐu⁴	høy⁵	kɔ³-tou⁶	
s/he	EXIST	go	there	's/he went there'

k'øy⁴	sɪk⁸-kɐn³	fan⁶	
s/he	eat-PROG	rice	's/he is eating'

k'øy⁴	høy⁵-kwɔ⁵	kɔ³-tou⁶	
s/he	go-EXP	there	's/he has been there'

The perfective aspect may also be expressed with tonal change in Cantonese, although this is no longer the preferred marking. Just like the *pin⁵ jɐm¹* for nouns, all tones except the high-level/ falling (1) and high-rising (3) tones will change into the high-rising tone in this function:

k'øy⁴	høy⁵ᐳ³	kɔ³-tou⁶	
s/he	go.PERF	there	's/he has gone there'

With stative verbs, degree of intensity may also be expressed by the same kind of tonal change, in conjunction with reduplication. Depending on word order, the degree of intensity is either increasing or decreasing; when the tonal change precedes the root it signifies increasing intensity, and when the tonal change follows the root it signifies decreasing intensity:

hʊŋ²ᐳ³	hʊŋ²	hʊŋ²	hʊŋ²ᐳ³-tei³
red	red	red	red-slight degree
'very red'		'a little red'	

Unlike Northern Chinese and like Southern Sinitic languages such as Hakka and Min, the Yue passive is expressed by a marker *pei³* that is associated with the agent and not the verb; the same marker expresses the causative, and it is identical with the verb 'to give'.

ŋɔ⁴	pei³	køy⁴	ta³	
I	let	s/he	hit	'I let him/her hit me.'

ŋɔ⁴	pei³	køy⁴	ta³søŋ¹	
I	PASS	s/he	hit-injure	'I was hit and hurt by him/her.'

Basic Syntax

The preferred word order in unmarked declarative or interrogative sentences is Subject-Verb-Object:

pin¹kɔ⁵	ta³	mun²	a⁵
which-person	hit	door	FINAL PARTICLE

'Who is knocking at the door?'

An Object-Verb order indicates topicalization for emphasis or contrast:

k'øy^{4} mɐt^{7a}jɛ^{4} sy^{1} tou^{1} mai^{4}
s/he what book all buy
'S/he will buy any book.'

Within a noun phrase, nominal modifiers precede the noun they modify:

nei^{4} t'ɐi^{3}-kɐn^{3} kɔ^{3} pun^{3} sy^{1} hɐi^{6} ŋɔ^{4} kɛ^{5}
you look-PROG that CLASS book be I NOMINALIZER
'The book you are reading is mine.'

The general negative marker is *m̩*^{2}:

hɐi^{2} kɔ^{3}-tou^{6} m̩^{2} hɐi^{3} ni^{1}-tou^{6}
locate there NEG locate here
'It is there, not here.'

Negation of perfective verbs is indicated by *mei*^{6}:

k'øy^{4} høy^{5}-tʃɔ^{3}mei^{6} a^{5}
s/he go-PERF NEG FINAL PARTICLE
'Has s/he gone yet?'

Negation of perfective verbs is indicated by the particle *mei*^{1} while negation of the existential is indicated by *mou*^{4} and negation of the imperative is indicated by *mɐi*^{4} before the verb:

k'øy^{4} jɐu^{4} mou^{4} høy^{5} a^{5}?
s/he EXIST NEG.EXIST go FINAL.PART
'did s/he go?'

mɐi^{4} juk^{7}!
NEG move
'don't move!'

At least three more syntactic constructions differ from Northern Chinese. The comparative construction has the two terms of comparison flanking the verb of comparison, similar to Archaic Chinese:

k'øy^{4} kou^{1} (kwɔ^{5}) ŋɔ^{4} lʊk^{8} tʃ'yn^{5}
s/he be-tall (exceed) I six inch
's/he is six inches taller than me'

The double-object construction has the direct object preceding the indirect object unless the verb carries the semantic features of [+deprive]:

k'øy^{4} pei^{3}-tʃɔ^{3} jɐt^{7a} mɐn^{1} ŋɔ^{4}
s/he give-PERF one dollar I
's/he gave me a dollar'

k'øy^{4} t'ɐu^{1} -tʃɔ^{3} ŋɔ^{4} jɐt^{7a} mɐn^{1}
s/he steal –PERF I one dollar
's/he stole a dollar from me'

The attributive construction carries no attributive marker if the head noun contains a demonstrative:

tʃ'ɐm^{2}jɐt^{8} lɐi^{2} kɔ^{3} kɔ^{5} hɐu^{6}saŋ^{1}tʃɐi^{3} hɐi^{6} ŋɔ^{4} sɐi^{5}lou^{3}
yesterday come that CL young-chap be I younger-brother
'The young chap who came yesterday is my younger brother.'

Contact with Other Languages

The Yue people have lived for centuries as neighbors with speakers of other languages, and depending on the social status of these languages, different types of loanwords can be found. With respect to non-Sinitic languages such as Zhuang, Miao, and Yao, it is difficult to judge whether certain lexical items common to them and to the Yue dialect are loanwords or substratum cognates. These are all basic vocabulary items. For example:

From Miao: *-na*^{3} 'female suffix for animals', *hɐm*^{6}*plaŋ*^{6} 'all'
From Zhuang: *lʊk*^{7a}*(jɐu*$^{6>3}$*)* 'pomelo', *nɐŋ*^{1}*(kai*^{1}*)* 'skin' (> 'goose flesh'), *hɐi*^{1} 'vulva'

During the last century and a half, Cantonese came into contact with speakers of ENGLISH and, to a much lesser extent, FRENCH. Loanwords from these languages pertain to modern material culture:

From English: *pa*^{1}*si*^{3} 'bus', *pɔ*^{1} 'ball', *fei*^{1}*lɐm*^{3} 'film', *kei*^{6}*lim*^{1} 'cream', *sɔ*^{1}*fa*^{3} 'sofa'
From French: *laŋ*^{1} 'yarn'

Common Words

man:	nam^{2}jɐn$^{2>3}$, lou^{3}	long:	tʃ'øŋ^{2}
woman:	nøy^{4}jɐn$^{2>3}$	small:	sɐi^{5}
water:	søy^{3}	yes:	(repeat verb)
sun:	jit^{8}t'ɐu$^{2>3}$	no:	(neg + verb)
three:	sam^{1}	good:	hou^{3}
fish:	ɥy$^{2>3}$	bird:	tʃøk$^{7b>3}$
big:	tai^{6}	tree:	sy^{6}
dog:	kɐu^{3}		

Example Sentences

(1) ŋɔ^{6} søŋ^{3} t'ʊŋ^{2} nei^{4} k'ɪŋ^{1} jɐt^{7} tʃɐn^{6}
I want with you talk one moment
'I want to talk with you for a while.'

(2) k'øy^{4} m^{2} jɐp^{8} tɐk^{7a} høy^{5}
s/he NEG enter can away.from
'S/he cannot enter.'

(3) ŋɔ^{6} tɐk^{7a}tʃɐi^{6} sɪk^{8} tɔ^{1} loeŋ^{4} wum^{3} sin^{1} la^{1}
hungry too eat more two bowls first FINAL.PART
'Too hungry, eat two more bowls first.'

Efforts to Preserve, Protect, and Promote the Language

Since Cantonese has enjoyed a socially high status and has been adopted as a regional standard for centuries, there is a strong sense of loyalty, pride, and desire among Yue speakers to maintain the same status for their standard language, even after considerable governmental effort since the 1950s to promote standard Mandarin as the national language. Yue opera, popular songs, movies, television, cartoons, poetry, plays, novels, essays, etc. still appear in the Cantonese colloquial in spoken or written form.

Select Bibliography

Bridgman, E. C. 1841. *Chinese Chrestomathy*. Macao: S. Wells Williams.

Cen, Qixiang. 1953. "Observing Language Contact and Development from the Dialects in Guangdong." In *Zhongguo Yuwen (Chinese Language & Writing)* 10–4: 9–12.

Cheung, Yat-Shing and Yu'en Gan. 1993. *A Bibliography of Yue Dialect Studies*. Hong Kong: Linguistic Society of Hong Kong.

Hashimoto, Mantaro. 1978. *Linguistic Typogeography*. Tokyo: Kobundo

Li, Rong, *et al.* 1987. *Language Atlas of China*. Hong Kong: Longman.

Mei, Yi, *et al.* eds. 1988. *Chinese Encyclopedia: Language, Writing*. Shanghai: Chinese Encyclopedia Publisher.

Norman, Jerry L. 1988. *Chinese*. Cambridge: Cambridge University Press.

Ramsey, Robert S. 1987. *The Languages of China*. Princeton: Princeton University Press.

Tsuji, Nobuhisa. 1980. *Comparative Phonology of Guangxi Yue Dialects*. Tokyo: Kazama Shobo Publishing Co.

Wang, William S-Y, ed. 1981. *Languages and Dialects of China*. Journal of Chinese Linguistics Monograph No. 3

Yang, Paul and S.J. Fumien. 1981. *Chinese Dialectology: A Selected and Classified Bibliography*. Hong Kong: Chinese University Press.

Yuan, Jiahua, *et al.* 1983. *Hanyu Fangyan Gaiyao (Outline of Chinese Dialects*). 2d ed. Beijing: Wenzi Gaige Press.

Yue(-Hashimoto), Anne O. 1970. "The Liang-Yue dialect materials." In *Unicorn* 6: 35–51.

____. 1972. *Studies in Yue Dialects 1: Phonology of Cantonese*. Cambridge: Cambridge University Press.

____. 1987. "A Preliminary Investigation into the Subclassification Problem of the Yue Dialects." In *Computational Analysis of Asian and African Languages*. Tokyo, No. 30, 1–30.

____. 1991. "The Yue Dialect." In *Languages and Dialects of China*, edited by William S-Y. Wang, 294-324.

____. 1993. *Comparative Chinese Dialectal Grammar: Handbook for Investigators*. Paris: École des Hautes Études en Sciences Sociales, Centre de Recherches Linguistiques sur l'Asie Orientale.

Zhan, Bohui, and Yat-shing Cheung. 1987. *A Survey of Dialects in the Pearl River Delta, Vol. 1: Comparative Morpheme-Syllabary*. Hong Kong: New Century Publishing House.

____. 1988. *A Survey of Dialects in the Pearl River Delta, Vol. 2: Comparative Lexicon*. Hong Kong: New Century Publishing House.

____ 1994. *A Survey of the Yue Dialects in North Guangdong*. Guangzhou: Jinan University Press.

COPTIC

Antonio Loprieno

Language Name: Coptic is an adjective derived from the GREEK *Aigyptios* 'Egyptian,' ARABIC *qibṭī*. It is the term used to refer to the language written and spoken during the early Christian period of the history of Egypt (from about A.D. 300). The native expression indicating the language of the country was *mntrmnkême* (pronounced *mentremenkême*), 'the speech of the people of the Black Land,' i.e., of Egypt. In the neighboring Semitic languages, Coptic was originally called 'Egyptian (language),' for example HEBREW *miṣrīt*, but is now referred to as "Coptic," for example, Arabic *(al-luġa) al-qibṭiyya*.

Location: Coptic was spoken and written in Egypt, that is, in northeast Africa in the portion of the Nile Valley north of the first cataract, corresponding to the present-day city of Aswan in the Nile Delta, and in the oases immediately to the west of the Nile Valley.

Family: Together with its ancestor, Ancient EGYPTIAN, Coptic represents an autonomous branch of the Afroasiatic (formerly labeled Hamito-Semitic) family, which also comprises Semitic, Berber (corresponding to Libyan in antiquity), Cushitic, Chadic, and Omotic languages.

Related Languages: Within the Afro-Asiatic family, Coptic displays the closest connections to Semitic and Berber languages.

Dialects: Coptic is known through a variety of dialects differing mostly in the graphic rendition of Egyptian phonemes, and to a lesser extent also in morphology and lexicon. The most important dialect is Sahidic (from Arabic *al-ṣa'īd* 'Upper Egypt'), originally spoken in the Theban area. Sahidic is the first dialect of Coptic literature. Bohairic (from Arabic *al-buḥayra* 'Lower Egypt'), the dialect of Alexandria, eventually became the language of the liturgy of the Coptic church. Other important dialects of Coptic literature are Akhmimic from the city of Akhmim (Greek Panopolis) in Upper Egypt; Subakhmimic, also called Lycopolitan, spoken in the area of Asyut (Greek Lycopolis) in Middle Egypt; and Fayyumic, the variety of Coptic from the oasis of Fayyum, in the upper western corner of the Nile Valley.

Number of Speakers: At present, there are no native speakers of Coptic, Arabic being the only language of the Egyptian population, 10 percent of which are Coptic Christians. A fair estimate of the number of speakers of the language in early Christian times is between 5 and 7 million.

Origin and History

Coptic, the latest stage in the evolution of Ancient Egyptian, was spoken and written from around A.D. 300. After the Arabic occupation of 641, it was superseded by Arabic, first as language of the administration, and then gradually also as the only spoken language in the country. This evolution was probably completed by 1200; however, Coptic survives to the present in the liturgy of the Christian church of Egypt, which is also called the Coptic church.

Orthography and Basic Phonology

With the success of Christianity in Egypt during the second and third centuries, when a changed cultural and religious setting favored the adoption of an alphabetic system, the Ancient Egyptian writing system (hieroglyphs and Demotic) was superseded by the Coptic alphabet, which is written from left to right and consists of the Greek alphabet of 24 letters and of six (in some dialects seven) Demotic signs to indicate phonemes absent from Greek. These supplementary phonemes are in all dialects the alveopalatal *š*, the labiodental *f*, the laryngeal *h*, the palatal affricate *j*, the palatalized velar *c*, and the sign for a sequence of plosive dental followed by the vowel *ti*. In addition, Bohairic and Akhmimic each have a different sign for the fricative velar *x*.

The exact phonological value of some Coptic consonants is obscured by our imperfect knowledge of earlier Egyptian phonology on the one hand and of the pronunciation of the Greek letters at the time of the adoption of the Greek alphabet in Egypt on the other; for classical Sahidic, we can posit the phonological inventory found below .

Table 1: Consonants

	Labial	Dental	Palatal	Velar	Glottal
Stops					
Voiceless	p	t	j [c]	k	[ʔ]
Voiced	b	d		g	
Palatalized				c [ki]	
Ejective		t [t']	j [c']	k [k']	
Fricatives					
Voiceless	f	s	š	x	h
Voiced		z			
Nasals	m	n			
Resonants	(o)u	l, r	(e)i		

The voiceless stops /p t c k/ are presumed to have been aspirated /pʰ tʰ cʰ kʰ/.

The phoneme "glottal stop" /ʔ/ is not written at the beginning or at the end of a word, and is represented by a reduplication of the vowel sign within the word: *anok* /ʔanok/ 'I', *nto* /n̩toʔ/ 'thou (fem.)', *eet* /ʔeʔt/ 'to be pregnant'.

Table 2: Vowels

	Front	Central	Back
High	(e) i		ou
Mid	e, ê	ə	o, ô
Low		a	

The vowel /ə/ (written *e*) only occurs unstressed; *a* is the only other vowel that can appear unstressed. The high vowels *(e)i* and *ou* are long /i:/ and /u:/, respectively, while *a* is short /a/. Length is distinctive only for the midvowels *e* /e/ and *o* /o/ versus *ê* /e:/ and *ô* /o:/.

Basic Morphology

The basic Coptic morphological unit is the word, originally based on a root, for example *son* 'brother' < *sn* or *sôtm* 'to hear' < *stm*. In the course of the evolution of Ancient Egyptian, however, the alternation of stems based on a root became gradually less productive, until in Coptic the number of words derived from a single root is rarely higher than two, the old morphological patterns having been superseded by analytic constructions.

Nouns are classified according to gender: masculine (*noute* 'god') and feminine (*sône* 'sister'), and number: singular (*sêu* 'time') and plural (*snêu* 'brothers'). A few remnants of duals (*spotou* 'lips') are syntactically treated like singulars or plurals. There are no predictable inflectional patterns, so that gender and number of a noun can be detected only on the basis of its classifiers and syntactic behavior. While a few nouns preserve an evolved form of the Ancient Egyptian patterns of nominal derivations (masc. *sabe*, fem. *sabê*, pl. *sabeeu* 'wise'), in the vast majority of cases Coptic nouns display only one form for singular and plural (*p-rôme* 'the man', *n-rôme* 'the men').

Although one may detect rare remnants of the Afro-Asiatic case system in Coptic morphology, these do not play a productive role in the language.

Adjectives are morphologically and syntactically treated like substantives: *p-dikaios* 'the just one'.

Coptic has three sets of pronouns. Suffix pronouns are used as the subject of verbal forms (*a=f-sôtm* 'he heard'), to indicate the possessor with possessive articles and pronouns (*pe=k-eiôt* 'your father'), and as object of prepositions and of infinitives (*nmma=s* 'with her', *a=i-cnt=f* 'I found him'). Proclitic pronouns are used as the subject of the present tense (*tn-sooun* 'we know') and of adverbial sentences (*k-mpeima* 'you are in this place'). Independent pronouns are used in topicalizations and focalizations (*ntok de tinacntk* 'but I shall find you') and as subject of nominal sentences (*ntôtn hen-ergatês têr=tn* 'you are all workers'); in this latter case, when not topicalized, they display the unstressed form: *ang ou-rmnkême* 'I am Egyptian'.

Table 3: Coptic Pronouns

Form	Suffix	Proclitic	Independent	
			Stressed	Unstressed
1 Sg	=i, =t	ti-	anok	ang
2 M.Sg	=k	k=	ntok	ntk
2 F.Sg	=e, =te, Ø	te=	nto	nte
3 M.Sg	=f	f-	ntof	ntf
3 F.Sg	=s	s-	ntos	ntos
1 Pl	=n	tn-	anon	ann
2 Pl	=tn	tetn-	ntôtn	ntetn
3 Pl	=ou, =sou, =se	se-	ntoou	ntoou

Coptic has an indefinite article: sing. *ou-*, derived from the numeral *oua* 'one' (*ou-rôme* 'a man'), pl. *hen-*, derived from the quantifier *hoeine* 'some' (*hen-rôme* 'men'). It also has a definite article (masc. *p(e)-*, fem. *t(e)-*, pl. *n(e)-*), which is the clitic form of the corresponding deictic series: adjective *pei-*, *tei-*, *nei-* 'this, these', pronoun *pai, tai, nai* 'this one, these ones'. From the same morphological pattern one derives the copula *pe, te, ne*, which agrees in gender and number with the subject, and, in combination with suffix pronouns, possessive adjectives (*pe=k-êi* 'your house'), and pronouns (*nou=k ne m-pêue* 'heaven is yours').

The relative pronoun has the forms *et-*, *ete-*, or *nt-*, depending on the syntactic environment. It can only refer to specific (i.e., semantically determined) antecedents, indefinite antecedents being resumed by a circumstantial clause:

p-rôme nt-a-f-ei
the-man who-PAST-3M/SG-came
'the man who came'

ou-rôme e-a-f-ei
a-man while-PAST-3M/SG-came
'a man who came'

Interrogative pronouns are *nim* 'who?' *aš* 'what?, which?'

The most common numerals show etymological connections with other Afro-Asiatic languages: *oua* '1', *snau* '2', *šomnt* '3', *ftoou* '4', *tiou* '5', *soou* '6', *sašf* '7', *šmoun* '8', *psit* '9', *mêt* '10', *jouôt* '20', *maab* '30', *hme* '40', *taiou*'50', *se* '60', *šfe* '70', *hmene* '80', *pstaiou* '90', *še* '100', *šêt* '200', *šo* '1,000', *tba* '10,000'. The number 5 is etymologically derived from the word for 'hand', 20 and 200 are dual forms of 10 and 100 respectively, 50 through 90 represent the plural forms of the respective units 5 through 9. Ordinals are derived from cardinals through the prefixation of the participle *meh-* 'filling' to the cardinal number: *mehftoou* 'fourth'.

Nonfinite forms of the Coptic verb are the infinitive, which usually indicates activities (*ei* 'to come'), accomplishments (*ôô* 'to conceive'), or achievements (*cine* 'to find'), and the qualitative, which conveys states (*eet* 'to be pregnant'). While participial functions are analytically conveyed by relative constructions (*p-et-rime* 'the one who weeps'), there are still a

Table 4: Verbal Markers

Form	Marker	Example	Meaning
Circumstantial Present	e=, ere-	e=i-hkaeit	'while I am hungry'
Aorist of Habit	ša=, šare-	ša=i-ka pa-joinna=i	'I keep my ship for me'
Negative Aorist	me=, mere-	me=f-sôtm	'he cannot hear'
Prospective of Wishing	e=, e, ere-, e	e=s-e-šôpe	'may it happen', 'amen'
Negative Prospective	nn(e)=, nne-	nne=f-eibe ša-eneh	'may he never be thirsty'
Optative	mar(e)=, mare-	mare-pe=k-ran ouop	'hallowed be your name'
Final	(n)tare=, (n)tare-	aitei tar=ou-ti nê=tn	'ask, that you may be given'
Completive	šant(e)=, šant(e)-	šante-prê hôtp	'until the sun sets down'
Negative Completive	mpat(e)=, mpat(e)-	mpat=f-ei	'he has not yet come'
Preterite	a=, a-	a-ouša šôpe	'a festival took place'
Negative Preterite	mp(e)=, mpe-	mpi-raše	'I did not rejoice'
Imperfect	ne=, nere-	nere-tmaau n-iêsous mmau	'Jesus' mother was there'
Temporal	nter(e)=, nter(e)-	ntere=f-je nai	'when he said these things'
Conjunctive	n=, nte-	e=k-e-nau n=g-eime	'may you see and understand'

few remnants of Ancient Egyptian synthetic participles (*mai-noute* 'lover of god' > 'pious').

Finite verbal forms consist of a marker that conveys aspectual, temporal, or modal features, followed by the nominal or pronominal subject and by the infinitive (for actions) of the verb: *a-prôme sôtm* 'the man heard', *a=i-hmoos* 'I sat down'. In the present and imperfect tenses, which are treated as adverbial constructions, the infinitive can be replaced by the qualitative (for states): *ti-hkaeit* 'I am hungry'. The most important verbal markers are found in Table 4 (the double stroke indicates pronominal subjects, the simple stroke nominal subjects).

In addition to these so-called sentence (or clause) conjugations, Coptic has an inflected form of the infinitive (*p-tre=f-sôtm* 'the fact that he hears'), a special suffix conjugation for adjective verbs (*nanou=f* 'he is good'), and a marker for the future of the present and imperfect tense (*ti-na-sôtm* 'I shall hear'). When verbal forms are preceded by a relative marker (*e-* for the present and the majority of the other tenses, *nt-* for the past), the verbal form appears nominalized and the focus of the utterance becomes a circumstantial clause or an adverbial adjunct: *e=f-na etôn* 'that he goes (is) whither' i.e., 'where does he go?'

The bare infinitive is usually found for the expression of the imperative (*bôk* 'go!'), but a few verbs keep the Ancient Egyptian imperative form with a prefix: *a-*: *a-nau* 'see!' < *nau*. The negative imperative is built by means of a prefix *mpr-* followed by the infinitive: *mpr-rime* 'do not weep!'

The most frequent prepositions are *n-, na=* 'to'; *n-, mmo=* 'in'; *hn* 'in'; *e-, ero=* 'toward'; *etbe-, etbêêt=* 'because of'; *nsa-* 'after'. A very frequent conjunction is *je-*, which introduces object clauses and direct speech.

Negation is expressed in nominal and adverbial sentences by means of the negative morpheme *n-* followed by the fortifier *an* (*n-anok an pe pe-khristos* 'I am not the Christ'), and in verbal sentences by specific verbal conjugations (listed above) or by the particle *tm*, originally the infinitive of a verb meaning 'not to do', placed before the infinitive (*e=f-tm-sôtm* 'if he does not hear' < 'while he does not do the hearing').

Basic Syntax

Coptic exhibits three sentence types, which are classified according to the syntactic nature of their predicate, the subject being always a nominal phrase:

(a) *Nominal sentences*, in which the predicate is a noun (substantive or adjective). The normal order of constituents is Predicate-Subject when the latter is a noun, Subject-Predicate when it is a pronoun; a copula may anticipate or replace the Subject:

anok ou-šôs
I a-shepherd 'I am a shepherd.'

ou-me te te=f-mnt-mntre
a-truth it this-3M/SG-thing-witness
'His testimony is true.'

te=k-shime te
this-2M/SG-wife it 'She is your wife.'

The order Predicate-(Copula-)Subject is modified into Topic-Comment in identifying sentences, when both Subject and Predicate are semantically determined or specific:

t-arkhê n-t-sophia te t-mnt-mai-noute
the-beginning DETER-the-wisdom it the-thing-lover-god
'The beginning of wisdom is piety.'

p-noute p-et-sooun
the-god the-who-knows 'God is the one who knows.'

(b) *Adverbial sentences*, in which the predicate is an adverbial or prepositional phrase; the order is always Subject-Predicate:

ti-hm pa-eiôt
I-in this 1/SG-father 'I am in my father.'

ne=f-bal	côšt	ejn	t-oikoumêne
these-3M/SG-eye	look	on	the-world

'His eyes look upon the world.'

(c) *Verbal sentences*, in which the predicate is a verbal phrase built according to the patterns described in the preceding section:

a=f-eine	mmo=f	a=f-kaa=f
PAST-3M/SG-bring	object-3M/SG	PAST-3M/SG-place-3M/SG

'He brought him and placed him.'

našô=ou
be numerous-3PL 'They are many.'

ari-pa-meeue
do-this1/SG-memory 'Remember me.'

Contact with Other Languages

Coptic was the vehicle of a primarily religious literature, and its emergence as the form that the language of Egypt acquired in Christian times relied very heavily, from a lexical point of view, on the linguistic code in which the Christian Scriptures were transmitted in the eastern Mediterranean world, i.e., on Hellenistic Greek. The amount of Greek loanwords in Coptic is, therefore, very high: depending on the nature of the text, up to one-third of the lexical items found in a Coptic text may be of Greek origin. Most of these words stem from the sphere of religious practice and belief (*angelos* 'angel', *diabolos* 'devil', *ekklêsia* 'church', *agios* 'saint', *sôtêr* 'savior'), administration (*arkhôn* 'governor', *oikonomei* 'to administer'), and high culture (*anagnôsis* 'recitation', *logikos* 'spiritual'). In some texts translated from Greek, the influence of this language extends to the realm of syntax. A limited number of words from the military context are LATIN (*douks* 'general'), whereas documents from the end of the first millennium begin to display the adoption of loanwords from Arabic (*alpesour* < *al-bāsūr* 'hemorrhoids'). The terms comprising the basic vocabulary, however, usually remained those of Egyptian origin.

Common Words

man:	rôme	long:	ôou
woman:	shime	small:	koui
water:	moou	yes:	ehe
sun:	rê	no:	mmon
three:	šomnt	good:	nanouf, agathos
fish:	tbt	bird:	ôbt
tree:	še	dog:	ouhor

Example Sentences

(1)

ntok	ou-rôme	n-agathos	pe
you	a-man	this-good	copula

'You are a good man.'

(2)

ne=f-bouhe	jno	n-n-šêre
these-3M/SG-eyelid	ask	OBJECT-the/PL-child

n-n-rôme
these-the/PL-man
'His eyelids scrutinize mankind.'

(3)

te=k-mnt-rro	mare=s-ei
the-2M/SG-thing-king	OPTATIVE-3F/SG-come

'May your kingdom come.'

Effort to Preserve, Protect, and Promote the Language

After its productive life, which ended in the centuries following the Arabic invasion of the country, Coptic continued to function as the liturgical language of the Christian church of Egypt. Native concerns for its survival emerge in the 14th century with the appearance of the first grammar of Coptic written in Arabic. In the West, scholarly knowledge of Coptic was rediscovered during the Renaissance: Coptic became an important part of the study of early Christianity and of oriental philology, and proved a key factor in Champollion's decipherment of the Ancient Egyptian hieroglyphic writing. Starting in the second part of the 19th century, and increasingly in recent decades, Coptic clerics and intellectuals have increased efforts aimed at a revival of Coptic as a spoken language of the Christian community, but the linguistic and cultural position of Arabic would seem to condemn those endeavors to failure.

Select Bibliography

Crum, W.E. 1939. *A Coptic Dictionary*. Oxford: Clarendon Press.

Lambdin, Thomas O. 1983. *Introduction to Sahidic Coptic*. Macon, Georgia: Mercer University Press.

Loprieno, Antonio. 1995. *Ancient Egyptian. A Linguistic Introduction*. Cambridge: Cambridge University Press.

Osing, Jürgen. 1976. *Die Nominalbildung des Ägyptischen*. Two vols. Mainz: Philipp von Zabern.

Polotsky, Hans-Jacob. 1971. *Collected Papers*. Jerusalem: Magnes Press.

____. 1987–90. *Grundlagen des koptischen Satzbaus*. Two vols. American Studies in Papyrology 27, 29. Atlanta: Scholars Press.

Shisha-Halevy, Ariel. 1986. *Coptic Grammatical Categories*. Analecta Orientalia 53. Rome: Pontifical Biblical Institute.

____. 1988 *Coptic Grammatical Chrestomathy*. Orientalia Lovaniensia Analecta 30. Leuven: Peeters.

Till, Walter C. 1970. *Koptische Grammatik (Saïdischer Dialekt)*. Lehrbücher für das Studium der Orientalischen und Afrikanischen Sprachen 1. 2nd edition. Leipzig: Verlag Enzyklopädie.

Westendorf, Wolfhart. 1965–77. *Koptisches Handwörterbuch*. Heidelberg: Carl Winter.

CREEK

Jack B. Martin and Margaret McKane Mauldin

Language Name: Creek, Muskogee.

Location: Central Oklahoma and central Florida, formerly in Alabama and Georgia.

Family: Muskogean.

Related Languages: Hitchiti (no longer spoken), Mikasuki (spoken within the Seminole Tribe and the Miccosukee Tribe of Florida), Alabama (spoken in eastern Texas), Koasati (spoken in Louisiana and eastern Texas), Choctaw (spoken in Mississippi and southeastern Oklahoma), and Chickasaw (spoken in south central Oklahoma).

Dialects: The three main dialects of Creek are Muskogee (spoken in the Muscogee [Creek] Nation of Oklahoma), Oklahoma Seminole (spoken in the Seminole Nation of Oklahoma), and Florida Seminole Creek (spoken within the Seminole Tribe of Florida). There is close contact between the Oklahoma groups with only minor differences in vocabulary. Florida Seminole Creek is slightly more divergent, owing in part to its location, to differences in flora and fauna, and to different neighboring languages.

Numbers of Speakers: 3,000–5,000.

Origin and History

Creek (or Muskogee) is a member of the Muskogean family of languages. The Muskogean family is indigenous to the southeastern United States, and includes Choctaw, Chickasaw, Alabama, Koasati, Apalachee, Hitchiti, and Mikasuki as well as Creek. The name "Creek" is thought to have been applied by English settlers (referring to the Creek habit of residing near water). "Muskogee" (*Maskoke* /ma:skó:ki/ or *Mvskoke* /maskó:ki/ in Creek) is of uncertain origin.

Early records show the Creeks living along the Coosa, Tallapoosa, Flint, and Chattahoochee Rivers in what are today the states of Alabama and Georgia. Those living along the Coosa and Tallapoosa are referred to as Upper Creeks; those along the Flint and Chattahoochee are Lower Creeks. These two groups (in all, including some 50 to 80 towns and 11,000–24,000 people) were united in a loose confederation known as the Creek Confederacy. Smaller groups were incorporated or annexed, and the Creek Confederacy eventually came to include speakers of Alabama, Koasati, Hitchiti, Natchez, Shawnee, Yuchi, and Chickasaw in addition to Creek.

Creeks have had contact with Europeans or European Americans since 1540, when DeSoto's expedition passed through their lands. Between 1740 and 1750, some Hitchiti-speaking Lower Creeks began moving into Florida. Some Creek-speaking refugees joined them following the disastrous Creek War of 1813–1815, in which some Alabama Creeks (inspired in part by the Shawnee-Creek leader Tecumseh) fought against Anglo-American settlers. This new group of Hitchiti and Creek-speaking runaways was referred to in Creek as *semvnole* /simanó:l-i/'wild', from Spanish *cimarrón* 'wild'. These Seminoles kept in contact for a while with the Lower Creeks, but were gradually excluded from treaties made with Creeks in Georgia and Alabama. In 1819, the state of Alabama was created, and tribal governments were outlawed (in violation of earlier treaties). In 1830, Andrew Jackson signed the Indian Removal Act. Although the U.S. Supreme Court found it unconstitutional, Creeks, Seminoles, Cherokees, Choctaws, and Chickasaws were removed to Indian Territory between 1834–1842. These "Five Civilized Tribes" formed independent nations with laws, courts, and schools, but their land was later allotted and in 1907 the state of Oklahoma was created. The Creek language was dominant numerically and politically within the Creek and Seminole Nations, but speakers of Yuchi, Hitchiti, Alabama, Koasati, and Natchez were also present.

Missionary work among the Creeks began as early as 1735, when the Moravian Brethren briefly operated a school on an island in the Savannah River. Intensive missionary work began after removal, and readers, hymnbooks, and translations of books of the New Testament were published in a spelling system devised by missionaries and native speakers. The first book published in Indian Territory was in Creek. In 1860, H. F. Buckner published a grammar of the language, and a dictionary written by R.M. Loughridge and David M. Hodge appeared in 1890. Literacy in the traditional spelling was low following the Civil War, but in 1906 it was estimated that 90 percent of full-bloods could read their language. Versions of the traditional spelling system were used in correspondence, legal briefs, laws, newspaper articles, and advertisements. Literacy declined following Oklahoma statehood. Use of the language has steadily declined. Toward the close of the 19th century, some leaders argued that students would be more successful if they were educated in ENGLISH. It was common for children in boarding schools to be punished for using even a casual word in Creek. When these children grew up, they spoke to their own children in English to save them punishment.

At the close of the 20th century Creek is spoken in central Oklahoma and on the Brighton Reservation within the Seminole Tribe of Florida. Creek speakers in Oklahoma and Florida have little difficulty understanding each other, though words for modern items and for local flora and fauna naturally differ. Creek is no longer spoken in Alabama or Georgia. In Oklahoma, the language is still used at churches, at ceremonial grounds, and at one radio station, but there are few individuals under the age of 50 who are able to use the language fluently. While there are some thirty to forty thousand individuals of Creek or Seminole descent, only 6,213 reported on the 1990 census that they speak Creek or Seminole at home, and the number of fluent speakers is decreasing at an alarming rate. There is, however, growing interest in maintaining the language and in producing new language materials.

The terms "Creek" and "Muskogee" (sometimes spelled "Muscogee") are both in use currently, and have different meanings for different people. "Creek" is felt by some to be broader in meaning: one might be Yuchi, Alabama, or Hitchiti and still call oneself "Creek". "Muskogee" is thought to be more specific. Creek speakers within the Seminole Tribe of Florida, for example, are comfortable calling their language "Creek", but associate "Muskogee" with Oklahoma. Oklahoma Seminoles, however, refer to their language as "Seminole", reserving "Creek" or "Muskogee" for members of the Creek Nation. Some younger people seem to favor "Muskogee", while most older people continue to use "Creek".

Orthography and Basic Phonology

The traditional Creek alphabet is based in part on English spelling.

a father /a:/
c such /c/
e fit /i/
ē feed /i:/
f fish /f/
h hotel /h/
i hey (formerly as in pine) /ey, ay/
k skill /k/
l love /l/
m man /m/
n no /n/
o boat (short) /o/, bode (long) /o:/
p spot /p/
r athlete /ɬ/
s sew /s/
t step /t/
u put /o/
v sofa /a/
w will /w/
y yes /y/

Table 1: Consonants

	Labial	Dental	Palatal	Velar	Glottal
Plosives	p	t	c	k	
Fricatives	f	s; r /ɬ/			h
Approximants	w	l	y		
Nasals	m	n			

Table 2: Vowels

	Front	Central	Back
High	e /i/; ē /i:/		
Mid			u /o/; o /o:/
Low		v /a/; a /a:/	

For English speakers, the surprising letters are *c*, *i*, *r*, and *v*. *C* is generally pronounced like English *such*. *V* is pronounced like the final vowel in *sofa*. In the 19th century, the diphthong spelled *i* was pronounced like English *pine*. Because of a sound change, it is now generally pronounced like English *hey*. *R* is used for a voiceless lateral fricative, a sound not found in English. English *athlete* gives a rough approximation of the sound, but the sound is properly made by placing the tongue in the position for *l*, and then raising the sides of the tongue slightly so that friction results.

Creek has a rule of voicing that makes *p*, *t*, *k*, and *c* sound like the first consonants in English *bill*, *dill*, *gill*, and *Jill*. Voicing applies only when *p*, *t*, *k*, and *c* are: 1) at the beginning of a syllable; and, 2) between voiced sounds (vowels, diphthongs, *m*, *l*, *n*, *w*, *y*). Examples: *opv* /opá/ 'owl' (sounds like English *b*), *eto* /itó/ 'tree' (sounds like English *d*), *hvmken* /hámk-in/ (sounds like English *g*), *vce* /ací/ 'corn' (sounds like English *j*).

Most consonants can be doubled. Doubled consonants are held slightly longer than single consonants, and are not voiced. Vowels are divided into short vowels *v* /a/, *e* /i/, *u* /o/, and long vowels *a* /a:/, *ē* /i:/, *o* /o:/.

Creek words have stress, but stress is realized in terms of pitch rather than loudness or emphasis. Creek also has tone. Falling tone, high tone, rising tone, and level tone are found primarily on verbs, and indicate whether an activity is ongoing, completed, etc. Tone is not marked in the traditional spelling. Thus *a-hueris* /á:-hoyɬ-éy-s/ [— — —] means 'I am in the process of standing up', while *a-hueris* /a:-hôyɬ-ey-s/ [— ‾- —] means 'I have stood up'. Vowels are sometimes nasalized, usually to indicate intensity or a prolonged event.

Basic Morphology

A few nouns form plurals with *-vke* /-aki/ or *-take* /-ta:ki/: *mēkko* /mí:kko/ 'chief', *mēkkvke* /mi:kk-akí/ 'chiefs', *honvnwv* /honánwa/ 'man', *honvntake* /honan-tá:ki/ 'men'. Diminutives are formed by adding *-uce* /-oci/: *efv* /ifá/ 'dog', *efuce* /if-óci/ 'puppy'. Nouns are possessed with inalienable or alienable prefixes:

cvpuse /ca-pósi/ 'my grandmother'
cepuse /ci-pósi/ 'your grandmother'
epuse /i-pósi/ 'his/her grandmother'
pupuse /po-pósi/ 'our grandmother'

vm efv /am-ífa/ 'my dog'
cem efv /cim-ífa/ 'your dog'
em efv /im-ífa/ 'his/her dog'
pum efv /pom-ífa/ 'our dog'

Inalienable prefixes are generally used for kin terms, body parts, and positional nouns.

Verbs may take a large number of affixes. Verbs expressing deliberate actions agree with the subject using suffixes:

hompis /homp-éy-s/ 'I am eating'
hompetskes /homp-íck-is/ 'you (singular) are eating'
hompes /homp-ís/ 'he/she is eating'
hompēs /homp-í:-s/ 'we are eating'
hompatskes /homp-á:ck-is/ 'you (plural) are eating'

Verbs expressing nondeliberate actions or states agree with the subject using prefixes:

cvhaktēsikes /ca-hakti:sêyk-is/ 'I sneezed'
cehaktēsikes /ci-hakti:sêyk-is/ 'you sneezed'
haktēsikes /hakti:sêyk-is/ 'he/she sneezed'
puhaktēsikes /po-hakti:sêyk-is/ 'we sneezed'

These prefixes are similar in shape to the inalienable prefixes, except that there is no third-person marker on verbs. The same markers are used for objects:

cvnafkes /ca-na:fk-ís/ 'he/she is hitting me'
cenafkes /ci-na:fk-ís/ 'he/she is hitting you'
nafkes /na:fk-ís/ 'he/she is hitting it/him/her'
punafkes /po-na:fk-ís/ 'he/she is hitting us'

Verbs may also be marked for number, tense, aspect, commands, and questions, giving what Mary R. Haas has described as a "luxuriance of grammatical processes":

nesetv /nis-íta/ 'to buy'
nesvketv /nis-ak-itá/ 'to buy (plural)'
nesvrēs /nis-áɬ-i:-s/ 'he/she will buy it'
nēses /ni:s-ís/ 'he/she is buying it'
nehses /níhs-is/ 'he/she bought it (today)'
nēsvnks /nî:s-ánk-s/ 'he/she bought it (recently, but not today)'
nēsemvts /nî:s-imát-s/ 'he/she bought it (about a year ago)'
nēsvntvs /nî:s-ánta-s/ 'he/she bought it (long ago)'
nesvs /nis-ás/ 'buy it!'
nēsv? /ni:s-a´/ 'is he/she buying it?'

As these forms show, modifications in the shape of a stem are common, and are referred to as Grades. Thus from *nes-* /nis-/ 'buy', Creek forms a lengthening grade (*nēs-* /ni:s-/), an aspirating grade (*nehs-* /níhs-/), a nasalizing grade (*nēs-* /nǐ:ⁿs-/), and a falling-tone grade (*nēs-* /nî:s-/).

Some notions corresponding to English prepositions are also expressed on the verb:

hoccicetv /ho:cceyc-itá/ 'to write'
enhoccicetv /in-ho:cceyc-itá/ 'to write to (someone)'
eshoccicetv /is-ho:cceyc-itá/ 'to write with (something)'
ohhoccicetv /oh-ho:cceyc-itá/ 'to write on top of (something)'

Creek has no true passive voice, but it has a middle voice (*tvcetv* /tac-íta/ 'to cut', *tvckē* /tác-k-i:/ 'be cut'), an impersonal (*kicetv* /keyc-itá/ 'to say', *kihoces* /kéyho:c-ís/ 'they say, someone says'), and a causative (*hompetv* /homp-itá/ 'to eat', *hompicetv* /hompeyc-itá/ 'to feed').

Distinctions in number are important in Creek. Verbs describing motion or position frequently have different forms depending on whether one, two, or three or more individuals are involved:

vretv /aɬ-íta/ 'to go about (of one)'
welvketv /wilak-itá/ 'to go about (of two)'
fulletv /foll-itá/ 'to go about (of three or more)'

liketv /leyk-itá/ 'to sit (of one)'
kaketv /ka:k-itá/ 'to sit (of two)'
vpoketv /apo:k-itá/ 'to sit (of three or more)'

Basic Syntax

The two main parts of speech in Creek are noun and verb. A verb marked for person, tense, and mood forms a complete sentence in Creek. When noun phrases are present, they generally occur in the order subject, object, verb. An auxiliary verb always follows the main verb. Numbers and descriptive words translating as adjectives follow the noun modified:

Hoktvke	*hokkolet*	*vce*	*hocvkētt*	*welaken...*
/hoktakí	hokkô:lit	ací	hocakǐ:ⁿtt	wila:kín/
women	two	corn	pounding	were:going:about

'There were two women pounding corn...'

Subjects may be marked with *-t* /-t/ and objects may be marked with *-n* /-n/; the presence or absence of these markers appears to relate to specificity. Possessors and demonstratives precede the nouns they modify: *Cane em efv* /cá:ni im-ífa/ 'John's dog', *mv efv* /ma ifá/ 'that dog'.

Clauses are linked with the switch-reference markers *-et* /-it/ (generally used for sequential events sharing the same subject) or *-en* /-in/ (for clauses that are less closely linked).

Negation is expressed with a suffix: *hecetv* /hic-íta/ 'to see', *heceko* /hic-íko-:/ 'doesn't see, blind'.

Contact with Other Languages

Creek has engaged in borrowing with neighboring languages. The Creek word *kolvpaken* /kolapâ:k-in/ 'seven' was borrowed into Cherokee, for example, and Creek *toknawv* /tokná:wa/ 'money, dollar' (earlier form *cvto konawv* /cato-koná:wa/ 'stone/iron bead') was borrowed into Alabama and Koasati. The Creek word *penwv* /pínwa/ 'turkey' may be Fox in origin, while *pvkanv* /paká:na/ 'peach' is thought to come from Shawnee.

Creek borrowed a number of Spanish words from SPANISH colonies in Florida. Creek *halo* /há:lo/ 'tin can' is from Spanish *jarro*, *wakv* /wá:ka/ 'cow, bovine' is from Spanish *vaca*, *cowatv* /cowá:ta/ 'goat' is from Spanish *chivato*, Creek *fvlasko* /falá:sko/ 'bottle' is from Spanish *frasco*, Creek *kapv* /ká:pa/ 'coat' is from Spanish *capa*, Creek *tosēnv* /tosí:na/ 'bacon' is from Spanish *tocino*, and *soletawv* /solitá:wa/ 'soldier' is from Spanish *soldado*. English has borrowed a few plant names from Creek:

catalpa winged head (Creek *'kv-tvrpv* /ka-táɬpa/)
tupelo swamp tree (Creek *'to-pelwv* /to-pílwa/)
coontie (Florida Seminole Creek *kuntē* /kontí:/)

A number of place names in Alabama, Georgia, Oklahoma, and Florida are Creek in origin:

Tallahassee old tribal town (Creek *Tvlvhasse* /tal-ahá:ssi/)
Talladega border of the tribal town (Creek *Tvlvtēkv* /tal-atí:k-a/)
Chattahoochee decorated rock (Creek *Cvto Hocce*/ cato-hó:cc-i/)
Wewoka barking water (Creek *Ue-wohkv* /oy-wó:hk-a/)

Common Words

big:	*rakkē* /ɬákk-i:/
bird:	*fuswv* /fóswa/
dog:	*efv* /ifá/
fish:	*rvro* /ɬaɬó/
good:	*herē* /hiɬ-í:/
long:	*cvpkē* /cápk-i:/
man:	*honvnwv* /honánwa/
no:	*monks* /monks/
small:	*cutkē* /cótk-i:/
sun:	*hvse* /hasí/
three:	*tuccēnen* /toccî:n-in/
tree:	*eto* /itó/
water:	*uewv* /óywa/
woman:	*hoktē* /hoktí:/
yes:	*ehe* /ihí/

Example Sentences

(1) *Cvpose efuce vnnēsvnks.*
/ca-pósi ifóci an-nî:sanks/
my-mother puppy for:me-bought
'My mother bought me a puppy.'

(2) *Hompetv rakko ohocat vpeyetv ceyacvkv?*
/hompita-ɬákko ohô:ca:t apiy-itá ci-yâ:c-ak-a´/
food-big that:they're:having to:go do:you:want
'Do you want to go to the big meal they're having?'

Efforts to Preserve, Protect, and Promote the Language

Few people younger than 40 grow up speaking Creek at home, and every month gifted monolingual and bilingual speakers pass away. As a result, Creek falls into the category of endangered languages. Courses in the Creek language are currently being offered at the University of Oklahoma and by a few individuals in the Creek Nation. Head Start programs in Oklahoma and Florida introduce Creek to preschool children. Several public school districts in Oklahoma have recently begun teaching their students Creek as a way to broaden the learning experience. A number of public school teachers have attended the Oklahoma Native American Language Development Institute to develop curricula for this purpose. Unless drastic measures are taken (for example, by establishing separate schools where Creek is the medium of instruction), it seems likely that Creek will continue to lose ground to English.

Select Bibliography

Booker, Karen M. 1991. *Languages of the Aboriginal Southeast: An Annotated Bibliography.* Native American Bibliography Series, No. 15. Metuchen, NJ: Scarecrow Press.

Buckner, H.F., and G. Herrod. 1860. *A Grammar of the Maskwke, or Creek Language, to Which are Prefixed Lessons in Spelling, Reading, and Defining.* Marion, AL: Domestic and Indian Mission Board of the Southern Baptist Convention.

Haas, Mary R. 1945. "Dialects of the Muskogee Language." In *International Journal of American Linguistics* 11:69–74. Facsimile reprint (1987) in William C. Sturtevant, ed., *A Creek Source Book* (New York: Garland Publishing).

____. 1979. "Southeastern Languages." In *The Languages of Native America: Historical and Comparative Assessment.* Ed. Lyle Campbell and Marianne Mithun. Austin: University of Texas Press, 299–326.

Loughridge, Robert M., and David M. Hodge. 1890. *English and Muskokee Dictionary Collected from Various Sources and Revised* and *Dictionary of the Muskokee or Creek Language in Creek and English.* St. Louis: J.T. Smith. Reprinted 1914, Philadelphia: Westminster Press. Facsimile reprint 1964, Okmulgee, OK: Baptist Home Mission Board.

Martin, Jack B., and Margaret McKane Mauldin. 2000. *A Dictionary of Creek/Muskogee, with Notes on the Florida and Oklahoma Seminole Dialects of Creek.* Lincoln: University of Nebraska Press.

Charles E. Townsend

Language Name: Czech. **Autonym:** *čeština.*

Location: The so-called Czech Lands (Bohemia to the west, Moravia to the east) in the Czech Republic in Central Europe.

Family: West Slavic group of the Slavic branch of the Indo-European language family.

Related Languages: The most closely related language is SLOVAK, with which Czech is mutually comprehensible. More distant, though still closely related, are the remaining West Slavic languages: Upper and Lower Lusatian and POLISH. More distantly related are the East Slavic languages: RUSSIAN, BELORUSSIAN and UKRAINIAN, and the South Slavic languages: SLOVENE, SERBO-CROATIAN, MACEDONIAN, and BULGARIAN.

Dialects: Czech contains four main dialect groups: Bohemian, Hanák, Lachian (Silesian), and Moravian-Slovak (southeast Moravia). The basic spoken language is so-called General, or Common Czech (*obecná čeština*), based on the speech of Prague and its environs. It is an interdialect, in that it is being regularized by centripetal forces including influences from the literary standard, Literary Czech.

Literary Czech (*spisovná čeština*) is a written language distinct from the varieties of the spoken language. It has several phonetic archaisms and abounds in grammatical forms, words, and usages that most Czechs no longer use in normal speech. This situation has created a diglossia, an often uneasy coexistence of two codes, one literary and one colloquial. Many Czechs are adept at mixing the two codes, and value the potential for nuance that the diglossia offers, but some recent scholars have called for more or less far-reaching reforms. Certain piecemeal changes are in the offing, but it is unlikely that either Czech speakers or grammarians will totally abandon large traditional, even if archaic, parts of the language they regard as their *národní poklad* 'national treasure'.

Number of Speakers: 10–11 million in the Czech Republic and perhaps 1 million elsewhere.

Origin and History

Sometime in the middle of the first millennium, the West Slavs fanned out westward from the Slavs' original home (considered to be roughly modern western Ukraine and southwestern Belarus). The more southern Czecho-Slovak group moved into approximately their present homeland, although at first they occupied a larger territory (including parts of modern Hungary and Austria).

The first literary language to be used in the Czech Lands was Old Church Slavonic, a liturgical language introduced in the Grand Duchy of Moravia in the late ninth century by Cyril and Methodius, two monks from Salonika, who had been invited to Moravia to introduce their Byzantine Christianity and who translated biblical texts into their own South Slavic Bulgaro- Macedonian dialect. A few Czech fragments found their way into one or two of the original Old Church Slavonic texts (the *Kiev Fragments*, so called because they were discovered in Kiev). But the Slavic liturgy and influence were eroded and replaced by the Roman Church and the Latin liturgy pressed upon the Czechs by their Germanic neighbors to the west. From the 10th and 11th centuries on, the prevailing influence on both the Czech language and the Czech lands was Western and Catholic, mostly through German.

Although LATIN was the main language used in the Czech Lands until at least the 13th century, with only isolated Czech words appearing in texts, the growth of Czech political power in ensuing centuries fostered the development of an independent Czech literary language. This was marked by important early monuments, such as the *Hymn to St. Václav* in the 13th century and the *Chronicle of Dalimil* in the 14th. In the middle of the 14th century, the ascendance of Charles IV to the throne of the Holy Roman Empire and the founding of Charles University in 1348 (the first university in Central Europe) marked a huge upswing in the importance of Czech language and culture, which found its major expression in the life and work of the religious martyr Jan Hus (1369–1415). Hus converted the active language of Prague into a literary language and created a phonetic orthography with unique diacritical marks for marking Czech vowel length and replacing Polish digraphs (still used in Poland today); for example, *sz* and *cz* become *s* and *c* with a reversed circumflex over them, en route to *š* and *č* (pronounced like ENGLISH *sh* and *ch*).

During this whole period, the Czech language itself was developing into its more modern form. The so-called Czech vowel mutation (*česká přehláska*), in which *a* > *e* and *u* > *i* after soft consonants, and the shift of long, midvowels to long, high vowels (*ó* > *ů*, *é* > *ý*) and long, high vowels to diphthongs (*ú* > *ou*, *ý* > *ej*) gave Czech phonology its unique character that distinguishes it from all other Slavic languages; for example Czech *vůle* 'will (noun)' is Slovak *vôla*, Polish *wola*, Russian *volja*.

Czech religious and secular development were brought to an abrupt halt during the Thirty Years War (1618–1648), and the Czech language moved into a period of drastic decline. By the middle of the 17th century it had been replaced by GERMAN in schools and administration and was spoken mostly

Table 1: Consonants

		Labial	Dental	Palatal	Velar	Glottal
Stops	Voiceless	p	t	t'	k	
	Voiced	b	d	d'	g	
Fricatives	Voiceless	f	s	š	ch	h
	Voiced	v	z	ž		
Affricates	Voiceless		c	č		
Nasals		m	n	ň		
Liquid			l, r	ř		
Glides				j		

in the countryside or by the lower classes in small towns. Great educators and scholars such as Jan Komenský (Comenius) were forced to work and live abroad. Some scholars believe that during this period Czech came quite close to extinction.

The late 18th century ushered in a period of National Revival, or *Obrození,* in reaction to the centralizing and Germanizing influences of the Habsburg Empire and Austria- Hungary. The key figure in the new awakening was Josef Dobrovský (1753–1829), who wrote an influential Czech grammar that used as a model the classical literary Czech abandoned almost two centuries before. Modern Standard or Literary Czech is based on his codification. Dobrovský's work was characterized by the purging of Germanisms and the introduction of words from Russian, for example, Czech *vzduch* 'air' from Russian *vozdux.* Josef Jungmann's Czech-German dictionary from the middle of the 19th century, Jan Gebauer's historical grammar at the end of the century, and certain additional spelling reforms helped stabilize Czech and introduce into it a precision that had up to then been missing.

In the 20th century Karel Capek's writings created an impetus for a rich new literature that included remarkable poetry, notably that of Jaroslav Seifert. Even 6 years of German occupation and more than 40 years of Soviet-imposed Communism failed to thwart Czech literature entirely. This is demonstrated by the works of exiled writers Milan Kundera and Josef Škvorecký and also of the dramatist and first president of free Czechoslovakia and the Czech Republic, Václav Havel.

Orthography and Basic Phonology

Czech orthography is phonetic, with pronunciation, except in easily specifiable cases, quite predictable. For this reason, the letters in the alphabet can be used to specify the sounds (see Table 1).

Each of the consonants on the chart represents a single Czech sound. Czech has, in addition, two letters that represent sequences of sounds: *x* represents [ks] and is a relatively common letter; *q* represents [kv] and is quite rare; *w* and *v* represent the same sound, /v/.

The palatal nasal *ň* represents a sound like the *ni* sequence in English onion. The palatal stops *t'* and *d'* represent sounds intermediate in quality between English /k/ and /g/ and the sounds in tune and dune in those varieties of English (especially British) in which these are not pronounced toon and doon. The *ř* sound cannot easily be described in terms of English. It involves a simultaneous trilled *r* (as in Spanish *perro*) and voiced palatal fricative [ž] (as in English measure).

Table 2: Vowels

	Front	Central	Back
High	i í		u ú
Mid	e é		o ó
Low		a á	

The acute accent over vowels indicates vowel length, for example *dál* 'further' versus *dal* 'he gave', *pás* 'belt' versus *pas* 'passport', *být* 'to be' versus *byt* 'apartment'.

The letters *y* and *ý* represent the same sounds as *i* and *í* respectively. The letter *i* following *t, d,* or *n* indicates phonetic /t'i/, /d'i/, or /ňi/; *ě*, not traditionally regarded as a distinct letter, represents /e/ after /t'/, /d'/, or /ň/, or after the sequences *pj, bj, mj, vj, fj.*

The letter *ů* is the equivalent of *ú*, but reflects an *ó* in older stages of Czech.

Czech morphophonology is characterized by many vowel alternations, both in quality (e.g., *b<u>í</u>ly* 'white', *b<u>ě</u>lit* 'whiten') and in length (e.g., *chv<u>á</u>lit* 'to praise', *chv<u>a</u>l!* 'praise!'). The consonant alternations are either inflectional: *mazat* 'to smear', *mažu* 'I smear', or derivational: *ruka* 'hand', *ručni* 'manual'. Also important is the alternation in syllables involving nonsyllabic elements between the vowel *e* and zero: *sen* 'sleep, NOM.SG' versus *snu* 'sleep, GEN. SG', *beru* 'I take' versus *brát* 'to take'.

Stress is uniformly on the first syllable in Czech.

Basic Morphology

Czech nouns, adjectives, pronouns, and numerals are inflected for gender (masculine, feminine, neuter), number (singular, plural), and case (nominative, genitive, dative, accusative, locative, instrumental, vocative). In addition, the specific set of endings used may depend on whether the inflected word ends in a hard (plain) or soft (palatal) consonant. The singular forms of the feminine noun *žena* 'woman' are illustrated below.

Case	Form	Case	Form
Nominative	žen-a	Genitive	žen-y
Dative	žen-ě	Accusative	žen-u
Locative	žen-o	Instrumental	žen-ě
Vocative	žen-ou		

Czech verbs are inflected for tense (present, preterite); there is also a compound future tense. Present tense verbs agree with their subjects in person and number, while preterite (past) verbs agree in gender and number. These agreement patterns are illustrated here for the verb *dělat* 'to do':

Present

	Singular	Plural
1st	dělám	děláme
2nd	děláš	děláte
3rd	dělá	dělají

Preterite

	Singular	Plural
Masculine	dělal	dělali
Feminine	dělalu	dělaly
Neuter	dělalo	dělala

The periphrastic future of this verb is *budu dělat.*

In addition to tense, Czech verbs distinguish two aspects, perfective and imperfective. Use of a perfective verb involves an implicit claim that the action described has been completed, while use of an imperfective verb involves no such claim: *on udělal* 'he did' means 'he did it, got it done', while *on dělal* means 'he did it, was doing it'.

As illustrated above, perfective verbs may be derived from imperfective verbs by prefixation; in the case of *udělat*, the prefix *u-* does not involve semantic change other than the change of imperfective to perfective aspect. Other prefixes may involve a change in meaning: *předělat* 'to redo', *vydělat* 'to earn', *rozdělat* 'to make (a fire)', *oddělat* 'to remove'. From these perfective verbs, new imperfectives are ordinarily formed (e.g., *předělávat* 'to redo [imperfective]').

The particle *se* is used to mark passive verbs:

on děl-á prác-i
he do-3SG work-ACC
'he does the work'

prác-e se děl-á
work-NOM PASS do-3SG
'the work is being done'

Se can also be used in simple intransitive sentences: *on se vrací* 'he is returning'. The verbal classifying suffix *-i* can act as a causative when opposed, for instance, to a stative in the suffix *-ě*: *posadit* 'seat, make sit' versus *sedět* 'sit, be sitting'.

Basic Syntax

The basic word order is Subject-Verb-Object, but there are many exceptions. For existential sentences, the order is reversed: *delegace přijela* 'the delegation arrived', *přijela delegace* 'there arrived a delegation'.

Adjectives generally precede nouns: *dobr-á vod-a* (good-FEM water-FEM) 'good water'. Longer modifiers, such as relative clauses, may follow the nouns they modify:

Tady je vod-a, kter-á je dobr-á pro všechny
here water-FEM which-FEM good-FEM for everyone
'Here is water which is good for everyone.'

Contact with Other Languages

Throughout its history, many loanwords have entered Czech, some directly, some through intermediary languages. Older borrowings, such as from Latin and Middle German, are completely naturalized. The huge number of international words such as *restaurace* 'restaurant', *restituce* 'restitution', *opera* 'opera', and *oáza* 'oasis' doubtless feels no more foreign to Czechs than their English equivalents do to us. Attempts to cleanse Czech of loanwords have sometimes been successful, particularly in the case of Germanisms, but hundreds of Germanisms still remain in use in ordinary Czech, particularly in colloquial style. Note the words for 'father': *otec* (formal), *tatínek* or *táta* (familiar), and *fotr* (familiar, ironic) from German *Vater.*

From Latin: *kostel* 'church'
From Middle German: *říše* 'empire, reich'
From German: *flaška* 'bottle', *furt* 'still, continually'
From FRENCH: *angažmá* 'engagement (theater)'

Common Words

man:	muž	long:	dlouhý
woman:	žena	small:	malý
water:	voda	yes:	ano
sun:	slunce	no:	ne
three:	tři	good:	dobrý
fish:	ryba	bird:	pták
big:	velký	dog:	pes
tree:	strom	cat:	kočka

Example Sentences

(1) Dobr-ý den, pane profesore.
good-MASC day Mr. professor
'Good day, (Mr.) Professor.'

(2) Co tím chce-te říct?
what this.INSTR want-2PL say.INF
'What do you mean?' (lit., 'What do you want to say by that?')

(3) Séstra prácuje na záhrad-ě.
sister work-3SG in garden-LOCATIVE
'(My) sister is working in the garden.'

Select Bibliography

Short, David. 1993. "Czech." In *The Slavonic Languages*, ed. Bernard Comrie and Greville G. Corbett. London and New York: Routledge, 455–532.

Townsend, Charles E. 1990. *Spoken Prague Czech.* Columbus: Slavica Publishers.

DAGAARE

Adams B. Bodomo

Language Name: Dagaare. **Alternates:** Dagaare-Waale, Dagarti, Dagara. **Autonym:** *Dagaare*.

Location: Mainly in the northwestern parts of Ghana but also in the adjoining areas of Burkina Faso and Ivory Coast.

Family: Dagaare is a member of the Mabia (western Oti-Volta) group of the Gur branch of the Niger-Congo language family.

Related Languages: Waale, Birifor, Frafra, Dagbane, Mampruli, Kusaal, Buli, MOORE.

Dialects: There are four main regional dialects: (1) Northern Dagaare, also known as Lobr or Dagara, is spoken in Nandom, Lawra, Dissin, Diebougou, Gaoua, and their areas of influence. A greater number of the speakers of this dialect group live in Burkina Faso. (2) Central Dagaare is spoken in Jirapa, Ullo, Daffiama, Nadawli, and their spheres of influence. This group is so called because it occupies approximately the middle of the Dagaare-speaking area and it enjoys a considerable degree of intelligibility with other dialects. It is the version of Dagaare used in church literature, educational material, and for mass communication in Ghana. (3) Southern Dagaare is the dialect of Kaleo, metropolitan Wa, and their surrounding villages. Southern Dagaare is widely spoken in markets and other trading centers. (4) Western Dagaare, sometimes called Birifor, is found mainly on the western side of the Black Volta River in Burkina Faso and Ivory Coast, but speakers of this dialect group have recently also moved into the area south of Wa.

Number of Speakers: 1.5–2 million.

Origin and History

The migration history of the Dagaaba (speakers of Dagaare) is most uncertain. The general discussion points to the fact that the ancestors of the Dagaaba are a splinter group from either the Mossi or the Dagomba or both who moved into the present area and assimilated, or were assimilated by earlier settlers and/or new arrivals.

In all probability the Dagaaba, the Mossi, the Dagomba, the Kusaasi, the Frafra, the Mamprusi, and many others are all directly descended from a common ancestral ethnolinguistic group, the Mabia.

The Dagaaba evolved a highly decentralized traditional system of government. This has been inappropriately described as acephalous, suggesting a weak and incohesive structure in the absence of a central authority. Unlike the highly centralized systems of government found among some ethnic groups in Ghana and other parts of Africa, where a distant monarch may appoint representatives to various towns and villages and exercise control from a central headquarters, every Dagaare village or group of villages was virtually autonomous as far as the day-to-day administration of natural resources are concerned.

The British policy of Indirect Rule between 1890 and 1957 substantially altered this decentralized political system and the Dagaaba are now organized into various paramountcies or chiefdoms. At the head of each paramountcy is a *Naa* who exercises authority over divisional chiefs. Prior to the advent of colonial rule, political decentralization was a democratic system of government that worked for the Dagaaba, and since political decentralization is now a democratic goal in many parts of Africa and beyond, a closer study of the Dagaaba traditional system of government may be a worthwhile exercise in the search for an appropriate democracy.

Orthography and Basic Phonology

The standard orthography used by the church in Ghana is based on the Central dialect but there are several alternative orthographies. All of these are basically phonemic. Dagaare is a two-tone language, but tone is not marked in the standard orthography. However, high tone and low tone are indicated in this chapter. Here is the Standard Dagaare alphabet:

P, B, M, F, V, T, D, R, N, S, Z, KY, GY, NY, K, G, NG,
p, b, m, f, v, t, d, r, n, s, z, ky, gy, ny, k, g, ng,

KP GB, NGM, L, Y, W, H, I, E, Ɛ, A, O, Ɔ, U
kp, gb, ngm, l, y, w, h, i, e, ɛ, a, o, ɔ, u

Dagaare has 25 consonants as shown in Table 1 and two glides (semiconsonants) in underlying representation. The glottal counterparts of *h*, *l*, and *m* are attested only in the Northern dialect of the language. Two additional consonants, [r] and [ɣ], are found at surface level, occurring as allophones to /d/ and /g/ at initial positions and intervocalically, respectively. Consider: [đi] 'to eat', [điré] 'eating', [górí] 'dowry', [pɔɣɔ] 'woman'. In these examples /d/ and /g/, when they appear, are at the primary word/syllable initial position.

The sounds [r] and [ɣ], on the other hand, occur intervocalically or at secondary syllable initial position. Voiceless plosives are usually aspirated when they occur in primary syllable initial position. The phonetic transcriptions [t^hàllI] 'to

Table 1: Consonants

	Bilabial	Labio-dental	Dental	Alveolar	Alveo-palatal	Palatal	Velar	Labio-velar	Glottal
Stops									
Voiceless	p		t				k	kp	ʔ
Voiced	b		d				g	gb	
Fricatives									
Voiceless		f		s					h
Voiced		v		z					
Affricates									
Voiceless					ky				
Voiced					gy				
Lateral				l					
Nasals	m			n		ɲ		ŋm	ŋ
Implosives	‘m			‘l					ɦ
Glides						y		w	

walk fast’ and [p^{h}àllI] ‘to weave’ illustrate aspiration. As can be seen from the table, Dagaare has labio-velar consonants, such as /kp, gb, and ŋm/, produced simultaneously with the velum and the lips as active organs of sound production. These sounds are known as double articulations or coarticulations. Examples are /ŋmámá/ ‘calabashes’ and /gbɛ́rI/ ‘cŕipple’.

Table 2: Vowels

		Front	Back
High	+ATR	i	u
	-ATR	ɪ	ʊ
Mid-high	+ATR	e	o
Mid-low	-ATR	ɛ	ɔ
Low		a	

Nine oral vowel phonemes may be established for Dagaare as shown in Table 2. The + and - signs in the chart show that the relevant distinctive features: High, Low, Round, and ATR (Advanced Tongue Root) are present or absent, respectively. These are then the basic vowel phonemes of Dagaare, but processes such as vowel lengthening, nasality, harmony, and sequencing make the system a bit more complex. Each of the nine short vowels has a long counterpart, and the opposition of short and long vowels of the same quality brings about differences in meaning, as in the following minimal pairs:

/tɔ̀ŕ/ ‘-self’ : /tɔ̀ɔ̀ŕ/ ‘far’
/kùŕ/ ‘tortoise’ : /kùùŕ/ ‘hoe’
/bà/ ‘fix to the ground’ : /bàà/ ‘grow up’

On the basis of this evidence, we may say that vowel length is phonemic in Dagaare. Each of the nine oral vowels may be nasalized. An interesting type of co-occurrence restriction in Dagaare involves the distinctive feature [∀ATR]. In a Dagaare phonological word, only vowels of the same ATR value must occur. The following will briefly illustrate the point:

/đìré/ ‘eating’ +ATR vowels
/dɪ́rɛ́/ ‘taking’ -ATR vowels
/púò/ ‘farmland’ +ATR vowels
/pʊ́ɔ́/ ‘stomach’ -ATR vowels

This co-occurrence restriction involving both contiguous and noncontiguous vowels is called vowel harmony. Dagaare is a register-tone language with two levels of tone, high and low, and a downstepped high unit. Downstep is said to occur when in a given phonological unit the second of two high tones (with a relatively low tone in between them) happens not to be as equally high as the first high tone. However, downstep can also occur with two successive high tones. Below is a list of words showing high and low tonal contrasts:

tú ‘to dig’ tù ‘to follow’
dá ‘to push (many items)’ dà ‘to buy’
nɔ́ŋ ‘to massage’ nɔ̀ŋ ‘to like, love’

Basic Morphology

The basic verbal morphology comprises a verb root and a number of aspectual suffixes. There are basically two aspectual forms in Dagaare: the perfective (completive) and the imperfective (progressive). A paradigm with the verb *nyu* ‘to drink’ is given below:

nyú dictionary form
nyu- verb root
nyú-Ø perfective aspect [zero morph] (transitive use)
nyú-é perfective aspect (intransitive use)
nyúú-rò imperfective aspect
nyú-é-ńg focus particle on perfective aspect

Dagaare is a noun class language. An intricate system of number suffixes divides Dagaare nouns into about 10 classes. Each of the following Dagaare nouns represents a noun class:

Stem	Singular		Plural
pɔg-	/pɔ́g-ɔ́/	'woman'	/pɔ́g(í)-bɔ́/
zi-	/zí-é/	'place'	/zíí-rí/
gyi-	/gyı̀-lí/	'xylophone'	/gyı̀-lé/
pı-	/pí-rʊ́ʊ́/	'sheep'	/píí-rı̀/
zu-	/zú-Ø/	'head'	/zú-rí/
bi-	/bí-rì/	'seed'	/bí-é/
gan-	/gán-ı̀/	'book'	/gá-mà/
gbıngbıl-	/gbíngbíl-áa/	'drying spot'	/gbíngbíl-lí/
di-	/dí-íú/	'food'	(no plural)
buul-	(no singular)	'porridge'	/búúl-ú/

Basic Syntax

Dagaare is basically an SVO language although there are some complications when we deal with more complex sentences. Verbal elements in most unmarked cases come after the subject NP and before the Object NP if there is any, schematically: Subject NP |preverbal particles—main verb—postverbal particle| Object NP. The following sentence further illustrates the point:

Dàkóráá dà nyúú-ró lá à kɔ̀ɔ́ à ɗìè pɔ́ɔ́
Dakoraa PAST drink-IMP FOC DEF water DEF room inside
'Dakoraa was drinking the water in the room.'

In the sentence, *Dàkóráá* is the subject NP. This is followed by the preverbal particle *dà*, which expresses the temporal features of the construction. We then have the main verb, *nyúú-ró*. The suffixal parts of the main verb express the aspectual features of the construction. The postverbal particle is *lá*, which functions as a focus particle. Finally *à kɔ̀ɔ́* is the object NP of the sentence. This is followed by an adverbial phrase comprising an NP, *à ɗìè,* and a locative postposition, *pɔ́ɔ́*.

This basic declarative sentence provides the basis for a number of syntactic alternations expressing aspect (perfective/imperfective), mood (imperative), polarity (negation/positivity), and voice (medio-passive), as well as more complex thought with constructions such as relativization, serialization, and serial verb nominalization:

Imperative:
nyú!
'Drink!'

Negative declarative:
Dàkóráá dà bá nyú à kɔ̀ɔ́
Dakoraa PAST NEG drink DEF water
'Dakoraa did not drink the water.'

Negative imperative:
Tá nyú!
NEG drink
'Don't drink!'

Medio-passive:
À kɔ̀ɔ́ nyú-é lá
DEF water drink-PERF FOC
'The water has been drunk.'

Relativization:
A dɔ́ɔ́ ná nàng zȁȁ wà kyɛ̀ nyú
DEF man that who yesterday come here drink

lá à kɔ́ɔ̀
FACT DEF water
'The man who came here yesterday drank the water.'

Serialization:
Dàkóráá ná dé lá à kùùrí zá lɔ́ɔ́
Dakoraa FUT take FACT DEF stone throw cause-fall

èng à kɔ̀ɔ́ pɔ́ɔ́
put DEF water inside
'Dakoraa will throw the stone into the water.'

Serial verb nominalization:
À kɔ̀ɔ́ dé nyú-ù
DEF water take drink-NOM
'The drinking of the water'

Contact with Other Languages

Besides their immediate neighbors, speakers of Dagaare have had trade and other kinds of contact with people speaking HAUSA, Bambara (Djula), AKAN, ENGLISH, and FRENCH.

From Hausa: *sènkááfá* 'rice', *lààféɛ̀* 'health, well-being', *pìtóò* 'guinea corn beer'
From Akan: *dàn̄séɛ̀* 'witness', *bɔrbɛ́* 'pineapple' *bɔ̀ɔ̀dɔ́wáá* 'towel'
From Bambara (Djula): *mìí* 'rice', *gyìlí* 'xylophone', *lòńŋò* 'hourglass'
From English: *mònsún* 'machine', *sákèrè* 'bicycle', *sàkúúrì* 'school'
From French: *sô* 'bucket', *vèlô* 'bicycle', *mótɛ́ɛr* 'machine, motorbike'

Common Words

man:	dɔ́ɔ́	long:	wógì
woman:	pɔ́gɔ́	small:	bílé
water:	kɔ̀ɔ́	yes:	òó
sun:	ngmenaa	no:	àí
three:	átà	good:	vèlàà
fish:	zòmmó	bird:	nuulee
big:	kpóñg	dog:	báá
tree:	tèɛ́		

Example Sentences

(1) Ǹ gɛ̀-rɛ́ lá a dàá.
I go-IMP FOC DEF market
'I am going to the market.'

(2) Bòńg lá ká fó è-rɛ́?
what FOC that you do-IMP
'What are you doing?'

(3) Ò dà nyɛ́ lá à tè téngɛ́ nàá.
s/he PAST see FOC DEF our land chief
'S/he saw the chief of our land/village/town.'

Efforts to Preserve, Protect, and Promote the Language

Because of relatively early European missionary settlements in Dagao (home of the Dagaaba) in the 1920s, Dagaare, especially the Central dialect, spoken around Jirapa, was one of the first languages in the region of Ghana and Burkina Faso to get a script. There exists a Dagaare Language Committee, started by the Roman Catholic Church in Ghana, which attempts to promote the language in various ways. Youth associations in Dagao also have strategies for the promotion of Dagaare under their cultural development programs. Dagaare is also promoted by the national governments in both Ghana and Burkina Faso. In Ghana it is one of the nine so-called government-promoted/sponsored languages. These are languages earmarked by the Bureau of Ghana Languages for the publication of educational materials in indigenous languages. Dagaare is studied and examined from lower levels of formal education to the university and is featured in radio and television broadcasting stations in the two countries. Many functional-literacy programs have been launched in the language in both Ghana and Burkina Faso.

Select Bibliography

Bodomo, A.B. (in press). *The Structure of Dagaare*. Stanford Monographs in African Linguistics, CSLI publications.

____. 1994. "Language, History and Culture in Northern Ghana: An Introduction to the Mabia Linguistic Group." In *Nordic Journal of African Studies*, 3: 2, 25–43.

Dagaare Language Committee. 1982. *A Guide to Dagaare Spelling*. Wa: Catholic Press.

Delplanque, A. 1983. *Phonologie Transformationnelle du Dagara*. Paris: SELAF.

Girault, L. 1967. "Description phonologique de la langue Dagara." In *Documents Linguistiques* 12. Université de Dakar.

Goody, J. 1967. *The Social Organization of the LoWiili*. London: IAS.

Hall, E. 1973. "Dagaare." In *West African Language Data Sheets*. ed. M.E.K. Dakubu. University of Ghana, Accra.

Herbert, J. 1975. "Esquisse d'une Monographie Historique du Pays Dagara." MS, Diebougou, Burkina Faso.

Kennedy, J. 1966. "Collected field reports on the phonology of Dagaari." In *Collected Language Notes* 6. Institute of African Studies, University of Ghana, Accra.

Nakuma, Constancio. 1999. *Phonie et graphie tonale Dagaare: Langue voltaïotue du Ghana*. Edition Harmatton.

Swadesh, M., *et. al.* 1966. "A Preliminary Glottochronology of the Gur Languages." In *Journal of West African Languages*, 3: 2.

Tuurey, G. 1987. *Introduction to the Mole-Speaking Community*. Wa: Catholic Press.

Zakpaa, B.B. 1978. *Te kɔɔbo yɛlɛ*. Accra: Bureau of Ghana Languages.

DANISH

Robin Allan and Tom Lundskær-Nielsen

Language Name: Danish. **Autonym:** *dansk*.

Location: The Kingdom of Denmark, which comprises Denmark, the Faroe Islands and Greenland. In Denmark, it is the native language of the whole population apart from some recent immigrants and foreign nationals. In the Faroe Islands and Greenland, Danish is the second language for the majority of the inhabitants and enjoys equal status with Faroese and Greenlandic, respectively, in all official communication. It is also the first language of a Danish minority of about 50,000 people in the Flensburg area of Schleswig-Holstein, north Germany, which formed part of Denmark until 1864. In Iceland, it has been taught as the first foreign language in schools since Iceland gained independence from Denmark in 1944. Approximately 45,000 Danes currently live in Norway and Sweden, and a few small emigré communities in the United States, Canada and Argentina still use Danish.

Family: North Germanic group of the Germanic branch of the Indo-European language family.

Related Languages: NORWEGIAN and SWEDISH (with a high degree of mutual comprehension among the three, "semicommunication"); more distantly related to Faroese and Icelandic.

Dialects: In terms of morphological gender distinctions, there are three main dialect groups: (1) those in the islands Djursland and North Jutland operate with three genders, (2) those in West Jutland distinguish between individual items and mass or collective nouns, (3) only those in East and South Jutland have the same two-gender systems as standard Danish.

Regarding pronunciation, there are a number of dialects, which are in theory mutually intelligible; however, people on the islands often have difficulty understanding their compatriots in North, South and West Jutland.

Number of Speakers: More than 5 million.

Origin and History

Tribes of Indo-European speakers are thought to have settled in the southern Baltic region about 1000 B.C. There they encountered a population of non-Indo-European speakers and their own Proto-Indo-European language developed into what we now call Common Germanic. From the southern Baltic region, the Germanic tribes later moved into some of the surrounding areas. These migrations are probably responsible for the further development of Common Germanic, for which there are no existing records, into three main branches: East Germanic (GOTHIC, now extinct), West Germanic (DUTCH, ENGLISH, Frisian, GERMAN), and North Germanic (Danish, Faroese, Icelandic, Norwegian, Swedish).

Records of Common or Ancient Scandinavian (c. 200–600) are found in the form of a number of runic inscriptions from as early as the beginning of the third century A.D. There are important differences among these, on the one hand, and the fourth-century Gothic Bible translations; the sixth-century runic inscriptions found in Germany and England; and the earliest written records in Old English, Old High German, and Old Saxon, on the other. Whereas Ancient Scandinavian does not seem to have had any dialect distinctions, Old Scandinavian (c. 600–1400) soon split into a West Scandinavian branch (Old Icelandic and Old Norwegian) and an East Scandinavian branch (Old Danish and Old Swedish). (Old West Scandinavian is also known as Old Norse.)

Historically, the Danish language may be divided into three main periods: **Old Danish** (c. 800–1100), approximately spanning the Viking Age; **Middle Danish** (c. 1100–1500), roughly covering the late Middle Ages; and **Modern Danish** (from c. 1500 onwards), from the Reformation to the present day.

During the Old Danish period, the Danish Vikings conquered and ruled over large areas of north and east England (the so-called Danelaw). Together with the introduction of Christianity, this caused the first major influx of loanwords into Danish. Most of them derived from GREEK or LATIN and reached Danish through Old English, Old Frisian or Old Saxon.

From the ninth century onwards, some sound changes took place exclusively in East Scandinavian (Danish and Swedish). Among the most prominent of the early changes are monophthongization of certain diphthongs (*ai*/*ei* > *e* and *au*/*øy* > *ø*; for example, Old Norse *steinn, rauðr* vs. Dan. *sten, rød* 'stone, red'), and the loss of *h* in front of *l, n* and *r* (such as Old Norse *hlið, hnefi, hrár* v. Dan. *led, næve, rå* 'gate, fist, raw').

During the Middle Ages, Danish conquests temporarily expanded the kingdom to the south and east to include some of the Baltic areas of present-day Germany and Poland plus Estonia, and to the north where Norway came under the Danish Crown and became part of a dual monarchy from 1380 until 1814. For some time Sweden, too, was a member of this Nordic Union. The Middle Danish period witnessed some major sound changes that removed Danish further from the other

Table 1: Consonants

		Labial	Alveolar	Palatal	Velar	Uvular	Glottal
Stops	Aspirated	p	t		k		
	Nonaspirated	b	d		g		
Fricatives	Voiceless	f	s				h
	Voiced	v	ð				
Nasals		m	n		ŋ		
Resonants			l			r	
Semi-vowels				j			

Scandinavian languages, including Swedish. The three most important changes were:

1. The weakening of the vowels *a, i,* and *u* to *e* in unstressed syllables (for example, Swedish *kasta* versus Danish *kaste* 'throw'). 2. Changes of the fricatives *d, g,* and *v* after certain vowels. Thus *d* [ð] often disappeared (even in the spelling) (e.g., Sw. *bida* versus Dan. *bie* 'wait'); *g* became *j* after front vowels (as in Swedish *öga* versus Danish *øje* 'eye'), *v* after back vowels (as in Swedish *skog* versus Danish *skov* 'forest'), and was lost after *i* and *u* (as in Swedish *stig, fluga* versus Danish *sti, flue* 'path, fly'); while *v* often disappeared in intervocalic position (such as Swedish *snuva* versus Danish *snue* 'head cold'), and became part of a diphthong in final position as in *hav* [hɑu] 'sea'). 3. The stops *p, t, k* became *b, d* [ð], *g* [j] after a vowel (for example, Swedish *köpa, gata, söka* versus Danish *købe, gade, søge* 'buy, street, seek').

At the syntactic level, word order was standardized during this period. The finite verb was increasingly attached to the subject, even in subordinate clauses where previously it often occurred in clause-final position. However, the old type of word order can be found up to about 1700.

At the same time the vocabulary was extended by over 1,500 loanwords. The vast majority came from Low German, owing to the extensive trade (and wars) with the Hanseatic League. Even loanwords of Latin origin were mostly introduced via Low German. This wave of borrowing had a lasting effect on Danish.

The total area of Denmark began to diminish in the 17th century with the loss of Scania, Halland, and Blekinge to Sweden. In 1814, at the end of the Napoleonic Wars, Denmark was forced to cede Norway to Sweden, and in 1864 it lost Schleswig-Holstein to Germany, although North Schleswig did return in 1920, following a referendum in the two Duchies. In 1944, Iceland gained independence, and both Greenland and the Faroe Islands, which are still part of the kingdom, have now obtained home rule status.

In the wake of the Reformation came a wealth of new loanwords, in particular from High German, French and Latin. A "purist" counter-movement in the middle of the 18th century attempted to create new "native" words in order to oust, or at least stem the flood of, the foreign imports, which were still dominated by German and FRENCH loanwords. In many cases this merely provided alternatives that existed alongside the foreign loanwords. In the 20th century, and especially after World War II, loanwords from English proliferated in all fields.

Orthography and Basic Phonology

The first attempt at establishing official rules for Danish spelling was made in 1775, but the first official spelling dictionary did not appear until 1872. The second official spelling dictionary was published in 1891, in conjunction with a major spelling reform, and the third one was issued in 1923. The next large spelling reform came in 1948 with the abandonment of capital letters at the beginning of nouns and the official introduction of the letter *å*, which until then had been represented by *aa*. These changes were reflected in the fourth official spelling dictionary, *Retskrivningsordbogen*, in 1955, published by the recently established Danish Language Council (*Dansk Sprognævn*), which has since then been responsible for the supervision of Modern Danish.

Today Danish has 29 letters: *a b c d e f g h i j k l m n o p q r s t u v w x y z æ ø å*, the same 26 letters as in English plus the three vowels *æ, ø,* and *å*. Of these, *q, w, x,* and *z* appear in foreign loanwords only.

The Danish consonant system is relatively simple, whereas the number of vowels and diphthongs is greater than in most other European languages (see Table 1). In the case of both consonants and vowels there is far from always a one-to-one correspondence between letters and sounds.

Danish has 17 consonant phonemes. All stops are voiceless. The letters *p, t, k* are only pronounced [p, t, k] in word-initial position and at the beginning of a stressed syllable elsewhere in the word. In other positions they are pronounced [b, d, g], while the letters *b, d, g* in the latter positions often become [w, ð, j]. The letter *r* is pronounced as a frictionless, uvular sound before a vowel (as in *ride* 'ride'), and as a semi-vowel [ɐ] after a vowel, with which it often merges, as in the ending *-er*. /ŋ/ is usually written *ng*.

All back vowels are rounded (see Table 2 on the next page). Apart from the vowel phonemes /a/ and /ʌ/, each of the short vowels has a long counterpart. Danish has two "schwa" sounds, [ə] and [ɐ], in unstressed syllables only. They bring the number of vowel phonemes up to 27, not counting allophonic variants, which are particularly common before and after *r*.

In addition, there are two sets of diphthongs, each with at least 19 members. One set has a short vowel as the first element and [i], [u], or [ɐ] as the second, as in *mig* [mɑi] 'me' and *syv* [syu] 'seven'. The other set has a long vowel as the first element and also [i], [u], or [ɐ] as the second, as in *ord* [o:'ɐ] 'word' and *sorg* [sɒ:u] 'sorrow'.

Table 2: Vowels

	Front		Back
	Unrounded	Rounded	
High	i	y	u
	e	ø	o
	ɛ	œ	ɔ
	a		ɒ
Low	ɑ		ʌ

A special Danish feature is the so-called *stød* (marked [']), which is a kind of glottal stop but without complete closure. It is a prosodic feature that can occur in stressed syllables that have a "*stød* base", as in a long vowel or a short vowel followed by a sonorant. Some words that would otherwise be homophones are only distinguished by the presence or absence of *stød* (as in *mand* [man'] 'man' versus *man* [man] 'one, you').

Danish has no sentence accent, so in sentences without special contrast or focus there is no particularly prominent stress or stress group. Intonation is marked by a level or falling pitch contour, with unstressed syllables rising between two stressed syllables. Range and variation of pitch are much narrower than in Norwegian and Swedish, for example.

Basic Morphology

Nouns are inflected for case, number, and gender. There are two cases (a common or unmarked case and the genitive), two numbers (singular and plural), and two genders (common gender and neuter).

Apart from a separate genitive form ending in *-s*, all other previous case endings in nouns have disappeared to leave a common, neutralized form. Nouns thus have the same form whether they function as subject, (direct or indirect) object, or (subject or object) complement. However, there are still examples of old genitive and dative case endings (*-s* and *-e*) in fossilized prepositional phrases (such as *til lands/søs* 'at land/sea'; *i live* 'alive').

The native plural endings are *-e*, *-(e)r*, and -zero, which may occur with both common gender and neuter nouns. In addition, some loans have a plural ending of foreign origin, often as an alternative to a native ending (as in *jeeps/jeeper* 'jeeps').

Gender distinctions occur in the singular, but are neutralized in the plural. Common gender is a conflation of previously distinct masculine and feminine forms. Gender is marked by means of articles, determiners, and/or adjectives. Natural gender, which may be marked by means of (often feminine) suffixes, is only important for the choice of corresponding personal pronouns, since in terms of grammatical gender both masculine and feminine forms are usually common gender.

There are two sets of articles: indefinite and definite. The indefinite article is *en* in front of common gender nouns and *et* in front of neuter nouns as in *en stol* (a chair), *et bord* (a table). It always appears as a separate word preceding the noun. The definite article has two forms (a front article and an end article) in both genders. If the noun is preceded by one or more modifying adjectives, the independent front article (common gender *den*, neuter *det*) is placed before the adjective(s), as in *den store stol* (the big chair), *det store bord* (the big table). If the noun has no modification, the end article (common gender *-en*, neuter *-et*) is added to the noun as an inflectional ending as in *stolen* (the chair), *bordet* (the table). The definite article in the plural is *de* (front article) or *-(e)ne* (end article) as in *de store stole/borde* (the big chairs/tables), *stolene/bordene* (the chairs/tables). There is no indefinite article in the plural. Unlike Norwegian and Swedish, Danish does not allow "double definiteness", that is, the use of both front and end article with the same noun.

Personal pronouns have one form in the first-person (singular and plural), two forms (formal and informal) in the second-person (singular and plural), four forms in the third-person singular (masculine, feminine, common gender [nonperson], and neuter), and one form in the third-person plural. Unlike nouns, personal pronouns have separate case forms in the nominative and the accusative/oblique case. In addition, there is a set of possessive pronouns (some of which inflect for number and gender) with genitive function.

Adjectives agree with articles and nouns in number and gender, although (as with articles and nouns) gender is neutralized in the plural. There are three possible adjective endings: -zero, *-t*, and *-e*, but some adjectives do not, for various reasons, add *-t* and/or *-e*. The choice of ending depends on a combination of factors, such as number, gender, definiteness, and position. Thus the *-e* ending occurs after a definite article and in the plural. The -zero ending occurs in the singular after the indefinite article *en* (common gender), in predicative position agreeing with a singular common noun, and in front of an articleless singular uncountable noun (common gender). The *-t* ending occurs in the singular after the indefinite article *et* (neuter), in predicative position agreeing with a neuter noun, and in front of an articleless singular uncountable noun (neuter).

Adverbs are either "pure" adverbs, that is, words that can only occur as adverbs, or derived from adjectives. Pure adverbs have a fixed form, while those derived from adjectives can have the ending *-t*, which (in accordance with rather complex rules) may be compulsory, optional, or not possible, mainly depending on the type and function of the individual adverb.

Verbs in Danish show no person or number distinctions, so that each tense has only one form. Agreement with the subject is thus neutralized. Two tenses (present and past) are expressed synthetically, whereas the rest (perfect, past perfect, future, future perfect, future of the past, and future perfect of the past) are formed analytically by means of auxiliary verbs such as *have* (have) or *være* (be) in the past tenses and *ville* (will/would) in the future tenses.

There are four conjugations: three weak ones and one strong one. In the past tense, the weak conjugations have the endings *-ede*, *-te*, and *-de*, respectively, such as *legede* (played), *sendte* (sent), *gjorde* (did), whereas the strong conjugation has the ending -zero or (occasionally) *-t*, often with vowel mutation as in (*synge* -) *sang* (sang), (*finde* -) *fandt* (found), but in contrast to weak verbs there is only one syllable in noncompound verbs. The infinitive ends in *-e*, except for a small number of vowel stems ending in another vowel as in *bo* (live, dwell), *dø* (die), and *få* (get). The past participle ending is *-(e)t* as in *sendt* (sent) or *fundet* (found); the present participle ending is *-ende* as in *syngende* (singing).

There are two passive forms; a synthetical one with the ending *-s* (the *-s* passive) and an analytical one formed by means of the auxiliary *blive* 'be, become' plus the past participle of the main verb (the *blive* passive) (*Kampen spilles/bliver spillet/ i København* 'The match is played in Copenhagen').

Negation is mainly expressed by the negative particle *ikke* 'not' or by means of negative prefixes (*mis-*, *u-*, *van-* as in *misforstå* 'misunderstand', *uvilje* 'unwillingness', or *vanskabt* 'misshapen').

Basic Syntax

In Danish, adjectives normally precede the noun they modify: *den store mand* (the big man) 'the big man'.

As subject complements, they appear after the verb, and as object complements they appear directly after the object:

Byen er blevet større
'The town has become bigger.'

Vi malede byen rød
'We painted the town red.'

The order of objects is always indirect object + direct object:

Jeg sendte ham bogen/den
'I sent him the book/it.'

Han gav Tom brevet/det
'He gave Tom the letter/it.'

Danish is a verb-second language, and clausal word order in Danish is relatively fixed; a distinction needs to be drawn, however, between main and subordinate clauses.

In main clauses, the finite verb is usually the second element:

Drengen fik en gave af sin mor
'The boy got a present from his mother.'

The only exceptions to this are yes/no questions and imperatives, where the finite verb comes first (in other words, the first position is empty):

Kommer han i morgen?
Comes he tomorrow?
'Is he coming tomorrow?'

Har du gjort det?
'Have you done it?'

Kom her!
'Come here!'

In questions introduced by an interrogative, the finite verb remains in second position:

Hvorfor har du gjort det?
'Why have you done it?'

Indeed, in sentences beginning with an element that is not the subject, the finite verb will still come second but is immediately followed by the subject (so-called inversion):

I går regnede det meget
Yesterday rained it much
'Yesterday it rained a lot.'

Inversion also occurs in main clauses when following a subordinate clause:

SUBORDINATE MAIN
Da jeg så ham, blev jeg glad
When I saw him became I happy
'When I saw him I became happy.'

Sentences where the first element is not the subject represent a common type of construction in Danish; it is possible to begin a main clause with most major sentence elements (= so-called "topicalization," which is done for emphasis or stylistic reasons). Further examples are:

Direct object:
Ham så Peter ikke
Him saw Peter not
'Peter didn't see him.'

Indirect object:
Hende gav jeg pengene
Her gave I the money
'I gave her the money.'

Non-finite verbs:
Synge kan han heller ikke
Sing can he either not
'He can't sing either.'

Place adverbial:
Her har han boet længe
Here has he lived a long time
'He has lived here a long time.'

Time adverbial:
I går sendte jeg ham et brev
Yesterday sent I him a letter
'I sent him a letter yesterday.'

This last pair of sentences demonstrates the normal positions occupied by adverbials in Danish main clauses, namely clause initial or clause final. There is one other position where adverbials may appear, namely immediately after the subject in sentences with inversion, or after the finite verb in sentences beginning with the subject; this position is usually filled by negative elements as in *ikke* (not), *aldrig* (never), or other "clausal adverbials":

Ham	har	jeg	ikke/ofte	set
'Him	have	I	not/often	seen.'

Jeg	har	ikke/ofte	set	ham
I	have	not/often	seen	him

'I haven't/ I've often/ seen him.'

In sentences with a simple verb, reflexive pronouns, unstressed and non-topicalized object pronouns and the adverbs *her* (here) and *der* (there) will appear directly after the finite verb where there is no "inversion", or immediately after the subject where there is "inversion"; these are known as "light elements":

Jeg	vaskede	mig	ikke	i	morges
'I	washed	myself	not	this	morning.'

I morges	vaskede	jeg	mig	ikke
This morning	washed	I	myself	not

'I didn't have a wash this morning.'

Jeg	kender	ham	ikke
I	know	him	not

'I don't know him.'

Desværre	er	Jens	her	ikke
Unfortunately	is	Jens	here	not

'Jens is unfortunately not here.'

When such sentences also contain a non-finite verb form, these "light elements" will (if not topicalized in the case of object pronouns and *her* and *der*) come after the non-finite verb:

Jeg	har	ikke	vasket	mig	i dag
I	have	not	washed	myself	today

'I haven't washed today.'

Han	har	ikke	set	hende	længe
He	has	not	seen	her	a long time

'He hasn't seen her for a long time.'

Hun	har	aldrig	været	der
She	has	never	been	there

'She's never been there.'

The order of the main sentence elements in Danish may be briefly summarized as follows:

1. The initial position may be occupied by either the subject or some other sentence element, including a subordinate clause (but excluding the finite verb).
2. The second position is occupied by the finite verb (present, past, or imperative).
3. The third position is occupied by the subject (if it is not in the first position, in which case this position is unfilled), and this may be followed by reflexive or unstressed object pronouns.
4. The fourth position may be occupied by clausal adverbials.
5. The fifth position is occupied by non-finite verbs (such as participles or infinitives).
6. The sixth position is occupied by noun phrases as objects, reflexive and object pronouns, and subject and object complements.
7. The seventh and final position is occupied by adverbials.

In subordinate clauses, too, most of the above applies. Subordinate clauses will often be introduced by a subordinator; after that, the main differences are that topicalization of elements other than the subject to the first position after any subordinator is not possible (the subject is normally always the first element), and that negative and clausal adverbials appear between the subject and the finite verb:

...selv	om	det	regnede	i går
...even	though	it	rained	yesterday

'...even though yesterday it rained.'

...selv	om	det	ikke/ofte	regner
...even	though	it	not/often	rains

'...even though it doesn't rain/often rains.'

Contact with Other Languages

From Latin: *museum* 'museum', *skole* 'school'
From Low German: *bager* 'baker', *fragt* 'freight', *købmand* 'merchant', *slot* 'castle'
From French: *ambassadør* 'ambassador', *bøf* 'beef', *kusine* '[female] cousin', *trist* 'sad', *vulgær* 'vulgar'
From English: *bacon*, *bus*, *drink*, *jeans*, *radio*

Common Words

man:	mand	long:	lang
woman:	kvinde	small:	lille (sg)/små (pl)
water:	vand	yes:	ja
sun:	sol	no:	nej
three:	tre	good:	god
fish:	fisk	bird:	fugl
big:	stor	dog:	hund
tree:	træ		

Example Sentences

(1)

Han	hav	de	aldrig	vær	et	i	Danmark.
3s.MASC	had	AUX	never	been	PART	PREP	Denmark.

'He had never been to Denmark.'

(2)

Syng	er	jeres	barn	dansk	e	sang	e?
Sings	PRES	2pl.POSS	child	Danish	PL	songs	PL

'Does your child sing Danish songs?'

(3)

Den	stor	e	mand	elsk	ede	at	spis	e	fisk.
the	big	DEF	man	loved	PAST	INFM	eat	INF	fish

'The big man loved eating fish.' (INFM=infinitive marker)

Efforts to Preserve, Protect, and Promote the Language

In 1955 the body called *Dansk Sprognævn* (Danish Language Council) was established to monitor the development of Danish by collecting and registering new words and expressions, and to provide information and guidance on Danish-language usage in general and on Danish spelling and punctuation in particular. It is now the highest authority on Modern Danish. As well as regularly publishing information booklets on current trends in Danish it also periodically updates the official dictionary of Danish spelling (*Retskrivningsordbogen*), the latest edition of which appeared in 1996. In 1997, *Dansk Sprognævn* was given official legal status through an act of parliament.

Select Bibliography

Allan, Robin, Philip Holmes and Tom Lundskær-Nielsen. 1995. *Danish: A Comprehensive Grammar*. London and New York: Routledge.

_____. 2000. *Danish: An Essential Grammar*. London and New York: Routledge.

Becker-Christensen, Christian and Peter Widell. 1996. *Politikens Nudansk Grammatik* (2nd ed.). Copenhagen: Politiken.

Brink, Lars, and Jørn Lund. 1975. *Dansk Rigsmål 1–2*. Copenhagen: Gyldendal.

Brink, Lars, Jørn Lund, Steffen Heger, and Jens Normann Jørgensen, eds. 1991. *Den Store Danske Udtaleordbog*. Copenhagen: Munksgaard.

Dahlerup, Verner. 1921. *Det danske Sprogs Historie* (2nd ed.). Copenhagen: J.H. Schultz.

Diderichsen, Paul. 1962. *Elementær dansk Grammatik* (3rd ed.). Copenhagen: Gyldendal.

Grønning, Nina. 1998. *Fonetik og Fonologi. Almen og Dansk*. Copenhagen: Akademisk Forlag.

Hansen, Aage. 1967. *Moderne dansk 1–3*. Copenhagen: Grafisk Forlag.

Hansen, Erik, and Jørn Lund. 1994. *Kulturens Gesandter. Fremmedordene i dansk*. Copenhagen: Munksgaard.

Haugen, Einar. 1976. *The Scandinavian Languages: An Introduction to their History*. Cambridge: Harvard University Press.

Jacobsen, Henrik Galberg, and Peter Stray Jørgensen. 1997. *Håndbog i Nudansk* (3rd ed.). Copenhagen: Politiken.

Jacobsen, Henrik Galberg and Peder Skyum-Nielsen. 1996. *Dansk sprog. En grundbog*. Copenhagen: Schønberg.

Jarvad, Pia. 1995. *Nye ord - hvorfor og hvordan?* Copenhagen: Gyldendal.

Karker, Allan. 1993. *Dansk i tusind år*. Modersmål-Selskabet. Copenhagen: C.A. Reitzel.

____. 1996. *Politikens Sproghistorie. Udviklingslinjer før nudansk*. Copenhagen: Politiken.

Karker, Allan, Birgitta Lindgren and Ståle Løland, eds. 1997. *Nordens Språk*. Nordisk språkråd. Oslo: Novus.

König, Ekkehard, and Johan van der Auwera, eds. 1994. *The Germanic Languages*. London and New York: Routledge.

Mikkelsen, Kristian. 1911. *Dansk ordföjningslære med sproghistoriske tillæg*. Copenhagen: Lehmann & Stage. (Reprinted 1975. Copenhagen: Hans Reitzel.)

Nielsen, B. Kjærulff. 1991. *Engelsk-Dansk Ordbog* (4th ed.). Copenhagen: Gyldendal.

Ordbog over det danske Sprog. 1–28. 1918–56. Copenhagen: Gyldendal.

Politikens Store Nye Nudansk Ordbog 1–2. 1996. Copenhagen: Politiken.

Retskrivningsordbogen (2nd ed.). 1996. Dansk Sprognævn. Copenhagen: Aschehoug.

Skautrup, Peter. 1944–1970. *Det danske sprogs historie. 1–5*. Copenhagen: Gyldendal.

Sørensen, Knud. 1973. *Engelske lån i dansk*. Copenhagen: Gyldendal.

____. 1995. *Engelsk i dansk–er det et must?* Copenhagen: Munksgaard.

DUTCH

Theo A.J.M. Janssen

Language Name: Dutch. **Autonym:** *Nederlands*. In former days the self-denomination of Dutch was *Diets/Duuts*, i.e., 'belonging to the people'. Later *Vlaams* 'Flemish' was used to name the language spoken in the northern part of Belgium, and *Hollands* was used to name the language spoken in the Netherlands. The Latinized name of Dutch is *theodiscus*.

Location: Dutch is spoken in the Netherlands and in the northern part of Belgium. It is also spoken in the Netherlands Antilles (Bonaire, Curaçao, St. Eustatius, St. Martin, Saba), Aruba, and Suriname.

Family: Dutch is a member of the West Germanic subgroup of the Germanic group of the Indo-European language family.

Related Languages: Dutch is closely related to the Low German dialects (spoken in northern Germany). Other closely related languages are Frisian (spoken in Friesland, a province of the Netherlands), the High German dialects, and, somewhat more distantly, ENGLISH. A daughter language of Dutch is AFRIKAANS.

Dialects: The map of the Dutch dialects in the Netherlands, Germany, Belgium, and France can roughly be divided into northern and southern zones, with the boundary formed by the basin where the rivers Lek, Waal, and Maas flow nearly parallel to the North Sea. The northern and southern zones each have three subdialects for a total of six. In the north are (1) Northwest, (2) Middle, and (3) Northeast zones. In the south one can distinguish the (4) Southwest, (5) Middle, and (6) Southeast zones.

Number of Speakers: 20.75–21.25 million.

Origin and History

Before A.D. 1150–1200 various Old Dutch ('Low Franconian') dialects were spoken in northern France, Belgium, the southern half of the Netherlands, and the lower Rhenic region in Germany (the region round the present Kleve, Xanten, and Krefeld).

From about 1200 to 1550, Middle Dutch expanded to the northern provinces of the Netherlands (first to Holland and Utrecht; later, mainly in written form to Overijssel, Drente, and Groningen).

The 16th century brought forth various (contrastive) grammars and numerous vocabularies, for example, the quadrilingual dictionary *Tetraglotton* (1561) and the *Thesaurus Theutonicae linguae* (1573), both by Christoffel Plantijn, and the *Dictionarium Teutonico-Latinum* by Cornelis Kiliaan (1574), as well as translations of the Bible, for example, the Liesveldt Bible (1526) and the Deux-Aes Bible (1561–1562).

In 1637 the *Statenbijbel* "States Bible", produced by order of Holland's government, the States of Holland, introduced a supraregional language standardized by the translators. This language had a major influence in particular on the speakers of the dialects in the northern, predominantly Protestant, part of the Netherlands. Children learned this supradialect because of their fathers reading the Bible aloud; hence, this language is called the "father tongue".

In the 19th century the codification process of Dutch took shape in the orthographic and lexicographic fields. Official spelling regulations were the "Spelling-Siegenbeek" (1804) and the "Spelling-De Vries & Te Winkel" (1864 in Belgium, 1883 in the Netherlands). In 1882 the first volume of the scientific dictionary *Woordenboek der Nederlandsche taal* 'Dictionary of the Dutch language' was published. The cultural and scientific status of Dutch, the third most spoken Germanic language, was enhanced by the development of the *Middelnederlandsch woordenboek* 'Middle Dutch Dictionary', whose first volume of a series of eleven was brought out in 1885.

In the 20th century the most important step to the codification of Dutch was the publication of the *Algemene Nederlandse spraakkunst* 'Standard Dutch Grammar' (1985). This grammar, rather descriptive than prescriptive, was thoroughly revised and enlarged in its second edition (1997).

Orthography and Basic Phonology

Dutch has a spelling that basically hinges on the LATIN tradition. The main spelling rule says that graphemes must represent audible sounds (phonemes). Because of this rule Dutch spelling is basically phonemic. The main exceptions to the phonemic principle are the following rules.

In all of its occurrences a lexeme is preferably spelled in one way. For instance, the *d* in *hoed* 'hat' is pronounced as [t], but is written as *d* because in the plural form, *hoeden*, the *d* is pronounced as [d].

Words with the same morphology are spelled analogously. For instance, the noun *grootte* 'bigness' is spelled in conformity with derivations such as *hoogte* 'height' and *diepte* 'depth'. Here the type of derivation is: adjective (*groot, hoog, diep*) + suffix *-te*. Thus, these uniform spellings are based on the uniform morphology. Exceptions to this analogy rule are inflected adjectives, such as *grote* and the comparative *groter*.

In a number of cases the etymology determines the spelling. This explains why, for instance, the spelling of the diphthong [ɛi] can be *ei, ij,* or *y*, and the spelling of the diphthong [ɔu] is *ou* or *au*.

Table 1: Consonants

		Bilabial	Labio-Dental	Alveolar	Velar	Palatal	Glottal
Stops	Voiceless	p		t	k, c, q		
	Voiced	b		d			
Fricatives	Voiceless		f	s, c	g, ch		h
	Voiced		v	z	(g)		
Nasals		m		n	ng		
Liquids				l, r			
Glides		w				j	

Dutch spelling shows two types of twin graphemes. First, a consonant must be written twice when the preceding vowel is a short one. The first of these two consonants marks the coda of the syllable involved. Second, the long vowels [u, e, o, a] are spelled as "uu", "ee", "oo", and "aa" if the coda consists of at least one consonant. If a consonant is missing, the long vowel is spelled with one letter. See, for instance, the contrast between the one-syllable word *draad* [drat] 'thread' and the two-syllable word *draden* [dra + də(n)].

A diaeresis signals that a new syllable starts with the letter the dots are written over; it is used where two consecutive vowels must be read as a digraph if the mark were missing. In compounds a hyphen is used to mark the border between the constituents if it is necessary or advisable to prevent reading problems. Diacritics such as the grave, acute, and circumflex accents are mainly used in FRENCH loanwords. The acute accent may be used to indicate stress.

q represents [k], *g* represents [χ, ɣ], *ch* represents [χ], *c* represents [k, s], and *w* represents [ʋ]. Loanwords can show the grapheme 'x', which represents [ks].

i(e) represents [i]; *eu* represents [ø]; *u(u)* represents [y]; *u* represents [ɵ]; *oe* represents [u]; *o(o)* represents [o]; *o* represents [ɔ, ʊ]; *a(a)* represents [a]; *a* represents [ɑ]; *ei* and *ij* represent [ɛi]; *ui* represents [ʌy]; and *au* and *ou* represent [ɔu].

Dutch has a phonemic long-short vowel opposition: *maan* 'moon' vs. *man* 'man'. Short vowels, except schwa, cannot occur in word-final position. Syllables feature final devoicing of the stops [b,d] and the fricatives [v,z,ɣ]. In words such as *eb* 'ebb' and *hoed* 'hat' the final consonants are voiceless in spite of the graphemes *b* and *d*.

Basic Morphology

Dutch has lost most of its inflectional endings and therefore more closely resembles English than GERMAN. The only morpheme that reflects case is the genitive *-s*, applied to proper nouns, some common nouns, and some pronouns: *Peters boek* 'Peter's book', *mijn vaders pen* 'my father's pen', and *ieders* 'everyone's'. Number is reflected in nouns with various suffixes: *-en, -s,* (and less frequently) *-eren, -ers.*

Nouns may be divided into two classes: nouns with common gender which take the definite determiner *de*, and nouns with neuter gender, taking the definite determiner *het*. Some nouns belonging to the *de* class may be considered feminine, as they take the feminine anaphoric pronoun *zij/ze*. These include words with, for example, the suffixes *-te, -heid,* and *-erij.* (In the northern zones, this masculine/feminine distinction does not exist.)

Dutch has definite articles, indefinite articles, and demonstratives. *Een* 'a' and *geen* 'no' are indefinite articles. The definite articles are *het ('t)* 'neuter' and *de* 'common'. Demonstratives are *dit* 'this', *dat* 'that' (neuter), and *deze* 'this', *die* 'that' (common). Gender and number are indicated in the articles and adjective agreement as follows:

	a/the big city	a/the big house
sg. def.	de grote stad	het grote huis
sg. indef.	een grote stad	een groot huis
pl. def.	de grote steden	de grote huizen

Dutch verbs inflect for the present and past tense and the present and past participles. Finite verb forms agree with the person and number of the subject. The following table illustrates the verbs *nippen* 'nip' and *dubben* 'waver'.

Person	Number	Present tense	Past tense
1	singular	nip, dub	nipte, dubde
2	unspecified	nipt, dubt	nipte, dubde
3	singular	nipt, dubt	nipte, dubde
1, 2, 3	plural	nippen, dubben	nipten, dubden

Table 2: Vowels

	Front		Central		Back	
	Unrounded	Rounded	Unrounded	Rounded	Unrounded	Rounded
High	i (e), e (e)	u (u)				oe
Mid	e, i	eu	e	u		o (o), o
Low			a (a)		a	
Diphthongs	ei, ij			ui		au, ou

Table 3: Full and Reduced Pronouns

Person	Number	Subject		Non-Subject	
		Full	Reduced	Full	Reduced
1	singular	*ik, ikke*	*'k*	*mij*	*me*
2	singular	*jij*	*je*	*jou*	*je*
2 polite	unspecified	*u*	-	*u*	-
3	singular	*hij, zij, (het)*	*-ie, ze, 't*	*hem, haar, (het)*	*'m, 'r, 't*
1	plural	*wij*	*we*	*ons*	-
2	plural	*jullie*	*je*	*jullie*	*je*
3	plural	*zij*	*ze*	*hen, hun*	*ze*

Pronouns have subject and object forms, both full and reduced. Reduced forms are more commonly used in spoken language, as full forms are reserved for emphasis (see Table 3 above).

Adjectives and adverbs denoting gradual properties may take the comparative suffix *-er*: *groter* 'bigger', *vaker* 'more often', and the superlative suffix *-st*: *grootst* 'greatest, biggest', *vaakst* 'most often'.

The diminutive suffix *-tje* and its allomorphs (*-je* after obstruents, *-etje* in some cases after liquids and nasals, and *-pje, -kje,* assimilated variants) not only occur with nouns, but also with adjectives *groentje* 'greenhorn', numerals *tientje* 'tenner', verbs *moetje* 'shotgun marriage', prepositions *uitje* 'outing', pronouns *ietsje* 'a bit', and phrases *onderonsje* 'private chat'.

Other affixes include the prefix *on-* as in *onbekend* 'unknown', the suffix *-ig* as in *schuldig* 'guilty', and the combination *ge—t/d* used to form past participles as in *genipt* 'nipped', *gedubd* 'wavered'.

Basic Syntax

Dutch is a verb-second language with a nominative/accusative syntax. Subjects (that agree with the verbs) can precede finite verbs in declarative sentences. In questions, requests, and certain types of conditionals, the finite verb is sentence-initial. The main verb is placed at the end of a clause with a finite auxiliary verb. Finite verbs appear at the end of the clause in dependent clauses.

Zal hij haar dat vertellen?
will he her that tell
'Will he tell her that?'

Ik heb het al geschreven.
I have it already written
' I have written it (already).'

Ik wed dat Fred haar morgen alles openhartig
I bet that Fred her tomorrow everything frankly

zal vertellen
will tell
'I bet that tomorrow Fred will tell her everything frankly.'

Dutch passives are periphrastic, formed with the verbs *worden* 'become' or *zijn* 'to be' and the past participle: *Peter wordt gekust; Peter is gekust;* 'Peter is kissed'; 'Peter has been kissed'.

Sentential negation is expressed by means of the adverb *niet* 'not' or other negative words such as *geen* 'no', *niemand* 'nobody', and *niets* 'nothing.'

Rita slaapt niet
Rita sleeps not
'Rita doesn't sleep.'

Rita heeft geen zere teen
Rita has no sore toe
'Rita does not have a sore toe.'

Rita ziet niemand
Rita sees nobody
'Rita does not see anyone.'

Verscheidene mensen willen niet komen
several people want not come
'Some people don't want to come'

Contact with Other Languages

Belgium and the Netherlands have a long merchant marine tradition because of their being situated on the North Sea coast, where various navigable rivers flow out. Their trading vessels put in at ports all over the world. In the 16th and 17th centuries the Dutch set up trading posts in South America, West Africa, India, China, and Japan. They founded colonies in New Netherlands (the current area of New York and its hinterland), the Netherlands Antilles, South Africa, Ceylon, and Indonesia.

Belgium and the Netherlands were influenced by many cultures through their merchant marines' activities. They, for their part, influenced a number of languages. Various Dutch marine words are borrowed, even by RUSSIAN and JAPANESE. For example, Russian has *botsman* (< Dutch *bootsman*) 'boatswain', *gavan* (< D. *haven*) 'harbor', *matrós* (< D. *matroos*) 'sailor', *bakport* (< D. *bakboord*, 'port'.

From Arabic: *sandaal* (< Ar. *sandal*) 'sandal', *schaakmat* (< Ar. *shah mat*) 'checkmate'

From English: *bietser* (< Eng. beachcomber) 'scrounger', *biefstuk* (< Eng. beefsteak) 'rump steak'

From French: *balans* (< Fr. *balance*) 'balance', *banaal* (< Fr. *banal*) 'banal', *baai* (< Fr. *baie*) 'bay'
From German: *bewust* (< Ger. *bewusst*) 'conscious', *buks* (< Ger. *Büchse*) 'rifle'
From Latin: *benedijen* (< Lat. *bene dicere*) 'bless', *biet* (< Lat. *beta*) 'beet'

Common Words

man:	man	long:	lang
woman:	vrouw	small:	klein
water:	water	yes:	ja
sun:	zon	no:	nee
three:	drie	good:	goed
fish:	vis	bird:	vogel
big:	groot	dog:	hond
tree:	boom		

Example Sentences

(1)

Ik	weet	het	niet.
1SG	know:VERB	it:3SG	not:ADVERB

'I don't know.'

(2)

Gisteren	heb	ik	hem
yesterday:ADVERB	have:VERB	1SG	him

zien	aankomen.
see:VERB:INF	come:VERB:INF

'I saw him come yesterday.'

(3)

Ik	heb	het	paard
I	have:VERB [AUX]	the:NEUTER.ART	horse:NOUN

over	het	hek	zien
over:PREP	the:NEUTER.ART	fence:NOUN	see:VERB.INF

springen.
jump:VERB.INF

'I saw the horse jump over the fence.'

Efforts to Preserve, Protect, and Promote the Language

In 1980 Belgium and the Netherlands made the treaty of *De Nederlandse Taalunie* 'The Dutch Language Union'. They accepted the responsibility of promoting Dutch as the official language in all social spheres. The institute of *De Nederlandse Taalunie* got the authority to regulate Dutch spelling, grammar, lexicon, and terminology.

De Nederlandse Taalunie supports lectureships at approximately 250 universities outside the Dutch language area. Once a year it organizes an international examination to be taken by students learning Dutch as a foreign language.

Select Bibliography

Bakker, D.M., and G.R.W. Dibbets, eds. 1977. *Geschiedenis van de Nederlandse taalkunde*. Den Bosch: Malmberg.

Booij, G.E. 1995. *The Phonology of Dutch*. Oxford: Clarendon.

Brachin, P. 1985. *The Dutch Language: A Survey*. Translated by P. Vincent. Cheltenham: Stanley Thornes/Leiden: E.J. Brill.

de Haas, W., and M. Trommelen. 1993. *Morfologisch handboek van het Nederlands. Een overzicht van de woordvorming*. Den Haag: SDU.

de Vries, J.W., R. Willemyns, and P. Burger, 1993. *Het verhaal van een taal. Negen eeuwen Nederlands*. Amsterdam: Prometheus.

de Vries, *et al.* 1882–1998. *Woordenboek der Nederlandsche taal* (Volumes 1–40), Den Haag: M. Nijhoff, [reprint Den Haag: SDU, 1992. CD-ROM version, Rotterdam: AND Electronic Publishing, 1995].

Donaldson, B.C. 1983. *Dutch: A Linguistic History*. Leiden: M. Nijhoff.

____. 1997. *Dutch: A Comprehensive Grammar*. New York and London: Routledge.

Geerts, G., *et al.* 1999. *Groot woordenboek der Nederlandse taal* (Volumes 1–3), Utrecht, Antwerpen: Van Dale Lexicografie [first edition 1864].

Haeseryn, W., K. Romijn, G. Geerts, J. de Rooij, and M.C. van den Toorn. 1997. *Algemene Nederlandse spraakkunst* (Volumes 1–2), Groningen: HM. Nijhoff Uitgevers/Deurne: Wolters Plantyn, [first edition 1984].

van den Toorn, W.J.J. Pijnenburg, J.A. van Leuvensteijn, and J.M. van der Horst, eds.1997. *Geschiedenis van de Nederlandse taal*. Amsterdam: Amsterdam University Press.

van Veen, P.A.F. *et al.*1989. *Etymologisch woordenboek*. Utrecht, Antwerp: Van Dale Lexicografie.

Vandeputte, O. 1981. *Dutch: The Language of Twenty Million Dutch and Flemish People*. Rekkem: Ons Erfdeel.

Verwijs, E., *et al.* 1885–1952. *Middelnederlandsch woordenboek* (Volumes 1–11), Den Haag: M. Nijhoff [reprinted 1969].

ANCIENT EGYPTIAN

Antonio Loprieno

Language Name: Ancient Egyptian, or simply Egyptian, is the general modern term for the language written and spoken during the Pharaonic (ca. 3000–323 B.C.), Ptolemaic (323–30 B.C.), and Roman (30 B.C.–third century A.D.) periods of the history of Egypt. The native expressions that indicated the language of the country were *r3 nj km.t* ('the language of the Black Land,' i.e., Egypt) or *md.t km.t* ('the speech of the Black Land'). In the neighboring Semitic languages, the language of Ancient Egypt is called "(Ancient) Egyptian (language)", for example, ARABIC *(al-luġa) al-misriyya (al-qadīma).*

Location: Ancient Egyptian was spoken and written in Egypt, i.e., in the northeast corner of Africa, in the Nile Valley north of the first cataract, corresponding to the present-day city of Assuan, in the Nile Delta, and in the oases immediately to the west of the Nile Valley.

Family: Ancient Egyptian represents an autonomous branch of the Afro-Asiatic (also called Hamito-Semitic) family, which also comprises Semitic, Berber (corresponding to Libyan in antiquity), Cushitic, Chadic, and Omotic languages.

Related Languages: Within the Afro-Asiatic family, Ancient Egyptian displays the closest connections to Semitic, especially AKKADIAN, and to Libyan-Berber.

Dialects: Because of the strongly centralized nature of the Egyptian administration, the unitary state ideology underlying the use of writing, and the peculiarities of the hieroglyphic system, which did not indicate vowels, dialectal differences tend to remain opaque. Nonetheless, on the basis of the different outcome of a few Afro-Asiatic phonemes in "earlier" as opposed to "later" Egyptian (see Origin and History below), one can regard Old and Middle Egyptian as representing a Lower Egyptian, i.e., a northern variety of the language, as opposed to Late Egyptian, which exhibits a prevalence of Upper Egyptian, i.e., southern features.

Number of Speakers: A fair estimate of the number of speakers of the language in antiquity is between 1 million during the Old Kingdom (c. 2800–2150 B.C.) and 5 million in Roman times.

Origin and History

Including its latest form, called COPTIC, Egyptian remained in use over four millennia (from about 3000 B.C. to around A.D. 1000) as the language of the northern Nile Valley and the delta. After the Arab invasion of 641, it was gradually replaced by Arabic, the only present-day language of the country. The history of Egyptian can be divided into two main stages, each of which can be further subdivided into three historical phases, which affect primarily the graphic sphere.

Earlier Egyptian. The language of all written texts from 3000 to 1300 B.C., surviving in religious texts until the second century A.D. Its main phases are: **Old Egyptian**, the language of the Old Kingdom and the First Intermediate Period (3000 B.C.–2000 B.C.). Its main documents are the religious corpus of the Pyramid Texts and a sizeable number of autobiographies on the walls of the rock tombs of the administrative elite; **Middle Egyptian**, also termed Classical Egyptian, from the Middle Kingdom to the end of Dyn. XVIII (2000B.C.–1300 B.C.). Middle Egyptian is the classical language of Egyptian literature: historical inscriptions, instructions addressed from a father to a son, narratives relating the adventures of a specific hero, and religious texts; **Late Middle Egyptian**, the language of rituals, mythological inscriptions, and hymns from the late New Kingdom to the end of Egyptian civilization: it maintains the linguistic structures of the classical language, but especially in the Greco-Roman period (fourth century B.C.–third century A.D.), it shows an enormous expansion of its set of hieroglyphic signs.

Later Egyptian. Later Egyptian is documented from Dyn. XIX down to Coptic (1300 B.C.–A.D. 1000). Its main phases are: **Late Egyptian** (1300 B.C.–700 B.C.), the language of written records from the second part of the New Kingdom. It conveys a rich entertainment literature consisting of traditional forms and of new literary genres, such as the mythological tale or love poetry. Late Egyptian was also the vehicle of bureaucracy, archival documents and school texts; **Demotic** (7th century B.C.–5th century A.D.), the language of administration and literature during the Late Period. While grammatically it closely continues Late Egyptian, it differs radically from it in its graphic system; **Coptic** (4th–12th centuries A.D.) the language of Christian Egypt, written in a variant of the GREEK alphabet with six or seven Demotic signs to indicate Egyptian phonemes absent in Greek. As a spoken language, Coptic was superseded by Arabic, but it survives to the present in the liturgy of the Coptic church.

Unless otherwise specified, the following grammatical sketch refers to Earlier Egyptian, more specifically to the language of classical Middle Egyptian literature.

Orthography and Basic Phonology

The language of Ancient Egypt was written in a monumental script and its cursive varieties. The monumental script is known as "Hieroglyphs". These are pictographic signs that represent living beings and objects, such as gods or people, animals,

Table 1: Consonants

		Labial	Apical	Alveo-palatal	Palatal	Velar	Uvular	Pharyngeal	Glottal
Stops	Aspirated	p	t	ṯ	k				
	Voiced/ Glottalized	b	d	ḏ	g	q, ḳ			i, j
Fricatives	Voiceless	f	s	š	ẖ	ḫ		ḥ	h
	Voiced							ʕ	
Nasals		m	n						
Lateral			3, n, r						
Resonants		w	r		y, jj		3		

parts of the human or animal body, plants, stars, buildings, furniture, containers, etc. The number of hieroglyphic signs varied from approximately 1,000 in the Old Kingdom down to about 750 in the classical language, but, following the decline of a centralized school system, it increased to many thousands during the Hellenistic and Roman periods.

In this writing system, phonological and ideographic principles appear combined; a written word consists of a sequence of signs, called "phonograms," which convey a substantial portion of its phonological structure: normally all the consonants, occasionally also the semivocalic phonemes. Each phonogram can express one, two, or three consonants of the language. The sequence of phonograms is usually followed by a "determinative", which indicates iconically the semantic sphere of the word, for example, a sitting god expresses the lexical sphere of "god, divine", a scribe's outfit indicates the semantic realm of "writing", a stylized desert landscape denotes the word as a foreign toponym. Although some words in common use may be written only with phonograms, many items of the basic vocabulary are expressed by hieroglyphic signs that represent, evoke, or symbolize their own meaning; these are called "logograms" or "ideograms": for example, the hieroglyphic sign representing a human head is used to signify the lexeme "head". The use of a hieroglyphic sign as logogram or ideogram is made visually explicit through a vertical stroke following the sign.

As part of its inventory of phonograms, hieroglyphic writing displayed a set of 24 "alphabetic" signs corresponding to the consonantal or semiconsonantal phonemes of Egyptian; in this way, we can obtain an insight into the complete phonological system of the language, the only exception being the consonant /l/, for which a distinct grapheme appears only in Demotic. In spite of the presence of this exact correspondence between monoconsonantal signs and the phoneme inventory, hieroglyphs never developed a genuine alphabetic system. In later periods, especially in Ptolemaic and Roman Egyptian, one can observe the emergence of hitherto unknown signs, of new phonological values for known signs, and of cryptographic solutions.

The hieroglyphic system was used mainly for monumental purposes, more rarely in a cursive form for religious texts in the Middle and the New Kingdom. During the three millennia of their productive use, hieroglyphs developed two manual forms: while Hieratic (2600 B.C.–third century A.D.) represents a direct cursive rendering of individual hieroglyphs (with ligatures and diacritic signs), Demotic (7th century B.C.–5th century A.D.) modifies completely the writing conventions by introducing a simplification of hieratic sign-groups. The hieroglyphic-based system was superseded in Coptic by an alphabet derived from that of Greek, with the addition of six or seven Demotic signs for the indication of phonemes absent from Greek.

The basic orientation of the Egyptian writing system—and the only one used in the cursive varieties—is from right to left; in epigraphic, i.e., monumental texts, this order is often inverted for reasons of symmetry or artistic composition.

The exact phonological value of many Egyptian consonants is obscured by difficulties in establishing reliable Afro-Asiatic correspondences; vocalism and prosody can only be reconstructed by combining the contemporary Akkadian transcriptions of the second millennium B.C. with Greek transcriptions of the Late Period (corresponding roughly to spoken Demotic) and the Coptic evidence of the first millennium A.D. Table 1 above uses the transcriptions of hieroglyphic signs that are generally used by Egyptologists.

The Egyptian phonological system does not include the "emphatic" phonemes common in the Semitic languages. The phoneme conventionally transcribed *3* (*aleph*), originally a uvular trill probably articulated like the FRENCH *r*, corresponds to Afro-Asiatic **r* or **l*. The existence of a phoneme /l/ in Egyptian is well established on the basis of Afro-Asiatic correspondences and of its presence in Coptic; yet, unlike all other consonantal phonemes, /l/ shows no unequivocal graphic rendering, being expressed in different lexemes by *3*, *n*, *r*, or *nr*.

The palatals *ṯ* and *ḏ* were probably affricates /č^{h}/ and /č'/.

While *b* was most likely a voiced bilabial stop, *d*, *ḏ*, *g*, and *q*/*ḳ* were voiceless glottalic /t'/, /č'/, /k'/, and /q'/, respectively.

The voiceless fricatives *ẖ*, *ḫ*, and *ḥ* were palatal /ç/ (as in GERMAN *ich*), velar /x/, and pharyngeal /ħ/, respectively.

During the second millennium BCE, the following sound changes took place: (a) the uvular vibrant /R/ acquired the articulation /ʔ/ (glottal stop); (b) the point of articulation was progressively moved to the front: velar to palatal, palatal to apical; (c) oppositions between fricatives in the palatal region (/š/, /ç/, /x/) tended to be neutralized into /š/; (d) word-final /r/ and /t/ tended to become /ʔ/, then to disappear. During the first millennium B.C., the opposition between *'ayin* /ʕ/ and *aleph* /ʔ/ was also neutralized.

Table 2: Vowels

	Front	Central	Back
High	i		u
Low		a	

The Egyptian vowels could be either long or short.

The original set of vowels underwent a certain number of historical changes. Already during the second millennium B.C., short-stressed /i/ and /u/ merged into /e/, while long /u:/ turned into /e:/. Around 1000 B.C., long /a:/ became /o:/, a phonetic evolution similar to the "Canaanite shift" in nearby Northwest Semitic. There was also a change of the short-stressed /a/ to /o/, but Coptic shows that this affected only a portion of the Egyptian linguistic domain. Egyptian unstressed vowels progressively lost phonological status and became realized as schwa.

Stress. In the classical language, the stress could lie only on the final or penultimate syllable. While both closed and open syllables are found in syllables before the stressed syllable, the only possible structure in syllables following the stress is the closed syllable with short vowel. The stressed vowel of a penultimate open syllable is long; some scholars suggest that word-final stressed syllables were extra long. In addition to final /j/, /w/, /t/, and /r/, unstressed vowels were dropped between 2000 B.C. and 1600 B.C.

Basic Morphology

The basic Egyptian morphological unit is a biliteral or triliteral root, for example *sn* 'brother' or *sḏm* 'to hear', which together with a vocalic and semivocalic pattern, forms a *stem*: **san-*, **sanuw-*, **saḏma-*, **saḏim-*, etc. An unmodified stem may serve as a word, or suffixes may be added to the stem to form a word: **san* 'brother', **sanūwaw* 'brothers', **saḏmaf* 'may he hear', **saḏimnak* 'you heard'.

Nouns are built by adding to the stem the following suffixes, indicating gender and number:

Nouns	Masculine	Feminine
Singular	.Ø, .w	.t
Dual	.wj	.tj
Plural	.Ø, .w, .ww	.t, .jjt, .wt

Although remnants of the Afro-Asiatic case system can be detected in the Egyptian nominal paradigm, the syntactic structure of historical Egyptian was so rigid that cases did not play a productive role in the language.

Adjectives are morphologically and syntactically treated like nouns. Very common is a derivational pattern called *nisbation*, in which a morpheme *-j* is added to a nominal stem, which may be different from the stem of the noun, to form the corresponding adjective: *nṯr* *nāṯar 'god', *nṯrj* *nuṯrij 'divine'.

Egyptian has three sets of pronouns. Independent pronouns are used for the topicalized subject of sentences with nominal or adjectival predicate in the first person (*jnk jtj=k* 'I am your father') and for the focalized subject of cleft sentences: *ntf sʕnḫ rn=j* 'he is the one who makes my name live'; *jnk jny=j sj* 'it is I who shall bring it'. Dependent pronouns are used as the object of a transitive verb (*sḏm=f wj* 'he will hear me'), as the subject of a qualifying nominal sentence (*nfr ṯw ḥnʕ=j* 'you are happy with me'), and of an adverbial sentence (in the first and second persons only after an initial particle): *mk wj m-b3ḥ=k* 'Look, I am in front of you'. Suffix pronouns are used as the subject of verbal forms, as a possessive pronoun, and as the object of prepositions: *ḏj=k r=k n=j ḫ.t=j* 'you shall truly (lit.: to-you) give me (= to-me) my possessions'.

All three sets of pronouns are inflected for person (first, second, third), number (singular, dual, plural), and, in second and third person singular, gender (masculine, feminine).

	Singular	Dual	Plural
Independent			
1st person	jnk		jnn
2nd person, masc	ntk	nttnj	ntṯn
2nd person, fem	ntṯ	ntṯnj	ntṯn
3rd person, masc	ntf	ntsnj	ntsn
3rd person, fem	nts	ntsnj	ntsn
Dependent			
1st person	wj	nj	n
2nd person, masc	ṯw	ṯnj	ṯn
2nd person, fem	ṯn	ṯnj	ṯn
3rd person, masc	sw	snj	sn, st
3rd person, fem	sj, st	snj	sn, st
Suffix			
1st person	=j	=nj	=n
2nd person, masc	=k	=ṯnj	=ṯn
2nd person, fem	=ṯ	=ṯnj	=ṯn
3rd person, masc	=f	=snj	=sn
3rd person, fem	=s	=snj	=sn

The relative pronoun is masc. *ntj*, fem. *nt.t*, pl. *ntj.w* 'who, which, that'. It only refers to specific (i.e., semantically determined) antecedents since, in Egyptian, indefinite antecedents are not resumed by a relative, but by a circumstantial clause:

rmṯ ntj rḫ.n=j sw
man that know-1SG/SUF 3M/SG/DEP 'The man whom I know'

rmṯ rḫ.n=j sw
man know-1SG/SUF 3M/SG/DEP 'A man that I know'

Egyptian also has a relative pronoun that semantically incorporates negation: masc. *jwtj*, fem. *jwt.t*, pl. *jwtj.w* 'who/which/that not'.

Finite verb forms are built by adding a suffix pronoun to the root, either directly or after an infix indicating tense, aspect, or voice features. The most important of these morphemes are as follows:

Suffix	Value	Example	Meaning
.n	past tense	sḏm.n=j	'I heard'
.t	perfective,	n sḏm.t=f	'he has not heard'
	prospective	jw.t=f	'he will come'
.w	prospective, passive	jrj.w=f	'it has/will be done'
.tw	passive	sḏm.tw=k	'you are heard'

Classes of so-called weak verbal roots, whose third radical

is a semiconsonant *j* or *w*, show the reduplication of the second radical and the presence of a stressed vowel between the two consonants; this form, which is conventionally called "emphatic", fulfills the function of pragmatic theme of the sentence in which it appears:

mrr=s wj
love-3F/SG/SUF 1SG/DEP '(the fact that) she loves me'

Egyptian also has a verbal form, variously called Old Perfective, Stative or Pseudoparticiple, which indicates the wide semantic range of verbal "perfectivity", from perfective aspect (with intransitive verbs) to passive voice (with transitive verbs). This form uses a set of suffix pronouns that are etymologically linked to the forms of the Semitic suffix conjugation. Examples: *prj.kw* 'I have come forth', *ḫpr.tj* 'you have become', *rḏj.w* 'it has been given'.

Especially in Later Egyptian, verbal predications can also be expressed by prepositional constructions:

sw ḥr sḏm
3M/SG/DEP on hearing 'He is hearing.'

jw=f r mrj=f
PART-'verily'-3M/SG/SUF toward loving
'He is going to love.'

The most frequent prepositions are *m* 'in, with'; *n* 'to, for'; *r* 'toward'; *mj* 'as, like'; *ḥr* 'on'; *ẖr* 'under'; *ḥnʕ* 'with'; *ḫft* 'according to'; and *ḥntj* 'before'. Particularly noteworthy is the presence of the preposition *ẖr* 'near', whose original meaning (A *ẖr* B 'A is near B') was applied to any situation in which the two participants A and B belong to different hierarchical levels, A being socioculturally higher or lower than B:

sḏd=f ẖr msj.w=f
speak-3M/SG/SUF near child-PL-3M/SG/SUF
'He will speak to his children.'

jm3ḫy ẖr nṯr ʕ3
honored near god great 'honored by the Great God'

Basic Syntax

Egyptian has three sentence types, which are classified according to the syntactic nature of their predicate, the subject being always a nominal phrase:

(a) *Nominal sentences*, in which the predicate is a noun (substantive or adjective). In categorical statements or qualifying adjectival sentences, the normal order of constituents is Predicate-Subject; a demonstrative *pw* 'this' functioning as copula may be inserted between predicate and subject:

nfr mṯn=j
good path-1SG/SUF 'My path is good.'

dmj.t pw jmn.t
town-F/SG COPULA West-F/SG
'The West is a place of residence.'

The order Predicate-(Copula-)Subject is modified into Topic-Comment in identifying sentences, when both subject and predicate are semantically determined or specific:

sn.t=f spd.t
sister-F/SG-3M/SG. Sirius-F/SG 'His sister is Sirius.'

or when the subject is focalized:

jn sn.t=f sʕnḫ rn=f
FOCUS-sister-F/SG-3M/SG/SUF make-live name-3M/SG/SUF
'It is his sister who causes his name to live.'

(b) *Adverbial sentences*, in which the Predicate is an adverbial or prepositional phrase; the order is always Subject-Predicate: *ḥr.t=k m prw=k* (ration-F/PL-2M/SG/SUF in house-2M/SG/SUF) 'Your rations are in your house'.

(c) *Verbal sentences*, in which the Predicate is a verbal phrase; the order is Predicate-Subject(-Complement): *jj.n=j m njw.t=j* (come-PAST-1SG /SUF from city-1SG/SUF) 'I came from my city'.

Prepositional phrases follow the noun or the verb they modify.

The basic Egyptian negative particle is *n*: *n rḫ.n=f* (NEG know-PAST-1SG/SUF) 'He does not know'.

A variant of this morpheme, conventionally transcribed *nn*, is used as predicative negation: *nn m3ʕ.tjw* (NEG trustworthy-PL) 'There are no trustworthy people'.

Contact with Other Languages

Due to Egypt's geographically protected location, Ancient Egyptian does not display in its earlier phase detectable influences from other languages, although the neighboring Semitic, Nubian, Libyan, and also Indo-European languages certainly contributed, both grammatically and lexically, to the development of historical Egyptian. During the New Kingdom (ca. 1500 B.C.–1100 B.C.), contacts with the Asiatic world led to the adoption of a considerable number of especially West Semitic loanwords, many of which remained confined to the scholarly and administrative sphere:

From Hebrew: *ṯpr* 'scribe' (<*sôpēr*); *mrkbt* 'chariot' (Coptic *berecôout*) (<*merkābâ*)
From Mitanni: *mryn* 'chariot-fighter' (<*maryannu*)

In the Late Period, after the seventh century B.C., when the productive written language was Demotic, a limited number of (mostly technical) Greek words entered the Egyptian domain: *gʕwmʕ* < *kauma* 'fever', *wynn* < *hoi Iōnes* 'the Ionians', i.e., the Greeks.

Common Words

(The forms in the third column are reconstructed pronunciations.)

man:	rmṯ	*rāmaṯ
woman:	ḥjm.t	*ḥijmat
water:	mw	*maw

sun:	rʕw	*rīʕuw
three:	ḫmtw	*ḫamtaw
fish:	rmw	
tree:	ḫt	*ḫit
long:	3w	
small:	šrj	*šūrij
yes:	tj	*tij
no:	m-bj3t	
good:	nfr	*nāfir
bird:	3pd	*3āpid
dog:	ṯzm	

Example Sentences

(1) ḥr-ntt ntk jtj n nmḥw h3j
on-that 2M/SG/INDEP father to orphan husband

n ẖ3r.t.
to widow-F
'For you are a father to the orphan, a husband to the widow.'

(2) gmj.n=j ḥf3w pw jw=f m
find-PAST-1SG/SUF snake it situation-3M/SG/SUF in

jj.t.
come-INFINITIVE
'I found that it was a snake coming.'

(3) h3b n=f jm
send-IMPERATIVE to-3M/SG/SUF give-IMPERATIVE

rḫ=f rn=k.
know-3M/SG/SUF name-2M/SG/SUF
'Send (a message) to him! Let him know your name!'

Efforts to Preserve, Protect, and Promote the Language

With the Christianization of Egypt, knowledge of Ancient Egyptian was lost for 15 centuries. After the first decipherment by Jean-François Champollion in the 1820s on the basis of a trilingual text (the Rosetta Stone in hieroglyphs, Demotic, and Greek), a solid understanding of morphology and basic syntax was reached by the end of the 19th century (the Berlin school of A. Erman and K. Sethe, whose achievements were standardized in A.H. Gardiner's *Egyptian Grammar*). The reconstruction of the lexicon reached its apex in the 1920s with the *Wörterbuch* of A. Erman and H. Grapow, whereas in the latter portion of our century research has mostly concentrated on syntax (H.J. Polotsky and his followers). The nature of hieroglyphic writing and the limited amount of bilingual material, however, doom our understanding of Egyptian phonology to remain very tentative.

Select Bibliography

Allen, James P. 1984. *The Inflection of the Verb in the Pyramid Texts.* Bibliotheca Aegyptia 2. Malibu: Undena.

Černý, Jaroslav, and Sarah I. Groll. 1984. *A Late Egyptian Grammar.* 3rd edition. Studia Pohl Series Maior 4. Rome: Pontifical Biblical Institute.

Erman, Adolf, and Hermann Grapow. 1925–71. *Wörterbuch der ägyptischen Sprache.* 7 vols. Berlin: Akademie-Verlag.

Faulkner, Raymond O. 1962. *A Concise Dictionary of Middle Egyptian.* Oxford: Oxford University Press.

Gardiner, Sir Alan H. 1957. *Egyptian Grammar, Being an Introduction to the Study of Hieroglyphs.* 3rd edition. Oxford: Clarendon Press.

Hannig, Rainer H.G. 1995. *Großes Handwörterbuch Ägyptisch-Deutsch: die Sprache der Pharaonen (2800–950 v. Chr.).* Kulturgeschichte der Antiken Welt 64. Mainz: Philipp von Zabern.

Johnson, Janet H. 1976. *The Demotic Verbal System.* Studies in Ancient Oriental Civilization 38. Chicago: Oriental Institute.

Loprieno, Antonio. 1995. *Ancient Egyptian. A Linguistic Introduction.* Cambridge: Cambridge University Press.

Osing, Jürgen. 1976. *Die Nominalbildung des Ägyptischen.* 2 vols. Mainz: Philipp von Zabern.

Peust, Carsten. 1999. *Egyptian Phonology.* Monographien zur Ägyptischen Sprache 2. Göttingen: Peust & Gutschmidt.

Polotsky, Hans-Jacob. 1971. *Collected Papers.* Jerusalem: Magnes Press.

____. 1976. "Les transpositions du verbe en égyptien classique." In *Israel Oriental Studies*, 6: 1–50.

Schenkel, Wolfgang. 1990. *Einführung in die altägyptische Sprachwissenschaft.* Darmstadt: Wissenschaftliche Buchgesellschaft.

English

Jon Erickson

Language Name and Autonym: English.

Location: Spoken as a first language primarily in Great Britain and Ireland, the United States, Canada, Australia, New Zealand, and South Africa. As a second language, English is used worldwide. In over 70 countries, including Ghana, Nigeria, India, and Singapore, English has the status of an official language, where it may be used in administration, the courts, the media, and in education.

Family: Low German subgroup of West Germanic. The West Germanic languages constitute a subgroup of Germanic, a branch of Indo-European.

Related Languages: English is most closely related to the other Low German languages—DUTCH, Frisian, and Low German (*Plattdeutsch*)—and then to High German. It is less closely related to the North Germanic languages (DANISH, NORWEGIAN, SWEDISH, and Icelandic).

Dialects: English shows substantial geographic variation, whereby a speaker can be identified as speaking, for example, British, American, or Australian English. Within each English-speaking nation, there are traditional regional differences involving phonology, vocabulary, and grammar. For example, in England, northern speakers pronounce words such as "luck" and "hub" with the same vowel sound as in "look" and "good", while southern speakers pronounce the two sets of words with different vowel sounds. In the United States, speakers from cities along the eastern seaboard tend to pronounce *r* as a consonant only when it precedes a vowel, while inland speakers pronounce *r* wherever in a word it occurs. Superimposed upon such regional variations are the norms of what is considered in each English-speaking country to be the standard language. Standard English shows a high degree of similarity from region to region in grammar and vocabulary, and varies mainly on the basis of pronunciation. The standard language is the variety normally used in writing.

Number of Speakers: The number of people who speak English as a first language has been estimated at over 337 million, with an additional 235 million speaking it as a second language.

Origin and History

English developed from the speech of Low German speakers who migrated to Britain from what is now southern Jutland (Denmark) and northern Germany after the middle of the fifth century (the traditional date is after 449). These Low German peoples are traditionally said to have been comprised of Angles, Saxons, and Jutes. The Low German of Britain came to be designated "English" (the language of the Angles). English is attested in names from the seventh century, and literary remains are attested from somewhat before 750. The language of texts from the earliest period to the end of the 11th century is designated **Old English** (earlier, Anglo-Saxon). On the basis of textual evidence Old English is said to have existed in four regional dialects: Kentish, Northumbrian, Mercian, and West Saxon. The vast majority of Old English texts are written in a standardized West Saxon orthography that was used in the monasterial scriptoria. Old English has grammatical gender (masculine, feminine, and neuter), and nouns may show two numbers—singular vs. plural—and four grammatical cases: nominative, accusative, genitive, and dative. Adjectives and determiners show agreement with the noun in gender, number, and case, as can be seen in the following noun phrase 'the old man':

Singular		Plural
sē ealda mann	NOM	þā ealdan menn
þone ealdan mann	ACC	þā ealdan menn
þæs ealdan mannes	GEN	þara ealdra manna
þǣm ealdan menn	DAT	þǣm ealdum mannum

Verbs are inflected for two tenses: past and nonpast, in singular and plural, whereby the singular distinguishes three persons. As in modern GERMAN, dependent clauses are verb final, main clauses are verb second with topic in the first position:

sē mann sægde þǣm cyninge þæt spell.
'the man told the king the story'

but:

þæt spell sægde sē mann þǣm cyninge
'The story told the man (to) the king.'
þǣm cyninge sægde sē mann þæt spell
'(to) the king the man told the story.'

Questions are formed by inversion as in German.

At the time of the Norman Conquest (1066), the English ruling dynasty was replaced by a Norman French dynasty. Over the next century the West Saxon orthography was replaced by an orthography based on the French model. The language rep-

Table 1: Consonants

		Labial	Interdental	Alveolar	Palatal	Velar	Glottal
Stops	Voiceless	p		t		c, k, ck [k]	
	Voiced	b		d		g	
Fricatives	Voiceless	f, ph [f]	th [θ]	s	sh [ʃ]		h
	Voiced	v	th [ð]	z	g(e), s [ʒ]		
Affricates	Voiceless				ch [tʃ]		
	Voiced				j, dg(e) [dʒ]		
Nasals		m		n	ng [ŋ]		
Lateral				l			
Approximants		w		r [ɹ]	y [j]		

resented in texts, referred to as **Middle English**, shows substantial differences from Old English. Middle English occupies the period from approximately 1100–1500. Early in this period, noun gender disappeared and nominal inflection was virtually reduced to the system in Modern English: singular vs. plural, with secondary genitive marker. "The" was generalized as the definite article: *the old(e) man*. The loss of case marking and agreement also fostered the development of the subject/verb/object order characteristic of Modern English. The texts of the period allow for the distinction of three primary Middle English dialect areas: Northern, Midland (East v. West), and Southern. It was the Middle English East Midland dialect (specifically, of London) that came to be the model for what is now designated standard English.

The subsequent periods in the development of English are designated **Early Modern English** (1500–1650) and **Modern** or **New English** (1650–present). Early Modern English saw the results of what is called the Great Vowel Shift and the generalization of the use of the auxiliary *do* for the formation of negatives and questions in constructions lacking modal or primary auxiliary. The Great Vowel Shift affected the earlier long vowels of English, diphthongizing the high vowels and successively raising mid and low vowels:

ME	MdE	ME	MdE
wyf /wi:f/	wife /waɪf/	hous /hu:s/	house /haʊs/
see /se:/	see /si/	to /to:/	too /tu/
see /sæ:/	sea /si/	hoom /hɔ:m/	home /hom/

The raised /æ:/ subsequently raised again and merged with /i/. Modern English standard orthography represents pre-vowel shift English.

From the 16th century on, English was carried to North America, South America, South Africa, Australia, and other areas, in conjunction with British colonial expansion.

Orthography and Basic Phonology

A Roman-type alphabet has been used to represent English since the seventh century, when it was introduced in conjunction with the Christianization of Britain. The English alphabet has 26 symbols: a, b, c, d, e, f, g, h, i, j, k, l, m, n, o, p, q, r, s, t, u, v, w, x, y, z. The language is written from left to right, with word boundaries indicated by spaces; each symbol has two forms, one occurring at the beginning of a sentence or at the beginning of a name, and the other elsewhere. Each word has a standard orthographic representation (spelling), although very minor variation exists between British and American English (for example, British *grey*, *honour*, *realisation* vs. American *gray*, *honor*, *realization*). The American spellings largely date from the spelling reforms advocated by Noah Webster in the late 18th century as part of his efforts to foster the development of a distinctively American language.

The consonantal system indicated in Table 1 is reflected in all major varieties of English. The vowel system may vary from one major variety to another. Table 2 on the next page represents the system of standard British.

With the exception of /h/, which occurs only at the beginning of a syllable (prevocalic, before /j/, and, in some dialects, before /w/), the obstruents (stops, fricatives, and affricates) are paired for voice. The dental pair /θ/:/ð/ carries a very light contrastive load; both dental fricatives are represented orthographically <th>. Word initially, /ð/ occurs only in function words (e.g, *their*, *this*); medially and finally there are diminishingly few minimal pairs (e.g., *ether*/*either*, *wreath*/*wreathe*). The palatal fricative /ʒ/ has a restricted distribution. It appears initially and finally only in French borrowings (e.g., *genre*, *garage*), where it competes with /dʒ/, and is generally represented <g(e)>. In medial position, there are a few contrastive pairs of the sort *pleasure*/*pressure* (/ʒ/:/ʃ/) and, for some dialects, *major*/*measure* (/dʒ/:/ʒ/); in this position, /ʒ/ is generally spelled <s>. The sonorants (nasals, lateral, and approximants) are all voiced. The velar nasal /ŋ/ occurs only post-vocalically and typically before a velar stop (*single*, *sinker*). It occurs without a following velar stop only at the end of a word (*sing*) or before a derivational affix (*singer*).

The representation of some consonants may vary according to the etymological subset of the vocabulary that a word belongs to; for example, /f/ is normally represented <f>, but, in words of Greek derivation, such as *telephone*, it is represented <ph>. In other instances, the representation of a consonant varies according to the environment in which it occurs in a word; /k/ is spelled <c> in *call*, <k> in *kill*, and <ck> in *back*.

Table 2: Vowels

	Front		Central		Back	
	Tense	Lax	Tense	Lax	Tense	Lax
High	i	ɪ			u	ʊ
High Mid	e	ɛ	ɜ	ə	o	ʌ
Low Mid					ɔ	ɒ
Low		æ			ɑ	

The basic vowel pattern for English is traditionally said to contrast a set of "short" vowels and a set of "long" vowels. The distinction essentially involves *tension*, where short vowels are lax and long vowels tense.

With the exception of /ɑ/, back vowels are rounded; rounding distinguishes the tense vowels /ɔ/ and /ɑ/. The mid-tense vowels tend to be pronounced with offglides: /e/ [eɪ], /o/ [oʊ] or [əʊ], depending on dialect. Of the two schwa-type vowels, /ɜ/ occurs only before /r/, in words like *burr*, *bird*, *her*. The shorter /ə/ occurs only in unaccented syllables, often alternating morphophonemically with a corresponding stressed vowel (e.g., *telegraph* /tέləgræf/, *telegraphy* /təlέgrəfi/).

English has three diphthongs: /aɪ/, /aʊ/, /ɔɪ/. In non-rhotic dialects—dialects in which /r/ is realized as [r] only before a following vowel—sequences corresponding to /ɪr/, /ɛr/, /ʊr/ will be realized as centering diphthongs [ɪə], [ɛə], [ʊə] (e.g., *scary* [skɛri] vs. *scarse* [skɛəs]).

The actual realization of the basic vowel pattern may vary from dialect to dialect, and contrasts may be missing. For instance, the British English three-way contrast /ɔ/:/ɑ/:/ɒ/ is reduced in American English to /ɔ/ : /ɑ/; in Canadian English and in some varieties of American English, only /ɑ/ is used.

The English vowels and diphthongs are represented orthographically using the vowel symbols *a*, *e*, *i (y)*, *o*, *u* and combinations of these symbols with each other or with *w* or *y*. Each vowel symbol may represent either of two vowel phonemes depending on the structure of the syllable in which it occurs. For instance, <a> in a closed syllable will represent the short vowel /æ/, as in *pat*; in an open syllable it represents /e/, as in *paper* (*pa.per*). A similar pattern occurs with <i> as well: in a closed syllable it represents /ɪ/ as in *big*, and, in an open syllable, the diphthong /aɪ/ as in *tiger* (*ti.ger*). Since it is also possible for lax vowels to occur in open syllables and for tense vowels to occur in closed syllables, an open syllable may be closed orthographically by doubling the postvocalic consonant, as in *hitting*, or a closed syllable may be opened orthographically by using a "silent" <e>, as in *mete*; in earlier stages of English, this <e> was pronounced as a separate syllable, so *mete* was a two-syllable word. In addition to the use of silent <e>, a tense vowel in a closed syllable may be represented by a combination of vowel symbols, as in *meet* or *meat*. The diphthongs /aʊ/ and /ɔɪ/ are typically represented by <ou>/<ow> (*house*, *cow*) and <oi>/<oy> (*boil*, *boy*) respectively.

The orthographic representation is morphological insofar as morphophonemic variation in derivation bases is generally not indicated, e.g., *educate*/*education* (/έdʒəket/, /ɛdʒəkéʃn). Predictable variation in affixes is also ignored, as, for example, the past tense marker *-ed* in *wanted* (/əd/), *asked* (/t/), *opened* (/d/). Monosyllabic homophones, on the other hand, are generally not also homographs, as can be seen in the examples above: *mete*, *meat*, *meet* (all /mit/). Since each word has a characteristic representation, the spellings are not, however, interchangeable.

Basic Morphology

Nouns in English have no grammatical gender. Most nouns may appear as singular or plural (e.g., *book*, *books*). Possessor NPs may occur with a genitive marker, homophonous with the normal plural marker but marked orthographically with an apostrophe (e.g., *Bill's books*). The genitive marker differs from noun inflection like the plural in that it can be attached to a phrase rather than only to a single noun (e.g., *the neighbor down the road's dog*).

English personal pronouns are marked for number (singular, plural), person (first, second, third), and, in the third-person singular, for gender (masculine, feminine, neuter). Pronouns also show distinctions of case (nominative, objective, and genitive), according to their syntactic position: nominative forms appear as the subjects of finite clauses, genitive forms as nominal modifiers, and objective forms as verbal and prepositional objects and as the subjects of non-finite clauses.

She (3SG/FEM/NOM) saw him (3SG/MASC/OBJ).
He (3SG/MASC/NOM) gave a book to her (3SG/FEM/OBJ).
Their (3PL/GEN) car is in the garage.

Pronouns that are marked for gender reflect biological gender only: *he*/*him*/*his* refer only to male beings, and *she*/*her*/*her* only to female beings; in both cases, reference is generally to humans only. Sexless references require *it*/*it*/*its*, which are also used by most speakers for non-human animates: *Where's the dog? It's on the porch.*

Verbs may be marked for tense (past or non-past). The typical indication of past tense is the marker *-ed*; in the non-past, the third person singular is marked by *-s*; otherwise the base form is used. The base form is also found in the imperative (e.g., *Sit!*). There are three non-finite forms of the verb: the base form as infinitive, a first participle marked with *-ing*, and a second participle generally marked with *-ed* and thus homophonous with the past. Thus there are potentially five forms of any verb: *open, opens, opened, opening, opened.* The various non-finite forms may combine with auxiliary verbs to form complex verbal expressions: (e.g., *will sleep*, *is sleeping*, *was sleeping*, *had slept*, *will have slept*, *will have been sleeping*).

The adjective may appear in the comparative (*-er*) or superlative (*-est*): *big*, *bigger*, *biggest*. This paradigm is limited to adjectives of one or two syllables. For many speakers, only those two-syllable adjectives where the second syllable, such as *pretty* or *shallow*, are inflected. Other two-syllable adjectives and those adjectives with three or more syllables can only be compared periphrastically, with *more* or *most*: *basic*, *more basic*, *most basic*.

The English lexicon includes both single-morpheme root words and morphologically complex words. The complex words are the result either of derivation or of compounding. Derivation may involve either suffixation or prefixation; in both cases, the result is a new word. English complex words are right-headed, so that the complex word's category is determined by the entity on the right. In the case of suffixation, the suffix selects a base that it can be added to, and the derived word has the category of the affix. Thus, the noun affix *-er* is added to a verb and produces a noun: *open, opener*; and the noun affix *-ness* is added to an adjective to produce a noun: *light, lightness*. Suffixes vary in terms of productivity, that is in terms of the relative size of the sets of words they relate, and in terms of the meaning transparency of the derived form. The affix *-ness* may be used to form the abstract noun of virtually any adjective, e.g., *active, activeness*, with the latter referring to the state or quality of being active, whereas a comparable noun suffix *-ity* can only be added to Latinate adjectives, and the resultant meaning is more idiosyncratic, e.g., *active, activity*, with the latter having the more concrete and specific meaning of something that one does.

Prefixes in English also select particular bases, but are modifiers only; they do not change the word class of the derived word. Thus, the prefix *re-* is added to verb bases and produces a repetitive verb: *paint, repaint*; a prefix *un-* selects adjective bases and produces a negative adjective: *fair, unfair*.

Compounds may be formed by uniting two words, with the result having a single main stress: compare *bláckbòard* with *bláck bóard*. The word class of the compound is determined by the class of the last element: *headstrong*, formed from the noun *head* and the adjective *strong* is, itself, an adjective.

Basic Syntax

In terms of the order of major sentence constituents, English is typically Subject-Verb-Object, where the subject position must be filled. Predication in English requires the use of a noun phrase subject and a verb phrase predicate. The predicate may include an auxiliary indicating finiteness, tense and subject agreement. In the following examples, the auxiliary appears in italics.

Bill *might* open the window.
Bill *has* opened the window.
Bill *was* opening the window.
Mary wanted Bill *to* open the window.

The negative is indicated by the particle *not*, which either occurs at the beginning of the verb phrase (following any auxiliary) or is cliticized as *n't* onto the preceding auxiliary.

Bill could *not* open the window.
Bill could*n't* open the window.

If there is no overt auxiliary in the non-negative, the auxiliary *do* must appear in the negative: Bill didn't open the window.

In questions, the auxiliary appears before rather than after the subject: Bill can open the window. > Can Bill open the window?; Bill has opened the window. > Has Bill opened the window? Where no overt auxiliary appears in the non-question, a form of *do* must appear in the question: Bill opened the window. > Did Bill open the window?

Constituent questions involve the use of special interrogative words—*who, what, when, where, why, how*—which are placed before the inverted auxiliary: Bill opened the window. > What did Bill open?; Bill gave it to you. > Who did Bill give it to?

Contact with Other Languages

English speakers have had contact with all of the major languages of Europe, with French and LATIN contributing the most words. Borrowing into English took place in the Old English period subsequent to the Christianization of the British Isles with the importation of vocabulary from Latin (or from Greek via Latin). Examples of words borrowed in this period include *apostle, circle, demon, paper*. In the later Old English period, extensive borrowing took place from the Scandinavian languages as a result of Norse settlements in Britain. These borrowings, e.g., *skin, shorts, kick, give, window*, have been completely integrated into the English vocabulary. After the Norman Conquest (1066) there was a large influx of words from Norman French in such areas as government and social organization. Examples include *parliament, state, country, court, crime, army*. In the later medieval period, extensive borrowing again took place from French, this time from Parisian French, as a result of the large French cultural influence in the Europe of the 13th and 14th centuries. These words include the large number of abstract terms ending in *-ance, -ant, -ence, -ity, -ment, -ion*. The early modern and modern English periods show extensive borrowing from Latin (and from Greek either directly or by way of Latin). During the century after 1500, for example, the following words were imported into English: *compensate, lapse, medium, notorious, ultimate, vindicate*. The modern period has also seen borrowing from French for general cultural vocabulary (*liaison, plateau, revue, souvenir, vignette*) and from various other, mainly European, languages, including ITALIAN (examples include musical vocabulary such as *piano, concerto, cadenza*). Most borrowings are fully integrated into the English lexicon, although the degree to which recent borrowings from French are fully anglicized in pronunciation is partially speaker dependent. In the course of its global expansion, English has also taken over designations for places and geographical features—e.g., *Chicago, Texas*, and *Mississippi* (from Native American languages) and for local flora and fauna and cultural artifacts as in *bamboo, mangrove* (from Pacific Island languages), *kangaroo, budgerigar* (from Australian Aboriginal languages), and *mocassin, toboggan* (from Native American languages). Many terms have also been taken over—first into American English—from New World Spanish: *adobe, bronco, canyon, lasso, mesa, patio*.

Efforts to Preserve, Protect, and Promote the Language

In the 18th century there was interest in England in the establishment of an English academy for the official regulation of the language, although no such institution ever evolved. In the late 18th century, American Noah Webster presented the case for the development of a distinctively American language, the main result of which was the fostering of the American spelling conventions institutionalized in his dictionary of English. The codification of what has come to be seen as standard English results from the establishment of the standard dictionaries and grammars of the language, and the standard orthography is essentially that which has been used since the late medieval period. The learning of English was fostered by British and American colonial policy, and in some now independent former colonies it remains the medium of instruction in schools, for example, in Nigeria and the Philippines. In recent years, British and American government organizations like the British Council and the U.S. Information Services (USIS) have encouraged the use of English as a second language around the world.

Select Bibliography

Bauer, Laurie. 1983. *English Word Formation.* Cambridge: Cambridge University Press.

Brown, Lesley, ed. 1993. *The New Shorter Oxford English Dictionary on Historical Principles.* Oxford: Clarendon Press.

Crystal, David. 1997. *English as a Global Language.* Cambridge: Cambridge University Press.

Giegerich, Heinz J. 1993. *English Phonology. An Introduction.* Cambridge: Cambridge University Press.

Görlach, Manfred. 1997. *The Linguistic History of English. An Introduction.* Basingstoke, Hants: Macmillan.

Hogg, Richard, ed. 1992–1997. *The Cambridge History of the English Language.* 6 vols. Cambridge: Cambridge University Press.

Huddleston, Rodney. 1984. *Introduction to the Grammar of English.* Cambridge: Cambridge University Press.

McArthur, Tom, ed. 1992. *The Oxford Companion to the English Language.* Oxford: Oxford University Press.

Pyles, Thomas, and John Algeo. 1993. *The Origins and Development of the English Language,* 4th ed. Fort Worth: Harcourt Brace Jovanovich.

Quirk, Randolph, Sidney Greenbaum, Geoffrey Leech, and Jan Svartvik. 1985. *A Comprehensive Grammar of the English Language.* London and New York: Longman.

Trudgill, Peter. 1983a. *On Dialect. Social and Geographical Perspectives.* Oxford: Blackwell.

____ 1983b. *Sociolinguistics. An Introduction to Language and Society.* Harmondsworth: Penguin.

Venezky, Richard L. 1970. *The Structure of English Orthography.* The Hague: Mouton.

ETRUSCAN

Larissa Bonfante

Language Name: Etruscan.

Location: Etruscan was spoken in Etruria, an ancient district in present-day central Italy, which comprised Tuscany and northern Latium, between the Tiber and the Arno Rivers, as well as beyond, to the Po Valley in the north and Campania to the south.

Family: None known (non-Indo-European).

Related Languages: None. Etruscan had no genetic connection with any other language of the world known to us today. In Italy, where it was spoken for at least 1,000 years, it had cultural connections with LATIN, Italic (Osco-Umbrian), and GREEK, and it absorbed numerous words from these other languages. These languages may even have had a morphological influence on Etruscan. But a common origin is out of the question.

Dialects: Small differences between northern and southern areas.

Origin and History

The Etruscan people arose in what is now central Italy from a local Bronze Age population (dated archaeologically to about 1300 B.C.). At the height of its power between the seventh and the fourth centuries B.C. there were about 15 thriving Etruscan city-states. The Etruscan civilization survived until the end of the Roman Republic, or about 100 B.C.

The Etruscans called themselves *Rasna*. The Greeks called them *Tyrrhenoi* and the Romans called them *Tusci*. The origin of the language is unknown. Ancient authors claimed the Etruscans were a colony from Lydia in Asia Minor. Scholars today deny this; there is no relationship of the language to Lydian, and archaeological evidence shows clear continuity between the prehistoric populations and the Etruscans in every major Etruscan city.

The Etruscan language must then have been spoken from at least the 10th century B.C. in Italy in the area where Etruscan texts have been found.

There are about 13,000 inscriptions written in Etruscan, ranging in time from the seventh to the first century B.C. About 75 inscriptions date from the seventh century, a respectable quantity when compared to the Greek inscriptions from this period. Some 200 words are understood. In addition, many personal and divine names are known.

There is no extant Etruscan literature, although from Roman tradition, confirmed by archaeological and linguistic evidence, we know they had a rich religious literature. There is archaeological evidence that drama was performed, implying that there was a body of dramatic literature although none has been discovered (Bonfante and Bonfante 1983: 9).

Orthography and Basic Phonology

Etruscan does not have to be deciphered. Nor is there any spelling problem, since Etruscan writing is phonetic. Changes in pronunciation, during the approximately seven centuries when Etruscan was spoken and written, were regularly reflected in the spelling (so when *ai* became *ei*, and eventually *e*, it was spelled the way it was pronounced: *Aivas > Eivas > Evas.*

Like archaic Greek, archaic Etruscan was written right to left, left to right, or boustrophedon; but it settled down in a right-to-left direction, like PHOENICIAN and other Semitic languages. The Etruscan alphabet was adopted from the Euboean Greek script of 26 letters, probably from the Greek settlers at Pithecoussai (Ischia), but it was adapted to the Etruscan language.

Table 1: Consonants

	Labial	Dental	Palatal	Velar	Glottal
Stops					
Voiceless	p	t		c	
Aspirated	ph	th		kh	
Fricatives					
Voiceless	f	s	ś		h
Voiced					
Affricate		z			
Resonants	v	r, l			

Consonants are arranged in Table 1 according to the traditional transliterations used by scholars working on Etruscan. In addition to these consonants, early Etruscan inscriptions used two additional letters, traditionally transliterated *q* and *š*.

Z represents a voiceless dental affricate [ts].

Table 2: Vowels

	Front	Central	Back
High	i		u
Mid	e		
Low		a	

Etruscan did not use a distinct symbol for the vowel sound /o/, representing /o/ in Greek borrowings with *u*. Some scholars believe that Etruscan did, indeed, distinguish /o/ from /u/ in pronunciation, but there is no written indication of such a distinction.

Around 500 B.C., Etruscan developed a strong stress accent (at approximately the same time, Latin did as well). As a result, some vowels were deleted: For example, the name *Klutaimestra* (borrowed from Greek *Klytaiméstra*) became *Clutumusta*, and then *Clutmsta*. In this form, the second syllable is *tm*; that is, as in the English word "rhythm", [m] is a syllabic consonant.

Basic Morphology

Because of the limited size of the Etruscan corpus, many aspects of Etruscan grammar are poorly understood.

Etruscan nouns were inflected for number and case, but not gender. Plural nouns are marked with the suffix *-ar/-er/-ur* following the noun stem. The various forms of the noun *methlum* 'nation' are:

	Singular	Plural
Nominative	methlum	methlumer
Accusative	methlum	methlumer
Genitive	methlumeś	methlumerś
Dative	methlumi	
Locative	methlumthi	methlumerthi

There are variant forms of many of these endings; this apparent variability may reflect our incomplete knowledge of the language.

No Etruscan personal pronouns are known, except for the first-person singular nominative *mi* and accusative *mini*.

Unlike common nouns, personal names in Etruscan indicate gender: masculine names end in consonants or *-e*, while feminine names generally end in *-a* or *-i*. For example, the Greek name of one of the Fates, Atropos, appears in Etruscan as *athrpa*. The Fates were all female.

Because Etruscan is known primarily from inscriptions, our understanding of its verbal system is limited. For instance, virtually all known Etruscan verbs appear in the third person. As far as can be determined from the inscriptions, present tense verbs either have no ending or end in *-a*, as *tva* 'shows'. Past tense verbs end in *-ce* or *-ke*: *turuce* 'gave', *urthanike* 'made'. Future tense verbs end in *-ne*: *turune* 'will give'. In addition, there are some forms ending in *-che* that appear to be the first person singular passive verbs in the past tense: *menache* 'I was offered'.

Etruscan also appears to have had a range of participles, including the passive participle: *mul-u* 'offered', *ces-u* 'lying', *tur-u* 'given'; the active participle: *sval-thas* 'having lived', *zilachn-thas* 'having been praetor'; and another active participle: *sval-as* 'living', *ar-as* 'making, doing'.

Basic Syntax

Etruscan inscriptions tend to use set phrases according to the type of inscription (votive, funerary, etc.). Typically, the word order is SOV; however, if the object is a pronoun (as in Example Sentence 1), the order is OVS.

Within noun phrases, genitives (possessives) precede the nouns they modify: *tin-as clinii-ar-as* (Jupiter-GEN son-pl-DAT) 'Jupiter's sons'. Likewise, demonstrative adjectives precede their head nouns: *cal-ti śuthi-ti* (this-LOC tomb-LOC) 'in this tomb'.

Contact with Other Languages

There was a strong influence from Greek in Etruscan. The Etruscans' material and religious life changed radically from the eighth century B.C. on because of their contact with the Greeks. Greek gods, myths, ideas, and customs invaded the Etruscan world and their language to such an extent that it is not always easy to distinguish what is really Etruscan from the Greek. The demon *Tuchulcha* and his name are both authentically Etruscan. Many gods, however, have Etruscan names that are used to identify Greek gods—Zeus becomes *Tinia*, Aphrodite becomes *Turan*.

In addition, the Etruscans borrowed words for ordinary things from Greek, Umbrian, and Latin.

From Greek: *qutun* 'jug' (< Greek *kōthōn*), *culichna* 'cup with handles' (< Greek *kýlix*)
From Umbrian: *etera* 'client, stranger', *cletram* 'basket', *tuthi* 'city, community'
From Latin: *fanu* 'sacred place, sanctuary', *tura* 'incense', *cupe* 'cup', *macstre* 'master' (< Latin *magister*), *nefts* 'grandson' (< Latin *nepōs*), *-c* 'and' (< Latin *que*)

Common Words

gods:	aisar	wife:	puia
wine:	vinum	sun:	usil
three:	ci	father:	apa
mother:	ati	son:	clan
daughter:	sech, sec [both spellings are found]		

Example Sentences

(1) tn turu-ce vel sveitus.
this-ACC give-PAST Vel Sveitus
'Vel Sveitus gave this.'

(2) laris aule laris-al clen-ar sval
Laris:NOM Aulus:NOM Laris-GEN son-PL.NOM living

cn suthi cerichun-ce.
this:ACC tomb:ACC make-PAST
'Laris and Aulus, sons of Laris, while living made this tomb.'

(3) apa-c ati-c sanisva thui ces-u.
father-and mother-and deceased here lie-PAST PART
'Both father and mother, deceased, lie here.'

Efforts to Preserve, Protect, and Promote the Language

Since Etruscan is a dead language, there are no efforts to preserve or promote it, although scholars have been studying it and making progress in understanding and translating it.

Select Bibliography

Bonfante, Giuliano, and Larissa Bonfante. 1983. *The Etruscan Language: An Introduction*. Manchester, New York: Manchester University Press. Revised edition forthcoming.

Bonfante, Larissa. 1990. *Reading the Past. Etruscan*. London and Berkeley: British Museum Publications.

Corpus Inscriptionum Etruscarum (CIE). 1987. Begun in 1893 by Pauli. Latest volume is M. Cristofani, *CIE*, III, 2. Florence: Centro di Studio per l'Archeologia Etrusco-Italica del CNR.

Pallottino, M. with M. Pandolfini Angeletti, C. de Simone, M. Cristofani and A. Morandi, eds. 1978. *Thesaurus Linguae Etruscae*. Edited by Rome: Consiglio nazionale delle ricerche.

Pallottino, Massimo. 1968. *Testimonia Linguae Etruscae (TLE). 2d ed.* Florence: La nuova Italia editrice.

Pfiffig, A.J. 1969. *Die Etruskische Sprache*. Graz: Akademische Druck und Verlagsanstalt.

Ewe

Felix K. Ameka

Language Name: Ewe or Ewegbe, written in the indigenous orthography as E*v*e or E*v*egbe. It is pronounced depending on one's dialect as əβə or ɛβɛ or eβe.

Location: The Ewe homeland occupies the area between River Volta in Ghana as far as and just across the Togo-Benin border and from the Atlantic coast to about 7°N. There are Ewe communities outside this area in Ghana and elsewhere in West Africa as well as in Europe and America.

Family: Kwa branch of the Niger Congo family.

Related Languages: Ewe is, in fact, a major dialect cluster of the language cluster that has come to be known as Gbe or Tadoid (Capo 1991). The other major members of the Gbe cluster that are the closest relatives of Ewe are Gen (spoken in Togo and Benin), Aja (spoken in Togo and Benin) and Fon (spoken in Benin and southwestern Nigeria). The ethnonym "Ewe" used to be applied to both Ewe proper and to the Gbe language cluster. (The name Gbe for the cluster is derived from the word for "language" in each of these dialect clusters. It can be adjoined to each of the terms as in Fongbe, Ajagbe, Gengbe or Ewegbe). Other non-Gbe relatives of Ewe are Ga-Dangme, AKAN, (both Kwa languges and spoken in Ghana) and YORUBA (a Benue-Congo language spoken in Togo, Benin and Nigeria). Ewe is also related to the Ghana-Togo Mountains or Togo Restsprachen, which are classified as Kwa. Some of these languages, e.g., Akpafu, Lolobi, Likpe, and Avatime, border on the Ewe-speaking area. Ewe is also used as a second language in some of the Ghana-Togo Mountains languages communities.

Dialects: The distinguishing feature for all Ewe dialects as opposed to other Gbe dialects is the bilabial fricatives *f* [ɸ] and *v* [β]. However, as is the case with many languages the speech in every group of villages differs from the speech of the neighboring villages. For instance there are distinct differences between the dialect spoken in Anfoega—120 km north of Accra and Kpando, which is only 10 km away from Anfoega. Similarly the speech of Sovie, which lies between them and is 7 km from Anfoega and 3 km from Kpando, is distinct from the speech of these two places. Thus the Kpando Ewes say *mbéxĩ́* 'I say' while the Anfoega say *mebaaxe* 'I say'. In the Peki dialect, which is some 30 km from Anfoega one hears *mbalólo* 'I say'. Thus individual groups of villages that constitute local government traditional areas can each be thought of as having their own dialects, which can, in turn, be made up of subdialects. Some of the dialects that correspond to groups of villages are: Aŋlɔ, Avenɔ, Tɔŋú, Waci [Watʃí], Kpele, Dzodze, Kpedze, Dodóme, Ho, Awudome, Pekí, Aŋfɔe, Sovie, Botoku, Kpándo, Gbi and Fódome. Dialect variation in Ewe is quite great. But these dialects may be grouped geographically into coastal or southern dialects (Avenɔ, Tɔŋú etc.) central (Ho, Kpedze, Dodóme) and northern dialects (Gbi, Kpando, Fódome, etc.) The central and northern dialects are collectively characterized indigenously as *Ewedomegbe* and may be referred to as the inland dialects as opposed to the coastal dialects. Nevertheless speakers from different localities understand each other and are aware of the peculiarities of the different areas.

In addition to phonological differences, there are slight differences in patterns of greeting as well. In the coastal dialects the one who initiates greetings continues to ask questions until all the topics are exhausted and then the interlocutor also assumes the role of the questioner. In the inland dialects the initiator and responder alternate the roles of questioner and responder throughout the greeting.

Apart from these spoken varieties, a written standard variety was developed in the middle of the 19th century by Norddeutsche Missions-Gesellschaft (Bremen) missionaries (Ansre 1971; Adzomada 1979). It is a hybrid of the variants spoken at the missionary centers and contains a high proportion of the coastal Aŋlɔ dialect. With it has also emerged a standard colloquial variety (spoken usually with a local accent), that is very widely used in cross-dialectal contact situations such as in schools, markets, churches, etc. The principles of the orthography especially with respect to word division continue to be debated and revised (see Bureau of Ghana Languages 1997 for the most recent rules).

Number of Speakers: 3–5 million in the west African region.

Origin and History

It has been suggested in some quarters that the Ewes migrated from Egypt and Mesopotamia. There does not seem to be much basis for this and such claims are difficult to support. The Ewe oral traditions, however, support the claim that before the Ewes migrated to their present homeland they lived in Ketu, a town in present-day People's Republic of Benin. They stopped in other places before coming to their present home. Ketu is today a Yoruba settlement. This suggests that the Ewes or rather the Gbe-speaking people were not the only settlers in Ketu. In fact, the Gbe-speaking peoples moved from Ketu because of Yoruba expansion.

As they left Ketu, the Gbe-speaking peoples divided into

Table 1: Consonants

	Voi	Labial	Labio-dental	Dental	Alveolar	Post-Alveolar	Alveo-palatal	Palatal	Velar	Labio-velar
Stops	-	p		t					k	kp
	+	b		d		ɖ			g	gb
Fricatives	-	*f*	f		s				x	
	+	*v*	v		z				h	
Affricates	-				ts		tsy			
	+				dz		dzy			
Nasals		m			n			ny	ŋ	
Approximants								y	ɣ	w
Trill					r					
Lateral					l					

groups: two subdivisions of one group went due south, one to Tado near River Mɔnɔ, the other founded a settlement in ŋɔtsie. The second group, which includes the present-day Aŋlɔs first went to settle in Adele in Togo before joining the rest in ŋɔtsie later. Of the people that settled in Tado a group moved later to form the Alada Kingdom whose political nucleus was Agbome and Xɔgbonu. Historically then, there were three kingdoms associated with the Gbe-speaking peoples around each of which evolved a name for the major dialect clusters of Gbe: Tado is associated with Aja, Alada with its centers of Agbome and Xɔgbonu associated with Fon, and ŋɔtsie associated with Ewe.

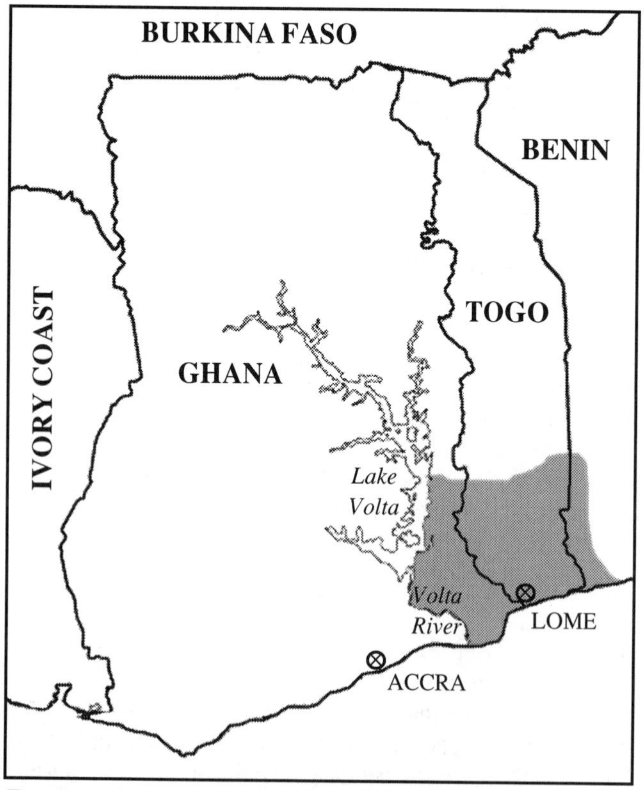

Ewe is spoken in the area between the River Volta in Ghana to just across the Togo-Benin border (shaded area).

It is believed that ŋɔtsie, the last ancestral home of the Ewes, was founded in the 16th century. The Ewes seemed to have lived there in peace until the cruelty of one king, Agorkorli, forced them to migrate to their present settlements in Ghana and Togo. From ŋɔtsie the Ewes dispersed in three groups. One group moved and settled in the northern parts of present day Ewe homeland. This group includes settlements such as Peki, Hohoe, and Alavanyo. A second group settled in the central parts of Eweland and include places such as Ho, Sokode, Abutia, and Adaklu. The third group moved southwards and includes Aŋlɔ and Bɛ (in present-day Togo). It is estimated that the Ewes settled in their present homeland in the period between the late 16th century and early 17th century. Many Ewe communities have traditions and festivals to commemorate their migration and settlement. The Anlos, for instance, refer to the ancestral homes of Ketu and ŋɔtsie as Hogbe and have an annual festival to celebrate the movement from Hogbe called *Hogbetsotso*.

Orthography and Basic Phonology

Ewe is written with the African alphabet devised in the 1920s based on the LATIN alphabet. The consonants are presented in their orthographic representation in Table 1 above.

Some of these sounds are in complementary distribution with one another. In general, nasals only occur before nasalized vowels. Thus [b] and [m] and [ɖ] and [n] are in complementary distribution. Similarly *ny* and *y* are allophones of the nasal phoneme. In the northern dialects the palatal approximant '*y*' may be nasalized and in this case it alternates in free variation with the palatal nasal. Thus the word for 'be/become black' may be either [j̃ɔ̃] or [nyɔ̃].

[ŋ] and [ʋ] occur before front vowels, and [w] occurs before oral nonfront vowels. There is some dialect variation with respect to these sounds. In the southern dialects [w] only occurs before back vowels but in the northern dialects it may occur before the central vowel [a]. Thus the word meaning 'do' is *wɔ* in Aŋlɔ and the standard dialect, but *wa* in the inland dialects. There is also a nasalized allophone of the labial velar approximant, which alternates in some contexts with the velar nasal in the northern dialects. For instance, the word for 'worm' in the southern dialects is *ŋɔ́* while in the northern dialects it may be realized as *w̃ã*. [l] has a nasalized allophone [l̃]. They complement each other in distribution along the oral nasal dimension: e.g., *ló* 'leopard' vs. *lõ̌* 'remove from fire'. Both laterals are in complementary distribution with the trill. First, the trill does not occur as an initial consonant in a syllable, while the laterals do as in the examples above. Second, when they occur as the second consonant in a cluster, the laterals occur after grave sounds (bilabials, labio-dentals, velars and labial-velars), while the trill occurs after non-grave sounds (dentals, alveolars, palatals). However, the laterals and the trill do not occur after the apical postalveolar plosive ɖ. /p/ occurs only in loanwords and ideophones.

There are seven oral and seven nasalized vowel phonemes in Ewe:

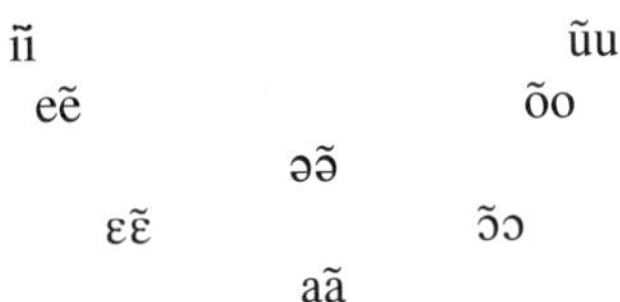

In some dialects such as Peki the high midvowels are not nasalized. Thus *lõ̌* is *lɔ̃́* 'remove from fire'. [ə] and [ə̃] are in complementary distribution with [e] and [ẽ] respectively. The latter pair of sounds occur after [+high] sounds. In the orthography, 'e' is used to represent these phonemes. Historically speaking, [ə] and [ə̃], are innovations in the Ewe dialects and some of the words with original /ɛ/ have merged with them. In the southern dialects the original /ɛ/ sound has disappeared and is replaced by the /ə/ sounds. In these dialects a word like */pɛpɛɛpɛ/* is pronounced *[pepeepe]* 'exactly'. In other dialects the /ə/ and /ɛ/ have merged into /ɛ/.

Tones. Ewe is a tone language. From a pan-Ewe dialectal point of view, one can say that there are five level tones: Low, Mid, High, Extra High and Extra Low. These five tones do not occur in all dialects. The Extra High occurs in Anlo in predictable environments (Clements 1977a and b). The Extra Low tone occurs in the Adangbe dialect and is specifically linked to the utterance, final interrogative particle/clitic *a*, which has a low tone in other dialects (Sprigge 1967). This leaves three level tones that are used in all dialects. Combinations of these lead to six surface contour tones: High-Low Falling, High-Mid Falling, Mid-Low Falling Low-High Rising, Mid-High Rising, and Low-Mid Rising. However all these surface tones reduce to two basic tonemes: a High and a non-High. The non-High may be realized as Low or Mid, while the High may be realized as High or Mid or Rising. Typically Mid tones at sentence final position become Low. A Mid tone also becomes Low after another Low tone.

The tones of nominals are affected to some extent by the consonant of the stem. Thus nominals with a non-high toneme may be realized as Mid if the nominal root has a sonorant or a voiceless obstruent. For example: *āmē* 'person'; *āmī* 'oil, pomade'; *á-fī* 'mouse'. It is low if the consonant of the nominal root is a voiced obstruent, for instance, *è-dà* 'snake'. For high tone nominals, the tone of the nominal root is high if the consonant is a voiceless obstruent or a sonorant as in *ā-tí* 'tree' and *ā-yí* 'skin'. If the stem consonant is a voiced obstruent the tone is a low-high rising tone as in *a-vɔ̌* 'cloth'. In context, this rising tone may change to low tone. This may happen when the word occurs before another syllable that is high. For example, note that the tone of the noun in the following is low as opposed to rising: *avɔ̀ lá* 'the cloth'.

Typically when morphemes come together, the tones of the two morphemes may be fused in much the same way that the vowels may fuse. To express first or second person singular possession, in the order of possessor followed by possessum, the link is expressed by a high tone which is a relic of the possessive marker *fé*. This high-tone possessive morpheme fuses with the low tone of the independent forms of the pronouns to yield a rising tone, for example, *nyě agbalẽ* 'my book' *wǒ srɔ̃ɖeɖe* 'your marriage', etc.

Tone is not customarily marked in the traditional orthography except on a few items with identical segmental forms. Thus the second person singular pronoun is written as *è* to distinguish it from the third person singular pronoun *e*, which has a high tone. Similarly the word for 'catch' or 'hold' is written as *lé* to distinguish it from the locative 'be' verb *le*, which has a low tone. A practice to mark all High tones in addition to the customarily marked low tones in the orthography introduced by Duthie (e.g., 1996) is gaining currency in academic linguistic writings. Whether this practice will catch on in non-academic circles is questionable.

Basic syllable structure in Ewe is: (C1) (C2) VT (C3). Each syllable has a tone that may be analyzed as being carried by the V element. C1 may be filled by any consonant in the language except r. C2 may be filled by a liquid as in *vlẽ* [βlẽ] 'struggle', *trɔ́* 'turn', or a palatal or a labial velar approximant as in *sjá* 'to expose something to the sun to dry it' and *sue* [swə] 'small'. V may be filled by any of the vowels or the bilabial or velar nasal, in which case they carry tone, for example, *ŋ̀dí* 'morning', *yɔ́-m̀* 'call me'. The nucleus may also be filled by two vowels that are the same, yielding a long vowel, or different, yielding a diphthong, for example: *dzáà* 'welcome', *kpáò* 'no', *yoo* 'OK'. C3 is only filled by a nasal as in the following words in which the syllable boundary is indicated by '=' where relevant: *sɔ́ŋ* 'several', *kam=pé* 'scissors', *kran=té* 'cutlass, machete'. The last two types, the double nucleus and the closed-syllable types, occur in borrowed words, ideophones or interjections.

Vowels may be elided or assimilated to other vowels in context. Vowel elision typically occurs in the formation of words involving nouns, where the vocalic prefix of a noun is dropped. For example, when the three forms *ame* 'person', *fo* 'beat', *atí* 'stick, tree' are compounded to form one noun meaning 'whip, cane', the vocalic prefix on *atí* is elided, as is evident in the word: *amefotí*. The vowel of a root can also be elided. The vowel of the word *gbe* 'day' is elided when it is in construction with *áɖé* INDEF and the word *gbe* is iterated after it as in the form *gbaɖégbe* 'some day'.

The third person singular object pronoun has the underlying form *-i* (Capo 1985). This vowel is either assimilated to the vowel of the predicate, or the vowel of the predicate is assimilated to it. Roughly speaking, when the assimilating vowel is a high vowel, the object pronoun vowel stays high, for example, *ɖu-i* 'eat it', *dí-i* 'look for it'. When the assimilating vowel is half close, the object pronoun is realized as the front half close vowel [e], for instance, *ɖó-e* 'planned it', *se-e* 'heard it'. In the southern dialects, the object pronoun vowel assimilates the half close stem vowel to itself making it high. Thus these words would be *ɖú-i* 'planned it' and *si-i* 'heard it' in *Aŋlɔ*, for example. When the vowel of the stem is low the object pronoun is realized as [ɛ], for example, *dɔ́-ɛ* 'send him/her/it'.

In the southern dialects, palatalization of alveolars in the environment of a high front vowel occurs as shown in the correspondences in the chart below.

Northern	Southern	
tsi	tʃi 'tsyi'	'water'
azi	aʒi	'peanut'
atí	atʃí 'atsi'	'tree'

Basic Morphology

Ewe is an isolating language with agglutinative features. As such most morpho-semantic features are expressed by lexical items or markers and by syntactic periphrasis.

Noun Morphology. Nouns as opposed to nominals have a vocalic prefix *à-* or *è-*, which are relics of Proto Niger Congo noun class markers. The *è-* prefix tends to be elided when the noun is said in isolation, e.g., *a-me* 'person', *a-tí* 'stick', *(e-)te* 'yam', *(e-)tsi* 'water'.

The nominal prefix bears a non-high tone with the following exceptions: (1) two temporal nouns in which the prefix bears a High tone and they are never elided, *égbe* 'today', and *ázɔ̃* 'now'; (2) the prefixes in some borrowed words retain their high tone, e.g., *áko* 'parrot', *Áma* 'name of a female born on a Saturday'.

Most categories pertaining to the noun are expressed by elements within the noun phrase. The order of elements in a simple noun phrase is: Noun/Pronoun - Adj - Quantifier - DET1 - DET2/DEM - Plural – Intensifier. Nominal plurality, for instance, is expressed by the morpheme *wó*, which is cliticized onto the immediately preceding element:

ame (kɔ́kɔ́) (má)-wó ko
person tall that-PL only
'only those people; only those tall people etc.'

There is a co-occurrence dependency between the Numeral, the Determiners and the Plural morpheme. A noun phrase containing a quantified noun that does not take a determiner is not marked with the plural morpheme *wó*. If a noun is quantified by a numeral and is modified by a determiner, then the plural marker is obligatory. Compare [NB (*x) = ungrammatical if x included; *(x) = ungrammatical if x omitted): *atí etɔ̃ (*wó)* (tree three PL) 'three trees', *atí etɔ̃ má *(wó)* 'those three trees'.

Numeration may be indicated within the noun phrase using a UNIT COUNTER *ame* which is related to the noun *ame* 'person' although as a unit counter *ame* is used to individuate not only humans but any countable entity. For example,

atí wó ame etɔ̃ (*wó)
tree 3PL COUNTER three PL
lit: tree, they three units/individual, i.e. 'three (units of) trees'

The Determiner1 slot can be filled by the definite article (*lá ~ a* 'the') or the particularized indefiniteness marker *áɖé* 'a certain'. The Determiner 2 slot is filled by demonstratives that vary in form from one group of dialects to the other. However, all Ewe dialects have two basic Demonstratives, as shown in the table below. The elements in italics are truncated forms of the corresponding forms, which have specific uses. A third demonstrative term for YONDER is derived from the THAT terms by either the suffixation of *-i* 'deictic' to *kema* to get *kemɛ* or by the addition of a particle *ɖá* 'in the distance', e.g. *kemi ɖáa* 'that further away in the distance'. In the Inland dialects the definiteness marker and the demonstratives can co-occur. In the Southern and Standard dialects, however, they are mutually exclusive.

Table 2: Ewe Demonstratives

	Standard Dialect	Southern (Aŋlɔ) Dialect	Northern Dialect
THIS	sia, *(ési)*	yia; yi, *(-i)*	ke; kelɛ́; xe; tsyi [ci]
THAT	má, kema	má, kema, *-m*, *-kem*	mí; kemí

A simple noun phrase may be preceded by a closed class of items labeled 'identifier'. There are three synonymous terms in this class, all of which can be glossed as 'such, the same', namely: *álé*, *neném*, *sigbe*. The identifier has a co-occurrence dependency with the items in the Determiner2 slot.

Verb Morphology. Most categories of the verb are expressed by markers that occur in the following order in a verb phrase:

(IRR)	(REP)	(MODAL)	-VERB-	(ASPECT)
(l)a FUT/POT	ga	kpɔ́! 'not yet'		[n]a HAB
(n)á SUBJV		xa 'in vain' etc.		

The only affixal element that occurs on the verb is the toneless *-(n)a* habitual aspect marker. It assumes the tone on the last syllable of the verb. Compare: *dí-(n)á* 'want-HAB' and *dze-(n)a* 'land-HAB'. The alternation between *na ~ a* tends to be syntactically determined. If the verb is followed by an object the habitual is realized as *-a*, but if it is not, then it is realized as *na*. A verb marked with the habitual signals an event that is customarily performed, a habit, or a disposition of the participant. The Progressive and Ingressive or Prospective aspect 'to be about to do something' are expressed by nominalizing the event whose unfolding in time is being described and then this functions as the complement of a verb that models the deictic and temporal frame of the situation. The aspectual markers are placed after the event complement: *é-le akɔ́nta fiá-m* (3s-be arithmetic teach-PROG) 'She is teaching arithmetic'.

Perfective aspect is signaled by three adverbial markers, which have evolved from verbs: *vɔ* 'finish' for completed or imminent completion situations, *sé* 'stop' for cessative perfective situations, and *kpɔ́* 'see' for experiential perfective (Ameka 1988).

The irrealis markers, the future or the potential and the subjunctive markers, both have allomorphs *a* and *á* respectively. *ga* is the marker of repetitive action or process. It can co-occur with any of the other elements in the verbal phrase.

A closed class of items function in the verbal phrase and express various modal meanings, e.g., *nye-mé kpɔ́ wɔ dɔ lá o* (1S-NEG MOD do work DEF NEG) 'I have not had the opportunity to do the work'.

General Rules. Ewe has very little inflectional morphology. It makes use of compounding as well as reduplication and triplication and affixation processes in the formation of new words, especially nouns, adjectives and adverbs. There are no morphological means for forming new verbs. Verbs can be reduplicated to form an adjective or a verbal noun. If the original begins with a consonant cluster, the cluster is simplified and the first consonant is retained in the copy. If the stem vowel is nasalized, it is replaced by its oral counterpart in the reduplicative. However, if the stem consonant is a nasalized approximant and the vowel is also nasalized then the whole form is copied without any change in nasalization. As far as tones are concerned, the copy retains the tone of the original when an adjective is being formed. If a noun is being formed, then a high tone in the original is changed to a low tone in the reduplicative form:

Verb	Nominal	Adjectival
sí 'to escape'	*sì-sí* 'escape, -ing'	*sí-sí* 'escaped'
sẽ́ 'be strong'	*sè-sẽ́* 'strength'	*sé-sẽ́* 'strong'
lɔ̃́ 'to love'	*lɔ̃́-lɔ̃́* 'love'	*lɔ̃́-lɔ̃́* 'beloved'
blá 'to tie'	*bà-blá* 'tying, tied'	*bá-blá* 'tied'
nyrɔ̀ 'to sink'	*nyɔ̀-nyrɔ̀* 'sinking'	*nyɔ̀-nyrɔ̀* 'sinking'
súbɔ́ 'to worship'	*sùbɔ̀-súbɔ́* 'worshipping'	*súbɔ́-súbɔ́* 'worshipping'

However, if the formation of a verbal noun involves the verb and its complement, then the tone and nasality of the stem vowel of the original is maintained in the reduplicative form: *sí du* 'run' > *du-sí-sí* 'running'; *lɔ̃́ Máwú* 'love God' > *Máwú-lɔ̃́-lɔ̃́* 'loving God'.

Ewe has two types of triplication: a plain triplication and a triplication with internal modification. In a triplicative construction involving internal modification, the vowel of the second syllable is lengthened. In some dialects, there is a further emphatic modification of the second syllable in the construction, by the insertion of an /*i*/ vowel. There are no tonal changes. Sometimes the feature of nasalization in the stem is left out in the first syllable: *ko* 'only' > *kokooko* 'only, only, only'; *gbã* 'first', *gbãgbããgbã* 'the very first', *gbãgbiããgbã* 'the very first of the first'.

Word repetition or syntactic iteration that could be open, ended is used for the expressive modification of meaning as well as indicating iterative numerals, e.g., *kábá* 'quickly' > *kábá kábá kábá* 'very very quickly'. Complex nominal duplication involves duplication of the nominal head or repetition of the entire nominal phrase with intervening morphological material between the two instances of the nominal base. It is used for the expression of specific syntactic semantic functions, such as distributive, deprecatory, superlative, etc.

ame síáa ame
person INT person
'everybody'

ame gbɔ́ mě
person near person
'a non-real person'

Nominal compounds abound in Ewe. They are formed by the juxtaposition of two nouns or a verb and a noun as in *yetrɔ́* 'sun-turn', i.e., 'late afternoon.' A verb and its complement may be permuted and compounded as in *nú-nyá* 'thing know', i.e., 'knowledge.' Permutation, compounding and repetition can all serve as input to affixation. Thus an agent nominal can be formed by suffixing *-lá* to a stem, *nú-fíá* 'thing-teach' formed by permutation and compounding to get *núfíálá* 'teacher'. A tonal prefix may be used to form a noun from a basic adjective as in *gã́* (ADJ) 'big' > *gǎ̃* (N) 'bigness'. Adjectives may also be derived from verbs by suffxation, e.g., *nyó* (V)' be good' > *nyúí* (ADJ) 'good'. Morphologically, Ewe is right headed.

Basic Syntax

Ewe is a grammatical word order language with basic SVO syntax (and subject and object are morphologically unmarked). Typically, weather clauses have a full subject NP which denotes a meteorological element. Ewe does not use dummy subjects in such sentences:

tsi dza;
water ooze
'It rained'

ŋdɔ ʋu sésíe etsɔ
sun shine hard yesterday
'The sun shone hard yesterday.'

Ewe also has a number of utterance final particles which signal the illocutionary force or the attitude of the speaker. For instance propositional questions are marked by an utterance final clitic *à:*

Áma *fle* avɔ etsɔ-a?
A. buy cloth yesterday-Q
'Did Ama buy a piece of cloth yesterday?'

In general, the possessor precedes the possessum. 'Alienable' possession is indicated by a possessive marker *fé*, which is interposed between the possessor and possessum. Inalienable possession is expressed by merely juxtaposing the possessor and the possessed. Body parts have 'alienable' syntax. Relative clauses and other modifiers generally follow the noun head.

Ewe is a serializing language. In a serial verb construction, each verb in the series has the same subject and shares the same tense, mood and aspect. The subject is only expressed with the first verb. In some of the serial verb constructions, serializing connectives may be used to link the verbs: *hé* for simultaneous or sequential relations and *ɖa* for purpose relations.

é-fɔ do go le zã me dzáá ɖa-ku
3SG-arise go outside at night in quietly PURP-dig

te ɖa ɖu.
yam cook eat
'He got out quietly at night, dug up yams, cooked them and ate them.'

In serial verb constructions in which the first verb is one of accompaniment such as *kplɔ* 'lead', or instrument such as 'take' etc., there is an optional element that may be called SERIAL-*i*, which occurs with the second verb to show that the events are concomitant or simultaneous rather than consecutive or consequential: *é-kplɔ Ama dzó-é* ('3SG-lead A leave-SERIAL) 'S/he led Ama away'.

Another verbal concatenative construction is the overlapping clause, in which the subject of the second clause is coreferential with a nonsubject argument of the first clause. Typically it is used to express simultaneous events: *é-da tú-í wò-kú* (3SG-throw gun-3SG 3SG-die) 'S/he shot it dead'.

The language has both prepositions, which evolved from verbs, and postpositions, most of which have evolved from body part nominals, for expressing relational meanings.

There are particles for indicating the status of the information units and for framing discourse. An NP or AP that sets the scene for the rest of the clause may be preposed to it. Typically such a constituent is separated from the rest of the clause by a pause and /or marked by a discourse framing particle *lá* or *ɖé*. If the preposed constituent is coreferential with a core argument of the clause, the relationship between the constituent and the argument is indicated by an anaphoric pronoun in the clause: *Kofí lá papá ná dɔ ɛ* (Kofi TOPIC father give work 3SG) 'Kofi, father gave him work.'

An argument of the clause may be front shifted to the precore clausal position for focus, that is, before the subject slot but after the preposed constituent slot. The fronted element is marked by an argument focus marker *-(y)é*. Typically a gap is left in the slot within the clause structure where the fronted element would have occurred. *Ga-é Papá ná Kofí* (money-FOC father give Kofi) 'MONEY father gave to Kofi.'

There are two dialectally varying strategies for verb or predicate focus. The verb may be copied, as happens in the *Aŋlɔ* dialect: *Kofí sí* 'Kofi escaped' vs. *Sí Kofí sí* 'Escape Kofi did'. In the standard and other dialects, the verb is focused by the use of a predicate focus marker *ɖè*: *Kofí ɖè wò-sí* (Kofi FOC 3SG-escape) 'Kofi did escape.'

Dependent and embedded clauses may be introduced by various conjunctions and connectives. They fill the first position in the clause preceding all the other elements.

Negation. Standard or clausal negation is marked by a discontinuous negative morpheme *mé...o*. *Mé* occurs just before the VP and tends to be cliticized onto the first element in the VP, while *o* occurs at the end of the clause but before the sentence-final particles. In a serial verbal construction, *mé* occurs before the first VP in the series, while the *o* occurs at the end of the serial clause.

Kofí	mé-	vá	afí	sia	o-a?
Kofi	NEG-	come	place	this	NEG-Q

'Did Kofi not come here?'

Mé-	ga-wɔ-e	o.
NEG:2SG	REP-do-3SG	NEG

'Don't do it.'

In this last example, the *mé* part of the negative morpheme has fused with the second person pronoun leading to a low tone on the form.

There are different kinds of nonclausal or constituent negation. One of these is the negative cleft construction. This construction is used to emphatically negate a particular constituent in a clause, an NP or a predicate. The constituent that is thus negated is focus marked, either by the argument focus marker or the predicate focus marker.

Mé-nyé	etsɔ-	é	me-	dzɔ	o
3SG:NEG-be	yesterday	AFOC	1SG	happen	NEG

'It wasn't yesterday I was born.'

Derivational negation is marked by the affix *ma-* 'un', the privative marker. This affix is used in the derivation of adjectives and adverbials. It is usually prefixed to a verbal element and reduplicated together with it when necessary: *ma-vɔ* (NEG-finish) 'everlasting', *nu-ma-ɖu-ma-ɖu* (thing-NEG-eat-NEG-eat) 'without eating'. These may occur with or without standard negation.

Transitivity. There are two types of transitive clauses in Ewe: a highly transitive one in which the subject is an Effector or an Agent and the Object a Theme, and a less-transitive one in which the Subject is a Theme (or Undergoer) and the Object a Locative including properties. Some verbs can occur in either construction. For instance *fo* 'hit, strike'

Núfíálá	*fo*	ɖeví-á		Effector -Theme
teacher	hit	child-DEF	=	'The teacher beat the child.'

Awu	lá	*fo*	ɖi		Theme -Locative
garment	DEF	hit	dirt	=	'The garment is dirty.'

Inversion. A grammatical process of inversion can apply to the Effector/Theme but not the Theme/Locative construction. The Inversion construction, which is a passive-like construction involves the introduction of a modal *nyá*, which forces the reorganization of the argument structure of the clause. The Effector is demoted to a dative object position or deleted and the Theme is promoted to Subject position. It is used to express the ability or the experience of the Effector in relation to the Theme:

ɖevi-a	nyá	*fo*	ná	nufiala
child-DEF	INV	hit	to	teacher

'The teacher was able to hit/enjoyed hitting the child.'

Reported Speech. The language also has a logophoric pronoun *ye* (plural *yewó*), which is used in reportive contexts to designate the individual(s) (except for the first person) whose speech, thoughts, feelings and so on are reported or reflected in the linguistic context. It occurs in grammatical or discourse dependent contexts ususally in clauses introduced by the dependent clause introducer *bé(ná)* 'that'.

Contact with Other Languages

Contact with various languages has yielded quite a few loanwords: *sini* < ENGLISH 'cinema'; *sukúù* < English 'school'; *bókiti* < Eng. 'bucket'; *súkli* 'sugar' < FRENCH *sucre*; *gáflo* 'fork' < GERMAN *Gabel*; *sabála* 'onion' < PORTUGUESE *cebola*; *atrakpoe* 'stairs' < DUTCH *trappe*; *ɖúku* 'headkerchief' < Dutch? DANISH *doek; abladzó* 'plantain' < Akan (Fante) *abrɔ dzo*; *ablegɔ́* 'chair' < Akan Twi *aburoguo*; *káfra* 'I beg your pardon' < Hausa *gafara*; *alafá* 'hundred' < Arabic '*alf* 'thousand'.

Common Words

man:	ŋútsu	small:	ví; sue; túkui
woman:	nyɔ́nu	yes:	ee; ẽẽ
water:	etsi	no:	ao; oo
sun:	ŋdɔ; ɣe	good:	nyó (Verb) nyúí (Adj)
three:	etɔ̃	bird:	xeví
fish:	tɔmelã; akpa	dog:	avŭ
big:	gã́	tree:	atí
long:	didi		

Example Sentences

(1) Máwúli nyé ŋútsu tsralɛ yibɔ-e áɖé.
M. COP man tall.slender black-DIM INDEF
'Mawuli is a slender, tall black man.'

(2) Du sue áɖé nɔ Eve-nyígbá dzí
town small INDEF be.at:NPRES Ewe-land upper.surface

le Ghana *fé* ɣedze*fé* lɔ*fo* kpɔ́.
at Ghana POSS east direction PFV
'There was once a small town in the east of Eweland in Ghana.'

(3) Ezuagba lɔ̃ é-xɔ́lɔ̃ Nyuiemedi ŋútɔ gaké
E. love 3SG-friend N. much but

ŋubiabiã ɖé ga ŋú trɔ́ é-*fé* lɔlɔ̃.
envy ALL money side change 3SG-POSS love
'Ezuagba loved his friend Nyuiemedi very much, but envy because of money changed his love.'

Efforts to Preserve, Protect, and Promote the Language

Ewe is used in Ghana as a second language in most of the Ghana-Togo Mountains–languages area. It is also one of the three most important languages in southern Ghana, Ga and Akan being the other two. Ewe is taught in primary, secondary and university institutions. It is used for radio and TV broadcasting and in some community newspapers, e.g., *Kpodoga*. It is also used in adult literacy programs. There is a fair amount of published material in the language (see Duthie and Vlaardingerbroek 1981: part 2).

In Togo, Ewe has been declared one of the two indigenous languages being promoted for official use as well as for use in education, mass media, etc. Ewe is thus an important language in that region of West Africa where it is in contact with English and French and other indigenous African languages. There is a commission in Togo that has been working to devise Ewe words for new technological terms. In Ghana there is an Ewe Language Committee that offers advice on the promotion and use of Ewe in Ghana. There is also an Ewe Section of the Bureau of Ghana Languages, which publishes some materials on and in the language.

Select Bibliography

Adzomada, Jacques K.1979. *L'Ewe Standard*. Lome: Institut National de Recherche Scientifiques.

Agbodeka, Francis K., ed. 1998. *A Handbook of Eweland. Vol. 1: The Ewe of Southeastern Ghana*. Accra: Woeli.

Ameka, Felix K. 1988. "The grammatical coding of the terminal viewpoint of situations in Ewe." In *Australian Journal of Linguistics*, 2: 185–217.

____. 1998. "Les particules énonciatives en ewe." In *Les langues d'Afrique Subsaharienne*. S. Platiel and R. Kabore, eds. pp. 179–204. Faits de Langues 11–12. Paris: Ophrys.

____. 1999. "The typology and semantics of complex nominal duplication in Ewe." In *Anthropological Linguistics* 41–1: 75–106.

Ansre, Gilbert. 1971. "Language standardisation in Sub-Saharan Africa." In *Current Trends in Linguistics. Vol. 7: Linguistics in Sub-Saharan Africa*. T. Sebeok, ed. pp. 680–698. The Hague: Mouton.

Asamoa, Ansa K.1986. *The Ewe of South-East Ghana and Togo on the Eve of Colonialism*. Tema: Ghana Publishing Corporation.

Capo, Hounkpati B.C.1985. "Determining the third person singular object pronoun in Gbe." In *West African Languages in Education*. K. Williaamson, ed. pp. 106–131. Wien: Afro Publishers.

____. 1991. *A Comparative Phonology of Gbe*. Berlin and Garome: de Gruyter (Foris) and LABOGBE.

Clements, George N. 1977a. "Four tones from three: The extra high tone in *Aŋlɔ* Ewe." In *Language and Linguistic Problems in Africa*. P.F. Kotey and H. Der-Houssikian, eds. pp. 168–81. Columbia: Hornbeam Press.

____. 1977b. "Tone and syntax in Ewe." In *Elements of Tone, Stress and Intonation*. J. Napoli, ed. pp. 21–99. Washington DC: Georgetown University Press.

Duthie, Alan S. 1996. *Introducing Ewe Linguistic Patterns*. Accra: Ghana Universities Press.

Duthie, Alan S, and R.K. Vlaardingerbroek.1981. *Bibliography of Gbe (Ewe, Gen Aja, Fon Xwla Gun, etc)*. Basel: Basler Afrika Bibliographien.

Essegbey, James. 1999. *Inherent Complement Verbs Revisited: Towards an Understanding of Argument Structure in Ewe*. Ph.D. Dissertation: Leiden University.

Ring, Andrew J. 1981. *Ewe as a Second Language: A Sociolinguistic Survey of Ghana's Central Volta Region*. Legon: Institute of African Studies, University of Ghana.

Rongier, Jacques. 1995. *Apprenons l'ewe*, (9 volumes) Paris: L'Harmattan

Sprigge, Robert G.S. 1967. *Tone in the Adangbe dialect of Ewe*. Legon: Institute of African Studies, University of Ghana.

Stahlke, Herbert F.W. 1971. *Topics in Ewe phonology*. Ann Arbor MI: University Microfilms.

Westermann, Diedrich. 1973a. [1928] *Ewefiala: Ewe -English dictionary*. Nendeln: Kraus Thompson.

____. 1973b. [1930] *Gbesela yeye: English-Ewe dictionary*. Nendeln: Kraus Thompson.

____. 1930. *A Study of the Ewe Language*. London: Oxford University Press.

Finnish

Erika J. Mitchell

Language Name: Finnish. **Alternates:** *Finsk* (in Swedish, Norwegian, and Danish); *some* (in Estonian); *Finskij* (in Russian). **Autonym:** *Suomi.*

Location: Finland. Smaller speech communities in northern Sweden (particularly Norrbotten Province), northern Norway (Finnmark Province and Troms), Russia (Karelian Autonomous Region and St. Petersburg area), the United States (northern midwestern states), and Australia.

Family: Baltic-Finnic subgroup of the Finno-Ugric branch of the Uralic language family.

Related Languages: Finnish is most closely related to the Balto-Finnic languages: Karelian, Estonian, Vepsian, Votian, Ingrian, and Livonian. Also related to Saame (Lappish), Mari, Komi, Mordvin, Mansi, Khanty, and HUNGARIAN.

Dialects: There are three major dialect regions comprising as many as eight distinct dialect areas: (1) Southwest: Southwest, Häme, Transitional Southwest, South Ostrobothnian; (2) Northeast: Mid and North Ostrobothnian, Northern, Savo; and (3) Karelian (Southeast). The literary standard is based upon the Southwest dialect.

Number of Speakers: 5.4–5.6 million.

Origin and History

Finnish is a descendant of an ancestral language spoken by Uralic tribes living in the Volga River Basin between 3000–2000 B.C. Around 2000 B.C. the Uralic peoples are believed to have split. One group migrated southwest toward modern-day Hungary and the other group headed northwest toward the Baltic Sea. About 2000 years ago Finnic tribes from the south and east are believed to have begun settling the area now known as Finland, pushing the related, but earlier-arriving Saame north.

By the ninth century, Swedish settlers had begun to appear on the western shores of Finland; Sweden established formal rule over the region in the 12th century. During the time of Swedish rule, SWEDISH served as the language of law, culture, and education. Mikael Agricola, a Swedish bishop, is credited with publishing the first book in Finnish, an ABC-primer in 1543. Agricola chose to use the Southwestern dialect with which he was most familiar; as a result this dialect ultimately became the literary standard. Except for the Bible and other religious texts that appeared after the Reformation, however, vernacular Finnish was not commonly used in printed material during this period.

With the rise and strengthening of the Russian empire to the east, considerations of economics and security made Finland a prime region of contention between Sweden and Russia and the source of numerous battles for territory. Portions of eastern Finland were ceded to Russia in 1721 and eventually the entire country came under Russian rule as an autonomous duchy in 1809. It was not until 1917 that Finland was established as an independent nation.

Shortly after Finland became a part of the Russian empire, two major factors conspired to bring the language into both common and official use: the growing nationalist movement in Europe and an official Russian effort to loosen Finnish ties with Sweden (which coincided with a Finnish determination to retain the relative independence that had been gained in the transition while avoiding assimilation with Russia). In the 1820s, Dr. Elias Lönrrot scoured the Karelian countryside to record the traditional tales of the common people. Out of this project came his *Kalevala*, published in 1835, which came to be known as the national epic of the Finnish people. The Finnish Literary Society (*Suomalaisen Kirjallisuuden Seura*) was established in 1831. Growing cries led by people such as Professor Johan Vilhelm Snellman urged the recognition of Finnish alongside the established Swedish in official government proceedings and education. A Finnish Department was established at the University of Helsinki in 1851, and the first Finnish language high school was begun in Jyväskylä in 1858. In 1863, Finnish was given equal legal status with Swedish by the Finnish diet. The first class of Finns educated in their own language began to emerge a generation later.

The first novel written in Finnish was Alexis Kivi's *Seitsemän veljestä* (The Seven Brothers) (1870). Frans Eemil Sillanpää won the 1939 Nobel prize for literature for his novel *Silja*. The best known modern Finnish novelist is Mika Waltari, author of *Sinuhe-Egyptiläinen* (Sinuhe the Egyptian) and many other books.

Outside of Finland, around the 17th century the Norrbotten area of Sweden had seen a migration of Finns to work in the mines. Large pockets of this area remain Finnish-speaking or bilingual to this day although the present generation is becoming more consistently monolingual in Swedish. Crop failures and other economic hardships precipitated migration of Finns to Finnmark Province (Norway), the United States, Canada, and Australia in the 1870s. In the U.S. these people settled in north-central Massachusetts (Fitchburg), central New York, and the northern Midwest states (particularly in Michigan's Upper Peninsula and Minnesota). Although largely monolingually Finnish or bilingual in the years following migration, this population has become more monolingually

Table 1: Consonants

	Labial	Dental	Alveolar	Palatal	Velar	Glottal
Stops	p	t	d		k	
Fricatives	v	s				h
Nasals	m	n			n (k)	
Resonants		l, r		j		

ENGLISH-speaking in the past 20–40 years. The Winter War with the Soviet Union (1939–1940) and World War II brought 450,000 Finnish and Karelian-speaking refugees from formerly Finnish Karelia into Finland proper. Since that time the number of Finnish speakers across the Russian border has decreased markedly, although a significant minority remains. Some efforts are being made to revive the language in the area.

Orthography and Basic Phonology

Finnish uses the Roman alphabet with two additional vowel symbols *ä* and *ö*. Of these, *b, c, f, g, q, x,* and *z* do not represent native sounds in Finnish and are only used in the spelling of foreign words. *w* is pronounced as [v], but it occurs only in foreign words and in older manuscripts. *n* before *k* represents the sound of English *ng* as it occurs in 'sink'. *g* is only written in the Finnish cluster *ng*, which represents a double occurrence of the [N] sound. For example, compare *Helsinki* [hel.sing.ki] with *Helsingin* [hel.sing.ngin].

An unwritten glottal stop (like the sound separating *uh'oh* 'no' in English) also occurs, but in entirely predictable environments. Among the consonants, /p, t, k/ are unaspirated. The consonants /t/ and /d/ are distinct in that /t/ is voiceless, dental and /d/ is voiced, alveolar (voicing is not distinctive). The native stop and nasal consonants and /s, l, r/ may appear long or short (geminate or plain).

Table 2: Vowels

	Front		Back	
	Unrounded	Rounded	Unrounded	Rounded
High	i	y		u
Mid	e	ö		o
Low	ä		a	

All vowels appear either long or short. In the standard orthography this is represented by one vowel for long and two for short: *sinä* 'you', *siinä* 'in that'.

Finnish word structure is most prominently characterized by a system of vowel harmony in which suffixes must occur with vowels that match those of the root in terms of the feature of frontness or backness. Front vowels are /y, ö, ä/. Back vowels are /u, o, a/. The vowels /i/ and /e/ are transparent to harmony and can appear in words with either front- or back-vowel harmony, but if a root only contains /i/ or /e/, front-vowel suffixes must occur. Examples with the adessive suffix *-lla/-llä* 'on':

Back: muna-lla	'on the egg'
Back: muovi-lla	'on plastic'
Front: pää-llä	'on the head'
Front: käde-llä	'on the hand'
{i,e}: tie-llä	'on the road'

Relatively few foreign borrowings violate vowel harmony since foreign words ordinarily contain only front vowels, /i/ and /e/. The few foreign words that do contain a mixture of back and front vowels are pronounced as their spelling would dictate but are tongue twisters for the Finns: *olympiakisat*. Compounds maintain harmony within each stem element, but do not have to maintain harmony between the stem elements: *yliopisto* 'over academy, i.e., university'.

Finnish also possesses a remarkably symmetric set of 18 diphthongs:

Table 3: Diphthongs

	Onset	Second Element					
		Unrounded			Rounded		
Front	High	ie		yi	iy		yö
	Mid	ei		öi	ey		öy
	Low		äi			äy	
Back	High	ie		ui	iu		uo
	Mid	ei		oi	eu		ou
	Low		ai			au	

Finnish syllable structure is subject to a rhythmic phenomenon called "consonant gradation". If the final syllable in a word ends in a consonant, the consonant at the beginning of that syllable appears in the "weak" grade. However, if the final syllable ends in a vowel, the consonant at the beginning of the syllable is in the "strong" grade. Pairings of strong- and weak-grade consonants are illustrated below. Words in the left column are in the nominative case (see below), and words in the right column are in the genitive case, indicated by the final *-n*.

Strong	Weak	Meaning
seppä	sepän	'smith'
matto	maton	'mat'
lukko	lukon	'lock'
parempi	paremmin	'better'
kulta	kullan	'gold'
rapu	ravun	'crayfish'
luku	luvun	'number'

Word stress always falls on the initial syllable. A weak secondary stress may also be heard on following odd-numbered syllables. Compound words also have a weak secondary stress on the first syllables of noninitial elements: *auringonpalovja* [OW.ring.ngon.PAHL.voh-yah] 'sun worshipper'.

In everyday speech many final vowels and syllables are lost; for example, *miks* is substituted for *miksi* 'why', *talos* for *talossa* 'in the house', *kauhee* for *kauhea* 'terrible'. In "correct" formal Finnish, however, all of the sounds that are written are retained and pronounced.

Most sentences have intonation patterns whose general pitch contours fall over the duration of the sentence. Constituents bearing information new to the discourse and focused words are usually associated with intonational peaks, but the general falling pattern of the sentence is still maintained.

Basic Morphology

The major classes of words in Finnish are noun, verb, adjective, adverb, postposition, preposition, and conjunction. The minor word classes include the personal pronoun, interrogative pronoun, relative pronoun, demonstrative adjective, and auxiliary verb.

The Finnish nominal system is characterized by an elaborate set of 15 grammatical case distinctions; 12 of these are commonly used and productive. Four structural cases—nominative, accusative, genitive, and partitive—express the grammatical relations such as subject, direct object, and possessor borne by major constituents in different types of sentences. The genitive case is also usually required of nouns governed by postpositions, while the partitive also expresses a partial effect of the predicate on the object. Six local cases—illative, inessive, elative, allative, adessive, and ablative—express motion and location with respect to an object. Two state cases—translative and essive—express the change in or temporariness of the state of an object. The three lesser-used cases—absesive, comitative, and instructive—express the notions "without", "with, accompanied by", and "with, by means of" which are now primarily expressed by prepositions and postpositions.

Except for the nominative, which has no marker, and the accusative, which sometimes has no marker, case is marked by a suffix that follows the noun stem and any plural marker. Modifying adjectives agree in case and number with the nouns they modify and take the same set of endings. There is no system of gender in the language. The following sentences illustrate some of the forms in which number and case appear:

Nominative:
Tuo iso talo on kaunis
that big house is beautiful

Genitive:
Tuo-n iso-n talo-n ovi on auki
that-GEN big-GEN house-GEN door is open
'The door of that big house is open.'

Illative:
Hän juoksi iso-on talo-on
s/he ran big-ILL house-ILL
'S/he ran into the big house.'

Translative:
Hän teki nuo vanhat laudat iso-ksi talo-ksi
s/he made those old boards big-TRANS house-TRANS
'S/he made those old boards into a big house.'

There are no articles in Finnish. However, definiteness can be expressed in plural direct objects and nominal and adjectival predicates: definite plural direct objects and predicates take nominative case form while indefinite plural direct objects and predicates appear in the partitive:

Nominative:
Hän näki talo-t
s/he saw house-PL
'S/he saw the houses.'

Partitive:
Hän näki talo-j-a
s/he saw house-PL-PART
'S/he saw houses.'

Finnish nouns, but not their modifying adjectives, also agree with pronominal possessors. An agreement suffix follows a vowel-final nominal stem (noun root plus any number and case suffixes) or, with some exceptions, replaces the final consonant of a consonant-final nominal stem. The following examples illustrate the first-person singular possessor agreement marker *-ni* and the second-person singular possessor agreement marker *-si*:

min-un iso talo-ni
my-GEN big house-1SG
'my big house'

sin-un iso-t talo-si
your-GEN big-PL house-2SG
'your big houses'

Finnish verbs agree in person and number with their subjects. There is no object agreement. The subject-agreement suffixes appear on the first element—verb stem or auxiliary—of the verbal complex. The third person singular has no overt marker in the past tense or with many verbs in the nonpast tense.

There are two tenses in Finnish, nonpast and past (called the imperfect). The nonpast is unmarked. The imperfect suffix *-i* occurs between the verb stem and the agreement suffix (here *-vat*):

He tul-i-vat eilen
they come-PAST-3PL yesterday

The Finnish verb also has four moods—indicative, conditional, potential ('may possibly'), and imperative—a perfect aspect, and four forms of the infinitive.

Roots and stems primarily associated with one word class may, through the use of derivational suffixes, occur in other words of the same or different word class. Rules governing the realization of vowels at the boundaries between morphemes can be complicated in derivation, as well as in the inflectional morphology discussed above and in compound formation. Some examples of derivatives formed from simple stems of the same word class include collective nouns, transitive or causative verbs, durative or frequentative verbs, intransitive verbs, and attenuative adjectives:

kirja	'book'	*kirja-sto*	'library'
kasva-a	'to grow (intr.)'	*kasva-tta-a*	'to grow (tr.)'

Some examples of cross-category derivations include the relationships between adjectives and abstract nouns, adjectives and adverbs, instrumental nouns and verbs, and locational nouns and locational adjectives:

kylmä	'cold'	*kylm-yys*	'coldness'
nopea	'fast'	*nopea-sti*	'quickly'

Compounding is extensive and productive in the creation of new words and the translation of loanwords. The head of the compound occurs finally, preceded by a form that may or may not be inflected:

auringo-n-palvoja
sun-GEN-worshipper
'sun-worshipper'

Basic Syntax

The basic order of major constituents in Finnish clauses is SVO. This order may vary as major constituents acquire the discourse functions of topic or focus. Topics (items previously known in the discourse) usually appear early in the sentence, before new information. The first example below offers commentary on the discourse topic.

Leena söi jäätelöä
Leena ate ice.cream
'Leena ate ice cream.'

Jäätelöä söi Leena
ice.cream ate Leena
'It was Leena who ate the ice cream.'

Constituents bearing special focus or emphasis may occur before the subject, or, in the case of objects, before the verb: *Jäätelöä hän söi* 'it was ice cream that s/he ate', *Hän jäätelöä söi* 'it was ice cream that s/he ate'.

The structure of the phrase in Finnish is inconsistently head-initial. In the noun phrase possessors, adjectives, numbers, and participles precede the noun they modify. Relative clauses follow the head noun; the relative pronoun occurs in clause-initial position: *hyvä kirja jonka hän kirjoitti* (good book which s/he wrote) 'The good book which s/he wrote'.

First names usually precede last names: *Leena Suominen.* However, the last name may precede the first name if the last name is in the genitive case: *Suomisen Leena.*

The truth of a statement as a whole is questioned through the use of an interrogative word order in which the verb appears in initial position, followed by the question particle *-ko/-kö*. An individual constituent questioned for reasons of confirmation appears in initial position before the subject, again followed by the question particle. Constituents being questioned for identity appear in initial position; the verb remains in its postsubject position:

Söi-kö hän jäätelöä
ate-Q s/he ice cream
'Did s/he eat ice cream?'

Jäätelöä-kö hän söi
Ice cream-Q s/he ate
'Was it ice cream that s/he ate?'

Mitä hän söi
What s/he ate
'What did she eat?'

Negation of the sentence is expressed with a negative verbal auxiliary. This auxiliary is the first element in the verbal complex; thus when it is present, it carries the subject-agreement suffix. It does not vary with tense. Aspectual auxiliaries or main verbs that follow the negative auxiliary appear in the present tense in the form of the simple stem. In the past tense these elements appear in the past participle, which agrees in number with the subject. The stem of the negative auxiliary is *e*; in the following example it is followed by the third-person singular subject-agreement marker *-i*:

Hän e-i vielä ole puhunut
s/he not-3SG yet has spoken
'S/he hasn't spoken yet.'

Contact with Other Languages

Long contact with the Germanic languages, particularly Swedish, is reflected in Finnish by many borrowed words and several grammatical structures (e.g., SVO word order and prenominal binding patterns). Signs of substantial but lesser contact with RUSSIAN include some vocabulary (e.g., Finnish *sininen* 'blue', Russian *sinij* 'blue') and grammatical features such as partitive of negation (cf. Russian genitive of negation) and the question particle *-ko/kö* (cf. Russian *li*). The Southwest dialect of Finnish spoken in the Helsinki area shows a greater effect of language contact with both Swedish and Russian, particularly in the realm of vocabulary.

Relatively few Finnish words have entered into international usage; the best known of these is *sauna.*

Early loans:
From Indo-European: *mesi* 'honey', *sata* 'hundred'
From Baltic: *meri* 'ocean', *hammas* 'tooth'
From Germanic: *rauta* 'iron', *leipä* 'bread'
From Slavonic: *saapas* 'boot', *vapaa* 'free'

Later loans:
From Swedish: *lääkäri* 'doctor' (< *läkare*), *katu* 'street' (< *gata*)
From Russian: *toveri* 'buddy' (< *tovarishch*)

Modern loans:

From ENGLISH: *auto* 'car', *takki* 'jacket', *rekka* 'truck' (<*wrecker*), *mikroprosessori* 'microprocessor'

Common Words

man:	mies	small:	pieni
woman:	nainen	yes:	kyllä (indeed)
water:	vesi	no:	ei (3sg)
sun:	aurinko	good:	hyvä
three:	kolme	bird:	lintu
fish:	kala	dog:	koira
big:	iso	tree:	puu
long:	pitkä		

Example Sentences

(1) Aurinko paista-a.
sun shine-3SG
'The sun is shining.'

(2) E-n tiedä.
not-1SG know
'I do not know.'

(3) Terveis-i-ä sauna-sta.
greeting-PL-PART sauna-ELATIVE
'Greetings from the sauna!'

Efforts to Preserve, Protect, and Promote the Language

Finnish is one of the two official languages of Finland (Finnish is 94 percent of the population; Swedish, 6 percent) and as such receives official sanctions in education, government, and services. The spread of the mass media in the last 40 years has led to the lessening and leveling of the major dialectal differences, with the Helsinki and the general Southwest dialect prevailing.

Outside of Finland, some efforts are being made to maintain the language in historically Finnish-speaking areas. In the Norrbotten province of Sweden and the Finnmark province of Norway, some services are available in Finnish and there are limited possibilities for Finnish-language instruction in schools. In Russian Karelia, there are possibilities for Finnish-language instruction, and there are several newspapers in Finnish.

Select Bibliography

Aaltio, Maija-Hellikki. 1984. *Finnish for Foreigners.* Helsinki: Kustannusosakeyhtiö.

Abondolo, Daniel Mario. 1998. *Colloquial Finnish: The Complete Course for Beginners.* London: Routledge.

Atkinson, John. *Finnish Grammar.* 1981. Helsinki: The Finnish Literature Society.

Branch, Michael. 1987. "Finnish." In Bernard Comrie, ed., *The World's Major Languages,* 593–617. London: Oxford University Press.

Hakulinen, Lauri. 1961. *The Structure and Development of the Finnish Language*, translated by John Atkinson. Bloomington: Indiana University Press.

Jutikkala, Eino. 1988. *A History of Finland*, translated by Paul Sjöblom. (Rev. ed.) New York: Dorset Press.

Karlsson, Fred. 1983. *Finnish Grammar.* Porvoo: Werner Söderström.

Karlsson, Fred, and Andrew Chesterman. 1999. *Finnish: An Essential Grammar.* London: Routledge.

____. 1992. "Finnish." In *International Encyclopedia of Linguistics.* New York: Oxford University Press.

Lehtinen, Meri K. 1967. *Basic Course in Finnish.* Bloomington: Indiana University Publications.

Sulkala, Helen, and Karjalainen, Merja. 1992. *Finnish.* London: Routledge.

French

Cynthia A. Fox

Language Name: French. **Autonym:** *le français*. **Alternates:** *Cadien* or *Cajun* (for French spoken in the state of Louisiana), *Acadian* (French of the Maritime provinces of Canada), *Québécois* (French of the province of Quebec, Canada).

Location: France, Monaco, Belgium, Switzerland, Luxembourg, the Aosta Valley of Italy, and the Channel Islands. In Canada: the provinces of Quebec, New Brunswick, Nova Scotia, Newfoundland, Prince Edward Island, Ontario, Manitoba, Saskatchewan, and the (French-owned) islands of Saint-Pierre-et-Miquelon. In the United States: the state of Louisiana and the Northeast region. South America: French Guyana. Caribbean: Martinique, Guadeloupe, and the Republic of Haiti. Africa: 5 to 10 percent of the population of Benin, Burkino-Faso, Burundi, Cameroon, the Central African Republic, Chad, the Comoro Islands, the Congo, Djibouti, Gabon, Guinea, Ivory Coast, Mali, Mauritania, Niger, Rwanda, Senegal, Chad, and Zaire; a large portion of the populations of Morocco, Algeria, and Tunisia. The Middle East: Syria and Lebanon. Asia: Laos, Kampuchea, and Vietnam. Oceania: New Caledonia, Vanuatu, and French Polynesia. Indian Ocean: Madagascar, Reunion, and Mauritius.

Family: Romance group of the Italic branch of Indo-European.

Related Languages: ITALIAN, PORTUGESE, ROMANIAN, SPANISH, CATALAN, Corsican, OCCITAN.

Dialects: The term *français régional* 'regional French' refers to varieties that are particular to specific geographical regions of France and that contain dialectal features of pronunciation, vocabulary, and, to a lesser extent, syntax. The term is also used for varieties of French spoken outside of France (in Belgium, Haiti, Algeria, Canada, etc.), all of which exhibit varying pronunciation, vocabulary, morphology, and syntax and are generally even more noticeably different from standard French.

Within France there are two main dialect areas, the north (*langue d'oïl*) and the south (*langue d'oc*), both of which contain subdialects, or *patois*, local remnants of various dialects that developed out of LATIN. Generally speaking, those found in the north are considered dialects of French, although mutual intelligibility with standard French does not always obtain. In the south, a number of dialects are grouped under the name Occitan (q.v.) which is considered a sister Romance language to French, although this is controversial as some scholars do not view Occitan as a distinct linguistic reality. Dialects containing features in common with both northern (*langue d'oïl*) and southern (*langue d'oc*) speech are spoken in a zone extending east- and westward from the mid-Rhone region and are known collectively as Franco-Provençal.

Number of Speakers: 109–123 million.

Origin and History

French is descended from Vulgar Latin, which was brought into France—then known as Gaul—by the Romans beginning in the second century B.C. The inhabitants encountered by the Romans were primarily Celts, an Indo-European people who had arrived from central or eastern Europe some 300 years earlier, displacing the Iberians and Ligurians. The legacy of Gaulish, their native tongue, is evident today in some thousand Gaulish place-names primarily in the north of France, as well as numerous common words. Latin gradually displaced Gaulish, and by the end of the fifth century, Gaulish became extinct.

After the unifying political influence of Rome eroded, about the start of the fourth century A.D., there began a series of invasions, the most important of which were those of the Germanic tribes. The Visigoths established their presence in the southwest, the Burgundians in the Rhone Valley, and the Franks in the north. These groups had a profound impact on the language.

The major dialect division that was to emerge in France was between the northern dialects, grouped under the term *langue d'oïl,* and the southern dialects, the *langue d'oc*, (*oïl* and *oc* are corresponding words from the north and the south respectively, that mean 'yes'). In the north, where the Franks held sway, the language changed most radically and eventually gave rise to what would become French as we know it, although it must be emphasized that the evolution from Latin to French was a very gradual process.

The realization that Latin had "deteriorated" prompted Emperor Charlemagne to import from England and Ireland monks who were Latin scholars. Through their efforts, the purity of Classical Latin was, to some extent, restored to the written language. They advocated a "letter-by-letter" pronunciation of Latin that conformed more closely to the new written standard. However, by the late eighth century, the spoken language in Gaul had diverged so much from Latin that in 813 at the Council of Tours, French clergymen were directed to preach their sermons in the vernacular, rather than in Latin, so that they could be understood by the people. The emergence of early Old French can be dated from this period.

Table 1: Consonants

	Labial	Dental	Alveolar	Alveo-palatal	Palatal	Velar	Uvular
Stops	p b	t d				k g	
Fricatives	f v		s s [z]	ch [š] j [ž]			 r [ʀ]
Lateral			l				
Nasals	m	n			gn [ɲ]		

The language that would become modern French arose from one of the dialects of the *langue d'oïl*. Modern scholars have termed this dialect *Francien*. It was spoken in the Ile-de-France region, roughly the area bounded by the Marne, the Oise, and the Seine, which includes the city of Paris. This region had assumed increasing political and cultural importance when Hugh Capet, Duke of Ile-de-France, became king of France in 987. Other dialects, however, continued to be spoken, and these have left their mark in the regional varieties of contemporary French.

From the 12th century onward, the language was increasingly being written down, and since *Francien* was the preferred spoken form, the writings strove to approximate it. During this period, there was a burgeoning of literature. The masterpiece *Chanson de Roland* is an example from the Old French period, which lasted until about 1300.

The Middle French period extended from roughly the first half of the 14th century to the first half of the 17th century. Words from Latin and later, Italian, continued to enter the language. The first printing press in France was located in Paris in 1470 and produced French texts in the language of Paris to the exclusion of other French dialects. By the 16th century, French was beginning to dominate Latin in official documents such as public records and legal documents.

During the French Revolution there was a sense that the lack of linguistic unity within France was a serious threat to the political unity of the country. In 1790, Abbé Grégoire, the bishop of Blois, prepared a detailed questionnaire concerning language use in the provinces; this yielded a count of 30 local speech varieties. He submitted his findings to the convention in 1794 and recommended the "sole and invariable use of the language of liberty in a Republic one and indivisible". State-sponsored primary education was advocated, although it was neither free nor compulsory until 1882.

Dialects declined at a steady pace until the last third of the 19nth century, when the rate of their loss greatly accelerated and scholars began to fear that the dialects might die out altogether. Jules Gilliéron and Edmond Edmont published the first dialect survey, *Atlas linguistique de la France* (1902–1910) which revealed that many dialect terms had ceased to be used. Today, the remnants of dialects that have flourished since the medieval period may be found among the oldest members of isolated rural communities. However, they are dying out, especially in the north where dialect areas have been described as being in a state of extreme disintegration. The term *patois*, which reflects a negative evaluation of these dialects, is popularly used to refer to them.

Orthography and Basic Phonology

French uses the 26 letters of the Roman alphabet plus two digraphs (œ and æ), as well as five diacritics in combination with certain letters (acute, grave, and circumflex accents; dieresis and cedilla). These additional elements bring the number of symbols used in spelling French to 41. Originally phonetically based, French orthography changed over the course of centuries, sometimes for ease of reading, sometimes for (real or imagined) etymological reasons until it was finally codified in the 17th century. Spelling rules have remained essentially unchanged since the 18th century. There is considerable divergence between spoken and written French today, so that the orthography is insufficient to represent the phonetics. For example, the sound [s] is represented by eight different spellings: *son, caisse, cerf, leçon, descendre, douceâtre, ration,* and *dix,* while in other cases the same letter or group of letters can represent different sounds as does *en* in *chien, quotient, solennel, hennir,* and *parlent.*

Mastery of the system is notoriously difficult. Numerous attempts at reform have been made since the mid-19th century, but the prestige accorded the written language is such that the proposals have met with much resistance.

French consonants (see Table 1 above) are either voiced (pronounced with vibration of the vocal cords) or voiceless (no vibration). When two successive consonants that differ with respect to this feature occur within a word or across a word boundary, the first will tend to assimilate to the second with respect to voicing; that is, the first will take the voicing of the second: *anecdote* 'anecdote' is pronounced [anɛgdɔt]; *une jupe bleue* 'a blue skirt' [yn žyb blø].

The consonants *l* and *r* will frequently not be pronounced if they conclude a consonant cluster that occurs at the end of a word: *une table* 'a table' is frequently pronounced [yn tab]; *notre ami* 'our friend' [nɔt ami].

French has 11 phonemic oral vowels and four nasal vowels, /ɛ^{n} œ^{n} ɑ^{n} o^{n}/, which are phonemic. *Beau* /bo/ 'handsome' and *bon* /bo^{n}/ 'good' are distinguished only in the quality of the vowel (oral vs. nasal).

Table 2: Vowels

	Front		Back	
	Unround	Round	Unround	Round
High	i	y		u
Upper Mid	e	ø		o
Lower Mid	ɛ	œ		ɔ
Low	a			ɑ
Nasal Vowels	ɛ^n	œ^n	ɑ^n	o^n
Semi-Vowels	j	ɥ		w

French vowels are generally short. All vowels except [e], [a], and [ɑ] may be lengthened, however, if they are in the last syllable of a word or rhythmic group and the syllable ends in a consonant. The 12th oral vowel, conventionally represented as schwa (ə), is troublesome. In terms of its pronunciation, it seems to fluctuate between [ø] and [œ]. Its status as an independent phonetic and/or phonemic entity has been called into question and it is most often not included on summary charts. However, the vowel has behavioral properties that distinguish it from all other French vowels. For example, it is either pronounced as a full vowel or it is not realized at all. Also, it can bear stress only in very limited contexts.

Lengthening will be automatic if the final consonant is *r, z, s, v,* or the cluster *vr*. The nasal vowels and [ø], [œ], and [ɑ] automatically lengthen before any final consonant.

The basic rhythm of French is a function of the syllable. Syllables occur at regular time intervals and are of equal duration. Syllables tend to be open; that is, to end with a vowel rather than a consonant. Stress is predictable, occurring on the final syllable before a pause. In connected speech, pauses tend to occur at major syntactic breaks rather than between words. The result is that there are no boundaries between words within a rhythmic group. There are three important linking phenomena: *élision, enchainement,* and *liaison.*

Élision involves the disappearance of certain word-final vowels when the following word begins with a vowel sound. For example, the full form of the masculine singular determiner *le* occurs before *garçon, (le garçon)* but the elided form *l'* occurs before a word such as *ami (l'ami).* Most common is *élision* of the vowel *e* [ə] in monosyllabic words such as determiners and pronouns. *Élision* also occurs before words beginning with a silent h but not the so-called "aspirate h", and before certain but not all semi-vowels, or glides, as illustrated in the contrasting pairs *l'homme* 'man', *le héros* 'hero'; and *l'oiseau* 'bird', *le whiskey* 'whiskey'.

Enchainement is the rhythmic linking of a pronounced word-final consonant with the initial vowel of the following word. As can be seen in the following example, *enchainement* results in resyllabification: *il écoute* (i.lé.coute). The same conditions that block *élision* also block *enchainement.*

Liaison is a special type of *enchainement.* In this case, a word-final consonant (which appears in the spelling of the word) will be pronounced *only* if the following word begins with a vowel. When the word is spoken in isolation or occurs before a word beginning with a consonant, the *liaison* consonant is silent: *les* 'plural article' [le] > *les garçons* 'the boys' [le garso^n]; *les amis* 'the friends' [le zami]. The small group that makes up the *liaison* consonants includes *s, t, n, p, r,* and *g. Liaison* is blocked by the same conditions that block *enchainement* and *élision.*

The intonational pattern of French sentences consists of subpatterns associated with the rhythmic groups of the sentence, which are generally determined by sentence type (declarative, interrogative, imperative).

Basic Morphology

The major classes of words in French include noun, determiner, adjective, pronoun, verb, adverb, preposition, conjunction, and interjection.

French nouns belong to one of two gender classes: masculine and feminine. Class assignment correlates partially with natural gender (nouns referring to males are generally masculine), reference (names of languages, trees, and geometric figures are masculine), or a combination of form and reference (nouns ending in *té* and referring to abstract concepts are feminine). Research suggests that native speakers of French associate gender with the noun's phonological form. Nouns are inflected for singular or plural number, e.g., *la voiture* 'the auto (feminine)' > *les voitures* 'the autos'; *le livre* 'the book (masculine) > *les livres* 'the books'.

With few exceptions, nouns are accompanied by determiners that are inflected for gender and number, to agree with the noun they modify. The class of determiners includes words traditionally called articles; demonstrative, possessive, and interrogative adjectives; and some quantifiers.

Distinct paradigms for subject, object (with direct and indirect object forms being identical except in the third person), and disjunctive pronouns are all that remain of case in Modern French.

Traditional treatments of French morphology are based on distinctions preserved in the orthography, many of which have been lost in the spoken language. Descriptive accounts based on the spoken language may depart significantly from what most people have been taught. This is particularly true in the treatment of French verbs.

French verbs may be simple or compound. In their simple form, verbs are inflected with a suffix that indicates tense/mood and agrees with the person of the subject (first, second, third, singular and plural). The suffix is attached to the verb root; verbs are traditionally classified into three conjugations (*-er*, *-ir*, and *-re*) according to the spelling of infinitive and present tense endings, leaving many apparently irregular verbs.

A regrouping of simple verbs into one of four categories based on the number of phonological roots they exhibit in the present tense—one, two, three, four or more—brings out the underlying regularity of the system. Verbs that have one root make up the largest and only productive group. An example from this group is the verb *chanter* 'to sing', which is conjugated adding appropriate endings to the root [ša^{n}t]. The verbs *partir* 'to depart' and *finir* 'to finish' have two roots in the present, [par] and [part], [fini] and [finis]. A three-root verb is *boire* 'to drink': [bwa], [buv], and [bwav]. The verb *aller* 'to go' is a four-root verb: [vɛ], [va], [al], [vo^n]. Verbs with more than four roots include *avoir* 'to have', *pouvoir* 'to be able', and *être* 'to be'.

Like the present tense, the imperfect, the simple past, the imperative, and the subjunctive are also formed by adding the appropriate suffix to the root morpheme. The future and the present conditional consist of the root plus an appropriate extension, and then the inflectional suffix. In the example *je chanterai* 'I will sing', the verb includes the root *chant* [ša^{n}t], extension *er* [ər], and suffix *ai* [ɛ].

Compound tenses are made up of an auxiliary verb inflected for person and tense/mood and a past participle. The past participle is composed of the verb stem plus a participle ending. In spoken French, compound tenses/mood are the indicative past indefinite, present perfect, pluperfect, future perfect, the past conditional, and the past subjunctive. The imperfect subjunctive may be used in the written language.

The auxiliary will either be a form of the verb *avoir* 'to have', or *être* 'to be'. A small number of intransitive verbs of motion or state and all reflexive verbs are conjugated with *être*. All other verbs are conjugated with *avoir*. The past participle of an intransitive verb conjugated with *être* must agree in number and gender with the subject of the sentence. The past participle of a verb conjugated with *avoir* and of reflexive verbs must agree in number and gender with the direct object if the object precedes the past participle in the sentence. If the direct object follows the past participle, no agreement is made. Since most past participles end in a vowel sound, agreement is rarely heard in the spoken language.

Basic Syntax

The basic constituent order of the French sentence is SVO. The simple declarative sentence with a nominal object exhibits this order: *Un chien mange de la viande.* (a dog eats PARTITIVE the meat) 'A dog eats meat'. However, the corresponding sentence with a prenominal object deviates from this order with the object in preverbal position: *Un chien la mange.* (IND.ART.MASC dog OBJ.FEM.SG eat.PRES.3S) 'A dog eats it'.

The truth of a statement as a whole may be questioned in standard French by means of the clause-initial question words *est-ce que*, by interrogative intonation, or inversion of the SVO word order:

Est-ce qu'il vient? 'Is he coming?'
*Il vi*ent? 'Is he coming?'
Vient-il? 'Is he coming?'

A fourth type, very common in North American spoken varieties of French, involves the inclusion of a morphological marker suffixed to the verb: *Il vient-tu?* 'Is he coming?' The rules for use of one form or another are subject to a complex number of syntactic, social, stylistic, pragmatic and discursive factors.

Negation of a statement is expressed with a construction of two elements that surround the verb or verbal auxiliary, if any, and any preceding object pronouns. The first negative element is the particle *ne*. The second element is one of several negative adverbs (*pas* 'not', *jamais* 'never', *plus* 'no longer') or pronouns (*rien* 'nothing' or *personne* 'no one'): *Je ne l'-ai pas fait.* (I NEG it-have NEG done) 'I didn't do it'. A sentence may include more than one following negative element: *Je n'ai jamais rien fait à personne.* 'I never did anything to anyone'. The first negative element is frequently omitted in the spoken language.

Contact with Other Languages

When William, duke of Normandy, defeated Harold, king of England, at the Battle of Hastings in 1066, he established himself as King of England, set up a new order of nobles, and made Norman French the language of the aristocracy, the court, law, and religion. Eventually ENGLISH triumphed over French, but French had a profound influence on English.

With French expansionism, the French language was exported to Canada, the Antilles, Senegal, and India. The prestige of French continued to mount in the 18th century when it became the language of diplomacy and of the courts of Prussia, Piedmont, Austria, Sweden, and Russia. In the 19th and early 20th centuries, the language spread further afield as France went into (and subsequently withdrew from) northern Africa, west Africa, the Middle East, Asia, and the Pacific.

Today there are French-based Creoles in various parts of the world where French is also spoken, including the United States (Louisiana); Africa; and the islands of Mauritius, Seychelles, and Réunion in the Indian Ocean; and Martinique, Guadeloupe, and Haiti in the West Indies. In most of these areas, the creoles are spoken by many more people than speak French.

Standard French has borrowed words from many languages. Latin forms the core of the language, but there are approximately 200 words of Gaulish origin, including common words such as *chemin* 'road', *mouton* 'sheep', and *sapin* 'pine tree'. The legacy of the Germanic invasions is evident in words such as *bleu* 'blue', *jardin* 'garden', *guerre* 'war'. Sample borrowings from regional speech include *amour* 'love' and *ballade* 'ballad' from Provençal, and *canevas* 'canvas' and *tricoter* 'knit' from Picard.

Internationally, French has incorporated vocabulary from many sources:

From English: budget, jury, verdict, wagon, tunnel
From Italian: *banque* 'bank', *credit* 'credit'
From Spanish: *nègre* 'negro', *tabac* 'tobacco'
From Portugese: *cobra* 'cobra', *banane* 'banana'
From DUTCH: *havre* 'harbor', *matelot* 'sailor'
From ARABIC: *hasard* 'hazard', *jupe* 'skirt'

French has been an important source of vocabulary in English: bachelor, caterpillar, duty, envelope, foreign, fuel, moustache, purchase, restaurant, and toast are all fully naturalized, while expressions like carte blanche, femme fatale, deja vu, double entendre, faux pas, and coup d'etat are more obviously French in origin.

Common Words

man:	homme	long:	long
woman:	femme	small:	petit
water:	eau	yes:	oui

sun:	soleil	no:	non
three:	trois	good:	bon
fish:	poisson	bird:	oiseau
big:	grand	dog:	chien
tree:	arbre		

Example Sentences

(1) Elle est américaine.
she is American.FEM.SG
'She is American.'

(2) Parl-ez-vous francais?
speak-2p.PRES-2p.PRO French
'Do you speak French.' (*Vous* may encode a plural or formal addressee).

(3) Nous avons regardé un film.
we have watched a.MASC movie
'We watched a movie.'

Efforts to Preserve, Protect, and Promote the Language

The most famous official body concerned with legislating language matters is the *Académie Française*. Founded in 1635 to oversee the development of the language and to create an official dictionary, grammar, rhetoric, and treatise on poetics, the academy's judgment in language matters was highly influential until the time of the French Revolution, when it was disbanded. Brought back into existence in the early 19th century, its power has declined substantially. However, it remains an important force in the awarding of subsidies to literary associations and journals and in its awarding of literary prizes.

The status of French as a world language has changed radically in the last hundred years, as English has largely become the language of choice in world trade and diplomacy. Yet, French continues as an official language in many former colonies, serving as an alternative to competing local languages as well as a vehicle for communication with the world at large. An international movement advocating a worldwide French-speaking community known as *la francophonie* has founded several organizations in support of this idea. The *Alliance Française*, formed in 1883, is active in some 96 countries teaching French language and culture.

In France, the *Délégation générale à la langue française* and the *Conseil supérieur de la langue française* serve to study general problems of French and to find solutions and advise the government, respectively. A major recent concern has been the development of technical vocabulary to insure against the adoption of Anglicisms.

Many other countries where French is spoken have seen the need to legislate linguistic matters as well. Among these, the efforts made in Quebec over the last 30 years are generally regarded as having been highly successful in stemming the flow of language shift toward English in that Canadian province.

Select Bibliography

Atkins, Beryl T., *et al.* 1993. *Collins-Robert French-English, English-French Dictionary*. London: Harper-Collins.

Battye, Adrian, and Marie-Anne Hintze. 1992. *The French Language Today*. London: Routledge.

Brunot, Ferdinand, and Charles Bruneau. 1949. *Précis de grammaire historique de la langue française*. Paris: Masson & Cie.

Catache, N. 1988. *L'orthographe*. 3rd ed. Paris: Presses Universitaires de France.

Chaudenson, Robert. 1979. *Les créoles français*. Paris: Nathan.

Deniau, X. 1983. *La francophonie*. The Hague: Mouton.

Grevisse, Maurice. 1993. *Le bon usage*. 13th ed. Paris and Gembloux: Ducrot.

Guiraud, Pierre. 1963. *Patois et dialectes français*. 3rd ed. Paris: Presses Universitaires de France.

____. 1978. *Les mots savants*. Paris: Presses Universitaires de France.

Hagège, Claude. 1987. *Le français et les siécles*. Paris: Odile Jacob.

Lodge, R. Anthony. 1993. *French: From Dialect to Standard*. London: Routledge.

Lodge, R. Anthony, Nigel Armstrong, Yvette M.L. Lewis, and Jane F. Shelton. 1997. *Exploring the French Language*. London: Arnold.

Price, Glanville. 1971. *The French Language: Past and Present*. London: Edward Arnold.

Rickard, Peter. 1989. *A History of the French Language*. 2nd ed. London: Unwin Hyman.

Sanders, Carol, ed. 1993. *French Today: Language In Its Social Context*. Cambridge: Cambridge University Press.

Valdman, Albert, ed. 1979. *Le français hors de France*. Paris: Champion.

Walter, Henriette. 1994. *French Inside Out*. London: Routledge.

Fula

Carole Paradis

Language Name: Fula. **Alternates:** Fulbe. In French: Peul or Poular (from Wolof *Pøl*). **Autonyms:** *Pulaar* (in Mauritania, Senegal, and Gambia); *Pular* (in Guinea, Guinea Bissau, and Sierra Leone); *Fulfulde* (in Mali, Nigeria, Niger, Chad, Cameroon, Sudan, Burkina Faso, Ghana, Togo, Benin, and the Central African Republic). The Hausa call the language Filani and the Kanuri call it Fulata or Felata. It is called several other names, depending on the neighborhood.

Location: Fula is spoken in west Africa between the 7th and 17th parallels, encompassing the 17 countries listed above.

Family: West Atlantic subgroup of the Niger-Congo (formerly West Sudanic) group of the Niger-Kordofanian language family.

Related Languages: Serer and WOLOF.

Dialects: Fula is divided between two main linguistic groups: Western and Eastern. Classification into one or the other is largely based on the infinitive class marker: *de* for the Western group and *gol* for the Eastern one. Nonetheless, all Fula dialects are mutually intelligible to a reasonable extent, regardless of what people call their language (*Pulaar*, *Pular*, or *Fulfulde*) or whichever dialect they speak. Divergences among dialects are mainly lexical, due mostly to differences in borrowings.

Western dialects are: (1) Pulaar (northern Senegal and southern Mauritania), (2) Central Senegal (central Senegal and Gambia), (3) Fulakunda-Gabu (southern Senegal, Guinea Bissau), (4) Fuuta-Jaloo (Guinea Bissau, Guinea and Sierra Leone), (5) West Maasina (western Mali), (6) East Maasina (eastern Mali), (7) Duentza (eastern Mali), (8) Seeno (eastern Mali and northern Burkina Faso, (9) Barani (eastern Mali and northern Burkina Faso), (10) South Tugan (western Burkina Faso), (11) Yatenga (western Burkina Faso), (12) Mossi-Gurma (central Burkina Faso), (13) Djelgooldji (central Burkina Faso), (14) Liptaako (eastern Burkina Faso and western Niger, (15) Gaobes (northeastern Mali), and (16) Say-Urorgelaadjo (eastern Burkina Faso and western Niger).

Eastern dialects are (17) Dallol (southwestern Niger), (18) Benin (northern Benin and northern Togo), (19) Zarma-Kabi (western Niger), (20) Central Niger, (21) Eastern Niger, (22) Sokkoto (northwestern Niger), (23) Nigeria (central dialects), (24) Bautchi (eastern Nigeria), (25) Bornu (eastern Nigeria), (26) Adamawa (eastern Nigeria, northern Cameroon, western Central African Republic, western Chad), (27) Dageeja (Cameroon), (28) Bagirmi (western Chad), (29) Lame (Chad), and (30) Gombe (Nigeria and Sudan). There are other Eastern dialects spoken in Cameroon, Chad, the Central African Republic, and Sudan. However, these cannot be located precisely because of the lack of documentation.

Number of Speakers: UNESCO estimated the number of speakers of Fula in 1985 to be between 12 and 15 million. However, because Fula speakers are so widely scattered in small groups across west Africa, it is hard to assess their exact numbers. Estimates of the number of Fula speakers who reside east of Cameroon are either unavailable or less reliable. Their being so scattered might explain the low political power of the Fulbe nowadays in most countries, and the fact that Fula does not have official status in any country.

Origin and History

There have been several controversial hypotheses concerning the origins of the Fulbe. Some scholars argue that they are the descendants of ancient Egyptians, others of the Basques, and still others of India's Dravidians. None of these hypotheses has been adequately proved. Instead, it is currently generally believed that the Fulbe have come in successive waves from west to east, mainly during the past 10 centuries. Their early habitat was somewhere in the eastern part of what is now Senegal or the western part of present-day Mali. They were essentially pastoral people, who herded their cattle in the west African savanna until the Fulbe jihads, which occurred over the past three centuries.

The Fulbe are divided into castes. The *Toorodɓe*, who are from the dominant Fulbe strata of Futa Toro, have been the conquerors who have participated in the Fulbe jihads, and who have subsequently formed the first real Islamic states in west Africa. Most of the Fulbe conquerors settled and developed intimate socioeconomic relationships with their captives, and entered into a new commercial economy. Unlike other African peoples, the Fulbe were producers of cattle, which are endowed with high economic and political value.

At present, some Fulbe are nomadic or seminomadic with rather frequent migrations, while others are transhumant, migrating between rainy and dry season camps or villages. Most Fulbe, however, have settled in villages or more recently in cities. This is the case of the *Toorodɓe*, who do not identify with the Fulbe anymore. In fact, they call themselves *haalpulaar'en* ('Fula speakers'), not Fulbe.

Table 1: Consonants

		Labial	Alveolar	Palatal	Velar	Glottal
Stops	Voiceless	p	t		k	' [ʔ]
	Voiced	b	d		g	
	Prenasalized	ᵐb	ⁿd	ᶮj	ᵑg	
Fricatives		f	s			h
Affricates	Voiceless		c [tʃ]			
	Voiced		j [dʒ]			
Implosives		ɓ	ɗ			
Nasals		m	n	ny [ɲ]	ŋ	
Trill			r			
Lateral			l			
Glides		w (ɥ)		y [j]		

Orthography and Basic Phonology

Fula has been written in the LATIN alphabet—following diverse conventions—since the 19th century. The orthography was unified in 1966 by a group of linguists of UNESCO at a conference in Bamako.

Fula has 27 consonants, as shown in Table 1 above. There is some phonological variation between dialects. For instance, the glottal stop, which is represented as an apostrophe in the written language, is not lexically distinctive in Pulaar, although it seems to be distinctive in other dialects. It is systematically realized before a word-initial vowel and productive suffixes such as *-ɛn* in *Aali-ʔɛn*. Consonant geminates and long vowels are written with two identical graphemes. The affricates *tʃ* and *dʒ* are spelled *c* and *j*, respectively, and the palatal nasal *ɲ* is usually written *ny*, although we use *ɲ* here.

Consonant geminates are permitted in Fula, although continuant ones (e.g., *rr*, *ww*, *yy*, etc.) are rare in *Fulfulde*, and plainly disallowed in Pulaar. Vocalic and consonantal geminates are written with two identical graphemes. Some examples from Pulaar include: *lepp-u-dɛ* 'wet', *abb-aa-dɛ* 'to rejoin', *yett-u-dɛ* 'to praise', *lacc-iri* 'couscous', *majj-ɛrɛ* 'ignorance', *ɗokk-uru* 'one-eyed', *taɓɓ-ɛrɛ* 'fruit', *wull-u-dɛ* 'to shout', *kaŋŋɛ* 'gold', and *hɛllɔ* 'slap'.

Consonantal geminates cannot occur after a long vowel (*V:C:), unless the consonantal geminate results from assimilation (e.g., Pulaar *fɔɔd-n-a* > *fɔɔnna* 'to make someone pull'). Nonetheless, a consonant sequence can occur after a long vowel (e.g., Pulaar *kaakt-ɛ* 'saliva').

Table 2: Vowels

	Front	Back
High, +ATR	i	u
Mid-High, +ATR	e	o
Mid-Low, -ATR	ɛ	ɔ
Low, -ATR		a

There are seven oral vowels in Fula. Each of the vowels shown in Table 2 has a long counterpart. Vowel length is distinctive although alternations are predictable in most cases: a long vowel, unless it belongs to the first syllable of a word, is shortened before a closed syllable. The mid-ATR vowels *e* and *o* are mostly phonetic variants of non-ATR *ɛ* and *ɔ*, which harmonize in tenseness with a following high tense vowel, such as Pulaar 'antelope' where the singular is *kɔɔb-a,* but the plural is *koob-i*. The non-ATR mid-vowels *ɛ* and *ɔ* are written *e* and *o*, respectively, and pronounced like 'e' in ENGLISH 'ten' and 'o' in English 'born'. The other vowels are written as in the above inventory.

In contrast to many west African languages, Fula is not a tonal language. The syllable structure of Fula is (C)V(V)(C). Stems are generally monosyllabic, although words can be much longer.

It is traditionally maintained that stress falls on the first syllable. This might be due to the fact that stress was often confused with high pitch (see Breedveld). If we assume that it is the amplitude that marks a stressed syllable, it is the syllable structure of a word that determines the place of stress. For instance, McIntosh shows that the stress in Fula falls on the last non-final heavy syllable (CVC or CVV) of nouns. It is only when such a syllable is absent that the stress is placed on the first syllable.

Basic Morphology

Fula has a complex nominal class system of about 25 class markers. The exact number of classes may vary from one dialect to another. For instance, Pulaar has 21 class markers, 17 in the singular and 4 in the plural. Nominal class is an abstract concept to which semantic features can sometimes be attached. These semantic features characterize, in most cases, subsets of the class but not the whole class. As such, nominal classes are as arbitrary as the feminine and masculine in FRENCH or the animate and inanimate in Amerindian languages.

What makes the marker system of Fula so complex is that markers have variants, which are traditionally distributed into grades. Grade A refers to the marker shortened form, Grade B to the marker continuant form, Grade C to the marker noncontinuant form, and Grade D to the marker prenasalized form (when the marker-initial consonant can be prenasalized). Atypical variants also exist, which are given in parentheses. Nonetheless, the nominal class-marker system of Pulaar might be less complex than it appears at first sight. Paradis (1992) has shown that if the Grade C form is taken as the basic one, the other marker variants are predictable on phonological and morphological grounds.

Nominal classes:

GRADES	A	B	C	D
1	ɔ	jɔ	ɗɔ	ɗɔ
2	ɓɛ [ɛn]	ɓɛ	ɓɛ	ɓɛ
3	ɛl	yɛl	gɛl	^{ŋ}gɛl
		wɛl		
4	al	wal	kal	kal
		yal		
5	ɔn	wɔn	kɔn	kɔn
		yɔn		
6	a	wa	ba	ba
7	ɔ	wɔ	kɔ	kɔ
8	(ɛ)rɛ	rɛ	dɛ	^{n}dɛ
	dɛ			
9	(i)ri	ri	di	^{n}di
	di			
10	(u)ru	ru	du	^{n}du
	du			
11	ɛ	wɛ	gɛ	^{ŋ}gɛ
12	ɔ	wɔ	gɔ	^{ŋ}gɔ
13	u	wu	gu	^{ŋ}gu
14	al	wal	gal	^{ŋ}gal
15	ɔl	wɔl	gɔl	^{ŋ}gɔl
16	a	wa	ka	ka
17	i	wi	ki	ki
18	am	jam	ɗam	ɗam [^{n}dam]
19	um	jum	ɗum	ɗum
20	ɛ	jɛ	ɗɛ [lɛ]	ɗɛ [lɛ]
21	i	ji	ɗi [li]	ɗi [li]

Examples with the class marker ^{ŋ}gel:

Grade A	paɗɛl	'small shoe'
Grade B	ɔtɔyɛl	'small car' (from French)
	dɔgɔwɛl	'small runner'
Grade C	gaɓugɛl	'small cheek'
Grade D	dawa^{ŋ}gɛl	'small dog'

Adjectives take the same class-marker variant (grade) as the noun they qualify: *nɔf-ru ɲaam-ru* (ear right) 'right ear'.

Fula is also reputed for the alternations the class markers can cause at the beginning of nouns, verbs and adjectives. Some class markers, the EFFECT-0 markers, trigger no change while some others, the EFFECT-1 and EFFECT-2 markers, cause, respectively, the occlusivization of a noun-initial consonant, or the prenasalization of the consonant.

Marker classification:

	EFFECT-0	EFFECT-1	EFFECT-2
singular	du	ɗum	ɗam
	dɛ	gal	ba
	gɛ	gɛl	di
	gɔ	gɔl	gu
	kɔ	ki	ka
		kal	
		ɗɔ	
plural	ɓɛ	ɗɛ	kɔn
		ɗi	

Examples (class markers are indicated in brackets):

EFFECT-0	EFFECT-1	EFFECT-2	gloss
w > b, ^{m}b			
wɛcc-ɔ [gɔ]	bɛcc-ɛ [ɗɛ]	^{m}bɛcc-ɔn [kɔn]	'rib'
wɔj-ɛrɛ [dɛ]	bɔj-ɛ [ɗɛ]	^{m}bɔj-ɔn [kɔn]	'hare'
wukk-uru [du]	bukk-i [ɗi]	^{m}bukk-ɔn [kɔn]	'pompom'
r > d, ^{n}dɛ			
ruul-dɛ [dɛ]	duul-ɛ [ɗɛ]	^{n}duul-ɔn [kɔn]	'cloud'
s > c			
sɛkk-ɔ [gɔ]	cɛkk-ɛ [ɗɛ]	cɛkk-ɔn [kɔn]	'mat'
h > k			
hɛll-ɔ [gɔ]	kɛll-ɛ [ɗɛ]	kɛll-ɔn [kɔn]	'slap'
y > j, ^{ɲ}j			
yim-rɛ [dɛ]	jim-ɛl [gɛl]	^{ɲ}jim-ɔn [kɔn]	'poem'
yɔnt-ɛrɛ [dɛ]	jɔnt-ɛ [ɗɛ]	^{ɲ}jɔnt-ɔn [kɔn]	'week'
yaaɓ-rɛ [dɛ]	jaaɓ-ɛ [ɗɛ]	^{ɲ}jaaɓ-ɔn [kɔn]	'jujube'
wɔ > gɔ, ^{ŋ}gɔ			
wɔr-ɓɛ [ɓɛ]	gɔr-k-ɔ [ɗɔ]	^{ŋ}gɔr-ɔn [kɔn]	'man'
wu > gu, ^{ŋ}gu			
wur-ɔ [gɔ]	gur-ɛ [ɗɛ]	^{ŋ}gur-ɔn [kɔn]	'village'
yi > gi, ^{ŋ}gi			
yiit-ɛrɛ [dɛ]	giit-ɛ [ɗɛ]	^{ŋ}giit-ɔn [kɔn]	'eye'
yɛ > gɛ, ^{ŋ}gɛ			
yɛrt-ɛrɛ [dɛ]	gɛrt-ɛ [ɗɛ]	^{ŋ}gɛrt-ɔn [kɔn]	'peanut'
a > ga, ^{ŋ}ga			
abb-ɛrɛ [dɛ]	gabb-ɛl [gɛl]	^{ŋ}gabb-ɔn [kɔn]	'seed'

Adjectives take the same classmarker as the noun they qualify. Definite articles and nonpersonal subject pronouns used in the perfective are identical to the Grade D variant of class markers (e.g., marker: *du*; definite article ^{n}*du*; pronoun (perfective): ^{n}*du*), e.g., *nɔf-ru ɲaam-ru* ^{n}*du* (ear right the) 'the right ear'.

Fula exhibits an aspectual system. Nonpersonal subject pronouns have perfective and imperfective forms. Personal pronouns can also have two forms, a short one (used with the perfective) and a long one (used with the imperfective). Short-form pronouns do not vary much across dialects in contrast to long-form pronouns, which differ more (see Miyamoto 1993 for a dialectal comparison). Here is a list of personal pronouns in Pulaar:

	Short form	Long form
1s.	mi	miɗɔ
2s.	a	aɗa
3s.	ɔ	ɔmɔ
1p. exclusive	min	amin
1p inclusive	ɛn	ɛɗɛn
2p.	ɔn	ɔɗɔn
3p.	ɓɛ	aɓɛ

Basic Syntax

Fula is a Subject-Verb-Object language. As such the above pronouns and other subjects precede the verb, as in: *mi ron-ii* (I inherit-PAST) 'I inherited'.

Fula also has a system of derivational suffixes. The most common derivational suffixes in verbs are:

-(i)r instrumental	*-kin* simulator
-(o)^{n} dir reciprocal	*-t* repetitive or inversive
-n causative	*-ɗ* inchoative
-w associative	*-an* benefactive

For example, the verb *ɗɔjj* 'to cough' can be causativized as *ɗɔjj-i-n* 'make cough'. The vowel *i* is epenthesized in order to prevent the formation of a disallowed complex coda or onset. Many of these suffixes can agglutinate (in a more or less strict order) and yield long verbal forms, e.g., *ɓutt-iɗ-it* 'become fat again'.

Fula has three voices: active, middle, and passive. There is an interesting interaction between voice and aspect. The perfective and imperfective aspects are cover terms for a total of seven aspectual categories, called subaspects and indicated with numerical indices in the table below:

Aspect	Voice		
Perfective (P)	Active (A)	Middle (M)	Passive (P)
P1	-	i	a
P2	i	ii	aa
P3	ii	iima	aama
Imperfective (I)			
I1	-	ɔ	ɛ
I2	a	ɔɔ	ɛɛ
I3	at	ɔtɔ	ɛtɛ
I4	ata	ɔtɔɔ	ɛtɛɛ

Here are some sentences from Pulaar based on the above table:

P1A Aali suuɗ sawru ^{n}du 'Ali hid the stick.'
P2A kɔ Aali suuɗ**i** sawru ^{n}du 'It is Ali who hid the stick.'
P3A Aali suuɗ**ii** sawru ^{n}du 'Ali hid the stick.'

I1A yɔɔ Aali suuɗ sawru ^{n}du 'Let Ali hide the stick.'
I2A maa Aali suuɗ**a** sawru ^{n}du 'Ali must hide the stick.'
I3A Aali suuɗ***at*** sawru ^{n}du 'Ali is hiding the stick.'
I4A kɔ Aali suuɗ**ata** sawru ^{n}du 'It is Ali who is hiding the stick.'

P1M Aali suuɗ**i** 'Ali hid.'
P2M kɔ Aali suuɗ**ii** 'It is Ali who hid.'
P3M Aali suuɗ**iima** 'Ali hid.'

11M yɔɔ Aali suuɗ**ɔ** 'Let Ali hide.'
12M maa Aali suuɗ**ɔɔ** 'Ali must hide.'
13M Aali suuɗ**ɔtɔ** 'Ali is hiding.'
14M kɔ Aali suud**ɔtɔɔ** 'It is Ali who is hiding.'

P1P Aali suuɗ**a** 'Ali was hidden.'
P2P kɔ Aali suuɗ**aa** 'It is Ali who was hidden.'
P3P Aali suuɗ**aama** 'Ali was hidden.'

I1P yɔɔ Aali suuɗ**ɛ** 'Let Ali be hidden.'
I2P maa Aali suuɗ**ɛɛ** 'Ali must be hidden.'
I3P Aali suuɗ**ɛtɛ** 'Ali is being hidden.'
I4P kɔ Aali suuɗ**ɛtɛɛ** 'It is Ali who is being hidden.'

There are three negative suffixes in the perfective aspect depending on which of the active, middle, and passive voices are involved. Here are some examples:

Active	mi suuɗ**aani**	'I did not hide.'
	mi an ^{n}**daa**	'I don't know.'
Middle	mi suuɗ**aaki**	'I am not hidden.'
Passive	mi suuɗ**aaka**	'I was not hidden (by someone).'

There are two types of negatives in the imperfective aspect: the periphrastic one and the suffixal one. The periphrastic one is used in the imperative:

haal! 'talk' > wɔtɔ haal! 'don't talk'

As in the case of the perfective, the suffixal negation in the imperfective aspect depends on which of the active, middle, and passive voices are involved.

Active:	mi suuɗ**ataa** comci di	'I will not hide the clothes.'
Middle	mi suuɗ**ɔtaakɔ**	'I will not hide.'
Passive	mi suuɗ**ɛtaakɛ**	'I will not be hidden (by someone).'

Contact with Other Languages

Fula has borrowed extensively from French and English since the beginning of the colonization in the 19th century. It has also borrowed from ARABIC, especially for religious items referring to Islam, and the neighboring west African languages, depending on the country where the Fula dialect is spoken. The following borrowed words are found in many dialects spoken in Mauritania, Senegal and Mali:

From French: *bɛrɛ* 'beret', *birɔ* 'desk', *kartal* 'card', *sɛ(ɛ)f* 'chef', *kalaas* 'class'
From Wolof: *^{m}balit* 'garbage', *^{m}bɛdda* 'road', *^{m}buru* 'bread', *kuddu* 'spoon'
From Arabic: *alkulal* 'letter (alphabet)', *annabi* 'prophet', *asamaan* 'sky', *anniya* 'conviction', *hakkillɛ* 'intelligence', *fajiri* 'dawn'

Common Words

man:	gɔrkɔ
long:	juutɔ (juut + marker)
woman:	dɛbbɔ
small:	tɔkɔsɔ (tɔkɔs + marker)
water:	^{n}diyam
yes:	eey
no:	ala

sun:	naa^{ŋ}gɛ
three:	tati
fish:	lii^{ŋ}gu
bird:	son^{n}du
big:	ɓuttɔ (ɓutt + marker)
dog:	rawaa^{n}du
tree:	lekki

Example Sentences

(1) miɗɔ ɲaam-a maarɔ
I:IMPERFECTIVE eat-IMPERFECTIVE rice
'I eat rice.'

(2) mi sood-i kɔsam
I buy-PERFECTIVE milk
'I bought milk.'

(3) ma-mi yɛɛy rawaa^{n}du ^{n}du
FUT-I sell dog DEF.ART
'I will sell the dog.'

Efforts to Preserve, Protect, and Promote the Language

The Fulbe are very protective of their language. Nevertheless, there is no one Fulbe organization that protects and promotes Fula, but there are several local associations. The Association for the Rebirth of Pulaar in the Islamic Republic of Mauritania (*Association pour la renaissance du Pulaar en République islamique de Mauritanie*) is one of these.

Select Bibliography

Arnott, D.W. 1970. *On the Nominal and Verbal Systems of Fula.* London: Oxford University Press.

Breedveld, J.O. 1995. *Form and Meaning in Fulfulde: A Morphophonological Study of Maasinankoore.* Leiden: Research School CNWS.

Kane, Moustapha, and David Robinson. 1984. *The Islamic Regime of Fuuta Toro.* Michigan State University: African Studies Center.

Labatut, Roger. 1973. *Le parler d'un groupe de peuls nomades, Nord Cameroun.* Société d'études linguistiques et anthropologiques de France. Paris: Selaf.

Lacroix, Pierre Francis. 1981. "Le peul." In Jean Perrot, ed., *Les langues dans le monde ancien et moderne*, 19–31. Paris: Éditions du centre national de la recherche scientifique.

Miyamoto, Ritsuko. 1993. "A Study of Fula Dialects: Examining the Continuous/Stative Constructions." In Paul Eguchi and Victor Azarya (eds.), *Unity and Diversity of a People: The Search for Fulbe Identity*, 215–230. Senri Ethnological Studies 35. Osaka: National Museum of Ethnology.

Paradis, Carole. 1992. *Lexical Phonology and Morphology: The Nominal Classes in Fula.* New York: Garland Publishing.

Prunet, Jean-François. 1992. *Spreading and Locality Domains in Phonology.* New York: Garland Publishing.

Seydou, Christiane. 1977. "Bibliographie générale du monde peul." In Études nigériennes, Institut de recherche en sciences humaines, Niamey University. Published with the help of the Centre national de la recherche scientifique (CNRS), France.

Sylla, Yero. 1982. *Grammaire moderne du Pulaar.* Dakar: Les novelles editions africaines.

Galician

Henrique Monteagudo

Language Name: Galician. **Alternate:** Galician-Portuguese. **Autonym:** *Galego.*

Location: Galicia (northwest Spain), as well as border areas in neighboring Asturias, León and Zamora (Spain). There are several nuclei of Galician emigration in other Spanish regions including Madrid, Barcelona and the Basque Country, as well as in France, Switzerland, Germany, United Kingdom, Holland, and the Americas including Argentina, Uruguay, Brazil, Venezuela, Cuba, Mexico, and the United States.

Family: Romance group of the Italic branch of Indo-European.

Related Languages: Galician is most closely related to PORTUGUESE; it is also related to the other Romance languages.

Dialects: There are three main dialect groups: (1) Eastern Galician, including dialects spoken outside Galicia proper, the most important being the Galician from Asturias; (2) Central Galician, including Central-Northern or "Mindoniense" and Central-Southern or "Lucu-Auriense"; and (3) Western Galician, including Northwestern and Southwestern.

The main dialectal features are: (1) in phonemics: *gheada* (pronunciation as H voiceless back fricative of *g* in words like *gato* 'cat', *pagar* 'pay'), characteristic of Western and a large part of Central Galician; and *seseo* (pronunciation as /s/ of elsewere dental *c* or *z* in words like *cen* '100', *cazar* 'hunt'), characteristic of Western Galician; (2) in morphology: in nouns, final *-án* (<LATIN *-anu* & *-ana*: *irmán* 'brother' < Latin *-germanu, germana*) in Western dialects against final *-ao* (< Latin *-anu*) as distinct from *-á* (<Latin *-ana*) (*irmao*/*irmá* ("brother/sister") in Central-Eastern dialects; in verbs, personal suffix *-is* for the fifth person (*andais* 'you walk') in Eastern dialects against general *-des* (*andades* 'you walk'). Eastern dialects (especially Galician from Asturias) offer several other particularities.

Number of Speakers: 2.5–3 million.

Origin and History

The history of Galician is usually divided into the following periods: Vulgar Latin and proto-Romance (approximately 1st to 8th centuries), Galician-Portuguese or medieval Galician (approximately 8th to 15th centuries), middle Galician (approximately 16th to 18th centuries), and contemporary Galician (19th century to the present).

Galician evolved from Vulgar Latin, introduced into the northwest Iberian Peninsula (today the region of Galicia in Spain) in the first century A.D. by the Romans. August (the conqueror of this area) incorporated what is now Galicia into the Hispania Citerior, or Tarraconensis, which included the northern and eastern parts of the peninsula. At the end of the third century Dioclecianus created the province of Gallaecia, which embodied the northwestern part of the Iberian Peninsula north of the Douro River. At the beginning of the fifth century, the Germanic Suevi settled there and created the first Catholic German kingdom in the Roman Empire, which lasted until the end of the sixth century, when the powerful Visigothic Hispanic Kingdom gained control of it. At this time, the Latinization of Gallaecia was probably almost complete because of the intense influence of the Christian Church.

At the beginning of the 8th century, the Moors invaded and occupied most of the Iberian Peninsula, although they were quickly expelled from the north, so their stay in Galicia was brief. In fact, the Galician area served as a refuge for the Hispanic-Visigothic aristocracy and Mozarabic clergy, and as a consequence many present Galician place names are Germanic in origin. Neither the Arabic-speaking Moors nor the Germanic speakers who preceded them influenced the local language to any degree. According to the extant evidence, until the end of the 12th century the only written language in Galicia was Latin, but the spoken language evolved more and more distinctly from it.

Nevertheless, Galician-Portuguese (the denomination commonly used by academics for Galician in its primitive and medieval form) counts among the most conservative of the Romance languages. For instance, it preserved both the Latin vowels without diphthongalization (Latin *petra* 'stone' > Gal. *pedra*; Latin *novu* > Gal. *novo*), and several Latin and Proto-Romance diphthongs that have been reduced elsewhere (Western Proto-Romance **teito* 'roof', **noite* 'night', **primairo* 'first' > Gal. *teito*, *noite*, *primeiro*). In addition to this, the main features that characterize Galician Portuguese among the Hispanic languages were fixed between the 8th and 12th centuries: reduction of intervocalic *ll* and *nn* to *l* and *n*, respectively (Latin *capillu-* 'hair', *canna* 'reed' > Galician *cabelo*, *cana*), and the dropping of *l* and *n* intervocalically (Latin *volare* 'fly', *luna* 'moon' > Galician *voar*, *lũa*). One feature genuinely distinctive of Galician-Portuguese is the nasalization of vowels caused by a dropped intervocalic *n*: *lũa* 'moon', *irmão* 'brother', *têer* 'to have', etc.

In the 11th century the territory of Gallaecia split into two polities: the independent kingdom of Portugal, and the kingdom of Galicia, which was federated with Leon and Castile. Eventually, these and other kingdoms would make up the country of Spain.

Table 1: Consonants

		Labial	Labio-dental	Dental	Alveolar	Palatal	Velar
Stops	Voiceless	p		t			c (a, o, u), qu (e, i)
	Voiced	b		d			g (a, o, u), gu (e, i)
Fricatives	Voiceless		f	z (a, o, u) c (e, i)	s	x	
Affricates						ch	
Nasals		m			n	ñ	-nh-, -n
Laterals					l	ll	
Tap					r		
Trill					r-, rr, -(l, n)r-		
Glides		u					

Toward the end of the 12th century Galician-Portuguese began to be written as the administrative and literary language of Galicia and Portugal. In the 13th century, Galician-Portuguese became the poetic language par excellence in the Iberian Peninsula, used in the feudal and royal courts throughout the north and west.

Since the political fragmentation of the Galician-Portuguese linguistic domain, Galician and Portuguese had been diverging. While the Portuguese variety was elevated as the official and cultivated language of the kingdom of Portugal, the Galician variety was under severe pressure from Castilian. Castilian, which was to become the basis for modern SPANISH, gained prestige during the 15th century because of the growing importance of the central region of the Iberian Peninsula and because of Castile's role in the reconquest of the south from the Moors.

From the 16th century to the 18th century, Castilian was imposed as the only official language of Galicia and Galician ceased almost completely to be used as a written language. As a consequence, Galician was not popularized through printing. The main features that characterize modern spoken Galician crystallized during this period.

In the 19th century, especially after the Napoleonic invasion of Spain, Galician reemerged as a literary language, although with moderate pretensions. The publication of *Cantares Gallegos*, by Galicia's most important writer, Rosalia de Castro (1837–1885), was the first modern literary event. Between 1916 and 1936 there was a large number of publications in Galician including fiction, civil oratory, essays, and research on the humanities and social sciences. The flowering was because of the work of organizations such as the *Irmandades da Fala* (Brotherhood of the Galician Language), *Seminario de Estudos Galegos* (Seminary of Galician Studies), and *Partido Galeguista* (Galicianist Party). Note must also be made of the efforts of the periodical *A Nosa Terra* (Our Land), the cutural review *Nós* (Us), and the editorial houses Céltiga, Lar, and Nós. Today, literary production in Galician is very much alive, with more than a thousand titles published annually. The same may be said of the essay and the social sciences and humanities. However, the use of Galician in the mass media, business, and in research in natural sciences is not as prevalent.

From the middle of the 19th to the middle of the 20th centuries large numbers of Galicians emigrated to Latin America, especially Cuba, Argentina, and Uruguay, and more recently to Europe and the United States For many years there had been movement to the industrialized areas of Spain including Madrid, Barcelona, and Basque Country, but emigration attained exodus proportions during this period (Galicia lost population in absolute terms).

The Spanish Civil War (1936–1939) and the subsequent Franco regime (1939–1975) brought new setbacks to the Galician language. Franco imposed the compulsory and exclusive use of Castilian in the official, educational and public domains. After the democratic restoration (1975), the new constitution recognized the official status of Galician at the regional level (1978), and the Statute of Autonomy of Galicia (1980) created the conditions for the recovery of the language, regulated by a regional law (*Lei de Normalización Lingüística*, 1983). Nevertheless, a lot of work remains to be done.

Orthography and Basic Phonology

The Galician alphabet has 23 letters (*a, b, c, d, e, f, g, h, i, l, m, n, ñ, o, p, q, r, s, t, u, v, x, z*) and six digraphs (*ch, gu, ll, nh, qu, rr*). The letters *ç, j, k, w* and *y* are used only in foreign words. The accent acute ´ is used to indicate the stressed syllable in polysyllabic words, and it is also used as a diacritic to distinguish pairs of words differentiated orally either because one of them is tonic and the other atonic (*dá*, verb *dar* 'give' / *da*, prep. *de* + article *a* 'of the, from the'), or because one has a lower midvowel and the other one has the corresponding upper midvowel (*vés*/*ves*). In writing, *é* and *ó* may represent both the upper mid- and the lower-mid vowels.

The distinctive consonant sounds in Galician are represented in Table 1 above by their typical orthographic spellings.

The vast majority of Galician speakers pronounce *ll* as a voiced palatal H stop.

Depending on the dialect *g* can be pronounced either as a voiced velar stop or as a voiceless velar, pharyngeal or glottal fricative. In the majority of Galician dialects *g* is pronounced as an H voiceless back fricative.

In word-final position, *-n* (as in *un* 'masculine indefinite article', *can* 'dog', *canción* 'song') is pronounced as a velar nasal.

The distinctive vowel sounds in Galician are represented in Table 2 below by their typical spellings.

Table 2: Vowels

	Front	Central	Back
High	i		u
Upper-Mid	e		o
Lower-Mid	é		ó
H Central		a	

*Note: In general *é* and *ó* may render the upper midvowels as well. The accent signs are used as diacritics in Table 2 for purposes of contrast.

Basic Morphology

Other than the three gender-neutral singular demonstrative pronouns *isto* 'this', *iso* 'that, medial', and *aquilo* 'that, distal', all articles, adjectives, nouns and pronouns are classified as either feminine or masculine in gender and as singular or plural in number. The plural is formed by adding *-s* or *-es* to the singular form, and may sometimes create new lexical items: *miolo* 'crumb' versus *miolos* 'brains'. Masculine nouns typically end in *-o* and feminines in *-a*, as in *neno/nena* 'child', *lobo/loba* 'wolf'. A pair of nouns opposed in gender may indicate a difference in sex, size (feminines usually denote larger objects than do masculines) or shape (*poza/pozo* 'well/pool'; *machada/machado* 'axe/hunting knife'). Nouns require morphological agreement with modifiers that they govern and with coreferential pronouns.

Galician is spoken in northwest Spain (shaded area) and also border areas in León and Zamora. It has also spread to areas as far as Madrid and Barcelona.

The indefinite articles are *un*, *unha* (feminine and masculine singular), and *uns*, *unhas* (feminine and masculine plural). The definite articles are *o*, *a*, *os*, and *as*. In speech, after words ending in *-r* or *-s*, these articles usually take the form *lo*, *la*, *los*, and *las*. In writing, *lo*, *la*, *los*, and *las* are frequently combined with preceding words. For example, they may combine with the prepositions *por* 'through' and *tras* 'after' to yield *polo(s)*, *pola(s)*, *tralo(s)*, and *trala(s)*, respectively. A hyphen is used if the preceding word is a verbal form (*levar os nenos* 'carry the children' > *leva-los nenos*).

Galician has a set of reflexive pronouns and five sets of personal pronouns: subject, direct object, indirect object, prepositional, and "company" pronouns. "Company" pronouns are pronouns of accompaniment, but note that *consigo* (below) is reflexive: we distinguish between *estabamos con el* 'we were with him' from *levaba unha pistola consigo* literally 'he/she had a gun with him/herself'. All six sets of pronouns have singular and plural forms for first, second and third persons. There are informal- and formal-address forms: informal *ti* (second person singular) and *vós* (second personal plural) and formal *vostede* (second person singular) and *vostedes* (second person plural). Subject, prepositional and "company" pronouns are stressed since they are used mainly for emphasis.

	Subject	Prepositional	Company
1 sg.	eu	min	comigo
2	ti	ti	contigo
3	el/ela	el/ela	consigo
1 pl.	nós	nós	connosco
2	vós	vós	convosco
3	eles/elas	eles/elas	consigo

Direct object, indirect object and reflexive pronouns are unstressed. In declarative affirmative independent sentences they are enclitic, i.e., they attach to the end of the verb; otherwise they are proclitic (placed before the verb).

	Direct Object	Indirect Object	Reflexive
1 sg.	me	me	me
2	te	che	te
3	o, a	lle	se
1 pl.	nos	nos	nos
2	vos	vos	vos
3	os, as	lles	se

The Galician verb (in its fullest forms) is constructed of a verb root, a verb class indicator, a mood/tense/perspective marker, and person agreement with the subject. A form like *andaremos* 'we will walk' is analyzed as follows: *and* (root 'walk') *-a* (1st class) *-re* (future indicative) *-mos* (1st pl). There are three verb classes, the indicators of which are *-a-* (*andar*), *-e-* (*bater*), and *-i-* (*partir*). There are a few irregular verbs: *dar* 'give', *dicir* 'say', *estar* 'be', *haber* 'have', *ir* 'go', *poder* 'be able', *pór* 'put', *querer* 'want', *saber* 'know', *ser* 'be', *ter* 'have', *traer* 'bring', *ver* 'see', and *vir* 'come'.

Only in the indicative are verbs inflected for tense and perspective (aspect): present (*ando*), past (*andei*), future (*andarei*); past perfect (*andara*), perfect (*andaba*), future perfect (*andaría*). In the subjunctive, verbs appear in either the present tense (*ande*) or past tense (*andase*). The future subjunctive (*andar*) is used only in legal and highly formal texts. Galician has two kinds of infinitives, the impersonal and the personal or inflected. The personal infinitive agrees with the subject in the second person singular and plural, first person plural and third person plural. Galician verb paradigms include two other impersonal forms: the gerund (invariable) and participle (variable in gender and number). Compound verbal forms exist only for the future (*hei andar*) and the future perfect (*había andar*).

Basic Syntax

Galician syntax is of the general southern Romance type. The basic word order is SVO, with direct objects preceding indirect objects (although the principles governing the positions of weak (clitic) pronouns are quite complex). Pronoun subjects that are not stressed or focused are indicated by verb morphology alone. In general, the language exhibits a head-initial nature in simple declarative sentences: auxiliaries precede verbs; verbs precede their objects and clausal complements; prepositions precede their terms; and within noun phrases nouns generally precede genitives, adjectives, and relative clause modifiers (although some adjectives do precede their head nouns; articles, possessives, demonstratives, numerals and indefinites generally precede their head nouns). Inversions of verb and object are common for thematization and emphasis of the object, however.

The true passive voice, formed with the auxiliary verb *ser* 'to be' plus the participle of the main verb, is rarely used in Galician except in legal, journalistic, and scientific writing. Instead, other constructions are used to convey a passivelike interpretation: the habitual word order can be inverted (*Ese libro lino eu cando era pequeno* 'This book was read by me when I was a child'; *Esa película rodárona na Coruña* 'This film was recorded in Coruña'); an active form of the verb can be used with a third person reflexive pronoun (*Esa película rodouse na Coruña*); and there is an impersonal construction in which an active third person singular form of the verb is used without an overt (spoken) subject, but is preceded by the pronoun *se*.

Absolute questions are usually formed by inverting the subject and finite verb (*¿Veu Antón?* 'Did you see Anton?'). Emphasis may be added with a final tag question (*¿Veu Antón ou non?*). In partial questions, an interrogative word is placed in sentence-initial position (*¿Cando veu Antón?*, *¿Como veu Antón?*, *¿Onde está Antón?*, *¿Quen é Antón?*, *¿Que di Antón?*, etc.). An expected answer, either positive or negative, may be anticipated with a final tag question (*Veu Antón, ¿non si?*—a positive answer is expected; *Non veu Antón, ¿a que non?*—a negative answer is expected). Positive answers are usually expressed via the repetition of the verb, reinforced on occasion with the adverb *si*:—*¿Veu Antón?* —*Veu*; —*¿Fostes á festa?* 'Did you go to the party?'—*Fomos, si* 'Yes, we did'. For negative answers, the adverb *non* is used.

Negation is generally expressed with *non* before the verb: *Carme non dixo nada interesante* (Carmen not said nothing interesting) 'Carme did not say anything interesting'. Galician uses "double negation".

Contact with Other Languages

The influence of Castilian (Spanish) on the Galician lexicon is well documented from the final Middle Ages. A great deal of the vocabulary related to the areas of law, religion, and literature was Castilianized, and later a new wealth of Castilian vocabulary was introduced relating to education, the sciences, trade, industry, technology, and the mass media. This invasion has reached such a proportion that in many cases, because of the lack of formal learning of Galician until very recently, spontaneous Galician-speakers fail to recognize traditional words as Galician, and consider the substituted Castilianisms to be the vernacular forms. At present, lexical substitution is so advanced that Castilianization extends as far as the everyday vocabulary, ranging from parts of the human body to family relations, the names of days of the week and months, and domestic life.

There is, in addition, Castilianization of grammatical gender of cognate words and irregular verbal forms, and placing of weak personal pronouns according to the Castilian rules. It must be said that the promotion of Galician in recent years has facilitated the learning of the "correct" norms of the two languages, and particularly the resurrection of patrimonial Galician words, the revitalization of the obsolescent ones, and the popularization of autonomous neologisms.

So far, the contact of Galician with languages other than Spanish has attracted little attention, although some work has been done in the case of the influence of ENGLISH on the Galician spoken by emigrants in New York.

Common Words

man:	home	long:	longo
woman:	muller	small:	pequeno
water:	auga	yes:	si
sun:	sol	no:	non
three:	tres	good:	bo
fish:	peixe	bird:	paxaro
big:	grande	dog:	can
tree:	árbore		

Example Sentences

(1) Temos un fillo e dúas fillas.
we.have DEF.ART.MASC son and two.FEM.PL daughters
'(We) have a son and two daughters.'

(2) O Xoaquín é che moi bo rapaz, pero está
the Joachim is 2s very good boy but is

un pouco tolo.
a little crazy

'Joachim is a very good guy, but he is a little crazy (colloquial style).'

(The definite article *o* is used with proper names to indicate familiarity. The weak pronoun of second person [*che*; formal *lle*] or fifth person [*vos*; formal *lles*] is used in conversation to implicate the interlocutor[s] in the opinion expressed by the locutor).

(3) Cando chegastes, xa remataran a
when arrived.2PL already finished:3PL DEF.ART.FEM

festa.
party
'When (you/plural) arrived (they) already had finished the party.'

Efforts to Preserve, Protect and Promote the Language

After the Spanish Constitution (1978) and the Autonomous Statute of Galicia (1980) were promulgated, Galician was recognized as the "natural language of Galicia" and an official language (together with Spanish) at the regional level. The Law of Linguistic Normalization (1983) forbids discrimination on linguistic grounds and establishes the legal framework for using Galician in schools, recognizing the right of children to receive instruction in their first language and the goal that students should have similar proficiency in Spanish and Galician. In addition, it specifies the creation of an autonomous radio and television network broadcasting in Galician, the *Galeguization* of institutions and the training of administrative employees and officials in Galician.

The Royal Galician Academy (RGA), created in 1906, promotes research in the fields of sociolinguistics and lexicography. The main center for the scientific study of the language is the University *Instituto da Lingua Galega* (Institute of the Galician Language), established in 1971. In 1982, the RGA and the *Instituto da Lingua Galega* elaborated orthographic and morphological norms, which were made official by the autonomous government in the following year. Since their promulgation, the main editorial houses and publications follow the proposed norms, which are used as well in academia. Nevertheless, alternative proposals, generally meant to bring written Galician closer to Portuguese, have been supported by private associations and individual writers.

Galician has been recognized as a language to be promoted by several European institutions, namely the European Parliament and those related to the European Union.

Select Bibliography

Entwistle, W.J. 1936. *The Spanish Language Together with Portuguese, Catalan and Basque*. London: Faber & Faber.

Fernandez Salgado, B., and H. Monteagudo. 1993. "The standardization of Galician: The state of the art." In *Portuguese Studies, 9*: 200–13.

Monteagudo, H. 1993. "Aspects of corpus planning in Galician." In *Plurilinguismes, 6*: 121–53.

Monteagudo, H., and A. Santamarina. 1993. "Galician and Castilian in contact: Historical, social and linguistic aspects." In *Trends in Romance Linguistics and Philology. Volume 5: Bilingualism and Linguistic Conflict in Romance*, eds. R. Posner and J. Green. Berlin and New York: Mouton de Gruyter.

Williams, E.B. 1938. *From Latin to Portuguese*. Philadelphia: University of Pennsylvania Press.

Williamson, R.C., and V.L. Williamson. 1984. "Selected factors in bilingualism: The case of Galicia." In *Journal of Multilingual and Multicultural Development, 5*: 401–12.

Monica S. Devens

Language Name: Ge‘ez. **Alternate:** Geez, classical Ethiopic, Ethiopic.

Location: Ethiopia.

Family: Ge‘ez is a member of the Ethiopic subgroup of the South Semitic group of the Semitic subfamily of the Afro-Asiatic language family.

Related Languages: Ge‘ez is most closely related to the other languages in the Ethiopic subgroup: AMHARIC, Argobba, Gafat, Gurage, Harari, Tigre, and TIGRINYA. Within the larger South Semitic group, South Arabian is Ethiopic's closest relative. ARABIC, HEBREW, ARAMAIC, and AKKADIAN, among others, make up the rest of the Semitic subfamily.

Dialects: There is very little information concerning the possible existence of dialects.

Number of Speakers: Ge‘ez ceased to be a spoken language around the year 1000. Approximately 40 percent of Ethiopia's current population is Ethiopian Orthodox Christians and would have some use of Ge‘ez as their church's liturgical language.

Origin and History

It is generally assumed that a Semitic language—or possibly several different Semitic languages—was brought to Africa by traders from South Arabia sometime in the first millennium before the current era, and established on an originally Cushitic (a different Afro-Asiatic subfamily) substratum. From this beginning developed the entire spectrum of Ethiopian Semitic.

The earliest written evidence of Ge‘ez—which is the earliest of any Ethiopian Semitic language—are the inscriptions found at Axum, Ethiopia's ancient capital, dating from the third or fourth century of the common era. Not long thereafter, sometime around the fifth century, the Bible was translated into Ge‘ez, followed by translations of other religious works.

Although Ge‘ez ceased to be spoken around 1000, its use as a literary language survived, analogous to the survival of LATIN in the Western church. In fact, Ge‘ez literature had a second, and far more productive, flowering after 1270, with the establishment of the so-called Solomonic Dynasty, a royal line claiming descent from the earliest rulers of Ethiopia and ultimately from the assumed union of King Solomon and the Queen of Sheba. This period saw the composition of numerous liturgical and religious works, saints' lives, theological treatises, and royal chronicles, in addition to the continued translation of religious works from other languages. It is from this literary corpus, which continues to serve the Ethiopian Orthodox Church in the modern period, that Ge‘ez derives its importance. However, the revolution of 1974 abolished the Christian monarchy, and since then the power of the Ethiopian Orthodox Church has been greatly curtailed.

Orthography and Basic Phonology

Ge‘ez employs a syllabary system of writing. Each grapheme has seven different shapes which represent a different vowel (or zero) added to the same consonant. Thus, the symbol በ stands for the syllable *ba*, ቡ for *bu*, ቢ for *bi*, ቤ or *be*, ባ for *bā*, ቦ for *bo*, and ብ for *bə* or *b*. Traditionally, these seven shapes are called "orders". The consonantal base of this syllabary is probably derived from the South Arabian writing system. The same syllabary is used by all the Ethiopian Semitic languages that have a written tradition.

The syllabary is deficient in two ways. First, there is no marking for geminated, or lengthened, consonants. Second, the "sixth-order" symbol, the sign for consonant + shwa, can also stand for consonant + zero vowel; therefore, it is ambiguous.

Disparities between Ge‘ez and Amharic phonology, plus the fact that most Ge‘ez texts were written after it ceased to be a spoken language, account for the fact that the spelling in Ge‘ez manuscripts is completely inconsistent. /s/ and /š/; /x/, /ḥ/, and /h/; and /’/ and /‘/, among other sets, are interchangeable. Only by comparing the Ge‘ez vocabulary to that of other Semitic languages can one determine—and even then only precariously—what the "original" spelling was.

The phonological inventory given below is one possible historical reconstruction based largely on comparison with other Semitic languages.

When Ge‘ez is spoken today, it is pronounced according to the phonological inventory of the speaker's native language. For example, if that language is Amharic, then the voiceless pharyngeal fricative /ḥ/ and the voiceless velar fricative /x/ are both pronounced as a voiceless glottal fricative /h/. The voiced pharyngeal fricative /‘/ is pronounced as a glottal stop or ignored altogether. Furthermore/ both /s/ and /š/ are pronounced /s/.

The sound given here as /š/ is often transcribed as /ś/, and it is understood to have been lateralized at some point in time. The glottalized dental fricative /s’/ given here obscures the fact that there are actually two different written letters that, presumably, were originally pronounced differently, whose pronunciation fell together at such an early time that any phonetic representation of their difference would be too conjectural.

The glottalized sounds /t’/, /p’/, /q’/, and /s’/ are unlike anything familiar to speakers of European languages. They are pronounced by simultaneously producing the corresponding

Table 1: Consonants

		Labial	Dental	Palatal	Velar	Pharyngeal	Glottal
Stops	Voiceless	p	t		k		'
	Voiced	b	d		g		
	Glottalized	p'	t'		q		
Fricatives	Voiceless	f	s	š	x	ḥ	h
	Voiced		z			'	
	Glottalized		s'				
Nasals		m	n				
Liquids			l, r				
Glides		w		y			

voiceless consonant and a glottal stop, so [t] and a glottal stop results in /t'/.

In addition, geminate (long) consonants may occur in word-medial or word-final position. Geminates are not distinguished from short consonants in the orthography.

Table 2: Vowels

	Front	Central	Back
High	i		u
Mid	e	ə	o
Low		a, ā	

The vowels /i/, /e/, /u/, and /o/ are understood to have been long. Only /ā/ is so marked in this transcription, since it is the only Ge'ez vowel to have a surviving contrasting short vowel, namely /a/.

Vowels often shorten in syllables closed by two consonants. This is particularly common in words with the feminine suffix *-t*. Thus *kə bur* + *t* 'mighty (feminine)' becomes /kəbərt/.

The glottals (/h/, /'/), the pharyngeals (/ḥ/, /'/), and the voiceless velar fricative (/x/) cause changes in adjacent vowels. When one of these consonants closes a syllable, a preceding short /a/ becomes long /ā/. When these consonants come between /a/ and any nonlow vowel (/i/, /e/, /u/, /o/, /ə/), the first vowel becomes /ə/. When they come between /ə/ and /a/, the first vowel changes to /a/.

Basic Morphology

Ge'ez nouns may be masculine or feminine and singular or plural. While gender is clearly a feature of Ge'ez nominal morphology, it is inconsistently marked on the noun itself. Furthermore, gender agreement between nouns and their accompanying adjectives, demonstrative pronouns, and verbs is often inconsistent. Thus, nominal gender cannot be determined by looking at any one single example, but rather must be deduced by examining a preponderance of cases.

Nominal plurals are formed in many different ways, sometimes by adding a plural suffix (-/ān/ or -/āt/) and sometimes by changing the pattern of the singular word to one of numerous plural patterns. Sometimes a plural is double marked, showing a plural pattern and a subsequent plural suffix.

There is no definite or indefinite article.

The only distinct case is the accusative, marked by the addition of short -/a/. If the noun ends in a vowel, then some modifications in the vowel pattern are made. The primary use of this case marker is as one common indicator of direct objects of transitive verbs.

Ge'ez, like most Semitic languages, makes use of a modifying relationship between nouns called the "construct" state. The accusative marker is also employed on the first element in a construct pair. A rough translation of a construct pair can be accomplished by using the preposition *of*.

ba-'af-a xas's'in
with-edge/CONSTRUCT-ACC sword
'with (the) point of a sword'

The Ge'ez verbal system consists of a system of root consonants that carry a basic meaning and that are then manipulated through a set of basic and derived stems, the latter generally expressed as prefixes, to refine the basic meaning. All roots do not occur in all stems, however.

The resulting verb forms can be conjugated in the perfect, imperfect, jussive (subjunctive), imperative, gerundive, and participial forms, using a system of prefixes and suffixes. Furthermore, the prefix/suffix system marks the verb distinctly for person, number, and gender.

For example, the root /q-t-l/ expresses the basic meaning 'kill'. The paradigm for the basic stem perfect is:

	Singular	Plural
3masc	qatal-a 'he killed'	qatal-u 'they (masc) killed'
3fem	qatal-at 'she killed'	qatal-ā 'they (fem) killed'
2masc	qatal-ka 'you (masc) killed'	qatal-kəmu 'you (pl/masc) killed'
2fem	qatal-ki 'you (fem) killed'	qatal-kən 'you (pl/fem) killed'
1st	qatal-ku 'I killed'	qatal-na 'we killed'

In the derived *ta-* stem, where the concept of passive is added, the third person masculine singular perfect form is *taqatla* 'he was killed'. In the derived *'a-* stem, where the concept of causative is added, the third person masculine singular perfect form is *'aqtala* 'he caused to kill'. The third person feminine singular perfect counterparts of these forms are *qatalat* 'she killed' and *'aqtalat* 'she caused to kill'.

The third person masculine and feminine singular imperfect forms are:

Stem	
Basic	Masculine: yəqattəl 'he kills/will kill'
	Feminine: təqattəl 'she kills/will kill'
ta	Masculine: yətqattal 'he is/will be killed'
	Feminine: tətqattal 'she is/will be killed'
'a-	Masculine: yāqattəl 'he causes/will cause to kill'
	Feminine: tāqattəl 'she causes/ will cause to kill'

Basic Syntax

As a rule, the word order in Ge'ez is VSO. Adjectives and other modifiers may precede or follow the noun. Word order may change if a particular emphasis is desired.

Sentence negation is expressed by the prefix *'i-* added to a verb. Thus, 'he did not kill' is *'i-qatala*.

Contact with Other Languages

Since our knowledge of Ge'ez is derived exclusively from a literary corpus, many of whose works are translations from other languages, we observe loanwords—or at least, transcribed foreign words—from GREEK, Hebrew, Arabic, Aramaic, and COPTIC.

From Greek: *falāsfā* 'philosopher', *galāmewos* 'chameleon'
From Hebrew: *'adonāy* 'name of God', *'adār* 'name of month'
From Arabic: *dibāg* 'brocade', *həlāl* 'new moon'
From Aramaic: *'abbā* 'Father (title for religious leaders)'
From Coptic: *'abib* 'name of a month'

True loanwords from various Cushitic languages and from Amharic can be observed. These include:

From Cushitic: *soson* 'kind of tree', *qāmā* 'necklace', *bez* 'shiny star'
From Amharic: *galado* 'knife', *t'all* 'beer', *gomāri* 'hippopotamus'

Today, as a strictly liturgical language, Ge'ez is in constant contact with the vernacular languages of its users, most commonly—but not restricted to—Amharic and Tigrinya.

Common Words

man:	bə'əsi	long:	nawwāx
woman:	bə'əsit	small:	nə'us
water:	māy	yes:	'əwwa
sun:	s'aḥāy	no:	'albo*
three:	salās	good:	xer
fish:	'asā	bird:	'of
big:	'abiyy	dog:	kalb
tree:	'ə		

*'*albo* literally means '(there is) not in it'

Example Sentences

(1) ba-qadāmi gabr-a
in-beginning make/PERFECT-3M/SG

'əgzi'abəḥer samāy-a wa-mədr-a.
God (lit. Master of the Land) heaven-ACC and-earth-ACC
'In the beginning, God created the heaven and the earth.'

(2) mənt 'a-s'haq-o la-'əgzi'abəḥer
what CAUS-yearn/PERF/3M/SG-him ACC-God

yə-ft'ər fət'rat-āt-a?
3M/SG-create/JUSSIVE creation-PL-ACC
'What urged God to create the creations?'

(3) wa-s'ab'-əw-omu wa-qatal-əw-omu
and-fight/PERFECT-3M/PL-them and-kill/PERFECT-3M/PL-them

ba-'af-a xas's'in.
with-edge-ACC sword
'And they fought them and they killed them with the point of a sword.'

Efforts to Preserve, Protect, and Promote the Language

There are no specific efforts to preserve, protect, or promote this language.

Select Bibliography

Dillmann, C.F.A. 1907 (1899). *Ethiopic Grammar*. Second edition enlarged and improved by Carl Bezold. James A. Crichton (Trans.) London: Williams and Norgate.

____. 1970 (1865). *Lexicon linguae Aethiopicae, cum indice Latino*. Osnabrück: Biblio Verlag.

Lambdin, T. 1978. "Introduction to Classical Ethiopic (Ge'ez)." In *Harvard Semitic Studies*, 24. Missoula, Montana: Scholars Press.

Leslau, W. 1987. *Comparative Dictionary of Ge'ez (Classical Ethiopic)*. Wiesbaden, Germany: Harrassowitz.

Makonnen Argaw. 1984. *Matériaux pour l'étude de la prononciation traditionelle du guèze*. (Mémoire, 44). Paris: Editions Récherche sur les Civilisations.

GEORGIAN

Karina Vamling

Language Name: Georgian. **Autonym:** *kartuli ena.*

Location: The Republic of Georgia. Outside of Georgia it is spoken in western Azerbaijan, northeastern Turkey, and Iran (Iranian Azerbaijan and the Gilan and Fereidan provinces).

Family: Kartvelian (or South Caucasian).

Related Languages: Svan and Mingrelian-Laz (Chan), spoken in the western part of Georgia. (Speakers of these languages in Georgia use Georgian as their literary language.)

Dialects: Regional dialects include, but are not limited to, the following: (1) Eastern (lowland dialects such as Kartlian and Kakhetian, and mountaineers' dialects such as Khevsurian, Mokhevian, Tushian, Pshavian, and Mtiulian); and (2) Western (Rachan, Gurian, Imeretian, and Acharian). The regional dialect spoken in Azerbaijan is Ingilo; in Turkey, it is Imerkheulian; and in Iran, it is Fereidanian.

The most archaic dialects are found in the mountaineers' dialects of northeastern Georgia, where many features of Georgian of the 9th through 13th centuries have been preserved.

The standard language is based on the Kartlian dialect.

Number of Speakers: According to the 1989 Soviet census there are just under 4 million Georgians, who make up 70.1 percent of the total population of Georgia.

Origin and History

The Kartvelian or South Caucasian languages constitute a small group of languages that is distributed over a very limited geographic area. Kartvelian shows typological similarities with other Caucasian languages. However, it has not been possible to reconstruct Proto-Caucasian, and the genetic relationship to other families is uncertain. Reconstruction of the Kartvelian languages shows that Mingrelian-Laz has more closely followed Georgian than Svan.

In the second millennium B.C. the Kartvelian tribes formed two cultures: an eastern and a western. Mingrelian-Laz and Svan tribes inhabited the western part of the country, and today those languages are still spoken there. In the sixth century B.C. the kingdom of Colchis, based on the western culture, was established on the Black Sea coast. About this time, Greek settlements appeared on the coast. The GREEK influence on the Georgian states was particularly strong during the Hellenistic period.

Christianity spread to Georgia in the first century and was established as the state religion in the first half of the fourth century. The earliest examples of Georgian writing—inscriptions in the Georgian Monastery of the Holy Cross in Palestine, the Bolnisi church south of Tbilisi, and the hagiographic work *Martyrdom of St. Shushanik*—date from the fifth century and may still be read by speakers of present-day Georgian.

The language is divided into three periods. **Old Georgian** spans the 5th through 11th centuries, Middle Georgian, the 12th through 18th centuries, and Modern Georgian begins in the 19th century. No major changes have taken place in Georgian during its 1,500 years of known written history.

Periods of Persian, Byzantine, Arab, and TURKISH domination preceded the unification of the western and eastern Georgian states in the 11th century. The golden age of Georgian history lasted only up to the mid-13th century, when Georgia was devastated by Mongol invaders. A second short period of revival and unification took place in the 14th century, followed by new invasions from Turks and Iranians.

During the period from the 15th to the 18th centuries, Georgia disintegrated into a number of small kingdoms and principalities, subsequently annexed by the Russian Empire (1801–1858). A united Georgian state emerged in 1918 after the Russian Revolution, but was abolished by a Bolshevik invasion in 1921. After the fall of the Soviet Union, an independent Georgian state was established once more.

The Kartvelian-speaking core area has been stable for a very long time, although there has been a conspicuous area of loss in the southwestern part (northeast of present-day Turkey), where the population is mixed Kartvelian, more Laz than Georgian proper. These languages have lost ground to Turkish. In the south of Georgia the percentage of Georgian speakers has decreasd because of immigration from the neighboring republics of Armenia and Azerbaijan. As a result of ethnopolitical events in South Ossetia and Abkhazia in the beginning of the 1990s, the Georgian-speaking population has been driven out of these regions of the country.

Orthography and Basic Phonology

The origin of the Georgian writing system is unclear. According to one source it is connected to ARAMAIC writing. Another source points out that the Greek model is evident in the alignment of the script. It is believed to have been created in the fourth century, at the time of the adoption of Christianity. However, according to Georgian chronicles, the script was created by the Geor-

Table 1: Consonants

		Labial	Dental/ Alveolar	Post- Alveolar	Velar	Uvular	Glottal
Stops	Voiceless	p	t		k		
	Voiced	b	d		g		
	Glottalized	p’	t’		k’	q’	
Fricatives	Voiceless		s	š		x	h
	Voiced	v	z	ž		ɣ	
Affricates	Voiceless		c	č			
	Voiced		ʒ	ǯ			
	Glottalized		c’	č’			
Nasal		m	n				
Lateral			l				
Flap			r				

gian king Parnavaz in the third century B.C. The inventory of Georgian phonemes is given in standard transcription of the Georgian letters. The orthography is strictly phonemic.

Georgian has 28 consonant phonemes and 5 vowel phonemes as represented in Tables 1 and 2.

Table 2: Vowels

	Front	Central	Back
High	i		u
Mid	e		o
Low		a	

A characteristic feature of Georgian is a three-way opposition among voiced-voiceless-glottalized consonants, as in b-p-p’. Glottalized (ejective) phonemes are thus found both among stops and affricates. They are marked by an apostrophe in the above consonant phoneme chart.

A salient feature of Georgian phonotactics is heavy initial-consonant clusters, as in *brc’q’invale* ‘excellent’, *mc’vrtneli* ‘trainer’, *vprckvni* ‘I peel it’. Another type of cluster found in Georgian is the so-called harmonic clusters, where the consonants agree in voicing, aspiration, or glottalization and are pronounced with one release. The first consonant is a prevelar and the second one a velar *bg-pk-p’k’*, *ʒg-ck-c’k’* or a uvular *bɣ-px-p’q’*, *ʒɣ-cx-c’q’*.

The Georgian Alphabet

ა	a	კ	ḳ	ს	s	ჩ	čh
ბ	b	ლ	l	ტ	ṭ	ც	ts
გ	g	მ	m	უ	u	ძ	dz
დ	d	ნ	n	ფ	ph	წ	ṭs
ე	e	ო	o	ქ	kh	ჭ	tʃ
ვ	v	პ	p	ღ	ɣ	ხ	x
ზ	z	ჟ	ž	ყ	q	ჯ	dž
თ	th	რ	r	შ	ʃ	ჰ	h
ი	i						

Stress is weak and nonphonemic. There is no general agreement on which syllable it falls. In disyllabic and trisyllabic words it falls on the initial syllable. In words with more than three syllables, secondary stress occurs.

An important morphophonological rule in declension applies to the oblique cases. The vowels *a* and *e* are dropped in nouns ending in *m, n, l, r* (*a* also drops before root-final *v* (Shanidze 1980: 27): *bal-i* > *bl-is* ‘cherry’; *mt’er-i* > *mt’r-ad* ‘enemy’; *katam-i* > *katm-it* ‘hen’. The vowel *o* may also drop, as in *potol-i* > *potl-is* ‘leaf ’. A similar rule applies to the thematic marker of verbs: *av*, *am*.

Basic Morphology

The dominating morphological type is agglutinative. Nominal morphology is predominantly suffixal. Verbal morphology uses both prefixes and suffixes.

Case and number (plural) are marked by suffixes: *k’ac-eb-ma* (man-PL-ERG). Georgian has seven cases: ergative (or narrative), nominative (or absolutive), dative, genitive, instrumental, adverbial and vocative. The cases are listed with their traditional labels, as shown in the table below:

	‘house’	‘father’	‘big house’
Nominative	saxl-i	mama	did-i saxl-i
Ergative	saxl-ma	mama-m	did-ma saxl-ma
Dative	saxl-s	mama-s	did saxl-s
Genitive	saxl-is	mam-is	did-i saxl-is
Instrumental	saxl-it	mam-it	did-i saxl-it
Adverbial	saxl-ad	mama-d	did saxl-ad
Vocative	saxl-o	mama-(v)	did-o saxl-o

Table 3: The Transitive Verb *damalva* 'hide'

Series		'hide': PreV-	subject Pers-	1SG, Rel-	object Root-	3SG/PL Th-	TP
I	Present		v-		mal-	av-	Ø
	Imperfect		v-		mal-	av-	d-i
	Conjunctive (pres.)		v-		mal-	av-	d-e
	Future	da-	v-		mal-	av-	Ø
	Conditional	da-	v-		mal-	av-	d-i
	Conjunctive (fut.)	da-	v-		mal-	av-	d-e
II	Aorist	da-	v-		mal-		e
	Optative	da-	v-		mal-		o
III	Perfect	da-	m-	i-	mal-	av-	s
	Pluperfect	da-	m-	e-	mal-		a
	Perfect conjunctive	da-	m-	e-	mal-		o-s

Note in particular "dative". The term covers dative/accusative in familiar European languages. Georgian has no gender distinctions and no articles. Agreement in case is found when the noun is modified by a preceding modifier, which is the basic order: *or-ma did-ma k'ac-ma* (two-ERG big-ERG man-ERG), *did-ma k'ac-eb-ma* (big-ERG man-PL-ERG). A postposed adjective agrees also in number: *kal-eb-ma lamaz-eb-ma* (woman-PL-ERG beautiful-PL-ERG). A noun modified by a numeral appears in the singular: *čem-ma or-ma megobar-ma* (my-ERG two-ERG friend-ERG) 'my two friends'.

Personal pronouns are found in first and second persons; demonstrative pronouns are used in the function of third person. First and second person are not marked for case in the syntactic cases (ergative, nominative, dative), whereas third person pronouns are.

The paradigm of the transitive verb *damalva* 'hide' is given in Table 3 above.

Note, in particular, the division of tense/aspect forms into three series. There are morphological differences in the series, for instance, the presence of the thematic marker (Th) in Series I and its absence in Series II. The tense and person markers (TP) also come in different sets. Verbs may take agreement prefixes of subject *da-v-male 'I* hid it', direct object *da-m-mala* 'he hid *me*' and indirect object *gamo-m-igzavna* 'he sent it to *me*'. However, there are restrictions on the co-occurrence of these prefixes; generally only one prefix is present. Third person number is reflected in a suffix position as well (TP): *damal-a*, *damal-es 'he* hid it/him/her, *they* hid it/him/her'. Georgian has morphological causatives, marked by the affixes *a-...-in-*, *a-...-evin*: *davac'erineb* 'I will make him write it'. By adding the vowel prefixes *a-*, *i-*, *e-*, *u-*, a large number of different verbal forms are derived, mainly marking change of valency. This is illustrated with the verb root *tb* 'warm' as follows:

ø-tb-eba	'it warms up'
u-tb-eba	'something of his warms up'
i-tb-obs	'he warms his something (e.g. hands)'
a-tb-obs	'he warms something'
u-tb-obs	'he warms something for someone'

Basic Syntax

Basic word order is SOV, with SVO as a common alternative order. Head-final constructions dominate in the language. The verb is usually preceded by its objects, even if VO is a common order. PPs are represented as postpositional phrases. The attribute usually precedes its head in NPs, although attributes may follow the head noun in poetic or archaic style. Relative clauses follow the head noun.

Active/passive verbal pairs are found in the language but the agent is preferably not expressed in the passive. The following sentences illustrate this active/passive syntactic alternation:

otari	c'erils	c'ers
Otari.NOM	letter.DAT	s3SG.o3.write.PRES

'Otari is writing a letter.'

c'erili	ic'ereba	(otar-is	mier)
letter.NOM	s3SG.write.PASS.PRES	(Otari-GEN	by)

'A letter is being written (by Otari).'

Case marking of subject and objects exhibits complex patterns depending on verb type, tense, and aspect. Case marking in transitive clauses depends on the choice of tense/aspect (see Example Sentences below). The same applies to certain mainly intransitive activity verbs such as *tamašobs* '(s)he plays', *t'iris* '(s)he cries', and *cek'vavs* '(s)he dances'. Emotive verbs have dative marked subjects (experiencers). Other verbs mark subjects by the nominative case and any object(s) by the dative.

Negation is marked by the particles *ar*, *nu*, or *ver*. The particle *ar* has the widest use, whereas *nu* is found in negated imperatives and *ver* corresponds to 'can't, not be able'. Double negation occurs with negative pronouns: *aravin ar mova* (nobody NEG come) 'Nobody will come'.

Contact with Other Languages

The Near East, the eastern Mediterranean, and the Black Sea regions have been the traditional contact areas for the Georgians. Contacts with the Greek culture occurred at a very early time and were particularly intense during the Hellenistic period. At monasteries in Georgia and in Georgian monasteries abroad, important translations of religious works were made from Greek, Syriac, and other languages into Georgian. Examples of loanwords below are from Jorbenadze (1991).

From PERSIAN: *amxanagi* 'friend', *navti* 'oil', *t'ani* 'body', *bevri* 'many/much', *k'aba* 'dress'
From ARABIC: *ekimi* 'doctor', *saati* 'hour', *tariɣi* 'date', *ruk'a* 'map'
From Greek: *ek'lesia* 'church', *k'alami* 'pen', *k'anoni* 'law'
From Turkish: *otaxi* 'room', *tepši* 'plate'

RUSSIAN has been the mediator of recent international loanwords.

Common Words

man:	k'aci	small:	p'at'ara (mcire)
woman:	kali	yes:	diax
water:	c'q'ali	no:	ara (nu, vera)
sun:	mze	bird:	čit'i
three:	sami	dog:	ʒaɣli
fish:	tevzi	tree:	xe
big:	didi	long:	grʒeli

Example Sentences

Case marking of subjects and objects is complex in Georgian. One has to take into consideration both verb class and choice of tense/aspect, as the following sentences illustrate.

(1) k'ac-i ʒma-s c'eril-s sc'ers.
man-NOM brother-DAT letter-DAT s3SG.o3.IO3.write.PRES(I)
'The man writes a letter to his brother.'

(2) k'ac-ma ʒma-s c'eril-i misc'era.
man-ERG brother-DAT letter-NOM s3SG.o3.IO3.write.AOR(II)
'The man wrote a letter to his brother.'

(3) k'ac-s ʒm-is(a)-tvis c'eril-i miuc'eria.
man-DAT brother-GEN-for letter-NOM s3SG.o3.write.PERF(III)
'(Apparently) the man has written a letter to his brother.'

Efforts to Preserve, Protect, and Promote the Language

Georgian is the official language of the Georgian Republic and the dominant language of all spheres of life. Even during the Soviet period, Georgian had a strong position compared to other minority languages of the Soviet Union. The Georgians actively (and successfully) defended the status of their language against the introduction of Russian as the official language.

The position of Georgian has grown stronger during the recent years of independence, in particular as a language of administration and business. Over 98 percent of Georgians consider Georgian to be their mother tongue, with only one-third claiming fluency in Russian. The use of ENGLISH as the first foreign language has increased at the expense of Russian.

Select Bibliography

Anderson, S.R. 1984. "On representations in morphology: Case, agreement and inversion in Georgian." In *Natural Language and Linguistic Theory 2:* 157–218.

Aronson, H.I. 1990. *Georgian; A Reading Grammar.* Corrected Edition. Chicago: Slavica.

Birdsall, J.N. 1991. "Georgian paleography." In A.C. Harris, ed. *The Indigenous Languages of the Caucasus.* Vol. 1, pp. 85–128. Delmar, NY: Caravan Books.

Harris, A.C. 1981. *Georgian Syntax; A Study in Relational Grammar.* Cambridge: Cambridge University Press.

Hewitt, B.G. 1995. *Georgian: A Structural Reference Grammar.* Amsterdam and Philadelphia: John Benjamins.

Jorbenadze, B. 1991. *The Kartvelian Languages and Dialects.* Tbilisi: Mecniereba.

Shanidze, A. 1980. *kartuli enis gramat'ik'is sapuʒvlebi* [*The Foundations of Georgian Grammar*]. Tbilisi: Tbilisi University Press.

Tschenkéli, K. 1958. *Einführung in die Georgische Sprache.* Zürich: Amirani Verlag.

Vogt, H. 1971. *Grammaire de la langue géorgienne.* Oslo: Universitetsforlaget.

Terrence C. McCormick

Language Name: German. **Autonym:** *Deutsch.*

Location: Germany, Austria, Switzerland (northeastern cantons), Luxembourg, Liechtenstein. German settlement in Slavic-speaking areas and the expansion of the Prussian state over the centuries led to a considerable expansion of the German-speaking area in Eastern Europe, and although many German speakers were resettled at the end of World War II, there remain pockets of German speakers in the Czech and Slovak republics. Relatively long-established settlements of German speakers are still found today in France (Alsace), Belgium, northern Italy, Romania, and Hungary. Due to emigration, German-speaking communities are found in the United States and Canada, in South America (primarily in Brazil and to a lesser extent in Argentina and Paraguay), in Africa (Republic of South Africa and Namibia), and in parts of the former Soviet Union.

Family: West Germanic subbranch of the Germanic branch of Indo-European.

Related Languages: DUTCH, ENGLISH, YIDDISH, DANISH, SWEDISH, NORWEGIAN, Icelandic.

Dialects: The German-speaking areas are divided into three broad dialect regions, each containing several subdialects which vary in their phonology, morphology, syntax, and lexicon. (1) Upper, or High German, spoken in the southernmost part of the German-speaking territory, includes the Alemanic dialects of Switzerland, Swabia, and Alsace, and the Bavarian and Austrian dialects of the southeast. (2) Low German dialects are found in the northern part of the German-speaking area, defined by a linguistic boundary stretching from Aachen in the west to Frankfurt in the east, crossing the Rhine at the town of Benrath. (3) Central German, or Franconian dialects are located between Upper and Low German.

Pennsylvania Dutch is an example of a dialect spoken outside of the German-speaking area.

Today standard German (based on East Central German), which has a prescribed orthography, pronunciation, and grammar, may be considered a linguistic convention that bridges the gap among mutually incomprehensible dialects.

In addition to the regional dialects and the standard language, there is a third form of spoken idiom known as *Umgangssprache*, which is a blending of features of a regional dialect into the standard language.

Number of Speakers: 90–100 million.

Origin and History

By 750 B.C. Germanic tribes had settled along the coasts of the North Sea and Baltic Sea in present-day southern Scandinavia, the Netherlands, Germany and Poland. Members of these tribes spoke mutually comprehensible dialects of Proto-Germanic. Germanic had separated from Indo-European by about 500 B.C. as a result of the First (or Germanic) Sound Shift. This shift involved only consonants, i.e., a restructuring of the Proto-Indo-European obstruent system, whereby:

PIE voiceless stops > Gmc. voiceless spirants (p > f)
PIE voiced stops > Gmc. voiceless stops (b > p)
PIE voiced aspirated stops > Gmc. voiced spirants (b^{h} > ƀ)

In addition, there were other linguistic changes including a shift in word-stress accent from variable to fixed on the first syllable, which in turn led eventually to the reduction of unstressed syllables.

There are three main branches of Germanic: West Germanic, which gave rise to the modern languages of German, English, Frisian, Netherlandic (Dutch-Flemish), AFRIKAANS, and Yiddish; North Germanic, from which arose modern Icelandic, Norwegian, Danish, and Swedish; and East Germanic, whose languages are all extinct, including GOTHIC, the oldest Germanic language preserved in manuscript (from the fourth century).

By A.D. 250 the East Germanic tribes moved south to the Black Sea. By the fourth century East Germanic tribes began to penetrate the Roman Empire while West Germanic peoples expanded their territory southwards. This movement/expansion is generally referred to as the *Völkerwanderung*. Some tribes crossed the North Sea to England, and English is the linguistic legacy of that conquest.

At the time the tribes moved into southern Germany they used the voiceless stops (or plosive consonants) *p, t,* and *k* in the same way they are used in English today. But between the fifth and seventh centuries what was to become the High German language underwent a Second, or High German Consonant Shift. West Germanic voiceless stops **p, *t, *k* changed to fricatives *f, s, ch* medially and affricates *pf, z, kch* in word initial position.

The cause of the High German Consonant Shift is strictly a matter of scholarly speculation, with no prevailing consensus. The theory claiming contact with Celtic/Illyrian/Rhaetian as a cause is "weak" because no one knows anything about the languages of these peoples at this time and in this place.

WGmc	*p-	*t-	*k
English	pepper	tin	cook
Low German	pepper	tinn	koken
Central German	**pf**effer	**z**inn	kochen
Upper German	**pf**effer	**z**inn	(k)**ch**ochen

The High German Consonant Shift, c. A.D. 400–500, resulted in German dialectal division. English (as well as Dutch and Frisian) and the Low German dialects did not participate in the shift. Upper German dialects participated most fully, altering the original stops in every position. The varying degree of participation of the various dialects may be illustrated by the above chart, which shows the differing outcomes of the West Germanic stops in word-initial position.

The earliest attestations of High German date from around 700, when Latin-German glossaries appeared. This marked the onset of the Old High German (OHG) period, which lasted to about 1050. The Latin alphabet was modified for depicting some OHG sounds, which did not exist in Latin. This is especially true of OHG fricatives and affricates, where *h* was added to a Latin stop symbol to indicate a fricative or affricate: thus *th, dh* (*thu, dhu* 'thou') represents a fricative in the dental range. No such accommodation was made, however, for those vowel sounds that differed from Latin. Only the basic Latin vowels *a, e, i, o, u,* and combinations thereof were employed, although comparative and dialect evidence indicate that the OHG vowel system was more complex than this.

The impetus for writing in the vernacular was the conversion to Christianity of the various Germanic peoples and the propagation of the religion throughout the domain of the Frankish (Carolingian) Empire. This is borne out by the fact that the majority of what is termed OHG literature has an ecclesiastical theme. A number of the earliest OHG documents arose from Charlemagne's proclamation (*Admonitio generalis*, 789) that basic prayers and tenets of faith, such as the *Pater Noster, Credo* and the baptismal vows, be translated into OHG dialects so they would be readily understood by the people. Study of OHG manuscripts reveals that there is no uniformity in OHG orthography. In fact, no two works of surviving OHG literature can be said to employ the same scribal practice.

Old Saxon, the precursor to Low German, appears in written form in the ninth century after Charlemagne's conquest of the Saxons.

The Middle High German (MHG) period is usually dated from 1050 to 1350. During this period unstressed vowels were reduced to ə (like the *a* of English 'about'). The reduction of unstressed syllables had a significant influence on the history of German inflectional morphology. Thus, any morphological distinction, which in the OHG period depended solely on unstressed vowel quality, was lost in the MHG period.

Verb endings lost some person/number and mood distinctions, and the three classes of OHG weak verbs were reduced in most dialect areas to a single class. Other phonological developments of the MHG period that had significance for the development of Modern Standard German are: (1) the merging of spirantal OHG *z* (from WGmc **t*) and OHG *s*; (2) *sk* > *sch*: OHG *scif* > MHG *schif* 'ship'; (3) initial *s* > *sch* before *l, m, n, w*: OHG *snēo* > MHG *schnē* 'snow'; and (4) devoicing of final stops and fricatives: OHG *liob* > MHG *liep* 'dear'; OHG *tag* > MHG *tac* 'day'.

	Old High German	Middle High German
Sg. Nom.	namo	name
Gen.	namin	namen
Acc.	namun	namen
Pl. Nom.	namun	namen
Gen.	namōno	namen
Dat.	namōm	namen
Acc.	namun	namen

Some noun declensions that had distinctive case endings in OHG lost their distinctiveness by the MHG period.

The MHG period, especially from 1170 to 1250, is marked by a blossoming of a distinctly secular literature reflecting the ideals of the courtly and knightly classes. Myths of the Germanic past were cast in the *Nibelungenlied.* Walter von der Vogelweide, Wolfram von Eschenbach, Hartmann von Aue, and Gottfried von Strassburg authored classic works. There is a high degree of FRENCH loanwords found in the literature of this period.

Because of greater political and cultural fragmentation in the German-speaking areas, a standard language took longer to emerge than in France or England. In the 13th century the so-called German Chancery Language (*Kanzleisprache*) was developed in which charters, deeds and various legal transactions were recorded in the vernacular as opposed to Latin. This type of document, known in German as an *Urkunde*, was originally a Roman practice. It was continued in the German-speaking area after the political collapse of the Roman Empire, but only in the 13th century was German first used for these legal documents. Between 1350 and 1650, which is referred to as the Early New High German period, there was a tendency for the various *Kanzleisprache*, which differed considerably from each other, to become more uniform. Under Charles IV (1347–1378) an orthography was devised in the imperial Prague chancery that combined dialect elements of Upper German and East Central German. It was this orthography in which Martin Luther (1483–1546) composed his German Bible, and the dissemination of the Bible in print greatly enhanced the prestige of this form of German and led to its becoming the basis of the modern standard. Modern German is said to begin after 1650.

Orthography and Basic Phonology

German is written in the Latin alphabet. Starting already in the OHG period, modifications were made in order to represent German sounds without Latin equivalents. Thus, *h* following a consonant letter is used to represent fricatives. During the MHG period it became an increasingly common orthographic practice to represent front-rounded vowels by superimposing a small *i* over a letter that would otherwise represent a back rounded vowel. This superimposed letter is the origin of the umlaut symbol in *ä, ü, ö,* and *äu* in Modern German orthography. An unusual feature of Modern German orthography is that all nouns—not merely proper nouns—are capitalized.

Table 1: Consonants

		Labial	Dental	Alveo-palatal	Palatal	Velar	Glottal
Stops	Voiceless	p	t			k	ʔ
	Voiced	b	d			g	
Fricatives	Voiceless	f	ss/ß	sch	ch	ch	h
	Voiced	w	s				
Affricates		pf	(t)z	tsch			
Nasals		m	n			ng	
Lateral			l				
Trill						r (uvular)	
Glide				j			

German *w* is a voiced labio-dental fricative [v].

A single *s* is generally pronounced [z]; in initial clusters *sp, st, s* is pronounced [š]: *spielen* [špilən]; in final position it is voiceless [s].

The pronunciation of *ch* depends on the preceding vowel: following *a, o, u,* or *au, ch* is a voiceless velar fricative. Otherwise *ch* is a voiceless palatal fricative.

J is pronounced [y] except in French loanwords, where it is pronounced [ž] as in *Journal.*

In most dialects of German, *r* is a voiced uvular trill; some speakers use instead an alveolar trill. A salient feature of German consonant articulation is the devoicing of stops and fricatives in word final position. This devoicing gives rise to alternations between voiced and voiceless consonants in noun, adjective, and verb paradigms. For example, the plural of *Tag* [ta<u>k</u>] is *Tage* [ta<u>g</u>ə].

Table 2: Vowels

	Front		Central	Back
	Spread	Rounded		
High	i	ü		u
Mid	e, ä	ö	e	o
Low			a	

German vowels may be either tense or lax. The difference between the two types of vowels is not consistently represented in the orthography. The symbol *i* may represent either tense /i/ or lax /ɪ/; but *ie* can only be tense /i/. For most vowels, a following *h* can be used to indicate that the vowel is tense: *eh, oh, öh; ah* and *uh* are also possible, with only *ih* impossible. Vowels followed by a doubled consonant (*Bett* 'bed') or by a consonant cluster are generally lax, and vowels followed by only a single consonant (*beten* 'ask') or by no consonants are generally tense. Finally, vowels written double are always tense (*See* 'sea').

German has three diphthongs, *ei, au,* and *äu*/*eu,* pronounced [ɔi].

Word stress in German generally falls on the root syllable: *béten* 'ask', *verstéhen* 'understand'. Stressed tense vowels are also long. These long vowels are always monophthongs.

Basic Morphology

Despite some simplifications over the centuries, Standard German today remains a highly inflected language, betraying its origins as an Indo-European language. A general characteristic of German morphology is umlaut. Many times, the addition of a suffix brings about a change in the vowel of the stem to which it is added: *a, u, o, au* become *ä, ü, ö, äu* respectively; more rarely, umlaut alone signals a morphological change (e.g., from singular to plural in nouns).

German nouns are inflected for case, gender, and number. There are three genders: masculine, feminine, and neuter. It is often arbitrary what gender a noun belongs to (*Wand* 'wall' is feminine, *Tisch* 'table' is masculine, and *Kind* 'child' is neuter), but there are some regularities. The gender of nouns representing human beings usually is predictable, and feminines can be formed from masculines by the addition of the suffix *-in*: *Student* 'student (m)', *Studentin* 'student (f)'.

The two numbers in German are singular and plural. Plural nouns are formed from singulars in several different ways; *-e* may be added, with or without umlaut: *Tag* 'day', pl. *Tag-e; Fuss* 'foot', pl. *Füss-e*. Plurals may also be formed by adding *-en, -er* or *-s* (*Uhr* 'hour', pl. *Uhr-en; Lamm* 'lamb', pl. *Lämm-er; Hotel* 'hotel', pl. *Hotel-s*). In addition, some nouns may be pluralized by a change in vowel: *Mantel* 'overcoat', pl. *Mäntel.* Finally, the forms of some nouns are the same whether singular or plural: *Fenster* 'window', pl. *Fenster.*

Adjectives agree with the nouns they modify and bear endings, which mark the noun phrase for gender, number, and case.

German verbs are inflected for tense. There are two simple tenses, present and past, and several compound tenses. The future is formed from inflected forms of the verb *werden* 'will' and the infinitive. In addition, perfect tenses are formed from inflected forms of the verbs *haben* 'have' or *sein* 'be' and the past participle. The past participle, together with forms of the verb *werden* 'become', is also used in the passive voice.

It is customary to describe German verbs in terms of their principal parts: the infinitive (*-en* added to the present stem), the third person singular past tense, and the past participle.

There are two general classes of verbs: "weak" verbs and "strong" verbs. The weak verbs form the principle parts only by means of affixation, while the strong verbs may alter the root vowel also.

Class	Infinitive	Past	Past Participle
Strong	si̲ng-en	sa̲ng	ge-su̲ng-en 'sing'
Weak	mach-en	mach-te	ge-mach-t 'make, do'

German verbs agree with their subjects in person and number. There are three moods: indicative, imperative, and two forms of subjunctive. In addition to distinguishing second person singular and plural familiar forms, German has a second person formal form, as illustrated in the following sentences, all meaning 'Are you doing that?' (literally, 'do you that?')

Singular, familiar:	Mach-st du das?
Plural, familiar:	Mach-t ihr das?
Formal, singular + plural:	Mach-en Sie das?

German has an extensive set of verb prefixes that modify the verb's meaning. For example, from the verb *stehen* 'stand' are derived *abstehen* 'be distant', *anstehen* 'line up', *aufstehen* 'get up', *ausstehen* 'be outstanding', *beistehen* 'help', *bestehen* 'endure', *einstehen* 'enter upon', *entstehen* 'originate', *überstehen* 'endure', *unterstehen* 'stand under', *verstehen* 'understand', *vorstehen* 'jut out', *zurückstehen* 'be inferior', *zusammenstehen* 'stand together', and *zustehen* 'pertain'.

Basic Syntax

German has different word order patterns for main and subordinate clauses. In indicative main clauses, the inflected verb, which may be the main verb or an auxiliary, appears in the second position in the sentence. It may be preceded by its subject or by an adverb; if the verb is preceded by an adverb, the subject follows the verb. In addition, some verb prefixes are found at the end of the clause.

Er steh-t um 7 Uhr auf
he get-3SG at 7 hour up

Um 7 Uhr steh-t er auf
at 7 hour get-3SG he up
'He gets up at 7 o'clock.'

If the sentence contains an auxiliary verb, the auxiliary, which agrees with the subject, is in second position, and the main verb is at the end of the sentence.

Er muss um 7 Uhr auf-stehen
he must:3SG at 7 hour up-get
'He must get up at 7 o'clock.'

In questions to which a "yes" or "no" answer is expected, the verb appears in sentence initial position. The verb is also sentence initial in commands.

In subordinate clauses, all verbs appear at the end of their clause; thus, the subordinate clause word order is SOV.

Ich weiss dass er um 7 Uhr auf-steh-t
I know that he at 7 hour up-get-3SG
'I know that he gets up at 7 o'clock.'

Adjectives precede the nouns they modify.

German sentences are negated by the word *nicht*, which follows the inflected verb in main clauses and precedes the verb in subordinate clauses. If there are other adverbs, *nicht* follows a time adverb and precedes a place adverb.

Er geh-t heute nicht in die
he go-3SG today NEG in the:ACC.FEM.SG

Schule
school:ACC.FEM.SG
'He's not going to school today.'

Contact with Other Languages

In various periods of the history of the language, German has borrowed concepts from other languages, especially Latin, and formed a word with native German prefixes, roots, and suffixes, based on the morphological structure of the foreign word. This is called a "loan translation". Whereas English has borrowed words wholesale from Latin, there is often an equivalent loan translation in German:

English: circum-stance, in-fluence, ab-brevi-ation, ex-it
German: Um-stand, Ein-fluss, Ab-kurz-ung, Aus-gang

Following are examples of simple loanwords:

From Latin: *Kloster* 'monastery', *schreiben* 'write'
From French: *tanzen* 'dance', *falsch* 'false'
From ITALIAN: *Bank* 'bank', *Risiko* 'risk'
From Slavic: *Grenze* 'border', *Peitsche* 'whip'
From ARABIC/PERSIAN: *Kaffee* 'coffee', *Atlas* 'atlas'
From English: export, partner, bluejeans, computer, teenager, jet

Common Words

man:	Mann	long:	lang
woman:	Frau	small:	klein
water:	Wasser	yes:	ja
sun:	Sonne	no:	nein
three:	drei	good:	gut
fish:	Fisch	bird:	Vogel
big:	groß	dog:	Hund
tree:	Baum		

Example Sentences

(1) Er hat mein-em Bruder die
he has my-DAT brother:DAT the:ACC.FEM.SG

ganz-e Geschichte erzähl-t.
whole-ACC.FEM.SG story:ACC.FEM.SG tell-PARTICIPLE
'He told my brother the whole story.'

(2) Das Buch lieg-t auf dem Tisch.
the:NEUT.SG book lie-3.SG on the:DAT.M.SG table:DAT.M.SG
'The book is on the table.'

(3) Sie hatt-e dem Kind(e) ein-e
she has-PAST the-DAT.SG child-DAT.SG a-ACC.F.SG

Decke über-ge-leg-t.
blanket-ACC.SG over-lay-PARTICIPLE
'She had laid a blanket over the child.'

Efforts to Preserve, Protect, and Promote the Language

Since the 19th century, German has been viewed as an international language for the natural sciences, technology, and business. It is taught in schools throughout the world. In the United States it is the third most frequently taught foreign language.

The German government promotes language study with scholarships and funding. At various times there have been efforts to "purify" the language of foreign words (as during the Nazi era) but this has not had much of a lasting effect.

Select Bibliography

Clyne, M. 1984. *Language and Society in the German-Speaking Countries.* Cambridge: Cambridge University Press.

Hawkins, J. 1987. "German." In *The World's Major Languages*, ed. B. Comrie, 110–38. New York: Oxford University Press.

Keller, R.E. 1961. *German Dialects.* Manchester: Manchester University Press.

Lederer, H. 1969. *Reference Grammar of the German Language.* New York: Charles Scribner's Sons.

Lohnes, W., and Strothmann, F. 1967. *German: A Structural Approach.* New York: W.W. Norton.

Moulton, W. 1962. *The Sounds of English and German.* Chicago: University of Chicago Press.

Priebach, R., and W. E. Collinson. 1962. *The German Language.* London: Faber & Faber.

Waterman, J.T. 1966. *A History of the German Language.* Seattle: University of Washington Press.

Gĩkũyu

Kimani Njogu

Language Name: Gĩkũyũ. **Alternates:** *Gĩgĩkũyũ, Kikuyu.* **Autonym:** *Gĩkũyũ.*

Location: Kenya and especially in central Kenya (north of Nairobi to the slopes of Mount Kenya), west to the Nyandarua Mountains and the Rift Valley.

Family: Thagicu subgroup of the Central Bantu group of the Benue-Congo subbranch of the Niger-Congo branch of the Niger-Kordofanian language family. Gĩkũyu is numbered E-51 in Guthrie's *Comparative Bantu.*

Related Languages: Meru, Embu, Kamba in Kenya, and Segeju in Tanzania.

Dialects: Alternate names are given in parentheses: (1) Kĩambu (Kabete), area nearest Nairobi to the northwest; (2) Mũrang'a (Metumi), north of Nairobi; (3) Nyeri (Gaki), north of Mũrang'a, (4) Kĩrĩnyaga (Ndia), on the southwestern slopes of Mount Kenya.

Number of Speakers: 8–9 million. This represents about 27 percent of the population of Kenya (including those who speak Gĩkũyu as a second or third language).

Origin and History

Gĩkũyu is one of five languages of the Thagicu subgroup of Bantu that stretches from Kenya to Tanzania (between the Aberdare Forest, Mount Kenya, and Mount Kilimanjaro). Around the 16th century, central Kenya was sparsely inhabited by the Gumba hunters and Athi berry gatherers, the predecessors of the Gĩkũyu in the area. These groups have since been absorbed by the majority Gĩkũyu and other neighboring ethnic groups.

According to Gĩkũyu oral traditions, the Manduti and Cuma generations (from the mid 17th century to the first half of the 18th century) are remembered for their raiding and fighting with hostile neighboring ethnic groups. During the Cuma generation, immigration into northern Metumi (present-day Mũrang'a) and southern Gaki (present-day Nyeri) took root. It was around this time that the Gĩkũyu evolved as a distinct ethnic group with a clearly defined culture and a language distinguishable from that of their cousins, the Meru and Embu. The Gĩkũyu had, prior to this time, migrated as hunters and pastoralists. However, the new ecology was more suited to agriculture; around the 17th century, the Gĩkũyu became a farming community.

Thus the popular myth that the Gĩkũyu grew out of Gĩkũyu and Mũmbi can be viewed within the context of their settlement in the new fertile land. According to Gĩkũyu mythology, Mgai (God) appeared to Gĩkũyu and Mambi (father and mother of the tribe) at Makũrwe wa Gathanga (in present-day Marang'a) and gave them all the land to the southwest of Mount Kirinyaga (Mount Kenya). Gĩkũyu and Mũmbi settled around Mũkũrwe wa Gathanga and gave birth to nine daughters. The daughters became the ancestors of the nine Gĩkũyu clans. The myth, while legitimizing the community's ownership of land in the region, also acted as a symbol of unity and cultural cohesion.

Orthography and Basic Phonology

The Gĩkũyu writing system was developed by missionaries in the 1910s under the auspices of the Gĩkũyu Language Committee, whose membership was predominantly missionary. However, there existed two competing orthographies, one spearheaded by Protestant missionaries and the other by Catholics. The orthographies differed primarily on how to represent long vowels and the seven vowel qualities in the language. The orthography in current use is the one advocated by the Protestants.

Gĩkũyu is written in the Roman alphabet using LATIN vowel conventions and simplified ENGLISH conventions for consonants. Long vowels are written as double. Tonal features are not marked in the orthography.

Table 1: Consonants

		Labial	Dental	Palatal	Velar
Stops	Voiceless		t		
	Voiced		d		k
	Prenasal	mb	nd	nj	ng
Fricatives		b	th	c	g
Nasals		m	n	ny	ng'
Resonants		w	r	y	

b is a voiced bilabial fricative [ß], *th* a voiced interdental fricative [ð], and *g* a voiced velar fricative [ɣ]. *c* is a voiceless fricative, [s] in some Gĩkũyu dialects, and [š] in others. *Ng'* is a velar nasal [ŋ], as in English 'sing', and *ny* is a palatal nasal [ñ].

The prenasalized consonants *mb, nd, nj,* and *ng* are not clusters, but rather single consonants with a nasal component in addition to their oral articulations.

A characteristic phonological alternation in Gĩkũyu is called Dahl's Law (after the person who first observed the pattern in Bantu): /k/ becomes [ɣ] (spelled *g*) when the following syllable begins with *t*, *th*, *c*, or *k*. The process is evident in verbs with the infinitival prefix *k*: compare *kũruma* 'to insult' with *gũkoma* [gokoma] 'to sleep'.

Table 2: Vowels

	Front	Central	Back
High	i		u
Mid-High	ĩ		ũ
Mid-Low	e		o
Low		a	

Vowels may be short (written single) or long (written double). *ĩ* and *ũ* are phonetically [e] and [o], while *e* and *o* are phonetically [ɛ] and [ɔ].

Gĩkũyu is a tone language. There are two underlying tones, H(igh) and L(ow). Like those of many other African tone languages, the Gĩkũyu tone system involves downstep: in a sentence containing several H's, each H is lower in physical pitch than the H's that precede it. An additional feature of Gĩkũyu tone is 'tone shift'. A tone that is lexically associated with a given syllable is realized in pronunciation on the following syllable. For example, in the verb *tòmàkórìré* 'we found them', the syllable *ma* is realized with the Low tone lexically associated with the prefix *to*, and the verb stem *kor* is realized with the High tone lexically associated with the prefix *ma*. Tone is not represented in the Gĩkũyu writing system.

Basic Morphology

Like other Bantu languages, Gĩkũyu has an elaborate system of noun classes. There are 16 classes, paired singular and plural. Each class has a characteristic prefix that appears on all nouns in that class (see Table 3 below).

Each class has a distinct agreement pattern; adjectives take the class prefix of the nouns they modify (sometimes with phonological modification):

mũ-ndu mw-ega
CL1-person CL1-good 'good person'

ma-timũ me-ega
CL6-spear CL6-good 'good spears'

Gĩkũyu verbs agree with their subjects in person and number; if the subject is in the third person, the verb agrees with it in class as well. Transitive verbs are also marked for the person, number, and class of their direct object. Verbs are also inflected for tense (indicated by a prefix between the subject and object agreement markers) and aspect (indicated by a suffix following the verb stem).

ka-mwana nĩ ka-raa-teng'er-a
CL11-boy FOCUS CL11-PRES-run-FINAL VOWEL
'The boy is running.'

tu-mwana nĩ t-raa-teng'er-a
CL12-boy FOCUS CL12-PRES-run-FINAL VOWEL
'The boys are running.'

Table 3: Noun Classes

Noun Class	Concept	Number	Example	Gloss
1.	Human	Singular	mũ-ndũ	'person'
2.	Human	Plural	a-ndũ	'people'
3.	Tree, plant, disease			
4.	Tree, plant, disease	Plural	mũ-tĩ	'trees'
5.	Ceremonial & religious objects, liquids	Singular	i-timũ	'spear'
6.	Ceremonial & religious objects, liquids	Plural	ma-timũ	'spears'
7.	Inanimate	Singular	kĩ-ondo	'bag'
8.	Inanimate	Plural	ci-ondo	'bags'
9. & 10.	Birds, Insects	Sing./Pl.	n-yoni	'bird(s)'
11.	Long, wavy	Singular	rũ-hiũ	'sword'
12.	Diminutive	Singular	ka-hiĩ	'boy'
13.	Diminutive	Plural	tũ-hiĩ	'boys'
14.	Abstract concepts		ũ-thaka	'beauty'
15.	Infinitive		kũ-he	'to give'
16.	Locative		kũ-ndũ	'place (indefinite)'
17.	Locative		ha-ndu	'place definite)'

ka-mwana nĩ ka-raa-teng'er-ag-a
CL11-boy FOCUS CL11-PRES-run-COMPLETE-FINAL VOWEL
'The boy was running.'

Causative and passive verbs are derived by the use of suffixes. There is also an applicative form, indicating that the action denoted by the verb is on someone's behalf: *tema* 'cut', *temera* 'cut for'; *ruta* 'remove', *rutĩra* 'remove for'. The vowel in the suffix is *ĩ* or *e*, depending on the vowel in the verb stem.

Basic Syntax

The basic word order in Gĩkũyu is SVO. Auxiliaries precede the main verb, and noun modifiers follow the nouns they modify.

Sentences are negated either by the prefix *nd-* attached to the main verb or by the particle *ti* replacing the focus marker *nĩ*.

Kamau nĩ a-gaa-thi-ĩ mũciĩ
Kamau FOCUS CL1-FUT-go home
'Kamau will go home.'

Kamau nd-a-gaa-thi-ĩ mũciĩ
Kamau NEG-CL1-FUT-go home
'Kamau will not go home.'

Contact with Other Languages

Gĩkũyu has greatly influenced language groups such as Meru, Tharaka, Embu, Kamba and to a certain extent, Maasai, because of contact through intermarriage and business. Although it is only taught during the first three years of primary school in predominantly Gĩkũyu-speaking areas, it has been slowly exerting a presence through its use on the radio and in newspapers. Gĩkũyu books are being translated into other world languages and vice versa.

From SWAHILI: *ngari* 'vehicle' (<*gari*), *burana* 'sweater' (<*fulana*), *ndini* 'religion'(<*dini*)
From English: *ngabana* 'governor', *ibuku* 'book', *mũrengeti* 'blanket'

Common Words

man:	mũ-ndũmũrũme
woman:	mũ-tumia
water:	maaĩ
sun:	ri-ũa
three:	ithatũ
fish:	kĩ-ũngũyũ
big:	kĩ-nene (noun class 7)
long:	kĩ-raaya (noun class 7)
small:	kĩ-niini (noun class 7)
yes:	ĩĩ
no:	aca
good:	mw-ega (noun class 1)
bird:	nyoni
dog:	ngui
tree:	mũ-tĩ

Example Sentences

(1) Mwangi nĩ a-reehe i-buku rĩ-rĩa
Mwangi FOCUS CL1:PERFECT-bring CL5-book CL5-which

rĩ-ega.
CL5-good
'Mwangi has brought the good book.'

(2) A-tumia aa ka-nitha nĩ mo-oka.
CL2-woman of CL12-church FOCUS CL2:PERFECT-come
'Church women have come.'

(3) Kamau a-raa-thi-ire kũ.
Kamau CL1-PRES-go-PERFECT where
'Where did Kamau go?'

Efforts to Preserve, Protect, and Promote the Language

Gĩkũyu is being promoted through music, newspapers such as *Inooro*, and radio broadcasts. A Gĩkũyu Language Committee was formed in the late 1910s to help standardize the language and orthography. Its work was halfhearted and by the late 1940s the committee was inoperative.

In postindependent Kenya, the foremost fiction writer in Gĩkũyu has been Gakaara Wanjau. Kenya's most famous novelist, Ngũgĩ wa Thiong'o (who has been a professor of comparative literature at New York University), stated in his book *Decolonizing the Mind* that he would write all of his creative works in Gĩkũyu. As a way of preserving and promoting the language, the Gĩkũyu Language Committee was revived in the late 1970s. The committee currently publishes a quarterly journal, *Mũtiiri*, and encourages Gĩkũyu, speaking scholars to study the language, the oral history of the people, and their literature. The journal carries articles on literature, politics, modern technology, and linguistics. It is contributing to the standardization of Gĩkũyu orthography and to lexical expansion so that the language can express concepts associated with advances in science and technology.

Gĩkũyu has been closely associated with the community-based popular theater movement in Kenya. Such Gĩkũyu plays as *Ngaahika Ndenda* ('I Will Marry When I Want'), on which peasants and workers around Limuru worked with intellectuals from the University of Nairobi, set in motion similar community-based theater activities in Botswana, Zimbabwe, and Tanzania.

Select Bibliography

Armstrong, Lilias E. 1940. *The Phonetic and Tonal Structure of Kikuyu*. London: Oxford University Press.
Barlow, A. Russell. 1960. *Studies in Kikuyu Grammar and Idiom*. Edinburgh: Blackwood and Sons.
Barlow, A. (compiler), and T.G. Benson, ed. 1975. *English-Kikuyu Dictionary*. London: Oxford University Press.
Benson, T.G., ed. 1964. *Kikuyu-English Dictionary*. London: Oxford University Press.
Kabĩra, Wanjikũ, and Karega Mũtahi. 1988. *Gĩkũyu Oral Literature*. Nairobi: Heinemann.

Goṇḍi

Rosanne Pelletier

Language Name: Goṇḍi. **Autonym:** *Goṇḍi.*

Location: Goṇḍi is spoken in Central India, in the states of Maharashtra, Madhya Pradesh, Andhra Pradesh, and Orissa.

Family: South-Central subgroup of the Dravidian language family.

Related Languages: Goṇḍi is most closely related to the six other South-Central Dravidian languages spoken in Andhra Pradesh, Madhya Pradesh, and Orissa, namely TELUGU, Koṇḍa (also called Kūbi), and the "Kondh" languages, so-called because they are spoken mainly in the Kondhmal Hills in Orissa: Kūi, Kūvi, Maṇḍa, and Pengo. Goṇḍi, along with all other members of the South-Central Dravidian subgroup except Telugu, belongs to the set of "tribal", or nonliterary, languages of India.

Dialects: Although the Goṇḍi dialect boundaries are not fully understood, the language is considered to have three regional dialect groups—Northern, Southeastern, and Southwestern—containing numerous dialects (with numerous subdialects), scattered over four Indian states: Maharashtra, Madhya Pradesh, Andhra Pradesh, and Orissa. Noncontiguous dialects are not mutually intelligible. By far, the best-studied dialect is Muria Goṇḍi (Southeastern), spoken in the Bastar District of Madhya Pradesh; if not otherwise noted, illustrative material will be from this dialect. Other dialects that have been studied are Maṛia (including Abujhmaṛia) and Koya (both Southeastern), and Adilabad (Southwestern).

Adilabad is considered to lie between Koya and the subdialect of Muria. One notable pronunciation difference between Adilabad and Muria is that where the former has initial /s/, the latter does not. For example, for the suppletive negative verb 'not.be', Adilabad has *sill-*, whereas Muria has *ill-*. In fact, a common feature of the Southeastern dialects is a historical change of initial /s/ to /h/, followed in certain dialects such as Muria Goṇḍi by deletion of the /h/ at a later historical period. The grammar of Adilabad also appears to have periphrastic tense forms that Muria lacks.

Number of Speakers: Approximately 1.5 million.

Origin and History

Because Goṇḍi is an unwritten language, its history is not documented, either through literary works or grammars. Several word lists and sketchy grammars were written by government officials and missionaries, but even these works were not produced until the very early 20th century. In fact, until the early 1960s, very little was written on Goṇḍi by linguists. Therefore, any conclusions regarding the history of Goṇḍi have necessarily been based on comparative methods.

It appears that Goṇḍi speakers are indigenous to the regions of India where Goṇḍi is currently spoken, where they have long practiced hunting and gathering or agriculture.

Orthography and Basic Phonology

Goṇḍi is an unwritten language. Since it lacks its own alphabet, recent transcriptions of Goṇḍi have utilized the Devanagari, LATIN, or Telugu alphabets.

The symbols in Tables 1 and 2 basically correspond to their IPA values. The symbol /R/, however, requires explanation. /R/ sounds like a post-velar fricative, but is accompanied by slight tremulance of the uvula. It is thus actually a combination of a trill and a fricative, and so is called a "scrape", a term coined by Kenneth Pike for this sound, which has more turbulence than a fricative but which is not clearly a trill. (Such a sound can only be produced at the uvula.)

Several general rules relating to syllable structure follow. First, the initial syllable of a word always receives primary stress. Second, before either a single intervocalic consonant or the last of a sequence of consonants preceding a vowel, a syllable break is made.

Table 1: Vowels

	Front	Central	Back
High	i		u
Mid	e		o
Low		a	

There are numerous specific phonological and morphological rules in Goṇḍi. One is the rule of vowel harmony in deictics, by which the height of a preceding low vowel (*a*) raises to assimilate to a following vowel, as in:

all-or	>ollor
THAT-MASC.PL	'those very persons (MASC)'

Although it is asserted that all Dravidian languages have a phonemic (underlying) long-short distinction with respect to vowels, no Goṇḍi dialect has a vowel length distinction in non-

Table 2: Consonants

	Bilabial	Labio-dental	Dental-alv.	Retro.	Palato-alv.	Palatal	Dorso-velar	Uvular	Glottal
Stops	p, b		t, d	ṭ, ḍ	c, j		k, g		
Nasals	m		n				ŋ		
Fricative			s						
Approx.		v				y			h
Lateral			l						
Trill			r					R	
Flap				ṛ					

initial syllables. In addition, many dialects of Goṇḍi lack a vowel length distinction in initial syllables as well. For example, Andres (1977) shows that vowel length in Muria Goṇḍi is completely predictable. Vowels are long before single consonants but short before consonant sequences. This lack of a phonemic contrast in vowel length makes Goṇḍi unique in the Dravidian language family.

Basic Morphology

Goṇḍi is an agglutinative-inflectional language whose morphology is largely suffixal. The order of morphemes is: ROOT + derivational suffix + inflectional suffix. There are two lexical classes in Goṇḍi: nouns and verbs.

Goṇḍi nouns may inflect for six cases. The nominative case is morphologically unmarked, and is used for sentential subjects, nominal predicates, or indefinite direct objects. The vocative case varies little or not at all from the unmarked nominative noun stem. The other cases consist of overt morphemes, attaching to the oblique form of the noun. These cases are the genitive (*-a*); the dative-accusative (*-un*), which marks the recipient or definite direct object; the instrumental/agentive/locative (*-e*); and the comitative/ablative *-ah*.

There are three number distinctions in nouns: singular, plural, and honorific (the latter of which triggers plural agreement on predicates). A two-way gender distinction, based on natural gender, exists in both singular and plural: masculine is the gender of all nouns representing human males, and non-masculine is the gender of all other nouns.

Within the pronominal system, there are four person distinctions: first person inclusive (including addressee), first person exclusive (excluding addressee), second person and third person.

While Goṇḍi has no articles, there are demonstrative elements that function either as determiners or nouns. There are five deictic categories: proximal, e.g. *idd* 'this (NON-MASC)', distal, e.g., *add* 'that (NON-MASC)', ultradistal, e.g., *hadd* 'that, distant (NON-MASC)', speaker-proximal, e.g., *illid* 'this close to me (NON-MASC)', addressee-proximal, e.g., *allad* 'that close to you (NON-MASC)', and also the interrogative category, e.g. *bodd* 'which (NON-MASC)'. The third person pronouns are, in fact, forms of the demonstratives that are inflected to bear affixes for person, number, gender, and case.

Sentential predicates and attributes bear agreement morphology for person, number, and gender, as in:

or kariyal-or
they.MASC black-3PL.MASC
'Those men are dark skinned.'

ikkeḍ-or leyy-or ann-o-r
here-3PL.MASC young.man-PL go-NEG-3PL.MASC
'The young men of this place won't go.'

The verbal system of Goṇḍi is very rich. Some notions that are expressed by adverbs or adjectives in other languages are expressed in Goṇḍi within complex verbal constructions. For example, instead of negative adverbs (as in ENGLISH), Goṇḍi uses a negative verbal suffix:

ann-v-i
go-NEG-2SG
'Aren't you going?'

This negative suffix apparently "competes" with tense/aspect morphology for the verb stem, since tense/aspect morphology and negation cannot both occur in the same word. Goṇḍi has six tense/aspect complexes. With respect to agreement morphology, the same distinctions of person, number, and gender which exist inherently in the Goṇḍi noun, and which are reflected in the nominal predicates, are reflected in the verbal predicates as well.

A perfective paradigm for the verb *oll-* 'bend over' illustrates morpheme order: *olltan* 'I bent over', *ollti* 'you bent over', *olltu* 'she/it bent over', *olltoR* 'he bent over', *olltom* 'we.EXCL bent over', *olltal* 'we.INCL bent over', *olltir* 'you.PL bent over', *olltuŋ* 'they.NON.MASC bent over', *olltur* 'they.MASC bent over'.

A passivelike construction is formed by suffixing a perfective element to the verb stem, in a process somewhat similar to English adjectival passive such as "uninhabited". Like the English construction, the Goṇḍi forms involve both transitive and intransitive verbs, and thus are not "true" passives. To derive a causative verb, the suffix *-ih* is suffixed to the verb stem: i.e., *malliy* 'to move about' vs. *malliy-ih* 'to cause to move about'. Verbs become transitive via a similar process.

Goṇḍi has three types of compounds: general classificatory, kin classificatory, and possessive. An example of kin classificatory is *ma-a-avva* 'our/my (HONORIFIC)-GENITIVE-mother'. A series of morphophonemic rules applies to the compound, yielding *mevva* 'our/my mother'.

Modern Goṇḍi has a vestige of a plural-action morpheme, a morpheme that signifies repeated performance of one action or performance of more than one action. For example, the form *kas-k-in-tan* (bite-PL.ACTION-PRES-3SG.NON.MASC) means 'they.NON.MASC. nibble'. While the plural-action form *kas-k* 'bite all over, nibble' remains in Goṇḍi, the simple verb base *kacc-* 'bite' itself no longer exists. Although there remains no productive morphological process of plural-action marking in Goṇḍi, apparently phonological rules indicate a morpheme boundary between the verb stem and a plural marker such as *-k* in a group of Goṇḍi verbs. This fact, combined with comparative data from sister languages, indicates that earlier stages of Goṇḍi had a productive morphological process of plural-action verb formation.

One interesting fact regarding the Goṇḍi lexicon is the bounty of relational terms for time. Goṇḍi has a single word for the following references to time: *onne* 'the day before yesterday', *ninne* 'yesterday', *neṇḍ* 'today', *naṛ* 'tomorrow', *monne* 'the day after tomorrow', *paRRne* 'two days from tomorrow', and *veyyne* 'three days from tomorrow'.

Basic Syntax

Goṇḍi is an SOV language, and is head-final at all levels of structure. Although there is some flexibility with respect to the major constituents, the verb (or nominal predicate) is virtually always last. There is no copula in sentences with nominal predicates, unless tense/aspect or negation must be expressed.

Negation in Goṇḍi is expressed by means of a negative suffix. However, when tense/aspect and negation must both be encoded, a periphrastic construction, employing a tensed form of the auxiliary verb *ava* 'be, become' in combination with the negative form of the main verb, is necessary. Thus, the first person singular tenseless negative of the Muria Goṇḍi verb *oll-* 'bend over' is *oll-on* 'I didn't/don't/won't bend over/am not bending over', but the first person singular perfective past negative is *oll-on atan* 'I didn't bend over', literally 'I not bend over, I was'. In other words, the main verb expresses the negation, while the auxiliary verb expresses the tense. Since both verbs in such a construction are fully inflected with first person agreement morphology, the construction is referred to as a "serial verb formation".

Additional noteworthy syntactic features of Goṇḍi are the use of dative subjects, e.g. *ven surta ille* (HIM.DAT/ACC thought NEG) 'He has no intelligence'. This sentence also illustrates the use of a suppletive negative verb *ill* 'not.be'. Verbs in dative-subject constructions do not inflect for agreement. Also, subjects may drop freely in Goṇḍi, as is the case with many highly inflected languages.

Contact with Other Languages

Being spoken in Central India, Goṇḍi is in contact with Indo-Aryan languages, mainly HINDI and Halbi, as well as Dravidian languages, mainly Telugu. Furthermore, Goṇḍi speakers are in contact with speakers of other Goṇḍi dialects. Many of the borrowings into Goṇḍi are of Hindi origin. English words originally borrowed into Hindi thus make their way into Goṇḍi. Telugu is also a source from which Goṇḍi borrows.

Since word-initial consonant clusters are not permitted in Goṇḍi, phonological modification of four types occurs with borrowed words: (1) consonant deletion: 'tractor' becomes /ṭakṭer/; (2) vowel insertion: 'glass' becomes /gillas/; (3) vowel preposing: 'school' becomes /iskul/; and (4) metathesis: 'clip' becomes /kilpi/.

Common Words

man:	muytoR	long:	laṭ
woman:	muytaṛ	small:	cinna (Koya dialect)
water:	eR	yes:	iṇgo
sun:	poṛd	no:	ille (negative verb)
three:	muṇḍu	good:	bennek
fish:	min	bird:	piṭṭe
big:	mayi	dog:	neyy
tree:	marra		

Example Sentences

(1) undi nattur-to-rom undi pen-to-rom
one blood-of-1 PL.EXCL one god-of-1 PL.EXCL

undi puṭṭul-to-rom.
one offspring-of-1 PL.EXCL
'We are of one blood, of one god, of one ancestral line.' (Andres 1977: 420)

(2) nava dada-lor ille-r.
my elder.brother-PL NEG-3 PL.MASC
'I have no elder brothers.' (Andres 1977: 380)

(3) loh-k here avv-tek nand-o-R
house-PL. some arrive-if get wet-NEG-3 SG.MASC

ay-e-R.
become-SUBJ-3 SG.MASC
'If he got near some houses, he would not get wet.' (Andres 1977: 296)

Efforts to Preserve, Protect, and Promote the Language

Goṇḍi lacks prestige of a political/economic type in India and the world in general. Thus, there appears little likelihood that the language will spread. On the contrary, if any change were to be expected, it would be contraction. One stage of this contraction would be the bilingualism reported at least for most male Koya Goṇḍi speakers (Tyler 1969).

These male Koyas speak either Koya and Telugu or Koya and a Hindi dialect. Nevertheless, since most female Koya speakers in remote regions are mainly monolingual Goṇḍi speakers, with proficiency only in Goṇḍi and "bazaar" Telugu, Hindi, or ORIYA, a high degree of Goṇḍi language maintenance seems likely.

There do not appear to be any active efforts to preserve or promote the language. Furthermore, without an established standard dialect, Goṇḍi does not seem likely to take on any important function in the political/legal life of India.

Select Bibliography

Natarajan, G.V. 1985. *Abujhmaṛia Grammar*. CIIL Grammar Series, 14. Mysore: Central Institute of Indian Languages.

Steever, Sanford. 1988. *The Serial Verb Formation in the Dravidian Languages*. Delhi: Motilal Banarsidass.

____. 1993. *Analysis to Synthesis: The Development of Complex Verb Morphology in the Dravidian Languages*. New York: Oxford University Press.

Subrahmanyam, P.S. 1968. *A Descriptive Grammar of Goṇḍi*. Annamalainagar: Annamalai University.

Tyler, Stephen. 1969. *Koya: An Outline Grammar, Gommu Dialect*. Berkeley and Los Angeles: University of California Press Publications in Linguistics 54.

GOTHIC

Charles M. Barrack

Language Name: Gothic. **Alternates:** *Ulfilian Gothic* (after Ulfilas, see below), not to be confused with Crimean Gothic.

Location: Now an extinct language, Gothic was formerly spoken in lower Romania, near the plains of the Danube River.

Family: East Germanic group of the Germanic branch of Indo-European.

Related Languages: Other members of the East Germanic group: Vandalic, Burgundian, Rugian, and Herulian (all extinct).

Origin and History

Gothic is the only well-documented language of the East Germanic group (now entirely extinct) of the Germanic branch of Indo-European. Around the beginning of the Christian era, the Goths migrated from southern Scandinavia, the heart of the Germanic homeland, crossed the Baltic Sea, and temporarily settled near the mouth of the Vistula. By the third century, they eventually migrated further southeast to the Black Sea, whence they staged periodic raids on Roman settlements.

Perhaps as early as the pre-Christian era, they had been known as belonging to two ill-defined groups, the Visigoths, i.e., the "good, noble Goths", and the Ostrogoths, i.e., the "Goths of the east". The Ostrogoths settled in the area of modern Ukraine whereas the Visigoths settled in what is now southern Romania on the plains of the lower Danube River. Eventually the term "Visigoth" was construed to be synonymous with "West Goth", and the terms are now used interchangeably.

Although there were several other dialects of East Germanic (including Vandalic and Burgundian), relatively little is known about them except what can be gleaned from personal and place names. Gothic was spared this anonymity through the efforts of one man, Ulfilas, born in 311 of a Greek-Cappadocian mother and a Visgothic father. Not long after being converted to Arian Christianity by Bishop Eusebius, Ulfilas was consecrated bishop to his tribe, the Visigoths. In order to facilitate their conversion to Christianity, Ulfilas created an alphabet suitable for the Gothic language.

Among his many writings (most of which have been lost), including one apparently written on his deathbed (ca. 385), he translated the Bible from GREEK into Gothic for his people. Although little of Ulfilas's translation of the Old Testament has come down to us, much of the New Testament has been preserved, a fact that renders Ulfilas' Bible translation the oldest surviving literary text in any Germanic language. It must be noted, however, that all fragments of Ulfilas's Bible translation come down to us in manuscripts composed in northern Italy by East Gothic scribes of the fifth and sixth centuries, a fact that becomes manifest in some of the deviant spellings.

During a diplomatic mission to Constantinople between the years 1560 and 1562, a Belgian nobleman from Flanders, Ogier Ghiselin de Busbecq, succeeded in eliciting and transcribing 68 words, the names of a few numerals, and a few sentences in what appeared to him to be a Germanic language, now recognized to be a descendant of the Gothic spoken in the Crimea. Known as Crimean Gothic, it is believed to have died out in the 18th century. It is quite possible that Crimean Gothic descended from a form of Gothic closely related to Ulfilian Gothic.

Orthography and Basic Phonology

Bishop Ulfilas created an alphabet for Gothic by adding a few letters from the LATIN alphabet to the Greek uncial alphabet as well as adding a few of the Germanic runes. (It is a matter of controversy as to exactly how much Ulfilas borrowed from the Latin alphabet or the runes.)

No diacritics occur in the original manuscript (except for those insignificant for our purposes here). Hence, both long and short *u, a, ai* /ɛ/, and *au* /ɔ/ are written with no indication of length. Comparative linguistics and internal reconstruction allow us to reconstruct these as long or short. Ulfilas used separate symbols for *ē* (transliterated *e* or *ē*), *ī* (transliterated *ei*), *ō* (transliterated *o* or *ō*). In this article diacritics have been added on *u, a, ai, au, e*, and *o* in accordance with the traditional practice.

Intervocalically, the voiced stops *b, d*, and *g* were probably fricatives [ß], [ð], and [ɣ], respectively. The velar nasal [ŋ] occurred exclusively before the other velars, *k, g*, or *q*, and was spelled *g*. Thus, *gk* represented the sequence /ŋk/.

Gothic fricatives were devoiced wordfinally and before voiceless consonants. The original voiced pronunciation was maintained in other environments. Thus, alongside *hlaibis* [hlɛ:ßis] 'bread (genitive)' with a voiced fricative [ß] (from the voiced stop /b/), we find the accusative form *hlaif* and the nominative form *hlaifs*.

Table 1: Vowels

	Front	Back
High	i, ei [i:]	u, ū [u:]
High-Mid	ē [e:]	ō [o:]
Mid	aí [ɛ], ái [ɛ:]	aú [ɔ], áu [ɔ:]
Low		a, ā [a:]

The short vowels *i* and *u* were lowered to *aí* and *aú* before the

Table 2: Consonants

		Labial	Dental	Alveolar	Palatal	Velar	Labio-velar	Glottal
Stops	Voiceless	p	t			k	q	
	Voiced	b	d			g		
Fricatives	Voiceless	f	þ	s				h, hʷ
	Voiced	β	ð	z		ɣ		h, hʷ
Nasals		m	n			ŋ		
Liquids								
Glides					j		w	

apical trill *r* and the glottals *hʷ* and *h*. For example, one class of strong verbs (see below) typically has the vowel *i* in the stem syllable in the infinitive form (e.g., *hilpan* 'to help', *lisan* 'to read'). However, before *r*, the stem vowel is *aí* (e.g., *waírpan* 'to throw'). Similarly, in the past participle, the stem vowel is *u* in this class (e.g., *hulpans* 'helped'). However, before *r*, the stem vowel is *aú* (e.g., *waúrpans* 'thrown').

Liquids and nasals that were not adjacent to a vowel were syllabic. For example, in the nominative plural form *bagmos* 'trees', the *m* was not syllabic, while in the nominative singular *bagms* [bag.m̩s] and the accusative singular *bagm* [bag.m̩], *m* was syllabic.

Basic Morphology

Gothic nouns and adjectives were inflected for case (nominative, vocative, genitive, dative, accusative), number (singular and plural), and gender (masculine, feminine, neuter). Adjectives (including demonstratives) agreed with the nouns they modified in these categories:

Hlaif	unsar-ana	þ-ana	sintein-an
bread/ACC/M/SG	our-ACC/M/SG	the-ACC/M/SG	daily-ACC/M/SG

gif	uns	hi-mma	dag-a
give	1PL:DAT	this-DAT/M/SG	day-DAT/M/SG

'Give us this day our daily bread.' (Matthew 6:11)

An adjective that modifies nouns of different genders was inflected as neuter plural:

Jah	qām-un	þan	áiþei	is	jah
and	came-3PL	then	mother-NOM/F/SG	his	and

brōþr-jus	is	jah	ūta	standand-ōna
brothers-NOM/M/PL	his	and	outside	standing-NOM/NEUT/PL

insandi-dēd-un	du	i-mma
send-PRETERITE-3PL	for	3SG/DAT/M

'And then came his mother and his brothers, and, standing outside, they sent for him.' (Mark 3:31)

The basic structure of nouns and adjectives followed the pattern: Root + Stem Suffix + Inflection. The inflection provided information on case, number, and gender. Stem-forming suffixes (identified because they recurred in many nouns), ended in vowels (*-a-*, *-ja-*, *-wa-* [masculine or neuter]; *-o-*, *-jo-*, *-wo-* [feminine]; *-i-*, and *-u-*), or consonants, usually *-n-*.

This structure is evident in the following dative plural nouns; in all of them, *-m* indicates dative plural:

Stem-class	Form	Gloss
a-stem	barn-a-m	'to/for the children'
ja-stem	haírd-ja-m	'to/for the shepherds'
ō-stem	sáiwal-ō-m	'to/for the souls'
i-stems	gast-i-m	'to/for the guests'
u-stem	sun-u-m	'to/for the sons'

In other cases, the stem suffix might not be visible as a distinct component in the noun.

Unlike nouns and adjectives, first and second person pronouns occurred in dual as well as singular and plural forms: eg., *wit* 'we two' vs. *weis* 'we (plural)'; *igqis* 'to/for you two' vs. *izwis* 'to/for you (plural)'.

Like nouns and adjectives, Gothic verbs followed the pattern: Root + Stem Suffix + Inflection. The inflection consisted of tense and mood markers and, in the case of the finite verb, person agreement with the subject of the sentence:

rōd-	i-	dēd-	ei-	na
speak ROOT	STEM SUFFIX CLASS 1 WEAK	PRETERITE TENSE	OPTATIVE MOOD	3PL

'they might speak'

The overwhelming majority of Gothic verbs fell into two subgroups, "weak" and "strong". Weak verbs formed the preterite and the perfect participle by means of a dental suffix (*-d-*, *-dēd-*, *-t-*), as in *rōdidēdeina*, from *rōdjan* 'to speak'. Strong verbs employed no suffix to express the preterite, but rather exhibited a systematic vowel change in the stem (called *ablaut*) and formed the perfect participle with the suffix *-an*: *drinkan* 'to drink', *drank* 'drank' [preterite, 1,3 sg], *drunkans* 'drunk' [perfect participle].

Gothic verbs agreed with their subjects in person and number. In the third person, singular and plural were distinguished, while in first and second person, singular, dual, and plural were distinguished, as illustrated in the following forms of the verb *baíran* 'to bear':

	Singular	Dual	Plural
1st person	baír-a	baír-ōs	baír-am
2nd person	baír-is	baír-ats	baír-iþ
3rd person	baír-iþ	--	baír-and

New words were freely derived by means of affixes:

háiþi 'heath' [noun]	>	háiþi-wisks 'wild' [adj.]
diups 'deep' [adj.]	>	diup-iþa 'depth' [noun]
handus 'hand' [noun]	>	handu-gs 'wise' [adj.]; handu-gei 'wisdom' [noun]
andáugi 'face' [noun]	>	andáugi-ba 'openly' [adverb]

Basic Syntax

Little direct knowledge of Gothic word order is available because existing documents are virtually all word-for-word glosses of original Greek sources. Nevertheless, Ulfilas's translations systematically deviate from the Greek originals at times, providing limited insight into other aspects of Gothic syntax.

For example, Gothic often employed the genitive and dative cases to express various thematic or syntactic roles in place of accusative case or prepositional phrases in the original Greek:

jabái hʷas matj-iþ þis hláib-is
eat-3sg this-GEN/SG bread-GEN/SG
'If anyone eats of this bread ...' (John 6:51)

The negative particles *ni* 'not' and *nih* 'neither' generally preceded the finite verb:

ni sai-and nih sneiþ-and nih lis-and in
NEG sow-3PL nor reap-3PL nor gather-3PL into

banst-ins
barn-ACC/PL
'they do not sow, nor reap, nor gather into barns' (Matthew 6:26)

The particle *ni* is often extended by the interrogative clitic *-u*: *niu* 'is it not the case that?':

ni-u sáiwal-a máis is-t fōdein-ái
NEG-Q soul-NOM/SG greater-than is-3SG food-DAT/SG

jah leik wastjō-m
and body-NOM/SG cloth-DAT/PL
'Is not the soul greater than food and the body greater than clothing?' (Matthew 6:25)

Contact with Other Langauges

Gothic incorporated words from Celtic, Greek, and Latin.

From Celtic: *sipōneis* 'disciple' (<**sepānios*)
From Greek: *aíwaggēljō* 'gospel' (< *euangélion*)
From Latin: *karkara* 'jail' (< *carcer*)

Common Words

man:	manna, waír	long:	laggs
woman:	qinō	small:	leitils
water:	watō	yes:	ja
sun:	sauil	no:	nē
third:	þridja	good:	gōþs
fish:	fisks	bird:	fugls
big:	mikils	dog:	hunds
tree:	bagms		

Example Sentences

(1) att-a unsar þu in
father-VOC/M/SG our 1pl/VOC/M/SG 2SG/NOM in

himina-m weih-n-ái
heaven-DAT/M/PL blessed-become-PRESENT/OPTATIVE/3SG

nam-ō þein.
name-NOM/NEUT/SG 2SG/NOM/NEUT/SG
'Our father who art in heaven, blessed be thy name.'

(2) qim-ái þiudinassu-s þein-s.
come-PRES/OPT/3SG kingdom-NOM/M/SG 2SG/NOM/M/SG
'Thy kingdom come.'

(3) waírþ-ái wil-ja þein-s swē
become-PRES/OPT/3SG will-NOM/M/SG 2SG/NOM/M/SG as

in himin-a jah ana aírþ-ái.
in heaven-DAT/M/SG and on earth-DAT/F/SG
'Thy will become, in heaven as it is on earth.'

Select Bibliography

Bennett, William Holmes. 1980. *Introduction to the Gothic Language*. New York: Modern Language Association of America.

Lehmann, Winfred P. 1986. *A Gothic Etymological Dictionary*. With bibliography prepared under the direction of Helen-Jo J. Hewitt. Leiden: E.J. Brill.

Vogel, Petra. 1995. *Minimalgrammatik des Gothischen*. Goppingen: Kummerle.

Wright, Joseph. 1975. *Grammar of the Gothic Language, and the Gospel of St. Mark*. Oxford: Clarendon Press.

ANCIENT GREEK

Brian D. Joseph

Language Name: Ancient Greek, Classical Greek, Greek (without reference to time period, the ancient form of the language is usually taken as the unmarked value, and within Ancient Greek, the Attic dialect [see **Dialects** below] is the usual point of reference). **Autonym:** *hellēnikē* (actually an adjective derived from *Héllēn*, the word for a 'Greek' in general (as opposed to a member of one of the Greek dialect groups); as an adjective, it is modifying an understood noun 'language').

Location: Ancient Greek in its earliest attested forms (14th century B.C.) was spoken in the southern Balkan peninsula, in territory that is now the modern nation of Greece, both on the Greek mainland and on some of the Aegean islands, most notably Crete. By relatively early in the 1st millennium B.C., Greek was spoken over all of the Aegean islands and Cyprus, and there were Greek-speaking colonies in Asia Minor, along the west coast of what is now Turkey, in Southern Italy, in parts of the western Mediterranean, and in the Black Sea area. Colonization continued during the Archaic and pre-Classical periods up to the 7th century B.C. and into the Classical period, but it was during the Hellenistic period, as part of the expansion of the empire of Philip of Macedon and especially of his son, Alexander the Great, both of whom adopted Greek as the official language of their court, that Greek achieved its greatest geographic distribution, spreading all over the eastern Mediterranean, with a major cultural center in Alexandria, and the Levant, and extending as far east as India. The demarcation between Ancient and the beginnings of MODERN GREEK is considered to be at the end of the Hellenistic period, roughly in the 4th century A.D.

Family: Ancient Greek is generally taken to be the only representative of the Greek or Hellenic branch of Indo-European. There is some dispute as to whether Ancient MACEDONIAN (the native language of Philip and Alexander), if it has any special affinity to Greek at all, is a dialect within Greek (see below) or a sibling language to all of the known Ancient Greek dialects. If the latter view is correct, then Macedonian and Greek would be the two subbranches of a group within Indo-European that could more properly be called Hellenic.

Related Languages: As noted above, Ancient Macedonian might be the language most closely related to Greek, perhaps even a dialect of Greek. The slender evidence is open to different interpretations, so that no definitive answer is really possible; but most likely, Ancient Macedonian was not simply an Ancient Greek dialect on a par with Attic or Aeolic (see below). Despite some suggestive affinities to ARMENIAN and Indo-Iranian, the general consensus is that these connections are not so strong as to warrant treating these branches as part of a larger subgroup within Indo-European. Although culturally there are close ties in the Classical and post-Classical periods between speakers of Greek and speakers of LATIN, and this has been reflected in Western academic circles (where courses on comparative Greek and Latin grammar are taught as part of classical linguistics), Greek and Latin are not closely related within Indo-European.

Dialects: The main dialects of Ancient Greek, identifiable in the end of the Archaic period, are (1) Attic-Ionic, comprising Attic and Ionic; (2) Aeolic, consisting of Boeotian and Thessalian on the mainland and the Greek of the island of Lesbos and of adjacent northwest Asia Minor; (3) Arcado-Cypriot, taking in Arcadian, in the Peloponnesos, and Cypriot, and (4) West Greek, covering not only Northwest Greek, such as Aetolian and Locrian, but also Doric, which includes Laconian (the dialect of Sparta), Corinthian, Megarian, Cretan, and Rhodian. Attic-Ionic and Arcado-Cypriot are sometimes classed together as East Greek, with Aeolic being seen as intermediate between East and West Greek. The ancients themselves were aware of some of these dialect differences, as indicated by the existence of verbs such as *aiolízein* 'to speak Aeolic', *dōrízein* 'to speak Doric', and *attikízein* 'to speak Attic', all of which can be contrasted with *hellēnízein* 'to speak (common) Greek' (cf. the autonym *hellēnikē* noted above).

Prior to the Archaic period, the earliest attested dialect is Mycenaean Greek, preserved mainly on clay tablets inscribed with syllabic characters commonly referred to as "Linear B"; these tablets have been found primarily at sites of major Mycenaean palaces, with the earliest coming from Knosos on Crete (where Mycenaeans had overcome the local Minoan rulers) dating from the 14th century B.C., and others coming from sites on the mainland somewhat later, e.g., Mycenae and Pylos from the 13th and 12th centuries B.C., the dates being a function of the adventitious preservation of the tablets in fires that destroyed the palaces. The relationship of Mycenaean Greek with the dialects of the later Archaic period is uncertain, since it shows some innovative features in common with both Arcado-Cypriot and (at least part of) Aeolic; moreover, considerable uniformity is evident in Mycenaean both during its two centuries of attestation and over its geographic range of mainland Greece, the Peloponnesos, and some Aegean islands, especially Crete. Thus it has been suggested that Mycenaean Greek may represent a supraregional koine in use in the 2nd millennium B.C. Also, although not a distinct dialect, the language of the Homeric epics, especially the *Iliad* and the *Odyssey,* represents an archaic form of Greek, largely based on Ionic but with a significant overlay of Aeolic. In the Hellenistic period, a dialect known as Pamphylian is found in southwest Asia Minor, but it may not be a separate dialect so much as a local variety heavily influenced by the Hellenistic Koine. The Hellenistic Koine refers to the form of the language that spread extensively in the Hellenistic and Roman periods, roughly from 300 B.C. to A.D. 300, based mainly on Attic and Ionic, with some input, to a much lesser extent, from other dialects; it shows some degree of simplification of certain structural features and innovative pronunciations as compared with Greek of the Classical period.

Number of Speakers: With the spread of Greek during the Hellenistic period, the number of speakers grew accordingly over Alexander's empire, and surely numbered above several million (though not all in the empire spoke Greek as their first language) at its peak.

Origin and History

The earliest stages of the prehistory of Greek, from the conventional date of reconstructed Proto-Indo-European, roughly 4500 B.C., to the first attestation in the Mycenaean period, c. 1400 B.C., are somewhat obscure. Still, it is generally agreed that Proto-Greek speakers first entered southeastern Europe, and the Balkans in particular, sometime between 2200 B.C. and 1600 B.C., most likely coming in several different migratory waves. The earliest of these migrations may well have been speakers of what in the first millennium B.C. became Arcado-Cypriot, and in the second millennium B.C. is represented by Mycenaean Greek (note the affinities referred to above between Mycenaean and Arcado-Cypriot), settling in the southern part of the Greek mainland and in the Peloponnesos. A later wave brought Ionic speakers into Attica as well as other parts of central Greece and the Peloponnesos. At this point, still in the second millennium B.C., West Greek speakers are believed to have been grouped in the northwestern part of the southern Balkan peninsula.

The next major historical event that had important linguistic consequences is the Dorian invasions of 12th century B.C., in which West Greek speakers from the northwest moved into the Peloponnesos, leading to the end of the Mycenaean civilization and thus to the establishment of a new dialect base in Greece. The small pocket of Arcadian speakers in the central Peloponnesos is presumed to be a remnant of a more widespread Arcado-Cypriot-like dialect from the 2nd millennium B.C. (note the affinities Mycenaean Greek shows with later Arcado-Cypriot). The Dorians moved as well into many of the Aegean Islands, including Crete, so that the dialect picture in 1st millennium B.C. Greece is quite different from that of the 2nd millennium B.C.

Somewhat later, in the eighth century B.C., a period of massive colonization began, spreading Greek throughout the eastern Mediterranean, with colonists from mainland localities transplanting their dialect abroad, sometimes with different dialects in neighboring settlements (as in southern Italy, for instance).

The Classical period, during which Athens established itself as the political, cultural, and economic center of the Greek world, was still a period in which the various dialects were able to thrive, though increasingly Attic was being used as a common language throughout much of Greece. This expansion of Attic led to the adoption of some non-Attic features by users of the dialect, even in Attica. This dialect mixing represented the beginnings of the *koinē diálektos*, or 'common dialect', more usually referred to simply as the Koine, as Koine Greek, or as Hellenistic Greek (after the historical period in which it arose). With the rise of the Macedonian Empire in the fourth century B.C. and the decision of Philip II of Macedonia to adopt (the modified) Attic as the official administrative language of his state, and with the subsequent expansion of Macedonian influence under his son Alexander the Great, the Greek language, in its emerging Koine Greek form, was spread throughout Asia Minor, Egypt, Syria and the Levant, Mesopotamia, and Persia. The resulting language was remarkably uniform throughout this territory, but, due in part to influences from substratum languages in the areas it came to be spoken in, as local populations shifted to the new variety of Greek, including speakers of any older dialects of Greek that were eventually ousted (especially in the eastern Mediterranean), there was some variation as well. What might be (somewhat artificially) characterized as a standard form of the Koine was the language used for the Septuagint and the Greek New Testament, and as the medium for a vast array of literary, philosophical, religious, historical, and scientific documents from the Hellenistic period. In addition, there are numerous official inscriptions in stone written in the Koine, and thousands of informal personal letters and documents written on papyrus. The Koine also is the basis for the development of Medieval and Modern Greek.

Orthography and Basic Phonology

The earliest writing system for Greek was the so-called Linear B syllabary, adapted from another system originally designed for an entirely different language; the source system probably was that now known as "Linear A", found all over Crete and at other Minoan sites from the second millennium B.C. Greek Linear B was in use at the various Mycenaean palaces in the second millennium B.C., most notably Pylos in the Peloponnesos and Knosos on Crete (after the Mycenaean invasion there), and has been found mostly inscribed onto clay tablets for record-keeping purposes, though, more rarely, the signs have been found painted onto vases as well. In Cyprus in the first millennium B.C., inscriptions occur that are written in a syllabary, entirely different from, but surely related to, the Mycenaean one, with both most likely having a common source, presumably Minoan Linear A.

Still, the most significant and enduring writing system for Greek is the Greek alphabet. Adapted from the West Semitic (probably

Table 1: Consonants

		Labial	Dental	Palatal	Velar	Glottal
Stops	voiceless, unaspirated	p	t		k	
	voiceless, aspirated	p^h	t^h		k^h	
	voiced	b	d		g	
Fricatives			s (z)			h
Nasals		m	n		(ŋ)	
Liquids			l, r (r̥)			
Glides		w		j		

PHOENICIAN) consonantal writing system and embellished with separate signs for vowel sounds, the Greek alphabet first appears in inscriptions in the eighth century B.C. The paths of transmission from Phoenician and of diffusion within the Greek world are obscure, but there is considerable variation in local ("epichoric") varieties of the alphabet all over Greece, both in the shapes of and the phonetic value attached to various letters. The Ionian alphabet came to predominate, ultimately becoming the standard medium in Athens and most Greek states.

The Greek Alphabet (Ionian Version)

Capital Letter	Small Letter	Transliteration
Α	α	a
Β	β	b
Γ	γ	g
	γ before γ κ χ ξ	n
Δ	δ	d
Ε	ϵ	e
Ζ	ζ	z
Η	η	e:, ē
Θ	θ	th
Ι	ι	i
Κ	κ	k
Λ	λ	l
Μ	μ	m
Ν	ν	n
Ξ	ξ	x
Ο	ο	o
Π	π	p
Ρ	ρ	r
Σ	σ (ς in final position)	s
Τ	τ	t
Υ	υ	y, u
Φ	φ	ph
Χ	χ	kh, ch
Ψ	ψ	ps
Ω	ω	o:, ō
	# '	h
	# '	—

The phonological descriptions in this article are of the Attic dialect, unless otherwise specified (see Table 1 above).

The sounds given in parentheses are conditioned variants of other phones: [ŋ] is an allophone of /n/ before velars; the voiceless trill [r̥] occurs in initial position, while the voiced variant [r] occurs elsewhere; [z] is an allophone of /s/ that occurs before voiced consonants.

There may have been a voiced dental affricate [d^z], corresponding to the letter <ζ> (see above), but most of the evidence concerning the pronunciation of <ζ> suggests it represented a true cluster of [z] + [d] (thus phonemically /s/ + /d/).

Dialectally, [w] had a wider distribution, being found in most dialects outside of Attic-Ionic in positions other than postvocalic; [j] occurs in Mycenaean in initial and intervocalic position. Mycenaean also had a series of labio-velar stops (g^w, k^w, k^{wh}) that correspond, under different conditions and in various words, to labials, dentals, or velars in first millennium B.C. Greek. In addition, one set of signs (the "z-series") in the Mycenaean Linear B syllabary seems to represent a series of affricates, writing sounds that derive from clusters of dental and velar stops with a palatal glide. Generally, differences from Attic in the other dialects are not so much in the phonemic inventory but rather in the lexical distribution of sounds; still, some spellings in non-Attic inscriptions may point to segmental differences, e.g., Central Cretan (Doric) <ζ> / <θθ> and Ionic <σσ>, corresponding to Attic <ττ>, may indicate a [t^s] if not still in the dialects at least in a stage not far removed in time from the attested spellings.

Table 2: Vowels

	Front	Central	Back
High	i ī y ȳ		
High-Mid	e ē		o ō
Low-Mid	ε̄		ɔ̄
Low		a ā	

By contrast to the relatively straightforward consonant inventory, the vowel system of Ancient Greek was quite complex. As illustrated in the preceding table, length was distinctive. The front-rounded vowels /y ȳ/ are found only in the Attic-Ionic dialect; the other dialects have back-rounded /u ū/ instead. In addition to the vowels above, Ancient Greek had the following diphthongs: *aj, oj, ew, aw, yj, ēj, āj, ōj, ēw, āw.*

The Ancient Greek accentual system was pitchbased, with three distinctions: high pitch (acute) and low pitch (grave), possible on long or short vowels, and, only on long vowels, and contour (high-low) pitch (circumflex). Accent placement was predictable generally only in finite verb forms and some noun forms, and in certain morphologically definable formations; otherwise it was unpredictable, and placement of accent served to distinguish words, e.g., *nomós* 'district' vs. *nómos* 'low'. Similarly, accent type on a given syllable also could signal lexical distinctions, e.g., *oíkoi* 'at home' vs. *oĩkoi* 'houses'. Generally, only one high pitch was allowed per word and it had to fall on one of the last three syllables; in certain groups of clitic elements, multiple high pitches on a single prosodic group were possible.

A basic phonological process involving consonants was the iterative deletion of all word-final consonants other than [s r n], the only final consonants therefore allowed on the surface; thus underlying /gálakt/ 'milk NOM.SG' surfaced as [gála], and /kléptōnts/ 'stealing NOM.SG.M' surfaced as [kléptōn]. Other morphophonemic alternations include *t* appearing as *s* before *i* (e.g., *ploût-os* 'wealth' / *ploús-ios* 'wealthy'), devoicing/deaspiration before *s* (e.g., *ág-ō* 'I lead' / *ák-s-ō* 'I will lead', *é-graph-e* '(s)he was writing' / *é-grap-s-e* '(s)he wrote'), and intervocalic loss of /s/, e.g., *alēthés* 'true NOM.SG.NEUT' / *alētheØ-a* 'true NOM.PL.NEUT' (which, in Attic, contracts to *alēthē̃*), among others. Contractions of vowel sequences are quite usual, even across word boundaries when the first element is a prosodically weak word such as the definite article or *kai* 'and'; the outcomes of these contractions vary from dialect to dialect and constitute one of the major isoglosses distinguishing the dialects.

The Classical Attic system given above underwent several changes in the post-Classical period, not all of which were completed by the end of the Hellenistic period, around the fourth century A.D. In the consonants, earlier *b d g* fricativized, giving *v ð γ*, as did *ph th kh*, yielding *f θ x*, and *h* was lost (a change found in several ancient dialects other than Attic). New instances of the voiced stops *b d g* were provided by loanwords and possibly also as variants of voiceless *p t k* after nasals. In addition, the once-allophonic [z] took on phonemic status. In the vowels, earlier [ō] raised to [ū], distinctive vowel length was lost, and the movement of several vowels to [i] was under way; the long palatal diphthongs lost their offglide, the *w* offglide became [v] or [f] depending on the voicing of the following sound, and each of the other diphthongs merged with some short monophthong. The ultimate result is the (considerably simplified) vowel system:

	Front	Central	Back
High	i y		u
Mid	ɛ		ɔ
Low		a	

These changes in the phonology were the beginnings of the developments that characterize Modern Greek in contrast to Classical Greek.

Basic Morphology

For the most part, Ancient Greek was a fusional inflecting language morphologically, with relevant grammatical information generally being indicated through the endings of inflected words, i.e., nouns, pronouns, adjectives, articles (which, in Homeric Greek, were clearly pronouns, with the determiner function developing by the Classical period), and verbs. Each ending typically encoded values for several categories simultaneously.

Nominal forms in Ancient Greek, comprising nouns, pronouns, adjectives, and determiners (specifically, the definite article), showed markings for five cases (nominative, accusative, genitive, dative, and vocative), three numbers (singular, dual, and plural), and three generally arbitrary noun classes ("genders", usually referred to as masculine, feminine, and neuter). In addition, cutting across the gender classes were different inflectional ("declensional") classes for nouns and adjectives, based on phonological characteristics of the final segment(s) of the stem, thus giving *o*-stems (in the nouns mainly masculine but with some feminines, as well as neuters with a different nominative/accusative form), *ā*-stems (mostly feminine but with some masculines), *i*-stems (mostly masculine and feminine, though some neuters occur), various consonant stems (*s*-stems, *n*-stems, *t*-stems, etc., in all genders), and so on. In most accounts, the *ā*-stems are considered one inflectional class (though the feminine and masculine *ā*-stems have different endings in some cases), the *o*-stems a second, and consonant stems (subsuming *i*- and *u*-stems, largely for historical reasons) a third.

The actual endings that realized these various categories were thus quite diverse, so that, since agreement in gender, number, and case was required between heads and modifiers, the actual form that these agreeing elements took could be very different. Some of these possibilities are illustrated below:

	Masculine	Feminine
Meaning	'the wise divinity'	'the worthy hope'
Singular:		
Nominative	ho sophòs daímōn	hē axíā elpís
Accusative	tòn sophòn daímona	tḕn axíān elpída
Genitive	toû sophoû daímonos	tē̂s axíās elpídos
Dative	tō̂i sophō̂i daímoni	tē̂i axíāi elpídi
Vocative	sophè daîmon	axíāèlpí
Dual:		
Nom/Acc/Voc	tō sophṑ daímone	tṑ axíā elpíde
Gen/Dat	toîn sophoîn daimónoin	taîn axíain elpídoin
Plural:		
Nom/Voc	hoi sophòi daímones	hai áxiai elpídes
Accusative	toùs sophoùs daímonas	tā̀s axíās elpídas
Genitive	tō̂n sophō̂n daimónōn	tō̂n axíōn elpídōn
Dative	toìs sophòis daímosi	taîs axíais elpísi

The same phonological segments could signal very different categories, depending on the gender and inflectional class they occurred in. For instance, *-es* signaled, neuter singular nominative/accusative of *s*-stem adjectives (e.g., *alēthés* 'true') and nominative plural masculine/feminine for consonant stems (e.g., *daímones*/*elpídes* above); *-os* could mark masculine nominative singular of *o*-stems (e.g., *sophòs* above), genitive singular of consonant stems (e.g., *daímonos*/*elpídos* above), or nominative/accusative singular of neuter *s*-stems (e.g., *génos* 'race'), etc. Personal pronouns had special forms, while demonstrative and other pronouns generally followed some other nominal declensional pattern. Adjectives also showed inflection for comparative and superlative degree.

The verbal system of Ancient Greek encoded many more categories than did the nominal system. The categories of tense (present, past, and future), aspect (distinguishing continuous action [imperfective] from simple occurrence [so-called "aoristic"] from completed action [perfective]), and voice (active, passive, and so-called "middle") are relevant for all verbs, whether finite, i.e., those that show the encoding of three persons and three numbers (singular, dual, plural), in agreement with the subject and of mood (indicative, subjunctive, imperative, and optative), or nonfinite, i.e., without person, number, and mood marked, covering the participles (11 in all) and the infinitives (11 in all). Not all combinations of categories have distinct realizations or even any realization at all; for instance, there are no first person dual active forms, there are no moods other than the indicative for the past imperfective (the so-called imperfect), and passive and middle voice forms are identical in the present tense and the imperfect as well as in the present and past perfective (the so-called present perfect and pluperfect).

The value of some of these categories and their interactions with one another require some comment. With regard to voice, middle is used to mark actions that a subject performs on him- or herself (e.g., reflexives), or for his or her own benefit, though in some instances, especially verbs that have only middle voice forms (so-called deponent verbs), such as *ergázomai* 'I work' (not 'I work for myself'), middle voice seems to be simply a different inflectional class. With regard to the various tense and aspect categories, the interrelationships among the categories are noteworthy, and are summarized below, giving the conventional names for the different tense-aspect combinations:

Tense	Present	Past	Future
Aspect			
Continuous	present	imperfect	future
Simple	———	aorist	future
Completed	perfect	pluperfect	future perfect (generally only passive)

The verbal inflectional picture is complicated further by the fact that a variety of formations existed for different combinations of categories, and that the endings could be different for each formation. For example, some verbs formed the aorist tense with an *-s* suffix, in which case the first person singular ending was *-a* (e.g. *égrap-s-a* 'I wrote'), while others modified the root vocalism, in which case the first person singular ending was *-on* (e.g., *élip-on* 'I left', vs. present *leíp-ō*). Similarly, a few verbs have a first person singular ending *-mi* in the present, while most have *-ō*, with further differences in other person/number endings. Finally, phonological differences in verbal stems could lead to surface differences in the realization of categories; for instance, stems ending in a consonant or the front-rounded vowel *-y-* marked their third person singular imperfect with the ending *-e* (e.g., *égraph-e* '(s)he was writing') while those ending in *-a-* had a third person singular imperfect in *-ā*, from a contraction of /ae/ (e.g., *etímā* '(s)he was honoring').

A full synopsis of the verb *gráphō* 'I write' is given on the next page, with first person singular forms for all tense, aspect, voice, and all moods but imperative, for which second singular is used, as well as nonfinite participial and infinitival forms; not all forms given here are actually attested, but they were, in principle, possible. In the table, past tense forms are Aorist unless otherwise marked, and perfect forms are present perfect unless otherwise marked.

Several changes in morphological categories took place between Classical Greek and Hellenistic Greek. In both the noun and the verb, dual number became increasingly restricted in use, and ultimately was lost. In the noun, the dative case was being replaced in Hellenistic times by various prepositional alternatives and in some functions by the genitive case. In the verb, the optative mood was increasingly on the wane, partly the result of sound changes that led to partial homophony in several forms in the paradigm, with the subjunctive and, less so, with the indicative. Similarly, the various forms of the perfect (present perfect, pluperfect, and future perfect) were used less and less, eventually being lost. In a change that affected both the morphology and the syntax, the infinitive began to give way in this period to finite subordinate-clause substitutes. There were also several changes in the actual form of grammatical endings, due to sound changes and analogical changes within the various systems of endings.

Basic Syntax

The order of major constituents in a sentence was generally free, so that both Subject-Verb and Verb-Subject orders are found. Similarly, the object may precede or follow the verb or even the subject, though weak pronominal objects generally occurred as clitics in second position within their clause, often as part of a string of clitic elements, including sentence connectives. These possibilities are illustrated in the example sentences at the end of this chapter.

Elements that make up constituents, however, are subject to tighter ordering restrictions. For example, the definite article always precedes a noun it occurs with, and adjectives generally occur between the article and the noun. In fact, Greek shows a systematic word-order difference between attributive adjectives, which follow the article (possibly repeated after the noun) and determine a noun phrase, and predicative adjectives, which occur outside the article and determine a copular sentence (with zero-copula), as illustrated below with *ho* 'the', *sophós* 'wise', and *basileús* 'king':

a. ho sophòs basileús	'the wise king'
b. ho basileús ho sophós	'the wise king'
c. sophós ho basileús	'the king is wise'
d. ho basileùs sophós	'the king is wise'

Within the noun phrase, the article afforded great flexibility, with extended prenominal modifiers possible, even multiple "embeddings" of articulated nouns (see Example Sentence 3).

A Full Synopsis of the Verb *gráphō*

A. Active Voice	Present	Past	Future	Perfect
Indicative	gráphō	égraphon IMPERF égrapsa	grápsō	gégrapha egegráphē PLUPERF
Subjunctive	gráphō	grápsō	———	gegráphō
Optative	gráphoimi	grápsaimi	grápsoimi	gegráphoimi
Imperative	gráphe	grápson	———	gégraphe
Infinitive	gráphein	grápsai	grápsein	gegráphenai
Participle	gráphōn	grápsas	grápsōn	gegraphṓs
B. Middle Voice				
Indicative	gráphomai	egraphómēn IMPERF egrapsámēn	grápsomai	gégrammai egegrámmēn PLUPERF
Subjunctive	gráphōmai	grapsōmai	———	gegramménos
Optative	graphoímēn	grapsaímēn	grapsoímēn	gegramménos eíēn
Imperative	gráphou	grápsai	———	gégrapso
Infinitive	gráphesthai	grápsasthai	grápsesthai	gegráphthai
Participle	graphómenos	grapsámenos	grapsómenos	gegramménos
C. Passive Voice				
Indicative	gráphomai	egraphómēn IMPERF egráphthēn	graphḗsomai	gégrammai egegrámmēn PLUPERF gegrápsomai FUT PERF
Subjunctive	gráphōmai	graphthṓ	———	gegramménosô
Optative	graphoímēn	graphtheíēn	graphēsoímēn	gegramménos eíēn gegrapsoímēn FUT PERF
Imperative	gráphou	gráphthēti	———	gégrapso
Infinitive	gráphesthai	graphthēnai	graphḗsesthai	gegráphthai gegrápsesthai FUT PERF
Participle	graphómenos	graphtheís	graphēsómenos	gegramménos gegrapsómenos FUT PERF

Nominative case is used to mark the subjects of finite verbs, while accusative is the usual case for the subject of an infinitive. Accusative is also the typical case for the direct object, though some verbs idiosyncratically govern objects in other cases (e.g., *árkhomai* 'begin' takes a genitive object). The dative case marks indirect objects as well as parties with an interest in some action, possession with 'be', agent with some passives, instrument or cause, accompaniment, time at which, and place in which. The genitive marks a variety of relations between nouns, including possession, and can be used for partitive verbal objects, e.g., (Thucydides 1.30) *tê̄s gê̄s étemon* 'they ravaged some of the land' (literally: 'of-the land they ravaged'). The vocative is essentially an asyntactic case, being used for direct address.

Accusative, dative, and genitive can also be assigned by prepositions; although some prepositions govern just a single case (e.g., *en* 'in' always takes the dative), in many instances a preposition can govern more than one case, with differences in meaning associated with the differential case assignment. For example, *epí* 'on, upon' occurs with the dative or genitive to denote place on which, but with the accusative for place toward which.

Greek negation is marked by one of two separate (adverbial) words, distributed mainly according to verbal mood: *ou* occurs with the indicative and the optative moods, whereas *mḗ* occurs with the subjunctive and the imperative. The two negation markers can co-occur, with their relative order correlating with different functions; for example, *ou mḗ* is an emphatic negator with a future tense, but *mḗ ou* can be used in an interrogative sentence that implies a negative answer. The negative marker tends to precede the main verb but need not be adjacent to it.

As with phonology and morphology, so too with syntax are various changes to be found between Classical and Hellenistic Greek. Besides changes with moods and with the dative (see Basic Morphology), a striking change in the syntax was the increased use of finite complementation in place of infinitival forms. Although the infinitive is still very much in use in Hellenistic Greek, it often competes with finite expressions; thus both *áxios lûsai* 'worthy to loosen (INFINITIVE)' and *áxios hína lúsō* 'worthy that I loosen (FINITE)' occur in the New Testament.

Contact with Other Languages

Ancient Greek shows a long history of the results of contact with speakers of other languages, and as noted above, the Koine period was characterized by extensive contacts between Greek speakers and non-Greek speakers, with a considerable number of Latin words entering the language. There are some words in Greek that seem to come from "pre-Greek" (sometimes referred to as "Pelasgian"), i.e., from an indigenous language of the Balkans before the coming of the Greeks, e.g., *plínthos* 'brick', where the cluster *-nth-* is otherwise unusual in Greek.

Also, the Ancient Greek lexicon contains some early loanwords from Anatolian languages, e.g., *eléphas* 'ivory' (attested in Mycenaean Greek) and Semitic languages, e.g., *khitṓn* 'tunic', *kúminon* 'cumin', etc. (both attested in Mycenaean).

Other loanwords entered in the Classical period, mostly cultural loans from languages such as PERSIAN (e.g., *satrapeía* 'satrapy'), but it was in the later Hellenistic period that large numbers of loanwords from Latin made their way into Greek. In addition, derivational suffixes from these words came to have a wider use within Greek. Some examples include *magístōr* 'master' (Latin *magister), dēnárion* 'small coin' (Latin *denarius),* and *títlos* 'title' (Latin *titulus*), as well as the adjectival suffix *-ianos,* the agent noun suffix *-ários,* and the instrumental noun suffix *-árion.*

Common Words

Nouns are cited in the nominative singular form, adjectives in nominative singular masculine; all forms cited are taken from the Classical Attic dialect as (somewhat artificially) representative of all of Ancient Greek:

man: anḗr (male person); ánthrōpos (human being)
woman: gunḗ
water: húdōr
sun: hḗlios
three: treîs (NOM.M&F), tría (NOM.NEUT)
fish: ikhthús
big: mégas
long: makrós
small: mikrós
yes: naí, málista*;* ge (and other affirmative adverbs as well)
no: ou (more usually, 'not')
good: agathós
bird: órnis
dog: kúōn
tree: déndron

Example Sentences

The following sentences provide instances of several of the verbal and nominal categories discussed above, and illustrate some aforementioned aspects of Greek syntax, e.g., possible placements of subjects and objects relative to the verb, negation, use of moods, use of cases, and the versatility provided by the definite article through the placement of modifiers between the article and the noun (multiple times in [3]) within the noun phrase.

(1) ô Sôkrates, nûn mèn anút-ōi ou
O Socrates.VOC now but Anutos-DAT.SG NEG

peisó-metha all' aphíe-men se.
believe-1PL.FUT.MID but acquit-1PL.PRES you.ACC
'O Socrates! At this time, we will not believe Anutos, but we (will) acquit you.' (Plato *Apology* 29c)

(2) ei oûn me epì toút-ois aphí-oite,
if indeed me.ACC on this-DAT.PL acquit-2PL.PRES.OPT

eíp-oimi àn hu-mîn hóti "egô
say-1SG.AOR.OPT PARTICLE you-DAT.PL that I.NOM

hu-mâs aspáz-omai mèn kaì phil-ô
you-ACC.PL salute-1SG.PRES.MID but and love-1SG.PRES

peís-omai dè mâllon t-ôi the-ôi
obey-1SG.FUT.MID but rather the-DAT.SG god-DAT.SG

ê hu-mîn."
than you-DAT.PL
'If indeed you were to acquit me on these terms, I would say to you (that) "I salute and love (you), but I will obey the god rather than you." (Plato *Apology* 29d)

(3) t-à gàr t-ês t-ôn
the-NOM.PL.NEUT for the-GEN.SG.F the-GEN.PL.M

poll-ōn psukh-ês ómmat-a
many-GEN.PL.M soul-GEN.SG.F eye-NOM.PL.NEUT

karter-eîn pròs t-ò
endure-PRES.INFIN toward the-ACC.SG.NEUT

theî-on aphor-ônta adúnat-a.
divine-ACC.SG.NEUT looking-NOM.PL.NEUT powerless-NOM.PL.NEUT
'For the eyes of the soul of the multitude are powerless to endure looking towards the divine.' (Plato *Sophist* 254a)

Select Bibliography

Blass, Friedrich, and Albert Debrunner. 1961. A *Greek Grammar of the New Testament and Other Early Christian Literature.* Chicago: University of Chicago Press.

Buck, Charles D. 1955. *The Greek Dialects.* Chicago: University of Chicago Press.

Horrocks, Geoffrey. 1997. *Greek: A History of the Language and its Speakers.* London: Longman.

Liddell, Henry G., Robert Scott, and Henry S. Jones. 1968. *A Greek-English Lexicon.* Oxford: Clarendon Press.

Palmer, Leonard. 1980. *The Greek Language.* Atlantic Heights, NJ: Humanities Press.

Schwyzer, Eduard. 1939. *Griechische Grammatik I: Lautlehre, Wortbildung, Flexion.* Munich: C. H. Beck.

Schwyzer, Eduard, and Albert Debrunner. 1950. *Griechische Grammatik 2: Syntax und syntaktische Stilistik.* Munich: C.H. Beck.

Smith, H. 1920. A *Greek Grammar for Colleges.* New York: American Book Co.

Ventris, Michael, and John Chadwick. 1973. *Documents in Mycenaean Greek* (2nd ed.). Cambridge: Cambridge University Press.

Modern Greek

Brian D. Joseph

Language Name: Modern Greek (note that "Greek" by itself, without reference to time period, usually refers to ANCIENT GREEK). **Autonym:** *eliniká* (compared with the Ancient Greek autonym *hellēnikē*, the neuter plural nominative/accusative of which is the source, via sound changes, of the modern term), also *neoeliniká* (literally, 'new [that is, Modern] Greek'), and *roméika* (literally, 'Romaic', because of the affinities [Orthodox Christian] Greeks felt after the fourth century A.D. with the Eastern Roman [= Byzantine] Empire based in Constantinople).

Location: Prior to the late Hellenistic period, as noted in the article on Ancient Greek, there were Greek speakers all over the eastern Mediterranean, including southern Italy, the Black Sea coasts, Egypt, the Levant, Cyprus, and much of Asia Minor. This distribution continued throughout the Hellenistic period and on through the Byzantine and Medieval periods, and is valid even into the Modern era, although Greece and Cyprus are the main venues for the Greek language today. Most of the Greek inhabitants of Asia Minor (what is now Turkey) were removed to Greece after the population exchanges of the early 1920s that came in the aftermath of the Turkish defeat of Greece's expansionist forays. New diasporic communities arose in the 20th century, quite robustly in Australia (especially Melbourne) and in North America (especially in major cities in the United States and Canada), and to a lesser extent in parts of Europe and Central Asia, the latter in part because of emigration brought on by the Greek civil war after World War II.

Family: As a descendant of Ancient Greek, Modern Greek has the same family affiliation, namely, part of the Greek or Hellenic branch of Indo-European.

Related Languages: The linguistic affinities noted for Ancient Greek are relevant for Modern Greek, although perhaps not as obvious as for the ancient language. Depending on how one judges the difference between "dialects of a language" and "separate languages", the highly divergent modern form of Greek known as Tsakonian, spoken still in the eastern Peloponnesos in Greece, could well be considered now a separate language from the rest of Modern Greek, and the Pontic dialects once spoken in Asia Minor along the Black Sea coast and now spoken in many parts of Greece because of the 1923 population exchanges are divergent enough also to warrant consideration as a separate language from the rest of Greek now.

Dialects: The dialect complexity of Ancient Greek was to a large extent leveled out during the Hellenistic period with the emergence of the relatively unified variety of Greek known as the Koine (see Ancient Greek). While somewhat oversimplified, since there were differences in the realizations of Koine Greek in different parts of the Hellenistic world, this view is essentially accurate. The dominant basis for the Koine was the ancient Attic-Ionic dialect though there was some limited input from the other dialects. For the most part, the Hellenistic Koine, or actually the version of it that took hold in the Byzantine period, was the starting point for the modern dialects, and it is conventional to date the emergence of Modern Greek dialects to about the 10th to 12th centuries A.D. The main exception to this characterization is Tsakonian, which derives more or less directly from the ancient Doric dialect, although with an admixture of standard Modern Greek in recent years; in addition, the Greek of southern Italy, still spoken for instance in some villages in Apulia and Calabria, seems to have Doric roots. The Pontic dialects may derive more directly from the Hellenistic Koine.

The main modern dialects that derive from the later Byzantine form of the Koine are: Peloponnesian-Ionian, Northern, Cretan, Old Athenian, and Southeastern (including the islands of the Dodecanese and Cypriot Greek). The major features distinguishing these dialects include deletion of original high vowels and raising of original mid-vowels when unstressed in the Northern varieties, loss of final *-n* in all but the Southeastern varieties, palatalizations of velars in all but Peloponnesian-Ionian, use of the accusative for indirect objects in the Northern dialects instead of the genitive, among others. Peloponnesian-Ionian forms the historical basis for what has emerged in the 20th century as Standard Modern Greek, and is thus the basis for the language of modern Athens, now the main center of population, Old Athenian being the dialect of Athens before the 1821 War of Independence, still found in other parts of Greece because of various relocations.

Number of Speakers: At present, there are approximately 13 million Greek speakers, about 10 million in Greece, with about 500,000 in Cyprus, and the remainder in the modern Hellenic diaspora including over 1 million in Australia.

Origin and History

Temporally, Modern Greek has its origins in the Hellenistic Koine, since many of the changes that constitute the key differences between Ancient and Modern Greek are evident in nascent form in the Koine (although some ran to completion only later). While it is customary to divide post-Classical and post-Hellenistic Greek into the early Byzantine period (about A.D. 300 to 1000) and the later Byzantine/Medieval period (1000 to 1600), with the (truly) modern period starting after 1600, in fact vernacular Greek of the 12th century seems quite modern in many respects.

A key feature in the development of the modern language is the fact that throughout the history of post-Classical Greek, the language and its speakers could never really escape the influence of the Classical Greek language and Classical Greece itself. The important position that Classical Greece held culturally throughout the Mediterranean, the Balkans, parts of the Middle East, and even parts of western and Central Europe, in the post-Classical period and on into the Middle Ages, meant that Greek speakers bore a constant reminder of the language and linguistic "monuments" of their ancestors. Classical Greek thus formed the prescriptive norm against which speakers of later stages of Greek generally measured themselves. This situation led to a "two-track system" for the language, in which a high-style consciously archaizing variety that speakers and writers modeled on Classical Greek was set against a vernacular innovative variety. While in the Medieval period this distinction was more a matter of a learned variety reserved for official (usually church-related) and many literary uses opposed to a colloquial variety that only occasionally found its way into literary expression, after the War of Independence from the Ottoman Empire in 1821, Greeks, confronted with the creation of a new nation-state of Greece, sought to codify and establish a national language as part of the nation-building process. At this point, the distinction became politicized, and the distinction arose between what came to be known as *katharevousa* ('Puristic', literally '[the] purifying [language]') as the high-style variety associated with official functions such as those pertaining to government, education, religion, and such, and *dimotiki* ('Demotic', literally '[the] popular [language]') as the language of the people in ordinary, day-to-day, mundane affairs. This sociolinguistic state of affairs was one of the paradigm cases that Ferguson (1959) used in developing the notion of diglossia, and the struggle between proponents of each variety, representing as well various concomitant social attitudes and political positions, continued into the latter half of the 20th century. Currently, by various acts and actions of the government in 1976, *dimotiki* is now the official language, and the diglossic situation is resolved, at least officially. Throughout the periods of diglossia, official and unofficial usage was actually somewhat mixed, with speakers often borrowing from one variety and, for instance, incorporating Puristic forms into Demotic usage, and the present state of Demotic what has emerged as "Standard Modern Greek" (the Greek of everyday life in the largest city and capital of Greece, Athens) reflects a number of such borrowings from *katharevousa*, involving both grammar (morphology and syntax) and pronunciation, as well as the lexicon.

Orthography and Basic Phonology

Throughout post-Classical Greek and on into the Modern era, the Greek alphabet has been the primary medium for writing Greek, although in the Medieval period, the ARABIC and HEBREW alphabets were occasionally used in certain communities, for

Table 1: Modern Greek Alphabet

Greek (Capital/Small)	Modern Phonetics	Transliteration
Α α	[a]	a
Β β	[v]	v
Γ γ	[j] before i/e	y, j
	[ɣ]before o/a/u	ɣ, g, gh
γ before γ κ χ ξ	[ŋ]	n
Δ δ	[ð]	dh, th, d, ð
Ε ε	[ɛ]	e
Ζ ζ	[z]	z
Η η	[i]	i
Θ θ	[θ]	th, θ
Ι ι	[i]	i
Κ κ	[k]	k
Λ λ	[l]	l
Μ μ	[m]	m
Ν ν	[n]	n
Ξ ξ	[ks]	x, ks
Ο ο	[o]	o
Π π	[p]	p
Ρ ρ	[r]	r
Σ σ	[s]	s
Τ τ	[t]	t
Υ υ	[i]	i, y, u
Φ φ	[f]	f
Χ χ	[x]	h, x
Ψ ψ	[ps]	ps
Ω ω	[o]	o

Table 2: Modern Greek Diagraphs

Consonant Combination	Phonetics	Transliteration
γγ	[ŋg, ^{ŋ}g, g]	ng, g
γκ	[ŋg, ^{ŋ}g, g] (medially)	ng, g
	[g, ^{ŋ}g] (initially)	g
γξ	[ŋks]	nks, nx
γχ	[ŋx]	nx, nh
μπ	[mb, ^{m}b, b] (medially)	mb, b, mp
	[b,^{m}b] (initially)	b, mb, mp
ντ	[nd, ^{n}d, d] (medially)	nd, d, nt
	[d,^{n}d] (initially)	d, nd, nt
τσ	[ts, t^{s}]	ts
τζ	[dz, d^{z}]	dz, tz
ει	[i]	i, ei
οι	[i]	i, oi
υι	[i]	i, yi
αι	[ɛ]	e, ai
ου	[u]	u, ou
αυ	[af] before voiceless sounds	af, au
	[av] before voiced sounds	av, au
ευ	[ɛf] before voiceless sounds	ef, eu
	[ɛv] before voiced sounds	ev, eu
ηυ (rare)	[if] before voiceless sounds	if, eu
	[iv] before voiced sounds	iv, eu

example, Hebrew by the Jewish community of Constantinople. The form of the alphabet is essentially that of the ancient Ionian alphabet (see Ancient Greek), with some additional letter combinations not found in ancient times, and moreover, the value of some of the letters and letter combinations is different because of sound changes. An official orthographic reform in 1982 by the government of Greece eliminated the ancient breathing marks and the grave and circumflex accents; thus, only the acute accent is used now, and only, for the most part, in polysyllabic words. Some variation is evident in the spelling of some words whose sounds have more than one representation, such as κοιταζω versus κυτταζω 'look at' ([kitázo]), αβγο versus αυγο 'egg' ([avɣó]).

Table 3: Modern Greek Diacritics*

Type	Mark	Phonetics	Transliteration
Breathings (on initial vowels): rough smooth	 # ʽ # ʼ	 Ø Ø	 h or nothing nothing
Accent (on vowels): acute grave circumflex	 ´ ` ˆor ˜	 main stress Ø main stress	 ´ ` or ´ ˆ or ˜ or ´

*For pre-1982 texts; post-1982, only the acute accent is used.

As noted earlier, the Classical Attic phonological system began to undergo several changes in the post-Classical period that ultimately characterize the differences between Ancient Greek and Modern Greek. These included, for the consonants, the fricativization of earlier *b d g* to *βðγ* (with *β* later becoming *v*) and of p^h t^h k^h to *fθx*, the loss of *h*, and the reduction of the *zd* cluster (represented orthographically by <ζ> [zeta]) to *z*, which then took on phonemic status. New instances of the voiced stops *b, d,* and *g* were provided by loanwords and possibly also as variants of voiceless *p, t,* and *k* after nasals.

Table 4: Consonants of Koine Greek

		Labial	Dental	Velar
Stops	Voiceless, unaspirated	p	t	k
	Voiced[1]	b	d	g
Fricatives	Voiceless	f	θ s	χ
	Voiced	v	ð z	γ
Nasals		m	n	(ŋ)[2]
Liquids	Trill		r	
	Lateral		l	

[1]These sounds were quite possibly not distinctive, but rather interpreted as positional variants of the voiceless stops.

[2]This sound was an allophone of /n/ before velars.

Not all of these changes were completed within the Hellenistic Koine period; the conservative pronunciation [p^h t^h k^h] for the Classical Greek voiceless aspirated stops, for instance, was maintained as a sociolinguistically conservative high-prestige pronunciation in the Byzantine scholastic tradition into the 10th century. Moreover, even though all members of whole classes of consonants eventually were affected by these changes, each sound in a class seems to have undergone the change at a different time, for example, in the Egyptian variety of the Koine, *g* > *γ* was completed by the 1st century B.C., *b* > (*β* >) *v* by the 3rd century A.D., and *d* > *ð* by the 7th century A.D.

The consonantal inventory of the late Koine is given in Table 4 below.

Several further changes took place in the consonants to give the inventory found in Standard Modern Greek, and all of these changes were such that they have led to analytic ambiguities for the resulting segments in the modern language. Their controversial status for the Modern Greek, where a full range of data is available, means that status of these new sounds cannot be adequately resolved for earlier stages.

From around the 10th to 12th centuries, affricate(-like) sounds *ts* and *dz* began to emerge as distinctive elements, partly in loanwords from neighboring languages, partly as a regular sound change of *k* and/or *t* before front vowels in some dialects, and partly as a sporadic outcome (possibly lexically induced or because of dialect borrowings) of *s, θ, z, ks, ps,* and other sounds in various contexts. The Medieval Greek spelling for these sounds is consistently with <τ ζ>, which is used in Modern Greek just for the voiced [dz]; the modern outcomes, however, suggest that it stood for [ts] as well as [dz] in Medieval Greek. Their status as unit affricates as opposed to clusters is controversial.

Similarly, in the post-Koine period, pure voiced stops continued to establish themselves in the language, through loanwords and through sound changes, not just post-nasal voicing of *p, t,* and *k*, but that together with the loss of unstressed initial vowels and nasality in complex syllable onsets, creating contrasts such as Ancient *en-trépomai* 'be ashamed' > *endrépome* > *ndrépome* > Modern *drépome*, with initial [dr-] opposed to *#ðr* (as in *ðrepáni* 'sickle') and *#tr* (as in *trépo* 'turn'); still, some modern speakers lightly nasalize even initial voiced stops (medially nasalization is more variable although apparently on the wane for younger speakers) and even loanwords show some variability, so that the status of *b, d,* and *g* in contemporary Greek is controversial, with some analysts arguing for underlying nasal + stop clusters even word-initially.

In addition, the palatal semivowel [j] arose in the post-Koine period, and this segment too offers analytic ambiguities. Its two historical sources, [γ] before front vowels and unstressed [i] before a vowel, are synchronically recoverable in some modern words because of morphophonemic alternations, for example, *spíti-Ø* 'house' / *spítj-a* 'houses'; *aníγ-o* 'I open' / *aníj-i* 's/he opens'.

With regard to vowels, in the Koine period, earlier [o:] raised to [u:], distinctive vowel length was lost, and the movement of several vowels to [i] was underway; in addition, the long palatal diphthongs lost their offglide, the labial offglide *w* became

[v] or [f] depending on the voicing of the following sound, and each of the other diphthongs merged with some short monophthong. The ultimate result in late Koine is the vowel system, considerably simplified from Classical Greek, given in Table 5 below.

Table 5: Late Hellenistic Vowel System

i	y	u
є		ɔ
	a	

The main additional change that took place to give the system found in Standard Modern Greek was the unrounding of *y* to *i* after the 10th century, although in certain environments such as around labials and/or velars and in some dialects *y* yielded *u*. Note also the loss of unstressed initial vowels mentioned above.

The final noteworthy phonological development was one that was clearly underway in the Hellenistic Koine, namely a change in the accent to a stress accent, as opposed to the pitch accent of Classical Greek; the main stress in Modern Greek words falls on the syllable that in earlier stages had the high pitch (acute or circumflex). Modern Greek still observes a restriction of the main stress to one of the last three syllables in the word (the modern realization of the Classical moraically based restriction), but accent placement is distinctive (compare *nómos* 'law' versus *nomós* 'prefecture'), being predictable only with regard to certain morphological classes and grammatical categories, such as recessive in *-ma(t)*-stem neuter nouns and end stressed in neuter *i*-stem genitive singulars in *-u*.

Many of the same phonological generalizations and processes discussed in the chapter on Ancient Greek apply as well to later stages of Greek, although with some alterations because of sound changes, borrowings, and such. The restriction on possible word-final consonants (only *-s*, *-n*, and *-r* permitted) held during the Koine and Middle Greek periods, though the loss of final *-n* via a regular sound change and the gradual restructuring of the nominal system away from consonant stems to vowel stems, for example, earlier *patér-* 'father' becoming *patéra-*, *léont-* 'lion' becoming *léonda-*, removed most word-final instances of *-r*, *-n*, and potential clusters; moreover, it is still valid today really just for native Greek vocabulary, for modern loans have brought in many words, relatively unaltered, with other final consonants, for example, *tsek* 'check', *mats* '(football) match', and *básket* 'basketball'.

The survival of groups of related words from Ancient Greek has led to the survival of various morphophonemic alternations in later stages, although in some instances in a somewhat different form because of sound changes, such as (unaltered) *t* ~ *s* before *i* (as in *plút-os* 'wealth' / *plús-ios* 'wealthy'), (altered) fortition of fricatives (from earlier aspirated stops) to stops before *s*, as in *é-γraf-e* '(s)he was writing' / *é-γrap-s-e* '(s)he wrote'), among others.

A post-Classical innovation that has led to significant morphophonemic alternations involves the voicing of voiceless stops after a nasal, word internally but also in article plus noun combinations and weak pronoun plus verb combinations. Thus, just as earlier *pénte* 'five' and *lámpō* 'shine' have yielded to later *pénde*, *lámbo* (with variants *pénde* / *péde*, *lámbo* / *lábo* found as well in the modern standard language), so too *ton tónon* 'the tone/ACC', *(au)tòn etáraksa* 'him I-disturbed' have yielded *to(n) dóno* (with loss of word-final *-n* as well), *to(n) dáraksa* (with loss of the unstressed initial vowel), and, with place assimilation of the nasal, *ton pónon* 'the pain/ACC', *(au)tòn epeísamen* 'him we-persuaded' have yielded *to(m) bóno*, *to(m) bísame*.

The weak pronominal forms, including direct and indirect object forms as well as possessives, provoke accentual readjustments when attached after their host noun (the usual position for possessives) or host verb (the usual position for object pronominals with nonfinite [imperatival and participial] forms). In particular, as a (transformed) continuation of accentual effects shown by Ancient Greek enclitic elements, effects that are evident in much of post-Classical Greek but in flux during the Medieval period, the weak pronominals trigger the addition of an accent, which for many speakers becomes the primary accent, on the syllable just before the pronominal when the host is otherwise accented on the antepenult, for example, *ónoma* 'name' / *ònomá mu* 'my name', *kítakse* 'look!' / *kìtaksé tus* 'look at them!'.

Basic Morphology

Like its ancient ancestor, Modern Greek is basically a fusional inflecting language morphologically, with relevant grammatical information generally being indicated through the endings of inflected words, i.e., nouns, pronouns, adjectives, articles, and verbs. Each ending typically encoded values for several categories simultaneously.

Still, compared to Ancient Greek, post-Classical Greek, from the Koine through to the modern language, shows a greater number and use of analytic structures, supplanting some of the earlier synthetic ones in Middle Greek. This trend is found to some extent in nominal morphology but is especially robust in the verb.

Interestingly, many of these changes in the direction of analytic structures, for example, with adjectival degree, indirect object marking, periphrastic futures (especially based on the verb 'want'), and finite replacements for the infinitive, are found in several of the Balkan languages that are neighbors to Greek, including ALBANIAN, BULGARIAN, MACEDONIAN, and ROMANIAN. While the relationship between the emergence of these changes in Greek and similar developments in these other languages is controversial—many of these changes were underway relatively early in post-Classical Greek and their spread may have been facilitated by contact with speakers of these other languages not caused by the contact (and in some instances, Greek may have been the source of these features in the other language)—no history of the development of Modern Greek can ignore the larger Balkan context for these changes.

The nominal forms and categories discussed in the chapter on Ancient Greek are valid as well into the Koine period, though the dative case and all dual-number forms begin to fall into disuse during that time, and are completely absent from colloquial Modern Greek. In addition, starting in the Koine period and continuing on into the Medieval period, most noun paradigms came to be restructured, with the basis for their organization becoming gender (masculine, feminine, and neuter) rather than the formal stem classes (*i*-stem, consonant-stem, *o*-stem, etc.) of Ancient Greek. The resulting division, for the most part, has most masculine nouns with a nominative singular in *-V-s* opposed to an accusative and genitive in *-V-Ø*, and most feminine nouns with a nominative and accusative singular in *-V-Ø* opposed to a genitive in *-V-s*; the neuters are rather diverse but, as in Ancient Greek, the nominative and accusative are always identical.

As in Ancient Greek, there is agreement in gender, number, and case within noun phrases between adjectives and head nouns, and definiteness is marked by the presence of an article as the first element in the noun phrase. The sample paradigms given in the Ancient Greek article are valid for the Koine nominal declension, except that the dative and the dual are moribund; some examples of article-adjective-noun combinations for Modern Greek are given in Table 6.

Table 6: Examples of Nominal Inflection

'the good father' (MASCULINE)
NOM SG o kalós patéras
ACC SG ton kaló patéra
GEN SG tu kalú patéra
VOC SG kalé patéra
NOM/VOC.PL i kalí patéres
ACC.PL tus kalús patéres
GEN.PL ton kalón patéron

'the good mother' (FEMININE)
NOM SG i kalí mitéra
ACC SG tin kalí mitéra
GEN SG tis kalís mitéras
VOC SG kalí mitéra
NOM/VOC.PL i kalés mitéres
ACC.PL tis kalés mitéres
GEN.PL ton kalón mitéron

'the good baby' (NEUTER)
NOM SG to kaló moró
ACC SG to kaló moró
GEN SG tu kalú morú
VOC SG kaló moró
NOM/VOC.PL ta kalá morá
ACC.PL ta kalá morá
GEN.PL ton kalón morón

As in Ancient Greek, the personal pronouns in Koine, Medieval, and Modern Greek have special forms, while demonstrative and other pronouns generally followed some other nominal declensional pattern. Adjectives show comparative and superlative degree forms, which, by Medieval Greek and on into the modern language, are generally formed analytically (comparative via *pjo* + adjective, superlative via definite article + pjo + adjective), although the synthetic adjectival inflections of Ancient Greek are still used, particularly with a few especially common adjectives.

As with the noun, the categories and forms of the verbal system of Ancient Greek are generally valid for the Koine, although with some changes, and even, to some extent, for Medieval and Modern Greek as well. As with the nouns, all verbal dual forms go out of use. Future periphrases begin to arise in the Koine in place of the earlier synthetic future, and by Medieval Greek one based on the use of the verb *thélō* 'want' as an auxiliary holds sway as the primary type, ultimately resulting in the Modern Greek future marker *θa* (from earlier third person singular *thélei* with the subjunctive marker *na*). In the early Koine, the perfect is on the wane and eventually disappears altogether as a category in the late Koine, only to be reconstituted as a category several centuries later in Medieval Greek through a periphrastic construction with "have" as an auxiliary together with the sole productive remnant of the earlier infinitive. Also, as noted in the previous section, the infinitive in the Koine period begins to retreat, being replaced by finite periphrases with subordinating conjunctions; the infinitive continued as a marginal category into the Middle Greek period (about the 15th century), and in Modern Greek now, all functions that might be thought of as typical for infinitivals in various languages, such as complementation, nominalization, purpose clauses, and control structures are expressed with fully finite (indicative or subjunctive) clauses. Similarly, the numerous participles of Ancient Greek diminish considerably in use, and although they were more prevalent in the Koine and Medieval Greek, there are now in Standard Modern Greek just two participial forms, an active and a medio-passive imperfective.

The system of verbal moods also underwent some changes, with the optative mood becoming moribund in the Koine period and ultimately disappearing from use altogether. Further, although the subjunctive mood has continued throughout the history of Greek, in the Koine period and on into Medieval and Modern Greek it comes to be used increasingly obligatorily with an introductory element, for example, a conjunction, of some sort; the most common of these was *hína*, originally a final conjunction ('in order that, that'), which became Medieval and Modern Greek *na* and now arguably functions solely as the marker for the subjunctive as a category (see Table 7, footnote 1).

Aspect continues to be a significant category in the Koine and on into Modern Greek, and owing to the emergence of a periphrastic future with the infinitive, a form that participated in aspectual distinctions, the aoristic/imperfective distinction is extended into the future. Moreover, with the re-emergence of the perfect in Medieval Greek, the relevant aspectual oppositions in the Modern language become imperfective, perfective (= aoristic), and perfect.

Voice too continues as an important category in the language, with essentially the same values for the forms as in Ancient Greek. One formal change is that there comes to be no distinction between passive and middle in any of the tenses.

Negation in the Koine and into Medieval Greek was marked as in Ancient Greek, that is, by syntactic means with a separate word for "not" associated with but not necessarily adjacent to the verb. Increasingly, though, the negative element came to stand obligatorily before the verb, and in Modern Greek the negators *ðe(n)* (for finite, indicative forms) and *mi(n)* (for subjunctive)—a pair that continues an Ancient Greek distinction—attach to the left of the verb and can only be separated from it by weak pronominal forms and/or the future marker (all of which are arguably affixal in contemporary Greek). The Ancient Greek ability of imperatival forms to be negated to yield a prohibitive is lost, however, and in Modern Greek, *mi(n)* with the subjunctive (with omission of *na* possible) forms a negative command.

Finally, as in Ancient Greek, the situation is similar in later stages with regard to marking for causative, frequentative, and iterative, in that there is in general no regular inflection for these categories; in Modern Greek causatives are expressed via periphrastic constructions parallel to the use of "make" in ENGLISH.

A full synopsis of the Modern Greek verb *γráfo* 'write' is given in Table 7, with first person singular forms for all tense, aspect, voice, and all moods but imperative, for which second singular is used, as well as the few nonfinite participial forms.

Word-formation processes in post-Classical Greek and on into Modern Greek remain essentially the same as in Ancient Greek. Some minor changes evident in the modern language include greater numbers of coordinative compounds, such as *maxero-píruna* 'cutlery' (literally: 'knife-[and]-forks') or *aniγo-klíno* 'open and close', and the emergence of multiply-inflected compounds, possibly through borrowing, for example, *peðí-θávma* 'child prodigy' (literally 'child-wonder') with a plural *peðjá-θávmata* (literally 'children-wonders'); note the multiple accents, suggesting that the individual words in this type retain their individual integrity.

Basic Syntax

What was said about basic word order for Ancient Greek—essentially free ordering of major constituents in a clause—holds for all later stages of the language as well. All permutations of ordering of subject, object, and verb can be found, though Modern Greek shows a preference for SVO ordering in neutral contexts. Similarly, the ordering of elements within constituents, as within the noun phrase, is virtually unchanged, so that the remarks in the previous section hold for later stages of Greek, too.

One main area of difference, however, is in the placement of weak pronouns, generally referred to as "clitics". In Ancient Greek, these elements, as well as various sentence connectives, were positioned in relation to the clausal unit that contained them, and they usually appeared in second position within that unit. In Modern Greek, however, their positioning is relative to the verb—before finite verbs and after nonfinite verbs (imperatives and participles) in the standard language—so that weak pronouns can now occur sentence initially. The Ancient Greek positioning was valid throughout the Hellenistic period and on into Byzantine Greek, but in the Medieval period, the orientation of the weak pronouns toward the verb, as opposed to the clause, began to emerge, with the modern distribution developing after the 16th century. The verbal complex that results from the combination of the verb with weak pronouns is the core of the Modern Greek clause structure, since tense, mood, and negation markers also form part of this complex (see above in Basic Morphology and below regarding negation and the Example Sentences).

The essentials of case-marking remained the same in Post-Classical Greek and on into the Medieval and Modern periods as those found in Ancient Greek. Subjects are still marked with the nominative case, and accusative marks direct objects; there

Table 7: Synopsis of *γráfo* 'write'

	Present	Past	Future	Perfect
Active				
Indicative	γráfo	éγrafa/IMPFVE éγrapsa/AOR	θa γráfo/IMPFVE θa γrápso/AOR	éxo γrápsi íxa γrápsi/PLUPRF θa éxo γrápsi/FUT.PRF
Subjunctive	na γráfo/IMPFVE na γrápso/AOR	**[1] **[1]	——	na éxo γrápsi
Imperative	γráfe/IMPFVE γrápse/AOR	——	——	éxe γrápsi
Participle	γráfondas	——	——	éxondas γrápsi
Medio-Passive				
Indicative	γráfome	γrafómun/IMPFVE γráftika/AOR	θa γráfome/IMPFVE θa γraftó/AOR	éxo γraftí íxa γraftí/PLUPRF θa éxo γraftí/FUT.PRF
Subjunctive	na γráfome/IMPFVE na γraftó/AOR	**[1] **[1]	——	na éxo γraftí
Imperative	γráfu/IMPFVE γrápsu/AOR	——	——	éxe γraftí
Participle	γrafómenos			γraménos

[1] The marker *na* can combine with indicative past forms to give various subtle shades of modality, for example, *na érafa* 'I should have written'; it is not clear, though, if these constitute a legitimate category of "past subjunctive" or instead derive from the combinations of the element *na*.

is, however, no idiosyncratic marking of direct objects with other cases in Modern Greek, though some instances are to be found in the Koine period. The loss of the dative case in the Koine period has led to the marking of indirect objects by the genitive case (accusative in some dialects) and by the preposition *s(e)* (earlier *eis*). The genitive is thus used now in ways it was not in earlier stages, but some earlier uses of the genitive no longer occur; the partitive, for instance, is expressed periphrastically rather than by the genitive case. Accusative is the only case found for the object of virtually all prepositions, except that pronominal objects with some prepositions are usually in the genitive case. Compare, for example, *mazí mu* '(together) with me/GEN' with *me eména* 'with me/ACC'.

As noted above in the section on morphology, negation in Modern Greek is marked primarily by morphological means, with the two markers *ðen* and *min* forming part of the verbal complex; the free word for 'no', *óxi*, is used with constituents in elliptical negation, as in *θélo to mov óxi to ble* 'I-want the mauve-one not the blue-one'. Negation in the pre-Modern period, from the Koine up through Medieval Greek, was mixed, being transitional from the Ancient Greek purely syntactic clause-based expression of negation to the modern verb-based, essentially morphological system.

From the Koine on into Medieval Greek, complementation was increasingly with finite clauses only, in place of the earlier infinitival complementation. After the 15th century, complementation is essentially only with finite clauses headed by the subjunctive marker *na* or by indicative complementizers *óti*, *pos*, or *pu*.

Similarly, the use of participles of Ancient Greek decreased in the post-Classical period, and the one productive participle of Modern Greek, the active imperfective participle, is now used more like a clausal adjunct, its subject, when unexpressed, being interpreted as coreferent with the main clause subject.

Increasingly in the Medieval period and on into Modern Greek, relative clauses are marked with an invariant relative marker—in the modern language *pu*, homophonous with one of the indicative complementizers—with resumptive pronouns in the relative clause being fairly common. The use of inflected relative pronouns, however, has always been possible, but is restricted now mainly to higher stylistic registers.

The definite article, which in Ancient Greek, among other functions, served as a means of nominalizing virtually any part of speech, continues in that use in later stages of the language, and provides a way in Modern Greek for nominalizing clauses (see the Example Sentences).

Finally, the weak object pronouns serve important discourse functions, and frequently co-index full noun-phrase objects, among other things to signal emphasis and topicality (note their use in relative clauses mentioned above).

Contact with Other Languages

As noted in the chapter on Ancient Greek, the language absorbed many loanwords from LATIN during the Koine period, some of which have stayed in the language since, such as Latin *hospitium* 'lodgings, house'—> post-Classical Greek *hospítion*—> (via regular sound changes) Modern *spíti* 'house'. In the Byzantine period, and on through Medieval times, Latin is still a major source of loanwords, but some enter through the medium of Balkan Latin, shown by various telltale phonological characteristics, for example, *pe(n)dziménton* 'baggage' from Latin *impedimentum* with Balkan Latin affricatization. In the later Medieval period, numerous loanwords from the Venetian dialect of ITALIAN enter Greek, including the verb-forming suffix *-ar-* (compare Italian infinitival *-are*), as do various technical feudal terms from FRENCH, as *rói* 'king' (French *roi*). Moreover, as speakers of Greek came into contact in this period with Slavic, Albanian, Vlach (Aromanian), and increasingly also TURKISH speakers, loanwords from all these languages permeate the language, with Turkish, especially after the 14th century, providing the greatest number by far. Turkish loanwords range over a variety of semantic domains and lexical categories, including ordinary day-to-day life, like *jeléki* 'vest', *piláfi* 'rice', *kafés* 'coffee', *tsái* 'tea', *boyá* 'paint'; military, as *tuféki* 'rifle', *askéri* 'soldier'; arts, like *baɣlamás* 'a musical instrument'; verbs, like *baildízo* 'faint', from Turkish *bayil* with a Turkish past tense suffix *-d-* and a Greek derivational suffix *-iz-*; and interjections such as *amán* 'for mercy's sake!', *de* 'marker of impatience with imperatives', among others; further, some Turkish derivational suffixes have become productive in Greek, especially the suffix *-dzis*, which forms nouns of occupation, like *taksi-dzís* 'taxi driver'.

This period of contact with neighboring Balkan languages also played a critical role in the ultimate shaping of Greek structurally, in that, as noted above, many of the structural features that characterize Modern Greek and distinguish it from Ancient Greek are shared by the other languages of the Balkans, including the formation of the future tense, the use of finite complementation, the merger of the genitive and dative cases, and analytic expression of adjectival comparison. Even if the appearance of these features in Greek was not caused directly by contact—and while the chronology might speak against that for some of them, for others it is still an open question—it may be that their presence in languages Greek speakers were in contact with facilitated their spread within Greek. And, at the very least, the lexical and phrasal parallels among all these languages, including Greek, are striking and speak to a period of intense and intimate contact among their speakers.

Finally, in the 20th century, French—especially in the first half of the century—and English—especially in the latter half—provided an abundance of loanwords, for example, from French *asensér(i)* 'elevator', *betón* 'concrete', *ble* 'blue', *kombinezón* 'petticoat', *majó* 'bathing suit'; and from English *fútbol* 'football', *gol* 'goal', *mats* '(football) match', *víntsi* 'winch', and *yot* 'yacht', among numerous others.

Common Words

Nouns are cited in the nominative singular form, adjectives in nominative singular masculine; all forms listed here are from Standard Modern Greek:

man:	á(n)dras (i.e., male person); ánθropos (i.e., human being)
woman:	jinéka
water:	neró
sun:	ílios

three: tris
fish: psári
big: meɣálos
long: makrós
small: mikrós
yes: ne; málista
no: óxi
good: kalós
bird: pulí
dog: skilí
tree: ðéndro

Example Sentences

Inasmuch as Koine syntax did not differ appreciably from Classical Greek syntax in kind, but rather more in the extent of use of certain forms, the examples in the Ancient Greek entry give an idea of the essentials of Koine syntax. Thus a few sample sentences are given here from Medieval Greek, following Ancient Greek transliteration to allow for recovery of the orthography, and Modern Greek to illustrate some of the characteristics discussed above (the Medieval periphrastic future; the Modern verbal complex with weak pronouns, future marker, and negation; relativization; co-indexing of objects with weak pronouns; finite complementation and nominalization of clausal complements in both periods with the definite article, etc.):

(1)

kaì	tóte	thélō	nà	idō̃
and	then	want1SG.PRES	that	see:1SG.AOR.SUBJ

tò	pō̃s	tòn	théleis
the:NTR.SG.ACC	how	him:MASC.SG.ACC.WEAK	will:2SG

súrein.
drag:INF

'And then I want to see how you will drag him.' (Literally: 'And then I-want that I-see the how him you-will drag.')

(2)

ðen	θa	tis	to
NEG	FUT	her:GEN.SG.WEAK	it:NTR.SG.ACC.WEAK

púme	to	jatí	borésame
say:1PL.AOR.	the:NTR.SG.ACC	why	could:1PL.AOR.INDIC

na	tin	afísume	s	tin
that	her:ACC.SG.WEAK	leave:1SG.SUBJ.AOR	at	the

paralía	xorís	leftá	ke	paréa.
beach:ACC	without	money	and	company:ACC

'We won't tell her why we could have left her at the beach without money or friends.' (Literally: 'We won't tell her it the why we-could that we-leave her ...')

(3)

o	meɣálos	ánθropos	pu	xθes
the	big	man:NOM.SG.MASC	that:COMP	yesterday

to	vraðí	milúsame	me
the	evening:ACC	spoke:1PL.IMPFVE	with

aftón	íxe	érθi	s	to
him:ACC.SG.STRONG	had:3SG	come:AOR	to	the

maɣazí	mas	na	mas
store:NTR.SG.ACC	our:GEN	that	us:ACC.WEAK

rotísi	an	tin
ask:3SG.AOR.SUBJ	if	her:ACC.SG.WEAK

ɣnorísame	tin	kiría	Moraíti.
knew:1PL.ACT.INDIC.AOR	the	lady	Moraitis:ACC.SG.FEM

'The big man that yesterday in the evening we were talking with had come to our store to ask us if we knew Mrs. Moraitis.' (Literally: 'The big man that yesterday the evening we-were talking with him had come to the store of-ours that he-might-ask us if we-knew her the Mrs. Moraitis.')

Select Bibliography

Browning, Robert. 1983. *Medieval and Modern Greek.* Cambridge: Cambridge University Press.

Ferguson 1959. "Diglossia." In *Word 15*, 325–340.

Holton, David, Peter Mackridge, and Irene Philippaki-Warburton. 1997. *Greek. A Comprehensive Grammar of the Modern Language.* London and New York: Routledge.

Horrocks, Geoffrey. 1997. *Greek. A History of the Language and its Speakers.* London and New York: Longman.

Householder, Fred W., Kostas Kazazis, and Andreas Koutsoudas. 1964. *Reference Grammar of Literary Dhimotiki.* (*International Journal of American Linguistics* 30.2/Publication 31 of the Indiana University Research Center in Anthropology, Folklore, and Linguistics). Bloomington: Indiana University.

Joseph, Brian D. 1990. *Morphology and Universals in Syntactic Change. Evidence from Medieval and Modern Greek.* New York and London: Garland Publishing, Inc.

Joseph, Brian D. and Irene Philippaki-Warburton. 1987. *Modern Greek.* London: Croom Helm Publishers.

Mackridge, Peter. 1985. *The Modern Greek Language.* Oxford: Clarendon Press.

Mirambel, André. 1959. *La langue grecque moderne, description et analyse.* Paris: Librairie C. Klincksieck (Collection Linguistique publiée par la Société de Linguistique de Paris).

Newton, Brian. 1972. *The Generative Interpretation of Dialect.* (*Cambridge Studies in Linguistics*, 7). Cambridge: Cambridge University Press.

GUARANÍ

Maura Velázquez-Castillo

Language Name: Guaraní. **Autonym:** *Ava ñe'e* 'the language of man(kind)'.

Location: Central area of South America, especially Paraguay, where the language is most widely spoken. It is also spoken in northern Argentina and southwestern Brazil.

Family: Tupi-Guaraní branch of the Tupian family.

Related Languages: The exact number of related languages and the degree of their relationship has not yet been precisely determined. Work on the classification of the languages of the Tupian stock is ongoing and the results attained so far are tentative. The following are some of the languages that have been determined to be related to Guaraní: Kaiwa, Chiripa, Kamaiura, Chiriguano, Guarayu, Tapirape, and Urubu.

Dialects: The dialects have not been precisely classified, but most Guaraní speakers are conscious of the following regional dialects: (1) Paraguayan, spoken by most of the white and *mestizo* ('mixed') population of Paraguay; (2) Northeastern Argentinean, spoken in the provinces of Misiones, Corrientes, Formosa, and Chaco; and (3) Mbya (considered by some a separate language), spoken by the native communities of eastern Paraguay and southwestern Brazil.

Number of Speakers: 5–7 million.

Origin and History

Several varieties of Guaraní were spoken by the native communities of a wide region south of the Amazon upon the arrival of the Europeans in South America. The first written records of the language come from Jesuit missionaries, notably Antonio Ruiz de Montoya whose *Catecismo, Arte y Vocabulario* and *Tesoro de la Lengua Guaraní* appeared in 1640.

Today in Paraguay the language is spoken by the majority of the population, both white and *mestizo*. In rural areas, Guaraní is the predominant and in many cases the only language. It is widely spoken along with SPANISH in towns as well as in the capital city. Only approximately 4 percent of the population does not speak any Guaraní.

Orthography and Basic Phonology

Until the arrival of the Spaniards, Guaraní had been an exclusively spoken language, with no written tradition. All attempts to provide an orthography for the language have been based on the LATIN alphabet. Even though there still is more than one competing orthography, the one with the best chance of becoming standard is the orthography adopted by the Ministry of Education. With a few exceptions, this orthography contains letters with almost identical values to the Spanish orthography.

Guaraní *ch* is an alveo-palatal fricative like ENGLISH 'sh'. *J* is a voiced alveo-palatal affricate like the initial sound in English 'just'. *Ñ* is a palatal nasal stop like its Spanish equivalent and like the English nasal in 'o<u>ni</u>on'. *G* is a voiced velar fricative as in Spanish *agua*. *L* occurs almost exclusively in loanwords from Spanish.

Table 1: Consonants

		Labial	Alveolar	Palatal	Velar	Glottal
Stops	Voiceless	p	t		k	' [ʔ]
	Prenasal	mb	nd		ng	
Fricatives	Voiceless		s	ch [ʃ]		h
	Voiced	v			g [ɣ]	
Affricates				j [dʒ]		
Nasals		m	n	ñ		
Resonants			(l), r			

Table 2: Vowels

	Unrounded		Rounded
	Front	Central	Back
High	i	y	u
Low	e	a	o

All Guaraní vowels may be oral (*i y u e a o)* or nasal (*ĩ ỹ ũ ẽ ã õ)*. The difference between oral and nasal vowels is phonemic: *potĩ* 'clean', *poti* 'defecate'; *tupã* 'God', *tupa* 'bed'. The vowel *y* is an unrounded vowel, either central [ɨ] or back [ɯ].

The most distinctive phonological feature of Guaraní words and phrases is 'nasal harmony'. Nasality tends to spread from stressed nasal vowels to other sounds of the basic root and onto suffixes and prefixes, creating some predictable consonant alternations: prenasalized consonants alternate with plain (voiceless) stops, and pure nasals alternate with voiceless and prenasalized stops. For example, the causative prefix *mbo-*

becomes *mo-* in words such as *mo-kã* 'to (make) dry', and the totalitative suffix *-pa* becomes *-mba* in words such as *mokã-mba* 'to dry completely'.

Stress in Guaraní generally falls on the final syllable in a word; accent marks are used to indicate a deviation from this pattern

Basic Morphology

Guaraní nominal morphology includes affixes that may indicate number, such as *-kuéra* 'plural', for example, *kuimba'e-kuéra* 'the men'; and *-eta,* such as *mitã-eta* 'a multitude of children'; or time relevance, such as *-kue* 'former', for example, *ména-kue* 'former husband'; and *-rã* 'nominal future', for example, *ména-rã* 'future husband'.

Nouns are not obligatorily marked for gender or number, although this is changing in Paraguayan Guaraní, which has incorporated a version of the Spanish definite article that indicates number as well as definiteness: *la-* indicates definite singular, for example, *la-karai* 'the gentleman,' *la-kuñã* 'the woman)'; and *lo-* indicates definite plural, for example, *lo-karai* 'the gentlemen', *lo-kuñã* 'the women'. Caselike relations are expressed by postpositional affixes and particles: *mitã* 'child', *mitã-me* 'to the child', *mitã-ndive* 'with the child', *mitã-rehe* 'about the child'.

Guaraní has a rich verbal morphology that can be expressed by both prefixes and suffixes. In general, prefixes indicate personal reference, and suffixes indicate tense/aspect and modality. Although there is a well-defined class of verbs in the lexicon, words belonging to most other major categories can function as sentential predicates and bear verb morphology. There are two sets of personal reference prefixes, active and nonactive. Action-oriented verbs take the active set, while descriptive verbs and nouns acting as predicates take the nonactive set. The paradigms of active and nonactive predicates are illustrated below:

Active: *jeroky* 'dance'

	Singular	Plural
1st	a-jeroky	ro-jeroky (excl)
		ja-jeroky (incl)
2nd	re-jeroky	pe-jeroky
3rd	o-jeroky	o-jeroky-(hikuái)

Nonactive: *porã* 'be pretty'

	Singular	Plural
1st	che-porã	ore-porã (excl)
		ñane-porã (incl)
2nd	ne-porã	pene-porã
3rd	i-porã	i-porã-(hikuái)

For both the active and the nonactive paradigms, there is a distinction between first person plural exclusive: "we, excluding you"; and inclusive: "we, including you".

The grammar of Guaraní is not oriented toward the expression of the subject/object distinction, but rather toward participant roles defined by their degree of agentivity. Depending on the particular verb, the subject may be either active or non-active.

Reflexive, reciprocal, and causative morphemes are also expressed by prefixes. Tense/aspect suffixes include a future tense, a recent past tense, a remote past tense, a habitual past, a habitual present, a progressive, a totalitative, a perfective, and an imperfective. Present tense is indicated by lack of any other tense marker. Some of the modality suffixes are the desiderative and the volitive (both of which express wishes), the imperative, and some evidentials. Some of these affixes are illustrated in the following examples:

che-porã-se-te-piko
1SG/INACT-pretty-VOLITIVE-EMPHATIC-EXCLAMATION
'How I want to be pretty!'

a-mbo-jeroky-mi-vaekue chu-pe
1SG/ACT-CAUS-dance-HAB/PAST-REMOTE/PAST 3SG-to
'I used to dance with him/her.' (literally, 'I used to make him/her dance.')

Basic Syntax

Word order in Guaraní is relatively flexible, and varies according to discourse structure. In multipropositional discourse, objects and subjects are predominantly coded by pronominal affixes (the personal-reference prefixes), but when noun phrases do occur in discourse or when decontextualized sentences are made up as examples, the default order of elements is generally Object-Verb, with the subject occurring either before or after the verb. As for other structural characteristics associated with basic word order, Guaraní presents mixed characteristics. Consistent with the OV word order, there are postpositions rather than prepositions. However, most nominal modifiers follow the nouns they modify.

Sentences are negated by a discontinuous morpheme *n- -i* surrounding the verb complex:

n-a-mbo-jeroky-i chu-pe
NEG-1SG/ACT-CAUS-dance-NEG 3SG-to
'I do not invite him/her to dance.' (literally, 'I do not make him/her dance.')

Contact with Other Languages

Guaraní has been in close contact with Spanish and PORTUGUESE and has numerous borrowings from both languages. The following examples are all Spanish loans in Paraguayan Guaraní, the main dialect. All the borrowings have been adapted to the final stress pattern of native Guaraní words.

From Spanish: *sapatu* 'shoe', *kavaju* 'horse', *mesa* 'table', *havõ* 'soap' *korasõ* 'heart'

Common Words

man:	kuimba'e	woman:	kuñã
water:	'y	sun:	kuarahy
three:	mbohapy	fish:	pira
big:	tuicha	tree:	yvyra

long:	puku	small:	michi
yes:	hee	no:	nahãniri
good:	porã	bird:	guyra
dog:	jagua		

Example Sentences

(1) Che ai-nupã María rymba-jagua petei yvyra-pe.
I 1SG/ACT-hit Maria pet-dog one stick-with
'I beat María's dog with a stick.'

(2) Pe-mitã-kuña o-u-va hína
that-child-woman 3SG/ACT-come-RELATIVE PROGRESSIVE

che-nupã-se kuri.
1SG/INACT-hit-VOLITIVE RECENT/PAST
'That young woman who is coming wanted to hit me.'

(3) Yvoty pyahú-icha i-porã pe-mitã-kuña.
flower new-COMPAR 3SG/INACT-beautiful that-child- woman
'That young woman is as beautiful as a new flower.'

Efforts to Preserve, Protect, and Promote the Language

Although Guaraní is an important symbol of identity for most Paraguayans, it had long been regarded as somewhat inferior to Spanish, which was until recently the official instrument of written communication and instruction. Apart from some literary works (mainly poetry), and occasional documents (mostly unpublished) written in Guaraní, the language remained primarily a spoken means of communication until the late 1970s/early 1980s, when the Paraguayan government instituted Guaruaní as an obligatory subject in public schools. The language went from being the "national language" to achieving "official language" status in the early 1990s and is now increasingly used as a literary medium.

Select Bibliography

Bolaños, Luis de. 1607. *Catecismo en la Lengua Guaraní*. In Fr. Luis Oré's *Rituale seu Manuale Peruanum*. Naples.
Gregores, Emma, and Jorge Suárez. 1967. *A Description of Colloqual Guaraní*. The Hague: Mouton.
Guash, Antonio. 1976a. *Diccionario Castellano-Guaraní y Guaraní-Castellano*. Asunción, Paraguay: Ediciones Loyola.
____. 1976b. *El Idioma Guaraní*. Asunción, Paraguay: Ediciones Loyola.
Morínigo, Marcos A. 1931. "Hispanismos en el Guaraní." *Coleccion de Estudios Indigenistas 1*. Buenos Aires: Universidad de Buenos Aires, Instituto de Filología.
Payne, Doris, ed. 1990. *Amazonian Linguistics: Studies in Lowland South American Languages*. Austin: University of Texas Press.
Ruiz de Montoya, Antonio. 1640a. *Arte y Vocabulario de la Lengua Guaraní*. Madrid:
_____. 1640b. *Catecismo de la Lengua Guaraní*. [Reprinted in 1870]. Leipzig: Oficina y Fundería de W. Drugulin.
Saguier, E. 1946. *El Idioma Guaraní. Método Práctico*. Buenos Aires: Padilla y Contreras.

GUJARATI

P.J. Mistry

Language Name and Autonym: Gujarati. **Alternates:** *Gujerati, Gujarathi, Guzratee, Guujaratee.*

Location: Spoken in the state of Gujarat, located on the western coast of India, with mountains and forest as its southern and eastern boundaries, the Aravalli Mountain Range and the Kaccha Desert as its northern boundary, and the sea coast as its western boundary. It is spoken in communities of Gujaratis in various parts of India, Asia, Africa, Great Britain, and North America.

Family: Central group of the Indo-Aryan branch of the Indo-Iranian subfamily of the Indo-European language family.

Related Languages: Having SANSKRIT as an ancestor, Gujarati is a sister language of BANGLA, HINDI, NEPALI, SINHALA and other Indo-Aryan languages.

Dialects: There are four major regional dialects: (1) Kathiawadi (the peninsular Saurashtra), (2) Pattani (north of the Sabarmati River), (3) Surati (south of the Tapti River), and (4) Charotari (the in-between region). The variety around the state capital, Ahmedabad, is considered Standard Gujarai (SG).

Number of Speakers: 42–45 million.

Origin and History

Gujarati evolved from Sanskrit, and there are various accounts of the historical development through which Gujarati has become distinct in the Indo-Aryan (IA) branch. The traditional practice is to differentiate the IA languages on the basis of three historical stages: (1) Old IA (Vedic and Classical Sanskrit), (2) Middle IA (various Prakrits and Apabhramshas), and (3) New IA (modern languages such as Bangla, Hindi, Kashmiri, etc.). Another view can be presented in terms of successive family, tree splits. According to this view, Gujarati is assumed to have separated from other IA languages in three stages: (1) IA languages split into Northern, Eastern, and Central divisions based on the innovative characteristics such as stops becoming voiced in the Northern and dental and retroflex sibilants merging with the palatal in the Eastern; (2) Central, into Gujarati/RAJASTHANI, Western Hindi, and PUNJABI/Lahanda/SINDHI, on the basis of innovation of auxiliary verbs and postpositions in Gujarati/Rajasthani; and (3) Gujarati/Rajasthani into Gujarati and Rajasthani through the development of such characteristics as auxiliary *ch-* and the possessive marker *-n-* during the 15th century (Dave 1948: 2–7; Pandit 1966: 156–177).

In the development of the modern IA languages, Gujarati is conservative in several features. For example, languages used in Asokan inscriptions (third century B.C.) display contemporary Northern, Western, and Eastern regional variations. Bhayani (1951) reports that words found in the Girnar inscription (located in Gujarat) containing consonant clusters with *-r-* as the second member do not have *-r-* in their occurrence in inscriptions found at other places. Interestingly, even in modern times such clusters are still retained in Gujarati. Corresponding to Gujarati *traṇ* (< Skt. *trayas*) 'three', *bhatrijo* (< Skt. *bhrātṛjah*) 'nephew', and *chatri* (< Skt. *chatram*) 'umbrella', Hindi has *tin, bhattijā,* and *chatti*, respectively.

Gujarati is customarily divided into the following three historical stages: Old Gujarati (from the mid-twelfth century to the fifteenth century), Middle Gujarati (from the mid-fifteenth century to the beginning of the 19th century), and Modern Gujarati. What is labelled as Old Gujarati, however, has been referred to differently by different scholars. Tessitori (1914–1916), on the basis of 14th and 15th century literary texts, came to the conclusion that at that time there was only a single language covering the region currently occupied by Gujarati and Rajasthani. He termed the common language the Old Western Rajasthani.

Changes have affected phonology, morphology and syntax of the language. Old Gujarati *miliu* '(he) met' has changed to *maḷyo* showing that except for the initial segment, all other sounds have gone through changes. Simplified case system for nouns and pronouns, use of auxiliaries and verbal compounds in place of the morphologically differentiated tense/aspect system, and complex gender based agreement patterns are the major grammatical innovations in the linguistic history of Gujarati.

Orthography and Basic Phonology

The Gujarati writing system exists in manuscripts from the 14th century onward. The earliest manuscripts are in Devanagari, a formal alphabet used in writing Indo-Aryan languages such as Sanskrit, Hindi, and MARATHI. Around the middle of the 19th century a modififed version of Devanagari emerged, known as the Gujarati script. It is a semi-syllabary. The writing system is basically phonemic; however, it retains certain Devanagari notations (long-short *i, u*; *ṛ, ru*; and *š, ṣ)* and has no notations for phonemic innovations (*e* vs. *ɛ*, *o* vs. *ɔ*; and the contrast between clear and murmured vowels) (Mistry 1996).

Consonantal characters have an inherent a̲ present except in word-final position. Other postconsonantal vowels are indicated by diacritics. Nasalization is shown by a dot above a character.

The Gujarati Script

Vowels

	Short		Long	
Central	અ	a	આ	ā
High Front	ઇ	i	ઈ	ī
High Back	ઉ	u	ઊ	ū
High Back Vibrant	ઋ	ṛ		
Mid Front			એ	e
Mid Front Diphthong			ઐ	ai
Mid Back			ઓ	o
Mid Back Diphthong			ઔ	au

Consonants

	Voiceless		Voiced				
	Unaspirated	Aspirated	Unaspirated	Aspirated	Nasals	Semi-vowels	Sibilants
Velars	ક k	ખ kh	ગ g	ઘ gh			
Palatals	ચ c	છ ch	જ j	ઝ jh		ય y	શ š
Retroflex	ટ ṭ	ઠ ṭh	ડ ḍ	ઢ ḍh	ણ ṇ	ર r	ષ ṣ
Dentals	ત t	થ th	દ d	ધ dh	ન n	લ l	સ s
Labials	પ p	ફ ph	બ b	ભ bh	મ m	વ v	

Four additional symbols are હ h, a guttural; ળ ḷ, a retroflex lateral; and two conjuncts ક્ષ kṣ and જ્ઞ gn.

The palatal stops *c, ch, j,* and *jh* are phonetically affricates, but they pattern like the other stops. /v/ has [v] and [w] as allophones.

The four consonant types, voiceless unaspirated, voiceless aspirated, voiced unaspirated, and voiced aspirated, are all phonemic; changing either voicing or aspiration can change the meaning of a word: *kāl* 'tomorrow', *khāl* 'leather', *gāl* 'cheek', *ghāl* 'insert!'. Gujarati *kh* is pronounced like ENGLISH 'k' at the beginning of a word; *k* is pronounced like the second consonant sound in 'school'; *g* is fully voiced, like the initial sound in Spanish *gato* 'cat'. Gujarati *gh* does not have a close equivalent in English. The vocal cords vibrate during the production of *gh*, but in a different way than they vibrate for *g*. This second type of vibration is like that found for English 'h' when it occurs between vowels, as in 'ahead'.

Retroflex consonants, indicated with a dot beneath, are produced with the tongue tip curled back. In English, this articulation only occurs for stops followed by *r* (e.g., 'tree'), but in Gujarati, it is not restricted in this way; *tāṇe* '(he) pulls' and *ṭāṇe* 'on the occasion' are two different words.

Table 1: Vowels

	Front	Central	Back
High	i		u
Mid	e	a	o
Low	ɛ	ā	ɔ

Gujarati *a* vs. *ā* distinction is close to vowel differences in "lust" vs. "last".

All Gujarati vowels can appear plain or nasalized. In addition, vowels can be murmured. Murmured vowels (indicated here by two dots under the vowel) have a breathy quality to them. Like the differences among voiced and voiceless aspirated and unaspirated stops, the differences among plain, nasalized, and murmured vowels are also phonemic; changing the vowel changes the meaning of a word: *karo* 'do!', *ka̤ro* 'wall'; *has* 'laugh', *hā̃s* 'swan'.

Roots ending in *-aC* loose their *a* before a suffix beginning with a vowel: *utar-še* '(he) will descend', *utr-iš* '(I) will descend'. Roots ending in *-āC* have their *ā* reduced to *a* before a suffix containing *-ā-* (Mistry 1997):

Table 2: Consonents

		Labial	Dental	Retroflex	Palatal	Velar	Glottal
Stops	Voiceless	p	t	ṭ	c	k	
	Aspirated	ph	th	ṭh	ch	kh	
	Voiced	b	d	ḍ	j	g	
	Aspirated	bh	dh	ḍh	jh	gh	
Fricatives			s		š		h
Resonants			r, l	ḷ			
Nasals		m	n	ṇ			
Glides		v			y		

kar-še '(he) will do'*: kar-āsĕ* '(he) will be able to do'
lāv-še '(he) will bring'*: lav-āsĕ* '(he) will be able to bring'

Basic Morphology

Gujarati has a three-way gender distinction: formally marked as in *chokro* 'boy' masculine, *chokri* 'girl' feminine, and *chokrũ* 'child' neuter. The distinction is inherently present as in masculine *baḷad* 'bull', *popaṭ* 'parrot'; feminine *gāy* 'cow', *koyal* 'cuckoo bird'; and neuter *batak* 'crane', *kabutar* 'pigeon'. The gender markers in some instances are indicators of difference in size: masculine *charo* 'big knife', feminine *chari* 'knife'. There is a two-way distinction for number: singular and plural. The singular is unmarked and plural is marked by *-o*: *māṇas* 'man', *māṇaso* 'men'.

Gujarati nouns are inflected for case. There are six cases: nominative, agentive, accusative/dative, instrumental, genitive, and locative, illustrated below with *šikšak* 'teacher'.

Nominative	šikšak
Agentive	šikšak-e
Accusative/Dative	šikšak-ne
Instrumental	šikšak-thi
Genitive	šikšak-n-
Locative	šikšak-mā̃

Case endings follow the plural marker: *šikšak-o-ne* 'teachers (dative)'.

Gujarati pronouns are inflected for agentive, accusative/dative, and genitive (see Table 3 below). There are two sets of first person plural pronouns. The inclusive set is used when the person being addressed is included in the *we*, and the exclusive set is used when the addressee is not included. The second person plural is also used to refer to a single individual to indicate respect. A special third person plural form exists for a similar function.

The instrumental and the locative forms of pronouns have the genitive form as a base: *mārāthi* 'by me', *mārāmā̃* 'in me'.

A verb form typically consists of three components: stem, tense/aspect suffix, and agreement suffix. The verb stem is a root optionally combined with one or two layers of causative suffixes, and/or a passive suffix. The root *dor* 'to draw (a picture)' can occur as *dor, dor-ā, dor-āv, dor-āv-ā, dor-āv-dāv,* and *dor-āv-dāv-ā*, where *-āv* and *-dāv* are causative suffixes, and *-ā* is the passive suffix. The present and future tense forms are inflected for person and number (PN), while the perfect, imperfect, and pluperfect forms (and some other forms) inflect for gender and number (GN). Imperatives only agree in number (N). The following table lists the inflected forms for one of the six possible stems with *dor* as the root.

Future	dor-š-PN
Present	dor-PN
Imperfect	dor-t-GN
Perfect	dor-y-GN
Pluperfect	dor-el-GN
Imperative	dor-N
Imperative Future	dor-j-N
Desiderative	dor-v-GN
Obligatory	dor-vān-GN
Conditional	dor-at, dor-te
Infinitive	dor-vũ
Conjunctive	dor-i-(ne)

Basic Syntax

Gujarati is an SOV language. Subjects occur in various case forms according to different constructions: dative with certain verbs, agentive with certain tense/aspect, instrumental in the passive, and locative for certain types of "have" constructions. There are three negation markers: *nā, nahi* and *nathi. Nā* varies with *nahi*; but *nā* can only occur before the verb, while *nahi* can occur before or after the verb. *Nathi* represents a combination of *nā* with a present tense auxiliary verb.

Table 3: Inflected Pronouns

	1sg.	2sg.	3sg.	1pl-exc.	1pl-inc.	2pl.	3pl.	3pl/hon
Nominative	hũ	tũ	te	ame	āpaṇe	tame	teo	
Agentive	mẽ	tẽ	teṇe	ame	āpaṇe	tame	teoe	temṇe
Acc/Dat	mane	tane	tene	amne	āpaṇne	tamne	teone	temne
Genitive	mār-	tār-	ten-	amār-	āpaṇ-	tamār-	teon-	temn-

Gujarati is a head-final language. It has postpositions, and relative clauses and adjectives precede nouns (see Example Sentences 1 and 2 below). It has relative-correlative as well as adjectival-type relative clauses. The basic word order can be freely scrambled for focusing and stylistic purposes.

Contact with Other Languages

Sanskrit as a prestige language has remained a continuous source of words in Gujarati. In many instances, the same Sanskrit word has been adopted at different times, leading to different pronunciations: the name of the deity *kṛšṇa* exists in three pronunciations; modified (*krašṇa*), recently borrowed from Sanskrit (*krušṇa*), and borrowed from neighboring languages: (*krišṇa*). The same phenomenon has resulted in *krapā*, *krupā*, and *kripā* from the Sanskrit *kṛpā* 'favor'. Gujarati speakers through their contact with speakers of PERSIAN, ARABIC, and Portuguese have many borrowed words from these languages. In recent years, English has become a major source of words.

From Persian: *hajār* 'thousand', *kharid-* 'to buy'
From Arabic: *duniā* 'world', *insāf* 'justice', *khabar* 'news'
From Portuguese: *cāvi* 'key', *pistol* 'gun', *mistri* 'craftsman'
From English: *kabāṭ* 'cupboard', *rasid* 'receipt', *koraṭ* 'court', bank, college, pencil, vitamin, minute, visit, colony

Common Words

man:	puruš	long:	lāmbũ
woman:	stri	small:	nānũ
water:	pāṇi	yes:	hā
sun:	suraj	no:	nā
three:	traṇ	good:	sārũ
fish:	māchli	bird:	pankhi
big:	moṭũ	dog:	kutro
tree:	jhāḍ		

Example Sentences

(1) pel-o ũc-o chokr-o ghaṇ-o vahel-o āv-y-o.
that tall boy-MASC very early come-PERFECT
'That tall boy came very early.'

(2) je chokr-o mā̃d-o hato te sāj-o
which boy-MASC sick was that recovered

tha-y-o.
become-PERFECT
'The boy who was sick has recovered.'

(3) pel-ā mā̃d-ā chokr-ā-thi vahel-ā nā av-ā-y-ũ.
that sick boy-MASC early not come-PASSIVE.PERFECT
'That sick boy was unable to come early.'

Efforts to Preserve, Protect, and Promote the Language

Among hundreds of languages in India, Gujarati is one of the 16 official languages recognized by the Indian constitution, and is seventh in numbers of speakers. It is used as a medium of instruction in schools, colleges, and universities, and also for public media and in movies and plays. It has also served as the medium of expression for the thoughts, feelings, experiences, and ideals of many gifted individuals, including Mahatma Gandhi, which has resulted in a varied and rich literary tradition extending approximately a thousand years.

Scores of Gujarati societies outside of Gujarat are devoted to maintaining identity and thereby their language through cultural activities, language classes, lectures, plays, and songs in Gujarati by literary figures and performers invited from Gujarat. Particularly noteworthy are the activities of the London-based Gujarati Literary Academy, and their literary annual, *Asmitā*. In certain regions in Great Britain and in Canada, Gujarati is taught in schools as a second language.

There is, however, a reverse trend prevailing in the home state. Although the number of Gujarati speakers is increasing, the overall percentage of Gujarati speakers in the national population of India is decreasing: from 5.3 percent in 1971 to 5 percent in 1981 (India 1991: 19). This is attributable to significant numbers of parents sending their children to English medium schools. No significant efforts against this trend are being undertaken either by government agencies or other associations in Gujarat.

In the United States, there are Gujarati societies in every medium-sized town and several in major cities. Some of these societies publish an annual literary volume, and a literary quarterly, *Gurjari Digest*, has been in existence since 1987.

Select Bibliography

Allen, Sheila. 1971. *New Minorities, Old Conflicts*. New York: Random House.

Bhayani, Harivallabh C. 1951. "Middle Indo-Aryan Groups of Consonants With Unassimilated *-r-*" In *Annals of Bhandarkar Oriental Research Institute, 31*, 225–232.

Cardona, George. 1965. *A Gujarati Reference Grammar*. Philadelphia: University of Pennsylvania Press.

Dave, Jagdish. 1995. *Colloquial Gujarati*. New York: Routledge.

Dave, Radhekant. 1977. *Studies in Gujarati Phonology and Phonetics*. Ph.D. dissertation, Cornell University.

Deshpande P.G. 1982. *A Modern English-Gujarati Dictionary*. Bombay: Oxford University Press.

Dwyer, Rachel. 1995. *Teach Yourself Gujarati*. London: Hodder and Stoughton.

Gajendragadkar, Shrikrishna N. 1972. *Parsi Gujarati*. Bombay: University of Bombay.

Lambert, H.M. 1972. *Gujarati Language Course*. Cambridge: Cambridge University Press.

Mistry, P.J. 1969. *Gujarati Verbal Constructions*. Ph.D. dissertation, University of California, Los Angeles.

____. 1992. Gujarati. *International Encyclopedia of Linguistics*, ed. William Bright. New York: Oxford University Press.

____. 1996. "The Gujarati Script." In *The World's Writing Systems*. Peter Daniels and William Bright, eds. Oxford: Oxford University Press.

____. 1997. "Gujarati Phonology." In *Phonologies of Asia and Africa*, ed. Alan S. Kaye, pp. 653–673. Winona Lake: Eisenbrauns.

GUSII

Lee S. Bickmore

Language Name: Gusii. **Alternates:** *Kisii, Guzii.* **Autonym**: *Ekegusii.*

Location: Southwestern Kenya, encompassing the area south of Kavirondo Gulf, Kisii District, in Nyanza Province.

Family: Gusii is a Bantu language of the Bantoid subgroup of the Benue-Congo group of the Niger-Congo subfamily of the Niger-Kordofanian family.

Related Languages: Logoori, Kikuria, Zanaki, and Sonjo.

Dialects: Gusii has little dialectal variation (Whitely 1956).

Number of Speakers: 1,386,000.

Origin and History

It is believed that the Gusii moved to their present location from the north some 400 to 500 years ago, first separating from the related Logoori in north Nyanza, and then from the Tende and abaSweta, who moved even further south. The entire Gusii people trace their genealogies back to a common ancestor, Mogusii, who is thought of as the founder of the society and the person after whom it was named. Despite the recognition of this common ancestry, however, the modern Gusii descend from seven ethnic subgroups who combined together for various reasons, including military operations against the Kipsigis (Maxon 1989). In 1907, the lands of these Gusii groups came under British administration, and became part of the South Nyanza District along with adjacent Luo areas. Kenya achieved its independence from Great Britain in December 1963.

The Gusii, currently occupying a fertile area of high country, are both pastoral and agricultural, providing a substantial part of Kenya's maize and an increasing quantity of coffee. The Gusii represent the fifth largest ethnic group in Kenya and have had a strong sense of national identity, largely because of their ethno-linguistic isolation as they are surrounded by non-Bantu groups. On the west and the south are the Luo (Nilotic) and on the northeast and southeast are the Masai and Kipsigis (Nilo-Hamitic). With the Luo there has been peaceful trading and some intermarriage. However, the Masai and Kipsigis have attacked the Gusii regularly, and therefore relations with them remained negative even after colonial pacification.

Orthography and Basic Phonology

The Gusii alphabet, which has 19 graphemes, is based on the LATIN alphabet as shown below. Digraphs, representing specific sounds, are also included.

A, B, CH, D, E, G, I, K, M, N, NG, NY, O, R, S, T, U, W, Y
a, b, ch, d, e, g, i, k, m, n, ng, ny, o, r, s, t, u, w, y

Gusii has 14 consonant phonemes as represented in Table 1 below. The consonants /č/, /ɲ/ and /ŋ/ are written in the orthography as *ch, ny,* and *ng'* respectively. The consonants /b/, /d/ and /g/ each have two allophones. They are realized as [b], [d] and [g] after nasals, and as [ß], [r] and [ɣ] elsewhere.

Table 1: Consonants

	Labial	Alveolar	Palatal	Velar
Stops Voiceless Voiced	 b	 t d		 k g
Fricatives		s		
Affricates			č	
Nasals	m	n	ɲ	ŋ
Tap		r		
Glides	w		y	

Gusii exhibits Dahl's Law, which turns a voiceless velar stop into a voiced fricative when the following consonant is voiceless. This can be seen in the following examples where the consonant in a verbal infinitive prefix alternates between [k] and [ɣ], conditioned by the following consonant:

ɔkɔ-rɔɔt-a 'to dream'
oko-ɣor-a 'to buy'
oko-nyw-a 'to drink'

oɣo-kaan-a 'to deny'
oɣo-tuu-a 'to be blunt'
ɔɣɔ-sɛk-a 'to laugh'

Table 2: Vowels

	Front	Central	Back
High	i		u
Mid-High	e		o
Mid-Low	ɛ		ɔ
Low		a	

Gusii has seven vowel phonemes as represented in Table 2 on the previous page. The language has a vowel harmony process by which mid-vowels in prefixes become lax when the first vowel of the root is lax:

oko-biimba	'to swell'
oko-ruga	'to cook'
oko-mera	'to swallow'
oko-roka	'to name'
oko-raama	'to abuse'

ɔkɔ-mɛra	'to sprout'
ɔkɔ-rɔɔta	'to dream'

ɛkɛ-rɛɛma	'lame person'
eke-roongo	'porcupine'

ɛ-ŋɔɔmbɛ	'cow'
e-siimba	'lion'

While there is a phonemic distinction between tense and lax mid vowels, this is not reflected in the orthography. Both /e/ and /ɛ/ are written as *e* and /o/ and /ɔ/ are written as *o*.

While vowel length is lexically contrastive in the language, for example, *omocheere* 'rice' but *omochere* 'calabash', it can also be derived by two quite productive processes. The first process compensatorily lengthens a vowel after the devocalization (gliding) of an immediately preceding nonlow vowel:

/omo-ana/	'child'	>	[omwaana]
/obo-ato/	'canoe'	>	[obwaato]

The second process lengthens a vowel before a nasal-consonant sequence:

/omo-nto/	'person'	>	[omoonto]
/e-mbori/	'goat'	>	[eembori]
/chi-nderu/	'beard'	>	[chiinderu]

Gusii is a tonal language, exhibiting a tonal contrast of high and low pitches on short vowels, and low-low, high-high, and high-low (but not low-high) pitches on long vowels.

The following minimal pairs indicate that tone is lexical in the language:

ríúgà	'flower'	but	rìùgà	'bone'
èèndá	'lice'	but	èèndà	'stomach'

Basic Morphology

The nominal morphology is based on a system of noun classes. In this system, nouns are organized into singular/plural pairs. The prefixes for each class (numbered in the traditional Bantu fashion) are given below. The singular/plural pairings most commonly found are: 1/2, 3/4, 5/6, 7/8, 9/10, 11/10, 12/8, 14/6, 15/6.

Class	Prefix	Example	Gloss
1	omo-	omo-remi	'farmer'
2	aba-	aba-remi	'farmers'
3	omo-	omo-te	'tree'
4	eme-	eme-te	'trees'
5	(e)ri-	ri-bururu	'grasshopper'
6	ama-	ama-bururu	'grasshoppers'
7	eke-	eke-baki	'eagle'
8	ebi-	ebi-baki	'eagles'
9	e(n)-	ri-gwaari	'zebra'
10	chi(n)-	ama-gwaari	'zebras'
11	oro-	oro-saana	'forest'
12	aka-	aka-gena	'small stone'
14	obo-	obo-gima	'life'
15	oko-	oko-goro	'leg'

Adjectives and possessives must always agree in class with the noun they modify:

omo-chi omo-ke — 'small village'
C3-village C3-small

eme-chi eme-ke — 'small villages'
C4-village C4-small

eke-baki ki-ane — 'my eagle'
C7-eagle C7-my

ebi-baki bi-ane — 'my eagles'
C8-eagle C8-my

Like most Bantu languages, Gusii has a rich verbal morphology. Verbal infinitives are expressed as Class 15 nouns:

oko-Root-Final Vowel, e.g.:

ogo-sab-a	'to ask, pray'
ogo-tam-a	'to run away'
oko-book-a	'to wake up'

Table 3: Suffixal "Extensions"

-er	Applicative	ogo-soom-a	'to read'	ogo-soom-er-a	'to read for'
-i	Causative	oko-genda	'to go'	oko-gend-i-a	'to cause to go'
-ek	Stative	oko-bun-a	'to break'	oko-bun-ek-a	'to be broken'
-w	Passive	ogo-soom-a	'to read'	ogo-soom-w-a	'to be read'
-an	Reciprocal	ogo-koony-a	'to help'	ogo-koony-an-a	'to help each other'
-or	Reversive	oko-ring-a	'to fold'	oko-ring-or-a	'to unfold'

The morphological structure of finite verbs is the following:

Subject-Tense/Aspect(T/A)-Object-Verb Root-Extensions-T/A-Final V

Suffixal "extensions" can modify both the semantics and number of arguments of the verb (see Table 3 on the previous page).

Gusii expresses the following tense/aspects:

Future: Near (by tomorrow), Far (after tomorrow), Future Progressive
Past: Recent (earlier today), Near (yesterday), Far (before yesterday), Sequential, Habitual, Perfective, Progressive
Other: Potential, Persistive, Desiderative, Inceptive, Present Habitual, Subjunctive, Present Progressive, Imperative

The following are examples of the sequential (Seq.), past (P) and far future (FF) tense/aspect forms in Gusii:

to-ga-timok-a
we-SEQ-rest-FV 'and we rested' (Sequential Past)

to-raa-timok-a
we-FF-rest-FV 'we will rest' (Far Future)

tw-aa-timok-et-e
we-P-rest-P-FV 'we rested' (Yesterday)

Basic Syntax

Gusii is an SVO language, as illustrated by the following sentences:

Omwaana naruta omopira
child threw ball
'The child threw the ball.'

Omoremi naareeta chinyeni
farmer brought vegetables
'The farmer brought the vegetables.'

Phrases are generally head initial as illustrated below (A = Associative marker):

VP > V ADV
Naache bwaangu
he-come quickly
'He will come quickly.'

VP > V NP PP
tobeeka ekarataasi ime y egetaabu
we-put paper in A book
'We put the paper in the book.'

NP > N ADJ POSS
ebitaabu ebike biane
books small my
'my small books'

PP > P NP
ime y egetaabu
in A book
'in the book'

Contact with Other Languages

The two main languages that Gusii has had contact with are ENGLISH and SWAHILI. During the time that Kenya was a British colony, Gusii borrowed many lexical items from English. Swahili has been a lingua franca in Kenya as well as other East African countries for centuries. Today, most speakers of Gusii are in fact trilingual, also speaking English and Swahili. Gusii is quite unusual in having relatively little influence from other Bantu languages. This is primarily because the Gusii-speaking population is largely surrounded by non-Bantu-speaking peoples. To the west and the south are the Nilotic Luo, to the northeast and southeast the Nilo-Hamitic Masai and Kipsigis.

Common Words

man:	omosaacha	woman:	omokuungu
water:	amaache	sun:	omogaso
three:	isato	fish:	eenswe
big:	-nene	long:	-tambe
small:	i-ke	yes:	ee
no:	yaaya	good:	-ya
bird:	enyoni	dog:	eseese
tree:	omote		

Example Sentences

(1) A-tag-ete ko-ror-a chi-nyoni chi-nene.
3SG-want-PERF INF-see-FV c10-bird c10-big
'(S)he wants to see the big birds.'

(2) Ekero n-daa-kor-e eme-remo igo n-daa-ch-e
when I-FUT-do-FV c4-job CFOC I-FUT-come-FV

ko-buuch-a ama-ache.
INF-fetch-FV c6-water
'When I have done this job, I'll come and fetch water.'
(FV = final vowel termination; CFOC = Continuation of Focus [i.e., Focus of 2nd clause is same as first])

(3) Omo-nto o-ta-a-ch-ete n-omo-tambe.
c1-man REL-NEG-PAST-come-PERF COP-c1-tall
'The man who hasn't come is tall.'

Efforts to Preserve, Protect, and Promote the Language

The Gusii language is used in the classroom in the first few years of elementary school in the region where it is spoken. At subsequent levels, it is replaced with Swahili and then English. While communication with government officials often takes place in Gusii, all formal written documents are only in Swahili and English. The Bible has been translated into Gusii, and it is the language used in local religious services. At the provincial level, every morning and evening there is a news and entertainment broadcast in Gusii on the radio.

Select Bibliography

Bickmore, L. 1997. "Problems in constraining High tone spread in Ekegusii." In *Lingua, 102*: 4, 265–290.

_____. 1999. "High Tone Spread in Ekegusii Revisited: An Optimality Theoretic Account." In *Lingua 109*: 109–153.

Harkansson, Thomas. 1998. *Bridewealth, Women and Land: Social Change Among the Gusii of Kenya.* Stockholm: Uppsala Studies in Cultural Anthropology 10.

Maxon, Robert. 1989. *Conflict and Accommodation in Western Kenya.* London and Toronto: Associated University Press.

Mayer, Philip. 1950. *Gusii Bridewealth Law and Custom.* Capetown and New York: Oxford University Press.

Ochieng, William R. 1991. *People of the South-Western Highlands: Gusii.* Nairobi and London: Evans Brothers Limited.

Whiteley, W.H. 1956. *A Practical Introduction to Gusii.* Nairobi: East African Literature Bureau.

____. 1960. *The Tense System of Gusii.* Kampala: East African Institute of Social Research.

HAITIAN CREOLE

Flore Zéphir

Language Name: Haitian Creole. **Autonym:** *Kreyòl.*

Location: The Caribbean country of Haiti, which is located on the western part of the island of Hispaniola. Haiti shares that island with the Dominican Republic.

Family: French-based Creoles.

Related Languages: Haitian Creole is related to other FRENCH-based Creoles of the American-Caribbean region that are spoken in Louisiana in the United States, Guadeloupe, Martinique, Dominica, St. Lucia, and French Guyana, and also to those of the Indian Ocean region, spoken in Seychelles, Reunion, and Mauritius.

Dialects: Haitian Creole is divided into three regional dialects: Northern (region of Cap-Haitian), Southern (region of Les Cayes), and Western (region of Port-au-Prince). The relatively small number of variants that exist occur mostly at the lexical and morphosyntactic levels. For example, the Northern variety uses the relator *a* to express possession, as in *zafè a mwen* 'my things', realized as *zafè an m*; the other varieties would say *zafè m*, without the relator. The Southern variety expresses progression through the use of the progressive marker *ape/pe*, as in *m ape manje* or *m pe manje* 'I am eating'. In the other varieties, the same statement would be rendered as *m ap manje*.

With regard to social stratification, two major sociolects of Haitian Creole can be identified: the rural variety that is presumably spoken by the uneducated, monolingual Creole speakers who constitute the bulk of the Haitian population, and the urban variety spoken by the privileged, educated bilingual (in French and Creole) minority. The former variety is known in Haiti as *kreyòl rèk*, or *gwo kreyòl* ('coarse Creole'). The characteristics—coarse, vulgar, unrefined—that are sometimes attributed to individuals belonging to the lower social echelons explain the labels. The latter variety is referred to as *kreyòl swa* ('refined Creole'). Again, the label seems to reflect the more positive attributes (refinement, education, cultural sophistication) associated with this group. Paradoxically perhaps, there appears to be a consensus that the rural variety contains fewer Frenchified features and, as such, is considered "purer" than the urban dialect which exhibits a stronger French influence. This explains why it is sometimes called *vrè kreyòl* or *bon kreyòl* ('real Creole' or 'good Creole'). The most salient distinctions between the two sociolects are found at the phonological level. The urban variety has three additional front-rounded vowels that are not, generally speaking, typical of the rural variety. They are *u* contrasting with *i* as in *etud* versus *etid* 'studies' (*études* in French), *eu* contrasting with *é* (written *e*) as in *paskeu* versus *paske* 'because' (Fr. *parce que*), and *eù* contrasting with *è* as in *peù* versus *pè* 'afraid', 'fear' (Fr. *peur*). Additionally, at the lexical level, some words have two variants, one considered more typical of the speech of the bilinguals than the other one. However, it needs to be cautioned that dialect contact does occur. In consequence, certain features commonly associated with one sociolect may well be produced by speakers of the other.

Number of Speakers: 6–8 million. This figure includes the number of Haitians living in Haiti, estimated at roughly 6 million, and the Haitian diaspora living abroad, mostly in the United States in New York, Miami, and Boston; Canada in Montreal; and in other Caribbean islands, primarily the Dominican Republic and the Bahamas. The Haitian population in the U.S. alone is about 1 million.

Origin and History

Haitian Creole is a language that arose in the French colony of Saint Domingue during the 17th and 18th centuries. Creolists suggest that this language developed during the expansion phase of the plantations after 1697, the date of the Treaty of Riswhick by which Spain gave the western part of the island of Hispaniola to France. From that date, French colonization consolidated itself in Saint Domingue, and the French introduced new crops such as indigo, coffee, cotton, and sugar, which required more intensive forms of cultivation. As a result of this expansion, this period witnessed the massive arrival of slaves from Africa, who outnumbered the white population. Many believed that the speech of these slaves evolved into what is known today as Haitian Creole.

Various theories have been proposed in an attempt to characterize the speech of the slaves. These can be grouped into two major positions: the monogenetic (one source) hypothesis and the polygenetic (many sources) hypothesis. The striking structural similarities between the various Creoles led to the appeal of the monogenetic hypothesis. According to this theory, all Creoles, including Haitian Creole, are derived from one source, identified as an Afro-Portuguese pidgin that would have developed in the 15th century on the western coast of Africa because of the presence of Portuguese traders. This Afro-Portuguese pidgin was itself a contact language originating from the lingua franca used at that time by sailors and traders from a variety of regions in the Mediterranean basin.

Table 1: Consonants

		Labial	Dental	Alveolar	Palatal	Velar
Stops	Voiceless	p	t			k
	Voiced	b	d			g
Fricatives	Voiceless	f		s	ch	
	Voiced	v		z	j	
Affricates	Voiceless				tch	
	Voiced				dj	
Nasals		m	n			gn
Liquids				l		r
Glides					y	w

Presumably, the Afro-Portuguese pidgin was the first European language that African slaves acquired while they awaited their shipment from the coast of Africa to the New World. Then, in the 16th century as Portuguese influence faded in Africa and as the pidgin was used in more and more contact situations, pidgin speakers drew on the dominant languages present for vocabulary expansion. The grammatical base of the Afro-Portuguese pidgin remained, but the vocabulary was replaced. This process is known as "relexification". Thus, according to this theory, Haitian Creole has managed to retain the grammar of the original Afro-Portuguese pidgin that underwent relexification because of the contact with the language of the French traders and colonizers, which intensified in the 17th century.

According to the polygenetic view, the Haitian language is a hybrid or "mixed" language consisting primarily of French words strung together according to the syntax of one (EWE) or more than one African language. There is evidence to suggest that slave owners deliberately grouped slaves on plantations who did not share a common tongue in order to minimize the chances of revolt. As a result of this linguistic heterogeneity, slaves had to resort to some form of common language to communicate among themselves, and this language was based on the reduced variety of French spoken by their masters. (The white colonizers, believing that the African slaves were too "primitive" to understand a language as "complex" as French, deliberately simplified their speech.) Haitian Creole, which retained some features of pronunciation and grammar from the various African languages, was the result.

It is beyond the scope of this article to resolve the controversy among the different views pertaining to the origin of Creoles in general and Haitian Creole in particular. Perhaps a complementary hypothesis, which takes into account all possible sources, may well be the correct one. What is certain is that Haitian Creole is a contact language that developed in the context of French colonization of Saint Domingue in the late 17th century. It is the consensus that French is the superstrate language (the language from which the bulk of the vocabulary is derived). With regard to the substrate language (that upon which the grammar is based), heated debates persist.

In any event, historical evidence suggests that Haitian Creole was widely used both among masters and slaves throughout the colonial period (1697–1803). Further, the first written account of Haitian Creole goes back to the 18th century. It consists of a poem titled "Lisette quitté la plaine", written around 1757 by Duvivier de la Mahotière, a "habitant" of Saint Domingue.

Orthography and Basic Phonology

Haitian Creole has an alphabet of approximately 34 symbols that represent the basic sounds of the language. The orthography used to represent these symbols corresponds to the standard orthography proposed in 1979 by the *Institut Pédagogique National* (IPN). Owing to a presidential decree issued in September 1979, this orthography was declared the official spelling for Haitian Creole, and as such it supersedes the previous spellings that have been used. Those are, respectively, the McConnell-Laubach devised in 1943 by an Irish Protestant missionary, Ormonde McConnell, and an American literacy expert, Frank Laubach; and the Pressoir in 1947 by the Haitian scholar Charles-Fernand Pressoir.

In addition to the consonants included on Table 1 above, Haitian Creole has two additional, marginal consonants. *H* appears in a very limited set of words such as *hougan* 'voodoo priest' and *housi* 'voodoo priestess'; *ng*, a velar nasal like that of English "thing", appears in a few words like *pinga* 'do not' and *ping pong*.

There is also a third glide, *u*, the front-rounded equivalent of back-rounded *w*. It appears in a few words, such as *uit* 'eight' and *uityèm* 'eighth'.

Table 2: Vowels

	Front		Central	Back
	Unrounded	Rounded		
High	i	u		ou
High-Mid	e	eu		o
Low-Mid	è	eù		ò
Low			a	
Nasal	en	(un)	an	on

The front-rounded vowels *u*, *eù*, and *eu* seem more common in the urban variety of Haitian Creole. In addition to the three

Table 3: Tense/Aspect Markers

Marker	Tense/Aspect	Example	Gloss
ap	Progressive	m ap manje	'I am eating'
va/a	Future	m a vin pita	'I'll come by later'
te	Past	m te wè Mari yè swa	'I saw Marie yesterday evening'
ta	Conditional	m ta renmen vwayaje	'I would like to travel'

nasal vowels listed on the Table 2, there is a marginal front rounded nasal vowel *un* that occurs only in four or five words, such as *pafun* 'perfume' and *lundi* 'Monday'.

Basic Morphology

In Haitian Creole, nouns and adjectives are invariable. They are not inflected for number or gender, and there are no case markers. Adjectives (except for a limited set) follow the nouns they modify. This is also the case for possessives and demonstratives. Like adjectives, definite articles always come after nouns. The singular definite article appears in several forms, depending on the nature of the preceding element. For example, in *tab la* 'the table', the determiner is *la*, which begins with a consonant, reflecting the preceding consonant, *b*. Similarly, in *radyo a* 'the radio', the determiner is *a*, reflecting the preceding vowel. The feature of nasalization is also reflected in the variants of the definite article, as in *chanm lan* or *chanm nan* 'the bedroom' or *chen an* 'the dog'.

Like nouns, personal pronouns are not inflected for case. They occur in either full or short forms. The short forms are very frequent in the spoken language. Subject pronouns precede the verb, and object pronouns follow it.

In Haitian Creole, verbs have one base form that does not change for person, modality, or tense. There is no subject agreement. Tense and aspect are expressed by markers that occur before the verb. The major markers are presented in Table 3 above.

The absence of a marker usually indicates a habitual fact, as in *m pale kreyòl* '(it is a fact that) I speak Creole', or an immediate past action, as in *m manje maten an* 'I ate this morning'. Haitian Creole, like many other languages, creates new words through affixation (the use of both prefixes and suffixes) as in *pwòp, pwòple* ('clean', 'cleanliness'). In addition, there are certain other processes of word formation deserving of mention. Onomatopoeic productivity allows a concept to be represented by the noise it represents:

li toup pou li
3sg for 3sg
'S/he punched him/her.'

kè m fè bipbip
heart 1sg make
'My heart was really pounding.'

Reduplication is also a very productive process of word formation, conveying emphatic force: *zwitzwit* 'extremely small', *vitvit* 'extremely fast' (< *vit* 'fast'). Compounding is another way of forming new words: *sanpwoblèm* 'an easy going person' (< *san* 'without' + *pwoblèm* 'problem').

Basic Syntax

Haitian Creole is a SVO language, with one striking particularity (for a language of that type): determiners, as mentioned above, follow the words they determine. In addition, they have a much wider semantic range than in French, since they occur with possessives and demonstratives. They can also modify elements other than nouns, such as relative and subordinate clauses, verbs, and adverbs:

kay sa a
house this DET 'this house'

pitit mwen an
child 1SG DET 'my child'

kay la mwen achte a gen anpil pyebwa
house DET 1SG buy DET have a lot tree
'The house I (just) bought has a lot of trees.'

depi Mari marye a, nou pa wè l(i) menm
since Marie marry DET 1PL NEG see 3SG at all
'Since Marie got married, we do not see her at all.'

kouche a va bon pou ou
to.lie.down DET FUTURE good for 2
'To lie down will be good for you.'

Negation is expressed by the particle *pa* placed before the tense marker and verb:

m pa ap manje
1SG NEG PROGRESSIVE eat
'I am not eating.'

Contact with Other Languages

In addition to French, which is the major source of its vocabulary, Haitian Creole contains loanwords from SPANISH and American Indian languages that extend back to the 17th century. With the Spanish invasion that lasted from 1492 (when Christopher Columbus first sailed to the island of Hispaniola) until 1697 (when Spain gave the western part of the island to France), several Spanish words came into Haitian Creole. ENGLISH has given many loanwords to Haitian Creole. On Tortuga Island, located in the northwestern part of Haiti, there was a considerable number of English freebooters throughout the 18th century. In fact, the southern city of Jeremie was once occupied by the English. American English is also a lexical contributor. Throughout the colonization period, Saint Domingue traded with the United States. Furthermore from 1915 to 1931, Haiti was under American occupation. More recently, the presence of a sizeable number of Haitians—approximately one million—currently living in the United States has contributed and continues to contribute to the infiltration of English words into Haitian Creole. In fact, many words dealing with science and technology come from English and are now part of the Haitian Creole repertoire.

From American Indian (Arawak): *kannòt* 'canoe', *patat* 'sweet potato', *gwayav* 'guayava'
From Spanish: *mawon* 'wild', *mantèg* 'vegetable shortening'
From English: *djòb* 'job', *tcheke* 'to check', *konpyoutè* 'computer', *bipè* 'beeper'

Common Words

man:	msye	long:	long
woman:	madanm	small:	piti, ti
water:	dlo	yes:	wi
sun:	solèy	no:	non
three:	twa	good:	bon
fish:	pwason	bird:	zwazo
big:	gwo	dog:	chen
tree:	pyebwa		

Example Sentences

(1) ki jan ou rele.
how 2SG call
'What is your name?' (lit. 'How do you call yourself?')

(2) m pa konprann sa l(i) ap di m lan.
1SG NEG understand what 3SG PROG say 1SG DET
'I don't understand what s/he is telling me.'

(3) Mari renmen machin l(i) achte a.
Marie like car 3SG buy DET
'Marie likes the car she bought.'

Efforts to Preserve, Protect, and Promote the Language

The Haitian constitution of March 1987 promoted Haitian Creole to the status of official language on a par with French. In recent years, it has expanded its domains of use, and it is accepted and introduced, to a certain extent, in the government and in the schools. The media are undoubtedly the main conveyors of the Haitian Creole into domains that have been traditionally reserved for French. There exist various newspapers, periodicals, brochures, and advertisements written in Creole. The recognition of a standard orthography in 1979 may have contributed to an increase in Creole-written production. Additionally, Haitian Creole is used in a number of radio and television broadcasts and commercials. Government leaders also choose to deliver their public statements in this language. Moreover, there is a fairly extensive literature in Haitian Creole. The best known of these writers is Félix Morisseau-Leroy who endeavored to translate into Creole the masterpieces of French and Greek literatures, in addition to writing poetry, plays, and novels. Morisseau-Leroy is considered by many to be the "father of Haitian Creole poetry, literature, and play writing". Finally, even in the United States, which has the largest number of Haitian Creole speakers outside of Haiti, Haitian Creole is promoted and is, in fact, used in urban bilingual education programs in New York, Miami, Boston, and Chicago.

Select Bibliography

Chaudenson, R. 1979. *Les Créoles français*. Paris: Fernand Nathan.

De Graff, M. 1999. *Language Creation and Language Change: Creolization, Diachrony and Development*. Cambridge: MIT Press.

Dejean, Y. 1980. *Comment écrire le créole d'Haiti?* Quebec: Collectif Paroles.

Fattier, D. 1998. "Contribution à l'étude de la genèse d'un créole: L'Atlas linguistique d'Haiti, cartes et commentaires." Doctoral dissertation. Université de Provence.

Freeman, B., and J. Laguerre. 1998. *Haitian-English Dictionary*. Lawrence, KS: Institute of Haitian Studies, University of Kansas.

Lefebve, C., H. Magloire-Holly, and N. Piou. 1982. *Syntaxe de l'haïtien*. Ann Arbor, MI: Karoma Publishers.

Romaine, S. 1988. *Pidgins and Creole Languages*. New York: Longman.

Schieffelin, B., and R. Charlier Doucet. 1994. "The 'real' Haitian Creole: Ideology, Metalinguistics, and Orthographic Choice." In *American Ethnologist, 21* (1): 176–200.

Valdman, A. 1978. *Le Créole: Structure, statut et origine*. Paris: Klincksieck.

_____. 1981. *Haitian-Creole-English-French Dictionary*, 2 vols. Bloomington: Indiana University Creole Institute.

Valdman, A., with C. Pooser and R. Jean-Baptiste. 1996. *A Learner's Dictionary of Haitian Creole*. Bloomington, IN: Indiana University Creole Institute.

HAUSA

Paul Newman

Language Name: Hausa. **Autonym:** *hausa.*

Location: Spoken in northern Nigeria and southern Niger, and by a small community in the Blue Nile area of Sudan. It is widely spoken as a second language in parts of Ghana, Togo, and Benin.

Family: West Chadic branch of the Chadic family of the Afro-Asiatic language phylum.

Related Languages: Within the Chadic family, Hausa is most closely related to other West Chadic languages such as Angas and Bole. It is distantly related to languages in the other branches of the Afro-Asiatic family, including, for example, Semitic (ARABIC, HEBREW, AMHARIC), Cushitic (OROMO, SOMALI), and Berber (Tuareg, Kabyle, TAMAZIGHT).

Dialects: Hausa is broadly divided into two regional dialect groups, Western and Eastern, which exhibit differences in pronunciation and grammar. The Standard Dialect (SH), which predominates in the written language and which is used in radio and TV broadcasts in Nigeria and abroad (e.g., BBC, Deutsche Welle, and Voice of America), is that of Kano, Nigeria, within the Eastern group. Western dialects (WH), are marked by the use of syllable-final [p], [b], and sometimes [m] instead of Standard Hausa [u], and in the use of [h] or [hw] instead of /f/; e.g., (SH) *sàuka laafiyàa* = (WH) *sàpka laahiyàa* 'arrive safely!'.

Crosscutting the East/West distinction is a North/South distinction corresponding to the line between Niger and Nigeria. In Niger, formerly a French colony, FRENCH was the source of the numerous loanwords that entered the language in the early to mid-20th century, while in Nigeria, which was an English colony, ENGLISH was the source of such loanwords; e.g., *shûu* (< French *chou*) vs. *kaabeejì* (< English 'cabbage').

Southeastern dialects are similar to other peripheral and second-language dialects in essentially doing away with lexical/grammatical gender distinctions found in regular Hausa.

A creolized offshoot of Hausa called Gwandara is spoken in the midbelt of Nigeria in the vicinity of Abuja, the federal capital. Gwandara and Hausa are no longer mutually intelligible.

Number of Speakers: 40–50 million.

Origin and History

Based on linguistic subgrouping and the present-day distribution of Chadic languages, we can assume that Proto-Chadic was spoken on the southern shores of Lake Chad in what is now northeastern Nigeria and northern Cameroon. Speakers of the Chadic subgroup to which Hausa belongs migrated gradually westward, the speakers of Proto-Hausa representing the furthest extent of this movement. From a core area located along the present Nigeria-Niger border, where the towns of Katsina and Maradi now exist, Hausa speakers fanned out in a westward and south-southeast direction. (When Kano, the major Hausa city, was settled by Hausa speakers, it probably already existed as a town occupied by speakers of the Plateau branch of the Niger-Congo family.) In the 20th century, Hausa continued to spread to the southeast, with the result that many communities where other languages were formerly spoken are now monolingual Hausa.

Hausa is the most important Chadic language. In addition to a large number of mother-tongue speakers, it serves as the lingua franca of trade and commerce in many parts of west Africa. Hausas have traditionally been traders who traveled long distances beyond the borders of the original seven Hausa states (Daura, Kano, Rano, Zazzau [Zaria], Gobir, Katsina and

Hausa is spoken mainly in northern Nigeria and southern Niger (shaded area). It is also spoken by a small community in the Blue Nile area of Sudan (not shown above).

Table 1: Consonants

	Labial	Alveolar	Palatal	Velar	Labio-velar	Palatal-velar	Glottal
Stops							
Voiceless		t	c	k	kw	ky	
Voiced	b	d	j	g	gw	gy	’
Glottalized	ɓ	ɗ	’y	ƙ	ƙw	ƙy	
Fricatives							
Voiceless	f, fy	s	sh				h
Voiced		z					
Glottalized		ts					
Nasals	m	n					
Liquids							
Lateral		l					
Flap		r					
Tap/Roll		r̃					
Glides			y		w		

Biram), and had permanent settlements in major cities of North and west Africa.

The Hausa language has been studied since the mid-19th century and books on Hausa grammar have been written in English, French, GERMAN, and RUSSIAN, as well as in Hausa itself.

Hausa has a rich tradition of oral and written stories, myths, and poetry. The poetry has been strongly influenced by Arabic traditions, but modern poetry is moving away from the classical style.

Orthography and Basic Phonology

Hausa orthography uses the normal letters of the English alphabet plus the three hooked letters ɓ, ɗ and ƙ the apostrophe ’ (indicating noninitial glottal stop); and ’y (a laryngealized semivowel). The English letters have normal English values except for *c*, which represents [ch], and *ts*, which represents an ejective sibilant [s’]. Tone and vowel length are not indicated in orthography. An attempt in Niger in the 1960s to indicate vowel length (by means of double letters) was subsequently dropped.

The writing of Hausa in LATIN script (termed *bookòo*) was introduced by colonial officers (British and French) at the beginning of the 20th century. Prior to that, Hausa had been written for a century (perhaps somewhat longer) using Arabic script, with minor modifications. Hausa in Arabic script (termed *àjàmi*) is still commonly employed by people with a good Islamic education.

Hausa has 32 consonants, as shown in Table 1 above. The letters *c* and *j* represent the affricates [tʃ] (as in English "church") and [dʒ] (as in English "judge") respectively. The /f/ phoneme is variably pronounced as [ɸ] (the norm), [f], [p], [h], or [hw], depending on dialect and phonological environment. There is no contrast between /f/ and /p/ in the language. The glottalized series includes both laryngealized and ejective obstruents. The "hooked" letters *ɓ* and *ɗ* are laryngealized, sometimes implosive, stops; *ƙ* (with its labialized and palatalized counterparts) is an ejective stop and the diagraph *ts* is an ejective sibilant or affricate. The symbol /’y/ represents a glottalized approximant, which is limited to a few very high frequency words. It is a historically recent phoneme, having developed from the sequence /ɗiy-/ via / ɗy/, cf. SH *’yaa* with WH *ɗìyaa* ‘daughter’. In word-final position, /n/ is pronounced [ŋ], e.g., *cân* ‘there’ = [câŋ]. Speakers of Standard Hausa usually also pronounce final /m/ as [ŋ], thereby resulting in the merger of the two phonemic nasals, e.g. *maalàm* ‘teacher’ = [maalàm] or [maalàŋ]. The symbol *r̃* is used to distinguish the apical tap or roll from the retroflex flap *r*. (This distinction is *not* indicated in standard orthography.) The apostrophe /’/ is used in standard orthography to indicate glottal stop, e.g., *saa’àa* ‘luck’, *jam’ìi* ‘plural’. It is not employed orthographically in word-initial position.

Table 2: Vowels

	Front		Back
High	i		u
Mid	e		o
Low		a	

There are five basic vowels, all of which have long and short counterparts, and two diphthongs, *ai* and *au*. The vowel-length contrast is only found in open syllables; in closed syllables, all vowels are short. Long vowels generally have typical IPA values, whereas the corresponding vowels are more lax and centralized. Vowel-length distinctions are not marked in standard orthography.

Hausa is basically a two-tone language. The two basic tones are low and high. The low tone is marked by a grave accent while the high is left unmarked. Examples are *kwàrii* ‘quiver (for arrows)' and *kwarìi* 'valley, lowland'. There is also a falling tone (indicated by a circumflex), which represents a combination of high plus low on a single (heavy) syllable. Examples are *mâi* 'oil' and *yâaraa* 'children'. There is no rising tone.

There are three types of syllables in the language: CV, CVV, and CVC. The first type is light and the other two are heavy. The vocalic part of the second type can be either a long vowel or a diphthong. Syllables may not contain both a long vowel (or a diphthong) and a final consonant. All Hausa syllables and words begin with a consonant. Words that appear in the orthography with an initial vowel begin phonemically with a glottal stop, e.g., the orthographic *aure* 'marriage' is phonemically represented thus: /*'auree*/. True consonant clusters are not allowed, although two consonants may abut across a syllable boundary, e.g., *han.tàa* 'liver'. Most words end in a vowel, the exceptions being ideophones, e.g., *wulik* 'emphasizing blackness'; recent loans e.g., *kyât* 'cake'; or the result of vowel apocopation, e.g., *kâr̃* = *kadà* 'don't'.

Syllable-final /n/ automatically assimilates to the position of following abutting consonants. In SH (but not in WH), syllable, final /m/ also usually does so. Coronal obstruents change to /r̃/ in syllable-final position, e.g., *'yar̃-sà* = *'yaa-ta-sà* 'his daughter' (lit. 'daughter-of-his'); *mar̃màtsaa* < //matsmàtsaa// 'push, pester repeatedly', cf. *matsàa* 'push, pester'. Syllable-final labial and velar obstruents assimilate fully and form a geminate with following abutting consonants, e.g., *zàzzaafaa* 'hot'< //zàfzaafaa//, cf. *zaafii* 'heat', *daddàkaa* 'pound repeatedly' < //dakdàkaa//, cf. *dakàa* 'pound'. When followed by a front vowel, either *i* or *e*, the alveolars *s*, *z*, and *t* palatalize to *sh*, *j*, and *c*, respectively. The voiced stop *d* also palatalizes to *j*, with resultant neutralization of the *z*/*d* contrast, but less regularly than with the above consonants. The semivowel /w/ palatalizes to *y*, e.g., *kàasuwaa* 'market', *kaasuwooyii* 'markets' (<//kaasuwoowii//). In closed syllables (resulting from the addition of morphological elements), long vowels automatically shorten and diphthongs reduce to short monophthongs. In normal speech tempo, short /e/ and /o/ are generally pronounced as schwa (thereby merging with each other and with short /a/), e.g., *kàree* 'dog', *kàre-n-sà* [kàrə-n-sà] 'his dog', *dòodoo* 'goblin', *dòodo-n-sà* [dòodə-n-sà] 'his goblin'.

Basic Morphology

There are two genders: masculine and feminine, in the singular only. There is no gender distinction in the plural. Feminine nouns almost all end in *–aa* (apart from recent loanwords); masculine nouns end in all five vowels, including *-aa*, e.g., feminine: *hantàa* 'liver', *raanaa* 'sun, day', *sàraunìyaa* 'queen'. masculine: *hancìi* 'nose', *watàa* 'moon, month', *sarkii* 'king'. Feminine nouns and adjectives are generally derived from the corresponding masculine forms by the addition of *-aa* (plus transitional /y/ or /w/ glides), e.g., *kàree* 'dog', *kàryaa* 'bitch', *saaboo* 'new (masc.)', *saabuwaa* 'new (fem.)'. The essence of Hausa morphosyntax is the genitival linker, which occurs in *N* of *N* constructions of various kinds. The linker occurs either as a particle (*ta* feminine, *na* not feminine [i.e. plural or masculine singular]), or as a vowelless clitic (*-r̃* feminine, *-n* not feminine [i.e., plural or masculine singular], e.g., *yaarò-n Muusaa* 'Musa's boy'; *raana-r̃ kàasuwaa* 'market day' (lit. 'day of market'); *dawaakin nàn na Muusaa* 'these horses of Musa' [lit. 'horses-of here of Musa']). There is no indefinite article. The definite article (which is really a previous reference marker indicating that the item in question has already been referred to in the discourse) is segmentally identical to the clitic form of the linker except that it has intrinsic low tone (which, when added to a word ending in high tone, produces a fall), e.g., *gidaa* 'house', *gidâ-n* 'the house', *raanaa* 'day' *raanâ-r̃* 'the day we were talking about'.

At a shallow surface level, there are some 40 different ways of forming purals. These include suffixation, (partial) reduplication, and infixation (internal *-a-*), or a combination thereof. Examples are: *rìigaa*/*rìigunàa* 'gown(s)'; *taagàa*/*taagoogii* 'window(s)'; *gulbii*/*gulàabee* 'stream(s)'; *daajìi*/*daazuzzukàa* 'forest(s)'; *dumaa*/*dumàamee* 'gourd(s)'; *fuskàa*/*fusàakaa* 'face(s)'.

Pronoun sets other than the "weak subject pronouns" have eight forms, namely 1sg, 2m.sg, 2f.sg, 3m.sg, 3f.sg, 1pl, 2pl, and 3pl (illustrated by the direct-object pronouns).

Personal pronouns (weak direct object set):

	Singular	Plural
1st	nì	mù
2nd.m	kà	kù
2nd.f	kì	
3rd.m	shì	sù
3rd.f	tà	

Weak subject pronouns have, in addition, an impersonal/indefinite pronoun /a/ 'one', comparable to French *on*, e.g. *à taashì* 'One should get up'.

Tense, aspect, and mood are components of a single conjugational system. They do not serve as independent crosscutting categories. They are indicated, not by changes in the form of the verb per se (except in those TAMs that require a verbal noun), but rather by a preverbal pronoun-aspect-complex (PAC) that occurs between the subject (if expressed) and the verb, e.g., *maataa* [*sunàa*] *dafà ruwaa* 'The women [they-CONTINUOUS] are boiling water'; *Faatimà* [*taa*] *dafà ruwaa* 'Fatima [she-PERFECTIVE] boiled water'. This PAC consists of a weak subject pronoun (WSP), and a TAM marker (in some cases segmentally distinct, in some cases consisting of tone and vowel length only, and in others phonologically zero). Examples (illustrated with the 3rd pl pronoun): *sun* PERFECTIVE; *sukà* PRETERITE (=RELATIVE-PERFECTIVE); *sunàa* CONTINUOUS; *sukèe* RELATIVE-CONTINUOUS; *sâa* (=*swâa*) POTENTIAL; *zaa sù* FUTURE; *sukàn* HABITUAL; *sukàa* RHETORICAL; *sù* SUBJUNCTIVE.

The essential morphological category reflected in the verb is its "grade". Each of the eight grades in Hausa has a distinct phonological specification, defined in terms of tone pattern and final vowel (or *-aC*), and a general grammatical/semantic characterization. Within a grade, the verb has various forms, depending on whether the verb occurs without an object (Form A), with a personal-pronoun object (Form B), or with any other direct object (Form C). Table 3 on the following page presents the forms of two- and three-syllable verbs (monosyllabic in the case of Grade 0).

Table 3: The Hausa Grade System

	Form A	Form B	Form C
Grade 0	-i/-aa H	-ii/-aa H	-i/-aa H
Grade 1	-aa HL(H)	-aa HL(H)	-a HL(L)
Grade 2	-aa LH(L)	-ee (L)LH	-i (L)LH
Grade 3	-a LH(L)		
Grade 4	-ee HL(H)	-ee HL(H)	-e HL(L) or -ee HL(H)
Grade 5	-ar̃/-as HH(H)	-ar̃/-as HH(H)	-ar̃/-as HH(H) or -shee HH(H)
Grade 6	-oo HH(H)	-oo HH(H)	-oo HH(H)
Grade 7	-u (L)LH		

Grade 0 contains the few basic high tone monosyllabic verbs that exist in the language, e.g., *ji* 'feel' *jaa* 'pull'. Grade 1 contains basic *a*-final verbs, e.g., *dafà* 'cook', as well as derived "applicatives" (often required with indirect objects). Grade 2, an exclusively transitive grade, contains basic verbs with final *-i*, e.g., *sàyi* 'buy', as well as derived verbs with a partitive sense. Grade 3 is an exclusively intransitive grade containing *a*-final basic verbs, e.g., *fita* 'go out'. Grade 4 ("totality") indicates an action totally done or affecting all the objects, e.g., *sayè(e)* 'buy up'. With many verbs, especially intransitives, Grade 4 is increasingly being used as a semantically neutral basic form. Grade 5 ("efferential"), traditionally termed "causative", indicates action directed away from speaker, e.g., *sayar̃* 'sell'. It also serves to transitivize certain inherently intransitive verbs, e.g. *fitar̃* 'take out'. Its direct object nouns are expressed obliquely using the preposition *dà* 'with', e.g., *naa zubar̃ dà mâi* 'I poured out the oil'. Grade 5 is unique among the grades in having considerable internal complexity as well as a great amount of dialectal variation. Grade 6 ("ventive") indicates action in the direction of or for the benefit of the speaker, e.g., *sayoo* 'buy and bring'. Grade 7 ("sustentative") indicates an agentless passive, middle voice, action well done, or the potentiality of sustaining action, e.g., *dàfu* 'be well cooked', *yanàa sàyuwaa* 'it is buyable'.

Most derivation/inflection is accomplished by the addition of suffixes. One also finds some derivation/inflection using prefixes or reduplication. In the case of suffixation (or partial reduplication to the right), the stem normally drops its final vowel. If the suffix is "toneintegrating" (as most are) the tone melody of the suffix is spread from right to left and overrides the lexical tone, e.g., *rìigaa* 'gown' + *-unaa* HL 'pl' > *riigunàa* 'gowns'. Two common derivational suffixes are *-(an)cii* H 'language or dialect', e.g., *Jaamusancii* 'German' from *Jaamùs* Germany, and *-ayyaa* LHL 'mutuality' e.g., *bùgayyàa* 'beating one another' from *bugàa* 'to beat'. The main prefixes are *bà-* 'ethnonym', e.g., *bàhaushèe* 'a Hausa person' < *Hausa*, and *ma-*, indicating agent, instrument, or location depending on the final vowel and tone, e.g., *manòomii* 'a farmer' < *noomàa* 'to farm', *magirbii* 'a harvesting tool' < *girbèe* 'to harvest', *marinaa* 'a dyeing place' < *rinàa* 'to dye'. Reduplication with verbs produces "pluractional" verb stems, i.e., verbs indicating that an action has been done multiple times or individually by multiple people, e.g., *ginàa* 'build' *gingìnaa* (pluractional) 'build many or often'. Compounding is extensive and productive. The two most common types of compounds are *N* of *N* compounds, e.g., *gàashì-n-bàaki* 'moustache' (lit. 'hair-of-mouth') and V-N compounds, e.g., *hànà-sallà* 'baseball cap' (lit. prevent prayer).

Basic Syntax

The basic order of verbal sentences in Hausa is SVO. If there is an indirect object, it normally precedes the direct object: *Muusaa yaa kaawoo matà ruwaa* (Musa he brought to her water) 'Musa brought her water'. The language is prepositional, e.g. *à Kanoo* 'at Kano'.

Equational sentences have the structure X Y STABILIZER (where the stabilizer is a gender sensitive grammatical particle), *cee* (with polar tone) with feminine singular items, *nee* (with polar tone) with plural and with masculine singular items, e.g., *shaahòo tsuntsuu nèe* (hawk bird STAB) 'A hawk is a bird'.

If the subject X is not expressed, one has an identificational sentence, e.g., *Kànde cèe* 'It's Kande (woman's name)'; *dookìi nee* 'It's a horse'.

Existential sentences have the structure there-is (or there-is-not) Y: *àkwai ruwaa* 'There is water'; *baabù ruwaa* 'There isn't any water'. There is no overt case. Normally the head noun precedes modifiers (such as numerals, possessives, and adjectives), e.g., *kèeke ɗaya* 'one bicycle', *kèeke na ukù* 'third bicycle', *kèeke-n yaaròo* 'boy's bicycle', *kèeke-n nàn* 'this bicycle', *kèeke farii* 'white bicycle'. Nouns may be preceded by an adjective plus a genitive linker or by a long-form demonstrative, e.g., *wannàn kèeke* 'this bicycle', *fari-n kèeke* 'white bicycle', *wannàn fari-n kèeke* 'this white bicycle'. With exceptions, indicated below, negation is indicated by a discontinuous morpheme *bà(a)...ba*, e.g., *bà tà daawoo ba* (NEG she return NEG) 'She did not return'; *ita bàa likità ba cèe.* (she NEG doctor NEG STAB) 'She is not a doctor'.

The negative continuous (progressive) uses only a single *baa* in the front, e.g., *baa tàa dafàawaa* 'She is not cooking (it)'. The negative subjunctive (and imperative) uses a negative prohibitive marker *kadà*, e.g., *kadà kù daawoo* 'Don't you (pl.)

return'. The negative existential uses *baabù* = *bâ* in place of the affirmative marker, e.g., *baabù tî* 'There isn't any tea', cf. *àkwai tî* 'There is tea'. Yes/no questions have normal word order. The question is indicated by question intonation, sometimes with a final question particle as well, e.g., *zaa kà sàyi mootàa (koo)*? 'Are you going to buy a car?' Q-word questions generally involve fronting of the questioned item, e.g.:

mèe zaa kà sàyaa?
what FUTURE you buy
'What will you buy?'

su-wàa sukà jee sìniimàa
they-who they:PRETERITE go cinema
'Who (pl.) went to the cinema?'

Contact with Other Languages

Hausa has borrowed extensively from other languages, including Arabic, Mande, Tuareg, and KANURI (not to mention the loanwords in this century from English and French). Arabic loans are the most numerous and some have come via the African languages listed. Arabic loanwords are found especially pertaining to religion (particularly Islam), government, law, warfare, horsemanship, literature and mathematics. Such words are well integrated into Hausa morphology. Recently technical words from Arabic have been imported into Hausa.

From Arabic: *bayyànaa* 'explain', *illaa* 'except', *mulkìi* 'rule, control, power', *sallàa* 'prayer', *tàmàanin* 'eighty', *wàsiyyàa* 'will, last testament'

From English: *biizàa* 'visa', *Dìsambàa* 'December', *fàr̃feesàa* = *fùr̃òofeesàa* 'professor', *tikitì* 'ticket'

Common Words

man:	mùtûm	long:	doogoo
woman:	màcè	small:	ƙàramii
water:	ruwaa	yes:	ii
sun:	raanaa	no:	aa'àa
three:	ukù	bird:	tsuntsuu
fish:	kiifii	dog:	kàree
big:	bàbba	tree:	bishiyàa

Example Sentences

(1) maalàmi-n-mù yaa sàyi saabuwa-r̃ mootàa baƙaa.
teacher-of-us he:PERFECTIVE buy new-of car black
'Our teacher bought a new black car.'

(2) su-wàa sukà ga yaarò-n dà ya
they-who they:PRETERITE saw boy-the that he:PRETERITE

saacè zoobè-n?
stole ring-the
'Who (plural) saw the boy who stole the ring (in question)?'

(3) leebur̃oor̃ii sunàa ciccìkaa
laborers they:CONTINUOUS fill:PLURACTIONAL

manà buhunhunàa dà gyàɗaa.
for.us sacks with peanut(s)
'The laborers are continuing to fill the sacks with peanuts for us.'

Efforts to Preserve, Protect, and Promote the Language

Hausa is one of three official indigenous languages of Nigeria. (The other two are YORUBA and IGBO.)

Hausa continues to spread as a lingua franca throughout northern Nigeria, especially in urban areas. Many speakers of small minority languages are now giving up their own languages and are switching to Hausa.

In northern Nigeria, Hausa is commonly used as a language of instruction in elementary schools, especially in the lower grades. Before Nigerian independence in1960, most Hausa language study was in Europe and the U.S.; today it is also active in Nigeria. The main institution for promoting research on and publications in Hausa is the Centre for the Study of Nigerian Languages, Bayero University, Kano. In the U.S., Hausa language and literature courses are taught in major universities such as Boston University, Columbia University, Indiana University, the University of Kansas, Ohio State University, Stanford University, UCLA, and the University of Wisconsin.

Select Bibliography

Ahmed, Umaru, and Bello Daura. 1970. *An Introduction to Classical Hausa and the Major Dialects.* Zaria, Nigeria: NNPC.

Bargery, G.P. 1934. *A Hausa-English Dictionary and English-Hausa Vocabulary.* London: Oxford University Press. [Reprint with supplement and new introduction by Neil Skinner, Ahmadu Bello University Press (Zaria), 1993].

Gouffé, Claude. 1981. "La langue haoussa." In *Les langues dans le monde ancien et moderne,* Part I, ed. Gabriel Manessy, 415–428. Paris: CNRS.

Newman, Paul. 1987. "Hausa and the Chadic Languages." In *The World's Major Languages*, ed. Bernard Comrie, 705–723. London: Croom Helm.

____. 1991. "A Century and a Half of Hausa Language Studies." In *Nigerian Languages: Yesterday, Today, and Tomorrow*, ed. Abba Rufa'i, 1–18. Kano: CSNL, Bayero University.

____. 1992. "Hausa." In *International Encyclopedia of Linguistics.* Vol. 2, 103–109. New York: Oxford University Press.

____. 2000. *The Hausa Language: An Encyclopedic Reference Grammar.* New Haven: Yale University Press.

Newman, Paul, and Roxana Ma Newman. 1977. *Modern Hausa-English Dictionary (Sabon Kamus na Hausa zuwa Turanci).* Ibadan, Nigeria: Oxford University Press.

Newman, Roxana Ma. 1990. *An English-Hausa Dictionary.* New Haven: Yale University Press.

Parsons, F. W. 1981. *Writings on Hausa Grammar: The Collected Papers of F.W. Parsons,* ed. Graham L. Furniss. Ann Arbor, MI: UMI Books on Demand.

Skinner, Neil. 1968. *Hausa Readings: Selections from Edgar's Tatsuniyoyi.* Madison: University of Wisconsin Press.

Wolff, H. Ekkehard. 1993. *Referenzgrammatik des Hausa.* (Hamburger Beiträge zur Afrikanistik, 2). Münster & Hamburg: LIT.

Biblical Hebrew

Gary A. Rendsburg

Language Name: Biblical Hebrew. **Autonyms:** In the Bible the language is called *Śəpat Kənaʕan*, literally 'lip (that is, language) of Canaan', reflecting no distinction between Hebrew and other Canaanite dialects (see below); the specific dialect of Judah is called *Yəhûdît* 'Judahite'. In the early postbiblical period we encounter the name *ʕIvrît* 'Hebrew', and this name continues to be used in MODERN HEBREW when referring to the Hebrew language, whether ancient or modern. Jews of the early postbiblical period also called the language *Ləšôn haq-qōdeš,* literally 'the holy tongue', a term that continued to be used in later periods.

Location: Israel. Also, because of the unique circumstances of the Diaspora of the Jews, Biblical Hebrew spread throughout the world. With the Babylonian conquest of Israel in general and Jerusalem, in particular, in 586 B.C., and even more so after the Roman destruction of Jerusalem in A.D. 70, Jews settled in other countries. In all cases they adopted the languages of these countries for everyday usage, both spoken and written, but they continued to read the Bible and other classical texts in Hebrew. (An important exception is the Jews of Ethiopia who read the Bible in GE'EZ.) Thus, Hebrew spread as the language of Judaism into areas of Asia, North Africa, and Europe, and in more modern times to the Americas, South Africa, and Australia.

Family: Northwest Semitic subgroup of the West Semitic group of the Semitic branch of the Afro-Asiastic language family.

Related Languages: Most closely related to the other dialects of Canaanite (see below), then to ARAMAIC, ARABIC, AKKADIAN, South Arabian and Ge'ez.

Dialects: Biblical Hebrew is one of a number of closely related dialects of the Canaanite language, which, along with Aramaic constitutes the Northwest Semitic language group. Other dialects of Canaanite include Ugaritic[1] (attested at a slightly earlier time), PHOENICIAN, Ammonite, Moabite, and Edomite (all attested contemporaneously with Bibical Hebrew).

Biblical Hebrew, in turn, can be divided into two subdialects: Judahite, referring to the subdialect of Judah in southern Israel, and Israelian, referring to the subdialect or dialect cluster of northern Israel (including the areas settled by those Israelite tribes east of the Jordan River). The evidence for these different varieties stems from an analysis of the biblical books themselves: about 80 percent of the Bible was written in Judah and reflects Judahite Hebrew, while approximately 20 percent was written in northern Israel and reflects Israelian Hebrew.

There is also evidence for the existence of diglossia in ancient Hebrew. The Bible is written in a classical literary register (whether Judahite or Israelian), but divergences from the grammatical standard are often colloquial uses that have crept into the text.

Origin and History

Hebrew is the dialect of Canaanite used by the people of Israel. The early history of Hebrew is thus part of a larger picture, the history of Canaanite. The earliest evidence for Canaanite comes from two sources: (a) Ugaritic, referring to the texts found at Ugarit (modern Ras Shamra on the Syrian coast), and (b) the Amarna letters (found at modern Tell el-Amarna, Egypt).

Ugarit was destroyed about 1200 B.C., so the majority of its texts, mainly administrative in nature, clearly come from the 13th century. The literary texts, mainly myths and epics, are probably older, and we can date their composition to the 14th century B.C., if not earlier. The Amarna letters are several hundred epistles written by local Canaanite kings to the pharaohs of Egypt in the mid-14th century B.C. They were written in Akkadian, but the scribes responsible for these letters typically used a pidgin Akkadian. The morphology and syntax frequently follow Canaanite grammar rather than Akkadian grammar, and often Canaanite words are used instead of their Akkadian equivalents.

About a century and a half after the Ugaritic literary texts and the Amarna letters come our earliest biblical texts. Biblical Hebrew is typically divided into three chronological periods: Archaic (about 1100–1000 B.C.), Standard (about 1000–550 B.C.), and Late (550–200 B.C.). Archaic Biblical Hebrew is represented by only a handful of ancient poems in the Bible. Standard Biblical Hebrew makes up most of the corpus and includes such familiar works as the Torah; the books of Joshua, Judges, Samuel, and Kings; prophets such as Amos, Isaiah, and Jeremiah; and poetic compilations such as Psalms and Proverbs. Late Biblical Hebrew, which is characterized most of all by influences from Aramaic, the lingua franca of that period, is represented by books such as Chronicles, Esther, Ezra, Nehemiah, and Qohelet (Ecclesiastes).

Archaeological fieldwork in the last century has uncovered hundreds of Hebrew inscriptions from the biblical period, most extremely short.

[1]Many scholars consider Ugaritic to be an independent language and not a dialect of Canaanite.

Table 1: Consonants

		Labial	Dental/ Alveolar	Alveo-palatal	Velar	Pharyngeal	Glottal
Stops	Voiceless	p	t ṭ		k, q		ʔ
	Voiced	b	d		g		
Fricatives	Voiceless		s ṣ	š	x	ḥ	h
	Voiced		z		ǵ	ʕ	
Nasals		m	n				
Laterals	Voiceless			ś			
	Voiced		l				
Trill			r				
Glides		w		y			

Technically, Biblical Hebrew should refer only to the Hebrew of the Bible (and perhaps the contemporary inscriptions). But postbiblical compositions are written in the same language, typically in the natural continuation of Late Biblical Hebrew. Among these are the literary work Ben Sira (Ecclesiasticus), dated about 180 B.C., and most importantly, the Dead Sea Scrolls (found at Qumran), dated about 150 B.C. to about A.D. 50. Eventually Hebrew died out as a spoken language; the best estimate is approximately A.D. 220. But Jews continued to write texts in Hebrew, although not in Biblical Hebrew, even in its latest stage, but in a more colloquial variety known as Mishnaic Hebrew (named after the Mishna, a classic text of law and practice dated about A.D. 220).

Orthography and Basic Phonology

Hebrew is written in a 22-letter alphabet that was invented by the Phoenicians. The 22 letters indicate consonants only, and the direction of writing is right to left.

The letter forms evolved over time. In the alphabet table appear both the ancient Hebrew letters, as originally borrowed from the Phoenicians, and the more familiar Hebrew alphabet still in use to this day. The latter alphabet includes five additional graphemes used in final position only.

At first, Biblical Hebrew orthography did not express the vowels. In time, the letters *y, w,* and *h* came to be used to indicate final vowels (quite regularly) and medial long vowels (sporadically). When used in this manner, these letters are called *matres lectionis*, or 'vowel letters'. This process is seen more fully developed in the Dead Sea Scrolls, where almost all long vowels are marked by vowel letters. In the transliteration system adopted in this chapter, *matres lectionis* are indicated by superscript letters.

In about A.D. 850 Jewish scholars known as the Masoretes (tradents) developed a series of markings to indicate the vowels. These markings typically are dots and dashes placed either above or below the line. Actually, three different systems were invented, although in time the one developed at Tiberias (in northern Israel) became the standard system utilized by Jews. In addition, the Masoretes developed diacritical marks to indicate distinctions not shown by the 22-letter alphabet, such as a dot inside a letter to indicate a doubled consonant. The text that the Masoretes produced is known as the Masoretic Text. It reproduces in writing the traditional pronunciation of the received biblical text of the late first millennium A.D. At the same time, however, scholars agree that the traditional pronunciation harks back to a much earlier period.

There were 25 distinct consonants in Biblical Hebrew, even though the alphabet had only 22 letters. A single letter *ḥ* was used to indicate both /ḥ/ and /x/; ʕ was used to indicate both /ʕ/ and /ǵ/; and *š* was used to indicate both /š/ and /ś/. In the other 19 instances, there is a one-to-one correspondence between orthography and consonantal phonology. In the course of time, /ś/ merged with /s/. When scribes wished to use a historical orthography, they continued to write *ś*; when they wished to use a more phonetic orthography, they used *s*. Also, /x/ eventually merged with /ḥ/, and /ǵ/ with /ʕ/.

The phonemes /ṭ/ /q/ /ṣ/ are known as emphatics. The exact articulation of these consonants in Biblical Hebrew is unknown. The corresponding consonants in Arabic are velarized or pharyngealized; the corresponding consonants in South Arabian and Ethiopian Semitic are glottalized.

At some point in ancient Hebrew, the six stops /b/ /p/ /d/ /t/ /g/ /k/ developed a two-fold realization. Following vowels, they came to be pronounced as fricatives /v/ /f/ /ð/ /θ/ /ǵ/ /x/; otherwise, they remained stops.

Consonant gemination was phonemic in ancient Hebrew. In theory all consonants could be single or geminate except that in the Masoretic Text, /ʔ/ /h/ /ʕ/ /ḥ/ /r/ can occur only single. When morphological processes would have geminated one of those seven consonants, the quality of the vowel in the preceding syllable generally changed instead.

Table 2: Vowels

	Front	Central	Back
High	i î		u û
Mid	ê		ô
Low		a â	

Historically, there were three simple vowels in Semitic, short /a/ /i/ /u/ and long /â/ /î/ /û/. In the course of time, the Hebrew

Table 3: The Hebrew Alphabet

Ancient Form	Familiar Form	Value	Ancient Form	Familiar Form	Value
𐤀	א	ʔ	𐤋	ל	l
𐤁	ב	b	𐤌	מ (final ם)	m
𐤂	ג	g	𐤍	נ (final ן)	n
𐤃	ד	d	𐤎	ס	s
𐤄	ה	h	𐤏	ע	ʕ, ǵ
𐤅	ו	w	𐤐	פ (final ף)	p
𐤆	ז	z	𐤑	צ (final ץ)	ṣ
𐤇	ח	ḥ, x	𐤒	ק	q
𐤈	ט	ṭ	𐤓	ר	r
𐤉	י	y	𐤔	ש	š, ś
𐤊	כ (final ך)	k	𐤕	ת	t

short vowels developed various allophones, depending on the kind of syllable in which the vowel occurred (open or closed) and depending on syllable stress. The Masoretic notation system (described above) indicates all these fine differences. In the transliteration system used in this chapter, some of these allophones are marked by a macron (for example, *ā*). The original long vowels, marked by a circumflex, are not affected by type of syllable or by placement of accent.

Ancient Hebrew also had two diphthongs, *ay* and *aw*. Generally in unaccented syllables and occasionally in accented syllables, these diphthongs became monophthongs /ê/ and /ô/.

Stress in Biblical Hebrew was generally on the final syllable in a phrase. Short vowels in unstressed open syllables typically were reduced to [ə].

Basic Morphology

As with all Semitic languages, Hebrew morphology is characterized by the interplay of root and pattern. Most roots consist of three consonants, and they may occur in any number of typical verbal and nominal patterns. For example, the root Z-K-R appears as a simple verb *zākar* 'he remembered'; in a derived verb *hizkî^{y}r* 'he caused to remember, he reminded'; in a participial form of the latter *mazkî^{y}r* 'recorder, secretary'; and in the noun forms *zēker* 'remembrance', *zikkārô^{w}n* 'memorial', and *ʔazkārā^{h}* 'memorial-sacrifice'.

Hebrew nouns are inflected for number (singular, plural [and, in some cases, dual]), gender (masculine, feminine), and definition (definite, indefinite). There are numerous nominal patterns, often with associated semantic qualities. For example, $C_1iC_2C_2\bar{e}C_3$ is used for nouns representing people with bodily defects (such as a blind person, lame person, or hunchback); $C_1aC_2C_2\hat{a}C_3$ is used for professions (such as a cook, archer, or horseman).

The definite article is *ha-* with the following consonant geminated: *melek* 'king', *hammelek* 'the king'. There is no indefinite article.

Hebrew adjectives agree with the nouns they modify in number, gender, and definition:

mište^{h}	gādô^{w}l
feast:MASC.INDEF	large:MASC.INDEF

'a large feast' (Genesis 21:8)

hā-ʕî^{y}r	hag-gədô^{w}l-ā^{h}
the-city:FEM	the-large-FEM

'the large city' (Jonah 1:1)

The Hebrew verb can appear in two conjugations, one utilizing suffixes and one utilizing mostly prefixes (accompanied by a few suffixes). Scholars still debate whether these conjugations reflect different tenses (present/future versus past) or aspects (imperfect versus perfect). Hence, they are often simply referred to as the suffix and prefix conjugations, respectively. The suffixes and prefixes indicate the person, number, and gender of the subject (gender distinctions are not made in the first person).

Hebrew verbs occur in a limited number of patterns, with the following the most common. The simple pattern is, as with *zākar* above, $C_1\bar{a}C_2aC_3$. A pattern $C_1iC_2C_2\bar{e}C_3$, with the middle root consonant doubled, often has a resultative meaning. The pattern $hiC_1C_2\hat{\imath}C_3$, with prefixed *hi-*, generally has a causative meaning, as with *hizkî^{y}r* above. The pattern $hitC_1aC_2C_2\bar{e}C_3$, with prefixed *hit-*, has a reflexive force. (All forms cited are third person masculine singulars from the suffix conjugation, the typical citation form.)

Hebrew has two sets of pronouns: free or independent forms, and bound or suffixed forms. They are inflected like the verb. The free forms serve as subjects. The bound forms have possessive meaning when suffixed to nouns and objective meaning when suffixed to verbs or prepositions. An unusual feature of Biblical Hebrew is the presence of two first person singular pronouns *ʔ^{a}nî^{y}* and *ʔānôkî^{y}*, apparently used interchangeably, although some scholars have detected syntactic or stylistic criteria determining which form is used.

The conjunction *wa-* 'and' and several common prepositions (*lə-* 'to, for', *bə-* 'in', *kə-* 'as, like') do not appear as independent forms, but instead are prefixed to the following word.

Basic Syntax

The basic word order in Biblical Hebrew was VSO. However, for emphasis, the subject or object could occur in initial position.

Biblical Hebrew has a special compound verb form used regularly for past-tense narration. Its third person masculine singular form appears as *wayyi*C_1C_2*ō*C_3, comprised of the conjunction *wa-* (serving here as a copula), the agreement marker *y* (doubled, most likely because a special past-tense marker *n* has been absorbed), and the verbal stem.

Verbless clauses and sentences (for identification or classification) occur frequently because there is no copula. For example:

hûʔ	ʔ^{a}dôn-î^{y}	
he	master-my	'He is my master.' (Genesis 24:65)

Adjectives follow the nouns they modify (see examples below).

Two nouns are often juxtaposed to create a construct phrase. This construction may indicate possession, or it may best be rendered by an adjectival phrase in ENGLISH. If the construct phrase is definite, the definite article is prefixed to the second of the two nouns only. If the construct phrase is plural, only the first of the two nouns is so marked:

bigəd-ê^{y}	haq-qōdeš
garment-PL.CONSTRUCT	the-holiness

'the holy garments' (Exodus 29:29)

A special form *ʔet*, with no translation equivalent, appears before definite nouns serving as the direct object.

Negation is accomplished by placing one of three different words, *lôʔ*, *ʔal*, or *ʔê^{y}n*, all essentially 'no' or 'not', before the word or phrase being negated. The choice depends on which part of speech follows.

Contact with Other Languages

Israel is at the crossroads of the ancient world, situated on the land bridge uniting Egypt and Mesopotamia, and with access to both the Mediterranean Sea and the Red Sea. In addition, mighty empires such as the Egyptian, Persian, and Greek ones ruled the land for centuries. Accordingly, Hebrew is in a unique position to have borrowed loanwords from a variety of languages. Among the best examples are the following:

From EGYPTIAN: *gômeʔ* 'papyrus', *ʔētû^{w}n* 'linen'
From SUMERIAN: *kissēʔ* 'chair', *mallāḥ* 'sailor'
From Akkadian: *sārî^{y}s* 'eunuch', *šēgal* 'queen, consort'
From Aramaic: *k^{e}tāb* 'writing', *q^{e}rāb* 'battle'
From PERSIAN: *dāt* 'law', *pardēs* 'garden'
From GREEK: *lappî^{y}d* 'torch', *məkērā^{h}* 'sword'

The Sumerian loanwords require a special comment. By the time of the earliest attestation of Hebrew, Sumerian was already a dead language for centuries. These loanwords presumably reached the West Semitic world at a very early date, in the third millennium B.C., and Hebrew simply inherited them from earlier Canaanite. Alternatively, although less likely, they might have entered Hebrew through Akkadian.

The Greek loanwords above are early borrowings into Hebrew, the result of trade and contact in the east Mediterranean during the Late Bronze and Early Iron Ages. Later, after the conquests of Alexander the Great, many more Greek words entered Hebrew. And still later, although well beyond the biblical period, LATIN loanwords entered Hebrew.

Also, trade contacts to the east brought the names of exotic spices, gems, woods, and animals into Hebrew. Most of these probably came from SANSKRIT, such as *tukkî^{y}* 'type of bird (parrot?)', while for others the exact origin cannot be determined, for example, *qinnāmô^{w}n* 'cinnamon'.

In the opposite direction, hundreds of Canaanite words entered the Egyptian language during the Late Bronze Age when many West Semites settled in the Egyptian delta. The biblical portrayal of the Israelites in Egypt (end of the book of Genesis and beginning of the book of Exodus) is part of this picture. Clearly the Israelites were not responsible for the introduction of all the words into Egyptian since they were but one among many groups of West Semites resident in Egypt then. But Hebrew is the best-attested Canaanite dialect. In the same way, we are able to point to a considerable number of Hebrew words present in the ancient Greek lexicon, probably transmitted by the Phoenicians through their contacts in the Aegean. Examples include (in their familiar English forms) *griffin, nectar, and balsam.*

In more recent times, Hebrew words were borrowed into numerous languages of the world, because of the Jewish Diaspora, and perhaps more importantly resulting from the spread of Christianity. Since Christianity adopted many ideas of Judaism and canonized the Bible of Judaism (to which it added other books, most importantly the New Testament, itself containing many Hebraisms), Hebrew words naturally entered the languages of Europe and elsewhere. Examples in English are *amen, jubilee, manna, Sabbath*, and of course many familiar personal names.

Common Words

man:	ʔî^{y}š	long:	ʔārôk
woman:	ʔiššā^{h}	small:	qāṭān
water:	mayim	tree:	ʕēṣ
sun:	šemeš	three:	šālôš
good:	ṭô^{w}b	fish:	dāg
bird:	ṣippôr	big:	gādô^{w}l
dog:	keleb	no:	lôʔ
yes:	no true equivalent; ʔāk = 'indeed'		

Example Sentences*

(1) wa-y-y-iqqaḥ	ʔabrām	ʔet	śāray	ʔišt-ô^{w}
and-PAST-3M.SG-takes	Abram	ACC	Sarai	wife-his

wə-ʔet	lô^{w}ṭ	ben	ʔāḥ-îw.
and-ACC	Lot	son:CONSTRUCT	brother-his

'Abram took Sarai his wife and Lot his brother's son.'

(2) wa-y-y-irʔ-û^{w} ʔôt-ā^{h} śār-êy parʕôh.
and-PAST-3M-see-PL ACC-her officer-PL.CONSTRUCT Pharaoh
'Pharaoh's officers saw her.'

(3) wə-śāray ʔēšet ʔabrām lôʔ yāləd-ā^{h} l-ô.
and-Sarai wife:CONSTRUCT Abram NEG bear-3F.SG to-him
'And Sarai the wife of Abram had not borne to him (a child).'

*All sentences are from the book of Genesis.

Efforts to Preserve, Protect, and Promote the Language

Throughout their history Jews have continued to read the Bible in Hebrew, thus transmitting the language without interruption for 3,000 years. In the Middle Ages, Jewish scholars wrote grammars and dictionaries of Biblical Hebrew. Christian scholars also learned Hebrew during different historical epochs and made important contributions to the study of the language.

Hebrew was revived as a language for everyday use in the late 19th and early 20th centuries. Individuals such as Eliezer Ben-Yehuda looked to the Biblical Hebrew lexicon for roots from which to build new words necessary to express modern concepts and technological advances. For example, Biblical Hebrew *bārāq* 'lightning' provided the root for Modern Hebrew *mivrāq* 'telegram'. The Academy of the Hebrew Language, an official arm of the State of Israel, is responsible for monitoring linguistic development and for coining new words today, and it continues the same process of mining the ancient Hebrew lexicon.

Select Bibliography

Blau, J. 1976. *A Grammar of Biblical Hebrew*. Wiesbaden, Germany: Otto Harrassowitz.

Clines, D.J.A., ed. 1993–. *The Dictionary of Classical Hebrew*. 8 vols. Sheffield, England: Sheffield Academic Press.

Joüon, P., and T. Muraoka. 1991. *A Grammar of Biblical Hebrew*. Rome: Pontificio Istituto Biblico.

Kutscher, E.Y. 1982. *A History of the Hebrew Language*. R. Kutscher, ed. Jerusalem: Magnes Press.

Sáenz-Badillos, A. 1993. *A History of the Hebrew Language*. Cambridge: Cambridge University Press.

Waldman, N.M. 1989. *The Recent Study of Hebrew*. Cincinnati: Hebrew Union College Press.

Waltke, B.K., and M. O'Connor. 1990. *An Introduction to Biblical Hebrew Syntax*. Winona Lake, IN: Eisenbrauns.

Modern Hebrew

Monica S. Devens

Language Name: Modern Hebrew, Israeli Hebrew. **Autonym:** *Ivrit* 'Hebrew', *Ivrit Meduberet* 'Spoken Hebrew'.

Location: Israel, plus limited usage by Jews throughout the world.

Family: Canaanite subgroup of the Northwest Semitic group of the Semitic subfamily of the Afro-Asiatic language family.

Related Languages: Most closely related to other members of the Canaanite subgroup: Ugaritic, PHOENICIAN, Ammonite, Moabite, and Edomite. ARAMAIC is the other main branch of the Northwest Semitic group.

The unusual history of Hebrew has, however, rendered these closest genetic relationships relatively meaningless. To all intents and purposes, Modern Hebrew is the only living descendant of any of these languages. More important, Modern Hebrew has been so extensively influenced by the Germanic and Slavic languages that its affinities are unclear to some.

For these reasons, the closest relative to Modern Hebrew among the surviving Semitic languages is undoubtedly ARABIC.

Dialects: There are two principal dialects of Modern Hebrew: General Israeli Hebrew (GIH) and Oriental Israeli Hebrew (OIH). As the name implies, GIH is spoken by a broad spectrum of Israeli society. OIH is spoken by a subset of those whose families trace their origins to the countries of the Middle East and North Africa.

The differences between these two dialects are largely phonetic. OIH speakers maintain the phoneme /ħ/, (represented by the letter ח) as a voiceless pharyngeal fricative [ħ], while GIH speakers render it as a velar [x]. Furthermore, OIH speakers often pronounce some form of the phoneme /ʿ/ (represented by the letter ע), whether as a voiced glide or as an effect on the surrounding vowels, while GIH speakers do not.

Although GIH and OIH began their existence as geographically based dialects, there is some evidence that they are shifting to dialects representative of different social classes, with GIH representing a more affluent or educated population.

Number of Speakers: 4–5 million.

Origin and History

While the Jews never stopped using Hebrew for written composition, by the 3rd century at the very latest there were no living native speakers of the language. This situation held until the end of the 19th century.

In the 1880s, as part of the nationalist push toward the settlement of the Jews in Palestine, a movement to revive Hebrew as the spoken language of the Jewish people began. It was spearheaded by Eliezer Ben-Yehuda (Perlman), a European Jew who moved to Jerusalem with his family, and advanced largely by the teachers of the Jewish settlements who began to use the developing spoken language as the language of instruction (*Ivrit be-Ivrit*).

A concerted effort was made on the part of Ben-Yehuda and the newly established *Va'ad Ha-Lashon* ('Language Committee') to create new vocabulary, suitable for modern times. They searched earlier stages of the language for roots, words, and constructions that could be reformed to modern needs, and borrowed both vocabulary and morphological patterns from the sister languages of Arabic and Aramaic, even at times from GREEK or LATIN.

For almost 75 years, Modern Hebrew existed in a state of flux. New vocabulary words introduced by language planners were often rejected by the actual speakers of the language, many in favor of pan-European replacements. Factions promoting different pronunciations flourished for a time in various parts of the country. Debates raged as to the relative worth of Biblical or Rabbinic Hebrew or both as a base for the new language.

In 1953 the Academy of the Hebrew Language was established, replacing the *Va'ad Ha-Lashon*, and by 1960 Modern Hebrew had become solidified as a language. While most scholars would accept that it is still a Semitic language, all would agree that it is not simply Classical Hebrew reborn, but rather a new construct all its own.

Orthography and Basic Phonology

Modern Hebrew is written from right to left, using a system of 22 consonantal letters (see the chart on the next page). Five of these consonants have a special shape used in word-final position only. Vowels are indicated sporadically by using the consonant *y* to signify /i/ or /e/, the consonant *v* to signify /o/ or /u/, and a final *h* to indicate a preceding /a/. When the *y* or *v* is truly a consonant, two are written, such as *yy* or *vv*. The system of dots and dashes used in earlier stages of the language is rarely used for Modern Hebrew.

Most Hebrew consonants are pronounced essentially the same as they are in ENGLISH (see Table 1). Hebrew /c/ corresponds to English 'ts' as in 'nuts', while Hebrew /š/ is the 'sh' sound of English 'short'. The glottal stop /'/, infrequent in both Hebrew and English, is the sound between the two syllables of 'uh-oh'.

Otherwise, Hebrew /x/ is the same as the combination 'ch' in GERMAN *Bach*, while Hebrew /r/ is similar to the FRENCH.

Table 1: Consonants

		Labial	Dental	Palatal	Velar	Uvular	Glottal
Stops	Voiceless	p	t		k		ʼ
	Voiced	b	d		g		
Fricatives	Voiceless	f	s	š	x		h
	Voiced	v	z			r	
Affricate			c				
Nasals		m	n				
Lateral			l				
Glide				y			

The Hebrew Alphabet

א	ʼ	ל	l
ב	b or v	מ	m
ג	g	נ	n
ד	d	ס	s
ה	h	ע	ʽ
ו	v or vowel	פ	p or f
ז	z	צ	c
ח	x	ק	k
ט	t	ר	r
י	y or vowel	ש	š or s
כ	k or x	ת	t

Final forms are:

ך	x	ף	f
ם	m	ץ	c
ן	n		

Modern Hebrew exhibits a truncated version of the older Hebrew system of spirantization of stops /b/ /p/ /k/. While in earlier stages of Hebrew, the fricatives [/v/ /f/ /x/] were found following vowels and the stops [/p/ /t/ /k/] everywhere else, in Modern Hebrew this system remains in a state of flux.

/h/ is generally not pronounced except at the beginning of an utterance.

Table 2: Vowels

	Front	Central	Back
High	i		u
Mid	e	ə	o
Low		a	

Hebrew stress is commonly word final, although there are classes of nouns and specific verbal conjugations that exhibit penultimate stress. In addition, proper names are generally given penultimate stress, most often ascribed to the influence of YIDDISH. Thus, *tová* is a noun 'favor', while *tóva* is a woman's name.

Basic Morphology

Nouns may be masculine or feminine, singular or plural, definite or indefinite. The feminine gender, plural number, and definite state are the marked forms. The feminine singular most often carries a final *-a* or *-t*, while the plural is formed by a final *-im* (masculine) or *-ot* (feminine). There are sometimes changes in the noun stem as well, as illustrated by the forms of the noun 'child' below:

	Singular	Plural
Masculine	yéled	yəladím
Feminine	yaldá	yəladót

The definite article is *ha-*: *hayéled* 'the child'.

There is no true case system, but definite direct objects are marked by the word *et*.

The pronominal system exhibits gender differentiation in the second and third persons, and number differentiation in all persons. Subject pronouns are free forms, but object pronouns are suffixes that may be found either on the direct object marker *et* or on a preposition (for example, *l-* 'to' in the chart below).

	Subject	Object
1sg	ani	l-i
2m/sg	ata	l-əxa
2f/sg	at	l-ax
3m/sg	hu	l-o
3f/sg	hi	l-a
1pl	anáxnu	l-ánu
2m/pl	atem	l-axem
2f/pl	aten	l-axen
3m/pl	hem	l-ahem
3f/pl	hen	l-ahen

Adjectives follow the nouns they modify and agree with them in number, gender, and definiteness:

yeled	katan	
child:M	little:M	'little boy'

ha-yald-a	ha-ktan-a	
DEF-child-F	DEF-little-F	'the little girl'

The Modern Hebrew verbal system, like those of all Semitic languages, is a system of root consonants that carry a basic meaning, and that are then manipulated through a set of derived stems to refine the meaning. Hardly any roots appear in all stems, however. While classical Hebrew roots mostly contained three consonants, Modern Hebrew has verbs of four, five, and even six root consonants.

Unlike older stages of the language, Modern Hebrew exhibits a straightforward system of tenses. Verbs are conjugated in the past, present, future, imperative, and infinitive, using a system of prefixes and suffixes. Furthermore, the prefix/suffix system marks the verb distinctly for all persons, numbers, and genders, with minor overlap.

For example, the root *rxc* expresses the basic meaning of 'wash'. In the basic stem (or *pa'al*), the third person masculine singular past-tense form is *raxac* 'he washed'. In the derived *nif'al* stem, which often expresses the passive, the third person masculine singular past is *nirxac* 'it (m.) was washed'. In the derived *pi'el* stem, where the concept of intensiveness is sometimes added (there are verbs that occur in *pi'el* without having a corresponding basic form), the third person masculine singular past form is *rixec* 'he washed clean'. In the *hif'il* stem, where the concept of causative is generally added, the third person masculine singular past form is *hirxic* 'he bathed someone' (that is, 'he caused to wash'). The derived *hitpa'el* stem, which often expresses reflexivity, has its third person masculine singular past as *hitraxec* 'he washed himself'. The third person feminine singular past tense forms of these verbs would be, correspondingly, *raxca* 'she washed', *nirxaca* 'it (f.) was washed', *rixca* 'she washed clean', *hirxica* 'she bathed someone', and *hitraxca* 'she washed herself'.

The corresponding third person masculine and feminine singular future-tense forms are:

basic stem:	yirxac	'he will wash'
	tirxac	'she will wash'
nif'al stem:	yeraxec	'it (m.) will be washed'
	teraxec	'it (f.) will be washed'
pi'el stem:	yəraxec	'he will wash clean'
	təraxec	'she will wash clean'
hif'il stem:	yarxic	'he will bathe someone'
	tarxic	'she will bathe someone'
hitpa'el stem:	yitraxec	'he will wash himself'
	titraxec	'she will wash herself'

Present-tense forms are not inflected for person. The masculine and feminine singular present-tense forms of the basic stem are *roxec* and *roxecet*.

Words that consist of a single consonant, and a following vowel, cannot be written alone, but rather are prefixed to the following form. Thus, *ha-* 'the' is always written as a prefix to the noun it defines. This is the case also with *ve-* 'and', *be-* 'in', *le-* 'to', etc.

Basic Syntax

As a rule, Hebrew word order is SVO. If the object is definite, and therefore marked, word order can be OSV for emphasis. As already noted, definite direct objects are preceded by the word *et*:

ra'i-ti	yeled	
see:PAST-1SG	child	'I saw a child.'

ra'i-ti	et	ha-yeled	
see:PAST-1SG	OBJECT.MARKER	DEF-child	'I saw the child.'

The negative is expressed by the word *lo* 'no, not' placed before the verb:

lo	ra'i-ti	yeled	
NEG	SEE:PAST-1SG	child	'I didn't see a child.'

A negative command is expressed by the element *al* before the future form of the verb:

al	ti-t-raxc-i	
NEG	2SG:FUT-REFLEX-wash-2F.SG	'Don't wash yourself.'

Possession is expressed by the construction '[possessed object] exists to [possessor]':

yeš	l-i	sefer	
there.is	to-me	book	'I have a book.'

Such sentences are negated by the element *en* replacing *yeš*:

en	l-i	sefer	
NEG	to-me	book	'I don't have a book.'

Modern Hebrew expresses the conditional by combining the appropriate past tense form of the verb 'to be' with the present tense form of the verb in question:

hayi-ti	holex	l-a-kolnoa	aval	lo	haya
be:PAST-1SG	go.M.SG	to-the-movie	but	NEG	be:PAST.3M.SG

l-i	kesef
to-me	money

'I would have gone to the movies, but I didn't have any money.'

Contact with Other Languages

Modern Hebrew has innumerable loanwords, early on from related Semitic languages, then from what is often termed Common European words that exist in similar form in Yiddish, German, French, RUSSIAN, and most recently specifically from English. In part this borrowing frenzy has been fueled by the need for an instant vocabulary capable of handling modern requirements and in part by the fact that the first speakers of the language were all native speakers of something else. As loanwords are absorbed into Hebrew they are often molded to the Hebrew morphological system. In particular, consonants may be extracted from foreign verbs to form stems like those described above under Basic Morphology. For instance, from the loanword *telefon* is formed the *pi'el* verb stem *tilfen* 'he telephoned'.

From Arabic: *garbayim* 'socks', *ta'arix* 'date (time)', *laxan* 'melody', *maxsan* 'storeroom'
From Common European: *telefon* 'telephone', *irgun* 'organization', *mivrešet* 'brush', *proyekt* 'project'
From English: *breksim* 'brakes', *super* 'supermarket', *tremp* 'ride', *ğinsim* 'jeans'

Common Words

man:	iš	long:	arox
woman	iša	small:	katan
water:	mayim	yes:	ken
sun:	šemeš	no:	lo
three:	šaloš	good:	tov
fish:	dag	bird:	cipor
big:	gadol	dog:	kelev
tree:	ec		

Example Sentences

(1) ha-kelev nošex et ha-yeled.
the-dog bite:PRES.M.SG OBJECT.MARKER the-child:M.SG
'The dog is biting the boy.'

(2) kše-yosi haya yeled katan hu tamid
when-Yossi be:PAST.3M.SG child small he always

ša'al šə'el-ot.
ask:PAST.3M.SG question-F.PL
'When Yossi was a small boy, he always asked questions.'

(3) sara ta-gid-i l-i ma ha-ša'a?
Sarah 2SG.FUTURE-tell-2F.SG to-me what the-time
'Sarah, tell me, what time is it?'

Efforts to Preserve, Protect, and Promote the Language

The Academy of the Hebrew Language continues its work to preserve, protect, and promote Hebrew. It publishes lists of newly coined words in an attempt to use classical Hebrew roots and patterns for the expression of modern technical concepts and to prevent the wholesale borrowing of foreign words.

The academy has tried for many years to influence the pronunciation of Hebrew. General scholarly opinion holds that the OIH dialect is closer to older stages of the language than the GIH dialect, and pressure has been put on government radio and television announcers to use this form. This campaign has had no apparent success among the general public.

Select Bibliography

Alcalay, R. 1965. *The Complete Hebrew-English, English-Hebrew Dictionary*. 2v. Tel Aviv: Massada.
Ben-Abba, D. 1994. *The Meridian Hebrew-English, English-Hebrew Dictionary*. New York: Meridian.
Ben-Yehudah, E. 1908–1958. *Thesaurus totius hebraitatis*. 16 volumes. Berlin and Jerusalem.
Fellman, J. 1973. *The Revival of a Classical Tongue: Eliezer Ben Yehuda and the Modern Hebrew Language*. The Hague: Mouton.
Glinert, L. 1989. *The Grammar of Modern Hebrew*. Cambridge: Cambridge University Press.
____. 1994. *Modern Hebrew: An Essential Grammar*. New York: Routledge.
Sáenz-Badillos, A. 1993. *A History of the Hebrew Language*. (J. Elwolde, tr.). Cambridge: Cambridge University Press.

Hiligaynon

R. David Zorc

Language Name: Hiligaynon. **Alternate:** *Ilonggo* (a term that is sometimes applied to the entire dialect chain).

Location: Hiligaynon is spoken in the Philippines throughout Negros Occidental (the western half of the island of Negros), the eastern and southern portions of Panay Island, and most of Guimaras Island, and by immigrants in large pockets on Mindanao (e.g., the Davao area) and Palawan (in and around Puerto Princesa).

Family: Bisayan subgroup of the Central Philippine group of the Western Malayo–Polynesian branch of the Austronesian language family.

Related Languages: Most closely related to Romblomanon (spoken in the Philippine Islands of Romblon and Tablas islands), Masbateño (of Masbate), Samar-Leyte, and Waray Bisayan, all comembers of the Bisayan subgroup of Central Philippine languages.

Dialects: Hiligaynon has many dialects. For example, the alternate language name *Ilonggo* originally referred only to the dialect of Iloilo City. Almost every town, especially those along language borders with CEBUANO, Kinaray-a and Aklanon, has some variation in lexicon and intonation. Those dialects that have notable differences include Capiznon (which is spoken in Capiz Province on central eastern Panay; it has several lexical idiosyncrasies) and Kawayan (which is spoken in the town of Cauayan, south of Bacolod City on Negros; it has a phonological idiosyncracy wherein an [l] between vowels is often replaced by a [y], e.g., Hil *ulán*, Kaw *uyán* 'rain').

Number of Speakers: 4.5 million (fourth largest Philippine language)

Origin and History

When the Spanish arrived in the Philippines, Hiligaynon was (and indeed still is) a major trade language in the western Visayas. Legends recorded in the *Maragtas*, a book by Pedro Alcantara Monteclaro, tell of 10 *datus* ('chieftains') who left Borneo to found settlements on the island of Panay in the central Philippines, but these have been critically analyzed by Scott (1984: 91–103) and shown to be well-intentioned fabrications. More serious still was the purported discovery of a law code and pre-Hispanic calendar, but Scott (104–135) has shown these to be forgeries by Jose E. Marco, a Filipino chemist. Each of these has unfortunately made its way into postwar Philippine history books. As Scott concludes: "The summary above discloses a considerable discrepancy between what is actually known about the pre-Hispanic Philippines and what has been written about it. The popular texts present a picture of law codes, membership in Asian empires, and political confederations projected against a background of 250,000 years of migrating waves of Filipino progenitors, almost complete with their points of departure, sailing dates and baggage."

Archeological and linguistic evidence, as well as a few Chinese reports are all we have to determine the prehistory of any Philippine group. Written history starts with the advent of the SPANISH. Thus, Kobak (1969: 22) reports that the Spanish researcher Alzina recorded the fact that the Hiligaynons of Oton (and elsewhere on Panay) traced their origin to Leyte. Zorc (1977: 45f) concludes that based on order of diversity, Hiligaynon (as well as all of the 35 other Bisayan speech varieties) developed in either the eastern Visayan region or on northeastern Mindanao.

The name Visayan was the Spanish rendition of the adjective *bisayá'* referring to a person or item from the central Philippine islands and the verb *binisayá'* meaning 'to speak Bisayan'. It applies to 36 different speech varieties, the most well-known of which include Cebuano, Waray, Hiligaynon, and Aklanon. Together, these groups represent over 40 percent of the Philippine population, almost double that of any other language in the archipelago. The word probably derives from a dialect variant of a MALAY loan *bicara* 'to speak', based on the propensity of many Filipinos to name their language based on some idiosyncrasy of that language, e.g., Waráy 'there is none,' Ja'ún 'over there', The Kinaray-a say *bisára'* 'to mention,' Aklanon has *bisáła'* 'to utter' and *bilisad'un* 'saying, maxim,' while the Banton, Odiongan, Surigao, Kawayan, and Romblon dialects use *bisáya'* 'to say, speak'. [See Zorc 1977: 42–45 for more details.]

After the arrival of Magellan in 1521, the Spanish conquest introduced Christianity through Roman Catholicism (which still coexists with the indigenous animistic beliefs), hundreds of loanwords, and a Western outlook on the world. The United States introduced a widespread elementary and high school education program, whereby own-language and ENGLISH literacy became the norms. The legal system and the press follow U.S. language and traditions. It is not uncommon for the wealthy to have had higher education in Manila, Cebu, or the U.S.

Orthography and Basic Phonology

The Hiligaynon writing system currently follows that established for the Philippine National Language based upon TAGALOG. Previously, a quasi-Hispanic orthography was fol-

Table 1: Consonants

		Labial	Dental	Palatal	Velar	Glottal
Stops	Voiceless	p	t		k	ʔ
	Voiced	b	d		g	
Fricatives	Voiceless	f	s			h
	Voiced	v				
Nasals		m	n		ng	
Resonants		w	l, r	y		

lowed, which is still in use by an older generation of authors, e.g., <icao> = *ikáw* 'you, thou'. The glottal stop is written as a hyphen before or after another consonant, e.g., *ba'ba'* = <ba-ba> 'mouth', *búg'at* = <bug-at> 'heavy'. However, it is never written in word-initial position before a vowel, whereas in word-final position it is not indicated in the vast majority of Hiligaynon publications apart from a convention of writing a final [u'] or [o'] as <u>. Following the tradition for Tagalog, it may be indicated with an acute accent over the vowel, e.g., *bisáya'* = <bisayà>, *binisayá'* = <binisayâ>. Punctuation (use of the period, comma, semicolon, question mark, and exclamation mark) is as established for English.

The voiceless stops are all unaspirated. The digraph <ng> represents the velar nasal [ŋ], which occurs in all positions (at the beginning, middle and end of words); *c, j, f, v, e,* and *o* occur mostly in borrowings from English and Spanish. *R* is trilled, as in Spanish *perro*.

The glottal stop is a very important sound in distinguishing words, e.g., [basá'] 'wet' as opposed to [básа] 'read' or [kíta'] 'see' as opposed to [kitá] 'we all [inclusive]'. When a word ends in a glottal stop and is followed by the linker *nga*, the two forms may be fused together, such as: *balíta'* + *nga* = <balitang> 'news (of)'. Some linguists, such as Wolfenden (1971), write the glottal catch with a <q>, e.g., <basáq> 'wet', but an apostrophe is used herein.

Word accent is very important in distinguishing forms in Hiligaynon. Roots generally have accent on either the second last or final syllable, as in: *ámo* 'master' (Sp.) vs. *amó* 'the same, thus', *áyaw* 'satisfaction' vs. *ayáw* 'don't', *bála* 'bullet' vs. *balá* 'is it?, really?' *báti'* 'feel, perceive' vs. *batí'* 'hear, catch sound of *bílin* 'remain, stay' vs. *bilín* 'leftovers', *dúlot* 'offer' vs. *dulút* 'penetrate', *súbong* 'like, similar' vs. *subóng* 'now, today', and *útud* 'sibling' vs. *utúd* 'cut'.

If the accent falls on the second last syllable (penult) and that syllable is not closed by a consonant (i.e., if the syllable is "open" or of the shape CV), the vowel is pronounced long. Thus [*á:mo, á:yaw, bá:la ... ú:tud*] in the above examples. If the accent falls on the final syllable, then that syllable receives stress (is pronounced louder and with a slight change in pitch), while the penult is pronounced with a short vowel. Thus [*amó, ayáw, balá ... utúd*] in the above.

Accent also plays an important role in distinguishing certain related pairs of words, such as noun or verb roots from their stative or adjective-like counterparts: *báli'* 'break' vs. *balí'* 'broken', *búhi'* 'live vs. *buhí'* 'alive', *kúsog* 'strength' vs. *kusóg* 'strong', *lútu'* 'to cook' vs. *lutú'* 'cooked', *pílas* 'to wound' vs. *pilás* 'wound, injury'.

Basic Phonological Rules. All words are formed from syllables of the shape CV(C), that is always an initial consonant (a word that appears to begin with a vowel, actually begins with a glottal stop), followed by any vowel, and optionally ending in a consonant, thus *sa* [CV] locative marker, *sang* [CVC] oblique marker, *matá* [CV.CV] 'eye', *takúp* [CV.CVC] 'cover', *támbuk* [CVC.CVC] 'fat', etc.

Morphophonemic Changes. The phoneme /d/ has a word-final allophone of [r], so when a root word ending with *d* receives a suffix, the *-d* changes to *-r-*, as in *báyad* 'pay' + *-an* = *bayáran* 'be paid' or *idád* / *edád* 'age' + *pang—on* = *pangidarón* 'be of a certain age'. In inflecting verbs borrowed from Spanish that end in *r*, the *-r* changes to *-h-*, as in *preparár* 'to prepare' + *-un* = *preparahón* 'be prepared' or *probár* 'to try out' + *-an* = *probahán* 'be tried out'.

After the distributive prefixes like *maN-* or *paN-* NASAL ASSIMILATION takes place:

	Example	Root	Gloss
b > m	*himánwa*	*bánwa*	'civic-mindedness'
	ginpamalibáran	*balíbad*	'was denied'
	památi'	*batí'*	'listen to'
p > m	*pamáhug*	*páhog*	'threaten, scare off'
	pamúgon	*púgon*	'work for a daily wage'
s > n	*panílag*	*sílag*	'observe, watch'
	panumbungon	*súmbong*	'accusation'
t > n	*panindugan*	*tíndog*	'stand, position'

Vowel loss is a common process affecting many words that receive a suffix: *dálhon* (from *dalá*) 'be brought', *kagamhánan* (from *gahóm*) 'powers', *madákpan* (from *dakóp*) 'can be caught', *pagkalímtan* (from *límot*) '(not) be forgotten', *pamálhon* (from *malá*) 'let become dry', *súndon* (from *sunúd*) 'be followed'.

Table 2: Vowels

	Front	Central	Back
High	i		u
Mid	e		o
Low		a	

Basic Morphology

Grammatical relations are shown either by particles (*ang* or *si* topic markers, *kag* 'and', *na* 'now, already', *mga* plural marker, *kaysa sa* 'than', *man* 'also, too', *lang* 'only,' etc.) or by the following kinds of affixes:

Prefixes (which come before a root word), e.g., *i-* instrumental verb, *inug-* instrumental noun, *ma-* future stative verb, *mag-* active contingent, *nag-* past active, *pa-* causative verb.

Infixes (which come after the first consonant but before the first vowel of a stem), e.g., *-in-* in *linuthang* 'was shot' and *-um-* in *pumulúyo'* 'resident'. Note that glottal stop begins all words that appear to have a vowel first, e.g., *'inagíhan* 'was passed', *'ináway* 'was fought'.

Suffixes (which come after the root), e.g., *-an* (in *baligyá'an* 'was sold to') or its alternate *-han* (after vowels, as in *listáhan* 'list'), *-i* (in *tilawí* 'taste it!'), *-on* (in *buháton* 'be made') or its alternate *-hon* (after vowels, as in *dálhon* 'be brought').

Circumfixes (which consist of a prefix and suffix or an infix and suffix that belong together), e.g., *paga—an* (in *pagahambálan* 'be discussed'), *-in—an* (in *ginikánan* 'parents', *tinindúgan* 'was stood upon'), *ka—an* (in *ka'ayuhán* 'goodness', *kahamtángan* 'situation'), *ka—ánan* (as in *ka'angtánan* 'connection, relationship').

Reduplications (which may be partial or full, and involve either the first consonant and the first vowel of the root or a repetition of the whole stem), e.g., *Culo-* (*bulobánta'* 'guess'), *-Vl-* (*balatí'an* 'disease'), full reduplication, denoting a diminutive (*basa'basá'on* 'be moistened', *kakikakíhon* 'brownish').

Noun Morphology. Nominals are of four kinds: common nouns (with *ang*-type markers), proper nouns (marked with *si*), demonstratives (e.g., *iní* 'this', *dídto* 'there'—also called deictics), and pronouns (e.g., *akó* 'I', *ikáw* 'you'). Common nouns are distinguished for three cases: a topic or subject form (equivalent to the nominative case), an oblique form (equivalent to both a genitive and an accusative, marking a direct relationship to a verb or head noun), and a locative form (marking location or an indirect object). Plurality is generally shown by *mga* [pronounced *mangá*], which indicates a "variety" or "assortment" of what the noun signifies. Personal names are also distinguished for three cases, but are marked for singular or plural. The plural here (e.g., *sanday Pedro*) is the equivalent of 'Peter and family' or 'Peter and his/her companions', etc.

Noun Markers

	Common Nouns		Personal Names	
	Singular	Plural	Singular	Plural
Topic/Focus	*ang*	*+ mga*	*si*	*sanday*
Oblique - definite	*sang*	*+ mga*	*ni*	*nanday*
- indefinite	*sing*	*+ mga*		
Locative	*sa*	*+ mga*	*(sa) kay*	*kanday*

Nouns are linked to adjectives or other parts of speech by means of a ligature or linking particle, *nga*, which has an alternate *-ng* after vowels, e.g., *matahúm nga babáyi* 'beautiful woman' or *ma'áyo-ng babáyi* 'good woman'.

Demonstratives (deictics) show three different locations (near me, near you, far away); they can also indicate time:

Deictics

	Near Me	Near You	Far Away
Topic	*iní*	*iná'*	*ató*
Oblique	*siní*	*siná'*	*sádto*
Locative	*dirí*	*dirá'*	*dídto*
Existential	*yári*	*yára'*	*yádto*
Verbal	*karí*	*kará'*	*kádto*

Pronouns are generally like their English equivalents, but there are inclusive vs. exclusive forms for "we", and a singular vs. plural form for "you":

Pronoun	Topic	Oblique		Locative
		Before	After	
I	*akó*	*ákon*	*-ko/nákon*	*sa'ákon*
you [singular]	*ikáw/ka*	*ímo*	*-mo/nímo*	*sa'ímo*
he / she	*si(y)á*	*íya*	*níya*	*sa'íya*
we [+ you / incl]	*kitá*	*áton*	*-ta/náton*	*sa'áton*
we [- you / excl]	*kamí*	*ámon*	*námon*	*sa'ámon*
you [plural]	*kamó*	*ínyo*	*nínyo*	*sa'ínyo*
they	*silá*	*íla*	*níla*	*sa'íla*

Numerals are not a separate part of speech, since they fall within the noun class. However, there is a native set as opposed to a Spanish set. This can cause some confusion as to pronunciation when an ARABIC number (such as 3 or 10) is encountered. As a general rule, phrases that involve time, dates, years, money and compound numbers use Spanish loans, while counting in a series (usually up to 10) or naming simple numbers is done with the original system: (1) *isá*; (2) *duhá*; (3) *tátlo*; (4) *ápat*; (5) *limá*; (6) *ánom*; (7) *pitó*; (8) *waló*; (9) *siyám*; (10) *napúlo'*; (11) *napúlog isá*; (22) *duhá ka púlo kag duhá*; (100) *isá ka gatós*; (1,000) *isá ka líbo*, etc.

When a noun follows a number (or the interrogative *pilá* 'how many?', the enumerative marker *ka* is used instead of the linker *nga*. Note that this is found in all the original numbers (above) from 20 upwards.

Verb Morphology. Verbs are inflected for the following categories:

VOICE

ACTIVE emphasizes an actor or a meteorological event
PASSIVE emphasizes an object totally affected or taken in
INSTRUMENTAL emphasizes an object moving away from the agent or doer
LOCAL emphasizes an object partially affected or a beneficiary ("for/to whom")

TENSE

PAST / action already begun = past-time statements
PROGRESSIVE = ongoing action (e.g., present)
CONTINGENT / action not yet begun (e.g., infinitive)
FUTURE = action expected to occur

ASPECT

PUNCTUAL / action viewed as a single event (*-um-*)
DURATIVE / action viewed as an ongoing process (*mag-*)
DISTRIBUTIVE / complex process or plural object (*maN-*)

MOOD

FACTUAL ("is Xing," "does X" or "did X" = unmarked)
POTENTIAL = "can/could", stative, or accidental

Examples with the verb root *balígya'* 'sell' include: *nagabalígya'* 'is selling [active progressive]', *nagbalígya'* 'sold [active past]', *magabalígya'* 'will sell [active future]',

Table 3: Verb Morphology

	Past	Progressive	Contingent	Future	Command
Active					
Punctual	*-um-*		*-um-*	*ma-*	*mag-*
Durative	*nag-*	*naga-*	*mag-*	*maga-*	*pag-*
Distributive	*naN-*	*nagapaN-*	*maN-*	*magapaN-*	*magpaN-*
Potential	*naka-*	*naka-*	*maka-*	*maka-*	
Passive					
Punctual	*-in-*		*-(h)on*	*-(h)on*	*-a*
Durative	*gin-*	*gina-*	*pag—on*	*paga—on*	*pag—a*
Distributive	*ginpaN-*	*ginapaN-*	*paN—on*	*paN—on*	
Potential	*na-*	*na-*	*ma-*	*ma-*	
Instrumental					
Punctual	*-in-*		*i-*	*i-*	*i-*
Durative	*gin-*	*gina-*	*i(g)-*	*iga-*	*ipag-*
Distributive	*ginpaN—an*	*ginapaN—an*	*ipaN—*	*ipaN-*	
Potential	*(ki)na-*	*na-*	*ika-*	*ika-*	
Local Passive					
Punctual	*-in—an*		*-an*	*-an*	*-i*
Durative	*gin—an*	*gina—an*	*pag—an*	*paga—an*	*pag—i*
Distributive	*ginpaN—an*	*ginapaN—an*	*paN—an*	*paN—an*	
Potential	*na—an*	*na—an*	*ma—an*	*ma—an*	

magbalígya' 'sell [active command]', *nakabalígya'* 'was able to sell; could sell [active potential past]', *makabalígya'* 'can sell [active potential future]', *nagapamalígya'* 'sell lots [distributive active progressive]', *namalígya'* 'sold lots [distributive active past]', *ginbalígya'* 'was sold [instrumental past]', *ginabalígya'* 'is being sold [instrumental progressive]', *ibalígya'* 'will be sold [instrumental future]; sell it! [object focus command]', *ikabalígya'* 'can be sold [instrumental potential future]', *ginabligya'án* 'is being sold to [local passive progressive]', *ginbaligya'án* 'was sold to [local passive past]', *nabaligya'án* 'was able (could) be sold to [local passive past potential]'.

The verb system also has some other frequently used affixes:

-ánay	Reciprocal	*patyanáy*	'killing each other'
pa-	Causative	*pakíta'*	'show, cause to see'
pakig-	Mutual Activity	*pagpakigkíta'*	'meeting with someone'
		nakighámbal	'talked with'
magka-	Stative	*nagkabuhí'*	'lived one's life out'

General Rules. In Hiligaynon, a part of speech is best assigned from the context or actual use of a form. Thus, a root word may be a noun or a verb (e.g., *ulán* 'rain') or a noun or an adjective (e.g., *támbuk* 'fat'). Some roots, depending on affixation, can serve as nouns, adjectives, verbs, and adverbs, e.g., *áyo* 'good; to repair' = *ma'áyo* 'good' [adjective] or 'well' [adverb], *ka'ayúhan* 'goodness' [abstract noun], *nangáyo* 'improved' [distributive verb], *ginka'áyo* 'was repaired' [stative verb]. Compounding is not a common process, but when it does occur, it involves the simple juxtaposition of two roots, e.g., *sakít'úlo* 'headache' [noun; also said as *masakít ang 'úlo ko* 'my head aches'].

Basic Syntax

Although there is relatively free word order due to the clarity provided by the case-marking particles and verb-subject (focus) agreement, standard word order follows the pattern VSO.

Case marking of major constituents is accomplished by focus; that is, having an appropriate voice affix on the verb that agrees with the grammatical role of the subject noun (in the nominative) plus any optional oblique or locative nouns.

Departures from the standard VSO word order generally indicate a kind of emphasis. *Nagʔabút akó kahápon* (arrived I yesterday) 'I arrived yesterday', *Kahápon akó nagʔabút* (yesterday I arrived) 'It was yesterday that I arrived'.

Despite the VSO sentence word order, Hiligaynon noun phrases are usually head final: *matahúm nga babáyi* (beautiful LINK woman) 'beautiful woman'.

There are three main negative markers in Hiligaynon. *Waláʔ* 'none' negates any existential statement: *Waláʔ kitá sing bugás* (NEG we:TOP OBL rice) 'We have no rice'. It also negates past tense verbs.

waláʔ	níya	pagbákla	ang	reló
NEG	he	buy.PASSIVE.NEG	the:sg:TOP	watch

'He did not buy the watch.'

Waláʔ has an alternate *waláy* if the word order is NEG-O-S: *Waláy bugás kitá* (NEG rice we) 'We have no rice'. Future tense verbs are negated with *díliʔ* 'not'.

díliʔ	níya	pagbáklun	ang	reló
NEG	he	buy-FUT	the:sg:TOP	watch

'He will not buy the watch.'

Díliʔ also negates nouns and adjectives in standard Hiligaynon: *díliʔ siyá abogádo* (NEG he lawyer) 'He is not a lawyer'. Negative imperatives are marked with *ayáw* 'don't!' *Ayáw pagbákla*! (don't buy.DURATIVE.PASSIVE) 'Don't buy it!'

Contact with Other Languages

The Hiligaynon dialects of Panay border on Kinaray-a (along the province of Antique) and Aklanon (along the province of Aklan); both of these are members of the West Bisyan group. The dialects of Negros border on Cebuano (the largest of the Bisayan dialects). Furthermore, the airwaves (television and radio channels) broadcast Tagalog (the basis for the Philippine national language). To the degree that Hiligaynon speakers are involved in these contacts, their vocabulary and grammar will differ from the standard dialect. Due to education and the media, the average person is trilingual (Hiligaynon, Tagalog and English) and thus everyday speech reflects a great deal of language mixture (called *halo-halo* or 'mix-mix').

There are a number of words borrowed from SANSKRIT, PERSIAN, and Arabic via Malay or INDONESIAN contacts during the pre-Hispanic era. More recently there are hundreds of words assimilated from Spanish and English.

From Sanskrit: *puʔása* 'to fast'
From Persian: *álak* 'alcoholic beverage'; *báyoʔ* 'shirt, dress'
From Arabic: *hukúm* 'judge', *salámat* 'thank you'
From English: *ayskrim* 'ice cream', *hayskul* 'high school', *bir* 'beer'
From Spanish: *pwéde* 'possible', *siémpre* 'of course'

Today television and radio channels broadcast in Tagalog (the basis for the Philippine National Language), and the average Hiligaynon speaker knows Tagalog and English. In addition, the Hiligaynon dialects of Panay border on Kinaray-a (along the province of Antique) and Aklanon (along the province of Aklan); both of these are members of the West Bisayan language group. The dialects of Negros border on Cebuano (the largest of the Bisayan dialects). Everyday speech reflects a great deal of language mixture, called *halo-halo* or 'mix-mix'.

Common Words

man:	laláki	long:	malábaʔ
woman:	babáyi	small:	gamáy
water:	túbig	yes:	húʔo
sun:	ádlaw	no:	díliʔ
three:	tátlo	good:	maʔáyo
fish:	ísdaʔ	bird:	píspis
big:	dakúʔ	dog:	idóʔ
tree:	káhoy		

Example Sentences

(1) sínʔu ang ngálan mo.
who TOP name your
'What is your name?'

(2) sa kíndat sa ímo matá na-sayúr-an ko
LOC wink LOC your eye be.known by.me

ang ímo pag-higúgma.
TOP your love
'By the look in your eye, I can know your love.'

(3) gin-píliʔ níya ang mangá maʔáyo.
PAST/PASSIVE-select by.him TOP PLURAL good
'He picked the good ones.'

Efforts to Preserve, Protect, and Promote the Language

Hiligaynon is taught in the schools from Grades 1–3 (thereafter, the medium of instruction is in the Philippine national language based on Tagalog). There are numerous publications (periodicals, newspapers, poetry and other literature journals) as well as movies and radio broadcasts in the language emanating from the regional centers (Bacolod City and Iloilo). The Roman Catholic Mass and Protestant Church services are in Hiligaynon, and there is a Hiligaynon translation of the Bible in wide use. The Hiligaynon-speaking population is strong and growing, as the census figures over the last few decades attest.

Select Bibliography

Constantino, Ernesto. 1975. *An English-Hiligaynon Dictionary.* Quezon City: University of the Philippines.

Kaufmann, Rev. John. 1939. *Pinciples of Visayan Grammar.* Manila: Catholic Trade School.

Kobak, Cantius, O.F.M.1969–1970. "Alzina's Historia de las Islas E Indios de Bisayas," *Leyte-Samar Studies*, Chapters 1–3, 3/1: 14–36, Chapters 4–5, 4/1: 17–28.

McFarland, Curtis D. 1980. *A Linguistic Atlas of the Philippines.* Study of Languages and Cultures of Asia and Africa, Monograph Series, No. 15. Tokyo: Institute for the Study of Languages and Cultures of Asia and Africa.

Motus, Cecile. 1971a. *Hiligaynon Dictionary.* PALI Language Texts: Philippines. Honolulu: University of Hawaii Press.

____. 1971b. *Hiligaynon Lessons.* PALI Language Texts: Philippines. Honolulu: University of Hawaii Press.

Scott, William Henry. 1984. *Prehispanic Source Materials for the Study of Philippine History* (revised edition). Quezon City: New Day Publishers.

Sunio, Delicia, and R. David Zorc. 1992. *Hiligaynon Reader.* Kensington, MD: Dunwoody Press.

Wolfenden, Elmer P. 1971. *Hiligaynon Reference Grammar.* PALI Language Texts: Philippines. Honolulu: University of Hawaii Press.

____. 1975. *A Description of Hiligaynon Syntax.* Summer Institute of Linguistics Publications in Linguistics and Related Fields, Pub. No. 46. Norman: University of Oklahoma Press.

Yap, Jose E. 1983. *English-Visayan (Ilonggo) Dictionary (Kapulungan Iningles-Binisaya).* Iloilo: Apostol Printers, Inc.

Zorc, R. David. 1967. *Peace Corps Primer for the Western Visayas.* Washington: Government Printing Office.

____. 1968. *Peace Corps Western Visayas Dialect Field Book.* Kalibo, Aklan: R.M. Trading.

____. 1977. *The Bisayan Dialects of the Philippines: Subgrouping and Reconstruction.* Pacific Linguisitics C.44. Canberra: The Australian National University.

Michael C. Shapiro

Language Name: Hindi. **Autonym:** *hindī; KhaRī bolī* (the modern standard language).

Location: Hindi is widely spoken as a first language in north India, with speakers concentrated heavily in the states of Uttar Pradesh, Madhya Pradesh, Delhi, Haryana, Rajasthan, and Bihar. Distinct nonstandard regional varieties of Hindi are found in many parts of India, with those spoken in Bombay, Calcutta, and Hyderabad most well known. Hindi is spoken as a second or subsidiary language throughout all of north India and as a lingua franca by emigrant Indian populations throughout the world. Dialectal forms of Hindi, for the most part based upon eastern varieties of the language, are spoken in Mauritius, South Africa, Trinidad, Fiji, and Guyana. Hindi is, along with ENGLISH, one of the two co-official languages of India. Hindi's "twin sister" language, URDU, is the official language of Pakistan, in addition to being widely spoken in the so-called Hindi belt of north India.

Family: Indo-Aryan group of the Indo-Iranian subfamily of the Indo-European language family.

Related Languages: Hindi is most closely related to Urdu. The nature of the relationship between Hindi and Urdu is the topic of much debate. Some scholars consider the two to be entirely separate languages. Most linguists, however, consider Hindi and Urdu to constitute different literary styles based on the same subdialect (Masica 1991: 27). The subdialectal base of the standard language (or *khaRī bolī*, literally 'standing language') is the language of the Delhi region (known by various names, including Dehlavi and Vernacular Hindustani), which is itself a dialectal composite.

There are other speech forms that, although counted by some as varieties of Hindi, are properly considered distinct languages. These include a number of RAJASTHANI languages (of which Marwari is the most widely spoken) and the so-called Bihari languages: MAITHILI, Magahi, and BHOJPURI.

Hindi is also related to the other Indo-Aryan languages such as BANGLA, MARATHI, KONKANI, PUNJABI, ASSAMESE, ORIYA, NEPALI, SINHALA, Kashmiri, and ROMANI. More distantly related are members of the Iranian group of the Indo-Aryan subfamily of Indo-European: PERSIAN, PASHTO, Ossetic, KURDISH, and BALOCHI. Hindi is even more remotely related to other Indo-European languages, especially the Satem languages (ALBANIAN, ARMENIAN, Baltic, and Slavic) as well as to GREEK and LATIN.

Dialects: Hindi is divided into two main groups, Western and Eastern. Western dialects include (1) Braj (western Uttar Pradesh and adjacent districts of Haryana, Rajasthan, and Madhya Pradesh), (2) Bundeli (north-central Madhya Pradesh and southwestern Uttar Pradesh), (3) Kanauji (west-central Uttar Pradesh), (4) Bangaru (Haryana), and (5) Kauravi (Uttar Pradesh northeastward from Delhi and including northeastern Haryana). Eastern dialects include (1) Avadhi (north-central and central Uttar Pradesh), (2) Bagheli (north-central Madhya Pradesh and south-central Uttar Pradesh), and (3) Chattisgarhi (east-central Madhya Pradesh). The so-called Pahari languages Garhwali and Kumauni are sometimes counted as Hindi dialects for census or administrative purposes, but are considered by linguists to be autonomous languages.

This chapter gives examples in Modern Standard Hindi unless noted otherwise.

Number of Speakers: Estimates vary widely depending upon which dialects and speech varieties are subsumed under the term 'Hindi', as well as upon whether second-language speakers are counted. The 1991 census of India gives a figure of 337,272,114, inclusive of the so-called Rajasthani, Bihari, and Pahari languages, but exclusive of Urdu. Worldwide, an estimate of between 300 and 400 million speakers for Hindi, depending on what speech varieties one subsumes under the term, is not unreasonable.

Origin and History

The term *hindī*, along with earlier variant forms *hinduī* and *hindavī*, is in origin an adjectival form signifying 'connected to or having to do with [the geographical area] Hind', which originally referred to the regions of the Indus River system, but gradually came to refer to an increasingly large area of the northern portion of the south Asian subcontinent. In its broadest sense, the word *hindī* is used today to refer to the language or languages of a huge central portion of the northern part of India, the so-called Hindi belt where Modern Standard Hindi (*KhaRī bolī*) is spoken alongside numerous regional languages and dialects of the area, including those cited under Dialects above. Some of these languages and dialects are also referred to as "Hindi" by their speakers.

The Indo-Aryan family of languages to which Hindi belongs is commonly divided into three stages of development: Old Indo-Aryan (OIA), consisting of various forms of Sanskrit, including Vedic Sanskrit; Middle Indo-Aryan (MIA), comprising Pali and the Prakrits; and New Indo-Aryan comprising Hindi; Urdu; and their sister languages Bangla, Punjabi, Marathi, etc. Straddling the divide between MIA and NIA is a language (more properly thought of as a set of languages or dialects) referred to as *Apabhraṃśa* (or the *Apabhraṃśas*). The immediate precursors

Table 1: Consonants

		Labial	Dental	Retroflex	Palatal	Velar	Glottal
Stops	Voiceless	p	t	ṭ	c	k	
	Aspirated	ph	th	ṭh	ch	kh	
	Voiced	b	d	ḍ	j	g	
	Murmured	bh	dh	ḍh	jh	gh	
Fricatives			s	ṣ	ś		h
Nasals		m	n	ṇ	ñ	ṅ	
Resonants			l	r			
Glides		v			y		

Supplemental Consonants

Flaps	R simple, Rh murmured
Stops	q uvular, voiceless
Fricatives	χ velar, voiceless
	ɣ uvular, voiced
	z dental, voiced sibilant
	f labio-dental, voiceless

of the set of dialects that comprise modern Hindi are generally considered to be a set of Prakrits and *Apabhraṃśas*.

Although the periodization of the stages of development of the Indo-Aryan languages presupposes that the stages can be arranged in a chronological sequence, it is not possible to impose strict time frames for each of the three stages. This is largely because throughout much of the course of south Asian history, languages and dialects representing different purported stages of development may have coexisted at the same time. Thus, for example, in much of classical Indian drama, some characters speak in OIA languages, while others speak in a MIA Prakrit. Likewise, the boundaries between late Prakrits and *Apabhraṃsas* on the one hand and early forms of the NIA language Hindi on the other are quite hazy, thus making the assigning of a specific date for the start of Hindi and other NIA languages (the date A.D. 1000 is commonly given) a gross approximation at best. The difficulty in establishing a satisfactory time frame for the emergence of Hindi is further complicated by the fact that the earliest extant texts of early Hindi works of literature date from many centuries after the periods in which these works were originally composed.

Although both Hindi and Urdu literary traditions can, with some justification, trace their origins to poems ascribed to Amir Khusrau (d. 1325), when speaking of early stages of Hindi and its literatures, the term "Hindi" is today understood as referring to a set of five literary dialects, each associated with a distinct literary and religious culture: (1) Ḍingal, associated with the Bardic traditions of Rajasthan and adjoining areas; (2) Braj, connected to Vaishnava traditions of Krishna worship; (3) Avadhi, associated with Sufi allegorial romances dating from the 13th century, and with the single greatest work of Rama worship, the *Rāmacaritamānas* of Tulsidas (1532–1623); (4) Sādhū Bhāṣā, seen in the texts of the western recension of the poet-saints of the *nirgua bhakti* traditions; and (5) Maithili, seen in the devotional tradition of north Bihar, particularly that written by the Vaishnava poet Vidyapati.

The origins of Modern Standard Hindi (*khaRī bolī*), as opposed to the earlier (sometimes called "medieval" literary dialects) can be traced to a combination of factors, no single one of which can be seen to have uniquely led to the creation of the modern standard. The first of these was the forging of a literary Urdu, based upon the grammatical core of the vernacular dialect of Delhi and its environs, at first in the 16th and 17th centuries in the courts of Golconda and Bijapur in South India, but later in such cultural centers as Aurangabad, Lucknow, and Delhi. The second factor was the cultivation in the mid-19th century, in part under British patronage, of a vernacular prose literature. This movement was given impetus by the establishment of Fort William College in Calcutta in 1800 and the subsequent commissioning of prose texts, which by the second half of the 19th century were frequently written in the *devanāgarī* (as opposed to Perso-Arabic) writing system. The third factor was the emergence of a movement for the propagation of a Sanskritized style of Hindi, championed by such organizations as the *Nāgarīpracāriṇi Sabhā* of Benaras (founded 1893), whose efforts can be viewed as having culminated in the acceptance of Hindi, written in *devanāgarī*, as the national language of the independent Republic of India.

Orthography and Basic Phonology

Modern Standard Hindi is generally written in the *devanāgarī* (or sometimes simply *nāgarī*) writing system, which is also used for writing Sanskrit and many MIA and NIA languages. In earlier periods, Hindi was also written in several related scripts, of which *kaithī* is the most important. The use of Perso-Arabic script, standard for Urdu, was also frequently employed for various forms of Hindi prior to Indian independence.

The *devanāgarī* writing system is a modified syllabary. The basic units of this system typically represent syllables; however, the symbols can be decomposed relatively easily into parts representing individual consonant and vowel sounds. The *devanāgarī* system comprises 33 basic symbols for consonants and 11 symbols for vowels not preceded by consonants. Vowels preceded by consonants are represented by smaller marks (called *mātrās*) written on or about the sign for the preceding consonant. There are, in addition, a substantial number of symbols for sequences of consonants. Through the addition of diacritics, seven basic consonant signs are modified so as to represent phonemes not present in Sanskrit's core phonemic inventory. They include sounds introduced into Hindi by loanwords from such non-Indo-Aryan languages as ARABIC, Persian, English, and PORTUGUESE, and two so-called flaps, which are indigenous NIA developments of earlier OIA and NIA phonemes.

Hindi distinguishes among four types of stops. Voiceless aspirated stops like *ph* are comparable to the voiceless stops of English in word-initial position. In contrast, neither the voiceless unaspirated stops nor the voiced stops are exactly comparable to English voiced stops. Hindi voiced stops are fully voiced in all positions in a word, unlike English voiced stops, which are sometimes fully voiced and sometimes have a delayed onset of voicing. Hindi murmured stops, sometimes inaccurately referred to as voiced aspirated stops, are breathier than the voiced stops.

Hindi retroflex consonants, generally indicated in transcription by a dot under the symbol for the corresponding dental, are produced with the tongue tip curled backward toward the rear part of the alveolar ridge. The retroflex fricative ṣ and the nasal ṇ are found almost exclusively in learned borrowings from Sanskrit.

The palatal fricative *ś* is very similar to English *sh* in words like *ship*. The palatal nasal *ñ* is similar to the sequence *ni* in English *onion*.

The glide *v* ranges in pronunciation from [v] (as in English *victory*) to [w] (as in English *water*).

Hindi *r* is a tongue tap comparable to the sound represented *dd* in English *ladder*. The flaps *R* and *Rh* are pronounced with the tongue curled back as for the production of retroflex consonants. However, instead of touching the roof of the mouth, it is rapidly rolled (or 'flapped') forward until the front part of the tongue comes to rest at the bottom of the mouth behind the front teeth.

Table 2: Vowels

	Front	Central	Back
High	i, ī		u, ū
Mid	e	a	o
Low	ai		au, ā

The Hindi long vowels *ā ī ū* differ from their short counterparts *a i u* in quality as well as in quantity: *i* and *u* are phonetically [ɪ] and [ʊ], respectively the vowels in English *fit* and *foot*, while *ī* and *ū* are [i] and [u]. Unlike the English vowels in *feet* and *boot*, the Hindi vowels are always monophthongs. The difference between *a* and *ā* is even greater; *a* is phonetically [ʌ], as in English *cut*, while *ā* is phonetically [ɑ], as in English *pot*.

The low front vowel *ai* is [æ] in Western Hindi; however, in many Eastern dialects it is a diphthong [ɑɪ] like that of English *bike*. Likewise, *au* is in Western Hindi a low back rounded monophthong [ɔ], while in Eastern Hindi it is a diphthong [ɑʊ] like that of English *cow*.

Hindi also has an *r*-colored vowel *ṛ* whose pronunciation varies depending on region. One common version consists of a tapped *r* followed by a short *i*. The occurrence of this vowel phoneme is almost entirely limited to learned borrowings from Sanskrit.

All Hindi vowels except *ṛ* can occur either oral or nasal. Nasal vowels are indicated by a tilde (~) over the symbol for the corresponding nonnasal vowel. In *devanāgarī*, the nasalization of vowels is indicated by either of the diacritics *anusvāra* (a superscript dot) or *candrabindu* (ँ).

Vowel nasalization leads to minimal pairs like *hai* 'be (third person singular, present tense)' vs. *hãĩ* 'be (third. person plural, present tense)'; *mās* 'month' vs. *mā̃s* 'meat, flesh'.

Basic Morphology

Hindi nouns are inflected for gender, number, and case. There are two genders, masculine and feminine; two numbers, singular and plural; and two inflected case forms, direct and oblique. Both masculine and feminine nouns occur in two classes, depending on the form of their stems. In general, oblique forms of nouns are used when a postposition follows, and direct forms are used in all other circumstances. In addition, distinct vocative forms of nouns are found in all plural paradigms, and in the singular for masculine I nouns. Some representative forms are illustrated below.

Singular:

	Direct	Oblique	Vocative	Gloss
Masc. I	laRkā	laRke	laRke	'boy'
Masc. II	ādmī	ādmī		'man'
Fem. I	laRkī	laRkī		'girl'
Fem. II	aurat	aurat		'woman'

Plural:

	Direct	Oblique	Vocative	Gloss
Masc. I	laRke	laRkõ	laRko	'boy'
Masc. II	ādmī	ādmiyõ	ādmiyo	'man'
Fem. I	laRkiyā̃	laRkiyõ	laRkiyo	'girl'
Fem. II	auratẽ	auratõ	aurato	'woman'

Hindi has two basic kinds of adjectives, declinable and indeclinable. Declinable adjectives agree with the nouns they modify in gender, number, and case:

khaRā laRkā
standing boy 'standing boy' (MASC.SG.DIRECT)

khaRe laRke ko
standing boy to 'to the standing boy' (MASC.SG.OBLIQUE)

khaRī laRkiyõ ko
standing girl to 'to the standing girls' (FEM.PL.OBLIQUE)

Hindi personal pronouns also distinguish three persons (first, second, and third), two numbers (singular and plural), and two cases (direct and oblique). Special possessive and ergative forms also exist for some personal pronouns. Second person plural pronouns further distinguish two degrees of respect (familiar and polite), and third person plural pronouns (in origin demonstrative pronouns) have both proximate and non-proximate forms. Both second and third person plural pronouns can be used to refer to individuals to indicate respect. For many speakers, the first person plural personal pronoun can be used with singular reference. The direct forms of the personal pronouns are illustrated below:

	Singular	Plural
1st person	mā̃ī	ham
2nd person	tū	tum (familiar)
		āp (polite)
3rd person		
proximate	yah	ye
nonproximate	vah	ve

The second person singular pronoun *tū* is used in situations of maximal intimacy, such as in calling a small child, addressing God, addressing close friends of equal status, and expressing anger or disgust. The second person plural familiar pronoun *tum* is used among family members, and generally by friends and colleagues in informal situations. The polite form *āp* is used to address individuals who the speaker respects or in formal situations. In situations of social inequality, *āp* is used to address the "superior" party and *tum* to address the "inferior" party.

The third person proximate pronouns are used to refer to persons or things physically close to the speaker or to the most recent of a number of items mentioned. The nonproximate forms are used to refer to items or things conceptualized as distant from the speaker or to an item (among two or more) mentioned earlier in a discourse.

The Hindi verbal system is primarily structured around the category of aspect, with distinctions based upon the category of tense limited to the copula *honā*. Present-tense forms of *honā* agree with their subjects in person and number:

	Singular	Plural
1st person	hū̃	hā̃ī
2nd person	hai	ho (familiar)
		hā̃ī (polite)
3rd person	hai	hā̃ī

Past-tense forms of *honā* agree with their subjects in number and gender:

	Masculine	Feminine
Singular	thā	thī
Plural	the	thī̃

There are two additional simple tenses, the presumptive and the subjunctive, the former agreeing with the subject in person and number, and the latter agreeing in person, number, and gender.

There are three aspects in Hindi: the habitual, the progressive, and the perfective. Verbs in each of these aspects are also secondarily marked for tense: present, past, presumptive, and subjunctive, with the tense indicated by the use of the appropriate form of *honā* as a verbal auxiliary. There is also a simple perfective form. Various aspects are formed by the addition of verbal auxiliaries and suffixes to the verb stem. Some forms of the verb *jānā* 'to go' are illustrated below:

tum aksar dillī jāte ho
2PL.FAM.DIR regularly Delhi go be:2PL.FAM
'You go to Delhi regularly.' (present habitual)

laRkī aksar banāras jātī thī
girl:SG.DIR regularly Benares go be:PAST.FEM.SG
'The girl used to go to Benares regularly.' (past habitual)

A notable feature of Hindi is the fact that the perfective forms of transitive verbs agree not with their subjects, but with their direct objects. In this so-called ergative construction, the logical subject is marked with the postposition *ne* and placed in the oblique case.

us bacce ne mez par kuch papīte
that boy-M.SG.OBL table on some papayas-M.PL.DIR

dekhe
see:PERFECTIVE.M.PL
'That boy saw some papayas on the table.' (perfective)

This sentence, in which *dekhe* agrees with *kuch papīte* 'some papayas', can be compared with the following sentence, in which the verb *dekhtā hai* agrees with the subject *vah baccā:*

vah baccā mez par kuch papīte
that boy:M.SG.DIR table on some papayas-M.PL.DIR

dekhtā hai
see be:3sg
'That boy sees some papayas on the table.' (present habitual)

Basic Syntax

The preferred word order in Hindi is Subject-Object-Verb, as illustrated above. Consistent with that order, verbal auxiliaries follow the main verb. If two objects are present, the direct object precedes the indirect object:

mā̃ī laRkī ko khānā khilātā hū̃
1SG girl:F.SG.OBL to food-M.SG.DIR give.to.eat be:1SG
'I feed food to the girl.'

Likewise, adjectives and other modifiers precede the nouns that they modify: *catur laRkā* (clever boy) 'clever boy', *sāt bahut amīr ādmī* (seven very rich men) 'seven very rich men'.

In addition, relations of nouns to verbal actions are indicated by postpositions rather than by prepositions, as in English. Hindi postpositions include: *ko* 'to', *mẽ* 'in, among', *par* 'on, at', *se* 'from, by means of ', *tak* 'until, as far as'. In addition to simple postpositions like those just illustrated, there are also many compound postpositions such as *ke liye* 'for, for the benefit of', *ke bād* 'after', *kī taraf* 'towards', and *se pahle* 'before (in time)'.

Sentences in Hindi are negated by the particles *nahī̃*, *na*, or *mat* preceding the verb:

vidyārthī ab skūl mẽ nahī̃ hai
student:M.SG.DIR now school in NEG be-3SG
'The student is not in school.'

Relative clauses in Hindi are introduced by one of a number of relative markers, each beginning with the phoneme *j-* (such as *jo* 'who, which', *jab* 'when', *jahā̃* 'where'). Relative clauses may either precede or follow the matrix clauses to which they are subordinate.

jo ādmī sigreṭ pī rahā hai vah merā choṭā
which man cigarette smoke be:3SG he my younger

bhāī hai
brother be:3SG
'The man who is smoking a cigarette is my younger brother.'

vah ādmī merā bhāī hai jo sigreṭ pī rahā
that man my brother be:3SG who cigarette smoke

hai
be:3SG
'The man who is smoking a cigarette is my brother.'

Contact with Other Languages

The vocabulary of Modern Standard Hindi is both rich and diverse. In addition to its large stock of native Hindi vocabulary items (referred to as *tadbhava* forms by Hindi grammarians), the language also contains numerous Sanskrit forms (referred to as *tatsama* forms), both borrowings of ancient attested words and neologisms coined from Sanskrit roots, prefixes, and suffixes. In addition to these Indo-Aryan sources of lexical items, Hindi has absorbed over the centuries loanwords from other languages: Arabic, Persian, Turkic, Portuguese, and English. The loanwords from Arabic, Persian, and Turkic are to a great extent the legacy of centuries of Muslim rule over large portions of north India. The Portuguese influence on Hindi vocabulary results from both Portuguese colonial and missionary activities in India, and from the role served by Portuguese as a commercial lingua franca. In the past two centuries, both as a result of British colonialism and of the central role of English in the 20th century in the expansion of worldwide economic and cultural networks, English has served as a major source of lexical borrowings into Hindi.

From Sanskrit: *pakṣī* 'bird', *jal* 'water', *kārya* 'work, deed', *agni* 'fire', *pradhān mantrī* 'prime minister'
From Arabic: *kursī* 'chair', *qilā* 'fort', *χayāl* 'thought, idea', *imtahān* 'examination, test', *istīfā* 'resignation'
From Persian: *rāstā* 'road, way', *bādām* 'almond', *gulābī* 'having to do with roses, pink', *tezāb* 'acid' [lit. 'sharp water']
From Turkic: *begam* 'woman of status', *top* 'field gun, cannon', *urdū* 'camp, encampment, the Urdu language'
From Portuguese: *kamrā* 'room, chamber', *almārī* 'cupboard', *girjā* 'church, chapel', *mistrī* 'artisan, mechanic', *cābī* 'key'
From English: *hoṭal*, *ḍākṭar*, *sāikil*, *skūl*, *kampyūṭar*, *reḍiyo*

Common Words

man:	ādmī	long:	lā̃bā
woman:	aurat, strī	small:	choṭā
water:	pānī	yes:	hā̃
sun:	sūraj	no:	nahī̃
three:	tīn	good:	acchā
fish:	machlī	bird:	ciRiyā
big:	baRā	dog:	kuttā
tree:	peR		

Example Sentences

(1) yah laRkī āp-kī bahan
this girl:F.SG.DIR you:POLITE-POSSESSIVE sister

hogī.
be:PRESUMPTIVE.3SG.FEM
'This girl must be your sister.'

(2) mãĩ kal hī bābaī gaī.
I yesterday only Bombay go:SIMPLE PERFECTIVE.F.SG
'I (fem.) went to Bombay only yesterday.'

(3) rājū apn-ī bahan-õ kī madad
Raju:M own-F.PL sister-F.PL.OBL of:F.SG.DIR help:F.SG.DIR

karegā.
do:3M.SG.FUTURE
'Raju will help his sisters.'

Efforts to Preserve, Protect, and Promote the Language

Hindi is, with English, the co-official language of the Republic of India and one of the 18 official languages (in addition to English) listed in Schedule VII of the Indian Constitution. The government of India has made extensive efforts to promote the language and to encourage its use in the public and private sectors, in Hindi-speaking states and in India as a whole. Particular emphasis has been placed on Hindi language education and promulgation, which although controversial, particularly in non-Hindi-speaking areas, has figured prominently in the various language policies endorsed by the government of India and legislated in the constitution of India.

Select Bibliography

King, Christopher R. 1994. *One Language, Two Scripts: The Hindi Movement in Nineteenth Century North India*. Delhi: Oxford University Press.

Masica, Colin P. 1991. *The Indo-Aryan Languages*. Cambridge: Cambridge University Press.

Rai, Amrit. 1984. *A House Divided: The Origin and Development of Hindi/Hindavi*. Delhi: Oxford University Press.

Shapiro, Michael C. 1989. (Reprint 1994) *A Primer of Modern Standard Hindi*. Delhi: Motilal Banarsidass Publishers.

HITTITE

Kenneth Shields, Jr.

Language Name: Hittite. **Autonym:** *Neši (Nišili)*.

Location: Originally spoken in the central plateau of what is now Anatolia and Turkey. With the expansion of the Hittite Empire during the period of the New Kingdom from 1350–1200 B.C., Hittite came to be spoken in the area bounded by the Aegean Sea in the west, Armenia in the east, upper Mesopotamia in the southeast, and Syria and Lebanon in the south. Although the ultimate origin of the Hittites is unknown, they invaded and conquered central Anatolia about 1900 B.C., saw their maximum expansion about 1300 B.C., and themselves succumbed to invaders known from Egyptian records as the Sea Peoples about 1200 B.C.

Family: Anatolian branch of the Indo-European language family. The entire Anatolian branch is extinct, leaving no modern descendants.

Related Languages: Hittite is related to two Anatolian languages that were contemporary with it: Luwian (attested in both cuneiform and hieroglyphic texts) to the Southwest, and Palaic to the northwest. Fragmentary records in the Anatolian languages Lycian and Lydian postdate Hittite by 700–900 years. Lycian is generally assumed to be a latter-day descendant of a western dialect of Luwian, while Lydian is, with much less certainty, sometimes viewed as a descendant of Hittite. As a result of recent textual discoveries, it is now believed by some scholars that Carian, an ancient language of the western coast of Asia Minor, belongs to the Anatolian family.

Dialects: Because information about Hittite is limited to written texts of great antiquity, its dialectal variants are unknown. The language is divided into three historical periods: Old (1800–1500 B.C.), Middle (1500–1350 B.C.), and Late Hittite (1350–1200 B.C.), largely parallel to the division of Hittite history into the Old Kingdom and the New Kingdom.

Origin and History

Although the Hittite people were known from references in Egyptian and Assyrian records and in the Bible, any information about their language comes from discoveries made in the 20th century. During the late 19th century, a large number of cuneiform records were found in Middle Egypt at Tell el-Amarna. Most of this material was written in AKKADIAN, a well-known Semitic language that became, in its more recent forms, Assyrian and Babylonian; but several official letters were in a heretofore unrecognized language that some scholars tentatively identified as Hittite. This suggestion was received with much skepticism until 1906 when the archives of the Hittite kings of the 14th and 13th centuries B.C. were excavated at Boğazköy, located about 90 miles east of Ankara. Some of the cuneiform tablets excavated at Boğazköy were written in Akkadian and Assyrian but the vast majority were in a third, unknown language. It was then recognized that these documents were written in the same language as those found at Tell el-Amarna: Hittite.

Approximately 25,000 cuneiform tablets were eventually excavated at Boğazköy, the earliest dating from 1800 B.C. and the most recent from about 1200 B.C. The content of these texts, along with others that have been subsequently discovered at such sites as Inandik and Eskiyapar, is generally religious, legal, historical, or social. Because the tablets were written in the cuneiform (wedge-shaped) script originally devised by the Sumerians and transmitted widely throughout Asia Minor, decipherment was accomplished rather quickly.

In 1915, Bedřich Hrozný proposed that the Hittite language was actually an Indo-European language on the basis of core vocabulary and inflectional similarities between Hittite and other early Indo-European languages. Such similarities, of course, are rarely the result of borrowing, implying instead genetic relationship. For example, Hittite *genu-* 'knee' corresponds to LATIN *genu* 'knee', while the first person singular present indicative suffix *-mi* of Hittite is clearly cognate with the functionally equivalent SANSKRIT ending *-mi*. However, it was noted that Hittite appeared to preserve a number of archaic features no longer or only residually retained in these other dialects. The most famous of these features is the preservation of so-called laryngeal consonants. In 1879, the Swiss linguist Ferdinand de Saussure proposed that certain vowel alternations (for example, GREEK *hístāmi* 'I stand' *~statós* 'stood') attested in early Indo-European dialects result from the influence of a "coefficient sonantique" now lost in those dialects. Saussure posited two of these phonological elements, about whose phonetic properties he refused to speculate. One element had the effect of lengthening adjoining vowels, while the other affected adjoining vowel color. In 1927, the Polish linguist Jerzy Kuryłowicz proposed that the consonant ḫ attested in Hittite texts occurred in certain positions where Saussure had hypothesized a "coefficient sonantique." Thus, Gk. *pūr* 'fire', with long vowel, stands beside Hitt. *paḫur* 'fire', with short vowel plus ḫ. Although it is still debated whether Hittite shows one or two of these sounds, now called "laryngeals," the importance of Hittite data in the formulation of reconstructions of Proto-Indo-European was established beyond doubt.

Among other archaisms frequently ascribed to Hittite are the lack of a feminine gender and a dual number, the presence of just two moods (indicative and imperative without subjunctive, optative, and others) and two inflected tenses (present-future and past without the aorist or perfect) in the conjugational system, the frequency of nouns with variable stem elements, and expression of the comparative and superlative degrees through an adjective inflected in the dative-locative (or ablative) case. Debate continues, however, about the status of such features, for some scholars prefer to see them as Hittite innovations, not archaisms. Their identification as archaisms prompted a view popular in the 1940s and 1950s that the Anatolian language group was actually derived, along with the Indo-European group, from a common ancestor known as Indo-Hittite. Popularized by the American linguist Edgar Sturtevant, the Indo-Hittite hypothesis gained little currency outside the United States, although contemporary supporters continue to argue its validity. Today most scholars who accept the archaic structure of the Anatolian family of languages propose that it is simply a conservative branch of Indo-European that may have separated from the main stock somewhat before other dialect groups. More recently, the view that Hittite is an archaic Indo-European language has played some role in the identification of eastern Anatolia, not the oft-proposed Pontic-Caspian steppes, as the homeland of the Indo-Europeans themselves (cf. Gamkrelidze & Ivanov 1995: 757 ff.). Again, this assertion remains highly controversial. In any event, because the oldest Hittite records constitute the earliest attested forms of any Indo-European language, Hittite data today play a central role in any attempts to reconstruct Proto-Indo-European.

Orthography and Basic Phonology

The Hittite language is written in a cuneiform script derived directly from the Babylonian-Assyrian or Akkadian cuneiform, a script originally devised by the Sumerians in the fourth millennium B.C. The written symbols of cuneiform are produced by making wedge-shaped impressions into a clay tablet by means of a stylus. In Hittite cuneiform, there are four types of written signs. The first type represents phonetic syllables; for example, ⟨cuneiform sign⟩ can denote the syllable *an*. Unfortunately, the same syllabic sign can denote several different syllables, making reading of texts difficult. The second type of sign is a logogram, used to encode an entire word. Some of the logograms come from SUMERIAN (Sumerograms), and others come from Akkadian (Akkadograms). It seems that such logograms were to be read in Hittite even if they were derived from these other languages. Of course, the phonetic character of such items is impossible to determine without parallel attestation in syllabic signs. In addition, some signs were phonetic complements, syllabic signs (from Hittite or Akkadian) attached to logograms as a means of specifying in more detail their pronunciation. For example, the attachment of the syllabic sign *-aš* to a nominal logogram could indicate that it is to be construed as a nominative singular. Finally, determinatives were logograms used to specify the semantic class of a (usually) following logogram because logograms frequently had very general meanings (for example, 'sky' and 'god'). Such signs have no phonetic value; they serve to disambiguate other logograms, as in the case of the logograms 'man' and 'woman' specifying the sexual references of proper names. Luwian words also occur in Hittite texts and are preceded there by a special sign known by the GERMAN name *Glossenkeil.* Again, it can be assumed that these words were originally read in Hittite. A total of eight different languages provide orthographic material for Hittite documents: Hittite, Sumerian, Akkadian, Luwian, Hattic, Palaic, Hurrian, and Mitanni (an Indo-Iranian language).

Contemporary practice in the transliteration of Hittite utilizes the Latin alphabet and indicates syllabic signs (including phonetic complements) in lowercase italics; Sumerograms, in uppercase nonitalics; Akkadograms, in uppercase italics; and determinatives in raised, small uppercase letters in full or abbreviated form. Sequences of Sumerograms are joined by periods; Hittite syllabic signs and Akkadograms are joined by hyphens.

Table 1: Consonants

	Labial	Dental	Velar
Stops	p (p b)	t (t d)	k (k g)
Fricatives		s (š)	x (ḫ)
Nasals	m	n	
Liquids		l, r	
Glides	w		y

Table 1 above lists the consonant phonemes most commonly ascribed to Hittite. Symbols in parentheses represent the way these sounds are transliterated, based on transliterations of Akkadian. For example, standard practice differentiates *p* from *b*, *t* from *d*, and *k* from *g* on the basis of Akkadian cuneiform, but spelling variation implies that Hittite made no phonemic distinction between the elements in these pairs.

A major difficulty in phonemicization of Hittite involves "double letters": for example, *ma-aḫ-ḫa-an* 'when'. According to the view adopted here, all such double consonants are nonfunctional artifacts of the juxtaposition of two syllabic signs whose consonants are used in reference to the same sound. Thus, *me-ik- ki-iš* 'large' is phonemicized /mekis/. However, other scholars see in at least some of these doublings evidence for a distinction between voiced and voiceless stops.

Table 2: Vowels

	Front	Back
High	i	u
Mid	e	
Low		a

Some scholars believe that the vowel transcribed here as *u* was /o/ and posit an additional vowel phoneme *ú* /u/. Hittite also had two diphthongs, *ai* and *au*.

The vowel system delineated above does not distinguish long from short vowels. Yet, it is the opinion of other Hittitologists that some vowels written double were, in fact, long. More recently, such doubling has been alternatively interpreted as a means of specifying primary stress placement or as a result of contraction (VCV > VV).

Basic Morphology

Hittite nouns are inflected for gender, number, and case. Instead of the three genders (masculine, feminine, and neuter) commonly found in older Indo-European languages, Hittite has two genders, animate (common) and neuter. Similarly, within the number category, only a singular and plural are found; the dual traditionally ascribed to Common Indo-European is lacking. However, Hittite frequently shows free variation in the number specification of suffixes, implying that the singular-plural distinction was not as well defined as in other Indo-European languages.

The Hittite case system is characterized by an asymmetry in the two numbers. In the singular, nouns assume inflection for nominative, vocative, accusative, genitive, dative, ablative, and instrumental cases. In the plural, nominative, accusative, genitive, and dative are attested. In addition, in Old Hittite, one special form of the dative singular appears to have been limited to directional meaning.

Hittite adjectives are inflected like nouns and agree with the nouns they modify in gender, number, and case.

Hittite has two inflected verb tenses, a present/future and a past; a periphrastic perfect and pluperfect are formed with the auxiliary *ḫar-* 'to have' and the nominative-accusative singular neuter participle: *mar-kan ḫar-te-ni* 'cut have', *ḫa-ni-eš-ša-an ḫar-ta* 'favored had'. There are, in addition, two moods (indicative and imperative) and two voices (active and mediopassive). Active verbs are assigned to two general conjugation classes named for the first person singular present active suffix that they assume:

	mi-conjugation	*ḫi*-conjugation
1sg	e-eš-mi 'I am'	da-aḫ-ḫi 'I take'
2sg	e-eš-ši 'you are'	da-at-ti 'you take'
3sg	e-eš-zi 'he is'	da-i 'he takes'

Derivational suffixes are added to verb stems to form an iterative (*-šk-*: *da-aš-mi* 'I take' ~*da-aš-ki-mi* 'I take repeatedly') and a causative (*-nu-*: *ar-nu-ut-ti* 'you bring').

Basic Syntax

The typical word order pattern of Hittite sentences is SOV. Hittite consistently shows the implicational patterns typically associated with this pattern: adjectives precede the nouns they modify, auxiliaries follow main verbs, and postpositions rather than prepositions are attested.

Hittite manifests an extensive system of enclitic pronouns and particles, marking such functions as sentence conjunction, indirect discourse, subject-referent reflexivity, ongoing activity, and completion of activity. An extremely rigid order among pronoun and particle types is maintained in the language, with six syntactic positions available for enclitic attachment.

Sentence negation is accomplished by means of one of the particles *le* and *natta* or the Akkadogram *UL* normally placed before the verb as in other Indo-European languages, but with possible sentence-final position, perhaps to mark emphasis.

Contact with Other Languages

Aside from orthographic influences, Hittite shows heavy substratal influences from a variety of other languages. Especially significant sources of loanwords in Hittite are:

From Hattic: *-umna-* suffix of origin, as in *Ḫattušumnaš* 'man from Hattus'
From Akkadian: *tuppi* 'writing table' (< *ṭuppu*)
From Caucasian languages: *puri* 'lip' (< **p'ir-i* [cf. GEORGIAN *p'ir-i* 'mouth', Svan *p'il* 'lip'])

Although the precise means of transmission is disputed, loanwords from the Indo-Iranian language Mitanni are also attested in the Hittite records (for example, *turiya-* 'to yoke to, to hitch' [cf. Vedic *dhur-* 'the act of yoking, hitching']). EGYPTIAN borrowings represent only a minor influence on the Hittite lexicon (for example, *nitri* 'sodium carbonate' < *ntr*).

Common Words

man:	antuḫšaš	small:	tepuš
woman:	lataš	yes:	(unknown)
water:	watar	no:	natta
sun:	Ištanu- 'Sun God'	good:	aššuš
three:	teriyan 'third'	bird:	ḫaraš 'eagle'
big:	mekkiš	dog:	(unknown)
long:	talukaeš (pl.)	tree:	taru

Example Sentences*

(1) DUMU.É.GAL šuppi+ø watar+ø
nobleman pure-ACC/NEUT/SG water-ACC/NEUT/SG

para ep+zi.
PREVERB bring-3SG/PRES
'The nobleman brings pure water.'

(2) man LUG[A]L-w+aš piran se+šk+anzi
when king-GEN/COM/SG before sleep-ITERATIVE-3PL/PRES

kui+š hazziz+zi
who-NOM/SG act appropriately-3SG/PRES

nu+šše geštin+an akuw+anna
PARTICLE-him-3SG/DAT wine-ACC/SG drink-INF

pi+anzi.
give-3PL/PRES
'When they sleep repeatedly before the king, then they give wine to the one who acts appropriately.'

(3) atta+š+maš ḫaršan+i ᴰÍD+ya
father-GEN/SG/COM-my person-DAT/SG river god-and

mekk-eš papri+šk+ir
many-NOM/PL be unclean-ITERATIVE-3PL/PRET

nu-uš *ABI* LUGAL natta
PARTICLE-them:ACC/PL my-father king not

ḫuiš+nu+šk+et.
live-CAUSATIVE-ITERATIVE-3SG/PRET
'My father, the king, had many of them killed who sinned with reference to the person of my father and the river god.'

*Taken from Lehmann 1974

Select Bibliography

Friedrich, Johannes. 1952–1954. *Hethitisches Wörterbuch.* Heidelberg: Winter.

Gamkrelidze, Thomas, and Vjačeslav Ivanov. 1995. *Indo-European and the Indo-Europeans.* Translated by J. Nichols. Berlin: Mouton de Gruyter.

Gurney, O.R. 1952. *The Hittites.* Melbourne: Penguin.

Güterbock, Hans, and Harry Hoffner. 1980. *The Hittite Dictionary of the Oriental Institute of the University of Chicago.* Chicago: Oriental Institute.

Held, Warren, William Schmalstieg, and Janet Gertz. 1988. *Beginning Hittite.* Columbus: Slavica.

Hoffner, Harry. 1967. "An English Hittite Glossary." In *Revue hittite et asianique* 25.

_____. 1973. "Studies of the Hittite Particles." In *Journal of the American Oriental Society 93*: 520–526.

Houwink ten Cate, P. 1970. "The Records of the Early Hittite Empire." In *Publications de l'Institut historique et archéologique néerlandais de Stamboul* 26.

Josephson, Folke. 1972. *The Function of the Sentence Particles in Old and Middle Hittite.* Uppsala: Uppsala University.

Lehmann, Johannes. 1975. *The Hittites.* Translated by J.M. Brownjohn. New York: Viking.

Lehmann, Winfred. 1974. *Proto-Indo-European Syntax.* Austin: University of Texas Press.

Macqueen, J.G. 1975. *The Hittites and Their Contemporaries in Asia Minor.* Boulder, CO: Westview.

Puhvel, Jaan. 1984. *Hittite Etymological Dictionary.* Berlin: Mouton.

Sturtevant, Edgar. 1951. *A Comparative Grammar of the Hittite Language.* New Haven: Yale University Press.

____. 1962. "The Indo-Hittite Hypothesis." In *Language 38*: 105–110.

HUNGARIAN

Robert Hetzron

Language Name: Hungarian. **Autonym:** *Magyar.*

Location: Hungary, Transylvania (Romania), Slovakia, Voivodina (Yugoslavia), Carpathic Ukraine, and spoken by the Hungarian diaspora around the world.

Family: Ugric subgroup of the Finno-Ugric group of the Uralic language family.

Related Languages: No close relative. The other two Ugric languages are Manyshi (older term: Vogul), and Khanty (older term: Ostyak), which differ greatly from Hungarian in phonology, syntax and vocabulary. FINNISH is a very distant relative.

Dialects: (1)Western (Transdanubian) dialects; (2) Northern (Palóc) dialects; (3) Eastern dialects; (4) Southern dialects; and in Transylvania (5) Meadowlands (Hung. Mezoség, Rom. Cîmpia) dialects and (6) Székely (Szekler) dialects. In addition, there are transit dialects and dialect islands (enclaves). There is relatively little variation among dialects and that which exists is in pronunciation. The standard language is roughly equivalent to the speech of Budapest. For /e/ of the standard language, many speakers (scattered) have /e/ [=ɛ] and /ë/ = [e]. In the south, /ë/ merges with /ö/; in the west, /e/ becomes [æ]. In the east, long vowels may become diphthongs. Some dialects in Romania and Slovakia-Hungary have separate morphological categories.

Number of speakers: 14–16 million.

Origin and History

Hungarian is a Finno-Ugric language that separated from its closest relatives, the other two Ugric languages (see above), at least two thousand years ago.

Leaving the ancestral land near the Urals, the Proto-Hungarian speakers moved southward to the Black Sea area, then westward, until they reached the Carpathic Basin, their present habitat. In their wanderings, Hungarians were subjected to Turkic, Iranian and other cultural and linguistic influences. According to one theory, which is found in works of Hungarian chroniclers of the Middle Ages, the date of arrival in present-day Hungary was 896. Led by their chieftain, *Árpád*, the newcomers consisted of a confederation of seven tribes whose élite were Hungarian speakers, the rest using Turkic and Iranian (Osset) tongues. The aboriginal population that was conquered and assimilated consisted of Slavs (Moravians), Turkic speakers, Goths, and many others.

The Turkic influence was especially pronounced and began with contact with Turks still in the east and included assimilation of Turkic people who arrived in Hungary with the Hungarians in 896 or so. In the 13th century came the Cumanians, and later, Turks invaded and occupied a good portion of Hungary from 1526–1686/87. German, Slavic and Romance languages were also important influences.

Evidence of an early Hungarian language can be found in Arab and other writings that contain Hungarian names. The word *Magyar* (in the form of *Majyeríja*) referring to the Hungarian people, is found in a book by Ibn Rusta, an Arab geographer, *The Book of the Precious Stones* (c. 930). In 1181 King Béla III established the royal chancery, which functioned as a legal and administrative office of the court, and ordered that all cases be recorded. Thus, there is from that date on a large body of legal documents written in LATIN and containing various amounts of Hungarian words and passages.

The first text wholly in Hungarian appears around 1200, the *Halotti Beszéd és Könyörgés* ('Funeral Oration and Prayer'), translated from the Latin. It amounts to 190 lexical entries. This and other documents of the language show what are probably recent innovations, such as the adoption of an article, the loosening of word order (from Subject-Object-Verb) and the development of preverbs.

The Hungarian language underwent a great deal of modernization in the 19th century, its vocabulary enriched with numerous neologisms. The precursor to the Hungarian Academy of Sciences, the Hungarian Learned Society (*Magyar Tudós Társaság*) published a booklet of spelling rules in 1832 that remained standard for almost a century. Grammmar and vocabulary were also codified by publications of the Hungarian Learned Society. In 1904 the Hungarian Linguistic Society was founded, uniting linguists and publishing a journal, the *Magyar Nyelv*.

Orthography and Basic Phonology

Hungarian orthography is basically a morphophonemic system. A stroke or a double stroke over a vowel indicates length; umlaut or double stroke denotes a front-rounded vowel (like *u* in English "Dude!"). *O* and *ö* do not occur at the end of a word. Before suffixes, *a* and *e* become *á* and *é*; word-final *á* and *é*, with very few exceptions, only occur in suffixes, not roots. *á* is very open, while *a* is labialized, properly *å*. (See Table 1 on the next page.)

Hungarian *sz* is similar to English *s*, while Hungarian *s* is similar to English *sh*; Hungarian *cs* and *dzs* are similar to English *ch* (as in *church*) and *j* (as in *judge*) (*dzs* occurs primarily in borrowed words), respectively; *ty* and *gy* are similar to the initial sounds in some varieties of English *tune* and *dew*, and *c* is similar to the sequence *ts* in English *cats* or *tsetse*. Hungarian *ny* is similar to Spanish *ñ* as in *cañon*. Finally, Hungarian *ly*, which merged with *j*, is like English *y*. Even though often listed as a separate phoneme, *dz* is better accounted for as a cluster of *d* and *z*.

Table 1: Vowels

Front		Back
Unrounded	Rounded	
i, í	ü, ű	u,ú
é	ö	o
e	ő	ó
		a, á

Table 2: Consonants

	Bilabial	Alveolar	Palatalized Alveolar	Alveo-palatal	Velar	Glottal
Stops/ Affricates	p b	t d	ty gy	cs [tʃ] dzs [dʒ]	k g	
Fricatives	f v	sz, c z	s zs			h
Nasals	m	n	ny			
Resonants		l, r		ly [j]		

Any Hungarian consonant can occur doubled, in which case it is written twice (doubled *t* is written *tt*, but doubled *ty* is written *tty*). Hungarian doubled consonants are actually pronounced double (unlike in English, where there is no difference between the *d*'s in *middle* and *sidle*). The doubled *mm* in *semmi* 'nothing' is prolonged like the sequence of *m*'s in careful pronunciations of English *some more*.

An important feature of Hungarian is vowel harmony. In principle, front and back vowels do not occur in the same word. However, the front vowels *i, e (=ë)* and *é* may occur in back-harmonic words. Vowel harmony is violated in foreign words, and, more importantly, in preverb-verb combinations where the two may belong to different classes. Most suffixes have two forms, some three (labial assimilation to the preceding syllable). Examples of the triple form: *tó**hoz*** '[going] to the lake', erd*ő**höz*** 'to the forest', *hegy**hez*** 'to the mountain'.

Stress falls on the first syllable of the word, but the pitch level of stressed syllables is grammatically important; four pitch levels can be distinguished: Ultrahigh + is used for contrast, High " for focus, Mid ' marks semantic head, and low for other words in the same phrase. Grammatical particles and phrases following a focus element are unstressed (°). See below for examples.

Basic Morphology

Most verb and noun inflection is expressed through suffixes. In addition to nominative, accusative, dative, and instrumental cases, there are nine local cases ("at", "in", "on", etc.), each with a distinct form for location, movement toward someone or something, and movement away. More complicated case functions are expressed by postpositions (like English *ago*).

Hungarian has no genders. Nouns can be singular or plural; singular nouns can be nonspecific, indefinite or definite, while plurals can be only definite or indefinite. Within noun phrases, definite demonstratives must agree in number and case with the following head noun. More generally, within a noun phrase, elements occur in the following order: Demonstrative + Numeral + Adjective + Noun,

eb-ben a két ház-ban
this-in the two house-in
'in these two houses'

There are three verb tenses: past, present, and future. Future-tense forms are compounds of the infinitive with a future auxiliary. There are two aspects, punctual and descriptive, and three moods, indicative, imperative, and conditional.

The verbal conjugations fully mark the person and number of the subject. In addition, they show agreement with the definiteness of the object: the indefinite form is used when there is no object or when the object is indefinite: *látok* 'I (can) see', *látok egy házat* 'I see a house'; the definite form either implies a pronominal object or agrees with a definite object: *látom* 'I see [him/her/it/them]', *látom a házat* 'I see the house'. There is a special form for a first person singular subject and a second person object: *látlak* 'I see you' (pronoun added for plural object).

Verbal derivation is very rich, although sometimes idiosyncratic: *olvas* 'he reads' *olvasgat* 'he reads from time to time', *olvastat* 'he makes (someone) read'.

A rich source of derivation is the preverb system. Preverbs are separable preverbal particles of locative-adverbial origin. In neutral sentences, they precede the verbs with which they are associated, but in focus sentences (see below) they are moved elsewhere. For the base *ír*, one finds *megír* 'finish writing', *felír* 'note down, give a prescription or a ticket', *kiír* 'write in a conspicuous place, spell out, (physician) allow sick leave', *beír* 'inscribe', *elír* 'make a mistake in writing', *átir* 'rewrite', *körülír* 'circumscribe', *aláír* 'sign', etc. The meaning of a preverb + verb compound is not always predictable from the meaning of the individual verb and preverb; the literal meaning of *felír*, for example, is 'write to a high place'.

Basic Syntax

Hungarian word order is SOV when the object is nonspecific, and SVO when the object is definite or indefinite. Other than this, word order is quite flexible.

Focus is an important feature of ordinary Hungarian discourse. It expresses the communicational importance of the component that carries it, while the rest of the sentence might as well be presupposed. There can be no more than one focus per sentence, marked by high stress.

No focus: *°A 'gyerek 'meg-ette °az 'almá-t*
the child up-ate the apple-ACC
'The child ate the apple.'

Subject focus: °*A Ogyerek °ette 'meg °az 'almát*
'It was the child who ate/has eaten the apple'

Object focus: °*Az Oalmá-t °ette 'meg °a 'gyerek.*
'It was the apple that the child ate/What the child ate was the apple'

Verb focus: °*A 'gyerek Omeg-ette °az °almá-t.*
The child up-ate the apple-ACC
'The child ate the apple'

Negation is expressed by means of preposed articles, *ne* for prohibition, otherwise *nem*. Negation always involves focus, either of the element the negative precedes or of the negative itself.

The first word in the sentence is usually the topic, the component the statement is made about (independently of what part of the speech it is).

Contact with Other Languages

Due to the domination of Austria, Hungarian historically had much contact with GERMAN. The modern boundaries of Hungary were established in 1919 after the fall of the Austro-Hungarian Empire (in 1914). The Treaty of Trianon attached parts of Hungary to Romania, Yugoslavia, Austria, Czechoslovakia and Ukraine, according to the ethnic majority. Consequently, Hungarian is today spoken in these countries.

Hungarian has borrowed words from a number of sources. The earliest borrowings are probably from Iranian, from the time when the Proto-Hungarian people came in contact with various Iranian peoples (during the Finno-Ugric and the Ugric periods). Turkic words entered Proto-Ugric and continued to enter the language (which would become Hungarian) for several thousand years, culminating in the 16th and 17th centuries when the Turks occupied Hungary. Both Eastern and Western Turkic contributed to Hungarian vocabulary, leading to such duplicates as *gyűszű* 'thimble' (Western), *gyűrű* 'ring (on the finger)' (Eastern), cf. Turkish *yüzük* 'ring'. Slavic words entered the language when the Proto-Hungarians settled in the Carpathic basin and came into contact with the Slavs who were living there. Ever since that time, there has been linguistic contact with Slavic neighbors to the north and south. In some cases, certain words have been identified as coming from specific Slavic languages (i.e., BULGARIAN, SERBO-CROATIAN, SLOVENE, SLOVAK, or POLISH). Germanic words began to enter Hungarian at a steady rate from the time the Hungarian kingdom was established. There are over 300 German words in Hungarian standard usage. Latin has contributed about 200 loanwords; most entered during the Middle Ages and Reformation.

From Iranian: *tehén* 'cow', *tej* 'milk', *arany* 'gold'
From Slavic: *macska* 'cat', *lapát* 'oar', *kalács* 'cake'
From Latin: *iskola* 'school', *tábla* 'blackboard'
From Romanian: *cimbora* 'fellow', *tokány* 'meat dish with pepper'
From Turkic: *kender* 'hemp', *alma* 'apple', *eke* 'plough'
From German: *hercëg* 'prince', *pék* 'baker', *tánc* 'dance'

Common Words

man:	ferfi	long:	hosszú
woman:	nő	small:	kicsi (kis before noun)
water:	víz	yes:	igen
sun:	nap	no:	nem
three:	három	good:	jó
fish:	hal	bird:	madár
big:	nagy	dog:	kutya
tree:	fa		

Example Sentences

(1) A diák level-et ír.
The student letter-ACC writes
[Aw di-ahk leh-veh-let eer] (*i* as in thin, *eh* as in let)
'The student is writing a letter.' ("letter" not specific)

(2)A diák ír- ja a level-et.
The student writes-it the letter-ACC.
[Aw di-ahk eer-yaw aw leh-veh-let]
'The student is writing the letter.'

(3) Hogy érz-ed maga-d?
How feel-sg.2. self-sg.2.
w/focus sub.
stressdef.obj.
[hody airzed mawgawd] (*dy* as in dew)
'How do you feel?'

Efforts to Preserve, Protect, and Promote the Language

Although Hungary was formerly multilingual, after the First World War and the redrawing of national borders, Hungarian became virtually the only language spoken there. During the Communist rule (1948–1989), the state discouraged the use of languages other than Hungarian.

However, the constitution of the Hungarian Republic, which was proclaimed on October 23, 1989, specified that "The national language minorities are under the protection of the Hungarian Republic. They have the right to take part collectively in public life, to foster their own culture, to use their mother tongue, and to receive education in their mother tongue, and to use their personal names in their own language." (Article 68, paragraph 2)

Today, reflecting the new tolerance for multiculturalism, bilingual education is available in Hungary whereby children are taught both in their mother tongue and in Hungarian.

Select Bibliography

Abondolo, Daniel. 1987. Hungarian. In *The World's Major Languages,* ed. Bernard Comrie, 577–592. London: Croom Helm.

Benkő, László, and Samu Imre, eds. 1972. *The Hungarian Language.* The Hague: Mouton.

Kiefer, Ferenc, ed. 1982. *Hungarian Linguistics.* Amsterdam: Benjamins.

IBIBIO

Okon Essien

Language Name: Ibibio. **Alternates:** *Ibibio-Efik, Efik-Ibibio* (obsolete); *Agbisherea* (19th century European name, no longer used), *Kwa/Qua* (name formerly used by the Bonny, a people in the Rivers State of Nigeria), and *Ndi mmọñọ* (name formerly used by the Igbo). **Autonym:** *Ibibio.*

Location: Spoken as the major and dominant local language in Akwa Ibom State of Nigeria and as a competing language (with Efik) in many parts of the Cross River State of Nigeria, both of which are in southeastern Nigeria.

Family: Lower Cross subgroup of the Delta group of the Cross River subbranch of the Benue-Congo branch of the Niger-Congo subfamily of the Niger-Kordofanian language family.

Related Languages: There are some differences of opinion and analysis regarding related languages. It is generally agreed that the following languages are closely related: Efik, Annang, Oron, Eket, Ibeno, Okobo, Mbo, Itu Mbon Uso, and Andoni (Obolo). Of these, Efik and Annang are mutually intelligible with Ibibio. The rest are unilaterally intelligible with Ibibio in that speakers of these tongues understand Ibibio without learning it, but the Ibibio do not understand nor speak their languages readily without learning them (Essien 1987).

Dialects: The above languages are regarded as dialects of Ibibio by Jeffreys, Forde and Jones, Kaufman, Welmers, and Essien. Assigning these languages the status of dialects of Ibibio is based on mutual intelligibility as well as vocabulary, phonological, and morphological similarities. Forde and Jones divide Ibibio into the following regional dialects: Eastern Ibibio or Ibibio Proper, Annang or Western Ibibio, Enyong or Northern Ibibio, Eket/Oron or Southern Ibibio, Andoni-Ibeno or Delta Ibibio, and Efik or the Riverain Ibibio. Since all these subgroups are very closely related linguistically and culturally, they are referred to as "Ibibiod", a term comparable to Edoid, Igboid, Yoruboid and others.

Within Ibibio proper, or Central Ibibio, which constitutes our focus, the following are the major regional subdialectal divisions: Eastern Ibibio Ikono, Ibiono Ibom, Itam, Uyo, Etinan, Ibesikpo, Asutan, Eket, and Mkpat Enin/Ikot Abasi. These correspond to either clan (for example, Ibiono, Ibom, and Itam) or administrative/political division referred to as Local Government Area (LGA) (for example, Uyo and Etinan). In both cases, the dialects are regional variants. This entry gives examples in Ibibio Proper, as spoken in Akwa Ibom State of Nigeria.

Number of Speakers: 4–4.5 million based on the projections of the 1963 census, considered the most reliable since independence in 1960.

Origin and History

Ibibio is one of the four major Nigerian languages after HAUSA, YORUBA, and IGBO.

Recent studies in Ibibio oral tradition (folktales, legends, songs, proverbs, and riddles) seem to provide internal evidence of migration from the areas around Egypt, Palestine, and East Africa, westward to west Africa a very long time ago. According to this tradition, the Ibibio passed through Abyssinia and Cameroon and entered what is now Nigeria through Usakedet.

Linguists and archaeologists believe that the ancestors of the Ibibio probably migrated from the central Benue Valley in what is now Nigeria to southeastern Nigeria between 600–200 B.C. (Abasiattai 1991).

In the sixteenth century came European traders, beginning with the Portuguese. The Ibibio, who had long produced palm oil, began trading on a large scale with the Europeans. The Ibibio produced "native iron reckoned better than the English" (Waddell 1863), and were great road builders. "Instead of the narrow customary native path ... the Kwos of Ibibio took great pride in making broad and smooth roads from village to village. These were kept clean of weeds and bordered with fine shady trees and neat hedges which enclosed plantations." (Jeffreys 1935)

When the British colonized what is now Nigeria in the 1840s, the Ibibio were the first to realize the importance of the new Western education for their society. They formed the legendary Ibibio Union that not only sent Ibibiod (not just Ibibio) people abroad in the 1930s for education in the key areas of the economy including medicine, law, agriculture, and science, but also built a community grammar school called Ibibio State College.

The British contact with what is now Nigeria was almost disastrous for the Ibibio language because beginning in the 1840s Efik, a numerically smaller dialect of the language, was written and used alongside ENGLISH by the early Christian missionaries. This led to the use of Efik as the literary dialect of Ibibio, eclipsing Ibibio. M.D.W. Jeffreys, a onetime District Officer of Colonial Nigeria, produced an orthography for the Ibibio language and made a passionate plea to the missionary authorities that Ibibio be used officially in the Ibibio territory, but his orthography was rejected. The attempt to write and make Ibibio an official language failed. Ibibio was to remain unwritten and unofficial until 1983 when, with the sponsorship of an Ibibio cultural organization known as *Akwa Esop*

Table 1: Consonants

		Labial	Dental	Palatal	Labio-velar	Velar	Uvular
Stops	Voiceless	p	t		kp	k	
	Voiced	b	d				
Fricatives		f	s				
Nasals		m	n	ny		n̄	
Approximants			r	y	w		h, gh

Imaisong Ibibio ('The Great Parliament of the Ibibio People'), an orthography was produced and presented to the Ministry of Education of the then Cross River State, of which what is now Akwa Ibom State was a part. Both the Ministry of Education and the Cross River State Government-in-Council officially approved the orthography. In 1985 it was approved by the Federal Ministry of Education.

Orthography and Basic Phonology

Ibibio orthography is partly phonemic and partly phonetic (see Table 1 above).

Ny represents the palatal nasal [ɲ], and *n̄* the velar nasal [ŋ]. *R* represents an alveolar tap similar to the sound in the middle of the English word "ladder". *H* is a uvular approximant [ʁ], similar to the *r* sound of FRENCH. *Gh* is a uvular flap [ʀ]. *Kp* is a doubly articulated stop [k͡p], with simultaneous velar and labial closures. Both oral and nasal stops can be single or geminate.

/n/ becomes syllabic when immediately followed by a consonant to which it assimilates in place of articulation.

Table 2: Vowels

	Front	Central	Back
High	i, ị		ụ,u
Mid	e	ə	o
Mid-Low		ʌ	ọ
Low		a	

The vowels /ị/ and /ụ/ are lower and somewhat centralized relative to /i/ and /u/, respectively.

Ibibio has two basic-level tones, high and low. Other tones involve a combination or modification of these basic tones. One such modification involves a high tone, which can be lowered by an abstract phenomenon known as "downstep". Such a slightly lowered tone is referred to as a downstepped high tone and contrasts phonemically with both the basic high and low tones. Other significant tones are rising and falling, which, although combinations of the high and low tones phonetically, do nonetheless contrast with these two basic-level tones. These tones are represented in standard transcription as follows:

Tone	Example
High (H)	dép 'buy'
Low (L)	dèp 'rain (verb)'
Downstepped (DH)	úkȯ 'yonder'(2nd syl)
Rising (LH)	kpăp ideophone, sudden 'seizure'
Falling (HL)	ùtâ̂n 'worm'

Each syllable of an Ibibio word has its own tone associated with it. Syllabic nasals also have tones.

There are tonal modifications of various kinds. Phonologically, preceding low tones affect all high tones, producing a falling intonational phenomenon known as "downdrift", in that the last high tone cannot be as high as the first tone in a phonological phrase. Downstepped high tones similarly affect all following high tones.

Some syntactic constructions contain tone indications that cannot be associated with a particular element in the construction. Such "floating" tones are identified by the effects they have on other, lexical tones. For example, associative or possessive constructions involve two nouns and a floating high tone. The floating high tone has no effect on the tones of the first noun. However, some tone combinations on the second noun are affected: sequences of high-high, low-low, and high-falling become high-low, and a sequence of low-high becomes high-downstepped-high.

Except in academic and technical works, tones are not normally indicated in Ibibio.

Basic Morphology

Nouns in Ibibio typically have two syllables, a prefix and a base. The prefix is either a vowel or a nasal. Prefixes may perform a variety of functions like *i-*, *u-*, *edi-* for abstractness of various sorts, *a-* for agency, and *e-* for animacy; there are many exceptions.

Ibibio has vestiges of nominal classification, by which vowels generally alternate with nasals for the singular/plural distinction:

Singular	Plural	Meaning
è-dídèm	ǹ-dídèm	'king'
á-yéyịn	ń-yéyịn	'grandchild'
á-bíâ	ḿ-bíâ	'expert'

Sometimes pluralization may be indicated by a change of prefix vowel (sometimes with additional changes):

Singular	Plural	Meaning
á-n̄wáàn	í-báàn	'wife'
à-bọ́íkpà	ú-bọ́íkpá	'girl'

Adjectives agree with nouns in number: *à-nyán ó-kúku* (tall chief) 'a tall chief', *-nyán ń̄-kúkú* (PL-tall PL-chief) 'tall chiefs'. There is no case marking for nouns. However, case distinctions are marked on pronouns. Where free forms are not indicated, the subject form is used.

	Subject	Object-bound	Object-free	Possessive
1sg	àmì	-ǹ-	mîn	ḿmì
1pl	ǹyị̀n	-î-	ńnyị̀n	
2sg	àfò	-û-	fîn	ḿfò
2pl	ǹdùfò			
3sg	ènyé			ọ́mọ̀
3pl	ọ̀mmộ			

Ibibio verbs agree with their subjects in person and number, as illustrated in the following present-tense forms of *-béd* 'wait':

	Singular	Plural
1	ḿ-bèd	ì-bèd
2	à-bèd	è-bèd
3	á-bêd	é-bêd

Verbs also exhibit a process called "pluriaction", by which they take on a plural form because the object is plural or because the action of the verb is performed repeatedly or frequently:

Ènyé â-dép ǹ́wèd kèed
he 3SG/PERF-buy book one
'He has bought one book.'

Ènyé â-déem-é ùwák ǹ́wèd
he 3SG/PERF-buy-PLUR many book
'He has bought many books.'

Pluriaction is expressed by a number of morphological processes including vowel doubling and counsonant nasalization.

Verbs are marked morphologically for tense and mood. Ibibio has three basic tenses including past, present, and future:

ḿ-màá-yàiyá 'I was pretty'
ḿ-mé-yàiyá 'I am pretty'
ń-yàá-yàiyá 'I will be pretty'
ń-yáà-yàiyá 'I will be pretty'

The difference between the two future-tense forms is that *–yàá-* marks an indefinite future while *–yáà-* marks an immediate or proximate future.

Tense morphemes are syntactically conditioned by negation, emphasis, and mood. The following examples illustrate the effects of negation:

ǹ́-ké-nyàiyá-ké 'I wasn't pretty'
ń-yàiyá-ké 'I'm not pretty'
ń-dî-yàiyá-ké 'I won't be pretty'

Ibibio verbs can be marked for inceptive/inchoative, habitual, or completive aspect:

ń-yé-nàm ǹ́kpọ́ ńtè ọ́bọ̀ọn̄
1SG-INCEPT-do something like chief
'I now begin to behave like a chief.'

ń-sí-nám ǹ́kpọ́ ńtè ọ́bọ̀ọn̄
1SG-INCEPT-do something like chief
'I often behave like a chief.'

ḿ-mé-nȧm ǹ́kpọ́ ńtè ọ́bọ̀ọn̄
1SG-PERF-do something like chief
'I have done something like a chief.'

Ibibio has a set of verbal extensions similar to those found in Bantu languages. These include markers for reflexive, reversive, and reciprocal verbs, and also a marker indicating the absence of an agent.

Reciprocals involve a prefix and a suffix: *È-dú-kòp-pò* (IMPERATIVE-RECIPROCAL-listen-RECIPROCAL) 'Listen to each other'.

The other extensions are suffixes: *Ǹ́síkàn á-máà-díb-bé* (Nsikan 3SG-PAST-hide-REFLEXIVE) 'Nsikan hid himself', *fʌ́k-kọ́* (cover-REVERSIVE) 'uncover'.

Basic Syntax

The normal or unmarked order of constituents in an Ibibio sentence is SVO. Both direct and indirect objects can be topicalized by movement to the beginning of the sentence and insertion of the partical *ké* immediately after it:

Òkón á-màá-wèd Âkòn détà
Okon 3SG-PAST-write Akon letter
'Okon wrote Akon a letter.'

Détà ké Òkón á-ké-wėd Âkòn
letter TOP Okon 3SG-PAST-write Akon
'It was a letter that Okon wrote Akon.'

Âkòn ké Òkón á-ké-wėd détà
Akon TOP Okon 3SG-PAST-write letter
'It was Akon that Okon wrote a letter to.'

Within the noun phrase, adjectives and quantifiers precede the noun while possessors, numerals, determiners, and relative clauses follow:

Ǹ-dìtò Êtị̀m ìtá ódò é-nàm-mà útóm
PL-child Etim three the 3PL-work-RELATIVE work
'The three children of Etim who are working...'

Ibibio verbs may be serial or nonserial. In serial constructions, two or more verbs can occur in one simple or nuclear clause; one of these is a main or controlling verb and the other(s) what Essien (1974) refers to as quasi-verbal. These verbs occur as a unit verb, attract the same agreement marker, and form a unitary construction syntactically and semantically. Tense, aspect, and mood affixes are borne only by the main verb:

Ímá á-màá-sàñá á-kpèré Inėm
Ima 3SG-PAST-walk 3SG-near Inem
'Ima walked near Inem.'

Èmèm í-dî-fèghé-ké inyʌñ-ñọ í-bọñ mkpo
Emem 3SG-FUT-run- 3SG-and-NEG 3SG-shout shout

'Emem will not run and will not shout.'

Negation in Ibibio is extremely complicated; it is expressed by a combination of prefixation, suffixation, selection of other grammatical affixes from a different set, and tonal change, and is conditioned by syllable structure and by sentence type.

In simple declarative sentences, negation is expressed by a suffix whose form depends on the verb stem. Roots consisting of a CV take a suffix of the form *-hV* or *-ghV*, where the V is determined by the vowel of the verb root. CVC roots take a CV suffix, where the C is a repetition of the second root consonant, and the V is determined by the vowel of the verb root.

Verbs that contain more than one syllable have invariant *-ké* as the negative suffix. Some examples of negative verbs include: *ńyị̀ppé* 'I have not stolen' (< *yị̀p* 'steal'), *ḿmànná* 'I have not given birth to' (< *màn* 'give birth'), *ńséeghé* 'I'm not looking at' (< *sé* 'look at'), *ńdàkkáké* 'I haven't gone away' (< *dàkká* 'go away'). Other negatives are illustrated in the immediately preceding example, in which the third person singular agreement prefix *á-* is also replaced by *í-*.

Contact with Other Languages

Ibibio has been in contact with other Nigerian languages (Igbo, Yoruba, Hausa), but the greatest number of loans has come from English with which there has been contact for over a century.

From English: *títìà* 'teacher', *bébà*, 'paper', *bêd* 'bed', *sìmét* 'cement', *bòdísè* 'police', *àkrâsì* 'glass'
From Igbo: *òsúsú* (or *àsúsú*) 'contribution'
From Hausa: *àdàfíà* 'enjoyment' (< Hausa *alafia* 'well-being')
From Yoruba: *àkàmù* 'kind of porridge'
From Efik: *èwrọ̀* 'kind of gown'

The English contact brought not only loanwords (which are generally assimilated into the phonology of the language) but also the phenomenon of codemixing among bilinguals, where English words are introduced on the spur of the moment, as the following examples illustrate: My car *í-fọ́n-n* (3SG-good-NEG) 'My car is not good', Those people *é-dòn̄n̄ò* (3PL-are) stupid. 'Those people are stupid'.

Common Words

man:	ówódèen	sun:	útín
woman:	ówón̄wàan	three:	ìtá
water:	ḿmóon̄	fish:	íyák
long:	ànyán	big:	èkámbá
small:	ètə̀k	no:	ìiyó
yes:	íi	good:	étî
bird:	ínúèn	tree:	étó

Example Sentences

(1) Ǹsíkán à-yàá-démmé í-dáp.
Nsikan 3SG-FUT-wake sleep
'Nsikan will be awake.'

(2) Yíé í-dém.
Wash body
'Have your bath.'

(3) À-kǎ úkè?
2SG-go where
'Where are you going?'

Efforts to Preserve, Protect, and Promote the Language

The Ibibio Language Writers Association (ILWA) is at the center of activities to promote and protect *ọ̀bʌ̀p-àtìib Íbìbìò*, that is, proper, not mixed, Ibibio. It acts as liaison between the government and the people in these endeavors. The association tries to discourage code mixing Ibibio not only with English but also with Efik. It insists that "Efik-Ibibio" or "Ibibio-Efik" is a dead concept and counterproductive.

To a large extent the discouragement of code-mixing Ibibio and Efik is effective, but code mixing English and Ibibio is very common, particularly among young bilinguals in informal situations. Government officials being interviewed on radio or television, for example, will restrain themselves from English code mixing.

The ILWA is also trying to keep loanwords to a minimum. Preferably, native words are coined before resorting to borrowing from another language. Thus, words such as *úkárá* 'government' and *úfộkn̄wèd-tàìfíọ̀k* 'university' are preferred to their loan counterparts *kọ̀fùmèn* and *yùnìfésìtì*, respectively.

In cases where a loanword must be adopted, it must be completely assimilated to the Ibibio sound system. Partial assimilation is viewed as inelegant and unacceptable.

The ILWA has been most successful in promoting scholarship in Ibibio. It publishes a premier series, *Kufre Mme Ndifreke*, anthologies of poems, short stories, plays, and novels. It has produced literacy charts, such as *Abisi Ibibio* ('Ibibio Orthography') and it has conducted innumerable workshops for teachers of Ibibio. Within a decade of its being written, ILWA has succeeded in transforming Ibibio from a preliterate to a literate language.

Select Bibliography

Abasiattai, Monday, ed. 1987. *Akwa Ibom and Cross River States: The Land, The People and Their Culture*. Calabar: Wusen Press Ltd.

Brann, C.M.B. 1993. "Democratisation of Language Use in Public Domains in Nigeria." In *Journal of Modern African Studies 31*, 4: 639–656.

Cook, T.L. 1985. *An Integrated Phonology of Efik, Vol. I: The Earlier Stages of the Phonological Derivation, With Particular Attention to the Vowel and Tone System*. Ph.D. Thesis, University of London.

Essien, Okon. 1974. *Pronominalization in Efik*. Ph.D. Thesis, University of Edinburgh.

____. 1983a. *The Orthography of the Ibibio Language*. Calabar: Paico Press & Books Ltd.

____. 1983b. "Verbal Derivation in Ibibio." In *Work In Progress 16*: 117–130.

____. 1990. *A Grammar of the Ibibio Language*. Ibadan: University Press Ltd.

____. 1995. "The English Language and Code-Mixing: A Case Study of the Phenomenon in Ibibio." In *New Englishes: A West African Perspective*. Ayo Bamgbose, Ayo Banjo, and Andrew Thomas, eds. Ibadan: Mosuro Publishers and Booksellers.

____. Forthcoming. "The Concepts of Minority and Majority Languages." In *Current Trends in Language Learning and Teaching*. M. Anyanwu, ed. Owerri: AICE.

Forde, Daryll, and Jones, G.I. 1950. *The Igbo and Ibibio-Speaking Peoples of Nigeria*. London: International African Institute.

Jeffreys, M.D.W. 1935. *Old Calabar and Notes on the Ibibio Language*. Calabar: H.W.T.I. Press.

Kaufman, Elaine. 1985. *Ibibio Dictionary*. London: African Studies Centre.

Udo, Edet. 1983. *Who Are the Ibibio?* Onitsha: Africana-Fep. Publishers Ltd.

Udoma, Sir Udo. 1987. *The Story of the Ibibio Union*. Ibadan: Spectrum Books.

Waddell, Hope. 1863. *Twenty-Nine Years in West and Central Africa*. Edinburgh: Nelson and Son.

Welmers, William. 1968. *Efik* (Occasional Publication No. 11). Ibadan: Institute of African Studies Publication.

ÌGBO

Éjíke Ezè and Victor Manfredi

Language Name and Autonym: Ìgbo [formerly spelled "Eboe" or "Ibo"].[1]

Location: Ìgbo is the second most populous indigenous language of southern Nigeria.

Family: Ìgbo belongs to the Niger-Congo family. Greenberg (1963) classified it in the Kwa group along with six other big clusters: Àkán, Gbè, Yorùbá-Ìgálà, Nupe-Èbìrà, Ẹ̀dó and Ìdọmà. Williamson (1989a) redrew this picture, reducing "Kwa" to Àkán and Gbè, and shifting the rest including Ìgbo to an enlarged "Benue-Congo" group (the aggregate that includes Bantu). Williamson's evidence does not go beyond lexicostatistics—a shortcut method rejected by orthodox comparativists.

Related Languages: The Ìgbo-speaking area is surrounded by dozens of closely related Niger-Congo languages, representing at least five large subgroups: Ẹdoid (to the west), Defoid (to the northwest), Idọmoid (to the north), Lower Cross (to the east and south) and Ịjọ (to the south).

Dialects: Ìgbo has dozens of geographic dialects. Williamson (1989b: 92f.) holds that the oldest linguistic division stranded the southwest periphery, including Ẹ̀hwụ́dà ["Ahoada" or "Ekpeye"] and Ọ̀gbakịrị ["Ikwerri"], but her conclusion may be an artefact of lexicostatistics that mix together innovations, archaisms and borrowing (Ọ́nwụejíọgwụ̀ 1975). Judging by sound change and morphosyntax, the oldest division is between a contiguous northern area, and a southern area that is still self-contiguous except for the old Ágbọ̀ ["Abwor", "Agbor" or "Ika"] Kingdom at the western end (Manfredi 1989). All northern dialects denasalized [cn] clusters—still found as such in Ágbọ̀—while many southern dialects including Òweré and Ńgẖwà ["Ngwa"] (but not Ágbọ̀) developed them to aspirated stops (Armstrong 1972; Ladefoged *et al.* 1976). Many southern dialects (including Ágbọ̀) glottalized *t* and *d* before expanded pharynx vowels (Ánọ̀ká 1985). Northern dialects have more auxiliary verbs, and fewer verb-inflecting suffixes, than do southern dialects (Éménanjọ 1984)—indicating a shift in the north from agglutination to a more isolating morphosyntactic type. Northern dialects also developed a new perfective suffix *-gea /-gu /-go /-gwo /-wo* (from a verb meaning 'finish') vs. southern *-(o)le* (related to Bantu *-ile*) and a new type of *wh*-question (described below, cf. Goldsmith 1981). This picture is consistent with ecological and oral evidence that northern Ìgbo started to develop on its own in hilly terrain between Ụ̀lụ́ ["Orlu"], Ọ́ka ["Awka"] and Ǹsụ́ká ["Nsukka"] after southern-Igbo speakers had dispersed to cultivate lowland forests that are today oil-palm savannah (Ọ́nwụejíọgwụ̀ 1972; Áfaìgbo 1981).

Number of Speakers: Official census figures since the 1960s have been controversial but subregional trends projected from four million Ìgbo speakers in 1921 and five and a half million in 1953 suggest an estimate of 20 or 25 million in the year 2000. Ìgbo is also widely spoken as a second language in the Niger Delta and the Cross River Basin. Probably between half a million and a million Ìgbo speakers died after the two *coups d'état* of 1966 and during the civil war of 1967–1970.

Origin and History

Whichever protolanguage led to Ìgbo was probably spoken near the confluence of the Niger and Benue Rivers between two and three thousand years ago, contemporaneous with a Nok-type iron technology (Armstrong 1964; Greenberg 1972; Cookey 1980; Williamson 1989b). Proto-Ìgbo speakers must have reached the present Ìgbo-speaking area long before the artistically rich Ìgbo Úkwu burials, which are iconographically related to the Ǹri Kingdom and which are "about a thousand years old" (Shaw 1970: 262; cf. Ọ́nwụejíọgwụ̀ 1980).

One synchronically salient gloss of the term "Ìgbo" is "community", as in personal names like *Òdénìgbo* 'The news has spread to the community' and *Ọ́nwụzùrúìgbo* 'Death reaches everyone' (Ọ́nwụejíọgwụ̀ 1972: 40f.). The first syllable [ì-] is an ancient prefix for the human, plural noun-class, attested in countless ethnic and place-names across Kwa and in archaic common noun plurals like the Ọ̀nịcha ["Onitsha"] forms for 'men' and 'women' (listed below; cf. Williamson 1976). Some speakers contrast *Ìgbo* with *Óru* (or *Ólu*) to distinguish inland dwellers from communities near the Niger's banks. The noun *Óru*/*Ólu* is transparently related to the verb *-rú*/*-lú* 'flood, overflow'—a predicate aptly describing riverine ecology. *Dioscorea* yam, the original Ìgbo staple crop, was probably domesticated in a floodplain setting, where still today the best yields are obtained. By the 18th century, the *Óru* network had developed a distinct identity as long-distance traders of foodstuffs, ivory, cloth, guns and slaves. According to a characteristic Ìgbo phrase structure for universal quantification, the Ọ̀nịcha phrase *Ólu nà Igbo* 'riverine and inland people' means, in effect, "the entire ethnolinguistic community" (Ífemésia 1979: 115) or indeed 'the inhabited world'. If this dichotomy is old, then the

[1]Throughout this article, following the first occurrence of an ethnic or place name, we cite its traditionally anglicized spelling (if any) in double quotes and within square brackets.

lexical root *-gbò* may be related to the verb for 'cover, protect' as in instrument nouns like *ḿgbòchí* 'veil' and *ḿgbòdó* 'shield' (Williamson 1972: 150). On these grounds, *Ì-gbo* would etymologically mean 'people of the covered (forested/sheltered/remote) interior'—a term coined in the Niger Riverbank trade some 300 years ago.

Orthography and Basic Phonology

The current official orthography—basically just a list of 36 symbols in less than a double-spaced typed page of text—was accepted from the Ọ́nwụ Committee by the Eastern Nigerian government in 1961. The main innovation is the rejection of non-Roman symbols and the adoption in their place of a subdot diacritic for vowels, a superdot diacritic for a nonsyllabic velar nasal, and digraphs for 9 consonants. (Eighteen monographic consonants were retained from previous orthographies.) Ọ́nwụ's 36 symbols, listed below, obviously represent a compromise between the low end of phonological endowment in the Ìgbo-speaking area—Ọ̀nịcha with 31 segmental phonemes—and the high end—Òweré ["Owerri"] with around 48.[2] For this reason, no standard variety of the language is defined.

4 "long" vowels	i, e (formerly "ɛ"), o, u
4 "short" vowels[3]	ị (formerly "e"), a, ọ (formerly "ɔ"), ụ (formerly "θ")
nonsyllabic velar nasal	ṅ (formerly "ng")
9 consonant digraphs	gb, gh, kp, sh, ch, gw, kw, nw, ny
18 consonant monographs	b, d, f, g, h, j, k, l, m, n, p, r, s, t, v, w, y, z (retained unchanged)

The Ọ́nwụ report did not consider tone or word division, and avoided dialect-specific features like aspiration and nasality.[4] One committee member later justified the exclusion of dialect-specific sounds as "a worthy sacrifice for the development of a de-dialectalised Ìgbo" (Ọ́gbàlụ́ 1975: 151). At the other extreme, some literary figures still reject the Ọ́nwụ framework (Nwáọ̀ga 1990; Échèrúó 1998). A middle road was taken by Green & Ígwè (1963), who added consonantal diacritics to the Ọ́nwụ symbols in order to accommodate the Ọ́màáhyá ["Umuahia"] dialect (which is phonologically close to Òweré). Green and Ígwè used the subdot plus [h] to mark the aspirated velar stop [gḥ]; we can extend this to the other aspirates [pḥ, bḥ, tḥ, dḥ, cḥ, jḥ, kḥ]. Equally, Ọ́nwụ's use of plain [h] in the digraph [gh] for the voiced velar fricative (found in many dialects both north and south) can be extended to other dialect-specific fricatives where needed.[5] Ánọ̀ká (1985) employs a plain subdot for the glottalized voiceless alveolar stop[ṭ].[6] Green and Ígwè write distinctively nasalized vowels with a superscript tilde [˜]—not above the vowel but on the preceding consonant [c̃v] where it doesn't interfere with tone marks; we prefer to write them [vn], following the lead of closely related languages like Ẹ̀dó and Yorùbá so as to avoid one more diacritic. Again on the model of Ẹ̀dó and Yorùbá, the subdot has wide current usage to indicate a ninth vowel [ẹ] in dialects where this sound is distinctive, e.g., Ẹ̀hwụ́dà, Ọ̀gbakịrị, Ágbọ̀, Ǹsụ́ká, Àbánkeléke ["Abakaliki" or "Izi"] and Ẹ́hụgbò ["Afikpo"].[7]

[`] and [´] indicate low and high tone, respectively. Downstep is no tone at all but a "juncture", specifically in Ìgbo it is a nonautomatic pitch drop between high tones (Green & Ígwè 1963: 6–7). In Ìgbo, downstep is part of the basic structure of infinitives, negatives, perfectives and genitives, and also occurs in a few underived nouns as well as in countless lexicalised phrases.[8] Following Swift, *et al* (1962), Welmers and Welmers (1968a,b) and Nwáchukwu (1976), we adopt the economy rule that an unmarked syllable shares the tone of the syllable to its left; in this way, any sequence of two high marks with no pause in between indicates a downstep before the second mark, e.g., the tonal melody of the phrase [*ọ̀wụ́wají*] 'new yam festival' (lit. 'splitting' plus 'yam.GEN') is LHH!H (where [!] is the phonetic downstep symbol). Williamson (1972) and Éménanjọ (1978) use a different system, with no high mark at all (i.e. every unmarked syllable is high), every low marked individually, and a macron on the first syllable after a downstep; accordingly they write 'new yam festival' as [*ọ̀wụwajī*].[9]

Some scholars argue that tone-marking is unnecessary in materials destined for a purely monolingual audience "except to resolve ambiguity where context is unclear" (Ùgonnà 1980:

[2]Not counting the syllabic nasal, which is homographic with the corresponding nasal stop. Slightly different numbers of segments are counted by Armstrong (1972: 4), based on slightly different assumptions.

[3]The subdotted vowels—which the Ọ́nwụ report called "short" on analogy to English lax vowels in closed syllables—are more accurately described as members of the [-ATR] or expanded-pharynx set. In roots, [a] has the distribution of a subdotted or [-ATR] vowel in all dialects, but in some northern dialects like Ọ̀nịcha [a] is neutral to [ATR] harmony in a few noun prefixes.

[4]After the Nigerian Civil War, various nongovernmental bodies have addressed some of these points with tacit official backing (see for example Society for Promoting Ìgbo Language & Culture (1977)).

[5][sh] contrasts with [s] in northern dialects like Ìgboúzọ̀ ["Ibusa"] and Àbáàgana where it corresponds to Ọ̀nịchạ [r] as in *áshọ̀* 'year', the name Ǹshi and the indicative negative suffix *-shọ̀*, cf. Ọ́gbàlụ́ (1982), Éménanjọ (1984). The alternative, to simply use [r] in such dialects, would be technically possible but seems overly abstract. Other dialect-specific fricatives may be allophonic. [sh] and [zh] occur only before front vowels and apparently never contrast with [s] and [z] (Green & Ígwè 1963: 6). (ß) occurs in Ọ̀nịcha and some other northern dialects as an intervocalic variant of [f]; Àzụ́ónye and Ùdéchukwu (1984) spell it [v], although [bh] would be more accurate. [ph] and [kh], reported in northern dialects like Àbánkeléke (Meir, *et al.* 1975) and Nsụ́ká, may be allophonic.

[6]Glottal stop as a syllable onset is an allophone of [ṭ]; if necessary, it can be written with a word-internal apostrophe, as in the Òweré verb *-wè'é* 'bring' (=Ọ̀nịcha *-wètá*, Ḿbàisén *–wèṭé*).

[7][ẹ] occurs, but redundantly, in some Ọ̀nịcha roots and affixes.

[8]Especially in proper names, cf. footnote 14 below. Also note that in proverbs, where some grammatical affixes are conventionally elided, downstep is the sole cue for negation, e.g., *Ìgbo énwé ezè* literally, 'Ìgbo has no king'.

[9]We prefer the Welmers-Nwáchukwu tone-marking to handle downstep in Ìgbo because it dispenses with the macron—a diacritic that has proven difficult to write legibly by hand and which, we observe, encourages the mistaken idea that Ìgbo downstep is a "mid-tone". If that were the case, then an immediately following high tone should be *higher* in pitch, but it is not. Syntactic antidownstep (reversal of a preceding downstep) does occur phonetically in all Ìgbo dialects, in a variety of contexts, but its predictability means that it need never be marked, even in Àbánkeléke and Ágbọ̀ where it is frequent (Manfredi 1992, *pace* Meir *et al.* 1975).

Table 1: Consonants

		Labial	Alveolar	Palato-alveolar	Velar	Labialized velar	Glottal
Non-Continuants	Voiceless Unaspirated	p	t	tʃ	k	k^{w}	(ʔ)
	Voiceless Aspirated	(p^{h})	(t^{h})	(tʃ^{h})	(k^{h})	(k^{hw})	
	Voiced Unaspirated	b	d	dʒ	g	g^{w}	
	Murmured Aspirated	(b^{h})	(d^{h})	(dʒ^{h})	(g^{h})	(g^{hw})	
	Voiceless Implosive	(p<)	(t<)				
	Voiced Implosive	ɓ					
	Nasal	m	n	ŋ	ŋ	ŋ^{w}	
Continuants	Voiceless Fricative	f	s	(ʃ)	(χ)		h
	Voiced Fricative	(β, v)	(z)		(ɣ)		
	Trill			r			
	Lateral			l			
	Glide	w		y			

147). The late Prof. D.I. Nwáọga asked: "To what extent is writing an attempt at an exact reproduction of the sounds of a language and to what extent may it be taken as a symbolic system that is quite effective by pointing rather than incorporating the total sense?" (letter, 30/5/90). Our answer: tone marks, too, are "pointing" devices, not acoustic recordings. For example, every Ìgbo speaker pronounces the third syllable of *ázịzá* 'response' at a lower pitch than the first syllable (this is the phonetic downdrift phenomenon), but both are marked as high tones because that information is what matters to the lexicon, e.g., to distinguish 'response' from 'broom' (which is either *àzịza* or *ázịzà*). Similarly, every Ìgbo speaker produces the low tone of the gerund prefix ò- at a much higher pitch in *òchíche* 'waiting' than in *òchiche* 'thinking'. Abraham (1967) devised different tone marks for both of these distinctions, but such detail *need* not be written because it doesn't affect sense, and it *should* not be written because it distracts from sense (Armstrong 1967). On the other hand, to apply Ùgo̍nnà's approach requires a working definition of ambiguity, and indeed of context, usable by a nonlinguist. With the advent of machine-based text processing, the equivalent task would be to devise spell-checking software to insert partial tone marks automatically by referencing an on-line dictionary and a context buffer with limited look-ahead. The great difficulty of such a procedure can only increase as the dictionary grows by coinage and by borrowing across dialects. Compared to these two extremes, full tone marking seems easy.

Depending on the dialect—and not counting coarticulation effects in *Cy* clusters or nasalized syllables—Ìgbo has eight or nine vowels[10] and one syllabic nasal that assimilates to a following consonant; between 12 and 24 nonnasal stops; five nasal stops and 6 to 12 continuant consonants (fricatives, rhotics, laterals and glides).

Table 2: Vowels

		Nonback	Back
Oral	High	i, ɩ	u, ʊ
	Nonhigh	i, (ɛ), a	o, ɔ
Nasal		m	

Basic Morphosyntax

Ìgbo is SVO and prepositional; a noun precedes its modifiers; inflection and derivation are prefixal in nouns, suffixal in verbs. However, each of these points needs to be qualified. As to basic word order, some southern dialects like Èchíè ["Etche"], Àvụ and Òweré depart from VO when they place a direct object in between the future auxiliary *-gá* with an obligative sense and the lexical verb (Éménanjọ 1984: 198).

(1a) Ọ́ gà e-lí nní. (Ọ̀nịcha)
3s AUX NOM-eat food.GEN
'S/he is going to eat/have a meal.'

(1b) Ọ́ gà í-rí rin. (Ḿbàisén)
3s AUX AGR-eat food
'S/he is going to eat, have a meal.'

(2a) Ọ́ gà a-tá akḥụ́. (Èchíè)
3s AUX NOM-chew palm.kernel.GEN
'S/he is going to chew palm kernels.'

(2b) Ọ́ gà ákḥụ a-ta. (Èchíè)
3s AUX palm.kernel NOM-chew
'S/he must (certainly) chew palm kernels.'

[10] A 10th vowel, [ə], occurs in some northern dialects including Ǹsụ́ká; research has not established whether it is a centralized variant of [ɩ] or a separate phoneme.

Example (2) shows that tone is not just a property of lexical items, but also marks some kinds of inflection (Welmers 1970b; Goldsmith 1976; Clark 1989; Déchaine 1993; Manfredi 1993). In nouns, genitive case is masked in some prosodic contexts; for purposes of this chapter it can be identified as a downstep before the rightmost syllable of a noun that bears only lexical high tone and has at most two syllables. By the tone-marking convention explained above, *akḥụ́* in (2a) has a downstep on the second syllable and is thereby genitive, while *akḥụ* in (2b) lacks the downstep and so is not. Overall, genitive occurs in the dependent noun of a complex noun phrase, the notional object of a subject-relative clause, the notional object of a nominalized verb (1a, 2a), and the notional object of a perfective verb. This pattern is expected if Ìgbo has a split-ergative case system (Déchaine & Manfredi 1998).

Still on basic word order, the direct object is not necessarily final in a monotransitive predicate. Most dialects allow a bound nominalization of a transitive verb to follow the direct object, adding an event presupposition as suggested by the italicized part of the gloss of (3b). Descriptively, this nominalized form is the same as the form that occurs in auxiliary constructions like those in (1a) and (2) above. If the direct object is suppressed, the nominalized verb copy is required; the pattern is similar if the verb takes a locative complement. If the verb is intransitive, the nominalized verb copy is required; but there is no corresponding presupposition, e.g., from Ḿbàisén:

(3) a. Ó rí-ri ji.
3s eat-TNS yam
'S/he ate (some) yam.'

b. Ó rí-ri ji e-ri.
3s eat-TNS eat NOM-eat
'S/he ate (some) yam *as expected/contra expectation*'

c. Ó rí-ri e-ri.
3s eat-TNS NOM-eat
'S/he ate (something) *as expected/contra expectation*'

(4) a. Ọ́ fụ̀-rụ n'úzọ̀.
3s out-TNS LOC-road
'S/he exited to/from the road.'

b. Ọ́ fụ̀-rụ a-fụ́.
3s out-TNS NOM-out
'S/he exited *from some presupposed place*'

(5) Ọ́ kụ̀-wa-ra a-kụ́-wa.
3s knock-split-TNS NOM-knock-split
'It split as a result of being knocked.'

Examples (4) and (5) show lexical prepositions and adjectives (*-fụ̀*, *-wá*) inside inflected verbs (Welmers 1970a; Hale, *et al.* 1995). The only preposition-like item that does not incorporate into the verb in this way is the locative marker *nà*. Notice, however, that *nà* in (4a) is ambiguous between the meanings of 'to' and 'from'—vagueness improbable in a lexical predicate.

The obligatory bound, nominalized verb in (3c) and (4b) led Éménanjọ to claim that "all Ìgbo verbs are transitive" (1975: 166). Indeed, most English intransitive predicates translate into Ìgbo as full verb phrases including an obligatory, free nominal complement. The verb root may be cognate with the noun as in (6), but the examples in (7) show that this is not necessary. In the latter case, it is difficult to perceive the semantic contribution of the verb root over and above the complement, hence the label "light verb". The following examples are from Ḿbàisén:

(6) a. Ọ́ chị̀-rị ọchị̀.
3s laugh-TNS laughter
'S/he laughed.'

b. Ó vù-ru ívù.
3s fat-TNS bulk
'It is big', 'S/he is plump.'

(7) a. Ọ́ kụ́ ilu.
3s V bitterness
'It is (intrinsically) bitter.'

b. Ọ́ thị́-rị ogologo.
3s V-TNS length
'It is long', 'S/he is tall.'

Attributive adjectives are limited to items for "big", "black", "good" and their opposites (Mádụ̀ká-Dúruǹze 1990), e.g., from Ḿbàisén: *ánya ukwu* (eye big) 'greed', lit. 'big eyes'; *ńkwụ ọcḥa* (oil palm white) 'palm-wine'; *áfọ ọma* (stomach good) 'kindness'. A few attributes are prenominal, as in (8), but most of these are nouns, as seen by the genitive case of their complement—(8a) may be the sole exception. Most attributes are postnominal nouns or relative clauses, as in (9). Examples (8)–(9) are from Ḿbàisén:

(8) a. ájọ(ọ́) hyen
bad thing
'something bad'

b. ézigbo hyén
goodness thing.GEN
'good/true thing'

c. ógologo okwú
length talk.GEN
'long discussion'

(9) a. íshi ikḥé
head strength.GEN
'stubbornness' (lit. 'strong head')

b. áhwán kwéshị-rị e-kweshị
name.H fit.REL-TNS NOM-fit
'a suitable name'

c. hyén wé-re anyá
thing take.REL-TNS eye.GEN
'something obvious'

Ìgbo has no word class corresponding to either the definite or indefinite articles of English, and there is no obligatory marking of number on count nouns. Thus, depending on discourse as well as grammatical context, a count noun like *éwu* 'goat' may be translated either as 'a goat', 'some goats', 'goats (in general)', 'the specific goat in question', or even as a proper noun 'Mr. Goat (the personified character in a story)'. To disambiguate some of these, deictic demonstratives, optionally combined with the plural classifier *ńdị*, compel a definite interpretation: *éwu à* 'this goat' or 'Mr. Goat here', *éwu ndị à* 'these goats', *éwu ahụ̀n* 'that goat', *éwu ndị ahụ̀n* 'those goats'. As was also the case in older stages of English, the numeral "one" compels an indefinite reading for a count noun: *òfú ewú* means either 'one goat' or 'some goat'.

All affixes on nouns are prefixes (Williamson 1972; Ànagbọ́ọ̀gụ 1987), cf. (10). In (10), the gloss DEF.GEN indicates the "specific construction". In verbs, by contrast, all affixes whether derivational (11) or inflectional (12) are suffixes—assuming that the items glossed as AGR in (13) are not prefixes but rather phrasal proclitics marking subject agreement (Ézè 1995). Note, however, that the orthography mostly writes these proclitics as part of the verb word.

(10) a. ò-gwú ú ji
AGT-dig DEF.GEN yam
'[human] digger of yams'
b. ǹ-gwú ú ji
INST-dig DEF.GEN yam
'digging tool for yams'
c. ò-bú íbu (Ọ̀nịcha)
ò-vú ívu (Ḿbàisén)
AGT-carry load.DEF.GEN
'[human] load carrier'
d. m̀-bú íbu (Ọ̀nịcha)
m̀-vú ívu (Ḿbàisén)
INST-carry load.DEF.GEN
'beast of burden'

(11) a. -lá-cha (Ọ̀nịcha)
-ńụ́-cha (Ḿbàisén)
drink-thorough
'drink up'
b. -kú-pụ̀-tá (Ọ̀nịcha)
-kú-fụ̀-ṭá (Ḿbàisén)
scoop-out-towards
'ladle out [a liquid]'

(12) a. Ó lì-li ńni. (Ọ̀nịcha)
Ó rí-ri rin. (Ḿbàisén)
3s eat-TNS food
'S/he ate, had a meal.'
b. Ó nà e-lí nní. (Ọ̀nịcha)
3s PROG NOM-eat food.GEN
Ó rí-ghe rin. (Ḿbàisén)
3s eat-PROG food
'S/he is eating.'
c. Ó lí-go nní. (Ọ̀nịcha)
Ó rí-ele rín. (Ḿbàisén)
3s eat-PERF food.GEN
'S/he has eaten.'

(13) a. Ànyị́ e- lí-rọ nni. (Ọ̀nịcha)
Ányị e- rí-ghi rin. (Ḿbàisén)
1P AGR eat-NEG food
'We didn't eat.'
b. í- lí nni (Ọ̀nịcha)
í- rí rin (Ḿbàisén)
AGR eat food
'to eat a meal'
c. É- lí-na nni! (Ọ̀nịcha)
É- rí-le rin! (Ḿbàisén)
AGR eat-NEG food
'Don't eat!'
d. Ànyị́ é- li-go nní. (Ọ̀nịcha)
Ányị̀ e- rí-ele rín. (Ḿbàisén)
1P AGR eat-PERF food.GEN
'We have eaten.'

Questions are formed by a range of strategies including movement, tone change and affixation. Yes/no questions involve either a low-toned subject clitic as in (14), or else a periphrastic strategy where the whole sentence is preceded by *Ọ̀ (bụ) kwa...*, abbreviating an embedding clause 'Is it the case that...?' as in (15).

(14) a. Ì je-kọ ọ́lụ? (Ọ̀nịcha)
L.2s go-PROG work
'Are you en route to work?'
b. Ì jịjhe ọ́rụn? (Ḿbàisén)
L.2s go.PROG work
'Are you en route to work?'

(15) a. Ọ̀ kwa í jè-kọ ọ́lụ? (Ọ̀nịcha)
Q 2s go-PROG work
'Is it the case that you are en route to work?'
b. Ọ̀ kwa í jịjhe ọ́rụn? (Ḿbàisén)
Q 2s go.PROG work
'Is it the case that you are en route to work?'

Content (or *wh*-type) questions impose the same L tone on subject AGR if basic word order is preserved (16a), but not if the question word is fronted (16b–d). If the subject is questioned, there is no fronting (17). If the question word is sentence initial and is also a complex phrase, the sentence has the tones of a relative clause; (17c) shows this for subject questions, and (18) shows it for object questions with a lexical subject, cf. (9b) above.

(16) a. Ì rí-ri gịrị́? (Ḿbàisén)
L.2s eat-TNS what
'What did you eat?'
b. Òléé hyen i rí-ri? (Ḿbàisén)
which thing 2s eat-TNS
'What did you eat?'
c. Gịnị́ kà í lì-li? (Ọ̀nịcha)
what that 2s eat-TNS
'What did you eat?'
d. Kèdụ́ ife i lì-li? (Ọ̀nịcha)
what thing 2s eat-TNS
'What did you eat?'

(17) a. Gịrị́ mè-re Úgḥ wu? (Ḿbàisén)
what do-TNS Úgḥ wu
'What happened to Úgḥwu?'
b. Ònyé gà-ra áhya? (Ḿbàisén)
L.person go-TNS market

'Who went to the market?'
c. Kèdụ́ ife mé-lụ Ugwú? (Ọ̀nịcha)
what thing do.REL-TNS Úgwu.GEN
'What happened to Úgwu?'
(lit. 'What is the thing that happened to Úgwu?')

(18) a. Òléé hyen Uché rí-ri? (Ḿbàisén)
which thing Úché.H eat-TNS
'What did Úchè eat?'
(lit. 'Which is the thing that Úchè ate?')
b. Kèdụ́ ife Uché lì-li? (Ọ̀nịcha)
what thing Uché.H eat-TNS
'What did Uché eat?'
(lit. 'What is the thing that Úchè ate?')

Contact with Other Languages

In the last 400 years, peripheral Ìgbo-speaking communities have borrowed words and social institutions from neighboring Ẹ̀dó, Ìgálà and Èfịk-Ìbibio among others. Ẹ̀dó loans like *ìdumu* 'village ward', *ósisi* 'gun' and numerous personal names and chieftaincy titles were adopted in Ágbọ̀, which, in turn, influenced Ọ̀nịcha and other northwestern riverine Ìgbo settlements through the Ụ́mụ̀ Ézè Chímà lineage of a 17th-century Ágbọ̀ emigrant, Nwádéin Kimẹ̀ (Èjiọfọ̀ 1982; Íjèọma 1984; Ọ̀hádiké 1994). In the 19th century, some of these Àniọ́cha and Óru towns inflated the Ágbọ̀ link to a more prestigious, direct descent from the Ẹ̀dó ("Benin") Kingdom, which, in Ìgbo, is called either *Ìdúù* or *Àdó*. (A case of reverse adoption, from Ìgbo to Ẹ̀dó, is the *íkeǹga* 'cult' of the right hand, cf. Bradbury 1961) Throughout the 18th century and until the Fulani *jihad*, the Ìgálà Kingdom influenced northern Ìgbo religion, notably in the *ọ̀mábe* masked ancestral dance (Boston 1960a,b; Shelton 1971). From the Cross River Basin came politically powerful oracles and male initiation groups. Ọ̀kọnkọ and Èkpe male title societies, and the associated Ékpo masked ancestral dance, derive from the Ékpè ('Leopard') Society of the Ekoi, Èfịk and Ìbibio-speaking area. These institutions spread through the eastern Ìgbo-speaking area via the Árụ̀ ["Aro"] oracular and slave-trading network between the 17th and 19th centuries (Green 1958; Áfaìgbo 1987; Díké & Ékèjiụbá 1990).

While Ìgbo predominates in the home, English is more widely used in commerce, mass media and formal education—even between or among Ìgbo speakers themselves. Rapid urbanization in Nigeria in the past half century has also brought Ìgbo speakers into more settings where English bilingualism is the default communication strategy. However, negative attitudes toward language mixture are common, and prescriptive views are often voiced.[11] Ézè (1997) shows that Ìgbo-English contact phenomena take two main forms: code switching and lexical borrowing. Code switching can occur either at a sentence boundary or within one sentence:

(19) *It's an opportunity* [$_S$ PRO ị́-gwá gị màka yá].
AGR-tell 2s about 3s
'It's an opportunity to tell you about it.'

(20) Ọ́ bụ̀ *a big disappointment to everyone.*
3s be
'He/she/it is a big disappointment to everyone.'

Most lexical loans from English are "nonce borrowings" (Poplack 1993), i.e., spontaneous uses of an unintegrated lexical item from one language in the discourse of another, as in (5), rather than stable expansions of the Ìgbo lexicon: *Ànyị́ jì-cha* <u>*paper*</u> *ànyị́*. (1P hold-complete paper 1P) 'We have all of our papers'.[12]

Common Words

	Northern	Southern (if different)
man:	nwóké	(nwá) nwokḥẹ́, *pl.* ụ́mụ̀ nwókḥé
	ókènye, *pl.* íkènye	(nwá) nwokḥọ́, *pl.* ụ́mụ̀ nwókḥọ́
woman:	nwáàyị, ónyenyè	(nwá) nwáànyị, *pl.* ụ́mụ̀ nwáànyị
	òkporó, *pl.* ìkporó	
water:	ṁmị́lị	mírin, míni
sun:	ánwụ, ánya anwụ́	
three (counting):	ìtọ́	àtọ́, àtọ́
fish:	ázụ̀	ázụ̀n
yes: (to a question)	ée, éèyi	
yes: (to a statement)	ịya	
yes: (to a command)	óo	
no:	é'è, ḿbà, wáà	Ọ̀ dịghị́ (lit: 'It's not [so]'), ḿ'm̀
bird:	ńnụ̀nụ	
dog:	ńkịtá/ńchịtá	
tree:	ósisi	óshishi

Efforts to Preserve, Protect, and Promote the Language

To date, there is no clearly defined 'Standard Ìgbo' (*Ìgbó Ìzugbé*), despite prescriptive efforts throughout colonial times (Dennis, *et al.* 1923; Adams 1932; Ward 1936, 1941, cf. Àchebé 1976; Éménanjọ 1995). As Schön remarked over a century ago, a project of standardizing Ìgbo by translating received English texts—rather than by collecting "a native literature of stories, proverbs and sayings"—is doomed to "inaccuracies, inconsistencies and contradictions" (1861: 1–3). Published oral texts from different locales include Green (1958), Ègúdu and Nwáọ̀ga (1971), Éménanjọ (1977), Ùgoǹnà (1980, 1983), Àchebé and Ùdéchukwu (1982), Àzụ́onye and Ùdéchukwu (1984) and Àmádiúme (1995). Ògbo (1994) observes two supra-dialectal varieties in spontaneous writing and cosmopolitan speech. One of these reflects forms current in the northern

[11]For example, Àhụ́kàńnà (1990: 179) quotes a radio announcer as describing the mixture of Ìgbo and English as "linguistic sabotage". The term "saboteur" was a potentially dangerous accusation during the Nigerian civil war, hence its use by language purists is particularly emotive in the Ìgbo context.

[12]For the example of 'paper', Ìgbo already has an indigenous neologism: ákwụkwọ (literally, 'leaf').

cities of Ọnịcha and Énugwú ["Enugu"]; the other represents especially the large rural communities of Ḿbàisén and Ọ́màáhyá in the southern area.

After two centuries of effort, continued low rates of literacy in Ìgbo call for historical explanation. Àchebé accuses "egoistic schoolmen" (1984: 95), while Áfàìgbo (1981) blames colonial policies encouraging labor migration and English-medium schools. Mission schools turned confessional rivalry into policy conflict; most northern literacy was carried out by Catholic authorities, while southern literacy was largely in the hands of Anglicans. Since the civil war, the state sector has sponsored little Ìgbo publishing besides examination textbooks. At war's end, several peripheral dialects were given idiosyncratic orthographies, hindering harmonization (Wugo 1970; Clark 1971; Meir, *et al.* 1975). To date there are two linguistically adequate Ìgbo dictionaries: Welmers and Welmers (1968)—a Peace Corps primer with 2,500 entries drawn from a variety of dialects—and Williamson (1972) with 5,000 entries from Ọnịcha. Échèrúó (1998) updates and modifies the unpublished compilation whose preface was published as Abraham (1967). In recent decades, efforts to preserve and promote Ìgbo have diminished in step with infrastructural collapse in state-sponsored schools and colleges, and also more generally as a result of diminished leverage by Ìgbo-speaking political brokers over resources from the national state.[13] Thus in the near-to-medium term, pro-Ìgbo linguistic activism will depend on the economic and intellectual capital of Ìgbo speakers in the private sector, including the Nigerian diaspora overseas.[14]

Select Bibliography

Abraham, R.C. 1967. *The Principles of Ìgbo; Archival Edition of Typescript.* Occasional Publication 5, Institute of African Studies, University of Ìbàdàn.

Àchebé, C. 1976. "The Bane of Union: An Appraisal of the Consequences of 'Union Ibo' for Ìgbo Language and Literature." In *Añụ 1*: 33–41.

_____. 1984. "Editorial and Linguistic Problems in '*Áka Wètá*'; A Comment." In *Ụ̀wá Ndị Ìgbo; A Journal of Ìgbo Life & Culture* 1: 94–95.

Àchebé, C., and O. Ùdéchukwu. 1982. *Áka Wètá; Égwu A Gùlụ Agụ́ nà Égwu E Dère Edé.* Òkike Magazine, Ǹsụ́ká.

Adams, R.F.G. 1932. *A Modern Ìgbo Grammar*. London: Oxford University Press.

Áfàìgbo, A.E. 1981. *Ropes of Sand; Studies in Ìgbo History & Culture.* Ìbàdàn: University Press Ltd.

_____. 1987. "The Ìgbo and their Neighbours in the Pre-colonial Period." In *The Ìgbo & their Neighbours*, 29–52. Ìbàdàn: University Press Ltd.

Àmádiúme, S. 1995. *Ílu Ndị Ìgbo; A Study of Ìgbo Proverbs.* Énugwú: Fourth Dimension.

Ànagbọ́ọ̀gụ, P.N 1995. "A Grammar of Ìgbo Nominalizations." Dissertation, University of Port Harcourt.

Ánọ̀ká, G.M.K. 1985. "The Phonology of the Three *t*'s of Ìgbo." In *West African Languages in Education*, edited by K. Williamson. *Beiträge zur Afrikanistik* 27, 99–105. Vienna: Institut für Afrikanistik und Ägyptologie.

Armstrong, R.G. 1964. *The Study of West African Languages.* Ìbàdàn University Press.

_____. 1967. "A Note on Marking Ìgbo Tones." In *The Principles of Ìgbo; Archival Edition of Typescript*, 1–2. Occasional Publication 5, Institute of African Studies, University of Ìbàdàn.

_____. 1972. *A Comparative Wordlist of Five Ìgbo Dialects.* Occasional Publication 5, Institute of African Studies, University of Ìbàdàn.

Boston, J.S. 1960a. "Notes on Contact between the Ìgálà and the Ìgbo." In *Journal of the Historical Society of Nigeria 2*: 52–58.

_____. 1960b. "Some Northern Ìgbo Masquerades." In *Journal of the Royal Anthropological Institute 90*: 54–65.

Bradbury, R.E. 1961. "Ézọmọ̀'s ìkẹ́gà obọ̀ and the Benin cult of the hand." In *Man 165*: 129–138.

Clark, D.J. 1971. *Reading & Writing Ẹ̀kpẹyẹ.* Rivers Readers Project, Ìbàdàn & Port Harcourt.

Clark, M.M. 1989. *The Tonal System of Ìgbo.* Foris, Dordrecht.

Cookey, S.J.S. 1980. "An Ethnohistorical Reconstruction of Traditional Ìgbo Society." In *West African Culture Dynamics*, edited by B.K. Swartz & R.E. Dummett, 327–346. Mouton, The Hague.

Déchaine, R.M. 1993. "The Syntax of Ìgbo Tone." In *Predicates across Categories; Towards a Category-neutral Syntax*, 497–520. Dissertation, University of Massachusetts, Amherst.

Déchaine, R.M., and V. Manfredi. 1998. "SVO Ergativity and Abstract Ergativity." In *Recherches Linguistiques de Vincennes* 27: 71–94.

Dennis, T.J., *et al.* 1923. *Dictionary of the Ìgbo Language: English-Ìgbo.* C.M.S. Bookshop, Lagos.

Díké, K.Ọ., and F.I. Ékèjiụbá, 1990. *The Árụ̀ of Southeastern Nigeria, 1650–1980.* Ìbàdàn University Press.

Échèrúó, M.J.C. 1998. *Dictionary of the Ìgbo Language.* New Haven: Yale University Press.

[13]Today, the two main ethnolinguistic interest groups in Nigerian politics are the Hausa-Fulani and their "middle-belt" clients on the one side (who now dominate the army), and Yorùbá speakers plus aggrieved "southern minorities" from oil producing areas on the other (Ọmọ́ruyì 1997). Some oil is produced from wells in Ìgbo-speaking areas in the present Ímò, Delta and Ábịa states, but a larger share has come from Ògoni, Ìzọ̀n ("Ijaw") and other non-Ìgbo speaking territory—all of which has been lumped into the category of "Southern Minorities" since the Nigerian civil war.

[14]But privatized policy has its own risks. Échèrúó (1998)—an Ìgbo-English dictionary compiled by a professor of English literature—suppresses tone marks, citing two erroneous grounds: (i) only words "in isolation from other syntactical processes" can constitute lexical items, and (ii) downstep is not found within lexical items. Counterexamples include lexicalized phrases like *nwánné* (H-downstep juncture-H), which is the ordinary gender-neutral kin term for 'sibling' (etymologically, 'mother's child', with a downstep of genitive case), as well as many personal and place-names that are no longer analyzable as phrases, e.g., Ǹsụ́ká (L-H-downstep juncture-H) and Ǹnééwi (L-H-downstep juncture-H-H), cf. Éménanjọ (1984). Minimal pairs abound like *ísí* (H-downstep juncture-H) 'to boil' versus *ísi* (H-H) 'head'. Another unilateral decision in Échèrúó's dictionary is to convert the vowel diacritic from the subdot (officially adopted in 1961, and currently used by nearly all neighboring and historically related languages in Nigeria) to an umlaut (once used in a few tiny, neighboring languages in the Cross River Basin). His explicit reason is to separate Ìgbo from "a script group to which, by the very nature of its sound system, it does not belong" (1998: x), but this sounds like rationalizing. Neither of these steps has been accepted by Nigerian language professionals.

Ègúdu, R.N., and D.I. Nwáọ̀ga. 1971. *Poetic Heritage; Ìgbo Traditional Verse*. Énugwú: Nwáńkwọ Ífejìka.

Èjiọfọ́, L.U. 1982. *Ìgbo Kingdoms; Power & Control*. Ọ̀nịcha: Africana Publishers.

Éménanjọ, E.'N. 1975. "Aspects of the Ìgbo Verb." In *Ìgbo Language & Culture 1*, edited by F.C. Ọ́gbàlụ́, & E.'N. Éménanjọ, 160–173. Ìbàdàn: Oxford University Press.

_____. 1977. *Ọ́málịnze; A Book of Ìgbo Folk-tales*. Oxford University Press, Ìbàdàn.

_____. 1978. *Elements of Modern Ìgbo Grammar*. Ìbàdàn: Oxford University Press.

_____. 1984. *Auxiliaries in Ìgbo Syntax*. Bloomington: Indiana University Linguistics Club.

_____. 1985. "Language Engineering in Present-Day Ìgbo." In *West African Languages in Education*, edited by K. Williamson. *Beiträge zur Afrikanistik* 27, 85–95. Vienna: Institut für Afrikanistik und Ägyptologie.

_____. 1995. "Issues in the Establishment of Standard Ìgbo." In *Language in Nigeria; Essays in Honour of Ayọ̀ Báḿgbóṣé*, edited by K. Owólabí, 213–29. Ìbàdàn: Group Publishers.

Ézè, E. 1995. "The Forgotten Null Subject of Ìgbo." In *Theoretical Approaches to African Linguistics 1*, edited by A. Akinlabí, 59–82. Trenton, New Jersey: Africa World Press.

_____. 1997. "Aspects of Language Contact: A Variationist Perspective on Code Switching & Borrowing in Ìgbo-English Bilingual Discourse." Dissertation, University of Ottawa.

Goldsmith, J. 1976. "Autosegmental Phonology." Dissertation, M.I.T., Cambridge, Massachusetts.

_____. 1981. "The Structure of *wh*-questions in Ìgbo." In *Linguistic Analysis 7*: 367–393.

Green, M.M. 1958. "Sayings of the Ọ̀kọnkọ Society of the Ìgbo-speaking People." In *Bulletin of S.O.A.S. 21*: 157–173.

Green, M.M., and G.E. Ígwè. 1963. *A Descriptive Grammar of Ìgbo*. Berlin: Akademie Verlag.

Greenberg, J.H. 1963. *The Languages of Africa*. The Hague: Mouton.

_____. 1972. "Linguistic Evidence Regarding Bantu Origins." In *Journal of African History 13*: 189–216.

Hale, K., Ụ. Íhìọnụ́, and V. Manfredi. 1995. "Ìgbo Bipositional Verbs in a Syntactic Theory of Argument Structure." In *Theoretical Approaches to African Linguistics 1*, edited by A. Akinlabí, 83–107. Trenton, New Jersey: Africa World Press.

Ífemésia, C.I. 1979. *Traditional Humane Living among the Ìgbo; An Historical Perspective*. Énugwú: Fourth Dimension.

Íjèọma, J.O. 1984. "The Evolution of Kingship among the West Niger Ìgbo Chiefdoms, with Particular Reference to Benin Influence." In *Íkenga 6*: 34–46.

Ladefoged, P., M.A. Ụwaláàka, K. Williamson and B.O. Elugbe 1976. "The Stops of Òweré Ìgbo." *Studies in African Linguistics, Supplement 6*: 146–163.

Mádụ̀ká-Dúruṅze. O.N. 1990. "Ìgbo Adjectives as Morphologised Relatives." In *Studies in African Linguistics 21*: 237–51.

Manfredi, V. 1989. "Igboid." In *The Niger-Congo Languages*, edited by J. Bendor-Samuel, 337–358. Lanham, Maryland: University Press of America.

_____. 1992. "The Limits of Downstep in Ágbọ̀ Sentence Prosody." In *IRCS Report* 92–37, edited by M. Liberman & C. Maclemore, 103–115. Institute for Research in Cognitive Science. Philadelphia: University of Pennsylvania.

_____. 1993. "Spreading and Downstep: Prosodic Government in Tone Languages." *The Phonology of Tone; the Representation of Tonal Register*, edited by H. van der Hulst & K. Snider, 133–84. Berlin: Mouton/de Gruyter.

Meir, P., I. Meir and J. Bendor-Samuel. 1975. *A Grammar of Ìzíì, An Ìgbo Language*. Normal, Oklahoma: Summer Institute of Linguistics/Wycliffe Bible Translators.

Nwáchukwu, P.A. 1976. *Noun Phrase Sentential Complementation in Ìgbo*. Dissertation, University of London.

Nwáọ̀ga, D.I. *et al.* 1990. *The Nwágụ́ Ánéke Research Project Proposal*. Institute of African Studies. Ǹsụ́ká: University of Nigeria.

Ògbo, O. 1994. "Saving the Ìgbo Language." In *Uwá Ndị Ìgbo; A Journal of Ìgbo Life & Culture 1*: 103–04.

Ọ́gbàlụ́, F.C. 1975. "Ìgbo Spelling." In *Ìgbo Language & Culture 1*, edited by F.C. Ọ́gbàlụ́, and E.'N. Éménanjọ, 138–59. Ìbàdàn: Oxford University Press.

_____. 1982. "Towards Standard Ìgbo: The Case of the Àbáàgana Dialect." In *Ìgbo Language & Culture 2*, edited by F.C. Ọ́gbàlụ́ and E.'N. Éménanjọ, 98–101. Ìbàdàn: Oxford University Press.

Ọ̀hádiké, D.C. 1994. *Ànịọ́ma; A Social History of the Western Ìgbo People*. Ohio University Press.

Ọ̀mọ́ruyì, Ọ. 1997. "The Mistake of 1914: North-South Anomalies in Nigerian Federalism." In *Wilberforce Conference on Nigerian Federalism*, edited by P. Ékèh, E. Ọ́nwụdíwe and E. Ọsaghae. Ohio: Central State University.

Ọ́nwụejíọgwụ̀, M.A. 1975. "Some Fundamental Problems in the Application of Lexicostatistics in the Study of African Languages." In *Paideuma 21*: 6–17.

_____. 1980. *An Ìgbo Civilization: Nri Kingdom & Hegemony*. London: Ethnographica.

Poplack, S. 1993. "Variation Theory and Language Contact." In *American Dialect Research*, edited by D. Preston, 251–286. Amsterdam: Benjamins.

Schön, J.F. 1861. *Ókwu Ìgbo; Grammatical Elements of the Ìgbo Language*. London: Watts.

Seligman, C.G. 1930. *The Races of Africa*. London: Butterworth.

Shaw, T. 1970. *Ìgbo Úkwu: An Account of Archaeological Discoveries in Eastern Nigeria*. London: Faber.

Shelton, A. 1971. *The Ìgbo-Ìgálà Borderland; Religion & Social Control in Indigenous African Colonialism*. Albany: S.U.N.Y. Press.

Swift, L.B., A. Àhághotù and E. Ùgọ́jị̀ 1962. *Ìgbo Basic Course*. Washington: Foreign Service Institute.

Ùgoṅnà, N. 1980. *Ábụ̀ na Égwuregwu Òdinalá Ìgbo*. Ìkẹjà: Longman.

_____. 1983. *Mmọ́nwụ́, a Dramatic Tradition of the Ìgbo*. Lagos University Press.

Ward, I.C. 1936. *Introduction to the Ìgbo Language*. London: Heffers.

_____. 1941. *Ìgbo Dialects & the Development of a Common Language*. London: Heffers.

Welmers, W.E. 1970a. "The Derivation of Ìgbo Verb Bases." In *Studies in African Linguistics* 1, 49–59.

_____. 1970b. "Ìgbo Tonology." In *Studies in African Linguistics*, 255–78.

Welmers, B.F. and W.E. Welmers. 1968a. *Ìgbo: A Learner's Dictionary*. Los Angeles: U.C.L.A.

_____. 1968b. *Ìgbo: A Learner's Manual.* Los Angeles: U.C.L.A.
Williamson, K., ed. 1972. *Ìgbo-English Dictionary, Based on the* Ọnịcha *Dialect.* Ethiope, Benin City.
_____. 1976. "Noun-class Prefixes in Proto-Lower Niger." Presented at the 12th West African Languages Congress, Ilé-Ifẹ̀.
_____. 1989a. "Niger-Congo Overview." In *The Niger-Congo Languages*, edited by J. Bendor-Samuel, 3–45. Lanham, Maryland: American Universities Press.
_____. 1989b. "Linguistic Evidence for the Prehistory of the Niger Delta." In *The Early History of the Niger Delta*, edited by E.J. Alagoa *et al*, 65–119. Hamburg: Buske.
Wugo, S.A. 1970. "Ọ̀kwukwō kè m̀bọm̄ nụ Ìkwere." Rivers Readers Project, Rivers State Government, Port Harcourt and Institute of African Studies, University of Ìbàdàn.

Ilocano

Carl Rubino

Language Name: Ilocano. **Alternates:** *Ilokano, Iloko, Iluko, Samtoy.*

Location: Ilocano is native to northwestern Luzon Island, Philippines. It is used as a second language in the interior and northwest coast of northern Luzon Island. There are also sizeable Ilocano communities on the islands of Mindanao, Palawan, and Mindoro and throughout Hawaii.

Family: Cordilleran group of the Northern Philippine subgroup of the Philippine subgroup of the Western Malayo–Polynesian branch of the Malayo-Polynesian subfamily of the Austronesian language family.

Related Languages: Ilocano has special status among the Cordilleran languages, having its own branch with no close sister languages. Other Cordilleran languages include Kalinga, Itneg, Alta, Balangao, Ifugao, Itawis, Kallahan, Isinay, PANGASINAN, Dumagat, Bontok, Yogad, Kankanaey, Ibanag, Gaddang, Ilongot, Isneg, Paranan, and Ibaloi.

Dialects: Unlike most of the major languages of the Philippines, dialectal variation in Ilocano is minimal. There are two main dialects, Northern and Southern, easily distinguishable by slight lexical differences, intonational patterns and the pronunciation of the native phoneme /e/.

Number of speakers: 9 million.

Origin and History

Little is known about the Ilocano people prior to Spanish contact in the 16th century. During early Spanish contact, the Ilocanos were confined to the present day provinces of Ilocos Norte, Ilocos Sur, and La Union, but in the last few centuries the Ilocano people have populated many other areas in the Philippines and even predominate in provinces such as Abra, Pangasinan, Benguet, Nueva Ecija, and Tarlac. There are sizable Ilocano communities in many other Philippine provinces and the islands of Mindoro and Mindanao. As the original Ilocano region borders the mountainous interior of Luzon, where members of linguistic minority groups prevail, Ilocano has been used for centuries as the lingua franca of the region and in legal documents and proceedings of the various mountain peoples. Many of these ethnic groups still use Ilocano today to communicate among themselves. For this reason, Ilocano has been unofficially considered the national language of the north.

Ilocanos are the most migratory of the Philippine ethnic groups. They have settled in many other parts of the world, forming rather large communities in Brunei, Singapore, Hong Kong, Saudi Arabia, Kuwait, and most urban centers in the United States and Canada. The largest concentrations of Ilocanos in the United States are in California, Alaska, and especially Hawaii where nearly one-fifth of the total population can claim Ilocano heritage.

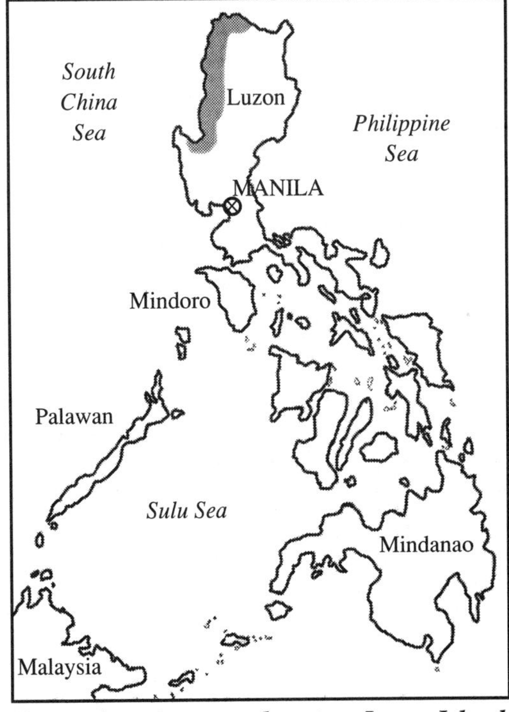

Ilocano is native to northwestern Luzon Island, Philippines (shaded area). There are also Ilocano communities on the islands of Mindanao, Palawan and Mindoro.

Orthography and Basic Phonology

Prior to the Spanish arrival, Ilocanos employed an Indic syllabary similar to that described for TAGALOG. The Ilocano innovation to the syllabary reflected consonantal syllable codas that were not represented in Tagalog. The Roman alphabet is used today in two forms. The SPANISH system (including the symbols *c*, *z*, *ch*, *ñ*, and *qu*) is preferred by the older generations. The alphabet employed in modern publications, however, is based upon the Tagalog system, which employs 20

Table 1: Consonants

	Labial	Dental/ Alveolar*	Alveo-palatal/ *palatal	Velar	Glottal
Stops	p b	t d	(ts, ti + V) [tʃ] (dy, di+ V) [dʒ]	k [k, x] g	- [ʔ]
Fricatives		s*			(h)
Nasals	m	n		ng [ŋ]	
Laterals		l*			
Trills/Flap		r*			
Glides	w		y*		

letters in the following order: A B D E G H I K L M N NG O P R S T U W Y.

Ilocano has the following contrastive consonant sounds (shown in Table 1 above by their orthographic symbols). Stops are unaspirated, and unreleased in final position. The voiceless velar stop (k) is slightly fricated. The alveolar trill (r) has various pronunciations from a simple flap to a trill, closely resembling its Spanish counterpart. The orthographic sequences /ts/ and /dy/ represent voiceless and voiced alveo-palatal affricates, respectively. Their origin usually involves sequences of two phonemes. The glottal fricative [h] only occurs in one native word, *haán*, the nonstandard variant of *saán* 'no'.

Unlike in Tagalog, the glottal stop phoneme does not occur word finally. When it occurs after a consonant, it is represented by a hyphen in the orthography › *salun-át* 'health' [sa.lun.ʔat]. It is not written between sequences of two vowels > *saán* 'no' [sa.ʔan], *rabií* 'night' [ra.bi.ʔí], *láud* 'west' [lá:.ʔud], or word initially where it is pronounced since all Ilocano syllables include a consonantal onset > *áso* 'dog' [ʔá:.so].

Table 2: Vowels

	Front	Central	Back	
			Unrounded	Rounded
High	i		e [ɯ]	u
Mid	e [ɛ]			(o)
Low		a		

Ilocano has six vowel phonemes (for the southern dialect), four of them /a, e, i, u/ are native to the language, while [o] and [ɛ] were incorporated after Spanish contact. Vowels are represented orthographically by five symbols [a, e, i, o, u], which closely represent their equivalents in Spanish. In the northern dialect the orthographic symbol '*e*' represents one sound, a front, mid, lax vowel similar to the *e* in the English *let*. In the southern dialect, however, the orthographic symbol *e* is used for two separate phonemes. In native words, *e* is pronounced as a high back unrounded vowel, while in Spanish loans its pronunciation is identical to that of the northern dialect. The high back vowel /*u*/ has a phrase-final allophone [*o*] that is reflected in the orthography. The vowel *o*, however, may also be considered to have phonemic status due to a few recent loanwords that differentiate *o* and *u*: *púso* 'heart' vs. *póso* 'well (from Spanish)'.

Stress is phonemic in Ilocano. Vowels are lengthened in stressed open syllables (those that have no consonantal coda) > *ások* 'my dog' ['á:.sok], ≠ *asók* 'smoke' ['a.sók], *síka* 'dysentery' [sí:.ka], ≠ *siká* 'you, familiar' [si.ká].

All single consonants may be geminated. Gemination may result from a derivational process or may be underlying > *ammó* 'know', *ittíp* 'rice crust', *lengngá* 'sesame', *innála* 'took', *galláki* 'boys' (plural of *laláki* 'boy'), *agattakkí* 'smell like excrement' (root word *takkí* 'excrement').

Syllable structure is C(C)V(C) where the second consonant of the onset may be a liquid or glide. Complex onsets and codas appear in loanwords, e.g., *lip.stik* 'lipstick', *klats.bag* 'handbag'.

Basic Morphology

Ilocano is an agglutinating language. There are many productive morphemes in the language that may derive both nouns and verbs from all lexical roots. From *lagíp* 'remember, memory', we may derive *ipalagíp* 'to remind', *palagipán* 'to advise, remind', *palagíp* 'prayer in memory of the dead', *nakallalagíp* 'memorable', *pakalaglagipán* 'souvenir', *malagíp* 'to remember', *lagipén* 'think of, recall', and *silalagíp* 'mindful', among many others. From *táo* 'man' we may derive *pagattáo* 'to be the height of a man', *agattáo* 'smell like a man', *tattáo* 'people', *sinantatáo* 'scarecrow', *itáo* 'to deliver a child', *agpakatáo* 'to be humane', *katatáo* 'ancestry, personality', *di katataoán* 'evil spirits', and *kinatáo* 'humanity', among others.

Pronouns inflect for three cases: genitive/ergative (ERG), absolutive (ABS), and oblique (OBL). The ergative and absolutive pronouns are enclitic. There are also two sets of independent possessive pronouns and one set of reflexive pronouns that are morphologically complex. Three categories are distinguished for the first person plural: *-ta* dual inclusive ('you and I'), *-kamí* exclusive ('we, not you'), and *-tayó* inclusive ('we and you'). Pronominal enclitics attach to the first constituent of their domain: *Napán-da idiáy* 'went-they there' = *Idiáy-da napán* 'there-they went'.

Table 3: Pronouns

Person			Case				
1	2	3	Independent	Ergative	Absolutive	Oblique	Gloss
+	-	-	*siák*	*=k(o)*	*=ak*	*kaniák*	1s
-	+	-	*siká*	*=m(o)*	*=ka*	*kenká*	2s familiar
-	-	+	*isú(na)*	*=na*	-	*kenkuána*	3s
+	+	-	*datá*	*=ta*	*=ta*	*kadatá*	1 dual incl
+	-	+	*dakamí*	*=mi*	*=kamí*	*kadakamí*	1 pl excl
+	+	-	*datayó*	*=tayó*	*=tayó*	*kadatayó*	1 pl incl
-	+	+	*dakayó*	*=yo*	*=kayó*	*kadakayó*	2 pl, (2 formal)
-	-	++	*isúda*	*=da*	*=da*	*kadakuáda*	3p

Articles are inflected for case (CORE vs. oblique [OBL]), number (singular, plural), and personal distinctions (common vs. personal [PA]). Articles in the core case mark nouns that would be in the ergative or absolutive case if pronominalized. *Diay*, an abbreviated form of the distal demonstrative *daydiáy* 'that' is also used in Ilocano discourse as a definite article for identifiable referents.

Table 4: Articles

ARTICLES	Non-personal		Personal	
	Singular	Plural	Singular	Plural
Core	*ti* (neutral), *diay*	*dagití*	*ni*	*da*
Oblique	*ití*	*kadagití*	*kenní*	*kadá*

The nontemporal Ilocano demonstratives mark three degrees of spatial orientation, proximal (near the speaker), medial (near the addressee, or near both speaker and addressee), and distal (far from both interlocutors), and the out of sight demonstratives have two degrees of temporality (recent vs. remote). The demonstratives inflect for two cases and two numbers, while their shortened article forms do not. In most dialects of Ilocano, the singular oblique forms are formed with the singular form preceded by the oblique article *iti*, but only the dialectal prefixed variants are given in Table 5.

The recent and remote articles and demonstratives are used for referents that are not visible in the speech event. They mark referents that may be dead, more specific, nonactual, or somehow distanced from the speech event. Referents that are recently activated into the consciousness of the speaker may also appear with a nonvisible demonstrative. Compare *N-ag-paráng ni Sinting.* (PERF-AGENT.VOICE-appear CORE.PERS Sinting) 'Sinting appeared/showed up' vs. *Nagparáng daydi Sinting* 'The late Sinting appeared (as a ghost)'; *Ania ti nágan=mo?* (what CORE name=your) 'What is your name' vs. *Ania tay náganmo (manén)*? 'What was your name (again), [I used to know it]?'

Nouns do not inflect for gender or case but may reduplicate in various ways to express plurality or distributiveness > *ubíng* 'child' vs. *ubbíng* 'children', *amá* 'father' vs. *ammá* 'fathers', *kaarúba* 'neighbor' vs. *kakaarúba* 'neighbors', *pusa* 'cat' vs. *puspusa* 'cats'. The circumfixes *pag- -an* and *ka- -an* are used to form locative nouns > *ka-darat-an* 'sandy place', *pag-adal-an* 'place where one studies'. The resemblance prefixes *mara-* 'like' and *sinan-* 'fake' often form new lexical items: *mara-gatas* (like-milk) 'kind of tree', *sinan-allawagi* (fake-carpenter) 'unskilled carpenter'.

Verbs derive for focus (see Basic Syntax) and inflect for aspect. All verbs are marked for transitivity based on the affixes they take. Aspectual distinctions appear morphologically as shown in Table 6 on the following page.

There are hundreds of affixes and affixal combinations in the morphological inventory of Ilocano, some of them more

Table 5: Demonstratives

		Article	Demonstrative			
Visibility	Range		Core		Oblique	
			Singular	Plural	Singular	Plural
Visible ↓ Neutral	Proximal	toy	daytóy	dagitóy	kadaytóy	kadagitóy
	Medial	ta	daytá	dagitá	kadaytá	kadagitá
	Distal	diay	daydiáy	dagidiáy	kadaydiáy	kadagidiáy
Out of sight	Recent	tay	daytáy	dagitáy	kadaytáy	kadagitáy
	Remote	ti	daydí	dagidí	kadaydí	kadagidí

Table 6: Ilocano Aspect

Infinitive Verb class (e.g., eat)	Complete n-/-(i)n- ate	Incomplete CVC- is eating	Future =(n)to will eat
	Intransitive (Actor Focus) Verbs		
*ag*surat 'write' (Actor)	nagsurat	agsursurat	agsuratto
g*um*atang 'buy' (Actor)	gimmatang	gumatgatang	gumatangto
*mang*an 'eat' (Detransitive)	nangan	mangmangan	manganto
	Transitive (Nonactor Focus) Verbs		
*i*kabil 'put' (Theme)	inkabil	ikabkabil	ikabilto
surat*en* 'write' (Patient)	sinurat	sursuraten	suratento
punas*an* 'wipe' (Directional)	pinunasan	punpunasan	punasanto
*ka*sao 'speak with' (Comitative)	kinasao	kasasao	kasaonto

productive than others. All focus/voice affixes exhibit selectional restrictions so they have been traditionally considered derivational. Aspectual morphology follows regular paradigms and is therefore inflectional. Among the distinctive affixes in the language are the following > *agaC-* 'smell like', *agabbáwang* 'smell like garlic', *agattsíko* 'smell like sapodilla fruit'; *pagat, pagaC-* 'reaching up to', *pagattáo* 'the height of a man', *pagatlapáyag* 'ear to ear (smile)' *pagabbarúkong* 'up to one's chest'; *-inn-* 'reciprocal infix' *Nagl{inn}emméngda.* 'They hid from each other', *p{inn}itakan* 'throwing mud at one another'; and *aginCV-* 'to pretend', *aginsisingpét* 'to pretend to be virtuous', *agimbabaknáng* 'to pretend to be rich'.

Adjectives are like stative verbs in their formation but they do not inflect for aspect. They have simple, equalitative, comparative, and various superlative forms. From the root *dakkél* 'big' we may derive *agkadakkél* 'as big as', *dakdakkél* 'bigger', *kadaklán* 'biggest', *nakadakdakkél* 'quite big', *nagdakkelen* 'how big!' *panakkelén* 'rather big', *sumangkadakkél* 'even bigger', and *naindaklán* 'very big, important'. Verbs inflect for aspect and they encode focus (see Basic Syntax), and mood (dynamic vs. potentive). Dynamic verbs are unmarked, and potentive verbs, which denote actions that are involuntary, accidental, coincidental, or abilitative, take a form of the prefix *ma(ka)-*.

Numeral morphology is highly developed in Ilocano. From the root *dua* 'two', we may derive the following words: *maikadua* 'second', *sumagdudua* 'about two', *kagudua* 'one half', *mamindua* 'twice', *kapamindua* 'second time', *sagdudua* 'two each', *dudua* 'only two', *pidua* 'second crop, second time', *kapidua* 'second cousin', and *paminduaén* 'do twice'.

Basic Syntax

Like the other Philippine languages, Ilocano is a head-marking, predicate-initial language. When two nominals appear post-predicately, the agent normally precedes the patient: *Nakita ni Maria ti baró* (saw PA Maria ART young.man) 'Maria saw the young man'.

Constituents in initial position are predicative. *Na-pangláw ti kabsát-na.* (ADJ-poor ART sibling-3SERG) 'Her sibling is poor'. *Tukák.* 'frog; It is a frog'.

Most syntactic structures follow a head + modifier pattern. Genitives follow their nouns > *ti balay-ko* 'my house', *ti balay ni Maria* 'Maria's house'.

Typical of the native languages of the Philippine archipelago, there is a rigid focus/voice distinction in which the semantic relationship between the pivot (absolutive argument) and the verb is signaled by the verb's morphology. The following sentences show this relationship with the absolutive argument underlined.

Actor focus (AF):

N-ag-dáit ti balásang ití saya.
PERF-AF-sew CORE maiden OBL skirt
'The maiden sewed a skirt.'

Patient focus (PF):

D{in}áit-na ti saya.
sewed{PERF.AF}-3SERG CORE skirt
'She sewed the skirt.'

Theme focus (TF) (absolutive argument is physically or psychologically conveyed):

In-y-áwid-ko ti dágum.
PERF-TF-to.home-1SERG CORE needle
'I brought home the needle.'

Benefactive focus (BF):

In-daít-an-na ni Maria iti saya.
PERF-sewed-BF-3SERG PA Maria OBL skirt
'She sewed a skirt for Maria.'

Comitative focus (CF):

K{in}a-saó-k ni Erlinda.
CF{PERF}-speak-1SERG PA Erlinda
'I spoke with Erlinda.'

Directional focus (DF):

S{in}agád-an-na ti datár.
sweep{PERF}-DF-3SERG CORE floor
'S/he swept the floor.'

Existence and possession are expressed with existentials *addá* (positive) and *awán* (negative). With the existentials, the possessor appears in the ergative case. In existential constructions, the nominal takes absolutive case marking.

Adda-kamí-n! = EXIST-1pEXCL.ABS-now
'We are here!'

Awán ti ka-buténg-mi.
NEG.EXIST CORE NML-fear-1pEXCL.ERG
'We have no fear (we are not afraid of anything).'

Declarations are negated with the adverb *saan* 'no' or *di* 'negative particle' preceding them. The linker *nga* joins *saan* to the negated phrase, but is not used with *di*. *Saán* is preferred when negating noun phrases. Pronominal enclitics, if any, attach to the negative adverb.

Saan-da	*nga*	*immay*. (*Di-da immay*)
NEG-3pABS	LINK	came
'They didn't come.'		(*Immayda* = 'They came'.)

Contact with Other Languages

Most Ilocano speakers under 30 years of age are proficient in Tagalog, the language of primary-school education in the country. Colloquial Ilocano of the younger generations may have sprinklings of Tagalog loans: i.e. *dápat* 'should/must '[Ilk: *rumbéng*]', *baká* 'might, maybe' [Ilk: *ngatá*], *kailángan* 'need' [Ilk: *masápol*].

Spanish loanwords, especially those over two syllables, are often recognized as foreign although fully incorporated into the language: *kalésa* 'horse-drawn carriage', *késo* 'cheese', *tsokoláte* 'chocolate', *sapátos* 'shoes', *kamás* 'jicama', *masétas* 'potted plant', *lamisáan* 'table', *libre* 'free'.

ENGLISH is the language of higher education and the largest source of new lexical items: *kompyúter* 'computer', *dyíp* 'jeep', *ísyu* 'issue', *naitklab* 'nightclub'.

CHINESE and SANSKRIT loans were incorporated into the language before the Spanish occupation. Most speakers are unaware of their foreign origin, or may attribute their origin to Tagalog. Chinese loans include *bíko* 'rice cake', *pansít* 'noodle', *petsáy* 'kind of cabbage'. Words of Sanskrit origin are not as prevalent in Ilocano as they are in Tagalog and may have perhaps been borrowed from Tagalog. These include *kalapáti* 'dove', *suká* 'vinegar', and *lasuná* 'onion'.

There are communities in northern Luzon where Ilocano predominates over the original language(s) of the area. In these areas, the minority language often contributes to the regional lexicon. Such languages are Pangasinan, Ibanag, and Itnég (Tinguian).

Common Words

person:	táo	long:	atiddóg
water:	danúm	world:	lúbong
sun:	ínit	yes:	wen
moon:	búlan	no:	saán
fish:	sidá	bird:	billít
child:	ubíng	tree:	káyo
day:	aldáw	night:	rabií
big:	dakkél	small:	bassít
eat:	mangán	sleep:	matúrog
pretty:	napíntas	ugly:	naalás

Example Sentences

(1) Ania ti nágan-mo?
what CORE name-2SERG
'What is your name?'

(2) Maka-pa-salun'át ti pan-ag-katáwa.
INVOL-CAUS-health CORE NML-INTRANS-laugh
'Laughing is healthy.'

(3) N-ag-kita-kamí ití ka-pinia-an.
PERF-AF-see-1pINCL OBL LOC-pineapple-NML
'We (exclusive) saw each other in the pineapple field.'

Efforts to Preserve, Protect, and Promote the Language

Ilocano does not have official status in the Philippine Republic. It is not used in schools past the first-grade level. Young pupils in the Ilocano provinces are immersed in the national language, Tagalog, in first grade with mininal or no reading proficiency in their native language.

There are, however, many regional newspapers that publish in the language. There is an association of Ilocano writers (GUMIL: *Gunglo dagiti Mannurat nga Ilokano*) dedicated to preserving the language through literature. Chapters of this group exist all over the Philippines with foreign branches in California and Hawaii.

The weekly magazine *Bannáwag* 'Dawn' and the quarterly webmagazine *Burnáy* 'Earthen Jar' are the best examples of language preservation, publishing short stories, news, serial novels, and poetry in Ilocano. Novels and literary compilations are also regularly published in the Philippines and in Hawaii, many of them serialized on Ilocano radio. The Ilocano *Bukanegán* 'poetical joust' is still practiced in some areas where authors can practice their impromptu literary skills.

As the lingua franca of northern Luzon and native tongue of many immigrants worldwide, Ilocano is not in danger of extinction.

Select Bibliography

Espiritu, Precy. 1984. *Let's Speak Ilokano*. Honolulu: UH Press.

Foronda, Marcelino, and A. Juan. 1972. *Samtoy: Essays on Iloko History and Culture*. Manila: United Publishing Co., Inc.

Jocano, F. Landa. 1982. *The Ilocanos: An Ethnography of Family and Community Life in the Ilocos Region*. Diliman, Quezon City: Asian Center, University of the Philippines.

Rosal, Nicolas. 1982. *Understanding an Exotic Language: Ilokano*. New Jersey: Edison.

Rubino, Carl. 1997. A reference grammar of Ilocano. PhD dissertation, University of California, Santa Barbara.

____. 1998. *Ilocano Dictionary and Phrasebook*. New York: Hippocrene.

____. 2000. *Ilocano Grammar and Dictionary*. Honolulu: UH Press.

____. *to appear*. "Iloko." In *The Austronesian Languages of Asia and Madagascar* edited by Nikolaus Himmelmann and Sander Adelaar. London: Curzon Press.

IRISH

James McCloskey

Language Name: Irish. **Autonym:** *Gaeilge*. **Alternates:** (Irish) *Gaelic*; *Erse* (archaic).

Location: Ireland.

Family: Irish belongs to the Goidelic branch of the Insular Celtic language group, which, together with the Continental Celtic group makes up the Celtic family, a branch of Indo-European.

Related Languages: Scots Gaelic, Manx, WELSH, and Breton.

Dialects: There are three major dialects of Irish, corresponding largely to the three provinces in which the language is still spoken. Ulster Irish is spoken in County Donegal in the extreme northwest. Connacht Irish is spoken in the west, in Counties Galway and Mayo and on the Aran Islands. Munster Irish is spoken in the south in Counties Kerry, Cork, and Waterford.

Number of Speakers: There are perhaps 30,000–35,000 native speakers in the rural western communities (*Gaeltachtaí*) in which Irish continues to be the vernacular. In addition, there are large numbers of people (estimates vary from 100,000–200,000) who have achieved some degree of second-language competence and who use the language regularly in their daily routines.

Origin and History

The Celtic family consists of two groups: Continental and Insular. In pre-Classical times, the various languages of the Continental Celtic group were spoken over most of Central Europe (France, Belgium, Holland, Northern Italy, the Iberian Peninsula, southern Germany, Austria, and Switzerland). These languages were quickly supplanted by LATIN as Roman influence expanded in the course of the first century B.C. and the first century A.D. Something is known of Continental Celtic languages because of the short phrases that survive in monumental inscriptions and on pottery shards, principally from Gaul and Iberia.

The Insular Celtic languages represent the Celtic family as it was exported to the British Isles circa 700–500 B.C. Insular Celtic consists of two branches: Brythonic and Goidelic. Originally, Brythonic was spoken in the easternmost of the two islands (present-day England, Scotland, and Wales), and Goidelic was spoken in Ireland. This simple pattern was changed by various population movements. For example, around the time of the collapse of the Roman Empire (between A.D. 400–600) large numbers of speakers of a Brythonic dialect migrated from southern England to the Gaulish province of Armorica (present day Brittany), seeking the protection of Roman garrisons and administration. The languages of these groups survive as Breton. Breton, although spoken now exclusively in France, is thus in origin an Insular Celtic language of the Brythonic branch. The other main survivor of the Brythonic branch is Welsh, spoken in Wales. Cornish, a related language that was spoken in the South of England, became extinct some two hundred years ago. Welsh and Cornish are found in written sources from A.D. 900, and these sources become extensive in the 12th century.

The Goidelic branch of Insular Celtic is known from the end of the sixth century, in the very large corpus of literature written in the literary standard that we now call Old Irish. A northern variety of this language was brought to western Scotland by raiders and colonizers from Ireland. From this movement derives modern Scots Gaelic and also Manx, a Gaelic language spoken in the Isle of Man until this century.

Irish and Scots Gaelic were united by a common literary standard and by a common literary culture until the 16th century. With the destruction of that literary culture and the social classes and institutions that supported it, the standard language was lost, and the two varieties developed along separate paths. They are conventionally thought of as distinct languages today.

With the extension of English colonial administration to all parts of Ireland at the beginning of the 17th century, Irish was banished from the domains of power and prestige (law, written literature, civil administration, and scholarship). Bilingual ability in Irish and ENGLISH became steadily more widespread at the close of the 17th century and especially in the 18th. However, at the beginning of the 19th century, Irish was still the everyday language of the vast majority of Irish people.

The precipitous decline in the fortunes of the language which followed is usually attributed to the calamitous social and economic conditions prevailing in 19th century Ireland: famines, increasing poverty, and emigration on a large scale. Irish was associated with poverty, deprivation, and illiteracy; relinquishing the language in favor of English was seen as a key to escape. By the end of the 19th century, Irish was thoroughly marginalized and was the language of an impoverished minority living in those parts of the country most remote from commercial and administrative centers. The census of 1891 put the number of speakers of Irish at 700,000 in a population of roughly 4 million.

Table 1: Consonants

	Voi	Labial	Dental	Alveolar	Palatal	Velar	Glottal
Stops	-	p [p p']	t [t]	t [t']	c [k']	c [k]	
	+	b [b b']	d [d]	d [d']	g [g']	g [g]	
Fricatives	-	ph/f [f f']		s [s ʃ]	ch [ç]	ch [χ]	th/sh/h [h]
	+	bh/mh [w, v']			dh/gh [j]	dh/gh [ɣ]	
Nasals	+	m [m m']	n/ nn [n]	n/ nn [n']	ng [ŋ']	ng [ŋ]	
	-						
Laterals	+		l /ll [l]	l/ ll [l']			
	-						
Flaps	+		r/ rr [r]	r/ rr [r']			
	-						

Language issues were important in the revolutionary nationalist politics of the late 19th and early 20th centuries, which culminated in partial independence in 1922. At independence, Irish was declared to be the first official language of the state, and efforts to revivify it became a part of the official national agenda.

Orthography and Basic Phonology

Irish is written today almost exclusively in the standard Latin alphabet. A distinctive "Gaelic script" was also in use until the 1950s. The Gaelic script derived ultimately from a typeface designed to print the earliest Irish books—religious texts used in official Protestant proselytism in the late 16th and early 17th century.

Vowel length is distinctive, indicated orthographically by an acute accent. Most varieties have long and short variants of [i], [e], [a], [o], and [u], as well as [ə] and two diphthongs, [iə] and [uə]. Southern and Western varieties in addition have a set of diphthongs that have developed from sequences of short vowel followed by long sonorant.

Table 2: Vowels

	Front	Central	Back
High	í [i:] i [i]		ú [u:] u [u]
Mid	é [e:] e [e]	unstressed a, e, ea, i, ai [ə]	ó [o:] o [o]
Low		á [a:] a [a]	
Diphthongs	Basic	ia [iə] ua [uə]	
	Derived from loss of fricative consonant; orthography preserves consonant	[au] [ai] [ei] [əi] [əu]	

The most distinctive aspect of the consonant system is that it is organized in two series, such that each basic consonant comes in two varieties. The traditional terms for these two series are 'broad' (*leathan*) and 'slender' (*caol*). Broad consonants are realized as velarized, labialized or neutral depending on details of the phonetic context; slender consonants are palatalized or neutral depending on the context. These distinctions play an important role in the morphology of the language, in that many morphological rules manipulate them. The plural (nongenitive) of the first declensional class, for instance, is formed by making a final broad consonant slender. A fairly large class of verbs (such as *buail* 'strike') forms deverbal nouns by making a final slender consonant broad and adding the suffix *-adh* (variously realized as [u:], [u], or [ə] in the different dialects): [buəl^y] > [buələ].

Also noteworthy is the system of sonorant consonants. Historically, the language possessed two series of sonorant consonants: one was long, tense and dental, and the other was short, lax and alveolar. The long sonorants are indicated orthographically by doubling: [ll], [nn], [rr]; in widely used transcription systems they are indicated with a capital letter: [L], [N], [R].

This system of sonorant consonants is now preserved only in the northernmost dialects (Mayo and Donegal). In other dialects, the distinction between long and short sonorants has been lost, and short vowels have undergone a process of compensatory lengthening (or diphthongization) before previously long sonorants. This is one of the most distinctive of the contrasts among the dialects and can be seen, for instance, in the various forms of the word *gleann* 'valley':

Spelling	Historical Form	Munster	Connacht	Ulster
gleann	[g^yl^yaN]	[g^yl^yaun]	[g^yl^ya:n]	[g^yl^y aN]

Historically, stress is on the initial syllable (with a secondary stress on the third). Most dialects preserve this system, but one of the most characteristic features of Munster Irish is that heavy syllables of various kinds attract the stress rightwards in complex circumstances, often resulting in weakening or loss of the vowel of the initial syllable.

Basic Morphology

The morphological system of Irish is predominantly, but not exclusively, suffixal. Nouns are inflected for number (singular or plural) and case (common, genitive or vocative). The distinction between masculine and feminine genders is important for determining inflectional class and also plays a role in the system of initial mutations.

Verbs are inflected for tense (past, present, future, conditional and past habitual); in formal registers a subjunctive (present or past) is also available (as an optative and to express indefinite time in the future). Progressive aspect is periphrastic. It is signaled by auxiliary 'be' (*tá*) and a nominal form of the verb (called the "verbal noun") that is preceded by a particle *a'* (which derives historically from the preposition meaning 'at').

Tá	sí	a'	tógáil	tithe.
be.PRES	she	PTC	build.VN	houses

'She is building houses.'

Perfective aspect is expressed by means of the preposition meaning 'after' (which has different forms in different dialects):

Tá	siad	i ndiaidh	teach	a thógáil.
be.PRES	they	after	house	build[-FIN]

'They have just built a house.'

Verbs inflect for the person and number of their subject. If a suitable inflected form is not available (as is frequently the case), a default form (known as the "analytic form") is used:

Thógadar	teach.
build.PAST.3PL	house

'They built a house.'

Tógfaidh	siad	teach.
build.FUT	they	house

'They will build a house.'

The subject of a verb is unexpressed when the verb is inflected.

Many prepositions inflect for the person and number of their object:

Thóg	siad	teach	dúinn.
build.PAST	they	house	for:1.PL

'They built a house for us.'

When prepositions are inflected, the associated object noun phrase must be unexpressed.

One of the most distinctive and celebrated aspects of Irish morphology is its system of initial mutations—systematic changes induced on the initial consonant of a word by morphosyntactic and lexical factors of various kinds. Historically, the mutations develop from regular phonological processes that happened to apply across word boundaries. With the loss of unstressed final syllables in pre–Old Irish, the phonological-conditioning environment was lost and the triggering environment for the process was reinterpreted in morphosyntactic terms. Irish has two such mutations: 'lenition' (*Séimhiú*) and 'nasalization' (*Urú*), also known as eclipsis.

Lenition, as its name suggests, is a weakening of an initial consonant (prehistorically in intervocalic position). More specifically, the following changes occur under lenition:

[p]→[f]	[b] → [w]	[f] → Ø
[t] → [h]	[d] → [ɣ]	[s] → [h]
[k] → [χ]	[g] → [ɣ]	[m] → [w]

A typical rule of lenition would require, for instance, that an adjective be lenited if it follows a feminine singular nongenitive noun. Lenition is indicated orthographically by placing *h* after the lenited consonant.

Lá	fuar [la: fuər]
day[MASC]	cold

'A cold day'

Oíche	f<u>h</u>uar [i:χ^{y}ə uər]
night[FEM]	cold

'A cold night'

Nasalization derives historically from a sandhi process in which initial consonants were assimilated to a preceding final nasal. It induces the following changes on an initial consonant.

[p] → [b]	[b] → [m]	[f] → [w]
[t] → [d]	[d] → [n]	
[k] → [g]	[g] → [ŋ]	

Nasalization is indicated orthographically by placing the derived consonant in front of the base form. The article in the genitive plural induces nasalization on a following noun.

na	daoine
the	people

eagla	na	<u>n</u>daoine
fear	the:GEN.PL	people:GEN.PL

'the people's fear'

Basic Syntax

Irish is a thoroughly head-initial language: heads precede complements, there are prepositions rather than postpositions, modifiers follow the head noun, possessors follow the head noun, the object of comparison follows the comparative adjective, and titles precede names. It is also VSO in finite clauses:

Thóg	siad	teach	i	nDoire	bliain	ó shin.
build.PAST	they	house	in	Derry	year	ago

'They built a house in Derry a year ago.'

More generally, Irish is predicate initial, since in clauses headed by nonverbal predicates (copular clauses), the phrasal predicate precedes the subject:

Is	col ceathrar	liom	í.
COP	cousin	with.me	her

'She is a cousin of mine.'

Is	de	bhunadh	na	h-Éireann	an	ghirseach	seo.
COP	of	people	the[GEN]	Ireland.GEN	the	girl	DEM

'This girl is of Irish extraction.'

In nonfinite clauses (clauses headed by verbal forms that are, historically at least, deverbal nouns), different word order patterns obtain. If the subject of the nonfinite clause is expressed (a possibility more freely available in Irish than in most languages), it is in initial position and precedes the verbal form:

B'fhearr liom iad fanacht sa bhaile.
I.would prefer them remain(-FIN) in.the home
'I would prefer for them to remain at home.'

When the subject is not expressed, the direct object precedes the verb:

D'iarr siad orainn bia na maidne
ask.PAST they on.us food the.GEN morning.GEN

a réiteach.
ready(-FIN)
'They asked us to prepare breakfast.'

When both the subject and the object are expressed, the dialects show different patterns. In northernmost dialects, both subject and object precede the verb (all other complements and adverbials follow):

Is éadóiche iad teach a cheannach anois.
COP.PRES unlikely them house buy(-FIN) now
'It is unlikely that they would buy a house now.'

Southernmost varieties barely allow the possibility, but when it is allowed, the subject precedes the verbal form and the object follows in the genitive case.

Ar mhiste leat mise do phlé mo chúise féin?
would you mind me plead(-FIN) my case.GEN REFLEX
'Would you mind if I pleaded my own case?'

Contact with Other Languages

In the first two centuries after the arrival of Christianity in the fifth century, several waves of loanwords from Latin were incorporated, mostly in learned domains (theology, philosophy, grammar, and civil and ecclesiastic administration). Around the end of the first millennium, when Scandinavian influence was at its height, a certain number of terms having to do with seacraft, commerce, and dress was borrowed from Norse languages. In the Middle Ages, the strongest lexical influence was Norman FRENCH, from which large numbers of words were borrowed in the domains of civil administration, law, and warfare. Since the late Middle Ages, the dominant lexical influence has been English, from which numerous words in all domains have been borrowed.

From Latin: *sagart* 'priest' (< *sacerdos*), *spiorad* 'spirit' (< *spiritus*), *aidiacht* 'adjective' (<*adiectivum*), *cathaoir* 'chair' (< *cathedra*), *pobal* 'community' (<*populus*)

From Norse: *stiúir* 'rudder', *margadh* 'market', *scilling* 'shilling'

From Norman French: *réasún* 'reason', *príosún* 'prison', *giústís* 'justice', *baile* 'town'

Common Words

man:	fear	long:	fada
woman:	bean	small:	beag
water:	uisce	yes:	*
sun:	grian	no:	*
three:	trí	good:	maith
fish:	iasc	bird:	éan
big:	mór	dog:	madadh
tree:	crann		

*Irish has no words for 'yes' and 'no'. To express 'Yes' in an answer to a question, an ellipsis is used that reduces a sentence so that it consists only of a finite verb (the verb used in the question). To express 'no' the same ellipsis process is used, but the verb is preceded by the negative particle.

Example Sentences

(1) Cá raibh tú anocht.
where were you this.evening
'Where were you this evening?'

(2) An bhfuil Gaeilge agat?
INTERROG is Irish at.you
'Do you speak Irish?' (lit. 'Do you have Irish?)'

(3) Cad is ainm duit?
what COP name to.you
'What is your name?'

Efforts to Preserve, Protect, and Promote the Language

Unofficial but enthusiastic efforts to revivify Irish began in the second half of the 19th century (just as it came close to extinction), and achieved clear organizational focus with the founding of *Conradh na Gaeilge* ('The Gaelic League') in 1893. Language issues were central to nationalist and anti-imperialist politics in the late 19th and early 20th centuries, and *Conradh na Gaeilge* was an important mobilizing force in those politics. As a consequence, when partial independence was achieved in 1922, Irish was recognized as the "first official language" of the newly independent state. The language continues to have that legal status (English is recognized as the second official language).

Every national government since 1922 has been committed, at least nominally, to language advocacy policies. The official aims have been to preserve those communities (*Gaeltachtaí*) in which Irish is still the vernacular, and to broaden knowledge and use of the language in the general population. Irish is a required subject of study at every level in every school (a policy that is widely resented), and financial subsidies of various kinds have been available to *Gaeltacht* communities. These policies seem to have had very little effect on the decline of *Gaeltacht* communities (from 700,000 in 1891 to perhaps 35,000 at present), and English has encroached steadily in all domains and in all age groups (there now are probably no monolingual speakers of Irish).

On the other hand, these losses have been offset at least in part by the development of a substantial community of speakers who have learned Irish as a second language to varying degrees of competence and who use it regularly in their daily routines.

There is a substantial modern literature (a recent flourishing in poetry, in particular) produced partly by people from *Gaeltacht* communities and partly by people from the learner community. *Raidió na Gaeltachta* is the national radio service in Irish, and a national TV service (*Teilifís na Gaeilge*) began broadcasting in October 1996. The language has also played an important role in the recent flourishing of traditional music and song. Although Irish today has a marginal role in Irish life, it is a role of some ritual and symbolic importance. Pessimism about the current state of the language and its future, however, is one of the enduring staples of political and cultural life.

Select Bibliography

De Bhaldraithe, Tomás. 1959. *English-Irish Dictionary.* Dublin: Government Publications Office.

Greene, David. 1966. *The Irish Language.* Dublin: Cultural Relations Committee of Ireland.

McKone, Kim, Damian McManus, Cathal Ó Háinle, Nicholas Williams, & Liam Breatnach, eds. 1994. *Stair na Gaeilge.* Maynooth: Department of Old Irish, St. Patrick's College.

Ó Dónaill, Niall. 1977. *Foclóir Gaeilge-Béarla.* Dublin: Government Publications Office.

Ó Siadhail, Mícheál. 1989. *Modern Irish: Grammatical Structure and Dialect Variation.* Cambridge: Cambridge University Press.

Thurneysen, Rudolf. 1946. *A Grammar of Old Irish.* Dublin: Dublin Institute for Advanced Studies.

Wagner, Heinrich. 1958. *Linguistic Atlas and Survey of Irish Dialects.* Dublin: Dublin Institute for Advanced Studies.

ITALIAN

Lori Repetti

Language Name: Italian. **Autonym:** *l'italiano*.

Location: The Italian language, and/or an Italian dialect, is spoken in the Republic of Italy, the Republic of San Marino, Vatican City, southern France in the area around Nice, Corsica, the Principality of Monaco, southern Switzerland where it is one of the country's four official languages, Croatia (in Istria and along the Dalmatian coast), and Slovenia. In addition, Italian is still spoken in Africa in the ex-colony of Eritrea, and Italian and/or a dialect is commonly used in the large communities of Italian immigrants outside of Italy, most notably in the United States, Canada, Australia, Brazil, and Argentina.

Family: The Romance branch of the Indo-European language family.

Related Languages: PORTUGUESE, SPANISH, CATALAN, FRENCH, OCCITAN, Franco-Provençal, Ladino, and ROMANIAN.

Dialects: The term "dialect" in the Italian tradition refers to a group of sister languages of Italian and other Romance languages, and not to different varieties of the same language, as it does, for example, in the ENGLISH tradition. Some dialects in Italy differ so much from the standard language (based on the dialect of Florence) that they are mutually unintelligible with it. Sicilian and Friulian are sometimes classified as Italian dialects, and sometimes they are accorded the status of separate languages. Sardinian is usually classified as a separate language. This degree of linguistic variety has survived because Italy was not politically united until 1861 so there was no national language that people had to use, and while Italian has long been the literary language of the peninsula, very few people could read and write until the beginning of the 20th century.

There is a linguistic boundary marker that transects Italy, the La Spezia–Rimini line, which divides the Romance languages into Western and Eastern groups according to specific traits found in each region. Italian dialects that are north of this line, including Piedmontese, Ligurian, Lombard, Emilian, Friulian, and Venetian are on the whole closer to French and Occitan than they are to dialects south of the line. Dialects south of the line include Tuscan, Umbrian, Laziale, Central Marchigiano, Abruzzese, Neapolitan, Pugliese, Calabrese, and Sicilian.

There are also regional varieties of the standard language that are marked in phonology and to a lesser extent in the lexicon, morphology, and syntax. Because of recent social changes including compulsory education, increased opportunities for travel, internal migration, and exposure to the media, the use of standard Italian, at the expense of the dialects, is rapidly becoming the norm.

Number of Speakers: Republic of Italy: 57.7 million; Republic of San Marino: 15,000; France: 150,000; Switzerland: 1 million; Croatia: 25,000; Slovenia: 4,000; United States: 2.5 million; Canada: 500,000; Brazil: 1.5 million; Argentina: 1 million; Australia: 400,000.

Origin and History

Italian, like the other Romance languages, is a direct descendent of LATIN, the language of the Roman civilization, which arose in what is now Italy.

Latin replaced the indigenous Indo-European languages including Lepontic Celtic, Oscan, and Umbrian, and the non-Indo-European languages including ETRUSCAN and Ligurian, spoken in Italy before the period of Roman domination of the peninsula.

Following the fall of the Roman Empire, a long period of political and cultural disunity, marked by numerous invasions of the Longobards, the Franks, the Arabs, and the Normans, resulted in the linguistic fragmentation of the peninsula. The lack of political unity meant that there was no centripetal force acting on the neo-Latin dialects, and they continued to develop and evolve in their own unique ways.

It was not until the 13th and 14th centuries that the dialect of Tuscany, or more specifically, Florentine, began to predominate over the competing dialects as the norm for literary production. The predominance of Tuscan is due in part to the political and economic importance of Tuscany during this period; to the superior quality of literary production in this dialect by such eminent writers as Dante, Petrarch, and Boccaccio who wrote in Tuscan; and to the linguistic characteristics of the Tuscan dialects that contain traits found in both the Northern and Southern dialects.

During the 15th and 16th centuries, a literary-linguistic debate arose regarding the nature of the variety of language to be used in literary production. The *Questione della lingua* 'question of language' was a popular topic of debate and had ideological as well as political implications. Some people saw the Italian language as a supraregional *lingua cortigiana* ('language of the courts'), others saw it as a variety of contemporary Tuscan, and still others preferred 14th-century Tuscan as the Classical Italian language. It was the last group that prevailed, supported by the literary and linguistic *Accademia della Crusca*, which published the first great dictionary of Italian in 1612.

The choice of 14th-century Tuscan as the model for literary

Table 1: Consonants

		Bilabial	Labiodental	Dental	Alveolar	Palatal	Palato-alveolar	Velar
Stops	Voiceless	p		t				c [k]
	Voiced	b		d				g
Fricatives	Voiceless		v		s		sc [s]	
	Voiced		f					
Affricates	Voiceless				z [ts]		c [tʃ]	
	Voiced				z [dz]		g [dʒ]	
Nasals		m			n	gn [ɲ]		
Liquids					l, r	gl [ʎ]		

production had profound implications on the linguistic history of Italy. The Italian language is unique among modern national languages in that it has changed little in its eight centuries of documented history; this is due in part to the fact that the literary language was a written and somewhat static model until quite recently. It was not until political unity was achieved in the second half of the 19th century that linguistic unity and vitality became possible.

The changes that have taken place in Italy over the past century are nothing short of astonishing. In 1861 when the country was first formed, only 2.5 percent of the population spoke Italian, although some scholars argue that it was closer to 10 percent. Today, virtually every Italian can understand the national language, and the vast majority can speak it with varying degrees of fluency.

Orthography and Basic Phonology

Italian orthography is very close to its phonetic form. This is because of the peculiar history of Italian, which has rendered it a relatively conservative language. Although most symbols represent in a one-to-one fashion the sounds they stand for, certain graphemes do represent more than one sound: *e* [e]/[ɛ], *o* [o]/[ɔ], *s* [s]/[z] (in those varieties that permit this sound), and *z* [ts]/[dz]. Moreover, palatal consonants, which did notexist in Latin, are represented not by single graphemes but by series of two or three letters: *ci*/*ce* [yi]/[ye], *gi*/*ge*-[dʒi]/[dʒe], *gn* [ɲ], *gli* [ʎi], and *sci*/*sce* [ʃi]/[ʃe]. An accent mark is only used to indicate a word-final stressed vowel: *città* 'city', *più* 'more'.

Italian has 20 consonants, seven vowels and two semi-vowels.

Consonants (see Table 1 above) can be single or geminate, except for [ʎ], [ɲ], [ts], [dz], and [ʃ], which are always long intervocalically, and [z], which is always short (in those varieties that permit this sound).

Table 2: Vowels

	Front	Mid	Back
High	i		u
Upper mid	e		o
Lower mid	e[ɛ]		o[ɔ]
Low		a	

Table 3: SemiVowels

Front	Back
i[j]	u[w]

All seven vowels (see Tables 2 and 3) can occur in stressed position, but only five are found in unstressed position; [ɛ] and [ɔ] are not permitted atonically. Vowels can be long or short depending on syllable structure and on the position of stress. Long vowels are found only in nonfinal, open, stressed syllables; vowels in all other positions are short.

Final stress is never predictable. When the final syllable of a word is not stressed, however, the penultimate syllable is stressed if it is heavy, consisting of a short vowel plus coda. If the penultimate syllable is light, either the penult or the antepenult is stressed.

There is an interesting and unique phonological phenomenon in Italian known as *raddoppiamento fonosintattico* 'phono-syntactic doubling'. This is a process whereby a stressed vowel in word-final position (or a stressed monosyllable ending in a vowel) triggers lengthening of the initial consonant of the following word: *a casa* [akka:sa] 'home', *metà torta* [metattorta] 'half a cake'. Historically, the origin of *raddoppiamento fonosintattico* may be found in the assimilation of the final consonant (now lost) of the first word and the initial consonant of the second word: *ad casam* [adkasam] > [akkasa]. Synchronically, it is due to the structure of stressed syllables, which must be heavy: the spreading of the [k] in [akka:sa] provides a coda for the stressed vowel preceding it, making the preceding syllable heavy.

The phonological system of Italian is relatively conservative in that it has retained many of the characteristics of Latin with few changes. Some of the changes include the increase in the number of vowels from five to seven (with the addition of *e* [ɛ] and *o* [ɔ]), the replacement of Latin's lexical (not predictable) vowel length distinctions with a new system of vowel length based on prosodic structure, the loss of a totally predictable system of stress assignment, the assimilation of obstruents (*lacte* > *latte* 'milk'), the palatalization of *l* following stops (*clamare* > *chiamare* [kjama:re] 'to call'), and random cases of sonorization (voicing) of intervocalic obstruents (*lacu* > *lago* 'lake', but *amicu* > *amico* 'friend').

Table 4: The Present Indicative Paradigm

Infinitive		parlare 'to speak'		credere 'to believe'		partire 'to depart'	
1sg	1pl	parlo	parliamo	credo	crediamo	parto	partiamo
2sg	2pl	parli	parlate	credi	credete	parti	partite
3sg	3pl	parla	parlano	crede	credono	parte	partono

Basic Morphology

Italian nouns and adjectives are marked for gender, either masculine or feminine, and number, either singular or plural. Masculine singular nouns typically end in *-o* with the plural form ending in *-i* (*piatto/piatti* 'dish/dishes'); feminine singular nouns usually end in *-a* with the plural form ending in *-e* (*casa/case* 'house/houses'); masculine and feminine nouns may end in *-e* with the plural form ending in *-i* (masculine: *cane/cani* 'dog/dogs'; feminine: *chiave/chiavi* 'key/keys').

Italian is known for its widespread use of descriptive suffixes. One or more suffixes may be added to a noun or adjective to alter its meaning. For example, *ragazzo* 'boy', *ragazzino* 'small boy', *ragazzone* 'big boy', *ragazzaccio* 'bad boy'; *fiore* 'flower', *fiorellino* 'small flower'.

Compounding is a productive process in Italian. For example, we find noun + noun compounds (*capo* 'head' + *luogo* 'place' > *capoluogo* 'capital'), noun + adjective compounds (*terra* 'land' +*fermo* 'still' >*terraferma* 'dry land'), verb + noun compounds (*asciuga* 's/he dries' + *mano* 'hand' > *asciugamano* 'hand towel'), and preposition + noun compounds (*senza* 'without' + *tetto* 'roof' > *senzatetto* 'homeless').

Although Latin had a rich case system, the use of noun inflections to express case functions decreased as the use of prepositions increased. The only remnant of case in Italian is found in the pronominal system: nominative, accusative, and dative forms of the pronoun may differ for some persons and numbers. For example, *io* is the first person singular nominative pronoun, whereas *me/mi* are the corresponding oblique (non-nominative) forms. The pronominal system includes free pronouns like *me* and *io*, which are stressed and occupy the same syntactic positions as do noun phrases, and clitic pronouns like *mi*, which are unstressed and have fixed positions next to the verb; compare *ha dato il regalo a me* 's/he gave the gift to me' and *mi ha dato il regalo* 's/he gave me the gift'. Italian and Italian dialects have accusative and dative clitics, but only some dialects have nominative clitics. Italian also has reflexive clitic pronouns in addition to free reflexive pronouns as well as a locative clitic, *ci*, (*ci vado* 'I go there'), a partitive-genitive clitic, *ne*, (*ne compro due* 'I buy two [of them]', *ho bisogno di un caffé* > *ne ho bisogno* 'I need a coffee' > 'I need one'), and a passive/impersonal clitic pronoun *si*.

Italian verbs are traditionally classified into three conjugations according to the ending of the infinitive form. The first conjugation consists of verbs ending in *-are* in the infinitive (*parlare* 'to speak'), the second consists of verbs ending in *-ere* in the infinitive, with stress either on the root (*credere* 'to believe') or on the suffix (*temere* 'to fear'), and the third consists of verbs ending in *-ire* in the infinitive (*partire* 'to depart').

Verbs are inflected with a suffix that indicates person (first, second, third) and number (singular, plural) of the subject and that also indicates tense and mood. Examples of the present indicative of three verbs are given in Table 4 above.

Some third conjugation verbs, for example, *finire* 'to finish', have another affix, *-isc*, found in the first, second, and third person singular; and the third person plural forms of the present indicative and subjunctive.

The future and conditional tenses of verbs of all three conjugations have an additional affix (*-er-* or *-ir-*) added before the inflectional suffix. Compound tenses are neo-Latin innovations and are made up of an inflected auxiliary verb plus a past participle, formed by the verb stem plus a participial suffix. Generally, the auxiliary *avere* 'to have' is used with transitive verbs, whereas *essere* 'to be' is used with ergative and reflexive verbs. The past participle of a verb conjugated with *essere* must agree in number and gender with the subject. The past participle of a verb conjugated with *avere* must agree with the preceding direct object clitic pronoun, if there is one.

Basic Syntax

The free word order system of Latin was replaced by a more fixed word order in Italian, generally Subject-Verb-Complement. The order of elements within the complement is Object–Prepositional Phrase: *Chiara vede il gatto nel giardino* 'Chiara sees the cat in the garden'. At the phrasal level, Italian is generally head medial. Within noun phrases, an adjective generally follows the noun it modifies, while definite and indefinite articles, demonstratives, ordinal and cardinal numbers, possessives, and quantifiers regularly precede the noun: *studenti intelligenti* 'intelligent students', *questi studenti* 'these students'. Italian is considered a pro-drop (or null subject) language; that is, it is a language in which the subject of the sentence need not be overtly expressed: *io mangio la frutta/mangio la frutta* 'I eat fruit'.

Interrogative sentences are formed by changing the intonation and/or word order of the declarative sentence or by introducing the sentence with an interrogative word: *Gianni mangia la frutta?/ Mangia la frutta Gianni?* 'Does John eat fruit?', *cosa mangia Gianni?* 'What does John eat?'

A negative sentence is formed by putting *non* before the verb: *Gianni non mangia la frutta* 'John does not eat fruit', or by putting *non* before the verb and a negative word after the verb: *Gianni non mangia mai la frutta* 'John never eats fruit', *Gianni non mangia niente* 'John does not eat anything'.

Contact with Other Languages

Since the Italian language has such a well-documented history dating from its Latin origin, we have a nearly complete record of words borrowed from other languages. Many loanwords entered into Latin from the languages spoken by the people that the Romans conquered, such as Etruscan, Osco-Umbrian, and Celtic.

During the Renaissance, Italian was influenced primarily by French and Spanish, although there are some borrowings from other languages as well, such as DUTCH and GERMAN. French remained the main source of loanwords until the last century when English took over its role as principal loaning language. Today, Italian has numerous partially and completely integrated English loans. Many have already become the basis for newly formed Italian words: *rock/rock-accio* 'rock/hard rock', and *manager/mangerialità* 'manager/quality of a manager'.

Italian played a significant role in the formation of the lingua franca used in the ports of the Mediterranean during the Middle Ages and Renaissance. It is also the basis for pidgins spoken (now or in the past) in Eritrea, Argentina, Brazil, Canada, and the United States.

From Etruscan: *persona* 'person', *taverna* 'tavern'
From Osco-Umbrian: *bufalo* 'buffalo', *casa* 'stable' > 'house'
From Celtic: *cammino* 'road', *montone* 'ram'
From Greek: *melo* 'apple tree', *poesia* 'poem'
From Germanic:
GOTHIC: *guardia* 'guard'
Longobard: *banca/panca* 'bench', *stucco* 'stucco'
Frankish: *barone* 'baron', *guadagnare* 'to earn'
From ARABIC: *limone* 'lemon', *algebra* 'algebra'
From French: *galleria* 'gallery', *massacro* 'massacre'
From Spanish: *complimento* 'compliment', *flotta* 'fleet'
From Dutch: *schizzo* 'sketch'
From German: *brindisi* 'toast'

Common Words

man:	uomo	long:	lungo
woman:	donna	small:	piccolo
water:	acqua	yes:	sì
sun:	sole	no:	no
three:	tre	good:	buono/bravo
fish:	pesce	bird:	uccello
big:	grande	dog:	cane
tree:	albero		

Example Sentences

(1) È americana.
s/he is American/FEM SG
'She is American.'

(2) Parli l' italiano?
you/SG speak the Italian
'Do you speak Italian?'

(3) Siamo andati a vedere un bel film.
we are gone/MASC PL to see a beautiful film
'We went to see a good movie.'

Efforts to Preserve, Protect, and Promote the Language

The use of Italian has spread significantly over the past century. When Italy was first united, only 2.5 percent of the population spoke Italian; nearly everyone spoke a "dialect". Today, every Italian has some degree of fluency in the national language. The government, concerned about the potential demise of the dialects, has taken some steps to promote their study in schools and to support cultural efforts aimed at increasing their prestige. In addition, the government promotes the study of Italian abroad by making materials and funds available to schools for teaching Italian.

Select Bibliography

Gensini, S. 1988. *Elementi di storia linguistica italiana.* Bergamo: Minerva Italica.

Harris, M., and N. Vincent, eds. 1987. *The Romance Languages.* London: Croom Helm.

Holtus, G., M. Metzeltin, and C. Schmitt, eds. 1988. *Lexicon der Romanistischen Linguistik: Italienisch, Korsisch, Sardisch* (vol. 4) Tübingen: Max Niemeyer.

Lepschy, A.L., and G. Lepschy. 1977. *The Italian Language Today.* London: Hutchinson.

Maiden, M. 1995. *A Linguistic History of Italian.* London and NewYork: Longman.

Maiden, M., and M. Parry. 1996. *The Dialects of Italy.* London: Routledge.

Renzi, L., ed. 1988. *Grande grammatica italiana di consultazione* (vol. 1). Bologna: Mulino.

Renzi, L., G. Salvi, and A. Cardinaletti, eds. 1991. *Grande grammatica italiana di consultazione* (vol. 2). Bologna: Mulino.

Renzi, L., G. Salvi, and A. Cardinaletti, eds. 1995. *Grande grammatica italiana di consultazione* (vol. 3). Bologna: Mulino.

JAPANESE

Timothy J. Vance

Language Name: Japanese. **Autonym:** *Nihongo.*

Location: The Japanese archipelago. Also spoken by emigrant communities in Hawaii, North America, and South America.

Family: Japanese-Ryūkyūan. This family may be a branch of Altaic, but some scholars consider Japanese-Ryūkyūan to be an isolated group or the result of a creolization of an Altaic-Austronesian contact language.

Related Languages: Ryūkyūan, which is sometimes treated as a subfamily consisting of three closely related languages. Japanese is possibly related to KOREAN, Manchu, and MONGOLIAN.

Dialects: There is wide regional dialect variation, although a standard based on the Tokyo dialect serves as a lingua franca throughout Japan. A crude geographical classification labels all dialects to the east of the Japan Alps on Honshū and Hokkaidō as Eastern, those to the west of the Japan Alps on Honshū and Shikoku as Western, and those on Kyūshū as a third group. The varieties spoken in Okinawa Prefecture or the Ryukyu Islands are popularly considered dialects of Japanese, but they are better treated as dialects of a Ryūkyūan subfamily within Japanese-Ryūkyūan.

Number of Speakers: 125 million.

Origin and History

The Japanese archaeological record shows the sudden appearance about 300 B.C. of a new cultural pattern including wet-rice agriculture and metal tools. The archipelago had been occupied by hunter-gatherers for several thousand years before this, and the new pattern was presumably introduced by immigrants. It is widely believed that these immigrants came from the Korean peninsula and spoke the common ancestor of Japanese-Ryūkyūan, but there is no direct evidence for this scenario. Some scholars maintain that the Japanese-Ryūkyūan languages are descended from a language of some of the earlier inhabitants. Still others suggest that the ancestor of Japanese-Ryūkyūan originated as a creole derived from contact between an Altaic language spoken by the immigrants and an Austronesian language spoken by the earlier inhabitants.

The oldest substantial written records of Japanese date from the eighth century A.D., and these reflect mostly the dialect of the aristocracy in Nara, a city in western Honshū that was the capital at the time. The language in these documents is commonly called Old Japanese. The imperial capital moved to nearby Kyōto in 794, and the grammars and dictionaries produced by Jesuit missionaries in the late 16th and early 17th centuries described the contemporary dialect of the Kyōto aristocracy. Tokyo has been the de facto political capital of the country since the 17th century, and the imperial court moved there in 1868. As a result, the Modern Standard language is based on the eastern Honshū dialect of upper-class Tokyo residents.

Orthography and Basic Phonology

The Japanese writing system is generally regarded as the modern world's most complex. Roughly speaking, native and Sino-Japanese nouns are written with Chinese characters (*kanji*), as are the invariant portions of most inflected words (verbs and adjectives). Inflectional endings, postpositions, and many adverbs are spelled out in a cursive syllabary (*hiragana*), and non-Chinese loanwords are spelled out in a squareish syllabary (*katakana*). There are, however, many exceptions to these broad generalizations. A single Chinese character often has two or more possible readings, the intended reading being determined by the context. The *hiragana* and *katakana* symbols originated as abbreviated versions of certain Chinese characters that had come to be used as phonograms.

There are two principal systems of Romanization, and a variant of the more popular Hepburn system is used here, with long vowels indicated by double letters (except in place-names mentioned in the text, where macrons are used instead). The chart on the next page shows the individual symbols of *hiragana* and *katakana* in the traditional right-to-left arrangement of top-to-bottom lines. The pronunciation of each symbol is given in Romanization. The many possible Japanese syllables not included in the chart are written by using diacritics and/or by combining two or three symbols.

All consonants listed in the Table 1 occur initially in CV syllables, and many can also occur initially in CyV syllables. A syllable-final consonant must be one of the two moraic consonants, which count as separate beats in poetic meter. The moraic nasal is always Romanized as *n*, but its pronunciation assimilates to the immediately following sound and varies widely, such as a bilabial [m] before bilabials, as in *onpa* 'soundwave', a nasalized glide [ɰ̃] before *s*, as in *kansa* 'inspection'; before a pause, it is usually uvular [N]. Before a vowel or *y*, a moraic nasal is followed by an apostrophe in Romanization to distinguish it from a syllable-initial alveolar nasal: *an'i* 'easy', *ani* 'older brother'. The moraic obstruent combines with an immediately following obstruent to form a phonetically long obstruent and is Romanized as a copy of that following obstruent, as in *rappa* 'bugle' and *dassen* 'derailment'. Except in recent loanwords, the moraic obstruent occurs only before voiceless obstruents.

Hiragana

ん	わ	ら	や	ま	は	な	た	さ	か	あ
[moraic]n	wa	ra	ya	ma	ha	na	ta	sa	ka	a
		り		み	ひ	に	ち	し	き	い
		ri		mi	hi	ni	chi	shi	ki	i
		る	ゆ	む	ふ	ぬ	つ	す	く	う
		ru	yu	mu	fu	nu	tsu	su	ku	u
		れ		め	へ	ね	て	せ	け	え
		re		me	he	ne	te	se	ke	e
	を	ろ	よ	も	ほ	の	と	そ	こ	お
	(w)o	ro	yo	mo	ho	no	to	so	ko	o

Katakana

ン	ワ	ラ	ヤ	マ	ハ	ナ	タ	サ	カ	ア
[moraic]n	wa	ra	ya	ma	ha	na	ta	sa	ka	a
		リ		ミ	ヒ	ニ	チ	シ	キ	イ
		ri		mi	hi	ni	chi	shi	ki	i
		ル	ユ	ム	フ	ヌ	ツ	ス	ク	ウ
		ru	yu	mu	fu	nu	tsu	su	ku	u
		レ		メ	ヘ	ネ	テ	セ	ケ	エ
		re		me	he	ne	te	se	ke	e
	ヲ	ロ	ヨ	モ	ホ	ノ	ト	ソ	コ	オ
	(w)o	ro	yo	mo	ho	no	to	so	ko	o

Table 1: Consonants

	Bilabial	Alveolar	Alveo-palatal	Velar	Glottal
Stops Voiceless Voiced	 p b	 t d		 k g	
Fricatives	f	s	sh		h
Affricates Voiceless Voiced		 ts z	 ch j		
Nasals	m	n			
Liquid		r			
Glides			y	w	

The voiceless stops and affricates are unaspirated. Some speakers can substitute a velar nasal [ŋ] for a word-medial voiced velar stop *g* in a large subset of the vocabulary. The alveolar affricates are *ts* [ts] and *z* [dz], but *z* is pronounced as a fricative [z] word-medially unless preceded by the moraic nasal. The alveo-palatal affricates are *ch* [cç] and *j* [ɟʑ]. The fricative *f* [ɸ] was until recently an allophone of *h*, occurring only before *u*, but *f* now appears before all vowels in loanwords, for example, *ferii* 'ferry'. The fricative *h* is pronounced as palatal [ç] before *y* or *i*. The alveopalatal fricative is *sh* [ɕ]. The liquid is a tap *r* [ɾ], and the velar glide *w* is often described as unrounded [ɰ], although it shows lip compression (not protrusion) in careful pronunciation. Even in recent loanwords, *t* and *d* do not occur before *u*, *s* and *z* do not occur before *y* or *i*, *h* does not occur before *u*, *y* does not occur before *i*, and *w* does not occur before *u*.

Table 2: Vowels

	Front	Back
High	i	u
Mid	e	o
Low		a

The high back vowel *u* is often described as unrounded [ɯ], but like the glide *w* it shows lip compression in careful pronunciation. All five vowels occur both short and long, and a syllable with a long vowel counts as two moras. All two-vowel sequences are possible, although some are quite rare; if the second vowel is *e*, *o*, or *a*, it is in a separate syllable from the first, but if the second vowel is *i* or *u*, it may be the second mora of a long syllable. Short *i* and *u* are frequently devoiced

Table 3: Honorific Morphology

	VERB 'eat'	ADJECTIVE 'high'	COPULA
Formal Nonpast Affirmative	tabe-masu	taka-i desu	desu
Formal Past Affirmative	tabe-mashita	taka-katta desu	deshita
Formal Nonpast Negative	tabe-masen	taka-ku na-i desu	ja na-i desu

between voiceless consonants or between a voiceless consonant and a pause.

Japanese has a pitch-accent system, and the location of accent, manifested as a drop from high to low pitch, is the contrastive feature of the system. The presence or absence of an accent and its location in a word are essential to determining the intonation contour of a phrase containing that word. The possible locations for accent are least constrained in nouns. A noun may be accented on any syllable, or it may be unaccented as in *ha'shi* 'chopsticks', *hashi'* 'bridge' and *hashi* (unaccented) 'edge'. Accent is not marked in Japanese orthography or in Romanization.

Basic Morphology

Japanese verbs and adjectives are inflected for many of the same categories, including those illustrated by the affirmative forms below. Verb negation is expressed by a derived form that inflects like an adjective, and adjective negation is expressed periphrastically.

	VERB 'eat' Affirmative	Negative
Nonpast Indicative	tabe-ru	tabe-na-i
Past Indicative	tabe-ta	tabe-na-katta
Gerund	tabe-te	tabe-na-kute
Conditional	tabe-reba	tabe-na-kereba

	ADJECTIVE 'high' Affirmative	Negative
Nonpast Indicative	taka-i	taka-ku na-i
Past Indicative	taka-katta	taka-ku na-katta
Gerund	taka-kute	taka-ku na-kute
Conditional	taka-kereba	taka-ku na-kereba

The copula manifests most of the same categories as verbs and adjectives and is probably best thought of as a third type of inflected word. There are alternatives for all of the forms listed below, but these are the most frequent in colloquial speech.

	COPULA Affirmative	Negative
Nonpast Indicative	da	ja na-i
Past Indicative	datta	ja na-katta
Gerund	de	ja na-kute
Conditional	nara	ja na-kereba

Verbs, adjectives, and the copula also have forms that express deference. Forms that indicate deference toward the addressee are commonly labeled "formal" or "distal." The forms in Table 3 are formal counterparts of some of the examples given above.

Forms that indicate deference toward the subject of the sentence are commonly labeled "honorific". There is a regular pattern for forming a periphrastic honorific counterpart of a verb, but for many common verbs a completely different verb or phrase is used as an honorific substitute. The verb for "eat" is unusual in that both the regular formation and a substitute verb are possible as honorific forms (see Table 4).

There are also forms that indicate deference indirectly by humbling the subject of the sentence. There is a regular pattern for forming the humble counterpart of a verb, but for many common verbs a completely different verb or phrase is used as a humble substitute (see Table 5).

Japanese also has fairly well-developed derivational morphology, and forms based on verb roots can be quite long. An extreme example is *tabe+sase+rare+ta+gar-u* 'show signs of wanting to be made to eat', which exhibits productive causative (*sase*), passive (*rare*), desiderative (*ta*), and evidential (*gar*) suffixes between the root (*tabe*) and the informal nonpast indicative inflection (*u*).

Compounding is also very common, and in contrast to ENGLISH, compound verbs are abundant. Compound verbs play much the same role in Japanese as verb+particle combinations play in English. The following examples all have the root of the verb *mi-ru* 'look' as their first element: *mi+age-ru* 'look up at' (compare *age-ru* 'raise'), *mi+okur-u* 'see off' (compare *okur-u* 'send'), *mi+kaes-u* 'look back at' (compare *kaes-u* 'return'), *mi+sage-ru* 'look down on' (compare *sage-ru* 'lower'), *mi+har-u* 'watch over' (compare *har-u* 'stretch'), *mi+mawas-u* 'look around' (compare *mawas-u* 'rotate'), *mi+wake-ru* 'tell apart' (compare *wake-ru* 'divide').

Japanese also has a very extensive sound-symbolic vocabulary, that is, items in which the relationship between pronunciation and meaning is not entirely arbitrary. These mimetic words typically function as manner adverbs, and many of them imitate motion instead of or in addition to sound. Reduplication is very common in the sound-symbolic vocabulary, and it carries an obvious meaning of repetition or continuation: *pyon* 'with a hop', *pyon-pyon* 'hop-hop'.

Basic Syntax

Japanese has nominative-accusative syntax with SOV as the basic order of clause constituents. Nouns do not inflect, and the case relations of noun phrases are marked by postpositions. The order of major constituents other than the predicate is quite free. Japanese is a prototypical SOV language in that it consistently exhibits modifier-head order. For example, adjectives

Table 4

	'eat'	'read'	'go'
Regular Honorific Informal Nonpast Affirmative	o-tabe ni naru	o-yomi ni naru	—
Substitute Honorific Informal Nonpast Affirmative	meshiagaru	—	irassharu

Table 5

	'read'	'go'
Regular Humble Formal Nonpast Affirmative	o-yomi shimasu	—
Substitute Humble Formal Nonpast Affirmative	—	mairimasu

precede nouns, relative clauses precede head nouns, and main verbs precede auxiliaries.

In a simple transitive sentence the subject noun phrase is marked with the nominative postposition *ga* and the direct-object noun phrase with the accusative postposition *o*: *A ga B o tabeta* 'A ate B'. Some stative predicates, however, allow or require a double nominative pattern. One example is the verb *wakaru* 'understand': *A ga B ga wakaru* 'A understands B'.

The topic postposition *wa* marks a noun phrase as old information or as contrastive. When that noun phrase is nominative or accusative, *wa* appears instead of *ga* or *o*; otherwise *wa* follows whatever postposition marks the case relation. Compare *A wa B ga tabeta* 'As for A, B ate it' with *A de wa B ga tabeta* 'At A, B ate', where *de* is a locative postposition.

There are three predicate types in Japanese: verbal, adjectival, and nominal. A nominal predicate consists of a noun phrase followed by the copula, and unlike verbs and adjectives, the nonpast form of the copula is different in a modifying clause than in a main clause. Furthermore, there are two different modifying-clause forms, and which of the two appears is determined by the preceding noun. For example, the nonpast copula *da* appears both in *byooki da* 'is sick' and in *genki da* 'is well', but it appears as *no* in *byooki no hito* 'person who is sick' and as *na* in *yuumei na hito* 'person who is famous'. Nouns that take *na* denote qualities and are typically translated into English as adjectives; some of them, including *yuumei*, cannot occur as nominatives or accusatives. Most nouns that take *no* are more prototypical; *byooki* can occur as a nominative or accusative in the meaning 'sickness'. Many nouns combine with the verb *suru* 'do' to form verbs. A typical example is *shookai+suru* 'introduce' (compare *shookai* 'introduction').

When the identity of a clause participant is clear from context, any noun phrase referring to that participant is simply omitted, as is the associated postposition. This phenomenon is sometimes called "zero pronominalization". Honorific and humble forms can be important contextual clues to identity, since the subject of an honorific predicate cannot be the speaker, and the subject of a humble predicate cannot be the addressee. The commonly used verbs of giving and receiving provide similar clues because each such verb is restricted to certain directions of transfer. For example, *kureru* 'give' ordinarily denotes a transfer to the speaker, whereas *ageru* 'give' ordinarily denotes a transfer to someone other than the speaker. These verbs of giving and receiving are included in the small set of verbs that can be used as auxiliaries following verb gerunds. In their auxiliary use they indicate explicitly that the action denoted by the gerund is done as a favor to someone, and the same restrictions on direction apply.

One salient characteristic of spoken Japanese is the heavy use of sentence-final particles, which convey as part of their meaning the speaker's attitude toward the content of the sentence. The most common are *ka*, which marks a sentence as a question; *ne*, which solicits agreement from the addressee; and *yo*, which communicates the speaker's assurance.

Contact with Other Languages

In historical times since about A.D. 400 CHINESE has had a far greater impact on Japanese than any other language. Chinese vocabulary was borrowed over the course of several centuries in three major waves, and Sino-Japanese vocabulary items in modern Japanese occupy a niche very similar to that occupied by GREEK and LATIN vocabulary in modern English. A Sino-Japanese word is typically more formal or bookish than a native Japanese word of similar meaning, for example, Sino-Japanese *konchuu* 'insect' versus native *mushi* 'bug'. Sino-Japanese elements can be combined productively as Japanese without reference to Chinese models, as in the 19th century coinage *sha + shin* 'reflection'+'reality' = 'photograph' (compare Greek-based *photo+graph* 'light'+ 'writing'). Long Sino-Japanese compound nouns are common, especially in technical vocabulary. A typical example is *genshi+ryoku+sensui+kan* 'atom'+'power'+'diving'+'ship' = 'nuclear submarine'.

Active trade with several European countries began in the mid-16th century, and a few words borrowed from PORTUGUESE at that time are still in use such as *pan* 'bread', *botan* 'button'. From the mid-17th century until the mid-19th century, Japan was closed to foreigners except for Dutch and Chinese traders at a post in Nagasaki harbor, but a number of DUTCH loanwords filtered in, and many are still in use such as *biiru* 'beer' and *penki* 'paint'. Since the mid-19th century, English has been the primary source of loanwords, and the rate of borrowing from English accelerated dramatically after the end of World War II.

Common Words

man:	otoko	long:	nagai
woman:	onna	small:	chiisai
water:	mizu	yes:	hai
sun:	hi	no:	iie
three:	san	good:	ii
fish:	sakana	dog:	inu
big:	ookii	tree:	ki

Example Sentences

(1) Tomodachi ga tsukut-te kure-ta keeki
friend NOM make-GERUND give-PAST cake

wa oishi-i yo.
TOP delicious-NONPAST ASSURANCE.PARTICLE
'The cake that my friend made for me is delicious!'

(2) Soroban de rishi o keisan-shi-masu
Abacus INST interest ACC calculation-do-FORMAL.NONPAST

ka.
QUESTION
'Do (you) calculate interest with an abacus?'

(3) Shashin o jiro-jiro mi-te i-ru
Photo ACC stare-stare look-GERUND be-NONPAST

hito wa gakusei da ne.
person TOP student COP CONFIRM
'The person who is staring at the photo is a student, right?'

Efforts to Preserve, Protect, and Promote the Language

Japanese ranks ninth in the world in terms of the number of native speakers, but it is not widely used as an international language. It was imposed as the language of education in Taiwan and Korea when these areas were under Japanese colonial rule, and there were efforts to teach it in areas conquered during World War II, but all of this ended in 1945. More recently, Japan has attracted large numbers of foreign students, especially from nearby Asian countries, and for most of these students Japanese language training is the first step in their work in Japan. The Japan Foundation, a government agency established in 1972, promotes language training both in Japan and abroad. Government language policy in the 20th century has focused almost exclusively on orthography. Several significant reforms were adopted after World War II, although some have been partially reversed in more recent years.

Select Bibliography

Alfonso, Anthony. 1966. *Japanese Language Patterns*. 2 vols. Tokyo: Sophia University.

Backhouse, A.E. 1993. *The Japanese Language: An Introduction*. Melbourne: Oxford University Press.

Beckman, Mary E., and Janet B. Pierrehumbert. 1988. *Japanese Tone Structure*. Cambridge: MIT Press.

Gottlieb, Nanette. 1995. *Kanji Politics: Language Policy and Japanese Script*. London: Kegan Paul International.

Habein, Yaeko Sato. 1984. *The History of the Japanese Written Language*. Tokyo: University of Tokyo Press.

Haig, John, ed. 1997. *The New Nelson Japanese-English Character Dictionary: Based on the Classic Edition by Andrew N. Nelson*. Rutland: Tuttle.

Hinds, John. 1986. *Japanese*. London: Croom Helm.

Jorden, Eleanor Harz, and Mari Noda. 1987–90. *Japanese: The Spoken Language*. 3 vols. New Haven: Yale University Press.

Kuno, Susumu. 1973. *The Structure of the Japanese Language*. Cambridge: MIT Press.

Martin, Samuel E. 1975. *A Reference Grammar of Japanese*. New Haven: Yale University Press.

____. 1987. *The Japanese Language through Time*. New Haven: Yale University Press.

Masuda, Koh, ed. 1974. *Kenkyusha's New Japanese-English Dictionary*. 4th ed. Tokyo: Kenkyusha.

Miller, Roy Andrew. 1967. *The Japanese Language*. Chicago: University of Chicago Press.

Ono, Hideichi, ed. 1984. *A Practical Guide to Japanese-English Onomatopoeia and Mimesis*. Tokyo: Hokuseido Press.

Seeley, Christopher. 1991. *A History of Writing in Japan*. Leiden: E.J. Brill.

Shibatani, Masayoshi. 1990. *The Language of Japan*. Cambridge: Cambridge University Press.

Soga, Matsuo. 1983. *Tense and Aspect in Modern Colloquial Japanese*. Vancouver: University of British Columbia Press.

Tagashira, Yoshiko, and Jean Hoff. 1986. *Handbook of Japanese Compound Verbs*. Tokyo: Hokuseido Press.

Unger, J. Marshall. 1996. *Literacy and Script Reform in Occupation Japan: Reading between the Lines*. Oxford: Oxford University Press.

Vance, Timothy J. 1987. *An Introduction to Japanese Phonology*. Albany: State University of New York Press.

JAVANESE

Hein Steinhauer

Language Name: Javanese. **Autonym:** *cara Jawa* or *basa Jawa* (in *ngoko* style [see Dialects below]); *cara Jawi* or *basa Jawi* (in *basa* style).

Location: Javanese is spoken in Indonesia (with Central and most of East Java as its core area, but with large communities all over the country), and by sizeable communities in Malaysia, Suriname, New Caledonia, and the Netherlands. All these communities speak varieties of Modern Javanese. Old Javanese still functions as a ritual theatrical and traditional scholarly language on the Indonesian islands of Bali and Lombok.

Family: Javanese belongs to the Western Malayo–Polynesian branch of the Austronesian language family. The subdivision of that branch is still a matter of debate.

Related Languages: The closest relatives of Javanese are (not in order) SUNDANESE, BALINESE, Sasak, MADURESE, and MALAY.

Dialects: The language variety of the Central Javanese sultanates of Yogyakarta and Surakarta is the basis of standard Javanese.

Geographical dialect surveys and dialect studies have been conducted on a very limited scale. Minor isoglosses are lexical. They may involve the particular value of cognates of words that are marked for formality or reverence in the standard dialect. The degree of Islamization, ranging from thoroughly and early along the northern coasts of Java to not yet in the Tengger area in the southeast, has its reflection in the vocabularies of the dialects. Language contact is another source of lexical variation: in the west (Banten, Krawang, Cirebon), Sundanese influence may be observed in the east, Madurese; in the Banyuwangi area also Balinese. Major isoglosses concern the extent to which the allophonic and phonemic splits and mergers have occurred, which are typical of standard Javanese.

The extent to which speech styles (see section below) are distinguished is another parameter for dialect differentiation. In the western and eastern peripheries (Banten, Banyumas, Banyuwangi), and in the Tengger area speech styles are less elaborate.

In Suriname the original dialects are in the process of developing into a koine. The majority of its speakers has its roots in the western parts of Central Java. Many speakers originate from the Kedu area, some come from Banyumas. A few even have a Sundanese background, although they now have shifted to Javanese. A pronunciation that reflects a Banyumas origin is stigmatized. Speech styles have been preserved, albeit with different parameters and with lexical differences as compared to standard Javanese.

No research has been done on the Javanese in New Caledonia and in Malaysia. Those in the Netherlands probably do not yet deviate much from their relatives in Suriname, apart from DUTCH lexical influences.

Speech Styles. What has sometimes erroneously been described as different social dialects, namely "High" and "Low" Javanese, are in fact inseparable speech styles that belong to one and the same language variety. In Javanese these styles are called *basa* (*krama*) and *ngoko*, respectively; the words and morphemes characterizing them are referred to as *krama* and *ngoko*. According to a recent calculation there are over 600 pairs of lexical items and three pairs of inflectional morphemes whose only semantic difference is a matter of courtesy; one of them is *ngoko*, the other *krama*. The former indicates that the speaker judges the speech situation to be informal, the latter that he qualifies it as formal. Parameters for his judgment are setting, topic, and social status of his audience in comparison with his own (measured by age, birth, relationship, and/or position). The speaker may steer a middle course by using basically *krama* vocabulary, but replacing this vocabulary where possible, by so-called *madya* 'middle' equivalents, of which there are several dozens, mostly for pronouns and function words; the *krama* inflectional morphemes are usually replaced by their *ngoko* counterparts, a possibility that contributes to the fluid character of the *madya* speech style. All morphemes that are not participating in a *ngoko-(madya-) krama* opposition may be called "neutral".

Over 220 among these neutral lexical morphemes are called *krama inggil*. They are opposed to one or two other neutral lexemes or to a *ngoko-krama* pair, which are referentially synonymous, by an extra semantic feature: the speaker expresses reverence vis-à-vis the referent of the lexeme in question. Some 20 neutral lexemes, known as *krama andhap*, are opposed to referentially synonymous lexemes by the additional semantic feature of downgrading the referent (most typically the speaker and his actions or belongings). Other neutral roots are unmarked in these respects.

Some examples of possible lexical sets, in phonemic transcription, are presented in the chart on the next page.

The majority of the morphemes are unmarked for reverence and/or formality. All marked lexical morphemes, however, refer to common, everyday aspects of life. They consequently have a high text frequency. The same holds for the non-neutral inflectional morphemes, which are involved in the construction of a very high number of word groups. The

Examples of Lexical Sets in Standard Orthography

		say	eat	go with	visit	nose
Non-neutral	*ngoko*	kandha	mangan	melu		
	madya	sanjang				
	krama	criyos	nedha	tumut		
Neutral	*krama inggil*	ngendika	dhahar		pinarak	grana
	krama andhap	matur		ndherek	sowan	
	unmarked				mampir	irung

elaborate vocabulary for speech style differentiation is one of the most salient features of standard Javanese. The lexical choices a speaker makes are a measure of proper conduct, but may also be a means to manipulate his audience. Examples here will be in *ngoko* style unless otherwise indicated.

Number of Speakers: According to the census of 1990 there are over 60.2 million speakers of Javanese over four years old in Indonesia, comprising 38.8 percent of the population of the same age group. In Suriname, the Javanese community is estimated to number about 70,000 speakers, of which some 20,000 have come to live in the Netherlands. In Malaysia there are a few Javanese villages in Johor and Selangor. In the late 1990s tens of thousands of Indonesians, among them many Javanese, sought employment in Malaysia as contract workers, but for the most part they have not settled permanently, but have repatriated. In New Caledonia there were nearly 7,000 Javanese in 1987.

Origin and History

Austronesian-speaking people populated insular Southeast Asia in a succession of waves, originating probably from southeast China. When and where Proto-Javanese separated itself from the other Austronesian branches is unknown. The oldest known specimen of a language identified as (Old) Javanese is the stone inscription of Sukabumi, dated March 25, 804. Older (dated) inscriptions, all from the eighth century are written in SANSKRIT. The feudal Indianized states that succeeded each other in Central and East Java became the centers of empires whose spheres of power and influence reached far beyond the Java coasts.

Old Javanese prevailed in stone and copper plate inscriptions from the 9th century onwards. It was riddled with Sanskrit loanwords and was the carrier of the Hindu-Buddhist culture, which was to be gradually replaced by a more Islam-inspired culture from the 15th century onwards, a process that is still continuing today. Where the Hindu-Buddhist cultural inheritance prevails in Bali and parts of Lombok, Old Javanese is still alive as a ceremonial language.

In Java, Old Javanese literature was produced from the 9th until the second half of the 15th century. In Bali original literature in Old Javanese was produced even in the 19th century. The relationship between Old Javanese and the language varieties known as Middle Javanese and Modern Javanese is unclear. Middle Javanese literature in all likelihood had its roots in East Java, but is known from Bali only, where it flourished after the direct Hindu-Javanese influence had waned, as in the 16th century. Together with a few East Javanese inscriptions from the 14th and 15th centuries this literature shows some lexical and phonological innovations that are also found in Modern Javanese. Yet, Middle Javanese cannot be considered the bridge between Old and Modern Javanese. Two Muslim 16th century manuscripts from the north coast of Java are more similar in language to the literary Modern Javanese that flourished around 1800, and which does not differ essentially from refined standard Javanese today, than they are to Middle Javanese.

The intensified colonial exploitation of Java by the Dutch in the 19th century resulted in the forced cultivation of export crops. The consequences were famine, land shortage, and population growth that caused "superfluous" Javanese to move to other areas. This was the beginning of the Javanization of the sparsely populated Lampung districts of South Sumatra, where the Javanese now outnumber the originally indigenous population.

Within Indonesia the Javanese have become a sizeable minority in most of the 27 provinces, having limited contacts with the indigenous local population. The Javanese in the Netherlands are mainly former inhabitants of Suriname who opted to become Dutch citizens after Suriname became independent in 1975.

Orthography and Basic Phonology

Various alphabets have been used in writing Javanese. The traditional Javanese script, called *carakan* or *hanacaraka,* is a semisyllabary, derived from a southern Indian prototype, and through history appearing in a variety of shapes. The printed version has not been used since World War II, except in exercise books. For publications with a strong Muslim inspiration an adapted variety of ARABIC, called *pegon* was already used in the 17th century; in Islamic circles it is still used today, both in writing and in printing. The LATIN alphabet was introduced in the beginning of the 20th century. It replaced the other scripts. The standard spelling, reformed (with the exception of proper names) in 1972 after the model of the Indonesian standard orthography, is basically a transliteration of the *hanacaraka* spelling; consequently it reflects an archaic pronunciation, which has been largely preserved in the western dialects of Central Java, but it stands in a rather complicated relation to the phonology of the standard language, especially with regard to the vocalism.

Table 1: Consonants

		Labial	Alveolar	Retroflex	Palatal	Velar	Glottal
Stops	Voiceless	p	t	th [ʈ]	c	k	(k) [ʔ]
	Voiced	b	d	dh [ɖ]	j [ɟ]	g	
Nasals		m	n		ny [ɲ]	ng [ŋ]	
Fricatives			s				h
Lateral			l				
Trill			r				
Glides		w			y		

The consonant system does not deviate dramatically from the current standard orthography. For some phonemes digraphs are used. Glottal stop, whose phonemic status is marginal, is written as *k*.

Palatal, retroflex, and "voiced" consonants do not occur word finally. In writing, lexical roots *may* end in *b,d,* or *g,* but in pronunciation they are not distinguished from their voiceless counterparts. In *non*-final position, the "voiced" stops are voiced only when they are preceded by a (homorganic) nasal, otherwise they are unvoiced with lowered larynx, lending a breathy quality to the following vowel. Most consonant clusters consist of a stop preceded by a homorganic nasal. Nasals before retroflexed stops are analyzed as /n/. Before palatal stops /ny/ is written as *n*. There are no consonant clusters in word-final position. Word-final *k* is always pronounced as a glottal stop, as it usually is in other syllable-final positions.

The analysis of the vowel system is more controversial. Standard orthography reflects an older stage of the language (maintained in several dialects), in which there were only six vowels: *i, e, a, o, u,* and *ə* (schwa). Originally mere allophonic alternations, however, have become phonemic in closed-final syllables of lexical roots, resulting in a system of eight vowels in modern Javanese. The orthographic representations are added in parentheses below.

Table 2: Vowels

		Front	Central	Back
High		i		u
Mid	Higher	é (i, e) [e]	e [ə]	o (u, o) [o]
	Lower	è (e) [ɛ]		ò (o, a) [ɔ]
Low			a	

Most roots are bisyllabic. In trisyllabic roots, the antepenultimate syllable can only contain one of the following vowels: *i, u, a,* and *ə*. The rare roots with four syllables are treated as if they consisted of two roots of two syllables each. Stress is not phonemic, and it is subject to paralinguistic variation.

In the examples below the standard orthography is used where this deviates from the phonemic spelling, the latter is added in square brackets in the next two sections, using the symbols of the consonant and vowel tables above.

Basic Morphology

Productive morphological processes are prefixation, suffixation, circumfixation, root or word reduplication, modification, and combinations of these. Infixation is archaic and nonproductive, as is partial reduplication. There is never more than one prefix; suffix combinations are highly restricted.

Most roots are bisyllabic. Monosyllabic roots are confined to some loanwords and onomatopoetic roots. Suffixation is often accompanied by root modification.

Nouns may be simple or derived. Illustrative derivations include *pastur* [pastor] 'minister' > *pastur-pasturan* 'imitation minister, play by imitating a minister', *kayu* 'wood' > *kayon,* [kayòn], *kayonan* 'finding or storing place for wood', *bumbu* 'herb' > *bumbon* [bumbòn] 'herbs', *gitar* 'guitar' > *gitar-gitaranku* 'the way I am accompanied on the guitar', *lurah* 'village head' > *kalurahan* 'administrative village', *ratu* 'king' > *kraton* [kratòn] 'palace', *mlarat* 'poor' > *kamlaratan* 'poverty', *loyo* 'weak' > *loyoku* 'my weakness'.

Nouns may be interpreted as singular or nonsingular when referring to countable entities. Duplicated forms indicate plurality and variety. The third-person suffix *-(n)e* [(n)é] is required if the possessor is expressed by a noun phrase and is also very frequently used as a definite marker: *omah* 'house(s)' > *omahe* 'his/her/its/the house(s)' > *omahe guru* 'the house(s) of the teacher(s).'

Modification, duplication, prefixation, and suffixation are also productively used in adjectival derivation: *galak* 'wild' > *galik* 'very wild'; *gatel* 'itching' > *gatel-gatel* 'all itching in various degrees, tending to be itching on all occasions'; *luwe* [luwé] 'hungry' > *luwenan* [luwénan] 'of a hungry nature'; *gampang* 'easy' > *sagampang-gampange* [sa(k)gampanggampangé] 'as easy as possible, as easy as it may be'; *lemu* 'fat' > *kelemon(en)* [kelemòn(en)] 'too fat'.

Morphological processes associated with numbers are as follows: *lima* [limò]'five' > *lima-lima* [limòlimò] 'in groups of five'; *loro* 'two' > *ngloro* 'two each'; *telu* 'three' > *pingtelu* [péngtelu] 'three times' > *mingtelu* [méngtelu] 'three times each'; *sanga* [sòngò] 'nine' > *sanga-sangane* 'all nine'; *puluh* [puloh] 'unit of ten' (bound form), se*puluh* [sepuloh] 'ten', *limang puluh* [limang puloh] 'fifty' > *puluhan* 'approximately ten'.

Verbs are divided into two major subclasses, dependent on the transitive or intransitive character of the verbal root. Inflectional distinctions, mostly marked by prefixes, include two voices, active and passive, and the following distinctions: declarative, imperative, and intentional. In the passive, the declaratives may be further subcategorized by whether or not they are agentive. Agentive forms differ as to first, second, or other person. All these forms occur in three parallel sets: without a suffix (indicating that the object is just a patient), with a suffix *-i* or variants (indicating that the object is a location), and with a suffix *-ke* [ké] or variants (indicating that the object is moved, that it is a causee or that it benefits from the action, or that the object is just a patient but that a beneficiary is somehow involved). With reduplicated root, repetition is expressed; additional root-vowel modification indicates irritation of the speaker. Adjectives and nouns may be verbalized with derivational morphology. Verbs are unmarked for tense.

Basic Syntax

Javanese sentences usually consist of a sequence of one or more intonationally marked topics, followed by a comment (usually consisting of or containing a predicate), and possibly one or more intonationally marked tails or afterthoughts. What would translate as a subject is usually (one of) the topic(s). Subjects may be left out where they are clear from the context. They may also fill a tail slot. Spoken Javanese is characterized by a relative abundance of interjections and modal particles, which seems to be in line with the information structure of Javanese sentences: segmentation of the sentence into intonationally marked trunks of information (topics, comment, afterthoughts).

Apart from pronominal affixes (agent in passive verb forms, possessor), the only case of case marking is the phonemically restricted prenasalization to indicate that the following noun is a location.

Attributes most commonly follow the head except in the core of the predicate, which has the following order of constituents: ±Aspect ±Negator ±Auxiliary + Predicate head, for example: *aku wis turu* [aku wés turu] 'I slept already'; *aku ora turu* 'I did not sleep'.

The predicate head may be a numeral expression, a noun phrase, an adjective phrase, a preposition + noun phrase, or a verb phrase. Some degree adverbs precede gradable adjectives; others do not, resulting in two types of adjective phrases:

rada gedhe	'rather big'
gedhe banget	'very big'

Noun phrases are of two types: (1) +Noun ±Adjective ±Numeral expression ±Relative clause ±Determiners or (2) +Noun + Possessive construction ±Relative clause ±Determiners.

A relative clause consists of the relator *sing (krama: ingkang)* followed by a predicative phrase or clause: *sing turu wae* [séng turu waé] 'who just sleeps'; *sing adhine turu wae* [séng adhiné turu waé] 'whose younger sibling just sleeps'.

The determiner slot has the structure: ±Demonstrative (DEM) ±Anaphoric marker (AN) ±Topic marker (TOP). A possessive construction consists of a personal pronominal form (a suffix or a free form), or of the third-person pronominal suffix *-(n)e* [(n)é] (*krama: -(n)ipun*) [(n)ipon]) followed by a noun phrase.

Examples of noun phrases:

omah	gedhe	loro	kuwi	mau	ki.
[omah	gedhé	loro	kuwi	mau	ki]
house	big	two	DEM	AN	TOP

'that mentioned big house now'

omahe	guruku	sing	diambrukke
[omah-é	guru-ku	séng	di-ambruk-ké]
house-his	teacher-my	REL	PASS-collapse-CAUS

lindhu
lindhu]
earthquake
'the house of my teacher was destroyed by an earthquake'

There are a number of negativizing words in Javanese. Nonparadigmatic negation is expressed with *ora (krama: mboten* [mbòten]*)* 'not, no', which is typically used with other than nominal constructions. Paradigmatic negation, the only possibility with nominal constructions, is expressed with *dhudhu (krama: sanes* [sanès]*)*. Prohibitions are marked with aja [òjò (*krama: sampun* [sampon]) 'don't'. Aspectual polar oppositions are indicated with *wis* 'already' versus *durung* [durong] *(krama: dereng* [dèrèng]*)* 'not yet.'

Aku durung turu.	'I did not sleep yet.'
Aja turu [òjò turu].	'Don't sleep.'
Dhudhu aku sing ora turu.	'It wasn't I who didn't sleep.'

Contact with Other Languages

From the earliest periods, the Old Javanese kingdoms were in contact with the Malay-speaking empire of Srivijaya in Sumatra. Long before the European expansion, varieties of Malay functioned as a trade language in Southeast Asia and beyond. To what extent Malay and Javanese have influenced each other in precolonial times is difficult to ascertain, but it is certain that they have.

Religious and political developments brought Javanese in contact with four waves of foreign (other than Austronesian) languages: the influence of Sanskrit on Old Javanese has been mentioned above. With the Islamicization of Java form the 15th century onwards Arabic and PERSIAN vocabulary entered the language. The period of European expansion is reflected in loanwords from PORTUGUESE (16th century) and Dutch (17th century until the 1940s). Since independence, foreign influences in the lexicon are ENGLISH, international vocabulary (through Indonesian), and (neo-)Sanskrit. The latter elements suggest remote ancestral respectability and are popular as names of companies, foundations and government institutions. At the same time Javanese influences Indonesian.

From Sanskrit: *estri* 'wife', *arta* 'money', *asma* 'name', *asmara* 'romantic love'; proper names such as *Soeharto* and *Dewi*
From Arabic: *Islam* 'Islam', *makmur* 'prosperous', *halal* 'permissible', *magrib* 'time (sunset) for the fourth daily prayer'
From Portuguese: *meja* 'table', *lemari* 'cupboard'
From Dutch: *makelar* 'broker', *pos* 'post', *simpanse* 'chimpanzee', *pasfoto* 'passport picture', *indhekos* 'to take room and board', *om* 'uncle', *branwir* 'fire brigade', *pulisi* 'police', *bredel* 'gag on the press'
From English (possibly through Malay): *carter* 'charter', *aksesori* 'accessory'
International vocabulary (through Dutch and Malay/Indonesian): *teknologi* 'technology', *dhemokrasi* 'democracy'

Common Words

	NGOKO	KRAMA	NEUTRAL
man:	wong lanang	tiyang jaler	
woman:	wong wadon	tiyang estri	
bird:	manuk	pesi	
dog:	asu	segawon	
fish:	iwak	ulam	
sun:			srengenge
tree:			wit
water:	bangu	toya	
three:	telu	tiga	
big:	gedhe	ageng	
good:	becik	sae	
long:	dawa	panjang	
small:	cilik	alit	

Example Sentences

The following sentences illustrate the use of some of the transitive verbal forms in wider contexts. The first two sentences are in *ngoko* style. The last sentence gives the *basa* equivalent of the second sentence.

(1) pit iki taktuku neng tokone pegawe sing
[pit iki tak-tuku nèng toko-né pegawé séng
bike this I-buy in shop-POSS civil.servant REL

ditahan merga korupsi kuwi mau.
di-tahan mergò korupsi kuwi mau]
be-arrested because corruption that mentioned
'I bought this bike in the shop of that mentioned civil servant who was arrested for corruption.'

(2) adhiku sing koktukokke pit iki.
[toko-né pegawé ki wes kòk-tukòn-i pit iki]
younger.sibling-my REL you-buy-for bike this
'It is my younger sibling that you bought this bike for.'

(3) adhi kula ingkang sampeyan-tumbas-aken
[adhi kulò éngkang sampéyan-tumbas-aken
younger.sibling my REL you-buy-for

pit kae.
pit kaé]
bike this
'It is my younger sibling that you bought this bike for.'

As Example Sentences (2) and (3) show, the *ngoko* and *krama* sentences are completely parallel, but for the fact that the pronominal affixes in *ngoko* are bound morphemes, whereas their *krama* equivalents are free forms used as clitics.

Efforts to Preserve, Protect, and Promote the Language

All over Indonesia, and with very few exceptions, a language shift can be observed from the regional languages to Indonesian, the national language. This is also evident in Java. Speakers using Javanese as their daily language are still on the increase; however, in terms of percentage, Javanese is losing ground to Indonesian, both in urban and rural surroundings. Mobilization and urbanization have increased interethnic contact, and consequently the use and spread of Indonesian or varieties of it. Bilingualism is common today, and that is apparent in the language and vocabulary of the average Javanese. Especially where speakers experience difficulties in determining which speech style is appropriate for the occasion, they will be inclined to shift to Indonesian.

While the Indonesian constitution obliges the government to foster the regional languages if their speakers wish it, the official language policy aims at a stable situation of diglossia: all official communication, including education should be in Indonesian. Regional languages are excluded from these domains, with the exception that, where feasible, they may be used as the language of instruction in the first three grades of elementary education, to be gradually replaced by Indonesian, with all instruction in Indonesian from the fourth grade onwards. Teaching materials, even for the first grades, are all in Indonesian.

Some of the larger languages are taught as a subject, in the area where they are indigenous, in grades 4–6 of elementary schools, and in the three years of lower high schools. This is also the pattern for Javanese. At university level, Javanese can be studied as a major subject only at Universitas Indonesia in Jakarta and at several universities and teacher training colleges in Central and East Java and at Leiden University in the Netherlands.

Javanese is one of the few regional languages that is regularly used in books and periodicals and in local broadcasting. A flourishing cassette industry contributes to the spread of plays and songs in Javanese. With strong governmental support, so far two prestigious international congresses on Javanese have been held, in 1991 and 1996. On the occasion of the first one, an Indonesian-Javanese dictionary and a standard grammar (Sudaryanto 1991) were published. The government body for the standardization and promotion of Indonesian, the Jakarta, based National Center for Language Development and Cultivation, has a branch in Yogyakarta that has the same function with regard to Javanese.

Select Bibliography

Arps, B. 1996. "Javanese Language, Literature and Theatre." In Kratz, E.U., ed. *Southeast Asian Languages and Literatures: A Bibliographical Guide to Burmese, Cambodian, Indonesian, Javanese, Malay, Minangkabau, Thai and Vietnamese.* London: Tauris Academic Studies. 112–164.

Errington, J.J. 1985. *Language and Social Change in Java: Linguistic Reflexes of Modernization in a Traditional Royal Polity.* Athens: Ohio University Center for International Studies.

____. 1988. *Structure and Style in Javanese: A Semiotic View of Linguistic Etiquette.* Philadelphia: University of Philadelphia Press.

Gericke, J.F.C., and T. Roorda. 1901. *Javaansch-Nederlandsch Handwoordenboek vermeerderd en verbeterd door Dr A.C. Vreede, met medewerking van Dr J.G.H. Gunning.* Amsterdam and Leiden: Mueller.

Keeler, W. 1984. *Javanese: A Cultural Approach.* Athens: Ohio University Center for International Studies.

Robson, Stuart. 1992. "Javanese Grammar for Students." Clayton, Victoria: Monash Papers on Southeast Asia. No. 26.

Sudaryanto, ed. 1991. *Tata Bahasa Baku Bahasa Jawa* (A standard grammar of Javanese). Yogyakarta: Duta Wacana University Press.

Suhamo, Ignatius. 1982. A *Descriptive Study of Javanese*. Pacific Linguistics D-43. Canberra: Research School of Pacific Studies, Australian National University.

Uhlenbeck, E.M. 1964. A *Critical Survey of Studies on Languages of Java and Madura*. Koninklijk Instituut voor Taal-, Land-en Volkenkunde. Bibliographical Series 7, 's-Gravenhage: Martinus Nijhoff.

____. 1978. *Studies in Javanese Morphology*. The Hague: Martinus Nijhoff.

____.1983. "Two Mechanisms of Javanese Syntax: The Construction with *sing* (*kang, ingkang*) and with *olehe (enggone, anggenipun)*." In Halim, A., Carrington, L., Wurm, S.A., eds. *Papers from the Third International Conference on Austronesian Linguistics. 4. Thematic Variation*. Canberra. Pacific Linguistics C–77: 9–20.

Zoetmulder, P.J. 1974. *Kalangwan. A Survey of Old Javanese Liuerature*. The Hague: Martinus Nijhoff.

Zoetmulder, P.J. (with S.O. Robson). 1983. *Old Javanese-English Dictionary*. The Hague: Martinus Nijhoff.

Kam

Jerold A. Edmondson

Language Name: Kam. **Autonym:** *Kam.*

Location: Spoken in the southern part of southeast Guzihou Miao-Kam Autonomous Prefecture, Guizhou Province, northeast Guangxi Province at Sanjiang, Longsheng, and Rongshui counties, and southwest Hunan Province at Tongdao and adjoining counties, all in southwest-central China.

Family: Kam is the largest representative of Kam-Sui, a sister branch of Tai. Tai and Kam-Sui are regarded as distinct but rather close phonologically and lexically and together form Kam-Tai. There are two names for the next higher level of affiliation, *Kadai* and *Tai-Kadai*, where in the latter tradition *Kadai* would refer to a group of smaller languages within overall *Tai-Kadai.*

Related Languages: The related Kam-Sui languages are found along the Guizhou-Guangxi border to the west. Most closely related to Kam is Mulam of Luocheng County in Guangxi (pop. 160,000). In addition to Kam and Mulam is the western subgrouping of Kam-Sui: Sui, Maonan, Mak, Ai-Cham, and Zau (Then). Lakkja (Lakkia) and Biao may be in Kam-Sui or closely related to the Kam-Sui subbranch, although they are regarded officially as belonging to the Yao and Han nationalities.

Dialects: Kam is one of China's officially recognized 55 minority nationalities and is divided linguistically, culturally, and geographically into two varieties, Northern and Southern. There is a strong sense of common identity between the two groups. Communication between the two varieties with some difficulty is possible.

Number of Speakers: The official population of the Kam nationality (1990 census) is 2,514,014. Of this number perhaps one half may speak the language. The Northern variety, which has had more influence from Chinese, has perhaps 40 percent of the speakers and the more conservative Southern variety has 60 percent.

Origin and History

Chinese scholars agree that the precursors of the *Kadai* (*Tai-Kadai*) were the Bai Yue (Bak Viet) "The Hundred Viets or The Hundreds of the (Southern) Margin (of the Chinese Empire)", who lived in east-central and southeast China about 2,500 or more years ago. Indeed, the Yue are thought to have been a group diverse enough to be called the Bai Yue, a name that signifies many subgroups. The Yue were first mentioned in 870 B.C. when some of them became tributaries of the Chinese emperor. Their territory extended from just south of the Yangtze River into the southeast coastal areas that today include Fujian, Guangdong, and Guangxi Provinces, and northern Vietnam. The subgroup of special interest here is the Luo Yue or Western Yue. They were the only group among the Yue to survive later sinification by descending armies. They included different kinds of people that, when they separated into distinct groups, became the Thai/Zhuang as well as Kam/Sui, and the Jiaozhi (the colonial rulers of the Vietnamese precursors, who called themselves *Giao-chi*).

A few words of the Yue language are recorded in the *Yueren Ge* ('The Song of the Yue Boatman'). It is a song sung by a governess entertaining a young Yue prince by rowing him in a boat in the sunshine. She says how happy she is and that she secretly admires this young prince. This language is recorded in Chinese characters but, while the general jist of the song is decipherable from the judiciously chosen Chinese characters, it is equally clear that these characters were recording sounds of another language. That other language is recognizable even today by Tai and Kam-Sui speakers. One example may serve to illustrate; the Chinese character recording the word 'boat' in the ancient Yue language was *la*^{2}. Today in THAI it is *rua*^{2}, in ZHUANG *ru*^{2} or *lu*^{2} and in Kam it is *lo*^{2}. It is a common inheritance found in all daughter languages today.

The Lao (Liao) were descended from the Luo Yue. They came to the attention of Han historians in the Han dynasty (116 B.C.) and figured prominently in all Chinese histories of the area up to the Tang, usually being afforded a separate chapter. In the Jin dynasty (A.D. 265–420) the Liao are found in profusion in Sichuan, entering that territory from the southeast and driving out the inhabitants. The Liao reached the pinnacle of their power in Liang times, when the Chinese garrisons in Shu (today's west-central Sichuan, Yunnan, and Guizhou) had to fight with them virtually every year. By A.D. 525, it was said, 200,000 Liao families were paying tribute to the Chinese emperor. By the time of the Song dynasty names for individual groups within the Lao emerged. One of these groups was known as the *Keling* or the *Kelam* (cf. Beauclair 1986: 372).

The earliest recorded use of the ethnonym "Kam" is in the Song dynasy before the year 1210 when it is said that the Kelam lived in areas corresponding to eastern Guizhou and western Hunan Provinces, where the Kam still live. The Kam largely escaped the interest of Western scholars until the 1940s, when the French-German anthropologist Inez de Beauclair visited their territory in 1952.

Table 1: Consonants

		Bilabial	Alveolar	Palatal	Velar	Uvular
Stops	Vcls asp.	ph	th		kh	(qh)
	Vcls usasp.	p	t		k	(q)
	Palatalized	pj phj	tj thj			
	Labialized				kw khw	
Fricatives		f	s			
Affricates	Vcls asp.		ts			
	Vcls unasp.			tsh		
Nasals		m	n		ŋ, ŋʷ	
Laterals				l, lj		

Orthography and Basic Phonology

Until 1957 the Kam did not have a writing system. For many centuries they had been using Chinese characters to record their songs and stories. However, Chinese writing was not especially well suited to this task, as Kam possesses more tones than Chinese and several sounds not found in Han. Chinese characters were viewed as an auxiliary form of recording information, because much of their tradition was transmitted orally through rhymed verse and song. This oral tradition along with their remote location may be responsible for the survival of the language today.

In the 1950s an investigative study of the Kam language was undertaken to determine its distinctive phonology, lexicon, and variation. From that study, which remains unpublished today, the current orthography was developed. It is based on characters of the LATIN alphabet. Since Kam in most places, like Modern Standard Chinese (MSC), possesses no voiced-stop initial consonants, the conventions of Chinese romanization, Hanyu Pinyin, were easily recruited for many sounds. Innovations were necessary only for sound segments and tones unlike those of the Han language. The variety of Kam on which the writing is based is Rongjiang Zhanglu, Guizhou Province; it is also described in the following basic Kam phonology.

In regard to tone, Kam is extraordinarily rich, possessing nine contrastive tones in open CV syllables and six contrastive tones in closed CVC/CVVC syllables (where the final C of these syllables can be only /-p -t -k/). Just as in the case of Zhuang and other new orthographies, it was decided to use a final consonant to mark the tone of a syllable. Thus, tone 1 was marked with a final -l; tone 2 by -c; tone l' by -p; tone 3 by -s; tone 4 by -x; tone 3' by -t'; tone 5 by -v; tone 6 by -h; and tone 5' by -k. The tones 7, 7', 8, 9, 9', and 10 occur only in CVC and CVVC syllables, but to keep the symbols for the syllable final stops distinct from the markers for tones, it was decided to use the orthographic forms <-b -d -g> in parallel to the use of <b- d- g-> for the unaspirated initial consonants /p- t- k-/.

As is generally the case for Tai and Kam-Sui languages, tones for the CVC/CVVC syllables have the pitch shape of some of the CV syllables (tone 1 = tone 7; tone 2 = tone 8; tone 1' = tone 7'; tone 3 = tone 9; tone 10 = tone 4; and tone 3' = tone 9') and the symbols for the tones in open syllables are used again in closed syllables. Specifically, tones for the CVC/CVVC syllables are written after the final consonant, e.g., *lagx* 'child' is used to represent /lak^{10}/ with the pitch the same as tone 4.

In regard to other consonants and vowels, we have just noted that <b d g> were used for unaspirated stops, and as in Hanyu Pinyin, <p t k> represent the aspirated forms. And in a manner like Hanyu Pinyin, <j q ny x y ng pi mi li gu ku ngu> correspond, respectively to /t th n ç j ŋ pj mj lj kw khw ŋw/. More recently, speakers at the nonstandard locations with retained uvular stops have taken to writing <kg> for /q- qh-/, although the official orthography is based on a kind of Kam that does not possess uvulars. Only the vowel /a/ and only the /a/ in CVC/CVVC syllables contrasts for vowel length. To indicate the long vowel, <a> is used, and for the short vowel, which is usually realized as [ɐ], the symbol <ae> is used. Thus, for example, [kɐm1] 'Kam' is written *Gaeml*, where the -l represents the first tone. Other examples are: *nyac* 'you sg.' *na*^{2}; *leec* 'language' le^{2}; and *bas* 'paternal aunt' pa^{3}, *lagx* 'child' lak^{10}, *bædl* 'duck' pɐt^{7}, and *padt* 'blood' phat^{9}.

Kam has basically three types of tones, which may be called high, low, and rising. Any of the original five tones of the Proto-language can appear in these three categories. In Zhanglu even-numbered tones came from vocabulary that once possessed a voiced-consonant initial; odd-numbered tones came from vocabulary that once possessed a voiceless-consonant initial; and the tones with prime marks, 1', 3', etc., came from vocabulary that once possessed and still possesses an aspirated initial stop or once possessed an original voiceless continuant.

Thus, the linguistic feature that caused the rising tone set is still preserved in stops but not in vocabulary with original voiceless sonorants, such as nasals, for example, *pha*$^{1'}$ 'ashes' but *ma*$^{1'}$ 'to come', both contrasting in tone with *pa*^{1} 'fish'. Kam is thus of considerable interest in matters relating to tonogenesis. There is little tone change in context.

High	Low	Rising
tone 1 = 55	tone 2 = 11	tone 1' = 35
tone 3 = 323	tone 4 = 31	tone 3' = 13
tone 5 = 53	tone 6 = 33	tone 5' = 453
tone 7 = 55	tone 8 = 11	tone 7' = 35
tone 9 = 323	tone 10 = 31	tone 9' = 13

We can illustrate the use of the orthography in the song:

Ngaemc sius keip wap pap jenc jemh.
Dens lagx nyenc Gaeml lyangp dos kgal.
Saemh xonc saemh map kgal menh dos.
Soh emv jenc nyangt yungt angl hac.

'As wild flowers bloom on the mountainside,
So the Kam in their hearts love to sing.
From long past time are linked with this gift,
So melody in mountain and brook side will ring.'

Table 2: Vowels

i		u
e		o
	a	

There are basically five vowels in Kam /a/ /e/ / i/ /o/ /u/. In Chinese loans one also finds [ɐ]. Originally, all vowels distinguished length. Today only *a* keeps a vestige of this difference. Proto /aa/ is today [a]; Proto /a/ is [ɐ]. The other vowels express this contrast as a tone difference, i.e., tone 7 (short) vs. Tone 9 (long), etc.

Basic Morphology

Kam does not exhibit any inflectional morphology. There is reduplication to express a plethora or intensity of something, for example, *wanp wanp* 'peaceful' and *mongl mongl* 'vast'. There are, of course, several types of word formation: (1) same category formation such as *jaix nongx* older siblings-younger siblings, that is, 'sibling, household'; (2) head-modifier formation *biol qemp* navel-needle 'eye of needle'; and (3) head + suffix formation (most of the cases of head + suffix occur with the head being an adjective) as in *yak* 'red', but *yak liids liids* (red-SUFFIX-SUFFIX) 'gorgeous shade of red'.

Basic Syntax

Kam is an SVO language. Any of these sentence parts may be omitted based on the communication situation. Question words are found in situ. The following are some construction types:

yaoc miac meix
1SG plant tree
'I plant a tree.'

Yaoc heemx maoh map xas leec
(subject-verb-object-comp)
1SG call 3SG come write book
'I will call him to come and write characters.'

maenl mus nyac bail nup (gil)
day tomorrow 2SG go which (place)
'Where will you go tomorrow?'

In noun phrases all nouns being modified by a numeral must have the combination numeral + classifier as modifier. The numeral + classifer comes before the noun, for example:

siik jiuc nyal
four CL river
'four rivers'

yac nongx
two younger.brother
'two younger brothers'

The Southern variety of Kam has some disyllabic proper place-names, but most of the proper place-names are monosyllabic, for example, *Xaih Xap* 'East Village'. It is likely that Kam proper place-names originally were all monosyllabic, and there is a tendency toward change to disyllabic forms.

When pronouns modify nouns, the Southern variety places the pronoun after the noun; the Northern variety places the pronoun before the noun. In the Southern variety, except for kinship terms, locative nouns, or proper nouns, the morpheme *dis* is added between the noun and its modifying pronoun.

Northern dialect:	Southern dialect:
yaoc dis bieedl 'my pen'	biedl yaoc 'my pen'
nyac maix 'your wife'	maix nyac 'your wife'

Contact with Other Languages

The language that has influenced Kam the most is Chinese. In fact, some original words of Kam have today been replaced by words borrowed from the Han language even in domains where Han loanwords are comparatively rare. Thus, we find *xaih* 'village' from Han *zhài; myinc* 'cotton' from Han *mián*; and *louc* 'tower' from Han *lou*. All words from the domains of tools (except those connected with wet-paddy rice farming), shoes and socks, study and learning, and all aspects of modern life are loaned from Han.

Common Words

man:	nyenc banl	woman:	nyenc myeegs
water:	naemx	sun:	dal maenc
three:	samp	fish:	bal
big:	laoc		

Example Sentences

(1) maoh sunx yaoc il bags guanl.
3SG give 1SG one CL axe
'He gave me an axe.'

(2) nyac bail aol naemx xih maoh bail?
2SG go get water or 3SG go
'Will you go get water or will he?'

(3) duil naih kuanp gueec kuanp?
pear this sweet NEG sweet
'Is this pear sweet or not?'

Efforts to Preserve, Protect, and Promote the Language

There is an official effort to promote literacy among Kam speakers. In southeast Guizhou Province some progress has been made to promote the use of the new script among children. Nevertheless, it is still not used very widely except among Kam scholars and educators in official publications.

Select Bibliography

Most of the information about Kam is found in Chinese-language sources, such as *Minzu Yuwen* and *Wang Jun* (ed.) 1984. *Zhuang-Dong yuzu yuyan jianzhi*. Beijing: Nationalities Publishing House.

Beauclair, Inez de. 1982. *Ethnographic Studies*. Taipei: Southern Materials, Inc.

Benedict, Paul K. 1975. *Austro-Thai: Language and Culture*. New Haven: HRAF Press.

Edmondson, Jerold A. 1992. "A Study of Tones and Initials in Kam, Lakkja, and Hlai." In Carol J. Compton and John R. Hartman, eds. *Papers on Tai Languages, Linguistics, and Literatures: In Honor of William J. Gedney on His 77th Birthday*. (Occasional Paper No. 16. 1992). DeKalb, IL: North Illinois University Center for Southeast Asian Studies, Monograph Series on Southeast Asia, 77–100.

Edmondson, Jerold A., and David B. Solnit, eds. 1988. *Comparative Kadai: Linguistic Studies beyond Tai*. Dallas: SIL/UTA Series in Linguistics.

Li Fang, Kuei. 1977. *A Handbook of Comparative Tai*. Honolulu: The University Press of Hawaii.

Ramsey, S.R. 1987. *The Languages of China*. Princeton: Princeton University Press.

Shangfant, Zhengzhang. 1991. "Decipherment of the Yue-Ren-Ge (Song of the Yue Boatman)". *Cahiers de Linguistique Asie Orientale* 22:2.159–68.

Yaohong, Long, and Zheng Guogiao. 1998. *The Dong language in Guizhou Province, China*. Translated by Geary, N. Dallas: SIL/UTA Series in Linguistics.

KANNADA

Sanford B. Steever

Name: Kannada. **Alternates:** *Kannarese, Canarese.* **Autonym:** *kannaḍa.*

Location: Indian state of Karnataka and neighboring states of Tamil Nadu, Andhra Pradesh and Maharashtra; also overseas communities in the United States and England.

Family: Belongs to the Southern branch of the Dravidian language family of India.

Related Languages: TAMIL, MALAYALAM, Kodagu, Tulu, TELUGU.

Dialects: Geographical dialects: (1) Southern (Mysore, Bangalore), (2) Western (Mangalore), (3) Northern (Dharwar), (4) Northeastern (Bijapur). Caste dialects: (1) Brahmin, (2) non-Brahmin, (3) Harijan. Diglossia: "high", formal register and "low", informal register. Further gradations are possible in each category of variation. This chapter is based on the Brahmin dialect spoken in the cities of Mysore and Bangalore, which has close parallels with the written language.

Number of Speakers: Kannada is the native language of approximately 25 million people; adding those who speak it as a second language may raise the total number of speakers to nearly 40 million.

Origin and History

Kannada belongs to the Southern branch of the Dravidian language family, and is closely related to Tamil, Malayalam, Irula, Kodagu, Toda and Kota. Badaga, spoken in the Nilgiri Mountains to the south of Karnataka, is thought to be a recent offshoot of Kannada (16th century). The name of the language most likely comes from the words *karu* 'black' and *nāḍu* 'country, land'; hence, '(language spoken in the) country of the black soil'.

Kannada varies primarily along four dimensions: history, geography, society and register. The historical record attests three distinct stages: Old (450 to 1200), Middle (1200 to 1700) and Modern Kannada (1700 to the present). Old Kannada is first attested in a rock inscription from Halmidi Village in Hassan District dating to about 450. Kannada has produced a continuous literary tradition from the ninth century to the present.

Throughout its history, Kannada has influenced and been influenced by a variety of languages, mainly of Dravidian and Indo-European stock. The earliest strata show the influence of SANSKRIT and Tamil the medieval period shows that of Telugu, PERSIAN and ARABIC and the modern stage shows that of PORTUGUESE and ENGLISH. As a further example, the influence of the modern Indo-Aryan language MARATHI can be discerned in the structure of the Northern dialect.

Modern Kannada has four main geographically based dialects, which grade into finer subdialects. The southern dialect area includes the varieties spoken in and around the cities of Bangalore and Mysore (Bright 1958, Sridhar 1990), and forms the basis of this description. The northern dialect area centers on the city of Dharwar (Hiremath 1980, McCormack 1966); the western dialect on Mangalore District; and the northeastern in and around the city of Bijapur.

Social dialects in Kannada reflect the historical fact that traditional social and economic interaction respected the caste structures of Hindu society. The primary distinction appears to be among Brahmin, non-Brahmin and Harijan varieties of the language. However, under the influence of modernization, which includes universal education, social dialect differences are shifting from a caste to a class basis.

Finally, Kannada exhibits a variation in register between an informal and a formal variety, known to linguists as "diglossia". The informal variety is used in virtually all face-to-face communication, while the formal variety appears in writing and many formal occasions such as political oratory and radio broadcasts. Examples of diglossia are presented below in the discussion of verb paradigms.

Orthography and Basic Phonology

Standard Kannada has 11 vowels: *a, ā, i, ī, u, ū, e, ē, o, ō, ǣ*; and 34 consonants (see Table 1 on the next page).

Of these sounds *ǣ*, *f* and *z* occur only in loanwords; in other dialects *æ* occurs in native words. The 10 aspirated and breathy voice stops occur only in loan words. Many of these are completely assimilated in Modern Kannada; in rapid speech, and in some dialects, these modified stops have been assimilated to their unmodified counterparts.

Kannada suprasegmental patterns are based on the length of segments and syllables; stress, which is nondistinctive, typically falls on the first syllable of each word. Intonation patterns are distinctive (for example, a question such as *ninna hesaru ēn(u) appa*? 'what$_3$ is your$_1$ name$_2$, sir$_4$?' is uttered with a steadily rising intonation) but they have yet to be adequately studied.

Kannada is written in an alphasyllabic system, and has evolved from the same source as modern Telugu writing. The script is adequate to represent the phonemic distinctions of the language. Where graphs do not exist to represent borrowed or innovated sounds, certain writing conventions have arisen, so that *ǣ* in /bǣnku/ 'bank', for example, is represented by a combination of the conjunct graph for *y* and the graph for *ā*.

Table 1: Consonants

		Labial	Dental	Retroflex	Palatal	Velar
Stops	Voiceless	p	t	ṭ	c	k
	Aspirated	p	th	ṭh	ch	kh
	Voiced	b	d	ḍ	j	g
	Breathy Voice	bh	dh	ḍh	jh	gh
Fricatives	Voiceless	f	s	ṣ	ś	h
	Voiced		z			
Nasals		m	n	ṇ		
Lateral			l	ḷ		
Glide		v			y	
Tap			r			

Basic Morphology

Kannada morphology distinguishes at a basic level between words and clitic particles. Words are independent forms; clitics are dependent. Independent words may be pronounced in isolation, and consist of a lexical base and one or more inflections. Clitics always combine with a host to form a phonological word; however, they make take an entire constituent in their scope. Clitics are generally monomorphemic, involving such notions as conjunction, quantification and emphasis; in this description, they are preceded by the symbol =.

Kannada morphology is agglutinating and primarily suffixal. Unlike the majority of Dravidian languages, however, Kannada has developed productive patterns of prefixation due to the influx of loanwords that have been resegmented into prefix and base and applied beyond their original scope. For example, the Kannada word *apanambike* 'mistrust' consists of the Sanskritic prefix *apa-* 'not' and the Kannada noun *nambike* 'trust'.

Nouns in Kannada include proper names, common nouns, pronouns, as well as other forms often translated as adjectives. They mark case, number and gender. There are seven cases that signal a variety of grammatical relations within the clause: nominative, accusative, genitive, dative, locative, source (which combines instrumental and ablative functions) and vocative. Unmarked singular contrasts with marked plural number. Gender is marked in pronoun choice, declensional patterns and, secondarily, certain derivational patterns; the basic gender categories include masculine, feminine and neuter.

The declension of nouns is regular; given the phonological shape of the noun and its gender, all other forms may be readily derived. Consider the three nouns *mara* 'tree', *mane* 'house', and *huḍuga* 'boy' below. Note that the distribution of the oblique base is not uniform across cases; for the inanimate noun *mara* 'tree', it is used in only the genitive, locative and source cases of the singular, while for the animate noun *huḍuga* 'boy', the oblique occurs in all singular, nonnominative cases.

<u>Singular</u>

Nominative			
	mara	*mane*	*huḍuga*
Oblique			
	mara.d-	*mane-*	*huḍuga.n-*
Accusative			
	mara.v-annu	*mane.y-annu*	*huḍuga.n-annu*
Dative			
	mara-kke	*mane-ge*	*huḍuga.n-ige*
Genitive			
	mara.d-a	*mane.y-a*	*huḍuga.n-a*
Locative			
	mara.d-alli	*mane.y-alli*	*huḍuga.n-alli*
Source			
	mara.d-inda	*mane.y-inda*	*huḍuga.n-inda*

Plural

Nominative			
	mara-gaḷu	*mane-gaḷu*	*huḍuga-ru*
Accusative			
	mara-gaḷ-annu	*mane-gaḷ-annu*	*huḍuga-r-annu*
Dative			
	mara-gaḷ-ige	*mane-gaḷ-ige*	*huḍuga-r-ige*
Genitive			
	mara-gaḷ-a	*mane-gaḷ-a*	*huḍuga-r-a*
Locative			
	mara-gaḷ-alli	*mane-gaḷ-alli*	*huḍuga-r-alli*
Source			
	mara-gaḷ-inda	*mane-gaḷ-inda*	*huḍuga-r-inda*

Personal pronouns form an important subset of nouns. Unlike more familiar Dravidian languages, such as Tamil, standard Kannada makes no distinction between first-person plural inclusive ("we and you") and exclusive pronouns ("we but not you") although some regional dialects preserve this very Dravidian feature (see Table 2 on the next page).

Additionally, Kannada has demonstrative pronouns that commonly function as third-person anaphoric pronouns. The modern language has a proximal series marked with *i-* 'this' and a distal series marked with *a-* 'that'. The distal series is unmarked and has the broadest range of occurrence, e.g., in the head of a relative clause. Those noted below do not exhaust the range of third-person proforms: the masculine pronoun *ātanu* 'that male' and the feminine *āke* 'that female', which have direct counterparts in Telugu, are frequently heard (see Tables 3 and 4).

Interrogative pronouns closely parallel the deictic pronouns, and include the following (which appear in their nominative forms): *yāru*

Table 2: Personal Pronouns

	First		Second	
	Singular	Plural	Singular	Plural
Nominative	nānu	nāvu	nīnu	nīvu
Accusative	nannannu	nammannu	ninnannu	nimmannu
Dative	nanage	namage	ninage	nimage
Genitive	nanna	namma	ninna	nimma
Locative	nannalli	nammalli	ninnalli	nimmalli
Source	nanninda	namminda	ninninda	nimminda

'who', *yāvudu* 'which (thing)', *entha* 'what kind', *ēnu* 'what', *yāke* 'why' (literary *ēke* 'id'). These may be combined with certain quantifiers to form indefinite pronouns, e.g., *yāru* 'who' combines with the clitic *=ō* 'or, any' to form *yār=ō* 'someone'.

Kannada has a broad set of postpositions that supplement the case system; they express more specific semantic relations than the simple case forms do. Postpositions that historically descend from nouns or nonfinite verb forms govern specific cases. For example, the postposition *-ōskara* 'for the sake of' in *avanig-ōskara* 'for his sake', governs the dative case, but has a more specific meaning than the simple dative in *avanige* 'for him, to him', which conveys the general notion of recipient.

Kannada verbs mark such categories as tense and mood. The verb consists of a lexical base and a set of suffixes. The lexical base may contain a simple root, or a root plus a suffix such as the causative marker *-isu*. Kannada has two basic conjugations: the first includes most verbs whose stem ends in *-u*, e.g., *māḍu* 'do, work'; the second includes most verbs whose stem ends in *-e* or *-i*, e.g., *kare* 'call', *kuḍi* 'drink'. Kannada also has a number of irregular verbs; the irregularity centers primarily on how they form their past stems.

Verb forms in Kannada are finite or nonfinite. Finite forms mark tense/mood and subject-verb agreement. Their distribution in the Kannada sentence is strictly limited by rule so that the majority of forms are nonfinite. Modern literary, or "high", Kannada has five finite paradigms: past, present, future, contingent and negative. The first three convey tense, the second two mood. The corresponding spoken, or "low", register has three: past, nonpast and contingent. The future finite paradigm is largely absent from the spoken register; the literary present formally corresponds to the spoken nonpast. The spoken dialect expresses negation through the use of specific compound verbs, e.g., *māḍal illa* 'did not, does not do, make'.

These paradigms are illustrated in Table 5 on the next page with the verb *māḍu* 'do, make'. Note that in all paradigms there is one form for the third-person human plural.

Besides these full paradigms, Kannada has other finite forms, among them the imperative, the optative and the hortative. The imperative, for example, has familiar and polite forms, *māḍu* 'do, make' and *māḍiri* 'please do', respectively. Modern Kannada lacks a simple negative imperative form, and uses instead such modal compound verbs as *māḍa bēḍa* 'don't do, make' and *māḍa bāradu* 'one shouldn't do, make'.

Nonfinite verbs encompass two sets of forms: those that combine with a following verb and those that combine with a following nominal. The first set include the conjunctive, infinitive and conditional forms; the second set includes the adnominal forms and certain verbal nouns.

Nonfinite verb forms that combine with a following verb appear in complex structures such as compound verb constructions and complex clause structures. In the sentence, *avanu*

Table 3: Third Person Distal Demonstrative Human Pronouns

	Singular		Plural
	Masculine	Feminine	
Nominative	avanu 'he'	avaḷu 'she'	avaru 'they'
Accusative	avanannu	avaḷannu	avarannu
Dative	avanige	avaḷige	avarige
Genitive	avana	avaḷa	avara
Locative	avanalli	avaḷalli	avaralli
Source	avaninda	avaḷinda	avarinda

Table 4: Third Person Nonhuman Pronouns

	Distal		Proximal	
	Singular	Plural	Singular	Plural
Nominative	adu 'this (one)'	avu 'that'	idu 'these'	ivu 'those'
Accusative	adannu	avannu	idannu	ivannu
Dative	adakke	avakke	idakke	ivakke
Genitive	adara	avugaḷa	idara	ivugaḷa
Locative	adaralli	avalli	idaralli	ivalli
Source	adarinda	avugaḷinda	idarinda	ivugaḷinda

Table 5: Finite Paradigms

		Literary Past Tense		Colloquial	
		Singular	Plural	Singular	Plural
1st		māḍidenu	māḍidevu	māḍide	māḍidivi
2nd		māḍide	māḍidiri	māḍide	māḍidiri
3rd	m	māḍidanu	māḍidaru	māḍida	mādidaru
	f	māḍidaḷu	māḍidaru	māḍidaḷu	māḍidaru
	n	māḍitu	māḍidavu	māḍitu	māḍidavu
		Literary Present Tense		Colloquial Nonpast Tense	
1st		māḍuttēne	māḍuttēve	māḍuttīni	māḍuttīvi
2nd		māḍuttī	māḍuttīri	māḍuttīya	māḍuttīra
3rd	m	māḍuttāne	māḍuttāre	māḍuttāne	māḍuttāre
	f	māḍuttāḷe	māḍuttāre	māḍuttāḷe	maḍuttāre
	n	māḍuttade	māḍuttave	māḍatte	māḍuttave
		Literary Future Tense		Contingent	
		Singular	Plural	Singular	Plural
1st		māḍuvenu	māḍuvevu	mād (iy)ēnu	māḍ (iy)ēvu
2nd		māḍuve	māḍuveru	māḍīye	māḍīri
3rd	m	māḍuvanu	māḍuvaru	māḍiyānu	māḍiyāru
	f	māḍuvaḷu	māḍuvaru	māḍiyāḷu	māḍiyāru
	n	māḍuvudu	māḍuvavu	māḍītu	māḍiyāvu
		Negative			
		Singular	Plural		
1st		māḍe(nu)	māḍevu		
2nd		māḍe	māḍari		
3rd	m	māḍa(nu)	māḍaru		
	f	māḍaḷu	māḍaru		
	n	māḍadu	māḍavu		

bandare, nānu hōguttīni 'if he$_1$ comes$_2$, I$_3$ (will) go$_4$' the conditional verb form *band-are* 'if (one) comes' joins an if-clause to a then-clause. In sentence (5a) below, the anterior conjunctive verb *kaṇḍu* 'seeing, having seen' joins two clauses in a coordinate structure.

Nonfinite verbs that combine with nouns help to generate relative clauses and similar structures. For example, the relative clause *banda hengasu* 'the woman$_2$ who came$_1$' consists of the adnominal verb *banda* 'which came' and the common noun *hengasu* 'woman', while *banda hāgē* 'manner$_2$ in which (one) came$_1$' adjoins *banda* to the adverbial noun *hāgē* 'manner'.

Kannada lacks articles. The numeral 'one', *ondu*, may function as an indefinite article in some circumstances. Further, the presence or absence of the accusative case marker on an inanimate noun may signal definite vs. indefinite reference (in 7c) the nominative form for the direct object *hālu* 'milk' conveys 'some'. Two minor parts of speech may be recognized primarily by appeal to their function rather than to any formally distinct morphology: adjectives and adverbs.

All clitics in Kannada are postclitic: they attach at the extreme right of their host constituent. While they form a phonological word with their host, they often take a full constituent, clause, or sentence in their scope. Their functions range from emphasis, to quantification (*=ū* 'all' in 7b), to discourse markers (*=ō* in 7b). One of the most common is the interrogative clitic *=ā*, which makes a yes-no question out of a declarative sentence (1a) when it appears at the end of the sentence (1b). When a particular constituent within the sentence (2a) is questioned, the clitic is attached to the questioned constituent and the sentence is transformed into a cleft structure in which the finite verb is transformed into a verbal noun (2b).

Basic Syntax

Kannada is a left-branching, head-final language. The canonical word order is subject, object, verb, which forms the basis of several word-order permutations. In keeping with basic SOV word order, complements precede matrix clauses, genitives precede their nouns, and main verbs precede their auxiliaries.

The simple sentence consists of a subject and a predicate. The subject generally occurs in the nominative case (3, 4), but certain predicates, typically verbs of cognition and feeling, take a subject in the dative case (5). The predicate may be a finite intransitive or transitive verb (1, 2). In another important pattern, the predicate may be a predicate nominal without any copula (3, 5a). A sentence with a predicate nominal such as (3a) is negated with the verb form *alla* 'not become' (3b), the negative of the verb *āga* 'become'. The most common simple sentence, however, consists of a nominative subject and a finite verb as predicate (4); this is the structure in terms of which constituent structure generalizations are framed. The dative-subject construction aside, the agreement pattern in Kannada is nominative-accusative.

Complex sentences are formed through three basic methods, in order of increasing markedness: (i) the use of nonfinite verb forms, (ii) certain embedding verbs and clitics, and (iii) conjunctions. In Example Sentences (5a) and (6a), the anterior conjunctive form of the verb in the first clause joins it to the second clause, which has a finite verb. In (7a), the verb *endu* 'having said' subordinates a clause that has a finite verb; in (7b) the clitic *=ō* 'or, whether' embeds a finite verb; and in (7c), the conjunction *mattu* 'and' conjoins two clauses with finite verbs

Contact with Other Languages

The core vocabulary of Kannada contains words of Dravidian origin, inherited directly from older stages of the language or borrowed from sister languages. It also contains words borrowed from Indo-Aryan languages such as Sanskrit (*prāyatna* 'attempt'), Prakrit and Marathi (*cunāvane* 'election'). Other languages have contributed to its lexical growth, as well: Persian, HINDI (*jōru* 'forceful'), Portuguese and English (*kālēju* 'college').

Common Words

small:	cikka	man:	gaṇḍasu
house:	mane	woman:	hengasu
yes:	haudu	no:	illa, alla
three:	mūru	tree:	mara
boy:	huḍuga	water:	nīru
sun:	sūrya	big:	doḍḍu

Example Sentences

(1) a. *avaḷu alli iddāḷe.*
she:NOM there be:PRES:3FM
'She is there.'

b. *avaḷu alli iddāḷ=ā?*
she:NOM there be:PRES:3FM=INT
'Is she there?'

(2) a. *rangana ī pustaka koṇḍa.*
Rangana:NOM this book buy:PST:3SM
'Rangana bought this book.'

b. *rangan=ā ī pustaka koṇḍiddu.*
Rangana:NOM=INT this book buy:PST:VN
'Is it Rangana who bought this book?

(3) a. *avaru olleya mēstru.*
he:H:NOM good teacher:NOM
'He (is) a good teacher.'

b. *avaru olleya mēstru alla.*
he:H:NOM good teacher:NOM not.become
'He (is) not a good teacher.'

(4) a. *nānu ninne manege bande.*
I:NOM yesterday house:DAT come:PST:1S
'I came home yesterday.'

b. *nīvu ā pustaka tōrisuttir=ā?*
you:P that book show:NPST:2P=INT
'Will you show (me) that book?'

(5) a. $_{S0}$[$_{S1}$[*avaḷannu kaṇḍu*]$_{S1}$ $_{2}$[*āḷugaḷige kutūhāla*]$_{S2}$]$_{S0}$.
she:ACC see:ANT.CNJ man:P:DAT curiosity:NOM
'Seeing her, the men were curious.'

b. *adu nanage sariyāgi tiḷiyal illa.*
that:NOM I:DAT really know:INF be.not
'I didn't really know that.'

(6) $_{S0}$[$_{S1}$[*maḷe bandu*]$_{S1}$ $_{2}$[*hole heccitu*]$_{S2}$]$_{S0}$.
rain:NOM come:ANT.CNJ river:NOM increase:PST:3SN
'The rain fell and the river rose.'

(7) a. $_{S0}$[*śāstrigaḷu pisumātinalli* $_{S1}$[*ēnu āḍa bēḍi.*
Sastri:NOM whisper:LOC anything say:INF must.not

yāra kivig=ādarū biddītu]$_{S1}$ *endu*
who:GEN ear:DAT=some fall:CNT:3SN say:ANT.CNJ

eccarisidaru]$_{S0}$.
warn:PST:3HP
'Sastri warned (her) in a whisper, "You mustn't say anything. It might fall in someone's ear." '

b. $_{S0}$[$_{S1}$[*ellige hōdan*]$_{S1}$*=ō yārig=ū*
where:DAT go:PST:3SM=OR who:DAT=AND

gott(u) illa]$_{S0}$.
knowledge:NOM not.be
'No one knew where he went to.'

c. $_{S0}$[$_{S1}$[*dineśa tiṇḍi tiṇḍa*]$_{S1}$ *mattu*$_{S2}$ [*hālu*
Dinesh:NOM snack eat:PST:3SM and milk:NOM

kuḍida]$_{S2}$]$_{S0}$.
drink:PST:3SM
'Dinesh ate a snack and drank (some) milk.'

Efforts to Preserve, Protect, and Promote the Language

Cultivated as a literary language for over a millennium, Kannada has produced a great body of literature, ranging from epics to devotional hymns, from short stories to novels, from dramas to lyrics. Such activity continues today, and is supported by an active publishing industry.

Unlike many of the smaller, nonliterary Dravidian languages, Kannada is not threatened with extinction. The Eighth Schedule of the Indian Constitution, which reorganized states along linguistic lines, confers the status of national language on Kannada. The state government of Karnataka promotes the use of Kannada through its Directorate of Kannada and Culture. These efforts include education, publishing and media (radio, cinema and television).

Recent proposals have been offered by politicians to ensure that Kannada is made the primary language of instruction at every level of education, often displacing English from that role.

Select Bibliography

Bright, William. 1958. *An Outline of Colloquial Kannada.* Pune: Deccan College.

Hiremath, R.G. 1980. *The Structure of Kannada.* Dharwad: Prasaranga.

Kittel, F. 1903. *A Grammar of the Kannada Language.* Reprinted in 1982. Delhi: Asian Educational Service.

McCormack, William. 1966. *Kannada: A Cultural Introduction to the Spoken Styles of the Language.* Madison: University of Wisconsin Press.

Nayak, H.M. 1967. *Kannada Literary and Colloquial: A Study of Two Styles.* Mysore: Rao and Raghavan.

Schiffman, Harold. 1983. *A Reference Grammar of Spoken Kannada.* Seattle: University of Washington Press.

Spencer, Harold. 1950. *Kannada Grammar.* Mysore: Wesley Press.

Sridhar, S.N. 1990. *Kannada.* London: Routledge.

Steever, Sanford B. 1998. "Kannada." In Sanford Steever (ed.), *The Dravidian Languages.* London: Routledge.

Kanuri

John P. Hutchison

Language Name: Kanuri. **Alternate:** *Kanembu.* (Kanuri and *Kanembu* are the names of sister languages that actually represent dialect extremes of the same language).

Location: Kanuri and Kanembu are spoken by the peoples of the same names who are today concentrated in the area to the west, north, and east of Lake Chad in Central Africa. Kanuri speakers are concentrated in Borno State in northeastern Nigeria.

Although for the major part of their history Kanuri and Kanembu were linked in various ways as one linguistic unit in a common political entity, today they occupy parts of four different African nations. In a great variety of dialect forms, the Kanuri and Kanembu languages are spoken by substantial numbers of people in Nigeria, Niger, Chad, and by a smaller group in the Cameroon.

This is a description of the Kanuri language as it is spoken in Yerwa, the traditional Kanuri name for what is known today outside of the Kanuri world as 'Maiduguri', the capital of the Borno State, Nigeria.

Family: Western Saharan subbranch of the Saharan branch of the Nilo-Saharan family.

Related Languages: Kanembu, Tubu (Teda/Dazaga), Zaghawa, Berti.

Dialects: The dialect picture reveals several different dialect clusters around specific languages or language varieties in the Kanuri branch of Western Saharan. Today, based on linguistic evidence, Kanuri and Kanembu are considered to constitute a dialect continuum running through a dialect cluster, with Kanuri and Kanembu as distinct points perhaps at the extremes of that continuum, but not as discrete and separate entities. The two are linked along the continuum through a series of morphophonological processes and rules.

The major dialects are listed here by country, with the traditional Kanuri/Kanembu labels.

Niger:	Kanuri: Bilma, Dagara, Fachi, Jetko, Manga, Mobar
	Kanembu: Kuburi, Sugurti, Tumari
Nigeria:	Kanuri: Fadawu, Jetko, Karda, Kwayam, Manga, Mobar, Ngumatiwu, Yerwa
	Kanembu: Kuburi, Sugurti
Chad:	Kanembu: Kogono, Kuburi Kura

Based on a recent comparative analysis of the verbal system, it appears that the Kanuri dialects of northern Nigeria and eastern Niger represent a cohesive, larger dialect grouping, and that the Kanembu dialects of the western shores of Lake Chad represent a second dialect grouping, with the Kanembu dialects of that area north and east of Lake Chad constituting a third grouping. There are certainly exceptions to this.

Despite the fact that different colonial traditions have resulted in greater borrowing of ENGLISH in some dialects, and FRENCH in others, the result has not affected the uninterrupted and enduring mutual intelligibility of the various forms of the language.

Number of Speakers: There are probably 2–3 million Kanuri speakers. Considering the Kanuri-Kanembu dialect cluster as one language, the total population is approximately 4 million speakers.

Origin and History

Historians have used the term "Kanem" to refer to the vast empire that dominated the central Sudan region from about A.D. 1000 until its collapse during the 14th century. The empire was concentrated in the Sahel region north of Lake Chad, and the historical term has been preserved today to refer to that region; it is also the official name of the large prefecture in present-day Chad that occupies a portion of the realm of the Kanem empire. The term *Kanembu* is derived from Kanem through the application of the plural form +*wú* of the agentive suffix +*ma*, and thus means literally 'people of Kanem, owners of Kanem'. Also in historical treatments, the term "Bornu" (today stripped of its colonial spelling and pronunciation and changed to "Borno" to reflect its actual pronunciation in the Kanuri language) is used to refer to the region southwest of Lake Chad, and to the offshoot of the failing Kanem empire that was founded there during the 14th or 15th century A.D. The members of the royal family, as well as other elements of the failing Kanem empire who left it and founded the Borno empire, are commonly referred to as the "Kanuri". It is believed that this name was originally applied to the conquering people from Kanem. The commonly espoused etymology of the term "Kanuri" is that it is morphologically a place-name,

Table 1: Consonants

	Bilabial	Labio-dental	Alveolar	Palatal	Velar	Laryngeal/ Glottal
Stops	(p) b		t d		k g	ʔ
Prenasalized Stops	mb		nd		ng [ŋ]	
Fricatives	(f) [ɸ] (v) [β]	f	s z	sh [ʃ]	g [ɣ]	h
Nasals	m		n	ɲ	ng [ŋ]	
Liquids			r [ɾ] l	ɬ		
Glides	w			y		

formed through the application of the suffix + *ri*, a morpheme used to derived nouns of place when applied to a noun referring to the occupant of that place. Thus, it is possible that *kànúrì* is derived from *kanem* + *ri*, which might literally translate as 'the place of Kanem'. It might have originally been used by the invaders from the north to refer to the area that they had conquered in Borno. Thus, historically speaking, the Kanembu language was once much more widely spoken than Kanuri, as the language of the Kanem empire, while Kanuri is basically the language of its successor state, Borno. Today, in referring to the history of both the Kanembu and the Kanuri peoples, historians talk of the history of the Kanem-Borno empire.

Given the ever-increasing importance of the HAUSA language in Niger and Nigeria, indeed throughout west Africa, smaller language groups like the Kanuri are seriously threatened. Prior to colonialism, when the Kanuri and Kanembu-speaking peoples were united in the Kanem-Borno Empire, they represented a powerful and significant cultural, political, and economic force. With the advent of colonialism and the decline of the empire, there occurred a bifurcation of these peoples, at least politically, and today they are divided among four different countries. The people have been able to maintain strong sociocultural, economic, marital, and traditional links in spite of the modern borders, but nevertheless, they have minority status in each of the four countries. In Niger and Nigeria the Hausa language is becoming increasingly dominant. These facts, combined with the bleak economic and ecological outlook in the region, may well mean a loss of Kanuri speakers.

Orthography and Basic Phonology

The Standard Kanuri Orthography (SKO) was developed during 1974–75 in Maiduguri by the research staff of Bayero University Kano's Centre for the Study of Nigerian languages, in collaboration with the Kanuri Language Board and the local representatives of the Borno State Ministry of Education. The Orthography Committee of the Kanuri Language Board put the finishing touches on an earlier proposed orthography, and the finished product was finally unanimously approved by the Kanuri Language Board for adoption in late 1975.

In general, the overriding principle applied in the development of the SKO was that the orthography should reflect the pronunciation of the Kanuri word in a systematic and predictable way, with as few exceptions as possible. In addition, wherever possible, an attempt was made to retain the historical CV(C) structure of the Kanuri syllable in the written word. In applying this principle, the already existing Kanuri (Roman) alphabet was used. This was done in order to avoid the educational and the financial costs that would have resulted from the creation of new letters and symbols, the use of diacritics such as tone markings, or the addition of new and unfamiliar vowel and consonant symbols. All of the latter were rejected as possible ways of standardizing the writing of Kanuri.

Below is an example of the kind of problem that the SKO had to resolve since marking tone was not retained as an orthographic convention:

SKO	Phonetic Realization	Meaning
fər	[fə̂r]	horse
fərwa	[fə̀rrá]	horses
fərra	[fə̀rrà]	having a horse
fərwaa	[fə̀ráà]	having horses

The alphabet of the SKO includes the following letters: *p, t, k, b, d, g, mb, nd, ng, c, j, f, s, sh, g, h, w, z, m, n, ɲ, ng, r, l, y, i, e, a, o, u,* and ´.

Kanuri has 28 consonant phonemes, including glides as shown in Table 1 above. The letters *c* and *j* represent the affricates [tʃ] (as in English "church") and [dʒ] (as in English "judge") respectively. Although the consonant *p* is not normally considered a phoneme, it is nevertheless included as a letter of Kanuri in the SKO. It occurs as an allophone of *b* when *b* is followed by a voiceless plosive. The voiceless bilabial fricative occurs as an allophone of *f*, and in apparent free variation with *f*, on all open vowel-final syllables that begin with *f*. It is also an allophone of /b/ when *b* occurs intervocalically. In SKO, this weakened *b* is written as a *w*. The palatal consonants occur both as phonemes and also as allophones. For example, the status of the phoneme ʃ, written as the diagraph *sh*, might be questioned since it normally occurs initially either in borrowed words or preceding the high front vowel *i*, and thus may be seen as an allophone of *s*. Consonant assimilation is also a widespread process in the language, as typified in some of the following examples. Clearly, assimilation can be either progressive or regressive:

búskìn	>	búkkìn > búkìn	'I eat'
yàskə́	>	yàkkə́	'three'
náb+ngìn	>	námngìn	'I sit down'
fàl+nə́mìn	>	fàllə́mìn	'you change'

There are seven basic vowels, as shown in Table 2 below.

Table 2: Vowels

	Front	Central	Back
High	i	ə [ɨ]	u
Mid	e	a [ʌ]	o
Low		a [ɑ]	

Basic Morphology

Kanuri has no gender, either lexical or grammatical, and thus no nominal classifier system. Number is added to nouns through suffixation. The plural of the noun is formed through changing its tone and applying the high-tone plural suffix always written as *-wa* (SKO). This suffix actually assimilates to a final consonant in pronunciation as shown phonetically here:

bàbúr	'motorcycle'	baburwa [bàbùrrá]	'motorcycles'
férò	'girl'	ferowa [fèròá]	'girls'

The articles include a definite article (anaphora marker) *-də*, which is suffixed to both singular and plural nouns, and four demonstratives: *ádə* 'this', *túdù* 'that', *ányí* 'these', and *túnyì* 'those'. The independent pronouns are six in number, and do not distinguish gender in any person:

	Singular		Plural	
First person	wú	'I'	àndí	'we'
Second person	nyí	'you'	nàndí	'you' (pl)
Third person	shí	's/he'	sàndí	'they'

The finite verb form of Kanuri is agglutinative. That is, the verb form carries all of the required inflectional morphemes like person, number, tense/aspect, and the optional morphemes like causation, negation, and reflexivization. Thus it is sentential:

Nzə̀kkə̀làdə̀kìnbâ 'I will not sell (it) to you.'

The verb carries a verb root, plus inflectional morphemes indicating a first-person singular subject and imperfect aspect interpreted here as future. It also carries a second-person singular indirect object, an applied morpheme, and negation. Thus, in neutral unmarked environments where nouns/pronouns are in no way emphasized or questioned and an independent subject is not expressed, they are carried only in the verb form and not manifested independently.

nzə̀-kkə̀-làd-k-ìn-bâ > nzə̀kkə̀làdə́kìnbâ
2S-APPLIED-sell-1S-IMPERFECT-NEGATIVE

Kanuri essentially has two verb classes that correspond to similar verb groupings in other Saharan languages. Every finite verb form must contain a verb root, and must be fully inflected for person of the subject, number of the subject, and tense/aspect. The inflection for the person of the subject is not simply a morpheme indicating person agreement, but rather is a subject pronoun carried within the finite verb form. When the subject of any sentence is a pronoun and is in no way questioned, focused, or emphasized, then it is only manifested inside of the verb form and not independently in the typologically predicted S-initial SOV position. Therefore the first-person singular imperfect form of the verb *lè+* 'go', which is *lèngîn*, constitutes a complete sentence meaning 'I go/am going/will go'. Likewise *lèngə́nà*, the first-person singular perfect form of the same verb constitutes a sentence meaning 'I have gone'.

The morphological processes that operate in the derivation of words include affixation, tone change, epenthesis, and reduplication. The following are some examples of these:

Affixation:	Basic word	Meaning	Derived word	Meaning
prefix kər+	mâi	king	kə̀rmâi	reign
prefix nəm+	bâ	there isn't	nə̀mbâ	absence, lack
suffix +la	bútù	cheap	bùtùlá	something cheap
suffix +ma/wu	àlîn	indigo	àlînmà/wù	dyer/s
suffix +mì	Aisâ		Aisâmì	son of Aisa
tone change:	Kànúrì	Kanuri person	Kànùrí	Kanuri language
	fátò	house	fàtó	of the household
compounding:	hùndúli	hair	cìkùndùlí	moustache
epenthesis:	bák+	beat, bit	bágə̀	stumbling block
reduplication:	fú+	blow	fùfú	lungs
	fù+	swell	fùfú	puffy bundle of cola nuts
	sáp+	collect	sàbsàwí	collection

Basic Syntax

The typological categorization of Kanuri as an SOV language is made in recognition of the basic order of the major constituents in the verbal structure. SOV represents the most natural and commonly occurring order of the declarative sentence:

S O V
Alì Músà+gà lèfàwónò
'Ali greeted Musa.'

* Alì lèfàwónò Músà+gà (SVO)
* lèfàwónò Músà+gà Alì (VSO)

In the following acceptable variant of the above example, notice that the order of the elements preceding the verb has been reversed so that the direct object precedes the subject. It is apparent that in this variant the subject is obligatorily marked by a postposition indicating its role as agent:

O S V
Músà+gà Alì+yè lèfàwónò
'Ali greeted Musa/Musa was greeted by Ali.'

* Músà+gà lèfàwónò Alì+yè (OVS)
* lèfàwónò Músà+gà Alì-yè (VSO)

As would be expected in an SOV language of this kind, Kanuri has a full set of postpositions that have been referred to in some treatments of Kanuri grammar as case markers or case suffixes. A postposition is a monomorphemic word or particle that is placed after a noun or pronoun, to mark it as an oblique constituent indicating place, direction, source, method, means, etc. The Kanuri postpositions and other suffixes, because they assimilate phonologically to their preceding head word, are written as part of the word they modify according to the Standard Kanuri Orthography:

Agent postposition: Músà+yè, 'Musa+by'
Associative postposition: kúngə́nà+à, 'money+with/having'
Indirect postposition: Músà+rò, 'Musa+to/for'
Genitive postposition: Músà+bè, 'Musa+of/'s'
Directional postposition: kàsúwù+mbèn, 'market+via'
Locative/means postposition: kàsúwù+làn, 'market+at' jánà+làn, 'knife+with'

The above set of postpositions is used to mark all oblique (adverbial) modifiers of the language, as well as major constituents in certain environments.

The Kanuri verb is negated by means of two negative particles. The first, *bâ,* is a negative predicate of existence, and is used to negate the imperfect or continuous aspect. The second, *gə̀nyí,* is a negative predicate of identification, and is used to negate the completive aspect, as well as the future:

Shí bâ	'S/he is not there'
Lèjin+bâ	'S/he is not going'
Adə̀ kàkkê (g)ə̀nyí	'This is not mine'
Nâ ádə̀rò ísə̀nyí	'S/he did not come here (to this place)'

Kanuri is a head-final language.

Contact with Other Languages

Most significant borrowing in Kanuri comes from ARABIC. Less significant sources for borrowing are from English, Hausa, and French.

From Arabic: *lùwásàr* 'onion', *sàkân* 'kettle', *líwú* 'pocket'
From English: *fə́rémàrè* 'primary', *kíshə̀n* 'kitchen', *kófreti* 'cooperative'
From French: *fàrtòmànê* 'purse'
From Hausa: *gòdèngə́nà* 'I thank (you)', *rèké* 'sugar cane'

Common Words

man:	kwâ, kwângâ	long:	kùrúwù
person:	kâm	small:	gàná
woman:	kámú	yes:	àâ
water:	njî	no:	á'à
sun:	kə̀ngâl	good:	ngə́là
three:	yàskə́	bird:	ngúdò
fish:	búnyì	dog:	kə́rì
big:	kúrà	tree:	kə̀ská

Example Sentences

(1) Álì bàrèmá.
'Ali is a farmer.'

(2) Álì bàrèmá gə̀nyí.
'Ali is not a farmer.'

(3) Ámmá búltù dâ+də́ bârò súrùnyí.
but hyena meat+DET not+PP 3SG:see+NEG.PAST
'But the hyena did not see that there was no meat.'

Efforts to Preserve, Protect, and Promote the Language

In the 1970s, when Kanuri was named as one of the 12 national languages of Nigeria selected for use in the proposed Universal Free Primary Education system, there was a great deal of enthusiastic effort exerted to preserve, protect, and promote the language. The mid-1970s saw a plethora of efforts directed at standardizing the language and developing materials for the education system. This period saw the establishment of the Kanuri Language Board (1974), which worked closely with researchers from Bayero University Kano's (then Abdullahi Bayero College) Center for the Study of Nigerian Languages. The Kanuri Language Board was selected by the local authority and worked closely with the Shehu of Borno in carrying out its work. The then Waziri of Borno was the chairman of the committee for developing the standard Kanuri orthography. These efforts resulted in the establishment of the standard orthography as well as a great many publications. A few years later the Northeastern College of Arts and Sciences was transformed into the University of Maiduguri, and researchers were hired to set up a certificate program for the training of Kanuri teachers for the educational system. This program survives today within the Department of Nigerian Languages & Linguistics where it is possible to obtain a doctorate degree in Kanuri language studies. These efforts continue to enhance the status of Kanuri in Nigeria, in spite of political or economic problems. The language has not been similarly honored in the sister francophone countries of Niger and Chad.

Select Bibliography

Awoboluyi, Oladele. 1968. *Introductory Kanuri.* Washington, DC: Centre for Applied Linguistics.
Bailey. 1911. *Kanuri-English Vocabulary.* Journal of the Royal Asiatic Society.

Benton, P. Askell. 1911. *Kanuri Readings Including Facsimiles of MSS., Transliteration, Interlinear Translation and Notes; Also a complete English-Kanuri Vocabulary and a Partial Kanuri-English Vocabulary*. Oxford.

____. 1917. *English-Kanuri and Kanuri-English Vocabularies Supplementary to those in Koelle's African Literature in Kanuri and Benton's Kanuri Readings, in Primer of Kanuri Grammar*. Oxford.

Cohen, Ronald. 1967. *The Kanuri of Bornu*. Chicago: Holt, Rinehart and Winston.

Cyffer, Norbert. 1976. "Bibliography of Saharan Languages." In *Harsunan Nijeriya* Vol. VI: 75–93. Kano: Centre for the Study of Nigerian Languages, Bayero University Kano.

Cyffer, Norbert, and John P. Hutchison. 1979. *The Standard Kanuri Orthography*. Lagos: Thomas Nelson.

Ellison, R.E. 1937. *An English-Kanuri Sentence Book*. London: Crown Agents for the Colonies.

Hutchison, John P. 1981. *The Kanuri Language: A Reference Grammar*. Madison: African Studies Program, University of Wisconsin.

Hutchison, John P., and Norbert Cyffer. 1990. *Dictionary of the Kanuri Language*. Providence: Foris Publications, and Maiduguri: University of Nigeria.

Jarrett, Kevin A., and Mustapha Maina. 1981. *The Standard Manga Orthography*. Kano: Centre for the Study of Nigerian Languages, Bayero University Kano.

Koelle, Sigismund Wilhelm. 1854. *Grammar of the Borno or Kanuri Language*. London: Church Missionary House.

Lukas, Johannes. 1937. *A Study of the Kanuri Language, Grammar and Vocabulary*. Oxford.

KAPAMPANGAN

Hiroaki Kitano

Language Name and Autonym: Kapampangan. It has also been called Pampanga, Pampango, Pampangan, or Pampangueño, but the name "Kapampangan" has been used most often in the linguistic literature, and is also preferred by native Kapampangans.

Location: Kapampangan is spoken mainly in Pampanga Province, but also in parts of Tarlac, Nueva Ecija, Bulacan, and Bataan Provinces, Central Luzon, the Philippines.

Family: Austronesian language family, Malayo-Polynesian branch, Western Malayo–Polynesian subbranch, Northern Philippine, Bashiic-Central Luzon-Northern Mindoro, Central Luzon, Kapampangan.

Related Languages: Kapampangan is classified as one of the Northern Philippine languages, although this classification is by no means definitive, since Kapampangan is not similar to TAGALOG to the south, nor to ILOCANO to the north in many respects.

Dialects: There are at least two major dialects; in the Western dialect, final *-ay* has frequently changed to *-e*, final *-aw* to *-o* (Forman 1971a). Anicia Del Corro has worked on Kapampangan dialects in the 1980s, and classified the dialects into Northern, Eastern, Central, Western, and Southern. Both Forman (1971a) and Gonzalez (1981) assert that there are only minor differences among the dialects.

Number of Speakers: 2 million.

Origin and History

Little is known about the pre-Hispanic history of the language, except the existence of a Kapampangan syllabary (Forman 1971a). The first recorded pedagogical grammar in Kapampangan was *Arte, Vocabulario, y Confesionario Pampango* by Diego Ochoa (circa 1580). Augustinian friar Diego Bergaño wrote several important works, including *Arte de la Lengua Pampanga* (1729) and *Vocabulario de la Lengua Pampanga en Romance* (1732).

One remarkable style of Kapampangan literature is called the *crissotan*, named in honor of famous playwright and poet Juan Crisostomo Soto (1867–1918), which is a debate in Kapampangan verse (Zapanta-Manlapaz 1981).

Orthography and Basic Phonology

Generally, the Tagalog-based orthography is used for writing Kapampangan, although the SPANISH-based orthography may sometimes be considered authentic and preferred. In addition, one may find minor spelling variations mostly due to personal preferences. The Tagalog alphabet consists of the following letters (in alphabetical order): A B K D E G H I L M N NG O P R S T U W Y.

Kapampangan consonants and vowels are shown in Tables 1 and 2 by their orthographic symbols. The voiceless velar stop may get voiced and fricativized between vowels in some words (e.g., *kéka* '2SG oblique pronoun'). The glottal stop is not always indicated in writing or publication, but in this overview, it is represented with a grave accent (`) on the final syllable, or a circumflex accent (^) if the word has final stress.

Two pairs of vowels, [i, e] and [u, o], may be contrastive or may be alternants in the same word (e.g., *ku* '1SG pronoun' vs. *ko* '2PL pronoun'; *kuya* ~ *koya* 'elder brother'). The midvariants [e] and [o] may occur word finally in interrogative or exclamatory utterances (e.g., *E ku balù.* 'I don't know' vs. *E me balò?* 'Don't you know him?').

Stress in Kapampangan is contrastive. A stressed vowel is pronounced long unless it is in the final closed syllable (e.g., /masá:kit/ 'difficult' vs. /ma:sakít/ 'sick').

Table 1: Consonants

		Bilabial	Dental	Alveo-Palatal	Velar	Glottal
Stops	Voiceless	p	t		k	- [ʔ]
	Voiced	b	d		g	
Fricatives			s			h
Affricates	Voiceless			ts, ch, ty, ti [tʃ]		
	Voiced			dy, di [dʒ]		
Nasals		m	n		ng [ŋ]	
Lateral			l			
Flap			r			
Glides		w				

Table 2: Vowels

	Front	Central	Back
High	i		u
Mid	e		o
Low		a	

Basic Morphology

Kapampangan verbs can be classified either as intransitive or transitive, depending on what affixes and enclitic pronouns they take. Verbs derive for focus (see Basic Syntax) and inflect for aspect. There are three aspects in Kapampangan: contingent (contemplated, future), perfective (completed, past), and imperfective (incompleted, progressive, present). Table 3 shows the most frequently used affixes (Forman 1971a; Mirikitani 1971). (CV = reduplication of the first syllable of a root.)

There are irregular verbs that conjugate through the vowel alternations and reduplication of the first syllable (see Table 4 below).

Other notable verbal affixes include aptative (abilitative, accidental, or coincidental actions), distributive (states or actions distributed over space, time, or participants, e.g., repetitive actions), and causative affixes (see Table 5).

Adjectives may be monomorphemic or formed with a root and affixation. A large number of adjectives are formed by adding the prefix *ma-* (plural *manga-*). The comparative degree is marked by *mas*, borrowed from Spanish (e.g., *mas maragul* 'bigger'). Superlative adjectives are formed with the prefix *peka-* (*pekamaragul* 'biggest'). Adjectives may be intensified by the prefix *ka-*, in place of *ma-* (*karagul* 'so big'), or by the repetition of an adjective (*Matas yang matas.* 'He/she is very tall.')

Case marking in Kapampangan is on an ergative/absolutive basis (Mithun 1994). Absolutive forms (better known as "topic", "nominative" or "subject" in Philippine linguistics) are used to mark the only core argument in an intransitive clause and a more patient-like argument in a transitive clause. Ergative (or "genitive") forms are used to mark a more agentlike argument in a transitive clause and a possessor in an NP.

Nouns may be case marked (absolutive, ergative or oblique) or not case marked (indefinite bare nominal). Case-marked nouns may be modified by one of the following prenominal

Table 3: Verb Affixes

		CONTINGENT	PERFECTIVE	IMPERFECTIVE
Intransitive affixes	Actor focus	-um-	-in-	CV-
		mag-	mig-, meg-	ma:g-
		maN-	meN-	ma:N-
		ma-	me-	ma:-
Transitive affixes	Patient focus	i-	-in-	CV-
		(zero)	-in-	CV-
		-an	-in-	CV- -an
	Directional focus	-an	-in- (-an)	CV- (-an)
		pag- -an	pig- -an	pa:g- -an
		paN- -an	piN- -an, peN- -an	pa:N- -an
	Beneficiary focus	(i)pag-	pig-	(i)pa:g-
		(i)paN-	piN-, peN-	(i)pa:N-
	Instrumental focus	(i)paN-	piN-, peN-	pa:N-

Table 4: Irregular Verbs

CONTINGENT	PERFECTIVE	IMPERFECTIVE	Examples
-a-	-i-, -e-	CV-	makó - mekó - mámakó ('leave')
-u-	-i-	CV-	muntá - mintá – mumuntá ('go')

Table 5: Other Verb Affixes

		CONTINGENT	PERFECTIVE	IMPERFECTIVE
Aptative	Intransitive	maka-	meka-	ma:ka-
		makapag-	mekapag-	ma:kapag-
		makapaN-	mekapaN-	ma:kapaN-
		makapa-	mekapa-	ma:kapa-
	Transitive	a-	a-	a-
Distributive	Intransitive	maN-	meN-	ma:N-
	Transitive	paN- (-an)	peN- (-an)	pa:N- (-an)
Causative	Intransitive	magpa-	migpa-	ma:gpa-
	Transitive	papa-, pa-	pe:pa-, pe:-	pa:pa-, pa:-

articles (= case markers, determiners). Note that the absolutive singular form *ing* often gets contracted to an enclitic *=ng* in natural speech.

Articles.

		ABS	ERG	OBL
Common nouns	SG	ing, =ng	ning	king, keng
	PL	deng/reng	reng	karing
Personal names	SG	i	=ng	kang
	PL	di/ri	ri	kari

There are enclitic personal pronouns (absolutive and ergative) and free pronouns (absolutive and oblique). The enclitics usually occupy the second position of the clause and the NP. Some pronouns have shortened variants (see Table 6).

Enclitic combinations (ergative + absolutive) may often be fused, as shown below:

	ABSOLUTIVE	
ERGATIVE	ABS.3SG (ya)	ABS.3PL (la)
ERG.1SG (ku)	ke, kya	ko
ERG.2SG (mu)	me, mya	mo
ERG.3SG (na)	ne, nya	no
ERG.1DUAL (ta)	te, tya	to
ERG.1PL.INCL (tá)	(táya)	(tála)
ERG.1PL.EXCL (mi)	mya	(mila)
ERG.2PL (yu)	ye, ya	yo
ERG.3PL (da/ra)	de/re, dya/rya	do/ro

For example *Íkit ke* (saw ERG.1SG+ABS.3SG) 'I saw him/her/it'; *Á-pangan ke itá=ng bútol.* (APTATIVE-eat ERG.1SG+ABS.3SG that.ABS=LK seed) 'I accidentally ate the seed'; *Kanínu me pa-gawâ?* (who.OBL ERG.2SG+ABS.3SG CAUS-make) 'Who will you ask to make it?'

Kapampangan has a three-way spatial demonstrative system (proximal = near the speaker; medial = near the listener; distal = far from both). However, spatial demonstrative adverbs distinguish two degrees of distals (visible vs. invisible).

Demonstrative Pronouns.

		ABS	ERG	OBL
Proximal	SG	iní	niní	kaníni
	PL	déni/réni	daréni	karéni
Medial	SG	iyán	niyán	kanyán
	PL	dén/rén	darén	karén
Distal	SG	itá	nitá	kaníta
	PL	déta/réta	daréta	karéta

Demonstrative Adverbs.

	LOCATIVE (here, there, over there) DIRECTION (to this/ that place)	TEMPORAL
Proximal	kéni	kaníni (immediate future)
Medial	kén	kanyán (future)
Distal (visible)	kéta	kaníta (past)
Distal (invisible)	karín	

Basic Syntax

Like other Philippine languages, Kapampangan is a predicate-initial language, i.e., verbs and adjectives usually occupy the initial position, but various elements may also appear initially when they function as a predicate (e.g., NPs and question words) or for discourse-pragmatic reasons.

Pronominal and adverbial clitics usually occupy the second position of a clause and an NP. Unlike many other Philippine languages, Kapampangan pronominal clitics are almost always obligatory. In the following example, the third-person singular absolutive pronoun *ya* is coreferential with *i Dan.*

Masantíng	ya	i	Dan.
handsome	ABS.3SG	ART.ABS.SG	Dan

'Dan is handsome.'

Here are some examples of the noun phrase. (LK = linker, which is realized either as *=ng* [after vowels, n, and the glottal stop] or *a*): *ing kótse ku* (ART.ABS.SG car ERG.1SG) 'my car'; *ing báyu ku=ng kótse* (ART.ABS.SG new ERG.1SG=LK car) 'my new car'; *iní=ng anák na=ng Jun* (this.ABS.SG=LK child ERG.3SG=ART.ERG.SG Jun) 'this kid of Jun's'; *ing dimdám ku kang Aida* (ART.ABS.SG heard ERG.1SG ART.OBL.SG Aida) 'what I heard from Aida'.

The morphology of the verb indicates the semantic relationship between the predicate and the absolutive argument. Thus, in a patient-focus construction, for example, the absolutive argument is semantically a patient, and the verbal predicate takes appropriate patient-focus affixes. The following are examples of each focus construction. (The underlined argument is absolutive.)

Table 6: Personal Pronouns

	ABS (clitic)	ABS (free)	ERG (clitic)	OBL (free)
1SG	ku	yáku, áku	ku	kanáku, káku
2SG	ka	íka	mu	kéka
3SG	ya	íya	na	kaya
1DUAL	kata	íkata	ta	kékata
1PL.INCL	katámu, támu, katá, tá	íkatámu, ítamu, íkatá, ítá	támu, tá	kékatámu, kékatá
1PL.EXCL	kami, ke	íkami, íke	mi	kékami, kéke
2PL	kayu, ko	íkayu, íko	yu	kékayu, kéko
3PL	la	íla	da/ra	karéla

Actor focus (AF)
Mámangan ya=ng manúk.
eating.AF ABS.3SG=LK chicken
'He/She is eating chicken.' (Root: *kan* 'eat')

Patient focus (PF)
Kakanán ke ing manúk.
eating.PF ERG.1SG+ABS.3SG ART.ABS.SG chicken
'I am eating the chicken.' (Root: *kan* 'eat')

Directional focus (DF)
Dínan me=ng péra itá=ng anák.
give.to.DF ERG.2SG+ABS.3SG=LK money that.ABS.SG=LK child
'(You) give some money to that kid.' (Root: *din* 'give')

Beneficiary focus (BF)
Pangadî me.
pray.for.BF ERG.2SG+ABS.3SG
'(You) pray for him/her/it.' (Root: *adî* 'pray)

Instrumental focus (IF)
Penyúlat ke ing lápis.
wrote.with.IF ERG.1SG+ABS.3SG ART.ABS.SG pencil
'I wrote with the pencil.' (Root: *súlat* 'write')

Negation is expressed by the predicate-initial *e*.
E ra na ta burí.
NEG ERG.3PL already ABS.1PL.INCL like
'They don't like us any more.'

Both existence and possession are expressed by the existential particles *atin, ating* or *atiu* ('there is, be present, have') and *alâ* ('there is not, be absent, do not have').

Atíng métung a árì a maburí king kwéntu.
EXIST one LK king LK fond ART.OBL.SG story
'There was a king who likes (to hear) stories.'

Alá=ng pámangan keng balé.
NEG.EXIST=LK food ART.OBL.SG house
'There is no food in the house.'

Alá yu.
NEG.EXIST ABS.3SG
'He is absent.'
(The special third-person form *yu* is used instead of *ya*)

Atín ya=ng kapatád a laláki i Tony.
EXIST ABS.3SG=LK sibling LK man ART.ABS.SG Tony
'Tony has a brother.'

Contact with Other Languages

Like many other Philippine languages, Kapampangan has a considerable number of Spanish and English loanwords. It is common to use Spanish, English and Tagalog words in daily Kapampangan conversation. One such example from natural conversational data is: *I-seal ke ságuli.* 'I will just seal it first'.

Common Words

man:	laláki (PLURAL la:lá:ki)	flower:	sampága
woman:	babái (PLURAL ba:bá:i)	tree:	dútung
water:	danúm	sun:	aldó
three:	atlú	fish:	asán
long:	makábà	good:	máyap
yes:	wa	no:	alî
big:	máragul	small:	malatî
bird:	áyop	dog:	ásu
town:	balén	house:	balé

Example Sentences

(1) Atín ku=ng balíta=ng tínggap ku nápun.
EXIST ABS.1SG=LK news=LK received ERG.1SG yesterday
'I have news that I received yesterday.'

(2) E ku bálu=ng dínatang ka kéni.
NEG ERG.1SG know=LK came ABS.2SG here
'I didn't know that you came here.'

(3) Nung bísa kayú=ng mulí atád da kayú.
if want ABS.2PL=LK go.home escort ERG.1SG ABS.2PL
'If you want to come home, I can take you (home).' (The first-person singular ergative pronominal form is *da* only when combined with the second-person pronouns *ka* and *kayu*.)

(4) Kítang da nung nánu=ng milyári kayá.
asked ERG.3PL COMP what=ART.ABS.SG happened OBL.3SG
'They asked what happened to him.'

(5) Magpa-ragúl ya=ng kamátis.
CAUS-big ABS.3SG=LK tomato
'He grows tomatoes.' (causative)

Efforts to Preserve, Protect, and Promote the Language

Throughout the region, children still learn Kapampangan as the first language, but in urban cities, such as San Fernando and Angeles, and nearby towns, children are being taught to speak Tagalog to cope with preschool and primary school education.

The pioneering organization promoting the perpetuation of Kapampangan literature and the research on Kapampangan history and language is the *Akademyang Kapampangan* (AKKAP), founded in 1937 by Zoilo J. Hilario, Monico R. Mercado and Amado M. Yuzon. The AKKAP's periodical is titled *Ing Susi* ('The Key').

Today, there are many individuals and various groups interested in preserving and promoting Kapampangan language and culture. One of these groups is the Batiauan Foundation, whose mission is to launch and fund projects aimed against the decline in the prestige and use of the Kapampangan language. Kapampangan people's efforts are also centered on some Web sites (e.g., Kapampangan Homepage: www.balen.net).

Select Bibliography

Bergaño, Diego. 1732 [1860]. *Vocabulario de la Lengua Pampanga en Romance*. Manila: Imprenta de Ramirez y Giraudier.

Forman, Michael L. 1971a. *Kapampangan Grammar Notes*. Honolulu: University of Hawaii Press.

_____. 1971b. *Kapampangan Dictionary*. Honolulu: University of Hawaii Press.

Gonzalez, Andrew B. 1981. *Pampangan: Towards a Meaning-based Description*. Pacific Linguistics, Series C - No. 48. Canberra: Department of Linguistics, the Australian National University.

Mirikitani, Leatrice T. 1971. *Speaking Kapampangan*. Honolulu: University of Hawaii Press.

_____. 1972. *Kapampangan Syntax*. Honolulu: University of Hawaii Press.

Mithun, Marianne. 1994. "The Implications of Ergativity for a Philippine Voice System." In *Voice: Form and Function*, ed. by Barbara Fox and Paul J. Hopper, 247–77. Amsterdam: John Benjamins.

Zapanta-Manlapaz, Edna. 1981. *Kapampangan Literature: A Historical Survey and Anthology*. Quezon City, Metro Manila: Ateneo de Manila University Press.

Zorc, R. David. 1992. "Grammatical Outline." In *Kapampangan Reader: Philippine Language Series*. Alma M. Davidson and Leonardo Aquino Pineda, ed. by Pamela Johnstone Moguet, ix–xxviii. Kensington, MD: Dunwoody Press.

Lars Johanson

Language Name: Kazakh. **Alternates:** *Kazak, Qazaq.* **Autonym:** *Qazaq tili, qazaqša.*

Location: Spoken in the Republic of Kazakhstan (*Qazaqstan Respublikasï*). Also spoken in parts of China (Xinjiang), Uzbekistan, Mongolia, Turkmenistan, Kyrgyzstan, Russian Federation, Tajikistan, and Afghanistan.

Family: Northwestern (Kipchak) branch of the Turkic family.

Related Languages: Karakalpak, Noghay.

Dialects: In spite of its huge extension, the Kazakh linguistic area exhibits relatively little local variation. The standard language is based on the Northwestern dialects as distinct from the ones spoken in the southern and western regions. The Easternmost dialects spoken in China and Mongolia display some special features. The Karakalpaks of Uzbekistan speak a slightly Uzbekized variant of Kazakh.

Number of Speakers: About 10 million.

Origin and History

The titulary nation of Kazakhstan goes back to separatist Uzbek tribes that founded a huge steppe empire in the area from the second half of the 15th century on. This empire later disintegrated into three so-called hordes. After century-long Russian advances into the territory, Kazakhstan was incorporated into Russia in the middle of the 19th century. In 1920, a Kazakh constituent republic of the Soviet Union was established. Kazakhstan declared its sovereignty in 1990, and full independence in 1991.

Orthography and Basic Phonology

In Kazakhstan, a LATIN-based alphabet was introduced in 1929, and a variant of the Cyrillic alphabet was adopted in 1940. There are now plans to adopt a Latin-based script again. In China (Xinjiang), Kazakh is written with the ARABIC script again, after an unsuccessful experiment with a Latin-based (*pinyin*) alphabet in the 1970s. The Karakalpaks of Uzbekistan use a new Latin script based on a different system.

Table 1: Vowels

	Front		Back	
	Unrounded	Rounded	Unrounded	Rounded
High	i	ü	ï	u
Mid	e	ö		o
Low	ä		a	

Vowel length is not distinctive, but found at a subphonemic level. Word-initial /e/ often exhibits a prothetic *y*-, for example, *yeki* 'two'. Word-initial /ö/ and /o/ can also be realized with a prothetic bilabial glide. The vowel /i/ is usually shorter than its TURKISH counterpart. Reduction of high vowels is very common.

Table 2: Consonants

	Labial	Alveolar	Alveo-palatal	Velar	Glottal
Stops	p b	t d		k g	’
Fricatives	f v	s z	š ž	x ɣ	h
Affricates		č ǰ			
Nasals	m	n		ŋ	
Liquids		l r			
Glides	w		y		

The phoneme /g/ occurs as a fronted stop [g] in front environments (next to front vowels) and as a back-velar (uvular) fricative [ɣ] in back environments (next to back vowels). The phoneme /k/ occurs as a mid-velar stop [k] in front environments and as a backvelar (uvular) stop [q] in back environments. The phoneme /l/ occurs as [l] in front environments and as a backed variant [ł] in back environments. The phonemes /f/, /v/, and /x/ are restricted to loanwords and are not present in all spoken varieties. Thus, /f/ is often substituted for by /p/, as in *avtobus* [aftobus] ~ [aptobus] 'bus', and /x/ by /q/, as in *xat* [qat] 'letter'. While /y/ is almost restricted to noninitial positions, such as *ay* 'moon', /ž/ is almost restricted to word-initial positions, such as *žer* 'land'. The phoneme /f/ occurs as a bilabial [ɸ], but may be a labiodental [f] in words borrowed from RUSSIAN. Between vowels, /b/ may be pronounced as [w].

Word-final obstruents are voiceless. This is reflected in the orthography except in some loanwords ending in б [b], в [v], г [g], and д [d], for example, клуб *klup* 'club'. In front of suffix-initial vowels, stem-final /p/, /q/, and /k/ are mostly weakened and become /b/, /ɣ/, and /g/, respectively, for example, *köp* 'much' versus *köbi* 'much of it', *qayïq* 'boat' versus *qayïɣï* 'his boat', *žürek* 'heart' versus *žüregim* 'my heart'. Between vowels, /b/ may be further weakened to [w].

In loanwords, high epenthetic vowels are inserted to dissolve nonpermissible consonant clusters, as in *xalïq* 'people' < Arabic *xalq* (but *xalq-ïm* 'my people'). Also certain native bisyllabic stems lose the high vowel of their final syllable in front of a suffix-initial vowel, such as *murïn* 'nose' versus *murnïm* 'my nose'.

The combinability of stem-final and suffix-initial consonants is relatively restricted. Suffix-initial voiced stops are devoiced after voiceless consonants, and /m/, /n/, /l/, and /d/ undergo certain changes. In the following examples, capital letters indicate variation. Thus, in the case of the negation marker *-MA*, /m/ is used after vowels and voiced consonants except after /z/ and /ž/, where the corresponding stop /b/ appears. The stop /b/ may also appear after /l/, /m/, /n/, and /ŋ/. The voiceless /p/ appears after voiceless consonants. Examples are: *kör-me-* 'not to see', *žaz-ba-* 'not to write', *kes-pe-* 'not to cut'. With the genitive marker *-NIŋ*, /n/ is used after vowels and nasals, whereas the corresponding stops /d/ and /t/ appear elsewhere, for example, *adamnïŋ* 'of the man', *közdiŋ* 'of the eye', *qazaqtïŋ* 'of the Kazakh'. With the plural marker *-LAr*, /l/ is used after vowels, [r], [y] and [w], whereas the corresponding stops /d/ and /t/ appear elsewhere, as in *žer-ler* 'places', *köz-der* 'eyes', and *at-tar* 'horses'. With the ablative marker *-DAn*, /n/ is used after nasals, whereas the corresponding stops /d/ and /t/ appear elsewhere, as in *adamnan* 'from the man', *üyden* 'from home', *žaqtan* 'from the side'. There are several other types of consonant assimilation.

According to the front-versus-back harmony, the vowels assimilate to the frontness-backness of the preceding syllable. The vowel is back if the preceding syllable has a back vowel, as in *toy-da* (feast-LOCATIVE) 'at the feast', and it is front if the preceding syllable has a front vowel, as in *üy-de* (house-LOCATIVE) 'in the house'. This harmony is well developed in suffixes and adequately represented in the orthography. The high-suffix vowels are /i/ and /ï/, and the low-suffix vowels are /e/ and /a/, for example, *iyt-ter-imiz-den* (front) 'from our dogs' versus *at-tar-ïmïz-dan* (back) 'from our horses'. Some consonant phonemes, in particular /k/ and /l/ (see above), are clearly affected by the front-versus-back harmony, exhibiting different realizations in front and back environments, as in /kol-da/ [qoł-da] 'in the hand' and /köl-de/ [köl-de] 'in the lake'.

Table 3: Kazakh Cyrillic Alphabet

Cyrillic-based	Value	Cyrillic-based	Value
Аа	a	Өө	ö
Әә	ä	Пп	p
Бб	b	Рр	r
Вв	v	Сс	s
Гг	[g]	Тт	t
Ғғ	γ	Уу	w, uw, üw
Дд	d	Ұұ	u
Ее	e, ye	Үү	ü
Ёё	yo	Фф	f
Жж	ž	Хх	x
Зз	z	hh	h
Ии	iy, ïy	Цц	c
Йй	y	Чч	č
Кк	[k]	Шш	š
Ққ	[q]	Щщ	šč
Лл	l	Ыы	ï
Мм	m	Ii	i
Нн	n	Ээ	e
Ңң	ŋ	Юю	yu, yuw, yüw
Оо	o	Яя	ya

Spoken Kazakh shows roundedness-unroundedness harmony both in low and high vowels, although this is not represented in the orthography. Written Kazakh only shows a, e, и, and ы and y in suffixes; the vowels /ö/, /o/, /ü/, and /u/ are not represented. The strength of the roundedness-unroundedness assimilation decreases with the distance from the first syllable, for example, *üyde* [üydö] 'in the house' and *üyimizde* [üyümüzde] 'in our house'. It is weaker in low vowels, /o/ not being admitted, as in *qolda* [qoł-da], not *[qoł-do] 'in the hand'.

As a rule, a pitch accent falls on the last syllable of words of Turkic origin.

Basic Morphology

Kazakh is an agglutinative language with suffixing morphology. Nouns and adjectives are formed from verbal and nominal stems by means of various derivational suffixes, for example, *aγ-ïm* 'flow' (*aq-* 'to flow') and *tuz-dï* 'salty' (*tuz* 'salt'). Nouns take the plural suffix *-LAr*, possessive suffixes such as *-(I)m* 'my', *-(I)ŋ* 'your', and case suffixes: genitive *-NIŋ*, accusative *-NI*, dative ('to') *-GA*, locative ('in', 'at', on') *-DA*, ablative ('from') *-DAn*. An example is: *žol-das-tar-ïm-nan* (road-DERIVATION-PLURAL-POSSESSIVE. 1P.SG.-ABLATIVE) 'from my comrades' (*žol-das* < 'fellow traveller', 'sharing the same road). Secondary verbal stems are formed from verbal and nominal stems by means of various suffixes. Deverbal suffixes include passive, cooperative, causative, frequentative and other elements, for example, *žaz-ïl-* 'to be written', *žaz-ïs-* 'to write to one another', *žaz-γz-* or *žaz-dïr-* 'to make write' (*žaz-* 'to write'). Verbal negation is expressed with the suffix *-MA*, as in *kör-me-* 'not to see'. Denominal and deverbal suffixes may be combined to form long chains, like *qam-sïz-dan-dïr-ïl-ma-γan-dïq-tan* (care-PRIVATIVE-VERBAL DERIVATION-CAUSATIVE-PASSIVE-NEGATION-PARTICIPLE-DERIVATION-ABLATIVE) 'since (s)he was not insured'.

Finite and infinite verb forms consist of a simple or expanded lexical stem plus aspect/mood/tense suffixes and often person and number suffixes, such as *al-ma-γan e-d-iŋiz-der* (take-NEGATION-PAST PARTICIPLE be-SIMPLE PAST-2P. PL.-PLURAL) 'you (formal address) had not taken [it]'. There is a wide variety of simple and compound aspect/mood/tense forms, as well as numerous converbs and participles. Like other Turkic languages, Kazakh has evidential categories of the type *kelgen eken* 'has obviously arrived'. A number of auxiliary verbs ("postverbs") express modifications of actionality, such as the manner in which an action is carried out, for example, *žanïp ket-* (burn-CONVERB go) 'burn down'.

Kazakh has numerous postpositions, corresponding to ENGLISH prepositions, such as *keš-ke deyin* (evening-DATIVE until) 'until the evening', *stol üst-in-de* (table top-POSSESSIVE 3P. SG.-LOCATIVE) 'on the table'.

Basic Syntax

Kazakh is syntactically very similar to other Turkic languages. It has a head-final constituent order, SOV, for example, *Asan üy sal-d-ï* (Hasan house build-PAST-3P.SG.) 'Hasan built a house'. The order of elements in a nominal phrase is Demonstrative-Numeral-Adjective-Noun, and the head of a relative clause follows the relative, as in *men-iŋ ayt-qan söz-im* (I-GENITIVE speak-PARTICIPLE word-POSSESSIVE.1P.SG.) 'the word I uttered'.

Relative and complement clauses in Kazakh are left branching, using various nonfinite verb forms. Complement clauses are embedded by means of nonfinite forms and case markers.

Contact with Other Languages

Like all Turkic languages of the Islamic cultural sphere, Kazakh displays a fair amount of Arabic and PERSIAN loanwords. Because of close language contacts there are also words of MONGOLIAN origin. The Russian influence upon spoken and written Kazakh has been very strong. The literary language of the Kazakhs living in China has been relatively little influenced by Chinese. Examples of loanwords are:

From Persian: *apta* 'week', *künä* 'crime', *nan* 'bread'
From Arabic: *ïlïm* 'science', *maïna* 'meaning', *waqït* 'time'
From Russian: *stol* 'table', *kerewet* 'bed'

Loanwords are mostly pronounced according to indigenous phonotactic rules, for example, *ras* [ïras] 'true' (from Persian *rast*). This is also valid for loanwords written according to Russian orthography, as in процент [pïratsent] 'percent'.

Common Words

man:	adam	woman:	äyel
water:	su	sun:	kün
three:	üš	fish:	balïq
big:	ülken	long:	uzïn
small:	kiškene	yes:	iyä
no:	žoq	good:	žaqsï
bird:	qus	dog:	iyt
tree:	terek		

Example Sentences

(1) Kel-me-gen kisi-ni küt-pe.
come-NEG-PART. person-ACC wait-NEG
'Do not wait for the person who has not arrived.'

(2) Poyez ket-ip bar-a žat-ïr.
train leave-CONVERB go-CONVERB-lie-PROGR
'The train is about to leave.'

(3) Siz-de mašina bar ma?
you-LOC car existing Q
'Do you have a car?'

Efforts to Preserve, Protect, and Promote the Language

Prior to independence, Russian had a dominant status in public life in Kazakhstan. In 1989, Kazakh was declared the official language of the republic, although in the 1995 constitution Russian was also officially acknowledged. There is now a strong tendency toward public communication in Kazakh.

Select Bibliography

Johanson, L. & É.Á. Csató, eds. 1998. *The Turkic Languages*. London and New York: Routledge.
Kirchner, M. 1998. "Kazakh and Karakalpak." In Johanson and Csató, 318–332.
Krueger, J.R. 1980. *Introduction to Kazakh*. Bloomington: Indiana University.
Menges, K.H. 1959. "Die aralo-kaspische Gruppe." In J. Deny *et al.*, eds. *Philologiae Turcicae Fundamenta* 1, Wiesbaden: Steiner, 434–488.
Mïrzabekova, Q. ed. 1992. *Qazaqša-nemisše sözdik* (Kazakh-German dictionary'). Almatï: Rawan.
Shnitnikov, B.N. 1966. *Kazakh-English Dictionary*. London, The Hague, and Paris: Mouton.

Robert K. Headley

Language Name: Khmer. **Alternate:** *Cambodian.* **Antonym:** *Khmer* (*/khmae/*).

Location: Cambodia, adjacent Thailand, Laos, and Vietnam. There are sizeable Khmer-speaking communities in France, the United States, Canada, and Australia.

Family: Mon-Khmer family of the Austroasiatic phylum.

Related Languages: Within its family, Khmer is a language isolate, not closely related to any other Mon-Khmer languages.

Dialects: Modern Khmer dialects differ mainly in their vowel systems and to a lesser extent in their lexicons. There has been no systematic study of Cambodian dialects, but the following dialects are broadly known: (1) Modern Standard Khmer. This is the generally recognized dialect of Khmer spoken throughout southeastern Cambodia; (2) Northwestern Khmer (composed of several subdialects), spoken in Siem Reap and Oddar Mean Chey Provinces in northwestern Cambodia, and in Surin, Sisaket, and Buriram Provinces in Thailand; (3) Western Khmer, spoken in Battambang Province and possibly parts of Pursat and Koh Kong Provinces in Cambodia and in Trat, Chantaburi, and Prachinburi Provinces in Thailand. Both the Northwestern and Western dialects are characterized by the retention of final /r/; (4) Southeastern Khmer, spoken in Takeo and Kampot Provinces south of Phnom Penh, characterized by the pronunciation of the Standard Khmer clusters /sk/ and /ck/ as /ck/ and /sk/, e.g., Standard /skɑɑ/ 'sugar' > Takeo /ckɑɑ/; (5) Southern Khmer, spoken by the Khmer Kampuchea Krom in the Mekong Delta of southern Vietnam; (6) Phnom Penh Khmer. The spoken Khmer of the capital and adjacent provinces has developed some phonetic innovations, notably the change of /r/ #___ vowel into a voiced pharyngeal spirant with some modifications of the following vowel, which set it apart from the other dialects. For example, the word /pram/ 'five' is pronounced /peam/ in the Phnom Penh dialect.

Number of Speakers: Approximately 8 million.

Origin and History

Khmer is one of the major Mon-Khmer languages; it is second in number of speakers only to Vietnamese. Khmer has been spoken in the area centered on present-day Cambodia since as early as A.D. 611, the date of the earliest known Khmer inscription.

The language has three historical stages: Old Khmer (up to 1431), Middle Khmer (1431 to the 18th century), and Modern Khmer (18th century to the present). Old Khmer was the language used in many of the inscriptions found throughout Cambodia and in neighboring countries.

Neolithic peoples were in what is now Cambodia in the second millennium B.C. Scholars believe they may have been Austroasiatic, with Mon-Khmer people arriving somewhat later, perhaps from southeastern China.

The Mon-Khmer of Southeast Asia were in contact with India from very early times. The Khmers adopted the Indian religions of Hinduism and Buddhism, and their writing system is adapted from an Indian script. Khmer mythology, political thought, and art were influenced by their Indian counterparts.

In the first half of the first millennium A.D., the first Khmer kingdom, Funan, arose on the Mekong Delta in what is now Vietnam. During the sixth century a neighboring kingdom, the Chenla, gained ascendancy and dominated its neighbors. The Khmer Empire was at its "time of greatness" between 802–1431, during the rule of the Kambujadesa Kingdom. (The name "Cambodia" comes from the Hindi variant of that kingdom's name, *Kambuja.*) During this period, the Khmers conquered a vast area of Southeast Asia, including what is now Laos, parts of Thailand, and the Malay Peninsula. Their society had hospitals, an elaborate system of canals and reservoirs, and an extensive network of roadways. At its capital at Angkor in western Cambodia the rulers built magnificent stone and brick temples. The greatest of these is the temple city complex of Angkor Wat, which is the largest religious edifice in the world.

Wars with the Thais led to the abandonment of Angkor, and a new capital was established on the site of the present capital, Phnom Penh, a location that was advantageous for commerce. By the 16th century, European traders were a presence in the area. In the 17th century, Cambodia came to be dominated by Thailand and Vietnam. In the 19th century a period of French colonialism began, during which Cambodia, Laos and Vietnam were joined in the Indochina Union. In 1953 Cambodia achieved independence, but in 1965 it became embroiled in the Vietnam War as well as being racked by civil wars.

In 1970 there was a military coup that deposed Prince Sihanouk. The country was declared a republic and General Lon Nol was installed as leader. Beset by constant and increasing military pressure from the Khmer Rouge, now allied with Prince Sihanouk, the Lon Nol government collapsed in 1975. The Khmer Rouge entered Phnom Penh in April 1975, beginning four years of brutal rule during which the population was subjected to mass oppression and arbitrary executions. The Communist Khmer Rouge attempted to make radical changes in all levels of Cambodian society and it has been estimated that as many as one million Cambodians died as a result of their policies. In response to continued Khmer Rouge provocations, Vietnam invaded Cambodia in December 1978 and a month later Vietnamese armed forces expelled the Khmer Rouge from Phnom Penh and installed Heng Samrin as head of state. In June 1982 a loose coalition of the three major anti-Vietnamese factions, including the Khmer Rouge, formed the Coalition Government of Democratic Kampuchea (CGDK) with the goal of driving the Vietnamese out and restoring Cambodian independence. Over the next nine years, despite military pressure from the CGDK, Vietnam controlled Cambodia. In October 1991, Vietnam signed the Paris Peace Accords and agreed to withdraw its forces from Cambodia. After a period of UN supervision, national elections were held in May 1993. The result was the formation of a coalition government with two prime ministers, one from the Communist Cambodian People's Party and one from the pro-Sihanouk FUNCINPEC party. Cambodia is now officially the Kingdom of Cambodia with Norodom Sihanouk as its king, but the country is effectively controlled by the two prime ministers.

Orthography and Basic Phonology

Khmer is written in a form of the Pallava script from South India that was adapted to write Khmer during the first half of the first millennium A.D. There are several styles of script: the straight style, the slanted style, and the round style, which is used especially for titles. The Khmer alphabet is organized into consonants, dependent vowels, independent vowels, and diacritics. More recently, the independent vowel symbols are disappearing as part of a campaign by the government. They are being replaced by the corresponding dependent vowel symbols.

Khmer Script: Consonants

ក	ខ	គ	ឃ	ង			
k	kh	k	kh	ng			
ច	ឆ	ជ	ឈ	ញ			
c	ch	c	ch	nh			
ដ	ឋ	ឌ	ឍ	ណ			
d	th	d	th	n			
ត	ថ	ទ	ធ	ន			
t	th	t	th	n			
ប	ផ	ព	ភ	ម			
b	ph	p	ph	m			
យ	រ	ល	វ	ស	ហ	ឡ	អ
y	r	l	v	s	h	l	ʔ

There are normally no spaces between words in Khmer text. When a space does occur, it may correspond to an ENGLISH comma.

Table 1: Consonants

	Labial	Dental	Palatal	Velar	Glottal
Stops					
Voiceless	p	t	c	k	ʔ
Voiced	b	d			
Fricatives	v	s			h
Nasals	m	n	ɲ	ŋ	
Lateral		l			
Flap		r			
Glide			y		

The voiceless stops /p t c k/ are unaspirated, and in word-final position they are unreleased. The voiced stops /b d/ are usually preglottalized [ʔb ʔd], respectively.

/v/ is a bilabial fricative in syllable-initial position before vowels; in syllable-final position, it becomes an unrounded high-central vowel [ɯ]. Khmer has, in addition, three fricatives that occur only in borrowed words: /f z ž/.

The only consonants that are permitted in word-final position are /p t c k ʔ; m n ɲ ŋ; h l y v/. There are numerous initial- and medial-consonant clusters.

Table 2: Vowels

	Front	Central	Back
High	i	ɯ	u
Mid-High	ei		
Mid	e	ə	o
Mid-Low	ɛɛ		ɔ
Low		a	ɑ

All Khmer vowels with the exception of /ei/ and /ɛɛ/ may occur either long or short. In addition to the above vowels, Khmer has short diphthongs /ʊə/, /ea/, and /oa/, and long diphthongs /ie/, /wə/, /uə/, /əɯ/, /ae/, /aə/, and /ao/.

The complex vowel system in Modern Khmer results from the historical devoicing of a series of voiced stops /b d j g/, which existed in Old Khmer. Vowels that followed these originally voiced consonants were pronounced with a breathy voice quality, while their counterparts following voiceless consonants were pronounced with a clear voice quality. Some dialects of Khmer retain this breathy-clear distinction. After the voiced stops became voiceless and merged with the voiceless stops, this difference between breathy and clear vowels became phonemic; in modern Khmer, it may be reflected as vowel height differences or as a difference between a simple vowel and a diphthong. For example the Old Khmer *daa* 'duck' is *tie* in Modern Khmer, and Old Khmer *taa* 'grandfather' is *taa* in Modern Khmer.

Basic Morphology

Nouns in Khmer are not normally marked for number or gen-

Table 3: Khmer Basic Pronouns

1st Person:	kɲom	'I', neutral, polite, male or female speaker
	kɲom preah kaʔruʔnaa	'I', layperson addressing Buddhist monk
	ʔaɲ	'I', intimate, male or female speaker
	ʔatmaa	'I', Buddhist monk addressing layperson
	yəəŋ	'we', neutral, polite
2nd Person:	louk	'you', polite, male or female speaker to male
	louk srəy	'you', polite, male or female speaker to female
	neak	'you', less respectful than *louk*
	neak srəy	'you', less respectful than *louk srəy*
	preah dac preah kun	'you', to Buddhist monk
3rd Person:	koat	's/he', respectful
	vie	'it', referring to child, animal, or inanimate object

der. If necessary, the words *srəy* 'female' and *proh* 'male' (for humans) and *ŋii* 'female' and *chmoul* 'male' (for animals) can be used to specify gender.

Plurality may be marked by various postnominal particles or by doubling the adjective, the noun *ckae* 'dog' may be modified as follows: *ckae bəy* 'three dogs', *ckae thom thom* 'large dogs', *ckae khlah* 'some dogs', and *ckae teaŋ ʔah* 'all the dogs'.

The pronominal system of Khmer is highly complex and contains true pronouns, kinship terms, and honorifics. The choice of first and second person pronouns, especially, is made based on the social status of the speaker and the social status of the hearer. There are special pronouns for addressing Buddhist monks and members of the royal family. Table 3 above shows the basic pronouns.

Tense and person are not marked on the verb in Khmer, and may not be marked in the clause. When necessary, tense may be marked by "time" words (e.g., *msəl mɯɲ* 'yesterday'), by preverbal particles (e.g., *baan* 'to have completed an action' or *nɯŋ* 'will'), or by sentence-final particles (e.g., *haəy* 'already'). Person may be marked by the use of pronouns. There is a class of preverbal particles that express various modal and tense meanings and a class of initiating verbs (e.g., *caŋ* 'to want to') that precede main verbs.

Older stages of Khmer had a very rich derivational system that involved prefixes and infixes, and possibly suffixes, as well as compounding. Nearly all of these affixes are no longer productive in Modern Khmer. Some idea of the extent of the historic Khmer derivational system can be seen in some of the derivatives of the root *kaət* 'be born':

k-omn-aət	'birth' (with nominalizing infix *-omn-*)
baŋ-kaət	'to create, cause to be born' (with causative prefix *baN*, where *N* indicates a nasal that assimilates to a following consonant)
k-n-aət	'period of the waxing moon' (with nominalizing infix *-n-*)

Basic Syntax

The basic word order in Khmer is Subject-Verb-Object. Within noun phrases, adjectives, numerals, and demonstratives follow the nouns they modify: *srəy lʔaa nuh* (girl pretty that) 'that pretty girl'. Verbal auxiliaries precede verbs.

Phrases are negated by use of two particles. One of the preverbal negative particles *mun*, *pum*, or *ʔat* is used in conjunction with the phrase final negative particle *tei*: *kɲom mun cɯə tei* (I NEG believe NEG) 'I don't believe'.

There are other negative preverbal particles, but all are compounds containing *mun*, *pum*, or *ʔat*, e.g., *mun dael* 'never'. Questions are marked by interrogative words, e.g., *ʔvəy* 'what', *haet ʔvəy baan cie* 'why?', or by phrase-final interrogative particles, e.g., *tei*, *rɯɯ tei*.

nih cie ʔvəy
this is what
'What is this?'

louk cool cət mhoop khmae rɯɯ tei
you enter heart food khmer Q
'Do you like Cambodian food?'

Contact with Other Languages

Khmer has borrowed extensively from the Indo-Aryan languages SANSKRIT and PALI (and perhaps other Prakrit languages). These borrowings are often words associated with the monarchy and with the Buddhist religion. More recent borrowings are from Chinese, THAI, and FRENCH.

From Pali: *vɯccie* 'field of learning' (< *vijjā*)
From Sanskrit: *srəy* 'woman' (< *satrī*)
From Sanskrit and Pali: *kbaal* 'head' (< *kapāla*)
From Chinese: *kav ʔəy* 'chair' (< *kau yi*)
From French: *paŋsəmaŋ* 'bandage' (< *pansement*), *komplee* 'suit of clothes' (< *complet*)

The Indic elements *kara* 'act; state or quality of ' (Khmer *kaa*), *kamma* 'action, deed, Karma' (Khmer *kam*), *kicca* 'affair, task' (Khmer *kəc*), and *bhava* 'state, condition' (Khmer *phiep*) are common nominalizing elements in Khmer nominal compounds, e.g., *kaa slap* 'death' (< *slap* 'die'), *serəyphiep* 'freedom' (< *serəy* 'be free').

Common Words

man:	proh	long:	vɛɛŋ
woman:	srəy	small:	tooc
water:	tɯk	yes:	baat, caah*
sun:	preah ʔaatɯt	no:	tei
three:	bəy	good:	lʔɑɑ
fish:	trəy	bird:	sat slaap
big:	thom	dog:	ckae
tree:	daəm chəə		

*The words for "yes" are really polite response particles and acknowledge that the hearer has heard what the speaker has said.

Example Sentences

(1) kɲom trəv kaa sac kou chaa krɯəŋ.
I need meat cow stir.fry spice
'I would like spicy beef.'

(2) kɲom nɯŋ coon thnam khlah tɯv louk.
I will give medicine some to you
'I'll give you some medicine.'

(3) nɯv khnoŋ voat mien preah sɑŋ
be.located.in temple there.are monks

ponmaan ʔɑŋ?
how many CLASS
'How many monks are in the temple?'

Efforts to Preserve, Protect, and Promote the Language

Following the disastrous four years of Khmer Rouge rule, during which Khmer lost about one-seventh of its speakers, the language has gradually returned to its former numbers. Little formal teaching of Khmer was provided to children during this time, but there was some effort to continue teaching outside the country. Various international organizations assisted native teachers by providing classroom supplies and by reprinting textbooks. The current government is pursuing the teaching of Khmer and numerous new textbooks have been written. Computers that can handle the Khmer script have been introduced and there are efforts to develop ways to sort Khmer text.

Select Bibliography

Headley, Robert K., Jr., Kylin Chhor, Lam Kheng Lim, Lim Hak Kheang, and Chen Chun. 1977. *Cambodian-English Dictionary*. Washington, DC: The Catholic University Press.

Headley, Robert K., Jr., Rath Chim, and Ok Soeum. 1997. *Modern Cambodian Dictionary*. Kensington, MD: Dunwoody Press.

Henderson, Eugénie J.A. 1952. "The Main Features of Cambodian Pronunciation." In *BSOAS* 14:149–74.

Huffman, Franklin E. 1967. *An Outline of Cambodian Grammar*. Ph.D. Dissertation, Cornell University.

____. 1970a. *Cambodian System of Writing and Beginning Reader*. New Haven and London: Yale University Press.

____. 1970b. *Modern Spoken Cambodian*. New Haven and London: Yale University Press.

____. 1972. *Intermediate Cambodian Reader*. New Haven and London: Yale University Press.

Huffman, Franklin E., and Im Proum. 1977. *Cambodian-English Glossary*. New Haven and London: Yale University Press.

____. 1978. *English-Khmer Dictionary*. New Haven and London: Yale University Press.

Jacob, Judith M. 1968. *Introduction to Cambodian*. London: Oxford University Press.

____. 1974. *A Concise Cambodian-English Dictionary*. London: Oxford University Press.

Jenner, Philip N. 1969. "Affixation in Modern Khmer." Ph.D. dissertation, University of Hawaii.

Jenner, Philip N., and Saveros Pou. 1980–81. *A Lexicon of Khmer Morphology*. Honolulu: University of Hawaii Press.

KIKONGO KITUBA

Salikoko S. Mufwene

Language Name: Kikongo Kituba. **Alternates:** *Kituba, Kikongo* (outside the Bakongo area), *Munu Kutuba, Kikongo ya Leta, Kikongo ya Bula Matadi, Kikongo Kikwango.*

Location: Western part of the Democratic Republic of the Congo, (in Bandundu and Bas Congo regions, south of the Kasaï River), southern part of the Republic of the Congo, and apparently in northern Angola.

Family: Restructured variety of Kikongo Kimanyanga (a member of the Kikongo language cluster, Bantu H) under contact with other Bantu languages.

Related languages: Lexified by Kikongo Kimanyanga; therefore related to other languages of the Kikongo cluster. Influenced by contact of the lexifier with other languages of the region, especially of Bantu B.

Dialects: There are three main dialects: (1) Northern Dialect, spoken in the Republic of the Congo, (2) Eastern Dialect, spoken east of the Kwango River in the Democratic Republic of the Congo, and (3) Western Dialect, spoken west of the Kwango River (in the DRC and in northern Angola). The Eastern Dialect may be subdivided into the Kikwit and Bandundu varieties.

Number of Speakers: 5–8 million, including second-language speakers. Kikongo Kituba is one of the major lingua francas of the region.

Origin and History

Kikongo Kituba apparently developed during the last quarter of the 19th century, after the Berlin Treaty (1885), by which the Congo became a property of King Leopold II of Belgium. Kikongo Kimanyanga, the language of Manyanga, which was already a main precolonial trade center between the coast and the interior, was adopted as the lingua franca of the colony. West African escorts were expected to learn this lingua franca and interpret to Belgian and other European colonists. During 1891–1898, when the railroad was being built between Matadi on the coast and Kinshasa in the interior, labor was brought to the Bakongo region from as far east as Zanzibar and from different parts of the Congo. Usage of Kikongo Kimanyanga by this Bantu-speaking multilingual labor force, especially in the developing urban centers (*centres extra-coutumiers*), and in the evangelization missions led to the language's restructuring into Kikongo Kituba, now identified by some linguists as a Creole. It spread from the Bakongo area to other places thanks to the colonial administration, the evangelization missions, and commercial industry and developed into three main dialects identified above. The Catholic missionaries also developed a different kind of religious lingua franca, called Kikongo Kisantu, which is richer in morphosyntax and may be a koine of traditional languages of the Kikongo cluster. However, this variety was used in the same way as LATIN is today for religious purposes; it was not spoken. Even the missionaries themselves spoke to their parishioners in Kikongo Kituba.

Orthography and Basic Phonology

There are 14 consonants (p, b, t, d, k, g, m, n, f, v, s, z, l, and r) and two semivowels (w and y). The preconsonantal nasals are not syllabic in word-initial position; they are homorganic. The liquids /l/ and /r/ merge into /l/ in the speech of some speakers. This may explain why the PORTUGUESE word *arroz* 'rice' has become *loso* in Kikongo Kituba. *Biro* and *bilo* 'office', from FRENCH *bureau* 'office', are normal, free variants.

Table 1: Consonants

	Labial	Dental/ Alveolar	Palatal	Velar
Stops	p b	t d		k g
Fricatives	f v	s z		
Nasals	m	n		
Liquids		l, r		
Glides	w		y	

Syllables are open, never ending with consonants. The only consonant clusters there are consist of a nasal and obstruent, or of an obstruent and a semivowel, or a combination of the three, as in *nkweso* 'rubber ball'. Nasal + obstruent clusters occur also word initially, as in *nda* 'long, tall', *mvula* 'rain'. Interestingly, *nda,* like some other monosyllabic words, has an HL tone pattern, with the floating H tone borne by the nasal in this case. However, the same tone pattern is also attested in the imperative form of *kudia* HL 'to eat' (infinitive), *dia* HL (imperative), in which the H tone is produced before *d.*

Kikongo Kituba has five vowels: i, e, a, o, and u. (Orthography is phonetic; tones are not indicated.) There is no length distinction. Long vowels are typically disyllabic, having usually resulted from the deletion of a consonant between two short vowels. There are two tones, identified also as accents: H and L. Most Bantuists have claimed that in Kikongo Kituba the high tone/accent usually falls on the penultimate syllable. However, there are several words that diverge from this norm, such as *munoko* LLL 'mouth, opening', *dibulu* LHH 'hole', *nzila* LH "way, road'.

Basic Morphology

The morphosyntax of Kikongo Kituba diverges from the Bantu canon in the following respects. (1) There are fewer active-noun class prefixes; several nouns that would belong to classes lower than 8 according to the Bantu canon have been reassigned to higher classes, on the pattern *Ø-/ba-* (1a/2), or *Ø-/mi-* (3a/4), or *Ø-/ma-* (5a/6). (2) There is no subject-verb concord, nor head-modifier agreement. The latter has been changed to head + connective + modifier construction, as in *mw-ana ya ki-toko* 'beautiful/good child' (literally: 'child' + CON. + 'goodness/beauty') and *nzo ya nda* 'big house/building' (literally: 'house/building' + CON. + 'big size'). Person and number distinctions for the verb are expressed exclusively by the form of the subject personal pronouns. (3) Relative clauses are also invariably introduced by the same connective *ya*. (4) There are no agglutinated object pronomial forms, whereas verbal derivational extensions are preserved. (5) The main tense suffixes are Ø for narrative (if one does not count the final vowel of the verb form), as in *yandi dia* 'he/she ate/eats' and *aka* (HL) for anterior, as in *andi diaka* 'he ate/had eaten'. The future is expressed periphrastically, with the preverbal marker *(a)ta* (LL), as in *yandi (a)ta dia* 'he/she will eat'. Aspect is likewise expressed periphrastically with *me(n)e* (HL) for perfect, as in *yandi me(n)e dia* 'he/she has eaten', and *ke(l)e* (HL) for progressive, as in *yandi ke(l)e dia* 'he/she is eating'.

Basic Syntax

The major constituent order is SOV, as in *yandi nata mono* 'he/she carried me'. When the verb is in applicative form, the dative object precedes the direct object, as in *yandi nat-il-a mono mu-kanda* 'he/she brought me [the] book' or 'he/she carried the book for me'. The marker of negation is *ve* (H) which occurs clause finally, as in *yandi natila mono mukanda ve*. Yes/no questions are marked by the word *nki* (HL), which occurs clause initially, as in *nki yandi nat-il-aka mono mukanda?* 'Did he/she bring me the book?' A WH constituent remains in situ in questions: *yandi nat-aka <u>nani</u>*? 'Who did he/she carry?' or *yandi nat-il-aka <u>nani</u> mu-kanda*. Whom did he/she carry the book to/for?' Kikongo Kituba is head initial.

Contact with Other Languages

One may want to investigate the nature of the contacts between the Bantu populations and the non-Bantus through the kinds of words borrowed in Kikongo Kituba. Some of these words predate the development of *Kituba* and were selected into its lexicon from the more traditional Bantu languages.

From Portuguese: *Ø-mesa/ba-mesa* (LLL) 'table' (< Port. *mesa*), *Ø-sabatu–sampatu/ba-sabatu–sampatu* (LLHL) 'shoe' (< Port. *sapato*)
From French: *Ø-komi/ba-komi* (LLH) 'secretary' (< Fr. *commis*), *Ø-leta* (LH) 'government/administrator' (< Fr. *l'etat* 'the state')
From ENGLISH: *Ø-buku* (HL) 'book'
From ARABIC: *di-sasi/ma-sasi* (LHL) 'bullet' (< Arabic *risas* (?))

Common Words

man:	mu-ntu/ba-ntu (LL)
long/tall:	nda (HL)
woman:	Ø-nkento/ba-nkento (LHL)
small:	fioti (HL)
water:	ma-sa (HL)
yes:	e (HL, with a floating H)
sun:	Ø-ntangu (HL)
no:	ve (H)
three:	tatu (HL)
good:	mbote (HL)
fish:	m-bisi/m-bisi (HL)
bird:	Ø-ndeke/ba-ndeke (LLL)
big:	nene (HL)
dog:	Ø-mbwa/ba-mbwa (LHL)
tree:	Ø-nti/ba-nti (LHL)

Example Sentences

(1) Maria mene tinda mi-kanda na bwala.
Mary finish send CL4-letter CONN village
'Mary has sent letters to the village.'

(2) Maria kwis-aka na nani?
Mary come-PAST CONN who
'Who did Mary come with?'

(3) Maria kele sumb-il-a mono n-kisi.
Mary be buy-APPL-ENDING me CL9-medicine
'Mary is buying me medicine.'

Select Bibliography

Fehderau, Harold. 1966. *The Origin and Development of Kituba*. Ph.D. dissertation, Cornell University.
Mufwene, Salikoko S. 1997. "Kituba." In *Contact Languages: A Wider Perspective*. Sarah G. Thomason, ed. 173–208. Amsterdam: Benjamins.
Ngalasso, Mwatha M. 1991. "Tons ou accents? Analyse des schèmes intonatifs du kikongo véhiculaire parlé dans la région de Bandundu (Zaïre)." In *Etudes Créoles* 14.147–162.
Samarin, William J. 1990. "The Origins of Kituba and Lingala." In *Journal of African Languages and Linguistics* 12.47–77.

Kinyarwanda

Alexandre Kimenyi

Language Name: Kinyarwanda. **Alternates:** *Runyarwanda* (used by some speakers in Uganda because of the influence of other neighboring languages which start with the prefix *ru-*, such as Runyankore, Rukiga, and Rutoro.) Some linguists call the language 'Rwanda', without the prefix, but its speakers resent this.

Location: Rwanda. Also spoken in some parts of eastern Zaire, southern Uganda, Burundi, and western Tanzania.

Family: The Northeast subgroup of the Bantu group of the Niger-Congo language family.

Related Languages: Kinyarwanda is related to a number of languages in Guthrie's (1971) classification of the Northeast zone of Bantu languages: Mashi, Kifurero, Kibembe, and Kilega in southern Kivu (the eastern province of Zaire); Rukiga, Runyankore, Lutoro, and Runyoro in southern Uganda; and Kinyambo in Kihaya in western Tanzania. It is more distantly related to SWAHILI and LUGANDA.

Dialects: There are five dialects of Kinyarwanda. They are, in Rwanda (1) Gitwa, spoken by the Batwa; (2) Kirera, spoken in Mulera; and (3) Kigoyi, spoken in Bugoyi. Dialects of Kinyarwanda are also spoken in Burundi and in western Tanzania; they are (4) Kirundi; and (5) Kiha, respectively.

Number of Speakers: 20 million in Rwanda, Burundi, and Tanzania. In Rwanda, Kinyarwanda has more speakers than any other Bantu language.

Origin and History

Very little is known about the history of the Kinyarwanda language since it was not written before the turn of the 20th century. The first and only dictionary was written in 1984. No reference grammar exists yet.

Orthography and Basic Phonology

The official orthography for Kinyarwanda is based on the LATIN alphabet. However, many features of Kinyarwanda are not represented in writing. These include vowel length and tone. In addition, many consonants are written with combinations of letters. Thus *sh* normally represents the same sounds as in ENGLISH "ship". However, when followed by *y* it represents /ç/, the final sound in GERMAN *ich* or the initial sound of English "huge". And, when followed by *w*, it represents the cluster /škw/, as in English "school".

Table 1: Consonants

		Labial	Alveolar	Alveo-palatal	Velar	Glottal
Stops	Voiceless	p	t	k^y	k	
	Voiced	b	d	g^y	g	
Fricatives	Voiceless	f	s	š, ç		h
	Voiced	ß	z	ž		
Affricates		pf	ts	tš		
Nasals		m	n	ñ	ŋ	
Liquids			r			
Glides		w		y		

Almost all consonants can be labio-velarized (e.g., plain /d/, /pf/; labio-velarized /dgw/, /fk/) or palatalized (e.g., plain /g/, /s/; palatalized /g^y/, /sk^y/). Stops and nasals can undergo both modifications: /bg^ygw/ is the labio-velarized, palatalized equivalent of /b/. In addition, there is a series of aspirated nasals, corresponding to the simple, labio-velarized, and palatalized nasals.

Table 2: Vowels

	Front	Central	Back
High	i		u
Mid	e		o
Low		a	

Vowels can be either short or long. Only short vowels occur in the first or last syllable of a word. Kinyarwanda also has open syllables only. No consonant occurs in syllable-final position.

Kinyarwanda tone rules are straightforward. A word can have at most one high tone (indicated in linguistic treatments but not in the Kinyarwanda orthography with an accent: *á*). Other surface tones are obtained by tone rhythm rules.

Basic Morphology

Kinyarwanda, like other Bantu languages, is an agglutinative language. Words (verbs or nouns) consist of stems and affixes. There are 16 classes of nouns, each with its own characteristic prefix. Classes 1 and 2 are exclusively for human beings. Classes 7/8, 11, 12/13 and 14 happen to be derivational classes also. Any noun from any class can take the prefix of these classes. Other class prefixes also serve for metonymic derivation. A noun then is made of a preprefix (a vowel that echoes the vowel of the prefix), a prefix, and a stem. The stem *-ntu* is used for illustrative purposes.

1. u-mu-ntu	'person'
2. a-ban-ntu	'people'
7. i-ki-ntu	'thing'
8. i-bi-ntu	'things'
11. u-ru-ntu	'a big thing'
12. a-ka-ntu	'a small thing'
13. u-tu-ntu	'small things'
14. u-bu-ntu	'generosity/personhood'
15. u-ku-ntu	'a way'
16. a-ha-ntu	'place'

The verb consists of a stem and a large number of affixes. Verbs always agree in class with their subjects. There are five tenses (present, recent past, distant past, near future, and distant future). Aspectual affixes indicate whether the event being described is still in progress or has not yet taken place, or whether events are consecutive. The verb can also have multiple object pronouns, multiple extensions (suffixes showing intensity, neutrality, etc.), and multiple derivational suffixes indicating causation, reciprocity, etc.

The order of the verb stem and its affixes is illustrated in the following example:

nti-tu-záa-na-ha-bi-mu-ba-som-eesh-er-ez-a
NEG-we-FUT-also-there-it-him-them-read-CAUS-APPLIC-CAUS-IMPERFECT
'we will not even make him read it for them there'

Basic Syntax

The basic word order of Kinyarwanda is Subject-Verb-Object. The verb always agrees with the subject; the class marker of the subject is prefixed to the verb. Modifiers are also prefixed with the class marker of the head noun:

a<u>ba</u>gabo	<u>ba</u>biri	<u>ba</u>gufi	<u>ba</u>fite	ubwanwa	<u>ba</u>vuze
men	two	short	who have	beard	said

ko	<u>ba</u>za	ku-ku-reba
that	come	to-you-see

'Two bearded short men just said that they are coming to see you.'

Contact with Other Languages

Kinyarwanda has borrowed much from other languages because of its colonial history and trade with neighboring countries. Before World War I, Rwanda was a German colony. Loanwords from German were replaced when German colonization ended. One of the survivors is *ishuri* [ishuúri] 'school' (German *Schul*). After the Belgians took over, most of the words having to do with the new political and judicial systems were FRENCH. In commerce many words from many languages such as English, HINDI, PERSIAN, PORTUGUESE, and ARABIC (via Swahili) have entered the language.

From French: *shefu* 'chief', *perezida* 'president', *ubunani* 'New Year' (< Bonne Année), *urumbeti* 'trumpet' (< trompette), *amangazini* 'store' (< magasin)
From Arabic: *umusirimu* 'cultivated', *abarimu* 'teachers' (< malim)
From Portuguese: *ameza* 'table' (< mesa)
From English: *radiyo* 'radio', *imashini* 'machine, engine', *telefoni* 'telephone'

Common Words

man:	umugabo	long:	-ree/-re
woman:	umugore	small:	-to(ya)
water:	amazi	yes:	yego
sun:	izuba	no:	oya
three:	-tatu	good:	-iza
fish:	ifi	bird:	inyoni
big:	-nini	dog:	imbwa
tree:	igiti		

Example Sentences

(1) umu-gore a-ra-ha-a aba-na ibi-ryo.
CL1-woman CL1-PRES-give-IMPERF CL2-child CL8-food
'The woman is giving food to the children.'

(2) w-it-w-a nde.
you-call-PASSIVE-IMPERF who
'What is your name?'

(3) aba-kobwa ba-ra-ryam-ye.
CL2-girl CL2-PRES-lie down-PERFECTIVE
'The girls are in bed.'

Efforts to Preserve, Protect, and Promote the Language

The Rwandan government has issued regulations in an effort to standardize the orthography of Kinyarwanda. Kinyarwanda is the national language and, together with French, one of the two official languages of the country. All newspapers published in Rwanda are written in Kinyarwanda. In addition, there are many books published in Kinyarwanda.

Because of the cyclic massacres of the minority Tutsi group in Rwanda that started in the early 1960s after decolonization, there have been successive waves of refugee movements to the neighboring countries. The refugees have been trying to promote their language and culture in the asylum countries.

Select Bibliography

Kimenyi, Alexandre. 1979. *Studies in Kinyarwanda and Bantu Phonology*. Edmonton, Alberta: Linguistics Research, Inc.

____. 1980. *A Relational Grammar of Kinyarwanda*. Berkeley and Los Angeles: University of California Press.

____. 1989. *Kinyarwanda and Kirundi Names: A Socio-linguistic Analysis of Bantu Onomastics*. New York: The Edwin Mellen Press.

KIRGHIZ

Lars Johanson

Language Name: Kirghiz. **Alternate:** *Kyrgyz*. **Autonym:** *qïrγïz tili, qïrγïzǯa.*

Location: Spoken in the Kyrgyz Republic or Kyrgyzstan (*Qïrγïz Respublikasï, Qïrγïzstan*). Also spoken in parts of Uzbekistan, Tajikistan, China (Xinjiang), Russian Federation, Kazakhstan, etc.

Family: Northwestern (Kipchak) branch of the Turkic family.

Related Languages: KAZAKH, Altay Turkic.

Dialects: The Northern dialects form the base of the standard language. The Southern dialects, mainly spoken in the Ferghana Basin, show Uzbek influence. The variety of Kirghiz spoken in Xinjiang exhibits numerous Chinese loanwords.

Number of Speakers: About 3 million; in Kyrgyzstan over 2.5 million.

Origin and History

It is unclear to what extent today's Kirghiz are successors of the Old Kirghiz, a Turkic-speaking people that settled on Upper Yenisey and established a huge steppe empire (840–920). The exodus of Old Kirghiz groups into West Turkestan and the Tienshan region was caused by the Mongol expansion in the 13th century. In the following centuries, the tribes referred to as Kirghiz were gradually pushed back by the Mongolian Oyrats and Dzungars. After the breakdown of the Dzungar Empire in 1758, the Kirghiz definitively settled in their present territory. In the 18th and 19th centuries they were subordinate to the Uzbek Khanate of Kokand. In 1880 their territory was incorporated into the Russian Empire. Under the Russian and Soviet rule numerous Kirghiz emigrated to China. In 1991 the Kirghiz Republic was proclaimed an independent state.

Orthography and Basic Phonology

Kirghiz was established as a literary language in the Soviet period. The ARABIC script was introduced in 1924, but given up after four years in favor of a Roman-based alphabet. In 1941, a variant of the Cyrillic alphabet was adopted. In the post-Soviet era a new Roman-based alphabet has been created, but has not yet replaced the Cyrillic-based script (see Table 1 below).

Table 2: Vowels

	Front		Back	
	Unrounded	Rounded	Unrounded	Rounded
High	i	ü	ï	u
Mid	e	ö		o
Low			a	

There are also six long-vowel phonemes, resulting from consonant loss in native words and from diphthongs in loanwords: *ā, ē, ō, ȫ, ū* and *ǖ*. Word-final *iy* and *ïy* are occasionally pronounced as long vowels, *ī* and *ï̄*, respectively. Kirghiz has no relics of early Turkic vowel length.

All vowels occur in the first syllable of words, whereas their

Table 1: Kirghiz Cyrillic Alphabet

Cyrillic-based	Value	Cyrillic-based	Value	Cyrillic-based	Value
Аа	a	Лл	l, ł	Фф	f
Бб	b	Мм	m	Хх	x
Вв	v, w	Нн	n	Цц	c
Гг	g, γ	Ңң	ŋ	Чч	č
Дд	d	Оо	o	Шш	š
Ее	e	Өө	ö	Щщ	šč
Ёё	yo	Пп	p	Ъъ	(non-palatalization sign)
Жж	ǰ	Рр	r	Ыы	ï
Зз	z	Сс	s	Ьь	(palatalization sign)
Ии	i	Тт	t	Ээ	e
Йй	y	Уу	u	Юю	yu
Кк	k, q	Үү	ü	Яя	ya

Long vowels are represented by digraphs, e.g., *oo* for *ō*.

number in the following syllables is reduced. The short *e* is somewhat higher in first syllables than in others. Initial *ö* and *o* tend to be pronounced with a prothetic bilabial glide. Unstressed high vowels are frequently reduced.

Table 3: Consonants

	Voice	Labial	Dental-Alveolar	Alveo-palatal	Velar
Stops	-	p	t		k
	+	b	d		g
Fricatives	-	(f)	s	š	(x)
	+	(v)	z	(ž)	ɣ
Affricates	-		č		
	+		ǰ		
Nasals	+	m	n		ŋ
Liquids	+		l, r		
Glides	+			y	

The consonants in parentheses are found in loanwords. The phonemes /g/, /k/ and /l/ have clearly discernible front and back variants, not distinguished in the orthography. Thus /g/ occurs as a fronted-stop [g] in front environments (next to front vowels), and as a back-velar (uvular) fricative [ɣ] in back environments (next to back vowels). The phoneme /k/ occurs as a mid-velar stop [k] in front environments, and as a back-velar (uvular) stop [q] in back environments. The phoneme /l/ occurs as [l] in front environments, and as a backed variant [ɫ] in back environments. A nonphonemic glottal stop ['] occurs before initial vowels. Voiceless stops are mostly aspirated. Voiced stops tend toward fricative pronunciation between vowels, e.g., [b] > [β], [d] > [ð].

Devoicing of word-final and suffix-initial consonants after voiceless consonants is reflected in the orthography, e.g., китеп *kitep* 'book', КYТТY *küttü* 'waited'. Suffix-initial *l* and *n* are assimilated to *t* after voiceless consonants, and mostly to *d* after voiced consonants, e.g., *at-tar* 'horses', *kün-dör* 'days'; cf. *alma-lar* 'apples'. Certain bisyllabic stems lose the high vowel of their final syllable when a suffix with an initial vowel is added, e.g., *erin* 'lip' vs. *erd-im* 'my lip'. In front of suffix-initial vowels, stem-final *k, q* and *p* become *g, ɣ* and *b*, respectively, e.g., *baɣ ïm* 'my garden' vs. *baq* 'garden', *čeg-i* 'its boundary' vs. *ček* 'boundary', *tob-um* 'my ball' vs. *top* 'ball'.

Kirghiz suffixes display both front vs. back harmony and rounded vs. unrounded harmony. The high-suffix vowels are *i, ü, ï, u*; the low-suffix vowels are *e, ö, a, o*. The vowel of the suffix depends on the vowel of the preceding stem syllable, e.g., *ǰol-dor* 'roads', *köl-dör* 'lakes', *üy-lör-übüz-dö* (house-PLURAL-POSS.1p-LOC) 'in our houses', *ǰer-ler-ibiz-de* (place-PLURAL-POSS.1p-LOC) 'in our places'. There are several exceptions from the rounded vs. unrounded harmony. For instance, *u* in stem syllables is not followed by *o*, e.g., *qum-da* 'in the sand', and certain long-suffix vowels only have rounded variants.

The optimal Kirghiz syllable is of the form CVC; CV and VC syllables also exist: *iš-ter* 'works', *ayt-pa* 'don't speak'.

Basic Morphology

Kirghiz is an agglutinative language with exclusively suffixing morphology. Nouns and adjectives are formed from verbal and nominal stems by means of various derivational suffixes, e.g., *ǰaz-ū* 'writing' (*ǰaz-* 'write'), *tuz-dū* 'salty' (*tuz* 'salt'). Nouns take the plural suffix *-LAr*, possessive suffixes such as *-(I)m* 'my', *-(I)ŋ* 'your', and case suffixes: genitive *-NIn*, accusative *-NI*, dative ('to') *-GA*, locative ('in', 'at', 'on') *-DA*, ablative ('from') *-DAn*. (Capital letters indicate variation.) Example: *ǰol-doš-tor-um-dan* [road-DERIVATION-PLURAL-POSSESSIVE 1 P. SG.ABLATIVE] 'from my friends' (*ǰol-doš* < 'fellow traveler', 'sharing the same road').

Secondary verbal stems are formed from verbal and nominal stems by means of various suffixes. Deverbal suffixes include passive, cooperative, causative, frequentative and other elements, e.g., *ǰaz-ïl-* 'to be written', *ǰaz-dïr-* 'to make write' (*ǰaz-* 'to write'). The reciprocal form in *-(I)š* is also used for the third person plural, e.g., *ǰaz-ïš-at* 'they write'. Verbal negation is expressed with the suffix *-BA*, e.g., *öl-bö-* 'not to die'.

Finite and infinite verb forms consist of a simple or expanded lexical stem plus aspect/mood/tense suffixes and often person and number suffixes, e.g., *iš-te-š-sin* [work-DERIVATION-RECIPROCAL/PLURAL-OPTATIVE] 'may they work'. There are numerous simple and compound aspect/mood/tense forms, as well as converbs and participles. Like other Turkic languages, Kirghiz has evidential categories of the type *bar-ɣan eken* (go-PAST EVIDENTIAL) 'has obviously gone'. A number of auxiliary verbs ('postverbs') express modifications of actionality, i.e., the manner in which an action is carried out, e.g., *ičip ket-* [drink-CONVERB go] 'to drink up'. Kirghiz has numerous postpositions, corresponding to ENGLISH prepositions, e.g., *kečke čeyin* [evening-DATIVE until] 'until the evening'.

Basic Syntax

Kirghiz is syntactically very similar to other Turkic languages. It has a head-final constituent order and is SOV, e.g., *Ata-ŋ saɣa qat ǰaz-d-ï* (father-POSS.2sg to.you letter write-PAST-3sg) 'Your father has written you a letter'. The order of elements in a nominal phrase is Demonstrative-Numeral-Adjective-Noun, e.g., *bul üč čoŋ üy* 'these three big houses'. The head of a relative clause follows the relative, e.g., *ešik-ti ač-qan qïz* [door-ACCUSATIVE open-PARTICIPLE girl] 'the girl who opened the door'.

Nominal and some verbal predicates are negated with *emes* '(is) not', e.g., *doktor emes-min* (doctor not-1sg) 'I am not a doctor'.

Contact with Other Languages

Older contacts with MONGOLIAN are reflected in a certain amount of loanwords. Numerous lexical elements have been copied from Arabic and PERSIAN via Chaghatay and UZBEK, particularly into Southern dialects. Kirghiz has been strongly influenced by Kazakh. The RUSSIAN impact on the vocabulary began at the end of the 19th century. Examples of loanwords include:

From Persian: *apta* 'week', *baqča* 'garden', *gül* 'flower', *šār* 'city'

From Arabic: *ǰōp* 'answer', *pikir* 'thought', *qabar* 'message'
From Russian: *stakan* 'glass', *vrač* 'doctor, physician'
From Mongolian: *belen* 'ready', *dülöy* 'deaf', *qara-* 'to look'

Common Words

man:	erkek	woman:	ayal
water:	sū	sun:	kün
three:	üč	fish:	balïq
big:	čoŋ	long:	uzun
small:	kičine	yes:	ōba
no:	ǰoq	good:	ǰaqšï
bird:	quš	dog:	it
tree:	ǰïɣač		

Example Sentences

(1) Dükön-dön nan sat-ïp al-d-ïm.
shop-ABLATIVE bread sell-CONVERB take-PAST-1P.SG.
'I bought bread in the shop.'

(2) Erteŋ tō-ɣo qar ǰa-y-t,
Tomorrow mountain-DAT. snow fall -PRESENT-3P.SG.

ĵe borōn bol-o-t.
or storm become-PRESENT-3P.SG.
'Tomorrow it will snow or storm in the mountains.'

(3) Kečik-kendig-im-e kečirim
be late-VERBAL NOUN- POSS.-1P.SG.-DAT. pardon

sura-y-m.
ask-PRESENT-1P.SG.
'I beg your pardon for being late.'

(4) Bar-ba-ɣan ĵer-i
go-NEGATION-PARTICIPLE place-POSSESSIVE-3P.SG.

qal-ba-d-ï.
remain-NEGATION-PAST-3P.SG.
'There is no place left where he hasn't gone.'

Efforts to Preserve, Protect, and Promote the Language

Kirghiz was proclaimed the official language of Kyrgyzstan in 1989. Since then it has consolidated its position, acquiring more social functions. Efforts are made to reduce the huge amount of Russian terms by creating neologisms. In 1996 the constitution was amended to make Russian an official language, along with Kirghiz, in territories and workplaces where Russian-speaking citizens predominate.

Select Bibliography

Hebert, R.J. and N. Poppe, 1963. *Kirghiz Manual*. The Hague: Mouton.
Imart, G. 1981. *Le kirghiz*. 1–2. Aix-en-Provence: Publications de l'Université de Provence.
Johanson, L. and É.Á. Csató (eds.), 1998. *The Turkic Languages*. London and New York: Routledge.
Kirchner, M., 1998. "Kirghiz." In *The Turkic Languages*, pp. 344–356. Johanson, L. and É.Á. Csató (eds.). London and New York: Routledge.
Wurm, S. 1949. "The (Kara-)Kirghiz Language." In *Bulletin of the School of Oriental Studies 13*, 97–120.

Konkani

Rocky V. Miranda

Language Name: Konkani. Referred to as *Canarim* by the Portuguese in 16th and 17th century literature.

Location: Spoken in Goa, a state in Western India on the Malabar coast; and in parts of the neighboring states of Maharashtra, Karnataka, and Kerala, where Konkani speakers from Goa have migrated during the last five centuries.

Family: Southwest group of the Indo-Aryan subbranch of the Indo-Iranian branch of the Indo-European language family.

Related Languages: Konkani is related to the other Indo-Aryan languages, the closest relatives being MARATHI and GUJARATI, which are also in the Southwest group.

Dialects: Numerous regional and social dialects. Major dialects are (1) Goa Hindu (the standard), (2) Goa Christian, (3) North Kanara Kindu, (4) South Kanara Hindu, and (5) South Kanara Christian.

Number of Speakers: 1.5 million

Origin and History

The name of the language comes from the area Konkan, which includes Goa and the neighboring coastal areas, where it is spoken. It is not known who introduced this name. When the Portuguese came to India in the 16th century, the script used for Konkani was the KANNADA or Canarese script. The Portuguese called the language *Canarim*, perhaps mistaking Konkani for Kannada. They must have realized their mistake soon afterwards, but they continued to use the term *Canarim* for Konkani.

The earliest Konkani writings are from the 16th and 17th centuries. The Portuguese missionaries who came to Goa in the wake of the Portuguese conquest in 1510 prepared several Konkani grammars and dictionaries, and they also wrote various religious treatises in Konkani. Some indigenous Old Konkani literature such as stories from the Ramayana and the Mahabharata, transcribed in the LATIN script by the Portuguese, have also been preserved.

Almost all Konkani settlements outside Goa are known to have resulted from migrations from the 16th century onwards. Following their conquest of parts of Goa, the Portuguese spread Christianity among the Hindus with considerable coercion. Hindu temples were demolished and the people unwilling to accept Christianity were threatened with expulsion. This resulted in the first great wave of migration. Among the Hindus that were converted to Christianity, many observed various native customs that were perceived as pagan customs by the Portuguese. These Christians were persecuted by the Inquisition. There was a mass migration of Christians in the 17th and 18th centuries that appears to be due mainly to the Inquisition. During the 19th and 20th centuries, a large number of Konkanis from Goa as well as other areas, who went to the city of Bombay seeking employment, have settled there.

Orthography and Basic Phonology

Different Konkani dialects use different scripts. For example, the Goa Christian dialect uses the Roman script, the North Kanara Hindu and the Goa Hindu dialects use the Nagari script, and the South Kanara Hindu and South Kanara Christian dialects use the Kannada script. However, the Nagari script, which is used for the SANSKRIT, HINDI, and Marathi languages as well as the above-mentioned dialects of Konkani, has now been adopted as the official script. This reflects the fact that Goa Hindu has emerged as the standard dialect.

In the Nagari script, as in other Indic scripts, CV sequences are represented by a primary consonant character and a diacritic for the vowel that may appear before, after, above, or below the consonant character. There is no diacritic for the vowel [ə]. Therefore, a consonant character stands for the consonant followed by [ə] in some environments, such as the word-initial position, and for the consonant alone in other environ-

Characters of the Nagari Alphabet

अ		आ	इ	ई	उ	ऊ	ए	ऐ	ओ	औ
a [ə]		ā	i	ī	u	ū	e	ai	o	au
क	ख	ग	घ							
k	kh	g	gh							
च	छ	ज	झ							
č	čh	ǰ	ǰh							
ट	ठ	ड	ढ	ण						
ṭ	ṭh	ḍ	ḍh	ṇ						
त	थ	द	ध	न						
t	th	d	dh	n						
प	फ	ब	भ	म						
p	ph	b	bh	m						
य	र	ल	व	श	स	ह	ळ			
y	r	l	w	š	s	h	ḷ			

Table 1: Consonants

	Voicing/ Aspiration	Labial	Dental	Alveolar	Palatal	Retroflex	Velar	Glottal
Stops	-voi, -asp	p p^y	t t^y	c	č	ṭ ṭ^y	k k^y	
	-voi, +asp	p^h	t^h	c^h	č^h		k^h	
	+voi, -asp	b b^y	d d^y	j	ǰ	ḍ ḍ^y	g g^y	
	+voi, +asp	b^h	d^h	j^h	ǰ^h		g^h	
Fricatives				s	š			h h^y
Nasals	-asp	m m^y		n n^y		ṇ ṇ^y		
	+asp	m^h		n^h				
Flaps				r r^y				
Laterals	-asp			l l^y		ḷ ḷ^y		
	+asp			l^h				
Glides	-asp	w w^y			y			
	+asp	w^h			y^h			

ments, such as the word-final position. There are independent characters for the vowels, but these are used only when the vowel does not follow a consonant. In the case of consonant clusters, usually the preceding consonants are represented by partially written characters and the final consonant is represented by a full character. However, there are many exceptions to this general rule. There are special characters for many consonant clusters.

Like other languages of India, Konkani has a four-way contrast among voiceless unaspirated, voiceless aspirated, voiced unaspirated, and voiced aspirated stops. The alveolar and palatal sounds listed as stops are phonetically affricates.

Dental and alveolar consonants become retroflex when they immediately follow retroflex consonants.

Table 2: Vowels

	Front	Back	
		Unrounded	Rounded
High	i		u
Mid High	e	ə	o
Mid Low	ɛ	ʌ	ɔ
Low		a	

All nine of the oral vowels in Konkani have nasal equivalents /ã/, etc. The difference between an oral and a nasal vowel can signal the difference between singular and plural for nouns: *kir-a* 'parrot', *kir-ã* 'parrots'.

Basic Morphology

Konkani nouns are divided into three classes and they are inflected for gender, case, and number. There are three genders: masculine, feminine, and neuter. There are five cases: absolute, dative/accusative, instrumental/ergative, genitive, superessive, and inessive. Case marking is indicated by suffixes on pronouns and by postclitics on nouns. Nouns have two stems, the direct stem, which may be singular (*pak-ɛ̃* 'roof') or plural (*pak-in* 'roofs'), and the oblique stem (*pak-^{y}a* 'roof', *pak-^{y}ã* 'roofs'). As illustrated below, the direct forms serve as the absolute case forms with no additional endings. Other case endings are added to the oblique stem.

	'you'		'roof' (neuter)	
	Singular	Plural	Singular	Plural
Absolute	tũ	tum-i	pak-ɛ̃	pak-i
Dat/Acc	tu-ka	tum-kã	pak-^{y}a-k	pak-^{y}ã-k
Inst/Erg	tu-wɛ̃	tum-in	pak-^{y}a-n	pak-^{y}ã-nin
Genitive	tu-jɔ	tum-cɔ	pak-^{y}a-cɔ	pak-^{y}ã-cɔ
Superess	tu-jer	tum-čer	pak-^{y}a-r	pak-^{y}ã-čer
Inessive			pak-^{y}ã-t	pak-^{y}ã-nin

Adjectives agree with the nouns they modify in gender, number, and case:

w^{h}əḍḷ-ɛ̃ pak-ɛ̃
big-DIR roof-DIR
'big roof '

w^{h}əḍḷ-^{y}a pak-^{y}a-r
big-OBL roof-OBL-SUPERESSIVE
'on the big roof '

Konkani verbs are inflected for aspect and tense, person, number, and gender. There are two bases for each verb: perfect, indicated by a suffix *-l*, and imperfect, indicated by a suffix *-t*. This base can be followed by a tense marker and an agreement marker.

apəy-t-a
call-IMPERFECT-3SG.PRES 'he/she called'

apəy-t-əl-ɛ
call-IMPERFECT-FUTURE-3PL.MASC 'he will call'

apəy-l-ĭ	
call-PERFECT-3SG.FEM	'she is called'

apəy-l-l-ĭ	
call-PERFECT-PAST.PERFECT-3PL.NEUT	'they had been called'

Konkani verb agreement is partly ergative. Transitive verbs in perfect forms (those with an *-l* marker) agree with their objects in number and gender; the subject of such a sentence appears in the ergative case.

t-i-ṇɛ	ãb-ɔ	mag-l-ɔ
that-F.SG-ERG	mango-M.SG.ABS	request-PERFECTIVE-M.SG

'She asked for the mango.'

When these same verbs appear in imperfect forms, they agree with their subjects in person, number, and gender.

t-i	ãb-ɔ
that-F.SG.ABS	mango-M.SG.ABS

mag-t-al-i
request-IMPERFECTIVE-PAST-3SG.FEM
'She was asking for the mango.'

The subjects of intransitive verbs occur in the nominative case, and the verbs agree with their subjects in person, number, and gender.

t-i	has-l-i
that-F.SG.ABS	laugh-PERFECTIVE-3SG.FEM

'She laughed.'

t-i	has-t-al-i
that-F.SG.ABS	laugh-IMPERFECTIVE-PAST-3SG.FEM

'She was laughing.'

Basic Syntax

As is evident from the examples above, Konkani syntax is strongly SOV. In addition to the verb-final clause order, auxiliary verbs follow main verbs, and adjectives and other modifiers follow nouns.

[tũ	wac-t-a	t-ɛ̃]	pustɔk
[you:SG	read-IMPERF.PRES-3SG	that-NEUT/SG]	book

magir	haḍ
later	bring

'Bring the book you are reading later.'

In addition to the clitic case suffixes described above under Basic Morphology, Konkani also has some postpositions.

pak-^{y}a	bhitɔr	
roof-OBL.SG	inside	'inside the roof'

pak-yã	səkər	
roof-OBL.PL	below	'below the roofs'

Konkani sentences are negated by a special negative auxiliary verb that follows the main verb.

t-ɔ	apəy-t-a
that-M.SG	call-IMPERFECTIVE.PRES-3SG

'He calls.'

t-ɔ	apəy-n-a
that-M.SG	call-NEG.PRES-3SG

'He doesn't call.'

Contact with Other Languages

Being on the Indo-Aryan/Dravidian border, Konkani has been profoundly influenced by Kannada. Goa, the Konkani homeland, was under Kannada rule for several centuries before the arrival of the Portuguese. Consequently, Old Konkani documents from the 16th and 17th centuries already show considerable Kannada influence in grammar as well as vocabulary.

In addition to its native Indo-Aryan vocabulary, Konkani has numerous loanwords from Sanskrit, Perso-Arabic, Kannada, and PORTUGUESE. The Portuguese loans in the Goa Christian dialects and the Kannada loans in the Hindu dialects of Karnataka are conspicuous. The dialects in South Kanara and Kerala have Tulu and Malayalam loans as well.

From Sanskrit: *əkšər* 'letter', *sə̃k^{hy}a* 'number', *yog^{y}ə* 'fit', *sur^{y}ə* 'sun', *udək* 'water'
From Persian: *badša* 'king', *šar* 'city', *dər^{y}a* 'sea'
From Arabic (via Persian): *hukum* 'order', *sʌwal* 'question', *jʌwab* 'reply', *nəšib* 'fate'
From Kannada: *bərəy* 'write', *niṭ* 'straight', *daṭ* 'thick'
From Portuguese: *wɔr* 'hour', *wɔkl* 'reading glasses', *mɛj* 'table', *jʌnɛl* 'window', *kʌdɛl* 'chair'

Common Words

man:	mənis	long:	lãb
woman:	bayl	small:	l^{h}an
water:	udək	yes:	w^{h}əy
sun:	sur^{y}ə	no:	n^{h}əy
three:	tin	good:	bərɛ
fish:	masli	bird:	səwnɛ
big:	w^{h}əḍ	dog:	sunɛ
tree:	ruk		

Example Sentences

(1) h-ɔ	ǰɔni-ɔ-ø	dhakṭ-ɔ	čɛḍ-ɔ.
this-M/SG	John-GEN-(M.SG)	little-M.SG	boy-M.SG

'This is John's younger son.'

(2) t-i	hanga	kəš-i	paw-l-i?
that-F.SG	here	how-F.SG	reach-PERFECTIVE-F.SG

'How did she get here?'

(3) t-i-ṇɛ	ãb-ɔ	khɛ-l-ɔ.
that-F.SG-ERG	mango-M.SG	eat-PERFECTIVE-M.SG

'She ate the mango.'

Efforts to Preserve, Protect, and Promote the Language

In Goa, Portuguese and Marathi were once the dominant languages, and Konkani had no official status. In recent years, there has been a dramatic improvement in the status of Konkani. It is taught in the educational institutions of Goa and a chair has been established for Konkani at Goa University. In 1976, Konkani was recognized by the Sahitya Akademi as one of India's literary languages. It became the official language of the state in 1987 and was included in the Eighth Schedule of the Indian Constitution as one of India's national languages in 1992. Marathi is still an influential language in Goa, but, after the departure of the Portuguese, the Portuguese language declined rapidly. Goa was ceded to India in 1962. The place of Portuguese has been taken by English.

Konkani speakers, particularly those outside Goa, have to use other languages in most situations. They are mostly multilingual (64.8 percent as calculated from data reported in Census of India, 1981b: 150), since they must learn other languages used in educational and other official spheres in the various regions: Kannada and Malayalam in the southern states, Marathi in Maharashtra and, to a considerable extent, in Goa; English in all the areas. Konkani speakers also need to communicate with their non-Konkani neighbors in a different language where the majority of the people speak other languages: for example, Marathi or Bazaar Hindi in metropolitan Bombay, Kannada or Tulu in the coastal districts of Karnataka, and MALAYALAM in Kerala.

Select Bibliography

Almeida, Mathew. 1985. *A Description of Konkani*. Ph.D. dissertation, Georgetown University. Ann Arbor, MI: University Microfilms International.

Census of India, 1981a. Series 1, Paper 1 of 1987. *Households and Household Population by Language Mainly Spoken in the Household*. Delhi: Office of the Registrar General.

Census of India, 1981b. Series 1, Part IVB(ii). *Population by Bilingualism*. Delhi: Office of the Registrar General.

Census of India, 1981c. *A Portrait of Population: Goa, Daman, & Diu*. Directorate of Census Operations, Goa, Daman, & Diu.

Katre, S. M. 1966. *The Formation of Konkani*. 1942. Poona: Deccan College.

_____. 1968. *Indo-Aryan Family: Southern Group*. Vol. VII of *Linguistic Survey of India*. George A Grierson, ed. 1905. Delhi: Motilal Banarsidass. 7:163-94.

Maffei, A.F.X. 1882. *A Konkani Grammar*. Mangalore, India: Basel Services.

_____. 1883. *An English-Konkani and Konkani-English Dictionary*. New Delhi, India: Asian Educational Services.

Miranda, Rocky. 1994. "Konkani." In *A Handbook of Indian Languages*. P.P. Giridhar and Rekha Sharma, eds. Mysore, India: Central Institute of Indian Languages.

Pereira, José. 1971. *Konkani, a Language*. Dharwar, India: Karnatak University.

Rangel, V.J.J. 1933. *Grámatica da lingua Concani*. Bastora, Goa, India: Tipografia Rangel.

KOREAN

Young-mee Yu Cho

Language Name: Korean. **Autonym:** *hankuko.*

Location: The Korean Peninsula. Also northeast China, the former Soviet Union, Japan, and North America.

Family: Altaic; alternatively, some scholars consider Korean to be a language isolate.

Related Languages: Manchu, MONGOLIAN; more distantly, JAPANESE.

Dialects: The seven major dialect areas generally correspond to provincial boundaries: (1) Hamgyŏng, (2) P'yŏngan (the standard dialect of North Korea), (3) Central (the standard dialect of South Korea), (4) Ch'ungch'ŏng, (5) Kyŏngsang, (6) Chŏlla, and (7) Cheju.

Number of Speakers: 65–73 million. Of these, approximately 42 million live in South Korea, 23 million in North Korea, and 5 million in about 100 countries outside the Korean Peninsula.

Origin and History

Ancestors of the Korean people are believed to have migrated to the general area of Manchuria and the Korean Peninsula around 4,000 B.C. Earlier occupants, known as the Paleosiberians, were either driven northward or assimilated by the new arrivals.

The Korean language has been divided into five stages, as established by Ki-Moon Lee. Prehistoric Korean was the ancestral language spoken from about 4,000 B.C. until the beginning of the Christian Era.

Between the first century B.C. and first century A.D., small tribal states became established, and the language entered a second stage called Old Korean, during which it seems to have divided into two dialects: Puyŏ, spoken in the states of Manchuria and the northern peninsula; and Han, spoken in three southern states of the peninsula. Around the 4th century A.D. the tribal states were consolidated into three kingdoms: Puyŏ-speaking Kokuryŏ of the north, Han-speaking Silla in the southeast, and Paekche in the southwest. It is uncertain which dialect was used in Paekche because this southern kingdom was ruled by Puyŏ-speaking northerners.

In the seventh century the Korean peninsula was unified under the Silla Kingdom and Han became the dominant form of Old Korean. For the next 300 years the Han speech of Kyŏngju, the Silla capital, served as the standard dialect of the language. Chinese vocabulary began to enter the language during the Old Korean stage; in the middle of the eighth century place names were sinicized.

In 936 the Silla dynasty was succeeded by the Koryŏ dynasty, which continued to favor the Han dialect over Puyŏ. The Koryŏ capital shifted to the city of Kaegyŏng in the central part of the peninsula, whose variety of Han became the standard dialect of the Middle Korean period. The use of the Chinese system of writing brought an increase in Chinese words to the lexicon.

The Yi (Chosŏn) dynasty succeeded Koryŏ in 1392. The spoken language of Seoul, the new capital, became the standard form of Korean. In 1443, King Sejong authorized an alphabetic script called *Hangŭl* for writing Korean. Although Chinese characters would continue to be used as the main form of writing Korean until the 20th century, records written in the *Hangŭl* orthography during this period provide the first substantial documentation of spoken Korean.

In the 17th century the language evolved to the stage called Modern Korean, with considerable phonological differences from Middle Korean.

The current stage in the development of the language, Contemporary Korean, began in the 20th century. Contemporary Korean is relatively homogeneous, even though there are seven major dialects.

The overseas Korean-speaking population is largely a result of emigration that began in the late 19th century. During the Japanese occupation, emigration to Japan, China, and the former Soviet Union proceeded until liberation in 1945. Koreans in the United States are currently the fastest growing segment of the overseas Korean population.

Orthography and Basic Phonology

Beginning in the Old Korean period and extending to the 20th century, Chinese characters were used to write Korean. This system had no intimate relationship to spoken Korean because Korean is essentially unrelated to Chinese either genetically or typologically, and it proved inadequate to represent the spoken language.

The orthography called *Hangŭl* was indigenously created in the Middle Korean period in response to the need for a writing system that reflected the nature of the spoken language. Devised on phonological principles, *Hangŭl* consists of 40 symbols: 10 vowels, 11 compounds of semivowel plus vowel, 14 consonants, and 5 double consonants. The *Hangŭl* alphabet is illustrated in Table 3.

There are several ways of romanizing *Hangŭl*; the McCune-

Table 1: Consonants

		Bilabial	Dental	Palatal	Velar	Glottal
Stops	Lax	p/b	t/d	ch/j	k/g	
	Aspirated	p'	t'	ch'	k'	
	Tense	pp	tt	tch	kk	
Fricatives	Lax		s			h
	Tense		ss			
Nasals		m	n		ng	
Liquid			l			
Glides		w		y		

Reischauer romanization is the most widely used and is followed here.

Lax stops are voiceless except when they occur between vowels and voiced consonants; for example, the *k* of *aki* 'baby' is pronounced [g]: [agi]. In word-final position or before other stops and fricatives, all stops of each series are pronounced identically, without releasing the articulators before the next sound: *p/b*, *p'*, and *pp* are pronounced [p]; *t/d*, *t'*, *tt*, *s*, *ss*, *ch/j*, *ch'*, and *tch* are pronounced [t]; and *k/g*, *k'*, and *kk* are pronounced as [k]. *L* is a dental lateral at the end of a word (approximating the ENGLISH "l" at the beginning of a word like "let") and before another "l", and as a flap elsewhere, represented as [r].

One of the most prominent features of Korean phonology is assimilation, in which sounds take on the qualities of neighboring sounds. For example, in nasal assimilation in Korean, a stop consonant is realized as its corresponding nasal consonant when it precedes a nasal of any kind: *kukmul* 'soup' is pronounced [kungmul], *patnunta* 'receive' is pronounced [pannunda].

Table 2: Vowels

	Front		Back	
	Unround	Round	Unround	Round
High	i	wi	ŭ	u
Mid	e	oe	ŏ	o
Low	æ		a	

Basic Morphology

The major classes of words in Korean include noun, verb, adjective, adverb, particle, and interjection. Of these, the verb (which can be subclassified into action verb, stative verb, existential, and copula) shows an elaborate system of agglutinative inflectional suffixes.

There are two case markers potentially carried by noun phrases, namely *-ka/i* 'nominative' and *-(l)ŭl* 'accusative'. In addition, the topic marker *-(n)ŭn* may appear after practically any phrase. In addition to the two case markers, there are additional postposed markers to indicate other relationships: *-eke* and *-e* mark goals, beneficiaries, or directions; *-e* marks location of a stative relation, while *-esŏ* marks location of an activity or a source; and *-(u)lŏ* marks direction, instrument, or means.

Verb stems consist of a root followed by derivational suffixes, such as passive or causative: *anc-hi* 'sit-causative' i.e., 'seat'; *kkakk-i* 'cut-passive' i.e., 'be cut'. To this verb stem, also called the "verb base", is suffixed an ending, which comprises suffixes occurring in up to seven sequence positions, as illustrated in the following pattern:

Stem >	Honorific >	Tense >	Aspect
	Comp1	Comp2	Comp3
			Conjunction
Speech Level >		Mood >	Comp4

The honorific suffix conveys the speaker's social attitude toward the subject of the sentence, while the suffix indicating speech level expresses the degree of the speaker's intended politeness toward the addressee. The Comp suffixes bear various functions; representative examples include Comp1, -ŏ 'continuative'; Comp2, *-ci* 'negative', *-ko* 'gerundive'; Comp3, *ŏya*, *-na*, 'prenominal modifiers'; Comp4, *-ko* 'quotative'.

cap-hi-si-ŏss-kes-ta-ko-yo
hold-PASSIVE-HONORIFIC-PAST-ASPECT-DECLARATIVE-QUOTATIVE-POLITE.SPEECH.LEVEL
'It is said that the honored person must have been captured.'

Roots and stems primarily associated with one word class may, through the use of derivational affixes, occur in other words of the same or different word class. Only suffixes may change the class of word in which the stem appears; derivational prefixes do not. Among the patterns of category-changing derivation, the most common is a variety of verb formation in which the light verb *hata* 'to do' is attached to a noun root of any origin, including Chinese and Western loans as well as native nouns.

The most productive word formation process is the compounding of more than one root or stem. This is particularly common with Sino-Korean words, most of which consist of more than one morpheme. A compound is a complex word consisting of two or more morphemes whose syntactic and semantic relations are of the type modifier-head, as in *pam-pi*

Table 3: The *Hangŭl* Alphabet

ㅂ	p,b	ㅉ	tch	ㅟ	wi	ㅕ	yŏ
ㅍ	p'	ㄱ	k,g	ㅔ	e	ㅝ	wŏ
ㅃ	pp	ㅋ	k'	ㅖ	ye	ㅏ	a
ㄷ	t,d	ㄲ	kk	ㅞ	we	ㅑ	ya
ㅌ	t'	ㅁ	m	ㅚ	oe	ㅘ	wa
ㄸ	tt	ㄴ	n	ㅐ	ae	ㅜ	u
ㅅ	s	ㅇ	-ng	ㅒ	yae	ㅠ	yu
ㅆ	ss	ㄹ	l,r	ㅙ	wae	ㅗ	o
ㅈ	ch,j	ㅎ	h	ㅡ	ŭ	ㅛ	yo
ㅊ	ch'	ㅣ	i	ㅓ	ŏ	ㅢ	ŭi

'night rain'; coordinate, as in *pam-nac* 'day and night'; or noun-predicate, as in *ton pŏli* 'money-making'.

Basic Syntax

The basic order of major constituents of the clause in Korean is Subject-Object-Verb. However, most of the constituents, other than the verb in a clause, can be permuted rather freely for stylistic purposes without affecting the grammatical acceptability of the result.

Korean possesses several hundred independent and affixal particles that express such syntactic functions as case relation, subordination and coordination, relativization, verbal complementation, passivization, causativation, honorification, tense, aspect, mood, and sentence type.

In accordance with the usual situation in languages with SOV basic constituent order, particles in the noun phrase are all postpositional, following the head noun of the phrase. Modifiers such as determiners, adverbs, possessive constructions, relative clauses, and verbal complement clauses must precede the modified elements.

Korean has a highly developed system of honorifics, in which the speaker expresses the relative social status between himself and a person denoted in the sentence through the use of an honorific particle in the verb phrase. There are subject and nonsubject honorifics. Subject honorifics also require the occurrence of an agreeing honorific suffix in the verb ending.

There are two types of negation, a short form and a long form. The short form construction involves the occurrence of a negative adverb (*an* 'not', or *mos* 'cannot') immediately before a verbal stem. In the long form, the verb being negated occurs with the suffix as the complement of the negative verb *anh-ta*. With the imperative and propositive ('let's ...') moods, the negative verb *malda* 'stop doing' is used. In addition, there is lexical negation, which involves inherently negative verbs; e.g., *ŏpsta* 'not exist', *anida* 'negative copula', and *molŭda* 'not know'.

Korean is a discourse-oriented language, in that contextually understood elements, regardless of their grammatical functions, are left unexpressed, or introduced by a topic marker, and need not be initial in the clause. The topic marker *(n)ŭn*, which may mark almost any element, has two main functions—to mark old (given) information and to indicate contrast.

Contact with Other Languages

Korea is a small country. Throughout the centuries it has been invaded by a number of foreign peoples including Chinese, Mongols, Huns, Manchu, and Japanese, all of whose languages have had varying degrees of influence on Korean. The most important has been Chinese. The influence of Korean on other languages has been minimal.

The massive influx of Chinese words resulted in a lexicon containing dual sets of vocabulary. Alongside indigenous sets of numerals and common nouns, for example, are parallel sets of Chinese origin. Sino-Korean words make up more than 50 percent of the Korean lexicon. In addition to the items of parallel vocabulary, Sino-Korean words are found in abstract and technical areas. Chinese loans also made their way into Korean grammar; one example is a form of noun phrase construction.

In contemporary Korean, a new wave of borrowings is coming from the West, mostly from English. A number of these words begin with *r*, which has resulted in the establishment of an initial *r* phoneme in Korean, which, prior to the adoption of these words, did not exist in the language.

From Chinese: *kongbu* 'study', *il* 'one', *i* 'two', *sam* 'three'
From Japanese: *sŭsi* 'sushi'
From Portuguese: *tambae* 'tobacco'
From English: *rak'et'ŭ* 'racket', *k'ŏmp'yut'a* 'computer', *enjin* 'engine'

Common Words

man:	namja	long:	kin
woman:	yŏja	small:	chagŭn
water:	mul	yes:	ne, ye
sun:	hae	no:	aniyo
three:	ses	good:	chohŭn
fish:	mulkogi	bird:	sae
big:	k'ŭn	dog:	kae
tree:	namu		

Example Sentences

(1) Annyŏng ha-se-yo?
peace do-HONORIFIC-SEMIFORMAL
'How are you?'

(2) Abŏji-ga pang-e tŭl-e
father-NOM room-to enter-CONTINUATIVE

ka-si-n-ta.
go-HONORIFIC-PRESENT-PLAIN
'Father goes into the room.'

(3) Na-ege c'aek han-gwŏn chu-se-yo.
me-to book one-CLASSIFIER give-HONORIFIC-SEMIFORMAL
'Please give me a book.'

Efforts to Preserve, Protect, and Promote the Language

The early years of the 20th century witnessed the publication of systematic studies on Korean, although such activity was suppressed during the Japanese colonial period. After the division of Korea following World War II, the governments in the South and the North established different policies on language. In South Korea, the Seoul or Central dialect continued in use as the standard, while the P'yŏngan dialect was made the standard in North Korea. In the North, the use of Chinese characters was abandoned in favor of the Korean alphabet. Instruction using Chinese characters was prohibited as was the publication of newspapers, magazines, and books. The government has also actively discouraged the use of Korean words of Chinese origin and promoted the spread of newly created indigenous terminology to wide audiences through government media.

Policy in the South has varied with changes in government. The use of Chinese writing in instruction alongside *Hangŭl* has generally been tolerated, although there have been short periods in which it has been discouraged. The government has encouraged attempts to purify the language of foreign elements that have been advocated by some scholars and organizations in the media and academic discussion.

Select Bibliography

Chang, Suk-Jin. 1996. *Korean.* Amsterdam: John Benjamins.

Cho, Young-mee, and Peter Sells. 1995. "A Lexical Account of Inflectional Suffixes in Korean." In *Journal of East Asian Linguistics* 4.2:119–174.

Kim, Chin-Wu. 1974. "The Making of the Korean Language." In *Korea Journal* 14.8:4–17. Honolulu: Center for Korean Studies, University of Hawaii.

Kim, Nam-Kil, ed. 1986. *Studies in Korean Language and Linguistics.* Los Angeles: East Asian Studies Center, University of Southern California.

____. 1987. "Korean." In Bernard Comrie, ed., *The World's Major Languages,* 881–898. London: Oxford University Press.

Kim-Renaud, Young-Key. 1986. *Studies in Korean Linguistics.* Seoul: Hanshin Publishing Co.

Korean National Commission for UNESCO, ed. 1983. *The Korean Language.* Seoul: Sisayongo-sa.

Ledyard, G.K. 1966. *The Korean Language Reform of 1446: The Origin, Background, and Early History of the Korean Alphabet.* Ph.D. dissertation, Berkeley: University of California.

Lee, Hansol H.B. 1989. *Korean Grammar.* Oxford: Oxford University Press.

Lee, Ki-Moon. 1976. *Kayceng Kwukesa Kaysel.* ('History of Korean Language') Seoul: Minjung Sogwan.

Lukoff, Fred. 1982. *An Introductory Course in Korean.* Seoul: Yonsei University Press.

Martin, Samuel E. 1992. *A Reference Grammar of Korean.* Rutland, VT and Tokyo: Charles E. Tuttle Co.

Miller, R. A. 1971. *Japanese and Other Altaic Languages.* Chicago: University of Chicago Press.

Sohn, Ho-Min. 1994. *Korean: Descriptive Grammar.* London: Routledge.

Kurmanjî Kurdish

Geoffrey Haig and Ludwig Paul

Language Name: The term "Kurdish" is a cover term applied to a group of closely related western Iranian dialects spoken across a large contiguous area of the Middle East. Speakers of these dialects are united by a common perceived ethnicity and refer to themselves collectively as Kurds. However, a politically defined and recognized Kurdish state corresponding to the Kurdish ethnic and linguistic unity does not exist; Kurds are officially citizens of the various countries they inhabit. Two regional varieties of Kurdish have emerged as the basis for more or less standardized written languages, Kurmanjî and Sorani. Kurmanjî (also spelled Kurmanji, Kurmancî, Kurmânjî, Kermânjî), also called Northern Kurdish, on which this entry is based, is the most important in terms of numbers of speakers. The other important standardized version of Kurdish is Sorani, also called Central Kurdish, used by most Kurds in Iraq. Although traditionally Kurmanjî and Sorani are called dialects of Kurdish, from a purely linguistic point of view they could be described as two distinct languages. There are nevertheless good reasons for maintaining the traditional terminology. First, it more accurately reflects the perceived common origin and ethnic unity of the Kurds, both of which are important factors in Kurdish self-determination. Second, Kurmanjî and Sorani represent points on a North-South dialect continuum, with no clear cutoff point between them. **Autonym:** *Kurmanji/Kurmanci* (the most general term, accepted by most speakers); *Bahdinanî* (used by speakers in north Iraq); and the term "here were" (parts of Centrol Anatolia).

Location: The traditional homeland of Kurmanjî is a rugged inland triangle straddling Turkey, Iran, Armenia, and Iraq. It stretches eastward from the Turkish town of Malatya and extends to the westward shores of Lake Urmia in Iran and the western part of Armenia as far as Yerevan, but excluding the Black Sea coast. Southward it extends to the northeastern tip of Syria and north of Iraq around the town of Mosul. There is also a sizeable Kurdish community in Syria, and smaller pockets of Kurmanjî speakers live in Georgia and Lebanon.

As a result of recent political and economic pressure, there has been a massive exodus of Kurmanjî speakers from their traditional rural settlements to the large cities of Turkey, in particular Istanbul (with an estimated Kurdish population of 2.5 million), Ankara, Adana, and Diyarbakir. Furthermore, at least 700,000 Kurds, mostly Kurmanjî speakers, emigrated to western Europe in the 20th century.

Family: Kurmanjî belongs to the Western Iranian group of the Iranian branch of Indo-European. Within Western Iranian, Kurmanjî occupies an intermediate position between northwest and southwest Iranian.

Related Languages: Apart from the other varieties of Kurdish, other languages closely related to Kurmanjî are Lori-Bakhtiari (Iran), Gorani (northwest Iraq), and Zazaki (also called Dimili, central-east Anatolia). See also the BALOCHI and PERSIAN entries. Although according to linguistic criteria Zazaki does not belong to Kurdish (e.g., certain sound changes, differences in morphology and in items of core vocabulary). Zazaki speakers themselves feel that ethnic, geographic, and religious ties weigh more heavily than linguistic ones and many consider themselves Kurds. Furthermore, Zazaki and Kurmanjî have been in contact for centuries, which has led to considerable structural convergence, thus blurring the boundaries further.

Dialects: Reliable data for most of the Kurmanjî dialects spoken in Turkey, for example, in Hakkari, are not available, so any account of Kurmanjî dialectology is of necessity sketchy and tentative. A number of grammatical features distinguishes the Northern dialects of Turkey and the Caucasus from those of north Iraq, but it should be noted that the various dialects constitute a north-south continuum rather than two clearly distinguished varieties. There are several isoglosses between the dialects of north Iraq (Bâdînânî) on the one hand and those of Turkey and the Caucasus on the other hand, for example:

Dialectal Differences	Bâdînânî	Turkey, Caucasus
3sg present	*-it/-ît*	*-e*
1pl present and past	*-ît*	*-in*
Formation of future tense	participle *dê* + indicative present of verb	particle *ê* + subjunctive form of verb
Oblique case of masc. sg noun	*-î*	*-î*, -Ø, raising of stem-final vowel: *â/a>ê*

Other isoglosses divide the dialects of north Iraq, thereby connecting some Bâdînânî dialects with those of Turkey, for example, the form of the second person plural pronoun, *hûn* in the dialects of Turkey and in the Zakho and Sheykhan dialects of Iraq, but *hing(ô)* in Amadiya and Akre (Iraq).

Number of Speakers: Because none of the states in which Kurds live has any particular interest in releasing accurate demographic statistics on its minorities, any estimates of the numbers of Kurdish speakers must be treated with caution. One recent scholar put the number of Kurds at 25 million. Subtracting the estimated 5 million Kurds in Iraq (Nezan 1996: 8) who make up the bulk of the Sorani speakers, it can be roughly estimated that there are 20 million Kurmanjî speakers. Figures of a similar dimension are obtained by adding the numbers of Kurds in Turkey, where estimates range from 15–20 million, to the estimated 400,000–500,000 Kurmanjî speakers in the ex-Soviet republics and the million speakers in Syria. However, these are probably optimistic estimates because many of those wishing to call themselves Kurds no longer have an active command of the language.

Origin and History

Since the speakers of Kurmanjî and Sorani share the same Kurdish ethnicity and history, it is appropriate to treat them together. The origins of the Kurds are obscure. Whether they can be identified with the "Cyrtii" who, according to historians such as Polybius and Strabo, inhabited the mountainous regions of west Iran from the second century B.C. onwards, is uncertain. A further hypothesis is that the Kurds stem from the Carduchi, living at the beginning of the fourth century B.C. in southeast Anatolia, but this can be ruled out on the basis of historical sound changes. Nor is there any positive evidence for the still widely held belief that the historical Medians are the ancestors of the Kurds (although they may well have been the Medians' neighbors). If the speakers of Zazaki, living to the northwest of the current Kurmanjî area, originally moved from the Caspian to their present territories, then it would seem likely that the Kurds arrived in Anatolia at a later date, arriving from the southwest and driving the Zaza toward the northwest. But this process must have started at the latest in the middle of the first millennium A.D.

From the time of the Arab conquest in the 7th century onwards, the Kurds are frequently mentioned in Arab written sources. However, the first extant historiographical work devoted exclusively to the Kurds is the *Sharaf-nâma* written by Sharaf al-Dîn Bidlîsî in Persian in 1596. At about the same time written Kurdish poetry began to flourish through the work of, among others, Melayê Cizrî (c. 1570–1640); Feqîyê Teyran (c. 1590–1660); and Amedî Xanî (1650–1707), the author of the epic poem *Mem û Zîn*. Nevertheless, the bulk of Kurdish literature was transmitted orally up until the early 20th century. Only after the Kurdish cultural and national movements between 1910 and 1930 did the Kurdish written language expand in scope, encompassing journalistic and scientific writing as well as novels. In the 1930s and 1940s an alphabet for Kurmanjî, based on the TURKISH version of the Roman alphabet, was developed by Emir Djeladet Bedir Khan. It achieved rapid acceptance, largely through the vehicle of the journal *Hawar*, and has remained the major medium for written Kurmanjî outside the Soviet sphere. In the 1930s, forms of Kurmanjî Kurdish were used as an official language of education in Soviet Transcaucasia, and in the 1960s Sorani Kurdish achieved some official status in northern Iraq.

Orthography and Basic Phonology

There is no standardized form of Kurmanjî Kurdish used by all speakers, and considerable cross-dialect differences in pronunciation exist. However, a reasonably standardized Roman-based writing system has gained widespread acceptance in Kurmanjî publications in Turkey and in the diaspora, and this chapter will use this system throughout. Table 1 gives the approximate phonetic values of the letters used in that system, as well as noting some additional phonemic contrasts that are not consistently reflected by the writing system.

The phonemic status of several consonant segments is arguable and varies from dialect to dialect. These segments are not uniformly treated in written Kurmanjî. The voiced velar and pharyngal fricatives occur mostly in ARABIC loanwords and are generally rendered <x> and <h> respectively. The table records both the voiceless aspirated and the voiceless unaspirated stops, a distinction found in most Kurmanjî dialects, possibly because of ARMENIAN influence. This distinction is recorded in the Cyrillic-based script and in some grammars and dictionaries

Table 1: Phonetic Values of Letters for Consonants

	Bilabial	Labio-dental	Dental/ Alveolar	Palatal	Palatal-alveolar	Velar	Uvular	Pharyngal	Glottal
Stops	p^h p b		t^h t d			k^h k g	q		
Nasals	m		n						
Laterals			l						
Fricatives		f v	s z		ş j	x (ɣ)		(ħ)	h
Affricates					ç c				
Glides	w			y					
Flap			r						
Trill			(r r)						

using the Roman-based alphabet, but most modern texts ignore it. Similarly, the emphatic consonants found in some Arabic-influenced dialects are generally not recorded in the orthography. Finally, [r] is always trilled in word-initial position and in a small number of words in other environments as well. Again, the distinction between flapped and trilled [r] is only recorded sporadically in the orthography (e.g., the trilled [r] is sometimes rendered via two *r* symbols.)

Table 2: Vowels

	Front	Central	Back short/long
High	î		u / û
High Middle	ê		o
Middle	e	i	
Low			a

The use of the circumflex ^ to indicate length with /û/, but height elsewhere, is an unfortunate feature of this system. Some publications have adopted Turkish usage, introducing <ı> for <i>, and using <i> instead of <î>.

Basic Morphology

There is relatively little productive derivational morphology in Kurmanjî. The most productive adnominal derivatives create abstract nouns from nouns and adjectives. There is a variety of phonetically and semantically similar suffixes employed for this function:*-î, -yi, -îtî,-tî, -atî*: *cotkar* m. 'farmer', *cotkar-î* 'agriculture, the occupation of the farmer'; *heyvan* m. 'animal', *heyvan-tî* 'brutishness', *adan* 'fertile', *adan-î* 'fertility', *bedbext* 'unhappy', *bedbext-î* 'unhappiness', *dujmin* 'enemy', *dujmin-atî* 'enmity'.

Another productive process in word formation is compounding: *avrû* 'honor' (<*av* 'water'+*rû* 'face'); *çakrût* 'immodest' (of women); (<*çak* 'back of knee'+*rût* 'naked'); *dilkoçer* (adj.) 'fickle, carefree' (<*dil* [m.] 'heart' + *koçer* m. 'nomad'); *dotmam* 'cousin' (girl), (<*dot* [f.] 'daughter'+*mam* [m.] 'uncle'); *keskesor* (f.) 'rainbow' (<*kesk* 'green'+*sor* 'red'). The bare present verb stem also occurs as the second element in compounds, where it creates agentive nominalizations: *bangbêj* 'one who calls to prayer' (<*bang* [m.] 'call to prayer' + *bêj* present stem of the verb *gotin* 'speak'); *dermanfiroş* 'one who sells medicine, chemist' (<*derman* [f.] 'medicine' + *firoş* present stem of *firotin* 'sell'); *agiravêj* 'flame thrower' (*agir* [m.] 'fire' + *avêj* present stem from *avêtin* 'throw').

Kurmanjî nouns inflect for the following categories: case (direct versus oblique), number (singular versus plural), gender (masculine versus feminine), and definiteness (definite versus indefinite). Table 3 below illustrates case, gender, and number inflections for nouns and pronouns.

The most common form of masculine singular oblique is suffixal *-î*, but a small group of nouns diverge from this pattern, for example, *hingiv* (dir./obl.) 'honey', or with stem-vowel raising *bajar* (dir.) ~ *bajêr* (obl.) 'town', *nan* (dir.) ~ *nên* (obl.) 'bread'. Generally, oblique marking of masculine singular nouns is characterized by considerable dialectal and even idiolectal variation. Definiteness is also a factor, the *-î* suffix being obligatory, for example when the noun is qualified by a demonstrative.

Pronouns occur in suppletive pairs:

	Direct	Oblique
1s	ez	min
2s	tu	te
3s	ew	wî / wê (masc./fem.)
1pl	em	me
2pl	hûn	we
3pl	ew	wan

Note that number and gender are not explicitly marked on nouns or third-person singular pronouns when they are in the direct case. In the following examples, neither gender nor number is made explicit on the noun, although plural number is reflected by number agreement on the verb: *heval hat* (friend come:PST(3s) 'the friend (male or female) came (default reading is male)'; *heval hat-in* (friend come.PST-3PL) '(the) friends (male or female) came'.

There is no definite article in Kurdish. Indefiniteness is signalled by an unstressed suffix, or if singular and in the sense of 'just one', the numeral *yek* 'one', preposed to the noun, may be used. For singular nouns, the indefinite suffix is *-ek;* for plurals it is *-in*: *jin-ek hat* (woman-IND came) 'a woman came'; *hesp-in hat-in* (horse-IND:PL came-PL) 'horses came'.

The direct case is used: (1) for all intransitive subjects, (2) for the subjects of transitive verb forms based on the present stem, (3) for the direct objects of transitive verb forms based on the past stem, and (4) for some types of adjunct. Elsewhere, the oblique case is used.

Kurmanjî nouns have two genders, masculine and feminine. However, unlike more familiar gender languages, many nouns for animate beings do not have a fixed gender. Rather, they have fluid gender, taking the respective masculine or feminine inflectional endings depending on the biological sex of the intended referent. Thus one and the same word, for example, *heval* 'friend' can be used to refer to both males and females and takes either masculine or feminine agreement (the default

Table 3: Case, Gender and Number (Dialect of Cizre-Botan)

	MASCULINE	FEMININE	PLURAL
DIRECT	-Ø	-Ø	-Ø
OBLIQUE	*-î* -Ø -raising of stem-final vowel	*-ê* *-e* (after the indefinite marker)	*-an* *-a(n)* after the indefinite marker

Table 4: Different Types of Gender Assignment

Fluid gender: Referent-dependent	Fixed gender: lexical pairs	Fixed gender for generic noun
mamoste 'teacher'	*mîh* f. 'ewe', *beran* m. 'ram'	*pîrê* f. 'spider'
heval 'friend'	*çêlek* f. 'cow'; *boxe* m. bull	*dûpişk* f. 'scorpion'
cotkar 'farmer'	*mirîşk* f. 'hen', *dîk* m. 'rooster'	*werdek/ordek* f. 'duck'
karker 'worker'		
ker 'donkey'		

meaning is, however, male). Compare this to, for example, GERMAN, where the word *Freund* 'friend' is always grammatically masculine and a secondary feminine form (*Freund-in* 'friend-FEM') must be derived from it when it is intended to express 'female friend'. Most Kurmanjî words with fluid gender refer to humans and large mammals. Insects and less significant animates have a fixed gender, as do inanimates. For some culturally relevant animals, lexical pairs exist for male and female (see Table 4 above).

The gender of nouns only surfaces in certain constructions: when a noun is in the singular of the oblique case, and when a noun is modified by an attribute (see *Ezâfe* constructions below). All nouns in the absolute form, assuming they have no attributes, have no overt signal of gender.

Ezâfe *Constructions.* Kurdish, like most Western Iranian languages, is characterized by the *ezâfe* construction, a particular means of linking attributes to the head noun in the noun phrase. Within the noun phrase, modifiers follow the head and are linked to it via an unstressed vocalic particle traditionally termed *ezâfe* (EZ). The form of the *ezâfe* varies according to the number, gender, and definiteness of the head noun as shown in Table 5 below.

Post-head modifiers include genitive attributes, adjectives, prepositional phrases, and relative clauses. Demonstratives and quantifiers, however, precede the head noun, and there is no *ezâfe*: *mêr-ê mezin* (man-EZ:masc tall) 'the tall man', but *ew mêr* 'this man'. The head noun itself remains in the direct case, regardless of its function within a particular clause. In other words, the presence of an *ezâfe* in a noun phrase neutralizes any case distinctions on the head of that noun phrase. Possessors go into the oblique case, while adjectival attributes remain uninflected. The following examples illustrate these principles:

ap-ê min kur-ê mezin di-bîn-e
uncle-EZ:M 1s:OBL boy-EZ:M large AFF-see:PRES-3s
'My uncle sees the tall boy.'

kur-ê mezin ap-ê min di-bîn-e
boy-EZ:M large uncle-EZ:M 1s:OBL AFF-see:PRES-3s
'The tall boy sees my uncle.'

In these two examples the direct/oblique case distinction on the NPs has been neutralized by the presence of the *ezâfe*. This means that only the word order is available to express who saw whom. Examples of prepositional phrases and relative clauses in *ezâfe* constructions are given below:

keç-a bi kinc-ên nû
girl-EZ:F with clothes-EZ:PL new
'the girl with new clothes'

mêr-ê ku min dît mezin e
man-EZ:M that 1s:OBL see:PST(3s) tall COP:3s
'The man I saw is tall.'

Verb Morphology. Each verb has two distinct stems, a past and a present stem. Each stem is used as the basis for two different sets of tense and aspect forms. For example, the present stem is used for simple present tense and the subjunctive, while the past stem is used for a variety of past verb forms, and as the basis for verbal nouns (participle and infinitive).

For most of the textually frequent verbs, there is no means of predicting one stem from the other; some of them look like suppletive pairs, others are clearly related, but the patterns that relate them do not extend over large numbers of lexemes. Examples of common verbs can be found in Table 6 on the next page.

The only moderately productive derivational process is a causative suffix, *-and*, used for deriving transitive verbs from intransitive stems: from *gerîn* 'walk, stroll' *gerandin* 'lead', from *herikîn* 'flow' *herikandin* 'move (trans.), make flow'.

Finite verbs take agreement suffixes, indexing the verb for person and number of a single core argument, the intransitive subject in all tenses, the transitive subject in present tenses, and the transitive object with past tenses. There are three sets of person agreement markers: Type 1, used with forms based on the present stem and after participial or nominal predicates; Type 2, used with forms based on the past stem, except subjunctive forms; and Type 3, used with past subjunctive forms (see Table 7 on the next page).

Verb forms based on the present tense (simple present, sub-

Table 5: The Form of *ezâfe*

Head noun is:	Masculine Definite	Masculine Indefinite	Feminine Definite	Feminine Indefinite	Plural Definite	Plural Indefinite
Form of *ezâfe*:	*-(y)ê*	*-î*	*-(y)a*	*-e*	*-(y)ên*	*-e*

(Note: The forms given as "indefinite" occur after the indefinite suffixes *-ek* (singular) and *-in* (plural))

Table 6: Common Verbs

Past Stem	Present Stem	Meaning
bir-	*-b-*	carry
hişt-	*-hêl-*	leave
bihîst-	*-bihîz- / -bihîs-*	hear
girt-	*-gir-*	grasp, hold, take
got-	*-bêj-*	say
kuşt-	*-kuj-*	kill
rûnişt-	*-rûn-*	sit (down)
kir-	*-k-*	do, make
dâ- / day-	*-d-*	give
çû-	*-ç-*	go
jî- / jiy	*-ji-*	live
ket-	*-kev-*	fall
xwar-	*-xw-*	eat
xwast-	*-xwaz-*	want
avêt-	*-avêj-*	throw
dît-	*-bîn-*	see

Table 7: Person Agreement Markers

Person	Type 1		Type 2	Type 3
	after consonants	after vowels		
1s	*-im*	*-me*	*-(i)m*	*-(a)ma*
2s	*-î /-e*	*-yî*	*-î*	*-(y)ayî*
3s	*-e*	*-ye*	*-Ø*	*-(y)a*
1,2,3plural	*-in*	*-ne*	*-(i)n*	*-(a)na*

(The 2s *-e* ending of Type 1 is used in the imperative)

junctive, imperative, future) obligatorily take a prefix, either the unmarked simple present prefix *di-* (glossed AFFirmative), or the subjunctive prefix *bi-* (see *Negation* below). Verb forms based on the past stem, however, are not necessarily prefixed. The paradigms for the simple present and the simple past are given in Table 8.

Negation. Negation of present verb forms uses the prefix *na-*, which replaces the prefix *di-*: *ez na-bêjim* 'I'm not saying/ I don't say' (the negative imperative takes the prefix *ne-* or *me-*). In the past, *ne* simply precedes the affirmative verb form: *ez ne-hatim* 'I didn't come'.

Basic Syntax

The pragmatically neutral order of main constituents in the clause is SOV, for example, *tu çû-yî* (you(DIR) go:PST-2s) 'you went'; *ez te dibînim* (I(DIR) you (OBL) AFF-see:PRESS-1s) 'I see you'. However, Kurmanjî is not a strictly verb final language because indirect objects and goals come after the verb when they are not adpositional. Compare *min da wan* (I(DIR) gave them (OBL)) with *min je wan re da* (I(OBL) ADP them(OBL) ADP gave), both of which express 'I gave (it) to them'.

Kurmanjî is predominantly prepositional: *bê min* 'without me', *bi kera* 'with the knife', but combinations of preposition and postpositional particles are also found: *ji te re* 'for you' (*te*=you(OBL).

With all verb forms based on the past stem, direct objects are in the direct case and the verb agrees with them in person and number (ergative alignment): *min tu dît-î* (I(OBL) you(DIR) see(PST)-2s) 'I saw you'. However, regardless of the differences in agreement patterns between the past and the present tenses, the order of constituents remains identical in both. Finally, we should note that violations of the canonical ergative alignment are well attested. For example, when the transitive subject of a past-tense verb is third-person plural, the verb will often agree in number with the transitive subject rather than with the direct object. Another pattern found, particularly in the speech of Kurmanjî-Turkish bilinguals, is for transitive subject *and* direct object to take the oblique case, while the verb remains invariant third-person singular: *min wan dît* I(OBL) they(OBL) saw(PST:3s) 'I saw them'.

Contact with Other Languages

Kurmanjî has always been in contact with the other languages of the area, particularly Turkish, Persian, Armenian, and Arabic. Unlike these languages, Kurmanjî has never achieved the status of a national language, so Kurmanjî speakers have generally been under greater pressure to learn the prestige language of the political unity in which they live rather than the other way around. Particularly today, probably most Kurmanjî speakers are bi- or trilingual. Modern Kurmanjî has been influenced by its neighboring languages, not only through bor-

Table 8: Sample Verb Paradigms

	simple present *gotin* 'say'	simple past (intransitive) *hatin* 'come'	simple past (transitive) *xwarin* 'eat'
1 sing.	*ez dibêjim* 'I say'	*ez hatim* 'I came'	*min xwar* 'I ate (it)'
2 sing.	*tu dibêjî*	*tu hatî*	*te xwar*
3 sing.	*ew dibêje*	*ew hat*	*wî* (masc.) *xwar* *wê* (fem.) *xwar*
1plural	*em dibêjin*	*em hatin*	*me xwar*
2plural	*hûn dibêjin*	*hûn hatin*	*we xwar*
3plural	*ew dibêjin*	*ew hatin*	*wan xwar*

rowing words, but also in phonology, morphology, and syntax. For example, the distinction found in many Kurmanjî dialects between aspirated and nonaspirated voiceless stops is probably because of Armenian influence, and several Kurmanjî dialects use a conditional marker *-se*, borrowed from Turkish. The process of structural convergence with neighboring languages is likely to accelerate in the future as more and more Kurds are obliged to leave their traditional homelands for urban centers or overseas.

Common Words

man:	mêr	small:	biçûk
woman:	jin	yes:	belê/erê
water:	av	no:	ne
sun:	roj	good:	baş
three:	sê	bird:	çivîk, çûçik
fish:	masî	dog:	se, kûçik
big:	mezin	tree:	dar
long:	dirêj		

Example Sentences

(1) hezar dost kêm e, dijmin-ek pir e.
thousand friend little COP:3s enemy-IND much COP:3s
'A thousand friends is little, a single enemy is a lot.'

(2) piştî ku di-ya min çêlek doti-bû-n
after that mother-EZ:F 1s:OBL cow(PL) milk:PP-be:PST-PL

hat mal-ê.
come:PST(3s) home-OBL
'After my mother had milked the cows she came home.'

Efforts to Preserve, Protect, and Promote the Language

The current situation of Kurmanjî is complex and changes rapidly along with the volatile politics of the region. In the states traditionally inhabited by Kurmanjî-speakers, the use of Kurmanjî is at best tolerated, at worst actively repressed. With the exception of Armenia, nowhere has it been possible to establish a stable environment in which the language is used in education or broadcasting or where it has any official status. In Turkey, where most Kurmanjî speakers live, the use of Kurmanjî was actively repressed and indeed the very existence of the language denied up until the early 1990s. It is now possible to openly purchase a wide range of Kurmanjî publications and cassettes in Turkey, but the use of Kurmanjî in broadcasting or any official capacity remains forbidden. Similarly, there is virtually no scholarly interest in the language at any official Turkish institute of higher education. In those other countries where dialects of Kurmanjî are spoken, they constitute linguistic minorities (Armenia, Georgia, Syria, Lebanon) with little official support. In Iraq and, less so, Iran, where most Kurds speak central (Sorani) or southern Kurdish dialects and where literary standards based upon these have evolved, the Kurmanjî dialects are becoming increasingly influenced by them. However, since the establishment of the United Nations protectorate in north Iraq in 1991, Kurds have enjoyed a short spell of comparative autonomy.

In the European diaspora, however, pilot projects with Kurmanjî in education have been started in Sweden, and in some states of Germany. Kurmanjî is also published extensively, and Kurdish is the subject of growing scholarly interest at a number of universities. Of particular significance was the establishment of MED-television, a broadcasting company based in Brussels that broadcasted television and radio programs in various Kurdish dialects to Europe and the Near East until it was forced to close under pressure from the Turkish government. The Kurds now make extensive use of the Internet for their publication activities, for example, the newspaper *Azadiya Welat*.

Despite these efforts, the long-term future of Kurmanjî is by no means secure. Probably at least one-third of all Kurmanjî speakers now lives outside the traditional borders of Kurdistan, most with no prospect of returning. Without a stable speech community in which Kurmanjî is an accepted means of communication for all functions of everyday life, including official communication outside the domestic sphere, it is difficult to see how the unbroken transmission of the language from one generation to the next can be guaranteed. Thus the future of the language depends to a large extent on positive political action to create the kind of stable community in which the language could flourish.

Select Bibliography

Blau, J. 1989. "Le kurde." In Schmitt, R., ed., *Compendium linguarum iranicarum*. Wiesbaden: Reichert: 327–335.

Dorleijn, M. 1996. *The Decay of Ergativity in Kurmanci. Language Internal or Contact Induced?* Tilburg: Tilburg University Press.

Hassanpour, A. 1992. *Nationalism and Language in Kurdistan, 1918–1985*. San Francisco: Mellen Research University Press.

Kreyenbroek, P. 1992. "On the Kurdish language." In Kreyenbroek, P., and S. Sperl, eds. *The Kurds: A Contemporary Overview*. London: Routledge/SOAS: Politics and Culture in the Middle East series: 68–83.

Kreyenbroek, P., and C. Allison, eds., 1996. *Kurdish Culture and Identity*. London: Zed Books Ltd.

Kurdoev, K.K. and Z.A. Jusupova. 1983. *Kurdsko-Russkij Slovar'/Ferhenga Kurdî-Rusî*. Moscow: Gosudarstvennoe Izdatel'stvo Inostrannykh i Natsional'nykh Slovarei.

MacKenzie, D.N. 1961. *Kurdish Dialect Studies, Vol. I–II*. London: Oxford University Press.

McDowall, D. 1996. *A Modern History of the Kurds*. New York: Tauris.

Nezan, K. 1996. "The Kurds: Current position and historical background." In Kreyenbroek, P., and C. Allison, eds., *Kurdish Culture and Identity*. London: Zed Books Ltd.: 7–19.

Paul, L. 1998. "The position of Zazaki among West Iranian languages." In Sims-Williams, N., ed., *Societas Iranologica Europaea. Proceedings of the Third European Conference of Iranian Studies, Cambridge, September 11–15, 1995. Part 1: Old and Middle Iranian Studies*. Wiesbaden: Reichert: 163–177.

Rizgar, B. 1993. *Kurdish-English, English-Kurdish Dictionary*. London: M.F. Onen.

LAKOTA

David S. Rood

Language Name: Lakota. **Alternates:** Mostly used by ENGLISH speakers: Dakota, Sioux, Teton. **Autonym:** *Lakhota.*

Location: United States and Canada (North and South Dakota, Manitoba, Saskatchewan, Montana, Alberta).

Family: Siouan.

Related Languages: Assiniboine, Stoney, Winnebago, Ioway, Otoe, Osage, Omaha, Ponca, Kansa, Quapaw, Mandan, Hidatsa, Crow, Biloxi, Ofo, Tutelo.

Dialects: Dakota/Lakota/Nakota. L = D = ⁿD = N in different dialects. Generally Lakota = Teton, Dakota = Santee, Nakota = Stoney, Assiniboine, Yankton, but both Dakota and Nakota have intermediate subgroups that use *ⁿd* instead of *n* or *d*.

Number of Speakers: 7,000–10,000.

Origin and History

Although Europeans have known about some of the Siouan languages since around 1650, the earliest useful records of the Lakota language date from the early 19th century. In 1819, as Minnesota was being settled and Ft. Snelling established, missionary and educational work began among the Santee. The Santee called themselves *Dakota*, and that name was then extended by Europeans to all the related dialects. The term "Sioux" is also applied to the group, but because of its FRENCH and/or Ojibwa origin, it is disliked by modern speakers.

A description published in 1852 concerning the speakers of Dakota stated that "they are scattered over an immense territory, extending from the Mississippi River on the east to the Black Hills on the west, and from the mouth of the Big Sioux River on the south to Devils Lake on the north" (Riggs 1852, *A Grammar and Dictionary of the Dakota Language*, Smithsonian Institution, reprinted in Riggs 1893a: 155). But by the 1890s, the group had been confined to reservations in Minnesota and the Dakotas.

The history of Dakota-U.S. relations is complex and bloody, involving massacres, flight to and return from Canada, confinement to ever-shrinking reservations, frontier justice and injustice, rebellion, and subjugation.

Early accounts of the group describe many divisions and subdivisions; whether and how these correspond to linguistic divisions is largely a matter of conjecture. Today, however, there is a small group of *d* speakers (Santee, Sisseton) in Minnesota and eastern South Dakota, and a much larger group of *l* speakers (Teton, with many subdivisions) in western South Dakota and scattered further north. All the historical records indicate that the *l* speakers, or Tetons, have always been the largest group. Another group is often called "Nakota" but is more properly divided into three or four languages and dialects: Assiniboine in Montana and Alberta, and Stoney in Alberta and Manitoba, are separate languages; Yankton and Yanktonais in North Dakota and Saskatchewan are Dakota dialects, but the diagnostic sound (*d/l/n*) is often pronounced *ⁿd* in those dialects. The correspondences are actually quite complex, since both *d* and *l* dialects have *n* in addition to the characteristic *l* or *d*, and exactly which words are pronounced which way divides the languages into even finer subdialects. See Parks and DeMallie (1992) for details.

Since there is no native recognition of the unity of these dialects, there is no native term for the language. Scholars use either "Sioux" or "Dakotan" for the complex, but both terms are offensive to at least some speakers of some of the dialects. Taken as a single language, "Dakotan" is related to other languages in the Siouan family, the ancestor language of which was probably spoken in the woodlands of the upper Midwest. There are some apparently Siouan languages attested in the Appalachians very early after European settlement began, but the records are very scanty. The more secure distribution of the languages, from the early 19th century, puts one group (Biloxi, Ofo, Tutelo) in the southeast (present states of Mississippi and Arkansas); some scholars think they migrated there from the Ohio Valley fairly recently. A larger group, called "Mississippi Valley Siouan", was found from northern Arkansas northward and westward, and included Dhegiha (in four dialects: Quapaw or Arkansas, Kansa or Kaw, Osage, Omaha-Ponca), Chiwere (Ioway, Otoe, Missouria), Winnebago, and Dakotan. Mandan forms a coordinate branch with Mississippi Valley Siouan; the combination is called "Central Siouan". The other group, "Missouri River Siouan", is found further north and west; it consists of Hidatsa and Crow.

The divergences within Dakotan are reminiscent of those within Slavic, and may therefore be about 1,000 or so years old. Central Siouan distinctions are more like those of Germanic, and therefore may be about 2,000 years old. These numbers are my personal intuitions, however, and I do not expect other scholars to agree with them; nor would I be willing to guess about anything further back.

More distant relationships are more controversial. Catawba is likely a distant relative of the family; Yuchi has also been said to be a distant relative, but the evidence for that is very weak. Beyond that, various scholars have proposed that Keresan, Iroquoian and/or Caddoan are related to Siouan, but now we are in the realm of intuition by linguists who study the groups (based on similar patterns in the syntax and morphol-

Table 1: Consonants

	Voice	Bilabial	Dental	Palatal	Velar	Post-velar	Glottal
Stops	-	p	t	č	k		ʔ
Fricatives	-		s	š		ȟ	
	+		z	ž		ǧ	
Nasals		m	n		ň		
Lateral			l				
Glides		w			y		

ogy, patterns that are very unlikely to be accidental similarities) rather than hard evidence.

Orthography and Basic Phonology

Lakota is primarily used for conversation and for oral transmission of traditional knowledge; it is not normal for Lakota speakers to write to anyone or for anything. In recent years several different attempts to teach the language to nonspeakers have required written material, but the writing systems devised have varied from class to class and teacher to teacher, and are chiefly memory devices for the students; literature in this language is oral, except when prepared by or for scholars or others who live outside the community.

There is no single accepted spelling system for the language. The letters used here are standard in most scholarly discussions, and are very close to those used by Lakota scholar Ella Deloria in her published and typed material; the difference is that we use just one diacritic, the "hacek", where she uses different marks (acute accent, raised dot), depending on the letter. Moreover, she continues to write *p* and *k* at the ends of words, even when they are pronounced [b] and [g], and she writes consonant clusters that have a brief vowel between the members with a dot between them; thus for her 'water' is *m.ní* rather than *mní*.

Other writers of Lakota use a GREEK eta following vowels to indicate nasalization (instead of the hook), and the letter *j* instead of our *ž*. Some other writers use nasal *o* instead of *ų*, and there are various schemes for marking the difference between aspirated and unaspirated stops, and for indicating glottalization and the glottal stop.

The orthographic conventions employed in this chapter are as follows. The hook under a vowel indicates nasalization: ǵ[ã], į [ĩ], ų [ũ]. A hacek indicates that the letter has a non-English value:

č = English 'ch' [tʃ]
š = English 'sh' [ʃ]
ž = French 'j' (*Jacques, jour*) [ʒ]
ȟ = GERMAN 'ch' (*ach, machen*) [x]
ǧ = Greek gamma, or SPANISH 'g' between vowels (*pagar*) [ɣ]
ň = English 'ng' of "singer", not "finger" [ŋ]

Note that in written words, every letter is pronounced, including *h* after consonants: *akhé* 'again' is pronounced with an aspirated *k*, *aké* '-teen', (in numbers like *akétopa* 'fourteen') is pronounced without the aspiration. Similarly, *č*, *p*, and *t* differ from *čh*, *ph*, and *th*. After *p*, *t*, or *k* and before the vowels *a*, *e*, *o*, *ą*, and *ų*, this "h" sounds like Lakota "*ȟ*".

Table 2: Vowels

		Front	Central	Back
High	Oral	i		u
	Nasal	į		ų
Mid		e		o
Low	Nasal		ą	
	Oral		a	

Syllable structure is (C)(C)V(C); the consonants that can close a syllable are limited to *b*, *g*, *l*, *n*, *s*, *š* and *ȟ*. A very large number of consonant clusters can appear syllable initially, including stop-stop clusters such as *pt*, *kt*, *pč*, *kp*, etc. When both members of the cluster are voiced, one hears a short transition vowel between them, so *mní* 'water' sounds a little like *miní*, and *bló* 'potato' sounds like English "below". This accounts for English spellings of Lakota words in place-names such as Minnesota (Lakota: *mnísòta* 'cloudy water')

Accent is always on either the first or the second syllable.

k often becomes *č* when *i* or *e* precedes it.

Word-final vowels are often lost when final in first members of compounds, or elsewhere in fast speech. When the vowel is lost, a preceding fricative becomes voiceless, but a preceding stop becomes voiced (and the voiced equivalent for /t/ and /č/ is /l/). If the vowel preceding the stop is nasal, the stop may in turn become nasal (/l/ becomes /n/ in this case).

Many verbs have a variable final vowel. Either *e*, *į*, or *a* may occur, depending on the next word. Nasalization of vowels often spreads in either direction across *y*, *w*, or *h*, but there are restrictions on this rule.

In fast speech, unstressed vowels and *y*, *w*, and h are often lost.

When inflectional morphemes occur before verb stems beginning with /y/, some unexpected changes occur: *wa-y* becomes *bl*; *ki-y* becomes *gl*; *ya-y* becomes just *l*.

Basic Morphology

Noun Morphology. There is no inflectional morphology on nouns to indicate case or number. Possession may be marked by prefixes showing person and an enclitic showing the number of the possessor, but the prefix can be used only with nouns that are apt to be possessed: words like "rock" or "water" do not take these prefixes.

The words that translate as adjectives are actually verbs in

Lakota. Compounds of noun + modifier may be formed freely, providing the collocation is normal or expectable ("big rock", "pretty woman", etc.); otherwise a construction like a relative clause is used. Modifiers of plural and mass nouns are often reduplicated.

There are two definite articles and several indefinite ones. The definites, *ki* and *kʔų*, distinguish between merely known entities (ki or, for some speakers and in the older language, *kį*), and "the aforementioned" (*kʔų*). Indefinite articles differ depending on (1) whether the noun is singular and countable vs. plural or mass; (2) whether the noun is human, nonhuman animate or inanimate; and (3) whether the noun is in a "real" sentence (one that states a known and objectively demonstrable fact), an "irrealis" sentence (where the existence of the object cannot be known for certain), or a negative sentence. For example, the singular article *wą* (real) would be used with 'book' in 'I have a book' or 'we found a book' or 'there's a book on the table', but the article would change to *wąží* (irrealis) in 'give me a book' or 'I want a book' or 'did you find a book?' or 'they will write a book' and to *wąžíni* (negative) in 'I don't have a book' or 'she can't find a book'.

Personal pronouns are almost never used. For third persons, sometimes the demonstratives can substitute for nouns; otherwise, there are two sets of independent pronouns, one derived from a verb 'to exist' (e.g., *miyé* 'it's me'), used to answer a question or as the object of a postposition, or emphatically, as we use reflexives in expressions like "she sang it herself"; and one used in contrastive contexts, such as *míš* 'as for me...'.

Lakota distinguishes first, second, and third person singular and plural, and in addition there is a special form when a first person and one second person are the subjects of the verb ("you and I"); this is called the "dual inclusive".

Demonstrative pronouns distinguish three degrees of distance, and singular, dual and plural number: near the speaker (*lé*, *lenáʔųs*, *lená*), far from the speaker (*ká*, *kanáʔųs*, *kaná*), and intermediate between them (*hé*, *henáʔųs*, *hená*). The presence of the plural demonstrative is often the only indication of noun number in the noun phrase, and it is the only plural marker that ever occurs with inanimate nouns.

Verbal Morphology. Verb morphology is very complex. Prefixes (or infixes, depending on the verb) indicate all the case relationships in the sentence (subject, object, indirect object, possessor of object), as well as some kinds of location and instrument. Enclitics indicate aspect; subject number; object number for first and second persons; negation; and many modal properties such as imperative, interrogative, doubt, certainty, possibility, pleading, sarcasm, rhetorical question, strong assertion, etc. There are probably 200 to 300 of these postverbal enclitics. There is no distinction between present and past tense, and the translation of the English future is accomplished with an enclitic that really means "unrealized" or "irrealis".

There are compelling linguistic arguments for considering the verbal person markers to be the real pronouns of the language, and not "agreement" morphemes.

A verb stem without any inflection or enclitics is understood to be the third person singular indicative, either present or past tense. Any deviation from that is marked morphologically.

In transitive verbs, prefixes or infixes indicate subject, object, and, if necessary, indirect object and possessor of object. Third person singular is always zero; third person plural is indicated only for animate nouns. There are two kinds of indirect object: those who know about and give permission for the event, and those for whom the event is undertaken without their knowledge and permission. Examples: *ičú* 'he or she took it' (this is the citation form, the simplest possible form); *iwáču* 'I took it'; *iwákiču* 'I took it on him/her; I took it (or his/hers) for/from him/her without permission'; *iwéčiču* 'I took it for him or her, or I took his/hers, and he/she knew about it'; *iwékču* 'I took my own'.

Intransitive verbs divide into two classes. One, called "active", uses the same morphemes for subjects as do transitive verbs. Most of these verbs express actions over which the subject has some control, such as "sing" or "walk" or "stand".

The other, called "stative", uses for the subject the same morphemes that express objects of transitive verbs. The verbs generally describe states or situations where the subject has little control. Many, but far from all, of these translate into adjectives in English. Examples are "be happy", "die", "fall down", and "fear". Both classes of intransitives can take indirect objects and the reflexive possessive if the situation is appropriate.

There is no passive; instead, the verb form with third person plural subject is used ("they found it" rather than "it was found").

Causatives are formed in three ways. Two of these involve auxiliary verbs, one of which means something like "force or make", while the other means something more like "let". Both of these verbs occur as the final elements in a compound, and speakers do not recognize them as independent; the main verb plus the causative verb is a new word.

The third causative device involves one of a set of seven prefixes that indicate the instrument involved in the causation. Observe these forms derived from *wačhí* 'dance': *yuwáčhi* 'to cause to dance by pulling out onto the dance floor' (*yu-* 'by means of the hands'), *nawáčhi* 'to cause to dance by kicking' (*na-* 'by means of the feet'), *yawáčhi* 'to cause to dance by talking (*ya-* 'by means of the mouth'), *pawáčhi* 'to cause to dance by pushing out onto the dance floor' (*pa-* 'by pressure exerted away from the body, by pushing'), *kawáčhi* ' to cause to dance by another kind of physical force' (*ka-* 'by sudden, often violent, force').

Two other prefixes (which don't occur with this verb) are *wo* 'by means of a pointed object' and *wa* 'by means of a blade'. An eighth, *pu* 'by means of general pressure, e.g., by sitting on' is no longer productive, but occurs in a number of fossilized stems.

These prefixes are extremely productive, and occur with many noncausative stems as well, indicating the means for the activity's accomplishment.

Besides the instrumentals just mentioned, Lakota has three vocalic verbal prefixes, *a*, *o*, and *i*. These are generally called "locative prefixes" in Lakota studies. Usually *a* means 'on' or 'because of'; *o* means 'in'; and *i* means 'with', but like all derivation, the precise meaning of the prefix is often obscure in a given form. These can combine with each other and with the instrumentals.

Pronoun inflections are either prefixes or infixes. They precede some of the instrumentals and follow others; they follow the locatives; and there are many synchronically unanalyzable stems into which they are inserted.

Both noun and verb compounds, and combinations of them, are frequent and productive. Verbs follow nouns in almost all cases, and modifiers follow modified; e.g., *maza-ska-ša* 'penny, copper' involves *ša* 'red' modifying the preceding combination, *maza-ska* 'money', which, in turn, is composed of *maza* 'metal' and *ska* 'white'.

Verbs are often reduplicated (one syllable of the verb is repeated) to show that their inanimate subjects are plural or mass, or that the action occurred distributed over an area or through a period of time. It is impossible to predict, synchronically, which syllable of the stem will be copied in reduplication.

Basic Syntax

Unmarked word order in transitive clauses is SOV; nouns occur after verbs only as afterthoughts, for clarification of a preceding pronoun, but S and O can change places to indicate that the object is the topic of the discourse. Adverbs may precede, interrupt, or follow the SO sequence, and both subordinating and coordinating conjunctions follow the verb. The most important phrase comes just before the verb.

Most other constructions are headfinal, too: postpositions head postpositional phrases, subordinating conjunctions end their clauses, and possessors precede possessed, but determiners follow nouns. Relative clauses are headinternal, but the head usually occurs first in the clause, and the whole relative clause precedes the rest of the sentence.

Wičáša	wǵ	wįyǵ	ki	hé	theȟíla	čha	wǵbláke
man	a	woman	the	that	3.loves.3	REL	I.saw.him/her

'I saw a man who loves that woman' *or* 'I saw a man whom that woman loves.'

Wičáša	wǵ	wįyǵ	ki	theȟíla	čha	wǵmáyǵke
man	a	woman	the	3.loves.3	REL	he/she.saw.me

'A man whom the woman loves saw me' *or* 'A man who loves the woman saw me.'

If the head is definite ('the man' instead of 'a man' above, the REL marker changes from *čha* to *ki hé*. Both *čha* and *ki hé* are also complementizers, so the first of the above sentences could also mean 'I see/saw that a man loves that woman'.

Negation is marked by the postverbal enclitic *šni*. Compare also the indefinite article discussion. Indefinite pronouns in a negative sentence must also be negative: "nobody didn't see him" or "he didn't see nobody" is the obligatory way of expressing this kind of negative clause.

Questions are marked by a clause-final enclitic *he*, whether they are yes/no or information questions. Question words do not come at the beginning of the sentence unless they would be there anyway; they occur in the place where the answer would occur.

Contact with Other Languages

All speakers of Lakota also speak English, and in Canada, many also speak Cree. Lakota is the everyday language of a few thousand people and many still speak it better than they do English, yet children are learning the language in ever decreasing numbers; schools report a sharp decrease in the number of non-English speakers entering kindergarten. The language is the vehicle for passing on traditional culture among its speakers, however, and history, philosophy, religion, folklore, and general social norms are taught (usually, if possible, by grandparents to grandchildren) using it.

Everyday Lakota is full of English words, but to call them "loanwords" rather than "code switching" could be the subject of a lengthy sociolinguistic debate. English has, however, borrowed quite a few Lakota words, generally as place-names (cf. Minnesota, above). Several have *mni* 'water' (Minneapolis, Minnihaha 'laughing water', really *mniȟáȟa*). Compare also *tipi* (*thípi* 'house').

Common Words

man:	wičháša	woman:	wįyǵ
water:	mní	sun:	wí
three:	yámni	fish:	hó
big:	thǵka	long:	hǵske
small:	čík?ala	yes:	hǵ
no:	hiyá	good:	wašté
bird:	zįtkála	dog:	šų́ka
tree:	čhǵ		

Example Sentences

(1)

Wǵčhį́yǵke	kį	lé	wašté.
I.see.you	the	this	good

'It's good to see you.'

(2)

Agnes	mni-píǧa	yatké	kį	waȟtéwala	šni.
Agnes	beer	drink	the	I.like	not

'I don't like (for) Agnes to drink beer.'

(3)

Wičháša	etǵ	wǵníyǵg	ú	pi	kte.
man	some	see.you	come	PL	POTENTIAL

'Some men will come to see you.'

Efforts to Preserve, Protect, and Promote the Language

Lakota is one of the few viable native languages left in North America. Nevertheless, it is endangered; recent years have seen ever decreasing numbers of Lakota-speaking children entering reservation schools.

All the schools on the reservations, from elementary through college, offer Lakota language courses, but their efforts are most successful with those who can also use the language at home. Teachers and administrators who do not understand much about how language works tend to equate school language teaching with reading and writing, and because there is no standard written form, everyone learns something a little different. Some of the community colleges that serve the reservations require some degree of fluency as a condition for graduation.

There is a radio station on Pine Ridge that broadcasts primarily in Lakota, and there are constant efforts by individuals to see to it that the language is used and learned.

Select Bibliography

Boas, Franz, and Ella Deloria. 1941. *Dakota Grammar. Memoirs of the National Academy of Sciences 23, Part 2.* Washington, DC: U.S. Government Printing Office.

Buechel, Eugene. 1939. *A Grammar of Lakota, The Language of the Teton Sioux Indians.* St. Francis, SD: St. Francis Mission.

_____. 1983. *Dictionary of Teton Sioux.* Pine Ridge, SD: Red Cloud Indian School.

de Reuse, William J. 1987. "One Hundred Years of Lakota Linguistics (1887–1987)." In *Kansas Working Papers in Linguistics* 12: 13–42.

_____. 1990. "A Supplemental Bibliography of Lakhota Language and Linguistics." In *Kansas Working Papers in Linguistics* 15.2:146–165.

Deloria, Ella. 1932. "Dakota Texts." *Publications of the American Ethnological Society, Vol. 14.*

Parks, Douglas R., and Raymond J. DeMallie. 1992. "Sioux, Assiniboine, and Stoney Dialects: A Classification." In *Anthropological Linguistics.* 34: 233–255.

Riggs, Stephen R. 1893a. *Dakota Grammar, Texts and Ethnography.* Washington: U.S. Government Printing Office.

_____. 1893b. *A Dakota-English Dictionary.* Washington, DC: U.S. Government Printing Office.

Rood, David S., and Allan R. Taylor. 1996. "Lakhota." In *Vol. 17, Handbook of North American Indians.* Washington: Smithsonian Institution.

University of Colorado Lakhota Project. 1976. *Beginning Lakhota* [two volumes]. Boulder, Colorado: Univ. of Colorado Linguistics Department.

Lao

Thomas W. Gething

Language Name: Lao. **Alternate:** *Laotian.* **Autonym:** *Lao.*

Location: Laos (Lao People's Democratic Republic) in Southeast Asia.

Family: Southwestern branch of the Tai family.

Related Languages: THAI (Siamese), SHAN, Ahom, Lu, Black Tai, White Tai.

Dialects: Vientiane, Luang Phrabang, Campasak.

Number of Speakers: 2.8–3.0 million in Laos, with additional speakers of the related Isan dialect in northeastern Thailand.

Origin and History

Lao exhibits a long history of exposure to Indic culture, as revealed by the numerous SANSKRIT and PALI loanwords in Lao. While Tai languages are principally monosyllabic, the polysyllabic Indic loans in Lao are significant, especially in scientific, academic, and religious terminology. The Tai language family is believed to have originated in what is now southern China, with migration of the antecedents of the Lao commencing in the 9th and 10th centuries.

The political unification of the Lao peoples was accomplished by Prince Fa Ngum in 1353 with the founding of the Lan Xang Kingdom. Some three centuries later, Lan Xang split into three centers and in the late 1700s Thai (Siamese) suzerainty was established. From the late 18th century to the mid 20th century, French control brought European influence to bear on the Lao, although traditional cultural values and mores proved resistant to that presence. Independence from France came in 1954.

Orthography and Basic Phonology

Lao uses a unique Indic-derived script, similar to, but distinct from Thai script. There are 30 consonant symbols, classified as middle, low, or high, which with vowel length and syllable final sound, and (in some morphemes) tone symbols determine the tone of each syllable. There are 19 vowel and 3 tone symbols.

ຮຽນ ແລະ ລົງພາກປະຕິບັດ

The above sample phrase translates to: *hían lɛ̄ lóŋphàakpatibát* 'study and practice'.

Table 1: Vowels

	Front	Central	Back
High	i	ʉ	u
Mid	e	ə	o
Low	æ	a	ɔ

All vowels can be either short or long. Vowel length is indicated in this chapter by doubling of the vowel symbol.

The high-central vowel *ʉ* is phonetically [ɯ], and *ə* is phonetically [ə]. In contrast to the central vowels, which are unrounded, the back vowels are all rounded: *ɔ* is phonetically [ɔ].

The voiced stops /b d/ are fully voiced, *ŋ* represents the velar nasal, and *c* represents a palatal stop [ts] (see Table 2 on the following page).

In addition, there are diphthongs *ia, uea,* and *ua.*

Lao is a tone language. There are six distinct tones, three level tones (low, mid, high), and three contour tones (rising, high falling, low falling). Tone in Lao serves to distinguish among words: the sequence /suea/ can mean 'tiger', 'mat', or 'shirt', depending on whether it occurs with rising, middle, or low-falling tone. In this chapter tones are marked for each syllable with superscript numbers as follows:

	Phonetic	Value	Diacritic
Low	1	22	a
Mid	2	33	ā
High falling	3	42	à
Low falling	4	21	â
High	5	45	á
Rising	6	24	ǎ

Linguists' transcriptions of these tones vary, but many scholars use accent diacritics above the vocalic in place of the numbers (^{1} is unmarked, ^{2} is –, ^{3} is ˋ, ^{4} is ˆ, ^{5} is ˊ, and ^{6} is ˇ).

Basic Morphology

Lao is an isolating language. Thus, there is very little inflectional morphology. In general, there is no overt plural marking and there is no subject-verb agreement. There is no gender marking except in compounds: for example, *phuu*^{2}*usaay*^{5} 'man' (literally, 'person-male') vs. *phuu*^{2}*usaaw*^{6} 'woman ('person-female'); *phɔɔ*^{2}*khaa*^{3} 'businessman' (literally, 'father-trade') vs. *mææ*^{2}*khaa*^{3} 'businesswoman' ('mother-trade').

Lao has a system of noun classifiers used in counting constructions and in several other constructions. There are several

Table 2: Consonants

		Labial	Dental	Palatal	Velar	Glottal
Stops	Unaspirated	p	t	c	k	ʔ
	Aspirated	ph	th		kh	
	Voiced	b	d			
Fricatives		f	s			h
Nasals		m	n	ñ	ŋ	
Lateral			l			
Glides		w		y		

dozen classes of nouns. Some count nouns are simply repeated as their own classifier, while others use a particular classifier assigned on a semantic basis; often the specific classifier used depends on the shape of the object represented. A comprehensive list of Lao classifiers would include many that are unique to a particular noun, but by Kerr's (1972) calculation, there are 85 that can be considered "common". Typical of these more common classifiers are the following: *baj* 'round shape', *hɔɔ*^{2} 'package shape', *kabɔɔk*^{4} 'tubular shape', *lam*^{5} 'rolled shape', *sen*^{4} 'slender, stringlike shape', *bɔɔn*^{2} 'places', *duaŋ* 'stars and round shapes', *khon*^{5} 'people', *lam*^{5} 'boats', *met*^{2} 'seeds, gems', *sabap*^{2} 'printed matter', *ton*^{4} 'trees', *too* 'animals; articles of clothing', *khuu*^{2} 'pairs', *sut*^{2} 'sets', and *ʔan* a catch all, meaning 'item' or 'each'.

There is no tense marking on verbs in Lao. Temporal reference is frequently made by use of overt "time" words or phrases like "yesterday" or "last year" or adverbials like *khəəy*^{5} 'ever'.

Basic Syntax

The basic word order in Lao is SVO; a noun phrase preceding the verb represents the subject under all circumstances:

khɔj^{4} phɔɔ^{2} muu^{2}
I meet/see friend
'I saw my friend.'

Adjectives in Lao generally follow the nouns they modify. However, in more complicated noun phrases, a topic and comment structure prevails:

kææ^{3}w ñay^{2}
bottle large 'large bottle'

bia^{1} kææw^{3} ñay^{2} sɔɔŋ kææw^{3}
beer bottle large two CLASS
'two large bottles of beer'

Verbs are negated by *bɔɔ*^{2} preceding the main verb in a sentence:

bɔɔ^{2} pay — bɔɔ^{2} mææn^{2}
NEG go — NEG true
'doesn't go' — 'not true'

When the same segmentals with first tone occur in sentence-final position, *bɔɔ*^{1} indicates a question.

Lao has a range of serial verb constructions, in which verbs occur in sequence with a composite meaning; an example occurs in Example Sentence (3).

Contact with Other Languages

Loanwords in Lao are mainly of Indic origin, although some KHMER, FRENCH and CHINESE loans are also found. In recent times THAI has been the source for some borrowings.

From Sanskrit: *see*^{4}*thakit*^{5} 'economics'
From Pali: *mahaa*^{6}*kasat*^{5} 'king'
From French: *kaa*^{1}*fee*^{5} 'coffee', *sinee*^{3} 'movie theater', *lii*^{5}*see*^{3} 'school'
From Chinese: *kəə*^{4}*ptɛ*^{5} 'slippers'
From Khmer: *phʔəən* 'accidentally'
From Thai: *lew*^{5} 'fast'

Common Words

man:	phuu^{2}saay^{5}	long:	ñaaw^{5}
woman:	phuu^{2}saaw^{6}	small:	nɔɔy^{3}
water:	nam^{3}	sun:	ta^{1}wen^{5}
three:	saam^{6}	good:	dii^{1}
fish:	paa^{1}	bird:	nok^{2}
big:	ñay^{2}	dog:	ma:
tree:	kok^{5}may^{3}	no:	bɔɔ^{2}
yes:	{confirm usually w/ verb repetition}		

Example Sentences

(1) caw^{3} khəəy^{5} khii^{5} hʉa^{5}bin^{1} bɔɔ^{1}?
you ever ride boat-fly Q
'Have you ever ridden in an airplane?'

(2) khɔɔp^{4}cay^{1} caw^{3} laay^{6} thii^{5} ʔaw^{1} naŋ^{6}sʉʉ^{6}
thank you much that bring letter

maa^{5} hay^{4}.
toward me give
'Thank you very much for bringing the letter.'

(3) khaa^{4}laa^{3}sa^{1}kaan^1 pay^1 sɔɔy^2 ʔop^{5}lom^5 bɔɔ^2 day^3.
civil-servant go help train NEG able
'The civil servant can't go help out in the training.'

Efforts to Preserve, Protect, and Promote the Language

Lao is the national language of the Lao People's Democratic Republic and is the home language of approximately two-thirds of the 4.6 million residents of the nation. Despite the French colonial presence and the disruption caused by the Vietnam War (from the mid-1950s through the mid-1970s), the Lao language has remained relatively untouched by Western influence. It is the language of government, commerce, and public education. It is used in the schools throughout the nation and has an extensive and rich literary tradition. Literacy is estimated at approximately 84 percent (*Asiaweek*, May 4, 1994).

Select Bibliography

Bunnyavong, Duangduon. 1995. *Vatchananukom Pakop Hup/ Luakfen Khamsap lae Hiaphiang*. Vientiane, LPDR: Phainam.

Gething, Thomas W. 1975. "Two Types of Semantic Contrast between Thai and Lao." In *A Tai Festschrift for William Gedney*. Honolulu: University of Hawaii Press.

Hoshino, Tatsuo, and Russell Marcus. 1981. *Lao for Beginners: An Introduction to the Spoken and Written Language of Laos*. Rutland, VT: Charles E. Tuttle Co.

Kerr, Allen D. 1972. *Lao-English Dictionary*. Washington, DC: Catholic University of America Press.

Koret, Peter. 1999. "Books of Search: The Invention of Lao Literature as a Subject of Study." In *Lao: Culture and Society*. Chiang Mai, Thailand: Silkworm Books.

Marcus, Russell. 1983. *English-Lao; Lao-English Dictionary*, revised ed. Rutland, VT: Charles E. Tuttle Co.

Rex E. Wallace

Language Name: Latin. **Autonym:** *lingua Latina.*

Location: Latin was spoken originally in many small towns scattered throughout the territory of Latium in central Italy. The variety of Latin spoken in Rome emerged as the standard because of this community's military and political prominence. By the first century B.C. Roman Latin had replaced most of the local dialects in Latium and had been carried by means of Roman colonies throughout the Italian peninsula. Roman conquests outside of Italy introduced Latin into western and Central Europe, Northern Africa, southern Britain, Germany, the Balkans as far south as Greece, Asia Minor and the Levant.

Family: Latin is the major representative of the Latino-Faliscan group within the Italic branch of the Indo-European language family.

Related Languages: Faliscan; more distantly, Oscan, Umbrian, South Picene, and other less well-attested Sabellian languages including Vestinian, Marrucinian, Paelignian, Marsian, Volscian, Aequian, and Hernican.

Dialects: Latin is a cover term for all of the different dialects of the Latin language. "Classical" Latin was used for the speech of the educated classes of Rome in the first century B.C. It is also the term applied to the Latin of literary compositions produced by the most notable authors of this social class, for example, Cicero, Caesar, and Virgil. The Latin of different areas, social levels, registers, and chronological periods is designated by other modifiers. Vulgar Latin is generally the label reserved for the speech of the common folk. Rural Latin refers to the speech of the inhabitants of the hill country in central and southern Latium, particularly as it was used in the last few centuries B.C. Rural Latin is contrasted with the Latin of Rome, so-called Urban Latin. Unless otherwise indicated, forms cited in this chapter are Classical Latin.

Origin and History

Speakers of the Italic branch of Indo-European moved into the Italian peninsula during the second millennium B.C. By the beginning of the Iron Age, about 900 B.C., Italic speakers had settled throughout central Italy.

Latin developed from the form of Italic spoken in Latium, a territory located south of the Tiber River in central Italy. Initially the term "Latin" was used to refer to the various regional varieties of the language, for example, the Latin of Praeneste, the Latin of Lanuvium, and others. After Rome became the foremost political and economic power in the region, Latin was used as a cover term for all of the geographical and social varieties of the language spoken and written throughout the Roman world.

The earliest evidence for Latin is a graffito incised on a fragment of an amphora base found near the sanctuary of *Mater Matuta* at Satricum, dated to the mid-seventh century B.C. The first complete text, a salutation scratched on a drinking vessel found at Gabii (present-day Osteria dell'Osa), is slightly later, circa 625 B.C. The oldest Latin inscription found at Rome, the so-called *Duenos* vase, is dated to the last half of the sixth century B.C. Inscriptions, most of which are dedications, epitaphs, or proprietary notices, are the sole source of our knowledge until the third century B.C., when contacts with Hellenistic Greeks led to the rise of Roman literary genres. The most important writers from the earliest period of Latin literature are the poets of Latin comedy, Plautus and Terence, and the Roman prose writer, Cato the Elder. After the third century B.C. the language is abundantly attested by both literary and epigraphical sources.

The first century B.C. was the most distinguished period of Roman literary activity. Literary compositions, many of which have no equal within the Western literary tradition, were published during this period: *De Rerum Natura* ('On the Nature of the Universe') by Lucretius, *Aeneidos* ('The Aeneid') by Virgil, *De Bello Gallico* ('The Gallic War') by Caesar, the corpus of political speeches and philosophical treatises authored by Cicero, and the *Carmina* (songs) of Catullus and Horace. The variety of Latin as it appeared in the prose and poetry of these authors was codified as the standard variety for literary composition. Thus, the Latin of the Roman educated classes served as the model for almost all later Latin literature.

The elaborate and complex sentence structures characteristic of the literary language diverged considerably from the more simple structures typical of spoken Latin, especially *sermo quotidianus* 'everyday speech' or *plebeius sermo* 'the speech of ordinary people'. This variety of Latin is often referred to, albeit unfortunately, as *lingua uulgaris* 'language of the crowd' or Vulgar Latin. Evidence for this variety of Latin is preserved in graffiti from the Campanian city of Pompeii, in funerary inscriptions, and in *defixiones*, which are curses incised on lead tablets and intended to bring harm to one's enemies. The *Satyricon*, a novel composed by Petronius, the arbiter of taste in the court of Nero, is an excellent source for information about Latin spoken during the first century A.D. The *Satyricon* presents the adventures of characters belonging to the lower social orders. Another source of information about spoken Latin is the *Appendix Probi*, a vocabulary list prepared by a schoolmaster in the third century A.D. The *Appendix* was apparently

Table 1: Consonants

		Labial	Dental	Palatal	Velar	Labiovelar	Glottal
Stops	Voiceless	p	t		k	qu [kʷ]	
	Voiced	b	d		g	gu [gʷ]	
Fricatives		f	s				h
Nasals		m	n				
Lateral			l				
Trill				r			
Glides				i [y]		u [w]	

designed to inform pupils about the most common misspellings of Classical Latin words. This list reflects Vulgar Latin pronunciation, 'mispronunciations' when measured against Classical Latin counterparts. The *Appendix Probi* is of particular importance because it is a barometer of the increasing divergence between Classical Latin, the literary register, and the language of everyday speech.

As the Roman Empire expanded beyond the bounds of the Italian peninsula, the Latin language followed. We know, from a census taken by the emperor Augustus (30 B.C.–A.D. 14), that the number of Roman citizens in A.D 14 was very near five million (4,973,000). During the height of the Roman Empire Latin was spoken in western and Central Europe, southern Britain, Northern Africa, the Balkans as far south as Greece, and portions of the Middle East. In most areas of the empire east of the Adriatic Sea, GREEK maintained its position as the primary spoken language, while Latin served as the language of civil administration. In the western provinces, however, Romanization was more thorough and the prestige and tenacity of Latin were such that it gradually replaced many of the native languages. The Romance languages of western Europe (SPANISH, PORTUGUESE, FRENCH) and of the northern Balkans (ROMANIAN) are descendants of varieties of provincial Latin.

After the collapse of the western half of the Roman Empire in the fifth century A.D., the varieties of Latin spoken in the provinces developed in relative isolation. Regional differences in spoken Latin widened. By the eighth century A.D. at the latest, it is no longer possible to speak of mutually intelligible varieties of Latin.

Despite the emergence of the Romance vernaculars, Latin survived in many areas as the language of education, administration, law, and religion. Latin was used actively as a literary language from the Middle Ages into the Italian Renaissance, particularly during those times when there was a revival of interest in Roman literature. Latin survived in the religious services of the Catholic Church until 1965, when the Second Vatican Council sanctioned the use of "vernaculars". Today masses are again being celebrated in Latin in some places and Latin remains the language of choice for the communication of papal encyclicals.

Orthography and Basic Phonology

The Latin alphabet was borrowed from the Etruscans who had established colonial outposts in northern Latium in the middle of the seventh century B.C. The earliest form of the Latin alphabet contained 21 letters. About 250 B.C. the letter *g* was created to represent the sound /g/ and this new letter took the place of *zeta* in the Latin *abecedarium*. The Greek letters *y* and *z* were added to the end of the Latin alphabet in the first century A.D. in order to write Greek words that had sounds not found in the Latin sound system (*z* = /z/, *y* = /ü/).

A B C D E F G H I K L M N O P Q R S T V X (Y Z)

The Latin alphabet, listed above, was in large part phonemic but evidence from metrics guarantees a contrast in vowel length that was not represented by the writing system. Each vowel sign stood for both short and long vowel phonemes; for example, *a* = /a, ā/. The Latin glides *y* and *w* were also represented by the corresponding vowel signs, so that the letter *i* could stand for any one of three phonemes /i, ī, y/.

The letter *g* regularly spelled a voiced velar stop /g/, but when it stood before a nasal it represented the velar nasal /ŋ/, for example, *agnus* 'lamb' = /aŋnus/.

The Etruscans spelled the voiceless velar *k* by means of the letters *gamma* (*c*), *kappa* (*k*), and *qoppa* (*q*). This manner of spelling the sound *k* was gradually phased out of the Latin writing system in favor of the spelling by means of the letter *c*, for example, *capio* /kapiō/. However, the letter *k* remained the sign of choice in a small set of words, such as *kalendae* 'Calends', and *kaeso* 'Kaeso' (proper name), and the letter *q* was reserved, in combination with the letter *u*, to spell the voiceless labio-velar /kʷ/. The voiced labio-velar /gʷ/ was spelled by the digraph *gu*. The letter *x* spelled the cluster *ks*, such as *rex* 'king' /rēks/.

Latin had a distinction between long and short consonants. Phonemically long consonants were spelled with double letters, for example, *agger* 'pile' /agger/ versus *ager* 'field' /ager/. Voiced stops were devoiced before voiceless sounds, such as *urbis* /urbis/ 'city (genitive singular)' but *urbs* /urps/ 'city (nominative singular)'; and *scrībit* 's/he writes' but *scrīpsit* 's/he wrote'. Dental stops were lost before *-s*, such as *sentit* 's/he feels' but *sēnsit* 's/he felt' < **sentsit*; *laudis* 'praise (genitive singular)' but *laus* < **lauds* 'praise (nominative singular)'.

The dental nasal *n* assimilated to /ŋ/ before a following velar or labiovelar, such as *tangō* 'touch' = /taŋgō/, *linquit*, and 's/he leaves' = /liŋkʷit/. The Latin *r* phoneme was phonetically a trill.

The *g* phoneme assimilated to /ŋ/ before a nasal, for example, *lignum* 'bundle of wood' = /liŋnum/.

The lateral liquid is velarized before back vowels, before consonants (except *l*), and in word-final position, as in *lātus* 'broad' = /ɫātus/, *uoltis* 'you wish' = /woɫtis/, *sōl* 'sun' = /sōɫ/; but *leuis* 'light' = /lewis/.

Table 2: Vowels

	Front	Central	Back
High	i		u
Mid	e		o
Low		a	

All Latin vowels could be either long or short. Phonetically, short mid and high vowels were qualitatively distinct from their long counterparts. Long vowels were higher and more tense, such as [ē vs. ɛ, and ō vs. ɔ]. In addition to the vowels listed, Latin had four diphthongs: *ui, oi, ai,* and *au*.

Vowels were shortened before all word-final consonants except -*s*; compare the variant pronunciations for the noun 'honor' *honor* vs. *honōs*.

Vowels were lengthened in nasal + *s* clusters. The nasal was not pronounced, even in Old Latin, but continued to be spelled in many words. As a result, during the Classical Latin period pronunciations influenced by spelling reintroduced the nasal before -*s*, such as *cōnsul* 'consul', but Old Latin *cōsol*.

In word-final position the sequence vowel + nasal was replaced by a long vowel, possibly nasalized, *ītaliam fātō* = /ītaliā fātō/ or /ītaliā̃ fātō/.

The diphthongs /oi/ and /ai/ were spelled *oe* and *ae* respectively. Classical Latin had a stress accent. Monosyllables were accented, except for a few clitics, such as *-que*, *-ue*, *-ne*, etc. For polysyllabic words the position of the accent was governed by the "law of the penultimate". Disyllabic words were accented on the penult, as in *dūcit* 's/he leads'. Words of more than two syllables stressed the penult, *unless* the vowel in that syllable was short and the syllable was open, in which case stress moved to the antepenultimate syllable, as in *dū́cimus* 'we lead' but *dūcēmus* 'we will lead', *dūcúntur* 'they are led'.

Basic Morphology

Latin is an inflecting language of the fusional type. All inflectional categories are marked by means of suffixes.

The nominal system, comprising nouns, adjectives, the cardinal numerals 1–3, pronouns, and pronominal adjectives, has the basic features of gender, number, and case. There are three genders (masculine, feminine, and neuter) and two numbers (singular and plural). Latin has six primary cases: nominative, accusative, genitive, dative, ablative, and vocative. Another case, the locative, is preserved for some nouns, such as *rūrī* 'in the country' and *Rōmae* 'at Rome'.

Nouns are organized into subsystems called "declensions" based on the stem type. Latin has five major vocalic-stem declensions, *a*- (*fēmina* 'woman'), *o*- (*seruos* 'servant'), *i*- (*fīnis* 'boundary'), *u*- (*exercitus* 'army') and *ē*- stems (*rēs* 'matter'), and four major consonant-stem declensions, stop stems (*prīnceps* 'chief'), *s*- stems (*genus* 'race'), *r*- stems (*pater* 'father'), and *n*- stems (*termen* 'limit').

Nouns were generally assigned to one of three genders on the basis of their stem type. For example, *a*- stems were feminine, *o*- stems and *u*- stems were either masculine or neuter, *-men*- stems were neuter, and so forth. But there were exceptions, particularly in the case of animate nouns, which were assigned gender based on sex, for example, *agricola* 'farmer', *a*-stem masculine.

Singular:

	A-STEMS	O-STEMS	CONSONANT-STEMS
NOMINATIVE	fēmin-a	seru-os	prīncep-s
ACCUSATIVE	fēmin-am	seru-om	prīncip-em
GENITIVE	fēmin-ae	seru-ī	prīncip-is
DATIVE	fēmin-ae	seru-ō	prīncip-ī
ABLATIVE	fēmin-ā	seru-ō	prīncip-e
VOCATIVE	fēmin-a	seru-e	prīncep-s

Plural:

	A-STEMS	O-STEMS	CONSONANT-STEMS
NOMINATIVE	fēmin-ae	seru-ī	prīncip-ēs
ACCUSATIVE	fēmin-ās	seru-ōs	prīncip-ēs
GENITIVE	fēmin-ārum	seru-ōrum	prīncip-um
DATIVE	fēmin-īs	seru-īs	prīncip-ibus
ABLATIVE	fēmin-īs	seru-īs	prīncip-ibus
VOCATIVE	fēmin-ae	seru-ī	prīncip-ēs

The inflection of the declensional classes of adjectives is the same as for nouns, except that there are fewer stem types. Latin does not have *u*- or *ē*-stem adjectives.

Demonstrative, anaphoric, emphatic, relative and intensive pronouns are inflected for gender, number and case. Latin personal pronouns are inflected for number and case but not gender.

First Person Pronoun:

	Singular	Plural
NOMINATIVE	egō	nōs
ACCUSATIVE	mē	nōs
GENITIVE	meī	nostrī/nostrum
DATIVE	mihi	nōbīs
ABLUTIVE	mē	nōbīs

Latin verbs are inflected for the following categories: tense (past, present, future), aspect (imperfective, perfective), mood (indicative, subjunctive, imperative), voice (active, middle-passive), person (1, 2, 3), and number (singular, plural). Alongside the finite forms of the verb, a number of nonfinite forms belonged to the system: infinitives (present, perfect), participles (present, perfect), supines, a gerundive, and a gerund.

The verb system was divided into two subsystems based on aspect: *infectum* (present system) vs. *perfectum* (perfect system). Each system had three tenses: present, future, and past.

	INFECTUM	PERFECTUM
Present	*dūcit* 'he is leading'	*dūxit* 'he led'
Future	*dūcet* 'he will lead'	*dūxerit* 'he will have led'
Past	*dūcēbat* 'he was leading'	*dūxerat* 'he had led'

The verb system was organized into inflectional types called "conjugations" based on the stem of the present-tense verb. There are five basic conjugations: *ā*- stems (*laudā*- 'praises'), *ē*- stems (*monē*- 'warns'), *i*- stems (*capi*- 'seizes'), *ī*- stems (*audī* 'hears') and *C*-/-*i*-stems (*dūc*-, *dūci*- 'leads'). The formation of the perfect stem was not (always) predictable based on present tense conjugation class.

Verbs in all conjugations agreed with their subjects in person and number, as illustrated below.

portā- 'carry' ā- stem, active

Present	Singular	Plural
1st	portō	portāmus
2nd	portās	portātis
3rd	portat	portant

Perfect	Singular	Plural
1st	portāvī	portāvimus
2nd	portāstī	portāstis
	portāvistī	portāvistis
3rd	portāvit	portārunt
		portāvērunt

monē- 'warn' ē- stem, passive

Present	Singular	Plural
1st	moneor	monēmur
2nd	monēris	monēminī
3rd	monētur	monentur

Perfect	Singular	Plural
1st	monitus sum	monitī sumus
2nd	monitus es	monitī estis
3rd	monitus est	monitī sunt

New words were generated in Latin by prefixation and suffixation.

Abstract nouns were formed by the suffixes -*tās*/-*tat*-, -*tūdō*/-*tūdin*-, and -*i(a)*: *audāc-ia* 'boldness', *uēri-tās*, *uēri-tātis* 'truth', *forti-tūdō*, *forti-tūdinis* 'strength'. The suffixes -*tr*-, -*c(u)l*-, -*cr*-, -*br*- and -*bul*- formed instrumental neuter nouns of the *o*-declension: *arā-trum* 'plow', *pō-c(u)lum* 'cup', *sepul-crum* 'tomb', etc. The most common agent noun suffix was -*tor*/-*tōr*-, such as *uictor* 'conquerer' and *genitor* 'parent'. The feminine suffix corresponding to masculine -*tor*/-*tōr*- is -*trīx*, -*trīcis*, as in *genitrīx*.

There were a handful of suffixes, -*āli*-, -*āri*-, -*ān*-, that were used to form adjectives from nouns: *ann-ālis* 'yearly', *argent-ārius* 'of silver', *urb-ānus* 'pertaining to the city'. Deverbative adjectives were built from the suffix -*bili*-, as in *amā-bilis* 'capable of loving'. The prefix *per*- was added to adjectives to form intensives: *facilis* 'easy' vs. *per-facilis* 'really easy'.

Verbs were productively formed from nouns by means of the suffix -*ā*, such as *nōmen*, *nōminis* 'name' *nōmin-āre* 'to call by name'. Latin also had an array of adverbial prefixes that were used to produce new verbs, for example, eō 'go' *trāns-eō* 'go across'; *ueniō* 'come' *per-ueniō* 'arrive at'.

Basic Syntax

The order of the major constituents of a Latin sentence varied according to style, register, and author. In the formal prose of Caesar and Cicero, SOV order is most common, although permutations of this order occur frequently and do not in any way affect the grammaticality of the sentence. In the less formal varieties of prose, however, as in, for example, the letters of Cicero, the SOV order is not as predominant, suggesting that the verb-final position typical of literary prose styles may not have been as characteristic of the spoken Latin of the period. The following examples are from Caesar's prose:

SOV:

hic	pāg-us	ūn-us
this/NOM/SG/MASC	district-NOM/SG/MASC	one-NOM/SG/MASC

L. Cassi-um	cōnsul-em
Cassius-ACC/SG/MASC	consul-ACC/SG/MASC

interfēc-era-t
kill-PAST/PLUPERF-3SG
'This one district had killed the consul, Lucius Cassius.'

OSV:

id	Helueti-ī	rat-ibus
this:ACC/SG/NEUT	Heluetiī-NOM/PL/MASC	raft-ABL/PL/MASC

ac	lintr-ibus	iūnctīs
and	canoe-ABL/PL/FEM	together-ABL/PL/FEM

trāns-ī-ba-nt
cross-go-IMPF.3PL
'The Helvetii were crossing this with rafts and canoes.'

This flexibility in word order was possible because the noun phrase constituents of the Latin sentence were marked by case: subjects were nominative, direct objects were accusative, and indirect objects were dative. Possession and partitive relations were marked by the genitive. The ablative case expressed adverbial notions such as time, place and manner. Vocative was the case of direct address. The locative, where it existed, specified the place where the action of the sentence occurred.

The order of elements within a noun phrase in the Latin of the classical period depended on the type of modifier. Adjectives and dependent genitives appeared in both pre-and post-nominal positions. Relative clauses typically followed the antecedent, while demonstrative modifiers like *hic* 'this' and *ille* 'that' were placed before the noun.

Adjectives agreed with their head nouns in gender, number, and case: *prim-ā noct-e* (first-ABL/SG/FEM night-ABL/SG/FEM) 'on the first night'.

The most common form of sentence negation was by means of the particle *nōn*, but certain syntactic structures required different forms of negation. For example, negative adjunct clauses of purpose were introduced by the particle *nē*:

nē mīlit-ēs oppid-um
so that-NEG soldiers-NOM/SG/MASC town-ACC/SG/NEUT

in-rumpe-re-nt port-ās obstru-it
into-break-IMPF/SUBJ-3PL gate-ACC/PL/FEM barricade-PERF/3SG
‘He barricaded the gates so that the soldiers would not break into the town.’

Contact with Other Languages

The earliest external influences on Latin came from neighboring peoples in central Italy. Several words were borrowed into Latin from a dialect of Oscan or Umbrian. A few Latin words may be of ETRUSCAN origin. Roman civilization throughout its history was most profoundly influenced by the Greeks. As a result, Greek loanwords constitute by far the most important source of borrowed words in Latin.

From Oscan or Umbrian: *bōs* ‘ox’, *popīna* ‘cookshop’
From Etruscan: *taberna* ‘shop’, *satelles* ‘bodyguard’
From Greek: *architectus* ‘architect’(< *architéktōn* ‘master builder’), *calx* ‘limestone’(< *chálix*), *machina* ‘engine’ (< *machaná*), *poeta* ‘poet’ (< *poiētēs*), *philosophia* ‘philosopher’ (< *philosophía* ‘lover of wisdom’)

Common Words

man:	uir, uirī, MASC
long:	longus, longa, longum
woman:	mulier, mulieris, FEM
small:	paruus, parua, paruum
water:	aqua, aquae, FEM
yes:	ita, vērō, certō, sic
sun:	sōl, sōlis, MASC
no:	nōn, minimē
three:	trēs, tria
good:	bonus, bonā, bonum
fish:	piscis, piscis, MASC
bird:	auis, auis, FEM
big:	magnus, magna, magnum
dog:	canis, canis, MASC/FEM
tree:	arbor, arboris, FEM

Example Sentences

(1) qu-ā dē caus-ā
this-ABL/SG/FEM for+ABL reason-ABL/SG/FEM

Helueti-ī quoque reliqu-ōs
Helvetians-NOM/SG/MASC also rest-ACC/PL/MASC

Gall-ōs uirtūt-e praeced-unt
Gauls-ACC/PL/MASC courage-ABL/SG/FEM surpass-PRES/3PL

quod fere cotidiān-īs proeli-īs
because almost daily-ABL/PL/NEUT battle-ABL/PL/NEUT

cum Germānīs contend-unt.
with+ABL German-ABL/PL/MASC fight-PRES/3PL
‘For this reason the Helvetians also surpass the rest of the Gauls in courage, because they fight in battles with the Germans almost daily.’ (Julius Caesar)

(2) h-ī ne-que uult-um
these-NOM/PL/MASC not-and expression-ACC/PL/MASC

finge-re ne-que interdum lacrim-ās
maintain-PRES/ACT/INF not-and at times tear-ACC/PL/FEM

tenē-re pot-era-nt.
hold back-PRES/ACT/INF be.able-IMPERF-3PL
‘These men were not able to maintain their expression and they were not able to hold back their tears at times.’ (Julius Caesar)

(3) sī scrībe-re-m ipse long-ior
if write-IMPF/SUBJ/1SG self:NOM/SG/MASC longer-NOM/SG/FEM

epistul-a fu-isse-t.
letter-NOM/SG/FEM be-PLUPF/SUBJ-3SG
‘If I myself were writing, the letter would have been longer.’ (Marcus Cicero)

Select Bibliography

Allen, W. Sidney. 1989. *Vox Latina*. 2d ed. Cambridge: Cambridge University Press.

Coleman, Robert. 1987. “Latin and the Italic languages.” In Bernard Comrie, ed., *The World's Major Languages*, 180–212. London: Croom Helm.

Ernout, Alfred, and Antoine Meillet. 1985. 4th ed. *Dictionnaire étymologique de la langue latine: Histoire des mots*. Paris: Klincksieck.

Ernout, Alfred, and François Thomas. 1984. *Syntaxe Latine*. Paris: Klincksieck.

Hofmann, J.B. 1951. *Lateinische Umgangssprache*. 3d ed. Heidelberg: Carl Winter.

Leumann, Manu., J.B. Hofmann, and Anton Szantyr. 1977. *Lateinische Grammatik*. München: Beck.

Meillet, Antoine. 1966. *Esquisse d'une histoire de la langue latine*. Paris: Éditions Klincksieck.

Niedermann, Max. 1985. *Phonétique historique du latin*. Paris: Éditions Klincksieck.

Palmer, Leonard R. 1954. *The Latin Language*. London: Faber & Faber.

Väänänen, Veikko. 1967. *Introduction au latin vulgaire*. Rev. ed. Paris: Klincksieck.

LATVIAN

Lalita Muizniece

Language Name: Latvian. **Alternate:** *Lettish.*

Location: Latvia. Enclaves in Russia and other former Soviet republics. After World War II Latvian-speaking groups emigrated to many major and some smaller cities around the world, primarily in Germany, Sweden, the United States, Canada, Venezuela, and Australia.

Family: (East) Baltic branch of the Indo-European family.

Related Languages: LITHUANIAN, East Prussian (now extinct).

Dialects: (1) Central dialect (the current standard and the basis for the literary language). It is geographically centrally located and the least influenced by neighboring foreign languages. (2) High Latvian dialect, spoken in the eastern part of Latvia. It has preserved the older grammatical forms and open syllables, but has changed the vowel quality in certain environments, devoiced consonants in the word-final position, and depalatalized certain consonant clusters. (3) Tamian dialect, spoken in the northwestern areas of Latvia. This dialect has been considerably influenced by Finno-Ugric dialects whose speakers have historically shared the same territory. Its chief grammatical differences include having only masculine gender, and the third person verb ending for all persons.

Number of Speakers: 2–2.5 million.

Origin and History

Together with Lithuanian, Latvian makes up the East Baltic branch of the Baltic language family. All members of the West Baltic branch are extinct.

Latvian has been spoken in approximately the same area (the geopolitical boundaries of Latvia) since at least the 13th century.

Influences on Latvian have come from three sources: the Western Finnic, Germanic, and Slavic languages. After the Latvian people's ancestors (Semigallian, Selian, and Latgalian speakers) came into contact with Finno-Ugric languages, their language developed some notable distinctions from its earlier state, including placing of the word stress on the first syllable, loss of short and shortening of long end vowels, development of low front vowel [e], regressive vowel harmony, etc. At some point Latvian lost the instrumental case ending, still active in Lithuanian. Lacking written records, it is impossible to date these changes, but we know they were established by the 13th century when isolated Latvian words are found incorporated into texts in other languages.

Later, since the first authors and translators into Latvian were Germans, a number of GERMAN syntactic patterns found their way into Latvian written texts from which some trickled into the spoken language and eventually into the literary language.

The first preserved written texts in Latvian come from the 16th century. These are exclusively religious texts written by non-Latvians in the GOTHIC script, which was inadequate for representing the Latvian sounds. Also the syntax and phraseology were literally transferred from the German language, resulting in fairly strange renderings. A systematization of spelling and "Latvianization" of expression was attempted by Georgius Mancelius (1593–1654), modeling the orthography on New High German writing and using a diacritical mark to indicate palatalized consonants. The translation of the Bible (1685–1694), both the New and Old Testaments, by a number of mainly German pastors, edited by Ernst Glück (1652–1705), exerted considerable influence on later texts. Some of the German syntactic patterns, established in this publication, lingered in the Latvian written language until the 20th century.

During the "National Awakening" period in the middle of the 19th century, Latvians themselves took charge of the development of their language, bringing it up to the standards of other modern languages. To accomplish that, many new terms were coined mainly by derivation process from existing Latvian words; borrowings from the Classical languages were brought into Latvian; and many unneeded Germanisms were eradicated. Modern Latvian was consciously forged out of three sources: folklore, especially the language of the folk songs; former written texts; and new coinage and borrowings. To prove that Latvian was capable of expressing any idea, Juris Alunāns (1832–1864) published a collection of original and translated poetry, 'Dziesmiņas' (1864); this little book is considered to be a milestone marking the beginning of Modern Latvian.

Around the turn of the century and thereafter, Latvian linguists, notably K. Mülenbachs and J. Endzelīns, studied the Latvian language extensively and published a large number of articles and several major works (grammars and dictionaries). They laid foundations for the present Standard Latvian or modern literary language. In 1922, the orthography was overhauled: the Gothic script was replaced by LATIN letters; a system of diacritics was established; the spelling of affixes was prescribed; and a system for transcribing foreign proper nouns and borrowed words based on pronunciation, rather than spelling in the source language, was laid out. The new orthography was fully adopted only in 1934. Meanwhile, under the leadership of J. Endzelīns, a full-scale language purification took place, and numerous prescriptive instructions regarding correct usage (lexical, morphological, syntactical, and phraseological) were published and became obligatory in publishing houses and schools.

After World War II, Latvia was incorporated into the Soviet Union and came under the political thumb of Moscow. A large number of RUSSIAN, UKRAINIAN, and BELORUSSIAN speakers were settled in Latvia; at one time, these speakers comprised almost half of the inhabitants of the country. The Soviets brought pressure to "internationalize" the language of their constituents to bring them closer to the "Great Russian Language". The Latvian linguists, still nominally headed by J. Endzelīns, resisted; but some spelling changes were prescribed and adopted. The 120,000 Latvian speakers who left the country and are now dispersed mainly in North America, Australia, and some European countries kept the orthography, which was sanctioned in the 1930s. With the regaining of Latvia's independence in 1991, Latvian has been reinstated as the official state language, and there is some stirring toward reevaluation of the changes enacted under Soviet authority.

Orthography and Basic Phonology

Latvian uses the Latin alphabet supplemented by three diacritical marks: a macron over a vowel to indicate length, and a cedilla under, or a wedge over, a consonant to indicate a palatal position of articulation.

Table 1: Consonants

	Labial	Dental	Alveo-palatal	Palatal	Velar
Stops					
Voiceless	p	t		ķ	k
Voiced	b	d		ğ	g
Fricatives					
Voiceless	f	s	š	ch	h
Voiced	v	z	ž		
Affricates					
Voiceless		c	č		
Voiced		dz	dž		
Nasals	m	n		ņ	
Laterals		l		ļ	
Trills		r		ŗ	
Glide				j	

The diacritic under or over a consonant indicates a palatal sound. *C* represents an alveolar affricate [t+s]. Latvian voiceless stops are all unaspirated.

The voiceless consonants /p t ķ k s š č/ are geminated when they occur between two short vowels: *cepa* 'baked' is phonetically [tseppa].

The difference between the vowels /e/ and /ę/ is not represented in Latvian orthography.

In Latvian, length is phonemic. All Latvian vowels can appear long or short; long /ā ē ī ū/ are indicated by a macron over the vowel letter, but /ō/ is generally written without the macron: *o*.

Table 2: Vowels

	Front	Central	Back
High	í i		u ū
Mid	é e		o ō
Low	ę̄ ę	ā a	

Long vowels in Standard Latvian carry one of two tones, level or nonlevel (broken or falling). Tone is not written in Latvian, but it is nonetheless phonemic. The two words *zāle* [zãle] 'hall, auditorium' and *zāle* [zâle] 'grass' differ only in tone; the former has a long level tone, and the latter a long broken (nonlevel) tone.

There are six basic diphthongs in Latvian: /ai au ei eu ia ua/. Additional diphthongs /iu oi ou ui/ are found in a few borrowed words. Like the long vowels, the diphthongs carry either level or nonlevel tone. In some instances, the diphthongs ending in /i/ and /u/ are spelled with *j* and *v*, respectively. If a suffix beginning in a vowel is added immediately following one of these diphthongs, the consonantal value of this letter reemerges: *tramvaj-s* 'tramway' [tramvais], *tramvaj-ā* 'in the tramway' [tramvajā], likewise, if a word ending in a diphthong is followed by a word starting in a vowel: *tev* 'to/for you' [teu], *tev ir* 'you have (literally, to you there is)' [tev ir].

Stress in Latvian generally falls on the first syllable of a word.

Basic Morphology

Latvian nouns consist of three parts: the noun stem, a thematic vowel, and a declensional ending. The declensional ending provides information about case, gender, and number.

Latvian has five cases: nominative, accusative, dative, genitive, and locative. An additional case, the vocative, is used for animate objects only. There are two genders, masculine and feminine; and two numbers, singular and plural. Adjectives agree with the nouns they modify in gender, number, and case:

maz-s bērn-s
small-NOM.M.SG child-NOM.M.SG
'a small child'

maz-i bērn-i
small-NOM.M.PL child-NOM.M.PL
'small children'

There are two sets of adjective endings, one for definite nouns and one for indefinite nouns.

biez-a grāmat-a	'a thick book' (NOM.F.SG)
biez-ā grāmat-a	'the thick book' (NOM.F.SG)
biez-ai grāmat-ai	'to a thick book' (DAT.F.SG)
biez-ajai grāmat-ai	'to the thick book' (DAT.F.SG)

Latvian has three simple tenses (past, present, and future), and three perfect tenses. Verb functions, momentary, iterative, and causative, are indicated by affixes. In addition, there are five moods (indicative, relative, conditional, imperative, and debitive) and three voices (active, passive, and middle/reflexive). Verbs agree with their subjects in person and number; there is no number distinction for the third person.

Latvian has two different passive affixes, one for present tense and the other for past tense.

ābol-s ir ēd-am-s
apple-NOM.M.SG be:3 eat-PASS-NOM.M.SG
'The apple can/should be eaten.'

ābol-s ir ēs-t-s
apple-NOM.M.SG be:3 eat-pass-NOM.M.SG
'The apple has been eaten.'

Latvian has an elaborate participial system. Two sets of participles, adjectival and adverbial, are derived from the present, past, or future verb stem by means of various affixes. The form and use of some participles derived from the verb *smiet' to* 'laugh' are illustrated below.

Adjectival participles:
smej-oš-s bērn-s 'a laughing child'
ap-smej-am-a grimas-e 'a grimace to be laughed at'
iz-smēj-ies bērn-s 'a child who has laughed'
ap-smie-ts bērn-s 'a laughed at child'

Adverbial participles:
bērn-am smej-ot 'while a child is/was/will be laughing'
bērn-s nāk smie-dam-s 'a child comes laughing'
redz-u bērn-u smej-am 'I see a child laughing'

Basic Syntax

The basic word order in Latvian sentences with nominal objects is SVO; with pronominal objects, SOV. In most sentences, the subject is in the nominative case and the direct object is in the accusative:

es redz-u māt-i
1SG.NOM see-1SG mother-SG.ACC
'I see (my) mother.'

māt-e man-i redz
mother-SG.NOM 1SG-ACC see:3
'Mother sees me.'

However, in the debitive mood, the subject switches to dative case and the object to nominative:

man jā-redz māt-e
1SG.DAT DEB-see:3 mother-SG.NOM
'I must see (my) mother.'

In addition, there are some verbs that inherently follow the debitive pattern, without being in debitive mood:

man patīk māt-e
1SG.DAT like mother-SG.NOM
'I like (my) mother.'

Adjectives generally precede the nouns they modify. Latvian sentences are negated by *ne-* prefixed to the verb.

māt-e man-i istab-ā ne-redz
mother-SG.NOM 1SG-ACC room-M.LOC NEG-see:3
'Mother doesn't see me in the room.'

If the verb is accompanied by an indefinite subject, object, and/or adverb, the latter also take the negative prefix, resulting in double or multiple negatives.

ne-vien-s ne-kur ne-ko ne-redz
NEG-one-NOM NEG-where NEG-what NEG-see:3
'Nobody sees anything anywhere.'

Contact with Other Languages

The first borrowed lexical items in Latvian came from Gothic and Old Norse, probably through the Old Prussian language (e.g., *alus* 'ale', *gatve* 'gate', *klaips* 'loaf ', *kviesis* 'wheat', etc.). In the 10th to 13th centuries, borrowings from Old Slavic included words referring to trading, Christianity, social affairs, and some household items. A number of words came from Finno-Ugric languages, chiefly those pertaining to the seashore and seafaring, but also some terms referring to marriage.

From Finno-Ugric: *laiva* 'boat', *puika* 'boy'
From German: *šķēres* 'scissors'
From Russian: *baznīca* 'church', *muita* 'customs'
From ENGLISH: *basketbols* 'basketball', *menedžeris* 'manager'
From FRENCH: *buržuā* 'bourgeois', *servīze* 'service (a set of dishes)'
From SWEDISH: *skola* 'school'

Latvian words, in turn, have been borrowed by the Finno-Ugric speakers and by the Baltic Germans, living for centuries in areas of Latvia and Estonia.

Common Words

man:	vīrietis	small:	mazs
woman:	sieviete	yes:	jā
water:	ūdens	no:	nē
sun:	saule	good:	labs
three:	trīs	bird:	putns
fish:	zivs	dog:	suns
big:	liels	tree:	koks
long:	garš		

Example Sentences

(1) Ir ruden-s.
be:3 autumn-M.NOM.SG
'It's autumn.'

(2) Mēs es-am šeit.
1PL be-1.PL here
'We are here.'

(3) Nāc māj-ā-s.
come:IMPERATIVE.SG house-LOC.PL
'Come home!'

Efforts to Preserve, Protect, and Promote the Language

Although spoken by a relatively small number of people in a small area of the world, Latvian has survived centuries of foreign occupations and natural disasters. During the Black Plague of 1710, the Latvian population declined to less than 240,000. Presently the Latvian lexicon consists of approximately 58 percent native Latvian words and 42 percent borrowed words; the latter have come mainly from international terms, e.g., *ğeogrāfija* 'geography', *chameleons/hameleons* 'chameleon', *kategorisks* 'categorical', *telefōns* 'telephone', etc. The phonology, morphology, and syntax have changed little since the first written records of the 13th century. To keep Latvian from becoming an international jargon, a terminology committee in the Latvian Academy of Sciences that consults with scientists and technicians is at work trying to find appropriate new coinages or derivations in the fields of sciences and technology.

Select Bibliography

Endzelīns, J. 1922. *Lettische Grammatik*. Rīga: Avots.

____. 1971. *Comparative Phonology and Morphology of the Baltic Languages*. The Hague and Paris: Mouton.

English–Latvian Dictionary. 1996. 2nd edition. Rīga: Jāna sēta.

Fennel, T. 1980. *A Grammar of Modern Latvian*. The Hague and Paris: Mouton.

Hauzenberga-Šturma, E. 1967. "Latvian Language." In *J. Rutkis, Latvia: Country and People*. Stockholm: Latvian National Foundation.

Lasmane, V. 1985. *A Course in Modern Latvian*. The American Latvian Association.

Lelis, J. 1984. *Basic Latvian I*. The American Latvian Association.

Turkina, E. 1982. *Latvian-English Dictionary*. 4th rev. ed. Rīga: Avots.

LINGALA

Salikoko S. Mufwene

Language Name and Alternate Name: Lingala.

Location: Northwestern part of the Democratic Republic of Congo, from Kinshasa to Kisangani, also in the northern part of the Popular Republic of Congo, west of the Congo River.

Family: Bantu.

Related Languages: Bobangi.

Dialects: Mankanza or standard Lingala, and urban Lingala. The two varieties differ mostly in their morphosyntactic features, especially regarding the Subject-Verb and Head Noun–Modifier agreement rules. For instance:

Lingala-Mankanza	Urban Lingala	Gloss
ba-to bá-nso (PL1-person PL1-all)	*ba-to nyɔ́nso* (PL1-person PL1-all)	'all (the) people'
mi-kolo mí-nso (PL4-day PL4-all)	*mi-kolo nyɔ́nso* (PL4-day all)	'all days, every day'
ma-lálá má-nso (PL6-orange PL6-all)	*ma-lálá nyɔ́nso* (PL6-orange all)	'all (the) oranges'

Number of Speakers: Over 10 million. Most speakers are nonnative. Most native speakers are in the urban population.

Origin and History

Lingala developed during the last quarter of the19th century or perhaps acquired its present form at the beginning of the 20th century. It is putatively a restructured variety of Bobangi, a Bantu language spoken south of the northwestern bend of the Congo River that functioned as a lingua franca among fishermen and traders along the river. Missionaries and colonial administrators adopted it as a lingua franca for colonial administration and evangelization in the northern part and in the capital city of the Belgian colony. Its use by privates in the army helped spread it around the country. It received more impetus from being the choice language of modern popular music diffused from the two Congos' capital cities, Kinshasa and Brazzaville, where it also functions as the vernacular of those born in the city. Here and in major cities of the whole of the northern and northwestern parts of both Congos, it functions as the main vernacular or the lingua franca.

Orthography and Basic Phonology

Lingala orthography is phonetic. Lingala has seven vowels represented in writing by 5 symbols *i, e, a, o, u*, which do not clearly show the differences between the higher midvowels /e/ and /o/ versus the lower midvowels /ɛ/ and /ɔ/. Thus, *ye* 'him/her' is pronounced with /e/ but *te* 'not' is pronounced with /ɛ/. In *moto* 'head', the first syllable has the lower mid /ɔ/, whereas the second syllable has the higher mid /o/. The other vowels have pronunciations corresponding to the relevant cardinal vowels:

```
i           u
e           o
ɛ           ɔ
      a
```

There are 17 consonants, /b, p, t, d, k, g, f, v, s, z, m, n, l/, and two glides, /j/ and /w/:

Table 1: Consonants

	Labial	Dental	Palatal	Velar
Stops	p b	t d		k g
Fricatives	f v	s z		
Liquids		l (alternates with r)		
Glides	w		y	
Nasals	m	p		

Consonant clusters consist almost exclusively of a nasal followed by a nonnasal consonant (NC). In word-initial position, the nasal of an NC cluster is not syllabic. The words *nzóto* 'body' and *mbóngo* 'money' have only two syllables. The vowel preceding a nasal consonant is not nasalized. Thus *mbóngo* is syllabified as *mbo.ngo*. There is no clear evidence that in word-initial position an NC cluster changes into a prenasalized consonant.

Lingala is a tonal language with two tones, high (marked with an acute accent) and low (unmarked). Verb inflection contrasts are sometimes indicated by tonal changes only. Thus *á-mɔ̃n-a* 'let him/her see' contrasts with *a-mɔ̃n-á* 'he/she saw a long time ago'. Some lexical items contrast only by their tones, e.g., *mɔto* 'person' contrasts with *mɔtó* 'head'.

Basic Morphology

A noun in Lingala consists of a prefix and a base. The prefix, which usually consists of the first syllable of the initial consonant at the very least, identifies the class and number of the referent. The noun classes are identified numerically by their forms (e.g., Cl 1 or Cl 2) but they are often also grouped in pairs of singular and plural forms (e.g., *mu-/ba-* or *mu-/mi-* instead of 1/2 or 3/4 classes). One may also argue that the noun classes have a derivational function, based on multiple forms derived from the same base, as in the case of *mo-bóti/ba-bóti* 'parent(s)', *ko-bóta* 'have children, give birth', *li-bóta/ma-bóta* 'family/families'.

The verb form varies according to subject prefix, whether or not it has a reflexive prefix, and derivational and tense suffixes, according the following template:

Subject Prefix—Reflexive prefix—Verb root—Derivational Suffix—Tense Suffix:

a-mi-tínd-él-í mo-kándá 'he had himself sent a book/letter'
3SG-REFL-send-APPL-near.PERFECT CL3-book/letter

The subject prefix varies according to the noun class of the referent. The reflexive prefix is invariant. Derivational suffixes include the applicative *-el*, the causative *-is*, the passive *-am*, and the reciprocal *-an*.

Among the possible derivations, a noun may be derived from a verb, as in *mo-sál-á* 'work, job' from the same base as *ko-sál-a* 'to work', and a verb may be derived from another verb, as in *ko-sál-is-a* 'to help (literally: to make somebody work)'. A noun can also be derived from a derived verb, as in *mo-tang-is-i* 'teacher (literally: he-who causes [somebody] to-read)'. There aren't many adjectives in Lingala and there are no rules for deriving adjectives from nouns or verbs, nor for deriving adverbs from adjectives. Concepts expressed adjectivally or adverbially in other languages are expressed by means of modifying nouns, e.g., *moto ya makási* 'strong person (literally: person of strength)'.

Compounding and reduplication are very productive processes for forming new nouns and verbs, as in *ki-mona mpási* 'a person who has experienced misery (literally CL7-see pain/misery)', *ku-dia ku-banza* 'a worried person (literally: INF-eat INF-think)', and *ku-loba-loba* 'talk a lot/too much/repeatedly'.

Basic Syntax

The basic major constituent order is Subject-Verb-Object-Adjunct. The subject can be a noun or an independent pronoun. The form of the noun phrase (noun or pronoun) is the same in the subject and object object positions. There is no case marking on nouns.

Ngái	*na-monák-í*	*yǒ/Eyenga*	*lóbi*
me	I-see-near.PERFECT	you/Eyenga	yesterday

'(Me) I saw you/Eyenga yesterday' (*yǒ* is an instance of rising tone)

When there are two objects and the verb is in the applicative, the dative object precedes the direct object:

Papá	*a-tínd-el-í*	*Eyenga*	*mo-kandá*
Daddy	he-send-APPL-near.PERFECT	Eyenga	Cl3-letter

'Daddy sent Eyenga [a] letter.'

Lingala is a head-initial language. All modifiers follow the head: *mw-ána ya mɔké* (Cl1-child CONNECTIVE small) 'a small child', *mw-ána ɔ́yo* (Cl1-child this) 'this child', *b-ána míbalé* (Cl2-child two) 'two children', *mw-ána ɔ́yo ɔ-món-ák-í* (Cl1-child this you-see-NEAR.PAST) 'the child that you saw'.

Negation is expressed sentence finally with the particle *tɛ́*.

Papá	*a-tínde-el-í*	*Eyenga*	*mo-kandá*	*tɛ́*
Daddy	he-send-APPL-NEAR.PERFECT	Eyenga	Cl3-letter	NEG

'Daddy did not send Eyenga [a] letter.'

Questions are identified by a rising intonation and/or by the presence of a question word in situ: *ɔ-mɔ́n-í níni?* (you-see-NEAR.PERFECT what) 'What have you seen?'

Contact with Other Languages

Urban Lingala has been affected by contacts with other lingua francas such as KIKONGO KITUBA and SWAHILI, as well as FRENCH. The evidence of French influence is most obvious in its vocabulary and constant language mixing by the educated. Influence from other languages that is not from the time of its initial development is not obvious.

Words related to modern technology and life have typically been borrowed from French, although there are a few that reflect the earliest precolonial contacts with PORTUGUESE, ARABIC, and ENGLISH:

From Arabic: *li-/ma-sási* 'bullet(s)', *sandúku* 'trunk/chest'
From Portuguese: *mesa* 'table', *sabátu* 'shoe'
From English: *búku* 'book', *mútuka* 'automobile'
From French: *dalapó* 'flag', *dilikitéli* 'director', *vwatíli* 'car', *aviɔ́* 'airplane', *dɔkitéli* 'doctor'

Common Words

man:	mobáli	woman:	mwási
water:	mái	sun:	likanga
three:	misátu	fish:	mbísi
big:	mɔnéne	long:	mɔlaí
small:	mɔké	yes:	ɛe
no:	tɛ́	good:	malámu
bird:	ndɛkɛ	dog:	mbwá
tree:	nzɛtɛ́		

Example Sentences

(1) Elóko elingí motéma okoluka yangó epaí nyónso.
thing likes heart you.FUT.look.for it place all
'What the heart wants, you will look for it everywhere (subject-verb inversion in relative clause).'

(2) Mwána abomelí ngái mótoka.
child killed.for me car
'The child broke down my car (adversative dative).'

Efforts to Preserve, Protect, and Promote the Language

Lingala does not count among the endangered languages. Much

of the momentum of its spread comes from urban life in Kinshasa and Brazzaville, the capital cities of the two Congo republics, and especially from its association with music. Its use by the armed forces has been an ambivalent factor in its spread.

Select Bibliography

De Boeck, Egide. 1904. *Grammaire et vocabulaire du lingala.* Bruxelles: Polleunis-Ceuterick.

Dzokanga, Adolphe. 1979. *Dictionnaire lingala-français, suivi d'une grammaire lingala.* Leipzig: Enzyklopadie.

Guthrie, Malcolm. 1935. *Lingala Grammar and Dictionary.* Léopoldville (Kinshasa): Conseil Protestant du Congo.

Guthrie, Malcolm, and John F. Carrington. 1988. *Lingala: Grammar and Dictionary.* London: Baptist Missionary Society.

Meeuwis, Michael. 1998. *Lingala.* Munich, Germany: Lincom Europa.

Lithuanian

Jules F. Levin

Language Name: Lithuanian. **Autonym:** *lietuvių kalba.*

Location: Spoken in Lithuania, an independent republic on the southeastern Baltic seacoast that is bounded by Latvia; Belarus; Poland; and Russia's Kaliningrad Oblast, the former East Prussia. There are also Lithuanian speakers in more or less contiguous communities across the borders in former East Prussia, Poland, Belarus, and Latvia. There is also a significant diaspora Lithuanian-speaking community with the usual problems of language and culture maintenance, found *inter alia* in Canada, Chicago, New England, Australia, Germany, and Sweden. About 80 percent of the population of Lithuania is ethnic Lithuanian; the remaining 20 percent is comprised of Poles, Russians, Belarusians, and a few less numerous groups who can communicate in the language with greater or lesser proficiency.

Family: Lithuanian belongs to the Baltic branch of the Indo-European language family.

Related Languages: LATVIAN (Lettish) is the closest living relative. Lithuanian and Latvian constitute East Baltic, and are the last living Baltic languages. The extinct (Old) Prussian language belonged to West Baltic. In addition, other related transitional dialects have been cited as separate Baltic languages at various times; none are extant as separate languages.

Dialects: The major dialect split is between Zhemaitian and Aukshtaitian, that is, "Low" and "High" Lithuanian, respectively. The former is spoken in the northwest 20 percent of the country, around Klaipeda (Memel). Aukshtaitian is divided into Western and Eastern Aukshtaition, the former being the basis of the literary language. There is considerable dialect variation. The many significant isoglosses involve phonetics and phonology—including tone-accent shifts; the loss of final short vowels; shortening of long vowels; fixing of stress; establishments of phonemic palatalization; loss of some nasal consonants; morphology, including the significant reshaping of the complex paradigms that characterize Lithuanian; syntax, including the contrasting use of grammatical devices involving case, aspect, tense, etc.; and lexicon/semantics, where the replacement of Slavic borrowings with native materials that has worked through the literary language has not fully engulfed the dialects.

Number of Speakers: 3.5–5 million.

Origin and History

Baltic, in the *satem* division of Indo-European, is closely related to the Slavic family, and some scholars unite them in a single superfamily. The next closest Indo-European family is probably Germanic, and a Baltic-Slavic-Germanic speech area within disintegrating Indo-European has been proposed. Written Lithuanian is attested from the 16th century, although place names and personal names are found in other sources much earlier. A common East Baltic must have been distinct from West Baltic by the beginning of the Christian Era. It was probably a fairly homogeneous language, since even now differences within East Baltic have a continuum character. East Baltic began to break up from around A.D. 600. The substantial changes leading to Latvian from Common East Baltic were analogous, although not identical, to changes breaking up Slavic unity simultaneously in A.D. 700–1100. The development of modern Lithuanian, especially the literary language, is characterized by resistance to macrophonological innovative isoglosses that swept over much of Europe and which ultimately caused the restructuring of the "classical" Indo-European languages. This resistance saved the synthetic character of the inflectional system, and even facilitated its strengthening, with changes that have been as much in the direction of agglutination as of analysis. Such developments contribute to Lithuanian's conservative appearance, and its characterization as "the only living Indo-European language".

Lithuanian has lost ground for centuries to BELORUSSIAN and POLISH along its borders. Belorussian clearly shows evidence of Baltic substrata in its border dialects, and Polish replaced Lithuanian among the Lithuanian higher classes after the union with Poland. The historic capital Vilnius was effectively Polonized, and adjacent rural areas were Slavic speaking. The languages of towns were YIDDISH, Polish, GERMAN, and RUSSIAN. The Lithuanian-speaking population was overwhelmingly rural and of the peasant class. During the period of Russian Empire rule, conscious policies to repress the Lithuanian language were pursued.

During the first period of independence between World Wars I and II, the non-Lithuanian-speaking minorities maintained their own languages, but there was some tendency to learn and use Lithuanian. After Lithuania was occupied by the Soviet Union, it was given Vilnius and the surrounding area, which had been kept by Poland in violation of the Treaty of Versailles. The Polish-speaking population was expelled and Vilnius became the capital and basically Lithuanian speaking. Surrounding rural areas retain a considerable Slavic-speaking population. During the Soviet period, knowledge of Russian was a requirement for social advancement, and there was a long-term policy of limiting the local language in the "international" area—science, etc. All dissertations had to be written or at least translated into Russian, and defended in Moscow. Non-Lithuanian ethnic minorities used Russian rather than Lithuanian if not their own languages. Still, Lithuanian was much more the dominant language spoken over a larger area than it had been in 1935. Since the recent independence in 1991, non-Lithuanian-speaking minorities are switching to Lithuanian, as use of Russian is now officially disfavored. Even so, Lithuania has not resorted to the stricter language policies of, for example, Latvia.

Orthography and Basic Phonology

Lithuanian is written in the LATIN alphabet. The orthography was originally based on Polish spelling (evident in the purely orthographic "nasal" vowels, not standing only for long vowels, which may in fact alternate with actual /V + n/ sequences morphophonemically), but has been reformed in the Czech style. The standard Lithuanian alphabet follows. The letters in parentheses are alphabetized with the preceding letter: Aa (ģ ģ) Bb Cc (Ch) Čč Dd Ee (Ģ) (ģģ) Ff Gg Hh Ii (Įį) Yy Jj Kk Ll Mm Nn Oo Pp Rr Ss Šš Tt Uu (Ūū) (Ųų) Vv Zz Žž

Table 1: Consonants

	Labial	Alveolar	Palatal	Velar
Stops				
Voiceless	p	t		k
Voiced	b	d		g
Fricatives				
Voiceless	(f)	s	š	(x)
Voiced		z	ž	(h)
Affricates				
Voiceless		(c)	č	
Voiced		(dz)	dž	
Nasals	m	n		
Liquids		r, l		
Glides	v		j	

Consonants in parentheses do not occur in the core native phonological inventory.

/f/ is found in relatively recent borrowings such as *elfas* 'fairy'; earlier, it was replaced by /p/ as in *Prancūzija* 'France'. Unlike other voiceless consonants, it does not alternate with its voiced counterpart ([v]).

/x/, spelled *ch*, is also limited to borrowings like *chaosas*. /h/, spelled *h*, is usually pronounced as a voiced pharyngeal fricative and is also limited to borrowings, as *haremas*.

/c/ and /dz/ are found in borrowings, for example, *cinkas* 'zinc'; affective vocabulary as *cypauti* 'to screech'; and the sporadic juxtaposition of phonological /t+s/ or /d+z/.

All consonants are phonetically palatalized when they precede a front vowel or /j/. A sequence of consonant + /j/ + back vowel (spelled *CiV*) thus results in a palatalized segment [C'V], contrasting with [CV]. When the dental stops /t/ and /d/ precede /j/ + back vowel, often at a stem-suffix boundary, they become affricates /č/ and /dž/. The stops and affricates regularly alternative within paradigms, for example, *medis* 'tree' *medžiai* 'trees'. This process is the main source for palatal affricates in Lithuanian. However, they also occur in loanwords, in other phonological environments, such as *čekas* 'Czech', *čekis* 'check', *čempionas* 'champion', and *čirkšti* 'twitter'.

Vowels:

	Front	Back
High	ī (y, į)	ū (ū, ų)
	ɪ (i)	u (u)
Mid	ē (e, ģ)	ō (ō)
Low	(e, ę)	ā (a,ģ)
	æ (e)	a (a)

The symbols in parentheses represent the orthographic representations of the preceding phonological transcriptions.

In addition, Lithuanian has diphthongs *ei, ai, ui, ie,* and *uo*. The combinations of a short vowel and a following sonorant /l/, /r/, /m/, and /n/ in the same syllable also function as diphthongs. /æ/ and /a/ (*e* and *a*) were originally the short counterparts of the long vowels /ē/ and /ō/, as is still evident in inflectional and derivational patterns. However, two phonological changes have resulted in the development of new long vowels /ǣ/ and /ā/. The first is the lengthening of /e/ in most open syllables: *nešti* 'to carry' [næšti] versus *nẽša* 'carries' [nǣša]. The second is the loss of /n/ before fricatives, with lengthening of the preceding short vowel. As a result, /ǣ/ and /ā/ contrast with both /æ/ and /a/ and with /ē/ and /ō/.

The morphophonemics of Lithuanian suggest a mora interpretation of vowel length and tone. All syllabic peaks have either one mora (a short vowel) or two (a long vowel or a diphthong). Sequences of more than two morae generated via morphological affixation are shortened by phonological rules.

Any given mora may potentially be stressed, although only one mora in a word will be. Thus, a syllable consisting of a single mora may be stressed, indicated by a grave accent, i.e., *è*, or not, indicated by lack of an accent mark. Likewise, a syllable containing two morae may have the stress on the first mora, indicated by an acute accent (*ái, ém*) or grave accent (*ìn, ùr*), on the second mora, indicated by a tilde (*añ, uõ*), or on neither (if unstressed).

Basic Morphology

Lithuanian is a highly inflected language, with extensive noun, adjective, pronoun, and verb paradigms. The categories expressed are the following: gender (masculine and feminine) and number (singular, plural, and some residual instances of dual). Nouns can appear in one of five declensions and are declined for case. The Lithuanian cases are: Nominative, Genitive, Dative, Accusative, Instrumental, Locative, and Vocative. Of the five declensions, three are quite productive and two are of limited productivity. A typical noun form consists of the following elements: stem + thematic vowel + case marker + number marker. Thus, the instrumental plural noun *rankomis* 'hands' can be analyzed as *rank + o + mi + s*. The first and second of the five declensions can occur with either front or back thematic vowels, and the third and fourth declensions can likewise be regarded as front and back variations on a single declension. The forms of a typical first declension noun, *výras* 'man', are illustrated below:

	Singular	Plural	Dual
Nominative	výras	výrai	výru
Genitive	výro	vrų	
Dative	výrui	výrams	výram
Accusative	výrą	výrus	výru
Instrumental	výru	výrais	výram
Locative	výre	výruose	
Vocative	výre	výrai	výru

Dual forms such as those listed above are, for the most part, obsolete.

Instrumental forms from various declensions are illustrated below, together with the nominative singular endings:

	Singular	Plural	Gloss
First, *-is*	bróliu	bróliais	'brother'
First, *-s*	árkliu	arkliaĩs	'horse'
Second, *-a*	várna	várnomis	'crow'
Second, *-ia*	valdžià	valdžiomis	'government'
Third, *-is*	dančiù	dantimìs	'tooth'
Fourth, *-ius*	skaĩčiumi	skaĩčiais	'number'
Fifth, *-uo*	vándeniu	vandenimis	'water'

Some of the declensions contain exclusively masculine or feminine nouns, while others contain both masculine and feminine nouns. There is no specific morphological marking for noun gender beyond that indicating declension.

Traditional grammars and dictionaries list four accent classes for the nominal declensions. There are over 40 paradigms in the introduction to the standard one volume Lithuanian dictionary, and entries are numbercoded to refer to these paradigms. However, a somewhat simpler analysis has been proposed, based on the mora analysis given above under Phonology. Most roots and affixes have a specific mora that may be accented. Moreover, noun, verb, and adjective roots are either fixed or mobile. Finally, Lithuanian has a strong tendency to avoid accenting the penultimate mora in a word. The various stress classes listed in standard references can all be accounted for by assigning surface accent in a given word, based on these three assumptions. Thus, nouns in stress class 2, such as *skaĩčius* 'number', are nouns with fixed accent on the last root mora, but when followed by a single-mora stressable ending, such as the accusative plural *-ùs*, the accent moves to the ending, in line with the third principle above: *skaičiùs*.

There are three basic productive adjective declensions. Adjectives agree with the nouns they modify in case and gender, and mark, in addition, whether the noun phrase is definite or indefinite. Some forms of the adjective *báltas* 'white' are illustrated below:

	Indefinite	Definite
Nominative, Singular, Masculine	báltas	baltàsis
Nominative, Singular, Feminine	baltà	baltóji
Locative, Plural, Masculine	baltuosè	baltuõsiuose
Locative, Plural, Feminine	baltosè	baltõsiose

Verbs agree with their subjects in person and number. There are three basic conjugation classes that differ in thematic vowel. Within a conjugation, stems may differ in the location of the accent. The present tense indicative forms of the first conjugation verb *dìrbti* 'to work' is illustrated below:

	Singular	Plural
1st person	dìrbu	dìrbame
2nd person	dìrbi	dìrbate
3rd person	dìrba	dìrba

In the verbs, in the indicative mode, there are three simple tenses, past, present, and future; two derived tenses, past and present frequentative; and three compound tenses, the present, past, and future perfect. The compound tenses consist of an auxiliary verb and a participle (see below). Verbal agreement is marked on the auxiliary, and the participle agrees with the subject in gender and number. Some second person forms of the second conjugation verb *tikėti* 'to believe' are illustrated below:

	Singular	Plural
Present	tikì	tìkite
Past	tikėjai	tikėjote
Future	tikėsi	tikėsite
Past frequentative	tikėdavai	tikėdavote
Present perfect (masc.)	esì tikėjęs	sate tikėję
Past perfect (masc.)	buvaĩ tikėjęs	bùvote tikėjusi

Lithuanian has a large number of participial forms, including, in Active Voice, present, past, frequentative past, and future participles; and, in Passive Voice, present, past, and future participles, as well as "participles of necessity". The perfect verb forms illustrated above are based on the past active participle.

Participles in many respects resemble adjectives in that they are inflected for number, gender, and case. In addition, they are marked for definiteness. Some feminine instrumental participles based on the verb *dirbti* 'to work' are illustrated below:

	Singular	Plural
Present active	dìrbančia	dìrbančiomis
Present active definite	dìrvančiąja	dìrbančiosiomis
Past active	dìrbusia	dìrbusiomis
Past active definite	dìrbusiąja	dìrbusiosiomis
Future active	dìrbsiančia	dìrbsiančiomis
Future active definite	dìrbsiančiąja	dìrbsiančiosiomis
Present passive	dìrbama	dirbamomìs
Past passive	dirbta	dirbtomìs
Future passive	dìrbsima	dirbsimomìs
Particple of necessity	dìrbtina	dirbtinomìs

In addition to their role in formation of the perfect tenses illustrated above, the participles are used in other derived verb forms. The present active participle, with *be-* prefixed, is used in the formation of the past progressive, as in *bùvo bedirbanti* 'she was working', the progressive frequentative past such as *būdavote bedirbą* 'y'all (masculine) used to be working', and the progressive future, for example, *bùs bedirvančios* 'they (feminine) will be working'. The passive participle is used in the formation of passive voice forms in various tenses. Some second person feminine forms of the verb *mùšti* 'to beat' are illustrated below:

	Singular	Plural
Present	esì mušamà	ẽsate mùšamos
Past	buvaĩ mušamà	bùvote mùšamos
Future	būsi mušamaà	būsite mùšamos
Past frequentative	būdavai mušamà	būdavote mùšamos
Present perfect (fem.)	esì bùvusi mušamà	ẽsate bùvusios mùšamos
Past perfect (fem.)	buvaĩ bùvusi mušamà	bùvote bùvusios mùšamos

Lithuanian is rich in derivational morphology, employing a large number of prefixes and suffixes, as well as compounding. It has also retained "class alternation" as a derivational device for nouns, adjectives, and verbs. An example of a cluster of words differing only in class membership is: *ìlgas* 'long', *ilgùs* 'boring', *ìlgis* 'tall man', and *ìlgė* 'tall woman'.

Basic Syntax

The neutral word order in Lithuanian is SVO, but, as with most inflectional languages, word order is easily changed for emphasis or poetic effect.

Vytas nor-i pirk-ti nauj-ģ automobil-į
Vytas want-3SG.PRES buy-INF new-ACC.SG car-ACC.SG
'Vytas wants to buy a new car.'

The most common variant is SOV, especially when the object is a pronoun.

Vytas man ją davė
Vytas me:1SG.DAT it give:3SG.PAST
'Vytas gave me a book.'

One of the most characteristic features of Lithuanian word order is that genitives precede the nouns they modify. This order is used for a variety of genitive functions, including possession such as *Vyto automobilis* 'Vyta's car' and attribution as in *lietuvos respublika* 'Republic of Lithuania'. The genitive noun can also stand for a relative adjective, for example, *aukso laikrodis* 'gold watch'.

Adjectives likewise generally precede the nouns they modify. This is so even when the adjective is formally a participle. In expanded noun phrases, the genitive element is generally closer to the head noun (which is phrase-final):

nauj-à seseȓ-s knyg-a
new-NOM.FEM.SG sister-GEN.SG book-NOM
'(my) sister's new book'

The usual negation is a prefix *ne-* attached to the head word:

Ji ne-suprant-a lietuviškai
she NEG-understand-3SG.PRES Lithuanian
'She doesn't understand Lithuanian.'

Other word classes also take *ne-* as a prefix: *nebrangus* 'inexpensive', *nedaug* 'a little' (lit. 'not much'), *nedora* 'immorality'. An independent negative particle *nė* adds an emphasis to a negated object, as in *nė vienas* 'not a one'.

Contact with Other Languages

Lithuanian has had extensive contact with the so-called Northern Slavic group for centuries, as well as with German. In the latter case, there was an important Lithuanian-speaking population in German East Prussia, as well as ancient contacts between Baltic and Germanic. There were probably Finnic-speaking groups in the eastern Lithuanian area, but this contact was less significant than it had been for Latvian. Along the northern and northeastern border there is more or less a continuum with Latvian dialects, although, in general, familiarity with Latvian is less than with other foreign languages. Before the 20th century, Polish and German were important avenues for the introduction of the Western international vocabulary; more recently (1940–1991) Russian played a more significant role. Examples of international vocabulary borrowings include: *Mylia* 'mile', *arena* 'arena', *karbolis* 'carbolic acid', *cechas* 'factory shop', and *chirurgas* 'surgeon'.

Common Words

man:	žmogus	long:	ilgus
woman:	motina	small:	mažiulas
water:	vanduo	yes:	taip
sun:	saulģ	no:	ne
three:	trys	good:	geras
fish:	žuvis	bird:	paukštis
big:	didis, didelis	dog:	šuo (šuns-GEN)

Example Sentences

(1) àš nė gatvės ne-mat-au.
I:NOM NEG street:GEN NEG-see-PRES.1SG
'I don't even see the street.'

(2) Okupant-ams svarbu kad tauta
occupier-DAT.PL important that people-NOM.SG

visai pamirštuv kas ji
entirely:ADV forget-SUBJUNCTIVE:3RD what it:NOM.SG.FEM

buv-o ir daryt-ų-si
be-PAST.3RD and become-SUBJUNCTIVE.3RD-REFLEX

lengviau jų pavald-oma.
more-easily them:GEN rule:PASSIVE PARTICIPLE-FEM.SG
'To the occupiers, it is important that the people entirely would forget what they were and would become more easily ruled by them.'

Efforts to Preserve, Protect, and Promote the Language

The great nationalist revival in the 19th century ensured the preservation of Lithuanian, once it culminated in national independence after the First World War. The modern literary language is based on the western Aukshtaitian dialects where most of the national movement leaders originated. Many of these individuals were university-trained philologists who consciously purged the language of Slavonisms and other "foreign" elements. During the Soviet period, Lithuanian linguists and philologists actively strove to promote Lithuanian through prescriptive articles in the popular press and education as well as the development of excellent reference materials, including a multi-volume dictionary that records dialectisms from all over the country.

Select Bibliography

Ambrazas, Vytautas. 1997. *Lithuanian Grammar*. Baltos Lankos.

Dambriūnas, L., A. Klimas, and W. Schmalstieg. 1966. *Introduction to Modern Lithuanian*. Brooklyn: Franciscan Fathers Press.

Levin, Jules F. 1979. "The Lithuanian Definite Adjective as Syntax and as Semiotic." In *Journal of Baltic Studies* X: 2. 152–161.

____. 1982. "Iconicity in Lithuanian." In *Proceedings of the Second Conference in Non-Slavic Languages*, University of Chicago. *Folia Slavica* V: 230–245.

____ . 1984. "Thematic Derivation as Evidence for Lexical Organization." In *Folia Slavica* VII: 1,2: 212–225.

____. 1990. "Lithuanian Accent as a Descriptive (Notational) Problem." In *Symposium Balticum*, Helmut Buske Verlag, Hamburg. 249–256.

____. 1994. "Sign of Jod (The Semiotic Function of /j/ in Lithuanian)." In *Baltistica* IV Priedas [IVth Supplement], Vilnius, Mokslo ir Enciklopedijų Leidykla, pp. 212–225.

Mathiassen, Terje. 1966. *A Short Grammar of Lithuanian*. Slavica Publishers, Inc.

Zinkevičius, Zigmas. 1996. *The History of the Lithuanian Language*. Mokslo ir enciklopedijų leidykla.

LUGANDA

Francis Katamba

Language Name and Autonym: Luganda (Ganda).

Location: Spoken in southeastern Uganda between Lake Kyoga to the north, the Tanzania border to the south and the northwest shore of Lake Victoria to the east.

Family: Luganda is a member of the Narrow Bantu subgroup of the Bantu subbranch of the Benue-Congo branch of the Niger-Kordofanian language family. It is classified as Zone J.15 in Guthrie's classification system for Bantu.

Related Languages: Bantu languages such as Nkore (E.13), KINYARWANDA (D.61), SWAHILI (G.42), BEMBA (M.40), SHONA (S.10), Nguni (S.40). (Guthrie's classification is given in parentheses.)

Dialects: (Standard) Luganda is spoken in the central counties of Buganda and a number of other dialects are spoken in peripheral areas. These include Lunnabuddu, spoken in Buddu county in the south, just north of the Tanzania border, Lukooki, spoken in Kooki County to the west of Buddu; Ruruuli spoken in northwest Buganda; Lunyala, spoken in northeast Buganda, as well as Lukoome, Lusese, and Luvuma, which are spoken in the three major groups of islands in the northern part of Lake Victoria. Because there is a very close relationship among the Bantu speech communities of the region of the Great Lakes, the distinction between language and dialect is a fluid one. So, this listing of Luganda dialects is inevitably controversial, both with regard to what is included and what is excluded.

Number of Speakers: Reliable figures showing the number of speakers are not available. According to the 1991 census, there are 3,015,980 first-language speakers of Luganda. Earlier, in a survey of language in Uganda, ENGLISH, Swahili, and Luganda were deemed the lingua francas of Uganda, and of the three, Luganda is the most widely used: 39 percent of Ugandans are capable of holding a conversation in Luganda, as opposed to 35 percent who can do so in Swahili and 21percent who are fluent in English. These figures include the 16 percent of the population who are mother tongue speakers of Luganda.

Origin and History

Historical records are recent. The early history of Buganda was passed down in oral tradition using folktales, legends, and songs. The Kintu legend is a generally accepted account of the founding of Buganda. In this legend fact and myth get intertwined. Kintu was not only the "First King" but also the "First Man", an Adam figure, and Nambi, his wife, the "First Woman". About A.D. 1200, Kintu came from the east, or from the sky in some versions of the legend, and established the kingdom of Buganda.

With the passage of time, the kings of Buganda presided over an increasingly well-organized, nation-state that many of them ruled with an iron fist. From small beginnings the kingdom expanded through encroachment on the territory of its neighbors until Buganda became the biggest and most powerful kingdom in the region by the middle of the 19th century.

In the 1840s Arab traders and slavers from Zanzibar started to penetrate the Great Lakes region. During this period Buganda made contact with the outside world of the Arabs and Islam. Not long afterward, European explorers seeking the source of the Nile arrived, soon to be followed by proselytizing missionaries. British traders and colonialists were not far behind.

Many in Buganda soon embraced the new foreign religions, with tragic consequences. The last 20 years of the 19th century were a period of great turmoil, fueled by religious zealotry and colonial ambitions. When the dust settled, Buganda was made a "British Protectorate" by an agreement signed in 1900. After that Buganda was used as a collaborator to colonize the surrounding territories, which became the modern state of Uganda. Until the 1920s, usually the lower echelons of the colonial administration were staffed by people from Buganda, as were the lower levels of the church. One important result of all this was that Luganda spread and was entrenched across many parts of Uganda as a second language.

The use of Luganda to colonize and evangelize other parts of Uganda was facilitated by the change of Luganda from a preliterate to a literate language which had taken place by the early years of the 20th century. To provide an instructional manual for incoming missionaries, Wilson of the Church Missionary Society published, in 1882, the first of several Luganda grammars that appeared between 1880 and 1914. The Bible, prayer books, and other religious literature were also among the first publications. Historical and anthropological works soon followed, the most notable of which were Sir Apollo Kaggwa's *Ekitabo kya Bassekabaka be Buganda* ('The Kings of Buganda') (1901) and *Empisa za Baganda* ('The Customs of the Baganda') (1905).

Orthography and Basic Phonology

The Luganda orthography is essentially phonemic. In Tables 1 and 2, IPA is given in brackets corresponding to the standard orthography where necessary.

There is one major case where the alphabet is not phonemic.

Table 1: Consonants

		Bilabial	Labio-dental	Alveolar	Palatal	Velar	Labio-velar
Stops	Voiceless	p		t	c	k	
	Voiced	b		d	j [ɟ]	g	
Fricatives	Voiceless		f	s			
	Voiced		v	z			
Nasals		m		n	ny [ɲ]	ng [ŋ]	
Approximants				l	y		w

Though [l] and [r] are allophones of the phoneme /l/, they are represented by separate letters in the orthography. The letter *r* is used after front vowels, and [l] elsewhere.

Nearly all consonants can be short or long (geminate). The contrast between short and geminate consonants is used to distinguish meaning. When short, consonants are written with a single letter; when geminate, they are written with double letters, as in *tutta* 'we kill'. Note, however, that the approximants *w*, *l/r*, and *y* are different. They are realized, respectively, as the stops *pp*, *dd*, and *jj*, when geminate. Likewise, when preceded by a nasal consonant, these same sounds are hardened into the stops *p, d,* and *j* as in *wala* 'scrape' versus *mpala* 'I scrape' *laba* 'see' versus *ndaba* 'I see'; *yiga,* 'learn' versus *njiga* 'I learn'.

Table 2: Vowels

	Front	Central	Back and Round
High	i		u
Mid	e		o
Low		a	

Any vowel can be long or short. The distinction between short and long (geminate) vowels—which is indicated in the orthography by doubling letters—is used to distinguish meaning. For instance, the verb *tuma* 'send' is contrasted with the verb *tuuma* 'name'.

Consonants may assimilate features of adjacent vowels. For instance, the front (palatal) vowel *i* causes strong palatalization when it immediately follows a velar, for example, /k/ is pronounced [c] in *kiki* 'which, what'.

The typical syllable is CV or CVV; that is, it starts with a consonant and ends in a short or long vowel, as an example, *tu.ma* 'send' and *tuu.ma* 'name'. (The dot marks a syllable boundary).

There are severe restrictions on vowels co-occurring with each other in a syllable. Sequences of nonidentical vowels are prohibited. Whenever vowels come together in the process of syllable formation, regardless of whether this happens within a morpheme, within a word, or across word boundaries, if the first vowel is low, it is deleted and the second one is lengthened in compensation. This is seen in *ba-oza* 'they wash (clothes)', which is syllabified as *boo.za* (the hyphen marks a morpheme boundary). In analogous circumstances, where the first vowel is high, it is not deleted. Rather, it becomes a semivowel and the second is again lengthened in compensation, as in *mu-ezi* 'moon' *mwe.zi*. As this vowel lengthening is both predictable, it is not shown in the standard orthography.

The maximal syllable has the structure CV(V). In the surface phonetic realization of words, vowel-initial syllables are only permitted at the start of a word after a pause, as in *a.tu.ma* 'he/she sends'. Consonant clusters are restricted to a nasal plus consonant (NC) sharing the same place of articulation. In such a cluster, the nasal is syllabic (indicated by underlining) and forms a syllable of its own if it is at the start of the word, as in *m.bu.zi* 'goat', *n .di.ga* 'sheep' and *n.kula* 'rhino'. But if the NC cluster is word internal, in which case it is always preceded by a vowel, the nasal forms a syllable with the preceding vowel, as in *ban.tuma* 'they send me'. The vowel preceding such a nasal is always long. Again, because this length is predictable, it is not indicated in the orthography.

The first consonant in the syllable onset may be followed by a *y* or *w* glide, for example, *mu.lyan.go* 'doorway' and *tu.lwa.na* 'we fight'. In a CGV (consonant-glide-vowel) sequence, the vowel is always predictably long and so its length is not shown in the orthography.

Another salient feature of Luganda syllabification is that syllables must have at least one mora and at most two morae. A mora is a phonological timing unit coinciding with a vowel position in a syllable, or a syllabic consonant, or the first part of a geminate consonant in the case of Luganda. Thus, a syllabic nasal has one mora as in *m.bula;* the first and third syllables in *a.tut.ta* 'he/she kills us' and *a.tuu.ma* 'she/she names' also have one mora each, while the middle syllable in each of these two words has two morae.

The fact that syllables cannot exceed two moras explains why long vowels are never followed by geminate consonants. The combination of a long vowel and a geminate would yield an overweight syllable with three morae. Mora trimming takes place to limit such a syllable to two morae. Thus *tu-a-tta* 'we killed' is pronounced as *twat.ta* (not **twaat.ta).*

Another context where vowel length is normally suppressed is at the end of a word. If there is underlying vowel length it shows through when an enclitic, such as *ki* 'which', is added and the long vowel ceases to be at the very end as in *muti* 'tree' versus *muti ki* 'which tree'. However, where the final vowel is truly short, it remains short even when an enclitic is present, compare *mubisi* 'banana juice' versus *mubisi ki* 'which banana juice'.

There is no phonemic difference between long vowels in

word-initial position. Length may fluctuate in this context, but such fluctuation has no contrastive function.

Tone. Although tone is phonemic in Luganda, it is not marked in the standard orthography. I have followed that practice—except in this section which is devoted to tone.

On the surface, Luganda shows a contrast between L(ow) (̀), H(igh) (́), and Falling (HL) (̂) tones. There are no rising tones.

a. kìsùmùlùzò (LLLL) 'key'
b. màtá (LH) 'milk'
c. kùléètá (LHLH) 'to bring'

As seen in (c) above, the falling tone is the result of H being immediately followed by an L in the same syllable.

Unlike other two-tone systems, however, there are severe restrictions on the tonal patterns that can characterize a Luganda word. Luganda is often regarded as a good example of a pitch-accent language because a Luganda word can have at most one pitch drop from H to L. This restriction is enforced through the interaction of a small number of tone rules that apply throughout the word-level phonology.

Luganda contrasts underlying H tone versus Ø (zero tone or toneless) morae. All instances of L tone must therefore be obtained by rule. As seen in the following examples, a rule known as Meeussen's Rule (MR) is applied to lower an H to L when it is immediately preceded by an H. The example in (d) below shows that MR applies again and again, going from right to left, whenever an H is preceded by another H so that only the first H survives unchanged.

a. Input a-túm-a 's/he sends'
H
Output à-túm-à

b. Input a-lí - túm-a 's/he will send'
Output à-lí - tùm-à (H, H > L)

c. bá-túm-a 'they send'
H H
bá-tùm-a (H H> L)

d. bá-lí - túm-a 'they will send'
bá-lì - túm-à (H, H > L, H > L)

The examples below show an H tone plateauing to prevent an H L H sequence within a word. Any vowels that occur between H tones within a word themselves become H, even those that would be expected to become L by MR, as [lí] in *bá-lí-tú-túm-à* 'they will send us' below:

à-tú-túm-à 's/he send us'
à-lí-tú-túm-à 's/he will send us'
bá-tú-tùm-à 'they send us'
bá-lí-tú-túm-à 'they will send us'

The two previous sets of examples show that any vowel that does not get a tone from another source, for example, by a tone rule, receives a default L tone. (See the Class 1 subject marker *à-* 'he/she' in the examples.)

There is strong interaction between tone and grammar. For instance, different tone patterns may be found in utterances depending on focus:

Subject focus: Àbáání bé bàvúmà 'His/her children insult (=are abusive)'
Object focus: Àbáání bè bàvùmâ 'It is the children that they insult'

The following example shows how differences between verbs in main clauses and subordinate clauses are signaled tonally:

àgùlà 'he/she buys' (main clause)
àgùlâ 'one who buys' (relative clause)

Basic Morphology

Luganda has rich, largely agglutinative morphology, in which tone plays a major role.

The simple noun has the following structure: Preprefix (PP), Class Prefix (CP), Stem = Root + Final Vowel (FV):

PP	CP	Root-FV	
o-	mu-	yimb- i	'singer'
o-	mu-	asajja	'man'

The PP does not appear in all syntactic contexts. For instance, while it is required when a noun phrase is in utterance initial position, it is not allowed to appear in an NP following a negative.

a. Omusajja alaba embwa
'The man sees the dog.'
b. Omusajja talaba mbwa
'The man does not see the dog.' (*Omusajja talaba embwa.)

The noun stem may consist of a bare root like *-sajja* 'man' or a root and a final vowel like the derivational suffix *-i* that is attached to verbs to give agentive nouns, for example, *ku-yimba* 'to sing' > *mu-yimb-i* 'singer'.

There are 21 noun classes in Luganda, each marked by a prefix. A sample of Luganda noun-class prefixes is given below. (The noun-class numbering system is standardized for all Bantu languages.)

	Class	PP	CP	Stem	
Singular:					
	1	o-	mu	sajja	'man'
	3	o-	mu-	ti	'tree'
	7	e-	ki-	muli	'flower'
	19	e-	n-	te	'cow'
Plural:					
	2	a-	ba-	sajja	'men'
	4	e-	mi-	ti	'trees'
	8	e-	bi-	muli	'flowers'
	10	e-	n-	te	'cows'

As the chart above shows, typically prefixes are paired for number, with the odd-numbered one marking the singular and

Table 3: Valence Changing Morphology

APPL(ICATIVE)	ROOT	APPL	FV	
-er-	gob-	er-	a	'chase for'
-ir-	kub-	ir-	a	'hit for'
CAUS(ATIVE)	ROOT	CAUS	FV	
-es-	gob-	es-	a	'cause to chase'
-is-	kub-	is-	a	'cause to hit'
PASS(IVE)	ROOT	CAUS	FV	
-ebu-	gob-	ebu-	a	(gobebwa) 'cause to chase'
-ibu-	kub-	ibu-	a	(kubibwa) 'cause to hit'

the even numbered one marking the plural. The classification system is a grammatical categorization system, with a residual semantic element based to some extent on animacy, for example, Classes 1 and 2 contain mostly humans, Classes 3 and 4 trees, etc. Male-female gender is not a factor.

The noun-class system is at the heart of the nominal concord system in Bantu. In a noun phrase, modifiers (such as adjectives, demonstratives, and numerals) agree with the head in number and class.

a. <u>omu</u>kazi	<u>omu</u>wanvu	<u>o</u>mu	'one tall woman'
woman	tan	one	
<u>aba</u>kazi	<u>aba</u>wanvu	<u>ba</u>biri	'two tall women'
women	tall	two	
b. <u>omu</u>ti	<u>omu</u>wanvu	<u>gu</u>mu	'one tall tree'
tree	tall	one	
<u>emi</u>ti	<u>emi</u>wanvu	<u>e</u>biri	'two tall trees'
tree	tall	two	

As the following template shows, the morphological structure of verbs is more complex than that of nouns: Negative Prefix + Subject Marker (SM) + Tense/Aspect Marker (TM) + Object Marker 1 (OM1) + Object Marker 2 (OM2) + ROOT + Extension Suffixes (DS) + Final Vowel (FV).

In common with other Bantu languages, Luganda has a rich tense system as well as having distinct paradigms for the negative and positive tenses.

Part of the tense paradigm:

	Positive	*Negative*
Past	nnasoma	saasoma
Near Past	nnasomye	saasomye
Immediate Past	nsomye	sisomye
Present	nsoma	sisoma
Near Future	nnaasoma	siisome
General Future	ndisoma	sirisoma

While nouns are not inflected for case, pronominal prefixes found in verbs have a different form depending on whether they are subject or object markers. In addition, they agree in number and class with the NPs they index:

a. A-li-gob-a   embwa.   's/he will chase the dog'
SM-GEN.FUT-chase-FV   dog

b. A-li-gi-gob-a   's/he will chase it'
SM-GEN FUT-OM-chase-FV

c. E-li-gob-a   abakazi   'it (dog) will chase the women'
SM-GEN.FUT-chase-FV   women

d. E-li-ba-gob-a   'it (dog) will chase them (women)'
SM-GEN.FUT-OM-chase-FV

Minimally the verb stem consists of the root and the final vowel (which is a mood/aspectual marker), as in *kub-a* 'hit'. A more elaborate stem can be constructed by including at least one derivational suffix as in Table 3 above.

The vowel of the extension is subject to vowel height harmony: if the root vowel is mid like *e* or *o*, then *e* or *o* is used in the suffix. If the root vowel is *i*, *a*, or *u*, the extension vowel is *i* or *u*.

A fuller example of verb structure is given in the following sentence:

NEG. PREF.	SM	TM	OM1	OM2	ROOT	EXT.	FV
te-	ba-	li-	ki-	mu-	kub-	ir-	a
not	they	GEN.FUT	it	her/him	hit	for	Mood/ Aspect

'They will not hit her/him for it.'

Basic Syntax

The typical word order in declarative sentences is SVO. But, as seen in the examples below, topicalization may result in a deviation from that order.

SVO: Omukazi   a-li-goba   embwa
woman   she-GEN.FUT-chase   dog
'The woman will chase the dog'

SOV: Omukazi embwa aligigoba.
'The woman will chase the dog'

OSV: Embwa omukazi aligigoba.
'As for the dog, the woman will chase it.'

Historically, SOV was the norm. Remnants of this earlier order can be detected within the verb itself when a topicalized object NP precedes the verb. Then the object marker pronoun follows the subject marker, but precedes the verb stem.

The unmarked SVO order is an instance of a general head-before modifier pattern that is also found in other constructions, for example, in NPs where the noun is followed by its modifiers.

Turning to interrogatives, we observe that yes/no questions are signaled in speech by rising intonation, while Wh-questions are indicated by a particle. Some interrogative particles appear at the beginning of the sentence as in (a) below and others are placed at the end as in (b).

(a) Ani a-li-genda? 'Who will go?'
who he/she-GEN.FUT-go

(b) Tu-li-genda wa? 'Where will we go?'
he/she-GEN.FUT-go where

Contact with Other Languages

Luganda has been in contact with neighboring languages, especially those belonging to the Bantu group, for many centuries. For instance, Runyoro, which is spoken to the west, has been the source of loanwords such as *kuwombeka* 'build' and *kikaali* 'chief's enclosure'. But because the relationship between Ugandan Bantu languages is very close, it is not easy to determine the extent of mutual influences.

Since the middle of the 19th century, first Swahili and then English have been strong influences on Luganda. Most of the vocabulary of modernization has come from one of these languages, albeit sometimes the ultimate source is a third language.

From Swahili: *ddiini* 'religion' (< Sw. *dini*, from ARABIC), *ggaali* 'bicycle, vehicle', (<Sw. *Gari*, from HINDI), *mmeeza* 'table' (< Sw. *meza*, from PORTUGUESE)
From English: *ddokita* 'doctor', *leerwe* 'railway' *kkooti* 'court' *sitenseni* 'station'

Among those who are fluent in English, code mixing is very common. The following example is not atypical:

Gamba secretary wa accountant axeroxinge report yange this afternoon.
'Tell the accountant's secretary to xerox my report this afternoon.'

Common Words

man:	musajja	yes:	ye
woman:	mukazi	no:	nedda
water:	mazzi	sun:	njuba
bird:	nnyonyi	three:	ssatu
dog:	mbwa	fish:	kyannyanja
tree:	muti	big:	-nene
long:	-wanvu	small:	-tono

Example Sentences

(1) A-ø-yimb-a.
He/she-PRES-sing-FV
'He/she sings.'

(2) Kintu ba-a-mu-kwat-a nga a-bb-a.
Kintu they-PAST-him-catch-FV while he-steal-FV
'Kintu was caught (while he was) stealing.'

(3) Te-ba-kya-gul-ir-a ba-wala bi-teeteeyi.
NEG-they-still-buy-APPL-FV CP-girls CP-dress
'They no longer buy dresses for the girls.' (CP = noun-class prefix)

Efforts to Preserve, Protect, and Promote the Language

The greatest champion of Luganda is *Ekibiina ky'Olulimi Oluganda* ('The Luganda Society'), a voluntary organization established in 1950 to defend the Luganda language and culture from the incursions of English and to combat wider British cultural imperialism. From the outset, the society campaigned against indiscriminate lexical borrowing, especially where an English word replaced a perfectly adequate Luganda word, such as *yelo* 'yellow' supplanting *kyenvu.* Code mixing has been considered the other major danger. Neither of these threats vanished with the end of colonialism. So, the society continued to pursue the same objectives after independence.

The most effective medium through which the society's work is promoted is a weekly Luganda-language and culture awareness raising radio program. In addition, the society organizes occasional literature and cultural festivals.

The society has cultivated the formal study of the Luganda language, literature and culture at all levels of formal education. It has also been a vigorous promoter of Luganda literature. Not only has it nurtured a growing body of original writing in Luganda, but it has also encouraged the translation of foreign literatures into Luganda. Another key objective, and one that has been pursued with a considerable measure of success, has been to foster basic literacy in Luganda through the production of basic literacy materials.

Today, Luganda is widely used on radio and television. Perhaps even more importantly, there are several Luganda daily newspapers, as well as weekly and monthly magazines, which all have a fairly large circulation. The future of Luganda as a written language is not in doubt.

Select Bibliography

Ashton, E.O., *et al.* 1954. *A Luganda Grammar.* London: Longmans, Green & Co.

Borowsky, Toni. 1983. "Geminate Consonants in Luganda." In *Current Approaches to African Linguistics* eds. Jonathan Kaye, *et al.*, 2:81–97. Dordrecht, Holland: Foris.

Clements, G.N. 1986. "Compensatory lengthening and consonant gemination in Luganda." In *Studies in Compensatory Lengthening*, eds. L. Wetzels and E. Sezer, 37–77. Dodrecht, Holland: Foris.

Cole, D.T. 1967. *Some Features of Ganda Linguistic Structure.* Johannesburg: Witwatersrand University.

Guthrie, M. 1967–71. *Comparative Bantu*, vols. I–IV. Hants: Gregg International Publishers.

Herbert, R.K. 1976. "A reanalysis of Luganda vowels." In *Afrika und Übersee, 59.* 113–124.

Hubbard, Kathleen A. 1995. "Prenasalized Consonants and Syllable-timing: Evidence from Runyambo and Luganda." In *Phonology* 12:235–256.

Hyman, Larry M. and Francis X. Katamba. 1990. "Final Vowel Shortening in Luganda." In *Studies in African Linguistics* 21:1–59.

____. 1993a. "A new Approach to Tone in Luganda." In *Language* 69:34–67.

____. 1993b. "The Agment in Luganda: Syntax or Pragmatics?" In *Theoretical Aspects of Bantu Grammar,* ed. Sam Mchombo, 209–256. Stanford: C.S.L.I.

Kaggwa, A. 1901 (1971). *Ekitabo kya Bassekabaka be Buganda* ('The Kings of Buganda') (Translated and annotated by M.S. Kiwanuka). Nairobi: East African Publishing House.

____. 1905 (1934). *Empisa za Baganda* ('The Customs of the Baganda') (Translated by E.B. Kalibala). New York: Columbia University Press.

Katamba, F.X. 1984. "A Nonlinear Analysis of Vowel Harmony in Luganda." In *Journal of Linguistics* 20:57–76.

Katamba, F.X., and Larry M. Hyman. 1991. "Nasality and Morpheme Structure Constraints in Luganda." In *Africanistische Arbeitspapiere* 25:175–211. Institut für Afrikanistik. Universität zu Köln.

Kiwanuka, S.M.S. 1971. *A History of Buganda*. London: Longman Group Limited.

Ladefoged, P., R. Glick, and C. Criper. 1972. *Language in Uganda*. Nairobi: Oxford University Press.

Meeussen, A.E. 1955. "Les phonèmes du Ganda et du Bantou Commun." *Africa* 25:170–180.

____. 1962. "Meinhof's rule in Bantu." In *African Language Studies* 3:25–30.

Snoxall, R.A. 1967. *Luganda-English Dictionary*. Oxford: Clarendon Press.

Stevick, E.W. 1969. "Pitch and Duration in Ganda." In *Journal of African Languages* 8:1–28.

Tucker, A.N. 1962. "The Syllable in Luganda: A Prosodic Approach." In *Journal of African Languages* 1:122–166.

MACEDONIAN

Victor A. Friedman

Language Name: Macedonian. **Alternate:** Modern Macedonian (to distinguish from Ancient Macedonian, a dead, non-Slavic language). **Autonym:** *makedonski.*

Location: The Republic of Macedonia, the Greek province of Makedhonia (Aegean Macedonia), the Blagoevgrad (Gorna Džumaja) district of Bulgaria (Pirin Macedonia), and 75 or more villages in eastern Albania. The Slavic dialects of Gora, northeast of the Republic of Macedonia in Kosovo and Albania have also been included with Macedonian. There are numerous Macedonian speakers in the rest of the former Yugoslavia as well as in North America, Australia, countries in western Europe with Balkan migrant workers (Sweden, Germany, etc.), and Macedonians who were sent to eastern Europe and the former Soviet Union as children during the Greek civil war (1948).

Family: South Slavic group of the Slavic branch of the Indo-European language family.

Related Languages: BULGARIAN, SERBO-CROATIAN; more distantly SLOVENE, then the other Slavic languages.

Dialects: Two major dialect regions, East and West, comprising 21 main dialects. The Kostur-Nestram dialects of western Greece and eastern Albania are now classed as a separate group.

Number of Speakers: 2–3.5 million.

Origin and History

The Slavs are an Indo-European people whose original homeland is the subject of scholarly debate but was probably somewhere in the general region of modern Poland, Belarus, and/or Ukraine. In the sixth and seventh centuries, large groups of Slavs crossed the Carpathian Mountains and settled throughout the Balkan peninsula. These became the South Slavs. The South Slavic tribes living on the territory of Macedonia (the region bounded in ancient times by Epirus, Thessaly, and Thrace on the southwest, south, and east, respectively) became the majority population in most districts, replacing or absorbing most of the earlier inhabitants. Their descendants became known as Macedonians (in Macedonian *makedonci*).

The earliest attested Slavic language, Old Church Slavonic, is very close to Common Slavic and is based on a dialect that was spoken on the territory of what is today Aegean Macedonia, namely Salonika (Macedonian Solun, GREEK Thessaloniki) in the ninth century. The brothers Methodius and Constantine (who took the monastic name Cyril on his deathbed), who were from Salonika, were sent in 863 on a Christianizing mission to Prince Rostislav of Moravia by the Byzantine emperor Michael III at the prince's request. The brothers invented an alphabet called *Glagolitic* (no longer in use except for symbolic purposes) probably based on Greek cursive, and they translated the Gospels and other liturgical works into what we now call Old Church Slavonic. The oldest surviving documents in this language are undated, but are presumed to be copies from the late 10th or early 11th century.

By the end of the 11th century, Slavic literacy had spread to many centers and Slavic dialectal differentiation had increased significantly. The language used by those centers that continued the Old Church Slavonic tradition is referred to as "Church Slavonic". The Church Slavonic produced on the territory of Macedonia can be referred to as Old Macedonian (not to be confused with Ancient Macedonian).

Koneski (1983) divides the history of Macedonian into two periods: Old, from the 12th through 15th centuries, and Modern, from the 15th century onward.

The Ottoman Turkish conquest of the Balkan peninsula in the 14th and 15th centuries caused a disruption of cultural continuity with regard to Slavic literacy in that region. Very few documents survived, and most of those that did continued the Church Slavonic written tradition despite changes in the spoken language.

Around the 15th century, the major structural changes characterizing Macedonian as a Balkan language became dominant, e.g., simplification of declension, loss of the infinitive, object reduplication, and the rise of a variety of analytic constructions. By that time the major phonological and morphophonological changes were also in place.

The history of Modern Literary Macedonian begins in the latter part of the 18th century with the birth of South Slavic nationalism. This history can be divided into five periods:

(1) c. 1794–1840. Ecclesiastical and didactic works using Macedonian dialects were first published during this period. Their authors' concern was with establishing a vernacular-based Slavic literary language in opposition to both the archaizing influence of those who would have based the Slavic literary language on Church Slavonic and the Hellenizing attempts of the Greek Orthodox Church, to which the majority of Macedonians and Bulgarians belonged. The authors of this period in both Macedonia and Bulgaria called their vernacular language "Bulgarian".

(2) c. 1840–1870. Secular works using Macedonian dialects began to appear. The struggle over the dialectal base of the

emerging vernacular literary language became manifest. Two principal literary centers arose on Macedo-Bulgarian territory: one in northeastern Bulgaria and the other in southwestern Macedonia. Some Macedonian intellectuals envisioned a Bulgarian literary language based on Macedonian dialects or a Macedo-Bulgarian dialectal compromise. Bulgarians, however, insisted that their eastern standard be adopted without compromise. It was during this period that increasing sentiment for a separate Macedonian literary language was expressed in private correspondence.

(3) 1870–1912. The establishment of the Bulgarian Exarchate in 1870 marked the definitive victory over Hellenism. (The rank of exarch in Eastern Orthodoxy is above that of metropolitan and below that of patriarch, but in this context the term came to denote the head of the autocephalous Bulgarian Church.) It is from this period that we have the first published statements insisting on Macedonian as a language separate from both Serbian and Bulgarian. In his book *Za makedonckite raboti* (1903) ('On Macedonian matters'), Krste Misirkov outlined the principles of a Macedonian literary language based on the Prilep-Bitola dialect group, precisely the dialects that later served as the basis of the Macedonian standard language. Thus, although most copies of the book were destroyed at the press by pro-Bulgarian activists, its existence belies the claim that literary Macedonian was created ex nihilo by Yugoslav fiat at the end of World War II.

(4) 1912–1944. In 1912 the kingdoms of Bulgaria, Greece, and Serbia united against Turkey in the first Balkan War. Less than a year later Macedonia was partitioned among these three allies. This essentially marked the end of the development of Literary Macedonian outside the borders of Yugoslavia, except for the period 1946–1948, during which the Macedonians of Pirin Macedonia were recognized as a national minority in Bulgaria with their own schools and publications in Literary Macedonian. In accordance with Article 9 of the Treaty of Sèvres (August 10, 1920) concerning minority-population language rights in Greece, a Macedonian primer entitled *Abecedar* was printed in Athens in 1925, but the book was never used and most copies were destroyed. In Yugoslavia, Macedonian was treated as a South Serbian dialect, which was consistent with claims that had been advanced since the 19th century, but the Yugoslav government permitted Macedonian literature to develop on a limited basis as a dialect literature. It was during this interwar period that linguists from outside the Balkans published studies in which they emphasized the distinctness of Macedonian from both Serbo-Croatian and Bulgarian.

(5) 1944–present. On August 2, 1944, Macedonian was formally declared the official language of the Republic of Macedonia. Literary Macedonian is based on the West Central dialects, whose major population centers are Prilep, Bitola, Kičevo, and Veles. The standardization of Literary Macedonian proceeded rapidly after its official recognition, in part because an interdialectal koine was already functioning. The west central region, which was the largest in both area and population, supplied a dialectal base to which speakers from other areas could adjust their speech most easily. In many respects these dialects are also maximally differentiated from both Serbo-Croatian and Bulgarian, but differentiation was not an absolute principle in codification.

Orthography and Basic Phonology

Macedonian is written in a form of the Cyrillic alphabet. The Cyrillic alphabet was developed, probably sometime after 885, by the disciples of Saints Cyril and Methodius on the basis of Greek uncial letters. Macedonian also has a standard form of LATIN transcription that was official when the Republic of Macedonia was part of Yugoslavia. This transcription is still used for international official purposes, except that the sequences *lj* and *nj* have been replaced by *ĺ* and *ń*.

Table 1: The Cyrillic Alphabet

Cyrillic	Transcription	Cyrillic	Transcription
Aa	a	Нн	n
Бб	b	Њњ	nj/ń
Вв	v	Оо	o
Гг	g	Пп-	p
Дд	d	Рр	r
Ѓѓ	ǵ	Сс	s
Ее	e	Тт	t
Жж	ž	Ќќ	ḱ
Зз	z	Уу	u
Ss	dz	Фф	f
Ии	i	Хх	h
Jj	j	Цц	c
Кк	k	Чч	č
Лл	l	Џџ	dž
Љљ	lj/ĺ	Шш	š
Мм	m	('	ə)

Table 2: Consonants

	Bilabial	Dental/ Alveolar	Alveo-palatal	Palatal	Velar
Stops					
Voiceless	p	t		ḱ	k
Voiced	b	d		ǵ	g
Fricatives					
Voiceless	f	s	š		h
Voiced	v	z	ž		
Affricates					
Voiceless		c	č		
Voiced		dz	dž		
Nasals	m	n		nj/ń	
Laterals		l			ł
Trill		r			
Glide				j	

All voiceless stops are unaspirated.

Under the influence of Serbo-Croatian and the Macedonian of Skopje, the capital, the clear alveolar /l/ is often realized as a palatal and [lj] > palatal [ĺ].

Final voiced consonants are devoiced, and there is regressive assimilation of voicing, e.g., *zob* [zop] 'oats', *zobta* [zopta] 'the oats', *zobnik* [zobnik] 'oat sack', *sretne* [sretne] 'meet', *sredba* [sredba] 'meeting'.

Table 3: Vowels

	Front	Central	Back
High	i		u
Mid	e	(ə)	o
Low			a

The five vowels are simple, not diphthongs. Schwa is phonemic in some dialects but marginal in the literary language. Stress in Macedonian usually falls on the antepenultimate syllable: *vodéničar* 'miller', *vodeníčari* 'millers', *vodeničárite* 'the millers'. Exceptions are lexical, usually unadapted loanwords or suffixes; if a phrase acts as a single accentual unit, stress will be on the antepenultimate syllable in this unit, e.g., *štó sakaš* 'what do you want?' Stress is never earlier in the word than the antepenultimate syllable.

Basic Morphology

Macedonian has lost case except in the pronoun (accusative and dative, e.g., *toj* 'he', accusative *nego*, dative *nemu*) and, in the west, a few masculine personal names and nouns (e.g., *Ivan* 'John', *od Ivan-a* 'from John'). There is also a vocative case form for some nouns, but it is always optional (e.g., *Ivan-e!* 'O John' *ženo!* 'O woman/wife!').

There are two numbers (singular and plural) and three genders: masculine (usually ending in a consonant but sometimes in *-a* or another vowel, but only to denote a human being), feminine (usually in *-a* but in a few old nouns in a consonant), and neuter (usually in *-o* or *-e* but sometimes in another vowel as in recent loanwords).

There are three definite articles that are postposed to the first inflected element of the noun phrase and agree in gender/number or form, depending on the grammatical category of the item: masc. *-ot* (neutral), *-ov* (proximate), *-on* (distal), feminine singular and neuter plural *-ta, -va, -na*, neuter *-to, -vo, -no,* other plural *-te, -ve, -ne,* e.g., *volk-ot* 'the wolf', *volci-te* 'the wolves', *vladika-ta* 'the bishop' (masculine), *žena-ta* 'the woman', *ženi-te* 'the women', *ljubov-ta* 'the love' (feminine), *selo-to* 'the village', *sela-ta* 'the villages'. Articles in *-v-* and *-n-* have a nuance like ENGLISH "this" and "that" respectively.

Verbs agree with their subjects. The aspectual opposition perfective/imperfective is inherent in the verb stem. Verbs can switch aspect by means of derivation. The accusative reflexive pronoun *se* is used to mark passives, reflexives, reciprocals, and plain intransitives.

Macedonian has three simple tenses and seven compound tenses. The simple tenses are the present, the aorist, and the imperfect. Of the compound forms, the old perfect (*sum* 'be' + l-participle) can carry a nuance of not vouching for the truth of the statement (inference, disbelief, surprise), and the new form using the old perfect of *ima* 'have' as an auxiliary with the neuter verbal adjective always carries this nuance: *moliš* 'you are asking', *zamoli* '(I am certain) you asked', *si zamolil* '(apparently/supposedly/to my surprise) you asked' or 'you have asked', *si imal zamoleno* '(apparently/supposedly/to my surprise) you have/had asked'. Sentence 2 gives a third-person example of the old perfect (the auxiliary is never used in the third person). The old pluperfect (imperfect of *sum* + l-participle, *beše zamolil* 'you had asked') and the new perfect (present of *ima* 'have' + neuter verbal adjective, *imaš zamoleno* 'you have asked') do not participate nuances of vouching or not vouching.

Basic Syntax

The basic word order in Macedonian sentences is SVO. However, this order can be modified in order to focus on or topicalize a particular element in the sentence.

kuče-to ja kasa mačka-ta
dog-the.NEUT 3SG.F.ACC bite.3SG.PRES cat-the.FEM
'The dog bites the cat.' (neutral)

mačka-ta ja kasa kuče-to
cat-the.FEM 3SG.F.ACC bite.3SG.PRES dog-the.NEUT
'The dog bites the cat.' (*mačka-ta* is topic)

kuče-to mačka-ta ja kasa
dog-the.NEUT cat-the.FEM 3SG.F.ACC bite-3SG.PRES
'The dog bites the cat.' (*mačka-ta* is topic and focus)

Case relations are only obligatorily marked in pronouns. If there is a definite (accusative) direct or indirect (dative) object, a clitic pronoun referring to that object will occur with the verb:

Jas ne mu ja dad-o-v kniga-ta
I NEG 3SG.M.DAT 3SG.F.ACC give-AORIST-1SG book-the

na momče-to.
to boy-the
'I did not give the book to the boy.'

As illustrated in the preceding example, sentence negation is expressed by placing *ne* before the verb complex (including any clitics). Constituents can also be negated by *ne*.

Nina dojde ne včera tuku
Nina come.3SG.AORIST NEG yesterday but

zavčera
day.before.yesterday
'Nina came not yesterday but the day before.'

A sentence can have more than one negative element:

Ni-ko-j ni-ko-mu ni-što ne
NEG-who-NOM.MASC NEG-who-DAT NEG-what NEG

reč-e
say-3SG.AORIST
'No one said anything to anyone.'

Absence is signaled by the impersonal *nema* 'it is not' (literally: 'it does not have'):

Nema ni-kakv-i direktor-i tuka
not.have.3SG NEG-what.kind.of- PL director-PL here
'There aren't any directors here at all.'

If the entity is definite, the verb takes an accusative clitic pronoun:

Direktor-ot	go	nema
director-the.SG	3SG.M.ACC	not.have.3SG

'The director isn't here.'

Macedonian adjectives generally precede the nouns they modify.

Contact with Other Languages

A major problem now for Literary Macedonian is the fact that Skopje—the capital and principal cultural and population center—is outside the West Central dialect area, whose dialects form the basis of the literary language, and the republic as a whole has been subject to considerable Serbo-Croatian influence. While the Republic of Macedonia was part of Yugoslavia, Macedonian was in a subordinate position to Serbo-Croatian. Now that the Republic of Macedonia is independent, the language is threatened only by the territorial and political pretensions of Macedonia's neighbors.

Macedonian has a very large component of borrowings from TURKISH dating from 500 years of Ottoman rule. It shares many of these words with other Balkan languages, and since many of these words are actually of Arabo-Persian origin, they occur in languages spoken throughout the Muslim world. There are also loanwords from Balkan Romance, Greek, and ALBANIAN. More recently, Macedonian has borrowed from English, FRENCH and GERMAN.

From Turkish: *džep* 'pocket', *tavan* 'ceiling' (in a house)
From Greek: *oti* 'that' (relativizer)
From Balkan Latin: *klisura* 'gorge'
From Albanian: *čupa* 'girl' (dialectal)
From Italian: *mandža* 'main-course meal'
From German: *šteker* 'electric plug'
From French: *plafon* 'ceiling' (e.g., price ceiling)
From English: *super* 'terrific', *lider* 'political leader'

Macedonian is the source for many words in the dialects of other languages that are in contact with it (Albanian, Turkish, Arumanian, ROMANI, etc.), e.g., Albanian *dërzhava* 'state', Turkish *odmor* 'vacation', Romani *vozinav* 'drive', Arumanian *ciudosi* 'be surprised'. These are strictly local-dialect phenomena, however, and not part of the respective literary languages, although insofar as Romani and Arumanian are still in the process of codification, the status of Macedonian borrowings in them is not settled. There are numerous South Slavic borrowings in Albanian and Greek, but these are often difficult to date and can go as far back as the period when the South Slavs settled in the Balkans.

Common Words

man:	mаž	long:	dolg
woman:	žena	small:	mal
water:	voda	yes:	da
sun:	sonce	no:	ne
three:	tri	good:	dobar
fish:	riba	bird:	ptica
big:	golem	dog:	kuče
tree:	drvo		

Example Sentences

(1) mu rek-ov na brat mi deka
3SG.DAT say-1SG.AORIST to brother 1SG.DAT that

[molba-ta bil-a potpišan-a od tatko-to
request-the was-FEM signed-FEM from father-the

na učenik-ot so moliv].
to pupil-the with pencil
'I said to my brother that [the request had been signed by the father of the pupil with a pencil].'

(2) toj rabote-l papudžija.
3SG.M work-3SG.PERF slipper.maker
'(Apparently) he worked/He has worked as a slipper-maker.'

(3) dali be-vte vo soba-ta?
INT be-2PL.IMPERFECT in room-the
'Were you in the room?'

Efforts to Preserve, Protect, and Promote the Language

The Republic of Macedonia has a Linguistics and Literature section of its Academy of Sciences, the Krste P. Misirkov Institute for the Macedonian Language, and the Macedonian Department of the Cyril and Methodius University of Skopje, which are responsible not only for linguistic research but also for developing and defining literary norms and for publishing grammars, dictionaries, and other authoritative works. The institute has a yearly journal, *Makedonski jazik*, the academy section has a biannual publication, *Prilozi*, and the humanities faculty to which the Macedonian department belongs has a yearbook (*Godišnik*), in which both theoretical and practical linguistic questions are addressed. These are not the only sources of language cultivation, however. There are also teachers' unions and other language organizations that publish linguistic or language-oriented journals on a more popular level, e.g., *Literaturen zbor* 'Literary Word.' Similar linguistic topics are also discussed in the daily press, and there are many popular books on "language culture," i.e., normative usage. As a result, the codification of the literary language has developed in part through dialogue between codifiers and users.

Select Bibliography

Čašule, Ilija. 1990. *Let's Learn Macedonian*. Sydney: Macquarie University, School of Modern Languages.
Crvenkovski, Dušan, and Branislav Grui. 1989. *Macedonian-English English-Macedonian Dictionary*. Skopje: Prosvetno Delo.

de Bray, Reginald G.A. 1980. "Macedonian." In *Guide to the South Slavic Languages (Guide to the Slavic Languages), 137–308*. 3rd ed., rev. Columbus, OH: Slavica.

de Bray, Reginald G.A. [compiler], Peter Hill, Sunčica Mirčevska, and Kevin Windle (eds.). 1998. *Routledge Macedonian-English Dictionary*. London, New York: Routledge.

Friedman, Victor A. 1975. "Macedonian Language and Nationalism during the Nineteenth and Early Twentieth Centuries." In *Balkanistica* 2:83–98.

____. 1985. "The Sociolinguistics of Literary Macedonian." In *International Journal of the Sociology of Language* 52:31–57.

____. 1989. "Macedonian: Codification and Lexicon." In *Language Reform* vol. IV, I. Fodor and C. Hagège, eds. 299–334. Hamburg: Helmut Buske.

____. 1993a. "Language Policy and Language Behavior in Macedonia: Background and Current Events." In *Language Contact, Language Conflict*. Eran Fraenkel and Christina Kramer, eds. 79–99. New York: Peter Lang.

____. 1993b. "Macedonian." In *The Slavonic Languages*, ed. B. Comrie and G. Corbett, 249–305. London: Routledge.

____. 1993c. "The First Philological Conference for the Establishment of the Macedonian Alphabet and the Macedonian Literary Language: Its Precedents and Consequences." In *The Earliest Stage of Language Planning: The "First Congress" Phenomenon*. Joshua Fishman, ed. 159–80. Berlin: Mouton de Gruyter.

Koneski, Blaže. 1983. *Macedonian Historical Phonology*, translated by Victor A. Friedman. (*Historical Phonology of the Slavic Languages, 12,* series ed. George Shevelov). Heidelberg: Carl Winter.

Koneski, Blaže, *et al.* 1978. *About the Macedonian Language*. Skopje: Institut za makedonski jazik.

Kramer, Christina. 1985. *Makedonsko-angliski razgovornik/ Macedonian-English phrasebook*. Skopje: Univerzitet Kiril i Metodij, Seminar za makedonski jazik, literatura i kultura.

____. 1993. "Language in Exile: The Macedonians in Toronto, Canada." In Fraenkel, Eran, and Christina Kramer, eds., *Language Contact, Language Conflict*, 157–83. New York: Peter Lang.

____. 1999. *Macedonian: A Course for Beginning and Intermediate Students*. Madison: University of Wisconsin.

Lunt, Horace. 1952. *A Grammar of the Macedonian Literary Language*. Skopje: Državno knigoizdatelstvo.

____. 1953. "A Survey of Macedonian Literature." In *Harvard Slavic Studies* 1:363–96.

____. 1974. *Old Church Slavonic Grammar*, 6th ed. The Hague: Mouton.

____. 1984. "Some Sociolinguistic Aspects of Macedonian and Bulgarian." In *Language and Literary Theory* (Papers in Slavic Philology, 5), B. Stolz, I. Titunik, and L. Doležel, eds. 83–132. Ann Arbor: University of Michigan.

____. 1986. "On Macedonian Language and Nationalism." In *Slavic Review* 45:4, 729–34.

Marinkoviḱ, Slavomir. 1991. *Let's Talk. Macedonian-English-French Picture Dictionary*. Skopje: Detska radost.

Mišeska-Tomiḱ, Olga, Natka Gogova, Mirka Mišiḱ, Zoze Murgoski, and Ljupčo Stefanovski. 1994. *English-Macedonian Dictionary*. Skopje: Kultura.

Misirkov, Krste P. 1974. *On Macedonian Matters*. Skopje: Macedonian Review Editions, (trans. from 1903 original).

Murgoski-Zafiroski, Zoze. 1993. *English-Macedonian Dictionary of Idioms*. Skopje: Matica makedonska.

Rossos, Andrew. 1994. "The British Foreign Office and Macedonian National Identity 1918–41." In *Slavic Review* 53, 369–94.

____. 1997. "Incompatible Allies: Greek Communism and Macedonian Nationalism in the Civil War in Greece, 1943–49." In *Journal of Modern History* 69:42–76.

Simeonova, Madedonka (transl.) 1990. *Renyi Macedonian Picture Dictionary*. Editions Renyi.

MADURESE

Alan M. Stevens

Language Name: Madurese. **Autonym:** *Basa Madura.* **Alternates:** *Bahasa Madura* (in Indonesian); *Madoerees(ch)* (in Dutch).

Location: Madurese is spoken in the Republic of Indonesia, especially on the island of Madura; it is also spoken on the Kangean Islands and Sapudi, and in parts of the province of East Java.

Family: The Sundic group of the Polynesian subbranch of the Western Malayo-Polynesian branch of the Austronesian family.

Related Languages: Most closely related to MALAY/INDONESIAN and JAVANESE; more distantly related to SUNDANESE and BALINESE.

Dialects: (1) West Madurese, (2) Central Madurese, (3) East Madurese (the standard), and (4) Kangean (islands to the east of Madura). These dialects differ from each other primarily in lexicon and in phonology and less so in morphology and syntax.

A characteristic that Madurese shares with its neighboring languages of Javanese, Sundanese, Balinese, and Sasak (spoken on Lombok, the island just east of Bali) is the system of language levels, in which many common meanings are expressed by two, three, or even more totally or partially different words. The choice of word depends on the social relations (i.e., socially superior, socially inferior, or socially equal) among the speaker, the person spoken to, and the person spoken about. There is also a special set of words to be used in reference to someone who is to be respected, and there is also a small set of self-denigrating words. This complex system contains hundreds of such pairs and triplets for pronouns, everyday nouns, verbs, adjectives, numbers, etc. (see Stevens 1965). Throughout this chapter, if there is a choice of language levels, the "low" forms are used.

Number of Speakers: 9–10 million.

Origin and History

Indonesia, of which Madura is part, consists of an archipelago in the Indian and Pacific Oceans off the coast of mainland Southeast Asia. Madura is one of the larger islands and lies off the northeast coast of Java. Indonesia was formerly called the Dutch, or Netherlands, East Indies. The name "Indonesia", which was given to it by a German geographer in 1884, may derive from the term *Indos Nesos* 'Indian Islands' used in the ancient trading language of the region.

The population of Indonesia originally came from areas outside of Indonesia, but the exact location is disputed; it was perhaps the Asian mainland or the Pacific Islands.

Madurese originated on the island of Madura, but because of population growth and the problems connected with growing enough food for that population, there was early—perhaps during the 14th century—movement to the eastern part of Java (province of East Java), where there is a sizeable Madurese population, which, in some areas is mixed with Javanese speakers.

Orthography and Basic Phonology

Madurese has been written with a syllabary (based on an Indian syllabary) similar to the one used for Javanese and Balinese. It is distantly related to the other syllabaries used in Southeast Asia. Madurese has also been written in an ARABIC-based alphabet and it has been written in Romanized form. Few people use or know the first two any more. In the Romanized form most of the vowels are written as pronounced and follow current Indonesian orthographic conventions. Unfortunately, the Romanized form does not show all the phonemic contrasts in the consonants; in particular, the aspirated series is written with the same symbol that is used for the voiced series, so that /p^hao/ 'shoulder' and /bao/ 'smell' are both written *bau.* It also does not usually mark the difference between the dental and alveolar series. Finally, some of the variation between vowel qualities is not indicated (even though some is). Madurese is not used much for writing. Most Madurese who are literate prefer to write in Indonesian.

As a result of the lack of orthographic distinctness for many important phonological characteristics, forms are given in Table 1 on the next page in both the orthography and phonetic transcription.

Madurese has a larger set of consonants than the neighboring languages because it has a three-way contrast, unusual in this group of languages, among voiceless unaspirated, voiceless aspirated, and voiced. Like Javanese, it also has a contrast between dental and alveolar (or slightly retroflex) stops. In most dialects the /w/ and the /h/ are limited to borrowings. Some of these phonemic differences are not marked in the Romanized form in current use.

All consonants besides the glottal stop /ʔ/ can occur single or geminated.

Table 1: Consonants

		Bilabial	Dental	Alveolar	Palatal	Velar	Glottal
Stops	Voiceless	p	t	ṭ	c	k	ʔ
	Aspirated	pʰ	tʰ	ṭʰ	cʰ	kʰ	
	Voiced	b	d	ḍ	j	g	
Fricatives			s				h
Nasals		m	n		ñ	ŋ	
Liquids			r, l				
Glides		w			y		

Table 2: Vowels

	Front	Central	Back
Mid	e	ə	o
Low		a	

Madurese is unusual in that it does not have any phonemically high vowels. However, the midvowels, which are phonetically [ɛ ə ɔ] have phonologically conditioned high variants [i ɨ u]; the vowel /a/ likewise has two variants, [a] and [ɤ]. The higher, tense variants [i ɨ u ɤ] occur following voiced or voiceless aspirated consonants; the lower, lax variants [ɛ ə ɔ a] occur word-initially and following other consonants. The second syllable of *bato* 'stone' has the lax variant [ɔ] because *t* is unaspirated; in contrast, the second syllable of *pʰakʰos* 'good' has the tense variant [u] because *kʰ* is voiceless aspirated. Vowel tensing can spread toward the end of the word across liquids and glides and through sequences of vowels. (For purposes of this rule, the glottal stop /ʔ/ and fricative /h/ count as glides.) In the word *baras* 'healthy', the first syllable has the tense variant [ɤ] because the initial consonant is voiced; the second syllable has the tense variant [ɤ] because of the [ɤ] in the first syllable.

Madurese has a phonological rule in which the form of a nasal consonant in a prefix is determined by the initial sound in a word. This nasal, which can be represented as *N*, appears as /ŋ/ before a vowel. Before consonants, its form varies depending on the specific consonant:

Stem Type	N+stem	Pronunciation	Meaning
voiceless	N-totop	nɔtɔp	'close'
aspirated	N-tʰaar	aṭʰɤʔɤr	'eat'
voiced-a	N-bəle	məllɛ	'buy'
voiced-b	N-baleʔ	abɤliʔ	'turn over'
nasal	N-ñata-akʰe	añataʔakʰi	'prove'
liquid	N-rosak	arɔsak	'break'

Basic Morphology

Madurese nouns are not inflected for case or gender. Nouns are made plural via reduplication. The most usual form of reduplication is rather unusual; the reduplicated element is an exact phonetic copy of the final syllable of the root: for example, the plural of *bato* 'stone' is *to-bato* [tɔ-bɤtɔ] 'stones'. Likewise, the plural of *bua* [buwɤ] 'fruit' is *wa'-buwa'-an* [wɤʔbuwɤʔɤn], in which reduplication is combined with addition of a suffix *-an*. Only after the *a* in the second syllable of the stem *bua* is tensed to [ɤ] (by the tensing rule described above), the phonetic syllable [wɤʔ] is copied to the front of the word.

In Madurese, verbs do not agree with their subjects and are not inflected for tense. However, there is a rich system of verbal derivation in which affixes are added to a verb stem to create new meanings. One of these affixes is similar to passive marking in languages like ENGLISH. For example, if the recipient of the action is focused on, the verb is marked with the passive prefix *e-*. In addition, verbs can be marked as causative, as benefiting someone, as representing an involuntary action, as specifically transitive, and as focusing on the location where something takes place, among others; further, multiple affixes can be added to a single verb. Some of these possibilities are illustrated in the Example Sentences below.

Basic Syntax

The basic word order in Madurese is SVO. Consistent with this order, within phrases, modifiers tend to follow their heads: in the phrase *oreng rowa* 'that man', the demonstrative *rowa* follows the noun *oreng*.

Negation is expressed by placing a negative word before the verb/adjective or before a noun phrase. As in closely related languages, there are different negative words for different kinds of negation.

There is one negation for noun phrases, e.g., *banne rea* 'it's not that one' where *banne* is the negative, and a different negation for other types of phrases, e.g., *taʔ masoʔ sakola* 'doesn't go to school' where *taʔ* is the negative.

Contact with Other Languages

Madurese has been in contact with Malay/Indonesian and Javanese for many centuries. It has borrowed heavily from these languages as well as from SANSKRIT and Arabic, although its contact with Arabic was largely limited to religious contexts. Madurese has fewer borrowings from DUTCH and English than Indonesian has.

From Dutch: *sapeda* [sapeḍɤ] 'bicycle'

From Javanese: *(anak) ontang-anteng* ‘only (child)’
From Indonesian: *susu* ‘milk’
From Arabic: *pekker* ‘think’
From PORTUGUESE: *candila* [canḍilɤ] ‘window’
From English: *gojer* ‘bicycle tire’ (from *Goodyear)*
From Sanskrit: *basa* [pʰɤsa] ‘language’

Common Words

man:	lalake	[lalakɛ]
woman:	babine	[bɤbinɛ]
yes:	iya	[iyɤ]
no:	enja’	[ənjɤʔ]
water:	aeng	[aɛŋ]
sun:	are	[arɛ]
good:	bagus	[pʰɤkʰus]
three:	tello’	[təllɔʔ]
bird:	mano’	[manɔʔ]
fish:	juko’	[cʰukɔʔ]
dog:	pate’	[patɛʔ]
big:	raja	[rajɤ]
small:	kene’	[kɛnɛʔ]
tree:	bungka	[pʰuŋka]
long:	lanjang	[lancʰɤŋ]

Example Sentences

(1)

Ebu	ngangka’agi	geṭṭang	guring	ḍa’
[ɛpʰu	ŋ-aŋkaʔ-akʰi	kʰɨṭṭʰɤŋ	kʰuriŋ	ḍɤʔ
Mother	ACTIVE-serve-BENEFACT	banana	fried	to

tamoy.
tamɔy]
guest.
‘Mother served fried bananas to the guest.’

(2)

Aeng	songay	jareya	agili	neng	babana
[aɛŋ	sɔŋay	jɤreya	a-kʰili	nəŋ	bɤbɤ-na
Water	river	that	INTRANS-flow	at	under:of-it

galaḍak.
kʰɤlɤṭʰɤk]
bridge
‘The river flows under the bridge.’

(3)

Oreng	rowa	etolare	panyaket.
[ɔrɛŋ	rowa	ɛ-tɔlar-ɛ	pañakɛt]
person	that	PASSIVE-infect-LOC	AGENT:sick

‘That man was infected by a disease.’

Efforts to Preserve, Protect, and Promote the Language

Some grammatical and lexicographical work on Madurese has been done at the *Pusat Pembinaan dan Pengembangan Bahasa* (‘Center for Language Promotion and Development’) of the Indonesian *Departemen Pendidikan dan Kebudayaan* (‘Department of Education and Culture’), but there has been little effort, either nationally or within the Madurese-speaking region, to promote the use of Madurese as a written language or even to devise a more accurate Romanization for it. Most literate Madurese prefer to write in Indonesian. Indonesian is introduced in schools as early as the second grade and has largely become the language of written communication. Many speakers are bilingual in Madurese and Indonesian, Madurese and Javanese (those living in Java), or even trilingual in Madurese, Indonesian, and Javanese.

Select Bibliography

Almost all pre–World War II literature was written in Dutch. Most recent literature in English has been highly technical. Recent descriptive work has been in Indonesian.

Blust, R.A. 1981. “The reconstruction of Proto-Malayo-Javanic: An appreciation.” In *The Bulletin of the School of Oriental and African Studies 45*: 284–299.

Cohn, A. 1991. “Voicing and Vowel Height in Madurese, a Preliminary Report.” Paper presented at 6ICAL, Honolulu, Hawaii.

Davies, William. 1999. *Madurese*. Languages of the World/ Materials 84. Munich: Lincom Europa.

Stevens, A.M. 1965. “Language Level in Madurese.” In *Language 41*: 294–302.

____. 1968. *Madurese Phonology and Morphology*. American Oriental Series #52. New Haven: American Oriental Society.

____. 1980. “Formative Boundary in Phonological Rules.” In M. Aronoff and M-L. Kean, eds. *Juncture*, Studia Linguistica et Philologica 7, Saratoga, California: Anma Libri.

____. 1985. “Reduplication in Madurese.” In Choi, *et al*, eds. *Proceedings of ESCOL 1985*. Ohio State University, 232–43.

____. 1991. “Madurese Reduplication Revisited.” Paper presented at *Workshop on Madurese Culture and Society: Continuity and Change*. Leiden, the Netherlands, October 7–11.

Uhlenbeck, E.M. 1964. *A Critical Survey of Studies on the Languages of Java and Madura*. ’s-Gravenhage: Martinus Nijhoff.

MAITHILI

Yogendra P. Yadava

Language Name: Maithili. **Alternate Names:** *Tirhutiyā*, *Dehāti*, *Avahaṭa*, or *Apabhraṁśa*.

Location: The Maithili language is spoken mainly in the northeastern part of the Indian state of Bihār and the eastern part of Nepal's Terai region. There are also Maithili-speaking minorities in adjoining Indian states like West Bengāl, Mahārāshtra and Madhya Pradesh and the central Nepal Terai.

Family: Maithili belongs to the Eastern subgroup of the Indo-Aryan group within the Indo-Iranian branch of the Indo-European language family.

Related Languages: Maithili forms a subgroup with BHOJPURI and Magahi and is linguistically closer to ASSAMESE, BANGLA, and ORIYA than to its more contiguous languages, namely, HINDI and NEPALI, which belong to the Central and Western subgroups of Indo-Aryan, respectively.

Dialects: According to S. Jha (1958:5–6), there exist seven regional dialects of Maithili. They are the standard, southern, eastern, Chikāchiki, western, Jolhi, and the central colloquial dialects. Of them, standard Maithili is spoken in the north of Darbhangā district (Bihār state, India), which now forms the part of the Madhubani district. So far little attempt has been made to study the social dialects of the language. It may, however, be suggested that Maithili exhibits social variations in its pronunciation, vocabulary and grammar in terms of the speaker's caste, sex, education, interpersonal relationship, and other social factors.

Number of Speakers: The Maithili language is spoken by more than 30 million people as a first language and by many others as a second language in the northeastern part of the Indian state of Bihār and the eastern part of Nepalese terai region. In Nepal, it is the language of approximately 12 percent (approximately 2.3 million) of the total population and figures second in terms of the number of speakers—next only to Nepali, the language of the nation, spoken by a little over 50 percent of the population.

Origin and History

Like other Indo-Aryan languages, Maithili is believed to have evolved from Vedic and Classical SANSKRIT through several intermediate stages of *Magadhi Prākrit*, Proto-Maithili and *Apabhraṁśhas*. It emerged as a distinct modern Indo-Aryan language between A.D. 1000 and 1200.

Maithili has had a long rich tradition of written literature in both India and Nepal. The earliest written record can be traced back as early as *Verṇaratnākara*, the oldest text in Maithili written by Jyotiriśvara Kaviśekharāchārya in the 14th century. The most famous Maithili writer is Vidyāpati Ṭhākur, popularly known as Mahākavi Vidyāpati. Apart from being a great Sanskrit writer, he composed melodious poems in Maithili, entitled *Vidyāpati Padāvali*, which mainly deal with the love between Rādhā and Krisṇa. It is this anthology of poems that has made him popular and immortal to the present day.

Maithili also flourished as a court language in the Kāṭhmāndu Valley during Malla period. Several literary works (especially dramas and songs) and inscriptions in Maithili are still preserved at the National Archives in Kāṭhmāndu.

In the present context there have been literary writings in all literary genres, especially poetry, plays, and fiction, from both Indian and Nepalese writers. Apart from literature, Maithili writers have also been contributing to other fields like culture, history, journalism, linguistics, etc.

In addition to written texts, Maithili has an enormous stock of oral literature in the forms of folktales in both prose and verse, ballads, songs, etc. Of them the ballads of Rās Lilā (expressing the love between Rādhā and Krisṇa) and Salhes (a prehistoric king) are well-known specimens.

As its name implies, Maithili is, properly speaking, the language of *Mithilā*, the prehistoric ancient kingdom, which was ruled by King Janak and was the birthplace of Jānaki or Sitā (Lord Ram's concubine). This region was also called *Tairabhukti*, the ancient name of Tirhut comprising both Darbhangā and Muzaffarpur districts of Bihār, India.

In both Nepal and India, Maithili has been taught as a subject of study from school to university levels of education. Especially in India, however, it has been hampered by the lack of official recognition as a medium of instruction. In Nepal, there has recently been made a constitutional provision for introducing all the mother tongues spoken in Nepal, including Maithili, as mediums of instruction at the primary level of education. This is, no doubt, a welcome step for their promotion, but in spite of speakers' zeal there has not been much headway in this regard in the dearth of official initiatives and basic requirements like teaching/reading materials and trained manpower. Both PEN (Poets, Essayists, Novelists) and *Sahitya Akademi* have recognized Maithili as the 16th largest language of India, though it has not yet been included in the Eighth Schedule of the Indian constitution despite the unceasing efforts made by the Maithili-speaking community in India.

Orthography and Basic Phonology

Previously, Maithili had its own script, called *Mithilākshar* or *Tirhutā*, which originated from *Brahmi* (of the third century B.C. Asokan inscriptions) via the proto-Bengāli script and is similar to the modern Bengāli and Oriya writing systems. Besides the *Mithilākshar* script, the *Kaithi* script was also used by *Kāyasthas* (belonging to a caste of writers and clerks), especially in keeping written records at government and private levels. These two scripts are now almost abandoned. For the sake of ease in learnability and printing (and also perhaps under the influence of the Hindi writing system), they have been gradually replaced by the *Devanāgari* script used in writing Hindi, Nepali and some other languages of both Indo-Aryan and Tibeto-Burman stocks spoken in adjoining areas.

Not all the characters in this script are distinctive and phonemic. For example, the *Devanāgari* alphabet makes short/long vowel contrasts, but they are not distinctive at the phonological level of the Maithili language; that is to say, Maithili has only short vowels and no long ones. Besides, each consonant in writing incorporates the inherent vowel [ə], which is pronounced with the consonant in isolation but dropped if it occurs with other vowels in the sequence of a word.

Except for a few, all consonants are pronounced like their symbols. The consonants that are spoken differently are: <s, sh, s.> =[s]; <kr> =[kri];<jna>=[gya]; and <ksa>=[kcha]. Maithili writing also uses diacritical marks like the *candrabindu* [ँ] or *anuswār* [°] for nasalization of a vowel.

There exist 26 consonants and eight oral vowels in Maithili:

Table 1: Consonants

	Bilabial	Dental	Retroflex	Palatal	Velar	Glottal
Stops	p pʰ b bʰ	t tʰ d dʰ	ṭ ṭʰ ḍ ḍʰ		k kʰ g gʰ	
Affricates				c cʰ j jʰ		
Nasals	m	n				
Tap		r				
Fricatives		s				h
Lateral		l				
Approximants	(w)			(y)		

Table 2: Vowels

	Front	Central	Back
High	i		u
Mid	e	ə	o
Low	æ	a	ɔ

The gemination of consonants is an important feature of the Maithili sound system. A consonant is geminated intervocally if the preceding vowel is stressed, e.g., *'sukkhā* 'draught', but **gi'rrā* (*gi'rā*) 'cause to fall' (Yadav 1996: 29–30). Stress is, however, not very significant in Maithili and has a marginal role in differentiating words. The morphophonemic alternations that are very productive in Maithili include schwa /ə/ deletion (e.g., *sərək-e* → [*sərk-e*] 'only the road') and *ā* → *ə* (e.g., *kām-āi* → *kəm-āi* 'salary').

Basic Morphology

Noun Morphology. The pronouns of Maithili distinguish person, honorificity (glossed in the article as "hh" for high honorifics, "mh" for mid-honorifics, and "nh" for non-honorifics), proximity and case:

	Nominative	Dative	Genitive
1	*ham*	*hamrā*	*hamar*
2nh	*tũ*	*torā*	*tohar*
2mh	*tõ*	*torā*	*tohar*
2h	*ahā̃*	*ahā̃-kẽ*	*ahā̃-k*
2hh indirect	*apne*	*apne-kẽ*	*apne-k*
3nh proximate	*i*	*ekrā*	*ekar*
3nh remote	*u*	*okrā*	*okar*
3h/hh proximate	*i*	*hinkā*	*hinak*
3h/hh remote	*o*	*hunkā*	*hunak*

With regard to most categories, pronouns are equally or less differentiated than verbal inflections. They are less specific with regard to the "honorific" vs. "high-honorific" distinction among third persons, which are registered as *-aith* and *-athinh*, respectively, on the verb. In either case, the pronoun is *o*. Moreover, if third person reference is proximate, all honorificity (h) distinctions are neutralized to *i*. Among second persons, pronouns are equally discriminatory as verb forms. However, the distinction between honorific *ahā̃* and high-honorific *apne* is not encoded synthetically. Rather, *apne* combines with a periphrastic passive-like construction that contrasts with the active form agreeing with *ahā̃*: *apne paḍh-al ge-l-aik.* (2hhN read-P PASS.AUX-PAST-3) 'Youʰʰ were reading', vs. *ahā̃ paḍh-ait cha-l-āuh.* (2hN read-IP AUX-PAST-2hN) 'Youʰ were reading'.

Mid- and non-honorific second persons are differentiated by *tũ* vs. *tõ*, respectively, but this contrast is not always maintained. It is neutralized especially among lower-caste speakers (Bickel, *et al.* 1999).

The distinction between honorific degrees is not limited to pronouns. Proper nouns can be marked by an honorific (h) suffix (*-ji*) or a non-honorific (nh) suffix (*-yā, -bā, -mā*), triggering corresponding verb inflection. *Hari-ji bhajan gab-ait ch-aith* (H.-h religious.song sing-IP AUX-3hN) 'Hariʰ is singing a *bhajan*, honorific form', *Hari-yā bhajan gab-ait ai-ch* (H.-nh religious.song sing-IP 3-AUX) 'Hariⁿʰ is singing a *bhajan*, non-honorific form'. Without such marking, a name has a neutral to mid-honorific value. Common nouns sometimes differentiate an honorific and a non-honorific lexical form, such as *bauā* 'boyʰ' vs. *chaurā* 'boyⁿʰ', or *daiyā* 'girlʰ' vs. *chauri* 'girlⁿʰ'.

Another feature restricted only to nominals is number. This category, however, is not fully grammaticalized with nominals either. It is expressed by the suffix *-sabh* or, with honorific reference only, the suffix *-lokain* (Singh 1989: 88). Notice that *-sabh* also occurs as a free word in the sense of 'all', which attests to a low degree of grammaticalization (R. Yadav 1996: 69). In verb agreement, no number distinctions are made. This fact, which makes Maithili quite different from other Indo-Aryan languages such as Hindi or Nepali, is the result of reanalyzing inherited number differentiation into honorificity distinctions.

Grammatical gender in Maithili nouns is rather very much restricted both as a morphological category and as a syntactic category. There exist declensions like *-i (chaurā* 'boy'*/ chauri* 'girl'), *-āin (guru/guruāin* 'teacher masculine/feminine'), etc., but they are confined to a limited number of nouns and do not apply across the board. Maithili pronominals do not encode gender distinctions at all. But in highly formal speech, Maithili verbs encode, as a syntactic category, the feminine gender associated with third person honorific nouns and pronouns in past and future tenses: *o daur-l-ih/daur-t-ih.* (3h run-PAST-3hN:FEM run-FUT-3hN:FEM) 'She ran/will run', *o daur-l-aith/ daur-t-āh.* (3h run-PAST-3hN run-FUT- 3hN) 'He ran/will run'. It is to be noted, however, that unlike Hindi and Nepali, possessive modifiers do not agree with their nominal heads in gender: *okar pati/patni* 'his/her husband/wife'. However, if the modifier is an adjective it does agree with its human head noun in gender: *okar pahilkā betā/ okar pahilki beti* 'his/her first son/ his/her first daughter'.

Like other south Asian languages, Maithili nominals involve a rich case system. They encode three types of case markings: zero-marking, clitics and *-(a)k* +postpositions. There are two cases in Maithili that are zero-marked, viz. nominative and accusative with nonhuman nouns: nominative *u daur-l-ak* (he-NOM run-PAST-3nh) 'he ran', accusative *u kitāb kin-l-ak.* (he-NOM book-ACC buy-PAST-3nh) 'he bought a book'.

Maithili is spoken mainly in the northeastern part of the Indian state of Bihār and in eastern Nepal (shaded area).

The clitic *-kẽ* marks accusative/dative case. *Rām chaurā-kẽ mār-l-ak* (Ram boy-ACC beat-PAST-3nh) 'Ram beat the boy', hari-kẽ bhukh lāg-al (Hari-DAT hunger feel-PAST) 'Hari felt hungry'. The clitics *–(a)k* (on nouns and honorific pronouns) and (*-(a)r* with non-honorific pronouns) mark the genitive case: *ham rām-ak ghar dekh-l-i-ainh* (Ram-GEN house see-PAST-1-3h) 'I saw Ram's house', *ham ahā̃-k ghar dekh-l-aũh* (I 2h-GEN house see- PAST-1) 'I saw your[h] house', *ham-ar ghar dur ai-ch* (my-GEN house far 3-AUX) 'My house is far away'.

The clitic *-sã* marks instruments or sources: *hari pensil-sã likh-l-ak* (Hari pencil-INS write-PAST-3nh) 'Hari wrote with a pencil', *hari-ji apan gām-sã ai-l-āh* (Hari-h self village-SRC come-PAST-3h) 'Hari came from his village'. The clitics *-me* and *-par* mark locatives: *hari-ji kothari-me ch-aith* (Hari-h room-LOC AUX-3h) 'Hari is in the room', *hari-ji ghar-par ch-aith* (Hari-h home-LOC AUX-3h) 'Hari is at home'. It is to be noted, however, that in contrast to many other Indo-Aryan languages including Hindi and Nepali, Maithili has no ergative case marking.

An example of the genitive case marker with a postposition is: *ham kitāb-ak-lel/bāste ae-l ch-i* (I book-GEN-P come-PARTICIPLE AUX-1) 'I have come for the book'.

Like Nepali, Hindi and several other south Asian languages, there is no one-to-one correspondence between cases and grammatical relations in Maithili. For example, the subject of a clause may take non-nominative case marking and appear in the following cases: dative(DAT), instrumental(INS), genitive(GEN) and locative(LOC), as well as logical subject in a passive construction: *hunkā bhukh lag-l-ain(h)* (3h-DAT hunger feel-PAST-3h) 'He felt hungry', *hunkā ciṭhi likhai-kẽ cha-l-ain(h)* (3h-DAT letter to write be-PAST-3HNN) 'He had to write a letter', *hunkā-sã i kitāb padh-al nahi bhe-l-ain(h)* (3h-Ins this book read-PARTICIPLE not become-PAST-3HNN) 'He couldn't read this book', *hunak paisā harā ge-l-ain(h)* (3h-GEN money lose go-PAST-3HNN) 'He lost his money', *hunkā-me sāphe dayā nahi ch-ain(h)* (3h-LOC at.all mercy not be-PRES3HNN) 'He has no mercy at all', *hunkā-sã i cithi likh-al ge-l-ain(h)* (3h-by this letter write-PARTICIPLE go-PAST-3HNN) 'This letter was written by him'.

Verb Morphology. The most striking feature of Maithili grammar is the extremely complex verbal system. Like other Indo-Aryan languages, Maithili has a polymorphomic verb paradigm. It consists of several elements normally to the right of the verb stem. Its structure may be expressed as follows: Verb → Stem (Asp) (Suff be) (Asp Suff) (Aux) Tense Agr_1 (Agr_2) (Agr_3), as illustrated in:

hari-ji daur-ait rah-ait cha-l- āh.
Hari-3h run-IP be- IP AUX-PAST-3h
'Hari had been running.'

Unlike most of the Indo-Aryan languages, however, Maithili encodes one of the most complex agreement systems of Indo-Aryan languages. In this language, not only nominative and non-nominative subjects, but also objects, other core arguments, and even non-arguments are cross-referenced, allowing for a maximum of three participants encoded by the verb affixes. An example of an intransitive clause where one argument is marked on the verb is *ham sut-l-aũ(h)* (1N sleep-PAST-1N) 'I slept'. In a transitive clause, two arguments may be marked on the verb: *ham hun-kā madat kar-l-i-ainh* (1N 3h-ACC help do-PAST-1N-3HACC) 'I helped him'. And a ditransitive verb may have three cross-referenced arguments: *ham to-rā hun-ak kitāb de-l-i-au-nh* (1N 2mh-ACC 3h-GEN book give-PAST-1N-2MHACC-3HGEN) 'I gave his book to you'.

The controllers of verb agreement in all the three types of verb agreement include not only the arguments of a predicate and the possessors but also non-arguments like nominals in postpositional phrases and possessors therein, as well as deictic referents in discourse: *tõ hun-kā-lel kāj kai-l-ah-unh* (2mhN 3h-OBL-for work do-PAST-2mhN-3HOBL) 'You worked for him (agreement with a non-argument)', *ham toh-ar ghar-par ge-l ch-al-i-ah* (1N 2mh-GEN house-at go-pcl AUX-PAST-1N-2MHGEN) 'I had been to your house (agreement with a possessor)', and *ham o-krā mār-l-i-ah* (1N 3nh-ACC beat-PAST-1N-2mh) 'I beat him (who is related to you, etc., agreement with a deictic referent)'. However, it has been found that the system is partly reduced by lower caste speakers, who are least interested in maintaining this style, especially its emphasis on hierarchy.

The categories reflected in the morphology are three persons with four honorific degrees and, in the case of third persons only, masculine vs. feminine gender, proximate vs. remote spatial distance and in focus vs. out of focus reference. However, not all combinations of category choices are equally represented, and there are many cases of neutralization.

A related issue in Maithili grammar is the optionality of pronouns. Not only the subject pronoun, but also the direct object and possessive within the direct object may be dropped. *Ham torā mār-b-au* (I-[1] you-[2nh] beat-FUT-1SUB+2nhDO) 'I will beat you' may have the following realizations: *torā mārbau*, *ham mārbau*, or *mārbau*.

Like Hindi but unlike Nepali, a verb in Maithili employs two types of causative verbs, e.g., *kaṭā-/kaṭbā-* 'have cut by someone/cause someone to have cut by someone'. Furthermore, the first causative is derived from its transitive counterpart *kāṭ-* 'cut something', which is further derived from its intransitive form *kaṭ-* 'cut' (as in 'the tree is cutting well').

A verb in Maithili, as in other south Asian languages, can be expanded in another way also, namely, in the form of a serial verb construction (often referred to as "compound verb") which involves a sequence of two verbs. The first of these verbs is in the form of conjunctive participle (CP) and may be referred to as a "host", while the second one is in the finite form and may be called a "light verb", e.g., *hari-ji kitāb paidh le-l-aith* (Hari-h book read-CP take-PAST-3h) 'Hari completed the reading of the book'. Apart from aspectual functions, serial verbs in Maithili also express other semantic functions, e.g., volitionality and control of the action by the agent as well as the speaker's attitude.

In addition to causativization and verb serialization, there exist other types of complex predicates in Maithili. For example, a verb can combine with a noun or adjective to form a complex verb:

rām cor-ak pichā kai-l-ak. (Noun + Verb)
Ram thief-GEN pursuitN do.IP-PAST-3nh
'Ram chased the thief.'

rām ghar sāph kai-l-ak. (Adjective + Verb)
Ram house clean do-PAST-3nh
'Ram cleaned the house.'

Basic Syntax

The normal order of constituents in a Maithili sentence is S(ubject) V(erb) O(bject), e.g., *rām kitāb kinat* (Ram book will.buy) 'Ram will buy a book (SVO)'. However, these constituents can be permuted in any order: *kitāb rām kinat* (OSV), *kitāb kinat rām* (OVS), *kinat rām kitāb* (VSO), *kinat kitāb rām* (VOS), and *rām kinat kitāb* (SVO).

The order SOV is unmarked and stylistically neutral, whereas the various permuted orders are generally accompanied by phonological and semantic effects like topicalization, focussing, afterthought, definiteness, etc.

The freedom of word order also extends to Indirect Object and adverbials of various types. What is more interesting about Maithili word order is that even elements like adjectives within NPs and auxiliaries within verbal sequences can be permuted with other elements of the sentence: e.g., *gitā hariyar sāri pahirne a-ich* (Geeta green sari wearing AUX-PRES3) 'Geeta is wearing a green sari' may have the following permutations: *gitā hariyar pahirne aich sāri* and *gitā sāri pahirne aich hariyar*), and the sentence *rām khā-it ai-ch* (Ram eat-IP PRES3-AUX) 'Ram is eating' may be said as *khā-it ai-ch rām*, *rām ai-ch khā-it*, or *ai-ch rām khā-it*.

The change in word order is not only restricted to simple sentences and phrases in Maithili but also extends to complex sentences. Consider the unmarked order of the constituents in the complex sentence and how the elements of both main and subordinate clauses can be juxtaposed with one another: *rām hari-kẽ kitāb padh-bāk-lel kah-l-ak* (Ram Hari-ACC book read-INF tell-PAST-3nh) 'Ram told Hari to read the book' = *hari-kẽ rām padh-bāk-lel kitāb kah-l-ak*, etc.

Taking the unmarked order into consideration, Maithili, like all languages of the south Asia *sprachbund* ('linguistic area'), is a head-final language, whereby we mean that the head of a phrase follows its complement. Thus, the head of a verb phrase (VP) is a verb (V) and it follows its complement (object NP); the head of a postpositional phrase (PP) is a postposition (P) and it follows its complement (object NP); and the head of a noun phrase (NP) is a noun (N) and it follows its complement (genitive marker *–ak*): *rām* [VP *hari-kẽ mār-l-ak*] (Ram3nhN Hari-ACC beat-PAST-3nhN) 'Ram beat Hari', [PP *nepāl me*] (Nepal in) 'in Nepal', [NP *rām-ak kitāb*] (Ram-GEN book) 'Ram's book'.

Contact with Other Languages

Most of the foreign words in Maithili have been borrowed from Sanskrit. Technical terms are mostly loanwords from ENGLISH.

From Sanskrit: *adatt* 'extreme', *anargal* 'improper', *abasthā* 'age', *ār* 'and'
From PERSIAN: *adnā* 'not related', *adālat* 'civil court', *ādmi* 'human being'
From English: *ṭisan* 'station', *pen* 'pen', *kāpi* 'copy; notebook', *ṭebul* 'table'

Common Words

man:	purus	woman:	istri
long:	namhar	small:	choṭ
water:	pāin	big:	namhar
no:	nai/nahi	sun:	suruj
good:	nik	three:	tin
bird:	cirai	fish:	māch
dog:	kuttā	tree:	gāch

Example Sentences

(1) hari-ji daur-ait rah-ait cha-l-āh.
Hari-3hN run-IMP be-IMP AUX-PAST-3hN
'Hari had been running.'

(2) ham hun-kā madat kar-l-i-ainh.
1N 3h-ACC help do-PAST-1n-3H.ACC
'I helped him.'

(3) ham to-rā hun-ak kitāb de-l-i-au-nh.
1N 2mh-ACC 3h-GEN book give-PAST-1N-2MH.ACC-3H.GEN
'I gave his book to you.'

Efforts to Preserve, Protect, and Promote the Language

Maithili possesses a rich heritage of both literary writings and linguistic studies and has sufficient potential for its further growth and development. Coupled with this, it has a large number of speakers with a strong sense of language loyalty, which is essential for language maintenance. Maithili speech communities in both India and Nepal have been active in promoting the cause of their mother tongue. For example, several initiatives have been taken to include Maithili in the Eighth Schedule of the Indian constitution. Similarly, Maithili speakers in Nepal, in collaboration with speakers of other indigenous languages, have recently launched a concerted effort to introduce their languages as official languages at least at the level of local administration.

Select Bibliography

Bickel, Balthasar, Walter Bisang, and Yogendra P. Yadava. 1999. "Face vs. Empathy: The Social Foundation of Maithili Verb Agreement." In *Linguistics* 39:37:3:481–518.

Burghart, R.1992. *Introduction to Spoken Maithili in Social Context Parts 1–3*. Universität Heidelberg, Südasien-Institut Abteilung für Ethnologue, MS.

Davis, A.I. 1973. "Maithili Sentences." In Hale, A. (ed.), *Clause, Sentences and Discourse Patterns*, Vol. 1, Kāṭhmāndu: SIL Tribhuvan University Press.

_____. 1984. *Basic Colloquial Maithili: A Maithili-Nepali- English Dictionary*. Delhi: Motilal Banarsidass.

Grierson, G.A. 1881. *An Introduction to the Maithili Dialect of the Bihāri Language as Spoken in Bihār Part I: Grammar*. Calcutta: The Asiatic Society of Bengal.

_____. 1885. *Bihār Peasant Life*. [second and revised edition 1926] Patna, Superintendent, Government Printing, Bihār and Orissa.

_____. 1903. *A Linguistic Survey of India 5/2* [reprinted 1968], Delhi: Motilal Banarsidass.

Hoernle, A.F.R. and G.A. Grierson. 1885. *A Comparative Dictionary of the Bihāri Language 1*. Calcutta: Bengal Secretariat Press.

Hoernle, A.F.R. and G.A. Grierson. 1889. *A Comparative Dictionary of the Bihāri Language 2*. Calcutta: Bengal Secretariat Press,.

Jha, D. 1950. *Maithili Bhāṣā Koṣ* ('The Dictionary of Maithili language'). Patna: Sri Rambhajan Press.

Jha, G. 1968. *Maithili Udgam o Vikās* ('The Origin and Development of Maithili'). Calcutta, Maithili Prakashan Samiti.

Jha, G. 1979. *Uccatara Maithili Vyākaranī* ('Higher Maithili Grammar'). Patna, Maithili Academy.

Jha, S.1958. *The Formation of the Maithili Language*, London: Luzac & Co.

Mishra, J. 1973, 1995. *Bṛhat Maithili Sabdkoṣa* ('A Comprehensive Maithili Dictionary'). Fascicule I (1973), Fascicule II (1995). Simla, Indian Institute of Advanced Study.

Singh, U.N. 1989. "How to Honor someone in Maithili." In *International Journal of the Sociology of Language* 75. 87–107.

Trail, R.L. 1973. *Word Lists*. Kāṭhmāndu: SIL Tribhuvan University Press,.

Williams, J. 1973. "Clause Patterns in Maithili." In Trail, ed. *Patterns in Clause, Sentence, and Discourse in Selected Languages of Nepal and India*, Oklahoma: SIL.

Yadav, R. 1984. *Maithili Phonetics and Phonology*. Mainz: Selden and Tamm.

_____. 1996. *A Reference Grammar of Maithili*. Berlin and New York: Mouton de Gruyter.

Yadav, S.K. 1989. "Language Planning in Nepal: An Assessment and Proposal for Reform." Unpublished doctoral dissertation, Jaipur, University of Jaipur,.

Yadava, Y.P. 1982. "Maithili Sentences: a Transformational Analysis." In *Indian Linguistics*, 7–28.

_____. 1998. *Issues in Maithili Syntax*, Munich: Lincom Europa.

_____. 1999a. *Readings in Maithili Language, Literature and Culture*. Kathmandu: Royal Nepal Academy.

_____. 1999b. "The Complexity of Maithili Verb Agreement." In Singh, R. (ed.), *The Yearbook of South Asian Languages and Linguistics 1999*, Vol.2., Delhi: The Sage Publications.

MALAGASY

Edward L. Keenan and Roger-Bruno Rabenilaina

Language Name: Malagasy. **Autonym:** *malagasy.*

Location: Spoken throughout the island of Madagascar, the large island across the Mozambique Channel from Mozambique in southeast Africa.

Family: The (East) Barito subgroup of the Barito group of the Borneo subbranch of the Western Malayo-Polynesian branch of the Malayo-Polynesian subfamily of the Austronesian language family.

Related Languages: Malagasy is most closely related to Maanyan, an East Barito language from Borneo. Better-known languages to which it is more distantly, but still obviously, related are INDONESIAN and TAGALOG.

Dialects: Phonological differences divide the dialects into two major groups: Western and Eastern. There are in all 21 dialects that correspond to distinct ethnic groups: Bara, Betsileo, Betsimisaraka, Bezanozano, Mahafaly, Makoa, Masikoro, Merina, Sakalava, Sihanaka, Tambahoaka, Tanala, Tandroy, Tankarana, Tanosy, Tefasy, Temoro, Tesaka, Tsimihety, Vezo, and Zafisoro. The dialects are generally mutually intelligible, typically sharing between 70 and 90 percent of their basic vocabulary. They are comparable with respect to morphological and syntactic structure, differing mainly with regard to lexical items (local customs, and flora and fauna tend to have local names) and phonology.

The Merina dialect, with vocabulary additions from other dialects, forms the basis for "official Malagasy", that variety used in most newspapers and government documents. The capital of Madagascar, Antananarivo, is located within the Merina dialect area. All examples in this chapter are in official Malagasy.

Number of Speakers: About 14 million.

Origin and History

Linguistic evidence supports that the Proto-Malagasy moved into what is now Madagascar during the first four centuries A.D. They came from southeast Borneo and had sufficient contact with Indic-influenced languages for there to be a detectable SANSKRIT influence on Proto-Malagasy phonology. They then made contact with the east coast of Africa, as witnessed by a certain number of Bantu loanwords (see Contact with Other Languages) and Bantu influence on Proto-Malagasy phonology: specifically, Malagasy syllables never end in consonants but always have the form V or C+V, where V is a vowel or diphthong and C is a single consonant. This is a pattern characteristic of eastern Bantu but not of the Austronesian languages Malagasy is genetically related to.

The major incursion into Madagascar came from the African coast via the Comoro Islands into the northern part of Madagascar. It is likely that traffic was maintained for many generations between the Proto-Malagasy and an Indonesian source. Eventually, perhaps in the seventh century, contact with Indonesian peoples ceased and the future Malagasy spread from the northern part of Madagascar throughout the island.

The Western dialects of Malagasy show a somewhat more direct phonological correspondence with Maanyan than do the Eastern dialects, suggesting that the west of Madagascar, the coastal regions facing Africa, were peopled first, and then the Malagasy population spread eastward. *Kibosy*, the dialect of Malagasy spoken in the Comoro Islands, is also Western.

It is interesting to note in this regard that the names of the cardinal points in Malagasy exhibit a 90-degree rotation compared with the corresponding terms in Indonesian languages. Thus, the Malagasy word for 'north', *avaratra*, is etymologically *barat* 'west' in Indonesian. Equally, Malagasy *atimo* (*atsimo*) 'south' corresponds to *timor* 'east'. This is explicable if we consider these terms to pertain originally to the character of prevailing winds. Thus, on the northwest coast of Madagascar the north winds bring the 'storms' (*varatra*) and correspond to the humid west winds of Indonesia, while the dry winds of the south correspond to the trade winds of East Indonesia (which have given their name to the Island of Timor).

Both British and French missionaries were active in Madagascar in the 19th century. In carrying out their work, they did a great deal to codify and disseminate what became the standard language, based on the Merina dialect, the one spoken by the major government institutions when the missionaries arrived. (Madagascar had had a succesion of kings and queens, and the majority of the island was under single rule when the British missionaries arrived in the early 1800s.)

The first English-Malagasy dictionary appeared in 1835. The standard and excellent French-Malagasy, Malagasy-French dictionary by Abinal and Malzac appeared in 1888.

Orthography and Basic Phonology

The Malagasy alphabet is borrowed from the Roman one, minus the letters *c, q, u, x,* and *w*. This alphabet was officially adopted by the Malagasy king Radama I in 1820. Prior to this, there had been some writing in ARABIC script.

Table 1: Consonants

		Labial	Dental	Alveolar	Velar
Stops	Voiced	b	d		g
	Voiceless	p	t		k
Pre-nasalized Stops	Voiced	mb	nd		ñg
	Voiceless	mp	nt		ñk
Nasals		m	n		ñ
Africatives	Voiced			j, dr	
	Voiceless			ts, tr	
Pre-nasalized Africatives	Voiced			nj, ndr	
	Voiceless			nts, ntr	
Fricatives	Voiced	v		z	
	Voiceless	f		s	h
Liquids			l	r	

Orthographic *j* is pronounced [dz], and is the voiced counterpart of /ts/. /tr/ is a single voiceless phoneme somewhat like the initial consonant sound in ENGLISH 'church', except that the blade of the tongue for the Malagasy sound is against the alveolar ridge, not the palate; and /dr/ is the voiced counterpart of /tr/.

The Malagasy /s/ has a somewhat different quality than its English counterpart; the front part of the tongue is a little further back in the mouth for the Malagasy sound than for its English equivalent, making it intermediate between English /s/ and /š/.

Ñ, phonetically [ŋ], does not occur in the Malagasy of Merina, but it does occur in most other dialects.

Consonants preceded by *m*, *n*, or *ñ* are prenasalized consonants. In general, the distinction between plain consonants and the prenasalized equivalents is phonemic.

R does not occur directly following /n/, but rather is replaced by /dr/: *amina* 'with', *amin-dRabe* 'with Rabe'.

Table 2: Vowels

	Front	Central	Back
High	i, y		o
Mid	e		
Low		a	

Both *i* and *y* are used for the vowel /i/; *y* is used word finally (as in English), *i* elsewhere. *O* is the high back vowel /u/. In borrowings from English or FRENCH, [o] is rendered *ao* or *ô*. Common diphthongs with the expected pronunciations are *ai*/*ay*, *oa*, and *oi*/*oy*.

Stress is phonemic in Malagasy. Generally, stress is penultimate in roots of two or more syllables, unless the root ends in one of the weak syllables *-na*, *-ka*, or *-tra*, in which case stress is usually antepenultimate, as in *lálana* 'path, way'. There are rare exceptions, such as *lalána* 'law', which yield minimal pairs.

Many derived verb forms are built by adding suffixes to roots or to derived forms, and this suffixing uniformly shifts stress to the right: *vídy* 'price', *vidína* 'is bought'. Occasionally stress shift alone functions to indicate a change in category as in the difference between the simple active present tense form *manása* 'washes' and the imperative *manasá* 'wash!' (but usually imperatives suffix an extra vowel as well as shifting stress).

Basic Morphology

Nouns in Malagasy do not inflect for number, gender, or, more generally, noun class. However, Malagasy presents a rich variety of determiners, including articles and article-like expressions.

Personal names are often built from a predicate phrase prefixed with the proper noun prefix *ra-*. Thus, from the adjective *be* 'big' the name *Rabe* 'Mr. Big' is formed; from *soa* 'fortunate', *Rasoa* 'Ms. Fortunate' is formed.

Malagasy distinguishes two definite articles: *ny*, whose uses include all those of English 'the', and *ilay*, used when the noun specified designates a referent already established in the discourse.

In contrast with the two-term demonstrative system of English ("this" versus "that"), Malagasy has a seven-term system, with different forms indicating different distances between the speaker and the object indicated: *ity*, *ito*, *io*, *itsy*, *iny*, *iroa*, *iry*; the plurals of these demonstratives are formed by infixing *re* after the initial *i* of the demonstrative: *irety*, *ireto*, *ireo*, *iretsy*, *ireny*, *ireroa*, and *irery*. Syntactically, the demonstratives frame the noun they modify: *olona* 'person', and *ireo olona ireo* 'those people'.

Malagasy also has seven forms covering the range from "here" to "there": from closer to farther, *ety*, *eto*, *eo*, *etsy*, *eny*, *eroa*, and *ery*. These forms are used for visible locations; for nonvisible locations, *e* is replaced by *a*: *aty*, *ato*, *ao*, *atsy*, *any*, *aroa*, and *ary*.

Malagasy, like English, distinguishes three grammatical cases in the pronoun system: nominative *aho* 'I', accusative *ahy* 'me', and genitive *-ko* 'my'. Case marking is quite systematic for pronouns. The nominative is used for subjects and some objects of comparison; the accusative for objects of verbs and a few adjectives and prepositions; and the genitive for possessors, nonsubject agent phrases with nonactive verbs, and most objects of prepositions.

	Nominative	Accusative	Genitive
1sg	aho	ahy	-ko
2sg	ianao	anao	-nao
3sg	izy	azy	-ny
1pl excl	izahay	anay	-nay
1pl incl	isika	antsika	-(n)tsika
2pl	ianareo	anareo	-nareo
3pl	izy (ireo)	azy (ireo)	-ny/n'izy ireo

The first person plural exclusive pronouns are used when the addressee is not included ("we" not including "you"), while the inclusive pronouns are used when the addressee is included ("we" = "I" + "you").

The third person plural forms are basically the same as the

third person singular ones. Commonly, however, a plural interpretation is forced by the addition of the overtly plural demonstrative *ireo*.

With regard to nouns as opposed to pronouns, nominative nouns do not carry any distinctive morphological markings. In the accusative, proper nouns, which are usually built from an article like *Ra-* or *i-*, prefix *an-*: *Manaja an-dRabe Rasoa* (respect ACC-Rabe Rasoa) 'Rasoa respects Rabe.' Some kin terms and, optionally, demonstratives (which also begin with *i-*) also prefix *an-* when accusative.

In the genitive, noun phrases are bound to their hosts in a morphologically complicated way: *tahotra* 'fear', *ny tahodRabe azy* 'Rabe's fear of him'.

Malagasy has a rich verbal morphology, in particular a rich voice system. Verbs are marked according to the semantic role of their syntactic subjects:

n-an-olotra	vary	hoan'ny	vahiny	t-amin-ny	lovia
PAST-ACTIVE-offer	rice	for-the	guests	PAST-on-the	dishes

vaovao	Rabe
new	Rabe

'Rabe offered the guests rice on the new dishes.'

In the above sentence, the verb *nanolotra* (from the base *tolotra*) contains the active voice marker *-an-*, indicating that the agent (*Rabe*) is the subject.

no-tolor-a+n-dRabe	vary	t-amin-ny	lovia
PAST-offer-PASSIVE+GEN-Rabe	rice	PAST-with-the	dishes

vaovao	ny	vahiny
new	the	guests

'The guests were offered rice on the new dishes by Rabe.'

In contrast, in the above sentence, the subject *ny vahiny* 'the guests' is the recipient of the action. The verb incorporates the passive marker *ana* and the genitive form of *Rabe* (indicated by the change to *dRabe*).

n-an-olor-an-dRabe	vary	hoan-ny	vahiny
PAST-ACTIVE-offer-CIRCUMSTANCE-Rabe	rice	for-the	guests

ny	lovia	vaovao
the	dishes	new

'The new dishes were served rice on by Rabe to guests.'

Finally, in the above sentence, the subject is *ny lovia vaovao* 'the new dishes' and the verb is in the circumstantial form that is used when the subject represents the place, time, or location of an action; the instrument by which the action is brought about; or the beneficiary of the action. The verb incorporates the circumstantial marker *ana* and the genitive form of *Rabe*; while the circumstantial and passive markers do not differ when affixed to 'offer', with other verbs they do differ. These sentences also illustrate that prepositional phrases (including the forms meaning "here" and "there" cited earlier) must have *t-* prefixed if they occur with verbs marked for past tense.

In addition to the past tense forms marked with *n-* or *no-*, Malagasy verbs may occur in present tense (marked with *m-*) or future tense (marked with *h-* or *ho-*).

Derived verbs are formed by affixes indicating causative, inchoative ("becomes X"), and reciprocal meanings among others.

Despite this extensive verbal morphology, however, Malagasy verbs do not agree with their subjects in such categories as person and number.

Malagasy makes quite productive use of reduplication in derivational morphology. In Malagasy, the most usual semantic effect of reduplication is one of attenuation rather than intensification. Thus, from *sarotra* 'difficult' is formed *sarotsarotra* 'somewhat difficult'. In this form, the weak syllable *-tra* is dropped, and the initial *s-* in the second half of the reduplicated form becomes the corresponding affricate *ts-*. In general, in these circumstances, alveolar fricatives become affricates, and labial fricatives become stops.

If the word to be reduplicated ends in *-na*, the *-a* is dropped; before *b* or *p*, the *n* becomes *m*, and it drops if it precedes a nasal: *miverina* 'returns', *miverimberina* 'goes back and forth' (*m-* is the present tense marker).

Basic Syntax

The basic word order in Malagasy is VOS. Within a noun phrase, adjectives, genitives, and relative clauses follow the nouns they modify, while articles precede:

ny	lobaka	fotsy	izay	no-sas-a+n-dRasoa
the	shirt	white	that	PAST-wash-PASSIVE+GEN-Rasoa

'the white shirt that was washed by Rasoa'

Malagasy sentences are negated by *tsy* before the verb. The form of the verb is not otherwise affected.

N-amaky	ilay	boky	Rabe
PAST-read	that	book	Rabe

'Rabe read that (aforementioned) book.'

Tsy	n-amaky	ilay	boky	Rabe
NEG	PAST-read	that	book	Rabe

'Rabe didn't read that (aforementioned) book.'

Contact with Other Languages

The biggest single outside influence on Malagasy in modern times has been contact with European languages: PORTUGUESE, French, DUTCH, and English. Such contacts began in the 15th century and assumed linguistically very significant proportions beginning in the early 19th century. The two major influences at the time were English from Christian missionaries in the early part of the 19th century and French, both from missionary activity from the 19th century onward and then at an institutional level during the period of colonization (1896–1958) as well as during the First Republic (1958–1972).

Malagasy borrowings from English tend to cluster around religious or instructional notions (see examples below).

The overall number of borrowings from the European languages is relatively few, and the reason for this can be seen in the nature of the Malagasy language. It is a root and affixing language. Words, especially verbs (which, in turn, feed the nominal system) are built by affixing roots, which often are not themselves words in the language. Thus, faced with a new piece of technology or social institution, it is rather easy to find a root and combine it with the appropriate affixes to construct a word with approximately the right sense. Here are two illustrative examples: from the root *anatra* 'admonition, advice', form the intransitive verb *mianatra* 'studies, learns' (also the transitive verb *mananatra* 'admonishes'); from that we may build the agent nominalization *mpianatra* 'student'. So, neither English "student" nor French *étudiant* were borrowed.

A second, less elaborate but perhaps also less obvious, example involves the root *varotra* 'sale, commerce, goods', from which is formed the active verb *mivarotra* 'sell, engage in commerce'. From this is built the circumstantial form *ivarotana* and thence the nominalization *fivarotana* 'place, means, instrument, of selling'. In practice, this noun is used to mean 'store, shop'. To specify the type of store, the verb is nominalized with its object. That is, *mivarotra boky* 'sells books' nominalizes to *fivarotam-boky* 'place of selling books, bookstore'.

From Arabic: *sikidy* 'divination', *alahady* 'Sunday (day one)' *alarobia* 'Wednesday (day four)'
From Bantu: *vahiny* 'foreigner', *amboa* 'dog', *omby* 'zebu, cow', *akoho* 'chicken'
From English: *boky* 'book', *sekoly* 'school', *penina* 'pen', *pensily* 'pencil', *baiboly* 'bible'
From French: *divay* 'wine', *latabatra* 'table', *egilizy* 'church'

Common Words

man:	lehilahy	small:	kely
woman:	vehivavy	yes:	eny, eka
water:	rano	no:	tsia
sun:	masoandro	good:	tsara, soa
three:	telo	bird:	vorona
fish:	trondro, hazandrano	dog:	alika, amboa
big:	be, lehibe	tree:	hazo
long:	lavo		

Example Sentences

(1) Heverin-dRabe fa m-i-resaka amin-dRakoto Rasoa.
think-by-Rabe that PRES-ACTIVE-talk with-Rakoto Rasoa
'It is thought by Rabe that Rasoa is talking with Rakoto.'

(2) Tsy h-i-anatra teny vahiny intsony Rasoa.
NEG FUT-ACTIVE-study language foreign any longer Rasoa
'Rasoa won't study foreign languages any more.'

(3) M-amp-i-homehy azy izy.
PRES-CAUSE-ACTIVE-laugh him he
'He's making him laugh.'

Efforts to Preserve, Protect, and Promote the Language

Malagasy is the unique language of Madagascar. By the Second Republic, beginning in 1972, there was a conscious effort to promote Malagasy as opposed to French. Much of the school instruction that had been in French was switched to Malagasy at elementary and high school levels, although university level education remained largely in French. The constitution of the Third Republic, adopted by referendum in August 1992, instituted Malagasy as "the national language" of the Republic of Madagascar.

There are many newspapers and novels published in Malagasy, and the national radio station broadcasts country-wide in Malagasy. There are many institutions concerned with the development of Malagasy as a national language; among them are the Malagasy Academy and the FIMPAMAMA (National Federation of Defenders and Promoters of the Malagasy Cultural Identity), and, at the University of Antananarivo, the Department of Language and Literature. These instutions are concerned with establishing the diverse technical terminologies appropriate to each discipline and each general sector of activity. In addition, the new Interdisciplinary Department of Professional Education is concerned with translation and interpretation among English, French, and Malagasy. Work is beginning on the establishment of electronic dictionaries, both monolingual and bilingual, with the goal of assisted translation among these three languages.

Select Bibliography

Dahl, Otto. 1966. *Les Débuts de l'Orthographe Malgache.* Oslo: Universitetsforlaget.
____. 1988. "Bantu Substratum in Malagasy." *Etudes Océan Indien no. 9.* Paris: INALCO.
Hollanger, F. 1969. *English-Malagasy Dictionary.* Antananarivo: Trano Printy Loterana.
Keenan, Edward L. 1976. "Remarkable Subjects in Malagasy." In Ch. Li. ed., *Subject and Topic.* New York: Academic Press.
Rabenilaina, R.B. 1996. *Le verbe malgache: constructions transitives et intransitives.* Montreal: Greslet, Aupelfuref.
_____. 1997. "Voice and Diathesis in Malagasy." In *The Structure of Malagasy, Volume II.* Los Angeles: UCLA, Department of Linguistics.
Stark, Elsie L. 1969. *Malagasy Without Moans.* Antananarivo: Trano Printy Loterana.

Malay/Indonesian

Hein Steinhauer

Language Names: Malay and Indonesian. Indonesian is a standardized variety of Malay. **Autonym:** *Bahasa Indonesia* 'the language of Indonesia'. The proper ENGLISH equivalent is Indonesian rather than *bahasa* 'language'. Before 1928 Indonesian was called *bahasa Melayu* 'Malay', which is also the official name of the national language of Malaysia.

Location: Indonesian is a standardized variety of Malay. In Malaysia, Singapore, and Brunei Darussalam, another standardized variety of Malay is used as the national language.

Family: Malay and Indonesian belong to the Western Malayo-Polynesian branch of the Austronesian language family. The subdivision of that branch is still a matter of debate.

Related Languages: All varieties of Malay including Indonesian, standard Malaysian, standard Bruneian, as well as local Malay and Malayic vernaculars (for example, Ambonese Malay, Jakarta Malay, MINANGKABAU, Banjarese, Iban, and Salako) are closely related. Other regional Western Malayo-Polynesian languages have long been in contact and are also related; these include SUNDANESE, JAVANESE, and MADURESE.

Dialects: Those Malay varieties in Indonesia that were similar enough not to be considered another language became dialects of Indonesian. Varieties of Malay spoken in Malaysia, although possibly quite similar to those in Indonesia, are obviously not dialects of Indonesian, but dialects of the standardized variety of Malay in Malaysia. Local vernaculars can also be qualified as varieties of Malay in east and central Sumatra, along the coasts of Borneo, in mainland Malaysia, in old centers of colonial presence in East Indonesia, in southern Thailand, and in a few villages in Sri Lanka.

The most conspicuous differences between both standard languages are functional, lexical, and phonetic. The position of Indonesian as national and official language is unchallenged at all levels of education and in all official domains. In Malaysia the national language has to compete with English, which is prominent in higher education, jurisdiction, and business. For many Malaysians English is a second language, and code switching between English and Malay(sian) is common.

Within Indonesia the regional varieties of Malay are used in nonformal communication among members of the local speech community and in ceremonies related to the local culture. The modern domains of formal education, technology, politics, and military and civil service belong to Indonesian. This functional difference is reflected in the lexicon. Also for the domains for which the local varieties are the appropriate vehicle, lexical differences with Indonesian are more or less conspicuous, as between Indonesian and Malaysian The differences also may include function words and derivational affixation.

Indonesian has a very conservative sound pattern. The only standard for the pronunciation of Indonesian is that it should not betray a regional origin. The dialects often have undergone sound changes that have caused more or less radical changes in the structure of the word and the morpheme. Recurrent changes are change of the central vowels, lowering of high vowels in final closed syllables, simplification of intervocalic clusters, and mergers and/or loss of final consonants. In Malaysia, the pronunciation typical of the Malay dialects of the state of Johor used to be propagated as normative: most typical of Malaysian pronunciation is that word-final *a* is realized as schwa [ə].

Number of Speakers: There are over 10 million speakers of Malay in Malaysia, excluding second-language speakers. According to the latest census figures for Indonesia (1990), 24 million people claimed to use Indonesian as their first language. Including those for whom Indonesian is a second language, there are over 131 million speakers.

Origin and History

The high geographical density of relatively divergent Malay-like languages until deep into the interior of West Borneo justifies the assumption that the homeland of the Malay language must be sought there. A few centuries before Christ, speakers of proto-Malay started to populate the islands in and the shores around the Straits of Malacca. Since maritime traffic between the Far East on the one hand and India and the Middle East on the other, had to sail through this passage or wait there for the change of trade wind, the Malay language came to play a pivotal role in precolonial trade in the whole of Southeast Asia, including the spice trade. It is possible that a form of Malay already functioned as a trade language before the Christian Era. Certainly what is now called Old Malay was the official language of the first state in the area of the Straits of Malacca, the Buddhist Srivijaya empire. Old Malay was the language of a number of inscriptions found in southeast Sumatra and the island of Bangka, dating from the seventh and eighth centuries. The non-SANSKRIT elements in these inscriptions are Austronesian, which have a greater resemblance with Malay than with any other Austronesian language known today. The importance of Old Malay as an official language is underscored by the existence of some 10th century inscriptions, found in West and Central Java.

Sriwijaya declined with the spread of Islam in Southeast Asia. In the 15th century, on the eve of the European expansion, the Muslim sultanate of Malacca was the major trade center in the area, where Chinese, Indians, Arabs, and other Asians met, and a pidginized variety of Malay must have been the means of interethnic communication, while a predecessor of what is now called "Classical Malay" was presumably the language of the court. This prominent position of Malay in interethnic and international contacts made it the natural vehicle for the spread of Islam. As such, it also became the court language of the Islamic sultanates that arose in various coastal city-states throughout the archipelago and the Malay Peninsula, even where the local population spoke different languages, such as Banjarmasin, Bima, and Ternate. The importance of Malay in international trade is reflected in the fact that the oldest sources on the language are a Malay-Chinese word list from the middle of the 15th century: a PERSIAN grammar from the middle of the 16th century; two letters from the sultan of the non-Austronesian island Ternate in the north Moluccas to the king of Portugal, dated 1521 and 1522 and a word list by Pigafetta, the Italian companion of Magelhaens from the same period. The earliest PORTUGUESE sources mention that Malay was known all over Southeast Asia.

As a consequence, Malay became the major language of contact between the indigenous population and the European colonialists. Being the language of Islam in the archipelago, it was used by the Portuguese Catholics in the 16th century and subsequently by the Dutch Protestants in the propagation of their religions. However, the question of what variety of Malay had to be used kept dividing the Protestant minds up to the end of the 19th century. Meanwhile, after the Napoleonic Wars, the Malay world had been divided by treaty into a Dutch and an English sphere of influence, which resulted finally in the double standard for Malay: Malaysian and Indonesian.

With the intensification of colonialism in the course of the 19th century, the demand for locally trained administrative staff in the Dutch Indies grew, and a governmental education system could no longer be avoided. In most schools for the indigenous population, Malay became the language of instruction. As Malay remained the main vehicle of contact between colonialist and colonized, it was taught in the Netherlands to colonial civil servants as well as the military. The importance of Malay increased even more toward the end of the 19th century, when the Dutch widened their control over areas outside Java.

For nearly three centuries Malay had been used in a large number of local and individual varieties, but now the need for its standardization became a government concern. Being the most powerful Malay state at the time of the arrival of the Europeans in the area, precolonial Malacca was perceived as the cradle and center of the "original" and "pure" Malay culture. The mythical-historical genealogy of the Malaccan sultans, which ended with the account of the Portuguese conquest of the city and the flight of the court to Johor, was considered by both Dutch and English scholars the most important Malay text. It was this "Malay Annals," as Europeans later called it, that was used as the standard for the major 19th century descriptions of Malay.

Most authoritative among them became the grammar by Van Ophuijsen (1910), who was also the author of the first standard spelling. It was basically his language, colored by his Minangkabau pupils, that was used in the Malay publications of the 1920s and 1930s of Balai Pustaka, the government publishing house for popular literature. And it was this variety of Malay that in 1928 the nationalist movement proclaimed the national language of the future independent state of Indonesia, henceforth to be called *bahasa Indonesia,* Indonesian.

In 1942 Dutch colonial rule ended with the occupation of the Dutch Indies by the Japanese. An Indonesian elite had been educated in DUTCH, but since that was the language of the colonialists, it was forbidden by the Japanese on all levels of communication. And as JAPANESE could not realistically be promoted as the national language of the occupied state, it was Malay that was officially proclaimed as such. Serious efforts to enrich and modernize the language with new terminology already started under the occupation. These efforts vigorously continued after the proclamation of independence in 1945.

Today the position of Malay/Indonesian is unchallenged. It is the major binding factor of the country, uniting speakers of nearly 500 different languages. Indonesia is the only former colony in which the language of the former colonizer has not become the national language and in which an indigenous minority language now successfully fulfills that role.

The success of Indonesian affects most of the other languages of the country in that the younger generations are shifting toward Indonesian. The combined effects of urbanization, nationwide institutionalized education and the mass media are expected to cause this shift toward Indonesian only to increase. Consequently in the 21st century, many of the approximately 500 local languages that had been spoken in Indonesia in the 1990s will disappear.

Orthography and Basic Phonology

The oldest forms of Malay, dating back to the seventh century A.D. were written in the *pallawa*-script, a semisyllabary of south Indian origin. With the introduction of Islam, adaptations of the Persian-Arabic script, the so-called *jawi* script, became the preferred tool of writing Malay. The oldest appearance dates from the early 13th century. In the Dutch Indies it was officially replaced by the LATIN script in 1901 with the introduction of standardized spelling. A variety of non-standardized spellings in Latin script, often transliterations of the Persian-Arabic script, had been used by Europeans ever since the early 17th century. After a minor reform in Indonesia in 1948, called the *Soewandi* spelling, a unified orthography was introduced officially in both Indonesia and Malaysia in 1972. This spelling, which has been adopted also by Singapore and Brunei Darussalam for writing Malay, is nearly phonemic. The only deviations are that the front and central mid vowels are not distinguished, that syllable-final *b*, *d*, and *g* (mainly occurring in loanwords from Arabic and Javanese) represent their voiceless counterparts (*p*, *t*, and *k*), that *f* and *v* (occur-

Table 1: Consonants

	Voicing	Labial	Dental-Alveolar	Palatal	Velar	Glottal
Stops/ Affricates	-	p	t	c	k	k [ʔ]
	+	b	d	j [ɟ]	g	
Fricatives	-	f*	s	sy* [ʃ]	kh* [x]	h
	+		z*			
Nasals	+	m	n	ny [ɲ]	ng [ŋ]	
Trill	+		r			
Lateral	+		l			
Glides	+	w			y	

Loan phonemes are marked with *

ring in European loanwords) both represent /f/, and finally that glottal stop is written as *k* in syllable-final position, whereas before a vowel (in a few loanwords only) it is not written at all.

The examples in Table 1 and Table 2 are in the standard orthography, with the only exception of the mid-front vowel. In the standard spelling this is not differentiated from the mid-central vowel, below it is: *é* (mid-front) versus *e* (mid-central). Some of the consonants are written as digraphs. Glottal stop is phonemic only in some loanwords in syllable-final position; in the orthography it is not distinguished from the voiceless velar: *k*.

Table 2: Vowels

	Front	Central	Back
High	i		u
Mid	é	e	o
Low		a	

The vast majority of lexical roots are bisyllabic. The canonical shape is $C_1V_1C_2V_2C_3$, in which two consonant positions may be empty. In the original vocabulary and in fully adapted loanwords C_1 and C_3 cannot be clusters; C_2, if it is a cluster, consists of a nasal followed by a homorganic stop. Recent loanwords and acronyms complicate this picture to some extent.

Stress is non-phonemic. Words in isolation tend to be stressed on the final syllable if the penultimate syllable contains a schwa, otherwise it is the penultimate that bears the stress.

Basic Morphology

Productive morphological processes include prefixation, suffixation, circumfixation, and word or root reduplication. Voiceless initial root consonants may turn into nasals as a consequence of certain prefixation processes (indicated by *N-* below).

Nouns referring to concrete countable entities can be reduplicated, unless they have the shape of a reduplicated form, in order to indicate plurality in diversity. The non-reduplicated form indicates an unspecified number of entities: *rumah* 'unspecified number of houses', *satu rumah* 'one house', *banyak rumah* 'many houses', *rumah-rumah* 'houses in diversity'. (Glosses of non-reduplicated nouns below will be given in the singular.) Definiteness and indefiniteness are expressed syntactically or remain a matter of context.

All nouns, including derived nouns, as well as the reduplicated forms can in principle be followed by the following personal pronominal suffixes: *-ku* 'my (familiar)', *-mu* 'your (familiar)', *-nya* 'his/her/its'. The latter suffix can be interpreted as 'belonging to the situation' and translated as 'the': *rumahku* 'my (familiar) house(s)', *rumahmu* 'your (familiar) house(s)', *rumahnya* 'his/her/its/the house(s)', *rumah-rumahku* 'my (various) houses'.

Derivation of nouns from other nouns include: a) *mata* 'eye' > *mata-mata* (1) 'eyes in variety', (2) 'spy, spies (either or not in variety)'; b) *laut* 'sea' > *lautan* 'ocean'; c) *buah* 'fruit' > *buah-buahan* 'all kinds of fruit'; d) *kebun* 'garden' > *perkebunan* 'plantation'; *guru* 'teacher' > *perguruan* 'school, educational institution'; *désa* 'village' > *pedésaan* 'countryside'; e) *raja* 'king' > *kerajaan* 'kingdom'; *réktor* 'rector', *keréktoran* 'rectorate'; f) *présidén* 'president' > *keprésidénan* 'presidency'; *wanita* 'woman', *kewanitaan* 'femininity'; g) *telur* 'egg' > *(ayam) petelur* 'laying-hen'; *bowling* 'bowling', *pebowling* 'bowling player'; h) *kilo* 'kilogram/kilometer', *sekilo* 'a kilogram/kilometer'; *ékor* 'tail'; and classifier noun for counting animals, *seékor kuda* 'a horse'. Derivations from other word classes will be discussed below.

There is no sharp difference between adjectives and intransitive verbs. Only gradable adjectives have some distinctive morphological characteristics. Patterns are: *terbesar* 'biggest' (also of small things); *(A) sebesar B* '(A) is as big as B', *sebesar mungkin* 'as big as possible', *sebesar-besarnya* 'as big as possible', *sebesar-besarnya X* 'as big as X may be', *A dan B sama besarnya* 'A and B are equally big'; *hijau* 'green' > *kehijau-hijauan* 'greenish'.

Adjectives and intransitive verbs may be derived by the following productive pattern: *besar* 'big' > *membesar* 'get big, grow up'; *hijau* 'green' > *menghijau* 'turn green, make the impression of being green'.

Many intransitive verbs are derived from precategorial bases by means of prefixation of *ber-*, or *meN-*: *berjuang* 'fight, struggle', *berteriak* 'shout'; *menangis* 'cry, weep' (root *tangis*); *melompat* 'jump'. Root reduplication (expressing continued/repeated action) is possible with some of these verbs: *berteriak-teriak* 'shout repeatedly'; *menangis-nangis* 'keep weeping'.

With the small class of monomorphemic intransitive verbs the following patterns of derivations may be found: *datang* 'come' > *berdatangan* 'come from all directions', *datang-datang (dia sudah mulai berkelahi)* 'no sooner had he arrived (than he began to quarrel)', *kedatangan tamu* 'be affected by the coming of a guest, have an unexpected visitor'.

From nominal bases adjectives/intransitive verbs are formed by the following processes: a) *topi (hitam)* '(black) hat' > *bertopi (hitam)* 'with a (black) hat'; *isi* 'content' > *berisi* 'have content, corpulent', *berisi air* 'contain water'; b) *telur* 'egg' > *bertelur* 'lay an egg'; *anak* 'child' > *beranak* 'give birth'; *bunyi* 'noise, sound' > *berbunyi* 'make a noise'; c) *guru* 'teacher' > *berguru* 'behave like a teacher'; d) *dasar* 'base' > *berdasarkan (hukum)* 'on the basis of (the law)'; e) *batu* 'stone' > *membatu* 'fossilize, turn into stone'; f) *gunung* 'mountain', >*menggunung* 'rise up like a mountain'; g) *rumput* 'grass' > *merumput* 'graze, collect grass'; h) *siang* 'day(light)' > *kesiangan* 'overslept' (lit. 'be negatively affected by daylight'); i) *Jawa* 'Java' > *kejawa-jawaan* 'behaving too Javanese'; j) *kelas* 'class', *sekelas* 'of the same class'; k) *Asia* 'Asia', *se-Asia* 'pan-Asiatic'; *Jawa, Bali, dan Sumatra* 'Java, Bali and Sumatra' > *se-Jawa , Bali, dan Sumatra* 'from all of Java, Bali and Sumatra'.

All adjectives and intransitive verbs can be nominalized by suffixation of *-nya*; preceding attributes are maintained: *besar* 'big' > *besarnya* 'his/her/its volume'; *cukup besar* 'big enough' > *cukup besarnya mobil itu* 'the sufficient volume of that car', *membesar* 'get big' > *membesarnya* 'his/her/its getting big', *membesarnya luka itu* 'the growing of that wound'.

Other nominalizations on the basis of adjectives and intransitive verbs include: a) *adil* 'just, fair', *tidak adil* 'unjust, unfair' > *ke(tidak)adilan* '(in)justice'; *mau* 'want', *kemauan* 'wish'; *aksara* 'graphic symbol, letter', *beraksara* 'literate' > *keberaksaraan* 'literacy'; b) *besar* 'big' > *pembesar* 'big shot, authority'; *tidur* 'sleep' > *penidur* 'someone who sleeps a great deal'; c) *meletus* 'explode' > *letusan* 'explosion'.

Most patterns of numeral morphology can be illustrated by derivations of *tiga* 'three' and *puluh* 'unit of ten' in an appropriate syntactic frame: a) *(masuk) tiga-tiga* '(enter) in groups of three'; b) *rumah ketiga itu* 'that third house'; c) *ketiga rumah itu* 'those three houses'; d) *ketiga-tiganya (masuk)* 'all three of them (came/went in)'; e) *sepertiga* 'one-third'; *dua pertiga* 'two thirds'; f) *kami bertiga* 'the three of us; we are three'; g) *sepuluh* 'ten', *tiga puluh* 'thirty'; h) *berpuluh-puluh rumah* 'tens of houses'; i) *tahun tiga puluhan* 'the (19)30s (*tahun* 'year'); *tiga puluhan tahun* 'about thirty years'.

Transitive verbs are inflected for voice including active, and agentive and non-agentive passive; mood including indicative and imperative; and to some extent for person of the non-subject such as the actor in the agentive passive voice and the patient in the active voice. Where semantically possible there is a reciprocal form. By reduplication of the root, repeated or prolonged action is indicated. Transitive verbs are derived from all other major word classes by suffixation of *-kan*, or *-i*, and/or by prefixation of *per-*.

With nominal, adjectival, and transitive and intransitive verbal bases the suffix *-i* indicates that the patient of the verb is spatially affected, which may imply repetition: *bulu* 'feather, fur' > *bului* 'feather (v.), apply fir', and also 'pluck, deplume'; *ibu* 'mother' > *ibui* 'mother (v.); *marah* 'angry' > *marahi* 'be angry at'; *panas* 'warm' > *panasi* 'apply heat to'; *cium* 'kiss, smell', *ciumi* 'kiss all over, sniff all over'; *jatuh* 'fall' > *jatuhi* 'fall on'.

With transitive verbal bases the suffix *-kan* may indicate that the patient is moved in the process, and/or that some entity benefits from the action (which may be specified by a prepositional phrase); or that the patient itself is the benefactive (in which case there is another nominal complement): *gantung* 'hang' > *gantungkan* '(take and) hang; hang (for someone)'; *tanam (bunga)* 'plant (flowers)' > *tanamkan (bunga [untuk saya])* 'plant (flowers [for me])'; *baca (buku)* 'read (a book)', *bacakan (saya buku)* 'read (me a book)'.

With nominal bases *-kan* may indicate that the patient is turned into whatever the base expresses, and/or that the patient is moved into the direction of the referent of the base: *primadona* 'primadona' > *primadonakan* 'put in the first place'; *rumah* 'house' > *rumahkan* 'make into a house', or 'send home, fire'.

With adjectival and intransitive verbal bases, *-kan* indicates causativity: *panas* 'warm' > *panaskan* 'make warm'; *jatuh* 'fall' > *jatuhkan* 'cause to fall'.

Even some prepositional phrases may be the base of a causative derivation with *-kan: atas nama* 'in the name of' > *atasnamakan* 'act in the name of'; *ke bumi* 'to the earth' > *kebumikan* 'inter'.

The prefix *per-*, sometimes in combination with a suffix, derives causative verbal stems from adjectives with the meaning 'make more <adjective>': *panjang* 'long' > *perpanjang* 'extend, prolong'; *baik* 'good' > *-perbaiki* 'repair, improve'.

With some verbal and nominal roots, usually in combination with a suffix, *-per* also adds a causative meaning: *dengar* 'hear' > *perdengarkan* 'let be heard, perform' (for example, a song); *senjata* 'weapon' > *bersenjata* 'be armed' > *persenjatai* 'provide with arms; cause to be armed'.

The agentive passive verb form, marked by the prefix *di-*, can be nominalized by suffixation of *-nya*; preceding auxiliaries and aspect words are maintained; compare: *mahasiswa akan ditémbak oléh polisi* 'the students will be shot by the police'; *berita tentang akan ditémbaknya mahasiswa oléh polisi* 'the news about the forthcoming shooting of the students by the police'.

Other productive nominalizations on the basis of transitive verb stems, of which a possible suffix is dropped in the process, are: a) *besar* 'big', *besarkan* 'make big' > *(kaca) pembesar* 'magnifying (glass)'; *tulis* 'write' > *penulis* 'writer'; b) > *besarkan* 'make big' > *pembesaran* 'enlargement, expansion'; *tulis* 'write' > *penulisan* 'manner/process of writing'; c) *tulis* 'write', *tulisan* 'something written, script' (result of action); d) *makan* 'eat', *makanan* 'food' (typical patient); e) *tutup* 'close', *tutupan* 'lid, cover' (instrument); f) *baik* 'good' > *perbaiki* 'repair, improve' > *perbaikan* 'reparation, improvement' (result and activity).

Nominal compounds are productively formed from a noun followed by a verbal root, usually transitive, indicating that there is an unspecified relation between the referent of the noun and the activity expressed by the verb: *méja* 'table', *tulis* 'write' > *méja tulis* 'writing desk'; *mesin* 'machine', *cuci* 'wash' >

mesin cuci 'washing machine'; *pisang* 'banana', *goréng* 'fry' > *pisang goréng* 'fried banana'; *air* 'water', *minum* 'drink' > *air minum* 'drinking water'; *tidur* 'sleep', *tempat* 'place' > *tempat tidur* 'sleeping place, bed'.

A limited set of forms with the prefix *ter-* are derived from transitive verbal roots, often stems that lose their suffix in the process; the resultant meaning is usually perfective and non-agentive, but lexically unpredictable: *masuk* 'come/go in' > *masukkan* 'put in' > *termasuk* 'including, belong to'; *batas* 'border' > *batasi* 'form the border of, limit' > *terbatas* 'restricted, limited'; *menjadi* 'become' > *jadikan* 'create, bring about' > *terjadi* 'occur'.

Basic Syntax

Indonesian has prepositions and a basic head-attribute syntax. Exceptions are: (1) some adverbs of degree; (2) numeral expressions (consisting of a cardinal numeral, optionally followed by a classifier noun), which precede the expression for the counted entity; (3) aspect words and negations:

(1) *lebih besar* 'bigger', *sangat besar* 'very big', *terlalu besar* 'too big', *paling besar* 'biggest (of big things)';
(2) *satu (ékor) kuda* 'one (tail = classifier for counting animals) horse', *seékor kuda* 'a horse' (lit. 'one-tail horse'), *dua (ékor) kuda* 'two horses';
(3) *Ali sudah merokok* 'Ali smokes already'
Ali sedang merokok 'Ali is smoking'
Ali tidak merokok 'Ali does not smoke'
Ali tidak pernah merokok 'Ali never smokes'

Examples of head-attribute word order are: *rambut (pirang) itu* (hair blond that) 'that (blond) hair'; *bahu bapak saya* (shoulder father my) 'my father's shoulder'; *rambut pirang di bahu bapak saya itu* 'that blond hair on my father's shoulder'.

Neutral word order in clauses is Subject-Predicate, but in the description of a sequence of events the inverted order is frequent, especially in the passive voice.

An intonational break may separate subject and predicate (predicate and subject), marking the subject as a topic (or afterthought). Any noun phrase other than the subject may be made into a topic by left-dislocation, but there has to be a pronominal trace (*-nya*) in the subsequent clause; compare:

Adik Ali sakit.
'Ali's younger sibling is ill (*sakit*)'
Ali, adiknya sakit..
'Ali, his younger sibling is ill'
Ada ular di dalam gua itu.
'There is (*ada*) a snake (*ular*) inside (*di dalam*) that (*itu*) cave (*gua*)'
Gua itu, ada ular di dalamnya.
'That cave, there is a snake inside it'

A predicate may be a noun phrase, an adjective phrase, a verb phrase, a prepositional phrase, or a numeral expression.

Noun phrases have the following structure:
± Numeral expression +Noun ± Adjective ± Possessive ± Prepositional phrase ± Relative phrase ± Demonstrative

Relative phrases consist of *yang* followed by a predicate of which the antecedent usually functions as the subject: *rumah yang rusak* 'the house which is damaged', *rumah yang dibongkar polisi* 'the house which was demolished by the police'.

If the antecedent is not the subject, *yang* is followed by a clause in which the third person pronominal suffix *-nya* represents the antecedent: *rumah yang atapnya rusak* 'the house of which the roof is damaged'.

An adjective phrase consists of an adjectival head, either or not preceded and/or followed by an adverb of degree: *sangat kecil* 'very small', *kecil sekali* 'very small', *sangat kecil sekali* 'extremely small'.

An adjective phrase may also be preceded by an expression implying a comparison, and followed by an expression for the standard thereof:

sama kecilnya (dengan X)	'just as small (as X)'
lebih kecil (daripada X)	'smaller (than X)'
sekecil X	'as small as X'

The latter construction (*se-*<adjective>Standard), an ordinal numeral, or a single adjective are the only adjectival phrases that are freely used attributively.

A prepositional phrase consists of a preposition (either or not compounded) and a noun phrase: *di atas atap rumah* 'on top of the house [on/at above roof house]'.

The only phenomenon that could be classified as case marking is the fact that in positions other than subject or predicate, bound forms may be used of the singular personal pronouns (only the familiar variants of the first and second person, and the neutral one for the third), whereas the corresponding free forms may be used in all positions: *Dia menciumku/mencium aku* 'He kissed me'; *Dia mencium tanganku/tangan aku* 'He kissed my hand'; *Aku cinta padamu/pada engkau* 'I love you'; *Engkau cinta padanya/pada dia* 'You love him'; *Aku yang pergi* 'It was I who went'.

Negation with *bukan* implies an alternative. Consequently, *bukan* has to be used when nouns and numerals are negated. *Bukan* also functions sentence finally as a tag, 'isn't it?'.

If an adjective, verb, or prepositional phrase is negated, without the implication of there being an alternative (merely in the sense of indicating the absence of the quality, a process or action) *tidak* has to be used. A contracted form of the latter, *tak*, may be used in some frequent collocations. Compare:

Dia guru? Bukan! Dia bukan guru.
'Is he a teacher? No! He is not a teacher.'
Dia guru, bukan?
'He is a teacher, isn't he?'
Bukan tiga, melainkan dua.
'Not three, but two'
Dia tidak pulang.
'He did not come home'
Itu tidak adil.
'That is not fair'
Dia tidak dari Bali.
'He is not from Bali'
Itu tidak/tak mungkin.
'That is not possible'

Contractions of collocations are *tiada* alongside *tidak ada* 'there is not', and *takkan* alongside *tidak akan* 'shall/will not'. Adjectives negated with *tidak/tak* can be negated again with *bukan*: *Bukan tidak/tak mungkin* 'not impossible'.

Morphologically expressed negation is found in a number of euphemisms on a Sanskrit basis, such as *tunanétra* 'blind, deprived of vision', *tunasusila* 'amoral', *tunawisma* 'homeless'. Prefixation with *non-* to derive adjectives from nominal bases is productive, for example, *pendidikan nonuniversitas* 'non-university education'.

Contact with Other Languages

As a language of interethnic contact, as a vehicle of world religions, and as an administrative language in colonial times, Malay has been subject to many foreign influences. These are still reflected in modern Indonesian. Being the language of mass education and the media only strengthens this open attitude toward foreign lexicon. Through the ages Malay/Indonesian has been in contact with many other languages. The close ties in early Malay history with Indian culture are reflected in many old loanwords from Sanskrit or later Indo-Arian languages: *bumi* 'world', *kepala* 'head', *menteri* 'minister', *negara* 'state', *putra* 'prince, son', *raja* 'king'; *asmara* 'love', *istri* 'wife', *senggama* 'copulation', *susila* 'morality', *suami* 'husband'; *agama* 'religion', *biara* 'cloister', *pendéta* 'priest, minister', *pura* 'temple'; *aksara* 'letter, character', *bahasa* 'language', *guru* 'teacher', *mahasiswa* 'student', *pustaka* 'book', *sastra* 'literature'; *antara* 'between', *asrama* 'dormitory', *harta* 'wealth', *utara* 'north'. Some Indian loanwords have a Dravidian (TAMIL) origin, e.g. *kapal* 'ship', *kolam* 'pond', *macam* 'species, kind'.

Loanwords from CHINESE are probably more recent, and are related to the economic role of Chinese immigrants; for example, *tauké* 'shop proprietor, employer', *toko* 'shop', *capcai* 'stir-fried vegetables'.

Many loanwords from the Middle East are related to Islamic religion, and not a few of them have found their way into Christian vocabulary: *Allah* 'Allah, God', *doa* 'prayer', *Alkitab* 'the Bible', *haji* 'someone who has fulfilled the pilgrimage to Mecca'. But there are Arabic, and to a lesser degree Persian, loanwords in all spheres of life: *adil* 'just, fair', *dakwa* 'accusation', *hakim* 'judge', *hukum* 'law', *jaksa* 'public prosecutor', *musim* 'season', *adat* 'custom', *roh* 'spirit', *aljabar* 'algebra', *huruf* 'letter', *jawab* 'answer', *zakar* 'penis'. More than in Indonesia, Islam in Malaysia is considered part of Malay identity, with the consequence that in Malaysian, Arabic loanwords are more frequent and less assimilated in pronunciation.

Older European loanwords reflect the different colonial history of the two countries: many of these loanwords betray an English origin in Malaysia, whereas in Indonesia they can be traced back to Dutch *brédel* 'gag on the press', *haatzaai artikelen* 'law against sedition', *sepéda* 'bicycle' (< FRENCH *vélocipède*), *sado* 'two-wheeled horse carriage' (< French *dos-à-dos*). The global influence of English is also felt in Indonesia: *mencarter* 'to charter', *difollowupi* 'be followed up'.

Within Indonesia, Indonesian is in contact with all 500 regional languages. It is language planning policy to look for Austronesian words if there is no acceptable international equivalent available to fill a lexical gap, and Javanese is the first option. Spontaneous Javanisms are always immediately understood and accepted by the largest ethnic minority supporting the language. Javanese, moreover, are well-represented among the speechmaking elite. Other languages of the country at best contribute a single expression or a word for a typically local phenomenon in culture or nature.

Common Words

man:	laki-laki
woman:	perempuan
bird:	burung
dog:	anjing
fish:	ikan
sun:	matahari (lit. 'eye of the day')
tree:	pohon
water:	air
big:	besar
good:	baik
long:	panjang
small:	kecil
yes:	ya
no:	tidak, bukan

Example Sentences

The following sentences illustrate some of the morphological verbal forms in context. Abbreviations used are: ACT = active, AG = agent marker, PASS = passive, PL = plural, REL = relative clause marker, SG = singular.

(1) *Anjing itu menggigitku*
'That dog bites me (familiar)'
Anjing itu menggigitmu
'That dog bites you (SG/PL, familiar)'
Anjing itu menggigitnya
'That dog bites him/her/it'
Anjing itu menggigit saya/meréka/ayam
'That dog bites me/them/the chicken'
Ayam itu kugigit
'That chicken is bitten by me'
Ayam itu kaugigit
'That chicken is bitten by you'
Ayam itu digigitnya
'That chicken is bitten by him/her/it'
Ayam itu digigit (meréka/anjing)
'That chicken is bitten (by them/a dog)'
Ayam itu saya/kamu/meréka gigit
'That chicken is bitten by me/you (SG/PL,familiar)/them'
Gigit ayam itu!
'Bite that chicken!'
Dia menggigit-gigitku
'He/she bites me (familiar) repeatedly'
Ayam itu digiti-gigit
'That chicken is bitten repeatedly'
Kucing dan anjing gigit-menggigit
'The cat and the dog bite each other'
Lidah saya tergigit
'My tongue got bitten'

(2) Bantal yang se-besar kasur itu ber-isi
cushion REL one-big mattress that qualified.by-content

bulu ayam.
feather chicken
'That cushion which is as big as a mattress is filled with chicken feathers.'

(3) Ayam besar yang baru saya bulu-i itu
chicken big REL just I feather-on that

hampir di-makan anjing tetangga.
nearly be-eaten dog neighbor
'That big chicken which I just had plucked was nearly eaten by the neighbor's dog.'

(4) Pem-bantu sudah mau mem-bulu-i ayam
AG-help already want ACT-feather-on chicken

itu ketika anjing tetangga me-makan-nya.
that moment dog neighbor ACT-eat-3SG
'The maid was about to pluck that chicken when the neighbor's dog ate it.'

Efforts to Preserve, Protect, and Promote the Language

When Japan occupied the Dutch Indies in 1942, it forbade the use of Dutch at all levels of official communication. Unable to replace it by decree with Japanese, they proclaimed Malay as the official language, to be used in government, in the mass media, and at all levels of education and science. This was in agreement with one of the resolutions of the first Indonesian Language Congress (Solo 1938), and implied the immediate implementation of some others: there had to come a "new grammar representing the reality of the language", and the necessary terminology had to be developed for Malay to fulfill its new functions. These efforts were continued after independence. The government body responsible for that standardization and propagation of the language is since 1975 the *Pusat Pembinaan dan Pengembangan Bahasa* ('National Center for Language Development and Cultivation'). Its main branch is in Jakarta; in several provincial capitals it has daughter subsidiary branches. Its main tasks include the production of monolingual dictionaries; a standard grammar, terminologies, weekly television and radio broadcasts on Indonesian; coordination of studies on the regional languages and standardization of the major ones; the organization of upgrading courses in correct language use for government officials on all levels; counseling; and publishing. Each year during the month of October the center coordinates the *Bulan Bahasa* ('Language Month') activities, such as contests in writing, poetry reading, and television program presentation, commemorating the proclamation of Malay as the future national language of Indonesia by the nationalist movement in October 1928. Finally the center regularly organizes and coordinates workshops and meetings on language and literature, culminating in the National Language Conferences, which, since 1978, have been held every five years.

After the Sixth National Language Conference (1993), the center launched a campaign against the extensive use of English for prestige projects, on billboards and in advertisements. Since the end of the 1960s the center cooperates with its sister organization in Malaysia, especially in terminology development. Since the 1980s they have formed, together with their Bruneian counterpart the *Majelis Bahasa Brunei Darussalam-Malaysia-Indonesia* ('Language Council of Brunei Darussalam-Malaysia-Indonesia').

Select Bibliography

Alieva, N.F. *et al.* 1972. *Grammatika Indonezijskogo Jazyka.* Moskwa: Nauka.

Alwi, Hasan, *et al.* 1998. *Tatabahasa baku bahasa Indonesia. Edisi ketiga.* Jakarta: Departemen Pendidikan dan Kebudayaan Republik Indonesia.

Echols, John M., and Hassan Shadily. 1989. *An Indonesian-English Dictionary.* Revised and edited by John U. Wolff and James T. Collins, in cooperation with Hassan Shadily. Ithaca and London: Cornell University Press.

Halim, Amran. 1981. *Intonation in Relation to Syntax in Indonesian.* Canberra. Pacific Linguistics, D–36.

Kaswanti Purwo, Bambang. 1984. *Deiksis dalam bahasa Indonesia.* Jakarta: Balai Pustaka.

Labrousse, Pierre. 1984. *Dictionnaire Général Indonésien-Français.* Paris: Association Archipel.

Moeliono, A.M. 1986. *Language Development and Cultivation: Alternative Approaches in Language Planning.* Canberra. Pacific Linguistics, D–68.

Moeliono, Anton M., and Soenjono Dardjowidjojo (eds). 1988. *Tatabahasa baku bahasa Indonesia.* Jakarta: Balai Pustaka; Yogyakarta: Gadjah Mada University Press.

Ophuijsen, A. van. 1910. *Maleische Spraakkunst.* Leiden: S.C. van Doesburgh. [2d edition 1915].

Simatupang, M.D.S. 1979. *Reduplikasi morfemis bahasa Indonesia.* Jakarta: Djambatan.

Sneddon, J.N. 1996. *Indonesian Reference Grammar.* St Leonards, NSW: Allen & Unwin.

Teeuw, A. 1961. *A Critical Survey of Studies on Malay and Indonesian.* The Hague: Martinus Nijhoff.

_____. 1996. *Indonesisch-Nederlands woorden-boek.* Leiden: KITLV Uitgeverij.

Tim Penyusun Kamus Pusat Pembinaan dan Pengembangan Bahasa. 1993. *Kamus besar bahasa Inonesia. Edisi kedua.* Jakarta: Balai Pustaka.

Wolff, J.U., Dede Oetomo, and Daniel Fietkiewicz. 1987. *Beginning Indonesian through Self-instruction.* Jakarta: Gramedia.

MALAYALAM

Rodney F. Moag

Language Name: Malayalam. **Autonym:** *MalayāLam.*

Location: Homeland: Kerala State in Southwestern India and the Laccadive (Lakshadweep) Islands in the Indian Ocean, west of Kerala. Outside of homeland: in large Malayali communities in Delhi, Mumbai (Bombay), and Chennai (Madras), in Dubai and other Arabian Gulf states where Malayalis form a large part of the expatriate labor force, and also major North American cities.

Family: South Dravidian subbranch of Dravidian.

Related Languages: TAMIL, the other major South Dravidian language, is the closest relative; all 22 known Dravidian languages in the three major branches—South, Central, and North Dravidian—are related.

Dialects: The language of South Central Kerala is the basis for standard Malayalam. There are social dialects within each region, and several recognized regional variants. The most divergent is that of Northern Kerala. It is both a regional and social dialect, being associated with the Muslim community, which is largest in North Kerala. An off-shore regional variant is that of the Laccadive Islands.

Dialects are distinguished mainly by lexical and phonological differences. Variations exist between the major communities—Hindu, Christian, and Muslim in order of greatest numbers. Within the Hindu community dialects are caste-based, with those of Brahmins and Izhavas providing the extreme examples. Kinship terms is a prime area of communal variation.

In addition, Malayalam has a very formal written style called *maNiprabhāLam*, which utilizes many SANSKRIT words.

Number of Speakers: 30 million (Kerala is 98 percent Malayalam-speaking.)

Origin and History

Malayalam is acknowledged to have split off from Tamil. The first evidence of distinct linguistic forms appears in stone inscriptions in Kerala in the 10th century. Earlier written records, both on copper plates and in stone, are in forms of Old Tamil. The Hindu revival in the 10th century brought literally thousands of Sanskrit words into the vocabulary. The earliest literature, epic poems, date from this period. In the 19th century the ruler of Travancore State (now the southern part of Kerala) instituted mass education. As a result Kerala today is unique among Indian states in having nearly 100 percent literacy. The Malayalam newspapers have the highest circulation figures in all of India. The modern literature contains all possible genres, and Kerala's creative writers have won many national and international prizes.

The first grammars of the language were written by Europeans. The best known of these was the German missionary Dr. Hermann Gundert, who also produced a highly respected Malayalam-English dictionary. The most authoritative grammar in Malayalam itself was written by the so-called Kerala Panini, Rajaraja Varma.

Malayalam has a full range of registers as well as dialects. It has long had specialized vocabularies in traditional subjects such as philosophy, homeopathic medicine, architecture, martial arts, and so forth. In the last century it has developed registers and lexicons for administrativese, journalese, legalese (the proceedings of the Kerala Supreme Court are conducted in Malayalam), and others. Technical subjects still tend to be taught and carried out in English, though books on science are increasingly written in Malayalam at the secondary school level.

Orthography and Basic Phonology

The Malayalam writing system, like most others in South Asia, is systemically patterned on the Devanagari alphabet used for Sanskrit. It is a syllabary writing system, meaning that a consonant contains an inherent short /a/ vowel unless otherwise marked. Furthermore, each vowel has two separate symbols—an independent symbol used when it forms the initial syllable in a sequence and a dependent symbol when it serves as nucleus for a syllable with a consonant onset. Typical of Indian scripts the symbols for vowels /e/ and /ē/ are written to the left of the consonant, and /o/ and /ō/ are written with a double symbol—the long or short /e/ symbol to the left of the consonant, and the long /ā/ symbol to its right.

Consonant symbols are marked in one of several ways to indicate absence of vowel, i.e., no phonetic release. A few use completely different symbols to indicate syllable-final status, either within or at the end of a word, but most modify or superscribe the normal symbol in some way to show this condition.

In addition there are a number of special symbols for double consonants and consonant clusters. Nasal, plus stop, sequences are of Dravidian origin, and all other consonant clusters are of Sanskrit origin. The orthographic symbols for some of these clusters were eliminated in the 1982 script reform.

Malayalam has a strong preference for writing two or more words together as a graphic unit. This is conditioned by a hier-

Table 1: Consonants

	Bilabial	Dental	Alveolar	Palato-Alveolar	Retroflex	Palatal	Velar	Glottal
Stops	p ph b bh	t̪ t̪h d̪ d̪h	t	c ch j jh	T Th D Dh	k' k'h g' g'h	k kh g gh	
Fricatives			s š		S			h
Nasals	m	n̪	n	n	N	ñ	ŋ	
Laterals			l		L			
Taps			r r̃					
Frictionless continuant					R			
Glides	w					y		

archy of phonetic and syntactic constraints. Words are written together only within major constituents of a sentence, provided those constituents are of sufficient length. In short sentences major constituent boundaries may be crossed, provided they fall within a natural-breath group. In orthographic conjoining, the independent vowel symbols are replaced by the dependent ones written either on the final consonant of word one, or, on the phonotactically conditioned [y] or [w] used as a joining device when the preceding word ends in a vowel. When a stop-initial word is joined to a preceding vowel-final one, the initial consonant is doubled to preserve its voiceless character in the new intervocalic environment. When a stop-initial word or suffix is joined to a preceding stop-final word, the required epenthetic vowel at the end of word one becomes short [u]. If word one ends in a sonorant consonant, vowel-initial words are joined to it, but consonant-initial words are not normally attached.

Malayalam has an extremely elaborated consonant system with 38 members. It is the only known language having a six-way phonemic opposition in stops: labial, dental, alveolar, palatal, retroflex, and velar. A similar six-way opposition exists in nasals, though the dental/alveolar distinction is partly allophonic. The Dravidian languages have only voiceless stops, but both voiced-voiceless and aspirated-unaspirated oppositions have come into the language through Sanskrit borrowings. Length is phonemic in both vowels and Dravidian consonants. Stops of Sanskrit origin behave differently. Voiced stops double only across syllable boundary, while double aspirates do not occur at all.

Table 2: Vowels

	Front	Central	Back
High	i ī		u ū
Mid	e ē		o ō
Low		a ā	
Syllabic vibrant		•	

The distinction between alveolar and dental nasals is neutralized in word-final position in favor of the alveolar place of articulation. Alveolar /t/ is systemically the double or geminate of trilled /r/, hence is represented orthographically with double *r*.

There are two laterals, one alveolar, and one retroflex. The /r̃/ is a lamino-palatal tap, while /r/ is an apico-alveolar trill. The most unique sound is the /R/, which is a retroflex continuant, which Malayalis claim no foreigner can pronounce.

Malayalam does not permit final unreleased stops. Therefore, stop-final sequences have an epenthetic vowel [ʉ], which is realized as a raised schwa somewhere near the bottom of the high-central range. It contrasts both in length and position with phonemic final /a/. Single stops become lightly voiced between vowels, and after a nasal. Dental /t̪/ becomes a voiced fricative intervocalically. The palatal series, though phonetically affricates, are systemically stops. The alveolar trill /r/ is also regarded as a stop with its geminate version realized as /t/.

The basic Dravidian syllable structure is (C)V(C). Consonant clusters, both initial and final, are found in words of Sanskrit origin and in more recent English borrowings. Unlike Sanskrit, Dravidian does not permit two vowels to adjoin. The glide [y] is inserted between two vowels except where the first vowel is /u/, which takes [w] instead. This is reflected in the orthography as well. All Malayalam words (except English borrowings) contain two or more syllables. In casual and rapid speech several processes normally operate to modify the cardinal structure of words: elision of unstressed syllables, assimilation across syllable boundaries, etc. The seven-syllable name of the capital city /t̪iruwanan̪t̪apuram/ can reduce to the four-syllable form, [tir̃antoor̃am].

Basic Morphology

Nominal Morphology. Malayalam has seven cases of the noun: nominative, accusative, dative, genitive, associative, instrumental, and vocative. Each case marker has two or three allomorphs. Case markers and particles of Dravidian origin for nouns are postposed. Sanskrit loans carry prefixes, but these are not particularly productive, e.g., *nyāyam* 'justice', *anyāyam* 'injustice'; *āgraham* 'desire', *atyāgraham* 'intense desire'. All save the vocative and instrumental end in the vowel *e*, long or short, or in the epenthetic vowel represented by [ʉ]. There is a hierarchy of cases such that generally when the experiencer is shown by the dative, the object cannot appear in the accusative, but must be in the associative case.

Malayalam has no grammatical gender, hence there is no agreement rule for modifiers. In terms of natural gender, native Dravidian items, kin terms, pronouns, etc., show final *-aL* for feminine and *-an* for masculine. Sanskrit-derived kin terms have taken on Malayalam *-an* for masculine, but show Sanskrit final *-i* for feminine. Number is optional, thus the plural marker *-kaL* is used mostly in written text and in formal speech. It is often deleted in everyday conversation.

In the NP head words occur phrase finally with postposed case markers. The plural marker attaches directly to the noun before the case marker. Particles indicating conjunction ("and"), disjunction ("or"), indefiniteness ("and such"), follow all other markers. Typical of languages with SOV word order, modifiers precede the head noun. There is no definite article, only demonstratives. Within the NP the indefinite article may optionally follow the possessive pronoun yielding phrases such as *enre oru kuTTukaran* (my one friend) 'a friend of mine'.

The pronoun system shows several levels along a dual axis of social status and familiarity. Masculine third person has three ranked pronouns while feminine third person has only two. The second-person repertoire includes five pronouns, though the upper two are reserved for highly exalted personages. There is only one first-person singular pronoun, while the plural has separate items for inclusive and exclusive "we".

Verbal Morphology. The Malayalam verb system marks neither gender nor number. Unlike its sister language Tamil, there is also no marking of person, though the marker *–ām* in its intentive meaning can only be used with first-person subjects.

Paradigm:

Root:	para	'to say, tell'
Present	parayunnu	'says, is telling'
Pres. Prog.	parayukayāNʉ	'is/are telling, saying'
Intentive (with nom. subject)	parayām	'(I, we) will tell, say'
Potential (with dative subject)	parayām	'can say, tell'
Future/habitual	parayum	'will say, tell; always says, tells'
Past	paraññu	'told, said'
Past prog.	parayukāyirunnu	'was saying, telling'
Remote past	paraññirunnu	'Had told, used to say'
Modal (with dative subject)	parayaNam	'want(s), need(s) to say, tell'
Modal (with nom. subject)	"	'must/has to/is required to say'

Basic Syntax

Malayalam is an SOV language with head-final clause construction. Thus all modifiers in an NP are to the left of the headword. There is a strong tendency for interrogative phrases to occur immediately before the verb. Direct objects normally appear right before the verb with other case roles to their left in the VP.

Negativization of most verb tenses is done with the suffix *–illa*, but there are a few exceptions. The verb 'to be' in the simple present, *āNʉ*, requires the separate negative *alla*. The defective verb *vēNam*, 'to want, need' becomes *vēNTa*. The modals, formed by adding a form of *vēNam* to other verbs take a form of *veNTa* in the negative. The distinction between intentive and future/habitual is lost in the negative:

parayunnilla	'is/are not saying, telling, talking'
parayukayilla	'will not, do/does not say, tell'
paraññilla,	'didn't say, tell'
parayeNTa	'not want to, ought not to say, tell'

Causativization is done by a set of processes whose conditioning is complex and not easily explained. The two most common causativizing strategies are: the infix *-ippi-* and doubling or other modification of the root consonant, e.g.,*paThikkuka* 'to study, learn' > *paThippikkuka* 'to teach'; *māruka* 'to change (intran.)' > *mārruka* 'to change, move (trans.)'.

The passive idea, i.e., focus on the object and how it is affected, is accomplished in several different ways, most commonly through subject deletion (see Example Sentences). This is routinely done in Malayalam and accounts for the high frequency of passive statements heard when Malayalis speak English. The language does have a construction much like the English passive, used mostly in newspapers and other reports, in which the object of an active verb becomes subject (nominative case) and the agent, if included, is rendered by the instrumental case. The so-called dative construction is very common. It is used to show possession (both alienable and inalienable), physical and emotional states, ability, desire, knowledge, etc., *enikkʉ mūnn cēTTan-mār uNTʉ* (to.me three older.brother-pl exist) 'I have three older brothers'.

Zero pronominalization (or zero anaphora) is endemic. Topics once established tend not to be reiterated in the discourse. In fact, nouns in any and all case roles in the sentence may be deleted in the following discourse. Thus, subsequent comments on a topic and responses to questions often consist of a verb alone.

Contact with Other Languages

Some 40 percent of everyday vocabulary is of Sanskrit origin. The words are highly nativized in that the nouns take regular Malayalam case endings and the verbs accept all the Malayalam markers of mood, tense, and aspect. Examples: *āhlāḓam* 'ecstasy', *nirbandhikkuka* 'to compel, force'.

Malayalam is in contact with Tamil in both the south and east. Two districts are particularly bilingual, Nagarcoil in the south and Palaghat in the east. Malayalam speakers in north Kerala are in touch with speakers of both Tulu and KANNADA. English enjoys high prestige, and English loans are increasingly common. In contrast to Sanskrit verbs, however, they normally do not accept Malayalam affixes directly, but require a carrier verb, "do" for active or transitive processes and forms of "to be" for passive processes. English nouns accept case endings readily. For example, *kōppi ceyyuka* 'to copy (something)', *kōppi ākuka* 'to be copied', *kampyuTarinre skrīNile immējukaL* 'the images on the computer screen'. A great number of English-medium schools have sprung up in the past two decades as a backlash to the nativization of upper primary and secondary school curricula. The growing availability of satellite-fed programs and movies from native English-speaking countries is also helping to spread English and English competence. HINDI is a required subject in most schools. The younger generation can generally manage some Hindi, but it lags behind English in interest and impact.

Common Words

man:	puṟušan
woman:	strī
water:	veLLam
sun:	sūryan
three:	mūnnʉ
fish:	mīn
big:	weliya
long:	nīNTa
small:	ceriya
yes:	no direct equivalent, varies according to verb, all yes/no questions can be answered with the positive of the verb.
	aṯe (for copula only),
	ūwwʉ (for existive and some other verbs)
no:	illa for most verbs
	alla for copula only
	vēNTa for modals (want, have to, etc.)
good:	nalla
bird:	kiLi (Dravidian, everyday), pakSi (fancy)
dog:	paTTi, nāy
tree:	maṟam (everyday), wrakSam (fancy)

Example Sentences

(1) pulisʉ avane piTiccu.
police him:ACC grab:PASS
'The police caught him.'

(2) avan pulisināl piTikka peTTu.
he:NOM police:INSTR grab:PASS AUX:PAST
'He was caught by the police.'

Efforts to Preserve, Protect, and Promote the Language

Malayalis settled in other countries have struggled with the issue of how to keep their language alive. There is a Malayalam library in Singapore, and until recently a Malayalam daily newspaper was published there. The majority of Malayali immigrants to the United States are Christians. Malayali associations exist in many large U.S. cities or, in some cases, on a statewide basis, as in Oklahoma. A number of these have attempted to run language classes for children, and several have established libraries and activity centers. At least two international umbrella organizations exist: the World Malayali Association, and the Federation of Kerala Associations of North America (FOKANA), both of which seek to preserve Malayalam language and culture. Writers groups are found in Houston and other U.S. cities, and there is a small but active expatriate literature movement. A Malayalam newspaper is published from New York City, and every few years a World Malayalam Conference is held. Venues have varied from New York to India. In the main, the second generation does not learn the language sufficiently well to participate in these movements.

Select Bibliography

Arnospadre. 1795. *Vocabularium Malabarico lusitanum, Malayalam-Portuguese Dictionary*. [Reprinted 1988] Trichur: Kerala Sahitya Academy.

Gundert, Rev. H.A. 1872. *Malayalam and English Dictionary*. Reprinted by J. Jetley for Asian Educational Services, New Delhi.

Moag, Rodney F. 1997. *Malayalam: A University Course and Reference Grammar*. Center for Asian Studies, University of Texas. Austin, TX. Third Edition.

Mohanan, K.P. 1986. *The Theory of Lexical Phonology*. Dordrecht, Holland: D. Reidel Publishing.

Pillai, T. Ramalingam. 1988. *English-English-Malayalam Dictionary*. D.C. Books, Kottayam, 1983, Twelfth Edition.

Varma, Rajaraja. 1994. *A. R. Keralapaniniyasangraham: Codyottararupattilulla punarakhyanam*. [Reprint] Gopikkuttan (ed.) Plavelil, Cannannur: Kalyani Books.

Zacharias, Tobias. 1933. *English-Malayalam Dictionary*. [Reprinted 1989] J. Jetley for Asian Educational Services, New Delhi.

Maninka-Bambara-Dyula

Jessica A. Barlow

Language Name: Bambara, Dyula, Maninka, and Khasonke (Xasonke) are considered dialects of Mandekan, or Manding. The people who make up the majority of the population in the core area where the language is spoken are called the Bambara in the northeastern section; Dyula in the southern and southeastern sections; and Maninka, Malinke, or Mandinka in the western section of the core. Basically the same language is spoken and understood by all of these peoples, and the language area is often referred to as the Maninka-Bambara-Dyula complex. The linguistic descriptions in this entry are based on Bambara, which is considered the standard. **Autonym for Bambara:** *Bamanakan*. **Alternate:** *Mandekalu* 'people of the Mande; from where all dialects have stemmed'.

Location: Mali, in west Africa, but also in an area from Senegal extending north to the Mauritanian border, south through central Guinea to the northwestern corner of the Ivory Coast, and east to Burkina Faso. The core area extends from Ségou, Mali, in the north, and into the Ivory Coast.

Family: East Mandekan subgroup of the Northern Mande group of the Niger-Congo branch of the Niger-Kordofanian family.

Related Languages: Soninke, Susu, Yalunka, Vai, Kono, Hwela-Numu, Khasonke, Western Malinke.

Dialects: Some of the differences between Bambara, Maninka, Dyula, and Khasonke lie in variation in pronunciation. For example, the word 'five' is *duuru* in Bambara, *loolu* in Maninka and Dyula, and *lolu* in Khasonke. There are several other examples of this /d/-/l/ variation.

The plural marker in the official Malian orthography is represented by w̲, but it is pronounced as /u/. In most Southern Maninka dialects, the plural marker is pronounced as /i/, and in some Western dialects, the plural marker is /lu/: Bambara: *mu̲sow̲*; Southern Maninka: *mu̲soi*; Gambian Mandinka: *mu̲solu* 'women'.

Number of Speakers: 8–10 million, the vast majority of whom live in Mali (80 percent of Mali's population, which was 9.82 million in 1992).

Origin and History

ARABIC chronicles that go back to the 11th century refer to two antagonist empires, the Ghana Empire and the Mali Empire, which most likely spoke Soninke and Mandingo, respectively. The Mali Empire was concentrated around its initial area, Upper Niger, between what is now Mali and Guinea. Over the centuries this empire expanded and contracted. At the beginning of the 15th century it began to decline, especially in the east and north. In the early 16th century the Songhai or Gao Empire gained power and limited the power of the Mali Empire on the east side, as did the Fulani kingdom of Macina. Through the centuries the Mandingo fragmented due to war and other factors.

Before the colonial period, Mandingo-speaking people experienced a political and territorial spread, which led to non-Maningo-speaking people speaking the language. After colonization, although Mandingo was denied use at the administrative and educational levels in favor of FRENCH, it was recognized by the colonial administration as a vehicular language, and thus was recognized as the most useful intermediate language between French and local languages.

Orthography and Basic Phonology

Bambara is written in the LATIN alphabet, with some modification. The spelling used here was adopted in 1967 by the members of the *Commission Technique du Bambara* for use in functional literacy programs in the Republic of Mali.

Table 1: Consonants

	Labial	Dental	Alveo-Palatal	Velar	Glottal
Stops					
Voiceless	p	t		k	
Voiced	b	d		g	
Fricatives					
Voiceless	f	s	sh [ʃ]		h
Voiced		z			
Affricates					
Voiceless			c [tʃ]		
Voiced			j [dʒ]		
Nasals	m	n	ny [ɲ]	ŋ	
Resonants		l, r [ɾ]			
Glides	w		j		

In addition, Bambara has a series of prenasalized consonants *np*, *nb*, *nf*, *nt*, *nd*, *ns*, *nk*, *ng*; in these consonants, the nasal assimilates in place of articulation to the oral component.

Vowels. Vowels can be short, long, or nasalized.

Table 2: Vowels

	Front	Central	Back
High	i		u
Mid-High	e		o
Mid-Low	è [ɛ]		ò [ɔ]
Low		a	

Contraction of juxtaposed vowels is obligatory. Generally, it is the first of the two vowels that drops out. In the orthography, it is replaced by an apostrophe.

Bambara is a tone language, so words can be distinguished from each other not only by consonants and vowels but also by relative pitch of the voice. A word can have one of two tones, high or low. In writing, words associated with low tones are represented by underlining the first vowel of the word. High tones are not marked.

The basic tones associated with words can be modified by the tones in adjacent words.

If a high-tone word follows another high-tone word, they will have the same level of pitch. A low-tone word following a high-tone word will occur on a lower level of pitch. A high-tone word following a low tone word will rise slightly in pitch.

A low-tone word followed by another low-tone word will rise in pitch so that a one-syllable word (with a low tone) will have a rising tone, a two-syllable word will be low-high, and a three-syllable word will be low-low-high.

In a sequence of three tones, high-low-high, the second tone will not be as high as the first. This phenomenon is called "downdrift".

When a vowel is contracted with another vowel, the tone of the contracted vowel will remain. If the first vowel is high and the second one is low, the contracted vowel will be high, but the following high-tone words will be pronounced on a slightly lower level of pitch.

Basic Morphology

Bambara does not have noun classes or any other sort of grammatical gender. There are two numbers (singular and plural). The singular is not specifically marked, but the plural is formed by a suffix on the last element in the noun phrase: *muso* 'woman', *musow* 'women', *muso dòw* 'some women'.

The definite article is expressed by a low tone following the noun and its modifiers. Definite low-tone nouns will rise in tone. With definite high-tone nouns, following high-tone words will occur on a slightly lower pitch.

muso tè	muso_tè
woman is-not	woman-the-is not
'it's not a woman'	'it's not the woman'

Neither nouns nor pronouns are inflected for case. The personal pronouns are:

	Singular	Plural
1st	n'/ne	anw
2nd	i/e	aw
3rd	a/ale	u/olu

Bambara distinguishes two kinds of possession, alienable (separable) and inalienable (inseparable). For example, *n'fa* 'my father' is an example of inalienable possession, while *n' ka mobili* 'my car' is an example of alienable possession. As illustrated by these examples, alienable possession is indicated by the particle *ka* between the pronoun and the possessed noun.

Bambara verbs do not agree with their subjects in any way. Most tense and aspect marking is provided by auxiliaries that occur as separate words from the verb. The tenses are past, present, and future, and the aspects are imperfect, habitual, perfect, progressive, conditional, and hortative. Passives are formed by placing the object in subject position in the sentence and suffixing *-len* to the verb. Causatives are formed by adding the prefix *la-* to any verb.

Verbs can be formed from nouns by using the action nominal form (indicated by the suffix *-li*) with the verb *kè* 'do': *foli* 'greeting', *foli_kè* 'to greet'.

Basic Syntax

The order of major constituents in Bambara is Subject-Auxiliary-Object-Verb:

N'-bè	baara_kè
1SG-AU	work-do
'I work'	

Adjectives and other modifiers follow the nouns they modify:

nègèso	nyu-man
bicycle	good-ADJ
'good bicycle'	

The suffix *-man* indicates that the adjective is used as a modifier rather than as a predicate.

Relative-clause formation in Bambara is unusual and is often cited in typological studies. The morpheme *min* occurs in the interior of the relative clause and serves either as a relative-clause marker or as a relative pronoun.

[i	ye	Fanta	min	ye	kunun]	taara	Bamako]
[2SG	AUX	Fanta	REL	see	yesterday]	go–PAST	Bamako]

'Fanta, whom you saw yesterday, went to Bamako.'

Bambara, like most OV languages, has postpositions. Many of the postpositions are identical to words for body parts and are considered to be homophones with them:

kun	'head' or 'on'
kònò	'stomach' or 'in'
nyè	'eye' or 'before, in front'

Negation in Bambara is expressed by using one of the specifically negative auxiliaries *tè*, *ma*, *man*, or *kana*.

Karamògò_bè	bamanakan	_sèbèn	tabulo	_la
teacher AUX	Bambara	write	blackboard	on

'The teacher writes on the blackboard.'

Ka̱ramògò_tè bamanakan_sèbèn ta̱bulo _la
teacher AUX-NEG Bambara write blackboard on
'The teacher does not write on the blackboard.'

Contact with Other Languages

Bambara has had much borrowing from French, Arabic, and WOLOF.

From French: *ambasadi* 'embassy', *anglopu* 'envelope', *dute* 'tea', *ta̱bali* 'table'
From Arabic: *sa̱n* 'year', *famu* 'understand', *hakili* 'thought, memory, mind, spirit', *kitabu* 'book'
From Wolof: *tu̱babu* 'white, European, French', *tu̱babukan* 'French language', *alikati* 'police agent', *kudu* 'spoon'

Common Words

man: cè̱
woman: mu̱so
water: ji
sun: ti̱le
three: sa̱ba
fish: jègè
big: bo̱n/be̱lebele
long: ja̱n/ja̱manjan
small: misèn/misènman
yes: a̱wò/o̱wò/o̱nhòn
no: a̱yi
good: di/duman
bird: ko̱nò
dog: wulu
tree: jiri

Example Sentences

(1) I tu̱n bè yòrò min n tu̱n bè ye̱n.
you PAST AUX place REL I PAST AUX there
'I was at the place that you were.'

(2) I bè mu̱n kè?
you AUX what do
'What are you doing?'

(3) N'ye ki̱tabu di Safi ma.
I-AUX book give Safi to
'I gave the book to Safi.'

Efforts to Preserve, Protect, and Promote the Language

Since Mali's independence in 1960, attempts have been made to promote literacy for adults. The variety of Bambara spoken around the city of Bamako was chosen by the Malian government to be used in their literacy program, which is being implemented by the Ministry of Education. This dialect is the most widely understood throughout the area; it is also a trade language for several million people in the surrounding area.

The policy of functional literacy was an effort to impart literacy to people in their mother tongue and also to give them technical training in that language within the framework of a national development campaign. Of four languages that were selected for this program—Bambara, Fulani, Tamashek (Tuareg), and Songhai—only in Bambara has there been a system of large-scale literacy training.

In addition to promoting literacy in national languages, Mali also chose to keep French as the national language and impose it in education and government. Senegal and the Ivory Coast also maintained French as the national language, while Guinea favored African languages for the national languages. There are newspapers, books, and magazines written in Bambara, as well as Bambara television stations.

Select Bibliography

Bird, Charles, ed. 1982. *The Dialects of Mandekan*. Bloomington: African Studies Program, Indiana University.

Bird, Charles, John Hutchison, and Mamadou Kante. 1977. *An Ka Bamanankan Kalan: Beginning Bambara*. Bloomington: Indiana University Linguistics Club.

Bird, Charles, and Mamadou Kante. 1976. *An Ka Bamanankan Kalan: Intermediate Bambara*. Bloomington: Indiana University Linguistics Club.

____. 1977. *Bambara-English English-Bambara Student Lexicon*. Bloomington: Indiana University Linguistics Club.

Calvet, Louis-Jean. 1982. "The Spread of Mandingo: Military, Commercial, and Colonial Influence on a Linguistic Datum." *Language Spread: Studies in Diffusion and Social Change*, Edited by R. L. Cooper. Bloomington: Indiana University Press.

Kone, Kassim. 1996. *Bamana Verbal Art: An Ethnographic Study of Proverbs*. Doctoral dissertation, Indiana University.

Welmers, William E. 1971. "Niger-Congo, Mande." *Current Trends in Linguistics VII: Linguistics in Sub-Saharan Africa*. T.A. Sebeok, J. Berry, J.H. Greenberg, D.W. Crabb, and P. Schachter, eds. 113–140. The Hague: Mouton.

Manipuri/Meithei

Shobhana L. Chelliah

Language Name: Manipuri. **Alternate:** *Meithei.* **Autonym:** *Meitheirón.*

Location: Manipuri is spoken predominantly in Manipur State, India. Smaller populations exist in Assam, Tripura, Myanmar, and Bangladesh.

Family: Tibeto-Burman. Manipuri belongs to Kamarupan (from the SANSKRIT word *Kāmarūpa* for Assam). It has generally been recognized that Manipuri does not readily fit into the Kuki-Chin-Naga, Abor-Miri-Dafla and Bodo-Garo subgroups postulated for this area. Pending the collection of more data on other languages in the group, the exact position of Manipuri within Kamarupan remains uncertain.

Related Languages: Major languages related to Manipuri and spoken within Manipur are the Naga languages, for example, Angami Naga, Rongmei Naga, and Tangkhul Naga and Kuki-Chin languages for example, Mizo (Lushai), Hmar, Thadou, and Paite.

Dialects: Standard Manipuri is spoken in Imphal, the capital of Manipur. The documented dialects of Manipuri are Sekmai, spoken 19 kilometers north of Imphal; Pheyeng, spoken 2 kilometers south of Imphal; and the Kwatha dialect spoken at the southeastern Indo-Burmese border. Separate Brahmin Manipuri and Muslim Manipuri dialects exist but have not yet been documented. Other undocumented dialects are Kakching, Thanga, Nongmaikhong, Ngaikhong, Moirang, Langthel, Palel, and Tokcing. It is difficult to say if these are truly distinct dialects or simply geographical labels. All dialects are mutually intelligible and differ mainly at the phonological and lexical levels.

Number of Speakers: According to the 1991 national census, the population of Manipur is 1,837,000. Of this number, 1,180,000 are native speakers of Manipuri. Many of the remaining 657,000 Naga or Kuki speakers use Manipuri as a lingua franca. ENGLISH and Manipuri are the official languages of the state.

Origin and History

The earliest written records of Manipuri are from A.D. 900. Before the advent of British rule in Manipur in 1762, the state was ruled by members of the Ningthouja clan. Members of six other prominent clans vied for the status of the most powerful group in the state. War with Myanmar occurred sporadically between 1700 and 1800. In 1752, and then again in 1824, the British assisted Manipur in repelling invading Burmese. In 1891 Manipur became a princely state of the British Empire. In 1949, two years after India won independence from the British, Manipur was integrated into the Indian Union. It was made a full-fledged state in 1972. Manipuri was given national language status in 1987.

Orthography and Basic Phonology

Manipuri is written in either the Meithei Mayek or BANGLA scripts. Both scripts are syllabic. Meithei Mayek is part of the TIBETAN group of Gupta Brahmi scripts. Each vowel grapheme has two representations, a grapheme for syllable-initial position and a diacritic that combines with a consonant grapheme in syllable-medial or -final position. Consonants are represented by syllable-initial and -medial graphemes. These occur with a vowel diacritic. A separate set of graphemes is used to represent consonants in word-final position. Tone distinctions are not uniformly indicated through this script. Samples of handwritten Meithei Mayek can be found in Grierson (1919: 32–39) and Chelliah (1997: 361–364).

The Bangla alphabet used for Manipuri developed from the Proto-Bangla script, which is a Northern Brahmi Gupta script of the Kutila group. As in Meithei Mayek, vowels have two representations depending on whether the vowel is in syllable-initial or -noninitial position. Conventions for indicating tone include the use of long vowels to indicate high tone; however, these conventions are not universally followed and do not adequately represent all tonal distinctions. There is an effort underway toward spelling standardization. Difficulties in standardization persist with regard to the indication of tone, the quality of word-final vowels, and the representation of geminate consonants and consonant clusters. A sample of Manipuri written in the Bangla script can be found in Chelliah (1997: 375–376).

There are no indigenous words beginning with /a/. The vowel /e/ occurs in initial position in a few words. The vowels *ə, a,* and *o* combine with semivowels to form diphthongs as in *tə́w* 'dig', *táy* 'smear', *taw* 'float', *táy* 'hears', and *tóy* 'be often'.

Table 1: Vowels

	Front	Central	Back
High	i		u
Mid	e	ə	o
Low		a	

The aspirated affricate /čʰ/ is phonetically realized as [s],

Table 2: Consonants

	Labial	Alveolar	Palatal	Velar	Laryngeal
Stops	p b ph bh	t d th dh		k g kh gh	
Affricates			č čh ǰ ǰh		
Fricatives		s			h
Nasals	m	n		ŋ	
Lateral/Flap		l			
Trill		r			
Semivowels	w		y		

[s^h], [ʒ] or [$ʒ^h$] in native words. /l/ has a flapped [r] allophone in intervocalic position. The unaspirated and aspirated voiced series are due to large scale borrowing of Indo-Aryan words. In native words, voiceless stops contrast with the voiced stops in word medial position only. In suffixation, voiceless unaspirated stops in syllable-initial position are voiced between voiced segments. Consonants are deaspirated when the previous syllable onset is an /h/ or an aspirated consonant. For example, *thin* 'pierce' + *-khət* 'V upward' is *thingət* 'pierce upward'. The lateral *l* assimilates in place and manner of articulation with a preceding nasal as in *yeŋŋəmmi* 'looking' from *yeŋ* 'look' + *-ləm* 'indirect evidence' and *-li* 'progressive'.

The Manipuri syllable consists of a nucleus and an onset and may include a coda. The nucleus consists of a vowel. Onsets may be simple or complex. For native words, in word initial position, onsets may be: *p, ph, t, th, č, čh, k, kh, m, n, ŋ, w, y, h, l.* Voiced stop onsets occur word medially through voice assimilation following affixation and word initially only in ideophones. Vowel-initial syllables of prefixes and roots are always preceded by a glottal stop: *əibə* [ʔəʔibə] 'writer' from *ə-* 'attributive' and *ibə* 'to write'. Complex onsets may consist of a voiced unaspirated stop, fricative or voiceless aspirated stop and a liquid or glide. Onsets of borrowed words may consist of voiced unaspirated or aspirated stops, affricates and fricatives in both word-initial or -medial position. Complex onsets are limited to consonant-liquid or consonant-glide sequences. The coda in native words may consist of *p, t, k, m, n, ŋ,* and *l.* In borrowed words, *s* may also occur as the coda. There are no complex codas.

A syllable without an onset has one created for it. When a root is followed by a suffix that begins with a vowel, a diphthong is formed. For example, *ú-* 'see' + *-í* 'declarative' result in *úy* 'sees'. Other ways that onsets are created are: (1) the insertion of a glide when the first vowel is front and high. For example, *pí* 'give' + *-u* 'imperative' results in *píyu* 'Give!'; (2) the insertion of a glottal stop when the first vowel is back. For example, *pu* 'carry' + *-o* 'solicitive' results in *puʔo* 'Won't you carry?' Syllables without onsets also arise when stems ending in consonants are followed by vowel-initial suffixes. In such cases the final consonant is geminated and provides the required onset. For example, *thəm-* 'keep'+ *-u* 'imperative' results in *thəmmu* 'keep!' In sequences of identical oral stops the second stop may be dissimilated. Thus in *čə́t* 'go' + *-u* 'imperative', gemination results in *čə́ttu*, which is followed by dissimilation of the second consonant to *l*, resulting in *čə́tlu!* 'go!'.

Manipuri exhibits contrast on roots between low and high tone. Suffixes and prefixes have no tone associated with them; instead, the pitch values observed for these are derived through the spreading of lexically specified root tone through rules of downstep and upstep. Low-tone roots trigger upstep, which results in an augmentation of pitch through the word. High-tone roots trigger downstep, which results in a downscaling of pitch through the word.

Basic Morphology

Manipuri is an agglutinative and primarily suffixing language. Nouns and pronouns are free forms with optional derivational suffixes that mark gender and number, and optional prefixes that mark possession. Nominal inflection is indicated through semantic role clitics.

Principal nominal affixes, derivational and inflectional:

Gender: *-pi* 'feminine' and *-pa* 'masculine', as in *hənuba* 'old man' and *hənubi* 'old woman'

Number: *-siŋ* 'plural', as in *əŋáŋsiŋ* 'children'

Possession: *i-* 'first-person possessive', as in *imít* 'my eye', *nə-* 'second-person possessive', as in *nəkhóŋ* 'your foot' and *mə-* 'third-person possessive' as in *məmā* 'his mother'

Semantic role: *-nə* 'agentive/instrumental', as in *nupanə* 'by the boy', *-pu* 'accusative', as in *nupabu* 'the boy (patient)', *-tə* 'locative', as in *nupadə* 'at/to the boy', *-təgi* 'ablative', as in *nupadəgi* 'from the boy', *-ki* 'genitive', as in *nupagi* 'of the boy', and *-kə* 'associative', as in *nupagə* 'with the boy'

Verb roots are bound forms and are also the basis for adjectives, adverbs, and verbal nouns. Verb derivational affixes can be classified into category changing and noncategory changing. Verb inflectional suffixes are discussed in the Basic Syntax section.

Category-changing verb derivational affixes:

ə- 'attributive': adjectives are derived from nominalized verbs through prefixation of the attributive, such as *əpikpə* 'small' from the verb root *pik-* 'be small'

-nə 'adverbial': manner adverbs are formed through the suffixation of *-nə* 'adverbial' to a verb root, such as *loynə* 'completely, all' from the verb root *loy-* 'complete, finish'

-pə 'nominalizer': verbal nouns that take clause-subordinating morphology are derived through affixation of this nominalizer to a verb root, such as *lakpə* 'to come, coming' from the verb root *lak-* 'come'

mə- 'nominalizer': nouns are derived from state verbs, as in *məčá* 'small one' from the verb root *čá-* 'be small'; locative adverbs are also derived from verbs, as in *məkhá* 'below, underneath' from *khá* 'be south' and *mətuŋ* 'behind' from *tuŋ-* 'be in back'

khut- 'nominalizer': nouns are derived from nonstate verbs as in *khutká* 'manner of climbing' from the verb root *ká-* 'climb'

First-level derivational suffixes occur immediately after the verb root. Only one first-level suffix can occur with a verb. All suffixes in this category are grammaticalized roots. They are *-khay* 'totally affect' from *kháy-* 'cut with a knife'; *-thət* 'partially affect' from *thət-* 'break by pulling'; *-hət* 'affect with undue psychological or physical influence' from *hát-* 'kill'; *-sin* 'V inward' from *sin-* 'be in', *-thok* 'V outward' from *thók-* 'be out', *-thə* 'V downward' from *thə-* 'be down', and *-khət* 'V upward' from *khət-* 'be up'. Examples are *phúgay-* 'beat till bones are broken' from the verb root *phú* 'beat' and the suffix *-khay* and *lawhət-* 'shout down' from the verb root *law-* 'shout' and the suffix *-hət.*

The second-level derivational suffixes consist of 19 morphemes that belong to 1 of 10 categories. The order of categories as 1–10 is the most common order in which the suffixes appear in the stem; however, these numbered positions do not represent position classes because the order of second-level derivational suffixes is free. Many of these suffixes have their origin in the grammaticalization of verb roots. These semantically defined categories predict co-occurrence restrictions among members of the same category since morphemes that signal analogous meanings never co-occur. For example, a verb will never be suffixed by two markers from the "direction" category: if a verb is marked by *-lə* 'proximal' (which indicates that an action takes place near the speaker), it would be anomalous for that same verb to be marked by *-lək* 'distal' (which indicates that an action was performed at a distance from the speaker).

Category 1:	*-min*	'comitative', *-nə* 'reciprocal'
Category 2:	*-pi*	'V for someone other than self', *-čə* 'V for sake of self'
Category 3:	*-hən*	'causative'
Category 4:	*-niŋ*	'wish to V'
Category 5:	*-mən*	'V to excess', *-kən* 'V habitually, repeatedly'
Category 6:	*-həw*	'V in the nick of time', *-khi* 'V ahead or behind expected time'
Category 7:	*-ləm*	'indirect evidence'
Category 8:	*-lə*	'proximal', *-lək* 'distal', *-lu* 'action away from speaker'
Category 9:	*-tə*	'negative'
Category 10:	*-lə*	'prospective aspect'

The third-level derivational suffixes are aspectual or modal. The three categories, 11 to 13, occur in their numerical order only and there can be only one instantiation of each category.

Category 11:	Mood 1	*-kə*	'potential'
		-loy	'nonpotential'
Category 12:	Mood 2	*-tə*	'necessity'
		-təw	'obligation, probability'
		-toy	'intention'
Category 13:	Aspect	*-li*	'progressive'
		-lə	'perfect'

Nominal compounding is highly productive, resulting in both right- and left-headed endocentric or exocentric compounds. Verbal compounds are exocentric only. Lexical collocations are formed through a variety of processes of reduplication and echo word formation. A constituent or part of a constituent can be either partially or fully duplicated, or a constituent or part of a constituent can be paired with a rhyming word. For example, *čə́tphə́m lakphə́m* 'place of much activity', literally 'go place come place', or *həway čeŋway* 'things to eat', literally 'lentils and rice and such'.

Basic Syntax

Sentences may be copulative where an uninflected verb or verbal noun is followed by *-ni* 'copula'. In finite clauses, illocutionary mood suffixes indicate sentence type: declarative *-í*, assertive *-e*, optative *-ke*, imperative *-u*, prohibitive *-nu*, solicitive *-o*, supplicative *-si*, and permissive *-sənu*. The mood suffixes, which constitute the only verb inflection, may be preceded optionally by three derivational categories.

There is no evidence in Manipuri for a verb-phrase constituent; the Manipuri clause consists of a verb and the arguments this verb subcategorizes for. There is no particular order imposed on the arguments; instead, word order is determined by pragmatic factors. The maximum number of noun phrases that may occur with a verb is restricted by the subcategorization frame of that verb. Since Manipuri allows for the omission of arguments, the minimum number of noun phrases that may occur with a verb is zero.

A verb may take an agent, defined as the instigator of an action, (marked by *-nə*), actor (marked by *-ø*), patient (marked by *-pu*), experiencer/goal (marked by *-tə*), path (marked by *-ø*), and theme (marked by *-ø*). In the default case the correct interpretation of the status of arguments in a sentence can be read off of semantic role markers and real-word semantics, for example, in *əy layrik ləyrukhini* I.book.will buy there 'I will buy books there,' even though neither *əy* or *layrik* are marked, it is understood that *əy* is the actor.

Morphologically encoded grammatical information is often obscured through the overlay of a system of pragmatic marking that may delete or replace the semantic role marker with one of the following enclitics: *-tə* 'exclusive', *-ti* 'delimitative', *-tu* 'distal', *-nə* 'contrastive', *-pu* 'adversative', *-si* 'proximate', or *-su* 'inclusive'. Pragmatic information can also be signaled by adding one of these enclitics to a semantic role and/or changing canonical agent/actor-patient verb word order. In some instances, the pragmatic system makes recovery of grammatical relations difficult so that sentences may often have more than one interpretation. In these cases the larger discourse context must be used to recover the intended meaning. For example, *əydi Ramnə phúniŋŋí* (I-Ram-wish to beat) can mean either 'It is Ram (not Chaoba) who wants to beat me (over all of you)', or 'It is Ram (not Chaoba) that I (over all of you) want to beat'.

Verbs with the nominalizer *-pə* suffix serve as heads of relative clauses. The relativized argument occurs to the right of a nominalized verb. A nominalized clause can also be suffixed by the locative, genitive, associative or ablative marker, which then acts like an adverbial subordinator. Thus *-kə* 'associative' is used to mean 'at the same time as Ving', *-ki* 'genitive' is used to mean 'for the purpose of Ving', *-tə* 'locative' is used to mean 'after Ving', *-təgi* 'ablative' is used to mean 'resulting from Ving', *-nə* 'instrumental' is used to mean 'by Ving, because of Ving'.

Contact with Other Languages

Between 1709 and 1748 Manipur was ruled by a monarch who converted from the traditional animistic religion to Hinduism and instigated a mass conversion of the Meitheis. The conversion to Hinduism exposed Manipuri speakers to Indo-Aryan languages, which resulted in extensive borrowing of Indo-Aryan words into Manipuri. The literate strata of Meithei society were eager to integrate themselves into the Hindu cosmological hierarchy, and so all literary genres used the scriptural languages, Old Bangla, Sanskrit and Brajabuli (an artificial mixture of Bangla and Maithili, a language of the Eastern Bihari Group, closely related to BHOJPURI and Magahi). The ancient period of Meithei literature, from the 16th-18th centuries, included political and civic chronicles, legends and creation stories, and botanical descriptions. In the 18th century there was an eclipsing of traditional genres and Meithei literature consisted mostly of translations to and from Bangla. Manipuri poets wrote in Bangla. Bangla was made an additional official language of Manipur and was used as the medium of instruction in schools. The influence of Bangla was so strong that Meithei Mayek, the script originally used for writing Manipuri, was replaced with the Bangla script. Borrowing from Bangla into Manipuri was extensive.

More recently, Manipuri borrowed from English, HINDI and ASSAMESE. English is an obligatory subject through 12th grade, in addition to being one of the official languages of the Manipur state. Hindi is also a required subject until the 8th grade. Hindi and English movies and television programs are popular in Manipur. Through trading and tourism in neighboring Assam, Manipuri also borrowed words from Assamese. Examples of loans are: from Sanskrit *dan* 'donation', from Bangla *ərtha* 'meaning', from Assamese *pukhri* 'tank, pond' and from English *kemera* 'camera'.

Common Words

be big:	čaw-	be good:	phə́-
be long:	saŋ-	be small:	pik-
bird:	učék	dog:	húy
fish:	ŋá	man:	nipa, mí
no:	nətte	sun:	numit, nóŋ
three:	əhum	tree:	u
water:	išiŋ	woman:	nupi
yes:	hóy, mane, čumme		

Example Sentences

(1) *əy* *layrik* *lə́yrukhini*
əy layrik lə́y-lu-khi-ni
I book buy-AWAY.-still-COP
I book will buy there
'I will buy books there.'

(2) *əydi* *yamnə* *pígənbə* *míni*
əy-ti yam-nə pí-kən-pə mí-ni
I-DEL lot-adverb give-repeat-NML man-COP
I a lot always giving man-be
'I am a very generous man.'

(3) *əydi* *Ramnə* *phúniŋŋí*
əy-ti Ram-nə phú-niŋ-í
I-DEL Ram-CONTR beat-wish-DECL
I Ram wish to beat
'It is Ram (not Chaoba) who wants to beat me (over all of you).' or
'It is Ram (not Chaoba) that I (over all of you) want to beat.'

(4) *tebəl* *məthə́ktə* *ləyribə*
tebəl mə-thə́k-tə ləy-li-pə
table NML-top-LOC be-PROG-NML
table on top of being

layriktəgi *wáhəypəreŋsiŋdu* *iyu*
layrik-təgi wáhəypəreŋ-siŋ-tu i-u
book-ABL sentence-PL-DET write-IMP
from the book those sentences write
'Write out the sentences in the book that is on the table.'

Efforts to Preserve, Protect, and Promote the Language

Manipuri, along with English, is a state language of Manipur and is officially recognized as a major Indian language in the Indian constitution. In 1996 the Manipuri legislative assembly commissioned a group of experts to promote the use of Manipuri in government documents, compile a learner's dictionary, and document the major Manipuri social and geographical dialects. The group of experts, the Language Cell, is also interested in the promotion of textbooks in Manipuri as well as in the minority languages of Manipur. The study of the Manipuri language and literature is flourishing at Manipur University in Imphal. Additionally, Professor Anvita Abbi at Jawaharlal Nehru University, Delhi, and Professor K.V. Subbarao at Delhi University both encourage students to engage in descriptive and theoretical work on Tibeto-Burman languages. Several Meithei students have graduated from linguistics programs in Delhi. Manipuri courses are occasionally offered by the Modern Languages Department of Delhi University.

Select Bibliography

Bhat, D.N.S., and M.S. Ningomba. 1997. *Manipuri Grammar*. Munchen: Lincom Europa.

Chelliah, S.L. 1997. *A Grammar of Meithei*. Berlin: Mouton.

DeLancey, S. 1987. "Sino-Tibetan Languages." In *The World's Major Languages*, ed. Bernard Comrie. London: Croom Helm, 797–810.

Grierson, G.A. 1919. *Linguistic Survey of India and the Census of 1911*. Calcutta: Superintendent Government Printing, India. [Reprinted 1967 by Motilal Banarsidass: Delhi, Varanasi, Patna].

Hodson, T.C. 1908. *The Meitheis*. Delhi: B.R. Publishing Corporation.

Matisoff, J. 1991. "Sino-Tibetan Linguistics: Present State and Future Prospects." In *Annual Review of Anthropology*. 20: 469–504.

Pettigrew, R.W. 1912. *Manipuri (Mitei) Grammar*. Allahabad: Pioneer Press.

Primrose, A.J. 1887. *Manipuri Grammar*. Manipur: Government Press.

Sharma, H.B. 1998. "The Role of Borrowing (Loan Words) and its Etymology in Manipuri Dictionary." In *On Compilation of An Advanced Learner's Dictionary. Language Cell Working Paper Series* 2, 204–241, India: The Government of Manipur.

Singh, C.Y. 1984. *Some Aspects of Meiteilon (Manipuri) Syntax*. Unpublished Ph.D. dissertation New Delhi: Jawaharlal Nehru University.

Singh, H.S. 1988. *A Comparative Study of Meiteiron Dialects (Compounding)*. Unpublished M.Phil. dissertation. Imphal: Manipur University.

Singh, K.S., and S. Manoharan. 1993. *Languages and Scripts*. Delhi-Oxford: Anthropological Survey of India, Oxford University Press.

Singh, N.K. 1964. *Manipuri to Manipuri and English Dictionary*. Imphal: Government of Manipur.

Singh, N.N. 1987. *A Meitei Grammar of Roots and Affixes*. Unpublished Ph.D. dissertation. Imphal: Manipur University.

Singh, W.R. 1989. "The Kwatha dialect of Meitei." In *Linguistics of the Tibeto-Burman Area* 12.2: 101–122.

Sen, Sipra. 1992. *Tribes and Castes of Manipur*. New Delhi: Mittal Publications.

Thoudam, P.C. 1980. *Grammatical Sketch of Meiteiron*. Unpublished Ph.D. dissertation. New Delhi: Jawaharlal Nehru University.

Marathi

Franklin C. Southworth

Language Name and Autonym: Marathi (*marāṭʰi*). The name is probably derived from Old Indo-Aryan *mahārāṣṭrī*, a derivative of *mahā-rāṣṭra*, or 'great country'. Because of the existence in early texts of alternate forms such as *marahaṭṭe* and *maragʰaṭṭe*, it is suspected that *mahārāṣṭra* may be a "Sanskritization" or a pre-Indo-Aryan form.

Location: Marathi is the official language of the state of Maharashtra, India (capital: Mumbai, formerly Bombay). The state is one of those formed on a linguistic basis in 1956 and numbers among its population speakers of other languages including KANNADA and TELUGU (both Dravidian languages) near its southern borders, and Khandeshi (Ahirani) in the northern districts of Dhule and Jalgav.

Family: Marathi belongs to the Indo-Aryan subgroup of the Indo-Iranian subfamily of the Indo-European language family.

Related Languages: Most scholars consider Marathi to belong to a "Western" or "Southwestern" regional subgroup of Indo-Aryan, along with GUJARATI and SINHALA. On the other hand, there is evidence to link Marathi with the Eastern group of Indo-Aryan (BANGLA/Bengali, ASSAMESE, ORIYA.). Within Maharashtra, Khandeshi/Ahirani has been considered by some to be a variety of Gujarati. It is probably best regarded as a distinct (nonliterary) language. The situation is different with respect to the dialect continuum known as KONKANI, which is spoken in the coastal strip of Maharashtra known as the Konkan (the districts of Thane, Raigad, Ratnagiri, and Sindhudurg) as well as in Goa, and from there southward in pockets along the coast as far as Trivandrum District, Kerala, in extreme southwest India. In fact, the whole of Marathi-Konkani is best treated diachronically as a single unit of Indo-Aryan, and synchronically as a single dialect continuum, although the names "Marathi" and "Konkani" are used for political reasons. Some of the southern varieties of Konkani are heavily influenced by Dravidian languages.

Dialects: The "standard" literary and educational language of Maharashtra is based on the high-caste/class speech of the Pune-Mumbai region. Apart from the regional varieties mentioned above, the regional speech of Varhad (eastern Maharashtra) known as Varhadi (*varhāḍi*) has some distinctive features, mainly morphological. Varhad, known officially by the SANSKRIT name *Vidarbha*, was part of the Central Provinces in colonial times and shows some links with HINDI. Social dialects form a continuum from this high-caste "standard" to the speech of uneducated rural speakers, with minor regional variants and no particular correlation with specific castes. Katkari, a language spoken by a "tribal" group in the Western Ghats, looks like a very aberrant form of Marathi, and is probably the result of a shift from an earlier unrelated language (of which no direct traces have been found).

Diglossia. Like other South Asian languages such as Hindi and MALAYALAM, the formal and literary varieties of Marathi use a highly Sanskritized vocabulary, eschewing words of ENGLISH and URDU origin that are common in colloquial speech. Some verbal constructions, which would be archaic in conversational Marathi, also occur in written and formal registers. Sanskritization and avoidance of "foreign" words is an old trend in literary Marathi, going back at least to the 15th century.

Number of Speakers: The Census of India 1991 records 41.7 million speakers, making Marathi the fourth-largest Indian language.

Origin and History

Marathi is mentioned as one of the *deśabhāsas* or regional languages in Sanskrit works as early as 500, and poetry in Maharashtri Prakrit (a Middle Indo-Aryan literary language) of the same period shows words characteristic of Marathi. A Sanskrit text of the eighth century quotes words belonging to the language of the *Marahatthe*, which are similar to Old Marathi words. Inscriptions and literary texts in Old Marathi are attested from the 11th century on, and possibly slightly earlier, although the actual manuscripts are of later date. From this period on a number of writers, apparently motivated by a desire to reach the common people, composed religious and other works in Marathi instead of Sanskrit. The *Yādavas* of Devagiri and other local kings patronized Marathi literature. The prose of the *Mānbhāv* (Sanskrit *Mahānubhāva*) sect was written in a near-colloquial style. Later, the poetry of the "poet-saints" seems to have been important in the linguistic unification and expansion of the Marathi area, helping to carry Marathi into the Khandeshi-speaking region and into southern Maharashtra, which was at that time Kannada speaking.

Orthography and Basic Phonology

Marathi is written in the *Devanāgari* (or *Nāgari*) script, a semi-syllabic script that uses diacritical marks for vowels following

Table 1: Consonants

		Labial	Dental	Alveolar	Retroflex	Palatal	Velar
Stops	Voiceless	p	t	c	ṭ	č	k
	Voiceless asp.	p^h	t^h		ṭ^h	č^h	k^h
	Voiced	b	d	j	ḍ	ǰ	g
	Voiced asp.	b^h	d^h	j^h	ḍ^h	ǰ^h	g^h
Fricatives		(f)		s	(ṣ)	š	
Nasals		m	n		ḷ		ŋ
Laterals			l		ṇ		
Flap				r			
Glides		v				y	h

consonants or semivowels. There are special characters for syllable-initial vowels. In the absence of any other vowel, consonants are read with a following *a* (known as the "inherent a"), except: (1) in final position, and even here, certain sequences of consonants (such as *kt, tr*) are read in Marathi with a final (nonphonemic) *a*; (2) in the environment $VC_1\_C_2V$, where C_1C_2 is one of a number of "permitted" clusters. This rule is applied starting from the end of the word; thus, the written sequence *sa-ma-ja-la* 'understood' (Nsg.) is pronounced [samaȷla], while *sa-ma-ja-va-la* 'persuaded' (Nsg.) is pronounced [samȷavla].

Even though vowel length is (mostly) noncontrastive for *i* and *u*, long vowels are written long in monosyllables or final syllables except when followed by consonant sequences; otherwise they are written short, except when representing words with contrastive length borrowed from Sanskrit or other languages; thus, long vowels in *ti* 'she', *tu* 'thou', *tin* 'three', *sun* 'daughter-in-law', *māṇus* 'man', *gaṇit* 'mathematics', *sītā* 'Sita', *sūtra* 'thread'; short in *tilā* 'to her', *tulā* 'to thee', *tine* 'by her', *tuj*^{h}*ā* 'thy', *čitr* 'picture', *k*^{h}*unt* 'stump'.

Segments in parentheses are relatively marginal in Marathi, occurring mostly in loanwords and in some highly constrained phonological environments.

Palatal and alveolar affricates (listed with the stops) tend to be in complementary distribution; except in loanwords, palatals occur before /i/ and /y/, and alveolars occur before other vowels. The loss of *y* has led to contrast in a few cases.

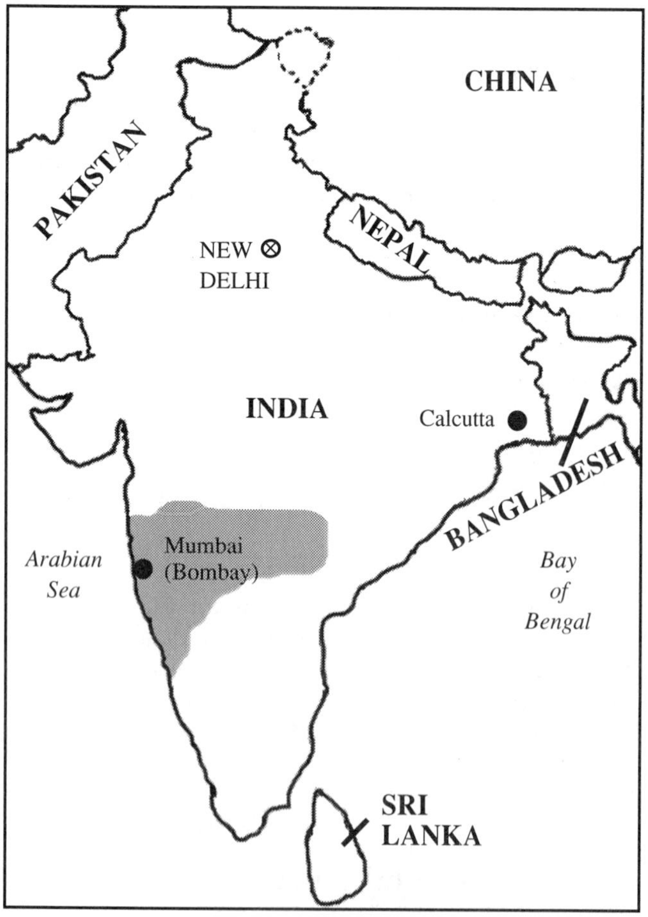

Marathi is the official language of the Indian state of Maharashtra (shaded area).

Table 2: Vowels

	Front	Central	Back
High	i		u
Mid	e	a	o
Low	(æ)	ā	(ɔ)

The vowels /a/ and /ā/ differ in height rather than length. The vowels /i/ and /u/ have long variants [ī] and [ū] that are, for the most part, phonologically conditioned. Length distinctions occur in Sanskrit-derived words in the usage of some highly educated speakers. The vowels /æ/ and /ɔ/ occur only in English-derived words, in the speech of English-educated speakers.

Basic Morphology

Marathi nouns are inflected for gender (masculine, feminine, neuter), number (singular, plural), and case (direct, oblique, locative). Oblique-case forms occur with a following postposition.

Table 3

	Singular			Plural		Gloss
Gender	Direct	Oblique	Locative	Direct	Oblique	
Masc	g^{h}oḍa	g^{h}oḍā-		g^{h}oḍe	g^{h}oḍyā(n)-	'horse'
Fem.	g^{h}oḍi	g^{h}oḍi-		g^{h}oḍyā	g^{h}oḍyā(n)-	'mare'
Neut.	g^{h}oḍa	g^{h}oḍyā-		g^{h}oḍi	g^{h}oḍyā(n)-	'horse'
Masc.	divas	divsā-	divši	divas	divsā(n)-	'day'
Fem.	bahiṇ	bahiṇi-		bahiṇi	bahiṇi(n)-	'sister'
Neut.	g^{h}ar	g^{h}arā-	g^{h}ari	g^{h}ara	g^{h}arā(n)-	'house'

Within each gender, there are several classes of nouns, depending on what segment the direct singular form ends in (see Table 3 above).

Variable adjectives agree with the nouns they precede in gender, number, and case:

h-ā	g^{h}oḍ-ā
this-M/DIR/SG	horse-M/DIR/SG

'this horse'

h-yā	g^{h}oḍ-yā
this-F/DIR/PL	horse-F/DIR/PL

'these mares'

h-yā	ghoḍ-yā-lā
this-N/OBL/SG	horse-N/OBL/SG-to

'to this horse'

t-yā	divš-i
that-M/LOC/SG	day-M/LOC/SG

'on that day'

Personal pronouns distinguish person (first, second, third), number (singular, plural), and case (direct, oblique, possessive, ergative). Additional distinctions are made for each person: there are first-person plural inclusive ('we [including you]') and exclusive ('we [not including you]') pronouns; in the second person, the primary distinction is among formal, neutral, and intimate addressees; and third person pronouns are inflected for gender.

Marathi verbs can be marked for tense in two ways, simple inflection and by use of an auxiliary verb, for example:

Future:	to jā-il	'he will go'
Habitual:	to jā-to	'he goes'
Perfect:	to ge-lā	'he went'
Present:	to jāt(o) āhe	'he is going'
Past:	to jāt hota	'he was going'

There are, in addition, some compound tenses: *gelā āhe* 'has gone, present perfective', *gelā hota* 'had gone, past perfective'.

Marathi has a number of "impersonal" verbs that (from the point of view of western European languages) appear to reverse the relationship between subject and object: ma-lā dud^{h} pāhiȷe (me-to milk want) 'I want milk'.

Marathi has the ergative feature found in Hindi and other Indo-Aryan languages, in which the verb agrees with the object rather than the subject in the perfect, and in compound tenses based on the perfect:

tyā-ne	āmbā	k^{h}āl-l-ā
he-ERGATIVE	mango/M/SG	eat-PERF-3M/SG

'He ate a mango.'

tyā-ne	miṭ^{h}āi	k^{h}āl-l-i
he-ERGATIVE	sweet/F/SG	eat-PERF-3F/SG

'He ate a sweet.'

ti-ne	āmbā	k^{h}āl-l-ā
she-ERGATIVE	mango/M/SG	eat-PERF-3M/SG

'She ate a mango.'

An unusual feature of Marathi among Indo-Aryan languages is the occurrence of numerous negative verbs: *nako* 'not wanted', *nasṇe* 'to be not', *navhe* 'is not', *naye* 'should not', *nalage* 'is not fitting'.

Basic Syntax

Marathi has Subject-Object-Verb as the unmarked word order in sentences (see the examples above). Adjectives generally precede the nouns they modify, and postpositions are used to the exclusion of prepositions.

Sentences with the same subject can be conjoined by means of a participle ending *-un*:

bass	g^{h}e-un	posṭā	pāši	utr-un	čāl-at	yā
bus	take-PART.	post office	near	descend-PART.	foot-on	come

'Take a bus, get down near the post office, and come on foot.'

Marathi has two types of relative constuctions. One uses the relative pronoun jo/ǰi/je 'who, which':

ȷo	māṇus	kāl	ā-lā	hotā
who	man	yesterday	come-PERF	had

'The man who came yesterday...'

The other relative construction, more commonly used in conversation, uses verbal participles instead of relative pronouns:

kāl ā-lel-ā māṇus
yesterday come-PAST PART.-M/SG man
'The man who came yesterday...'

Contact with Other Languages

Apart from lexical borrowings (see below), Marathi (along with Gujarati and SINDHI) has borrowed from Dravidian a distinction between exclusive and inclusive in the first-person plural pronouns, though this distinction is expressed with inherited Indo-Aryan surface forms: *āmhi* 'we (excl.)': *āpaṇ* 'we (incl.)'. A number of syntactic constructions are borrowed from Dravidian or other pre-Indo-Aryan sources; examples are: (1) negative verbs (noted above) probably from Kannada or other Dravidian sources; (2) the second relative construction mentioned above; (3) a third relative construction, perhaps the most common in colloquial speech: *kāl ālā hotā to māṇus* (yesterday came-past was, that man) 'the man who had come yesterday'; (4) clause-final question particle. Direct evidence of early contact with speakers of Dravidian languages is provided by the occurrence of Dravidian place-name suffixes (most notably the suffix *-v(a)li* as in *Borivli, Kandivli*), found especially in western Maharashtra and forming a continuum with similar suffixes in the Dravidian south. The area in which this suffix is found extends northward into Gujarat and probably beyond.

Marathi has enriched its lexicon with material from PERSIAN, ARABIC, TURKISH (these three from the language of Muslim rulers), PORTUGUESE, English, and Kannada and other Dravidian languages, as well as Sanskrit and Prakrit.

From Sanskrit/Prakrit: *prāṇi* 'animal', *kāraṇ* 'because', *pakśi* 'bird', *rakt* 'blood', *śvās* 'breath', *divas* 'day', *kutrā* 'dog', *hruday* 'heart', *puruś* 'man, male', *anek* 'many', *mās* 'meat', *parvat* 'mountain', *nadi* 'river', *samudr* 'sea', *ākāś* 'sky', *hima* 'snow', *viār* 'thought, intention', *sang* 'with'
From Persian: *janāvar* 'animal', *k^harāb* 'bad', *arbi* 'fat, grease', *kam* 'few, less', *k^hup* 'very, much/many', *lāl* 'red', *rastā* 'road', *dur* 'far', *barp^h* 'ice', *garam* 'hot'
From Arabic: *śikār* 'hunting', *barobar* 'alike', *jangal* 'forest'
From Kannada (or other Dravidian languages): *ḍoka* 'head', *$ṭ^h$āuk* 'known', *ḍāvā* 'left' (or Austric?), *āi* 'mother'
From Portuguese: *pagār* 'pay, salary', *mistri* 'artisan'
From English: *hɔṭel/haṭel* 'restaurant', *lɔǰ* 'lodging house', *jankśan* 'road junction', *sāykal* 'bicycle', *moṭār* 'motorcar', *ɔfiss/hap^{h}is* 'office'

Common Words

man:	māṇus	small:	lahān
woman:	bāi	yes:	ho
water:	pāṇi	no:	nāhi
sun:	sūry	good:	čānglā
three:	tin	bird:	pakši
fish:	māsā	dog:	kutrā
big:	moṭʰā	tree:	ǰʰāḍ
long:	lāmb		

Example Sentences

(1) mi visr-un ge-l-o.
I forget-PARTICIPLE go-PERFECT-1M/SG
'I completely forgot.'

(2) ma-lā čahā nako.
I/OBL-to tea unwanted-3M/SG
'I don't want tea.'

(3) tu-lā pustak sāpaḍ-l-a kā.
you/2SG/OBL-to book find-PERF.-3M/SG QUESTION
'Did you find the book?'

Efforts to Preserve, Protect, and Promote the Language

Marathi speakers tend to have relatively high levels of language loyalty (though not excessively high for the South Asian context). The quality of contemporary Marathi writing and the language's long literary history are sources of pride for educated Maharashtrians. Many publishing houses in Pune and Mumbai are devoted to producing the work of Marathi poets and writers, and it is not unusual for even English-educated Maharashtrians to publish memoirs and essays in Marathi. The State Board for Literature and Culture has produced numerous literary and linguistic studies. For Konkani, various organizations are active in Maharashtra and Goa, and the *Konkani Bhasha Samsthan* in Cochin is active in promoting educational and cultural activities there.

Select Bibliography

Berntsen, Maxine. 1978. "Social Stratification in the Speech of Phaltan." In *Indian Linguistics* 39: 233–51.

Deshpande, Madhav M. 1979. *Sociolinguistic Attitudes in India: An Historical Reconstruction.* Ann Arbor, Michigan: Karoma Publishers.

Feldhaus, Anne. 1983. *The Religious System of the Mahānubhāva Sect: The Mahānubhāva Sūtraphāṭha.* Manohar, Delhi.

Gumperz, John J., and Robert Wilson 1971. "Creolization without pidginization: a case from the Indo-Aryan/Dravidian border." In Dell Hymes (ed.), *Pidginization and Creolization of Languages,* pp. 151–67. Cambridge, at the University Press.

Kavadi, Naresh B., and F.C. Southworth. 1964. *Spoken Marathi: First-Year Intensive Course.* Revised edition. University of Pennsylvania Press, Philadelphia.

Master, Alfred. 1964. *A Grammar of Old Marathi.* Oxford: Clarendon Press.

Nadkarni, Mangesh. 1975. "Bilingualism and Syntactic Change in Konkani." In *Language* 51(3): 672–83.

Southworth, Franklin C. 1969. "Marathi." In *Current Trends in Linguistics: Vol. V. Linguistics in South Asia* (ed. M.B. Emeneau *et al.*, Series Editor: T.A. Sebeok). Mouton & Co.

____. 1971. "Detecting Prior Creolization: An Analysis of the Historical Origins of Marathi." In Hymes 1971: 255–74.

____. 1976. "The verb in Marathi-Konkani." In *International Journal of Dravidian Linguistics* 5(2): 298–326.

MAYA

Gary Bevington

Language Name and Autonym: Maya. **Alternate:** *Mayan.* The great Maya civilization flourished in southern Mexico, Guatemala, Belize, and Honduras, beginning around 200 B.C., with the Classic Maya civilization spanning the period A.D. 300–900. Its people presumably spoke languages antecedent to several of the modern Mayan languages, and the emerging consensus is that the epigraphic material reflects primarily antecedents of Chol and Yucatec. This chapter describes Yucatec Maya.

Location: Yucatan Peninsula including the entire Mexican states of Yucatan and Quintana Roo, and all but the southeastern corner of Campeche. Also found in the Central American countries of Belize (northern region) and Guatemala (Peten region).

Family: Member of the Yucatecan branch of the Mayan family. The Mayan language family is made up of five branches comprising about 30 language varieties: Yucatecan, Huastecan, Cholan-Tzeltalan, Kanjobalan-Chujean, and Quichean-Mamean.

Related Languages: Of the approximately 30 Mayan languages, those with the most speakers include Quiché (the largest number of speakers of any Mayan language), Cakchiquel, Kekchi, and Mam (all in Guatemala). In highland Chiapas, Tzeltal and Tzotzil are the best known; in Veracruz it is Huastec (an isolate), and in Chiapas it is Chol.

Dialects: Although Yucatec Maya has a large number of speakers distributed over a large geographic area, there is relatively little variation in speech forms. Further study may reveal some patterns in variation but the little social and regional variations that exist are not prominent.

Number of Speakers: The Mayan family has a total speakership of about 3 million. The 1990 Mexican census figures show that 713,520 citizens claimed to be speakers of Yucatec Maya. The census shows that the number of people monolingual in Yucatec Maya has decreased from 15.1 percent of the total in 1970 to 7.7 percent in 1990.

Origin and History

Maya is an indigenous New World language, spoken in essentially the same area today that it was at the time of the Spanish conquest in the 16th century. The Mayans possessed a hieroglyphic writing system, one of only two known in the New World. The other is the so-called *La Mojarra* (or 'epi-Olmec') script that survives in just two texts. (Although similar to and related to the Maya, its language base is apparently Mixe-Zoque.)

In 1512 a small group of Spaniards was shipwrecked off the coast of the Yucatan Peninsula and two men, Jerónimo de Aguilar and Gonzalo Guerrero, survived and lived among the Maya. Aguilar joined Cortés and his army when they passed through on the way to the conquest of Mexico and served as an interpreter to that expedition (1519). Later in Tabasco, Cortés picked up an Indian woman, the famous Doña Marina or Malinche, who had learned Maya although her native tongue was NAHUATL, the language of the Aztecs. Through the combination of Aguilar and Malinche, Cortés was able to communicate with the objects of his conquest. The other Spaniard, Guerrero, stayed with the Maya and helped them resist early Spanish attempts at conquest. He married the daughter of a Mayan chief, and their children are considered the beginning of the Mexican tradition of *mestizaje*, 'mixing' of indigenous and Hispanic peoples and cultures.

In 1517 the explorer Hernández de Córdoba landed in the northeast corner of the Yucatan Peninsula. The locals, misunderstanding the Spaniards' attempts to ascertain the name of the land, replied *ka otoche* ('it's our home'), and the place became known as Cabo Catoche, *cabo* being SPANISH for 'cape'.

After the conquest of the peninsula by Francisco de Montejo the Younger in 1542, the Franciscans arrived to convert the people to Christianity. The Franciscans learned Maya and developed an orthography using LATIN letters that they taught to the sons of the old preconquest elite, along with Spanish and Latin. The earliest known Maya document in the Latin alphabet dates from 1557, and there is a continuous written tradition in it from that time through the 19th century, which is referred to as Colonial or Classical Maya. Substantial changes in vocabulary and some in grammar distinguish it from Modern Maya, roughly the language of the 20th century.

The Mayan civilization gave rise to the most important native writing system of the New World, Hieroglyphic Maya. The epigraphic record is largely from the Classic period (300–900) and is found in a large number of archeological sites principally in the south (Palenque, Tikal, Copan, Quiriguá) and also in the north (Chichén Itzá, Uxmal, Cobá). There are two main sources of the written language: the stone inscriptions of the ceremonial centers (stelae, lintels and tablets) and screenfold codices on sized bark from fig trees (*amatl*). Minor sources of Hieroglyphic Maya include painted pottery and incised

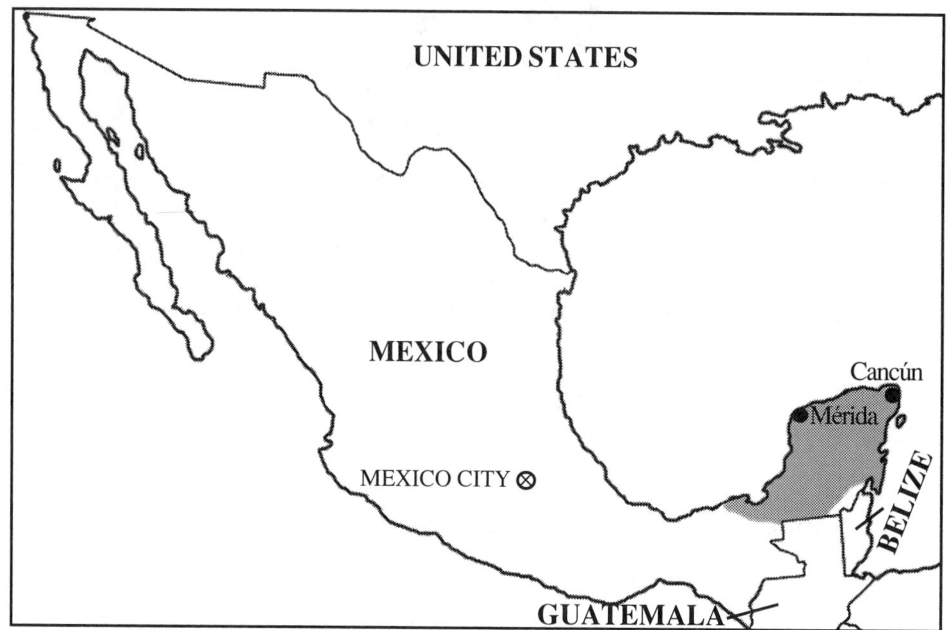

Yucatec Maya is spoken in the Mexican states of Yucatan, Quintana Roo and all but the the southeastern corner of Campeche (shaded area). It is also spoken in certain regions in the countries of Belize and Guatemala.

materials such as bone. Four codices, or books, also survive, three of which were taken to Europe, apparently quite soon after the conquest. They are now in Madrid, Paris, and Dresden respectively. The fourth, the Grolier Codex, was discovered in this century and is in Mexico City. Only the Dresden Codex is clearly preconquest, perhaps dating to the 13th century.

The system of calendrics and dating in the hieroglyphics was quickly understood with the help of information provided in *Relación de las cosas de Yucatán,* written by an early Franciscan, Diego de Landa. However, the balance of the material remained largely undeciphered until a series of breakthroughs by scholars beginning slowly in the 1950s and then picking up momentum in the 1970s. Interpretation and increasingly transliteration and translation of many of the hieroglyphic texts is still under way.

The notational system of Hieroglyphic Maya is a complex mixture of more than 800 ideographic, logographic, and syllabic elements. The syllabic elements make Maya hieroglyphics a true writing system (a direct representation of a language). The atomic signs (glyphs) represented a consonant followed by a vowel and were placed together in blocks to make words. Thus the sign

represented the syllable *chu* and appears in glyph block such as

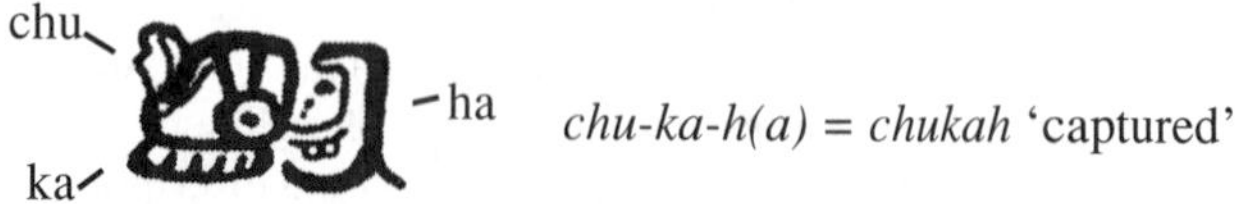

chu-ka-h(a) = *chukah* 'captured'

The reading order of the symbols within the block is basically top to bottom and left to right. Because many Mayan words end in a consonant, the final vowel (often the same or similar quality to the preceding vowel) of the last sign could be "silent" (like "silent e" in ENGLISH) as in the example above.

Using the same sign as the final one we have:

u- ku chu *u-ku-ch(u)* = *u kuch* 'his burden'

and

yo- to chu *yo-to-ch(u)* = *yotoch* 'his home'

The important conclusion is that Maya has a very long written history, more or less continuous for about 1,500 years, far longer than any other New World language and indeed longer than many European languages, including English.

Orthography and Basic Phonology

There are two broad alphabetic traditions for Maya. One is the colonial alphabet established by the Franciscans after 1542 and modified into several variants. The colonial alphabet was used exclusively until the middle of this century. Then experimentation began with a modern alphabet, to be based either on the idea of a unified alphabetic system for the indigenous languages of Mexico, including many non-Mayan languages, or on the idea of a pan-Mayan alphabet for all the Mayan languages, including those spoken outside of Mexico.

It is relatively easy to establish whether a text is in colonial or modern orthography by looking for the presence or absence of the letter *c* (except in the digraph *ch*). All colonial variants use *c* invariantly as the plain velar stop contrasting with *k* as

Table 1: Consonants

		Labial	Dental	Alveo-palatal	Velar	Glottal
Stops	Voiceless	p	t		k	
	Voiced Glottalized	b				
	Voiceless Glottalized	p'	t'		k'	
Fricatives			s	x		h
Affricates	Voiceless		ts	ch		
	Glottalized		ts'	ch'		
Nasals		m	n			
Resonants			l, r			
Glides		w		y		

the glottalized velar stop, while modern variants eschew the *c* because of the bivalent pronunciation associated with it in Spanish in favor of *k* for the plain and *k'* for the glottalized stop.

For the monumental Maya dictionary of 1980, the modern alphabet approved at the time by the Maya Academy in Mérida was used, and this is the alphabet used herein.

The differences among the colonial variants center on the use of diacritics and ad hoc symbols on the one hand, or the apostrophe and digraphs for the glottalized sounds on the other. Vowel quantity is usually poorly represented in colonial writings. Some of the most recent modern variants have reintroduced some colonial notations such as *dz* for *ts'*. Maya place and family names are still spelled with colonial spelling in Mexico but are sometimes mispronounced. For example, *Xcacel*, a resort development on the Caribbean coast is pronounced /ška-sel/ and the family name *Cen* is pronounced /sen/, even by the Maya, at least for public purposes.

The resonant /r/ is a marginal phoneme, occurring in a small number of native words, where it does not contrast with /l/, as well as in many Spanish loanwords.

In addition to the sounds listed above, Maya also has *d*, *g*, and *f* in Spanish loanwords.

The sounds marked with ' are glottalic pressure sounds, produced with a glottal closure accompanying their main constriction.

Following the spelling of premodern Spanish, *x* represents an alveopalatal fricative /š/ as in English "shoe".

Table 2: Vowels

	Front	Central	Back
High	i		u
Mid	e		o
Low		a	

Each vowel quality occurs in four contrasting forms: short (*a*), long (*aa*), interglottalized (*a'a*), and postglottalized (*a'*). The long vowels also occur with contrasting rising and falling tones.

Basic Morphology

Nouns in Maya are not marked for gender or for case. Nouns are marked as definite by a combination of the article *le* preceding the noun and a deictic particle following it: *peek'* 'dog', *le peek'a'* 'this dog', *le peek'o'* 'that dog'.

Nouns are marked as plural by the suffix *-o'ob*. This suffix is optional and usually omitted in contexts where the plurality is evident, either linguistically (after quantifiers) or physically: looking at a pack of dogs, and wanting to bring this to someone's attention, a Maya would say *peek'*.

There are two sets of clitic pronouns, generally referred to in grammatical treatments as set A and set B. In the examples below, *in* and *a* are A pronouns, and *-ech* and *-en* are B pronouns:

tan in hats'-ik-ech
AUX I hit-TRANS-you
'I am hitting you.'

tan a hats'-ik-en
AUX you hit-TRANS-me
'You are hitting me.'

Maya verbs are morphologically marked as transitive, intransitive, or passive and occur in one of three aspects: incompletive, completive, or subjunctive. Both subjects and objects are marked by means of pronominal clitics according to a split ergative system. For incompletive aspect, agreement is transitive (intransitive arguments use the same clitic set as transitive subjects), while agreement is ergative for completive and subjunctive aspects (intransitive arguments use the same clitic set as transitive objects).

Thus, *tan in bin* 'I am going' uses an A pronoun (*in*) because it is in incompletive aspect. In contrast, *bin-en* 'I went' uses a B pronoun (*-en*) because it is in completive aspect.

Aspect is marked by a combination of affix, such as the transitive incompletive *-ik-* in the examples above; auxiliary; and choice of pronoun set. The following sentence should be compared with *tan in hats'ikech* 'I am hitting you':

t-in	hats'-ah-ech
AUX-I	hit-COMP/TRANS-you

'I hit you.'

The difference between the present reference of incompletive aspect and the past reference of completive aspect is indicated both by the change in auxiliary (*t-* versus *tan)* and by the change in aspect affix (*-ah-* versus *-ik-).*

Basic Syntax

Maya is a VOS language, but arguments are frequently placed before the verb for discourse purposes, for example, topicalization or focus.

Maya is generally a head-initial language although adjectives precede the nouns that they modify. There is only one true preposition, *ti'*, expressing both location and direction. Other apparent prepositions are constructed out of nominal elements:

t-u	taan-il	le	nah-o'
in-its	front-POSS	the	house-this

'in front of the house'

y-et-el	le	maak-o'ob-o'
its-accompaniment-POSS	the	person-PL-this

'with the people'

Direction of motion, particularly away from a point of reference, is expressed by various verbs rather than by prepositions.

Negation in Maya is expressed by a negative particle *ma'* preceding the verb and an extensive set of negative indefinites incorporating the prefix *mix.*

ma'	t'u	y-il-ah	mix-ba'al	mix-maak
NEG	AUX	he-3-see-COMP/TRANS	NEG-thing	NEG-person

'Nobody saw anything.'

Contact with Other Languages

Maya contains a small number of Nahuatl loans from pre- conquest contact with the peoples of Mexico.

There are a small number of very early loans from Spanish that are not readily identifiable as such. Spanish borrowings have been used increasingly with a concomitant loss of native vocabulary. Modern spoken Maya uses many Spanish words and expressions, and frequent code switching is prevalent in the speech of most bilinguals. This kind of Maya is referred to as *mestizo maya.* There is also a largely fictive entity called *maya puro*, which avoids, to the extent possible, gratuitous Spanish and attempts to bring back native terms that have fallen into disuse such as the native numeration above four.

In the other direction, there is one English word of possible Maya origin, although the etymology is not certain: the word 'shark' may be from Maya *xok.*

From Nahuatl: *iipil* 'native woman's dress' (<*huipilli*); *xiw* 'herb' (<*xiuitl*)

From Spanish: *wakax* 'cattle' (<*vacas*), *kaax* 'chicken' (<*castellano*)

Common Words

man:	winik	small:	chichan, mehen
woman:	ko'olel	yes:	he'ele'*
water:	ha'	no:	ma'
sun:	k'iin	good:	uts, ma'aloob
three:	oxp'el	bird:	ch'iich'
fish:	kay	dog:	peek'
big:	nohoch	tree:	che'
long:	chowak		

Example Sentences

(1)

Hwebes-ak	bin-en	Saki'
Thursday-preceding	go-I	Valladolid

y-et-el	inw-atan.
her-accompaniment-POSS	my wife

'Last Thursday I went to Valladolid with my wife.'

(2)

Ba'ax	k-a	w-a'al-ik?
what	AUX-you	you-say-COMP/TRANS

'What do you say?' (greeting)

(3)

Dyos	bó'ot-ik.
God	pay-TRANS.INCOMP.

'Thank you.' (literally, 'God pays it.')

Efforts to Preserve, Protect, and Promote the Language

Efforts to promote Maya in Mexico are modest at best. Besides the Maya Academy, there is also a system of so-called bilingual schools. These four-year schools are located only in the most remote areas with a substantial monolingual Maya population. Despite the name, the goal of the instructional program is for students to make a transition from Maya to Spanish. Literacy skills are taught in Maya, usually by means of a single primer, and students are then taught to read Spanish. There are plans to teach content, such as social studies, in Maya but as yet no texts exist.

There is very little public presentation of the language. A few agricultural notices are the only signs in Maya. There are few books, and attempts to launch Maya periodicals have been unsuccessful. There is no television and only a minuscule amount of radio broadcasting in the language.

Nevertheless, Maya remains the dominant spoken language of most of the rural peasantry and a portion of the urban proletariat in traditional Maya areas. People speak Maya freely and openly anywhere they choose throughout the peninsula, although one is careful never to address someone in Maya who might not speak it or wish to speak it.

While Maya is not endangered in the short term, its long term prospects are perhaps somewhat bleaker. Negative pres-

*There is no simple way of giving affirmation in Maya. *He'ele'* means roughly 'that's the way it will be'.

sures include the dominance of Spanish in the educational system, the heavy migration from other parts of Mexico—particularly of middle-class technocrats from the capital—and the lure of the Anglophone modern material culture, or at least its Mexican variant.

Select Bibliography

Barrera Vasquez, Alfredo, *et al.* 1980. *Diccionario maya Cordemex: maya-español, español-maya.* Merida: Ediciones Cordemex.

Bevington, Gary. 1995. *Maya for Travelers and Students: A Guide to Language and Culture in Yucatan.* Austin: University of Texas Press.

Bricker, Victoria, Eleuterio Po'ot Yah, and Ofelia Dzul de Po'ot. 1998. *A Dictionary of the Maya Language as Spoken in Hocabá, Yucatán.* Salt Lake City, Utah: the University of Utah Press.

Coe, Michael D. 1992. *Breaking the Maya Code.* New York: Thames and Hudson.

Harris, John F., and Stephen K. Stearns. 1992. *Understanding Maya Inscriptions: A Hieroglyph Handbook.* Philadelphia: The University Museum of Archaeology and Anthropology.

Mende

David J. Dwyer

Language Name: Mende. **Alternates:** *Mendi, Boumpe, Hulo/Huro, Kossa/Kos(s)o.*

Location: A large part of the southern half of Sierra Leone and also spoken to a limited extent in adjacent border areas of Liberia.

Family: The Southwestern Mande (SWM) group of the Mande subbranch of the Niger-Congo branch of the Niger-Kordofanian language family.

Related Languages: Mende is very closely related to Loko (spoken in northern Sierra Leone) and Bandi (Liberia), so much so that they could be called dialects. Mende is also closely related to two other SWM languages, Lorma and Kpelle. Among the other Mande languages (some 27 in all) are: Bamana (BAMBARA), Malinke, Soninke, Sembla, Bobo, and Mano.

Dialects: While Mende represents a fairly homogeneous language, two dialects are often mentioned: Kpa Mende, spoken in the western area, and *Kɔɔ* spoken in the eastern area with the town of Kenema being the approximate point of division. While recognized as dialects, their differences are minor.

Number of Speakers: 1–1.5 million.

Origin and History

The Southwestern Mande languages, to which Mende belongs, currently occupy both the savanna-forest borderland and forested (historically at least) areas of southern Sierra Leone, northern/western Liberia, and southwestern Guinea. The movement into the forest area is considered more recent, having begun at least 500 years ago. This movement may have been in response to changing environmental conditions (declining rainfall), to changing technology (the development of rice agriculture and iron tools), and to changing economic conditions (the appearance of European traders on the coast), or some combination of the three. The name "Mende" does not appear in pre-1700 historical accounts, and its emergence may have been related to the Mane invasions in the mid-16th century that displaced some of the West Atlantic–speaking peoples from the area now occupied by the Mende.

Orthography and Basic Phonology

The majority of Mende literature has been published by the Provincial Literature Bureau in Bo, Sierra Leone. Consequently, this orthography is considered to represent the standard, even though it does not represent lexical tone. Most of the alternative orthographies have been developed by linguists and language teachers to present the intricacies of this tonal system for analytical or pedagogical purposes.

The sequences *kp* and *gb* represent doubly articulated stops, with simultaneous labial and velar closure. *Ny* is a palatal nasal, like *ñ* in SPANISH *piñata* and the *ni* sequence in ENGLISH "onion".

The prenasalized voiced stops *mb, nd, nj, ng,* and *ngb* act as units in the phonology of Mande especially with regard to initial consonant alternations. In each case, the nasal is homorganic to the following stop: *nj* is [ñj] and *ng* is [ŋg].

Mande consonants participate in a well-developed system of initial consonant alternations. When prenasalized stops, voiceless stops, and fricatives are not the first element in certain nominal constructions, they weaken, as shown below:

Voiceless		Prenasalized	
Strong	Weak	Strong	Weak
p	w	mb	b
f	v		
t	l	nd	l
s	j	nj	y
k	g	ng	y or w
kp	gb	ngb	gb

Mende has a rule of vowel assimilation, in which nonfront vowels usually become front before the specific suffix *-í*: *u* becomes *i*, *o* becomes *e*, and *ɔ* and *a* becomes *ɛ*.

Table 1: Vowels

	Front	Central	Back
High	i		u
High-Mid	e		o
Low-Mid	ɛ		ɔ
Low		a	

Tone. Mende has four basic tones, illustrated here on the vowel *e*: *é* high tone, *è* low tone, *ê* falling tone, *ě* polarized tone. (Tones, while extremely important in the language, are not represented in the orthography.)

An important phenomenon affecting Mende tones is "downstep". In sequences of high tone-low tone-high tone, the second high tone is lower than the first, and it is said to be downdrifted. In some cases, the intervening low tone has been

Table 2: Consonants

		Labial	Dental	Palatal	Velar	Labio-velar	Glottal
Stops	Voiceless	p	t		k	kp	
	Voiced	b	d		g	gb	
	Prenasalized	mb	nd	nj	ng	ngb	
Fricatives	Voiceless	f	s				h
	Voiced	v		j			
Nasals		m	n	ny		ŋ	
Resonants			l				
Glides				y		w	

lost, leading to a sequence of high tone-lower high tone. In such cases, the lower high tone is said to be "downstepped", and is marked with an apostrophe before the downstepped high tone in the following example, *Nyá yɛ̀-'í* (H H'H) 'my water'.

There are other rules affecting tone realization. For instance, a polarizing tone is realized as a low tone when it is followed by a high tone, and by a high tone when it is followed by a low tone and at the end of an utterance.

In noun compounds, the tones of all elements (morphemes) except the first one become low.

Basic Morphology

Mende, like other Mande languages, lacks a gender or noun-class system along with an agreement system depending on noun-class membership. Neither is there a case system. Pluralization is marked for noun phrases as a whole, not for the noun head:

ndópò	nyàndɛ̀	í	nà	sìà
girl	nice	SPECIFIC	that	PLURAL

'those nice girls'

The precise expression of possession in Mende depends on the nature of the object possessed. Mende possessives fall into three categories: kinship, body parts, and other.

Type	Example	Meaning	Noun base
Kinship	nyá njé-'í	'my mother'	njě
Body part	nyá wómbì-í	'my knee'	ngómbì
Other	nyá wùlì-í	'my tree'	ngúlú

Kinship possession involves nothing more than juxtaposition of the possessive pronoun *nyá* with the "possessed" noun; body part possession involves change of the initial consonant *ng* to *w*, in accord with the consonant alternations described above; and other possession involves, in addition to the consonant change, change of the tones on the possessed nouns to low tone, as if it were a nominal compound.

Mende subject pronouns have coalesced with various following morphemes, giving a well-developed array of personal pronouns, including distinct sets for negative sentences, future-tense sentences, future-tense negatives, and others.

	Base	Negative	Future Neg.	Possessive	Emphatic
1sg	ngí	ngî	ngɛ́ɛ̀	nyá	nyáá'á
2sg	bí	bî	bɛ́ɛ̀	bí	bíá'á
3sg	ì	ì	ɛ̀	à	tá'á
1pl	mŭ	múù	mɛ́ɛ̀	mŭ	mùá'á
2pl	wŭ	wúù	wɛ́ɛ̀	wŭ	wùá'á
3pl	tŭ	tî	tɛ́ɛ̀	tĭ	tìá'á

Mende verbs do not agree with their subjects in person, number, or gender. Neither are verbs inflected for tense. Tense is expressed through a combination of postverbal particles and choice of subject pronoun. For example, present tense verbs take subject pronouns from the emphatic set, followed by *'lɔ́*, and are followed by the suffix *-mà*.

In contrast, negative present tense verbs take subject pronouns from the negative set followed by the particle *ì*, and have no postverbal particle. Besides the present tense postverbal particle *-mà*, there is a positive emphatic particle *lɔ́* that follows the verb in nonnegative past and future tense sentences, a past tense suffix *-nì*, a perfect suffix *-ngɔ̀*, and a stative suffix *-ngà*.

Basic Syntax

Mende sentences are normally in SOV order; adverbial elements may follow the verb. As noted above, there is no obligatory subject-verb agreement in Mende. However, anaphoric pronouns may occur between the subject and verb phrase:

hìíndò-í	ì	lí-nì	pɛ́ɛ́-bù	lɔ́
man-SPECIFIC	he:BASE	go-PAST	house-in	EMPHATIC

'That man went home.'

Basic word order can be altered from SOV through the use of emphatic markers:

nɔ̀nì-í-jí-sìà-mìà	mú-à	tì	lɔ́lí	à
bird-SPEC-THIS-PLU-EMPH	we-FUT	them:BASE	call	to

yùbɛ́-í
vulture-SPEC
'These birds are called vultures.'

The Mende negative marker *ì* follows the subject and precedes the verb phrase. As noted above, this marker coalesces with preceding subject pronouns. In addition, the emphatic particle *lɔ́* does not occur in negative sentences.

Contact with Other Languages

Mende, being an important lingua franca of Southern Sierra Leone, has both influenced and been influenced by surrounding languages. Turay in one of the few published analyses of such contact demonstrates that Temne, the major language of northern Sierra Leone, has acquired a large number of words from Mende, particularly in the area of "secret societies" known as *Bondo* and *Poro*. (The following examples are from Turay, 1978: 58.)

Mende

sówó	high official in Bondo or Poro
pàlî	inner part of poro bush

Temne

ù-sókó	1. ordinary member of Poro
	2. high official in Bondo
à-pàlî	grave for Poro or Bondo official.

It is also likely that Mende has influenced Krio, an ENGLISH-based creole language spoken as a first language on the Sierra Leone peninsula and as a lingua franca throughout the country. Many Krio words containing the vowel *ɛ* are cognate English words containing the diphthong *ay*.

Krio	English	English Phonemic
rɛs	'rice'	/rays/
wɛf	'wife'	/wayf/
lɛk	'like'	/layk/

This may well reflect the adoption of the Mende rule (see vowels) in which *a* becomes *ɛ* before *i*. In addition, Krio, like Mende, marks the present continuous using a locative construction.

Krio	Mende
i de pan wɔk	tá'á yèngè-má
he there on work	he is work-on
'He is working'	'He is working'

PORTUGUESE, ARABIC, Temne, and Manding have contributed to the lexicon of Mende, but the largest source of borrowed words is English, primarily through Krio. In addition to borrowing, Mende makes extensive use of nominal compounding to capture new meanings: *hálé-wɛ́lɛ̀* (hh-hl) 'medicine house' = 'hospital'; *hálé-mɔ̂* 'doctor'.

Mende is known to have contributed significantly to Gullah, an English-based Creole of the Sea Islands of South Carolina and Georgia.

Common Words

man:	hìíndò	woman:	nyàhâ
water:	nja	sun:	fóló
three:	sàwá	fish:	nyɛ
big:	wáá	long:	kúhà
small:	ngóló	yes:	mm
no:	m'm	good:	nyàndě
bird:	ŋɔní	dog:	ngílà

Example Sentences

(1) nyá ló-ngɔ̀ ngí lì pɛ́ɛ́-bù.
My want-STATIVE I:BASE go house-in
'I want to go home.'

(2) Ngáà lápí lɔ́ ngí téé.
I:FUTURE swim EMPH I:BASE it:cross
'I will swim across it.'

(3) nyáá-'á kùlɛ̀-í-ná yéyá-mà nyá-njé-và.
I-EMPH cloth-SPEC-that buy-on my-mother-for
'I am buying that cloth for my mother.'

Efforts to Preserve, Protect, and Promote the Lanugage

Mende is one of the five official languages of Sierra Leone; the others are Temne, Kono, Limba and Krio. Mende is a major lingua franca (particularly in the area of commerce) in the southern half of Sierra Leone. In some communities, it has even replaced other languages (e.g., Vai) as the first language of the community. In this area, Mende also competes with two other linguae francae: Krio and English. Although there is little literature beyond the publications of the literacy-oriented Bunumbu Press of Bo in Sierra Leone, there are plans to expand publishing in Mende.

Select Bibliography

Dwyer, D. 1974. "The Historical Development of Southwestern Mande Consonants." In *Studies in African Languages*, 5: 59–93.

____. 1978. "What sort of a tone language is Mende?" In *Studies in African Linguistics* 9: 167–208.

____. 1985. "The Evolutionary Morphology of Southwestern Mande Definite Articles." In *Current Approaches to African Linguistics*, ed. G. Dimmendaal, 149–70. Dordrecht: Foris Publishers.

Innes. G . 1962. *A Mende Grammar*. London: MacMillan.

____. 1969. *A Mende-English Dictionary*. London: Cambridge University Press.

Spears, R.A. 1967. *Basic Course in Mende*. Evanston, Ill: Northwestern University.

____. 1970. "Toward a Mende Lexicon." In *Journal of West African Languages* 7: 15–28.

Turay, A.K. 1978. "Language Contact: Mende and Temne: A Case Study." In *Afr. M.*, 55–73.

Minangkabau

Ismet Fanany

Language Name: Minangkabau. **Autonyms:** *Bahaso Minang, Bahaso Awak, Bahaso Padang.*

Location: The Indonesian province of West Sumatra with groups of speakers as far north as Padang Sidempuan in the province of North Sumatra, as far east as Bangkinang and Kuantan in the province of Riau, and as far south as Mount Kerinci, which forms the border with speakers of Rejang Lebong. Further, significant Minang-speaking communities are found in the Sumatran cities of Bengkulu, Curup, Lubuklinggau, Lubukjambi, Muarobungo, Bangkinang, and Pekanbaru, where Minang speakers are estimated to make up as much as 65 percent of the population. Large communities of Minangkabau speakers also reside in most major Indonesian cities, including Jakarta, Bandung, Surabaya, Medan, Ujungpandang, and Palembang, as well as in the Malaysian state of Negeri Sembilan which was originally settled by migrants from Minangkabau and whose descendants still speak a Minang dialect.

Family: Minangkabau is a Malayic language in the Western Malayo–Polynesian subfamily of the Austronesian family.

Related Languages: Varieties of MALAY, including standard Bahasa INDONESIA, Bahasa Malaysia, Bahasa Melayu (spoken in Singapore and Brunei), and other Sumatran languages such as Bahasa Kerinci and Bahasa Kubu, spoken by isolated, jungle-dwelling populations.

Dialects: There are four main dialects with many subdialects. The major dialects are: (1) Tanah Datar, spoken in the highland region, the traditional *darek* area (*darek* refers to the interior region of the province of West Sumatra considered to be the original home of the Minangkabau people), around the cities of Batusangkar and Padang Panjang; (2) Lima Puluh Kota, used in the *darek*, around the city of Payakumbuh; (3) Agam, spoken in the *darek*, around the city of Bukittinggi; and (4) Pasisia, spoken along the coast of West Sumatra, the traditional *rantau* area, where Minang settlers spread in historical times, outside the Minangkabau heartland. Linguistic surveys have suggested, however, that at least 25 regional subdialects can be identified on the basis of a range of phonological characteristics. While there is no standard dialect of Minangkabau, the dialect spoken in Padang, the provincial capital of West Sumatra located on the coast in the *rantau*, is widely viewed as the prestige dialect and may serve as a lingua franca among Minangkabau speakers. Minangkabau speakers living outside West Sumatra in other parts of Indonesia or elsewhere generally communicate using this Padang dialect. Additionally, the Minangkabau speakers of Negeri Sembilan, Malaysia, speak a distinctive dialect that has been described in the context of varieties of Bahasa Malaysia.

Number of Speakers: 6.5 million

Origin and History

There can be no doubt that a connection exists between Minangkabau and Malay. This relationship has been extensively discussed. The two languages share many linguistic characteristics and cognate vocabulary, but Minangkabau cannot be understood by native speakers of Malay without study and exposure and vice versa. Some of the early scholars who wrote about language use in the Malay world, incorporating the modern nations of Indonesia, Malaysia, Singapore, and Brunei, suggested that there were only two "dialects" in the region, Minangkabau and Malay, which included all the other variants, dialects, and languages related to Malay spoken in the area (see, for example, Marsden 1811; Crawfurd 1852; de Hollander 1893). More recently, linguists have postulated an earlier split from Proto-Malay for Minangkabau compared with other Malay dialects which might account for the situation that exists today (Dyen 1965; Notofer 1988). It is not possible to determine the chronology or exact nature of the ancient language communities of the Malay world, including Minangkabau, but it is clear that Minangkabau has a place within the framework of languages related to modern Malay and Indonesian that come from the same Proto-Malay origins, and it may in fact be the dominant part of a single dialect complex shared with Kerinci (Blust 1988).

As these historical linguistic studies suggest, the Minangkabau language has long been used in the region and displays characteristics that may have once been more widespread. This is the case with respect to Minangkabau societal structure as well as to the language itself. Of the major Malay cultural groups, it is only the Minangkabau who are matrilineal. Matrilineal cultures have been viewed by anthropologists as being among the earliest forms of social organization (Aberle 1961), indicating that the Minangkabau language has a long, if mostly undocumented history, in its region of origin.

Orthography and Basic Phonology

There is no Minangkabau script, but until the early 20th century, an adapted form of ARABIC script was used to write the language. This required the creation of five letters to accommodate sounds not present in Arabic (*ca, nga, ga, pa, nya*). In

Table 1: Consonants

		Labial	Dental	Alveolar	Palatal	Velar	Glottal
Stops	Voiceless	p	t		c	k	ʔ
	Voiced	b	d		j	g	
Nasals		m	n		ny	ng	
Fricatives	Voiceless	(f)		s	(sy)	(kh)	h
	Voiced			(z)			
Liquid			l				
Trill			r				
Glides		w			y		

the 1930s, a system of writing using the Roman alphabet was developed. Following the standardization of Indonesian spelling and adopting the same system of sound representation, Minangkabau spelling was simplified and standardized in 1976.

The phonological system described in Table 1 is based on the Minangkabau spoken in Padang.

The phonemes /*f*, *z*, *sy*, and *kh*/ are loan phonemes occurring in loanwords mainly from Arabic.

Minangkabau has five vowel phonemes:

	Front	Central	Back
High	i		u
Mid	e		o
Low		a	

Minangkabau has the following diphthongs:

/ay/	/sampay/	sampai 'arrive, until'
/au/	/lapau/	lapau 'shop [noun]'
/uə/	/buluəh/	buluah 'bamboo'
/uy/	/kuruyh/	kuruih 'thin'
/iə/	/putiəh/	putiah 'white'

In Minangkabau, all consonants can occur in initial position. Only five can occur in final position, however. These are /*ʔ*, *ng*, *m*, *n*, and *h*/. All vowels can occur in final position. Consonants cannot occur together, except in combination with nasals, frequently in the context of affixation.

Syllable structure may be open, CV, or closed, CVC. Native Minangkabau roots (as opposed to loanwords from Arabic, SANSKRIT, ENGLISH, and so forth) take the form CV-CV or CV-CVC.

Basic Morphology

Minangkabau makes use of several morphological processes, including prefixation, suffixation, and root reduplication. The grammatical function and syntactic behavior of affixed forms tend to be predictable based on the nature of affixation. Case, number, and gender are not signaled in most classes of words. Some pronouns, however, indicate gender and number and frequently level of intimacy and relative status as well. First person plural pronouns denote interlocutor inclusion.

Nominal Morphology. The root noun in Minangkabau indicates an unspecified number of the item in question. Duplicated forms mean a variety or diversity of the item in question. Definiteness may be determined from context or indicated through use of *iko* (*ko*) 'this' or *itu* (*tu*) 'that'.

Nouns may be formed through several processes of affixation: suffixation with *-an* forms a noun from a verb; prefixation with *paN-* (*pa-* for roots beginning with vowels) forms a noun from a verb; affixation with *ka- -an* forms a noun from an adjective; affixation with *paN- -an* (*pa- -an* for roots beginning with a vowel) forms a noun from a verb. In the case of *paN-*, the form of the prefix depends on the initial sound of the root. The sound changes that occur with *paN-* also apply to the prefix *maN-* described under verbal morphology below. Table 2 on the next page shows these sound changes.

Verbal Morphology. Minangkabau has a number of verbal affixes that signal transitive vs. intransitive status as well as voice in the case of transitive verbs. Verb roots may be verbs but may also be other parts of speech that are made into verbs through affixation.

The major verbal prefixes are: *maN-*, *ba-*, *di-*, and *ta-*. The prefix *maN-* signals an active transitive verb. The form of the prefix depends on the initial sound of the root and follows the same pattern of change as the nominal prefix *paN-* (see Table 2). *Di-* occurs with transitive verbs in the passive voice. *Ba-* indicates an intransitive verb. *Ta-* shows a perfective form indicating an existing state or condition or an instance where the action occurred unintentionally. The agent is generally not specified. The prefix *pa-* occurs with verbs in a causative meaning and may be used in conjunction with other prefixes.

The major verb suffixes are *-kan* and *-i* which occur in various combinations with the verbal prefixes. Examples of affixation of verbs include:

a. salang 'borrow', basalang 'be borrowed'
b. jua 'sell', manjua 'sell [st]'
c. bali 'buy', dibali '[st] is bought'
d. campak 'throw, scatter', tacampak 'strewn'
e. elok 'good'; mampaelok 'fix, repair [st]'
f. kalah 'lose', mangalahkan 'defeat [st, so]'
g. jalan 'go', manjalani 'undergo [st]'
h. lapeh 'free, loose', dilapehkan '[st] is freed'

Verb roots may come from all other major word classes, with verbs formed through affixation. Reduplication of the root

Table 2: Prefix *paN*- Morphophonemic Change

Initial sound of root	Form of affix	Notes and examples
b	pam-	*bali* 'buy' > *pambali* 'buyer'
c, d, j	pan-	*cari* 'look for' > *pancari* 'person who looks for [st] or tool used to look for [st]'
g, h	pang-	*galeh* 'trade' > *panggaleh* 'trader'
k	pang-	initial of root dropped: *kaik* 'hook [v]' > *pangaik* 'hook [n]'
l, m, n, ng, ny, r, w, y, vowels	pa-	*lawan* 'challenge' > *palawan* 'habitual contradictor'; *aleh* 'place [a place mat]' > *paaleh* 'place mat'
p	pam-	initial of root dropped: *pukek* 'dragnet' > *pamukek* 'fisherman'
s	pany-	initial of root dropped: *saok* 'cover [v]' > *panyaok* 'cover [n]'
t	pan-	initial of root dropped: *tuai* 'reap by hand' > *panuai* 'hand reaper'

is also possible indicating repeated action. Reduplicated forms may also be affixed.

Basic Syntax

Minangkabau uses a basic subject-predicate construction. Noun phrases, verb phrases, adjective phrases, numbers and prepositional phrases may act as predicates. Verbs are not inflected for tense or other inflectional categories.

The language is head initial with some exceptions, including expressions of number, negation, and adverbs of degree, e.g., *rumah gadang* (house big) 'big house', *rumah kawan kami* (house friend we) 'our friend's house', *rumak kawan kami dakek sungai* (house friend we near river) 'our friend's house near the river'. Exceptions to head-initial syntax include: *labiah rancak* (more nice) 'nicer', *sangek rancak* (very nice) 'very nice' (*rancak bana* is also possible), *talampau jauah* (too far) 'too far', *ciek buku* (one book) 'one book', *sabuah buku* (one+COUNTER book) 'one book', *banyak buku* (many book) 'many books', *Ambo indak nio pai* (I NEG want go) 'I am not going to go', *Ambo alah pai* (I already go) 'I already went', and *Ambo alun pai* (I NEG go) 'I haven't gone yet'.

Negation. All types of predicate are negated with *indak* with the basic meaning 'no, not.' *Alun*...(*lai*), where *alun* precedes the predicate while *lai* generally follows it, negates with the meaning 'not yet': *Rumah kami indak dakek musajik* (house we NEG near mosque) 'Our house is not near a mosque'; *Anak Nuriah alun pai sikolah* (child Nuriah NEG go school) 'Nuriah's child hasn't gone to school yet'; *Kawan awak alun tibo lai* (friend we NEG arrive NEG) 'Our friend hasn't arrived yet'.

Word Order. Word order at clause level is predominantly subject-predicate, but an inverted order may occur, particularly in passive constructions.

Relative phrases consist of *nan* followed by a predicate-type phrase. Relative phrases may refer to their antecedent or stand alone as subjects or predicates: *rumah nan gadang tu* (house REL big DEF) 'that big house', *Rumah ambo nan gadang di sabalah kida tu* (house I REL big PREP side left DEF) 'My house is the big one on the left', *Banyak anak nan baraja di siko* (many child REL study PREP here) '[There are] a lot of children [who are] studying here', *Urang nan duduak di sinan tu kawan Samsir* (person REL sit PREP there DEF friend Samsir) 'The person who is sitting over there is Samsir's friend', *Nan duduak di sabalah suok Bidin tu urang Amerika* (REL sit PREP side right Bidin DEF person America) '[The one] who is sitting on Bidin's right is an American'.

Adjective phrases have an adjective head that may be preceded or followed by an adverb of degree, e.g., *elok bana*, *elok sakali*, *elok amek* (good very) 'very good', *sangek elok* (very good) 'very good'. It is possible to have a string of adjectives with the resulting phrase incorporating a relative, e.g., *Rumah nan elok bana* (house REL good very) 'a very good house'. Adjective phrases may also indicate comparison using *labiah* 'more' or *paliang* 'most': *Rumah itu labiah elok dari rumah ambo* (house DEF more good than house I) 'That house is better than my house', *Rumah itu nan paliang elok* (house DEF REL most good) 'That house is the best', *Rumah nan elok bana tu nan paliang gadang* (house REL good very DEF REL most big) 'That very good house is the biggest'.

Prepositional phrases consist of one or more prepositions followed by a noun phrase: *di rumah* 'at the house, at home', *di dalam rumah* 'in(side) the house', *pai ka sikolah* 'go to school', *agiah ka(pado) ambo* 'give to me'.

Contact with Other Languages

Through the long-standing practice of *marantau* ('voluntary migration'), Minangkabau speakers have come in contact with speakers of many other languages throughout the Malay world. Additional contact with other languages came through the spread of religion (Islam) to the region by traders from India and the Arab world as well as through colonial experience. Today exposure to foreign languages is promoted by television as satellite dishes allowing viewers to see a range of foreign programs are common throughout West Sumatra and Indonesia in general. Additionally, the influence of Indonesian, which, as the national language, is the language of instruction in schools as well as the language of the press throughout the nation, cannot be underestimated as a source of loanwords for Minangkabau speakers.

A great many loanwords used commonly in Minangkabau come from Arabic and relate to religious concepts and philosophy. Some refer to ordinary objects related to religious practice for which the language did not have a native term. Examples include: *musajik* 'mosque', *iman* 'faith', *ibadaik* 'religious practices', *sadakah* 'contributions to charity', *faham* 'understand'. In many cases, the pronunciation of these words has been altered to accommodate the phonological system of the language.

In the first half of the 20th century, a number of DUTCH loanwords were common in Minangkabau due to the influence of colonizing efforts in the region. Today, however, the most important source of loanwords is English. English words are frequently borrowed into the Indonesian press, for example. Many of these have to do with technological fields, politics, entertainment, and other "new" fields. Examples include: *telepon* 'telephone', *tifi* 'TV', *telefisi* 'television', *radio* 'radio'.

An interesting phenomenon among Minangkabau speakers today is the use of Indonesian loanwords, some of which have cognates in Minangkabau while others do not. Because virtually all Minangkabau speakers can at least understand Indonesian through exposure in school, from the press and television, or by necessity for communication with non-Minangkabau speakers, the availability of Indonesian vocabulary is very high among the population. Code switching often occurs between Minangkabau and Indonesian depending on the topic of conversation, and it is not uncommon for Minangkabau speakers to use Indonesian words when discussing public, rather than personal, matters such as government, education, business, and so forth. Even today, Minangkabau is used by most speakers in an almost exclusive manner to discuss day-to-day issues and personal subjects.

Common Words

man:	laki(-laki)	long:	panjang
woman:	padusi	small:	ketek
water:	aia	yes:	iyo
sun:	matoari	no:	indak
three:	tigo	bird:	buruang
fish:	ikan	dog:	anjiang
big:	gadang	tree:	batang kayu

Example Sentences

(1) Rumah ambo ciek.
house I one
'I have one house.'

(2) Bagindo jo Rusli sadang bakarajo di sawah.
NAME and NAME PROG work PREP rice field
'Bagindo and Rusli are working in the rice fields.'

(3) Anjiang nan itam tu punyo ambo.
dog REL black DEF have I
'The black dog is mine.'

(4) Umua Ani alah limo baleh taun.
age NAME PERF fifteen year
'Ani is already 15 years old.'

Efforts to Preserve, Protect, and Promote the Language

The ability to speak Minangkabau is viewed as an integral part of identity in the Minangkabau ethnic group. It is generally recognized and accepted in the community that children raised in the *rantau* (anywhere outside the traditional Minangkabau homeland in West Sumatra) often do not speak the language. Within West Sumatra, almost everyone speaks Minangkabau as their first language. Those who do not, often because their parents, or one of the parents, came from outside the region, generally develop some facility through social interaction outside the home due to the very high level of use in the community.

Perhaps because of its close association with group membership, Minangkabau is not viewed as threatened in the community, although concerns are occasionally voiced in the community that the quality of young people's language is deteriorating. This is manifested in a declining ability to understand very formal, rhetorical and literary language among young people. This situation has come about primarily through changes in lifestyle and the trend toward nuclear families that has removed young people from the traditional environment where there would be more opportunities for exposure to this kind of language. The ability to use the language in ordinary contexts is very high and does not appear to be adversely affected by influence from other language sources.

Over the past decade, there has been a resurgence of interest in Minangkabau traditions and customs, evidenced by the publication of a large number of books on *adaik* ('traditional law and customs'), culture, and history. Many of these works have been reprinted from originals that first appeared in the early part of the century. Interestingly, as Minangkabau remains primarily a spoken language, the text of these works tends to be in Indonesian with passages and examples in Minangkabau. The regional press also caters to this deepening interest in Minangkabau culture by publishing short stories in Minangkabau in otherwise Indonesian-language newspapers and running comic strips with a Minangkabau theme. Additionally, the Sunday editions of the provincial newspapers regularly publish opinion and commentary pieces by *adaik* leaders discussing issues that may be unfamiliar to readers, many of whom now live in cities and work in modern jobs.

Select Bibliography

Aberle, D.F. 1961. "Matrilineal Descent in Cross Cultural Perspective." In Schneider, D.M. and Gough, K. eds. *Matrilineal Kinship*. 655–730. Berkeley: University of California Press.

Anwar, K. 1990. *Indonesian: The Development and Use of a National Language*. Yogyakarta: Gadjah Mada University Press.

Blust, R. 1988. "Malay Historical Linguistics: A Progress Report." In Ahmad, M.T. and Zain, A.M., eds., *Rekonstruksi dan Cabang-cabang Bahasa Melayu Induk*. 1–33. Kuala Lumpur: Dewan Bahasa dan Pustaka.

Crawfurd, J. 1852. *Malay Language: Grammar and Dictionary with a Preliminary Dissertation*. London: Smith, Elder & Co.

Dyen, I. 1965. "A Lexico Statistical Classification of Austronesian Languages." In *International Journal of American Linguistics*, Memoir 19, 13 (1).

Emeis, M.C. 1932. *Lakeh Pandai: Kitab Batjoan Bahaso Minangkabau Oentoea' Ana' nan Baroe Moelai Baradja Mambatjo*. Groningen: Den Haag.

Fakultas Sastra Seni, IKIP Padang. 1978. *Struktur Bahasa Minangkabau: Dialek Lima Puluh Kota, Agam, Tanah Datar, dan Pesisir Selatan*. Padang: Departemen Pendidikan dan Kebudayaan.

Hakimy, I. 1994. *Pegangan Penghulu, Bundo Kanduang, dan Pidato Alua Pasambahan Adat di Minangkabau*. Bandung: Penerbit PT Rosdakarya.

Hollander, JJ de. 1893. *Handleiding bij de Beofening der Maleische Taal en Letterkunde*. Breda: Van Broese & Co.

Kasim, Y., *et al*. 1987. *Pemetaan Bahasa Daerah di Sumatera Barat dan Bengkulu*. Jakarta: Pusat Pembinaan dan Pengembangan Bahasa, Departemen Pendidikan dan Kebudayaan.

Marsden, W. 1811. *History of Sumatra*. London. Reprinted 1986, Kuala Lumpur: Oxford University Press.

Medan, T. 1985. *Bahasa Minangkabau Dialek Kubang Tigo Baleh*. Jakarta: Pusat Pembinaan dan Pengembangan Bahasa, Departemen Pendidikan dan Kebudayaan.

Medan, T., *et al*. 1986. *Geografi Dialek Bahasa Minangkabau: Suatu Deskripsi dan Pemetaan di Daerah Kabupaten Pasaman*. Jakarta: Pusat Pembinaan dan Pengembangan Bahasa, Departemen Pendidikan dan Kebudayaan.

Medan, T. 1988. *Antologi Kebahasan*. Padang: Angkasa Raya.

Moussay, G. 1998. *Tata Bahasa Minagkabau*. Jakarta: Kepustakaan Populer Gramedia.

Naim, M. 1984. *Merantau: Pola Migrasi Suku Minangkabau*. Yogyakarta: Gadjah Mada University Press.

Notofer, B. 1988. "A Discussion of Two Austronesian Subgroups: Proto-Malay and Proto-Malayic." In Ahmad, M.T. and Zain, A.M., eds. *Rekonstruksi dan Cabang-cabang Bahasa Melayu Induk*, Dewan Bahasa dan Pustaka, Kuala Lumpur, 34–58.

Omar, A.H. 1993. *Susur Galur Bahasa Melayu*. Kuala Lumpur: Dewan Bahasa dan Pustaka.

Pamoentjak, M.T.S. 1935. *Kamoes Bahasa Minangkabau-Bahasa Melajoe Riau*. Batavia: Balai Poestaka.

Said, C., *et al*. 1986. *Struktur Bahasa Minangkabau di Kabupaten Kampar*. Jakarta: Pusat Pembinaan dan Pengembangan Bahasa, Departemen Pendidikan dan Kebudayaan.

Zainil, *et al*. 1986. *Sistem Pemajemukan Bahasa Minangkabau*. Jakarta: Pusat Pembinaan dan Pengembangan Bahasa, Departemen Pendidikan dan Kebudayaan.

MONGOLIAN

Robert I. Binnick

Language Name: Mongolian. **Alternate:** *Mongol.* **Autonym:** *Mongol khel* 'the Mongolian language'.

Location: The majority of Mongolian speakers are in the Inner Mongolian Autonomous Region of China as well as adjacent areas of China (Gansu, Sinkiang, etc.). The language is also spoken in the Mongolian People's Republic (Outer Mongolia).

Family: Mongolic branch of the Altaic family.

Related Languages: Most closely related to other members of the Mongolic branch: Buriat, Kalmuck, Oirat, and Dagur. Also related to languages in the other two branches of Altaic, such as TURKISH of the Turkic branch, and Evenki (Tungus) of the Tungusic branch. Mongolian is also likely related to KOREAN and is conjectured to be related to JAPANESE.

Dialects: Mongolian dialects are generally mutually intelligible and differ principally in phonetic detail and vocabulary. The standard is the Khalkha dialect, which is spoken by approximately 90 percent of Mongolian speakers in Outer Mongolia. In Inner Mongolia there are a number of dialects, including Chakhar, Kharchin, Dariganga, Urat, Ordos, and Barga. Forms of Mongolian that are significantly different from Khalkha, for example, Monguor or Dagur, are usually accounted different languages from Mongolian proper.

Number of Speakers: 4.5–5 million.

Origin and History

In the first few centuries of the current era, the Chinese encountered many nomadic peoples speaking Altaic languages. Some of these undoubtedly belonged to the Mongolic branch of the Altaic language family.

The "Mongols" were in origin one of several related nomadic tribes living in what is now Outer Mongolia. Several of these tribes were united by Genghiz Khan and his successors as the "Mongols" and amalgamated with groups of Turkic and Tungusic speaking groups to form the Mongol hordes. By about 1350 the Mongols had conquered most of northern Eurasia. Their dynasties did not long survive, however, and by about 1450 they had been expelled or absorbed in most of these territories and were largely limited to Mongolia itself.

Since then they have generally maintained a traditional nomadic, herder lifestyle. Conversion to Lamaistic Buddhism had a tremendous impact on their culture and lives. Politically they have had great difficulty in retaining their independence, caught between China and Russia, whom they have traditionally sought to play off against each other. By the end of the 17th century all of Mongolia had fallen under the control of the Chinese Empire. At various times the Mongols tried to use Japan or the United States as a lever of power, but with little success. Following the Chinese Revolution of 1912, Outer Mongolia regained independence but by 1924 had become a Soviet satellite, virtually a republic of the Soviet Union. The Stalinist purges in Mongolia were even more ruthless than those in the Soviet Union. During the period of the Sino-Japanese War (1931–1945) Outer Mongolia was remarkably successful in fighting off Japanese attack. Since the fall of the Soviet Union, the Mongolian People's Republic has slowly moved toward new politics and economics. Inner Mongolia continues to have little more than nominal autonomy within the Chinese People's Republic.

Orthography and Basic Phonology

Mongolian has a written history of approximately 800 years. During that time it has been regularly written in four different scripts: (1) the *hP'agspa* script (official script 1269–1368 of the Yüan or Mongol dynasty in China); (2) the vertical or Uighur script; (3) the LATIN alphabet (briefly in the 1940s); and (4) a modified Cyrillic script.

Of these writing systems, the vertical or Uighur and Cyrillic scripts are in use today. The vertical script was borrowed from the Uighur Turks around the year 1200 and has been in continuous use as the medium of the written literary language. It has always been in use in Inner Mongolia (China) and is currently being reintroduced in Outer Mongolia (the Mongolian Republic).

Both the vertical and Cyrillic scripts represent the spoken language. The vertical script, known as Classical or Literary Mongolian, has changed little in the last several centuries; its spelling reflects a form of the language perhaps older than Genghiz Khan. Archaic spellings are, however, given the modern pronunciation. Thus literary *aghula* 'mountain' would be read aloud the same way as Cyrillic *uul;* both are pronounced [ūlə].

The Cyrillic script adds the characters transliterated as *ü* and *ö* and attempts to reflect actual pronunciation in the Khalkha and related dialects. This is not completely successful because here, too, the spelling conventions are in some cases arcane. Actual pronunciation often differs markedly from the spelling. For example, *bid* 'we' has two syllables in pronunciation, but *bayna* 'is' has one.

Mongolian Vertical Script Samples: Vowels

Initial	Medial	Final	Transcription
ᠠ	ᠠ	ᠠ ᠠ	a
ᠡ	ᠡ	ᠡ ᠡ	e
ᠢ	ᠢ	ᠢ	i
ᠣ	ᠣ	ᠣ	o
ᠤ	ᠤ	ᠤ	u
ᠥ	ᠥ ᠥ	ᠥ	ö
ᠦ	ᠦ ᠦ	ᠦ	ü

The Mongolian vertical script has distinct letter shapes at different positions (beginning, middle, and end) of words. Furthermore, certain combinations of letters are run together as digraphs; these are not shown here because they are too numerous. In the middle of a word certain vowels, for example, *ü* and *ö*, and consonants including *t* and *d*, are not distinguished. Consequently words can be ambiguous in up to eight ways. Forms in this chapter are cited in transliteration of the Cyrillic script.

Table 1: Mongolian Cyrillic

Cyrillic	Transliteration	Cyrillic	Transliteration
Аа	a	Рр	r
Бб	b	Сс	s
Вв	v	Тт	t
Гг	g	Уу	u
Дд	d	Үү	ü
Ее	e/ye	Фф	f
Ёё	ë/yo/yö	Хх	kh/x
Жж	j	Цц	ts/c
Зз	z	Чч	č
Ии	i	Шш	š
Йй	y	Щщ	šč
Кк	k	ъ	"
Лл	l	ы	ii
Мм	m	ь	'
Нн	n/ng	Ээ	e
Оо	o	Юю	yu/yü
Өө	ö	Яя	ya
Пп	p		

Table 2 displays Mongolian consonants. The sounds marked with a * are distinct phonemes only in the modern language.

F, p, w, and word-initial *r* occur only in borrowings. In the modern language, *k* occurs only in borrowings. The literary written language has two sets of velar stops, distinguishing front *g* and *k* from back or deep-velar (uvular) *gh* and *q*.

Table 2: Consonants

		Labial	Dental	Alveo-palatal	Velar
Stops	Voiceless	p	t		k
	Voiced	b	d		g
Fricatives	Voiceless	f	s	sh*	kh*
Affricates	Voiceless		ts*	ch	
	Voiced		dz*	j	
Nasals		m	n		
Liquids			l, r		
Glides		w		y	

Table 3 shows Mongolian vowels. Some scholars consider the weak sound [ə] to be an independent phoneme. Mongolian originally had a high back unrounded vowel *ɨ* like that found in Turkish.

Mongolian vowels may be either short (written single) or long (written double). Short vowels when unstressed, especially in noninitial syllables, tend to weaken and under certain conditions become unvoiced or disappear altogether. Thus, *irekh* 'to come' may be pronounced something like [irkh].

The most striking phonological feature of Mongolian is the phenomenon of vowel harmony, found in many Altaic languages such as Turkish, as well as in Uralic languages including HUNGARIAN and FINNISH.

Table 3: Vowels

	Front		Back	
	Unrounded	Rounded	Unrounded	Rounded
High	i	ü		u
Non-high	e	ö	a	o

There are two aspects of Mongolian vowel harmony, front-back (palatal) harmony and labial (rounding) harmony.

For front-back harmony, all vowels and certain consonants (in the literary written language, the velars) are grouped into two mutually exclusive sets, front and back, and the two may not, in general, mix within the same word, although compounds like the name *Tserendulmaa* and loanwords like "professor" may violate this principle. The front vowels are *i e ü ö* and the back vowels are *a u o*. In the literary language, the velars *g k* are front, and the deep velars *gh q* are back.

When a suffix is added as an ending to a stem containing one of these sets, its vowels generally must match those of the stem; in noninitial syllables, the vowel *i* is neutral, occurring also in words with back vowels.

For rounding harmony, a vowel must be round under certain conditions and must not be under others. When a suffix is added as an ending to a stem ending in a nonhigh rounded vowel (*o ö*), it must match that vowel in rounding.

Consequently, endings must appear in different forms so as not to violate these principles. Some endings in Mongolian have up to four different forms as a result:

Front stem ending in nonhigh rounded vowel:
öls- 'hunger', *ölsööd* 'having hungered'
Front stem ending in other vowel:
ire- 'come', *ireed* 'having come'
Back stem ending in nonhigh rounded vowel:
ol- 'find', *olood* 'having found'
Back stem ending in other vowel:
gar- 'go out', *garaad* 'having gone out'

Basic Morphology

There is no grammatical gender in Mongolian. Although there are plural suffixes, their use is highly specialized and limited. 'I read books' is normally *bi nom üzne*, with singular *nom*; the plural *nomuud* is unidiomatic and suggests a special meaning, emphasizing the plurality. When indicating some definite set of books, the plural may be used with the accusative case: *bi nomuudiig üzne* 'I read the books'.

Mongolian nouns are inflected for case. There are eight cases, illustrated below with the endings used for front unrounded vowels:

Case	Meaning/Use	Suffix
Nominative	subject	— (unmarked)
Accusative	object	-g/-iyg
Genitive	'of'	-n/-iyn/-iy
Dative-Locative	'at, on, in, to'	-d
Ablative	'from'	-ees
Instrumental	'with, by'	-eer
Comitative	'together with'	-tey
Directive	'toward'	-rüü

In addition to the variation in forms caused by vowel harmony, other variations occur. For example, nouns ending in *n* may drop the *n* in the nominative and in some other cases. In addition, the dative ending *-d* may occur as *t* after some stem-final consonants.

Case endings occur after the plural ending and before an adjoined unemphatic possessive: *mori-d-oos-min'* (horse-PL-ABLATIVE-my) 'from my horses'.

An interesting peculiarity of Mongolian is the ability to double case endings: *man-ay-d* (place-GENITIVE-LOCATIVE) 'at our (place)', *ger-t-ees* (house-LOCATIVE-ABLATIVE) 'from home'. Mongolian pronouns are differentiated by person and number, but not gender. In the first person, the nominative case has a different stem from the other case forms.

	Singular		Plural	
	Nomin.	Other Cases	Nomin.	Other Cases
1	bi	min-/nada-/nama-	bide	biden-/man-
2	chi	chin-/chima-	ta	tan-

Originally there was a third-person pronoun, singular *i-*, plural *a-*, but these forms were lost in the nominative and other cases already in the older language. In the modern language, only fossils survive, and they have been supplanted by forms of *ene* 'this' and *ter* 'that'.

The second-person plural pronoun *ta* has become a formal singular; its plural is *tanar*.

There was a distinction in the older language between an inclusive "we" (you and I or you and we) versus an exclusive "we" (I and another or I and others, but not you). In the nominative, this distinction has all but disappeared, and it is disappearing in the other cases as well. In the previous table, *biden-* is the first-person plural inclusive form, and *man-* is the exclusive form.

Mongolian verbs do not agree with their subjects in any way. Nonetheless, there is a remarkably large number of forms. There are four basic types of verbs. Imperative forms occur without subjects. Indicative forms serve as the main verb in a statement or a question. Converbs occur in subordinate clauses and sometimes with auxiliary verbs. Participles occur with auxiliary verbs and in negative sentences. The indicative forms of the verb *yav-* 'go' are illustrated below:

Tense	Form	Approximate Meaning
Present	yav-na	'goes, will go'
Past	yav-av	'went'
Evidential	yav-laa	'has gone'
Perfect	yav-jee	'had gone'

One feature of Mongolian is that, as in ENGLISH, the present tense cannot be used of events occurring at the precise moment of speech. Instead, the imperfect converb is used, with the auxiliary "be". This construction is comparable to the English present progressive.

bi nom üz-ne
I.NOM books read-PRESENT
'I (generally) read books.'

bi üz-ej bay-na
I.NOM read-IMP/CON be-PRESENT
'I'm reading (now).'

Causative verbs are formed with a suffix, usually *-uula*: *yav-uula-kh* (go-CAUS-FUT/PARTICIPLE) 'to send' (lit. 'to cause to go').

Basic Syntax

Mongolian is a Subject-Object-Verb language; only the question particle *uu* can follow the verb. Modifiers precede the element that they modify: *ter ikh khot* (that big city) 'that big city'.

In negative sentences, the main verb occurs as a participle that is compounded with *-güy* (from *ügüy* 'without, no').

bi med-ev
I.NOM know-PAST
'I knew.'

bi med-sen-güy
I.NOM know-PERF/PARTICIPLE-NEG
'I didn't know.'

There is a special passive form of the verb, formed with a suffix *-gda*. The agent in a passive sentence occurs in the dative case:

deeremch tsagdaa-d buuda-gd-av
bandit-NOM police-DATIVE shoot-PASSIVE-PAST
'The bandit was shot by the police.'

Contact with Other Languages

Throughout its history, Mongolian has been affected by other languages. A number of prehistoric borrowings have been identified (some but not all of which remain controversial hypotheses), such as *nom* 'book' from GREEK *nomos* 'law,' via other Central Asian languages.

There are a large number of SANSKRIT and TIBETAN religious terms in Mongolian, including from Tibetan many personal names, astronomical terms, days of the week, etc. The long cultural dominance of the Chinese is reflected in many administrative and bureaucratic terms that are of Chinese and Manchu origin; in addition, many older scientific and technical terms are also from CHINESE. International words of Greek, Latin, English, FRENCH or other European origin came into Mongolian proximately from RUSSIAN.

From Russian: *kharandaa* 'pencil', *nomer* 'number', *prokuror* 'prosecutor'
From Chinese: *puujin* 'rocket', *luuzing* 'compass', *galt tereg* 'fire car', e.g., 'railroad train'
From Tibetan: *lama* 'lama'
From English: *pasport* 'passport', *sport* 'sports, sporting'

Common Words

man:	er (khün)	small:	baga
woman:	em (khün)	yes:	tiym
water:	us	no:	ügüy
sun:	nar(an)	good:	sayn
three:	gurav, gurban	bird:	shuvuu
fish:	zagas	dog:	nokhoy
big:	ikh	tree:	mod(on)

Example Sentences

(1) Bi önöödör doloon tsag-t bos-ov.
I.NOM today seven hour-DATIVE get up-PAST
'I got up today at seven o'clock.'

(2) cham-d zakhidl-iin tsaas bayna uu?
you-DATIVE writing-GEN paper.NOM be-PRESENT Q
'Do you have any writing paper?'

(3) bid gol-iin khoyt tal-d gar-aad
we.NOM river-GEN northern side-DAT get out-PERF/CONVERB

[tos-oj ir-üül-sen mor-iyg
[meet-IMPERF/CON send-PASSIVE-PERF/PARTICIPLE horse-ACC

un-aj] davkhi-n
mount-IMPERF/CONVERB] gallop-MOD/CONVERB

od-loo.
set.out-EVIDENTIAL

'We got out of the boat on the north side of the river, and mounting the horses that had been sent to meet us, set out at a gallop.'

Efforts to Preserve, Protect, and Promote the Language

In China, Mongolian has more or less faced the normal pressures on a minority language in a great, multinational state, albeit one with an overwhelming majority of Han Chinese.

In the Mongolian People's Republic, tremendous pressure was applied by Russian speakers during the Soviet period. Nonetheless, foreign borrowings were resisted, and only a fraction of those that entered into the closely related Buriat language, spoken in the Soviet Union's Buriat ASSR, were accepted into Mongolian. Russian had virtually no impact on any other aspect of the language. As soon as the Soviet period ended, the Cyrillic script was abandoned in favor of the old vertical or Uighur script still in use in Inner Mongolia (China). The vertical script will become the official standard in Outer Mongolia (the Mongolian Republic) in 2004.

Select Bibliography

Austin, William M., John G. Hangin, and Peter Onon. 1963. *Mongol Reader*. Bloomington, Indiana: University of Indiana and The Hague: Mouton. (Uralic and Altaic series, 29).

Bosson, James E. 1964. *Modern Mongolian: A Primer and a Reader*. Bloomington, Indiana: University of Indiana and The Hague: Mouton. (Uralic and Altaic series, 38).

Hangin, John G. 1968. *Basic Course in Mongolian*. Bloomington, Indiana: University of Indiana and The Hague, Mouton. (Uralic and Altaic series, 73).

_____. 1970. *A Concise English-Mongolian Dictionary*. Bloomington, Indiana: University of Indiana and The Hague: Mouton. (Uralic and Altaic series, 89).

Lessing, Ferdinand D., *et al.* 1973. *Mongolian-English Dictionary. Corrected Reprinting with a New Supplement*. Bloomington, Indiana: The Mongolia Society.

Peoples of China. July 1980. Map to accompany the *National Geographic Magazine*. (Shows the distribution of Mongolian dialects and related Mongolic languages in the Chinese People's Republic.)

Peoples of the Soviet Union. February 1976. Map to accompany the *National Geographic Magazine*. (Shows distribution of related Mongolic languages in the Soviet Union.)

Poppe, Nicholas. 1954. *Grammar of Written Mongolian*. Wiesbaden: Otto Harrasowitz.

_____. 1970. *Mongolian Language Handbook*. Washington, DC: Center for Applied Linguistics.

_____. 1955. *Introduction to Mongolian Comparative Studies*. Helsinki: Sumalais-Ugrilanen Seura. (Mémoires de la Société Finno-Ougrienne, 110).

Sanzheyev, G.D. 1973. *The Modern Mongolian Language*. Moscow: Nauka Publishing House.

Street, John C. 1963. *Khalkha Structure*. Bloomington, Indiana: University of Indiana and The Hague: Mouton, 1963. (Uralic and Altaic series, 24).

MOORE

Norbert Nikiema

Language Name: Mooré (autonym in current official orthography). **Alternative Names:** These names are found in the linguistic literature. Mõre, Mõre, Mole, Mo:re, Mʊ̀ʊré, Mossi, Mosi, Moisi, Moshi. Speakers of Mooré are called *Moose* (plural of *Moaaga*). They are also known as Mossi or Moshi.

Location: Spoken in Burkina Faso and parts of the Ivory-Coast.

Family: Western Oti-Volta, Northern branch of Central Gur, Niger-Congo family.

Related Languages: Kusaal, Yaana, Joore, Frafra, Dagbane, Nawdem, Gulmancema, Dagara.

Dialects: There are four major regional dialects that can be called central, northern, eastern and western. The central variety is spoken around Ouagadougou, the capital city of Burkina Faso and of the Empire of the Moose. It is composed of 3 other subdialects: làllwéoogò, Wùbrwéoogó, and Zũ̀ndwéoogó. The northern dialect is known as *yáadré* and is spoken around Ouahigouya; the western variety is known as *tàooléndé* and is spoken around Koudougou; the eastern variety is known as Sã̀ré and is spoken around Kougpéla. There is mutual intelligibility between those dialects. Malgoubri (1988) includes Yaana and Joore among the dialects of Moore although their understanding by speakers of the other dialects is much less obvious. The central dialect is often taken as the dialect of reference or the standard dialect. It is, for example, the one that is most widely described and the one that is heard most often on the radio.

The differences between the four mutually intelligible dialects are mostly phonetic (including segmental and tonal features) and lexical/morphological. Typical differentiating features include the treatment of vowel sequences, the rounding of stem vowels in words ending in *-go*, RTR harmony, the pronunciation of initial /r/ in a coronal or nasal context as opposed to other contexts, the pronunciation of medial /l/ preceded by a nasal(ized) vowel; the formation of imperatives, the use of suffixes in the gerund and variations in the use of certain lexical items, as illustrated below:

Dialect Feature	Central	Eastern	Western	Northern
ao oa ea ae	[ɔ] [wa] [ɛ] [ɛ], [a^j]	[ɔ] [wa] [ja] [ɛ], [a^j]	[ɔ] [wa] [ɛ] [ɛ], [a^j]	[a^w] [ɔ] [ɛ] [a^j]
Local seasoning	kaolgo [kɔ́lɣò]	kaolgo [kɔ́lɣò]	kaolgo [kɔ́lɣò]	kalgo [kálgɔ̀]
#r	[d], [r]	[d], [r]	[r]	[d], [r]
ãl-	[ãn]	[ãl]	[ãn]	[ãn]
Imperative 'come'	wà	wà	wà	wàabɔ́
Gerund 'beating'	pã́brè	pã́brè	pã́brè	pã́ppɔ̀
Lexical item 'child'	bíigá	bíiyá	bíigé	bíigó

Number of Speakers: 7–9 million native speakers.

Origin and History

Little is known about the origin and development of the Moore language. Evidence from oral tradition and comparative work have led historians to hypothesize that the Moose came from the Lake Chad area (which does not exclude that they may have originated elsewhere, and Egypt has been mentioned in that respect). Recent history has it that they conquered the northern part of Ghana and first established in the Tenkodogo area in the 11th century; from there they radiated further west and conquered the central part of Burkina Faso, making Ouagadougou the capital of their empire. The native populations have adopted the language of their conquerors, which probably explains the large number of speakers of Moore today.

Table 1: Consonants

	Bilabial	Labio-dental	Alveolar	Palatal	Velar	Glottal
Stops	p b		t d		k g	' [ʔ]
Fricatives		f v	s z			h
Nasals	m		n			
Lateral			l			
Flap			r			
Glides				y [j]	w	

The most detailed and authoritative research work on the language groups to which Moore belongs is Manessy (1975), who has tried a reconstruction of the ancestor of Moore and of other languages, viz. proto-Oti-Volta. A comparison between the features of this proto-language and those of present-day Moore shows, among other things, a simplification of the consonantal system by the loss of complex segments, most notably labio-velars and affricates. The morphology has also changed from a class system with a complex concord to a system of suffixes that is still complex but in which the suffixes have lost their original meaning and now play mostly a grammatical role.

Orthography and Basic Phonology

Because of its demographic importance Moore has attracted the attention of the colonial administration and of the Christian missionaries, Catholic or Protestant, who visited the area at the end of the previous century or the beginning of the current one. They used the symbols of the FRENCH alphabet (with the value they have in LATIN) and often with diacritics to write the language. The orthographic system that was used then is most notably illustrated in the mammoth work of Rvd. Father Gustave Alexandre prepared in the 1920s and the 1930s but published only in 1953: la langue mõre. It was modified substantially only in 1968. The current orthography, which was officialized by a governmental decree in 1986, is essentially phonemic and uses characters taken from a reference list of characters proposed for all the languages of Africa by an international conference held in Niamey (Niger) in 1978 under the auspices of UNESCO and the French *Agence de Coopération Culturelle et Technique* (ACCT).

The orthography uses the same symbols except that the apostrophe <'> is used to represent the glottal stop; <y> represents the palatal semiconsonant and <yn> its nasal counterpart found in some words as variants of /n/ and /m/.

All descriptions since the 1970s agree on the inventory of oral vowels presented here, although not necessarily on the values of [high] and [ATR] to be used for the vowels in the middle rows. It is also agreed that [ɛ], [ə] and [ɔ] only occur at the phonetic level. A few recent descriptions also include [ʌ] in the phonetic inventory, as a tense realization of /a/. The orthographic alphabet of Moore uses the symbols presented above but also includes <ɛ> as an equivalent notation for /ae/ or /ea/.

Vowels

Oral: Front	Cental	Back	Nasal: Front	Central	Back
i		u	ĩ		ũ
ɩ		ʊ	ɩ̃		ʊ̃
e		o			õ
	a			ã	

There are debates on the phonemic inventory of nasal vowels. The disagreements concern the vowels of intermediate aperture. The presentation above reflects this author's view that the northern dialects have /ʊ̃/ but that all other dialects have /õ/ instead. It is agreed that there is no evidence of ɩ̃/ẽ or ʊ̃/õ contrasts in any of the various dialects, so that in the orthography <ẽ> and <õ> are used to represent the nasal vowels of intermediate aperture, for all dialects.

There are surface contrasts between short and long vowels (represented in the orthography by double symbols), whether oral or nasal. Vowel length is, however, always predictable, essentially by a rule that lengthens the right-most vowel of the rightmost open syllable of the stem when it is followed by a consonantal suffix (bi+g+a > bíiga 'child'; liu+l+a > líuulá 'bird').

Moore is a terraced tone language with two basic tones, low and high. Both tones are lowered by downdrift and the high tone can be downstepped to mid. However, tone is not represented in the standard orthography. The 1986 decree recommends that it be noted by the grave and the acute accents in scientific work and in writing destined to foreigners. In this chapter only the initial tone and subsequent changes of register will be marked. The acute accent will mark high and downstepped high tone, as in *líuulá* (HH$_1$) 'bird'.

A good deal of the (morpho)phonological processes involving segments or tones are governed by an underlying hierarchy that can be represented as follows:

Segmental hierarchy:
Consonants: p t k > b d g > f s > h ' > l > r > y w
Vowels: u, i > ɩ, ʊ > a > o > e
Tonal hierarchy: high > low

Moore thus has strengthening as well as weakening processes: a strengthening process will cause an element at the bottom of the ladder to either resist deletion or "downgrading". A weakening process, on the other hand, will force an item to either assimilate entirely or partially to another item, or to alternate with an item lower in the hierarchy, or to be deleted altogether. For instance, a non initial g or s weakens to [ɣ] and [h] respectively, but g+g will strengthen to [kk] and ss will resist a change to [h]. /r/ is entirely assimilated by /l/ word internally; it becomes d after a nasal stop; it may vocalize and become /e/ (meaning that the weakest true consonant alternates with the vowel that is lowest in the hierarchy).

/ɩ/ and /e/ are changed to [i] and / ʋ, o/ changed to [u] by a preceding high closed and tense vowel (i, u), whether adjacent or not. A final /a/ is copied into the stem after the vowels it dominates: *bed+a* > *béadà* 'big'(pl); *ko+d+a* > *kǫ́aadà* 'farmer'; such copy is not possible when the root vowels are the ones higher than /a/ in the hierarchy.

A low tone can be raised to high by another high tone, but a high tone may never become low. A word final post-consonantal suffix vowel is deleted when phrase internal, except when it is a high vowel underlyingly; elision is also blocked before a pause when the vowel carries a high tone. A nasal suffix vowel is never elided.

The canonical syllable patterns are, superficially, CV(V), V, V(V)C, and CV(V)C. Epenthetic vowels are inserted to break unacceptable consonant sequences, notably in second position in a /CCC/ sequence. When an additional syllable is needed initially, such as in borrowed words beginning with two or more consonants, it is /e/ that is used as a syllable peak: éstati 'statute'(French: statue). The same applies in final position for borrowed words normally ending in a checked syllable: zɩ́lbɛɛrè 'Gilbert'. Verbs and all words not participating in the noun class system (cf. below), such as ideophones, end in /e/ (or in reduplicated consonants for some ideophones). /e/ is thus a typical prothetic or epithetic vowel in Moore.

Basic Morphology

Major class words have the structure Root + suffix(es). The stem is often monosyllabic. In (pro)nouns, adjectives and determiners, the final vowel (+a or +o underlyingly, e being the default at the surface), is a noun class marker while the preceding, generally consonantal, suffix marks number. Singular and plural numbers are marked by different suffixes. The most common, regular, pairings are as shown below:

Singular	Plural	Class Marker
Ø	b	a
g	s	a
g	d	o
r	e	a
f	Ø	o
m	ɩ	(a)

The determiner rã̀mbá is used as a plural marker in loan words that have not been fully integrated to this fundamental system. A noun generally has one number marker, although double singular suffixes may be used to express paucity/minimization: *kòóm* (ko+m) 'water; *kòomdé* (ko+m+r) 'a drop of water'; *béngré* (bén+g+r) 'a single grain of bean'.

The pronominal system distinguishes between strong/full forms and weak/reduced forms:

Singular		Plural	
Strong	Weak	Strong	Weak
máam,màm	mà	tɔ̃́ndò	dò
fóo(m)	fò	yɑ̃́mbà	yɑ̃́, y
yɛ̃́ndá	à	bɑ̃́mbà	bà

The final vowel may be elided, yielding monosegmental weak pronominal forms. There is no gender (i.e. masculine/feminine) distinction in nouns or in pronouns, and the concord between class markers and pronouns, which is typical of other Gur languages such as Gulmancema, is lost in Moore. There is no such agreement between typical modifiers such as adjectives and the class marker of the noun either. The noun actually looses its final suffixes (number and class markers) when followed by an adjective (or another noun in the case of compounds), and it is the variation in the suffixes of the adjective (or the second element of the compound) that distinguishes singular from plural nouns in such cases.

Verbs may be monosyllabic or take a consonantal suffix that generally indicates number. The same consonantal number suffixes used in the singular of nouns occur in verbs, although +r shows up as +l and +f as +b. Much fewer suffixes are used in the plural: the most common are s and Ø. A zero plural morpheme will trigger various morphophonological processes. Contrasts between singular and plural in verbs express notions such as "action performed once/several times, by one/several actors, on one/several thing(s)..." : *pàkke* (pàg+g) 'open one thing' vs. *pàgse* (pàg+s) open several things, or action of opening carried out by several persons.' Minimization can again be expressed: mòge (mòg) 'suck'; mògmde (mòg+m+r) 'suck in no time'. There can thus be a number agreement between subjects or objects and verbs. Number suffixes in verbs can also have other values, such as transitivity, often marked by +g.

Other verbal suffixes express declarative/indicative mode (+*la*(*me*), exclamative mode (Ø, a) or aspect: stative (Ø), imperfective/progressive (d), perfective (Ø, yɑ̃́), or durative (stative or imperfective + ɛ̃́). There is no morphological variation to express agreement in person or tense. Suffixes can also be used to derive nouns from verbs, nouns from nouns, adjectives from verbs, etc.

Reduplication is a frequently used process which may express number (lʋ̀mbə́rè/lʋ̀mbá-lʋ̀mbá 'big and round, sg/pl'); intensity (góme/góm n gome 'speak/speak a long time ~a lot'; wókkò/wókk-wokkò, 'long/very long'), reiterated action (pɩ̀ɩs-pɩ̀ɩse 'sweep here and there') etc. Partial reduplication is typical of ideophones (sɩ́ddd... 'silently', sòaa..., 'idea of pouring down'; báss... 'warm, hot').

Basic Syntax

Major sentence types with specific defining features include: declarative, imperative, interrogative, and exclamative sentences. Noun phrases exhibit Modifier-Head as well as Head-Modifier surface structures, although determiners, adjectives and clausal complements to an NP always follow the head (except in cases of relativization *in situ* where the head is clause internal). In verb phrases, auxiliary verbs (AV) precede the main verb. Negation is marked by a discontinuous morpheme, the first member of which is an AV placed before the main verb while the second member occurs at the extreme end of the sentence. In clause-mate verb chains (so-called serial constructions) where a head verb is modified by other verbs, most modifying verbs (MVs) may only precede while a number of others can only follow the head. Aspect markers (AMs) and sentence-type markers (STMs), namely the declarative marker, follow the verb and precede lexical and full-form pronominal objects. There is at most one negative AV and one STM per clause. The language has a few prepositions and a number of postpositions. The unmarked word order in the sentence is S(ubject)-V(erb)-O(bject) (meaning "direct object", but the term would be improper when applied to Moore since the link to the verb is not mediated by any morphological material in the case of what would be an "indirect object"). Subjectless sentences do occur in the language. In a string of (auxiliary) verbs with the same subject a preverbal conjunction (PVC), which is a trace of the subject, is used to link each of the verbs occurring after the one closest to the subject NP. In three place predicates the more definite of the two objects is placed closer to the verb. Otherwise the D(ative) object precedes the other object. The typical order in long simple sentences with prepositional phrases (PreP), postpositional phrases (PostP) and adverbials (Adv) would be (S)-(AV)-(MV)-V-AM-STM-(MV)-(D)-(O)-(PrepP)-(PostP)-(Adv), e.g., sékàmé (be enough+PERF.+decl) 'it is enough'; nòaamá (be.good+EXCL) 'it is good!'; *wà* (come+IMPERATIVE) 'Come'.

kàrem-saambã́ rág ǹ ná n zã̀msa
teach-father+the had PVC FUT PVC teach+DECL

násáarbã móor ń baas ne seb-kã̀ngã́
Europeans+the Moore PVC finish with book-this+the

lekollẽ wã́ béoogo
school+at the tomorrow
'The teacher was about to finish teaching Moore to the Europeans with this book at the school tomorrow.'

[Contrast the negative counterpart kàrem-saambã́ rág ǹ ká ná n zã̀ms nasáarbâ móor ń baas ne seb-kã̀ngã́ lekollẽ wã́ béoog ye. 'The teacher was not about to teach Moore to the Europeans with this book at the school tomorrow.']

pág ning fó sẽ́n yã́-á zàamẽ́ wã̀
[$_{NP}$woman det. [$_{RC}$you NOM. see-her yesterday] the]

yáa mám zóá
be+DECL I friend

fò sẽ́n yã́ pág ning záamẽ́ wã̀
[NP[RCyou NOM. see woman DET. yesterday] the]

yáa mám zóá
be+DECL I friend
'The woman you saw yesterday is my friend.'

Contact with Other Languages

Moore is surrounded by Koromfe, Fulfulde, Gulmancema, Joore, Yaana, Bisa, Kasim, Nuni, Lyele and San. Lexical analyses have revealed borrowings mostly from such languages as ARABIC, HAUSA, Songay, Jula, French and ENGLISH.

From Arabic: (the days of the week) árbà 'Wednesday', làmúsà 'Thursday', hátò 'Sunday'.
From Jula: tɛ̀gdɛ́ge 'peanut butter', pɔ̃̀gé 'slip'.
From French: mɔ́ntɛɛrè 'motor/moped', lìsabɛ́tà 'Elizabeth', lékollè 'school'
From English: lórè 'lorry'; kàrenzí̃ 'kerosene'; pĩ̀gní 'penny'

Common Words

man:	ráoa	long:	wókkò
woman:	pága	small:	bílfu
water:	kòom̃	good:	nòogó
sun:	wĩ́ntoogo	bird:	líuulá
three:	tã̀abó	dog:	báaga
fish:	zĩ́nfú	drink:	yṹ
big:	bédré	eat:	rì
tree:	tìgá	come:	wà

Example Sentences

(1) wà tɩ d kíili.
come+IMP and we go home
'Come home with me.'

(2) làafí la d bãaga.
health be we sickness
'We are in perfect health.'

(3) kʊ́ɩlg sá n gòlem bí yẽbg tũ̀ n golme
river if PVC twist then crocodile follow PVC twist
'One must not resist but adjust to change.'

Efforts to Preserve, Protect, and Promote the Language

Moore is one of the best studied of the 59 languages of Burkina Faso. It is used in all the media (radio, television, newspapers, cinema, etc.), at court and unofficially in the administration. Although it is not an official language—no national language is—presidential addresses to the nation and similar important messages are translated into Moore (and into two other major national languages). All political parties use it for political campaigning. Existing documents cover not only the various aspects of the language but also the history and the culture of the Moose. There are several Moore versions of (parts of) the New Testament and two versions of the whole Bible. In 1969, a government decree created a national language board to study the various national languages of Burkina and provide them with acceptable writing systems. Specific language subcommittees were created later. The national subcommittee for the Moore language (*Sous-commission nationale du mooré*) was the first to be created by a ministerial decree on January 23, 1970.

Moore was used for adult literacy soon thereafter and is today the first language of literacy among the national languages. It was selected along with two other national languages for an experimental use as a medium of instruction at school during the educational reform of 1978–1984. Since 1994 it is used in the first years of primary school in about a hundred schools in several districts in the country. The national language board for the Moore language has been quite active: the orthography of Moore as used by the missionaries was first revised in 1968 and again in 1975 and then officialized by a ministerial decree in September 1986. An orthographic dictionary of the Moore language with over 1,400 pages was published in 1997.

Select Bibliography

Canu, Gaston. 1973. "Description synchronique de la langue Mò:rẽ (dialecte de Ouagadougou)." In *Documents linguistiques* 45. Abidjan: Université d'Abidjan, ILA.

Froger, Fernand. 1910. *Etude sur la langue des Mossi (boucle du Niger) suivi d'un vocabulaire et de textes*. Paris: Ernest Leroux.

Hall, John F. 1938–48. *Dictionary and practical notes. Moshi-English*. Mission des Assemblées de Dieu, Ouahigouya, Haute-Volta.

Kaboré, Raphaël. 1985. "Essai d'analyse de la langue mʊ̀ʊré (dialecte de Waogdgo: Ouagadougou)." Paris: Laboratoire de linguistique formelle, Collection ERA 642.758p.

Kinda, Jules. 1980. "Réflexions sur quelques problèmes relatifs aux voyelles du moore: tension, notation graphique, distribution." Mémoire de DEA, Université de la Sorbonne Nouvelle, Paris III.

Kouraogo, Pierre. 1976. "Serial verb construction and some aspects of Moore grammar: towards a case grammar solution for serialization." Unpublished MA thesis, University of South Florida, Tampa, Florida.

Malgoubri, Pierre. 1985. "Introduction à la morpho-syntaxe du moore." Mémoire de DEA, Faculté de Lettres et Sciences Humaines, Université de Nice.

____. 1988. "Recherches sur la variation dialectale en mooré. Essai dialectométrique." Thèse de 3e cycle, Faculté de Lettres et Sciences Humaines, Université de Nice.

Manessy, Gabriel. 1975. "Les langues Oti-Volta." *Classification généalogique de d'un groupe de langues voltaïques*. Paris: SELAF.

Nikièma, Emmanuel. 1986. "Niveau syllabique et structures radicales en mooré." Mémoire de maîtrise, Université du Québec à Montréal.

Nikièma, Norbert. 1976. "On the linguistic bases of Moore orthography." Ph.D. thesis, Indiana University, Bloomington, Indiana. University Microfilms International, Ann Arbor, Michigan.

____. 1980. *Ed gom mooré: la grammaire du mooré en 50 leçons*. Université de Ouagadougou.

____. 1982. *Moor gulsg sebre/Manuel de transcription du mooré*. Ouagadougou: Presses africaines.

Nikièma, Norbert, and Kinda Jules. 1997. *Dictionnaire orthographique du mooré/ Moor gom-biis no-tũur gulsg sebre*. Ouagadougou: SOGIF.

Peterson, Thomas H. 1971. "Moore structure: a generative analysis of the tonal system and aspects of the syntax." Unpublished UCLA dissertation. University Microfilms International, Ann Arbor, Michigan.

NAMA

W. Haacke

Language Name: Nama; Nama/Damara (Hottentot). **Autonym:** *Khoekhoegowab* (autonym now used officially).

Location: Namibia: north-central (Damara and Hai||om) to south (Nama).

Family: Western Central-Khoesaan of Khoesaan phylum (Note: the spelling "Khoi-San" is to be avoided, and although "Khoisan" is in vogue, it is orthographically wrong).

Related Languages: Korana (!Gora), Grikwa (Xri) [extinct]; Naro, ||Ganakhoe; Kxoé.

Dialects: (1) Nama (in southern Namibia, with little internal variation); (2) Topnaar (a subvariety of Nama on the central coast); (3) Damara (central Namibia); (4) Namidama (Damara of the Namib desert periphery); (5) Sesfontein Damara (phonologically deviating old dialects in northwest, relatively close to Proto-Central-Khoesaan); (6) Hai||om, ǂĀkhoe (old dialects on northern periphery).

Number of Speakers: 175,554 (according to the 1991 census). It is spoken by the largest language community in Namibia (12.5 percent) after that of the Oshiwambo dialects (50.6 percent).

Origin and History

Khoekhoegowab (generally known as Nama) is the best documented Khoesaan language. It is the only Khoesaan language officially supported by the Namibian state for language planning purposes and also offered as a major university subject (University of Namibia). Khoekhoegowab is a unitary autonym that was recently revived for the language, meaning "language of the Khoekhoe". Khoekhoe in this nontechnical but authentic sense refers to the Khoesaanid Nama and the Negroid Damara mainly, including groups like the Hai||om and ǂĀkhoe in northern Namibia.

The historical origin of Khoesaan languages is still a matter of dispute, and reconstruction of protolanguages has as yet not been very successful. Affinity to "Hamitic" (Afroasiatic) languages has been disproved, while the relatedness of Khoe ("Hottentot") and Saan ("Bushman") languages is no longer contested. The phylum is now subdivided into Northern, Central, and Southern Khoesaan subfamilies, albeit considerably divergent (Oswin Köhler). Khoekhoegowab belongs to the Central Khoesaan subfamily, which is characterized mainly by gender distinctions applied to nouns (Voben 1997).

Elphick's (1977) hypothesis that the Khoekhoe (Hottentot) languages originated in or near Botswana and spread with the hunters turned pastoralists seems to be the least controversial.

The common assumption that the Damara acquired the language from the Nama in a process of complete language shift is fallacious. Damara dialects on the northern and northwestern periphery (Hai||om, Sesfontein, and Namib Damara) that were not exposed to the Nama dialects have retained old traits that link especially their lexicon to Naro of central Botswana, a language that according to Köhler (1975: 329) is closest to Proto-Western-Central-Khoesaan. The Damara thus must have been speakers of Khoekhoe dialects even before they encountered the Nama, who arrived from the south in Namibia only later. Of the Western-Central-Khoesaan group, the Nama dialects of Khoekhoegowab differ from the protolanguage more than most other languages do.

Orthography and Basic Phonology

Khoekhoe speakers have difficulty with the reading and spell-

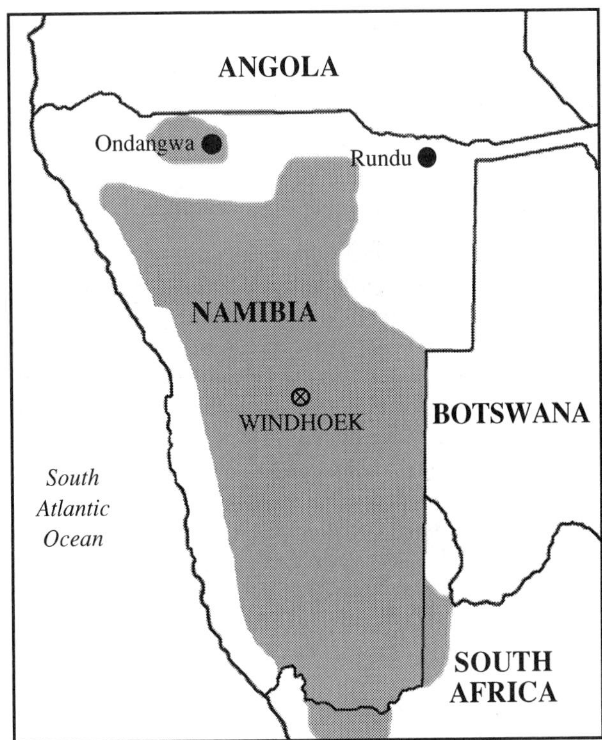

Nama is spoken in the north-central to southern area of Namibia (shaded area).

Table 1: Clicks

Influx	Efflux				
	Glottal Stop	Voiceless Velar Stop	Delayed Glottal Fricative	Voiceless Velar Affricate	Voiced Nasalization
Dental	| [|ʔ]	|g [|]	|h [|¯h]	|kh [|x^h]	|n [ŋ|]
Alveolar	! [!ʔ]	!g [!]	!h [!¯h]	!kh [!x^h]	!n [ŋ!]
Palatal	ǂ [ǂʔ]	ǂg [ǂ]	ǂh [ǂ¯h]	ǂkh [ǂx^h]	ǂn [ŋǂ]
Lateral	ǁ ʔ [ǁʔ]	ǁg [ǁ]	ǁh [ǁ¯h]	ǁkh [ǁx^h]	ǁn [ŋǁ]

ing of Khoekhoegowab. One reason for this may be that for the sake of simplicity tone is not marked, although the language relies heavily on it. Khoekhoegowab still uses the Lepsius symbols for the clicks (|, ǁ, ǂ, !). These had been agreed upon in 1856 by a conference of missionaries in consultation with Lepsius. In 1830 Khoekhoegowab became the first African language in Namibia to be reduced to writing.

Consonants. Khoesaan languages are also known as "click languages" because of their characteristic use of such ingressive consonants. Khoekhoegowab is comparatively moderate in comparison to Northern Khoesaan languages in that it employs only 20 clicks.

Table 2: Egressive Consonants

	Labial	Dental	Alveolar	Velar	Glottal
Stops	p/b [p], VbV	t/d [t]		k/g [k] kh	ʔ
Affricates		ts			
Trills			r		
Fricatives	VβV⇔VvV		s	x	h
Laterals			(l)		
Nasals	m	n			

Khoekhoegowab has lost the voicing distinction in stops as part of the development of additional tones. Prevocalic stops are voiceless and unaspirated. The standard orthography uses a distinction between letters used in other languages to represent voiced consonants and those used to represent voiceless consonants in or to indicate the tonal melody of the following vowels: *p, t, k* indicate a higher melody, and *b, d, g* a lower melody. The prevocalic glottal stop is not represented in the orthography. The voiced labial fricatives [β] and [v] and the voiced bilabial stop [b] occur only intervocalically in roots as variants of /p/. The intervocalic alveolar trill /r/ in roots is allophonic with the prevocalic alveolar stop [*t/d*], but is distinctive in grammatical formatives. The continuant [l] is a variant of /n/ occurring occasionally in Damara dialects.

Clicks. In Table 1 above, the standardized spelling is followed by a phonetic rendering. The clicks consist of four influxes (primary articulations) each having five variants determined by the effluxes (secondary articulations).

What all of the clicks have in common is that they are produced by at least two simultaneous closures; in addition to the primary closure, there is also a velar closure. During the articulation of the primary closure, the body of the tongue is moved down, so that when the primary closure is released, air rushes into the mouth, producing a characteristic "popping" sound; the sound represented as 'tsk-tsk' in ENGLISH is a dental click.

The spelling of some of the secondary articulations of the clicks is somewhat idiosyncratic, for historical reasons. A glottal stop following the primary articulation is not represented in the orthography: |*a* [ʔa]; the inaudible release of the (voiceless) velar closure is represented by *g*: |*ga* /|*a*/. The voiceless glottal fricative efflux is slightly delayed relative to the other effluxes, here indicated by a macron, e.g., *ha* [|¯]. Nasal accompaniment (e.g., |*n*) commences before the click articulation and continues throughout it, up to the vowel.

Vowels. Khoekhoegowab has five oral vowels *i, e, a, o, u*, with nasalized versions in certain combinations. Contrary to popular claims, all Khoekhoegowab vowels are of the same length, essentially short. Apparent long vowels and diphthongs arise through the elision of intervocalic consonants in roots, which are exclusively disyllabic C_1VC_2V in origin. Only the following sequences occur: /ii ee aa oo uu/, spelled with a macron for length: /ī, ē, ā, ō, ū/ and /ai ae ao au oe oa ui/. In addition, some nasalized vowel combinations occur: /ĩĩ, ãã, ũũ/, spelled *î â û*, and /ãĩ, ãũ, õã, ũĩ, (ĩã)/, spelled *âi âu ôa ûi (îa)*.

Root Structure and Tonology. Khoekhoegowab is a tone language. Tonal melodies consist of a sequence of two register (level) tonemes selected from a four-tone system. There are six main melodies. Tone is not marked in the practical orthography, other than using the letters for voiced and voiceless stop consonants to distinguish between lower and higher melodies, respectively, e.g.,: *doa* [tòà] 'tear (transitive)', *doa* [tòá] 'tear (intransitive)', *toa* [tőá] 'come to an end'. The articulation of initial stops is consistently voiceless, however.

All Khoekhoegowab roots are disyllabic and are historically based on the structure C_1VC_2V. Clicks can only occur as C_1, while C_2 is confined to the oral consonants *w* ([b], [v], or [β]) and *r*, and the nasals *m* and *n*. If C_1 is a glottal stop, then it is not represented in the practical orthography, e.g., *uri* 'jump' [ʔuri].

Roots that are conventionally considered to be monosyllabic (comprising so-called long vowels, nasal vowels, or oral/nasal diphthongs) are truly disyllabic, having the structure CVV, CṼṼ), or CVN. The first two structures arise through the deletion of the intervocalic C_2, and the third through deletion of the final vowel (apocope). When the final vowel is deleted, the nasal consonant N is syllabic. Depending on whether the deleted C_2 is oral or nasal and on whether the two vowels are identical or not, the following four patterns emerge from CV(C)V:

CV_1CV_1	ǀnowo	> *ǀnoo (slough skin), spelt ǀnō (long vowel)
CV_1CV_2	xora (scratch)	> xoa (write) (oral diphthong)
CV_1NV_1	ǂgana (inside)	> *ǂgãã (enter), spelt ǂgâ (nasal vowel)
CV_1NV_2	tomas	> *tõãs (wild cucumber), spelt tôas (nasal diphthong)

Deletion of the final vowel is only possible if the intervocalic consonant is a nasal, as it has to bear the tone of the second syllable. The following example is from the Haiǁom dialect: ǀama > ǀam (gnaw bones).

Syllables and morae are in isomorphic relation in roots. Tonal melodies consist of a sequence of two register (level) tonemes selected from a four-tone surface system. Six main melodies exist, apart from some residual melodies. Each melody consists of a primary and a sandhi version. Tonal sandhi occurs in lexical and postlexical phonology, while flip-flop perturbation is confined to compounds in lexical phonology. Khoekhoegowab tonology is typologically most akin to the Southeast Asian type, in that it makes use of paradigmatic displacement of melodies in cyclic application, rather than feature changing rules.

Basic Morphology

Khoekhoegowab is exclusively suffixing.

Noun Morphology. Typically for Central Khoesaan languages, Khoekhoegowab inflects not only pronouns but also nouns for person, gender, and number (singular, dual, plural). Conventional analyses hold that Khoekhoegowab nouns consist of a stem with a PGN (person/gender/number) suffix. This suffix is, historically, a cliticized pronoun, and the noun+suffix complex is historically a reduced relative clause (Haacke 1992). Some examples of nouns inflected for person are: *khoe-ta* (person-1SG) 'I, the person'; *khoe-ts* (person-2M/SG) 'You, the person', *khoe-b* (person-3M/SG) 'He, the person'.

Nouns can also be marked for tense and have internal negation:

gao tama-b
chief NEG-3M/SG
'a non-chief'

gao ge i-b
chief PAST STATIVE-3M/SG
'he who was chief'

gao tama ge i-b
chief NEG PAST STATIVE-3M/SG
'he who was not chief'

Khoekhoegowab has four definite articles. These determiners, which are conventionally misinterpreted as "pronoun stems", denote communicatory status in a way that is superficially similar, yet crucially different, to the category of person:

Stem	Refers to
ti	singular speaker
si	dual/plural speaker, excludes addressee
sa	addressee
ǁî	discussed

While *ti* and *si* can be interpreted as first-person singular and plural, respectively, and ǁî as third person, the crucial difference is that in *sa* the category speaker (first person) is overruled by addressee (second person). *Sa* can thus occur with PGN markers of first *or* second person: *sa-m* (1F/DUAL PGN) 'we two' (speaker included), *sa-ro* (2F/DUAL PGN) 'you two' (speaker excluded). In non-singular pronominal usage with PGN markers of the first person, *si* and *sa* denote exclusion and inclusion of the addressee, respectively: *si-khom* 'we two males (excluding you)', *sa-khom* 'we two males (you and I)'.

Khoekhoegowab noun phrases may also be marked for case. Nominative case is unmarked; genitive, oblique, agentive, and vocative cases are marked by suffixes (genitive *–di*, obl *-a*, agentive *-i*, vocative *-e*).

Verb Morphology. Khoekhoegowab verbs are not inflected; tense and aspect distinctions are indicated by means of particles. The tense/aspect system is simple with only four tenses (*ge* remote past, *go* recent past, *nî* future/compellative, and unmarked present), and four aspects (*rV* inchoative, *i/a* stative, *hâ* perfective, and unmarked semelfactive). For certain moods, modality is marked immediately after the subject-PGN marker, e.g., by indicative *ge*. The aspect marker follows the tense marker and may merge with it, as in the present indicative.

Axa-b ge ra kai
boy-3M/SG INDIC INCHOATIVE big
'The boy is getting big.'

Axa-b ge a kai
boy-3M/SG INDIC STATIVE big
'The boy is big.'

Axa-b ge kai hâ
boy-3M/SG INDIC big PERFECTIVE
'The boy has grown big.'

Verb valency can be modified by means of five verbal extensions/suffixes:

stem	mû	'see'
applicative	mû-ba	'see for or on behalf of'
reciprocal	mû-gu	'see one another'
passive	mû-he	'seen'
reflexive	mû-sen	'see oneself'
stem	ǂoa	'go out'
venitive	ǂoa-xa	'come out'

While derivational morphology makes use mainly of suffixes, tone is also employed extensively for derivational purposes. Tone alone may differentiate transitive from intransitive verbs and nouns from verbs: ǂgắń 'close, transitive' vs. ǂgàǹ 'close, be blocked, intransitive'; gȍá(s) 'foam(ing), intransitive' vs. gȍàs 'foam, noun'.

In compound verbs, flip-flop (the pairwise exchange of melodies) is triggered in the initial head verb (X) when the second verb (Y) acts as a modifier or result of the first verb, giving a generalized meaning "do (X) to the extent/with the result that Y", e.g., *!gàwì!khàrű* 'ride until past, ride past' comes from *!gáwì* 'ride' and *!khàrű* 'pass, go by'.

Infinitives are formed by appending the feminine singular PGN-marker to the verb (without tonal changes), e.g., *khomai* 'read' > *khomais* 'to read, reading'.

Khoekhoegowab makes extensive use of incorporation (Haacke 1995). Nouns, postpositions and postpositional phrases can be overtly incorporated: *khoe-e lapessa ra mā* (person advice PRES.INCH give) 'give someone advice' > *khoe-e ra lapemā*; *dai-e sūs !nâ ra ǁhō* (milk pot in PRES.INCH pour) 'pour milk into a pot' > *dai-e sūsa ra ǁhō!nâ*.

As noted above, more generalized derivation takes place via suffixes:

ǂai-b	'anger'	noun
ǂai-xa	'angry'	adjective
ǂai-xa-se	'angrily'	adverb
ǂai-xa-si-b	'irritability'	noun

Basic Syntax

The surface order of Khoekhoegowab sentences is Subject-Object-Verb, if the subject and object are lexically specified nominals.

Ao-b	ge	tara-sa	ra	hui
man-3M/SG	INDIC	woman-3F/SG	PRES.INCHOATIVE	help

'A/the man is helping a/the woman.'

However, object PGN-markers, pronominal in function, follow the verb as enclitics:

Ao-b	ge	ra	hui	si
man-3M/SG	INDIC	PRES.INCHOATIVE	help	3F/SG

'A/the man is helping her.'

Khoekhoegowab syntax is highly flexible in constituent order as topicalization occurs via moving the relevant constituent into the slot immediately preceding the subject PGN-marker. Should a constituent other than the lexical specification of the subject (i.e., the noun "stem", possibly with qualifiers) be topicalized, then this subject specification is deposed, normally to a slot behind the modality marker:

Tarasa	b	ge	ao-b-a	ra	hui
woman	he	IND	he.being.man	PRES.INCHOATIVE	help

'He, the man, is helping the *woman*.'

Within a noun phrase, all qualifiers (demonstratives, adjectives, numerals, possessives, relative clauses) precede the noun in attributive function, and without inflection. The head noun is marked by sandhi tone. Modifiers can also follow the head noun as appositions, with a copy of the PGN-marker. Modifiers in pronominal use are governed by the PGN-marker alone: *{nē audos}a* (this car+OBL) 'this car, attributive', *{audos nēs}a* (car this.one+OBL) 'this car, appositive', *{nēs}a* (this one) 'this, pronominal'. Genitive NPs are morphologically marked by a possessive particle: *taras di aob* (woman POSS husband) 'the woman's husband'. The possessive particle may be omitted in transparent NPs, as the qualifying (possessive) function of the first NP (*taras*) always manifests itself in the tonal sandhi of the head noun (*aob*) that follows.

Agentive NPs in passive sentences may be formed with the suffix *–i*, if the PGN-marker is not syllabic (does not end in a vowel); otherwise, and most commonly, they are formed with the postposition *xa* 'by'.

ǀGôas	ge	axab*i* (or axab *xa*)	ra	ǂgaihe.
girl	IND	boy-by	PRES.INCH.	call.PASSIVE

'A/the girl is called by a/the boy.'

The negative marker for past and present tense is *tama;* for future tense, the negative may be either *tide* or *tama*. These markers immediately follow the stem that is to be negated: Tita ge go ǂkhā (I IND PAST.SEMELF refuse) 'I did refuse', Tita ge ǂkhā tama go hâ i or Tita ge go ǂkhā tama hâ i 'I didn't refuse', Tita ge ǂkhā tide (I IND refuse FUT.NEG) 'I won't refuse'. As indicated earlier, surface nouns may indicate tense and negation.

Contact with Other Languages

Khoekhoegowab borrows extensively from European languages; earlier from GERMAN, then especially from AFRIKAANS. Phonological adaptation is minimal, with only some evidence of epenthesis.

From Afrikaans: *brōxos* 'bridge' (< Afr. *brug*), *kombis* 'kitchen' (< Afr. *kombuis*), *plū* 'plough (verb)' (< Afr. *ploeg*), *klīmâs* 'younger maternal aunt' (<Afr. *kleinma*), *tekmasins* 'typewriter' (< Afr. *tikmasjien*), *tûis* 'garden' (< Afr. *tuin*).
From German: *gemaindes* 'congregation' (< Ger. *Gemeinde*), *tsanges* 'pair of pliers' (< Ger. *Zange*), *t(u)rub* 'armed forces' (< Ger. *Truppe*, Afr. *troep(e)*)
From English: *stems* 'post-stamp' (< Eng. 'stamp')

Common Words

man:	aob	long:	gāxu
woman:	taras	small:	ǂkhari
water:	ǁgam-i	yes:	ā
sun:	sores	no:	hî-î
three:	!nona	good:	!gâi
fish:	ǁaub	bird:	anis
big:	kai	dog:	arib
tree:	hais		

Example Sentences

(1)	Nē	hoa	skolǁgôa-n	Khoekhoegowab-a
	these	all	schoolchildren-3PL	Khoekhoe.language-OBL

ra !hoa-n ge ||în di ǂkhani-de
INCHOATIVE speak-3PL INDIC they GEN book-PL

tūraxase ra khomai.
eagerly INCHOATIVE read
'All those students who speak Khoekhoegowab eagerly read their books.'

(2) Mati-ts sa ǂkham axa-ts-a a mîdan
how-2M/SG ART young boy-2m/sg STATIVE convince

gu ||khā?
them can
'How can you, small boy, convince them?'

(3) Buruxa gowa-b ge sida di ||gûsigowa-b-a!
wonderful language INDIC we GEN mother-language-OBL
'A wonderful language it is, our mother tongue!'

Select Bibliography

Elphick, R. 1977. *Kraal and Castle*. New Haven: Yale University Press.

Haacke, W.H.G. 1990. "Nama: Survival through Standardization?" In Fodor, I. and Hagège, Cl. (eds.) *Language Reform - History and Future* Vol. IV. Hamburg: Buske. 397–162.

_____. 1992. "Dislocated Noun Phrases in Khoekhoe (Nama/Damara): Further Evidence for the Sentential Hypothesis." In *Afrikanist. Arbeitspapier* no. 29 (1992), Cologne. 149–162.

_____. 1995. "Instances of Incorporation and Compounding in Khoekhoe (Nama/Damara)." In Traill, A., A. Vossen and M. Biesele (eds.) *The Complete Linguist. Papers in Memory of Patrick Dickens*. Cologne: Köppe. 125–209.

Haacke, W., E. Eiseb and L. Namaseb. 1997. "Internal and External Relations of Khoekhoe Dialects: A Preliminary Survey." In Haacke, W. and E.D. Elderkin (eds.) *Namibian Languages: Reports and Papers*. Namibian African Studies Vol. 4. Cologne: Rüdiger Köppe. 125–209.

Köhler, O. 1975. "Geschichte und Probleme der Gliederung der Sprachen Afrikas." In Baumann, H. (ed.) *Die Völker Afrikas und ihre raditionellen Kulturen*. Wiesbaden: Steiner. 135–373.

Voben, R. 1997. *Die Khoe-Sprachen: Ein Beitrag zur Erforschung der Sprachgeschichte Afrikas*. Quellen zur Khoisan-Forschung 12. Cologne: Rüdiger Köppe.

NAHUATL

Frances Karttunen

Language Name: Nahuatl. **Alternates:** *Aztec, Mexicano, Mexica.* **Autonym:** Most speakers today call their language *Mexicano* or *Mexica.* Less commonly, *mācēhuallahtolli* 'the speech of the common people'. The Aztecs referred to any speech mutually intelligible with their own as *nāhuatlahtōlli* 'clear speech' or just *nāhuatl.*

Location: Communities in the Federal District and the following states of the Republic of Mexico: Colima, Durango, Guerrero, Hidalgo, Jalisco, Mexico, Michoacan, Morelos, Nayarit, Puebla, San Luis Potosi, Tabasco, Tlaxcala, and Veracruz. Some Nahuatl speakers have become economic migrants to the United States.

Nahuatl and its close relatives, Pipil and Pochutec, were previously spoken in large areas of central Mexico with outposts as far south as modern El Salvador and Nicaragua. The language of the Aztecs of Tenochtitlan at the time of the Spanish conquest in the 16th century was a central dialect of Nahuatl.

Family: Nahuatl, together with Pipil and Pochutec (extinct), comprise the Aztecan branch of the Uto-Aztecan language family.

Related Languages: Other southern Uto-Aztecan languages are Cora, Huichol, Tarahumara, Northern and Southern Tepehuan, Yaqui-Mayo, and Pima-Papago (O'odham). The Northern Uto-Aztecan languages include Hopi, Tübatulabal, and the Takic and Numic languages groups. Among the Numic languages are Ute and Shoshone-Comanche, and among the Takic languages are Luiseño and Cupeño of the extreme southern-most part of California.

Dialects: The primary dialect division is between central dialects and peripheral dialects, with further distinctions among the peripheral ones. The central group includes dialects of the Valley of Mexico, the Huasteca region, central and north Puebla, Tlaxcala, Morelos, and central Guerrero.

Number of Speakers: 800,000–1.7 million.

Origin and History

The geographic distribution of Uto-Aztecan languages agrees with the migration myths of the Nahua peoples that they had their origin in the northwest and came via waves of migration south into Mesoamerica. Latecomers to an ancient cultural area and *Sprachbund*, they adopted much of what was already there, both in terms of material culture and grammatical structure. There is a Mesoamerican area well defined in terms of grammatical constructions and metaphors shared by many groups speaking genetically unrelated languages (MAYA, Otomanguean, Mixe-Zoquean, and others), and Nahuatl had become well established as part of it long before the first European contact in the 16th century. In spite of this, Nahuatl shows little evidence of lexical borrowing from other Mesoamerican languages. On the other hand, through domination of trade in the 15th century and continuing into the colonial period when Nahuatl speakers often served as agents of Spanish administrators, Nahuatl place-names were spread over the entire Mesoamerican area, coexisting with or replacing place-names in locally spoken languages. Populations in these areas continued to speak their own languages, however.

Soon after the conquest of Mexico, Franciscan friars adapted SPANISH and LATIN orthographic conventions to the alphabetic representation of Nahuatl. A massive educational effort was undertaken to teach reading and writing to young Nahua males (Anderson and Dibble 1982). Alphabetic writing was immediately adopted for community record keeping and legal documentation, and there are dated samples of written Nahuatl for every decade from the 1540s through the first decade of the 19th century (Karttunen 1982). From these records it appears that there was less dialect differentiation during the colonial period than presently, although an alternative explanation is that a type of administrative dialect was used for written documents that was more uniform than what was actually spoken from one community to the next.

Prior to the introduction of alphabetic writing, Nahuatl speakers had used a logosyllabic writing system similar to (and undoubtedly derived from) those used by the Zapotec, Maya, and Mixtec. It included symbols for entire words/concepts and other elements that indicated pronunciation in syllabic units. Large libraries of documents written in these symbols were reported by chroniclers of the Spanish conquest. From the little that remains of such writing on monuments and from new documents commissioned soon after the conquest, it appears that although Nahuatl speakers produced captions, they did not organize their logosyllabic elements into running text as the Maya did, but we cannot be sure.

With the aid of native-speaking assistants, the Franciscans, and later the Jesuits, compiled sophisticated grammars and dictionaries in the 16th and 17th centuries. Bernardino de Sahagún and his Nahua assistants compiled a 12-volume encyclopedia of Nahua history and culture in the language (Sahagún 1970–1982). In addition to legal documents—wills, property transfers, complaints, suits and countersuits—much literature was redacted in the language, especially in the 16th century. There

Table 1: Consonants (Orthography)

	Labial	Dental	Alveo-Palatal	Velar	Labialized Velar	Glottal
Stops	p	t		c, qu	cu, uc	h
Fricatives			c, z	x		
Affricates		tl	tz	ch		
Nasals	m	n				
Laterals		l, tl				
Glides	hu, uh		y			

are manuscripts of songs/poetry; histories organized by year from long before the Spanish Conquest on into the colonial period; origin and foundation myths; riddles and aphorisms; and a type of moral discourse known as "ancient words". Several Nahuatl speakers of the colonial period created compendia of earlier fragmentary works and wrote annals.

The vitality enjoyed by written Nahuatl throughout the colonial period, however, was profoundly undercut by the abolition of the Indian courts at the time of Mexico's independence from Spain. Prior to independence, documentation written in Nahuatl could be presented as evidence in court, and depositions could be recorded in Nahuatl. With the move to Spanish-language court proceedings, the single most pragmatic function of written Nahuatl was lost.

Modern linguistic study of Nahuatl began at the opening of the 20th century, was interrupted by the Mexican Revolution, and has continued since. The Summer Institute of Linguistics, an arm of the Wycliffe Bible translators, has created grammars and dictionaries for a number of communities, while academic linguists have also produced a large body of grammatical and lexical work.

Orthography and Basic Phonology

As mentioned above, within years of initial contact in the first quarter of the 16th century, Franciscan grammarians and lexicographers devised an orthography for Nahuatl based on Latin and Spanish orthographic conventions. Several diagraphs served to represent unitary consonants absent from these two languages: *tl* for laterally released /t^{l}/ and *tz* for /t^{s}/. The grammarians pointed out that orthographic *ll* (as in *calli* 'house') represented geminate /l+l/ across syllable boundary and not palatalized /ly/. By the 17th century, the inversion of the digraphs *cu* /k^{w}/ and *hu* /w/ to *uc* and *uh* in syllable-final position was generally accepted: *totē<u>cu</u>iyo* /to.te:.k^{w}i.yo/ 'our lord', *tē<u>uc</u>tli* /te:k^{w}.t^{l}i/ 'lord'; *cua<u>hu</u>*itl /k^{w}a.witl/ 'tree', *cua<u>uh</u>ti* /k^{w}aw.ti/ 'to stiffen, become like wood'.

Segmental glottal stop, which occurs only syllable finally, was sporadically represented with orthographic *h* but generally omitted. Distinctive vowel length was unmarked. Late in the 16th century the Jesuit grammarian Antonio del Rincón appended to his grammar (Rincón 1595) a list of minimal pairs contrasting in vowel length and presence versus absence of glottal stop. His fellow Jesuit, Horacio Carochi, expanded on Rincón's contrastive vocabulary list and used a set of diacritics for long vowels, short vowels, and vowels followed by *saltillo* ('glottal stop') in his 1645 grammar, but the diacritics were not adopted into general use.

In 1940 an "Aztec Congress" of Nahuatl speakers was held, and there a revision of the traditional orthography was adopted that replaced the Spanish conventions of *c/qu* for /k/ and *hu* for /w/ with orthographic *k* and *w*, while keeping the digraphs *tl*, *tz*, and *ch*: *tlakatl* for traditional *tlacatl*; *nawatl* for *nahuatl*. Glottal stop or its reflex is generally represented as *h* in modern orthography, but some areas have adopted *j*.

J. Richard Andrews in his grammar of Nahuatl, Frances Karttunen in her dictionary, and Karttunen and Campbell in their Nahuatl course book use a canonical orthography based on the traditional one enriched with macrons to mark long vowels. This canonical orthography is used throughout this chapter.

The letter *c* represents a dental fricative /s/ before front vowels and a velar stop /k/ elsewhere. *Tz* and *ch* represent affricates /t^{s}/ and /č/, respectively. *Tl* is likewise an affricate, but with a lateral release: /t^{l}/.

The Nahuatl obstruents are voiceless. The resonants are voiced in syllable-initial position and devoiced, sometimes to inaudibility, in syllable-final position.

The nasals /m/ and /n/ only contrast in syllable-initial position; /m/ delabializes in word-final position, and there is a further tendency to velarization of word-final nasals to [ŋ]. Word internally, both /m/ and /n/ assimilate to the place of articulation of a following consonant.

There are no initial or final consonant clusters. Two consonants can only be adjacent across a syllable boundary. If affixation or borrowing would result in a cluster, vowel epenthesis or consonant deletion occurs. The absence of consonant clusters is obscured in the orthography by the use of digraphs for some consonants; the first syllable of *mētztli* >'moon'= /mēt^{s}.t^{l}i/ ends in the single consonant /t^{s}/ and the second syllable begins with the single consonant /t^{l}/.

Table 2: Vowels (Orthography)

	Front	Central	Back
High	i		
Mid	e		o
Low		a	

All vowels can occur long or short. Because there is no high-mid contrast for back vowels, there is considerable nondistinctive variation with /ō/ sometimes perceived as higher than /o/.

Stress in Nahuatl is always on the penultimate syllable, except in masculine vocative forms ending in *-e* where stress is word final. Since Nahuatl makes heavy use of derivational and inflectional suffixes, the syllable that is stressed in the dictionary citation form of a word often is not the stressed syllable when that word is inflected in context: *'tepētl* 'hill', *te'pēmeh* 'hills', *tote'pēhuān* 'our hills', *tepētlānchā' nehqueh* 'dwellers among the hills'.

Basic Morphology

Nahuatl has two classes of morphemes: inflected stems and uninflected particles. The inflected stems include verbs, nouns, and locatives that are sometimes called relational nouns.

Relational nouns, which are never freestanding, can take possessive prefixes, or they can be compounded with noun stems: *ī-pan calli* and *cal-pan* both mean 'on/at the house'.

Nouns are either absolutive or possessed: *me-tl* 'maguey cactus' *no-me* 'my maguey cactus'. The most common absolute marker is *-tli* for stems ending in consonants, *-li* after stems ending in *l*, and *-tl* for stems ending in vowels. Animate and quasi-animate nouns have distinct plural forms, but inanimate nouns do not: *tōch-tli* 'rabbit', *tōtōch-tin/tōch-meh* 'rabbits'; *calli* 'house/houses'.

Adjectives are not morphologically distinct from nouns. Qualities of nouns are usually expressed in compounds in which the first element modifies the second: *cihuā-* 'woman' + *tōtolin* 'domestic fowl', *cihuātōtolin* 'turkey hen'.

When nouns are enumerated, the numbers may take noun classifiers, but they are not obligatory. The most common and neutral of the several classifiers is *-tetl* derived from the noun *tetl* 'stone': *nāuh-tetl tamalli* 'four tamales' (literally: four-lump classifier tamale).

There is no case or gender marking. There are no definite or indefinite articles.

Nahuatl verbs agree with their subjects in person and number. Person agreement is indicated by prefixes for first- and second-person subjects; there are no prefixes for third-person subjects. In addition, transitive verbs must have object prefixes, which must be specific or nonspecific. Nonspecific object markers are either human or nonhuman.

The order of elements within a verb is: SOV-derivational suffix-inflectional suffix-number suffix. Some uses of derivational suffixes are for forming causative, benefactive, and impersonal verbs. A common use of inflectional suffixes is to indicate tense and number marking on verbs.

Transitive verbs can incorporate nouns in place of the object prefix providing the action is generic rather than specific: *cac-chīhua* 'he engages in shoemaking', *qui-chīhua cac-tli* 'he makes a specific shoe/shoes'.

Basic Syntax

Although the prefix order is SOV, the neutral order of verb and noun phrases in a sentence is VOS. Focus on a noun phrase is accomplished with the particle *in*, which has the sense of 'as for X'. This particle is ubiquitous in Nahuatl.

Syntactic relations are expressed morphologically by obligatory prefixing of subject and object markers to the verb. Because there is no case marking on nouns, where subject, direct object, and oblique object are all third person, there is ambiguity of reference between the prefixes and noun phrases in a sentence.

Negation is formed with the particle *ahmō*, the negative prefix *ah-*, negative forms of clause-introductory particles, and the use of the vetitive form of verbs ("beware lest X").

Ahmō	qui-chiya	Malia	in	īoquich.
NEG	SG.OBJ.SPEC-wait:PRES	María	FOCUS	POSS.husband

'Maria isn't waiting for her husband.'

Contact with Other Languages

In some areas Nahuatl speakers live in contact with speakers of other indigenous languages. In the Huasteca, Nahua communities are interspersed with Huastec communities. Elsewhere there are neighboring communities of Totonacs, Otomí, and others.

All indigenous languages in Mexico, however, have been primarily engaged with Spanish since the first quarter of the 16th century, and Nahuatl has borrowed massively from Spanish. The borrowing falls into three clear stages. Spanish nouns that end in vowels are borrowed as if they end in a glottal stop, which is reflected in the morphology. Borrowed nouns that take Nahuatl absolutive suffixes take *-tli*, the one used with consonant-final stems: Spanish *camisa* 'shirt' > Nahuatl *camixah-tli*. After an initial period of assimilating Spanish vocabulary to Nahuatl morphology, the small Nahuatl class of absolutiveless nouns was expanded to accommodate the incoming loans, so most Spanish loan nouns do not take *-tli*: Spanish *sábado* 'Saturday' > Nahuatl *xapatoh*. Spanish verbs are borrowed by adding the suffix *-oā* to the Spanish infinitive form: Spanish *firmar* 'to sign one's name' > Nahuatl *firmaroā*. Spanish locational and temporal particles were borrowed very early in the contact period: Spanish *hasta* 'up to, until' > Nahuatl *asta*.

Common Words

man:	oquichtli	small:	tepitzīn
woman:	cihuātl	yes:	quēmah
water:	ātl	no:	ahmō
sun:	tōnatiuh	good:	cualli
three:	ēyi	bird:	tōtōtl
fish:	michin	dog:	chichi
big:	huēi	tree:	cuahuitl
long:	huēiyac		

Example Sentences

(1) Ni-c-nequi
1SG.SUBJ-3SG.SPEC.OBJ-want-PRES

ni-c-cuāz	tlaxcal-li.
1.SG.SUBJ-3SG.SPEC.OBJ-eat:FUT	tortilla-ABSOLUTIVE

'I want to eat a tortilla/tortillas.'

(2) Qui-chiya-ni	Malia	in	Xuan.
3SG.SPEC.OBJ-wait-customarily	María	as.for	Juan

'As for Juan, he customarily waits for Maria.' or 'As for Juan, Maria customarily waits for him.'

(3) ō-ni-quin-tla-maca-c.
ANTECESSIVE-1SG.SUBJ-3PL.SPEC.OBJ-NONSPEC.OBJECT-give-PRETERITE
'I gave something to them.' (This could also mean 'I gave them to something', but it would be hard to make sense of the latter reading.)

Efforts to Preserve, Protect, and Promote the Language

During the presidency of Lázaro Cárdenas (1934–1940) and for some years thereafter, efforts were made to promote literacy in Nahuatl and active use of the language through Nahuatl newspapers, local theatricals, and political action meetings. More recently, a seminar on the Nahuatl language at the National Autonomous University of Mexico has encouraged Nahuatl speakers to create a new Nahuatl literature that is showcased in a section of the journal *Estudios de cultura náhuatl* entitled *Yancuic tlahtolli* ('new words').

Today, the absolute number of Nahuatl speakers is on the increase, but as a percentage of the Mexican population they are diminishing. In many communities, only middle-aged and older speakers command the language, and among younger speakers who use the language, there are signs of language death (restricted vocabulary, reduced number of grammatical constructions in use, heavy calquing on Spanish sentence structure, and massive lexical borrowing).

As Nahuas feel ethnically overwhelmed by the majority culture, they seek solidarity through special clothes, crafts, rituals, and their language. However, this has proven problematical. Puristic efforts to purge Nahuatl of Hispanicisms have led to discouragement and abandonment of the language by speakers who are convinced that it is irreparably contaminated or that they are not competent to speak it elegantly. The massive body of colonial-period Nahuatl literature is unavailable to most speakers and not obviously relevant to economic or even cultural survival in Mexico at the close of the 20th century.

Select Bibliography

Anderson, Arthur J.O., Frances Berdan, and James Lockhart. 1976. *Beyond the Codices: The Nahua View of Colonial Mexico.* Berkeley, Los Angeles, and London: University of California Press.

Anderson, Arthur J.O., and Charles E. Dibble. 1982. *Florentine Codex. Introductory Volume: Introductions, Sahagūn's Prologues and Interpolations, General Bibliography, General Indices.* Salt Lake City: University of Utah Press and School of American Research.

Andrews, J. Richard. 1975. *Introduction to Classical Nahuatl.* Austin: University of Texas Press.

Bierhorst, John. 1985. *Cantares Mexicanos: Songs of the Aztecs.* Stanford: Stanford University Press.

____. 1992. *History and Mythology of the Aztecs: The Codex Chimalpopoca.* Tucson: The University of Arizona Press.

Carochi, Horacio. 1983. *Arte de la lengua mexicana. Facsímiles de lingüistica y filología náhuas: 2.* Mexico City: Universidad Nacional Autonoma de Mexico, Instituto de Investigaciones Filológicas, Instituto de Investigaciones Históricas. [Originally published in 1645]

H. de León-Portilla, Ascensión. 1988. *Tepuztlahcuilolli: Impresros nahuas, historia y bibliografía.* 2 vols. Mexico City: National University of Mexico Press.

Hill, Jane H., and Kenneth C. Hill. 1986. *Speaking Mexicano: Dynamics of Syncretic Language in Central Mexico.* Tucson: University of Arizona Press.

Karttunen, Frances. 1982. "Nahuatl Literacy." In *The Inca and Aztec States 1400–1800: Anthropology and History.* George Collier, *et al.*, eds. New York: Academic Press. 395–417.

_____. 1990. "Conventions of Polite Speech in Nahuatl." In *Estudios de cultura náhuatl* 20: 281–296.

_____. 1995. "The Roots of Sixteenth-Century Mesoamerican Lexicography." In *Cultures, Ideologies, and the Dictionary: Studies in Honor of Ladislav Zgusta.* Braj B. Kachru and Henry Kahane, eds. Tübingen: Max Niemeyer Verlag. 75–88.

Karttunen, Frances, and R. Joe Campbell. 1994. *Foundation Course in Nahuatl Grammar.* Austin: University of Texas, Institute of Latin American Studies.

Karttunen, Frances, and James Lockhart. 1976. *Nahuatl in the Middle Years: Language Contact Phenomena in Texts of the Colonial Period.* University of California Publications in Linguistics. 85. Berkeley and Los Angeles: University of California Press.

_____. 1987. *The Art of Nahuatl Speech: The Bancroft Dialogues.* Los Angeles: UCLA Latin American Center, Nahuatl Studies Series 2.

León-Portilla, Miguel. 1991. "Have We Really Translated the Mesoamerican 'Ancient Word'?" In *On The Translation of Native American Literatures.* Brian Swann, ed. 313–338. Washington and London: Smithsonian Institution Press.

Lockhart, James. 1991. *Nahuas and Spaniards: Postconquest Central Mexican History and Philology.* Stanford: Stanford University Press.

_____. 1992. *The Nahuas after the Conquest: A Social and Cultural History of the Indians of Central Mexico, Sixteenth through Eighteenth Centuries.* Stanford: Stanford University Press.

Molina, Alonso de. 1945. *Arte de la lengua mexicana y castellana.* Madrid: Ediciones Cultural Hispanica. [Originally published in 1571.]

_____. 1970. *Vocabulario en lengua castellana y mexicana y mexicana y castellana.* Mexico City: Editorial Porrua. [Facsimile edition. Originally pub. 1571.]

Olmos, Andrés de. 1985. *Arte de la lengua mexicana y vocabulario.* Thelma D. Sullivan, ed. Mexico City: Universidad Nacional Autonoma de Mexico. [Composed in 1547.]

Rincón, Antonio de. 1967. *Arte mexicana, en Mexico, en casa de Pedro Bali, 1595.* Guadalajara: Oficina Tipográfica de la Secretaría de Fomento. [Originally published in 1595].

Sahagún, Bernardino de. 1970–82. *Florentine Codex: General History of the Things of New Spain.* Arthur J.O. Anderson and Charles E. Dibble, eds. and transl. 13 vols. Salt Lake City: School of American Research and University of Utah Press.

Navajo

Margaret Field

Language Name: Navajo (Navaho). **Autonym:** *Diné*.

Location: The northeastern part of the state of Arizona, northwestern New Mexico, southeastern Utah, and a few speakers in Colorado.

Family: Athabaskan (Athapaskan, Athabascan).

Related Languages: Navajo is part of the Na-Dene language stock, and is related to other Northern Athabaskan languages spoken in the state of Alaska and Canada, as well as several nearly extinct or extinct Athabaskan languages of the Pacific Coast. It is most closely related to other Apachean languages in the Southwest, including Jicarilla, Mescalero-Chiricahua, and Western Apache.

Dialects: The Navajo language is spoken over a very wide geographic area, and dialect variation does exist, although it is not very well documented to date. The most salient example that is often cited is *yas* versus *zas* 'snow.' Alternations have been documented between syllable-initial consonants *t/k/x*, *x/h*, *s/ts*, and *gh/w/y*. In addition there is some variation in the use of *s/sh* in first-person possessive prefix that is not always because of sibilant assimilation but rather appears to be from dialect difference. Saville-Troike (1974) also discusses some lexical variation.

Number of Speakers: According to the 1990 U.S. census, there are 148,530 speakers including 7,616 monolinguals, out of 219,198 ethnic Navajo (Grimes, *et al.* 1998).

Origin and History

Although the exact time of arrival of the first Athabaskans in the Southwest, as well as their route of travel from groups farther north (in Canada) is not entirely clear, most scholars from varying fields agree that it was approximately 1,000 years ago, and the Navajo and other Apachean groups separated from each other after this date. Whether early Apacheans traveled as one group or in bands is not clear either, but it appears that they migrated southward due to famine or other ecological disasters, arriving in the area which is now occupied by the current Navajo tribe (*Dinetah*, meaning 'Navajo homeland') around A.D. 1300. The name "Navajo" is most likely derived from the early Spanish appellation Apaches de Nabajó, as the Spanish observed that Apachean languages and Navajo were mutually intelligible and thus referred to the Navajo as the "Apaches" who lived in the "Nabajó region." The Spanish *Nabajó* appears to be borrowed in turn from the Tewa *navahuu* meaning 'field + wide valley' (Harrington 1940, in Brugge 1979). Early Spanish records dating from approximately 1630 also indicate that Navajos were more agricultural than other Apachean groups, and in this way more like their Puebloan neighbors. These records describe a semisedentary people who planted maize but also hunted, traded with the Pueblos around them, had many local headmen including both peace and war chiefs, and were skillful warriors (Brugge 1979). Horses were not introduced to the Navajo until the arrival of the Spanish. During the 18th and 19th centuries the Navajo people continued to live in *Dinetah*, fighting sporadically with Mexican colonists and Ute Indians from the north, and eventually with American colonists and military representatives. In 1863 Kit Carson was instructed by the U.S. government to round up all members of the Navajo tribe and incarcerate them at Fort Sumner, New Mexico. About 6,000 people were forced to make the trek of several hundred miles and then kept against their will at Ft. Sumner, where many died of hunger and illness. In 1868, the U.S. government agreed to allow them to return to their traditional homeland. Today the Navajo tribe numbers well over 200,000 (Grimes *et al.* 1998) and is the second largest Native American tribe in the United States, after Cherokee.

Orthography and Basic Phonology

The now standardized Navajo orthography was developed by Robert Young and William Morgan in the 1930s, combining the systems used by earlier Franciscan and Protestant missionaries (Lockard 1996). See Tables 1 and 2 on the following page.

Tone. Navajo has tone as a distinctive feature. Short vowels and diphthongs may have high or low tone; long vowels and vowel clusters may have rising or falling tone.

Basic Phonological Rules. The stems of Navajo nominal, postpositional, and verbal elements almost always have the syllable structure CV, or CVC; prefixes have the form CV or C (Young 1979; Young and Morgan 1987). The Navajo language has an extremely complex phonology that I will not attempt to encapsulate here, as even a "basic" description would require several pages.

Basic Morphology

Noun Morphology. Navajo nouns range from the simplest nominal forms, stem nouns, such as *dił*, 'blood,' or *gah* 'rabbit,' to complex nominalizations such as *bee 'ił 'ada' agizí tsin*

Table 1: Consonants

	Voicing	Labial	Alveolar/dental	Alv-pal affricates	Lateral	Palatal	Velar	Labio-velar	Glottal
Stops	+	b	d	dz	dl	j	g		
	-		t	ts	tł	ch	k	kw	ʻ
Ejectives	-		t'	ts'	tł'	ch'	k'		
Fricatives	+		z		l	zh	gh		
	-		s		ł	sh	x		h, hw
Nasals	+	m	n						
Glides	+					y		w	

Table 2: Vowels*

	Front	Central	Back
High	i, ii, į, įį		o, oo, ǫ,ǫǫ
Mid	e, ee, ę, ęę		
Low		a, aa, ą, ąą	

*Oral 'a', nasal 'ą', long oral 'aa', long nasal 'ąą'.
Diphthongs: ei, ai, ao, oi

bighą́ąh dé' áhígįį 'screwdriver,' lit. 'that which is used to twist things away out of sight that is attached to wood.' Between these two extremes are various combinations that are today fully lexicalized for speakers as a single noun, including historically compound forms such as *kék'eh ké-* 'foot' plus *k'eh* 'place': 'footprint', as well as nominalized verbs such as *nímasii*: *nímaz*, 'it is round' plus *-ii* (nominalizing enclitic). Whatever the historical path of grammaticization, Navajo nouns are not marked for much grammatical information except possession, which may be for first, second, third, or fourth person, or indefinitely possessed (by "someone"). Some nouns, such as body parts, are inalienably possessed. Some may also be pluralized with the distributive (DIST) plural prefix along with a possessive prefix, such that they are possessed by several: *danihima* 'our mother', although otherwise plurality is always marked on the verb. There are also a few kinship terms that may be pluralized through the addition of the suffix *-ké*: *ashiiké* 'boys', *at'éédké*, 'girls', etc.

Verbs may be nominalized through the addition of various nominalizing/relativizing enclitics, including (1) *-ii* 'one which is (has the inherent quality of being)': *mą'ii* 'the roamer, e.g., coyote'; (2) *-í* 'one which is'; and (3) the more particularizing *-ígíí* 'the one in particular which is', thus: *sidá* 's/he sits', *sidáhí* 'sitter', *sidáhígíí* 'the one who is sitting'. There is also another enclitic *-yę́e*, meaning 'that (previously mentioned) one,' or 'the one which is gone': *dine'iyę́e* 'those people'.

Nouns may also be modified through the addition of a small set of directional enclitics, such as *-góó* 'towards', *-dę́ę́* 'from', etc.

There are also interrogative suffixes: *-sh* and *-shą́ą́* 'how about X', as well as a modal enclitic of uncertainty *-shįį* 'maybe X', and a negative circumfix *doo- ... -da* 'not X'. The subordinating enclitic *-go*, which typically goes on verbs, may also attach to nouns, yielding the meaning 'being X', as in *dinék'ehgo* 'being Navajo, in the Navajo way'.

Verbal Morphology. The Navajo verb typically consists of a stem preceded by two or more (up to nine) prefixes in a sequential order that produce a lexical unit. Verb prefixes may be divided into two broad classes: paradigmatic and derivational-thematic (Young and Morgan 1987). Paradigmatic prefixes identify verbal arguments, mode, aspect, degree of transitivity, and number. Derivational-thematic prefixes include a wide range of elements that contribute to lexical meaning, including direction, manner, location, and aspect. Many thematic prefixes have lost their historical meaning and have simply become part of a verb theme, and may be separated from the stem by other more productive prefixes, as in *yá- ...łti'* 'to speak': *yáshti'* 'I speak', *yáníłti'* 'you speak', *yáłti'* 's/he speaks' (see Tables 3 and 4 on the next page).

Navajo verbs are divided into two classes: "active" and "neuter". Active verbs may be conjugated in three to six different "modes" or paradigms, including the imperfective, perfective, future/progressive, usitative/iterative, and optative. Neuter verbs may only be conjugated in one paradigm, either imperfective or perfective. Imperfective neuters denote attributes or qualities of their subject, as in the following examples: *łibá* 'it is gray', *nidaaz* 'it is heavy', *'ałhosh* 'one is asleep'. Perfective neuters denote a completed action, as in the subject being in position, or in a state of rest resulting from some action. Both active and neuter paradigms (especially in the perfective) may be further subdivided into as many as four different conjugations depending on which prefix, if any, they take in position 7 (0, *yi-*, *ni-* or *si-*).

Transitivity is marked on the verb through a set of prefixes (four of them: *0, ł, l, d*) called "classifiers" (Young and Morgan 1987), or "transitivity indicators" (Kibrik 1993, 1996). The literature does employ the term "passive" for constructions involving detransitivizing classifiers (*l, d*) that encode a suppressed agent. Similarly, much of the literature discusses the use of the classifier that signals increased transitivity as a causativizing device. For phonological reasons, and due to the fact that a "peg" prefix (prefix that fills out the CVC structure at the beginning of verb stems when necessary) often appears in either subject or object positions, active and "passive" constructions often appear identical. Both active and neuter verb classes may be "passivized" in this way:

Table 3: Basic Prefix Position Template

1	2	3	4	5	6	7	8	9	Stem
Adverb	Repet.	Distrib. Pl.	Dir. obj.	4th pers., deictic subj., indef. subj.	Adverb	Mode	Subject	Classifier	

Decreased transitivity or "simple passive" examples:

1)*Mósí yoołteeł* 'S/he is carrying the/a cat'
cat obj.themat.classif.carry.animate.obj

Mósí yiltééł 'The/a cat is being carried'
peg.classif.carry.animate.obj

2)*Gish yis(ł)tą́* 'S/he keeps the/a cane'
cane obj.classif.hold.cylindrical.obj

Gish yis(l)tą́ 'The/a cane is kept'
peg.classif.hold.cylindrical.obj

In the second example the classifiers (ł, l) disappear at the surface level.

Increased transitivity:

3)*yi(0)béézh* 'it's boiling'
peg.classif.boils

yiłbeezh 's/he's boiling it'
obj.classif.boils

Negation is achieved through the use of the negative frame *doo...da* around the verb (or noun) phrase, as in the following examples:

doo łikan da 'it's not sweet'
not sweet not

doo shił yá'át'ééh da 'I don't like it'
not to.me pleasant not

díí ch'ah doo shí da 'this hat isn't mine'
this hat not me not

Basic Syntax

When both subject and object are represented by nouns in addition to the subject and object prefixes marked on the verb, the order is generally SOV. When the subject is other than third person it is generally represented by the verb-incorporated pronoun alone. It has been suggested that Navajo has an animacy hierarchy in which humans must precede animals (Young and Morgan 1987), followed by several finer levels of discrimination (Creamer 1974), in sentence order, resulting in inverted subject/object order. Inversion is mandatory when the subject is inanimate and the object is animate. When inversion occurs, it is marked by the replacement of the unmarked *yi-* 3rd person object prefix with the marked *bi-* 3rd person object prefix, as in the following (examples from Young and Morgan 1987):

ashkii dzaneez bishhash 'The mule bit the boy.'
boy mule it-bit-it

Table 4: Sample Verb Paradigm of the Verb 'to make'

Tense + stem form	**Imperfective** *-lééh/-nééh* X makes it	**Perfective** *-laa/-yaa* X made it	**Future** *-nííł/-lííł* X will make it	**Usitative** - '*įįd* X makes it	**Optative** *-le'/-ne'* X would make it
I	áshłeeh	áshłaa	ádeeshłííł	ásh'į	óoshłe
You	áníléeh	íinilaa	ádíílííł	áníł'į́	óóle
He/she	íílééh	áyiilaa	íidoolííł	ííł'į́	ayóle
One	ájílééh	ájiilaa	ázhdoolííł	ájíł'į	ájole
We	íílnééh	íilyaa	ádiilnííł	íil'í	óolne
You (pl)	óhłééh	óohłaa	ádoohłííł	ół'į	óohłe
They	íílééh	áyiilaa	íidoolííł	ííł'į	ayóle
Ones	ájílééh	ájiilaa	ázhdoolííł	ájíł'į	ájóle
Distributives (Multiple/distributed agents or patients)					
We	ádeiilnééh	ádeiilyaa	ádadiilnííł	ádeiil'į	ádaoolne
You	ádaohłééh	ádaohłaa	ádadoohłííł	ádaoł'į	ádaoohłe
They	ádajilééh	ádayiilaa	ádeidoolííł	ádeł'į	ádayóle
Ones	ádajilééh	ádajiilaa	ádazhdoolííł	ádajíł'í	ádajóle

Adverbs typically precede the verbs they modify :

tsį́į́ łgo yishwoł 'I'm running fast.'
fast-sub I-run

Adjectives and postpositions follow the nouns they modify:

chidí łichíí' nahálnii'
car red-one I-bought-it
'I bought the red car.'

Ch'ah shaa yiní'ą́
hat me-to he-gave-it
'He gave the hat to me.'

Contact with Other Languages

Historically, the Navajo language has been in close contact with several other Native American languages, including Keresan and the Tanoan languages, Hopi, Zuni, and Ute, as well as SPANISH (post-1600). Most recently, the Navajo speech community has been inundated with ENGLISH, especially since the establishment of universal education, the development of roads on the reservation, and the introduction of radio and television, all in the latter half of the 20th century.

With the exception of a few verbs in phrases borrowed wholesale from English ("ready, set, go") borrowings are limited to nouns for the most part (and other discourse particles such as "gosh",). Until very recently the Navajo speech community has been very resistant to borrowing even of nouns, but this is attitude is changing rapidly in the second half of the 20th century, especially among younger speakers. Here are a few examples of relatively older borrowed nouns.

From Spanish: *béeso* (Spanish *peso*) 'money', *Bilagaana* (Spanish *americano*) 'white man', *dééh* (Spanish *té*) 'tea'
From English: *késhmish* 'Christmas', *gááboleita* 'carburetor'

Common Words

man:	hastiin	long:	nineez
woman:	asdzáán	small:	yázhí
water:	tó	yes:	aoo'
sun:	Jóhonaa'éí	no:	ndaga'
three:	táá'	good:	yá'át'ééh
fish:	łóó'	bird:	tsídii
big:	tsoh	dog:	łééchą́ą́'í
tree:	tsin íí'áii		

Example Sentence

Ashiiké t'óó diigis léi' "tółikaní ła' ádiilnííł
Boys foolish certain wine some we'll make

dóó nihaa nahidoonih" nínigo yee hodeez'ą́
and us-from it will be bought saying it-with they planned

jiní. Ako t'áá ał'ąą́ ch'il na'atł'o'ii
it is said. So then separately grapevines

k'iidiilá dóó hááhgóóshį́į́ yinaalnishgo
they planted them and diligently they working on them

t'áá áłah ch'il na'atł'o'ii néineest'ą́ jiní.
both grapevines they raised them it is said.

Aádóó tółikaní áyiilaago t'áá bíhígíí t'áá ał'ąą́
And then wine having made it each their own separately

tł'ízíkágí yii' haidééłbį́įd jiní.
goatskin in it they filled it it is said.

'Some foolish boys decided to make some wine to sell, so they each planted grapevines and, working hard on them, they raised them to maturity. Then, having made wine, they each filled a goatskin with it.' (Young and Morgan 1987:205)

Efforts to Preserve, Protect, and Promote the Language

Although speakers of Navajo currently make up the largest Native American speech community in the United States (with approximately 148,000 speakers, representing about 45 percent of all Native North American Language speakers, according to the 1993 census, cited in Crawford 1994), their number is shrinking, as fewer children speak the language every year. A shift from Navajo to English as the dominant language in many Navajo communities, especially those closer to urban centers, is now in progress (Field 1998).

Currently, most schools on the reservation provide at least minimal Navajo-language instruction, although many are not able to provide as much as might be desired. On the other hand, there are a handful of schools where instruction truly is bilingual and children are immersed in Navajo. Dine College (previously Navajo Community College) also provides instruction in Navajo language and particularly Navajo literacy, helping dozens of native-Navajo-speaking teachers every year to attain certification in Navajo bilingual education.

Select Bibliography

Brugge, David. 1979. "Navajo Prehistory and History to 1850." In Sturtevant, William, and Ortiz, Alfonso. 1979. *Handbook of North American Indians: Southwest. Vol. 8*. Washington, DC: Smithsonian Institution. 489–501.

Crawford, James. 1994. "Endangered Native American Languages: What Is to be Done, and Why?" American Educational Research Association, New Orleans.

Creamer, Mary H. 1974. "Ranking in Navajo Nouns." In *Navajo Language Review 1* (1) 29–38.

Field, Margaret. 1998. "Maintenance of Indigenous Ways of Speaking Despite Language Shift: Language Socialization in a Navajo Preschool." Ph.D. Dissertation, University of California Santa Barbara.

Grimes, Barbara, Richard Pittman, and James Grimes. 1998. *Ethnologue: Languages of the World*. Dallas: Summer Institute of Linguistics.

Haile, Fr. Berard. 1945. *Stem Vocabulary of the Navaho Language*. St. Michaels' Arizona: St. Michael's Press.

Holm, Agnes, Wayne Holm, and Bernard Spolsky. 1973. "English Loan Words in the Speech of Young Navajo Children." In Turner, P. (Ed.). *Bilingualism in the Southwest.* Tucson: University of Arizona Press. 227–239.

Kibrik, Andrej. 1993. "Transitivity Increase in Athabaskan Languages." In Comrie, B. and Polinsky, M., (Eds). *Causatives and Transitivity.* Amsterdam and Philadelphia: John Benjamins. (47–67).

_____. 1996. "Transitivity Decrease in Navajo and Athabaskan: Actor-affecting Propositional Derivations." In Jelinek, E., Midgette, S., Rice, K. and Saxon, L. (Eds.), *Athabaskan Language Studies.* Albuquerque: University New Mexico Press. (259–304).

Reichard, Gladys. 1945. "Linguistic Diversity Among the Navaho Indians." In *International Journal of American Linguistics.* v. 11(3) 156–168.

Saville-Troike, Muriel. 1974. "Diversity in Southwestern Athabaskan: A Historical Perspective." In *Navajo Language Review* v.1 67–84.

Sundberg, Lawrence. 1995. *Dinetah: An Early History of the People.* Santa Fe: Sunstone Press.

Young, Robert. 1979. "Apachean Languages." In Sturtevant, William, and Ortiz, Alfonso. 1979. *Handbook of North American Indians: Southwest.* v.8. Washington, DC: Smithsonian Institution. (393–405).

Young, Robert, and Morgan, William. 1987. *The Navajo Language: A Grammar and Colloquial Dictionary.* Albuquerque: University of New Mexico Press.

_____. 1992. *Analytical Lexicon of Navajo.* Albuquerque: University of New Mexico Press.

NEPALI

Manindra K. Verma

Language Name: Nepali. **Alternates:** *Gurkhali, Khaskura, Parbate.*

Location: Nepali is spoken in the kingdom of Nepal and in Sikkim, Bhutan, and the northern districts of West Bengal in India.

Family: Pahari group of the Indo-Aryan branch of the Indo-European language family.

Related Languages: Closest relatives are Kumauni and Garhwali, spoken in the immediate vicinity to the west of Nepal; more distantly related is HINDI (-URDU). All are languages of India.

Dialects: There are three geographically defined dialects: Eastern, Central, and Western. The Central dialect, spoken in Kathmandu Valley, is treated as the standard. The educated version of the language tends to be highly Sanskritized in its literary and administrative vocabulary.

Number of Speakers: 16 million; 10 million are in Nepal, 6 million are in India.

Origin and History

The Pahari group of languages, to which Nepali belongs, is found in the Himalayan region of south Asia. The exact place of the Pahari group of languages within Indo-Aryan is a moot question. It is possible that the Middle Indo-Aryan ancestor of Nepali was a variety of Shauraseni Prakrit (Middle Indo-Aryan of the midland region in India), which was the ancestor of Hindi and Urdu. Some scholars also believe that the Pahari languages are related to the Dardic group of languages to which Kashmiri belongs.

The name "Nepali" was officially adopted for the language in the early part of this century, when the term was used in the curriculum of Calcutta University. The Gorkha rulers of the kingdom of Nepal had a preference for the name *Gorkhali* or *Gorka Bhasha* ('Gorkha language'). The early inhabitants of the Nepal Valley, who identified it as the language of the Khasa people migrating from the west, give it the name *Khaskura* ('Khasa language').

The earliest known example of what may be called Old Nepali occurs in a series of epigraphs found in western Nepal and can be dated at about 1250. J.A. Ayton's *A Grammar of the Nepalese Language* (1820) is the first known grammar of modern Nepali.

Orthography and Basic Phonology

Nepali uses the Devanagari script, which provides for a generally very good fit between spelling and pronunciation. The script essentially expresses the phonemic inventory of SANSKRIT and very largely provides for the phonemic inventory of Nepali also. Nepali as a "Sanskritic" language retains the Sanskrit spellings in its formal learned vocabulary. Historical changes in the phonology do create some predictable discrepancies, though. For example, there is a loss of length distinction in the high vowels, and there is syncretism in the sibilants (only one /s/ in place of three) and syncretism in the nasals (only two, /n/ and /m/, in place of five). Also, characteristically, orthographic *w* is pronounced /b/ and the inherent vowel /a/ of the word-final consonant symbol is omitted. However, it is retained in some verbal forms where, in fact, its absence is indicated by a special sign called *halanta* put under the final consonant symbol.

The plain stops such as /p b/ are unaspirated, while the stops represented by /ph bh/ are aspirated. /R/ is a retroflex flap. It is similar to the ENGLISH sound written "dd" in "ladder" in that it is extremely short; it differs from the English sound in that the tongue tip touches the alveolar ridge, the area immediately behind the upper front teeth, for the English sound; but for the Nepali sound the tongue tip is curled back slightly toward the rear of the mouth. *T, Th, D, Dh* are also retroflex.

Even though it might be assumed on the basis of their conventional transliteration that /a/ and /aa/ differ primarily in length, they actual differ more in quality: /a/ is similar to the vowel sound in the English word "putt", while /aa/ is similar to the first vowel sound in the English word "father". The vowels *ii* and *uu*, distinct in the orthography, are pronounced as /i/ and /u/, respectively.

Table 1: Vowels

	Front	Central	Back
High	i		u
Mid	e	a	o
Low		aa	

Nepali also has diphthongs /ai/ and /au/. All of the vowels and diphthongs have their phonemically distinguished nasalized counterparts. Nasalization is expressed in this presentation by the use of /N/ following a vowel.

Basic Morphology

Nepali nouns come in two genders, masculine and feminine.

Table 2: Consonants

		Labial	Dental	Retroflex	Palatal	Velar	Glottal
Stops	Voiceless	p, ph	t, th	T, Th	c, ch	k, kh	
	Voiced	b, bh	d, dh	D, Dh	j, jh	g, gh	
Fricatives			s				h
Nasals		m	n				
Resonants			r, l	R, Rh			
Glides		w			y		

Nouns referring to females are feminine, and all other nouns are masculine. There may be some derivationally related masculine and feminine animate nouns in which the masculine ends in *-aa* and the feminine ends in *-i*, such as *keTaa* 'boy' *keTi* 'girl'.

Plurality can be expressed by the particle *haru* attached to the nouns, for example, *khet* 'field', *khetharu* 'fields', *keTaaharu* 'boys', *keTiharu* 'girls'. More often than not, in colloquial Nepali, plurality is implied by the context or by verbal agreement, if any. Nepali has no equivalent of the English articles, but definiteness can be expressed through topicalization involving word order variation, as in *koThaa maa saap cha* (room in snake is) 'There is a snake in the room' but *saap koThaa maa cha* (snake room in is) 'The snake is in the room'. Numerals preceding a noun take a classifier to express countability: *-janaa* for human, and *-waTaa* for an animal or inanimate noun, as in *tinwaTaa saanaa kukur* 'three small dogs', *paaNcjanaa calaak keTi* 'five intelligent girls', *saatwaTaa naraamraa kitaap* 'seven boring books'. The noun remains singular in such a construction.

Nepali adjectives, including the pronominal ones, that end in *-o* change their ending to *-aa* to have plural agreement with nouns they modify, *buRho maanche* 'an old man', *buRhaa maancheharu* 'old men', *mero keTaa* 'my son', *meraa keTaaharu* 'my sons'. Feminine agreement is shown by changing the ending to *-i: buRhi aaimaai(haru)* 'old woman (women)', *meri keTi(haru)* 'my daughter(s)'. Comparison of adjectives is accomplished by the use of the postposition *-bhandaa,* as in *niuyaark sikaago bhandaa Thulo cha* 'New York is bigger than Chicago'. The superlative is accomplished by the phrase *sab bhandaa* to imply 'than all', as in *kaaThmaaRauN nepaalko sab bhandaa Thulo sahar ho* 'Kathmandu is the biggest city of all in Nepal'.

Nepali has personal pronouns in three persons. They may have inflected plurals that are essentially used for honorificity. Plurality is ensured by adding *haru* to these inflected forms (almost like the colloquial English "y'all"); for example, second person singular *taN* 'you', *timi* 'you honorific' *timiharu* 'you plural honorific or nonhonorific', third-person singular *tyo* 'he, she', *tini* 'he, she honorific', *tiniharu* 'they honorific or nonhonorific'. In addition, there are more formal honorifics, both for second person *tapaaiN* 'your honor', and third person *yahaaN/wahaaN* 'their honor', used in everyday conversation and not necessarily restricted to ceremonial occasions. They have corresponding agreement forms in verbs, and their plurality can be ensured by adding *haru.* Third-person pronouns are distinguished for proximity also: *u/tyo* 'he, she it there', and *yo* 'he, she, it here'. There are no separate gender-distinguished pronominal forms even though they might affect verbal agreement, as in *u garcha* 'He does' but *u garche* 'She does'. Personal pronouns in Nepali are listed below:

Person	Singular: Nonhonorific	Singular: Honorific	Plural
First	ma		haami (haru)
Second	taN	timi tapaaiN	timi (haru) tapaaiN (haru)
Third	u/tyo, yo	uni/tini, yini uhaaN, yahaaN	uni/tini, yini (haru) uhaaN, yahaaN (haru)

Nepali verbs agree with their subjects in number, person, gender, and honorificity. The finite verb forms have various combinations of tense, mode, and aspects. There are eight single word verb forms that provide for the following tenses and modes. Examples are for the verb *gar-* 'to do' in third person, singular, masculine, nonhonorific. The structure of the form in present indefinite *garcha* below is the verb stem *gar-*, an affixed auxiliary *-ch-*, and the third-person, singular, masculine, nonhonorific present tense suffix *-a*.

Present Indefinite	gar-ch-a	'does'
Past Simple	gar-yo	'did'
Past Habitual	gar-thyo	'used to do'
Presumptive Future	gar-laa	'will probably do' (potential)
Injunctive	gar-os	'May he do, let him do'
Imperative (2p.sg.)	gar-a	'Do!'
Narrative Present	gar-e-cha	'has done (Oh, I see)'
Narrative Past	gar-e-thyo	'had done (I find)'

It may be noted that "habitual" is an important aspect in Nepali, as in most Indic languages, and has a separate form in the past tense. The present habitual is expressed by present indefinite, which is a multipurpose verb form. The injuctive and imperative are clearly modes, and the future form above is essentially the presumptive-potential mode as opposed to predictive future given further below. The last two have the force of a comment on a situation and essentially have the stative aspect.

Table 3: Compound Tenses

Imperfective-Progressive	Present	gar-dai cha	'is doing'
Imperfective-Progressive	Past	gar-dai thiyo	'was doing'
Imperfective-Progressive	Future	gar-dai hunecha	'will be doing'
Imperfective-Progressive	Presumptive	gar-dai holaa	'may be doing'
Perfective-Stative	Present	gar-eko cha	'has done'
Perfective-Stative	Past	gar-eko thiyo	'had done'
Perfective-Stative	Future	gar-eko hunecha	'will have done'
Perfective-Stative	Presumptive	gar-eko holaa	'may have done'
Infinitival-Factitive	Present	gar-ne cha	(Predictive Future)
Infinitival-Factitive	Past	gar-ne thiyo	(Counterfactual)

Two-word finite forms provide for what may be called compound tenses consisting of a participial form of the main verb followed by an auxiliary that expresses tense or mode and is the essential carrier of agreement features. The participial generally expresses the aspect, such as progressive, stative.

It may be noted that Nepali has two kinds of future, one predictive (infinitival-factitive present) as noted just above with a somewhat emphatic assertion of what is to happen in the future, and the other the presumptive in *-laa*. In fact, the presumptive-potential nature of the *-laa* ending can be seen in the presumptive constructions with the auxiliary *holaa* with nonfinite participials as noted above. It is also true that the auxiliary form *holaa* can be added to fully finite forms to add the mode of presumptive-potential in such constructions as *u garcha holaa* 'It is probable he will do it', *usle garyo holaa* 'It is probable, he did it; He must have done it'. The infinitival-factitive in the past tense provides for the counterfactual, something like 'would have done, but ...' in the form *garne thiyo* cited above.

Nepali has a very rich system of morphologically related verb stems in which a causative suffix *-aa*, a passive suffix *-i*, or both, can be used to derive morphologically complex verb stems.

Basic: gar- nu
do- INFINITIVE 'to do'

Causative: gar- aau- nu
do- CAUS- INFINITIVE 'to have someone do'

Passive: gar- i- nu
do- PASS- INFINITIVE 'to be done'

Causative + Passive: gar- aa- i- nu
do- CAUS- PASS- INFINITIVE
'to have something be done'

Basic: ru- nu
cry- INFINITIVE 'to cry'

Causative: ruw- aau- nu
cry- CAUS- INFINITIVE 'to make someone cry'

Passive: ro- i- nu
cry- PASS- INFINITIVE 'to be mourned'

Causative + Passive: ruw- aa- i- nu
cry- CAUS- PASS- INFINITIVE
'to have/make someone cry'

Basic Syntax

The unmarked word order in Nepali is SOV, as can be seen in the example sentences below.

tyo maanche dinahuN kaam gar-ch-a
that man everyday work do-AUX-3SG.PRES
'That man works everyday.'

ma maasu khaan-ch-u
I meat eat-AUX-1SG.PRES.
'I eat meat.'

Within a noun phrase, adjectives and other modifiers precede their head nouns. Relations among nouns are expressed via postpositions rather than prepositions, as in *sahar-maa* (city-in) 'in the city' and *khaaT-muni* (bed-under) 'under the bed'.

Verbs are negated with the particle *na*. This particle is typically incorporated into the verbal paradigm: *taN cha-i-na-s* (you be-STEM.EXTENSION-NEG-2SG) 'You aren't'.

Verb stems may have morphophonemic variations depending on whether they end in consonants or vowels, and the shape of the suffix, as seen above. With certain verb forms, particularly the imperative, the infinitive, and the potential future, the *na* is prefixed to the verb stem rather than being suffixed immediately before the subject agreement suffix: *na-jaa* (NEG-go) 'Don't go', *na-gar-laa* (NEG-do-FUTURE.POTENTIAL) 'will probably not go'.

Contact with Other Languages

Like most other south Asian languages, Nepali uses a very large proportion of Sanskrit loanwords in its formal and literary variety, although most educated speakers and writers of Nepali do not even think of them as loanwords. As in most south Asian languages, it creates a situation of diglossia. In addition, because of its close academic and literary contact with Hindi, Nepali tends to use quite a few Hindi words of common south Asian currency. Another source of non-Nepali vocabulary in its colloquial varieties is its contact with Magadhi languages (an Indo-Aryan group) such as MAITHILI and BHOJPURI, spoken in its foothills region. Nepali also has its share of ARABIC/PERSIAN loanwords, coming essentially through the Hindi route, and English loanwords, phonologically reshaped according to its own system.

From Sanskrit: *pradhaanmantri* 'prime minister', *widyaarthii* 'student', *wis'wawidyaalay* 'university'
From Perso-Arabic: *kitaap/kitaab* 'book', *kalam* 'pen', *mausam* 'climate', *darbaar* 'court'
From English: *juu* 'zoo', *bhiijaa* 'visa', *sinemaa* 'cinema, film', *Tebul* 'table'

Common Words

man:	maanche	long:	laamo
woman:	aaimaaii	small:	saano
water:	paanii	yes:	ho/cha
sun:	ghaam	no:	hoina/chaina
three:	tiin	good:	raamro
fish:	maachaa	dog:	kukur
big:	Thuulo	tree:	rukh

Example Sentences

(1) tim–ro naauN ke ho?
you–POSS name what is
'What is your name?'

(2) me–ro kitaap kahaaN cha?
I–POSS book where is
'Where is my book?'

(3) KaaThmaaRauN Thuulo sahar ho tar pokhraa
Kathmandu big city is but Pokhra

dherai saano ho.
much small is
'Kathmandu is a big city but Pokhra is very small.'

Efforts to Preserve, Protect, and Promote the Language

Apart from being the lingua franca in the kingdom of Nepal, Nepali is also the official language of the country and is the beneficiary of government patronage and national pride. The most important organization in this regard is the Royal Nepal Academy. Besides publishing journals and books, it holds seminars and symposia on Nepali language and literature and has installed literary awards. *Nepali Sahitya Samsathana* (Nepali Literary Institute) and *Nepal Bhasha Parishad* (Nepali Language Society) are two other such organizations. The *Madan Puraskar Guthi* is a trust that publishes a scholarly quarterly *Nepali* and has instituted an award for the best literary work in Nepali.

The promotion and support for Nepali in India has been remarkable. It was recognized as a modern literary language of India by *Sahitya Akademi* (the Indian Academy of Literature) in 1975. Subsequently it was given the status of a national language of India by including it in the Eighth Schedule of the Indian Constitution through the 77th Amendment of the Constitution in 1992. The Government of the State of West Bengal in India founded the Nepali Academy in 1979 and brought out a journal and instituted a literary award called *Bhanu Puraskar*. Some of the earliest literary organizations for Nepali in India include the *Nepali Sahitya Sammelan* (Literary Association) founded in Darjeeling in 1924 publishing a journal Diyalo, the *Nepali Sahitya Parishad* (Literary Council) founded in Darjeeling in 1963 publishing the journal *Malingo*, the *Sahitya Adhyayan Samiti* (Study Circle) of Kalimpong, and *Nepali Sahitya Parishad* of Shillong in India.

Select Bibliography

Clark, T.W. 1963. *Introduction to Nepali*. London: SOAS, University of London.

Devakota, Grishamabahadur. 1967. *Nepaalko Chaapaakhaanaa Ra Patra Patrikaako Itihaas* (In Nepali, The History of the Nepali Press and Journals). Kathmandu: Sajha Prakashan.

Grierson, G.A. 1916. *Linguistic Survey of India, Vol. IX, Part IV, Nepali*. Delhi: Motillal Banarsidass (Reprint 1968).

Matthews, David. 1984. *A Course in Nepali*. London: SOAS, University of London.

Pradhan, Krishna Bhai. 1989. *The Structure of Spoken Nepali*. Madison: SAS, University of Wisconsin.

Pradhan, Kumar. 1984. *A History of Nepali Literature*. Delhi: Sahitya Akademi.

Pradhan, Paras Mani. 1970. *Nepaali Bhaashaa Ra Saahityako Vivaran* (In Nepali, An Account of Nepali Language and Literature). Kalimpong: Bhagyalakshami Publications.

Regmi, Chudamani Upadhyay. 1963. *Nepaali Bhaashaako Utpatti* (In Nepali, The Origin of the Nepali Language). Lalitpur: Jagdamba Publications.

Srivastava, Dayanand. 1962. *Nepali Language: Its History and Development*. Calcutta: Calcutta University Press.

Turner, R.L. 1931. *A Comparative and Etymological Dictionary of the Nepali Language*. London: K. Paul.

Verma, Manindra K. 1976. "The Notion of Subject and the Data from Nepali." In Manindra K. Verma (ed.) *The Notion of Subject in South Asian Languages*, 270–285. Madison: SAS, University of Wisconsin.

____. 1992. "Nepali." In William Bright and Bernard Comrie (eds.) *International Encyclopedia of Linguistics*, 3: 76–79. New York: Oxford University Press.

Verma, Manindra K. and T.N. Sharma. 1979. *Intermediate Nepali Structures*. Delhi: Manohar Publications. (Revised Second Edition 1992).

____. 1983. "Nepali Literature." In *Encyclopedia of World Literature in the Twentieth Century*, III: 366–368. New York: Frederick Unger Publishing Co.

Nivkh

Johanna Mattissen

Language Name: Nivkh, Gilyak. **Autonym:** *N'ivx* (on the Amur), *N'iɣvŋ* (on Sakhalin).

Location: The Nivkh live in scattered settlements in the Far East of the Asian Continent in the territory of the Russian Federation. They reside in the lower Amur basin, along the estuary north and south of the Amur River delta, and in the north and east of the offshore island of Sakhalin, with some minor settlements in the south of the island.

Family: Nivkh is a language isolate, but is included in the Paleosiberian language group consisting of the Chukotko-Kamchatkan language family (Chukchi, Koryak, Alyutor, Kerek, Kamchadal or Itelmen) and the genetically unaffiliated and mutually unrelated isolates Ket (the only surviving Yeniseian language), Nivkh, and for some scholars, Yukaghir.

Related Languages: None. Comparative approaches examined the alleged relatedness to the neighboring Tungusic languages, Manchu, MONGOLIAN, and Ainu, to Uralic, Chukotko-Kamchatkan, Almosan-Keresiouan, even Southeast Asian languages and to KOREAN. For lexical and grammatical morpheme correspondences to neighboring languages borrowing cannot be excluded. Abstracting from lack of diachronic data and daring comparisons, lexical resemblances to Uralic languages are quite impressive. From the typological perspective, however, Nivkh shows affinities to Chukchi, Ainu, and American Indian languages in morphological type.

Dialects: Within the Nivkh language, four dialects are distinguished: the Amur dialect on the continent and the East Sakhalin dialect are substantially different in phonology, grammar, and lexicon, and mutual intelligibility is claimed to be very low by native speakers. The North Sakhalin dialect is intermediate between these two, but closer to the Amur variety. The South Sakhalin (Poronaisk) dialect is again distinct from the East Sakhalin dialect and at the other extreme of the Amur variety. The Sakhalin dialects are generally more archaic, in preserving, for instance, a word final nasal and more complex consonant clusters.

	Amur dialect	East Sakhalin dialect
'cow'	*eʁa*	*eʁaŋ*
'child'	*ōla, oɣla*	*eʁlŋ*
'house'	*təf*	*taf*
PL	*-ɣu ~ -ku*	*-ɣun(u) ~ - kun(u)*
IND	*-d̜ ~ -t̜*	*-d ~ -nd ~ -nt*

Number of Speakers: According to the 1989 census, 2,008 out of 4,681 ethnic Nivkh lived on Sakhalin, but only 447 of these gave Nivkh as their native language. On the continent, the number is estimated to be even lower. The mother tongue of those younger than 40 years of age is RUSSIAN.

Origin and History

The Nivkh are considered to be descendants of an original neolithic population on the lower Amur. They are presumed to be first referred to in a Chinese chronicle of the 12th century and remained under Chinese, then Mongol and later Manchu authorities for several centuries.

In the 17th century, Russian Cossack expedition records mention them as *Giliatski*. At that time, the Nivkh resisted annexation but tribute was extorted from them. They lived in scattered settlements and shared their territory with Tungusic peoples: the Ulch, Nanai, Evenki, Oroch, Udighe, and Negidal; on the Amur, and with the Orok, Evenki, and Ainu on Sakhalin. The Nivkh continue to live in these areas to the present day. They were fishermen, hunters, and dog breeders, and maintained trading relations with their neighbors as well as with the Chinese. Since the early 19th century, the Nivkh have also traded with the Japanese.

After 1850 the territory became part of the Russian Empire, and Nivkh people came to be employed as guards and trackers in the penal colonies on Sakhalin. With increasing technological and economical impact from Russia, the Nivkh were able to preserve their original culture until the end of the 19th century. The study of the Nivkh began in this epoch with the expeditions of L. von Schrenck and P. von Glehn, whose materials were published between 1880 and 1900. The rich materials collected by L. Sternberg around the turn of the century are important contributions to the study of the Nivkh.

Between 1905 and 1945, South Sakhalin, where slightly more than 100 Nivkh lived in Poronaisk, was in Japanese hands and called *Karafuto*.

During the Soviet regime, the Nivkh underwent mass collectivization in the 1920s and 1930s. They abandoned their system of moving between summer and winter settlements and began to give up their traditional profession as fishermen. After a phase of recognition of ethnic communities, during which

Table 1: Consonants in Roman and Cyrillic Transcription

		Labial	Dental	Palatal	Velar	Uvular	Pharyngeal
Stops	Voiceless	p/п	t/т	t̡/ть	k/к	q/ӄ	
	Aspirated	p‘/п’	t‘/т’	t̡‘/ч’	k‘/к’	q‘/ӄ’	
	Voiced	b/б	d/д	d̡/дь	g/г	ɢ/ӷ	
Fricatives	Voiceless	f/ф	s/c		x/x	χ/ӽ	h/x
	Voiced	v/в	z/з		ɣ/ғ	ʁ/ӷ	
Trills	Voiceless		ř/р̌				
	Voiced		r/p				
Nasals		m/м	n/н	ñ/нь	ŋ/ӈ		
Laterals			l/л				
Approximants			j/й		w		

a Nivkh writing system was introduced, Russification set in. Between 1950 and 1980 the Nivkh suffered forced resettlement into larger towns of mixed population. Furthermore, their children attended Russian boarding schools and lost contact with their language background. Under these conditions the number of native speakers has continually been decreasing. Census figures of Sakhalin show that between 1970 and 1979, the Nivkh population dropped from 1,021 speakers to only 597.

Since the end of the last century, linguistic research on Nivkh has produced text anthologies, several grammatical sketches, a grammar, a dictionary, and a considerable number of studies on single domains, including comparative work.

Orthography and Basic Phonology

The first official Nivkh alphabet, based on Roman characters, was introduced in 1931. A written language developed out of the Amur dialect, in which several primers and schoolbooks as well as 11 editions of a newspaper were published. In 1953, a new orthography in Cyrillic letters was promulgated and replaced the Roman-based primers. Since then, the alphabet has been partly modified; the characters are displayed in the consonant and vowel tables to the right of the slashes (see Tables 1 and 2). Among linguists, different versions of Cyrillic orthography are in use that differ as to the imitation of Russian syllabic writing conventions and to special signs for phonemes that do not exist in Russian. Roman transliteration systems are very heterogenous. In this presentation, an IPA based transliteration is used.

Consonantal phonemes are displayed in Table 1. The palatal stops are actually affricates: /t̡/ = [tʃ], /t̡‘/ = [tʰʃ], /d̡/ = [dʒ]; the voiceless trill /ř/ is [r̥].

The phoneme /w/ does not exist in the Amur dialect, where it has merged with /v/. In the South Sakhalin variety, there is a two-way tense vs. lax distinction in plosives instead of the three-way voiceless, aspirated and voiced system. Nivkh is rich in consonant clusters.

The vowel system presented in Table 2 is shared by all Nivkh dialects.

Long vowels are distinctive, but resulted from compensatory lengthening in origin and rarely occur. There are residues of a high (/i/, /ə/, /u/) vs. low (/e/, /a/, /o/) vowel-harmony system in the pronoun allomorphy.

Table 2: Vowels

	Front	Central	Back
High	i/и		u/y
Mid	e/э	ə/ы	o/o
Low		a/a	

Nivkh has a remarkable system of morphophonological alternations of consonants that dominates morphology and syntax. Whenever two morphemes, be they lexical or grammatical, are adjacent and stand in a dependent-head or head-affix relation, an initial consonant of the following morpheme alternates in dependence of the final sound of the preceding morpheme, roughly speaking according to partly a dissimilation and partly an assimilation mechanism. Within this system, the consonants involved in it form homorganic sets, as compiled below.

Alternation Set A:

p	t	t̡	k	q	voiceless plosives
v	r	z̡	ɣ	ʁ	voiced fricatives
b	d	d̡	g	ɢ	voiced plosives
f	ř	s̡	x	χ	voiceless fricatives

Alternation Set B:

p‘	t‘	t̡‘	k‘	q‘	aspirated plosives
f	ř	s̡	x	χ	voiceless fricatives

Voiceless plosives and voiced fricatives out of each homorganic column in Set A alternate with all other consonants of their respective column within this set. Homorganic aspirated plosives and voiceless fricatives in Set B alternate with each other. Other consonants and vowels do not mutate. Alternation conditions in the Amur dialect are shown in Table 3 on the next page.

They are also illustrated below for a verb and a noun, respectively.

Table 3: Alternation Conditions for Consonant Mutation

Final sound of preceding morpheme	Initial sound of following morpheme	
	Alternation Set A	Alternation Set B
Plosive, vowel, /j/, /l/, /ñ/	voiceless fricative	voiced fricative
Fricative	aspirated plosive	voiceless plosive
Nasal		voiced plosive

Citation form: *vəkzd̜* 's.o. loses sth.'
t̜aqo-vəkzd̜ 's.o. loses a knife'
taj-vəkzd̜ 's.o. loses his pipe'
mot-vəkzd̜ 's.o. throws away a pillow'
puñd̜-vəkzd̜ 's.o. loses his bow'
ŋas-pəkzd̜ 's.o. loses a strap'
nux-pəkzd̜ 's.o. loses a needle'
ŋir(ŋ)-bəkzd̜ 's.o. loses a dish'

Citation form: *pəñx* 'soup'
t̜'o-vəñx 'fish soup'
k̜'əŋrai-vəñx 'kəŋraj-duck soup'
həjk-vəñx 'hare soup'
t̜xəf-pəñx 'bear soup'
eʁa-bəñx 'beef soup' (/ŋ/ elided in Amur dialect)

With very few exceptions, an occlusive initial sound of transitive verbs is a fricative, while an occlusive initial of intransitive verbs and nouns is a plosive. The initial consonants of transitive verbs and nouns alternate, the initial sound of intransitive verbs does not.

Basic Morphology

Nivkh distinguishes nouns, pronouns, verbs, and (invariable) particles. Both nouns and verbs form complex word forms.

Nouns and pronouns are inflected for number, case, and focus. The cases are causee, comparative, allative, locative, ablative, perlative, terminative, instrumental, and vocative; there are no central or adnominal cases. Postpositions encode further peripheral relations. Focus markers comprise "also", "even", "only", highlighting, constituent-question marker, etc.

The personal pronouns are *ñi* 1s, *t̜'i* 2s, *if ~ i ~ jaŋ* 3s, *megi ~ meŋ* 1d, *mer ~ min ~ miřn* 1p incl, *ñəŋ ~ ñin* 1p excl, *t̜'əŋ ~ t̜'in* 2p, *imɣ ~ imŋ ~ jivŋ ~ in ~iřn* 3p and *p'i* 'self'.

Nouns form highly complex word forms that include determiners (deictic roots), possessors (pronominal or nominal) and attributes (verb roots or nouns). For a nominal word form the following template can be established:

(determiner/possessor)-(quantifier)-(attribute)-nominal root-(number)-case-(focus)

The tight unit is evidenced by morphophonological alternations of consonants in comparison to the citation forms:

t̜'-vila-ɢan eʁa-d̜uz-ñi-d̜
2s-big-dog cow-meat-eat-IND
'your big dog ate (the) beef'

Citation forms:
t̜'i 2s *pild̜* 'big' (attr. *pila(ŋ)-*) *qan* 'dog'
eʁa(ŋ) 'cow' *t̜uz* 'meat' *iñd̜* 'eat'

For numerals from one to five there is a system of numeral classification with 26 classes based on animacy, shape, collection and salient items of everyday life, e.g., nets, sleds, portions of dog food, etc.

	person	long object	boat	bundle of dried fish
1	*ñin*	*ñex*	*ñim*	*ñar*
2	*men*	*mex*	*mim*	*mer*

Verbs are inflected for mood, temporal and aspectoid (completive, resultative, progressive, habitual, iterative, degree) categories, modalities, and causative. Polarity and phases of events are encoded with the help of auxiliaries. There is no passive. Furthermore, the object is marked on (di)transitive verbs, which leads to the following template:

object-verb root-(aspectoid)-(causative)-(aspectoid/temporal)-(modal verb root)-mood

The morphological distinction of transitive and intransitive verbs is due to the object reflex, a fricative or /i ~ e ~ j/, on the former. The person of the subject is not marked on finite verbs, except for optional plural marking on the indicative form.

j-uski-ivu-gu-inə-t'əɣm-d-ɣun
3s-pay-PROG-CST-INT-seem-IND-PL
'they seem to be going to make him pay [for sth.]'

Part of the considerable number of converbs are person marked in that they have one allomorph for 1s or plural subject, and another for nonfirst singular subject. In the Sakhalin varieties, there is a separate allomorph for the first-person singular.

Nivkh possesses seven roots denoting local concepts related to environmental landmarks, as well as six deictic roots for various distances.

Landmark roots:
a- 'downriver'
k'e- 'upriver'
t'a- 'from the bank/shore out onto the water, from one bank/shore to the opposite one'
he- 'from the river/open sea to the bank/shore, from the bank/shore up into the interior'
qo- 'down from a mountain, from the interior down to the bank/shore'

k'i- 'up (onto a mountain/into the sky)'
t'a- (interrogative)

They can be derived to form nominal, verbal or adverbial lexemes, or are components of nominal and verbal word forms. Word formation makes use of composition and, less so, of derivation.

Basic Syntax

Nivkh is a head-marking SOV language in which dependents precede their heads, and syntax is organized according to an S/A pivot. Central syntactic relations (subject, primary and secondary objects) are not case marked, and nominal participants or subject pronouns are not obligatory. Case-unmarked nominal word forms are used as predicates without a copula. The most frequently occurring finite predicate form (indicative) is originally of nominalized nature and is also used as a complement form. Clausal nexion otherwise works on converbs.

The most interesting characteristic of Nivkh is that dependents are generally marked on their heads, i.e., dependents and heads form complex synthetic units, recognizable because of the morphophonological alternations occurring within these complexes. Thus primary objects are incorporated into (di)transitive verbs, and attributes and determiners are "incorporated" into their nominal heads.

t̨'o-ŋəŋ-ñivx k'e toqo-xro-d̨
fish-hunt-person net fence-hang-IND
'the fisherman hung the net on the fence'
eɣrod̨ ~ -k'rod̨ ~ -xrod̨ 's.o. hangs sth. on sth.'

if hə-ula-bal-dox mər-jiki-d̨
3s that-high-mountain-ALL go_up-cannot-IND
'he cannot climb that high mountain'
pal(n) ~ -val(n) ~ -bal(n) 'mountain', *-rox ~ -tox ~ -dox* ALL

There are no relative clauses. Most strikingly, incorporated elements can be inflected (see Example Sentences), except for case or mood, and even proper names can be incorporated as possessors (*Sarat-rəf* 'Sarat's house' with *təf ~ -rəf ~ -dəf* 'house') or as objects (*Seus-tod̨* 's.o. helped Seus' with *rod̨ ~ -tod̨ ~ -dod̨* 's.o. helps s.o.').

The subject is not marked on the finite verb form, but any finite verb form is a minimal sentence as such. This makes Nivkh a language with "word-phrases" that are structurally comparable to "word-sentences" in polysynthetic languages. Thus Nivkh bears a resemblance to Chukchi and American Indian languages.

The morphological type of Nivkh is not yet agreed upon. After an animated debate about the existence of incorporation between Russian scholars in the 1950s and 1960s, the topic was neglected. At the base of the old discussion, however, were opposed definitions of the word, and the arguments against incorporation departed from the conception of the word as a semantic, not a morphophonological, unit.

Contact with Other Languages

Nivkh has been in close contact with its neighboring Tungusic languages Ulch, Nanai, Evenki, Oroch, Udighe, Negidal, Orok, and with Ainu, as well as with the languages of the political powers, Chinese, Mongolian, Manchu, Russian and JAPANESE. The influence of Altaic, Ainu and, of course, Russian is manifest in loanwords and through phonetic interference. Most Russian technological, political, and cultural terms have been taken over as foreign words without any adaptation to Nivkh phonology, and even Russian word order patterns made their way into the syntax. Most terms of Chinese origin exist in the Altaic languages of the region as well, obscuring the source of the borrowing. The impact on Nivkh has always been greater than Nivkh influence on other languages, and bilingualism or even trilingualism was common among the Nivkh.

From Tungusic: *pitɣə* 'book' (Nanai: *bitxə*), *oxt* 'medicine' (Nanai: *okto*), *t̨'am* 'shaman' (Nanai: *saman*), *siŋgrud̨* 'torture' (Nanai: *siŋgərə*)
From Ainu: *qoj* 'larch' < *kui*, *osk* 'hare' < *osuke*, *t̨'arb* 'silk' < *sarampe*
From Russian: *lep* 'bread' < *xleb*, *karandas* 'pencil' < *karandaš*
From Chinese: *t̨'aj* 'tea' < *chá*, *seta* 'sugar' < *shātáng* (Chin.), *šatan* (Manchu), *šata* (Nanai)
From Mongolian: *pəx* 'ink' < *beke*, *t̨'afq* 'chopsticks' < *sabqa*, *xota* 'town' < *qota*

Common Words

man:	*utku* (Amur), *utkun* (North Sakhalin), *azmət̨* (East Sakhalin)
woman:	*umgu* (A), *řak* (NS), *řaŋq* (ES)
water:	*t̨'aχ*
sun:	*k'eŋ* (A, NS, ES), *keŋ* (South Sakhalin)
three:	*t̨-* *t̨aqr* 'three things', *t̨raχ* 'three flat things', *t̨or* 'three animals', *t̨em* 'three boats', *t̨eř* 'three sleds' etc.
fish:	*t̨'o*
big:	*pild̨* (A), *piland* (ES)
long:	*kəld̨* (A)
small:	*mat̨kid̨* (A)
yes:	*hə*
no:	*q'aukra*
good:	*urd̨* (A), *urlad* (ES)
bird:	*pəiŋa* (A, NS), *pujŋa* (ES) ('fly-animal')
dog:	*qan* (A, NS), *qanŋ* (ES), *ɢanŋ* (SS)
tree:	*t̨iɣr* (A), *t̨iɣř* (NS), *t̨'xař* (ES)

Example Sentences

(1) *ñi mu-lət-ivu-ñivx-ñřə-d̨*
1s boat-make-PROG-person-see-IND
'I saw a man building a boat.'

(2) *i-ŋəñf-ku-bark-uvr-ñřə-nə-d̨-ō*
3s-bone-PL-only-maybe-see-PRJ-IND-EXCL
'Oh! If only I could see his bones.'

(3) *vo-ñlami əlt̨'-ɣo verax-ko imŋ-k'im-d̨*
village-half servant-COM.PL slave-COM.PL 3p-give-IND
'Half the village gave them servants and slaves.'

Efforts to Preserve, Protect, and Promote the Language

Since the 1960s ethnic awareness arose among the northern peoples and with it concern about the decline in use of the native languages. As a result, in the early 1980s the Ministry of Education initiated a Nivkh language teaching program for primary and secondary schools. New primers and dictionaries were written for both the Amur and the East Sakhalin dialects, and literature was even produced by a Nivkh writer. Nivkh native speakers received formation as teachers. Today, however, Nivkh is taught in two schools on Sakhalin up to the third form. In 1987, Nivkh elders started a discussion group on Nivkh language and culture in a Sakhalin village as a means to pass on the language to the participating children. Since 1990, a monthly newspaper *Nivkh Dif* ('Nivkh Word') is being published. The recognition of ecological problems resulting from commercial exploitation of their forests and rivers led the Siberian nations in the time of *glasnost* to promote their interests, including language and culture revival, culminating in the foundation of the Association of Peoples of the North in 1989 with a Nivkh as chairman.

Select Bibliography

Beffa, Marie-Lise. 1982. "Présentation de la Langue Nivx suivie de l'analyse linguistique d'un paragraphe du conte." In *Études mongoles et sibériennes* 13: 49–98.

Black, Lydia. 1973. "The Nivkh (Gilyak) of Sakhalin and the Lower Amur." In *Artic Anthropology* X (1): 1–117.

Bondarko, L.V. and L.R. Zinder. 1962. "Fonetičeskaja xarakteristika različnyx tipov sintaksičeskix sočetanij v nivxskom jazyke." In *Voprosy Jazykoznanija* 11 (4): 84–89.

Comrie, Bernard. 1981. *Languages of the Soviet Union*. Cambridge: CUP.

Forsyth, James. 1992. *A History of the Peoples of Siberia*. Cambridge: CUP.

Gruzdeva, E. Ju. 1998. *Nivkh*. Munich: LINCOM.

Hattori, Takeshi. 1988. "Giriyâkugo." In *Gengogaku Daijiten*. Vol. I. Tokyo: Kenkyûsha. 1408–1414.

Jakobson, Roman. 1971. "Notes on Gilyak" and "Texte guilyak." In Jakobson, Roman: *Selected Writings* II. The Hague: Mouton. 72–97, 98–102.

Korsakov, G.M. 1939. "Inkorporirovanie v paleoaziatskix i severo-amerikanskix indečskix jazykax." In *Sovetskij Sever* 4: 27–51.

Krejnovič, E.A. 1934. "Nivxskij (giljackij) jazyk." In Al'kor, Ja.P. (ed.): *Jazyki i pis'mennost' narodov Severa* III. Leningrad: Institut Narodov Severa (= Trudy po Lingvistike, Vol. 3). 181–222.

_____. 1937. "Fonetika nivxskogo jazyka." Moscow-Leningrad: Institut Narodov Severa (= Trudy po Lingvistike, Vol. 5). 7–102.

_____. 1966. "Ob inkorporirovanii i primykanii v nixvskom jazyke." In *Voprosy Jazykoznanija* 15 (3): 36–51.

Mattissen, Johanna. 1999. "Dependent-Head synthesis in Nivkh—with an outlook on polysynthesis in the Far Northeast." In *Sprachtypologie und Universalienforschung* (STUF) 52 (3/4): 298–319.

Mattissen, Johanna and Werner Drossard. 1998. "Lexical and syntactic categories in Nivkh (Gilyak)." In *Theorie des Lexikons, Arbeiten des Sonderforschungsbereichs* 282 Nr. 85. Düsseldorf: Heinrich-Heine-Universität.

Nedjalkov, V.P., G.A. Otaina and A.A. Xolodovič. 1974. "Diatezy i zalogi v nivxskom jazyke." In Xolodovič, A.A. (ed.): *Tipologija passivnyx konstrukcij. Diatezy i zalogi.* Leningrad: Nauka. 232–251.

Otaina, G.A. 1978. *Kačestvennye glagoly v nivxskom jazyke.* Moscow: Nauka.

Panfilov, V.Z. 1962, 1965. *Grammatika nivxskogo jazyka.* 2 Vols. Moscow and Leningrad: Nauka.

Savel'eva, V.N. and Č.M. Taksami. 1965. *Russko-Nivxskij Slovar'*. Moscow: Sovetskaja Enciklopedija

_____. 1970. *Nivxsko-Russkij Slovar'*. Moscow: Sovetskaja Enciklopedija.

NORWEGIAN

John Weinstock

Language Name: Norwegian. There are two official languages in Norway and each is called *norsk* (Norwegian) by its supporters. One is *bokmål* ('book language'), also called *riksmål* ('official language'). *Bokmål* was formerly known as Dano-Norwegian. The other is *nynorsk* ('new Norwegian'), formerly *landsmål*. These varieties are mutually intelligible with each other.

Location: Norway. Most of the descendants of Norwegian immigrants to the United States, Canada, and elsewhere from the 19th and early 20th centuries have lost their Norwegian language.

Family: North Germanic group of the Germanic branch of Indo-European.

Related Languages: DANISH, SWEDISH (both are mutually intelligible, with some difficulty, with Norwegian), Icelandic and Faroese.

Dialects: Both varieties of Norwegian have minor dialect differences, although not enough to hinder communication. For *bokmål*, coastal towns influenced by the Hanseatic League, such as Bergen and Stavanger, have uvular *r*, as found in Danish and GERMAN. For *nynorsk*, the Aasen norm can be considered to be a written norm.

Number of Speakers: About 80–85 percent of the Norwegian population of about 4.5 million have *bokmål* as their mother tongue; the remaining 15–20 percent have *nynorsk*.

Origin and History

Norwegian is descended from the Germanic languages that must have begun to branch off from the other Indo-European languages in the northwestern part of Europe as early as 2000 B.C. The heartland was the area around the Baltic that is now Denmark and southern Sweden. From the Baltic, Germanic peoples migrated north into Norway and Sweden, east along the Baltic, and south into what is now Germany. In time, the Germanic languages broke up. East Germanic (GOTHIC) groups were the first to depart, leaving the Scandinavian peninsula in the second and first centuries B.C. The remaining peoples must have formed a Northwest Germanic branch (they have a number of linguistic features in common not shared by East Germanic) before splitting into North Germanic (eventually the Scandinavian languages) and West Germanic (eventually German, DUTCH, and ENGLISH).

Runic inscriptions, the earliest indigenous texts from roughly A.D. 200 and later, show a fairly uniform, largely hypothetical language that can be called Proto-Scandinavian. From 550–1050 one can speak of Common Scandinavian as the language of the peoples of the area. During the Viking era there were more and more contacts with peoples to the south, and linguistic innovations moved from south to north along the Baltic or North Sea leading to a split between Old West Scandinavian, the forerunner of modern Norwegian, Icelandic, and Faroese, and Old East Scandinavian, the forerunner of modern Danish and Swedish. Old Norse is the name of the classical literary language until 1350 when it breaks apart into Old Norwegian, Old Danish, etc. This is the time when the current Scandinavian dialects began developing.

The Kalmar Union of Denmark, Norway and Sweden from 1397 to the early 16th century brought Danish hegemony over Norway. Although the union dissolved, the Danes retained control over Norway until the end of the Napoleonic Wars in 1814. This meant that Danish became the written language of Norway, the language of the officials, the cultivated and educated classes, and the urban population. Official pressure toward a Danish pronunciation, however, never succeeded, so that when Danish rule ended in the early 19th century, the written language of the urban areas was Danish but with a Norwegian pronunciation. The Danish influence was less in rural areas.

The Danes were forced to hand Norway over to Sweden after the Treaty of Kiel in 1814, and the Norwegians were not to gain their independence until 1905. The Swedes allowed a good measure of local autonomy to the Norwegians so that there were few influences on the language of Norway. During the 19th century, nationalism flourished in the wake of romanticism, and for Norway this meant that a national language was needed. There were two approaches taken, each of which had the goal of creating a national language; both were eventually successful to the extent that by the end of the 19th century there were two official languages in Norway: *bokmål* and *nynorsk*.

The conservative approach took as its point of departure the language of the cultivated classes, which was, in effect, written Danish with Norwegian pronunciation. Knud Knudsen, an educator and linguist, was the main force behind this movement that sought to Norwegianize Danish spelling so that it conformed more with what people were speaking in the urban areas. He advocated a series of spelling changes that would gradually change the written language, and he published a grammar in 1856. His ideas were supported by Bjørnson and Ibsen and came to fruition in official spelling reforms that were adopted in 1907, 1917 and 1938.

The incentive for the other more radical approach came from Ivar Aasen, the linguist and poet, who sought a language that would be more appropriate for the common people of rural Norway. He traveled the country, especially the western parts, recording the dialects he came in contact with. He then created a normalized language based on the dialects and on Old Norwegian, which he called *landsmål* ('country language'). He created a grammar in 1848 and a dictionary in 1850, and re-established a definitive language in his grammar of 1864 and dictionary of 1873; and he then proceeded to use the language in a number of areas including poetry, translation, and technical discourse. Some of Norway's finest writers including Vinje, Garborg, Duun and Vesaas helped lend prestige to this new language. It also served a nationalistic purpose as Norway was moving toward its independence at the turn of the century. It attained official equality in 1885 and became an option for use in local schools in 1892; a professorship in *landsmål* was established at the University of Oslo in 1899. After 1902 future teachers had to learn *landsmål*, and it was required for admission to the university in 1907. Yet never more than 20 percent of the population were native speakers of *nynorsk*, and the numbers seem to be decreasing very gradually. In 1927 the name of the language changed to *nynorsk* ('new Norwegian').

During the 20th century there have been a number of attempts to bring the two languages, *bokmål* and *nynorsk*, closer together. For example, the feminine gender has been introduced into *bokmål*, and the official spelling reforms mentioned above helped bring them closer to one another. Yet they remain separate languages. A certain percentage of television and radio programs must be broadcast in *nynorsk*. Students whose mother tongue is *bokmål* must study some *nynorsk* in school. *Bokmål* speakers generally refuse to read *nynorsk*, preferring to read Danish translations of it instead. It is not clear what the future will bring what with ever increasing social mobility, but the long term prospects for *nynorsk* are not sanguine.

Orthography and Basic Phonology

Both *bokmål* and *nynorsk* are generally pronounced the way they are written. There are a few silent letters, most frequently *d*, but also *g* (e.g., *nynorsk heldigvis* 'fortunately', *bokmål -ig* '-y' *lykkelig* 'happy') and *t*.

Table 1: Consonants

	Labial	Alveolar	Alveo-palatal	Velar	Glottal
Stops					
Voiceless	p	t		k	
Voiced	b	d		g	
Fricatives					
Voiceless	f	s	sj, kj		h
Voiced	v				
Nasals	m	n		ng	
Lateral		l, r			

Sj and *kj* represent a voiceless alveo-palatal fricative, like English "sh"; *s* is a voiceless alveolar fricative, like English "s". *Ng* is, as in English, a single phoneme, not a sequence of nasal followed by velar stop.

Table 2: Vowels

	Front		Central	Back
	Unrounded	Rounded		
High	i	y	u	
Mid	e	ø		o
Low	æ			å

The central vowel *u* and the back vowels *o* and *å* are all rounded. *Bokmål* has one unstressed vowel that varies from [ə], as in *bakke* 'hill', to no vowel, as in the second syllable of *middel* 'means'. *Nynorsk* has four unstressed vowels *e, a, o, i*, as in three inflected forms of the word *nokon* 'someone' (*nokre, noka, noko*) and the participle *teki* 'taken'.

In both varieties of Norwegian, the stressed syllable in a word must contain either a long vowel or a long consonant (including clusters). Thus, the first syllable of *nynorsk baka* 'bake' has a long [a:], while the first syllable of *bakke* 'hill' has a short [a] and a geminate (doubled) [kk]. It is mainly the vowel length that the listener perceives.

In east Norway and the Trøndelag area, the usual pitch on a stressed syllable is low, the opposite of the English pattern. The pitch falls to the stress and then rises to the end of the word. This pattern does not indicate a question, contrary to the perception of some foreigners. In the rest of Norway, the pattern is similar to that of English, with the usual pitch on a stressed syllable being high.

Norwegian is a tone language. Lexical pitch is used to distinguish otherwise identical words. Tone contrasts occur only on stressed syllables followed by at least one more syllable. Words without tone are said to have Accent 1 or monosyllabic tone. Words with Accent 2 or polysyllabic tone often show a second rise in pitch, although this varies throughout the country. For example, *bokmål bønder* 'farmers' and *bønner* 'beans' are identical phonetically except that the former has Accent 1 while the latter has Accent 2. Accent is not systematically represented in the orthography.

Basic Morphology

Norwegian nouns are marked for number and gender. *Nynorsk* has three genders: masculine, feminine, and neuter. *Bokmål* has two systems of gender, depending on the speaker. Common (a merger of masculine and feminine) and neuter genders were part of the system taken over during the period of Danish rule. In the past century, the feminine gender has been reintroduced as part of an attempt to bring *bokmål* closer to *nynorsk*. The plural endings in *bokmål* are *-(e)r* and, occasionally, *-e* or change of the stem vowel for masculine and feminine nouns, and no ending and, occasionally, *-er* for neuter nouns: *kvinne* 'woman', *kvinner* 'women' (feminine); *trykker* 'printer', *trykkere* 'printers' (masculine); *mann* 'man', *menn* 'men' (masculine); *skip* 'ship, ships' (neuter). In *nynorsk*, the plural endings are *-ar*, *-er*, and no ending (occasionally with a change of the stem vowel in the plural form): *bygd* '(rural) district', *bygder* 'districts' (feminine); *by* 'city', *byar* 'cities' (masculine); *våpen* 'weapon, weapons' (neuter).

In the nominal system, the only case marker is the genitive *-s*, as in *manns hår* 'man's hair' and in several fixed phrases after the preposition *til* 'to'.

The definite article varies depending on whether there is an adjective in the noun phrase or not. Without an adjective, the article is suffixed to the noun and has three forms: *mann-en* 'the man', *kvinn-a* 'the woman', *hus-et* 'the house'.

In noun phrases containing an adjective, the definite article is preposed. In *bokmål* there may be a suffixed definite article as well (double definite form): *den store mann(en)* 'the strong man'; in *nynorsk*, the double-definite form predominates: *det lange skip-et* 'the long ship'.

Noun modifiers are inflected for gender and number and usually have both strong and weak forms depending on whether they are preceded by an article or other determiner (definite form) or not (indefinite form): *den store mann* 'the large man', *en stor mann* 'a strong man'.

Norwegian verbs are strong or weak depending on how they are inflected. Verbs do not agree with their subjects in person or number. Thus verb inflection concerns derivation of the principle parts of the verb (present tense, preterite [past], and participle). Strong verbs usually have vowel changes in the preterite and participle forms, as well as monosyllabic preterites: *nynorsk* present *bita* 'bite', preterite *beit* 'bit', participle *bite* 'bitten'; *bokmål* present *bite*, preterite *bet*, participle *bitt*. Weak verbs form their preterites and participles with an alveolar suffix: *nynorsk* present *tenkja* 'think', past *'tenk-te* 'thought', participle *tenk-t* 'thought'; *bokmål* present *tro* 'believe', preterite *tro-dde* 'believed', participle *tro-dd* 'believed'. The present tense in *nynorsk* has four forms, depending on the stem of the verb: ending *-ar*, *-er, or -r*, or no ending.

The present perfect in both varieties of Norwegian is formed with the auxiliary verb *ha* 'have' plus the participle:

han	har	gå-tt
he	have:PRES	walk-PARTICIPLE

'he has walked'

The passive voice in *bokmål* is formed with the auxiliary verb *bli* 'become' plus the participle:

han	ble	døm-t
he	be:PRETERITE	sentence-PARTICIPLE

'he was sentenced'

In *nynorsk*, the passive auxiliary may be *bli* or *verta*:

port-en	var-t	steng-d
gate-the	be-PRETERITE	close-PARTICIPLE

'the gate was closed'

Both varieties of Norwegian also have a mediopassive form, created with the suffix *-s* in *bokmål* and *-st* in *nynorsk*:

avis-er	selja-st	hver	dag
newspaper-PL	sell-PASS	every	day

'Newspapers are sold every day.'

Basic Syntax

Word order in Norwegian is quite rigid. In statements, the verb is the second major constituent:

I går	drakk	han	vin
yesterday	drink:PRETERITE	he	wine

'Yesterday he drank wine.'

In conditional statements, the verb is the first major constituent:

Drikk	vi	vin	kan	vi	ikkje	køyre
drink:PRES	we	wine	can	we	NEG	drive

'If we drink, we can't drive.'

Alternatively, if the conditional is marked by the particle *om* 'if', the verb is in third position:

Om	han	ikkje	kjem
if	he	NEG	come:PRES

'If he doesn't come.'

As is illustrated above, negation is marked by the negative adverb *ikkje* (in *bokmål ikke*) preceding the inflected verb.

Adjectives precede the nouns they modify:

den	pene	kvinn-a
the	pretty	woman-the

'The pretty woman.'

Contact with Other Languages

Norwegian vocabulary reveals the cultural transformations through which the country has passed. Influences include Christianity, which was brought in and spread by a new clerical class using LATIN. New political institutions such as governments were created by the king and his nobles, whose technical language was also Latin, but with influence also from FRENCH and German feudal models. Increasing commercial contacts brought a Low German technical vocabulary. Foreign influences on the language were greater in urban areas:

From Latin: *skole* 'school', *museum* 'museum'
From Low German: *krig* 'war', *betale* 'pay'

Common Words

(All words below are identical in *bokmål* and *nynorsk* except those for water.)

man:	mann	long:	lang
woman:	kvinne	small:	liten
water:	vann (B) vatn (N)	yes:	ja
no:	nei	sun:	sol
three:	tre	good:	god
fish:	fisk	bird:	fugl
big:	stor	dog:	hund
tree:	tre		

Example Sentences

Bokmål sentences from Bjørg Vik's *Elsi Lund*:

(1) Noen pik-er la man aldri særlig merke
some girl-PL pay:PRETERITE one never special attention

til enda man ha-dde kjen-t dem
to although one have-PRETERITE know-PARTICIPLE them

i mange år.
for many years
'Some girls you never really noticed even though you had known them for many years.'

(2) Han ha-r med en pose med frukt.
he have-PRES with a bag of fruit
'He is carrying a bag of fruit.'

Nynorsk sentence from Kjartan Fløgstad's *Kniven påa strupen*:

(3) Lik ein fisk bak akvarie-glas-et opna
like a fish behind aquarium-glass-the open:past

og lukka far-en munn-en.
and close:PAST father-the mouth-the
'Like a fish behind the aquarium glass his father opened and closed his mouth.'

Efforts to Preserve, Protect, and Promote the Language

There is an ongoing effort to protect and promote the Norwegian (*bokmål*) language in Norway through such groups as the *Norsk Språkråd*, which is in its 23rd year. There are also groups devoted to the promotion of *nynorsk*, such as the *Det Norske Samlaget*, which has published a number of books in and about *nynorsk*.

In an effort to control the number of loanwords coming into Norwegian, all groups suggest loan translations that make use of already extant Norwegian vocabulary, and they occasionally have some success. Parents' choice of names for their children is tightly controlled with many foreign names not allowed. But, the onslaught of English words and phrases continues, especially in certain areas such as commerce and science.

Select Bibliography

Aasen, Ivar. 1864. *Norsk Grammatik*. Christiana: P.T. Malling.

Beito, Olav. 1970. *Nynorsk grammatikk*. Oslo: Det Norske Samlaget.

Halland, Hils. 1955. *Engelsk-nynorsk ordbok*. Oslo: Gyldendal Norsk Forlag.

Hallaråker, Peter. 1983. *Norwegian-Nynorsk: An Introduction for Foreign Students*. Oslo: Universitetsforlaget.

Haugen, Einar. 1965. *Norwegian English Dictionary*. Madison: University of Wisconsin Press.

_____. 1966. *Language Conflict and Language Planning: The Case of Modern Norwegian*. Cambridge: Cambridge University Press.

_____. 1976. *The Scandinavian Languages: An Introduction To Their History*. Cambridge: Harvard University Press.

Kirkeby, Willy A. 1989. *English-Norwegian Dictionary*. Oslo: Norwegian University Press.

Landrø M., and B. Wangensteen, eds. 1986. *Bokmålsordboka: Definisjons-og rettskrivningsordbok*. Oslo: Universitetsforlaget.

Larsen, Amund B. 1968. *Oversigt over de norske bygdemål*. Oslo: Aschehoug.

Knudsen, Trygye, and Alf Sommerfelt, eds. 1937–57. *Norsk Riksmålsordbok*. Oslo.

Popperwell, R.G. 1963. *The Pronunciation of Norwegian*. Cambridge: Cambridge University Press.

Seip, Didrik Arup. 1955. *Norsk språkhistorie til omring 1370*. Oslo: Aschehoug.

Skard, Vemund. 1968–73. *Norsk språkhistorie I–III*. Oslo: Universitetsforlaget.

Slette, Theodore. 1977. *Norsk-engelsk ordbok*. Oslo: Det Norske Samlaget.

Vikør, Lars S. 1975. *The New Norse Language Movement*. Oslo: Novus.

Occitan

Thomas T. Field

Language Name: Occitan. **Alternates:** *Langue d'oc, Provençal.* (The latter term more properly refers to one dialect of Occitan.)

Location: The southern third of France, along with small parts of Italy and Spain.

Family: Romance group of the Italic branch of Indo-European.

Related Languages: Occitan is closely related to CATALAN; it is more distantly related to SPANISH, ITALIAN, AND FRENCH.

Dialects: There are six dialects: (1) Languedocian, (2) Provençal, (3) Limousin, (4) Auvergnat, (5) Alpine, and (6) Gascon.

Number of speakers: 2–5 million.

Origin and History

Occitan is a Romance language, descended from LATIN. Vulgar Latin was brought to Gaul (present-day France) by the Romans in the second century B.C., and after about 500 years the native language, Gaulish, became extinct. Over time there emerged two distinct linguistic areas in Romanized Gaul: north and south. This may be due in part to the fact that the north and south of France are different in climate and vegetation, and therefore in agriculture and culture. In addition, the populations of the north at the time of the Roman conquest were exclusively Celtic, while the south also included Aquitanian, Iberian, Greek, and Ligurian populations. Rome colonized the south earlier and more intensely than it did the north. Cities like Narbonne were large, cosmopolitan places from which a very "Roman" Latin spread out to most of the areas that were to become Occitania. Northern Gaul, on the other hand, was colonized largely via Lyon, which was less thoroughly Romanized and was considered to have a more "rustic" form of Latin. Later, the Germanic invasions brought different peoples to the north and the south. The Franks in the north had a far deeper influence on Gallo-Roman culture and language than did the Visigoths and Burgundians in the south. These different influences led to a divergence between the languages spoken in the north and south, which from medieval times have been known as the *langue d'oïl* and the *langue d'oc*, respectively (*oïl* and *oc* being corresponding words meaning 'yes').

With the Carolingian Renaissance in the 9th century, the learned segments of the populations of Romance Europe began to accept the fact that their spoken languages had become too different from the Latin of classical texts to be noted with traditional Latin spelling. Although Latin continued to be the language of serious writing, French and Occitan texts began to appear for the first time in this period. The earliest texts in Occitan appear in the 10th century, first in the form of marginal notes and poetic fragments, and then in the religious poem *Boecis*, a reworking of Boethius' *Consolation of Philosophy*. Although very little else remains from the period, the language of this 10th-century work is clearly Occitan and suggests that a tradition of written vernacular language was being formed.

The 12th and 13th centuries represent the classical period of Occitan. The most innovative use of the language—and the one that seems to have provided the first impetus for a kind of standardization—was the poetry of the troubadours, the first vernacular poetic tradition of medieval Europe. The standard poetic language used by these poets was a *koiné* known at the time as *roman*, *lemosi*, or *proensal*, adopted by writer-performers from Spain to Italy. There are works of about 400 named poets of the troubadour tradition, both male and female. From the late 12th century on, Occitan was also used extensively in administration, as the cities and courts of the south flourished. An administrative *koine*, based largely on the Languedocian dialect of the region of Toulouse, was in use from Navarre to Provence.

The rise of French royal power in Paris, however, conflicted with the independence and prosperity of the Occitan courts and the culture they maintained. The Albigensian Crusade (1208–1229), ostensibly launched to combat the Cathar heresy, quickly became a war of conquest and competition for the riches of Occitania. The most powerful lords of Languedoc and Provence were defeated and replaced by French princes or by puppet rulers. While this political event had very little immediate effect on the use of Occitan, it destroyed the foundations of the society that had developed the troubadour lyric, and it made French a useful communicative tool, at least for the upper class, for the first time in the south.

The 14th and 15th centuries can be characterized as the Middle Occitan period. The disappearance of final consonants that characterizes Provençal and North Occitan can be dated to this time, as can the regularization of a number of previously irregular verb paradigms. During this period the range of uses of Occitan actually expanded and came to include even such forms as encyclopedias and manuals of medicine, law, and carpentry. The written language adopted styles that were

Table 1: Consonants

		Bilabial	Labiodental	Alveolar	Alveo-palatal	Palatal	Velar
Stops	Voiceless	p		t			c
	Voiced	b		d			g
Fricatives	Voiceless		f	s			
	Voiced			z			
Affricates	Voiceless		tz		ch, tg		
	Voiced				j/ tg/ g		
Nasals		m		n/-nh		nh	
Liquids				l/-lh		lh	
Flap				r			
Trill				rr			

syntactically more elaborate. But French was increasingly present. In Auvergne, administration switched abruptly to French with the appearance of administrators from the north. By the beginning of the 15th century the higher nobility of Occitania was thoroughly familiar with French, and French influence in word choice and in spelling was becoming increasingly evident in nearly all written Occitan.

In 1539, King Francis I commanded that all administrative documents in his kingdom be written in French. From this point on, official use of Occitan declined dramatically. Only in the principality of Bearn in the Pyrenees were administrative functions of Occitan consistently maintained beyond the 16th century. Although the language experienced a literary Renaissance in this period, its structure and the linguistic consciousness of its speakers were fragmenting into regional forms, and writers tended to gain success only within their areas of origin.

By the 17th century, although Occitan was the only language spoken by the vast majority of the population in the south, French had become the language of respectability and culture there, and what writing was done in Occitan tended to be occasional and popular in nature. During the French Revolution those in power promulgated the elitist notion that Parisian French was the language of logic, clarity, and reason, and a policy was adopted to replace all the *patois* of France, including Occitan, with the language of Paris. Even ordinary Occitan soldiers in Napoleon's armies struggled to use French (and only partly succeeded) when they wrote to their parents.

During the 19th century Occitan continued its decline as a cultural language. Although the majority of the population was probably still monolingual, urban areas were gradually adopting French as the spoken language. Today, monolingual speakers of Occitan are nearly nonexistent. Nevertheless, Occitan is not yet close to extinction. Movements dating from the latter half of the 19th century have actively sought to revive the language (see Efforts to Preserve, Protect, and Promote the Language).

Languedocian, the form of Occitan spoken in the former province of Languedoc between Toulouse and Nîmes, is phonetically the most conservative, and for this reason has been proposed as the basis for a standard modern form of Occitan. Languedocian has retained final consonants, for example, that have been dropped in Provençal. Gascon, spoken in the southwest between Toulouse and the Atlantic Ocean and from Bordeaux to the Pyrenees, is remarkably different from the other dialects in both phonology and grammar. Some have suggested that it ought to be considered a separate language because it is at least as different from the other dialects as Catalan is.

Orthography and Basic Phonology

Occitan uses the Roman alphabet minus *x*, with *k*, *w*, and *y* used rarely. It employs grave and acute accents as well as the cedilla.

There are two widely used spelling systems for Occitan. The one adopted here is the Occitanist orthography. Its goal is to unify the many dialects of the language under one general system of spelling rules. Occitan orthography writes word-final consonants, for example, even in dialects where they are no longer pronounced.

The set of 19 distinctive Occitan consonants is represented in Table 1 above by their orthographic spellings.

All consonants that occur in voiced/voiceless pairs allow only the voiceless variant in word-final position. For example, *b*, *d*, *g* appear as *p*, *t*, *c*.

lop	'wolf'	*loba*	'she-wolf'
pòt	'she can'	*pòden*	'they can'
pauruc	'fearful (masc.)'	*pauruga*	'fearful (fem.)'

The palatalized consonants *lh* and *nh* are pronounced *l* and *n* in word-final position.

The set of vowels in Occitan is represented in Table 2 on the next page by their spellings.

The high rounded front vowel *u* is quite similar to French *u* or GERMAN *ü;* its closest equivalent in ENGLISH is in the phrase "cool, dude". Occitan has seven stressed vowels but only six unstressed vowels. In unstressed position *è* and *ò* do not occur: only *e* and *o* are possible (pronounced [e] and [u]). In addition, in final unstressed syllables, *a* is pronounced [o]; thus *boca* 'mouth' is pronounced [buko].

Table 2: Vowels

	Front		Central	Back
	Unrounded	Rounded		
High	i	u		o
Upper mid	e			
Lower mid	è			ò/-a
Low			a	

Basic Morphology

Occitan nouns are inflected for number (singular and plural) and gender (masculine or feminine) and require morphological agreement with pronouns that replace them and modifiers that they govern. Modern Occitan has no noun case.

The Occitan verb (in its fullest form) is constructed of root, verb-class indicator, tense/aspect/mood marker, and person agreement with subject.

cant + a + ra + i = cantarai 'I will sing'
root verb + class1+
future tense + 1st sing.

Occitan has a rich series of derivational suffixes that form diminutives (expressing smallness, cuteness, fondness) and augmentatives (expressing largeness, crudeness, disdain).

ausèl	'bird'	*ausel<u>on</u>*	'little bird'
fòl	'crazy'	*fol<u>et</u>*	'a little crazy'
ostal	'house'	*ostal<u>às</u>*	'a big ugly house'

Basic Syntax

Occitan syntax is of a general Southern Romance type. Basic word order is SVO. Pronoun subjects that are not stressed or focused on are marked with verb morphology (suffixes) alone (like Spanish, unlike French): *canti* 'I sing', *canta* 'he/she sings' etc. Constituents are head initial, as in Romance in general:

Noun + Adjective	*un dròlle san*	'a healthy child'
Auxiliary + Verb	*aviá acabat*	'he had finished'
Preposition + Noun	*per Pèire*	'for Peter'

Negation is effected with insertion of a negative form (*pas* in most dialects) after the conjugated verb form:

plòu <u>pas</u>	'It's not raining.'
aurà <u>pas</u> compres	'He will not have understood.'

Pronominal complements of the verb appear as preverbal clitics:

<u>la</u> conèissi	'I know <u>her.</u>'
<u>li</u> respondèt que non	'She answered <u>him</u> no (i.e. she refused).'
<u>me'n</u> mandaràs	'You will send <u>me some.</u>'

Pronominal clitics of infinitives climb to a position preceding the conjugated verb:

<u>li</u> voliái balhar d'argent	'I wanted to give <u>him</u> some money.'

Contact with Other Languages

Occitan dialects contain loanwords that extend back to the pre-Latin period. For example, Gascon has *esquèr* 'left' (from Ibero-Aquitanian), Provençal has *empurar* 'to stir up a fire' (from GREEK). Because of the dominant role of French in the Occitan region, Occitan as it is traditionally used is full of French loanwords. Modern puristic models of the language are attempting to eradicate most of these. For example:

Occitan	French	Purist Form
mèma 'same'	*même*	*meteis*
citoièn 'citizen'	*citoyen*	*ciutadan*

One of the interesting examples of loanwords from French is the use of *oui* and *nani* (borrowed from earlier colloquial French) for polite 'yes' and 'no.' In many traditional dialects, these are the forms used with those whom one addresses politely or respectfully (with *vos*, as opposed to *tu*), while the traditional Occitan forms *òc* and *non* signal familiarity and casual usage. Modern puristic prescriptions are attempting to extend the familiar forms (the ones that were originally Occitan) to all uses.

In its period of glory, the 12th and 13th centuries, Occitan was a cultural language for much of western Europe. Dante actually considered writing his *Divine Comedy* in Occitan. The language was one of the most important models for the development of literary languages in northern France, Catalonia, Castile, Portugal, Italy, and Germany. During this period a number of Occitan loanwords entered these languages. In French, for example, even the word *amour* is an Occitan borrowing (the French equivalent would be *ameur*), a fact that is certainly related to the prestige of the literary tradition of courtly love in southern France.

Prior to the Renaissance, Occitan played a large role in Navarre, where Occitan colonies often enjoyed commercial monopolies. It also served as an official language for the Basque Country on the north side of the Pyrenees.

Common Words

man:	òme	long:	long
woman:	femna	small:	pichon
water:	aiga	yes:	òc
sun:	solelh	no:	non
three:	tres	good:	bon
fish:	peis	bird:	ausèl
big:	grand	dog:	can
tree:	arbre		

Example Sentences

(1) Cossí va?
How go-it
'How are you?'

(2) Aquel ostal m'agrad-è-t pas.
that house me please-PAST-3.SG not
'I didn't like that house.'

(3) Los joves son partits totes e
The.M/PL young-PL are leave.PAST PART/PL all-PL and

l'escòla es barrada.
the-school be.3rdSG close.PAST PART/FEM/SG
'The young people have all left and the school has closed.'

Efforts to Preserve, Protect, and Promote the Language

In the 19th century, as France became increasingly centralized and industrialized, a movement to revitalize Occitan developed, primarily in Provence. The group that called itself the *Felibrige* attempted to revive and promote Provençal as a source of regional pride. It succeeded in developing an orthography for the language and in launching a veritable Renaissance of Provençal literature. The culmination of this movement was the awarding of the Nobel Prize to poet Frederic Mistral in 1904. But the *Felibrige*, which focused on the beauties of the land and the life of the peasantry, had little impact on the general process of a language shift toward French, especially in the face of ever-increasing centralization of French society after 1871 and the effectiveness of obligatory French-language schooling. Each succeeding generation had fewer speakers of Occitan. This process has accelerated in the 20th century.

In 1919, the *Escola Occitana* launched the Occitanist movement, the second major attempt at reviving the language. Grouped around the *Institut d'Estudis Occitans* after World War II, Occitanism intended to replace the *Felibrige*'s largely conservative attempts at maintaining the language with new initiatives designed to reconquer a linguistic space for Occitan in southern France. A new spelling system is at the heart of these attempts. In the 1970s, Occitanism stimulated a flourishing of song, poetry, novels, and journalism. Classes and workshops were set up all over southern France attracting participants from around the world.

Today the most promising developments for the future of the language are the *Calandretas* (monolingual Occitan schools), the increased presence of the language in the rest of the school system, and the recent officialization of Occitan in the Spanish territory of the Val d'Aran (part of the *Generalitat de Catalunya*). Nevertheless, it seems certain that the decline of Occitan will continue.

Select Bibliography

Ager, D. 1990. *Sociolinguistics and Contemporary French*. Cambridge: Cambridge University Press.

Akehurst, F.R.P. and J. Davis. 1995. *Handbook of the Troubadours*. Berkeley: University of California Press.

Alibert, L. 1966. *Dictionnaire occitan-français d'après les parlers languedociens*. Toulouse: Institut d'Etudes Occitanes.

Edwards, J. 1985. *Language, Society, and Identity*. Oxford: Basil Blackwell.

Field, T. 1980. "The Sociolinguistic Situation of Modern Occitan." In *The French Review* 54: 37–46.

____. 1981. "Language Survival in a European Context: The Future of Occitan." In *Language Problems and Language Planning* 5: 251–263.

Grillo, R. 1989. *Dominant Languages: Language and Hierarchy in Britain and France*. Cambridge: Cambridge University Press.

Hall, R. 1974. *External History of the Romance Languages*. New York: Elsevier.

Harris, M., and N. Vincent. 1988. *The Romance Languages*. Oxford: Oxford University Press.

Jacob, J. 1980. "Ethnic Mobilization and the Pursuit of Post-industrial Values: The Case of Occitanie." In *Toqueville Review* 2–3: 52–85.

Jacob, J., and D. Gordon. 1985. "Language Policy in France." In Beer, W. and J. Jacob, eds. *Language Policy and National Unity*. Totowa, NJ: Rowman & Allanheld.

Jensen, F. 1972. *From Vulgar Latin to Old Provençal*. Odense: Odense University Press.

Lodge, R.A. 1993. *French: From Dialect to Standard*. London: Routledge.

Paden, W. 1998. *An Introduction to Old Occitan*. New York: Modern Language Association of America.

Pei, M. 1976. *The Story of Latin and the Romance Languages*. New York: Harper and Row.

Price, G. 1964. "The Problem of Modern Literary Occitan." In *Archivum Linguisticum* 16: 34–53.

Schlieben-Lange, B. 1977. "The Language Situation in Southern France." In *International Journal of the Sociology of Language* 12: 101–109.

Wolff, P. 1971. *Western Languages AD 100–1500*. London: Weidenfeld and Nicolson.

Oriya

Subhadra Ramachandran

Language Name: Oriya. **Alternates:** *Oḍri*, *Utkali*. **Autonym:** *Oḍiya*.

Location: Oriya is the language of the Indian state of Orissa.

Family: The Eastern (or Magadhan) group of the Indo-Aryan language family.

Related Languages: Oriya is most closely related to other members of the above-mentioned group: BANGLA, ASSAMESE, MAITHILI, Magahi, and BHOJPURI.

Dialects: According to the Linguistic Survey of India (1987), Oriya has only one dialect, Bhaṭri, which represents a transitional stage tending toward MARATHI. However, many other dialects have been recognized; one of the most important is Sambalpuri, spoken in the districts of Sambalpur, Sundergarh, Kalahandi, Bolangir, and Bauda. It is a mixture of SANSKRIT, Oriya, HINDI, Chattisgarhi, and many other languages of the Austro-Asiatic group.

Number of Speakers: 19.7–24 million.

Origin and History

The origin of Oriya has not been determined. It is said that before the conquest of Kalinga (ancient Orissa) by King Ashoka of Magadha, a language of Sanskritic origin prevailed. During the conquest, several categories of people—officers, monks, and merchants—entered Kalinga in large numbers and imposed their language, believed to be PALI (also of Sanskritic origin), on the Kalingans. After the Magadhan rule, a king of the Chedi dynasty (first century B.C.) ruled over Orissa and during this time, the language of the official documents (determined on the basis of stone inscriptions) was Prakrit and remained so until the end of the fourth century A.D. Dynasties that succeeded the Chedis used Sanskrit for their official records. Even though Pāli, Prakrit, and Sanskrit were never the spoken languages of Orissa, copperplate inscriptions show that the earlier form of Oriya must have been derived from them all.

When the Somavamsis came to power in the 10th and 11th centuries, three political units existed in Orissa, namely Utkal (Oḍra), Kosala, and Kongoda. The Somavamsis united the three units, and this political change fostered the growth of a common language in Orissa. The people of western Orissa originally spoke a language akin to the Bhojpuri Prakrit while the people of coastal Orissa spoke a language that resembled Magadhi Prakrit. These two branches of Prakrit met and mingled in Orissa and formed a new language that came to be known as Oriya. The name "Oriya" seems to have derived from the fact that the elements of the language of the coastal strip (Magadhi Prakrit)—the land of the Oḍras—predominated in it.

In the year 1514, Portuguese traders set foot in Orissa and established their first settlement on the coast of the Bay of Bengal at Pipli. There was one more settlement in Balasore, and the Portuguese continued their trade and commerce for a considerable period of time in Orissa and involved themselves in the internal political affairs of Bengal. PORTUGUESE words crept into Oriya during the 16th and 17th centuries because, although there were only two Portuguese settlements in Orissa, Portuguese was the lingua franca in all the European settlements in Orissa and Bengal.

According to a recent census, one-fifth of Orissa's population consists of tribespeople (called *adivasis*) who speak a number of languages that possess no records or written literature. Some of these languages belong to the Austro-Asiastic group: Bhumij, Bhuyan, Gond, Gadba, Ho, Kondh, Kol, Kui, Kisan, Laria, Munda, Mundari, Orang, Patua, Saura, and SANTALI. Most of these languages have not been linguistically analyzed, except for Mundari, which was identified as one of the most important tribal languages of the region and studied by the American linguist John Gumperz. However, some of these tribal languages are gradually dying as a result of increased interaction among the tribes living in the hills and the Oriya-speaking "city dwellers".

Orthography and Basic Phonology

Like many of the other languages of India, Orissa is written in a quasi-syllabic script, probably descended from the early Indian Brahmi script. In these scripts, each symbol represents a consonant and the following vowel (if any). The oldest inscriptions in Orissa date to the Maṭhara period (A.D. 350–550).

Like other languages of India, Orissa distinguishes among four classes of stops: voiceless aspirated (*ph*), voiceless unaspirated (*p*), voiced unaspirated (*b*), and voiced aspirated (*bh*).

The alveo-palatal nasal *ɲ* is similar to the "ny" sequence in ENGLISH words like "canyon".

The retroflex sounds represented by letters with dots beneath them (*ṭ*, *ḍ*, etc.) differ from their dental counterparts in the position of the tongue tip during their articulation. For the dentals, the tongue tip is touching the upper teeth, while for the retroflexes, it is curled back along the roof of the mouth. The closest English equivalent to the retroflex sounds occurs when an alveolar consonant precedes /r/ (e.g., "d̲ream").

All consonants, except /n/, /n/, and /l/ may occur word initially. *J* ([y]) is often pronounced ǰ.

The distinction among the three fricatives *s*, *š*, and *ṣ* is preserved only in literary pronunciation; in colloquial speech, all three are pronounced [s].

Table 1: Consonants

	Bilabial	Dental	Alveo-palatal	Retroflex	Velar
Stops	p ph b bh	t th d dh		ṭ ṭh ḍ ḍh	k kh g gh
Fricatives		s	š	ṣ	h
Affricates			č čh ǰ ǰh		
Nasals	m	n	ɲ	ṇ	ŋ
Laterals		l		ḷ	
Semivowels			j		

Table 2: Vowels

	Front	Back
High	i	u
Mid	e	o
		ɒ
Low	a	

The difference between oral and nasal vowels is phonemic in Oriya: /a/ 'come', /ã/ 'open mouthed'; /ui/ 'termite' /ũi/ 'having risen'; /pɒhɒrɒ/ 'fraction of the day', /pɒhɒ̃rɒ/ '(you) swim'.

Basic Morphology

Oriya has a rich case system, marking nominals for accusative/dative (*-ku)*, instrumental (*-re*), ablative (*-ru*), genitive (*-rɒ*), and locative (*-re*/*-ri*) cases. Nouns in the nominative are not marked. Case markers may be preceded by plural markers, or by the definite marker (*-ṭi* or *-ṭa*).

gɒčɒ-ru phɒlɒ-ṭi pɒḍila
tree-ABL fruit-the fell
'The fruit fell from the tree.'

The accusative case is used only when the direct object is specific.

mu bɒhi-ru pɒd-ili
I book-ACC.SPEC read-pres.
'I'm reading a (specific) book.'

Oriya nouns can be singular or plural: *pila* 'child' *pila-maane* 'children'.

Oriya also has a rich distribution of pronouns—first-, second- and third-person pronouns; the remote demonstrative; the proximate demonstrative pronouns; the correlative and the relative pronouns; the reflexive pronoun; and the honorific and the interrogative pronouns.

Oriya verbs are inflected for tense and agree with their subjects in person and number, but not in gender, as illustrated in the conjugation of the verb *jaa-* 'go' in the present continuous tense, formed by combining the participle with inflected forms of the auxiliary *-ɒčh* 'to be'.

	Singular	Plural
1st person	mu jaa-učh-i	ame jaa-učh-u
2nd person	tu jaa-učh-u	
3rd person	se jaa-učh-i	se mane jaa-učh-ɒnti

The past continuous is based on the auxiliary *thiba* 'to stay':

mu bɒhi pɒdhu-thili
I book read-was
'I was reading a book.'

Other tenses (past, present, and future) are formed without auxiliaries.

Basic Syntax

The unmarked word order in Oriya is Subject-Object-Verb. Because verbs agree with their subjects in person and number, sentences can appear without the subject:

(mu) iskul jibi nãhi
I school go won't
'I won't go to school.'

In standard Oriya the negative particle *nãhi* is suffixed to the verb (as illustrated above), but in the Sambalpuri dialect, as in Hindi, the negative particle is prefixed to the verb. The nonfinite past participle is formed by adding the suffix *-i* to the verb stem. A series of past participles, one followed by another also occurs in Oriya, as seen below. Such formations are referred to as serial verb constructions.

mu jaṇi deli
I known gave
'(I), having known, gave.'

Causative verbs in Oriya are formed by adding *-a* to verb roots: *pi-a* 'cause to drink', *ji-a* 'cause to live', *khu-a* 'cause to eat'.

Contact with Other Languages

Even though the dialects of Oriya are marked by the rich influence of the languages of the neighboring states, standard Oriya itself seems to have a lexicon that is composed of loanwords from Hindi, GUJARATI, NEPALI, Sanskrit, and even Portuguese. It is not surprising that a language such as Oriya, which has evolved from Sanskrit, should have loanwords from other Indo-Aryan languages, and it is interesting that Portuguese has so richly contributed to its vocabulary.

From Portuguese: *girija* 'church' (<*igreja*), *balti* 'bucket' (<balde) *kakatua* 'parrot' (<*catatua*)
From Hindi: *bɒrɒfɒ* 'ice/snow' (<*varfa*), *khɒrap(ɒ)* 'bad' (<*kharab*), *dhuli* (<*dhul*)
From Sanskrit: *pɒtrɒ* 'leaf' (<*patra*), *sɒtru* 'enemy'(<*satru*)

Common Words

man:	purusɒ	long:	lɒmba
woman:	nari	small:	čhoṭɒ
water:	paṇi	yes:	hɒ̃
sun:	surjɒ	no:	nãhi
three:	tĩni	good:	bhɒlɒ
fish:	mačhɒ	bird:	čiḍija
big:	bɒḍɒ	dog:	kukurɒ

Example Sentences

(1) mu mɒndirɒ kali jibī nãhi.
I temple tomorrow go:1SG will.not
'I will not go to the temple tomorrow.'

(2) Bijɒjɒ ambɒ khai sarila.
Bijoy mango eat:PAST.PART finished:3SG.
'Bijoy has eaten the mango.'

(3) tu kɒṇɒ kɒr-uč h-u?
you what doing-PRES.CONT-2SG
'What are you doing?'

Efforts to Preserve, Protect, and Promote the Language

As promulgated in the Indian constitution, many states have an official or "regional language", the language spoken by the majority (all Indian states are multilingual). Oriya is the regional language of Orissa as well as being one of 18 "scheduled languages", which means it is used for official government purposes.

There are a number of literary awards that recognize an author's contribution toward promoting the Oriya language; two of the most important are the Orissa Sahitya Academy Award, and the Phakir Mohan Award. The latter award is special in that it promotes literary works in nonstandard Oriya (dialectal varieties) and was instituted in honor of a writer who wrote many works in regional varieties of Oriya.

Select Bibliography

Campos, J.J.A. 1919. *History of the Portuguese in Bengal*. Calcutta.

Das, Biswarup. 1985. *Orissa: Social, Cultural and Religious Aspects*. Delhi: Sundeep Prakashan.

Dhall, G.B. 1959. "The Languages and Dialects Spoken in Orissa." In *Indian Linguistics* 20: 87–92.

Sebeok, Thomas, ed. 1968. *Current Trends in Linguistics 5: Linguistics in South Asia*. The Hague: Mouton.

Tripathi, K.B. 1957. "Western Oriya Dialect." In *Indian Linguistics* 18: 76–85.

OROMO

Robbin Clamons

Language Name: Oromo. **Autonyms:** *Oromo*, *Afaan Oromo*. **Alternates:** *Oromiffa*, *Galla* (obsolete pejorative).

Location: Spoken in southern Ethiopia: in the west, between the Blue Nile and Gojeb Rivers, throughout the central Shoan region and northward into Wollo, eastward as far as Harar, and south into Kenya, in the northern regions and in communities extending southward through the Tana River Valley to the coast of the Indian Ocean, and southward to Kilifi. Also nomadic herding communities of Oromo are found in northern Tanzania.

Family: Lowland East Cushitic branch of the Afro-Asiatic Language Family.

Related Languages: Within Lowland East Cushitic, the closest linguistic relatives are the Konso languages, Afar-Saho, Rendille, SOMALI and Boni.

Dialects: In Ethiopia: (1) Western: Macha, (2) Central: Tulama, (3) Northern: Wollo and Raya, (4) Eastern: Harar, and (5) Southern: Arssi, Gugi, Gabra, Garre, and Boraana. Boraana, Orma, and Waata in Kenya form a dialect cluster. Oromo is mutually intelligible across the range of dialects.

Number of Speakers: 15–26 million in Ethiopia; 100,000 in Kenya, and a smaller number in Tanzania.

Origin and History

The ancient homeland of the Oromos is identified by scholars as the southeastern highlands of the Horn of Africa. Settled regions as far north as Harar are ancient. Oromos from the southeastern highlands migrated north into the areas of Shoa, northwards into Wollo, and westwards into the areas south of the Blue Nile following the 16th century depopulation of these regions during religious wars. This migration located the Oromo in their modern lands and led to certain dialectal differences. Oromo is closely related to the Konso languages spoken in the Rift Valley, west of the Oromo, Rendille and Boni, spoken in the north of Kenya, and Afar-Saho and Somali spoken to the east and north.

Although Oromo is the mother tongue of one of the largest speech communities in Africa, it is relatively unknown internationally. This is because of political isolation and repression of the language almost continuously from the late 19th century through most of the 20th century. Nonetheless, Oromo is spoken widely as a second language in all of southern Ethiopia and is used extensively as a lingua franca in the Horn of Africa, in spite of the long-term political repression of the language. For example, Oromo appears to be replacing Burjii, a Highland East Cushitic language of northern Kenya.

Orthography and Basic Phonology

There is no traditional writing system for Oromo. However, an adaptation of the LATIN writing system is now used by Oromos in the diaspora and in Ethiopia for literary materials and for newspapers. In this system, some letters are used in ways that would not be expected in terms of European alphabets. For instance, *x* is used to represent an alveolar ejective [t']. In addition, digraphs with *h* have very different meanings: *ph* represents a bilabial ejective [p'], *dh* an alveolar implosive [ɗ], *ch* a palatal affricate [č] (as opposed to *c*, which represents an ejective palatal affricate [č']), and *sh* and *kh* represent palatal and velar fricatives [š] and [x]. In addition, the ' is used both to indicate a glottal stop and to signal elision.

All consonants except *h* and ' can appear doubled, which indicates length or duration. In the case of a digraph, only the first letter is doubled in writing: *ny* is single, and *nny* doubled. The ejective consonants *ph, x, c,* and *q* are produced with simultaneous oral and glottal closures. Thus, for example, *x* is *t* with a simultaneous glottal closure. The palatal ejective *c* is phonetically an affricate.

The alveolar implosive *dh* differs from its voiced counterpart *d* in the direction the air is flowing through the larynx during its production. For *d*, air is flowing out from the lungs through the larynx. In contrast, for *dh*, air is flowing down from the mouth into the larynx; sometimes this is brought about by raising, then lowering the larynx during the articulation of the consonant so that the air is *effectively* flowing downward through it.

The consonants *p, v,* and *z* are found only in borrowings. Some consonants do not occur freely in words: *ch* and *ph* do not occur word initially, and *h* is not found word finally.

Table 1: Vowels

	Front	Central	Back
High	ii, i		u, uu
Mid	ee, e		o, oo
Low		aa, a	

Oromo vowels can be either long or short. Short vowels tend to be centralized relative to their long counterparts. Thus, *ii* is phonetically [i], and *i* is phonetically more nearly [ɪ].

In Oromo there are regular pitch patterns associated with certain grammatical meanings; tone is not lexically distinc-

Table 2: Consonants

		Labial	Alveolar	Palatal	Velar	Glottal
Stops	Voiceless	p	t		k	'
	Voiced	b	d		g	
	Ejective	ph	x	c	q	
	Implosive		dh			
Fricatives	Voiceless	f	s	sh	kh	h
	Voiced	v	z			
Affricates	Voiceless			ch		
	Voiced			j		
Nasals		m	n	ny		
Tap			r			
Lateral			l			
Glides		w		y		

tive. Morphological tone patterns (marked with an accent over a vowel, such as *ó*) are largely predictable: for example, high tone is found only on final or penultimate syllables of nouns and patterns to mark case.

There are widespread systematic morphophonological processes in Oromo. For instance, alveolar and velar obstruents assimilate to a following consonant: *beekh* 'know' + *-ne* > *beenne* 'we knew'. Sonorants assimilate to a preceding *l* or *r*: *walal* 'fight' + *ne* > *walalle* 'we fought'. Obstruents assimilate in voicing to a preceding consonant: *gabaab-* 'short' + *tuu* > *gabaabduu* 'short (FEM)'.

Basic Morphology

Oromo nouns may be masculine or feminine, with gender marked by suffixes: *jar-ti* 'old woman', *jar-sa* 'old man'.

A characteristic feature of Oromo morphology is that gender in demonstratives, possessive pronouns, and some other forms is distinguished by the initial consonant of the form: *t-* for feminine, and *k-* for masculine. First- and second-person possessive pronouns from Boraana, a southern variety, are illustrated below:

	Feminine	Masculine
First-Person Singular	tiyya	kiyya
Second-Person Singular	(tán)té	(kán)ké
First-Person Plural	teenna	keenna
Second-Person Plural	teésaní	keésaní

In Wollega (Western Oromo), all of these forms, both masculine and feminine, begin with *k*, so that there is no gender differentiation for these forms.

The Oromo case system distinguishes the following cases: topic subject, nontopic subject, absolute, and possessive, as illustrated in the following third-person pronouns from Wollega, a Western variety of Oromo:

	Feminine	Masculine
Topic Subject	iseen	inni
Nontopic Subject	isee	isaa
Absolute	isee	isa
Possessive	see	isa

Other cases include dative, instrumental, and locative, which are marked only phrase finally.

Plurality can be indicated by an elaborate inflectional system, including reduplication: *guddoo* 'big (singular)', *gurguddoo* 'big (plural)'. However, most often a general form is chosen, and plurality is contextually indicated by use of adverbs like *hedduu* 'many' or numerals.

Oromo verbs agree with topic subjects in gender, person, and number. The following forms represent the imperfective paradigm for *dhuf-* 'come'.

	Singular	Plural
First-Person Singular	n'-dhuf-a	dhuf-na
Second-Person Singular	dhuf-ta	dhuf-tan
Third-Person Singular Male	dhuf-a	dhuf-an
Third-Person Singular Female	dhuf-ti	dhuf-an

Oromo verbs are negated with a combination of prefixes and suffixes. The prefix *hin-* is used, together with *-ne*, *-ni*, or *-nin*, in main clauses (as illustrated in Example Sentence 1), and *-u* or *-tu* in subordinate clauses.

Basic Syntax

The main-clause word order in Oromo is the typical Cushitic SOV. Only afterthoughts or exceptions can follow the final verb. The relative order of subject and object phrases is determined on the basis of their relative topicality. Phrases are not uniformly head final.

Nominal modifiers (adjectives, demonstratives, possessives)

follow the nouns they modify. There are very few prepositions in the language, most of which are relatively transparently derived from nouns; adpositional relations are mostly conveyed by postpositions.

Subject-verb agreement is based on topicality of the subject.

Contact with Other Languages

The borrowing pattern in the Horn of Africa is very complex: Gragg (1980) explains the complicated (12 simple paths) borrowing situation. This alone makes determining the language of origin sometimes difficult. Words may be borrowed among different Cushitic languages, or different Semitic languages, or from one group into the other. There has been an ancient contact between Oromo and ARABIC in the east and in some Moslem centers in the western areas of southern Ethiopia, such as Jimma. During the period of migration there was extensive contact with Highland East Cushitic, as well as Semitic and Omotic languages. There has also been contact with SWAHILI in the south. Many lexical items were borrowed during the Italian occupation years. Some borrowings, and in fact a large percentage from Arabic in all varieties, are clear. For example *kitaba* 'write' has made its way into the lexicon of all varieties from Arabic and is used productively as a root form.

From Arabic: *zabiba* 'raisins', *zeytuna* 'guava'
From ITALIAN: *pizza*

Common Words

man:	namiccha, dhiira
woman:	naddheen, dubartii
water:	bishaan
sun:	aduu
three:	sadii
fish:	qurxummii
big:	guddaa, guddoo
long:	dheera, dheertuu
small:	xiqqaa, xinnoo
yes:	ee (ingressive airstream commonly used for emphasis, agreement)
no:	lakki
good:	gaari
bird:	simbira
dog:	saree
tree:	mukha

Example Sentences

(1) buddee-na oww-aa kha hin-nyaa-n-e
bread-M fresh-M who:M NEG-eat-NEG-PERFECTIVE

gowwa.
fool
'Who doesn't eat fresh bread is a fool.'

(2) haa-ti tiyya [intala ta habb-oo te
mother my:F [girl who:F aunt-F your:F

beet-t-u] gaafat-t-e.
know-3SG.F-PERFECTIVE/SUBORDINATE] ask-3SG.F-PERFECTIVE
'My mother asked the girl who knew your aunt.'

(3) namni lama tokkoo'raa gaarii?
person two one-than good
'Aren't two heads better than one?'

Efforts to Preserve, Protect, and Promote the Language

Although language repression (use of Oromo in public was punishable—and punished—by imprisonment) was carried out against the Oromo language for a century, the Oromo alphabet has been actively taught in the schools in the Oromo areas during the past couple of years. Onesimus Nesib translated the Bible into Oromo during the 19th century. In addition, Oromo has been studied in the diaspora by missionary groups who have translated sections of the Bible into at least two dialect versions; and by Oromo community groups publishing bilingual Oromo/ENGLISH newspapers, pedagogical materials, poetry collections, and dictionaries. Within Ethiopia, literacy materials have been produced by Oromo organizations wishing to promote Oromo literacy.

Select Bibliography

Ali, Mohammed, and Andrzej Zaborski. 1990. *Handbook of the Oromo Language*. Wroclaw: Polska Akademia Nauk.

Andrzejewski, B.W. 1976. "The Introduction of Written Oromo." In *IAI Bulletin* 46,3: 6–7.

____. 1980. "Some Observations on the Present Orthography for Oromo." In *L'Ethiopie Moderne/Modern Ethiopia*. Joseph Tubiana, ed. 125–132. Rotterdam: A.A. Balkema.

Baxter. P.T.W. 1978. "Africa's Unacknowledged Problem: The Oromo." In *African Affairs* 77: 283–296.

Bender, Marvin Lionel, Mulugeta Eteffa, and Lloyd D. Stinsin. 1976. "Two Cushitic Languages." In *Language in Ethiopia*. M.L. Bender *et al.*, eds. 130–154. London: Oxford University Press.

Gamta, Tilahun. 1989. *Oromo-English Dictionary*. Addis Ababa.

Gragg, Gene B. 1976. "Oromo of Wellega." In *The Non-Semitic Languages of Ethiopia*. M.L. Bender, ed. 166–195. East Lansing, MI: African Studies Center, Michigan State University.

____. 1980. "Lexical Aspects of Oromo-Amharic Language Contact: Amharic Loanwords in Western Oromo." In *L'Ethiopie Moderne/Modern Ethiopia*, Joseph Tubiana, ed. 107–121.

____. 1982. *Oromo Dictionary*. East Lansing, MI: African Studies Center, Michigan State University.

Hassen, Mohammed. 1990. *The Oromo of Ethiopia: A History 1570–1860*. Cambridge: Cambridge University Press.

Muudee, Hamid. 1995. *Oromo Dictionary, Vol. 1*. Atlanta: Sagalee Oromo Publishing Co.

Owens, Jonathan. 1985. *A Grammar of Harar Oromo (Northeastern Ethiopia)*. Hamburg, Germany: Buske.

Stroomer, Harry. 1987. *A Comparative Study of Three Southern Oromo Dialects in Kenya*. Hamburg: Buske.

PALI

John Michael Peterson

Language Name: Pali (*pāli*). The language in which the holy texts of the *Theravādin*—Buddhists of Sri Lanka and Southeast Asia—are written. The name "Pali" was almost certainly not the name used for the language by its own speakers, but rather appears to be the result of a centuries-old misinterpretation. The word *pāli* means "row, series" and came to be used to designate a row of canonical text as opposed to that of the commentaries. The designation *pāli-bhāsā* or 'language of the row (of canonical text)' was most likely reinterpreted as 'the Pali language' and came to be applied to the language of both the canon and its commentaries.

Location: Pali was most likely based on a dialect that was spoken in what is now Central India in the last centuries B.C. However, the language as we know it is the product of centuries of use as a lingua franca and a vehicle for culture and literature and shows many signs of contact with other related dialects. With the spread of Buddhism to Sri Lanka and Southeast Asia, Pali was also transplanted as a religious language, a function that it still has today in these regions outside India. In India itself, the religious functions once filled by Pali and other Middle Indo-Aryan dialects generally came to be filled exclusively by SANSKRIT and later by the modern languages.

Family: Pali belongs to the Indo-Aryan branch of Indo-Iranian, a subfamily of Indo-European. Within Indo-Aryan it is located in the early Middle Indo-Aryan (MIA) period.

Related Languages: Pali is most closely related to the other Middle Indo-Aryan dialects of its time, of which very few are known to us. Its closest affiliation is with the dialects of the West, such as the dialect represented in the Ashokan inscription from Girnār in present-day Gujarat. These Western dialects in turn show a number of common characteristics which clearly set them apart from the Eastern dialects of the time, such as Magadhi.

Being a Middle Indo-Aryan language, Pali occupies an intermediate position between Old Indo-Aryan, best represented by pre–Classical Sanskrit, and the New Indo-Aryan languages, such as HINDI, MARATHI, and NEPALI.

Dialects: Pali is one of a number of Middle Indo-Aryan dialects that were once spoken across large portions of northern and Central India and which, in time, developed into the New Indo-Aryan languages. Some of these Middle Indo-Aryan dialects are only known to us through the Ashokan inscriptions found throughout India, while others, such as Ardha-Māgadhī, Śaurasenī, and Māhārāṣṭī, are well known to us through the literature. These Middle Indo-Aryan dialects are often collectively referred to as *prākṛt*-s or 'natural' languages, as opposed to *saṃskṛt*, the 'polished' or 'refined' language of literature and culture, that is, Sanskrit. With the exception of the Ashokan inscriptions, Pali represents the first well-documented Middle Indo-Aryan dialect.

Also, although Pali is based primarily on a Central-to-Western Indo-Aryan dialect, it came into contact with and absorbed elements from other dialects of the time. This influence has been shown for the language of the canon, where a large number of Eastern forms coexist side by side with the expected Central and Western forms.

Origin and History

According to tradition, the Pali canon, which contains the oldest literature we have in Pali, was passed on orally in India in the centuries following the death of the Buddha and was brought by Buddhist missionaries to Sri Lanka, where it was written down in the first century B.C.

Before being brought to Sri Lanka, the language, which later came to be called Pali, had grown naturally out of the dialects of what is now western and Central India. It thus shows more similarities with the Vedic language, which originated in the northwest, than with Classical Sanskrit, which is based on a more Eastern dialect.

Pali also has an especially interesting chronological relationship to Sanskrit. Given the fact that Pali is a Middle Indo-Aryan dialect and Sanskrit belongs to Old Indo-Aryan, one would naturally expect that most texts in Sanskrit would be older than the oldest texts in Pali, at least those that have survived to the present. However, the exact opposite is true. This is because Classical Sanskrit literature reached its zenith long after the language it comes closest to representing had ceased to be a spoken language. The case is very different for Pali, since the early Buddhists chose to translate their texts into the vernaculars of the time. Thus the oldest Pali texts we possess, while perhaps not written by true native speakers, are nevertheless written in a language that comes much closer to the spoken dialects of the time than does the literature written in Classical Sanskrit, which was composed almost entirely by nonnative speakers of a much later period.

It should also be stressed here that, whatever the exact location of the origin of Pali, and whatever language the Buddha may have spoken or preached in, there is almost unanimous agreement in the scientific community today that Pali was not this language.

Orthography and Basic Phonology

Pali is written today in any number of different scripts, de-

Table 1: Consonants

		Labial	Dental	Alveolar	Retroflex	Palatal	Velar
Stops	Voiceless	p	t		ṭ	c	k
	Voiceless aspirated	ph	th		ṭh	ch	kh
	Voiced	b	d		ḍ	j	g
	Voiced aspirated	bh	dh		ḍh	jh	gh
Fricatives				s			
Nasals		m/mh	n		ṇ	ñ	(ṅ)
Flap				r			
Glides		v	l/lh		(ḷ /ḷh)	y	h

pending on where it is written, whether in India, Sri Lanka, Burma, Thailand, Europe, or elsewhere. Thus, whatever script(s) may originally have been used to write the language, one cannot speak today of a Pali script.

Table 1 lists the consonant phonemes. The status of consonant segments in parentheses as independent phonemes is uncertain.

Table 2: Vowels

	Front	Central	Back
High	i/ī		u/ū
Mid	(e/) ē	a	(o/)ō
Low		ā	

e/*ē* and *o*/*ō* are not differentiated in script, because of the fact that *e* and *o* are traditionally considered in most Indian script systems, at least those of northern India, to be inherently long. Short *e* and *o* should probably not be considered separate phonemes. With other vowels, however, vowel length is phonemic. What is representented as short *a* in the script was probably spoken as [ʌ] or [ə].

In addition, all short vowels can be nasalized and are then transliterated with a following *ṃ* nowadays, written as *ṁ* in older Western texts. Also in older texts, long vowels are generally indicated by a circumflex over the vowel instead of a macron, for example, *â* for *ā*.

Pali has the basic syllable structure (C)V(C). There are strict rules governing the quality of the consonants and vowels. They are briefly summed up here.

The most pervasive phonotactic rule of the language is undoubtedly the so-called Law of Morae. All syllables in Pali may contain at most two morae. In practice this means that a syllable may end in either a long or short nonnasalized vowel but, if it ends in a consonant or a nasalized vowel, the vowel of that syllable must be short.

While virtually any consonant may appear in the word-initial position, there are severe restrictions as to the types of consonant clusters that may appear within words containing more than one syllable. For example, assuming that a word consists of two syllables with the structure C_1VC_2-C_3V, C_2 and C_3 must have the same point of articulation. If C_2 and C_3 are both plosives, their voicing must be identical, that is, both must be voiced or both must be voiceless. Only C_3 may be aspirated. Also, if C_3 is a plosive, C_2 may also be a homorganic nasal, that is, produced at the same point of articulation as C_3.

The fricative *s* may be geminated but does not combine with other consonants.

Finally, all words in Pali end in a vowel.

Basic Morphology

Pali is a predominantly fusional language. That is, it is not generally possible to clearly separate case and verb endings from the stem.

Nouns and adjectives in Pali mark for case, number, and gender. Altogether there are eight cases: nominative, accusative, instrumental, dative, genitive, ablative, locative, and vocative; two numbers: singular and plural; and three genders: masculine, feminine, and neuter. There are a number of different declensions for each gender, depending on the stem final.

The following is an example of the masculine and neuter *a*-declensions, which differ only in the nominative singular and the nominative, accusative and vocative plural. As can be seen, a number of cases have alternate forms:

dhamma- 'Dharma' (m.), *rūpa-* 'form' (n.)

	Singular	
Nominative	dhammo	rūpaṃ
Accusative	dhammaṃ	rūpaṃ
Instrumental	dhammena, dhammā	rūpena, rūpā
Genitive	dhammassa	rūpassa
Dative	dhammassa, dhammāya	rūpassa, rūpāya
Ablative	dhammā, dhammamhā	rūpā, rūpamhā
Locative	dhamme, dhammamhi	rūpe, rūpamhi
Vocative	dhamma	rūpa

	Plural	
Nominative	dhammā	rūpā, rūpāni
Accusative	dhamme	rūpe, rūpāni
Instrumental	dhammehi	rūpehi
Genitive	dhammānaṃ	rūpānaṃ
Dative	dhammānaṃ	rūpānaṃ
Ablative	dhammehi	rūpehi
Locative	dhammesu	rūpesu
Vocative	dhammā	rūpā, rūpāni

In contrast, the feminine *ā*- declension:

kaññā- 'girl' (f.)

	Singular	Plural
Nominative	kaññā	kaññā, kaññāyo
Accusative	kaññaṃ	kaññā, kaññāyo
Instrumental	kaññāya	kaññāhi
Genitive	kaññāya	kaññānaṃ
Dative	kaññāya	kaññānaṃ
Ablative	kaññāya	kaññāhi
Locative	kaññāya, kaññāyaṃ	kaññāsu
Vocative	kaññe	kaññā, kaññāyo

There are several more declensions in all three genders and a number of irregular forms. Adjectives inflect the same way as the nouns of the corresponding class.

The first- and second-person pronouns inflect for case and number, but not gender. The third person is expressed by demonstrative pronouns that inflect for case, number, and gender.

Formally speaking, there are two types of verbal constructions in Pali. In the first group, the verb marks for person and number. All verbal categories in this group have both active and passive forms and operate on a nominative-accusative basis. They contain the following indicative categories: present, future, and past, which consists of the remnants of the Old Indo-Aryan "imperfect", "perfect", and "aorist". To these indicative categories can also be added the conditional and the imperative.

Active:

bhagavā rājānaṃ sandassesi.
Lord:NOM.SG.M king:ACC.SG.M instruct:3.SG.PAST
'The Lord instructed the king.'

nisīdi bhagavā paññatte
sit:3.SG.PAST Lord:NOM.SG.M appointed:LOC.SG.N

āsane.
seat:LOC.SG.N
'The Lord sat down on the appointed seat.'

Passive:

tāni cīvarāni nassanti.
that:NOM.PL.N robe:NOM.PL.N destroy:PRESENT.3.PL
'These robes are (= become/get) destroyed.'

Verbal constructions in the second group are based on participial forms, which, in Pali, are in the process of being reinterpreted as full verbs. The participles used in these constructions agree with their subject in terms of case, number, and gender.

This group consists of two different verbal categories. The first is the perfect, formed by the (inappropriately named) "past passive participle" (PPP) and optionally the copula. The PPP agrees with the nominative-case transitive patient and the nominative-case intransitive subject in an ergative-like pattern. Hence, it is not a passive form. The transitive agent generally appears in the instrumental. It is this construction that led to the emergence of ergativity in most modern Indo-Aryan languages.

mahā bhikkhusaṃgho
big:NOM.SG.M community.of.monks:NOM.SG.M

sannipatito hoti.
assemble:PPP.NOM.SG.M COPULA:3.SG.PRESENT
'A large community of monks has assembled.'

upāsakena attano atthāya nivesanaṃ
layman:INST.SG.M 'for oneself' dwelling:NOM.SG.N

kārāpitaṃ hoti.
build:CAUS.PPP.NOM.SG.N COPULA:3.SG.PRST
'A layman has had a dwelling built for himself.'

The second category consists of the so-called gerundival construction, which denotes obligation. Here, similar to the marking pattern of the PPP, the gerundive also agrees with the nominative-case transitive patient in terms of case, number, and gender. However, unlike the PPP, it does not agree with the intransitive subject. In intransitive clauses, the gerundive has default marking, that is, nominative, singular, and neuter. Both the transitive agent and the intransitive subject appear in the instrumental.

tehi bhikkhūhi
this:INST.PL.M monks:INST.PL.M

uposatho kātabbo.
uposatho.ceremony:NOM.SG.M do:GERUNDIVE.NOM.SG.M
'These monks should perform the *uposatho*-ceremony.'

gilānena na gantabbaṃ.
sick:INST.M.SG NEG go:GERUNDIVE.NOM.SG.N
'One who is sick should not go.'

Neither the perfect nor the gerundival construction has an active/passive distinction.

Finally, if a sentence has two or more clauses that share a common "subject", a special nonfinite form called the "conjunctive participle" or "sequential converb" may be used to join them. This form usually has the ending *-tvā*.

Devadattena pabbajitvā
Devadatta:INST.SG.M become.a.monk:SEQUENTIAL

saṃgho bhinno.
community:NOM.SG. divide:PPP.NOM.SG.M
'Devadatta has divided the community, after having become a monk.'

Basic Syntax

Word order in Pali is relatively free and is regulated primarily by the discourse status of the various arguments of the clause, with the topic appearing at the beginning of the clause and preceding noncontrasted new information. In addition to the topic, a contrasted focused NP or a focused verb may also appear at the beginning of the clause.

sammatā sīmā
determine:PPP.NOM.SG.F boundary:NOM.SG.F

saṃghena.
community:INST.SG.M
'The community has determined the boundary.'

Word order is not at all dependent on the case marking of the NPs of the clause nor on semantic criteria such as agent or patient. Thus, one cannot speak of "SOV order" in Pali but merely of an unmarked verb-final position.

Also, the passive in Pali simply denotes that the agent of the clause is unknown—it is not used to make a topical patient the grammatical subject, as in english. Instead, when the patient is the topic and the agent is known, the topical patient merely precedes the agent in the sentence, and the active is used.

aññataraṃ bhikkhuṃ ñātakā
certain:ACC.SG.M monk:ACC.SG.M relatives:NOM.PL.M

gaṇhiṃsu.
grab:PAST.3.PL
'Relatives grabbed a certain monk (to take him away).' (or, more colloquially: 'A certain monk was grabbed by [his] relatives.')

In unmarked word order, adjectives precede the nouns they modify, although this order is not rigidly fixed.

The language has adpositions, which, as a general rule, may either precede or follow the noun, that is, the majority of adpositions may function as either pre- or post-positions. Nevertheless, the individual adpositions generally have a preferred unmarked position either before or after the noun, such as *saddhiṃ* 'with', which virtually always follows the noun.

Nouns and adjectives may be negated in Pali by the prefix *a-* before consonants or *an-* before vowels. Sentential negation is indicated by the particle *na* 'not'. This particle may also be used to negate a verb. In the following attested example, all three forms are used.

Mahāvagga II:17,6
na … a-gilānena na gantabbaṃ.
NEG NEG-sick:INST.SGM NEG go:GER.NOM.SGM
'One who […] is not sick should not "not-go" (= "should go").'

Contact with Other Languages

Although there are undoubtedly a large number of loanwords in Pali from various sources, identifying them is not an easy task because this depends on a correct etymology of the word in question, which, in Pali, often means determining whether the word is of Indo-Aryan origin or not. There is also the problem of determining whether a word has been borrowed into Pali from a closely related dialect.

Nevertheless, there are a few words that are easily recognizable as loanwords from Sanskrit because these violate the phonotactic rules of the language, such as *brāhmaṇo* 'Brahman'.

Much more common than loanwords is the practice of loan orthography, such as writing the ablative ending *-amhā* as *-asmā* or the spelling of the locative ending *-amhi* as *-asmiṃ*, since the consonant cluster *-sm-* is not allowed elsewhere in Pali, although it is found in Sanskrit.

Common Words

In the following list, nouns are given in the nominative singular; adjectives are given in their stem.

man:	naro
woman:	itthī
long:	lamba-
small:	khudda-
water:	udakaṃ
yes:	(āma 'indeed'); repeat verb
no:	repeat verb in negative
sun:	suriyo
three:	tayo (m.), tīṇi (n.), tisso (f.)
good:	bhadda-
fish:	maccho
bird:	pakkhī
big:	mahant-
dog:	kukkuro

Example Sentences

(1) Mahāvagga II: 2,1
atha kho te bhikkhū bhagavato etam atthaṃ ārocesuṃ.
'and then' this:NOM.PL.M monk:NOM.PL.M Lord:DAT.SG.M this:ACC.SG.M matter:ACC.SG.M tell:3.PL.PAST
'And then the monks told the Lord this matter.'

(2) Mahāvagga III: 9,1
a. […] bhikkhū siriṃsapehi ubbāḷhā honti,
monk:NOM.PL.M serpent:INST.PL.M trouble:PPP.NOM.PL.M COPULA:3.PL.PRESENT

b. ḍasanti pi paripātenti pi.
bite:3.PL.PRESENT also attack:3.PL.PRESENT also
'[…] Monks have been troubled by serpents. [The serpents] bite [the monks] and attack [them].'

(3) Mahāvagga II: 11,1
tehi […] bhikkhūhi sabbeh' eva ekajjhaṃ sannipatitvā
this:INST.PL.M monk:INST.PL.M all:INST.PL.M FOCUS together come.together:SEQENTIAL CONVERB
uposatho kātabbo […]
uposatha-ceremony:NOM.SG.M do:GERUNDIVE.NOM.SG.M
'[…] These monks should all come together and perform the *uposatha*-ceremony.'

Select Bibliography

Basham, A.L. 1967. *The Wonder That Was India.* [Reprint: Calcutta/Allahabad/Bombay/Delhi: Rupa & Co., 1989].

Brough, John. 1980. “Sakāya Niruttiyā: Cauld kale het.” In: Heinz Bechert, ed. *Die Sprache der ältesten buddhistischen Überlieferung*. Göttingen: Vandenhoeck & Ruprecht. (Symposien zur Buddhismusforschung, II) Abh. der Akad.d.Wiss. in Göttingen, Phil.-hist. Kl., 3. Folge, Nr. 117.

Childers, Robert Caesar. 1875. *A Dictionary of the Pali Language*. London: Trubner & Co. [Reprint: New Delhi/Madras: Asian Educational Services, 1993].

Fahs, Achim. 1985. *Grammatik des Pali*. Leipzig: VEB Verlag Enzyklopädie.

Gair, James W., and W.S. Karunatillake. 1998. *A New Course in Reading Pali: Entering the Word of the Buddha*. Delhi: Motilal Banarsidass.

Geiger, Wilhelm. 1978. *Pāli Literature and Language. Authorised English Translation by Batakrishna Ghosh*. New Delhi: Munshiram Manoharlal. (Third Reprint of the 1943 edition by Calcutta University).

Hendriksen, Hans. 1944. *Syntax of the Infinite Verb-Forms of Pāli*. Copenhagen: Munksgaard.

Hinüber, Oskar von. 1986. *Das ältere Mittelindisch im Überblick*. Wien: Österreichische.

_____. 1994. *Selected Papers on Pali Studies*. Oxford: Pali Text Society.

Masica, Colin P. 1991. *The Indo-Aryan Languages*. Cambridge/New York/Port Chester/Melbourne/Sydney: Cambridge University Press (Cambridge Language Surveys).

Norman, K.R. 1983. *Pāli Literature. Including the Canonical Literature in Prakrit and Sanskrit of All the Hīnayāna Schools of Buddhism*. Wiesbaden: Harrassowitz (A History of Indian Literature, Volume VII, Fasc. 2).

Peterson, John M. 1998. *Grammatical Relations in Pāli and the Emergence of Ergativity in Indo-Aryan*. München/Newcastle: Lincom Europa (LINCOM Studies in Indo-European Linguistics, 1).

Rhys Davids, T.W. and William Stede, eds. 1925. *Pali-English Dictionary*. [Reprint of London edition: Motilal Banarsidass, 1993].

Trenckner, V. 1925. *A Critical Pāli Dictionary*. Begun by V. Trenckner. Copenhagen: The Royal Danish Academy of Sciences and Letters.

Warder, A.K. 1963. *Introduction to Pali*. London: Pali Text Society.

PANGASINAN

Carl Rubino

Language Name and Autonym: Pangasinan. The term *Kaboloan* was used during Spanish occupation, and *Panggalató* is used pejoratively.

Location: Lingayen Gulf, Philippines, in much of the province of Pangasinan and parts of southern La Union.

Family: South-Cordilleran branch of South-Central Cordilleran group of the Meso-Cordilleran subgroup of the Northern Philippine subgroup of the Philippine subbranch of the Western Malayo-Polynesian branch of the Malayo-Polynesian subfamily of the Austronesian language family.

Related Languages: Pangasinan is most closely related to the Southern Cordilleran languages in the Philippines: Ilongot, Inibaloi, Karao, and Kallahan.

Dialects: Dialect diversity is minimal in the Pangasinan region. Pangasinan spoken in Southern La Union (municipality of *Santo Tomás*) is marked with Ilocano influences. The purest form of the language is spoken in the Binalatongan region of the province around the towns of Urbiztondo, Santa Barbara, and San Carlos, the historical center of Pangasinan culture.

Number of Speakers: 2 million.

Origin and History

The exact origin of the Pangasinan people is still unknown. We can speculate that the homeland of the Pangasinan people in the Philippines was on the southern shores of the Lingayen Gulf between the sea and *Agno* river from where they spread southward. Their terms for direction *dapit ilog* 'south—to river' and *dapit baybay* 'north—to sea' contribute to this assumption.

The province of Pangasinan was created by the Spanish conquistadors that included lands dominated by Pangasinenses: present-day Pangasinan, Northern Tarlac and Nueva Ecija, and Southern La Union. After the uprising of Serrat in 1816, much of the Pangasinan area was settled by Ilocano settlers. Many regions of present-day Pangasinan province, which has considerably decreased in size since Spanish colonial times, are dominated by ethnic Pangasinenses whose mother tongue is ILOCANO.

Orthography and Basic Phonology

The Roman alphabet is used today in two forms. The SPANISH system (including the symbols c, ch, ñ, ñg, qu, and z) is preferred by most writers. Because of the TAGALOG-based educational system, some speakers employ the Tagalog system which employs 20 letters: A B D E G H I K L M N NG O P R S T U W Y. This outline employs the latter system.

The alveolar trill (*r*) does not occur word initially; it is an intervocalic variant of the phoneme /d/. The orthographic sequences /ch, ti + V/ and /dy, di + V/ represent voiceless and voiced alveo-palatal affricates, respectively. Stops are unaspirated and unreleased in final position, and the voiceless velar stop (*k*) often fricates between vowels (see Table 1).

Pangasinan has four native vowel phonemes /a e i u/, and two phonemes /o/ and /ɛ/, introduced after Spanish contact. Vowels are represented orthographically by five symbols /a e i o u/. The orthographic symbol *e* stands for two separate phonemes. In native words *e* is pronounced as a centralized high back unrounded vowel, while in Spanish loans it is pronounced as a front mid unrounded vowel like its Spanish counterpart. The other vowels of the language closely resemble their Spanish equivalents (see Table 2 below).

Table 1: Consonants

	Labial	Dental/ Alveolar	Palatal	Velar	Glottal
Stops Voiceless Voiced	 p b	 t d		 qu, k g	 ', (-)
Fricatives		s			
Nasals	m	n		ng	
Lateral		l			
Trill/Flap		(r)			
Glides	w		y		

Table 2: Vowels

	Front	Central	Back	
			Unrounded	Rounded
High	i		e [ɯ]	u
Mid	(e [ɛ])			(o)
Low		a		

Stress is phonemic in Pangasinan. Vowels are lengthened in stressed open syllables (those that have no consonantal coda) → *láki* 'grandfather' [lá:.ki], ≠ *lakí* 'male' [la.kí]; *bálo* 'new' [bá:.lo] ≠ *baló* 'widow' [ba.ló]; ≠ *naáwat* 'will receive', ≠ [na'.á:.wat] *naawát* 'received' [na'.a.wát].

Basic Morphology

Pangasinan is an agglutinating language. There are many productive morphemes in the language that may derive nouns and verbs from the same root. Verbal morphology is quite elaborate, as verbs encode mode (indicative or potentive), orientation (focus), transitivity, and aspect. From the root *nengnéng* 'see', the following forms may be derived: *akanengnéng* 'happened to see', *akanengnengán* 'happened to see at (locative)', *anengnéng* 'was seen', *nannengnéng* 'saw', *mannengneng* 'will see', *nanengnéng* 'can be seen', *makanengnéng* 'can see', *mannengnengán* 'will see each other', *ninengnéng* 'was seen', *nannengnengán* 'saw each other', and *ipanengnéng* 'show (make see)'.

There are two sets of enclitic pronouns and one set of independent pronouns as shown in Table 3. Genitive pronouns are used to express both possessors and agents of transitive verbs, the ergative category. Topic pronouns represent single arguments of intransitive verbs, nominal and existential predicates, and also patients of transitive verbs, the absolutive category. There are three first-person plural categories in Pangasinan: *sikatá* 'you and I', *sikamí* 'we, not you', and *sikatayó* 'we and you'. Gender is not indicated in the pronouns, but respect is encoded.

Table 3: Pangasinan Pronouns

Person	Topic Enclitic	Genitive Enclitic	Independent
1s	ak	ko, -k	siák
2s	ka	mo, -m	siká
3s	-, -a	to	sikató
1p dual (you and I)	(i)tá	ta	sikatá
1p inclusive	(i)tayó	tayó	sikatayó
1p exclusive	kamí	mi	sikamí
2p, 2SPOLITE	kayó	yo	sikayó
3p, 3SPOLITE	(i)rá	da	sikará

The first-person singular enclitic genitive pronoun *ko* changes to *ta* before the second-person topic enclitics *ka* and *kayo*: *Inaro ta ka.* (TRANS-love 1SGEN 2SABS) 'I love you', *Kaaro ta ka* 'You are my friend'. The enclitic pronouns *kayo* 'you', and *tayo* 'we' often change to *ki* and *ti*, respectively when followed by an enclitic adverb or linker: *la ki la* (go 2p(*kayo*) already) 'go already', *say abóng ti-n marutak* (ART house 1p.INCL.GEN-LINK dirty) 'our dirty house'. Third-person singular topics are usually not pronominalized, except after the negative particle *ag-*, in which the pronoun is realized as *–a*. After vowels, the first- and second-singular genitive enclitics *ko* and *mo* become suffixes *–k*, and *–m*, respectively, unless they are preceded by another enclitic: *Ala-m ya-y belás* (take-2SGEN this-LINK rice) 'Take this rice', *Kaaro mo ak* (friend 2SGEN 1STOP) 'I am your friend'.

Pangasinan has proclitic noun markers that inflect for number, personal versus common nouns, and three cases: topic/nominative, attributive (genitive + notional object of intransitive for common nouns), and oblique (see Table 4 below). Nominal case for common nouns does not follow an ergative/absolutive pattern as pronominal case does. Like the genitive case in the pronouns, the attributive case is used with both possessors and agents of transitive verbs: *say kapút na abung* (ART door ATTRIB house) 'the door of the house', *Pinatéy na duég so asó* (killed ATTRIB carabao TOP dog) 'The carabao killed the dog'. Unlike the pronominal genitive case, the attributive case for common nouns is also used to designate notional patients of intransitive verbs in antipassive constructions: *Analiw ak na aysing* (bought.INTRANS 1STOP ATTRIB dress) 'I bought a dress'.

Nouns may derive plural/distributive forms with various morphological means including stress shift and different types of reduplication: *anák* 'child' > *ának* 'children', *toó* 'man', > *totóo* 'people', *amígo* 'friend' > *amimígo* 'friends', *báley* 'town' > *balbáley* 'towns', *plato* 'plate' > *papláto* 'plates', *manók* 'chicken' > *manómanók* 'chickens', and *duég* 'carabao' > *deréweg* 'carabaos'.

Demonstratives mark three degrees of distance and inflect for case and number. For example, in the topic/nominative case Pangasinan has *saya/saraya* 'this/these', *satan/saratan* 'that (medial)/those', and *saman/saraman* 'that (distal)/those'. The demonstrative radicals are maintained with the locatives, *dia* 'here', *ditán* 'there (medial)', and *dimán* 'there (distal)', as well as the predicative locatives, *niá* 'here it is', *nitán* 'there (medial) it is', *nimán* 'there (distal) it is', and comparative demonstratives, *onyá* 'like this', *ontán* 'like that (medial)', and *onmán* 'like that (distal)'.

There is also a complex morphological system developed for numbers. From the root *duá* 'two', the following forms may be derived: *duára* 'two individuated items', *sanderuá* 'two

Table 4: Pangasinan Noun Markers

Case	Personal		Non-Personal	
	Singular/ Familar	Plural/ Respectful	Singular/ Neutral	Plural
Topic	si	di	say, imáy, so, -y	saray, irámay, iray, ira so
Genitive	nen	di	Attributive: na (-y nongenitive)	na saray, day, daray
Object of intransitive	kínen	kindí		
Oblique			ed, -d	ed saray

each', *maminduá* 'twice', *pídua* 'second time', *amidua* 'twice, past', *komaduá, mikaduá* 'second', *duágduára* 'only two', *kaduá* 'companion', and *kapalduá* 'half'.

Basic Syntax

Like its sister Philippine languages, Pangasinan is predicate-initial. Word order is more rigid than in languages like Tagalog. For post-predicate nominals, the agent normally precedes the patient in a phrase.

I-batík nen Elena may itik.
PF-run GEN Elena TOP duck
'Elena will run away with the duck.'

Nominals may appear in predicate position in identificational constructions where they are contrastive: *Maermén ak.* (sad 1S.TOP) 'I am sad'; *Siák so maermén.* (1S TOP sad) 'I am the one who is sad'.

Like other Philippine languages, Pangasinan has a focus system in which the semantic relationship between the "topic" (absolutive argument) and the verb is reflected in the morphology of the verb. The topic nouns are underlined below.

Actor focus (AF)
Man-tanem si Beng na kiew diman.
AF-plant TOP Beng ATTRIB tree there
'<u>Beng</u> will plant a tree there.'

Patient focus (PF)
Agámil-en mo 'ya.
use-PF 2S.GEN this.TOP
'Use <u>this.</u>'

Directional focus (DF)
Kawes-an mo'y ogaw
dress-DF 2S.GEN-TOP child
'Dress <u>the child</u>.'

Theme focus (TF)
I-tanem nen Beng may kiew diman.
TF-plant ATTRIB.PERS Beng TOP tree there
'Beng will plant <u>the tree</u> there.'

Benefactive focus (BF)
I-tanem-an nen Beng si Dexina na kiew
BF-plant-BF ATTRIB.PERS Beng TOP Dexina ATTRIB tree

diman.
there
'Beng will plant the tree for <u>Dexina</u> there.'

Instrumental focus (IF)
Pan-tanem nen Beng imay lima-to.
IF-plan ATTRIB.PERS Beng TOP hand-3S.GEN
'Beng will plant with his <u>hands</u>.'

There are a few ways in Pangasinan to express negation. For nonexistential phrases, the negative particle *ag* is used with enclitic pronouns, while the particle *aliwa* is used without enclitics to negate phrases.

Ag ko kaaro si Bering.
NEG 1SGEN friend TOP Bering
'Bering is not my friend.'

Aliwa-n siak so nan-luto.
NEG-LINK 1S TOP AF.PAST-cook
'I am not the one who cooked.'

Itik ya, aliwa-n manók.
duck this NEG-LINK chicken
'This is a duck, not a chicken.'

Existential phrases (which express both existence and possession) are negated with *andí* or *anggapó*. *Anggapó-y nilotó, tinapay so walá.* (NEG.EXIST-TOP cooked.rice bread TOP EXIST) 'There is no rice, bread is what we have', *Angappó-y iba-k.* (NEG.EXIST-TOP companion-1S.GEN) 'I have no companion'.

The linker *ya* is another prominent feature in the syntax of Pangasinan. It has three realizations: *ya* (before vowels), *-n* (after vowels), and *a* (everywhere else). It is used to connect various dependent constituents to their heads including nouns and adjectives, appositives, and various types of complement constructions: *sakey ya agew* (one LINK day) 'one day', *toó-n lakséb* (person-LINK naked) 'naked person'.

Ag ta ka in-abóloy-an a mang-galáw.
NEG 1S.GEN 2S.TOP PERF-allowed-TRANS LINK AF-play
'I did not allow you to play.'

Contact with Other Languages

Very few Pangasinan speakers are monolingual. In most areas of the original homeland province of the Pangasinan people, the Ilocanos actually predominate. Many Pangasinenses are well-versed in Tagalog, ENGLISH, and Ilocano, which is reflected in their speech in the streets and on the Pangasinan airwaves.

Spanish and English are the largest sources of foreign loanwords. Most Spanish loanwords have been incorporated natively into the language. Among the Spanish loanwords are suffixes that are still productive with native roots *-eño/eña* designating origin *Pampangueño* 'person from Pampanga', *-ero/era* indicating agent of action *kusinero* 'cook', *kahero* 'cashier', *kartero* 'mailman', and *-eriá* like English "-ery": *pansiteriá* 'noodle house', *panaderiá* 'bakery'. Many words for clothing, occupations, and technical terms are borrowed from Spanish: *abogádo* 'lawyer', *pantalón* 'pants', *kótse* 'car', *sombréro* 'hat', *sine* 'cinema', and *makinílya* 'typewriter'. Spanish numbers usually replace native ones in computation and counting over 10.

English loanwords, on the other hand, have a separate status in the lexicon of Pangasinan speakers. They are usually recognized as foreign since many of them violate native phonological patterns: *pinggerprint* 'fingerprint', *sekso* 'sex', *obertaym* 'overtime'. They nevertheless may participate in most derivational processes available to native roots.

The degree to which Ilocano and Tagalog are used by Pangasinan speakers is determined by social factors.

Common Words

man:	toó	small:	melág
woman:	bií	yes:	ikan
water:	danum	no:	andi
sun:	ágew	good:	maong
three:	talo	bird:	manok
fish:	ikan	dog:	asó
big:	báleg	tree:	kiew
long:	andukey		

Example Sentences

(1) Inér so laen mo?
where TOP go 2SGEN
'Where are you going?'

(2) Ag ko amta no anto'y a-gawa.
NEG 1SGEN know SUB what-TOP PAST-done
'I don't know what happened.'

(3) T{in}akew-an da ak na dueg.
rob{PAST}-TRANS 3PGEN 1SABS ATTRIB.OBJ water.buffalo
'They stole a water buffalo from me.'

Efforts to Preserve, Protect, and Promote the Language

Since there are two million speakers of Pangasinan, very little has been done in the area of language preservation. Pangasinan is categorized as one of the eight major languages of the Philippines. Nevertheless, Pangasinan speakers do not have access to much printed material in their native language. The few works available in the Pangasinan language are evangelical in nature and often products of English translation for proselytizing purposes.

The *Awiran na Pangasinan* ('Pangasinan Academy') was established in 1912 by several writers to develop and standardize the language. The academy is no longer active today. There are no newspapers or magazines available in Pangasinan and all adequate reference materials on the language are out of print. There are, however, a few AM radio stations that broadcast in Pangasinan.

Select Bibliography

Amurrio, Fidel. 1970. *Pangasinan Grammar*. Published by the author in the Philippines.

Benton, Richard Anthony. 1971. *Spoken Pangasinan*. Honolulu: University of Hawaii Press.

_____. 1971. *Pangasinan Reference Grammar*. Honolulu: University of Hawaii Press.

_____. 1971. *Pangasinan Dictionary*. Honolulu: University of Hawaii Press.

Cortes, Rosario Mendoza. 1974. *Pangasinan 1572–1800*. Quezon City: University of the Philippines Press.

Rayner, Ernest A. 1923. *Grammar and Dictionary of the Pangasinan Language* (*Gramatica tan Diccionario na salitay Pangasinan*). Manila: Methodist Publishing House.

PASHTO

Igor Inozemtsev

Language Name: Pashto, Afghan. **Autonym:** Pašto (eastern), Paxto (western). **Alternates:** Pushtoo, Pushtu, Pukkhto, Pukhto, Pushto, Pooshtoo, Afghan, Avgan.

Location: Afghanistan, Northwestern Frontier Province of Pakistan, tribal areas and Baluchistan.

Family: Pashto is the largest member of the East Iranian Group of the Indo-European family.

Related Languages: Dari, PERSIAN, URDU.

Dialects: The many dialects of Pashto may be classified into two large groups. The Western group is widespread in the area close to Kandahar, while the Eastern group is spoken in the Peshawar and Jalalabad regions. Neither the Western nor the Eastern dialect group has developed into a literary language, but a tendency exists to standardize Pashto on an inter-dialect basis.

Number of Speakers: 10–27 million.

Origin and History

Pashto has long been spoken in the present-day territory of Afghanistan, the homeland of the Pashtuns (*Pathans* in Pakistan), or Afghans. Although at present the language does not have a so-called literary norm, historical tendencies in its development led to the formation of two main dialects claiming to be the literary norm. Because of the lack of sources, there are numerous gaps in the history of the language that up until now have partially been filled with theories of European origin, as well as tales and legends elaborated by Afghan scholars.

One of the earliest sources of written Pashto is *Pəṭa-xazāna* ('Hidden Treasure') and it contains some information about 8th-century Afghan poets, but its date has not been established precisely. At any rate, the name "Pashtuns" appears as early as the 980s in the geographical work *Hudūd al-'ālam*. The first reliable description of the Pashtuns appears in the *Bābur-nāma*, 16th century. At that time the Pashtuns existed as tribal unions and were not united into one state. Their location, at the crossroads between East and West Asia, exposed them to influences from all the surrounding language environments: ARABIC, Persian and Urdu. The Perso-Arabic script became the basis for Pashto writing. Their closest neighbors, the Kurts and Timurids (14th-15th centuries) and later, the Safavids and Moguls (15th-18th centuries) were politically opposed to them, but provided the most important cultural influences. The first reliably dated written Pashto source is *Xair āl-bayān* ('The Happy News'), written by Bayazid Ansari in the 16th century.

Between the presumed date of the formation of the Pashtun nation and the first reliably dated written piece there is a five hundred year gap during which very little written work is found. Probably at that time, the Pashto oral tradition had been the inner engine of development of literature and language. Literature, anonymous for the most part, existed in the form of songs, quite voluminous and popular, which have preserved their significance up to today. Afghan songs like the *lanḍəy* served Afghans as mass media and books. Genres such as *čārbait* ('rhyming couplet') dated precisely all the events mentioned by them. Nowadays multivolume collections of Afghan songs have been published.

The literary talent of Khoshhal Khan Khattak (1613–1689) introduced the most significant changes into Pashto, and after his time the language took a form, sometimes called "Classical Pashto". Khattak consciously introduced foreign words into Pashto, saturated his writings with folk elements, and standardized verb usage. During the 19th and 20th centuries the language acquired the form that can be referred to as modern Pashto.

Orthography and Basic Phonology

Pashto, like Persian, uses Arabic consonant characters modified to the language needs. The extra letters, representing Pashto phonemes are: ṭ, ḍ, ṇ, ṛ, ʒ, ẓ̌, ṣ̌, ey. These letters differ from their Arabic counterparts only by a diacritic (see the samples of the Pashto alphabet on the next page).

Some consonants may be subject to transformation, depending on dialect and on the speaker's knowledge of Dari, which is also widespread in the country. Afghanistan natives who are not familiar with Dari, for example, may replace the *f* of borrowed words with *p*. Most of the Pashto-specific phonemes, especially the retroflex ones, for example *ṇ*, usually can be found in the middle or the end of the word. Non-retroflex affricates *c* and *ʒ* may be allophones within the same dialect. In addition, the retroflex affricates ṣ̌ and ẓ̌ of western Pashto dialects correspond to velar affricates *č* and *ǰ* of eastern Pashto, though writing is the same (see Table 1).

Long vowels are represented by separate letters in written Pashto (ā, ē, ū, o, ī), while short vowels (a, i, ə, u) can be omitted or are represented by diacritic symbols over or under the letter representing the preceding consonant. These diacritics in general resemble those of Persian, the only one specific to

Table 1: Consonants

		Labial	Alveolar		Palatal	Velar	Uvular	Pharyngeal
			Non-Retroflex	Retroflex				
Stops	Voiceless	p	t	ṭ		k	q	ʻ [ʕ]
	Voiced	b	d	ḍ		g		γ
Fricatives	Voiceless	f	s	(ṣ̌ W)	ṣ̌		x	ḥ
	Voiced	w	z	(ẓ̌ W)	ẓ̌			
Affricates	Voiceless		c		č	(x̌ E)		
	Voiced		ʒ		ǰ	(γ̌ E)		
Nasals		m	n	ṇ				
Lateral			l					
Trills			r	ṛ				
Glide					y			

Pashto *ə* (*zwarakai*) can be found at the end of words. The long back vowel *ā* may be slightly labialized by Dari-speaking persons; *o* is a stable labialized back vowel, opposed to *ā*, the opposition *u:o* is weak; *e* is stable opposed to *i*, if unstressed is almost neutralized; *u* is labialized. There are no real diphthongs in Pashto, though the combination of a vowel plus the following glide *y*, appearing word finally, can be treated as such.

Table 2: Vowels

	Front	Central	Back
High	i		u
Mid	e	ə	o
Low	a		ā

Basic Morphology

Pashto nouns occur in one of four declensions, and may be masculine or feminine. Nouns are inflected for number (singular, plural) and case (direct, oblique). The declension that a particular noun occurs in depends partly on phonological factors, but classification is, to a certain extent arbitrary.

Declension	Semantic class	Singular ends in	Plural
1st	masculine, nonhuman	-C, -ə,	-ūna
2nd	mostly humans	-C, -ə, -a, -u, -i,	-ān
3rd		-ay	-ī
4th		-oC, -uC	change in vowel in final syllable

The plural of feminine nouns is formed with *-āni or –gāni:*

Singular	Plural	Meaning
lās	lasūna	'hand(s)'
poh	pohān	'scholar(s)'
zmaray	zmarī	'lion(s)'
ṣ̌a	ṣ̌agāni	'back(s)'

The oblique case of singular nouns of the first and second declension has no inflection (but sometimes can produce the second oblique case); three and four mostly are homonymous to plural direct; oblique plural nouns end in *-o*.

Verbs are inflected for tense, mood, voice (active or passive), and aspect (perfective or imperfective), and may be transitive or intransitive: simple, compound (the auxiliary is inflected), or semicompound (inflected, but in certain terms breaks up into stem + auxiliary, which undergoes inflection).

Samples of the Pashto Alphabet

ا	alif	a, ā	چ	če	č
ب	be	b	ځ	ʒe	ʒ
پ	pe	p	څ	ce	c
ت	te	t	ح	hā-yi hutti	h
ټ	ṭe	ṭ	خ	xe	x
ث	se	s	د	dāl	d
ج	ǰim	ǰ	ډ		

Table 3: Pashto Verb Classes

Class	Group	Subgroup	Sample	Translation
I. Primary	1. 1-stem		baləl	'to call'
	2. 2-stem(past-present)		wuz-, watəl	'to exit'
	3. 2-4 stem(perf.-imp.) 6 verbs:		tləl	'to go'
			rātləl	'to come'
	(the most used verbs)		kawəl	'to do'
			kedəl	'to become'
			biwəl/botləl	'to take away'
			wṛəl	'to carry, move'
II. Prefixed (prefix+I class)	1. with prefixes: nəna-, pore, kṣ̌e-, pre-		nənawatəl	'to enter'
	2. with prefixes: rā-, war-, dar-		rābaləl	'to invite'
			rāaxistəl	'to take with'
III. Suffixed:	intransitive, 2 stem, suffix -ed- past; -eẓ̌- present			
	transitive, 1 stem, suffix -aw- past/present			
	1. compound:	- primary	gərzawəl	'to rotate'
		- sound imitating	trəngedəl	'to chime'
		- causative (I1 and I2)	xurawəl	'to force to eat'
		- from nouns	blosedəl	'to collide (blos = collision)'
	2. semicompound	- from nouns	obawəl	'to water (obə = water)'
		- from adjectives	narmawəl	'to soften (narm = soft)'
			ṛandawəl	'to make blind (ṛund = blind)'
IV. Compound	1. with nouns		imzā kawəl	'to sign (imzā = signature)'
	2. with adverbs		wṛānde kedəl	'to move forward'
	3. with verbal nouns		lidəna kawəl	'to meet (lidəl = see)'

By structure of the lexic component, verbs can be grouped into four classes, as shown in Table 3 above.

Future tense is usually formed by the clitic *be*, which is always in the second position in the sentence, and can also denote the conditional mood. The perfective aspect can be produced: (1) by the perfective prefix *-wu*; (2) by using the suppletive stem; (3) by stressing the first syllable, or (4) by the combination of the above. Verbal prefixes can be separated from the host by various clitics and particles.

Sample of the verb conjugation in the present tense:
'to go' (present imperfective stem *tləl*, perfective stem *wlār*)

	Singular	Plural
'to go' stem	tləl (imperfective stem)	
1st person	tlələm, tləm	tlǝlu
2nd person	tləle, tle	tlələy
3rd, masculine	tə, təy	tləl
3rd, femenine	tləla, tla	tləle

	Singular	Plural
'to go' stem	wlāṛ (perfective stem)	
1st person	wlāṛəm	wlāṛu
2nd person	wlāṛe	wlāṛəy
3rd, masculine	wlāṛ	wlāṛəl
3rd, femenine	wlāṛa	wlāṛe

Basic Syntax

There are two basic types of subject-object relations in Pashto, nominative and ergative. A nominative type of sentence generally uses all intransitive and present tense of transitive verbs as a predicate. The ergative construction is required when a transitive verb is in any form of a past tense. The nominative construction uses a noun or pronoun as a subject in a nominative (direct) case, and the predicate agrees with its subject in number and person.

Sample nominative sentence:

ẓ̌almay	xpəl	kor	ta	ṣ̌ayista
pers.name:NOM.	his	home	to(POSTPOSITION)	beautiful

guluna	wṛi
flowers	bring:3SG

'Zalmay brings home the beautiful flowers.'

In the ergative construction, the subject usually is a noun or an enclitic in the oblique case, and agrees with the predicate in number, gender and person; and the object has to be represented by a noun in the nominative case. Therefore a noun used as an object in Pashto is as a rule in the nominative case.

Sample ergative sentence:

awdas	aw	lmunʒ	me	zda
ablution	and	prayer	I:ENCLITIC:1SG:OBL	learn:STEM

kəṛ
AUX:3SG.PERF

'I learned to do an ablution and prayer.'

Since both object and subject in a nominative sentence are in the direct case, the word order is mostly SOV, though because of the frequent usage of the enclitics this is not always true.

Adjectives in most cases precede the nouns they modify, and they agree with them in most grammatical categories for example:

də	kəli	co	kasa	spinẓ̌iri	də
of	village:SG:OBL	few	person:OBL	old.man	under:PREP.

čarmāɣz	tər	yawe	loye	wane
walnut	under:PREP	one:OBL	big:OBL	tree:OBL

lānde	nāst	wə
under:POSTP	sit:STAT.ADJ.	AUX

'a few village's old men were sitting under a big walnut tree'

Pashto sentences are negated by the particle *–na-* immediately preceding the verb, which is not to be confused with the prefix *ṇa-* (for example *nāpoh* 'ignoramus, fool' from *poh* 'clever, knowledgeable'); in imperative sentences by the stressed prefix *ma-,* for example, *má-kawa* - 'don't do !'

Contact with Other Languages

The best description of modern Pashto vocabulary is that of MacKenzie: "The Pashto lexicon is as fascinating as an archaeological museum. It contains side-by-side words going back to the dawn of Iranian, neologisms of all ages and loanwords from half a dozen languages acquired over a couple of millennia".

The Greeks occupied Bactria (in present-day Afghanistan) in the third century B.C. and there are GREEK loanwords dating from that time. The modern language developed in close contact with Persian and languages of India and Pakistan. Many Persianized Arabic words penetrated Pashto along with Persian words. Arabic and Persian words are borrowed along with some of their grammatical categories; for example, the Pashto word *pə nisbat* 'relative to' includes the Pashto preposition *pə* and the Arabic word *nisbat*, and can also be used in the Arabic native form *nisbatan*, which is also common in Persian. In the modern language, sometimes even Persian rules can apply to word construction; for example, *tər ṭol ǰahān-na kawitara* 'the most powerful in the world', where a superlative is formed with the help of the Persian suffix *-tar*. Since contact with the Western world has increased, Western words are more and more being incorporated into Pashto: *reumatism*, *trazedi*, *trafik*.

Common Words

man:	saṛay	small:	kučnay
woman:	ṣ̌əʒa	yes:	nā, yā
water:	obə	no:	ho
sun:	lmar	good:	ṣ̌ə
three:	dre	bird:	murɣ̌əy
fish:	kab, māhay	dog:	spay
big:	loy	tree:	wəna
long:	uẓ̌d		

Example Sentences

(1)

munẓ̌	tāsu	ṣ̌ə	pežan-u	xo	tāse	munẓ̌
1PL.DIR	2PL.OBL	good	know-1PL	but	2PL.DIR	1PL.OBL

na-pežan-əy.
NEG-know-2PL

'We know you well, but you don't know us.'

(2)

də	duy	žwand	yaw	də	bəl	farq
of	his	life	one	of/from	another	difference

larī.
have:3SG

'[The conditions] of their life were different from each other.'

(3)

halta	ye	xpəla	mahbuba	wu-lidəla.
there	he(clitic)	his	lover:FM:SG	PRF-see:3FM.SG

'There he has seen his lover.'

Efforts to Preserve, Protect, and Promote the Language

Pashto has always been the important language of Afghanistan and the North-West Frontier Province of Pakistan, but received state recognition only in 1936, when it was declared the national language of Afghanistan. In 1937 the Pashto Academy (Paṣ̌to Toləna) was established with the purpose to develop and preserve Pashto. It published numerous articles and reports on syntax, morphology, phonology and all other aspects of the language, adopted special decrees regarding the literary norm, and introduced new words.

The Philology Department of Kabul University was another center of Pashto studies, and published numerous articles in the journal "Waẓ̌ma". There was also the International Center of the Pashto Study in the Academy of Sciences, publishing the "Pashto" quarterly (in European languages, from 1977). The journal "Də Jumhuri Palwasa" started in 1976 as a publication of the Department of Pashto Development of the Ministry of Culture and Information of Afghanistan, though just a few issues were published. In 1950–1980 Pashto linguistics moved forward with the notable Afghan scholars from the Academy of Sciences like S. Ristin and M. Zyār, especially in their efforts to standardize the literary Pashto; their colleagues like A. Palwāl, H. Tegey, G. Ulfat, A. Helāli, and A. Habibi contributed significantly to the studies of various aspects of Pashto and promoting the language.

The most important European studies were accomplished by G.J. Raverty, H.W. Bellew, and J. Darmesteter (19th century); historic-linguistic studies by E. Trumpp, D. Lorimer, W. Geiger, and G. Morgenstierne. After World War II, other landmark studies were conducted by H. Penzl, J. Meyer-Ingversen, C. Kieffer, and D. N. McKenzie.

Russian scholars such as N. Dvoriankov, A. Ganiyev, Z. Kalinina, M. Aslanov, I. Oransky, K. Lebedev, V. Livshiz and A. Grünberg have made outstanding contributions to the study of Pashto. The *Ocherk Grammatiki Afganskogo Yazyka* (Study of the Pashto Grammar) by A. Grünberg is the most comprehensive and developed grammar of Pashto today.

Select Bibliography

Bellew, Henry Walter. 1980. *A Dictionary of the Pukkhto or Pushto Language*. Karachi: Pakistan Publishing House.

Bellew, Henry Walter. 1983. *A Grammar of the Pukkhto or Pukshto Language*. Peshawar: Saeed Book Bank & Subscription Agency.

Darmesteter, James. 1890. *Chants Popularies des Afghans*. Paris: Imprimerie nationale, E. Leroux.

Grünberg, Alexandr Leonovich. 1987. *Ocherk Grammatiki Afganskogo Yazyka (Pashto)*. Leningrad: Izdatel'stvo "Nauka", Leningradskoye Otdeleniye.

Lorenz, Manfred. 1979. *Lehrbuch des Pashto(Afghanisch)*. Leipzig: VEB Verlag Enzyklopädie (In German).

Lorimer, John Gordon, 1902. *Grammar and Vocabulary of Waziri Pashto*. Calcutta: Office of the Superintendant of Government Printing, India.

MacKenzie, D.N. 1959. "A Standard Pashto." In *Bulletin of the School of Oriental and African Studies, No. 22*. London: School of Oriental and African Studies.

_____. 1987 "Pashto." In *World's Major Languages*. Bernard Comrie, ed. 547–565. New York: Oxford University Press.

Penzl, Herbert. 1955. *A Grammar of Pashto: A Descriptive Study of the Dialect of Kandahar, Afghanistan*. Washington, DC: American Council of Learned Societies.

Raverty, Henry George. 1856. *A Grammar of the Pukhto, Pushto or Language of the Afghans*. Calcutta: J. Thomas.

Tegey, Habibullah. 1978. *The Grammar of Clitics*. Kabul: International Center for Pashto Studies.

Trumpp, Ernst. 1873. *Grammar of the Pashto or the Language of the Afghans*. London: Messrs. Trübner & Co.

PERSIAN

John R. Perry

Language Name: Persian. **Alternates:** *New Persian, Farsi.* **Autonym:** *fārsi.*

Location: Iran; northern and central Afghanistan (where it is also known as *Dari* or *Kāboli*); Tajikistan, Bukhara, and Samarkand (where it is also known as *Tajik/Tājikī*).

Family: The West Iranian group of the Iranian (Iranic) branch of the Indo-European family.

Related Languages: KURDISH and BALOCHI; more distantly, PASHTO. Persian has close affinities with URDU, which developed under the influence of Persian (same alphabet, much Persian loan vocabulary).

Dialects: There are three main dialect areas of Persian, each containing a number of dialects: (1) the Persian of Iran (West), (2) the Persian of Afghanistan (East), and (3) the Persian of Tajikistan (Northeast). Standard Persian, based on the dialect of the Iranian capital, Tehran, is widespread in Iran. There is no essential difference between spoken and written standard Persian. However, there are a number of minor differences between Tehran Persian pronunciation and the written standard. Most commonly, the object marker *-rā* is realized as /ro/ or /o/, and the segments *ān* and *ām* as /un/ and /um/. Provincial dialects exhibit small differences in pronunciation and vocabulary. A number of so-called dialects of Persian (e.g., Luri, Gilaki, and Semnāni) are actually distinct Iranian languages, heavily Persianized in vocabulary but with quite different verb systems and other syntactical features. In Afghanistan, the metropolitan dialect of Kabul, called Dari, has joint official status with Pashto as national language. TAJIK, embracing Persian dialects of northeast Afghanistan, the Pamirs foothills, and the Oxus basin, is also the state language of Tajikistan. This chapter gives examples in Standard Persian, reflecting educated speech of Tehran.

Number of Speakers: At least 50 million. Iran, 40 million (nonnative but fluent speakers of Persian as a second language account for several millions more); Afghanistan, 6 million; Tajikistan and Uzbekistan, 4 million.

Origin and History

Persian takes its ENGLISH (and European) designation from Iran's southwestern province of Pārs (modern Fārs), known to the ancient Greeks as *Persē*, 'Persia'. This was the home of two powerful dynasties (the Achaemenians, 546–331 B.C., and the Sassanians, circa A.D. 226–642) that came to dominate the rest of Iran and much of the ancient Near East. In each case their regional dialect became an imperial language, and the name of their home province was usually applied to Iran as a whole.

Old Persian survives in Achaemenian inscriptions from the sixth century B.C. It used a cuneiform syllabary. The Sassanians used **Middle Persian**, also known as Pahlavi, which spans the period of the Sassanian Empire. It was written in a script derived from ARAMAIC. **New Persian** arose after the Arab Muslim conquest in the seventh century; it is characterized by the use of a modified ARABIC alphabet and a large Arabic loan vocabulary.

Old Persian was a typical early Indo-European language, almost as highly inflected as LATIN, GREEK, and SANSKRIT. By the end of the Middle Persian period, however, nearly all traces of the case and concord systems, and many of the primitive verbs, had disappeared; syntactic relationships were determined largely by word order and prepositions, and new compound verbs were being created from nouns and adjectives with the aid of auxiliaries (a process that is continuing today). Structurally, Persian has changed little in the past 1,000 years.

Historically, Persian was a primary vehicle of Islamic literature and culture. Also, Iran was a great transmitter of Indian culture to the West (e.g., the "Fables of Bidpay" cycle and the game of chess). The nucleus of the Arabian Nights cycle, which is mainly of Indian origin, is a Middle Persian collection, *Hazār Afsāna* 'The Thousand Stories', which was translated into Arabic in the 8th century. Firdausi of Tus' epic, *Shāh-nāmah* 'Book of Kings', written in the early 11th century, reflects the emergence of Iranian nationalism after Muslim domination. It marked the flowering of New Persian literature that continued even after the Mongol conquests in the mid-13th century.

Persian was widely used as a language of administration and diplomacy throughout western, central, and southern Asia, well into the 19th century. Its range as an auxiliary language in these areas began to diminish with the establishment of state Shi'ism in Iran in the 16th century because of estrangement from surrounding Sunni Muslim regions. Further causes of Persian's contraction include the expansion of the Western powers in the 19th century, including Russia in central Asia and Britain in India, and the postcolonial devolution into nation-states with national languages.

In the 1930s, Reza Shah required foreign diplomats to refer to the country by its self-designation of Iran, instead of Persia. In recent years, popular confusion over nomenclature (Iran is ignorantly confused with Iraq, (New) Persian with Old Persian), has contributed to a tendency in English to use the autonym of the modern language, *Farsi* (an Arabicized variant of *pārsi*).

Table 1: Consonants

		Labial	Alveolar	Palatal	Velar	Uvular	Glottal
Stops	Voiceless	p	t	č	k		ʿ
	Voiced	b	d	j	g		h
Fricatives	Voiceless	f	s	š	x		
	Voiced	v	z	ž		ḡ	
Resonants			l, r	y			
Nasals		m	N				

Orthography and Basic Phonology

Persian uses the Arabic alphabet with the addition of 4 modified letters to represent sounds not found in Arabic (/p/, /č/, /ž/, /g/) for a total of 32 characters.

The Arabic alphabet is, strictly speaking, a universal syllabary; so-called short vowels are not indicated, and long vowels are indicated only by means of the polyvalent letters *vāv* (/u/, /w/, and /v/), *ye* (/i/, /y/), and *alef* (for /ā/ medially and finally, but in initial position it may stand for any of three other vowels). Together with the consonant *he*, used to indicate a "short" vowel word finally, there are thus a total of four characters available to represent the eight vowels and diphthongs of Persian. However, Persian syllables and syllable boundaries are predictable CV(V), CV(V)C, CVCC), so ambiguities in reading are rare in practice. Diacritics are available for the short vowels, but rarely used.

Arabic loanwords are mostly spelled as in Arabic. Since some of the sounds of Arabic are not found in Persian, at least eight of the Arabic letters are redundant (e.g., there are four letters all pronounced /z/ in Persian); this makes for spelling difficulties in writing Arabic words, similar to the problems of etymological spelling in English. Otherwise Persian orthography is simple and regular.

The palatals /č/ and /j/ are phonetically affricates. There is wide allophonic variation in the phoneme /ḡ/, which can be a voiceless uvular stop /q/, a voiced uvular stop /ɢ/, a voiced uvular fricative /ʀ/, or a voiced affricate [gʀ].

Table 2: Vowels

	Front	Back
High	i	u
Mid	e	o
Low	a	ā

The vowels /i/, /u/, and /ā/ are considered long, and /e/, /o/, and /a/ are considered short. However, short and long vowels are distinguished more by quality than by duration. The short vowels, in particular, are subject to environmental variation.

Long /ā/ is an open back vowel [ɑ] and may be somewhat rounded [ɔ]; short /a/ is open [a], tending toward [æ].

There are also two diphthongs, /ei/ and /ou/.

The midfront vowel /e/ tends to be somewhat higher than /e/ in other languages, tending toward [ɪ].

Stress in Persian nouns and noun phrases falls on the final syllable unless that syllable is a clitic: *barādár* 'brother', *barādár-am* 'my brother', and *barādár-am-rā* 'my brother' (obj.). All have stress on the syllable *-dár*. In verbs, however, stress tends to move to the first syllable.

Basic Morphology

Persian nouns are not inflected. There is no grammatical gender, with the exception of a limited distinction between a third-person pronoun representing human beings and one for both persons and things. The third-person singular pronoun *u* is used to refer to masculine and to feminine humans. Persian does not have a formal case system. However, definite direct objects are marked with the suffix *-rā*. In addition, possessed nouns are marked with the clitic *-e*: *māšin* 'car', *māšin-e barādar-am* 'my brother's car'.

The suffix *-i* acts to derive nouns from adjectives (*xub* 'good', *xub-i* 'goodness') and adjectives from nouns (*irān* 'Iran', *irān-i* 'Iranian').

Persian verbs have two stems, one for past tense (always ending in an alveolar) and one for present tense. Verbs in both tenses are inflected for person and number, as illustrated in the following past tense forms of the verb *kardan* 'to do, make':

	Singular	Plural
First	kard-am	kard-im
Second	kard-i	kard-id
Third	kard	kard-and

In addition to being formed with a different stem, present tense forms are characterized by the prefix *mi-*; unlike in the past tense, third person singular present tense verbs take the ending *-ad*: *mi-kon-ad* 's/he's doing'. The prefix *mi-* is replaced by *be-* in the subjunctive mood. There is a periphrastic future formed similarly to that of English: an auxiliary verb *xāh-* 'will' (from the verb *xāstan* 'to wish, want') is followed by the "short infinitive" (=past stem) of the main verb, as *xāham raft* 'I will go'.

Persian has an extensive system of compound verbs. These verbs are readily formed from nouns, adjectives, and participles, combined with an auxiliary verb with minimal semantic content. The verbs *kardan* 'to do, make' and *šodan* 'to become' are especially productive in the formation of compound verbs: *zekr kard* 'he mentioned', *zekr šod* 'it was mentioned'.

Causative verbs are formed by the addition of a suffix *-ān* to the present stem: *rasidan* 'to arrive', *ras-ān-idan* 'to deliver'.

Basic Syntax

The word order in Persian sentences is generally SOV. However, modifiers generally follow the nouns they modify (except for demonstrative adjectives and numerals, which precede). Head nouns are generally connected to following modifiers by an unstressed *-(y)e* known as *ezāfe*: *irān-e bāstān* 'ancient Iran', *olāḡ-e mollā* 'the Mullah's donkey'.

Relative clauses are introduced by the particle *ke* 'that', and the noun modified by a restrictive relative clause takes the (unstresed) clitic *-i*. The relative clause may contain a pronominal copy of the head noun:

mard-i-ke	az	u	gereft-ám-aš
man-REL-that	from	him/3SG	get/PAST-1SG-it/3SG

'The man from whom I got it ...'

Sentences are negated by the addition of the prefix *na-* to the main verb.

Contact with Other Languages

Despite a common alphabet, Iran today has little in common with the Arab countries, linguistically or culturally. Historically, however, a high proportion of nouns and adjectives (including action nouns and participles of verbs) has been borrowed from Arabic. Addition of a Persian auxiliary verb to many of these produces new verbs: *montazer budan/šodan*, literally 'to be/become waiting', i.e., 'to wait'; *entezār dāštan*, literally 'to have expectation', e.g., 'to expect'.

Speakers of Persian and TURKISH have been in direct contact, with a high degree of bilingualism, for centuries, and have greatly influenced one another's vocabulary and idioms. Although modern Turkey now uses the Roman alphabet, there is a large Turkish-speaking population in Iran (related dialect, adjacent populations); political and cultural ties in modern times have been excellent. Since the dissolution of the Soviet Union, Iran's contacts with Persian-speaking Tajikistan and Shi'i, (though Turkish speaking) Azerbaijan, have increased. Cultural and commercial relations with Pakistan and India, where Persian is a valued Classical language, have remained active; Indian, PORTUGUESE, Arabic, and Persian maritime vocabulary is widely shared among the coastal dwellers and seafarers of the Persian Gulf.

In modern times, words have been borrowed freely from European languages, particularly FRENCH (19th to mid-20th centuries), and English (mid-20th century on).

From French: *sinemā* 'cinema', *teātr* 'theater', *žāndarm* 'policeman'
From English: *kuler* 'air-conditioning unit/air-conditioner', *kompyuter* 'computer', *sāndvič* 'sandwich'

These, too, may be made into verbs, as *telefon kardan* 'to telephone'. With native neologisms, Persian thus has a rich store of near synonyms; e.g., *xetāb* and *xetābe* (Arabic), *konferāns* (French), *soxanrāni* (Persian) for 'a talk, address, speech, lecture'.

Persian has contributed to the vocabulary of English and other European languages in four phases. Old Persian terms came in through Greek during the period of Athenian and Achaemenian rivalry in the Aegean; some of these terms were *parasang, satrap,* and *paradise*, which referred to an enclosed hunting park. Via Arabic, during the Islamic hegemony in Spain and the Mediterranean, we have "chess", "checkmate", "rook" (the chess piece), and "vizier". From the Elizabethan era of direct commerce with Iran came "caravan", "caravanserai", and "scimitar". And through Indian languages during the period of the British Raj came "durbar", "Parsee", and "sepoy" (as also French "spahi", by way of Turkish).

Common Words

man:	mard	small:	kuček
woman:	zan	yes:	bale; āre
water:	āb	no:	na; naxeyr
sun:	āftāb	good:	xub
three:	se	bird:	parande
fish:	māhi	dog:	sag
big:	bozorg	tree:	deraxt
long:	darāz		

Example Sentences

(1)

pesar-i-rā	[ke	ān-jā	bud]	na-did-am.
boy-REL-OBJ	[that	that-place	was-3SG]	NEG-saw-1SG

'I didn't see the boy who was there.'

(2)

če-vaḡt	mi-tavān-id	xāne	be-y-ā-īd?
what-time	PRES-can-2PL	house	SUBJ-come-2PL

'When can you come home?'

(3)

māšin-e	jadid-e	barādar-am	xarāb	šod.
car-EZAFE	new-EZAFE	brother-my	broken	became-3SG

'My brother's new car broke down.'

Efforts to Preserve, Protect, and Promote the Language

Persian is the official language of Iran, but only about half the population speaks it as their mother tongue; Turkic dialects, notably AZERBAIJANI (Azeri), are widely spoken. However, almost all Iranians can use Persian as a contact language. About 79.5 percent of the population over the age of six are literate.

From the 1930s to the 1950s a language reform movement in Iran (largely inspired by that of Ataturk in Turkey) sought to purge Persian of Arabic loanwords and other foreign influences. This was embodied officially in a language academy, *Farhangestān*, but with a less radical agenda. Scores of Arabic loanwords were replaced by Persian neologisms, although the bulk of the assimilated Arabic vocabulary survived. Today, a low-key 'Iranian Language Academy', *farhangestān-e zabān-o adabe fārsi*, still suggests neologisms and attempts to put the brakes on indiscriminate borrowing from English and other foreign languages.

There are forms of the language (terms of address, special pronouns, and verb forms applicable to both speaker and addressee) for addressing a perceived social superior ("perceived" because the other promotion or self-demotion may be an ad hoc social strategy rather than a reaction to conventional status); this system, known as *ta'ārof*, is becoming less elaborate and less frequently used as Iranian society becomes more egalitarian.

Iranians think of Persian as an elegant and refined language, the vehicle of a renowned lyrical and mystical poetry. It is highly regarded even by the poorly educated, who often know many poems and proverbs by heart, and is thus a major factor in national identity and cultural pride.

Select Bibliography

Beeman, William O. 1986. *Language, Status, and Power in Iran*. Bloomington: Indiana University Press.

Haïm, S. 1975. *New Persian-English Dictionary*. 2 vols. Teheran: Béroukhim, 1934–36. Reprint, Teheran: Béroukhim.

____. 1993a. *Haïm's Persian-English Dictionary*. New York: Hippocrene.

____. 1993b. *Haïm's One-Volume English-Persian Dictionary*. New York: Hippocrene.

Lazard, Gilbert. 1975. "The Rise of the New Persian Language." In *Cambridge History of Iran IV*, 595–632.

____. 1992. *A Grammar of Contemporary Persian*. Costa Mesa: Mazda.

Meskoob, Shahrokh. 1992. *Iranian Nationality and the Persian Language*. Washington, DC: Mage.

Perry, John R. 1985. "Language Reform in Turkey and Iran." In *International Journal of Middle East Studies* 17: 295–311.

____. 1991. *Form and Meaning in Persian Vocabulary: The Arabic Feminine Ending*. Costa Mesa: Mazda.

Thackston, Wheeler M. 1993. *Introduction to Persian*. Bethesda: Iranbooks (audio tapes available).

Windfuhr, Gernot L. 1987. "Persian." In Bernard Comrie, ed., *The World's Major Languages*, 523–546. New York: Oxford University Press.

Phoenician/Punic

Charles R. Krahmalkov

Language Name: Phoenician/Punic. **Alternates:** (1) Tyro-Sidonian, referring to the standard based on the dialect of the cities of Tyre and Sidon; (2) Byblian, referring to the dialect of the city of Byblos; and (3) Punic, referring to the Tyro-Sidonian subdialect of Carthage and Western Phoenicia. **Autonym:** *Ponnīm*.

Location: Phoenician was spoken in the original homeland of the Phoenicians, which corresponds to the coastal region of what is today Syria, Lebanon, and northern Israel. During the Persian period (538–333 B.C.) Phoenicians spread from Acco to Dor, Joppa (modern Yafo-Tel Aviv), and Ascalon. The language spread further as the Phoenicians established colonies in Cyprus, North Africa (Libya to Morocco), southern Spain (Cartagena to Cadiz), the Balearic Islands, Sardinia, northern and western Sicily (Palermo to Motya), Malta, and Gozo. The language was also spoken in Phoenician communities in Greece, Egypt, and throughout the ancient and classical world.

Family: Canaanite subgroup of the ancient Northwest Semitic group of the Western branch of the Semitic language family.

Related Languages: Phoenician is closely related to the other members of the Canaanite subgroup of the Northwest Semitic group: Ugaritic, HEBREW, "Ephraimite", Edomite, Moabite and Ammonite. It is more distantly related to ARAMAIC.

Dialects: The four major dialects of Phoenician were: (1) Tyro-Sidonian, the standard literary language of all Phoenicians, spoken in Lebanon, Palestine, Cyprus, and the Tyrian and Sidonian communities of Greece and Egypt; (2) Punic or Western Phoenician (the language of Carthage and its empire), a dialect of Tyro-Sidonian, spoken in North Africa, southern Spain, the Balearic Islands, Sardinia, Sicily, Malta and Gozo; (3) Neo-Punic, the Punic of the Roman period, differing from Punic principally in (a) minor aspects of phonology and (b) orthography; and (4) Byblian, spoken in and limited to the northern Lebanese city of Byblos, differing from Tyro-Sidonian mainly in the pronominal system but also in other, minor aspects of morphophonology.

Origin and History

The Phoenicians called themselves *Canaanites*, Canaan being all of Lebanon and Palestine. Although politically the Phoenicians controlled only parts of the region, it may be that the entire coastal area of Canaan was populated by Phoenician speakers from a very early period.

Phoenicians were already settled in their historical city-states—the most famous were Tyre, Sidon, and Byblos—in the second half of the second millennium B.C. In this period the first specimens of the Phoenician languages are attested, in the form of (1) Tyro–Sidonian and Byblian glosses in the 14th century B.C. cuneiform documents from Tell el-Amarna in Egypt (the diplomatic correspondence of the courts of Amenophis III and Amenophis IV); (2) loanwords in Egyptian documents of the 18th, 19th, and 20th dynasties; and (3) the first inscriptions in alphabetic script, from around 1200 B.C.

In the first half of the first millennium, Phoenician alphabetic inscriptions appeared in increasing numbers in Canaan (Phoenicia) proper, Cyprus, and in the western Mediterranean, where the cities of Tyre and Sidon had begun to establish colonies. The two primary dialects of Phoenician, Tyro-Sidonian and Byblian, were fully and clearly attested from this time onward. The earliest inscriptions, dating from about 1000–900 B.C., are in Byblian; in the ninth century inscriptions in Tyro-Sidonian appeared in northern Syria, Cyprus, North Africa, and Sardinia, although one inscription from Sardinia may well date to about 1200–1100 B.C. These early materials show Byblian and Tyro-Sidonian already clearly differentiated on the linguistic level, but the Tyro-Sidonian of the Levant and that of the West was still undifferentiated.

With the emergence of the Suffetic Republic of Carthage on the north coast of Africa in about 500 B.C., the center of Phoenician political and cultural life shifted west from the Levantine motherland, and Punic (Western Phoenician) asserted itself as the dominant Phoenician dialect. The differences between Phoenician and Punic were already manifested in the fifth century: (1) in phonology, the characteristic dissimilation *nt* for Phoenician *tt* (for example, Punic *yinten* =Phoenician *yitten*); (2) in morphology, the unaspirated definite article *ʔa-* and the pronoun *-im* 'his, her' alongside or in place of Phoenician *ha-* and *-i*, respectively; (3) in orthography, the use of word-final *ʔaleph* to express the presence of a vowel (such as *yadó* 'his hand', written <*ydʔ*> in Punic but <*yd*> in Phoenician).

The Punic language survived the Roman destruction in 146 B.C. of Carthage, its cultural center. Punic remained the preferred language of Africans well into the fifth century of the Christian period. After the destruction of Carthage, Rome planted a colony on the site, and Roman Carthage became one of the greatest cities of the empire. During the Roman period the language, called Neo-Punic, differed from the language of the time of Carthaginian hegemony in some important respects, including in phonology, morphology, and orthography.

Orthography and Basic Phonology

Phoenician was written in a 22 letter alphabet reflecting its distinctive 22 consonant repertory; no vowel letters were part

Table 1: Consonants

		Labial	Dental	Palatal	Velar	Uvular	Pharyngeal	Glottal
Stops	Voiceless	p	t		k	q		ʔ
	Voiced	b	d		g			
Fricatives	Voiceless		s	ś			ḥ	h
	Voiced						ʕ	
Affricates	Voiceless		ts					
	Voiced		dz					
Nasals		m	n					
Lateral			l					
Trill			r					
Glides		w		y				

of this alphabet although occasionally <y> was used to indicate word-final *-i* and <w> was used for word-internal *o* or *u*. Historically, the Phoenician alphabet was a regional version of the linear alphabet invented (perhaps in Sinai) about 1700–1500 B.C. In the Classical period (1000 B.C. and later), Phoenician was written from right to left; earlier it was also written from right to left or "boustrophedon" (in both directions).

Punic employed the Phoenician alphabet and orthography, with the sole difference of using (optionally) the letter *ʔaleph* to indicate any word-final and, more rarely, word-internal vowel. Neo-Punic used the Punic system but made extensive use of the obsolete letters <ʔ h ḥ ʕ> to express vowels although never in a coherent, systematic manner. Neo-Punic formal inscriptions, however, adhered to the conservative Punic orthography. In the first century A.D. Roman Tripolitania (Libya), the Phoenician-Punic alphabet was replaced by the LATIN; inscriptions (including literary texts) in Latin-letter Punic were written in the province as late as the fourth century. Tripolitanian Punic bears the distinction of being the only Semitic language other than modern Maltese (ARABIC) to have used the Latin alphabet.

The Classical Phoenician 22 letter alphabet already displayed a fixed order in the 13th century B.C.; this order is preserved, along with the Phoenician names of the letters, in the Hebrew, Syriac, and GREEK alphabets, all early adaptations of the Phoenician.

Within this chapter, cited forms from Latin-letter Punic are identified as such; other forms are transliterated from the Phoenician alphabet.

Table 1 represents the consonant system of Classical Phoenician.

The bilabial stop *b* had the allophones [b] and [v] in Neo-Punic, the latter (written *f* in Roman orthography) before a following consonant: *efsem* [evsem] 'in the name of', *lifnim* [livnīm] 'for his son', *myntsyfth* [mintsivt] 'stele'.

The voiceless bilabial stop *p* had the allophones [p] and [f] in Punic. The conditioning of the latter is unclear, but perhaps before a following consonant or, as in Hebrew, after a vowel: for example, Latin-letter *Ponnim* 'Phoenician' but *liful* [lif'ūl] 'to do'. The situation in Phoenician is unknown. In Neo-Punic, *p* is replaced by *f* in all positions: Roman-letter *fel* 'he made', *felioth* 'work' (both sentence initial).

The palatal fricative /ś/, written <ś> had already merged with /s/ in Classical Phoenician.

The fricatives /h ḥ ʕ/ and the stop /ʔ/ were entirely lost in Neo-Punic.

The phoneme represented by the grapheme <z> was realized as an affricate /dz/ or as a double sound of the shape /zd/ or /zz/; for example, the demonstrative pronoun *z-* is found in Latin-letter transcriptions *esde* and *esse* in Punic. In Neo-Punic, this phoneme was a simple /s/.

The phoneme represented by the grapheme <ṣ> was either an affricate /ts/ or a double sound of the shape /st/ or /ss/, as inferable from the transcriptions *atzir*, *astir,* and *atir* for <ḥṣr> 'herb' and *iussim* for <yṣʔm> 'those coming out'.

Phoenician consonants could appear single or geminate (double).

Vowels

	Front	Mid	Back
High	i		u
Mid	e		o
Low		a	

The high and midvowels /i e u o/ could appear long or short; the low vowel /a/ only occured short.

The original short vowels remained short in closed unstressed syllables. However, they were lengthened in open unstressed syllables and in stressed syllables.

In Punic and Neo-Punic, the original short vowel *a* had several allophones: [i] in a closed unstressed syllable (for example, *qiddīs* 'holy' [< Proto-Canaanite **qaddīš*); [ā] in an open unstressed syllable and [ō] in a stressed syllable (for example, *adom* [ʔādōm] 'person' [<Proto-Canaanite *ʔadam]); and under certain conditions, stressed *a* was [ā] (for example, *fela* [fēʕlā]).

Phoenician had four original long vowels: ē ī ō and ū. The original long vowel ō had the allophone [ū] in an open unstressed syllable (such as *duber* [dūbér] 'he says', versus *dobrim* [dōbrīm] 'they say') and in a stressed syllable (such as *liful* [lifʕūl] 'to do').

Basic Morphology

Phoenician/Punic nouns were inflected for number (singular and plural) and gender (masculine and feminine). There was also a vestigial dual form. Dual and plural masculine nouns have a special construct form (used when preceding another noun).

	Masculine	Feminine
Singular	sūs 'horse'	sūs-ot, yod 'hand'
Plural	sūs-īm (bound: sūs-ē)	sūs-ūt
Dual		yad-ēm (bound: yad-ē)

Case inflection was vestigial, observed only in third-person and first-person plural possessive suffixes attached to singular nouns; nominative and accusative *-o* 'his', *-on* 'our', and *-om* 'their' were opposed to genitive *-i(m)*, *-en*, and *-nom*.

	Masculine singular 'horse'	Masculine plural 'horses'
1st person, singular	sūs-ī	sūs-ay
2nd person, masculine singular	sūs-ka	sūs-ēka
2nd person, feminine singular	sūs-ki	sūs-ēki
3rd person, masculine singular	sūs-o, sūs-i(m)	sūs-ēyo
3rd person, feminine singular	sūs-a, sūs-i(m)	sūs-ēya
1st person, plural	sūs-on, sūs-en	sūs-ēn
2nd person, plural	sūs-kom	sūs-ēkom
3rd person, plural	sūs-om, sūs-nom	sūs-ēnom

Periphrasis of the possessive pronouns was common. Thus, *sūs-o* 'his horse' could be expressed (1) *sūs lo* (literally, 'horse to-him'), (2) *(his)sūs ʔīs lo* (literally, 'the horse that is to-him'), (3) *(ʔis)sūs sill-o* (literally, 'the horse of-him').

Phoenician/Punic is unique among the Canaanite languages in having a reflexive possessive pronoun *bitt-/binat-*:

bi-milkat-i(m)	bitt-i(m)	
AT-expense-his	REFLEX.-his	'at his own expense'

The Phoenician definite article was *hi-* prefixed to a noun, the first consonant of which was geminated. The variant *ha-* (with no gemination) occurred before a pharyngeal or glottal consonant. In Punic and Neo-Punic, *h* of the definite article was replaced by *ʔ*.

Phoenician verb roots, like those of other Semitic languages, characteristically consist of three consonants that occur in various stems. Phoenician verbs are attested in five stems: *Qal* (simple), *Niphʕal*, *Piʕʕel*, *Yiphʕil*, and *ʔitpaʕʕel*. The *Niphʕal* stem is characterized by a prefixed *ni-*, Yiph'il by a prefixed *yi-*, and *ʔitpaʕʕel* by a prefixed *ʔit-*. The middle consonant of *Pi'el* and *Hitpa'el* verbs is geminate. Each stem can occur in a suffix conjugation, three prefix conjugations, imperative, active participle, passive participle, and two infinitives.

Verbs in the prefix and suffix conjugations agree with their subjects in person and number, and, in the case of third person singular suffix conjugation, gender. Imperatives and participles agree with their subjects in number and gender, and infinitives are uninflected.

Some forms of the verb *K-T-B* 'write' (*Qal* stem) are illustrated below:

Suffix conjugation:

	Singular	Plural
1st person	katáb-ti	katáb-nu
2nd person masculine	katáb-ta	k^etab-tím
3rd person masculine	katób	kitb-ū
3rd person feminine		kitb-á

Prefix conjugation (indicative):

	Singular	Plural
1st person	ʔe-któb	ni-któb
2nd person masculine	ti-któb	ti-ktob-ūn
3rd person masculine	yi-któb	yi-ktob-ūn

Subjunctive forms of the prefix conjugation have the augment *-a(n)*: *ʔe-ktob-an*, etc. Jussive and subjunctive forms in second- and third-person plural end in *-ū* rather than *-ūn*: *ti-ktob-ū*.

Active participle:

	Singular	Plural
Masculine	kūtéb	kōtb-īm
Feminine	kūtéb-it	kōtb-ūt

There is no one-to-one correlation between the specific conjugations and meaning; no form is in and of itself marked for mood, tense, or aspect. Rather, the mood/tense/aspect reference of any given form is a function of the larger syntactic structure in which it is embedded. For example, in Classical Phoenician, the suffixing form *katob* has past-perfective reference when it is the principal verb in an independent clause (in which it is restricted to clause noninitial position), jussive/optative or present-perfective reference when clause-initial in an independent clause, and future-imperfective reference in clause-initial position in the result ('then ...') clause of a conditional sentence or in the main clause of a sentence with an anticipatory clause.

Phoenician has four moods including indicative, subjunctive, jussive/optative, and imperative; three general narrative tenses including past, present, and future; and two aspects, perfective and imperfective; but, as already noted, no specific form correlates with any single mood or tense/aspect. For instance, the indicative past perfective 'he wrote' may be expressed in Phoenician by *(w)katōb hū* (clause-initial infinitive absolute + nominal or pronominal subject), *hū katob* (clause noninitial suffixing verb), or *(way)yiktob (hū)* (prefixing form, restricted to clause-initial position). In a similar manner, the future imperfective 'he will write' can be expressed *yiktob* (prefix conjugation, indicative), *liktōb* (the infinitive construct), or *(w)katob* (suffix conjugation, in a main clause following an anticipatory clause).

Basic Syntax

The word order of Punic and Neo-Punic is remarkably free: SVO, VSO, and OVS all occur. Phoenician, on the other hand, is somewhat more restrictive; for example, when the verb has past perfective meaning, SVO and OVS require that the verb be in the suffix conjugation, but VSO requires that the verb be in the infinitive absolute.

Modifying adjectives follow the noun they modify, agreeing with it in number and gender. If the noun is definite, it may or may not receive the definite article, but the article is obligatory with the adjective:

hib-bēt	hik-kibbir;	bēt	hik-kibbir
the-house	the-big	house	the-big

'the big house'

In Standard Phoenician/Punic, the demonstrative pronouns follow the noun, which may or may not receive the definite article:

hib-bēt	ᵉdze	bēt	ᵉdze
the-house	this	house	this

'this house'

The narrative tenses are negated by any of the negative particles: *bal*, *ʔī*, or *ʔībal*. The infinitive construct is negated by *bal*: *bal liftūḥ* 'Do not open!' The jussive/optative is negated by the particle *ʔal*: *ʔal tiftaḥ* 'Do not open!'

Contact with Other Languages

Phoenician and Punic show a small number of Greek, Latin, and Libyan (Berber) technical terms but little wholesale borrowing of functional vocabulary. Neo-Punic, on the other hand, shows the heavy impact of Latin; for instance, lacking a true neuter-gender pronoun, the language borrowed the Latin neuter *hoc* 'this'. Also, in the numerals 11–19, in replacement of Standard Phoenician/Punic TEN–and–NUMERAL we find NUMERAL–TEN after the Latin numerals: for example, *sys asar*, 'sixteen' after Latin *sedecim*; and again, after Latin, numerals ending in feminine *-t* are construed with feminine nouns, and numerals ending in *zero* are construed with masculine nouns; in Standard Phoenician/Punic, numerals in *-t* are masculine and those in *zero* are feminine.

Common Words

man:	ʔīs	long:	ʔarrīk
woman:	ʔísat (bound: ʔist-)	small:	tsaʕīr
water:	mēm	yes:	not attested
sun:	sámis (sémis)	no(t):	ʔal, ʔī, bal, ʔībal
three:	salūs	bird:	tsoppūr
fish:	not attested	dog:	kalb
big:	ʔiddīr	tree:	ʕets

Example Sentences

(1) Classical Phoenician (sixth century B.C.):

my	ʔt	kl	ʔdm	ʔš	tpq	ʔyt	ʔrn
[mī	ʔát	kil	ʔadóm	ʔīs	ta-pūq	ʔet	ʔarūn
who	you	any	person	who	2SG-acquire	ACC	coffin

z	ʔl	tpth	ʕlty.
ᵉdze	ʔal	ti-ftaḥ	ʕaltēyo]
this	NEG	2SG-open	it

'Whoever you are, any person who shall acquire this coffin, do not open it!'

(2) Punic (Latin letters, ca. third century B.C.):

Itt	esde	anec	nasote	hers	ahelicot.
[ʔitt	ᵉzde	ʔanīk	nasó-ti	ḥers	a-helīkót]
with	this.man	I	carry-1SG	shard.of	DEF-hospitality

'With him I shared a shard of hospitality.'

(3) Neo–Punic (Latin letters, ca. A.D. 350):

BAdnim	garasth	is	on
[b-adnīm	garás-t	īs	ōn
from-Adnim	expel-1SG	man-of	evil

MySyrthim	bal	sem	ra.
mis-sírtim	bál	sem	rá]
from-Syrtis	possessor.of	name	evil

'From Adnim I expelled the evil fellow, // from the Syrtis, the infamous fellow.'

Select Bibliography

Friedrich, J., and W. Roellig. 1999. *Phoenizisch-Punische Grammatik.* 3 Auflage, neu bearbeitet von Maria Giulia Amadasi Guzzo. Analecta Orientalia 55. Rome: Pontificium Institutum Biblicum.

Harris, S.Z. 1936. *A Grammar of the Phoenician Language.* American Oriental Series, Vol. 8. New Haven: American Oriental Society.

Krahmalkov, C.R. 1992. "Phoenician. s.v. Languages." In D. N. Freedman, ed., *The Anchor Bible Dictionary.* Vol. 4: 222–223. New York: Doubleday.

_____. 2000a. *Phoenician-Punic Dictionary.* Studia Phoenicia XV. Orientalia Lovaniensia Analecta. Leuven: Peeters.

_____. 2000b. *Phoenician and Punic Grammar.* Leiden: Brill.

Segert, S. 1976. *A Grammar of Phoenician and Punic.* Munich: Beck.

Tomback, R.S. 1978. *A Comparative Semitic Lexicon of the Phoenician and Punic Languages.* Missoula: Scholars Press.

Van den Branden, A. 1969. *Grammaire phénicienne.* Beirut: Librairie du Liban.

Polish

Katarzyna Dziwirek

Language Name: Polish. **Autonym:** *polski.*

Location: Poland. Also spoken in neighboring countries of Lithuania, Belarus, Ukraine; less so in Russia. Also spoken by emigrants in the United States, Canada, Brazil, France, and territories of the former Soviet Union.

Family: Lechitic subgroup of the West Slavic group of the Slavic branch of the Indo-European language family.

Related Languages: CZECH, SLOVAK, Upper Lusatian (Sorbian), Lower Lusatian (Sorbian), RUSSIAN, UKRAINIAN.

Dialects: In addition to standard Polish there are five main dialect groups, each of which contains subdialects: (1) Kashubian (north, near the Baltic Sea); (2) the Great Poland dialects (west-central); (3) the Little Poland dialects (southeast); (4) Mazovian (northeastern and central); and (5) Silesian (southwest). Most speakers of these dialects also speak standard Polish. Kashubian differs the most from standard Polish and is the only dialect that is not mutually intelligible with the others; it is, in fact, considered by some scholars to be a separate language. The speakers of Kashubian, however, do not seem to have a separate national identity; they identify themselves as either Poles or Germans.

Number of Speakers: 40–50 million.

Origin and History

The Polish tribes that gave rise to the Polish nation were a confederation of people sharing a culture and language who occupied the basins of the Oder and Vistula Rivers. By A.D. 800, these tribes were organized into small states, each with its own leader and fortified towns. Proto-Slavic, the ancestor of Polish, is believed to have undergone dialect division around the end of the sixth century, and by the ninth century three groups of Slavic languages, South Slavic, East Slavic, and West Slavic, had coalesced. The tribes who would become the Poles spoke a West Slavic dialect of the Lechitic subgroup, of which Polish is the only surviving language. Extinct members of the Lechitic subgroup are Polabian, Pomeranian, and Slovincian. Another member, Kashubian, is generally classified as a dialect of Polish (see Dialects, above).

The history of Polish is typically divided into four periods: (1) **Preliterary**, until 1136, (2) **Old Polish**, from 1136 to the beginning of the 16th century when the first books were printed in Polish, (3) **Middle Polish**, from the beginning of the 16th century to the middle of the 18th century, and (4) **Modern Polish**, from the middle of the 18th century until the present.

Relatively little is known of the preliterary period. The earliest written records of the Polish language are individual words found in medieval LATIN texts describing the lives of the saints and in legal documents such as founding acts of churches, monasteries, towns, etc. These words are primarily names and vocabulary relating to tributes, levies, and taxes. The *Papal Bull of Gniezno* of 1136, which contains 410 names of people and places from the Gniezno Archdiocese, is the most important of the early documents.

By the Old Polish period there are texts documenting the language written mostly or entirely in Polish. Some of the earliest are books of sermons appearing in the first half of the 14th century. Other written documents from this era include court records (the earliest one from 1386); poetry (e.g., *Bogurodzica*); and chronicles of towns, churches, monasteries, etc.

The texts of the Old Polish period were written using the Roman alphabet which lacked symbols to represent many Polish sounds: nasal vowels, soft and hushing consonants, etc. Consequently, the orthography of that era is very unsystematic. The scribes used either simple letters or digraphs to represent Polish sounds (e.g., *a, an, am* for the nasal vowel ą). Attempts at standardization were unsuccessful until the 1551 publication of Stanisław Murzynowski's translation of the Bible.

The turn of the 16th century marks the beginning of the Middle Polish period, the "golden era" in the history of Polish when it emerged as a national language with its own linguistic traditions and literature. The main factors that contributed to this development were the trends of humanism and the reformation, prompting the use of Polish as the language of instruction in schools, publication of books printed in Polish, wider use of Polish in public life, and the development of Polish literature (e.g., Mikołaj Rej, Jan Kochanowski). The Middle Polish period is also the time when Polish spread significantly to the east (Russia and Lithuania) and north (East Prussia).

In the middle of the 18th century, when the Modern Polish period begins, there are renewed efforts to purify and preserve the language. In 1771 the 'Commission on National Education' *(Komisja Edukacji Narodowej)* was created. It officially established Polish as the language of instruction in schools and sponsored and encouraged the publication of grammars and other linguistic texts. The remarkable flourishing of Polish literature contributed to the establishment of Polish as a national language. This process was not stopped by the fact that Poland practically ceased to exist from 1795 to 1918. Since regaining

Table 1: Consonants

	Labial	Labiodental	Dental	Alveolar	Alveo-palatal	Palatal	Velar
Stops	p, pi b, bi		t d				k, ki g, gi
Fricatives		f, fi w [v], wi	s z	sz [ʃ] ż/rz [ʒ]	ś [ɕ] ź [ʑ]		h/ch [x], hi, chi
Affricates			c [ts] dz [dz]	cz [tʃ] dż [dʒ]	ć [tɕ] dź [dʑ]		
Nasals	m, mi		n			ń [ɲ], ni	
Liquids				r	l		
Glides	ł [w]					j	

independence in 1918, and especially after World War II, concerted governmental efforts toward universal access and uniformity in basic education, the elimination of illiteracy, and the influence of radio and television have led to the establishment of the literary dialect as the standard language, which most dialect speakers also use.

The territory where Polish is spoken has changed considerably in the course of history. In the Middle Ages, the western boundary of that territory was pushed steadily eastward because of German expansion. At the same time, losses in the west were compensated by gains in the east. The union between Poland and Lithuania (1385) caused significant extension of Polish influence in Lithuania and Russia. This eastward expansion of Polish continued until the 19th century when (especially after the failed November uprising of 1830) the Russian authorities closed down Polish schools and began concerted efforts to Russify the Polish-speaking population. The second half of the 19th century was a bad time for Polish both in the east and in the west where deliberate attempts at Germanization significantly diminished the number of speakers. It was also the period of massive migrations of Poles to the Americas, where the emigrants tried to preserve their Polish heritage and language. The borders established after World War II gave Poland land in the west previously occupied primarily by GERMAN-speakers and reduced the Polish territories in the east. Most Polish speakers from the formerly Polish eastern areas were resettled in the west and north, but pockets of concentrated Polish population still remain in Lithuania, Belarus, and the Ukraine.

Orthography and Basic Phonology

When the Polish language was written down it was in the Roman alphabet, which had been brought to Poland by Christian monks in the ninth century. Gradually the orthography was adapted to fit Polish with the use of diacritics and digraphs. Standardization was achieved in 1551 with Stanisław Murzynowski's translation of the Bible. This became the foundation of modern Polish orthography.

Polish consonants (see Table 1 above) are of two main types, soft (e.g., *pi, bi, ki, gi*) and hard (e.g., *p, b, k, g*). The soft consonants are phonetically palatalized. For example, hard *f* is similar to the *f* in the ENGLISH word "food", and soft *f* is similar to the *f* in the word "few". The soft consonants are written with a following *-i* in the above chart, or with an accent (e.g., *ś*). In addition, *l* and *j* (which is pronounced like the initial sound in English "yes", not the initial sound in "jeep") are soft. Hardened or functionally soft consonants (*c, dz, sz, ż/rz, cz, dż*) fall in between the soft and hard groups. For the most part they behave like soft consonants in inflection (e.g., *afisz-afisze* 'poster/s'), but are like hard consonants phonetically (must be followed by *y* and not by *i*).

Ch/h is a voiceless velar fricative. *W* is a fricative, as in the English word "vague", and *ł* is phonetically [w], as in the English word "wag".

The most striking feature of the Polish consonant system is the existence of three sets of fricatives and affricates produced with the front part of the tongue. *S* and *z* are dental fricatives that are quite similar to the English sounds at the beginning of "sip" and "zip". *Sz* and *ś* (and their voiced counterparts *rz/ż* and ź) are somewhat similar to English *sh*, but both sounds are noticeably different from English "sh".

Table 2: Vowels

	Front	Central	Back
High	i		u, ó [u]
Mid	e [ɛ]		o [ɔ]
Low		a	

The vowel /i/ has two variants: *i* [i] occurs following soft consonants, and *y* [ɨ] (as in English "bit") occurs following hard consonants. The vowel /u/ can be spelled either *u* or *ó*. *E* and *o* are lower midvowels, [ɛ] and [ɔ] respectively, as in English "bed" and "fall". Polish also has two nasal vowels, *ę* /ɛ̃/ and *ą* /õ/, though frequent in the orthography they are consistently pronounced as nasal only before fricatives: *Wałęsa* [vawɛ̃sa].

The most salient phonological rules of Polish involve consonant voicing. Obstruents assimilate in voicing to a following obstruent: e.g., *wódka* [vu<u>tk</u>a] 'vodka', *jakby* [ya<u>gb</u>ɨ] 'as if'. All obstruents are devoiced in word-final position: e.g., *kod* [kɔd] 'code nominative' (compare *kodu* [kɔdu] 'code genitive'), *staw* [staf] 'pond' (compare *stawy* [stavɨ] 'ponds').

Polish words are stressed on the penultimate syllable.

Basic Morphology

Polish nouns are inflected for gender, number, and case. There are two numbers (singular and plural) and seven cases (nominative, accusative, genitive, dative, locative, instrumental, and vocative). In the plural, there are two genders, "masculine human" and other.

The gender of a noun is largely predictable from its phonological form. Nouns whose nominative singular form ends in a consonant are masculine; nouns ending in *a* are feminine, and nouns ending in other vowels are neuter. There are some exceptions (e.g., *muzeum* 'museum' is neuter), and meaning usually overrides form for nouns denoting human beings (e.g., *mężczyzna* 'man' is masculine). Each gender class has its own set of case endings.

Adjectives agree with nouns they modify in gender, number, and case: *mił-a kobiet-a* (nice woman) 'nice woman, feminine nominative singular', *mił-y chłopak* (nice boy) 'nice boy, masculine nominative singular', *mił-e kobiety* (nice women) 'nice women, nominative plural (nonmasculine)', *mił-emu chłopak-owi* 'to a/the nice boy, masculine dative singular'.

Polish verbs are of two types, perfective and imperfective. Most verbs have both an imperfective and a perfective form. Perfectives are often derived from imperfectives by one of a number of prefixes: *pisać* is the imperfective form of 'to write' and *napisać* is the perfective form. Perfective forms generally are used for completed actions and do not occur in the present tense.

Present-tense and perfective-future-tense verbs agree with their subjects in person and number. Imperfective-future-tense verbs are compounds of forms of the auxiliary verb *być* 'to be', inflected for person and number, and a main verb either in the infinitive or agreeing with the subject in number and gender (but not person). Past-tense verbs agree with their subjects in person, number and gender.

Ewa	pisz-e	list-y.
Eve-NOM	write-3rd PRES/SG	letters-ACC

'Eve writes/is writing letters (PRESENT).'

Ty	pisa-łaś	list-y.
you.NOM/SG	write-2ND PAST/FEM	letters-ACC

'You were writing letters (PAST IMPERFECTIVE).'

Ty	na-pisa-łaś	list-y.
you:NOM/SG	PERF-write-2ND PAST/FEM	letters-ACC

'You wrote/have written letters (PAST PERFECTIVE).'

Ewa będzie	pisa-ła	list-y.
Eve be:3RD FUT/SG	write-3RD PAST/FFM	letters-ACC

'Eve will be writing letters (FUTURE IMPERFECTIVE).'

Ewa	na-pisz-e	list-y.
Eve:NOM	PERF-write-3RD PRES/SG	letters-ACC

'Eve will write letters (FUTURE PERFECTIVE).'

One unusual feature of the past-tense morphology is that the first- and second-person endings need not appear on the verb, but may attach to another constituent, as long as it precedes the verb. This so-called floating inflection is illustrated below with the first-person plural ending *-śmy* which shows up on the verb, the adverb, or on the direct object:

Wieczorem	czyta-li-śmy	książk-i
evening	read-PAST-1ST/PL	books-ACC

Wieczorem-śmy	czyta-li	książk-i
evening-1ST/PL	read-PAST	books-ACC

Książk-i	wieczorem-śmy	czyta-li
books-FEM/ACC/PL	evening-1ST/PL	read-PAST

Książk-i-śmy	wieczorem	czyta-li
books-FEM/ACC-1ST/PL	evening	read-PAST

Wieczorem	książk-i-śmy	czyta-li
evening	books-FEM/ACC-1ST/PL	read-PAST

'In the evening we read books.'

Basic Syntax

As can be seen in the immediately preceding examples, the word order in Polish sentences is relatively free, though SVO is most natural, and the indirect object tends to precede the direct object.

Subjects of transitive and intransitive verbs are marked with nominative case, indirect objects are dative, and the case of the direct object depends on the verb. Most verbs select accusative, but some may govern genitive or instrumental. Adverbials are expressed by means of prepositional phrases or nominals marked with instrumental, genitive, or accusative case. The verb agrees with the subject in all features relevant for a given tense. In nonemphatic sentences, first- and second-person subject pronouns are usually omitted.

Sentences are negated with preverbal *nie*.

Direct objects that take accusative case in affirmative sentences must take genitive case in negative sentences.

Ewa	czyta	książk-ę.
Eve:NOM	reads-3RD-PRES/SG	book-FEM/ACC

'Eve is reading a book.'

Ewa	nie	czyta	książk-i.
Eve-NOM	NEG	reads:3RD.SG	book-FEM/GEN

'Eve is not reading a book.'

Contact with Other Languages

In the course of its history, Polish has borrowed numerous lexical items from several languages. Although the majority of the general Polish vocabulary is of Slavic origin, non-Slavic borrowed words comprise a high percentage of the language of various specialized disciplines (e.g., engineering, technology, sports, etc.) The 1983 edition of Władysław Kopaliński's *Dictionary of Borrowed Words* lists 16,000 words and phrases of foreign origin.

All of the borrowings listed here, even the most recent ones, are completely naturalized and behave like Polish words phonologically (i.e., undergo final devoicing) and morphologically (i.e., decline like Polish nouns of similar shape).

From Latin (via Czech): *anioł* 'angel', *msza* 'mass', *biskup* 'bishop'
From Czech: *hańba* 'disgrace', *obywatel* 'citizen'
From German: *cegła* 'brick', *papier* 'paper', *bawełna* 'cotton'
From Ukrainian: *druh* 'friend', *bohater* 'hero'
From ITALIAN: *molo* 'pier', *pomidor* 'tomato'
From FRENCH: *fotel* 'armchair,' *bilet* 'ticket'
From English: *radio, radar, laser, stres, relaks, komputer, faks, modem*

Common Words

man:	mężczyzna	small:	mały
woman:	kobieta	yes:	tak
water:	woda	no:	nie
sun:	słońce	good:	dobry
three:	trzy	bird:	ptak
fish:	ryba	dog:	pies
big:	duży	tree:	drzewo
long:	długi		

Example Sentences

(1) Tamt-a kobiet-a by-ł-a
that-FEM SG NOM woman-FEM SG NOM be-PAST-3RD SC FEM

głodn-a.
hungry-FEM SG NOM
'That woman was hungry.'

(2) Co to jest.
what it be:3RD PERS SG
'What is it?'

(3) Da-li-śmy mu prezent.
give-PAST-1ST. PL him:DAT.SG present:ACC
'We gave him a present.'

Select Bibliography

Brooks, Maria. 1975. *Polish Reference Grammar*. The Hague: Mouton.

Bulas, Kazimierz, Lawrence T. Thomas, and Francis J. Whitfield. 1961. *The Kościuszko Foundation Dictionary*. The Hague: Mouton.

Dziwirek, Katarzyna. 1994. *Polish Subjects*. New York: Garland Publishing.

Fokker, A.A., and Emilia Smolikowska. 1971. *Anatomy of a Word-Class. A Chapter of Polish Grammar*. The Hague: Mouton.

Gladney, Frank Y. 1983. *A Handbook of Polish*. Urbana, IL: G & G Press.

Klemensiewicz, Zenon. 1985. *Historia języka polskiego*. Warszawa: PWN.

Kopaliński, Władysław. 1983. *Słownik Wyrazów Obcych*. Warszawa: Wiedza Powszechna.

Puppel, Stanisław, Jadwiga Nawrocka-Fisiak, and Halina Krassowska. 1977. *A Handbook of Polish Pronounciation for English Learners*. Warszawa: PWN.

Schenker, Alexander M. 1964. *Polish Declension: A Descriptive Analysis*. The Hague: Mouton.

Stieber, Zdzisław. 1973. *A Historical Phonology of the Polish Language*. Heidelberg: Carl Winter.

POLYNESIAN LANGUAGES

Jeff Marck

Language Names: There are about 30 distinct Polynesian languages comprised of about 60 named languages and dialects. All are named after the island or island group where they are found except for Maori, the language of Polynesians native to New Zealand, and Mooriori, the (extinct) language of the Chatham Islands off New Zealand.

Those for which at least some linguistic data are available are: Aitutaki (East Polynesian, Southern Cooks), Aniwa (Outlier, Southern Vanuatu), Anuta (Outlier, Solomon Islands, Santa Cruz area), Atiu (East Polynesia, Southern Cooks), East Futuna (Western Polynesia), East Uvea (Western Polynesia), Easter Island (see Rapanui), Ellice Islands (see Tuvalu), Futuna (see: East Futuna and West Futuna), Hawaii (East Polynesia), Kapingamarangi (Outlier, Micronesia), Luangiua (Ongtong Java) (Outlier, Solomon Islands, some distance north of the center of the chain), Mae (Outlier, Central Vanuatu), Manihiki-Rakahanga (East Polynesia, Northern Cooks), Maori (East Polynesia, New Zealand), Mele-Fila (Outlier, Central Vanuatu), Mangaia (East Polynesia, Southern Cooks), Mitiaro (East Polynesia, Southern Cooks), Mauke (East Polynesia, Southern Cooks), Mooriori (East Polynesia off New Zealand, Chatham Islands), Marquesas (East Polynesia, dialects: Northern and Southern), Mangareva (East Polynesia, southeast of Tuamotus), Mele-Fila (Outlier, central Vanuatu), Nanumea (Western Polynesia, Tuvalu), Niuafo'ou (Western Polynesia), Niuatoputapu (Western Polynesia, a language of the Samoan type in the early historical period but then replaced by Tongan prior to substantial documentation), Niue (Western Polynesia), Nukumanu (Outlier, Solomon Islands, some distance north of the center of the Solomon chain), Nukuoro (Outlier, Micronesia), Nukuria (Outlier, Solomon Islands, north of Bougainville), Ongtong Java (see Luangiua), Paumotu (see Tuamotu), Pileni (Outlier, Santa Cruz area), Pukapuka (East Polynesia, Northern Cooks), Rakahanga (see Manihiki), Rapa (East Polynesia, Australs), Rapanui (East Polynesia), Rarotonga (East Polynesia, Southern Cooks), Rennell and Bellona (Outlier, Solomon Islands), Rangiroa (Northern Tuamotus), Rurutu (East Polynesia, Australs), Samoa (Western Polynesia), Sikaiana (Outlier, Solomon Islands, some distance north of the southeastern tip of the chain), Tahiti (East Polynesia), Takuu (Outlier, Solomon Islands, some distance north of the main northwestern islands of the chain), Taumako (Outlier, Solomon Islands, Santa Cruz area), Tikopia (Outlier, Santa Cruz area), Tokelau (Western Polynesia), Tonga (Western Polynesia), Tongareva (East Polynesia, Northern Cooks), Tuamotu (East Polynesia, numerous islands and dialects), Tubuai (East Polynesia, Australs), Tuvalu (Western Polynesia, formerly the "Ellice Islands"; better described dialects: Nanumea, Vaitapu), Uvea (see: East Uvea and West Uvea), Vaitupu (Western Polynesia, Tuvalu), Wallis Island (see East Uvea), West Futuna (Outlier, Southern Vanuatu), West Uvea (Outlier, New Caledonia, Loyalty Islands).

Location: All the languages found within the "Polynesian Triangle", defined by Hawaii, New Zealand and Rapanui, are of the same family of Oceanic Austronesian, thus the name for the group. Polynesian languages (the "Polynesian Outliers") are also found scattered on small islands from southernmost Melanesia (West Uvea in the Loyalty Islands north of New Caledonia), up through Vanuatu, off the Santa Cruz Islands, among the small islands north of the main Solomon Islands and into south-central Micronesia (Nukuoro and Kapingamarangi).

Family: Austronesian.

Related Languages: The Oceanic subgroup of Eastern Malayo-Polynesian. Most immediately related to Fijian and Rotuman, these languages together may have originally emerged out of Northern Vanuatu but the relationship is not well marked by shared innovations.

Dialects: Islands separated from others by more than a single night's voyaging in traditional craft have, in most instances, developed such distinctions as to be beyond the language limit with their neighbors. East Uvean, East Futuna, the Outliers, the Tokelaus and the Southern Cooks (versus Tahiti and the Societies) follow this pattern, and Tongarevan versus Manihiki-Rakahangan in the Northern Cooks may follow this pattern as well. Dialects exist(ed) for those languages spread over archipelagoes consisting of islands less than a day's voyaging apart: Tuvalu (Ellice Islands: northern and southern dialects); Samoan (Manu'a versus Savai'i), New Zealand Maori (North Island and South Island (now extinct), and numerous dialects internal to North Island: a general East-West division and local subdialects: Bay of Plenty, Taranaki-Wanganui, North Auckland); Marquesan (well-marked Northern and Southern dialects); the Tuamotus (dozens of inhabited atolls, probably very distinct when comparing the furthest northwest to the furthest southeast but not well described and being replaced, from northwest to southeast, by Neo-Tahitian); and Hawaiian (one of the most recently settled Polynesian Islands whose dialects were not well marked (and not well described before becoming extinct). Dialects are not reported for Tongan and a highly unified language apparently extends through the whole archipelago, which lies at a convenient angle to the prevailing winds (and through which easy voyaging to all destinations within the archipelago is possible through most of the year).

Number of Speakers: Recent census information is available for few of the islands and groups and those censuses that have been taken have not always reported on language use. In most instances there are significant numbers of speakers in other Polynesian or Pacific Rim localities, especially Marquesans in Tahiti, Cook Islanders in New Zealand, Samoans in New Zealand and California, and so on. From east to west: 2,645 Rapanui people were counted in 1986, 1,717 of whom lived on Rapanui. Not all were able to speak the language. Presently the number of speakers is about 2,000. While the language is in daily use by adults, this is not so true of children who communicate with each other in Chilean Spanish. In 1988 there were 4,557 people living in the Northern Marquesas and 2,801 in the Southern Marquesas, the great majority of both were native speakers. In that same year, 620 people were counted on Mangareva and 11,173 in the Tuamotus. Mangerevans and southeast Tuamotuans have continued using their traditional languages but, from the northwest Tuamotus, Neo-Tahitian is encroaching toward the others. Also in 1988, 6,509 people were counted on the Austral Islands as were 162,573 for the Societies, 140,069 of those living on Tahiti and its immediate neighbors, 22,232 living on the "leeward" islands: Ra'iatea and its immediate neighbors. About 115,000 of the people enumerated in the Societies identified themselves as native Tahitians and 80 percent of those were speakers of Tahitian. The population of the Cooks was 18,128 in 1983, the vast majority were native Cook Islanders and speakers of one or more of the "Cook Maori" dialects. There are presently over 250,000 native Hawaiians in Hawaii and another 100,000 living elsewhere, only a few hundred of whom speak Hawaiian. Western Samoans numbered about 160,000 in the late 1980s while American Samoa had a population of about 34,000 in those years. The 1991 Tokelau census enumerated 1,538 people and a 1979 census of Tuvalu found 5,887 persons, most native speakers in both instances. A 1976 census of Tonga found 90,085 persons. Estimates of population about 10 years later put 100,000 people in Tonga itself and about 30,000 Tongans in other localities, particularly New Zealand, Australia, the United States, Samoa, and Fiji. There are some hundreds of thousands of New Zealanders of Maori extraction but fewer than 30,000 speakers of Maori remain, most of them over 50 years old. The Outliers are generally single islands or atolls and commonly support populations of only a few hundred, although some of the "Futunic" Outliers are small volcanic peaks or good-sized raised-coral formations and can support populations closer to a thousand. Although individual Outlier islands have very few people, they are typically all or nearly all active speakers of the traditional language. The typical Polynesian age pyramid resembles a low mountain (because of the large family size) and population doubles about every 25 years. So estimates of populations above that are dated may reflect only 50 to 70 percent of the number of native speakers today. Migration streams from the small islands to larger ones and from larger islands to metropolitan centers reduce native speakers in residence on any given island. Hawaii and New Zealand are exceptions: family size is smaller but the general social and language-use contexts are atypical.

Origin and History

Fiji and Western Polynesia were first settled by people more or less at once at a time archaeologists now put at about 850 B.C. The "synthetic" model of prehistory for the area, a result of archaeological, linguistic, human genetic, ethnobotanic, and other evidence, attributes the appearance of people at that time to speakers of Oceanic Austronesian. They arrived as part of the emergence into Oceania of seafaring Austronesian-speaking horticulturalists who had earlier established themselves in Western and then Eastern Melanesia, having come to Western Melanesia from Eastern Indonesia.

Populations grew slowly around Fiji and Western Polynesia and more or less intense social contacts between Fiji and Western Polynesia centered in the large islands of Tonga and Samoa are implied by innovations shared between Fijian and Polynesian during the early period of settlement. The period of common development between Fijian and Polynesian was short relative to the common development of Tongan, Samoan and other Western Polynesian speech. About a thousand years of cohesive Polynesian linguistic and cultural development largely distinct from other Oceanic is implied by the massive innovations of Polynesian language and culture as compared to Fijian and other Oceanic. Social contacts with Fiji can be assumed through that period because of the short distance and demonstrable loanwords, but Tonga and Samoa lie in a more favorable relationship to the main seasonal winds and the sea between them was a regular highway for social and linguistic continuities. Contacts with Fiji were more difficult and the period of linguistic unity between Polynesia and eastern Fiji (the Laus in particular) apparently broke down a few centuries after settlement.

By the early first millennium A.D., perhaps by about A.D. 250, there were substantial local populations in the Tongan and Samoan archipelagoes and the period of shared linguistic innovations seems to have ceased. The disintegration of a continuous language between the two groups would appear to have been due to a declining ratio of internal (within Western Polynesia) migrants as a portion of overall population, because of a decline in absolute numbers of internal migrants or both. The islands of East Polynesia were settled at about this time by people speaking the progenitor language of modern East Polynesian languages. Some centuries of common development ensued in the east, the resulting language being Proto East Polynesian, which carried a predominance of specifically Samoan rather than Tongan innovations, marking the main source of its origin. The Outliers were also settled by people speaking languages marked by innovations originating in the Samoa area rather than Tonga. Thus the genetic grouping of Polynesian languages has languages other than Tongan (and Niuean) in a subgroup called "Nuclear Polynesian" and Tongan and Niuean in another first-order group called "Tongic". Outlier languages from Santa Cruz south ("Futunic" Outliers) seem to have come from East Futuna and/or East Uvean (both just west of Samoa) and Outliers west and northwest of Santa Cruz ("Ellicean" Outliers) seem to have come from Tuvalu (northwest of Samoa, the former Ellice Islands), Tuvaluan having previously emerged specifically from Samoan. Linguistic phylogeny suggests the Futunic Outliers were settled at about the same time as East Polynesia and the Ellicean Outliers slightly later. However, the archaeology of the Outliers presently shows dates for Polynesian material culture in the Outliers only from many hundreds of years later.

East Polynesian linguistic dispersals began with the divergence of Rapanui (Easter Island) speech some hundreds of years after the establishment of a uniquely "East Polynesian" linguistic community. The archaeology is controversial and the linguist can only guess but settlement of Rapanui at about A.D. 500 is implied by the general linguistic and archaeological relations of East Polynesian. Other East Polynesian languages, called "Central–East Polynesian," continued their common development for some hundreds of years and then developed varieties centered in the Marquesas ("Marquesic"), from which Hawaiian emerged in the late first millennium A.D. and Tahiti ("Tahitic"), from which New Zealand Maori emerged in the early second millennium A.D. Some time after the divergence of Hawaiian, Mangarevan diverged from Marquesan. The speech of the Tuamotus and Cooks appears to have diverged from Tahitian after the divergence of New Zealand Maori, probably resulting from the gradual growth of population through the area and a declining ratio of internal migrants to total population in a manner similar to the disintegration of early Tongan and Samoan as a continuous language. This type of slow end to linguistic sharing through an area after settlement has been termed "network breaking" (with diminishing linguistic impact of internal migration) in the Oceanic context, as contrasted with the relatively abrupt language splits of "radiation" (stream migration to a distant place and early isolation of speech after initial settlement).

East Polynesian languages are quite similar to one another and East Polynesians find it remarkable how much they understand of East Polynesian languages other than their own. But internal divergences began over a thousand years ago; isolation was often profound and the major languages of Rapanui, Marquesan, Tahitian, Hawaiian, and New Zealand Maori, are not mutually intelligible for practical purposes. They, for instance, only score about 50 percent with each other on the 200-word lexicostatistical list. Tongan and Samoan score in the same range, about 50 percent on the 200-word list, and are not mutually intelligible. East Uvean, west of Samoa, is more or less mutually intelligible with Tongan but this is because of massive Tongan loanwords in East Uvean that occurred all at once in the late prehistoric period and overlaid deeper historical connections having more to do with Samoan.

Orthography and Basic Phonology

Proto-Polynesian and all its daughters had/have five vowels of the LATIN type. Vowel length was/is phonemic and long vowels occur/red in all the languages and protolanguages. There were 13 Proto-Polynesian consonants (see Table 1 below).

Proto-Tongic had lost Proto-Polynesian **r* and merged **s* and **h* as Proto-Tongic **h*. Proto–Nuclear Polynesian had lost Proto-Polynesian **h* and merged **r* and **l* as Proto–Nuclear Polynesian **l*. Most Nuclear-Polynesian languages have lost the Proto-Polynesian glottal stop and many East Polynesian languages are characterized by further reductions because of mergers, for example, Hawaiian of **n* and **ng* to *n*, Tahitian of **k* and **ng* to glottal stop, and a general tendency in East Polynesian to merge **f* and **s* as *h*. Proto-Polynesian **k* has become glottal stop in Samoan, Luangiua, Tahitian, Southern Marquesan, and Hawaiian; **t* has become *k* in colloquial Samoan, Luangiua, and Hawaiian; **s* has often become *h* in Tongic, East Uvean, some Outliers and, mainly independently of one another, all but one East Polynesian language; and **h* has in several instances become glottal stop in Mangarevan and Austral Island dialects, and some Southern Cook Island dialects.

Table 1: Consonants

	Labial	Apical	Velar	Glottal
Stops	p	t	k	q
Fricatives	f	s		h
Nasals	m	n	ng	
Trill/Flap		r		
Liquid		l		
Glide	w			

Polynesian vowels are primarily stressed penultimately and secondarily every second vowel toward the beginning of the word working back from the penultimate vowel. Vowels may occur in diphthongs or longer sequences uninterrupted by consonants, for example, Hawaiian *uai* 'to move, as an object' and Tahitian *aie* 'plant sp.', but Proto-Polynesian had no consonant clusters nor do any of the living languages other than in the instance of certain Outliers, which have developed clusters through vowel deletion. All words end in vowels.

No living Polynesian language has productive morphophonemic assimilatory processes and none can be attributed to any of the Polynesian protolanguages back to Proto-Polynesian itself. Diachronically, assimilation of unstressed or secondarily stressed low vowels to following high vowels is important in the history of Tongic and Nuclear-Marquesic (Marquesan and Mangarevan). Marquesan, and other languages more sporadically, has regularly raised **a* to *e* where -*Ca*(C)V# followed, for example, Proto-Polynesian **mataku* > Marquesan *meta'u* 'afraid'. Another common outcome, especially in Nuclear-Polynesian, for words of that form is lengthening to #(C)*aa*C*a*(C)V#. Kapingamarangi has assimilated large numbers of word-final vowels to preceding vowels, like Proto-Polynesian **malo* > Kapingamarangi *mala* 'loin garment'. Otherwise, living Polynesian languages tend to faithfully follow the Proto-Polynesian pattern except for sporadic changes, mainly assimilations, some of which mark the various subgroups.

Orthographic conventions are normally simple. Linguists have long represented the glottal stop as **q* for the protolanguages and with an apostrophe in the living languages. East Polynesians are often indifferent to its representation in their own, even official, writing, and are less inclined to mark vowel length than in Tonga or Samoa. The velar nasal is variously represented as *g* and *ng*. Other sounds have ENGLISH equivalents and are spelled with single letters as seen above in the Proto-Polynesian consonant table. No living Polynesian language has any sound not found in Proto-Polynesian with the exception of some nonphonemic voicing of the stops in some Outliers (and their spelling as voiced rather than voiceless in Nukuoro) and the presence of an affricate "*j*" in West Futuna–Aniwa and "*ts*" in Niuean. Tongan recently had an affricate, (e.g., *Fiji*, the Tongan pronunciation in the early historic period) but it became [s] before the language was much recorded.

Basic Morphology

Polynesian languages are isolating rather than agglutinative, especially so the East Polynesian subgroup. Few grammatical morphemes are bound and those that are generally consist of small sets of verbal prefixes marking such things as continuity, causation, plurality of events, capability, and plurality of patients. Verbal suffixes are relatively rare and generally change the case frame of the verb. The main causative prefix is very productive in all Polynesian languages and commonly the source of pages of distinct words, many with their own idioms, and other special usages in the dictionaries. Inalienable possessives are suffixed to nouns. Nouns and their associated adjectives or modifying nouns are often spelled as separate words even when they are fixed terms with their own lexical entry, such as seen in the ambivalence of scholars over whether to use "Rapa Nui" or "Rapanui". Highly productive reduplication patterns are typical of all Polynesian languages.

Some of the prefixes that have been reconstructed for Proto Polynesian are:

**aa-*	ligative particle, like, as, after the manner of
**fai-*	prefix deriving noun performer from certain verbs
**faka-*	causative prefix (very productive)
**faa-*	causative prefix (less common)
**fe-*	reciprocal prefix
**fia-*	verbal prefix indicating desire, wish
**ka-*	stativizing prefix (fossilized)
**ma-*	stativizing prefix (productive)
**pa-*	stativizing prefix (moderately productive)
**taki-*	numeric distributive prefix
**toko-* or **toka-*	human numerical prefix
**tuqa-*	ordinal prefix

Some of the suffixes reconstructed are:

*-*a*	expressing abundance or infestation by N-
*-(C)*anga*	a noun-forming suffix, substantivizer
*-(C)*ia*	passivizing/ergativizing suffix
*-*ina*	passivizing/ergativizing suffix
*-*a*	passivizing/ergativizing suffix
*-*nga*	gerundive suffix
*-*ngataqa*	with difficulty
*-*ngaofia*	with ease
*-*qaki*	verbal formative suffix
*-*qi*	ligative enclitic of possession
*-*qi*	transitivizing suffix

Possessive pronouns were:

	First	Second	Third
Singular	*-*ku*	*-*u*	*-*na*
Dual	*-*ta* (incl.) *-*ma* (excl.)	*-lua	?
Plural	*-*tau* (incl.) ? (excl.)	?	?

Demonstrative formatives included *-*ni* 'this', *-*na* 'that' and *-*a* 'that (particular one)'.

Samoan, and especially Tongan, rather than East Polynesian languages, retain more of the morphological complexity that was probably current in Proto Polynesian, and Samoan is the better described. Morphological processes are derivational, never inflectional, and most bound grammatical morphemes are nonproductive. The list of non-relic prefixes for Samoan is short and "heterogenous":

(')*a-*	future	*ma-*	de-ergative
ana-	past	*maa-*	de-ergative
au-	lacking something	*ta-*	plurality of patients
au-	continuous/repeated activity	*ta-*	verbal derivation
fa'a-	causative	*taa-*	verbal derivation
fe-	plurality of events	*ta'i-*	distributive
ma-	able to	*to'a-*	human

The list of suffixes is similarly short and heterogenous:

-*a*	being affected by N-
-*a*	ergativizing suffix (productive)
-*ina*	ergativizing suffix (productive)
-(C)*ia*	ergativizing suffix (fossilized)
-(C)*a'i*	intensifier
-*e*	vocative suffix
-*ga*	gerundive suffix (more productive)
-(C)*aga*	gerundive suffix (fossilized)
-(C)*i*	forms words with more specific meanings

Reduplication in Samoan is of the common Polynesian formations: it may be partial or the whole word may be reduplicated. In form, partial reduplication in Samoan consists of reduplicating the primarily stressed penultimate syllable (which is also the first syllable in those many words which are disyllabic):

atamai	clever	*atamamai*	clever, plural subject
'emo	blink	*'e'emo*	blink, plural
motu	break, nonergative	*momotu*	break, ergative

As can be seen, the semantic results of this kind of reduplication vary. While reduplication is productive, reduplicated words fixed in the lexicon generally have their own specific sense from among various possible outcomes. Pluralization and ergativization are shown above. Other usages disambiguate verbal from nominal use, create frequentives, create an opposite, and create a verb of application from the noun being applied. This is not an exhaustive list. Thus, there is an emphasis on such words being lexicalized and having meanings one can guess at but not predict according to one single shift in function and meaning.

Disyllabic words may be reduplicated in full and a disyllable, from the beginning or end of the word, may be reduplicated from trisyllabic and longer roots. Disyllabic reduplication may form plurals, as seen above in single-syllable reduplication: (*fitifiti* 'flick, plural' from *fiti* 'flick') or, more commonly, create a frequentative or intensified verb:

a'a	kick	*a'aa'a*	kick repeatedly
ala	awake	*alaala*	sit up and talk
'etu	limp	*'etu'etu*	frequentative of *'etu*
lele	fly	*lelelele*	flutter

While the last form immediately above has a result of intensification, disyllabic reduplication may also result in less of something:

'ata	laugh, laughter	*'ata'ata*	smile, grin
galu	rough (of sea)	*galugalu*	ripple
mili	rub	*milimili*	rub gently

As with single-syllable reduplication, disyllable reduplication may form a verb from a noun or clarify whether a noun or verb is meant:

isu	nose	*isuisu*	inquisitive
miti	sip (n.)	*mitimiti*	sip (v.)
pepe	butterfly	*pepepepe*	flutter

Another kind of morphological variation is found in certain plurals, mostly verbs, where the first vowel of the singular has lengthened. These are said to be archaic or very formal usages and occur in a limited number of words, for example:

'aiate	cowardly	*'aaiate*	cowardly, plural
matua	parent	*maatua*	parents
punitia	blocked	*puunitia*	blocked, plural

Basic Syntax

Proto-Polynesian morphosyntax was the subject of Clark's 1976 study as were earlier and subsequent works by Clark and Chung. Amongst other things, their work continues work by Hohepa, which considers whether there has been an accusative-to-ergative drift in Polynesian languages or vice versa.

In terms of transitive constructions, Clark posits a Proto-Polynesian system more like Tongan and Samoan than New Zealand Maori. He attributes the main differences in Maori to changes that occurred at the time of Maori's common development in East Polynesia with Rapanui, Marquesan, Hawaiian, Tahitian and other East Polynesian languages (after their divergence from Samoan and before their divergence from each other). All Polynesian languages have constructions where subjects of intransitive verbs are marked as in the nominative case by the absence of a preposition. In their passive/ergative equivalents the agent is marked by *e* and Proto-Polynesian **e* is reconstructed. The two patterns can be observed in the following two Samoan sentences:

Pattern I

Saa	alofa	le	tagata	le	teine.
TENSE	love	ART.	man	ART.	girl

'The man loved the girl.'

Pattern II

Saa	alofa-gia	e	le	tagata	le	teine.
TENSE	love-ERG.	NOM.	ART	man	ART.	girl

'The girl was loved by the man.'

A third type of construction in Tongan, Samoan, Rapanui and many other languages, Pattern III, is one in which the Erg. suffix is omitted and ergativity signaled only by the **e* marker. Clark posits a situation where Type A verbs, such as "eat" or "hit" and Type B verbs, such as "see" or "listen to" have had shifting relations with respect to Patterns I, II and II since Proto Polynesian. In Proto-Polynesian, Pattern I occurred only with Type B verbs, Pattern II occurred with Type A verbs and some Type B, while Pattern III only occurred with Type A verbs. Both examples above are VSO, which was the Proto Polynesian pattern in such constructions. Subject pronouns preceded the verb and object pronouns followed the verb but did not occur, except for emphasis, when the subject or object noun was expressed.

Contact with Other Languages

Prior to Western contact, borrowing of non-Polynesian words was extremely limited within the Polynesian triangle. It has long been assumed that Early East Polynesian **kumara* 'sweet potato' is a pre-European loan from QUECHUA, probably by way of Rapanui, which shows other South American cultural influences, but more recently there has been the observation that Quechua is not spoken on the coast where Polynesian and South American contacts most probably occurred. Other possible links between South American and Polynesian vocabulary have not been supported by modern linguistic analysis.

In the west there was borrowing from Fijian, especially by Tongan, and the most convincing cases thus far demonstrated have been names of plants and other useful materials and objects.

There was much intra-Polynesian borrowing, mainly between neighboring islands, for example, between Tongan and Samoan; Samoan loanwords in East Futunan, East Uvean, Tuvalu, and Tokelauan; massive Tongan loanwords in East Uvean and Niuafo'ou and total replacement of a distinct Niuatoputapu language by Tongan; East Polynesian loanwords in Niuean; Tahitian loans in Southern Cook, Austral and Tuamotuan languages and dialects; and Tahitic loanwords in Hawaiian overlaying a Marquesic base.

All Polynesian languages, however isolated, have large numbers of borrowings from European languages. This may involve material-culture terms or more, depending on the size and isolation of the island; the interest the Europeans have taken in the island and the interest of the Polynesians in the Europeans. Colonial histories have been Spanish then Chilean in Rapanui, with the consequent importance of the Spanish language; FRENCH through the center of East Polynesia (the Societies, Tuamotus and Marquesas), East Futuna, East Uvea, and West Uvea; and English language countries elsewhere (Ameri-

Table 2: Common Words

	Hawaiian	Tahitian	Samoan	N.Z. Maori	Rapanui
man:	kaane	taane	taane	kaane	taane
woman:	wahine	vahine	fafine	wahine	tamahahine
water:	wai	vai	vai	wai	vai
sun:	laa	raa	laa	raa	ra'a
three:	kolu	toru	tolu	toru	toru
fish:	i'a	i'a	i'a	ika	ika
big:	nui	nui	tele	nui	nui
long:	loa	roa	loa	roa	roa
small:	li'i, iki	ri'i, iti	lili'i, itiiti	riki, iti	riki, iti
yes:	'ae, 'ee, oo	'ae, 'ee	'ioe, 'ii	aae	eee
no:	'a'ole, 'a'ohe	'aima, a'ore	leai	kaore	ina
good:	maika'i	maita'i	lelei	pai	riva-riva
bird:	manu	manu-rere	manu	manu	manu
dog:	'iilio	'uri	maile	kurii	kuri
tree:	laa'au	ra'au	laa'au	raakau	tumu

can in Hawaii and Eastern Samoa, and British in Western Samoa, the Cooks, and New Zealand). Outliers other than West Uvea have been more heavily influenced by English than French. Bilingualism with European languages led to extensive borrowings in Hawaii, New Zealand, Tahiti, and Rapanui. Hawaiian was almost lost and, through the middle of the 20h century, used mainly on an island (Ni'ihau) privately owned and traditionally managed by native Hawaiians. French influence has been profound on some of the large islands of the Societies (Tahiti). French loanwords are common in modern Tahitian and 20 percent of native Tahitians now speak only French. The dialects of the Tuamotus, from the northwest and moving southeast, have been overwhelmed in recent generations by a shift to Neo-Tahitian, and the local atoll dialects being replaced have never been well described.

Outlier Polynesian languages have had other kinds of influences. Because they are so small and isolated, they have been largely insulated from Western influences of a profound sort. Rather, as one might expect, they show varying degrees of borrowing from neighboring Melanesian languages and, now, depending on locality, Neo-Melanesian (pidgin English). Anutan and Tikopian have substantial loanwords from East Uvean and Tongan from the prehistoric period.

Example Sentences

(1) Samoan:

Ona laa a'e ai lea 'i Tutuila e i ai
so 3rd dual go there it to Tutuila who at there

Pagopago i ona luga a'e.
Pagopago at to over ascent
'Then they went on to Tutuila, and to the place on which Pagopago looks down.'

(2) Rapanui:

Ana noho au i Hiva, he topa hakaou
when stay I at/on continent ART. get occasion

mai te mana'u mo toou.
hither tea remember for my
'When I'm on the Continent, I drink tea (idiom for habitual action).'

(3) Hawaiian:

Hanau o Maaui he moku, he 'aina, na kama
birth of Maaui INDEF island INDEF land for child(ren)

o Kamalalawalue noho.
of Kamalalawalue dwell
'Maui was born an island, a land, a dwelling place for the children of Kamalalawalue.'

(4) Tahitian:

Tae i hiti'a, i te Tua Motu e i Ma'areva.
arrive at east, to DEF Tuamotus and to Mangareva
'They went to the east, to the Tuamotus and Mangareva.'

(5) Maori:

Tangihia e Apakura ki te whanau a
lament by Apakura with DEF. family of

Kuru-Tongia, he roroa Wai-Rerewa kau.
Kuru-Tongia, INDEF. tall Wai-Rerewa ancestor
'Apakura lamented with the family of Kuru-Tongia, all tall of stature, descendants of Wai-Rerewa.'

Efforts to Preserve, Protect, and Promote the Languages

Aside from Hawaiian, New Zealand Maori, and Rapanui, Polynesian languages are generally so isolated from outside influences that language death has not occurred nor is it likely to occur. Endangered languages are mainly those just mentioned and some Tuamotuan and Austral languages, which are being replaced by Neo-Tahitian. French influences are substantial around Tahiti but 80 percent of native Tahitians speak the language; radio, television and newspapers use Tahitian; and strong sentiments toward cultural survival and revival among many young Tahitians (and their use of the language with their children) result in an overall situation where the language cannot be said to be in immediate danger.

On modern Hawaii, it has become popular for people of the various ethnic groups to study and now use the language and one can hear it colloquially around some of the schools and universities and even out around the towns and cities. Immersion schools exist but in very small numbers. There are presently 11 such preschools and a few primary schools leading to two such high schools (grades 7–12). Total enrolment is 1,700+ including Ni'ihau children. University students studying Hawaiian as a second language now number over 2,000.

New Zealand Maori language programs have been in place for about 20 years. By 1989 such programs included 400 "nests", Maori preschools. As in Hawaii, it is a revival program rather than a preservation program, there being almost no native speakers under 40 years of age. The object of these programs has been to produce fluent second-language speakers among preschool children and then to support their use and continuing learning of the language as they come of school age.

Select Bibliography

Bayard, Donn T. 1976. *The Cultural Relationships of the Polynesian Outliers*. Dunedin: University of Otago Department of Anthropology.

Biggs, Bruce. 1965. "Direct and indirect inheritance in Rotuman." In *Lingua* 14(I):383–445.

_____. 1971. "The languages of Polynesia." In *Current Trends in Linguistics, Vol. 8*, ed. T.A. Sebeok, 466–505. The Hague: Mouton.

_____. 1978. "The history of Polynesian phonology." In *Second International Conference on Austronesian Linguistics: Proceedings, Fascicle 2: Eastern Austronesian*. eds. S.A. Wurm and Lois Carrington, 143–152. Canberra: Pacific Linguistics C-61.

_____. 1994. "Does Maori have a closest relative." In *The Origins of the First New Zealanders*, ed. Douglas G. Sutton, 96–105. Auckland: Auckland University Press.

Biggs, Bruce, and Ross Clark. 1999. *Pollex: Comparative Polynesian Lexicon*. Computer database. Auckland: Department of Anthropology, University of Auckland.

Chung, Sandra. 1978. *Case Marking and Grammatical Relations in Polynesian*. Austin: University of Texas Press.

Clark, Ross. 1976. *Aspects of Proto-Polynesian Syntax*. Auckland: Linguistic Society of New Zealand.

_____. 1979. "Language." In *The Prehistory of Polynesia*, ed. Jesse D. Jennings, 249–227. Canberra: Australian National University.

_____. 1981. "Inside and outside Polynesian nominalizations." In *Studies in Pacific Languages and Cultures in Honour of Bruce Biggs*. eds. Jim Hollyman and Andrew Pawley, 65–81. Auckland: Linguistics Society of New Zealand.

_____. 1981b. Review of S. Chung, "Case Marking and Grammatical Relations in Polynesian Languages." In *Language* 57(2): 198–205.

Condax, Iovanna D. 1989. "Tongan definitive accent." In *Journal of the Polynesian Society* 98(4): 425–450.

_____. 1990. "Locative accent in Samoan." In *Oceanic Linguistics* 29(1): 27–48.

Geraghty, Paul A. 1983. *The History of the Fijian Languages*. Honolulu: University of Hawaii Press.

_____. 1995. "Prehistoric exchange between Fiji and Western Polynesia: Some evidence from linguistics." In *Rongorongo Studies* 5(1): 3–14.

Green, Roger C. 1966. "Linguistic subgrouping within Polynesia: the implications for prehistoric settlement." In *Journal of the Polynesian Society* 75(1): 6–38.

_____. 1988. "Subgrouping of the Rapanui language of Easter Island in Polynesian and its implications for East Polynesian prehistory." In *First International Congress, Easter Island and East Polynesia, Volume 1: Archaeology*. eds. Claudio Cristino, Patricia Vargas, Roberto Izaurieta, and Reginald Budd, 37–57. Isle de Pascua (Easter Island): Universidad de Chile, Facultad de Arquitectura y Urbinismo, Instituto de Estudios.

Harlow, Ray. 1994. "Maori dialectology and the settlement of New Zealand." In *The Origins of the First New Zealanders*, ed. Douglas G. Sutton, 106–122. Auckland: Auckland University Press.

Hohepa, P.W. 1969. "The accusative-to-ergative drift in Polynesian languages." In *Journal of the Polynesian Society* 78(3): 295–329.

Hovdhaugen, Even. 1992. "Language contact in the Pacific: Samoan influence on Tokelauan." In *Language Contact: Theoretical and empirical studies*. ed. Ernst H. Jahr, 53–69. Berlin and New York: Mouton de Gruyter.

Krupa, Viktor. 1982. *The Polynesian Languages: A guide*. London: Routledge and Kegan Paul.

Marck, Jeff. 2000. *Topics in Polynesian Language and Culture History*. Canberra: Pacific Linguistics.

Mosel, Ulrike, and Even Hovdhaugen. 1992. *Samoan Reference Grammar*. Oslo: Scandinavian University Press.

Pawley, Andrew. 1966. "Polynesian languages: A subgrouping based upon shared innovations." In *Journal of the Polynesian Society* 75(1): 39–64.

_____. 1967. "The relationships of Polynesian Outlier languages." In *Journal of the Polynesian Society* 76(3):259–296.

_____. 1996. "On the Polynesian subgroup as a problem for Irwin's continuous settlement hypothesis." In *Oceanic Culture History: Essays in honour of Roger Green*. eds. Janet Davidson, Geoffrey Irwin, Foss Leach, Andrew Pawley, and Dorothy Brown, 387–410. Dunedin North: New Zealand Journal of Archaeology.

Pawley, Andrew, and Malcolm Ross. 1993. "Austronesian historical linguistics and culture history." In *Annual Review of Anthropology* 22: 425–459.

Tryon, Darrell. 1991. "The French language in the Pacific." In *Journal of Pacific History* 26(2):271–287.

Wilson, William H. 1982. *Proto-Polynesian Possessive Marking*. Canberra: Pacific Linguistics.

_____. 1985. "Evidence for an Outlier source for the Proto Eastern Polynesian pronominal system." In *Oceanic Linguistics* 24(1&2): 85–133.

PORTUGUESE

Karin Van den Dool

Language Name: Portuguese. **Autonym:** *português.*

Location: Portugal; Brazil; the Atlantic Archipelagos of Madeira and the Azores; Angola, Cape Verde, Guinea-Bissau, Mozambique and São Tomé e Príncipe in Africa; Goa, Damao, Diu, Macao in Asia; Timor in Oceania; and in several nuclei of Portuguese emigration in France, Germany, the United States and Canada.

Family: Romance group of the Italic branch of Indo-European.

Related Languages: GALICIAN, SPANISH, CATALAN, ITALIAN, FRENCH, OCCITAN, Ladino, Sardinian, and ROMANIAN.

Dialects: There are three varieties of Portuguese: (1) European Portuguese, spoken in Portugal (with three main dialect areas: Northern, Central, Southern [speech of Lisbon considered the standard]); (2) Brazilian Portuguese (two main dialect regions: Northern and Southern); and (3) the dialects of other areas including the Atlantic Archipelagos of Madeira and the Azores.

Number of Speakers: 177–185 million, the vast majority of whom live in Brazil.

Origin and History

European Portuguese. Portuguese evolved from Vulgar LATIN, which was introduced into the Iberian Peninsula in the second century B.C. as a result of the Roman occupation that followed the defeat of the Carthaginians in the Second Punic War. In 197 B.C., the Romans divided the Iberian Peninsula into two provinces: Hispania Citerior and Hispania Ulterior. Later, in 27 B.C., probably taking into account certain ethnocultural characteristics of the native population, Augustus subdivided Hispania Ulterior into Baetica and Lusitania. The latter extended along the Atlantic coast and included all of modern Portugal south of the River Douro. While Baetica was characterized by its linguistic and cultural conservatism, Lusitania became intensely romanized. Latin came to predominate because of the continued presence and traffic of merchants, soldiers, and civil servants from Rome.

In the fifth century there were invasions by Germanic tribes; these do not seem to have influenced the language to any great degree, except in what is now northern Portugal and Galicia. There Visigoths, fleeing the invading Moors from North Africa, settled in fortified towns around the year 700. Although the Moors occupied the Iberian Peninsula in the eighth century, the influence of ARABIC on the local language was restricted.

The transformation of Vulgar Latin into the different forms of Romance languages and then into separate languages was gradual, and it is difficult to date. Portuguese Romance seems to have come into being at some time between the Germanic invasions during the fifth century and the appearance of the first written documents in the ninth century.

Scholars have divided the history of Portuguese into four broad stages. The **Galician-Portuguese period** extended from the end of the 12th century to around 1350, during which time Oporto served as the linguistic center. This stage of the language was characterized by a number of phonological, morphological, and syntactic changes from Latin. For example, many Latin intervocalic consonants were lost, resulting in Galician-Portuguese forms such as *dor* from the Latin *dolorem* 'pain, grief, distress'. In the early 13th century, various documents as well as poetry written partially or totally in Galician-Portuguese started to appear. The oldest documents are said to be *Noticia de Torto* (probably before 1211) and the *Testament of Alfonso II* (1214).

In the **Preclassical period** (about 1350/85–1540) Portuguese became differentiated from Galician when the linguistic center of Portuguese shifted to Lisbon. Texts written during this period document noticeable differences between Galician and Portuguese language varieties. Morphological structure became more fixed, especially noun and verb endings. Some words come into the language from Spanish (*castelhano, mantilha).*

The **Classical period** extended from 1540 to the middle of the 18th century. During the 15th and 16th centuries, Portuguese explorers sailed to Africa, Asia, Oceania, and America, and the Portuguese developed intense commerce in these regions followed by permanent settlements. As the language was taken into different parts of the world, many foreign words, especially referring to plants, animals, costumes, and objects, entered Portuguese and later other European languages. Examples include *manga* 'mango', *bambu* 'bamboo', *zebra* 'zebra', and *pagode* 'pagoda'. Variations of these words are found in Spanish, Italian, and French.

During the 16th and 17th centuries an abundance of vocabulary entered the language from Italian and Spanish. The prestige of Latin was high during this period, although many Latin words that came into the written language at this time never extended into popular speech. The first grammars setting the linguistic norms for Portuguese are from the 16th century, of which the earliest is Fernão de Oliveira's *Gramatica da lingoagem portuguesa* (1536).

The **Modern period** began in the middle of the 18th century. During the 18th century the scientific and philosophic lexicon was renovated with a large infusion of Latin terms, and many phonological changes occurred that are not reflected in the orthography. At the end of the century the *Academia Real das Ciências* published the first volume of its dictionary and the *Dicionario* of Morais Silva appeared, both helping to consolidate the language. In the 19th century more words entered the language from Spanish, Italian, and for the first time, ENGLISH. A modern change in the phonology is the velarization of the double *r*, in contrast with the simple *r*, which remains alveolar.

The division of the country into three dialectal regions is based mainly on phonetic traits: sibilants, pronunciation of the letter *v*, and the transformation or nontransformation of diphthongs into vowels. Morphological and syntactic differences show much more variation. Where lexical differences exist, the Central and Southern dialects often prefer terms of Arabic origin and accept more innovations, while the northern areas will prefer a word of Latin or Visigothic origin and maintain more archaic terms. The Northern dialect is the oldest and closest to Galician; the Central dialect has considerable prestige, because of the standing of the University of Coimbra and the relative uniformity of the language spoken by the different social classes. Since Lisbon, the capital of the country, is situated in the southern region, its dialect is usually taken as the norm.

Brazilian Portuguese. The Portuguese language came to the New World in 1500 with the discovery of Brazil by Pedro Álvares Cabral. Settlers came from different linguistic regions of Portugal bringing their own dialects, while administrators and nobles imported the Lisbon norm. As the Portuguese occupied the Atlantic Coast, they came into contact with tribes of the Tupi group, which were quite homogeneous linguistically. Tupi, with borrowings from Portuguese, became the basis of the so-called *língua geral*, which first evolved along the coast. It was spoken quite well by the general population and also by merchants and Jesuit missionaries, who wrote it as they translated prayers and composed hymns and plays. It was later taken to the hinterland. The use of this *língua geral* started to decline in the middle of the 17th century and was prohibited in 1759 when the Jesuits were expelled from Portugal and its colonies.

Up to the middle of the 19th century, African slaves from different groups, mainly Bantu and YORUBA, came to Brazil in ever-increasing numbers. Since they were forced to learn the language of the whites, a creolized Portuguese evolved. This creolized Portuguese, occasionally mixed with the *língua geral*, which the Africans also tended to learn, had an impact on the development of Brazilian Portuguese.

Despite the country's size, there is on the whole considerable uniformity in the language spoken throughout Brazil. Although a precise documentation of the dialectal map of Brazil is yet to be undertaken, a generally accepted pattern based on phonological traits divides the country into two general areas: north and south.

The Atlantic Archipelagos. The third main group of dialects includes Portuguese variants spoken in the Atlantic Archipelagos of Madeira and the Azores. Although the dialect spoken in each island of these groups has its own characteristics, which, to some degree, depends on the speaker's level of education, the most differentiated are the dialects of Madeira and of São Miguel in the Azores. Besides other phonological differences, the most striking characteristic of the Madeira dialect is the long vowels and its intonational pattern, while the São Miguel dialect is noted for retaining several sounds from early Portuguese.

The Portuguese spoken in Angola and Mozambique in Africa is quite similar to that of Portugal although it displays some phonological differences, uses the preposition *em* with verbs of motion, and deviates from the Continental norms in the placement of object pronouns.

Orthography and Basic Phonology

The Portuguese alphabet has 23 letters: *a, b, c, d, e, f, g, h, i, j, l, m, n, o, p, q, r, s, t, u, v, x, z*. The letters *k, w*, and *y*, which are not part of the alphabet, are used in symbols and in foreign words and their derivatives, such as *km* 'kilometer', *washingtoniano* 'Washingtonian', and *yd* 'yard'.

A cedilla written beneath the letter *c* indicates that the letter represents the sound [s]. When it is not written with a cedilla, c represents the sound [s] only if it precedes *i* or *e*; if it precedes *a, o*, or *u* it represents the sound [k].

Portuguese has four accent signs, two of which are used to indicate that a syllable is stressed. Words ending in *-a(s), -e(s), -o(s), am, -em*, and *-ens* are usually stressed on the penultimate syllable, whereas for most other words stress falls on the last syllable. When the stress does not follow this pattern, either an acute or a circumflex accent is placed on the vowel of the stressed syllable: *café* 'coffee', *último* 'last', *avô* 'grandfather'. The particular accent used depends on which vowel occurs in the stressed syllable. A circumflex is used when the vowel is *a* in *am/an* or semiclosed *e* or *o*; otherwise an acute accent is used.

The acute and circumflex accents have other uses in addition to indicating stress. An acute accent is placed on an *i* or *u* that follows another vowel to indicate that the *i* or *u* is fully syllabic: *aí* (bisyllabic) versus *pai* (monosyllabic). The circumflex is used to differentiate an upper midoral vowel (*pôde* 'could') from a phonologically distinct lower midoral vowel (*pode* 'can'). The nasal vowels in *tem* 'he has' and *têm* 'they have' are both upper midfront vowels since the phonological contrast between upper mid and lower mid has been lost for nasal vowels; the distinction between *tem* and *têm* is now purely lexical.

A tilde over a vowel indicates that the vowel is nasalized even though it is not followed by a nasal consonant: *são* 'saint'. The grave accent is used to indicate contractions of the preposition *a* with the definite feminine determiner singular or plural *-a* or *as*, yielding *à* or *às*; and the demonstratives *aquele, aquilo, aquela* yielding *àquele, àquilo, àquela*.

The governments of countries in which Portuguese is the official language concluded an orthographic agreement in 1993 that standardizes the spelling of Portuguese (while taking into account some differences in pronunciation). This agreement has not yet been put into effect.

The set of distinctive consonant sounds in Portuguese is represented in Table 1 on the following page by their typical orthographic spellings.

Table 1: Consonants

	Bilabial	Labiodental	Dental	Alveolar	Alveo-palatal	Palatal	Velar
Stops	p b		t d				c, qu g, gu
Fricatives		f v		s-/ç/c(i,e)/ss z/-s-/x	x/-s*/ch j/g (i,e)		
Nasals	m		n			nh	
Laterals			l			lh	
Tap/trill			r				r-/-rr-

* Not all dialects palatalize *-s*.

The set of distinctive vowel sounds in Portuguese is represented in the following tables for monophthongs and diphthongs by their typical orthographic spellings:

Table 2: Monophthongs

	Front		Central		Back	
	Oral	Nasal	Oral	Nasal	Oral	Nasal
High (closed)	i	im/in			u	um/un
Upper Mid (semi-closed)	e/ê	em/en		ã/am/an	o/ô	õ/om/on
Lower Mid (semi-open)	e/é				o/ó	
Low (open)	a		a			

Table 3: Diphthongs

	Front	Central	Back
High (closed)	iu		ui ui
Upper Mid (semi-closed)	ei eu	ãi/ãe ão	oi oe/õe
Lower Mid (semi-open)	éi éu		ói
Low (open)	ai au		

In some words *em* and *en* are pronounced as nasal diphthongs: [ẽ] plus *a* [y] glide, and in some words *am* is pronounced as [ã] plus *a* [w] glide.

In general, Portuguese sentences display the following patterns of relative pitch level (intonational contours): midhigh-low for statements and for questions that include a question word, midhigh for questions that do not include a question word, and mid-high-mid for unfinished utterances.

Basic Morphology

All articles, adjectives, nouns, and pronouns are classified as feminine or masculine in gender, and as singular or plural in number. The three gender-neutral singular demonstrative pronouns, *isto*, *isso*, and *aquilo*, are the only exceptions to this rule.

The definite articles are *a* and *o* (feminine and masculine singular), and *as* and *os* (feminine and masculine plural). The indefinite articles are *uma* and *um* (feminine and masculine singular), and *umas* and *uns* (feminine and masculine singular). Within noun phrases, articles agree in gender and number with the head noun.

Adjectives agree in number and gender with the nouns they modify. Predicate adjectives agree in gender and number with their subjects. Most adjectives ending in unstressed *-a* are feminine, while most ending in *-o* are masculine.

Most nouns ending in unstressed *-a* are feminine, most ending in *-o* are masculine. Abstract nouns ending in *-ão* are generally feminine while concrete nouns ending in *-ão* are generally masculine. Many nouns can have either a feminine ending or a masculine ending: *vizinha, vizinho* 'neighbor' (feminine, masculine), but many are invariable: *imigrante*, *intérprete*, and nouns ending in *-ista* (English "-ist"). The grammatical gender of animate nouns tends to correlate with natural gender, with the exception of nouns such as *criança* ('child'), a feminine word used for both boys and girls. Some homonyms are semantically distinguished on the basis of their gender: *capital* (feminine) 'capital city'; *capital* (masculine) 'capital, money'. Plural number is typically marked orthographically with one of the suffixes *-s*, *-es*, or *-is*.

Portuguese has a set of reflexive pronouns and four sets of personal pronouns: subject, direct object, indirect object, and prepositional pronouns. All five sets of pronouns have singular and plural forms for first, second, and third persons. There are also a number of address forms. Two of these, *você* and *vocês* 'you' (singular and plural, respectively), are considered informal in Brazil and semiformal in Portugal. Subject pronouns are generally stressed since they are used mainly for emphasis, whereas direct-object and indirect-object pronouns are unstressed, unless they are objects of prepositions. In Brazilian Portuguese, subject pronouns are used more often than in European Portuguese and not always for emphasis, maybe to compensate for the fact that some verbal inflections are being lost in the spoken language.

Verbs belong to one of three conjugations depending on their infinitive ending: *-ar*, first conjugation; *-er*, second conjugation; and *-ir*, third conjugation. Most verbs are regular and follow the paradigm for their class, but there are a number of irregular ones such as *pôr* 'to put', *ir* 'to go', *ter* 'to have' and *ser* 'to be'.

Portuguese has two kinds of infinitives, the impersonal and the personal (or inflected) infinitive. Personal infinitives show agreement with their subjects (*comeres*, *comermos*, see below), whereas impersonal infinitives do not.

É bom tu comer-es fruta.
is good you.SG to eat-2SG fruit
'It is good for you to eat fruit.'

É bom nós comer-mos fruta.
Is good we.1PL to eat-1PL fruit
'It is good for us to eat fruit.'

In addition to these infinitive forms, Portuguese verb paradigms include gerund and participle forms as well as forms for the present, imperfect, preterit, perfect, pluperfect, conditional, and future tenses in the indicative mood; present, imperfect, and future tenses in the subjunctive mood; and the imperative. In the indicative, the pluperfect, future and conditional all have compound forms that use the auxiliary *ter* (or *haver*) and *ir* with a participle or infinitive, respectively. In the subjunctive, compound forms exist for the perfect, pluperfect, and future tenses.

Basic Syntax

The predominant word order in declarative sentences, affirmative or negative, is SVO (with direct objects preceding indirect objects). In general, the language exhibits a head-initial nature in simple declarative sentences: auxiliaries precede verbs, verbs precede their objects and clausal complements, there are prepositions, and within noun phrases nouns generally precede genitives and adjective and relative-clause modifiers (although some adjectives do precede their head nouns; articles also precede their head nouns). However, numerous variations are possible in the orders of elements.

Inversions are common for emphasis: to emphasize the subject, it may follow the verb; to emphasize predicates, direct or indirect objects, and adverbial adjuncts, these elements may be placed before the verb.

Onde é que a Helena trabalha?
Where is.it that DEF ART. Helen work-3SG
'Where does Helen work?'

Onde (é que) trabalha a Helena?
Where (is.it that) work-3SG DEF ART. Helen
'Where does Helen work?'

The verb can precede the subject when a verb is in the subjunctive mood and the sentence expresses a command or desire.

Weak object pronouns can generally precede or follow the verb. There are many prescriptive rules governing the order of verbs and their object pronouns, although Brazilian Portuguese speakers tend to allow more freedom of order to these elements than do European Portuguese speakers. In Brazilian Portuguese, third-person accusative clitics are disappearing from the spoken language, and it is very common to find speakers using the nominative form *ele/ela* or *eles/elas* in the object position. In both dialects, a future-indicative verb allows a weak object pronoun to be placed between the verb and its ending. In Brazilian Portuguese this is only found in very formal written styles.

Questions are usually formed by inverting the subject and finite verb and placing an interrogative word in sentence-initial position, or by maintaining normal declarative order and adding a tag question such as *não é*? 'isn't it?'. In Brazilian Portuguese the inversion with transitive verbs is much less common than in European Portuguese and is found only in formal styles.

There is no morphological case marking, except in the pronominal systems. Subject pronouns are used when the subject is being emphasized. When no emphasis is needed, subject pronouns, especially first- and second- person subject pronouns, are usually omitted from the sentence.

The most common pattern of negation is with *não* 'not' placed before the verb. Negative adverbs and indefinite pronouns such as *nunca* 'never', *nada* 'nothing', *ninguém* 'nobody', *nenhum(a)* 'none', are used with *não*. When the negative adverbs or indefinite pronouns precede the verb, *não* is omitted (although it may be present in popular speech). Negative answers to yes/no questions start with *não* 'no' followed by a pause or comma, with the negative marker *não* 'not' before the verb and occasionally another at the end of the answer for emphasis: *Você é português? Não, não sou (não)* 'Are you Portuguese? No, I am not'.

The true passive voice is formed with the auxiliary verb *ser* 'to be' plus the participle of the main verb. A reflexive construction also exists that makes use of an active form of the verb plus a third-person reflexive pronoun to yield a passive-like interpretation. An impersonal construction, in which an active third-person singular form of the verb is used without an overt (spoken) subject, but instead is preceded by the pronoun *se*, is also used to convey a passivelike interpretation.

Contact with Other Languages

During the 16th and 17th centuries, Portuguese formed the basis for the lingua franca of commerce along the African coast and in parts of India and Southeast Asia (Sumatra, Java, Timor, Japan, Thailand, China). In many places, a Creole language (*crioulo*) developed from Portuguese. Although these diverse Creoles share some parallel characteristics, they are best considered as separate languages. In Africa, three groups of Portuguese-based Creoles are spoken on the islands of the Gulf of Guinea, the archipelago of Cape Verde, and on the mainland in Guiné-Bissau and the Casamance region of Senegal. In Asia, Portuguese Creoles exist in the Malacca region of Malaysia, Macao, Hong Kong, Sri Lanka, India, Singapore, Java, Borneo, and Timor.

Most Portuguese words are of Latin origin. There is a large number of borrowings from GREEK used in cultural, technological, and scientific terminology: some came via Latin, others are direct borrowings, frequently composed of compound words. Nevertheless, a sizeable number of words have entered Portuguese as a result of contact with other languages.

From BASQUE: *esquerdo* 'left', *cachorro* 'dog'
From Germanic: *luva* 'glove', *elmo* 'helm'
From French: *jardim* 'garden', *loja* 'store'
From Arabic: *arroz* 'rice', *bairro* 'neighborhood'
From Spanish: *caudal* 'abundant', *velar* 'to keep vigil'
From Italian: *soneto* 'sonnet', *sentinela* 'sentinel'

A dictionary recently published on African borrowings in Brazilian Portuguese contains more than 2,000 entries. Examples include *samba* 'samba', *quitanda* 'vegetable market', *banana* 'banana', and *cachimbo* 'pipe'. Also in Brazilian Portuguese there are many borrowings from indigenous languages, mostly Tupi, often referring to fauna and flora, including, for example, *maracujá* 'passion fruit' and *piranha* 'piranha fish'.

There is a very large number of borrowings from English today, especially in Brazilian Portuguese. Some are written in their English forms and spoken with a Portuguese pronunciation such as "software", "marketing", "freezer", "jeans", and "shopping center". Others have had their spelling adapted to Portuguese including *futebol*, *hamburguer*, and *coquetel* 'cocktail'.

Common Words

man:	homem	long:	longo, comprido, extenso
woman:	mulher	small:	pequeno, miúdo, limitado
water:	água	yes:	sim
sun:	sol	no:	não
three:	três	good:	bom
fish:	peixe	bird:	pássaro
big:	grande	dog:	cão, cachorro
tree:	árvore		

Example Sentences

(1) Eu sou brasileiro.
I am Brazilian
'I am Brazilian.' (male speaker)

(2) Eu convidei-o mas ele não quis ir[1]
Eu convidei ele mas ele não quis ir[2]
I invited(-)him but he not wanted to.go
'I invited him, but he didn't want to go.'

The nominative form of the pronoun is used productively in informal styles. Educated speakers of BP will avoid the nominative form of the pronoun *ele* as substandard. At the same time they will avoid the accusative clitic pronoun since it is a form learned at school and not part of regular spoken language. However, there is a third option used productively by educated and uneducated speakers alike: speakers may drop the object pronoun of regular transitive verbs in order to avoid the nominative form. The object drop is subject to syntactic constraints, and therefore not always possible.

Efforts to Preserve, Protect, and Promote the Language

Portuguese is the official language of Portugal, Brazil, and the former Portuguese colonies in Africa: Angola, Cape Verde, Guinéa-Bissau, Mozambique, and São Tomé e Príncipe. It is also the official language of Macao, which Portugal administered until 1999.

The Portuguese have put a greater effort than the Brazilians into preserving and promoting the language, especially in Africa, in regions to which the Portuguese have emigrated, and in Europe. This includes the creation of language courses and didactic materials, sponsoring lecturers, promoting exhibits and conferences, translations of literary works, and granting scholarships.

Recently an agreement has been reached, but not yet put into effect, among Portugal, Brazil, and the PALOP (*Países Africanos de Língua Oficial Portuguesa*) to standardize the orthography of the language. There has been an increase in cultural contacts among these countries. In 1994, they formed the Community of Portuguese-Speaking Nations. In Portugal, the *Instituto Camões* has been founded to promote Portuguese language and culture, and in Brazil, there is the *Instituto Internacional de Língua Portuguesa* ('International Institute of Portuguese Language').

Select Bibliography

Asher, R.E. 1994. "International Languages." In *The Encyclopedia of Language and Linguistics*. Oxford: Pergamon Press.

Camargo, S., and M. Steinberg. 1989. *Dictionary of Metaphoric Idioms: English-Portuguese*. São Paulo: Editoria Pedagógica e Universitária.

Campbell, G.L. 1991. "Portuguese." In *Compendium of the World's Languages*. New York: Routledge.

Chamberlain, B.J. and R.M. Harmon. 1983. *A Dictionary of Informal Brazilian Portuguese*. Washington: Georgetown University Press.

Green, J.N. 1987. "Romance Languages." In *The World's Major Languages*. New York: Oxford University Press.

Harris, M., and Vincent Nigel. *The Romance Languages*. 1988. Oxford: Oxford University Press.

Houaiss, A., and C.B. Avery. 1993. *Dicionário Brasileiro*. Rio: Enciclopédia Britânica do Brasil. (2 vols., Portuguese-English and English-Portuguese).

Mattoso Câmara, Jr., J. 1972. *The Portuguese Language* (trans. by A.J. Naro). Chicago: University of Chicago Press.

Schneider, J.T. 1991. *Dictionary of African Borrowings in Brazilian Portuguese*. Hamburg: Helmut Buske Verlag.

Williams, E.B. 1938. *From Latin to Portuguese*. Philadelphia: University of Pennsylvania Press.

[1]Spoken EP and written BP.
[2]Spoken BP nonstandard.

Pulaar

Fallou Ngom

Language Name: Pulaar. **Alternates:** Many varieties of Pulaar—known under the umbrella term of *Fulani*—are spoken in several west African countries (see Location, below). This chapter gives examples in the Pulo Futa dialect.

Location: West Africa. Pulo Futa, the dialect that is presented in this chapter, is primarily spoken in the mountains and plateaus of Futa Jalon in Guinea Conakry. Many other varieties are spoken in Senegal, Sierra Leone, Mali, Mauritania, Guinea-Bissau, Gambia, Niger, Cameroon, Nigeria, Chad, Central African Republic, Burkina Faso and Togo. Thus, Pulaar (also known as Futa Fula or Peul Futa) is the language of a large group of people mostly located in the western African nations. The spreading of the language in West Africa is due to the fact that the Fulani people are mostly herders, and thus are a nomadic people.

Family: Although the Bantu-like features of the language (e.g. consonant mutations) caused controversies among early scholars for its classification in the Atlantic language group, it is now accepted that the language belongs the West-Atlantic branch of the Niger-Congo phylum (*Ethnologue*, 1995). The Niger-Congo phylum is the most widely distributed language family in West Africa (Over 70 percent of Africans speak a language of this family).

Related Languages: The major languages related to Pulaar are others of the West-Atlantic branch, especially WOLOF and Seereer. These two languages share more phonological, morphological and lexical properties with Pulaar than any other language in the Atlantic language group. In addition, due to their long coexistence, these languages engage in mutual influence and borrowing relationships with Pulaar.

Dialects: In addition to Pulo Futa, the most important dialects of the language are the following: Tukulor, spoken in the northern part of Senegal; Fulakunda, spoken in the southeastern part of Senegal and Guinea Bissau; Fulfulde/Fulfulbe, also spoken in the southeastern part of Senegal and influenced by Mandinka; Peul Jolof (or Pulo Jeeri), spoken in the region of Louga in Senegal, the Adamawa Fulani of Cameroon; the Bagirmi Fula of Chad and the Central African Republic; the Bauchi Fulani of Nigeria; the Benin/Togo Fulani of Togo; the Bororo Fulani of Cameroon; the Gurma Fulani of Burkina Faso; the Krio Fula of Sierra Leone; the Fula Kita of Mali and Mauritania; the Sokoto Fulani of Niger and Nigeria; the Liptako Fula of Burkina Faso; the Toroobe Fulani of Nigeria; and the Western Fulani of Niger.

The percentage of common vocabulary of these varieties is very high (over 60 percent) and they are mutually intelligible and share similar morphological and syntactic properties despite some lexical differences.

Number of Speakers: According to *Ethnologue* (1995), about 3,000,000 people speak the language in all west Africa: there are 2,550,000 speakers in Guinea Conakry, i.e., 40 percent of the population of the country; in Sierra Leone, there are 178,400 speakers; in Mali, 50,000 in 1991; in Senegal, 100,000; in Gambia, about 214,000; and in Guinea-Bissau, 180,000 people speak the language.

Origin And History

The Pulo Futa people (Fulani) settled in the Futa Jalon region in Guinea Conakry over two centuries ago, and have since spread throughout western Africa. The region of Futa Jalon is considered to be the water tower of Africa. Various west African rivers, such as the Senegal, the Gambia and the Tinkisso, which runs toward eastern Niger and the coastal river in the south, take their source in that region (Mancher 1987). Whether in Guinea Conakry, Mali, Senegal or in other parts of west Africa, the cultural beliefs, practices and the language of Pulo Futa speakers are all similar. Pulo Futa is influenced by classical ARABIC and FRENCH. The Fulani people are almost all Muslim. They became rooted in the Islamic faith centuries ago. The early Islamization of the Pulo Futa speakers allowed them to use Classical Arabic scripts of the Koran to write poems (Ngom 1999). Thus the contact between Pulo Futa and Arabic dates back from the Islamization era of west Africa (around the 13th century). The influence of French on Pulo Futa results from the French colonization of west Africa in the 19th century.

Orthography and Basic Phonology

The Pulo Futa has a classical five-vowel system. All vowels have equal status in the language; they can appear in all positions in a word, initial, medial or final.

Table 1: Vowels

	Front	Central	Back
High	i		u
Mid	e		o
Low		a	

Table 2: Consonants

		Labial	Alveolar	Palatal	Velar	Glottal
Stops	Voiceless	p	t		k	ʔ
	Voiced	b	d		g	
Affricates	Voiceless			c		
	Voiced			ĵ		
Fricatives		f	s			h
Nasals		m	n	ñ	ŋ	
Lateral			l			
Trill			r			
Glides		w		j		
Prenasalized Stops		mb	nd	nj	ŋg	
Implosives		ɓ	ɗ			

Vowel length is phonemic in the language as shown in the following minimal pairs: *sekude* 'to be angry' vs. *seekude* 'to tear off'; *walude* 'to flow' vs. *waalude* 'to spend the night'; *hirude* 'to be jealous' vs. *hiirude* 'to be late at night'.

The language has 24 consonants and 2 semiconsonants (glides). Voicing is a distinctive feature in the language. The voiced consonants contrast phonemically with their voiceless counterparts. All consonants except the semi-consonants, the lateral /l/ and the velar nasal /ŋ/, can only occur word initially and word medially in the language. As for /l/, /n/, /w/ and /j/, they occur in all three of these positions of the word in the language. The frequent occurrence of the velar nasal [ŋ] at word final position makes the language sound nasal in comparison to other varieties spoken in west Africa. Thus the nasal phoneme [ŋ] is a phonological characteristic of Pulo Futa as spoken in the Futa Jalon region. In Tukulor and in Fulakunda, the alveolar nasal [n] or the bilabial [m] are generally substituted in contexts where Pulo Futa would use the velar nasal /ŋ/, as shown in the following three sets of examples:

Pulo Futa: [duŋ] (this), [miñaŋ] (brother)
Tukulor: [dum] (this), [miñam] (brother)
Fulakunda: [dun] (this), [miñam] (brother)

In Pulo Futa, the velar nasal [ŋ] also undergoes assimilation processes in certain contexts. /ŋ/ becomes /n/ or /m/ when followed by an alveolar or a bilabial consonant, respectively. The following examples show this Pulo Futa nasal assimilation.

/noŋ+tigi/	>	[nontigi]	('that's really it')
/miñaŋ+tigi/	>	[miñantigi]	('real brother')
/duŋ+tigi/	>	[duntigi]	('this is really it')
/duŋ+moĵĵi/	>	[dummoĵĵi]	('this is good')

Similarly, the velar nasal /ŋ/, the lateral /l/, and the semi-consonants occur frequently in word-final position. The lateral /l/ is mostly found in word final position in the aspectual morpheme /-gol/, which is generally attached to verbs to indicate the state of the verb, as shown in the following examples:

[ñaamugol]: 'the act of eating from' [ñaamu] ('to eat')
[laamugol]: 'the act of asking from' [laamu] ('to ask')
[jahugol]: 'the act of going from' [jahu] ('to go')

As for the semiconsonants /w/ and /j/, they occur word finally in various contexts in the language. It is important to emphasize that in Pulo Futa, only /ŋ/, /l/ and the semiconsonants have a normal distribution in the language. Geminates are also very common in the language. The most common geminates found in the language are the following: *mm*, *nn*, *ññ*, *ŋŋ*, *bb*, *dd*, *ĵĵ*, *gg*, *pp*, *tt*, *cc*, *kk*, *ll*, and *jj*.

Syllable Roots. The canonic structure of Pulo Futa is like most Niger-Congo languages: CVCV. However, VC structures also occur occasionally in the language. As shown earlier, except for the velar nasal /ŋ/, the lateral /l/ and the semi-consonants /w, j/, all other consonants can only occur at word initial and medial position, thus making the CVCV syllable root more common in the language. Thus, the only possible coda consonants are /ŋ/, /l/ and the semiconsonants.

Pulo Futa syllable structure generally consists of a nucleus (a vowel) and an onset and may not include a coda consonant other than those mentioned. Onsets may consist of a single consonant, a semiconsonant, or a prenasalized unit. The most common prenasalized onsets are /mb/, /nd/, /nj/ and /ŋg/ as in the following words: *mbaba* ('pig'), *ndijan* ('water'), *njaafugol* ('the act of forgiving'), and *jaŋgo* ('tomorrow').

Diphthongs. There are five common diphthongs in the language. Following are the diphthongs attested in the language as seen in the following words: *r<u>iw</u>* 'to chase', *c<u>ew</u>do* 'thin', *k<u>ow</u>le* 'fence', *l<u>aw</u>* 'early', and *b<u>uj</u>* 'a lot'.

Stress. In Pulo Futa, stress is not phonemic. Stress generally falls on the penultimate syllable. However, if the antepenultimate syllable is heavier than the penultimate, the stress falls on the antepenultimate.

Basic Morphology

Nouns. Pulo Futa has a complex noun-class system. There are 20 noun classes in Pulo Futa, just like in the Senegalese variety (Tukulor). The most common classes found in the language are the following: *o, nde, ndu, nge, ngo, ngol* (for singular nouns), and *be, de, di,* (for plural nouns) (Diop, 1989). Pulo Futa also uses inflectional morphology to derive certain nouns:

[cuka]	('kid')	[cukalel]	('small kid')
[boobo]	('baby')	[boobojel]	('small baby')
[ĵiwo]	('girl')	[ĵiwel]	('small girl')

There are two epenthesis rules that insert the lateral /l/ and the semiconsonant /j/ in [cukalel] and [boobojel], respectively. There is also a vowel apocope rule that deletes the vowel of the root morpheme /o/ in the last example. These phonological processes represent ways in which the language preserves its basic syllabic structure.

The morpheme /-gol/ is used as an aspectual unit to indicate the state of the verb. In general Pulo Futa marks aspect (perfective and imperfective) rather than tense by inflecting the main verb. The /-el/ morpheme is used to show how small the referent is. Just like Wolof and many other Niger-Congo languages, Pulo Futa does not mark gender distinctions with morphological inflections. The language only marks number agreement where the morphological form is determined by the noun class, e.g., *mbaalu* 'sheep, singular', *mbaali* 'sheep, plural'; *puccu* 'horse', *pucci* 'horses'. Suppletive plural forms also exist:

[sehil]	('friend')	[sehilaabe]	('friends')
[neddo]	('person')	[jimbe]	('people')
[cukalel]	('kid')	[sukaabe]	('kids')
[gorko]	('man')	[worbe]	('men')
[debbo]	('woman')	[rewbe]	('women')
[lekki]	('tree, wood')	[ledde]	('trees, woods')

The presence of /-be/ in the examples above in plural nouns suggests that the referents have the feature [+human]. When the plural noun refers to things, /-de/ is used in the plural nouns as in [lekki] and [ledde]. Similarly, gender differences are not expressed morphologically in the language. Just like the plural nouns discussed above, gender difference is conveyed by means of particular lexical units. Each masculine noun has a particular feminine counterpart as shown in the following examples.

Masculine		Feminine	
[cikili]	('goat')	[mbeewa]	('she goat')
[gorko]	('man')	[debbo]	('woman')
[njawdi]	('sheep') masc.	[mbaalu]	('sheep') fem.

Pronouns. In Pulo Futa, subject pronouns are free. However, object pronouns are generally suffixes. Subject pronouns found in Pulo Futa are the following: *miŋ/mi, aŋ/a, kaŋko/o, eneŋ/eŋ, onoŋ/oŋ, kambe/ɓe*. The first set of subject pronouns is generally used for emphatic reasons while the second set is used in nonemphatic sentences in the language. The object pronouns are the following: *-aŋ, -ma, -mo,-eŋ, -oŋ*, and *-be*. These object pronouns are always suffixed in a verb. The glottal stop /ʔ/ is often introduced by means of an epenthesis rule to avoid the occurrence of certain vowel clusters as in [okkiiʔeŋ] and [okkiiʔoŋ] in the examples below. The glottal epenthesis rule is very common in Pulo Futa to fulfill the phonotactic requirement of the language as it favors CV syllable structures.

Subject pronouns			Object pronouns
miŋ/mi	ñaami('I eat')		Falu okkiilaŋ ('Falu gave me')
aŋ/a	ì	('You eat')	Falu okkiima ('Falu gave you')
kaŋko/O	ì	('S/he eat')	Falu okkiimo ('Falu gave him/her')
eneŋ/En	ì	('We eat')	Falu okkiiʔeŋ ('Falu gave us')
onoŋ/On	ì	('You eat')	Falu okkiiʔoŋ ('Falu gave you.pl')
kambe/ɓe	ì	('They eat')	Falu okkiibe ('Falu gave them')

Verbs. In Pulo Futa, verbal forms generally indicate two aspects: the perfective aspect (for completed actions) with the suffix /-iino/ and the imperfective aspect (for noncomplete actions) with morpheme /ay/, e.g., *Mi yahiino Chicago* (I go.PERF Chicago) 'I went to Chicago', *O faaliino kaalisi buj* (S/he want.PERF money a.lot) 'He wanted lots of money', *Mi yahay Chicago* (I go. IMPERF Chicago) 'I will go to Chicago', *Be haalay buj* (they speak.IMPERF a.lot) 'They will speak a lot'.

Beside affixation, reduplication is also a commonly used morphological process in Pulo Futa. It is derivational in nature and derives new words: *seeda* 'little' > *seeda-seeda* 'slowly'; *ĵooni* 'now' >*ĵooni-ĵooni* 'right now'; *gorko-tigi* 'real man' > *gorko-tigi-tigi* 'very strong man'.

Basic Syntax

Pulo Futa has a basic head-driven SVO syntactic structure. The language has the following phrase-structure rules: Sentence > [Noun Phrase] [Verb Phrase] in declarative constructions. The internal structure of a VP in the language consists of a verb followed by a noun phrase, e.g., *Falu ñaami ñiiri mako* (Falu eat rice his) 'Falu eats his rice'. However, the language allows VSO sentences in certain constructions.

In addition to such NP constructions attested in Pulo Futa, adjectival phrases (AP) of the language generally consist of a noun followed by an adjective (AP > N ADJ): *Needo moĵĵo* (person good) 'good person', *Worbe moĵĵube* (men good) 'good men', *Cukalel moĵĵeel* (small.kid good) 'good small kid'.

There are two major negative morphemes in Pulo Futa for declarative sentences: *-aani* and *-aa*. The latter is a variant of the former as suggested by Sylla (1982). These two morphemes are generally attached to verbs. The *-aa* morpheme is only used with certain types of verbs such as: *andu* ('to know'), *yiidu* ('to want'), *siwu* ('to be ready'), etc., and the more general *-aani* morpheme is used with all other verbs. The following examples show the use of the two negation morphemes *-aani* and *-aa* in Pulo Futa: *Mi Jogaani pucci* (I have.NEG horses) 'I do not have horses'. *A yiidaa-mo* (you like.NEG-him/her) 'You do not like him/her'. *O andaa saare-mako* (s/he know.NEG country-his/her) 'S/he does not know his/her country'.

Contact with Other Languages

Beside the West-Atlantic languages, the major noncontiguous languages that have influenced Pulo Futa are, respectively, Classical Arabic and French. Pulo Futa has borrowed various words from both French and Arabic because of the long contact with the French and especially Arabic language and culture. Most of the borrowed words are fully adapted to the Pulo Futa linguistic system. However, given that the overwhelming majority of the Pulo Futa speakers are Muslim, the percentage of words (constantly used in speakers' daily lives) borrowed from Classical Arabic is higher than the percentage of French words in Pulo Futa. This is due to the fact that religion is very important in the life of Pulo Futa speakers. Consequently, most words borrowed from classical Arabic belong to the religious register of Pulo Futa. Following are some words borrowed from Classical Arabic and commonly used in Pulo Futa:

almaami 'spiritual leader', from the Arabic word *aliimaam* 'the leader of prayers';*ĵuma* 'mosque', from the Arabic word *ĵaami?*; *alla* 'God', from the Arabic word *allaah*; *sallugol* 'act of praying', from the Arabic word *sallaatu*; *ĵamaano* 'time period', from the Arabic word *zamaan*

While words that Pulo Futa borrows from Arabic are mostly used in the religious sphere, those borrowed from French are generally used for modern items, which came along with the French culture, as shown by the following examples:

telewisijoŋ 'television', from the French word *televiziõ*; *ekol* 'school', from the French word *ekol*; *peresidaŋ* 'president', from the French word *prezidã*; *iniwersite* 'university', from the French word *yniversite*; *abijoŋ* 'plane', from the French word *avjõ*

Common Words

person:	neddo	man:	gorko
woman:	debbo	study:	ĵangu
yes:	eey	no:	o?owoje/o?oje
good:	moĵĵi	bird:	sondu
dog:	raawandu	water:	ndijaŋ
sea:	maajo	father:	baaba
mother:	neene	elder brother:	koto
elder sister:	ĵaaĵa		

Example Sentences

(1) O sikkino o waaway wadude piyi buy.
s/he PAST-think s/he PAST-can do thing every (a lot)
'He thought he could do everything.'

(2) Mi faalano nanude Pulo Fuutaare
I want-PAST INF-understand Pulo Futa

tigi-tigi.
Adv.really(well)
'I wanted to understand Pulo Futa really well.'

(3) Be yiidii haala.
3rd. PERS.PL. present.want INF-speak
'They like to speak.'

Efforts to Preserve, Protect, and Promote the Language

Although linguists have long discussed the classification of West-Atlantic languages in Africa, it is only since the 1970s that serious research was conducted on these languages.

The Center of Applied Linguistics of Dakar (CLAD: *Centre de Linguistique Appliquée de Dakar*) was commissioned by the Senegalese government to develop, beside French, didactic materials for the promotion of Senegalese national languages. CLAD has developed writing systems for the six major spoken languages in Senegal: Wolof, Pulaar, Mandinka, Soninke, Joola, and Seereer. Thus, nowadays, various textbooks are developed in all national languages. Today, the study of national languages, especially Wolof and Pulaar, is flourishing in Senegal as the Senegalese Ministry responsible for the promotion of national languages and several other nongovernmental organizations are involved in the teaching and the promotion of local languages and cultures.

In addition, several Pulaar speakers now hold doctoral degrees in linguistics and are actively involved in linguistic research for the preservation, protection and promotion of their language. Although the efforts provided for the promotion of national languages in Senegal are remarkable, it still remains that a lot has to be done in its neighboring countries with respect to the promotion, preservation and protection of their languages.

Select Bibliography

De Wolf, Paul P. 1995. *English-Fula Dictionary: Fulfulde, Pulaar, Fulani: A Multidialectal Approach.* Berlin: D. Reimer.

Diop, Amadou Hamady. 1989. *Language Contact, Language Planning and Language Policy: The Study of a Bilingual Community in Northern Senegal.* Pennsylvania: Pennsylvania State University.

Mancher, Christian, and Henri Moniot. 1987. *Les Civilisations de l'Afrique.* Paris: Universite Paris VII.

Niang, Mamadou Ousmane. 1997. *Pulaar-English/English-Pulaar Dictionary.* New York: Hippocrene Books.

Ngom, Fallou. 1999. *A Sociolinguistic Profile of Senegal.* Urbana: Department of Linguistics, University of Illinois at Urbana-Champaign.

Sylla, Yero. 1982. *Grammarie Moderne Du Pulaar.* Dakar: Les nouvelles Editions Africaines.

Wilson, A.A. 1989. "The Atlantic." In J. Bendor (ed.) *Niger-Congo Languages: A Description of Africa's Largest Language Family.* New York: University Press of America, pp. 82–97.

PUNJABI

Tej K. Bhatia

Language Name: Punjabi. **Alternate:** *Panjabi.*

Location: Punjab, the land of five rivers (the Jehlam, the Ravi, the Chanab, the Vyas, and the Satluj). The name "Punjab" represents a geographical approximation of the Punjabi-speaking area; that is, primarily in the Punjab states of both India and Pakistan.

Family: Indo-Aryan.

Related Languages: HINDI, URDU, Lahanda, SINDHI, and Kashmiri.

Dialects: Punjabi has several national, regional, and social varieties. The geographical distribution of the four major dialects of Punjabi is as follows: (1) Majhi is spoken in the districts of Amritsar and Gurdaspur; (2) Malwi is dominant in the districts of Ferozpur, Bhatinda, Ludhiana, the western parts of Patiala, and Sangrur; (3) Doabi is spoken in the districts of Jallandar, Kapurthala, and Hoshiarpur; and (4) Powadhi is found in the district of Ropar and the eastern parts of Patiala and Sangrur. There are four additional traditionally recognized dialects of Punjabi (Rathi, Ludhianwi, Patialwi, and Bhattiani) whose status as independent dialects is now questioned by linguists. The status of Lahanda is another point of disagreement; it is classified as Western Punjabi by some language authorities, but other linguists do not include Lahanda and Dogri as varieties of Punjabi.

The Punjabi of Pakistan is more influenced by Perso-Arabic than the Punjabi of India. The high Punjabi of India favors SANSKRIT influence whereas the high Punjabi of Pakistan favors Perso-Arabic influence. As regards informal varieties of Punjabi, retroflexion is an important source of regional and social dialect differentiation. For example, the Majhi dialect maintains a phonemic difference between the retroflex *r* [R] and nonretroflex *r* [r]. In Lahanda, particularly in its Multani dialect, however, this contrast is neutralized in favor of the nonretroflex *r*. Similarly, the Punjabi spoken in Ludhiana (India) and in Lahore (Pakistan), a few miles away from the standard Majhi-speaking area, is sensitive to a phonemic contrast between retroflex [L] and nonretroflex [l]. As regards grammar, here are some differences in verbal forms. For example, 'I used to do': *kardaa sii* (standard Majhi), *kardaa siigaa* (Doabi), *kardaa saaii* (Lahanda).

Number of Speakers: 40–45 million.

Origin and History

Punjabi has been in use as a literary language since the 11th century. As an independent language, Punjabi has three distinct historical stages: **Old** (10th-16th century), **Medieval** (16th-19th century), and **Modern** (19th century to the present).

It is unanimously agreed that the golden period of the language begins with "the age of Nanak" (beginning from the 15th century to the 18th). The most important treatise of this period is *Aadi Grantha*, the sacred scripture of the Sikhs. In addition to the hymns by the prominent Sikh gurus such as Nanak, Angad, Arjun, and Amardas Ramdas, the hymns by Hindu and Muslim saints are also included in this work. Some linguists contend that a very large portion of the collections incorporated in this work are from the various dialects of Western Hindi, MARATHI, and Lahanda. Muslim Sufi poets also contributed significantly during this period. The modern literature of Punjabi departs from its traditional religious literature in a number of ways, most importantly in being influenced by Western literature, mainly ENGLISH and RUSSIAN.

With the partition of the Indian subcontinent came the partition of the state of Punjab. So massive was the migration in 1947 that it is viewed as the greatest migration in the history of humanity. About 10 million people were uprooted from both sides of what is now India and Pakistan. Consequently, the population of the Punjabi-speaking area underwent radical reorganization, which had and continues to have an impact on the language. Multidialectism became the rule rather than the exception in the Punjabi-speaking area.

Orthography and Basic Phonology

Punjabi is primarily written in Gurmukhi in India. The Gurmukhi script is a descendant of the Brahmi script of Ashoka. It is syllabic in nature and written from left to right. There is no special symbol for tones or retroflex [L].

Punjabi also exhibits religion-based linguistic differentiations in the employment of script. Hindus and Sikhs generally use the Gurmukhi script, but these days Hindus have also begun to use the Devanagari script used for Hindi. Moslems tend to write Punjabi in the Perso-Arabic script, which is also employed for Urdu.

The voiceless stops *p, t, T, c,* and *k* are unaspirated. For example, Punjabi *p* is like English "p" in "spot", not like "p" in "pot". In contrast, *ph, th, Th, ch,* and *kh* are aspirated.

The Punjabi dental consonants are similar to their English equivalents, except that the tongue tip touches the upper front teeth.

The retroflex consonants *T, Th, D, N, sh, R,* and *L* are pronounced with the tongue tip curled up and back. English does

Table 1: Consonants

		Labial	Dental	Retroflex	Palatal	Velar	Uvular	Glottal
Stops	Voiceless	p	t	T	c	k	(q)	
	Aspirated	ph	th	Th	ch	kh		
	Voiced	b	d	D	j	g		
Fricatives	Voiceless	(f)	s	sh			(x)	h
	Voiced		(z)				(G)	
Nasals		m	n	N	ñ	ŋ		
Resonants			r, l	R, L				
Glides		w (v)			y			

not have contrastive retroflex consonants, although English "t" and "d" may be retroflex when they precede "r", as in "drip" or "trap". All consonants except *N, L, R, h, y,* and *w* may be geminate (doubled).

The consonants *f, z, x, q,* and *G* only occur in borrowings from Perso-Arabic and English. Some speakers distinguish between /ph/ and /f/, /j/ and /z/, /k/ and /q/, /kh/ and /x/, and /g/ and /G/, while most speakers do not. Such differentiation is more common in Pakistan than in India.

The consonant *v* occurs only in borrowings from English. In addition, *w* can be pronounced as English /v/ (such as a labiodental fricative rather than as a labio-velar glide), depending on the nature of the following vowel.

The mid-low back vowel *au* is not a diphthong, but rather [ɔ].

Punjabi vowels may be oral or nasal. The distinction is phonemic: *gaa* (oral) 'sing' versus *gãã* (nasal) 'cow'.

Punjabi is spoken in the Punjab region of India and Pakistan (shaded area).

Table 2: Vowels

	Front	Central	Back
High	ii, i		uu u
Mid-High	e		o
Mid-Low	æ	a	au
Low		aa	

Punjabi is the only modern Indo-Aryan language that has developed tonal contrasts. It has three tones: low, mid, and high. High and low tones are indicated here with accents, /´/ and /`/ respectively. Tone in Punjabi is fully phonemic: *kòRaa* 'horse', *koRaa* 'whip', *kóRaa* 'leper'.

There is a close correlation between the *h* and voiced aspirates of Hindi and the Punjabi tones. In place of Hindi voiced aspirates, Punjabi shows voiceless unaspirated segments in word-initial position followed by low tone (for example, Hindi *gha* = Punjabi *kà*); in noninitial position, it shows voiced stops either preceded by high tone or followed by low tone (as Hindi *agh* = Punjabi *ág*; Hindi *agha* = Punjabi *gà*).

Although stress is not a prominent feature of Punjabi, nevertheless, it seems that its existence and phonemic status cannot be denied. Stress is utilized in disyllabic words to distinguish among grammatical categories. In nouns, stress falls on the initial syllable, and in verbs (particularly imperatives and causatives), stress falls on the final syllable: for example, *'galaa* 'throat', *'talaa* 'sole' versus *ga'làà* 'cause to melt', *ta'làà* 'cause to fry'.

Basic Morphology

Punjabi nouns are inflected for number, gender, and case. There are two numbers (singular and plural), two genders (masculine and feminine), and three cases (simple, oblique, and vocative). Nouns are declined according to their gender class and the phonological structure of their final segments. The three main patterns of nominal declensions in Majhi Punjabi are:

Pattern I: masculine nouns ending in *-aa*:

	Singular	Plural	
Direct	muNDaa	muNDe	'boy'
Oblique	muNDe	muNDiãã	
Vocative	muNDiaa	muNDio	

Pattern II: masculine nouns ending other than in *-aa*:

	Singular	Plural	
Direct	aadmii	aadmii	'man'
Oblique	aadmii	aadmiiãã	
Vocative	aadmiiaa	aadmiio	

Pattern III: all feminine nouns:

	Singular	Plural	
Direct	kuRii	kuRiiãã	'girl'
Oblique	kuRii	kuRiiãã	
Vocative	kuRie	kuRio	

The syntactic and semantic functions of noun phrases can be expressed by case suffixes, postpositions, and derivational processes.

Adjectives are primarily of three types: (1) simple adjectives such as *sóNaa* 'handsome'; (2) derived adjectives employing various parts of speech, for example, *mardaanaa* 'masculine' (< *mard* 'man'), *mandaa* 'slow' (< *mand* 'slow'), and *dillii vaalaa* 'from Delhi' (< *dillii* 'Delhi' + *vaalaa* '-er'); and (3) participial adjectives, as in *caldii* 'moving' (*cal-* 'walk' + *dii* present participle [feminine singular]), and *nasdaa* 'running' (< *nas-* 'run' + *daa* present participle [masculine singular]).

Simple adjectives agree with the nouns they modify in number and gender.

soN-aa muND-aa
handsome-M.SG.DIR boy-M.SG 'handsome boy'

soN-e muND-aa
handsome-M.SG.OBL boy-M.SG 'handsome boy'

soN-ii kuR-ii
handsome-F.SG girl-F.SG 'beautiful girl'

soN-iãã kuR-iãã
handsome-F.PL girl-F.PL 'beautiful girls'

There are three tenses in Punjabi: present, past, and future.

ó aa-nd-aa e
he come-PRES-M.SG is:3SG 'He comes.' (present)

ó aa-i-aa
he come-PAST-M.SG 'He came.' (past)

ó aa-e-g-aa
he come-3SG-FUTURE-M.SG 'He will come.' (future)

Verbs are inflected for number, gender, and person.

Verbs can be made causative by a very productive process of suffixation. Two suffixes, *-aa-* (called the 'first causative') and *-vaa-* ('second causative') can be attached to the root of a verb:

Intransitive: pakNaa 'to be cooked'
Transitive (Causative I): pakaaNaa 'to cook something'
Causative II: pakvaaNaa 'to cause someone to cook something'
(In the examples above, *-Naa* is the infinitive ending.)

Basic Syntax

Punjabi is an SOV language. Its word order is fairly fixed, although some variation in phrase order is permitted. Adjectives precede the nouns they modify. However, relative clauses may precede or follow their head nouns.

The verb generally agrees with the subject. In transitive perfective sentences, where the subject is overtly or underlyingly marked with the postposition *ne*, the verb agrees with the direct object. The general rule is that the verb never agrees with a noun phrase marked with a postposition.

Any positive sentence can be negated by placing the particle *nàii* 'not' before the verb:

ò nàĩĩ aa-e-g-aa
he NEG come-3SG-FUTURE-M.SG 'He will not come.'

Contact with Other Languages

There have been borrowings from SANSKRIT, PERSIAN/ARABIC, and recently, English.

From Sanskrit: *panDat* 'scholar' (< *pundit*), *guru* 'teacher' (< *guru*)
From Perso/Arabic: *khariid* 'buy' (< *xariid*), *jaraa* 'little' (< *zaraa*)
From English: *teshion* 'station', *sakuul* 'school'

Common Words

man:	aadmii, mard	long:	lambaa
woman:	aurat, janaanii	small:	nikkaa
water:	paaNii	yes:	aaho, hãã
sun:	suuraj	no:	nàĩĩ
three:	tinna	good:	caŋgaa
fish:	macchii	bird:	parindaa
big:	vaDDaa	dog:	kuttaa
tree:	draxat		

Example Sentences

(1) mãĩ jaaN-d-aa hãã ki ó
I:NOM know-PRES-M.SG be:1SG that he

aa-e-gaa.
come-3SG-FUT-M.SG
'I know that he would come.'

(2) ó ne é gall aakh-ii.
he SUBJ this matter:F.SG say-PAST.F.SG
'He told me this thing/matter.'

(3) ó nũũ katab pasand e.
he DATIV book choice is:3SG
'He likes the book.'

Efforts to Preserve, Protect, and Promote the Language

Punjabi is the sacred language of the Sikhs. Many Sikh organizations around the world are especially active to protect and promote the Punjabi language outside India.

Select Bibliography

Arun, V.B. 1961. *A Comparative Phonology of Hindi and Punjabi*. Ludhiana: Punjabi Sahitya Akademi.

Bahl, K.C. 1969. "Panjabi." In *Current Trends in Linguistics*, T.A. Sebeok, ed. V: 153–200. The Hague: Mouton.

Bhatia. M. 1985. *An Intensive Course in Punjabi*. Mysore: Central Institute of Indian Languages.

Bhatia, T.K. 1993. *Punjabi: A Cognitive-Descriptive Grammar*. London: Routledge.

Dulai, N.K., and O.N. Koul. 1980. *Punjabi Phonetic Reader*. Mysore: Central Institute of Indian Languages.

Gill, H.S., and H.A. Gleason. 1969. *A Reference Grammar of Panjabi*. Patiala: Punjabi University.

Kachru, Y., B. Kachru, and T.K. Bhatia. 1976. "On the Notion of 'Subjecthood' in Hindi, Punjabi, and Kashmiri." In *On the Notion of Subject in South Asian Languages*. M.K. Verma, ed. 79–108. Madison: University of Wisconsin.

Shackle, C. 1972. *Punjabi*. London: English University Press.

PWO KAREN

Atsuhiko Kato

Language Name: Pwo Karen or Pho Karen. Pwo Karen call themselves [phloʊ̃11] in the Eastern dialects, and [phloʊ̃55] in the Western dialects. The ENGLISH appellation "Pwo" or "Pho" comes from the Sgaw Karen appellation for Pwo Karens, [pɣo31], while "Karen" comes from the old form of the present BURMESE word /kayin_/, which is the general term for all Karen groups. The Burmese appellation for Pwo Karen is /po:kayin_/; in THAI they are called /kariaŋ_poo/.

Location: The Burma-Thai border area (Eastern dialects) and the Irrawady Delta in lower Burma (Western dialects). Their distribution overlaps that of Sgaw Karen in many districts, but usually the two groups do not live in the same villages.

Family: Pwo Karen is one of the languages of the Karen group. The view that the Karen group belongs to the Tibeto-Burman branch of the Sino-Tibetan family is now widely supported. However, Karen languages are SVO in their syntactic typology, which is thus different from the other Tibeto-Burman languages, almost all of which are SOV. Consequently, genetic relations are not yet firmly established. For example, one view is to divide Sino-Tibetan first into Chinese and Tibeto-Karen, and then further subdivide the latter into Karen and Tibeto-Burman.

Related Languages: The most closely related languages are the languages of the Karen group spoken in Karen State, Kaya State, Shan State, and the other districts of lower Burma and northern Thailand. There are more than 10 of these, among which Sgaw Karen, Pa-O (Taungthu), and Kaya (Red Karen) are most well known. The linguistic subgrouping of the Karen languages is not yet completely clear, because many of them have not been sufficiently researched. In Burma, the appellation /kayin_/ sometimes refers to only Pwo Karen and Sgaw Karen, leaving out the other Karen people. From the linguistic point of view also, Pwo Karen and Sgaw Karen are in a quite close relationship. Although Pa-O has been closely placed to Pwo Karen, judging from the resemblance in their vocabulary and syntax, Sgaw Karen may have to be put in the nearest position to Pwo Karen.

Dialects: Pwo Karen can be roughly divided into two groups: Eastern (Karen State, Mon State, Tenasserim Division of Burma, and the northwestern part of Thailand); and Western (distributed over the Irrawady Delta of Burma). The Eastern and Western dialect groups are hardly intelligible to each other, mainly because of differences in phonology and lexicon. For instance, the Eastern word [tɕaĩ55] means 'to walk', but the corresponding Western word is [saĩ11], meaning 'to run'. The dialect treated in this chapter is the Hpa-an dialect (Eastern group), spoken in Hpa-an, the capital of Karen State.

Number of Speakers: The precise number of Pwo Karen speakers is not known. In 1992, it was estimated by the Burmese government to be about 2.86 million Karen in Burma. Although it is not obvious how many of these are Pwo Karen, they probably number more than 1 million. Since they also live in Thailand, the total number of speakers is probably between 1 and 2 million.

Origin and History

The history of the Karen group is poorly understood except that they seem to have moved down from the north like the other peoples of Southeast Asia. But it would be safe to say that their ancestors came into eastern Burma at a very early period, because various Karen peoples are concentrated in this "narrow" area.

Orthography and Basic Phonology

Several writing systems have been created for the Pwo Karen dialects. Of these, the Monastic script and the Mission script are used more widely than the others in Burma.

The Monastic script was created for one of the Eastern dialects (perhaps the Hpa-an dialect) and is mainly based on the Mon script. Its oldest surviving record is a palm-leaf inscription about Buddhism written in the middle of the 19th century, but its history is not clear. This script is used most widely today by the Pwo Karens of Karen State.

The Mission script was originally invented in the middle of the 19th century by a missionary for one of the Eastern dialects, but is not in vogue in the eastern areas where Buddhists overwhelmingly outnumber Christians. It is, however, presently popular in the delta where there are relatively more Christians. But the Mission script does not suit the phonological systems of the Western dialects very well.

Based on the Hpa-an dialect, Pwo Karen has 24 consonant and 11 vowel phonemes as indicated in the charts below.

/θ/ is a voiceless unaspirated interdental stop.

/c/ and /ch/ are affricates [tɕ] [tɕh].

/b/ and /d/ are implosives [ɓ] [ɗ], but /d/ is sometimes pronounced as an egressive [d]. /s/ is [s~ɕ].

As a C2, each of /w/ /l/ /r/ /j/ can appear. For example, /ʔəkhwa./ 'male'; /phlɛ=/ 'disciple'; /krɨ_/ 'should'; /phja./ 'market'.

As a C3, only /n/ can appear, which is, in this environment, the element that nasalizes preceding vowels. For example, /ʔan:/ 'to eat', /jain_/ 'be far'. In some other Eastern dialects, such as the Tavoy (Dawe) dialect of Tenasserim Division, /ʔ/ can also appear as a C3, but the Hpa-an dialect has lost it.

Table 1: Consonants

		Labial	Dental	Alveolar	Palatal	Velar	Uvular	Glottal
Stops	Plain	p	θ	t		k		ʔ
	Aspirated	ph		th		kh		
	Implosive	b [ɓ]		d [ɗ]				
Fricatives	Voiceless			s		x		h
	Voiced					ɣ	ʁ	
Affricates	Plain				c			
	Aspirated				ch			
Nasals		m		n	ɲ			
Liquids				l, r				
Glides		w			j			

Vowels

i	ɨ	ɯ
ɪ		ʊ
e	ə	o
ɛ		ɔ
	a	

The vowels /a/, /ə/ and /o/ can each be nasalized as /an/, /ən/ and /on/. In addition to these basic vowels, there are diphthongs, including /ai/, /aʊ/, /ei/, /əɯ/ and /oʊ/. Besides /aʊ/ each of the four remaining diphthongs can be nasalized as /ain/, /ein/, /əɯn/, and /oʊn/.

There are four tonemes. The tone transcription below follows the method of the Pwo Karen monastery script:

high level	/CV:/ [55]
mid level	/CV=/ [33(4)]
low level	/CV_/ [11]
falling	/CV./ [51]

The syllable structure of the Hpa-an dialect can be represented as C1(C2)V1(V2)(C3)/T, where C is a consonant, V a vowel, and T a tone. This dialect has atonic syllables. In atonic syllables, the only vowel that can occur is /ə/. If there is a word boundary after an atonic syllable, it is shown as /Cə-/ with a hyphen.

Basic Morphology

Pwo Karen has no inflection for parts of speech. Verbs make no distinction regarding tense or person. Determination of word classes depends entirely on syntactic criteria. Below are processes that could be treated within the morphology of Pwo Karen grammar:

Compounding:

khan: + phai_ → khan:phai_ 'sandal, shoe'
foot skin

me: + thi. → me:thi. 'tear'
eye water

Nominalization using prefix:

chə- + ma_ → chəma_ 'job'
prefix to.do

Adverbialization using duplication:

phlɛ: → phlɛ: phlɛ: 'quickly'
quick

Adverbialization using prefix:

ʔe_ + thi. → ʔe_thi. 'exactly'
prefix exact

Basic Syntax

Pwo Karen is an SVO language. Grammatical relations are mainly represented through word order. The following sentences illustrate various word orders involving subjects, object and verbs, nouns and adpositions, and nouns and stative verbs.

The order of subjects, objects, and verbs is SUBJECT + VERB + OBJECT, for example:

θa_ʔwa_ thɛ_ thwi:
Thawa kick dog
'Thawa kicked a dog.'

jə- phɪ:lan. ʔəwe. lai:ʔaʊ_
1SG give 3SG book
'I gave him a book.'

The order of nouns and adpositions is ADPOSITION + NOUN, as in:

jə- ʔan: mɪ_ de= nʊ:thoʊn_
1SG eat rice with spoon
'I eat rice with a spoon.'

The order of nouns and stative verbs is NOUN + STATIVE VERB, such as: *phloʊn_ ɣɪ_ jo_* (person good this) 'This good man.'

Nouns representing possessors precede possessed nouns. A corresponding pronoun (possessive form) to the possessor is often attached to the possessed noun, for example: *θa_ʔwa [ʔə-]ɣein:* (Thawa [3SG] house) 'Thawa's house', *ʔə- ɣein:* (3SG house) 'his house'.

Two types of relative clauses exist in Pwo Karen.

1. Relative clause follows head noun (relative marker appears):

khan:phai_	lə:	jə-	thaʊ:	lə:	daʊ_	phən_	(nɔ:)
shoe	REL	1SG	wear	at	room	inside	that

'The shoes that I wear in the room'

2. Head noun follows relative clause (no relative marker):

jə-	thaʊ:	lə:	daʊ_	phən_	khan:phai_	(nɔ:)
1SG	wear	at	room	inside	shoe	that

'The shoes I wear in the room'

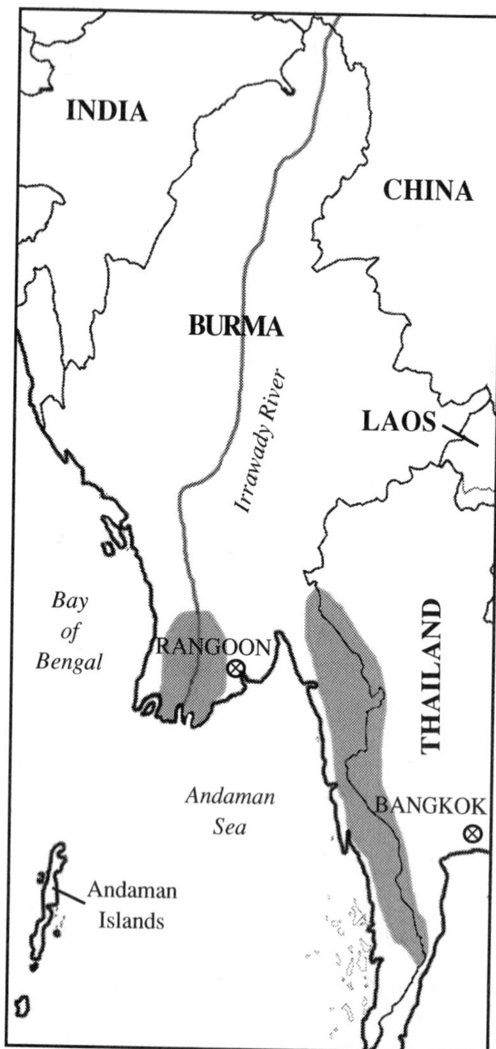

Pwo Karen is spoken on the Burma-Thai border and around the Irrawady Delta in lower Burma (shaded areras).

In specifier phrases, the numeral and classifier follow the noun: *ɣein: nɪ. phloʊn:* (house two CL [round thing]) 'two houses'.

The order of proper and common nouns can be PROPER NOUN + COMMON NOUN or vice versa: *pəjan_ khan=* (Burma country), or *khan= pəjan_* (country Burma) 'Burma'.

There are two types of auxiliaries: those that precede main verbs and those that follow them, for example: *jə- ba: lɪ_* (1SG must go) 'I must go'; *ə- lɪ_ jʊ=wa=* (1SG go try) 'I tried to go'.

Pwo Karen has two negative markers.

1. /ʔe:/ is used in main clauses and put in sentence-final position:

ʔəwe.	lɪ	ʔe:	
3SG	go	NEG	'He didn't/won't go.'

2. /lə-/ is used in subordinate clauses and placed immediately before verbs:

ʔəwe.	ʔe_	lə-	lɪ_	wa:	nɔ:	jə_	θi:	lɪ_	ʔe:
3.SG	if	NEG	go	can	that	I	also	go	NEG

'If he cannot go, I will not go, either.'

Adverbial elements follow verbs (including stative verbs):

jʊ=	ʔe_thi.
look	carefully

'(I) looked carefully.'

ɣɪ_	cha.
good	very

'(It is) very good.'

Adverbial clauses of all types usually precede main clauses:

be.	mə-	θɪ:	θo_,	ʔəwe.	klɨ_cɨ_
SUB	IRR	able	SUB	3SG	make.an.effort

'He made an effort so that he could do (it).'

Contact with Other Languages

Hpa-an dialect has many loanwords from Mon and Burmese.

From Mon: *phja.* 'market' (< phya), *təmjan.* 'strange' (< təmeaŋ)
From Burmese: *con=* 'school' (< *caun:*), *pai_chan.* 'money' (<Burmese *paiʔshan_*)

Common Words

man:	ʔəkhwa.	long:	thɔ.
woman:	ʔəmɯ:	small:	pɪ.
water:	thi.	yes:	mwɛ=
sun:	mɯ=	no:	mwɛ= ʔe:
three:	θən.	good:	ɣɪ_
fish:	ja:	bird:	thʊ:
big:	dʊ:	dog:	thwi:
tree:	θein:		

Example Sentences

(1) pə- təwan. nɔ: ʔəmein_ mwɛ= we. boʊn:kətai: lɔ=
1PL village that name be AUX (name) POL
'The name of our village is Bonkatai.' (*nɔ*: 'that' denotes topics.)

(2) chə- ma_ θi. ʔəwe.
thing CAUS die 3SG
'He was killed.' (Literally, 'Something killed him'.)

(3) jə ʔan: ja: jɛ= bein: ɣon_ jaʊ_
1SG eat fish five CL[flat things] finish PERF
'I have finished eating five fish.'

Efforts to Preserve, Protect, and Promote the Language

The dialects of the Irrawady Delta (Western dialects) are declining because of the influence of Burmese, and the number of Pwo Karen who cannot speak Pwo Karen is increasing. The most important reason is that more Burmese than Karen live in the delta.

The Eastern dialects, including the Hpa-an dialect, are holding their own because Karen State and the neighboring districts where the dialects are spoken are inhabited overwhelmingly by Karen.

In Burma, it is difficult to teach the minority languages to children in the schools because of Burmese government policy. Therefore, the number of Pwo Karen who can read and write any of the Pwo Karen scripts is fairly low. Since not a few Pwo Karen wish to learn their own script, some monasteries in the eastern areas occasionally teach people the Monastic script, and in the delta some churches teach the Mission script.

Select Bibliography

Benedict, Paul K. 1972. *Sino-Tibetan: A Conspectus*. Cambridge: Cambridge University Press.

Chappell, Hilary. 1992. "The Benefactive Construction in Moulmein Sgaw Karen." In *Linguistics of the Tibeto-Burman Area* 15.1: 11–30.

Cooke, Joseph R., Edwin Hudspith, and James A. Morris. 1976. "Phlong (Pwo Karen of Hot District, Chiang Mai)." William A. Smally, ed., *Phonemes and Orthography: Language Planning in Ten Minority Languages of Thailand,* 187–220. Pacific Linguistics Series C-No. 43, The Australian National University.

Jones, Robert B., Jr. 1961. *Karen Linguistic Studies*. Berkeley and Los Angeles: University of California Press.

Kato, Atsuhiko. 1993. "Sugoo-karengo no doosirenzoku. (Verb serialization in Sgaw Karen)." In *Journal of Asian and African Studies* 45:177–204, Tokyo University of Foreign Studies.

____. 1995. "The Phonological Systems of Pwo Karen Dialects." In *Linguistics of the Tibeto-Burman Area.*

Purser, W.C.B. 1922. *A Comparative Dictionary of the Pwo-Karen Dialect*. Rangoon: American Baptist Mission Press.

Shafer, Robert. 1974. *Introduction to Sino-Tibetan*. Wiesbaden, Germany: Otto Harrassowitz.

Solnit, David B. 1997. *Eastern Kayah Li: Grammar, Texts, Glossary*. Honolulu: University of Hawaii Press.

Stern, Theodore. 1968. "Three Pwo Karen Scripts: A Study of Alphabet Formation." In *Anthropological Linguistics* 10 (1): 1–39.

QUECHUA

Serafín M. Coronel-Molina

Language Name: Quechua. **Alternates:** *Quichua, Qqichua, Kichua, Kichwa, Kičua, Khetsua, Kechwa, Kkechuwa, Keshua, Keswa, Qheswa, Q"eswa, Qhexwa, Cjeswa, Runa-simi, Runa-shimi, Ingano, Napeño, Almaguero, Almagrao, Llamista* or *Llácuash, Inga, Quichiua-Aimara* and *Quechumara*. Some of these variants are clearly nothing more than orthographic variations, that came into being during the Spanish conquest and colonization of Latin America and are now out of use. Some, such as *Quechumara*, are more modern designations. The notations *Keshua, Keswa, Q"eswa, Qhexwa* and *Cjeswa* are modern attempts to more faithfully represent the various interpretations of the word as pronounced in modern Cuzco Quechua. The terms *Runa-simi* and *Runa-shimi* are Quechua in origin and came into use during colonial times. They literally mean "human speech," and were used to indicate any indigenous language in pejorative contrast to the SPANISH language. These terms are becoming almost as common as the term "Quechua" and have lost their pejorative connotations.

Location: Quechua is currently spoken in the region ranging between the Andes Mountains and the Amazonian jungles of six Latin American countries: Argentina, Bolivia, Brazil, Colombia, Ecuador, and Peru. In Argentina, it is spoken in two areas of the northwestern provinces, where it is more commonly known as Quichua. The two areas are (1) the territory from Salta to Chañi in the province of Jujuy (where it is currently in the process of becoming extinct) and (2) the north and central regions of the province of Santiago de Estero. In Bolivia, Quechua is spoken in six of the nine provinces: Potosí, Cochabamba, Chuquisaca, Oruro, Santa Cruz and La Paz. In Brazil, linguists believe it to be spoken in the region of Acre, on the banks of the Chandless River down to where it joins with the Alto Purús River. It is thought that there are also Quechua speakers in the area of Tabatinga, near the Amazon River. In both cases, absolute confirmation is not available. In Colombia, it is spoken in various towns in the provinces of Nariño, Cauca, Huila, Caquetá and Putumayo. In Ecuador, where it is known as Quichua, it is primarily found in the provinces of Imbabura, Pichincha, Cotopaxi, Tungurahua, Bolívar, Chimborazo, Cañar, Azuay, Loja, Napo and Pastaza. In Peru, Quechua speakers are distributed in irregular patterns throughout 21 of the 24 departments: all across the Andes, on the eastern flanks of the Andean Mountain Range, and in the Amazon region. The three Peruvian provinces where Quechua is *not* found are Tacna in the far south, and Tumbes and Piura in the far north. The greatest concentration of speakers is found in Peru, Bolivia and Ecuador.

Family: Quechuan.

Related Languages: There is new evidence to support the hypothesis that Quechua and AYMARA may be related languages. However, the field is divided between those who believe there is a genetic relationship between the two languages and those who espouse a theory of linguistic convergence due to sustained contact.

Dialects: According to contemporary historical linguistic research (dating from the early 1960s), two branches of Quechua arose from Proto-Quechua. These two branches are Quechua I (QI), also known as Huáihuash, spoken principally in Peru, and Quechua II (QII), also known as Huámpuy, extending into all other countries where Quechua is spoken. Regarding the question of mutual intelligibility among dialects, it might be possible to understand the basic message when communicating across dialects, but many of the specifics and nuances will be lost, as is true in many languages.

The dialects that fall under Quechua I include Pacaraos, a single dialect that stands by itself, and all the Central dialects: Huáilay (a group comprised of Huáilas and Conchucos), Alto Pativilca-Alto Marañón-Alto Huallaga (a complex of dialects that is grouped together because they share a great number of morphological similarities), and Huáncay (a group which includes Yaru, Jauja-Huanca and Huangáscar). Quechua II is divided into three subgroups: (1) QIIA (also known as Yúngay), which is comprised of seven dialects that have essentially disappeared or are in the process of becoming extinct: Laraos, Lincha, Apurí, Chocos and Madeán, which comprise Central Yúngay; and Cañaris-Incahuasi or Ferreñafe, and Cajamarca, which comprise Northern Yúngay; (2) QIIB (Northern Chínchay); and (3) QIIC (Southern Chínchay). The latter two are collectively known as Chínchay, which is the subgroup that has the widest geographical distribution. Its spread surrounds the territories of the other varieties of Quechua.

Number of Speakers: 8–10 million. This number includes bilingual Quechua-Spanish speakers. Accurate numbers are difficult to obtain, since numbers of Quechua speakers are notoriously under-reported on traditional censuses. Therefore, some experts assert that the numbers may actually be higher than 10 million, but none have ventured to suggest a number above that figure.

Origin and History

The history of Quechua can be divided into three stages: pre-Inca, Inca, and colonial. While there is a reconstructed language known as Proto-Quechua from which the various branches and dialects of Quechua are posited to have arisen, no strong evidence has been found to trace Quechua further back than Proto-Quechua. There are four regions that have been identified as the place of Quechua's origin: the Peruvian highland, the Peruvian coast, the Peruvian jungle, and Ecuador. Historically, the most widely accepted notion has been that of highland origins, but recent research now casts doubt on the validity of this idea. The historical, linguistic and archeological evidence supports much more strongly the hypothesis of a coastal origin.

During the reign of the Incas, Quechua, especially the Cuzco dialect, spread rapidly throughout the territory that they conquered, although the more than 200 ethnic groups under their rule also continued to use their own languages or dialects. Because of its widespread use as the official language of the empire and lingua franca, Cuzco Quechua came to be something of a "general language", considered almost as a supradialectal, "pure" Quechua. However, because individual communities continued to also speak their own languages and dialects, bilingualism or bidialectism was the accepted societal norm.

This bilingualism was also accepted, and even encouraged, at the beginning of the colonial period. In fact, at the First Council of Lima in 1552, it was established that the only effective way to complete the military and spiritual conquest of the indigenous peoples was to communicate with them in their own language to the extent possible. As a result of the Third Council of Lima in 1582–1583, missionaries and clerics were required to learn the native languages of the populations with whom they worked, and a Quechua language program was established at San Marcos University as early as 1579. But within less than 100 years (by the reign of Philip IV), the Spanish government began to insist that Spanish be the primary means of communication, with a goal of eventually making it the only means of communication. By 1783, the Quechua program at San Marcos had been shut down, not to be reopened until the republican period. Then began a long period of linguistic persecution, not just of Quechua speakers, but of speakers of all indigenous languages. Thus, although Quechua was originally used for the establishment of colonial power, it was eventually despised and devalued as "backward" and inadequate for the needs of colonial rule.

After independence from the Spanish in the early 19th century, the situation continued to worsen for indigenous languages. Despite official recognition of Quechua and other languages, societal attitudes were frequently so unfavorable to its use that no official efforts ever survived beyond the printed page, especially in Peru. In Colombia, Brazil and Argentina, the three countries where it is spoken only in small, isolated pockets, Quechua is in the process of becoming extinct, despite some small-scale efforts to preserve it.

Orthography and Basic Phonology

The history of the orthographic system used for Quechua dates back to the Spanish conquest. Prior to that time Quechua had been an unwritten language. With the Spanish written tradition well established by the time of the conquest, the Spaniards felt an immediate need to transfer the Quechua oral traditions into written texts. In 1560, Fray Domingo de Santo Tomás wrote the *Grammática o arte de la lengua general de los Indios de los reynos del Perú*, the first such work to be produced. Diego González Holguín wrote another one in 1607, the *Gramática y Arte nueva de la lengua general de todo el Perú llamada lengua qqichua o lengua del Inca*; and in 1608, he produced a dictionary, the *Vocabulario de la lengua general de todo el Perú llamada lengua qqichua o del Inca*. In addition, many anonymously written grammars and dictionaries exist from colonial times. However, since the Spanish alphabet was not adequate to represent all the sounds present in Quechua, their efforts were not entirely successful.

Over the years, several alphabets have been proposed by different groups working with the Quechua language. Many of these alphabets have failed for reasons ranging from not taking the Quechua phonological system into account to attempting to use alphabets that were so complex they were nearly impossible to manage.

The alphabet used in this chapter is the Pan-Quechua Alphabet. It was approved in 1983 by the First Workshop on Quechua and Aymara Writing convened in Lima, Peru, and was developed specifically with the intention of being able to represent the major sound variants in all Quechua dialects. Results of this workshop included establishment of orthographic rules, how to incorporate Spanish loanwords into the Quechua orthographic system, and the use of only three vowels (*a*, *i*, *u*) in both the Quechua and Aymara official alphabets. Despite the existence of the Pan-Quechua Alphabet, there are some groups that still debate the issue of an effective orthography and use their own preferred orthographic systems, usually for political or ideological reasons.

In Quechua, accentuation in polysyllabic words is normally placed on the penultimate syllable (grave accentuation) and so is not orthographically indicated. However, a very few words have acute accentuation; that is, the stress falls on the last syllable. In these cases, as established by the rules of the Pan-Quechua alphabet, an orthographic accent mark identical to that used in Spanish is placed over the vowel in question. Likewise, when a word carries what is known as an "emphatic stress", the final syllable is marked with the orthographic accent mark. Emphatic stress is used when a word ends with the enclitics *-ya* or *-ma*, and sometimes with *-cha* and *-sa*, and their equivalents in other dialects. It is also used on the final word of a question or emphatic statement, and when the *-y* marker indicating first person nominal is used to form the vocative.

Both consonant and vowel segments in Quechua tend to be fairly stable, especially in syllable-initial position and in stressed syllables. Unifying tendencies across dialects include (1) the absence of voiced plosives, (2) the use of the uvular region as a point of articulation, (3) the phonemic distinction (mainly in some QII dialects) of the plosives between simple, aspirated and glottalized (see below), and (4) the use of two types of affricates expressed in the alveopalatal region (simple and retroflex). It should be noted that these are merely tendencies, and not all dialects reflect all of these characteristics.

Table 1: Consonants

		Bilabial	Labio-dental	Alveolar	Retroflex	Palatal	Velar	Uvular	Glottal
Stops	Unaspirated	p, b*		t, d*		ch	k, g*	q	
	Aspirated	ph		th		chh	kh	qh	
	Glottalized	p'		t'		ch'	k'	q'	
Fricatives			f*	s		sh			h
Affricates				ts	tr				
Nasals		m		n		ñ			
Laterals				l		ll			
Trill				r					
Semivowel		w				y			

*Used only in loanwords.

The basic phonemes of all Quechua dialects are outlined in Tables 1 and 2.

The consonants *ch*, *chh*, and *ch'* are listed in the table above as plosives, but they are also frequently classified as affricates. Plosive consonants followed by /h/ are strongly aspirated, as in *khamuy* [kʰamuj] 'to chew'. This explains the apparent doubling of the letter *h* in the palatal plosive character *chh*. Likewise, an apostrophe after a plosive consonant indicates a strong glottal closure produced in conjunction with the consonant, as in the word *k'umuy* [k'umuj].

In many southern dialects of QII, the consonant *q* is expressed as a uvular plosive [x] in some environments, and as a velar fricative [χ] in others, for instance, in syllable-final position. In Huanca Quechua (QI), the pronunciation of this phoneme has undergone lenition to the point that it is now nearly inaudible, manifested as little more than a glottal stop.

The character *sh* is pronounced as a normal palatal fricative [ʃ]. In Huanca Quechua, however, it also manifests as a retroflex apical sibilant. It is pronounced like a palatal fricative when in contact with the vowel /i/ and after the semivowel /y/, and as a retroflex in all other cases.

The Quechua /r/ manifests two allophones: it is a retroflex alveolar sonorant when it is word final, pronounced almost like *rzh* (*r* together with a voiced palatal fricative). It is a simple vibrant, or flap, in all other positions.

Regarding syllable formation, open syllables are preferred, as in Spanish. However, all of the following syllable configurations are permitted (where V=vowel or syllable nucleus, and C=consonant or syllable margin): V, VC, CV and CVC. In Quechua, it is impossible to have either a series of consonants or one of vowels; in other words, syllables such as *CCV or *VCC do not exist, nor do words with series of vowels next to each other (except in denoting long vowels). There will always be at least one mediating consonant between any two vowels. In the case of loanwords such as *maestro* ('teacher'), this is manifested through the employment of the semivowel /y/ to separate the syllables: [ma-yis-ru].

Vowels. In Quechua, /i/ is pronounced [e] and /u/ is pronounced [o] when they precede or follow the uvular consonant /q/ or its counterparts /qh/ (aspirated) and /q'/ (glottalized). This allophonic variation occurs in all Quechua dialects. During the efforts to develop a writing system for Quechua, at least two groups of language planners proposed using a five-vowel system to reflect the pronunciation of these allophones. However, such a move seems to indicate that [e] and [o] are phonemes in their own right, which is not the case. In utilizing only three vowels, the Pan-Quechua alphabet reflects the allophonic nature of the [e] and [o] sounds.

Table 2: Vowels

	Front	Central	Back
High	i, ii		u, uu
Low		a, aa	

The double vowels listed above indicate relative duration of the vowel sound. These long vowels are a feature only of QI dialects. Long vowel usage has both phonological and morphological implications. Phonologically speaking, long vowels are conditioned by syllable type: they occur only in open syllables (that is, those ending in a vowel), and are automatically shortened if they are constrained by a consonant. The morphological aspect will be treated below in the discussion on morphology. Long vowels are also employed in many loanwords; that is, where the original word may have had either a free accented vowel or a diphthong, Quechua interprets those as a single, long vowel. For instance, the Spanish word *aceite* 'oil' becomes [asi:ti] in Huanca Quechua (QI) and [asiti] in Cuzco Quechua (QII). In this and remaining sections, I will represent the Cuzco-Collao dialect from QII, since it is one of the most widely recognized dialects of Quechua.

Basic Morphology

Quechua is an agglutinative language. Most syntactic functions are performed through the addition of inflectional, derivational and independent suffixes added to the noun (nominal derivatives) or the verb (verbal derivatives), or often to both. There are two principal nominal derivatives used throughout all of the Quechua dialects: the transformative *-ya* and the factive *-cha*. The specific verbal derivatives can vary from dialect to dialect.

The independent suffixes exhibit enclitic behavior. They can be attached to any part of the sentence, not just to the noun or verb. They tend to be the last suffix added to a word, serving in the nature of a means of closure for the word or sentence. They fall into four general classes: (1) topical enclitics, (2) focal enclitics, (3) relational enclitics, and (4) enclitics that specify the state or frequency of an action.

Most Quechua dialects do not have articles, conjunctions or prepositions, contrary to both ENGLISH and Spanish, with the following exceptions: *huk* 'one; some'; and *icha* 'or'. Huanca Quechua (QI) is the only dialect that has an article, *kaq* 'the'. There are 12 cases in Quechua and 11 case suffixes: Genitive *-pa*, Accusative *-ta*, Illative *-man*, Ablative *-manta*, Locative *-pi*, Instrumental-Agentive *-wan*, Benefactive *-paq*, Terminative *-kama*, Causal *-rayku*, Interactive *-pura*, and Comparative *-hina*. The nominative case is unmarked.

Quechua does not grammatically mark gender in nouns. Rather, there are words that are generally used to explicitly indicate gender, but only in the case of people and animals. For human beings, the word *qhari* means 'man', and *warmi* means 'woman'. For animals, *urqu* means 'male' and *china* means 'female'. There are also other specific words for male or female of different ages and relationships, such as *paya* 'old woman', *machu* 'old man', *ñaña* or *pana* 'sister', and *turi* or *wawqi* 'brother'. The lack of grammatical gender extends also to pronouns.

Traditionally, Quechua did not grammatically mark number, but in modern times, the suffix *-kuna* has been adopted to indicate plurality. Again, there is an explicit manner of indicating number, by the simple expedient of saying the number of items being discussed: *suqta wasi* 'six houses', or by using the less specific *ancha* (adv.)/*ashka* (adj.) 'much', 'many', 'a lot', or *pisi* (adj.)/*as* (adv.) '(a) little' or 'few': *ashka qulqi* 'a lot of money'. Note that if the number is explicitly stated, the plural marker *-kuna* is not used, contrary to either English or Spanish. In addition, similar to English (but contrary to Spanish), there is no requirement for agreement between nouns and their modifiers: *yana kuchi**kuna*** 'black pigs' (in Spanish, 'cerdos negros').

The pronominal system consists of subject, object and possessive pronouns. Since the pronouns are so tightly interwoven with verbs, the two will be treated together.

The subject pronouns are separate words in their own right. Object and possessive pronouns are suffixes attached to the verb. Conjugated verbs also reflect the subject of the sentence, so the subject pronouns are sometimes omitted. Table 3 summarizes the pronouns in relation to verbs. The verb *yanapay* 'to help' is used to illustrate how verbs and pronouns work together.

It should be noted that the first-person plural subject pronoun has two forms, inclusive and exclusive. The "we" inclusive is used when the speaker is including all listeners in his interaction; e.g., "we [all of us here] help". The "we" exclusive is used when one or more listeners is not considered to be included in the interaction; e.g., "we [over here on this side of the room] help, but you [over there] do not."

Table 3: Pronominal Morphology

	Subjects	Objects	Possessives
I	***nuqa** yanapa-**ni*** 'I help'	-wa. *Pay yanapa-**wa**-n* 'She helps me.'	*llaqta-**y*** 'my town'
you (singular)	***qan** yanapa-**nki*** 'you help'	-yki (with 1st p. subject) -su (with 3rd p. subject) *Pay yanapa-**su**-nki* 'She helps you.'	*llaqta-**yki*** 'your town'
he/she	*.**pay** yanapa-**n*** 'he/she helps'	-Ø *Nuqa yanapani* 'I help him.'	*llaqta-**n*** 'his/her town'
we (inclusive)	***nuqanchis** yanapa-**nchis*** 'we help'	-wa *Pay yanapa-**wa**-nchis.* 'She helps us.'	*llaqta-**nchis*** 'our town'
we (exclusive)	***nuqayku** yanapa-**yku*** 'we help'	-wa *Pay yanapa-**wa**-yku* 'She helps us.'	*llaqta-**yku*** 'our town'
you (plural)	***qankuna** yanapa-**nkichis*** all of you help'	-yki (with 1st p. subject) -su (with 3rd p. subject) *Pay yanapa-**su**-nkichis.* 'She helps all of you.'	*llaqta-**ykichis*** 'your town'
they	***paykuna** yanapa-**nku*** 'they help'	-Ø *Nuqa yanapani.* 'I help them.'	*llaqta-**nku*** 'their town'

There is no specific suffix for third-person object pronouns. Nor is there a word exclusively for the English pronoun "it", although the demonstrative adjectives *kay* 'this' and *chay* 'that' can fulfill that function in certain instances: ***Kay**-ta waqaychay* 'Keep this (it)'; ***Chay**-ta allinta t'aqsanki* 'Wash that (it) well'. Note also that singular and plural forms of object pronouns are the same for all persons (first, second, third).

Possessive pronouns are usually combined with genitive flexions on the noun, thus in a sense creating a double possessive: *qanpa llaqtayki*, literally translated 'of you your house'.

The basic inflection of present-tense verbs can be seen in Table 3 on the previous page. Note that verbs are inflected to agree with both subject and object; the plural subject markers are the suffixes *-nchik*, *-yku*, *-nkichis* and *-nku*. Suffixes are used to perform most other verbal functions as well, such as negation (see Basic Syntax).

Other grammatical aspects of verbs are inflected through the use of suffixes as well. The verbal inflectional system of Quechua reflects the following tenses, aspects and moods: present, present progressive, simple preterite, pluperfect, habitual past (imperfect), future, conditional, obligative and imperative.

Causatives are constructed through the use of the suffix *-chi*: *llank'a-**chi**-y* 'to cause to work'; *rima-chi-y* 'to cause to talk'.

Basic Syntax

The basic word order in Quechua is Subject-Object-Verb, which holds true across all dialects of Quechua, e.g., *Satuku t'anta-ta ranti-shan* (Satuku bread-D.O. buy-PRES. PROG) 'Satuku is buying bread'. In noun phrases, the adjective generally precedes the noun, e.g., *hatun llama* 'big llama'.

There can be up to seven modifiers complementing a noun, each serving a different function, and each falling in a specific order in the noun phrase:

Demons.	Quant.	Num.	Neg.	Preadj.
7	6	5	4	3
chay	*llapan*	*chunka mana*	*ancha*	*alli*
that	all	ten	not	very

Adj.	Attrib. NUCLEUS
2	1
sara	*chakra(-kuna)*
good	corn field(-plural)

'all 10 of those not very good corn fields.'

Verbs are formed generally to indicate person, mood, and tense with the suffixes being attached in that order, although there are exceptions. Note that even though the verb carries a person marker, the personal pronoun can still be used in the subject position if desired.

(Qan)	*puklla*	*-nki*	*-man*	*karqa.*
You	to.play	2nd.p.SING.PRES.	COND.	to.be:PAST (participle)

'You would have played.'

There are two negative formulas in Quechua. If one is negating a statement or forming a yes/no question (regardless of whether it is phrased positively or negatively), one simply begins the statement with the word *mana* and adds the negative suffix *-chu* to either the verb or the noun: ***Manam** wawachay**chu*** 'he is not my son'. In the case of the question, *mana-chu* can also be used as the opening word of the question.

Commands are negated by using the word *ama* at the beginning of the sentence with the negative suffix *-chu* affixed to the verb: ***ama** chayta ruway**chu*** 'don't do that'.

Quechua does not manifest a passive voice.

Contact with Other Languages

The language with which Quechua has been most in contact in modern times is Spanish, although in recent decades English has had some influence as well, especially in the area of proper names. There has historically been contact with Aymara, predating the Spanish conquest. The influence of Aymara is reflected most notably in the lexicon, although there are also some phonological, morphological and syntactic similarities between the two languages. Often loanwords fill a genuine need, such as when it becomes necessary to express a new concept for which Quechua does not have any adequate glosses. In many cases, however, already existing Quechua words have been replaced by Spanish equivalents, which are then nativized.

Loanwords from Spanish include: *asiti* 'aceite' ('oil'); *iskuyla* 'escuela' ('school'); *karpintiru* 'carpintero' ('carpenter'); *sini* 'cine' ('movie theatre'); *latanus* 'plátanos' ('bananas'); *kampana* 'campana' ('bell'); *simana* 'semana' ('week'); *liwru* 'libro' ('book'); *inhiniru* 'ingeniero' ('engineer'); *kumputadura* 'computadora' ('computer').

Common Words

These words come from the Cuzco-Collao dialect.

man:	qhari	long:	suni
woman:	warmi	small:	huch'uy
water:	unu	yes:	arí
sun:	inti	no:	manan
three:	kinsa, kimsa	good:	allin
fish:	challwa, chawlla	big:	hatun
tree:	sach'a, mallki	dog:	alqu
bird:	pisqu, pichiku, pichinchu		

Example Sentences

(1) Mana	pi-	-pas	qispi-	-nqa
no	who	ADDITIVE	to free oneself	3rd P. FUTURE

wañuy	-manta.
death	ABLATIVE

'No one escapes death.'

(2) Misi	-ta	yarqa	-sha	-rqa
cat	ACCUSATIVE	be hungry	PROGRESSIVE	SIMPLE PAST

-n.
3rd P. SING.

'The cat was hungry.'

(3) ¿Satuku ri -nqa -chu?
Satuku to go 3rd P. FUTURE INTERROGATIVE
'Is Satuku going to go?'

Efforts to Preserve, Protect, and Promote the Language

At the beginning of the 20th century, a broad-based pro-indigenous movement began that found its way into not only the literary and artistic life of society, but also into the political realm. It purported to support the indigenes and incorporate them into mainstream society, and was ultimately more successful in some countries than in others. However, very often the cost of this assimilation was loss of the ancestral culture and language.

In both Bolivia and Ecuador, Quechua has fared somewhat better than in Peru. While the Quechuas of all three countries have suffered linguistic persecution over the centuries, Bolivia and Ecuador somehow developed and maintained organized social and cultural resistance movements that have fought for and won some linguistic rights for Quechua speakers. Peru, on the other hand, has never been successful at uniting the indigenous peoples, so any grassroots struggles to maintain Quechua have been diffused and regional at best, and few efforts have met with any long-term success. In 1975 Quechua had been made an official language of Peru, supposedly coequal with Spanish, but official status was rescinded in the 1979 constitution and limited to "official-use zones." The current situation of Quechua in Peru is clouded, and its future is uncertain.

In all three countries, Spanish is codified in the constitutions as the only official language, although in all cases Quechua receives recognition in "official use zones." The organized grass-roots movements in Ecuador and Bolivia have kept the issue of Quechua language use before the public. In Bolivia, as of 1994, the official language question was being debated in the parliament. The Confederation of Indigenous Nationalities in Ecuador has achieved considerable political presence, which has benefited revitalization efforts and the actual spread of the language in that country.

As part of the effort to preserve Quechua, several bilingual education efforts are under way, with purported intentions of maintenance bilingualism rather than the previous function of transitional bilingualism. Perhaps part of the reason for this is the recognition of the extremely high illiteracy rate among Quechua native speakers, and the need to find a way to bring them into schools and keep them there.

There are numerous programs in several of the Andean countries that offer courses in Quechua and in Andean linguistics. Perhaps the best known of these is the *Colegio Universitario Andino*, sponsored by the Centro "Bartolomé de las Casas" in Cuzco, Peru. In addition, linguists, language planners, and scholars from a broad range of fields from around the world are also working with the Quechua language.

With the support of UNESCO, a radio program has been established that is disseminated to radio stations not only in the Andean countries where Quechua is spoken, but around the world via e-mail and the Internet. With projects such as this, and the multitude of home pages on the World Wide Web dedicated to Quechua culture and language, high technology has now been officially employed as a means of combating the extinction of the language. The Web pages range from simple travel-type promotions of the Andean region to cultural displays to self-study courses, and many of them include multimedia elements such as video and audio clips, and the capacity to record and play to practice pronunciation. In addition, computing in Quechua is now possible due to a broad array of Quechua software, from on-line dictionaries to graphics packages, desktop publishing, OCR (optical character recognition) software for scanners, even a Windows system package.

If Quechua is finally extinguished, it will not be due to a lack of interest and efforts from a variety of interested parties, both grassroots (the so-called bottom-up effort) and institutional, or "top-down." A collaboration between bottom-up and top-down will be the most beneficial and effective for the ultimate preservation of the language.

Select Bibliography

Adelaar, W. F. H. 1997. *Morfología del quechua de Pacaraos*. Lima: Centro de Investigaciones de Lingüística Aplicada, Universidad Nacional Mayor de San Marcos.

_____. 1977. *Tarma Quechua Grammar, Texts, Dictionary*. Lisse: Peter de Ridder.

Ballón Aguirre, E., R. Cerrón-Palomino, and E. Chambi Apaza. 1992. *Vocabulario Razonado de la Actividad Agraria Andina. Terminología Agraria Quechua*. Cuzco: Centro de Estudios Regionales Andinos "Bartolomé de las Casas."

Bravo, D.A. 1977. *Diccionario castellano-quichua santiagueño*. Buenos Aires: Ed. Universitaria de Buenos Aires.

Calvo Pérez, J. 1993. *Pragmática y gramática del quechua cuzqueño*. Cuzco: Centro de Estudios Regionales Andinos "Bartolomé de las Casas."

Campbell, L. 1995. "The Quechuan Hypothesis and Lessons for Distant Genetic Comparison." In *Diachronica, XII 2*: 157–200.

Cerrón-Palomino, R. 1994a. *Quechumara: Estructuras paralelas de las lenguas quechua y aimara*. La Paz: Centro de Investigación y Promoción del Campesinado.

_____. 1994b. *Quechua sureño: Diccionario unificado*. Lima: Biblioteca Básica Peruana, Biblioteca Nacional del Perú.

_____. 1987. *Lingüística quechua*. Cuzco: Centro de Estudios Rurales Andinos "Bartolomé de las Casas."

_____. 1976a. *Diccionario quechua-castellano/castellano-quechua Junín-Huanca*. Lima: Ministerio de Educación and Instituto de Estudios Peruanos.

_____. 1976b. *Gramática quechua: Junín-Huanca*. Lima: Ministerio de Educación and Instituto de Estudios Peruanos.

Colegio de Propaganda FIDE del Perú. 1905. *Vocabulario políglota incaico*. Lima: Tipografía del Colegio de PFP. Versión actualizada y normalizada 1998. Lima: Ministerio de Educación.

Coombs, D., H. Coombs, and R. Weber. 1976. *Gramática quechua: San Martín*. Lima: Ministerio de Educación and Instituto de Estudios Peruanos.

Coronel-Molina, S.M. 1999. "Functional domains of the Quechua language in Peru: Issues of status planning." In *Bilingual Education and Bilingualism, 2* (3): 166–180.

Cusihuamán G.A. 1976a. *Diccionario quechua Cuzco-Collao.* Lima: Ministerio de Educación.

_____. 1976b. *Gramática quechua Cuzco-Collao.* Lima: Ministerio de Eduación.

Godenzzi, J.C., ed. 1992. *El quechua en debate: ideología, normalización y enseñanza.* Cuzco: Centro de Estudios Regionales Andinos "Bartolomé de las Casas."

Godenzzi, J. C. and I. Vengoa Zúñiga. 1994. *Runasimimanta Yuyaychakusun: Manual de lingüística quechua para bilingües.* Cuzco: Centro de Estudios Regionales Andinos "Bartolomé de las Casas."

Hornberger, N. H., ed. 1997. *Indigenous Literacies in the Americas: Language Planning from the Bottom Up.* Berlin: Mouton de Gruyter.

_____. 2000. "La enseñanza de y en quechua en el PEEB." In I. Jung and L.E. López (eds.), *Abriendo la Escuela.* Madrid: Morata.

_____. 1988. *Bilingual Education and Language Maintenance.* Dordrecht: Foris.

Hornberger, E., and N.H. Hornberger. 1983. *Diccionario trilingüe quechua de Cusco: Quechua/English/castellano.* La Paz: "Qoya Raymi."

Lastra, Y. 1968. *Cochabamba Quechua Syntax.* The Hague: Mouton.

Lira, J.A. 1944. *Diccionario kkechuwa-español. Universidad Nacional de Tucumán.* Tucumán: Instituto de Historia, Lingüística y Folklore. Pub. n. 12.

López Quiroz, L.E., ed. 1988. *Pesquisas en lingüística andina.* Lima-Puno: CONCYTEC/UNA-P/GTZ.

Mannheim, B. 1991. *The Language of the Inka since the European Invasion.* Austin: University of Texas Press.

Middendorf, E.W. 1970 [1890, Germanic]. *Gramática keshwa.* Trans. E. More. Madrid: Aguilar.

Parker, G. J. 1976. *Gramática quechua: Ancash Huailas.* Lima: Ministerio de Educación and Instituto de Estudios Peruanos.

_____. 1963. La clasificación genética de los dialectos quechuas. *Revista del Museo Nacional, 32*: 241–252.

Quesada Castillo, F. 1976. *Diccionario quechua: Cajamarca-Cañaris.* Lima: Ministerio de Educación and Instituto de Estudios Peruanos.

Santo Tomás, Fray Domingo. 1992. *Gramática quichua.* Quito: Proyecto Educación Bilingüe Intercultural, Corporación Editora Nacional.

Soto Ruiz, C. 1976. *Diccionario quechua-castellano/castellano-quechua Ayacucho-Chanca.* Lima: Ministerio de Educación and Instituto de Estudios Peruanos.

_____. 1976. *Gramática quechua Ayacucho-Chanca.* Lima: Ministerio de Educación and Instituto de Estudios Peruanos.

Stark, L.R. 1969. *Bolivian Quechua Dictionary.* Madison: University of Wisconsin, Dept. of Anthropology.

Torero, A. 1974. *El quechua y la historia social andina.* Lima: Universidad Ricardo Palma.

_____. 1964. "Los dialectos quechuas." In *Anales Científicos de la Universidad Agraria 2 4*: 446–478.

von Gleich, U. 1994. "Language Spread Policy: The case of Quechua in the Andean Republics of Bolivia, Ecuador and Peru." In *International Journal of the Sociology of Language, 107*: 77–113.

Weber, D.J. 1989. *A Grammar of Huallaga Huánuco Quechua.* Los Angeles: University of California Press.

Wolck, W. 1987. *Pequeño breviario quechua.* Lima: Instituto de Estudios Peruanos.

RAJASTHANI

John D. Smith

Language Name: Rajasthani.

Location: Rajasthani is spoken in the Indian state of Rajasthan, which lies to the west of Delhi; Rajasthan's western border coincides with the international border between India and Pakistan.

Family: Rajasthani is a member of the Central group of the Indo-Aryan branch of the Indo-Iranian subfamily of the Indo-European family.

Related Languages: Most closely related to HINDI and GUJARATI.

Dialects: The culturally dominant dialect has always been Marwari, spoken in the largely desert area to the west of the Aravali Mountain Range that runs SW-NE through the state. Morphologically, Marwari is characterized by a substantive verb in *h-*, a possessive postposition in *r-*, and a future in (or deriving from forms in) *-s-*. Phonologically/phonetically, its chief characteristics are implosive articulation of the voiced stops /g/, /ḍ/, /d/, and /b/ articulation of the palatals /c(h)/, /j(h)/ as [ts(h)], [dz(ɦ)] and articulation of /s/ as unvoiced [h] (contrasting with /h/, articulated [ɦ]).

The smaller eastern area divides into a number of dialects, of which the chief are Mewari in the southwest, Harauti in the southeast, and Jaipuri or Dhundhari in the north. Mewari lies closest to Marwari and shares some of its features (although not the implosive stops). Harauti and Jaipuri are closer to each other and more clearly distinct from Marwari. Morphologically they have a substantive verb in *ch-*, a possessive postposition in *k-*, and future forms in *-g-* or *-l-*; phonologically, they show none of the characteristic Marwari traits, but share the feature of loss of all noninitial aspiration.

Number of Speakers: In the 1991 census a total of 23,013,383 Indians declared that their mother tongue was one or another form of Rajasthani (which was grouped for the purposes of the census under the "scheduled language" Hindi).

Origin and History

By the 13th century, even Apabhraṁśa, the latest and least SANSKRIT-like of the Middle Indo-Aryan languages, was apparently too remote for comfort from the forms of language in contemporary use in Western India. Works now began to appear in a clearly new Indo-Aryan form of speech: geminate consonants were typically replaced by a single consonant following a lengthened vowel; a new, more analytical morphology was preferred, including new complex tenses and greatly increased use of postpositions; and loanwords were relatively freely used. By about 1300, a fairly standardized form of language had emerged, which was used throughout what are now Rajasthan and Gujarat; this language (which, like Gujarati, has three genders) is normally referred to as Old Gujarati, but some scholars have argued that at this stage Gujarati and Rajasthani had not yet separated, and have preferred the term "Old Western Rajasthani".

By the 15th century, more distinctively Rajasthani works began to appear, characterized by a two-gender noun morphology as well as by other linguistic features indicating Rajasthani provenance. During the Mughal period these early beginnings developed into a major literature that continued into the 19th century.

Rajasthani has never been much used outside Rajasthan (the wealthy Marwari merchant community in Calcutta is the only major exception). The language is not recognized under the Indian constitution and since independence has lost much ground to its larger and more prestigious neighbor, Hindi, which is the official language of the entire country. It is often erroneously claimed that Rajasthani is a dialect of Hindi.

Orthography and Basic Phonology

Like Hindi, NEPALI, and MARATHI, Rajasthani is normally written in the Nāgarī (or Devanāgarī) script, although other local or caste-specific scripts have sometimes been used in the past. The inventory differs little from that of Hindi (see Tables 1 and 2).

Table 1: Vowels

	Front	Central	Back
High	i ī		u ū
Mid	e ai [ɛ]		o au [ɔ]
Low		a ā	

Of the vowels there is little to be said, save to note that /ai/ and /au/ are always monophthongal: [ɛ] and [ɔ]. In some areas nasalized /ā̃/ has come to be pronounced [ɔ̃]; in others, final *-o* after a nasal consonant has come to be pronounced [ũ], leading some early scholars to believe (on the analogy of the Gujarati neuter termination *-ũ*) that the language contained "sporadic instances of the use of a neuter gender"; this was a factor in the adoption of the term "Old Western Rajasthani" for the language generally known as Old Gujarati (see above).

Among the consonants, the retroflex series (/ṭ/, /ṭh/, etc.) differs from Hindi in not containing an aspirated /ṛh/ and in containing the lateral /ḷ/ (found also in Gujarati). Both /ṛ/ and /ḷ/ occur only medially and finally. /y/ does not occur in initial position except in pronouns.

There are constraints on aspiration in many Rajasthani dialects, though written forms of the language from a few centu-

Table 2: Consonants

	Voi	Asp	Labial	Dental	Retroflex	Palatal	Velar	Glottal
Stops	-	-	p	t	ṭ	c	k	
	-	+	ph	th	ṭh	ch	kh	
	+	-	b	d	ḍ	j	g	
	+	+	bh	dh	ḍh	jh	gh	
Fricatives				s				h
Nasals			m	n	ṇ			
Laterals				l	ḷ			
Tap/Trill				r	ṛ			
Glides			v			y		

ries ago suggest that these may have come into being relatively recently. In Marwari, initial voiced aspirates are de-aspirated if another voiced aspirate occurs later in the word. In Mewari and Harauti, noninitial voiced aspirates are de-aspirated.

In Mewari and some forms of Marwari where /s/ is articulated as unvoiced [h], this constraint on aspiration extends to forms of the future tense that were historically marked by terminations in *s*-. In these dialects, the *s*- is lost, and the radical vowel is lengthened and pronounced with raised tone: [vo kə́:ri] 'he will do' from *kar*- ([kər]) 'do'.

In word formation, a final *-ā* (and also the final *-e* or *-ai* of certain verbs) inserts *-v-* before a vowel.

Basic Morphology

Noun morphology shows two genders (masculine and feminine) and two numbers (singular and plural). Nouns (and adjectives, whose inflexion is identical) are either extended or unextended: masculine extended nouns end in *-o*, while the equivalent feminine forms end in *-ī*; unextended nouns have no distinctive ending. Nouns are inflected to three cases, direct, oblique/vocative and instrumental/locative; note that the distinction between the latter two cases is nowadays maintained only in the singular of extended masculine nouns.

	Direct	Obl./Voc.	Instrumental/ Locative
m. extended sg.	-o	-ā	-ai
pl.	-ā	-ā̃	-ā̃
m. unextended sg.	-Ø	-Ø	-Ø
pl.	-ā̃	-ā̃	-ā̃
f. extended sg.	-ī	-ī	-ī
pl.	-(i)yā̃	-(i)yā̃	-(i)yā̃
f. unextended sg.	-Ø	-Ø	-Ø
pl.	-Ø/-ā̃	-ā̃	-ā̃

Extended attributive adjectives show full agreement in the singular; in the plural they always remain in the direct-case form.

Personal pronouns show direct, objective, instrumental and possessive forms; there is no oblique form as such, the obl.pl.possessive being used instead (e.g., *mhārā̃ū̃* 'by me'). Demonstratives, relatives and interrogatives have only direct and oblique.

As in other Indo-Aryan languages, a range of pronominal adjectives and adverbs exist whose initial alternates analogically with those of the pronouns, as evidenced, for example, by the simple adverbs of place: *aṭhai* 'here', *uṭhai*/*vaṭhai* 'there', *jaṭhai* 'where' (rel.), *kaṭhai* 'where?' (interrog.).

The present stem of the substantive verb in Marwari and Mewari is *h*-; in Harauti and Jaipuri it is *ch*-. The inflection is as follows:

	Singular	Plural
1	hū̃/haū̃ [hɔ̃]	hā̃
2	hai	ho
3	hai	hai

The simple present tense of every verb is inflected in the same manner. In many dialects the future is identical with the present save for the addition of a final affix *-lā* (or, in some cases, with distinction of number and gender: *-lo*/*-lā*/*-lī* or *-go*/*-gā*/*-gī*). However, many dialects have future forms in *-s-* (or derivatives of such forms). The imperative is typically in *-Ø*/*-jai* (s.), *-o*/*-jo* (pl.).

Other tenses are formed with participles (imperfective *-to*/*-tā*/*-tī*, perfective *-yo*/*-yā*/*-ī*), or with the simple present itself, together with forms of the substantive verb (e.g., *vo āvai hai* 'he comes', *vo āyo* 'he came', *vo āyo hai* 'he has come').

The substantive verb has a past tense that shows distinction of number and gender rather than person: *ho*/*hā*/*hī* or *tho*/*thā*/*thī*.

Passives are formed by affixing *-īj* to the root before adding inflectional endings. There is also a secondary passive, normally formed from the perfective participle followed by forms of *jā* 'go'. It is used only in contexts where the impossibility of the action is stated or implied: *o kāgad mhārā̃ ū̃ vā̃cyo konī jāvai* 'This paper cannot be read by me'.

Causative stems may be formed from many verbs. There are two distinct formations, whose distribution among verbs is unpredictable, and there are also numerous irregularities.

(1) In verbs ending in *-a-*, *-ĭ-* or *-ŭ* + consonant, the vowel is strengthened: -a- → *-ā-*, *-ĭ* → *-e*, *-ŭ* → *-o-*.

(2) *-ā* is suffixed, with optional shortening/weakening of a long strong radical vowel.

As an example, the verb *ḍhaḷ-* 'be spread' employs both formations: *ḍhaḷai* 'it is spread', *ḍhāḷai* or *ḍhaḷāvai* 'he/she spreads'.

Basic Syntax

The verb is normally the final item of the sentence; linking words aside, the subject is normally the first item. In between these two, the commonest order is nonfinite verbal phrase(s) + adverbial of time + adverbial of place + indirect object + direct object + adverbial of manner. The internal sequence of nonfinite verbal phrases resembles that of the sentence.

ar pābūjī hiraṇ lenai pāchlai pohar ḍerai āyā
And Pābūjī deer taking last:LOC watch:LOC tent:LOC came
'And during the last watch Pābūjī took the deer and came to his tent.'

The direct case may be used for the subject and the direct object of a sentence. Like Hindi, most Rajasthani dialects use an agentive construction if a past tense of a transitive verb is used; the instrumental case is substituted for the direct case of the subject, and the verb agrees with its direct object. Thus *choro sā̃ḍ dekhai* 'the boy sees a she-camel', but *chorai sā̃ḍ dekhī* 'the boy saw a she-camel'. In some dialects, however, other usages are found. If the objective postposition is used to mark the direct object, the verb nonetheless agrees with that object in number and gender (*chorai sā̃ḍ nai dekhī* 'the boy saw the she-camel'); this is different from Hindi.

A major divergence between Rajasthani and most other Indo-Aryan languages is its usage in relative constructions. Here the Indo-Aryan norm is for there to be two nonembedded clauses, one marked with a relative, the other with a correlative pronominal form. In Rajasthani this general syntactic pattern is maintained, but the marking of the clauses differs. The relative clause may be marked with a relative pronominal form or not marked at all, while the correlative clause may be unmarked or marked with a demonstrative, but is often itself marked with a relative form. Thus:

jehī din thā̃ pīcho sambhāḷyo jehī
On.which day you (my-)back watch on.which

din hū̃ jāīs
day I shall.go
'On the day you spy on me I shall leave.'

Contact with Other Languages

Like Hindi and other Indo-Aryan languages, Rajasthani borrows from three main sources: Sanskrit, PERSIAN, and ENGLISH. Such vocabulary is normally little changed save for the resolution of "difficult" consonant clusters (e.g., *dharam* for Sanskrit *dharma*) and the normalization of letters that do not exist in the target language (for example, *khusī* for Persian [χʊʃi]. However, favored word "shapes" or other less obvious forces sometimes distort the borrowed word rather more, as with *siṇgār* for Sanskrit *śr̥ṅgāra*, *jināvar* for Persian *jānvar*, or Harauti *salīmo* ([həlimo]) for English 'cinema'.

Common Words

man:	māṇas	long:	lambo
woman:	lugāī	small:	naino
water:	pāṇī	yes:	hā̃
sun:	sūraj	no:	nī
three:	tīn	good:	cokho
fish:	māchḷo	bird:	caṛkalo
big:	moṭo	dog:	gaṇḍak

Example Sentences

(1) ghaṇā dinā̃ ū̃ mhārī gāyā̃ pyāsī hai.
ghɦəɳa dɪnɔ̃ ũ mɦari gayɔ̃ pyasi hɛ
Many days from my cows thirsty are
'My cows have been thirsty for many days.'

(2) Mhāro kaiṇo mānnai pācho jā paro.
mɦarɔ kɛɳɔ mɔnnɛ patshɔ dza pərɔ
My speaking acknowledged back go! away
'Heed my words and return!'

(3) āgai thanai nīkaḷtā̃ ī mail mẽ khī̃cī
agɛ thənɛ nikəɭtɔ̃ ĩ mɛl mẽ khĩtsi
Ahead to.you emerging (emphatic) palace in Khī̃cī

sūtoṛo lād jāvailā.
hutoɽɔ lad javɛla
sleeping accrue will.go.
'As soon as you go on ahead you will find Khī̃cī sleeping in his palace.'

Efforts to Preserve, Protect, and Promote the Language

Many works of earlier Rajasthani literature have been published by a variety of scholarly institutions in Rajasthan over the past few decades; there has also been a steady trickle of modern works in both prose and verse. Sītārām Lāëas' great dictionary provided users of the language with a vital tool. In the 1970s a Rajasthani department opened at the University of Jodhpur, and at about the same time efforts to win the language more air time on All India Radio met with success. All these initiatives have strengthened the position of Rajasthani within Rajasthan; however, it is unlikely ever to make much headway elsewhere, and even within Rajasthan the impact of Hindi will continue to be very great.

Select Bibliography

Allen, W.S. 1975. "Some Phonological Characteristics of Rājasthānī." In *Bulletin of the School of Oriental and African Studies* 20, 5–11.

Lāḷas, Sītārām. *Rājasthānī sabad kos*. Jodhpur: Caupāsnī Śikṣā Samiti, 4 vols. In 9 parts, n.d.

Smith, John D. 1975. "An Introduction to the Language of the Historical Documents from Rājasthān." In *Modern Asian Studies* 9, 4: 433–464.

____. 1976. *The Vīsaḷadevarāsa: A Restoration of the Text*. Cambridge: Cambridge University Press.

____. 1992. "Epic Rajasthani." In *Indo-Iranian Journal* 35, 251–269.

ROMANI

Ian F. Hancock

Language Name: Romani. **Alternates:** *Romany, Romanes, Gypsy, Gipsy.* **Autonym:** *Rromances.*

Location: Romani is a diaspora language spoken on every continent, with the greatest concentration of speakers in the Balkans in southeastern Europe. From there the population has spread into all western and northern European countries, and eastwards as far as the Pacific Coast. From western Europe, Rroma have migrated (or been forcibly transported) to ex-colonial territories overseas, and are found in sizeable numbers today in North and South America and Australia, and in smaller numbers in New Zealand and the Republic of South Africa. Romani communities have also been reported from the Caribbean, Singapore, Tokyo, Hong Kong, and Harbin (in northern China).

Family: Indo-Aryan branch of Indo-European.

Related Languages: HINDI, RAJASTHANI, Dumaki, PUNJABI, Phalura.

Dialects: About 60 separate dialects have been documented. There appear to be four major dialect divisions: Northern, Central, Balkan, and Southern, although because of the historically diasporic nature of the speech community, these are not distributed geographically; for example, descendants of speakers of Balkan dialects are found in central Iran and in Egypt, and the Romani population in Spain appears to have spoken a Northern dialect. In each case, these groups have been affected to a greater or a lesser degree by the lexicon, phonology, idiom, and structure of the languages surrounding them. The Vlax or Danubian group, for example, which are Southern dialects, are heavily influenced by ROMANIAN; the Sinti dialects, which are Northern, by GERMAN, and so on. Most Rroma in North and South America speak varieties of Vlax Romani, specifically Kalderash and Machvano. This chapter describes Vlax Romani, the basis for the international written standard.

Number of Speakers: About 5 million people speak one or another variety of Romani. Some dialects have only a few surviving speakers (for example, those in the Baltic states where there was massive destruction of the Romani population during the Holocaust), while others, such as Vlax, account for over half of the entire Romani-speaking population. Some Romani ethnolects survive only as lexicons (for example, in Britain and Spain) and can no longer be typologically classified as Indic.

Origin and History

Although Romani is an Indic language, it has developed outside of India, and speakers found in Asia today are there because of migration back into the region from Europe. The Indian origin of Romani was recognized in the 1760s, but its investigation did not begin until the following century, when scholars attempted not only to determine its precise linguistic affinity, but also to identify the ethnic origin of its speakers, and the time and place of their exodus out of India.

For a very long time, it was believed that some of the answers lay in the *Shah Nameh,* an epic poem by the Persian Firdausi, which told of a gift of 10,000 musicians and entertainers from King Shankal of Sindh (in India) to Bahram Gur, ruler of Persia, in the fifth century. The poem describes how this population had disappeared after a year. Scholars assumed that its disappearance was in the direction of Europe. It was hypothesized that on their way west the population split into at least three groups, the descendants of which include the Domari-speaking Dom of the Middle East, the Lomavren-speaking Lom of eastern Turkey, and the Romani-speaking Rrom throughout Europe. The presumed link among these groups was reinforced by their shared ethnonym, which also pointed to a possible origin in India from the *Ḍom,* a social class of low and outcaste persons in India who were entertainers, and also such people as cesspit emptiers, slaughterers, and prostitutes. *Ḍom* is demonstrably the etymological source of the three names Dom/Lom/Rrom.

Recent scholarship generally rejects both the *Shah Nameh* explanation and the *ḍom* theory, at least in unmodified form. Linguistic and historical factors argue convincingly against such an early migration out of India, and against all three groups originating in the Sindh. Only the Domari-speaking Doms of the Middle East, whose language has more linguistic affinity to SINDHI than does Romani, might plausibly have roots in the Sindh. Therefore, if the *Shah Nameh* account is accurate, it would seem to refer to the Doms alone, and have no bearing on Romani. It is further unlikely that the different populations described above have a common ancestor since while there are PERSIAN words in all three languages (including over 100 in Romani), not a single one is shared by all of them. The speech of the Loms is only a lexicon today, operating in a wholly ARMENIAN grammatical framework, so it is impossible to classify Lomavren structurally. That lexicon, however, seems to be much closer to Romani than to Domari, so it is possible that the Loms descend from Romani speakers who remained in the eastern Byzantine Empire instead of coming west into Europe. The form "Lom" instead of "Rrom" is easily explained by interference from Armenian.

Current research suggests that the ancestors of the Rroma were not one people but a composite population speaking several different Indic and Dardic languages, and that they were Dravidian, Pratihara, and possibly African (from the Siddhis,

Table 1: Consonants

		Labial	Dental	Alveo-palatal	Velar	Uvular	Glottal
Stops	Voiceless	p	t	tj/kj	k		
	Aspirated	ph	th		kh		
	Voiced	b	d	dj/gj	g		
Fricatives	Voiceless	f	s	š		x	h
	Voiced	v	z	ž		rr	
Affricates	Voiceless		c	č			
	Aspirated			čh			
	Voiced			dž			
Nasals		m	n	nj			
Resonants			r	j, lj	l		

or African mercenaries recruited to fight for both the Hindu and the Muslim armies). It appears that members of various groups were recruited and trained as a military force to resist the eastern encroachment of Islam and the Ghaznavid forays into India between the years 1001 and 1027.

Because of the Dardic element in Romani, and because of the presence of what appear to be a few lexical items from Burushaski, the route out of India could only have taken place through the Hindu Kush. And because of the heavy Iranic element in Romani, but the virtual nonexistence of Turkic or ARABIC items, the route appears to have been from the Pamir across to the southern shore of the Caspian Sea, then north along its coastline to the southern Caucasus, where words from this area were accreted (e.g., from Armenian, GEORGIAN, and Ossetic), thence across the southern Caucasus to the northern coastline of Turkey (then the Byzantine Empire), which was followed along into Europe. During this period, heavy lexical and structural influence was acquired from Byzantine GREEK. The move out of India, which was probably stimulated by a succession of armed conflicts with the Islamic troops, occurred during the first quarter of the 11th century; arrival in Europe probably took place during the last quarter of the 13th century. The reason for the move into southern Europe was also because of the expansion of Islam, this time by the Seljuk Turks, whose defeat of Byzantium led to the establishment of the Ottoman Empire, which lasted until 1918.

Upon arrival in Europe, the Romani population began to fragment, a large part of it being held in slavery in Moldavia and Wallachia (hence "Vlax"), a condition that lasted until the mid-19th century, while the rest of the population moved on into northern and western Europe, reaching every part by about 1500. Rroma whose ancestors were slaves are today the most numerous and (since abolition) the most widely dispersed throughout the world.

Orthography and Basic Phonology

In part because of the scattered nature of the Romani population and the fragmented dialect situation, writers have used the orthographic conventions of their relevant national language, thus Romani speakers in the United States have attempted to spell it using ENGLISH graphemes (e.g., 'rye' for /raj/). This is still the case to some extent. Because of its numerical strength and widespread geographical existence, Vlax Romani has tended to become the dialect of choice, and since it is spoken extensively in Slavic-speaking lands, an orthography based on romanized Slavic is at present the most widely employed.

The language commission of the International Romani Union has proposed an orthography that differs from the one based on romanized Slavic in several respects. Reactions to this system have been mixed; at present, some of its conventions are being used (e.g., use of a grave accent to indicate a stressed syllable: *lìndra* 'sleep'), while others are not.

The affricates *čh* and *dž* are realized as retroflex fricatives [ʂ] and [ʐ] in Vlax.

Nj represents the palatal nasal /ɲ/, similar but not identical to the "ni" in English "onion". Likewise, *lj* is a palatal lateral /ʎ/, similar but not identical to "lli" in English "William". *Tj* and *kj* represent a palatal stop /c/, while *dj* and *gj* represent its voiced equivalent /ɟ/. In contrast to *lj*, Rrom *l* is always velar as in English "fool". *R* is either a alveolar tap or a trill, and is to be distinguished from *rr*, a voiced uvular fricative.

The distinction between voiceless unaspirated and voiceless aspirated obstruents is phonemic in Romani. However, a single word (stem + affixes) can only contain one aspirated sound. In addition, final voiced sounds tend to become voiceless unaspirated at the end of a phrase.

Table 2: Vowels

	Front	Central	Back
High	i		u
Mid	e		o
Low		a	

Vowels are frequently centralized in Vlax. In the International Romani Union orthography, this centralization is indicated by two dots over the vowel symbol: *ü*, *ë*, etc. Also in the International Romani Union Orthography, a haček over the vowel (e.g., ǎ) indicates that the preceding consonant is palatalized.

Basic Morphology

Romani grammar falls into two distinct paradigms, called "thematic" and "athematic". Thematic grammar, which is mainly Indic and Dardic in origin, applies to those items that formed the language before the European period, including, for example,

Iranic and Armenian items; athematic grammar, derived mainly from Byzantine Greek (and to a lesser extent South Slavic and Romanian) applies to everything else, including lexical adoptions from English.

Romani nouns and pronouns are marked for gender (masculine and feminine), number (singular and plural), and case (subject, oblique, and vocative). Masculine nouns usually end in *-o* or a consonant, and feminine nouns end in *-i* or a consonant. The plural of monosyllabic or high-frequency nouns may not be marked. Masculine and feminine nouns ending in a consonant form their subject plural in *-a*: *Rrom* 'Gypsy man', *Romà* 'Gypsy men'. The various forms of *rakl-* 'child' (thematic) and *frèno* 'friend' (athematic) are illustrated below:

	Masculine		Feminine	
	Singular	Plural	Singular	Plural
Subject	rakl-ò	rakl-è	rakl-i	rakl-ja
Oblique	rakl-ès	rakl-en	rakl-ja	rakl-jan
Vocative	rakl-èja	rakl-àle	rakl-ìjo	rakl-jàle
Subject	fren-o	fren-ura	fren-aki	fren-ača
Oblique	fren-os	fren-a	fren-akja	fren-ačan
Vocative	fren-eja	fren-ale	fren-ako	fren-akona

Definite articles precede the nouns they define and agree with them in case, gender, and number. A total of four forms are used: *o* nominative, masculine, singular; *e* nominative, feminine, singular; *la* oblique, feminine, singular; *le* plural or oblique, masculine, singular. There are four postpositions that may be affixed to the oblique stem:

le rakl-ès-ke
the child-M.SG.OBL-for 'for the boy'

la rakl-jà-tar
the child-F.SG.OBL-from 'from the girl'

le rakl-en-sa
the child-M.PL.OBL-with 'with the boys'

le rakl-ja-n-de
the child-F.PL.OBL-with 'at the girls'

Adjectives agree with the nouns they modify in person, number, and gender:

lošen-ès khel-èl o xurd-ò rakl-ò
happi-ly play-3SG the short-M.SG.SUBJ child-M.SG.SUBJ

lès-k-e dil-è amal-ès-sa
his-GEN-M..SG.OBL silly-M.SG.OBL friend-M.SG.OBL-WITH
'The short boy is playing happily with his silly friend.'

The above example represents the thematic paradigm. The athematic equivalent is (glossing conventions: AAV: athematic adverb marker, IAV: *i*-category athematic verb marker, UAV: universal athematic verb marker):

vesolo-n-ès plej-i-sar-el o skùrt-o
happy-AAV-ADV play-IAV-UAV-3sg the short-M.SG.SUBJ

bòj-o lès-k-e divij-o-n-è
boy-M.SG.SUBJ his-GEN-M.SG.OBL silly-M/F.SG-OBL-M/F.OBL

fren-ò-s-sa
friend-M-SG.OBL-ABLATIVE

Verbs have two tenses, present and aorist, from which all other verb forms are derived. In almost every case, the aorist stem is derived from the present root. There is no infinitive, the equivalent being formed with *te* (roughly 'that'):

puč̌h-l-em te beš-es
ask-AORIST-1SG that sit-2SG
'I asked you to sit.'

Romani verbs agree with their suffixes in person and number, as illustrated in the thematic present tense conjugation of the verb *dikh* 'see':

	Singular	Plural
1st	dikh-av	dikh-as
2nd	dikh-es	dikh-en
3rd	dikh-el	dikh-en

Thematic roots that end in *-a* drop the vowel of the suffix: e.g., *asa* 'laugh', *asa-v* 'I laugh'.

The aorist stem almost always consists of the present root plus an affix, usually *-l-* or *-d-* (phonologically determined): thus, *dikh-l-* 'saw', *čhor-d-* 'poured'. Different endings are used in the aorist from in the present:

	Singular	Plural
1st	dikh-l-em	dikh-l-am
2nd	dikh-l-an	dikh-l-an
3rd	dikh-l-as	dikh-l-e

The imperfect and the pluperfect are formed by affixing *-as-* to the present and the aorist, respectively. Stress remains on the person/number marker:

Tense	Form	Gloss
Present	čhor-àv	'I pour'
Imperfect	čhor-àv-as	'I was pouring, I used to pour'
Aorist	čhor-d-èm	'I poured'
Pluperfect	čhor-d-èm-as	'I had poured'

The future is constructed by suffixing *-a* to the present tense form (*dikh-àv-a* 'I will see') or by using the independent particle *kam* before it (*kam dikh-àv* 'I will see'); the latter construction is modeled on Balkan grammar.

The present causative is constructed by incorporating the unstressed particle *-av-* after the root: *ač̌h-àv* 'I stay', *ač̌h-av-àv* 'I detain (literally, cause to stay)'. The past causative incorporates *-ad-* after the root: *ač̌h-ad-èm* 'I detained'.

Athematic verbs fall into two groups, those that take an *-o-* after the root, and those that take an *-i-*. This is then followed by the particle *sar* and the appropriate present or aorist suffixes: *vol-i-sar-ès* 'you love', *fač-o-sar-d-èm* 'I wrapped'.

Basic Syntax

The unmarked word order in Romani is Subject-Verb-Object. As illustrated above, adjectives precede the nouns they modify. The negative marker is preverbal *či:*

či	dikh-àv	
NEG	see-1SG	'I don't see.'

Contact with Other Languages

Romani is in constant contact with non-Romani languages, and with the exception of very small children, monolingualism is extremely rare. Romani adopts lexicon and idioms freely from the languages with which it is in contact, but the last acquired are usually the first to be abandoned when the community moves into a new language area. The core vocabulary serves to maintain a means of common expression when Romani-speaking populations from different areas encounter each other. Historically, Romani has been in contact with the languages of areas through which the people traveled in their migration from India to Europe.

From Dardic: *džamutro* 'son-in-law', *phabaj* 'apple', *lìndra* 'sleep'
From Iranian: *ambrol* 'pear', *xulaj* 'host', *buzno* 'goat'
From Armenian: *grast* 'horse', *kočak* 'button', *patjiv* 'honor'
From Georgian: *khoni* 'suet', *čamčali* 'eyebrow', *khilav* 'plum'
From Ossetic: *vurdon* 'wagon', *orde* 'here', *feder* 'better'
From Greek (Byzantine): *petalo* 'horseshoe', *oxto* 'eight', *savato* 'Saturday'
From Burushaski: *cird-* 'pull', *sulum* 'straw', *khurmin* 'grain'

Common Words*

water:	panì	sun:	kham
three:	trin	fish:	mačho
big:	barò	long:	lùngo
small:	ciknò	yes:	ava, va
no:	na, nìči	good:	lačh
bird:	čhiriklò	dog:	džukèl
tree:	rukh		
man:	Rrom (Gypsy man); gadžò (non-Gypsy man) manùš (male individual); murš (male human being)		
woman:	Rromnì (Gypsy woman); gadžì (non-Gypsy woman); manušnì (female individual); džuvlì (female human being)		

*All Indic, except for *lùngo* 'long'.

Example Sentences

(1) me kin-àv e klìšk-a le rakl-ès-ke.
I buy-1SG the book-SG.OBL the child-M.SG.OBL-for
'I buy the book for the boy.'

(2) si le rakl-ès-te bar-ò kher.
be:3SG the child-M.SG.OBL-with big-M.SG.SUBJ house
'The child has a big house.'

(3) tu mukh-ès o lil le rakl-jàn-sa.
you.SG leave-2SG the letter the child-F.SG.OBL-with
'You leave the letter with the girls.'

Efforts to Preserve, Protect, and Promote the Language

The International Romani Union, an umbrella body that coordinates a great number of regional and national Romani organizations in over 30 countries, has set up a language commission that is engaged in the creation of a unified dialect and orthography. A number of publications in this endeavor have already appeared. The language is also being more widely used because of the greatly increased involvement of Romani organizations in various international bodies (such as the United Nations, UNICEF, UNESCO, the Council of Europe, and the Organization for Security and Cooperation in Europe), as is use of the written language for official documentation, and as the common medium of interaction at international conferences.

For the past five years the Romani Union has established annual summer schools in different European countries to teach the language to Rroma who do not speak it, and it is now being taught at a number of universities (including in Austin, Prague, Budapest, Moscow, London, Paris, and Bucharest). Because of the large-scale movement of Rroma westwards from former Eastern bloc countries, the language is being introduced into communities where it had died out, and indications are that the global Romani speech community is, in fact, getting bigger. In Spain, where the language has disappeared as a result of anti-Rroma legislation in past centuries, it is being revived and is supporting a small but growing body of literature. In New York, the growing population of post–Communist Romani immigrants from Hungary who never spoke the language (again as a result of historical legislation) are also planning classes in Romani.

Select Bibliography

Boretzky, Norbert, and Birgit Igla. 1995. *Wörterbuch Romani-Deutsch-English, mit einer Grammatik der dialektvarienten.* Berlin: Harrassowitz.

Calvet, Georges. 1993. *Dictionnaire Tsigane-Français.* Paris: L'Asiathèque.

Demeter, R.S., and P.S. Demeter. 1990. *Gypsy-English Dictionary (Kalderash Dialect).* Moscow: Russky Yazyk Publishers.

Hancock, Ian. 1995. *A Handbook of Vlax Romani.* Columbus: Slavica Publishers.

Matras, Yaron, ed. 1995. *Romani in Contact: The History, Sociology, and Structure of a Language.* Amsterdam: John Benjamins.

Sampson, John. 1926. *The Dialect of the Gypsies of Wales.* Oxford: The Clarendon Press.

ROMANIAN

Charles M. Carlton

Language Name: Romanian (spelling recommended since the 1989 Revolution). **Alternates:** *Rumanian, Roumanian* (British following French tradition); *Daco-Romanian* (referring to the national language of Romania).

Location: Romania, Republic of Moldova, parts of Ukraine and other regions in the former Soviet Union such as Siberia. Also spoken in eastern Hungary and former Yugoslavia (the Banat, Vojvodina). Emigré speakers in France, Germany, Israel, United States, Canada, Australia, Scandinavia, and elsewhere.

Family: Eastern subgroup of the Romance family of the Italic branch of Indo-European.

Related Languages: ITALIAN, with features specific to other Romance languages (FRENCH, SPANISH, etc.); lexical affinity with Slavic languages via Old Church Slavic.

Dialects: Romanian has four main varieties: (1) Daco-Romanian; (2) Aromanian or Macedo-Romanian, spoken in Macedonia, northern Greece, southern Albania, Bulgaria, Turkey, and the United States (about 333,000); (3) Megleno-Romanian (derived from Aromanian), spoken in northern Greece and Macedonia (a few thousand speakers); and (4) Istro-Romanian, spoken in Croatia (fewer than 2,000 speakers). Communication among the respective speakers is difficult; however, speakers of Daco-Romanian and Aromanian quickly achieve mutual intelligibility.

Daco-Romanian, the national language of Romania and the variety described here, has two main subdialects: Muntenian, the language of Bucharest and the basis of the literary language in the late 18th-early 19th centuries, and Moldavian, spoken in northeastern Romania and Moldova. Both Muntenian and Moldavian features are found in Transylvania. There are numerous regional variations, especially in the lexicon and phonology.

Number of Speakers: About 23 million.

Origin and History

The four varieties of Romanian are thought to have a common protolanguage (Common Romanian) that probably split between the 7th and 10th centuries, owing partly to Slavic influence.

The account favored by most Romanians is that they—and their language—are the descendants of the Vulgar LATIN–speaking Roman soldiers (*veterani*) and settlers who occupied the Roman province of Dacia, in particular after military campaigns under the Emperor Trajan, from 101 until about 271 or 274 when the army and administration, at least, under Emperor Aurelian were obliged, under pressure from the Visigoths, to cross the Danube. Supported by archeological evidence and folk customs, it is held that the common people persisted in their Latinity/"romanitate" down through the ages.

A rival theory states that the Romanians are latter-day arrivals from south of the Danube, where Latin continued to be spoken after the exodus of the Romans from Dacia, and that these migrants known as *Vlachs*, a sheepherding people, reintroduced their Latin into the former Roman province.

In any event, the Latin origin of Romanian is not disputed, even though much of its Latinate aspect has been achieved through re-Latinization via French (see below); historically speaking, the lexicon has had numerous Slavic words, and it shows some grammatical similarities (for example, the numerical system) with Slavic. In addition, Romanian and ALBANIAN share a number of terms that may reflect a Daco-Thraco-Illyrian substratum.

Unlike the other Romance languages, Romanian, the easternmost of the Romance languages, shares non-Romance features with some of its genetically unrelated Balkan neighbors, such as the postposed definite article (Albanian, BULGARIAN, MACEDONIAN), and also a predilection for the "subjunctive" vis-à-vis the infinitive.With the demise of the last speaker of Dalmatian (Vegliote) in 1898, Romanian is the only Romance language extant in the Balkans.

Two Greek writers of the seventh century mention the words *Torna, torna, fratre* ('turn back, brother'), spoken by a soldier in the Byzantine army during a campaign in Thrace in 587. While this may be the first written evidence of Romanian, solid attestation is very late and dates to 1521 in a letter to Mayor Benckner of Braşov, Transylvania.

Orthography and Basic Phonology

The Cyrillic alphabet was replaced by the Latin alphabet after the union of the principalities Moldavia and Wallachia in 1859, and was only recently adopted in Moldova. Hence, with the principal exception of <i>, it offers an excellent "fit" between sound and grapheme. Three diacritics (ş ţ ă â î) extend the spelling system.

Romanian has a productive phonological process whereby voiceless and velar stops /k/ and /g/ before /i/ and /e/ give affricates /č/ and /ğ/. This palatalization is not indicated directly in the orthography; /k/ and /č/ are both written *c*: *copac* [kopak] 'tree', *copaci* [kopač] 'trees'; /g/ and /ğ / are written *g*: *fag* [fag] 'beech (tree)', *fagi* [fağ] 'beechtrees'. Palatalization of dental stops /t/ and /d/ before /i/ gives, respectively,

Table 1: Consonants

		Labial	Labiodental	Dental	Alveo-palatal	Velar	Glottal
Stops	Voiceless	p		t		k	
	Voiced	b		d		g	
Fricatives	Voiceless		f	s	š		h
	Voiced		v	z	ž		
Affricates	Voiceless			c=ts	tš		
	Voiced				dž		
Nasals		m		n			
Resonants				l, r			
Glides		w			j		

voiceless dental affricate *ţ* /c/=/ts/ and voiced dental fricative *z* /z/: *bărbat* [bərbat] 'man', *bărbaţi* [bərbacị̥] 'men'; *aud* [a(w)ud] '(1sg) hear', *auzi* [a(w)uzị̥] '(2sg) hear'. Palatalization of dental fricative /s/ before /i/ yields alveo-palatal *ş* /š/: *pus* [pus] '(past part) put, placed'. Complex palatalizations also occur in {-esc} adjectives and verbs: *vorbesc* [vorbesk] '(1sg) speak', *vorbeşti* [vorbeštị̥] '(2sg) speak'.

Table 2: Vowels

	Front	Central	Back
High	i	ɨ	u
Mid	e	ə	o
Low		a	

The central vowels /ə/ and /ɨ/ are written *ă* and *â* or *î*, respectively.

Among the Romance languages, Romanian is unusual for its internal vocalic modifications produced via umlaut, the most common of which are the accented front and back midvowels /é/ and /ó/, alternating with /e̯á/ (or /já/) and /o̯á/ (or /wá/) respectively, before final schwa and schwa or /-e/, e.g., *des, deasă* 'thick', *fereastră* 'window' (pl. *ferestre*), *vostru* 'your', (*voastră* fem., *voastre* fem-neut. pl.).

With a preceding labial or palatal consonant the diphthong is reduced to, e.g., *fată* 'girl', vs. **feată*, *fete* pl., *iarnă* 'winter', *ierni* pl. In word-final position high vowels may elide before low, for example, *nu am fost* ~ *n-am fost* 'I wasn't', *mă întreb* ~ *mă-ntreb* 'I wonder'.

Basic Morphology

Romanian nouns are considered to occur in either of three genders (masculine, feminine, neuter) or two (neuter sin-gular = masculine, neuter plural = feminine). Unlike all the other modern Romance languages, Romanian nouns inflect for case (nominative/accusative, genitive/dative, and, to a lesser extent, vocative) via a postposed definite article. As in Italian, Romanian plurals are formed with vocalic endings.

Masculine singulars usually end in a consonant or *-e*; they are pluralized by adding *-i*, phonetically voiceless [ị̥] (e.g., *bărbat* 'man' *bărbaţi* 'men', *domn* 'gentleman' *domni* 'gentlemen', *frate* 'brother' *fraţi* 'brothers'). Feminine singulars usually end in a schwa or, occasionally, in *-á*; they are pluralized by *-e* or *-i* , or, occasionally, *-le* (e.g., *casă* 'house' *case* 'houses', *carte* 'book' *cărţi* 'books', *stea* 'star', *stele* 'stars'). Neuter plurals commonly end in *-e* or in *-uri*, the latter a reflection of Latin *-ora* and characteristic of some feminine plurals as well (e.g., *treabă* 'business, affair', *treburi*).

The genitive/dative forms of singular and plural masculine and neuter nouns are identical to the nominative/accusative forms. In contrast, the genitive/dative of *both* the singular and plural of the feminine nouns is like the nominative/accusative plural.

The definite article is postposed to nouns, as shown below, and also to adjectives.

		Nominative/Accusative	Genitive/Dative
Singular	Masc	-l	-lui
	Neut	-l	-lui
	Fem	-a	-i, -ei
Plural	Masc	-i	-lor
	Fem	-le	-lor
	Neut	-le	-lor

A transitional *-u-* ([u] or [w]) links a masculine/neuter noun stem ending in a consonant or a feminine noun in *-á* with the definite article (e.g., *domn* 'gentleman' *domnul* 'the gentleman' *domnului* 'to/of the gentleman', *stea* 'star' *steaua* 'the star'). In masculine/neuter nouns ending in *-e*, an additional riming *-e* is added to the definite article (e.g., *frate* 'brother' *fratele* 'the brother').

The genitive/dative articles *lui, ei, lor,* etc. also exist as free forms meaning 'of/to him', 'of/to her', 'of/to them'. The phrase *domnul lui* 'his master' differs from *domnului* 'of/to the master' in that the latter has diminished stress on *lui*.

In the popular language, the oblique synthetic cases are rivaled by prepositions:

geam-ul	uşi-i	
glass-the/NOM	door-the/GEN	'the glass of the door'

geam-ul de la uşă
glass-the/NOM from door/NOM 'the glass from the door'

Personal pronouns are marked for person, number, and case (nominative, accusative, dative). Third-person pronouns also code gender. Subject pronouns are used, as in Italian, PORTUGUESE, and Spanish, for emphasis:

	Singular		Plural	
First person	eu	'I'	noi	'me'
Second person	tu	'you'	voi	'you'
Third person, masc	el	'he, it'	ei	'they'
Third person, fem	ea	'she, it'	ele	'they'

Romanian also has alternate subject pronouns whose use depends on degree of politeness, intimacy, etc.:

	Singular	Plural
Second person	dumneata mata, matale	dumneavoastră
Third person, masc	dumnealui, dânsul	dumnealor, dânşii
Third person, fem	dumneaei, dânsa	dumnealor, dânsele

The first ones mean literally 'your/his/her/their dignity'.

Apart from such subject forms, Romanian personal pronouns are renowned for their morphophonemically determined variants, as in the various functions of *el* [jel] 'he, it': accented/unaccented, direct/indirect object, before/after a vowel, as indirect object combined with a direct object, as object of a preposition, as a reflexive.

	Use	Form
Unaccented	Direct Object	îl [ɨl]
	Before a vowel	l-
	After a vowel	-l
	Indirect Object	îi [ɨj]
	Before a vowel	i- [j-]
	After a vowel	-i [-j]
	Indirect, with direct *se*	i [i]
Accented	Direct Object	(pe) el [jel]
	Indirect Object	lui [luj]
	Object of preposition	(*cu*, etc.) el [jel]
Reflexives Unaccented	Direct Object	se
	Before a vowel	s-
	Indirect Object	îşi [ɨši]
	Before a vowel	şi- [šj-]
	After a vowel	-şi [-ši]
Accented	Direct Object	sine
	Indirect Object	sie(şi) [sije(šj)]

Romanian verbs occur in four conjugation classes. Infinitives in all classes are marked by the preposition *a*: I *a cânta* 'to sing', II *a vedea* 'to see', III *a merge* 'to walk', IV *a vorbi* 'to speak'. Verbs agree with their subjects in person and number, as illustrated below with the present tense of *a vedea* 'to see':

	Singular	Plural
First person	văd	vedem
Second person	vezi	vedeţi
Third person	vede	văd

Additional tenses are both simple (imperfect, pluperfect, and, regionally, simple past) and compound (present perfect, future perfect, and the future [three constructions]). There are also compound conditional and conditional perfect forms. The first person singular forms of *a merge* 'to walk' in these various tense forms appear below:

Form	Indicative	Subjunctive
Present	merg	să merg
Imperfect	mergeam	
Pluperfect	mersesem	
Simple Past	mersei	
Present Perfect	am mers	să fi mers
Future Perfect	voi fi mers o să fi mers	
Future	voi merge o să merg am să merg	
Conditional	aş merge	
Conditional Perfect	aş fi mers	

The present perfect consists of an auxiliary from *avea* 'have' (in the above example, *am*) followed by the past participle. This participle is also part of the future perfect and conditional perfect forms. *Fi* in the future perfect and conditional perfect forms illustrated is the verb 'be', here also in the sense 'have'. *Voi* and *o* in the future and future perfect are reduced forms of *a vrea* 'to wish, will'.

Basic Syntax

Word order in Romanian is somewhat free, and can be varied for emphasis.

Eu nu ştiu
I NEG know:1SG 'I don't know.'

Ştiu eu
know-1sg I
'How am I supposed to know?' (lit. 'I know?')

Adjectives generally follow the nouns they modify: *noapte bună* (night good) 'good night'. Demonstratives may precede the nouns they modify, but more usually follow, in which case the noun also has a definite article and the adjective a deictic particle:

această carte cartea aceasta
this book book-the this-DEICTIC PART
'this book'

The possessive must follow the noun and the noun also has a postposed agglutinated definite article: *mam-a mea* (mother-the my) 'my mother'.

Negative sentences are formed with *nu* (*nu pot* 'I can't'), which also means 'no'. Other negatives include adverbs *nicăieri* 'nowhere' and *niciodată* 'never', and pronouns *nimeni* 'nobody' and *nimic* 'nothing', *nimeni nu mi-a spus nimic* 'nobody told me anything'.

Contact with Other Languages

External influence is most felt on the lexicon of Romanian, although the effect was often exaggerated in past claims that the Slavic element was as high as 40 percent, leaving out of the equation the concept of "circulation" (= relative frequency) of the vocabulary. Basic word lists show the weighted Latin basis to be over 90 percent.

Words cognate with Albanian and thus possibly from the substratum include Romanian *copac* 'tree', *rață* 'duck'.

Adstratum Slavic loans came from two groups, popular words from South Slavic (Bulgarian), starting in the 6th century, and literary terms from the 13th, many of which, especially the religious terms, are themselves of GREEK origin. Other Greek terms entered Romanian in the Phanariot period (18th–early 19 century). In terms of frequency (not necessarily cultural value) the lexical contributions of Turkish and Hungarian to Romanian are low.

Western Romance influence was particularly strong, especially as exerted by the "Transylvanian School," which greatly contributed to the language by combining French with Classical Latin, e.g., Romanian *echilibru* (< French *équilibre* + Latin *aequilibrium*), and countless others.

From Latin: *arbore* 'tree' (< Lat. *arbore*), *câine* 'dog' (< Lat. *cane*), *fapt* 'deed' (< Lat. *factu* 'done')
From Slavic: *nevastă* 'wife', *drag* 'dear'
From Greek: *dascăl* 'teacher', *drum* 'road'
From Turkish: *odaie* 'room', *dușman* 'enemy'
From Hungarian: *oraș* 'city', *gând* 'thought'

Common Words

man:	bărbat	long:	lung
woman:	femeie	small:	mic
water:	apă	yes:	da
sun:	soare	no:	nu
three:	trei	good:	bun
fish:	pește	bird:	pasăre
big:	mare	dog:	câine
tree:	arbore		

Example Sentences

(1) Du-te și te plimbă prin
lead-2SG and 2SG/IMPERATIVE/REFL walk through

curte, însă bagă de seamă să nu
courtyard however observe that NEG

cazi.
2SG/SUBJUNCTIVE. fall
'Go take a walk in the courtyard, but be careful not to fall.'

(2) Acest lucru e mai ușor de făcut în România
this thing be:3SG more easy of done in Romania

datorită faptului că toate editurile
owing fact-the-to that all publishing houses-the

nu mai sânt ale statului.
NEG more be-3PL of state-the-of
'This thing is more easily done in Romania owing to the fact that all the publishing houses no longer belong to the state.'

(3) Această înlocuire a vocativului cu
this replacement of vocative-the-of with

nominativul o găsim și la alte cuvinte.
nominative-the it find:1PL also at other words
'This replacement of the vocative by the nominative we also find in other words.'

Efforts to Preserve, Protect, and Promote the Language

Standard Romanian is the language of administration and most higher education, although minority languages (such as Romany, Hungarian, and GERMAN) thrive in some communities where the latter two, especially, have been used in primary and secondary education, newspapers, theater, etc.

Since about 1970 there have been efforts to make the Romanian language better known in the United States. Modest programs have depended largely on the presence of Romanian scholars on the Fulbright-Hays program. By far the most successful attempt has been at Ohio State University.

Select Bibliography

Agard, Frederick B. 1958. "Structural Sketch of Rumanian." *Language* monograph no. 26, July–Sept.

Carlton, C.M. 1993–1995. "Romanian and its Place in 'The Romania.'" In *Revue romaine de linguistique*, 38:6, 531–546.

Close, Elisabeth. 1974. *The Development of Modern Rumanian-Linguistic Theory and Practice in Muntenia 1821–1838*. Oxford: Oxford University Press.

Juilland, Alphonse, *et al.* 1965. *Frequency Dictionary of Rumanian Words*. The Hague: Mouton.

Lombard, Alf. 1974. *La Langue roumaine: Une présentation*. Paris: Klincksieck.

Mallinson, Graham. 1986. *Rumanian*. London and Dover, NH: Croom Helm.

Sala, Marius, *et al.* 1989. *Vocabularul reprezentativ al limbilor romanice*. Bucharest: Editura Științifică și Enciclopedică.

Rundi

Patrick R. Bennett

Language Name: Rundi. **Alternates:** *Kirundi, ikiRuúndi.*

Location: Burundi, where it is the language of nearly the entire population. It is also spoken in parts of Tanzania.

Family: Central Bantu group (classed by Malcolm Guthrie as D62; reclassified by Belgian researchers as J62) of the Benue-Congo subbranch of the Niger-Congo branch of the Niger-Kordofanian language family.

Related Languages: The closest relatives are KINYARWANDA and Ha. More distant relatives include LUGANDA and Nyankore. Most of the neighboring languages in Tanzania and Zaire are Bantu and are at least distantly related.

Dialects: There is only minimal dialect variation within Rundi, mostly involving lexical differences and some variation in tonal behavior.

Number of Speakers: 4–5 million.

Origin and History

It is clear that Rundi's closest connections are to the north and east of Burundi; it is generally agreed that the origins of the Bantu languages are to be sought further north and west, from somewhere in the area where Nigeria and Cameroon meet. However, our understanding of how the present-day languages developed is still minimal. The earliest grammatical work was *Eléments d'une grammaire kirundi*, by J.M. van der Burgt, published in 1902; his *Dictionnaire français-kirundi* appeared in 1903. Since the first records we have, Rundi has changed very little. The major changes observed are, as might be expected, in vocabulary. In addition to the constant change found in every language, there has been impact from FRENCH, SWAHILI, and other languages, in part related to the great changes in culture and technology since the turn of the century.

For the origins and history of the people, we rely in large part on oral tradition. A problem for reconstructing origins has been the division of the Rundi into three groups: Batwa, Bahutu, and Batutsi, which some take to reflect three ethnic groups that came to be in the same area. The Batutsi have been seen as relatively recent Cushitic invaders from Ethiopia. While the area of Burundi was inhabited by an Iron Age population as early as about 500 B.C., there is no way to tell how, if at all, that population was related to the Rundi speakers of today, and, of course, we have no indication of their language. The oral traditions indicate the rise of kingdoms in the 16th and 17th centuries, with expansion in the 18th century. By the end of the 19th century European penetration had begun. Burundi was the Belgian colony of Urundi until independence in 1962.

Orthography and Basic Phonology

Rundi is written in an alphabet based on that of LATIN. Some spelling conventions are based on French orthography, while others are based on ENGLISH.

Rundi affricates are voiceless; however, the voiced fricatives are sometimes slightly affricated.

The voiced bilabial stop /b/ is realized as a bilabial fricative [β] between vowels; this [β] is distinct from the labio-dental fricative /v/.

The pronunciation of /w/ and /y/ following a consonant depends on the place and manner of articulation of the consonant. After labials, /w/ is a velar stop: *imbwá* 'dog' [imbgá]; a velar stop is inserted between an alveolar stop and a following /w/: *gutwáara* 'carry' [gutkwáara]. A velar stop is likewise inserted between /r t d s/ and a following /y/; the sequences *fy* and *vy* are pronounced [fsy] and [vzy], respectively (see Table 2 on the following page).

Velar stops are palatalized before front vowels.

Rundi voiceless stops are aspirated; following nasals, little or no stop element is audible: *impú* 'hide' is pronounced [im^{p}hú].

The palatal nasal *ny* [ñ] is phonemically distinct from a sequence of *n* + *y* [ny].

Table 1: Vowels

	Front	Central	Back
High	i		u
Mid	e		o
Low		a	

Rundi vowels can be either long or short.

Rundi has four tones, high, low, falling, and rising. Tone and vowel lengths are not always marked. When they are marked, long vowels are written double (*aa* = [ā]), and tones are marked with accents (*á* high tone, *à* low tone, *â* falling tone, *ǎ* rising tone).

Basic Morphology

Most Rundi nouns consist of a stem and a prefix. A few nouns, like *sé* 'father', consist of a stem without a prefix. The stem

Table 2: Consonants

		Labial	Alveolar	Alveo-palatal	Palatal	Velar	Glottal
Stops	Voiceless	p	t			k	
	Voiced	b	d			g	
Fricatives	Voiceless	f	s	sh	shy		h
	Voiced	v	z	j	jy		
Affricates		pf	ts	c	cy		
Nasals		m	n		ny		
Tap			r				
Glides					y	w	

may be a single morpheme, a compound, or a derived noun. The prefix in most cases indicates which of 16 noun classes the noun belongs to. There is a tendency for nouns with related meanings to fall into the same class. Thus, most nouns representing human beings are in Class 1 in the singular and Class 2 in the plural. However, it would be wrong to speak of the "meaning" of a particular class.

The same noun can occur in more than one class, with changes of meaning. Thus, *umw-áana* 'child' is in Class 1; its plural, *ab-áana* is in Class 2. Other forms based on this stem are: *am-áana* 'childish prattle' (Class 6), *ic-áana* 'young (singular) of an animal' (Class 7), *ivy-áana* 'young (plural) of an animal' (Class 8), *iny-ánà* 'calves' (Class 9/10), *rw-áana* 'childishly' (Class 11), *utw-áana* 'babies' (Class 12), *ak-áana* 'baby' (Class 13), and *ubw-áana* 'childhood' (Class 14).

Adjectives agree in class with the nouns that they modify.

Rundi verbs typically agree with their subjects in person and number, and in the case of third person, in class. This agreement is indicated by a subject prefix comparable to the noun class prefixes discussed above: *m-bariira* 'I'm sewing', *u-bariira* 'you're sewing', *a-bariira* 's/he's sewing'. Each Rundi verb has an imperfective stem, usually ending in *-a*, and a perfective stem, ending in the suffix *-ye*; the /y/ of this stem may cause change in or loss of the stem-final consonant. Thus, the perfective equivalent of *abariir-a* is *abarir-iye*.

Rundi has a complex system of verbal inflection marking four tenses, two aspects, and six moods. These categories are marked by combinations of prefixes, suffixes, and tonal patterns. For example, *ntuuzóobáriira* 'you will not sew' is made up of *nti-* 'negative', *u-* 'you', *-zoo-* 'future', *-bariir-* 'sew', and *-a* 'imperfective'. The overall tone pattern is determined by the set of components in the form.

Rundi has a set of derivational suffixes that function to indicate changes in case relationships of nouns in the sentence. For instance, in addition to *kurima* 'cultivate', we have *kurimwa* 'be cultivated', *kurimira* 'cultivate for someone', *kurimiisha* 'make/help someone cultivate', and *kurimana* 'cultivate together'.

Basic Syntax

The basic word order in Rundi is SVO. If there are two objects, the beneficiary or recipient will precede the direct object.

Within noun phrases, demonstratives precede nouns; adjectives and numerals follow. In possessive phrases, the noun denoting the possessor follows the noun denoting that which is possessed.

In addition to prefixal markers like *ku-* 'at, to', *mu-* 'in', *na-* 'with', Rundi has a number of independent markers of positional or temporal relationships. Most of these, like *mbere* 'before', are structurally nouns; *inyuma y'inzu* 'behind the house' could be translated literally 'back of the house'.

Negative verbs have *nti* prefixed to the subject marker; there may also be changes in tone pattern. The negative of *u-zoo-bariir-a* 'you will sew' is *ntu-u-zóo-báriir-a* 'you won't sew'. (In this form, the /i/ of *nti* has been assimilated to the *u* of the second person singular subject marker.)

Contact with Other Languages

In addition to neighboring Bantu languages and non-Bantu languages met far back in prehistory, we know that Rundi has had contact with ARABIC (mostly trade), Swahili (trade, education, ongoing communication with Tanzania), GERMAN (missionaries and expeditions from German East Africa), French and to a lesser degree Flemish (missionaries, Belgian colonial administration, education), and English (ongoing communication with East Africa).

Although there have been recent attempts to eliminate most obvious borrowings from colonial languages, Rundi has absorbed numerous loanwords from French and Swahili. There are items that derive from Arabic or English, but it is usually impossible to determine whether these entered Rundi directly from the source language or through Swahili. A noun like *poolisí* 'policeman' could be from Swahili *polisi*, English "police" or French *police*. Borrowings from Bantu languages other than Swahili almost certainly exist, but cannot readily be identified.

Recent borrowings are often unassimilated in phonology and morphology. Thus *leeta* 'state' (<French *l'état)* may be heard either with a non-Rundi *l* or with *r*; unlike normal nouns, it has no class prefix. The tendency, however, is to assimilate; *umusuguti* 'scout' is indistinguishable from a native Rundi word.

From French: *ibitalo* 'hospital' (<*hôpital*), *perezidá* 'president' (<président)
From Swahili: *igitabu* 'book' (<*kitabu*), *umucúungwá* 'orange' (<*chungwa*)

Common Words

man:	umugabo	small:	-tó
woman:	igì'ti	yes:	eegó
water:	amáazi	no:	oya
sun:	izúuba	good:	-iizá
three:	-tatu	bird:	inyoni
fish:	ifí	dog:	imbwá
big:	-níni	tree:	igǐti
long:	-ree- -re (e.g., *igǐti kireekire* 'a tall tree')		

Example Sentences

(1) mu-ra-tú-zi-báriir-i-ye.
2PL-DISJUNCT-1PL/CL10-sew-BENEFIC-PERFECTIVE
'You have sewn them for us.'

(2)

a-vuz-e	ngw'-iki-báanza	n'-ícy-iizá.
CL1-say-PERFECTIVE	QUOT-CL7-site	AFFIRMATIVE-CL7-good

'He said that the place is good.'

(3)

uru-kúund-o	ru-ta-rí-mw-ó	umu-kúunz-i	ntí-ru-raamb-á.
CL11-love-ACTION	CL11-NEG-be-LOC-NOM	CL1-love-AGENT	NEG-CL11-last-IMPERFECTIVE

'Love where there is no lover does not last.'

Efforts to Preserve, Protect, and Promote the Language

The principal movement is an attempt, as has been seen in other languages of the area, to expand the vocabulary to accommodate new technology without drawing on loanwords, although this is something of a wasted effort; technological vocabulary is best created by its users, and some pseudonative neologisms are much more awkward than a borrowing would be.

Select Bibliography

Bigangara, Jean-Baptiste. 1982. *Eléments de linguistique burundaise.* Bujumbura: Collection, Expression et valeurs africaines burundaises.

Meeussen, A.E. 1959. *Essai de Grammaire Rundi.* Tervuren: Annales du Musée Royale du Congo Belge .

Mioni, Alberto M. 1970. *Problèmes de linguistique, d'orthographe et de coordination culturelle au Burundi.* Naples: Istituto Universitario Orientale.

Mworoha, Emile, *et al.* 1987. *Histoire du Burundi des origines a la fin du XIXe siècle.* Paris: Hatier.

Rodegem, F.M. 1970. *Dictionnaire Rundi-Français.* Tervuren: M.R.A.C.

RUSSIAN

Thomas R. Beyer

Language Name: Russian. **Autonym:** *russkij jazyk.*

Location: The Russian Federation (*Rossijskaja federacija*) and also in many of the former republics of the Soviet Union. Russian was frequently used as the language of communication between Russians and citizens in eastern European countries where Russian was a required language in most schools.

Family: Russian is the Northeastern subgroup of the Eastern Slavic group of the Slavic branch of Indo-European.

Related Languages: BELORUSSIAN and UKRAINIAN, both of the Eastern Slavic group.

Dialects: Universal education and a system of norms of language dictated from Moscow have resulted in a fairly standardized language among educated people. Standard modern Russian is most closely related to that spoken in and around Moscow. Dialectical differences occur across the broad expanse of Russia and are often distinguished by the pronunciation of certain vowel sounds in unstressed positions: so-called *akan'je, okan'je, ikan'je, jakan'je.* Another dialectical feature is the replacement of the velar stop [g] with a laryngeal fricative [h], mostly in southern areas.

Since Russian was also a required second language in the former Soviet republics, it was and is often spoken with distinctive national accents, such as ARMENIAN, GEORGIAN, and Estonian.

Number of Speakers: 154 million ethnic Russians. 250–300 million, including inhabitants of Russia and the former Soviet Union.

Origin and History

The Slavs were some of the last Indo-Europeans to migrate into Central and southern Europe, where their presence is confirmed in the 6th century. Precise dating of early movements is complicated because of the lack of early Slavic written records. The language used by the Slavs was mutually comprehensible as late as the 9th century even as the tribes had separated into distinctive political groupings and three major linguistic families had emerged: South Slavic, Western, and Eastern Slavic (these latter two are sometimes referred to as Northern Slavic). The political center of the Eastern Slavs was Kievan Rus' from the 9th to the 12th centuries. This unity was destroyed by the invasions of the Mongols in the 13th century and subsequent occupation that resulted in an isolation of Russian from what developed as the Ukrainian and Belorussian languages.

The literary language was heavily influenced by Old Church Slavic (based on Southern Slavic), and debates in the 18th and the beginning of the 19th centuries over the composition of a Russian literary language were resolved only with the emergence of Alexander Pushkin as a national poet in the first quarter of the 19th century. Also during that century, writers such as Pushkin, Chekhov, Tolstoy, Dos-toyevsky, Turgenev, and Gogol wrote enduring masterpieces of world fiction in the Russian language.

Orthography and Basic Phonology

Russian used the Cyrillic alphabet dating to the 9th century. Kievan Rus' officially accepted Christianity in 988 along with the Cyrillic alphabet used primarily for the Old Church Slavic of religious texts. Modest reforms to the writing system were made under Peter the Great. The last reform of the Russian orthographic system occurred in 1918 after the 1917 Great October Socialist Revolution. The alphabet consists of 21 consonant letters, 10 vowel letters and two signs: the hard and soft signs.

Table 1: The Cyrillic Alphabet

Cyrillic	Transcription	Cyrillic	Transcription
Аа	a	Рр	r
Бб	b	Сс	s
Вв	v	Тт	t
Гг	g	Уу	u
Дд	d	Фф	f
Ее	je, e	Хх	x
Ёё	jo, o	Цц	c
Жж	ž	Чч	č
Зз	z	Шш	š
Ии	i	Щщ	šč
Йй	j	Ъъ	"
Кк	k	Ыы	y
Лл	l	Ьь	'
Мм	m	Ээ	e
Нн	n	Юю	ju
Оо	o	Яя	ja
Пп	p		

Most Russian consonants come in pairs, palatalized (soft) and nonpalatalized (hard). The palatalization of a consonant is indicated in the orthography either by the following vowel or by the use of a soft sign. In phonetic transcription, palatalized consonants are indicated by a following ': *ugol* 'corner' vs. *ugol'* 'coal'. The consonant /c/ is always hard, and /č/ is always soft.

Table 2: Consonants

	Labial	Dental	Palatal	Velar
Stops				
Voiceless	p	t		k
Voiced	b	d		g
Fricatives				
Voiceless	f	s	š	
Voiced	v	z	ž	x
Affricates				
Voiceless		c	č	
Nasals	m	n		
Resonants		l, r	j	

Voiced stops and fricatives are devoiced at the end of a word. In addition, Russian has progressive voicing assimilation: before a voiced consonant (except /v l m n/) a voiceless stop or fricative becomes voiced, and before a voiceless consonant a voiced stop or fricative becomes voiceless.

Table 3: Vowels

	Front	Central	Back
High	i	y	u
Mid	e		o
Low		a	

Russian has six vowel sounds, which are represented by 10 vowel letters. The vowels /u e o a/ are spelled differently depending on whether they follow a soft or a hard consonant. The soft vowel letters, when they occur at the beginning of a word, after another vowel, or after a hard or a soft sign, represent /ju je jo ja/. /y/ is a high, central, unrounded vowel.

Russian has only one stress per word, and unstressed vowels are reduced. Unstressed /o/ becomes [ʌ] if it is one syllable before the stress; two syllables before the stress or following the stress, it becomes [ə]. Unstressed /e/ is reduced to [i].

While not generally recognized as separate phonemes, /i/ and /y/ are clearly distinctive in modern Russian.

Basic Morphology

Russian nouns occur in three genders (masculine, feminine, and neuter) and are inflected for number (singular and plural) and case (nominative, genitive, dative, accusative, instrumental, and prepositional). The inflected forms of *studént* 'student' (masculine), *pis'mó* 'letter' (neuter), and *žénščina* 'woman' (feminine) are illustrated below.

A. Singular

Nominative	studént	pis'm-ó	žénščin-a
Genitive	studént-a	pis'm-á	žénščin-y
Dative	studént-u	pis'm-ú	žénščin-e
Accusative	studént-a	pis'm-ó	žénščin-u
Instrumental	studént-om	pis'm-óm	žénščin-oj
Prepositional	studént-e	pis'm-é	žénščin-e

B. Plural

Nominative	studént-y	pís'm-a	žénščin-y
Genitive	studént-ov	písem	žénščin
Dative	studént-am	pís'm-am	žénščin-am
Accusative	studént-ov	pís'm-a	žénščin
Instrumental	studént-ami	pís'm-ami	žénščin-ami
Prepositional	studént-ax	pís'm-ax	žénščin-ax

In the masculine accusative singular, a distinction is made between animate and inanimate nouns, e.g., *televizor* 'television, nominative and accusative', but *student* 'student, nominative' vs. *studenta* 'student, genitive and accusative'. A similar distinction is made for masculine and feminine nouns in the plural, where the inanimate accusative is identical to the nominative and the animate accusative is identical to the genitive, e.g., nominative *televizory, telegrammy*, Accusative *televizory, telegrammy*; nominative *studenty, studentki*, Accusative *studentov, studentok*.

Adjectives and other modifiers agree with the nouns they modify in gender, number, and case: *novyj student* 'new student' *o novom studente* 'about a new student', *staraja dama* 'old lady', *s staroj damoj* 'with an old lady'.

Russian verbs belong to one of two conjugations, and to either imperfective or perfective aspect. There are three tenses, present, past, and future. Imperfective verbs may occur in all three tenses, while perfective verbs may occur in past or future tense only.

Some perfective verbs are formed by adding a prefix to an imperfective verb: *govorít' -pogovorít* 'to speak/talk', *délat'-sdélat'* 'to do'. Many pairs have an imperfective in the first conjugation with the perfective verb belonging to the second conjugation: *končát'-kónčit* 'to finish', *povtorját'-povtorít'* 'to repeat'. Many imperfective verbs were derived from perfective verbs by adding *-yva-* after the stem and before the ending: *pokázyvat'-pokazát* 'to show', *proígryvat'-proigrát'* 'to lose'.

Present tense forms of the first conjugation verb *znát* 'to know' and the second conjugation verb *govorít'* 'to speak' are illustrated below.

Infinitive	znat'		govorít'	
	Singular	Plural	Singular	Plural
1st per.	zná-ju	zná-em	govor-jú	govor-ím
2nd per.	zná-ěš'	zná-ete	govor-íš'	govor-íte
3rd per.	zná-et	zná-jut	govor-ít	govor-ját

The verbs *znát* and *govorít'* are imperfective. When perfective stems occur in this paradigm, they are future tense. Thus, inflected forms of *yznát'* 'to recognize' (derived from *znát'*) such as *yznáj-u, yzná-em* mean 'I will recognize', 'we will recognize'.

The past tense is formed by the addition of the marker *-l* to the infinitive stem. Past tense verbs agree with their subjects in number and, in the singular, in gender. Unlike present and future tense verbs, past tense verbs do not indicate first, second, or third person. *Olég zna-l* (Oleg know-PAST.M.SG) 'Oleg knew', *Maša skazá-la* (Masha say-PAST.F.SG) 'Masha said', *Oknó bý-lo otkrýt-o* (window be-PAST.NEUT.SG open-NEUT.SG) 'The window was open', *Oní priéxa-li* (they arrive-PAST.PL) 'They arrived'.

The compound future tense is formed by combining a conjugated form of the verb *byt'*: *Ja búd-u slúšat'* (I be-1SG listen-INFIN) 'I will listen'.

Basic Syntax

Russian word order is relatively free; the function of a word is determined by its ending and not by its position in the sentence. As a general rule, old or known information is followed by the new information, sometimes resulting in the subject appearing after the predicate: *Priexal v gorod novyj student* (arrived in town new student) 'A new student arrived in town'.

Adjectives usually precede the nouns they modify, and adverbs generally precede verbs: *Novjy student ploxo govorit po-russki* (new student poorly speaks Russian) 'The new student speaks Russian poorly'.

Negation in Russian is relatively simple, formed by preceding any word with the negative particle *ne*, e.g., *On ne znaet urok* (He NEG knows lesson) 'He doesn't know the lesson', *On znaet ne pervyj urok, a vtoroj urok* (He knows NEG first lesson but second lesson) 'He doesn't know the first lesson, but the second lesson'. Russian does permit what appears to be a double negative: *On nikogda ne znaet urok* (He never NEG knows lesson) 'He never knows the lesson'.

Contact with Other Languages

Historically, Russian has been enriched by its neighbors (GREEK, TURKISH, and in the 17th century, POLISH). During the 18th century Western European languages were an influence, in particular GERMAN, FRENCH, and DUTCH.

From German: *láger'* 'camp'
From French: *pljaž* 'beach', *ètáž* 'floor'
From Chinese: *čaj* 'tea'
From ENGLISH: *ófis* 'office', *komp'júter* 'computer'

One of the official languages of the United Nations, spoken in the largest country in the world and by millions in the now neighboring countries, Russian continues to be a language of communication for hundreds of millions. Yet since the use of Russian was propagated by the former Soviet Union, the impact of local languages upon it has been minor. The major influence on Russian in most recent years has been the large-scale influx of English words in order to provide a vocabulary for Western-style market economy, management, and governance that has been newly introduced into Russia. The increasing use of computer technology has likewise expanded the use of English cognates significantly.

Common Words

man:	mužčína	small:	málen'kij
woman:	žénščina	yes:	da
water:	vodá	no:	net
sun:	sólnce	good:	xoróšij
three:	tri	bird:	ptíca
fish:	rýba	dog:	sobáka
big:	bol'šój	tree:	dérevo
long:	dlínnyj		

Example Sentences

(1) Včerá ja víde-l Maksím-a i
yesterday I see-PAST.M.SG Maxim-M.SG.ACC and

Nín-u v nóv-om restorán-e.
Nina-F.SG.ACC in new-M.SG.PREP restaurant-M.SG.PREP
'Yesterday I saw Maxim and Nina in the new restaurant.'

(2) čto vy déla-ete pósle závtrak-a?
What you.PL do-IMPERF-2PL after breakfast-M.SG.GEN
'What are you doing after breakfast?'

(3) Kogdá oná priéd- et, s kem my
when she arrive.PERF-3SG with who:INST we

búd-em igrát'?
be-1PL play:INFIN
'When she arrives, with whom will we play?'

Efforts to Preserve, Protect, and Promote the Language

Far from being preserved or supported, the teaching of Russian in many countries has declined since its peak at the end of the Gorbachev era (1990). In countries freed from Soviet domination, people have chosen to replace Russian with English as the language of choice for their acquisition of a second language.

Select Bibliography

Comrie, Bernard, and Greville Corbett. 1993. *The Slavonic Languages*. London and New York: Routledge.
Falla, P.S. 1992. *The Oxford English-Russian Dictionary*. Oxford: Clarendon.
Schenker, Alexander M. 1995. *The Dawn of Slavic*. New Haven: Yale University Press.
Wade, Terrence. 1992. *A Comprehensive Russian Grammar*. Oxford and Boston: Blackwell.
Wheeler, Marcus. 1992. *The Oxford Russian-English Dictionary*. 2nd ed. Oxford: Clarendon.

SANGO

William J. Samarin

Language Name and Autonym: Sango. In the past Sango was called "vehicular Sango" or *Sango véhiculaire* in FRENCH. In Sango itself rural people called it *Sango ti turugu* 'soldier's Sango' or *Sango ti gara* 'marketplace Sango'.

Location: Sango is spoken in the Central African Republic (CAR) and known by small numbers of people across the political boundaries with Chad, Cameroon, and Zaire. A Sango-speaking community is also found in Brazzaville.

Family: Ubangian subgroup of the Adamawa-Ubangian group of the Niger-Congo branch of the Niger-Kordofanian language family.

Related Languages: Sango is directly related to a cluster of languages, including Ngbandi, Yakoma, and Dendi. It is more distantly related to Banda, Gbaya, and Zande.

Dialects: No distinct dialects characterize the language on a national scale. However, when used as a second language, speakers may have an accent based on their ethnic languages. Recent changes, moreover, are making the speech of Bangui, the capital and largest city, different in many ways from rural speech, but not enough to make comprehension difficult for Central African speakers. Creole, or creolized Sango, as spoken by native speakers of the language, is fundamentally the same language as Pidgin Sango.

Number of Speakers: About 2.5 million as first or second language. In CAR the percentage speaking Sango as a mother tongue is estimated, on the basis of the census of 1988, at about 17 percent, about 4/5 of whom live in Bangui; about 4/5 of the preschool children in Bangui in 1994 used Sango as their mother tongue.

Origin and History

Sango is in origin a pidgin language, one of few well-studied pidgins in the world based on a non-European language. (See, for an example of an ENGLISH-based pidgin, TOK PISIN). Sango developed in the last two decades of the 19th century when representatives of the Congo Free State (Belgians) and the French government took possession of the two sides of the Ubangi River. Alphonse Van Gele of Belgium spent a year among the Yakoma people buying ivory and establishing the claims of the Congo Free State in the region. The French established themselves in what came to be known as Bangui in 1889 and quickly made forays on the river and northward into the hinterland.

Since the Yakoma and their coethnics were riverine people, possessing canoes 20 meters in length and capable of carrying two tons of merchandise, these people figured importantly in the occupation of the territory. They provided canoes and canoers. It was therefore natural that the African employees and militiamen brought by the Europeans—men who came from as far away as Zanzibar and Senegal, among many others—should use (and imperfectly learn) this indigenous language. The pidgin that emerged was reduced in grammar and in lexicon. Some words from foreign languages were introduced including African as well as PORTUGUESE and French.

Once the language had become stable as a lingua franca, it did not appear to have changed very much until independence. Of course, first, Catholic missionaries and then Protestant ones employed it for religious purposes. They accepted the language for what it was and enriched it only with some religious terminology. They prepared the first dictionaries and grammars, and they published the first literature, religious naturally, in Sango. Since literacy in French in the colonial period was very limited, most of the literate people were literate in Sango.

Orthography and Basic Phonology

Up until recently there was no official orthography. The Protestants and Catholics had their own standard forms. An official orthography was adopted in 1991. However, there is no standardization of spelling. Tone is marked in the following manners: circumflex (^) is for high tone, umlaut/dieresis/trema (¨) for mid tone, and absence of diacritic for low tone. However, it has been argued that tone marking will be difficult to learn and will impede the acquisition of literacy. Because only a small number of people will become competent in the use of tone marking, it is elitist.

The labio-velar stops /kp/ and /gb/ involve a simultaneous labial and velar closure. The prenasal stops /mb nd ng ngb/ and fricatives /mv nz/ act as units in terms of the phonology; they are not clusters of a nasal followed by an oral stop (see Table 1 on the following page).

There is a certain amount of variation in pronunciation. For instance, /h/ is realized as a glottal stop in some parts of the country and in Bangui. Likewise, /z/ is [ž] in some regions.

R is an alveolar tap, as in SPANISH *pe*r̲*o*. For some speakers, however, under the influence of French, it is a uvular, as in French.

All of the vowels except the high-mid /e o/ can appear oral or nasalized. The distinction between the high-mid vowels /e o/ and their low-mid counterparts /ɛ ɔ/ is not represented in Sango

Table 1: Consonants

		Labial	Dental	Velar	Labio-velar	Glottal
Stops	Voiceless	p	t	k	kp	
	Voiced	b	d	g	gb	
	Pre-nasal	mb	nd	ng	ngb	
Fricatives	Voiceless	f	s			h
	Voiced	v	z			
	Pre-nasal	mv	nz			
Resonants			l, r			
Glides			y		w	

writing; the letters *e* and *o* are used both for high-mid and low-mid vowels.

Table 2: Vowels

	Front	Central	Back
High	i		u
High-Mid	e		o
Low-Mid	ɛ		ɔ
Low		a	

The contemporary pronunciation of many young people in Bangui is characterized by frequent contractions and other changes, as *sus* from *susu* 'fish', *âa* from *âla* 'they' in Example Sentence 1, and in Sentence 2, *sâa* from *sâra* 'do'.

Basic Morphology

Sango nouns may be marked as plural by the prefix *â-*, although this is not obligatory. In Bangui, a pattern of number agreement is emerging whereby all elements in a noun phrase are pluralized:

mbênî kôtâ zo
some large person 'an adult'

â-mbênî â-kôtâ â-zo
PL-some PL-large PL-person 'some adults'

There is no morphological marking of gender. However, gender can be marked syntactically, using the word *wâlï* 'woman': *kôndo* 'chicken', *wâlï kôndo* 'hen' (literally, 'woman chicken').

Sango has distinct pronouns for first person singular (*mbï*), second-person singular (*mo*), third-person singular (*lo*), and first-person plural (*ï*). In addition, *âla* is used for second- and third-person plural as well as for second-person singular deferential. There is no case marking.

Sango verbs are invariant in form. There is a predicate-marking prefix *a-* (distinguished from the plural prefix by its tone) that is used following a noun subject or for an unspecified subject, but not following a pronominal subject:

ngû a-pîka
water SUBJ-strike 'it's raining'

Verb aspect is marked with words rather than by affixation. There are three basic aspectual forms: preterite, irrealis (continuative, durative, future), and perfective.

mbï pîka lo
I hit 3-SG Preterite
'I hit him/her'

mbï ke pîka lo
I be hit 3-SG Irrealis
'I'm hitting him/her'/'I'm going to hit him/her'

mbï pîka lo awe
I hit 3-SG (it is) finished Perfective
'I've hit him/her'

Basic Syntax

The basic word order in Sango, as illustrated above, is SVO. Adjectives precede the nouns they modify. Sango has prepositions rather than postpositions.

Sentences in Sango are negated by the word *äpe* at the end of the clause:

lo mû na mbï äpe
s/he give to me neg
'She didn't give it to me.'

Contact with Other Languages

Sango acquired words from coterritorial languages and from Bantu and west African languages spoken by those who accompanied colonial government representatives, military personnel, traders, and missionaries into the area starting around 1887. Several of the names for wild animals and for food products are Banda in origin.

French influence on Sango was extensive during the colonial period, and its influence continues today with increased education. Whereas some speakers pronounce French words, even the older borrowings, in a close approximation of standard French, others continue to adapt them to Sango phonology. Code switching between French and Sango goes on among those fluent in French.

From French: *pûsu* 'push' (<*pousse*), *kumäsi* 'begin' (<*commencer*), *depîi* or *dipîi* 'for a long time' (<*depuis* 'since')
From Banda (or other Central African languages): *bâmarä* 'lion', *dambá* 'tail', *ndaramba* 'rabbit'
From Bantu: *bongö* 'cloth, clothing (of any kind)', *mafuta* 'oil, grease', *pîka* 'to hit, strike'

Common Words

man:	kôlï	long:	yongöro
woman:	wâlï	small:	kêtê
water:	ngû	yes:	ï̧ï̧
sun:	lâ	no:	î̧'i̧
three:	otä	good:	nzönî
big:	kôtâ	bird:	ndeke
dog:	mbo	tree:	këkë

Example Sentences

(1)

mo	bâa	â-susu	nî	a-sïgï	â-kôtâ	â-vokö
you	see	PL-fish	the	SUBJ-appear	PL-big	PL-black

susu	sô	âla	sïgï.
fish	this	they	appear

'The next thing, the fish appear, these big black fish; they appear.'

(2)

mbï	sâra	tî	mbï	mbeto	tî	gwe	mü-ngö	â-susu
I	do	of	me	fear	of	go	take-NOM	PL-fish

nî	awe.
the	have

'Me, I was afraid to go get the fish.'

(3)

â-îtä	tî	mbï	nî	a-tûku	na	terë	tî	mbï
PL-sibling	of	me	the	SUBJ-pour	on	body	of	me

a-hë	mbï.
SUBJ-laugh	me

'My sisters surrounded me and laughed at me.'

Efforts to Preserve, Protect, and Promote the Language

In 1960, immediately after independence from France, Sango was considered constitutionally the national language of the nation, and in 1994 co-official with French. In January 1965, a decree established the *Commission National pour l'Etude de Sango* ('National Committee for the Study of Sango'). In 1974 the *Institut Pédagogique National* (IPN, the 'National Pedagogical Institute') was established whose purpose was to initiate research on Sango and promote the teaching of the language in schools. It was replaced in 1983 by the *Institut National d'Education et de Formation* (INEF).

With help from UNESCO and other agencies, attempts have been made in the last decade or so to use Sango in the first grades of primary school and to increase literacy in the language. Plans are under way to teach Sango grammar in some schools. For this purpose linguistic terminology has been created, and there are designs to produce a Sango-Sango dictionary.

Sango is used on radio and television, the latter limited to the capital, for broadcasts of various kinds including news, practical advice, religious programs, etc. New terminology to replace French loans has been introduced on the radio. A considerable amount of commercially produced popular music is in Sango. Sango versions of indigenous folktales and proverbs have been published by the missions, but no indigenous literature has yet appeared.

Select Bibliography

Samarin, William J. 1966. "Self-annulling prestige factors among speakers of a creole language." In *Sociolinguistics: Proceedings of the UCLA Sociolinguistics Conference, 1964*, ed. William Bright, 188–213. The Hague: Mouton.

____. 1967. *A Grammar of Sango*. The Hague: Mouton.

____. 1971. "Salient and Substantive Pidginization." In *Pidginization and Creolization of Languages*, ed. Dell Hymes, 117–140. Cambridge: Cambridge University Press.

____. 1982a. "Colonization and Pidginization on the Ubangi River." In *Journal of African Languages and Linguistics*, 4: 1–42.

____. 1982b. "Goals, Roles, and Language Skills in Colonizing Central Equatorial Africa." In *Anthropological Linguistics* 24: 410–422.

____. 1989. "The Colonial Heritage of the Central African Republic: A Linguistic Perspective." In *The International Journal of African Historical Studies* 22: 697–711.

Sanskrit

Michael Witzel

Language Name: Sanskrit (*saṃskṛtam* 'the polished [language]'), traditionally also *devabhāṣā* 'the language of the gods'; in the oldest texts, sometimes *āryā vāk* 'the Aryan speech'.

Location: Originally, as Vedic Sanskrit, only in the greater Panjab (c. 1500 B.C.); subsequently all over South Asia, from Eastern Afghanistan to Assam, and from Kashmir/Nepal to Sri Lanka. As the language of culture and religion and lingua franca of the learned, it was also used outside south Asia, in Central and east Asia and especially in Southeast Asia, from Burma to Bali. Today, it is still spoken as a second (learned) language by many students, scholars and priests.

Family: A member of the Indo-Aryan branch of the Indo-Iranian subfamily of Indo-European, where it belongs to the Eastern Indo-European languages (Satem group). Sanskrit is the only representative of a number of Old Indo-Aryan dialects that have not extensively been preserved (Mitanni Indo-Aryan in northern Syria, Iraq c. 1400 B.C., etc., and various old northern Indian dialects).

Related Languages: Sanskrit is the historical ancestor (or close to the Old Indo-Aryan ancestor) of all Northern, i.e., New Indo-Aryan, languages of southern Asia, from PUNJABI and URDU to BANGLA, and from Kashmiri and NEPALI to HINDI, MARATHI, SINHALA and Gypsy (ROMANI); ditto, for all Middle Indo-Aryan languages (PALI and the various *Prākṛts*).

Outside Indo-Aryan, it is most closely related to Iranian, i.e., the Old Iranian languages Avestan and Old PERSIAN, the Middle Iranian languages (Pahlavi, SOGDIAN, Khotanese, Scythian, etc.), and to modern Iranian (Persian, TAJIK, KURDISH, BALOCHI, PASTHO, Ossete, etc.). More distant relationships within Indo-European (IE), of various degrees, exist with Baltic and Slavic, ARMENIAN and GREEK.

Dialects: The fiction of Indian (and some Western) grammarians is that Sanskrit has no dialects and is unchangeable in the form it has been described by the ingenious grammarian Pāṇini, a native of the extreme northwest, a place at the confluence of the Kabul and Indus Rivers. He formulated his grammar in some 4000 brief rules. In his work, he contrasted some features of the local Sanskrit (*bhāṣā*) of northwest Pakistan with some eastern forms and the (earlier) sacred form, Vedic, which he calls *chandas* ('meter').

Historically speaking, there are a number of forms of Sanskrit with several dialects and styles. The oldest and most archaic form is Vedic (c. 1500–500 B.C.), with some five subsequent layers from the language of the *Ṛgveda* down to that of the late Vedic Sūtras. Other, Old Indo-Aryan dialects are not well documented: Mitanni Indo-Aryan (IA), other non-*Ṛgvedic* IA, Pāṇini's northwestern *bhāṣā*, local forms of Vedic (Kuru-Pañcāla, *Prācī* 'eastern,' and subdialects such as that of Kurukṣetra).

A local form of Vedic Sanskrit was actively spoken by the educated down to the time of the Buddha (c. 500/400 B.C.) and Patañjali (c. 150 B.C.). At this time, the popular language (various forms of early Middle Indo-Aryan) was used in all sections of society, including the royal court. Indeed, the first inscriptions of southern Asia are in Middle Indo-Aryan (MIA) (Asoka's edicts, c. 250 B.C.), not in Sanskrit, which was only reintroduced in official documents about the beginning of our era (first in Mathura, later in Gujarat). When one refers to Sanskrit one usually thinks of its Epic-Classical form, while other varieties are specified (Vedic, Buddhist Sanskrit, etc.)

The Epic form of Sanskrit (beginning in the last centuries B.C.) was a lingua franca, the koine of traditional bards of northern India. It included eastern and western peculiarities and was heavily influenced by Middle Indo-Aryan in vocabulary, grammatical forms and syntax. The Great Epics, the *Mahābhārata* and the *Rāmāyaṇa*, are composed in this form of Sanskrit. The little studied language of the great medieval religious texts, the Purāṇas and Tantras, is similar.

The same applies to Buddhist Sanskrit (since the beginning of our era); it has several variants, from an almost MIA form with superficial Old Indo-Aryan (OIA) phonetic adjustment, to what we refer to now as Classical Sanskrit.

Classical Sanskrit is not directly based on any Vedic dialect. It first appears in the last centuries B.C.; around 150 B.C., in Patañjali's *Mahābhāṣya*, a commentary on Pāṇini's grammar that was composed a few centuries earlier. Classical Sanskrit follows the rules of Pāṇini's grammar closely though it does not make use of all forms he teaches (no subjunctive, or pitch accent). This has been the standard form since and has been used in poetry, handbooks of the indigenous sciences, in inscriptions, day-to-day administration and some official documents, including diplomatic ones. This form of Sanskrit is still used in modern articles and books, government publications and news broadcasts. Like medieval LATIN, it served and still serves as the lingua franca of the learned (*śiṣṭa*) all over the subcontinent and beyond. However, with the increasing distance of MIA, (and from the end of the first millennium onwards, of New Indo-Aryan [NIA]), Sanskrit became a second language that had to be actively learned in school. Sanskrit, always the dominant form of OIA, is still spoken as a second (learned) language by a small minority of South Asians, especially by students, scholars and priests who cannot communicate with each other in ENGLISH.

Even then, there are many very little studied medieval and modern local forms of Sanskrit. Some of them were clearly less educated varieties. Frequently, they are more or less heavily influenced by the local languages. For example, Nepalese Sanskrit has been subjected to a TIBETO-BURMESE language, Old Newari, resulting in loss of gender; North Indian Sanskrit is a calque on (early) NIA, imitating its participle-based verb forms; South Indian Sanskrit has been influenced by Dravidian languages and has negative verbs expressed by the prefix *a-* 'non-'.

Number of Speakers: Present statistics for the Indian Union, from the 1991 census, have 49,736 speakers of the then 846 million Indian nationals. Such data are not very reliable as traditional people will give Sanskrit as their first language, even though it virtually never is. The number will also differ per state, depending upon the percentage of Brahmins in their population.

Origin and History

Sanskrit, in its archaic Vedic form, originated from a common Indo-Iranian parent language in the greater Afghanistan/Panjab area during the early to mid–second millennium B.C. through a series of phonetic and grammatical developments, such as *ć*, > *ś*, *j̑* > *j*, *jh*> *h*, loss of *z*; several new formations, such as NOM.PL.INTR. *-āni*; new perfect forms without reduplication with medial *-e-* as in *sazde* > *sede* 'he has sat', *mene* 'he has thought'; the addition of *-u* in the third singular perfect, *jaga-u* 'he has gone'; and development of the absolutive, which is missing even in Iranian. Indo-Iranian itself is separated from common IE by a series of changes, some of which are common to the eastern IE Satem languages, such as labiovelars and velars resulting in velars (*k*, k^w > *k*) while palatals changed to affricates (*k̑* > *ć*), or the palatalization after high vowels, *is, us* > *iš, uš*.

The manner of the introduction of Vedic Sanskrit into the subcontinent is still a matter of much discussion. Clearly, the close relationship with Old Iranian (found between the Danube and Mongolia, the Urals and the Persian Gulf) and with the rest of IE indicates an origin outside the greater Panjab. The same is also shown by the more archaic Mitanni IA, as it lacks typical Indian features such as retroflexes and certain grammatical innovations. Rather, it is the actual model of introduction that should be updated. Research over the past few decades has indicated that, instead of the 19th-century "invasion model," it was a complicated pattern of a (repeated) introduction of an IA language and culture by pastoral bands and tribes that was followed by quick acculturation in the Panjab of *some* of the members of the localized cultures that succeeded the great Indus Civilization (2600–1900 B.C.). Some of these developments precede even the texts of the *Ṛgveda*. (Much of present Indian historiography regards the "Aryans" and the IA language, improbably, as autochthonous.)

Sanskrit is first extensively documented in an ancient collection of 1,028 hymns addressed to the gods, the *Ṛgveda* (c. 1500–1200 B.C.). A slightly earlier form is preserved in names of kings and divinities, and in terms connected with horses and horse racing as a relict among the non-IA Mitanni of northern Iraq and Syria (and some of their neighbors in Mesopotamia, Syria, and Palestine) from about the middle of the second to the beginning of the first millennium B.C. It must have split off from early IA a little earlier than Vedic but, due to the existence of the word for 'chariot' (*ratha*) and horse racing, after 2000 B.C. The Vedic dialect is still very closely related to Avestan, the Old Iranian language of Zoroaster and his followers, so that certain sentences look like two dialect variants: *tam mitram yajāmahe; təm miθrəm yazamaide* 'we worship (God) Mitra'.

Though Ṛgvedic Sanskrit was the educated koine of the poets of greater Panjab, it has some indications of popular speech as well (the wives of the gods use a popular and later on, common, form *kuru* 'do!' instead of the correct *kṛṇu*, etc.) Like other languages, Vedic underwent changes in phonetic shape, grammatical formations, and vocabulary. There are five stages from the RV down to the latest level, that of the *Upaniṣads* and *Sūtras*. The major features of changes include: phonetic simplification such as *gh* > *h* , C + *uv* > C + *v;* loss of forms and grammatical categories such as the injunctive, the moods of the perfect and of the aorist; development of new periphrastic forms for the aorist and perfect; for a certain time, coalescence of the genitive/dative; loss of many old words and change of meanings, e.g., *bṛhat* 'high' > 'big'.

It is important to note that all Vedic texts were composed orally and transmitted orally. This *exact* oral transmission, including the pitch accent that has been dead for some two thousand years, is unique among that of traditional texts of India and is ensured by orally transmitted devices (Padapāṭha, Kramapāṭha, etc.), which countercheck on accuracy of sounds, order of words, etc.

By the middle of the first millennium B.C., Sanskrit as a widely spoken language was already largely superseded by the various dialects of MIA (Prākṛt, Pāli). But it did not die out as a living language; it continued as the educated speech of Brahmins and other high castes, as is clearly visible in Patañjali's grammatical commentary *Mahābhāṣya* (c. 150 B.C.) on Pāṇini's grammar, who expressively states that one has to learn proper Sanskrit not to become barbarian or "demonic."

Another form of Sanskrit continued as the lingua franca of the Bards who composed and transmitted the great Indian Epics (*Mahābhārata*, *Rāmāyaṇa*); these texts are multilayered and undatable; they begin sometime in the first millennium B.C. but were redacted only in the mid–first millennium A.D. Nevertheless the epics (and to some degree the medieval religious texts), the *Purāṇas* and *Tantras*, employ a less formal version of Sanskrit, heavily influenced by MIA. That this reflects social reality can be observed in the coexistence, in the Mathura inscriptions from the beginning of our era of various forms of Sanskrit: those of a few Brahmins or kings are in correct Sanskrit, others have various degrees of Sanskritization or simply follow local MIA, which for several hundred years was also the official language of administration, beginning with the edicts of Emperor Asoka, c. 250 B.C.

Classical Sanskrit was reintroduced by a foreign Kṣatrapa king, Rudradāman of Gujarat, as the official language around A.D. 150. Around the beginning of our era, Classical Sanskrit also began to be used by the Buddhists to supplement their use of MIA in their sacred texts. Classical Sanskrit, from then on, remained in official use, especially under the Guptas (c. A.D. 300–500) and their successors, and well into the Muslim period (after 1200). The case differs from area to area: in Kashmir it was given up around 1420, but it was retained in Nepal well into the 19th century.

Classical Sanskrit, based on Pāṇini, is a highly polished language with a large degree of specialized terminology for the various fields of administration, the sciences, religion, etc. The Gupta period, with the great poet Kālidāsa, is regarded as the Classical period as far as Sanskrit literature is concerned. It is in this period that the high-flown *kāvya* style of poetry was fully developed; due to the many homonyms in Sanskrit and other poetical tricks it abounds in puns and rhetorical devices. In some of the most elaborate cases, a verse has to be read twice with different word divisions to make sense in the context, and there are even complete dramas in which this device has been used to provide two different sectarian meanings to tell both epics at the same time.

By Gupta time, the scientific language (*śāstra* style) that was already clearly in evidence in Patañjali in 150 B.C. was fully developed. It is characterized by a stark nominal style (see examples below) and by enormously long nominal compounds. Both features, *kāvya* and *śāstra*, are retained to this day and are the marks of a well-trained scholar.

The first and second millennium saw the use of Sanskrit in all fields, besides the familiar ones of poetry and religion: in philosophy, education (including general cultural and sexual: *Kāmasūtra*), medicine, mathematics, astronomy, astrology, medicine, agriculture, forestry, law, arts, the all-important grammar and lexicography, and even in discussing specialties such as cooking, gems, falconry, wrestling, and thievery.

Though English was introduced as an official language in India in 1835, the use of Sanskrit continued in administration in some areas.

Since Sanskrit was recognized as one of the 15 official languages of India, there have been occasional government publications as well as regular radio broadcasts. The Sanskrit Commission of the Central Government, in 1956–57 traveled throughout the country in order to investigate the state of the language and its instruction. Some of their recommendations have been implemented and several Sanskrit universities and research centers (*Kendriya Sanskrit Vidyāpīṭh*) have been founded, as suggested in the 1958 government report of V. Raghavan. Nepal, too, has recently established a Sanskrit university at Dang, where Sanskrit education, including boarding, is free.

Orthography and Basic Phonology

Sanskrit has no orthography in the usual sense of the word. All words are written phonetically, with the very well attuned North/West Indian Devanāgarī alphabet (and regionally, other scripts from the Panjab to Bali). They all derive from the Asokan Brahmī script of c. 250 B.C. (Recent finds in Sri Lanka improbably assume that the script was used around 500 B.C.). However, it has no predecessor in the Indus script of 3300–1900 B.C., with its nearly 800 mostly logographic signs.

The Brahmī and Nāgarī script represent a real alphabet, however, with the unusual but ingenious invention of not writing the short vowel *a*. This is the most common vowel in all North Indian languages, and one can thereby shorten the length of texts remarkably.

All other vowels are marked by diacritics that are added to the consonants. Syllable-initial vowels have their own signs, and consonant groups are marked by combination or by a small diacritic sign to avoid vocalization.

The little there is of orthography is based on medieval interpretation of Pāṇini's rules, most common: doubling of consonants after *r*; thus, *karman* :: *karmman* 'work', *varman* :: *varmman* 'protection'. (An official orthographic reform was carried out by King Aṃśuvarmman of Nepal in 605 A.D. who wrote his name, after his coronation, as Aṃśuvarman).

There is no punctuation beyond marking the end of sentences or verses by strokes. All other speech marks, if written, have been introduced during the last century or so (? " ! parenthesis, and occasionally also ; ,).

The sounds of Sanskrit have been traditionally ordered in the following way; it underlies Pāṇini's system and perhaps goes back, in light of the attention paid early to grammatical features, even to the Middle Vedic period.

vowels	a ā i ī u ṛ ṝ ḷ ḹ e ai o au (ṃ m̐ ḥ ẖ ḫ)
velars	k kh g gh ṅ
palatals	c ch j jh ñ
retroflexes	ṭ ṭh ḍ ḍh ṇ (ḻ ḻh)
dentals	t th d dh n
labials	p ph b bh m
"semivowels"	y r l v
sibilants	ś ṣ s
fricative	h (also, ḥ, ẖ, ḫ)

The sounds given in parenthesis are allophones, not separate phonemes; indeed, they are not part of the Paṇinean tables but are inserted in the alphabet at the given locations, with the exception of *ñ* (which is only an allophone) and *ḻ*, *ḻh*, which are in some areas placed after *h*. Further, *ṃ* is an allophone of *m* (originally found before *y*, *r*, *v* only), *m̐* for *n* (before *l*, *ś*, *ṣ*, *s* inside a word and in certain endings), *ḥ* in pause in words ending in *-s* (and a few ending in *-r*) and now also before *k*, *kh*, *p*, *ph*, while in Vedic and at first even in Classical Sanskrit *-s* became velar fricative *ẖ* before *k*, *kh* and bilabial fricative *ḫ* before *p*, *ph*. The sounds *-ḻ-*, *-ḻh-* occur since Middle Vedic as allophones for intervocalic *-ḍ-*, *-ḍh-* but disappear in most parts of India, along with ẖ, ḫ, at the end of the first millennium A.D.

Note that *ṛ*, *ḷ* are true vowels (as in American English "read<u>er</u>", "bott<u>le</u>"), that *e*, *o* (< older *ai*, *au*) are long vowels, and *ai*, *au* (< *āi*, *āu*) are true diphthongs, nowadays, however, often pronounced [ɛ, ɛi] and [ɔ, ɔu], respectively; *-ḥ* as [h] is now pronounced with the preceding vowel briefly repeated, thus *-aḥ* [ah^{a}]; *ṃ* and *m̐* nowadays nasalize preceding vowels, while in modern Veda recitation, *m̐* often appears as [gũ]. Originally it must have been a velar nasal.

Table 1: Consonants

		Labial	Dental/ *Alveolar	Retroflex	Palatal	Velar
Stops	-voi	p	t	ṭ	c	k
	-voi, +asp	ph	th	ṭh	ch	kh
	+voi	b	d	ḍ	j	g
	+voi, +asp	bh	dh	ḍh	jh	gh
Fricatives			s	ṣ	ś	
Nasals		m, ṃ	n	ṇ	ñ	ṅ
Flap			*r			
Glides		v	l	ḻ, ḻh	y	

Table 2: Vowels

	Front	Central	Back
High		i/ī ḷ ṛ	uū
Mid	e, ai	a [ə]	o, au
Low		ā	

Pronunciation all over southern Asia is fairly uniform, some regional, frequently old, peculiarities include: northern India: *ṣ* [x], *v* [b], *jñ* [gy], *ṛ* [ri]; Maharashtra: *v* [w], *jñ* [dny], intervocalic *-l-* [ḷ], *ṛ* [ru]; Tamil Nadu: *ś* [s], *ṛ* [ra]; Kashmir, Bengal and Kerala have even more deviant pronunciations with rather involved, little-studied substitutions.

Accent. Vedic accent was pitch based, and it still is in the recitation of Vedic texts, although it has disappeared from common speech and the pronunciation of Classical Sanskrit for at least two thousand years. It is taught, with special mnemotechnical devices, such as hand movements, in Veda school. There are three main tones, somewhat similar to the Greek ones. Syllables with the rising tone (*udātta*) mostly agree with those accented in Greek, Proto-Germanic and reconstructed IE. The Udātta is regularly preceded by a lower tone (*an-udātta* 'not raised') and followed by a falling tone (*svarita* 'the sounded one'), which, nowadays, is pronounced as first slightly rising higher than the Udātta and then sharply falling, giving it the "sounding" quality. Completely unaccented syllables are called *ekaśruti* or *pracaya.*

Normally, each Vedic word has one rising tone; the rest depends on the surrounding syllables; there also is sandhi of tones when they occur in certain surroundings, i.e., rising tone immediately followed by low tone before another rising tone. Successive Udāttas belonging to several words are allowed. Unaccented words are rare; they include certain particles and unstressed pronouns; they often take the typical second, unstressed position in a sentence, irrespective of the word they belong to.

The position of high pitch (Udātta) in a word depends on a large number of rules that go back to IE, e.g., *ás-ti* 'he, she is', *s-ánti* 'they are', or shift of accent within a paradigm, as in *vāc* 'voice, speech': nom. *vā́k,* acc. *vā́cam,* instr. *vācā́,* gen./abl. *vācáḥ,* loc. *vācí,* etc. In other cases, accent remains fixed on one syllable. Homonyms are often distinguished by accent: *divā́* 'by, through heaven, day'; *dívā* 'during daytime', *vára* 'wish; excellent, better;' *vará* 'wooer'.

In Classical Sanskrit pitch accent has been replaced by something that usually is described as stress on the penultimate, and if short on the third last syllable; however, closer observation shows that in spite of this, long vowels, especially *ā,* carry pitch accent.

Sandhi. Euphonic combinations between words (*sandhi*) are very frequent in Sanskrit. Usually, the second word influences the shape of the last sound of the preceding word, somewhat in the manner of FRENCH *il est* [ile], but *est-il* [etil] where *-t-* reappears in pronunciation before a vowel. In Sanskrit, usually just a change of articulation is involved, and only in some cases reappearance of an old historically lost sound. There must have been much less sandhi in early Vedic than what now appears in our texts (redacted before the middle of the first millennium B.C.). By the time of Pāṇini, sandhi rules of Sanskrit, though not yet of all Vedic recitation, were fixed. Thus, *tasmāt + agnis > tasmād agniḥ, agnis + adhyasṛjyata > agnir adhyasṛjyata; yat + lohitam > yal lohitam.* Vowels coalesce or change to "semivowels" (resonants): *apa + amṛṣṭa > apāmṛṣṭa; ca + ekadhā > caikadā; adhi + asṛjyata > adhyasṛjyata* (for translations, see Basic Syntax). Some sandhi forms retain millennia-old states of (pre-)Vedic pronunciation, such as the dual forms in *-ī*, etc., that go back to IE laryngeal *-h2* that still are represented by a hiatus before a following vowel, similar to the retention in French of hiatuses before originally Germanic words: *Le Havre :: l' homme.*

It must be noted that only certain single consonants are allowed as word finals (i.e., in pause), *k, p, ṭ, t, n, m, r/ḥ,* rarely *ṅ, l*; all others are changed, thus *-bh > -p*, etc. Any double- or triple-consonant clusters occurring at the end of a word are deleted, only the first one is kept, thus: *gacchants > gacchan* 'going', *aprākṣṭ > aprāk* 'he asked' (from *pṛch*). (Such consonants 'reappear' in non-final forms, acc. *gacchant-am, aprākṣam* 'I asked'.) Vowel sandhi and that of words ending in *-s/ḥ/r* is seriously affected by the disappearance of the pre-Vedic sounds *ž, z* which mostly result in *-r* or *zero*, sometimes with compensatory lengthening.

The syllable structure of Sanskrit is close to that of IIr and IE and far from the simple one of modern MIA and NIA lan-

Table 3: Nominal Morphology

	Singular	Dual	Plural
NOM	sá vásus devás	táu vásū deváu	té vásavas devā́s
ACC	tám vásum devám	táu vásū deváu	tā́n vásūn devā́n
INST	téna vásunā devéna	tā́bhyām vásubhyām devā́bhyām	táis vásubhis deváis
DAT	tásmai vásave devā́ya	tā́bhyām vásubhyām devā́bhyām	tébhyas vásubhyas devébhyas
ABL	tásmāt vásos devā́t	tā́bhyām vásubhyām devā́bhyām	tébhyas vásubhyas devébhyas
GEN	tásya vásos devásya	táyos vásvos deváyos	téṣāṃ vásūnām devánām
LOC	tásmin vásau devé	táyos vásvos deváyos	téṣu vásuṣu devéṣu
VOC	- váso déva	- vásū dévau	- vásavas dévās
NOM	sā́ kalyānī́ kanyā̀	té kalyānyàu kanyè	tā́s kalyānyàs kanyā̀s
ACC	tā́m kalyānī́ m kanyā̀m	té kalyānyàu kanyè	tā́s kalyānyàs kanyā̀s
INST	táyā kalyānyā̀ kanyàyā	tā́bhyām kalyānī́ bhyām kanyā̀bhyām	tā́bhis kalyānī́ bhis kanyā̀bhis
DAT	tásyai kalyānyài kanyā̀yai	tā́bhyām kalyānī́ bhyām kanyā̀bhyām	tā́bhyas kalyānī́ bhyas kanyā̀bhyas
ABL	tásyās kalyānyā̀s kanyā̀yās	tā́bhyām kalyānī́ bhyām kanyā̀bhyām	tā́bhyas kalyānī́ bhyas kanyā̀bhyas
GEN	tásyās kalyānyā̀s kanyā̀yās	táyos kalyānyòs kanyàyos	tā́sām kalyānī́ nām kanyā̀nām
LOC	tásyām kalyānyā̀m kanyā̀yām	táyos kalyānyòs kanyàyos	tā́su kalyānī́ ṣu kanyā̀su
VOC	- kályāni kánye	- kályānyau kánye	- kályānyas kányās
NOM	tád mahát dānám	té mahatī́ dāné	tā́ni mahā́nti dānā́ni
ACC	tád mahát dānám	té mahatī́ dāné	tā́ni mahā́nti dānā́ni
INST	téna mahatā́ dānéna	tā́bhyām mahádbhyām dānā́bhyām	táis mahádbhis dānáis
DAT	tásmai mahaté dānā́ya	tā́bhyām mahádbhyām dānā́bhyām	tébhyas mahádbhyas dānébhyas
ABL	tásmāt mahátas dānā́t	tā́bhyām mahádbhyām dānā́bhyām	tébhyas mahádbhyas dānébhyas
GEN	tásya mahatás dānásya	táyos mahatós dānáyos	téṣāṃ mahatā́m dānā́nām
LOC	tásmin mahatí dāné	táyos mahatós dānáyos	téṣu mahátsu dānéṣu
VOC	- máhat dā́na	- máhat dā́ne	- máhhānti dā́nāni

guages. IE/IA roots ordinarily have three consonants, and can only have the structure: +/- prefixes {(s) (C) (R) (e) (R) (C/s)} +/- suffixes +/- ending), where ( ) indicates possible appearance, and C = consonant (including the laryngeal sounds, H = h_1, h_2, h_3); *e* = standard IE vowel (> Skt. *a*); it can change to *o* (> Skt. *a*), *ē*, ō (> Skt. *ā*) or disappear (*zero* forms); R = resonants, the "semi-vowels" *i, ṛ, ḷ, u, m, n,* which can also appear as *y, r, l, v, m, n*; the consonant *s* when found at the beginning of roots, is unstable and can disappear (as in *spaś* 'spy' : *paś-ya-ti* 'sees'). Possible are, e.g., Skt. *ad* (IE eC), *pat* (CeC), *śrath* (CReC), *bandh* (CeRC), *kṛ* (CR), *śru* (CRR), *kram* (CReR), *krand* (CReRC), *i* (R), *iṣ* (RC), *man* (ReR), *manth* (ReRC), *tras* (CRes), *tvakṣ* (CReCs), *stambh* (sCeRC), *svap* (sReC), *sas* (ses), etc.; and with laryngeals: *bhū* (CRH), *brū* (CRRH), *īkṣ* (HRCs), *as* (Hes), etc. Sounds inside a root are arranged according to the following order of preference: C/s-R-e..., thus: CRe- (Skt. *śram*), sRe- (Skt. *srav*). Not allowed are the types RCa- or Rsa- (Skt. **ṛka*, **usa*, etc.), and the types: Skt. **bad*, **bhat*, **tabh*, **pap*, **tork/takt*.

Sometimes up to five consonants can cluster in Sanskrit words: *viśvapsnya, bibhaṅkṣya-, bhuṅkṣva,* etc., and complex groups appear even in initial position, *kṣnauti, kṣvedati,* but there is considerable simplification at the end of words (see above).

Basic Morphology

Nominal Morphology. Most of the nouns and verbs of Sanskrit are, as in all older IE languages, composed of three elements, the monosyllabic root (carrying the lexical meaning), one or two stem suffixes (specifying some grammatical or semantic relationship with, or derivation from, the root), and the endings that indicate certain grammatical categories such as case, number, gender (in nouns), and person, number and voice (in verbs).

The combination of root, stem and endings is of the inflectional or fusional type: the three constituents cannot always be separated at first sight, though the matter was so much clearer in Sanskrit than Greek or Latin that Pāṇini could actually set up these three categories. In so doing, Pāṇini became the father of grammatical analysis used by the early IE scholars of the 19th century.

Nouns and adjectives (including declinable verbal adjectives or participles) distinguish case, number and gender, which are often expressed by a single, fused ending. There are seven cases plus the vocative, which is outside the paradigm. The traditional (Pāṇinean) order is nominative, accusative, instrumental, dative, genitive, ablative, locative (and vocative). The main functions of the cases are similar to those in other old IE languages: nominative indicates the subject, accusative the direct object (and direction of travel, length of time, space), INSTR. the means or instrument (or in whose company ones moves), dative the indirect object (and the aim for which something is done), genitive possession or beneficiary, ablative the place or time of origin (or cause), locative the location (or end point of movement) and the vocative the person addressed.

Sanskrit has three genders; the masculine and neuter forms usually are quite closely related while the feminine has a separate set of endings. There are three numbers: singular, dual and plural. The dual is not only used for items that occur in pairs, but for any two items, such as two books, two friends; plural therefore means "three or more", for example: *pitā* 'a father', *pitarau* 'two fathers, parents',*pitaras* '(3+) fathers, ancestors'.

The combination of nominal stems with case endings results in a large number of "declensions" that tended to become somewhat simplified in post-Vedic times but still exceed the number of the Greek or Latin ones.

The most important ones are given in Table 3. It should be noted that the very common stems, in *-a, ā*, are comparatively recent in IE and have been heavily influenced by pronominal declension, while the others reflect the older nominal declension. A large number of "irregular" forms can be explained by historical developments such as the declension of *pathi (pathās, panthāsas* 'path', etc.) from various ablaut forms of IE **penth2-*. There was considerable change in some individual forms from the RV down to Epic/Classical Sanskrit; especially in the multifunctional ending *-ā*, for example, nom. pl. *dānā*, nom. dual *devā* > later Vedic, Epic, Classical Sanskrit *dānāni, devau*; such archaic forms cannot be detailed here. Common stems are those in *-a-, -ā-, -i-, -u-, -ī-, -ū-, -tṛ-, -an-, -in-, -ant-, -mant-, -vant-, -īyaṃs-, -añc/ak-*, and other consonant stems.

The two most common stems, the MASC./NTR. *-a-* stem and the FEM. *-ā-* stems are given in Table 3, accompanied by the congruent forms of adjectives and of the demonstrative pronoun (in Vedic functioning also as article); all are given with the Vedic accents, which need to be deleted for Classical forms. Declension of the masculine, feminine, neuter pronouns, adjectives and nouns: *sá / vásu / devá* 'the/this good god'; *sā́ / kalyāṇī́ / kanyā̀* 'the/this beautiful young woman,' *tát / mahát / dānám* 'the/this large gift'. (All forms are given without Sandhi between the words involved.)

Pronouns. There are a considerable number of pronouns. They all share a clear distinction between the nominative and the oblique cases, which usually are built on a different stem. A comparison with the *-a-, -ā-* stems shows their influence on these declensions. There are, besides the personal pronoun, two deictic ones, referring to close and nonproximal items (*ayam :: asau*), and the anaphoric *eṣa-* 'the one mentioned before, the well-known'; the third person of the personal pronoun in reality is a demonstrative pronoun (and article in Vedic) and it is also used as such; it is closely related to Latin *is, (ea), id*, and Greek *ho, hē, to*, as well as to English ("he"), "she", "it". First and second personal pronouns do not distinguish gender (enclitic forms follow after the comma).

In addition, there is the relative pronoun *ya-s/yā/yad* (m., f., n.) and the interrogative *ka-s/kā/kim* and indefinite versions of it. Vedic has (remnants of) some more pronouns that are not employed later on. A number of common adjectives (such as *uttara-* 'northern') follow the pronominal declension.

Articles. Sanskrit does not have an article; however, in the Vedic period, the proximal demonstrative pronoun *sa, sā, tad* 'this' was used, just as in Greek (*ho, hē, to*), as an article indicating identifiability (definiteness); this practice disappeared by the time of the Epic and Pāṇinean/Classical Sanskrit

Verbal Morphology. The verb is, as in all other older IE languages, the most complex of word forms, comprising many categories: aspect, tense, mood, voice, person, number and, apart from these, the nonfinite forms such as the participles.

Any verb form consists of a root, stem and ending. The endings distinguish person, number and voice (diathesis). There are three voices: active, the so-called middle (medium), and the passive. The middle indicates actions that are carried out by oneself, not for someone else (active) or variously experienced by oneself (passive), but are carried out in one's own interest or done by oneself to oneself (reflexive); thus, *yajati* 'he offers (for a king)', *yajate* 'he offers (for himself, in his own interest)', [tena] *ijyate* '(something) is being offered [by him]'. Some verbs have only middle but no active forms (cf. the Greek and Latin deponents), though the reason for this is no longer visible in each case, e.g., *bhuj* 'to enjoy' pres. *bhu-ṅ-k-te* (cf. the corresponding Latin deponent *fung-or*), *bhāṣ-a-te* 'speaks', *bādh-a-te* 'oppresses'.

In order to properly understand the older Sanskrit (Vedic) verbal morphology one has to forget the common division into several "tenses". Rather, the verb system is based on the classification of all verbal roots into two sets: those that signify continuous action, formalized by the grammatical category imperfective aspect and expressed by the present stem, and those signifying noncontinuous action (with a beginning, ending, repetition, or being momentative, etc.), formalized as perfective aspect and expressed by the aorist stem. From these stems, we have the present tense and past tense (imperfect) in the present stem, and the aorist past tense in the aorist stem. Past tenses are characterized, as in Greek, by the augment that is added in front of the verb form, *bhar-a-ti* 'he carries, brings', impf. *a-bhar-a-t* 'he carried', aor. *a-bhār(-t)* 'he (just now) carried'; verbs beginning in a vowel have unexpected lengthening: *et-i* 'goes' :: *ait* 'went', *ṛdh-no-ti* 'obtains' :: *ārdhnot* 'obtained'.

Outside this system, there is the perfect stem built on the reduplicated root (*ba-bhār-a* 'he has brought', or the irregular, analogical form, *jabhāra,* from *bhṛ* 'to carry, bring'); it indicates a state that has been attained through action in the past, as in the English perfect. (There also is the rare pluperfect, *a-ja-bhār-a-t* and there are a few remnants of a special stative category: *veda* 'he knows', *śaye* 'he lies, rests').

Table 4: Personal Pronouns

nom.	aham 'I'	tvam 'you, sg.'	vayam 'we'	yūyam 'you, pl.'
acc.	mām, mā	tvām, tvā	asmān, nas	yuṣmān, vas
instr.	mayā	tvayā	asmābhis	yuṣmābhiḥ
dat.	mahyam, me	tubhyam, te	asmabhyam, nas	yuṣmabhyam, vas
abl.	mat	tvat	asmat	yuṣmat
gen.	mama, me	tava, te	asmākam, nas	yuṣmākam, vas
loc.	mayi	tvayi	asmāsu	yuṣmāsu

Present and aorist verb stems are formed, according to the original meaning of the root, either directly by the root or with special suffixes that are based on a no longer attainable meaning; for example, reduplication indicating repetition, *bhṛ* 'to carry', pres. stem *bi-bhar-ti* 'brings' :: aor. *bhār-ṣ-*, or with the stem suffix *-ccha-* (IE *sk'e*), *pṛ-ccha-* :: aor. stem *prāk-ṣ-* of *pṛ-ch* 'to ask' (= Latin *posc-o*, GERMAN *forsch-en*). Pāṇini has classified the two dozen present stems into 10 categories; and the aorist has seven formations, including the root, reduplicated, *s*-Aor. (*dṛś* 'to see': *a-drāk-ṣ-t* > *adrāk; a-gā-s-ī-t* 'he sung'), etc.

These three verbs stems originally had five moods each: indicative (description), injunctive (mentioning, found only in the oldest text, *Ṛgveda*), subjunctive (prescription, future), optative (wish, possibility, condition, irrealis), imperative (order). Examples, in third person singular (he, she, it) of to 'become, to be' (*bhū, as*):

	Present	Aorist	Perfect	Meaning (Present Stem)
ind.	as-ti	a-bhū-t	ba-bhūv-a*	'he/she/it is'
inj.	as-t	bhū-t	ba-bhūv-at**	'is, as you know'
subj.	as-a-ti	bhuv-a-t***	ba-bhūv-a-t**	'wants to/must be'
opt.	s-yā-t	bhū-yā-t	ba-bhū-yā-t	'wishes/ought/might be'
imp.	as-tu	bhū-tu	ba-bhū-tu	'(he better) be'

*also from the root *as*: *āsa*, etc.; **not attested of this verb; ***for expected *bhav-a-t*.

Because of the different function (based on the lexical meaning of the roots involved) of the aorist and present stems, the verb "to be/to become" is built, like the English one, on two roots, *as* (English "we are") and *bhū* (English "be"). In Classical Sanskrit, much of this wealth of forms has disappeared, and only the indicative, optative and imperative of the present stem and only the indicative of the aorist and perfect stems are used. An exception is the "negative imperative" (prohibitive, inhibitive) of the type *mābhūt* = *mā* + *bhūt* 'don't become, don't be,' i.e., the particle *mā* (= Greek *mē*) and the injunctive, usually the injunctive of the aorist stem.

There are separate verb endings indicating present and non-present: active *ti* :: *t*, middle (= passive) *te* :: *ta*. The basic sets are given below (imperative and optative have separate sets). See Table 5 below.

A special development in Sanskrit is the clear distinction in function of the three past tenses: the past (imperfect) *a-gacch-a-t* 'he came (long ago)', the aorist *a-gan-(t)* 'he came (just now)' (final *-t* disappears, see above), *ja-gām-a* 'he has come.' The meaning of these three tenses is clearly visible in Vedic, Pāṇinean and good Classical Sanskrit, but the three are conflated in the heavily MIA-influenced Epic.

In addition, there is a large number of other verb stems, such as a separate future stem (*bhavi-ṣya-*), passive (*bhū-ya-*), desiderative (*bu-bhū-ṣ-a-*), intensive (*bo-bhavī-*), and most importantly, the causative stem (*bhāv-aya-*). Many actions are expressed in Sanskrit by causatives, thus not "Caesar built a bridge", but "Caesar caused (his soldiers) to build a bridge". All of these additional verb stems have moods and tenses.

In addition to the finite forms listed so far, Sanskrit also has nonfinite forms, i.e., those that do not include the category "person". These unconjugated verb forms include the infinitive (*bhavi-tum*) and the absolutive (*bhū-tvā*, [*sam*]-*bhūya*, roughly: 'having been'), which can stand for a whole secondary sentence ("after he had been...").

A special category, as in other IE languages, is the verbal adjectives, that is, the participles of the present, past and future, which are declinable like adjectives, e.g., 'been' *bhū-ta-s, bhū-ta-m, bhū-tā* (m., n., f.; others in *-na* such as *pūr-ṇa* 'filled, full'), *bhav-ant-* 'being'; *bhavi-ṣya-nt* or *bhavitṛ-* 'becoming, being in the future' (decl. as *-tṛ* stems); middle forms: pres. (*sam-*)*bhava-māna-*, fut. (*sam-*)*bhavi-ṣya-māna-*. There are separate forms for the passive (pres. *bhū-ya-māna-*) and perfect active (*ba-bhūvāṃs-*). Finally there is a gerundive/particle, of necessity (*bhavya-, bhavitavya-, bhavanīya-* 'must be').

Even this long enumeration does not exhaust the list of possible verb forms, some of them periphrastic; Vedic has many more forms and categories (injunctive, subjunctive, etc.) that have disappeared.

Word Formation. Almost all nouns are derived from verbal roots, with primary (*kṛt*) and secondary (*taddhita*) suffixes, thus: *kṛ*/ *kar* 'to do, make', primary: *kar-man* 'action' or *kar-tṛ* 'actor', *kṛ-ti* 'action, work'; secondary, *kar-tṛ-tva, kar-tṛ-tā* 'the being an actor', *kār-man-a* 'pertaining to an action, bewitching', etc. There is a large number of such suffixes, such as the

Table 5: Verb Endings

Active Pres.	Non-present.	Middle/pass. Present	Middle/pass. Non-present	Perfect act., Middle	(Person)
mi	m	e	e	a, e	'I'
si	s	se	thās	tha, se	'you'
ti	t	te	ta	a, e	'he, she, it'
vas	va	vahe	vahi	va, vahe	'we two'
thas	tam	ethe	thām	athus, āthe	'you two'
tas	tām	ete	tām	atus, āte	'the two'
mas	ma	mahe	mahi	ma, mahe	'we'
tha	ta	dhve	dhvam	ta, dhve	'you'
nti	n(t)	nte	nta	us, re	'they'

abstract suffixes in *-ti, tva, tu, tā, as, is, us*, agent nouns in *-tṛ*, nouns of action *-ana, -man,* diminutive, and later a general purpose suffix in *-ka*, adjectives in *-ya, ra*, etc.

The principle underlying word formation is the IE one of ablaut or gradation. Any syllable, whether in roots, stem suffixes, or endings, can change from plain full grade vowel (Pāṇini's *guṇa*, IE *e/o* > Skt. *a*) to long vowel (*vṛddhi*, IE *ē/ō* > Skt. *ā*) to zero vowel (no Pāṇinean name, as this is the starting point of his discussion). In short, the vowel *ṛ* in the root *bhṛ* 'to bring, to carry' can occur as zero grade 0+*ṛ* (*bhṛ-ta-* 'brought'), full grade *ar* in *bhar-a-ti* 'carries' or long grade *ār* in *ba-bhār-a* 'has brought,' the same can be seen in nouns (see above, the grades of *u*, i.e., *0+u, *au > o, *āu > au*) in the declension of *vasu-* 'good': *vasus, vasos, vasau.*

The other elements of word formation have been discussed above, under nouns and verbs: they include prefixes (reduplication, augment, prepositions), suffixes (stem suffixes, endings) and the singular case of an infix, *-na/n-* in the present class typified by the verb *yuj, yu-na-k-ti* 'yokes, joins,' *yu-ñ-j-mas* 'we yoke.'

Compounds. Nouns, but not verbs, can be combined into sets of originally two or three, and subsequently with a limitless number of members (the longest one in literature is said to be 10 pages long). Thus, even in the supposedly early drama *Pratimā* by Bhāsa, one of eight members:

> *vana-gaja-bṛṃhita-anukārita-śabda-samputpanna-vana-gaja-śaṅkayā*
> wood-elephant-augmented-resembled-sound-originated-wood-elephant-by supposition
> '[the boy was killed by the king] who (thought) that (the noise) had come from the sound [of the jar that the boy filled in the pond] which imitated the noise of a wild elephant and who thought that it was a wild elephant.'

As seen here, all members of a compound but the last ordinarily take the stem form; the last member is declined according to syntactical meaning required by the syntax of the sentence in question (i.e., sg. number, fem. gender, instr. case). Indian grammarians have classified nominal compounds extensively according to form and meaning. The two most common types are: *tat-puruṣa-* 'servant of X, his servant', *bahu-vrīhi-* 'someone who has/is characterized by much rice', (examples identical with the names of these compounds); other categories (indigenous names in parentheses) are seen in the following examples: *mātā-pitarau* 'mother and father' (*Dvandva*), *triyuga* 'three ages' (*Dvigu*), *śveta-ketu-* 'white banner' (*Karmadhāraya*), *anu-gaṅgam* 'along the Ganges' (*Avyayībhāva*), *ahaṃ-śreṣtha-* 'competition for preeminence' (from: 'I am the best', sentence compound like "forget-me-not"), etc.

The *Bahuvrīhi* compound differs from the other compounds in that it is exocentric; its referent is elsewhere, as in English "blockhead" '(somebody) who has a head of wood, a stupid (person)'; basically, it functions as an adjective that is sometimes, especially in (nick)names, nominalized.

As has been indicated above, Sanskrit has been relatively stable since Pāṇini's grammar, even if colloquialisms, regional features and loanwords intervene. In that sense, it has enjoyed the stable, fixed form of a language of literature, similar to that of Greek koine or to (post–) Classical Latin. However, before the emergence of Classical Sanskrit, its archaic form, Vedic, differed in many respects. Classical Sanskrit has seen the loss of the Vedic pitch accent, a sharp reduction of verb forms, and a tendency to reduce some of the many nominal declensions, giving preference to forms of the *a-* and *ā-* stems. Even then, many of the forms of Classical and modern Sanskrit remain the same as Epic and Vedic Sanskrit.

Basic Syntax

The basic syntax of Sanskrit can be first observed, outside of the relatively free word order of metrical texts, in Vedic prose. Sentences consist of noun phrase (subject) and verbal phrase (predicate), such as abundantly seen in the simple prose of the *Yajurveda* texts. The objects come in between the N and P phrase; basically, there is preference for SOV order. In other words, the topic appears at the beginning of the clause.

prajāpatir	vā	idam	āsīt.
lord.of.creation:NOM	verily	this.here	he.was:3.ACT.PAST

'Prajāpati ("the lord of creation") encompassed this universe.'

There also are slightly more complex sentences of paratactic form (from the same passage, *Kaṭha Saṃhitā* 6.1):

tasya	yal	lohitam	āsīt,	tad
his:DEM	what:REL	blood:NOM	was:3S.PRES	that

apāmṛṣṭa
he.wiped.away:ABS
'What was red (blood), that he wiped away'

In Epic and Classical Sanskrit, sentence structure becomes more complex, and the sentences much longer, especially by using the absolutives (see Example Sentences).

Nominal clauses have inverted word order, not SV, but VS (rather, as these contain nominal forms only, not Subject-Predicate but Predicate-Subject); one may interpret this in terms of the new topic, which, again, appears at the beginning of the clause as to introduce new information: *andhó hí bhágaḥ* 'Blind indeed is (God)' *Bhaga* ('share'), i.e., 'Luck is blind' (the verb 'to be' is not used in nominal clauses). Or, *paśavo vai pūṣā, paśavo 'ntarikṣaṃ* '(God) *Pūṣan*' is cattle, the interspace (between heaven and earth) is cattle. Such cases go against the basic SOV word order. The same feature is seen in prose when a new topic is stressed: *rudrám vái devā́ḥ nírabhajan* 'The gods excluded Rudra (from sacrifice)' (OSV), that is 'it was Rudra whom the gods excluded from sacrifice,' while the normal word order would be: *devā́ vái rudrám nírabhajan* (SOV). In verse, of course, various transpositions of words are seen.

Adjectives as well as (possessive) genitives normally precede the nouns they qualify.

Adpositions, that is the prepositions of Western IE languages, appear in Sanskrit as postpositions from Vedic onwards (*ati* 'beyond', *adhi* on top', *anu* 'along', *apa* 'away', *(a)pi* 'close to', *abhi* 'to, against', *ava* 'down', *ā* 'to, at', *ud* 'up', *upa* 'towards', *ni* 'at the proper place', *nis* 'out', *parā* 'away', *pari* 'around', *pra* 'forward', *prati* 'back again', *vi* 'apart', *sam* 'together'). In later Sanskrit, their number is augmented by a number of secondary formations (*madhye* 'in the middle = in', *dvārā* 'through a gate = by'). The old Sanskrit prepositions are also combined with verbs, for example *pra-* 'forward', *pari-* 'around', etc., and with nouns (see nominal compounds, above).

In later Sanskrit passive constructions are often preferred, for example, *grāmeṇa mārgeṇa gamyate*, 'by a path the village is being gone' (INSTR.SG.M.INSTR.SG-3RD.SG.PASS), which does not mean, as one might think, 'the village is forced to go by a path', but '(the people of) a village travel on a path'.

In Classical Sanskrit the desire for brevity in technical literature (*Śāstra*) has led to a new style of sentences with extreme, nominal constructions (with a few verbs only), with long nominal compounds, and with a particular syntax of its own that is not met outside this learned style. The whole clause depends on the NP (subject), usually positioned at the end of the sentence, e.g., *parvato vahnimān, dhūmavattvāt* 'of the mountain, having fire, from having-smoke-ness'. However, the genitive is usually translated, for convenience sake, as the subject and the NP (here not expressed) by a verb: 'There is fire on the mountain because there is smoke'. As seen here, the ablative is used as substitution for a causal secondary clause ("because of"). Similarly, the instrumental denotes an equivalence or characterization: *hetur liṅgatvena nibadhyate* 'the reason, by sign-ness, it is bound' = 'reason is represented as the sign (of a syllogism)'. The locative stands for a conditional or concessive clause: *ācāra-svarūpasya pratyakṣa-siddhatvena mūlāntarānapekṣaṇāt* 'of the self-nature of custom, by the validity-ness of perception, from the disregard of another justification' = 'because "custom" does not demand another justification, insofar as it is fully demonstrated by perception'.

Negation is normally expressed by *na* 'not,' put at the beginning of the sentence or immediately before the verb. It can also be expressed by the prefix *a-* /*an-* (= English, variously, "un-", "in-", "a/an-") prefixed before nouns, adjectives and participles and as such is found in abundance in technical works in *Śāstra* style. As pointed out above, prohibitive and inhibitive orders are expressed by *mā* (= Grk. *mē*) 'don't!' which is not found, however, when *na* used in conjunction with the optative as this indicates "one ought not, should not, may not (do)".

Vedic and Classical Sanskrit have a fairly "straightforward" way of telling stories and linking clauses with each other. There is no indirect speech, just direct speech whose end is indicated by *iti* 'thus' (which is also used for quotes and definitions, such as *deva iti* 'the word "devas"). Also, there is nothing such as the complicated way of indicating various levels of previous and later temporality in western classical languages. Instead, one can say "while he is one who lusted for meet, he went.' Few conjunctions are used, the most important ones derived from the relative pronoun.

Contact with Other Languages

The various forms of Sanskrit have been in direct contact with the other languages spoken inside south Asia (Dravidian, Munda, Tibeto-Burmese), but also—not unlike Latin and Greek in medieval and modern Europe—with the later forms of IA, that is MIA and NIA. All these languages are full of ancient (often heavily phonetically changed, *tadbhava*) or more recent and phonetically more correct loans (*tatsama*). The cultural influence of Sanskrit and its speakers has been enormous, and is comparable to that of Latin in Europe. There has been increasing convergence of the languages of south Asia, similar to the Balkan *sprachbund,* which originally formed a very heterogeneous linguistic area.

Furthermore, Sanskrit has had an extraordinary impact on Southeast Asia so that, for example, the language of Indonesia is called *bahasa* (Skt. *bhāṣā*); in Indonesia, a minister is *menteri* (*mantrī*), a priest *pendeta* (*paṇḍita*), religion *agama* (*āgama*), the country *negeri* (*nagarī* 'town') or *desa* (*deśa*), charitable *dermawan* (*dharmavant*), human *manusia* (*manuṣya*), effort *usaha* (*utsāha*), work *kedja*, (*karya*, [locally, *karja*]), color *warna* (*varṇa*), or, *Megawati Sukarnoputri* ('the cloudy one, daughter of Sukarno, Good-ear'), *Suharto* ('Good-hearted'), etc. Many such terms have even penetrated down to the tribal level. The same or a very similar situation exists in Malaysia (*Mahathir* 'the great steadfast one', *bumiputra* 'sons of the earth', aboriginal people), Thailand (*Bhumibol* 'the protector of the earth'), and phonetically less recognizably, in Cambodia, Burma and medieval Vietnam.

In Central Asia, Buddhism has provided a high number of loans as well (M. Iranian, Uighur Turkish, etc.), and the translation of the canon into Chinese and Tibetan during the first millennium A.D. has transmitted Sanskrit words and Indian concepts to these areas, and indirectly so, also to Vietnam, Korea, and Japan (JAPANESE *zen* < Chinese *chan* < Sanskrit. *dhyāna* 'meditation', *bosatsu* < *Bodhisattva*, or *danna* 'husband', which is supposed to come from *dampati* 'lord of the house, husband'). The order of the present Japanese syllabary (*Hiragana, Katakana*) is based on the Indian order: *a, i, u, e, o, ka, ki..., sa* (< *ca*), *ta, na, ha* (< *pa*), ma, ya, ra, wa (see above). Some teaching of Sanskrit persisted in Japan down to the beginning of the modern period.

Western contacts took place directly with Iran, and have left their traces in M. Persian and modern Iranian, as well as indirectly, via Iranian, in ARABIC. Due to the strong influence of Indian storytelling (*Arabian Nights*) or mathematics, many Indian concepts and names wandered further westward, into Europe; however, they have often left only indirect traces: *cipher*, 'zero' < Arabic *çifr* 'empty' < Sanskrit *śūnya* 'empty', or 'square root' < Sanskrit *mūla* 'root'). Many other terms of culture and commerce took the same route: Late Vedic *nāraṅga* 'orange tree' > Arabic *naranj* > SPANISH *naranja*, Latin *arancia*, English, French *orange*, or 'beryll' < Sanskrit *vaiḍūrya* / Pkt. *verul-* < Drav. place name *Vēḷūr*.

However, there was no direct contact of Sanskrit with Europe until the beginning of the 16th century, the period of the European expansion into Indian Ocean. Even the brief Greek contact with India at the time of Alexander and his first few successors, and with the Bactrian Greeks to the beginning of our era, and that of commerce with Rome resulted in relatively little direct knowledge and influence. (Note, India, Indus < Grk. *Indos* < O.Pers. *Hinduš* < Skt. *Sindhu-* 'Indus river and province', Grk. *karpasos* < *karpāsa* 'cotton', *brakhmanes* < *brāhmaṇa* 'Brahmins', etc.).

Loanwords. Sanskrit was from its beginnings in close contact with various languages of southern and western Asia. The tribes speaking Vedic Sanskrit encountered, on arrival in the greater Panjab, a population that spoke a variety of unknown, lost prefixing languages resembling but not identical to modern Munda. They have left a residue of some 4 percent of foreign words even in the strictly hieratic *Ṛgveda*, such as *kapard-in* 'with hair knot', *kilāsa* 'spotted, leprous', *kīkasā* (dual) 'rib bone', *kīnāśa, kīnāra-* 'ploughman', *kuliśa* 'axe', *pippala* 'pipal tree', *kulpha* 'ankle'. Some of them go back to a so far unnoticed Central Asian substrate that is also found in the closely related Old Iranian languages, which indicates the route of immigration: *uṣṭra*/Avest. *uštra* 'camel', *khara*/Avest. *xara* 'donkey', *iṣṭi, iṣṭikā*/Avest. *ištiia* 'brick', O. Pers. *išti*; *sthūna*/Avest. *stūnā, stunā*, O. Pers. *stūnā* 'pillar'; *yavyā*/O. Pers. *yauviyā* 'channel' (not from exactly the same source); *godhūma* /Avest. *gantuma* 'wheat' from a Near Eastern language, cf. PSemitic **ḥnṭ*, Hitt. *kant* and EGYPTIAN *xnd*; *kaśyapa*/Avest. *kasiiapa* 'turtle'; **pard/pandh* 'spotted animal, panther' : Ved. *pṛdāku* 'panther snake' RV; N. Pers. *palang* 'leopard' < O. Iran. **pard-*, cf. Greek *párdalis, párdos, léo-pardos* 'leopard'; **kapauta* 'blue': Ved. *kapota* 'pigeon', O. Pers. *kapauta* 'blue'; **kadru* 'brown': Ved. *kadru* 'red-brown', Avest. *kadruua-* 'brown', etc.

A few of the loans from the middle and later *Ṛgveda* onwards go back to old Dravidian words, though not always uncontested, such as *ukha*[-child] 'hip[-breaking]'; *phalgu* 'minute', *āṇi* 'lynch pin', *phala* 'fruit', *kuṇāru* 'lame in the arm', *daṇḍa* 'stick', *ulūkhala* 'mortar'. These sources (with the exception of the Central Asian substrate) continued to influence Sanskrit during the post-Vedic period as well; some of the loans have even come in only in recent times.

Perhaps greater than the foreign influence on Sanskrit, was the influence Sanskrit exercised on the local southern Asian languages. They all are full of Sanskrit loan words, from their earliest sources onwards. For Example, TAMIL has such words as *arahan* < *rājan* 'king,' *araicu* < *rājā* 'king', *kālai* < *kāla* 'time, season', *tūtu* < *dūta* 'messenger', *maṇi* < *maṇi* 'gem, precious stone'.

Among the other languages that exercised influence on Sanskrit are mostly those of India's western neighbors, to begin with the Achaemenid Empire of Persia: O. Pers. *Yauna* 'Greek' > Skt. *Yavana*, S.W. Iranian/O. Pers. *siça* 'white' > Ved. (AV+) *sīsa* 'lead'(?), O. Pers. *dipi* 'script' > Pāṇini's *dipi*, otherwise found in its E. Iranian form *lipi*.

The next source is the Greek used in Alexander's realm and the sucessor states: *khalīna* 'bridle, bit' < *kalīnós, paristoma* 'blanket' < *perístoma, sauṭīra* 'nobleman' < Pkt. *soṭīra* < Grk. *sotḗr* 'savior', the title of the Bactrian Greek kings, *kastīra* 'tin', < *kassíteros, marakata* 'emerald' < *(s)máragdos, kalama* 'pen' < *kálamos*, etc. Many are related to the introduction of Greek-Babylonian astronomy: *hṛdroga* 'Aquarius', with popular etymology 'heart illness' < Gr. *hudrokhóos*, *heli* < *hḗlis* 'sun', *horā* < *hṓra* 'hour', *kendra* 'center of a circle' < Gr. *kéntron*, *jāmitra* < *diámetron* 'diameter'.

After the emergence of the new Arsacide and Sasanide empires, Middle Iranian words entered: *kṣatrapa* < Iran. **xšaθrapa* (cf. Greek Satrápēs); *khola* 'helmet' < Avest. *xaoδa*; *bandī* 'prisoner, slave' < M./N. Pers. *banda*; *gañjavara* 'treasurer, divira 'scribe' < M. Pers. *ganjwar* < O. Pers. **ganzabāra*, cf. O. Pers. *dipi* > Skt. *dipi, lipi* 'script', *Mihira* 'sun deity' < M. Pers. *mihr* < Avest. Miθra (cf. Latin Mithras). Some Greek words entered via M. Pers.: *kaisara*/*keśara* < Greek *Kaisar* < Caesar, *Roma(ka)* < M. Pers *Hrōm* < Greek *Hrōmē* 'Constantinople', *dīnāra* 'a coin' < M. Pers. *dēnār*, < Gr. *dēnarion* < Lat. *denarius*. Other words came from other M. Iranian dialects such those of the Saka relatives of the Scythians: *horaka* 'donor' < Khot. Saka *haur, hor* 'to give,' or from Sogdian: *bakanapati* 'temple attendant' < *bynpt*, and even later medieval loans introduced by the Iranian "Maga Brahmins", such as *abhyaṅga* < *aiβiiåŋhana* 'sacrificial girdle'.

After the Muslim conquest of Iran and by 1200, Arabic and then Turkic words came in: *khāna* 'Khan', *bega* 'Bey' as titles, *Mahāmuda* 'Muhammad', *sūratrāṇa* 'sultan', *Turuṣka* 'Turk, foreigner, Muslim'. Many words ending in *-āha* signify colors of horses, such as *ukanāha, urāha, kiyāha*, etc. From MONGOLIAN comes *bahadūra* 'audacious', still a common name. And finally, from English, we find words such as *Aṅgla-* 'English', *ḍākṭara* 'doctor', or *moṭara-yāna* or *mṛttara-yantra* 'motor car' and many other, barely Sanskritized terms.

As a reaction to modernization over the past two centuries, a lot of new formations have been coined, often in imitation of English Graeco-Roman vocabulary, but in other cases drawing on older words and concepts and filling them with new content. Loan translations include such terns as: *mudrālaya* 'printing press' < *mudrā* 'coin, impression' + *ālaya* 'place, abode', *jala-vidyud-āyoga* 'water-lightning undertaking, hydro-electricity project', *dūra-darśana* 'far-seeing, television', *vāyu-seva* 'wind service, airline', *viśvavidyālaya* 'all-knowledge-abode, university', *pradhāna-mantrī* 'principal advisor, prime minister', *rāṣṭra-pati* 'lord of the realm, president', *ākāśa-vāṇī* 'voice from the ether, radio', *vimāna-seva: vimāna* 'flying car of the gods' + *seva* 'service' = 'airline'.

Common Words*

man:	nṛ́-, nára-, manuṣyà-
woman:	strī́-, gnā́-
water:	udaká-, jalá-, tóya-
sun:	sū́rya-, ādityá-
three:	tri-; tráyas (m.), trī́ṇi (n.), tisrás (f.)
fish:	mátsya-
big:	mahánt-
tree:	vṛkṣá-
long:	dīrghá-
small:	kṣudrá-, kṣullaká
yes:	táthā, evá, (sacred speech: óṃ)
no:	ná, negated verb, and neg. nominal forms in: a-, an-; in prohibitive/inhibitive phrases: mā́
good:	vásu-, bhadrá; su- in nominal formations
dog:	śván-, kurkurá-

* With Vedic accents.

Example Sentences

(a) Vedic Prose (forms without sandhi in parentheses)

(1) prajāpatir	vā	idam
(prajā-pati-s	vai	idam
creator:NOM.SG	verily	this.one/universe:NOM.SG.NTR,

āsīt.
a-as-īt)
he.was:3SG.ACT.INDIC.PST
'Prajāpati ("the lord of creation") encompassed this universe.'

(2) tasmād agnir
(tasmāt agni-s
from.him:ABS.SG fire.NOM.SG

adhyasṛjyata.
adhi+a-sṛj-ya-ta)
on.top-emanated-3SG.PAST.PASSIVE
'By him (God) fire was created.'

There also are slightly more complex sentences of paratactic form (from the same passage, *Kaṭha Saṃhitā* 6.1):

(3) tasya yal lohitam āsīt,
(tasya tat lohita-m a-as-īt
of.him:GEN.SG which:NOM red/blood-NOM was-3SG.PAST

tad apāmṛṣṭa.
tat apa+a-mṛṣ-ṭa)
that away+wiped-3.PAST
'What was red (blood), that he wiped away.'

(b) In Epic and Classical Sanskrit, sentence structure becomes more complex, and the sentences much longer, especially by using the absolutives (PTC = participle).

(1) sa caikadhā māṃsalubdhaḥ san,
(sas ca+ekadhā māṃsa+lubdha-s san
he and+once flesh-lusted-PST.PTC.NOM.SG being:PTC,

dhanur ādāya, vindhyāṭavīmadhyaṃ
dhanuṣ ā+dā-ya Vindhyā+atavī+madhya-m
bow:NOM on-put-ABS V.mountain+forest+middle-ACC.SG.NTR

gataḥ.
ga-ta-s)
gone:PST.PTC:SG:M
'Desiring meat, he strung (his) bow, (and) went into the Vindhyā forest.' (*Hitopadeśa*)

(c) Scientific style (*Śāstra*)

(1) notpatti-mātraṃ sva-bhāva-pratibaddhaṃ
PTL-noun.stem PRON-NOM.SG.NTR
not.origin-measure own-existence-bound.to

buddhimad-dhetutvena kiṃ-tu
ADJ.STEM-INTR.SG.NTR PTL.S
by.having.intelligence-cause-ness, but

tad-viśeṣo yad-dṛṣṭer a-kriyā-darśino
PRON-NOM.SG.M PRON-GEN.SG.F NEG-STEM.GEN.SG.M
that-special of.which.seeing. of.non.action.seer

'pi kṛta-buddhir utpadyate.
PTL PAST.PTC-NOM.SG.F 3SG.PRES.PASS
also the created.notion comes into existence
'The simple fact of having been produced is not in a natural connection with the presence of a natural intelligent cause; but, only a special type of (production) by the perception of which a person without having seen the act itself, acquires the notion that an object has been created.'

Efforts to Preserve, Protect, and Promote the Language

Sanskrit precariously hangs on among the priestly class and the traditionally learned, and it is still spoken today as second language by many students, scholars and priests in India and Nepal. Its position has been like that of Latin in the European Middle Ages, and just like this, its position has waned. The neglect of Sanskrit is due, however, to Islamic domination after 1200 in wide parts of northern India, and secondly, due to the spread of Persian and English.

There have been sporadic efforts to promote a (simplified) Sanskrit as a national language, but nothing much has come of it. Instead, the position of Sanskrit has been indirectly strengthened by the increasing Sanskritization of Hindi, Nepali, Bangla and other NIA (and Dravidian) languages so much so that modern newspapers, broadcasts or Government publications are barely understandable by the average person. Modern Hindi (etc.) often is Sanskrit without endings and with native (auxiliary) verbs attached.

This is the case even in Muslim Bangladesh, whose very name is Sanskritic (*deśa* 'country', or note the airline, Bangla Viman, from *vimāna* 'chariot of the gods'). But not in Pakistan, where there is an increasing trend to supplement the vocabulary of Hindustani (in its Urdu form) with Persian and Arabic words. And also not in Tamil Nadu, where the past few decades have seen strong anti-Brahmin and anti-Sanskrit campaigns, a cult of "Dravidianness" (i.e., of Tamil language and culture). Here, teaching of Sanskrit has been cut back.

There have been sporadic, but futile, attempts dating back to the Middle Ages to promote spoken Sanskrit. One of the more recent attempts to reintroduce Sanskrit as a spoken language has been that of Krishna Shastri, the founder of *Hindu Seva Pratisthanam* in Bangalore, Karnataka, who now offers clases all over India and the United States Due to his efforts, in the village of Mattur/Muttur in Karnataka, 80 percent of the people reportedly speak in Sanskrit. Similar reports come from a handful of other villages in Karnataka. Also, the national media in India broadcast some Sanskrit though a daily Sanskrit newscast. Occasionally, a Sanskrit drama will be produced. There also have been some films in Sanskrit.

Select Bibliography

Apte, V.M. 1890. *The Practical Sanskrit-English Dictionary, Containing Appendices on Sanskrit Prosody and Important Literary & Geographic Names in the Ancient History of India, for the Use of Schools and Colleges.* Poona: Shiralkar.

Bloch, J. 1934. *L'indo-aryen du Veda aux temps modernes.*

Paris: Adrien-Maisonneuve. English translation: *Indo-Aryan from the Vedas to Modern Times,* largely revised by the author and translated by Alfred Master. Paris: Adrien-Maisonneuve.

Burrow, T. 1955. [1973]. *The Sanskrit Language.* London: Faber & Faber.

Böhtlingk, O., and R. Roth. 1990. *Sanskrit-Wörterbuch.* St. Petersburg (7 vols., pp. 4756) 1852–1875. (reprint, Osnabrück 1966, Delhi).

Capeller, C. 1992. *A Sanskrit–English Dictionary.* Strassburg 1887; reprint Berlin 1966, Varanasi: Chowkhamba.

Delbrück, B. 1888. *Altindische Syntax.* Halle, reprint, 1968, Darmstadt: Wissenschaftliche Buchgesellschaft

Houben, J.E.M. ed. 1996. *Ideology and Status of Sanskrit. Contributions to the History of the Sanskrit Language.* Leiden and New York: E.J. Brill.

Kuiper, F.B.J. 1991. *Aryans in the Rigveda.* Amsterdam-Atlanta: Rodopi.

Mayrhofer, M. 1956–1976. *Kurzgefasstes etymologisches Wörterbuch des Altindischen.* Heidelberg: C.Winter.

____. 1966. *Die Indo-Arier im Alten Vorderasien. Mit einer analytischen Bibliographie.* Wiesbaden: Harrassowitz.

____. 1972. *A Sanskrit grammar.* Translated from the German with revisions and introduction by Gordon B. Ford. University of Alabama Press.

Monier-Williams, M. 1899. *Sanskrit English Dictionary.* Oxford: Clarendon Press 1872, revised edition.

MacDonell, A.B. 1966. *Vedic Grammar for Students.* Oxford: Oxford University Press 1916. Repr. Bombay.

Masica, C.P. 1991. *The Indo-Aryan Languages.* Cambridge and New York: Cambridge University Press.

Nakamura, H. 1973. *A Companion to Contemporary Sanskrit.* Delhi: Motilal Banarssidas.

Renou, L. 1962. *Grammaire de la langue védique.* Lyon: Editions IAC.

____. 1956. *Histoire de la langue sanskrite.* Lyon: Editions IAC.

Speijer, J.S. 1974. *Sanskrit Syntax.* Leiden: E.J. Brill 1896, repr. Delhi: Motilal 1973, (Graz 1974, Kyoto)

Wackernagel, J. (and B. Debrunner). 1896–1954. *Altindische Grammatik.* (Vols. I–III) Göttingen: Vandenhoek & Ruprecht.

Werba, Ch. 1997. *Verba indoarica: die primären und sekundären Wurzeln der Sanskrit-Sprache.* Wien: Verlag der Österreichischen Akademie der Wissenschaften.

Whitney, W. D. 1975. *A Sanskrit Grammar.* Leipzig : Breitkopf & Haertel 1879, reprint, (revised ed. 1889) Cambridge: Harvard University Press.

____. 1963. *The Roots, Verb Forms and Primary Derivatives of the Sanskrit Language.* Leipzig: Breitkopf & Haertel 1885, reprint: New Haven: American Oriental Society 1988; Delhi: Motilal Banarssidass.

Witzel, M. 1999. "Early Sources for South Asian Substrate Languages." In *Mother Tongue* Oct. 1999: 1–70.

Santali

Gregory D.S. Anderson

Language Name: Santali is an Anglicized form of Bengla *sãotal* < *Sāmanta-pāla* 'dweller on the frontier'. Only Christianized Santals refer to themselves as such. Otherwise, their self-designation is *hɔṛ* 'man' or *hɔṛ hɔpɔn* 'sons of man' (also *mañjhi/mãjhi* 'headman'); they call their language *hɔṛ ṛɔṛ*. In north Bengal their language is known as *jaŋli* or *paharia*, in south Bengal and Orissa as *ṭʰaṛ*, and in Bihar as *parsi* (Ghosh 1994: 2).

Location: Santali is spoken primarily in the eastern-central Indian states of West Bengal, Bihar, and Orissa. There are also significant groups of Santals found in Bangladesh, Nepal and Assam (on tea garden plantations), as well as a few thousand each in the northeastern Indian states of Tripura and Mizoram. The most compact area of Santal settlement is in the Sadar subdivision of Bankura, the Jhargram subdivision of Midnapur, and Purulia in West Bengal; south of Bhagalpur and Monghyr, in the Santal Parganas; Hazaribagh and Dhalbhum in Bihar; and Baleshwar, Mayurbhanj, and Keonjhar in Orissa. In Bangladesh, the Santals are found mainly in Rajshahi, Rangpur and the Chittagong Hill tracts (Ghosh 1994).

Family: Santali belongs to the Munda language family, the westernmost branch of the far-flung Austroasiatic phylum, which includes such languages as MON, KHMER, VIETNAMESE, Nicobarese, Bahnar, Khasi, etc. (ca. 150 total). These are spoken by predominantly so-called hill tribes scattered throughout geographically and politically inaccessible regions of mainland Southeast Asia (Malaysia, north Thailand, Myanmar, south China, Laos, Cambodia, and Vietnam) and on the Nicobar Islands as well.

Related Languages: The Munda language family consists of North Munda and South Munda, each with their own internal subdivisions. Santali is the major/sole member of a subgroup[1] of the Kherwarian branch of North Munda, which also includes such languages as Mundari, Ho, Bhumij, Korwa, Turi, Birhor, etc., with around 2 million total speakers. In addition to Kherwarian, North Munda also includes the westernmost Austroasiatic language, Korku, spoken by 300,000 people primarily in the Indian states of Madhya Pradesh and northern Maharashtra. The South Munda languages consist of seven languages spoken mostly in Orissa and adjacent parts of northern Andhra Pradesh. There are three subgroups of South Munda, Kharia-Juang, Sora-Gorum, and Gutob-Remo-Gtaʔ, with around a half million total speakers, the vast majority of whom speak Kharia or Sora. South Munda shows far greater internal time depth than do the North Munda languages, and thus presents a relatively heterogenous picture (Anderson 1999). The Munda languages represent the oldest known linguistic layer in the east-central parts of India, predating Indo-Aryan and Dravidian-speaking elements there.

Dialects: Dialect studies of Munda languages in general are in great need. Roughly speaking, Santali seems to divide into a Northern and Southern dialect sphere, with slightly different sets of phonemes (Southern Santali has six phonemic vowels in contrast with 8 or 9 in Northern Santali), different lexical items, and to a certain degree, variable morphology as well (e.g., the *-ič'* : *–rɛn* singular/plural opposition in animate genitive case markers).[2]

Number of Speakers: There are approximately 5,000,000 speakers of Santali, 4.8 million of whom live in India, over 100,000 in Bangladesh, and around 40,000 speakers in tea districts in Nepal. In India, over 2 million Santals live in Bihar, nearly 2 million in West Bengal, several hundred thousand in Orissa, and around 100,000 in Assamese tea gardens. Given the high self-reported levels of bilingualism and the relatively low language-retention rate in some areas where Santals live, the actual number of speakers of Santali may be somewhat lower (Ghosh 1994).

Origin and History

Little is known of the pre-history of the Santals (before the mid-18th century). They may have occupied an area somewhat to the northwest in southern Uttar Pradesh and parts of the Gangetic Plain. There were two Santal rebellions, after the second of which (1855–56), they pushed farther into northern Bengal, and the diaspora to the tea plantations in Assam began.

[1] This group may also include the Santalized or mixed Santali-Mundari Karmali and Mahali [Mahle] (cf. texts in the LSI) that share with Santali the use of the *–kan-* copula and progressive marker in contrast with the Mundari/Ho/Bhumij *–tan-* form. The former group are iron smiths found in Manbhum, Hazaribagh, and Santal Parganas, Bihar; the latter group are outcaste palanquin bearers, basket makers, and drummers. They both may have resulted from intermarriage between otherwise endogamous groups of Mundari and Santali clans (Parkin 1991: 16).

[2] According to Ghosh (1994: 7–8) who conducted several years of fieldwork on Santali in a number of locations, the border between the N. and S. dialect areas is the Chhatna and Saltora subdivisions of north Bankura in West Bengal (N. dialect) into Birbhum, Malda, and west Pinajpur and the Santal Parganas, Bhagalpur and Munghyr districts of Bihar (N. dialect) and the Khatra, Ranibandh, Raipur, Simlipal, etc., subdivisions of south Bankura (West Bengal) and the districts in Orissa (S. dialect). Among the features separating the two dialects are the loss of nasals before consonants (but preserving the nasalization of the vowel) in the Southern dialect *pɔ̃ṛ* 'white' (vs. *ponḍ*) , *mãjhi* (vs. *mañjhi*) 'village headman', *cãdo* (vs. *cando*) 'sun', etc., and the correspondence of the inanimate genitive markers: S. Santali *–aŋ* and N. Santali *–a'k*.

This was followed by moves to Nepal in the late 1920s (Parkin 1991). There is no written material in Santali before the mid-19th century.

The traditional homeland of the Santali may have extended somewhat beyond the boundaries of the area of densest settlement mentioned above (Wesr Bengal, north Orissa, Bihar), but Santali was probably not dispersed much further than this area up until recent times. There has been a general diaspora of Santali speakers over the past century and half, predominantly due to migrating laborers who left to work in the tea garden industry in Assam and Nepal.

Orthography and Basic Phonology

The Santali language has been written in a number of different scripts, depending on the locale of production and the purpose of the written material. There have been Santali publications in at least five alphabets, Devanagari (HINDI), ORIYA, Bengla, Roman, and the *ɔlčɛmɛt'* (*ɔl čiki* or simply now usually just *ɔl*) (Zide forthcoming). This last named script was created by Raghunat Murmu, a Santal pandit. It is based on the Mayurbhanj (S. Santali) dialect, with six vowels, etc. According to Zide (Ibid.), among the positive features of the *ɔl* script are the diacritics for deglottalization, aspiration, vowel nasalization, etc. There is apparently some desire among Santal intellectuals, cooly received to date, to use this script for other Munda and tribal Dravidian groups of the area (Ibid.).

Santali has a relatively small number of total phonemes, but nevertheless some interesting phonological (and phonetic) phenomena are encountered. The minimal vocalic inventory is as in (1). There are nasalized variants of all the vowels as well. In addition to the basic inventory, there is an allophone of /a/ or phoneme of limited distribution [ə] in both N. and S. Santali.

Table 1: Vowels

i		u
e	ə	o
ɛ		ɔ
	a	

According to Zide, there is a degree of laryngeal tension (phonation type) associated with certain Santali vowels. This gives Santali (and Mundari) its characteristic sound.

A wide range of vowel combinations can be found in Santali. These include *ae, eo, ao, ɛo, ɛi, ɛɔ, əi, əu, iu, oe, ɔe ɔi, ui, ea, iə, oa, uə, iəu eae oao*, etc. Large vowel sequences can also be encountered, e.g. *kɔeaeae* 'he will ask for him'.

The consonantal system of Santali recognizes five places of articulation, labial, dental, alveolar-retroflex, palatal, and velar (see Table 2). Stops are found at all places, both voiceless and voiced/checked series; nasals are found at four (*ṇ* occurs only as an allophone of *n* before *–ḍ*). There is no word-initial ***ŋ* - or ***ṛ*- in Santali, though these may be initial in word-medial syllables (see Table 2).

Examples of checked (preglottalized) consonants in final position include *sɛč'* 'towards', *rit'* 'grind', *selep'* 'antelope', *dak'* 'water', etc. (Bodding 1923: 79). Contrasts of various vowels and consonants can be seen in *daṛe* 'strength' vs. *dare* 'tree' vs. *dãṛɛ̃* 'sacrificial animal'.

There are also aspirated consonants, as in Indo-Aryan, which appear primarily in loanwords: *k*^{h}*ɛt* 'rice field', *g*^{h}*ugri* 'mole-cricket', *č*^{h}*al* 'tree bark', *j*^{h}*ĩk* 'porcupine', *kuṭ*^{h}*ri* 'cabin', *lat*^{h}*ak'* 'lumpy', *badha* 'clogs', *bhuk'* 'hole', etc. (Bodding 1923).

Table 2: Consonants

	Labial	Dental	Alveolar-Retroflex	Palatal	Velar
Stops Voiceless Voiced	 p b	 t d	 ṭ ḍ	 č ǰ	 k g
Fricatives		s			h
Nasals	m	n		ñ	ŋ
Lateral		l			
Trills		r	ṛ		
Glide				y	

Hetero-syllabic consonant clusters appear relatively frequently and of many differing types in word-medial position. The only tautosyllabic clusters found in onset position in word-medial syllables (or in word/syllable-final position in general) are homo-organic nasal + stop clusters. This phonotactic distribution, as well as various metathesis phenomena, suggest that these nasal + stop clusters function as unitary segments, and therefore that a set of prenasalized stops should be considered part of Santali phonology as well. Examples include *k*^{h}*okṇḍo* 'ill conditioned', *məñj*^{h}*lə* 'fourth of six brothers', *mɔ̃ñj* 'beautiful', *oṭ*^{h}*ŋgao* 'to steady on', *gaṇḍke* 'log', *oṇḍga* 'ogre', *b*^{h}*osṇḍo* 'slovenly', *beṛmbak'* 'incorrectly', *telŋga* 'stick'; also *k*^{h}*əṛnduŋ* ~ *k*^{h}*əndṛuŋ* 'deep', *kɔṛñjɛ* (~ *kɔñjṛɛ*) 'crooked' and *d*^{h}*aṛŋga* ~ *dhəŋgra/i* 'strapping' (Bodding 1923).

Basic Phonological Rules. One of the characteristic aspects of Santali phonology is the "checking" or preglottalization of final stops. This occurs at the end of words and before certain morpheme boundaries. Before vowels (generally speaking) these alternate with voiced stops, e.g., *dal-aka-'t-ko-a-e* 'he has beat them' vs. *dal-aka-d-e-a-e* 'he has beaten him'.

There is a regressive assimilation to place of articulation of a (derivationally added or epenthetic) nasal to a following stop found in such forms as *no* 'this' > *nɔ-ṇ-ḍɛ* 'this place' or *no-ŋ-ka* 'this way'.

Vowel harmony in Santali is morphologically triggered. Some affixes show variants dependent on the nature of the vowel(s) in the stem, while others do not. Harmonic ("weak") affixes include the locative *–rE* [-rɛ/e] (*oṛak'-re* vs. *hɔr-rɛ*) and allative case *-tE* [-tɛ/e] (*oṛak'-te* vs. *hɔr-tɛ*) markers (Bodding 1923)[3], or the third singular agreement marker when found enclitic to the word preceding the verb. Nonharmonic ("strong") affixes include the transitive aorist marker—*ke*: *ɛṛɛ -yɛ rɔṛ-a* (lie-3 speak-FIN) 'he lies'; *səri-ye rɔṛ-a* (truth-3 speak-FIN) 'he tells the truth'; *ba-e rɔṛ-a* (NEG-3 speak-FIN) 'he won't speak'; *hɔ̃ ṛũ -i dəṛ-ke-t'-a* (hanuman-3 run.away-AOR-TR-FIN) 'the hanuman monkey ran away'.

[3] These are being generalized with the vowel *–ɛ*, but harmonic variation is found in earlier sources.

Basic Morphology

Noun Morphology. The basic dichotomy in Santali nouns is between the classes animate and inanimate. Generally speaking, everything living is animate, as are a number of important inanimate things (e.g., *ñindačãdo* 'moon', *ipil* 'star', *ǰənum* 'thorn', *ɛ̃rgɔt'* 'earwax', *putul* 'doll'); everything else is considered inanimate (Ghosh 1994). The animate/inanimate distinction is not marked on nonderived (i.e., root) nouns at all, but rather this is marked morphosyntactically through such means as the differing genitive case forms for animate and inanimate nouns, the lack of locative and allative case forms for animate nouns, or the triggering (or not) of particular types of verb agreement. Santali makes no use of modifier noun agreement, adjectives appearing in an unmarked form. Adjective as a form class in Santali is definable only as an element used as a modifier in prenominal position.

The case inventory of Santali is relatively small, though several postpositional elements seem to be moving into becoming new case forms. The cases of Santali include the locative in *–rE* and the allative in *–tE*, both used only with inanimate nouns, and the ablative*–k^{h}on* (SS)/*-k^{h}oč'* (NS), which occurs with both animates and inanimates, e.g., *bir-rɛ* 'in the forest' *bir-tɛ* 'to the forest' *gidrə-k^{h}on hatao-me* 'take it from the child' (cf. NS *gidra-k^{h}oč'*) (Ghosh 1994). Homophonous with the allative, but probably to be treated separately, is the instrumental in *–tə*: (Ibid.) *ḍaŋ-tɛ tiyɔk'-mɛ* (stick-INS pull.down.INTR-2) 'pull it down with a stick'.

The most complicated aspect of Santali nominal morphology is the wide range of suffixes functioning as genitive case markers. In Southern Santali, they have the following distribution: *–ič'* is used with animate singular-governed nouns, *–rɛn* with animate plural nouns, and*–ak'* ~ *-aŋ* with inanimate nouns (Ibid.); Northern Santali shows only*–rɛn* for animates, whether singular or plural, and *–ak'* for inanimates: *Birsə-rɛn hɔpɔn* 'B's son', *iñ-ič'* (*iñ-rɛn*) *gəi* 'my cow', *am-ič' mɛrɔm* 'your goat', *am-ak' kat^{h}a* 'your word', *am-aŋ ti* 'your hand', *Lɔk^{h}ɔn-ak' oṛak'* 'L's house'. Note that the genitive form may also attach to a form already marked in the locative case*: dare-rɛ-ak' jc* 'the fruit of the tree' (~ *dare-rɛ-ŋ-ak'*) or *bir-rɛ-n-aŋ dare* 'tree of the forest'.

A small number of basic kin terms may appear in a bound form with a suffixed pronominal possessor (Ibid.) *hɔpɔn-iŋ* 'my son', *eŋga-m* 'your mother', *kimin-tet'* 'his/their daughter-in-law'. The suffix *-rɛn* may be an adjectival form derived from a locative case form. The *–ič'* and *–ak'* are derivational class-determinative suffixes borrowed into the genitive case function in modern Santali.

Enclitic postpositions are also found in Santali; these include *–são* 'with' (~ *-são-tɛ*), *-(i)hɛn* 'near', and *–ləgit'* 'for'.

The pronominal system of Santali contrasts first, second, and third singular, first inclusive, first exclusive, second- and third-person dual and plural (11 total forms).

	sg	dl/incl	dl/excl	pl/incl	pl/excl
1	iñ	alaŋ	aliñ	abo	alɛ
2	am		aben/abin		apɛ
3	uni		unkin		onko/unku

Santali has a complicated demonstrative system (Zide 1972). Its basic three-way system is a straightforward proximal, distal, remote system coming in animate (*-i*/*kin*/*ko*) and inanimate forms (*-a*/*-akin*/*-ako*) [singular, dual, and plural].

	sg	dl	pl
Proximal:			
anim	nui	nukin	noko/nuku
inan	noa	noakin	noako
	'this'	'these two'	'these'
Distal:			
anim	uni	unkin	onko/unku
inan	ona	onakin	onako
	'that'	'those two'	'those'
Remote:			
anim	hani	hankin	hanko
inan	hana	hanakin	hanako
	'that yonder'	'those (two) yonder'	

Alongside of these are intensive forms (marked by infixation of *–k'-*), 'just' forms (marked by a shift of (*o*/*u*>)-*i*-), as well as forms adding connotations of "things seen" and "things heard":

Intensives:

nuk'ui	'this very one'
nik'i	'just this very one'
nɔk'ɔy	'this very thing'

	sg	dl	pl
'Just' Proximal:			
anim	nii	nikin	neko/niku
inan	nia	niakin	niako
	'just this'	'just these 2'	'just these'
'Just' Distal:			
anim	ini	inkin	enko/inku
inan	ina	inakin	inako
	'just that'	'just those 2'	'just those'

	sg	dl	pl
'Seen' Distal:			
	ɔnɛ	ɔnɛkin	ɔnɛko
	'that seen '	'those (two) seen'	
'Seen' Remote:			
	hanɛ	hanɛkin	hanɛko
	'that yonder seen'	'those yonder seen'	
'Heard' Distal:			
	ɔtɛ	ɔtɛkin	ɔtɛko
	'that heard'	'those (two) heard'	

The operation of various types of vowel harmony that apply in a local and morphologically triggered fashion can be seen in the demonstrative stem alternations above. Thus, *o* > *u* when an adjacent syllable has an *i*: *on* 'that' > *uni* 's/he'. Also, *o* > *ɔ* when the word contains *ɛ*: *no* 'this' > *nɔnḍɛ* 'this place', *on* 'that' > *ɔnḍɛ* 'that place'. Similarly, *e* alternates with *i* and *ɛ*, though less regularly. The plural variants arise from either the plural suffix being considered dominant (e.g., *enko* 'just those ones', *onko* 'those') or the demonstrative stem being considered dominant (*inku* 'just those ones', *unku* 'those') in terms of triggering particular vowel harmonic patterns.

Verb Morphology. Verb as a lexical category in Santali (and in Munda languages in general) is loosely defined (Bhat; Cust). One and the same root may be used as a noun, as a modifier (adjective/participle), and as a predicate. Even a noun root like "house" may be used verbally with verbal inflection. *kombro* 'thief', *kombro mɛrɔm* (stolen goat) 'a stolen goat', *mɛrɔm-ko kombro-ke-d-e-a* (goat-PL steal-ASP-TR-3-FIN) 'they stole the goat'; *oṛak-ke-d-a-e* (house-ASP-TR-FIN-3) 'he made a house'.

Among the unusual characteristics of Santali is the fact that the person/number of the subject of the verb frequently is realized on the word immediately preceding the verb; on occasion, subject is marked at the very end of the verb form itself.

uni dal-iñ-kan-a-e	
he beat-1-PROG-FIN-3	'he is beating me'
hɛ̃ iñ-iñ čala'k-a;	
yes I-1 go.INTR–FIN	'yes I will go'
iñ am-iñ ñɛl-mɛ-a;	
I you-1 see-2-FIN	'I will see you'

In addition to subject, the Santali verb marks the person/number of the object of a transitive action, either direct objects, indirect objects, causees, or beneficiaries ("applicatives"). Santali also has an unusual system where the possessor of the logical subject or object may be marked with a special set of suffixes in the verb form: *ba-ko sap'-le-d-e-a* (NEG-PL catch-ANT-TR-3-FIN) 'they did not catch him'; *hɛč'-očo-ke-d-e-a-ko* (come=CAUS-AOR-TR-3-FIN-PL) 'they let/made him come'; *sukri-ko gɔč-ke-d-e-tiñ-a* (pig-PL die-ASP-TR-3-1POSS-FIN) 'they killed my pig'; *hɔpɔn-e hɛč'-en-tiñ-a* (son-3 come-PAST.INTR-1.POSS-FIN) 'my son came'; *kɔe-a-e-a-e* (ask-BEN-3-FIN-3) 'he will ask for him'.

The tense-aspect system of Santali is also complicated. The various forms can be split into two basic sets of inflections, roughly speaking a nonpast/durative and a past/completive. Verb stems themselves are either transitive/active or intransitive/detransitive/neutral. In the first set of forms, we find the durative/noncompletive endings *–kan-* [progressive] and *tahɛ̃kan* [imperfect] used with both transitive and intransitive stems. These also function as the present and past copulae, respectively. A stem may be further marked as passive (or intransitive/detransitive) by the suffix *–ok'* in the first set of forms as well. Note that *–ok'* is lacking in series-2 forms, where it alternates with (*–o*/Ø) the intransitive marker *–n-*: *kan-a-ñ* (COP-FIN-1) 'I am'; *tahɛ̃kan-a-m* (PAST.COP-FIN-2) 'you were'; *dal-e-kan-a-e* (beat-3-PROG-FIN-3) 'he is beating him'; *dal-ed-e-a-e* (beat-PRES-3-FIN-3) 'he is beating him'; *dal-ed-a-e* (beat-PRES-FIN-3) 'he is beating'; *dal-et'-me-tahɛ̃kan-a-e* (beat-PRES(.TR)-2-IMPERF-FIN-3) 'he was beating you'; *dal-ok'-kan-a-e* (beat-DETR-PROG-FIN-3) 'he is being beaten'; *dal-ok'-a-e* (beat-DETR-FIN-3) 'he is beaten'; *čalak'-ə-ñ* (go.INTR-FIN-1) 'I will go'; *ɔṇtɛ-yɛčalao-en-a* (there-3 go.INTR-AOR.INTR-FIN) 'he went there'.

The second set of forms consists of an aspect marker followed by a transitivity marker. These come in the following sets, *-aka-t'*/*-aka-n* (perfect) and *-le-t'*/*-le-n* (pluperfect; anterior). In addition, there is an aorist form in *–ke-t'*/*-en* for transitives and intransitives, respectively.[4] The *–n-* forms occur with intransitive roots; with transitive roots, these create forms with passive meanings. As mentioned above, in the nonpast/durative series, the affix *–ok'* is found instead of *–n-* in this function: *dal-ked-a-e* (beat-AOR.TR-FIN-3) 'he beat'; *dal-led-e-a-e* (beat-AOR.II-3-FIN-3) 'he beat him'; *dal-en-a-e* (beat-AOR.INTR-FIN-3) 'he was beaten'; *dal-akad-a-e* (beat-PERF.TR-FIN-3) 'he has beaten'; *dal-akad-e-a-e* (beat-PERF.TR-3-FIN-3) 'he has beaten him'; *dal-akan-a-e* (beat-PERF.INTR-FIN-3) 'he has been beaten'; *dal-led-e-a-e* (beat-PLUPERF.TR-3-FIN-3) 'he had beaten him'; *dal-len-a-e* (beat-PLUPERF.INTR-FIN-3) 'he had been beaten'; *dal-hɔčɔ-m-a-e* (beat-CAUS-2-FIN-3) 'he will cause you to beat'; *dal-an-a-e* (beat-BEN-INTR-FIN-3) 'he beat for himself'. Note that the future tense is unmarked in Santali.

Subjunctive mood is marked by the suffix *–ke-* occupying the same position in the template as the tense/aspect markers. In the imperative, which lacks a formal marker (unlike most South Munda languages, at least with intransitive stems), the order of elements is verb.stem-(aspect.marker)-<obj>-subj. The conditional is marked by the suffix *-k^{h}an,* which occupies the same position in the verb as the finite marker *–a-;* note that the conditional generally includes the anterior aspect suffix (-*l(e)-*) as well: *uni dal-k-iñ-a-e* (he beat-SBJNCTV-1-FIN-3) 'he might beat me'; *mɛrɔm-em kiriñ-k-e-a* (goat-2 buy-OPT/SBJNCTV-3-FIN) 'would you care to buy the goat'; *ɛm-ke-ko-a-m* (give-OPT/SBJNCTV-PL-FIN-2) 'would you give it to them'; *ɛm-l-iñ-me* (give-ANT-1-2) 'give it to me first, then…'; *iñ-em ñɛl-l-iñ-k^{h}an* (I-2 see-ANT-1-COND) 'if you see me'.

The negative is formed by the preverbal particle *ba*. The prohibitive is marked by the preverbal particle *alo*. Both of these generally have the subject clitic attached to them: *ba-ko sap'-le-d-e-a* (NEG-PL catch-ASP-TR-3-FIN) 'they did not catch him'; *alo-m lai-a-e-a* (PROHIB-2 tell-APPL-3- FIN) 'don't tell him'; *ba-ñ sɛn-le-n=k^{h}an uni ba-e hij-uk-a* (NEG-1 go-ASP-INTR=if he NEG-3 come-INTR/PASSV-FIN) 'if I do not go, he will not come'.

Thus, the basic template for a Santali verb (phrase) is as follows:

Series-1: NEG-subj Vb.Root-Voice/Valence-obj-tense/aspect-finite.marker-subj

Series-2: NEG-subj Vb.Root-tense/aspect-transitivity-obj-finite.marker-subj

Inflection, Derivation, Compound Formation. A number of different derivational affixes are made use of in Santali. These include animate and inanimate noun suffixes, *-ič'* and *-ak'*: *ɔl-ič'* 'writer', *kiriñ-ič'* 'buyer'; *jɔm-ak'* 'food', *ak^{h}riñ-ak'* 'that which is sold'; *arak'* 'red' > *arak'-ič'* 'red one (anim)', > *arak'-ak'* 'red thing (inan)', *boge* 'good' > *boge-ič'* 'good one', > *boge-ak'* 'good thing'; a number of different noun-forming infixes (*-tV-, -nV-, -mV-, -pV-, -ṛV-*), e.g., and a single noun-forming prefix *ma-*; examples include: *bɔr* 'fear (v)' > *bɔtɔr* 'fear (n)' > *bɔtɔr-an* 'fearful'; *rɔk'* 'sew' > *rɔtɔk'* 'seam';

[4] This represents two paradigms historically: the transitive form corresponding to *–en*, that is, *–et'*, has shifted to a general or progressive present meaning; the intransitive form corresponding to *–ke-t', -ke-n,* is mainly obsolete in Modern Santali. It has been preserved in various formations (see Bodding 1929: 220ff. for more discussion). When the verb is marked strongly transitive, *-le-t'* may be used in the aorist instead of *-ke-t'*.

ñum 'name' > *ñutum* 'name'; *ɛhɔp'* 'begin' > *ɛtɔhɔp'* 'beginning'; *sarɛč'* exceed'> *satarɛč'* 'excess'; *jɔk'* 'sweep' > *jɔnɔk'* 'broom'; *rakap'* 'rise, ascend' > *ranakap'* 'up, development'; *dapal* 'cover' > *danapal* 'lid'; *goč'* 'kill' > *gonoč'* 'killing'; *bar* 'two' > *banar* 'both'; *pɛ* 'three' > *pɛnɛ* 'all three'; *čɛt'* 'teach' > *čɛmɛt'* 'teaching material'; *čɛ̃* 'squeak' > *čɛ̃ṛɛ̃* 'bird'; *mañǰhi* 'village chief' > *mapañǰhi* 'village chiefs'; *raǰ* 'king' > *rapaǰ* 'king and his retinue'; *marak'* 'peacock < *rak'* 'cry'; *mačɛt'* 'teacher' < *čɛt'* 'teach'. A few other noun formants can be isolated from lexicalized forms. These include *–ḍɛ* 'place', *-ka* 'way, manner', etc.: *ɔnḍɛ* 'that place', *hanḍɛ* 'that yonder place'; *noŋka* 'this way', *onka* 'that way'. The productive modifier-forming suffix in Santali is *–an: dare* 'strength' > *dare-an* 'strong', *kaḍa* 'buffalo' > *kaḍa-van* 'one having a buffalo'. Nominal forms with more than one derivational affix are also found in Santali, though not with great frequency: *nɔ-n-ḍɛ-n-ič'* (this-ADJ/EPENTHETIC-NOM.LOC-ADJ-NOM.ANIM) 'one who belongs in this place'. Note that the animate formant *–ič'* is replaced by number markers in the dual and plural: *ɔl-ič'* 'writer' > *ɔl-kin* 'two writers', *dadal-ič'* 'one who beats' > *dadal-ko* 'many who beat'.

The derivation of new verbs is mostly limited to causative and reciprocal voice formations. The former category, more accurately causative-permissive, is formed by the suffix *–očo* (NS) or *–hɔčɔ* (SS): *ǰɔm* 'eat' > *ǰɔm-očo/ǰɔm-hɔčɔ* 'make eat' cf. *dalo-čo ~ dal-hɔčɔ* 'cause/allow to beat'; *ñu-očo ~ ñu-hɔčɔ* 'make drink'. In a small number of verbs, there is a lexicalized causative prefix *a-*, with cognates in South Munda and throughout the Austroasiatic family (Anderson and Zide 1999): *a-ǰɔ* 'feed', *a-ñu* 'give to drink'. Reciprocals are marked by infixed *–p-: ñɛpɛl* 'see each other, meet', *ñapam* 'get together, meet', *ñɛpɛl-hɔčɔ* 'cause/allow to see each other'.

Passive is marked inflectionally in Santali, either through the Series-1 marker in *–ok'* or the Series-2 intransitive marker in *–n* (see above). Other middle or detransitive meanings can be marked by adding *–ǰɔŋ* to the stem. Benefactive voice may be marked by the derivational suffix *–ka* in N. Santali, or *–ka* with animate objects and *–kak'* with inanimate objects or in antipassive constructions in S. Santali. Indirect (and often benefactive) objects may also be marked with the inflectional benefactive (BEN) aspect marker in the verb (*-a-*): *silpiñ sinkak'-me* (door close-BEN-INTR-2) 'close the door (for me)'; *dal-ǰɔŋ* 'beat/thrash for oneself'; *dal-ka* 'beat/thrash for someone else'; *dal-ok'* 'be beaten'; *ɛhɔp'* 'begin' > *ɛhɔbɔk'* 'be begun' [note voicing of checked consonant]; *alo-m lǝi-a-e-a* (PROHIB-2 tell-ben-3-fin) 'don't tell him'. Other verbal derivational processes are found in Santali: *–dare* 'be able to X', e.g., *ɛm-dare* 'able to give', etc. There is also a gerund in Santali in *–katɛ* that attaches to stems of various types: *dal-katɛ* 'having beaten'; *dal-ok'-katɛ* (beat-PASSIVE-GERUND) 'having been beaten'. It is used primarily when there is subject co-reference between parts of a complex sentence (see also Anderson and Boyle).

An intensive or repetitive verbal base may be formed by CV- reduplication in Santali, e.g., *dadal* 'beat intensively, repeatedly', *sesen* 'go intensively, repeatedly'. With VC- stems, a *–k'*- is inserted and the vowel alone reduplicated: *ɔk'ɔl* 'write repeatedly, intensively'. Reduplicated stems can form derived nominals as well: *gɔgɔč' ič'* 'killer', *dadalak'* 'striking thing', etc. With numerals, reduplication creates distributive numbers 'X each, by Xs': *gɛgɛl* '10 each, by tens'.

A number of auxiliary verbs are used in Santali as well. These frequently are found in constructions marking a range of complex aspectual nuances[5]: *jɔm baṛa-ke-t'-a-ko* (eat AUX-AOR-TR-FIN-PL) 'they are done eating'; *ǝgu hɔt'-ke-t'-ko-a-e* (bring AUX-AOR-TR-PL-FIN-3) 'he brought them quickly'.

Among the other noteworthy aspects of Santali morphology is the presence of expressive formations. These generally are formed by deforming a basic root: changing its vowels and keeping its consonants, or vice versa, and/or various combinations thereof, to form sets of related forms with (more or less) the same lexical meaning but differing connotative or expressive semantics. An example of this can be found in the many words meaning 'fat' listed in Macphail: *itil, ahal ɛhɛl, ehel; lɔbdhɔ, lɔbhɔk', lɔbɔ dhɔrɔk', lodo dhɔrɔk', lɔdhɔr, lodhṛo, lodrok'*, etc. Similarly, forms meaning 'awry, askew, flat, slanting': *lač(a) lača, lɛč(ɛ) lɛčɛ, lɔč lɔčɔ, liča lače, ličo lɔčɔ, lǝčuk' lǝčuk', lǝčuk' lučuk', lɔčɔk' lɔčɔk'*, etc. (Bodding 1923). The specifics of this lexicalized subsystem of expressive formation in Santali have not yet been thoroughly investigated.

Basic Syntax

Santali is a predominantly head-marking, agglutinative language with Subject-Object-Verb word order within the clause in unmarked discourse contexts. As mentioned above, one of the peculiar characteristics of Santali clauses is the placement of the subject marker on the word immediately preceding the verb. Overt subject nouns and most nominal objects of verbs appear in their basic form; directional cases maybe found on inanimate nouns. Negation is marked through a preverbal particle; note that verbal subject markers generally attach to the negative (and prohibitive) particle in Santali.

ba-ko sap'-le-d-e-a NEG-PL catch-AOR.II-TR-3-FIN	'they did not catch him'
alo-m lǝi-a-e-a PROHIB-2 tell-APPL-3- FIN	'don't tell him'
iñ am-iñ ñɛl-mɛ-a I you-1 see-2-FIN	'I will see you'

Relative pronouns are generally not known in Santali. Verbs of most types used without the finitizer suffix *–a* can be used in Santali syntactically as a prenominal modifier, corresponding to relative clauses (or adjectives) in languages like ENGLISH. These preserve all the morphology of the corresponding finite verb form, marking objects, tense-aspect, etc., except lack the finitizer *–a-;* they may even appear with a class-determinative affix, e.g., *–ak'*: *lǝi-aka-wa-d-e-ak'* (tell-PERF-BEN-TR-3-INAN) 'what has been told to him'.

Temporally subordinate clauses may appear in a finite form,

[5] Unlike the related South Munda language Gorum, where inflection of both the main verb and the lexical verb component is the norm, the main verb appears in an uninflected form (and in Santali the subject clitic generally is found word finally on the auxiliary, suggesting this is becoming a unitary form phonologically).

or may be marked in the locative case to form a subordinate clause of the "when" type.

Contact with Other Languages

Santali speakers are in contact with speakers of various modern Indo-Aryan languages. These differ according to the locale where the Santali speakers find themselves. Thus, for example, the contact language may be local versions of standardized Hindi or Sadani/Nagpuria dialects in Bihar, Bengali in West Bengal and Bangladesh, Oriya in Orissa, ASSAMESE in the tea gardens of Assam, etc.

Santali has been strongly influenced by local Indo-Aryan languages in its vocabulary. Of the many loanwords in Santali are kin terms, cultural items, etc., as well as noun and adjective pairs marking masculine and feminine like IA rather than the animate/inanimate distinction that is characteristic of Santali:

dal 'beans', *panahi* 'shoes', *pukʰri* 'pond', *utar* 'north', *bhagna* 'nephew', *bhagni* 'niece', *kala* 'deaf' (m), *kali* 'deaf' (f)

Common Words

man:	hɔṛ	long:	jeleñ
woman:	maejiu	small:	huḍiñ (or kəṭič')
water:	dak'	yes:	hɛ̃
sun:	(siñ)čando	no:	ba(ŋ)
three:	pɛ(a)	good:	boge
fish:	hako	bird:	čɛ̃ṛɛ̃
big:	maraŋ	dog:	seta

Example Sentences*

(1) ɔkɔe-ko-ko čalao-en-a.
who-PL-PL go-AOR.INTR-FIN
'Who all went?'

(2) Kandna iñ-ren barea gəi-ye gupiy-et'-kin-tiñ-a.
Kandna I-GEN two cow-3 herd-PRES.TR-DL-1.POSS-FIN
'K is herding my two cows.'

(3) ɔṇḍɛ-ko atoe-ləgid-ok'-kan-tahɛ-kan-re
that.place-PL found(village)-ABOUT.TO-DETR-PROG-IMPERF-LOC

ək'yurič' dɔ-e gɔč'-en-tako-a.
leader EMPH-3 die-AOR.INTR-PL.POSS-FIN
'When they were about to found a village, their leader died.'

*All sentences from Bodding (1929).

Efforts to Preserve, Protect, and Promote the Language

Santali is spoken by people of all ages and is not an endangered language. Its status may increase in the future, as there are efforts to have Santali be considered one of the official state languages of India (or some not-yet-defined Kherwarian [Santali-Mundari-Ho] quasi standard. This would create numerous opportunities for the expansion of the existing efforts in the publication of literature, pedagogical materials, etc. in Santali.[6]

Select Bibliography

Anderson, G.D.S. 1999. "A New Classification of the Munda Language Family: Evidence from Comparative Verb Morphology." Presented at the 209th American Oriental Society Meeting.

Anderson, G.D.S. and N.H. Zide. 1999. "Recent Advances in the Reconstruction of the Proto-Munda Verb." To appear in L. Brinton, ed. *Historical Linguistics 1999*. Amsterdam: Benjamins.

Bhat, D.N.S. 1997. "Noun-Verb Distinction in Munda Languages." In A. Abbi [ed.] *Languages of Tribal and Indigenous Peoples of India: The Ethnic Space*. pp. 227–251. Delhi: Motilal Banarsidass.

Bodding, P.O. 1923. *Materials for a Santali Grammar (Mostly Phonetic)*. Benegaria: Santal Mission Press.

____. 1925–29. *Santal Folk Tales*. 3 vols. Oslo: Institutet for Sammenlignende, Kulturforsning.

____. 1929. *Materials for a Santali Grammar (Mostly Morphological)*. Benegaria: Santal Mission Press.

Cust, R.N. 1878. *A Sketch of the Modern Languages of the East Indies*. London: Trübner.

Ghosh, A. 1994. *Santali: A Look Into Santali Morphology*. New Delhi: Gyan Publishing House.

Grierson, G.A. 1906. *Linguistic Survey of India. Vol IV: Munda and Dravidian*. Calcutta: Office of the Superintendant of Government Printing.

Macphail, R.M. 1954. *Campbell's English-Santali Dictionary*. 3rd ed. Benegaria: Santal Mission Press.

Parkin, R. 1991. *A Guide to Austroasiatic Speakers and Their Languages*. Oceanic Linguistics Special Publication No. 23. Honolulu: University of Hawaii Press.

Sebeok, T. 1943. "Phonemic Analysis of Santali." In *Journal of the American Oriental Society* 63: 66–67.

Soren, S.S.K. 1999. *Santalia: Catalogue of Santal Manuscripts in Oslo*. Copenhagen: NIAS.

Troisi, J. 1976. *The Santals: A Classified and Annotated Bibliography*. New Delhi: Manohar Book Service.

____ 1979. *Tribal Religion: Religious Beliefs and Practices among the Santals*. Columbia, MO: South Asia Books.

Zide, N.H. 1958. "Final Stops in Korku and Santali." In *Indian Linguistics* 19: 44–48.

____. 1967. "The Santali Ol Cemet Script." In *Languages and Areas: Studies Presented to George V. Bobrinskoy*, 180–189. Chicago.

____. 1972. "A Munda Demonstrative System: Santali." In J. Barrau *et al.* [eds.] *Langues et Techniques, Nature et Société I* (Papers for A. Haudricourt), pp. 267–274. Paris: Klincksieck.

____. forthcoming. "Three Munda Scripts." To appear in *Linguistics in the Tibeto Burman Area*.

[6] According to Parkin (1991: 15) "...(the Santals) have a strong tribal identity, marked by hostility to Hindus, advancement of the Santali language and traditional culture, and political activity through the Jharkhand Party...".

Serbo-Croatian

Wayles Browne

Language Name: Serbo-Croatian, Serbo-Croat. Self-denomination: *srpskohrvatski jezik* (српскохрватски језик). **Alternates:** (1) Croatian, especially referring to the standard form used in Croatia. Self-denomination: *Hrvatski jezik* (хрватски језик). (2) Serbian, referring to the standard used in Serbia. Self-denomination: *Srpski jezik* (срп ски језик). (3) Bosnian, as used in Bosnia-Hercegovina. Self-denomination: *Bosanski jezik* (босански језик).

Location: Spoken in the southeast European countries of Croatia, Serbia, Bosnia-Hercegovina, and Montenegro; widely known as a second language in Slovenia and Macedonia. (These were the six republics of the former Yugoslavia.) Serbo-Croatian is spoken by many hundreds of thousands of foreign workers in western Europe, including Germany, Sweden, France, and by immigrants to the United States, Canada, Chile, and Australia.

Family: West South Slavic subgroup of the South Slavic group of the Slavic branch of the Indo-European language family.

Related Languages: Serbo-Croatian is related to the other South Slavic languages, the closest being Slovenian (=SLOVENE); MACEDONIAN and BULGARIAN are less close.

Dialects: The three major dialects are (1) Kajkavian, (2) Čakavian, and (3) Štokavian, which is broken down into the subdialects Ekavian, Jekavian (=Ijekavian), and Ikavian. The Štokavian subdialects are the basis for the standard languages in all parts of the former Yugoslavia: Što.-Ekavian in Serbia and Što.-Jekavian in Croatia, Bosnia-Hercegovina, and Montenegro. This chapter presents examples in Jekavian.

Number of Speakers: 17–18 million.

Origin and History

In the sixth and seventh centuries A.D., South Slavs (including tribes of Croats and Serbs) came to the Balkans perhaps from Poland by crossing the lower Danube. There they encountered Illyrians (perhaps ancestors of modern Albanians), Vlachs, and other peoples, some of whom spoke LATIN as a legacy of the area's Roman occupation.

By the seventh century there were two main Slavic dialect groups in the Balkans: one (East South Slavic) gave rise to Bulgarian and Macedonian, and the other (West South Slavic) gave rise to Slovene and Serbo-Croatian. Serbo-Croatian eventually split into three dialect groups: Kajkavian, spoken in the north; Čakavian in the west; and Štokavian in the east, center, and southwest.

The area where Serbo-Croatian is spoken has long been the site of unstable political boundaries and hegemonies, and it has been divided between western and eastern influence in religious matters. In 803 the Croats accepted the suzerainty of Charlemagne and became Christianized through the Roman Church. The Serbian region came under the dominion of the Byzantine emperor and became Christianized through the Orthodox Church. In 862, at the request of the prince of Moravia (present-day Czech Republic), the Byzantine emperor sent two monks, Constantine (later called Cyril) and Methodius, who translated and disseminated the teachings of Christianity in a written language known as Old Church Slavonic, which was based on a Slavic dialect spoken in Salonika (today northern Greece). The two monks created the Glagolitic alphabet for this language. Later their followers brought the language to South Slavic areas and developed a second alphabet, the Cyrillic.

Old Church Slavonic marks the beginning of Slavic writing, there being no hard evidence of any writing system prior to it. Old Church Slavonic gave rise to local vernacular writing forms that were influenced by the prevailing languages. One of the oldest documents written in the vernacular in 1189 is a Cyrillic charter by which the ruler of Bosnia granted certain commercial privileges to merchants of Ragusa (Dubrovnik). In the Middle Ages literature was written in vernacular Croatian, using Glagolitic. The Roman alphabet was introduced into Croatia through the Catholic Church.

The Serbian literary language evolved from a Serbian variety of Old Church Slavonic using Cyrillic. Books were printed in this language in Belgrade, Skadar, Goražde, Mileševo, and other cities in the first half of the 16th century, but from the second half of that century until the mid-18th century, all printing ceased under the control of the Turks, who took over large parts of the Balkans beginning in the 14th century. When the production of books resumed, it was in a new language called Slavenoserbian, a combination of Russian Church Slavonic and the Serbian vernacular.

At the beginning of the 19th century there were literatures in at least three dialects of Croatian. With GERMAN and HUNGARIAN being forced upon them by the Austro-Hungarian Empire, the Croats were moved to develop a single Croatian literary language.

The work of two scholars in particular stands out as contributing to the development of the modern Serbo-Croatian language as a standard, unifying language. In 1818 the Serb Vuk Karadžić published a grammar and a dictionary based on Štokavian and suggested that a new literary language be based upon it. His language accurately reflected the sounds of Serbo-

Table 1: Consonants

		Labial	Dental	Palato-Alveolar	Palatal	Velar
Stops	Voiceless	p	t			k
	Voiced	b	d			g
Fricatives	Voiceless	f	s	š		h
	Voiced	v	z	ž		
Affricates	Voiceless		c	č	ć	
	Voiced			dž	đ	
Nasals		m	n		nj	
Laterals			l		lj	
Trill			r			
Glide					j	

Croatian speech and used a new version of Cyrillic. In 1830 Ljudevit Gaj, a Croat, reformed the Roman alphabet of Croatian Kajkavian, later endorsing the more widely spoken Štokavian. The idea of a joint Serbo-Croatian literary language, based on Štokavian, gained impetus when the Literary Accord was signed in 1850 by Croat and Serb men of letters. The new language could be written either in the Cyrillic or Roman alphabet, but the linguistic picture has remained complex, mirroring the intense factionalism that exists.

Yugoslavia as a unified state for South Slavs—the "Kingdom of Serbs, Croats and Slovenes"—came into being after World War I. After World War II, it was reestablished as a Communist federal republic, consisting of the republics of Croatia, Bosnia-Hercegovina, Serbia, Montenegro, Macedonia, and Slovenia. The Štokavian-Ekavian standard of Serbia and the Štokavian-Jekavian standard of Croatia, Bosnia-Hercegovina, and Montenegro continued to be used side by side although people were discouraged from calling them "Serbian" and "Croatian". It has been argued that Croatian and Serbian are not merely different varieties, but separate languages. In the 1990s the country of Yugoslavia broke up and four of the six republics petitioned for international recognition as independent states. Serbia and Montenegro reformed into a new Yugoslavia in 1992. Since then the region has been torn by fierce wars.

Orthography and Basic Phonology

The two orthographies of Serbo-Croatian, Cyrillic and Roman, have almost complete conformity with each other, having practically a one-to-one correspondence between the letters. The Roman alphabet is used for Croatian, and the Cyrillic alphabet (together with the Roman) is used for Serbian. Bosnians mostly use Roman (see Table 2).

H is phonetically either a velar [x] or glottal [h] fricative. *J* is a palatal glide. It is similar to the initial sound in ENGLISH "yes", not the initial sound in "jeep". *Dž* represents the voiced affricate in English "jeep".

There is no exact English equivalent to the Serbo-Croatian palatal affricates *ć* and *đ*. The closest English sounds to them are the "ch" of "cheap" and the "j" of "jeep" (pronounced with the tongue close to the roof of the mouth).

Table 2: Serbo-Croatian Cyrillic

Cyrillic	Roman	Cyrillic	Roman
А, а	A, a	Л, л	L, l
Б, б	B, b	Љ, љ	LJ, lj
Ц, ц	C, c	М, м	M, m
Ч, ч	Č, č	Н, н	N, n
Ћ, ћ	Ć, ć	Њ, њ	NJ, nj
Д, д	D, d	О, о	O, o
Џ, џ	DŽ, dž	П, п	P, p
Ђ, ђ	Đ, đ	Р, р	R, r
Е, е	E, e	С, с	S, s
Ф, ф	F, f	Ш, ш	Š, š
Г, г	G, g	Т, т	T, t
Х, х	H, h	У, у	U, u
И, и	I, i	В, в	V, v
Ј, ј	J, j	З, з	Z, z
К, к	K, k	Ж, ж	Ž, ž

Sequences of obstruents must all agree in voicing. The voicing of the last consonant in a sequence is transferred to all earlier consonants in the sequence. (The only exception is *v*, which can be preceded or followed by voiceless obstruents.) 'To travel' is *putovati*. 'Away, from' is *od*. 'To depart' ('travel away') is *otputovati*. 'To count' is *brojati*. 'Together' is *s*. 'To add' ('count together') is *zbrajati*.

In addition, *r* can serve as the nucleus of a syllable in a word like *drvo* 'tree', which has two syllables, *dr* and *vo*.

Table 3: Vowels

	Front	Mid	Back
High	i		u
Mid	e		o
Low		a	

Older Serbo-Croatian had an extra vowel that linguists transcribe as *ě*. This vowel yielded *e* in the Ekavian subdialect (*čovek* 'man', *peva* 'sings') but *je* or *ije* in the Jekavian (*čovjek, pjeva*).

Serbo-Croatian is characterized by pitch accent. An accented syllable can have a rising pitch or a falling pitch. Falling accent occurs only on the first syllable of a word. Since a rising accent places a high pitch on the syllable following it, rising accent does not occur on a word-final syllable. Accent distinctions are not represented in the orthography.

Basic Morphology

Serbo-Croatian nouns are inflected for case, number, and gender. The cases are nominative, accusative, genitive, dative, locative, instrumental, and vocative. Only some nouns have vocative forms, and the dative and locative are almost completely identical. In addition to singular and plural forms, there is a separate form used with the numerals 2, 3, and 4. The 2/3/4 forms are not inflected for case. Thus 'one dog' is *jedan pas* in the nominative, *jednog psa* in the genitive and accusative, etc. 'Dogs' are *psi* nominative, *pasa* (with inserted vowel) genitive, *pse* accusative, etc. 'Three dogs' are *tri psa;* it is the same for all cases. The genders are masculine, feminine, and neuter. Modifiers agree with the nouns they modify in case, number, and gender, and also in animacy; animate masculine singular objects have an accusative case form identical to the genitive.

There are no articles. However, adjectives show a remnant of a definite-indefinite distinction: *dobar pas* 'a good dog', *dobri pas* 'the good dog'.

Serbo-Croatian verbs, like those of other Slavic languages, are of two types: perfective and imperfective. Imperfective verbs are derived from perfectives by means of suffixes, and perfective verbs are derived from imperfectives by prefixes. The perfective equivalent of the imperfective verb *čitati* 'to read (in general, repeatedly)' is *pročitati* 'to read (and finish) something, read through'. *Pro* + *pisati* 'to write' yields *propisati* 'to prescribe (something)', which is perfective. From this we can make *propis-iva-ti* 'to prescribe (in general, repeatedly)', which is imperfective.

Serbo-Croatian verbs agree with their subjects in person and number, and, in the compound tenses, in gender. Of the commonly used (not rare or archaic) tenses, only the present is morphologically simple. The perfect and conditional are compound tenses formed of a participle combined with an inflected auxiliary verb.

Present:

	Singular	Plural
1st pers	čita-m	čita-mo
2nd pers	čita-š	čita-te
3rd pers	čita	čita-ju

Perfect (third person):

	Singular	Plural
Masculine	čita-o je	čita-li su
Feminine	čita-la je	čita-le su
Neuter	čita-lo je	čita-la su

Future:

	Singular	Plural
1st pers	čitat ću	čitat ćemo
2nd pers	čitat ćeš	čitat ćete
3rd pers	čitat će	čitat će

Outside of Croatia, the future-tense forms are spelled as single words even though these forms are infinitives with an inflected auxiliary. Thus, outside of Croatia, *čitat ću* is spelled *čitaću.*

Serbo-Croatian has a second future form used exclusively in subordinate clauses:

Kad	budem	znao,	reći	ću	ti.
when	be-1:SG.AUX	know:PART	tell.INF	will	you.DATIVE.SG

'When I know [in the future], I will tell you.'

Here *budem znao* is the second future, and the main clause has the regular future tense.

Basic Syntax

The basic word order of Serbo-Croatian is SVO, although other orders are possible when required by discourse structure. Regardless of what comes first in a sentence, clitic auxiliary verbs and clitic genitive/dative/accusative pronouns are required to be in the second position in a clause.

Within noun phrases, nouns follow demonstratives, numerals, and adjectives. Relative clauses follow the nouns they modify.

Sentences are negated by a prefix *ne-* added to the inflected verb; any indefinite pronouns receive the prefix *ni-*.

ni-tko	ni-šta	ne	radi	
no-who	no-what	not	do	'Nobody does anything.'

Contact with Other Languages

Serbo-Croatian has influenced Slovenian, Macedonian, and the languages of other groups in the former Yugoslavia, including ALBANIAN, Hungarian, ROMANIAN, SLOVAK, and earlier German. It in turn was influenced by neighboring German, Hungarian, GREEK, other Balkan languages, Latin, ITALIAN, FRENCH, RUSSIAN, and now English.

The Latin and Dalmato-Romanic, which was spoken by the native population in the Balkans, contributed words in certain fields such as fishing, maritime pursuits, and stoneworking. After the Turkish conquest there were many loanwords from TURKISH.

From Greek: *kaluđer* 'monk', *manastir* 'monastery', *trpeza* 'table', *hiljada* 'thousand'
From Italian: *pijaca* 'market' (< It. *piazza*), *škola* 'school'
From Hungarian: *varoš* 'town'
From Turkish: *lula* 'pipe', *rakija* 'brandy', *boja* 'color', *sokak* 'alley'
From German: *kuhinja* 'kitchen'
From English: *folklor* 'folklore'

There is a long Croatian tradition of finding native equivalents for foreign words: *tajnik* 'secretary' made from *tajna* 'secret'. Since World War II English has been the leading source of loans.

Common Words

man:	čovjek/čovek	long:	dugi
woman:	žena	small:	mali
water:	voda	yes:	da
sun:	sunce	no:	ne
three:	tri	good:	dobar
fish:	riba	bird:	ptica
big:	velik	dog:	pas
tree:	drvo		

Example Sentences

(1) Tko pjeva, zlo ne misli.
Who:NOM sing:PRES.3s evil:NEUT.ACC not think:PRES.3s
'He who sings, thinks no evil.'

(2) Tko laže, taj i krade.
Who:NOM lie:PRES:3s that also steal:PRES:3s
'He who lies, also steals.'

(3) Sestra je kupila bratu
Sister:FEM is:3RD SG buy:PART brother:MASC:DAT

poklon.
present:ACC
'The sister bought the brother a present.'

Efforts to Preserve, Protect, and Promote the Language

As part of the Croatian tradition of purism, Croatian linguists have sought to find domestic replacements for foreign words. In the 1980s, Yugoslav government authorities began supporting the provision of schooling in Serbo-Croatian for the children of "guest workers" in western European countries. The wars among the different factions of Serbo-Croatian speakers will undoubtedly cause divergence in the language's standards through killing, mass expulsions, and resettlement of refugees.

Select Bibliography

Benson, Morton. 1990a. *An English-Serbo-Croatian Dictionary*. Cambridge: Cambridge University Press.

____. 1990b. *A Serbo-Croatian-English Dictionary*. Cambridge: Cambridge University Press.

Browne, Wayles. 1993. "Serbo-Croat." In *The Slavonic Languages,* ed. Bernard Comrie & Greville Corbett, London: Routledge, 306–387.

Corbett, Greville. 1987. "Serbo-Croat." In *The World's Major Languages*, ed. Bernard Comrie. London: Croom Helm, 391–409.

Filipović, Rudolf, ed., 1968–; 1975–. *Publications of the Yugoslav Serbo-Croatian- English Contrastive Project*; *Publications of the Zagreb English-Serbo-Croatian Contrastive Project*. Zagreb: Institute of Linguistics.

Kordić, Snježana. 1997. "Serbo-Croatian." In *Series Languages of the World, Materials 148*. Munich: LINCOM EUROPA.

Naylor, Kenneth. 1980. "Serbo-Croatian." In *The Slavic Literary Languages: Formation and Development,* ed. Alexander M. Schenker and Edward Stankiewicz. New Haven: Yale Concilium on International and Area Studies, 65–83.

Sesotho

Katherine Demuth and 'Malillo Machobane

Name: Sesotho. **Alternates:** *Southern Sotho, Sesuto, Sutu.*

Location: Lesotho and adjacent central parts of South Africa including urban centers around Johannesburg.

Family: Southern Bantu group of the Bantu branch of Niger-Khordofanian.

Related Languages: Other Sotho languages, including various dialects of Setswana (spoken in Botswana and adjacent parts of South Africa), Sepedi, or Northern Sotho (spoken to the north of Johannesburg), and Silozi, or Lozi (spoken in southeastern Zambia). In general, there is much mutual intelligibility among these languages. Sesotho is also related to other southern Bantu languages of Guthrie's zone 30, which include the Nguni languages (ZULU, XHOSA, Ndebele, SISWATI) as well as Venda, Tonga, and Shangaan.

Dialects: Sesotho is generally considered to be relatively homogeneous, especially within Lesotho. Even within Lesotho, however, there is an ideolectal difference with respect to a rule of verb-tone sandhi. Sesotho as spoken in South Africa contains another tonal rule affecting verb stems, and shows the influence of Setswana in the tense/aspect system.

'Deep Sesotho', or *Sesotho se tebileng*, is a more formal speech register used for special purposes such as storytelling and the like. This more ritualized use of Sesotho is generally maintained in rural areas by older generations, and is being lost by the young and the urban, especially with the spread of television and radio, as well as an increasing number of lexical items from ENGLISH, AFRIKAANS, Zulu, and other languages in the area.

Number of Speakers: About 5 million as a first language, split approximately equally between South Africa and Lesotho, and in addition many more speak it as a second language.

Origin and History

It is thought that speakers of contemporary Southern Bantu languages migrated south from the northern lake regions. Speakers of the Sotho languages were subsequently dispersed in the mid-1800s, fleeing the armies of Shaka Zulu that were based in what is today the province of Kwa Zulu Natal, South Africa. This Sotho dispersion accounts in part for the Silozi presence in Zambia to the north. It is also responsible for the creation of one major Sesotho linguistic group, where speakers of various Sotho regional dialects came to be politically united under the protection of Moshoeshoe in the mountains of what is today Lesotho. Interestingly, Sesotho seems to have lost some of the morphological richness found in other Sotho languages. It is possible that morphological leveling arose as a result of this political upheaval and subsequent national and linguistic incorporation and consolidation.

Orthography and Basic Phonology

Sesotho is written with two different orthographic systems, one used in Lesotho, the other used in South Africa. The major difference between the two is that in Lesotho orthography phonemic /l/ is used for the [d] allophonic variant before high vowels (e.g., /li/ is pronounced [di]), and the mid vowel graphemes /e/ and /o/ are used for front and back glides respectively. In addition, Lesotho *ch, kh, tš, 'n,* and *'m* = South African *tjh, kg, tsh, nn,* and *mm*, respectively. Several different orthographic conventions were used by different missionaries in the 1800s and early 1900s, generally resulting in no orthographic representation of aspiration on aspirated stops, and high mid vowels being represented as high vowels. Lesotho orthography will be used here unless otherwise indicated.

Sesotho has a rich inventory of consonants—as many as 45—including an extensive array of affricates and laterals, as shown in the consonant table. Word-internal syllabic laterals and nasals are orthographically represented with a double consonant *nn, ll*, whereas word-initial nasals are represented with an apostrophe, *'n*. Sesotho also demonstrates phonemic use of aspiration, indicated by *h* after the voiceless stops /p/ and /t/, the click /q/, and the lateral affricate /tl/. Aspirated /k/ is realized as /k'h/, the aspirated affricate /ts/ as /tš/, and the aspirated lateral fricative /tl/ as /tlh/. Sesotho has no /d/ or /g/ phoneme. [d] occurs only as an allophonic variant of /l/ before high vowels /i/ and /u/, as in *mosali* /mʊsɑdi/ 'woman' and *lumela* / dumɛlɑ/ 'hello, agree'.

In Table 1, consonants found in foreign acquisitions are written in brackets [ ], and (*z*), (*r*), and (*o*) indicate alternate positions for *j, r,* and *o*, respectively. Orthographic *g* is /x/.

Vowels:

	Front	Back
High	i	u
Mid-high	e	o
Mid	e	o
Mid-low	e	o
Low	a	

While most Bantu languages have five or seven vowel sys-

Table 1: Consonants

		Labial	Labio-dental	Alveolar	Pre-palatal	Velar	Uvular	Glottal	Compounds
Stops	Voiced	b							bj
	Ejective	p		t		k			pj
	Aspirated	ph		th		k'h			psh
Fricatives	Voiced		[v]		(z)				
	Voiceless		f	s	sh	[g]		h	fsh
Affricates	Voiced				j				
	Voiceless			ts	tj				
	Aspirated			tš	ch	kh			
Lateral Affricates	Ejective			tl					
	Aspirated			tlh					
Laterals	Voiced			l, ll					
	Fricative			hl					
Nasals		m		n	ny	ng			
	Syllabic	'm, mm		'n, nn	'ny	'ng			
Trill				r			(r)		
Glides		(o)			e	(o)			
Clicks	Ejective				q				
	Aspirated				qh				
Nasal					nq				

tems, Sesotho has a nine-vowel system, with three different heights of mid vowels as indicated in the vowel chart. Orthographically, all mid vowels /i/, /e/, /ɛ/, and /u/, /o/, /ɔ/ are written with the graphemes *e* and *o*, respectively.

Tone is not marked in Sesotho orthography. The tonal system can be described as containing a two-way tonal contrast between (H)igh tone and the lack of high tone, the latter being realized as L(ow) tone. Tone functions both lexically and grammatically in the language. Verbs can be classified as H or L toned and this basic tone then interacts with tone-spreading phenomena to produce a specific tonal pattern or tonal melody.

Basic phonological rules include "strengthening" (n + *ruta* > *nthute* 'teach me'), palatalization (*roba* 'break' > *rojoa* 'be broken'), and alveolarization (*laela* 'order' > *laetsa* 'cause to order').

Sesotho has no phonemic vowel length, but the penultimate syllable of phonological phrases is somewhat lengthened. Open class word roots are generally disyllabic. Monosyllabic verbs in the imperative must therefore be lengthened to form two syllables or a minimal prosodic word, e.g., *ja* 'eat' > *eja*! ~ *jaa*!

Basic Morphology

Like most other Bantu languages, Sesotho has a rich noun-class gender and agreement system. Nouns fall into several singular/plural class pairs, and verbs and nominal modifiers 'agree' with these nouns through the use of fairly phonologically regular agreement prefixes.

The Sesotho noun-class system has 14 productive noun classes, as shown below. Although much of the productive semantics of Bantu noun-class systems have been lost, some of the core semantics remains, especially in the derivation of new nouns.

Class	Singular	Class	Plural	Gloss
1	mo-tho	2	ba-tho	'person'
1a	Ø-rakhali	2a	bo-rakhali	'aunt'
3	mo-se	4	me-se	'dress'
5	le-tsatsi	6	ma-tsatsi	'day/sun'
7	se-fate	8	li-fate	'tree'
9	Ø-ntja	10	li-ntja	'dog'
14	bo-phelo			'health'
15	ho-pheha			'to cook'

Nouns agree with a wide range of nominal modifiers, as well as relative pronouns and verbs. The use of noun class and agreement morphology is illustrated in the following sentence (SM =

subject agreement, ADJ = adjective, PERF = perfect tense/aspect, and numerals = respective noun classes). Note that Sesotho does not use case marking or articles.

Lesela le-lecha le-taboh-ile
5-cloth 5ADJ-5new 5SM-torn-PERF
'The new cloth is torn.'

Unlike other Bantu languages that use noun class prefixes in the formation of locatives, Sesotho uses only the invariant locative suffix *-(e)ng*:

tafoleng 'to, at, on, by the table'
bukeng 'by, in, near the table'

As in other Bantu languages, the Sesotho "verb" is a highly inflected entity composed of the verb root, an obligatory subject agreement marker, the possibility of a tense/aspect marker (FUT = future), and a final vowel (FV) that generally marks mood. If the object is pronominalized (OBJ) it occurs immediately prior to the verb root, as shown below:

Ke-tla-ba-bon-a
1s.SM-FUT-OBJ-Verb-FV 'I will see them.'

In addition to this inflectional morphology, Sesotho verbs also exhibit a productive system of derivational morphology, where grammatical function–changing morphemes (verbal extensions) are infixed between the verb root and the final vowel. These infixes include the passive, applicative, reversive, reciprocal, etc. In general, verbal extensions occur immediately after the verb root, followed by the perfect tense/aspect (Perf) and then the passive (Pass), if applicable:

rek-is-its-o-e
Verb-CAUS-PERF-PASS-FV
'caused to have bought'

The reflexive *-i-* however, occurs immediately prior to the verb stem, and is in complementary distribution with a pronominal object, for example, *ipona* 'see oneself'.

Deverbal nouns can be productively created from most verbs, and derive slightly different meanings depending on the noun class to which they are assigned. Suffixal diminutive and augmentative/feminine morphology is also productive. Although noun-class prefixes are generally considered to be obligatory, those from Classes 5, 7, 8 and 10 can be omitted when a nominal modifier or subject agreement marker follows:

(le)tsatsi lena 'this day/today'
(le)tsatsi le chabile 'the sun shown'

Basic Syntax

Sesotho is an SVO language. However, because Sesotho maintains obligatory subject marking on the verb, and because the pronominal object prefixes to the verb root, subject and object can be extraposed under appropriate discourse situations, giving rise to any surface order of lexical items:

SVO Thabo o-rat-a nama
T. 1SM-Verb-FV 9meat
'Thabo likes meat.'

VOS o-rat-a nama Thabo
OVS nama o-a-e-rat-a Thabo
SOV Thabo nama o-a-e-rat-a
VSO o-a-e-rat-a Thabo nama
OSV nama Thabo o-a-e-rat-a

In locative inversion and expletive constructions, the subject comes after the verb, and the subject marker is *ho-* (Class 17–locative):

(Maseru) ho-je-o-a nama
Maseru 17SM-Verb-PASS-FV 9meat
'(In Maseru) meat is eaten.'

Main-clause negation in simple tense constructions occurs after the lexical subject, but prior to the verb complex:

Thabo ha a-rat-e nama
Thabo NEG 1SM-Verb-FV 9meat
'Thabo doesn't like meat.'

In main clauses with complex tense constructions, and in subordinate clauses including relative clauses, negation is embedded within the verbal complex itself: (REL = relative complementizer, RL = relative suffix).

nama eo Thabo a-sa-e-rat-e-ng
9meat 9REL T. 1SM-NEG-OBJ-Verb-FV-RL
'The meat that Thabo doesn't like'

The third-person subject marker, final vowel, and tonal melody all change in negative, subjunctive, and participial/embedded constructions.

Contact with Other Languages

Sesotho has borrowed various lexical items from surrounding languages, including Zulu, Afrikaans, and English. Sesotho has incorporated many words from Zulu along with their accompanying clicks (e.g., *ho-qala* 'to begin', *ho-qeta* 'to finish'). The relatively large number of borrowings from Zulu accounts for many of the differences in vocabulary between Sesotho and TSWANA. Verbs from other languages are incorporated morphologically with a final vowel *-a* (e.g., *pusha* < [English] 'push'). Nouns are incorporated into noun classes on the basis of either phonology or semantics, or assigned to the "default" Noun Class 9.

"Semantic classification"

1/2 From English: *mo-lepera* (< *leper)* 'leper'
1a/2a From Afrikaans: *base* (< *baas*) 'boss'
7 From FRENCH: *se-fora* (< *français*) 'French')

"Phonological classification"

3/4 From English: *mo-chini (< machine)* 'machine, engine'
5/6 From Afrikaans: *le-lente* (< *lint)* 'ribbon'

"Default classificaton"

9/10 From Afrikaans: *tafole* (< *tafel)* 'table'
9/10 From English: *ofisi* (< *office*) 'office'

Common Words

Adjectives require an agreement prefix in order to agree with the noun they modify.

man:	monna	long:	-lelele
woman:	mosali	small:	-nyane
water:	metsi	yes:	e
sun:	letsatsi	no:	e-e
three:	-raro	good:	-tle
fish:	tlhapi	bird:	nonyana
big:	-holo	dog:	ntja
tree:	sefate		

Example Sentences

(1) Lintja tsena li-noele lebese.
10:dog 10:DEM 10:SM-eat.PERF.FV 5:milk
'These dogs drank the milk.'

(2) Re-batla lebese leletle.
1PL.SM-want.FV 5:milk 5:ADJ.5:good
'We want good milk.'

(3) Ba-batla lebese le-beiloeng tafoleng.
2SM-want.FV 5:milk 5:REL-put.PERF.PASS.FV.RL 9:table:LOC
'They want the milk that was put on the table.'

Efforts to Preserve, Protect, and Promote the Language

Sesotho is one of the Southern African Bantu languages with a relatively long literary history, with epic novels being written and read during the late 19th century. The Sesotho Academy, established in Lesotho in 1972, has the broad aim of preserving, protecting, and promoting the use of the Sesotho language and has worked together in pursuit of these goals with a similar body in South Africa. Although many rural speakers of Sesotho are monolingual, much of the urban population in both Lesotho and South Africa is multilingual, and all of the Bantu languages spoken in South Africa now have official status. The impact this will have on the preservation and promotion of Sesotho in its spoken and written form, both within the educational system as well as more informally, is still to be determined.

Select Bibliography

Demuth, Katherine. 1989. "Maturation and the Acquisition of Sesotho Passive." In *Language* 65: 56–80.

_____. 1990. "Locatives, impersonals and expletives in Sesotho." In *Linguistic Review* 7: 233–249.

_____. 1993. "Issues in the Acquisition of the Sesotho tonal system." In *Journal of Child Language* 20: 275–301.

_____. 1998. "Argument structure and the acquisition of Sesotho applicatives." In *Linguistics* 36 (4): 781–806.

Demuth, Katherine and Carolyn Harford. 1999. "Verb raising and subject inversion in comparative Bantu." In *Journal of African Languages and Linguistics* 18: 1–19.

Doke, C.M., and S.M. Mofokeng. 1957. *Textbook of Southern Sotho Grammar*. Cape Town: Longman.

Machobane, 'Malillo. 1989. "Some restrictions of transitivizing morphemes in Sesotho." Unpublished Ph.D. dissertation, McGill University: Montreal.

_____. 1993. "The ordering restriction between the Sesotho applicative and causitive suffixes." In *South African Journal of African Languages* 12 (4): 129–137.

_____. 1995. "The Sesotho locative constructions." In *Journal of African Languages and Linguistics* 16: 115–136.

_____. 1997. "The Sesotho control verbs with applicative suffix." In *South African Journal of Liguistics* 15: 59–64.

Paroz, R.A. 1974. *Southern Sotho-English Dictionary*. Morija: Morija Printing Works. [Revision of A. Mabille & H. Dieterlen.]

SHAN

David B. Solnit

Language Name: Shan. **Autonym:** Speakers of the language call themselves *Tai táj* often followed by a specifying word like *long lŏŋ* 'great' or *Mao máaw*, a place-name. The ENGLISH word "Shan" is a rendition of the Burmese name for the people, spelled *hram* and pronounced *hjan~hjã* (this word is cognate with "Siam"). Shan speakers in China are considered to be part of the Dai nationality, which also includes the Tai Lue of Xishuangbanna in southern Yunnan; therefore in the Chinese scheme both Shan and Lue (plus Neua; see below) are considered 'dialects' (*fangyan*) of the 'Dai language' (*daiyu*).

Location: The center of the Shan-speaking area is more or less the western half of Shan State, Burma. Shan speakers also live in adjoining areas of Thailand, Laos and Yunnan Province of China.

Family: Shan belongs to Southwestern Tai, a large group of closely related languages found across a wide area of southern China and northern Southeast Asia. Such a distribution, in which languages cover a broad area separated by small linguistic differences, is sometimes called a "dialect continuum" and typically results from an expansion that is relatively recent and relatively rapid. This sort of distribution also makes it hard to draw linguistic boundaries: languages differentiate most clearly when they are widely separated by both time and geography, but the Southwestern Tai languages have been neither. Therefore lines are hard to draw both inside and outside of Shan, and this fact must be kept in mind when considering the topics of location, related languages, and dialects. Adding to the complexity are recent migrations and other sociocultural factors, such as the attitudes and concepts held by the people themselves about their own and other languages.

Tai is itself a branch of the Kadai (or Tai-Kadai) family. The further affiliations of Kadai are uncertain: the older view of Tai as a Sino-Tibetan language has lost favor, although the alternative proposal placing Kadai with Austronesian and Miao-Yao in an Austro-Tai stock has gained a few adherents.

Related Languages: There are languages that may be considered either varieties of Shan or distinct but closely related languages. These include Khamti in northernmost Burma, Khuen *khɯn*, centered on the city of Kengtung in eastern Shan State, and Neua *nɯa*, *nə*, spoken in the Dehong area and other parts of southwestern Yunnan Province. All of these have been called "Shan" in various contexts; for example, Neua is called "Chinese Shan" in older English-language sources.

After these, Shan's closest relatives are other Southwestern Tai languages such as Tai Yuan (Northern Thai, Khammuang, Lanna Thai), Central or Standard Thai (Siamese), Lao, and White and Black Tai. Not as close are other Tai languages of the Central and Northern subgroups such as Nung (Tay) of northern Vietnam, and Zhuang and Buyi of Guangxi and Guizhou Provinces (respectively) of China. More distant relatives are all found in China, including the Kam-Sui languages of Guizhou and Guangxi such as Sui, Kam, and Mulam; the Hlai (Li) languages of Hainan; and the Gelao languages of Guizhou.

Dialects: In general Shan varies along a north-south axis. The southern half of Shan territory has definite boundaries: on the southeast it is clearly differentiated from Tai Yuan, and on the south and southwest it is fully distinct from Burmese and the Karen languages. In spite of a few references (mostly older) to Khuen as a type of Shan, this language is also distinct from Shan, having more affinities with Tai Yuan and Lue, so Khuen may be taken as an eastern boundary of this southern Shan area. (Inclusion of Khuen in discussions of Shan may also be prompted by the sociopolitical fact of its incorporation in the Shan states–Burma political system). The dialects of this southern area are most clearly Shan, while to the north there is a gradual transition through Northern Shan varieties into Nuea and Khamti.

Phonological variation in Shan and its near kin is most notable in (1) tonal systems and (2) development of certain initial consonants (data are insufficient to make any generalizations about lexical or other types of variation).

Comparative Tai Tones: Terminology and Display. In comparing the tone systems of Tai and other Asian tonal languages it has been found most useful to compare the ways that the original three tones of the protolanguage have split and recombined under the conditioning influence of initial consonants. Proto-Tai had three tones in smooth syllables (those with final sonorant or vowel), conventionally labeled A B C. Checked syllables (with final voiceless stop) were atonal, but since they later acquired tonal contrasts they are labeled D, and since vowel length is a further conditioning factor in these later tones of the checked syllables they are subdivided into DS(hort) and DL(ong). The features that conditioned tonal development define four classes of Proto-Tai initial consonants:

1-voiceless sonorants, fricatives, and aspirated obstruents, e.g., *hm hn f s ph kh*
2-voiceless unaspirated obstruents, e.g., *p t k*
3-glottal stop and voiced glottalized stops (probably implosive), i.e., *ʔ ɓ ɗ* (the latter are usually written *ʔb ʔd* in diachronic studies of Tai)
4-voiced sonorants and obstruents, e.g., *m n ŋ b d g*

It is convenient to display the historical origins of the tones of modern Tai languages in a matrix, with the prototones on the horizontal axis and the protoinitial consonants on the vertical. The consonants are listed in terms of the Classes 1–4 as defined above, each class numeral followed by examples from the labial place of articulation:

	A	B	C	DS	DL
1 (*hm f ph)					
2 (*p)					
3 (*ʔ ʔb)					
4 (*m b)					

As an example, the five-tone system of Siamese (i.e., modern Standard Thai) is displayed below:

	A	B	C	DS	DL
1 (*hm f ph)	24	21	52	11	11
2 (*p)	33	21	52	11	11
3 (*ʔ ʔb)	33	21	52	11	11
4 (*m b)	33	52	453	55	52

The following points are to be noted:
1. The Siamese writing system for the most part reflects the Proto-Tai tones: syllables written with *maj eek* are from Tone B, those with *maj thoo* are from Tone C, and those with no mark are Tone A if smooth or D if checked.
2. Each prototone splits into two Siamese reflexes. This is typical, although some Tai languages show three-way splitting of one of the tones and some retain one unsplit tone.
3. The modern falling tone represents a merger of parts of two prototones: Tone B with *voiced initials, and Tone C with *voiceless aspirated, voiceless unaspirated, and glottalic initials. This merger can be given a shorthand representation in terms of coordinates in the matrix: B4=C123.
4. The new tones developed in checked syllables are all identifiable with one of the smooth-syllable tones (the 11 and 55 tones are considered to be variants of the 21 and 453 tones, respectively).

Southern Shan. Southern varieties of Shan have a merger of the Proto-Tai initials **f* *v* *ph* as *ph*, and a five-tone system with B4=C123 merger. Dialects of this type are spoken in such locations as Taunggyi, Panglong, and Hsipaw of Burma, and Mae Hong Son of Thailand, and are found in locations as far north as Kut Kai, about 60 kilometers south of Namkham (Jerold Edmondson, personal communication).

An example of the consonant merger is Hsi Paw (Gedney) *phaa*^{24} 'wall', *pha*^{21} 'flat of hand', *pha*^{41} 'sky', *pha*^{21} 'split', *pha*^{31} 'cloth'. Compare the Standard Thai cognates *fǎa fâa fáa phàa phâa.*

A representative tone system is that of Mae Hong Son Shan:

	A	B	C	DS	DL
1 (*hm f ph)	24	21	33ʔ	55	21
2 (*p)	24	21	33ʔ	55	21
3 (*ʔ ʔb)	24	21	33ʔ	55	21
4 (*m b)	45	33ʔ	52	52	33

The midlevel tone representing a merger of B4 with C123 is notated 33ʔ, indicating that it terminates in glottal stop.

Tai Neua. Tai Neua is spoken mainly in the area of Mangshi (Luxi), the capital of the Dehong Dai Autonomous Prefecture in Yunnan, China; it is also found in scattered pockets eastwards. Neua (*nüa, nɯa*[1]) means 'above, north, upstream'.

Neua differs from Shan consonantally in keeping **ph* distinct from **f* and **v*, and tonally in having a six-tone system with A23=B4 merger. Consonant examples in Meng Vo (Gedney) are *faa*^{24} 'wall', *faa*^{11} 'palm', *faa*^{31} 'sky', but *phaa*^{13} 'cloth'. A representative tone system is that of Mangshi (Edmondson and Solnit 1997):

	A	B	C	DS	DL
1 (*hm f ph)	25	21	31ʔ	31	13
2 (*p)	33	21	31ʔ	31	13
3 (*ʔ ʔb)	33	21	31ʔ	31	13
4 (*m b)	51	33	52ʔ	55	55

[1]Note that the diphthong /ɯa/ indicates that the source of this English neologism is not Shan, which would be /ñə/, but Siamese or perhaps Tai Yuan, Khuen, or LAO.

Northern Shan: A Transition Zone. The Tai languages spoken in between Neua and Shan, in an area straddling the Burma-China border, resemble Shan in having the **f-*v-*ph* merger but resemble Neua in showing the A23=B4 tone merger. These places include Namkham and Mu-se in Burma, and Ruili, Gengma, and Menglian in Yunnan, China (Mu-se and Ruili are directly across from each other on the Shweli River). Namkham is a center of the people and speech known as *Tai Mao tǎj máaw*. The term "Northern Shan", used occasionally and inconsistently in the English-language literature, could be appropriately used for these dialects.

Khamti. (A Burmese-style spelling, *Hkamti*, is also seen). This term applies to Tai languages spoken in areas of northernmost Burma such as Putao, Singkaling Khamti, and the Hukawng Valley. These languages are quite similar to the transitional Shan dialects just described, in that **f *v *ph* are merged as *ph*, and the tone system exhibits the A23=B4 merger. However, some sources indicate an additional merger of A1 with B23 or B123, which differs from anything reported for Neua.

Summary. There is an area, relatively discrete in linguistic terms, that we may call "Southern Shan", covering Shan State west of Kengtung and as far north as Kut Kai. The Tai languages well to the north of this area known as Khamti and Neua may be classed as Shan in the broad sense. That leaves Tai Mao and other languages that I have listed under Northern Shan and described as transitional. Whether to call these Shan in the broader or narrower sense is a question that cannot be answered on purely linguistic grounds, so I will leave it open. I would point out that using terms based on the full self-designations would both avoid a decision and make the close kinship explicit: Tai Long (for Southern Shan[2]), Tai Khamti, Tai Mao, Tai Neua.

Number of Speakers. The 1983 Census of Burma lists ethnicity rather than language, giving a figure of 2.89 million for people of Shan ethnicity. It is not known how many of these actually speak Shan. There are surely ethnic Shan whose first language is non-Shan (most likely Burmese), but on the other hand-members of other ethnicities speak Shan to varying degrees including bilingualism, so the 2.89 million figure is probably not far off for Shan speakers. In China, the members of the Dai nationality speaking dialects fitting the present definition of Shan in the narrow sense probably number only in the thousands.

Origin and History

The language ancestral to the Southwestern Tai languages was probably spoken in the China-Vietnam border region late in the first millennium A.D. The relative rapidity of the spread of speakers of these Tai languages is attested by the appearance of the name "Shan" in a Pagan (Burma) inscription dated 1120.

Although moving from Vietnam to Burma means an east-to-west direction of migration, there is much Shan tradition of entering Burma from the north. Of course an overall westward movement does not exclude the possibility of significant southerly movements in particular times and areas.

The Shan-dominated state of Ava ruled Upper Burma during the 14th and 15th centuries, and extensive Shan-Burman interaction has continued up to the present.

Orthography and Basic Phonology

The Shan writing system is closely related to those of Burmese and Mon, hence is ultimately of Indic origin. In its traditional form it marks tone only in limited circumstances and does not distinguish certain vowels that differ from each other by one degree of height, such as *i e* and *u o*. Cushing's *Shan and English Dictionary* supplements the Shan script with numerals for the tones, and for the vowels a letter code that cannot be easily summarized (see Egerod's 1957 article for an interpretation). In 1955 the script was reformed with a set of additional symbols marking the tones and all vowel distinctions.

The following phonological sketch applies to Southern Shan and is based on Egerod's (1957) description of the "educated speech" of Taunggyi, the capital of Shan state, supplemented by my own observation of Shan as spoken in the vicinity of Mae Hong Son town in northwestern Thailand.

Of the two starred initials, *s* is unaspirated and is realized as an affricate *ts* in some locations; *sh* is aspirated; both may be slightly palatalized. In Mae Hong Son *s* is an alveo-palatal affricate *tɕ*, and *sh* is an ordinary *s*. The Proto-Tai antecedents of these initials are palatal or prepalatal affricates, and they are retained as such in most modern Tai languages. The distinctive Shan treatment of these consonants has a geographic connection, since similar developments are found in both Burmese and many Karen languages.

Note also that initial *r* occurs mostly in PALI and (older) Burmese loanwords.

Table 1: Initial Consonants

	labial	dental	*	palatal	velar	glottal
voiceless unaspirated	p	t	s*		k	ʔ
voiceless aspirated	ph	th	sh*		kh	
nasal	m	n			ŋ	
fricative						h
liquid, glide	w	l, r		j		

Table 2: Vowels

	Front Unround	Central	Back Unround	Back Round
High	i		ɯ	u
Mid	e		ɤ	o
Low	æ	aa a		ɔ

[2]Although it is possible that Tai Long may be used by or for speakers of Northern/transitional Shan dialects as well.

æ and *ɤ* are herein transcribed *ɛ ə*, respectively, following common practice in comparative Tai studies. However, we will not follow the similar practice of rendering *ɯ* as *y* here. The contrast *aa a* includes both quantity and quality, with *a* usually higher than *aa*, approaching IPA *ə*. The peripheral vowels *e o ɛ ɔ* may be diphthongalized to various degrees.

Final consonants are *p t k m n ŋ w j ɰ*. w does not occur after back vowels, *j* does not occur after front vowels, and *ɰ* occurs only in the rhyme *aɰ*.

Tones. This is one of the areas in which locations differ noticeably, both in number of tones and their pronunciation (unfortunately the latter may differ even in different descriptions of a single dialect). The Southern dialects have five tones. The following is common to Egerod's Taunggyi, Gedney's Hsi Paw, and my Mae Hong Son. Each tone listing includes (1) parentheses enclosing an indication of the portion of the Proto-Tai tone matrix (see above) that the tone occupies, (2) a description, (3) the Chao pitch-level transcription, and (4) the diacritic for that tone in Egerod's transcription, shown over the vowel *a*:

(A123) low rising, 24, *ă*
(B123, D123L) low, level or slightly falling, 11 or 21, *à*
(B4=C123, D4L) mid, level or slightly falling, 33 or 31 (Hsi Paw "glottalized," Mae Hong Son ends in creak + glottal stop), *a* (unmarked)
(A4, D123S) high, level or slightly rising, 55 or 45, *á*
(C4, D4S) high falling, 41 or 52, *â*

Basic Morphology

There is no inflectional morphology (case marking, number/gender agreement, inflection of verbs for voice/tense/aspect, etc). Word formation is largely by compounding, e.g., *saaŋ lék* 'skilled, artisan' + 'iron' = 'blacksmith', *ti naŋ* 'place' + 'sit' = 'chair, seat'. The functions that in other languages are served by inflectional morphology are served in Shan by compounding, by word order, by phrasal formations such as verb serialization, or by particles: small but phonologically independent morphemes affixed to entire phrases or sentences.

Basic Syntax

Although little has been published that directly analyzes Shan syntax or discourse, the following generalizations can be made.

Word order is generally Subject-Verb-Object, with heads preceding their modifiers. *hə́n kăw* 'house' + 'I/me' = 'my house', *kón lĭ* 'person' + 'good' = 'good person', *lɛn pháɰ* 'run' + 'quick' = 'run quickly', *səm tók kwà* 'melt' + 'fall' + 'go' = 'melt down completely'. Possible exceptions to this rule include the negative *ʔám ~ ḿ*, which precedes the verb it negates; and numerals, which precede classifiers, as in *ŋú săam tŏ* 'snake' + 'three' + 'classifier for animals'—note, however, that the numeral+classifier construction as a whole follows the head noun 'snake'.

Prepositions exist, e.g., *nə̆ pháj* 'above' + 'fire' = 'over the fire', *náɰ hə́n* 'in' + 'house' = 'in the house'. However some of the locative/directional function served by prepositions in other languages is in Shan covered by verbs, e.g., *khaw hə́n* 'enter' + 'house' = 'go into a house'.

Adverbial expressions often follow the verb-object construction, as in *hə́t năj tík tík* 'do' + 'this' + 'continuously' = 'it went on like this without end'.

Contact with Other Languages

Like all Tai languages, Shan has inherited words borrowed from Chinese into Proto-Tai, perhaps most notably the numerals 3 through 10. Much more recent in date are large numbers of words of Burmese origin and a body of learned vocabulary borrowed from Pali and SANSKRIT.

Examples from Burmese include *pwé* 'festival' and *thí* 'umbrella'; Indic examples are *kàm phàa* 'age, era, cosmic cycle' and *pâthâmâ* 'basis'.

Common Words

man:	kón sáaj, phu sáaj
woman:	kón jíŋ, mɛ jíŋ
long:	jáaw
small:	ʔɔ̀n, nɔ̂j, lêk
water:	nâm
yes:	saɰ jâw ('it is so')
no:	ʔám saɰ kɔ́j ('it's not so')
sun:	kăaŋ wán
three:	săam
good:	lĭ
fish:	păa
bird:	nôk
big:	jáɰ, lôŋ
dog:	mă
tree:	ton mâj

Example Sentences

(1) ʔám lăj hôp kăn hɯ̆ŋ nà jâw.
not get meet together long.time along PERFECTIVE
'Long time no see.'

(2) hə́n nâj mí tĕm wâj táŋ mɛ́ŋshàap táŋ mát
house this have full put and cockroach and flea

ʔəə.
PARTICLE
'This house is full of cockroaches and fleas.'

(3) kamnâj mə phái maj nân kăaŋwán nâj ʔɔ̀ɔk
here(then) when fire burn that sun this emerge

jù cét pĭ păaj cét lŏn păaj cét
dwell seven year more seven month more seven

wán năj.
day this
'Then when the fire came [and destroyed the world], the sun stayed out for seven years, seven months and seven days.'

Efforts to Preserve, Protect, and Promote the Language

Shan is under pressure from the national majority languages Burmese, Chinese, and Siamese, and probably also from the regional majority language of Northern Thailand, Tai Yuan. The pressure in Burma is mitigated at present by the disordered political situation, which allows continuation of premodern conditions of communications and transportation. But by the same token, the political disorder has impelled a certain number of Shan speakers to move to Thailand. Political improvement will surely entail a drastic increase in pressure from Burmese, and in some cases, English.

Some efforts to counteract these pressures may be mentioned. There exists a Shan culture journal published by Rangoon University, and a certain number of Shan magazines and books are published in Burma using the reformed script.

Select Bibliography

Cushing, Josiah Nelson. 1888a. *A Shan and English Dictionary*. 1st. ed. Rangoon. Reprinted in 1971, by Gregg International Publishers Limited, Westmead, Farnborough, Hants., England.

____. 1888b. *Elementary Handbook of the Shan Language*. Rangoon. Reprinted in 1971, by Gregg International Publishers Limited, Westmead, Farnborough, Hants., England.

Edmondson, Jerold A. and David B. Solnit. 1997. "Comparative Shan." In Edmondson, Jerold A. and David B. Solnit (eds.), *Comparative Kadai: The Tai Branch. Publications in Linguistics 124*. Arlington: Summer Institute of Linguistics and University of Texas at Arlington.

Glick, Irving, and Sao Tern Moeng. 1991. *Shan for English Speakers: Dialogues, Readings, and Vocabulary*. Wheaton: Dunwoody Press.

Li Fang-kuei. 1977. *A Handbook of Comparative Tai*. Honolulu: the University Press of Hawaii.

Mix, H.W. 1920. *An English-Shan Dictionary*. Rangoon: American Baptist Mission Press, F.D. Phinney Supt.

Saimong Mangrai, Sao. 1965. *The Shan States and the British Annexation*. Cornell University Southeast Asia Program Data Paper No. 57. Ithaca: Cornell University Dept. of Asian Studies.

Young, Linda W.L. 1985. *Shan Chrestomathy: An Introduction to the Dai Mau Language and Literature*. Lanham: University Press of America.

SHONA

Hazel Carter

Language Name: Shona. **Autonym:** *chi-Shóna* or *chi-vanhu* ('language of the [indigenous] people').

Location: Principally spoken in Zimbabwe, central Mozambique (down to the coast), northeastern Botswana and southern Zambia.

Family: Bantu.

Related Languages: Most closely related to the Bantu languages Tonga in Zambia and Zimbabwe, and Nyanja/Chewa in Zambia and Malawi.

Dialects: Principal dialects are: Zezuru, in the vicinity of Harare, the capital; Manyika, in the eastern highlands, around Mutare (Umtali); Karanga, south of Zezuru, centered in Masvingo (formerly Ft. Victoria); Ndau, in southeast Zimbabwe and central Mozambique; Korekore, north and northwest along Zambezi; and Kalanga, spoken by groups, mostly in Botswana, cut off during Ndebele invasions (distinguished by having [l] where other dialects have [r]).

Each of these has a number of subdialects, and all have differences of pronunciation, phonology (including tonal system), morphology, and vocabulary. An interesting recent variety is *chi-Haráre*, based principally on Zezuru, with massive lexical input from ENGLISH.

Number of Speakers: 7–10 million in Zimbabwe.

Origin and History

The Shona have a tradition of migration from the north, possibly from Tanganyika. They, or more specifically the Karanga, are descendants of the inhabitants of the empire of Monomotapa (or Mwene-mutapa); the name was recorded by the Portuguese in 1506, and the most famous holder of the title ruled in the 17th century. It is this Monomotapa who is thought by some to have ordered the construction of much of the famous (now ruined) buildings at Great Zimbabwe. The Karanga were known at one time as Rozvi (*va-rozví* 'destroyers') from their depredations among other groups, including the Mbire (now called the Zezuru).

Ndebele incursions of the 19th century drove a wedge through the Shona, isolating the Western dialects from the main body. A former name for the language is *chi-Swína*, said to be from the verb *-svina* 'squeeze', in reference to the partiality of the Shona for eating caterpillars, and their way of extracting the contents.

A vocabulary of Ndau (called "Sofala") was included in a work of 1856, but more substantial work on the language began from the 1890s onward. In 1929, Clement M. Doke undertook a comparative phonetic study of the dialects, and made proposals for a unified orthography. The most detailed and comprehensive published studies of the language are by George Fortune, who became first head of the Department of African Languages and Literature at what is now the University of Zimbabwe at Harare.

The *Standard Shona Dictionary*, basically a Shona-English dictionary, compiled by a Shona Language Committee under the direction of the late Michael Hannan, was first published in 1959. It has gone through several editions, each time with improvements, such as the recording of tone patterns, additional entries, and special sections on botanical names and ideophones. Other smaller but useful dictionaries are those by Desmond Dale that include a Shona-Shona version. Of particular note is the new (1996) *Duramazwi rechiShona*, a comprehensive Shona-Shona dictionary, edited by Herbert Chimhundu, the current head of the University Department.

Many of the early publications in Shona were by missionaries, including, as one would expect, much didactic material such as readers for schoolchildren and instructional manuals. The establishment of a literature bureau in 1954 "to promote a supply of literature for Africa through commercial publishers", and including the holding of literary competitions, did much to stimulate the production of novels, short stories, and poetry, both modern and traditional. The first novel to appear was *Feso* by Solomon Mutswairo. There is now a flourishing literature, which also includes plays, newspaper articles and scripts for radio and TV. Poetry has always figured largely in traditional Shona life (it has been said "every Shona is a poet"), and the output of poetry on both traditional and imported models has been phenomenal. Collection of oral literature is in progress.

Orthography and Basic Phonology

The first serious attempts to write Shona were made in the 19th century, principally by missionaries. Several different systems were developed, most of which attempted phonetic rather than phonemic representation. As mentioned above, Clement Doke, a South African linguist, was commissioned to undertake an analytic comparison of the Shona dialects, and in 1933 made recommendations for a unified orthography based on the three central dialects of Zezuru, Manyika, and Karanga.

Table 1: Consonants

		Bilabial	Labio-dental	Alveolar	Palato-Alveolar	Palatal	Velar	Glottal
Stops	Voiceless	p		t			k	
	Voiced	(b)		(d)			(g)	
	Murmured	bh		dh			g	
Implosives		b		d			g	
Fricatives-plain	Voiceless		f	s	sh			
	Voiced		(v)					
	Murmured		vh	z	zh			h
Fricatives Retroflex	Voiceless			sz				
	Murmured			zv				
Affricates-plain	Voiceless		pf	ts	ch			
	Murmured		bv	dz	j			
Affricates-Retroflex	Voiceless			tsv				
	Voiced			dzv				
Nasals	Voiced	m		n		ny	n' (n)	
	Murmured	mh		nh		ny		
Trill	Voiced			r				
	Murmured			r				
Approximants	Voiced	w	v			y		
	Murmured	hw						

This became known as the Standard Shona Orthography, which has undergone several revisions since, the most radical being that of 1955. The first version used six special characters, now discarded; the current form uses Roman letters only, with 16 digraphs, two trigraphs and one apostrophized character.

Shona speakers interpret the spelling in terms of their own dialects; for example, the character *v,* unless followed by *h* represents the labiodental approximant [ʋ], found in Zezuru but not Manyika, where it is replaced by [w]; a Manyika reader therefore interprets written *v* and *w* both as [w]. The spelling is largely phonemic; e.g., the phoneme /w/ has several allophones, but not all are pronounced [w].

Among the digraphs, *dy* and *ty* represent sounds that differ among the dialects, but are pronounced as the sequences [ɟg] as in "lodge gate" and [čk] as in "latch key" respectively in Zezuru. [ɟg] is accompanied by murmur or breathy voice. Examples are *kudyá* 'to eat' and *kutyá* 'to fear'.

The implosives [ɓ ɗ ɠ], shown as *b d g* without parentheses on the chart, differ from their plain voiced (ex-)plosive counterparts in their manner of production. For the plain voiced plosives, the vocal cords vibrate with the air coming from the lungs; for the implosives, the larynx is lowered and the air is momentarily drawn down while the vocal cords vibrate. Murmured consonants, represented by a voiced consonant letter preceded or followed by *h*, are distinguished from other voiced consonants by the vocal cords being held partially apart during vibration; murmur is also known as breathy voice. The plain voiced consonants /b d g v/ (shown in parentheses in the table) are of limited distribution, occurring only after nasals. The velar nasal [ŋ], as in the English word "sing", is represented by the character *n* before *g* and elsewhere by *n'*.

As indicated in Table 1 above, Shona orthography does not distinguish all consonants in the language: *g*, for example, can represent a plain voiced, murmured, or implosive velar stop. Further, tone is not normally represented, except in linguistic works.

Table 2: Vowels

	Front	Central	Back
High	i		u
Mid	e		o
Low		a	

Shona does not distinguish long from short vowels phonemically. However, in ordinary speech, as opposed to poetic delivery or greeting mode, the vowel of the penultimate syllable of a word is lengthened.

Tone. Shona is a tone language, with two basic tones, high (H) and low (L). H is marked here with an acute accent (for example, *é*), and L left unmarked, except that lowered H tones are marked with a grave accent (for example, *è*), and raised L tones underlined (for example, *é*). There are differences among Shona dialects in the details of their tonal systems; the description in this chapter refers principally to the Zezuru dialect.

Tone has both lexical and grammatical functions. Lexically, *gótsí* 'chief's councillor' and *gotsi* 'back of the head' are two different words, distinguished only by their tone patterns. Grammatical distinctions are exemplified by the contrast between *áénda* 's/he went', *aénda* 's/he who went', and *áendá* 's/he having gone'. Likewise, *murúmé* 'man' and *múrume* 'he/it is a man' differ only in tone pattern.

Some Shona dialects have two rules of tone sandhi:

(1) A word-final sequence of HH is replaced by HL if the following word begins with H:

kuténgá + *hárí* > *kuténgà hárí* 'to buy pot(s)'

(2) If a word ending in H is followed by one beginning with LL, the first L is usually raised:

kuténgá + *nyama* > *kuténgá nyáma* 'to buy meat'

A further characteristic of the Shona tonal system is "downdrift". This refers to the gradual lowering of the pitch range in the course of a sentence. A high tone at the end of a sentence can be lower in pitch than a low tone at the beginning of the sentence. A sequence of L's descends in pitch throughout.

Consonants with murmur cannot be uttered on a high pitch and tend to lower the pitch of even a low surface tone; for this reason they are known as "depressors". They also partially or completely lower the pitch of an adjacent H vowel; *mukádzí* 'woman', containing the depressor *dz*, is pronounced with a falling pitch on the second syllable and a rising pitch on the final syllable.

Basic Morphology

Shona does not have a gender system such as is found in European languages. Instead, there are as many as 21 nominal classes (the exact number varies by dialect). The class is a system of agreement, within both nominal and verbal systems, such as:

ichi	*chinhu*	*chínondífádzá;*	*ndinódá*	*kuchíténga*
this	thing	(it) pleases me;	I want	to buy it

izvi	*zvinhu*	*zvínondífádzá;*	*ndinódá*	*kuzvíténgá*
these	things	(they) please me;	I want	to buy them

Typically the noun consists of a class prefix and a stem: *mu-nhu* 'person' (Class 1), *va-nhu* 'people' (Class 2). However, some classes do not have a syllabic prefix as a class marker: the singular of *ma-pángá* 'knives' (Class 6) is *bángá* (Class 5).

As shown in the above examples, some classes are paired singular/plural. To some extent, class and meaning can be correlated. Classes 1/2 are limited to nouns representing human beings, although not all nouns denoting persons are in these classes. Classes 3/4 contain most names of trees, Classes 9/10 include many animal names, and Class 14 abstract nouns. Class 15 consists of verbal infinitives only, such as *ku-téngá* 'to buy' in the examples above.

Some classes have a secondary function; their prefixes can replace, or be prefixed to, the basic class prefix to give additional meaning:

mu-kómaná	'boy'	Class 1
ka-kómaná	'little boy'	Class 12
tu-kómaná	'little boys'	Class 13
gómaná	'lout, ugly or unpleasant boy'	Class 5
zí-gómaná	'great, ugly or ungainly lout'	Class 21
ma-zi-gómaná	'great ugly louts'	Classes 21 + 6

Shona verbs are mostly divided between two major tonal classes, High and Low: *ku-téngá* 'to buy' but *ku-enda* 'to go.' Verb roots may be expanded by the addition of *verbal extensions,* which add to or modify the meaning (passive, causative, relational, reciprocal, etc.). More than one extension can appear in a given verb: *ku-téngá* 'to buy', *ku-téng-ér-á* 'to buy for/at', *ku-téng-ér-w-á* 'to have bought for one' (literally, 'to be bought for').

Inflected verbs typically have the following elements: +/- subject prefix + tense/aspect/mood marker (TAM) +/- adverbial infix +/- object concord + root +/- extension + final vowel +/- suffixes.

Of these, the subject prefix, the root, and the final vowel are the obligatory elements, except for the Imperative, which has no subject prefix. The final vowel varies; it is part of the TAM marker.

ti-nó-téng-á
we-PRES.HABIT-buy-TAM2 'we buy'

ti-nó-wanzo-téng-á
we-PRES.HABIT-often-buy-TAM2 'we often buy'

kuti	*tí-téng-é*	
that	we-buy-SUBJUNCTIVE	'that we may buy'

Shona distinguishes between a recent past tense (past of today) and a more distant past tense (past of before today).

t-a-téng-a	'we bought (today)'
t-aká-teng-a	'we bought (before today)'

However, a group of verbs known as statives use the past of before today for a present meaning: *t-aká-gár-a* 'we are seated'.

Outside both nominal and verbal systems is the category of "ideophones". These are vivid expressions of various qualities and actions, including color, sound (and absence of sound). An ideophone is often "said" by the entity to which it refers, and there may also be an accompanying verb expressing the same meaning in a more prosaic way:

mwedzí wákátí 'mbée' kuchena
'the moon said "mbee" to be white = the moon is snow-white' (stative use of tense)

yákánzí 'dzvi' némbwa
'it was said "seizing" by the dog = it was seized by the dog'

Basic Syntax

The basic word order in clauses is SVO. Objects can precede the verb for purposes of emphasis. In this case, the verb form usually contains an object concord.

t-a-ón-a *mu-rúmé*
we-PAST.TODAY-see-TAM2 CL1-man
'we saw a/the man'

mu-rúmé t-a-mú-on-a
CL1-man we-PAST.TODAY-him-see-TAM2
'we saw the man' (literally, 'the man, we saw him')

Verbs may have a relational extension to indicate that the following noun is an indirect object; there is no case marking on the noun.

t-a-téng-a *nyama*
we-PAST.TODAY-buy-TAM2 meat
'we bought meat'

t-a-téng-er-a *vaná* *nyáma*
we-PAST.TODAY-buy-REL-TAM2 children meat
'we bought meat for the children'

Sentences are negated by negative affixes forming part of the verb. The specific negative marker used depends on the verb form.

ku-téngá 'to buy'

ku-sa-téngá
INFINITIVE-NEG-buy 'not to buy'

vá-no-téng-á 'they buy'

ha-vá-téng-í
NEG-they-buy-TAM2 'they don't buy'

Contact with Other Languages

Shona has adopted many words from neighboring languages, including Ndebele (from ZULU, of the Nguni group) and the South African pidginized Zulu known variously as Fanigalo, Kitchen Kaffir, *chi-ráparápa* or *chiróóróo.*

With European contact, Shona adopted words from PORTUGUESE and AFRIKAANS; many words of Afrikaans origin are related to farming. These are now being replaced by English derivatives, especially in the variety called *chiHaráre*, spoken in the capital and based on Zezuru with a large admixture of English; 'window' is now more often *hwíndo* (plural *mahwíndo*) than *fáfitera or fásitera* (< Afrikaans *venster*), and 'dress' is more often *dhirési* than *rókwe* (< Afrikaans *rok*).

From Ndebele: *-geza* 'wash', *-vhura* 'open', *mufúndisi* 'missionary, teacher'

From Afrikaans: *purázi* 'farm' (< *plaas*), *dhézibhomu* 'disselboom', *gwaímani* 'trek ox' (< *kwaai man*), *karukúni* 'turkey' (< *kalkoen*)

From Portuguese: *fódya* 'tobacco' (< *folha* 'leaf')

From English: *bhébhi* 'girlfriend' (< *baby*), *chi-támbi* 'postage stamp', *fóni* 'telephone', *rábha* 'thief' (< *robber*)

Common Words

man:	murúmé
woman:	mukádzí
sun:	zúvá
bird:	shiri
dog:	imbwá
water:	mvúrá
tree:	mutí
fish:	hóvé
big:	-kúrú (adj. stem; murúmé mukúrú 'big/elderly/important man')
tall, long:	-refú (adj. stem; murúmé múrefú 'tall man')
small:	-dúku (adj. stem; mwaná mudúku 'small child')
three:	-tatú (adj. stem: vanhu vatatú 'three people')
good:	-naka (stative verb; munhu akánáka 'good person')
yes:	hóngu
no:	kwéte

Example Sentences

(1) Ma-ngwánaní*, m-a-rár-a
CL6-morning, you.PL-PAST.TODAY-sleep-TAM2

heré*?
QUESTION MARKER
'Good morning, have you slept?'
(*The final vowel is lengthened in greeting mode.)

(2) Áiwa, t-a-rár-a, kana
no we-PAST.TODAY-sleep-TAM2 if

m-á-rár-a-wó.
you:PL-PAST.TODAY-sleep-TAM2-too.
'Yes, we have slept, if you have also slept.'

(3) Fámb-á-ì zvé-nyú
walk-IMPERATIVE-PL ADVERBIAL/POSSESSIVE-you:PL

zv-aká-nák-a.
ADVERBIAL-STATIVE/RELATIVE-become.good-TAM2
'Travel well (said to person going away).'

Efforts to Preserve, Protect, and Promote the Language

Debate has continued for many years as to whether Shona should be promoted or allowed to "die". Those in favor of its promotion cite studies showing that children learn best in their first language. They emphasize the beauty of the language, its poetry, its function as a carrier of culture, and the respect that is due to the ancestors and their heritage. Those in favor of letting it die out point to the geographical limitations of Shona, the need to expand vocabulary to meet modern situations, the usefulness of an international language for communication even with other African countries, and the advantage of exposing children to such a language as early as possible. Meanwhile, the Shona Language Committee collects and disseminates new vocabulary, literature flourishes, and many point to the role Shona songs have played in the war of independence. Moreover, the rapidly expanding population means that now there are more Shona speakers than ever before in history. The death of Shona will not be soon or sudden.

Select Bibliography

Carter, H., and G.P. Kahari. 1986. *Kuverenga chiShóna: An Introductory Shona Reader, with Grammatical Sketch (in two parts).* Rev. ed. London: School of Oriental & African Studies, University of London.

____. 1987. *Shona Language Course.* Rev. ed. African Studies Program, University of Wisconsin.

Chimhundu, Herbert, ed. 1996. *Duramazwi rechiShona.* Harare: College Press.

Dale, D. 1975. *A Basic English-Shona Dictionary.* Gwelo (Gweru): Mambo Press.

____. 1978. *Shona Companion.* 4th ed. Gwelo (Gweru): Mambo Press.

Doke, C.M. 1931a. *Comparative Study in Shona Phonetics.* Johannesburg: University of the Witwatersrand.

____. 1931b. *Report on the Unification of the Shona Dialects.* Hertford: Stephen Austin.

Fortune, G. 1955. *An Analytical Grammar of Shona.* Cape Town and New York: Longmans, Green & Co.

____. 1967. *Elements of Shona (Zezuru Dialect).* 2d ed. Salisbury (Harare): Longman Rhodesia (Zimbabwe).

____. 1969. "Seventy-Five Years of Writing in Shona." In *Zambezia* 1/1: 55–67.

____. 1970. "Some Speech Styles in Shona." In *African Language Studies.* 172–182.

____. 1977. *Shona Grammatical Constructions.* Harare: University of Zimbabwe.

Hannan, M. 1984. *Standard Shona Dictionary.* Rev. ed. with Addendum. Harare: College Press and Literature Bureau.

Tucker, A.N. 1971. "Orthographic Systems and Conventions in Sub-Saharan Africa." In T. Sebeok, *Current Trends in Linguistics* 7: 618–653. The Hague: Mouton.

SINDHI

Jennifer S. Cole

Language Name: Sindhi.

Location: Sindhi is spoken in the lower Indus Valley region of the Indian subcontinent, and is a primary language of Sindh Province, Pakistan. The Sindhi-speaking region is bounded on the north by the Sukkur Dam on the Indus River and extends south to the Arabian Sea. It is bounded on the east by the Great Indian Desert (Thar) and on the west by the Kirthar Mountain Range.

In India Sindhi is spoken by large populations in those cities where Hindu Sindhi speakers located after the 1947 partition of India and Pakistan, including Mumbai (Bombay), Pune, Ajmer, Delhi, Ahmedabad, Ahmednagar, among others. There are also sizeable populations of emigrant Sindhi speakers in Singapore, the United Arab Emirates, the United States, Canada, and many other cities around the world.

Family: Northwestern subgroup of Indo-Aryan, under the Indo-Iranian branch of Indo-European.

Related Languages: Sindhi is closely related to SIRAIKI, a literary standard for the "South Lahnda" dialects[1], including Multani and Bahawalpuri, spoken to the north of Sindh Province. Other Lahnda dialects assigned to the Northwestern subgroup of Indo-Aryan include Potohari and Hindko.

Dialects: The Vicholi (< Sindhi *vicu* 'middle') dialect of Sindhi, spoken in Hyderabad (Sindh), is recognized as the standard variey. Other dialects include Thareli (spoken in the Thar Desert region), Lāsī (in Kohistan and Las Bela), Laṛī (in the lower Sind delta and coastal areas), and Kachchi (in the Rann of Kutch). Siraiki (< Sindhi *siru* 'north') is listed among the Sindhi dialects by Trumpp (1872) and Yegorova (1971), but Grierson rejects the claim of a distinct Siraiki Sindhi dialect. Confusing the matter is the fact that the term "Siraiki" is used to refer to a variety of "South Lahnda" that has emerged as a modern literary standard (Masica 1991: 443). In any case, there is scant published material available that describes the differences between the Sindhi dialects. Many scholars rely on Trumpp's very brief observations that Laṛī is pronounced with more contracted vowel qualities and a greater degree of consonant assimilation, Siraiki is the more "pure" form, and Thar pronunciation is influenced by Marwari.

More information is available for the Kachchi dialect. Rohra (1971) reports that Kachchi has lost the series of voiced aspirated stops, which have been neutralized with the simple voiced stops. A related observation is that the voiced fricatives /f, z, x, ʃ/ are realized as /pʰ, j, kʰ, s/. The Kachchi dialect has also lost the final very short vowels characteristic of the standard dialect. Since these vowels form an important basis for gender classification, and also serve to mark number and case distinctions, those aspects of the grammar are rendered more opaque, and thus more abstract in Kachchi. Rohra suggests that at least some of these innovations in Kachchi may result from contact with GUJARATI. Another feature of Kachchi is noted by Khubchandani (1981), who describes the subvariety Maṇḍvi as retaining only two implosives, /ɓ, ɗ/. Vagai, another subvariety, has only /ɓ/.

Sindhi speakers report salient differences in pronunciation between the various dialects, though as noted above, linguistic descriptions are lacking. More obvious are lexical differences, including differences in some pronouns and inflectional markers, some of which are noted in the sections below.

Number of Speakers: The 1961 census of Pakistan lists 4.9 million Sindhi speakers. These numbers are strongly disputed within Pakistan, however. The 1991 census (which was cancelled before completion) produced an initial estimate of close to 40 million. The 1971 census of India lists 1.2 million Sindhi speakers in India (a number that is close to the estimated number of Hindu Sindhi emigrants, 1.25 million). Including speakers of the Kachchi dialect would raise the figure, based on census data, to 1.7 million speakers. This number must be further inflated to account for population growth over the past three decades.

Origin and History

Sindhi has developed, alongside the other modern Indo-Aryan languages, from an earlier Prakrit form of Indo-Aryan. The Vedic variety of *Vrācaḍa Apabhraṃśa* is often cited as the source of Old Sindhi. The earliest literary reference to Sindhi appears to be Bharartamuni's *Nāṭyaśāstra* in the 2nd century A.D. (Khubchandani 1981). Evidence from 9th century Persian history texts suggests that a writing system was firmly in place in Sindhi by that time. Literature dating from the 8th to the 15th centuries includes legends of saints, kings and epic heroes; however, literary Sindhi really flourished in an era start-

[1] "Lahnda" is the term used by Grierson (1919) in his *Linguistic Survey of India* to refer to a group of dialects, sometimes also called "Western Punjabi." Masica (1991: 18) notes that the name "Lahnda" is used by language scholars and not by speakers of the various dialects. He cites Shackle (1979, 1980) as rejecting the "Lahnda" grouping in favor of four distinct groups for the dialects spoken to the north of the Sindhi-speaking territory in Pakistan: Siraiki, Hindko, Potohari, and Punjabi.

Table 1: Consonants

	Labial	Dental	Alveolar	Post-alveolar	Palato-alveolar	Velar	Glottal
Stop —Plosive	p b	t d		ʈ ɖ		k g	
	p^h b^h	t^h d^h		ʈ^h ɖ^h		k^h g^h	
—Implosive	ɓ		ɗ		ʄ	ɠ	
Affricate					c c^h		
					j j^h		
Nasal	m		n	ɳ	ñ	ŋ	
	(m^h)		(n^h)	(ɳ^h)			
Fricative	f		s (z)		(ʃ)	(x ɣ)	h
Rhotic			r	(ɽ)			
				ɽ^h			
Lateral		l					
		(l^h)					
Glide	w				y		
	(w^h)						

ing in the 16th century with a vast literature of Sufi poetry. The major Sufi poets of that period include Shah Abdul Latif (1680–1752), Sachal Sarmast (1739–1828), and Sami (1743–1850), who remain very popular even today.

Orthography and Basic Phonology

There is a conventionalized transcription system widely used for Indo-Aryan languages, the primary features of which are listed here: vowel length: marked with the macron (*ā*); nasalization: marked with a superscript tilde (*ã*); retroflexion: marked with a subscript dot (*ṭ*), Palato-alveolar nasal: /ñ/; aspiration: consonant + *h* (*ph*); affricates: /j, jh/ and either /c, ch/ or /ch, chh/. The presentation here departs somewhat from this tradition, in adherence to International Phonetic Association (IPA) standards in the following features: vowel length: marked with *:* (*a:*); retroflexion: marked on the consonant symbol by a rightward bottom hook (*ʈ, ɖ, ɽ*); aspiration: marked with a subscript ^{h} (p^h).

The non-IPA conventions preserved here are the representation of affricates as /c, ch, j, jh/, the palatal glide as /y/, and the palatal nasal as /ñ/. The decision to retain these transcription symbols was made to facilitate ready comparisons with other material on Sindhi. Place-names and language or dialect names are presented with conventional spelling (Romanic alphabet) when such a standard exists. Thus, the language name is represented here as Sindhi, instead of the IPA standard transcription, which would be Sind^{h}i:.

Sindhi is written today using a modified Perso-Arabic script. Extra diacritic dots are added to represent implosives and some aspirates as unitary symbols. The Nagari script is in current use by some Sindhi speakers in India; however, there is a trend to return to the Perso-Arabic script to promote unity of the language and access to the older literature.

The earliest written specimens of Sindhi are believed to be in a proto-Nagari script. Samples of Sindhi writing in Nagari script have been found dating back to at least the 15th century. Ancient manuscript samples also suggest that between the 11th and 13th centuries a variant of a script called Khojaki was used (so-called because the scriptures of the Khojas, an Islamic heterodoxy, have been written in this script). This script is related to Nagari. Some time after the Arab invasion in the 8th century, an ARABIC script was in use. Over time new letters were invented by adding dots to account for the additional sounds in Sindhi. In the late 19th century, the British colonialists decreed a standardization of the modern Sindhi script based on Arabic orthography. Although the decision was controversial at the time, virtually all Sindhi literature has since been published in this script. The Arabic script contains several letters that represent the same sound (e.g., four letters for /z/) in Sindhi.

Consonants. The sound inventory for Sindhi consonants is shown in Table 1 (adapted from Nihalani 1995). Sounds marked in parentheses are of questionable phonemic status (the aspirated sonorants and *ɽ*), or restricted to borrowings (*z, ʃ, x, ɣ*).

The most notable feature of the Sindhi consonant inventory is the occurrence of the implosive stops, found among Indo-Aryan languages exclusively in Sindhi and a few of its neighbors (Siraiki, Marwari). The implosives derive from Middle Indo-Aryan geminate voiced stops in medial position, and singleton voiced stops in initial position. Instrumental phonetic studies demonstrate that these sounds are genuine glottalic ingressives in Sindhi (Nihalani 1986).

Sindhi displays a full series of voiceless, voiced, voiceless aspirated and voiced aspirated stops at five places of articulation. The post-alveolars are apical, and the palato-alveolars are laminal; these are referred to as retroflex and palatals, respectively, in the terminology traditionally used for Indo-Aryan. Among the implosives, there is only the single alveolar stop corresponding to the pair of dental and post-alveolar stops in the plosive series. Sindhi has retained the full set of five phonemic nasals from SANSKRIT. The other sonorants include an alveolar and post-alveolar rhotic tap, the latter of which is a marginal phoneme at best, in complementary distribution with the retroflex stop [ɖ]. [ɽ] occurs only in intervocalic position and in the clusters [dɽ, ʈɽ], with the exception of a few loan words such as *lo:ɖiŋga* 'truck' (from ENGLISH "loading"). The retroflex [ɖ, ʈ] in the Northern dialects freely vary with the clusters [dɽ, ʈɽ].

Aspirated sonorants, /mʰ, nʰ, ɳʰ, lʰ, ɽʰ, wʰ/, occur intervocalically, but since they don't contrast with a sonorant + /h/ cluster, no strong claim can be made for their phonemic status. Some native speakers describe them as being unitary sounds and are reluctant to separate them in syllable-by-syllable pronunciation, even though the /h/ component is written as a separate letter in the orthographic system. (In comparison, nearly all the aspirated voiced and voiceless stops are rendered as a single letter.)

The glide /w/ is produced as a weak labio-dental approximant [ʋ], with a vocalic allophonic variant [w], and is transcribed variously in published sources as *w* or *v*.

Vowels. The Sindhi vowel system represents the standard Indo-Aryan symmetrical 10 vowel system. The system can be construed in terms of a basic length contrast over five vowel qualities: /i, i:, e, e:, u, u:, o, o:, a, a:/. All the vowels have counterparts with nasalization, though the phonemic status of short nasal vowels is not clear.

Table 2: Vowels

High	i i: (ĩ) ĩ:		u u: (ũ) ũ:
Mid	e e: (ẽ) ẽ:		o o: (õ) õ:
Low		a (ã) a: ã:	

The phonetic values for the (oral) vowels are shown below, based on Nihalani (1995).

i: [i]	e: [e]	a: [ɑ]	o: [o]	u: [u]
i [ɪ]	e [ɛ]	a [ə]	o [ɔ]	u [ʊ]

The vowels [ɛ] and [ɔ] are realized as diphthongs [ɛə] and [əʊ], respectively, by some speakers. Northern dialects lack the diphthongs, and realize only [e] and [o]. A distinctive feature of the vowel system is the extremely short duration of short vowels in word-final position. Only the peripheral short vowels /i, u, a/ occur contrastively in final position, and as they are barely audible to nonnative speakers, they are not reliably transcribed in descriptions of the language. Nonetheless, important grammatical information is expressed in the final vowel, including grammatical gender, number and case. The final short /i/ is transcribed variously in published sources as /i, e, $^{i, ε}$/.

Sindhi displays a rich system of morphophonological vowel alternation in the formation of verbs and nouns with inflectional and derivational affixes. Especially affected are stem-final short vowels in combination with a vowel-initial suffix, though the stem-final long vowels are also subject to change (including shortening) in this environment. The exact nature of the change is idiosyncratic to the specific morphological construct and often restricted by gender class as well, and the full set of morphophonological vowel alternations are too numerous to mention in this presentation. The reader may consult Trumpp (1872) or Grierson (1919) for more comprehensive treatments.

More robust aspects of the phonological system concern syllable structure and restrictions on consonant clusters. Syllable structure in Sindhi is maximally CCVC, though codas are prohibited in word-final position. The onset consonant is optional, words may begin in a vowel, but vowel hiatus within words is frequently resolved through glide insertion or glide formation. Word-medial –CC– clusters may consist of any combination of obstruent and/or sonorant consonants. In –CC– clusters with an initial obstruent, there is typically an alternative pronunciation with a vowel inserted between the two consonants. For example, *hikɽo* 'one' and *j^hupɽi* 'shack' have free variants in *hikaɽo* and *j^hupiɽi*, respectively. The identity of the intrusive short vowel can be difficult to determine, and native speakers can disagree, perhaps in part because the short vowels are not represented in the orthography. One restriction on –CC– clusters is the exclusion of geminates; historical geminate consonants are reduced to singleton –C– in Sindhi. Word-initial consonant clusters consisting of a consonant + glide (*y*, *w*) occur, as do the clusters [ʈɽ, dɽ].

Basic Morphology

Noun Morphology. Nouns are grouped into gender classes, which are only partially phonologically determined. As with all Sindhi words, nouns must end in a vowel (long or short), and the final vowel of a noun in the nominative singular form, referred to as the "thematic vowel" here, generally serves to determine the gender class assignment of the noun. There are basic patterns of gender class assignment for most thematic vowels; however, alongside these there are numerous exceptions for which the gender class must simply be stipulated. The gender class of a noun determines vowel alternations that occur under declension; masculine endings are *–u, -o:*, and *u:* (*g^haru* 'house', *p^hi*:to: 'wheel', *raha:ku:* 'resident'); feminine endings are *–a, -i, -a:*, and *–i:* (*k^haʈa* 'cot', *ra:ti* 'night', *duniya:* 'world', *ɓili:* 'cat').

Sindhi nouns are marked for number and case through a complex system of noun-stem modification and through the use of postpositions. Noun-stem modification involves a change in the thematic vowel with or without overt suffixation. Number is marked for plurals by noun-stem modification. Regarding case, the nominative, oblique, ablative and vocative are expressed through noun-stem modification, while other cases are expressed through the use of a postposition that follows the noun in the oblique case.

The thematic vowel changes as a function of number and case marking. For the nominative plural of the masculine nouns and the oblique singular of both masculine and feminine nouns, the change in thematic vowel is the only mark of number and case. For the other cases, in both singular and plural, the thematic vowel is followed by a corresponding number/case suffix. The ablative plural is formed by attaching the ablative suffix to the suffix marking oblique plural. For the smaller number of nouns whose gender class does not follow the regular pattern based on thematic vowel (e.g., masculine nouns ending in /-i:/), there are slightly different patterns of thematic vowel change. For a detailed discussion, see Trumpp (1872) or Grierson (1919).

Below are example paradigms of number/case marking by gender class:

Masculine	-u *'house'*	-o: *'wheel'*	-u: *'resident'*
Nom.sg.	g^{h}aru	p^{h}i:to:	raha:ku:
Nom.pl	g^{h}ara	p^{h}i:ta:	raha:ku:
Obl.sg.	g^{h}ara	p^{h}i:te:	raha:kui, raha:ku:a
Obl.pl.	g^{h}arani	p^{h}i:tani	rahakuni, raha:kuani
Abl.sg.	g^{h}arã:	p^{h}i:tã:	raha:kuã:
Abl.pl.	g^{h}araniã:	p^{h}i:taniã:	raha:kuaniã:
Voc.sg.	g^{h}ara	p^{h}i:ta:	raha:ku:
Voc.pl.	g^{h}ara:	p^{h}i:ta:	raha:kua:

Feminine	-a *'cot'*	-i *'night'*	-a: *'world'*	-i: *'cat'*
Nom.sg.	k^{h}aʈa	ra:ti	duniya:	ɓili:
Nom.pl	k^{h}aʈũ:	ra:ti	duniya:ũ:	ɓiliũ:
Obl.sg.	k^{h}aʈa	ra:tiũ:	duniya:	ɓiliùa, ɓilia
Obl.pl.	k^{h}aʈuni	ra:tiuni	duniya:uni	ɓiliuni
Abl.sg.	k^{h}aʈã:	ra:tiã:	duniyã:	ɓiliã:
Abl.pl.	k^{h}aʈuniã:	ra:tiuniã:	duniya:uniã:	ɓiliuniã:
Voc.sg.	k^{h}aʈa	ra:ti	duniya:	ɓili:
Voc.pl.	k^{h}aʈũ:	ra:tiũ:	duniya:ũ:	ɓiliũ:

These examples are illustrative of the standard dialect. Dialect variation affects especially the short vowels /i, a/ in feminine number-case endings, which vary with one another and may disappear in vowel sequences in some varieties. Other variation occurs in the choice of suffix vowel, e.g., /-o:/ as the plural vocative in place of /-a:/.

The remaining cases are each marked through the use of a postposition following the noun in the oblique form. These include the dative, ablative, comitative and locative. The genitive postposition is declined like an adjective, and is described immediately following. There is no accusative postposition, and instead the nominative or dative form is used (depending on the animacy of subject and object). Also, the oblique case forms substitute for a distinct ergative case form (see Basic Syntax below).

Adjectives. Adjectives are declined just as the nouns, and like nouns the final (i.e., thematic) vowel determines the declension pattern. In general, when the adjective precedes the noun it modifies it must agree with the noun in gender, number and case. The older grammars indicate an ablative form for the adjectives, but in current varieties (confirmed for northern and standard dialects) the oblique form replaces the ablative for adjectives, though the ablative marking on nouns is maintained. The thematic vowel of the adjective may change for the purpose of gender agreement. Thus, in adjectives masculine /-o:/ changes to /-i:/. Note in the following example that even though the adjective agrees with the noun in gender, number and case, the thematic vowels of the adjective and noun may yet be different, e.g., *suʈ^{h}o: puʈʈu* 'good son' (Nom., sg.).

Below are adjectives marked for number and case in agreement with a following noun:

	Masculine 'good son'	Feminine 'good girl'
Nom.sg.	suʈ^{h}o: puʈʈu	suʈ^{h}i: c^{h}o:kri:
Nom.pl.	suʈ^{h}a: puʈʈa	suʈ^{h}iũ: c^{h}o:kriũ:
Obl.sg.	suʈ^{h}e: puʈʈa	suʈ^{h}ia c^{h}o:kri:a
Obl.pl.	suʈ^{h}ani puʈʈani	suʈ^{h}iuni c^{h}o:kriuni
Abl.sg.	suʈ^{h}e: puʈʈã:	suʈ^{h}ia c^{h}o:kriã:
Abl.pl.	suʈ^{h}ani puʈʈaniã:	suʈ^{h}iuni c^{h}o:kriuniã:
Voc.sg.	suʈ^{h}a: puʈʈa	suʈ^{h}i: c^{h}o:kri:
Voc.pl.	suʈ^{h}a: puʈʈa:	suʈ^{h}iũ: c^{h}o:kriũ:

The genitive postposition follows the possessor noun and precedes the possessed noun, and agrees with the possessed noun in gender, number and case. Thus, *b^{h}e:ɳa jo g^{h}aru* (sister:FEM.SG.OBL. gen: MASC.SG.NOM house: MASC.SG.NOM) 'sister's house'.

Pronouns. Pronouns are declined for number and display nominative and oblique case marking. Pronouns lack ablative and vocative forms, and mark gender only in Nom. third-person forms. Personal pronouns are given below, with some of the dialectal variants shown (forms following the semicolon are from the northern dialect). The genitive is shown with MASC.SG. features; genitive concordance is determined by the possessed noun. The third-person pronouns are identical to the demonstratives. Third-person forms shown in the table are proximal; distinct forms are used for distal and emphatic pronouns. This same pattern of declension is found with the relative and corelative pronouns and indefinite pronouns. There is also a set of interrogative pronouns, most of which are undeclinable. The exception is the pronoun "who?", which displays the same limited pattern of case/number marking as the relative, co-relative, and indefinite pronouns.

Table 3: Personal Pronouns

		First person	Second person	Third person (proximal)
Singular	Nom.	a:ũ:, ã:; mã:, mũ:	tũ:	(MASC.) hi:, he:, hi:u, hiu (FEM.) hi:, he:, hi:a, hia
	Obl.	ã:, mũ:, mũ ; mã:	to:	hina
	Gen.	ã:-jo:, mũhũ-jo:, mũ:-jo:	tũhũ-jo:, tũhĩ-jo	hina-jo:
Plural	Nom.	asĩ:	tavahĩ:, tavĩ:, tahĩ: ; avahĩ:	hi:, he:
	Obl.	asã:, asã:hĩ, asã:hũ:	tavahã:, tahã:; avahã:, ahã:	hina, hinani
	Gen.	asã:-jo, asã:hĩ-jo	tavhã:-jo; avhã:-jo	hinani-jo:

Pronominal Suffixes. Sindhi is one of only a few Indo-Aryan languages that employ pronominal suffixes, which can appear on nouns that refer to humans or properties of humans, on postpositions, and on verbs. There are three sets of pronominal suffixes, though several forms are common to two sets. The nominative suffixes attach only to verbs in the definite Future tense or intransitive verbs in the Unspecified Imperfective tense, where they serve to mark the nominative subject of the verb. The oblique suffixes attach to nouns, postpositions or verbs. On nouns, the oblique suffix marks a genitive possessor, as in *akʰiu-mi* 'my eyes', but is never marked for the first person plural. On a postposition the oblique suffix replaces the oblique case pronoun governed by the postposition, as in *kʰe:-mi* for *mũ: kʰe:* 'to me' and *mã:ũ:* for *asã: mã:* 'from us'. On verbs, the oblique suffix marks the direct or indirect object, or the goal/source of motion, as in *ɓudʰa:yã:-va* 'I shall tell you', for *tavahã: kʰe: ɓudʰa:yã*. The third set of pronominal suffixes are termed the "agentive suffixes" by Grierson (1919) and are used to mark the oblique-case (i.e., ergative) subjects of transitive verbs in the perfective aspect (formed from the adjectival perfective participle). The pronominal suffixes are declined for person and number, and with two exceptions, do not mark gender.

On transitive verbs in the perfective aspect the oblique and agentive suffixes may occur together, with the agentive suffix preceding. (In that situation, the first singular Agentive suffix /-mi/ is realized /-mã:/.)

Verb Morphology. The verb form in Sindhi is a complex construction that may include up to three parts: adverbial participle—primary verb—auxiliary verb. These components appear in various combinations determined by the aspect, tense and mood of the verb. The system of verb forms as a whole expresses the following distinctions:

Aspect:	Perfective; Imperfective (habitual/continuous); Unspecified
Tense:	Past; Present; Future
Mood:	Subjunctive; Imperative; Presumptive; Counterfactual
Valence:	Transitive; Causative
Voice:	Active; Passive
Concordance:	Gender; Number

The morphological form of the verb includes six nonfinite forms, including nominal, adjectival and adverbial participles. There are 17 finite verb forms that mark the aspect, tense, mood and concordance distinctions noted above. Valence and voice features are expressed in the verb stem, in nonfinite and finite forms alike.

Verbs are divided into two conjugation classes: the "a-conjugation" class includes all intransitives, passives and some transitives, and the "i-conjugation" class includes most transitives and all causatives. Some verb endings differ in the two conjugation classes. There are six nonfinite forms of the verb, which function either as nominal, adjectival or adverbial forms: infinitive, unspecified (=future), imperfective, perfective, imperfective participle, and perfective participle. Adjectival non-finite forms are declined as all other adjectives, with changes in the final vowels expressing number and gender agreement. For example, the imperfective adjectival form of *halaɳu* 'to go' yields *halando:* 'MASC.SG.,' *halandi:* 'FEM.SG.,' *halanda:* 'MASC.PL.,' *halandiũ:* 'FEM.PL.' Note also that the adjectival unspecified form has a passive meaning, and as such is used only with transitive verbs.

Voice and Valence Distinctions. Finite verb forms express voice and valence features through stem derivation. An underived verb stem is in the active voice and is inherently either intransitive or transitive. There are two passive forms, one used with the unspecified aspect in the future tense, and one used with the imperfective aspect in the present and past tenses. The primary causative suffix derives transitives from inherent intransitives, and causatives from inherent transitives. The secondary causative suffix derives a causative from a transitive that is itself derived through primary causative suffixation, e.g., *sikʰaɳu* 'to learn (underived verb)', *sikʰijaɳu* 'to be learned (passive, unspec.)', *sikʰibo:* 'being learned (passive, imperfective)', *sikʰa:iɳu* 'to teach, cause to learn (primary causative)', and *sikʰa:ra:iɳu* 'to cause to teach (secondary causative)'.

Aspect. Finite verb forms are built from a verb base, typically in combination with an auxiliary verb. The form of the verb base is determined by the choice of aspect: perfective, imperfective (habitual or continuous), or unspecified. The verb base is built from the verb root through suffixation in the unspecified aspect, and is built from a participle verb form in the perfective and imperfective aspects. While most finite verb forms express tense, mood and concordance features on the auxiliary verb, in two finite forms there is no auxiliary and the verb participle itself expresses concordance through the attachment of the pronominal suffixes. Note the unusual mark of the imperfective-continuous aspect, which takes as it base a perfective participle form of the primary verb followed by the perfective participle of the verb /rahaɳu/ 'to remain, to stay'.

Table 4: Aspectual Features

Aspectual feature	*Base form*	*Participle ending*
Perfective	Adjectival Perfective participle	- yo
Imperfective—habitual	Adjectival Imperfective participle	- ando/- i:ndo
Imperfective—continuous	Adverbial Perfective participle	- i:/- e: + "rahaɳu"
Unspecified	Root + "Old Present" suffix	(Nominative pronominal suffixes)

Combining Tense/Mood and Aspect. Aspect combined with tense and mood yield 17 distinct forms of the finite verb. The aspect/tense/mood distinction is, for the most part, independent of the voice and valence distinctions, although some restrictions exist, such as the restriction of the passive /ij/ form to the present and past tense unspecified forms. As already noted, tense and mood are expressed through the auxiliary verb for most finite forms. There are three auxiliary verbs, which have partial or full conjugation, *a:hyã:*, *tʰo* and *huaɳu*. In addition, there are two nonconjugating auxiliary particles: *ha:* and *the:*. The choice among these auxiliaries is determined by the tense and aspect of the verb form: *a:hyã:* and *tʰo* are used only in the present tense and are distinguished by aspect. These two auxiliaries have defective conjugations. *Huaɳu* is used as an auxiliary only in the past tense, but also exists in all tenses as a primary verb meaning 'to be'.

Basic Syntax

Word Order. The basic word order in pragmatically neutral sentences in Sindhi is Subject-Object-Verb, or SOV, and with ditransitives the indirect object generally precedes the direct object, e.g., *cokria kuto: ɗiʈʰo:* (girl:OBL dog:NOM saw) 'The girl saw the dog'. Sindhi is a so-called free word order language; other sequences of subject, object, indirect object and verb are also possible, preserving the same overall (logical) meaning, and are quite common in spoken discourse. The alternate word orders have the effect of shifting, increasing, or decreasing focus of the "displaced" constituents. The pragmatic factors that govern word order have not been well studied.

Phrases in Sindhi are head final, which means that the noun, verb, and postposition are all final in their respective phrases, with modifiers and complements generally preceding the head. The order of individual words within a phrase is not subject to permutation, except under special conditions (e.g., phrases embedded within a noun phrase may be displaced rightward). In the noun phrase, a determiner is not required. Without it the noun may be interpreted as indefinite or generic, but a definite interpretation is also possible if the discourse context is already established. Examples of phrases containing modifiers and complements include *hi:a naĩ: ga:ɗi:* (this new car) 'this new car', *mũhĩnja: ʈre: puʈra* (my:MASC.PL.NOM three sons) 'my three sons', *tama:m vaɗo:* (very large) 'very large', and *hina naĩ:a ga:ɗiya mẽ:* (this:OBL new:OBL car:OBL in) 'in this new car'.

The verb phrase contains the verbal elements as well as the direct and indirect objects (Masica 1991: 373 includes as well the goal/source of motion). The verbal elements themselves have a complex structure, as seen in the previous section. The main verb is typically the leftmost element in the verb complex, followed by an auxiliary verb that marks tense and mood. Operator or modal verb elements may also occur, placed in between the main verb (in participle form) and the auxiliary verb.

One exception to the rule that the object precedes the verb in Sindhi arises with sentential objects, which are displaced rightward, conjoined with the main clause by a sentential subordinate particle.

Case Marking of Major Constituents. The canonical, neutral word order in Sindhi is SOV and the subject in the nominative case governs agreement with the verb. The direct object may be marked with the dative postposition or it may be left unmarked in the nominative case; there is no accusative case. The oblique case is marked on the direct object most typically when the direct object is a human or animate noun, or to express definiteness of an inanimate. The indirect object is marked with the dative postposition following the noun in the oblique case. The oblique case is also used to mark the erstwhile ergative subject of a transitive verb in a perfective aspectual form. There is no distinct case ending or postposition that expresses the ergative case. In ergative constructions, the verb agrees with a direct object in the nominative case if there is one, and otherwise expresses a default third person, sg., masc. concordance.

Nonnominative subjects also occur as the "dative" or "experiencer" subjects with a class of verbs that condition dative case marking (through the use of the dative postposition). The verbs in this class include verbs of physical sensation (such as feeling hunger or pain); verbs expressing psychological states (such as knowledge or pleasure); verbs of wanting, needing or obligation; verbs of receiving; and constructions expressing kinship relations. "Experiencer" verbs agree with a syntactic direct object if it is nominative, and otherwise take a default agreement, just as in the ergative tenses. This complicated situation of case marking and verb agreement makes the whole notion of subjecthood a murky issue in the linguistic analysis of Indo-Aryan languages, including Sindhi.

hu:	ciʈʰi:	paʈʰanda:
they.MASC.NOM	letter:FEM.NOM	will.read:3PL.MASC.

'They (masc.) will read the letter.' (verb agreement with nominative subject)

hunani	ciʈʰi:	paʈʰi:	a:he:
they:MASC.OBL	letter:FEM.NOM	read:PERF.3SG.FEM	AUX:3SG.

'They (MASC.) have read the letter (FEM.).' (verb agreement with oblique/ergative subject)

Negation. Negation is expressed through the use of the negative particle /na/ or /ko:na/, which can be placed either before the verb complex or within it, typically before the tense-marked verb or auxiliary. The negative particle also has fused forms with the auxiliary verb, e.g., *na:hiyã:*, (1sg.), or *ko:nhe:* (3sg.). Example sentences include *asã: ko:na halia:sĩ:* (we NEG go:PERF.3PL.MASC) 'We didn't go', *mũ: kʰe: bukʰa ko:nhe:* (me DAT hunger NEG:is) 'I'm not hungry'.

Question Formation. Questions are formed without any special syntactic devices. For yes/no questions, the interrogative particle /cʰa:/ may be placed at the beginning of the sentence. Questions can also be formed without the particle, just by using a question intonation with an ordinary declarative sentence form. Other kinds of questions are formed by using an interrogative pronoun, most typically placed in focal position before the verb (though subject to the same scrambling of constituent order allowed in declarative sentences):

cʰa	tavahĩ:	kʰai:	ve:ʈʰa:	a:hyo:?
INTERR	you:PL	eat	sit/done:2PL	AUX.2PL.NOM

'Did you eat?'

Contact with Other Languages

Sindhi is in contact with neighboring dialects and languages in every region where it is spoken. Sindh Province experienced a heavy immigration of non-Sindhi speakers after the formation of Pakistan in 1947, and the status of Sindhi as the official language of the province has been compromised. The radio and television media continue to be dominated by URDU, the language of the immigrants to Sindh and of the political elite. As a result, Sindhis experience close, daily contact with Urdu, which has led, not surprisingly, to an increase in the number of Urdu words in the Sindhi lexicon of urban dwellers, and the importation of other grammatical and stylistic features of Urdu.

Sindhi has many borrowed words of Persian, Arabic and Turkic origin, some of which are fully integrated into the language, as well as more recent borrowings from English. Some examples are:

From Persian: *guzar* 'passage' *kʰari:d, χari:d* 'purchasing'
From Arabic: *intiza:r* 'expectation' *za:limu* 'tyrant'
From English: *injiɳu* 'engine' *ɖa:kʈaru* 'doctor' *iskulu* 'school' *re:la* 'railway'

Common Words

man:	ma:ɳhũ:	long:	ɖrigʰo:
woman:	ma:i:	small:	nanɖʰɽo:
water:	pã:ɳĩ:	yes:	ha:
sun:	siʄu	no:	na, ko:nhe:
three:	ʈre:	good:	caŋo:
fish:	macʰi:	bird:	pakʰi:
big:	vaɗo:	dog:	kuto:
tree:	waɳu		

Example Sentences

(1) huna kʰã: kʰatu vartumi.
him:OBL ABL letter:NOM received:1SG
'I took a letter from him.'

(2) huna kʰe: cʰa: kʰape:?
him DAT what be.wanted
'What does he want?'

(3) tavahã: kʰe: hi: kʰatu paɽʰaɳo
you:PL.MASC.OBL DAT this letter:NOM read:INF.OBL

pavando.
must:3SG.MASC
'You (pl.) must read this letter.'

Efforts to Preserve, Protect, and Promote the Language

The status of Sindhi as a literary language was challenged by the immigration to India of a large educated population at the time of the partition of India. Subsequent serious losses in the Sindhi-language publishing and printing industries followed suit, along with the closure of many Sindhi-medium public schools. Efforts are currently under way to preserve and promote Sindhi in urban areas of Sindh Province. Key to this effort is the regeneration of the printing and publishing industries, which produce an increasing number of newspapers, magazines, and books in Sindhi.

In India, Sindhi was established as a medium of instruction in areas where Sindhis immigrated, but has seen a decline in the past few decades in areas other than Kutch (Kachchh) and Thar (Rajasthan). The Indian government recognized Sindhi as a national language in 1967 and has since established an autonomous National Council for Promotion of Sindhi Language with its headquarters in Vadodara, India. Indian Sindhis, especially of the older generation, express concern that future generations of Sindhis in India will have less access to and lesser command of the language as Sindhi competes with HINDI, English (among the educated), and other regional languages in their environment.

Select Bibliography

Grierson, Sir George A. 1919. *Linguistic Survey of India, Vol.VII, Part I: Indo-Aryan Family: Northwestern Group, Specimens of Sindhi and Lahnda.* Calcutta: Superintendent Government Printing.

Khubchandani, Lachman M. 1961. "The phonology and morphophonemics of Sindhi." Unpublished University of Pennsylvania M.A. thesis.

_____. 1981. *Sindhi Studies.* Studies in Linguistics Mimeograph Series, Number 7. Pune: Centre for Communication Studies.

Masica, Colin P. 1991. *The Indo-Aryan Languages.* Cambridge: Cambridge University Press.

Nihalani, Paroo. 1986. "Phonetic Implementation of Implosives." In *Language and Speech,* 29:253–62.

_____. 1995. "Sindhi." In *Journal of the IPA,* 25.2: 95–98.

Rohra, Satish K. 1971. "Sindhi, Kacchi, and Emigrant Sindhi." In *Indian Linguistics.* 32.2: 123–31.

Stack, Captain George. 1849. *Dictionary, English and Sindhi.* Bombay: American Mission Press.

Shackle, C. 1976. *The Siraiki Language of Central Pakistan.* London: School of Oriental and African Studies.

_____. 1977. "Siraiki: A Language Movement in Pakistan." In *Modern Asian Studies,* 11: 379–403.

Trumpp, Ernest. 1872. *Grammar of the Sindhi Language.* London: Trübner and Co. and Leipzig: F.A. Brockhaus.

Yegorova, R.P. 1971. *The Sindhi Language.* Moscow: "Naukua" Publishing House.

SINHALA

Sunil Kariyakarawana

Language Name: Sinhala. **Alternate:** *Sinhalese* (speakers of the language do not favor this term since it reminds them of their colonial experiences). **Autonym:** *siŋhala.*

Location: The island of Sri Lanka (formerly known as Ceylon).

Family: Sinhalese-Maldivian group of the Indo-Aryan subbranch of the Indo-Iranian branch of the Indo-European language family.

Related Languages: Other Indo-Aryan languages, the closest being Maldivian, BANGLA and ORIYA.

Dialects: There are about six regional dialects. Sinhala is a diglossic language, with different written and spoken varieties. While these share general typological features such as word order, they show differences at all levels of structure. There are varieties within both spoken and written. The most widely used standard literary variety makes considerable use of direct SANSKRIT borrowings; it is considered "high." It is used in all nonfiction writing, but rarely in formal speech applications. Spoken Sinhala ("low"), which is used in all face-to-face communication, has two main varieties: Formal Spoken and Colloquial Spoken. Formal Spoken shares some grammatical features and the lexicon of Literary Sinhala. It is the variety used in university lectures, and most often for parliamentary and other formal speeches, although these latter speeches are occasionally made in Literary Sinhala. Colloquial Sinhala displays further variety according to geographical area (Gair 1986).

This chapter is based on the Colombo regional dialect which is considered standard and formal. Examples reflect the spoken variety.

Number of Speakers: 12 million.

Origin and History

The island of Sri Lanka, off the southern coast of India, has been populated for over 2,500 years. The earliest settlers were tribes from India, who were followed by later migrations from India that occurred around the fifth century B.C. It is a matter of controversy whether or not the earliest settlers were from the western coast or the eastern coast of India.

Legend has it that the leader of one migration, Vijaya, was the grandson of a lion, *Sinha,* from Bengal. The descendants of these people were called "Sinhalese" and their language was named "Sinhala".

Sinhala has a long history. The oldest written evidence is found in the inscriptions in caves dated back to the second and third centuries B.C.

It has long been disputed whether Sinhala originated as a western or eastern Indo-Aryan language. One reason for the uncertainty is that the language left India before it underwent most of the linguistic changes that ultimately distinguished the subgroups of Indo-Aryan languages. While many competent scholars have argued for both eastern and western origins on both linguistic and cultural grounds, some work on the history of Sinhala phonology has provided evidence for an eastern origin (Karunatillake 1977).

Orthography and Basic Phonology

Sinhala has a syllabic writing system; i.e., vowel plus consonant cluster is represented by a single letter. The script evolved from Grantha, a south Indian version of the Brahmi script, influenced by Dravidian scripts such as those of KANNADA and TELUGU.

The sounds in parentheses in the consonant table on the next page are of limited distribution in Sinhala.

Prenasalized stops like <u>mb</u> are distinct from consonant sequences like *mb.*

The vowels written double (*ii, ee, ææ, əə, uu, oo*) are long.

Table 1: Vowels

	Front	Central	Back
High	i, ii		u, uu
Mid	e, ee	ə, əə	
Low	æ, ææ	a, aa	o, oo

Basic Morphology

Unlike the written variety, spoken Sinhala does not have subject-verb agreement, or any other type of verb agreement. Causative verbs are formed by suffixing *-və* to the verb stem: (*kərə* > 'to do' *kərəvə* 'cause or make to do'). Some syntactic operations such as focusing and sentence negation are shown morphologically by a verb suffix: (*kərənəva* 'do-INDICATIVE', *kəranne* 'do-FOCUS').

Table 2: Consonants

		Labial	Dental	Alveolar	Retroflex	Palato-alveolar	Velar	Glottal
Stops	Voiceless	p	t		ṭ		k	
	Voiced	b	d		ḍ		g	
Fricatives	Voiceless	(f)	s			š		h
Affricates	Voiceless					č		
	Voiced					ǰ		
Nasals		m		n		ñ	ŋ	
Pre-nasalized resonants		mb	nd	ṇd		ñǰ	ng	
Resonants				r				
Laterals				l				
Continuants		v				y		

Sinhala has five cases, inflected in both singular and plural. These are nominative, accusative, dative, genitive, and instrumental. Inanimate nouns occur only in the nominative, accusative, or dative. Case markers are suffixed to nouns. Articles do not occur as separate words, but the distinction between definite and indefinite nouns is conveyed by postpositions. Both case and definite/indefinite markers are illustrated in the following forms of *miniha* 'man'.

	Definite	Indefinite
Nominative	miniha	minihek
Accusative	miniha-və	minihek-və
Dative	miniha-tə	minihek-utə
Genitive	miniha-ge	minihek-ge
Instrumental	miniha-gen	minihek-gen

The number and gender systems in nouns are like those in ENGLISH. That is, nouns can be singular or plural. And, nouns are not specifically marked for gender, although the distinction between masculine and feminine nouns representing human beings is relevant to choice of pronouns.

The Sinhala pronominal system is very complex. In addition to the standard first, second, and third person pronouns that do not encode gender differences, Sinhala has a four-way pronominal system mimicking the demonstrative system: *oyaa* 'you', *meyaa* 'this person', *arəya* 'that man over there', *eyaa* 'man (previously mentioned in discourse)'.

Basic Syntax

Although Sinhala word order is SOV, the constituent order is relatively free. It is a postpositional language as opposed to prepositional languages such as English. Complements and modifiers precede their heads just like in any other right-branching language. Relative clauses, like other modifiers, also precede the nouns they modify.

There are two sentence negators: *nææ* 'no', which negates a predicate, and *nevey* 'not', which is a constituent negator.

Siri game yanne nææ
Siri village go-FOCUS not
'Siri doesn't go to the village.'

Siri game yanawa nevey
Siri village go-PRES not
'It is not that Siri goes to the village.'

Nææ negates the verb *yanne*, while *nevey* negates the whole sentence.

Contact with Other Languages

Sinhala, especially the standard spoken variety, has borrowed heavily from Sanskrit and PALI. Sanskrit borrowings are far more numerous than Pali borrowings. There are also many English, DUTCH and PORTUGUESE words since Sri Lanka had been under their various rules for many years. English is a "link language" widely used for business purposes in Colombo, the capital of Sri Lanka.

From TAMIL: *idam* 'land' (<*idəm*), *pādam* 'lesson' (<*pādam*), *jōdu* 'couple' (<*jōdu*)
From Sanskrit: *candraya* 'moon' (<*candra*), *sūryaya* 'sun' (<*surya*)
From Pali: *āsanaya* 'seat' (<āsana), *ānisamsaya* 'consequence' (<ānisamsa)
From English: *dxybar* 'driver', *wētər* 'waiter', *bæg* 'bag'
From Dutch: *notāris* 'notary', *advakāt* 'advocate'
From Portuguese: *janēlaya* 'window' (<*janela*), *kāmaraya* 'room' (<*camara*)

Common Words

man:	miniha	long:	digə

woman:	ææni	small:	kotə
water:	waturə	yes:	ov
sun:	irə	no:	nææ
three:	tunə	good:	honday
fish:	maalu	bird:	kurulla
big:	loku	dog:	balla
tree:	gaha		

Example Sentences

(1) laŋkaavə harimə lassənay.
Sri Lanka very beautiful
'Sri Lanka is very beautiful.'

(2) laŋkaave minissu kanne bat.
Sri Lanka-GEN man:PLURAL eat:FOCUS rice
'It is rice that the people of Sri Lanka eat.'

(3) bat kanəkotə særətə kanəva.
rice eat-when hot eat:INDICATIVE
'When they eat rice they eat it hot.'

Efforts to Preserve, Protect, and Promote the Language

Sinhala is one of the official languages of Sri Lanka, and it is the majority language except in the northern and eastern provinces where it is spoken by the minority (second to Tamil). Although English, the colonial language, is widely used in government and commerce, civil servants must speak and write in Sinhala, and education, with the exception of some fields such as medicine, is conducted in Sinhala (Gair 1986).

There are some projects at the national level to promote Sinhala, especially along the lines of introducing new terminology to teach subjects such as computer science, etc. The main idea is to expand the lexicon in order to be able to accommodate new knowledge coming through English and other languages. University-level language societies are a good example of this.

Select Bibliography

De Silva, M.W.S. 1979. *Sinhalese and Other Island Languages of South Asia*. Tubingen: Gunther Narr Verlag.

Fairbanks, G.H., J.W. Gair and M.W.S. De Silva. 1983. *Colloquial Sinhalese. Vols. I and II*. Ithaca, NY: South Asia Program, Cornell University.

____. 1986. "Sinhala Diglossia Revisited, or Diglossia Dies Hard." In *South Asian Languages: Structure, Convergence & Diglossia*. Edited by B. Krishnamurti, 322–336. Delhi: Motilal Banarsidass.

Karunatillake, W.S. 1977. "The Position of Sinhala Among the Indo-Aryan Languages." In *Indian Journal of Linguistics* 4: 1–6.

____. 1990. *Introduction to Spoken Sinhala*. Colombo: Gunəsena Publishers.

Masica, Colin P. 1991. *The Indo-Aryan Languages*. Cambridge: Cambridge University Press.

Sumangala, L. 1972. *The Syntax of Focus and WH-questions in Sinhala*. Ph.D. dissertation, Cornell University, DMLL.

Siraiki

Christopher Shackle

Language Name: Siraiki. **Alternates:** *Siraeki*; formerly *Multani*, *Western Panjabi*. Sometimes still called *Southern Lahnda*/*Lahndi* by linguists. **Autonym:** *sirāēkī, sirāikī.*

Location: Central Pakistan (encompassing the southwestern districts of Panjab Province and adjacent districts of Sind, Baluchistan, and North-West Frontier Province).

Family Northwestern subgroup of the Indo-Aryan branch of Indo-European.

Related Languages: PUNJABI, SINDHI.

Dialects: (1) Northern: Mianwali, Dera Ismail Khan; (2) Central: Multan, Dera Ghazi Khan, Northern Bahawalpur (the standard); and (3) Southern: Southern Dera Ghazi Khan, Southern Bahawalpur. The differences between the dialects are fairly minor ones of phonology and lexis. Peripheral varieties show influence of neighboring languages, for example, of Sindhi in the Siraiki of Sind.

Number of Speakers: Approximately 25–40 million.

Origin and History

Since PERSIAN, and later URDU and ENGLISH, were the administrative and cultural languages of the region, earlier records of Siraiki are confined to Muslim religious poetry, first in the verses attributed to Shai<u>kh</u> Farīd (d. 1266) in the Sikh scriptures (1604). Here as in later examples there is considerable confusion of parallel Panjabi and Siraiki forms. Unambiguously Siraiki poetry appears from the late 18th century, reaching its apogee in the Sufi hymns of <u>Kh</u>wāja <u>Gh</u>ulām Farīd (d. 1901), which have become the prime icon of modern Siraiki cultural identity.

The linguistic homogeneity of the region was severely disrupted in the partition of 1947 when the enforced migration of the Hindu minority population to India (where communities of Siraiki speakers are centered in the towns of Hariyana) was followed by the large-scale settlement of Muslim refugees from eastern Panjab who retained their own language.

A modern linguistic consciousness transcending historic dialectal divisions hardly predates the 1970s when it was developed as part of an increasingly broad local politico-cultural movement dedicated to promoting the interests of the region against what its leaders saw as exploitation by the central areas of Panjab.

Past dominance of other languages, continued with official use of Urdu in Pakistan, has severely inhibited development of Siraiki for formal purposes.

Orthography and Basic Phonology

Hindu businessmen formerly used local mercantile shorthands, called *ka'ṛikkī*. Otherwise local forms of the Perso-ARABIC script are used. Outside Sind, where the Sindhi alphabet contains letters to represent all Siraiki phonemes, the unmodified Perso-Urdu script formerly used elsewhere to write Siraiki does not indicate its distinctive implosives and nasal phonemes, but since the 1970s it has become normal to mark these with diacritics, most commonly with an additional subscript dot.

There is the usual Indic contrast between the dental sounds similar to those of ITALIAN and the retroflex sounds pronounced with the tip of the tongue curled up and back.

The marked contrast (shared with Sindhi) between the implosives, pronounced with in-drawn breath, and the corresponding explosives is a proudly maintained point of contrast with Panjabi.

All five nasal phonemes are in contrast, especially the dental *n* and the retroflex *ṇ*, pronounced as a nasalized version of the retroflex flap *ṛ*.

The aspirated stops are fully contrastive with nonaspirates. Other aspirated phonemes are not always so well established. They often result from displacements of (voiced) aspiration consequent on the characteristic breathy articulation of intervening vowels, such as historical *sōhṇā* 'beautiful' > Siraiki *sōṇhā*, versus Panjabi *sō^ṇā* (with high-falling tone). Some fricatives are largely restricted to loans, and the contrasts <u>*kh*</u>/*kh*, <u>*gh*</u>/*g*, or *f*/*ph* are often weak in ordinary speech.

Table 1: Vowels

	Front	Central	Back
High	i, ī		u, ū
Mid	ē	i	ō
Low	(ai)	a, ā	(au)

There is a notably large number of diphthongs in standard speech, including the pronunciation of /au/ as *aō*, reduced in southern dialects by closer and higher articulation, which therefore has *e* for the historical low front vowel /ai/, versus standard *aē*/*æ*. All vowels other than the short *a, i, u* may have contrastive nasalization, written as <u>*n*</u>.

There is a notable phonetic contrast between stressed *a* and the corresponding unstressed *ə*. Stress is normally on the first

Table 2: Consonants

		Labial	Dental	Retroflex	Palatal	Velar	Glottal
Stops	-voi, -asp	p	t	ṭ	c	k	
	-voi, +asp	ph	th	ṭh	ch	kh	
	+voi, -asp	b	d	ḍ	j	g	
	+voi, +asp	bh	dh	ḍh	jh	gh	
	Implosive	b̲		d̲	j̲	g̲	
Fricatives	Voiceless	f	s		s̲h̲	k̲h̲	
	Voiced		z			g̲h̲	h
Nasals	Plain	m	n	ṇ	ñ	ṇ	
	Aspirated	mh	nh	ṇh			
Lateral	Plain		l				
	Aspirated		lh				
Flaps	Plain		r	ṛ			
	Aspirated		rh	ṛh			
Glides	Plain	v			y		
	Aspirated	vh					

syllable, but a few well-defined types of words have second-syllable stress and weakened first syllable, e.g., *'kītā* 'did' >*ki 'tōnē* 'they did'.

Basic Morphology

The basic morphology is generally of the usual Indo-Aryan type, with the addition or inflection of suffixes, but also with some distinctive modifications of the stem, including internal vowel changes.

Nouns have two numbers, singular and plural. There are five case categories, including the usual Indo-Aryan direct and oblique. The others are ablative singular, and the semantically restricted vocative and locative-instrumental cases. The four main declensions are defined by gender and formation of plural direct: masculine *ghōṛā/ghōṛē* 'horse/s', *ghar/ghar* 'house(s)', feminine *ghōṛī/ghōṛiyā̲n̲* 'mare/s', *rāt/rātī̲n̲* 'night/s'. In one interesting class of disyllables, gender and number are marked by internal vowel contrast: *kukuṛ/kukaṛ* 'cock/s', *kukiṛ/kukṛī̲n̲* 'hen/s'. Adjectives with masc.sing. direct in *-ā* agree with the nouns they modify; others are invariable. A number of productive patterns exist for the formation of compound nouns and adjectives, and these are fully exploited for the coinage of neologisms by contemporary writers.

Verbs exhibit differing types of stems. Besides causative stems in *-'ā-*, there are passive stems in *-'ī-*, e.g., *kar-* 'do', *ka'rā-* 'cause to be done', *ka'rī-* 'be done'. Transitives have extended stems for present participle and future, for example, *ka'rē̲n̲dā* 'doing', *ka'rēsī* 'he will do', also with internal vowel change in the type *ma'roṛ-* 'twist', *mur'ṛēsī* 'he will twist'. Verbal inflection is of the usual Indo-Aryan type, but with many irregular past participles, such as *vañ-* 'go', *giā* 'went', *vas-* 'rain', *vuṭhā* 'rained'. A wide variety of modal auxiliaries is used.

Pronominal suffixes are very frequently used with many finite verbal forms, either to mark the object, e.g., *khāv-is* 'eat it!', or with the past participle to mark the direct subject of intransitives, e.g., *gi-um* 'I went' or ergative subject (agent) of transitives, e.g., *ākhi-us* 'he said'. Some suffixes involve shift of stress, e.g. *akhi-'ōsē* 'we said', including double suffixes, e.g., *akhi-'om-is* 'I said to him'.

Besides the negative markers *na, nahī̲n̲* 'not', there are inflected negative forms of the verb 'to be', e.g., *nimhī* 'I am not', *nisē* 'we are not'.

Basic Syntax

The basic order is SOV. Adjectives precede nouns. Postpositions follow nouns and pronouns. With respect to case marking, postpositions follow the oblique case (although direct objects of some verbs are unmarked). There are also ablative singular and locative-instrumental cases. Siraiki is basically head final, but with considerable latitude (probably from influence of both Persian and English syntax) in typical placement of, for example, relative and other subordinate clauses after headwords.

Contact with Other Languages

Except during the century of British rule from 1849–1947, Islam has been politically and culturally dominant in the Siraiki region since the early Middle Ages. So, like most other Pakistani languages, Siraiki contains very large numbers of

Perso-Arabic loanwords, including common items not used in Urdu, plus a considerable number of English loanwords.

From Arabic: *shai* (plural *shaīn̲*) 'thing' (Urdu *chīz* < Persian)
From Persian: *jā* (plural *jāīn̲*) 'place' (Urdu *jagah*)
From English: *bas* 'bus' (versus *b̲as* 'enough' < Persian)

Apart from enforced migration to India in 1947, the Siraiki region has not been an area of significant emigration. The language has largely been confined to its original locations in central Pakistan. Nearly all educated speakers have some knowledge of English, and they are also fluent in Urdu in addition to local regional languages, such as Panjabi, Sindhi, and PASHTO. In India Siraiki is now normally spoken bilingually with HINDI.

Common Words

man:	ādmī	small:	chōṭā
woman:	zāl	yes:	hā
water:	pāṇī	no:	na
sun:	sijh	good:	caṅā
three:	trai	bird:	pakhī
fish:	machī	dog:	kutā
big:	vaḏā	tree:	darak̲h̲t
long:	lambā		

Example Sentences

(1) ūn̲ kūn̲ hath na lāvēn̲ kiūn̲jō ūn̲-dē-vic
it:OBJ hand not apply:IMP.2SG because it-LINK-in

zahar ē.
poison is
'Don't touch it, because there's poison in it.'

(2) mā tē bhēṇ vī yād
mother and sister also memory

ā gi-ōn-is.
come-went-SUBJ.3PL.OBJ.3SG
'He also remembered his mother and sister.'

(3) hik bhiˈrā luˈṭīn̲dā piai hik
one brother rob:PASS.PRES.PTC lie:PRES.PERF.3SG one

bhiˈrā luˈṭēn̲dā khaṛai.
brother rob:PRES.PTC stand:PRES.PERF.3SG
'One brother is (down) being robbed, the other is up robbing.'

Efforts to Preserve, Protect, and Promote the Language

Since the 1970s considerable efforts have been made by local cultural and grassroots political organizations in Pakistan to secure increased recognition of Siraiki as a distinct language and ensure the rights of Siraiki speakers. There is a lively modern literature, and Siraiki speakers (now commonly called "Siraikis") are increasingly being recognized as a distinct ethnic group, with their own radio and television programs on the state-controlled media. Although Siraiki has yet to be officially recognized as a distinct language by the government, it seems likely that there will be increased recognition of the language in the future.

Select Bibliography

Grierson, G.A., ed. 1919. "Specimens of Sindhī and Lahndā." In *Linguistic Survey of India*, Vol. viii, Part I. Calcutta: Superintendent of Government Printing.

Jukes, A. 1900. *Dictionary of the Jatki or Western Punjábi Language*. Lahore: Religious Book Tract Society.

O'Brien, E. 1903. *Glossary of the Multani Language or (South-Western Panjabi)*. Edited by J. Wilson and H.K. Kaul. Lahore: Punjab Government Press.

Shackle, C. 1975. "Siraiki: A Language Movement in Pakistan." In *Modern Asian Studies*. 11: 379–403.

____. 1976. *The Siraiki Language of Central Pakistan: a Reference Grammar*. London: School of Oriental and African Studies.

____. 1979. "Problems of Classification in Pakistan Panjab." In *Transactions of the Philological Society*. 191–210.

____. 1983. "Language, Dialect, and Local Identity in Northern Pakistan." *Pakistan in its Fourth Decade*. Edited by W.P. Zingel and S.Z.-A. Lallemant, 175–187. Hamburg: Deutsches Orient-Institut.

____. 1984. *From Wuch to Southern Lahnda: A Century of Siraiki Studies in English*. Multan: Bazm-e-Saqafat.

Wagha, A. 1990. *The Siraiki Language: Its Growth and Development*. Islamabad: Dderawar Publications.

siSwati

Mpunga wa Ilunga

Language Name: siSwati.

Location: siSwati is one of the languages of the Nguni group employed as the national language of Swaziland, a state enclaved in the Republic of South Africa and bordered on the East by Mozambique.

Family: siSwati is a Bantu language belonging to a branch of the large Niger-Congo-Kordofanian family. Bantu languages are characterized by a system of nominal classification and tones.

Related Languages: siSwati is most closely related to languages belonging to the Nguni group: XHOSA, the language of Lesotho; ZULU, spoken in South Africa; Ndebele, spoken in Zimbabwe; and various languages between Mozambique and Tanzania and in the region of Lake Malawi.

Dialects: Various regional dialects are attested in siSwati, categorized by their four districts: Shisélwèni, Lúbòmbò, Hhohò, and Mandzinì. This chapter is based on the speech of the Mandzinì dialect.

Number of Speakers: 1 million.

Origin and History

Although the common origin of the Bantu peoples is speculative, most sources point out the modern-day border of Cameroon and Nigeria to be the starting point from which the Bantu peoples commenced their expansion, which is usually associated with the cultivation of the Malaysian food crops: banana, taro, and yam.

In the early 19th century, the Nguni group of Bantu languages was confined to Natal, the Cape of Good Hope, and the Transvaal state in South Africa. Three groups of Nguni are distinguished: the Southern Nguni, comprising the Zulu, Swati, and Xhosa peoples who are still settled in their original homeland; the Ndebele of southern Zimbabwe; and the Ngoni of northern Malawi, Zambia, south Tanzania, and the Gaza district in Mozambique.

The Swati people have been historically independent and did not suffer the fate of Zulu domination like other Nguni groups in South Africa. Their political and military organization is similar to that of the Zulus. The Swati are the dominant clan in Swaziland, a state composed of 70 clans that are 70 percent Nguni and 30 percent Sotho. Like all the languages of the Nguni group, siSwati is characterized by having clicks.

Orthography and Basic Phonology

siSwati has five vowels and two semivowels.

Table 1: Vowels

	Front	Central	Back
High	i		u
Mid	e		o
Low	a		
Glides	y		w

The high vowels /i/ and /u/ are nearly inaudible when they occur in the first syllable of a word: *sílèvù* 'beard' is pronounced and even spelled [śl̀è:vù] in modern siSwati.

In addition to the usual consonants employed by Bantu languages, siSwati also has clicks, lateral affricates, and lateral fricatives. The voicing distinction is minimal in siSwati. Prenasalized voiceless consonants /p, t, k, tf, ts, kl/ and /k/ in word-initial position are lightly voiced. Voiced consonants in intervocalic position are also slightly devoiced.

The consonants /t, p, k, kl/ are realized as ejectives. The voiced palatal fricative /ʒ/ is only attested in one word *kúʒìʒà* 'babble'. The phoneme /hh/ is voiced, whereas /h/ is voiceless. The /dl/ sequence in *kûdlà* 'eat' is realized phonetically as [lʒ]. The /hl/ in *síhlàhlà* 'tree' is realized as a voiceless lateral fricative [ɬ]. The click *c* in *cǎ* 'no' is a voiced dental click [ǀ], while the /gc/ phoneme represents a dorso-alveolar, murmured click.

One can notice that the /ny/ sequence is not admissible in siSwati; /ny/ is a simple phoneme. The double-articulated consonants /dl, dz, ts, tj, gc/ are also simple phonemes (see Table 2 on the next page).

Generally, consonant phonemes may appear before each vowel without distinction. However, certain consonants do not have the same realization before all the vowels. The phonemes /dz/ and /ts/ can be phonetically realized [dβ, tɸ̧] and transcribed as /dv, tf/ by speakers. These phonemes have conditioned variants. The phoneme /dz/ is realized [dβ] when followed by /u, o, w/ and [dz] in other environments. The phoneme /ts/ is realized as [tɸ̧] when followed by /u, o, w/ and as [ts] in other environments. We will dispense with the current orthographic practice employed in Swaziland and eliminate /dv/ and /tf/ from phonological notation: [índβɔ̀:dzà] 'men' /índzòdzà/, *bútɸɔ̀:ŋɔ̀* 'sleep' /bútsòngò/. The glide /y/ usually only occurs in word-initial position or intervocalically, except in the word *kúsháywà* 'be beaten'. The glide /w/ is not attested after labial consonants, with the exception of /f/ in *ínfwásáhlòbò* 'spring'.

Vowel length in siSwati is predictable. Clause finally, the vowel of a penultimate syllable is phonetically long, corresponding to dynamic accent: *lídàdà* 'duck' [lídà:dà], *lídàdà*

Table 2: Consonants

Mode of Articulation	Bilabial	Labio-dental	Dental	Dento-Alveolar	Dorso-Alveolar	Palatal	Velar	Glottal
Nasal	m		n			ny [ɲ]	ng [ŋ]	
Stops								
Voiced	b, bh		d				k	
Voiceless	p, ph		t, th				kh	
Fricatives								
Voiced		v	z			ʒ		
Voiceless		f	s			sh [ʃ]		h
Murmured								hh
Lateral				l				
Fricative								
Voiced			dl					
Voiceless			hl [ɬ]					
Affricate					kl [kx']			
Affricates								
Voiced			dz			j [dʒ]		
Voiceless			ts			tj [tʃ]		
Clicks								
Voiced			c [ǀ]					
Murmured			ch		gc [ǂ]			

lámì 'my duck' [lídàdà lá:mì], *lídàdà lámí lífílè* 'my duck is dead' [lídàdà lámì lífí:lè].

There are two tones in siSwati, high tone (*á*) and low tone (*à*). Tones can distinguish words on the lexical level *kúbútsà* 'bring back' versus *kúbùtsà* 'moisten', and also on the grammatical level to distinguish tense, mode, or person: *bèkàlímà* 'he cultivated' versus *békálímà* 'he had cultivated', *úbàlé* 'He counted (indicative)' versus *úbálé* 'that he counted (subjunctive)', *úyálìmà* 'you cultivate' versus *ùyálìmà* 'he cultivates'.

Tones can combine on the same vowel and constitute a tonal sequence LOW-HIGH as in *cǎ* 'no', or HIGH-LOW as in *înjà* 'dog'. Except in monosyllabic words, the LOW-HIGH and HIGH-LOW sequences are limited to prefinal vowels in a word. The sequence of three tones on a prefinal vowel indicates a verbal root of -VC- structure and is a variant of a high tone: *kwấtì* or *kwátì* 'know'. While two high tones follow each other in a word, the second tone, if it belongs to a prefinal syllable in phrase-final position, is realized as a mid-tone: /líkátì/ 'cat' [líkā:tì]. Although each siSwati word in isolation has a fixed tonal pattern, tones vary in discourse according to the place of a word in a phrase: *lúbîsí* 'milk' > *lúbísí lwé ŋkhòmò* 'cow's milk', *íŋkhòmó* 'cow' > *íŋkhòmò ìnàtsá lúbîsí* 'the cow drinks the milk'.

Syllable structure in siSwati is as follows (Nasal) {(Consonant)} (glide) vowel. All syllables in siSwati are open: *kú-bí-twà* 'be called', *í-ncò-là* 'wagon', *ú-mú-ntswà-nà* 'child,' *kú-bâ-njwà* 'be arrested'. Two vowels cannot occur in the same syllable. Syllables composed of a single vowel only appear word initially, and the number of syllables in a word can be from one to seven, rarely more: *ú-mú-sì-dlà-nyá-nyà-nà* 'a quite small tail'.

Basic Morphology

Like its sister Bantu languages, siSwati has noun classes, whose canonical classifying morphemes are shown in Table 3 on the next page. Asterisks indicate morphemes with variant forms, and hyphens indicate that the morpheme in question is identical to the morpheme form shown to the left. Empty boxes correspond to categories where no morpheme is present.

The augment is a vocalic morpheme with high tone whose form is identical to that of the nominal prefix of the same class. It is placed in preinitial position in nouns, adjectives, pronouns, and hybrid words. In some cases, the augment is a marker of definiteness: *àbá nà ímbûtí* 'they don't have the goat' versus *àbá nà mbûtí* 'they don't have a goat'. In other contexts, the augment is always present, notably after the associative *n'èbantswànà* 'with the children', the connective *y'ebántswànà* 'belonging to the children', the predicative *yǐndlòvù* 'it is the cow', or the deictic morpheme (*là*): *l'òmúlòmò* 'the mouth', In these cases, the augment is relatively fixed. It is absent in proper names of people: *lùsèkwànè* 'Madam Bamboo'.

Other classifiers include the nominal prefix: *úmûntsù* 'human', *bântsù* 'humans', the verbal prefix: *úyánàtsà* 'he drinks', the pronominal prefix: *kímì* 'towards me', the object prefix *úyábùnátsà* 'he drank', and the reflexive: *úyátìlìmátà* 'he blesses himself'.

The nominal prefix of Class 1 has a zero variant with terms of parenting: *bàbé* 'father', and the prefix of Class 2 has two secondary variants: the collective prefix *bó* as in *ká bóbàbé* 'in the clan of my father' and the variant *be* attested before the names of peoples: *béswâtì*.

Classes 16, 17a, 17b, 18, and 25 are locative classes. The prefix /e/ of Class 25 attaches to a noun or adjective with or without the suffix *-ìnì*: *éndlìnì* 'in the house', *ékhàyà* 'at home', *phánsì* 'by land', *kúsà* 'at dawn'. Locative agreement is found most often in Class 17 and rarely in Class 16: *phándlè kúhlè* 'outside it is

Table 3: Noun Classes

	Augment	Noun Prefix	Verb Prefix	Pronominal Prefix	Object Prefix
Tone	High	Low	Low	Low	High
Speech Participants					
1singular	*i		ngi	*ngi	-
2singular	*u		u	*u	ku
1plural	*i		si	*si	-
2plural	*i		ni	-	-
Tone	High	Low	High	High	High
Third Person					
Class 1	*u	*mu	*u	-	mu
Class 2	*a	*ba	-	-	-
Class 3	*u	*mu	u	*u	-
Class 4	*i	*mi	i	*i	-
Class 5	*li	*Ø	li	-	-
Class 6	*a	ma	a	*a	-
Class 7	*i	si	-	-	-
Class 8	*i	*ti	ti	-	-
Class 9	*i	*n	i	*i	-
Class 10	*i	*tin	ti	-	-
Class 11	*u	lu	-	-	-
Class 14	*u	bu	-	-	-
Class 15	*u	ku	-	-	-
Locative Classes					
16	*a	pha	ku	ku, ka/pha	ku
17a	*u	ku	-	ku, ka/pha	ku
17b	*u	ka	ku	ku, ka/pha	ku
18	*u	mu	ku	ku, ka/pha	ku
25		é	ku	ku, ka/pha	ku
Reflexive					ti

nice (weather)', *éndlìnì kúhlè* 'it is nice inside the house'. The prefix of Class 17 is placed before the nouns of Class 1a, the names of people, pronouns, and numeric adjectives. It has two forms: *kù-* from Class 17a, and *kà-* from Class 17b: *hâmbà kú málûmè* 'you are going to your maternal uncle' versus *hâmbà ká málûmè* 'you are going to your maternal uncle's house'.

Nouns, characterized by the presence of a nominal prefix, also include the class of adjectives. The root may be simple, derived, or complex, and comes from an open lexical class. There are a limited number of adjectives, consisting of a root that can take all classes: *sílèvù síhlè* 'the beard is beautiful,' *tílèvù tíhlè* 'the beards are beautiful'. Numeric adjectives express number from one to four; all other numbers are nouns. To express order, the numbers are preceded by a connective: *w'èsítsátsù* 'the second'.

There are various derivational affixes in siSwati: *hámb* 'leave' > *úmúhâmbì* 'traveler', *phèk* 'cook' > *úmúphèkì* 'chef', *hlèk* 'laugh' > *kúhlékáhlèkà* 'laugh a little', *bísí* 'milk' > *lúbísánà* 'a little milk', *kátì* 'cat' > *líkátányànà* 'quite small cat', *nyàwò* 'foot' > *lúnyáwókàtì* 'big foot'.

siSwati has a variety of pronoun types: connectives: *tîndlù tá bàbé* 'the houses of my father'; substitutives: *hâmbà nà bó* 'leave with them'; possessives: *líkátí lâbò* 'their cat'; demonstratives: *l'òlâ* 'far from us'; presentatives: *nâló lúbîsí* 'there's the milk'; indefinites: *l'àbântsù l'àbátsìté* 'some people'; and interrogatives: *bâphí bántswànà* 'where are the children?'

Verbal forms in siSwati are distinguished by their morphological complexity. They are composed of a verbal prefix, root, and an ending: *ú-fúndz-à* 'he learns'. All verbs have three morphemes, a verbal prefix, root, and ending, except the imperative, which is deprived of a prefix. Other morphemes associated with verbs are the preinitial negative *à-* as in *àbàfûndzì* 'he doesn't learn'; *ka-* as in *lítàlà kàlíbǒlì* 'crime doesn't go bad'; the temporal prefixes *à-, bé-,* and *bè-*: *àwúnâtsè* 'please drink'; *békánàtsé* 'he had drunk'; *bèkànátsà* 'he was drinking'; postinitial morphemes such as the negator: *àsínòcêlà* 'we will not request'; the formatives: *úsácélà* 'he requests again'; the reflexive prefix: *ùt̲ìl̲ìmátà* 'he blesses himself'; the suffixes: *kúbàmbè̲lê̲là* 'to seize forcibly'; the prefinal suffixes: *bánátsì̲l̲è* 'they have drunk'; and the postfinal suffixes *hàmbán̲ì̲* 'leave'.

Conjugation classes in siSwati are characterized by the form of the verbal conjunct (always followed by a complement) and the disjunct (not obligatorily followed by a complement).

Present conjunct: úlímá (ínsîmù) 'he cultivates the field'
Present disjunct: úyálìmà 'he cultivates habitually'
Recent perfect conjunct: úlìmé (ínsîmù) 'he has cultivated the field'
Recent perfect disjunct: úlímìlè 'he has cultivated'

Basic Syntax

The normal word order in siSwati is Subject-Verb-Complement:

l'àbántswànà bàfûndzà síSwàtì
children learn siSwati
'The children are learning siSwati.'

The verb can be enriched by several suffixes or extensions: *l'àbántsú bá-fùndz-ĭsá síswàtì* 'people teach siSwati,' *l'àbántswànà bà-bòn-èl-à gógò ímbûtí* 'the children watch the goats for grandmother', *l'àbántswànà bàbàmbèlélá úmúlèntè* 'the children clutch the leg strongly'.

Negation is expressed by means of a negative preinitial prefix and a final morpheme according to the conjugation class: 'we do not cultivate' *àsìlímì*.

Contact with Other Languages

siSwati speakers are in close contact with speakers of ENGLISH and AFRIKAANS, as seen in the following loanwords.

From Afrikaans and DUTCH: *íkhélì, émákhélì* 'address', *íŋkhómìshì* 'cup' (from *kommetje*)
From Dutch: *ìbhàyìsíkòbhò* 'cinema' (from *bioscoop*), *lìdòlôbhà* 'city' (from *dorp*)
From English: *ibhăsi* 'bus', *íngădzè* 'garden', *líhábhùlà* 'apple', *índĭshì* 'dish'

Common Words

human:	úmûntsù	woman:	úmúfâtì
water:	émântì	rain:	ímvûlá
three:	-tsátsù	bird:	ínyònì
drink:	kúnàtsà	eat:	kûdlà
long:	-dzĕ	go:	kúyà
eye:	lîsó	eyes:	émêhlò
become:	kúbà	read, understand:	kúfûndzà
goat:	ímbûtí	bosom:	líbĕlè

Example Sentences

(1) Ngìgcìné ngákúbôná.
'Hello.' (Literally: 'Finally I saw you.')

(2) Ngù njànì?
'How are you?'

(3) Sìtàbònánà.
'Goodbye.' (Literally: 'We will see each other again.')

Efforts to Preserve, Protect, and Promote the Language

Along with English, siSwati carries offical status in Swaziland. It is in no danger of extinction.

Select Bibliography

Davez, A.S. 1981. "Aspects of the Tonology of Swati." Unpublished Ph.D. thesis. Pretoria: University of South Africa.
DeBlois, K.F. 1970. "The Augment in Bantu Languages." In *Africana Linguistica* 4: 85–166.
Diyomi, S. Davis. 1992. "Verb Reduplication in siSwati." In *African Languages and Cultures* 5:2: 113–124.
Dlamini, J.V. 1980. "Luhelo lwe Siswati." The Naval Witness (PTY) Lid Pretermaritzburg.
Doke, C.M. 1926. *The Phonetics of the Zulu Language*. Johannesburg: Witwatersrand University Press.
____. 1990. "A Swati Comparative List." In *South Africa Languages* 10:4: 372–383.
Finlayson, R. 1987. "Southern Bantu Origin." In *South African Journal of African Languages* 7:2: 50–57.
Ginindza, T.T. 1962. *Kusile (Swati Tales)*. London: Longmans Group.
Herbert, R.K. 1990. "Labial Palatalisation in Nguni and Sotho Languages: Internal and External Evidence." In *South African Journal of African Languages* 10:2: 74–80.
Kunene, E.C.L. 1986. "Acquisition of siSwati Noun Classes." In *South African Journal of African Languages* 6:1: 34–37.
Rycroft, D.K. 1976. *siSwati-English Dictionary*. Oxford: Charendon Press.
____. 1979. *Say It In siSwati*. London: SOAS.
____. 1990. *Essential siSwati, a Phrasebook for Swaziland*. Pretoria: J.L. Van Schaik.
Schachter, P. 1976. "An Unnatural Class of Consonants in Swati." In *Studies in African Linguistics* Sup. 6: 211–220.
Setsuko, K. 1992. "Verb Reduplication in Swati." In *African Languages and Cultures* 5:2: 113–124.
Ziervogel, D. 1952. *A Grammar of Swazi*. Johannesburg: Witwatersrand University Press.
Ziervogel, D., and Mabuza. 1954. *A Grammar of the Swati Language*. Pretoria: J.L. Schaik.

SLOVAK

David Short

Language Name: Slovak. **Autonym:** *slovenský jazyk, slovenčina.*

Location: The Slovak Republic (Slovakia), pockets in Romania, former Yugoslavia (Vojvodina), Hungary, and Poland; emigré communities in the United States, Canada, Argentina, and Italy; and a dispersed minority in the Czech Republic.

Family: West Slavic group of the Slavic branch of the Indo-European language family.

Related Languages: CZECH and POLISH; more distantly related to the South and East Slavic languages.

Dialects: (1) Central (on which the standard language is based), (2) Western, and (3) Eastern.

Number of Speakers: 4.5 million in Slovakia; 308,000 in the Czech Republic; probably 500,000 in other countries.

Origin and History

Slovak is the official language of the Slovak Republic (Slovakia), which, up until January 1993, had been part of Czechoslovakia. Slovak enjoyed joint official status with Czech in Czechoslovakia.

Slovak constitutes with Czech a separate subgroup within the Western branch of the Slavic family of languages. It is no longer held to be merely an offshoot or historical dialect of Czech, with which it is about 90 percent mutually intelligible, but to have had a continuous evolution out of Proto-Slavic in parallel to the other Slavic languages.

In the early centuries of the Current Era, the inhabitants of what is now Slovakia were Illyrian, Celtic, and Germanic tribes. In the 6th and 7th centuries, Slavic tribes entered the area, probably from two different directions. Most of the area became part of the ninth-century Great Moravian Empire, which included some of the territory that is now the Czech Republic, part of southern Poland, and western Hungary. Great Moravia collapsed in the 10th century under Magyar pressure and with the shift of the Slavic power center to Bohemia, and "Slovakia" was subsequently absorbed into the Hungarian state, where HUNGARIAN and LATIN became the dominant languages, with Latin as the language of record.

Slovak place-names are found in some Latin texts of feudal Hungary. In the 14th and 15th centuries, Czech overtook Latin as the instrument of writing, and Czech was used in documents of law, sermons, and administration. The first document in the Slovak language is the Žilina town book from the late 15th century. For the most part, though, Slovak remained a spoken vernacular and was confined in print merely to glosses and sentences within Latin and Czech texts.

In the 16th century, the first true Slovak written texts appeared, although Czech (or Polish) additions were frequently made to express ideas not yet expressible in Slovak. Czech remained dominant as the language of the Lutheran Reformation. Slovak displayed considerable local variation in the absence of a cultural capital. The future Slovakia was still only upper Hungary, and the Slovaks "Slavs of Hungary", or indeed "Czechs".

By the 17th century a more or less unified form of Slovak ('Cultured West Slovak') became widely used in legal documents and public records. 'Cultured Central Slovak', without a particular urban focus, was even more widely used, while 'Cultured East Slovak' is best represented in the Zemplín version found in Calvinist printed books. In all three areas, there were conscious attempts to unify the local usage. Meanwhile, Latin continued to serve the nobility and higher clergy as well as scholarship and literature, while Czech became the language of both Protestants and those who would re-Catholicize the country. But Protestant Czech was becoming archaic, clinging to the standard set by the (Czech) Kralice Bible. Catholic Czech of this time shows many signs of the local Slovak vernacular.

In the late 18th century a Catholic priest, Anton Bernolák (1762–1813), attempted to shape an official Slovak standard, taking as his basis the cultured Southwestern Slovak of Trnava and Pressburg, with some recognition of Central Slovak features. He produced a Slovak grammar (1790) and a posthumous five-volume dictionary (1825–27). Some literature was written to this standard, but it failed to become accepted because of lack of support and because of the active efforts by some leading Slovak intellectuals to reinstate forms of Czech as the standard language.

During the 19th century, there was a Slovak national movement aimed at both political and cultural sovereignty. The publication of Ľudovít Štúr's *Nauka reči slovenskej* (1846) marked the beginning of the modern standard language, based on Central Slovak dialects. There were some refinements to his work, including incorporation of some elements of Western Slovak and changes to his spelling system. After the Austro-Hungarian Compromise of 1867, Slovak political activity and language were repressed, but after World War I, the Habsburg monarchy, which had ruled in Hungary since 1526, collapsed. The sovereign state of Czechoslovakia was established within the historic borders of the main Bohemian lands and Slovakia.

In the 1920s and 1930s there was concerted activity aimed at refining literary Slovak. The cultural institute *Matica Slovenská* began publishing a periodical devoted to the literary language, *Slovenská reč.*

The old regional differences in the Slovak language are not

entirely dead, and there is ongoing debate as to the acceptability of some forms or words as part of the literary standard. In practice, there is great tolerance for regionalisms, giving the modern literary language considerable lexical breadth and depth.

Slovak is broadly divided into three main dialect groups: Central, on which the standard language is based; Western, showing similarities to adjacent Moravian dialects of Czech; and Eastern, which shares with Polish penultimate stress and lack of phonemic quantity. Each of the three main dialect areas has subdialects, identified by the names of the old counties in which they are located.

Political and economic factors have driven Slovaks to the Americas and elsewhere abroad, where the language is sustained wherever there is a large enough community. The scattered Slovak towns and villages of the more local diaspora, especially in Romania, Hungary, and the former Yugoslavia, are at the mercy of the political whim of the host country and seem likely to decline (or be "cleansed" in some areas).

Orthography and Basic Phonology

The Slovak writing system is based on that of Latin. In addition to the basic 23 letters (*q, w,* and *x* are only used in words borrowed into Slovak), combinations of letters are used to represent some sounds, and other letters are modified by diacritics. For instance, *ch* is used to represent a voiceless velar fricative, *é* is used to represent the long equivalent of the vowel *e*, and the diacritics ˇ over a letter or ' after a letter are used to represent a palatal sound, e.g., *š* (*sh*).

Table 1: Consonants

	Labial	Dental	Palatal	Velar	Glottal
Stops					
Voiceless	p	t	ť	k	
Voiced	b	d	d'	g	
Fricatives					
Voiceless	f	s	š	ch	h
Voiced	v	z	ž		
Affricates					
Voiceless		c	č		
Voiced		dz	dž		
Nasals	m	n	ň		
Resonants		l, r	l', j		

The voiceless stops are all unaspirated.

Table 2: Vowels

	Front	Central	Back
High	i		u
Mid	e		o
Low	(ä)	a	

All vowels can appear either short (*i e a o u*) or long (*í é á ó ú*). The six-vowel system is now rather archaic. The letter *ä* is retained in the spelling, even if replaced in the pronunciation by /e/.

In addition, Slovak has four diphthongs *ie, ia, io,* and *uo* (spelled *ô*).

The resonants *l* and *r* can, like the vowels, serve as the core of a syllable. In the word *dlhý* 'long', *l* is the core of the first syllable. Like the vowels, syllabic resonants can also occur long, as in *vŕšiť* 'pile up', in which the *r* is significantly longer than that in *vrch* 'hill'. Similarly, *vlk* 'wolf', but *vĺča* 'wolf cub'.

A central characteristic of Slovak consonantism is "voice assimilation": voiceless consonants become voiced before voiced consonants, and voiced consonants become voiceless before voiceless consonants. Thus, even though there are sequences of consonants that are spelled *-dk-*, these are pronounced [tk], as in *hádka* 'quarrel', which is pronounced [hātka]. Voice assimilation occurs even when the two consonants are in two different words, as in *vlak mešká* 'train's late', pronounced /vlagmeškā/. There is no contrast between voiced and voiceless consonants word finally: both *stred* 'middle' and *stret* 'encounter' are pronounced /stret/. The complete pattern of assimilation and neutralization of consonants, which, at the word boundary may even involve vowels, as in *vlak ide* 'the train's coming', pronounced /vlagid'e/, is one of the most complex among European languages.

A feature unique to Slovak is the "law of rhythmical shortening", by which, of two morphonologically long syllables in sequence, the second one shortens.

Basic Morphology

Nouns are inflected for number, gender, and case. There are two numbers, singular and plural, and three genders, masculine, feminine, and neuter. In the singular, Slovak distinguishes between animate and inanimate masculine nouns. In the plural, the primary distinction among masculine nouns is between humans and all others. Apart from assignment according to natural gender in the case of living things, gender assignment is largely arbitrary; young animals are always neuter. There are six productive cases in Slovak: Nominative, Genitive, Dative, Accusative, Locative (or Prepositional, since it never occurs without a preposition), and Instrumental. There are isolated survivals of the vocative.

Personal pronouns are used in the nominative chiefly for stress or contrastive emphasis; the personal endings in the verb themselves are sufficient to mark person. In the other cases, the personal pronouns are either weak and enclitic (in the second grammatical slot in the sentence) or strong and mobile, like other major constituents. In many instances, there are formal differences between weak and strong forms. For instance, the strong second-person singular accusative pronoun *teba* contrasts with the weak form *ťa*. Only strong forms occur after prepositions.

Slovak has no articles, although the indefinite pronouns *nejaký, akýsi,* and the numeral *jeden* may sometimes function like an indefinite article, and the demonstrative pronoun *ten* may function somewhat like a definite article, especially before the antecedent of a relative clause. Adjectives, indefinite and demonstrative pronouns, and, although in a variety of patterns, also numerals, must agree with the noun they modify.

The Slovak verb carries the categories of tense and aspect.

Table 3: Conjugation of the Verb *Volat'* 'to call'

Present			Imperfective Future		Perfective Future	Past Participle	Auxiliary	
Form	*Ending*		*Auxiliary*	*Infinitive*				
volám	-m	1st person sg.	budem	volat'	zavolám	volal/-a	som	volal = mas. sg.
voláš	-š	2nd person sg.	budeš	volat'	zavolás	volal/-a	si	volala = fem. sg.
volá	—	3rd person sg.	bude	volat'	zavolá	volal/-a/-o	—	volalo = neuter sg.
voláme	-me	1st person pl.	budeme	volat'	zavoláme	volali	sme	
voláte	-te	2nd person pl.	budete	volat'	zavoláte	volali	ste	
volajú	-jú	3rd person pl.	budú	volat'	zavolajú	volali	—	

There are three main tenses: present, past, and future (with an inconsistently used, and redundant, pluperfect); and two aspects: imperfective and perfective. Verbs that can have the imperfective/perfective opposition have two distinct forms (for example: 'to wash [garments]' is *prat'*—imperfective, and *vyprat'*—perfective). Imperfective verb forms express the action as process (or repeated process), while perfective forms emphasize that the action is completed (the completedness is necessary or relevant). Contrast: "She washed the clothes and thought about what to cook for dinner"; and "She washed the clothes, then hung them to dry".

Verbs agree with the subject in person and number, and in the past tense, also in gender. A sample conjugation consisting of present, future, and past of the imperfective verb *volat'* 'to call', is in Table 3 above.

Negation is expressed by the prefixed *ne-*, attached to the inflected form in the present, the auxiliary in the future, and the participle in the past.

Basic Syntax

The order of constituents in the Slovak sentence is strongly governed by functional-sentence perspective. The general pattern is that old, given, or least-relevant information tends to be at the beginning of a sentence, while new, relevant, emphasized information tends to be at the end. Word order is, therefore, extremely flexible. One of the simplest visible contrasts is in existential sentences, which simultaneously show how Slovak may deal with definiteness:

Na stole je kniha
on table is book
'There's a book on the table.'

Kniha je na stole
book is on table
'The book is on the table.'

Within its flexible word order, the language has fairly strong rules on the positioning of enclitics, typically in the second constituent slot in the sentence (the first slot may be occupied by subject, object, the lexical part of a past tense or conditional verb, an infinitive, adverb, or adverbial phrase, subordinating conjunction, or disyllabic coordinating conjunction). To the extent that more than one enclitic is present, their order within the second slot is fixed: conditional particle, past tense auxiliary, and reflexive pronoun-particle, dative personal pronoun, nondative personal pronoun, and some sentence adverbs:

Báli by sme sa jej to
feared:PL COND.PART PAST AUX1.PL REFL her:DAT it:ACC

však povedat'
but tell:INF
'We would be afraid to tell her though.'

Contact with Other Languages

Slovak has long been in geographical and geopolitical contact with Czech, Polish, Hungarian, and Ruthenian (UKRAINIAN), and from the first three has drawn at least some of its borrowings. In the case of Polish and Ruthenian there are some mixed border dialects. Coexistence with and proximity to the Czechs has also had an inevitable effect on the Slovak lexicon. Contact with GERMAN and ROMANIAN has been largely occasioned by German (Saxon) and Wallachian in-migration in the Middle Ages; the Germans were chiefly miners and merchants; the Wallachians were upland sheep farmers.

Slovak is, and always has been, hospitable to loans. In early times many came from or through German and Latin. Later loans came from or through Hungarian. In the late 19th century, Slovak took some words from RUSSIAN (Russia was seen by many Slovaks as a possible counterweight to oppression from the Hungarians), and since World War II, many Soviet words passed into Slovak. General technical and cultural development has given Slovak a very broad range of "internationalisms", of both classical and modern European provenance.

From German: *almužna* 'alms', *krst* 'baptism', *richtár* 'magistrate', *cech* 'guild'
From Latin: *anjel* 'angel', *diabol* 'devil'
From Hungarian: *čižma* 'boot', *chýr* 'rumor, reputation', *gazda* 'farmer'
From Czech: *spor* 'dispute', *jednotlivý* 'individual'

From Russian: *dejstvovat'* 'to act', *jestvovat'* 'to exist'
from ENGLISH: *sejvnút'* 'save' (on computer disk; colloquial), *futbal* 'soccer', *džin* 'gin'

Currently, every sixth word in the press is a loan, with about 500 entrants added to the word stock every year.

Common Words

man:	muž	long:	dlhý
woman:	žena	short:	krátky
water:	voda	yes:	áno
sun:	slnko	no:	nie
three:	traja, tri	good:	dobrý
fish:	ryba	bird:	vták
big:	vel'ký	dog:	pes
small:	malý	tree:	strom

Example Sentences

(1) Kotlinka je malá dedinka,
Kotlinka is small:FEM.NOM.SG village:FEM.NOM.SG

ktorej hrozí zánik.
that:FEM.DAT.SG threaten:3.SG demise:MASC.NOM.SG
'Kotlinka is a small village that is threatened with disappearance.'

(2) Ako sa máte?
how self have:2D.PL
'How are you?' (Literally: 'How do you have yourself?')

(3) Milova-l-a ho.
love-PAST-she him:ACC
'She loved him.'

Efforts to Preserve, Protect, and Promote the Language

The *Ľudovít Štúr* Linguistics Institute of the Slovak Academy of Sciences is engaged in the description and evaluation of the dialects and the changing norm of Standard Slovak. The institute's work is dependent on the vagaries of central funding. The fruits of its labors are published in two journals (*Slovenská reč* and *Kultúra slova*) and a number of monograph series. Ongoing research is frequently reported through the Slovak Linguistics Association's newsletter *Zápisník slovenského jazykovedca*. The institute oversees the creation of neologisms to express new ideas, drawing on a mixture of native elements and modified internationalisms; it is also the sponsor of any orthographic reforms and the source of a modest output of dictionaries. The lexical standard is constantly being refined out of what the dialects have to offer, but also by active elimination of undesirable alien elements; this is one of the outcomes of 1990s language laws. These, largely sponsored by the national cultural foundation, *Matica slovenská*, were not only purist, but were also a dynamic, if not autocratic, assertion of the "state" status of Slovak. There were complex provisions for the use of languages in the public arena (visible notices, language qualifications of job seekers, etc.); a language inspectorate was instituted to oversee observance of the new legislation, with quite substantial fines for transgressors. Since the change of government in 1999, the more extreme provisions of some of the language legislation have been mitigated or withdrawn. The *Matica* has been traditionally concerned with fostering the use of Slovak among emigré communities, the life and language of which are described in contributions to its journal, *Slováci v zahraničí*.

Select Bibliography

Ďurovič, Ľ. 1980. "Slovak." In *The Slavic Literary Languages: Formation and Development*, ed. A.M. Schenker and E. Stankiewicz. New Haven: Yale Concilium on International and Area Studies.
Hammer, L.B. 1995/96. *Slovak Elementary 1/2: Student Manual*. Columbus, OH: Ohio State University.
Horálek, K. 1992. *An Introduction to the Study of the Slavonic Languages*. Trans. P. Herrity. Nottingham: Astra Press.
Mistrík, J. 1987. *A Grammar of Contemporary Slovak*. 2d ed. Bratislava: Slovenské pedagogické nakladatel'stvo.
Naughton, J.D. 1997. *Colloquial Slovak*. London: Routledge.
Oravec, J., and J. Prokop. 1986. *A Slovak Textbook for English-Speaking Countrymen*. Martin: Matica slovenská.
Rubach, J. 1993. *The Lexical Phonology of Slovak*. Oxford: Clarendon Press.
Short, D. 1993. "Slovak." In *The Slavonic Languages*, ed. B. Comrie and G.G. Corbett. London and New York: Routledge.
Swan, O.E., and S. Gálová-Lorenc. 1990. *Beginning Slovak: A Course for the Individual or Classroom Learner*. Columbus, OH: Slavica.

SLOVENE

Marc L. Greenberg

Language Name: Slovene. **Alternate:** *Slovenian.* **Autonym:** *slovenski jezik, slovenščina.*

Location: Spoken in the Republic of Slovenia. Significant minorities are found in neighboring territories in Italy, Austria, and Hungary. Diaspora communities are primarily in Argentina, Australia, Canada, and the United States.

Family: Together with SERBO-CROATIAN, Slovene makes up the West South Slavic subgroup of the South Slavic group of the Slavic branch of Indo-European.

Related Languages: Slovene is related to the other South Slavic languages, particularly to the Čakavian and Kajkavian dialects of Croatian; it is less close to the Štokavian dialect, which is the basis for the Croatian, Bosnian, and Serbian standard languages. Slovene is more distantly related to MACEDONIAN and BULGARIAN; it also shows correspondences to the central dialect of SLOVAK in the West Slavic branch.

Dialects: Slovene is traditionally divided into seven dialect bases, within each of which there is further dialect differentiation: (1) Littoral dialects (*primorsko narečje*), spoken partly in Italy; (2) Carinthian (*koroško narečje*), spoken largely in Austria; (3) Upper Carniolan (*gorenjsko narečje*); (4) Lower Carniolan (*dolenjsko narečje*); (5) Styrian (*štajersko narečje*); (6) Pannonian (*panonsko narečje*), spoken partly in Hungary; and (7) Rovte (*rovtarsko narečje*). Additionally, the Inner Carniolan dialect constitutes a transition between the Littoral and Lower Carniolan dialects.

Number of Speakers: Approximately 2 million.

Origin and History

In the sixth to seventh centuries A.D. Slavs began settling in the eastern Alpine regions, having employed the Danube, Sava, and Drava river systems to migrate westward, occupying lands abandoned by the Langobards; southward Slavic migrations of Proto-Croats, Serbs, Macedonians, and Bulgarians resulted in settlement of the Balkan hinterland. These settlements ultimately gave rise to the modern Slovene, Serbo-Croatian (now corresponding to the Croatian, Bosnian, and Serbian standard languages), Macedonian, and Bulgarian speech territories. The Proto-Slovene territory reached as far west as the Tagliamento River, the Gulf of Trieste, Linz, and the outskirts of Vienna to the north, and the southern end of Lake Balaton to the east. Features of South Slavic provenience in the Central dialect area of Slovak point to a time when Proto-Slovene was still contiguous with West Slavic. The Slavic state of Carantania, centered around modern Klagenfurt, Austria, was established in the seventh century. In the ninth century, the state came under Frankish domination, an alliance motivated by the Avar threat. Throughout the medieval period, the Proto-Slovene speech territory has gradually diminished as speakers shifted to Friulian, ITALIAN, GERMAN, and HUNGARIAN, leaving a southern core area today that is equal to the present-day republic of Slovenia plus border areas in Italy, Austria, and Hungary.

The earliest surviving written documents from the Proto-Slovene speech territory are the *Freising Folia*, consisting of liturgical formulae in the Western rite, and a sermon, composed around A.D. 1000. These constitute the oldest attestation of any Slavic language written in the LATIN (Carolingian) alphabet. From this time until the middle of the 16th century there are a few surviving documents in Slovene, mostly religious and legal texts. The first printed book in Slovene is Primož Trubar's (1508–1586) *Catechismus* (1550), which, along with Jurij Dalmatin's (1547–1598) translation of the Bible (1584), ushers in the first era in the creation of a Slovene standard language. Trubar was aware of the already considerable dialect differentiation of the Slovene speech territory and employed elements of the Central Slovene dialects, particularly the dialect of Ljubljana and his native Lower Carniolan as the basis for his written language. The Counter-Reformation put an end to this era, while the Protestants developed a regional literary language for use in Prekmurje, in the northeast. Štefan Küzmič's (1723–1799) translation of the New Testament (1771) remains the major achievement in the local Prekmurje literary language, which is still employed in Protestant churches in the region.

Although some important contributions were made to Slovene literacy by Catholic intellectuals (notably, the monk and grammarian, Marko Pohlin, 1735–1801), the Slovene language remained secondary to the state language, German and, in the western and northeastern peripheries, Italian and Hungarian. The beginning of the modern Slovene standard language can be dated to the work of Jernej Kopitar (1780–1844), whose *Grammatik der slawischen Sprache in Krain, Kärnten und Steyermark* (1809) marks the beginning of a language constructed from selected dialect elements and based on historically supported spelling. The literary language was raised in prestige by the literary efforts of the Romantic poet France Prešeren (1800–1849) and the literary circle around Baron Sigismund Zois (1747–1819). The orthographic system that makes up the modern standard, by and large in the form it is found today, was codified in the *Slovene-German Dictionary* of Maks Pleteršnik (1840–1923), published in 1894–95.

Orthography and Basic Phonology

The Slovene alphabet (*abeceda*) is a modification of the Roman alphabet, as adapted from CZECH by Ljudevit Gaj in the 19th century: A, a; B, b; C, c; Č, č; D, d; E, e; F, f; G, g; H, h; I, i; J, j; K, k; L, l; M, m; N, n; O, o; P, p; R, r; S, s; Š, š; T, t; U, u; V, v; Z, z; Ž, ž.

Several other letters are sanctioned in standard orthography to render direct citation of foreign words, for example, *Ç, ç; Ć, ć; Đ, đ; Q, q; X, x; Y, y; Ś, ś; Ź, ź; Ż, ż.*

Table 1: Consonants

		Labial	Dental	Palatal	Velar
Stops	vls	p	t		k
	vd	b	d		g
Affricates	vls		c	č	
	vd			dž	
Fricatives	vls	f		š	h
	vd			ž	
Nasals		m	n		
Lateral			l		
Trill/Tap			r		
Glides		v		j	

Č, dž, š, and *ž* are pronounced roughly as the ENGLISH sounds "ch", "j", "sh", and "s" as in "check", "jeep", "sheep", and "pleasure", respectively.

V is pronounced as English "v" only when it precedes a vowel; otherwise it is pronounced similarly to "w": *krava* 'cow'—*krav* [kraw] 'of cows' (genitive plural); *vlak* [wlak] 'train'; *navzgor* [nawzgor] 'upwards'. *L* is pronounced as *w* in final position and before a consonant (with some morphologically conditioned exceptions): *brala* 'she read'-*bral* [braw] 'he read'; *spremljevalec* [-ləc] 'companion' *spremljevalca* [-wca] 'companion' (genitive singular).

Obstruents are neutralized for the voicing feature before a pause, for example, *žaba* 'frog' -*žab* [žap] 'of frogs' (genitive plural). Obstruents (listed in the table with the opposition *vls- vd*) in clusters agree in voicing with the final obstruent of the cluster, such as *sladek* 'sweet' (masculine singular) -*sladka* [slatka] (feminine singular). The final-devoicing rule applies first: *brizga* 'syringe' -*brizg* [brisk] 'of syringes' (genitive plural).

Table 2: Vowels

	Front	Central	Back
High	i		u
High-mid	e	ə	o
Low-mid	ɛ		ɔ
Low		a	

The vowels *i, e, ɛ, a, ɔ, o, u* occur in long stressed syllables, whereas the stressed *ə* is always short (*pes* [pə̀čs] 'dog'). In unstressed syllables the distinctions between *e—ɛ* and *o—ɔ* are neutralized to *ɛ* and *ɔ*, respectively: *človek* [člɔ́vɛ̱k] 'person'—*človeka* [člɔvé̱ka] 'person' (genitive singular); *potok* [pɔ́tɔ̱k] 'stream'—*potoka* [pɔtó̱ka] 'stream' (genitive singular). The orthography has only one grapheme, *e*, for the sounds *e, ɛ, and ə*; it has only *o* for both the sounds *o* and *ɔ*.

A syllable nucleus represented by the grapheme *r* is pronounced as a sequence of the sounds *ə* + *r*, for example, *vrt* [vərt] 'garden', *srce* [sərce] 'heart'.

Accent. Standard Slovene pronunciation has two accentual norms, one characterized by pitch accent (based on the pattern of the Upper and Lower Carniolan dialects), the other by stress and vowel length. In the pitch-accent system, any long stressed syllable is characterized by either a low tone (traditionally, "rising" or "acute") or a high tone (traditionally, "falling" or "circumflex"). Excluding unstressed particles, prepositions, conjunctions, and certain pronouns (such as *se* [reflexive particle], *pri* 'by, near' *in* 'and', *ki* 'which', *en* 'a'), words that do not have a long stressed vowel are short stressed (redundantly high) on the final syllable. Examples are: *bráti* 'to read' (low), *brât* 'to go read', *bràt* 'brother' (short); *poskòk* 'hop' (short). In the non pitch stress system, the distinction between low and high tone is not realized. Pitch and stress marks are not included in Slovene orthography.

Basic Morphology

Slovene is an inflecting language. Nouns, pronouns, and adjectives agree in case, number, and gender. The cases are nominative, genitive, dative, accusative, locative, and instrumental. The locative and instrumental obligatorily occur with prepositions. In addition to plural and singular, Slovene has separate forms for dual. The genders are feminine, masculine, and neuter.

Singular

Case	Feminine	Masculine	Neuter
Nominative	punca 'girl'	fant 'boy'	mesto 'city'
Genitive	punce	fanta	mesta
Dative	punci	fantu	mestu
Accusative	punco	fanta	mesto
Locative	(pri) punci	(pri) fantu	(pri) mestu
Instrumental	(s) punco	(s) fantom	(z) mestom

Plural

Case	Feminine	Masculine	Neuter
Nominative	punce	fant	mesta
Genitive	punc	fantov	mest
Dative	puncam	fantom	mestom
Accusative	punce	fante	mesta
Locative	(pri) puncah	(pri) fantih	(pri) mestih
Instrumental	(s) puncami	(s) fanti	(z) mesti

Dual

Case	Feminine	Masculine	Neuter
Nominative, Accusative	punci	fanta	mesti
Genitive	punc	fantov	mest
Locative	(pri) puncah	(pri) fantih	(pri) mestih
Dative, Instrumental	puncama	fantoma	mestoma

In Standard Slovene, definiteness is not expressed by an article, as it is in English. Rather, the masculine adjective in the nominative and accusative case shows this distinction, for example, *lep paradižnik* '(a) beautiful tomato'—*lepi paradižnik* 'the beautiful tomato'. However, in the colloquial language, a definite article has developed from a demonstrative pronoun (in all genders and numbers): *lep* 'beautiful' (generic or indefinite)—*ta lep* 'the beautiful (one)'. An indefinite article has developed from the numeral 'one' (*eden*), as in *en lep paradižnik* 'a beautiful tomato'.

Slovene verbs distinguish imperfective and perfective aspect, roughly, incomplete versus completed action. Basic or simplex (unprefixed) verbs are generally imperfective (*misliti* 'to think') or bi-aspectual (*roditi* 'to give birth'). Prefixation creates additional, usually perfective meanings, such as *premisliti* 'to think something through', *prinesti* 'to bring'; imperfectives are derived by suffixation, as in *premišljevati* 'to be in the process of thinking something through', *prinašati* 'to bring (repeatedly), to be in the process of bringing'.

The present tense of the verb distinguishes person and number. Pronouns are usually dropped unless the person is emphasized or reference is switched in the discourse. Second-person plural is used also as an honorific for a single addressee. The personal pronouns are given in parentheses in the chart; where two are listed, the first is masculine, the second feminine.

Present:

	Singular	Plural	Dual
First person:	(jaz) misli-m '(I) think'	(mi) misli-mo	(midva, medve) misli-va
Second person:	(ti) misli-š	(vi) misli-te	(vidva, vedve) misli-ta
Third person:	(on, ona) misli	(oni, one) misli-jo	(onadva, onidve) misli-ta

The past and future are compound tenses, made up of an auxiliary verb that inflects for person and number and a participial form that distinguishes gender and number. The past-tense auxiliary is *sem, si, je...*; the future is *bom, boš, bo...* (see chart). For example, *Premislil sem to* 'I thought it through', *Premislil bom to* 'I shall think it through'. The conditional mood is made up of an uninflected particle *bi* + the same participle, thus, *Presmislil bi to* 'I/you/he should/would think it through'.

Auxiliaries:

	Singular		Plural		Dual	
	Past	**Future**	**Past**	**Future**	**Past**	**Future**
First person:	sem	bom	smo	bomo	sva	bova
Second person:	si	boš	ste	boste	sta	bosta
Third person:	je	bo	so	bodo	sta	bosta

Participles (third-person past used as an example):

	Singular	Plural	Dual
Masculine	mislil	mislil-i	mislil-a
Feminine	mislil-a	mislil-e	mislil-i
Neuter	mislil-o	mislil-a	mislil-i

Slovene also distinguishes the infinitive from a secondary infinitive, called the "supine", a form expressing intention to perform an action. The supine occurs after verbs of motion. Thus, *Moram kositi* 'I must mow' (infinitive)—*Grem kosit* 'I am going to mow' (supine).

Basic Syntax

Slovene word order is basically SVO, but word order is said to be free in that the elements may be rearranged for emphasis, as in the following examples:

Gospod je dve uri čakal.
man be:3s.AUX two hours waited
'The man waited for two hours.' [emphasizes "waited"]

Gospod je čakal dve uri.
Man be:3s.AUX waited two hours
'The man waited for two hours.' [emphasizes "two hours"]

Na postaji je čakal gospod.
At station be:3s.AUX waited man.
'There was a man waiting at the station.' [emphasizes "man"]

Generally, clitic elements follow the first verb or noun phrase in the main clause:

Bojimo se ga vznemirjati.
be.afraid:1p REFL.PART him:GEN.SG disturb:INF
'We are afraid to disturb him.'

In noun phrases the normal order is demonstrative + numeral + adjective + noun. Subordinate clauses are typically begun by *da* 'that', *ki*/*kateri* 'which', *ker* 'because', *ko(t)* 'as', *če* 'if':

Vem, da je pametna punca.
know:1s that 3s.AUX smart:FEM.SG girl:NOM.SG
'I know that she is a smart girl.'

Tam stoji vlak, ki smo ga
There stands:3SG train: NOM.SG which 1p.AUX it:ACC.MASC.SG
čakali.
waited:PL
'There is the train for which we were waiting.'

Contact with Other Languages

Slovene as a substratum language and as a language in contact has left its mark on Friulian, German (especially the Bavarian and Tyrolian dialects), Hungarian, and Croatian. Influences on Slovene have come from the same languages, as well as Venetian Italian, Dalmatian, and Istrian Romance. A number of languages, including Illyrian and continental Celtic, may have made up substrata to Proto-Slovene (or the Romance dialects that preceded it) and are recognizable as trace elements in the vocabulary, for example, from Celtic *Karavanke* 'Karawanken Alps', *Kranj(ska)* 'Carniola'.

From Romance: *pogača* 'cake' (cf. Ital. *focaccia*), *jota* 'type of thin soup' (< Friulian *jote*, in turn ultimately from Celtic)
From Italian: *briga* 'worry', *punca* 'girl'
From German: *reva* 'poor person' (< Old High German *riuwe*), *brihten* 'smart', *puška* 'shotgun'
From Hungarian: *gazda* 'landowner, boss'
From English: *gangster*

Common Words

man:	človek	small:	majhen
woman:	ženska	yes:	da (colloq., ja)
water:	voda	no:	ne
sun:	sonce	good:	dober
three:	tri	bird:	ptič
fish:	riba	dog:	pes
big:	velik	tree:	drevo
long:	dolg		

Example Sentences

(1) Vsak, ki jo je poznal,
everyone which her:ACC.SG.FEM 3s.AUX knew:MASC.SG

jo je imel rad.
her:ACC.SG.FEM 3s.AUX had:MASC.SG glad:MASC.SG
'Everyone who knew her liked her.'

(2) Sedeli smo za mizo in smo
sat:MASC.PL 1p.AUX behind table:INSTR and 1p.AUX

se pogovarjali.
REFL conversed:MASC.PL
'We sat at the table and conversed.'

(3) Prinesla sta očetu
brought.MASC.DUAL 3.DUAL.AUX father:DAT.SG

star časopis.
old:ACC.SG.INDEF newspaper:ACC.SG
'The two of them brought father an old newspaper.'

Efforts to Preserve, Protect, and Promote the Language

After the incorporation of the Slovene speech territory (minus the Carinthian area, which remained in Austria, the littoral area in Italy, and the Porabje region in Hungary) into the kingdom of Serbs, Croats, and Slovenes in 1918 (named Yugoslavia in 1929), Slovene was no longer a regional language subordinate to German, but now became subordinate to Serbo-Croatian, the de facto lingua franca of the Yugoslav state. The legal status and prestige of Slovene within the reconstituted, Socialist Yugoslavia, was raised after World War II. Its rights as the official language of the Socialist Republic of Slovenia as well as an official Yugoslav state language were reaffirmed by the Yugoslav Federal Constitution of 1974, in which it was declared to be on par with Serbo-Croatian. However, the real situation was markedly asymmetrical, with Slovene enjoying limited rights in Yugoslav state functions as well as some matters within the Republic of Slovenia itself (in particular, the military). In the 1980s leading Slovene intellectuals took issue with the discrepancy between the constitutionalized protection of Slovene and the encroachment of Serbo-Croatian, which they felt a threat to their national identity. Events leading up to the 1991 secession of Slovenia from Yugoslavia frequently centered on language issues, including a staged trial of four Slovenes accused of treason and sedition. This trial was held in Serbo-Croatian within the Slovene Republic, in violation of the sovereignty of Slovene in its own state and of the constitutional rights of the accused. Slovene is now the state language of the independent Republic of Slovenia. Additionally, Italian and Hungarian are accorded official status for administration and education in the coastal region and Prekmurje, respectively.

Slovenes continue to be concerned with the plight of Slovene-speaking minorities in Italy, Austria, and Hungary, where they have attempted to encourage the respective governments to accord language rights and foster Slovene-language education. These efforts have met with limited success.

In recent years, some intellectuals perceive a threat to the survival of Slovene from major world and European languages, especially English. This has led to some successful attempts to introduce native coinages and loan translations, for example, *strežnik* 'server', *svetovni splet* 'the World Wide Web', *zgoščenka* 'compact disk'.

Select Bibliography

Greenberg, Marc L., ed. 1997. *The Sociolinguistics of Slovene* (=*International Journal of the Sociology of Language* 124). Berlin: Mouton de Gruyter.

____. 2000. *A Historical Phonology of the Slovene Language* (=*Historical Phonology of the Slavic Languages, VII*). Heidelberg: Carl Winter Universitätsverlag.

Lencek, Rado L. 1982. *The Structure and History of the Slovene Language*. Columbus: Slavica.

Priestly, T.M.S. 1993. "Slovene." In *The Slavonic Languages*. B. Comrie and G. Corbett, eds. London: Routledge, 388–451.

Rigler, Jakob. 1986. "The Origins of the Slovene Literary Language." In J. Rigler, *Razprave o slovenskem jeziku*. F. Jakopin, ed. Ljubljana: Slovenska matica, 52–64.

Stankiewicz, Edward. 1980. "Slovenian." In *The Slavic Literary Languages*. Alexander M. Schenker and Edward Stankiewicz, eds. New Haven: Yale Concilium on International and Area Studies, 85–102.

Thomas, George. 1977. "The Impact of Purism on the Development of the Slovene Standard Language." In *Slovenski jezik–Slovene Linguistic Studies* 1, 133–152.

SOGDIAN

Yutaka Yoshida

Language Name: Sogdian. **Autonym:** Unknown, but cf. *swγδy'w* 'in the Sogdian language'.

Location: Sogdian was spoken in Sogdiana, the area along the Zarafshan and the Kashka-darya (part of modern Uzbekistan and Tajikistan). The main sites where Sogdian manuscripts have been discovered are Dunhuang (China), Turfan (Chinese Turkestan), and Mount Mug (Tajikistan). Manuscripts and inscriptions date from the 4th to the 10th centuries.

Family: The East Iranian group of the Iranian branch of Indo-European.

Related Languages: Yaghnobi is its (not direct) descendant and is sometimes called Modern Sogdian; neighboring Middle Iranian languages were Choresmian and Bactrian; Modern Iranian languages include PERSIAN and KURDISH.

Dialects: Linguistic variations found in the written material are comparatively trivial and are mainly chronological rather than dialectal. However, some of the differences observed among the manuscripts may reflect social as well as regional dialects.

Origin and History

The history of Sogdiana is largely obscure. It constituted a satrapy of the Achaemenian Empire, which was conquered by Alexander the Great in the fourth century B.C. Later it was governed by or under the influence of neighboring empires, such as Kushan (1st to 2nd centuries), Sassanian (3rd century), Ephtalite (5th to 6th centuries), Western Turks (6th to 7th centuries), and Chinese (7th to 8th centuries). However, until it was conquered by the Arabs in the 8th century it seemed to have enjoyed a degree of independence. During this period of relative independence the Sogdians played an active role as traders along the Silk Road between China and the West. The Sogdian language became a lingua franca in the region between Sogdiana and China where the Sogdians founded many colonies. Most of the Sogdian manuscripts have been discovered from this region, in particular from the oasis of Turfan and one of the caves of the Thousand Buddhas in Dunhuang. An important exception is the site at Mount Mug in Sogdiana proper (120 km east of Samarqand) where 70-odd documents were unearthed.

Apart from the so-called Ancient Letters of the early 4th century and inscriptions discovered in the upper Indus, the bulk of Sogdian manuscripts date back to the 7th through 10th centuries. While the Mug documents represent part of the archives of a local ruler just before the Arab conquest, almost all the manuscripts from Chinese Turkestan are religious texts translated from the originals in Chinese (Buddhist texts), Middle Persian, and Parthian (Manichaean), and Syriac (Christian).

While they were governed by nomadic peoples, Sogdians, being literate since the period of the Achaemenian Empire when the ARAMAIC script (predecessor of Sogdian script) was introduced, exercised a strong cultural influence upon their rulers. Consequently, Sogdian script was later employed to write Old TURKISH, i.e., UYGHUR. This Uyghur script, "late Sogdian script" as it were, in turn was refashioned to transcribe MONGOLIAN.

Since the language of Samarqand and Bukhara of the 10th century reported by Maqdisī is nothing but a local variation of Persian, Sogdian fell into disuse by that time. However, his statement that Sughd (the area between Samarqand and Bukhara) had its own language similar to that spoken in the suburb of Bukhara seems to indicate that at that time the employment of Persian was still restricted to the urban area. Later it gradually gave way to Persian and then to Turkish. A dialect still spoken in the valley of the Yaghnob, a tributary of the Zarafshan River, is a descendant of a variant of the Sogdian language; the language of texts known to us is believed to represent "the standard Sogdian" that used to be spoken in Samarqand.

Orthography and Basic Phonology

Sogdian texts are written in three scripts: Sogdian, Manichaean, and Syriac. While Manichaean script is restricted to Manichaean texts and Syriac to Christian, Sogdian script is a kind of national script employed for all kinds of text, regardless of the religious affiliation of the writer. Sogdian script is an adaptation of the Achaemenian chancellery script deriving from Aramaic, with the result that several Aramaic words appeared in their original spelling but were pronounced with their Sogdian equivalents. In the printed texts these ideograms are transliterated with capital letters, e.g., *CWRH* 'self, body' pronounced as /γrīw/. Because of its long history, texts written in Sogdian script contain many historical spellings from which those in Manichaean and Syriac scripts are virtually free, e.g., *'xš'y''δ* /əxšēθ/ 'king' < Old Iranian **xšāyaθya-*, cf. *xšyδ* in Manichaean script.

All three writing systems that ultimately originate from Aramaic are consonantal and hardly adequate for representing the Sogdian language. Vowels are indicated by means of three mater lectiones, i.e., ', *w*, and *y*: ' (initially ") representing [ā], *w* [w, ū̆, ō̆] and *y* [y, ī̆, ē̆], although the short vowel [a] is not represented except for the initial position where it is indicated by '-.

Sogdian being a dead language, the phonemic tables given on the next page are based largely on comparative phonology and internal reconstruction, and consequently phonetic values of certain sounds are speculative. In discussing phonology Sogdian material is cited in orthographic as well as in vocalized form but after that only orthographic forms are given (in Sogdian script if not stated otherwise).

Sounds in parentheses in the table are allophones (voiced stops and *ŋ*) and marginal phonemes (*ts*, *l*, and *h*), mainly employed in foreign words. The unbalanced system, with the lack of distinction between the voiced and voiceless feature in stops while the contrast is found in fricatives, is because of the sound change in which the Old Iranian voiced stops changed into voiced fricatives even in initial position. As a result, the voiced series occurs only after nasalized vowels, in which position the Old Iranian voiced and voiceless series have fallen together, as in *snk* [saṃg] 'stone' < **asanga-* vs. *znk* [zaṃg] 'kind, sort' < **zanaka-*.

Table 1: Consonants

	Labial	Dental	Alveolar	Palatal	Velar
Stops					
Voiceless	p	t	(ts)	č	k
Voiced	(b)	(d)		(ǰ)	(g)
Fricatives					
Voiceless	f	θ	s	š	x
Voiced	ß	δ	z	ž	γ
Nasals	m	n			(ŋ)
Glides	w	(l)	r	y	(h)

Table 2: Vowels

	Front	Central	Back
High	i, ī	(ɨ)	u, ū
Mid	e, ē	(ə)	o, ō
Low	a		ā

Sounds in parentheses are variants of phoneme /a/. In addition to the simple vowels shown above, Sogdian possessed three rhotacized vowels: $ə^r$, i^r and u^r and a nasal vowel *ṃ*. The morphophonemic process known as "rhythmic law" shows that a syllable containing a simple vowel followed by $ə^r$ or *ṃ* (e.g., *mrγ* [ma$ə^r$γ] 'forest', *knδ* [kaṃθ] 'city', etc.) is treated as "heavy", and that it is a diphthong rythmically equivalent to long vowels.

According to this law, the retention or loss of Proto-Sogdian final vowels depends on whether they bore a stress; in its turn, the position of the stress in words of more than one syllable is determined by the prosodic quantity of those syllables. Therefore, any stems in Sogdian, either nominal or verbal, containing a long vowel are heavy and bear a stress, while a stress falls on the endings of light stems that consist only of short vowel(s). In what follows, light stems are written with a final hyphen (*wn-* [wan-] 'to do') to distinguish them from heavy stems (*wyn* [wēn] 'to see').

Basic Morphology

Sogdian nouns and adjectives are inflected for number (singular, plural, and numerative), gender (masculine and feminine with marginal survival of neuter), and case (light stems: nominative, accusative, genitive-dative, locative, instrumental-ablative, and vocative; heavy stems: direct and oblique). The old dual forms have come to be used for nouns immediately following a numeral—not only "two" but also higher numbers. A remarkable feature of the Sogdian nominal inflection is that while light stems still retain the pattern of the classical Indo-European languages, heavy stems show simple agglutinative inflection with dir. sg. -*ø*, obl. sg. -*ī*, dir. pl. -*t*, and obl. pl. -*tī* regardless of gender. For example, a light-stem masculine noun *rm-* [ram-] 'people' inflects as follows (singular/plural):

ram-í/ram-tá	nominative
ram-ú/ram-tá	accusative
ram-é/ram-tyá	genitive-dative
ram-yá/ram-tyá	locative
ram-á/ram-tyá	instrumental-ablative
ram-á/ram-té	vocative
ram-á	nom.-acc. numerative

and a heavy stem: *myδ* 'day' declines as *mēθ* (dir. sg.), and *mēθ-ī* (obl. sg.), *mēθ-t* (dir. pl.), and *mēθ-tī* (obl. pl.).

The basic forms of the first- and second-person singular pronouns are:

(')zw 'I' (nom.)
mn' 'me, my' (non-nom.)
-my (enclitic)
tγw 'thou' (nom.)
tw' 'thee, thy' (non-nom.)
-ßy (enclitic)

The plural forms *m'x* 'we, us, our' and *šm'x* 'you, your' show no case distinction; their enclitic forms functioning as oblique case are *-mn* and *-βn* respectively.

Sogdian verbs have two stems, one present and the other past, the latter ending in *-t*, e.g., *kwn-/'krt-* 'to make, do'. Verbs in both stems are inflected for person (first, second, and third) and number (singular and plural). Apart from some isolated endings, the active has displaced the Old Iranian middle inflection. Forms derived from the present stem are indicative present, imperfect, subjunctive, optative, imperative, etc., and those from the past stem comprise preterite, perfect, potentialis, etc.

Present indicative forms of *kwn-* are:

	Singular	Plural
1st	kwn'm	kwnym
2nd	kwny	kwnδ'
3rd	kwnty	kwn'nt

The future tense is formed by the addition of the particle *-k'm* (later *-k'n, -q'* [Syriac script]) to the present indicative (e.g., *kwnty-k'm* 'he will do') and the durative particle *-(')skwn* (later *skn, -sk*, etc.) are most often suffixed to present indicative and imperfect (e.g., *mynt-skwn* 'he resembles').

In comparison with other Middle and Modern Iranian languages Sogdian is peculiar in that at least in the language of the majority of texts the preterite and perfect of transitive verbs employ an auxiliary verb *δ'r* 'to have, hold' (e.g., *δβrtw δ'rt* 'he gave' < *δβr-δβrt-* 'to give') in contrast with the intransitives, which are construed with enclitic forms of *x-* 'to be' (e.g., *tγt-ym* 'I entered' < *tys/tγt-* 'to enter'), and that Old Iranian imperfect forms survive as such, with the augment being preserved in the stems provided with preverbs (e.g., *npyst* 'he writes' vs. *nypys* 'he wrote' < Old Iranian **ni-paisati* vs. **ni-a-paisat*, cf. *βrty* 'he brings' vs. *βr'* 'he brought' < **barati* vs. **a-barat* without any trace of the augment).

The passive is formed by means of the past participle and forms of *β(w)-* 'to be(come)'. Sometimes transitive (or causative) and corresponding intransitive (or passive) stems are found in pairs, e.g., *βr-* 'to bring' vs. *βyr-* 'to be brought' and *ywc* 'to teach' vs. *ywxs-* 'to learn'. The potentialis is a periphrasis consisting of a past stem and auxiliary verb *kwn-, wn-* 'to make, do' (transitive) or *β(w)-* (intransitive). It expresses two senses, one "possibility" (e.g., *žγt' kwn'm* 'I can hold' < *δ'r/žγt-* 'to have, hold') and the other "anteriority" (e.g., *c'n'w xwrt'sptk xwrt wn'nt* 'when they had completely finished eating the food' < *xwr-/xwrt* 'to eat').

Basic Syntax

The bulk of Sogdian literature is sacred texts translated from other languages, and sentences often slavishly reproduce the word order of the originals. That being said, the basic word order in Sogdian is SOV, but sometimes, especially when an object consists of several juxtaposed elements, a verb precedes:

r-ty ZK mrɣ'rt-yh xypδ'w'nt ZKh 100 δyn''r zyrn tw'z
then-CONJ the pearl-OBL owner the 100 dēnār gold paid
'Then the owner of the pearls paid one hundred gold dēnārs'

r-ty-šn ''ßr 'xw rš'k pr''mn myδ'kw ZY wyx ZY wrkr...
Then-CONJ-them brought the seer Brahmin fruit and root and leaves
'Then the Brahmin seer brought them fruits, roots, leaves ...'

Adjectives precede the nouns they modify and agree with them, but the agreement is not compulsory. Possession is indicated by nouns in the genitive-dative or oblique case preceding the head noun:

pwtystß-y šyr'krtyh
bodhisattva-OBL good.deed 'The bodhisattva's good action'

Relative clauses follow the head noun:

wysph 'rkh cw-ZY-my tɣw prm'y-y
all work which-CONJ-me thou order-PRES.2SG
'all the works which you order me (to do)'

Sogdian employs prepositions but postpositions are not uncommon; sometimes the meaning of a preposition is reinforced by a postposition:

prw xypδ'w'nt-y prm'nh
on owner-OBL order 'According to the owner's order'

Negative and prohibitive forms are expressed respectively by means of the particles *ny* and *n'* prefixed to verbs:

'r-ty tym 'yδc mrɣ'rt nyy swmb-t (Manichaean script)
Then-CONJ still any pearl not bore-PRES.3SG
'He does not yet bore any pearls'

n' wy'ßr n' ptɣ'wš
not speak:IMPER not hear:IMPER 'Don't speak nor listen to'

Enclitic pronouns are placed after the first constituent of a sentence:

'r-t-šy 'zw w'nw ptyškwy
then-CONJ-him I thus say.IMP.1SG 'Then I said to him'

Contact with Other Languages

In the texts translated from other languages one naturally finds many foreign forms, but the majority cannot be regarded as naturalized in Sogdian, e.g., *šr'wk'* 'verse' from SANSKRIT *śloka-*. Fully assimilated loanwords are listed below with their etyma; their principal sources are Indian (mainly from Middle Indian forms) and Middle Iranian languages (Middle Persian, Parthian, and Bactrian). In spite of close contact with Chinese and Turkish, words borrowed from them are not many.

From Bactrian: *sxr-* 'wheel' (a Sogdian cognate *cxr-* is also attested)
From Turkish: *''rxyš* 'caravan' (in late texts) (< Tk. *arqïš*)
From GREEK: *δyδym* 'diadem' (< Gk. διαδημα)
From Sanskrit: *kwtr-* 'family' (< Skt. *gotra-*), *sm'wtr-* 'sea' (< Skt. *samudra-*), *rtn-* 'jewel' (< Skt. *ratna*)
From Middle Persian: *myr* 'Sunday' (< M. Per. *myhr*)
From Chinese: *tym* 'inn' (Middle Chinese **tiem*)

Common Words

man:	mrty	long:	ßrzy
woman:	'ync	small:	rync'k
water:	''p	good:	šyr-
sun:	xwyr	bird:	mrɣ-
three:	'δry	dog:	'kwt-
fish:	kp-	tree:	wn-
big:	mzyx		

Example Sentences

(1) r-ty 'xw zɣ'rt 'M ßwδ'ntk sm''δn ''pyh
then-CONJ he quickly with fragrant pomade water

ZKwh ɣryw syn'y.
the body wash:IMPERFECT.3SG
'Then he washed his body quickly with fragrant pomade-water.'

(2) r-t-xw δštw'n 'pw-pwrc š't
then-CONJ poor without-debt happy

xwyn-ty.
be.called-PRES.3SG.MID
'A poor man (when he is) without debt is regarded as happy.'

(3) r-ty-šn-ms 'wn'kw cw-ZY prw 'ßc'npδ
then-CONJ-them-again that which-CONJ on earth

wyty wm't wßyw šyrw wßyw ɣnt'kw r-ty
seen was both good both bad then-CONJ

''ɣ'z-'nt s't ZKn mrtxmy ywɣty ZY
begin-IMPERF.3PL all the man teach:INF and

ßs'ɣt.
instruct:INF
'Then again they began to teach and instruct to the man all that which, good and bad, was seen by them on the earth.'

Select Bibliography

Gershevitch, Ilya. 1954. *Grammar of Manichean Sogdian*. Oxford: Blackwell.
Gharib, Badresaman. 1995. *Sogdian Dictionary*. Tehran: Farhangan Publications.
Sims-Williams, Nicholas. 1989. "Sogdian." In *Compendium Linguarum Iranicarum*, edited by Rüdiger Schmitt, 173–92. Wiesbaden: Dr. Ludwig Reichert Verlag.

Somali

John I. Saeed

Language Name: Somali. **Autonym:** *Af soomaali.*

Location: Spoken in Somalia, Ethiopia, northeastern Kenya and the Republic of Djibouti.

Family: Eastern Cushitic branch of the Cushitic subfamily of the Afro-Asiatic language family.

Related Languages: Within Eastern Cushitic, Somali is most closely related to other languages in its Omo-Tana subgroup, including Rendille, Bayso, Dasenach, and Arbore. Other Eastern Cushitic languages include OROMO, Afar, and Sidamo. Other Cushitic languages include Beja, Agaw, and Iraqw. More distantly Somali is related to languages in the other branches of the Afro-Asiatic family, for example, Semitic (including ARABIC, HEBREW, AMHARIC); Berber (including Tuareg, Kabyle, TAMAZIGHT); and Chadic, (HAUSA).

Dialects: Somali shows considerable dialect variation. There are four main dialect groups: (1) Northern, (2) Benadir, (3) May; and (4) the Southern Interriverine dialects. The most widely differentiated dialects show considerable differences at all levels. The most geographically widespread of these is the Northern dialect group, which is a somewhat misleading term since, because of migrations, this dialect group is spoken in a broad sweep across the northern, western and southernmost parts of the Somali-speaking area. This dialect has been used as a lingua franca among other dialects; it enjoys the most prestige, not least because it has been the dialect used by the greatest Somali poets; and it formed the basis of the standard used for official purposes in the Somali Republic. Because of this the dialect is often called Standard Somali. It is used by external media such as the BBC. In comparison to the relative homogeneity of Standard Somali over its vast range, there is much greater dialectal variation in the more sedentary areas of the southern riverine region and the southern ports of Mogadishu, Merka, Brava, and Kismayo.

Number of Speakers: 8–10 million in the Horn of Africa, with sizeable expatriate communities in Arabia, Great Britain, France, Italy, Canada, and the United States.

Origin and History

Somali speakers consider themselves a single ethnic group. They occupy the northeastern corner of Africa, a region known as the Horn of Africa. Much of the land is arid with light seasonal rainfall and the dominant lifestyle is pastoral nomadism because the Somalis traditionally move great distances with their herds of camel, sheep, and goats on a seasonal cycle. The coastal towns of Berbera, Mogadishu, Merka, Brava, and Kismayo have been trade centers in the gulf and Indian Ocean for centuries.

From linguistic evidence it seems that the Horn and Ethiopian highlands have been the home of Cushitic languages since ancient times. Since medieval times there is foreign written evidence of Somali speakers in the region, from Zeila on the northwest coast to Mogadishu in the southeast. Somali society is traditionally organized along patrilineal clan lines and there is evidence of major migrations by Somali clans in recent history. Northern and Ethiopian clans have moved southward over the past centuries, pushing other clans and other ethnic groups before them. This movement was halted by the establishment of European protectorates and colonies from the late 19th century, leaving the southern limit of Somali speakers at the Tana River in what is now Kenya.

The Somalis have a rich tradition of oral poetry consisting of many genres characterized by complex metrical structures. Many foreign writers have commented on the Somalis' fierce independence and pride in their language and culture.

Orthography and Basic Phonology

Somali is written in the LATIN alphabet. Some letters, however, have very different values than in European languages.

The distinction between voiced and voiceless consonants is not very important in Somali. Thus, there is no *p* corresponding to /b/, and there is no *v* corresponding to /f/. Some sounds, like *j* and *q*, can occur either voiced or voiceless, depending on context. *J* represents a palato-alveolar affricate and is the only affricate in Somali. The two pronunciations [tʃ] and [dʒ] seem to be in free variation.

The digraph *sh* represents a voiceless palato-alveolar fricative /ʃ/. It is always voiceless.

The digraph *dh* represents /ɖ/, a voiced reflexive stop. In southern varieties of Standard Somali, the distinction between *dh* and the rolled liquid *r* is lost, except at the beginning of a word or where the Northern varieties have a double consonant *dhdh*, corresponding to Southern *dh*.

Somali has two pharyngeal fricatives, *c* /ʕ/, similar to Arabic *'ayn*, and *x* /ħ/; they are voiced and voiceless, respectively.

The digraph *kh* represents a voiceless uvular fricative /χ/ which is found only in loanwords from Arabic, for example, *khál* 'vinegar'. The letter *q* represents /ɢ/, a voiced uvular stop.

The symbol ' represents the glottal stop /ʔ/. It occurs between vowels, for example, *la'àan* 'being without' and word-finally, as in *ló'* 'cattle'. The sound /ʔ/ also occurs word initially, where it is not represented in the orthography. Thus, *íl*

Table 1: Consonants

		Labial	Dental	Post-Alveolar	Palato-Alveolar	Velar	Uvular	Pharyngeal	Glottal
Stops	Voiceless		t			k			' [ʔ]
	Voiced	b	d	dh [ɖ]		g	q [ɢ]		
Fricatives	Voiceless	f	s		sh [ʃ]		kh [χ]	x [ħ]	
	Voiced							c [ʕ]	h
Affricate					j				
Nasals		m	n						
Resonants			r	l					
Glides		w			y				

'eye' is pronounced in isolation [ʔíl], as part of a general requirement that word-initial syllables in Somali begin with a consonant.

Somali has 10 basic vowel sounds, all of which can be either short or long. Their principal pronunciations, in the transcription of the International Phonetic Alphabet, are shown below.

Table 2: Vowels

	Front	Central	Back
High	ɪ i		u ʉ
Mid	ɛ e		ɔ ö
Low		ɑ æ	

In each pair, the second vowel is pronounced with the tongue more forward in the mouth than the first. Each pair of vowels is represented by a single letter in the standard orthography:

Orthography	Back Series	Front Series
i	ɪ	i
e	ɛ	e
a	ɑ	æ
o	ɔ	ö
u	u	ʉ

Long vowels, represented by doubled letters, occur with very little change in quality. The distinction between short and long vowels is always significant: compare *tág* /tɑg/ 'to go' and *táag* /tɑ:g/.

The relationship between the sets of front and back vowels is important to the process of vowel harmony in the language. Words in the major lexical categories of nouns, verbs, and adjectives occur with a specific vowel quality, and words in other functional categories must agree with this quality, within a breath group.

Back series:	Ma	shabèel	bàa?	[mɑ ʃɑbɛ:l bɑ:]
	Q	leopard	FOCUS	'Is it a leopard?'
Front series:	Ma	libàax	bàa?	[mæ libæ:h bæ:]
	Q	lion	FOCUS	'Is it a lion?'

In addition to these short and long vowels, standard Somali also has the diphthongs *ay, aw, ey, oy, ow*, which also occur long as *aay, aaw, eey, ooy,* and *oow*. These diphthongs also occur in back and front variants.

The set of possible syllable structures in Somali is V, CV, VC, and CVC (where V is a short vowel, a long vowel, or a diphthong). Since the maximum number of consonants at the beginning and end of a syllable is one, the longest consonant sequence that can occur is two, across a syllable boundary. The sounds *t* and *k* do not occur syllable finally, nor does *j* in native Somali words. When two instances of *b, d, dh, g, q, l, m, n,* or *r* meet at a syllable boundary, they form phonetically long geminate consonants. The difference between single and geminate consonants forms minimal pairs like *wáran* 'spear' and *wárran* 'to tell'. There are no geminate fricatives in Somali.

Somali is a tonal accent language. The accentual pattern of words gives mostly grammatical information about gender, case, and number. The accents are a combination of tone (High, Mid, and Low pitch) and stress (Strong and Weak). Accents are not marked in the standard orthography.

The basic units are HIGH (high tone, strong stress) and LOW (low tone, weak stress), although there are many rules modifying these basic units. The accent-bearing unit is the mora rather than the syllable; a syllable consisting of a long vowel or a diphthong contains two morae. All roots of common nouns, verbs, and adjectives have one of three basic accentual patterns in their citation (or isolation) form: (1) HIGH on the last mora, LOW on all others; (2) HIGH on the next-to-last mora, LOW on all others; (3) LOW on all moras.

A sequence of HIGH-LOW on a long vowel or diphthong is realized as a falling tone with diminishing stress, while a sequence LOW-HIGH becomes a long, level HIGH. In linguistic descriptions, HIGH accent is marked with an acute accent (*á*), LOW accent is unmarked (*a*), and falling accent with a grave (*àa*).

The accentual patterns mark the declension, number, and gender of a noun, or the conjugation of a verb, as in the following contrasts: *èy* 'dog', *éy* 'dogs'; *ínan* 'boy', *inán* 'girl'. The case-marking system is largely accentual as well: *Cáli* 'Ali (absolutive case)', *Cali* 'Ali (subject case)', *Calí* 'of Ali (genitive case)'.

Basic Morphology

Inflectional and derivational information is marked by a combination of accentual pattern and the processes of suffixation, prefixation, and reduplication.

Nouns in Somali are either masculine or feminine. Gender is marked by accentual pattern and agreement with determiners and verbs. Most nouns reverse gender in the plural, for example, *náag* 'woman (f), and *naagó* 'women (m)'. There are seven basic noun declensions, differentiated by accentual pattern, gender, type of plural formation, and whether they reverse gender. Thus, a Declension 4 noun *áf* 'mouth' is masculine in singular, forms its plural *afáf* 'mouths' by reduplication, and does not reverse gender; and the Declension 6 noun *dáwo* 'medicine' is feminine in singular, forms its plural *dawóoyin* 'medicines' by a suffix *-oyin*, and reverses gender.

Nouns take a range of suffixed determiners that agree in gender but not number.

Form	Meaning
gèed	'tree'
gèed-ka	'the tree (nonremote)'
gèed-kíi	'the tree (remote in time or space)'
gèed-kán	'this tree'
gèed-káa(s)	'that tree (further away from speaker)'
gèed-kéer	'that tree (in the middle distance)'
gèed-kóo	'that tree (in the far distance)'
geed-kée	'which tree?'
gèed-kàyga	'my tree'
gèed-kàaga	'your tree'

Somali has two types of pronouns. The first are independent pronouns, which act like nouns and usually occur with a definite article.

	Singular	Plural
1st person	aníga	annága (exclusive)
		innága (inclusive)
2nd person	adíga	idínka
3rd person, m	isága	iyága
3rd person, f	iyáda	iyága

The second are weak or verbal pronouns, which occur as clitics in the verbal group. They occur in subject and object forms; the following are the subject forms:

	Singular	Plural
1st person	aan	aannu (exclusive)
		aynu (inclusive)
2nd person	aad	aydin
3rd person, m	uu	ay
3rd person, f	ay	ay

All verbs carry an inflectional marked combination of tense, aspect, and mood (TAM) information. It is not possible to segment a verb form into segments representing each of these elements; it is the unitary form that expresses the meaning. Thus it is convenient to identify 12 verbal paradigms: imperative, infinitive, past simple, past progressive, past habitual, present habitual, present progressive, future, conditional, optative, potential, and special subordinate clause forms. All forms have distinct negative forms that are used along with negative words.

There are two main morphological classes of verbs. First, there is a small archaic group of four prefix, or "strong" verbs: *yidhi* 'say', *yimi* 'come', *yiil* 'be (in a place)', and *yiqiin* 'know', all in their reference forms of third-person masculine singular, past simple. These verbs mark agreement by prefixes, and TAM distinctions by vowel changes in the root, as illustrated by the following forms of *yaqaan* 'know':

	PRESENT POSITIVE	PRESENT NEGATIVE	PAST POSITIVE	PAST NEGATIVE
1sg	aqaan	aqáan	iqiin	oqóon
2sg-3f.sg	taqaan	taqáan	tiqiin	[invariant]
3m.sg	yaqaan	yaqáan	yiqiin	
1pl	naqaan	naqáan	niqiin	
2pl	taqaanniin	taqaannìin	tiqiinneen	
3pl	yaqaanniin	yaqaannìin	yiqiinneen	

All other verbs in Somali, except the irregular verb *yahay* 'to be' are of the second type: suffix, or "weak", verbs, which show both agreement and TAM distinctions by suffixation, as illustrated by the following forms of the verb *súg* 'wait for':

	PRESENT POSITIVE	PRESENT NEGATIVE	PAST POSITIVE	PAST NEGATIVE
1sg-3m.sg	sugaa	sugó	sugay	sugín
2sg-3fsg	sugtaa	sugtó	sugtay	[invariant]
1pl	sugnaan	sugnó	sugnay	
2pl	sugtaan	sugtàan	sugteen	
3pl	sugaan	sugàan	sugeen	

Suffix verbs may take a set of derivational affixes, or "extensions", which are added to the root to modify the meaning of the verb. The applicability and effect of these affixes depend upon the semantics of the verb root to which they are attached. There are many such affixes; the most productive are causative *-is*, strong causative *-sii*, passive *-am*, and middle *-at*. See, for example, the effect of the causative *-is* (in its contextual form *-iy*):

Ardá-dii w-ày qosl-een
students-the DCL-3PL laugh-3PL.PAST
'The students laughed.'

Barí-hii ardá-dii w-uu ká
teacher-the students-the DCL-3SG ADP

qosl-iy-ey
laugh-CAUS-3M.SG.PAST
'The teacher made the students laugh.'

Other derivational affixes shift roots from category to category; for example, *-ow* creates verbs from nouns: *báraf* 'ice', *barafòw* 'freeze (turn into ice)'.

Basic Syntax

One of the most striking characteristics of Somali syntax is its sensitivity to pragmatic forces: word order, for example, does not depend on which noun phrase is the subject and which is object but on which are focused or topics. There are two particles, *bàa* and *àyaa*, which serve to focus a preceding noun phrase, that is, to mark it as prominent, typically because it represents new information or for contrastive emphasis.

nimán-kíi	ayàa	warqád-díi	keen-áy
men-the	FOCUS	letter-the	bring-3M.SG.PAST

'The men brought the letter.' or 'It was the men who brought the letter.'

Sentences with nominal focus like the above are very different from those without nominal focus:

nimán-kii	warqád-díi	w-ày	keen-een
men-the	letter-the	DCL-3PL	bring-3PL.PAST

'The men brought the letter.'

Comparing the two sentences, the first has some unusual characteristics: the subject, *nimán-kii* 'the men' is not subject marked, but occurs in the absolutive case; the verb shows singular agreement even though *nimán-kíi* is plural; the accentual pattern on the verb shows it to be a subordinate clause form; and finally, there is no coreferential subject clitic pronoun. The second sentence is different with regard to all of these features.

Focus affects word order, too: a noun phrase focused by *baa* or *ayàa* must precede the verb, while nonfocused noun phrases can occur anywhere and in any order. Thus, the second sentence has the following variants:

Warqáddíi nimánkii wày keeneen.
Warqáddíi wày keeneen nimánkii.
Nimánkii wày keeneen warqáddíi.
Wày keeneen nimánkii warqáddíi.
All meaning 'The men brought the letter.'

The accentual case marking (HIGH versus LOW on the final syllable) shows which nominals are subject (LOW) and object (HIGH); the choice of order in the above set depends on discourse context.

Different sentence types are identified by specific morphemes called classifiers:

w-ùu waa-3M.SG	keenay brought	declarative (DCL) 'he brought it'
má	keenín brought:NEG	negative declarative 'he didn't bring it'
miy-ùu ma-3M.SG	keenay brought	interrogative 'did he bring it?'
shòw	keenee	potential 'perhaps he'll bring it'
há	keeno!	optative 'may he bring it!'

Contact with Other Languages

The trading relations between the Horn and the Arabs of Yemen and Oman date from ancient times and the Somalis were converted to Islam very early in the religion's expansion. The influence of Islam, and of Arabic, on Somali culture has been very great and the population is almost totally Moslem with the majority being Sunni. Many of the Somali clans trace their lineage back to the Arab religious leaders who brought Islam to the region. In fact, the majority of personal names, especially of men, are Arabic. Despite this close religious and commercial attachment to the Arab world, the Somalis maintained their own language, their traditional laws alongside Islamic law, and in many areas, such as the social role of women, preserved their distinct identity. There are many loanwords from Arabic, including the days of the week, for example, *arbacá* 'Wednesday'; personal names, as *Cáli* 'Ali'; some animals and foods, such as *fáras* 'horse', *qáxwe* 'coffee'; and terms in the fields of religion, politics, and law: *jamhuuriyád* 'republic', *xísbi* 'political party', *jannó* 'heaven', *dìin* 'religion'. More recently some scientific and technological terms have been borrowed from ENGLISH, for example: *átam* 'atom', *batéri* 'battery', *kombiyúutar* 'computer'; and especially in the south, from ITALIAN: *bóosto* 'post office', *farmashíye* 'pharmacy', and *míino* 'land mine'.

Common Words

man:	nín	small:	yár
woman:	náag	yes:	hàa
water:	bíyo	no:	máya
sun:	qorráx	good:	wanaagsán
three:	sáddex	bird:	shimbír
fish:	kallùun	dog:	èy
big:	wèyn	tree:	gèed
long:	dhèer		

Example Sentences

(1)

Gaadhi	cusub	b-aan	soo	iibsaday.
car	new	FOCUS-1SG	VENITIVE	buy-1SG.PAST

'I bought a new car.'

(2)

In-tee	b-aad	joogtay	Muqdisho?
time-Q	FOCUS-2SG	stay:2SG.PAST	Mogadishu

'How long have you been in Mogadishu?'

(3)

Lambar-ka	telefoon-kaaga	i	sii	oo	w-aan
number-the	telephone-your	me	give:IMPER	and	DCL-1SG

sheegayaa	in-uu	kuu	soo	yeedho.
will.tell	that-3M.SG	you.to	VENITIVE	calls

'Give me your telephone number and I'll tell him to call you back.'

Efforts to Preserve, Protect, and Promote the Language

After years of heated debate about choosing among Roman,

Arabic, and indigenous orthographies, a Roman orthography was adopted for Somali in the Somali Republic in 1972, and Somali was adopted as the official language of the state. Great strides were made in the development of literacy and the introduction of Somali as the medium of government, education, and mass media. Arabic was adopted as the second language of the state. At this level of official state languages, Somali thus joined its neighbors Amharic to the west in Ethiopia and SWAHILI to the south in Kenya, making this region one of the most important in the development of African languages as official media. Although the development of Somali as an official language has been halted by the recent civil wars, it continues to be the written medium in all parts of the Somali-speaking Horn and among and between expatriate communities abroad.

Select Bibliography

Agostini, F., A. Pughelli, and Ciise Moxamed Siyaad, eds. 1985. *Dizionario somalo-italiano*. Rome: Gangemi.

Andrzejewski, B.W. and I.M. Lewis. 1964. *Somali Poetry: An Introduction*. London: Oxford University Press.

Laitin, D.D. 1977. *Politics, Language, and Thought: The Somali Experience*. Chicago: University of Chicago Press.

Loughran, Katheryne S., John L. Loughran, John William Johnson, and Said Sheikh Samatar, eds. 1986. *Somalia in Word and Image*. Bloomington: Indiana University Press.

Muuse Haaji Ismaa'iil Galaal, and B.W. Andrzejewski. 1956 *Hikmad Soomaali*. ['Somali Sayings']. London: Oxford University Press.

Puglielli, Annarita, ed. 1981. *Sintassi della lingua somala. (Studi somali 2)*. Rome: Mnistero degli afari esteri-Dipartimento per la cooperazione allo sviluppo.

____. ed. 1984. *Aspetti morfologici, lessicali e della focalizzazione. (Studi somali* 5) Rome: Ministero degli afari esteri-Dipartimento per la cooperazione allo sviluppo.

Saeed, John Ibrahim. 1984. The *Syntax of Focus and Topic in Somali*. Kuschitische Sprachstudien Band 3. Hamburg: Helmut Buske.

____. 1993. *Somali Reference Grammar*. Second Revised Edition. Kensington, MD: Dunwoody Press.

____. 1999. *Somali*. The London Oriental and African Language Library. Amsterdam: John Benjamins.

Zorc, R.D. and A.A. Issa. 1990. *Somali Textbook*. Kensington, MD: Dunwoody Press.

Zorc, R.D. and Madina M. Osman 1993. *Somali-English Dictionary with English Index*. Third Edition. Kensington, MD: Dunwoody Press.

Spanish

Luis López

Language Name: Spanish. **Alternate:** *Castilian* (in Spanish, *castellano*, preferred name in Peru, Chile, Argentina, Bolivia, and parts of Spain). **Autonym:** *español*.

Location: Spain, Equatorial Guinea, 18 countries in Latin America: Argentina, Bolivia, Colombia, Costa Rica, Chile, Cuba, Dominican Republic, Ecuador, El Salvador, Guatemala, Honduras, Mexico, Nicaragua, Panamá, Paraguay, Peru, Uruguay, and Venezuela. There are Spanish-speaking populations in numerous places in the United States especially Miami, New York, the Southwest, and the island of Puerto Rico. Judeo-Spanish is spoken in scattered places, and particularly in Israel.

Family: Italic group of the Romance branch of the Indo-European language family.

Related Languages: PORTUGUESE, GALICIAN, CATALAN, ITALIAN, FRENCH, Romansch, and ROMANIAN.

Dialects: Spanish is generally held to have two norms, one corresponding to the speech of Madrid and the other to the speech of Mexico City. Differences between these varieties of Spanish are slight.

The modern dialects of Spain fall into two dialect areas, North (containing Aragonese, Asturian, Leonese, Castilian, and Valencian) and South (Andalusian). This division roughly corresponds to the imaginary line dividing the northern half of the Iberian Peninsula from the southern. The dialects contain subdialects and are the remnants of Romance varieties that can be traced back to medieval and earlier times. Northern varieties are different from all other varieties of Spanish in that they have an interdental fricative /θ/, spelled *z* or *c*.

In Latin America, the dialects are relatively uniform, except for the Caribbean, which has more distinct dialect features. On the island of Puerto Rico, syllable-final [r] may become [l]: [puelto rico]. While both dialect areas of Spain have distinct pronouns and agreement markers for formal and informal second-person plural, Latin American varieties have only one form to address a plural interlocutor. Also interesting is the influence of aboriginal languages in areas where speakers are bilingual, particularly in the Andes and Central America, where adoption of loanwords from the indigenous languages occurs often. The linguistic base of Latin American Spanish was probably a koine, drawn from different dialects of the Iberian Peninsula, with a major influence from Andalusian speakers.

Sefardi (<*Sefarad*, Hebrew for Spain), also known as Judeo-Spanish, *Judezmo*, and *Ladino* (specifically the often archaic language of prayer and scripture), is the variety spoken by the descendants of the Jews who were expelled from Spain in 1492. It has maintained some features of 15th century Spanish that were lost in other varieties of Spanish. Many *Sephardim* lived in Portugal after the expulsion, and *Sefardi* has consequently undergone some influence from Portuguese. In the early years of the 20th century, tens of thousands of *Sephardim* emigrated to the United States, and many others died during the Holocaust. *Sefardi*, once the principal means of communication for thousands of Eastern European Jews, is now found mainly in Israel.

Number of Speakers: 150–250 million, with an additional 30 million who speak it as a second language.

Origin and History

Spanish is a direct descendant of Vulgar LATIN, which was brought to what is now Spain after 218 B.C. when the Romans invaded and defeated the Carthaginians and began colonizing the Iberian Peninsula. Vulgar Latin spread quickly over the eastern and southern parts of the Iberian Peninsula and more slowly to the other parts. BASQUE is the sole surviving language of the Iberian Peninsula from the pre-Roman period. Since a large proportion of the population was of Celtic origin, we can assume that one or more Celtic languages were spoken there. Another pre-Roman group, the Ibers, inhabited the eastern and southern parts of the Iberian Peninsula, leaving some as yet undeciphered writing.

In the sixth century, with the Roman Empire in full demise, the Visigoths took over the Iberian Peninsula. The Visigoths had been living inside the borders of the Roman Empire for some time and were bilingual when they arrived in Spain. While they introduced some words from their native Germanic language, they soon spoke Latin exclusively.

In 711 there was another invasion, this time by the Muslims of North Africa and Arabia—the Moors. Soon more than two-thirds of the peninsula was under Islamic rule. Romance speakers were split into two groups. In the northern part of the Peninsula, where the Moors did not penetrate, people lived under Christian rule, and one of the northern dialects was to become what we now call "Spanish". In the southern part, which was Islamicized, a variety of Romance called "Mozarabic" evolved. Many ARABIC words were introduced into Spanish via Mozarabic. However, Mozarabic gradually disappeared as the Christians from the north expanded southward.

In 1085, Toledo, the Moorish capital, fell to Castilians, and

Table 1: Consonants

		Labial	Dental	Alveolar	Palatal	Velar
Stops	Voiceless	p	t			c, qu [k]
	Voiced	b	d [d]			g [ɣ]
Fricatives	Voiceless	f	z, c [θ]	s		j [x]
	Voiced		d [ð]			g
Affricates	Voiceless				ch	
	Voiced				y, ll [dʒ]	
Nasals		m		n	ñ	
Laterals				l	ll [ʎ]	
Tap				r		
Trill				rr		
Glides					y	u

in 1492 Granada was defeated. At this time, Isabella, queen of Castile, and Ferdinand, king of Aragon, reigned over the entire Iberian Peninsula, with the exception of Portugal. Within Castile several languages were spoken in addition to the official language, Castilian: Galician, Basque, and (presumably) Mozarabic. In Aragon, Aragonese and the official language of Catalonia, Catalan, were spoken. In the following centuries, the Castilian dialect became dominant throughout the Iberian Peninsula and was destined to be the basis of standard Spanish, in part because of the prestige gained by the Castilians who reconquered the Moorish territories, and also because of the literary output in Castilian. During the 13th century Castilian was also the medium of scientific, legal, administrative, and other writing, and superseded Latin in documents issued from the royal chancery of Alfonso X the Learned, king of Castile and Léon (Penny 1991: 16).

The evolution of Spanish from Latin was a long and gradual process. A religious text from the monastery of San Millán in the Rioja region dated to the second half of the 10th century provides evidence of the transformation. The scribe translated Latin words and phrases that he feared might be unknown to speakers of the vernacular, which by this time could probably be called Spanish. As Latin evolved into Old Spanish, many changes took place in the language: the 10 vowels of Latin decreased to 5, and new diphthongs were created. Word stress moved from the antepenultimate syllable to the penult; as a consequence, many syllables were syncopated. New consonants *ll*, *j*, and *ñ* were added.

Radical changes took place in the morphosyntax. The Latin nominal case system was lost, and the free word order of Latin became slightly more constrained in Spanish. The neutral SOV of Latin bcame SVO in Spanish. There were some changes in the verbal morphology, though less radical than in the noun morphology: creation of periphrastic perfect tenses, periphrastic present passive, and new future and conditional tenses. In general, there was a tendency toward analytic forms.

In the 15th century, two historical events led to the expansion of the Spanish language far from its borders: the discovery and consequent invasion of America, and the expulsion of the Spanish Jews (*Sefardim*), who settled in scattered parts of the Ottoman Empire, especially Constantinople, Smyrna (Izmir), Salonica, and Rhodes. They spoke a variety of Spanish known as *Sefardi*.

The 15th century also saw the appearance of the first Spanish grammar by Antonio de Nebrija. Nebrija wrote the grammar in order to teach Spanish to the new subjects of Spain in America. Many more grammars would follow. The end of the 15th century marks the beginning of Modern Spanish, and the language has remained relatively stable since then.

At the beginning of the 17th century the Catalans lost a civil war for the throne and the new king issued the decrees of *Nueva Planta* which abolished the Catalan-Aragonese and Valencian judicial and administrative systems and imposed the Castilian ones. Consequently, Castilian replaced Catalan as the official language in Catalonia. From this point on, language homogenization became a political objective of the Spanish monarchy, leading to the progressive decline of the other languages, until the Romantic movements of the 18th century brought new attention to them.

Orthography and Basic Phonology

Spanish orthography is skewed so that although one may learn fairly easily to pronounce the written language by learning the orthographic conventions, the orthography does not accurately represent pronunciation in its current form. In addition, there are several instances in which the same sound has multiple spellings. For example, /k/ can be spelled *k*, *q*, or, before back vowels, *c*; *c* can also be pronounced /θ/ or /s/ (depending on region), and *b* and *v* are pronounced the same. *H* is mute. (See Table 1 above.)

In northern Spain, *z*, also spelled *c*, is a voiceless interdental fricative [θ]. In other varieties of Spanish, this sound is pronounced the same as *s* [s].

The alveolar lateral *l* is pronounced as in ENGLISH *leap*. The palatal lateral *ll*, phonetically [ʎ], is similar to the "ll" in English "billiard", with the exception that the [l] and [y] sounds are articulated simultaneously rather than sequentially as in English. Certain dialects also pronounce the *ll* and *y* as an alveo-palatal affricate or fricative.

The palatal nasal *ñ* is similar to the "ni" sequence in English "onion", again with simultaneous articulation of the nasal and the [y]. Spanish *r* is a flap, like the "t" in English "writer", In contrast, *rr* is a rapid sequence of three consecutive flaps.

The voiced stops /b d g/ are pronounced as fricatives [β ð ɣ] when they follow a vowel or some resonants. The vowel may be in the preceding word, as in *la vaca* 'the cow'. However, in utterance initially or after a nasal, they maintain their stop pronunciation.

Nasals assimilate to following consonants in place of articulation: *un balón* 'a ball' is pronounced [um ba'lon].

In many varieties of Spanish, both in Spain and in the Americas, syllable final *s* is pronounced [h].

Table 2: Vowels

	Front	Central	Back
High	i		u
Mid	e		o
Low		a	

Spanish also has diphthongs: *ai, au, ei, eu, oi, ue, ie*.

Stress in Spanish generally falls on the penultimate syllable in a word that ends in a vowel, *n*, or *s*, and on the final syllable of a word that ends in some other consonant. Regular stress is not marked in writing. If stress falls on some other syllable than that predicted by the preceding rule, an accent mark is used to indicate the stressed syllable: *largo* 'long' ['largo], *estómago* 'stomach' [es'tomago], *balón* 'ball' [ba'lon].

Basic Morphology

Spanish nouns appear in two genders, masculine and feminine. Male persons and some male animals are generally in masculine gender, and female persons and some female animals are in feminine gender. Inanimate beings and most animals are assigned to one or the other gender more or less arbitrarily from a semantic point of view, but rather depending on the last vowel of the word. Thus, most words that end in *-o* are masculine, and most words that end in *-a* are feminine. Examples are *casa* 'house' (feminine) and *libro* 'book' (masculine). Words that end in other vowels or in a consonant are unpredictable in gender: compare *puente* 'bridge' (masculine) with *fuente* 'fountain' (feminine). Nouns are pluralized by adding *-s*. The definite and indefinite articles also inflect for gender:

	Definite	Indefinite
masc.sg	el	un
fem.sg	la	una
masc.pl	los	unos
fem.pl	las	unas

Determiners and adjectives agree with the nouns they modify in gender and number:

el libr-o roj-o
the.M.SG book-M.SG red-M.SG
'the red book'

las cas-a-s roj-a-s
the.F.PL house-F-PL red-F-PL
'the red houses'

Spanish verbs agree with their subjects in person and number, as illustrated in the following present tense forms of the verb *cantar* 'to sing':

	Singular	Plural
First	canto	cantamos
Second	cantas	cantáis
Third	canta	cantan

The distinct second-person plural form is used only in northern Spain. Elsewhere in the Spanish-speaking world, the same verb form is used for second- and third-person plural.

In addition to the present, there are three simple tenses, illustrated below in their first-person singular forms:

Tense	Form
Preterite	canté
Imperfect	cantaba
Future	cantaré

In addition, there is a conditional mood, based on the future: e.g., *cantaría* 'I would sing'. Compound tenses are formed from an auxiliary verb and a participle or gerund. The perfect *ha cantado* 'I have sung' consists of a form of the verb *haber* 'to have' and the participle *cantado*, and the progressive form *estoy cantando* 'I'm singing' consists of an inflected form of the verb *estar* 'to be' and the gerundive *cantando*.

Direct and indirect object pronouns are clitics that form a morphological and prosodic unit with the verb complex. Clitics occur before conjugated verbs and following infinitives and gerundives:

La vi en la librería
3SG.F see.PRET.1SG in the.F bookstore.F
'I saw her in the bookstore.'

Será difícil compr-ar-lo
be.FUT.3SG difficult buy-INFINITIVE-3SG.M
'It will be difficult to buy it.'

Basic Syntax

In Spanish, the subject may be placed before or after the verb, giving three possible word orders: SVO, VSO, and VOS. The distribution of constituents within the sentence depends on their information load. Constituents expressing new information come late in the sentence, while constituents expressing old information come early in the sentence. Thus, *Vino Juan* 'John came', in which the subject follows the verb, is a good answer for the question *¿Quién vino?* 'Who came?', and *Juan* expresses new information. In contrast, *Juan vino con nosotros* 'John came with us', in which the subject precedes the verb, implicitly answers a question like *¿Qué hizo Juan?* 'What did John do?', and *Juan* expresses old, assumed information.

Objects may precede the verb if they express old information. In such an instance, an object clitic is obligatory:

Los	libr-o-s	no	sé	dónde
the:M.PL	book-M-PL	NEG	know.PRES.1SG	where

los	he	dej-ado
3PL.M	have.PRES.1SG	leave-PARTICIPLE

'As for the books, I don't know where I left them.'

Spanish is a head-initial language. It has prepositions rather than postpositions. Adjectives generally follow the nouns they modify. Some adjectives can either precede or follow the noun, with a change in nuance: *mi amigo viejo* 'my old friend (my friend, who happens to be old)', *mi viejo amigo* 'my old friend (the person who has been my friend for a long time)'.

As illustrated above, sentences are negated by the word *no* preceding the verb. Only object clitic pronouns can come between *no* and the verb.

Contact with Other Languages

In Spain, Spanish coexists with three other languages: Galician, Basque, and Catalan. All three languages receive strong institutional support from the local governments in the regions in which they are spoken. Most people in these areas are bilingual and tend to have "an accent", that is, they include features from their native language when they speak Spanish.

Spanish has borrowed from many sources. There are a few words from Basque, which was spoken in Iberia before the arrival of the Romans and is still alive today. A small number of words of Germanic origin (mainly Visigothic and Frankish) are present in the language. There are thousands of words from Latin and Arabic, and a smaller number from Mozarabic. There are also words of French, Catalan, Portuguese, and Italian origin. The 20th century has seen an infusion of hundreds of Anglicisms.

From Basque: *izquierda* 'left'
From Latin: *condición* 'condition', *apellido* 'surname', *proyección* 'projection'
From Germanic: *espía* 'spy', *ropa* 'clothing'
From Arabic: *naranja* 'orange', *alcalde* 'mayor'
From Mozarabic: *fideos* 'noodles', *gazpacho* 'gazpacho'
From Native American: *papa, patata* 'potato' (<QUECHUA)
From English: *champú* 'shampoo', *cámara, bikini, smoking*

Common Words

man:	hombre	long:	largo
woman:	mujer	small:	pequeño
water:	agua	yes:	sí
sun:	sol	no:	no
three:	tres	good:	bueno
fish:	pescado	bird:	pájaro
big:	grande	dog:	perro
tree:	árbol		

Example Sentences

(1)

Cuando	fui	a	España,	visité	a	mi
When	go.PAST.1SG	to	Spain,	visit.PAST.1SG	to	my

familia	y	le	llevé	un	regalo
family	and	to-him.her	bring.PAST.1SG	a	present

al	bebé.
to-the	baby

'When I went to Spain, I visited my family and brought a present for the baby.'

(2)

Soy	norteamerican-o.
be.PRES.1SG	North American-M.SG

'I am American (from North America).'

(3)

Hac-e	un	buen	día.
do-PRES.3SG	a.M.SG	good.M.SG	day.M.SG

'It is a beautiful day.'

Efforts to Preserve, Protect, and Promote the Language

In the 18th century the *Real Academia Española de la Lengua* (RAE) 'Royal Spanish Academy of Language' was created to standardize the Spanish language in Spain. The RAE is an institution of enormous prestige. About half of its members are linguists or philologists and the other half are writers of solid reputation. Its main function is the production of authoritative dictionaries and grammars. Unlike similar institutions in other countries, the RAE does not seem to be so concerned about Anglicisms and linguistic "purity" in general. Following the example of the RAE, Spanish-language academies were founded in Latin America during the 19th and 20th centuries and are functioning in Colombia, Mexico, Ecuador, El Salvador, Venezuela, Chile, Peru, Guatemala, Bolivia, Costa Rica, Cuba, Honduras, Panamá, Paraguay, Puerto Rico, and the Dominican Republic. They are all members of an association of Hispanic academies, with the intention of maintaining the unity of the Spanish language.

Spanish is expanding in Latin America at the expense of indigenous languages since fluency in Spanish is seen as a prerequisite for entering the middle class. Even well-established indigenous languages such as Quechua seem to be losing speakers, according to the surveys carried out in Bolivia by the sociolinguist Xavier Albo. This is despite the current Bolivian government's support for educating people in their native language.

Spanish is widely spoken in the U.S., which ranks as the fourth largest Spanish-speaking country in the world today after Mexico, Spain, and Colombia. However, the social status of Spanish in the U.S. is the opposite of what it is in Latin America, since it is regarded as a low status language. The defense of bilingual education programs by Latino political groups like

La Raza has found resistance among many monolingual English speakers. Spanish is the unstated target of those who urge that the U.S. declare English the official language of the nation; some states, including Arizona and Florida, already designate English as the official state language.

The situation with respect to Spanish language maintenance is different in different parts of the U.S. A recent study found that in the Southwest, Hispanics are giving up Spanish as they become more acculturated to U.S. life. The only exceptions are where there is "isolation from the mainstream or a considerable influx of Spanish speakers from Mexico". (Bills 1989) However, in many urban centers with Spanish-speaking populations such as New York, Miami, Los Angeles, and Chicago, there seems to be a situation of stable bilingualism, largely because of bilingual education.

The last representative of the Judeo-Spanish press in the U.S. was the weekly newspaper *La Vara* (printed in Hebrew characters) which ceased publication in 1948. In the 1980s there was a revival of interest in Sefardic culture in the U.S., especially in communities in New York, Miami, Atlanta, Portland, and Seattle.

Select Bibliography

Alvar, M., and J. Pheby. 1985. *The Oxford–Duden Pictorial English Dictionary.* New York: Oxford University Press.

Baron, D. 1990. *The English-Only Question: An Official Language for Americans?* New Haven: Yale University Press.

Barrutia, R., and A. Schwegler. 1994. *Fonética y Fonología Españolas.* New York: John Wiley and Sons.

Bergen, J., ed. 1990. *Spanish in the U.S.: Sociolinguistic Issues.* Washington, DC: Georgetown University Press.

Bills, G.D. 1989. "The U.S. Census of 1980 and Spanish in the Southwest." In *International Journal of the Sociology of Language* 79. Berlin, NY: Mouton de Gruyter.

Butt, J., and C. Benjamín. 1988. *A New Reference Grammar of Modern Spanish.* London: Arnold.

Campos, H. 1993. *De la Oración Simple a la Oración Compuesta.* Washington DC: Georgetown University Press.

Cotton, E. and J. Sharp. 1988. *Spanish in the Americas.* Washington, DC: Georgetown University Press.

Galimberti Jarman, B., and R. Russell, eds. 1994. *The Oxford Spanish Dictionary.* New York: Oxford University Press.

Jarvis, A.C.R. Lebredo and F. Mena-Ayllón. 1992. *Basic Spanish Grammar.* Lexington, MA: DC Heath and Co.

Lipski, J. 1994. *Latin American Spanish.* New York: Longman Linguistics Library.

Malinowski, Arlene. 1983. "Judeo-Spanish Language-Maintenance Efforts in the United States." In *International Journal of the Sociology of Language* 44: 137–151.

Penny, R. 1991. *A History of the Spanish Language.* Cambridge: Cambridge University Press.

Siguán, M. 1993. *Multilingual Spain.* Amsterdam: Swets and Zeitlinger.

Whitley, M. 1986. *Spanish/English Contrasts.* Washington, DC: Georgetown University Press.

Sukuma

Herman M. Batibo

Language Name: Sukuma. **Alternates:** *Kisukuma* (SWAHILI version, also official denomination). **Autonym:** *Kɪsukuma.* Formerly, the Sukuma did not refer to themselves by a single name as they saw themselves as a cluster of clan units. The use of the term "Sukuma" was popularized during the colonial period (1905–1961).

Location: The Sukuma speech community is located in an area that was traditionally known as Sukumaland or Busukuma, in the northwest of Tanzania. It is a generally savanna grassland area of around 16,000 square miles extending from the south and southeast of Lake Victoria to as far south as the river Manonga, which forms a rough boundary between the Sukuma and the Nyamwezi. To the east, it borders the Serengeti National Park plains, and to the west the Geita/Biharamulo woodlands. The Sukuma-speaking people are found mainly in the Mwanza and Shinyanga regions. However, due to population pressures many Sukuma people have migrated to the neighboring regions, particularly Tabora, Musoma, Singida and Bukoba.

Family: Sukuma is a member of the Bantu group of the Benue-Congo subfamily of the Niger-Congo Family. It is classified among the Eastern Bantu languages. Guthrie (1948) classifies it as F21. Nurse and Philippson (1980) classify it among the West Tanzania languages.

Related Languages: The closest language to Sukuma (with high intercomprehension) is Nyamwezi. Sukuma and Nyamwezi form a continuum without a clear boundary but with very distinct variations at the extreme ends. Sukuma, Nyamwezi, and a number of other smaller languages such as Sumbwa, Konongo and Kimbu together form a large linguistic cluster with remarkable intercomprehension at the areas of contact. This cluster is known as Greater Unyamwezi (Abrahams 1967). Its total population is roughly 20 percent of the Tanzanian population or about 7 million speakers. According to Nurse (1980), the degree of lexical similarity between Sukuma and the other languages is as follows: with Nyamwezi 84 percent, with Sumbwa 59 percent, with Nyaturu 57 percent, and with Kimbu 55 percent. In fact, Sukuma/Nyamwezi common lexical stock would be 98 percent, instead of 84 percent, if taken from the bordering varieties. All of the languages in the cluster belong to Guthrie's Zone F (Guthrie 1948) or Nurse and Philippson's West Tanzania Zone (Nurse and Philippson 1980).

Dialects: There are basically four dialects, which are directional and mainly due to influences from neighboring languages. (1) *Kimunasukuma* (the northern way of speaking), spoken in the northern parts of Busukuma. It is also spoken near Mwanza, the main town. It is therefore the most prestigious, and consequently the representative variety of the language; (2) *Kimunadakama* (the southern way of speaking), the dialect bordering the Nyamwezi language. It therefore has influences from the latter in terms of certain items of vocabulary and phonological rules, including tone rules. Kimunadakama is mainly spoken in Shinyanga and Kahama districts; (3) *Kimunang'weli* (the western way of speaking), the dialect bordering lacustrine languages such as Zinza, Subi and Ha. The only noticeable differences are in some items of vocabulary, and some expressions, such as the mode of greeting. This dialect is spoken mainly in Geita and Sengerema districts; (4) *Kimunakiiya* (the eastern way of speaking) This is the most conspicuous dialect of Sukuma. It is spoken in Bariadi, Meatu and Maswa districts. This dialect became distinct because of massive influence from the Datoga language over the last 300 years. Thus, one distinguishes a Kiiya speaker by the tendencies of voicing all initial voiceless plosives, laxing all tense vowels, and shortening all long syllables. Also, many items of vocabulary differ from those used in the other Sukuma dialects.

Number of Speakers: Recent estimates have ranged from 3.5 million to 5 million. Sukuma speakers were said to constitute 12.6 percent of the Tanzanian population in 1957, the last census in which there was a systematic mention of ethnic (linguistic) repartition. Given that the Tanzanian population is now around 35 million, we can deduce (assuming that Sukuma population growth equals national growth) that there are around 4.4 million Sukuma speakers.

Origin and History

The Bantu linguistic family, of which the Sukuma-Nyamwezi language cluster is a member, started to disperse from near the Benue River area west of Cameroon around 1,500 B.C. An Eastern Bantu branch of ancestral Bantu moved eastwards towards the Great Lakes. One subbranch of Eastern Bantu known as Western Pela Bantu (Ehret 1980) gave rise to Proto–West Tanzania Bantu, whose speakers are believed to have settled in the west-central parts of present-day Tanzania, probably in, or near, the upper reaches of the Wembere River (Batibo, 1992). The Proto–West Tanzania Bantu were presumably skilled in hunting, crop farming and stock raising, having gone through the experiences of the early Iron Age (Ehret 1974). In their movement northwards they presumably came into contact with the well-established West-Rift Southern Cushitic communities who were widely scattered in the north-central plains. From them, their socioeconomic life was enriched through the reinforcement of their knowledge of crop farming and stock raising.

The Proto–West Tanzania communities started to disperse

Table 1: Consonants

		Bilabial	Labio-dental	Alveolar	Palatal	Velar	Glottal
Stops	Voiceless	p		t	c	k	
	Voiced	ß		d	ɟ	g	
Fricatives	Voiceless		f	s			h
	Voiced		v	z			
Nasals	Unaspirated	m		n	ɲ	ŋ	
	Aspirated	mh		nh	ɲh	ŋh	
Glide					j	w	
Lateral				l			

into smaller groups from around A.D. 500 to form various varieties and languages. The first groups to branch off were Kimbu (to the south), then Nilyamba/Nyaturu (to the east) (Nurse 1988). This left the Proto-Sukuma/Nyamwezi cluster as the mainstream around the Gombe River, from which northward movement by the Sukuma (Northern) variety took place between 1000 and 1300. The northward movement toward the southern shores of Lake Victoria was presumably slow, but reinforced by more groups moving toward the same direction, thus enhancing their demographic dominance (Brandstrom 1986).

The earlier Bantu and non-Bantu communities in the area, which were integrated into the Sukuma language and culture, must have been bilingual, using Sukuma speech as a lingua franca, before eventually shifting to it. The earlier languages in the area formed both a linguistic substratum and a source of sociocultural diversity. Later on other Bantu groups and the pastoral Datoga (a Nilotic group that entered the Sukuma area in the 16th century) added to the linguistic and socio-cultural mixture in the area.

The various origins of the Sukuma people have given rise to a diversity in the structure and inventory of the Sukuma language. It is socioculturally described as an amalgam of semi-autonomous entities, known as *mabutemi* 'chiefdoms' (Itandala 1983). Each *butemi* (whether the ruling dynasty or the ruled subjects) would claim to have their own origin and history. The only features that characterize the identity or unity of the Busukuma are to be found in the broad linguistic and cultural homogeneity.

The Sukuma people have been described as a society with a mixed economy. Contrary to most of their neighbors, they engage in both crop farming and stock raising. This could be attributed to their diverse origins, since Sukumaland was both a natural corridor and a melting pot for many linguistic groups.

Sukuma has not spread or contracted much in recent years, except that Sukuma speakers have since the early 1950s migrated into neighboring districts, thus dominating the smaller groups like the Zinza, Subi, Sumbwa, Shashi, Ikizu and Isanzu, eventually forcing them to become bilingual.

Moreover, most Sukuma speakers are bilingual with Swahili, the national language (or trilingual with ENGLISH, the second official language of Tanzania).

Orthography and Basic Phonology

There is no formally agreed-upon orthography, except that missionaries have used an orthography based on English and Swahili to prepare Christian readers (including the Bible) and in printing a Sukuma newspaper *Lumuli.* The spelling is as explained below. The conjunctivist system is used in word division. Also tone is not marked in the current orthography, one of the reasons is that the tone pattern of a word is not fixed, but varies with tonological, morphological and syntactic context.

The following is a comprehensive list of graphemes that constitute the Sukuma alphabet. They are based on the LATIN alphabet as shown below. Digraphs, representing specific sounds, are also included: A, B, CH, D, E, F, G, H, I, J, K, L, M, MH, N, NH, NG', NG'H, NY, NY'H, O, P, S, SH, T, U, V, W, Y, Z; a, b, ch, d, e, f, g, h, i, j, k, l, m, mh, n, nh, ng', ng'h, ny, ny'h, o, p, s, sh, t, u, v, w, y, z.

Sukuma has 24 consonant phonemes, as represented in Table 1. The consonants /c/, /ß/, /ɟ/, /ç/ /ɲ/,/ŋ/ and /j/ are written in the orthography as *ch, b, j, sh, ny, ng'* and *y* respectively. Nyamwezi has no /ɟ/; it has /z/ where Sukuma would have /ɟ/. Also, the phoneme /w/ is realized as a bilabial rather than a velar in Nyamwezi.

Table 2: Vowels

		Front	Back
High	Tense	i	u
	Lax	ɪ	ʊ
Mid		ɛ	ɔ
Low		a	

Sukuma has seven vowel phonemes, as indicated in the above vowel table. The vowel phonemes /ɪ/, /ɛ/, /ɔ/ and /ʊ/ are represented in the orthography as *i, e, o,* and *u* respectively.

The following are some of the basic phonological rules of the language:

(1) ß > b / m_ ([ßɔnà] 'see' > [m-bɔ́na] 'witness')
(2) l > d / n_ ([laalá!] 'sleep' > [n-daaló] 'sleep (n)').
(3) m > ŋ / _w (mu + ana > [ŋwàànà] 'child' but *mwaaná* in Nyamwezi)
(4) [n + ph] > [mh] (e.g [n-pʊlI] > [mhʊlI] 'elephant')
[n + th] > [nh]
[n + ch] > [ɲh] <u>condition</u>:
[n + kh] > [ŋh] n = Noun cl. 9/10
(5) l > z / _u ([pɔla] 'cool down' > [pɔz-ù] 'cool')
(6) ß > Ø / _ w (e.g., [ßu + ana] > [wàànà] 'infancy')
(7) [u/ʊ] > [w] / _V and [i/ɪ] > [j] / _V

<u>Condition</u>: Vowel must be of different specification.

e.g., ʊ + a + ne [waanὲ] 'mine' (n.cl.3)
I + a + ne [jaanὲ] 'mine' (n.cl.9)

There is also a vowel harmony rule in which the stem vowel *a*, *i* and *u* must be followed by *i* in the applicative suffix, and *o* and *e* by *e*. Here are some examples:

-bin-a	'dance'	bin-il-a	'dance for'
-bon-a	'see'	bon-el-a	'see on behalf of'

With regard to consonant realization in the language, /p, t, c, k/ are strongly aspirated in realization, /w/ is realized more as a velar consonant than a bilabial consonant, and /v/ is usually found in ideophonic and onomatopoeic words, with the impression of squeezing, friction or constriction.

Sukuma is a tone-accent language. This means that although most syllables are toneless, some are high toned (H). The H tones are either fixed or displaceable. Where an H tone is displaceable, it falls on the second syllable to the right of the syllable it is associated with underlyingly, in the same word, or the second syllable of the next word, if there are not enough syllables. One important Sukuma tone rule is that any displaced H cannot surface with or across another H (whether fixed or displaceable). It will have to settle on the syllable preceding the one associated with H. Also where there are not enough syllables for the displaceable H to surface, it will be deleted and the syllables will be realized lower (i.e., extra-low) than the toneless syllables, which normally surface with a default L.

Sukuma syllables may be short (one mora) or long (two morae), except at word-final position where they are always short. For convenience's sake, length is shown by doubling the vowels. (In the current Sukuma orthography length is not indicated). The following are illustrations:

-seba	'get hot'	-seeba	'excavate'
-pala	'be angry'	-paala	'strike'
-bola	'rot'	-boola	'abduct'

In current Sukuma, the syllable is the tone bearing unit (TBU), except in a few cases, such as the verb radicals, where the second part is regarded tonally as a derivational suffix, e.g., *se.eba* 'to excavate'. There is evidence that historically the mora was the TBU.

Dahl's law, which, in its formulation, resembles Grassman's law in Indo-European, operates in Nyamwezi, just as in a number of languages in the area. According to this rule, no two voiceless stops can occur in successive syllables; when such a situation occurs, the first stop will be voiced, e.g., *ku+bɔna* [*kʊßɔnà*] 'to see', but *ku+toola* [gʊtɔɔlá] 'to marry' and *ku+kula* [gʊkʊlà] 'to grow up'.

Basic Morphology

Nouns comprise a stem (usually disyllabic) and a noun prefix that marks class and number. Just as in most Bantu languages, Sukuma has neither gender nor case markings in the noun. The noun prefixes are as follows:

1. mu-nhu 'a person'	2. ba-nhu 'persons'
1a. Ø-baaba 'father'	2a. baa-baaba 'fathers'
3. mu-eji 'month'	4. mi-eji 'months'
5. i-tale 'rock'	6. ma-tale 'rocks'
7. ki-kolo 'thing'	8. shi-kolo 'things'
9. n-dama 'calf'	10. n-dama 'calves'
9a. Ø-kuuli 'lizard'	10a. Ø-kuuli 'lizards'
11. lu-goye 'rope'	10. n-goye 'ropes'
12. ka-ana 'infant'	13. tu-ana 'infants'
14. bu-lugu 'war'	6. ma-lugu 'wars'
15. ku-kono 'hand'	6. ma-kono 'hands'
16. ha-kaaya 'at home'	
17. ku-kaaya 'to one's home'	
18. mu-kaaya 'in one's home'	

An initial vowel is used to mark definiteness, e.g., *mu-nhu* 'a person', but *u-mu-nhu* 'the person in question'. In Sukuma the vowels of noun-class prefixes 1 and 3 delete before consonants. The remaining nasal becomes homorganic with the following consonant. The noun agrees with all words that relate to it, i.e., adjectives, demonstratives, possessives, numerals, and verb subjects:

ba-kiima a-ba ba-bili ba-awiiza ba-kwiiza
women these two beautiful they-will come
'These two beautiful women will come.'

shi-kolo i-shi shi-bili shi-awiiza shi-kwiiza
things these two beautiful they-will come
'These two beautiful things will come.'

The verb is made up of prefixes and suffixes. The stem is composed of the root followed by derivational suffixes that may be one of the following: the causative (*-ish-*) or (*-y-*), applicative (*-il-*), reciprocal (*-an-*), neutral (*-ik-*), reversive (*-ul-*), passive (*-w-*) and repetitive (*-agul-*). The following are examples:

-fung-a	'close'
-fung-il-a	'close by means of', or 'close for'
-fung-ul-a	'open'
-fung-an-a	'go draw'
-fung-w-a	'be closed, be imprisoned'
-fung-agul-a	'close one door after another'

Pronominal and tense/aspect markers are indicated by prefixes. The order is as follows: Subject Marker + Tense/Aspect

Marker + Object Marker (Optional) + Verb stem, e.g., *a-ku-ni-tula* [akhʊnithʊlà] (he-FUTURE-me-beat) 'he will beat me'.

The tense/aspect markers include the future (*-ku-*), potential/remote future (*-laa-*), past (*-ka-*), distant past (*-a!-*), immediative (*-a-*), present (*-lii-*) and perfective (*-ile*). The last one is a suffix. The negative tense/aspect markers are, in some ways, different from the affirmative ones. The normal negative marker is (*-ta-*), e.g.:

a-ta-u-tul-aga [athʊthʊlagá]
he-NEG-PRES-beat-CONTIN.SUFF.
'he is not beating'

Generally, inflection is prefixal and derivation is suffixal. However, some noun-class prefixes can be used for derivation, e.g.:

mu-nhu	'person'
bu-mu-nhu	'humanity' (abstract noun)
ka-mu-nhu	'a dwarf' (diminutive)

Also nouns can be formed through the process of deverbativization:

(ku)-imb-a	'(to) sing'
mu-imb-i	'singer'
li-imb-o	'song'

Sukuma has few adjectives. However, many adjectival forms are derived through deverbativization:

-lih-a	'be long'	>	-lih-u	'long'
-pol-a	'cool down'	>	-poz-u	'cool'
-kal-a	'be dry'	>	-kaz-u	'dry'
-seb-a	'be hot'	>	-seb-u	'hot'

Basic Syntax

Sukuma is a head-initial SVO language. Elements of the noun phrase are in the following order: Noun (+ Possessive) (+ Demonstrative) (+ Numeral) (+ Adjective). This order is not rigid. It depends on individual speakers as well as on topic/focus. The verb phrase is composed of a verb followed by optional noun phrases, adverbials and prepositional phrases. This structure is illustrated by the following sentence:

Ba-ana	ba-ane	ba-lii-lya	shi-liiwa	shi-ngi	shi-a
2-children	2-my	they-pres-eat	8-food	8-many	8-of

mu-n-gunda
3-farm
'My children are eating much food from the field'

But it is possible to change this SVO order and say: *Shiliiwa shingi baliilya abaana baane* 'Much food, my children are eating'.

As remarked earlier, there is no case marking for the NP constituents in a sentence. But often the subject and object markers indicate the thematic roles of the respective nouns by their class agreement (SN = subject noun, SM = subject marker, OM = object marker and ON = object noun):

ba-ana	ba-lii-shi-lya	shi-liiwa
SN	SM-pres-OM-eat	ON

'The children are eating the food'

Unlike some other Bantu languages that allow more than one object marker, Sukuma allows only one. Negation is expressed by the prefix *ta-* which is associated with specific tense/aspect markers. In Sukuma some word categories are invariable. These include prepositions, conjunctions, ideophones/interjections, onomatopoeias, and adverbs. The definitive initial vowel and the demonstratives are used in the place of articles (which are nonexistent).

Contact with Other Languages

Sukuma has borrowed extensively from Swahili, Tanzania's lingua franca and national language. Many Swahili words originate from ARABIC. Some words have been borrowed from English, GERMAN, FRENCH and ITALIAN, the last two through missionary activities.

From Swahili: *shibiliiti/shilibiiti* 'matches', *shitabo* 'book', *ifulila* 'cooking pot', *ibakuli* 'bowl', *sahaani* 'plate'
From English: *batija* 'baptize', *teleeni* 'train', *ishaati* 'shirt'
From German: *shuule* 'school', *hela* 'money'
From French: *ndali* 'Catholic neck-medal', *nweele* 'Christmas'
From Italian/Latin: *ikelezia* 'church', *misa* 'Holy Mass'

In adapting foreign words to Sukuma, the canonical CVCV syllable structure has to be preserved by inserting vowels to clustered consonant sequences, adding vowels to final consonants or deleting all extrasyllabic consonants. Also nonexisting sounds are normally replaced by the nearest Sukuma sounds. All nouns must contain noun prefixes. Where the first syllable of the borrowed word resembles a noun prefix, it will be interpreted so (e.g., 'ecclesia'—*i-kelezia* (sg)/*ma-kelezia* (pl). Where the noun denotes a human being, it will belong to Noun Classes 1a/2a (e.g., *ø - paadili/baa-paadili* 'priest'). In all other cases, it will belong to Noun Classes 9/10, whose prefixes are generally ø- or zero. All words are completely nativized, except where speakers choose not to be typical.

Common Words

water:	miinzi
long:	-liihu
sun:	liimi
yes:	ehe!
no:	yaaya
fish:	ndilo
small:	-do
big:	-taale
good:	-awiza
bird:	noni (sg/pl)
dog:	nva (sg/pl)
tree:	nti/miti (sg/pl)

Example Sentences*

(1) Unke wa ng'u Masanja akuja kudaha miinzi.

u-mu-ke	u-a	mu-u
DEF-1sg-wife	1sg-of	3sg-DEF

ø – Masanja	a-ku-ja	ku-daha	ma-inzi.
1a.sg-M	she-FUT-go	to-draw	6.pl-water

'Masanja's wife will go to draw water.'

(2) naabona bakiima baliilima ngunda.

ni-a-bona	ba-kiima
I-IMMEDIATIVE-see	2pl-woman)

ba-lii-lima	n-gunda
they-PRES-cultivate	3sg-farm

'I have just seen women cultivating a farm.'

(3) bayaanda babili baliidiima ng'ombe.

ba-yanda	ba-bili	ba-lii-diima	n-g'ombe
2pl-boy	2pl-two	they-PRES-herd	10pl-cow

'Two boys are herding cattle.'

*Numerals correspond to noun classes.

Efforts to Preserve, Protect, and Promote the Language

Sukuma has not been accorded any official role in Tanzania. Although before independence in 1961 Sukuma identity and self-determination were strong and the language was used as a medium of education in missionary lower-primary schools, in recent years Sukuma has surrendered all public functions to Swahili, the national language. Sukuma is now considered a mere cultural language (spoken at village level within its geographical confines), just like the other remaining 120 or so languages in Tanzania, although given its strong demographic position, Sukuma is probably the least threatened indigenous language in Tanzania.

Efforts to preserve Sukuma language and culture are being made, especially by missionaries of the Catholic Church and the African Inland Church. These efforts include the creation of the Bujora Sukuma Museum (11 miles from Mwanza town) where Sukuma culture and traditions are kept. The museum is sponsored by Denmark and Canada. In addition, efforts have been made to revive the bimonthly newspaper *lumuli*, which became dormant in the late 1960s. Another regular publication is the newsletter known as *Bana Cecilia* ('Association of the followers of St. Cecilia'), published by Bujora Catholic Church. Some church materials, including the Holy Bible, have been translated into Sukuma. However, because of the difficulty of the current orthographic system, many Sukuma people prefer reading Swahili versions. A number of concerned local Sukuma people are attempting to preserve the language by collecting proverbs, sayings, stories, puzzles and even preparing dictionaries. Their major concern is to preserve botanical, wildlife and place-names. Such efforts, however, remain superfluous and amateurish.

Select Bibliography

Batibo, H.M. 1985. *Le Kesukuma, Langue Bantu de Tanzanie: Phonologie et Morpholigie*. Paris: CREDU Editions recherche sur les civilisations.

____. 1992. "The Peopling of Busukuma: A Linguistic Account." In *Journal of Linguistics and Language in Education* 6: 42–76. Department of Foreign Languages and Linguistics, University of Dar-es-Salaam.

Brandstrom, P. 1986, "Who is a Sukuma and Who is a Nyamwezi? Ethnic Identity in West Central Tanzania." In *Working Papers in African Studies* 27: 1–15. African Studies Programme, Department of Cultural Anthropology, University of Uppsala.

Ehret, C. 1974. "Agricultural History of Central and Southern Africa (c.a. 1000 B.C.–A.D. 500)." In *Transafrican Journal of History* 4, 1–2: 1–27.

____. 1980. "Historical Inference from Transformations in Culture Vocabularies." In *SUGIA* 2: 189–218, Cologne.

Goldsmith, J. 1990, *Autosegmental and Metrical Phonology*. Oxford and Cambridge, MA: Basil Blackwell.

Guthrie, M. 1948. *The Classification of the Bantu Languages*, Oxford University Press, I.A.I., Handbook of African Languages.

Itandala, B. 1983. "The History of Babinza of Usukuma." PhD Dissertation, Department of History, Dalhousie University, Halfax.

Nurse, D. 1988. "The Diachronic Background to the Language Communities of Southwestern Tanzania." In *SUGIA* 9: 15–115.

Nurse, D., and G. Philippson. 1980. "Historical Implications of the Language Map of East Africa." In L. Bouquiaux (Ed.) *Expansion Bantoue: Actes du Colloque international du CNRS*, Viviers, France, SELAF, Paris.

SUMERIAN

Daniel C. Snell

Language Name: Sumerian. *Šumerû* in AKKADIAN, *eme Kengir* in Sumerian.

Location: Southern Mesopotamia, ancient Iraq, Syria, and contiguous areas.

Family: Language Isolate.

Related Languages: None.

Dialects: Standard: *eme-gir*. Also, *eme-sal* 'thin dialect', used in some kinds of poetry.

Origin and History

Sumerian is the oldest attested written language, and the cuneiform writing system was perhaps devised to write it. The system uses signs that stand for whole words, but it was eventually supplemented by the use of some signs with only syllabic value. These were used to write foreign personal names and to show grammatical elements, which had earlier not been expressed in writing. For example, *ka* 'mouth' became used for *-ka* (sign of the genitive). Most cuneiform signs can be read more than one way, and so some ambiguity must remain.

The first period in the written history of the language, the Old Sumerian (3100 B.C. to c. 2400 B.C.) saw some archival texts and monumental texts produced with a minimum of grammatical elements shown. From about 2400 B.C. to 2150 B.C. few extended texts in the language are preserved, since the ruling dynasty preferred to use its own Akkadian language. A Neo-Sumerian period (2150 B.C.–2000 B.C.) saw a new, southern dynasty revert to Sumerian for official purposes. And in subsequent periods Sumerian texts were copied in schools, and the language was used for religious, and decreasingly, official purposes. It must have died out as a spoken language before 1600 B.C., and some would say much earlier.

Orthography and Basic Phonology

There are no spelling rules, but there is a standard orthography that may have been set in scribal circles in Nippur, the religious capital. Most cuneiform signs have logographic values as well as phonetic values, usually Consonant-Vowel or Vowel-Consonant. Scribes were usually free to spell names as they heard them, and other words had comon spellings from which to choose.

Because Sumerian is a dead language that was used over a fairly long period of time, it is difficult to know exactly how it was pronounced in any particular era. The values used in this chapter are standard transcriptions used by scholars working on Sumerian, and they are based on reasonable inferences from uses of similar signs in Akkadian, about whose pronunciation somewhat more is known.

dr represents a single phoneme, pronounced [dr]. *š* represents the sound of ENGLISH "sh". *g̃* is presumed to represent a velar nasal, [ŋ], the sound of English "ng".

Table 1: Consonants

	Labial	Dental	Alveo-palatal	Velar	Glottal
Stops Voiceless Voiced	 p b	 t d, dr		 k g	
Fricatives Voiceless Voiced		 s	 š z		 h
Nasals	m	n		g̃	
Resonants		r, l			

Final consonants are often omitted in writing, as in *umunadakure* for *umunadakuren* 'after you have entered before him'.

Table 2: Vowels

	Front	Back
High	i	u
Low	e	a

The vowel *i* could also be nasalized: ĩ. The other vowels apparently were only oral.

Some dialects of Sumerian have vowel harmony: verb prefixes *i-* and *bi-* appear as *e-*and *be-*before low vowels: *e-ak* appears instead of *ĩ-ak* 'he does'.

It has been suggested, based on the number of homonyms, that Sumerian was a tone language. But the writing provides no indication of such, so the idea is not provable.

Basic Morphology

Sumerian nouns were marked for the following cases: genitive, ergative, comitative, terminative, ablative/instrumental, locative-terminative, and equative. In addition, animate nouns could be dative, and inanimate nouns could be locative. Case was indicated by suffixes, the absolutive being characterized by absence of an ending.

In general, Sumerian was a highly agglutinative language, suffixing elements to nouns as needed:

kituš-dingir-galgal-ene-ak-a
dwelling-god-great-PL-GEN-LOC
'in the dwelling of the great gods'

Sumerian verb derivation is very subtle, and involves infixes that appear to have an adverbial force. There is also a distinction called in Akkadian *hamtû* 'quick' vs. *marû* 'fat' that seems to refer to aspect. But some verbs appear only in the *hamtû* form.

Sumerian has two basic verb conjugation patterns, one for intransitive verbs and one for transitive verbs:

Intransitive: *ikur* 'enter'

	Singular	Plural
1st	ikur-en	ikur-enden
2nd	ikur-en	ikur-enzen
3rd	ikur	ikur-eš

Transitive *inzig* 'raise'

	Singular	Plural
1st	i-zig	i-zig-enden
2nd	mue-zig	mue-zig-enzen
3rd	in-zig (animate)	in-zig-eš
		ib-zig (inanimate)

Basic Syntax

The basic word order in Sumerian was Subject-Object-Verb. In addition, the language is ergative; that is, intransitive subjects and transitive objects are treated alike by the syntax.

lu-e sag mun-zig
man-ERG head:ABS 3SG-raise
'The man raised the head.'

lu ikur
man:ABS enter:3SG
'The man entered.'

Adjectives in Sumerian precede the nouns they modify: *nam dug* (good fate) 'good fate'. Sentences in Sumerian are negated by the addition of *nu-* to the verbal chain:

nu-ba-ta-e
NEG-CONJ-ABL-go(out)
'shall not escape'

Contact with Other Languages

Long and intimate contact with Akkadian led to many borrowed words in each direction, and when Sumerian died as a spoken language, Akkadian replaced it.

From Akkadian: *arad* 'slave' (< *ardum*); *guza* 'chair' (< *kussu*); *buzur* 'secret' (< *puzru*) *damgar* 'merchant' (< *tamkār*)

Common Words

man:	guruš, lu	long:	gid
woman:	geme, dam	small:	sal
water:	a	yes:	ki
sun:	utu	no:	nu
three:	eš	good:	dug
fish:	ku	bird:	mušen
big:	gal	dog:	ur
tree:	giš		

Example Sentences

All of the example sentences are from *The Sumerian Language* by Marie-Louise Thomsen (1984).

(1) Gudea en Ningirsuk-e nam dug
Gudea:for lord:ABS Ningirsu-ERG good fate:ABS

mu-ni-tar.
toward 3SG/ERG cut
'The Lord Ningirsu has decided a good fate.'

(2) igib-a šembi ba-ni-gar.
their.eyes-LOC kohl:ABS LOC-3SG/ERG-put
'He placed kohl in their eyes.'

(3) g̃a-e Utu-gin i-a-dim-men.
I-ERG Utu-like VERB.PREF-also-build-1SG
'I also am created like Utu (the Sun God).'

Efforts to Preserve, Protect, and Promote the Language

As a scribal language, Sumerian was preserved in schools, and the dictionary tradition that started as lists of signs in the third millennium B.C. was simplified with Akkadian translations and pronunciations for the convenience of Akkadian-speaking scribes. It was written until the end of the cuneiform tradition in the first century, A.D.

Select Bibliography

Borger, Rykle. 1981. *Assyrisch-babylonische Zeichenliste*. Kevelaer und Neukirchen-Vluyn: Butzon and Bercker und Neukirchener.

Gragg, Gene B. 1973. *Sumerian Dimensional Infixes*. Neukirchen-Vluyn and Kevelaer: Neukirchener and Butzon and Bercker.

Landsberger, Benno, *et al.*, eds. 1937–. *Materialien zum Sumerischen Lexikon*. Rome: Pontificial Biblica Institute.

Sjöberg, Åke. 1992–. *The Sumerian Dictionary of the University Museum of the University of Pennsylvania*. Philadelphia: University Museum.

Thomsen, Marie-Louise. 1984. *The Sumerian Language*. Copenhagen: Akademisk.

Sundanese

Abigail C. Cohn

Language Name: Sundanese. **Alternates:** *Sunda, Priangan.* **Autonym:** *Basa Sunda.*

Location: Sundanese is spoken in West Java, Indonesia, in approximately the western third of Java, excluding Jakarta and surrounding areas and a narrow strip along the north coast. It is also spoken in other areas of Indonesia, especially South Sumatra due to migration of Sundanese speakers.

Family: Western Austronesian subfamily of the Austronesian language family.

Related Languages: JAVANESE and MADURESE, spoken in Java and neighboring Madura, respectively, are the most closely related languages. Also related is INDONESIAN (national language of Indonesia, dialect of MALAY) and possibly Lampung (spoken in S. Sumatra) and Iban (or Sea Dayak, spoken along the coasts in Kalimantan).

Dialects: The dialect spoken in Bandung, the capital of Sunda (the province of W. Java), is taken to be the standard (officially declared so by the government in 1918). This area, also referred to as Priangan, includes the south and south-central areas of W. Java. The other dialects (regionally defined) include the areas of Banten, all the way to the west; Bogor/Krawang, east of Banten, north of Priangan; and Cirebon to the east. While some phonological and morphological differences exist, the more noteworthy dialect differences are lexical. Much of this is due to waves of Javanese and Malay influences. In general, the Javanese influence is strongest in the northern dialects.

The Priangan dialect area is distinguished from the others in several respects (as are the other dialects from each other). For example, the word for 'water buffalo' is *munding* in the Priangan area and *kebo* (from Javanese *kerbau*) elsewhere throughout the dialects (Nothofer 1980, map 25). The word for 'sun' is also different in the Priangan dialect area, while showing the Javanese influence in Cirebon. The forms include variants of *panon poe* (in most of Priangan) and *matapoe* (in Banten and Bogor/Krawang and parts of Cirebon), vs. *sarengenge* (in parts of Cirebon). The element *poe* is the Sundanese descendant of Proto-Austronesian 'day, sun'; while *sarengenge* is from Javanese *srengenge* (Nothofer 1980, map 1).

Phonologically some differences are seen in the phoneme inventory. Two dialects spoken in the north—Parean and Lelea, which are surrounded by Javanese-speaking areas—show particularly marked variation. Here morphological variation is observed as well, e.g., the suffix *-keun* assimilates in place of articulation in Parean: Priangan *kirim* 'send', *kirim-keun* 'send for', Parean *kirim, kirim-peun*, Priangan *turun* 'descend', *turun-keun* 'lower', Parean *turun, turun-teun.*

Number of Speakers: 22–26 million.

Origin and History

While there is no consensus on where the original homeland of the Austronesian people was, it is clear that the Austronesians were a seafaring people who started to disperse throughout the Austronesian archipelago by at least 3000 B.C. The original homeland has been argued to have been somewhere in China, mainland S.E. Asia, Taiwan, or the Philippines. It is believed that the Austronesian people migrated southward, either through the Malay Peninsula or the Philippines, into Sulawesi and then west and east throughout the archipelago. (This migration continued as far west as Madagascar and as far east as Hawaii, Cribb 1992.)

The earliest inscriptions in W. Java (the stones of Ci Catih) date from 1030, although the first inscriptions identified as being in Old Sundanese, the *Batutulis*, date from the 14th century (de Casparis 1975). A number of these inscriptions are at the ancient site of the capital of Pajajaran, the last Hindu kingdom of W. Java, founded in 1344. These inscriptions and some manuscripts constitute the total extant materials in Old Sundanese. There are about 30 extant Old Sundanese *lontar* manuscripts; the language in these shows forms still current in Sundanese or its dialects (Noorduyn 1962). These texts are written in a syllabary, similar to the Javanese script, but distinct in certain respects (see de Casparis 1975).

More recent manuscripts exist which chronicle the history of Sunda from the 16th through 20th centuries. Several hundred such manuscripts are housed in the National Museum in Jakarta, archives in Holland, and regional museums and private collections in W. Java. Beginning in the nineteenth century, these texts have been studied in order to document the history, society and literature of Sunda. A number of individual texts have been analyzed and translated, but little systematic linguistic work has been undertaken. In a very useful survey of these texts, Ekadjati *et al.* (1985) provide summaries and basic descriptions of 30 of these texts, with examples taken from the 16th, 18th, 19th and 20th centuries. The texts are written in four distinct scripts: the Old Sundanese syllabary, the Sunda version of the Javanese syllabary, and ARABIC and Roman alphabets. These scripts can be used to roughly date the texts, with the Old Sundanese script being the oldest and the Roman script the most recent. Based on these texts spanning five centuries, preliminary historical observations have been made. There are some small phonological differences, but there are few differences in sentence structure. Interestingly, the degree of lexical influence from SANSKRIT vs. Arabic is useful in dating the texts. There is significant Sanskrit influence in the texts from the 16th and 18th centuries, while significant Arabic influence starts in the 19th century texts (even though the political and social influence of Islam dates to the 15th century).

Linguistic description of Sundanese did not start until the 19th century and, except for observations about the manuscripts mentioned above, little is known about the language before this period. There are a few word lists from the first half of the 19th century, but more substantive work did not appear until later. Dictionaries, grammatical sketches and Bible translations were produced by Dutch civil servants, missionaries and scholars (see Uhlenbeck for a survey of these works).

A study of the use of Sundanese in W. Java (Kartini *et al.* 1985) shows significant use of Sundanese by adults covering a full range of socioeconomic backgrounds in a wide range of contexts and settings. Sundanese is used both as a spoken and written language, the latter primarily for personal, but not professional matters. Most speakers of Sundanese are also fluent in Indonesian, the national language of Indonesia, which is used in education and business. But Sundanese remains very important in informal settings. The 1980 census data for W. Java, a geographic area roughly coextensive with the Sundanese speaking area, show that few people in W. Java speak only Indonesian (9 percent), while the majority speak both Sundanese and Indonesian (53 percent). The remaining population describe themselves as speaking only Sundanese (38 percent) (although many of these individuals probably have at least a passive knowledge of Indonesian).

Orthography and Basic Phonology

The current orthography (in Roman script) is modeled on the Indonesian standard orthography (following the spelling reform of 1972). The orthography is a systematic one that indicates almost all of the phonemic distinctions in the language. The values of the symbols correspond quite closely to the IPA use of the symbols. To clarify the difference between /ɛ/ and /ə/, an acute accent can be added to the former. Several digraphs are used, *ng* and *ny* for the nasals /ŋ/ and /ɲ/, and *eu* for the high central vowel /ɨ/.

Table 1: Consonants

		Labial	Dental/ Alveolar	Palatal	Velar	Glottal
Stops	Voiceless	p	t	c	k	q
	Voiced	b	d	j	g	
Fricatives			s			h
Nasals		m	n	ny	ng	
Liquids			l, r			
Glides				y	w	

A Roman orthography has been used since Sundanese materials started being printed in the 19th century. Although in the 19th century some materials were written in Arabic script and the Javanese script (syllabary) is also sometimes used, these are no longer very common.

The voiceless stops *p*, *t*, and *k* are unaspirated. *c* and *j* are lightly affricated voiceless and voiced palatal stops (less strongly affricated than their counterparts "ch" and "j" in ENGLISH). *r* is pronounced either as a trill or a tap. The glottal stop *q* is not usually represented in the orthography as its presence is largely predictable.

The vowels all have a clear, non-diphthongal quality. [é] is a midfront vowel, similar to "e" in "bet", although not always written with the accent; *e* is pronounced as a schwa, a mid-central vowel, similar to "a" in "about". /eu/ is the graph for the high central unrounded vowel.

Table 2: Vowels

	Front Unrounded	Central Unrounded	Back Rounded
High	i	eu	u
Mid	é	e	o
Low		a	

The sound patterns are quite similar to closely related languages, although in the vowel system the vowel *eu* is unusual, both for languages of this family and crosslinguistically.

There is a rule of nasalization in Sundanese with quite dramatic effects, as a nasal consonant may cause a whole sequence of vowels and glottal sounds to become nasalized, similar to *a* in the English word "band", as compared with "a" in "bad" (described in a now quite well-known article by R.H. Robins 1957): *ngatur* [ŋãtur] 'arrange', *niis* [nĩʔĩs] 'relax in a cool place', *nyiar* [ɲãr] 'seek', *mahal* [mãhãl] 'expensive'.

There is a pattern of liquid dissimilation, most systematically observed as the result of infixation of *=ar=* (marking the plural in verbs, see below) (Cohn 1992): *k{ar}usut* 'messy', *t{ar}iis* 'cold' but: *d{al}ahar* 'eat', *k{al}otor* 'dirty'.

Stress in Sundanese (marked ´) systematically falls on the penultimate syllable of a word, whether or not it is morphologically complex. In words of four syllables or longer, a secondary stress (marked `) appears on the initial syllable of the stem: *máhal* 'expensive', *m-ar-áhal* 'expensive, plural', *di-mahál-keun* 'be made expensive', *di-m-àr-ahál-keun* 'be made expensive, plural'.

Basic Morphology

There is little in the way of regular inflectional morphology in Sundanese, and even some of the inflectional marking that occurs appears to be optional.

In the nouns, there is no case marking nor gender marking, and no agreement between modifiers and nouns. The plural is indicated morphologically with full reduplication, e.g., *baju* 'clothes', *baju-baju* 'clothes, pl.'; *kertas* 'paper', *kertas-kertas* 'paper, pl.' However, marking of the plural is not obligatory. Plurality can be implicit or indicated through context, and if there is a separate explicit indication of plurality, e.g., a cardinal number, then the noun cannot be marked for plurality. The basic pronominal system is:

1sg.	L	kuring	1pl.	N	urang
	H	abdi			
2sg.	L	maneh	2pl.	L	maraneh
	H	anjeun		H	aranjeun
3sg.	L	manehna	3pl.	L	maranehna
	H	anjeunna		H	aranjeunna

Like Sundanese nouns, these pronouns are not marked for case; the same form is used as both subject and object, so *kuring* can mean either 'I' or 'me', depending on its role in a sentence.

Sundanese has a complex system of speech levels (indicating differing levels of formality, see below), and this is indicated in the pronominal system: N = neutral, L = low, H = high. Also of interest in the pronominal system is the fact that gender is not indicated; *manehna* can be used where English would use 'he' or 'she'.

While articles are not obligatory, definiteness can be marked with a suffix *-na*, e.g., *baju* 'clothes', *baju-na* 'the clothes'. In addition there is a class of "specifiers" that mark the size and shape of things, e.g., *keclak* 'a drop', *leunjeur* 'a pole', *tilu leunjeur awi* 'three, pole, bamboo = three sticks of bamboo'.

There is not much overt verbal morphology, and there is no morphological marking of tense, aspect or negation. The distinction between active and passive verbs is marked morphologically, *borong* 'buy (an entire stock)', *nga-borong* 'buy', *di-borong* 'be bought'. There is no person agreement between the verb and either the subject or object, although the verb may be marked for plurality, e.g., *nga-b-ar-orong* 'buy, active, pl.' *di-b-ar-orong* 'be bought, pl.' The infix *-ar-* also appears in plural pronouns and some very common nouns (see above). Some causatives are formed morphologically with the addition of a suffix, e.g., *sare* 'sleep', *nyare-keun* 'send to sleep'; *tenjo* 'see', *nenjo-keun* 'show'.

While there is not much inflectional morphology, Sundanese exhibits a rich pattern of derivational morphology (which is both systematic and productive). Most of the morphology (both inflectional and derivational) is marked through affixation, prefixation, infixation, suffixation, circumfixation and reduplication or a combination of affixation and reduplication (see Robins 1959, for a systematic overview of the morphological constructions of Sundanese). See examples of prefixation, suffixation and infixation above. Circumfixation consists of independently occurring prefixes and suffixes, but with distinct semantics, e.g., *ka-an, dahar* 'eat', *ka-dahar-an* 'food'; *pa-an, sare* 'sleep', *pa-sare-an* 'bed'.

One of the most pervasive prefixes, the active marker, varies systematically, depending on the first sound of the verb root it is prefixed to. It is *ng-* before words beginning with vowels, *nga-* before words beginning with *r, l* and some other consonants. When added to a word beginning with a voiceless stop, it changes the stop to the corresponding nasal, e.g., *t* becomes *n* (see Robins 1953).

inum	ng-inum	'drink, active'
borong	nga-borong	'buy (an entire stock), active'
liwat	nga-liwat	'pass, active'
nyaho	nga-nyaho(an)	'know, active'
pake	make	'use, active'
teunggeul	neunggeul	'beat, active'
kirim	ngirim	'send, active'

In addition to full reduplication marking plurals in nouns (see above), there are a number of other root and syllable reduplication patterns, e.g., *rame* 'friendly', *rame-rame* 'very friendly'; *buah* 'fruit', *buah-buahan* 'various types of fruit'; *kirim* 'send', *ki-kirim* 'what is sent'; *tangkal* 'tree', *ta-tangkal-an* 'plantation'.

There are both endocentric compounds, e.g., *kurung manuk* 'cage, bird = birdcage', as well as exocentric ones, e.g., *indung bapa* 'mother, father = parents'.

Sundanese, like neighboring Javanese, shows a complex system of speech levels. There are two basic levels: 'kasar' low (L) vs. 'lemes' high (H), which can be broken down into finer distinctions (Wessing 1974; Ajatrohaedi 1975). The high language is quite limited in its social use; it is used when speaking with individuals to whom deference should be shown. Written Sundanese is based on the low language. For the most part, the level differences are reflected in the use of completely distinct words; two parallel items exist for most pronouns (see above), terms of address, and many common nouns and verbs, e.g., *anak* 'child L', *putra* 'child H'; *inum* 'drink L', *leuleut* 'drink H'. It is generally agreed that the High Speech level developed through influence from the Javanese court high language, probably starting from the late 17th century. There are about 400 H-level lexical items in Sundanese.

Basic Syntax

Many of the following examples are drawn from Hardjadibrata's (1985) comprehensive discussion of the syntax of Sundanese (information in parentheses refers to his page and example numbers).

Sundanese is basically an SVO language; auxiliary verbs precede the main verb: *Kurin rek indit* (I will go) 'I will go', *Manehna mawa buku* (he, bring, book) 'He brings a book'.

However the passive is very common, resulting in an OV(S) pattern:

Buku teh dibawa ku manehna
book be-brought by he (*teh* is a phrasal marker)
'The book was brought by him'

There is no case marking; as noted above, there is very little inflectional marking in the language.

Sundanese is basically a head-initial language. This can be seen in the structure of the noun phrases: determiners and quantifiers precede nouns; and adjectives, relative clauses, prepositional phrases and possessive adjectives follow nouns. *Loba mahasiswa asing* (many, students, foreign) 'many foreign students', *imah butut manehna* (house, old, his) 'his old house', *rahayat di desa* (people, in, village) 'people of the village'.

In sentence negation, a negative particle, *teu lain* (L), or *sanes* (H), appears before the auxiliary verb: *Kuring teu rek indit* (I not, will, go) 'I will not go'.

There is no overt copula in Sundanese, e.g., *kuring gur* 'I, teacher = I am a teacher'.

In addition to the basic passive (mentioned above), there is an adversive passive, e.g., *kuring ka-hujan-an* (I, affected-by rain) 'I was caught in the rain'.

Contact with Other Languages

There is of course extensive contact with Indonesian, since most speakers of Sundanese are fluent in Indonesian, and the two languages are quite closely related. This results in borrowing from Indonesian. There is also close contact with Javanese—the neighboring language—also closely related.

Historically there was extensive influence from Javanese and Malay, due to the political domination of W. Java (the Sundanese-speaking area) over the centuries, by the Malay-speaking kingdom of Srivijaya (7th–14th centuries) and a succession of neighboring (and encroaching) Javanese empires. Sundanese shows borrowings from a number of languages. The influence of both Javanese and Indonesian continues to this day. Historically there was also influence from Sanskrit and Arabic, due to the Hindu and Muslim political influences, and to a lesser degree from PORTUGUESE and DUTCH.

Many doublets appear in Sundanese, but the borrowed item can often be identified by the lack of a certain systematic sound change. For example, the presence of *e* [ə] indicates a borrowing, e.g. *beuneur* 'full and good (of a rice grain)' vs. *bener* 'true, right', the latter borrowed from Javanese, cf. Javenese *bener* 'true, right' (Nothofer 1975: 39). Borrowings show up throughout the vocabulary, including quite common items. In some cases they tend to be specialized, for example, many of the borrowings from Arabic are either religious or legal terms. Since World War II, extensive borrowing from Indonesian is seen (see Prawiraatmaja *et al.* 1986).

From Javanese: *gedé* 'big', *lemes* 'smooth'
From Malay/Indonesian: *besar* 'big, great', *pidato* 'speech'
From Dutch: *kas* 'chest', *bon* 'receipt'
From Arabic: *haji* 'a person who has made the pilgrimage to Mecca'
From Sanskrit: *nagara* 'country', *angka* 'figure, letter'
From Portuguese: *pelor* 'bullet, ball for cannon or gun', *sapatu* 'shoe'

Common Words

man:	lalaki (L), pameget (H)
woman:	awéwé (L), istri (H)
yes:	enya (L), sumuhun (H)
no:	henteu, teu
water:	cai
sun:	panon poé
good:	alus (L), saé (H)
three:	tilu
bird:	manuk
fish (freshwater):	lauk cai
dog:	anjing
small:	leutik (L), alit (H)
big:	gedé (L), ageung (H)
tree:	tangkal
long:	panjang
sun:	panon po

Example Sentences

(1) Guru nu nampiling Rusdi pindah ka Bandung.
teacher who slap Rusdi move to Bandung
'The teacher who slapped Rusdi moved to Bandung.'

(2) Buku naon nu di-cokot ku manehna?
book what which be-taken by he
'What book did he take?'

(3) Tiasa anjeun sumping ka rorompok abdi enjing?
can you come to house my tomorrow
Can you come to my house tomorrow?

Efforts to Preserve, Protect, and Promote the Language

Very little material written in or about Sundanese was available before the second half of the 19th century. As discussed by Moriyama (1995), the first Sundanese book ever printed appeared in 1850, and the second half of the 19th century saw the publication of numerous works from Dutch, Arabic, Javanese and Malay, as well as some readers of Sundanese stories. The Sundanese language benefited from the creation of the *Balé Pustaka*, founded in 1908, responsible for the publication of numerous books in Sundanese. These included publication of traditional Sundanese fables and stories, a Sundanese language journal, as well as translations from Javanese, Dutch, and other languages. Sundanese literature per se dates from the beginning of publication of these materials and is still continuing today, in novels, newspapers and magazines. A number of congresses for the Sundanese language have been held; the first was in Bandung in 1924.

Preservation of the language is actively being undertaken at both the national and regional levels. The National Language Development Center, PPPB, has been engaged in describing and documenting the regional languages of Indonesia, while at the same time promoting Indonesian as a national language. Descriptions of various aspects of Sundanese grammar, as well as the dialects of and sociolinguistic uses of Sundanese, have been documented by the PPPB (Hardjadibrata 1985 provides a bibliography of many of these works). The *Lembaga Basa jeung Sastra Sunda* ('the Institute for Sundanese Language and Literature', founded in 1952) has sought to preserve and perpetuate the language through its publications, congresses and other activities. Its publications include a Sundanese-Sundanese dictionary, *Kamus Umum Basa Sunda*, now in its fifth printing. The Teacher College in Bandung and the Pajajaran University have departments of Sundanese. The Teacher College is responsible for teacher training and curriculum development for the teaching of Sundanese in the schools. Limited linguistic work continues in Holland, the United States and Australia.

This includes a recently published comprehensive Sundanese-Dutch dictionary (Eringa 1984).

There are weekly newspapers and magazines written in Sundanese and these have quite wide circulation. Sundanese is also used as the medium of instruction through the third grade in W. Java. After the third grade, Sundanese is taught as a subject in school. Data from the 1980 census show a broad age distribution of Sundanese, including a very significant and not diminishing population of young speakers.

Select Bibliography

Ajatrohaedi. 1975. "Bentuk hormat dalam basa Sunda." In *Budaja Djaja*. 4/43: 730–745.

Cohn, A. 1992. "The consequences of dissimilation in Sundanese." In *Phonology* 9: 199–220.

Cribb, R.B. 1992. *Historical Dictionary of Indonesia*. Metuchen, NJ: Scarecrow Press.

de Casparis, J.G. 1975. *Indonesian Palaeography: A History of Writing in Indonesia from the Beginnings to c. A.D. 1500*. Leiden and Köln: E.J. Brill.

Ekadjati, E.S., W. Wibisana, and A.K. Anggawisastra. 1985. *Naskah Sunda Lama Kelompok Babad*. Jakarta: Pusat Pembinaan dan Pengembangan Bahasa, Departemen Pendidikan dan Kebudayaan.

Eringa, F.S. 1984. *Soendaas-Nederlands Woordenboek*. KITLV. Dordrecht, Holland: Foris Publications.

Hardjadibrata, R.R. 1985. *Sundanese: A Syntactic Analysis*. Pacific Linguistics D-65. Canberra: The Australian National University.

Kartini, T., K.M. Saini, and Iyo Mulyono. 1985. *Kedudukan dan Fungsi Bahasa Sunda di Jawa Barat*. Jakarta: Pusat Pembinaan dan Pengembangan Bahasa, Departemen Pendidikan dan Kebudayaan.

Lembaga, Basa and Sastra Sunda. 1985. *Kamus Umum Basa Sunda, citakan kalima*. Bandung, Indonesia: Penerbit Tarate Bandung.

Moriyama, M. 1995. "Language Policy in the Dutch Colony: On Sundanese in the Dutch East Indies." In *Southeast Asia Studies* 33: 1. Kyoto University, the Center for Southeast Asian Studies.

Noorduyn, J. 1962. "Over het eerste gedeelte van de Oud-Soendase Carita Parahyangan." In *Bijdragen tot de Taal-, Land- en Volkenkunde* 118: 374–383.

Nothofer, Bernd. 1975. *The Reconstruction of Proto-Malayo-Javanic*. *VKI* 73. 's-Gravenhage: Martinus Nijhoff.

____. 1980. *Dialektgeographische Untersuchungen in West-Java und im westlichen Zentral-Java*, 2 vols. Wiesbaden: Harrassowitz.

Prawiraatmaja, D., A. Husen, and I.S.K. Sukandi. Yudibrata. 1986. *Perkembangan Bahasa Sunda sesudah Perang Dunia II*. Jakarta: Pusat Pembinaan dan Pengembangan Bahasa, Departemen Pendidikan dan Kebudayaan.

Robins, R.H. 1953. "The Phonology of Nasalized Verb Forms in Sundanese." In *Bulletin of the School of Oriental and African Studies* 15: 138–145.

____. 1957. "Vowel Nasality in Sundanese: A Phonological and Grammatical Study." In *Studies in Linguistics* (special volume of the Philological Society). Oxford: Basil Blackwell, 87–103.

____. 1959. "Nominal and Verbal Derivation in Sundanese." In *Lingua* 8: 337–369.

Uhlenbeck, E.M. 1964. *A Critical Survey of Studies on the Language of Java and Madura*. 's-Gravenhage: Martinus Nijhoff.

Wessing, Robert. 1974. "Language Levels in Sundanese." In *Man* 9: 5–22.

Swahili

Kimani Njogu

Language Name: Swahili. **Alternate and Autonym:** *Kiswahili.*

Location: Spoken mainly in the eastern African countries of Tanzania, Kenya, Uganda, and the Comoros; also spoken in Burundi, eastern Zaire, southern Somalia, and parts of northern Mozambique.

Family: Central Bantu subgroup of the Bantoid group of the Nyima subbranch of the Benue-Zambezi branch of the (Central) Niger-Congo subfamily of the Niger-Kordofanian language family.

Related Languages: Swahili is related to the other members of the Central Bantu subgroup, including SHONA. It is closely related to the Sabaki languages of the East African coast such as the Mijikenda languages, Giriama and Duruma.

Dialects: (1) Northern dialects (ChiMwini [around Brava, in Somalia], Bajuni [in southern Somalia and northern coastal Kenya], and the island dialects of Amu, Siyu, Pate, and Mvita [Mombasa]); (2) Central dialects (Chifundi, Vumba, Mtang'ata, Pemba, Tumbatu, Hadimu and Ngazija); (3) Southern dialects (Unguja, Dar-es-Salaam and Mgao).

Number of Speakers: 80–90 million.

Origin and History

The term "Swahili" is derived from ARABIC *Sawa:ħil* 'coasts'. A popular belief is that the Swahili language arose as a sort of lingua franca between traders from southern Arabia and indigenous Bantu language speakers on the east coast of Africa at the end of the first millennium. However, the scholarly consensus is that "Swahili is clearly an African language in its basic sound system and grammar and is closely related to Bantu languages of Kenya, northeast Tanzania, and the Comoro Islands, with which it shared a common development long prior to the widespread adoption of Arabic vocabulary" (Nurse and Spear).

Before the 9th century, indigenous peoples lived in small farming and fishing settlements along the East African coast. Gradually these settlements spread southward and towns grew up that included permanent structures made of coral blocks. There is speculation that some of the structures may have been mosques that might have served visiting Muslim merchants. Towns such as Muqdisho, Mombasa, Shanga, Malindi, and Kilwa were prosperous trading centers by the 14th century. In the early 16th century the Portuguese visited the East African coast and trading was disrupted.

Orthography and Basic Phonology

Traditionally, Swahili was written in a modified Arabic script and numerous poetic compositions existed in that script before the 17th century. Modern Swahili is written in the Roman alphabet, using LATIN vowel conventions and simplified ENGLISH conventions for consonants.

Although /ch/ and /j/ are charted as stops, they are affricates [č] and [ǰ], as in the English words "church" and "judge" respectively. The combination /ng/ represents the velar nasal [ŋ], as in the English word "song", not a sequence of [n] followed by [g]. The palatal fricative /ny/ does not occur in English. It is similar to the sound in the middle of English "canyon", but the nasal and palatal articulations are simultaneous rather than in sequence.

Table 1: Consonants

	Labial	Dental	Alveo-palatal	Velar	Glottal
Stops Voiceless Voiced	 p b	 t d	 ch j	 k g	
Fricatives Voiceless Voiced	 f v	 s z	 sh		 h
Nasals	m	n	ny	ng	
Resonants		r, l	y	w	

The interdental fricatives /th/ [θ] and /dh/ [ð] and the voiced velar fricative /gh/ [ɣ] occur exclusively in words borrowed from Arabic.

Table 2: Vowels

	Front	Central	Back
High	i		u
Mid	e [ɛ]		o [ɔ]
Low		a	

The midvowels /e/ and /o/ are phonetically [ɛ] and [ɔ].

Syllables in Swahili consist of a vowel nucleus, optionally preceded by a single consonant. The syllable peak may be occupied by a vowel or by a nasal consonant. Consonant clusters in loanwords are broken by a process of vowel epenthesis, for example, *gesi* 'gas'. Syllabic nasals appear in simplex forms as in *ta.m.ko* 'utterance' or as prefixes for Noun Classes 1 as in *m.to.to* 'child' and 3 *m.pi.ra* 'ball'. Finally, the third-person singular object marker may also be realized as a syllabic nasal as in *wa.li.m.pe.nda* 'they liked him/her'; when it precedes a vowel, it is *mu*/*mw* instead, as in *wa.ta.mw.a.mbi.a* 'they will tell him/her'.

With the exception of a few loanwords, Swahili words are stressed on the penultimate syllable.

Basic Morphology

Like other Bantu languages, Swahili is a highly agglutinative language. Nouns occur in 16 classes, some of which are intrinsically singular and some of which are intrinsically plural. Each class has its own characteristic prefixes and its own pattern of noun- and verb-phrase agreement.

wa-toto	wa-le	wa-tatu	wa-dogo
CL2-child	CL2-DEMONSTRATIVE	CL2-three	CL2-small

'those three little children'

vi-tabu	vi-le	vi-tatu	vi-dogo
CL8-book	CL8-DEMONSTRATIVE	CL8-three	CL8-small

'those three small books'

Some nouns, especially in Classes 5, 9, and 10, do not have the characteristic prefix of the class: *ji-na* 'name' (Class 5) has the prefix *ji-*, while *neno* 'word' does not.

Swahili is not a case language; the difference between nominative and accusative is indicated only by the syntactic position of the nouns. The applicative marker *-i-* suffixed to a verb indicates that the second of two following objects is an indirect object (see Example Sentence 1). The locative *-ni* is suffixed to the noun it marks: *mji-ni* 'in town', *kazi-ni* 'at work'.

Verbs agree with their subjects in noun class and, if it is relevant, person. The subject-agreement prefix is usually the first element in the verb, although it may be preceded by a negative prefix. To the right of the subject marker (SM), but before the verb stem, there is a tense/aspect marker, an optional relative marker, and an optional object marker (OM).

a-li-ni-fund-ish-a
SM.3SG-PAST-OM:1SG-teach-CAUSATIVE-INDICATIVE
'S/he taught me.'

Basic Syntax

Swahili is an SVO language. Auxiliaries precede main verbs and all modifiers (adjectives, numerals, demonstratives, and relative clauses) that follow the noun that they modify.

Sentences are negated by prefixing *ha-* or *si-* to the verb complex.

One way of forming questions is to use a focus construction along with the interrogative word.

ni	nani	a-li-ye-lal-a
FOCUS	who	SM.3SG-PAST-INTERROGATIVE-sleep-INDICATIVE

'Who is it who slept?'

Contact with Other Languages

Swahili's long contact with Arabic has meant that many religious (Islamic), cultural, and literary terms are borrowed from Arabic. However, "most basic farming vocabulary derives from proto-Bantu, pointing to an unbroken tradition of more than 3,000 years" (Nurse and Spear). Influence from Southern Cushitic languages is more obvious in the field of cattle husbandry. Swahili has greatly influenced coastal languages such as Mijikenda and Pokomo. More recently, the language has been borrowing scientific and technological terms from English.

From English: *motokaa* 'motorcar'
From PORTUGUESE: *gereza* 'prison' (< 'church')
From Arabic: *shughuli* 'business'; *alhamisi* 'Thursday'; *kitabu* 'book'

Common Words

man:	mwanamme	long:	ndefu
woman:	mwanamke	small:	ndogo
water:	maji	yes:	ndio
sun:	jua	no:	hapana
three:	tatu	good:	nzuri
fish:	samaki	bird:	ndege/nyuni
big:	kubwa	dog:	mbwa
tree:	mti		

Example Sentences

(1) Juma a-li-mw-andik-i-a
Juma SM.3SG-PAST-OM.CL9-write- APPLICATIVE-INDICATIVE

Asha barua.
Asha CL9.letter
'Juma wrote a letter to Asha.'

(2) M-walimu a-na-wa-fund-ish-a
CL1-teacher SM.3SG-PRESENT-OM.CL2-teach-CAUSATIVE-INDICATIVE

wa-toto shule-ni.
CL2-child school-LOCATIVE
'The teacher is teaching the children at school.'

(3) M-toto a-me-lal-a
CL1-child SM.3SG-PERFECT-sleep-INDICATIVE

ki-tanda-ni ch-angu.
CL7-bed-LOCATIVE CL7-1SG.POSSESSIVE
'The child has slept on my bed.'

Efforts to Preserve, Protect, and Promote the Language

Swahili is the most widely spoken Bantu language in Africa. It is the national and official language of Tanzania, the national language of Kenya, and one of the national languages of Zaire. Although most speakers of Swahili currently speak it as a second language, it is spoken as a first language on the East African coast, and first-language speakers of Swahili have been emerging in East African urban centers, where it is used as a lingua franca for commercial and interethnic communication.

Swahili is a compulsory language in national examinations at the primary and high school levels in Kenya, is used in the National Assemblies of Kenya and Tanzania, and in the law courts. Numerous daily newspapers are published in the language.

Monolingual and bilingual dictionaries exist and more are being developed. The Fort Jesus Museum in Mombasa and the Lamu Museum in Lamu are contributing to the preservation of Swahili culture. The Institutes of Swahili Research at the University of Dar es Salaam and in Zanzibar are involved in researching and developing the language. The journals *Swahili* and *Mulika* are vital in the promotion of Swahili.

Most universities in Kenya and Tanzania have departments of Kiswahili. The Kenya Kiswahili Committee (CHAKITA), the Institute of Kiswahili Research at the University of Dar-es-Salaam, and the Tanzania Kiswahili Council (BAKITA) are involved in modernizing the language through the development of technical vocabulary.

Select Bibliography

Allen, James de Vere. 1993. *Swahili Origins: Swahili Culture and the Shungwaya Phenomenon*. London: James Curry.

Heinebusch, T.J. 1979. "Swahili." In T. Shopen, ed., *Languages and Their Status*. Cambridge, MA: Winthrop.

Johnson, F. 1939. *A Standard English-Swahili/Swahili-English Dictionary*. Oxford: Oxford University Press.

Nurse, Derek, and Thomas Spear. 1985. *The Swahili: Reconstructing the History and Language of an African Society 800–1500*. Philadelphia: University of Pennsylvania Press.

Polomé, Edgar, E.C. 1967. *Swahili Language Handbook*. Washington, DC: Center for Applied Linguistics.

SWEDISH

Kersti Börjars

Language Name: Swedish. **Autonym:** *svenska*.

Location: Sweden and parts of Finland.

Family: Swedish is a member of the North Germanic subgroup of Germanic, in the Indo-European language family.

Related Languages: The North Germanic languages: NORWEGIAN, DANISH, Icelandic, and Faroese. They are often referred to as the Scandinavian languages, even though the geographic entity Scandinavia is a matter of dispute. Swedish, Norwegian, and Danish have a high level of mutual intelligibility.

Dialects: Most geographical regions of Sweden have their own dialects. Two of these dialects are very striking: that spoken in Finland (*Finlandssvenska*) lacks the tone of Standard Swedish (see under phonology); and *Älvdalsmål*, a dialect spoken in a small part of the county Dalarna (Dalecarlia, just below the middle of Sweden), is the most similar to older versions of Swedish. For instance, it has retained more morphological categories from older stages of the language.

Number of Speakers: 8–9 million in Sweden and about 250,000–300,000 native speakers in Finland.

Origin and History

Written fragments of the ancestor language Proto-Scandinavian exist in the form of short inscriptions from as far back as 200 A.D. Swedish as a language independent from the other East Scandinavian languages (Danish and Norwegian) is considered to have begun with the development of nation states toward the end of the Viking era (about the 9th to 11th centuries). Initially it was written with the Runic alphabet, but Christian missionaries brought the idea of writing on parchment and from this developed the new alphabet. The oldest book in Swedish is a legal code (*Västgötalagen*) from about 1220. A simplification of the inflectional system took place in the Middle Ages and 1526 is usually taken as the beginning of Modern Swedish. In this year, the first copies of a translation of the New Testament were circulated and it was also the year Sweden won its independence from Danish rule. A translated version of the whole Bible was published in 1541 (*Gustav Vasas Bibel*) and had considerable influence on the language.

Orthography and Basic Phonology

Swedish uses the LATIN alphabet. The Swedish alphabet has 28 letters, the same as the ENGLISH alphabet except that Swedish lacks "w" (it occurs only in names and a handful of loanwords and is treated as a variant of "v"). Swedish has the additional three letters *å, ä,* and *ö*. The Swedish spelling system is fairly regular; long consonants are usually spelled with two letters, a long vowel is one that is followed by only one consonant letter in the same syllable. The most notorious sounds are /ʃ/, which can be spelled in a number of ways: *sk-, sj-, stj-, skj-, ch-,* and *-sch-;* and /j/, which can be spelled as *j, gj-, hj-, dj-,* and *lj-*.

Swedish consonants may be short (plain) or long (geminate). /r/ is pronounced as a uvular fricative [R] in many southern dialects of Swedish. /ʃ/ is alveo-palatal in many northern dialects. The voiceless stops /p t k/ are normally aspirated [pʰ tʰ kʰ]. The velar stops /k g/ are palatalized to [ç] and [j] before front vowels. Compare *kaka* [ka:ka] 'cookie' with *känga* [çɛŋa] 'boot'.

Table 1: Consonants

	Labial	Dental	Alveo-Palatal	Palatal	Velar	Glottal
Stops	p b	t d			k g	
Fricatives	f v	s		ç	ʃ	h
Resonants		l	r	j		
Nasals	m	n			ŋ	

When the dentals /t d s n l/ are immediately preceded by /r/ the cluster will be realized as retroflex [ʈ ɖ ʂ ɳ ɭ]; for example, *bord* [bu:ɖ] 'table'.

Table 2: Vowels

	Front		Central	Back
	Rounded	Unrounded		
High	y, ʉ	i		u
Mid-High	ø	e		
Mid-Low		ɛ		ɔ
Low			a	

Swedish vowels can occur either long or short. The phonological length description may be reflected in differences in vowel quality as well as in duration. For example, /a:/ is phonetically long back [ɑ:], while /a/ is central [a]; and /e:/ is [e:], while /e/ is [e] or [ə].

Standard Swedish does not have phonemic diphthongs, but some speakers have a slight diphthongization of certain long vowels, so that /i:/ might be /i:/ or /ij/.

Swedish has a number of front-rounded vowels. The high front-rounded vowels /ʉ/ and /y/ are distinguished by the exact position of the lips. The lips are rounded and protruded ("out-rounded") for /y/ and rounded and compressed ("inrounded") for /ʉ/.

Swedish syllable structure is interesting in that only stressed syllables may contain long segments. A stressed syllable must contain either a long vowel or a long consonant, but not both. Thus *vit* [vi:t] 'white' and *vitt* [vit:] 'white (neuter)' occur, but not [vi:t:].

Swedish makes a distinction that is often referred to as "tonal". The pattern that can be found on words as well as on intonational units occurring in connected speech is usually called Accent I (*akut accent*). This would be the pattern most similar to English stress. Then there is Accent II (*grav accent*), usually marked with a preceding ˣ, which is to be found only on certain multisyllabic words. The difference is primarily one of pitch, but there is an effect of some secondary stress on the syllable imediately following the syllable with the main stress. The difference in tone can give rise to minimal pairs such as *'anden* 'the duck' (Accent I) vs. *ˣanden* 'the spirit' (Accent II).

Basic Morphology

Swedish nouns belong to one of two genders, neuter or nonneuter/common (sometimes referred to as "t-gender" and "n-gender"). The noun itself can be marked for number (singular vs. plural) and definiteness. Definiteness is always marked by an explicit ending, but pluralization may not be, depending on declensional class, of which there are five. The definite ending on a noun serves the same function as a definite article if there is no modifier present.

		Indefinite	Definite	Gloss
Singular:	Nonneuter	stol	stolen	'chair'
	Neuter	bord	bordet	'table'
Plural:	Nonneuter	stolar	stolarna	
	Neuter	bord	borden	

Most determiners agree in number and gender with their head noun, although the gender distinction is neutralized in the plural: *den stolen* 'that chair (nonneuter)', *det bordet* 'that table (neuter)', *de stolarna* 'those chairs', *de borden* 'those tables'. Adjectives may be marked for number, gender, and definiteness:

ett gul-t bord
a/NEUT/SG yellow-NEUT/SG table/NEUT/SG 'a yellow table'

en gul stol
a/NON.NEUT/SG yellow/NON.NEUT/SG chair/NON.NEUT/SG
'a yellow chair'

The gender distinction for adjectives is neutralized in definite noun phrases and in plural noun phrases.

det gul-a bord-et
the/NEUT yellow-DEF table-NEUT/DEF 'the yellow table'

den gul-a stol-en
the/NON.NEUT yellow-DEF chair-NON.NEUT/DEF
'the yellow chair'

några gul-a bord
some yellow-PL table/PL 'some yellow tables'

några gul-a stolar-na
some yellow-PL chair-PL 'some yellow chairs'

Swedish has no case marking on nouns other than personal pronouns. Personal pronouns have two forms, the subject form and the object form (e.g., *han* 'he', *honom* 'him'; *hon* 'she', *henne* 'her'). In the spoken language, the object form *dem* (pronounced /dɔm:/) of the third-person plural pronoun is also used in subject position in place of the subject form *de*.

Apart from reflexive pronouns, Swedish also has a reflexive determiner. In a noun phrase with a possessive determiner, that determiner will have a reflexive form when the noun phrase occurs in a position where a pronoun would occur in its reflexive forms.

Han måla-de sitt hus.
he paint-PAST his/REFL house
'He painted his (own) house.'

Han måla-de han-s hus.
he paint-PAST his house
'He painted his (=someone else's) house.'

Swedish infinitives usually end in *-a*, and present tense forms end in *-r*. Verbs do not agree with their subjects at all, not even for a verb like *vara* 'to be', which has the present tense form *är* regardless of subject (*jag är* 'I am', *han är* 'he is', etc.).

Swedish has only two simple tenses, present and past; the latter is regularly marked by *-te* or *-de*, but there are irregular verbs. The perfect is formed with the verb *ha* 'to have' and the supine, ending in *-t*.

The passive can be formed in either of two ways: morphologically, by the addition of *-s*, or, less commonly, with the verb *bli* 'become' and a passive participle (ending in *-d*).

Some representative forms of the verbs *köra* 'to drive' and *skriva* 'to write' occur below:

	köra 'drive'	skriva 'write'
Present	kör	skriver
Past	körde	skrev
Perfect	har kört	har skrivit
Passive	körs	skrivs
	blir körd	blir skriven

The present participle (ending in *-ande* or *-ende*) and past participle (ending in *-d*, *-t*, or *-en* and inflected like adjectives) have mainly adjectival functions.

den kör-d-a sträck-an
the/NON.NEUT driv-en-DEF distance-NON.NEUT/DEF
'the driven distance'

en skriv-en text
a/NON.NEUT written-NON.NEUT text/NON.NEUT
'a written text'

Basic Syntax

Along with most of the modern Germanic languages, Swedish can be described as a verb-second language. The verb occurs in second position in the sentence and can be preceded by any of the major constituents. All orders receive a fairly neutral interpretation.

Oscar gav henne en boll igår
Oscar give/PAST her a ball yesterday
'Oscar gave her a ball yesterday.'

Henne gav Oscar en boll igår.
En boll gav Oscar henne igår.
Igår gav Oscar henne en boll.

Swedish nominal modifiers precede the nouns they modify, while prepositional phrases follow: *den gröna stol-en i kök-et* (the green chair-DEF in kitchen-DEF) 'the green chair in the kitchen'.

Swedish has a clausal negation marker *inte* and a phrasal negation marker *ingen* (which inflects like an adjective).

Oscar tvättar inte sin bil.
Oscar wash/PRES NEG his car 'Oscar isn't washing his car.'

Oscar åt ingen kaka
Oscar eat/PAST NEG cookie 'Oscar didn't eat a cookie.'

Frequently, both options will be available.

Oscar såg inte någon kaka
Oscar saw/PAST NEG some cookie

Oscar såg ingen kaka
Oscar saw/PAST NEG cookie 'Oscar didn't see a cookie.'

The position of the clausal negative marker *inte* differs in main and subordinate clauses. In main clauses, as in the examples above, *inte* follows the verb; in subordinate clauses, *inte* precedes the verb:

Karl sa att Oscar inte gav henne en boll igår
Karl said that Oscar NEG gave her a ball yesterday
'Karl said that Oscar didn't give her a ball yesterday.'

Contact with Other Languages

With the introduction of Christianity came many Latin loanwords, e.g., *präst* 'priest' from Latin *presbyter* and *skriva* from Latin *scribere*. Since that time, Latin and GREEK words have often been borrowed, in particular for science and technology. In more recent times these loans have often come via English.

In the Middle Ages, Low German was the main source of loanwords frequently related to the town organization and crafts. GERMAN borrowings continued, with High German supplying, for instance, language related to the Reformation.

The influence from FRENCH started in the 17th century, but was at its strongest in the 18th century. Many loanwords pertained to concepts particularly associated with the aristocratic lifestyle, e.g., words for architecture and clothing. The pronunciation and spelling of these words have been adapted to the Swedish system.

Many English loanwords entered the language in the 19th century. In the 20th, English was the main source of borrowings, many of them related to popular culture.

From Low German: *borgmästare* 'mayor', *slaktare* 'butcher'
From French: *paraply* 'umbrella', *maräng* 'meringue'
From English: *rostbiff* 'roast beef; beef', *pop(musik), hamburgare, bestseller*

Common Words

man:	man	long:	lång
woman:	kvinna	small:	liten
water:	vatten	yes:	ja
sun:	sol	no:	nej
three:	tre	good:	bra
fish:	fisk	bird:	fågel
big:	stor	dog:	hund
tree:	träd		

Example Sentences

(1) Oscar-s mamma vill gärna ge sin son
Oscar-POSS mother want/PRES dearly give her.REFL son

ett ny-tt hus.
a/NEUT new-NEUT house
'Oscar's mother would very much like to give her son a new house.'

(2) Han trod-de att hon inte ha-de
he/SUBJ believe-PAST that she/SUBJ NEG have-PAST

sett den ny-a bil-en.
see/SUPINE the/NON.NEUT new-DEF car-NON.NEUT/DEF
'He thought that she hadn't seen the new car.'

(3) Efter middag-en gav pojk-en present-en
after dinner-DEF give/PAST boy-DEF present-DEF

till hans mamma.
to his mother
'After dinner, the boy gave the present to his (not the boy's) mother.'

Efforts to Preserve, Protect, and Promote the Language

The Swedish Academy was formed in 1786. It has long produced a dictionary of Swedish and has recently produced a major Swedish grammar. There was a spelling reform in 1906.

Select Bibliography

Holmes, Philip and Ian Hinchliffe. 1994. *Swedish—A Comprehensive Grammar*. London: Routledge.

Svenska akademien. 1898-1993. *Ordbok över svenska språket*. Lund: C.W.K. Gleerup.

Thorell, Olof. 1973. *Svensk grammatik*. Stockholm: Esselte Studium.

TAGALOG

Videa P. De Guzman

Language Name: Tagalog. **Alternates:** *Pilipino* or *Filipino*. **Autonym:** *Tagálog*.

Location: Republic of the Philippines. Tagalog is native to only the southern part of the island of Luzon and to the coastal areas of the islands of Marinduque, Occidental Mindoro, Oriental Mindoro, Masbate, and Palawan, but it has spread (as a second language) to most of the Philippine archipelago.

Family: Central Philippine group in the Philippine subgroup of the Western Malayo-Polynesian branch of the Malayo-Polynesian subfamily of the Austronesian language family.

Related Languages: BIKOL languages in the southeastern part of Luzon, and the North Bisayan languages.

Dialects: Regional: one in Manila (the standard) and its suburbs (Metro-Manila), Pasay City, Quezon City, and Caloocan City; and others in the provinces of Rizal, Bulacan, Bataan, Batangas, Laguna, Cavite, parts of Nueva Ecija, Quezon, Marinduque, Occidental Mindoro, Oriental Mindoro, Masbate, and Palawan. The dialects in the provinces named above differ primarily in pronunciation and intonation patterns, vocabulary items, and a few patterns of inflecting verbs. The dialect of educated speakers in Manila and suburbs is considered the standard. It contains a considerable number of SPANISH and ENGLISH loanwords; outside Manila, the language retains more of its native vocabulary and does not succumb as readily to English borrowings.

Number of Speakers: 10 million.

Origin and History

Tagalog is the dominant language of the Philippines out of a total of about 100 major and minor languages spoken there. Of the 8 major Philippine languages (Bikol, HILIGAYNON, ILOCANO, KAPAMPANGAN, PANGASINAN, CEBUANO, Tagalog, WARAY WARAY), Tagalog has the oldest and most extensive written literature, dating from the 16th century.

Very little is known and recorded about Tagalog and the other Philippine languages before the conquest of the islands by the Spaniards in the 16th century. Significant periods in the nation's political history by which the development of the languages may be defined are as follows.

Pre-Spanish (Before 1521). When the Spaniards arrived on Philippine soil in 1521, they discovered that the natives had had trade relations with Chinese, Indian, and Arabic seafarers. The prehistoric contact of the Philippines with the Chinese is said to go as far back as 3 B.C., while the earliest commercial intercourse occurred around A.D. 890 and continued until about the middle of the 12th century through Arab traders. By about the 13th century, the Chinese took over the trade almost completely from Arab merchants. Chinese merchants later settled at the chief ports and centers of native culture. Attesting to this contact is the existence of Chinese loanwords in Tagalog. Contact with traders from India is claimed to have occurred around 2 or 3 B.C., and with the Japanese as early as the 15th century.

Prior to the Spanish colonization of the Philippines, Tagalog and most of the other major languages such as Ilocano, Pangasinan, Kapampangan, and Cebuano, possessed a writing system that was a syllabary, purportedly of Indian origin. Others trace its early development from the West JAVANESE script. It is said to have been introduced between the 12th and 14th centuries. The Tagalog syllabary was called *Alibata*. It consisted of 17 symbols, of which 3 represented vowels and the rest represented consonants.

Tagalog Syllabary

pa	ᜉ	ta	ᜆ	ka	ᜃ
ba	ᜊ	da/ra	ᜇ	ga	ᜄ
sa	ᜐ	ha	ᜑ		
la	ᜎ	wa	ᜏ	ya	ᜌ
ma	ᜋ	na	ᜈ	ng	ᜅ
ʔa	ᜀ	ga	ᜄ	-g	ᜄ᜔
		ʔe, ʔi	ᜁ	ge/gi	ᜄᜒ
		ʔo, ʔu	ᜂ	go/gu	ᜄᜓ

Spanish Conquest (1521–1898). The Spanish missionaries learned the language of the natives so that they could preach the Christian gospel, and the first materials they translated into Tagalog were the *Doctrina Cristiana*, a catechism, a confessional, a grammar, and a dictionary. In the 17th century private schools were established by the missionaries, and Spanish was taught to Filipino students of the wealthy class. As literacy spread among the population, especially with the inception of parochial schools, writing in Tagalog progressively increased. Literary pieces, historical accounts, and other kinds of writings were recorded in Spanish and in Tagalog. This persisted until the end of the Spanish era. After three and a half

Table 1: Consonants

	Labial	Dental	Alveolar	Palatal	Velar	Glottal
Stops	p b	t d			k g	ʔ
Fricatives			s			h
Nasal	m	n			ŋ	
Lateral			l			
Tap/Trill			r			
Glides				y	w	

centuries of contact with Spanish, Tagalog contains an enormous number of loanwords that relate to every aspect of life.

American Conquest (1898–1946). By the end of the 19th century, Army officers of the American occupation (following the Spanish-American War) took up linguistic studies of the major languages of the Philippines, especially Tagalog. However, only a few works resulted from these efforts. Notable among them was MacKinley's handbook and grammar of Tagalog, written in 1905. The picture of the development of Tagalog became brighter when the military government was replaced by a civil government soon after 1901. This period marked the beginning of some 40 years of productive work on both descriptive and historical linguistics of Philippine languages. Foremost among the descriptive works on Tagalog were those writen by Frank Blake (1925) and Leonard Bloomfield (1917).

As for the selection of a language of instruction in the schools, the American government decided that it would be most efficient to continue with the use of English, which the army had been using. Thus, most scientific writings on the Tagalog language were written in English. Tagalog itself was used for newspaper and local weekly magazines, and to some extent, poetry and literary works. Later, Tagalog also became the language of radio, movies, and stage shows.

Period of Independence (1946–present). In 1937 when Pilipino was proclaimed the country's national language, the Institute of National Language was established and Tagalog experts produced materials for classroom instruction, including a grammar, a dictionary, and many circulars on relevant topics, all written in Tagalog/Pilipino. This work picked up momentum after the war. In order to assist in preparing teachers to meet the new mandate of teaching Pilipino, the universities began offering courses that led to Pilipino as a major field in the education degree program. The Philippine Branch of the Summer Institute of Linguistics, which was established in 1953, influenced the greater study of Tagalog.

Orthography and Basic Phonology

Tagalog is written in an alphabet based on that of LATIN, called *abakada*. Its inventory is as follows: *a, b, k, d, e, g, h, i, l, m, n, ng, o, p, r, s, t, u, w, y*. One additional consonant sound that is not indicated in the standard orthography is the glottal stop, /ʔ/. As with all other consonants, the glottal stop may occur in syllable initial or final position. In addition to the letters in the *abakada*, certain letters from the Spanish alphabet have been assimilated and are commonly used with loanwords, but especially with names of persons or places. In many cases, even the Spanish spelling system persists. Thus, we find the letters *c, f, j, ch, q, v, z* in orthographic practice as in *Corazon, Josefina, Conchita, Joaquin, Quirino, Velasquez, etc*. The same letters spill over English borrowings as in "Alex", "Jake", "jazz", "Audrey", "Mercy", "Phil-Am Life", "Quezon Bridge", "Roxas" Boulevard, etc. The corresponding sounds given to these symbols, however, are usually their Tagalog counterparts. That is, *z* in *Corazon* is pronounced the same as *s*.

The consonant *h* is not written when it occurs word finally; the sound itself is barely audible. However, the *h* "resurfaces" when a suffix is added: *bili* 'buy', *bilh-in* 'to buy something'. The velar nasal /ŋ/, written *ng*, is pronounced as in English in the words *sanga* 'branch' and *talong* 'eggplant'. Unlike in English, this sound also occurs in word-initial position, as in *ngipin* 'tooth'. *Ng* assimilates to the place of articulation of a following *p, b, t, d, s, l, r*: *pa<u>ng</u>+paligo?* > *pa<u>m</u>paligo?* 'something for bathing'; *ma<u>ng</u>+reyd* > *ma<u>n</u>reyd* 'to raid'.

<u>Vowels</u>

	Front	Central	Back
High	i		u
Mid	e		o
Low		a	

In native Tagalog words, the vowels *e* and *o* are variants of *i* and *u*, especially in final syllables. For example, *sakit* 'illness' has the variant *saket*. Because of the large number of loanwords from Spanish and English, Tagalog also has minimal pairs involving these vowels: *misa* 'mass', *mesa* 'table'; *uso* 'fad, currently used', *oso* 'bear'

Tagalog also has four phonemic diphthongs: *ay, aw, iw, uy*. *Ay* has the variant *ey*, and *uy* has the variant *oy*.

Tagalog syllables may be either stressed or unstressed. Stressed vowels are longer and higher pitched than unstressed vowels. Typically, the penultimate syllable in a word is stressed, but sometimes the final syllable is stressed; thus there are pairs of words distinguished only by stress:

<u>Penultimate</u>	<u>Final</u>
áso 'dog'	*asó* 'smoke'
bálat 'birthmark'	*balát* 'skin, peeling'
búhay 'life'	*buháy* 'alive'

Basic Morphology

Unlike nouns in other languages, Tagalog nouns are not inflected. Personal and demonstrative pronouns, however, are inflected for case (absolutive, ergative/genitive, and oblique). Personal pronouns are further distinguished in terms of person (first, second, and third) and number (singular and plural). There is also a distinction between inclusive and exclusive first person plural pronouns: *tayo* means 'we' (including the person spoken to), while *kami* means 'we' (excluding the addressee). Even though Tagalog nouns are not inflected, they are preceded by case particles depending on their function in the sentence. For common nouns, the particles are: *ang* (absolutive), *ng* (ergative/genitive), and *sa* (oblique); for personal names, the particles are *si/sina* (absolutive), *ni/nina* (ergative/genitive), and *kay/kina* (oblique).

Verbs generally exhibit inflectional features. The standard analysis of Tagalog considers voice and aspect as the characteristic features of Tagalog verbs. Voice is expressed by an affix that indicates which of the co-occurring nominals is selected to function as the absolutive, previously identified in the literature as the grammatical "subject", "focus", or "topic". For example, the root *hiram* 'borrow', which, conceptually, carries the meaning of an agent who does the borrowing, an object to be borrowed, and the person or place the object is to be borrowed from, has the following voice-inflected forms:

hiram-<u>in</u> objective voice (OV)
h-<u>um</u>-iram agentive voice (AV)
hiram-<u>an</u> dative/locative voice (DL/LV)

This type of verb may also freely take either an instrumental nominal and/or a benefactive nominal to indicate an instrument used for borrowing something and someone for whom the borrowing is done. Each of these nominals may likewise be chosen to function as the absolutive, in which case the verb will take the following forms:

<u>i</u>-hiram benefactive voice (BV)
<u>i</u>-pang-hiram instrumental voice (IV)

The above voice forms are in their infinitival forms. Each in turn inflects for three aspectual forms: (1) completed, (2) incompleted, and (3) contemplated. As their meanings suggest, they are analogous to perfective, imperfective or durative, and irrealis, respectively. When the voice and aspect systems are combined, there are 15 forms in the paradigm of a typical three-argument verb. These verbs do not have affixes indicating the person, number, or gender of their subjects (here equated with semantic agents, actors or experiencers). However, the voice affixes select a noun phrase bearing a specific semantic relation to the verb to be marked "absolutive".

Tagalog has several systematic ways of deriving verbs. Corresponding to the verb *bigay* 'give' are the causative *<u>pa</u>bigay* 'cause someone to give something to someone else' and the abilitative/involuntary/accidental form *<u>ma</u>bigay* 'be able to give something to someone'.

Tagalog is characteristically an agglutinating language. From a simple root, a word may expand to a complex structure by the addition of one or more affixes. Roots may be made up of one, two, or three syllables; four-syllable roots are less common than two-syllable ones. There are many disyllabic words that show reduplication of the same syllable. Words in Tagalog may then be either simple roots or complex words.

Besides affixation, the other morphological processes employed by Tagalog in constructing words are reduplication, stress shift, and compounding, or a combination of these. Reduplication may involve part of the stem—one or sometimes two syllables—or the full stem. The former is called "partial" reduplication and the latter, "full". Full reduplication corresponds to different meanings, e.g., intensive, accretion, diminution, based on the category of the stem involved. For example:

bahay 'house' > *bahay-bahay* 'every house; house after house'
butas 'pierced; having a hole' > *butas-butas* 'perforated, tattered'
payat 'thin' > *payat-payat* 'a little/somewhat thin'
ma-ganda 'beautiful' > *maganda-ganda* 'somewhat beautiful'
oto 'car' > *oto-otohan* 'toy car'
linis-in 'to clean' > *linis-linis-in* 'to clean something even slightly, not thoroughly'

A stress shift within the same word can produce a different word under another category. For example, adjectives may be derived from nouns in this manner:

búhay 'life' vs. *buháy* 'alive'
hílo 'nausea' vs. *hiló* 'nauseated'

Compound words are usually formed by combining two stems from the classes of nouns, verbs, and adjectives. Each compound stem according to its new category may in turn accept certain affixes to form other words. For example, the first compound below is created from two nouns, while the second is formed from a verb and a noun: *baboy-damo* (pig-grass) 'wild pig'; *kapos-palad* (short.of-palm/fate) 'poor, unfortunate'.

Basic Syntax

Tagalog is typologically classified as a VSO language, with "subject" referring to the semantic agent or doer of the action and "object" to the patient directly affected by the action. This is the preferred ordering of constituents although there is greater freedom in interchanging the positions of the postverbal nominals. The order becomes stringent when pronouns instead of full noun phrases are involved. The pronouns are placed right after the verb similar to adverbial particles; one-syllable pronouns come before two-syllable ones if they co-occur.

The grammatical subject of a sentence is generally indicated by the absolutive case. Tagalog is here considered as having an ergative structure. Thus, the noun phrase marked as the subject typically corresponds to the object in the English translation. To avoid the confusion pertaining to the identification of the so-called grammatical subject, we will adopt the alignment of the semantic agent/actor/experiencer with the grammatical term "object". It will be observed that Tagalog tends to express transitive clauses with verb forms that mark the object nominal "absolutive" and the agent "ergative". Both absolutive and ergative phrases serve as pivots in various syntactic operations. Thus, Tagalog has been more recently described as exhibiting some characteristics of ergative type languages.

tutugtug-in ng bata? ang paborito ko-ng piyesa
will play-OV ERG child ABS favorite my-LINKER piece
'The child will play my favorite music piece.'

matalino si Amanda
intelligent ABS Amanda
'Amanda is intelligent.'

Yes/no questions are formed by inserting the particle *ba* after the first major constituent and rendered with a rising intonation.

tutugtug-in ba ng bata? ang paborito ko-ng
will play-OV Q ERG child ABS favorite my-LINKER

piyesa?
piece
'Will the child play my favorite musical piece?'

Comparing the ABS phrase in the transitive clause and the ABS phrase in the intransitive clause that follows, they are marked differently from the agent (marked ERG or non-ABS) in the transitive.

In a Tagalog clause, the nominal that is generally required to co-occur with a predicate is marked "absolutive", indicated by the particle *ang* or *si/sina* before a noun or by the absolutive case form of a pronoun. In any given clause, the voice affix on the verb indicates which noun phrase takes the absolutive marker.

As noted above, the grammatical subject of a Tagalog sentence is signaled by the occurrence of the appropriate absolutive particle *ang* or *si/sina* before a noun or of the absolutive case form of a pronoun. In any particular sentence, which noun phrase functions as the grammatical subject is usually indicated by the voice of the main verb.

hihiram-in ng kaibigan ko ang libro sa
will borrow-OV ERG friend my ABS book OBL

aklatan ng ID niya bukas para sa akin
library OBL ID her tomorrow for OBL me
'My friend will borrow the book from the library for me with her ID tomorrow.'

In this sentence with a verb in the objective voice (OV), the most common of the Tagalog voices, the absolutive nominal *ang libro* 'the book' fills the semantic role of patient or undergoer of the action. In contrast, in the agentive voice (AV), the absolutive nominal is the agent of the action, *ang kaibigan ko* 'my friend':

hihiram ang kaibigan ko ng libro sa
will.borrow.AV ABS friend my ERG book OBL

aklatan ng ID niya bukas para sa akin
library OBL ID her tomorrow for OBL me

In the locative voice (LV), the absolutive nominal is the location of the action, *ang aklatan* 'the library'.

hihiram-an ng kaibigan ko ng libro ang aklatan
will-borrow-LV ERG friend my OBL book ABS library

ng ID niya bukas para sa akin
OBL ID her tomorrow for OBL me

In the benefactive voice (BV), the absolutive nominal is the person on whose behalf the action takes place, in this case, *ako* 'me', the absolutive equivalent of the oblique *sa akin*.

i-hihiram ako ng kaibigan ko ng libro
will borrow-BV me-ABS ERG friend my OBL book

sa aklatan ng ID niya bukas
OBL library OBL ID her tomorrow

Finally, in the instrumental voice (IV), the absolutive nominal is the instrument or means by which the action takes place, *ang ID niya* 'her ID'.

i-panghihiram ng kaibigan ko ng libro sa
will borrow-IV ERG friend my OBL book OBL

aklatan ang ID niya bukas para sa akin
library ABS ID her tomorrow for OBL me

In addition to the voice constructions described above, Tagalog has a variety of constructions in which a particular noun phrase is focused on (see Example Sentence 1). In addition, there are sentence types without an expressed absolutive phrase. Some of these are illustrated in Example Sentences 2 and 3.

Negation is expressed by using appropriate negative particles before the predicate. In ordinary verbal and nonverbal constructions, the particle *hindi?* 'not' is used. In commands, the particle is *huwag* 'don't'.

hindi? ba amerikano ang guro mo
NEG Q American ABS teacher your
'Isn't your teacher an American?'

Contact with Other Languages

The majority of loanwords in Tagalog are from the two conquerors' languages, Spanish and English. A few are from Chinese.

From Spanish: *siguro* 'maybe', *oras* 'hour', *Diyos* 'God', *mas* 'more', *sige* 'okay', *basta* 'provided', *kuwento* 'story', *lugar* 'place', *kotse* 'automobile', *pasiya* 'decision'
From English: *mister* 'Mr.', *radyo* 'radio', *bertdey* 'birthday', *riport* 'report', *atorni* 'attorney', *meyor* 'mayor'
From Chinese: *diko/sangko/sikong* 'second/third/fourth oldest brother', *siopao* 'steamed buns with meat fillings', *hopia* 'bean cake', *mami* 'noodle soup with meat and vegetables'

Many words borrowed from English are given either Spanish equivalent (where possible) or Tagalog pronunciation.

Common Words

man:	lalake	woman:	baba?e
water:	tubig	big:	malakí
small:	mali?ít	sun:	araw
yes:	o?o	good:	mabuti
no:	hindí?	three:	tatló
fish:	isdá?	bird:	ibon
dog:	aso	tree:	puno?
long:	mahaba?		

Example Sentences

(1) Ang paborito ko-ng piyesa ang tutugtug-in ng
ABS favorite my- LINKER piece ABS will play-OV ERG

bata?.
child
'It's my favorite piece that the child will play.'

(2) Gusto ng bata? ng saging.
wants ERG child OBL banana
'The child wants a banana.'

(3) May parada bukas.
have parade tomorrow
'There's a parade tomorrow.'

Efforts to Preserve, Protect, and Promote the Language

In 1937 Tagalog was proclaimed the linguistic base for the national language by the Commonwealth Government. That national language is called Pilipino, or Filipino. As Tagalog is the native language of Manila, which is the center of trade, commerce, and education, as well as the seat of the national government, Tagalog was the most plausible choice from among the major Philippine languages. However, Tagalog was adopted only after a series of bitter and passionate debates from the non-Tagalog sectors in the House of Representatives, especially the Cebuanos. Pilipino then became a part of the curriculum in the public schools. In the mid-1950s, Pilipino was already adopted as the medium of instruction from grades I to IV in the Tagalog-speaking regions, and English was taught as a second language. In the non-Tagalog-speaking areas, English and Pilipino were both taught as a second language, and the first language of the region was used as the medium of instruction. One significant undertaking started in the early 1970s was the experimental use of Pilipino as a medium of instruction at the university level. It is believed that extending the use of Pilipino as a medium of instruction from elementary through postsecondary schools will definitely secure the successful development of the national language.

In academic or professional meetings, court proceedings, government affairs, business meetings, and other formal gatherings where no foreigners are in attendance, the use of Pilipino/Tagalog rather than English is becoming preferred. The language is being used more and more in the press, radio, television, and films. Likewise, a remarkable growth in Tagalog literature is testimony to the development of this language and its popularity in the country.

Select Bibliography

Bellwood, Peter. 1991. "The Austronesian Dispersal and the Origin of Languages." In *Scientific American* (July), 88–93.

Blake, Frank. 1925. *A Grammar of the Tagalog Language*. New Haven: Yale University Press.

Bloomfield, Leonard. 1917. *Tagalog Texts with Grammatical Analysis*. University of Illinois, Studies in Language and Literature, 3: 2–4. Urbana: University of Illinois.

Blust, Robert. 1991. "The Greater Central Philippines Hypothesis." In *Oceanic Linguistics* 30:2, 73–129.

Brainard, Sherri. 1996. "Why the 'focused NP' is not the subject in Philippine languages: Evidence from Karoa." In *Philippine Journal of Linguistics* 27: 1–47.

Constantino, Ernesto. 1971. "Tagalog and Other Major Languages of the Philippines." In Thomas Sebeok, ed. *Current Trends in Linguistics,* Vol. VIII (Linguistics in Oceania), 112–154. The Hague: Mouton.

Cubar, Nelly I. 1984. "Cultural Change as Reflected in the Tagalog Language." In Andrew Gonzalez, ed. *Language Planning, Implementation and Evaluation*. 192–217. Manila: Linguistic Society of the Philippines.

English, Leo James, C.S.R. 1986. *Tagalog-English Dictionary*. Quezon City: Capitol Publishing House, Inc.

Francisco, Juan R. 1973. *Philippine Paleography*. Philippine Journal of Linguistics Special Monograph Issue No. 3.

McFarland, Curtis D. 1983. *A Linguistic Atlas of the Philippines*. Manila: Linguistic Society of the Philippines.

Panganiban, Jose Villa. 1972. *Dikyunaryo-Tesauro Pilipino-Ingles*. Quezon City: Manlapaz Publishing Co.

Phelan, John L. 1955. "Philippine Linguistics and Spanish Missionaries, 1565–1700." In *Mid-America* 37: 153–170.

Rubino, Carl. 1998. *Tagalog Standard Dictionary*. New York: Hippocrene Books.

Schachter, Paul, and Fe T. Otanes. 1972. *Tagalog Reference Grammar*. Berkeley: University of California Press.

Thomas, David, and Alan Healey. 1962. "Some Philippine Language Subgroupings: A Lexicostatistical Study." In *Anthropological Linguistics* 4: 9, 21–23.

Zorc, R. David. 1984. "The Philippine Language Scene—The Sociolinguistic Contributions of Historical Linguistics." In Andrew Gonzalez, ed. *Language Planning, Implementation and Evaluation*. 135–148. Manila: Linguistic Society of the Philippines.

TAJIK

John R. Perry

Language Name: Tajik. **Alternates:** *Tajik Persian, Central Asian Persian, Tadzhik.* **Autonym:** *zaboni tojik, (zaboni) tojikī, forsii tojikī.*

Location: Republic of Tajikistan, parts of Uzbekistan (especially Bukhara and Samarkand), and parts of Kirgizstan and Kazakhstan. Since the 1920s Tajik has been fostered as the national and literary language of the Soviet republic (from 1991, independent state) of Tajikistan.

Family: The West Iranian group of the Iranian (Iranic) branch of the Indo-European family.

Related Languages: Linguistically, Tajik is a variety of PERSIAN, from which it is differentiated by some features of phonology, vocabulary, and syntax, and especially in the writing system. Considered geographically and politically, however, it is a distinct language. The speech areas of Tajik and Persian are not contiguous, but are at opposite ends of a continuum, with Persian dialects of Afghanistan in between, and interrupted by areas of Turkic (TURKMEN and UZBEK) speech.

Tajik is also related to Dari (Kaboli) of Afghanistan, KURDISH, and BALOCHI; it is more distantly related to PASHTO. There is a close affinity with URDU that developed under the influence of Persian and the Persianate cultures of Central Asia.

Dialects: Spoken Tajik may be broadly subdivided into two dialect groups: (1) Northern, including the regions of Bukhara, Samarkand, and Khujand (formerly called Leninabad); one such dialect with a modest literature of its own is that of the Jews of Bukhara, many of whom emigrated to Israel in past decades; and (2) Southern, including the capital, Dushanbe, and the regions of Kūlob (Russian transcription, Kulyab), also called Khatlon, and Qurḡontepe (Kurgan-tyube) bordering Afghanistan.

Most of the peoples of Badakhshan, Tajikistan's mountainous eastern province, are speakers of distinct Iranian languages of the Pamir group (Shughni, Wakhi, Yazgulami, etc.), which are also represented in northern Afghanistan, Pakistan, and India, and southwestern Sinkiang (China). Of these so-called (Mountain) Tajiks, those in Tajikistan generally know Tajik Persian as well, but not necessarily those across the frontiers.

Number of Speakers: 4–5 million.

Origin and History

Literary Persian evolved during the 10th century at the Samanid court of Bukhara and its dependencies in what is now Uzbekistan and Tajikistan. In effect, it replaced the older Iranian languages of the region (notably SOGDIAN) with the dialect of the southwest Iranian province of Pars (*see* Persian), enriched with ARABIC vocabulary and expressed in Arabic script. As the imperial language of Islam in the east, New Persian soon spread south and west over the rest of Iran. Thus the classical literary language has a common history and identity whether in Iran, Central Asia, or Afghanistan; there was no such language as "Tajik" until the 1920s.

The spoken Persian of the northeast, however, evolved through the centuries as a distinctive dialect group, thanks to a Sogdian substratum, a Turkic superstratum, and increasing political and cultural separation from the rest of Iran. The medieval Persian-writing world of eastern Islam was increasingly dominated by Turkic-speaking invaders from Inner Asia; to distinguish them, Persian speakers in general—and especially those of the northeast, who were separated from their colinguals by areas of Turkish settlement—came to be called *Tājīk*, derived from a Middle Persian term meaning 'Arab'.

In 19th century Central Asia, both Uzbeks, whose language was called *Turkī* or *Turkistonja*, and Persian-speaking Tajiks were ruled by an Uzbek elite: the emirs of Bukhara. This state became a protectorate of Imperial Russia in 1868 and, after the Russian Revolution, a part of Soviet Turkestan. Stalin's nationalities policy carved it into the Uzbek and Tajik Soviet Socialist Republics (1929) and mandated the creation of modern literary languages ("Uzbek" and "Tajik") for the respective nationalities to be written in a modified LATIN alphabet.

Even before the Russian Revolution, reformist writers such as Sadriddin Ayni (1876–1954), a scholar of Bukhara and bilingual in Persian and Uzbek, had begun to publish works in a more vernacular style of Persian. The dialect base chosen by the state language commission for modern literary Tajik was in essence that of the northern group which had been heavily influenced by Uzbek vocabulary and syntax. Paradoxically, the traditional centers of this variety, the cities of Bukhara and Samarkand, were allocated to Uzbekistan; the capital of Tajikistan, Dushanbe, was a new city virtually created by Russian immigrants, and most of the territory of the republic was inhabited by speakers of the southern, less Uzbekized, dialects and of the non-Persian Pamir languages.

Translations from RUSSIAN and imitations of Marxist-Leninist literature in the new language soon introduced a stratum of Russian vocabulary and idiom. In 1940 Tajik, following the policy established for Uzbek and other Turkic languages of the Soviet Union, switched from Latin to a modified Cyrillic alphabet. Very little of Persian classical literature was made available in the new script. The Tajik language was now in every way separate and distinct from (literary) Persian of Iran or Afghanistan. From the 1950s into the 1980s, Russian steadily encroached on the written and spoken range of Tajik.

The reforms promised by *perestroika* and *glasnost* suddenly enabled the Tajiks to oppose many aspects of Sovietization, including the results of Moscow's language policy. An enthusiastic grassroots language movement led in 1989, as in most other Soviet republics, to the passage of a language-status law that declared Tajik to be the state language and enunciated a program of sociolinguistic "affirmative action". Journalists and younger writers have been introducing vocabulary and idioms from Persian of Iran. Following Tajikistan's declaration of independence, a new language law of 1992 committed the republic, among other measures, to reverting officially to the Perso-Arabic writing system "in the near future". Since then, however, a civil war, the establishment of a neo-Communist government, and Tajikistan's continuing economic weakness have relegated official-language reform to a low priority.

Orthography and Basic Phonology

Of the three writing systems that have been used for Tajik, only the 32-letter Latin alphabet, which was in use for less than a decade, was specifically designed for it. The current Cyrillic alphabet of 39 letters is Russian specific and, like Arabic, has 8 redundant letters. The 6 additional letters representing Tajik phonemes, modified by the addition of hooks or bars, are conventionally appended to the Russian order of the alphabet, as in Table 1 below.

Table 1: The Cyrillic Tajik Alphabet

Аа	a	Сс	s
Бб	b	Тт	t
Вв	v	Уу	u
Гг	g	Фф	f
Дд	d	Хх	x
Ее	ye, e	Чч	č
Ёё	yo	Шш	š
Жж	ž	Ъъ	’
Зз	z	Ээ	e
Ии	i	Юю	yu
Йй	y	Яя	ya
Кк	k	Ғғ	ḡ
Лл	l	Ӣӣ	ī
Мм	m	Ққ	q
Н, н	n	Ӯӯ	ū
Оо	o	Ҳҳ	h
Пп	p	Ҷҷ	j
Рр	r		

The Russian "hard sign" (ъ) represents the Arabic graphemes *hamza* or *'ayn*, which optionally trigger a "bookish" enunciation as a glottal stop; and *ī* is used in word-final position to distinguish stressed, i.e., morphological, *-i* (as in *dūstī* 'friendship') from clitic *-i* of *izofat* (as in *dūsti man* 'my friend').

Russian-language transcriptions of Tajik names (in which forms they are usually transmitted to Western languages) use approximations or digraphs to reproduce non-Russian sounds; hence, they are oddities such as *Kulyab* for *Kūlob*, *Akhmaddzhan* for *Ahmadjon*, and *Tadzhik* in ENGLISH. The latter results from a chain-reaction reanalysis of simple Tajik /j/ (=English /j/ as in "judge"): Russian has no /j/ affricate, and so substitutes the digraph дж; English has no /ž/, so substitutes the digraph *zh*, ending up with an unnecessary and misleading trigraph *dzh*.

Since 1989 there has been some simplification and de-Russification in Tajik (Cyrillic) orthography: the "soft sign" (ь) has been dropped from words of non-Russian origin (e.g., *bis'yor* 'much, very' is now *bisyor*), and non-Tajik letters are replaced by the nearest Tajik equivalent, even in Russian names: (Yel'tsin) Ельцин becomes Елсинь (Yelsin).

Soviet Tajik orthography was based on an analysis of the vowel system (see below) of dialects that did not systematically distinguish the "long" and "short" vowels of literary Persian, which are differentiated in the Arabic script. As a result, the prosody of traditional Tajik Persian poetry is obscured in the Latin or Cyrillic orthographies.

Table 2: Consonants

	Labial	Alveolar	Palatal	Velar	Uvular	Glottal
Stops						
Voiceless	p	t	č	k	q	‘
Voiced	b	d	j	g		
Fricatives						
Voiceless	f	s	š	x		h
Voiced	v ~ w	z	ž	ḡ		
Nasals	m	n				
Resonants		l, r	y			

The palatals /č/ and /j/ are phonetically affricates.

The labials [v] and [w] are in complementary distribution: [v] occurs in word-initial position and intervocalically (/varaq/ 'page', /beva/ 'widow'), and [w] occurs in word-final position, between rounded vowels, and preconsonantally after /a/ (/gow/ 'cow', /suwol/ 'question', /qawl/ 'speech').

Table 3: Vowels

	Front	Central	Back
High	i	ū	u
Mid	e		o
Low	a		

Tajik vowels are distinguished primarily by quality, although length and stress also play a part. Central and back vowels are rounded. The vowel sound /ū/ is intermediate in quality between high back-rounded [u] and high front-rounded [ü].

The three vowels /i/, /u/, and /a/ are classed as "unstable". That is, their articulation changes according to the phonetic environment. In stressed position and in unstressed closed syllables, they are the same length as the three "stable" vowels /e/, /ū/, and /o/. In unstressed open syllables, they may be shortened and reduced to [ə] or even lost: /did/ '(s)he saw', /d[i]gar/ 'other'; /dud/ 'smoke', /g[u]doz/ 'melting'; /bad/ 'bad', /b[a]dan/ 'body'.

Basic Morphology

As in Persian, there is no inflection for case or number in Tajik. There is also no grammatical gender. Whereas Persian has a limited gender distinction (animate vs. inanimate) in third-person pronoun forms, Tajik *ū* and *vay* both mean 'he/she/it', and the demonstratives *in* 'this', *on* 'that', and their plurals *inho* and *onho* may also have animate or inanimate referents.

Partly in response to the introduction of Soviet technology and bureaucracy, Tajik has considerably expanded the range of compound nominals, as compared with Persian, and readily coins neologisms by juxtaposing multiple morphemes:

avtomobil'-kor-karda-bar-or-ī
auto-work-done-out-bring-ing
'automobile production'

mablağ-jūdo- kun-ī
sum-separate- make-ing
'appropriation (of funds), disbursement'

The Tajik verb system is fundamentally the same as that of Persian. However, there are a number of compound forms peculiar to Tajik, expressive of durativity, inference, conjecture, etc. Many of these have analogies in, and have been influenced by, Uzbek usage. Thus, the present/future of the conjectural mood is composed of the following elements: present tense marker + past participle (characterized by a final *-ta* or *-da*) + (conjectural) suffix + copula + personal ending. The forms given below of the verb 'come' can be translated 'I'll probably come', 'I may well come', or 'I suppose I'll come', etc.

	Singular	Plural
1st	me-omada-gi-st-am	me-omada-gi-st-em
2nd	me-omada-gi-st-ī	me-omada-gi-st-ed
3rd	me-omada-gi-st	me-omada-gi-st-and

Tajik also has "serial verbs", in which an uninflected form of the main verb followed by an inflected auxiliary adds an adverbial nuance to the expression (here, self-benefactive and other-benefactive, respectively):

nivišta girift-am
write take:PAST-1SG 'I jotted it down (for my own use)'

nivišta me-dih-ad
write PRES-give-3SG 'S/he'll write it down (for you)'

Basic Syntax

As in Persian, sentence word order is generally SOV. Modifiers (except demonstratives and numerals) follow head nouns; the two are connected by an unstressed *-(y)i* known as *izofat*:

havo-i nağz
weather-IZOFAT nice
'nice weather'

korkunon-i kolxoz
workers-IZOFAT collective:farm
'the collective farmworkers'

Persian-style relative clauses may be replaced by phrases consisting of a verbal participle used attributively:

angur-i ovarda-gi-am
grapes-IZOFAT bring-SUFFIX-1SG 'the grapes I brought'

Tajik sentences are negated by *na* prefixed to the inflected verb, as illustrated in Example Sentence 2 below.

Contact with Other Languages

In pre-Soviet times, (Tajik) Persian became the contact vernacular among speakers of Pamir languages, and until the 1920s was the principal (written) language of government, diplomacy and serious literature throughout Central Asia. Tajiks have lived side by side with Uzbeks and other Turks for centuries with considerable intermarriage and bilingualism, so that each has influenced the other's language. The northern dialects of Tajik, and hence the (Soviet) literary language, show Uzbek influence not only in phonology and vocabulary but also in syntax.

Since the 1920s, however, the most active influence has been that of Russian, primarily on the lexicon. The vocabulary of Marxism-Leninism (*kolxoz* 'collective farm', *partiya*) and modern technology (*traktor, kosmonavt*) has infiltrated via Russian loanwords and calques, even into everyday life (*familiya* 'surname', *remont kardan* 'to repair'). This narrowly-channelled "evolution of modern literary Tajik" was facilitated by the changes of alphabet; official discouragement of direct contact with Iran, Afghanistan and Western countries; and a ban on the importation of Persian publications.

Since the onset of the language movement in 1989 (see below), efforts are being made to replace Russian vocabulary with native (Iranian) Persian, English, and other stock. Thus we currently find vacillating forms for, e.g., the adjective 'French': *fransuzī* (from Russian *frantsuzskiĭ*), *fransavī* (from Arabic), *faronsavī* (from Persian).

Common Words

man:	mard	small:	xurd, mayda
woman:	zan	yes:	ha, bale, ore
water:	ob	no:	ne, na
sun:	oftob	good:	nağz, nek, xub
three:	se	bird:	paranda
fish:	mohī	dog:	sag
big:	kalon	tree:	daraxt
long:	daroz		

Example Sentences

(1) šumo gazeta me-xon-da-ed, az
you newspaper DURATIVE-read-PST.PART-2SG from

siyosat gap me-za-da-ed — šikoyat
politics talk DURATIVE-struck-PST.PART-2SG complaint

karda guft.
make said:3SG
' "[From what I hear] you've been reading newspapers and talking politics," he complained.'

(2) marhamat karda na-dar-o-ed.
kindness do NEG-in-come-2PL
'Please don't come in.'

(3) man be-sabr-ī kard-am, rav-am
I without-patience-ness did-1SG go:SUBJUNCT-1SG

gufta, kampir na-mond.
say old.woman NEG-let:PAST:3SG
'I got impatient and wanted to go, but the old woman wouldn't let me.'

Efforts to Preserve, Protect, and Promote the Language

Few languages have undergone as much conscious, centralized planning as Tajik, or seen so many radical shifts in policy, within the space of two generations. The Communists' initial purpose in establishing a national literary language on a vernacular basis was to develop a native intelligentsia and bureaucracy for the newly created republic; Lenin (as today's Tajik-language activists point out) voiced support for the promotion of national languages and opposition to a privileged position for Russian. Latinization was accompanied by a concerted educational program that dramatically increased literacy. With the change to Cyrillic, however, the policy of "nativization" was reversed, and Russian came to dominate public life. The language movement of the 1980s evolved as one aspect of a general reassertion of Tajik ethnic and cultural identity, as members of a non-Slavic, non-Turkic, Iranian ethnos.

Beyond the basic goals of replacing Russian as the language of government and higher education, and reducing Russian (and Uzbek) borrowings in Tajik, there is a wide range of opinion on how to plan the future of Tajik Persian. Pan-Iranist and Islamicist sentiment would revert immediately to use of the Perso-Arabic script (in which part or all of some recent newspapers and periodicals have been printed). Many of the older bureaucrats and intellectuals, formed under the Soviet system, are more at home with Russian and have been slow to implement changes mandated by the language law. There is no language academy as such, but bodies set up to help publicize and implement language reform include the 12-member 'terminology committee' (*kumitai istilohot*), affiliated with the republic's Academy of Sciences, and the nongovernmental 'Tajik Persian Language Foundation' (*bunyodi zaboni forsii tojikī*).

Select Bibliography

Barakaeva, G.B. 1968. *Luḡati muxtasari tojikī-anglisī* [Concise Tajik-English Dictionary]. 2 vols. Dushanbe.

Bashiri, Iraj. 1994. "Russian Loanwords in Persian and Tajiki Languages." In Mehdi Marashi, ed., *Persian Studies in North America: Studies in Honor of Muhammad Ali Jazayery*. Bethesda: Iranbooks, 109–39.

Birnbaum, S.A. 1950. "The Verb in the Bukharic Language of Samarkand." In *Archivum Linguisticum* II, fasc. 1, 60–73; fasc. 2, 158–76.

Lazard, Gilbert. 1956. "Caractères distinctifs de la langue tadjik." In *Bulletin de la Société de Linguistique de Paris*, 52: 117–86.

Perry, John R. 1979. "Uzbek Influence on Tajik Syntax: The Converb Constructions." In P.R. Cline, W.F. Hanks and C.F. Hofbauer, eds., *The elements: A Parasession on Linguistic Units and Levels, Including Papers from the Conference on Non-Slavic Languages of the USSR*. Chicago: Chicago Linguistic Society, 448–61.

____. 1996. "From Persian to Tajik to Persian: Culture, Politics and Law Reshape a Central Asian Language." In *NSL.8. Linguistic Studies in the Non-Slavic Languages of the Commonwealth of Independent States and the Baltic Republics*, ed. Howard I. Aronson. Chicago Linguistics Society, the University of Chicago, 279–305.

Rastorgueva, V.S. 1963. *A Short Sketch of Tajik Grammar*. Translated and edited by Herbert H. Paper. Bloomington: Indiana University.

Tamazight

Ali Alalou and Patrick Farrell

Language Name: Tamazight. **Autonym:** *Tamazight* (also used as a generic name to refer to Berber languages in general).

Location: Tamazight is spoken by *Imazighen* 'Berbers' who live in Morocco in the region that extends from the Saghro Mountains south of the High Atlas to the north at the foothills of the Rif Mountains limited by the town named Taza. In the east, the limit would be the Moulwiyya River, and in the West, it would be the Grou River. The area comprises the Middle Atlas; the eastern part of the High Atlas, the valleys of Dades, Gueris; and Ziz and the region between the Mgoun Mountains and the Saghro Mountains from the west, and the Ayyachi Mountains and the Saghro Mountains in the northeast.

Family: Afro-Asiatic.

Related Languages: Tashelhit, Taqbaylit, Tashawit, Tarifit, and Tamashek.

Dialects: There are numerous tribes that occupy the region where Tamazight is spoken, each of which speaks a slightly different variety of the language. Some of these groups are: Ait Sedrat, Ait Atta, Ait Marghad, Ait Hdiddou, Ait Ayache, Imgoun, and Ait Seghrouchen. The differences are mainly phonological and lexical. For example, the dialect that we use for examples given here (Ait Marghad) has fricative realizations for the lax variants of the velar stops. The dialect of Imgoun, on the other hand, has fricatives for /b/ and /g/, but not /k/, which is realized as /kʷ/. These are all realized as stops in other dialects, such as Ait Seghrouchen.

Number of Speakers: The estimates of speakers of Berber languages in Morocco range from 40 percent to 60 percent of the population, which is roughly 30 million; the rest of the population speaks an ARABIC dialect as its first language. The numbers of speakers of each of the three individual Berber languages spoken in Morocco (Tamazight, Tashelhit, and Tarifit) are unavailable. Most speakers of Tamazight are bilingual or trilingual in Arabic and FRENCH.

Origin and History

The native people of North Africa and their language and culture were known to the Romans, the Greeks and later the Arabs as "Berber". Berbers established powerful kingdoms in the period 238–184 B.C. With the Islamization of the Berbers (7th century and 11th century and thereafter), Arabic became their written language, especially for those who attended traditional schools. Arabic also became more and more used as a spoken language, and many Berbers became Arabized or bilingual. It is, however, important to stress that Tamazight has survived centuries of invasions and continues to thrive.

Orthography and Basic Phonology

Although Tamazight is predominantly an oral language, there exists an ancient Berber alphabetic script, known as *Tifinagh*, which is still used by the Tuareg Berber tribes (mainly for inscriptions on pots, bracelets, shields, etc.). A contemporary form of this script has been used for Tamazight in Berber magazines. Roman and Arabic writing systems have also been adapted in numerous ways to transcribe Tamazight for various purposes.

All Tamazight consonants have phonemic tense and lax variants (see Table 1 on the next page). Thus, *as:a* 'today', with a tense /s:/ contrasts with *asa* 'liver', with a lax /s/. In general, tenseness is generally held to involve increased constriction and muscular tension, although, depending on segment type and phonetic context, tense phonemes may be longer and more aspirated than their lax counterparts. Subject to dialectal variation, the lax stops tend to be realized as fricatives or affricates. Moreover, the constriction for nonlabial tense stops is slightly retracted relative to that for their lax counterparts.

Pharyngealized (or "emphatic") consonants, indicated by a dot underneath, are pronounced with the tip of the tongue slightly further back in the mouth than with their plain counterparts and with a secondary constriction involving the root of the tongue. Pharyngealization is manifested acoustically in the quality of adjacent vowels.

Although labialization of back obstruents is often due to regular phonological processes of assimilation, the distinction is also phonemic (at least for the stops), as indicated by such minimal pairs as *ikrm* 'he ties' vs. *ikʷrm* 'he's cold'.

The digraphs *gh* and *kh* are often used for the uvular fricatives /ɣ/ and /x/, respectively, in French and ENGLISH texts containing transcriptions of Tamazight.

Each of the three vowel phonemes has several allophonic variants, the choice of which is determined in a complex way by position within the word (initial or final) and the nature of the surrounding consonants (see Table 2 on the next page). For instance, vowels that are adjacent to pharyngeal or pharyngealized consonants are lowered and/or backed relative to the position they would have adjacent to plain consonants only.

Table 1: Consonants

		Labial	Dental/ Alveolar	Alveo- palatal	Palato- velar	Uvular	Pharyngeal	Glottal
Stops	Voiceless		t ṭ		k kʷ	q qʷ		
	Voiced	b	d ḍ		g gʷ			
Fricatives	Voiceless	f	s ṣ	š		x	ḥ	h
	Voiced		z ẓ			ɣ	ʕ	
Nasals		m	n					
Resonants		w	r ṛ l ḷ		y			

Tamazight characteristically has words with long strings of consonants (as in *xmsṭaʔš* 'fifteen') and words without phonemic vowels (such as *rẓm* 'open'). Although some kinds of consonant clusters occur phonetically as syllable onsets and codas, a vocalic transition or "vowel excreschence" breaks up consonant clusters and creates syllable nuclei in a rule governed way. Thus, *rẓm* is phonetically [rẓᵊm].

Table 2: Vowels

	Front	Central	Back
High	i		u
Low		a	

Word stress in Tamazight falls on the final syllable in the word.

Basic Morphology

Tamazight nouns are inflected for number and gender. There are four prefix/suffix combinations that express both distinctions simultaneously, as illustrated in the following forms for 'chicken':

	Masculine	Feminine
Singular	a-ful:us	ta-ful:us-t
Plural	i-ful:us-n	ti-ful:us-in

There are also nouns that undergo stem modification and manifest other sorts of irregularities.

In addition, many nouns have a construct state singular form used if the noun is part of a compound or if it is the head of a noun phrase functioning as subject (in typical postverbal position; see below), as indirect object, or as a prepositional or genitive object. For example, the construct form of *aɣyul* 'donkey' (masculine singular) is *uɣyul*.

Demonstratives are expressed as suffixes on nouns: *tad:art-a* 'this house' (feminine singular), *tad:art-in* 'that house'.

Adjectives and quantifiers are inflected to agree in number and gender with the nouns they modify:

ta-mṭ:u-t ta-ws:ar-t
woman (F/SG) old (F/SG)
'old woman'

a-ryaz a-ws:ar
man (M/SG) old (M/SG)
'old man'

yuw-t tmṭ:u-t
one/a (F/SG) woman (F/SG/CONSTRUCT)
'a woman'

yuw-n uryaz
one/a (M/SG) man (M/SG/CONSTRUCT)
'a man'

Person, number, and gender are distinguished in pronominal forms. There is a set of freestanding independent subject pronouns, although these are normally omitted in running speech, given that the verb carries subject agreement.

Pronominal direct and indirect objects are expressed as affixes on the verb: *isal-t* 'he asked him', *isal-šm* 'he asked you (feminine singular)'; *isawl-as* 'he spoke to him', *isawl-am* 'he spoke to you (feminine singular)'.

Pronominal genitive phrases are expressed by a complex set of possessive suffixes on the head noun; such as *iful:usn-inu* 'my chickens (masculine plural)'.

Pronominal objects of prepositions are also expressed as suffixes on prepositions (e.g., *dig-s* 'in it'). A longer form of the preposition is used with a pronominal object than with a nominal object (*dig-s* 'in it' vs. *g ṭbsil* 'in the dish').

Tamazight verbs are inflected for mood (indicative vs. imperative), tense, and aspect. Verbs agree with their subjects in person, number, and gender. Agreement is indicated by prefixes, suffixes, and "circumfixes" (prefixes and suffixes combined). Differences in the form of these affixes indicate the distinction between indicative and imperative verbs. Verbs undergo internal segment changes and/or prefixation to indicate tense (realized vs. unrealized actions or states) and intensive aspect (habitual, repetitive, or continuing actions or states). (See Table 3 on the next page.)

Direct, and indirect, object pronominal affixes and orientation markers (*n:* denoting remoteness and *d* denoting proximity) precede the verb if there is a negative, tense/aspect, or interrogative particle; otherwise they follow the verb: *is d̲-id:a* 'did he come [= go proximate]?' vs. *id:a-d̲* 'he came'; *urš-isal* 'he didn't ask you' vs. *isal-š* 'he asked you'.

Prefixes may be added to verbs to derive causative, reci-

Table 3: Sample Paradigm for the Verb *d:u* 'go'

Subject	Unrealized	Realized	Intensive
1st-person singular	d:u-x	d:i-x	t:-d:u-x
2nd-person singular	t-d:u-d	t-d:i-d	t:-d:u-d
3rd-person feminine singular	t-d:u	t-d:a	t:-d:u
3rd-person masculine singular	i-d:u	i-d:a	it:-d:u
1st-person plural	n-d:u	n-d:a	nt:-d:u
2nd-person feminine plural	t-d:u-mt	t-d:a-mt	t:-d:u-mt
2nd-person masculine plural	t-d:u-m	t-d:a-m	t:-d:u-m
3rd-person feminine plural	d:u-nt	d:a-nt	t:-d:u-nt
3rd-person masculine plural	d:u-n	d:a-n	t:-d:u-n

procal and passive verbs: *gn* 'sleep' *s:-gn* 'make sleep', *wala* 'face' *m-wala* 'face each other', *srs* 'put down', *t:u-srs* 'be put down'.

Basic Syntax

Tamazight word order is strongly Verb-Subject-Object. Consistent with this pattern, nominal modifiers, including relative clauses, genitive phrases, and adjectives, follow the head noun within the noun phrase:

afus n talbr:at
handle GEN teapot
'the handle of the teapot'

tamṭ:ut d:a ta-n:ayḍ
woman REL 2SG-saw
'the woman you saw'

Negative sentences and yes/no questions are formed by placing particles in preverbal position:

is ur t:isal
Q NEG he ask her
'Didn't he ask her?'

Topicalization involves moving a constituent to sentence-initial position, adding topic stress, and, if this constituent is a noun phrase, placing an agreeing pronominal affix in its place within the main clause:

i-sawl Muḥa i Zaid
3M/SG-spoke Muḥa to Zaid
'Muḥa spoke to Zaid.'

Zaid i-sawl-as Muḥa
Zaid 3M/SG-spoke-3M/SG Muḥa
'Zaid, Muḥa spoke to him.'

Contrastive focus involves placing a constituent in preverbal position, followed by a relative pronoun and the remainder of the sentence minus the focused constituent:

Zaid ayd n-an:i
Zaid who 1PL-saw
'It was Zaid who we saw.'

If the affected constituent is the subject, the verb is in a participial form, with the circumfix *i- in* and without subject agreement marking:

nk^{w}ni ayd i-an:i-n Zaid
we who seen Zaid
'It was we who saw Zaid.'

Contact with Other Languages

When the French colonized North Africa they brought their language, and many Berbers, especially those in Algeria, Morocco, and Tunisia learned French and were educated in the French educational system. Tamazight has borrowed lexical items from the languages of the people who invaded North Africa, particularly Arabic and French. It has also borrowed some words from LATIN and SPANISH. In the other direction, Tamazight has enriched Moroccan Arabic, Algerian Arabic, and Tunisian Arabic with vocabulary and syntactic structures that were not available in the original Arabic language.

From Arabic: *taẓal:it* 'prayer' (< *ṣalā*), *tamdint* 'city' (< *madina*), *axam* 'ten' (< *xayma*)
From French: *biru* 'office' (< *bureau*), *stilu* 'pen' (< *stylo*)
From Spanish: *mutšo* 'little boy' (<*muchacho*), *sk^{w}ela* 'school' (< *escuela*)
From Latin: *urti* 'garden' (< *hortus*)

Common Words

man:	aryaz	long:	ayz:af
woman:	tamṭ:ut	small:	amẓ:an
water:	aman	yes:	y:eh
sun:	tafuyt	no:	uhu
three:	kraḍ	good:	iḥla
fish:	aslm	bird:	ažḍiḍ
big:	axatar	dog:	widi
tree:	tasklut		

Example Sentences

(1) sn-ɣ is i-m-sl:am Zaid d Buʕz:a
know-1SG that 3M/SG-RECIPROCAL-greeted Zaid with Buʕz:a
'I know that Zaid greeted Buʕz:a.'

(2) rẓa-nt tu-tm-in i-fšk-an d:a n-s:-ard
broke-3F/PL woman-F/PL dish-M/PL which 1PL-CAUS-clean
'The women broke the dishes that we washed.'

(3) t-ufid-n: lmuʕal:im-in-nš g lbar
2SG-found-REMOTE teacher-M/PL-2SG/POSS in bar
'You found your teachers at the bar.'

Efforts to Preserve, Protect, and Promote the Language

Standard Arabic and French have always been the languages of government, commerce, and education in Morocco. Consequently, Tamazight and other local Berber and Arabic language varieties are socially stigmatized to some extent. Despite its widespread use at home, Berber is rarely even mentioned in Moroccan schoolbooks. In recent years, however, news programs have begun to be broadcast in Berber. And journals, magazines, and many artistic productions are utilizing and promoting the use of Berber. Many Berber associations have been created throughout the world such as the ACAA. In some countries, such as Algeria, Berber languages are taught at the university level. There have been proposals to begin using them for instruction at the elementary school level in Morocco. The Internet, with its newsgroups and mailing lists devoted to Berber language and culture, has also contributed to their promotion.

Select Bibliography

Abdel-Massih, Ernest T. 1968. *Tamazight Verb Structure: A Generative Approach.* The Hague: Mouton.

____. 1971. *A Reference Grammar of Tamazight: A Comparative Study of the Berber Dialects of Ayt Ayache and Ayt Seghrouchen.* University of Michigan: Publications of the Center for Near Eastern and North African Studies.

Boukous, Ahmed. 1995. "La Langue berbere: maintien et changement." In *International Journal of the Sociology of Language.* New York: Mouton De Gryter.

Chaker, Salem. 1984. *Textes en linguistique berbère: Introduction au domain berbère.* Paris: Editions du Centre National de la Recherche Scientifique.

Cohen, Marcel. 1952. "Les langues chamito-sémitiques." In Antoine Meillet and Marcel Cohen, eds., *Les langues du monde, par un groupe de linguistes, sous la direction de A. Meillet et Marcel Cohen.* Paris: Editions du Centre National de la Recherche Scientique.

Hanouz, S. 1968. *Grammaire berbère: La langue, les origines du peuple berbère.* Paris: Libraire C. Klincksieck.

Harries, Jeanette. 1974. *Tamazight Basic Course.* Washington, DC: Institute of International Studies, U.S. Department of Health, Education, and Welfare.

Tamil

Sanford B. Steever

Language Name: Tamil. **Autonym**: *tamiẓ*.

Location: Southeastern India, northern and eastern Sri Lanka; also spoken in Malaysia and Singapore.

Family: Tamil-Irula subgroup of the Tamil-Kannada group of the South Dravidian branch of the Dravidian language family.

Related Languages: MALAYALAM, Irula, Kota, Toda, KANNADA; more distantly, TELUGU.

Dialects: Tamil has six regional dialects: (1) Sri Lanka; (2) Northern, spoken in the Chingleput, North Arcot, and South Arcot districts of India; (3) Western, spoken in the Coimbatore, Salem, and Dharmapuri districts of India; (4) Central, spoken in the Tirychirapalli, Tanjore and Madurai districts of India (the standard); (5) Eastern, spoken in the Putukottai and Ramanathapuram districts of India; and (6) Southern, spoken in the Nagercoil and Tirunelveli districts of India.

In terms of social dialects, Brahmin and non-Brahmin castes speak different varieties of Tamil. In addition, there is a strong distinction between "High" formal Tamil and "Low" informal Tamil. The High variety is used in public lectures, political speeches, radio and television broadcasts, and in most writing. The low variety, in contrast, is used in almost all face-to-face communication, in the movies, and in some modern fiction. The differences between High and Low Tamil are much more extensive than those between formal and informal ENGLISH. For example, all Low Tamil words end in vowels, while High Tamil words may end in consonants. All speakers of Tamil, regardless of their level of education, can use both varieties of Tamil in appropriate situations; High Tamil is not the specific language of more educated Tamil speakers.

Number of Speakers: 45–55 million.

Origin and History

Tamil is an autochthonous Dravidian language of south India and Sri Lanka, spoken since prehistoric times. It is one of 25 Dravidian languages extant on the south Asian subcontinent. A fragment of Proto-Dravidian, the prehistoric parent language, has been reconstructed by linguists.

The earliest records of Tamil are stone inscriptions dating from 200 B.C. Tamil has three distinct historical stages: Old (200 B.C. – A.D. 700), Medieval (700–1500), and Modern (1500–present). Old Tamil survives in inscriptions and in a vast literature. It developed into Tamil and, in the western Ghats, into Malayalam.

Tamil is one of India's two classical languages, the other is SANSKRIT. Tamil is one of the four literary Dravidian languages; the others are Malayalam, Kannada, and Telugu.

During the Chola Empire (10th to 12th centuries) Tamil spread to Southeast Asia (the Sri Vijaya Empire); it remains in Malaysia and Singapore. During the British Raj, it was transplanted to Burma, South Africa, Mauritius, Fiji, and other British possessions. The Raj also transported Indian Tamil to Sri Lanka.

Orthography and Basic Phonology

The traditional orthography is largely phonemic and can adequately represent the core phonology of Tamil. The basic unit of the Tamil writing system (*tamiẓ eẓuttu* 'Tamil letter') is a unit representing the combination of a consonant followed by the vowel *a*. Combinations of a consonant followed by a different vowel are represented by a modification of the basic shape:

க = ka   கி = ki

Special symbols can be used for vowels that occur at the beginning of the word, and a diacritic called, *puḷḷi*, attached to the basic form indicates that no vowel is pronounced.

Table 1: Consonants

	Labial	Dental	Alveolar	Retroflex	Palatal	Velar
Stops	p (b)	t (d)	ṟ	ṭ (ḍ)	c (j)	k (g)
Fricatives	(f)			(ṣ)	(ś)	
Nasals	m	n	<n̠>	ṇ	ñ	<ṅ>
Laterals		l		ḷ		
Tap		r				
Approximants	v			ẓ	y	(h)

Sounds in parentheses in the table are more characteristic of loans into Tamil; the sounds not in parentheses constitute the native Tamil phonological core. In speaking, the peripheral sounds are often pronounced like the most similar core sound; for example, *faiyal* 'file', which begins with the peripheral *f*, would be pronounced *paiyal*.

n̲ is pronounced the same as *n*, but it is differentiated from *n* in spelling.

The dental sounds *t* and *n* are similar to their English equivalents except that the tongue is touching the upper front teeth. *r* is similar to English "t" or "d" in the middle of a word like "middle".

The retroflex sounds are pronounced with the tip of the tongue curled up and back. The closest sound in English to a Tamil retroflex is "d" before "r" in words like "drip".

The palatal fricative *ś* represents a sound not ordinarily used in English. It is similar to both "s" and "sh", but not identical. Some English speakers pronounce words like "heel" and "huge" as if they start with a sound that is almost the same as Tamil *ś*.

Table 2: Vowels

	Front	Central	Back
High	i, ī		u, ū
Mid	e, ē	(ə)	o, ō
Low	(æ)	a, ā	(ɔ)
Diphthong	ai		au

Stops are voiced between vowels or after nasals. The dentals *t* and *nt* become palatal *c* and *ñc* when they follow *i, ī* or *ai*.

Tamil words are noncontrastively stressed on the first syllable.

Basic Morphology

Tamil morphology is expressed exclusively through suffixes. Nouns are marked singular or plural and inflected for case. Tamil has the following cases: nominative, accusative, dative, genitive, locative, instrumental, sociative, and ablative. There is no grammatical gender, but there are two different locative endings, one for nouns referring to human beings and another for all other nouns. Adjectives do not agree with the nouns they modify.

Tamil is spoken mainly in southeastern India and in eastern Sri Lanka (shaded areas).

Tamil has two different forms of the pronoun meaning 'we': *nām* means 'we (including you)', while *nāṅkaḷ* means 'we (not including you)'.

Tamil verb inflection is extremely complicated. There are two classes of verbs: affective verbs have subjects that undergo the action referred to by the verb, while effective verbs have subjects that bring about the action referred to by the verb. Verbs are inflected for person and number. There are three tenses: past, present, and future.

piri-nt-ār
separate-PAST-he
'He was separated.' (note: *piri* is an affective transitive verb)

piri-kir-āḷ
separate-PRES-she 'She is separated.'

piri-v-ōm
separate-will.be-we 'We will be separated.'

The negative of past and present tense verbs is expressed by *(v)illai* following the infinitive: for example, *piraya (v)illai* 'not separate'. The negative of future tense verbs is expressed by inflected forms of the negative auxiliary *piriya māṭṭ-ēn̲* 'I won't be separated'.

Noun compounding is very productive. For example, *maram* 'tree', *aṭi* 'foot', and *niḻal* 'shade' can be compounded into *maratt-aṭi-niḻal* 'shade at the foot of the tree'.

Basic Syntax

Tamil syntax is strongly head final. The basic word order is SOV, although constituents before the verb can sometimes be rearranged for emphasis; subordinate clauses precede main clauses, adjectives precede nouns, and main verbs precede auxiliaries.

The structure of relative clauses is very different in Tamil than in English:

aṅkē pō-kir̲-a vaṇṭi
there GO-PRES-RELATIVE cart
'The cart that is going there ...'

There is no explicit marker corresponding to the English relative pronoun "that"; instead, the verb 'go' is in the special relative form *pōkir̲a*, which does not include any marking of the subject. In addition the relative clause precedes the noun it is modifying.

Contact with Other Languages

Since the Middle Ages, Tamil has been transplanted to Southeast Asia, Malaysia, Singapore, and Burma, and more recently to South Africa, Fiji, Martinique, and Guyana. Tamil words in

English include "catamaran" (from *kaṭṭamaram* 'tied logs'), "mulligatawny soup" (from *miḷakaitaṇṇir* 'pepper water'), and "mango" (from *māṅkāy*).

Most loanwords come from Sanskrit; many words dealing with administration and commerce come from Perso-Arabic.

From PORTUGUESE: *mēcai* 'table'
From Sanskrit: *jaṉmam* 'rebirth'
From English: *lāri* 'lorry, truck'
From Perso-Arabic: *vakkīl* 'lawyer'

Common Words

man:	maṉitaṉ	long:	nīlamāṉa
woman:	peṇpiḷḷai	small:	ciṉṉa
water:	nīr	yes:	āmām
sun:	cūriyaṉ	no:	illai
three:	mūṉṟu	good:	nalla
fish:	mīṉ	bird:	paṟavai, pakṣi
big:	periya, periyatu	dog:	nāy
tree:	maram		

Example Sentences

(1) [avar [avaḷ-ukku oru makaṉ] eṉṟu ninai-kkiṟ-ār].
[he:NOM [she-DAT one son.NOM] say.and think-PRES-3SG]
'He thinks that she has a son.'

(2) maẓai pey-tu veyil aṭi-ttu vāṉavil
rain rain-and sun beat-and rainbow

tōṉṟ-i-(y)atu.
appear-PST-3SG.(NONHUMAN)
'It rained, the sun shone, and a rainbow appeared.'

(3) [nāṉ [appōtu va-nt-a] maṉitaṉ-ai pār-tt-ēṉ].
I.NOM [that-time come-PST-ADNOM] man-ACC see-PST-1SG]
'I saw the man who came then.'

Efforts to Preserve, Protect, and Promote the Language

Tamil is one of the 15 national languages of India and the first official language of Tamil Nadu State (English is the second). It is a national language in Sri Lanka (with SINHALA), Malaysia, and Singapore. The "Pure Tamil Movement" of the early 1900s succeeded in reducing borrowings from Sanskrit, replacing them with Ultra-Tamil, often reviving classical vocabulary. Language loyalty is strong, manifesting itself since Indian independence in agitations, language riots, and demonstrations against the imposition of HINDI.

Select Bibliography

Andronov, M.S. 1969. *A Standard Grammar of Modern and Classical Tamil.* Madras: New Century Book House.

____. 1970. *Dravidian Languages.* Moscow: Nauka.

Annamalai, E., and S.B. Steever. 1998. "Modern Tamil." In *The Draviian Langugaes.* ed. Sannford Steever, 100–128. London: Routledge.

Arden, A.H. 1942. *A Progressive Grammar of the Tamil Languages.* 5th ed. Madras: The Christian Literature Society.

Asher, R.E. 1985. *Tamil.* (Croom Helm descriptive grammars) London: Routledge.

Lehmann, Thomas. 1989. *A Grammar of Modern Tamil.* (Pondicherry Institute of Linguistics and Culture Publication No. 1). Pondicherry: Pondicherry Institute of Linguistics and Culture.

Meenakshisundaran, T.P. 1965. *A History of the Tamil Language.* Poona: Deccan College.

Pope, G.U. 1979. *A Handbook of the Tamil Language.* New Delhi: Asian Educational Services.

Schiffman, H. 1979. *A Grammar of Spoken Tamil.* Madras: Christian Literature Society.

Steever, Sanford. 1981. *Selected Papers on Tamil and Dravidian Linguistics.* Madurai: Muttu Patippakam.

____. 1987. "Tamil and the Dravidian Languages." In *The World's Major Languages.* ed. Bernard Comrie, 725–46. New York: Oxford University Press.

____. 1992. "Tamil." In *The Oxford International Encyclopedia of Linguistics.* ed. William Bright, 4: 131–36. New York: Oxford University Press.

Zvelebil, Kamil. 1969. "Tamil." In *Linguistics in South Asia.* eds. Murray Emeneau and Charles Ferguson, 343–71. (*Current Trends in Linguistics*, Vol. 5). The Hague: Mouton.

____. 1983. "Dravidian Languages." In *The New Encyclopedia Britannica. Macropedia.* 4: 988–92. Chicago: Encyclopedia Britannica.

TATAR

Lars Johanson

Language Name: Tatar. **Alternate:** *Kazan Tatar*. **Autonym:** *tatar tĕlĕ, tatarča*.

Location: Spoken in the Republic of Tatarstan (*Tatarstan Respublikasï*). Also spoken in parts of Bashqortostan, Kazakhstan, Uzbekistan, China, and Romania.

Family: Northwestern (Kipchak) branch of the Turkic family.

Related Languages: Bashkir, Crimean Tatar, KAZAKH.

Dialects: The central dialect is spoken in the Republic of Tatarstan. The western (Misher) dialect is spoken in the Volga region outside the republic. The so-called eastern dialects spoken in western Siberia are of partly different origin.

Number of Speakers: Over 6 million (including over 5 million in the Russian Federation).

Origin and History

Tatar is the official language of the multinational Republic of Tatarstan which occupies a large area between the Volga River and the Ural Mountains. The Turkic-speaking tribes of this and adjacent areas have, from the period of the Golden Horde (13th to 15th centuries) on, been referred to as "Tatar", originally a Mongolian tribal name. However, several of these tribes, for example the Volga Bulgars, had settled between Volga and Kama long before the Mongolian invasion. Later on, the Kipchak Turkic element became the dominant ethnic component, assimilating the Mongolian and parts of the Finno-Ugric population of the area. The Khanate of Kazan emerged in 1445 after the dissolution of the Golden Horde and was conquered by Russia in 1552. An "autonomous" Tatar Soviet republic was established in 1920. In 1990, the Republic of Tatarstan was declared a sovereign state, associated with (in fact, part of) the Russian Federation.

Orthography and Basic Phonology

The ARABIC script was used for Tatar until a Roman-based alphabet was introduced in 1927. In 1939, a variant of the Cyrillic alphabet was adopted. In the post-Soviet era a new Roman-based alphabet has been created, although it has not yet replaced the Cyrillic-based script.

The Cyrillic sign ъ indicates that the preceding consonant is syllable final and not palatalized. In loanwords, къ and гъ indicate /q/ and /ġ/, respectively. The sign ь indicates that the preceding consonant is syllable final. It can also indicate that the preceding consonant is palatalized or that the preceding syllable is a front syllable, as in ямь [yäm] 'beauty'. Rounding harmony is not consistently represented in the orthography. Thus, the letters *y* and *e* are written for /ŏ/ and /ö̆/ in noninitial syllables. In words of Arabic origin, word-internal glottal stops are marked with Cyrillic ь and Roman ', for example, Корьән, *Qŏr'än* 'the Koran'.

Since the high-mid vowels /ĕ/, /ŏ/, /ï̆/, and /ö̆/ are shorter and more centralized than the low and high vowels, they are often described as "reduced". The phonemes /ü/ and /ö̆/ often have a somewhat centralized pronunciation. The phoneme /a/ has a slightly rounded variant [ɒ] occurring in first syllables and in a syllable after [ɒ], as in *bɒlɒ* 'child'. It is otherwise unrounded, as in *uram* 'street'. A low-mid /o/, a low-mid /e/, and a high

Table 1: Tatar Cyrillic Alphabet

Cyrillic-based	Value	Cyrillic-based	Value	Cyrillic-based	Value
Аа	a	Нн	n	Ъъ	(see text)
Бб	b	Оо	ŏ	Ыы	ï, ɨ
Вв	w, v	Пп	p	Ьь	(see text)
Гг	g, ġ, ɣ	Рр	r	Ээ	ĕ, e, 'e
Дд	d	Сс	s	Юю	yu, yü
Ее	ĕ, yĕ, yï̆, e, ye	Тт	t	Яя	ya, yä
Жж	ž	Уу	w, uw, w	Әә	ä
Зз	z	Фф	f	Өө	ö̆
Ии	i	Хх	x	Үү	ü, üw, w
Йй	y	Цц	c	Җҗ	ǰ
Кк	k, q	Чч	ś, č	Ңң	ŋ
Лл	l	Шш	š	hh	h
Мм	m	Щщ	šč		

Table 1: Consonants

	Labial	Dental/ Alveolar	Alveo- palatal	Palato- alveolar	Front Velar	Back Velar	Glottal
Stops	p b	t d			k g	q	’
Fricatives	f	s z	ś ź	š ž		x ɣ	h
Nasals	m	n			ŋ		
Liquids		l r					
Glides	w		y				

Table 2: Vowels

	Front		Back	
	Unrounded	Rounded	Unrounded	Rounded
High	i	ü		u
Mid	ĕ	ŏ̈	ĭ̈	ŏ
Low	ä		a	

central /ɨ/ are found in modern loanwords from RUSSIAN. The sequence /ĭ̈y/ is sometimes considered to constitute a phoneme /ï/, that is, a back equivalent of /i/. Vowel length is not distinctive, but found at a subphonemic level, as in Arabic and PERSIAN loanwords. Unstressed reduced vowels alternate with zero in colloquial speech, for example, *kĕšĕ*, ~ *kšĕ*, ‘person’. The sequences /iy/, /uy/, /uw/, and /üw/ may be realized as long vowels /i:/, /u:/, /u:/, and /ü:/, respectively.

Russian loanwords may also contain /v/, /c/, /č/, and /šč/ = [šš’] and palatalized consonants. Russian /v/ is mostly replaced by /w/. A non-phonemic glottal stop [’] occurs in front of initial vowels. The phoneme /ɣ/ may also be realized as a back-velar voiced stop [ġ].

Voiceless stops are mostly aspirated. The consonant /f/ is realized as a bilabial [ɸ], but in loanwords from Russian as a labio-dental [f]. The consonants /ś/ and /ź/, which correspond to the affricates /č/ and /ǰ/ in most other Turkic languages, occur in Standard Tatar as fronted (palatalized) fricatives. They may also occur as palatalized affricates [t’ʃ’] and [d’ʒ’]. They are traditionally transliterated as *č* and *ǰ*; these symbols will be used in the examples below.

The vowels /i/, /ŏ/, /ŏ̈/, /u/, and /ü/ do not occur in suffixes. Certain bisyllabic stems lose the high vowel of their final syllable when a suffix with an initial vowel is added, as in *irĕn* ‘lip’ versus *irnĕm* ‘my lip’. Final /ä/ and /a/ of the verb stem is lost in some verb forms, for example, *ĕšli* ‘(s)he works’, present tense of *ĕšlä-* ‘to work’. In front of suffix-initial vowels, stem-final /p/, /q/ and /k/ mostly become /b/, /ɣ/ and /g/, respectively, for example, *taba* ‘finds’ versus *tap!* ‘find!’, *ayaɣïm* ‘my foot’ versus *ayaq* ‘foot’, *čigĕ* ‘its boundary’ versus *čik* ‘boundary’. Devoicing of word-final consonants and suffix-initial consonants after voiceless consonants is reflected in the orthography, as in *kitap* ‘book’, *kŏ̈ttĕ* ‘waited’. After the stem-final nasals /m/, /n/, and /ŋ/, the suffix-initial /l/ of the plural suffix and the /d/ of the ablative suffix are assimilated to /n/, as in *kŏ̈n-när* ‘days’ and *Qazan-nan* ‘from Kazan’.

Tatar suffixes display front versus back harmony, whereas rounded versus unrounded harmony is absent in Standard Tatar. The high suffix vowels are thus /ĕ/ and /ĭ/, and the low suffix vowels are /ä/ and /a/, for example, *ĕt-lär-ĕbĕz-dän* (front) ‘from our dogs’ versus *at-lar-ĭ̈bĭ̈z-dan* (back) ‘from our horses’. The vowel of the suffix depends on the frontness versus backness of the last stem syllable.

Basic Morphology

Tatar is an agglutinative language with suffixing morphology. Nouns and adjectives are formed from verbal and nominal stems by means of various derivational suffixes, for example, *kil-ĕš* ‘arrival’ (*kil-* ‘come’) and *toz-lĭ̈* ‘salty’ (*toz* ‘salt’). Nouns take the plural suffix *-LAr*, possessive suffixes such as *-(Ĕ)m* ‘my’, *-(Ĕ)ŋ* ‘your’, and case suffixes: genitive *-nĔŋ*, accusative *-nĔ*, dative (‘to’) *-(G)A*, locative (‘in’, ‘at’, ‘on’) *-DA*, ablative (‘from’) *-DAn*. (Capital letters indicate variation.) An example is: *yul-ďaš-lar- ïm-nan* [road-DERIVATION-PLURAL-POSSESSIVE 1 P. SG.-ABLATIVE] ‘from my companions’ (*yol-daš* < ‘fellow traveller’, sharing the same road).

Secondary verbal stems are formed from verbal and nominal stems by means of various suffixes. Deverbal suffixes include passive, cooperative, causative, frequentative and other elements, as in *yaz-ĭ̈l-* ‘to be written’ and *yaz-d ĭ̈r-* ‘to make write’ (*yaz-* ‘to write’). Verbal negation is expressed with the suffix *-mA*, e.g. *kit-mä-* ‘not to go away’.

Finite and infinite verb forms consist of a simple or expanded lexical stem plus aspect/mood/tense suffixes and often person and number suffixes, for example, *ĕš-lä-sĕn-när* [work-DERIVATION-OPTATIVE-PLURAL] ‘may they work’. There is a wide variety of simple and compound aspect/mood/tense forms, as well as numerous converbs and participles.

Like other Turkic languages, Tatar has evidential categories of the type *qaytqan ikän* ‘has obviously returned’. A number of auxiliary verbs (‘postverbs’) express modifications of actionality, that is the manner in which an action is carried out; for example, *yanĭ̈p bĕt-* [burn-CONVERB end] ‘burn down (to completion)’.

Tatar has numerous postpositions, corresponding to ENGLISH prepositions, for example, *kičkä taba* [evening-DATIVE towards] ‘towards the evening’.

Basic Syntax

Tatar is syntactically very similar to other Turkic languages. It has a head-final constituent order, SOV. The order of elements in a nominal phrase is Demonstrative-Numeral-Adjective-Noun, as in *bu ŏ̈č zur ŏ̈y* ‘these three big houses’, and the head of a relative clause follows the relative, like *běz söyläš-kän qı̆z* [we talk-PARTICIPLE girl] 'the girl we talked to'.

Contact with Other Languages

Tatar has been influenced by Russian, particularly in the lexicon. It has itself exerted strong influence on the neighboring Turkic languages, Bashkir and Chuvash, as well as on some Finno-Ugric languages of the area. Since it has been used as a written language by the small Turkic groups of western Siberia, it has had a strong impact on their dialects. Literary Tatar has to a certain extent also served as a model for Literary Kazakh.

From Persian: *zur* 'big', *aždaha* 'dragon', *baqča* 'garden', *atna* 'week', *gŏl* 'flower', *šähär* 'city'
From Arabic: *fikĕr* 'thought', *mäktäp* 'school', *taraf* 'side'
From Russian: *stakan* 'glass', *par* 'steam', *kuxnya* 'kitchen', *vrač* 'doctor, physician'
From MONGOLIAN: *uram* 'street', *dala* 'steppe'

Common Words

man:	ir	woman:	xatı̆n
water:	su	sun:	qŏyaš
three:	ŏč	fish:	balïq
big:	zur	long:	ŏzı̆n
small:	kĕčkĕnä	yes:	äyĕ
no:	yuq	good:	yaxšı̆
bird:	qŏš	dog:	ĕt
tree:	aɣač		

Example Sentences

(1) Bala-lar mäktäp-kä kit-t-ĕ-lär-mĕ älĕ?
child-PLUR school-DAT go-PAST-3P.PLUR-Q yet
'Have the children gone to school yet?'

(2) Bĕz yaz-ɣan xat-nı̆ uqı̆-ɣan.
we write-PAST.PART letter-ACC read-PERFECT
'(S)he has read the letter we wrote.'

(3) Uqı̆-ma-ɣan-ɣa bĕl-m-i.
read-NEG-PAST.PART-DAT know-NEG-PRESENT
'Since (s)he has not read it, (s)he does not know it.'

(4) Qazan šähär-ĕ Idĕl yı̆lɣa-sı̆
Kazan city-POSS.3SG Volga river- POSS.3P.SG

buy-ĕn-a urnaš-qan.
extent- POSS.3P.SG.-DAT be.located-PART
'The city of Kazan is situated on the Volga River.'

Efforts to Preserve, Protect, and Promote the Language

Tatar has long been one of the most firmly established Turkic languages. In the post-Soviet era, the language has consolidated its position further, acquiring more social functions than it had before.

Select Bibliography

Berta, Á. 1998. "Tatar and Bashkir." In *The Turkic Languages*, Johanson, L. and É.Á. Csató, eds. London and New York: Routledge. 283–300.

Johanson, L. and É.Á. Csató, eds. 1998. *The Turkic Languages*. London and New York: Routledge.

Poppe, N. 1963. *Tatar Manual. Descriptive Grammar and Texts with a Tatar-English Glossary*. Bloomington: Indiana University; The Hague: Mouton.

TAY-NUNG

Peter Ross

Language Name: Tay and Nung are names of two Tai people groups in northern Vietnam. The term 'Tay-Nung language', or *tiếng Tày-Nùng*, was coined in the late 1960s during debates on language standardization to refer collectively to the languages of the Tay and Nung people. Regional dialect distinctions are referred to by the name of the subgroup and locality: *Tay Dao Ngan* ('Tay of DN'), *Tay Thach An* ('Tay of TA'). Nung dialects are more frequently referred to by "clan" names such as *Nung Chao* or *Nung An* and it is suggested that these refer to their town of origin in China, *Ie Long Chau, Long An*. In dialect studies it may be necessary to refer to both the 'clan' name and the town of current location, *Ie Nung Fan Slinh Chi Lang* ('Nung of Van Thanh, China, now living in CL').

During and following the French colonial era, the terms "Tay" or "Tho" and "Nung" were also used to refer Tai speakers in southern China today called *Zhuang*. The name "Nung" was also used as a euphemism for Cantonese-speaking laborers brought into Vietnam by the French.The name *Tho* (*Thổ*) meaning 'native, indigenous' has been rejected in Vietnam since the 1960s on the grounds that it is derogatory. Tay speakers today may not be familiar with the term, though it remains a reference term for a small group of Muong (Vietic) speakers also called "Tay Poong".

Location: The Tay and Nung live interspersed in the northern border region of Vietnam from the Red River valley to the Gulf of Tonkin (Beibu Gulf). Previously called *Haut Tonkin* by the French, for some time after independence it was known as the Viet Bac Autonomous Region. Today, the Tay-Nung (TN) region encompasses the provinces of Ha Tuyen, Cao Bang, Bac Thai and Lang Son, along with a portion of Hoang Lien Son province. Tay and Nung who migrated to the south in 1954 form a southern population in the provinces of Thuan Hai, Lam Dong and Dong Nai.

Family: TN belongs to the Tai language family. The area that it occupies in Vietnam makes up roughly one half of a linguistic area. The other half spreads from the China-Vietnam border northwards to the You River in Guangxi Zhuang autonomous region as well as to the west in the Wenshan autonomous region, Yunnan. The language in these areas is Southern Zhuang. The area is marked by mountainous terrain, long-term settlement and village-to-village dialect variation, and lies between the two main branches of the Tai language family, Northern Tai or Dioi in southern China and Southwestern Tai or Thai proper, which spreads out across northern mainland Southeast Asia. The two outside branches have variously influenced or excluded from influence the Intermediate group or Central Tai. The number of Central Tai speakers has been put at around 3 or 4 million with estimates up to 8 million.

Tai languages were first categorized into two groups, Thai proper and Yai, by the French linguist Haudricourt on the basis of differences in vowels (T *rak* Y *riak* 'vomit') and some initials (T *nam* Y *ram* 'water'). On this basis TN is part of Thai proper. A third criterion of differences in initial aspiration (e.g., *phɔ/pɔɔ* 'father'), initially thought to be a fieldwork error, was soon also showed to hold. Later, detailed comparative study of initial consonants and shared words by Chinese linguist Li Fang Kuei suggested further that Central Tai and Southwestern Tai belonged to different subgroups. Li demonstrated that Central Tai dialects are sometimes like Southwestern Tai (N *kuk* SW/C *sɯa* 'tiger') and sometimes unique (N/SW *taa* C *thaa* 'eye'). Later, two Nung An dialects with features of both Northern and Central dialects (*kuk* 'tiger', *thaa* 'eye') became key in demonstrating that, while a two-way tree model might hold for the two main groups, some developments in Central Tai were better treated on the basis of areal influence.

Recently, a Northwestern Tai branch has been proposed on the basis of dialects identified as being "dislocated" among the Southwestern dialects. While having undergone a lot of the sound changes of the southwestern branch, these dialects have a number of words in common with the Northern branch and some shared by the Northern Tai and Central Tai branches.

Dialects: A major study by Hanoi University students using a 3,700 word list found an overall 75 percent phonetic resemblance for 33 Tay and Nung dialects. Nung may be characterized by its rarer use of diphthongs (*nựa/nự* 'meat', *lưang/lưng* 'yellow') and differences in initials (Tay [w, r, f] Nung [v , ɬ, ph]), but these features are not restricted to Nung dialects. Nung dialects have also been characterized with a higher percentage of Chinese loans, up to 80 percent by one early count. More conservative figures from a study using a 2,000 word list showed Tay dialects have 4 percent–21.8 percent Vietnamese loans and 0.2 percent–1 percent Chinese loans whereas Nung dialects have 1.2 percent–6.8 percent Chinese loans and only up to 6.1% Vietnamese loans. Nung or Tay dialects in the same or different areas may or may not be mutually intelligible, a factor that seems to have been influenced by migration.

Four dialect regions can be distinguished. The central region stretching east and west from Bac Thai is highly homogenous with a corresponding high degree of mutual intelligibility. Features here are usually found in other areas: the standard dialect was chosen from here. Moving southeast toward the trade route from Hanoi through Lang Son to China an increasing lack of homogeneity is found: W/N *tha* C *tha, ha,* S *tha, pha, ha, sa* 'eye'. To the north along the upper reaches of the Bang (Zuo) River, dialects share common features, W *haa* N *phuy* S *phuy, cang* 'to speak, say', but also have some distinctive features of their own. In particular, they show preservation of a four-way distinction in the stop consonant series with a breathy voiced consonant: /phaa/ 'to split', /pi/ 'year', /bi/ 'lard', /ʔbaa/ 'crazy'. On the border in the west, dialects have been characterized by least distributed phenomena, with influence of Northern Tai (*chəu* 'frog', *pik* [Tone DS]) and loans from Southwestern Chinese, for example the points of the compass, in contrast to the dialects in the east with loans from Cantonese.

Number of Speakers: The Tay are the largest minority ethnic group in Vietnam and the Nung the third largest, as well as the third largest Tai group after the Tay and the Thai. Statistics show a steadily growing population:

Year	Tay	Nung
1924	n/a	100,000
1959	437,019	270,810
1960	503,995	313,998
1979	870,000	540,000
1989	1,190,342	705,709

In 1924, the number of Nung in China were put at 200,000. Tay and Nung populations in the south of Vietnam in 1989 were put at 20,270 and 41,828, respectively.

Origin and History

"We Nung came here walking and carrying our firewood, but the Tay came riding horses; now the roles are reversed." This folk origin goes on to say that when the Nung arrived, the Tay were already farming the valleys and were forced to take to the hills. Through hard work, good trading and intermarriage, the situation changed. Some support for this account is found in demographic distribution.

Chinese expansion southwards beginning in the Qin (22–206 B.C.) and Han (206 B.C.–A.D. 220) dynasties increasingly exposed the Tai to Chinese culture and political control. For part of this time the Tai must have made up part of the population of the *Nam Viet* ('South Viet') empire (202–111 B.C.), which spread from Canton to Vietnam until it was defeated by the Han. The Tai were centred in mountain valleys between the You and Zou (Bang) Rivers in southwestern Guangxi and northern Vietnam where local chieftans established dependent clans and controlled land distribution. The Han dynasty extended direct control as far south as the Red River delta but their control was restricted to the larger cities and the Tai heartland remained outside Chinese influence. Tai people to the north of the You River who were affected by Han colonization today make up the Northern Tai branch.

In the Tang dynasty (A.D. 617–907) the Chinese came into the Tai heartland in force, developing waterways as communication routes and enforcing assimilation. The Tang system was oppressive and widely scattered resistance movements broke out on Tang southern borders. The Tai, under the leading Hoang clan, carried out a series of uprisings (756–824). Though allied with Yunnan (Nanzhao) and receiving occasional support from the Vietnamese in the south, disunity within foiled their attempts. Over the next century, this repeated pattern was to earn them the reputation of being "as easy to buy and divide as difficult to bring to submission and unify."

As Tang power declined, the frontier from Cao Bang to Lang Son was taken under Vietnamese control. In 939, the Vietnamese declared themselves independent and by 981 gained preliminary recognition from the Song dynasty (960–1126). The Tai now found themselves pressured from two sides. In 1038, the chieftan of the new leading Nung clan, allied again with Yunnan (Dali), declared himself an independent Tho or native ruler. The Vietnamese responded by executing him and most of his family, but his son, Nung Tri Cao, survived. In the following years, Nung Tri Cao, pursuing the vision of a Tai state, founded his own state of Dali, temporarily accepted Vietnamese vassalship, sought Chinese support, and finally, when it was not forthcoming, led his troops in 1052 in a campaign to Canton proclaiming himself king of *Dai Nam* ('Great South'). Unable to hold his position, he retreated and suffered a major defeat. The Chinese revived clan disunity. Nung Tri Cao and his remaining supporters fled to Yunnan, where it is suggested they stayed and formed the basis of the recently proposed Northwestern Tai branch.

Following Nung Tri Cao, the Nung clan declined as clan members sought to dissociate themselves with him. In 1084, Sino-Vietnamese affairs had settled sufficiently for demarcation of borders to be discussed. Innumerable successive invasions until as recent as 1979 inevitably involved the Tay and Nung. In the 13th century they were among those who, along with malarial mosquitoes, largely contributed to the Mongolian defeat. Frequently when Vietnam was invaded from China it was through the "China Gate", a narrow river valley pass between Lang Son and Cao Bang and a key peacetime trade route or through other key border towns dominated by Tais. Vietnam and China settled on a "loose-rein" policy, allowing local chieftans autonomy in return for yearly tribute paid to one or both powers. Vietnamese-appointed officials played varying roles in relation to those of the hereditary chiefs. Clan conflicts and the use of the area by rebels and bandits as a refuge left the area sufficiently turbulent to keep the two external powers on edge, but peaceful enough to only occasionally require their intervention.

In 1592 the Vietnamese Mac dynasty under Mac Kinh Cung was overthrown and retreated to Cao Bang. Remaining there until 1660, the Mac first operated a resistance base and later, under Chinese protection, gained status as a tributary province of Vietnam.

It is still difficult to say at what point the TN as part of the Central Tai group became distinguished from the Southwestern Tai. Some claim that as the Tang and Vietnamese tried to gain control they forced their way up the Red River valley separating the TN to the northeast from the Black and White Tai to the southwest. However, Vietnamese sources show a number of Tay to the south of the Red River, and the distribution of these Tay along with the Black and White Thai corresponds to three 18th-century administrative prefectures based on clan groupings. On the other hand early French sources call the Tay south of the Red River "White Tai", and make reference groups of White and Black Tai to the north of the Red River in the Chay and Lo (Clear) River valleys. At some point, however, the Tai to the southwest of the Red River watershed came into the Indosphere and developed an alphabetic writing system along the lines of Siamese and LAO, undergoing further sound changes at the same time.

In the late 1800s and early 1900s the Tay and Nung came under French colonial control. French missionaries and military officers in *Haut Tonkin* wrote bilingual dictionaries and language texts, grammars and catechisms for Tay and Nung using Romanized orthographies that were often a cross between FRENCH and the Vietnamese Romanized script. French policy highlighted ethnic diversity, by one report even attempting to set up an independent Nung state. In the late 1930s and 1940s scholars of the *École Française D'Extrême-Orient* were involved in dialect surveys of minority languages, including 10 Tay and 10 Nung dialects, and the first publication of Tay Nom texts was printed.

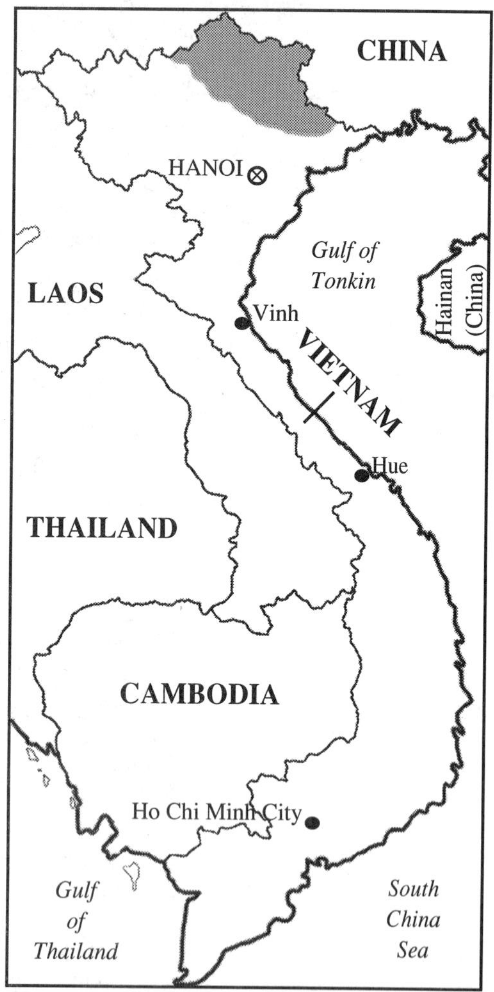

Tay-Nung is spoken in the northern provinces of Ha Tuyen, Cao Bang, Bac Thai, Lang Son and Hoang Lien Son (shaded areas). There are also some 60,000 speakers in the southern provinces of Thuan Hai, Lam Dong and Dong Nai.

In 1937 the Vietnamese Communist Party was founded. Under the direction of Ho Chi Minh, Cao Bang became the base for a resistance movement against the French in which the Tay and Nung played a major role and in which literacy was valued highly. After the French were ousted in 1954, Tay and Nung cadres went on to take senior positions in government. In 1956 the Viet Bac Autonomous Region was set up. In 1961, the government passed projects for the development of a Tay Nung script. From 1967–1969, dialect surveys were carried out by linguistics students from Hanoi University forced to take refuge in the mountains during U.S. bombing. Provisionally a decision was made to rely on the most widely spread features of pronunciation to create a standard for which the orthography was based on a modified Vietnamese Romanized script.

In 1969 the dialect on the axis between Dong Khe (Cao Bang) and That Khe (Lang Son) was officially accepted as the TN standard. Directions in developing a unified standard were discussed in newspapers and magazines, in particular a series of articles in *Independent Vietnam* from June 1969 to July 1970. A TN grammar was published in 1971. The government decision was further approved by a 1973 conference on standardization. Reading primers were published and students in lower elementary school were taught in TN. Bilingual dictionary preparation began immediately after the writing script projects were ratified, and a TN-Vietnamese dictionary was published in 1974. From 1960 to 1978, 20 volumes of literature were prepared. During the same period, linguistic work with the Tay and Nung southern population was also carried out by western scholars and missionaries in South Vietnam.

After reunification in 1975, the Viet Bac Autonomous region was dissolved. In 1980, after a decade of successful TN language education, the program was officially discontinued, although use of minority languages was still allowed in dealing with government offices and agencies. Lack of TN-speaking teachers and social pressure from the Tay and Nung for Vietnamese-language education have at different times been reported as problems. Some reports say TN language instruction continues in some schools. TN remains a lingua franca among minority groups in TN areas. A Vietnamese-TN dictionary was published in 1984. Literature in Tay-Nung is not readily available in bookshops though a collection of 50 Tay-Nom texts is now housed in the Han Nom Institute in Hanoi, and in the 1990s publications of traditional literature in Romanized script have reappeared.

Orthography and Basic Phonology

In the 17th century the first TN texts appeared, written in a character script called *Tày Nôm* in two works: *Bàn Về Tam Nguyên* ('Essay of Origins') by Be Van Phung, a Tay intellectual appointed under the Mac; and *Tứ Quí Slíp Sloong Bươn* ('Four Seasons Twelve Months') by Nong Quynh Van, under the pseudonym *Ca Dang* ('Dappled Crow'). The Tay-Nom in these works is already well developed, suggesting an earlier origin. The first characters in the equivalent Zhuang-character

Table 1: Consonants

	Bilabial	Labio-Dental	Alveolar	Palatal	Velar	Glottal
Stops	ph/pʰ/		th/tʰ/	ch/c/	c, k, q /k/	/ʔ/
	p/p/		t/t/		kh/kʰ/	
	b/ʔb/		đ/ʔd/			
Fricatives		f/f/	x/s/			h/h/
		v/v/	d/z/			
Lateral			sl/ɬ/			
Fricatives			l/l/			
Nasals	m/m/		n/n/	nh/ɲ/	ng/ŋ/	

script were recorded in 1175. However, Tay-Nom is usually thought to have been based on Vietnamese character script, for which the earliest date is a stone inscription from 1343.

Tay-Nom has three basic types of characters: those where a Chinese character is borrowed in full based on its sound; those where a Chinese character is borrowed with modifications because the Chinese sound only approximates the Tay sound; and those where a compound character is formed between one Chinese character, based on the sound, and another, based on the meaning. Tay-Nom has two innovations not shared with Vietnamese-character script. Small wormlike diacritics called *lục non* are placed before or after the character to signal an alteration in pronunciation from the original form. A further development involves a type of complex compound character, from which a bisyllabic form can be read. Tay-Nom is distinct from the Chinese characters Tay and Nung shamans still use today.

A modified version of the Vietnamese orthography was standardized in the 1970s and is in use today.

There are two descriptions of the TN standard phonological system based alternately on the provisional standard and the later-adopted standard of Tay from *Thạch An*. The provisional standard has received most exposure.

The syllable in TN consists of an initial and a rime. The initial consists of a simple initial with an optional medial. The rime is comprised of a main vowel or diphthong and a tone, with or without a final consonant or semivowel final. These possibilities can be summarized as $T / C^1 (S^1) V^1 (V^2) (C^2, S^2)$.

In standard TN, there are 21 consonants. In the orthography words beginning with a vowel have a glottal stop.

Any consonant can stand in initial position (C^1). Consonants in final position (C^2) are restricted to three stops /p, t, k/ and three nasals /m, n, ŋ/. As with Vietnamese, palatalization of /k/ and /ŋ/ may occur after a high front vowel /i/, signaled in the orthography as *ch* and *nh*; labiovelar coarticulation of /k/ and /ŋ/ may occur after back vowels /u/ and /o/.

Vowels and Diphthongs. TN has nine long vowels and two short vowels.

Short vowels cannot stand in final position. Short-long contrasts are *đăng* 'nose'; *đang* 'body' and *bân* 'sky'; *bơn* 'going along without looking at the road'. /e/ in final position is extremely limited, whereas /ɔ/ before a velar final is predominantly long and spelled with a double vowel: *sloong* 'two', *bjooc* 'flower'. There are three diphthongs, each with an offglide to a low central vowel with spelling dependent on context: /ia/ *mìa* 'wife', *riệc* 'to call'; /ʉa/ *slưa* 'tiger', *bươn* 'month'; /ua/ *hua* 'head', *sluôn* 'garden'.

Table 2: Vowels

	Front	Back	
		Unrounded	Rounded
Close	i/i/	ư/ʉ/	u/u/
Half Closed	ê/e/	â/ə/ ơ/əə/	ô/o/
Open	e/ɛ/	ă/a/ a/aa/	o/ɔ/

Semivowels. There are three semivowels corresponding to the vowels /i, ʉ, u/. These semivowels involve greater friction and a stronger stream of air than their vowel equivalents. Those corresponding to /i/ and /u/ can function as medials (S^1): *pja* (or occasionally *pia*) /pyaa/ 'fish'; *sloa* /ɬwaa/ 'right side', *quang* /kwaaŋ/ 'deer'. Medials are sometimes called "pretonals" because they precede tonal stress. All three semivowels can function in final position (S^2): *lai* 'much', *hâu* 'louse', *hẩư* 'give'.

Tones. The provisional dialect has five tones: level (unmarked) *ma* 'dog', high rising *má* 'type of rice seed', mid falling *mà* 'to come', low rising *mả* 'grave', and low glottalized *mạ* 'horse'. The names of these tones follow the Vietnamese names: *không, sắc, huyền, hỏi, nặng*. The official standard of *Thach An* has a sixth tone called the *lửng* tone: low-falling tone *ma̱ tha* 'magic trick'.

The *lửng* tone has proved difficult for TN orthography. Although Vietnamese also has six tones, use of the sixth tone mark is unintuitive for TN, because the tone it marks in Vietnamese is high. In printed manuscripts it is usually written in by hand as a line below the vowel. Dialects without this tone use the low rising tone in its place resulting in a number of homonyms: *ta* 'river'—> *tả : tả* 'to leave'. Tones are permitted with any syllable type with the exception that syllables ending in [p, t, k] can only take the low-rising and low-glottalized tones.

Basic Morphology

Word Formation. A word with no more than one meaningful unit is a simple word. Monosyllabic simple words make up much of the basic vocabulary, e.g. *chài* 'man', *nhình* 'woman', *eng* 'small', *chứ* 'yes'. There are a number of monosyllables that cannot stand independently but function as restricted-use intensifiers: *khao xoac* 'pure white' (*khao* 'white' + *xoac*), *rèng rạt* 'robust' (*rèng* 'strength' + *rạt*). Another group of monosyllables that cannot stand independently are linked to a leading syllable through rhyming or alliteration, resulting in a metaphoric extension with affective meaning: *lằn chằn* 'messy, complicated' (*lằn* 'fall down' + *chằn*), *đăc đí* 'silent, still' (*đăc* 'deep' + *đí*).

A word made up of two or more meaningful units is a compound. Compounds can be coordinative or attributive. Coordinative compounds are formed by two elements of similar or opposite meaning that instantiate a broader semantic category. Coordinate compounds with elements of similar meaning include *nộc nu* 'animals' (*nộc* 'bird' + *nu* 'mouse'); *hung hang* 'to cook' (*hung* 'to steam' + *hang* 'to stir-fry'). Coordinative compounds with elements of opposite meaning include *slao báo* 'young people' (*slao* 'girl' + *báo* 'boy'); *khai dự* 'to trade' (*khai* 'to sell' + *dự* 'to buy'). In attributive compounds, the second element narrows the semantic range of the first: *fặc đeng* 'pumpkin' (*fặc* 'squash' + *đeng* 'red'); *khóa cổm* 'shorts' (*khóa* 'pants' +*cổm* 'short').

Reduplication. Reduplication involves varying types of repetition in a word or syllable. Reduplication may indicate indeterminacy, *sluôn* 'garden' —> *sluôn sluôn* 'gardens (everywhere)'; it may lighten the base, *xup* 'to smell something' —> *xup xup* 'have a smell of something'; it may intensify, *tăc bjôp* 'to fall with a crash' —> *tăc bjôp bjôp* 'to fall with a thunderous crash'; or it may indicate continuity, *chêp dẹt* 'to throb' —> *chêp dẹt dẹt* 'to throb and throb'. A more complex type of reduplication with bisyllabic constructions involves repetition of the first syllable followed by alliteration of the second syllable plus *í* for elaborate emphasis: *đeng chit* 'bright red' —> *đeng chit đeng chí* 'bright shiny red'.

Emphatic tone involves reduplication with a tone change on the base word and intensifies meaning: *hom* 'fragrant' —> *hóm hom* 'wonderfully fragrant'.

Pronouns. Choice of pronouns in TN, as with other Southeast Asian languages, is often dependent on the social position of speakers in a given situation. First- and Second-person pronouns are illustrated below.

Situation	First Person	Second Person
1. Person of lower status with a person of higher status, a younger person with an older	*khởi*	
2. Equals in a familiar relationship, especially husband and wife	*ngỏ*	*nỉ*
3. Authorities addressing their inferiors; close friends or husband and wife; speaking to animals	*câu*	*mầư*
4. Speaking with familiars inclusive of the hearer or speaking of oneself	*hây, rầu*	

Third-person pronouns *te* and *mền* are used in referring to people or things and do not mark social position. Plurality is marked by prefixing *boong* to the relevant pronoun, *boong khởi, boong mầư, boong te*, etc. Kinship terms are often used in position as pronouns. *Mẹ* 'mother', *pú* 'grandfather', *chài* 'elder brother', *noọng* 'younger brother/sister' may be used by these people speaking of themselves, or by others in the family speaking about them or to them.

Demonstratives. Demonstratives include: *nẩy* 'here, this'; *tỉ, mến* 'there, that'; *đai, ứn* 'the other'. They may function as pronouns or as attributes in a noun expression. *Nẩy lẻ noọng Bình* (This is younger-sibling Binh) 'This is Binh', *Ăn rườn nẩy cải quá ăn rườn tỉ* (CLF house this big than CLF house that) 'This house is bigger than that house'.

Classifiers. Classifiers are obligatory in TN and the usual word order is quantifier + classifier + noun. Classifiers may be used independently to refer to previous subjects. Common classifiers include: *cần* 'people', *tua* 'animals, things', *ăn* 'things'. Classifiers for inanimate objects usually refer to general qualities of things. *Mạc* is used with things that are sharp and usually made of metal: *mạc khêm* 'a needle', *mạc pjạ* 'a knife'. *bâư* is used with wide, thin things: *bâư slửa* 'shirt' *bâư toong* 'large leaf (e.g., banana leaf)'.

Aspect and Tense. Verbs of aspect before the main verb are: *cỏi* 'intention to do something at a later time'; *đang slí* 'action in progress'; *ngám* 'action immediately preceding the reference time'; and *slén* 'action preceding the reference time by some time'. After the verb *dá* signals cessation of action. Loans from Vietnamese *đạ* (*đã* 'already') and *xẹ* (*sẽ* 'will') are used for more specific notions of past and future tense: *Vằn pjục cỏi hêt* (day-tomorrow ~ do) 'We'll do it tomorrow'.

Basic Syntax

The basic word order for a simple sentence in TN is Subject-Verb-Object: *Noọng hung khẩu* (Younger-sibling cook rice) 'Little brother/sister is cooking rice'.

Predicates. A complex predicate typically features a succession of verbs surrounding a main verb, called a "serial verb construction". Serial verbs can indicate things like temporal deixis, aspect, negation, modality, direction or causality. The position of a particular verb before or after the main verb depends on its role in the context of the event. The same verb in different positions may grammaticalize in different directions: *pây đảy* (go = able) 'can go': *đảy pây* 'had the chance to go'.

Interrogatives. Interrogatives in TN occur in the same position as nouns and can combine with nouns to form a compound or question. Words in this group include: *cầư* 'who', *tầư* 'where', *răng* 'what'. *Cầư mà liểu?* (who come play) 'Who came for a visit?', *Boọng te pây tầư?* (PLURAL 3P go where) 'Where are they going?'

Negation. The predicate can be negated by placing one of a range of words before the main verb: *bấu, mí, nắm* not'; *dá* 'don't'; *xằng, páy* 'not yet'. *Te nắm pây.* (3P not go) 'S/he didn't go', *Te xằng mà* (3P not-yet come) 'S/he didn't come back yet'.

Directionals. Directionals fall after the main verb. They include *pây* 'go', *mà* 'come', *mừa* 'return to', *ooc* 'out/away from', *khẩu* 'into/towards', *khửn* 'go up', *lồng* 'go down'. Where two directionals occur in succession the first refers to the movement of the subject in relation to its location and the second refers to direction in relation to the speaker's perspective. *Te lển khẩu rườn mà* (3P run into house come) 'S/he ran into the house'.

Particles. Particles in TN include question particles and attitudinal particles. These generally come at the end of the sentence. Some question particles require a yes/no response. Negator words such as *bấu* 'not', *xằng* 'not yet' are placed after the predicate: *Nọong mì chèn bâú?* (younger-sibling have money not) 'Have you got any money?' In this case the addressee responds either *bâú* 'No' or *mì* 'Yes, I have'. An extended form involves *rụ bấu* 'or not', to which the addressee responds similarly: *Pú hăn rụ bâú?*(Grandfather see or not) 'Can you see or not?'

Some question particles turn a statement into a question and signal attitude. *á, náo á* suggests dissatisfaction in the speaker. *lỏ, á lỏ, nớ, a rớ* suggests familiar respect: *Bấu pây náo á?* (not go PT) 'So you're not going, eh?'

Attitudinal particles signal attitudes or feelings of the speaker, usually in a statement. These include *ạ* "respect", *tằng nới* "reluctance", *nẻ, chầy* "assertion", *pây* "commanding", *a dè* "encouraging", *lố, a nè* "urging". *dè* and *chế* are used in a question after an interrogative or negative to show familiarity and respect.

Contact with Other Languages

While the number of Chinese loans in spoken TN has been put at not higher than 6.8 percent, the number of loans in traditional literature is much higher. Apart from an east-west distinction in borrowing, evidence also points to borrowing over several centuries. Chinese loans may have been loaned either directly from Chinese or indirectly via Vietnamese (Sino-Vietnamese). Direct loans include loans from spoken Chinese and literary loans. Direct loans are not found in Vietnamese or if they are their pronunciation in Vietnamese, is very different from that in TN. Their pronunciation is often similar to that in neighboring Zhuang languages. A Chinese syllable may be compounded with a word of Tai origin. The order of a compound may be reversed in borrowing. Semantic change often occurs though less in the case of literary loans.

Loanwords from Vietnamese include those of native origin, Sino-Vietnamese origin, or from other languages. Loans of native Vietnamese origin are found throughout traditional writing, poetry and proverbs. Prominent among them are a number of monosyllabic words with grammatical function, *xẹ* 'will', *vạ* 'and', *nhưng* 'but', *cụng* 'also', *đạ* 'already', but general vocabulary items are also included, *việc* 'work', *dờ* 'hour'. Sino-Vietnamese loanwords are bisyllabic abstract terms that maintain their Vietnamese meanings and are not used in constructing new forms in TN: *xạ hội chủ nghịa* 'socialism', *hợp tac xạ* 'cooperative', *huyện* 'district', *văn hoá* 'culture', *khao học* 'science', *chính phủ* 'government', *đảng ủy* 'party committee', *diều tra* 'survey'. Many of these have been introduced as part of the Communist enterprise over the last century. Several words from ENGLISH and French have also been borrowed through Vietnamese: *mít tinh* 'meeting', *xà phong savon* ('soap'), *ô tô* 'automobile'.

Generally Vietnamese forms are closely preserved. There are two tone-change rules. Vietnamese high-glottal (*ngã*) tone becomes TN low glottal (*nặng*) tone. Vietnamese high-rise (*sắc*) tone often becomes TN low-rising (*hỏi*) tone. Preserving Vietnamese forms may mean introducing a sound that is not in the TN phonological system: [*g*] in *rườn ga* 'train station'. Adaptation of such forms to the TN phonological system is officially encouraged, and a number of loans demonstrate this has been the natural course. Some loans suggest further sound changes may have taken place since borrowing.

Common Words

man:	chài	woman:	nhình
water:	nặm	sun:	tha vằn
three:	slam	fish:	pja
big:	cải	small:	eng
yes:	chử	not, no:	bấu
good:	đây	bird:	nộc
long:	rì	dog:	ma
tree:	mạy		

Example Sentences

(1) Nặm luây lồng rù pây.
water flow down hole go
'The water flowed down into the hole.'

(2) Kin a dè, lục!
eat ENCOURAGING.PARTICLE child
'Eat up, son!'

(3) Mì sloong tua vài, tua kin nhả, tua nòn.
have two CLF buffalo CLF eat grass CLF sleep
'There are two buffaloes, one eating grass and one lying down.'

Select Bibliography

Bế Viết Đệng, Nguyễn Văn Huy, and Chu Thái Sơn, eds. 1992. *Các Dân Tộc Tày Nẳng ở Việt Nam* ('The Tay-Nung Peoples of Vietnam'). Hanoi: Viện Khoa Học Xã Hội.

Barlow, J. 1987. "The Zhuang Minority Peoples of the Sino-Vietnamese Frontier in the Song Period." In *Journal of South-east Asian Studies* 18.2: 250–269.

Doan Thien Thuat. 1996. *Tay-Nung Language in the North (of) Vietnam.* Tokyo: Tokyo University of Foreign Studies.

Hoàng Văn Ma. 1971. *Ngữ Pháp Tiếng Tày-Nùng* ('Grammar of Tay-Nung'). Hanoi: Nhà Xuất Bản Khoa Học Xã Hội.

Hoàng Văn Ma and Lục Văn Pảo. 1970. "Các từ mượn trong tiếng Tày-Nùng ('Loanwords in Tay-Nung')." In *Ngôn Ngữ* ('Language') 1: 35–41.

Hoàng Văn Ma, Lục Văn Pảo and Hoàng Chi. 1973. *Từ Điển Tày-Nùng—Việt* ('Tay-Nung—Vietnamese Dictionary'). Hanoi: Nhà Xuất Bản Khoa Học Xã Hội.

Nguyen Khac Vien, ed. 1968. "Mountain Regions and National Minorities in the D.R. of Vietnam." In *Vietnamese Studies* 15. Hanoi: Xunhasaba.

Ross, P. 1996. "Dao Ngan Tay: A B-language in Vietnam." In *Mon-Khmer Studies* 25: 133–139.

Yongxian Luo. 1996. "The sub-group structure of the Tai languages." Doctoral Dissertation, The Australian National University, Canberra.

TELUGU

Rosanne Pelletier

Language Name: Telugu. **Alternates:** *Andhra, Talinga, Tailinga, Telinga, Teloogoo, Telungu, Tenugu Tenungu.* **Autonym:** *Telugu.*

Location: Telugu is spoken mainly in the south Indian state of Andhra Pradesh, with some speakers in the neighboring states Karnataka (to the west) and Tamil Nadu (to the south).

Family: South-Central subgroup of the Dravidian language family.

Related Languages: Telugu is most closely related to the six other members of the South-Central Dravidian subgroup spoken in Andhra Pradesh, Madhya Pradesh, and Orissa. These languages, all nonliterary, are: GONDI, Koṇḍa (also known as Kūbi), and the "Kondh" languages spoken in Orissa's Kondhmal Hills: Kūi, Kūvi, Maṇḍa, and Pengo.

Dialects: Telugu has four regional dialects. While the regional distinctions are more obvious among uneducated speakers of the language, the following dialect distinctions nevertheless exist for both educated and uneducated speakers: Northern, Southern, Eastern (bordering the ORIYA-speaking area), and Central. The phoneme /ǣ/, a long, low front vowel occurring in the ENGLISH word "cat", exists only in the Central and Eastern dialects.

Despite regional and caste differences, educational level distinguishes Telugu pronunciation to a great degree. Illiterate monolingual Telugu speakers lack the phonemes that standard Telugu has acquired through borrowings from SANSKRIT and English. Specifically, 10 aspirated consonants, 4 fricatives, and 2 retroflex consonants are lacking from the speech of uneducated speakers. Thus, while an educated Telugu speaker pronounces the word borrowed from English for 'coffee' as /kaafii/, an uneducated speaker, lacking the labiodental fricative /f/, pronounces this word using the labial stop /p/: /kaapii/. Consonant clusters are also absent from the grammar of uneducated speakers.

Number of Speakers: 55–60 million.

Origin and History

The Telugu-speaking people of south India, the Andhras, are indigenous to the Indian subcontinent. Literature in Telugu dates to the 11th century A.D. The earliest known work is Nannaya's *Mahaabhaarata*. The earliest inscription written entirely in Telugu dates to the 6th century A.D. While the Andhras demanded their own state as early as 1913, and Telugu is in fact now the official language of the south Indian state of Andhra Pradesh, until the mid-20th century, Telugu speakers occupied two different political units: the northern half of the former Madras presidency, and nine districts of the Nizam's Dominions called Telangana. Telangana Telugu, spoken in a region where the official language was URDU, was heavily influenced by the official language, as well as by PERSIAN and ARABIC.

Finally, in 1953, the northern districts of Madras were reorganized into the Andhra State, India's first linguistically defined state. In 1956 the nine districts constituting Telangana joined Andhra, and the resulting state was called Andhra Pradesh. This political reorganization changed the Northern group of Telugu speakers from a linguistic minority in Urdu-speaking territory to speakers of the official language of the state (Telugu was declared the official language in 1966). Not surprisingly, Telugu began to be used as a literary language in Telangana at this same historical period. Through the recent use of Telugu in mass media and popular literature, Modern Standard Telugu, a standard dialect based on the language of educated speakers of the Central dialect, has gradually developed.

Orthography and Basic Phonology

Telugu is the only literary language in the South-Central subgroup of the Dravidian language family. (Dravidian has three other literary languages: KANNADA, MALAYALAM, and TAMIL.)

The writing system of Modern Telugu is a syllabary based on the Southern variety of Brahmi, which then developed into the Telugu-Kannada script. Telugu writing developed further distinctions, and Telugu now has an alphabet that is different from, although still similar to, that of the South Dravidian language Kannada. In comparison with the alphabets used in Indo-Aryan languages, the characters of the Telugu and Kannada alphabet are very round. The fact that writing was done on a palmyra leaf with an iron style, and round characters produce few rips, has been cited as a primary reason for the development of the circular shape of Telugu and Kannada characters.

The chart on the next page shows samples of the 12 primary vowel symbols of Telugu. There are also 23 primary consonant symbols. Telugu also has 10 aspirated consonant symbols that are used mainly in words borrowed from Sanskrit and the modern Indo-Aryan languages.

In contrast to the arrangement of the LATIN alphabet, the order of the Telugu characters is based on phonological feature considerations. For example, after the vowel group, the consonants are then ordered according to place/manner of articulation in their unvoiced, then voiced, and if applicable, nasal realizations.

Table 1: Consonants

	Bilabial	Labio-dental	Dental-Alveolar	Retroflex	Palato-alveolar	Palatal	Dorso-velar	Glottal
Stops	p (ph) b (bh)		t (th) d (dh)	ṭ (ṭh) ḍ (ḍh)	c (ch) j (jh)		k (kh) g (gh)	
Nasals	m		n		(ṇ)			
Fricatives		(f)	s	(ṣ)		(ś)		(h)
Laterals			l	(ḷ)				
Trill			r					
Approx.	w					y		

When the primary consonant symbols are written as listed in the chart, they are pronounced with an accompanying vowel /a/. All vowels and consonants have secondary forms, the secondary consonant symbols being used in consonant clusters, including double consonants. Vowels that follow a consonant cluster are symbolized by the addition of this vowel's secondary form to the primary form of the first consonant (as is the secondary form of the second consonant). Thus, vertical as well as horizontal space is utilized in a way that differs from the linear representation of phonemes in, for example, IPA transcription. Strict rules govern the order in which the orthographic elements are read.

The Telugu symbol *o* is an unspecified nasal, whose point of articulation is determined by the following consonant. For example, in *pampu* 'to send', this nasal is pronounced as the labial nasal /m/, since /p/ is a labial stop; while in *mantsu* 'dew', the nasal is pronounced as the dental nasal /n/, since /t/ is a dental stop.

Table 2: Vowels

	Front	Back
High	i ii	u uu
Mid	e ee	o oo
Low	ǣ	a aa

Telugu has two diphthongs: /ai/ and /au/.

The phonemes in Tables 1 and 2 correspond rather closely to their IPA values. A few elements, however, require explanation. The symbol /ś/ indicates a palatal fricative. When /w/ occurs before the back vowels, it is pronounced as a bilabial approximant similar to the English /w/ but without lip rounding. However, it is pronounced as a labiodental fricative [v] when it precedes a front vowel. Vowel length is phonemic in Telugu: *paḍu* 'to fall' versus *paaḍu* 'to sing'. The long vowels are approximately twice as long as the short vowels. The phoneme /ǣ/ is present only in the Central and Eastern dialects. The consonants in parentheses occur only in Standard Telugu; Standard Telugu distinguishes aspirated consonants from non-aspirated ones.

Samples of Telugu Symbols: Vowels

అ	ఆ	ఇ	ఈ	ఉ	ఊ
a	aa	i	ii	u	uu
ఎ	ఏ	ఐ	ఒ	ఓ	ఔ
e	ee	ai	o	oo	au

Telugu has numerous phonological rules. For example, a vowel harmony process causes the noninitial high front vowel /i/ to assimilate in backness to the vowel in the plural suffix *-lu*: *puli* 'tiger' *-lu* > *pululu* 'tigers', *maniṣi* 'person' *-lu* > *manuṣulu* 'people'. Additionally, any short vowel is deleted before a vowel-initial suffix or word: *adi* 'that' + *-ee* 'emphatic suffix' > *adee* 'that itself'. This process is obligatory within words and preferred across word boundaries.

Basic Morphology

The morphology of Telugu is agglutinating and suffixal. Telugu has a rich case system; suffixes attach to a form of the noun called the "oblique stem". The language has singular, plural, and honorific nouns. Plural predicate agreement occurs with honorific subjects.

Telugu has a two-way gender system based on natural gender; however, the gender categories differ in the singular and plural. That is, while singular nouns are divided into the categories masculine (for nouns denoting male human beings) versus nonmasculine (all other entities), in the plural, nouns are divided into the categories human versus nonhuman. Notice that although there are several pronouns (below) that refer specifically to female human beings, a separate feminine gender category does not exist. Nouns denoting female human beings group with nouns denoting nonhumans in the singular and with nouns denoting humans in the plural with respect to pronominal choice as well as predicate agreement. Compare the singular *waaḍu weḷ-tunna-ḍu* (he go-DUR-3SM) 'he is going' versus *adi weḷ-tunnaa-di* (it/she go-DUR-3S.NOM.M) 'it/she is going' with the plural: *waaru weḷ-tunnaa-ru* (they[HUMAN] are going-DUR-3PL.HUMAN) 'they (M or F) are going' versus *awi weḷ-tunnaa-yi* (they[NONHUMAN] go-DUR-3PL.NON.HUMAN) 'they (NONHUMAN) are going.' Most common nouns do not carry a morpheme indicating gender.

Telugu has personal pronouns only in the first and second person. The personal pronouns are shown below in their nominative and oblique/genitive forms. Note the additional person distinction within the first-person plural forms: the inclusive form is chosen when the addressee is included in the reference of the pronoun, and the exclusive form is used otherwise. The inclusive/exclusive distinction is not reflected in predicate agreement; only a single first-person plural agreement morpheme occurs. The second-person plural pronoun is also used as a polite form.

	Nominative	Oblique-Genitive
Singular:		
first person	neenu	naa
second person	niiwu/nuwwu	nii
Plural:		
first person inclusive	manam(u)	mana
first person exclusive	meem(u)	maa
second person	miiru	mii

Third-person pronouns, with the exception of the reflexives, are all demonstrative pronouns. These forms are composed of a pronominal stem suffixed to forms of the demonstrative determiners *aa* 'that' and *ii* 'this'. The first broad cut to be made among such pronouns is proximal versus distal. Within these categories, gender, number, and various degrees of formality are distinguished. The following singular masculine distal forms all mean 'he, that man': *waaḍu* (he, very informal, intimate, impolite), *atanu* (informal, third degree of respect), *aayana* formal, second degree of respect), *waaru* (very polite, first degree of respect). The singular distal feminine forms meaning 'she, that woman' are *adi* (very informal, intimate, impolite), *aame* (formal or informal, second or third degree of respect), *aawiḍa* (informal, second or third degree of respect), and *waaru* (very polite, first degree of respect). The singular neuter form 'it, that thing' is *adi*, the same as the informal feminine form. Plural distal human forms are *waaṇḍlu/waaḷḷu* or *waaru* 'they, those people'; the nonhuman counterpart is *awi* 'they, those things'.

In the corresponding proximal forms meaning 'he, this man', etc., the forms differ only in having *i* or *ii* for *a* or *aa*, for example, *wiiḍu, itanu* instead of *waaḍu, atanu*, etc. There are fewer forms for the interrogative pronouns, but these forms are based roughly on the demonstrative stem forms as well. These pronouns have *e* or *ee* in place of *i/a* or *ii/aa*. The most commonly used forms are *ewaru* 'who', *eem* 'what', and *eemiṭi* 'what' (predicate nominal form). The reflexive pronouns are *tanu/taanu* 'himself, herself' and *tamu/taamu* 'themselves'. Only third-person reflexive forms exist; personal pronouns in an unusual syntactic construction are used to express reflexivity for first and second persons. All of the third-person forms express case distinctions by affixation of the case suffixes to their oblique stems.

Telugu has no indefinite or definite articles, but does have a set of demonstrative determiners: *aa* 'that', *ii* 'this' and *ee* 'which'. The numeral *oka* 'one' is sometimes used with the function of an indefinite article.

In Telugu, as in all Dravidian languages, there exist only two basic part-of-speech categories: nouns and verbs. While it is not inaccurate to refer to other categories, such other categories are in fact derived from combinations of nominal and verbal elements. Therefore, adnominal modification of nouns is accomplished by means of other nouns. In such structures, there is no overt agreement except with numeral nouns, in which a human/nonhuman distinction is made: *aydu kukka-lu* (five dog-PL) 'five dogs' versus *aydu-guru manuṣu-lu* (five-HUMAN person-PL) 'five people'.

On the other hand, in appositional structures, the head noun agrees in all features (number and person):

meemu	aaḍawaaḷ-ḷa-m	pani	cees-aa-mu
we.EXCL	woman-PL-1PL	work	do-PST-1PL

'We women worked.'

In verbless sentences headed by nominal predicates, the same agreement morphology appears on the nominal predicate: *meemu aaḍawaaḷ-ḷa-m* (we.EXCL woman-PL-1PL) 'we are women'.

Telugu verbs agree with their subjects in person, number, and in the third person, gender. With its rich variety of verbal suffixes, Telugu expresses many semantic notions that other languages express by parts of speech such as adverbs, for example, intensity of an action. Another example is negation, which is expressed by the negative suffix *-a* in the future-habitual tense: *amm-a-nu* (sell-NEG-1SG) 'I will not/do not sell'. Note that this form lacks a tense/aspect morpheme. As is typical of the language family, no Telugu word can contain morphology for both tense/aspect and negation; the negative suffix preempts the tense suffix.

Common tense/aspect suffixes are the past, future-habitual, and durative suffixes. In finite verbs, the order of morphemes is verb stem + tense/aspect (or negative) suffix + agreement suffix, as can be seen in the future-habitual paradigm of the verb *ammu* 'sell' with the future-habitual suffix *-taa/-tun*. Note the phonetic similarity between the agreement morpheme and the last syllable of the subject pronoun:

nee*nu*	ammu-taa-*nu*	'I will/do sell'
nuw*wu*	ammu-taa-*w(u)*	'you will/do sell'
waa*ḍu*	ammu-taa-*ḍu*	'he will/does sell'
a*di*	ammu-tun-*di*	'she/(it) will/does sell'
mana*m(u)*	ammu-taa-*m(u)*	'we will/do sell'
mii*ru*	ammu-taa-*ru*	'you will/do sell'
waa*ru*	ammu-taa-*ru*	'they (human) will/do sell'
(a*wi*	ammu-taa-*y(i)*	'they (non-human) will/do sell')

In Telugu, morphemes are ordered root + derivational suffix + inflectional suffix. To express kinship relations, a co-compound is used, with the final vowel of the first element often lengthened as a marker of coordination. For example, from *akka* 'older sister' and *cellelu* 'younger sister' is derived the following compound: *akka-a-celleḷ-lu* (older.sister-COORD-younger.sister-PL) 'sisters'. Such forms appear to have become lexicalized.

Telugu has a suffixal verbal reflexive consisting of an inflected form of the verb *kon* (literally 'to take') attached to the main verb: *aayana koṭṭu-konn-aa-ḍu* (he beat-REFL-PST-3SM) 'He beat himself'. This reflexive has a number of other related meanings, including 'self-benefactive': *aayana waṇṭa ceesu-koṇ-ṭaa-ḍu* (he cooking do-REFL-FUT-3SM) 'He will cook for himself'.

Causative verbs are formed by attaching the suffix *-inc*. This suffix is also one of the various transitivizing suffixes. In addition, Modern Telugu uses the auxiliary forms of the verbs *koṭṭ* 'to beat', *peṭṭ* 'to put', and *wees* 'to throw, strike' to form causatives/transitives. For example, *koṭṭ* 'to beat' attaches to *weḷḷ* 'to go' to form the causative *weḷḷagoṭṭ* 'to chase, drive out', voicing the *k* in this environment.

There are a number of clitics in the language. For example, the interrogative clitic *-aa* typically attaches to the right-most element of the clause to form a yes/no question.

Basic Syntax

Telugu is a typical Dravidian language in that it has many types of complex predicate constructions. The richness within the verb itself is multiplied when combined with other, similarly richly inflected elements.

The preferred order of major constituents is SOV, with the verb (or nominal predicate) virtually always fixed in final position. Nonpredicate elements display some variation in word order. Telugu is a head-final language.

Telugu expresses grammatical relations by means of case morphology as opposed to word order. Important case suffixes are the accusative suffix *-ni/-nu*, which marks the direct object (but occurs only on animates in colloquial Telugu); the dative suffix *-ki/-ku*, which generally marks the indirect object, or signifies 'to' or 'for', *-ninci/-nunci* 'from', *-koosam* 'for, for the sake of', *-too* 'with', *-kaṇṭe* 'compared with'. The nominative case is morphologically unmarked, and is the case of subjects, third-person predicates, and inanimate direct objects.

Telugu has two negative verbs. Nominal predicates are negated with *kaa* (which has a default, nonagreeing form *kaadu*): *neenu siita-ni kaa-nu* (I Sita-1SG NEG-1SG) 'I am not Sita'. *lee* negates other predicates: *neenu uuḷ-ḷoo lee-nu* (I town-in NEG-1SG) 'I am not/was not in town'. (*lee* is irregular in that it has an inherent nonfuture tense.)

The two sentences above do not morphologically express tense. Recall that Telugu disallows the morphological expression of both tense/aspect and negation within the same word. Nonetheless, Telugu does make tense/aspect distinctions in negative sentences, expressing negation syntactically within a complex verbal construction. For example, the following constructions involve a default auxiliary form of the negative verb *leedu* (note the lack of subject agreement) in combination with the infinitive or gerund of the main verb to express the past and durative negative, respectively. (Recall that in the absence of tense/aspect morphology, the verb is interpreted as future habitual.) *neenu raay-a leedu* (I write-INF NEG) 'I did not write', *neenu raay-aḍam leedu* (I write-GER NEG) 'I am not writing'.

Telugu makes extensive use of participles. In general, more than one finite verb per sentence is disallowed. Thus, even to express a sentence such as 'Ramu ate idlies and drank coffee', the first verb occurs as a participle:

raamu	iḍlii-lu	tin-i	kaafii	taag-ǣ-ḍu
Ramu	idlie-PL	eat-PERF.PART	coffee	drink-PST-3SM

(lit: 'Ramu, having eaten idlies, drank coffee.')

One situation in which multiple finite verbs are encountered is the quotative construction, but here the quoted material is embedded beneath a quotative complementizer:

nuwwu	naa-too	[nuwwu	reepu	was-taa-w(u)]
you	I-with	you	tomorrow	come-FUT-2S

ani	ceppǣwu
QUOT	say-PAST-2S

'You told me that you would come tomorrow.'

Numerous complex predicate constructions exist in Telugu, including "light-verb" constructions, in which a noun (usually borrowed from Sanskrit or English) occurs with a Telugu verb: *siita snaanam cees-in-di* (Sita bath do-PST-3S.NON.M) 'Sita took a bath'.

Relative clauses are formed using a relative participle rather than a relative pronoun. Only case (no verbal morphology) disambiguates the agent and patient in such constructions: *nannu pilic-ina abbaayi* (I.ACC call-PST.REL.PART boy) 'the boy who called me' versus *neenu pilic-ina abbaayi* (I.NOM call-PST.REL.PART boy) 'the boy who I called'.

Telugu uses dative-marked subjects with certain experiencer verbs. Also, in general, Telugu sentences are grammatical without an overt subject.

While there is a passive construction in Telugu, formed by combining the finite form of the verb *paḍu* 'to fall, suffer' and the infinitive of the main verb, this construction is rarely used. In fact, it is mainly used by Telugu writers translating the English passive. A construction used more commonly is the past participle in combination with the finite form of the verb *un* 'to be': *talupu teric-i unna-di* (door open-PERF.PART be-3SG.N) The door is open'.

Contact with Other Languages

Telugu is located at a very important crossroads within the Indian Linguistic Area. Being spoken in Central and South India, it is in contact with both Indo-Aryan languages (generally spoken to the north), as well as Dravidian languages (generally spoken to the south). Among the Dravidian languages with which Telugu has contact are Kannada, Tamil, and the Central Dravidian "tribal" languages Kolami and Parji. As for Indo-Aryan languages, along with Oriya, MARATHI, and Halbi, Telugu has a great deal of contact with Dakkhini Urdu, the variety of Urdu spoken in Andhra Pradesh and other southern states of India. Finally, in urban areas Telugu is in contact with varieties of English.

While Telugu has borrowed heavily from Sanskrit, in some cases Dravidian words are beginning to replace Sanskrit terms in Modern Telugu. However, the vocabulary of certain topics, such as religion, remains highly Sanskritized.

As mentioned above, certain borrowed nouns combine with the Telugu verb *cees* 'do' to form a "light-verb" construction. Similarly, many Sanskrit nouns combine with the causative-transitive suffix *-inc* (mentioned in the discussion of morphology) to form Telugu verbs; for example Sanskrit *preema* 'love' becomes Telugu *preeminc* 'to love'. Also, HINDI-Urdu *keeṭaanaa* 'to allot' becomes Telugu *keeṭaayinc* 'to allocate'.

Telugu contains very many borrowings from English, particularly in urban areas. English words ending in a consonant such as *pencil, mile*, and *road* generally end in the vowel /u/ when borrowed into Telugu, for example, *pensilu, mailu*, and *rooḍḍu*. Also, English words containing an alveolar stop contain the retroflex counterpart when borrowed into Telugu. For example, English 'tea' becomes *ṭii* and 'doctor' becomes *ḍaakṭaru*. Telugu, particularly Telangana Telugu, also contains vocabulary borrowed from Urdu, Persian, and Arabic.

Common Words

man:	maniṣi	long:	poḍugaaṭi
woman:	strii	small:	cinna
water:	niiḷḷu (plural)	yes:	awunu
sun:	poddu	no:	kaadu
three:	muuḍu	good:	manci
fish:	ceepa	bird:	pakṣi
big:	pedda	dog:	kukka
tree:	ceṭṭu		

Example Sentences

(1) manam telugu waaḷ-ḷa-m ay-i mana
we.INCL Telugu person-PL-1PL be-PERF.PART. our.INCL

bhaaṣa-ku eem ceesæ̃m.
language-DAT what do-PST-1PL
'What have we done for our language, we (being) Telugus?'

(2) raamu aalasyan-gaa waccæ̃ḍu ani
Ramu delay-become.INF (= late) come-PST-3SM that

kamala-ku koopam wacc-in-di.
Kamala-DAT anger come-PST-3S.NON.M
'Kamala got angry because Ramu came late.'

(3) meemu ninnu pilaw-aṭam leedu.
we.EXCL you.ACC call-GER NEG
'We are not calling you.'

Efforts to Preserve, Protect, and Promote the Language

Despite its official status, the actual role of Telugu in the legal, administrative, and advanced educational workings of the state has been limited. The lack of appropriate vocabulary and an "officialese" register have been cited as the major reasons for this limited role. Obviously, however, such a problem is self-solving, since necessary terms are coined (or borrowed) as soon as the need for such vocabulary arises.

In 1969 the *Telugu Akademi* decided that the Andhra Pradesh Education Department must use Modern Standard Telugu in its textbooks for all subjects. Previously, only textbooks for the Telugu language were in Telugu, and they were in a more archaic classical style differing from actual spoken Telugu.

The existence of a standard variety spoken by educated Andhras all over the state, and its use in the educational system seem likely to aid Telugu in maintaining a strong foothold not only as an official language of India, but also as India's second largest linguistic group (after Hindi). It appears extremely likely that the number of Telugu speakers will continue to increase.

Select Bibliography

Brown, Charles. 1985. *Dictionary Telugu English*. (Second edition of C.P. Brown's 1903 *Telugu-English Dictionary* revised by M. Venkata Ratnam, W.H. Campbell, and Rao Bahadur K. Veeresalingam.) New Delhi: Asian Educational Services.

Krishnamurti, Bhadriraju, and J.P.L. Gwynn. 1985. *A Grammar of Modern Telugu*. Delhi: Oxford University Press.

Lisker, Leigh. 1963. *Introduction to Spoken Telugu*. New York: American Council of Learned Societies.

Ramanarasimham, P. 1985. *An Intensive Course in Telugu*. Mysore: Central Institute of Indian Languages.

Thai

Alexander Robertson Coupe

Language Name: Thai (Standard Thai, Central Thai, Siamese). **Autonym:** *phaasăa thay.*

Location: Thai is the official and national language of Thailand. It is the language of government, the preferred medium of education, the language of mass media, and the language of wider communication within the country. Thai is based on Central Thai (*phaasăa klaaŋ*), a closely related regional variety spoken as the first language of people living in the central plains of the Chao Phrya River basin, including the capital, Bangkok.

Family: Thai belongs to the Tai language family, which Li (1977) splits into three branches: Northern, Central and Southwestern. Thai is a member of the Southwestern branch. The established spelling convention is that "Tai" (pronounced with an unaspirated dental stop *t*) is used for the family name, and "Thai" (pronounced with an aspirated dental stop *th*) is normally used to refer to the national language of Thailand.

Attempts have been made to connect Tai languages to the Sino-Tibetan family on the basis of typological characteristics shared with Chinese languages. The most controversial genetic classification links Tai with the Austronesian family in a superstock designated Austro-T(h)ai. There is strong evidence to support the claim that Tai is genetically related to the Kam-Sui languages of southern China and the Bê (Lin-gao) and Li (Hlai) languages of Hainan Island. This generally accepted grouping constitutes a family designated "Kam-Tai". Classification beyond this level is speculative and scholars remain divided over higher-level affiliations with other language families.

Related Languages: Languages most closely related to Thai are those that belong to the southwestern branch of the Tai family. Some of these are LAO (Laos, Thailand), SHAN (northern Burma), Khampti (northeastern India), Black Tai (northern Vietnam, northern Laos, Thailand), White Tai (northern Vietnam), Red Tai (northern Vietnam) and Lue (Yunnan).

Dialects: Four regional varieties of Thai are found within Thailand: Central Thai, spoken in the central region; Northern Thai, spoken in the mountainous region north of Sukhothai; Southern Thai, spoken in peninsula Thailand south of the provincial capital city of Prachuap Khiri Khan; and Northeastern Thai, spoken on the Khorat Plateau. Lexical and phonological (both segmental and suprasegmental) divergences differentiate the four varieties. Northeastern Thai is actually Lao according to phonological and lexical criteria, but is referred to by the Indic loanwords *phaasăa ʔiisăan* 'northeastern language' for political reasons.

Number of Speakers: It is difficult to state with absolute certainty how many of the estimated 53 million people of Thailand speak the national language. Smalley (1994) estimates that only 10.4 million people (20 percent) speak Standard Thai as their native language (figure based on 1980 census), but also notes that the estimation is complicated by the fact that Thai lacks clear-cut boundaries between registers. It is therefore best viewed as a continuum ranging from a codified normative variety closely associated with the written medium and characterized by initial-consonant clusters, a phonemic distinction between *r* and *l*, and many loanwords of KHMER or Indic provenance, to a regional variety characterized by initial consonant cluster reduction, the merger of *r* to *l*, and a vocabulary more reflective of an ancestral Tai origin. At one extreme is Standard Thai, which, for the most part, is acquired through formal education; at the other extreme is the regional dialect Central Thai, spoken by approximately 14 million people (27 percent) as their first language. Outside of the central region, proficiency in Standard Thai varies according to the amount of exposure to the national language. Speakers of the other regional varieties are most likely to have at least some ability in the national language, with degree of proficiency determined by factors such as age, schooling, occupation, and location.

Origin and History

Comparative-historical linguistic research demonstrates that the Tai languages are descended from a parent language designated Proto-Tai, estimated to have been spoken by a single group of people approximately 1,500 to 2,000 years ago. The geographical origin of this common ancestor is uncertain, but most linguists now believe that the Tai homeland was somewhere near the present-day Vietnam/China border. Tai speakers are believed to have migrated from this region to northern Vietnam, Laos, Thailand, the southern provinces of China, northern Burma, and Assam in northeastern India at a relatively rapid rate of dispersion. Speakers of early forms of Thai gradually moved into the central plains of Thailand between the 8th and 12th centuries and established political dominions in the Chao Phrya River Valley.

One of these polities was Sukhothai, which consolidated and extended its political power in the late 13th century under the rule of King Ramkhamhaeng. Sukhothai is regarded as the first ethnic Thai kingdom and its people are thought to have spoken a language quite close to Proto-Tai. Evidence of this language survives in the stone inscriptions of Sukhothai. These are written in a form of modified Indic script, the earliest dated 1292. The death of King Ramkhamhaeng in 1298 resulted in a rapid decline of the political power of Sukhothai as other Tai principalities sought to extend their spheres of influence. In the last half of the 14th century the Thai kingdom of Ayutthaya (1351–1767) established its ascendancy in the lower Chao Phrya River Valley. The increasing political influence of Ayutthaya also had the effect of enhancing the prestige of the Thai dialect spoken in this region.

Early Ayutthaya was heavily influenced by an Angkorian model of bureaucracy, and a Khmer-speaking elite employed by the royal court was responsible for an influx of Indic and Khmer loanwords into Thai, adding to those borrowed since the first contacts with Khmer civilization. There was an elaboration of terminology relating to court practices, administration and etiquette; the introduction of titles for nobility and officials reflecting rank and status; and the development of a special vocabulary drawn from SANSKRIT and Khmer called *raachaasàp* 'royal language', to be used when speaking to or of royalty. The expanding complexity of lexical registers in Thai was a reflection of the development of an increasingly stratified and sophisticated society during this period.

The register differentiation and codification of Thai continued on into the Bangkok era following the destruction of Ayutthaya by the Burmese in 1767 and the founding of a new capital in the same year at Thonburi. Much of the former culture of Ayutthaya was reestablished by the ruling class, who spoke a language significantly divergent from that of the commoners. This was not only because of the fact that it was a different dialect to the variety spoken by the inhabitants of the Bangkok region, but also because of the large number of Indic and Khmer loanwords that had now become an intrinsic part of the elite's linguistic register. In the 19th century a language prescriptivism developed as a result of European influence via missionaries and the normative language reforms of King Mongkut (Rama IV). This culminated in the publication of prescriptive grammars in the late 19th and early 20th centuries that were based on models of traditional ENGLISH school grammars. The traditional grammatical analysis was substituted for a classical Sanskritic morphophonemic analysis using neologisms coined from Indic languages; this was then applied to Thai in a manner analogous to the way that LATIN formed the framework of prescriptive grammars of English. Codification and standardization have continued under the direction and influence of government institutions such as the Ministry of Education and the Royal Institute of Thailand (see Diller 1988).

Historical Development of the Tone System. Historical-comparative Tai linguists have posited that the tonal systems of Tai languages originated from a single parent language that had three contrasting tones occurring on "unstopped syllables" (i.e., syllables ending in a nasal, a semivowel, or a vowel). In addition, there was a fourth category of "stopped syllables" (i.e., syllables ending in the voiceless stops *p*, *t*, *k*, including the glottal stop *ʔ*), which is generally believed to have had no tonal distinction in the parent language. The three contrasting tones of unstopped syllables are usually labeled A, B and C, and the tonally undifferentiated category of stopped syllables is usually labeled D. The D category is further divided into stopped syllables with a long vowel (DL) and stopped syllables with a short vowel (DS), as tonal contrasts can be motivated by syllable-nucleus length if a phonemic vowel length distinction existed prior to the development of modern tones.

Sometime between the 14th and 17th centuries a cataclysmic sound change swept through the tonal languages of China and Southeast Asia. Its effect was that each original tone underwent a split into two or more tones depending upon the phonetic characteristics of the initial consonant of the syllable at that particular time. In brief, linguists have identified a common pattern in the languages affected by these tone splits: voiceless initial consonants raised tones, and voiced initial consonants lowered tones. This resulted in each original tone having two or more noncontrastive pitch-level differences. Sometime after this the initial consonants of syllables also went through radical sound changes. For example, syllables with initial voiceless preaspirated sonorant sounds such as *hm*, *hn*, and *hl* lost their voiceless preaspirated component so that phonetically they were undifferentiated from their voiced counterparts *m*, *n* and *l*, respectively.

In yet another sound change, initial voiced stop consonants such as *b*, *d* and *g* lost their voicing and developed aspiration, so that they became phonetically identical to an already existent voiceless aspirated stop series *ph*, *th*, and *kh*. And following this, preglottalized sounds such as *ʔb*, *ʔd* and *ʔy*, which are considered to be voiceless because the glottal feature is voiceless, lost their glottal component to become voiced sounds *b*, *d* and *y* respectively. The previously noncontrastive tones created anew by the tone splits now took on an important contrastive function, since the phonemic difference that was formerly signaled by the phonetic nature of the initial consonant of the syllable had been lost. The tone splits also caused the erstwhile tonally undifferentiated stopped syllables to develop contrastive tone.

William Gedney presents the following collective evidence for proposing that the tone splits occurred in Thai during the Ayutthaya period, and as recently as the late 15th century. Firstly, the script King Ramkhamhaeng devised for writing the first stone inscription of Sukhothai (known as Inscription One) used a system of marking that indicated just three tones on unstopped syllables. Category A tones were unmarked, Category B tones carried a superscript tone marker called *máy ʔèek*, and Category C tones had a superscript tone marker called *máy thoo*. Another feature of the script was that letters representing voiced sounds in Indic languages were used to write sounds in Thai that are now voiceless. The implication is that these sounds were voiced in the language of Sukhothai, therefore the sound change must have taken place after the Sukhothai period. Secondly, Khmer loanwords were heavily borrowed by the Central Thai dialect of Ayutthaya, presumably around the time of the Thai conquest of Angkor in the 15th century. Because the voiced initial stops of these loanwords also underwent the sound changes that affected Thai, it is apparent that the Khmer loanwords were borrowed prior to the tone splits and sound changes. And lastly, there is evidence from forms of Thai poetry. Two early forms of Thai verse called *khlooŋ* and *râay* had rules of metrical composition that would only have been possible in the three-tone system assumed for Sukhothai. Another form of verse called *klɔɔn* became popular at the end of the Ayutthaya period, but this had rules of

Table 1: Historical Origin of the Five-tone System of Thai

<table>
<tr><th rowspan="3">Initial Consonants</th><th colspan="3">Unstopped Syllables</th><th colspan="2">Stopped Syllables</th></tr>
<tr><th>A</th><th>B</th><th>C</th><th>DS</th><th>DL</th></tr>
<tr><th>unmarked</th><th>máy ʔèek</th><th>máy thoo</th><th>unmarked</th><th>unmarked</th></tr>
<tr><td>voiceless friction sounds ph, f, hm etc.</td><td>rising</td><td rowspan="3">low</td><td rowspan="3">falling</td><td rowspan="3">low</td><td rowspan="3">low</td></tr>
<tr><td>voiceless unaspirated stops p, t, c, k</td><td rowspan="3">mid</td></tr>
<tr><td>preglottalized sounds ʔb, ʔd, ʔy, ʔ</td></tr>
<tr><td>voiced sounds b, d, g, m, l, y, etc.</td><td>falling</td><td>high</td><td>high</td><td>falling</td></tr>
</table>

composition that could only apply to the modern five-tone system of Thai; that is, after the sound changes had taken place.

The phonetic characteristics of initial consonants that originally conditioned the splits and sound changes resulting in the five-tone system of Modern Thai (as well as the tone systems of all the daughter languages of Proto-Tai) can be found in Table 1. Note that with the exception of Proto-Tai Tone A, a voicing opposition in the initial consonant appears to have provided the primary motivation for a two-way tone split and subsequent tonal mergers. This binary pattern is common in many languages and dialects of the Tai family, although subsequent splits and coalescences that occurred independently in daughter languages after the major historic tone splits have resulted in widely differing five-, six-, and seven-tone systems. A common pattern of distribution is for the Category D tones to correspond in terms of pitch onset height and contour to some of the tones occurring on the unstopped syllables, but to differ in duration in the case of syllables with short nuclei. In varieties demonstrating this pattern, Category D tones may be analyzed as being in an allotonic relationship to those occurring on unstopped syllables.

Modern Thai has a system of five contrasting tones. This is demonstrated by the following words, whose meanings are signaled by different pitch contours on segmentally identical syllables: *naa* 'rice field', *nàa* 'custard apple', *nâa* 'face', *náa* 'mother's younger sibling', and *nǎa* 'thick'. In continuous speech, tones may undergo changes called "tone sandhi". This occurs when particular sequences of adjacent tones form conditioning environments that affect the phonetic realization of a tone. For example, the rising tone on an initial syllable in a disyllabic word may be pronounced as a high tone when it is followed by a rising tone on the second syllable. Thus *sǐ khǎaw* 'white' is usually pronounced as *sí khǎaw* at the normal speed of conversation.

Orthography and Basic Phonology

The modern Thai writing system originates from an Indic script. This was borrowed from Khmer and modified by King Ramkhamhaeng of Sukhothai in the 13th century to account for the tone system and additional sounds of the language of Sukhothai. The alphabet contains 44 consonant symbols arranged in an alphabetical order commonly found in the scripts of Indic languages, viz. velars, palatals, retroflexes, dentals, and labials, followed by a miscellaneous group of continuants. Two symbols representing velar fricative sounds have been made redundant because of historical sound changes and are no longer used, although they continue to be included in the traditional consonant symbol inventory. Six symbols originally representative of Indic retroflex sounds are retained in the spellings of Indic loanwords but are pronounced as dentals in Thai, further contributing to the many-to-one relationship between symbols and sounds resulting from historical sound changes. Spellings tend to be conservative and therefore reflect the historical origin of words.

The historical tone splits and sound changes were accounted for orthographically by a codification made during the Ayutthaya period. Consonant letters were divided into three tone classes—*ʔàksɔ̌ɔn sǔuŋ* 'high consonants', *ʔàksɔ̌ɔn klaaŋ* 'middle consonants', and *ʔàksɔ̌ɔn tàm* 'low consonants'—according to the original phonetic features responsible for the genesis of their associated tones (cf. the tripartite division of initial consonants in Table 1). High consonants include those sounds that originated from voiceless friction sounds; middle

Figure 1: Thai Tone Contours on Unstopped Syllables in Isolated Utterances

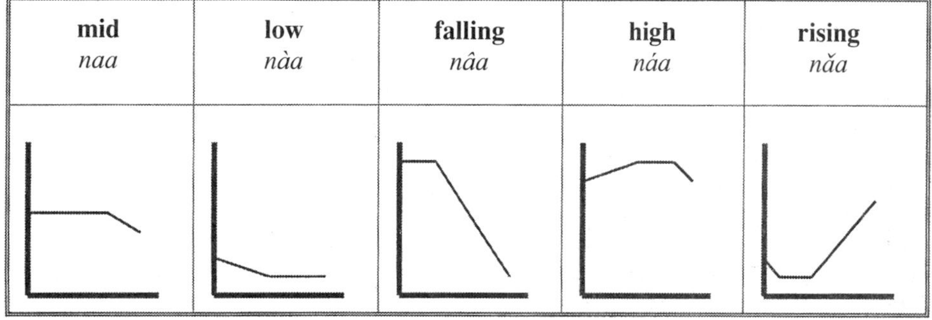

mid
naa
low
nàa
falling
nâa
high
náa
rising
nǎa

Table 2: Thai Consonants*

Velar		ก k^{M}		ข kh^{H}	ฃ kh^{H}	ค kh^{L}	ฅ kh^{L}	ฆ kh^{L}	ง ŋ^{L}
Palatal		จ c^{M}		ฉ ch^{H}	ช ch^{L}	ซ s^{L}	ฌ ch^{L}		ญ y^{L}
Retroflex	ฎ d^{M}	ฏ t^{M}		ฐ th^{H}	ฑ th^{L}	ฒ th^{L}			ณ n^{L}
Dental	ด d^{M}	ต t^{M}		ถ th^{H}	ท th^{L}	ธ th^{L}			น n^{L}
Labial	บ b^{M}	ป p^{M}		ผ ph^{H}	ฝ f^{H}	พ ph^{L}	ฟ f^{L}	ภ ph^{L}	ม m^{L}
Miscellaneous	ย y^{L}	ร r^{L}	ล l^{L}	ว w^{L}		ศ s^{H}	ษ s^{H}	ส s^{H}	
	ห h^{H}	ฬ l^{L}	อ ʔ^{M}	ฮ h^{L}					
Tone Markers		่ *máy ʔeek*		้ *máy thoo*		๊ *máy trii*		๋ *máy càttawaa*	

*Superscript H(igh), M(iddle) and L(ow) indicate the particular tone class of each consonant.

consonants encompass the originally voiceless unaspirated stops and glottalized sounds; and low consonants subsume those sounds that were originally voiced. The terms "high", "middle" and "low" are believed to have corresponded at the time of their coining (17th century) to the actual pitch levels of tones in the language of Ayutthaya after the historic tone splits had taken place, hence the traditional names; now they are no more than arbitrary labels because the tone system of Thai has gone through subsequent development. Nevertheless, they remain an essential codification for determining the spelling rules relating to the tones of Thai. The tone of a syllable is generally dictated by rules that take into account the class of initial consonant, the presence or absence of a tone marker, the syllable being unstopped or stopped, and if the latter, its vowel length. Two additional tone markers (*máy trii* and *máy càttawaa*) were introduced in the 18th century in order to write Chinese names and loanwords with high and rising tones respectively, on stopped and unstopped syllables having initial middle-class consonants (*b, d, ʔ, p, t, c, k*). High and rising tones on these types of syllables would otherwise be impossible to represent in the Thai orthography. The extra diacritics allow loanwords to be spelled in Thai with tones approximating their pronunciation in the source languages. Their use has since been extended in some cases to loanwords from nontonal languages, and the written expression of colloquial spoken language, onomatopoeia and speech-act particles.

The canonical syllable consists of an obligatory vowel and a tone with up to four optional elements having the following linear order: $(C_1\ (C_2))\ V_1\ (V_2)\ (C_3)$ plus tone. This allows for 12 possible syllable types: V, VV, VC, VVC, CV, CVC, CVV, CVVC, CCV, CCVV, CCVC and CCVVC.

Any of the 20 consonant phonemes may fill the C_1 position. The C_2 position is limited to the liquids *r* and *l* and the semivowel *w* if the C_1 position is filled, producing the following twelve consonant clusters: *pr, phr, tr, thr, kr, khr, pl, phl, kl, khl, kw* and *khw*. The cluster *thr* is extremely rare. The syllable-final C_3 position is restricted to the stops *p, t, k*, the nasals *m, n, ŋ* and the semivowels *w, y*. Stops are always unreleased wordfinally. Because the occurrence of the glottal stop is entirely predictable, it cannot strictly be considered a phoneme. It occurs utterance initially when the syllable-initial position ($C_1(C_2)$) is unfilled e.g., *ʔaray* 'what', and utterance finally after a short vowel when the syllable-final position (C_3) is unfilled e.g., *phɛ́ʔ* 'goat'. Its occurrence word-medially is dependent upon the speed of the utterance and it may be omitted at the speed of normal conversation, particularly when followed by a continuant e.g., *kraʔhǎay* ~ *krahǎay* 'to yearn for'.

Table 3: Thai Vowels*

short vowels		long vowels		short vowels		long vowels	
คะ	*khá?*	คา	*khaa*	คัวะ	*khúa?*	คัว	*khua*
คิ	*khí?*	คี	*khii*	เคียะ	*khía?*	เคีย	*khia*
คึ	*khɨ́?*	คื	*khɨɨ*	เคือะ	*khɨ́a?*	เคือ	*khɨa*
คุ	*khú?*	คู	*khuu*	เคอะ	*khə́?*	เคอ	*khɛɛ*
เคะ	*khé?*	เค	*khee*	คำ	*kham*		
แคะ	*khɛ́?*	แค	*khɛɛ*	ใค	*khay*		
โคะ	*khó?*	โค	*khoo*	ไค	*khay*		
เคาะ	*khɔ́?*	คอ	*khɔɔ*	เคา	*khaw*		

*A vowel symbol consists of from one to four separate graphemes written above, below, before, or after the consonant, depending upon their respective conventions.

The monophthongal vowel phoneme inventory demonstrates three degrees of height and two degrees of backness, with back vowels further specified for [± round]. Vowel length is phonemic for all nine vowels. There are three phonemic falling diphthongs *ia*, *ɨa*, *ua*, in which the syllabic element V_1 is a high vowel and the nonsyllabic element V_2 is a centering offglide. Some linguists include two short diphthongs *iə* and *ɨə* in the phoneme inventory.

Table 4: Vowels

	Front	Back	
	Unrounded	Unrounded	Rounded
High	i	ɨ	u
Mid	e	ə	o
Low	ɛ	a	ɔ

Basic Morphology

Morphology is limited to the derivational processes of affixation, compounding, and reduplication (see Haas 1964 for a good overview of types of derivation). Much of the derivational morphology has been borrowed from Khmer and Indic sources, although some is of Tai origin, such as the nonproductive prefix *ma-* occurring in some plant and fruit names, e.g., *mánaaw* 'lime', *malakɔɔ* 'papaya', and the productive prefixes *nâa-*'worthy of ...' and *khîi-* 'given to...' that create verb derivatives, e.g., *kin* 'to eat' ~ *nâa-kin* 'to be tasty looking', or *lɨɨm* 'to forget' ~ *khîi-lɨɨm* 'to be forgetful'. Another productive prefix of Tai provenance is *khwaam*, which also occurs as an independent noun meaning 'sense, substance, gist (of a matter)'. It derives abstract nouns from stative and adjectival verbs, e.g., *rúu* 'to know' ~ *khwaam-rúu* 'knowledge', *chûa* 'wicked' ~ *khwaam-chûa* 'wickedness', and is used to form abstract nominal phrases such as *khwaam pen thay* 'the state of being Thai, Thainess'.

The bound morpheme *kaan* 'work, affair, matter' of Indic origin occurs predominantly as a prefix 'affairs of ..., matters of ...' but may also function as a suffix in some derivatives, e.g., *càt* 'to arrange, manage' ~ *càt-kaan* 'to make arrangements' ~ *kaan-càt-kaan* 'management'. It can also nominalize whole subordinate clauses, e.g., *kaan thîi...* 'the fact that ...'. A prefix

Table 5: Thai Consonent Phonemes

		Labial	Dental	Palatal	Velar	Glottal
Stops	Voiced	b	d			
	Voiceless, unaspirated	p	t	c	k	
	Voiceless, aspirated	ph	th	ch	kh	
Fricatives		f	s			h
Nasals		m	n		ŋ	
Tap/Trill			r			
Lateral			l			
Semi-vowels		w		y		

borrowed from Khmer, *nák* 'expert, authority', forms agentive nouns when bound to nouns or verbs, e.g., *bun* 'merit' ~ *nák-bun* 'saint', and *rɔ́ɔŋ* 'to sing' ~ *nák-rɔ́ɔŋ* 'singer'. The infix *-am(n)-*, also borrowed from Khmer, often derives stylistic variants of Thai bases, e.g., *sǐaŋ* (common) 'voice' ~ *sǎmniaŋ* (elegant) 'accent', or *dəən* (common) 'to walk' ~ *damnəən* (elegant, of royalty) 'to proceed'. Similarly, the ubiquitous but now semantically indeterminable Indic prefixes *phrá-* and *krà-* can encode register differentiation in some words, e.g., *khun* (common) 'virtue' ~ *phrá-khun* (elegant) 'beneficence, benevolence' and *phǒm* (common) 'I (masculine)' ~ *krà-phǒm* (elegant) 'I (masculine)'.

Endocentric compounds of head-modifier structure are extremely common in Thai, some examples being *mɛ̂ɛ-khrua* (mother + kitchen) 'cook', *kamlaŋ-cay* (strength + heart) 'willpower', *rê-khǎay* (wander + sell) 'peddle', *tòk-yâak* (fall + difficult) 'to be impoverished, suffer hardship', and *thɔɔŋ-dɛɛŋ* (gold + red) 'copper'. In these types of compounds the head determines the word class.

Reduplication may take the form of repetition of the base, e.g., *ciŋ* 'true' ~ *ciŋ-ciŋ* 'really', or vowel ablaut, e.g., *ciŋ-caŋ* 'earnest'. Sometimes repetition of the base can imply repetitive action, e.g., *pay-pay maa-maa* (go + go come + come) 'to come and go continuously', or emphasis, with an emphatic high tone on the first syllable in the latter case, e.g., *di* 'good' ~ *díi-dii* 'extremely good'. For a small number of nominals, repetition of the base implies plurality, e.g., *khray* 'who, someone' ~ *khray-khray* 'everyone'. Another type of reduplication is found in elaborate expressions. These often have a four-part template based on compounds in an ABAC type of construction, such as *kháp-ʔòk-kháp-cay* 'to feel distressed, heavy hearted', which is made up of *ʔòk* 'chest', and *kháp* 'to be tight' and *cay* 'heart' occurring in the compound *kháp-cay* 'to feel distressed, troubled'. A semantic relationship often holds between the B and C constituents. Some elaborate expressions have an ABCD structure with no reduplication, but internal rhyme between components B and C. Component B may or may not bear a semantic relationship to the whole, e.g., *mǔu-hèt-pèt-kày* 'different kinds of meats', made up of *mǔu* 'pig', *hèt* 'mushroom', *pèt* 'duck', and *kày* 'chicken'.

Basic Syntax

Typologically, Thai can be described as an isolating language that relies on a fixed word order to demonstrate the syntactic function of constituents. The basic order of constituents is Subject-Verb-Object, although pragmatically determined, topic-first word order and heavy use of zero anaphora are common in colloquial language and have been well documented (see Diller 1988). An extensive system of particles is used to mark interrogative sentences and to express illocutionary force. Pronominal reference is sociolinguistically constrained and obligatorily encodes hierarchical social relationships. Attributes and demonstratives follow the nouns they modify, possessors follow entities possessed, and there is obligatory use of noun classifiers for quantification.

pàakkaa	*dam*	*sɔ̌ɔŋ*	*dâam*	*nán*
pen	black	two	CLASSIFIER	DEMONSTRATIVE

'Those two black pens'

A semantic link can often be found between nouns quantified by a particular classifier—e.g., *tua* 'body' is used for counting animals as well as objects having animal-like attributes such as heads, limbs and tails (subsuming tables, trousers, kites and orthographic symbols)—although aberrations in the system usually defy attempts at comprehensive semantic characterizations. An example is the classifier *lêm*, which quantifies such disparate entities as knives, carts, and combs.

Thai lacks tense, inflectional marking for person and number, and finite/nonfinite verb distinctions. Instead such grammatical categories find equivalent expression through independent words. Temporal reference is signaled by context, adverbial phrases, or by aspectual markers that have grammaticalized from verb concatenations. In some cases a grammaticalized function exists synchronically with a main verb function, e.g. *yùu* functions as a main verb with the meaning 'to stay' but also occurs in postverbal position to indicate progressive aspect.

nɔ́ɔŋ-sǎaw	*yaŋ*	*yùu*	*bâan*	*yùu*
younger sister	still	stay	house	PROGRESSIVE

'Younger sister is still at home'

The negative morpheme *mây* precedes the verb. Long strings of serial verbs demonstrating iconic ordering of events and elided noun phrases recoverable from context are a feature of spoken language. Prepositions are used sparingly as they are often made redundant by serial verbs that operate as direction markers. Some examples of verbs that can function as direction markers in verb concatenations are *khɨ̂n* 'ascend', *loŋ* 'descend', *khâw* 'enter', *ʔɔ̀ɔk* 'exit', *pay* 'go' and *maa* 'come'. Causation is signaled periphrastically by the verbs *tham* 'do, make' and/or *hây* 'give'. The functional equivalent of a passive construction has developed historically from verb concatenations involving *thùuk* 'to touch, hit' or *doon* 'to strike, collide'. This passive construction is generally constrained to infelicitous events.

khruu	*tham*	*hây*	*dèk*	*khɨ̂n*	*pay*	*khǐan*	*tɔ̀ɔ*
teacher	make	give	child	ascend	go	write	continue

'The teacher made the child go up (and) continue writing'

mǎa	*thùuk*	*ŋuu*	*kàt*	*taay*
dog	suffer	snake	bite	die

'The dog was bitten by a snake and died'

Contact with Other Languages

Indic and Khmer borrowings that are predominantly polysyllabic in structure constitute the majority of loanwords in Thai and make up a sizeable proportion of the lexicon. Gedney (1947) observes that they occur in Thai about as frequently as words of GREEK and Latin provenance occur in English. A large number of loanwords originate from Chinese languages. Some of these are believed to have been borrowed into Tai languages around the time of the Middle Chinese period approximately fourteen hundred years ago, and have since become part of the core vocabulary. Examples include number terms, e.g., *hâa* 'five'; nouns, e.g., *thùa* 'beans', *chiaŋ* 'city'; verbs, e.g., *lóo* 'to swing, to row', *thaa* 'to paint'; and classifiers, e.g., *tua* 'body'. In recent centuries Taechiw-speaking (*tɛ̂ɛcǐw* in Thai) Chinese immigrants from Swatow have contributed a few hundred loanwords to the Thai lexicon, mostly in the semantic domains of cuisine, e.g., *cɛɛ* 'Lenten fare', *ʔoolíaŋ* 'black iced coffee', *bamìi* 'egg noodles', and commerce, e.g., *chéŋ* 'to settle (accounts)', *yîihɔ̂ɔ* 'brand'. Other examples include terms relating to gaming, e.g., *tǎw* 'dice', *hǔay* 'lottery', and furniture, e.g., *tûu* 'chest of drawers', *kâw ʔîi* 'chair'. Since the 19th century English has become an important source of loanwords, particularly in the fields of science, industrial technology, sports and entertainment, and trade. At the upper echelons of the Thai register spectrum many English loanwords are replaced by neologisms coined from PALI and Sanskrit; e.g., the calque *thoorathát* 'television' (distant + view) replaces *thiiwii* 'TV' of lower colloquial registers. Pali and Sanskrit remain an important source of lexical roots for new coinages.

Common Words

man:	phûu chaay	long:	yaaw
woman:	phûu yǐŋ	small:	lék
water:	náam	yes:	chây
sun:	tawan	no:	mây chây
three:	sǎam	good:	dii
fish:	plaa	bird:	nók
big:	yày	dog:	mǎa
tree:	tôn máay		

Example Sentences

(1) phûak raw mák càʔ kin kǔaytǐaw pen
group we usually IRREALIS eat noodle be

ʔaahǎan thîaŋ.
food midday
'Our group would usually eat noodles for lunch.'

(2) khǎw chɨ̂ɨ ʔaray náʔ
s/he name what PARTICLE
'What's her/his name?'

(3) mây mii khray leey yàak pay rɔɔk.
NEGATIVE have anyone at all want go PARTICLE
'No one actually wants to go (contrary to what you think).'

Efforts to Preserve, Protect, and Promote the Language

Thai continues to occupy an important position, together with the monarchy and Buddhism, as one of the three pillars of Thai national identity. This symbolism is further reinforced by the Thai script, which is unique to the Thai language. The spread of the national language has been enhanced by national development and the impact of education in previously remote regions in the second half of the 20th century.

Select Bibliography

Brown, J. Marvin. 1967–1979. *AUA Language Center Thai Course (5 Vols.)*. Bangkok: The American University Alumni Association Language Center.

Diller, Anthony V. N. 1988. "Thai Syntax and National Grammar." In *Language Sciences* 10:273–312.

Gedney, William J. 1947. *Indic Loanwords in Spoken Thai*. Ph.D. Dissertation. Yale University.

_____. 1989. *Selected Papers on Comparative Tai Studies, Edited by Robert Bickner, John Hartmann, Thomas John Hudak, and Patcharin Peyasantiwong*. Ann Arbor: University of Michigan, Center for South and South-east Asian Studies.

Haas, Mary R. 1956. *The Thai System of Writing*. 2nd ed. Washington, DC: American Council of Learned Societies.

_____. 1964. *Thai-English Student's Dictionary*. Stanford: Stanford University Press.

Li, Fang-Kuei. 1977. *A Handbook of Comparative Tai*. Oceanic Linguistics Special Publications No. 15. Honolulu: University of Hawaii Press.

Noss, Richard B. 1964. *Thai Reference Grammar*. Washington, DC: Foreign Service Institute.

Smalley, William A. 1994. *Linguistic Diversity and National Unity: Language Ecology in Thailand*. Chicago and London: University of Chicago Press.

Wyatt, David K. 1984. *Thailand: A Short History*. New Haven: Yale University Press.

Tibetan

Christopher I. Beckwith

Language Name: Tibetan. Autonym: *phö̱ökää <bod-skad>*[1]

Location: Tibet (the Tibetan Autonomous Region [TAR] of the People's Republic of China [PRC]; Tibetan autonomous areas in Gansu, Qinghai, Sichuan, and Yunnan provinces of the PRC); Baltistan (Pakistani Kashmir); Ladakh, Lahul-Spiti, and neighboring regions (northwest India, including Indian Kashmir); Dolpo, Mustang, Sherpa, and neighboring regions (northern Nepal); Sikkim; Bhutan. Also an immigrant language in India, Nepal, Pakistan, and elsewhere.

Family: Tibetan (or "Bodish") subgroup of the Tibetic (or "Bodic") group of the Tibeto-Burman language family, thought by some to belong to a Sino-Tibetan language family.

Related Languages: Tibetan is related to hundreds of Tibeto-Burman languages, the most politically important being BURMESE, Lepcha (Sikkim), Newari (Nepal), and Tangut (extinct language of northeastern Tibet, northwestern China, and Inner Mongolia). The languages outside the Tibetan subgroup that are most closely related to Tibetan are the Kanauri group of languages spoken in the western Himalayas.

Dialects: There are five major dialect groups: Northeastern (Amdo), Eastern (Khams), Southern, Central, and Western.

Number of Speakers: 4–6 million.

Origin and History

So far as is presently known, Tibetan is genetically related to a large number of other languages that belong to the Tibeto-Burman family of languages. The Tibeto-Burman languages are in turn related to the Karenic languages, spoken mostly in Burma and Thailand.

Considering the great variety and number of daughter languages—hundreds are known, variously grouped into subfamilies (Matisoff 1986)—one may suggest that a Tibeto-Burman or Tibeto-Karenic protolanguage could have broken up around 3,000 years ago. Based on the present distribution of the speakers of these languages, and on the legends found in many related cultures in Southeast Asia relating the speakers' migration from a cold northern land (many are known to have moved south, or in the case of Tibetan, west, in historical times), one may further hypothesize that the speakers of the protolanguage lived in the vicinity of northeastern Tibet. This location would account for the introduction of a large number of loanwords into the proto-language from Sinitic (presumably from Chinese speakers in northeastern Tibet), Indo-European (from the speakers of Indo-Iranian and perhaps Tokharian and other early IE languages in the same region), and, possibly, from Austroasiatic languages to the southeast.

By the beginning of the present era at the latest, proto-Tibetan split off from its nearest relatives (the Himalayan languages), partly under the influence of the migratory movements of peoples known in Chinese historical sources as *Qiang* (who were perhaps Tibeto-Burman speakers) and *Yuezhi* (probably Tokharian speakers), as well as speakers of an early Indo-Iranic language. This was followed somewhat later (from the fifth century on) by an influx of Mongolic speakers (the *Tu-yü-hun*) into the northeastern Tibetan Plateau.

Old Tibetan (c. 650–950), the state language of the Tibetan Empire, was carried by its speakers across Tibet and into distant countries. As a literary language, Old Tibetan continued in use uninterruptedly in border states after the fall of the centralized Tibetan Empire in the mid-9th century. When an active Buddhist literary culture was revived in central Tibet in the 10th century, the Late Old Tibetan literary language was the chosen vehicle. With some later modifications, this became Classical Tibetan, the only form in which Tibetan was written until the 20th century. Old Tibetan (and its modified continuation, Classical Tibetan) may be characterized as a heavily prefixing, partly fusional and partly agglutinative SOV language with a strong-verb system, vestiges of an adjectival gender system such as seen today in the neighboring Himalayan language Limbu, and two sets of vocabulary for nonhonorific and honorific use (some of the latter perhaps unrelated to other vocabulary in the language).

Classical Tibetan literature is vast and rich, containing much of the wisdom of a great, unique civilization. Beginning in the 20th century, under Western influence, Tibetans began increasingly to write a somewhat more colloquial form of the language based on the existing epistolary style. Since the Chinese invasion of Tibet in 1950–51 and the subsequent Tibetan uprising in 1959, as a vast number of new loanwords (both Chinese and ENGLISH) and calques have entered the language, a new literary language known as Modern Literary Tibetan has developed, based partly on the spoken language and partly on

[1]Since there is no standardized system of transcription for either modern spoken Tibetan or any of the several forms of written Tibetan, for clarity's sake this entry uses a phonemic transcription of the standard Lhasa dialect followed by a transliteration of the modern written form (where the latter is not given, it would be identical to the phonemic transcription).

Table 1: Consonants

		Labial	Dental	Retroflex	Palatal	Velar	Glottal
Stops	Unaspirated	p	t	ṭ	k^y	k	ʔ
	Aspirated	ph	th	ṭh	kh^y	kh	
Fricatives	Voiceless		s		ś		h
	Voiced						ɦ
Affricates	Unaspirated		ts		c (tś)		
	Aspirated		tsh		ch (tśh)		
Nasals		m	n		ñ	ŋ	
Liquids	Unaspirated		l	r			
	Aspirated		lh				
Glides		w			y		

Classical Tibetan. The phonology of the modern spoken language is, however, largely ignored by the writing system, which continues to spell most words essentially as they are spelled in Classical Tibetan.

Despite the conservatism of the literary languages, it is possible to periodize the development of spoken Tibetan on the basis of foreign transcriptions and some internal evidence. Already by the early 9th century, the phonology of the language had begun to undergo some important changes, including the development of a retroflex consonant series from initial clusters of the shape (-)CrV, and of the rounded front vowel [ö], from *-oɦi* (vowel stems ending in *-o* plus the genitive case suffix). By the time of the Mongol conquest in the 13th century, a great deal of simplification had already taken place, including dropping of the majority of the consonants in initial clusters. By the 17th or 18th century, most, if not all, of the changes that characterize the modern spoken language of Central Tibet (especially the dialect of Lhasa, the capital and seat of the Tibetan government) had taken place. These changes among others include elimination of all word-initial consonant clusters, devoicing of initial voiced obstruents (compensated for by development of a low tone in such syllables), dropping of most syllable-final consonants, including all post-final consonants, and development of a rich inventory of vowel phonemes and a vowel harmony system. Morphosyntactically, the language has become almost completely agglutinative. The honorific system has been preserved, although it is much less in evidence in some Tibetan speech communities than in others, and the high elegant form of honorific language once spoken by Lhasa aristocrats is dying or already dead. Structurally speaking, modern spoken Tibetan seems now to be more akin to the Mongolic or the Turkic languages than to the neighboring languages of East, Southeast, or South Asia. However, phonologically and lexically Tibetan very clearly belongs with the languages of Southeast Asia.

Orthography and Basic Phonology

Tibetan is written in an alphabet created in the seventh century on the basis of the contemporaneous Northwest Indian Upright Gupta script. There are 30 consonant graphs and four vowel graphs. They are traditionally transliterated according to their Old Tibetan values, given here in Tibetan alphabetic order (read lines in each column from left to right).

Consonants

ཀ k	ཁ kh	ག g	ང ŋ
ཅ c	ཆ ch	ཇ j	ཉ ñ
ཏ t	ཐ th	ད d	ན n
པ p	ཕ ph	བ b	མ m
ཙ ts	ཚ tsh	ཛ dz	ཝ w
ཞ ź	ཟ z	འ ɦ	ཡ y
ར r	ལ l	ཤ ś	ས s
ཧ h	ཨ ʔ		

Vowels

འ	ི	ྀ	ུ	ེ	ོ
(a)	i	(ï)	u	e	o

If a consonant symbol is written without an accompanying vowel symbol, the vowel is assumed to be *a*; <m> by itself is *ma*, while <m> with an <i> written above it is *mi*.

The Tibetan letters for sounds in the same syllable can be arranged either horizontally or vertically, but the overall sequence of syllables in a line is from left to right, as in English.

Table 2: Vowels

	Front			Central	Back	
	Unrounded		Rounded	Unrounded	Rounded	
High	i	ė	ü	ə	ȯ	u
Low	e	ɛ	ö	a	ɔ	o

Table 2 does not consider the underlying vowel archiphonemes of root-syllable nuclei as they occur in fully inflected speech, where the vowel harmony system is operating, for example. The vowel leveling or "vowel harmony" system, which has been much studied, consists primarily of regressive vowel assimilation within words (note that consonant assimilation in Tibetan is progressive), in the majority of cases resulting in the raising of low vowels. See also the discussion of the "inquisitive" under Basic Morphology.

Tables 1 and 2 do not include sounds that are not separate phonemes in Lhasa Tibetan, even though some of these are represented in the script and occur in other dialects. In Lhasa Tibetan and in other Central Tibetan dialects, the primary consonantal contrast is between aspirated and unaspirated voiceless stops. However, in other dialects (particularly the most distant northeastern, northwestern, and southern dialects), the primary contrast is between voiced and voiceless stops as in Old Tibetan, where, however, the voiceless stops had both aspirated and unaspirated allophones.

The sounds [ŋh], [ñh], [nh], [mh], and [rh] are characteristic of the elegant sociolect of the old Lhasa aristocracy. They are not phonemic for most Tibetan speakers. Whispered vowel articulation is also common among Lhasa-dialect speakers.

Vowel nasalization is phonemic in Tibetan; oral and nasal /i/, /e/, /a/, /o/, and /u/ are the only vowels that occur in open syllables. All other vowels occur only geminate (long) or in closed syllables.

/ɦ/ represents a voiced, lax, glottal fricative (the voiced counterpart of /h/).

/ʈ/, /ʈh/, represent retroflex stops in the pronunciation of most speakers, including the Lhasa dialect, but in the elegant aristocratic sociolect, they are articulated as affricates: [ʈʂ], [ʈʂh].

/ė/ represents a high version of [e] that is allophonic (or absent) in the speech of most Tibetans, but phonemic in the Lhasa dialect.

Tibetan has two distinct tones, low and high. Low tone is marked by underlining in the transcriptions in this chapter. The contrast between low and high tone is only relevant for the first syllable of multisyllable words. (Many speakers of the standard Central Tibetan dialect, particularly those whose native dialect is from the far northeast or northwest, make no phonemic tonal distinctions whatsoever.) The historical phonology of Tibetan has been of great importance in formulation of theories and models of tonogenesis in East and Southeast Asian languages.

The minimal syllable shape is CV; the maximal is CVC or CVV (vowels may be nasal).

Any consonant can occur in the onset of any word-initial syllable, but only [k], [ŋ], [p], [m] can occur in the coda of any word-final syllable spoken in Lhasa Tibetan. In word-internal position in normal speech, and in citation style, especially in the reading style, several other consonants (which are still written) may be articulated.

An aspirated stop is deaspirated when it occurs in the onset position of any noninitial syllable.

All word-final stops are unreleased.

Words are mainly disyllabic, but monosyllabic words are common, trisyllabic words are not uncommon, and some quadrisyllabic (and very rarely, longer) words occur.

Basic Morphology

There are four nominal cases. Absolutive (in Old and Classical Tibetan, regularly used for the subject of an intransitive verb and the object of a transitive verb; in spoken Tibetan, it is used also for the "unmarked" subject of a transitive verb in all tenses except the past), ergative (used for the subject of a transitive verb and for causation and concession), genitive (in addition to expected uses, it is very productive in the formation of relative clauses), and dative-locative (distinct from the postposition *la* in Old and Classical Tibetan both in function and in semantics, but no longer distinct in spoken Lhasa Tibetan). The case suffixes are in the process of becoming postpositions phonologically. There is no case concord; cases are marked on the last independent word of a noun phrase (but may be followed by conjunctives).

Only personal pronouns and determiners (demonstrative pronouns) can be pluralized.

The third-person personal pronouns (except for the honorific third-person pronoun *khoŋ* 'he/she [hon.]' and derivatives) distinguish natural gender: *kho* 'he (nonhon.)', *khoraŋ* 'himself; he (neutral/hon.)' *mo* or *khomo* 'she (nonhon.), *moraŋ* 'herself; she (neutral/hon.)', etc. Other noun classification occurs within the honorific system, which, itself, constitutes a concord-triggering register class. In the latter system, the honorific class terms of honorific class nouns (compound nouns; see below) are distributed according to classifier-like categories. There are, however, no classifiers in Tibetan.

Demonstratives are a subcategory of the adjectives distinguished by pluralizability and by syntax (they cannot precede other adjectivals).

The enclitic indefinite article suffix *-ci* (<cig>, with several sandhi spellings), a reduced form of the numeral *cik* <gcig> 'one', indicates that the noun it qualifies is specifically indefinite, for example, *mici* <mi-źig> 'a (certain) person; someone'.

There is no true definite article in Tibetan, but the demonstrative *t̲i̲* <ɦdi> 'this' in the spoken language, and both <ɦdi> 'this' and <de> 'that' in the written language, are frequently used as definite articles.

Tibetan has a system of honorifics. Many words have honorific forms that are used under specific social circumstances. The use of an honorific form tends to trigger honorific agreement throughout a sentence, resulting in the use of honorific nouns, adjectives, verbs, adverbs, etc. The extent to which the agreement is realized in practice is partly a function of the register level intended as well as of the linguistic competence of the speaker. Many nouns, adjectives, and other parts of speech have no honorific forms. There is no other modifier-noun agreement other than pronominal natural-gender agreement (see above).

Subject agreement is indicated by verbal auxiliary selection, not by suffixes. In the declarative mood the second and third person, both singular and plural, take a different auxiliary than the first person, while in the interrogative mood, the first and second person (both singular and plural) take a different auxiliary than the third person. Compare *yĩĩ* 'I/we will go' with *ʈuki ree* 'You/he/she/it/they will go'. (The honorific equivalent of the latter is *phiiki ree*.)

Subjects and objects, particularly pronominals, are commonly omitted when the context is clear. See the Example Sentences below.

The negative precedes the main verb in imperatives; otherwise, it normally follows the main verb and precedes the auxiliary (in the latter case, phonologically it may be treated as a prefix). In Old and Classical Tibetan, the negative agrees in tense or mood with the verb: the negative *ma* is used with past and imperative verb forms, while the negative *mi* is used with present and future verb forms.

There are no morphologically distinct passives in Tibetan; the logical subject of a passive sentence is normally marked by the postposition *lää* <las>. The subjunctive mood is formed periphrastically utilizing tense and auxiliary changes.

In the written language, most causative verbs are marked by the prefix <s>, which is now silent in all but the far Western dialects.

The imperative may be formed by use of the bare verb root (extremely rude), but is usually followed by one of a large number of polite affixes such as *-ta* <daŋ>. Otherwise, the significant verbal affixes are the tense suffixes, *-k-* for present and future, *-p-* for past, followed by mood suffixes, *-ää* for interrogative, *-aa* for inquisitive (i.e., '*wh-*' interrogative), and *-i* (after *-k-*) or *-ə* (after *-p-*) for indicative, which requires an auxiliary to make a sentence finite. The inquisitive may, alternatively, be marked on the auxiliary, in which case either the vowel of the final auxiliary changes to a more open variant, or an inquisitive marker is suffixed to the auxiliary. (Note that the inquisitive requires a *wh-* question in the sentence.) For example:

Lä̲ä̲ka che̲eta
'Please work!' (imperative)

Lä̲ä̲ka chi̲gi yö̲ö̲
'I'm working.' (indicative)

Lä̲ä̲ka chi̲gi yö̲ö̲pee
'Are you working?' (interrogative)

Lä̲ä̲ka che̲egee
'Are you working?' (interrogative)

Kha̲re che̲egaa
'What are you doing?' (inquisitive)

Kha̲re chi̲gi yɔ̲ɔ̲
'What are you doing?' (inquisitive)

Kha̲re chi̲gi yö̲ö̲paa
'What are you doing?' (inquisitive)

Lexical derivation is accomplished almost exclusively by suffixing or compounding. The most productive suffix in Tibetan is *pa/pə*, a nominalizer (historical change in the verb system has given the unrelated suffix *pa/pə* for the past tense). Compounding is accomplished by dropping syllables (usually any after the first) of each word and joining them to form a disyllabic compound. Among several types of compounds (synonym, polar, etc.), both nonhonorific and honorific class nouns (i.e., noun-noun compounds) are formed in this way; on the special character of the honorific class nouns, see above.

Evidentiality plays a crucial role in the actual realization of the default-grammar rules, including major sentence constituent case assignment and auxiliary verb assignment. This feature must be borne in mind when reading descriptions of verb paradigms and ergativity in Tibetan.

Basic Syntax

Tibetan is an SOV language.

Tibetan phrases are head initial. The typical order of constituents in the noun phrase is: [((Noun) (Adjective) (Number) (Determiner)) Case]

In contrast, Tibetan words are typically head final; the typical order of constituents in noun-noun compounds is: (qualifier_head).

Negation is formed with *ma* (there are a few exceptions and some contractions with auxiliaries).

Typical verb phrase order: V-tense (negative) AUX-mood or (negative) V-tense-mood.

Imperative VP: *ma* V (few exceptions).

Contact with Other Languages

Among the ancient loanwords, many are from an unknown Indo-European language. On the basis of the word for "pig" and other examples, they would appear to have been borrowed into Common Tibeto-Burman from an unknown language belonging to a very early subfamily of IE akin to Indo-Iranian which retained the IE palatal velar stops as velars.

From IE: *phak* <phag> 'pig' (<early IE language akin to Indo-Iranic (O. Khotanese *pāsa*) <IE **pork-*)
From MONGOLIAN: *thep* <deb> 'book' (*debther* <Mongol *debter* <Persian *däftär* <GREEK διφθερα 'parchment')
From Chinese: *par* 'print, printing'

Recent loanwords (written forms of these are not given, as they are not standardized):

From Mongol: *ʔumusu* or *ʔomosu(lu)* 'socks'
From Chinese: *khaṭhə* 'truck'
From English: *pulis* 'police'
From HINDI: *peskop* 'movie' (<English)

In the other direction, Tibetan has had great influence in much of northern and eastern Asia, being learned by Mongols, Manchus, various Turkic peoples, Chinese, and other peoples of the Sino-Tibetan frontier, and in the Himalayan countries south of Tibet, because of its role as the holy language of Northern Vajrayana Buddhism, of which Tibetan Buddhism is the chief variety.

Common Words

man:	mi
woman:	kyeemä̲ä̲ <skye-dman>

long:	ri̱ŋgu <riŋ-po>
small:	chüncuŋ <chuŋ-chuŋ>
water:	chu (nonhonorific); chap <chab> (honorific)
yes:	ləs; ləsi; ləs ləs; 'ləsi ləsi; ɦõ̱õ
no:	(there is no equiv.; a negated verb is used)
sun:	ñi̱mə <ñi-ma>
three:	sum <gsum>
fish:	ña̱
good:	ya̱ko; ya̱kpo <yag-po>
big:	chempo <chen-po>
bird:	cha̱ <bya>
dog:	khi <khyi> (nonhon.); si̱mki <gzim-khyi> (hon.)
tree:	śiŋ

Example Sentences*

(1) aalee ŋä̱ä kya̱-mo re̱e sam-k-i tu̱u
Oh! I/ERG Chinese-FEM COP think-PRFUT/IND AUX

phu̱mo ya̱kpo tu̱u.
girl good exist.EVIDENTIAL
'Oh! I was thinking she is Chinese. She is a nice girl.' or: 'The girl is nice.'

(2) khyerãã lhääsa-a kha̱paa śu̱u-k-i
you$_{\{+HON\}}$ Lhasa-DL where dwell$_{\{+HON\}}$-PRFUT-IND

yɔ̱ɔ?
AUX/PR/1ST-2ND.PERSON/INQ
'Where do you live in Lhasa?' or: 'Where are you staying in Lhasa?'

(3) ma̱acä̱ä-ki śa ţhi̱ ti̱-i tup-k-i
cook-ERG meat knife this-ERG cut-PRFUT/IND

re̱-pää?
AUX/FUT/3RD.PERSON-INT
'Is the cook going to cut (the) meat with this knife?' or: 'Will the cook cut (the) meat with this knife?'

Note that the word *phu̱mo* 'girl' is etymologically a noun—*phu̱* [bu] 'child; boy'—with the feminine suffix *-mo*; thus the two sentences in Example Sentence 1 are an example of the occasional gender concord that occurs in Tibetan.

*These examples are taken from Hongladarom (1993) and Chang and Shefts (1964).

Efforts to Preserve, Protect, and Promote the Language

Tibetans, both in Tibet and in India, are expending effort to preserve and promote the use of Tibetan, but this effort is all at the private level, consisting either of individuals singly or in small groups. In India, a private foundation, the Amnye Machen Institute, has been attempting to obtain funding to support its proposed ventures in Tibetan publishing and other areas intended to protect and preserve the Tibetan language and Tibetan culture.

Select Bibliography

Chang, Kun and Betty Shefts. 1964. *A Manual of Spoken Tibetan (Lhasa Dialect)*. Seattle: University of Washington Press.

Goldstein, Melvyn C. 1984. *English-Tibetan Dictionary of Modern Tibetan*. Berkeley: University of California Press.

_____. 1991. *English-Tibetan Dictionary of Modern Tibetan*. Berkeley: University of California Press.

Hongladarom, Krisadawan. 1993. "Evidentials in Tibetan: A Dialogic Study of the Interplay Between Form and Meaning." Ph.D. dissertation, Indiana University.

Jäschke, H.A. 1972. *A Tibetan-English Dictionary, With Special Reference to the Prevailing Dialects. [1881]* London: Routledge and Kegan Paul.

Kitamura, Hajime. 1975. "The Honorifics in Tibetan." In *Acta Asiatica* 28: 56–74.

Kuløy, Hallvard, and Yoshiro Imaeda. 1986. *Bibliography of Tibetan Studies*. Narita: Naritasan Shinshoji.

Matisoff, James A. 1986. "The Languages and Dialects of Tibeto-Burman: an alphabetic/genetic listing, with some preliminary remarks on ethnonymic and glossonymic complications." In John McCoy and Timothy Light, eds. *Contributions to Sino-Tibetan Studies*. Leiden: E.J. Brill, 3–75.

Norbu, Thubten J., and Tsuguhito Takeuchi. 1991. "Mongolian Loan-Words in Tibetan and their Socio-cultural Implications." In E. Steinkellner, ed., *Tibetan History and Language*. Wien, 383–386.

Richardson, Hugh E. 1985. *A Corpus of Early Tibetan Inscriptions*. London: Royal Asiatic Society.

TIGRINYA

Tesfay Tewolde

Language Name: *Tigrinya, Tigrigna* (ITALIAN spelling). **Autonym:** *qwanqwa ħabəšša.*

Location: Tigrinya is the only modern Semitic language spoken in both Ethiopia and Eritrea. It is spoken in the highly concentrated highlands as well as the urban areas of Eritrea and in almost all of Tigray Province in Ethiopia. Different linguistic groups in Tigray and in Eritrea use it as a lingua franca. There are about 100,000 speakers in Israel.

Family: Tigrinya belongs to the Southwest Semitic language subfamily.

Related Languages: Tigrinya is related to the Ethiopian Semitic languages AMHARIC, Harari, Argobba, the Gurage cluster, and Gafat; GE'EZ and Tigre are its closest relatives.

Dialects: Tigrinya has two standard varieties: that of Tigray, and that of Eritrea, both of which have regional dialects, although no adequate study has been made yet to identify the regional linguistic boundaries among the regions. The Eritrean standard variety is basically that of Asmara while the Tigrean standard variety is very much related to the varieties spoken in Adwa, Shire, and Axum regions of Tigray.

There are no significant social dialect differences in Tigrinya.

Number of Speakers: 5.5–6 million.

Origin and History

Tigrinya is in many ways strikingly related to the ancient Northeast, Northwest, and Southwest Semitic languages.

The first written evidence of Tigrinya is from the 13th century. It was found in Logosarda in southern Eritrea and concerned the customary laws of the area. It is written in Tigrinya characters. Many of the words are similar to those in present-day Tigrinya. The Lazarist Catholic Mission established a printing press in Massawa, Eritrea, in 1863. In 1867 it was used to publish religious materials using Tigrinya characters.

Orthography and Basic Phonology

Tigrinya characters were basically taken from Sabean through Ge'ez. Ge'ez dropped some of the 29 Sabean characters, retained the rest, modified them, and added some of its own. Tigrinya in turn added characters not inherited from Ge'ez.

With certain exceptions, each consonant symbol occurs in seven forms, called "orders", depending on the following vowel. For instance, the symbol /b/በ can have the forms በ, ቡ, ቢ, ባ, ቤ, ብ, or ቦ, representing /bə/, /bu/, /bi/, /ba/, /be/, /b/ or /bɨ/, and /bo/, respectively.

Each individual symbol can thus represent a single consonant, a consonant+vowel sequence, or a sequence of a doubled (geminate) consonant+vowel.

Each of the consonants in Table 1 can occur single or geminate. Single velars /k/ and /q/ and labio-velars /kʷ/ and /qʷ/ become /x/, /x'/, /xʷ/, and /x'ʷ/ when preceded by a vowel.

/p/ and /v/ occur only in recent loanwords and are often replaced by /b/. /ž/ is very rare, and is often replaced by /j/.

There are no sequences of vowels in Tigrinya, and the only consonant sequences occur word internally. If the morphology of Tigrinya produces unacceptable sequences, a segment must be inserted or deleted. The vowel /i/ is inserted as needed in word-final position, and /ɨ/ is inserted as needed word medially. The consonants /ʔ/, /y/, and /w/ can be inserted in word-initial or word-medial position. For example, in the verb *səmiʕuwwa* 'he listened to her', the /ww/ is inserted between the affix *u*, indicating a third-person masculine singular subject, and the affix *a*, indicating a third-person feminine singular object.

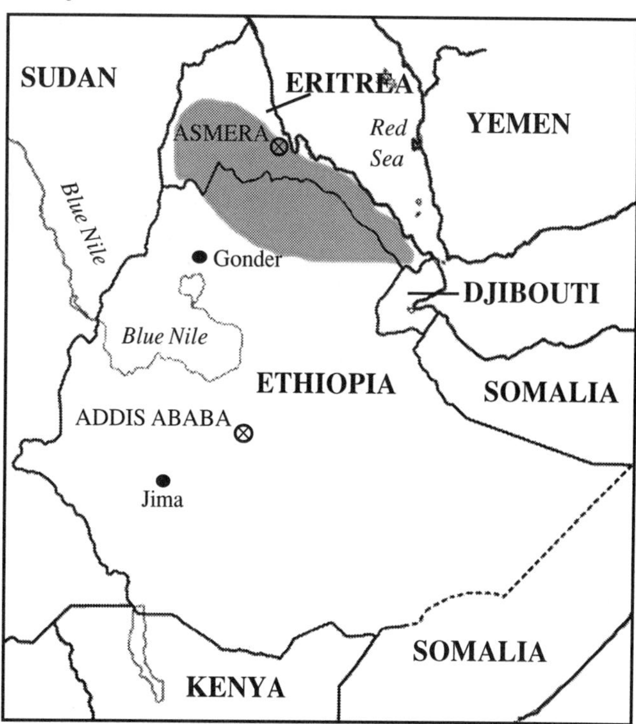

Tigrinya is spoken in the highlands and urban areas of Eritrea and in most of Tigray Province of Ethiopia (shaded area).

Table 1: Consonants

		Labial	Dental	Alveolar	Palatal	Velar	Labio-velar	Pharyngeal	Glottal
Stops	Voiceless	p	t			k	k^w		ʔ
	Voiced	b		d		g	g^w		
	Glottalized	p'	t'			q	q^w		
Fricatives	Voiceless	f		s	š			ħ	h
	Voiced	v		z	ž			ʕ	
Affricates	Voiceless				č				
	Voiced				j				
	Glottalized			s'	č'				
Nasals		m		n	ñ				
Resonants		w		l, r	y				

Table 2: Vowels

	Front	Central	Back
High	i	ɨ	u
Mid	e	ə	o
Low		a	

Basic Morphology

As in other Semitic languages, the most frequent method of word formation in Tigrinya is by changing the consonant-vowel template a root is used in. For instance, the verb *qətəl-* is formed from the root QTL, the vowel *ə*, and the template CVCVC. Roots can have three or four consonants. One of the consonants in quadriliteral roots is always alveolar. The alveolar consonant may be an extension added to a root, as in *mənkəra* 'suffering' (from *məkkəra*).

Tigrinya nouns are inflected for number (singular versus plural). All nouns are either masculine or feminine. The nouns themselves are not marked for gender, but their gender is reflected in the forms of associated determiners and adjectives:

ʔɨt-a qəyyaħ rɨsas
the-F.SG red(F) pencil 'the red pencil'

ʔɨt-ən qəyyaħ-ti rɨsas-at
the-F.PL red-.PL pencil-PL 'the red pencils'

Tigrinya plurals are formed by the addition of a suffix, as in *rɨsas-at* 'pencils' above, or by modification of the stem, for example, *ʔom* 'tree', *ʔaʔwam* 'trees'.

Tigrinya personal pronouns can occur as independent words or as affixes. Some independent personal pronouns, such as *ʔanə* 'I' and *nɨssɨxa* 'you (m.sg)', refer to a subject, while others, such as *nɨʔay* 'for me' and *nɨʔaxa* 'for you (m.sg)', indicate an object. The affixed personal pronouns can likewise refer to a subject or an object:

tɨmali rəxib-ə-yy-a
yesterday found-1SG- -3F.SG 'I found her yesterday.'

Possession is also indicated by an affixed pronoun: *gənzəb-ka* (money-your) 'your money'.

Typical verbs, such as *rəxibə* contain three or four root consonants. There are some verbs that look like biliterals or that seem to have more than four root consonants. However, there is ample evidence that this is not the case. For instance, verbs like *konə* 'it became/has become' appear to have only two consonants. But, some of its inflected forms, such as *yɨxəwwin* 'it becomes', show that the root consonants are actually KWN and not KN. There are also verbs such as *tənbərkəxə* 'he (has) knelt down' with prefixes *tə-* and *n-*, and verbs such as *ʔat'wəlwələ* 'he (has) vomited' with reduplicated root consonants *w* and *l*.

Verbs agree with their subjects and objects in person, number, and gender. In addition, verbs are marked for aspect (perfective and imperfective) and mood (realis and irrealis). The perfective aspect, which includes perfective *qətəl-ə* and gerundive *qətil-u*, both 'he (has) killed', indicates events that are completed; the imperfective aspect, for example, *yɨ-qəttɨl* 'he kills', represents events that are ongoing and/or repeated. The above three forms all represent realis mood; irrealis mood forms, such as the imperative *qɨtəl* 'kill! (2.m.sg) and the jussive *yɨ-qtəl* 'let him kill', represent potential actions. For imperfective and jussive forms, subject agreement is indicated via prefix (*yɨ-* in the above examples) and suffix, while for other forms, subject agreement is indicated via suffix only.

Tigrinya verbs are passivized by addition of a prefix *tə-* and causativized by addition of a prefix *ʔa-*.

fəs's'imu 'he (has) completed'
tə-fəs's'imu 'it is/was completed'
ʔa-fəs's'imu 'he made something/someone complete it'

Tigrinya has additional benefactive and malefactive forms; these indicate that the designated action benefits or disadvantages an additional person. For transitive verbs, both benefactive and malefactive forms are formed with the marker *-l-* followed by a possessive pronoun:

qətil-u-ll-əy
kill:GERUNDIVE-3M.SG-for-1SG
'He killed something for me.'

For intransitive verbs, benefactives are formed with the marker *-l-* followed by a possessive pronoun, while malefactives are formed by adding an object pronominal suffix to the verb:

məs'iʔ-u-ll-əy
come:GERUNDIVE-3M.SG-for-1SG 'he came (for my benefit)'

məs'iʔ-u-nni
come:GERUNDIVE-3M.SG-1SG 'he came (to my disadvantage)'

Basic Syntax

The basic word order in Tigrinya sentences is SOV:

ħaw-ka	tɨmali	fərəs	gəziʔ-u
brother-2M.SG	yesterday	horse	buy:GERUNDIVE-3M.SG

'Your brother bought a horse yesterday.'

Adjectives and other modifiers precede the nouns they modify:

ʔɨ-ta	nəwwaħ	bətri
the-F.SG	long(F.SG)	stick

Tigrinya expresses relations via prepositions rather than postpositions:

ʔab	may	bɨ	mɨbrax'
on	water	in	east

Sentences are negated by the morpheme *ʔay* prefixed to the main verb, which is reinforced by a suffix *-n*:

ʔay-fəs's'əm-ə-n
NEG-complete:PERFECTIVE-3M.SG-NEG 'he didn't complete'

The same elements can also be attached to nouns, adjectives, and phrases:

ʔay-səb-ɨn
NEG-man-NEG 'not a man'

ʔay-kɨfuʔ-ɨn
NEG-bad-NEG 'not bad'

ʔay-bɨ-fətəw-t-u-n
NEG-by-friend-PL-3M.SG-NEG 'not by his friends'

Contact with Other Languages

Tigrinya syntax has been heavily influenced by that of the Cushitic languages such as Agaw. But its lexical and morphological structure is clearly Semitic. Tigrinya has borrowed heavily from Ge'ez and, more recently, from Italian and ENGLISH.

From Ge'ez: *ħɨbrətəsəb* 'society'

From Italian: *sɨtanza* 'room', *ʔarranši* 'orange' (< It. *arrancia*), *cobborta* 'blanket' (< It. *copperta*)
From English: *tələfon* 'telephone', *jakət* 'jacket'

Common Words

man:	səb	long:	nəwwiħ
woman:	səbəyti	small:	nɨʔɨšto
water:	may	yes:	ʔɨwwə
sun:	s'əħay	no:	ʔaykonən
three:	sələstə	good:	s'ɨbbux'
fish:	ʕasa	bird:	ʕuf
big:	ʕabi	dog:	kəlbi
tree:	ʔom		

Example Sentences

(1)
ʔɨ-tu	bɨʕray	nɨ-ʔɨ-ta	saʕri
the-M.SG	ox (SG)	to-the-F.SG	grass (SG)

baliʕ-u-ww-a.
eat:PERFECT-3M.SG- -3F.SG
'The ox ate the grass.'

(2)
s'əħay	bɨ	mɨbrax'	tɨ-bərɨx'.
sun (SG)	in	east	3F.SG-rise:IMPERFECTIVE

'The sun rises in the east.'

(3)
ʕasa	ʔab	may	yɨ-nəbbɨr.
fish	in	water	3M.SG-live:IMPERFECTIVE

'Fish live in water.'

Efforts to Preserve, Protect, and Promote the Language

In the 19th and 20th centuries several phonological, morphological, and syntactic studies of Tigrinya were published. The Eritrean government in the 1940s and 1950s, the Eritrean Liberation Fronts from 1961 to 1991, and the Tigrean Liberation Front from 1974 to 1991 have all tried to develop the language. Currently, Tigrinya is used in the mass media, in schools, and in different government and nongovernment offices of Eritrea and Tigray. Unfortunately curriculum designers and teachers in both countries complain that they have acute shortages of modern grammar books.

Select Bibliography

Academy of Ethiopian Languages. 1997. *Məzgəbə qalat tɨgrinya bɨtɨgrinya*. Addis Ababa: Commercial Printing Press.

Leslau, W. 1941. *Documents Tigrigna*. Paris: C. Klincksieck.

Ouqubagebriel. Habtemariam. 1993. *Məzbə qalat ʔɨngliz tigrinya*. Addis Ababa: Commercial Printing Press.

Research and Information Centre on Eritrea (RICE). 1982. *Dictionary: English-Tigrigna*. Rome.

Tewolde, Tesfay. 2000. *A Grammar of Tigrinya*. Rome: Simmos Printing Press.

Ullendorff, E. 1965. *The Semitic Languages of Ethiopia: A Comparative Phonology*. London: Taylor's [Foreign] Press.

TOCHARIAN

Douglas Q. Adams

Language Name: Tocharian B. **Alternates:** *West Tocharian, Kuchean.* **Autonym:** *Kuśiññe.*

Location: Tocharian was spoken along the northern rim of the Tarim Basin and in the Qarashar and Turfan basins in the northeast, all in the central part of what is now the Chinese province of Xinjiang.

Family: Tocharian B was a member of the Tocharian branch of the Indo-European language family. The entire Tocharian branch is extinct with no modern descendants.

Related Languages: Tocharian B is closely related to its contemporary Tocharian A (both known from texts datable to the period A.D. 500 to 800). Tocharian A is attested coterritorially with Tocharian B in the Qarashar and Turfan basins. Also related is the more anciently (third century A.D.), but very fragmentarily attested "Tocharian C", spoken to the southeast, in the Loulan region of Xinjiang. Although attested at the same time and largely in the same place as Tocharian B, it is possible, and even likely, that Tocharian A was no longer a spoken language, but rather a written liturgical language, used alongside Tocharian B as a medium of Buddhist literature by a population that natively spoke UYGHUR, a Turkic language. Tocharian C is known only from a few loanwords recorded in texts otherwise written in the Kroraina (= Loulan) Prakrit used as the administrative language of the Loulan Kingdom. While the Kroraina Prakrit is a form of Middle Indic and thus imported into Central Asia as a literary language, the inhabitants of Loulan presumably spoke Tocharian C natively.

Dialects: The documents written in Tocharian B can be divided into three dialect groups, usually denominated Eastern, Central, and Western. The most plentifully attested variety is the Central dialect of the Qarashar region. This variety of Tocharian B seems to have been recognized as some sort of standard vis-à-vis the rest of the Tocharian-speaking world because documents showing the characteristics of the Central dialect have also been found in the east and west, while characteristically Eastern or Western documents are largely confined to those geographical areas. It seems likely that the relatively uniform Central dialect reflects the scribal norms of a large monastic center (Yurpa?) somewhere in the Qarashar area that were prestigious throughout the Tocharian-speaking world. It is significant that the documents in the Eastern and Central dialects, like documents in the coterritorial Tocharian A, are almost exclusively religious in content. Documents in the Western variety, on the other hand, treat administrative matters such as caravan passes, deeds, and religious materials.

Origin and History

The existence of the Tocharian languages was completely unsuspected until the first decade of the 20th century. French, Prussian, and Anglo-Indian expeditions into Chinese Central Asia, more particularly the Tarim Basin of southern Xinjiang, of the decade or so immediately preceding World War I, brought back a wealth of linguistic and cultural material representing a number of known ethnic groups including TIBETAN and Iranian and the remains of two unknown but obviously related languages. Since the texts were written in a variety of a well-known North Indian alphabet, they were easily read. To the surprise of the readers, they turned out to be obviously Indo-European (e.g.,Tocharian A *mācar*, Tocharian B *mācer* 'mother', and A *pācar*, B *pācer* 'father'; compare LATIN *māter*, *pater*).

Almost immediately after their Indo-European character was announced in 1907, Emil Sieg and Wilhelm Siegling identified them as Tocharian A and Tocharian B, equating them with the classical Tocharoi of Transoxiana, the equivalent of modern Uzbekistan and adjacent parts of Tadzhikistan and Kyrgyzstan. The Tocharoi comprised a people whose earliest known location was in the Chinese region of Gansu (where Chinese records label them as the *Yuezhi*). They were driven westward in the second century B.C., ending up in Transoxiana, where they formed a powerful kingdown that was to expand southward, eventually conquering, under the designation Kushana, a large portion of northwestern India in the first centuries of our era.

Sieg and Siegling's equation was largely based on the text of a colophon to the Uyghur version of a certain Buddhist drama. Uyghur is an unrelated Turkic language that ultimately replaced the Tocharian languages, but at the time the documents were found, was spoken in adjacent areas of Chinese Central Asia. The Uyghur colophon states that the Uyghur version of the drama was translated from the "Twgry language". Since this drama is otherwise known only in a Tocharian A version, it was Sieg and Siegling's contention that Twgry was the same as Tocharian A and, further, that Twgry should be equated with the Tocharoi because of the phonological similarity of the names. Others have argued that there is no reason that both the Uyghur and Tocharian A version of the drama could not be translations from Twgry, another language altogether. Also arguing against equating the Tocharians with the Tocharoi is the fact that the actual language of the Tocharoi, when attested to in the second and third centuries of our era, is indubitably Iranian. However, since the attestations of the language of the Tocharoi come so late, it may only mean that in the half millennium of their sojourn in Transoxiana the Tocharoi, whatever their original language, had become thoroughly Iranized linguistically. In any case, Sieg and Siegling's identification has probably more often been rejected than accepted but, in the absence of any more obviously appropriate designation, the name has stuck.

Nearly a century of research into the Tocharian languages has failed to answer conclusively the question of their origins. The linguistic evidence provides no particularly close relatives for Tocharian within the Indo-European family; certainly there appears to be no close relationship with Indo-Iranian, Tocharian's closest geographical neighbor of the Indo-European languages. Indeed, what special linguistic ties Tocharian may have with other Indo-European groups appears to be, disconcertingly, with Western groups such as Germanic or GREEK. However, the number of similarities is small, and it is possible that they reflect shared retentions or independent creations rather than shared innovations.

Since all reasonable theories of Indo-European origins, including, for example, the North Pontic Steppes, the northern Balkans, and Anatolia, place them to the west of Central Asia, the linguistic ancestors of the Tocharians must have come ultimately from somewhere west of the Tarim Basin. Since Chinese accounts of the region go back to the second century B.C. and record for that early period a settled political and economic situation and indicate no subsequent population changes, until the advent of Islam, towards the end of the first millennium A.D., the entry of the pre-Tocharians must be put before the middle of the first millennium B.C. It has often been supposed that the ancestors of the Tocharians should be looked for among the Andronovo cultural complex (2000 B.C.–900 B.C.) in ex-Soviet Central Asia and adjacent southwestern Siberia. The Andronovo cultures clearly hearken back to earlier cultures of the North Pontic Steppes, an area that was either the Proto-Indo-European homeland itself or a major staging area for eastern Indo-European peoples. However, it is increasingly clear that the Andronovo cultures were the precursors of the various Indo-Iranian groups, and the lack of any real linguistic connection between Tocharian and Indo-Iranian would seem to rule out any intimate, long-term association between the pre-Tocharians and the Andronovo peoples.

Another possible Western antecedent of the Tocharians is provided by the Afanasievo cultural complex. The best-known sites of the latter are in south central Siberia in the Minusink Basin but it, too, is clearly an eastern outlier of the cultures centered on the North Pontic Steppes. It is possible to see the Tocharians as originally a southern extension of the Afanasievo peoples who moved further south into the Tarim Basin.

All in all, it seems likely that the pre-Tocharians, plausibly of Afanasievo origin, entered the Tarim Basin about 2000 B.C., bringing with them irrigation, which first appeared in the Tarim Basin at that time and without which agriculture would have been impossible in so arid a climate. That significant Tocharian B irrigation terms, such as *newiya* 'canal', are Eastern Iranian in origin suggest that the pre-Tocharians learned the technology from eastern Iranians on the outskirts of the Tarim Basin, present-day northeastern Kazakstan. Less likely is the hypothesis that the pre-Tocharians learned of this technology from Iranians, such as the pre-Khotanese, already in the Tarim Basin since these terms are not attested in Khotanese and, in any case, how would the pre-Tocharians have supported themselves within the Tarim Basin without having known irrigation?

Tocharian was replaced by Uyghur around the end of the first Christian millennium. In all probability, the Uyghurization of Chinese Central Asia had been proceeding for some centuries, most likely having engulfed Tocharian A by the time of the attested texts. The replacement of Tocharian B, as well as the replacement of the Iranian languages in the southern part of the Tarim Basin by Uyghur, may have been hastened by the coming of Islam to Chinese Central Asia and the attendant realignment of social, economic, and, particularly, trade relationships.

Orthography and Basic Phonology

Tocharian B was natively written using a variety of the North Indian Brahmi alphabet that was widespread in Central Asia. This script is a syllabary and thus each symbol reflects a consonant and an inherent vowel. In the symbols inherited directly from the Indian script, the inherent vowel is *-a-*. The adaptation of this script used for Tocharian has certain new symbols whose inherent vowel is *-ä-*. If the vowel of the syllable was something other than *-a-* (or *-ä-*), that vowel was indicated by a diacritic, thus canceling out, as it were, the inherent vowel. Also symbolized by a diacritic was a syllable-final *-n*, which in transcription, is represented by *ṃ*. Otherwise syllable-final consonants were represented by the appropriate symbol, with another diacritic that canceled all vowels.

Table 1: Consonants

	Labial	Dental	Retroflex	Palatal	Velar
Stops	p	t, ts		c	k
Fricatives		s	ṣ		
Nasals	m	n			
Resonants		l, r		ly	
Glides	w			y	

Table 2: Vowels

	Front	Central	Back
High	i		u
High-Mid		ä	
Mid	e		o
Low-Mid		a	
Low		ā	

In the many loanwords from Buddhist Hybrid SANSKRIT, we find in transcription the following symbols: *b, bh,* and *ph* (all [p]); and in pronunciation, *d, dh, th, ṭ, ḍ, ṭh, ḍh* (= [t]), *j, jh, ch* (= [c], *g, gh, kh* (= [k]), and *v* (=[w]).

The symbols used in the transcription of Tocharian B have their expected values except in the following cases:

ś voiceless palatal fricative, like POLISH *ś* or Chinese *x*
c voiceless palatal affricate
ly voiced palatal lateral approximant
ṣ voiceless retracted (probably retroflex) alveolar fricative

Though word stress is not overtly noted, it is clear that it played an important role in Tocharian phonology. Underlying /ä/ becomes [a] when stressed and disappears entirely when unstressed in an open syllable: thus /räso/ 'span' and /räsontā/ 'spans', both with stress on the next to the last syllable, be-

Table 3: Two-Story Case Markings

Case	Singular	Dual	Plural	Gloss
Locative	enkw-eṃ-ne	enkwe-ne-ne	enkw-eṃ-ne	'to the man/men'
Allative	enkw-eṃ-śc	enkwe-ne-śc	enkw-eṃ-śc	'toward the man/men'
Commitative	enkw-eṃ-mpa	enkwe-ne-mpa	enkw-eṃ-mpa	'with the man/men'
Perlative	enkw-eṃ-sa	enkwe-ne-sa	enkw-eṃ-sa	'over/by the man/men'
Ablative	enkw-eṃ-meṃ	enkwe-ne-meṃ	enkw-eṃ-meṃ	'from the man/men'

come *raso* and *rsonta,* respectively. Similarly, medial /ā/ remains [ā] when stressed, but becomes [a] when unstressed. Also not noted in the spelling, but highly probable, is a rule that allophonically voices obstruents intervocalically.

Basic Morphology

Tocharian B, like most older Indo-European languages, shows many relationships within a sentence by means of inflection, both nominal and verbal, rather than by word order. Thus, Tocharian B nouns belong to one of three genders: masculine, feminine, and neuter, with the latter looking like the masculine in the singular and feminine in the plural, and are inflected for both number and case. Adjectives are inflected for gender, number, and case. Verbs are inflected for person, number, tense, aspect, and mood.

The Tocharian noun is characterized by gender; number including singular, dual, and plural; and a "two-story" case marking system. In the first story, nouns have (at least potentially, since not all nouns show all possible distinctions) a vocative, nominative, accusative or oblique, and genitive. The following examples reflect two common paradigm types. There are many others.

enkwe 'man' (masculine):

	Singular	Dual	Plural
Voc	enkw-a	enkw-ene	enkw-i
Nom	enkw-e	enkw-ene	enkw-i
Acc	enkw-eṃ	enkw-ene	enkw-eṃ
Gen	enkw-entse	enkw-enais	enkw-ents

aśiya 'nun' (feminine):

	Singular	Dual	Plural
Voc	aśiy-a	aśiy-ane	aśiy-ana
Nom	aśiy-a	aśiy-ane	aśiy-ana
Acc	aśiy-ai	aśiy-ane	aśiy-ana
Gen	aśiy-antse	aśiy-anais	aśiy-ants

The second-story cases are formed by the addition of further suffixes to the accusative forms of the singular, dual, and plural (see Table 3 above).

Certain nouns are also inflected for a causal case such as *lakle* 'suffering' and *läkle-ñ* 'because of suffering'. In noun phrases with more than one noun, the second-story case markers are typically added only to the last noun in the series.

Adjectives agree with the nouns they modify in gender, number, and case; in the latter instance, they agree only in terms of first-story endings.

The Tocharian gender system is typical of Indo-European gender systems. Animate nouns are usually masculine or feminine, depending on the sex of the referent of the noun; for example, *pācer* 'father' and *kattāke* 'householder' are masculine, while *mācer* 'mother' and *aśiya* 'nun' are feminine; inanimate nouns may be masculine as *taupe* 'mine', feminine as *kälymiye* 'direction', or neuter as *palsko* 'thought'. Unlike the general Indo-European pattern, neuter nouns in Tocharian do not have a special shape that is distinct from masculine and feminine nouns. Instead, owing to certain phonological changes, neuter nouns look like masculine nouns in the singular and show agreement with adjectives in their masculine singular forms, and feminine ones in the plural where they agree with feminine plural adjectives. Indeed, another, perhaps better, name for this gender would be the "alternating gender", but, for historical and comparative reasons, the designation "neuter" is usually preferred.

The Tocharian verb is inflected for person: first, second, third; number: singular, dual, plural; tense: present, past; aspect: imperfective, perfective (the latter occuring only in the past); mood: indicative, subjunctive (whose past tense is usually called the optative and used to express wishes or contrary-to-fact situations); imperative; and voice: active, mediopassive.

In addition there are numerous nonfinite forms: infinitive, a variety of participles, two verbal adjectives, and two verbal nouns.

The present indicative active imperfective paradigm of the verb *tarkatsi* 'to release' is illustrated below:

	Singular	Plural
First person	tärk-an-au	tärk-an-am
Second person	tärk-an-at	tärk-an-acer
Third person	tärk-an-aṃ	tärk-an-aṃ

The other tense, aspect, mood, and voice forms are characterized both by additional affixes and by selection of different suffixes for person and number agreement, as illustrated by the following second-person singular forms:

Form	Meaning
tärk-nā-tar	present, indicative, imperfective, mediopassive
tärk-an-oy-t	past, indicative, imperfective, active
cärk-ā-sta	past, indicative, perfective, active
tärk-an-oy-tar	past, indicative, imperfective, mediopassive
tärk-ā-tai	past, indicative, perfective, mediopassive
tark-a-t	present, subjunctive, imperfective, active
tark-a-tar	present, subjunctive, imperfective, mediopassive
tark-oy-t	past, subjunctive, imperfective, active
tark-oy-tar	past, subjunctive, imperfective, mediopassive

Basic Syntax

The unmarked order of sentence constituents in Tocharian was SOV.

cai	wat-e-sa	kwaṣ-ai-ś
they	second-time-ACC/ALLATIVE	village-ACC-PERLAT

päst	kam-eṃ	ostū-wa	yärpar-wa
back	come-PAST.3PL	house-ACC.PL	granary-ACC.PL

tsaik-ānte	omtek	papāṣṣorñe
build-PAST.PASSIVE.3PL	there	moral.behavior-ACC

paṣṣ-ānte
practice-PAST.PASSIVE.3PL

'They came back for a second time to the village and built houses and granaries and practiced moral behavior there.'

Within noun phrases, adjectives and genitives normally preceded the noun they modified.

cämpaññecc-eṃ	orocc-eṃ	wnolm-eṃ-mpa
capable-ACC.PL	great-ACC.PL	being-ACC.PL-COMIT

'with capable, great beings'

The ordinary negative element in Tocharian B is *mā*:

mā	su	nes-äṃ	kuse	onwaññe
NEG	one	be-PRES.3SG.IMPERF	who	immortal

tāk-oy
be-PAST.SUBJUNCT.IMPERFECT

'There is no one who is immortal.'

Contact with Other Languages

In the middle of the first Christian millennium, Tocharian B was probably the major vernacular language of Buddhism in central Asia. Through the medium of Tocharian B, Buddhist teachings were first propagated to the Turkic-speaking peoples and to the Chinese. Its own Buddhist terminology was borrowed first from Iranian and later directly from Indic sources. As an example of its role as intermediary between India and the rest of Asia, we might look at *ṣamāne* '(Buddhist) monk', itself a borrowing from Sanskrit *śramana*, which was borrowed into Turkic and then, from language to language, into Siberia, eventually by RUSSIAN from Tungus and thus, via GERMAN, into ENGLISH as 'shaman'.

From Proto-Iranian: *peri* 'debt' (< **parya* 'what must be paid, debt'
From Eastern Iranian: *newiya* 'irrigation canal' (< **nawiya*)
From Sanskrit: *pat* 'stupa' (< *buddha* 'Buddha'; the Tocharian B word for 'Buddha' is *pañäkte* < **pat-ñäkte* 'Buddha-god')
From Old Chinese: *cāk* '100 quarts (dry measure)' (< *d'iak*)

Common Words

man:	enkwe	small:	lykaśke
woman:	kliye	yes:	[not known]
water:	war	no:	mā
sun:	kauṃ	good:	kartse
three:	trey	bird:	[not known]
fish:	laks	dog:	ku
big:	orotstse	tree:	stām
long:	pärkare		

Example Sentences

(1)

ysāre	ri-ne	plyañc-tsi
grain:ACC.SG	city:ACC.M.SG-LOC	sell-INFINITIVE

wāya	Tonke	ṣarmire
bring:3SG.PAST.PERF	Tonke:NOM.M.SG	novice:NOM.M.SG

śak	cak-anma.
ten	cāk-ACC.PL

'The novice Tonke brought ten *cāks* of grain to sell in the city.'

(2)

se	ṣamāne	plāki-sa
what:NOM	monk:NOM.M.SG	agreement-PERL.SG

aśiya-na-mpa	olyi-ne	ṣam-äṃ
NUN-ACC.F.PL-COMIT	boat:ACC.M.SG-LOC	sit-3SG.PRES.INDIC

kaucū-wär	olyi	āś-äṃ
up-water	boat:ACC.M.SG	guide-3SG.PRES.INDIC

ñoru-wär	wat	parna	totte
down-water	or	except	opposite.bank:ACC.SG

katkalñe-sa	pāyti.
crossing:ACC.SG-PERL	sin-NOM.SG

'Whatever monk by agreement sits in a boat with nuns and guides the boat upstream or downstream, except to cross to the other shore, [commits a] sin.'

(3)

ṣle-taś	pink-äṃ
mountain-commander:NOM	write-3SG.PRES.INDIC

salyits-ai	yoñy-ai-ne
salt.having-ACC.F.SG	road-ACC.F.SG-LOC

Putatatt-eṃ-śco.
Buddhadatta-ACC.SG-ALLATIVE

'The mountain commander writes to Buddhadatta on the Salt Road.'

Select Bibliography

Adams, Douglas Q. 1988. *Tocharian Historical Phonology and Morphology*. (American Oriental Series, 71). New Haven: American Oriental Society.

_____. 1999. *A Dictionary of Tocharian B*. Amsterdam and Atlanta: Rodopi.

Krause, Wolfgang. 1952. *Westtocharische Grammatik*. Heidelberg: C. Winter.

Tok Pisin

Suzanne Romaine

Language Name and Autonym: Tok Pisin. **Alternates:** *Papua New Guinea Pidgin/Creole English, Neomelanesian, Melanesian Pidgin, New Guinea Pidgin, Tok Boi, Pidgin* (ENGLISH).

Location: Papua New Guinea.

Family: English-lexifier Pidgin/Creole.

Related Languages: Bislama (Vanuatu Pidgin/Creole English), Pijin (Solomon Islands Pidgin/Creole English).

Dialects: The most important dimension for variation in Tok Pisin today is the dichotomy between rural and urban. Rural and urban Tok Pisin represent two extremes of a continuum. Urban Tok Pisin is a more Anglicized variety reflecting the greater accessibility of town dwellers to English speakers and better educational facilities. Rural Tok Pisin is also now seen by many as the "real" Tok Pisin, while the urban variety is stigmatized as mixed and impure. Although the competence of most urban speakers includes rural Tok Pisin, the reverse is not true. Many of the items that are found in the media and commonly used in town speech are not intelligible to the average rural adult speaker. In town standard English, English spoken as second language with varying degrees of fluency, highly Anglicized Tok Pisin, more rural Tok Pisin of migrants, and the creolized Tok Pisin of the urban-born coexist and loosely reflect the emerging social stratification.

Regional dialects originally resulted from the influence of substratum languages in the speech of older speakers, but these are being dropped by younger, more proficient speakers (see Basic Phonology).

Number of Speakers: Estimated 2 million (+?) speakers out of a population of about 4 million in 1990.

National population census data are unreliable and not directly comparable from one period to the next due to the different questions asked about language and the different sectors of the population sampled. The 1980 census, the first after independence from Australia, asked respondents to say which language was spoken most at home and in the marketplace, but not all areas received the language question. Tok Pisin was by far the most often reported language of the home in urban areas, as well as of the marketplace (except in the capital, Port Moresby, where Hiri Motu is preferred).

Origin and History

Tok Pisin [Eng. "talk pidgin"], an English-based pidgin currently undergoing creolization and decreolization, has its roots in the late 19th century varieties of pidgin English first learned by New Guineans and other Melanesians working as contract laborers on plantations in Queensland, Samoa, Fiji and later in Papua New Guinea itself. Returning workers passed the language onto younger men and boys in their villages. Since Europeans usually referred to the indigenous males they employed as "boys", one of the early names given to the language was *Tok boi* [Eng: 'talk boy']. The term has strong colonial overtones and is little known or used today.

While the language was originally used for instrumental purposes in vertical, hierarchical, communicative encounters between Europeans and indigenous people, an expanded Tok Pisin later came to serve an integrative function at the horizontal level of communication among villagers within Papua New Guinea itself, a highly multilingual setting with as many as 800 languages belonging to two language families (Austronesian and Papuan or non-Austronesian). Amidst a highly linguistically diverse scene, Tok Pisin today stands as a lingua franca that cuts across the social spectrum, known by villagers and government ministers alike. Most government and church communication at the grassroots level is in Tok Pisin. Tok Pisin was the language used to make the public aware of voting, elections, and independence in 1975, and is the most frequently used language in the House of Assembly, the country's main legislative body. Tok Pisin has become the main language of the migrant proletariat and the first language of the younger generation of town-born children, i.e., a creole. The time frame in which Tok Pisin developed from its jargon roots to an expanded pidgin, then Creole, and now post-Creole, has been compressed into a period of 100 to 150 years. It is thus a young Creole, by comparison with most of the Atlantic Creoles such as Jamaican or Haitian Creole. Decreolization is already well under way in urban areas.

Tok Pisin is one of the few pidgin and Creole languages to have undergone considerable standardization because missionaries realized its potential early on as a valuable lingua franca for proselytizing among a linguistically diverse population and began using it for teaching. There were at least nine different spelling systems in use by different missions.

Orthography and Basic Phonology

The spelling conventions of present-day Tok Pisin derive from Hall's (1955) orthography. They were approved by the director of Education and the administrator of the Territory of Papua New Guinea and by the Minister for the Territories in Canberra. The standard is based on the rural variety of Tok Pisin spoken along the north coast of mainland New Guinea. Mihalic's (1957) grammar and dictionary of Melanesian Pidgin using Hall's orthography was adopted for use in 1963 and made compulsory for the production of written material in Tok Pisin and for teaching the Vernacular Education program. It is also widely used as a guideline in publications such as *Wantok*, the weekly newspaper in Tok Pisin (founded by the Catholics in 1967 and now run by Papua New Guineans), and *Nupela Testamen* (1966), the translation of the New Testament into Tok Pisin. All of the early written materials in Tok Pisin, dating from the 1920s, and the majority of published works today, are religious in nature. However, the past 20 or 30 years have seen the appearance of a number of manuals on health, hygiene, agriculture, carpentry, and cooking as well as creative writing, particularly poetry and drama, written in Tok Pisin. There are already indications that secular publications are setting a new standard for the written language. Wantok's *Stail Buk* (Mihalic 1986) is a more recent guide to orthographic conventions.

Tok Pisin orthography uses the letters of the LATIN alphabet, with the exception of *c*, *q*, *x*, and *z*. There are no diacritics.

The phonology of individual speakers of Tok Pisin varies depending on the degree to which an individual's phonology is Anglicized. All speakers share a core system that is similar to that of the indigenous substrate languages.

Table 1: Consonants

		Labial	Alveolar	Palatal	Velar
Stops	Voiceless	p	t		k
	Voiced	b	d		g
Fricatives			s		h
Nasals		m	n		ŋ
Liquids			l, r		
Glides		w		y	

Voiced stop consonants tend not to occur in word-final position.

Table 2: Vowels

	Front	Central	Back
High	i		u
Mid	e		o
Low		a	

There are also three diphthongs *ai*, *au*, *oi*. There is no distinction between long and short vowels.

Some speakers have a more Anglicized phonology, incorporating more of the consonant and vowel distinctions in English. In principle, the fluent bilingual speaker of Tok Pisin and English has the whole phonological inventory of English to draw on when speaking Tok Pisin.

Tok Pisin phonology reflects pressures from both substratum and superstratum as well as universal tendencies of first- and second-language acquisition. Non-Austronesian languages are generally not rich in fricatives. Allophonic variability in a speaker's substrate language will affect the number of contrasts made in varieties of Tok Pisin spoken as a second language. Many highland speakers have prenasalized stops, e.g., /ngut/ for /gut/ 'good'. Some rural speakers still do not distinguish between /r/ and /l/, in line with allophonic variability present in many of the indigenous languages, e.g., /lot/ for /rot/ 'road', /raik/ for /laik/ 'like' 'want to'. The elimination of marked segments, such as affricates, is a universal tendency of language acquisition as is a reduction in the overall number of phonological contrasts, and these tendencies are also reflected in the core system of Tok Pisin phonology. Yet fricatives and affricates are being added to the inventory of some speakers as new words are borrowed from English; e.g., /pis/ 'fish' is now realized variably by some speakers as /fis/, /fiʃ/, and /piʃ/. Younger speakers modify their phonology with increasing exposure to education in English. Less exposure to English leads to hypercorrection, e.g., /fikinini/ for /pikinini/ 'child', /fik/ for /pik/ 'pig'.

Epenthetic vowels often occur in rural varieties, e.g., /peles/ for /ples/ 'village' /sikin/ for /skin/ 'skin', while younger fluent speakers in urban areas often omit vowels and condense longer forms:

disla [<*dispela*] man na meri blem [<*bilong en*], ol
this man and woman of him they

sa [<save] lukautim pikinini blol [<*bilong ol*]
HAB take.care.of child of them

gutpla [<*gutpela*]
good
'This man and his wife take good care of their child.'

Basic Morphology

Like most pidgins and creoles, Tok Pisin has little morphology. When grammatical categories such as case, number, gender, tense, mood, and aspect are expressed at all, they are in general expressed with full lexemes rather than by inflectional morphology. Thus gender can be expressed for nouns by adding the words for male (*man*) and female (*meri*), *pik man/meri* 'boar'/'sow'. Possessive constructions are normally phrased in Tok Pisin by means of the preposition *bilong*, e.g., *bilong ol meri* 'women's', and the plurality of nouns is optionally marked by the use of the third-person plural pronoun *ol*, *ol diwai* 'trees'.

Tok Pisin has, however, acquired some derivational and inflectional morphology in the course of its expansion. An inflectional affix *-pela* is used to form the plural of the first- and second-person pronouns: *mi* 'I', *mipela* 'we' EXC (*yumi* 'we' INC); *yu* 'you', *yupela* 'you' (pl.); *em* 'he/she/it', *ol* 'they'.

-pela also marks a subset of monosyllabic attributive adjectives, demonstratives and cardinal numerals: *dispela tupela pis* 'these two fish(es)'; *gutpela kaikai* 'good food'; *wanpela liklik pikinini* 'a/one small child'.

The suffix *-im* is used as a transitive verb marker (although not with verbs such as *gat* 'have' and *save* 'know', even when they are followed by a direct object):

em	i	lusim	dispela	ples
3SG	PR	leave+TRANS	this	place/village

'He/she/it/left this place/village.'

The suffix *-im* is also used as a derivational affix that attaches to adjectives to form causative verbs: *bik* 'big' + *im* = *bikim* 'to enlarge'.

Following the preposition *long*, there is an oblique variant of the normally invariant third-person pronoun *em*:

em	karim	wanpela	pikinini	bilong	en
3SG	carry+TRANS	one	child	of	3SG

'He/she carried his/her child.'

There is a high degree of multifunctionality in Tok Pisin, so that many words are used as both nouns and verbs: *save* 'knowledge'/'to know', *askim* 'question'/'to ask'. Compounds can be formed in a variety of ways: noun + noun *skulboi* 'schoolboy'; noun + adjective *belhat* 'angry' (a condensation of *bel bilong mi i hat* 'my stomach is hot', i.e., 'I am angry').

Basic Syntax

Like many pidgins and creoles, Tok Pisin has SVO word order. There is no copula. Adjectives may function as intransitive predicates. The so-called predicate marker *i* appears preverbally following third-person and plural subjects, although it is being lost in many urban areas: *Em wanpela gutpela man* (3SG one good man) 'He's a good man'; *Pikinini (i) sik* (child (PR) sick) 'The child is sick'.

Tense, mood and aspect are optionally expressed by full lexemes, most of which occur in preverbal position. Thus, although the normal way of indicating past time is through use of the unmarked verb form, the lexeme *bin* can be used as a past-time marker.

ol	i	bin	adoptim	em
3PL	PR	PAST	adopt+TRANS	3SG

'They adopted him.'

The lexeme *pinis*, which occurs clause finally, indicates that an action has been completed, whereas postverbal *kam, go* and *stap*, usually preceded by the predicate marker, can be used to indicate continuous action, with *go* implying motion away from the speaker, and *kam* motion toward the speaker.

Nau	liklik	gel	ia	em	pikim	flaua	pinis	putim	go
Now	little	girl	FOC	she	pick	flower	COMP	put	go

insait	long	bag	bilong	en
inside	in	bag	of	her

'The little girl picked a flower and put it inside her bag.'

em	i	wokabaut	i	go.
he	PR	walk	PR	go

'He is/was walking (away from speaker).'

Bai (which has almost entirely replaced *baimbai* [<Eng. 'by and by']) expresses immediate and remote future, prediction, intention, and irrealis.

Sapos	neks	yia	yutupela	kam	bek	mipela
suppose	next	year	you.two-PL	come	back	2PL.EXC

bai	kam	lukim	yutupela
FUT	come	look+ TRANS	you two-PL

'If you both come back next year, we'll come to see you.'

Other markers of modality include *laik* desiderative/futurity (often shortened to *la*), *mas* obligation/possibility/probability, and *ken* permission/futurity/ability.

Normally only one preverbal marker may occur, although two particle combinations are beginning to be used: *OK, yu ken bai kisim* (ok you can FUT get) 'OK, you can take it'; *Yumi mas bai helpim* (2PL INC must FUT help) 'We'll have to help'.

Clauses are coordinated with *na* 'and', *nau* 'now', and *tasol* 'but'/'however'. There is little use of explicit markers of subordination in the spoken language, though the adverb *olsem* 'thus' and the conjunction *na* can be used as complementizers.

New markers of subordination such as *bikos* 'because' are being borrowed from English and used instead of or alongside native ones such as *long wanem*. For relative clauses the most frequent strategy is simple juxtaposition of clauses, although in the written language (and increasingly in speech) the interrogative pronoun *husat* 'who' can be used for subject relatives. The focus marker *ia* is sometimes used to bracket the relative clause, especially subject clauses.

Em	go	nau	luk	dispela	rebit	ia [0	stap	insait	long
3SG	go	now	look	this	rabbit	FOC	stop	inside	of

wanpela	hul.
one	hole

'He went and looked at the rabbit [(that) was inside the hole].'

Negation is preverbal: *Mi no save* (1SG NEG know) 'I don't know'; *Em i no gat mani* (3SG PR NEG have money) '(S)he doesn't have any money'.

There is no inversion for questions. Question particles and interrogatives are utterance final.

Yupela	gat	brus	a?
You (PL)	have	tobacco	Q

'Have you got any tobacco?'

yu	painim	husat
you	look	for who

'Who are you looking for?'

Contact with Other Languages

Increased contact with English is leading to greater differences between rural and urban Tok Pisin. In cases where Tok Pisin and English coexist as closely as they do in urban centers, and speakers code switch between them, new intermediate varieties have arisen that contain compromise forms. The existence of these intermediate varieties is a sign that decreolization is already advanced in urban areas like Lae even though 20 years previously it had been reported that the distinction between Tok Pisin and English was clear. Complaints about Anglicized Tok Pisin and the use of English to show off have become more frequent since the 1970s. Anglicization is seen to undermine the integrative function of Tok Pisin and its perceived value as a national language.

At the village level Tok Pisin is in contact with numerous vernacular languages, and in some areas Tok Pisin is seen as a threat to their purity. Frequent borrowing and code switching between vernacular languages and Tok Pisin is common. In some areas children are acquiring Tok Pisin instead of their vernacular language.

Using the not entirely reliable etymologies provided in Mihalic (1971), the lexical composition of Tok Pisin is mainly English (79 percent), while an indigenous language (Tolai) contributes 11 percent, other indigenous languages 6 percent, German 3 percent and Malay 1 percent. To this can be added a small set of words common to many pidgins and creoles throughout the world that have their origin in PORTUGUESE/SPANISH, e.g., *save* 'know'. The German element, a remnant from the German colonial regime in former German New Guinea (1884–1914), is now declining, although a few words are in very common use, e.g., *rausim* 'to get rid of/throw out'.

English provides the most important source for borrowings. For example, the following words appeared in a 1987 political broadside, *developmen* 'development', *underdevelopmen* 'underdevelopment', *praivet kampani* 'private company', *advaisa* 'adviser', etc. There are also anglicisms such as the use of *ov* instead of *bilong* e.g. *standat ov edukesen* 'standard of education'.

In many cases borrowing is resorted to as a means of filling a lexical gap, particularly where foreign institutions and ideas are involved. These concepts could be expressed in Tok Pisin but usually only by means of a lengthy circumlocution.

Most of these new borrowings are still conspicuous morphologically and semantically, even where some effort has been made to adapt them orthographically. The introduction of more anglicized spellings is a departure from the standard orthography and leads to inconsistency. In *Wantok* newspaper and other publications new English loans such as *reperi* 'referee' and *painal* 'painal' are now spelled as *referi* and *fainal*.

Even frequently used words like *kiau* from Tolai are increasingly replaced by or used alongside English 'egg'. New borrowings are disrupting the traditional lexical structure of rural varieties by introducing arbitrary new forms whose meanings are opaque and have to be learned. The borrowing of these terms has other syntactic consequences since some words such as *inning* then take English plurals, e.g., "innings". The English plural suffix now competes with the use of the traditional plural marker *ol* and is often used together with it in more recent English borrowings, *ol gels* 'girls'.

The most colloquial registers of Tok Pisin rely heavily on creative coinages, largely from English, and can sometimes be seen in printed form in comics. Many of the new idiomatic expressions derive from similar English ones, as in *single meri* 'single mother'. Here the English term "single" has been borrowed and used along with the Tok Pisin word *meri* 'woman' to form a hybrid collocation modeled on English.

Common Words

man:	man	long:	long(pela)
woman:	meri	small:	smol(pela)
water:	wara	yes:	yes
sun:	san	no:	nogat
three:	tri(pela)	good:	gut(pela)
fish:	pis, fis	bird:	pisin
big:	bik(pela)	dog:	dok
tree:	diwai		

Example Sentences

(1) Tasol man em putim kain hat olsem ol meri
however man 3SG put kind hat thus PL woman

bai respectim ol moa yet.
FUT respect+TRANS 3PL more even

'However, if men wore this kind of hat, the women respected them even more.' [Oral story told by elderly man in rural village, Morobe Province, 1986]

(2) Mipela yet i gat pawa na i gat rait, long
we.EXC EMPH PR have power and PR have right for

wanem, mipela i lain pipel i bin stap hia
what we.EXC PR line people PR PAST stop here

longtaim moa na mipela i fri na mipela i
long.time more and we.EXC PR free and we.EXC PR

independen.
independent

'We ourselves have the power and the right because we are the people who have been here a long time and we are free and independent.' [Preamble to the constitution of the independent country, Papua New Guinea, translated by Frank Mihalic, 1986]

(3) Bihain ol i kaikai inap pinis, ol i bungim
after 3PL PR eat enough COMP they PR gather

olgeta liklik hap i stap yet, na i pulapim 7-pela
all little half PR stop EMPH and PR fill seven

basket.
basket

'After they had eaten enough, they gathered together all the little pieces still remaining and filled seven baskets.' [*Nupela Testamen* 1966 'Jisas i givim kaikai long 4,000 man' (The story of the loaves and fishes, Mark 8:8).]

Efforts to Preserve, Protect, and Promote the Language

Since independence there has been considerable discussion over the question of whether Tok Pisin should become the national language of Papua New Guinea. The national constitution does not contain anything on the status of Tok Pisin and

Hiri Motu, which are frequently claimed to be national languages, but knowledge of one or the other is one of the indispensable prerequisites for granting of citizenship by naturalization. At the moment Tok Pisin has "official" status, along with English and Hiri Motu ('trade Motu'), an indigenous pidgin based on Motu, one of the languages of what used to be the Territory of Papua. The designation "official" means the language is accepted for use in the House of Assembly, where since independence it is the preferred language. Although simultaneous translation is provided for it, the Hansard transcriptions of debates appear only in English, which is the official medium of education. The name "Tok Pisin" was officially adopted in 1981. Even now Tok Pisin is spoken principally in the ex-German and Australian territory of New Guinea, while Hiri Motu is still largely confined to the ex-British territory of Papua. Hiri Motu has become, for some, a symbol of Papuan separatism.

Data from the national population census in 1980 indicates that literacy in any language is not widespread. Fewer than one third of the population over age 10 can read and write in any language. Post-independence governments have not committed themselves to any clear-cut policy on language. Because control of English was seen as essential for participation in national development, modernization of vernacular languages and Tok Pisin was not encouraged, although there have been small-scale efforts on a regional basis to use languages other than English as the medium of education. English will play an increasingly important role as a means of cross-cultural communication within and outside the Pacific, while the future of the indigenous languages and pidgins/creoles is less certain.

Select Bibliography

Dutton, Tom and Thomas, Dicks. 1985. *A New Course in Tok Pisin. Pacific Linguistics D-67.* Canberra: Australian National University.

Hall, Jr., Robert A. 1955. *A Standard Orthography and List of Suggested Spellings for Neomelanesian.* Port Moresby: Department of Education.

Laycock, Don C. 1970. *Materials in New Guinea Pidgin (Coastal and Lowlands). Pacific Linguistics D-5.* Canberra: Australian National University.

McElhanon, K.A., ed. 1975. *Tok Pisin i go we?* Special Issue of *Kivung 1*: Ukarumpa: Linguistic Society of Papua New Guinea.

Mihalic, Frank. 1957. *The Jacaranda dictionary and grammar of Melanesian Pidgin.* Milton: The Jacaranda Press. [2nd ed. 1971].

Mühlhäusler, Peter. 1979. *Growth and Structure of the Lexicon of New Guinea Pidgin. Pacific Linguistics C-52.* Canberra: Australian National University.

Mühlhäusler, Peter, Suzanne Romaine, and Tom E. Dutton, to appear. *Tok Pisin Texts. Varieties of English around the World.* Amsterdam: John Benjamins.

Romaine, Suzanne. 1992. *Language, Education and Development: Urban and Rural Tok Pisin in Papua New Guinea.* Oxford: Oxford University Press.

Sankoff, Gillian 1980. *The Social Life of Language.* Philadelphia: University of Pennsylvania Press. Chapters 1, 2, 5, 10, 11, 12.

Verhaar, John W.M. 1995. *Toward a Reference Grammar of Tok Pisin: An Experiment in Corpus Linguistics.* Honolulu: University of Hawai'i Press.

Wurm, Stephen A. 1971. *New Guinea Highlands Pidgin: Course Materials. Pacific Linguistics. D-3.* Canberra: Australian National University.

Wurm, Stephen A., and Peter Mühlhäusler. 1982. "Registers in New Guinea Pidgin." In *International Journal of the Sociology of Language* 35: 69–86.

Wurm, Stephen A., and Peter Mühlhäusler, eds. 1985. *Handbook of Tok Pisin. Pacific Linguistics* C-70. Canberra: Australian National University.

TSHILUBÀ

Mpunga wa Ilunga

Language Name: Tshilubà. **Alternate:** *Luba.*

Location: Tshilubà is one of the four national languages of Zaire. It is spoken in the provinces of East and West Kasaï.

Family: Tshilubà is a member of the Bantu group of the Niger-Congo-Kordofanian branch.

Related Languages: Lexicostatistics affirms that Tshilubà is most closely related to the other Bantu languages in Zone L: Kanyok, Luba Katanga, Sanga, Budya, Songye, Hemba, Bangubangu, Bwila, Kaonde, Zela, Dete, Salampasu, Bindi, Lwalwa, Mbagani.

Dialects: Regional variations in Tshilubà can be attested on the lexical and grammatical level. The word *mshìma* 'alimentary paste made from corn and manioc flower' has three regional variations: *bidyà, bidyàjì*, and *byajì*. Some verbs have regional variants that are recognized by their tones: *ngaafutshì* 'I paid' has a regional variant *ngăfutshì.*

Number of Speakers: Over 10 million.

Origin and History

A number of theories on the origin of Bantu languages and their spread have been proposed. African linguists trace Bantu-language expansion from Northwest Cameroon. The expansion was realized in two principal waves of migration, one course extending along the west coast, making its way toward the south following the course of the water; the other progressing toward the east, bordering the forest to descend toward the south along the interlacustre fault, undoubtedly in search of new land. These populations settled in the region of the great lakes in Kenya, in the Congo basin, in Shaba, Zambia, Angola, and a great part of Southen Africa. These migrations, begun near the first century of our era, continued until the 19th century. It was in this wave that the Baluba (speakers of Luba) came to their present home.

Archaeological records from the High Lwalaba region around Lake Kisale in Sanga attest traces of an ancient Iron Age civilization (Hiernaux 1958). The traces, dated 800 years A. are attributable to the ancestors of the Balubà speaking peoples (Nenquin 1958): the Luba Shaba and the Luba Kasaï who lived together during that period. Historical records also indicate that the Luba, and Lunda, speaking peoples had formed great empires in what is now Katanga (Verhulpen 1936). The Baluba have witnessed two great empires constituted of various communities: the first empire of Nkongolo Mwamba, a Musongye, and the second empire of Ilunga Mbidi, a Kunda.

The movement of the Baluba toward the north commenced around 1450. Various factors triggered the massive emigrations: a demographic explosion, food shortages, fraternal disputes, and a cataclysm. The waves of departure were by clan. The Beena Kanyok were the first to leave. The second group followed them and occupied the Luluwa River Basin. The third wave consisted of an important group that settled around the Lubilanji river. Oral tradition of the migrating populations makes reference to the term *Nsàngalubangu*, considered the origin of the Baluba and all of the communities that were a part of the Baluba Empire. Elikia Mbokolo (1985) asserts that by oral tradition confirmed by archaeological discoveries, the point of origin of the Baluba before the massive expansion is in Katangale, not far from the Kamina military base.

The first works on the Tshilubà language were by De Clercq who wrote *A Grammar of Luba* (1911), *A French-Luba, Luba-French Dictionary* (1914), *The Verb in Luba* (1925), and *A New Grammar of Luba* (1929). Burssens (1938–1939) and Willems (1943–1955) followed De Clercq. The Scheut missions published teaching manuals and reading materials in Tshilubà. These works were followed by those of native linguists, to cite a few: Mpoyi Mwadyamvita, Mbuyi Wetu, C. Faïk Nzuji, Kanyinda Lusanga, Mufuta Kabemba, Mabika Kalanda, Ngindu Mushete, and Lufulwabo F.M.

Orthography and Basic Phonology

The first written records in Tshilubà were the works of missionaries using the LATIN alphabet. Tshilubà orthography was modified several times. In 1964, a committee formed from the Catholic and Protestant churches created a unified orthography. Zairean linguists appoved the orthography in 1974.

Tshilubà has five vowels, and two glides (semivowels). Length is phonemic and represented in the orthography by a double vowel.

Table 1: Vowels and Glides

	Front	Central	Back
High	i, ii		u, uu
Mid	e, ee [ɛ, ɛɛ]		o, oo [ɔ, ɔɔ]
Low		a, aa	
Glides	y		w

Tshilubà has two distinctive tones, low and high. Diacritics on vowels in Luba represent the following tonal patterns: /á/

Table 2: Consonants

		Labial	Dental	Alveolar	Palatal	Velar
Stops	Voiceless	p	t			
	Voiced	b	(d)			k
Fricatives	Voiceless	f	s		sh [ʃ]	
	Voiced	v	z		j [ʒ]	
Affricates					tsh, c [tʃ]	
Nasals		m	n		ny [ɲ]	ng [ŋ]
Lateral				l		

high tone (also unmarked), /à/ low tone, /â/ falling tone, /ǎ/ rising tone, /â/ = [áà] or [â:], /ǎ/=/àá/ or [ǎ:]. A vowel carrying a complex tone will always be pronounced long, as will a vowel followed by a nasal consonant sequence, preceded by a consonant and glide sequence, or by word-initial glide, except in regional varieties and in the word *Yo'ura* = girl's name: *àbâsà* [àbâ:sa] *tshilumbù* 'that he dares to ask for the accounts', *kulonda* [kulo:nda] 'follow', *kwasa* [kwa:sa] 'construct'.

A rising tone a prefinal syllable preceded by a low tone is realized as a midtone: *muvyě̱lè* [muvyē̱lè] 'woman who has just given birth'. A high tone in prefinal position between two low tones is realized as a falling tone: *ùbambà* [ùbâmbà] 'you must tell them'. Tone is used on the lexical level and also as a grammatical marker: *kubala* 'count' vs. *kubàla* 'shine', *udi* 'you are' vs. *ùdi* 'he is'. A curious feature of Tshilubà tone is that the system is the inverse of the mother Bantu language; Proto-Bantu high tones are realized in Tshilubà as low tones, and vice versa.

The voiceless afficate [tʃ] is represented in the orthography as either /tsh/, /c/. The phoneme /p/ is realized as [h] when it is not preceded by a nasal. The lateral /l/ and the dental /d/ are in complementary distribution but are both represented in the orthography. The lateral *l* is represented as /d/ before the vowel /i/ and after the nasal /n/: *kulààla* 'sleep', *mulààdi* 'sleeper', *ndǎlà* 'that I sleep'. The palatal nasal /ny/ is a unique phoneme and not a sequence of *n-y*.

The morphophonemes *n, z, s, t* palatalize to /ny, j, sh, tsh/ if they are followed by *i* or *y*: *mu-fut-i* > /mufutshi/ 'he who pays'. One exception occurs in the word *tshîniinà* 'a small pit'.

Tshilubà syllable structure does not differ from that of the majority of Bantu languages. A syllable can consist of a single vowel or a syllabic nasal. The maximal syllable in Tshilubà is N-C-Glide-V: *nkwa-sa* 'chair', *ku-lo-nda* 'follow', *ndya-dya* 'eater', *ku-swa* 'want', *ù-bàmtù-mì-nè* 'send them to me'.

The following morphophonemic rules are attested in Tshilubà:
(1) Distance vowel-assimilation. In Kasaï Tshilubà, the morphophoneme *i* of a verbal suffix or the final suffix *-ile* is represented as /e/ if the preceding root vowel is *i* or *o*, *ku-bel-il-a* > /kubelela/ 'advise'. The *u* of a verbal suffix surfaces as /o/ after the vowel *o*. This rule does not apply with the passive suffix *-i:bu-*. The application of this rule is optional for the second suffix if the causative suffix *-ish-* is reduplicated or employed with other suffixes.
(2) Consonant assimilation. The morphophoneme *l* of a verbal suffix or the final suffix *-ile* is represented as /n/ if preceded by the morphophonemes *m* or *n* not followed by an intermediary consonant: *ku-tùm-il-a* = /kutùmina/ 'to send to'.

The nasal /n/ is always homorganic and assimilates to the following consonant. The morphophoneme *n* used as a verbal prefix or a predicative morpheme changes to /ng/ before vowels or the glide *w*: *N-wêwe* /ngwêwe/ 'it's you'. As a prefix to a resultative verb, *n* is represented as /ng/ and optionally /mb/: *n-a-fut-i* > /ngǎfutshì/ or /mbǎfutshì/ 'I paid'.
(3) Consonantal loss. The phoneme *l* or *n* in a verbal suffix is not represented before the suffixes *-il* or *-ile*: *ku-kàng-ul-il-a* > /kukàngwila/ 'to open for'. This rule does not apply if the applicative suffix *-il* is reduplicated: *ku-sèng-il-il-a* > /kusengelela/ 'to implore'.
(4) Vowel contact. In Tshilubà if two identical vowels follow each other, they are represented by a long vowel. If the two vowels are different, the contact between *a* and *e* surfaces as /ee/, and in some words, the vowel *a* raises to *i* with the final representation /ii/. In other contexts, *a* or *e* adapt to the following vowel: *ma-itu* > /meetu/ 'forests', *ba-ibi* > /biibi/ 'thieves', *ma-ùlu* > /mûlu/ 'nose', *ma-owa* > /moowa/ 'mushrooms', *ne-ùfikà* > /nûfikà/ 'you will arrive'. There are a few exceptions to this rule: /tshibau/ 'guilt'. The contraction does not take place if the second vowel belongs to an object prefix, pronominal prefix, or a verbal prefix representing future tense or eventual mode (except in regional varieties).
(5) Tones in succession. If two different vowels carrying the same tone follow each other without an intervening consonant, the tone of the first consonant elides: *mù-ètù* > /mwètù/ 'at our house'. Elision does not take place if the second vowel is in a prefix: *nèùbengà, neùmonà* 'If you dare to refuse, you'll see'. Two successive tones carried by a long vowel are directly represented: *bàfutààyi* 'pay them'.
(6) Tonal harmony. The connective vowel *-a*, the numeral pronoun *-mwe*, and the final relative object *-e* suffix do not carry their own tone, they carry the tone of the preceding vowel. The derivative suffix is in tonal harmony with the final tone of the verb: *ku-imb-ulul-a* > /kwimbulula/, *ku-tùm-ulul-a* > *kutùmununa* 'to send again' *imb-ùlùlà* 'to sing again'.
(7) Tonal contrast. The final tone of a verb is the opposite of that of the root vowel of the participle, imperative, resultative, and negative: *-fik-i* > /twâfikì/ 'We arrived'.
(8) Tonal contraction. If two different tones come in contact with each other in a word, they are represented by a complex (falling or rising) tone: *mu-àna* /mwâna/ 'child'. Word finally,

if two tones come in contact, only the first is represented: *ku-dì-a* > /kudyà/ 'eat'.
(9) Tonal assimilation. A high tone followed by a low tone is realized as a low tone if it is immediately followed by a relative, possessive, or connective form: *ba-àna* > /bânà bàà mukàjì/ 'the children of the woman'.

Basic Morphology

Tshilubà has 16 noun classes as indicated in Table 3 below.

Table 3: Noun Classes

Class	Noun class prefix	Pronoun	Verb	Object	Pronominal suffix
1/1a	mu-/ø,n-	u-	ù-	-mu-	-ye/-yi
2/2a	ba-/baa-	bà-	-	-	-bo/-bu
3/3a	mu-/ø	ù-/-wu	-	-	-wo/-wu
4/4a	mi-/n-	ì-/-yi	-	-	-yo/-yi
5	di-	dì-	-	-	-dyo/-di
6	ma-	à-	-	-	-wo/-wu
7	tshi-	tshì-	tshì-	-	-tsho/-tshi
8	bi-	bì-	bì-	-	-byo/-byi
9	n-	u-	ù-	-mu-	-ye/-i
10	n-	ì-	ì-	-	-ye/-i
11	lu-	lù-	-	-	-lo/-lu
12	ka-	kà-	-	-	-ko/-ku
13	tu-	tù-	-	-	-to/-tu
14	bu-	bù-	-	-	-bo/-bu
15	ku-	kù-	-	-	-ko/-ku
16	pa-	pà-	-	-	-po/-pu
17	ku-	kù-	-	-	-ko/-ku
18	mu-	mù-	-	-	-mo/-mu
IR	dì-				

The noun-class prefix occurs in all nominal forms (nouns or adjectives), ordinal numbers, and participles: *muntu munène* 'big person'. Noun-class agreement is also shown on the verb: *tshilàmbà etshi, tshìdi tshìmsànkisha, ùtshìnsùmbìlè* 'I like that fabric, buy it for me'. Classifying prefixes inflect for plurality: *muntu* 'person', *bantu* 'persons'.

Some classes have a semantic component. Classes 1 and 2 are usually associated with human beings, Classes 3 and 4 deal with parts of the body or diverse objects, Class 14 contains abstract words, and Class 15 infinitives. These semantic distinctions are only generalizations one can find words denoting humans in classes other than 1 and 2.

Some classifiers are used derivationally to form new lexemes. Classes 7 and 8 are used to form augmentatives: *nzùbu* 'house', *tshizùbu* 'a poorly constructed big house'. Classes 12 and 13 are used to form diminutives: *mwâna* 'child', *kâna* 'a beautiful little child'. Class 14 contains abstract words: *bwâna* 'childhood'. Nominal prefixes appear with a long vowel if they are employed as additive prefixes.

Nouns. The nominal category comprises adjectives and nouns. They are composed of a prefix and a theme that may be simple (*mu-kàndà* 'book') or derived (*bu-lààlu* 'bed' derived from *-lààl-* 'sleep'). Adjectives agree with their nouns in noun class and are always placed after the noun (except for the adjectives *-ànga* 'other', *-kwàbò* 'other', and *-inè* 'same', which can either precede or follow their nouns). Ordinal numbers from 2 to 6 are adjectival.

Pronouns. Pronouns are characterized by the presence of a pronominal prefix followed by a theme. Tshilubà has connective, substitutive, possessive, demonstrative, presentative, and determinative pronouns. Cardinal numbers from 1 to 6 are pronominal: *muntu umwe* 'a person'. Verbal relative forms also use a pronominal prefix.

Verbs. In Tshilubà, the temporal and aspectual distinction is strongly marked. Various verbal categories exist in Tshilubà. The **constative** expresses an action achieved in the past without reference to its term or consequences: *tulòmbèle* 'we asked for, we had asked for'. The **resultative** is used for perfective actions encoding result: *twâfutshì* 'We have paid', *twatùmì* 'we have sent'. The **durative** expresses actions in the process of being fulfilled: *tufuta* 'we pay'. The **subsecutive** indicates that the action expressed in the verb is a consequence of another past action: *pàfikìlàye wadya kakùyi lusa* 'when he arrived, he ate without pity'. Other verbal categories include **imperative** denoting commands: *tùma* 'send', the **subjunctive**, the **future**: *netùfutà* 'we will pay', and the **participle**: *budimi budima* 'the cultivated field', *wêwe mudyà* 'if you have eaten'.

Verbal forms consist of several elements, among which the verbal prefix, the root, and the final verbal suffix are the only obligatory elements.

Other verbal morphemes include the **preinitial** *ka-* morpheme of negation: *katùdimìne* 'we had not cultivated', the **initial** classificatory prefix: *tudi tudima* 'we cultivate', *bàdi bàdima* 'they cultivate', the **formatives** *-a-* 'resultative or subsecutive' and *-àka* 'constative', the **limitator** or **aspectual morphemes** *-ka-* 'movement towards', *-tshì-* 'durative', and *-kàà-* 'inceptive', the **object** or **reflexive** prefix: *tumutùma* 'we sent him', *kuditàpa* 'to hurt oneself', and the **extension**, or verbal suffix. Verbal suffixes include the causative *-ij*, *-ish-* (*kudìisha* 'to feed'), the passive *-i:bu-* (*kulàmbiibwa* 'be susceptible to being cooked'), the reciprocal *-angan-* (*kutùmangana* 'to send to each other'), the reversive *-uk-*, *-ul-* (*kubùmbuka* 'be destroyed') the repetitive *-ulul* (*kukwàtulula* 'catch again'), the associative *-an-* (*kusangana* 'find'), and the extensive *-akan-* (*kwalakana* 'send').

The final verb suffix varies according to time and mode, *-a* characterizes the infinitive, durative, subsecutive, passive participle, and is the final vowel of the nonextended imperative. The suffix *-à* appears in the extended imperative and subjunctive. The active participle is expressed with the atonal suffixes *-a* or *-e* the suffix *-i* denotes the negative (*katùmutùminyi* 'let's not send it to him'). The suffix *-ile* is used to express the constative (perfect): *tutùmìne* 'we had sent'.

There are also postfinal suffixes used for pronominal subjects or complements, and the suffixes -:*yi* 'plural imperative', -*ku* 'polite singular imperative', and -^{x}ku 'exhortation morpheme'.

Tshilubà has an auxiliary copular verb "to be". This defective verb is attested in the durative (*tudi* 'we are'), the habitual (*tutu* 'we are habitually'), the past (*tuvwa* 'we were habitually'), and in the negative (*katwèna* 'we are not', *katùvwa* 'we were not', and *katùtu* 'we are not [habitually]').

Basic Syntax

The normal word-order of a sentence is Subject-Verb-Complement. In order to emphasize an object, the object can be fronted to the head of the phrase in which it is also shown as an object prefix on the verb:

di-bànza ba-ntu bà-a-dì-fut-ù.
CLASS-debt PL.CLASS-person PL.CLASS-OBJ-pay-FINAL
'The people paid the debt.'

When two pronominal complements are employed in a verb, the complement of an indirect object appears as a prefix to the verbal root, and the complement of a direct object is realized by a pronominal suffix corresponding to the object class except when the indirect object prefix is in the first-person singular.

àtùmà tshilàmba. 'that he sends the cloth'

à-tshi-n-tùmìn-à
PREF-DO.PREFIX-IO-send-FINAL
'that he sends me it (the cloth)'.

à-ku-tùmìn-à-tshi
PREF-IO-send-FINAL-DO.CLASS
'that he sends it (the cloth) to you'.

Negation is rendered by the use of the preinitial negative prefix *ka-* and the final suffix *-i* or *-u*, in which the tone is high if there is no secondary prefix and in contrast to the tone of the root in the presence of a secondary prefix. The final *-u* is freely employed whenever the root is of a CVC or VC type with a back vowel. The general negative can be translated by the negative subjunctive or imperative.

ka-tù-dim-i budimi.
NEG-PREFIX-cultivate-FINAL field
'We don't cultivate the field; that we don't cultivate the field; Let's not cultivate the field'.

ka-tù-bà-tùm-i/u.
NEG-PREFIX-IO-send-FINAL
'Let's not send them; It is not necessary that we send them'.

Contact with Other Languages

Foreign loan words are adapted into Tshilubà phonology. These words take a classificatory prefix according to the nature of their initial consonant. In the absence of consonant resemblance, borrowed words are found in Classes 3a, 4a, 3, 4, 5, 6, 7, 8, 12, 13....

From SWAHILI: *kukùmbula* 'pay a visit', *kukombola* 'replace or substitute a work position' (from the Swahili word meaning "redeem")

From PORTUGUESE: *bisàbatà* Cl. 7,8 'shoe' < (*sapato*), *mputù* 'Europe' < (Portugal), *kabalù* Cl. 12,13 'horse' (*cavalo*)

From DUTCH: *dikopo* 'cup' < (*kop*), *bàzopù* 'attention' < (*pas op*), *matabishì* Cl. 6 'tip (for waiter)' < (*maatschapij*)

From FRENCH: *kàlàndê* cl.12 'pavement' < (*canal d'eau*), *kàlaasà* Cl.12,13 'class', *dìbàlaasà* 'a very big house' < (*dix bras*), *muzàbi* Cl. 3,4 'dress' < (*mes habits*) , *kàtàlôngà* Cl. 12,13 'type of skirt' < (*catalogue*), *nsùkaadì* Cl. 3a,4a 'sugar', and *mposù* 4a 'provisions distributed on the weekend' < (*portion*)

From ENGLISH: *mbùlankètà* Cl. 3a, 4a 'blanket'

Common Words

long:	-le/-la
man:	mulùme
woman:	mukàjì
water:	mâyi:
sun:	dîba
bird:	nyuunyi
dog:	mbwa
tree:	mutshì
elder:	-kùlù

Example Sentences

(1) Ba-ntu bà-a-fut-u di-bànzà.
PL.CLASS-people PL.CLASS-paid-FINAL CLASS-debt
'The people paid their debt.'

(2) ka-tù-tùm-i bâna.
NEG-PREF-send-FINAL children
'We didn't send the children.'

Efforts to Preserve, Protect, and Promote the Language

Speakers of Tshilubà make conscious efforts to promote Tshilubà language and culture. This can be seen in the province of Kasaï where the language is taught in the schools. Tshilubà-speaking families also make efforts to maintain the language even when residing abroad. There are newspapers in Tshilubà and a growing literature propagated by the native intellectuals. The beauty and richness of Tshilubà language and culture is also spread through the tales and songs promoted by Tshilubà cultural associations.

Select Bibliography

Burssens, A. 1938. "Tonologische onderzoek van de Copula di in het tshiluba." Kongo overzee 4, (275–285).

____. 1946. *Manuel de Tshiluba*. Kasayi, Congo Belge, (94).

Faïk-Nzuji Clémentine Madiya. 1967. *Essai de Méthodologie pour l'étude des proverbes luba*. Kinshasa: Ecole Supérieure Pédagogique.

____. 1976. "Variations vocaliques (luba-Kasayi)." n.1 (M.R. A.C. Tervuren).

Ilunga Mukubi. 1980. "Graphie anarchique des noms propres en luba." Mbujumayi, manuscrits. (27).

Kuperus J., et Mpunga wa I. 1990. "Locative markers in Luba." MRAC, Tervuren, Annales Sciences Humaines, Vol. 130 (45).

Lukusa M. 1991. "Affixation et sémantisme ciluba." Cas de quelques affixes usuels. Annales Aequatoria 12, (251–276).

Lukusa S. 1993. "Imbrication of extensions in Ciluba." Afrikanistische Arbeitspapiere 36 (55–77).

Madieson I. 1977. "Tone reversal in Ciluba: a new theory." Los Angeles, UCLA Working papers in phonetics 33 (9–11)

Morrison W.M. 1906. *Grammar of the Buluba-lulua Language*. Luebo, J. Leighton Wilson Press. (189).

Mpoyi Mwadtamvita. 1987. *Lwendu lwa Baluba, 2è éd.* Katoka, B.P. 21, Kananga.

Mutombo Huta. 1973. *Ebauche de grammaire de la langue bembe et du dialecte kalambaayi de la langue luba-kasayi*. Bruxelles (Université libre-, mémoire (211).

____. 1977. "Variations lexicales en luba-Kasayi." Lubumbashi (université du Zaïre), thèse (374).

Stuky S. 1976. "Locatives as objects in Tshiluba: a function of transitivity." Studies in the linguistic sciences 6, 2 (174–202).

Van Spaandonck M. 1971. "On the so-called reversing tonal of Ciluba: a case for restructuring." Studies in African Linguistics 2, 2 (131–163).

Yukawa Y. 1992. "A classified vocabulary of the Luba language." Tokyo, ILCAA, Bantu Vocabulary Series 7 (104).

Tswana

Karen Mistry

Language Name: Tswana. **Alternates:** *Chuana*, *Chwana*, *Tchuana*, *Coana*, *Cuana*, *Sechuana*, *Sichuana*, *Secwana*, *Secoana*; or *Beetjuans*, *Bootchuana*, *Bechuana Language*, and *Bootsuanna*. **Autonym:** *Setswana*.

Location: Southern Africa: Botswana, and adjacent areas in the western Transvaal, northern Cape, and northwestern Orange Free State Provinces of South Africa.

Family: Sotho subgroup of the South Eastern Bantu group of the Benue-Congo subbranch of the Niger Congo branch of the Niger-Kordofanian language family. Tswana is classified as Narrow Bantu S.30, based on the work of Bastin (1978) and Guthrie (1967–71) (Wald 1992).

Related Languages: Most closely related to SOTHO and Southern Ndebele. Tswana is largely mutually intelligible with Northern Sotho, but they have generally been considered separate languages. It is closely related to Southern Sotho, Tsonga, and ZULU. More distantly related are SHONA, Birwa, Manyika, Nambya, Ndau, Venda, Lozi, SISWATI, Northern Ndebele, XHOSA, Ronga, Tswa, and Chopi.

Dialects: (1) Hurutshe, (2) Ngwaketse, (3) Kwena, (4) Ngwato, (5) Kgatla, (6) Rolong, (7) Tlhaping, and (8) Tlharo (Tlhware). Considering how widely dispersed the various groups speaking Tswana are, it is surprising to find how uniform the language is throughout the Tswana-speaking area. Forms that previously had been characteristic of a given dialect now occur in nearly all the others. This is because modern social and economic conditions leading to population shifts and urbanization have more or less eliminated tribal, and therefore dialectal, boundaries. Nevertheless, there are differences in pronunciation, vocabulary, and to a lesser extent, grammatical structure. No one dialect of Tswana is taken as the literary or educational standard.

Number of Speakers: 2.5–3.5 million.

Origin and History

The earliest inhabitants of the region where Tswana is now spoken were Khoisan-speaking hunters and gatherers. Groups of Bantu-speakers who practiced agriculture gradually took over almost all of southern Africa, including the area where Tswana is spoken, over a period of many hundred years. The earliest archaeological remains of the newcomers in Botswana are dated to around 1,500 years ago. Today the majority of the population of Botswana is Bantu speaking, and the ancestors of this group moved into the country from the surrounding areas within the last 500 years or so.

The Sotho-Tswana people probably existed in the Transvaal as early as around 1200. From there several groups over time moved westwards into present Botswana. The first to arrive were the Bakgalakgadi. Later on, the Batswana moved into their present habitats in several migrations.

From the 17th or 18th century the Batswana lived in a number of states that functioned cooperatively in Botswana and adjacent parts of northern and northwestern South Africa. However, the Boers expanded continually north from the Cape of Good Hope in what is known as the Great Trek, resulting in the wars and large-scale migrations of 1820–1850 (*the Difaqane*). They gradually occupied the land of the eastern and southern Tswana states, and in the process, drastically reduced the political and economic status of the Batswana. In 1885, on the initiative of concerned Batswana chiefs, the British Protectorate Bechuanaland was formed, mainly in order to check the advance of the Boers; the present boundaries were established in 1891. The protectorate existed up to 1966 when it was peacefully transformed into the independent Republic of Botswana.

Since independence there are indications that some Batswana have experienced social changes of an unusual order of magnitude. People may now identify themselves primarily as a citizen of Botswana rather than as a member of one of the traditional states. This is especially true of those who have moved from the rural areas into the cities. The traditional society had and has a well-established and relatively permanent network of relations and a ranking order, both largely based on descent and kinship. The persons who move permanently out of the village and settle in places like Gaborone find themselves in an environment where no social relations are given beforehand. Success in school and in employment are now the most important factors in determining one's social position. There is some indication that since independence the rate of language change has accelerated. A generation gap is developing between young urban dwellers who may not understand their village-dwelling grandparents (Janson and Tsonope 1991).

Orthography and Basic Phonology

There are currently two orthographic systems for the writing of Tswana. In 1964, the Department of Bantu Affairs of the

Table 1: Consonants

		Labial	Alveolar	Aleveo-palatal	Velar	Glottal
Stops	Voiceless	ph	th		kh	
	Voiced	b	d			
	Ejective	p	t		k	
Fricatives	Voiceless	f	s	š	g	h
Affricates	Voiceless		tsh	tšh	kg	
	Voiced			j		
	Ejective		ts	tš		
Nasals		m	n	ny	ng	
Laterals	Voiceless		tlh			
	Voiced		l			
	Ejective		tl			
Trill			r			
Glides				y	w	

Republic of South Africa issued a handbook that is the most recent comprehensive exposition of the official orthography. The writing of Tswana is becoming increasingly conformed to this system, especially in schools where it is the only orthography permitted to be taught.

However, there is considerable variation in orthographic representation even within government publications. Furthermore, unlike ENGLISH, Tswana does not have any hard and fast rules of correct spelling.

The voiceless sounds /ph th kh tsh tšh tlh/ are all aspirated. In contrast, /p t k ts tš tl/ are all ejectives. That is, they are produced with a glottal closure simultaneous with their main oral constriction. The fricative *f* is a voiceless bilabial fricative [ɸ]. *L* has a variant *d* before the vowels /i u/. This variant is an alveolar flap like the sound in the middle of the English word "ladder".

Words that phonologically begin with a vowel often have a phonetic glottal stop [ʔ] in pronunciation, which is not represented in the orthography.

Table 2: Vowels

	Front	Central	Back
High	i		u
Mid-high	ê		ô
Mid-low	e		o
Low		a	

The vowels /ê/ and /i/ are often indistinguishable in speech, as are /ô/ and /u/. The difference is maintained in spelling, however, because they have different etymological sources.

Nasal consonants are homorganic with following consonants, although only changes to *m* are reflected in the orthography. (Because of this assimilation, there are prefixes containing nasals whose inherent place of articulation cannot be identified; here, these nasals will be written *N*.) In addition, some consonants are changed (strengthened) when they follow such a nasal.

N + b	mp	N + h	nkh
N + l	nt	N + ʔ	nk
N + w	nkw	N + s	ntsh
N + f	mph	N + g	nkg
N + r	nth	N + š	ntšh

Nasals before these strengthened weak consonants are often omitted. Nasals before other consonants than those listed above are likewise assimilated to the following consonant. However, the strong consonants like /p/ remain unchanged following the nasal, and the nasal is not omitted.

Basic Morphology

In Tswana, there are only two fully productive word classes, verbs and nouns. Like other Bantu languages, Tswana has an elaborate system of noun classes, indicated by prefix pairs, one for singular and one for plural. Nine classes are preserved in Tswana, with approximately 15 distinct prefixes (some prefixes are used with more than one class). For example, the plural of the Class 3 noun *letsatsi* 'sun' is *matsatsi*.

In most cases, it is fairly arbitrary which class a particular noun belongs to. But, some regularities are apparent. Nouns representing human beings tend to be in Class 1 (*mo-*/*ba-*) and all personal and proper names and most kinship terms belong to Class 1a (*-*/*bô-*). Nouns representing animals tend to be in

Class 5 (*N-/diN-*), and more abstract nouns tend to belong to Class 7 (*bo-/ma-*). In addition, a given stem can occur in different classes, with differences in meaning: *motswana* (Class 1) 'a Tswana tribesman', *setswana* (Class 4) 'the Tswana language', *botswana* (Class 7) 'the Tswana country'.

Table 3: Tswana Noun Classes

Class	Singular	Plural
1	*mo-* (1a —)	*ba-* (1a*bô*)
2	*mo-*	*me-*, *ma-*
3	*le-*	*ma-*
4	*se-*	*di*
5	*N-*	*diN-*
6	*lo-*	*diN-*
7	*bo-*	*ma-*
8	*go-*	
9	*fa-*, *go-*, *mo-*	

Differences among noun classes pervade the structure of Tswana. There are different third-person pronouns for each class and different concord markers:

ba-tho ba batla go dira
CL1/PL-person CL1/PL want to work
'The people want to work.'

In some Tswana dialects, especially in the east and north, there is a tendency for nouns of Class 6 (*lo-/diN-*) to be absorbed into Class 3 (*le-/ma-*). Personal nouns of Class 3 fall into three main categories: (1) national and tribal names of peoples of non-Sotho stock, (2) persons characterized by some habit, weakness or other peculiarity of character, usually undesirable and (3) names of Tswana tribal regiments or age-groups are all included in this class of nouns. Class 8 (*go-*) includes only the infinitive forms of verbs. There is no distinction between singular and plural nouns in this class. Class 9 (*fa-, go-, mo-*) includes only words having a locative significance, and which therefore function mainly as adverbs. Some nouns, mass nouns, collective nouns, and abstract nouns appear only in the plural form.

The basic Tswana verb consists of a stem and a suffix *-a*, which becomes *-e* or *-ê* under some circumstances. Verbs are generally preceded by a subject marker like the second underlined *ba* in the example above. For simple tenses (future, potential, and long present), the tense marker is interposed between the subject concord marker and the verb stem: *ke rêka* 'I buy', *ke a rêka* 'I am buying', *ke tla rêka* 'I will buy', *ke ka rêka* 'I can buy'. For perfect tenses, the stem suffix *-a* becomes *-ilê*: *ke rêkilê* 'I have bought', *ke nê ke rêkilê* 'I had bought'. Like the last of these examples, other past-tense forms involve an auxiliary verb *nê,* which takes its own subject marker in the past continuous: *ke nê ke rêka* 'I was buying'.

It is a matter of some dispute whether a verb like *ke tla rêka* is a single verb consisting of a stem preceded by two prefixes, or whether it is three separate words.

Derived verb stems are created by replacing the suffix *-a* with other affixes:

Passive: *-wa*, e.g., *rêkwa* 'be bought'
Causative: *-isa*, e.g., *rêkisa* 'sell'
Extensive: *-aka*, e.g., *rêmaka* 'chop to pieces' (<*rêma* 'chop')
Reciprocal: *-ana*, e.g., *ratana* 'love each other' (<*rata* 'love')
Reversive: *-o(lo)la*, e.g., *rêkolola* 'redeem, ransom'

Nouns can be derived from verbs by use of noun-class prefixes (sometimes with other changes): *mo-rêki* 'buyer (Class 1)', *thêkô* (< *N-rêkô*) 'purchase (Class 5)'.

Compared with most other Bantu languages, Tswana has a large number of adjectives, about 40 or 50. Adjectives, like other qualificatives, consist of two parts, a concord which shows agreement as to number and class of the qualified noun, and a stem. They always follow the nouns that they qualify and their form is identical to that of relative clauses: *mosetsana yo mosesane-nyane* (girl DEM CLASS.PREF-slender-ADJ.SUFFIX) 'very slender girl; girl who is very thin', *legodu le le-be* (thief DEM CLASS.PREF-bad) 'bad thief, thief who is bad'.

Basic Syntax

Tswana sentences tend to be SVO when the object is represented by a noun. If the object noun is not present, an object concord marker must precede the verb.

ba-simane ba bolailê nôga
CL1/PL-boy CL1/PL kill-PERF CL5/SG:snake
'The boys have killed a snake.'

ba-simane ba e bola-ilê
CL1/PL-boy CL1/PL CL5/SG kill-PERF
'The boys have killed it.'

Tswana sentences are negated by a *ga*, *sa,* or *se* in the verb complex; in addition, the final *-a* of the verb stem may change to *-e*: *ga ke rêke* 'I am not buying'.

Contact with Other Languages

Tswana borrows occasionally from AFRIKAANS and heavily from English. The British established themselves in the Cape colony during the Napoleonic Wars, and missionary activities and trade in the early decades of the 19th century brought English speakers in contact with the Batswana. In the mid–19th century, contact between the Boers and the Batswana became frequent. The Batswana in the Transvaal came under the domination of the Boers in the late 19th century, and that situation still persists. Only a small number of Boers settled permanently in Botswana. There is a long tradition of Batswana going to South Africa for paid work, especially in the gold mines in Johannesburg.

Many of the words borrowed into Tswana from English and Afrikaans are verbs, but the majority are nouns. The original word almost invariably undergoes phonetic modification so as to conform to the sound structure of Tswana, but sometimes the foreign sounds and sound combinations are retained.

From Afrikaans: *beke* 'week', *jase* 'coat', *gôuta* 'gold'
From English: *aena* 'iron', *phaka* 'park', *sopo* 'soup', *bokose* 'box', *kholetshe* 'college'

If the initial part of a borrowed word resembles one of the Tswana prefixes, it is often reinterpreted as a class prefix and replaced with the appropriate plural prefix. For example, the English word 'school' has been borrowed into Tswana as *sekole*, which looks like a native Tswana singular noun from Class 4. Accordingly, the plural of *sekole* is *dikole*.

Borrowed words from Tswana into English are rare. The most widespread use of a Tswana word in English is the term "tsetse fly". The word *Ntsi* in Tswana means 'fly'.

Common Words

man:	monna	small:	-nnye
woman:	mosadi	yes:	e, êê
water:	metse, metsi	no:	nya
sun:	letsatsi	good:	molemô, -ntle
fish:	tlhapi	bird:	nônyane
big:	-tonna, -tona	dog:	ntšha
long:	-lêlê	tree:	setlhare
three:	-raro (with prefix); tharo (without prefix)		

Example Sentences*

(1) Ke tla rema se-tlhare ka se-lepe sê
I will chop CL4/SG-tree with CL4/SG-axe CL4/SG-that

se bogale.
CL4/SG sharp
'I shall cut down the tree with a sharp axe.'

(2) Ba-tlhanka ba-ngwe ba-gago ke ba
CL1/PL-servant CL1/PL-one CL1/PL-of you I CL1/PL(=them)

ônye ba tšoma kwa nokê-ng.
saw CL1/PL(=they) hunt at river-LOC
I saw some of your servants hunting at the river.'

(3) N-ku n-ngwe ya gago ke
CL5/SG-sheep CL5/SG-one CL5/SG-of you I

e-bônye e fula kwa nokê-ng.
CL5/SG-it-saw CL5/SG-it graze at river-LOC
'I saw one of your sheep grazing at the river.'
*All Example Sentences are from Cole, 1955.

Efforts to Preserve, Protect, and Promote the Language

Botswana is predominantly monolingual. Tswana is spoken everywhere as the mother tongue by the dominant ethnic community and by other groups as a second language. However, under the previous colonial regime, English was introduced and subsequently gained a major role in formal communication. It remains dominant today at the national and regional levels, although Tswana is preferred at the local level by administrators and courts. The government has not initiated any significant changes in this situation. There exists a small group of fluent English speakers and a large proportion of Botswanans who speak English with little or no competency at all. Obviously, the latter are discriminated against by the official-language policy and are excluded from important discussions in national life as long as they are conducted in English.

Select Bibliography

Archbell, J. 1837. *A Grammar of the Bechuana Language*. Graham's Town, Cape of Good Hope: Meurant and Godlonton.

Brown, J.T. 1965. *Setswana Dictionary: Setswana-English and English-Setswana*. Lobatse, Bechuanaland: Bechuanaland Book Centre.

Cole, D.T. 1955. *An Introduction to Tswana Grammar*. London: Longmans Green and Co.

Cole, D.T., and D.M. Mokaila. 1962. *A Course in Tswana*. Washington, DC: Georgetown University.

Doke, C.M. 1954. *The Southern Bantu Languages*. London: Oxford University Press/International African Institute.

Doke, C.M., and D.T. Cole, eds. 1961. *Contributions to the History of Bantu Linguistics*. Johannesburg: Witwatersrand University Press.

Janson, T., and J. Tsonope. 1991. *Birth of a National Language: The History of Setswana*. Gaborone: Heinemann.

Sandilands, A. 1953. *Introduction to Tswana*. Tigerkloof: South Africa: London Missionary Society.

Schapera, I. 1980. "Afrikaans Loan Words in Tswana Languages." In *V.O.C.* 1: 5–14.

Tswana Language Committee. 1972. *Tswana Terminology and Orthography*. No. 3. South Africa Department of Bantu Education.

Wald, Benji. 1992. Bantu Languages. In *International Encyclopedia of Linguistics*, edited by William Bright, Vol. 1, 157–159. New York: Oxford University Press.

TURKISH

Robert Underhill

Language Name: Turkish. **Autonym:** *Türkçe.*

Location: Spoken in the republic of Turkey where it is the official language. Also spoken in small areas throughout the Balkans, notably in Greece, Bulgaria, and Macedonia; and on Cyprus, where it is the co-official language along with GREEK. There is a Turkish-speaking population in northern Iraq, in the area of Kirkuk, and smaller groups throughout the Middle East, particularly in Syria and Lebanon. Since the 1960s, there has been a major migration of Turkish workers and their families into Western Europe, particularly Germany and the Netherlands.

Family: Southwestern (Oğuz) group of the Turkic branch of the Altaic language family.

Related Languages: Other members of the southwestern Turkic group, including AZERBAIJANIAN (Azeri), TURKMEN, Qashqay, and Gagauz. More distantly, many of the Turkic languages of the newly independent Soviet republics, and languages of Siberia such as KAZAKH, UZBEK, TATAR, Tuvan (Tuvinian), and Yakut.

Dialects: Caferoğlu (1959) distinguishes the following dialect areas: (1) Southwestern dialects (spoken in the area from Bandırma to the Antalya region); (2) Central Anatolian dialects (widely spread from Afyon Karahısar up to Erzurum and Elazığ; (3) Eastern dialects (east of Erzurum and Elazığ up to the border, with close similarities with Azerbaijani); (4) the dialects from the north (Trabzon and Rize); (5) Rumelian (Balkan-Turkish) dialects; (6) Southeastern dialects (Gaziantep, Adana, Antalya and surroundings); and (7) the Kastamonu dialect, including dialects spoken by the Karamanlı and other tribes (Boeschoten 1991, 151). Modern standard Turkish is based on the speech of Istanbul.

Number of Speakers: 45 million in Turkey, about 120,000 in Cyprus, 1 million in the Balkans, and more than one million in Western Europe.

Origin and History

While Turkish speakers arrived in the area that is now Turkey in the 11th century, the earliest written materials in Anatolian Turkish date from the 13th century. Turkish scholars divide the history of Turkish into three periods. **Old Anatolian Turkish** (*Eski Anadolu Türkçesi*) includes the thirteenth through 15th centuries; **Ottoman Turkish** (*Osmanlıca*) includes the period of the height and decline of the Ottoman Empire. The most important characteristic of Ottoman that distinguishes it from Modern Turkish is the very heavy influence of ARABIC and PERSIAN, a consequence of Arabic and Persian influence on Turkish literature and culture during that period. Ottoman Turkish was written in Arabic script and used a higher proportion of Arabic and Persian words, particularly in literary or learned writing, and borrowed certain syntactic rules from Persian.

The transition from Ottoman to **Modern Turkish** (*Yeni Türkçe*) is given by the political events connected with the fall of the Ottoman Empire in the civil war of 1919–22, and by the language reform movement of the late 1920s and 30s. The language reform movement must be understood in the political and social context of the Kemalist revolution, a nationalist and secularist movement aimed at the modernization and Westernization of Turkey. The reduction of Arabic and Persian influence on the language thus coincided with the broader political goals of the reduction of Oriental and Islamic influence on Turkish culture in favor of native or Western influence.

Orthography and Basic Phonology

Turkish was written in Arabic script until the language reform of 1928, when it was replaced with a LATIN based orthography. It was claimed at the time that the Latin alphabet was easier to learn and to use; however, political motivations were equally important. Older people who knew both scripts continued to use the Arabic script in private correspondence. The Latin writing system for Turkish represents more predictable phonetic information than the Arabic system did (see Table 1).

The alveo-palatal "stops" *ç* and *c* are phonetically affricates [č] and [ǰ]. The fricatives *ş* and *j* are phonetically [š] and [ž].

In native Turkish words, the front velars /k̯ g̯ l̯/ occur only before front vowels, and their back equivalents /k g l/ occur elsewhere. Because of borrowing, however, there have come to be minimal pairs involving front and back velars before back vowels: *kar* /kar/ 'snow' *kâr* /k̯ar/ 'profit'. The accent over the *a* in *kâr* indicates that *k* is /k̯/ rather than /k/.

Turkish orthography contains an additional symbol *ğ*. This symbol, which formerly indicated a voiced velar fricative /ɣ/, is not pronounced in standard Turkish. Rather, it indicates that a preceding vowel is long (e.g., *dağ* [dā] 'mountain') or that two vowels occur in sequence (e.g., *eğer* [eer] 'if'). For some speakers, *ğ* in the neighborhood of front vowels (see below) is pronounced as *y:öğle* [öyle] 'thus', *eğer* [eyer] 'if'.

Turkish has a process of (morpheme-) final devoicing; that is, only voiceless stops can occur in morpheme (and word) final position: *sebep̲* 'reason (nominative)' *sebeb̲i* 'reason (objective)'.

Table 1: Consonants

		Labial	Dental	Alveo-Palatal	Front Velar	Back Velar	Glottal
Stops	Voiceless	p	t	ç	k̭	k	
	Voiced	b	d	c	g	g	
Fricatives	Voiceless	f	s	ş			h
	Voiced	v	z	j			
Nasals		m	n				
Resonants				r	ḽ	l	
Glide				y			

Table 2: Vowels

	Front		Back	
Rounding	-	+	-	+
High	i	ü	ı	u
Non-high	e	ö	a	o

ü and *ö* are front rounded vowels. *ı* is a back- unrounded vowel, phonetically [ɯ]; it has no easy equivalent in ENGLISH.

Turkish has a system of "vowel harmony". That is, all of the vowels in a word must agree in certain properties. For example, the objective case ending (see below) varies in quality depending on the vowel in the noun stem to which it is added: *eli* 'hand', *gözü* 'eye', *atı* 'horse', *kulu* 'slave'. In all four examples, the vowel is high, but it agrees in frontness and rounding with the stem vowel. This ending can be written *I*, with the understanding that *I* represents a high vowel that is unspecified for frontness or rounding. Endings containing a low vowel *A* alternate between *e* (after front vowels) and *a* (after back vowels).

Basic Morphology

Turkish nouns are inflected for number, case and possession; there is no explicit marking of gender. The numbers in Turkish are singular and plural, and the cases are nominative, objective, genitive, dative, locative, and ablative. A new comitative/instrumental case is in the process of developing, as a post position *ile* 'with' is suffixed to noun stems and becomes harmonic: *Hasan ile* 'with Hasan' > *Hasanla*. The singular has no marker, and the plural marker is *-lAr*. The other cases are illustrated with forms of *ev* 'house'.

	Singular	Plural
Nominative	ev	evler
Objective	evi	evleri
Genitive	evin	evlerin
Dative	eve	evlere
Locative	evde	evlerde
Ablative	evden	evlerden

An optional possessive marker may occur between the plural marker (if any) and the case marker: *evim* 'my house', *evlerim* 'my houses', *evlerimde* 'in my houses'.

A relative marker *-ki* may occur following genitive or locative suffixes: *evlerimdeki* 'that which is in my houses'. The result is a noun stem that can itself be inflected: *evlerimdekiler* 'those which are in my houses'.

Turkish verb inflection is more complex. Minimally, a finite verb form consists of a verb stem followed by a tense marker and a person/number marker. There are nine tenses: Past, General Present, Progressive, Future, Unwitnessed Past, Conditional, Necessitative, Subjunctive, Optative.

gel-iyor-um	gel-ecek-sin
come-PROGRESSIVE-1SG	come-FUTURE-2SG
'I am coming'	'you will come'

The past tense is normally used to describe events that the speaker has personal knowledge of, or are generally known; the unwitnessed (narrative) past is used for actions that the speaker has heard about or has inferred.

Git-ti-n	git-miş-sin
go-PAST-2SG	go-NARR-2SG
'you went'	'you supposedly went'

Auxiliary suffixes may occur before the person/number marker, and may be added to verbal or nonverbal predicates. One auxiliary puts the action or statement in the past:

Gel-iyor-um	gel-iyor-du-m
come-PROG-1SG	come-PROG-PAST-1SG
'I am coming'	'I was coming'

Other auxiliaries indicate contingency or doubt:

tembel-sin	tembel-miş-sin
lazy-2SG	lazy-DUBITATIVE-2SG
'you are lazy'	'they say you are lazy'

The verb stem can be expanded by adding reflexive, reciprocal, causative, or passive suffixes, or combinations of these, after the stem and before tense:

çocuklar yıka-n-dı-lar
Children wash-REFL-PAST-PL
'The children washed themselves.'

Hasan diş-in-i çek-tir-di
Hasan tooth-POSS-OBJ pull-CAUS-PAST
'Hasan had his tooth pulled (caused his tooth to be pulled).'

Yeni para bas-tır-ıl-ıyor
new money print-CAUS-PASS-PROG
'new money is being (caused to be) printed.'

Negation is also indicated by a suffix at the end of the verb stem and immediately before tense:

git-me-di-n
go-NEG-PAST-2SG
'You didn't go.'

gel-m-iyor-um
come-NEG-PROG-1SG
'I am not coming.'

Basic Syntax

The basic word order in Turkish is SOV, with anything else in the sentence coming between Subject and Object:

Ahmet şimdi mektub-u gönder-iyor
Ahmet now letter-OBJ send-PROG
'Ahmet is sending the letter now.'

Other orders, however, are possible; Turkish is a language with pragmatically controlled, or so-called free word order, where word order depends whether an entity is topic or focus, or whether it is new or old information. The topic of the sentence comes at the beginning. New, focused, or contrastive information comes right before the verb:

Mektub-u Ahmet şimdi gönder-iyor
letter-OBJ Ahmet now send-PROG
'The letter, Ahmet is sending (it) right now.'

Consistent with its status as an SOV language, Turkish modifiers precede the nouns they modify, and positional relations are expressed by postpositions rather than by prepositions. In possessive noun phrases, the possessed noun must have a suffix agreeing with the possessor:

Hasan-ın kedi-si
Hasan-GENITIVE cat-3SG/POSSESSIVE
'Hasan's cat'

Relative clauses in Turkish also precede the nouns they modify:

Çocuk mektub-u oku-yor
child letter-OBJ read-PROG
'The child is reading the letter.'

Mektub-u oku-yan çocuk
letter-OBJ read-PARTICIPLE child
'the child who is reading the letter'

Çocuğ-un oku-duğ-u mektup
child-GEN read-PARTICIPLE-3SG/POSS letter
'the letter which the child is reading'

Imperatives in their most informal form may lack any person/number marker: *Koş!* 'Run!'; *Koş-ma!* 'Don't run!' but more often have a marker for plurality and/or politeness:

Gid-in
go-PLURAL
'Go away (several people)'

Getir-iniz
bring-PL/POLITE
'Bring (polite)'

Contact with Other Languages

As mentioned above, during the Ottoman period there was a heavy influx of Arabic and Persian words into the Turkish lexicon. Despite the efforts of the language reform movement to reduce that component of the Turkish vocabulary, it has been by no means eliminated; a count of the basic vocabulary in one textbook (Underhill 1976) gives 35 percent Arabic or Persian against 62 percent Turkic and 3 percent European; the percentage would be higher in a more complete lexicon or in literary or learned text.

Some Greek and ITALIAN loans are very old. More recently, many FRENCH and English loans have accompanied the modernization and Westernization of Turkey (see Efforts to Preserve, Protect, and Promote the Language).

From Greek: *karides* 'shrimp', *pide* 'flat bread', *pırasa* 'leek', *papaz* 'priest'
From Arabic: *mektup* 'letter', *sebep* 'reason', *zaman* 'time' *cami* 'mosque'
From Persian: *renk* 'color', *dost* 'friend', *yegâne* 'only', *peygamber* 'prophet'
From Italian: *masa* 'table', *iskele* 'quay', *salata* 'salad', *lira* 'unit of money'

Common Words

man:	adam	small:	küçük
woman:	kadın	yes:	evet
water:	su	no:	hayır, yok
sun:	güneş	good:	iyi
three:	üç	dog:	köpek
fish:	balık	tree:	ağaç
big:	büyük	long:	uzun

Example Sentences

(1) mektub-u kim yaz-dı.
letter-OBJ who write-PAST
'Who wrote the letter?'

(2) Hasan-ın mektub-u gönder-me-sin-i
Hasan-GEN letter-OBJ send-INFINITIVE-3SG/POSS-OBJ

iste-mi-yor-uz.
want-NEG-PROG-1PL
'We don't want Hasan to send the letter.'

(3) Hasan-ın mektub-u gönder-diğ-in-i bil-iyor-uz.
Hasan-GEN letter-OBJ send-NOMINAL-OBJ know-PROG-1PL
'We know that Hasan sent the letter.'

Efforts to Preserve, Protect, and Promote the Language

During the decade following the orthographic reform, and continuing until the present time, the 'Turkish Language Society' (*Türk Dil Kurumu*) has supervised a steady program aimed at the reduction of the number of Arabic and Persian loanwords. Turkish replacements were taken from nonstandard dialects or other Turkic languages, constructed with Turkish derivational suffixes (some of which were revived for this purpose), or simply invented: *Okul* 'school' is a mixture of French *école* and Turkish *oku-* 'read, study'. Sometimes loanwords were replaced with simpler loanwords: *kütüphane* 'library', made of the Arabic plural *kütüp* 'books' plus Persian *hane* 'house of', has been replaced (in some quarters) with *kitaplik*, made of the Arabic singular *kitap* 'book' plus a Turkish abstract noun suffix *-llk*.

Over the intervening years the language reform program has blown hot and cold in different periods. A correlation between political outlook and linguistic views has developed: the political left tends to favor Turkicized neologisms, while the right is more tolerant of older and skeptical of newer forms. Thus, the vocabulary used in the press often indicates the political orientation of the writer.

Since 1980 those with a more conservative view of the language have dominated the Language Society, seeking to curtail radical activities in the field of standard language vocabulary. In February 1985, the national broadcasting organization TRT issued a regulation forbidding the use on the radio and television networks of 200 neologisms. This regulation was signed by a number of conservative linguists.

Select Bibliography

Boeschoten, Hendrik, and Ludo Verhoeven, eds. 1991. *Turkish Linguistics Today*. Leiden: E.J. Brill.

Hony, H.C., and Fahir Iz. 1984. *The Oxford Turkish-English Dictionary*. Oxford: Clarendon Press.

Kornfilt, Jaklin. 1987. "Turkish." In B. Comrie (ed.), *The World's Major Languages*. Oxford: Oxford U.P.

____. 1997. *Turkish*. London: Routledge.

Lees, R.B. 1961. *The Phonology of Modern Standard Turkish*. Bloomington: Indiana University Press.

Underhill, Robert. 1976. *Turkish Grammar*. Cambridge: MIT Press.

TURKMEN

Lars Johanson

Language Name: Turkmen. **Alternate:** *Turcoman* (obsolete). **Autonym:** *Türkmenče, türkmen dili.*

Location: Spoken in Turkmenistan as well as in Iran, Afghanistan, Kazakhstan, and Uzbekistan.

Family: Turkmen belongs to the Southwestern or Oghuz branch of the Turkic family, constituting the East Oghuz subbranch.

Related Languages: AZERBAIJANIAN, Khorasan Turkic, and TURKISH.

Dialects: The main dialects are those of the Teke, Yomut, Ärsarï, Salïr, Sarïq, Čowdur, Alili, Gökleŋ, Nohur, and Änew tribes. The standard language is based on the Teke dialect, in particular on the Ahal subdialect spoken in the region around the capital, Ašġabat.

Number of Speakers: Over 3,800,000.

Origin and History

The Turkmens go back to the Turkic-speaking Oghuz confederation of tribes, whose Inner Asian steppe empire collapsed in 744. One group migrated into the region between the Syrdarya and Ural Rivers. The Saljuk Oghuz left this region in the middle of the 11th century and reached Khorasan. Their modern descendants are the Khorasan Turks. Other descendants are the Turks of Azerbaijan and Turkey. During the Mongol conquests in the 13th century, the remaining non-Saljuk Oghuz tribes were pushed into the Karakum desert and the region east of the Caspian Sea. From the 13th century on, these Turkmen groups migrated to Khorezm, to the southern part of today's Turkmenistan, and to Khorasan, absorbing local Turkic and Iranian elements. The major migrations of the Salïr, Ärsarï, Sarïq, and Teke tribes took place in the 17th century. Finally, in the 18th century Merv was conquered. Most Turkmen tribes were controlled by the Uzbek khanates of Khiwa and Bukhara, and the Persian shahs tried to subdue the southern tribes. After the middle of the 19th century, the dependence of Khiwa and Persia came to an end, but only some decades later Russia encroached on the Turkmen territory and finally annexed it. From then on, many Turkmen groups emigrated to Afghanistan and Iran. In 1924, Turkmenistan was proclaimed a socialist Soviet republic. On October 27, 1991, the independent state of Turkmenistan (*Türkmenistan dövleti*) was established.

Modern Standard Turkmen was formed during the Soviet period, mainly between 1928 and 1940. Prior to 1917, the Chaghatay literary language written in ARABIC script was used.

Several nomadic groups in Iraq and Anatolia are referred to as "Turkmen" without being Turkmen in a linguistic sense.

Orthography and Basic Phonology

Turkmen was first written with Arabic script. After a Roman-

Table 1: Turkmen Alphabet

Cyrillic-based	Roman-based	Value	Cyrillic-based	Roman-based	Value	Cyrillic-based	Roman-based	Value
Аа	Aa	a ~ a:	Лл	Ll	l	Хх	Hh	x ~ h
Бб	Bb	b	Мм	Mm	m	Цц		c
Вв	Ww	v [ß ~ v], w	Нн	Nn	n	Чч	Çç	č
Гг	Gg	g ~ ɣ	Ңң	Ňň	ŋ	Шш	Şş	š
Дд	Dd	d	Өө	Oo	o ~ o:	Щщ		šč
Ее	Ee	ye ~ ye:	Оо	Öö	ö ~ ö	Ъъ		separation sign
Ёё		yo ~ yo:	Пп	Pp	p	Ыы	Yy	ï
Жж	Žž	ž	Рр	Rr	r	Ьь		softening sign
Җҗ	Jj	ǰ	Сс	Ss	θ	Ээ	Ee	e ~ e:
Зз	Zz	ð	Тт	Tt	t	Әә	Ää	ä: ~ ä
Ии	Ii	i	Уу	Uu	u ~ u:	Юю		yu ~ yu:
Йй	Ýý	y	Үү	Üü	ü	Яя		ya ~ ya:
Кк	Kk	k [k ~ q]	Фф	Ff	f			

Table 2: Consonants

	Labial	Dental	Alveolar	Alveo-palatal	Velar	Glottal
Stops	p b		td		k g	
Fricatives	f v	θð		š ž	x ɣ	h
Affricates				č ǰ		
Nasals	m		n			
Liquids			l r		ŋ	
Glides	w			y		

based alphabet had been in use in 1929–30, a variant of the Cyrillic alphabet was adopted in 1939–40. In 1993, a Roman-based alphabet, that is, a Turkmen version of the Common Turkic Alphabet, was adopted to replace the Cyrillic one. However, there was no sudden changeover; Turkmen had a dual system with the Cyrillic- and Roman-based alphabets appearing side by side. A modified version of the Roman-based alphabet became obligatory as of January 1, 2000.

The orthography represents the phonemes of the standard language rather closely. However, long-vowel phonemes are normally not marked as such. In words of Turkic origin, the high long vowel /ü:/ is written үй [üy], for example, сүйт /θü:t/ 'milk'. Rounding harmony is not consistently represented in the orthography, such as өе [öyö] 'to the house', өрдеклер [ördöklör] 'ducks', гөрди [gördü] 'saw', достумыз [do:θumuð] 'our friend'.

The phonemes /v/ and /ž/ occur only in words of non-Turkic origin and are not present in all spoken varieties. The phoneme /f/ has a similarly restricted occurrence and is frequently replaced by /p/.

Table 3: Vowels

	Front		Back	
	Unrounded	Rounded	Unrounded	Rounded
High	i i:	ü ü:	ï ï:	u u:
Mid	e e:	ö ö:		o o:
Low	ä ä:		a a:	

Vowel length is distinctive in Turkmen, the distinctions corresponding to the Old Turkic ones in a rather consistent way. The phonemes /ä/ and /e:/ occur only in a few words, /e:/ as a contraction product in *ge:r* 'will come' < *geler* and *be:r* 'will give' < *berer*.

The pronunciation of high long vowels tends to be diphthongoid. A striking feature of Turkmen pronunciation is the presence of the interdental fricatives /θ/ and /ð/ instead of /s/ and /z/. In back environments, /k/ is realized as back-velar [q], in front environments as front-velar [k]. In back environments, /g/ occurs as a back-velar [ġ], in front environments as a front-velar [g]. Similarly, /ɣ/ occurs as a back-velar [ɣ] or as a front-velar [ɣ´]. The labials /f/ and /v/ occur as bilabial [ɸ] and [ß], but may have labiodental variants /f/ and /v/ in words borrowed from RUSSIAN.

Most Turkmen suffixes are variable according to the rules of sound harmony. According to the front versus back harmony, the vowels assimilate to the frontness-backness of the preceding syllable. The vowel is back if the preceding syllable has a back vowel, for example, *toy-do* (feast-LOCATIVE) 'at the feast', and it is front if the preceding syllable has a front vowel, such as *öy-dö* (house-LOCATIVE) 'in the house'. Certain suffix vowels also assimilate to the roundedness-unroundedness of the preceding vowel. In this case, the vowel is rounded if the preceding syllable has a rounded vowel, as in *toy-do* 'at the feast', *öy-dö* 'in the house', and it is otherwise unrounded, as in *suw-da* 'in the water'. There are several types of consonant assimilation, such as, *mende* > *menne* 'in me', *ġïð-dan* > *ġïððan* 'from the girl'. In loanwords, high epenthetic vowels are inserted to dissolve nonpermissible consonant clusters, for example, *pikir* 'thought' < Arabic *fikr* (but *pikr-im* 'my thought'). In certain stems, high vowels are dropped when a suffix beginning with a vowel is added, such as *burun* 'nose' versus *burn-ï* 'his nose', *ömür* 'life' versus *ömr-üm* 'my life'.

Certain stems end in weak obstruents, which undergo syllable-final devoicing to [k], [q], [p], [t], [č], respectively, but are realized as voiced [g], [ɣ], [b], [d], [ǰ], respectively, before suffixes beginning in a vowel, for example, *dert* 'pain', *derd-i* 'its pain', *at* 'name', *adïŋ* 'your name', *aɣač* 'tree', *aɣaǰïm* 'my tree'.

As a rule, pitch accent falls on the last syllable of words of Turkic origin.

Basic Morphology

Turkmen is an agglutinative language with suffixing morphology. Nouns and adjectives are formed from nominal and verbal stems by means of various derivational suffixes. Nouns can take the plural suffix *-LAr,* possessive suffixes such as *-(I)m* 'my', *-(I)ŋ* 'your', and case suffixes: genitive *-(n)Iŋ,* locative ('in', 'at', 'on') *-DA,* accusative *-(n)I,* dative ('to') *-(G)A,* ablative ('from') *-DAn.* (Capital letters are used here to indicate harmonic variation.) Examples are: *at-lar-ïm-ïŋ* 'of my horses', *ġï:d-lar-ïmïð-ðan* 'from our girls'.

Secondary verbal stems are formed from nominal and verbal stems by means of various suffixes. Deverbal suffixes include passive, cooperative, causative, and other elements. Negation is marked with the suffix *-mA.* Finite and infinite verb forms consist of a simple or expanded lexical stem plus aspect/mood/tense suffixes and often person and number suffixes, for example, *plan-laš-tïr-ïl-dï* (plan-VERBAL DERIVATION-CAUSATIVE-PASSIVE-PAST) 'was planned'. There is a wide variety of simple and compound aspect/mood/tense forms, as well as numerous converbs and participles. Like other Turkic languages, Turkmen has evidential categories of the type *gelen eken* 'has obviously arrived'. A number of auxiliary verbs ("postverbs") express modifications of actionality, such as the manner in which an action is carried out, for example, *učup git-* (fly-CONVERB-go) 'fly away'.

Turkmen has postpositions of different kinds, corresponding to ENGLISH prepositions, such as *mašï:n bilen* 'with the machine'.

Basic Syntax

Turkmen is syntactically very similar to other Turkic languages. It has a head-final constituent order, SOV. The order of elements in a nominal phrase is Demonstrative-Numeral-Adjective-Noun, and the head of a relative clause follows the relative, for example, *gel-en adam* (come-PARTICIPLE man) 'the man who came'.

Contact with Other Languages

Turkmen has had intensive contacts with PERSIAN and, during the last century, with Russian. Within the Turkic family, Khorasan Turkic, UZBEK, and Karakalpak are the most important contact languages. The vocabulary contains numerous words of Arabic-Persian origin, borrowed from Persian, and words of Russian origin, including recent internationalisms borrowed through Russian.

From Persian: *xer* 'every', *gül* 'flower', *ša:t* 'glad', *ireŋk* 'color'
From Arabic: *emma* 'but', *ïnθa:n* 'human being', *xat* 'letter'
From Russian: *poθyolok* 'settlement', *gaðyet* 'newspaper', *fe:rma* 'farm'

Loanwords are often adopted to indigenous Turkmen phonology, for example, район [ïrayo:n] 'district', with a prothetic vowel in front of a consonant that does not occur in initial position in native words.

Common Words

man:	erkek a:dam	woman:	aya:l
water:	θuw	sun:	gün
three:	üč	fish:	ba:lïq
big:	ulï	long:	uðï:n
small:	kiči	yes:	xä:
no:	yo:q	good:	yaɣšï
bird:	ġuš	dog:	it
tree:	aɣač		

Example Sentences

(1) Ol erti:r gid-er di-yip pikir ed-yä:r-in.
(S)he tomorrow go-will-3P.SG saying think-PRESENT.1P.SG
'I think (s)he will leave tomorrow.'

(2) Men gel-mer-in, čünki waɣt-ïm
I come-will.NEG-1SG for time-POSSESSIVE.1P.SG

yo:q.
non:existent
'I will not come, for I have no time.'

(3) Bið-iŋ ya:ša-ya:n ǰa:y-ïmïð šäher-iŋ
We-GEN. live-PART. building-POSS.1P. PL city-GEN

merkeð-in-de yerleš-yä:r.
center-POSS.3P.SG-LOC be.situated-PRES.3P.SG
'The building we live in is situated in the center of the city.'

Efforts to Preserve, Protect, and Promote the Language

In the post-Soviet era, Turkmen has acquired more social functions than it had before.

Select Bibliography

Clark, Larry. 1998. *Turkmen Grammar*. (Turcologica, 34). Wiesbaden: Harrassowitz.
Dulling, G.K. 1960. *An Introduction to the Turkmen Language*. Oxford: Central Asian Research Centre in association with St. Anthony's College.
Johanson, Lars, and Éva Á. Csató, eds. 1998. *The Turkic Languages*. London and New York: Routledge.
Schönig, Claus. 1998. "Turkmen." In Johanson and Csató 1998, 261–272.

UKRAINIAN

Andrij Hornjatkevyč

Language Name: Ukrainian. **Alternates:** *Ruthenian, Little Russian* (archaic and obsolete). **Autonym:** *ukrajíns' ka móva.*

Location: Ukraine, Moldova, Romania, Slovak Republic, Belarus, Russian Federation. Also spoken in communities in Poland, Western Europe, the United States, Canada, Brazil, Argentina, Australia, the United Kingdom, Kazakhstan, and other states of the former Soviet Union.

Family: East Slavic group of the Balto-Slavic branch of the Indo-European language family.

Related Languages: BELORUSSIAN, RUSSIAN; other Slavic languages.

Dialects: There are three major dialect areas: Northern, Southwestern, and Southeastern. All have subdialects. Central Dnipro, a subdialect of the Southeastern dialect area, together with Kyiv usage, are the bases of the modern literary language. The Southwestern dialect area served as the basis for a vigorous literature in the 19th and early 20th centuries. All subdialects, although quite distinct with phonological, morphological, and lexical differences, have a high degree of mutual intelligibility.

Number of Speakers: 46–55 million.

Origin and History

Common Slavic, the ancestor of all Slavic languages, was probably spoken in present-day Ukrainian territory, the original homeland of the Slavs who began migrating from this area northward, westward and southward in the 6th century. By early historical times (ninth century) the language had spread to the left bank of the Dnipro (Dnieper) River and southward into the Steppes. In the South, settlers were exposed to invaders from the West and Asia who came through the Ural-Caspian Gap (Goths, Huns, Cumans, Tatars, to name but a few).

Old Ukrainian began to take shape before and during the Kyivan Rus' state (9th to the 13th centuries), formed from the dialects spoken by the Polyany, Derevlyany, and Siveryany (East Slavic tribes). The earliest written records (beginning with the 11th century) were strongly influenced by Old Church Slavic which had a literary tradition by the late 9th century, originally based on Macedonian Slavic dialects. After the fall of the Kyivan Rus' state (13th to 14th centuries), Ukraine came under the political control of the Grand Duchy of Lithuania and the Kingdom of Poland. The former had virtually no influence on the language, while the influence of the latter was significant during the Renaissance and Baroque periods.

In the mid-17th century the Muscovite Empire (soon to be renamed Russia) gained control of eastern (left-bank) Ukraine, and expanded its domain over much of right-bank Ukraine in the following century. The Tatar state in the Crimea, which incidentally had more Ukrainian than Tatar subjects, but which had been a constant threat with its plundering raids northward, was overcome and the steppes were soon settled by Ukrainians. As part of Russian imperial policy Ukrainians settled on the eastern shores of the Black Sea along the Kuban' River and later in many regions of Asia, notably the area on the lower course of the Amur River.

Beginning in the second half of the 19th century Ukrainians started emigrating to the New World. Emigration continued in the interwar period, when Ukrainian settlements were established in Bosnia as well. After World War II, emigration was chiefly to the Americas and Australia.

At the beginning of the 20th century, Ukrainian was spoken in an area much larger than the present political boundaries. There has been considerable contraction because of foreign colonization, especially by Russians in the Donets Basin and the Crimea, and by Poles in the west.

During and after World War II significant demographic changes took place. Many Poles and Czechs who had lived in western Ukraine were resettled to their respective countries, while Ukrainians who found themselves under Polish rule (west of the Curzon line) were forcibly resettled, either in Ukraine or in regions that Poland had acquired from Germany (Silesia, Pomerania, and East Prussia).

Orthography and Basic Phonology

Ukrainian uses the Cyrillic script as modified to the specific needs of the language. Inasmuch as Ukrainian uses the Cyrillic script the phonological inventory will be given here in both the traditional orthography and in transcription.

Table 1: The Ukrainian Alphabet

Аа	Єє	Кк	Сс	Шш
Бб	Жж	Лл	Тт	Щщ
Вв	Зз	Мм	Уу	Ьь
Гг	Ии	Нн	Фф	Юю
Ґґ	Іі	Оо	Хх	Яя
Дд	Її	Пп	Цц	
Ее	Йй	Рр	Чч	

Generally there is a very close connection between sound

Table 2: Consonants

		Labial	Dental	Palatal	Velar	Pharyngeal
Stops	Voiceless	p	t		k	
	Voiced	b	d		g	
Affricates	Voiceless		c	č	x	
	Voiced		ʒ	ǯ		h
Fricatives	Voiceless	f	s	š		
	Voiced	v	z	ž		
Lateral			l			
Trill			r			
Nasals		m	n			
Glide				j		

and letter. Ukrainian orthography is phonemic, and occasionally morphophonemic. The latter is significant in some nominal and verbal forms where certain consonant clusters are simplified in articulation but are written in such a way that all morphemes can be clearly distinguished.

While *f* is a voiceless labiodental fricative, its "partner" *v* has two allophones. Before vowels, it is a voiced bilabial fricative [ß], and in other contexts it is a voiced bilabial glide [w].

The fricative /h/ is a voiced pharyngeal fricative, not a glottal fricative as might be expected from the symbol *h*.

Voiced consonants do not undergo regressive devoicing before voiceless consonants or in word-final position.

Table 3: Vowels

	Front	Back
High	i, y	u
Mid	e	o
Low		a

Ukrainian /y/ is, like /i/, a high, front unrounded vowel; /i/ is like the vowel in ENGLISH "beet", differing only in that it is never diphthongized or long, and /y/ is like the vowel in English "bit".

Except for /j/, all Ukrainian consonants can occur either plain or palatalized, and the difference is phonemic: *s'ádu* 'I shall sit down', *sádu* 'orchard (gen.sg.)'. Consonants are generally palatalized before the vowel /i/, and may be palatalized before other vowels. Palatalized consonants are spelled two different ways. At the end of a word or before a consonant, a special letter is used to indicate that the preceding consonant is palatalized. Finally, there are two distinct letters for each of the vowels /e a u/; one set of vowel letters is used after palatalized consonants, and the other is used after plain consonants.

Ukrainian vowels can be stressed or unstressed; stressed vowels are indicated here with an accent, e.g., *é*.

Basic Morphology

Ukrainian nouns are inflected for number, gender, and case. The numbers are singular and plural, and the genders are masculine, feminine, and neuter; gender distinctions are made only for singular nouns. There are seven cases: nominative, genitive, dative, accusative, instrumental, locative, and vocative. There are four distinct noun declensions (classes), each with its own set of case endings. Gender and declension are interdependent: first declension nouns are overwhelmingly feminine; second declension nouns can be either masculine or neuter; third declension nouns are all feminine; and fourth declension nouns are all neuter. Furthermore, some endings occur in more than one class, so that it is impossible to predict solely from the form of a noun what class it belongs to; nouns ending in *-ja* may be first declension feminine (*vól'a* 'freedom') or fourth declension neuter (*imjá* 'name').

Adjectives agree with the nouns they modify in case, number, and gender.

Ukrainian verbs have two stems, perfective and imperfective. The perfective stem of a verb is generally related to the imperfective stem, but there is no one perfective morpheme; most commonly, one of a number of prefixes is used, but some imperfective stems incorporate suffixes.

All verbs, regardless of aspect, are inflected for tense. Perfective verbs can be either past or future tense; imperfective verbs can appear in past, present, or future tense.

Past tense verbs agree with their subjects in gender and number, but not in person; present and future tense verbs agree with their subjects in person and number, but not in gender. Thus, *báčy-v* 'saw (imperfective)' is masculine singular, and can be used with first, second, or third person subjects, and *báčy-la* is feminine singular. In contrast, the present tense imperfective *báč-u* is first person singular, and can be used with masculine and feminine subjects; the same is true of the future perfective *pobáč-u*.

Basic Syntax

The most conventional word order in Ukrainian is SVO, but major constituents can be rearranged because of the highly inflected nature of the language.

Ukrainian has a variety of prepositions, and adjectives generally precede the nouns that they modify.

The verb *búty* 'be' generally does not appear in the present tense.

Ukrainian sentences are negated by using the word *ne* before the verb. In addition, direct objects, which, in affirmative sentences, tend to be in the accusative case, are marked instead with the genitive in negative sentences.

ja ni-kóho ne báčy-la
I no-one NEG see:IMPERFECTIVE-PAST.SG.FEM
'I didn't see anyone.'

As the above example also indicates, Ukrainian has obligatory double negation; if a negative word marked with the prefix *ni-* occurs in a sentence, the verb must be negated.

Contact with Other Languages

Except in the south and southwest, Ukrainian is surrounded by Slavic languages: SLOVAK and POLISH (West Slavic) in the west, Belorussian in the north, and Russian (East Slavic) in the north, east, and southeast. In the latter regions it has some contact with the non-Indo-European languages of the Caucasus. In the Crimea, Ukrainian was, until the forced resettlement in the 1940s, in contact with Crimean Tatar. In the southwest Ukrainian borders with ROMANIAN (a Romance language) and HUNGARIAN (a Uralic language).

The earliest foreign acquisitions came from (Byzantine) GREEK in the ecclesiastical realm. Later some Turkic (along with ARABIC and PERSIAN) words came into the language. During the Renaissance and Baroque periods many neo-LATIN and neo-GREEK words made their appearance. Beginning with the 19th century, GERMAN, FRENCH, and English words appeared.

From Greek: *jevánhelij* 'Gospel'
From Turkic: *janyčár* 'janissary'
From Latin: *rácija* 'right'
From German: *gvalt* 'rape'
From French: *vernisáž* 'exhibit opening', *rezón* 'sense'

Common Words

man:	čolovík	woman:	žínka
water:	vodá	sun:	sónce
three:	try	fish:	rýba
big:	velýkyj	long:	dóvhyj
small:	malýj	yes:	tak
no:	ni	good:	dóbryj
bird:	ptax	dog:	pes
tree:	dérevo		

Example Sentences

(1) spokokonvíku bul-ó slóv-o.
since:eternity was-NEUT.SG word-NOM.NEUT.SG
'In the beginning was the Word.'

(2) iván-e kolý ty pro-čytáj-eš
Ivan-VOC.MASC.SG when you:NOM.SG PERF-read-FUT:2SG

c'u knýžku.
this:ACC.FEM.SG book:ACC.FEM.SG
'Ivan, when will you read this book?'

(3) xl'ib ø na stol'-í v
bread:NOM.MASC.SG is on table-LOC.MASC.SG in

jidál'n'-i.
dining room-LOC.FEM.SG
'The bread is on the table in the dining room.'

Efforts to Preserve, Protect, and Promote the Language

Until the law of 1989, which established Ukrainian as the official language of the Ukrainian SSR (and it was a very weak law at that), the language had almost no official protection in its own country. At times it was excluded from schools and official usage and relegated to the household and marketplace, thus, in effect, condemned to vegetation with no prospects for well-rounded development in all spheres of human endeavor. In Soviet times, although never officially prohibited, its use was essentially limited to *belles lettres*.

It seemed to be the diaspora that took the most resolute measures to protect and preserve the language. At first this was accomplished by the establishment of extracurricular courses for elementary and secondary school pupils. Then, particularly in western Canada and to some degree in Brazil, bilingual classes were established in public schools where not only the language but also some subjects are now taught in Ukrainian.

After World War II, Ukrainian language, literature, history, culture, and folklore courses were established at various universities in Slovakia, Poland, Romania, Germany, the United Kingdom, Canada, the United States, Australia, and Brazil.

One of the challenges facing the newly independent Ukraine is the reestablishment of Ukrainian in all spheres of life. To achieve this, Ukrainian must become a prestigious language in its own country.

Select Bibliography

Andrusyshen, C.H. and J.N. Krett. 1955. *Ukrajins'ko-anhlijs'kyj slovnyk* ('Ukrainian-English Dictionary'). Toronto: University of Toronto Press.

Podvez'ko, M.L. and M.I. Balla. 1988. *Anhlo-ukrajins'kyj slovnyk* ('English Ukrainian Dictionary'). Edmonton: Canadian Institute of Ukrainian Studies.

Shevelov, G.Y. 1951. *Narys sučasnoji ukrajins'koji literaturnoji movy*. München: Molode žyttja.

____. 1979. *A Historical Phonology of the Ukrainian Language*. Heidelberg: Carl Winter Universitätsverlag.

____. 1993. "Ukrainian." In *The Slavonic Languages,* ed. B. Comrie and G. Corbett, 947–998. London and New York: Routledge.

Žylko, F.T. 1958. *Hovory ukrajins'koji movy*. Kyjiv: Radjans'ka škola.

UMbundu

Thilo C. Schadeberg

Language Name: UMbundu; the people are called OviMbundu (sing. OciMbundu). The form of the name without a prefix, i.e., Mbundu, frequently leads to confusion with the neighboring but quite distinct language KiMbundu. Distortions of the name are common in the PORTUGUESE literature, e.g., *a língua bunda.*

Location: Central provinces of Angola: Bié, Huambo, Benguela.

Family: Bantu, which is part of Benue-Congo, which is part of Niger-Congo. Within Bantu, UMbundu belongs to the Southwestern zone ("Zone R" in Guthrie's referential classification) which includes the UMbundu group, the Kwanyama-Ndonga group and the Herero group in southern Angola and in Namibia.

Related Languages: Most closely related are Nkhumbi, Ndombe and Nyaneka, all spoken in southern Angola.

Dialects: The language appears to be relatively uniform.

Number of Speakers: About 4 million, or 38 percent of the population of Angola (*Ethnologue,* B. Grimes, 1996).

Origin and History

The language was first recorded in the 19th century; the time span is too short and the quality of the first recordings too poor to see any major changes. It is only by comparing UMbundu with other Bantu languages (the historical-comparative method) that changes linking the hypothetical proto-Bantu (estimated to be spoken several thousand years ago) and present-day UMbundu can be reconstructed. Some of these changes are not specific for UMbundu but also concern more or less closely related languages.

The OviMbundu originally lived in the highlands of central Angola. They engaged in long distance trade, and at the beginning of the 20th century, after the building of the railway line, their language spread to the coastal province of Benguela. UMbundu has gained a certain status as a trade language or lingua franca.

Orthography and Basic Phonology

		Labial	Dental	Palatal	Velar
Consonants:		p	t	c	k
		f	s		h
		v	l	y	
		ṽ	l̰	ỹ	ẖ
		m	n	nh	ng'
		mb	nd	nj	ng
Glides: y, (ỹ)	w, (w̃)				
Vowels:	i	e	a	o	u
	ḭ	(ḛ)	a̰	(o̰)	ṵ

UMbundu *c* is an affricate pronounced as "ch" in "chip"; UMbundu *nh* as "gn" in FRENCH *cognac* or in ITALIAN *lasagne;* UMbundu *ng'* as "ng" in "sing"; UMbundu *ṽ l̰ ỹ ẖ* are pronounced with nasalization; UMbundu *mb nd nj ng* are single phonemes and always belong to one and the same syllable: *ú-mbu-ndù; ó-nja-ngò* 'meetinghouse'.

Several morphemes (e.g., the verbal subject and object markers of the first person) consist of just a nasal that must be combined with the following consonant. This results in a prenasalized consonant in the case of a voiced obstruent, and in a nasal consonant in the case of a voiceless obstruent.

N + *v / l / y / Ø* > *mb / nd / nj / ng*
N + *p / t / c / k* > *m / n / nh / ng'*

óku-landà	'to buy'	*ndanda*	'I buy'
ókw-endà	'to go'	*ngenda*	'I go'
óku-túma	'to send'	*núma*	'I send'
óku-kwátà	'to take'	*ng'wátà*	'I take'
óku-limà	'to cultivate'	*nima*	'I cultivate'

The last example shows that a prenasalized consonant turns into a nasal when the second consonant in the stem is a pure nasal.

The vowels have about the same pronunciation as in Italian. Approximate ENGLISH equivalents would be: *i* as in *meet; e* as in *get; a* as in *father; o* as in *hot; u* as in *boot.* There is no distinction between short and long (or single and double) vowels. All vowels and glides may also be nasalized.

Any vowel immediately preceding or following a nasalized (not a nasal) consonant is nasalized; in this environment the tilde under the vowel is not written. The nasalized vowels *ḭ a̰ ṵ* also occur in monosyllabic stems without being conditioned by a neighboring nasalized consonant. Writing the tilde below the vowels leaves space for tone marks above the vowel symbols.

A kind of vowel and nasal harmony affects verbal suffixes containing a nonlow vowel (producing the alternations *i* ~ *e* and *u* ~ *o*) and one of the consonants *l* (alternating with *l̰*) and *k* (alternating with *ẖ*).

Glides are phonologically vowels in a position where they are not the nucleus of a syllable. The consonant *y* and the glide *y* are phonetically identical but phonologically distinct. Only the consonant *y* can be prenasalized, in which case it is represented as *nj*, and it may be followed by the glide *w* as in *éywí* 'crazy person'.

Most syllables consist of a consonant or glide followed by a vowel; word-initial syllables may lack the consonantal onset. The consonant may be prenasalized, and it may be followed by a glide. Word-internal orthographic vowel sequences are indistinguishable from a sequence vowel-glide-vowel: *ou* = *owu*. In most cases where morphology puts vowels into adjacent positions, one of two things happens: either the first vowel becomes a glide (*i, e* > *y; u, o* > *w*), e.g., °*óku-ímba* > *ókwímba* 'to sing', or the two vowels merge, e.g., °*óva-íva* > *óváva* 'water'.

Each syllable (vowel) bears a tone, either high or low. In addition, a high tone after another high tone may be either the same or slightly lower than the preceding high tone. This lowering of the tonal register affects all following (high) tones of the tonal phrase; it is called "downstep". The downstep can be analyzed as a "floating" low tone, i.e., a low tone not attached to any vowel.

When a downstep occurs between the last two syllables of a word, the last-but-one syllable is realized with a tone falling from high to downstepped-high, and the last syllable remains on that same level of downstepped-high. When two high tones at the beginning of a tonal phrase are immediately followed by a downstep the first of these two high tones is realized on a lower pitch than the second.

Tone is marked (on vowels) as follows:

(1) The first acute accent in a word marks a high tone.
(2) Each subsequent acute accent in a word marks a downstepped high tone, setting a new register for all following high tones.
(3) The grave accent marks a low tone.
(4) A vowel without a tone mark has the same tone as the preceding vowel in the word.
(5) An unmarked vowel at the beginning of a word is low.

There are two very general tonal processes: (1) a word-final sequence Hi-Lo is excluded and replaced by Hi-Hi; e.g., °*okutúm-a* (LL-H-L) > *okutúma* (LLHH) and (2) a high tone spreads over all following low tones except the last one in the word; if it encounters another high tone in the same word the deplaced low tone(s) provoke a downstep. Examples: °*óku-tuvik-a* (HL-LL-L) > *ókutuvikà* (HHHHL) 'to cover'; °*óku-súlis-a* (HL-HL-L) > *ókusúlisà* (HH!HHL) 'to finish' (the exclamation mark represents the downstep).

Tone as a feature of lexical items may distinguish words (e.g., *ókw-imbà* 'to throw' vs. *ókw-ímba* 'to sing'); tone as a feature of bound morphemes may distinguish different grammatical categories (*o-lila* 'you cry' vs. *ó-lilà* 's/he cries'; *tu-yév-é* 'hear us!' vs. *tú-yev-è* 'let us hear'; *óváva á-talalà* 'the water is cold' vs. *óváva átalalá* 'water which is cold' = 'cold water').

Basic Morphology

Each noun belongs to a noun class, and most nouns have a prefix. (The numbering of the noun classes is the one traditionally used in Bantu linguistics. The hyphens would normally not be written.)

1	*u-*	*ú-féko ú-na*	'that girl'
2	*a-*	*á-kwenjé vá-na*	'those boys'
3	*u-*	*ú-liví ú-na*	'that trap'
4	*ovi-*	*óvi-kánda ví-na*	'those letters'
5	*e-*	*é-púmbu lí-na*	'that knot'
6	*a-*	*á-kambà á-na*	'those friends'
7	*oci-*	*óci-nhamà cí-na*	'that animal'
9	*on-*	*ón-dalù í-na*	'that fire'
10	*olon-*	*ólon-dukò ví-na*	'those names'
11	*olu-*	*ólu-nhí<u>h</u>i lú-na*	'that bee'
12	*oka-*	*óka-lénge ká-na*	'that cat'
13	*otu-*	*ótu-válù tú-na*	'those horses'
15	*oku-*	*ókw-óko kú-na*	'that arm'

The longer nominal prefixes all start with the vowel *o-*, called the "pre-prefix" or "augment". The vowel of the augment—but not its tone—has been deleted before a vowel (Classes 1, 2, 3, 5, 6). Some nouns, especially proper names and some kinship terms, lack the augment; cf. *óngevé* 'hippopotamus' vs. *ngévé* 'Mr./Ms. Hippo'.

The singular and plural forms of countable nouns belong to different classes. There are 10 such pairs of classes ("genders"): 1/2 (*úféko/áféko* 'girl/girls'); 3/4; 3/6; 5/6; 7/4; 9/10; 11/10; 11/6; 12/13; 15/6. Infinitives belong to Class 15 (e.g., *óku-landà* 'to buy'). Most nouns of Classes 12/13 (sg/pl) are derived diminutives.

Classes 16–18 are locative classes; the locative nominal prefix (without an augment) is placed before the inherent (lexical) prefix.

16	*pa-*	*p-é-púmbu pá-na*	'near that knot there'
17	*ku-*	*k-ón-dalù kú-na*	'at that fire there'
18	*vu-*	*v-ú-liví mú-na*	'in that trap there'

Each noun appears in two tonal shapes: one with an initial high tone and one with an initial low tone (e.g., *úféko* - *uféko*, *ócinhamà* - *ocinhama*). The two shapes mark different syntactic functions.

Adnominal modifiers (adjectives; numerals; demonstratives; possessives; connexive or "genitival" noun phrases and various determiners such as "some", "other", "which?") agree with the class of the head noun. The agreement marking prefixes can be seen in the above chart preceding the demonstrative *-na*.

There are just five adjectives in UMbundu: "good", "bad", "big", "small", "short". The numerals 1 through 5 form a similar but separate word category; higher numerals are nouns.

There are four basic series of demonstratives, distinguishing degrees of closeness to speaker and hearer. For each series there are three kinds of demonstratives: simple ('*this* house', '*this* is his house'), predicative ('his house *is this one*') and presentative ('*look here, this is* his house'). There are special emphatic forms for predicative demonstratives. And finally, of course, each of these demonstratives agrees in class with its head noun.

Pronominal possessives agree with the noun class of the possessed as well as with the noun class of the possessor. Underived possessive stems exist for the first and second person singular and plural, as well as for Class 1. They are preceded by an agreement marking prefix and the linker *-a-*. Examples: *épyá ly-á-ẖé* 'her farm'; *ówisì w-á-ẖé* 'her pestle'. In these examples, *-ẖé* refers to a noun of Class 1, e.g., *úká̰yi* 'the woman'. If the possessor were a noun of another class, he/she/it/they would be referred to by the agreement marker followed by *-ó*; e.g., *ócinè l'ówisì w-á-c-ó* 'the mortar and its pestle'.

Finite verb forms (except imperatives) always include a subject marker that may refer to the first or second person singular or plural, or to one of the noun classes including the locative classes. The verb form may also include one or two object markers referring to a person or a class except the locative classes. Verb forms are further marked for tense (time/aspect/mood), negation, order (absolute/relative), and other categories. Here is a maximally complex verb form (TAM = tense; IT = itive):

ka-	*tw-*	*á-*	*ka-*	*va-*	*u-*	*pandwíl-*	*il-*	*ì-*	*kó*
NEG	SJ	TAM	IT	OJ	OJ	VERB	TAM	PL	LOC
not	we	PAST	go	them	you	thank:for	PAST	PL	there

'we did not go there to thank them for you (pl.)'

Verbal inflection includes simple affirmative and negative tenses such as Optative, Non-Past, Progressive and two different Past tenses. Negative and relative forms are tenses in their own right and not regularly derivable from affirmative and absolute tenses. In addition, there are complex tenses formed with the help of various auxiliary verbs.

Optative:	*tú-ci-landís-e*	'let us sell it'
Nonpast:	*tu-cí-landis-à*	'we sell it'
Past I:	*tw-a-cí-landís-a*	'we sold it'
Past II:	*tw-a-cí-landís-ilè*	'we had sold it'
Neg. Optative:	*ka-tú-ka-ci-landís-e*	'let us not sell it'
Neg. Nonpast:	*ka-tú-ci-landís-a*	'we don't sell it'
Neg. Past I:	*ka-tw-á-ci-landís-ilé*	'we had not sold it'
Neg. Past II:	*ka-tw-á-cí-landís-ilè*	'we had sold it'

Verbal derivation is a rich and productive system with affixes for deriving passive, causative, dative ("applicative"), stative, neuter, extensive, separative and other kinds of verbs. Example: *-landisiwa* 'be sold' = pass. < *-landisa* 'sell' = caus. < *-landa* 'buy'. Verb-to-noun derivation is also common. Example: *-lima* 'cultivate' > *ókulimà* (Cl. 15) 'cultivating'; *úlimì/álimì* (Cl. 1/2) 'farmer'; *úlimé/óvilimé* (Cl. 3/4) 'piece of land to be hoed in one day'; *úlimà/álimà* (Cl. 3/6) 'year'. Reduplication and various types of compounding are additional instruments of word formation.

Basic Syntax

The finite verb form constitutes a full verbal sentence. A lexical subject normally precedes the verb form and a lexical object normally follows it (SVO). Other word orders are possible to mark particular constellations of topic and focus. Adjuncts (generally nouns or noun phrases) may precede the subject or follow the object. The noun occupies the first position within the noun phrase; modifiers follow the noun. When a noun is modified by another noun (phrase), the construction parallels that of the pronominal possessive, e.g., *úká̰yi w-a-somá* 'the wife of the chief'.

Locative nouns are not necessarily adjuncts but may function as subjects and as objects. As subjects, they command agreement with the subject concord of the verb, e.g., *v-onjó mú-talalà* 'in the house [it] is cool'. (The subject noun is preceded by the locative prefix of Class 18 *vu-*, and the predicate, the verb *-tálala* 'to be cold' has the subject-agreement marker of Class 18 *mú-*.)

The object that directly follows an affirmative verb in a main clause has a high augment (pre-prefix); the augment is low in all other cases (subject, adjunct, displaced object, object of a negative verb form or in a subordinate clause). Words without an augment do not make this tonal distinction, which comes close to being a case marking.

ndasangá óngevé	'I came across a hippo'
ndasangá ngevé	'I came across Mr/Ms Ngeve'
ongevé yámḛ́la	'the hippo came closer'
ngevé wámḛ́la	'Mr/Ms Ngeve came closer'

When the predicate is a noun (with or without an augment) it is preceded by a floating high tone that spreads to the right as any other high tone: *óngevé* 'it is a hippo'; *ngévé* 'it is Ngeve'. When the subject of a sentence with a nominal predicate is a first or second person, the same prefix that serves as the subject marker of a verb form is attached to the noun: *(ame) nd-ulongisi* 'I am a teacher'.

In verbal sentences, negation is expressed in the verb form. In nominal sentences, the negative marker *ha-* (the same as occurs in verb forms) is prefixed to the nominal predicate, and a clitic *-kó* follows the noun or the noun phrase: *há-citelè cángè-kó* 'it is not my luggage'.

Contact with Other Languages

UMbundu has certainly had contact with neighboring languages, but borrowings between closely related Bantu languages are often difficult to recognize. In modern times, the most important donor language has been Portuguese. Many loanwords are nouns referring to things that were not part of traditional culture or have acquired a new significance; e.g., *élívulú* 'book' < *livro; ómba̰láw̃ù* 'aeroplane' < *balão* 'balloon'. In some cases, the initial syllable of a Portuguese word has been reanalyzed as a nominal prefix, e.g., *óvi-nénù* 'poison' < *veneno.* Most loanwords are nouns, but cf. *-tolokala* 'exchange' < *trocar; sésá* 'hello, may I come in' < *dá licença* 'give permission'. There has also been some borrowing in the opposite direction, particularly into regional varieties of Brazilian Portuguese, but it is often impossible to be certain of the exact donor language because the same word may occur in several Bantu languages of Angola and Zaïre; e.g., Port. *dendê* 'palm oil' < *óndendé*. The name of the language of Curaçao, *Papiamento,* may well be built on the UMbundu verb *-pópya* 'say, speak' and the Portuguese suffix *-mente.* Finally, *ómbambì*, the name of a small kind of gazelle, has become famous as the star of a Disney movie.

Common Words

woman:	úkáy̧i	big:	-nénè
man:	úlúme	small:	-titó
dog:	ómbwá	good:	-wá
bird:	ónjíla	be long:	-lepa
fish:	ómbísi	three:	-tátu
water:	óváva	yes:	óco ('that's it')
sun:	ékúmbi	no:	há-à; ndátì; syó

Example Sentences

(1) e-téke lí-mwe ka-n-dímba w-á-fetika ókw-endà.
5-day 5-one 1a-9-rabbit 1-PAST-start 15-go
'Once upon a time, Mr. Rabbit set out on a journey.'

(2) nóke w-á-fá v-ú-liví.
then 1-PAST-die 18-3-trap
'And then he fell into a trap.'

(3) w-á-fetika óku-téh̲a-teh̲à c-á-lwa óco
1-PAST-start 15-jump-jump 7-PAST-be:much 7:DEM2

á-tund-è-mó v-u-liví.
1-leave-OPT-18 18-3-trap
'He started jumping up and down a lot in order to get out of the trap.'

(The numbers in the interlinear translations refer to the nominal prefixes and the agreement markers of the noun classes. Morphemes consisting only of tone have not been separated by hyphens and not been glossed.)

Efforts to Preserve, Protect and Promote the Language

Until 1975, when Angola became independent, UMbundu was the medium of instruction at mission schools, and written literature was mainly religious (including Bible translations) and educational. Catholics and Protestants used somewhat different orthographies. None of the seriously proposed orthographies marks tone, and the marking of nasalization is haphazard.

After independence, Portuguese became the official language and UMbundu one of the six national languages. The national languages are used for radio broadcasts, but alphabetization programs could not gain much momentum due to the civil war. Large parts of the provinces where UMbundu is spoken were not controlled by the government. The National Language Institute at Luanda is engaged in efforts to develop UMbundu and other national languages.

Select Bibliography

Lecomte, E. 1963. *Método prático da língua mbundu falado no distrito de Benguela.* Coimbra.

Le Guennec, G., and J.F. Valente. 1972. *Dicionário Português-Umbundu.* Luanda: Instituto de Investigação Científica de Angola.

Schadeberg, T.C. 1982. "Nasalization in UMbundu." In *Journal of African Languages and Linguistics* 4: 109–132.

_____. 1986. "Tone Cases in UMbundu." In *Africana Linguistica X,* pp. 423–447. Tervuren: Musée Royal de l'Afrique Centrale.

_____. 1990. *A Sketch of UMbundu.* Cologne: Rüdiger Köppe.

Valente, J.F. 1964a. *Gramática Umbundu: A língua do centro de Angola.* Lisbon: Junta de Investigações do Ultramar.

_____. 1964b. *Selecção de provérbios e adivinhas em Umbundu.* Lisbon: Junta de Investigações do Ultramar.

_____. 1973. *Paisagem africana: uma tribo africana no seu fabulário.* Luanda: Instituto de Investigação Científica de Angola.

URDU

Tahsin Siddiqi

Language Name: Urdu. **Autonyms:** *Urdu; hindustani; hindvi/hindi.*

Location: People who speak Urdu as a first language are scattered all over south Asia, with the majority living in the Indian states of Uttar Pradesh, Bihar, Maharashtra, Andhra Pradesh and Karnataka. In Pakistan, Urdu is mainly spoken as a first language by the immigrant population from India. In Bangladesh, many people who migrated from Bihar and Uttar Pradesh speak Urdu as their first language. A sizeable number of Urdu-speaking people who migrated from India and Pakistan to other countries also use it as the first language at home. For these immigrants, Urdu is also the medium of entertainment and culture. Urdu is spoken as a second language in many regions of India, Pakistan, Afghanistan and Nepal. It is one of the official languages of Pakistan. (The other official language is ENGLISH.) It is also an official language of the state of Jammu and Kashmir, and has recently gained the status of the second official language in several Indian states (e.g., Bihar in north India, and some areas of Andhra Pradesh). Unlike most other languages of India and Pakistan, Urdu is not a majority language of any geographical region in these countries. It is, nevertheless, a lingua franca of south Asia.

Family: Urdu belongs to the Indo-Aryan branch of the Indo-European language family.

Related Languages: Urdu is closely related to other Indo-Aryan languages, such as PUNJABI, SIRAIKI, BANGLA, GUJARATI, MARATHI, SINDHI, Kashmiri, ORIYA, NEPALI, SINHALA, etc; and it is mutually intelligible with HINDI.

Dialects: Urdu is spoken in various linguistic environments and varies according to region and occupation. Studies have highlighted specific linguistic features of different social and regional variants of Urdu, for example *Karkhandari* (Narang: 1961).

Number of Speakers: The official figures vary from 104–127 million. See also figures for Hindi.

Origin and History

Urdu, like other modern Indo-Aryan languages, developed from spoken dialects called Prakrits. In the beginning, PERSIAN speakers called modern Urdu by the names of *Hindvi*, *Hindi*, *Rekhta*, and *Hindustani*. Around 1780, the term "Urdu" was used for the first time to refer to this language (Faruqi 1999: 17), yet poets and writers continued to use the term *Hindvi* or *Hindi* for their language until the end of the 19th century.

Urdu is a TURKISH word meaning "camp". Because of this, some scholars call it "the language of the camp". (Geijbels 1985: 3). In India, the term *Urdu* has been used to refer to many things, but, prior to the last quarter of the 18th century, *Urdu* was not used for the language. During the 18th century, the term *Urdu* was used to refer to the walled city of Delhi (Faruqi 1999: 37) as well as for the nobles and servants belonging to the Mughal court (Shairani 1966: 37). A few writers of this period used the terms *Zabān-i Urdū-yi mu'allā'* and *'Urdū-yi mu'allā'* to refer to the language, first for Persian and later for *Hindvi* (Faruqi 1999: 16), spoken in and around the court. By the end of the 19th century, the term *Urdu* gained dominance over all previous names—i.e., *Hindvi*, *Hindi* and *Rekhta* in the north; *Gujri* in Gujarat; and *Hindi*, *Dakani*, and *Zaban-i Hindustan* in Deccan—and was associated for the first time with the speech of Muslim elites and nobles.

Urdu is a continuation of the *Hindvi/Hindi* spoken in and around Delhi that absorbed many Persian, ARABIC, and some Turkish words in its lexicon due to the language contact and bilingualism that began during the 12th century and continued in subsequent centuries. In 1027, Muslim Turks attacked Panjab and annexed it to their rule. In 1193, they captured Delhi and established their rule there. This brought *Hindvi* speakers and the invaders, who spoke Persian, PASHTO, and Turkish, into close contact, whereas before they had interacted with one another only in limited situations such as trade and military contexts. Because the Muslim rulers did not force native *Hindvi* speakers to learn Persian, the cultural language of the Muslims who either settled in India at that time or immigrated at a later date, bilingualism occurred initially mostly among the Persian-speaking settlers, Sufis, poets, soldiers, and rulers, in particular, who had to learn *Hindvi* in order to enter and function within Indian society. After bilingualism spread among Muslims, Indian nobles and then other native *Hindvi* speakers became bilingual. The textbooks *Khāliq Bārī*, attributed to Amīr Khusrau (1253–1325) (Jalibi 1975: 1:29), and Ajay Chand Bhaṭnāgar's *Misl Khāliq Bārī* (1552) were written to teach *Hindvi* to the Persian-speaking settlers. Later, Mīr 'Abdul Wāsi' wrote *Ṣamad Bārī* (17th century) to teach Persian to *Hindvi* speakers. With both groups now acquiring some knowledge of each other's language, the resulting bilingualism mutually influenced both *Hindvi* and Persian. As commonly happens among bilinguals, Persian-speaking bilinguals started mixing *Hindvi* words as well as translations of Hindvi idioms into their speech, and at the same time they mixed Persian words into their Hindvi. Simultaneously, *Hindvi*-speaking bilinguals began to mix Persian words as well as translations of Persian idioms into *Hindvi*, and also started to mix *Hindvi* words into their Persian. At that time, *Hindvi* was also called *Rekhta*, which means 'scattered, mixed', probably due to the many new words and idioms that entered into the speech of native *Hindvi* speakers. This code-mixing is evident from the poetry of both groups of this time, in which a portion or full line of a couplet was in Persian, and the other line or portion of the other line was in *Hindvi*. It is also evident from the *Hindvi* utterances of the Sufis (Muslim mystics) recorded in Persian works of that period, from the language in Muhammad Afzal's (d. 1625) long poem *Bikaṭ kahānī*, and from the poetry and prose of Ja'far Zaṭallī (d. 1713), a great satirist of the 17th century.

With the Muslim conquest of Gujarat and Deccan in the early 14th century, Urdu, which, at that time, was called *Hindvi* or Hindi, also spread in these regions. Here Urdu came into close contact with the languages of these regions and borrowed words and idioms from them. In Gujarat, it was named *Gujri*, and in Deccan it was called *Dakani*. In these regions, Urdu flourished as a literary language. The first Urdu literary books were written in Gujarat and Deccan.

In Delhi and other parts of north India, Persian was the court language, but Urdu held the position of lingua franca. Urdu was used in trade and commerce, at home, and for teaching and entertainment. Sufis and Bhakti poets (Muslim and Hindu mystics, respectively) used Urdu to preach their teachings and carried the language to new regions as they traveled all over the country. Additionally, Mas'ūd Sa'd Salmān (1046–1121) is said to be the first bilingual poet who actually compiled a collection of his *Hindvi* and Persian poetry (Faruqi 1999: 61). Unfortunately, a sample of his poetry is not available to us. Another bilingual poet, Amīr Khusrau (1253–1325), said that he compiled a small collection of his own *Hindvi* poetry, but only a few couplets that definitely belong to him have been found. During the 17th century, two long poems in Urdu, *Bikaṭ Kahānī* by Muhammad Fazal (d.1625) and *'Āshūr Nāma* (1688) by Raušan 'Alī, were written in the north. A final important development was that Urdu was adopted as the medium of instruction in *madarsā* (Muslim religious schools). Mir Abdul Wasi' (17th century), who was a teacher by profession, wrote textbooks and compiled the first Urdu dictionary, *Gharāib-ul lughāt*, for teaching purposes.

During the 18th century, Urdu also gained the prestige of a literary language in Delhi perhaps because Emperor Shah Alam II (1759–1806) wrote *'Ajāib-ul qaṣaṣ*, a long tale in Urdu prose (Faruqi 1999: 17), or because Muslim nobles and elites began to speak Urdu as their first language and Persian as their second language. The language and style of poetry was also changing during this time. Previous to this time, Urdu literature was mostly produced by Sufis and Bhakti poets who wrote for the common monolingual audience. Most of the poets who started writing in Urdu during the 18th century were well versed in both Persian and Urdu, and their audience was also bilingual. Thus the poets began to naturally employ Persian similes and metaphors freely with Urdu similes and metaphors in their poetry. *Mušāi'rā*, a gathering of Urdu poets where the latter recited their poetry for an audience, became popular. A few Urdu prose books written during the 18th century have been discovered. Women's speech also was recognized as a distinct style of Urdu (Insha 1935: 171). In the 19th century when the British abolished the use of Persian for administrative purposes, Urdu took some of that role in certain parts of north India. During the British rule, Urdu became the medium of instruction in schools in a number of states, and it also became the judiciary language in some states. Osmani, a University with Urdu as its medium was founded in Hyderabad, Deccan, in 1918. However, in 1948 when the Republic of India abolished all princely states and brought them under her rule, the medium of instruction of the *Jamia Osmania* also changed from Urdu to TELUGU. After the partition of India in 1947, Urdu was declared one of two official languages of the Republic of Pakistan, and was instituted as one of the official languages of the Republic of India.

Orthography and Basic Phonology

Modern Urdu is written in a modified form (*Nasta'līq* style) of Arabic script, which is written from right to left. Urdu, Kashmiri and Sindhi, as well as all written languages in Pakistan use a form of modified Arabic script. Before the Arabic writing system came to India, it had already been modified for Persian, Turkish, and a few other languages. New letters were added to the Perso-Arabic script to represent the sounds particular to Urdu. Some early Hindi books written in Arabic script have been found.

The Urdu script has 36 letters, of which all represent consonantal sounds except *alif*—the only letter that exclusively indicates a vowel sound. Three other letters *vaao, choTii ye* and *baRii ye* indicate both vowel and consonant sounds. In addition to these letters, several diacritics are used to mark vowel sounds and gemination, but diacritics are rarely used in normal text. In most cases, one must guess the vowel sound and gemination from the context of the surrounding consonants in the word or from the other words in the sentence. In a few cases, a letter may represent more than one sound or, conversely, more than one letter can be used to indicate a single sound. In the modern Urdu writing system, a letter called *do chashmi he* is used to indicate aspiration in the preceding consonant.

Urdu has 10 vowels and 37 consonants, of which 31 are of Indic origin and 6 are of Perso-Arabic origin. Arabic sounds entered into Urdu via speakers of Persian.

There is a four-way contrast in stops: plain voiceless /p/, plain voiced /b/, and their aspirated counterparts, /ph/ and /bh/. The uvular stop /q/ is borrowed from Arabic, and its pronunciation varies regionally. The Urdu /v/ is pronounced with little friction; its pronunciation ranges between the English /v/ and /w/.

All Urdu consonants, except aspirated stops and /ž/ and /R/, may occur as geminates. In casual speech, Urdu voiceless aspirated stops lose their aspiration completely or are pronounced with less of a puff of air in word-final position. For example, *haath* 'hand' is pronounced as *haat*. /R/ and /Rh/ do not occur in the beginning of a word; /ph/ and /ž/ do not occur in word-final position. In Urdu, consonant clusters in word-initial position are not permitted. Such sequences in borrowed words are broken apart by the epenthesis of a vowel.

Voicing assimilation generally occurs in casual speech; e.g., *aag ke paas mat jaao* 'don't go near the fire', is pronounced *aakke paas mat jaao* in casual speech.

Urdu has 10 vowels that all have phonemic nasal counterparts; e.g., *hæ* 'is' vs. *hÆ* 'are'; *kahaa* 'said, third masc. singular' vs. *kahAA* 'where'. All Urdu vowels are pure with no diphthongization.

Table 1: Consonants

	Labial	Labio-dental	Dental	Alveolar	Retroflex	Palatal	Velar	Uvular	Glottal
Stops	p ph b bh		t th d dh		T Th D Dh	c ch j jh	k kh g gh	q	
Fricatives		f		s z		š ž		x G	h
Nasals	m		n						
Lateral				l					
Flaps				r	R Rh				
Glides		v				y			

Table 2: Vowels

	Front		Central	Back	
High	i	ii		u	uu
Mid	e	æ	o		
Low			a	au	aa
Nasalization: upper-case vowels					

/u, i, a/ do not occur in word-final position. /a/ occurs in word-final position only in one word: *na* 'not'. /y/ does not occur in word-final position. When /a/ is followed by /h/, its pronunciation changes from /a/ to /ɛ/. For example, *mahal* 'palace' is pronounced *mɛhɛl*. When /a/ occurs in the middle syllable of a word that contains three or more syllables, it is not pronounced; e.g., when /E/ is added to *aurat* 'woman' to form its plural, the /a/ is not pronounced and *auratE* becomes *aurtE* 'women'.

Basic Morphology

Urdu nouns express number (singular or plural) and gender (feminine or masculine). Feminine and masculine nouns are further classified into two types depending on their final phoneme. Masculine nouns terminating in *-aa* are categorized as Type I nouns. Masculine nouns not ending in *-aa* are categorized as Type II. Most Type I nouns are declinable. The final ending *-aa* in Type I masculine nouns changes to *-e* to mark plurality. However, a class of Type I masculine nouns exists that terminates in *-aa* but does not change to mark plurality, such as kinship terms; e.g., *caacaa* 'uncle'. The ending of Type II masculine nouns does not change to show plurality.

Feminine nouns terminating in *-ii* are Type I nouns. Feminine nouns not ending in *-ii* are Type II nouns. To make Type I feminine nouns plural, the *-ii* changes to *iyAA*. To make Type II feminine nouns plural, an *-E* is added to the singular form of the noun.

Urdu has three cases: direct, oblique, and vocative. A noun is in the oblique case when it is followed by a postposition. Most singular masculine nouns of Type I are inflected in the oblique or vocative case; i.e., the final *-aa* changes to *-e* to mark the oblique or vocative case. All other nouns, including Type II singular masculine nouns as well as Type I and Type II singular feminine nouns, do not change to mark the oblique or vocative case. All plural nouns, however, change in the oblique or vocative case.

Masculine Nouns:

	Direct	Oblique	Vocative
Type I			
Singular	baccaa 'child'	bacce	bacce
Plural	bacce	baccO	bacco
Type II			
Singular	aadmii 'man'	aadmii	aadmii
Plural	aadmii	aadmiyO	aadmiyo

Feminine Nouns:

	Direct	Oblique	Vocative
Type I			
Singular	beTii 'daughter'	beTii	beTii
Plural	beTiyAA	beTiyO	beTiyo
Type II			
Singular	aurat 'woman'	aurat	aurat
Plural	auratE	auratO	aurato

Like nouns, adjectives can also be categorized into two groups: Type I or Type II. Type I adjectives have an *-aa* ending, while Type II adjectives end in a sound other than *-aa*. With few exceptions, all adjectives terminating in *-aa* change to agree with the nouns they modify in respect to gender, number, and case.

Masc/Sg/Direct	acchaa baccaa	'good child'
Masc/Pl/Direct	acche bacce	'good children'
Masc/Sg/Oblique	acche bacce ko	'to a good child'
Masc/Pl/Oblique	acche baccO ko	'to good children'
Fem/Sg/Direct	acchii baccii	'good child'
Fem/Pl/Direct	acchii bacciyA	'good children'
Fem/Sg/Oblique	acchii baccii ko	'to a good child'
Fem/Pl/Oblique	acchii bacciyO ko	'to good children'

Postpositions and adverbs are invariant, except the possessive postposition *kaa*, which changes like a Type I adjective.

Urdu pronouns can be classified into personal, relative, correlative, possessive, demonstrative, definite, and reflexive pronouns. Personal pronouns are classified by person (first, second, or third person), by number (singular or plural), and by case (direct or oblique).

Table 3: Personal Pronouns

	Direct	Oblique	Possessive
1s	mÆ	muhj	meraa
1p	ham	ham	hamaaraa
2s	tuu	tuhj (intimate)	teraa
2p	tum	tum (familiar)	tumhaaraa
2p	aap	aap (polite)	aapkaa
3s	ye	is (proximate)	iskaa
	vo	us (distant)	uskaa
3p	ye	in (proximate)	inkaa
	vo	un (distant)	unkaa

The second-person pronoun has three forms: *tuu, tum* and *aap*. On an honorific scale, *aap* is the most polite, and *tuu* is the most informal. However, the use of these forms is rather complex. For example, the use of *tuu* in some regions is considered rude, whereas in other regions using *tuu* expresses intimacy. In some situations, the use of *tuu* expresses endearment, but in other situations it is used to show anger.

Similarly, in some regions the use of *aap* may be considered snobbish, but in other regions it may be considered sophisticated. *aap* also may be used to express respect or to express distance. The third-person plural may be used for single referents to indicate respect. Third-person pronouns function as demonstratives; *ye* is used for the persons and things that are present and physically close to the speaker, and *vo* is used for persons and things either absent or physically distant from the speaker.

Possessive pronouns are like Type I adjectives in that they change to agree with the gender and the number of the noun they modify.

Like other pronouns, the relative pronoun *jo* 'who' also has two numbers (singular or plural) and two cases (direct or oblique). Just like third-person direct pronouns, *jo* also is used for singular and plural in the direct case. But in the oblique case, it has two distinct forms: *jis* and *jin*. *jis* is used for singular, and *jin* is used for plural:

	Relative	Correlative
Direct Singular	jo	vo
plural	jo	vo
Oblique Singular	jis	us
plural	jin	un

The third person plural pronoun *vo* and the relative plural pronoun *jo* change to *unhO* and *jinhO* respectively before the postposition *ne*.

Verb stems in Urdu can be categorized as intransitive, transitive, and causative:

makaan banaa.	'A house was made/built.'
mÆ ne makaan banaayaa.	'I made/built a house.'
mÆ ne makaan banvaayaa.	'I had a house made/built.'

The derivation of these sets of verbs is complex and depends on the phonological form of the verb stem. The causative always has the suffix *-vaa*.

Verb constructions in Urdu can be divided into single-word and two-word constructions. Single-word constructions consist only of the verb stem and its endings; two-word constructions consist of the verb stem, its ending, and an auxiliary verb. The verb *honaa* 'to be' is used as an auxiliary, and its different forms mark tense (present or past) and mood.

Single-word constructions V-stem ending

1. Simple past: *(y)aa* (inflects to mark gender and number)
2. Imperative: unmarked, *o, iye*
3. Subjunctive: *UU, o, O, e, E* (indicate person and number)
4. Future: subjunctive ending plus *gaa* (*gaa* inflects to mark gender and number)
5. Past conditional: *taa* (inflects to mark gender and number)

Two-word constructions V-stem ending + auxiliary verb

1. Present perfect/past prefect: *(y)aa* (inflects to mark gender and number)
2. Habitual present/past: *taa* (inflects to mark gender and number)
3. Progressive present/past: *rahaa* (inflects to mark gender and number)

The verb *honaa* 'to be' plays a significant role in the verbal system. It is used both as a main verb and as an auxiliary verb. In its auxiliary function, *honaa* identifies tense (*hæ* present, and *thaa* past) and mood (*ho, hotaa, hogaa*). Imperative, future, and subjunctive constructions do not require an auxiliary. The simple past and perfective forms of transitive verbs frequently require the use of *ne* after the subject. In Urdu sentence constructions, the verb agrees with the subject in number and gender. However, if the subject is in the oblique case, i.e., if it is followed by a postposition, then the verb agrees with the direct object. In case the direct object also is followed by a postposition, the verb does not agree with the direct object and instead takes a third-person singular masculine ending. As a general rule, Urdu verbs never agree with a noun that precedes a postposition:

larkii	ne	kamr-e	saaf	k-ie.
girl	POSTPOSITION	room-3MASC.PL	clean	do-PAST.MASC.PL

'The girl cleaned the rooms.' (verb agrees with noun *kamre*)

larkii	ne	kamr-O	ko	saaf	k-iyaa.
girl	POSTPOSITION	room-OBL.PL	POSTPOSITION	clean	do-PAST.MASC.SG

'The girl cleaned the rooms.' (verb does not agree with either noun)

Tense forms of verb *honaa* 'to be':

Present	Singular	Plural
First	h-UU	h-Æ
Second	h-æ	h-o (informal)
		h-Æ (formal)
Third	h-æ	h-Æ

Past	Singular	Plural
Masculine	th-aa	th-e
Feminine	th-ii	th-II

Basic Syntax

Urdu is a Subject-Object-Verb (SOV) language. The normal word order of a sentence is: subject, adverb, indirect object, direct object, negation, verb. Like many other SOV languages, Urdu has postpositions that mark grammatical information and allow some word order variability.

tum	us-ko	pæs-e	mat
2s.INFORMAL	3s.obl	money-MASC.PL	don't
SUBJECT	INDIRECT OBJECT	DIRECT OBJECT	NEGATIVE

d-o.
give-2s.INFORMAL
VERB
'Don't give him money.' = *tum pæs-e usko mat do.*

In addition to simple-verb constructions, compound-verb constructions are common in Urdu. In compound-verb constructions, the first verb is in its root form and carries the basic meaning of the verb sequence. The second verb, which is used as an auxiliary verb, follows the rules of inflection: *caae pii l-o* (tea drink take-IMPERATIVE.FAMILIAR) 'drink tea'.

The passive is formed by adding the verb *jaanaa* 'to go' to the simple past form of the verb. The agent is rarely mentioned in passive constructions. If the object in the sentence is mentioned or understood, both the simple past form of the main verb and *jaanaa* agree with the object in number and gender. Otherwise, the verb takes the third-person singular form. *jaanaa* also changes to mark tense.

Active:

us	ne	ye	xabar
3s.OBL	POSTPOSITION	this.APPROX	news:SG.FEM

sunaa-ii
tell-PAST.SG.FEM
'S/he told this news.'

Passive:

ye	xabar	sunaa-ii-ga-ii
3.APPROX	news:SG.FEM	tell-PAST.SG.FEM-go-PAST.SG.FEM

'This news was told.'

Three words are used in negative sentences: *nahII*, *na*, and *mat*. *mat* is used only in imperative sentences; *na* is generally used in subjunctive and imperative sentences; and *nahII* is used in the many remaining types of sentences.

Contact with Other Languages

Urdu has a sizeable literary and cultural vocabulary that comes either directly or indirectly from Persian. Urdu also has adopted the Persian conjunction *ki* 'that' as well as the subordinate conjunctions *agar* 'if', *agarce* 'although', and several others.

The author of *Farhang-i Āsfiyā*, a standard dictionary of Urdu in four volumes published in 1908, included words from SANSKRIT, Arabic, Turkish, Persian, MALAYALAM, PALI, Punjabi, English, PORTUGUESE, and SPANISH in the Urdu lexicon. Contemporary Urdu freely borrows words from English. In India, more and more Sanskrit words are becoming a part of everyday Urdu speech. In Pakistan, several words from regional languages are used in Urdu speech. Urdu also has borrowed several suffixes from Sanskrit, Persian, and Arabic. In addition, Urdu also has derived several verbs based on borrowed words; e.g., *badalnaa* 'to change' from the Arabic word *badlaa*, *rangnaa* 'to dye' from the Persian word *rang* , and *filmaanaa* 'to shoot a movie' from the English word *film*. The following are some of the other words Urdu has borrowed from various languages:

From Arabic: *ilm* 'knowledge', *kitaab* 'book', *qalam* 'pen', *yaqiinan* 'surely', *duniyaa* 'world', *aurat* 'woman'
From English: *yunivarsiTii* 'university', *lækcar* 'lecture', *laaibrerii* 'library', *vižan* 'vision', *isTešan* 'station', *bas* 'bus'
From FRENCH: *burzvaa* 'bourgeois', *buurzaazii/buurzvaaii* 'bourgeoisie', *resturAA/resTurAAT* 'restaurant' *cimnii* 'chimney' *sanel* 'chenille'
From Persian: *baazaar* 'bazaar', *andešaa* 'suspicion', *afsos* 'sorrow', *xariidnaa* 'to buy', *ustaad* 'teacher', *raušnii* 'light'
From Portuguese: *kamraa* 'room', *paadrii* 'padre', *girjaa* 'church', *anannaas* 'pineapple', *almaarii* 'closet', *caabii* 'key'
From Sanskrit: *ang* 'limb', *paap* 'sin', *daršan* 'sight', *naag* 'cobra', *devmaalaa* 'mythology', *dhyaan* 'attention'
From Turkish: *bavarcii* 'cook', *jurraab* 'sock', *tamGaa* 'medal', *tamAAcaa* 'slap', *qÆcii* 'scissors', *top* 'canon'

Common Words

man:	aadmii	long:	lambaa
woman:	aurat	small:	choTaa
water:	paanii	yes:	hAA
sun:	suraj	no:	nahII
three:	tiin	good:	acchaa
fish:	machlii	bird:	ciRyaa
big:	baRaa	dog:	kuttaa
tree:	peR, daraxt		

Example Sentences

(1) ham aaj baazaar jaa-E-g-e.
we today market go-PL.FUTURE-MASC.PL
'We will go to market today.'

(2) vo šaayad dillii jaa-e.
3s perhaps Delhi go-3s.SUBJUNCTIVE
'S/he may go to Delhi.'

(3) vo dost-O se baat-E kar rah-e
they friend-PL.OBL with talk-FEM.PL do prog-3MASC.PL

h-Æ.
be-3p
'They are talking to friends.'

Efforts to Preserve, Protect, and Promote the Language

Both in India and in Pakistan, efforts are being made on official as well as individual levels to form a standard orthography, to develop a technical terminology, to prepare dictionaries, and to write standard textbooks in Urdu. Each year in India, the Central Government of India as well as several state governments and private institutions give awards to Urdu writers and poets for their literary achievements. These agencies also provide funds to various organizations to publish Urdu books and to develop the language. The National Council for Promotion of Urdu Language—Ministry of Human Resource Development, Government of India, has published a 6 volume English-Urdu dictionary. It also has prepared a 12-volume Urdu encyclopedia and has published a 5-volume history of Urdu literature. Recently, Maulana Azad National Urdu University was established in Hyderabad, India, with Urdu as its medium of instruction. At present, it teaches a limited number of courses in Urdu.

Ayyub Sabir (1985) has listed 63 institutions, both private and official, that are working to develop Urdu in Pakistan. Most of these institutions publish books in Urdu on various subjects. The University of Punjab has published an *Encyclopedia of Islam* in Urdu. The Urdu Dictionary Board, Karachi has prepared a multivolume dictionary categorized on the pattern of the *Oxford English Dictionary*. Twelve volumes of it have already been published. The Urdu Science Board has published over 80 books in Urdu on various scientific subjects in Urdu.

In 1979, the government of Pakistan formed *Muqtadra Qaumi Zaban* ('the National Language Authority') to promote Urdu as the national language of Pakistan. This organization has published an English-Urdu dictionary, an Urdu thesaurus, reference books in Urdu, and several books on Urdu technical terms. Recently, the Government of Pakistan started awarding Urdu writers for their literary contributions in the language. Though English continues to dominate in all official domains of prestige in Pakistan (Rahman 1997: 203), Urdu is used in mass media (radio and television) and in lower levels of administration. Urdu still holds the position of the link language between regions in Pakistan.

Select Bibliography

Ahmad, Kalimuddin (Chief ed.). 1994–1998. *English Urdu Dictionary*. 6 vols. New Delhi: National Council for Promotion of Urdu Language.

Barker, M.A., *et al.* 1967. *A Course in Urdu*. 3 Vol. Montreal: McGill University.

Beg, Mirza K.A. 1996. *Sociolinguistic Perspective of Hindi and Urdu in India*. New Delhi: Bahri Publications.

Chaterjee, Suniti Kumar. 1960. *Indo-Aryan and Hindi*. Calcutta: K.L. Mukhopadhyay.

Faruqi, Shamsur Rahman. 1998. "Unprivileged Power: The Strange Case of Persian (and Urdu) in Nineteenth-Century India." In *The Annual of Urdu Studies* 13: 3–30.

_____. 1999. *Urdu ka ibtidai zamana: Adabi tahzib-o tarikh ke pahlu* ('Urdu: Early Period of Urdu: Literary Culture and the Aspects of History). Karachi: Aj ki kitaben.

Geijbels, M. 1985. "The Rise and Development of the Urdu Language." *Al-Mushir* 27: 2. Reprinted in M. Geijbels and J.S. Addison. Undated. *The Rise and Development of Urdu and the Importance of Regional Languages in Pakistan*. Rawalpindi: Christian Study Center. (1–16).

Insha, Insha Allah Khan. 1935. *Darya-i latafat* ('Persian: Elegance of Ocean') Translated into Urdu by Pandit Braj Mohan Dattaraya Kaifi Dehlavi. Delhi: Anjuman Taraqqi-yi Urdu.

Jalibi, Jamil. 1975. *Tarikh-i Adab-i Urdu* ('Urdu: History of Urdu Literature'). 2 vols. Lahore: Majlis-i Taraqqi-yi Adab.

King, Christopher R. 1994. *One Language, Two Scripts: The Hindi Movement in Nineteenth Century North India*. Delhi: Oxford University Press.

Masica, Collins P. 1991. *The Indo-Aryan Languages*. Cambridge: University Press.

Narang, Gopi Chand. 1961. *Karkhandari Dialect of Delhi Urdu*. Delhi: Munshi Ram Manohar Lal.

Rahman, Tariq. 1997. "The Urdu-English Controversy in Pakistan." In *Modern Asian Studies* 31:1, 177–207.

Sabir, Ayyub. 1985. *Pakistan men urdu ke taraqqiyati idare* ('Urdu: Institutions for the development of Urdu in Pakistan'). Islamabad: Muqtadara Qaumi Zaban.

Sadiq, Muhammad. 1984. *A History of Urdu Literature*. New Delhi: OUP.

Saksena, Ram Babu. 1927. *A History of Urdu Literature*. Allhabad: Ram Narain.

Shairani, Hafiz Mahmud. 1966. "Urdu zaban aur uske mukhtalif nam (Urdu: Urdu Language and Its Various Names)." First published in 1929. Reprinted in *Maqalat-i Hafiz Mahmud Shirani*. ('Urdu: Hafiz Mahmud Shirani's essays') edited by Mazhar Mahmud Shairani; Vol.1. Lahore: Majlis-i Taraqqi-yi Adab. (10–44).

Uyghur

Arienne M. Dwyer

Language Name: Uyghur. **Alternates:** *Uigur/Uygur, Eastern Turki.* **Autonym:** *Uyghur* (pronounced "ooy-GUR" [ujǧhúr]).

Location: Spoken in the Xinjiang Autonomous Region (eastern Turkistan) in the People's Republic of China; also spoken in the former Soviet Central Asian Republics, Afghanistan and Mongolia.

Family: The Southeastern, or "Chaghatay" branch of the Turkic language family.

Related Languages: Uyghur is most closely related to UZBEK, although the two languages differ somewhat in pronunciation and vocabulary.

Some scholars consider the Turkic languages, including Uyghur, to be part of the larger Altaic family. At present it is unclear whether the three main Altaic language groups—Turkic, Mongolic, and Manchu-Tungusic—are of common origin or merely related by borrowings.

Dialects: Uyghur dialects are nearly identical in terms of syntax but differ in phonology, morphology, and vocabulary. The classification of Uyghur dialects is still under debate, but there are three main groups: (1) Central/Northern dialects, including areas north and east of the Tianshan mountains, as well as the oases immediately south of this range; (2) the Southern or Hotan (Khotan) dialects; and (3) the Lopnur dialect, an eastern Tarim basin isolate (with KIRGHIZ and MONGOLIAN influence).

The Uyghur spoken in the Uzbek and Kazakh areas to the west is considered to be similar to the Ghulja vernacular, and thus part of the Central dialect. Modern standard Uyghur is a standardization of the dialects of Ghulja and Ürümchi.

Two other Turkic languages spoken within the borders of modern China, Salar and *Sarïg Yuğur* ('Yellow Yuğur'), were formerly considered dialects of Uyghur. Both are independent languages preserving Old Turkic features; Salar stems likely from Western Turkic (Oghuz); Sarïg Yuğur may have evolved from a 9th century Old Uyghur dialect. Both are typologically distinct from the Southeastern Turkic now called Modern Uyghur.

Number of Speakers: 7–9 million.

Origin and History

The modern Uyghurs trace their lineage back to the great Uyghur kaghans who ruled south Siberia and inner Asia between A.D. 744–840, and to the subsequent Uyghur states in Eastern Turkestan, especially to the Uyghur kingdom at Turfan (9th–15th centuries). The modern Uyghur language is, however, typologically distinct from the Old Turkic of south Siberia and medival Eastern Turkestan; this largely reflects centuries of contact with speakers of Indo-European (SOGDIAN, TOCHARIAN, and Turkicized Iranic), whom the Eastern Turkestani Turks eventually assimilated, as well as contact with other Turkic speakers and Mongols.

The ethnonym "Uyghur", which had fallen out of use by the 16th century, was revived by intellectuals in 1921. From that time, the ethnonym has designated the modern Turkic-speaking oasis agriculturalists of the Tarim basin and the Ili Valley (as well as smaller populations in the Junggarian Basin, in the Ferghana Valley, and eastern Kazakhstan).

The ancient Uyghurs were first mentioned in Chinese records as one of the vassal tribes of the eastern Turkic steppe confederation, living near the Selenga River in what is now Mongolia. Around 744 the Uyghurs created a new political state from Lake Baikal to the Altai Mountains, with their capital at Ordubalig (later Qarabalgasun) on the upper reaches of the Orxon River. They ruled for a hundred years before being defeated in 840 by the historical Kirghiz tribal confederation. The Uyghurs and many of their Turkic subjects fled southward and settled in three main areas: the Ordos region, the Gansu corridor, and the Tarim basin. Those that fled southeast settled in the Ordos region of northern China and eventually assimilated with the Chinese and Mongols there. Those that fled directly south settled along the 'Gansu' (Héxī) corridor. (In constant contact with Buddhist Tibetans and, later, Mongols, these Uyghurs eventually converted to Lama Buddhism and became known as the *Sarïg Yuğur* or 'Yellow Yuğur', now defined as a distinct minority nationality in China.) By far the largest number of Uyghurs fled to Turfan, their southwesternmost possession. There they established Karakhoja, the capital of a kingdom, which, by the 11th century, extended from Kucha to Beiting to Qumue, the eastern part of modern Xinjiang. These Uyghurs likely absorbed Tocharian and Sogdian groups residing in these areas; portions of the Turpan-area Uyghur elite, in turn, adopted Tocharian Buddhism, the Sogdian's Manichaein religion, and the Sogdian script. It was not until the 14th and 15th centuries that Islam spread to the easternmost parts of the Uyghur region.

These oasis-states of the Tarim basin were drawn into a nearly constant series of hostilities as larger powers vied for political control of the area. Over the centuries, the oases of western

Uyghur is spoken in the Xinjiang Autonomous Region of China and in Eastern Kazakhstan(shaded area).

and eastern areas have been controlled by the Karakitay, the Mongols, the Junggars (Western Mongols), and a series of local rulers. In the last century, the Soviet Union, China, and Britain all vied for pieces of Eastern Turkistan in the "Great Game".

From the 13th to the 20th centuries, the sedentary residents of Eastern Turkistan (Xinjiang) strongly identified with their local oases, referring to themselves not by ethnonym ("Uyghur", "Qaraxanid") but rather by place-name, such as *Qäšqärlik* 'Kashgarian' and *Turfanlïq* 'Turfani'. Until the 20th century, residents of western Xinjiang (Kashgar, Khotan), who had adopted Islam several centuries earlier, had little in common with the Turfan Uyghurs to the east.

Orthography and Basic Phonology

Uyghur is written from right to left with an ARABIC-based script. The Uyghur alphabet contains 32 symbols and, unlike the Arabic alphabet, has 8 unique symbols that designate vowels. It distinguishes front-rounded from back-rounded vowels by means of diacritics except *i/ï*; both writen as *ï*. The hamza, denoting a glottal stop, is a mandatory diacritic preceding initial vowels.

In 1957 a Cyrillic script was introduced for five major Xinjiang languages, including Uyghur. By 1958, however, the formerly close relations with the Soviet Union had soured, and LATIN script (known as *yengi yezïq* or 'new script') was introduced. It was based on the Chinese (*pinyin*) transliteration system and was in official use between 1960 and 1983. The Arabic-based orthography was then revived. In Kazakhstan, Kyrgyzstan, and Uzbekistan, however, Uyghurs still use a Cyrillic standard.

The orthographic conventions are semiphonemic. Some predictable harmonic variations are represented such as the dative ka/qa/ğa/gä/kä *mäktäp<u>ka</u>* 'to the school' and *bazar<u>ğa</u>* 'to the market'. Others are not; *i* and *ï*, and long and short vowels, for example, are not distinguished orthographically.

The consonants *f* and *ž* (ž as in FRENCH '*jour*') occur only in non-Turkic vocabulary. *f* merges with *p* in the colloquial language: *Turfan* [turpan]~[turfan] 'Turfan', *fikir* [pikir] ~ [fikir] 'idea'. *l, x,* and *ğ* have front and back variants depending on the backness of the tautosyllabic syllable. *ğ*, the voiced uvular fricative in "Uyghur", is also realized as a velar fricative in front-vocalic words (*ğäm* 'worry'), and as a voiced uvular stop after nonlabial nasals (*bašlanğuč* 'elementary'). *q* and *ğ* are also realized as the voiceless uvular fricative χ before nonuvular consonants: *qulaq* 'ear', *qulaχta* 'in/on the ear'; *yağ* 'oil', *yaχsiz* 'without oil'. *h* is realized preconsonantally as *χ*, especially in men's speech (*rähmät-räχmät* 'thanks').

Table 1: Consonants

	Labial	Apical	Palatal	Velar	Uvular	Glottal
Stops	p b	t d	č dz	k g	q	ʔ
Fricatives	(f)	s z	š (zh)	x	 ğ	h
Nasals	m	n		ŋ		
Lateral		l				
Vibrant		r				
Glides	w		y			

As in TURKISH, Uyghur devoices syllable-final oral stops and affricates: *kitap-tan* 'from the book', but *kitab-i* 'his/her book'. Word-final *r*-devoicing occurs in the Kashgar dialect, for example, *bir* [biR] 'one'.

Uyghur has nine phonemic vowels, which may be grouped according to the features of backness and rounding.

No phonemic long vowels exist in the Turkic vocabulary of

modern Uyghur. In colloquial speech, however, consonant loss between sonorants in some Turkic words causes compensatory lengthening of a vowel: *körmidim* 'I didn't see (it)' [kö:midim], *muʔallim* 'teacher' [ma:llim]. The original vowel length of some Arabic and PERSIAN loanwords is sometimes preserved in Uyghur as phonemic: *dunya* [dunja:] 'world'.

Table 2: Vowels

	Front		Back	
	Unround	Round	Unround	Round
High	i	ü	ï	u
Mid	e	ö		o
Low	ä		a	

Uyghur suffixes have a number of harmonic variants: suffix vowels are specified for height and sometimes rounding, and their backness is determined by the preceeding element: *orun-da* place-LOC 'in place, on the seat', *öy-dä* home-LOC 'at home'. Velar and uvular consonants in suffixes show backness harmony (see Dative -GA in Basic Morphology below).

Rounding harmony in Uyghur is weaker than in many other Turkic languages. It occurs consistently in stems, but many suffixes do not have rounded allophones. The third-person possessive suffix, rounded in many Turkic languages, such as Turkish *göz-ü* 'her/his/its eye', is unrounded in Uyghur: *köz-i*. Rounding harmony occurs consistently in Uyghur suffixes with epenthetic (inserted) vowels, denoted here by °: as in the first-person possessive suffix -°*m*: *ata-m* 'my father', *qïz-ïm* 'my daughter', *dost-um* 'my friend'. Rounding harmony of epenthetic vowels is not reflected in the orthography: *dost+°m* is written as *dostim*. Otherwise, rounding and backness harmony are consistently represented in the orthography.

Uyghur's most unique phonological phenomena are undoubtedly vowel raising and vowel devoicing. In the former, unstressed *a* and *ä* are raised to *i* (or *ï*) in open syllables: *bala* 'child' + *-lAr* → *balïlar* 'children', *apa* 'mother', + *-(s) i* → *apisi* 'his/her/its mother'; in the latter, short high vowels are devoiced between voiceless consonants, often with spirantization: *i̥t* 'dog'.

Arabic and Persian loanwords with long vowels do not undergo this vowel-raising rule: /dunya/ [dunya:] 'world', /dunya + -(s)i/ [dunya:si] 'his/her world', not *dunyisi.

Uyghur strongly tends toward a CV(C) syllable structure. If a Uyghur stem has a nonpermissible syllable-final consonant cluster, a high vowel is inserted, which undergoes vowel harmony: *fikr-* 'idea' acc. *fikri*, nom. *fikir*. Certain other clusters in syllable-final position are broken up in speech by epenthesis or deletion: *xalq* 'the people' [xalïq], *dost* 'friend' [dos]. *l* and *r* are commonly deleted before obstruents, even across syllable boundaries (*er.zan* > [e:zan] 'cheap, inexpensive'). In colloquial speech, *r* and consonant clusters, common in loanwords, are disallowed in word-initial position; such segments are preceded by an epenthetic high vowel: *(i)radiyo* 'radio', *ayropilan* 'airplane'.

Stress generally falls on the last syllable and usually coincides with high pitch as in *bardí* 's/he went'. Some suffixed morphemes, however, are unstressed. In words containing such morphemes, stress is shifted onto the immediately preceding syllable: '*kắlmidi* 'did not come'. Borrowings with preserved long vowels bear primary or secondary stress: *asá:sij* (<*Ab. asāsī*) 'fundamental, basic', but *šärqíj* (<*Ab. šarqī*) 'east.'

Basic Morphology

Uyghur is an agglutinative language with suffixing morphology. It has one productive prefixing process, however, in which adverbs and adjectives are partially repeated (reduplicated) for an intensive effect: *qïzïl* 'red', *qïp-qïzïl* 'totally red'. Nouns are not distinguished by grammatical gender, nor are they accompanied by articles. Definiteness is indicated by the suffixation of the accusative *-ni* or by the use of a demonstrative pronoun: *u kitab-ni äwätti* (she/he book-ACC sent) 'she/he sent the book(s)', *u kitab äwätti* 'she/he sent a book(s)'.

Nouns are pluralized with the suffix *-lar/lär* as in *qïzlar* 'girls', *közlär* 'eyes', although the plural suffix is never used with numerals: *ikki kitab* 'two books' (not **ikki kitablar*).

The Uyghur case suffixes are as follows, with harmonic variants shown in parentheses:

Nom.	[zero suffix]	Bu yaxši adäm 'This is a good person.'
Gen.	-ning	Bu at mening. 'This horse is mine.'
Loc.	-DA(-da/ta/dä/tä)	Kitab ustäldä. 'The book is on the table.'
Acc.	-ni	Kitabni bering! 'Give me the book!'
Dat.('to')	-GA (-ğa/qa/gä/kä)	Män bazarğa bardim. 'I went to the market.'
Abl. ('from')	-Din (-din/tin)	Män bazardin keldim. 'I came from the market.'

Other more abstract case functions are expressed by postpositions, such as *keyin* 'after' (... *körgändin keyin*) 'after seeing...'; *toğrisida* 'according to' *uning gepi toğrisida* 'according to his/her words...'.

Personal and possessive pronouns have distinct familiar and polite forms for the second-person singular.

Uyghur verbs consist of a verb stem, a tense/aspect suffix, and person/number marking for the subject (which is derived from the personal pronouns). Uyghur distinguishes only two main tense forms, past and present-future. However, the past tense subdivides into definite and indefinite forms. The definite past form *-di-* corresponds to the ENGLISH simple past: *bardi* 'he went'. The indefinite (or experiential) past suffix *-GAn-* expresses an action at an unspecified time in the past: *bar-ğan* 'he went (at some time)'.

Most Turkic languages rigorously distinguish between reported information ("I heard that ...") and events witnessed by the speaker. Uyghur uses the copula *ikän* or the compound past suffix *-ptu* for this purpose: *u muʔallim ikän* 'I hear s/he's a teacher'; *u ürümčigä qaytiptu* 'I hear s/he's gone back to Urumchi'. It also has an indefinite past suffix *-GAn*.

In addition, Uyghur has a number of compound tenses, including the past perfect, the pluperfect, the habitual past, and the intentional. Conditional and imperative moods are expressed by means of suffixes; aspect is generally expressed by verb compounding.

Basic Syntax

Uyghur is syntactically very similar to other Turkic languages. It has a head-final constituent order, SOV. Thus the order of elements in a noun phrase is Demonstrative-Numeral-Adjective-Noun, and the head of a relative clause follows the relative: *äwätkän kitab* 'the book that (I) sent'.

Uyghur has a system of some 23 auxiliary verbs that express aspect (the manner in which an action is carried out). These auxiliaries are independent verbs that, when used with a main verb, lose their original meaning and express some aspect of the action. For example, the independent verb *čiq-* 'to emerge' expresses thoroughness when used as an auxiliary. The main verb takes a participial suffix *-ºp* and is followed by a conjugated aspect auxiliary:

u kitab-ni kör-üp čiq-ti
s/he book-ACC read-ºp CHIQ-p.t.
'S/he read the book from cover to cover'; cf.

u kitab-ni kör-di
s/he book-ACC read-p.t.
'S/he read the book.'

The Uyghur aspectual system is less developed than that of other Turkic languages, although grammaticization of aspect auxiliaries is more common in Uyghur than in KAZAKH and Uzbek. In Uyghur, several aspect auxiliaries have been reanalyzed as suffixes for main verbs (original forms shown in parentheses):

-iwat- 'do continuously' (< -ºp yat- 'lie')
-iwät- 'do suddenly' (< -ºp ät 'do')
-iwal- 'do for oneself' (< -ºp al- 'take')
-iwär- 'do as a benefit to others; do without interruption' (< -ºp bär 'give')

In interrogative utterances with question words (*nimä* 'what?' *qačan* 'when?'), the question word is usually sentence-initial (*nimä oquysiz?* 'What are you reading?'). But in copular sentences (see Example Sentence 1), or for emphasis, the question word is sentence final. Yes/no questions (see Example Sentence 3) are formed with the sentence-final particle *mu*. There are three main types of sentential negation. Negative copular sentences are formed with the sentence-final negated copula *ämäs*. Negative existential sentences are formed with the sentence-final word *yoq* (*umit yoq* 'There is no hope'). Verbs are negated morphologically with the suffix *-ma/mä* (*bar* 'go' + *mA* + PAST *-dI* + pers.suff. *-ºm* > *barmidim* 'I didn't go').

Contact with Other Languages

Since Eastern Turkistan has always been one of the major crossroads of Central Asia, the Uyghurs have had constant intercourse with speakers of other languages. Up to the ninth century, the ancient Uyghurs jostled for territory with other Turkic speakers and with Mongols. Later, settled firmly in the Tarim basin, the medieval Uyghurs had considerable contact with speakers of the Indo-European languages of the Tarim basin, whom they eventually absorbed. As Persian and Arabic merchants and mullahs traveled along the "Silk Road" through Eastern Turkistan to China, the lexicon of Islam spread eastwards. With the gradual adoption of Islam throughout the region, Persian and Arabic vocabulary enriched the Uyghur language. These loanwords were not confined merely to religious vocabulary, but also included many abstract philosophical terms. Today, approximately 20 percent of the vocabulary is from Persian and Arabic.

As powers great and small vied for control over the region through the centuries, the Uyghurs came into contact with speakers of other Turkic languages such as Kirghiz and Kazakh; traces of this contact can be seen in the phonology and lexicon of the eastern dialects today as in Qomul Uyghur *jigit* 'young guy', cf. Kazakh *jigit*, Standard Uyghur *yigit*. The Chinese presence in the area has waxed and waned with the Chinese dynasties, but the number of Chinese speakers there has increased dramatically since the 1950s. Contact with RUSSIAN speakers began early in this century and peaked in the 1950s with a great influx of Soviet advisors to Xinjiang. Hence, there is a large number of technical and administrative loanwords from Russian.

Since the mid-20th century the most intense and prolonged language contact has been with Chinese. Chinese neologisms have entered the Uyghur language at a great rate, particularly in the 1960s when the Chinese state required Uyghur to use Chinese scientific terminology. Since 1980, however, the Language and Script Committee has abandoned cumbersome Chinese terms in favor of international (via Russian) technical terms, such as *hidrogen* 'hydrogen'. Where possible, Turkic-language equivalents have been introduced, with varying success: Uyghur *temur yol* 'railroad' (cf. Chinese *tié-lù* [iron-road] 'id.') is in widespread use, while many Uyghurs use the Chinese *bīngxiāng* 'refrigerator' more frequently than the Uyghur neologism *tonglatğu* 'id'.

From Persian: *göš* 'meat', *bazar* 'market', *tawuz* 'watermelon'
From Arabic: *kitab* 'book', *siyasi* 'political', *adäm* 'person'
From Russian: *poyuz* 'train', *yanwar* 'January', *banka* 'bank'
From Chinese: *baysay* 'cabbage', *tongla-* (Ch. *dōng*) 'to freeze'

Common Words

man:	är	long:	uzun
woman:	ayal	small:	kičik
water:	su	yes:	hä'ä
sun:	kün, quyaš	no:	yaq
three:	üč	good:	yaxši
fish:	beliq	bird:	quš
big:	čong	dog:	it (pronounced *išt*)
tree:	däräx		

Example Sentences

(1) Ism-ingiz nimä? — Ism-im Bahargül.
name-2SG.POSS what name-1SG.POSS Bahargül.
'What's your name?' — 'My name's Bahargül.'

(2) Män apa-m-ğa xät yez-iwat-imän.
I mother-1SG.POSS-DAT letter write-PROG-1SG
'I'm writing my mother a letter.'

(3) Tursun oquğuchi mu? — Yaq, Tursun oquğuchi ämäs.
Tursun student INTERR — No, Tursun student not.be
'Is Tursun a student?' — 'No, he is not a student.'

Efforts to Preserve, Protect, and Promote the Language

Since 1954 the 'Minority Language and Script Work Committee' (*Til-yeziq xizmiti komiteti*) has been responsible for language standardization and implementation of government orthography policy. The committee has published spelling and pronouncing dictionaries that illustrate standard usage of the Arabic-based script. There are Uyghur-language newspapers, magazines, books, and television and radio shows. Uyghur is the official local language of Xinjiang; as such, government documents are required to be in both Uyghur and Chinese.

Schooling is available in Uyghur from preschool through the university level. Nonetheless, there are fewer Uyghur-language schools than Chinese-language schools, and competency in Chinese is required in tertiary institutions.

While institutional encouragement of Uyghur-language maintenance is rather tepid, Uyghur families provide strong and consistent support for language preservation. Most families take particular care to raise their children within the Uyghur language and culture. In Kazakhstan, where the Uyghur population is much smaller, there are, nonetheless, a handful of Uyghur schools; books are published in Uyghur, and a division of the Academy of Science in Almaty is devoted to Uyghur research.

Select Bibliography

Golden, Peter B. 1992. *An Introduction to the History of the Turkic Peoples.* Wiesbaden: Otto Harrassowitz.

Hahn, Reinhard F. 1989. *Modern Uyghur.* Seattle: University of Washington Press.

Ibrahim, Ablahat. 1995. *Usage and Meaning of Compound Verbs in Uighur and Uzbek.* Ph.D. dissertation, University of Washington.

Schwarz, Henry G. 1992. *An Uyghur-English Dictionary.* Bellingham: Western Washington University Press.

Uzbek

Lars Johanson

Language Name: Uzbek. **Alternate:** *Özbek*. **Autonym:** *Ȯzbek tili, ȯzbekčȧ*.

Location: Spoken primarily in the Republic of Uzbekistan, but also in parts of Tajikistan, northern Afghanistan, Kyrgyzstan, Kazakhstan, Turkmenistan, and China (Xinjiang).

Family: Southeastern (Chaghatay) branch of the Turkic family.

Related Languages: UYGHUR.

Dialects: Uzbek has numerous rather different dialects mirroring the complicated ethnic composition of the Uzbek nation. The dominant group of dialects goes back to varieties of the settled population in the oases of Samarkand, Bukhara, Tashkent, and the Fergana Valley, which have been heavily influenced by TAJIK (neo-PERSIAN) elements. Uzbek dialects of the Kipchak type (related to KAZAKH) have a weak status today. So-called Oghuz Uzbek dialects are spoken in Khwarezm and adjacent areas of Karakalpakistan and Turkmenistan.

Number of Speakers: Over 18 million.

Origin and History

The composition of the modern Uzbek nation is the result of highly complicated ethnic processes. First, there is an old settled population that has been living for a millennium in close symbiosis with originally Iranian elements and has assimilated them linguistically. Other groups go back to Turkic tribes that have remained nomadic or seminomadic up to modern times, both descendants of an older Turkic population of the area and descendants of the Kipchak tribes that moved into Transoxania in the 16th century and have been politically dominant ever since.

Orthography and Basic Phonology

Chaghatay, the literary predecessor of Uzbek, was written in ARABIC script. For Standard Uzbek, a Roman-based alphabet was applied from 1927 until the introduction of a Cyrillic-based script in 1938. The transition to a new Roman-based alphabet enacted by law in 1993 has so far been rather hesitant. The new script essentially represents a transliteration of the Cyrillic spelling.

Modern spelling applies a system of six vowel signs that does not reflect the distinctions between back and slightly front vowels, for example, the pairs /u/ versus /u̇/ and /o/ versus /ȯ/ are homographic. (The dot over the vowel signs in our transcription is used here and in Table 1 below to represent the slightly front character of the vowels in question.) The labialized /ɒ/ is written with the sign *o*. Some Cyrillic letters, such as ц and щ, only occur in RUSSIAN loanwords. No separate symbols for [ts] and [šč] exist in the new Roman-based alphabet.

The back and front consonants /q/ versus /k/ and /ɣ/ versus /g/ have phoneme status in Uzbek (see Table 2 on the next page). In some varieties, /l/ has a backed variant [ɫ] in back syllables and a fronted variant [l] in front syllables. Voiceless stops are mostly aspirated. A nonphonemic glottal stop [ʻ] occurs in front of initial vowels. The labials /f/ and /v/ are labio-dental.

Table 1: Uzbek Alphabet

Cyrillic-based	Roman-based	Value	Cyrillic-based	Roman-based	Value	Cyrillic-based	Roman-based	Value
Аа	Aa	a [ȧ, a]	Кк	Kk	k	Хх	Xx	x
Бб	Bb	b	Лл	Ll	l	Цц	Cc	c
Вв	Vv	w, v	Мм	Mm	m	Чч	Ch,ch	č
Гг	Gg	g	Нн	Nn	n	Шш	Sh, sh	š
Дд	Dd	d	Оо	Oo	å	Ээ	Ee	e
Ее	Ee	e, ye	Пп	Pp	p	Юю		yu, yu̇
Ёё		yå	Рр	Rr	r	Яя		ya [yȧ, ya]
Жж	Jj	ǰ	Сс	Ss	s	Ўў	Oʻoʻ	o,ȯ
Зз	Zz	z	Тт	Tt	t	Ққ	Qq	q
Ии	İi	i [i, ï]	Уу	Uu	u, u̇	Ғғ	Gʻgʻ	ɣ
Йй	Yy	y	Фф	Ff	f	Ҳҳ	Hh	h

Table 2: Consonants

	Labial	Dental/ Alveolar	Alveo-palatal	Front Velar	Back Velar	Glottal
Stops	p b	t d		k g	q	
Fricative	f (v)	s z	š (ž)		x ɣ	h
Affricate			č ǰ			
Nasal	m	n			ŋ	
Liquid		l r				
Glide	w		y			

The velar /ŋ/ is often produced with a following *g* sound, as in *köŋ*[g]*il* 'heart'.

The basic Turkic phonological system assigns the features front versus back to primary stems. Because of Tajik influence, the manifestations of sound harmony in whole word forms are less straightforward than in most other Turkic languages. Suffixes are very often invariable, their vowels (*i, ȧ, å*) not assimilating to the frontness-backness or the roundedness-unroundedness of the preceding vowels, for example, *yol-imiz-dȧ* 'in our road' (compare to TURKISH *yol-umuz-da*).

Devoicing of word-final consonants and suffix-initial consonants after voiceless consonants is usually not reflected in the orthography, as in ишда *iš-tȧ* 'at work'. Certain bisyllabic stems lose the high vowel of their final syllable when a suffix with an initial vowel is added, as in *burun* 'nose' versus *burnim* 'my nose'. In loanwords, high epenthetic vowels are inserted to dissolve nonpermissible consonant clusters, for example, *fik*[i]*r* 'thought' (written фикр) < Arabic *fikr* (but *fikr-im* 'my thought').

A number of stems display final weak obstruents that are voiced before suffix-initial vowels, as in *ešig-i* 'its door' versus *ešik* 'door'. Strong obstruents are not subject to this alternation, as in *yük-i* 'its burden' versus *yük* 'burden'.

As a rule, a pitch accent falls on the last syllable of words of Turkic origin.

Table 3: Vowels

	Front		Central	Back	
	Unrounded	Rounded		Less Rounded	More Rounded
High		u̇	i		
Mid	e	ȯ			o
Low			a	å	

The phonetic realizations of the vowels vary greatly, in particular the qualities of /a/ and /i/. The distinctions between back and front vowels have been largely preserved, for example, /u/ versus /u̇/ and /o/ versus /ȯ/ in *bol-* 'become, be' versus *bȯl-* 'divide' and *uč* 'end' versus *u̇č* 'three'. The phonemes /u̇/ and /ȯ/ tend toward a somewhat lowered and retracted pronunciation. The variants of /å/ are more or less labialized: [ɒ], [ɑ]. The two central phonemes /i/ and /a/ mostly occur as front [i] and [ȧ], but may also have backed variants [ï] and [a], for example, when adjacent to back-velar consonants. High unrounded vowels are lowered in open syllables, and reduced or lost in closed syllables before certain consonants, as in [b[i]r] 'one', [kʃɪ] 'man'.

Vowel length is not distinctive, but found at a subphonemic level. Long vowels appears in pronunciation of Arabic and Persian loanwords.

Basic Morphology

Uzbek is an agglutinative language with suffixing morphology. Nouns and adjectives are formed from verbal and nominal stems by means of various derivational suffixes, for example, *tuy-ɣu* 'feeling' (*tuy-* 'to feel'), *tuz-li* 'salty' (*tuz* 'salt'). Nouns take the plural suffix *-lȧr*, possessive suffixes such as *-(i)m* 'my', *-(i)ŋ* 'your', and case suffixes: genitive *-niŋ*, accusative *-ni*, dative ('to') *-(G)ȧ*, locative ('in', 'at', 'on') *-Dȧ*, ablative ('from') *-Dȧn*. (Capital letters indicate variation.) Example: *yol-dåš-lȧr-im-dȧn* (road-DERIVATION-PLURAL-POSSESSIVE 1 P. SG.-ABLATIVE) 'from my companions' (*yol-dåš* < 'fellow traveller', sharing the same road). In spite of the dominant suffixing morphology, the strong Iranian influence on Uzbek has led to the emergence of prefixes, as in *nåtoɣri* 'untrue' (with *nå-* 'non-' copied from Tajik plus native Turkic *toɣri* 'right').

Secondary verbal stems are formed from verbal and nominal stems by means of various suffixes. Deverbal suffixes include reflexive, passive, causative, cooperative, frequentative and other elements, for example, *yuw-in-* 'to wash oneself', *yuw-il-* 'to be washed', *yuw-dir-* 'to let wash', *yuw-in-tir-il-* 'to be caused to wash oneself' (*yuw-* 'to wash'). Verbal negation is expressed with the suffix *-mȧ*, as in *yåz-mȧ-* 'not to write'. Finite and infinite verb forms consist of a simple or expanded lexical stem plus aspect/mood/tense suffixes and often person and number suffixes, such as *iš-lȧ-måq-dȧ-lȧr* (work-DERIVATION-INFINITIVE-LOCATIVE-PLURAL) 'they are working'. There is a wide variety of simple and compound aspect/mood/tense forms, as well as numerous converbs and participles. Like other Turkic languages, Uzbek has evidential categories of the type *yåz-gȧn ekȧn* 'has obviously written'. A number of auxiliary verbs ("postverbs") express modifications of actionality, such as the manner in which an action is carried out, as in *ku̇l-ib yu̇bår-* (laugh-CONVERB send) 'burst out laughing'.

Uzbek has numerous postpositions, functionally corresponding to ENGLISH prepositions, as in *u̇ygȧ tåmån* (house-DATIVE side) 'towards the house'.

Basic Syntax

Uzbek is syntactically very similar to other Turkic languages. It has a head-final constituent order, SOV: *Qiz men-gȧ bir kitåb ber-d-i* (girl I-DAT one book give-PAST.3.P.SG). The order of elements in a nominal phrase is Demonstrative-Numeral-Adjective-Noun. As in other Turkic languages, possessor complements take genitive markers, as in *qiz-niŋ yüz-i* (girl-GEN face-POSS.3.P.SG) 'the girl's face'. The head of a relative clause follows the relative, as in *yåz-gan xat-im* (write-PART letter-POSS.1.P.SG) 'the letter I wrote'. Conjunctions and other functional words copied from Persian and Arabic (via Persian) are frequently used, as in *ki* (preceding complement and relative clauses), *gȯyå* 'as if'.

The particle *ėmȧs* is used to negate nominals but may also be used with verbal predicates for contrastive purposes. The existential particle *bȧr* 'existing' has a negative counterpart, *yoq*.

The enclitic *-mi* follows predicates to form polar (yes/no) questions. It precedes the copular suffix of nominal predicates, but follows the copula of verbal predicates.

Contact with Other Languages

Long-standing intensive contacts with Tajik have resulted in numerous copied Iranian features in phonology, morphology, lexicon, and syntax. Examples of loanwords:

From Arabic: *mümkin* 'possible', *nihåyȧt* 'at last', *quwwȧt* 'strength'
From Persian (Tajik): *gȯšt* 'meat', *låy* 'mud', *pȧrdȧ* 'curtain', *nån* 'bread'
From Russian: *plan* 'plan', *stul* 'chair', *stakan* 'tumbler, glass'

Common Words

man:	erkȧk	water:	suw
woman:	ȧyål	sun:	quyåš
three:	üč	fish:	baliq
big:	kȧttȧ	long:	uzun
small:	kičkinȧ	yes:	hȧ
no:	yoq	good	yaxši
bird:	quš	dog:	it
tree:	dȧrȧxt		

Example Sentences

(1) Håzir kel-gȧn qiz kim?
now come-PART girl who
'Who is the girl that arrived now?'

(2) Bu ǰåy boš-mi?
this place free-Q
'Is this place free?'

(3) Iš-ni tu̇gȧt-ib u̇y-gȧ ket-d-im.
work-ACC finish-CONVERB house-DAT go-PAST-1P.SG.
'I finished the work and went home.'

Efforts to Preserve, Protect, and Promote the Language

Uzbek is one of the most firmly established languages in the Turkic world and subject to systematic language-planning measures.

Select Bibliography

Boeschoten, Hendrik. 1998. "Uzbek." In Johanson and Csató. 1998. 357–378.

Johanson, L. and É. Á. Csató, eds. 1998. *The Turkic Languages*. London and New York: Routledge.

Raun, A. 1969. *Basic Course in Uzbek*. Bloomington: Indiana University and The Hague: Mouton.

Sjoberg, A.F. 1963. *Uzbek Structural Grammar*. Bloomington: Indiana University and The Hague: Mouton.

Waterson, N. 1980. *Uzbek-English Dictionary*. Oxford: Oxford University Press.

VIETNAMESE

Nguyễn Đình–Hoà

Language Name: Vietnamese. **Autonym:** *Việt-ngữ* [spoken]*; Việt-văn* [written]; or simply *tiếng Việt.*

Location: Vietnam, parts of Kampuchea (Cambodia), Thailand, and Laos; also overseas communities in the United States, Hong Kong, England, Germany, France, Pacific Islands, Canada, and Australia.

Family: Muong-Vietnamese subgroup of the Mon-Khmer subfamily of the Austro-Asiatic language family.

Related languages: Mường, KHMER, Mon, and other Mon-Khmer languages of Indochina; SANTALI, Ho, and other Munda languages of India; and groups of minor languages scattered throughout Southeast Asia.

Dialects: (1) Northern (Hanoi), (2) Central (Huê), and (3) Southern (Ho Chi Minh City [formerly Saigon]). The Vietnamese language of today is a continuum of regional dialects from north to south. Dialects spoken in the major urban centers of Hanoi, Huê, and Ho Chi Minh City represent rather special forms marked by the influence of more educated and cosmopolitan speakers. The Hanoi dialect has served as the basis for the literary language since the 11th century and carries the greatest social prestige.

This chapter's discussion of the basic structure and elements of the language is based upon the Hanoi dialect.

Number of Speakers: About 67 million; of this number, about 65 million live in Vietnam.

Origin and History

Vietnamese is the easternmost and largest of the approximately 150 languages of the Austro-Asiatic family. These modern-day descendants of the ancestral Austro-Asiatic language are currently distributed in an inland arc extending from Central India around the Bay of Bengal into Myanmar (Burma), Thailand, Laos, and Vietnam, then southward through Kampuchea (Cambodia) to the Malay Peninsula of Malaysia and westward to the Nicobar Islands northwest of the Indonesian island of Sumatra.

By 200 B.C. a community with an early but distinctive Vietnamese identity had developed in the Red River delta area of Nam Viet, an independent kingdom ranging between southern China to the north and the contemporary Vietnamese city of Da Nang to the south. From this early period until modern times, the language of these people has evolved through five identifiable phases: Proto-Vietnamese, Sino-Vietnamese, Ancient Vietnamese, Middle Vietnamese, and Modern Vietnamese.

Proto-Vietnamese persisted several centuries after the conquest of Nam Viet in 111 B.C. by the more powerful Chinese from the north. During this period, spoken Proto-Vietnamese, like its cousin Mon-Khmer languages, is believed to have been a nontonal language; that is, it did not rely upon differences of tone to distinguish the meanings of words or language structure.

The annexation of Nam Viet into China began a millennium of Chinese political and cultural domination over the region. During this period, a system of writing was introduced to the Vietnamese people for the first time in the form of the script of Chinese characters. Chinese terminology and pronunciation replaced and augmented extensive portions of the indigenous Vietnamese vocabulary, especially in administrative, technical, literary, and philosophical areas. By the 6th century, the language had entered the transition to its second phase, **Sino-Vietnamese**, as three tonal distinctions developed in the spoken language. In time, the Chinese contributions to the lexicon began to acquire a distinctive Vietnamese articulation. As this process stabilized in the 11th century, Buddhist scholar priests began developing a localized version of the written script called *chữ nôm*, 'southern characters'. Many characters of *chữ nôm* were composites of the original Chinese characters, with one component representing the character's meaning and a second added either to refine its meaning or more often to suggest its Vietnamese pronunciation. The three tonal distinctions of the spoken language expanded to six in the 12th century.

Literary works written in the *chữ nôm* script between the 14th and 17th centuries reveal that the language had evolved to its third phase. This stage of the language is documented in the 16th century Chinese-Vietnamese glossary, *Hua-yi Yi-yu.*

European traders and missionaries entered Vietnam in significant numbers in the 17th century. During this time, Catholic priests, including Alexandre de Rhodes, a French Jesuit, devised for the language a remarkable orthography based on the Roman alphabet. For the first time in world history, this alphabet, named *quốc ngữ* 'national script', systematically represented distinctions of tone. Rhodes's *Dictionarium Annamiticum-Lusitanum-et-Latinum*, published in 1651, presents the language in its fourth, or **Middle Vietnamese** phase.

Modern Vietnamese, which began in the 19th century, is characterized by the loss of the Middle Vietnamese consonant clusters *bl, tl, ml,* and *mnh*, which simplified to either *l* or *tr*. The French colonial government officially sanctioned the use of the *quốc ngữ* orthography in 1910.

Orthography and Basic Phonology

Quốc ngữ, often called chữ phổ-thông 'standard script', serves as the medium of written instruction at all three levels of schooling. Vietnamese was the first and remains one of the relatively

Table 1: Consonants

		Labial	Dental	Retroflex	Palatal	Velar	Glottal
Stops	Voiceless	p	t	tr	ch	c/k/q	
	Voiceless aspirated			th			
	Voiced	b	đ				
Fricatives	Voiceless	ph	x		s	kh	h
	Voiced	v	d	r	gi	g/gh	
Nasals		m	n		nh	ng/ngh	
Lateral			l				
Glides		o/u			y/i		

few Asian languages whose writing system is based on the LATIN alphabet. Diacritic marks are used to distinguish between certain phonemes, such as *e* vs. *ê*, and to indicate tone.

C, *k*, and *q* represent variant spellings of /k/; *k* is used before front vowels, *q* before *u* (in the cluster /kw/), and *c* elsewhere. Likewise, the voiced velar fricative /ɣ/ is spelled *gh* before front vowels and *g* before back vowels, and the velar nasal /ŋ/ is spelled *ngh* before front vowels and *ng* before back vowels.

Initial *p* occurs only in loanwords from FRENCH and ENGLISH. In the Hanoi dialect, both *s* and *x* are pronounced /s/; in other dialects, however, *x* is /s/ and *s* is /š/. Plain *d* represents /z/, and the D stop /d/. In Hanoi, *gi* and *r* are also pronounced /z/.

Table 2: Vowels

	Front	Central	Back	
			Unrounded	Rounded
High	i/y		ư	u
High-Mid	ê		ơ	ô
Low-Mid	e		â	o
Low		ă a		

Ă represents the short central vowel /a/. The hooked ("whiskered") vowels *ư* and *ơ* represent the back unrounded vowels /ɯ/ and /ɤ/, respectively.

Vietnamese has six tones, which serve to differentiate meaning:

Tone	Example	Gloss
level	*ma*	'ghost'
rising	*má*	'cheek; Mom'
falling	*mà*	'but'
dipping-rising	*mả*	'tomb, grave'
creaky	*mã*	'horse'
constricted	*mạ*	'rice seedling'

In syllables closed by a voiceless stop (one of /p t k/), only rising or falling tone can occur.

Basic Morphology

Vietnamese nouns and verbs are not inflected. Such categories as number, gender, case, and tense are expressed by means of function words and word order.

Nominal categories are reflected in counting expressions; depending on the nature and shape of the objects being counted, one or another classifier/counter-word will be used: *hai con gà* (two ANIMAL.CLASSIFIER chicken) 'two chickens', *hai cái bàn* (two THING.CLASSIFIER/table) 'two tables', *hai cuốn sách* (two roll book) 'two books', *hai cây nến* (two tree candle) 'two candles'. Some classifiers have independent meaning, while others do not.

Terms of relationship are used as personal pronouns. For example, the pair *bố-con* 'father-child' defines two participants in a conversation. *Bố* would be used by the father to refer to himself and by the child in addressing the father; thus it functions as the equivalent either to English 'I' or to English 'you'. Likewise, *con* is used by the child to refer to him- or herself and by the father addressing the child. Other such pairs include *mẹ-con* 'mother-child', *ông-cháu* 'grandfather-grandchild', and *bà-cháu* 'grandmother-grandchild'.

The pronominal use of kinship terms illustrated above is distinguished from a demonstrative use by tone: *anh* means 'you, my older brother', while *ảnh* means 'that elder brother'.

Reduplication, both partial and complete, plays an important role in Vietnamese derivational morphology. Among other functions, reduplication may express iteration or diminution:

năm-năm 'year after year' (< *năm* 'year')
to-to 'rather large' (< *to* 'large')
xanh-xanh 'bluish' (< *xanh* 'blue')
gầy-gầy 'skinny' (< *gầy* 'slim, slender')

Names of insects and fruits also show reduplicative patterns: *cào-cào* 'grasshopper', *chuồn-chuồn* 'dragonfly', *bươm-bướm* 'butterfly', and *chôm-chôm* 'rambutan fruit'.

Basic Syntax

The basic word order in Vietnamese is SVO: *X đi Sàigòn hôm-qua* (X go Saigon day) 'X went to Saigon yesterday', *Hôm-nay X đi ô-tô* (day-this X go car) 'Today X goes by car'.

Within noun phrases, most modifiers follow the nouns they modify numbers precede nouns: *tất-cả tám ngôi nhà gạch mà chú tôi tậu năm ngoái đó* (all eight throne house brick which uncle I buy year past those) 'all those eight brick houses which my uncle bought last year'.

The negatives *không* 'not' and *chưa* 'not yet' precede the main verb: *Tôi không đói* (I not hungry) 'I'm not hungry'.

Vietnamese has several final particles that convey the speaker's attitude, assumptions, and presumptions: *Anh đói không?* (you hungry not) 'Are you hungry (or not)?', *Anh đói chưa?* (you hungry not.yet) 'Are you hungry yet?', *Anh đói rồi chưa?* (you hungry already I.presume) 'You are hungry, I presume', *Tôi thổi cơm nhé!* (I cook rice shall.I) 'I will cook some rice, shall I?', *Ừ, anh thổi cơm đi!* (Yes you cook rice go.ahead) 'Yes, go ahead and cook some rice', *Cơm ngon quá nhỉ!* (rice tasty very right) 'The food is very tasty, don't you agree?'

Contact with Other Languages

During the period of French colonization of Vietnam in the 19th and 20th centuries, sustained contact occurred between French newcomers who could speak but a few words of the Vietnamese language, and Vietnamese who knew little French. Under these conditions a French-Vietnamese pidgin called *Tây bồi* developed for use as a limited vehicle of communication. After the French withdrawal from Vietnam, this pidgin gradually faded from use. Similarly, an English-Vietnamese pidgin arose in the south during the American presence there in the 1960s and 1970s, but it, too, has become obsolete.

Some Vietnamese who grew up under French rule became fully bilingual. The generations of 1945 and afterward, for whom French ceased to be the medium of instruction, have favored English as a second language, especially in the south. French remains the language of preference in diplomatic and political contexts. Chinese script continues to be taught as a classical language for studies in Eastern humanities.

From French: *phó-mát* 'cheese', *vét-tông* 'jacket', *xà-phòng* 'soap'
From English: *pích-ních* 'picnic'

Common Words

man:	đàn ông	small:	nhỏ
woman:	đàn bà	yes:	có
water:	nước	no:	không
sun:	mặt trời; nắng	good:	tốt
three:	ba	bird:	chim
fish:	cá	dog:	chó
big:	lớn	tree:	cây
long:	dài		

Example Sentences

(1) Con chó của ông Nam cắn thằng Tý.
animal dog property grandfather Nam bit boy Ty
'Mr. Nam's dog bit little Ty.'

(2) Gia-đình chúng tôi xin có lời chúc-mừng quý-vị được hưởng mọi điều tốt-lành.
house-court group I beg have words wish-congratulate distinguished-position get enjoy every thing good-auspicious
'Our family wish you all the best.'

(3) Ở nhà không có gì làm nên Chị ấy thường đi làm công-quả ở Chùa.
At.house not have anything do so older sister that often go do public-merit at Buddhist.temple
'At home she does not have anything to do, so she often goes to the Buddhist temple to do volunteer work.'

Efforts to Preserve, Protect, and Promote the Language

After gaining independence from France in 1945, Vietnam conducted a lengthy national campaign to spread literacy to workers and farmers. As the majority language, Vietnamese has gradually become the medium of instruction in schools at all levels, and it is the favored language of intercommunication by ethnic minorities.

The press has blossomed since World War II, and Vietnam can boast of a vigorous explosion of newspapers, magazines, learned journals, and technical reviews covering all disciplines.

Government initiatives have aimed at standardizing the language in regard to pronunciation, spelling, grammar, and terminology. Teachers of language, literature, and other subjects have cooperated with linguists, journalists, and translators working at universities, as well as the Institute of Linguistics (established in 1969) and the Linguistic Society of Vietnam (established in 1989). Both monolingual and bilingual dictionaries have been published, as well as technical glossaries and dictionaries in the natural and social sciences.

Select Bibliography

Emeneau, M.B. 1951. *Studies in Vietnamese (Annamese) Grammar*. Berkeley and Los Angeles: University of California Press.

Nguyễn, Đình-Hoà. 1966a. *Read Vietnamese*. Rutland, VT: Charles E. Tuttle.

____. 1966b. *Speak Vietnamese*. Rutland, VT: Charles E. Tuttle.

____.1974. *Colloquial Vietnamese*. Carbondale: Southern Illinois University Press.

____. 1980. *Language in Vietnamese Society*. Carbondale, IL: Asia Books.

____. 1995. *Vietnamese-English Dictionary*. Lincolnwood, IL: National Textbook Co.

____. 1997. *Vietnamese*. Amsterdam: John Benjamins Publishing Co. [London Oriental and African Language Library].

Ruhlen, Merritt. 1987. *A Guide to the World's Languages, Vol. 1: Classification*. Stanford: Stanford University Press, 148–158, 295, 334–337.

Thompson, Lawrence. (1965) 1987. *A Vietnamese Reference Grammar*. Honolulu: University of Hawaii Press.

WARAY WARAY

Carl Rubino

Language Name: Waráy-Waráy (or Waráy). Waray Waray is the common name of the language, although many speakers also refer to it as *Bisaya* or *Binisaya*, not distinguishing it from the dozens of other Visayan languages and dialects. The toponyms *Samar-Leyte* and *Lineyte-Samarnon* have also been used, reflecting the geographic location of the language. When referring to the dialects of the language, the terms *Samarnon (Samareño)* and *Leytehanon* are also employed.

Location: Waray is the native language of the people from the islands of Samar, Biliran, and northeast Leyte, Philippines.

Family: Central Bisayan branch of the Bisayan subgroup of the Central Philippine subgroup of the Philippine group of the Western Malayo-Polynesian branch of the Malayo-Polynesian subfamily of the Austronesian language family.

Related Languages: Waray Waray is most closely related to the Central Visayan languages: Sorsogon BIKOL, HILIGAYNON, and Romblomanon. Other closely related Visayan languages include Tausug, CEBUANO, Banton, Aklanon, Kinaray-a, and Kuyonon.

Dialects: There are several dialects of Waray Waray, often referred to by their place-name. The dialects of Northern Samar are the most conservative, maintaining [s] where other dialects have innovated [h]. Vowel length in the verb prefix paradigm (table shown in Basic Morphology) for the Northern Samar dialect is absent except in the active potentive form *náka-*. Zorc (1975) identifies the following three major dialects: Samar-Leyte spoken in Central Samar and the northern half of Leyte, Waray spoken in southern and eastern Samar, and the Northern Samar dialect.

Number of Speakers: 3 million.

Origin and History

The Westerners' first contact with Waray peoples was on March 31, 1521, when Magellan found the Leyte gateway. Very little is known about pre–Hispanic Waray history, but linguistic, ethnographic, and archeological evidence help to classify the Warays as the easternmost extension of the Visayan peoples (see Cebuano, Hiligaynon), a relatively homogeneous group inhabiting the central Philippine Islands named after the great Sumatran empire of *Sri Vijaya*.

Warays today are predominantly Roman Catholic, many practicing with a blend of pre-Hispanic animistic elements. They are the most culturally conservative of the Visayans.

Orthography and Basic Phonology

Roman script is used based on the TAGALOG system, which employs 20 letters: A B D E G H I K L M N NG O P R S T U W Y. Word-final glottal stop is rendered with a grave accent.

Waray Waray has the following contrastive consonant sounds (shown in Table 1 by their orthographic symbols). Stops are unaspirated, and unreleased in final position, and the voiceless velar stop (*k*) often fricates between vowels.

Waray Waray has three native vowel phonemes /i, a, u/, and two phonemes /o, e/ acquiring contrastive status after contact with SPANISH. Due to phrase-final high vowel lowering, word final /u/ is often written /o/ and /e/, respectively. Diphthongs include *aw*, *iw*, *ay*, and *uy*. Vowel sequences (except old spelling forms *ia*, *io*, *ua*) are produced as two syllables with an intervening glottal stop, e.g., *laon* 'original Waray deity' > [la.'on].

Table 1: Consonants

		Bilabial	Dental/ Alveolar	Alveo-palatal	Velar	Glottal
Stops	Voiceless	p	t	(ch/ ti+V)	k (qu)	',(-)
	Voiced	b	d	(dy, di+V)	g	
Fricatives			s			h
Nasals		m	n		ng	
Laterals			l			
Trill/Flap			r			
Glides		w		y		

Table 2: Vowels

	Front	Mid	Back
High	i (i, e) e		u (u, o) o
Low		a	

Basic Morphology

Waray Waray is a head-marking, agglutinating language with a complex morphological system of productive derivational and inflectional affixes.

Verbs in Waray Waray derive focus/voice (see ILOCANO) and inflect for aspect (perfectivity vs. imperfectivity). Waray Waray dialects have 72 categories of verbal inflection/derivation en-

Table 3: Waray Waray Verbal Affixes *

Aspect	Imperfective			Perfective		
Tense → VOICE ↓	Actual	Contingent	Aorist	Actual	Contingent	Aorist
Active punctual durative potentive	ná: nagCV:- nakáka-/ náka-	má: magCV:- makáka-/ máka-	CV:- pagCV:- pakáka-	{i(m)n} nag- naka-	{um} mag- maka-	0- pag- paka-
Instrument punctual durative potentive	iCinV:- iginCV:- nahíhi-/ ikinaCV- nahaCV:-	iCV:- igCV:- mahíhi-/ ikaCV:-/ mahaCV:-	iCV:- +CV --an igCV:- maCV--an/ ikaCV:-/ mahaCV:-	i- {in} igin- nahi-/ ikina-/ naha-	i- ig- mahi-/ ika-/ maha-/	i- -an ig- +ma--an ika- maha-
Pat/Goal punctual durative potentive	CinV- ginCV:- naCV:-	CV:--en pagCV:--en maCV--en	CV:--a pagCV:--a kaCV:--i	{in} gin- na-	-en pag--en ma--en	-a pag--a ka-
Local punctual durative potentive	CinV:--an ginCV:--an naCV:--an	CV:--an pagCV:--an maCV:--an	CV:--i pagCV:--an kaCV:--i	{in}-an gin--an na--an	-an pag--an ma--an	-i pag--i ka--i
USES:	present progressive future	future	with future preverbs	past, perfect	infinitive, polite commands	commands, with past preverb

*Accent or : denotes vowel length.

coded by 83 affixes as shown in Table 3 above (modified from Zorc 1975: 149). The three verb tenses in Waray can be summed up as follows. Actual tense endings reflect progressive actions in the imperfective aspect and past reference in the perfective. Contingent tense is used for future actions in the imperfective, and dependent actions in the perfective. Aorist verbs are used as subjunctives. They get their temporal reference from preverbs or other time clauses. The perfective aorist (past subjunctive) forms can be used in imperatives: *palit-á an pangasi* (buy-AORIST ART rice.wine) 'Buy the rice wine!'

The infix *-Vr-* is used with verbs to express plural actors or repeated action; from the root *bagtas* 'walk' one may say: *Nag-b{ar}ágtas hirá* (PERF-walk{PL} 3p) 'They walked and walked.' Mutual actions can be expressed with the secondary prefix *ka-*: *Nag-ka-dúrug kami* (PERF-MUTUAL-sleep 1p.EXCL) 'We slept together'.

The article system in Waray Waray dialects differs between the three main dialects. In all dialects, the articles inflect for three cases (topic, genitive, and oblique) and definiteness, but the Northern Samar dialect has lost the past/nonpast distinction with the definite articles.

Tagpíra	it	mangga?
how.much	NONPAST	mango

'How much are mangos?

Tagpíra	an	mangga?
how.much	PAST	mango

'How much were (the) mangos?

Articles also distinguish personal (names) vs. common nouns and personal articles inflect for number, which is shown in Table 4 on the next page (Zorc 1975: 107).

Demonstratives inflect for all three cases and encode four degrees of distance: near the speaker *adi(n)*, near the speaker and addressee *ini(n)*, near the addressee or not too far *itu(n)*, and far away from both speaker and addressee *adtu(n)*.

Pronouns also inflect for all three cases. They do not distinguish gender (*hiyá* = s/he, *hirá* = they) but make a distinction in the second person for singular (*ikáw*) vs. plural (polite) (*kamú*), and in the first-person plural there is an inclusive/exclusive distinction: *kitá* ('I/we and you'), *kamí* ('we not you').

Waray adjectives may be pluralized by adding [g] after the first vowel: *haráni* 'near' > *hagráni* 'near, pl'; *dakò* 'big' > *dagkò* 'big, pl'.

Basic Syntax

Waray Waray is a predicate-initial language. Nominals may appear in predicate position where they are contrastive or identificational.

Hini-higugmà	ko	ikáw.
PAT.FOC-love	1SGEN	2STOP

'I love you.'

Table 4: Waray Articles

	TOPIC			GENITIVE			OBLIQUE
PERSONAL singular plural	*si* (*hi* E. Samar) *sirá* (*hirá* E. Samar)			*ni* *níra* (*nirá* N. Samar)			*kan* *kánda*
COMMON	indef.	definite		indef.	definite		
		past	non-past		past	non-past	future
E. Samar	*in*	*an*	*it*	*hin*	*han*	*hit*	*ha*
Sam-Leyte	*in*	*an*	*it*	*sin*	*san*	*sit*	*sa*
N. Samar	*i*	*a*		*si(n)*	*sa(n)*		*sa*

Like other Philippine languages, Waray Waray has a focus system in that the semantic relationship between the topic (pivotal) argument and the verb is reflected in the morphology of the verb. Agents of actor focus verbs appear as "topics" (a term used in Philippine linguistics to describe the argument that is least marked morphologically and most syntactically privileged, previously referred to as the nominal in the nominative case). Agents of nonactor focus verbs appear in the genitive (GEN) case, as the nonactor argument of these verbs becomes the topic. The topic arguments below are underlined.

Actor focus (AF, topic nominal (TOP) is an actor in an action or process):

Mahinay lumakat an daraga.
slow walk.AF TOP lady
'The lady walks slowly.'

Theme focus (TF, topic is an instrument, conveyed object or benefactor):

Iginiíhaw han babayi hin manúk an batà.
kill.PROG.IF GEN girl INDEF chicken TOP child
'The girl is killing a chicken for the child.'

Patient/goal focus (PF/GF, topic is a goal or affected patient):

Giníhaw níra an manúk pára ha íyo.
killed.PF 3pGEN TOP chicken for OBL 2SOBL
'They killed the chicken for you.'

Local focus (LF, topic is a place or locus of action):

Pinagiháwan han daraga hin manók an kusinà.
killed.LF GEN lady INDEF chicken TOP kitchen
'The lady killed a chicken in the kitchen.'

There are three negators in Waray: negation of existence and possession are expressed with the negative existential particle *waráy*, as are negative past statements; negative commands are expressed with *ayáw*; and *dirì* is used to negate nonpast statements.

Waráy kamí inóm didto.
NEG we.EXCL drink here
'We didn't drink here.'

Ayáw pagdakpa an alibangbang.
NEG catch TOP butterfly
'Don't catch the butterfly.'

Dirì nahisasakót an tubig ha lana.
NEG mix TOP water and oil
'Water and oil don't mix.'

Existence and possession expressed with existential (EXIST) particles, *may* 'positive existential' and *waráy* 'negative existential': *Waráy lubí dínhi.* (NEG.EXIST coconut here) 'There are no coconuts here'; *Waráy hiyá lubí* (NEG.EXIST 3STOP coconut) 'He doesn't have a coconut'.

Contact with Other Languages

Spanish loans include the days of the week and months of the year, and words like *telepono* 'telephone', *sugal* 'play cards, gamble', *bintanà* 'window', *padí* 'godfather', *tíyu* 'uncle', *pára* 'for', *kusinà* 'kitchen', *basu* 'glass', and *purtáhan* 'door'. Spanish is no longer used in Waray communities.

ENGLISH, as the language of education, business, and the government, is the primary source of new words, e.g., *aysbaks* 'icebox', *dyip* 'jeep', *kompyuter* 'computer', and *haiskul* 'high school'.

Most Waray Waray speakers are proficient in Tagalog, the national language of the Philippines, and may borrow Tagalog words and expressions in their speech.

Common Words

man:	lalaki	woman:	babáyi
tree:	káhoy	water:	tubig
sun:	adlaw	three:	tuló
fish:	isdà	long:	halabà
good:	maópay	yes:	oo
no:	dirí	big:	dakò
small:	gutì	bird:	támsi
dog:	ayam		

Example Sentences

(1) Pagka-barú níya, na-lípay hiyá.
NML-know 3SGEN ADJ-happy 3STOP
'He was happy when he found out.'

(2) May pakla ba hi Weni?
EXIST frog QUES PA Weni
'Does Weni have a frog?'

(3) Makadto ako ha Tacloban buwás.
go 1s OBL Tacloban tomorrow
'I'll go to Tacloban tomorrow.'

(4) Maupay nga patron ha iyo ngatanan.
good LINK fiesta OBL 2p all
'Happy fiesta (Patron Saint's Day) to all of you!'

Efforts to Preserve, Protect, and Promote the Language

Although Waray Waray ranks among the top eight languages of the Philippines, there has been very little done in the way of propagating the language through literature or the media. No works of literature have been produced prior to the 1900s during the early American period of occupation, and nothing substantial is being produced in Waray to this day.

Norberto Romualdez was the first accomplished writer in Waray, staging his first play, *An Pagtabang ni San Miguel* 'The Assistance of St. Michael', in 1899 at the age of 24. In 1908 he produced a Bisayan Grammar, and organized the *Sanghiran san Binisaya* 'Bisayan Language Academy' the following year. The academy is no longer active.

Select Bibliography

Cruikshank. 1985. *Samar: 1768-1898*. Manila: Historical Conservation Society.

Luangco, Gregorio, ed. 1982. *Kandabao: Essays of Waray Language, Literature and Culture*. Tacloban City: Divine Word University Publications.

Tantuico, Francisco S., Jr. 1964. *Leyte: The Historic Islands*. Tacloban City, Philippines: Leyte Publishing Corporation.

Tramp, George Dewey, Jr. 1995. *Waray Dictionary*. Kensington, MD: Dunwoody Press.

Wolff, John U., and Ida O. Wolff. 1967. *Beginning Waray*. Cebu City.

Zorc, R. David Paul. 1975. "The Bisayan Dialects of the Philippines: Subgrouping and Reconstruction." PhD Dissertation, Cornell University.

Angela Terrill

Language Name: Warlpiri.

Location: The area associated with the Warlpiri language extends over a large area of the desert region of the central west of the Northern Territory of Australia, including much of the Tanami Desert. Warlpiri is the main language of the regional centers at Lajamanu, Willowra and Yuendumu, and there are also sizeable Warlpiri-speaking communities in Alice Springs and Tennant Creek.

Family: Warlpiri belongs to the Yapa subgroup of the Pama-Nyungan family of Australian languages. The Yapa subgroup is named for the words for "person" in all three languages; the subgroup is also known as the Ngarrga subgroup.

Related Languages: The most closely related languages to Warlpiri are the two other members of the Yapa subgroup, Warlmanpa and Ngardi. Similarities between Warlpiri, Ngardi and Warlmanpa are such that some have suggested they are in fact dialects of one language, although later views suggest that they are better considered separate, albeit closely related, languages. Other closely related languages include Mudbura, Gurindji, Djaru and Walmajarri.

Dialects: There are four geographically based dialects; names for these dialects differ, but Steve Swartz's online dictionary names them Lajamanu, Yurntumu, Wirliyajarrayi, and Alekerenge (Wakirti). There are only a handful of lexical differences between the dialects. It is possible that differences between the dialects were greater in the past, but today, social, political and educational factors have encouraged linguistic unity in the Warlpiri language.

Number of speakers: 3,000–4,000 speakers.

Origin and History

As far as the Warlpiri people are concerned, their ancestors have always been in the same area the people now call Warlpiri country. Probably the first European seen by Warlpiri people was the explorer J.M. Stuart, who traveled through Warlpiri territory on a voyage to cross Australia from south to north in the early 1860s. His journey was shortly afterwards followed by the arrival of workers on the construction of the Overland Telegraph Line, which reached north to Darwin in the 1870s.

The Warlpiri people traditionally lived a hunter-gatherer lifestyle. The nature of the desert terrain in which they lived meant that population density was very low, and clans hunted over a large area depending on the seasonal availability of game and plant foods. The Warlpiri people have long had close relations with the Gurindji and Mudbura groups to their north, and were involved in complex trading and ceremonial interchanges between many other groups. The Warlpiri, along with other Australian Aboriginal groups, have a very complex classificatory kinship system, with everybody in the society divided into 1 of 16 groups. The relationships between the groups determined not only marriage possibilities, but every relationship within the society. Belonging to a particular group, or "skin", determines a person's access to inherited land, rituals and stories. The skin names are shown in Diagram 1.

In Diagram 1, skin names beginning with *j* refer to males; skin names beginning with *n* refer to females. The equals signs represent ideal marriage partners in the system. Lines link father-child pairs. Thus the skin name of every individual is determined by the skins of that individual's parents.

Diagram 1: Skin Names

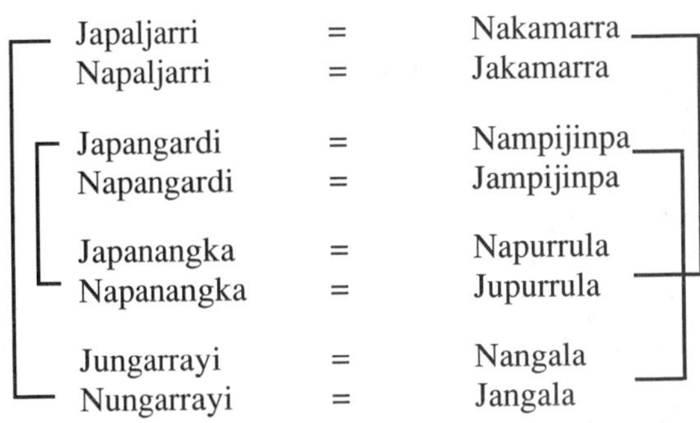

There is an "avoidance" style of language, used when a speaker is in the presence of certain proscribed relatives. The language style is called *Yikirrinyi*, and consists of about 80 special words, which are substituted for normal words when in the presence of certain relatives. There is also a secret language used for mens' initiation, which cannot be described in print.

There is also a well-documented Warlpiri sign language, used mainly as a bereavement language by women when their spouse, child or son-in-law dies. The sign language is used instead of speech, and can be the sole means of communication for a woman for over a year after the death of a spouse.

Orthography and Basic Phonology

The Warlpiri phonemic system, using the standard Warlpiri orthography, is presented on the following page.

Table 1: Consonants

	Bilabial	Apico-alveolar	Retro-flex	Lamino-alveolar	Dorso-velar
Stops	p	t	rt	j	k
Nasals	m	n	rn	ny	ng
Laterals		l	rl	ly	
Flaps		rr	rd		
Glides	w		r	y	

Vowels:

i u

a

There is a length distinction in each of the three vowels. Long vowels are relatively infrequent, and usually occur in the first syllable of noun and preverb roots. They are written /ii/, /aa/ and /uu/.

Warlpiri has a system of vowel harmony. There are two basic rules: one of regressive assimilation and one of progressive assimilation. Under regressive assimilation, a final /i/ of a verb stem assimilates to a /u/ in a verb suffix. Thus (all examples and analysis in this section are from Nash 1986, especially pp. 65–99): *pangi-rni* 'dig-NPast'; *pangi-ka* 'dig-IMPER'; *pangu-rnu* 'dig-Past'.

The assimilation applies to both vowels of a verb stem, if both are /i/: *kiji-rni* 'throw-NPast'; *kuju-rnu* 'throw-Past'. But the assimilation is blocked by an intervening /a/ vowel: *yirra-rni* 'put-NPast'; *yirra-rnu* 'put-Past'.

Under progressive assimilation, /u/ vowels in suffixes assimilate in quality to an /i/ vowel of a stem. In the following examples, the high vowels of the suffixes are underlyingly /u/: *kurdu-kurlu-lku-ju-lu* child-PROP-ERG-then-me-they; *maliki-kirli-lki-ji-li* dog-PROP-ERG-then-me-they.

As with the previous assimilation, this assimilation is blocked by an intervening /a/ vowel: *maliki-kirli-kirra-lku-ju-lu* dog-PROPrietive-ALLative-then-me-they. Some consonants, particularly /p/ and /w/, seem to block this assimilation: *ngamirni-puraji* mother's brother-your.

Primary stress appears on the first syllable of a word.

Basic Morphology

Warlpiri has an ergative/absolutive system of case marking for its nominals, and has a number of oblique cases. All case marking is indicated by suffixes on nouns and dependents. The suffixes are:

Ergative	*-ngku/-rlu*
Locative	*-ngka/-rla*
Dative	*-ku*
Allative	*-kurra*
Towards	*-purda* (only with certain nominals)
Elative	*-ngurlu*
Origin	*-jangka*
Source	*-warnu*
Perlative	*-wana*

Other nominal inflections include proprietive *-parnta*, *-kurlu*; privative *-wangu*; similar to *-piya*; dual *-jarra*, collective plural *-patu*.

Tense/Aspect/Mood suffixes attach to verbs. Their forms vary according to five conjugation classes. The forms are:

Table 2: Tense/Aspect/Mood

Conjugation Class	Non-Past	Past	Present	Immediate Future	Imperative
1	ø, -mi	-ja	-nya	-ju, -ji	-ya (-ka)
2	-rni	-rnu	-rninya	-ku	-ka
3	-nyi	-ngu	-nganya	-ngku	-ngka
4	-rni	-rnu	-rninya	-lku	-nja
5	-ni	-nu	-nanya	-nku	-nta

Other inflections include irrealis (formed with the imperative suffix plus *-rla*); infinitive (formed with the nonpast suffix plus *-nja*, or just *-nja*, depending on the conjugation class of the verb); inceptive (formed with the infinitive suffix, or the infinitive suffix plus *-nji*, or the infinitive suffix with final *i* instead of *a*, depending on the conjugation class of the verb); and the progressive, formed with the Inceptive plus *-na*. There are directional enclitics hither *-rni*, by *-mpa* and thither *-rra*.

Basic Syntax

Warlpiri has been much discussed in the literature as a non-configurational language. Apart from the fact that the auxiliary must always be the first or second element in the clause, order of all other elements is not syntactically fixed, but rather any element can occur anywhere in a sentence.

Warlpiri only has about 125 simple verbs, but it has a productive strategy of combining simple verbs with preverbs, which are uninflecting adverbial-like words that precede simple verbs to produce complex meanings. There are two kinds of preverbs: those that occur freely with any simple verb, and those that only occur with a small number of simple verbs, or only one. Some examples of preverbs in sentences:

Pirlangkiti-ji	jurnta-kuju-rnu	yarda.
blanket-me	away-throw-PAST	again

'He threw off my blanket again.' (Nash 1986: 49)

Ngapa	wiri-ngki-nganpa	pina	lani-ma-ni
rain	big-ERG-us	back	afraid-CAUS-NPAST

wirlinyi-kijaku
hunting-NEGPURP
'The big rain will deter us from hunting.' (Nash 1982: 180)

Auxiliaries carry pronominal cross-referencing clitics, and also carry information about Tense, Aspect and Mood. Auxiliaries are always the second word of a sentence. The auxiliary bases are as follows:

kapu, kapi, ngarra	Future
kalaka	Admonitive
kula	Negative
kaji	If, When
kuja, ngula	Relative
yungu, yinga	Causal
ka	Present
lpa	Imperfect
kala	Usitative
kaji-ka	Potential
kuja-ka	Present Presentational

Bound pronominal clitics operate under a nominative/accusative system. The forms are presented in the tables below.

Table 3: Subject (S/A) Clitics

	Singular	Dual	Plural
1 Inclusive	*rna*	*rli*	*rlipa*
1 Exclusive		*rlijarra*	*rnalu*
2	*r(pa)*	*n(pa)pala*	*nkulu*
3	*ø*	*pala*	*lu*

Table 4: Object (O) Clitics

	Singular	Dual	Plural
1 Inclusive	*ju*	*ngali(ngki)*	*ngalpa*
1 Exclusive		*jarrangku*	*nganpa*
2	*ngku*	*ngkupala*	*nyarra*
3	*ø, rla*	*palangu*	*jana*

Auxiliaries also carry the reflexive clitic *-nyanu*, and the dative clitic *-jinta*. The basic order of pronominal clitics is Subject-Object, although there are various rather complicated ordering rules with particular combinations of suffixes.

Contact with Other Languages

Warlpiri has long been surrounded by other closely related members of the Pama-Nyungan family of languages. Warlpiri and its neighbors have been in a stable situation of contact for some time, and borrowing of lexical items and grammatical morphemes has long been a feature of the languages. This is a feature of many Australian languages, so much so that, in synchronic studies of Australian languages, it is often extremely difficult to separate loans from inherited features.

Warlpiri has also borrowed from ENGLISH in more recent times, both in terms of lexical items and grammatical morphemes. Thus recent borrowings from English include common items such as *pulawa* 'flour' and *jati* 'shirt'. Words of English origin may be suffixed with Warlpiri morphology e.g., verbs if intransitive receive the inchoative bound verb, and transitive verbs receive the causative bound verb, thus creating well-formed Warlpiri verbs, which may then receive further morphology: for example, *grow-jarrimi* 'grow-INCH' and *hold-mani* 'hold-CAUS'.

Common Words

man:	ngarrka	small:	wita
woman:	karnta	yes:	yuwayi
water:	ngapa	no:	lawa
sun:	wanta	good:	ngurrju
three:	jirrama-kari-jinta	bird:	jurlpu
fish:	yawu	dog:	maliki
big:	wiri	tree:	watiya
long:	kirrirdi		

Example Sentences

(1) Kuyu ka-rlipa paka-rninja ya-ni.
meat PRES-we.pl.incl kill-INF go-PAST
'We are going along killing game.' (Nash 1986: 44)

(2) Wurulypa-rli ya-ni.
seclusion-we go-NPAST
'Let's go and hide.' (Nash 1986: 52)

(3) Japiya muku ka-lu panu-ngku nga-rni.
big all PRES-they many-ERG eat-NPAST
'Many of them are eating a whole lot.' (Nash 1986: 54)

Efforts to Preserve, Protect, and Promote the Language

Warlpiri is one of the healthiest indigenous Australian languages, and certainly one of the most studied. There has been a Bilingual Education Program in Warlpiri since 1974, first based at Yuendumu, and subsequently extended to Willowra, Lajamanu and Nyirrpi. This program has published many primers and reading materials, and a monthly newsletter, *Junga Yimi*. The Warlpiri Media Association produces radio, TV and video programs in Warlpiri. The Warlpiri Lexicography Group, involving Ken Hale, Mary Laughren and others, has been working for over 20 years on a comprehensive dictionary of Warlpiri, and has disseminated many work-in-progress versions of the dictionary over the years.

Select Bibliography

Hale, Kenneth. 1983. "Warlpiri and the grammar of non-configurational languages." In *Natural Language and Linguistic Theory* 1: 5–47.

Hale, Kenneth L., Mary Laughren, and Jane Simpson. 1995. *Warlpiri*. Joachim Jacobs (ed) Syntax: Ein Internationales Handbuch zeitgnössischer Forschung. Berlin: Walter de Gruyter. pp. 1430–1451.

Jagst, Lothar. 1973. "Ngardilpa phonology." In *Papers in Australian Linguistics 8*. Canberra: Pacific Linguistics. pp. 21–57.

Nash, David. 1986. *Topics in Warlpiri Grammar*. New York: Garland.

Simpson, J.H. 1991. *Warlpiri Morpho-Sntax: A Lexicalist Approach*. Dordrecht: Kluwer.

Warlpiri Links. http://www.anu.edu.au/linguistics/nash/aust/wlp/.

WELSH

Nicholas Kibre

Language Name: Welsh. **Autonym:** *Cymraeg*, /kəmráig/.

Location: Principally Wales in the United Kingdom. Welsh speakers constitute a large portion and in some areas a majority of the population in north and mid-Wales. Speakers are just as numerous but much more thinly spread in the more densely populated urban south. Small numbers of speakers also live in communities in Argentina.

Family: Welsh is a member of the Celtic branch of the Indo-European family.

Related Languages: The closest relatives to Welsh are Cornish (now extinct) and Breton. The three languages make up the Brythonic or British subgroup of Celtic, although Cornish and Breton are more similar to each other than either is to Welsh. More distantly related languages are IRISH and Scots Gaelic and long-vanished continental relatives such as Gaulish.

Dialects: A significant isogloss near the Dyfi River divides Wales into north and south dialect regions, each of which contains numerous local varieties. Dialect differences are not an extreme impediment to communication, although this may in part be due to Welsh-language media and education having a standardizing effect on the language.

Although much of modern written Welsh is reasonably close to the spoken language, a literary variety quite far removed from it was the medium of virtually all published writing into the 20th century, and register-based variation remains significant.

Number of Speakers: A 1991 census reported roughly half a million speakers in Wales. Unknown numbers of speakers live in other parts of the United Kingdom, but are not generally part of Welsh-speaking communities. The number of speakers in Argentina is probably not more than several thousand.

Origin and History

The emergence of Welsh and its siblings from British Celtic is identified with the Anglo-Saxon settlement of Britain, which separated their speakers into distinct communities, roughly A.D. 450–600. Written examples of Welsh exist from the 8th or 9th century onward. Significant recorded literature is attested beginning in the 12th century, although the earliest texts probably record much older oral traditions. Modern Literary Welsh dates from the 15th century. Adherence to this standard has left little record of the spoken language's subsequent evolution until the relatively recent acceptance of modern Colloquial Welsh as a written language.

Orthography and Basic Phonology

Welsh is written with the Roman alphabet, but native words do not use *j, k, q, v, x*, or *z*.

Consonants. The consonants of Welsh are listed in Table 2 on the next page.

The sounds marked * have an ambiguous status. In native words alveo-palatals might be analyzed as palatalized allophones of alveolars, but their use in many entrenched borrowings forces them into the status of phonemes. On the other hand *z* is a completely foreign sound that many speakers replace with *s*.

Dorsal sounds are velar, except that the voiceless fricative is /χ/ in North Welsh. Rhotic consonants are usually alveolar flaps or trills, but retroflex and uvular types are found in some areas.

Vowels. Table 1 lists the North Welsh vowel system, which is simplified in South Welsh by the merger of /ɨ, ɨ:/ into /ɪ, i:/.

Table 1: Vowels

	Front	Mid	Back
High	i [ɪ/i:]	y/u [ɨ/ɨ:]	w [ʊ/u:]
Mid	e [ɛ/e:]	y [ə]	o [ɔ/o:]
Low		a [a/a:]	

The letter *y* represents [ə] except in ultima syllables of open-class words, where [ə] does not occur; in this environment (regardless of stress) *y* represents the same vowel as the letter *u*.

All vowels except [ə] have distinctive length, but in native words length is often constrained by context (dialects vary, but stress, position in word, and following consonants play a role). In environments where both short and long vowels are possible, circumflex accents are used to indicate long vowels.

In most dialects diphthongs end exclusively in high vowels. The inventory of diphthongs in North Welsh is:

ei [ei], ai [ai], oi [oi]
ey/eu [eɨ], au [aɨ], ae [a:ɨ], oe [oɨ], wy [uɨ]
iw [iu], ew [eu], aw [au], ow [ow], yw [ɨw/əw], uw [ɨw]

This is reduced considerably in South Welsh by the loss of /ɨ/, and loss of the length distinction in *au* vs. *ae*. In all dialects many diphthongs are reduced to simple vowels.

Syllable Structure and Phonotactics. The maximal syllable is CCCVCC. Onset and coda clusters generally have their more sonorous members closest to the vowel. Exceptions to sonority sequencing in initial clusters include *s*-stop clusters, *gwl-*,

Table 2: Consonants

	Voi	Labial	Dental	Alveolar	Lateral	Palatal	Dorsal	Glottal
Stops/	-	p		t		tsi/ch*	c [k]	
Affricates	+	b		d		d/j*	g	
Fricatives	-	ff/ph [f]	th [θ]	s	ll [ɬ]	si/sh* [ʃ]	ch [x/χ]	h
	+	f [v]	dd [ð]	z*				
Nasals	+	m		n			ng [ŋ]	
	-	mh		nh			ngh [ŋh]	
Glides	+	w		r, rh	l	i [j]		

gwr-, *wl-*, and *wr-*. In coda position, northern dialects tolerate voiced obstruent-sonorant clusters such as in the words *cwbl* 'whole', and *cefn* 'back', a type that South Welsh eliminates with an epenthetic vowel echoing the one preceding, thus [kúbul] and [kéven].

Further phonotactic restrictions apply at the word level. Consonants are never geminate. Voiceless sonorants and /h/ only appear in onsets of stressed or initial syllables; in this respect *ll* patterns with other fricatives, appearing freely in codas as in *allt* 'hill' and *iarll* 'earl'. Several sets of consonants almost never appear initially in native open-class words citation forms, including voiced liquids, voiceless and/or velar nasals, voiced fricatives, *th*, and *ch*, other than in the cluster *chw-*; however, these segments do appear word initially as the result of consonant mutation rules, described below.

Consonant Mutation. Open-class and some closed class words in Welsh are subject to a process known as "mutation", in which initial consonants are altered from their citation forms. Mutation is usually triggered by a preceding grammatical particle; the type of mutation, if any, associated with a particle is an opaque phonological feature that cannot be determined from its phonemic content. Mutation is also applied without any triggering particle in some syntactic contexts.

There are three main classes of mutation, traditionally termed "lenition", "aspiration", and "nasalization". Lenition causes voicing of voiceless stops, elides *g*, turns oral voiced stops and *m* into oral voiced fricatives, and turns *ll* and *rh* into *l* and *r*. Aspiration turns voiceless stops into voiceless fricatives. Nasalization turns oral stops into nasals, with the voiceless/voiced feature preserved except in dialects that lack voiceless nasals. The chart below gives examples of the three mutation types, triggered by the possessive pronouns *ei* 'his' (lenition), *ei* 'her' (aspiration), and *fy* 'my' (nasalization), alongside *eu* 'their', which triggers no mutation. Note that these pronouns are accompanied by "copy"' pronouns in the regular postnominal position of genitive noun phrases.

	'their'	'his...'	'her...'	'my...
'father'	*eu tad nhw*	*ei dad e*	*ei thad hi*	*fy nhad i*
'clothes'	*eu dillad nhw*	*ei ddillad e*	*ei dillad hi*	*fy nillad i*
'garden'	*eu gardd nhw*	*ei ardd e*	*ei gardd hi*	*fy ngardd i*
'mother'	*eu mam nhw*	*ei fam e*	*ei mam hi*	*fy mam i*
'book'	*eu llyfr nhw*	*ei lyfr e*	*ei llyfr hi*	*fy llyfr i*

Of the three mutations, lenition is the most common and the most robust, and is for the most part the only one associated directly with certain syntactic contexts.

A fourth phonological process similar to mutation is traditionally termed "prevocalic aspiration". After certain particles, an *h* is prefixed to vowel and glide-initial words. *Ei*, 'her', in addition to triggering the aspiration mutation, has this effect, as seen in *ei hafal hi* 'her apple' and *ei hiaith hi* 'her language' from *afal* and *iaith* [jaiθ]. In northern dialects, this process is extended to nasals, so that *mam* 'mother' becomes *ei mham hi* 'her mother'; in small parts of the northwest, around Bangor and Aglesey Ynys Môn, it is further extended to words beginning with *l* and *r* (chiefly borrowings), so in the context 'her lamp', *lamp* becomes *ei lhamp hi*, (producing an aspirated *l* sound that is distinct from the lateral fricative *ll*).

Prosody. Stress is regularly in the penult of polysyllabic words, but in the ultima of a small class of exceptions.

Phonetically, an important correlate of stress is lengthening but not of the stressed vowel itself, rather of the following consonant. Intonational figures are often aligned with stressed vowels, but in penultimately stressed words the poststress ultima is sometimes just as or more intonationally prominent than the stressed syllable, and often considerably longer. The use of such patterns is not global, however, and may be a mark of emphasis.

Basic Morphology

Welsh inflection is realized principally by suffixes, although vowel shifts sometimes accompany suffixes or replace them. In some cases consonant mutation also plays an inflectional role. Where more than one feature is marked (chiefly verbs) inflection is fusional.

Nouns and Noun Phrases. Noun-phrase inflection distinguishes singular and plural number, and masculine and feminine grammatical gender.

Nouns indicate number through a variety of marking types. In most cases a plural form is derived from singular form through suffixing and/or a stem vowel shift: for example, *llong* 'ship', *mab* 'son', *ffordd* 'way' have the plurals *llongau*, *meibion*, and *ffyrdd*. Some nouns, however, have plural roots and derive singulars by the addition of a suffix *-en* (if femenine) or *-yn* (if masculine), which may also trigger a vowel change:

thus *plentyn*, 'child' and *pluen* 'feather' have the plurals *plant* and *plu*. A few nouns explicitly mark both singular and plural, as in *blodyn* 'flower' vs. *blodau* 'flowers'. Of all native number-marking strategies, suffixing *-au* for a plural is the most productive and by far the most likely to be applied to borrowings. Among the alternatives, some are associated with certain types of nouns, defined phonologically or semantically.

Dependent elements of a noun phrase indicate agreement with the number and gender of the head noun in a number of ways. Some numerals and a few adjectives take different forms with masculine singular, feminine singular, and plural nouns. The definite article *y(r)* and the numeral *un* 'one' do not reflect agreement in their own forms, but do so by causing lenition in whatever word follows if the head noun is feminine singular. Feminine singular nouns also trigger lenition of the initial word of any modifying adjective phrase. Examples of agreement through mutation are illustrated below.

	Singular Phrase	Plural Phrase
Masculine Noun *ci* 'dog'	*y ci bach*	*y cŵn bach*
Feminine Noun *cath* 'cat'	*y gath fach*	*y cathod bach*

It is interesting to note that, unlike the mutation triggered by particles such as possessive pronouns, adjectival agreement through lenition reflects grammatical structure rather than simple linear adjacency. This can be seen, for example, in the fact that multiple adjectives or adjective phrases can be affected, and in the fact that adjective phrases modifying head-initial noun+noun compounds are lenited if and only if the head noun feminine singular, regardless of the features of the immediately preceding nonhead noun:

rhaglen foreol boblogaidd 'a popular morning program' < *rhaglen* 'program' (FEM.), *boreol* 'morning-ADJ', *poblogaidd* 'popular'
yr orsaf radio fwyaf poblogaidd 'the most popular radio station' < *gorsaf* 'station' (FEM.), *radio* 'radio' (MASC.), *mwyaf* 'most', *poblogaidd* 'popular'
tŷ fferm coch 'a red farmhouse' < *tŷ* 'house' (MASC.), *fferm* 'farm' (FEM.), *coch* 'red'

Definiteness is marked by the article *y(r)*, but there is no indefinite article. The definite article is omitted in noun phrases that have dependent genitives, pronominal or lexical; *côt Rhodri* can mean either 'a' or 'the coat of Rhodri' and **y gôt Rhodri* is ungrammatical.

Verbs. The Welsh infinitive is a nominal form traditionally termed the "verb-noun". The nominal nature of this form is evident in the fact that it can be used in normal noun contexts, as in *yr hwylio* 'the sailing', and that pronominal objects take the form of genitives, as in *ei weld e* 'his seeing/seeing him'.

The verbal inflection of Literary and Colloquial Welsh differs considerably, primarily through the development of extensive periphrastic constructions in the latter and a corresponding reduction and reorganization of verbal conjugation (although the prevalence of conjugation in Literary Welsh may be stronger than was ever the case in the spoken language). Colloquial Welsh uses three conjugated tenses, future (the residue of a former present/future, sometimes still used as a present in very formal writing and fixed expressions), past, and (less robustly) conditional. On the other hand, periphrastic constructions, generally of the form Aux-Subject-(Particle)-Verb-Arguments, provide means of expressing a rich range of tense/aspect/mood distinctions, including alternatives to conjugated tenses.

Below are examples of the two types of constructions for present, past, and future:

dw i'n dysgu Cymraeg (be.1s 1s PRT learn Welsh)	'I am learning Welsh'
collod e'r arian (loose.3S.PAST 3M the money)	'he lost the money'
ddaru mi werthu hanner dwsin (PAST.AUX 1s sell half dozen)	'I sold half a dozen'
wela i chi (see.1S.FUT 1s 2p)	'I'll see you'
na i ddarllen (make.1S.FUT 1s read)	'I'm going to read'

The following illustrate additional periphrastic constructions, ranging from the highly grammaticalized perfect to types more resembling idioms:

dw i wedi neud y coffi
(be.1s 1s after make the coffee)
'I have made the coffee'

mae e heb brynu'r tocynnau
(be.3s 3m without buy the tickets)
'he has not bought the tickets'

maen nhw newydd gyrraedd
(be.3p 3p new(ly) arrive)
'they've just arrived'

w'i am dalu
(be.1s 1s about pay)
'I want to pay'

roedd e wrthi'n darllen y papur
(be.3S.PAST 3m by PRT read the paper)
'he was busy reading the paper'

Verbal conjugations have forms for all six person/number combinations, but verbal agreement is only with pronominal subjects; an inflected verb with a lexical subject takes a third person singular form regardless of the noun's actual number: thus *helpodd/*helpon y bechgyn* 'the boys helped'. All tenses have an additional impersonal inflection that takes no subject, which is attested in writing but for the most part replaced by periphrastic passives in the modern spoken language.

Pronouns and Prepositions. Pronouns distinguish the usual three persons, and singular and plural number, with a familiar/formal distinction overloaded on number for second, plus masculine vs. feminine grammatical gender for the third-person singular.

Genitive/possessive pronouns have special forms, which, as has been noted, are also used for objects of verb-nouns (often accompanied by trailing nongenitive copy-pronouns in both cases). Otherwise no case distinctions are made; some pronouns do have multiple forms, but these are selected according to local criteria that are specific to each. All pronouns also have phonologically elaborated "contrastive" forms, used for various types of contrast and emphasis, such as in *a finnau* 'me too' (vs. the simple *a fi* 'and me').

When they have pronominal objects, most core prepositions show agreement with their person and number. This inflection often takes the form of an ending reminiscent of corresponding agreement morphology in verbs, sometimes with a linker element intervening between it and the preposition root. Other prepositions are uninflected. The examples below illustrate the range of types:

am 'for/about' > *amdana i* 'for me', *amdanoch chi* 'for you'
o 'of/from' > *o(ho)non ni* 'from us', *o(ho)noch chi* 'from you'
wrth 'by' > *wrtha i* 'by me', *wrtho fe* 'by him'
gyda 'with' (uninflected) > *gyda hi* 'with her, *gyda nhw* 'with them'

A special preposition, *mo*, historically *ddim o* 'nothing of', is used for objects of negated finite verbs, as in *weles i mohonyn nhw* 'I didn't see them'.

Most simple prepositions cause mutation to the first word of a noun-phrase object; this is usually lenition, sometimes aspiration, while *yn* 'in' is one of two words that trigger nasalization. Note that, in parallel with the pattern of subject-verb agreement, prepositions never use inflected forms with non-pronominal objects. This consistency suggests that both types of inflection might best be analyzed not as agreement per se but as a morphological linker to the pronouns that follow, which is consistent with the fact that historically phonemes have sometimes shifted from endings to pronouns, as in *arna fi* 'on me' < *arnaf i*.

Basic Syntax

Welsh word order is thoroughly head initial; with a handful of exceptions, adjectives follow the nouns they modify, adpositions are exclusively prepositions, verbs precede their objects, and inflected verbs precede their subjects. At a clausal level Welsh is traditionally described as having verb-initial syntax, and while this is decidedly so for Literary Welsh, as noted earlier the prevalence of periphrastic constructions in the modern colloquial language has produced a dominant pattern of AUX-SUBJECT-(PARTICLE)-Verb-Arguments, which, even if technically still VSO, is SVO in spirit. Copular sentences have a parallel structure, "be"-SUBJECT-PARTICLE-PREDICATE.

In a number of constructions, main-clause constituents are fronted and appear before the finite verb, such as topical elements and question words; special forms of the copula are used in some of these. Complementized clauses by and large are syntactically like main clauses. Relativization is accomplished without relative pronouns; however, relative clauses can be morphosyntactically marked as such either by use of an initial relative particle, or when the relativized argument is a subject of "be" and the clause is present tense by a special relative form of the copula. Relativized core arguments are not realized, but relatived obliques can be expressed by pronouns. Examples can be found in the Example Sentences section below.

Contact with Other Languages

The Welsh vocabulary reflects contact with LATIN (as a spoken language), Irish and Old ENGLISH, while extensive contact with Middle and Modern English has had a significant impact on its lexicon and increasingly on idiom and probably grammar. Phonetic influence is also apparent in some areas, for example through the use of retroflex approximant *r*.

From Latin: *Chwefror* 'February', *ffenest* 'window', *eglwys* 'church'
From Irish: *bloneg*, 'lard/grease', *tolc* 'dent', *cerddin* 'rowan tree'
From Norse: *iarll* 'earl', *llong* 'ship', *ocr* 'usury'
From English (Old, Middle, Modern): *rhaca* 'rake', *gonest* 'honest', *bws* 'bus'

A few English words can be traced to Welsh or British Celtic, including *crag* and *coomb*/*cwm* (compare *craig* 'rock' and *cwm* valley).

Common Words

man:	gŵr, dyn
woman:	gwraig
water:	dŵr
three:	tri + aspiration (MASC.), tair (FEM.)
fish:	pysgodyn
big:	mawr
long:	hir
small:	bach, mân
yes:	ie, do (PAST), plus echo forms such as ydy '(yes it) is'
no:	nage, naddo (PAST), plus echo forms such as nag ydy 'NEG (it) is'
good:	da
bird:	aderyn
dog:	ci
tree:	coeden

Example Sentences

(1) Ond dw i 'n credu fod na le hefyd
but be.1s 1s PRT believe be there place also

i liwio...
to color
'But I also believe there's a place to add color...'

(2) Sut dych chi 'n ymateb i 'r hyn sydd yn
how be.2p 2p PRT respond to the this REL.be PRT

digwydd?
happen
'How do you respond to what's happening?'

(3) Mae ein cerrig milltir cynharaf yn dyddio o
be.3s 1P.GEN stones mile earliest PRT date from

oes y Rhufeiniaid.
age the Romans
'Our earliest milestones date from the time of the Romans.'

Efforts to Preserve, Protect, and Promote the Language

Adult Welsh speakers are almost exceptionlessly bilingual with English. In the decades for which language information is available from censuses, both a steady reduction of overall numbers of native speakers and erosion of areas in which the language dominates are evident, but also evident is a mild resurgence in areas such as urban centers where it has in the past been weakest. Today the language benefits from both a very active preservation movement and increasing institutional support in the form of Welsh-medium education, print and broadcast media. Its status must be regarded as endangered, but not hopeless, and its future cannot be predicted with certainty.

Select Bibliography

Aitchison, John, and Harold Carter. 1994. *A Geography of the Welsh Language*. Cardiff: University of Wales Press.

Ball, Martin, and Glyn Jones. 1984. *Welsh Phonology: Selected Readings*. Cardiff: University of Wales Press.

Kibre, Nicholas. 1997. *A Model of Mutation in Welsh*. Bloomington: Indiana University Linguistics Club.

_____. 1999. "Analysis of Terminal Contours in Welsh Intonation." Ph.D. Thesis, University of California, Santa Barbara.

King, Gareth. 1993. *Modern Welsh: A Comprehensive Grammar*. New York: Routledge. (Describes Colloquial Welsh)

Rouvert, Alain. 1994. *Syntax du Fallois: Principes Genesaux et Typologie*. Paris: CNRS Editions.

Thorne, David. 1993. *A Comprehensive Welsh Grammar: Gramadeg Cymraeg Cynhwysfawr*. Oxford: Blackwell. (Describes literary language.)

Williams, Briony. 1989. *Stress in Modern Welsh*. Bloomington: Indiana University Linguistics Club.

WOLAITTA

Azeb Amha

Language Name: Wolaitta. The name "Wolamo", with which both the speakers and the language were identified in the past by other speech communities, is now largely out of use.

Location: The Wolaitta area is found in Southern Ethiopia (in the North Omo Administrative Zone of the Southern Peoples, Nations and Nationalities Regional State). It is located between the Omo and the Bilate Rivers, bordering in the north the Kambatta and Hadiyya areas and in the South the Gamo and the Gofa areas. The people are mainly mixed farmers, with significant numbers of traders and craftsmen.

Family: Wolaitta belongs to the western branch of the Omotic language family, which, together with Cushitic, Semitic, Chadic, Berber and ANCIENT EGYPTIAN constitutes the Afro-Asiatic superfamily.

Related Languages and Dialects: Omotic languages are subdivided into two major branches: Eastern and Western, each with internal subdivisions (cf. Fleming 1976). Wolaitta belongs to the Ometo cluster of the western Omotic branch. It is closely related to Gamo, Gofa and Dawro (the latter is also known as Kullo), with which it shares 81 percent, 86 percent and 79 percent basic vocabulary, respectively (cf. Alemayehu Abebe 1994, and Bender (1971)). The attitude of speakers of one variety towards the other dialects fluctuates over time. Some 10 or 20 years ago, members of the four communities claimed they spoke different languages. In recent years, however, the elite of the Wolaitta, Gamo, Gofa and Dawro people conceded that they speak the same language. Indications of this shift in attitude include the publication of a collection of proverbs by the Ethiopian Language Academy in a book entitled *Wolaitta Proverbs with Amharic Translations*, edited by a team of researchers and native speakers of these dialects. In the introduction the editors write: "This language (i.e., Wolaitta) has different names because it has different dialects in different areas; that is, in the Wolaitta area it is called the Wolaitta language, in the Dawro area it is called the Dawro language; in the Gamo area it is called the Gamo or Dorze language; in the Gofa area it is called the Gofa language" (Ethiopian Language Academy 1995: 13). Thus, counting the speakers of the four lects, these authors state that the total number of Wolaitta speakers is 5.5 million. The Zone Administration in collaboration with the regional ministry of education has developed one writing system which is supposed to be used among the four groups in primary school education.

This writing system is called WOGAGODA (representing the first syllables of the four dialects). However, this effort has been met with strong resistence on the part of the common people. (See Efforts to Preserve, Protect and Promote the Language).

Despite the high rate of mutual intelligibility, the four dialects have some phonological and lexical variations. For instance, while Gamo has voiced and voiceless alveolar affricates *ts* and *dz*, Gofa and Kullo have only *ts*; Wolaitta replaced all cognate words with these affricates with *t*.

Other more distantly related languages are Basketo, Maale, Zayse and Koorete, which are spoken further south and which, together with the above four dialects, form the Ometo cluster of Omotic.

Number of Speakers: According to the 1994 national census, 1,210,235 million.

Origin and History

The original homeland of the Wolaitta people is said to be a small area known as Kindo (now the most southwestern part of the Wolaitta area). From there, they expanded their territory far toward the east and north. Tsehai Berhane Selassie (1975: 42) wrote that "The lands east of Kendo which are now settled by Wälamo were formerly inhabited by the Alaba, the Tämbaro, the Hadeya, the Kämbata (called Maräqo by the Wolamo) and by the Arussi Oromo." Until Emperor Menilek II of Shewa (central Ethiopia) invaded their country in 1894 and made it a tributary, the Wolaitta had a strong dynastic kingdom. It is also believed that the Wolaitta kingdom once had control over the independent territories of the Gamo, Gofa and Dawro people (cf. Tsehai 1975: 42).

Orthography and Basic Phonology

Early attempts to write the language were made in the 1950s and 1960s by missionaries using the Ethiopian script known as *fidäl*. Wolaitta was also one of the fifteen indigenous languages chosen for developing text books for adult literacy programs in the 1980s. The script used was also the *fidäl*. Since 1993 a modified LATIN script has been used. The change of script caused confusion for many people who participated in the earlier adult literacy programs conducted with the *fidäl* script.

Wolaitta manifests a contrast between two types of glottalized consonants, i.e., the ejective and implosive. The labial implosive is attested both in word initial and medial positions. The alveolar implosive on the other hand occurs only in word me-

Table 1: Consonants

		Labial	Dental	Alveolar	Palatal	Velar	Glottal
Stops	Voiceless	p	t		c	k	
	Voiced	b	d		j	g	
	Ejective	p'	t'		c'	k'	ʔ
	Implosive	ɓ		ɗ			
Spirants	Voiceless	ɸ	s		ʃ		h (ɦ̃)
	Voiced		z		(ʒ)		
Nasals		m	n				
Liquids	Lateral		l				
	Trill		r				
Glides		w			y		

dial position. The segments *p* and *ɸ* are free variant forms. The consonants given in brackets are rare: ʒ is attested only with ideophonic words, raising question on its phonemic status. The nasalized glottal fricative *ɦ̃* occurs only with a limited number of words: *ʔa ɦ̃a* 'corpse'. Gemination is contrastive; with the exception of *r*, all consonants occur geminated.

Vowels. Wolaitta has five short and five long vowels. Vowel length is phonemic, as the contrast between *mára* 'calf' and *maára* 'row' demonstrates. Thus, we have the following:

i, ii u,uu
e, ee o, oo
a, aa

Syllable Structure. The following syllable types are found in Wolaitta: CV, CVC, CVVC, CVV, as in *ka.ré* 'door', *bág.ga* 'half', *keet.tá* 'house', and *ʃoo.ró* 'neighbor', respectively. Gemination and consonant clusters consisting of a maximum of two consonants occur in intervocalic position. Geminate consonants and consonant clusters transcend two syllables. Morphophonemic processes include (1) vowel raising plus glide insertion when two nonidentical vowels occur in sequence, as in *geleʃʃúwa* 'the monkey (M:ACC)' from *geleʃʃó* 'monkey' plus the masculine accusative case marker *-a*; and *godar-íya* 'the hyena (M:ACC) from *godaré* 'hyena' plus the accusative suffix *-a;* (2) gemination of consonants, which occurs immediately before verbal inflectional markers (underlined), as in *kiitt-iísi* 'he sent', *kiit-iss-iísi* 'he made somebody send', *kiit-is-iss-iísi* 'he made somebody send somebody else'.

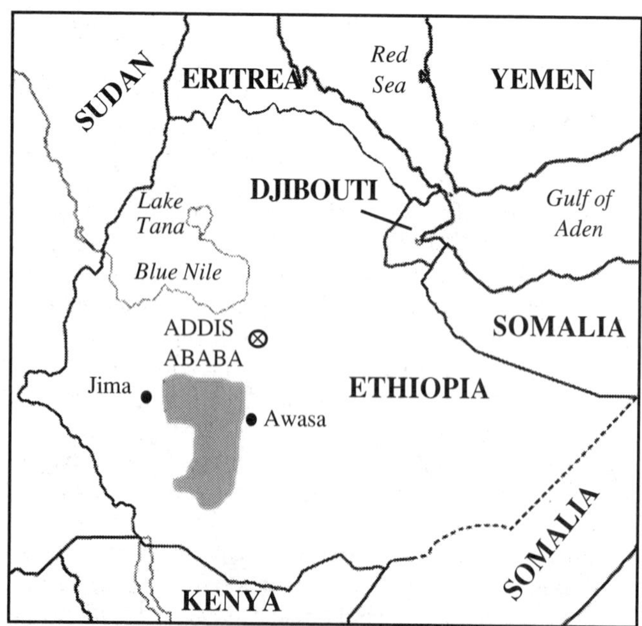

Wolaitta is spoken in southern Ethiopia (shaded area).

Tone Accent. The presence of words such as *záre* 'relative', *zaré* 'lizard'; *ʃaára* 'pregnant,' and *ʃaará* 'cloud', which are distinct only in tone, might suggest that Wolaitta is a tone language. However, the distribution of the low and high tones reveals that Wolaitta is a tone-accent language. Unlike tone languages, in Wolaitta all lexical items should have at least one high tone. The exceptions to this are the demonstratives *ha/hage* 'this', *he/hege* 'that', and possessive pronouns, such as *ta* 'my', *ne* 'your', which occur without a high tone. Otherwise, there are no simple or derived words that occur with just low tones on all tone-bearing units. Except for a few numerals and nouns, in which the high tone occurs on the antepenultimate vowel, high tone occurs either on the ultimate or penultimate vowel. Nominals with antepenultimate high tone are derived from historically complex forms. Because tone in Wolaitta is not fully predictable and since it has a significant role in differentiating various paradigms, examples are marked for tone: high tone with (´); low tone is not marked.

Basic Morphology

Wolaitta is an agglutinative language with fusional characteristics. That is, in most cases morpheme boundaries can be readily recognized. Thus, *kana-t-í* 'the dogs' can be segmented into three parts: the basic noun *kaná* 'dog', the plural marker *-t-*, and the nominative marker *-i*. In some cases, however, two or more categories can be expressed by one portmanteau morpheme, as in *kaná-y* 'the dog (M:NOM)' in which the morpheme *-y* expresses nominative case and masculine gender and contrasts with the morpheme *-a*, which marks nominative case and feminine gender. All inflectional and derivational categories are marked by suffixes; there are no prefixes in this language.

Nouns. Citation forms, i.e., uninflected and nonsegmentable nominals in Wolaitta are characterized in that they end in one of the three terminal vowels: *e*, *o*, or *a*. These vowels are often treated as noun classifiers:

e-class	*o*-class	*a*-class
mórke 'enemy'	*lóʔʔo* 'good'	*naʔá* 'child'
ʔecʻeré 'rat'	*migído*'ring'	*ʔazálla* 'lazy'

In context, the citation form of nouns is used only in nonverbal sentences and general statements. In the latter case, the final vowel of *o*- and *a*-class nouns is replaced by *-i*:

hage ʔecʻeré
this:M rat:BE 'this is a rat'

naʔi ʃemp-énna
child:NOM rest-NEG:IPF
'A child is restless/ children are restless'

Case and Gender. Morphologically, Wolaitta distinguishes nominative, accusative and genitive cases. Nominative case is marked by *-i* for masculine and by *-a* for feminine, while accusative is marked by *-a* for masculine and *-o* for feminine. Plural nouns take the same case markers as masculine singular nouns. As mentioned above, affixation of the nominative or accusative case marker may lead to a change in the vocalic quality of the terminal vowel and/or insertion of a glide consonant. For this reason, morpheme boundaries are not marked on the words in the following table (see example above for the translation of the words in Table 2). Notice in Table 2 that for *e*-class nouns the masculine accusative form is identical to the feminine nominative form.

The genitive case is marked by *-ee* in definite feminine nouns and by *-u* in plural nouns. In indefinite nouns and definite masculine nouns, the genitive and the accusative are formally identical. In all cases the possessor noun occurs before the possessed noun. Consider the form of *naʔá* 'child' and *keettá* 'house' in the following genitive constructions:

naʔá keetta	'a child's house'
naʔáa keetta	'the child's (M) house'
naʔée keetta	'the child's (F) house'
naatú keetta	'the children's house'

Along with the structural cases shown above, there are various suffixes marking semantic cases. These are, among others, the instrumental, the ablative and the dative, marked respectively by *-ra*, *-ppe*, *-yo* or *-ssi*. These morphemes are attached to a noun already marked with the genitive case. Compare the examples above with those below:

naʔá-ppe 'from a child'	*naʔá-ra* 'with a child'
naʔáá-ppe 'from the child (M)'	*naʔáá-ra* 'with the child (M)'
naʔéé-ppe 'from the child (F)'	*naʔéé-ra* 'with the child (F)'
naatú-ppe 'from the children'	*naatú-ra* 'with the children'

Number. Plural is marked by *-t-* on definite nouns. Indefinite nouns are not inflected for number. Singular is unmarked:

keettá	'house'
keetta-t-í	'the houses (NOM)'
keetta-t-á	'the houses (ACC)'
tóho	'foot'
tóho-t-i	'the feet (NOM)'
tóho-t-a	'the feet (ACC)'

Nominal Derivation. Nominal derivational suffixes include *-ta*, which derives state nouns:

lágge	'friend'	*laggé-ta*	'friendship'
siík'o	'loved one'	*siik'ó-ta*	'love'
zoré	'advice'	*zoré-ta*	'discussion'

The suffix *-tetta* can be suffixed to a noun or an adjective to derive abstract nouns, as in:

kawó	'king'	*kawó-tétta*	'kingdom'
ʃooró	'neighbor'	*ʃooró-tétta*	'neighborhood'
dúre	'rich'	*duré-tétta*	'richness'

Agent nouns are derived from verbs or nouns by affixing *-anca*, which is also used to derive "property nouns":

ʔoóso	'work'	*ʔoos-ánca*	worker'
goʃʃá	'farm'	*goʃ-ánca*	'farmer'
ʔéra	'knowledge'	*ʔer-ánca*	'wise person'
mála	'look, appearance'	*mal-ánca*	'good looking'

The suffix *-ama* derives adjectives from nouns:

wolkʻá	'power'	*wolkʻ-aáma*	'one with power'
wozaná	'heart'	*wozann-aáma*	'one with good memory, intelligent'

Table 2: Case and Gender Inflection

	Masculine Form			Feminine Form		
	class-e	class-o	class-a	class-e	class-o	class-a
Nominative	*mórkee*	*lóʔʔoy*	*naʔáy*	*mórkiya*	*lóʔʔiya*	*naʔíya*
	ʔecʻerée	*migídoy*	*ʔazállay*	*ʔacʻeríya*	*migídiya*	*ʔazálliya*
Accusative	*mórkiya*	*lóʔʔuwa*	*naʔáa*	*mórkiyo*	*lóʔʔiyo*	*naʔíyo*
	ʔecʻeríya	*migíduwa*	*ʔazállaa*	*ʔecʻeríyo*	*migídiyo*	*ʔazálliyo*

Table 3: Wolaitta Tense-Aspect and Polarity Inflection

	Affirmative			Negative	
Person	Perfective	Imperfective		Perfective	Imperfective
		PRES/HAB.	FUT.IPF		
1SG	*ʔod-aási/ʔod-ádisi*	*ʔod-áysi*	*ʔod-aná*	*ʔod-ábéyke*	*ʔod-íkke*
2SG	*ʔod-ádasa*	*ʔod-aása*	*ʔod-aná*	*ʔod-ábákká*	*ʔod-ákká*
3MS	*ʔod-iísi/ʔod-ídesi*	*ʔod-eési*	*ʔod-aná*	*ʔod-íbénná*	*ʔod-énná*
3FS	*ʔod-aásu/ʔod-ádusu*	*ʔod-áwsu*	*ʔod-aná*	*ʔod-ábéykú*	*ʔod-úkkú*
1PL	*ʔod-ída*	*ʔod-oósi*	*ʔod-aná*	*ʔod-íboókko*	*ʔod-ókko*
2PL	*ʔod-ídeta*	*ʔod-eéta*	*ʔod-aná*	*ʔod-íbékkétá*	*ʔod-ékkétá*
3PL	*ʔod-ídosona*	*ʔod-oósona*	*ʔod-aná*	*ʔod-íbókkóná*	*ʔod-ókkóná*

Verbs: Aspect and Polarity. Aspect in Wolaitta involves past and nonpast distinctions. Thus, while the perfective aspect has only one form, e.g., *ʔod-aási* 'I told', the imperfective distinguishes between present/habitual *ʔod-áysi* 'I am telling (now)' or 'I (usually) tell' and future imperfect *ʔod-aná* 'I will tell'. In the negative, the two-way division of the imperfective is neutralized. Except in the future imperfect, the verb shows subject agreement. In the perfective, first-person and third-person singular have two forms, e.g., *ʔod-aási* or *ʔod-ádisi* 'I told', which reflect only stylistic differences. There is no object agreement. Table 3 above shows the inflectional paradigm of *ʔod-* 'tell' for aspect and polarity.

Converbs. This verb type is formed by affixing to the verb root *-ada* (hereafter CNV$_1$) for first and second person and for third-person feminine; and *-idi* (hereafter CNV$_2$) for third-person singular masculine and for first-, second- and third-person plural forms:

táání	*ʔod-ada*	'I having told'
1SG:NOM	tell-CNV$_1$	
ʔí	*ʔod-ídi*	'he having told'
3MS:NOM	tell-CNV$_2$	

Often the converb functions as a temporal or manner adverb of a main verb as above. However, in complex predicates (compound verbs) a converb is used as a main verb. In this case, the converb marker is morphologically reduced, i.e., *-ada* is shortened to *-a*, while *-idi* becomes *-i*, as in the following examples:

márz-iya ʔúy-ada <u>haík'k'-a ʔagg-asu</u>
poison-ACC drink-CNV$_1$ die-CNV$_1$ give up-3FS:PF
'Having drunk the poison, she died instantly.'

márz-iya ʔúy-idi <u>haík'k'-i ʔagg-iiisi</u>
poison-ACC drink-CNV$_2$ die-CNV$_2$ give up-3MS:PF
'Having drunk the poison, he died instantly.'

In the above examples, the main verb is *haik'k'-* 'die'. However, for aspect and polarity distinctions, the converb is dependent on the second verb. The second member of complex predicates functions more like an auxilary verb; it does not express its basic lexical meaning. It carries aspect and/or polarity markers that it shares with the converb. There are about 14 verbs that are used as second members of such complex predicates, e.g., in the slot where *ʔagg-* 'give up' occurred in the above examples, whereas the first member can be any verb in the language. This shows that the compounding is more of a grammatical than a lexical phenomenon. Finally, the converb is also used to form complex sentences (clause chains), in which a series of converbs occur before the final main verb.

Mood. Apart from the Declarative (illustrated above), imperative and optative moods are distinguished. The imperative affirmative is marked by *-a* for second-person singular, and by *-(i)ite* for plural. These modal suffixes get high tone when attached to a verb root with low tone.

2SG:	*ʔod-á*	'tell!'	2PL:	*ʔod-ité*	'tell!'
	b-á	'go!'		*b-iité*	'go!'
	K'ér-a	'split'		*K'ér-ite*	'split'

The optative involves only third-person singular and plural forms. It is marked by *-o* for third-person singular masculine and by *-u* for feminine. For third-person plural, it is marked by *-ona.*

ʔod-ó	'Let him tell'	*fat'-ó*	'may he be cured'
ʔod-ú	'Let her tell'	*fat'-ú*	'may she be cured'
ʔod-óná	'Let them tell'	*fat'-óná*	'may they be cured'

Masculine and plural optative verbs take an identical negative marker as the negative imperative. Note also that the negative marker for imperative and optative sentences is distinct from that in declarative sentences.

ʔod-ópp-a	'Don't tell (2SG)!'
ʔod-ópp-ite	'Don't tell (2PL)!'
bo-ópp-a	'Don't go (2SG)!'
bo-ópp-ite	'Don't go (2PL)!'
ʔod-ópp-ó	'let him not tell!'
fat'-ópp-ó	'may he not be cured'
ʔod-úpp-ú	'let her not tell!'
fat'-úpp-ú	'may she not be cured'
ʔod-ópp-óná	'let them not tell'
fat'-ópp-óná	'may they not be cured'

Interrogatives. In Wolaitta, verbs are inflected for the subject of an interrogative sentence, as shown in Table 4 for the verb *ʔod-* 'tell'. Note also that, here, tense-aspect is differently marked from that in declarative sentences.

Table 4: Subject Agreement and Aspect Inflection in Interrogative Sentences

Interrogatives			
Person	Perfective	Imperfective	
		Pres/Hab.	Future
1SG	*ʔod-ádina* 'did I tell?'	*ʔod-aína*	*ʔod-ané*
2SG	*ʔod-ádi* 'did you tell?'	*ʔod-áy*	*ʔod-uúte*
3MS	*ʔod-íde* 'did he tell?'	*ʔod-í*	*ʔod-ané*
3FS	*ʔod-áde* 'did she tell?'	*ʔod-áy*	*ʔod-ané*
1Pl	*ʔod-ído* 'did we tell?'	*ʔod-íyo*	*ʔod-ané*
2PL	*ʔod-ideti* 'did you (PL) tell?'	*ʔod-eéti*	*ʔod-uúteti*
3PL	*ʔod-ídona* 'did they tell?'	*ʔod-íyona*	*ʔod-ané*

The following are content question words of Wolaitta: *ʔaí* 'what', *ʔai-gé* 'which (M)', *ʔai-nná* 'which (F)', *ʔaí-ssi* 'why', *ʔa-udé* 'when', *ʔá-wan* 'where', *ʔoóní* 'who'.

Verb Root Extension. Verb roots can be extended by suffixing valency increasing or decreasing morphemes to the basic verb root. Root extension also involves reciprocal, reflexive, and intensive marking.

Gloss	Verb root	Causative stem
'give'	*ʔim-*	*ʔim-is(s)-*
'buy'	*ʃam-*	*ʃam-is(s)-*
'break'	*ment-*	*ment-is(s)-*

Gloss	Passive/Recip	Intensive/Repetitive
'give'	*ʔim-étt-*	*ʔim-erett-*
'buy'	*ʃam-étt-*	*ʃam-erett-*
'break'	*ment-étt-*	*ment-erett-*

The passive and reciprocal are marked by the same morpheme: *naʔá-y k'áʃ-étt-iisi* (boy-NOM tie-PAS-PF) 'The boy is sentenced'; *naa-t-í ʔissó-y ʔissu-á-ra c'ey-étt-ósona* (child-PL-NOM one-NOM one-ACC-INST insult-RECP-3PL:IPF) 'The children insult each other'.

Pronouns. Wolaitta distinguishes nominative, accusative, and possessive pronouns (see Table 5).

Note the gender syncretism between third-person singular pronouns in the above forms. The shorter variants of first- and second-person singular and first-person plural in the nominative can be used in almost all contexts where the full pronouns are used. The pronoun *ba* is used when the subject of the sentence is coreferential with an object or possessive noun in the same sentence, as in:

ʔí *ba* *keettáa* *baizz-iisi*
3MS:NOM 3LOG house:ACC sell-3MS:PF
'He$_i$ sold his$_i$ house'

ʔi *ʔa* *keettáa* *baizz-iisi*
3MS:NOM 3MS/POS house:ACC sell-3MS:PF
'He$_i$ sold his$_j$ house'

Adjectives. Adjectives exhibit characteristics of both nouns and verbs. Like nouns, in the citation form adjectives end in one of the vowels *-e*, *-o* or *-a*. And, when the noun modified by the adjective is dropped, the adjective is affixed with case, gender and number markers that otherwise are affixed to the noun.

Adjective Basic Form	Attributive Function
lóʔʔo 'good'	*lóʔʔo keetta-y* 'good house (M:NOM)'
k'íta 'dirty'	*k'íta maay-iya* 'dirty cloth (F:NOM)
ʔadussá 'tall'	*ʔadussá ʔasa-t-i* 'tall people (PL:NOM)'

Inflected Adjectives
lóʔʔo-y 'the good one(D:NOM)'
k'ít-iya 'the dirty one(F:NOM)'
ʔadussa-t-í 'the tall ones (NOM)'

Adjectives behave like verbs in taking tense-aspect and mood markers in the inchoative, as in *loʔʔ-iísi* 'he became good'; *loʔʔ-aásu* 'she became good'; *loʔʔ-ídosona* 'they became

Table 5: Wolaitta Pronouns

Person	Possessive	Nominative	Accusative
1SG	*ta*	*taáníl tá*	*táná*
2SG	*ne*	*neéníl né*	*néná*
3MS	*ʔa*	*ʔí*	*ʔá*
3FS	*ʔi*	*ʔál ʔíyá*	*ʔól ʔíyó*
1Pl	*nu*	*nuúni/né*	*núná*
2PL	*ʔinte*	*ʔínté*	*ʔínténá*
3PL	*ʔeta*	*ʔetí*	*ʔetá*
3LOG	*ba*		*ba*

good'; *loʔʔ-íbénná* 'he did not become good'; *loʔʔ-ábékkú* 'she did not become good'; *loʔʔ-ó* 'let him be good!'

Adverbs. Most of the temporal notions are expressed by way of nonderived adverbs: *haʔʔí* 'now', *kasé* 'earlier', *hácci* 'today', *wontó* 'tomorrow'. However, manner and spatial adverbs are formed by affixing the locative suffix *-n*, the instrumental *-ra* or the ablative marker *-ppe* to nouns, adjectives, demonstratives or numerals.

digí-ni	*lódda-ra*	*ʔissí-ppe*
later-LOC	slowness-INST	one-ABL
'later'	'slowly'	'together'

Ideophones. There are two classes of ideophones: adjectival ideophones and verbal ideophones. Adjectival ideophones typically involve reduplication, and semantically they cover physical property, human propensity, color, value, etc., which can also be expressed in this language through nonideophonic, simple adjectives. The difference between these two types of adjectives is that the ideophonic forms are formally different in involving reduplication, in comprising several syllables in a word, and in being semantically very specific and more expressive. Adjectival ideophones include: *tiit'itiít'a* 'one with a hasty manner of walk, especially of teenagers or of a slim person', *gaʃáʃʃa* 'weak, slow and unhealthy', and *gaagaáno* 'very big, e.g., pots'.

Verbal ideophones typically express both the situation (mainly action) as well as the manner in which the action is carried out. Like converbs, verbal ideophones cannot take verbal inflection directly. Rather, they co-occur with the verb *g-* 'say' when they are intransitive and with *ʔoott-* 'do' when they are transitive:

c'úrúru g-	'to spill, of liquid coming out in a slow consistent manner (intransitive)'
púsku g-	'to scatter completely (intransitive)'
púsku ʔoott-	'to scatter completely, of small things, e.g., coins, grain (transitive)'
ʃóppu ʔoott-	'to spill at once for a large quantity of liquid (transitive)'

Both adjectival and verbal ideophones show sound symbolism by associating midvowels with largeness/heaviness and high vowels with smallness/lightness:

bort'ót't'a	'big and several, of eyes, some grain types e.g., maize'
pirc'ic'c'a	'small and several, e.g., of rush, chickenpox'
póʒʒu g-	'to tear suddenly of thick cloth' (e.g., 'garment': *kuta*)
píʒʒi g-	'to tear suddenly of thin cloth' (e.g., 'light shawl': *nat'ala*)

Basic Syntax

Wolaitta basically follows an SOV word order in sentences.

táání	*ʔá-ssi*	*kiíta*	*ʔod-aasi*
1SG:NOM	3MS:ACC-DAT	message:ACC	tell-1SG:PF

'I told him the message.'

However, this basic word order may be altered for pragmatic reasons. Subjects and objects can be omitted. In phrases, the modifying categories precede the head. In noun phrases with several modifiers the order of the modifiers is demonstratives, numerals, adjective:

AP *dáró keeha*
a lot kind 'very kind'

NP *hege-t-í naaʔʔú lóʔʔó ʔasa-t-i*
that-PL-NOM two good person-NOM
'those two good persons'

REL:Cl. *keettáa garsa-n deʔ-íya naʔ-ay*
house:DEF inside-LOC exist-IPF boy-NOM
'The boy who is inside the house'

In complex sentences, adverbial and complement clauses precede main clauses.

ʔí	*nabbab-íʃin*	*táání*	*ʔoóso*	*keetta*	*b-aasi*
3MS:NOM	read-TEMP	1SG:NOM	work	house	go-1SG:PF

'While he was reading, I went to my office.'

Contact with Other Languages

Wolaitta speakers have frequent contact in trade with their northern neighbors, the Kembata and Hadiyya, whose languages belong to the Cushitic family. However, the effect of this contact on the Wolaitta language is minimal (none known to this author, who comes from further south of the border area). On the other hand, many borrowed words have been integrated in the language from AMHARIC (Semitic), which was used as a medium of instruction for elementary schools in Wolaitta until 1994. Regular language contact situations involving trade and intermarriage exist among the Wolaitta and the other Ometo speakers, i.e., the Gamo, the Gofa, and Kullo people. In this case, obviously it is difficult to differentiate between borrowing and shared retention.

From Amharic: *bataskaána* 'church' (Amharic *betäkrïstian*), *mat'aáfa* 'book' (Amharic *mäs'ïhaf*), *hakíme* 'doctor' (Amharic *hakim*)

Common Words

person:	ʔasá	yes:	ʔee
man:	ʔattúma ʔasa	no:	cii
woman:	mác'c'a ʔasa	good:	lóʔʔo
water:	haattá	dog:	kaná
three:	heezzá	old:	c'eéga
fish:	molé	hand:	kúʃe
big:	gitá	bird:	kapó
tree:	mítta	sun:	ʔawá
long:	ʔadussá	small:	guútta

Example Sentences

(1) hegé	ta	naʔá	hinná	ta	naʔá.
that:M	1SG:POS	son	that:F	1SG:POS	daughter
'That is my son.'			'That is my daughter.'		

(2) ne keettáy ʔáwa-n deʔ-i.
2SG:POS house:NOM where-LOC exist-3MS:Q
'Where is your house?'

(3) neé-yyo keettí baáwa.
2SG-DAT house:IDF exist not
'You don't have a house.'

Efforts to Preserve, Protect, and Promote the Language

Wolaitta is one of the major languages of Ethiopia. It is widely used in the southern region of Ethiopia. Since 1994–95, the language has been used as a medium of instruction in elementary schools and in one of the higher educational institutions in the region (Arba Minch Teachers Training Institute). A few publications in the language have appeared recently, including the book on Wolaitta proverbs mentioned earlier. In the late 1990s the regional authorities devised a common writing system for Wolaitta, Gamo, Gofa and Dawro. In the process of making the orthography, some phonological, morphological and lexical differences among the four dialects were ignored and a choice for one or the other form was made. Many people were against such modifications, which they saw as a purposeful effort to make "the four languages" look alike. They also claimed that the use of the abbreviation WOGAGODA to refer to the writing system and WOGAGODASO to the languages involved was intended to deprive them of their very names, with which they have been identified for centuries. In some areas people expressed their anger by burning textbooks written in the new writing system and by holding large demonstrations. During these demonstrations clashes with security forces occurred and many casualties were reported (cf. "Human Rights Violations in North Omo" by Ethiopian Human Rights Council, 27th Special Report, December 13, 1999).

Select Bibliography

Adams, B.A. 1983. "A Tagmemic Analysis of the Wolaitta Language." Ph.D. thesis, University of London.

Alemayehu, Abebe. 1994. "Malo: An Unknown Ometo Language." In Marcus, Harold G. (ed.), *New Trends in Ethiopian Studies, Vol. I: 1064–1084*. Lawrenceville, NJ: Red Sea Press.

Amha, Azeb. 1996. "Tone-Accent and Prosodic Domains of Wolaitta." In *Studies in African Linguistics*. 25 (2): 111–138.

_____. (Forthcoming). "Ideophones and Compound Verbs in Wolaitta."

Bekale, Seyoum. 1989. "The Case System in Wolayta." M.A. thesis, Addis Ababa University.

Bender, M.L. 1971. "The Languages of Ethiopia: A New Lexicostatistic Classification and Some Problems of Diffusion." In *Anthropological Linguistics* 13 (5): 165–287.

Ethiopian Language Academy. 1995. *Wolaitatto Leemisuwa. Wolaitta Proverbs with Amharic Translations.* Edited by Getachew Talachew and Tsegaye Ammenu. Addis Ababa: Artistic Printers for Ethiopian Language Academy.

Lamberti, Marcello, and Roberto Sottile. 1997. *The Wolaytta Language*. Köln: Rüdiger Köppe Verlag.

Ohman, W.A. and Hailu Fulass. 1976. "Welamo." In Bender, M.L. *et al.* (eds.), *The Non-Semitic Languages of Ethiopia*. London: Oxford University Press.

Selassie, Tsehai Berhane. 1975. "The Question of Damot and Wälamo." In *Journal of Ethiopian Studies* 13 (1): 37–45.

Yitbarek, Ejigu. 1983. "The Phonology of Wolaitta: Generative Approach." M.A. thesis, Addis Ababa University.

WOLOF

Omar Ka

Language Name: Wolof. **Alternates:** *Walaf, Olof, Ouolof* (FRENCH spelling).

Location: Wolof is spoken primarily in Senegal and the Gambia (hereafter Senegambia), on the northwestern coast of Africa. It is also spoken on a smaller scale in the neighboring countries of Mauritania, Mali, and Guinea. Immigrant groups use it in West Africa (in Côte d'Ivoire and Gabon), Europe (in particular France), and the United States (mainly in New York City).

Family: Wolof belongs to the West Atlantic group of the Niger-Congo family, one of the four language families in Africa (according to Greenberg's classification).

Related Languages: Wolof is most closely related to other languages in the West Atlantic group such as PULAAR (the Senegambian variety of FULA), Serer (Seereer, Sereer), and Jola (Dyola, Diola).

Dialects: There are a number of regional varieties or dialects of Wolof, determined mainly by differences in pronunciation and vocabulary. The grammar, however, is very similar throughout the Wolof-speaking areas. Four major dialect groups can be identified within Senegambia: (1) Northern (including Waalo and Jolof); (2) Central (including Kajoor and Bawol); (3) Cap-Vert (including Lebu); and (4) Saalum (including the Gambian dialect). The Kajoor dialect is perceived as the "purest" form of Wolof, and has therefore been implicitly chosen as the standard dialect.

Number of Speakers: Wolof is spoken as a first language by aproximately 40 percent of the Senegalese and 16 percent of the Gambians. When nonnative speakers are included, the percentage soars to about 80 percent of the 10 million inhabitants of the two countries. Therefore, Wolof is considered as the lingua franca of Senegambia.

Origin and History

The origins of the language are not well known. Different hypotheses have been formulated, including Cheikh Anta Diop's linking of the language to ANCIENT EGYPTIAN.

According to one version of oral history (Malherbe and Sall 1989), the Wolof people and language originated from Njajaan Njaay, a wise man who emerged from the waters of the Senegal River, and founded the kingdoms of Waalo and Jolof around 1200.

Another version (Kane and Carrie-Sembène 1978) contends that Wolof is originally the language of the Lebu, who were until the 11th century one of the main ethnic groups living on the banks of the Senegal River, along with the Sereer, the Fulani, the Soninke, and the Moors. Together these groups established the Tekruur Empire in the 10th century. Migrating south, they founded the Jolof empire toward the end of the 14th century. The word "Jolof" would then come from the area, called Lof, in which the empire was established. Therefore the word "Wolof" would have originally been used for the inhabitants of Lof (*waa Lof*: literally "the people of Lof"). This would explain why the Wolof constitute a multiethnic society speaking the language of the Lebu. The original Jolof Empire was succeeded by several states, including Waalo, Jolof, Kajoor, and Saalum.

Even before the advent of political independence in 1960, Wolof had witnessed a rapid expansion because of three main factors: socioeconomic integration, urbanization, and interethnic marriages.

Orthography and Basic Phonology

The basic principle in the orthography of the language is that every symbol is pronounced and corresponds to the same sound in every word, except for complex consonants such as prenasals, which are transcribed with two letters (see Table 1). The doubling of vowels symbolizes long vowels; the doubling of consonants symbolizes geminates (long or strong consonants).

The present standard orthography of the language derives from the "Décret no. 71-566 du 21 mai 1971 relatif à la transcription des langues nationales," Dakar, 1972. That official decree of the Senegalese government standardizes the orthography of Wolof and five main Senegambian languages; it closely follows the recommendations of the 1966 UNESCO conference

Table 1: Standard Wolof Alpbabet

a	à	aa	b	bb	c	cc	d	dd	e	ee	é	éé
ë	f	g	gg	i	ii	j	jj	k	kk	l	ll	m
mm	mb	mp	n	nn	nc	nd	ng	nj	nk	nq	nt	ñ
ññ	ŋ	ŋŋ	o	oo	ó	óó	p	pp	q	r	s	t
tt	u	uu	w	ww	x	y	yy					

on the unification of African-languages alphabets, held in Bamako, Mali. Wolof had a LATIN alphabet as early as the 17th century, and prior to that the language had used an original script, and then ARABIC characters (*Wolofal*, in which an important body of literature has been written). Wolofal is still used by sizeable segments of the literate population.

Table 2: Consonants

	Labial	Alveolar	Palatal	Velar	Uvular
Stops Voiceless Voiced	 p b	 t d	 c j	 k g	
Fricatives	f	s		x	
Nasals	m	n	ñ	ṅ	
Approximants Lateral Central	 	 l r	 y	 w	
Prenasals Voiceless Voiced	 mp mb	 nt nd	 nc nj	 nk ng	 nq

Table 3: Vowels

	Front	Central	Back
High	i		u
High-Mid	e	ə	o
Low-Mid	ɛ		ɔ
Low		a	

The consonant system of Wolof contrasts simple consonants, prenasal consonants, and geminates. The simple and prenasal consonants are indicated on the above consonant table. In addition, each simple consonant, except *f, s, r,* and *x*, has a geminate counterpart. These three series of consonants have different distributions depending on their position within the word. Voiceless prenasal consonants, geminates, and consonant clusters do not appear word initially. In stem-medial and final positions, all consonants in the above table and geminates may appear, except *p,d,c,k* (which appear in these positions only in borrowed or derived words).

Wolof has eight simple vowel phonemes, as shown on the above vowel table. Each of these simple vowels, except the schwa *ə*, has a long counterpart. Vowel length is contrastive in the language. Some dialects, such as the Gambian dialect, do not have the schwa.

The most general phonological rules of Wolof involve gemination, degemination, glide insertion, vowel coalescence, vowel insertion, prenasalization, and vowel harmony.

Gemination strengthens (or lengthens) a simple consonant in root-final position, when the following derivational suffixes are added:

-i 'reversive':

ubbi	'to open'	(*ub*	'to close')
fecci	'to untie'	(*fas*	'to tie')

-anti 'corrective':

lijjanti	'to untangle'	(*lëj*	'to be tangled')
ruccanti	'to put at ease'	(*rus*	'to be ashamed')

-ali 'completive':

jottali	'To transmit'	(*jot*	'to obtain')

As the data above suggest, the pairing of simple and geminate consonants is not always the "expected" one, e.g., :*f ~ pp; s ~ cc; r ~ dd; ø ~ kk; x ~ qq*. These "unexpected" alternations result from a rule of spirantization, which, in postvocalic position, converts the underlying simple stop consonants /p c d k q/ into continuants (or zero in the case of *k*). The spirantization rule is accompanied by a shift in the point of articulation of the resulting continuant. Finally, note the changes in the quality of certain stem vowels when the reversive, corrective, and completive suffixes are added; this appears to be a morphologized phenomenon restricted to words derived through these suffixes.

Degemination converts a geminate (or strong, or long) consonant in stem-final position into a simple consonant before the following suffixes:

-al 'causative':

sonal	'to tire, to bother'	(*sonn*	'to be tired')
seral	'to cool'	(*sedd*	'to be cold')

-o 'nominalizing':

tofo	'younger sibling'	(*topp*	'to follow')
coono	'tiredness'	(*sonn*	'to be tired')

The subsequent spirantization rule as examined above converts a simple stop to the corresponding continuant after a vowel.

Glide insertion occurs between:

an open monosyllabic stem and a vowel-initial suffix:

jiwaat	'to plant again'	(*ji*	'to plant'; *-aat* 'iterative')
foyi	'to go and play'	(*fo*	'to play'; *-i* 'motion away')

-a vowel-final stem and a long vowel-initial suffix:

yónniwoon	'sent'	(*yónni*	'to send'; *-oon* 'past tense')
nuyuwaale	'to greet also'	(*nuyu*	'to greet'; *-aale* 'associative')

In general, the quality of the glide is determined by the following vowel.

The process of vowel coalescence collapses the final vowel of a polysyllabic stem and the initial short vowel of a suffix; the resulting long vowel has the back, round and ATR features of the first vowel, and the high feature of the second vowel:

yóbbóóti	'to carry away once more'
(*yóbbu*	'to carry away'; *-ati* 'reiterative')
pareel	'to be ready for someone'
(*pare*	'to be ready'; *-al* 'benefactive')
saagaal	'to cause to insult'
(*saaga*	'to insult'; *-al* 'causative')

Vowel insertion involves two types: schwa insertion and vowel epenthesis. The rule of schwa insertion applies between a stem ending in a geminate consonant and a consonant-initial suffix (the inserted *ë* is not noted in the orthography of the language): *làkk[ë]kat* 'speaker of a foreign language' comes from *làkk* 'to speak a foreign language' and *-kat* 'agent'; *sàmm[ë]kat* 'cattle raiser' comes from *sàmm* 'to raise cattle'.

The vowel epenthesis rule applies when some stems end underlyingly in a consonant cluster. In such a case, the second member of the cluster is unable to be syllabified; a vowel is then inserted in front of that unsyllabified consonant; the vowel has the same quality as the vowel in the preceding syllable:

xaraf	'to be circumcised'	(from: / #xarf# /)
sëlëm	'to wash someone's face'	(from: / #sëlm# /)

Prenasal consonants in Wolof are either underlying or derived. Underlying prenasals are found in all positions within the word. Derived prenasals result from the prefixation of a nasal segment to stop-initial stems. That nasal prefix is added to a verb stem to form derived nouns, or to a noun stem to form derived nouns having a diminutive or general meaning; the nasal assimilates in point of articulation with the initial voiced consonant of the stem:

mbokk	'relative'	(*bokk*	'to share')
ndugg	'shopping items'	(*dugg*	'to shop')
njàng	'study'	(*jàng*	'to learn')
ndoom	'little child'	(*doom*	'child')
ngarab	'small tree'	(*garab*	'tree')

If the stem-initial consonant is a voiceless stop, the nasal prefix is deleted:

póót	'laundry'	(*fóót*	'to do laundry')
caaf	'roasted peanuts'	(*saaf*	'to fry')
koor	'fasting'	(*woor*	'to fast')

Vowel harmony in Wolof is based on the feature [ATR]. Each vowel has a [+ATR] or [–ATR] counterpart, except for the high vowels (which do not have [–ATR] counterparts) and the low, long vowel (which does not have a [+ATR] counterpart):

[+ATR]	[–ATR]
i	-
ii	-
u	-
uu	-
é	e
éé	ee
ë	a
ó	o
óó	oo
-	aa

Within the domain of vowel harmony, only elements belonging to the same harmonic set may appear together. That domain may be:

the root:

jigéén	'woman'
junqóób	'crab'
doole	'strength'

the derived (or inflected) word:

dendandoo	'to be neighbors'	(*dend*	'to be next to')
xamadi	'to be impolite'	(*xam*	'to know')

the phrase:

nit kilé	'this person'	(*nit* 'person'; *Cile* 'demonstr.')
xar mile	'this sheep'	(*xar* 'sheep'; *Cile* 'demonstr.')

The vowel harmony rule can be defined as the spreading of the feature [+ATR] from left to right to all harmonizing vowels within a given harmony domain. However, the high vowels /i/ and /u/ in word noninitial syllables do not affect the harmonic category of subsequent vowels, and are compatible with either harmonic set. Conversely, the low, long vowel /aa/ not only is not affected by harmony, but also blocks the spreading of the [+ATR] feature.

Basic Morphology

Wolof nouns are divided into eight classes in the singular, and two in the plural. Each class is characterized by a separate class affix, which does not attach to the noun itself, but is found on the morphological elements dependent on the noun. In contrast with other West Atlantic languages such as Pulaar or Sereer, the class system in Wolof is in an advanced stage of lexicalization. Most new words entering the lexicon are assigned to Class b, regardless of their phonological or semantic makeup. Below are illustrations of the class affixes:

a. Singular:

-Class **b**:	tànk b-	'foot'
-Class **m**:	ndox m-	'water'
-Class **s**:	suuf s-	'sand'
-Class **l**:	cin l-	'dish'
-Class **j**:	doom j-	'child'
-Class **k**:	nit k-	'human being'
-Class **g**:	kër g-	'house'
-Class **w**:	sant w-	'last name'

b. Plural:

-Class **y**:	kër y-	'houses'
	cin y-	'dishes'
-Class **ñ**:	nit ñ-	'human beings'

Only four nouns (all referring to humans) are found in the plural Class **ñ**:

nit	'human being'
jigéén	'woman'
góór	'man'
gaa	'guy'

Noun-class affixes appear in noun determiners and are symbolized here by C. The following noun determiners exist in the language:

-the indefinite *aC*: *ab xarit* 'a friend'
ay kër 'some houses'

-the definites *Ci* (indicating closeness) and *Ca* (indicating remoteness):

xarit bi	'the friend'
jigéén ña	'the women'

-the demonstratives *Cii~Cile* (indicating closeness), *Cee~Cale* (indicating remoteness), *CooCu~CooCule* (indicating immediate reference), *CooCa~CooCale* (indicating remote reference):

xarit bii/bile	'this friend'
xarit yee/yale	'those friends'
kër googu/googule	'the house just mentioned'
kër yooya/yooyale	'those houses mentioned earlier'

-the quantifiers C*épp* ('any, all'), C*enn* ('one, some'), C*eneen* ('other'):

bépp xarit	'any friend'
benn xarit	'one friend'
ñeneen nit	'other people'

-the interrogative *Can*:

ban xarit ?	'which friend?'
kër yan ?	'which houses?'

-the possessives:

		One object possessed:	Many objects possessed:
sg.	1	sama xarit	samay xarit
	2	sa xarit	say xarit
	3	xaritam	ay xaritam
pl.	1	sunu xarit	sunuy xarit
	2	seen xarit	seeni xarit
	3	seen xarit	seeni xarit

Except for the indefinite and the possessives, noun determiners can be used as pronouns:

nit kii 'this person'	*kii* 'this'
kër yépp 'all houses'	*yépp* 'all'
kër gan? 'which house ?'	*gan?* 'which?'
sa kër 'your house'	*sa bos* 'yours'
këram 'his/her house'	*bosam* 'his/hers'

Gender distinctions are expressed by -noun + *Cu* + *góór* (male): *doom ju góór* 'son'; -noun + *Cu* + *jigéén* (female): *gaynde gu jigéén* lioness'.

Verbs in Wolof are generally uninflected (except for the negative marker in some cases, and the past-tense marker). Other markers, such as those indicating focus, aspect, tense, and person appear as separate words in the verb phrase.

Personal pronouns are divided into three series: independent pronouns, subject pronouns, and object pronouns:

		Independent Pronouns	Subject Pronouns	Object Pronouns
sg.	1	man	ma	ma
	2	yow	nga	la
	3	moom	mu	ko
pl.	1	nun	nu	nu
	2	yeen	ngeen	leen
	3	ñoom	ñu	leen

Subject pronouns are amalgamated with affixes indicating focus and aspect.

Focus may be placed on any of the main elements of the sentence: the subject, the verb, the complement, or on the whole sentence. No focus is also possible. In all cases, the focus marker appears in the main clause and is phonologically amalgamated with the subject pronoun of that clause.

Aspect in Wolof is divided into the perfective and the imperfective. The perfective aspect is marked by Ø and is used to describe a completed action or a particular state; the imperfective aspect is marked by *di~-y* and is used to describe an action not yet completed or still going on, or a permanent or habitual fact: *dama naan ndox* 'I drank water (perfective)', *damay naan ndox* 'I am drinking/will drink/usually drink water (imperfective)'.

Negation in the perfective is expressed by a suffix attached to the verb; and in the imperfective aspect, the negative suffix is attached to *di*: *duma naan ndox* 'I will not drink water or I do not usually drink water', *Naanuma ndox* 'I did not drink water'.

In terms of tense, Wolof marks a distinction between past and future tenses. The present tense is marked by Ø. The past tense is marked by the suffixes *-oon~woon* and *-aan~waan* (with an added meaning of habitual or repetition), which may be attached to the verb, the negative suffix *-ul*, the imperfective *di*, and the negative imperfective *dul*:

dama naanoon ndox	'I had drunk water.'
dama naanulwoon ndox	'I had not drunk water.'
dama doon naan ndox	'I had been drinking water.'
dama daan naan ndox	'I used to drink water.'
dama dulwoon naan ndox	'I had not been drinking water.'

The future tense is characterized by the following preverbal markers*: dinaa, dinanu; dinga, dingeen*; and *dina, dinañu* in the first-, second-, and third-person singular and plural, respectively.

Among the various processes used in the language to form new words are derivation, reduplication, and compounding. Most nouns and verbs are derived through the attachment of a suffix to a stem: some 40 derivational suffixes exist in the language. They include verbalizing, nominalizing, reversive, reflexive neutro-passive, instrumental-locative, comitative, depriving, depreciative, reciprocal, causative, iterative, benefactive, and agentive suffixes. (For an exhaustive account of Wolof derivational suffixes, see Ka 1981 and Fal, *et al.* 1990).

Reduplication allows one to derive nouns from verb, noun or ideophonic stems:

jam-jam	'cut, wound' (*jam* 'to pierce')
Jolof-Jolof	'inhabitant of Jolof' (*Jolof* 'central region of Senegal')
poto-poto	'muddy location'

Compounding is used to form nouns, verbs and adverbs:

diw-tiir 'palm oil' (*diw g-* 'oil', *tiir g-* 'palm tree')
yàq-der 'to tarnish reputation' (*yàq* 'to spoil', *der w-* 'skin')
wax-dëgg 'truly' (*wax* 'to say', *dëgg g-* 'truth')

Basic Syntax

The basic word order is Subject-Verb-Object (SVO). The only exception to this preferred order is constituted by the complement-focus mood, where the order is Complement + LA + Subject + Verb.

The Wolof sentence can be divided into a noun phrase and a verb phrase. A noun phrase includes a head noun that governs different types of complements (or nonheads) including the indefinite marker (preposed to the noun), the definite markers (postposed to the noun), the demonstrative markers (generally postposed to the noun), the interrogative marker (generally preposed to the noun), the possessive markers (preposed to the noun, except in the third-person singular), and the numerals (preposed to the noun).

A verb phrase includes a head verb that also governs different types of complements including inflectional markers and clitics. Inflectional markers are words in which aspect, mood, tense, and person are amalgamated. They generally appear to the left of the verb, except the NA-no focus marker, which appears to the right. Clitics include the object pronouns, the locative pronouns indicating closeness *ci* and *fi*, the locative pronouns indicating remoteness *ca* and *fa*, conjunctions such as *ag* 'and', and the verb linker *-a*. The object and locative pronouns immediately follow the inflectional markers.

Relevant sentences will obey the following patterns:

1. Verb + Inflection + Clitic:

naan na ndox
's/he drank water'

naan na ko
's/he drank it'

dem nga ca xew ma
'you went to the event'

dem nga ca
'you went to it'

2. Inflection + Clitic + Verb:

maa naan ndox
'I drank water.'

maa ko naan
'I drank it.'

maa ngi dem Ndar
'I went to Saint-Louis.'

maa ngi fa dem
'I went there.'

3. The imperfective marker is attached to the object or locative pronouns:

maay naan ndox
'I am drinking water.'

maa koy naan
'I am drinking it.'

maa ngiy dem Ndar
'I am going to Saint-Louis.'

maa ngi fay dem
'I am going there.'

Contact with Other Languages

Wolof has been in contact with Arabic through the trans-Saharan trade and Islam; this explains the great number of borrowings from Arabic, particularly in the religious domain. Contacts with European languages such as PORTUGUESE, ENGLISH, and French occurred as a result of European commercial and colonial expansion from the 17th to the 20th centuries. In the second half of the 20th century, migration trends to Western Europe and North America serve to reinforce these contacts.

Words borrowed from Arabic, English, and Portuguese are older and have been assimilated into the language. Borrowings from French are more recent, and are generally less integrated into the phonology of Wolof.

From Arabic: *aada j-* 'custom, habit', *àllaaxira j-* 'the hereafter', *bidaa b-* 'superstition'
From English: *koppar g-* coin', *jinjeer j-* 'ginger'
From Portuguese: *caabi j-* 'key', *gurmet b-* 'Christian'
From French: *fobeere* 'to clean the floor', *lempo b-* 'tax', *feebar* 'to be sick', *afeer b-* 'business'

Common Words

man:	góór g-	(to be) long:	gudd, njool
woman:	jigéén j-	(to be) small:	ndaw, tuuti, gàtt
water:	ndox m-	yes:	waaw
sun:	jant b-	no:	déédéét
three:	ñett	(to be) good:	baax
fish:	jën w-	bird:	picc m-
(to be) big:	mag, réy	dog:	xaj b-
tree:	garab g-		

Example Sentences

(1) Jàng xam-xamu Kocc Barma, walla xam-xamu
study knowledge-of Kocc Barma or knowledge-of

ku mel ni moom, war naa
one-who is like him should NA3p.S-verb connector

tax nu gëna góórgóórlu ci sunuy làkk.
cause we be better-VC try.hard in our-PL language

'Studying Kocc Barma's knowledge, or the knowledge of someone like him, should be a reason for us to put more effort into (studying) our languages.'

(2) Sunuy làkk ñoo ëmb xam-xamu
Our-PL language A 3p.p bundle up knowledge-of

démb xam-xamu démb moo jur
yesterday knowledge-of yesterday A 3p.s give birth to

bu tey.
that of today
'Our languages are the key to the knowledge of yesterday; yesterday's knowledge is at the origin of today's.'

(3) Kenn mënula xam làkku jaambur
Nobody can NEG.3p.s VC know language of the other

feeg nekkoo ag ñooña ba seey
as long as be-NEG2p.s with those(people) until melt

ca ñoom xam leen bu baax xam seeni
in them know them well know their PLURAL

melokaan.
trait
'Nobody can know someone else's language, unless they are with them, to the point of melting with them, knowing them well, knowing their traits.'

Efforts to Preserve, Protect, and Promote the Language

During the precolonial period, efforts to preserve and promote Wolof included the transcription of important pieces of oral literature in an original script, and then in Arabic characters. More recently, the Latin alphabet has been used to write literary works whose origins date as far back as the 15th century.

Among the more well-known writers who contributed to those efforts are the philosopher Kocc Barma, the jurist Majaxate Kala (who translated the Koran into Wolof), the storyteller Ndaamal Gosaas, the poet Musaa Ka, the Muslim leader and founder of the Murit *tariqa* Séëx Ahmadu Bàmba. Contemporary authors and advocates of the language include the scientist Séëx Anta Jóób (Cheikh Anta Diop in the French spelling), who translated Einstein's *Theory of Relativity* into Wolof; as well as political scientists, mathematicians, linguists, and filmmakers.

Senegal has officially recognized six languages as "national languages": Wolof, Sereer, Pulaar, Joolaa, Manding, and Soninke. The main purpose of these selections was to use them as media of adult literacy programs and primary education. As of today, however, none of these languages is taught in primary school, despite repeated recommendations by various committees, including the National Commission for Educational and Training Reform (CNREF). The lack of serious attention given by policymakers to the question of promoting the use of Senegambian languages in public domains can be explained by the persistence of language policies inherited from the French (or British in the case of the Gambia) colonial domination. These policies call for the use of French in Senegal and English in the Gambia as sole languages of administration and education, to the exclusion of Wolof and other Senegambian languages; this in spite of the fact that Wolof is widely used on radio and television, is taught as a subject at the University Cheikh Anta Diop of Dakar, and has recently started to be used in the Senegalese Parliament. Outside Senegambia, Wolof is also taught as a foreign language in some European and American universities (most notably the University of Paris-Sorbonne, the University of Illinois at Urbana-Champaign, the University of California-Los Angeles, the University of Maryland-Baltimore County, and Central State College in Ohio).

Recognizing the crucial role that Senegambian languages must play in the political, socioeconomic, and cultural development of Senegambian society, various research centers, nongovernmental organizations, and private cultural associations have been publishing a number of grammars, dictionaries, textbooks, and readers for use both in adult literacy and in formal education. It is likely that the increased availability of such materials, and greater political awareness, will bring about necessary changes in official language policies.

Select Bibiliography

Dard, J. 1825. *Dictionnaire français-wolof et français-bambara,* suivi du dictionnaire wolof-français. Paris: Imprimerie Royale.

Diagne, P. 1971. *Grammaire du wolof moderne.* Paris: Présence Africaine.

Diouf, J.L. and M. Yaguello. 1987. *Damay jàng wolof.* Dakar: Centre de Linguistique Appliquée.

Doneux, J. 1975. *Quelle phonologie pour le wolof?* Dakar: Centre de Linguistique Appliquée, 65.

Dunigan, M. 1994. *On the Clausal Structure of Wolof.* Doctoral dissertation, University of North Carolina at Chapel Hill.

Fal, A., R. Santos, and J.L. Doneux. 1990. *Dictionnaire wolof-français,* suivi d'un index français-wolof. Paris: Karthala.

Gaye, P.A. 1980. *Practical Course in Wolof: An Audio-Aural Approach.* Washington, DC: United States Peace Corps.

Ka, O. 1981. *La dérivation et la composition en wolof.* Dakar: Centre de Linguistique Appliquée, 77.

____. 1994. *Wolof Phonology and Morphology.* Lanham: University Press of America.

Ka, O., and M. Sarr. 1985. *Aywa ci Wolof.* Urbana: Center for African Studies, University of Illinois.

Kane, B. and R. Carrie-Sembène. 1978. *Manuel de conversation/Conversation Handbook: Wolof, Mandeng, Pulaar.* P. Diagne, ed. Dakar: Librairie Sankoré.

Kobès, A. 1923. *Dictionnaire wolof-français,nouvelle édition revue et considérablement augmentée par le R.P.O.* Abiven. Dakar: Mission Catholique.

Malherbe, M., and C. Sall. 1989. *Parlons wolof: Langue et culture.* Paris: Editions L'Harmattan.

Munro, P., and D. Gaye. 1991. *Ay Baati Wolof, a Wolof Dictionary.* Los Angeles: University of California at Los Angeles.

Njie, C. 1982. *Description syntaxique du wolof de Gambie.* Dakar: Nouvelles Editions Africaines.

Sauvageot, S. 1965. *Description synchronique d'un dialecte wolof: Le parler du Dyolof.* Mémoires de l'IFAN, 73. Dakar: Institut Fondamental d'Afrique Noire.

Stewart, W. 1966. *Introductory Course in Dakar Wolof.* Washington, DC: Center for Applied Linguistics.

Xhosa

Laura J. Downing

Language Name: Xhosa. **Autonym:** *(Isi)Xhosa.*

Location: Southwest Cape Province and Transkei in the Republic of South Africa. It is one of the official languages of the Republic of South Africa.

Family: Nguni group of the Bantu subbranch of the Benue-Congo branch of the Niger-Congo subfamily of the Niger-Kordofanian family.

Related Languages: Xhosa is a member of Guthrie's (1967) S30 group of Bantu languages. Other major languages in S30 (also called the Nguni group) are Zulu, siSwati and Ndebele. Closely related S group Bantu languages include Venda, Tswana, Sepedi, and Sesotho. Many Xhosa speakers speak and/or understand Zulu, siSwati, Sesotho, English, and/or Afrikaans.

Dialects: Xhosa has a number of regional dialects: Ngqika (Gaika), Ndlambe, Gcaleka (these are the basis for standard, written Xhosa), Thembu, Bomvana, Mpondo, Mpondomse, Mfengu, and Xesibe. There is virtually no detailed documentation available for the dialects that are not the basis of the standard language. Besides these traditional regional dialects, with urbanization there has arisen a rural-urban dialect split. The distinguishing characteristic of the urban dialects is the more frequent occurrence of words borrowed from English and Afrikaans.

Number of Speakers: 6.5 million in 1991, or about 18 percent of the population of the Republic of South Africa.

Origin and History

Xhosa is a member of the Bantu language family, which is the largest language family of sub–Saharan Africa. Xhosa has only been a written language since the early 19th century, and most of our knowledge of it, until very recently, is based on descriptions and studies written by Europeans and South Africans of European origin. The earliest extensive word list of Xhosa is found in an appendix to Heinrich Lichtenstein's *Travels in Southern Africa* (1803–6), although sketchy lists appeared in travel accounts as early as 1776, and the Xhosa people had been established in southern Africa for centuries before these early European contacts. The first published grammar of Xhosa is William B. Boyce's *Grammar of the Kafir Language* (1834). The first printing of a "reading sheet" in Xhosa was in 1824 by John Bennie, and the orthography used in this reading sheet formed the basis for standard Xhosa orthography. The current orthography was adopted in 1931.

Orthography and Basic Phonology

Xhosa is written using the Latin alphabet, with the letters *c*, *x*, and *q* used to represent the dental, lateral, and palatal clicks, respectively. (The clicks were borrowed from the neighboring Khoisan languages.) Combinations of consonants represent single sounds (not consonant sequences); Xhosa syllable structure is strictly CV.

Xhosa distinguishes four major initiation types: voiceless ejective, voiceless aspirated, voiced and breathy voiced. Voiceless aspirated /ph th kh/ are comparable to English /p t k/ in most contexts, and ejective /p t k/ are comparable to the strong versions of English /p t k/ in word-final position. The most salient feature of the breathy voiced consonants is that, in many varieties of Xhosa, they act to lower the tone of a following vowel.

Xhosa has an unusual inventory of lateral sounds. In addition to the voiced and breathy voiced resonants, there are voiceless and breathy voice lateral fricatives *hl* and *dl*, an ejective lateral affricate *tl*, and a breathy voice lateral affricate *(n)dl*.

The alveolar nasal *n* assimilates in place to a following consonant. The consonant following the nasal may also change its pronunciation: notably, aspirated consonants become ejectives, and fricatives become affricates. Before resonants and glides, the nasal drops.

In addition to the above consonants, Xhosa has 18 click consonants. Clicks are produced with a velar closure simultaneous to their main articulation. When the main closure is released, an inrushing of air produces the characteristic clicking sound. In English, click sounds are only used paralinguistically. For example, the "disapproval" sound generally written "tsk-tsk" involves two dental clicks. In Xhosa, as in Zulu and in the Xhoisan languages, clicks are ordinary consonants. The Xhosa clicks are listed in Table 1 below.

Table 1: Clicks

		Dental	Lateral	Alveo-Palatal
Oral	Voiceless	c	x	q
	Aspirated	ch	xh	qh
	Breathy	gc	gx	gq
Pre-Nasalized	Voiceless	nc/nkc	nx/nkx	nq/nkq
	Breathy	ngc	ngx	ngq

Table 2: Consonants (Orthography)

		Labial	Alveolar	Alveo-Palatal	Palatal	Velar	Glottal
Stops	Ejective	p	t		ty	k	
	Aspirated	ph	th		tyh	kh	
	Breathy	bh	d		dy	g	
	Implosive	b					
Pre-nasalized Stops	Ejective	mp	nt, nts, ntl	ntsh	nty	nk	
	Breathy	mb	nd, nz, ndl	nj	ndy	ng	
Fricatives	Voiceless	f	s, hl	sh		rh	
	Breathy	v	z, dl			rh	
Affricates	Ejective		ts	tsh		kr	
	Aspirated		ts	tsh			
	Breathy			j			
Nasals	Voiced	m	n		ny		
	Breathy	mh	nh		nyh		
Resonants			l, r				
Glides	Voiced	w			y		
	Breathy						h
	Voiceless						h

Vowel length is not contrastive in Xhosa. Long vowels (indicated by a : following the vowel letter) only occur in phrase-penultimate stressed syllables and in a few morphologically defined contexts.

Table 3: Vowels

	Front	Central	Back
High	i		u
Mid	e		o
Low		a	

Sequences of vowels are not generally permitted in Xhosa. When morphological processes would otherwise produce sequences of vowels, several resolutions are possible. One of the vowels may be deleted, the first vowel may become a glide, or features of the two vowels may be combined in a single vowel.

Tone. Tone is lexically contrastive in Xhosa (as in most Bantu languages). There are two contrastive tones, high tone (marked ') and low tone (unmarked). In addition, there is a falling (high-low) contour tone (marked ^), which may only occur on long vowels. These contrasts are illustrated by the following triple: *amá- tha:nga* 'pumpkins', *amá-tha:ngá* 'thighs', *áma-thâ:nga* 'cattle posts'.

The most striking tonal rule of Xhosa is that high tones shift toward the end of the word, so that the latest high tone in a word falls on the antepenultimate syllable. Note the changing position of the high tone on the following: *í-thanga* 'pumpkin', *i-thángana* 'small pumpkins', *i-thangányana* 'tiny pumpkins'.

Basic Morphology

Like other Bantu languages, Xhosa has a system of alliterative concord that pervades the morphology. All nouns have a prefix that identify it as belonging to one of 15 agreement classes. Some classes are used exclusively for singular nouns; each of these has a corresponding plural class.

Class	Singular	Plural	Gloss
1/2	úm-limi	abá-limi	'farmer(s)'
3/4	úm-lilo	imí-lilo	'fire(s)'
5/6	í-phiko	amá-phiko	'wing(s)'
7/8	isí-qhamo	izí-qhamo	'fruit(s)'
9/10	ím-pahla	í:m-pahla	'possession(s)'
11/10	ú-thuli	í:n-thuli	'dust(s)'

Adjectives and other nominal modifiers take similar agreement prefixes:

abá-ntu ába-khûlu
CL2-person CL2-big
'big people'

ín-doda én-kûlu
CL9-man CL9-big
'big man'

Verbs are composed of the following morphemes: Negative-Subject-Tense/aspect-Object-Root-Derivation-Final V.

Ndi-ya-yi-bon-ís-w-a
SUBJ-T/A-OBJ-see-CAUS-PASSIVE-FINAL.V
'I am being shown it.'

A-ndi-sá-bá-bón-i
NEG-SUBJ-T/A-OBJ/CL2-see-FINAL.V
'I don't see them any longer.'

Not all of these "slots" must be filled: only the root, final vowel, and a subject prefix (for an inflected verb) are obligatory in all forms. The others are optional, depending on the meaning or function of the verb. The subject and object prefixes agree with the class of the noun phrases that serve these functions and co-occur with the overt noun phrases they agree with.

The meaning of verb roots may be modified by adding derivational suffixes: *-thánd-a* 'love', *-thand-án-a* 'love each other', *-thand-ék-a* 'be loveable', *-thand-él-a* 'love for', *-thand-ís-a* 'cause to love', *-thánd-w-a* 'be loved.'

Like most Bantu languages, Xhosa has numerous verb tenses/moods/aspects. Doke (1954) lists five tenses (remote past, immediate past, present, immediate future, and remote future), three aspects (indefinite, continuous, and perfect), and four moods (indicative, potential, contingent, and participial). Each of these has distinct morphology. There are also a number of compound tenses, which are composed of "defective" verbs followed by a "nonfinite" verbal complement. Further, most of these affirmative verb forms have a corresponding negative form whose morphology and tone pattern are quite distinct from the affirmative. Some examples of forms of the verb *-bal-* 'count' follow:

Tense/aspect	Form	Gloss
present affirmative	ni-ya-bala	'you count'
present negative	a-ni-bál-i	'you don't count'
perfect	ni-bal-ile	'you counted'
remote past	nâ-bal-á	'you counted'
perfect negative	a-ní-bal-ánga	'you didn't count'
subjunctive	ni-bál-e	'that you count'
past negative subjunc.	a-nâ-bal-á	'that you did not count'

Basic Syntax

The preferred order of constituents in Xhosa sentences is SVO.

Ábá-ntwana bá-ty-a úku-tyá
CL2-child CL2-eat-FINAL.V CL15-food
'The children eat food.'

But this preferred word order is frequently modified in discourse:

Í-gusha úm-fûyi ú-ya-yi-xhél-a
CL9-sheep CL1-farmer CL1-PRESENT-CL9-slaughter-FINAL.V
'(As for) the sheep, the farmer slaughters it.'

W-á-phum-á ápho úMthunzíni
CL1-PAST-go-FINAL.V out Mthunzini
'Mthunzini went out.'

As illustrated above, adjectives follow the nouns they modify. Xhosa sentences are negated by use of morphologically distinct verb forms as illustrated in the description of verb morphology above.

Contact with Other Languages

Xhosa has some borrowings from Khoisan languages, for example, *í- cáwa* 'church, Sunday', but most recent borrowings are either from English or Afrikaans. The borrowings are fit into the morphological system of Xhosa by being assigned class agreement, if they are nouns. And they are adapted phonologically to fit the segment inventory and syllable structure of Xhosa:

From Afrikaans: *í-bhulúkhwe* 'trousers' (< *broek*), *ísí-túphu* 'verandah' (< *stoep*)
From English: *í-derí* 'dairy', *í-tshókhwe* 'chalk'

Common Words

person:	úm-ntu	woman:	úm-fâzi
water:	ám-ânzi	sun:	í-langa
three:	-thâthu	fish:	ín-tlanzi
big:	-khûlu	tree:	úm-thí
long:	-de	good:	-hlé
bad:	-bí	bird:	ín-taka
dog:	ín-já	to walk:	úku-hámba
to see:	úku-bôna	to cultivate:	ukú-lima

Example Sentences

(1) Úm-ntwana u-sík-a í-sónka ngé-méla.
CL1-child CL1-cut-FINAL.V CL9-bread with-knife
'The child cuts bread with a knife.'

(2) Úm-pheki ú-ph-a ábá-ntwana úku-tyá.
CL1-cook CL1-give-FINAL.V CL2-child CL15-food
'The cook gives the children food.'

(3) Úm-ntwana u-béth-w-a y-ín-doda.
CL1-child CL1-beat-PASSIVE-FINAL.V by-CL9-man
'The child is beaten by the man.'

Efforts to Preserve, Protect, and Promote the Language

Xhosa is an official language of the Republic of South Africa used for secondary education, on the radio and in newspapers, and is taught as a second language. Xhosa has a long-established literary tradition, with novels, poetry, and plays, as well as more traditional literary forms widely available.

Select Bibliography

Cassimjee, Farida. 1998. *Isixhosa Tonology: An Optimal Domains Theory Analysis*. Munich: LINCOM EUROPA.
Claughton, J. 1983. *The Tones of Xhosa Inflections*. Communication no. 13, Department of African Languages. Grahamstown: Rhodes University.

Doke, C.M. 1954. *The Southern Bantu Languages*. London: Oxford University Press for the International African Institute.

Downing, Laura J. 1990. "Local and Metrical Tone Shift in Nguni." In *Studies in African Linguistics* 21, 261–317.

Finlayson, Rosalie. 1992. "From Past to Present Dynamics in Xhosa." In Derek F. Gowlett, ed. *African Linguistic Contributions*, 104–121. Pretoria: Via Afrika Limited.

Guthrie, M. 1967. *The Classification of the Bantu Languages*. London: Dawsons of Pall Mall for the International African Institute.

Louw, J.A. 1975/76. "Palatalization of Bilabials in the Passive, Diminutive, and Locative in Xhosa and Tsonga." In *Afrika und Übersee* 59, 241–278.

Satyo, S.C. "Topics in Xhosa Verbal Extensions." Ph.D. dissertation. Pretoria: University of South Africa.

Traill, A., J.S.M. Khumalo and P. Fridhon. 1987. "Depressing Facts about Zulu." In *African Studies* 46, 255–274.

Ziervogel, D. 1967. *Handbook of the Speech Sounds and Sound Changes of the Bantu Languages of South Africa*. UNISA Handbook Series No. 3E. Pretoria: University of South Africa.

Yi

David Bradley

Language Name: Yi. Various self-denominations, mostly based on a compound (stative verb 'black' plus nominalizing suffix *-su* or similar) meaning 'black people', such as Northern Yi *Nuosy*, Eastern Yi *Nasu*, Southern Yi *Nisu*. **Alternates:** (1) Ancient self-denomination *Nì* (still used in traditional texts); (2) *Cuàn* (Ts'uan), originally the surname of a ruling family, in use from the 4th to about the 15th centuries; still used in modern Chinese historical writing about this period; (3) *Lolo*, Chinese term in use from about the 15th to the mid-20th centuries; now regarded as pejorative and not used in the People's Republic of China (PRC).

Location: Spoken in most areas of southwestern Sichuan, eastern and central Yunnan, western Guizhou, and the northwestern tip of Guangxi in southwest China; also by a small number in northernmost Vietnam, where they go under the names *Lolo* and *Phula*.

Family: Northern Loloish subgroup of the (southeastern) Burmese-Lolo group of the Tibeto-Burman branch of the Sino-Tibetan language family. (It is proposed that the terms "Lolo" and "Loloish" which come from the old pejorative exonym *Lolo* be replaced by *Ni*, from the ancient autonym; see Bradley, 1995.)

Related Languages: Most closely related to the Central Loloish languages of northwestern Yunnan such as Lalaw, Lisu/Lipo/Lolopo, with Lahu and Jinuo somewhat more distant. Further distant are the Southern Loloish languages such as Hani/Akha, Bisu/Phunoi/Coong, as well as other small groups.

Dialects: The Yi nationality (like many other post-1950 nationalities of China) represents an amalgamation of various distinct groups speaking diverse dialects and languages. Traditional Yi history suggests six subgroups of the Yi.

The Yi language is officially divided into (1) Northern Yi, or *Nuosy*; (2) Eastern Yi or *Nasu*; (3) Southern Yi or *Nisu*; and (4) Southeastern Yi. Although not mutually intelligible, they are closely related and share a traditional script (which has very extensive local differences). All also share very similar verb-final syntax, extensive use of verb serialization, N + numeral + classifier, and so on; but there are major lexical differences, some based on regular sound change over the last millennium or so. Two other groups now included in the Yi nationality in China, Western Yi, or *Lalaw*, and Central Yi, *Lipo* or *Lolopo*, speak languages that are linguistically related to the others.

Number of Speakers: 4.9–5 million, approximately, of which about 2.5 million speak Northern Yi.

Origin and History

Yi is one of 55 minority languages of China. Unlike the Chinese language, whose various members belong to the Sinitic branch of the Sino-Tibetan family, Yi is a member of the Tibeto-Burman branch.

Yi speakers are ethnically distinct from Chinese. They are one of a number of minority groups within China and have been described as having "Caucasoid features" and skin darker than that of the Chinese (Ramsey 1987: 252).

Around 500 B.C., the classic age of China, Chinese peoples and languages were largely confined to the area north of the Yangtze River. The Chinese referred to themselves as *Han* and to the southern peoples as *Mán* or 'Southern Barbarians' (Ramsey 1987: 31). Over time the Chinese moved southward, but they were unable to dominate the Yi. Chinese records dating from 2,000 years ago describe the Yi under a variety of names (Ramsey 1987: 251).

Presumed ancestors of the Yi lived in the area around Dian Lake (where Kunming, the present capital of Yunnan, is located) and had a relatively high culture by the first millennium B.C. (Rawson 1983). This culture was probably in contact with the contemporaneous Dongson culture of what is now northern Vietnam. Artifacts include the well-known Dongson drums decorated with frogs and bronze models of five pipe-gourd reed organs similar to those still used by modern Ni/Loloish groups but not by others in the area (Bradley 1979a).

The Dian Kingdom came into Chinese history as one of many non-Chinese groups in a tenuous "tributary" relationship from the mid-fourth century B.C. The connection consisted mainly of occasional Chinese raids, somewhat more regular visits by envoys of the local rulers to the Chinese court, and the granting of titles and seals to these rulers; some of these seals have been found in tombs of the Dian rulers. Chinese cultural influence gradually increased; indeed, all early inscriptions are in Chinese.

After a hiatus caused by Chinese disunity in the third century A.D. (the Three Kingdoms period), Chinese contacts with the area were renewed to find a new dynasty, the Cuan (Ts'uan) family, in control of what is now northeastern Yunnan. A probably fictitious Chinese origin was claimed by these rulers; but they and most of their subjects appear to have been pre-Yi. Increasing Chinese influence followed for several centuries, with Chinese garrisons at various strategic salt-producing areas. In the mid-fifth century, the indigenous Cuan rulers split into two dynasties, the Eastern Cuan (northeast of Dian Lake)

Table 1: Consonants

		Bilabial	Labio-dental	Alveolar	Retroflex	Alveo-palatal	Velar
Stops	Voiceless, unaspirated	b		d	zh	j	g
	Voiced, aspirated	p		t	ch	g	k
	Voiced	bb		dd	rr	jj	gg
	Prenasal	nb		nd	nr	nj	mg
Fricatives	Voiceless		f	s	sh	x	h
	Voiced		v	ss	r	y	w
Affricates	Voiceless, unaspirated			z			
	Voiced, aspirated			c			
	Voiced			zz			
	Prenasal			nz			
Nasals	Voiceless	hm		hn		hny	hx
	Voiced	m		n		ny	ng
Laterals	Voiceless			hl			
	Voiced			l			

and the Western Cuan (to the southwest, centered on what is now Jinning). This dynastic split may have triggered the earliest dialect split of Yi into Eastern and Western.

The earliest recording of a genuine precursor of modern Yi is in Fan Chou's book, *Man Shu* ("Book of the Southwestern Barbarians"), written after A.D. 780 and translated by Luce (1961). This contains six words of Eastern Cuan in a Chinese phonetic representation.

Orthography and Basic Phonology

Cuan rulers and their successors continued to write in Chinese, but at some point an indigenous writing system was developed, based on the character principle used in Chinese: some words were represented by ideographic characters, and others phonetically similar to these were represented by modified versions of the ideographic characters. While the principle and some of the characters are derived from Chinese, the Yi writing system is completely different and very rich, with over 10,000 distinct characters.

The main use for writing was religious; traditional male religious leaders, the *bimox*, transmitted literacy to their chosen son or nephew so that he would take over this religious leadership. The teaching consisted of rote recitations of the older man's texts. Books were mainly written on handmade paper, but some stone funerary inscriptions, and inscriptions on bronze bells, including some bilingual with Chinese, also survive (see Ma 1986). The contents were primarily religious and historical literature; prior to 1950, only a very small proportion of the male population was literate. In the early 20th century a Yi aristocrat in Sichuan had one book printed (for details, see d'Ollone 1912); but apart from this, prior to 1950, all books were handwritten.

Because of the method of transmission, the script appears to have diversified quite rapidly, with almost every *bimox* having his own version. General similarities persist, but because the books are in archaic language and use individual versions of many characters, it is impossible for one *bimox* to read another's book(s) with full understanding. The syntax of these books is stylized, usually with five-syllable lines (occasionally three, seven, or nine syllable lines are also encountered); the vocabulary is also often obscure.

The most successful and widespread of the modern adaptations of traditional orthography is the one for the *Shengza* variety of Northern Yi used in Sichuan and northwestern Yunnan, and is based on an 819-item syllabary plus one diacritic to represent a sandhi tone. Each of the 819 items was originally an ideographic character.

In addition to the syllabic script used in Sichuan, there is also a romanization used for pedagogical purposes with speakers of other dialects and languages (including a few foreigners who have learned this dialect at the Southwestern Institute of Nationalities in Chengdu, Sichuan).

Yi syllables consist of an initial consonant, a vowel, and a tone.

The prenasalized voiced stops are homorganic, *so nb* = [mb], *mg* = [ŋg], and so on. *Hx* is historically the voiceless velar nasal *hng*, but is pronounced as a nasalized [~h].

Table 2: Vowels

	Front	Back
High	i	e
Mid-High		o
Mid-Low	ie	uo
Low		a

The midlow vowels *ie* and *uo* are monophthongs /ɛ/ and /ɔ/.

There are two additional syllabic segments: *y* and *u*. *Y* is an alveolar approximant, produced with the tongue a little closer to the hard palate than it is for *i*. After stops, *u* is a voiced bilabial trill, somewhat like a Bronx cheer; after other initials, it is a voiced bilabial fricative [β].

Tones. In the standard transcription, Yi tones are written with consonant letters following the vowel. This practice does not lead to confusion, because, as noted above, no Yi syllables end in consonant sounds.

Final Consonant	Tone Represented (1 = low, 5 = high)
-t	55 (high)
-ø	33 (mid)
-p	21 (low falling)
-r	33 (mid creaky)
-x	44 (higher mid)

The underline with the *-r* tone indicates laryngeal constriction (creaky voice); this occurs only with *u* and *y* in standard Shengza, and with more or fewer vowels in other dialects.

In Shengza, nearly all instances of the [44] tone result from sandhi of various kinds:

(1) In compounds with the first syllable containing most vowels, [33] usually becomes [44] if the following syllable has [33] tone.

(2) If a verb with low falling ([21]) tone is negated (by a preceding *ap*), the [21] tone of the verb becomes [44].

(3) In four-syllable reduplicated poetic compounds, the first or second of two identical low-tone syllables changes to [44] tone.

(4) A direct object pronoun immediately before a low tone [21] verb changes to [44] tone.

In dialects of Northern Yi other than Shengza, this sandhi is less frequent or absent. The sandhi may be viewed as a reaction to historical processes that merged about 80 percent of all Shengza syllables to [33] tone (see Bradley, 1993).

Basic Morphology

There is little noun morphology, other than compounding; pronouns do show some paradigmatic oppositions, for example, between plural and singular and among subject, object, and possessor form. There are distinct subject pronouns for first-, second-, and third-person singular, dual, and plural. For first-person plural, there is a distinction between inclusive 'you and I' *nitngop* and exclusive 'we (but not you)' *ngopwox*. Reflexive object pronouns are reduplicated from the singular subject pronouns, with a change in tone: *nga* 'I', *ngatngat* 'myself'. Cases are marked on nouns (if at all) by nonobligatory postposed particles; number marking is absent from nouns.

There is also very little verb morphology, other than sandhi in midtone compound verbs or low-tone verbs in certain environments. In particular, there is no agreement of any kind between nouns and verbs.

Adverbs usually occur at the beginning of a sentence (or at least before the verb). Some adverbs are derived via reduplication of verbs or adjectives (see Example Sentence 3).

Basic Syntax

The order of constituents is verb-final; order of preceding noun phrases is determined by pragmatic considerations. As in most related languages, the question (WH) words are not necessarily fronted, as they are in ENGLISH (see Example Sentence 1).

Within the noun phrase, possessors, relative clauses, and other nominal modifiers precede the head, which may be followed by a numeral plus classifier. This numeral plus classifier also may act as a pronominal, without a head noun:

ngat tepyy
my book

The classifier system contains 186 classifiers; most are the usual semantically based categories: human, nonhuman animate, shape-based, function-based, autoclassifers (noun = classifier), and so on. Apart from counting, numerals do not occur without a following classifier:

co suo-yuo
person three-CLASSIFIER:HUMAN
'three people'

co cy-bot
person this-CLASSIFIER:MALE.HUMAN
'this (male) person'

Within the verb, some serial elements (such as negation) precede the head, but most modal-type serials follow the head. These may be followed by sentence-final markers of various types: aspect, evidential, and so on.

Pronouns are infrequent in running text; Yi sentences do not have to contain an overt subject or object or any noun phrase at all, if the context is clear.

As in most closely related Southeast Tibeto-Burman languages, there are postposed case-marking particles, mainly for non-core (i.e., not S or O) arguments. In some tonal environments, a pronominal object may be marked by the sandhi [44] tone.

Most compound nominals have the nominal head preceding a verbal attribute (so "house-white") but conversely a nominal specifier or attribute preceding the head nominal (so "spirit - house" a house for spirits; "house-spirit", the house spirit).

Sentences are negated by prefixing *ap* immediately before the verb. This triggers the [44] sandhi tone on a following low tone verb.

Contact with Other Languages

All Ni/Loloish languages of China, including Yi, have undergone extensive contact with Chinese; and Yi has been in contact with Chinese for more than two millennia. However, for those Yi who did not assimilate and become Chinese, until 1950 there was relatively little linguistic influence other than a few loanwords. In many areas of northern Yunnan and western Guizhou (and for the last three centuries in southwestern Sichuan), Yi was used by members of other groups such as the Miao. In many cases, the Yi were local feudal lords, and in some areas the Yi population was regularly augmented by captured Miao, Chinese, or other slaves, who by now have assimilated into the general Yi population.

Most loanwords in Northern Yi are rather recent and so are relatively less assimilated, especially in the speech of bilinguals between Yi and Chinese. Other varieties of Yi have a greater proportion of Chinese loanwords; for example, the Samei variety spoken southeast of Kunming in Yunnan uses about 40 percent Chinese loanwords in everyday speech; that is when Samei is spoken at all, which it rarely is by anyone under 50 years old.

Common Words

man:	co	long:	a sho
woman:	ap my sse	small:	iet zyr
water:	ie qyt	yes:	nge
sun:	hxo bbu	no:	ap zhot
three:	suo	good:	nbop
fish:	hxe mgot	bird:	hxie zyr
big:	ax yy	dog:	ke
tree:	syr		

Note: *ap my sse* 'woman' does not begin with the negative morpheme *ap*. 'Woman' has a basic tone sequence of [33]-[33]-[33]. The first-level tone changes to a low [21] tone via tone sandhi (see above). In *ap zhot* 'no', the [21] tone of *ap* is basic and not the result of tone sandhi.

Example Sentences

(1) Ne kat da la?
nɯ^{33} kha^{55} ta^{33} la^{33}
you where from come
'Where do you come from?' (a usual greeting)

(2) nry ndo!
nd^{33} ndo^{33}
whisky drink
'Drink whiskey!'

(3) iex ssa iex ssa bbo.
ɛ^{44} za^{33} ɛ^{44} za^{33} bo^{33}
slow slow go
'Go slowly.' (a usual farewell)

Efforts to Preserve, Protect, and Promote the Language

In some Yi communities, such as those around Kunming in Yunnan, spoken Yi is being replaced by Chinese.

At the county, prefecture, and provincial levels and in various research institutions in Beijing, Sichuan, Yunnan and Guizhou, extensive efforts are being made to preserve traditional Yi literature. Local language offices collect manuscripts; many also attempt to transcribe them phonetically as well as to translate them into MANDARIN. Some of this material is then published, mainly by the Sichuan Nationalities Publishing House, but also to a lesser extent by the Yunnan Nationalities Publishing House and at the Central University of Nationalities in Beijing. Unfortunately, due to the differences among individual versions of the traditional script, the *bimox* who wrote the text, or one of his trained descendants, is needed to read it, so many collected manuscripts cannot be fully read, and as most *bimox* regard their manuscripts as secret, few are willing to come forward and help. Traditionally trained *bimox* are mostly rather old men, but now many of the younger Yi language scholars are relatives of *bimox* partly or fully trained by their father or uncle prior to formal study.

Linguists have developed revised versions of the traditional script and taught these very widely. Unfortunately, each province with a substantial Yi population has taken a completely different approach to script reform (see Bradley 1995).

Select Bibliography

Most of the published dictionaries, grammars, and other descriptive materials on Yi are in Chinese, Chinese and Yi, or most recently, in Yi, and are not widely available outside China.

Backus, Charles. 1981. *The Nan-chao Kingdom and T'ang China's Southwestern Frontier.* Cambridge: Cambridge University Press.

Bradley, David. 1979a. "Speech through Music: The Sino-Tibetan Gourd Reed-Organ." In *Bulletin of the School of Oriental and African Studies* XLII, 3, 535–540.

____. 1979b. *Proto-Loloish.* Scandinavian Institute of Asian Studies Monograph Series No. 39. London: Curzon Press.

____. 1993. "Pronouns in Burmese-Lolo." In *Linguistics of the Tibeto-Burman Area* 16/1: 157–215.

____. 1995a. "Language Policy for the Yi." Paper given at the Yi Studies Conference, University of Washington, Seattle, March 16–19.

____. 1995b. "Grammaticalisation of Extent in Mran-Ni." In *Linguistics of the Tibeto-Burman Area* 18:1: 1–28.

Coblin, W. South. 1979. "A New Study of the Pai-lang Songs." In *The Tsing Hua Journal of Chinese Studies* 12, 1–2, 179–216.

d'Ollone, H.M.G. 1912. *Ecritures des peuples non chinois de la chine, quatre dictionaires Lolo et Miao Tseu* ('Writing systems of non-Chinese peoples of China: four Lolo and Miao Tseu dictionaries'). Paris: Ernest Leroux.

Luce, Gordon Hannington, trans. 1961. *Man Shu* ('Book of the Southern Barbarians'). Ithaca, NY: Data Paper Number 44, Southeast Asia Program, Department of Far Eastern Studies, Cornell University.

Ma Xueliang. 1986/1999. *Cuanwen Congke* ('Cuan Inscriptions, in Chinese and Yi'). 3 vol. Chengdu: Siichuan Nationalities Press.

Moseley, Christopher, ed. 1993. *Atlas of the World's Languages.* London: Routledge.

Ramsey, S.R. 1987. *The Languages of China.* Princeton: Princeton University Press.

Rawson, Jessica, ed. 1983. *The Chinese Bronzes of Yunnan.* London: Sidgwick and Jackson. Published in association with the Cultural Relics Publishing House, Beijing.

Wurm, S.A., *et al.*, eds. 1987/1991. *Language Atlas of China.* Hong Kong: Longman.

YIDDISH

Paul Glasser

Language Name: Yiddish. **Alternate:** *mame-lošn* (lit. 'mother tongue'). **Autonym:** *jidiš*.

Location: At its peak in the 18th century, the Yiddish-language area reached nearly across the whole width of northern Europe—Germany, Holland, Alsace, Switzerland, Bohemia, Moravia, Slovakia, Hungary, Poland, Lithuania, Latvia, Estonia, Belorussia, Ukraine, and Romania. By the early part of the 20th century, there were only pockets remaining in the western part of this area, with most speakers found in the eastern half. Since the Holocaust, the number of Yiddish speakers in Europe has shrunk dramatically, with most now found in France, Belgium, and the former Soviet Union. Because of immigration, there are sizeable Yiddish-speaking communities in Israel, the United States, Canada, Argentina, Mexico, and South Africa.

Family: West Germanic subbranch of the Germanic branch of Indo-European.

Related Languages: GERMAN, specifically High German. Like ENGLISH, Yiddish is a fusion language, and has integrated elements from Middle High German dialects, HEBREW, and the Slavic languages (primarily CZECH, POLISH, BELORUSSIAN, and UKRAINIAN). Hebrew and Slavic have influenced Yiddish primarily, but not exclusively, in its lexicon.

Dialects: Historically, Yiddish is divisible into two main dialects: Western Yiddish spoken in Germany, Holland, Alsace, Switzerland, Bohemia, Moravia, Slovakia, and western Hungary; and Eastern Yiddish spoken in Poland, Lithuania, Latvia, Estonia, Belorussia, Ukraine, Romania, and eastern Hungary. With the decline of Western Yiddish, most Yiddish speakers today use one of the subdialects of Eastern Yiddish: Northeastern Yiddish spoken in Lithuania, Latvia, Estonia, Belorussia, and northeastern Ukraine; Southeastern Yiddish spoken in the rest of the Ukraine and in eastern Romania; and Central Yiddish spoken in Poland, eastern Hungary and western Romania. The largest Yiddish-speaking communities today are found among Hasidic Jews in the United States, Canada, France, Belgium, and Israel, and nearly all use one form or another of Central Yiddish.

Standard Yiddish is the designation for the form of Yiddish used in Yiddish-language classes and in public speaking (speeches, radio); it most resembles Northeastern Yiddish in pronunciation and Southeastern-Central Yiddish in morphology-grammar, for example, grammatical gender and plural of nouns. Stage Yiddish is a form used in the Yiddish theater and film that resembles Southeastern Yiddish in both pronunciation and morphology-grammar.

Number of Speakers: At its height, before the Holocaust, there were 10–11 million. Since the Holocaust, there are probably a few hundred thousand who actually use Yiddish more or less full-time, mostly among Hasidim, and 1–2 million more who speak Yiddish fluently, but may not use it regularly.

Origin and History

Jews first arrived in the Rhineland about the year 1000, having passed through the Italian peninsula and the future territory of France. They presumably arrived speaking a Romance-based Jewish language, as is postulated based on knowledge of settlement history and on a number of Yiddish lexical items of Romance origin. Recent research now calls this hypothesis into question.

Over the next two centuries, the future Ashkenazim settled over most of High German territory and incorporated elements from the various urban dialects of Upper and Central German into their language. Low German has had virtually no effect on Yiddish. Contact with Slavs in the eastern part of this territory brought about the beginnings of a Slavic component, which, however, remained small in Western Yiddish and only came into full bloom with the advent of large Jewish settlements in the Slavic heartland in the following centuries.

A result of the mobility of German Jews and the close contact between Jewish settlements scattered throughout High German territory was the rise of a German component of Yiddish that was not identical to any particular German regional or local dialect. While attested Middle High German forms do shed light on the development of Yiddish, there are a number of items where the Yiddish form cannot be derived directly from the Middle High German form.

The periodization of Yiddish is as follows. **Earliest Yiddish** (1000–1250) was the language before contact with Slavic; **Old Yiddish** (1250–1500) developed after the encounter with Slavic and the speakers' eventual settlement in Slavic territory. During this period Slavic-speaking Jews already living in these areas began speaking Yiddish. The oldest surviving texts, a sentence in a Hebrew prayer book from 1272 and the *Cambridge Codex* from 1382, are in Old Yiddish. Also during this period the standard written language, based on what is now known as Western Yiddish, came into being. **Middle Yiddish** (1500–1700) was characterized by the shifting of the demographic weight from west to east. The written language re-

Table 1: Consonants

		Labial	Dental	Alveo-palatal	Palatal	Velar	Glottal
Stops	Voiceless	p	t		t'	k	
	Voiced	b	d		d'	g	
Fricatives	Voiceless	f	s	š	s'	x	h
	Voiced	v	z	ž	z'	r	
Affricates	Voiceless		c	č			
	Voiced		dz	dž			
Resonants			l	j	l'		
Nasals		m	n		n'	ŋ	

mained fixed on its western base as the eastern dialects developed. Finally, **Modern Yiddish** (1700–present) has been characterized by the decline of both spoken Western Yiddish sparked by the emancipation of the Jews in Germany and France, and by the collapse of the old literary standard. A new, eastern-based literary standard gradually took shape over the course of the 19th century. Yiddish began to acquire a measure of social prestige.

Orthography and Basic Phonology

Yiddish is written in the Hebrew alphabet with the addition of several vowel and consonant diacritics. Unlike Hebrew, vowels are regularly represented by separate letters, with or without diacritics. The letter *alef* represents /a/ and /o/, the letter *ajin* /e/, the letter *jud* /i/ (as well as /j/), and the letter *vov* /u/ (two *vovs* are /v/). The Hebrew rule that word-initial /i/ or /u/, as well as the diphthongs /aj/, /ej/ and /oj/, must be preceded by silent *alef*, that is, *alef* with no diacritics, has been retained in Yiddish. Morever, while words of the other components are written phonemically, words of Hebrew-ARAMAIC origin are written in the traditional manner, that is consonant letters only.

Standard Yiddish has the basic European-type consonants in voiceless and voiced series and unaspirated stops, as well as a palatal series because of Slavic influence; while these palatal consonants do occur in all etymological components, they are found primarily in the Slavic component, and they are the rarest of the consonants.

The sound represented by /r/ is a voiced velar or postvelar fricative for a majority of Yiddish speakers, although a large minority has an apical tap or trill. The location of the latter phone at the fringes of the Eastern Yiddish language territory in primarily western Poland, Hungary, Bessarabia, and eastern Belorussia leads to the inference that it is a survival, whereas the former is the innovation. In contrast to German, the phoneme /x/ is always phonetic [x].

Also in contrast to German, in Standard Yiddish, word- or morpheme-final voiced consonants are not devoiced; that is, voiced distinctions are maintained in final position. In various dialects, a rule of final devoicing does apply; it is more complicated than simple word-final devoicing—devoicing occurs in utterance-final position, but in certain syntactic contexts that are not yet defined, word-final devoicing is overridden and historical voiceless consonants may even acquire voicing. Moreover, in the easternmost dialects and in Standard Yiddish as spoken by speakers of those dialects, regressive voice assimilation occurs across morpheme boundaries.

Table 2: Vowels

	Front	Central	Back
High	i		u
Mid	e		o
Low		a	

Standard Yiddish has a five-vowel inventory of the usual European type, as well as three diphthongs, /ej/, /oj/, and /aj/. Most dialects have a larger vowel inventory; some have a full or nearly a full short-long series.

Stress generally falls on the root syllable in German-component words, on the penultimate in Hebrew-component words (which requires a stress shift between singular and plural in many cases), on the penultimate or antepenultimate in Slavic-component words, on the penultimate in modern borrowings that end in a vowel, and on the ultimate in modern borrowings that end in a consonant. Overall, this yields penultimate stress in the majority of lexical items.

Basic Morphology

Yiddish noun phrases are inflected for case, gender and number. Only a few nouns, most denoting male humans, are inflected for case: for example, *der tate* (nominative), *dem tatn* (accusative-dative) 'father', *der zejde* (nominative), *dem zejdn* (accusative-dative) 'grandfather'. Otherwise, the definite article and the adjective of the noun phrase carry the case, gender, and number markers.

There are three genders: masculine, feminine, and neuter. While nouns denoting animates generally fall into the appro-

Table 3: Verbs

Verb Type	Infinitive	Past Participle	Meaning
regular *-t*	zog-n	ge-zog-t	'say'
irregular *-t*	hob-n	ge-ha-t	'have'
	vel-n	ge-vol-t	'want'
	vis-n	ge-vus-t	'know'
	brengen	ge-brax-t/ ge-breng-t	'bring'
-n, -i-/-u-	vinč-n	ge-vunč-n	'wish'
-n, -i-/-o-	šis-n	ge-šos-n	'shoot'
-n, -i-/-oj-	farlir-n	farlojr-n	'lose'
-n, -e-/-o-	šext-n	ge-šoxt-n	'slaughter'
-n, -e-/-oj-	veg-n	ge-vojg-n	'weigh'
-n, -e-/-e-	ze-n	ge-ze-n	'see'
-n, -ej-/-oj-	hejb-n	ge-hojb-n	'lift'
-n, -aj-/-i-	šraj-en	ge-šrig-n	'shout'
-n, -o-/-o-	bod-n	ge-bod-n	'bathe'
-n, -a-/-a-	vaš-n	ge-vaš-n	'wash'
-n, -a-/-o-	špalt-n	ge-špolt-n	'split'

priate "natural" gender—*der man* 'man', *der bik* 'bull' (masculine), *di froj* 'woman', *di ku* 'cow' (feminine), *dos kind* 'child', *dos kalb* 'calf' (neuter, because indeterminate); but *dos vajb* 'wife, woman' (neuter)—gender of nouns denoting inanimates is distributed arbitrarily: *der tiš* 'table' (masculine), *di krajd* 'chalk' (feminine), *dos bux* 'book' (neuter). In general, nouns retain the gender of the source language, but there are numerous exceptions, for example, *der gopl* 'fork' (masculine), German *die Gabel*; *(der) šabes* 'Sabbath' (masculine), and Hebrew *šabat* (feminine).

The two numbers in Yiddish are singular and plural. There are several ways of forming the plural: *-n* (most frequent), as in *štul-n* 'chair(s)'; *-s*, as in *feter-s* 'uncle(s)', *mogn-s* 'stomach(s)', *majse-s* 'story, stories'; *-es*, as in *nudnik-es* 'pest(s)', *smi(či)k-es* '(violin) bow', *xolem, xalojmes* 'dream(s)'; *-er* (with vowel change when the root vowel is a back vowel), as in *kloc, klecer* 'wooden beam', *bret-er* 'wooden board'; vowel change only, as in *hant, hent* 'hand(s)'; syncretism of singular and plural, as in *fencter, fencter* 'window(s)', *šof, šof* 'sheep'; *-im*, as in *šabes, šabosim* 'Sabbath(s), Saturday(s)', *dokter, doktojrim* 'physician(s)'. Note that nouns that form the plural with the suffixes *-es* or *-im* frequently have stress shift and therefore a different vowel in the singular and plural, as in the aforementioned *xolem, xalojmes, šabes, šabosim, dokter, doktojrim*. While most nouns retain the historical plural suffixes, many do not, such as in nearly all the aforementioned nouns: *feters*, German *Vettern*; *mogns* or *megener*, German *Magen* or *Mägen*; *majses*, Hebrew *maase, maasim* 'deed(s)' (cognate with the Yiddish singular, *majse*); and *maasija, maasijot* 'story, stories' (cognate with, but not identical to, the Yiddish plural, *majses*); *nudnikes*, Polish *nudziarz-y*; *smi(či)kes*, Polish *smyczky* (the Yiddish *-es* plural does not have an equivalent in Polish, nor does the Polish *-y* plural have a Yiddish equivalent); *klecer*, German *Klötze, hent*, German *Hände*, *šof*, German *Schafe* (the German *-e* plural does not exist in Yiddish); *šabosim*, Hebrew *šabatot*; *doktojrim*, German *Doktoren*.

In the verb, all tenses and moods except for the present tense and the imperative are formed analytically. The past tense is formed from inflected forms of the verbs *hobn* 'to have' (over 90 percent) or *zajn* 'to be' (under 10 percent) and the past participle. The future tense is formed from the auxiliary stem *vel-* plus the infinitive; the habitual past from the auxiliary stem *fleg-* plus the infinitive; the conditional from the auxiliary stem *volt-* plus the past participle (regionally, the infinitive).

The past participle is formed by the addition of the prefix *ge-* (except if the verb has an unstressed prefix) and the suffix *-t* (over 80 percent) or the suffix *-n* (under 20 percent); many verbs that form the past participle with the suffix *-n* also alter the root vowel and, occasionally, a root consonant. On the whole, such verbs fall into patterns. In addition, there are four irregular *-t* verbs that have a different stem in the present and in the past participle. (See Table 3 above.)

Yiddish has a system of verbal prefixes and complements that modify the meaning of the verb, occasionally beyond recognition. The prefixes are *ant-, ba-, ce-, der-, far-, ge-*. Their meanings are generally quite abstract and hard to gloss. Once added to a verb, the prefixes remain attached in all forms and block the prefixation of *ge-* to the past participle: *max-n, ge-max-t* 'make, made', but *far-max-n, far-max-t* 'close(d)'.

The verbal complements, *afer-* 'out from under', *(ar-)ajn-* 'in', *baj-* '(approximate) by', *cu-* 'to(ward)', *curik-* 'back', *cuzamen-/cunojf-* 'together', *durx-* 'through', *for-* 'fore-', *(ar-)iber-* 'over, across', *(ar-)ojs-* 'out', *on-* '(approximate)

Table 4: Morphological Verb Types

Verb Type	Infinitive	First Person (Present/Past/Future)	Imperative
Simple Verb	*maxn* 'make'	*ix max/ hob gemaxt/ vel maxn*	*max(t)!*
Prefixed Verb	*farmaxn* 'close'	*ix farmax/ hob farmaxt / vel farmaxn*	*farmax (t)!*
Complemented Verb	*ibermaxn* 'change, redo'	*ix max iber/ hob ibergemaxt/ vel ibermaxn*	*max(t) iber!*
Periphrastic Verb	*xorev maxn* 'destroy'	*ix max xorev/ hob xorev gemaxt/ vel xorev maxn*	*max(t) xorev!*

on', *(ar-)op-* 'off, down', *(ar-)uf-* 'up', *(ar-)um-* 'around', *(ar-) unter-* 'under', generally have a rather concrete meaning. In the pairs with and without *(ar-)*, the form with *(ar-)* has a more concrete meaning, the form without *(ar-)* a more abstract meaning. Contrast, for example, *ar-ojs-gej-n* 'to go out, exit' and *ojs-gej-n* 'to go out, expire, lapse, be extinguished'. Once added to a verb, complements remain attached to the unconjugated forms (infinitive, past participle, present participle), but are detached from the conjugated forms (present tense, imperative): *ix bin arojsgegangen* 'I went out', *ix vel arojsgejn* 'I will go out', *ix gej arojs* 'I go out', *gej arojs!* 'go out!'.

Yiddish also has a series of periphrastic verbs, made up of an auxiliary, which is conjugated, and an invariant element; in most such verbs, the auxiliary is *zajn* 'to be' (but the past tense auxiliary is the hybrid *hobn* + *geven*, rather than the expected past tense form of 'to be', *zajn* + *geven*) and the invariant is derived from a Hebrew present participle, for example, *mojxl zajn* 'to forgive', *mekane zajn* 'to envy', *maskim zajn* 'to agree', *jojce zajn* 'to do just enough'.

Basic Syntax

In Yiddish, unlike in German, the word order of main and subordinate clauses is uniform. The verb generally occurs in the second position in the clause. In order to express continuity of discourse, the verb can be placed first in the clause and the subject is second. In the imperative, the verb is also sentence initial.

Yes/no questions are formed in Yiddish either by use of an interrogative intonation with the usual declarative word order or by placing the verb before the subject, with or without the interrogative particle *ci* (which otherwise means 'whether').

Adjectives generally proceed the nouns they modify; however, constructions such as *a mejdl a klugs* 'a clever girl, (literally) a girl a clever (one)', *a boxer a šejner* 'a handsome guy, (literally) a guy a handsome (one)' are also possible.

Sentences are negated by *ni(š)t*, which follows the inflected verb. *ni(š)t* follows adverbs of time and precedes adverbs of place and manner. In contrast to German and English, but similarly to the Slavic languages, Yiddish uses multiple negatives.

All such short adverbs appear between the two elements of a periphrastic verb (either the aforementioned periphrastic verb or periphrastic tenses of simple verbs—past and future), but adverbial and prepositional phrases will generally precede the first or follow the second element of the verb, as will noun phrases other than the subject:

in majn ganc lebn hob ix nox kejn mol
in my whole/DAT/NEUT/SG life have/1SG I yet no time

ništ ge-ze-n dem jam
NEG PAST-see-PAST the/ACC/MASC/SG sea
'I've never yet seen the sea in my whole life.'

Contact with Other Languages

Yiddish is a fusion language, made up of three historical components: German, Hebrew-Aramaic, and Slavic. It has a largely German-origin phonology, vocabulary, and grammar, and a substantial stratum of Hebrew and Aramaic lexical items, as well as Slavic lexical borrowings. There is strong Slavic influence evident in the phonology, grammar and syntax as well, especially in easternmost Yiddish. There is also a small number of words of Romance origin, presumably derived from the Old FRENCH– and Old ITALIAN–based languages spoken by the Jews before they arrived in what is now Germany; and a larger number of "internationalisms", scientific and other loanwords from LATIN and GREEK in the modern period, via German, Polish, or RUSSIAN.

Examples of words from each component (which may or may not occur in the given form in the language of origin):

From German: *tiš* 'table', *šnur* 'daughter-in-law'
From Hebrew-Aramaic: *šabes* 'Sabbath/Saturday', *balebos* 'landlord, boss'
From Slavic: *blote* 'mud', *pi(š)čevke* 'detail'
From Romance: *benčn* 'to bless', *čolnt* 'Sabbath stew'
"Internationalisms": *biologje* 'biology', *konferenc* 'conference', *kompjuter* 'computer'

An interesting subject is those words that are nearly identical in form in Yiddish and the source language and yet have completely different, occasionally even opposite, meanings: Yiddish *opšaj* 'reverence' versus German *Abscheu* 'disgust'; Yiddish *vorem* 'because' versus German *warum* 'why'. There is a whole series of Slavic-influenced Yiddish verbal prefixes that resemble their German cognates in form, but not in meaning: for example, Yiddish *unter-* 'under' is cognate with German *unter-* 'under', but the meaning is often 'stealthily; slightly', which does not appear in German but matches the Slavic prefix *pod-*; Yiddish *op-* 'off' is cognate with German *ab-* 'off', but the meaning is frequently 'back, to finish', which does not appear in German but matches the Slavic prefix *od-/ ot-*. Examples follow:

untervarfn 'to plant, for example, leave a baby on a doorstep', from *varfn* 'to throw', compared to Polish *podrzucać*
untervaksn 'to grow up imperceptibly', from *vaksn* 'to grow', compared to Polish *podróść*
unterganvenen zix 'to sneak up on', from *ganvenen* 'to steal' (a Hebrew-origin verb), compared to Polish *podkradać sie*
unterzingen 'to hum', from *zingen* 'to sing', compared to Polish *podspiewywać*
opgebn 'to give back', from *gebn* 'to give', compared to Polish *oddać*
oplojbn zix 'to praise sufficiently', from *lojbn* 'to praise', compared to Polish *odchwalić sie*

There are even some verbs of this type that have two meanings, one resembling the one in German and the other the one in Slavic as in:

opredn 'to agree, arrange; to finish speaking', from *redn* 'to speak', compared to German *absprechen* and Polish *odmówić* respectively.

Common Words

man:	man	long:	lang
woman:	froj, vajb	small:	klejn
water:	vaser	yes:	jo
sun:	zun	no:	nejn
three:	draj	good:	gut
fish:	fiš	bird:	fojgl
big:	grojs	dog:	hunt
tree:	bojm		

Example Sentences

(1) Nox-n benčn hot de-r
following-the/DAT/NEUT/SG blessing has the-NOM/MASC/SG

zejde ge-kojf-t a sejfer.
grandfather PAST-buy-PAST a religious.book
'Following the blessing after the meal, Grandfather bought a religious book.'

(2) Hajnt vel ix ništ gej-n cu de-r arbet.
today will I NEG go-INFINITIVE to the-DAT/FEM/SG work
'I'm not going to go to work today.'

(3) Es iz šojn ge-ve-n etlexe un
it is already PAST-be-past several and

zibecik jor nox di
seventy year/NOM/NEUT/PL after the-DAT/MASC/PL

Xmjelnicki- pogrom-en un jidiš lebn
Khmelnitski pogrom-PL and Yiddish life

iz nox alc ge-ve-n hefker.
is still all PAST-be-PAST unprotected
'It was already seventy some-odd years after the Khmelnitski pogroms, and Jewish life was still unprotected.'

Efforts to Preserve, Protect, and Promote the Language

Yiddish has benefited from government protection on rare occasions only, most notably during the 1920s in the Soviet Union, in particular in the Ukrainian and Belorussian Republics. From 1935 to 1937, Yiddish was an official language of the Jewish Autonomous Region (Birobidzhan); since 1937, it has been widely used in the region, but has been a language of government de jure only, not de facto. Most efforts to promote it have been private.

From its beginnings until the mid-19th century, Yiddish was used as a spoken language and in writings addressed to uneducated people, primarily women. Extant pre-19th century Yiddish literature was intended either to educate simple folk in following the commandments relevant to them or to entertain them in a wholesome fashion and thus discourage from seeking such entertainment outside the community. Serious works of scholarship were all written in Hebrew.

In 1864, the classic Yiddish writer Sholem-Yankev Abramovitsh (known as Mendele Moykher-Sforim) published his first Yiddish novel, *Dos klejne menčele* ('The Little Man'); this is considered to be the first work of Modern Yiddish literature, written for men and women. At this time, Jewish writers in Eastern Europe, the majority of whom had begun their careers writing in Hebrew, started to write serious works of literature and scholarship in Yiddish. This was done for practical reasons since the Yiddish-reading audience was much greater than the Hebrew-reading public, and also because of the conviction that Yiddish was worth cultivating for its own sake. Throughout the 20th century, Modern Yiddish poetry and prose continued to develop, culminating in the awarding of the Nobel Prize to the novelist and short-story writer Isaac Bashevis Singer in 1978.

The 'Jewish Labor Alliance' (*Bund*), founded in 1897, conducted most of its agitation in Yiddish, for the same practical reasons mentioned above. The *Bund* and other political organizations introduced much terminology into the language, mostly borrowed from German, and buttressed the principle that Yiddish was fit for higher spheres of endeavor, such as politics, not just for conversation and light entertainment. The Yiddish press began to blossom early in this century and reached a high point in interwar Eastern Europe and America. Yiddish school systems also flourished in this period, in particular the *TsIShO* ('Central Yiddish School Organization') schools in Poland as well as several competing systems in the U.S., each associated with a particular political movement.

In 1908, the first conference to promote Yiddish was held in Czernowitz, Austria (now Tshernivtsy, Ukraine), and served to galvanize the pro-Yiddish camp. The year 1925 brought the founding of the *Jidišer visnšaftlexer institut* ('Jewish Research

Institute'), in Vilna, then Poland. It is now known as the YIVO Institute for Jewish Research and located in New York. The YIVO undertook research in various fields, especially linguistics, history, economics, psychology, and sociology; conducted its business almost exclusively in Yiddish; sought to collect Yiddish terminology of all types and to create terminology where it was lacking; and promulgated a standard Yiddish orthography where there had been none before. It achieved a certain measure of success in these endeavors, both before World War II, in Poland, and after World War II, in New York.

Select Bibliography

Birnbaum, Solomon A. 1979. *Yiddish*. Toronto: University of Toronto Press.

Bratkowsky, Joan G. 1988. *Yiddish Linguistics: A Multilingual Bibliography*. New York and London: Garland Press.

Bunis, David M., and Andrew Sunshine. 1994. *Yiddish Linguistics: A Classified Bilingual Index to Yiddish Serials and Collections, 1913–1958*. New York: Garland Press.

Goldberg, David, ed. 1993. *The Field of Yiddish*, fifth collection. Evanston, IL and New York: Northwestern University Press and YIVO Institute for Jewish Research.

Harkavy, Alexander. 1928. *Yiddish-English-Hebrew Dictionary*. New York: Hebrew Publishing Co.

Herzog, Marvin I. 1965. *The Yiddish Language in Northern Poland*. Bloomington: Indiana University Press.

____. 1967. "A Bibliography of Uriel Weinreich." In *Language* 43, no. 2 (1967), 607–610.

Herzog, Marvin I., *et al.* eds. 1992, 1995. *Language and Culture Atlas of Ashkenazic Jewry*. 2 vols. (more forthcoming). New York: YIVO Institute for Jewish Research and Tübingen: Max Niemeyer.

____. 1980. *The Field of Yiddish*, fourth collection. Philadelphia: Institute for the Study of Human Issues.

Mark, Yudel. 1978. *Gramatik fun der jidišer klal-šprax* ('Grammar of Standard Yiddish'). New York: Congress for Jewish Culture.

Schaechter, Mordkhe. 1993. *Yiddish Two*. New York: League for Yiddish.

Stutchkoff, Nahum. 1950. *Der oycer fun der jidišer šprax* ('Thesaurus of the Yiddish Language'). New York: YIVO Institute for Jewish Research.

Weinreich, Max. 1964. *For Max Weinreich on his Seventieth Birthday: Studies in Jewish Languages, Literature, and Society*. The Hague: Mouton.

____. 1973. *Gešixte fun der jidišer šprax* ('History of the Yiddish Language'). 4 vols. New York: YIVO Institute for Jewish Research.

____. 1980. *History of the Yiddish Language* [translation of vols. 1–2 of *Gešixte fun der jidišer šprax*]. Chicago: University of Chicago Press. [translation of vols. 3–4 forthcoming]

Weinreich, Uriel. 1949. *College Yiddish*. New York: YIVO Institute for Jewish Research.

____. 1968. *Modern English-Yiddish Yiddish-English Dictionary*. New York: McGraw-Hill and YIVO Institute for Jewish Research.

Weinreich, Uriel, ed. 1954. *The Field of Yiddish*, first collection. New York: Linguistic Circle of New York.

____. 1965. *The Field of Yiddish*, second collection. The Hague: Mouton and Co.

Weinreich, Uriel, and Beatrice Weinreich. 1959. *Yiddish Language and Folklore: A Selective Bibliography for Research*. The Hague: Mouton.

Weinreich, Uriel, *et al.*, eds. 1969. *The Field of Yiddish*, third collection. The Hague: Mouton and Co.

YORUBA

Akinbiyi Akinlabi

Language Name: Yoruba. **Autonym:** *Aku, Anago.*

Location: Southwestern Nigeria, southern Benin, and eastern Togo. Varieties of this language are also found in Sierra Leone, the West Indies, Brazil, and Cuba.

Family: Yoruboid subgroup of the Defoid group of the Benue-Congo subfamily of the Volta-Congo family of the Atlantic-Congo subbranch of the Niger-Congo branch of the Niger-Kordofanian family.

Related Languages: The Defoid group consists of Yoruboid and Akokoid subgroups. Yoruboid consists of three closely related languages: Yoruba, Iṣẹkiri and Igala. The Akokoid subgroup includes Afa, Ahan, Arigidi, Ayere, Erushu, Igashi, Oyin, Udo, and Uro.

Dialects: The dialect areas of Yoruba are broadly classified as (1) Northwestern (NWY) including Ọyọ, Ẹgba, Ibọlọ, and Mọba ; (2) Southeastern (SEY) including Ondo, Ọwọ, Ijẹbu, and the dialects spoken in and around Okitipupa: Ikalẹ, Ilajẹ, Ijọ-Apọi, etc.; (3) Central (CY) including Ifẹ, Ijẹṣa, Irun, Ifaki, and Ekiti; (4) Northeastern (NEY) including Iyagba, Gbẹdẹ, Ikiri, Ijumu; and (5) Southwestern (SWY) including Tsabẹ, Ketu, and Ifẹ (Togo).

The linguistic characteristics of NWY include the merger of Proto-Yoruba (PYOR) *gw and *ɣ with w, the merger of *ĩ and *ũ with ĩ and ũ respectively, and the development of PYOR **c* to *ʃ*. Present-day standard Yoruba is largely derived from this dialect group. SEY is marked by the retention of PYOR **gw* and **ɣ*, and by the merger of PYOR **ĩ* and **ũ* with *ɛ̃*, and *ɔ̃* respectively. PYOR lenis **m'* has developed to *w̃* in this dialect group; and in the Okitipupa subgroup, PYOR **s* has become *h*. There is no distinction between the second- and third-person plural pronouns in SEY. In CY, the PYOR **gw* has changed to *w*, and **ɣ* and **w* have become *Ø*. CY retains PYOR **ĩ* and **ũ* in prefixes, and in nonfinal stem positions. In NEY, PYOR **gw* and **ɣ* have merged with *w*, as in NWY. However, PYOR **w* has shifted to *ɣ* before [el and [a]. PYOR **s* has also become *h* in this dialect group. Finally PYOR lenis **m'* has developed to *ŋ*. SWY is the only dialect where PYOR lenis **k'* has merged with its fortis counterpart. In all other dialect groups, it has merged with [g]. This dialect group retains PYOR **c*, which has shifted to either *ʃ* or *s* in all other dialects. Finally, SWY has lost vowel nasalization in all PYOR **gũ* sequences, and in some PYOR **kũ* sequences.

Number of Speakers: 20–25 million.

Origin and History

All the various tribes of the Yoruba nation trace their origin from a leader called Oduduwa and the city of Ile Ife in present-day southwestern Nigeria. Ile Ife is in fact fabled as the spot where God created man. The seven principal tribes that sprang from Oduduwa's seven grandchildren are the Oyos (from Oranyan) the Benins, Ilas, Owus, Ketus, Sabes, and the Popos. The other tribes are offshoots of one or the other of these seven tribes.

Linguistic evidence suggests that the Yoruba have always lived in their present habitat. Linguistic evidence further suggests that the area around Kaba (northeastern Yoruba) or a little south of it, may be the point of dispersion for the Yoruba, and the point where Proto-Yoruba-Igala (PYIG) was spoken.

As can be seen from the list of the main tribes, migration has taken place both eastward and westward, with some of the main tribes (Ketu and Sabe) located in the Benin republic, west of Nigeria. Other Yoruba tribes, including the Yoruba of Ife (Togo), Idaisa and Manigiri of the republics of Benin and Togo, may in fact not belong to the Oduduwa/Ile Ife tradition.

It was at Freetown, Sierra Leone, that Yoruba studies began in the early 19th century. The reason for this was that the African language most widely spoken among liberated slaves resettled in Freetown in the early 19th century was Yoruba, or 'Aku' (from *ọọkú* or *ẹẹkú*, a form of greeting), as it was then known. Interest in Yoruba studies was centered in Freetown until around 1840 when the British government decided to send an expedition to the Niger, and when the Church Missionary Society (CMS) paid attention to the appeals of the Christian converts who had returned from Freetown to their original homes in Yorubaland. On the 1840 expedition was a Yoruba missioner, Samuel Ajayi Crowther, a resettled slave who had received an education in Freetown. Crowther was trained and ordained as a priest by the CMS in 1843. The same year, the CMS published his first book on Yoruba, *Vocabulary of the Yoruba Language.* This was soon followed by a primer (1849), a grammar (1852), and a translation of the Bible (1867); all published by the CMS Crowther and the CMS could thus be credited with the founding of a written literature for Yoruba. Other prominent names in the development of Yoruba studies at that time were C.A. Gollmer, H. Kilham, T. King, J. Raban, and H. Townsend.

Orthography and Basic Phonology

The earliest formal attempts at devising an orthography for

Table 1: Consonants

		Labial	Alveolar	Palatal	Velar	Labio-Velar	Glottal
Stops	Voiceless		t		k	p [k͡p]	
	Voiced	b	d	j [ɟ]	g	gb [g͡b]	
Fricatives	Voiceless	f	s	ṣ [ʃ]			
Nasals		m	n				
Approximants	Lateral		l				
	Central		r	y [j]		w	h

the Yoruba language started around 1850 and involved an international cooperative effort of missionaries in Freetown and in Abeokuta (Nigeria) and linguistics experts in Europe, around 1850. Prominent among these were J.F. Schon, S. Lee, C.R. Lepsius, C.A. Gollmer, J. Raban, H. Townsend, and S.A. Crowther. This original orthography survived with little changes for over a century. In 1875, a conference on the Yoruba language chaired by Crowther, which primarily discussed and resolved a number of anomalies in the orthography, was held in Lagos, Nigeria. The orthography was further revised in 1963, 1966, 1969, and 1974. The current orthography is the one revised in 1974.

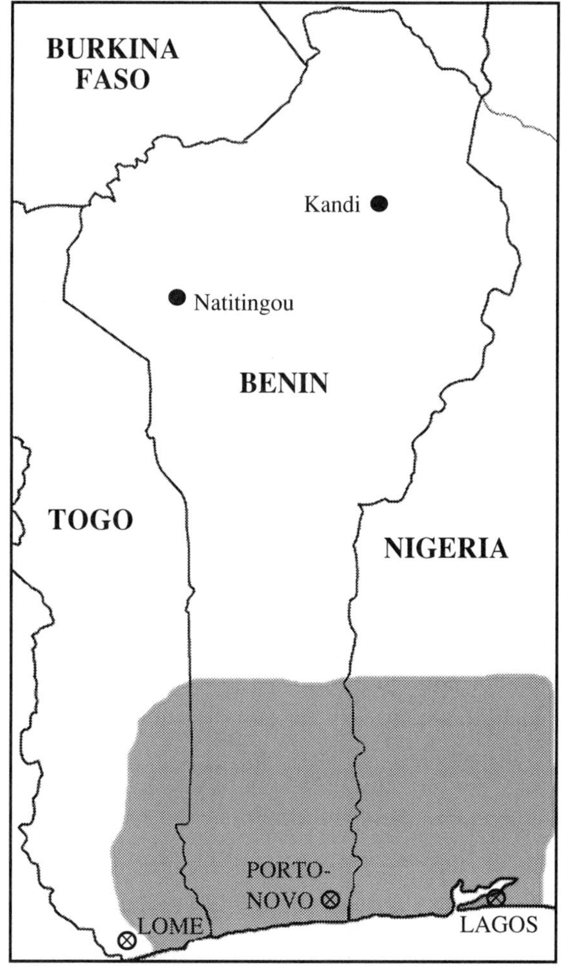

Yoruba is primarily spoken in southwestern Nigeria, southern Benin and eastern Togo (shaded area).

Yoruba has 18 basic consonants, which are listed in Table 1 as written in the orthography, with the IPA symbol indicated where both notations differ. The consonant [g͡b], written as *gb* in the orthography, is a doubly articulated voiced labio-velar plosive and not a consonant cluster. Its voiceless counterpart, [k͡p], is written as *p* in the orthography since the voiceless bilabial plosive [p] does not exist in the language.

Some Yoruba consonants have contextual or positional variants. First, Yoruba oral sonorants have nasalized variants when produced before nasal vowels. The sonorant consonants /l , r, w, y, h/ are pronounced respectively as [n, r̃, w̃, ỹ, h̃] before nasal vowels: /lũ/ → [nũ] 'to feed', /rĩ/ → [r̃ĩ] 'to walk', /wĩ/ → [w̃ĩ] 'to lend', /yũ/ → [ỹũ] 'to dispense', /hũ/→ [h̃ũ] 'to weave'. Except for the *n*/*l* alternation, nasalized variants of sonorants are not indicated in the orthography.

Secondly, when the nasal /n/ is syllabic, it has six variants whose places of articulation are based on the places of articulation of the following consonants. Therefore, it is a bilabial [m] before /b, m/, a labiodental [ɱ] before /f/, an alveolar [n] before /t, d, s, n, r, l/, a palatal [ɲ] before /ʃ, ɟ, y/, a velar [ŋ/ before the consonants /k, g, w, h/ and the vowel /o/, and a labiovelar [ŋ͡m] before /k͡p, g͡b/. This variation is not symbolized in Yoruba orthography, except that *m* is written before *b*, and *n* is written before other consonants, as indicated in the rightmost column.

[òròm̀bó]	'orange'	òròm̀bó
[bóɱ́fò]	'short skirt'	bónfò
[pan̄la]	'stockfish'	pan̄la
[ìɟáɲ̀ɟá]	'small piece (of meat)'	ìjáǹjá
[ògòŋ̀gò]	'ostrich'	ògòǹgò

Vowels

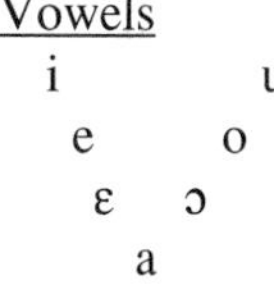

Yoruba has seven contrastive oral vowels: *i, e, ẹ, a, ọ, o, u*. The orthographic vowels *ẹ, ọ* are [ɛ], [ɔ], respectively, corresponding roughly to the vowels in the words "bet" and "bought" in American ENGLISH. All seven oral vowels are pronounced nasalized after nasal consonants. In this context, the midvowels [ẽ, õ] are perhaps the least nasalized: [mĩ́] 'to breathe', [mɔ̃̀] 'to know', [mṍwó] 'take money' (<*mú* 'to take' *owó* 'money'), [mũ] 'to drink'.

In addition, Yoruba has four inherently nasal vowels [ĩ] [ɛ̃] [ɔ̃] [ũ], whose nasalization is not caused by a preceding nasal consonant. Instead, these vowels occur following oral consonants, as in *ikın* 'palmnuts for Ifa divination', *ìyẹn* 'that one', *ìbọn* 'gun', *ikún* 'type of squirrel'. In the orthography, contrastive nasalization is indicated with the nasal consonant (*n*) after the nasal vowel. Predictable nasalization, as in the preceding paragraph, is not marked in the orthography. Two of these vowels, [ɔ̃] and [ɛ̃], require comments. [ɔ̃] is indicated in the orthography as *an* following nonlabial consonants: *ikán* 'white ants', and as *ọn* following labial consonants: *ìbọn* 'gun'. The nasal vowel [ã], however, occurs contrastively in some dialects, for example, the Ikalẹ̀ dialect. The remaining nasal vowel, [ɛ̃], is severely restricted, occurring only in a few related items: *ìyẹn* 'that one', and *yẹn* 'that'. Though long vowels occur phonetically in Yoruba, vowel length is not contrastive. Long vowels occur most commonly as a result of vowel assimilation (see discussion below): *egúngún* → *eégún* 'masquerade', *òrùka* → 'ring', *òrìṣà* → *òòṣà* 'god'.

Yoruba has vowel occurrence restrictions known as "vowel harmony". In simple (monomorphemic) words in Yoruba, the last vowel of the word determines the rest of the vowels in the word. If the last vowel is produced with retracted tongue root (RTR) (*a*, *ẹ*, *ọ*), then all the preceding vowels are RTR as well. However, in standard Yoruba only mid vowels (*e*, *o*, *ẹ*, *ọ*) are fully involved in the harmony. The high vowels (*i*, *u*) do not participate in the harmony at all; that is, the high vowels can occur with any vowel. The following are examples of permitted and nonpermitted mid vowel sequences:

Permitted			Permitted			Not Permitted
ọ ... ọ	ọjọ́	'day'	ẹ ... ẹ	ẹsẹ̀	'leg/foot'	*o ... ọ
ẹ ... ọ	ẹjọ́	'case'	ọ ... ẹ	ọ̀sẹ̀	'week'	*e ... ọ
ẹ ... a	ẹja	'fish'	ọ ... a	ọjà	'market'	*ẹ ... e
						*ọ ... e
o ... o	òjò	'rain'	e ... e	ètè	'lips'	*e ... a
e ... o	ejò	'snake'	o ... e	olè	'thief'	*o ... a

Another major phonological process in Yoruba is vowel assimilation. When two vowels are situated side by side without an intervening consonant, one of the vowels becomes completely assimilated to the other. Vowel assimilation in Yoruba is most commonly observed when two nouns are next to each other, one ending in a vowel and the other beginning with a vowel. In general, the first vowel of the second noun completely assimilates the preceding vowel, except when the second vowel is /i/, in which case it becomes completely assimilated to the first vowel. Examples of vowel assimilation include *owó adé* → *owáadé* 'Ade's money', *owó epo* → *owéepo* 'oil money', *owó ılé* → *owóolé* 'house rent'.

The most documented phonological process in Yoruba is perhaps vowel deletion. As in vowel assimilation, vowel deletion occurs when two words are placed side by side, one ending with a vowel and the other beginning with a vowel. However, vowel deletion is most commonly found when lexical classes other than two nouns occur next to each other; such as when a noun occurs after a verb, for example, verb + object. Leaving the well documented exceptions aside, it is the first vowel in the sequence that gets deleted, except if the second vowel is /i/.

wá (H) 'look (for)'	ẹ̀kọ́ (LH) 'education'	→	wẹ́kọ́ (HLH) 'look for education'
wá (H) + 'look (for)'	owó (MH) 'money'	→	wówó (HH) 'look for money'
wá (H) + 'look (for)'	ọkọ̀ (ML) 'vehicle'	→	wọ́kọ̀ (HL) 'look for a vehicle'
wá (H) + 'look (for)'	ọkọ (MM) 'husband'	→	wọ́kọ (HM) 'look for a husband'

Of crucial importance is the stability of tone in the processes of vowel assimilation and vowel deletion. When a vowel gets assimilated or deleted, its tone remains behind on the surviving vowel, except if the second vowel is a mid tone: *wá* (H) + *owó* (MH) → *wówó* (HH) 'look for money'. Tones are therefore independent from segments in Yoruba.

Finally, Yoruba has three contrastive tones: H(igh), M(id), and L(ow), which are generally realized on vowels and sometimes on nasal consonants, when they are syllabic as seen above. Tones carry a heavy functional load in Yoruba, since they distinguish the meanings of words like consonants and vowels do.

kọ́ (H)	'to build'
kọ (M)	'to sing'
kọ̀ (L)	'to reject'

However, there is a restriction on the distribution of the high tone; the high tone does not occur in word-initial position except in (marked) consonant-initial words. Thus, in vowel-initial words, while it is possible to have forms like *ọkọ̀* 'vehicle' and *ọ̀kọ̀* 'spear', it is impossible to have a form like **ọ́kọ̀* with a high tone on the initial syllable. Except for this minor restriction, tones occur freely in lexical representations, without apparent restrictions on word melodies.

Two of the three basic tones, the high tone and the low tone, have variants. The high tone (H) is pronounced as a low-rising tone (LH contour) after a low tone, and a low tone is pronounced as a high-falling one (HL contour) after a high one: *àlá* (LH) → *àlǎ* (L LH) 'dream', *rárà* (HL) → *rárâ* (H HL) 'elegy'. Contour tones are not indicated in the orthography except when they occur on long vowels, in which case the vowel is doubled and a single tone is indicated on each vowel.

Yoruba words result from a very simple syllable structure. Using the symbol C to stand for consonants and V to stand for vowels, Yoruba has only two types of syllables, V and CV (- marks syllable division):

V:	àlá	(à - lá)	'dream'
CV:	wá	(wá)	'come'

Other than pronouns that can be single vowels and so are representative of the V syllable, this syllable type is largely found as the initial vowel of nouns. The V also represents syllabic nasals, such as the *m* in *òrombó* (*ò-ro-m̀-bó*) 'orange', and *n* in *géńdé* (*gé-ńdé*) 'a sturdy young man', since syllabic nasals are the only consonants that are tone bearing like vowels.

Yoruba disallows consonant clusters. Thus it is impossible

to have a combination like [krim] (the pronunciation of the English "cream") which has the cluster *kr* at the beginning, or [sɪlk] (the pronunciation of the English "silk") which has the cluster *lk* at the end.

Basic Morphology

Yoruba nouns are minimally VCV. That is, a noun in standard Yoruba is at least two syllables beginning with a vowel and followed by a C(onsonant)-V(owel) sequence: *omi* 'water', *apá* 'arm'. The majority of Yoruba nouns have this structure. Among the major word classes only nouns can begin with vowels. But nouns can also begin with consonants: *rárà* 'dirge', *gèlè* 'head tie', *gẹ̀gẹ̀* 'goiter'. Simple nouns are in general not longer than four syllables: *ìkarahun* 'big snail shell', *ìjímèrè* 'brown monkey', *àjànọ̀kú* 'elephant'. When they are this long or when they are longer, they are often ideophonic: *ògúlúǹtu* 'sand block, clod of earth'.

The initial vowel of a noun cannot be a nasal vowel, and it cannot be the vowel [u]. Therefore, there are no such nouns as **inlé* or **ulé*; standard Yoruba has instead *ilé* 'house'. The word *ulé* 'house' occurs in some eastern Yoruba dialects such as the Ondo dialect, but a word like **inlé* does not occur in any dialect. Since only nouns can begin with vowels in Yoruba, it follows that no word can begin with a nasal vowel or the vowel [u]. The second restriction on vowel-initial nouns is that they cannot begin on a high tone. So initial vowels of nouns are either low-toned or mid toned. Yoruba does not have nouns like **íle, *áṣọ*.

Verbs are minimally CV. That is, the simple verb in Yoruba consists of a C(onsonant) followed by a V(owel). Except for a few disyllabic forms like *pàdé* 'to meet', all Yoruba verbs have the structure CV. Other major word classes begin with consonants, and are disyllabic or longer.

Word formation in Yoruba is the result of three derivational processes: prefixation, reduplication, and compounding. Nouns and verbs are not inflected for case, person, number, or gender.

Nouns may be formed from verb stems or from verb phrases through prefixation. Various kinds of nouns such as abstract, agentive, and instrument, are formed in this way. For example, the prefix /ì/ or /à/ may be attached to a verb, a verb plus object, or serial verbs to form an instrument nominal: *ìlu* 'opener' (< *lu* 'make a hole'), *àlòkù* 'used instrument' (< *lò* 'use', *kù* 'remain').

Abstract nominals and agentive nominals may be formed the same way, using other prefixes. Furthermore, negative nominals are formed by prefixing /àì/ to a verb or a verb phrase: *àìlọ* '(act of) not going' (*lọ* 'go'). Finally, possessor nominals are formed by prefixing /oní/ to a noun or to a noun phrase: *aláṣọ* 'owner of cloth or seller of cloth' (< *oni* + *aṣọ* 'cloth').

Nouns are also formed through reduplication, which may be partial or complete. Several forms of both types of reduplications exist. The most productive partial reduplication is one that forms gerundive nominals from verbs or verb phrases by reduplicating the first consonant of the stem followed by a "prefix" /í/: *lílọ* 'going' (< *lọ* 'go'), *jíjẹ* 'eating' (< *jẹ* 'eat').

Secondly, the first VCV of a noun may be reduplicated to form a word meaning "every (noun)". The first tone of the stem is spread onto the reduplicant, and the initial vowel of the stem assimilates the last vowel of the reduplicant: *oṣooṣù* 'every month' (< *oṣù* 'month'), *ìrìirọ̀lẹ́* 'every evening' (< *ìrọ̀lẹ́* 'evening').

One form of complete reduplication takes various lexical classes, including verbs, adverbs, adjectives, and numerals as input and produces an intensified output, or it can have a group meaning:

kíákíá	'very quickly'	kía	'quickly'
burúkúburúkú	'very bad'	burúkú	'bad'
dáradára	'good (adj.)'	dára	'good (verb)'

Another form of complete reduplication takes verb phrases as input to form agentive nominals.

woléwolé	'sanitary inspector'	(< *wò* 'look at', *ilé* 'house')
panápaná	'fireman'	(<*pa* 'kill/put out', *iná* 'fire')

Finally, reduplication may be combined with affixation. The formatives /kí/ and /ní/ may be inserted between a reduplicated noun base. /kí/ forms a nominal with the meaning 'any or bad (noun)' from a noun:

ọmọkọ́mọ	'any child, bad child'	(< *ọmọ 'child'*)
èròkerò	'any thought, bad thought'	(< *èrò* 'thought')
ọ̀pọ̀lọpọ̀	'abundance'	(< *ọ̀pọ̀* 'many'*)*

Basic Syntax

The basic word order is SVO, and word order is crucial in expressing grammatical relations such as subject, object, and indirect object, because nouns are morphologically uninflected.

olú rí adé	adé rí olú
'Olu saw Ade.'	'Ade saw Olu.'
olú fún adé ní aṣọ	adé fún olú ní aṣọ
'Olu gave Ade clothes.'	'Ade gave Olu clothes.'

Word order is also used in expressing pragmatic functions such as focus. In focus construction, the focused item is fronted and is followed by the formative *ni*, for emphasis. The subject, object, verb, or even the entire sentence may be focused, as in the following examples:

olú pa ẹran
'Olu killed an animal.'

olú ni ó pa ẹran
Olu FOCUS 3.SG kill animal
'It was OLU that killed an animal.'

ẹran ni olú pa
animal FOCUS Olu kill
'It was an ANIMAL that Olu killed.'

pípa ni olú pa ẹran
killing FOCUS olú kill animal
'Olu KILLED an animal.'

olú pa ẹran ni
'It is the case that Olu killed an animal.'

When the subject is focused, its vacated position is occupied by a pronoun clitic; and in the case of a focused verb, the verb itself is reduplicated and a copy of the verb retains its vacated position. If the subject is a pronoun clitic, an equivalent independent pronoun is fronted, but the original clitic or the clitic *ó* stands in its vacated position.

wọ́n pè wá
3.PL FOC. 1.PL
'They called us.'

àwọn ni wọ́n pè wá OR awọ́n ni ó pè wá
3.PL FOC. 3.PL CALL 1.PL 3.PL FOC. 3.SG call 1.PL
'It is THEY who called us.'

Other word classes that may be focused include adverbs and nominal qualifiers.

Another interesting phenomenon related to word order is that of serial verbs; these are constructions in which a sequence of verbs occurs within a clause. Word order is crucial in this case since a reverse order of the verbs gives a different interpretation.

olú gbé àga wá BUT olú wá gbé àga
Olu carry chair come Olu came carry chair
'Olu brought a chair.' 'Olu came to carry a chair.'

In a serial construction the second verb in the sequence may express directionality (or sequence), duration, or consequence.

olú gbé àga lọ (directionality)
Olu come carry chair
'Olu brought a chair.'

olú jìyà kú (duration)
Olu suffer die
'Olu suffered until he died.'

olú mu ọtí yó (consequence)
Olu drink wine be.full
'Olu is drunk.'

The subject of the second verb can be the same as that of the first verb, as in all of the preceding examples, or it may be the object of the first verb, as in:

olú lo aṣọ náà gbó
Olu use cloth DEICTIC be.worn.out
'Olu used the cloth until it was worn out.'
(*aṣọ* 'cloth' is subject of *gbó* 'be worn out')

Or it may be both the subject and object of the first verb:

olú lé ọmọ náà wá ilé
Olu chase child DEICTIC come home
'Olu chased the child home.' (Omo, or Olu and Omo can be the subject of *wá* 'come')

In a declarative clause, when the subject stands before the verb phrase, the end of the subject noun phrase is marked with a high tone, which is associated with the last syllable of this phrase. Thus, a final low tone is realized as a low-rising tone (LH), and a final mid tone is realized as a high tone. A final high tone remains unchanged. This tonal change is obligatory in the nonfuture tense, but optional in the future tense:

ọkọ̌ bàjẹ́ (*ọkọ̀* 'car') 'The car broke down.'

ọmọ́ lọ (*ọmọ* 'child') 'The child went.'

ajá gbó (*ajá* 'dog') 'The dog barked.'

Within the phrase, heads are initial. Thus in a noun phrase, determiners, adjectives, demonstratives, relative clauses, and others all come after the head noun:

ìwé mi
book my
'My book'

ìwé yẹn
book that
'That book'

ilé ńlá
house big
'Big house'

ilé ńlá yẹn
house big that
'That big house'

Contact with Other Languages

Because of British colonization, most of Yoruba's borrowed words are from English. There are also borrowings from ARABIC because of the influence of Islam. Hundreds of these words exist in the vocabulary, and they are regularly modified to fit the phonological constraints of the language, especially the syllable structure constraints. Consonant clusters are split with /i/ or /u/ and coda consonants are deleted: *dírẹ́bà* 'driver', *sùkúrù* 'school'. Very commonly, however, the vowel harmony pattern of the language is violated in the loan vocabulary: *télọ̀* 'tailor', *bébà* 'paper'. There are also a few borrowings from FRENCH and HAUSA.

From English: *ṣọ́ọ̀ṣì* 'church', *tíṣà* 'teacher', *kọ́ọ̀bù* 'cup', *títì* 'street'

From Arabic: *sábàbí sabab* '(cause)', *àdúrá al-du'ā* '(prayer)', *ṣẹ̀ríà shari'ah* '(punishment, law)'

Common Words

man:	ọkùnrin	(be) long:	gùn
woman:	obìnrin	(be) small:	kéré
water:	omi	yes:	hẹn
sun:	òòrùn	no:	rárá
three:	ẹ̀ta	(be) good:	dára
fish:	ẹja	bird:	ẹyẹ
(be) big:	tóbi	dog:	ajá
tree:	igi		

Example Sentences

(1) Olú rí adé.
Olu see Ade
'Olu saw Ade.'

(2) adé fún olú ní aṣọ.
Ade give Olu clothes
'Ade gave Olu clothes.'

(3) olú jìyà kú.
Olu suffer die
'Olu suffered until he died.'

Efforts to Preserve, Protect, and Promote the Language

Today, Yoruba is the official language in southwestern Nigeria, where it is used for government notices, radio, television, education through university level, and a thriving literature including books and newspapers. Yoruba was the first west African language in which a periodical was published (*Iwe Irohin Yoruba*, 1859–1867). Since the first grammar by Crowther in 1852, it has enjoyed excellent scholarship with studies on various aspects of the language, culture, and history. It is the most documented west African language.

Select Bibliography

Abraham, R.C. 1958. *Dictionary of Modern Yoruba*. London: Hodder and Stoughton.

Agiri, B. 1975. "Yoruba Oral Tradition with Special Reference to the Early History of the Oyo Kingdom." In Wande Abimbọla, ed., *Yoruba Oral Tradition*. Ifẹ African Languages and Literature Series, No. 1. 157–197.

Ajayi, J.F.A. 1960. "How Yoruba was Reduced to Writing." In *Odu* 8: 49–58.

Akinkugbe, O.O. 1978. *A Comparative Phonology of Yoruba Dialects, Isekiri, and Igala*. Ph.D. dissertation, University of Ibadan, Nigeria.

Awobuluyi, O. 1978. *Essentials of Yoruba Grammar*. Ibadan: Oxford University Press.

Bamgbose, A. 1966. *A Grammar of Yoruba*. London: Cambridge University Press.

____. 1967. *A Short Grammar of Yoruba*. Ibadan: Heinemann.

____. 1990. *Fonoloji ati Girama Yoruba*. Ibadan: Ibadan University Press.

Capo, H.B.C. 1989. "Defoid." In J. Bendor Samuel ed., *The Niger Congo Languages*. Lanham: University Press of America.

Fresco, E.M. 1970. *Topics in Yoruba Dialect Phonology. Studies in African Linguistics*. Supplement 1. Los Angeles: University of California.

Johnson, S. 1921. *The History of the Yorubas*. Lagos: C.S.S. Bookshops.

Owolabi, D.K.O. 1989. *Ijinle Itupale Ede Yoruba (1). Fonetiiki ati Fonoloji*. Ibadan: Onibonoje Press and Book Industries.

Ward, Ida. 1952. *An Introduction to the Yoruba Language*. Cambridge: W. Heffer and Sons Ltd.

Central Alaskan Yup'ik Eskimo

Carl Rubino and Kanaqluk George Charles

Language Name: Central Alaskan Yup'ik Eskimo. **Autonym:** Yup'ik or Yupiaq 'real person'.

Location: Central Alaskan Yup'ik Eskimo is spoken south of Golovin and Elim (Norton Sound), on Nunivak Island, on the Yukon (to Holy Cross) and Kuskokwim (to Sleetmute) Rivers, and the north coast of the Alaskan Peninsula.

Family: Yupik (Western Eskimo) branch of the Eskimo subfamily of the Eskimo-Aleut family.

Related Languages: Central Alaskan Yup'ik is most closely related to four other Yupik languages that compose the Yupik (Western Eskimo) branch of the Eskimo family. The other four Yupik languages are Aluttiq Alaskan Yupik, Central Siberian Yupik, Naukanski, and Sireniski. The other branch of the Eskimo family includes the Inuit languages that compose a dialect chain of very closely related languages spoken in northern Alaska, Canada and Greenland.

Dialects: Central Alaskan Yup'ik has five dialects with considerable phonological and lexical variation: Norton Sound, Hooper Bay and Chevak, Nunivak, General Central Yup'ik, and Egegik (Miyaoka 1993). Data in this chapter are from the General Central Alaskan Yup'ik language as spoken on Nelson Island and the Kuskokwim River by George Charles and Liz Charles Ali.

Number of Speakers: 13,000 out of a population of 18,000 in the ethnic group.

Origin and History

The four major indigenous groups of Alaska, the Eskimo, Aleut, Eskimo (Yup'ik and Inuit), Coastal Tlingit and Haida, and the Athabascan tribes crossed the Bering land bridge in successive waves 25,000 to 40,000 years ago.

The ancestral home of the Eskimo people is the Bering Sea area, and it is around this region (western Alaska) that the language family is most divergent. Maritime Eskimo (Thule) cultural traditions evolved during the first millennium A.D., most noted for the small subsistence economies and the harvest of large sea mammals, hunting with dog teams and semisubterranean houses in a region that is icebound for 9–10 months of the year. A warming trend in 900 suitable for the summer habitat of the bowhead whale was responsible for an eastward expansion of the Thule culture, but a cooling period between 1650 and 1800 led to a decline in whaling activities and the Eskimos turned to the seal for subsistence.

The Yup'ik live in southwestern Alaska and have occupied that area for at least 5,000 years. Prior to the arrival of the Russians and other Europeans they have led mostly a nomadic lifestyle. Family groups would occasionally gather together for brief periods of time before once again scattering to occupy hunting and fishing sites.

Alaska was colonized by Russia in 1745, after Bering discovered the Aleutian Islands in 1741. For the first 40 years, Russian colonization was heaviest in the Aleutian Islands, where the native (Aleut) population was decimated from 16,000 to 2,500. By the 1770s, Eskimo lands were also visited by the British, American, Spanish and French. In 1867, Alaska was ceded to the United States in the Treaty of Cession.

Orthography and Basic Phonology

The Russians and Americans were the first outsiders who attempted to write the Yup'ik language, motivated mostly in the spreading of the Christian gospel in the beginning of the 19th century. There was no coordinated movement to develop a unified orthography in those years. There was one Yup'ik man, Uyaquq, who developed his own orthography, which was learned by about a dozen Yup'ik men.

Nowadays, Central Alaskan Yup'ik is written in a practical orthography, devised principally by Irene Reed, Paschal Afcan, Osahito Miyaoka, and Michael Kraus between 1967 and 1972 for the bilingual-education program. Among the conventions is the use of double letters to represent underlyingly voiceless fricatives (not geminates). Voiced fricatives that devoice because of their phonological environment (next to a stop or a voiceless fricative, word initially or word finally) are written with one letter if they are the second consonant in a cluster. The labialized front velar fricatives are represented with unique symbols, *u͡g* (voiced), *u͡gg* (voiceless), with back velar counterparts *u͡r* and *u͡rr*. Phonemic /v/ and /w/ are both written with the letter *v*. Voiceless nasals are written with acute accents over them, unless they appear after a stop or voiceless fricative in which they are voiceless by environment.

All consonants in Yup'ik may occur geminate. Geminate consonants are indicated in the orthography by an apostrophe before a vowel unless the consonant is geminate due to its phonological environment. The hyphen is also used to signal a voiced fricative next to a voiceless stop, e.g., *qut'raaq* 'sandhill crane' [qutʀa:q], or when a rule of the general accentuation pattern is broken. The hyphen is also used to mark an enclitic boundary.

Table 1: Consonants (In Practical Orthography)

	Labial	Apical		Velar		Labio-velar	
		Dental	Alveo-palatal	Front	Back	Front	Back
Stops, affricate	p	t	c [tʃ]	k	q		
Voiceless fricatives	vv [f]	ll [ɬ]	ss	gg [x]	rr [χ]	u͡g [xʷ]	u͡gg [χʷ]
Voiced fricatives	v	l	s [z]	g [ɣ]	r [ʀ]	u͡r [ɣʷ]	u͡rr [ʀʷ]
Approximants	w		y				
Voiced nasals	m	n		ng			
Voiceless nasals	ḿ [m̥]	ń [n̥]		ń [ŋ̊]			

Among the consonants, the stops are unaspirated, except in word-final position. The back velar (uvular) stop and fricatives are labialized when preceded by the vowel *u*.

Table 2: Vowels

	Front	Central	Back
High	i	e [ə]	u
Low		a	

Yup'ik has four vowels, three of which (the prime vowels) may occur long, *aa, ii, uu*. The vowel *a* is considerably fronted to [æ] after the vowel *i*, e.g., *kaviaq* 'fox' [kav.væq]. The vowels *i* and *u* lower to *e* and *o* before back velars, e.g., *uquq* 'seal oil' [oqʷoqʷ]. The vowel *e* [ə] is devoiced when it is not next to a voiced sound, and word initially it is not usually pronounced.

Morphophonemics is rather complex in Yup'ik. Postbases (all post root) and endings (inflectional suffixes) are classified as to whether they delete the final velar fricative of their preceding host, or whether they delete or spirantize preceding apical stops, among other things.

Syllable Structure and Stress. Syllable types include open (C)V, closed (C)VC, light -V, heavy -VV. Jacobson (1984) postulates three kinds of stress in Yup'ik: inherent, rhythmic, and secondary (phonetically equivalent to primary stress). Inherent stress occurs in all heavy and initial closed syllables. Rhythmic stress follows every syllable following an unstressed syllable, and secondary stress occurs on a prime vowel (/i/, /a/, or /u/) before a heavy syllable.

Phonological Gemination. A consonant becomes geminate in Yup'ik under the following conditions: (1) as the onset of a heavy syllable preceded by a light open syllable or (2) as the onset of an unstressed light syllable preceded by a stressed syllable with the vowel /*e*/, *tamaani* /ta.maa.ni/ 'there' [tam.ma:.ni], *terr'a* /té.rra/ 'its anus' [tə́χ.χa].

Basic Morphology

Yup'ik Eskimo is a suffixing polysynthetic language and one of the most morphologically complex languages in the world today. Words fall into two main categories (1) uninflectable words including interjections, connectives, adverbial particles, and enclitics and (2) inflectable words, which include all nouns and verbs. Productive morphemes occurring in inflected words are exclusively suffixing, and are divided into four morpheme types: (1) the base, which carries most of the lexical meaning (except for the null root base *pi* 'do; thing', which is used when the primary meaning is to be designated by a postbase), (2) postbases, morphemes that vary in productivity that immediately follow their root and specify lexical derivational information (3) endings, inflectional grammatical suffixes; and (4) enclitics, attaching to full grammatical words at the boundary of the last inflectional grammatical suffix:

Base (Root)	Postbase (Derivational)	Ending (Inflectional)	=Enclitic

cali-vkar-a-a=gguq (orthographically: *calivkaraa-gguq*)
work-let/allow-TRANS.INDIC=3s/3s=HRSY
BASE-POSTBASE-ENDING-ENDING-CLITIC
'He is supposedly allowing her to work.'

kelipar-tur-tu-q (orthographically: *keliparturtuq*)
bread-eat-INTRANS.INDIC-3s
BASE-POSTBASE-ENDING-ENDING
'He is eating bread.'

The number of primary Yup'ik bases is quite small. Miyaoka (1997) gives the figure of an upper limit of 2,000. Postbases number about 400, and together with the primary bases can contribute to an impressive lexicon. Examples of words (many of them lexicalized) that include at least one postbase include *agayu-lir-ta* (pray-much-AGENT) 'priest', *teng-suun* (fly-device) 'airplane', *uitavig-kaq* (place.to.stay-future.N) 'future place to stay', *neqerrlug-kuaq* (dried.fish-leftover) 'leftover dried fish', *nuna-kuar-cuun* (land-go.by.way.of-device) 'automobile', *qimugte-linraq* (dog-product.of) 'dog feces; dog track', *nelernaq* (fart-CAUSATIVE) 'bean', *tuntute-nqigt-uq* (catch.caribou-do.again-3s INTR.IND) 'he catches caribou again', and *nut'-vialuk* (gun-worthless) 'beat-up old gun'.

Nominal Morphology. Yup'ik nouns may consist of a single root, or a root with inflectional endings indicating number, possession, and/or case. There are three degress of number in Yup'ik, singular, dual, and plural: *paluqtaq* 'one beaver', *paluqtak* 'two beavers', *paluqtat* 'more than two beavers'. In some nouns, number may function to lexicalize an entity: *ucuk* 'penis, singular genitalia' vs. *ucuuk* 'vagina, dual genitalia'.

Yup'ik has seven cases, two core (grammatical) cases, and five oblique cases. The grammatical cases are the relative (ergative), used to indicate possession or the agent of a transitive verb, and the unmarked absolutive case, which encompasses subjects of intransitive verbs and objects of transitive verbs.

The oblique cases are (1) localis, indicating location and sometimes time; (2) ablative-modalis, indicating the place or time from which an action is taking place, or an extra referent not core to the verb; (3) allative (terminalis), indicating the direction, place or time toward which an action takes place; (4) vialis (translocative), indicating the route or instrument of a verbal action, or part of a while; and (5) equalitative, used to show equivalence or express comparison or similarities between two referents:

Relative (ergative) and Absolutive cases:

arnassaaga-m *tang'aurluq* *qavar-cit-a-a*
old.woman-REL boy:ABS sleep-CAUS-INDIC.TRANS-3s/3s
'The old woman is putting the boy to sleep.'

arnassaagaq *qavar-tu-q.*
old.woman.ABS sleep-INDIC.INTRANS-3s
'The old woman is sleeping.'

Ablative modalis case:

.. *napa-mek*
tree-ABL
'(after filling the bucket, he climbed down) from the tree.'

Localis case:

marulussaagagtellriik *utia-qellriik* *ena-cuar-mi*
grandparent&child live-RECIP.DUAL house-small-LOCALIS
'A grandparent and grandchild living together in a small house.'

Allative/terminalis case:

Aya-llini-lria *ataam,* *Mamterriller-mun*
leave-EVIDENT-INTR.PARTICIPAL PART village.name-ALLATIVE
'So he left to Mamterilleq village.'

Vialis (Translocative) case:

Kuig-kun *anelrare-lria ..*
river-VIAL go.downriver-INTR.PARTICIPIAL
'He went by river.'

Equalitive case:

una *mikta-u-q* *tau-tun.*
this small-INTR.INDIC-3s that-EQ
'This is as small as that.'

The case endings for unpossessed nouns are summarized below:

Case	Singular	Dual	Plural
Absolutive	-	-k	-t
Relative –m	-m	-k	-t
Locative –ni	-mi	-gni	-ni
Allative –nun	-mun	-gnun	-nun
Ablative –nek	-mek	-gnek	-nek
Vialis –kun	-kun	-gkun	-tgun
Equalis –tun	-tun	-gtun	-ttun

Possession is expressed with transitive endings: *ila-nka* (relative-1s/3p) 'my relatives'. Table 3 includes information for absolutive and relative nouns only; localis, vialis, and equalis possession are not given. The variants given in the table reflect allomorphy, allomorphs starting with fricatives are used with vowel-ending bases only, while the allomorphs beginning in stops may be used with both, although they were originally only used with consonant-ending bases. The conventions of Jacobson (1984) used before the suffixes to capture morphophonemic processes are as follows: (+) suffix keeps final consonants of bases, (-) suffix drops final consonants from bases, (~) suffix drops final *e* from bases, (%) suffix keeps 'strong' final consonants such as *g* or *r* preceded by *e* or ending in a base of the form CVV*r*-, (:) suffix drops voiced velar continuants if they occur between single vowels of which at least the first is prime, (@) suffix affects the *t*, dropped from bases ending in *te*, (—) base drops both the final consonant and the vowel preceding it when in contact with the suffix.

Some of the derivational postbases used with nominal roots include: *-ssaar* 'to hunt N', *-ngqerr* 'to have N', *-lleq* 'former N', *-li-* 'make N', *-lquq* 'old broken N', *+qlikacaaraq* 'one that is farthest in the area denoted by N', *-rpallar-* 'to make the sound of N', and *-vaarrluk* 'huge N'.

Table 3: Absolutive and Relative Nouns

Number of Possessor	Absolutive Case			Relative Case		
	Number of Possessed					
Unpossessed	-	%t	%k	%m	%t	%k
3rd person sg.	:(ng)a	:(ng)i	%k	:(ng)an	:(ng)in	%gken
plural	:(ng)at	:(ng)it	%gket	:(ng)ata	:(ng)ita	%gketa
dual	:(ng)ak	-kek	%gkek	:(ng)agnek	-kenka	%gkenka
1st person sg.	-ka	%nka	%gka	-ma		%gma
plural	+vut/put	-put	%gput	-mta		%gemta
dual	+vuk/puk	-puk	%gpuk	-megnuk		%gmegnuk
2nd person sg.	%n	-ten	%gken	-vet/+pet		%gpet
plural	+si/ci	-ci	%gci	-vci/+peci		%gpeci
dual	+sek/tek	-tek	%gtek	-vtek/+petek		%gpetek
3rd Refl person sg.	-ni	-ni	%gni	-mi		%gmi
plural	+seng/teng	-teng	%gteng	-meng		%gmeng
dual	+sek/tek	-tek	%gtek	-mek		%gmek

Verbal Morphology. Yup'ik verbs consist of a root and an inflectional ending that encodes mood, transitivity, and person. There are six moods in Yup'ik, four independent moods used as main-clause predicates (indicative, interrogative, participial and optative), and the dependent moods (eight connective and one subordinative), usually used in subordinate clauses.

There are four persons distinguished on the verb: first, second, third, and reflexive third person, and three numbers distinguished for person: singular, dual, and plural. Reflexive third person only appears in the dependent moods, as it refers to the subject of the main clause.

Personal endings of intransitive verbs are found in Table 4. Allomorphy is fully explained in Jacobson (1984).

Transitive-mood affixes are given in Table 5, personal endings following the mood affixes are not shown.

A full transitive paradigm is shown in Table 6 for indicative verbs, verbs expressing a straight statement of an event or state. All personal indicative endings starting with *pe-* are stem retaining (*+pe...* in morphophonemic notation), and *m-* endings are stem dropping (*–m...*).

The interrogative mood is used for verbs in information questions. It is not used for polar (yes/no) questions with the yes/no question enclitic *=qaa*. The transitive paradigm is given in Table 7 on the next page.

Verbs in the participial mood (marked *–lria* for intransitives or *~-ke-* for transitives + the specific personal participial endings) express potential predications with less expressive force (Miyaoka 1997: 340), e.g., *mikelnguq kitur-lria* (child pass-PART.INTR) 'a child (who) passes by'. Nonpredicative participials are nominal in nature. The optative mood expresses wishes or requests, e.g., Pasgesgu 'Would you (please) take some food to him?'

The eight connective moods include: contemporative 1 ("when" in the past), contemporative 2 ("while"), contemporative 3 ("si-

Table 4: Personal Endings of Intransitive Verbs

Person	Indicative		Interrogative		Optative		Subordinative		Participial	
3rd sg		g	+' (g/ t) a-	-	@t~li-	-		ni		-
plural		t		t		t		teng		t
dual		k		k		k		tek		k
1st sg		:nga	+~(t)si	a		+~lii		:nga	-lria/ @+ngur	nga
plural	+' (g/ t) u	kut	@ce-	ta		%lta	@+~lu-	ta		kut
dual		kuk	@ce-	ńuk		@+~luk		nuk		kuk
2nd sg		ten	+~(t)si	t	@-	-/(g)i/		ten		ten
plural		ci	@ce-	ci		@u		ci		ci
dual		tek	@ce-	tek				tek		tek

Table 5: Transitive Mood Affixes

Person	Indicative	Interrogative	Optative	Subordinative	Participial
3rd person sg	+'(g)a-	+'(g)a-	+~li		
plural					
dual					
1st person sg		+~(t)si	+~la-	@+~lu-	-~ke-
plural					
dual	+'(g)ar-				
2nd person sg		+~(t)si-	@+		
plural		@+ce-			
dual		@+ce-			

Table 6: Transitive Paradigm for Indicative Verbs

Agent		Person of Object								
		3rd Person			1st Person			2nd Person		
		sg	plural	dual	sg	plural	dual	sg	plural	dual
3rd sg	+'(g)a-	a	i	k	anga	akut	akuk	aten	aci	atek
pl		at	it	gket	itkut	itkut	itkuk	atgen	iceci	icetek
dual		ak	kek	gkek	agkut	agkuk	agkuk	agten	agten	agtek
1st sg		-ka	%nka	%gka				mken	mci	mtek
pl		+put	-put	%gput				mteggen	mceci	mcetek
dual		+puk	-puk	%gpuk				megten	megci	megtek
2nd sg	+'(g)ar-	%n	-ten	%gken	penga	pekuk	pekuk			
pl		+ci	-ci	%gci	pecia	pecikut	pecikuk			
dual		+tek	-tek	%gtek	petegnga	petegkuk	petegkuk			

Table 7: Transitive Paradigm for Interrogative Verbs

Agent		Person of Object								
		3rd Person			1st Person			2nd Person		
		sg	plural	dual	sg	plural	dual	sg	plural	dual
3rd sg	+' (g/ t)a-	:gu	ki	kek	nga	kut	kuk	ten	ci	tek
pl		tgu	tki	tkek	tnga	tkut	tkuk	tgen	ceci	cetek
dual		gnegu	gki	gkek	gnga	gkut	gkuk	gten	gci	gtek
1st sg							ken			
pl	+~(t)si	None								
dual										
2nd sg	+~(t)si	u	ki	kek	a	kut	kuk	None		
pl	@+ce-	ciu	ciki	citkek	cia	cikut	cikuk			
dual		tegu	tegki	tegkek	tegnga	tegkut	tegkuk			

multaneously"), precessive ("before"), concessive ("though"), contingent ("whenever"), consequential ("because"), and conditional ("if"). An example of a contemporative verb is:

piyua-qcaara-ller-ani
walk-minding.own.business-CONT.1-3s/s
'while she was walking along, minding her own business.'

Verbs in the subordinate mood express events concomitant with the event expressed by the main verb but may also be used independently.

Elli-qar-lu=llu=gguq *aya-lria*
put-V.briefly-SUB-3s=and=HEARSAY leave-PART.INTRANS
'And after he placed it on, he went away.'

Among the hundreds of postbases that can be used with verbs include *–rrlluarar-* 'to be a little bit V', *-llru* 'past tense', *–nritarar-* 'to be almost V', *-nrir-* 'to stop V-ing', *+~naciar-* 'to V late', *-myag-* 'to not V enough', *+~nirqe-* 'to be pleasant to V', *-nrite-* 'to not V', *-qainaurte-* 'to be ready to V', *-rraar-* 'to V first', *-ssaag-* 'to try to V', *-~yuite* 'to never V', *-yunrite-* 'to not want to V', and *-~yunari-* 'to be the proper time to V'. Examples of verbs with postbases are given below with the postbase underlined:

...tangerr-yuumii-na-ku *tulukaru-cilleq.*
... see-not.care.to-SUB-R/3s raven-worthless
'... (and so that girl) did not care to see that dirty rotten raven.'

angya-minun *elli-qa-llini-k-ii*
boat-3RS/SP.ALL put.briefly-apparently-PART.TRANS-3s/3s
'He apparently quickly placed it upon his boat.'

Kitek tua-i tunu-mnun pi-yugnga-u-ten
well then back-1s/3s.ALL do-able-INTRANS.INDIC-2s
'Well, you can get on my back.'

Enclitics. Enclitics are phrasal affixes that occur after the inflectional endings. Words in Yup'ik rarely have over 2 enclitics. The 13 enclitics in the language are *=am* 'emphasis', *=ggem* 'contrast or reservation', *=gguq* 'hearsay, reported speech', *=i* 'verbal pointer used to form exclamations from demonstrative adverb bases', *=kin* 'optative', *=kiq* 'I wonder', *=llam* 'I wish it weren't so', *=lli* 'exclamative', *=llu* 'and', *=mi* 'on the other hand', *=qaa* 'polar questions', *=tuq* 'I wish', and *=wa/=gga* 'answers questions with a verb in the consequential mood'.

Basic Syntax

The basic word order in Yup'ik is SOV (Agent-Patient-Verb), but may vary for pragmatic purposes. The ergative/absolutive pattern permeates much of the nominal (possessive) and verbal system, but traces of accusativity may be found in clause combining strategies and by the pronominal suffixes of certain moods.

Negation is expressed by the postbases: *-nrite-* 'to not V', *-peke-* 'to not V', *-taite-* 'negative existential, not have', *+(s)ciigate-* 'to not be able to V', *-ate-* 'negates certain stative verbs', *-:(ng)ite-* 'to lack N or V, have no N or V', *-llrunrite-* 'to not have V'ed', *-yuite-* 'to never V, to habitually not V', *-yunrite-* 'to not want to V, to continue not to V', *+~yuumiite-* 'to not care to V', *+~yuumiirarte-* 'to no longer want to', and their combinations with other postbases.

Tangerr-suumiit-a-mken.
see-not.care/want-TRANS.INDIC-1s/2s
'I do not care to see you.'

Aya-sciiga-na-ni.
leave-not.able.to-SUBORD-3s
'It wasn't able to go (referring to an engine).'

Kap-suun-tait-lini-lrii-t.
poke-device-not.have-apparently-PARTICIP.INTRANS-3p
'They apparently have no quills.'

... camai-ar-peke-na-ku *tuai* *ayag-lu-ni...*
... hello-say-NEG-SUB-R/3s there leave-SUB-3s
'... he did not greet her but continued to go.'

Complement clauses usually precede main verbs.

Contact with Other Languages

The distribution of the native languages of Alaska in 1980 was not much different from that of the first contact with Europeans (Woodbury 1984). The infrequent cross-cultural travel between the Eskimos and their immediate neighbors has nevertheless resulted in a few loanwords.

Nouns and verbs incorporated into Yup'ik usually take the ending *–(a)r-/-(a)q*, from which they may take native morphology. Yup'ik has borrowed extensively from RUSSIAN and ENGLISH, and to a lesser extent from Inupiaq, Aleut, Athabascan, Siberian languages and Philippine languages (Jacobson 1984)

From Russian: *pasmakiq* 'shoe, boot', *uataq* 'cotton', *kuuniq* 'horse', *sumpaq* 'jacket', *miilaq* 'soap', *kantalaq* 'jail', *palatkaaq* 'tent', *sun'aq* 'ship', *suupaq* 'soup', *alatiq* 'fried bread', *kulutaq* 'whip', *kankiiq* 'ice skates', *kelup'aaq* 'rice'
From English: *piikinaq* 'pig (from bacon)', *suuq* 'movie (from show)', *selip'ussaaq* 'slipper', *milek* 'milk', *kelassaq* 'glass', *tiiviiq* 'television', *paatnaq* 'partner', *(e)skuulaq* 'school', *sainar-* 'to sign', *espaak* 'spark plug', *piipiq* 'baby'
From Inupiaq: *aakaq* 'mother', *nuya'illaq* 'bald person', *tupiq'uyaq* 'tent'
From Aleut: *arliaq* 'albatross', *taangaq* 'liquor', *cagiq*, 'halibut', *atgiaq* 'codfish'
From Filipino: *mantiikaq* 'lard, shortening', *Pilip'iinaq* 'Filipino'

Common Words

man:	angun	woman:	arnaq
water:	(e)meq	sun:	akerta
tree	napa, uqvik	three:	pingayun
dog:	qimugta	long:	aku, take-
yes:	ii-i	no:	agu, qang'a, qaang
small:	mikete-, -cuar(aq)	bird:	tengmiaq, yaqulek
fish:	neqa, iqalluk	sky:	qilak
big:	ange-, -rpak, -ruk, -vak, among others		
good:	assir-, cavaq-, -nike, among others		

Example Sentences

(1) Ak'a=gguq yuu-t curuka-lallru-u-t
past=HRSY person-PL feast.exchange-used.to-INDIC.INTR-3PL

kesianek.
always
'Long ago the people used to always go back and forth between villages exchanging gifts and feasts.'

(2) Ilaita=gguq cupegte-ngu-t.
some.of.them=HRSY homesick-INDIC.INTR-3p
'Some of them are apparently getting homesick.'

(3) Qerar-ciiq-a-mken tunu-mkun kuimar-lu-a.
cross-FUT-IND.TRANS-1s/2s back-VIALIS swim-SUBORD-1s
'I'll be able to swim across with you on my back.'

Efforts to Preserve, Protect, and Promote the Language

The Yup'ik have a rich and varied oral tradition of stories, myths, and songs, as well as dance. The male and female elders transmit these cultural artifacts to the younger generations who exhibit varying degrees of competency in storytelling and dancing. Philosophical oration by the elders is greatly respected and appreciated, and it is emulated by the younger generations. Oral competency remains to this day a mark of a knowledgeable elder.

In the 1960s the University of Alaska in Fairbanks began research that led to the development of a grammar and orthography for Yup'ik. The original research was headed by Michael Krauss with the assistance of Irene Reed and Martha Teeluk (Reed 1977). The Alaska Native Language Center grew out of these early efforts and has contributed to the preservation and promotion of the Yup'ik language through the Yup'ik Language Workshop based in Bethel, Alaska. There are a number of school districts in which Yup'ik is taught in the primary grades and English is taught as a second language.

There is a group of Yup'ik elders in the Lower Kuskokwim School District who help to create new Yup'ik words, with the advent of new state and federal programs, for such words as "boundary commission". Various museums have begun to use Yup'ik words to identify and describe the various material culture artifacts in their collections.

Krauss (1984) documents the decline of fluent Yup'ik speakers, noting in 1974 that out of the 23,000 ethnically Yup'ik people, 18,000 were fluent speakers. A decade later in 1984, only 10,000 fluent speakers were accounted for out of a population of 18,000. Despite the decline of native speakers, Yup'ik Eskimo remains to this day one of the most vibrant Native American languages.

Select Bibliography

Jacobson, Steven A. 1984. *Yup'ik Eskimo Dictionary*. Fairbanks, Alaska: Alaska Native Language Center.

_____. 1990. "Comparison of Central Alaskan Yup'ik Eskimo and Central Siberian Yup'ik Eskimo." *International Journal of American Linguistics* 56: 264–286.

_____. 1995. *A Practical Grammar of the Central Alaskan Yup'ik Eskimo Language*. Fairbanks, Alaska: Alaska Native Language Center.

Krauss, Michael E. 1973. "Eskimo-Aleut." In *Linguistics in North America. Current Trends in Linguistics*, Thomas A. Sebeok, ed. Vol. 10. Hague: Mouton.

_____. 1974. *Language Map of Alaska*. Fairbanks: Alaska Native Language Center.

Mithun, Marianne, ed. 1996. *Prosody, Grammar and Discourse in Central Alaskan Yup'ik*. University of California, Santa Barbara: Santa Barbara Papers in Linguistics, vol. 7.

Miyaoka, Osahito. 1997. "Sketch of Yup'ik, an Eskimo Language." In *Handbook of North American Indian Languages*, vol, 17. Washington DC: Smithsonian Institution.

Reed, Irene, Osahito Miyaoka, Steven Jacobson, Paschal Afcan, and Michael Krauss. 1977. *Yup'ik Eskimo Grammar*. Fairbanks: Alaska Native Language Center.

Woodbury, Anthony C. 1984. "Eskimo and Aleut Languages." In *Handbook of North American Indians, vol. 5: The Arctic*. ed. by David Thomas. Washington: Smithsonian.

ZHUANG-BOUYEI

Jerold A. Edmondson

Language Name: Zhuang and Bouyei. In the Tai languages of China there are some complexities regarding language names because official appellations and speech communities do not always coincide. Here we treat the groups Chinese scholars call Zhuang and Bouyei as a single entry even though they count officially as two of China's 55 recognized ethnic minorities.

There is no universally used autonym among the Zhuang-Bouyei. The Chinese name *Zhuang* [tʂuaŋ^{51}], formerly spelled *Chuang*, comes from *pou*^{43}*ɕu:ŋ*^{33} or *pou*^{43}*tsu:ŋ*^{33}, whereas the name *Bouyei* is from *pu*^{31}*jai*^{31}. Beyond these there are about 20 other self-designations among the Zhuang, such as (raised single numbers represent tone categories, which are invariant over the Tai branch, although they vary in value from place to place): *pu*^{4} *noŋ*^{2} (Yunnan Wenshan); *bu*^{6}*dai*^{2} (Yunnan Wenshan, Malipo, Kaiyuan); *pho*^{6}*thai*^{2} (Guangxi Longzhou); *kɯn*^{2}*tho*^{3} or *pu*^{4}*to*^{3} (Zuojiang); *pou*^{4}*ma:n*^{2} (Guangxi Hechi); *pou*^{4}*ba:n*^{3} ('village people' Guangxi Wuming); and *pou*^{4}*lau*^{2} (Guangxi Fengshan). In still other places they call themselves Bushuang, Butu (Gentu), Buyang, Buyue, Buna, Nongían, Bubian, Tulao, Gaolan, Buman, Buming, Bulong, and Budong, where *Bu-/pu-/* is a classifier meaning 'people'. The Chinese name *Bouyei* was formerly spelled *Pu-yi*. The Bouyei at various locations also call themselves Buna and Bunong. In the past the Bouyei were often called *Zhongjia*.

Location: Southern China. The Zhuang live mostly in the Guangxi-Zhuang Autonomous Region (with about 1 million also found in Yunnan to the west). The Bouyei are located in Guizhou Province just to the north of Zhuang.

Family: Zhuang-Bouyei is the largest representative of the Tai branch in China. Because the Zhuang and Bouyei dwell in different provinces and have thus been subject to two different provincial administrations over the centuries, some differences of designation, language, custom, and ethnic perspective have developed. The same kinds of factors have developed in the opposite direction in the case of the Zhuang. The Zhuang have for a very long time been regarded by the Chinese as a single group. But when Professor Li Fang Kuei conducted field investigations at various sites on the Zhuang language in the 1930s and 1940s, he found that the Northern Zhuang language resembled more the language of the Bouyei and that the Southern Zhuang language was rather different from both Northern Zhuang and Bouyei. Following Li, most scholars have assigned Northern Zhuang and Bouyei to the Northern Subbranch of Tai, and Southern Zhuang to the Central Subbranch of Tai (Thai is classified as belonging to the Southwestern Subbranch). Thus, although the official nomenclature for these Tai peoples is Zhuang = {Northern Zhuang + Southern Zhuang} and Bouyei, the linguistic evidence suggests rather a structure: {Northern Zhuang + Bouyei (Northern Tai Subbranch)} and Southern Zhuang (Central Tai Subbranch). Nevertheless, doubt concerning the litmus tests for a three-fold division of Tai into Northern, Central, and Southwestern subbranches has been arising of late with increasing frequency and thus the Tripartite Tai Hypothesis is perhaps apt to change in the future.

As for affiliation at the next higher level, Tai shows regular and unproblematic phonological and lexical correspondences to its sister branch, Kam-Sui, and the two branches can thus be joined with some confidence to form Kam-Tai. At a still higher level, Benedict (1975) unites Kam-Tai with the small languages Hlai, Gelao, Lachi, and others to form Kadai (others use the term Tai-Kadai for this whole, whereas in the latter tradition Kadai would refer to Hlai, Gelao, Lachi, etc.).

The most controversial of all issues, however, concerns ties of Kadai to other attested families in Asia. The traditional lore was to place Kadai (Tai-Kadai or possibly Kam-Tai) under the ensign of a "grand" Sino-Tibetan family. Benedict and others have argued for a new alignment that does not relegate Kadai to Sino-Tibetan despite some apparent similarities. The phonological and lexical resemblance of Kadai to Sino-Tibetan languages stems not from inheritance, Benedict says, but from long-term language contact.

Related Languages: The languages most closely related to Northern Zhuang and Bouyei are all small in population. Haudricourt (1963) and Gedney (1970) have reported on the northern Tai language Saek, of Laos and Nakhorn Phanom, Thailand. More recently, Chamberlain (1991) has claimed Northern Tai heritage for Mène of Lak Sao, Laos. Also, Edmondson (1992) has noted the Northern Tai features of E (Kjang E) of Rongshui and Luocheng Counties in northern Guangxi Province (population 10,000).

Regarding relatives of Southern Zhuang, there are the Central Tai languages Tày (formerly called Thô) (pop. 1.19 million in 1989) and Nùng (pop. 705,709 in 1989) of extreme northern Vietnam in the borderland provinces of Lang So'n, Bàc Thái, Cao Bàng, Hà Giang, Tuyên Quang, and Lào Cai. Tày and Nùng of Vietnam are not dramatically different from the Southern Zhuang spoken across the border in China; for example, the Nùng Cháo of Lang So'n say their blood relatives in China are the Longzhou Zhuang.

Dialects: In Northern Zhuang there are seven vernacular areas that share about 80 percent in common cognate vocabulary;

the kind spoken at Wuming is the basis of the new Zhuang orthography. Bouyei writing is based on the Bouyei spoken in Wangmo County in southern Guizhou. In all of Guizhou there are said to be three basic Bouyei areas with variation not warranting division into distinct varieties. The most prominent feature of Northern Zhuang and Bouyei is the loss of aspiration in initials and unremarkable tonal developments

In Southern Zhuang there are five vernacular areas that share about 68 percent common cognate vocabulary; the representative location for Southern Zhuang usually taken is Longzhou near the border with Vietnam. Zhuang at locations other than Wuming is written with the standard Zhuang script appropriately modified. Southern Zhuang's most prominent feature is retention of aspiration, indeed the development of aspiration in vocabulary that originally had **r* or clustered **r* as well as unusual secondary tone changes.

Of the three, Bouyei is the most homogeneous and Southern Zhuang is the most diverse. In all cases nonagreement in phonological contrasts and lexicon prevents understanding of running conversation, although comprehension of isolated words across areas is very easy.

Number of Speakers: The Zhuang-Bouyei have a sizeable populace, some of it urban or semiurban, some of it in mountainous areas, and some of it in flatlands. The combined numbers of Zhuang and Bouyei far outnumber all other minority groups in China. The Zhuang amounted to 15.4 million and the Bouyei to 2.5 million in the 1990 census. Indeed, the combined population of nearly 18 million constitutes the second largest group after the Thai in the entire Tai Branch.

Origin and History

About 2,000 years ago ancient documents say that in Lingnan (South China) lived the *Baiyue* or 'Hundred Yue'. The Han chroniclers reported in the *Lüshi Chunqiu* that the Hundred Yue inhabited land found south of the Yangtze River and were in fact so numerous that for a distance of 4,000 km there was a myriad and varied populace with many names. The peoples of contemporary Guangxi were called Wuhu, Lang, or Li. Originally the Zhuang and the Lang were not the same, and the Lang made up half the population of one county in Guangxi. But by the Ming Dynasty they were regarded as a single group. One writer from the time, Fan Dachen in Nandan, explicitly states there were Zhuang in that place and that they were successors of the Yue.

As for the Bouyei, in the Eastern Han (A.D. 220) there was a group called the Yelang who had a very large area under its control. It is closely related to the contemporary Bouyei of Guizhou. The center of its area was probably located in Anshun about 60 km to the southwest of the present capital of Guizhou Province at Guiyang. The Ye in Yelang is from Yue of the Hundred Yue, which, in Southwest MANDARIN and also in Bouyei, is simply pronounced Ye. And Lang (see above) is probably just Luo, the name of one of the major subgroups among the Hundred Yue. Note that the order of words here is Yelang, which is typical of the left-headed construction type used by Kadai speakers and not of the right-headed construction type of the Chinese; compare Han Bai-Yue and Kadai Yue-Luo.

From the Northern and Southern Dynasty to the Tang, the Bouyei and Zhuang were indiscriminately called Liliao, Manliao, or Yiliao (the Liao or Lao was one of the successor groups to the Yue that was not sinified). After the Five Dynasties (951), the Bouyei began to appear in Chinese history under the designation "Zhongjia"; this name has endured almost up to the present. The name "Zhuang" first appeared after the beginning of the Song Dynasty (960). But despite the use of different names—Zhuang or Zhongjia—from these periods onward, it is very likely from what we know of sound change in this part of China that Zhuang and Zhong represent only minor phonological variants of a common etymon written differently by Chinese scribes at different courts. Both of the names "Zhuang" and "Zhong" evolved naturally and are not the product of conscious decision.

In the course of the Qing (1644–1911) the autonym Lang gradually disappeared and was replaced by Zhuang or by one of the names used by the Zhuang: Puxiong, Buyi, Buyei, Buman, Buxia, Bunong, Butu, etc. In the 1950s all these groups were being called "Zhuang" and in 1965 the original Chinese character for Zhuang was replaced by the one in use today. In brief, the Zhuang-Bouyei people are the descendants of the Baiyue and remain in the area of Lingnan where their precursors once lived.

Orthography and Basic Phonology

The Zhuang-Bouyei are unlike the better-known Tai Lɯ of Sipsongpanna and the Chinese Shan of Dehong Prefectures in Yunnan Province in that they do not possess a traditional writing system. Chinese characters were used by Zhuang-Bouyei literati as a rough, and ready, system for recording traditional songs and household records. But, a standard was never established. Owing to their size and importance the Zhuang and Bouyei were among the very first minority languages provided with new orthographies in the post 1949 period. The new writing system was at first based on Latin letters with Cyrillic symbols for the tone marks, but later the Cyrillic tone marks were eliminated. The current system for Zhuang uses final consonants to mark tones in open syllables. In closed syllables Tone 7 and Tone 7S (S=short vowel) are written with a final voiceless stop symbol and Tone 8 and Tone 8S are written with final voiced stop symbol. All finals are, of course, pronounced as voiceless unreleased consonants and the choice of *-p* or *-b* is simply a writing convention for tone. In this chapter, tones will be transcribed using superscript numbers representing the tone class.

Tone 1 -Ø	Tone 2 -z
Tone 3 -j	Tone 4 -x
Tone 5 -q	Tone 6 -h
Tone 7 -p/-t/-k	Tone 7S -p/-t/-k
Tone 8-b/-d/-g	Tone 8S -b/-d/-g

Table 1: Consonants

		Bilabial	Alveolar	Palatal	Velar	Glottal
Stops	Voiceless, unaspirated	p	t		k	ʔ
	Voiceless, aspirated	#ph	#th		#kh	
	Voiced, preglottal	ʔb	ʔd			
Fricatives	Voiceless	f	s, #ɬ	ɕ	*x	h
	Voiced	v	*z		t	
Affricates			*ts	*tɕ		
Nasals		m	n	ɲ	ŋ	
Laterals			l			
Glides	Voiced			j		
	Preglottal	*ʔw		*ʔj		

Note: The sound systems of Wuming Zhuang and Wangmo Bouyei are provided here as points for comparison. Consonants marked with * are found only in Bouyei, and those marked with # are found only in Southern Zhuang.

Initials /t ts k ʔ ʔb ʔd f s ɕ h v ɣ m n ɳ ŋ l j pj mj kw ŋw/ are written <b d c g Ø mb nd f s x h v r m n ny l y py my kv ngv>. The vowels of Zhuang are written as follows: /i e a o u ɯ/ are <i e a o u w>.

Diphthongal forms are indicated by combinations: /iŋ iəŋ/ are <ing ieng>. Some examples are *haj* 'five'; *na* 'thick'; *roj* 'to know'; *daengz* 'to arrive'; and *bit* 'duck'.

In addition to the consonants in Table 1 above, Zhuang-Bouyei has palatalized bilabials /pj mj/; Northern Zhuang also has a palatalized velar /kj/. Zhuang-Bouyei also has labialized velars /kw ŋw/.

In Chinese loans, the "apical vowel" /ɿ/ may also occur. The vowel *a* is distinguished for length: /a:/ is phonetically [ɑ], and /a/ is phonetically /ɐ/.

Table 2: Vowels

	Front	Back	
		Unrounded	Rounded
High	i	ɯ	u
Mid	e	ə	o
Low		a	

Tone. The Zhuang-Bouyei language is relatively rich in tonal contrasts, possessing in most places six contrastive tones in open CV syllables and four contrastive tones in closed C_1V_2/ C_1VVC_2 syllables, where C_2 is *p, t,* or *k*.

In the chart below, sequences of identical numbers represent level tones (55 high, 33 mid, 11 low); sequences of unlike numbers represent rising (e.g., 24, 35) or falling (e.g., 53, 31) contours.

In Wuming Zhuang (WZ) and Wangmo Bouyei (WB) the tone values are as follows:

Class	WZ	WB
Tone 1	24	35
Tone 2	31	11
Tone 3	55	13
Tone 4	42	31
Tone 5	35	33
Tone 6	33	53
Tone 7	35	33
Tone 7S	55	35
Tone 8	33	53
Tone 8S	33	11

Basic Morphology

Zhuang-Bouyei does not exhibit any inflectional morphology. There is reduplication to express a plethora of something:

pit^{7}pit^7	kai^{5}kai^5	ɕuŋ^3	mi^2
duck-duck	chicken-chicken	all	have

'There were lots of chickens and ducks.'

Basic Syntax

The order of constituents in Zhuang-Bouyei is SVO. Question words are found in situ. Yes/No questions are generally formed by the strategy Verb-Neg-Verb.

Within the noun phrase the order of elements is usually Numeral-Classifier-Head noun, as in:

Zhuang:

ha^3	tu^2	mou^1	
five	CL	pig	'five pigs'

so:ŋ^1	bak^7	na^2	
two	CL	paddy	'two rice fields'

Bouyei:

va:ʔ^{8} kɯ^{5} ku^{1} ni^{4}
CL pan I this
'this pan of mine'

Modifiers basically follow the nouns they modify:

ɣa:n^{2} ɣau^{2}
house our
'our house'

na^{2} ɣam^{4}
paddy wet
'wet paddy'

ɣam^{4} na^{2}
water paddy
'(the) water of the paddy.'

Contact with Other Languages

The Zhuang-Bouyei have been in contact with several other groups, including KAM, Yao, Miao, and YI. But the language that has influenced Zhuang-Bouyei the most is clearly Chinese. In Guangxi, Cantonese was and remains an important vehicle to interact with petty merchants traversing Zhuang territory. In recent times Cantonese has been supplanted to some degree by Southwest Mandarin Chinese and recently by Modern Standard Chinese (MSC).

Common Words

	Wuming Zhuang	Wangmo Bouyei
man:	pou^{4}sa:i^{1}	pu^{4}sa:i^{1}
woman:	me^{6}bɯk^{7}	lɯʔ^{8}bɯkʔ^{7}
water:	ɣam^{4}	zam^{4}
sun:	taŋ^{1}ŋon^{2}	taŋ^{1}ŋon^{2}
three:	sa:m^{1}	sa:m^{1}
fish:	pja^{1}	pja^{1}
big:	huŋ^{1}	la:u^{4} ; ɣuŋ^{1}

Example Sentences

Zhuang:

(1) fa:k^{8} ɣa:u^{5} nei^{4} tɯk^{8}kou^{1} ɕoi^{6} dei^{1} ne^{3}?
CL harrow this be I repair good FINAL.PARTICLE
'I repaired this harrow well, didn't I?'

(2) mɯŋ^{2} pai^{1} kjaɯ^{2} ha^{6}?
you go where then
'Where are you going then?'

Bouyei:

(3) ti^{1} ma^{1} mi^{2} ma^{1}?
he come NEG come
'Is he coming?'

(4) lɯʔ^{8}sai^{5} ni^{4} di^{1}tɕai^{2} ta^{2}za:i^{4}
child this cute really
'This kid is really cute.'

Efforts to Preserve, Protect, and Promote the Language

Zhuang-Bouyei are at the forefront in regard to China's efforts to promote literacy in minority language speakers. There are at present large projects to teach the Zhuang script and the promotion in the use of Zhuang writing in Guangxi Province in children and in adults. It is still difficult to decide if these efforts will be powerful enough or rapid enough to stop an unmistakable language shift of Zhuang speakers to Chinese. Signs, books, and official documents are printed in both languages.

Select Bibliography

Benedict, Paul K. 1975. *Austro-Thai: Language and Culture*. New Haven: HRAF Press.

Chamberlain, James R. 1994. *Tai Mène, a New Northern Tai Language*. Paper presented at the 24 ICSIL, Bangkok, Thailand.

Edmondson, Jerold A. 1992. "Fusion and diffusion in E. Guangxi Province, China." In T. Dutton, *et al* (eds.), *The Language Game: Papers in Memory of Donald C. Laycock* (Pacific Linguistic Series, C-110). Department of Linguistics, Australian National University, Canberra, 131–40.

_____. 1994. "Change and variation in Zhuang." In K. Adams and T. Hudak (eds.) *Papers From the Second Annual Meeting of the Southeast Asian Linguistics Society 1992*. Tempe: Arizona State University. 147–85.

Edmondson, Jerold and David B. Solnit eds. 1997. *Comparative Kadai: The Tai Branch*. Dallas: SIL/UTA Series in Linguistics.

Haudricourt, André-Georges. 1963. "Remarques sur les initiales complexes de la langue Sek." In *Bulletin de la Société de linguistique de Paris* 58: 156–63.

Li Fang Kuei. 1977. *Handbook of Comparative Tai*. Honolulu: University Press of Hawaii.

Ramsey, S.R. 1987. *The Languages of China*. Princeton: Princeton University Press.

Snyder, Donna. 1995. "Variation in Bouyei." MA thesis, University of Texas at Arlington.

Snyder, Wil, and Lu Tianqiao. 1996. "Wuming Zhuang Tone Sandhi: A Phonological, Syntactic, and Lexical Investigation." In Edmondson and Solnit (eds.) *Comparative Kadai: the Tai Branch*. Dallas: SIL/UTA Series in Linguistics.

ZULU

Sandra Sanneh

Language Name: Zulu or IsiZulu. *Isi-* is the prefix denoting language.

Location: Eastern South Africa (KwaZulu-Natal Province) and urban centers in central South Africa, especially Gauteng province, also Swaziland, Lesotho, southern Zimbabwe and Malawi. Widely used throughout southern Africa as a lingua franca among speakers of Bantu languages.

Family: *Nguni* cluster of the Southern Bantu group of the Bantu branch of Niger-Kordofanian.

Related Languages: Zulu is highly mutually intelligible with other Nguni languages: Northern Nguni (Zunda) comprising Ndebele (Zimbabwe), IsiNdebele (Mpumalanga Province) and XHOSA (Western and Eastern Cape); Southern Nguni (Tekela) comprising SISWATI, Northern Ndebele (Northern Province) and Bhaca (Eastern Cape). It is also closely related to the other languages of the Southern Bantu group. These include the Sotho cluster (SESOTHO, Sepedi/Northern Sotho, TSWANA, Silozi), as well as Tsonga, Shangaan and, more remotely, Venda.

Dialects: The main regional dialects are so-called Zululand or northern Zulu, and Natal or southern Zulu. Dialectal differences affect tone and nasal consonants.

In urban centers of South Africa, Zulu is spoken with codeswitching into other languages. The extent of this codeswitching and the languages used depend on a range of variables such as age, education, gender and income level of the speaker, as well as other aspects of each speech event, including the identity of the interlocutor. In Durban and Pietermaritzburg (KwaZulu-Natal Province) code switching from Zulu is into ENGLISH, and, to a lesser extent, AFRIKAANS. In Soweto, Johannesburg, and Pretoria (Gauteng Province) Zulu speakers switch into English, Afrikaans and Sesotho/Setswana, all four languages often being used in a single conversation. A less widely spoken variety of this urban Zulu dialect is *Is'camtho*, an argot that originated as the language of one of the criminal gangs that operated on the Witwatersrand (Gauteng) in the 1920s (another being *Tsotsitaal*, which is Afrikaans based) and is now spoken in certain largely male Soweto subcultures. Is'camtho speakers codeswitch into Afrikaans, English and Sesotho/Tswana.

In the early decades of the 20th century, mining companies devised a pidgin called *Fanakalo* ('do like so') for communication in the mines. This pidgin combines Zulu lexical items with simplified English syntax. Much despised by Zulu language speakers, it is nevertheless still used by some white employers in urban areas and on farms.

Number of Speakers: 8.5 million, or 22.4 percent of South Africans give Zulu as their home language (Central Statistical Services 1998), making it the most widely used home language in the country (Xhosa is 17.5 percent, Afrikaans 15.1 percent, Sepedi 9.8 percent and English 9.1 percent). Zulu is also the lingua franca of the black community, and is estimated to be understood by well over 80 percent of that community. By contrast only a tiny fraction of white South Africans understand Zulu.

Origin and History

Scholars are convinced there is sufficient archaeological evidence to conclude that the Iron Age communities living in the area now known as KwaZulu/Natal Province after about 1500 were the cultural, linguistic and physical ancestors of the modern-day Nguni people (Laband). Since political organization was in the form of small and medium-sized chieftaincies, loosely but broadly allied through blood and marriage relationships, it is thought that a broad continuum of slightly differing Nguni dialects was spoken throughout the16th and 17th centuries, and that during this period the Nguni dialects acquired their distinctive click sounds through close contact with the neighboring San peoples—possibly via the innovation required by new wives and junior men in accordance with linguistic taboos (*ukuhlonipha*).

The Zulu people trace their own origins to Zulu, second son of Malandela, who lived with his clan north of the Tugela river in the early 17th century. On Malandela's death, his elder son, Qwabe, inherited the family compound (*umuzi*) and, as was the custom, Zulu moved away with his family and other dependents to establish a new clan. The *AmaZulu* ('people of the sky') seem to have been a relatively small and uninfluential clan, and little is known about them until the late 18th century, when changes in the slave, and more importantly, ivory trade at Delagoa Bay (Maputo) made certain chiefs wealthy, powerful and predatory, making it prudent for smaller clans to form alliances with and seek protection from them.

In the 1780s a Zulu king named Senzangakhona became prominent when, at the request of Dingiswayo, king of the powerful Mthethwa, he successfully led the Zulu army in defense of the Mthethwa's western flank against the equally powerful Ndwandwe. The Mthethwa king, Dingiswayo, rewarded Senzangakhona and his people with cattle and land. On Senzangakhona's death, Shaka, his son by a junior wife, Nandi, seized power by assassinating the rightful heir. Shaka had already distinguished himself as a military leader, and Dingiswayo supported his bid for the kingship. In 1817 the

Ndwandwe, still rivals of the Mthethwa, attacked their main army and killed Dingiswayo, leaving the Zulus under Shaka to face the Ndwandwe and their king, Zwide. After some initial defeats, Shaka's army fought off the Ndwandwe in 1818, and he retreated to regroup and strengthen his army. In 1819, Zwide attacked again, and this time Shaka defeated them and took the Ndwandwe capital. Between 1820 and his assassination by a half-brother in 1828, Shaka consolidated many northern Nguni clans to form the Zulu Empire, the largest ever seen in southern Africa.

The consolidation of clans into larger polities in the early 19th century, along with other factors, seems to have been accompanied by some consolidation of the previously large variety of Nguni dialects. The southern Nguni, for example, by then dominated by the powerful Xhosa kingdom, spoke a cluster of dialects that had a wider use of clicks than the Zulu (now including many vassal clans) and other northern Nguni.

From the1820s onward foreign envoys to the Zulu kingdom began to report and document its language and culture. From 1835 onward Protestant and Catholic missionaries established stations first in Zululand, and later in Natal, and set about creating orthographies and translating religious material, each one thereby standardizing a different dialect for the work of his mission. By 1860 several orthographies for Zulu were in use, prompting a lively discussion in the local newspaper of the merits of Lepsius's Standard Alphabet, and by the end of the century that number had doubled. By then Zulu had several detailed dictionaries, the most comprehensive being that compiled by Bishop John Colenso, numerous grammars, and a fledgling written literature consisting of autobiographies and accounts of Zulu history written by Christian converts, as well as transcriptions of the two major oral genres: *izinganekwane* ('folktales') and *izibongo* ('praise poetry'). Zulu was also the medium of instruction for the first three years of education in schools established by missionaries for Zulu speakers.

After 1910, the Union of South Africa adopted the languages of the two white communities, English and Afrikaans, as official languages. Education for white children was centralized and made mandatory, while only a small number of black children had access to education, which remained the responsibility of the mission organizations and the churches. These mission/church schools continued their policy of mother-tongue instruction for the first three years of education.

In 1948 an Afrikaner-led party was elected in whites-only elections and began passing legislation to separate the population by race, as part of a comprehensive policy termed *apartheid* ('separateness'). This policy had as its ultimate scenario the division of about one-fifth of South Africa into a number of separate semi-independent "homelands", one for each black ethnic group. The remaining four fifths would then be fully controlled by the white community. The promotion of narrowly defined ethnic identity was considered crucial to the success of this policy, and therefore large investments were made by the state in approved representations of the languages and cultures of the black community. Over the next 40 years Zulu (as well as Xhosa, Sesotho and other) language publications, radio stations, academic departments, and, later, Zulu television programs, a Zulu language board and a Zulu university were established with state funds.

In 1996, following free and fair elections in 1994, South Africa adopted a new constitution that recognized eleven official languages, including Zulu. A new Pan South African Language Board was charged with formulating a language policy for the country in accordance with the new constitution. While implementation was being debated, some changes in language use spontaneously followed adoption of the new constitution. These changes include a widespread embrace of English as the language both of liberation and of advancement; a widespread rejection of Afrikaans in schools and the media except for first language speakers; an increase in Zulu as Second Language courses in (historically) white schools; a dramatic increase in the use of Zulu in translated official and business documents; and a marked preference on the part of television producers and artists in general for productions in which the protagonists speak English and code switch into Zulu and other languages, over monolingual works in any language.

Orthography and Basic Phonology

Zulu orthography, standardized in 1921 and slightly modified since then, uses the Roman alphabet with no additional characters. Click phonemes are represented by the characters *c*, *q* and *x*. Lateral fricatives are represented by *hl* and *dl*. Aspiration is indicated by the addition of *h*. Voiced [h] *hh* is distinguished from voiceless *h*. Tone is not marked.

Vowels. Zulu has a system of five pure contrastive vowels. The mid vowels have allophonic mid-high before high vowels. There are no long vowels and no diphthongs with contrastive significance:

	Front		Back
High	i		u
Mid	e		o
Low		a	

Consonants. Voiced stops and affricates have delayed voicing. The alveolar nasal [n] too has delayed voicing in Natal dialect. The trill [r] occurs only in loanwords from Afrikaans. All obstruents, including clicks, can occur with prenasalization. All obstruents, including clicks, but excluding labials, can occur with postlabialization. Voiced obstruents, including clicks, have a depressor effect on tone. The alveolar nasal [n] is accompanied by voiced aspiration. (See Table 1 on the next page.)

Tone. 'Zululand' Zulu has a three-way tonal contrast: high (H), non-high (L), and falling (F). Natal Zulu has only a two-way H-L contrast. Tone patterns with spreading and downstep are associated with both lexical and grammatical items, and these patterns are modified by the morphology and the syntax. Voiced obstruents have a depressor effect on the onset of H, L and F tones. Examples of tone patterns:

-bóna! 'see' *-bonga* 'thank' *-bûka* 'watch'
Ngiyabóna. 'I see.' *Ngiyabonga.* 'Thanks.' *Ngiyabûka.* 'I'm watching.'
Sáwubóna. 'Hello.' *Sáwubonga.* 'We thanked you.' *Sáwubûka.* 'We watched you.'

Table 1: Consonants

		Bilabial	Labio-dental	Alveolar	Postalveolar	Velar	Glottal
Stops	Ejective	p		t		k	
	Aspirated	ph		th		kh	
	Voiced	bh		d		g	
	Implosives	b					
Fricatives	Voiceless		f	s	sh		h
	Voiced		v	z			hh
	Lateral vcls.			hl			
	Lateral vd.			dl			
Affricates	Ejective			ts	tsh		
	Voiced				j		
	Lateral ejective					kl	
Nasals		m		n	ny	ng	
Liquids	Lateral			l			
	Trill			[r]			
Glides		w			y		
Clicks	Voiceless			c	x	q	
	Aspirated			ch	xh	qh	
	Voiced			gc	gx	gq	

Basic Phonological Rules. Here are the basic phonological rules for Zulu.

1. Vowel Elision/Coalescence. If concatenation of morphological elements results in the juxtaposition of vowels, there is either elision, coalescence or epenthetic glide insertion, the choice of outcome being grammatically determined:

(1) Elision of V_1 occurs with CV or /a/ prefix, and with vowel-initial verb stems:
CV + a > Ca *Ngi-akha* > *Ngakha* 'I build/am building.'
CV + o > Co *Siya-osa* > *Siyosa* 'We're roasting.'
CV+ e > Ce *Ba-enzani?* > *Benzani?* 'What are they doing?'
a + V > V *A-enzani?* > *Enzani?* 'What are they (the men) doing?'
With /u/, /i/ prefix and vowel-initial verb stems V > glide:
u + V > *wV U-enzani?* > *Wenzani?* 'What are you doing?'
i + V > *yV I enzani?* > *Yenzani?* 'What is he (man) doing?'
(2) Coalescence occurs with Ca prefixes and initial V on nouns:
a + a > a *za - abantu* > *zabantu* 'of the people'
a + i > e *ba-indoda* > *bendoda* 'of the man'
a + u > o *wa-umfazi* > *womfazi* 'of the woman'
(3) Epenthesis occurs on affixes preceding the subject or object concord:
i + u = iwu *Angi-u-funi.* > *Angiwufuni.* 'I don't want it (the medicine).'
a + i = ayi *A-i-dli.* > *Ayidli.* 'He (man) isn't eating.'
a + a = awa *A-a-dli.* > *Awadli.* 'They (men) aren't eating.'

2. Palatalization. Concatenation of bilabial obstruents and glides, such as in locative construction, triggers palatalization:

ph + w = sh *impuphu-wini* > *empushini* 'in the maize porridge'
m + w = ny *emlomo-wini* > *emlonyeni* 'in the mouth'
b + w = tsh *ingubo-wini* > *engutsheni* 'on the dress'

3. Deaspiration. Concatenation of nasal and aspirated voiceless stops, as in deverbal nominalization and in pluralization, triggers loss of aspiration. Concatenation of nasal and aspirated/voiceless clicks triggers loss of aspiration and adds voicing:

n + th = nt *-thanda* > intando
m + ph = mp *uphondo* > izimpondo
n + kh = nk *ukhondo* > izinkondo
n + c = ngc *ucingo* > izingcingo

4. Lengthening of Monosyllabics. Uninflected monosyllabic verb stems and monosyllabic noun stems add a syllable:
-dla 'eat' > *Yidla!* 'Eat!'
cf: *-hamba* 'go' > cf. *Hamba!* 'Go!'
umuthi 'tree' cf. *umfana* 'boy'

Syllable Structure and Stress. Syllable structure is CV or, in word-initial position, V. Nasal *m* is syllabic before C. Stress is on the penultimate syllable. Monosyllabic words are rare:

(C)V	cha	'no'
(C)VCV	ye'bo	'yes'
(C)VCVCV	uku'dla	'food'
(C)VCVCVCV...	ukubo'na	'to see'

Ideophones have their own stress patterns.

Basic Morphology

Noun Morphology. Zulu exhibits the full noun-class and concord system that identify it as a Bantu language. Nouns fall into 14 classes (or grammatical genders), recognizable by prefix and paired consecutively for number. Descriptive grammars use Carl Meinhof's numbering system as follows:

1. sg.	**um**- fana	boy)
[1a. sg.	**u**- baba	(father)]
2. pl.	**aba**- fana	(boys)
[2a. pl.	**o**- baba	(fathers)]
3. sg.	**um**- fula	(river)
4. pl.	**imi**- fula	(rivers)
5. sg.	**i**- gama	(word, name)
6. pl.	**ama**- gama	(words, names)
7. sg.	**isi**- hlalo	(seat)
8. pl.	**izi**- hlalo	(seats)
9. sg.	**in**- komo	(head of cattle)
10. pl.	**izin**- komo	cattle)
11. sg.	**u**-phondo	(horn)
[10. pl.	izim- pondo	(horns)]
14.	**u**- tshani	(grass)
15.	**uku**- khala	(crying)

Classes such as 12, 13, 16, etc., that do not occur in Zulu, can be found in other Bantu languages. No single language has all the 23 classes for which Meinhof allocated numbers. Though there is no neat semantic cohesion to the noun classes, other than for Classes 1 and 2, the following features are associated with many members of each class:

Classes 1–2: Humans only.
Classes 1a–2a: Proper names, some humans, loan words.
Classes 3–4: Long or elongated objects, natural phenomena.
Classes 5–6: Loanwords, inanimate objects, liquids, mass nouns.
Classes 7–8: Humans singled out by skill/handicap; languages, ordinal numbers.
Classes 9–10: Humans singled out by age/position; animals.
Classes 11–10: Larger/weightier forms of concepts in Class 9–10.
Class 14: Abstracts.
Class 15: Verbal nouns.

All modifiers of a noun carry concordial agreement with that noun which is in most cases a recognizable echo of the noun prefix. In the following example the head noun is in Class 2:

<u>Bo</u>nke <u>aba</u>ntwana <u>aba</u>ncane <u>aba</u>thenge izincwadi <u>ba</u>hambile.
2-all 2-children 2-small 2-bought 10-books 2-are gone
'All the small children who bought books are gone.'

Nouns are not marked for case, but pronominal concords show partial accusative and full genitive case marking:

	Nominative	Accusative	Genitive
1st p.sg.	ngi-	-ngi-	-mi
1st p.pl.	si-	-si-	-(i)thu
2nd p.sg.	u-	-wu-/-ku-	-kho
2nd p.pl.	ni-	-ni-	-(i)nu
3rd p.sg.1	u-	-m-	-khe
3rd p.pl.2	ba-	-ba-	-bo

Zulu does not have articles. Definite-/indefiniteness is indicated through presence or absence of the objectival concord:

Bathenga izincwadi.	Bayazithenga izincwadi.
2-vbuy 10-Nbooks	2-ASP-OBJ10-vbuy 10-Nbooks
'They buy/are buying books.'	'They buy/are buying the books.'

Deverbal nouns can be productively created from verbs, and a single noun stem can occur in several classes:

-hamba	'go, walk, travel'
umhambi 1	'traveller'
isihambi 7	'stranger'
umhambo 11	'journey'
izulu 5	'sky, weather, heaven'
umZulu 1	'member of the Zulu nation'
isiZulu 7	'Zulu language'
uZulu 11	'Zulu nation'
KwaZulu 17	'Zululand'

Verb Morphology. The verb root is affixally inflected for tense, aspect, mood and affirmativity/negativity. It has an obligatory prefixal concord for the subject noun and an optional infix for the object noun.

A-ngi-ba-bon-a-nga
NEG-SUBJ(I)-OBJ(them)-verb-ASP-NEG+TENSE
'I did not see them.'

Derivational morphemes may be attached to verb stems to alter meaning and grammatical function, e.g., *-bona* 'see', *-bonela* 'see for, on behalf of', *-bonisa* 'cause to see, show', *-bonana* 'see one another', *-bonakala* 'be visible', *-zibona* 'see oneself', and *-zibonisela* 'show oneself for, on behalf of'.

There are four simple tenses:

(1) PRESENT TENSE (NEUTRAL ASPECT) *-bona* 'see'

	Affirmative	Negative
1st p.sg.	Ngiyabona 'I see/am seeing'	Angiboni
1st p.pl.	Siyabona	Asiboni
2nd p.sg.	Uyabona	Awuboni
2nd p.pl.	Niyabona	Aniboni
3rd p.:		
sg.1	Uyabona	Akaboni
pl.2	Bayabona	Ababoni
sg.3	Uyabona	Awuboni

	Affirmative	Negative
pl.4	Iyabona	Ayiboni
sg.5	Liyabona	Aliboni
pl.6	Ayabona	Awaboni
sg.7	Siyabona	Asiboni
pl.8	Ziyabona	Aziboni
sg.9	Iyabona	Ayiboni
pl.10	Ziyabona	Aziboni
sg.11	Luyabona	Aluboni
14	Buyabona	Abuboni
15	Kuyabona	Akuboni

When the verb is not clause final, the infix /-ya-/ is deleted:
Ngibona abantwana. 'I see children.'

(2) PAST TENSE (NON-CONTINUOUS ASPECT)

	Affirmative	Negative
1st p.sg.	Ngibonile 'I saw'	Angibonanga
1st p.pl.	Sibonile	Asibonanga
2nd p.sg.	Ubonile	Awubonanga
2nd p.pl.	Nibonile	Anibonanga
3rd p.:		
sg.1	Ubonile	Akabonanga
pl.2	Babonile	Ababonanga
...etc.		

When the verb is not utterance final, the suffix /-ile/ is shortened to /-e/:
Ngibone abantwana 'I saw children.'

(3) PAST TENSE (CONTINUOUS ASPECT)

	Affirmative	Negative
1st p.sg.	Bengibona 'I was/ have been seeing.'	Bengingaboni
1st p.pl.	Besibona	Besingaboni
2nd p.sg.	Ububona	Ubungaboni
2nd p.pl.	Benibona	Beningaboni
3rd p.:		
sg.1	Ubebona	Ubengaboni
pl.2	Bebebona	Bebengaboni
...etc.		

(4) FUTURE TENSE (NONCONTINUOUS ASPECT)

	Affirmative	Negative
1st p.sg.	Ngizobona 'I will see'	Angizubona
1st p.pl.	Sizobona	Asizubona
2nd p.sg.	Uzobona	Awuzubona
2nd p.pl.	Nizobona	Anizubona
3rd p.:		
sg.1	Uzobona	Akazubona
pl.2	Bazobona	Abazubona
...etc.		

Zulu has a wide range of complex verb structures that modify the base verb either aspectually or in some other way, e.g., *Ngize ngabona* 'I eventually saw', *Ngimane ngibone* 'I merely see', *Ngicishe ngabona* 'I almost saw', *Ngike ngambona* 'I saw him for a while'.

Adverbials. Adverbials are of three main types:

(1) Locatives (time and place)
emzini 'to/at/from the compound' < *umuzi* 'compound'
esontweni 'to/at/from the church' < *isonto* 'church'
ekuseni 'at dawn' < *ukusa* 'dawn'
ebusuku 'at night' < *ubusuku* 'night'
(2) Adverbs in *ka-*
kakhulu 'well' < *-khulu* 'large'
kancane 'a little' < *-ncane* 'small'
(3) Relic forms from Bantu locative Cl. 16 with Prefix *pha-*
phezulu 'up' < *izulu* 'sky'
phandle 'outside' < *indle* 'exterior'

Ideophones. Zulu has a large number of descriptive words conveying perceptions, and these have a morphology and grammatical function that differs from other word categories. They vary in length from one to many syllables, and do not have penultimate stress. They have no internal structure other than reduplication. Ideophones are widely used in general conversation, e.g., *swi* 'of being full to capacity' *ngci* 'of being tight or complete', *bhuqe* 'of being black or very dark', *gubhu* 'of waking up suddenly', *qoshosho* 'of squatting', *kalakatsha* 'of leaping'.

Ideophones are generally preceded by the verb *-thi* 'say, express, act, demonstrate, manifest':

Umfana wawela odakeni wathi bhalakaxa.
1-Nboy 1-PAST-vfall LOC-11-Nmud 1-vexpress ID-splat
'The boy fell splat in the mud.'

Bebeqala bathi ngqa ukumbona.
2-PAST-vbegin 2-vexpress ID-for the first time INFIN-vsee
'They saw him for the very first time.'

Ibhubesi belihlezi lathi khose emthunzini.
5-Nlion PERF-5-vsit 5-PAST-express ID-sheltering LOC-Nshade
'The lion was seated, sheltering, in the shade.'

Basic Syntax

Order of Constituents. Zulu is a head-initial, SVO language, but other surface orders are possible since the verb carries obligatory subject marking and optional object marking:

Head-initial syntax:
Abantwana ababili abancane abathanda amaswidi.....
2-Nchildren 2-ADJtwo 2-ADJsmall 2REL-vlove 6-Ncandy
'The two small children who love candy...'

SVO: Izinsizwa ziphethe amawisa.
10-Nyouths 10-PERF-vcarry 6-Nknobkerries
'(The) youths are carrying knobkerries.'

SOV: Izinsizwa ziwaphethe.
10-Nyouths 10-6OBJ-PERF-vcarry
'(The) youths are carrying them.'

OSV: Amawisa ziwaphethe.
6-Nknobkerries 10-6OBJ-PERF-Vcarry
'(The) knobkerries, they are carrying them.'

Negation. In matrix-verb simple tense constructions, negation follows the lexical subject, but precedes the verb complex:

Abafazi a - ba-phis - i tshwala namhlanje.
2-Nwomen NEG- 2-Vbrew-NEG/T Ø14-Nbeer ADV-today.
'The women are not brewing beer today.'

In periphrastic matrix-verb constructions and in subordinate clauses, including relative constructions, negation is embedded in the verbal complex:

...ukuze abafazi ba -nga - phis - i tshwala namhlanje
so that 2-Nwomen 2-NEG-Vbrew-NEG/T Ø14-Nbeer ADV-today
'...so that the women do not brew beer today'

...abafazi e - si -nga -bu - phuz - i tshwala ba - bo
2-Nwomen REL-1P-NEG-14OBJ-Vdrink-NEG/T Ø14-Nbeer 14POSS-2PRO
'...the women whose beer we are not drinking'

Contact with Other Languages

Zulu has a large number of loanwords and borrowed words from English and Afrikaans. Epenthetic vowels dilute consonant clusters. Loan nouns occur most frequently in Classes 5/6, but are also found in Classes 1a/2a. Borrowed nouns occur mainly in Classes 1a/2a. Loan nouns with initial /s/ or /sC/ tend to be in Classes 7/8, where the /s/ is incorporated into the prefix:

English

ibhayisikili	'bicycle'	amabhayiskili	5/6
unesi	'nurse'	onesi	1a/2a
isitimela	'train' (steamer)	izitimela	7/8
isiketi	'skirt'	iziketi	7/8
u-ice cream	'ice cream'		1a/2a
u-anti	'aunt(ie)'	o-anti	1a/2a

Afrikaans

ifasitela	'window' (venster)	amafasitela	5/6
isipoki	'ghost' (spook)	izipoki	7/8
-bhasobha	'watch out, over' (pas op)		

Common Words

man:	indoda	long:	-de
woman:	umfazi	small:	-ncane
water:	amanzi	yes:	yebo
sun:	ilanga	no:	cha
three:*	-thathu	good:	-hle
fish:	inhlanzi	bird:	inyoni
big:*	-khulu	dog:	inja
tree:	umuthi		

*Adjectives require a prefix that agrees with the class of the noun they modify.

Example Sentences

(1) Lezo zi-nja ezi-mbili zi-dl-e i(n)-nyama
10-DEM 10-Ndog 10-ADJtwo 10-Veat-PAST 10-Nmeat

yo-nke.
10-ENUMall
'Those two dogs ate all the meat.'

(2) Aba-fazi ba-zo-buy-el-a e-khaya
2-Nwomen 2-FUT-Vreturn-APP-AFFIRM LOC-5-Nhome

e-mini.
LOC-9-Nmidday
'The women will return home at midday.'

(3) E-ndl[u]-ini be-ku-thul-a
LOC-9-Nhouse-LOC PAST-17-Vbe.quiet-AFFIRM

kwa-thi cwaka.
17-PAST-Vexpress IDEOsilence
'There was absolute quiet in the house.'

Select Bibliography

Doke, C, Malcolm, Sikakana and Vilakazi. 1990. *English-Zulu Zulu-English Dictionary*. Johannesburg: WUP.

Gunner, Elizabeth, and Mafika Gwala, eds. 1991. *Musho! Zulu Popular Praises*. East Lansing: MSUP.

Laband, John. 1995. *Rope of Sand: The Rise and Fall of the Zulu Kingdom in the Nineteenth Century*. Jeppestown: Jonathan Ball.

Taljaard, P.C., and S.E. Bosch. 1988. *Handbook of IsiZulu*. Pretoria: van Schaik.

GLOSSARY

A: 1) Abbreviation for AGENT of a transitive verb; 2) Abbreviation for ADJECTIVE; 3) ARGUMENT in government-binding theory.

abessive: inflectional category of OBLIQUE CASE used to express the absence of a noun 'without.' In Estonian the abessive SUFFIX is *-ta* > *maa-ta-mes* land-ABESSIVE-man 'landless peasant' (Tauli 1973). See PRIVATIVE.

ablative: Inflectional category of OBLIQUE CASE used to express a range of meanings from LOCATIVE to INSTRUMENTAL, i.e. 'out of', 'away from.' In some languages, the general term for OBLIQUE CASE. Hungarian has an ablative suffix *-tól*: *fal* 'wall' > *fal-tól* 'away from the wall', *ajtó* 'door' > *ajtó-tól* 'from the door.'

ablaut: meaningful (morphological) change in vowel quality. Some English past tense verbs are formed by ablaut: *sing* > *sang, sit* > *sat, speak* > *spoke*.

absolute: 1) refers to a type of linguistic universal that applies to all languages without exception. See also UNIVERSAL. 2) variant of ABSOLUTIVE.

absolutive: A category of ERGATIVE languages which encompasses the SUBJECTS of INTRANSITIVE VERBS and OBJECTS of TRANSITIVE VERBS as they contrast to the ERGATIVE CATEGORY which encompasses AGENTS of transitive verbs. In many ergative languages, the absolutive category is UNMARKED.

abstract noun: noun which refers to a concept, idea, quality or emotion, anything lacking discernible physical attributes. Ilocano has an abstract nominalizing prefix *kina-*: *sadút* 'lazy' > *kinasadút* 'laziness.'

accent: 1) a feature of one's pronunciation which distinguishes origin and/or social class. 2) emphasis (defined by LOUDNESS, PITCH or DURATION) placed on a word or SYLLABLE. 3) DIACRITIC mark.

accentuation: see STRESS.

accompaniment clause: see COMITATIVE clause.

accommodation: 1) adapting to the speech of surrounding people. See CONVERGENCE. 2) modification in the articulation of a sound in order to ease the transition to a following sound.

accusative: An inflectional category of case and system of case marking in which OBJECTS of TRANSITIVE VERBS are formally distinguished from AGENTS of TRANSITIVE VERBS and SUBJECTS of INTRANSITIVE VERBS, the NOMINATIVE case. English pronouns demonstrate morphological **accusativity**. *He* = nominative case, *him* = accusative case. In **accusative languages**, the objects of transitive verbs are referred to as DIRECT OBJECTS. Contrast with ERGATIVE.

acoustic phonetics: the scientific study of the physical properties of speech sounds.

acquisition: the process of learning a language.

acrolect: term used in sociolinguistics to refer to the prestige variety of language. Contrast MESOLECT and BASILECT.

action: activity which typically involves movement or the exertion of energy. **Action verbs** are verbs which describe actions, activities, or events, while **action nouns** designate an activity as an abstract concept. *Run* is an action verb, *be* is not.

activation cost: term used to reflect the status of information in the consciousness of the addressee(s). Information can be classified as NEW (newly introduced in the speech context), GIVEN (previously introduced in the speech context and **activated** in the consciousness of the addressee), or accessible (information which has not been introduced but can be easily retrieved as relevant to the speech context).

active (active voice): term referring to a clause or verb form in which the grammatical SUBJECT corresponds to the SEMANTIC ACTOR of the PREDICATE. It contrasts with PASSIVE and middle VOICES. In English, *My friend hit me* is an active clause, its passive counterpart is *I was hit by my friend*.

active/stative language: Language which grammaticizes CONTROL in its CASE system, in which volitional actors (AGENTS) are encoded differently from non-volitional actors or EXPERIENCERS. TRANSITIVITY does not play a role in an **active case** system; AGENTS of intransitives are encoded the same as agents of transitives. See AGENT/PATIENT LANGUAGE.

actor: term used to comprise nouns that pattern like AGENTS grammatically, but do not necessarily share the semantic properties of agents.

actuation: the introduction of change into a language.

adessive: Inflectional category of case which expresses the meaning of 'at' or 'near' a location. Hungarian has an adessive SUFFIX *-nal/-nel*: *színház* 'theater' > *színház-nál* 'by (located near) the theater.' (Kenesei et al 1998: 239).

adjacency pair: minimal UNIT of conversation consisting of a single remark followed by a single response.

adjective: term used in word classification to apply to the set of items which specify attributes of NOUNS which share formal properties. The category of adjective is not UNIVERSAL. Morphological categories that are characteristic of adjectives include COMPARATIVES, SUPERLATIVES, EXCLAMATIVES, equalitatives, etc. In Rapanui (Polynesian, Easter Island), most adjectives can be formally distinguished by DUPLICATION: *roa roa* 'tall', *'ano 'ano* 'wide', *ve'a ve'a* 'hot' (DuFeu 1996: 72).

adjoined relative clause: RELATIVE CLAUSE placed at the end of the sentence, regardless of the position of the HEAD NOUN to which the clause refers.

adjunct: 1) optional or secondary element in a construction. adjuncts may be removed from a constituent without altering its structural identity. ADVERBIALS are **adjunctival**. In the sentence, *Tomorrow I will buy some ice-cream from Fred*, *tomorrow* and *from Fred* are adjuncts, leaving them out will not affect the integrity of the sentence. 2) nominal that does not function as a predicate ARGUMENT. See OBLIQUE.

admirative: grammatical category used to express surprise or admiration. In Caddo, the prefix *hús-* expresses surprise: *hús-ba-?a=sa-yi=k'awih-sa?* = ADMIR-1SBENEF.IRREALIS-name-know-PROGRESSIVE = 'My goodness, he knows my name!' (Chafe 1995: 356).

admonitive: grammatical MODE which expresses warning.

adnominal: [analogy to ADVERBIAL] any element of a NOUN PHRASE that modifies a HEAD NOUN. (See ADJECTIVES, PREPOSITIONAL PHRASES, RELATIVE CLAUSES, POSSESSIVES).

adoptive: linguistic UNIT or pattern that is borrowed form another language. In some languages, adoptive ROOTS take special morphology.

adstrate: a neighboring language that influences another language that is not more or less prestigious than the influenced language. Compare SUBSTRATE and SUPERSTRATE.

ADV: Abbreviation for ADVERB or ADVERBIAL.

advanced tongue root: DISTINCTIVE FEATURE in PHONOLOGY used to classify vowels produced with the ROOT of the TONGUE pushed forward [+ATR]. Some African languages distinguish vowels with this feature.

adverb: word class that shares formal and functional properties whose main function is to specify a characteristic of the action of the VERB. ADVERBS may be classified by their semantic properties designating 'manner', 'place', 'time', 'reason', 'condition', etc. **Adverbials** are elements of clause structure whose main function is to modify a PREDICATE. **Adverbial clauses** are subordinate modificational structures which expand off the VERB PHRASE as ADVERBS modify verbs.

adversative: said of a grammatical form which implies OPPOSITION or CONTRAST. *But* and *although* are adversative conjunctions which introduce **adversative clauses**.

affected patient: entity which is involved in some way with the event denoted by the verb that does not cause the event to come into being.

affective meaning: attitudinal element of meaning which results in emotional associations. See ADMIRATIVE.

affirmative: verb or clause which expresses an assertion and has no marker of NEGATION.

affix: a type of MORPHEME which is PHONOLOGICALLY BOUND. Affixes may never occur in isolation. Affixes may be classified into three main types, depending on the relative position between the ROOT morpheme and AFFIX. PREFIXES precede the root, SUFFIXES follow the root, and INFIXES are inserted within the root. Other types of **affixation** include CIRCUMFIXES, SUPRASEGMENTAL MORPHEMES or SUPERFIXES, and REDUPLICATION.

affricate: CONSONANTAL sound classified by the manner of its articulation, where complete closure is followed by a gradual release of air. AFFRICATES may be seen as complex sounds consisting of two units: a STOP and FRICATIVE. The initial sound [*tʃ*] in English *church* is an affricate.

agent: In grammatical description 1) the actor argument of a transitive verb or 2) the conscious INSTIGATOR of an action who performs or causes the action with VOLITION and/or CONTROL.

agent/patient language: Language which formally distinguishes AGENTS from PATIENTS as single ARGUMENTS of INTRANSITIVE VERBS and does not differentiate based on TRANSITIVITY. Also ACTIVE/STATIVE LANGUAGE. In Lakota, pronouns express this distinction; *wa* is the first singular agent pronoun and *ma* is its patient counterpart: *wahí* 'I came', ***wa**ktékte* 'I'll kill him', ***ma**xwá* 'I'm sick', ***ma**ktékte* 'He'll kill me.' (Mithun 1991: 514).

agglutinative: referring to a language with a morphologically complex typology (in which words may consist of many morphemes) whereby morphemic boundaries are easily discernible. Turkish is an **agglutinating** language; morphemes are easily recognized and delineated: *aç-a-ma-m* = open-ABILITATIVE-NEGATIVE-1s = 'I can't open it'. Contrast ISOLATING and FUSIONAL.

agreement: the formal relationship between elements, in which one form of one word requires the corresponding form of another word. In Spanish nouns **agree** with articles and adjectives in NUMBER and GENDER: (masculine singular: *el chico feo* 'the ugly boy' vs. feminine plural: *las chicas feas* 'the ugly girls'). In Maltese, adjectives agree with their nouns only in the singular. See CONCORD.

airstream mechanism: mechanism that controls airflow during speech. It can be PULMONIC, GLOTTALIC, or VELARIC.

Aktionsart: verbal ASPECT which is lexically distinguished, e.g. *cut* vs. *chop*.

alethic: referring to MODALITY which is concerned with the necessary or contingent truth of propositions (the degree of certainty of a proposition). Contrast DEONTIC and EPISTEMIC.

alienable: a type of possessive relationship in which the possessed item has a temporary or non-essential possessor. **Alienable possession** contrasts with **inalienable possession**, in which the relationship between the possessor and possessed is more permanent and important. In Loniu (Austronesian, Papua New Guinea), some nouns have different forms based on **alienability**: *purɛt* 'work, alienable' vs. *puriya* 'work, inalienable' (Hamel 1994: 48).

allative: inflectional case category which expresses motion towards a location. In Ao Naga (Nagaland, India), the allative case is marked by the suffixes *-tangi* or *-caki*: *kí-tangi* 'to the house'; *ayong-caki* 'to church'; *ayong-caki* 'to the river' (Gowda 1975: 41).

allomorph: any of the possible variants of a MORPHEME. Allomorphs may be determined by the ENVIRONMENT in which they occur, or can occur in FREE VARIATION. The English indefinite article has two environmentally-conditioned allomorphs: *a* before consonants, and *an* before vowels: *a house* vs. *an orange*.

allophone: in phonology, any of the possible non-CONTRASTIVE phonetic variants of a PHONEME. For the analogous term in morphology, see ALLOMORPH.

alpha notation: an abbreviatory convention in phonological rule writing which collapses two rules into one when the rules differ only in the values of certain features. Rules (1) and (2) may be collapsed into (3) using alpha notation.

alternant: a variant in form of a linguistic unit. Alternants can be grammatically conditioned, phonologically conditioned, socially conditioned, or exist in FREE VARIATION. Noun = **alternation**.

alternative: a lexical choice. In English the **alternative conjunction** is *or*.

alveolar: consonant sound classified by place of articulation. Alveolar consonants are made when the blade of the tongue touches the **alveolar ridge**, the bony prominence behind the upper teeth. English [t], [d], [l], [n], [s], and [z] are alveolar consonants.

alveo-palatal: consonant sound classified by place of articulation. Alveo-palatal consonants are produced when the front of the tongue hits the front of the PALATAL region in the direction of the ALVEOLAR RIDGE. Contrast PALATO-ALVEOLAR.

ambient verb: verb which denotes a meteorological event. Ambient verbs in English include *snow, rain, thunder,* etc.

ambiguous: expressing more than one meaning which is usually not discernible from the context. **Structural ambiguity** (or **grammatical ambiguity**) results from a POLYSEMOUS grammatical form. The scope of the adjective *cheap* in the noun phrase *cheap wine and cheese* is ambiguous; it may refer to the noun wine only, or both nouns wine and cheese.

ambisyllabic: belonging to two syllables at the same time.

amelioration: historical process of word change in which the meaning of the word changes into something more attractive or impressive. Contrast PEJORATION.

anacoluthon: breaking away from an utterance before completing it in order to say something else.

analogy: (from historical linguistics and language acquisition) process of regularization in which regular patterns are applied to irregular forms. Young children learning English apply the verb *goed* as the incorrect past tense of *went* by analogy to regular forms. Also called **analogical change**.

analytic: language type in which most words are invariable, and do not usually contain more than one morpheme (compare ISOLATING). Analytic languages contrast from SYNTHETIC ones.

anaphor: Noun with no independent reference that refers to another constituent previously mentioned in the discourse (the antecedent). Anaphors include REFLEXIVE PRONOUNS and RECIPROCAL PRONOUNS.

anaphora (anaphoric): linguistic unit that refers to an entity previously mentioned in the DISCOURSE. Contrast CATAPHORA.

anaptyxis: kind of EPENTHESIS in which a vowel is inserted to break a CONSONANT CLUSTER.

angma: the IPA symbol for the velar nasal [ŋ].

animate: grammatical term applied to nominals referring to living entities, as opposed to INANIMATE. In English, the pronouns *he* and *she* refer to animate beings, *it* is the inanimate equivalent. Noun = **animacy**. See also animacy HIERARCHY.

anomalous: said of linguistic forms that do not conform to the usual rules.

anomaly: incompatibility of meaning (said of two structures in a single construction).

antecedent: previously mentioned referent to which an ANAPHOR refers.

antepenult: the third syllable from the end. Contrast PENULT, ULTIMA.

anterior: DISTINCTIVE FEATURE in PHONOLOGY referring to CONSONANTS articulated further forward than the PALATO-ALVEOLAR region.

anticipation: type of ASSIMILATION in which a sound assimilates to a following sound: *in-* + *possible* > *impossible*.

antipassive: clause type common in ERGATIVE LANGUAGES in which the AGENT noun is promoted and expressed in ABSOLUTIVE CASE as a single argument of a detransitivized verb and the semantic PATIENT is DEMOTED and expressed in OBLIQUE CASE. The Ilocano *Nangán-ak iti sabá* = ateINTRANS-1sABS OBL.ART banana = 'I ate a banana' is the antipassive of *Kinnán-ko ti sabá* = ate.TRANS-1sERG CORE.ART banana = 'I ate the banana.' (As an analogy to PASSIVE as used in ACCUSATIVE languages).

antonym: term which denotes the opposite of another in meaning. Contrast SYNONYM. Noun = **antonymy**.

aorist: term used in the grammatical description of some languages to refer to simple past-tense verb forms that are unmarked for ASPECT.

apex: tip of the tongue. See APICAL.

aphaeresis: the loss of one or more sounds from the beginning of a word.

aphasia: language disability caused by brain damage.

apical: referring to the APEX of the tongue. The Spanish word *perro* 'dog' contains an apical trill.

apocope: the deletion of the final element of a word. Contrast SYNCOPE.

apodosis: the consequential part of a conditional. In the sentence *If she goes, I'll follow*, *If she goes* is the PROTASIS and *I'll follow* is the apodosis.

apophony: ABLAUT.

applicative: MORPHEME used with VERBS that increases their VALENCE by one. It creates di-transitive verbs from transitive verbs, and allows certain PERIPHERAL (or INDIRECT) OBJECTS to appear as CORE ARGUMENTS with respect to the APPLIED predicate. Compare the following Mwera forms in which the applied verb has a BENEFACTIVE OBJECT in its CASE FRAME: *kututawa* 'to bind us' vs. *kututawila* 'to bind something for us (with applicative)' (Harries 1950: 68).

applied verb: verb form which contains an APPLICATIVE morpheme.

apposition: the linking of two equated concepts. In the sentence *Mary, my teacher, is Indonesian*, the two nouns *Mary* and *teacher* are in apposition. Equational noun phrases that immediately followed the equated noun phrases are **appositives**.

approximant: a continuous speech sound that is produced without friction, in which one articulator approaches another without producing audible friction. GLIDES, VOWELS, and LIQUIDS are approximants.

arbitrary: said of linguistic forms without connection to the outside world. The relationship between sound and meaning is said to be arbitrary. Contrast ICONIC.

archaic: term used to describe a form that is no longer used. Old forms are called **archaisms**.

archiphoneme: the underlying representation of two or more PHONEMES that no longer contrast in a certain environment, the result of NEUTRALIZATION.

areal: pertaining to a geographical region. **Areal features** in a grammatical system are those that are common to languages in a given geographic area.

argot: special vocabulary of a close-knit group.

argument: nominal referent that is subcategorized by the VALENCE of a verb, bearing a GRAMMATICAL RELATION. Intransitive verbs have one argument (S), transitive verbs have two or more (A, O). ADJUNCTS are not arguments.

article: subclass of DETERMINERS whose primary role is to differentiate the use of NOUNS. English has DEFINITE and INDEFINITE articles.

articulation: the production of speech.

articulator: specific part of the vocal apparatus employed to produce a sound.

aspect: VERBAL CATEGORY referring to a type of ACTION, PROCESS, QUALITY or STATE, with reference to the internal structure of what is denoted by the verb. Different **aspectual** categories include: AUGMENTATIVE, CESSATIVE, completive, CONTINUATIVE, customary, DIMINUTIVE, FREQUENTATIVE, HABITUATIVE, INCHOATIVE, incompletive, momentaneous, punctiliar, REPETITIVE, and SEMELFACTIVE.

aspiration: the audible breath that may accompany a sound. In English, word-initial stops are **aspirated**, unlike in Spanish.

assimilation: (phonological term) process in which the articulation of a given sound is changed so as to become similar or identical to that of an adjacent of neighboring sound. In **regressive assimilation**, the sound change takes place because of the influence of a following sound. In **progressive assimilation** the sound changes due to the influence of a preceding sound. In **coalescent (reciprocal) assimilation**, there is mutual influence.

associative: grammatical term used to describe actions that are performed in conjunction with other people. Some languages have associative case marking on nouns.

assumptive mood: EPISTEMIC MODE for statements whose truth value is based on the assumptions of the speaker.

atelic: term used with regards to ASPECT denoting an action with no clear end point. *Sing, play,* and *run* are atelic verbs. Contrast TELIC.

attenuative: type of quantitative ASPECT, e.g., Tagalog *linisin* 'clean' vs. *linis-linisin* 'clean a little.'

attribute: something serving to MODIFY. The adjective *noisy* has an attributive function in the NOUN PHRASE *noisy men.* Noun = **attribution**.

augmentative: morphological category used with nouns that denotes the largeness of the noun. It may also be used to denote ugliness of awkwardness by metaphoric extension. Spanish has an augmentative suffix *-ón*: *silla* 'chair' > *sillón* 'large chair.' Contrast DIMINUTIVE.

autonomous: independent; having significance in its own terms.

autonym: self-designation.

AUX: abbreviation for AUXILIARY.

auxiliary: type of verb which usually denotes grammatical distinctions such as MOOD, VOICE, ASPECT, TRANSITIVITY, etc. Not all languages have auxiliary verbs. English has two main auxiliaries, *do* and *have*: I *did* go. I *have* been to Polynesia. Also called HELPING VERB. Contrast LEXICAL VERB.

back: (said of sounds) sounds articulated with the back part of the tongue or in the back part of the mouth. **Back vowels** include [o] and [u], **back consonants** include [k] and [g], among many others.

back formation: a type of word formation in which a shorter word is derived by deleting an imagined AFFIX from a longer form already present in the language. In English an example of back formation is the verb *edit* which comes from *editor*, and not the other way around.

bahuvrihi: (Sanskrit) term referring to EXOCENTRIC COMPOUNDS which describe a person or an object with a quality similar to that compound, e.g., *bird brain* refers to someone with a brain like a bird's.

base: alternative word for STEM, a morpheme or group of morphemes to which additional morphology may be applied. In Yup'ik Eskimo, *cali-vkar* = work-CAUSATIVE serves as the base for the word *cali-vkar-a-a* =work-CAUS-TRANS-3/3 = 'He made her work.'

basic structure: formula which illustrates the CANONICAL form. The basic structure of an English NOUN PHRASE is: DETERMINER - (ADJECTIVE) - HEAD NOUN.

basilect: the linguistic variety of a language which least resembles the PRESTIGE variety. Contrast MESOLECT and ACROLECT.

benefactive: term used to refer to a form or construction that denotes the action 'for the benefit of' or 'on behalf of.' English has a benefactive preposition *for*. In Ilocano, the benefactive focus verbalizer is *i- -an* : *dait* 'sew' > *idaitan* 'to sew for someone.'

bilabial: sound produced with the two lips. [b] is a voiced bilabial stop.

bilateral opposition: differing in a single feature. English [k] and [g] are in bilateral opposition because they differ only in voicing.

bilingual: competent in two languages. Compare MONOLINGUAL and MULTILINGUAL. Noun = **bilingualism**.

binary feature: property used to classify units in terms of two mutually exclusive possibilities. Nouns, for instance, may be classified in terms of binary features: [± animate], [± specific], [± referential], [± possessible], etc.

blade: the part of the tongue between the TIP and center. Also known as the LAMINA.

blend(ing): a process in which two elements which do not normally co-occur come together in a single linguistic unit. The English word *smog* is an example of blending *smoke* and *fog*. The Tagalog breakfast *tapsilog* is an example of blending from *tapa* 'dried beef', *sinangág* 'fried rice' and *itlóg* 'egg'.

borrowing: the use of linguistic forms from another language.

bound morpheme: a MORPHEME which cannot occur in isolation (meaningfully uttered alone). AFFIXES are bound morphemes. Contrast FREE MORPHEME.

bounded: 1) with a BOUND MORPHEME attached. 2) (referring to situations) with an endpoint. PERFECTIVE VERBS denote bounded situations.

brackets: symbols used in linguistics to elucidate formal STRUCTURE. In **bracket notation**, elements are grouped according to constituency and/or inter-dependency. **Curly brackets** are used to enclose alternative elements {Adjective, Noun}. **Square brackets** are used to enclose FEATURES, [+ round], and **round brackets** (parentheses) enclose optional elements.

breath group: utterance produced with a single expiration of breath.

breathy: referring to the vocal effect produced by allowing air to pass through a slightly open GLOTTIS. Breathy vowels are contrastive from non-breathy vowels in Gujarati.

buccal: alternative word for ORAL.

canonical: referring to a form which serves as the standard or norm for purposes of comparison. In many Polynesian languages, the canonical syllable structure is CV (CONSONANT-VOWEL) and the canonical morpheme is bisyllabic.

cardinal number: The class of numbers which denote quantity. Contrast ORDINAL numbers. In English *one, two, three,* etc. are cardinal numbers. *First, second, third* are ordinal.

cardinal vowel: One of a set of standard reference points devised by the British phonetician David Jones (1881–1967) used to identify VOWEL sounds of any language.

case: grammatical category which identifies the syntactic relationship between words in a sentence. English marks case in the pronouns: *he* 'subject, NOMINATIVE case', *him* 'object, ACCUSATIVE case', *his* 'possessor, GENITIVE.' In German, case is indicated by articles and noun endings. In Russian, case is represented morphologically.

cataphoric: referring forward to another unit. A pronoun is cataphoric if it marks the identity of something that is about to be expressed. Noun = **cataphora**. Contrast ANAPHORIC.

category: class of things which possess something in common, a way to organize human experience. Grammatical categories associated with nouns include NUMBER, CASE, GENDER, COUNTABILITY, POSSESSIBILITY, etc.

catenative: referring to a LEXICAL VERB which governs the non-FINITE form of another lexical verb. The verb *tried* in *I tried to escape* is catenative.

causative: a linguistic form in which the AGENT of the utterance is responsible for having an action done, or causing another entity to perform the action. Causative morphology usually increases the VALENCE of a verb. Fijian has a causative prefix *vaka-*: *mate* 'die' > *vakamatea* (with transitive suffix *-a*) 'to kill, make someone/something die.'

cavity: any of various chambers in the VOCAL TRACT, including the ORAL cavity, NASAL cavity, esophageal cavity, and PULMONIC cavity.

central vowel: vowel pronounced with the TONGUE in NEUTRAL position, neither advanced (as in FRONT VOWELS) nor retracted (as in BACK VOWELS). The English *schwa* is a central vowel.

cessative: ASPECTUAL distinction which indicates the ceasing of an action.

characterizational phrase: type of relational phrase which characterizes a preceding noun by describing its function, purpose, content, origin, etc. (Josephs 1975).

circumfix: AFFIX which has two parts which appear on both sides of the ROOT MORPHEME. Ilocano has a locative circumfix *pag- -an*: *adal* 'study' > *pagadalan* 'school, place where one studies'.

citation form: form of a linguistic unit as it can be produced in isolation. It is often the least MARKED morphologically Dictionaries are often organized by citation forms. The citation form of nouns in Finnish is the NOMINATIVE CASE. The citation form of verbs in Spanish is the INFINITIVE.

class: set of entities which share certain FORMAL or SEMANTIC properties. See **word class**.

classifier: morpheme which indicates the formal or semantic class to which an item belongs.

clause: grammatical unit containing a SUBJECT and a PREDICATE. All sentences contain at least one MAIN CLAUSE, and can be further expanded by **subordinate clauses**.

cleft: a linguistic structure that is put into FOCUS, usually by altering its order or using various syntactic devices to put it in a prominent position, e.g., I killed the tapir > (cleft) It was *I* who killed the tapir or It was the *tapir* I killed.

cline: continuum of potentially infinite gradation. See CONTINUUM.

clipping: shortening of a linguistic FORM, e.g., English *veggies* from vegetables.

clitic: morphological form which is phonologically dependent upon another and cannot be uttered in isolation. Clitics contrast from AFFIXES because their host is a WORD that does not have to belong to one LEXICAL CLASS. Clitics can be seen also as PHRASAL AFFIXES. Clitics are distinguished by relative position to their hosts. See PROCLITIC. Abstract idea = **clisis**.

close: (vowels) synonym for HIGH.

closed syllable: a SYLLABLE with a CODA CONSONANT. In English, *stop, air*, and *wing* consist of closed syllables, while *me, so,* and *tea* consist of **open** syllables.

cluster: sequence of like items. The ONSET of the English verb *try* is a **consonant cluster**.

coalescence: process in which two items become one.

co-articulation: an articulation involving two simultaneous constrictions in the vocal tract. In English, the glide [w] has both VELAR and LABIAL constrictions.

coda: element of a syllable which follows the syllable NUCLEUS. In the word *dog*, [g] is the coda. Contrast ONSET.

code-mixing: the transferring of linguistic elements from one language into another.

code-switching: the switching of two languages based on context and environment.

cognate: linguistic form that is historically derived from the same source as another form and whose sound correspondence is evident. Spanish *mano* 'hand' and Portuguese *mão* 'hand' are cognates.

cognitive: relating to mental processes.

coherence: the relation of a segment of discourse to one's understanding of the world. If a particular utterance does not make sense in its context, it is said not to be **coherent**.

cohesion: the binding of elements into CONSTRUCTIONS.

collective: noun which denotes a group of entities or collection of individual entities.

collocation: term used to express the frequent co-occurrence of individual LEXICAL ITEMS to from a standard expression.

comitative: linguistic category used to express companionship. In English, *with* is used to express both the INSTRUMENTAL and comitative categories, e.g., I ate *with* a fork vs. I ate *with* Percival.

command: grammatical form used to tell someone to do something. In many languages, commands are issued with verbs in the IMPERATIVE MOOD.

comment: The part of a sentence which expresses something about the TOPIC. In the sentence *Many people die of malaria every year*, *many people* is the topic, and *die of malaria every year* is the comment.

commissive: an utterance in which the speaker makes a commitment to a future course of action. *I promise to be faithful* is a commissive sentence.

common: the unmarked form of a grammatical category. In some languages, **common nouns** which designate any member of a general class contrast morphologically with **proper nouns** which designate named specific people, places, etc.

comparative: linguistic form or construction that expresses inequality. Many English adjectives have a comparative form with the suffix *-er*: *bigger, smaller, taller,* etc. See also SUPERLATIVE and EQUALITATIVE.

comparative linguistics: branch of linguistics that deals with genetic relationships between languages. Comparative linguists also reconstruct PROTO-LANGUAGES from the data they gather of related daughter languages.

competence: speaker's knowledge of the rules of his native language.

competing motivations: the interaction of two distinct functional MOTIVATIONS that conflict.

complement: a particular linguistic form whose presence is required by something else in the sentence. A **complement clause** is a CLAUSE which acts as an ARGUMENT of a PREDICATE, forming one grammatical unit with the predicate. '*me to go*' in the sentence *She wanted me to go* is an OBJECT complement clause, while '*smoking in the bathroom*' in the sentence *Smoking in the bathroom annoys her* is a SUBJECT complement clause.

complementary: 1) (semantics) referring to words that express sense relation with minimal gradation in which the assertion of one term entails the denial of the other. *Male* is the complementary of *female*. 2) (phonology) **complementary distribution** refers to the mutual exclusiveness of a pair of sounds in a certain phonetic ENVIRONMENT.

complementizer: SUBORDINATING MORPHEME which marks an EMBEDDED sentence.

complex: consisting of more than one UNIT. A **complex noun** is one which is formed with two or more MORPHEMES. Contrast SIMPLE.

componential analysis: semantic theory developed by anthropologists in the 1950s which claims that all lexical items can be analyzed using a finite set of **components**: [± male] [± animate] [± human], etc.

compound: linguistic unit composed of elements that function independently in other circumstances. The English words *bathroom, waterfall, nightlight,* and *wildlife* are compounds. Compounds display phonological unity, are uninterruptible and, in some cases, not predictable by the semantics of their constituent parts. Three different kinds of compounds are: ENDOCENTRIC, EXOCENTRIC, and COPULATIVE.

conative: expression used to achieve result in an addressee, in accord with the speaker's wishes. Contrast EXPRESSIVE and REFERENTIAL.

concatenation: process in which strings of elements are formed in linear succession. **Concatenative morphology** deals with the study of roots and affixes, not taking into account SUPERSEGMENTAL FEATURES.

concessive clause: subordinate clause which expresses a situation in which the information denoted by the main clause is surprising or unexpected. *Although* is a concessive subordinator.

concord: alternative word for AGREEMENT.

concrete noun: noun which identifies something that has discernible physical attributes. Contrast ABSTRACT NOUN.

condition: 1) factor that can be taken into account to evaluate a theory. 2) criteria which must be met to render truth value or adequacy.

conditional: expressing hypotheses or conditions. English has a conditional CONJUNCTION *if*. Spanish has a conditional mood: *lloró* 'he/she cried, INDICATIVE MOOD' vs. *lloraría* 'he would cry, CONDITIONAL MOOD.'

conditioned: determined by context. ALLOMORPHS can be conditioned by their ENVIRONMENT. Phonologically conditioned allomorphs are determined by their phonological environment, as in the English plural affixes: dog-*z*, cat-*s*, and bush-*es*. Grammatically conditioned allomorphs are determined by grammar. Lexically conditioned allomorphs are determined in the lexicon (conjugation or declension classes). In Spanish, for example, verbs take a set of affixes which are dependent upon the conjugation class of the verb, *-ar*, *-er*, or *-ir*.

conjunction: word whose primary function is to connect words or clauses. See COORDINATION and SUBORDINATION.

connected speech: spoken language analyzed as a continuous sequence.

connective: morpheme used to link linguistic units.

connotation: referring to the meaning with reference to the emotional associations suggested by a linguistic unit. The connotations of the word *Christmas* might include 'parties', 'relatives', 'presents', etc. Contrast DENOTATION.

consequent: event, action, or state which takes place as a result or consequence of some other event, action, or state. **Consequential clauses** express the consequent.

consonant: Sounds produced by manipulating airflow in the vocal tract which function as margins of SYLLABLES. Contrast VOWEL.

consonant cluster: series of two adjacent consonants in the same syllable.

consonant mutation: meaningful consonant modification, common in Celtic languages. Mutation patterns include fortition, SPIRANTIZATION, and LENITION. See Welsh phonology in this volume.

constative: descriptive statement. Contrast PERFORMATIVE.

constituent: linguistic unit which is a component of a larger CONSTRUCTION.

constraint: condition which restricts the application of a RULE.

construction: grammatical unit, as seen in its internal organization.

consultant: see INFORMANT.

contact: situation of close proximity which may result in language BORROWING.

content question: type of question which requests a response other than *yes* or *no*. Contrast YES/NO QUESTION.

content word: word with lexical meaning. Contrast FUNCTION WORD.

context: part of an utterance which is adjacent to the unit which is the focus of attention, the environment of a word, phrase, or sentence. Meaning sometimes must be determined from the context.

continuant: sound produced with incomplete closure of the VOCAL TRACT. VOWELS and FRICATIVES are continuants.

continuative: ASPECTUAL distinction which reflects actions that continue.

continuous: see DURATIVE.

contraction: the phonetic reduction of a linguistic form. In English, *can't* is **contracted** from *can not*.

contradictory: see COMPLEMENTARY.

contrafactive: said of verbs taking COMPLEMENT CLAUSES in which the PROPOSITION expressed in the complement clause is presupposed to be false. Contrast FACTIVE.

contrary terms: see ANTONYMS.

contrastive: serving to distinguish meaning. In English, [p] and [b] are contrastive, as seen in the MINIMAL PAIR *pat* vs. *bat*.

control: 1) grammatical category found in verbs which refers to the ability of an ACTOR to initiate or take charge of an action. The subject of *throw* is a controller, while the subject of *fall* is not. In Tagalog, notice the difference between the [+control] suffix *-in* and the [-control] prefix *ma-* in *pansin-in* 'to pay attention to' vs. *mapansín* 'to happen to notice'. 2) Relation of referential dependence between an 'controlled' unexpressed argument in an EMBEDDED CLAUSE and another argument in the MAIN CLAUSE.

convention: accepted practice in the use of language.

convergence: process in which languages or dialects become more like one another through CONTACT. Contrast DIVERGENCE.

conversation analysis (CA): discipline which investigates the STRUCTURE and COHERENCE of conversations.

converse: 1) opposite. 2) RECIPROCAL. *Smile* is the converse of *frown*; *payer* is the converse of *payee*.

conversion: DERIVATIONAL process in which an item changes lexical class without AFFIXATION. In English *itch* can be a noun or verb. See ZERO DERIVATION.

co-occur: (said of linguistic forms) appear together grammatically.

coordinate compound: COMPOUND which consists of two juxtaposed nouns and refers to a unitary concept, e.g., Sanskrit *mata-pitarau* mother-father 'parents'.

coordination: the linking of linguistic units of equivalent syntactic status. *And* is a **coordinating conjunction (coordinator)** in English. Coordinators can be CONJUNCTIVE (*and*), ADVERSATIVE (*but*), or ALTERNATIVE (*or*).

copula: verb whose main function is to relate elements of CLAUSE STRUCTURE. The English copula is *be*. Spanish and Portuguese have two copulas, *ser* and *estar*. Some semantic categories that may involve copulas include: identity, classification, attribution, presentation, existence, happening, location, possession, experience, pointing out, similarity, becoming, remaining, naming, and topicalization. Adjective = **copulative**.

copulative compound: compound whose meaning represents the sum of the meanings of its constituent parts. Consider Tok Pisin, *yu-mi* 'we', *brata-sista* 'siblings,' and *papa-mama* 'parents.'

core: 1) (phonology) the nucleus and coda of a syllable as one constituent. 2) grammatical (as opposed to OBLIQUE) CASE.

core argument: ARGUMENT which is required by the PREDICATE. Transitive verbs have two core arguments: AGENT and OBJECT. INTRANSITIVE VERBS have one core argument: SUBJECT.

co-referential: referring to constituents in a sentence that have the same REFERENCE. In the REFLEXIVE CONSTRUCTION *Grace saw herself in the mirror*, the reflexive pronoun, *herself*, is co-referential with the subject, *Grace*.

coronal: sounds produced when the BLADE of the tongue is raised from its NEUTRAL position. ALVEOLAR, DENTAL, and PALATO-ALVEOLAR consonants are coronal.

corpus: collection of linguistic DATA. Plural is **corpora**.

correspondence: similarity of form between structures in related languages.

countable nouns: NOUNS that can be treated as separable entities, as opposed to non-count or uncountable nouns.

counter-example: piece of data which falsifies a hypothesis.

counter-factual: not true, HYPOTHETICAL.

covert: said of properties of linguistic forms that are observable only by contrasting other forms, not by SURFACE STRUCTURE. Contrast OVERT.

creaky: vocal effect produced by the slow vibration of one end of the VOCAL CORDS. See LARYNGEALIZATION.

Creole: mother-tongue of a speech community that developed from a PIDGIN. A Creole may **de-Creolize** as the standard lexifier language begins to exert influence on the Creole.

data: material used in linguistic investigation. A collection of data is called a CORPUS.

dative: inflectional grammatical case associated with INDIRECT OBJECTS.

daughter language: language which is descended from another. Spanish, French, Portuguese, Romanian, and Catalán are among the daughter languages of Latin.

debitive: grammatical category which expresses obligation. Spanish has a debitive modal verb *deber* 'must.'

declarative: grammatical form (usually a verb or clause) used in the expression of statements. Contrast IMPERATIVE, INTERROGATIVE MOODS.

defective paradigm: paradigm that results when INFLECTIONAL morphology is not fully PRODUCTIVE.

definite: grammatical term used to refer to SPECIFIC or identifiable entities. English has a definite article *the*. Contrast INDEFINITE.

degree: grammatical category which expresses the extent of comparison. See COMPARATIVE, SUPERLATIVE, EQUATIVE.

deictic: morpheme which indicates DEIXIS (deictic REFERENCE). English demonstratives are deictics.

deixis: pointing, in linguistics. Deictic categories include PERSON: *I*, *you*, *he*, etc.; TENSE/TEMPORAL relationships: *now*, *later*, *today*; space/direction: *here*, *there*, *that*, *this*, and NUMBER, etc.

delayed imperative: a COMMAND to be carried out in the FUTURE.

delimitative: verbal ASPECt which reflects limited duration of an action, e.g. Russian *sidet'* 'sit' vs. *posidet'* 'sit for a little while.'

demotion: term used to express the grammatical phenomenon of a noun which obtains a grammatical RELATION that is lower down on the hierarchy from its previous position. In PASSIVE constructions, the AGENTIVE noun is **demoted** from SUBJECT role to OBLIQUE.

denotation: REFERENTIAL meaning. Contrast CONNOTATION.

dental: referring to speech sounds produced with the TIP of the TONGUE against the teeth. [t] and [d] are dental STOPS.

deontic: referring to the MODALITY of obligation and permission. Contrast ALETHIC and EPISTEMIC.

dependent clause: synonym for SUBORDINATE CLAUSE.

dependent marking: a grammatical pattern in which the grammatical relationship between a HEAD constituent and a dependent constituent is reflected by overt marking on the dependent constituent. Languages with CASE morphology on their nouns are examples of dependent marking languages, the morphology of the nouns reflect the relationship between the nouns and their head verb.

derivation: 1) (morphology) process of word formation which results in a new word. **Derivational affixes** may change the grammatical class of the MORPHEMES to which they attach and affect the overall meaning of the **derived construction**. They are also considered to vary in their productivity, and not be obligatorily governed by syntax. Contrast INFLECTION. 2) (historical linguistics) the historical development of a form.

descriptive linguistics: branch of linguistics that is concerned with describing natural languages in terms of their grammatical structure. Linguists who write grammars of languages are called **descriptivists**.

de-semanticization: process in which lexical meanings shift to grammatical ones.

desiderative: referring to linguistic forms that express wants and desires.

determiner: class of items that co-occur with NOUNS to express or grammatical contrasts such as quantity, CASE or NUMBER. Determiners in English include *a, the, each, every, some, any, this, that*, etc. ARTICLES are a subclass of determiners.

deviant: linguistic form which does not conform to the RULES of a GRAMMAR.

devoiced: said of sounds which are normally voiced in another environment, but are produced with less or no VOICING.

diachronic: referring to historical development over a period of time. Contrast SYNCHRONIC.

diacritic: mark added to a symbol in phonetic notation to alter its value.

dialect: regionally or socially distinctive variety of LANGUAGE. A subdivision of a LANGUAGE. Language varieties based on geographic location are called **regional dialects**, those based on social class are called **social dialects** or **class dialects**.

diglossia: situation in which two varieties of a language co-occur, each with a distinct range of use and social function.

diminutive: referring to an AFFIX which denotes smallness. Diminutive affixes are often used to LEXICALIZE terms of endearment.

diphthong: vowel sound with a noticeable change in quality in a SYLLABLE. Contrast MONOPHTHONG where no change is heard, and TRIPHTHONG where two changes are heard.

direct: 1) opposite of inverse. 2) (direct/inverse case) case system common in Algonquian languages, in which personal morphemes do not indicate case; a grammatical morpheme is used to distinguish the relationship between the personal arguments of a given verb, based on a language-specific hierarchy of participant roles. In Blackfoot the hierarchy is 2 > 1 > 3 proximate > 3 obviative (Frantz 1991:15, Mithun 1996:150). When the hierarchy is maintained, e.g. a first or second person acts on a third person, the direct case morpheme is used (*nit-sikákomimm-a-wa* = 1s-love-DIRECT-him/her = 'I love him/her'); when the hierarchy is violated, e.g. a third person acts on a first or second person, the inverse morpheme is employed (*nit-sikákomimm-ok-a* = 1s-love-inverse-3s = 'He/she loves me.')

direct object: object seen as the most directly involved in a transitive action. In many languages, direct objects take ACCUSATIVE case marking. In the sentence, *I sent the flowers to Jill, flowers* is the direct object, and *Jill* is the INDIRECT OBJECT.

direct speech: the reporting of another's words verbatim, e.g., *Peter said, 'Yes, I'll come.'* Contrast INDIRECT SPEECH.

directive: utterance whose purpose is to get someone to do something. COMMANDS are directives.

discontinuity: the splitting of a construction by another grammatical unit. French negation is **discontinuous**: *Ne fumez pas* = NEG smoke.2PL NEG = 'Don't smoke.'

discourse: continuous stretch of spoken language.

discrete: said of a form with definable boundaries.

disjunction: The grammatical expression of OPPOSITION or contrast, e.g., an 'either/or' relationship. *But* and *or* are **disjunctives**; they express opposition or contrast.

dissimilation: (phonology) process in which one sound segment causes another to change so that the two sound segments become less alike. Contrast ASSIMILATION.

distal: referring to entities that are far (physically and psychologically) from both the speaker and addressee. Contrast proximal and MEDIAL. Spanish has a distal demonstrative *aquel* 'that (far)' which contrasts with the medial counterpart *ese* 'that (near)'.

distinctive: CONTRASTIVE.

distribution: total set of contexts in which a UNIT can occur. See also COMPLEMENTARY DISTRIBUTION.

distributive: grammatical category found with the lexical class of numbers which specifies distribution of items. In Ao Naga, distributives are formed by REDUPLICATING the final syllable of the number: *ká* 'one' > *káká* 'one each', *asem* 'three' > *asemsem* 'three each', *ténet* 'seven' > *ténetnet* 'seven each' (Gowda 1975:39).

disyllabic: consisting of two syllables. (Compare MONOSYLLABIC, trisyllabic).

ditransitive: a verb that can take two objects. *Give* is a ditransitive verb as seen in the sentence *I gave her ten dollars*.

divergence: process in which two forms become less like one another. DIALECTS can **diverge** and become separate languages.

domain: the realm of application of any linguistic construct.

dorsal: said of sounds produced with the BACK of the tongue, i.e. VELAR and PALATAL sounds.

downdrift: the gradual descent of high-pitched tones in an INTONATION UNIT.

dual: referring to exactly two. Yup'ik Eskimo has three numbers encoded on nouns, SINGULAR, DUAL and PLURAL: *kaviaq* 'fox', *kaviak* '2 foxes', *kaviat* '3+ foxes.' Ilocano has a dual INCLUSIVE PRONOUN *datá* 'you and I.'

dubitative: grammatical category which expresses doubt.

dummy: said of a form which is SEMANTICALLY empty (with no meaning). In the sentence *It is freezing, it* is a dummy element.

duration: the length of time involved in the ARTICULATION of a sound.

durative: referring to an event involving a long period of time. Many languages have durative distinctions in their ASPECT system.

dvandva: (Sanskrit 'two and two') term used to refer to COORDINATE COMPOUNDS consisting of two juxtaposed nouns which refer to a unitary concept, e.g., Sanskrit *mata-pitarau* (mother-father) 'parents'.

dynamic: 1) referring to verbs that encode activities and processes, usually ones that can appear in PROGRESSIVE FORM. (Contrast STATIVE or STATIC). 2) involving a temporal dimension. Contrast SYNCHRONIC.

echo question: Type of question which repeats part of a previous utterance, e.g., *I swam in the ocean yesterday.* Echo question: *You swam in the ocean?*

economy: criterion in linguistic description which requires simplicity or brevity.

egressive: sounds produced with outwards-moving airflow. Egressive sounds may be PULMONIC or EJECTIVE. Contrast INGRESSIVE.

ejective: sound produced with the GLOTTALIC AIRSTREAM MECHANISM. The GLOTTIS remains closed during ARTICULATION, so only air in the mouth is employed to produce ejectives.

elative: case inflection which expresses the meaning of 'motion away from (inside) a place.'

elicitation: method of obtaining linguistic DATA from CONSULTANTS by asking questions.

elision: the omission of sounds in connected speech.

ellipsis: the omission of part of a structure.

embedding: a structure in which a CONSTITUENT is contained within a larger constituent of the same kind. In the NOUN PHRASE 'the cat in the closet', *in the closet* is a noun phrase embedded within the larger noun phrase.

emic: referring to the relationship between elements in a system for purposes of description. Illustrating how phonemes in a certain language contrast with each other in an example of an emic construction.

emotive: referring to expressions that have an emotional effect on the listener or speaker.

empty: 1) meaningless element. 2) (**empty morph**) meaning that cannot be attributed to a morpheme.

endocentric: referring to a group of syntactically related words where one of the words is the definable center or HEAD within the group. A NOUN PHRASE is an endocentric construction, because it will contain a HEAD NOUN. An endocentric compound denotes a subclass of items referred to by one of the elements in the compound, i.e. *boat-house* is a kind of house. Contrast EXOCENTRIC.

endophoric: referring to the relationships of COHESION that help define the structure of a TEXT. Endophoric relations are divided into ANAPHORIC and CATAPHORIC types. Contrast EXOPHORIC.

entailment: (from logic) relation between a set of situations in which the truth of the second follows from the truth of the first. Verb = **entail**.

enumerative: relating to numbers.

environment: 1) context of a linguistic form (referring to adjacent parts of a UNIT in question. 2) set of conditions in which a linguistic rule applies.

epenthesis: the insertion of an extra sound (vowel or consonantal). An inserted sound is called **epenthetic**.

epistemic: MODALITY which asserts or implies that a PROPOSITION is known or believed. Contrast ALETHIC and DEONTIC.

equational: referring to a construction in which two NOUN PHRASES are used in the relationship of identity. Verbs that link two NPs are **equational verbs**.

equative degree: grammatical category of ADJECTIVES in which two items are seen to possess the qualities of the adjective in equal amounts. Tagalog has an equative prefix *kasing-*: *ulól* 'crazy' > *kasing-ulól* 'as crazy as'. Compare COMPARATIVE and SUPERLATIVE.

equi NP deletion: the deletion of a NOUN PHRASE from a COMPLEMENT CLAUSE when it is CO-REFERENTIAL with another noun phrase in the main clause of the same sentence.

ergative: category of AGENTS of TRANSITIVE VERBS which is formally distinct from the ABSOLUTIVE category, which encompasses SUBJECTS of INTRANSITIVE VERBS and OBJECTS of TRANSITIVE VERBS. Languages which make this distinction are said to be **ergative languages**.

erosion: the shortening of a morpheme in length.

essive: inflection which expresses a state of being; being *at* a place.

eth: the character [ð] in IPA corresponding to a voiced interdental fricative. Compare THETA.

ethnolinguistics: branch of linguistics which studies language in relation to ethnic types and behavior.

etic: referring to the physical form of linguistic units in description. An etic description of [m] might note that it is a VOICED, BILABIAL NASAL. Contrast EMIC.

etymology: the study of word origins and history. A **folk etymology** is the assumption that a word derives from a particular ETYMON, when in fact it doesn't.

etymon: linguistic form from which a later form derives.

evidential: linguistic form that expresses the speaker's commitment to an utterance in terms of the available evidence. Evidentials designate the source of information from which the speaker obtains his knowledge and may vary in meaning from 'so I heard', to 'so I smelled', to 'I have seen evidence that it happened', etc.

excessive: grammatical category indicating excess. When used with VERBS, it usually encodes actions that are carried to excess or extended in space and time.

exclamation: an utterance that expresses strong emotion. See EXCLAMATIVE.

exclamative: linguistic form that encodes emotion.

existential: linguistic form that expresses the concept of existence. Some languages which have existentials also use them to express possession.

exocentric: referring to a group of syntactically related words that have no 'center' or HEAD (none of the words is functionally equivalent to the group as a whole). Exocentric compounds denote something which is not a subclass of their components, e.g. *egghead* 'type of intellectual' or Nicobarese *kúykuvɔ́əkə* from *kúy* 'head' + *kuvɔ́kə* 'basket.' Contrast ENDOCENTRIC.

exonym: name given to a SPEECH COMMUNITY by outsiders.

exophoric: relating to a linguistic UNIT that refers to the EXTRA LINGUISTIC SITUATION, e.g., *there, that, him.* Contrast ENDOPHORIC.

expansion: process in which a grammatical unit takes on an additional grammatical function.

experiencer: nominal entity that is affected by the action or state expressed by a VERB, usually without CONTROL.

expletive: DUMMY element with no semantic value. In the English sentence *It is raining*, the expletive *it* has no meaning.

explicit: (said of rules) specified fully and precisely.

exponent: a piece or morphological material which expresses grammatical information. The *s* in *cats* is an exponent of plurality.

expression: string of elements treated as a UNIT for purposes of analysis.

expressive: emotive, referring to the state of mind of the speaker. Some languages have an 'expressive' or 'interjectional' class of words.

external evidence: non-linguistic evidence, e.g., archaeological records.

extralinguistic: referring to anything outside the realm of language. Social class structure is extralinguistic.

extraposition: the process of moving (**extraposing**) an element from its normal position to a position at or near the end of a sentence.

ezafe: term used in Arabic and Iranian linguistics to describe the grammatical phenomenon of LINKAGE. In Persian ezafe is expressed with a linking vowel between the HEAD and its ATTRIBUTE: *dæst-e mæn* = hand-EZAFE 1s = 'my hand' (Mahootian 1997: 112).

factitive: referring to a form denoting an action in which a cause produces a result.

factive: verb which takes a complement clause in which the speaker PRESUPPOSES the truth of what the clause expresses. Noun = *factivity*. See CONTRAFACTIVE.

family: group of genetically related languages, usually represented with a **family tree**.

feature: a noticeable property of spoken or written language. See also DISTINCTIVE feature.

field: 1) place where FIELDWORK is obtained; 2) **semantic field** system of interrelated networks of meaning.

fieldwork: the manner of collecting data for linguistic analysis.

filled pause: non-silent pause.

final: last element of a linguistic unit.

finite: referring to a verb which can occur on its own in an independent sentence. All forms of the verb except the INFINITIVE and PARTICIPLES are finite. Finite verbs express distinctions that non-finite verbs do not.

fixed: not alterable. Contrast free. English is a language with fixed WORD ORDER.

flap: consonant sound produced by rapid contact between two organs of articulation. In American English, the second consonant of the word *butter* is a flap.

focus: 1) center of communicative interest. 2) (Philippine linguistics) the system of verbal encoding which reflects the privileged status of the TOPIC argument of a clause and its semantic relationship to the verb.

folk etymology: an arbitrary change in the form of a word to make it seem more familiar or transparent, e.g. the changing of the French *écrevisse* into *crayfish.*

foot: unit of rhythm in languages, used by PHONOLOGISTS.

foregrounding: relative prominence in DISCOURSE. Prominent referents are often **foregrounded** by means of a grammatical construction. Contrast backgrounding.

formal: referring to linguistic form, as opposed to meaning or function.

formant: concentration of acoustic energy which reflects the way air is manipulated in the vocal tract. Phoneticians study formants with the use of a SPECTOGRAPH.

fortis: referring to a sound made with considerable effort and force. Contrast LENIS.

fossilized: referring to a morpheme that is no longer used productively. The process is called **fossilization**. A word or construction that preserves an ancient linguistic feature is called a **fossilized form**.

fourth person: the OBVIATIVE category in some languages in which a non-focal referent in the discourse gets different marking than a focal third person referent.

frame: the structural context in which a class of items is used.

free morpheme: see WORD; morpheme which may be uttered alone with meaning.

free variation: (phonology) free substitutability of one sound for another without altering the meaning.

frequentative: expressing repeated action. In Ilocano frequentative numbers take the prefix *mamin-*: *mamin-dua* 'twice,' *mamin-limá* 'five times.'

fricative: consonant produced without complete closure in the mouth, causing audible friction. Also called SPIRANT.

friction: (phonetics) the audible sound produced when air passes a constriction in the vocal tract.

front: referring to speech sounds articulated in the front part of the mouth, as opposed to the BACK, or speech sounds made by the front part of the tongue.

fronting: 1) the process in which a speech sound is produced further forward in the mouth than usual. 2) the changing of position of a constituent to initial position.

full sentence: sentence with a PREDICATE that can stand on its own.

function word: word whose role is grammatical. ARTICLES are function words. See also FUNCTOR.

functional: referring to the relationship between form and the system in which it is used.

functor: bound MORPHEME whose role is fully grammatical.

fundamental frequency: the lowest frequency component in a complex sound wave, also called F_0 (F *nought*).

fusional: referring to a morpheme boundary which is not discernible. Languages with many fusional morpheme boundaries are called **fusional languages**.

future: grammatical term used for situations or entities that come into being subsequent to the speech event.

fuzzy: indeterminate, not clear-cut. **Fuzzy categories** are those with no readily definable boundaries.

gap: absence of a linguistic unit where one might have been expected.

geminate: sequence of identical adjacent segments. Ilocano expresses some animate plurals by **gemination**: *ubíng* 'child' > *ubbing* 'children.'

gender: grammatical category which expresses contrasts such as MASCULINE, FEMININE and NEUTER, or ANIMATE/INANIMATE. **Natural gender** refers to the sex of real-world entities, **grammatical gender** deals with grammatical categorization, which may be arbitrary. English specifies gender in SINGULAR PRONOUNS. Romance languages express gender in ADJECTIVES, NOUNS, ARTICLES, and demonstratives, e.g., Aragonese *ixe can ye royo* 'that male dog is red' vs. *ixa caña ye roya* 'that female dog is red.'

general: universally applicable.

generalization: statement aimed at reflecting the nature of data.

generic: referring to a CLASS of entities, not a SPECIFIC entity. Generic SUBJECTS in English are often expressed as PLURALS: *Dogs are friendly.*

genitive: inflectional CASE or CONSTRUCTION typically associated with possession or other similar close-connection.

gerund: a de-verbal NOUN (noun derived from a verb). A clause whose HEAD is a gerund is called a **gerund clause**, e.g., *sitting for long hours, smoking outside, eating too many beans.* Contrast PARTICIPLE.

given: term used to reflect the information status or ACTIVATION STATE of a referent as being previously introduced in the DISCOURSE. Contrast with NEW.

glide: sound produced when the vocal organs are in transition away from or toward an articulation. [w] and [y] are glides in English.

glottal: referring to the **glottis**, the aperture between the vocal cords. **Glottalization** refers to articulation which is accompanied by glottal constriction.

glottalic airstream mechanism: area between the PHARYNX and mouth from which EJECTIVE sounds are produced.

goal: the SEMANTIC ROLE which expresses the person or place towards which motion is directed. Compare SOURCE.

government: syntactic linkage between elements where one UNIT requires a specific morphological form of another.

gradability: the ability to differ in DEGREE. **Gradable** adjectives include *fat, big, small, high, shallow, narrow.* **Ungradable** adjectives include *pregnant, married, wrong,* etc.

gradience: having no clear boundaries between sets of analytic categories.

gradual: differing in DEGREE, along a scale of some kind.

grammar: 1) RULES of a language, known by native speakers. 2) linguistic description of the RULES of a language.

grammaticality: the conforming to the accepted RULES of the language. Native speakers of a language are often asked by linguists to give **grammaticality judgments** in which they tell if certain forms are **grammatically correct**.

grammaticization/grammaticalization: the process by which full lexical items become grammatical morphemes. Grammaticization is seen to be UNIDIRECTIONAL.

grapheme: CONTRASTIVE UNIT in a writing system of a language.

group: 1) a number of UNITS. 2) collection of entities.

habitual: ASPECTUAL category which indicates usual actions. In English, the past tense habitual is indicated by *used to* as in *I used to take drugs.*

habituative: expressing HABITUAL actions.

haplology: the omission of sounds in speech, usually referring to syllables which are similar or identical.

hard consonant: consonant which lacks PALATALIZATION.

harmony: (phonology) the effect of phonological influence, in which one phonological UNIT influences the pronunciation of another. Turkish is an example of a language with **vowel harmony**. If one vowel in a Turkish word is ROUND, all vowels in the word will be round.

head: the central element of a structure which is distributionally equivalent to the phrase as a whole. The head may determine AGREEMENT. In the NOUN PHRASE *the lady from Bulgaria*, the noun *lady* is the **head noun**.

headless relative clause: a relative clause which forms a complete NOUN PHRASE by itself.

head-marking: a construction in which the grammatical connection between two elements is marked overtly on the HEAD. Contrast DEPENDENT MARKING.

hearsay: relating to information that the speaker has not witnessed first hand, but rather has heard about from a secondary source.

hesternal: performed the day before the speech event. Contrast HODIERNAL.

heteroganic: said of sounds that are not produced in the same PLACE OF ARTICULATION. Contrast HOMORGANIC.

heteronymy: partial HOMONYMY in which words differ in meaning but are identical in form in one medium only (speech or writing). HOMOGRAPHS are identical in written form but have different meanings, and HOMOPHONES are identical in speech but not in writing.

hierarchy: classification of linguistic UNITS which recognizes a series of successively SUBORDINATE levels. In the **animacy hierarchy**, ANIMATE nouns are SUPERORDINATE to INANIMATE nouns, and among the animate nouns, HUMANS are SUPERORDINATE to animals.

high: term applied to sounds which are produced with the TONGUE above the NEUTRAL position in the mouth. CLOSE vowels and PALATAL consonants are high.

historical linguistics: the scientific study of the evolution of language. DIACHRONIC linguistics.

hodiernal: performed the day of the speech event. Contrast HESTERNAL.

homographs: lexical items that differ in meaning but are identical in written form. In Tagalog, the word *singáw* means both 'cold sore' and 'vapor.' Compare HOMOPHONE.

homonyms: lexical items with the same form but different meaning. See HOMOGRAPH and HOMOPHONE.

homophones: lexical items that differ in meaning but are identical in spoken form. In English, *there* and *their* are homophones.

homophora: reference that is dependent upon cultural knowledge.

homorganic: produced in the same place of articulation. [k], [g], and [ŋ] are homorganic. Contrast HETEROGANIC.

honorific: linguistic form that designates the higher social status and position of the addressee. Japanese and Korean have honorific verb endings.

hypercorrection: the practice of incorrectly applying the rules of standard language, usually said of speakers of substandard varieties of a language in an attempt to sound formal. The sentence *Will you go with Anita and I?* is an instance of hypercorrection.

hypocoristic: pertaining to nicknames.

hyponymy: the relationship between specific and general lexical items, in which the former is included in the latter. *Table* is a **hyponym** of *furniture*. The superordinate term is referred to as the **hypernym**.

hypotaxis: the linking of SUBORDINATE constructions with the use of SUBORDINATING CONJUNCTIONS, e.g., *I laughed because he tickled me.* Adj = **hypotactic**. Contrast PARATAXIS.

hypothetical: existing only as an idea or concept, in which the truth value is not assumed. Palauan has **hypothetical pro-**

nouns used to designate the AGENT of a hypothetical action (Josephs 1975: 105).

iconic: said of words or grammatical forms which resemble or are analogous to what they represent. Onomatopoetic words are thought to be iconic. Noun = **iconicity**, the relationship between linguistic form and linguistic function. Contrast ARBITRARY.

idiolect: linguistic system of an individual speaker, personal DIALECT.

idiom: sequence of words that function as a UNIT and whose MEANING cannot be easily deduced from the sum of its parts. *To let the cat out of the bag* is an **idiomatic expression**.

idiophone: speech sound that mimics a natural sound.

illative: case inflection which expresses motion into or direction towards a place.

illocutionary act: speech act; an act which is performed upon utterance, i.e., promising, baptizing, marrying two individuals, arresting, etc.

imperative: verb form used in the expression of COMMANDS. Contrast INDICATIVE, INTERROGATIVE, SUBJUNCTIVE MOODS.

imperfective: ASPECTUAL term referring to the internal time structure of a situation. Imperfective verbs denote actions and situations that are not viewed as being BOUNDED. Contrast PERFECTIVE forms, where the situation is seen as a whole, regardless of the time contrasts it may contain.

impersonal: unable to encode PERSON. In Spanish, the verb *llueve* 'it rains' is an impersonal verb, it cannot take a PERSON SUBJECT.

implosive: sound produced involving inward movement of air with a downwards movement of the LARYNX.

inalienable: referring to a type of possessive relationship in which the link between the possessor and possessed is seen as permanent or necessary. Contrast ALIENABLE.

inanimate: referring to a non-living referent. *It* is an inanimate PRONOUN.

inceptive: ASPECTUAL term referring to the commencing of an action: 'to start to', 'to be about to.' Contrast TELIC. See also INCHOATIVE.

inchoative: ASPECTUAL distinction which designates the beginning of an activity. See INCEPTIVE.

inclusive: included. **Inclusive pronouns** include the addressee. An **exclusive pronoun** does not include the addressee.

incorporation: see NOUN INCORPORATION.

indefinite: grammatical term referring to an entity that is not SPECIFIC or identifiable. English has indefinite ARTICLES, *a* and *an*. Contrast DEFINITE.

indicative: MOOD used in the expression of statements. Contrast IMPERATIVE, SUBJUNCTIVE.

indirect evidence: evidence not acquired first hand, see INFERENTIAL.

indirect object: the grammatical relation between the NOUN PHRASE expressing the person who receives something, which is grammatically distinct from the DIRECT OBJECT. In the sentence *I gave Mary the ball*, the ball is a direct object, and Mary is the indirect object.

indirect speech: reporting what a speaker has said without using his exact words.

individuated: referring to entities whose individuality is marked. In Pangasinan, numbers express individuation with the suffix *-ra*, e.g., *limá* 'five (units of)' vs. *limáran toó* 'five individual men.'

inessive: case inflection which expresses location or position within a place. Mising has an inessive suffix *-(a)rade*: *aina* 'heart' > *ainarade* 'inside the heart' (Prasad 1991: 63).

inferential: referring to a statement which is based on inference, and not direct observation. See EVIDENTIAL.

infinitive: NON-FINITE form of a VERB, usually cited as the unmarked or base form. In Spanish, infinitive verbs end in *-ar, -er,* or *-ir*: *platicar* 'to talk,' *comer* 'to eat', *decidir* 'to decide.'

infix: MORPHEME type which is inserted in the middle of a ROOT. Ilocano has a verbalizing infix *–um-*: *tugáw* 'chair' > *tumugáw* 'to sit'.

inflecting language: language which signals many GRAMMATICAL categories with INFLECTION.

inflection: MORPHOLOGICAL AFFIXATION which signals GRAMMATICAL meaning, as opposed to DERIVATION. Inflection is seen as an OBLIGATORY category, and inflectional affixes are always semantically predictable. Inflectional categories include TENSE, NUMBER, PERSON, ASPECT, etc.

informant: A natives speaker of a certain langugae who acts as a source of linguistic data for researchers. CONSULTANT is the term now generally used by modern linguists when describing such a person.

ingressive: 1) referring to air which flows into the mouth. IMPLOSIVE and CLICKS are ingressive sounds. Contrast EGRESSIVE. 2) verbal ASPECT which reflects a situation which is bounded at the start, e.g., Russian *pet'* 'sing' vs. *zapet'* 'start to sing, ingressive'. Compare INCEPTIVE and INCHOATIVE.

initial: occurring at the beginning. Tagalog is a predicate-initial language, predicates are the first constituents.

initiated: ASPECTUAL term referring to ACTIONS or PROCESSES that have started.

innate: inherent from birth, not acquired through experience.

instantaneous release: referring to sounds released suddenly, without turbulence (said of STOPS).

instigator: the conscious initiator of an ACTION. See AGENT.

instrument: the SEMANTIC ROLE which represents the thing used to do something. In the sentence *I killed the ant with my slipper*, *slipper* is the instrument.

instrumental: CASE term which refers to the form of the NOUN PHRASE that expresses the INSTRUMENT.

intensifier: class of words that have a heightening or lowering effect on the meaning of the CONSTITUENT they modify.

intensive: verbal category that refers to actions that are more intense than normal, repeated, or prolonged, e.g. Tukang Besi *rau* 'yell' vs. *no-heka-rau* 'cry out repeatedly, intensive' (Donohue 1999: 282).

intentive: grammatical MODE that indicates a plan to do something.

interdental: referring to sounds made between the teeth. The initial [ð] sound in the word *this* is a voiced interdental.

interjection: Class of words which express strong emotion. English interjections include *oh, wow, ouch*, etc.

interrogative: MOOD or form used with QUESTIONS. Contrast DECLARATIVE.

intervocalic: between VOWELS.

intonation: pattern of PITCH in spoken language.

intragenetic comparison: comparison of related languages in the same genetic group.
intuition: judgment made by speakers about their language.
invariable: unable to change form morphologically (take affixes). The English definite article *the* is invariable. Contrast VARIABLE.
invariant: word that cannot undergo morphological change. Unlike many verbs in English, the verb *put* is invariant (noninflecting).
inventory: unordered listing of items. English doesn't have a BILABIAL TRILL in its PHONEMIC inventory.
inversion: the changing of a specific SEQUENCE of CONSTITUENTS. In French, inversion is used for certain questions: *Il est laid* = 'He is ugly' > *Est-il laid?* = 'Is he ugly?'
IPA: abbreviation for International Phonetic Association and their conventions for transcribing speech sounds.
irrealis: grammatical category referring to events that have not been realized. In some languages, FUTURE verbs and NEGATIVES are marked with an irrealis morpheme.
irregular: said of a linguistic form that does not abide by a grammatical rule. See also SUPPLETIVE.
isogloss: line drawn on a map to show where a certain linguistic form is used.
isolated: referring to a language with no outside contact.
isolating language: language whose words are invariable (do not take affixes). Chinese is an isolating language. Also ANALYTIC language.
isolect: (sociolinguistics) linguistic variety that differs minimally from another.
isomorphism: the hypothesis that one form has one meaning; one-to-one correspondence.
item and arrangement: model of MORPHOLOGICAL description in which sequences of words are analyzed linearly: *Man+ cat+s live+d+in+this+house*. Contrast ITEM AND PROCESS and WORD AND PARADIGM models.
item and process: model of MORPHOLOGICAL description in which the relationships between words are seen as processes of DERIVATION. The word *sang* is derived from *sing* in a morphological process involving ABLAUT.
iteration: the repeated application of a rule, also recursion.
iterative: term used denoting verbal ASPECT which expresses the repetition of a situation, e.g., Tukang Besi *langke* 'sail' vs. *no-para-langke* 'sail regularly, iterative' (Donohue 1999: 284).
izafe(t): see EZAFE.
jargon: 1) technical terminology. 2) distinctive vocabulary of a certain group.
juncture: a phonetic feature whose presence signals the presence of a grammatical boundary. Differences in juncture account for the different pronunciations of *nitrate* and *night rate*.
jussive: a third person IMPERATIVE (directed at someone other than the speaker or addressee).
kinesis: grammatical category that reflects the ACTIVE nature of verbs. **Kinetic verbs** are those that denote actions in which energy is exerted and/or motion is involved.
kinship term: term used to express degree of kindred (blood relationship).
labial: referring to speech sounds produced with the lips. [p] is a VOICELESS BILABIAL STOP.
labialization: the process of rounding the lips when producing a sound.
labio-dental: referring to sounds produced with the teeth and lips. [f] is a voiceless labio-dental FRICATIVE.
labio-velar: referring to sounds that are produced at the VELUM with simultaneous lip ROUNDING.
laminal: referring to the **lamina**, or blade of the tongue.
language: linguistic system shared by a SPEECH COMMUNITY.
laryngeal: referring to speech sounds made in the LARYNX. **Laryngealization** refers to excess vibration of the vocal cords, resulting in CREAKY VOICE.
larynx: voice box, the part of the trachea that contains the VOCAL CORDS.
lateral: sound which is produced when air escapes around one or both sides of a closure in the mouth. [l] is a lateral sound.
lative case: CASE that expresses motion 'up to' a location or 'as far as' a location.
lax: sound produced with less movement and muscular effort, e.g., vowels in the center of the VOWEL area.
length: physical DURATION. In Finnish VOWEL length is CONTRASTIVE.
lenis: sound produced with weak muscular effort of force. See LAX.
lenition: the weakening of the strength of a sound, e.g., the reduction in voicing in a certain environment.
lexeme: abstract representation of a WORD, the minimal DISTINCTIVE UNIT in the SEMANTIC SYSTEM of a language.
lexical: referring to the LEXICON. A **lexical item** is another term for LEXEME.
lexicalization: referring to the situation in which a word develops to represent a meaning.
lexicography: the science of dictionary-making.
lexicology: the study of a language's vocabulary.
lexicon: vocabulary of a language. Also often called **lexis**.
liaison: the linking of sounds across WORD boundaries that are not pronounced word-finally. For example, in French, the *t* of *est* [ɛ]'is' is not pronounced unless it is followed by another word beginning in a vowel: *Il est_urgent*.
ligature: element which serves to link two constituents. Tagalog has a ligature *na/-ng* which, among other uses, links adjectives and nouns: *maganda-ng buhay* = beautiful-ligature life = 'beautiful life.'
light syllable: SYLLABLE where the RHYME contains only one segment (MORA). Contrast heavy syllable.
limitative: expressing a limit. In Pangasinan, REDUPLICATION is used to form limitative numbers, e.g., *sak-sakéy* 'only one,' *tal-talóra* 'only three.'
lingua franca: common language used to enable routine communication between two different groups of people.
lingual, linguo-: referring to speech sounds produced with the TONGUE.
linguist: 1) speaker of many languages (common sense). 2) student or practitioner of LINGUISTICS (linguistic sense).
linguistic: referring to LANGUAGE.
linguistic area: a geographical region containing several languages that share similar features, even though they may not be closely related. Also called SPRACHBUND.
linguistic sign: in the work of Saussure, the combination of a linguistic form with its meaning or function.

linguistics: the scientific study of language.

linkage: grammatical mechanism which serves to connect two constituents. In Philippine languages, this is done with an OVERT LINKER or LIGATURE. In Arabic/Persian linguistics the term used is EZAFE.

linker: element which serves to link two constituents. See LIGATURE.

linking: inserting a sound between LINGUISTIC UNITS for ease of articulation.

liquid: apico-alveolar consonantal sound of the [r] and [l] type.

loan: WORD or CONSTRUCTION that is BORROWED from another LANGUAGE.

locative: referring to location.

logogram: a symbol which represents a complete word. The Chinese writing system is an example of a **logographic script**.

long: (term used to describe certain vowels) articulated with greater length than the corresponding **short** vowel.

loudness: the intensity of sound, as measured in decibels.

low: referring to sounds that are pronounced with the tongue in the lowest position of the mouth. OPEN VOWELS and GLOTTAL FRICATIVES are low.

main clause: a clause which does not form a part of a larger clause. All sentences contain at least one main clause.

manner adverbial: adverb which qualifies the sense of a verb.

manner of articulation: any of the different ways of producing a consonantal sound. The chief categories are STOP (PLOSIVE), FRICATIVE, AFFRICATE, TAP, FLAP, TRILL, NASAL, LATERAL, and APPROXIMANT. The first three are called OBSTRUENTS and the rest are SONORANTS.

marked: referring to a form or construction which differs from another form in any of several respects: 1) it is morphologically more complex, 2) it is of more limited applicability, 3) it departs more noticeably from the ordinary patterns of language. The property that distinguishes a marked form from an unmarked form is called **markedness**.

markedness shift: a type of language change in which a MARKED form or construction becomes unmarked, or vice versa.

mass noun: a noun which is treated as a continuous entity and cannot be counted. *Water* is a mass noun.

medial: 1) said of a linguistic UNIT which occurs between to others. English is a verb medial language; the verb occurs between the SUBJECT and OBJECT. 2) In DEICTIC reference, referring to something which is neither near (PROXIMAL) nor far away (DISTAL). See MESIAL.

medial verb construction: construction common in Papuan languages in which verbs in a sequence take a different set of subject markers depending on their position in the sequence. The subject affixes of the first of the two verbs are called **medial verb affixes**, e.g., Hua *Rmi-na iftehi-e* 'go.down-3sSUBJ.MEDIAL get.lost-3s 'She went down and got lost' (Crowley et al 1995: 369).

mediopassive: VOICE construction with a STATIVE verb and an unexpressed, but understood, AGENT.

merger: process in which two linguistic units **merge** into one with a meaning or function that is different from that of the combined units. (Heine and Reh 1984: 44–45).

mesial: another term for MEDIAL when used for DEICTIC reference.

mesolect: intermediate variety of language between an ACROLECT and a BASILECT.

metathesis: alteration in the normal sequence of elements in a sentence. In Rapanui, the alternation between the two forms of the verb to give, *va'ai* and *'avai* exhibit metathesis (DuFeu 1996: 190). Metathesis can be contiguous, involving adjacent sounds, or non-contiguous, involving non-adjacent sounds.

meteorological verb: verb which describes an event of nature. See AMBIENT verb.

mid: referring to VOWEL sounds produced when the tongue is in a vertical position, as opposed to HIGH and LOW. [e] [ɛ], [ɔ] and [o] are **mid vowels**.

minimal pair: a pair of lexemes that differ in only one PHONOLOGICAL FEATURE and CONTRAST in meaning. Minimal pairs are gathered when investigating the PHONEMIC INVENTORY of a LANGUAGE. In Portuguese, *não* 'no' and *mão* 'hand' form a minimal pair; they contrast only in the PLACE OF ARTICULATION of the ONSET NASAL.

mirative: grammatical category expressing INFORMATION which is contrary to expectation; expresses surprise. Noun = **mirativity**.

mixed language: a language which originated from the combination of two (or more) different languages.

modality: the SEMANTIC contrasts in the category of MOOD. English has **modal** AUXILIARY VERBS *can, will, may, might.*

mode: verbal category which reflects the psychological atmosphere of an action in the eyes of the speaker. Different modes include INDICATIVE (DECLARATIVE), SUBJUNCTIVE, IMPERATIVE, NEGATIVE, CONDITIONAL, OPTATIVE, DESIDERATIVE, INTENTIVE, DUBITATIVE, quotative, POTENTIAL, ADMONITIVE, PERMISSIVE, and OBLIGATORY.

modifier: linguistic UNIT which serves to express information that can be attributed to a HEAD constituent.

modularity: referring to a set of systems, each with its own distinctive properties.

monitory: the grammatical category associated with warnings.

monolingual: speaking only one language. A monolingual person is called a **monoglot**.

monomorphemic: consisting of only one MORPHEME.

monophthong: VOWEL with no detectable change in quality. Contrast DIPHTHONG.

monosyllabic: consisting of only one SYLLABLE.

mood: linguistic category (sometimes called MODE) which relates the speaker's attitude to or involvement in an event. Common moods include the INDICATIVE (DECLARATIVE) mood used in making statements, the IMPERATIVE mood used for issuing commands, the SUBJUNCTIVE mood which indicates uncertainty or tentativeness, and the INTERROGATIVE mood used for asking questions.

mora: minimal UNIT of metrical time, equivalent to a short SYLLABLE.

moribund language: a language which is no longer passed down and is doomed to extinction.

morph: a piece of morphological material whose morphological status may or may not be determinable.

morpheme: minimal DISTINCTIVE UNIT with meaning. Morphemes can be BOUND AFFIXES or FREE (WORDS).

morphology: branch of linguistics concerned with the study of STRUCTURE and how it refers to meaning and GRAMMAR.

morphophoneme: an abstract phonological unit which is realized as one or two more different PHONEMES in different circumstances, especially during neutralization. In German *hund* 'dog' ends in [t], a separate phoneme from the German /d/; the morphophoneme [D] is used in certain analyses to represent both phonemes and how they interact in this environment.

morphophonemic alternation: the appearance of two or more different PHONEMES in the same position in the same MORPHEME in different circumstances, e.g., the alternation of the English plural marker /-s/ ~ /-z/ ~ /-iz/.

morphophonemics: the description of MORPHOPHONEMIC alternations.

morphosyntax: MORPHOLOGY and SYNTAX (as they apply together) Adj = **morphosyntactic**.

mother tongue: a language learned in childhood. An individual can have more than one mother tongue.

motherese: the special kind of language spoken by mothers to their babies.

motivation: the functional correlates that shape grammatical form. Grammar is seen to be **motivated** by communicative and discourse pressures.

multilingual: competent in many languages. Compare BILINGUAL, MONOLINGUAL.

multiplicative: grammatical category which expresses the number of times an action is performed. In Manipuri (Tibeto-Burman, India) the multiplicative suffix is *-lək*: *me-ri-lək* = NM-four-MULT = 'four times'.

mutation: a systematic change in certain consonants in a word for grammatical reasons.

mutative: ASPECT which indicates a change in status.

narrative: description of past events.

nasal: said of sounds that are produced when the ORAL CAVITY is closed because of a lowered SOFT PALATE which results in air escaping through the nose.

native speaker: a person is a native speaker of a language if he has acquired the language naturally in childhood and has exceptional command of the RULES of the language.

natural class: any class of linguistic objects which can be characterized using less information than is required to characterize any part of it, e.g. the class of nouns or nasal vowels.

natural gender: the case in which the GENDER of a noun is predictable from its meaning.

negation: the process of contradicting some or all of the meaning of a linguistic form, e.g., from *true* to *false*, or vice-versa. Words with **negative polarity** can only appear in a negative environment, e.g., *any*. Contrast AFFIRMATIVE.

negator: negating morpheme. French has two clause negators, *ne* and *pas*. Portuguese has one, *não*.

neurolinguistics: branch of linguistics which studies the neurological basis of language.

neutral: 1) said of the tongue when it is not raised, lowered, FRONT, or BACK. Also central. The mid-central **neutral vowel** *schwa* is articulated in a position which is least extreme in terms of tongue height and advancement. 2) said of the lips when unrounded, but rather in a relaxed position.

new: term applied to information which is supplied for the first time in an utterance, as opposed to GIVEN information that is previously ACTIVATED.

nominalization: the process of forming a NOUN from another word class.

nominative: term applied to INFLECTIONAL CASE which refers to the category encompassing SUBJECTS of INTRANSITIVE VERBS and AGENTS of TRANSITIVE VERBS, as opposed to the ACCUSATIVE CASE, PATIENTS of TRANSITIVE VERBS. Languages with a nominative category are called ACCUSATIVE LANGUAGES. The nominative case is usually morphologically UNMARKED.

non-configurational languages: languages with fairly free (pragmatic) word order.

nonfinite: referring to a verb which does not carry full marking for TENSE and AGREEMENT and which cannot serve as the only verb in a sentence.

normative: said of the standard practice in speech or writing.

notation: system of graphic representation, e.g. PHONEMIC notation.

noun: term applied to the grammatical class of words with time stability, i.e., names of people, places, things, concepts. Constructions which are headed by nouns are NOUN PHRASES.

noun class: language specific categorization of NOUNS according to their formal grammatical properties. French has two noun classes based on GENDER: masculine and feminine. Kickapoo has two noun classes based on ANIMACY: animate and inanimate. Nauruan has 39 noun classes based on inherent properties of the members of each class.

noun incorporation: the process in which a generic noun is syntactically and morphologically included within a verb.

NP: abbreviation for NOUN PHRASE.

nucleus: term applied to the phonetic segment which carries the maximal prominence in a SYLLABLE. The nucleus of the syllable [*kar*] is the vowel *a*.

null: EMPTY, ZERO.

number: grammatical category which expresses countability. See SINGULAR, DUAL, PAUCAL, TRIAL, PLURAL, COLLECTIVE.

object: 1) the PATIENT ARGUMENT of a TRANSITIVE VERB; the receiver, theme, or goal of an action. English distinguishes DIRECT and INDIRECT objects. The term **objective** is also used for ACCUSATIVE. Contrast SUBJECT.

object concord: the indexing of a grammatical OBJECT on a verb.

obligative: grammatical category which expresses obligations. In Caddo, the obligative prefix is *kas-*: *kas-sa-náy=aw* = OBLIG-3AGENT.IRREALIS-sing = 'He should/is supposed to sing.' (Chafe 1995:356).

obligatory: not OPTIONAL with regard to a RULE.

oblique: said of a NOUN PHRASE which is not a CORE ARGUMENT of a VERB, subcategorized by the VALENCE of the verb. All CASE forms that are not GRAMMATICAL are called oblique.

obstruent: sound which involves a constriction of airflow. STOPS, FRICATIVES, and AFFRICATES are obstruents.

obviative: the grammatical category which encodes FOURTH PERSON. It contrasts with the THIRD PERSON, the more TOPICAL of the referents not participating in the speech event.

obvitative: the grammatical category (usually modal) which expresses obvious information. Compare Kapau *qoenqa* 'I am obviously lying down (OBVITATIVE).' vs. *qoenga* 'I am lying down (INDICATIVE)' (Oates and Oates 1968: 72).

occlusive: STOP consonant.
onset: initial part of a SYLLABLE before the vowel. Contrast CODA.
ontology: the set of different kinds of things or situations that exist or that are posited in human minds or languages.
opaque: referring to FORMS whose derivations are not evident. Contrast TRANSPARENT.
open: referring to vowel sounds that are produced with the tongue in the lowest position. Contrast CLOSE.
open class: WORD CLASS into which new members may be added. In English NOUNS, ADJECTIVES and VERBS are open classes, PRONOUNS and DEMONSTRATIVES are **closed classes**.
opposition: CONTRAST between linguistic UNITS.
optative: category which expresses wishes, hopes, or desires.
optional: ANTONYM of OBLIGATORY, said of a RULE.
oral: referring to sounds produced in the mouth; opposed to NASAL.
order: underlying linear sequence. English has SUBJECT-VERB-OBJECT WORD ORDER.
ordinal: class of numbers denoting position. *First, second, third,* and *fourth* are ordinal numbers. Contrast CARDINAL.
overgeneralization: the process of applying a PRODUCTIVE RULE in an ENVIRONMENT where it doesn't belong. Children often **overgeneralize** the use of the English past tense suffix *-ed*, and utter *goed* instead of *went.*
overlap: referring to parts of a conversation in which more than one person is talking.
overt: referring to a FORM which is observable. Contrast COVERT.
oxymoron: a phrase containing contradictory words.
palate: roof of the mouth, divided into the hard palate behind the ALVEOLAR ridge and the SOFT PALATE (VELUM).
palatal: referring to sounds produced with the tongue in contact with the hard palate. The [y] is *yes* is a palatal GLIDE.
palatalization: Process involving the movement of the tongue towards the hard palate. Palatalization is a SECONDARY ARTICULATION. In speech, the [t] in *got you* often **palatalizes** to [tʃ] as in *gotcha* [gatʃa].
palato-alveolar: referring to sounds produced when the blade of the tongue touches the ALVEOLAR ridge while the FRONT of the tongue is raised towards the hard palate. The [ʃ] in *sure* is a VOICELESS palato-alveolar FRICATIVE.
palindrome: a word or phrase that reads the same in both directions, such as Malayalam.
pandialectal: occurring in all DIALECTS of a language.
paradigm: set of substitutable relationships a linguistic unit has with others in a specific CONTEXT. Adj = **paradigmatic**.
parasite vowel: extra vowel inserted in a sequence. See ANAPTYXIS.
parataxis: the linking of CONSTRUCTIONS of equal status without a grammatical MORPHEME expressing the linkage.
paronymy: the relationship between WORDS derived from the same ROOT.
parse: to break down a text grammatically. The word *deconstruction* may be parsed morphologically as *de-construct-ion.*
part of speech: see WORD CLASS.
participant: person taking part in a linguistic interaction.
participant role: the SEMANTIC ROLE that reflects how an entity participates in the action of situation denoted by the clause. Participant roles include AGENT, PATIENT, BENEFACTIVE, RECIPIENT, EXPERIENCER, etc.
participle: word derived from a VERB which is used as an ADJECTIVE. Contrast GERUND.
particle: 1) INVARIABLE FUNCTOR. 2) (in polysynthetic languages) member of a small class of morphemes which cannot take any affixes.
partitive: referring to a part or quantity, e.g., a piece of pie, a bar of soap.
passive: clause type (or verb form) where the grammatical SUBJECT is the PATIENT, RECIPIENT, or GOAL of the action denoted by the verb. Contrast ACTIVE, in which the SUBJECT of a passive construction appears as an OBJECT.
past: grammatical term used for entities or situation that have come into being prior to the speech event.
past perfect: a verb form which is PAST in TENSE and PERFECT in ASPECT.
path: route taken by an entity from the SOURCE to GOAL.
patient: entity that is affected by the action denoted by the verb. In the sentence *She spanked Henry*, *Henry* is the patient.
patois: regional speech form of low prestige.
pattern: systematic arrangement of units.
paucal: referring to a small number of items greater than two. Contrast SINGULAR, DUAL, TRIAL, and PLURAL.
pause: short interruption during the production of an utterance. Pauses can be silent or filled (with a filler or hesitation noise).
pejorative: with an insulting meaning.
penult: the second to last SYLLABLE of a word. Adj = **penultimate**.
perfect: term used to reflect a grammatical category that expresses a past situation, usually with some relevance at the moment of speech to another point of reference. *I have gone* is the English perfect of *I went.*
perfective: ASPECT term used to refer to actions that have been completed and seen as a whole, regardless of the internal time-structuring. Perfective verbs denote situations which are BOUNDED. Contrast IMPERFECTIVE.
performative: type of SENTENCE in which an action is performed by the uttering of the sentence. *With this ring, I thee wed* is a performative sentence.
periphrasis: the use of separate words instead of BOUND MORPHEMES to express a grammatical relationship. English equalitative adjectives are expressed periphrastically: *as happy as.*
permansive: term used for grammatical MODE which indicates universal or timeless truths. Mode often found in proverbs.
permissive: verbal MODE which indicates granted permission.
person: category which identifies entities according to their role in conversation. FIRST PERSON = speaker, SECOND PERSON = addressee, THIRD PERSON = third party not involved in conversation, FOURTH PERSON = a second third person.
pharynx: tubular cavity above the LARYNX. Hebrew has **pharyngeal** sounds (produced in the PHARYNX).
phatic communion: the use of language to establish or maintain social relations.
philology: HISTORICAL or COMPARATIVE LINGUISTICS.
phonation: the vocal activity in the larynx. **Phonation types**

include *breathy voice* (noisy airflow through an open glottis), *whisper* (airflow through an open glottis), *creaky voice* (very slow vibration of the vocal folds), *modal voice* (rapid vibration of the vocal folds), and *falsetto* (very rapid vibration of tensed vocal folds).

phone: smallest possible DISCRETE segment of sound.

phoneme: the smallest distinct unit in a given language. Noncontrastive variants of a phoneme are called ALLOPHONES. In English, [pʰ] and [p] are allophones of the phoneme /p/.

phonetics: the scientific study of speech sounds.

phonology: the scientific study of SOUND SYSTEMS in LANGUAGE.

phrase: element of structure with more than one WORD but lacking the SUBJECT-PREDICATE structure of CLAUSES.

pidgin: trade language formed when two speech communities come together with no common language. Once a pidgin acquires native speakers, it becomes a CREOLE.

pitch: the audible difference in sound which correlates to the frequency of the sound wave. Pitch may be used in INTONATION, and also on the lexical or grammatical level in TONE languages.

pitch accent language: a language which has a highly restricted use of lexical tone.

pivot: argument with a privileged syntactic status in a given construction. English has a subject pivot in coordinated phrases: He saw Mary and (he/*Mary) left.

place of articulation: location of the vocal apparatus during the production of a sound.

plosive: STOP consonant.

pluperfect: a tense used to frame a PAST action with reference to another past action. Also called PAST PERFECT.

plural: grammatical category of NUMBER which expresses more than one unit. See DUAL, PAUCAL. Contrast SINGULAR. Botolan Sambal employs various prefixes with pluralized verbs, e.g. *mog-alih* 'to leave (one person),' *mipog-alih* 'to leave (more than one person)' (Antworth 1979: 25).

polar question: YES/NO QUESTION.

polarity: the distinction between POSITIVE and NEGATIVE features in a form or language.

polyglot: a person who speaks several languages.

polysemous: having a range of different meanings. Noun = **polysemy**.

polysyllabic: consisting of more than one SYLLABLE.

polysynthetic: term used to describe morphologically complex languages, usually those that include NOUN INCORPORATION in their morphological inventories. See also AGGLUTINATIVE, ISOLATING.

portmanteau: single morph that may be analyzed into more than one morpheme. In Portuguese, the portmanteau form *no* 'in the' derives from *em* 'in' + *o* 'masculine definite article.'

position: place of a linguistic unit. In English, the velar nasal /ng/ does not appear in INITIAL position.

positive: 1) AFFIRMATIVE. 2) unmarked degree of an adjective, as opposed to COMPARATIVE and SUPERLATIVE.

possessive: form or construction that indicates possession or association. In many languages, possession is shown by the GENITIVE case.

postalveolar: referring to the region behind the ALVEOLAR RIDGE.

postposition: grammatical category which consists of a closed set of words which follow nouns to form a noun phrase. Japanese has postpositions, while English has PREPOSITIONS.

potential: grammatical category which refers to possibility rather than actuality.

potentive: (Philippine linguistics) verbal MODE that expresses coincidental, accidental, involuntary, or abilitative actions.

pragmatics: study of language and the influence SEMANTICS and extralinguistic factors have on interaction.

predicate: the part of a sentence which accompanies the SUBJECT. In English, all predicates minimally consist of a VERB. Ilocano, on the other hand, allows predicate nominals: *tukák* 'frog; it is a frog'.

predicate nominal: a noun which serves as a PREDICATE. In English, predicate nominals follow a COPULA.

predicate position: the position occupied by a PREDICATE. In English, ADJECTIVES may appear in predicate position. Compare attributive position.

prefix: AFFIX which attaches to a word before the ROOT. Contrast SUFFIX.

prepose: to move to the beginning of a constituent. Also called FRONTING.

preposition: grammatical category which consists of a closed set of items which precede nouns to form a NOUN PHRASE. In English, the words, *in, above, below, with,* and *of* are prepositions.

prescriptive: referring to RULES that express how a LANGUAGE should be spoken instead of how it actually is spoken. The rule in English that prepositions cannot be stranded (occur sentence-finally) is prescriptive.

presupposition: a proposition whose truth must be taken for granted for an utterance to be regarded as sensible.

pretentative: grammatical category which denotes feigned action. In Ilocano, the pretentative prefix is *aginCV-*: *singpet* 'virtue' > *aginsisingpet* 'pretend to be virtuous.'

preterite: the simple PAST TENSE form of a verb.

primary stress: the strongest degree of STRESS in a word.

primitive: a theoretical construct that is GIVEN as opposed to derived or provided for by rules.

privative: lacking the presence of a feature; grammatical term used to express the English concept *without*. Hungarian has a privative suffix *-telen*: *ízlés* 'taste' > *ízlés-telen* 'tasteless, without taste.' (Kenesei et at 1998)

proclitic: a CLITIC which precedes its host. *An* used before a word beginning with a vowel is and example of a proclitic. **Enclitics** are clitics that follow a word, such as can**not**.

productive: said of morphemes that are not very restricted in their application. The English plural suffix is productive, it applies to all countable nouns and is used synchronically to produce new forms, whereas the English verbalizing suffix *-en* is less productive. Noun = **productivity**. Compare FOSSILIZED.

pro-form: anaphor.

progressive: referring to an ASPECT which denotes situations that are in progress at a certain reference time. In English, *She is eating* is the progressive form of *she eats*.

prohibitive: a negative IMPERATIVE. The English prohibitive is *don't*.

promotion: grammatical method for changing the status of a noun from OBLIQUE to CORE. See APPLICATIVE.

pronoun: MORPHEME which can act as a SUBSTITUTE for a NOUN PHRASE. Types of pronouns: PERSONAL, POSSESSIVE, DEMONSTRATIVE, REFLEXIVE, RELATIVE, INTERROGATIVE, INDEFINITE, RESUMPTIVE.

pronunciation: a particular way of speaking.

proper noun: referring to the class of NOUNS which designate people or places. Contrast COMMON NOUN. The category of proper nouns may be language specific. In Tagalog, singular proper nouns (including names and vocative kinterms) in NOMINATIVE CASE take the article *si* while common nouns don't > *si Mary* 'Mary' vs. *ang bata* 'the child'.

proposition: a statement which can be considered either true or false.

prosody: SUPRASEGMENTAL language as reflected in PITCH, LOUDNESS, TEMPO, and RHYTHM.

prospective: an ASPECT form indicating an action or event which is likely to happen.

protasis: the CONDITIONAL constituent of a conditional statement. In an English *if..then..* sentence, the protasis follows the *if*, and the APODOSIS follows the *then*.

prothesis: type of EPENTHESIS in which an extra sound is inserted initially in a WORD.

proto-language: ancestral language. Historical linguists RECONSTRUCT proto-languages.

prototype: the typical member associated with a category. Adj = **prototypical**.

proximate: 1) term used to describe the location close to the speaker. 2) grammatical form used to mark a topical third person who is the center of interest. Contrast OBVIATIVE.

pulmonic: associated with the lungs. The pulmonic AIRSTREAM MECHANISM is used to produce most human speech sounds.

punctual: ASPECTUAL term referring to momentary events, with no temporal duration. Contrast DURATIVE and CONTINUOUS.

pure vowel: a VOWEL which retains the same quality from the beginning to end. Compare DIPHTHONG.

purism: the idea that languages should be preserved in a standard form and speakers should avoid innovations or substandard uses. People who adhere to this belief are called **purists**.

qualification: depending structurally on another unit. Dependent items **qualify** non-dependent ones (ADJECTIVES are said to qualify NOUNS).

quality: the characteristic, defining feature of a VOWEL.

quantifier: MORPHEME which expresses contrasts in quantity. English quantifiers include *some, all,* and *each.*

quantifier float: a construction in which a quantifier appears later in a sentence than its normal position.

quantitative: referring to the frequency and distribution of an analysis.

quasi-copula: a verb which resembles a copula but has semantic content, e.g., *become, remain, grow.*

question: speech act whose purpose is to elicit information. Contrast statement and EXCLAMATION.

raising: the movement of an item to a position in a higher clause.

r-coloring: see RETROFLEX.

range: semantic role that completes, further specifies, or is a product of an event.

realis: MOOD which encompasses factual (realized) events as opposed to non-factual or hypothetical. Contrast IRREALIS.

received pronunciation: neutral accent in British English.

recipient: term used to express the CASE ROLE of ANIMATE referents that receive something or are passively implicated by the verb, in English expressed as INDIRECT OBJECTS of verbs.

reciprocal: expressing a mutual relationship. Ilocano has a reciprocal infix *-inn-*: *N-ag-l{inn}emmeng-da* = PERF-INTRANS-hide{RECIP}-they = 'They hid from each other.' Maltese has a reciprocal pronoun *xulxin* 'each other.' See also (RECIPROCAL) ASSIMILATION.

reconstruct: to hypothesize an earlier form of the language from available evidence.

reduced: 1) simplified (consonant clusters) 2) centralized (vowels).

redundant: containing more information than necessary.

reduplicand: the constituent or string that is copied in a reduplicative construction. The actual copy is called the **duple**.

reduplication: repetition of a phonological segment. Reduplication can be partial or complete, e.g., Ilocano *tukak* 'frog,' *tuktukak* 'frogs,' *tukaktukak* 'wart.' See also REDUPLICAND.

referent: entity in the real world to which a linguistic expression relates.

referent tracking: device for keeping track of what is being referred to in discourse.

referential: referring to a specific entity in the real world.

referring expression: free NOUN PHRASES that do not function as ANAPHORS or PRONOMINALS.

reflex: (in reconstruction) A form which is derived from an earlier form. Spanish *lluvia* 'rain' and French *pluie* are reflexes of Latin *pluvia*.

reflexive: grammatical CONSTRUCTION in which the SUBJECT and OBJECT relate to the same entity. In the sentence *Joe loves himself, himself* is a reflexive pronoun CO-REFERENTIAL with the SUBJECT *Joe*.

register: 1) variety of language used in a certain social situation. 2) (phonetics) voice quality produced by the LARYNX.

regressive assimilation: ANTICIPATORY ASSIMILATION.

regular: 1) in conformity with the RULES of language. 2) predictable.

reiteration: repetition.

reiterative: grammatical category used to express repetition.

relation: connection between two or more linguistic elements.

relational adjective: an adjective derived from a noun which allows the noun to be used as a modifier.

relative clause: modificational clause that expands off a HEAD NOUN and is part of the NOUN PHRASE. The noun phrase *the man who comes from China* contains a relative clause: *who comes from China.* Relative clauses can be RESTRICTIVE (defining the head noun) or non-restrictive (non-defining).

relative pronoun: pronoun that introduces a RELATIVE CLAUSE. English relative pronouns include *that, who, whom, whose,* and *which.*

relativity: (linguistic relativity) the view that LANGUAGE influences thought.

release: type of movement made when the vocal organs move away from a place of ARTICULATION.
relic form: an archaic form in language which still survives in certain regions.
repair: attempt made by a speaker to correct an imagined deficiency in the interaction.
repetitive: indicating repeated action.
replacive: hypothetical morpheme used to account for problematic alternations. Some linguists can assert that the plural of *mouse* (*mice*) has a replacive morpheme *ou* > *i*.
reported speech: speech that is reported by the speaker as having originated from another person. See also HEARSAY.
residual morphology: unproductive morphology that can be seen to be fully productive in the past. Compare FOSSILIZED.
resonant: speech sound produced with an open GLOTTIS so no audible friction is discernable. VOWELS, NASALS, LATERALS, and frictionless CONTINUANTS are resonant.
restrictive: said of a MODIFICATIONAL structure such as a RELATIVE CLAUSE that is used to identify the modified structure. Contrast non-restrictive.
resultative: FORM which expresses the notion of effect or consequence.
resumptive: FORM which repeats or recapitulates the meaning of a prior element. In the sentence *That French boy, I bought him a doughnut*, *him* is a **resumptive pronoun**.
retracted: said of speech sounds that are produced a little further back than a given reference point.
retroflex: sound produced when the tip of the tongue is curled back towards the front part of the hard palate. Hindi distinguishes retroflex consonants.
reversive: grammatical category usually used with VERBS that specifies the entire reversal of an action. Contrast the Mwera forms *mata* 'plaster' vs. *matu(ku)ka* 'become unplastered (reversive)' (Harries 1950: 74).
rheme: part of the sentence responsible for providing the most new meaning. Contrast THEME.
rhetorical question: a question that does not expect an answer.
rhotic: said of English dialects that pronounce the /r/ as a consonant in CODA position.
rhyme: part of the SYLLABLE which comprises the NUCLEUS and CODA.
rigidification: process in which a rule starts to apply without exception. Free word order languages can evolve into languages with strict word order via this process.
rim: edge of the tongue.
rising: said of PITCH which moves from LOW to HIGH.
roll: older term for a TRILL.
rolled: movement of tongue during a TRILL.
root: 1) base form of a word which provides the lexical meaning and cannot be deconstructed. See ADVANCED TONGUE ROOT.
round: said of the lips when assuming a rounded position. The vowel [u] is a HIGH BACK ROUND vowel.
rule: formal statement that describes the behavior of ELEMENTS or STRUCTURES in GRAMMAR.
sandhi: phonological change associated with forms that are juxtaposed. See ASSIMILATION and DISSIMILATION.
Sapir-Whorf hypothesis: a theory of the relationship between LANGUAGE and thought. Also known as the theory of linguistic RELATIVITY.
saturative: verbal ASPECT which expresses fulfilment, e.g., Russian *yest'* 'eat' vs *nayest'sja* 'eat to one's heart's content, until one is full.'
schema: a mental picture of some area of experience.
schwa: CENTRAL, NEUTRAL vowel, as heard in the English word *rough*.
scope: stretch of words which is affected by the meaning of a particular form.
secondary articulation: when a sound is produced with two points of articulation, the one that involves less STRICTURE, i.e., PALATALIZATION, LABIALIZATION.
secondary stress: a noticeable difference in STRESS which has less force than PRIMARY STRESS.
secret language: specialized LANGUAGE known only to a select group of individuals of a SPEECH COMMUNITY. In Easter Island, the secret language was called *ponoko*.
secretive: category which refers to actions performed in secret. In Kokborok, the adverb *čɔm* can suffix to verb roots to indicate their secret nature: *ča* 'eat' > *čacɔm* 'eat secretively', *bɔ nay-čɔm-ɔ* = he look-SECRET-PRES.INDIC = 'He looks secretively (spies)' (Pai 1976: 80).
segment: DISCRETE UNIT.
segment inventory: an enumeration of the PHONEMES of a language.
segmentable affix: AFFIX that is delineated by clearly defined boundaries. The process of delineating morpheme boundaries is called **segmentation**. See also PORTMANTEAU and FUSIONAL.
selectional restriction: the limitation placed on what types of units may appear in a particular slot in an utterance.
semantic role: the way in which an entity is involved in an action or situation, i.e., AGENT, PATIENT, PLACE, GOAL, BENEFACTOR, RECIPIENT. Also called THETA ROLE.
semantics: the scientific study of meaning in language.
seme: minimal DISTINCTIVE SEMANTIC FEATURE.
semiotics: scientific study of signalling systems (signs).
semi-speaker: a person with limited command of a language. Most MORIBUND languages have semi-speakers.
semi-vowel: sound which functions as a consonant, but lacks the formal characteristics of a consonant (friction or closure). The [w] is *water* is a semi-vowel. See also GLIDES.
sentence: formal structure that consists minimally of a PREDICATE that can be uttered in isolation. In English, sentences have both a SUBJECT and PREDICATE.
sequence: order of UNITS.
sequence of tenses: a grammatical restriction on what TENSES may occur in a SUBORDINATE CLAUSE following a MAIN CLAUSE.
serial verb construction: grammatical construction in which a sequence of two or more verbs is used to express one concept with a single set of participants. In serial verb constructions, all the verbs share a single set of inflectional categories, e.g., Lewo *a-sape a-tove a-va a-la ika* (3pS-say 3pS-go.down 3pS-go 3pS-take fish) 'They said they were going down to get some fish' (Early 1993: 69).
shadow pronoun: RESUMPTIVE PRONOUN.

short: taking less time to pronounce. Languages with PHONEMIC LENGTH contrast long and short segments, e.g., Tagalog *gá:bi* 'taro' vs. *gabi* 'night.'
sibilant: FRICATIVE sound which is produced with a narrow groove-like stricture, resulting in a hissing sound. In English [s] and [ʃ] are sibilants.
significant sound: see CONTRASTIVE sound.
signified: (French *signifié*) the meaning of a LINGUISTIC SIGN.
signifier: (French *signifiant*) the form of a LINGUISTIC SIGN.
silent letter: in orthographic systems, a symbol that does not correspond to a sound.
simple: 1) monomorphemic (said of words that can take affixation); form which is least COMPLEX morphologically 2) UNMARKED member of an OPPOSITION.
simulfix: a discontinuous AFFIX with two separated parts. See also CIRCUMFIX.
singular: referring to a single entity. Languages that have a grammatical category of NUMBER contrast singular and PLURAL, and sometimes have even further distinctions like PAUCAL or DUAL.
singulative: grammatical form which expresses INDIVIDUATION.
sister language: language which is descended from a common ancestor, usually said of closely related languages only.
slot: place where a CLASS of ITEMS can be inserted.
sociolect: DIALECT which is shared by a certain SOCIAL class.
sociolinguistics: the scientific study of the relationship between LANGUAGE and society.
sonorant: sound which is produced with free airflow and possible VOICING. Sonorants include VOWELS, LIQUIDS, LATERALS, and NASALS. Contrast OBSTRUENTS.
sonority: the relative LOUDNESS of a sound. Adj = **sonorous**.
sound change: change in a language's SOUND SYSTEM. When a series of related sound changes takes place, this is called a **sound shift**.
sound symbolism: the association between the phonetic form and meaning in language. Compare onomatopoeia and SYNAESTHESIA.
sound system: network of phonetically related CONTRASTS in a language.
source: origin.
specific: referring to a particular entity or occasion. Tagalog has a specific ARTICLE *ang*.
spectrograph: instrument used to measure the acoustic features of sounds.
speech: the spoken medium of language.
speech community: group which shares the same linguistic SYSTEM.
spirant: FRICATIVE.
spirantization: a change in pronunciation in which a CONSONANT (usually a STOP) is turned into a FRICATIVE.
Sprachbund: (German) see LINGUISTIC AREA.
spread: said of stretched lips, the position of lips in close vowels.
static: 1) opposite of DYNAMIC. 2) STATIVE. 3) (said of tones) not varying in PITCH.
stative: said of VERBS that encode states of affairs, rather than ACTIONS, or inactive cognitive processes. In English, stative verbs cannot occur in PROGRESSIVE aspect. Contrast DYNAMIC.
stem: MORPHEME or series of MORPHEMES which serves as a base for AFFIXATION.
stop: CONSONANT sound produced with complete closure in the VOCAL TRACT. Stops can be INGRESSIVE or EGRESSIVE.
stress: degree of force used in producing a SYLLABLE. The most prominent syllable is called **stressed**. In English, stress is CONTRASTIVE: *récord* vs. *recórd*.
stress-timed: said of a language in which STRESSED SYLLABLES recur at regular intervals of time, following a particular rhythm, as in English. Contrast SYLLABLE-TIMED.
stricture: the restriction of the airflow during ARTICULATION. CONSONANTS are produced with stricture.
strident: referring to sounds produced with complex STRICTURE and high frequency and intensity. [f], [s], and [ʃ] are stridents.
string: linear sequence of elements.
strong verb: a VERB in Germanic languages that inflects by changing the VOWEL of its STEM: e.g., *sing*, *sang*, *sung*. Contrast WEAK VERB.
structure: any particular way of arranging smaller LINGUISTIC UNITS into larger ones.
subject: 1) In ACCUSATIVE languages, the privileged argument which represents the doer of a TRANSITIVE or INTRANSITIVE action, ARGUMENT in NOMINATIVE CASE 2) In Basic Linguistic Theory, the single ARGUMENT of an INTRANSITIVE VERB, or the AGENTIVE argument of a TRANSITIVE verb.
subjunctive: verbal MOOD connected with uncertainty or unreality.
subordination: grammatical dependency. Clauses which cannot stand on their own as complete utterances are called **subordinate clauses**. They must be attached to a MAIN CLAUSE to make a complete SENTENCE. Morphemes that mark subordinate clauses are called **subordinators** and lexemes fulfilling this function are called **subordinating conjunctions**.
substantive: NOUN.
substrate: a variety of a language which has influenced a more dominant variety.
subtractive morpheme: the meaningful loss of a phonological sequence. In Dyirbal, the imperative is formed by deletion of the final consonant of the root: *banij* 'come, root', vs. *bani* 'come, imperative.'
suction: inward direction of airflow.
suffix: AFFIX which is added after a ROOT or STEM.
superessive: CASE that expresses location 'on' or 'upon' the noun it modifies.
superfix: a SUPRASEGMENTAL affix, e.g., stress, vowel length or tone. Compare the Mbay forms *tèe* 'to come out' vs. *tée* 'to come out numerously (Keegan 1997: 40).
superlative: form of an ADJECTIVE or ADVERB which expresses the highest DEGREE. Tagalog has a superlative PREFIX *pinaka-*: *pangit* 'ugly' > *pinakapangit* 'most ugly'. Compare COMPARATIVE.
superordinate: referring to a linguistic UNIT which is higher up in a HIERARCHY than another. Contrast SUBORDINATE.
superstratum: DOMINANT variety of language which has influenced a less dominant variety.
suppletion: unrelated forms in the grammar of a language because two forms which correspond grammatically derive from

different ROOTS. English has a **suppletive** past tense form of *go*: *went*, which came from the old English verb *wende*.

supplicative: grammatical morpheme which encodes imploring or urging of an action. In Manipuri, the supplicative suffix is *-si*: *nók-kum-si* = laugh-refuse-SUP = 'let's not laugh! (Chelliah 1997: 136).'

suprafix: SUPERFIX.

supraglottal: the area of the VOCAL TRACT above the GLOTTIS.

suprasegmental: vocal effect which extends over a sound segment, i.e., STRESS, TONE, PITCH.

surface structure: minimally abstract representation of a linguistic form which most closely resemblance the spoken form.

svarabhakti vowel: see ANAPTYXIS.

switch reference: Grammatical device used in certain languages to disambiguate two third person referents. Switch reference morphemes are usually interclausal and encode whether the subject or actor of one clause is the same or different from the subject of the previous clause.

syllabary: writing system in which the minimal GRAPHEME represents a SYLLABLE.

syllable: UNIT of sound with one NUCLEUS. In the phonological systems of languages, syllables can be defined by their STRUCTURE. In many Polynesian languages, the syllable structure is (C)V. Adj = **syllabic**.

syllable-timed: referring to a language where SYLLABLES occur at regular intervals of time, as in French. Contrast STRESS TIMED.

synaesthesia: direct association between a form and its meaning. In English, the *sn-* sound is often associated with the nose: *sneeze, sniff, snout, snore, snooty, snot, snuff.* See SOUND SYMBOLISM.

syncategorematic item: a word which cannot be assigned to any WORD CLASS because of its peculiar behavior.

synchronic: referring to a state of a language at a particular moment in time. Contrast DIACHRONIC.

syncope: loss of a sound segment in the middle of a word, e.g. [*kamra*] for *camera*.

synonym: lexical item with the same meaning. Contrast ANTONYM.

syntagmatic: referring to the sequential, linear order, as applied to a STRING of CONSTITUENTS. Contrast PARADIGMATIC.

syntax: study of RULES which govern the structure of WORDS and SENTENCES in language.

synthetic: morphologically complex. **Synthetic languages** can be either AGGLUTINATING, INFLECTING, or POLYSYNTHETIC. Contrast ISOLATING.

system: network of patterned relationships.

taboo: prohibited linguistic form or practice. In some cultures, saying the name of a recently deceased relative is considered taboo.

tacit knowledge: unconscious knowledge native speakers have about their language.

tag: kind of QUESTION used to elicit response which is usually positive or negative: 'Maria is Esteban's sister, *isn't she*?'

TAM system: Abbreviation for the system in a language used for marking TENSE, ASPECT and MODALITY.

tap: sound produced with a single rapid contact of the tongue with the roof of the mouth. See also FLAP.

target: intended goal; can be an intended utterance or a language one intends to learn.

tautosyllabic: occurring in the same SYLLABLE.

taxeme: minimal feature of grammatical arrangement, i.e., WORD ORDER, meaningful INTONATION, AGREEMENT.

taxonomy: classification.

telic: ASPECTUAL term referring to events with a clear endpoint (*bake, punch, fall*). Contrast ATELIC.

template: chart showing structural properties.

tempo: speed of speech.

temporal: pertaining to time. *When I bought the car* is a temporal adverbial clause.

tense: grammatical category which marks the time in which an action takes place. See PRESENT, PAST, FUTURE.

terminative: referring to a TELIC situation which is bounded at the end.

text: stretch of language used for linguistic analysis.

theme: 1) term used to describe the topical element of a sentence which is of major importance. Contrast RHEME. 2) The semantic role of an entity which is passively involved in a state of affairs without being strongly affected. 3) In Philippine languages, nouns which are transferred or conveyed in some way occur with **theme focus** verbs.

theta: the IPA character [θ], corresponding to a VOICELESS INTERDENTAL FRICATIVE.

theta role: theoretical term for SEMANTIC ROLE.

third person: the category of PERSON which does not include the speaker or addressee. English has three third person subject pronouns: *he*, *she*, and *they*.

tier: level of PHONOLOGICAL representation in autosegmental phonology.

tip: end point of the tongue.

tip-of-the-tongue phenomenon: the phenomenon in speech where a speaker suddenly is unable to produce a familiar word. In many cases, the speaker has some recollection of the structure of the word s/he is trying to produce.

TMA system: the system for marking TENSE, MOOD, and ASPECT in a language.

token: an individual occurrence of a linguistic form in discourse.

tone: DISTINCTIVE PITCH level of a SYLLABLE. Languages in which TONE is CONTRASTIVE are called **tonal**.

tongue: organ of speech segregated into TIP (APEX), BLADE (FRONT), CENTER (top), BACK (DORSUM), and ROOT.

tonic: referring to the SYLLABLE with maximal prominence.

topic: 1) entity about which something is said. (Contrast COMMENT). 2) (Philippine linguistics) NOUN PHRASE in FOCUS. Adj = **topical**.

topicalization: assigning prominence to a constituent (so it functions as TOPIC), usually by preposing the constituent.

toponym: a place name.

transcription: method of writing down DATA.

transformative: grammatical category which encodes the transformation of one thing into another.

transitivity: grammatical category which deals with the relationship between a VERB and its dependent ARGUMENTS. Verbs that cannot take OBJECTS are said to be INTRANSITIVE, those that take one object are transitive, and those that take more than one, DITRANSITIVE. In English, *die* is an intransitive verb, it only takes a SUBJECT; *kill* is transitive, as it takes a DIRECT OBJECT.

transparent: obvious. Contrast OPAQUE.
tree: kind of diagram with hierarchical structure used to exhibit SYNTACTIC STRUCTURE (**tree diagram**) or genetic affiliation (**family tree**).
trial: referring to three items. Contrast SINGULAR, DUAL, and PAUCAL.
trigger: (Austronesian linguistics) syntactically privileged argument whose semantic properties with relationship to the verb are reflected by the verbal morphology.
trigraph: a sequence of three letters to represent a single sound.
trill: (consonant) series of two or three TAPS pronounced in rapid succession. The second consonant of the Spanish word *perro* 'dog' is an ALVEOLAR trill.
tripartite: containing three elements, as the Malagasy compound *sòlom-bodiakóho* (/sólo-vody-akóho/ = substitute-rump-chicken) 'a gift given to one's elder (different from the traditional chicken rump)'.
triphthong: vowel sound with two noticeable changes in the same SYLLABLE. In British English, *wire* is pronounced with a triphthong.
triplication: double reduplication of an element, resulting in three identical phonological sequences.
trope: figurative use of an expression.
truncation: the shortening of a morphological form. Morphological truncation is used to form plurals in the Upper Hessian dialects of German: *hond* 'dog' > *hon* 'dogs' (Schirmunski 1962).
turn: in a conversation, the contribution of one of the participants.
twang: informal label for persistent NASALIZATION.
typology: branch of linguistics which investigates the STRUCTURAL similarities between languages.
ultima: the final SYLLABLE. Contrast PENULT, ANTEPENULT.
umlaut: phonological process in which a VOWEL change serves a grammatical purpose. The plural of *louse* (*lice*) is an instance of umlaut.
unaccusative: INTRANSITIVE VERB CONSTRUCTION whose SUBJECTS originate as objects, e.g., *the glass broke.* **Unaccusative verbs** are sometimes called ERGATIVE VERBS, but this use is not common.
underlying: referring to the abstract level of representation. Contrast SURFACE.
unergative verb: an INTRANSITIVE VERB whose subject is an AGENT. Contrast UNACCUSATIVE.
ungrammatical: ill formed, not abiding by the rules of language that are accepted by NATIVE speakers. In English, *Went I to store* is ungrammatical; no dialect of the language would accept it as a well-formed English sentence. *I says*, on the other hand, is grammatical in some varieties of English; it is just not STANDARD.
unidirectional: occurring in only one direction. GRAMMATICIZATION is seen to be a unidirectional process.
unit: entity which constitutes the focus of an enquiry.
universal: common to all languages. **Absolute universals** are found in all languages; **relative universals** are general tendencies of language. An **implicational universal** is a statement in the form of 'if a language has X, it will also have Y.'
unmarked: said of a form which is more neutral, expected, or common and in many cases less COMPLEX MORPHOLOGICALLY. The singular form of nouns in English is unmarked. The term *small* in the opposition *big/small* is MARKED as seen in the contrast of the sentences: *How big are you*? and *How small are you*?
unproductive: referring to a process (syntactic or morphological) which is applied in a limited domain. In Spanish the infinitive endings *–er* and *–ir* are unproductive, as they cannot be applied to new verbs.
unrounded: referring to vowel sounds which are produced without rounding of the lips.
usage: habits of a speech community.
utterance: stretch of speech.
uvular: said of sounds produced with the back of the tongue touching the **uvula**, the small flap of tissue that hangs in the back of the throat and is an extension of the soft palate. The French /r/ is uvular.
valency: referring to the number of SYNTACTIC elements that can form with each other. A verb which cannot take COMPLEMENTS has no valency. A TRANSITIVE verb takes two or more ARGUMENTS, so it is bivalent, as opposed to an intransitive verb whose valency is less (1 or 0).
valency changing operation: grammatical means to increase or decrease the TRANSITIVITY of a VERB. APPLICATIVES are valency-increasing morphemes.
variable: able to change form morphologically. Words that cannot change form are INVARIABLE.
variant: a linguistic form which is one of a set of ALTERNATIVES.
velar: relating to the VELUM. English has two velar stops, *k* and *g*.
velaric airstream mechanism: the manner in which clicks are produced in which the back of the tongue presses against the VELUM and a second closure is made further back in the mouth to trap and manipulate air in the mouth.
velum: the membrane behind the soft palate which serves as the place of articulation for the stops *k* and *g*, the nasal *ng*, etc.
venitive: grammatical case which expresses motion toward, coming to the speaker, e.g. Zacapoaxtla Aztec *ničoka* 'I am crying' vs. *ničokaki* 'I am coming to cry.'
verb: member of a lexical word class of items that prototypically encode events, and sometimes states and conditions. Verbs may be subcategorized for TRANSITIVITY depending on the number of ARGUMENTS they may take. Verbs are usually defined by their morphological properties. In Spanish, for instance, verbs may encode PERSON, NUMBER, TENSE, and MOOD.
verb phrase: constituent which contains a VERB as its HEAD.
vernacular: indigenous LANGUAGE of a SPEECH COMMUNITY.
visible: referring to items that can be seen during the speech event.
vocabulary: LEXICON.
vocal cords: two muscular folds surrounding the GLOTTIS that are responsible for PHONATION of sounds. Vocal cords are responsible for VOICED, VOICELESS, BREATHY and CREAKY sounds.
vocal tract: the air passage above the PHARYNX involved with the production of sounds.
vocalic: 1) pertaining to VOWELS. 2) having the nature of a vowel. Syllabic nasals in Bantu languages are vocalic.

vocative: inflectional CASE category which functions to address. In Comanche, vocative terms often involve an *h* substitution for a stem-final glottal: *pia#* 'mother, nominative' vs. *piah* 'mother, vocative' (Robinson and Armagost 1990: 288).

vocoid: referring to VOWELS in the PHONETIC sense. Contrast CONTOID.

voice: 1) (phonetic) another term for VOICING. 2) (grammatical) means to align various PARTICIPANT ROLES (agent, patient, etc.) to the various GRAMMATICAL RELATIONS (subject, object, etc.). Different voices include ACTIVE, PASSIVE, REFLEXIVE, RECIPROCAL, CAUSATIVE and middle.

voiced: sound produced with the vibration of the VOCAL CORDS. The consonant *b* is a voiced BILABIAL STOP, as opposed to its VOICELESS counterpart, *p*. Contrast VOICELESS.

voiceless: produced without vibration of the VOCAL cords.

voicing: 1) vibration of the VOCAL folds. 2) changing a VOICELESS sound to a VOICED sound.

vowel: speech sound that is articulated without closure in the mouth that would produce audible friction. Vowels can be ORAL or NASAL depending on whether the air passes through the mouth or nose. Vowels can be defined by the position of the tongue (HIGH, MID, LOW, CENTRAL, BACK) and the position of the lips (SPREAD, ROUND, NEUTRAL). Contrast CONSONANT.

vowel harmony: a constraint in some languages by which only certain combinations of VOWELS may occur in a single word.

VP: abbreviation for VERB PHRASE.

Wackernagel clitic: CLITIC which appears in second position, attaching to the first word of a constituent.

weak verb: a VERB in Germanic languages that does not inflect by changing its STEM vowel. Contrast STRONG VERB.

weakening: another term for LENITION.

well formed: (generative grammar) referring to a sentence that can be generated by the RULES of GRAMMAR.

wh- word: (From English interrogatives) INTERROGATIVE word, typically the first constituent of a QUESTION.

whisper: a PHONATION type in which the front of the GLOTTIS is closed but the back part is wide open. Whisper is noisier than BREATHY.

word: linguistic UNIT that can occur in isolation, a minimal free form. Words may be further defined by grammatical or phonological criteria.

word and paradigm: model of MORPHOLOGICAL description which takes the WORD as a basic UNIT of analysis which operates under a set of variables which constitute a PARADIGM, e.g. Spanish present tense forms of *hablar* 'to speak' > *hablo, hablas, habla, hablamos, habláis, hablan*. Contrast ITEM AND PROCESS, ITEM AND ARRANGEMENT.

word class: any of the small number of grammatical classes into which WORDS may fall, e.g. NOUN, VERB, ADJECTIVE, ADVERB, PREPOSITION, DETERMINER, IDIOPHONE, etc.

word formation: the process of deriving WORDS from morphological RULES.

word order: the SEQUENTIAL arrangement of WORDS into UNITS. English is an SVO Word Order Language, as the typical word order is SUBJECT-VERB-OBJECT.

xenophone: PHONEME or sound borrowed from another language.

yes/no question: type of question named for the type of response solicited, *yes* or *no*. Contrast CONTENT QUESTIONS.

zero: linguistic category that is expressed by the absence of a linguistic form. When the absence of a morpheme is meaningful, it is often referred to as a **zero morpheme**.

zero derivation: see CONVERSION.

zero morph: the meaningful absence of a morpheme.

Ziph's Law: the idea that high frequency is the cause of small magnitude (Zipf 1935: 29). Frequent linguistic forms will be small in size due to pressures of economic motivation.

Glossary References

Antworth, Evan. 1979. *A Grammatical Sketch of Botolan Sambal*. Manila: Linguistic Society of the Philippines.

Bhat, D. N. S, and M. S. Ningomba. 1997. *Manipuri Grammar*. Munich: Lincom Europa.

Brown, Keith, and Jim Miller. 1999. Concise Encyclopedia of Grammatical Categories. Amsterdam: Elsevier.

Chafe, Wallace. 1995. "The Realis-Irrealis Distinction." In Joan Bybee and Suzanne Fleischman (eds.) *Modality in Grammar and Discourse*. Amsterdam: John Benjamins.

Chelliah, Shobhana. 1997. *A Grammar of Meithei*. Berlin: Mouton de Gruyter.

Comrie, Bernard. 1981. *Language Universals and Linguistic Typology*. Cambridge: Cambridge University Press.

Croft, William. 1990. *Typology and Universals*. Cambridge: Cambridge University Press.

Crowley, Terry, John Lynch, Jeff Siegel, and Julie Piau. 1995. *The Design of Language: An Introduction to Descriptive Linguistics*. Auckland: Longman Paul.

Crystal, David. 1980. *A Dictionary of Linguistics and Phonetics*. Cambridge: Blackwell Publishers.

Donohue, Mark. 1999. *A Grammar of Tukang Besi*. Berlin: Mouton de Gruyter.

DuFeu, Veronica. 1996. *Rapanui*. London/New York: Routledge.

Early, Robert. "Nuclear Layer Serialization in Lewo." In *Oceanic Linguistics* 32:1:65–94.

Frantz, Donald G. 1991. *Blackfoot Grammar*. Toronto: University of Toronto Press.

Gowda, K. S. Gurubasave. 1975. "Ao Grammar." Mysore: Central Institute of Indian Languages Grammar Series I.

Hamel, Patricia J. 1994. *A Grammar and Lexicon of Loniu, Papua New Guinea*. Canberra: Pacific Linguistics C-103.

Harries, Lyndon. 1950. *A Grammar of Mwera*. Johannesburg: Witwatersrand University Press.

Heine, Bernd and Mechthild Reh. 1984. *Grammaticalization and reanalysis in African languages*. Hamburg: Helmut Buske Verlag.

Keegan, John M. 1997. *A Reference Grammar of Mbay*. Munich: Lincom Europa.

Kenesei, István, Robert M. Vago, and Anna Fenyvesi. 1998. *Hungarian*. London: Routledge.

Josephs, Lewis S. 1975. *Palauan Reference Grammar*. Honolulu: University of Hawaii Press.

Klokeid, Terry J. 1969. *Thargari Phonology and Morphology*. Canberra: Pacific Linguistics B:12.

Mahootian, Shahrzad. 1997. *Persian*. London/New York: Routledge.

Matthews, Peter. 1997. *The Concise Oxford Dictionary of Linguistics*. Oxford: Oxford University Press.

Mithun, Marianne. 1991. "Active/agentive case marking and its motivations." In *Language* 67:3:510–546.

____. 1996. "Overview of General Characteristics." In Goddard, Ives, ed. *Languages. Handbook of North American Indians*. Vol. 17. Washington: Smithsonian, p. 137–157.

Nida, Eugene. 1946. *Morphology: The Descriptive Analysis of Words*. Ann Arbor: University of Michigan Press.

Oates, W. and L. Oates. 1968. *Kapau Pedagogical Grammar*. Canberra: Pacific Linguistics C:10.

Pai (Karapurkar), Pushpa. 1976. "Kokborok Grammar." Mysore: Central Institute of Indian Languages Grammar Series no. 3.

Prasad, Bal Ram. 1991. *Mising Grammar*. Revised and enlarged by G. Devi Prasada Sastry and P. T. Abraham. Mysore: Central Institute of Indian Languages.

Robinson, Lisa Wistrand, and James Armagost. 1990. *Comanche Dictionary and Grammar*. Arlington: Summer Institute of Linguistics.

Rubino, Carl. 1997. "A Reference Grammar of Ilocano." PhD Dissertation, University of California, Santa Barbara.

____. 2000. *Ilocano Grammar and Dictionary*. Honolulu: University of Hawaii Press.

Schirmunski, Viktor M. 1962. *Deutsche Mundartkunde. Vergleichende Laut- und Formenlehre der deutschen Mundarten,* trans. and rev. Wolfgang Fleischer. Berlin: Akademia-Verlag.

Sulkala, Helena, and Merja Karjalainen. 1992. *Finnish*. London: Routledge.

Tauli, V. 1973. *Standard Estonian Grammar. Part 1. Phonology, morphology, word formation*. Uppsala: Acta Universitatis Upsaliensis. Studia Uralica et Altaica Upsaliensia 8.

Trask, R. L. 1997. *A Student's Dictionary of Language and Linguistics*. London: Arnold.

Zipf, George. 1935. *The Psychobiology of Language: An Introduction to Dynamic Philology*. Cambridge: MIT Press.

Index of Languages by Country

Below is an index of the major countries in the world mentioned in this book. Following each country is a list of some of the more dominant languages spoken in each. This index includes only the languages with an entry in this book. Languages with official status or considered the language of the government are marked with an asterisk. In many African and South American countries, a language with official status may be spoken by only a small percentage of citizens or generally used only during government proceedings, in official literature or by the elite.

The remaining languages that follow the languages marked with an asterisk are ones spoken by a significant number of citizens. They are arranged alphabetically.

Afghanistan—*Pashto; Arabic, Balochi, Kazakh, Turkmen, Uzbek

Albania—*Albanian; Macedonian

Algeria—*Arabic; French

Angola—*Portuguese; Kikongo, Kituba, UMbundu

Argentina—*Spanish; German, Guarani, Italian, Quechua

Armenia—*Armenian; Azerbaijanian, Kurmanjî Kurdish

Aruba—*Dutch

Australia—*English; Finnish, Italian, Lithuanian, Serbo-Croatian, Ukrainian, Warlpiri

Austria—*German; Slovene, Serbo-Croatian

Azerbaijan—*Azerbaijanian; Armenian, Georgian

Bahrain—*Arabic

Bangladesh—*Bangla; English, Manipuri, Santali

Barbados—*English; Caribbean Creole English

Belarus—*Belorussian; Lithuanian, Ukrainian

Belgium—*Dutch, French, German

Belize—*English; Maya, Spanish

Benin—*French; Ewe, Fula, Yoruba

Bhutan—Tibetan

Bolivia—*Spanish; Aymara, Quechua

Bosnia Herzegovina—*Serbo-Croatian

Botswana—*Tswana, *English; Shona

Brazil—*Portuguese; German, Guarani, Italian, Polish, Quechua, Ukrainian

Bulgaria—*Bulgarian; Macedonian, Turkish

Burkina Faso—*French; Dagaare, Fula, Maninka-Bambara-Dyula, Moore

Burma (Myanmar)—*Burmese; Manipuri, Pwo Karen

Burundi—*French, *Rundi; Kinyarwanda, Swahili

Cambodia—*Khmer

Cameroon—*French, *English; Fula

Canada—*English, *French; German, Italian, Polish, Portuguese, Ukrainian

Central African Republic—*French, *Sango

Chad—*French; Fula, Kanuri

Chile—*Spanish; Aymara

China—*Mandarin, Arabic, Classical Chinese, Gan, Hakka, Kam, Kazakh, Korean, Min, Mongolian, Tatar, Tibetan, Tocharian, Uyghur, Uzbek, Wu, Xiang, Yi, Yue, Zhuang-Bouyei

Colombia—*Spanish; Quechua

Democratic Republic of the Congo—*French; Bemba, Kikongo Kituba, Kinyarwanda, Luba, Swahili, Tshiluba

Republic of the Congo—*French, *Lingala; Kikongo Kituba

Costa Rica—*Spanish

Croatia—*Serbo-Croatian; Italian

Cuba—*Spanish

Czech Republic—*Czech; German, Slovak

Denmark—*Danish

Djibouti—*French; Arabic, Somali

Dominican Republic—*Spanish

Ecuador—*Spanish; Quechua

Egypt—*Arabic; English, French

El Salvador—*Spanish

Eritrea—*Tigrinya

Ethiopia—*Amharic; English, Ge'ez, Oromo, Somali, Wolaitta, Tigrinya

Finland—*Finnish; Swedish

France—*French; Basque, Catalan, German, Italian, Occitan, Polish, Portuguese

French Guiana—*French; Hakka

Gabon—*French

Gambia—*English; Fula, Wolof

Georgia—*Georgian; Azerbaijanian

Germany—*German; Lithuanian, Portuguese, Romanian, Serbo-Croatian

Ghana—*English; Akan, Dagaare, Ewe, Fula

Greece—*Modern Greek; Albanian, Turkish

Greenland—*Danish

Guadeloupe—*French

Guatemala—*Spanish; Maya

Guinea—*French; Fula, Wolof

Guinea-Bissau—*Portuguese; Pulaar

Guyana—*English

Haiti—*French; Haitian Creole

Honduras—*Spanish

Hungary—*Hungarian; Bulgarian, German, Slovak

Iceland—Danish

India—*Hindi, *English; Assamese, Arabic, Bhojpuri, Gondi, Gujarati, Kannada, Konkani, Manipuri/Meithei, Marathi, Oriya, Punjabi, Rajasthani, Santali, Sindhi, Tamil, Telugu, Tibetan, Urdu

Indonesia—*Malay/Indonesian; Acehnese, Arabic, Balinese, Bugis, Javanese, Madurese, Minangkabau

Iran—*Persian; Arabic, Armenian, Azerbaijanian, Balochi, Georgian, Kurmanj Kurdish

Iraq—*Arabic; Azerbaijanian, Kurmanjî Kurdish, Turkish

Ireland—*English, *Irish

Israel—*Modern Hebrew, *Arabic; English, German, Romanian

Italy—*Italian; Albanian, French, German, Occitan, Slovene

Ivory Coast—*French; Akan, Dagaare, Maninka-Bambara-Dyula, Moore

Jamaica—Caribbean Creole English, English

Japan—*Japanese; Korean

Jordan—*Arabic

Kazakhstan—*Kirghiz; Tajik, Tatar, Turkmen, Ukrainian, Uzbek

Kenya—*Somali, *English; Gikuyu, Oromo, Swahili

North Korea—*Korean

South Korea—*Korean

Kuwait—*Arabic

Kyrgyzstan—Kirghiz

Laos—*Lao; French, Khmer

Latvia—*Latvian; Belorussian, Lithuanian

Lebanon—*Arabic; French, Turkish, Armenian

Lesotho—*English, *Sesotho; Zulu

Libya—*Arabic

Liechtenstein—German

Lithuania—*Lithuanian; Belorussian, Polish,

Luxembourg—*French; German

Macedonia—Albanian, Macedonian, Serbo-Croatian, Turkish

Madagascar—*Malagasy, *French

Malawi—*Chichewa; English

Malaysia—Javanese, Malay/Indonesian, Tamil

Mali—*French; Fula, Maninka-Bambura-Dyula, Wolof

Martinique—French

Mauritania—*French, *Arabic; Fula, Maninka-Bambara-Dyula, Wolof

Mauritius—*English; Caribbean Creole English

Mexico—*Spanish; Maya, Nahuatl

Moldova—Bulgarian, Romanian, Ukrainian

Monaco—French, Italian

Mongolia—*Mongolian; Uyghur

Morocco—*Arabic; French, Tamazight

Mozambique—*Portuguese; Chichewa, Shona, Swahili

Namibia—*Afrikaans, Nama

Nepal—Bhojpuri, Nepali, Santali, Tibetan

Netherlands—*Dutch

New Caledonia—French

New Zealand—*English

Nicaragua—*Spanish

Niger—*French; Fula, Hausa, Kanuri

Nigeria—*English; Arabic, Fula, Hausa, Igbo, Kanuri, Yoruba

Norway—*Norwegian; Danish, Finnish

Oman—*Arabic

Pakistan—*Urdu; Arabic, Balochi, English, Pashto, Punjabi, Sindhi, Siraiki, Tibetan

Panama—*Spanish

Papua New Guinea—*English; Arapesh, Tok Pisin

Paraguay—*Spanish; German, Guarani

Peru—*Spanish, *Quechua; Aymara

Philippines—*English, *Tagalog; Bikol, Cebuano, Hiligaynon, Ilocano, Kapampangan, Pangasinan, Spanish, Waray Waray

Poland—*Polish; Lithuanian, Slovak, Ukrainian,

Portugal—*Portuguese

Qatar—*Arabic

Romania—*Romanian; Bulgarian, German, Hungarian, Slovak, Ukrainian

Russia—*Russian; Bulgarian, Finnish, Nivkh, Ukrainian

Rwanda—*Kinyarwanda, *French

Saudi Arabia—*Arabic

Senegal—*French; Fula, Maninka-Bambara-Dyula, Wolof

Serbia and Montenegro—*Serbo-Croatian; Albania, Bulgarian,

Sierra Leone—*English; Fula, Mende

Singapore—*English; Mandarin, Tamil

Slovakia—*Slovak; German, Hungarian, Ukrainian

Slovenia—*Slovene; German, Italian

Somalia—*Somali; Arabic, Swahili

South Africa—*Afrikaans, *English; German, Sesotho, Xhosa, Zulu

Spain—*Spanish; Basque, Catalan, Galician, Occitan

Sri Lanka—*Sinhala; English, Tamil

Sudan—Arabic, Fula, Hausa

Surinam—*Dutch; English, Spanish

Swaziland—*siSwati, *English; Zulu

Sweden—*Swedish; Danish, Finnish, Serbo-Croatian

Switzerland—French, German, Italian

Syria—*Arabic; Armenian, French, Kurmanj Kurdish, Turkish

Tajikistan—*Tajik; Kazakh, Persian, Uzbek

Tanzania—*Swahili; Bemba, Kinyarwanda, Oromo, Rundi

Thailand—*Thai; Khmer, Pwo Karen

Togo—*French; Ewe, Fula, Yoruba

Trinidad and Tobago—*English; Caribbean Creole English

Tunisia—*Arabic; French

Turkey—*Turkish; Arabic, Armenian, Azerbaijanian, Georgian, Kurmanjî Kurdish

Turkmenistan—*Turkmen; Balochi, Kazakh, Uzbek

Uganda—*English, *Swahili; Kinyarwanda, Luganda

Ukraine—*Ukrainian; Bulgarian, Hungarian, Polish, Romanian, Russian

United Arab Emirates—*Arabic

United Kingdom—*English; Irish, Welsh

United States—*English; Cherokee, Creek, French, German, Italian, Lakota, Navajo, Polish, Spanish, Yup'ik Eskimo

Uruguay—*Spanish

Uzbekistan—*Uzbek; Kazakh, Tajik, Tatar, Turkmen

Venezuela—*Spanish

Vietnam—*Vietnamese; French, Khmer, Tay-Nung, Yi

Wales—Welsh, English

Yemen—*Arabic

Zambia—*English; Bemba, Chichewa, Shona

Zimbabwe—*English; Chichewa, Shona, Zulu

Index of Languages by Family

Below is a listing of the languages found in this book organized according to language family. Each language is listed alphabetically under its main family branch.

Index of Languages and Alternate Names

Below is an index of all of the languages mentioned in this book as well as the alternate names for some of the languages with full entries. The alternate name is shown in italics, with the language name following in parenthesis.

T